GRAND PRIX
PRIX
WHO'S
WHO

3rd Edition

Steve Small

GRAND PRIX WHO'S WHO

3rd Edition

Published in Great Britain by
Travel Publishing Ltd
7a Apollo House,
Calleva Park, Aldermaston,
Reading, Berkshire RG7 8TN

Text design and layout: Steve Small

Printed and bound in Great Britain by
J. H. Haynes & Co. Ltd., Sparkford

A catalogue record of this book is available from the
British Library

ISBN 1-902-00746-8

ACKNOWLEDGEMENTS

There have been many friends and colleagues who have given their encouragement and assistance during the many years it took for this project to reach fruition and in the preparation of this third edition. I can truly say that, without their help, this volume would not have been so complete.

There are two people who must be singled out for their sterling efforts on my behalf. Firstly, the late John Taylor, who was well known to serious followers of the sport for more than a decade as the statistical guru of the leading Grand Prix annual Autocourse. When I first discussed the idea for the first edition with him back in 1988, he willingly undertook the massive job of placing much of the contents of my folders onto a computer database, keeping his eagle eye out for the inevitable inaccuracies and omissions there and putting them to rights. Sadly, his early death from muscular dystrophy in 1991 meant he was not to see the finished article in which he had played such a major part. More recently, I have been fortunate indeed to enlist the help of Peter Lovering. His skills and patience have been stretched to the limits for a third time with this new edition, as he first brought some semblance of literacy to the biographical pieces, and then ran the rule over the massive bank of statistics, helping in the almost impossible task of filtering out the remaining inconsistencies and errors with a diligence that could hardly be matched.

Since the publication of the first edition in 1994, I have benefited from the encouragement and wisdom imparted by a number of distinguished motor sport writers. My thanks to Bernard Cahier, Adriano Cimarosti, Adam Cooper, Gérard 'Jabby' Crombac, Alan Henry, Hartmut Lehbrink, Doug Nye, Jimmy Piget, Murray Walker and Antonio Watson.

Very special thanks go to Sir Stirling Moss for so kindly contributing a foreword to this third edition. His deeds were indeed the stuff of legend, and an inspiration for this book.

Apart from the aforementioned, my gratitude goes to the following for their help, enthusiasm and forbearance over the past few years: Kathy Ager, Jean-Luc Alexandre, Simon Arron, Jocelyne Bia, Jeff Bloxham, Liz Le Breton, Diana Burnett, Paddy Driver, Simon Duncan, Paul Fearnley, Deirdre Fenney, George Greenfield, Soda Hayata, David Hayhoe, Peter Higham, David Holland, Bryan Kennedy, Christine Lalla, Ian Marshall, Marius Matthee, Wilfried Müller, Steven Palmer, Jimmy Piget, Eddie Pinto, Ivan Ponting, Richard Poulter, Charles Richards, Nigel Snowdon, Steve Tee, Sam Tingle, Paul Vestey, Christian Weber, Bryn Williams, Jo Wright and Tim Wright. Thanks also to Roland J Kraus for taking so much time and trouble to search out the inaccuracies which are inevitable in a work such as this. I hope they have been remedied in this edition.

The author is also grateful for permission to reproduce photographs. The vast majority are from the amazing collection of LAT Photographic, Diana Burnett and Nigel Snowdon, with additional but telling contributions from: Bernard Cahier, Tony Crook, Graham Gauld, Dick Gibson, GPL Library, Simon Hildreth, John James, Maurice Louche, The Ludvigsen Library, Teddy Mayer, Mercedes Benz Archive, MPS (Motoring Press Service, Japan), Brausch Niemann, Jürgen Nill, Yves Peyrouse, John Ross, Matthias Schneider, Jimmy Stewart, Roger Swann, Bob Tronolone and Christian Weber.

Efforts have been made to trace copyright holders of all photographs used in this book. We apologise for any omissions, which are unintentional, and would be pleased to include an appropriate acknowledgement in any subsequent edition.

FOREWORD by
Sir STIRLING MOSS

IT is hard for me to believe that there have been fifty seasons of Grand Prix racing since the start of the World Championship. I can clearly remember that sunny day back in May 1950 when the mighty Alfa Romeo team came to Silverstone to compete in the very first event to count towards the newly inaugurated Drivers' World Championship.

Way back then, I was just an ambitious twenty-year-old competing in a supporting race for 500 cc F3 cars, but I was given the honour of lining up with the international stars of the day to be presented to King George VI and other members of the royal family. The following year, I made my debut on the Grand Prix stage and have since witnessed the incredible technological developments which have turned my sport into the billion-dollar global spectacle of today.

I have been fortunate enough to have either raced against or been closely acquainted with the vast majority of the racing drivers who have graced the highest level of the sport over these past five decades, and Grand Prix Who's Who is the only book to chronicle the deeds of every one of them.

Steve Small has produced a hugely informative publication, which marries a wealth of easy-to-use statistics with carefully searched biographies. Illustrated by a fascinating selection of contemporary photographs, this enlarged third edition of Grand Prix Who's Who will undoubtedly become the standard work of reference on Grand Prix drivers past and present, and should find a place on the bookshelf of every motor racing enthusiast.

Sir Stirling Moss
London, January 2000

INTRODUCTION

The first seeds of Grand Prix Who's Who were sown in the mid-seventies, when I began piecing together records of Grand Prix drivers' careers, not just in Formula 1 but in all other types of racing as well. My files began to multiply at a disconcerting rate as trivial and minor, seemingly irrelevant, information about every driver was recorded. Even then I had in mind a volume of this sort, but not perhaps of this magnitude or detail.

As time passed I became increasingly aware of the need for such a book. There were few single sources of reference that enabled a reader to chart a driver's Grand Prix career, and even these were selective, usually concerning themselves merely with the upper strata who had scored championship points. It was this lack of completeness at even the most fundamental level that spurred me on. Through the eighties, with the huge upsurge of statistical works on sport in general, I genuinely believed that someone must be about to publish a book of this sort – but still nothing was forthcoming. So, as outlined in the acknowledgements, the first edition of Grand Prix Who's Who took shape over a span of some five years, and the initial concept has not been fundamentally altered for this new and fully revised and enlarged third edition.

The raison d'être is the statistics, which comprise an entry for every driver who has started a World Championship Grand Prix since the inception of the drivers' championship in 1950, arranged alphabetically. Each driver's Grand Prix career is then set out in chronological order on a race-by-race basis. Here you will find: the placing, the race, the circuit, the car number, the entrant, the car and engine, a commentary and a qualifying ranking from total entries. This recent addition shows the qualifying position attained by each driver plus the total number of drivers entered for that particular race. These are not necessarily final starting positions, because drivers who failed to make the grid have their position shown between brackets in the place they should have occupied. This of course means all slower drivers are moved one place down the order. The biographical details have also been expanded to include the driver's place of birth and death, and for this information I must thank both David Hayhoe and David Holland, who generously suggested I take advantage of the tireless research incorporated in their mammoth and highly recommended Grand Prix Data Book 3.

As this work is focused on the drivers, I have steered clear of the minefield that is individual chassis numbers; quite honestly, they have no place here, and would merely add to the clutter. What I have done, however, is to include additional lines where a driver competed in a different chassis/engine combination either in official practice or in the race itself, for example Alboreto in Austria in 1983 racing the Tyrrell 012, but practising in the 011 as well; or Arundell at Brands Hatch in 1966 driving two Lotus 33s, one with a BRM engine and the other a Climax. A word of warning regarding the race numbers, which are now allocated for a whole season, but were not so in earlier days. It was not uncommon for some Continental race organisers to change the numbers between practice and race, to try to defeat the wiles of pirate programme producers, so total accuracy here is next to impossible. The same applies to the comment column. Published reasons for retirements and so forth often proved to be contradictory, and teams were sometimes quite happy to give totally fictitious explanations of their cars' failures in an attempt to disguise any weaknesses. I have wherever possible followed the most generally held views, but out there someone probably knows different. Keen readers will notice a couple of new additions to this edition. Wherever possible I have included the make of tyre used by each driver (see page 624 for key) and above each season completed there is a running summary of that year's performances.

I have concerned myself solely with the core statistics as described; there are other authors whose books compare and analyse racing data, and I am happy to leave that field in their most capable hands. At the end of each driver's entry, however, I have included a line giving details of his total starts, wins, pole positions, fastest laps and points scored. The vexed question of starts should be addressed here. For when does a driver 'start' a Grand Prix? To my mind he does so only if he is on the grid when the flag drops or light goes green at the final start. Should a driver have failed to complete the parade lap, for instance (as was the case with Prost at Imola in 1990), he cannot truly be said to have started the race. In the case of restarted events such as the British GP in 1986, poor Jacques Laffite certainly did start the race, but this was declared null and void and he was not present to take the restart, which is the only one that counts. The different rules governing incidents of this sort over the years have led to inconsistencies that can probably never be resolved satisfactorily. I have decided wherever applicable to give two totals: the first, the true number of actual final race starts; and a second which includes any incidents of the kind outlined above. You pays yer money, you takes yer choice . . .

Although the statistics are the backbone of this work, on their own they tell only part of the story. As you will find, many drivers, particularly in recent times, have enjoyed Grand Prix careers of a length out of all proportion to their achievements, while there are literally dozens of other perhaps more worthy pilots over the years who maybe made only a minor mark and have been all but forgotten. This is due in part to the way motor racing has changed in the past forty years. In the fifties, it was possible for the amateur hopeful to participate in a Grand Prix and trundle round at the back of the field enjoying his big day as he rubbed shoulders with the greats. By the sixties, Formula 1 was the domain of the professional, but one could still compete quite usefully as an independent by purchasing a proprietary chassis and hope for the occasional placing, earning one's corn in the plethora of non-championship events that then abounded. By the seventies, the stakes had been raised, but the availability of the Ford-Cosworth engine still made it possible for those with enough talent and persistence to establish themselves. Since then the costs of producing a Grand Prix car, and the rule permitting only constructors who build their own machines to compete, have severely limited top Grand Prix opportunities to a select band who naturally dominate the scene.

In order to reflect the impact a driver has made not only on Grand Prix racing but also on motor racing as a whole, I have included biographies of virtually every driver to have started a World Championship race. Therefore for the first time in one volume you will be able to read about both the great champions and also literally hundreds of other hopefuls who have rarely been profiled in the past. As you will find, these essays are not necessarily just blow-by-blow accounts chronicling the subject's Grand Prix career, which is already fully documented in the statistics, but attempt to paint a wider picture, encompassing early racing achievements and pivotal successes as well as the trials and tribulations and all too often the tragedy. Using the biographies as a signpost, the reader can add detail to the picture by studying the statistics. As an addendum, there is a section at the back which lists all the non-starters, those unlucky souls who tried in vain to make the grid for a championship Grand Prix.

The third, and by no means least important, facet of this volume is the hundreds of photographs which have been painstakingly assembled. Some have never been used before, and countless others only saw the light of day in the dim and distant past. Now, as never before, you can put a face to the names: from the fifties, very fast and debonair Argentinian Carlos Menditéguy, or the scholastic Rudi Fischer; from sun-drenched Kyalami in the sixties, locals such as Trevor Blokdyk, Sam Tingle and Doug Serrurier; from the land of the rising sun the complete Japanese racing quartet of the mid-seventies, Takahara, Takahashi, Hasemi and Hoshino. One of the great sources of satisfaction in attempting a project of these proportions has been the opportunity to unearth – and use – photographs of such glorious obscurities as Alfredo Uria, Fred Wacker, Bernard Collomb, Oswald Karch, Mike Fisher, John Cordts, Albert Scherrer and Tom Jones. Now, together, they at last have their place in motor racing literature!

At this point I would particularly like to thank the publishers, Chris Day and Peter Robinson, my partners in this project, for they showed great enthusiasm from the start, and then gave me total freedom with which to work, a wonderful indulgence. I hope this enlarged third edition meets their expectations.

Steve Small
Windsor, Berkshire
January 2000

SELECTED BIBLIOGRAPHY

YEARBOOKS, MAGAZINES & PERIODICALS

AUTOCAR & MOTOR	AUTOCOURSE
AUTOSPORT	THE 'MOTOR' YEARBOOK 1948 to 1960
GRAND PRIX INTERNATIONAL	MARLBORO GRAND PRIX GUIDE 1972 to 1974
MOTORING NEWS	JOHN PLAYER MOTOR SPORT YEAR 1972 to 1976
MOTOR SPORT	INTERNATIONAL MOTOR RACING YEAR 1977 to 1978
ROAD & TRACK	MOTOR RACING AND RALLY DIRECTORY 1957
GRAND PRIX YEAR	AUTOCOURSE CART OFFICIAL YEARBOOK

BOOKS

DERRICK ALLSOP
**THE BRITISH RACING HERO
FROM MOSS TO MANSELL**
Magna Books

MICHAEL COOPER-EVANS
ROB WALKER
Hazleton Publishing

ROBERT CUTTER & BOB FENDELL
ENCYCLOPEDIA OF AUTO GREATS
Prentice Hall

ROBERT DALEY
THE CRUEL SPORT
Studio Vista

ROBERT DALEY
CARS AT SPEED
Foulis

ROBERT EDWARDS
ARCHIE AND THE LISTERS
PSL

LYLE KENYON ENGEL
JACKIE STEWART – WORLD DRIVING CHAMPION
Arco Publishing

JUAN MANUEL FANGIO
FANGIO
Temple Press

EMERSON FITTIPALDI & ELIZABETH HAYWARD
FLYING ON THE GROUND
William Kimber

GRAHAM GAULD
REG PARNELL
PSL

G N GEORGEANO (Ed)
ENCYCLOPEDIA OF MOTOR RACING
Ebury Press and Michael Joseph

DAVID HAYHOE and DAVID HOLLAND
GRAND PRIX DATA BOOK 3
Duke

ALAN HENRY
MARCH, THE GRAND PRIX & INDY CARS
Hazleton Publishing

ALAN HENRY
GRAND PRIX – DRIVER BY DRIVER
Crowood Press

PETER HIGHAM
**THE GUINNESS GUIDE TO
INTERNATIONAL MOTOR RACING**
Guinness Publishing

DENIS JENKINSON (Ed)
FANGIO
Michael Joseph

DENIS JENKINSON & CYRIL POSTHUMUS
VANWALL
Patrick Stephens

JENKINSON/ROEBUCK/HENRY/HAMILTON
THE GRAND PRIX DRIVERS
Hazleton Publishing

CHRIS JONES
ROAD RACE
George Allen & Unwin

MICHAEL KEYSER
THE SPEED MERCHANTS
Prentice Hall

GORDON KIRBY
EMERSON FITTIPALDI
Hazleton Publishing

RAYMOND MAYS & PETER ROBERTS
BRM
Pan Books

PETER MILLER
MEN AT THE WHEEL
Batsford

PETER MILLER
THE FAST ONES
Stanley Paul

CHRIS NIXON
**RACING WITH THE DAVID BROWN
ASTON MARTINS Vols 1 & 2**
Transport Bookman

DOUG NYE
**THE AUTOCOURSE HISTORY OF THE GRAND PRIX
CAR 1945-65 & 1966-91**
Hazleton Publishing

DOUG NYE
THEME LOTUS 1958-86
MRP

DOUG NYE
DINO – THE LITTLE FERRARI
Osprey

DOUG NYE
**RACERS: THE INSIDE STORY OF WILLIAMS
GRAND PRIX ENGINEERING**
Osprey

DOUG NYE
COOPER CARS
Osprey

DOUG NYE
THE UNITED STATES GRAND PRIX 1908-77
Batsford

DOUG NYE
THE BRITISH GRAND PRIX 1926-76
Batsford

JIMMY PIGET
F3 SUDAM FACT BOOK
Jimmy Piget

JIMMY PIGET
**COMPANION TO FORMULA 1 REGISTER
FACT BOOKS**
Jimmy Piget

JIMMY PIGET
**MEMENTO FOR GRAND PRIX, INDY CAR
and OTHER MAJOR SINGLE SEATER RACES**
Jimmy Piget

HEINZ PRÜLLER
JOCHEN RINDT
William Kimber

PETER REVSON & LEON MANDEL
**SPEED WITH STYLE – THE AUTOBIOGRAPHY OF
PETER REVSON**
William Kimber

NIGEL ROEBUCK
GRAND PRIX GREATS
Patrick Stephens

Dr K PAUL SHELDON with DUNCAN RABAGLIATI
**A RECORD OF GRAND PRIX AND VOITURETTE
RACING – Volumes 5, 6, 7 & 8**
St Leonard's Press

JOHN SURTEES
JOHN SURTEES – WORLD CHAMPION
Hazleton Publishing

HANS TANNER & DOUG NYE
FERRARI
Haynes

JONATHAN THOMPSON with DUNCAN
RABAGLIATI & Dr K PAUL SHELDON
THE FORMULA ONE RECORD BOOK
Leslie Frewin

THE AUTHOR

Steve Small has been a close follower of motor sport since the mid-sixties, when the likes of Clark, Hill, Rindt and Stewart seemed to be racing almost every weekend across the many categories of the sport.

Having gained a Dip. A.D. and M.A. in Graphic Design, he worked for more than a decade in advertising and design, before moving into the publishing world. The Art Editor of the prestigious motor sport annual AUTOCOURSE since 1986, he has been involved with many other acclaimed motor sport titles.

GRAND PRIX WHO'S WHO

FROM ABECASSIS TO ZUNINO

THE COMPLETE
GRAND PRIX CAREER RECORD
OF EVERY DRIVER TO HAVE STARTED
A WORLD CHAMPIONSHIP RACE
FROM 1950 TO 1999

KENNETH ACHESON

Following a rapid and spectacularly successful rise from his 1976 Formula Ford debut through to F3 in 1980, Grovewood Award winner Acheson's progress – interrupted by a broken leg sustained in the F2 Pau GP in 1981 – finally ran up a cul-de-sac with his fruitless attempts to make an impression in Formula 1 with the uncompetitive RAM team.

Although his subsequent career lacked continuity, the quiet and talented Ulsterman proved his ability in sports car racing, emerging as 1987 joint All-Japan champion in a Porsche 962. A works Sauber-Mercedes driver in 1989, he finished third at Le Mans in 1991 in a factory Jaguar.

Acheson survived a 180 mph crash at the 1996 Daytona 24-hour sports car race, when his Lister GT tangled with a slower competitor. Escaping with an eye injury and massive bruising, he subsequently retired from the sport.

GEORGE ABECASSIS

Having raced an Alta and an ERA before the war, Abecassis was involved in the development of the unsuccessful 1948 GP Alta before joining forces with John Heath to found the HW Motors team which ran their Alta-engined HWMs on a shoestring budget at home and abroad in the early fifties.

In the main Abecassis concentrated on sports cars, driving for the works Aston Martin team between 1951 and '53 and enjoying success in national events with the potent Jaguar-engined HWM from 1953 until 1956, when the death of his partner Heath in the Mille Miglia saw George cease driving and ultimately wind down the Walton team's racing activities.

PHILIPPE ADAMS

On paper Adams' record was good: three years in British F3 culminating in second place in the 1992 championship, and, after appeal, belatedly crowned 1993 Halfords British F2 champion. With the once dominant Lotus marque heading for oblivion, it was perhaps no surprise, given their parlous state in the autumn of 1994, that they were more than keen to run him for a reported cash injection of $500,000. The hapless Belgian looked out of his depth at Grand Prix level and must have been glad to return to the Belgian Procar series with Audi, where he was an extremely competitive proposition. Though often a race winner, he narrowly failed to land the title in both 1994 and 1995.

He has subsequently found success in a BMW M3, winning a group N race at Magione, Italy, in 1997.

ABECASSIS, George (GB) b 21/3/1913, Chertsey, Surrey – d 18/12/1991, Ibstone, nr High Wycombe, Buckinghamshire

	1951			Championship position: Unplaced				
	Race	Circuit	No	Entrant	Tyres	Car/Engine	Comment	Q Pos/Entries
ret	SWISS GP	Bremgarten	12	HW Motors Ltd	D	2.0 HWM-Alta 4	magneto	20/21
	1952			Championship position: Unplaced				
ret	SWISS GP	Bremgarten	16	HW Motors Ltd	D	2.0 HWM-Alta 4	hub shaft failure-crashed	10/21

GP Starts: 2   GP Wins: 0   Pole positions: 0   Fastest laps: 0   Points: 0

ACHESON, Kenneth (GB) b 27/11/1957, Cookstown, Co Tyrone, Northern Ireland

	1983			Championship position: Unplaced				
	Race	Circuit	No	Entrant	Tyres	Car/Engine	Comment	Q Pos/Entries
dnq	BRITISH GP	Silverstone	17	RAM Automotive Team March	P	3.0 March-RAM 01-Cosworth V8		29/29
dnq	GERMAN GP	Hockenheim	17	RAM Automotive Team March	P	3.0 March-RAM 01-Cosworth V8		27/29
dnq	AUSTRIAN GP	Österreichring	17	RAM Automotive Team March	P	3.0 March-RAM 01-Cosworth V8		29/29
dnq	DUTCH GP	Zandvoort	17	RAM Automotive Team March	P	3.0 March-RAM 01-Cosworth V8		29/29
dnq	ITALIAN GP	Monza	17	RAM Automotive Team March	P	3.0 March-RAM 01-Cosworth V8		29/29
dnq	EUROPEAN GP	Brands Hatch	17	RAM Automotive Team March	P	3.0 March-RAM 01-Cosworth V8		27/29
12	SOUTH AFRICAN GP	Kyalami	17	RAM Automotive Team March	P	3.0 March-RAM 01-Cosworth V8	6 laps behind	24/26
	1985			Championship position: Unplaced				
ret	AUSTRIAN GP	Österreichring	10	Skoal Bandit Formula 1 Team	P	1.5 t/c RAM 03-Hart 4	engine	23/27
dnq	DUTCH GP	Zandvoort	10	Skoal Bandit Formula 1 Team	P	1.5 t/c RAM 03-Hart 4		27/27
ret	ITALIAN GP	Monza	10	Skoal Bandit Formula 1 Team	P	1.5 t/c RAM 03-Hart 4	clutch	24/26

GP Starts: 3   GP Wins: 0   Pole positions: 0   Fastest laps: 0   Points: 0

ADAMS, Philippe (B) b 19/11/1969, Mouscron

	1994			Championship position: Unplaced					
	Race	*Circuit*	*No*	*Entrant*	*Tyres*	*Car/Engine*		*Comment*	*Q Pos/Entries*
ret	BELGIAN GP	Spa	11	Team Lotus	G	3.5 Lotus 109-Mugen Honda V10		*spun off*	26/28
16	PORTUGUESE GP	Estoril	11	Team Lotus	G	3.5 Lotus 109-Mugen Honda V10		*4 laps behind*	25/28

GP Starts: 2   GP Wins: 0   Pole positions: 0   Fastest laps: 0   Points: 0

ADOLFF, Kurt (D) b 5/11/1921, Stuttgart

	1953			Championship position: Unplaced					
	Race	*Circuit*	*No*	*Entrant*	*Tyres*	*Car/Engine*		*Comment*	*Q Pos/Entries*
ret	GERMAN GP	Nürburgring	34	Ecurie Espadon	P	2.0 Ferrari 166 V12			27/35

GP Starts: 1   GP Wins: 0   Pole positions: 0   Fastest laps: 0   Points: 0

AHRENS Jnr, Kurt (D) b 19/4/1940, Braunschweig, nr Hanover

	1966			Championship position: Unplaced					
	Race	*Circuit*	*No*	*Entrant*	*Tyres*	*Car/Engine*		*Comment*	*Q Pos/Entries*
ret	GERMAN GP (F2)	Nürburgring	25	Caltex Racing Team	D	1.0 Brabham BT18-Cosworth 4 F2		*gearbox*	22/30
	1967			Championship position: Unplaced					
ret	GERMAN GP (F2)	Nürburgring	26	Ron Harris Racing Team	D	1.6 Protos-Cosworth 4 F2		*split radiator*	=21/25
	1968			Championship position: Unplaced					
12	GERMAN GP	Nürburgring	17	Caltex Racing Team	D	3.0 Brabham BT24-Repco V8		*3rd works car/1 lap behind*	17/20
	1969			Championship position: Unplaced					
7*	GERMAN GP (F2)	Nürburgring	20	Ahrens Racing Team	D	1.6 Brabham BT30-Cosworth 4 F2		** 3rd in F2 class/1 lap behind*	19/25

GP Starts: 4   GP Wins: 0   Pole positions: 0   Fastest laps: 0   Points: 0

KURT ADOLFF

Adolff had enjoyed competition on home soil driving Mercedes 170 saloons along with Fritz Riess and Karl Kling. But his performances with the 2-litre Veritas RS sports between 1950 and 1952 brought him to the fore, his results including two third places at the Nürburgring.

In 1953 Kurt joined Ecurie Espadon, handling Swiss driver Rudi Fischer's Ferrari. After bringing it into a distant fourth place in the Eifelrennen, he retired the same car in that year's Grand Prix.

Adolff subsequently competed in hill-climbs with a Jaguar.

KURT AHRENS Jnr

Perhaps Germany's most promising young driver of the early sixties, Ahrens Jnr began racing in 1958, aged 18, driving an F3 Cooper. He was soon beating his father (a former 250 cc German speedway champion and accomplished national car racer), notching up a dozen wins by the end of 1959. After a rather barren 1960 season with a Formula Junior Cooper, Kurt made amends the following year, defeating Gerhard Mitter to win the German Formula Junior championship, a feat which he repeated in 1963 after returning from a six-month suspension imposed by the ONS for disputing the official result of a race the previous year.

The acquisition of a Brabham in 1965 provided him with the opportunity to race in both F3 and F2 but his outings in the latter category were restricted by his commitments at his father's garage and scrap metal business. Nevertheless he also found time to race the works Fiat-Abarth on occasion with success.

Backed by Caltex (who sponsored his only F1 ride in the German GP of that year), he enjoyed a full Formula 2 season in 1968, finishing second in the Eifelrennen and third at both Jarama and Hockenheim, relishing the chance to compete with Grand Prix stars such as Rindt and Stewart.

Having previously stated his dislike of long-distance racing, it is perhaps surprising that Ahrens chose to opt for this category in 1969, winning the Austrian GP with Jo Siffert in David Piper's Porsche 917. Racing a works Porsche, he proved a reliable partner for Vic Elford, the pair winning the Nürburgring 1000 Km in 1970, Kurt's final racing season before retirement.

MICHELE ALBORETO

A smooth and stylish driver without some of the more histrionic traits of his fellow countrymen, Alboreto's rise to the top was swift. Backed by Paolo Pavanello, he was runner-up in the 1979 Italian F3 championship and became the 1980 European F3 champion after a season-long battle with Thierry Boutsen. This led to a drive for the Minardi F2 team in 1981, which yielded an end-of-season win at Misano. With the financial backing of Count Zanon Michele had already leap-frogged this career stepping-stone by gaining a place in the Tyrrell team after an impressive Grand Prix debut at Imola which saw the curly-haired Italian smartly placed under a three-year contract.

The next two seasons were illuminated by wins at Las Vegas and Detroit but the naturally aspirated Tyrrells were increasingly uncompetitive against the turbo onslaught and it was no great surprise when Alboreto took up the offer of a Ferrari drive for 1984. After a promising start and a victory at Zolder in the Belgian GP, the season disintegrated amid a plague of engine failures, but a strong finish to the year boded well for 1985, which was to be the highwater mark of his career. For much of the season he held off the challenge of Alain Prost's McLaren, but the team lost momentum and Michele saw his title chance blighted by mechanical failure. Although three more years were spent at Maranello, somehow things were never the same. The arrival of Gerhard Berger in 1987 pushed the Italian to the margins and he opted out of the political turmoil that was Ferrari to return to Tyrrell for 1989.

It was to be a brief reunion, with a splendid third in Mexico in the new Tyrrell 018 the highlight, before Michele split with the team after a sponsorship clash. Thereafter his career began a swift decline in a succession of uncompetitive cars which included the disastrously overweight Porsche-engined Footwork. An Indian summer in 1992 with some revitalised performances in the Footwork-Mugen restored his credibility, but the nadir of his Formula 1 career came with a move to the Lola Scuderia Italia team. The wretched Lola-Ferrari could well have brought Alboreto's tenure in Grand Prix racing to an end, but he found himself a berth with the restructured Minardi team in 1994. A single point at Monaco was garnered from a year which saw the team struggling to meet the technical changes demanded in the wake of the Senna tragedy. Increasingly disenchanted with his lot, especially after a fine levied in the wake of the German Grand Prix first-lap crash, Alboreto finally bowed out of F1 at season's end.

With the enticing prospect of racing the Schübel-entered Alfa Romeo T155 in the high-profile DTM and ITC championships for 1995, Michele was looking forward to some competitive racing at last. Sadly, he rarely figured among the leading runners, finishing an anonymous year with just 22nd place in the DTM to show for his efforts.

Meanwhile selective appearances with the Dick Simon Scandia Ferrari 333SP sports car, which included a second place at Sebring in 1996, paved the way for Alboreto to race in the newly formed IRL single-seater oval series. Michele was one of a handful of 'name' drivers contesting the 1996 championship, and he scored three top-six finishes in his five starts, though a chance of victory in the Indianapolis 500 ended with a gearbox failure. When sponsor Agip withdrew their support at the start of the 1997 season, Alboreto was left without a regular drive, but his luck was about to turn at last. Rejoining Joest Racing for a second outing in their Porsche WSC95 prototype, Michele claimed an unexpected victory in the Le Mans 24-hour race partnered by Stefan Johansson and Tom Kristensen. Subsequently, he took a Joest Porsche LM1 to second place at Road Atlanta in 1998, and was part of Joest's squad handling the 1999 Audi R8R challenger. His two races yielded a third place in the Sebring 12 Hours (with Johansson and Capello) and a fourth place at Le Mans (with Aïello and Capello).

ALBORETO, Michele (I) b 23/12/1956, Milan

1981 — Championship position: Unplaced

	Race	Circuit	No	Entrant	Tyres	Car/Engine	Comment	Q Pos/Entries
ret	SAN MARINO GP	Imola	4	Team Tyrrell	M	3.0 Tyrrell 010-Cosworth V8	collision with Gabbiani	17/30
12	BELGIAN GP	Zolder	4	Team Tyrrell	M	3.0 Tyrrell 010-Cosworth V8	2 laps behind	19/31
ret	MONACO GP	Monte Carlo	4	Team Tyrrell	M	3.0 Tyrrell 010-Cosworth V8	spun-collision with Giacomelli	20/31
dnq	SPANISH GP	Jarama	4	Team Tyrrell	M	3.0 Tyrrell 010-Cosworth V8		25/30
16	FRENCH GP	Dijon	4	Team Tyrrell	M	3.0 Tyrrell 010-Cosworth V8	3 laps behind	23/29
ret	BRITISH GP	Silverstone	4	Team Tyrrell	M	3.0 Tyrrell 010-Cosworth V8	clutch	19/30
dnq	GERMAN GP	Hockenheim	4	Team Tyrrell	A	3.0 Tyrrell 010-Cosworth V8		29/30
ret	AUSTRIAN GP	Österreichring	4	Team Tyrrell	A	3.0 Tyrrell 010-Cosworth V8	engine	22/30
9/ret	DUTCH GP	Zandvoort	4	Team Tyrrell	A	3.0 Tyrrell 011-Cosworth V8	reserve starter/engine/-4 laps	25/30
ret	ITALIAN GP	Monza	4	Team Tyrrell	A	3.0 Tyrrell 011-Cosworth V8	hit Watson's wreckage	22/30
11	CANADIAN GP	Montreal	4	Team Tyrrell	A	3.0 Tyrrell 011-Cosworth V8	4 laps behind	22/30
13/ret	CAESARS PALACE GP	Las Vegas	4	Team Tyrrell	A	3.0 Tyrrell 011-Cosworth V8	electrical problems/-8 laps	17/30

1982 — Championship position: 7th= Wins: 1 Pole positions: 0 Fastest laps: 1 Points scored: 25

	Race	Circuit	No	Entrant	Tyres	Car/Engine	Comment	Q Pos/Entries
7	SOUTH AFRICAN GP	Kyalami	3	Team Tyrrell	G	3.0 Tyrrell 011-Cosworth V8	1 lap behind	10/30
4*	BRAZILIAN GP	Rio	3	Team Tyrrell	G	3.0 Tyrrell 011-Cosworth V8	*1st & 2nd place cars dsq	13/31
4*	US GP WEST	Long Beach	3	Team Tyrrell	G	3.0 Tyrrell 011-Cosworth V8	*3rd place car disqualified	12/31
3	SAN MARINO GP	Imola	3	Team Tyrrell	G	3.0 Tyrrell 011-Cosworth V8		5/14
ret	BELGIAN GP	Zolder	3	Team Tyrrell	G	3.0 Tyrrell 011-Cosworth V8	engine	5/32
10/ret	MONACO GP	Monte Carlo	3	Team Tyrrell	G	3.0 Tyrrell 011-Cosworth V8	suspension/6 laps behind	9/31
ret	US GP (DETROIT)	Detroit	3	Team Tyrrell	G	3.0 Tyrrell 011-Cosworth V8	accident at chicane	16/28
ret	CANADIAN GP	Montreal	3	Team Tyrrell	G	3.0 Tyrrell 011-Cosworth V8	gearbox and fuel starvation	15/29
7	DUTCH GP	Zandvoort	3	Team Tyrrell	G	3.0 Tyrrell 011-Cosworth V8	1 lap behind	14/31
nc	BRITISH GP	Brands Hatch	3	Team Tyrrell	G	3.0 Tyrrell 011-Cosworth V8	handling problems/-32 laps	9/31
6	FRENCH GP	Paul Ricard	3	Team Tyrrell	G	3.0 Tyrrell 011-Cosworth V8		15/30
4	GERMAN GP	Hockenheim	3	Team Tyrrell	G	3.0 Tyrrell 011-Cosworth V8	1 lap behind	7/30
ret	AUSTRIAN GP	Österreichring	3	Team Tyrrell	G	3.0 Tyrrell 011-Cosworth V8	spun off	8/29
7	SWISS GP	Dijon	3	Team Tyrrell	G	3.0 Tyrrell 011-Cosworth V8	1 lap behind	12/29
5	ITALIAN GP	Monza	3	Team Tyrrell	G	3.0 Tyrrell 011-Cosworth V8	1 lap behind	11/30
1	CAESARS PALACE GP	Las Vegas	3	Team Tyrrell	G	3.0 Tyrrell 011-Cosworth V8	FL	3/30

1983 — Championship position: 12th= Wins: 1 Pole positions: 0 Fastest laps: 0 Points scored: 10

	Race	Circuit	No	Entrant	Tyres	Car/Engine	Comment	Q Pos/Entries
ret	BRAZILIAN GP	Rio	3	Benetton Tyrrell Team	G	3.0 Tyrrell 011-Cosworth V8	incident with Baldi-oil cooler	11/27
9	US GP WEST	Long Beach	3	Benetton Tyrrell Team	G	3.0 Tyrrell 011-Cosworth V8	collision with Jarier/-2 laps	7/28
8	FRENCH GP	Paul Ricard	3	Benetton Tyrrell Team	G	3.0 Tyrrell 011-Cosworth V8	1 lap behind	15/29
ret	SAN MARINO GP	Imola	3	Benetton Tyrrell Team	G	3.0 Tyrrell 011-Cosworth V8	accident-collapsed suspension	13/28
ret	MONACO GP	Monte Carlo	3	Benetton Tyrrell Team	G	3.0 Tyrrell 011-Cosworth V8	collision with Mansell	11/28
14	BELGIAN GP	Spa	3	Benetton Tyrrell Team	G	3.0 Tyrrell 011-Cosworth V8	pit stop-gearbox/-2 laps	17/28
1	US GP (DETROIT)	Detroit	3	Benetton Tyrrell Team	G	3.0 Tyrrell 011-Cosworth V8		6/27
8	CANADIAN GP	Montreal	3	Benetton Tyrrell Team	G	3.0 Tyrrell 011-Cosworth V8	2 laps behind	17/28
13	BRITISH GP	Silverstone	3	Benetton Tyrrell Team	G	3.0 Tyrrell 011-Cosworth V8	2 laps behind	16/29
ret	GERMAN GP	Hockenheim	3	Benetton Tyrrell Team	G	3.0 Tyrrell 011-Cosworth V8	fuel pump drive	16/29
ret	AUSTRIAN GP	Österreichring	3	Benetton Tyrrell Team	G	3.0 Tyrrell 012-Cosworth V8	hit Johansson-spun off	–/–
dns	"	"	3	Benetton Tyrrell Team	G	3.0 Tyrrell 011-Cosworth V8	qualified in this car	18/29
6	DUTCH GP	Zandvoort	3	Benetton Tyrrell Team	G	3.0 Tyrrell 012-Cosworth V8	pit stop-fuel/1 lap behind	18/29
ret	ITALIAN GP	Monza	3	Benetton Tyrrell Team	G	3.0 Tyrrell 012-Cosworth V8	clutch	24/29
ret	EUROPEAN GP	Brands Hatch	3	Benetton Tyrrell Team	G	3.0 Tyrrell 012-Cosworth V8	engine	26/29
ret	SOUTH AFRICAN GP	Kyalami	3	Benetton Tyrrell Team	G	3.0 Tyrrell 012-Cosworth V8	engine	18/26

1984 — Championship position: 4th Wins: 1 Pole positions: 1 Fastest laps: 1 Points scored: 30.5

	Race	Circuit	No	Entrant	Tyres	Car/Engine	Comment	Q Pos/Entries
ret	BRAZILIAN GP	Rio	27	Scuderia Ferrari SpA SEFAC	G	1.5 t/c Ferrari 126C4 V6	brake caliper	2/27
11*/ret	SOUTH AFRICAN GP	Kyalami	27	Scuderia Ferrari SpA SEFAC	G	1.5 t/c Ferrari 126C4 V6	ignition/*11th place car dsq	10/27
1	BELGIAN GP	Zolder	27	Scuderia Ferrari SpA SEFAC	G	1.5 t/c Ferrari 126C4 V6		1/27
ret	SAN MARINO GP	Imola	27	Scuderia Ferrari SpA SEFAC	G	1.5 t/c Ferrari 126C4 V6	exhaust	13/28
ret	FRENCH GP	Dijon	27	Scuderia Ferrari SpA SEFAC	G	1.5 t/c Ferrari 126C4 V6	engine	10/27
6*	MONACO GP	Monte Carlo	27	Scuderia Ferrari SpA SEFAC	G	1.5 t/c Ferrari 126C4 V6	*3rd car dsq/half points/-1 lap	4/27
ret	CANADIAN GP	Montreal	27	Scuderia Ferrari SpA SEFAC	G	1.5 t/c Ferrari 126C4 V6	engine	6/26
ret	US GP (DETROIT)	Detroit	27	Scuderia Ferrari SpA SEFAC	G	1.5 t/c Ferrari 126C4 V6	engine	4/27
ret	US GP (DALLAS)	Dallas	27	Scuderia Ferrari SpA SEFAC	G	1.5 t/c Ferrari 126C4 V6	hit wall	9/27
5	BRITISH GP	Brands Hatch	27	Scuderia Ferrari SpA SEFAC	G	1.5 t/c Ferrari 126C4 V6	1 lap behind	9/27
ret	GERMAN GP	Hockenheim	27	Scuderia Ferrari SpA SEFAC	G	1.5 t/c Ferrari 126C4 V6	misfire	6/27
3	AUSTRIAN GP	Österreichring	27	Scuderia Ferrari SpA SEFAC	G	1.5 t/c Ferrari 126C4 V6		12/28
ret	DUTCH GP	Zandvoort	27	Scuderia Ferrari SpA SEFAC	G	1.5 t/c Ferrari 126C4 V6	engine	9/27
2	ITALIAN GP	Monza	27	Scuderia Ferrari SpA SEFAC	G	1.5 t/c Ferrari 126C4 V6		11/27
2	EUROPEAN GP	Nürburgring	27	Scuderia Ferrari SpA SEFAC	G	1.5 t/c Ferrari 126C4 V6	FL (shared with Piquet)	5/26
4	PORTUGUESE GP	Estoril	27	Scuderia Ferrari SpA SEFAC	G	1.5 t/c Ferrari 126C4 V6		8/27

1985 — Championship position: 2nd Wins: 2 Pole positions: 1 Fastest laps: 2 Points scored: 53

	Race	Circuit	No	Entrant	Tyres	Car/Engine	Comment	Q Pos/Entries
2	BRAZILIAN GP	Rio	27	Scuderia Ferrari SpA SEFAC	G	1.5 t/c Ferrari 156/85 V6		1/25
2	PORTUGUESE GP	Estoril	27	Scuderia Ferrari SpA SEFAC	G	1.5 t/c Ferrari 156/85 V6		5/26
ret	SAN MARINO GP	Imola	27	Scuderia Ferrari SpA SEFAC	G	1.5 t/c Ferrari 156/85 V6	electrics/FL	4/26
2	MONACO GP	Monte Carlo	27	Scuderia Ferrari SpA SEFAC	G	1.5 t/c Ferrari 156/85 V6	FL	3/26
1	CANADIAN GP	Montreal	27	Scuderia Ferrari SpA SEFAC	G	1.5 t/c Ferrari 156/85 V6		3/25
3	US GP (DETROIT)	Detroit	27	Scuderia Ferrari SpA SEFAC	G	1.5 t/c Ferrari 156/85 V6		3/25
ret	FRENCH GP	Paul Ricard	27	Scuderia Ferrari SpA SEFAC	G	1.5 t/c Ferrari 156/85 V6	turbo	3/26
2	BRITISH GP	Silverstone	27	Scuderia Ferrari SpA SEFAC	G	1.5 t/c Ferrari 156/85 V6	1 lap behind	6/26
1	GERMAN GP	Nürburgring	27	Scuderia Ferrari Spa SEFAC	G	1.5 t/c Ferrari 156/85 V6		8/27
3	AUSTRIAN GP	Österreichring	27	Scuderia Ferrari Spa SEFAC	G	1.5 t/c Ferrari 156/85 V6		9/27
4	DUTCH GP	Zandvoort	27	Scuderia Ferrari SpA SEFAC	G	1.5 t/c Ferrari 156/85 V6		16/27
13/ret	ITALIAN GP	Monza	27	Scuderia Ferrari SpA SEFAC	G	1.5 t/c Ferrari 156/85 V6	engine	7/26

ret	BELGIAN GP	Spa	27	Scuderia Ferrari SpA SEFAC	G	1.5 t/c Ferrari 156/85 V6	clutch	4/24
ret	EUROPEAN GP	Brands Hatch	27	Scuderia Ferrari SpA SEFAC	G	1.5 t/c Ferrari 156/85 V6	turbo	15/27
ret	SOUTH AFRICAN GP	Kyalami	27	Scuderia Ferrari SpA SEFAC	G	1.5 t/c Ferrari 156/85 V6	turbo	15/21
ret	AUSTRALIAN GP	Adelaide	27	Scuderia Ferrari SpA SEFAC	G	1.5 t/c Ferrari 156/85 V6	gear linkage	5/25

1986 Championship position: 8th= Wins: 0 Pole positions: 0 Fastest laps: 0 Points scored: 14

ret	BRAZILIAN GP	Rio	27	Scuderia Ferrari SpA SEFAC	G	1.5 t/c Ferrari F1/86 V6	fuel pump	– / –
dns	"	"	27	Scuderia Ferrari SpA SEFAC	G	1.5 t/c Ferrari 156/85 V6	set grid time in this car	6/25
ret	SPANISH GP	Jerez	27	Scuderia Ferrari SpA SEFAC	G	1.5 t/c Ferrari F1/86 V6	wheel bearing	13/25
10/ret	SAN MARINO GP	Imola	27	Scuderia Ferrari SpA SEFAC	G	1.5 t/c Ferrari F1/86 V6	turbo/4 laps behind	5/26
ret	MONACO GP	Monte Carlo	27	Scuderia Ferrari SpA SEFAC	G	1.5 t/c Ferrari F1/86 V6	turbo	4/26
4	BELGIAN GP	Spa	27	Scuderia Ferrari SpA SEFAC	G	1.5 t/c Ferrari F1/86 V6		9/25
8	CANADIAN GP	Montreal	27	Scuderia Ferrari SpA SEFAC	G	1.5 t/c Ferrari F1/86 V6	spin-Johansson/1 lap behind	11/25
4	US GP (DETROIT)	Detroit	27	Scuderia Ferrari SpA SEFAC	G	1.5 t/c Ferrari F1/86 V6		11/26
8	FRENCH GP	Paul Ricard	27	Scuderia Ferrari SpA SEFAC	G	1.5 t/c Ferrari F1/86 V6	stalled on startline/-2 laps	6/26
ret	BRITISH GP	Brands Hatch	27	Scuderia Ferrari SpA SEFAC	G	1.5 t/c Ferrari F1/86 V6	turbo	12/26
ret	GERMAN GP	Hockenheim	27	Scuderia Ferrari SpA SEFAC	G	1.5 t/c Ferrari F1/86 V6	transmission	10/26
ret	HUNGARIAN GP	Hungaroring	27	Scuderia Ferrari SpA SEFAC	G	1.5 t/c Ferrari F1/86 V6	hit Warwick	15/26
2	AUSTRIAN GP	Österreichring	27	Scuderia Ferrari SpA SEFAC	G	1.5 t/c Ferrari F1/86 V6	1 lap behind	9/26
ret	ITALIAN GP	Monza	27	Scuderia Ferrari SpA SEFAC	G	1.5 t/c Ferrari F1/86 V6	engine	9/27
5	PORTUGUESE GP	Estoril	27	Scuderia Ferrari SpA SEFAC	G	1.5 t/c Ferrari F1/86 V6	1 lap behind	13/27
ret	MEXICAN GP	Mexico City	27	Scuderia Ferrari SpA SEFAC	G	1.5 t/c Ferrari F1/86 V6	turbo	12/26
ret	AUSTRALIAN GP	Adelaide	27	Scuderia Ferrari SpA SEFAC	G	1.5 t/c Ferrari F1/86 V6	hit from behind on grid	9/26

1987 Championship position: 7th Wins: 0 Pole positions: 0 Fastest laps: 0 Points scored: 17

8/ret	BRAZILIAN GP	Rio	27	Scuderia Ferrari SpA SEFAC	G	1.5 t/c Ferrari F1/87 V6	spun off/3 laps behind	9/23
3	SAN MARINO GP	Imola	27	Scuderia Ferrari SpA SEFAC	G	1.5 t/c Ferrari F1/87 V6		7/27
ret	BELGIAN GP	Spa	27	Scuderia Ferrari SpA SEFAC	G	1.5 t/c Ferrari F1/87 V6	transmission	5/26
3	MONACO GP	Monte Carlo	27	Scuderia Ferrari SpA SEFAC	G	1.5 t/c Ferrari F1/87 V6		5/26
ret	US GP (DETROIT)	Detroit	27	Scuderia Ferrari SpA SEFAC	G	1.5 t/c Ferrari F1/87 V6	gearbox	7/26
ret	FRENCH GP	Paul Ricard	27	Scuderia Ferrari SpA SEFAC	G	1.5 t/c Ferrari F1/87 V6	engine	8/26
ret	BRITISH GP	Silverstone	27	Scuderia Ferrari SpA SEFAC	G	1.5 t/c Ferrari F1/87 V6	rear suspension	7/26
ret	GERMAN GP	Hockenheim	27	Scuderia Ferrari SpA SEFAC	G	1.5 t/c Ferrari F1/87 V6	turbo	5/26
ret	HUNGARIAN GP	Hungaroring	27	Scuderia Ferrari SpA SEFAC	G	1.5 t/c Ferrari F1/87 V6	engine	5/26
ret	AUSTRIAN GP	Österreichring	27	Scuderia Ferrari SpA SEFAC	G	1.5 t/c Ferrari F1/87 V6	started from pits/turbo/exhaust	6/26
ret	ITALIAN GP	Monza	27	Scuderia Ferrari SpA SEFAC	G	1.5 t/c Ferrari F1/87 V6	turbo	8/28
ret	PORTUGUESE GP	Estoril	27	Scuderia Ferrari SpA SEFAC	G	1.5 t/c Ferrari F1/87 V6	gearbox	4/27
15/ret	SPANISH GP	Jerez	27	Scuderia Ferrari SpA SEFAC	G	1.5 t/c Ferrari F1/87 V6	engine/5 laps behind	4/28
ret	MEXICAN GP	Mexico City	27	Scuderia Ferrari SpA SEFAC	G	1.5 t/c Ferrari F1/87 V6	engine	9/27
4	JAPANESE GP	Suzuka	27	Scuderia Ferrari SpA SEFAC	G	1.5 t/c Ferrari F1/87 V6		4/27
2*	AUSTRALIAN GP	Adelaide	27	Scuderia Ferrari SpA SEFAC	G	1.5 t/c Ferrari F1/87 V6	* 2nd place car disqualified	6/27

1988 Championship position: 5th Wins: 0 Pole positions: 0 Fastest laps: 1 Points scored: 24

5	BRAZILIAN GP	Rio	27	Scuderia Ferrari SpA SEFAC	G	1.5 t/c Ferrari F1/87/88C V6		6/31
18/ret	SAN MARINO GP	Imola	27	Scuderia Ferrari SpA SEFAC	G	1.5 t/c Ferrari F1/87/88C V6	started from back /engine/-6 laps	10/31
3	MONACO GP	Monte Carlo	27	Scuderia Ferrari SpA SEFAC	G	1.5 t/c Ferrari F1/87/88C V6		4/30
4	MEXICAN GP	Mexico City	27	Scuderia Ferrari SpA SEFAC	G	1.5 t/c Ferrari F1/87/88C V6	1 lap behind	5/30
ret	CANADIAN GP	Montreal	27	Scuderia Ferrari SpA SEFAC	G	1.5 t/c Ferrari F1/87/88C V6	engine	4/31
ret	US GP (DETROIT)	Detroit	27	Scuderia Ferrari SpA SEFAC	G	1.5 t/c Ferrari F1/87/88C V6	accident	3/31
3	FRENCH GP	Paul Ricard	27	Scuderia Ferrari SpA SEFAC	G	1.5 t/c Ferrari F1/87/88C V6		4/31
17/ret	BRITISH GP	Silverstone	27	Scuderia Ferrari SpA SEFAC	G	1.5 t/c Ferrari F1/87/88C V6	out of fuel/3 laps behind	2/31
4	GERMAN GP	Hockenheim	27	Scuderia Ferrari SpA SEFAC	G	1.5 t/c Ferrari F1/87/88C V6		4/31
ret	HUNGARIAN GP	Hungaroring	27	Scuderia Ferrari SpA SEFAC	G	1.5 t/c Ferrari F1/87/88C V6	engine cut out	15/31
ret	BELGIAN GP	Spa	27	Scuderia Ferrari SpA SEFAC	G	1.5 t/c Ferrari F1/87/88C V6	engine	4/31
2	ITALIAN GP	Monza	27	Scuderia Ferrari SpA SEFAC	G	1.5 t/c Ferrari F1/87/88C V6	FL	4/31
5	PORTUGUESE GP	Estoril	27	Scuderia Ferrari SpA SEFAC	G	1.5 t/c Ferrari F1/87/88C V6		7/31
ret	SPANISH GP	Jerez	27	Scuderia Ferrari SpA SEFAC	G	1.5 t/c Ferrari F1/87/88C V6	engine	10/31
11	JAPANESE GP	Suzuka	27	Scuderia Ferrari SpA SEFAC	G	1.5 t/c Ferrari F1/87/88C V6	collision with Nannini/-1 lap	9/31
ret	AUSTRALIAN GP	Adelaide	27	Scuderia Ferrari SpA SEFAC	G	1.5 t/c Ferrari F1/87/88C V6	collision with Caffi on lap 1	12/31

1989 Championship position: 11th= Wins: 0 Pole positions: 0 Fastest laps: 0 Points scored: 6

10	BRAZILIAN GP	Rio	4	Tyrrell Racing Organisation	G	3.5 Tyrrell 017B-Cosworth V8	2 pit stops-gearbox/-2 laps	20/38
dnq	SAN MARINO GP	Imola	4	Tyrrell Racing Organisation	G	3.5 Tyrrell 018-Cosworth V8		27/39
dnq	"	"	4	Tyrrell Racing Organisation	G	3.5 Tyrrell 017B-Cosworth V8		– / –
5	MONACO GP	Monte Carlo	4	Tyrrell Racing Organisation	G	3.5 Tyrrell 018-Cosworth V8	2 laps behind	12/38
dns	"	"	4	Tyrrell Racing Organisation	G	3.5 Tyrrell 017B-Cosworth V8	practice only	– / –
3	MEXICAN GP	Mexico City	4	Tyrrell Racing Organisation	G	3.5 Tyrrell 018-Cosworth V8		7/39
ret	US GP (PHOENIX)	Phoenix	4	Tyrrell Racing Organisation	G	3.5 Tyrrell 018-Cosworth V8	gearbox	9/39
ret	CANADIAN GP	Montreal	4	Tyrrell Racing Organisation	G	3.5 Tyrrell 018-Cosworth V8	electrics	20/39
ret	GERMAN GP	Hockenheim	29	Equipe Larrousse	G	3.5 Lola LC89-Lamborghini V12	electrics	26/39
ret	HUNGARIAN GP	Hungaroring	29	Equipe Larrousse	G	3.5 Lola LC89-Lamborghini V12	engine	26/39
ret	BELGIAN GP	Spa	29	Equipe Larrousse	G	3.5 Lola LC89-Lamborghini V12	collision with Patrese	22/39
ret	ITALIAN GP	Monza	29	Equipe Larrousse	G	3.5 Lola LC89-Lamborghini V12	engine	13/39
11	PORTUGUESE GP	Estoril	29	Equipe Larrousse	G	3.5 Lola LC89-Lamborghini V12	pit stop-tyres/2 laps behind	21/39
dnpq	SPANISH GP	Jerez	29	Equipe Larrousse	G	3.5 Lola LC89-Lamborghini V12		33/38
dnq	JAPANESE GP	Suzuka	29	Equipe Larrousse	G	3.5 Lola LC89-Lamborghini V12		28/39
dnpq	AUSTRALIAN GP	Adelaide	29	Equipe Larrousse	G	3.5 Lola LC89-Lamborghini V12		32/39

1990 Championship position: Unplaced

10	US GP (PHOENIX)	Phoenix	9	Footwork Arrows Racing	G	3.5 Arrows A11B-Cosworth V8	2 laps behind	21/35
ret	BRAZILIAN GP	Interlagos	9	Footwork Arrows Racing	G	3.5 Arrows A11B-Cosworth V8	handling-suspension	23/35
dns	"	"	9	Footwork Arrows Racing	G	3.5 Arrows A11-Cosworth V8	practice only	– / –
dnq	SAN MARINO GP	Imola	9	Footwork Arrows Racing	G	3.5 Arrows A11B-Cosworth V8		29/34
dnq	MONACO GP	Monte Carlo	9	Footwork Arrows Racing	G	3.5 Arrows A11B-Cosworth V8		27/34

ret	CANADIAN GP	Montreal	9	Footwork Arrows Racing	G	3.5 Arrows A11B-Cosworth V8	collision with Pirro	14/35
17	MEXICAN GP	Mexico City	9	Footwork Arrows Racing	G	3.5 Arrows A11B-Cosworth V8	power loss/3 laps behind	17/35
10	FRENCH GP	Paul Ricard	9	Footwork Arrows Racing	G	3.5 Arrows A11B-Cosworth V8	1 lap behind	18/35
ret	BRITISH GP	Silverstone	9	Footwork Arrows Racing	G	3.5 Arrows A11B-Cosworth V8	electrics	25/35
ret	GERMAN GP	Hockenheim	9	Footwork Arrows Racing	G	3.5 Arrows A11B-Cosworth V8	engine	19/35
12	HUNGARIAN GP	Hungaroring	9	Footwork Arrows Racing	G	3.5 Arrows A11B-Cosworth V8	pit stop-tyres/2 laps behind	22/35
13	BELGIAN GP	Spa	9	Footwork Arrows Racing	G	3.5 Arrows A11B-Cosworth V8	engine lost power/-1 lap	26/33
12/ret	ITALIAN GP	Monza	9	Footwork Arrows Racing	G	3.5 Arrows A11B-Cosworth V8	spun off/3 laps behind	22/33
9	PORTUGUESE GP	Estoril	9	Footwork Arrows Racing	G	3.5 Arrows A11B-Cosworth V8	1 lap behind	19/33
10	SPANISH GP	Jerez	9	Footwork Arrows Racing	G	3.5 Arrows A11B-Cosworth V8	2 laps behind	26/33
ret	JAPANESE GP	Suzuka	9	Footwork Arrows Racing	G	3.5 Arrows A11B-Cosworth V8	engine	25/30
dnq	AUSTRALIAN GP	Adelaide	9	Footwork Arrows Racing	G	3.5 Arrows A11B-Cosworth V8		27/30

1991 Championship position: Unplaced

ret	US GP (PHOENIX)	Phoenix	9	Footwork Grand Prix International	G	3.5 Footwork A11C-Porsche V12	gearbox	25/34
dnq	BRAZILIAN GP	Interlagos	9	Footwork Grand Prix International	G	3.5 Footwork A11C-Porsche V12		29/34
dnq	SAN MARINO GP	Imola	9	Footwork Grand Prix International	G	3.5 Footwork A11C-Porsche V12		30/34
ret	MONACO GP	Monte Carlo	9	Footwork Grand Prix International	G	3.5 Footwork FA12-Porsche V12	engine	25/34
ret	CANADIAN GP	Montreal	9	Footwork Grand Prix International	G	3.5 Footwork FA12-Porsche V12	engine	21/34
ret	MEXICAN GP	Mexico City	9	Footwork Grand Prix International	G	3.5 Footwork FA12-Porsche V12	started from pitlane/oil pressure	26/34
ret	FRENCH GP	Magny Cours	9	Footwork Grand Prix International	G	3.5 Footwork FA12-Cosworth V8	gearbox/transmission	25/34
ret	BRITISH GP	Silverstone	9	Footwork Grand Prix International	G	3.5 Footwork FA12-Cosworth V8	gearbox	26/34
dnq	GERMAN GP	Hockenheim	9	Footwork Grand Prix International	G	3.5 Footwork FA12-Cosworth V8		27/34
dnq	HUNGARIAN GP	Hungaroring	9	Footwork Grand Prix International	G	3.5 Footwork FA12-Cosworth V8		28/34
dnpq	BELGIAN GP	Spa	9	Footwork Grand Prix International	G	3.5 Footwork FA12-Cosworth V8		31/34
dnq	ITALIAN GP	Monza	9	Footwork Grand Prix International	G	3.5 Footwork FA12-Cosworth V8		27/34
15	PORTUGUESE GP	Estoril	9	Footwork Grand Prix International	G	3.5 Footwork FA12-Cosworth V8	3 laps behind	24/34
ret	SPANISH GP	Barcelona	9	Footwork Grand Prix International	G	3.5 Footwork FA12-Cosworth V8	engine	24/33
dnq	JAPANESE GP	Suzuka	9	Footwork Grand Prix International	G	3.5 Footwork FA12-Cosworth V8		27/31
13	AUSTRALIAN GP	Adelaide	9	Footwork Grand Prix International	G	3.5 Footwork FA12-Cosworth V8	wet race-stopped after 14 laps	15/32

1992 Championship position: 10th   Wins: 0   Pole positions: 0   Fastest laps: 0   Points scored: 6

10	SOUTH AFRICAN GP	Kyalami	9	Footwork Grand Prix International	G	3.5 Footwork FA13-Mugen Honda V10	gearbox trouble	17/30
13	MEXICAN GP	Mexico City	9	Footwork Grand Prix International	G	3.5 Footwork FA13-Mugen Honda V10	4 laps behind	25/30
6	BRAZILIAN GP	Interlagos	9	Footwork Grand Prix International	G	3.5 Footwork FA13-Mugen Honda V10	1 lap behind	14/31
5	SPANISH GP	Barcelona	9	Footwork Grand Prix International	G	3.5 Footwork FA13-Mugen Honda V10	1 lap behind	16/32
5	SAN MARINO GP	Imola	9	Footwork Grand Prix International	G	3.5 Footwork FA13-Mugen Honda V10	1 lap behind	9/32
7	MONACO GP	Monte Carlo	9	Footwork Grand Prix International	G	3.5 Footwork FA13-Mugen Honda V10	spin/1 lap behind	11/32
7	CANADIAN GP	Montreal	9	Footwork Grand Prix International	G	3.5 Footwork FA13-Mugen Honda V10	1 lap behind	16/32
7*	FRENCH GP	Magny Cours	9	Footwork Grand Prix International	G	3.5 Footwork FA13-Mugen Honda V10	*aggregate of two parts/-1 lap	14/30
7	BRITISH GP	Silverstone	9	Footwork Grand Prix International	G	3.5 Footwork FA13-Mugen Honda V10	1 lap behind	12/32
9	GERMAN GP	Hockenheim	9	Footwork Grand Prix International	G	3.5 Footwork FA13-Mugen Honda V10	1 lap behind	17/32
7	HUNGARIAN GP	Hungaroring	9	Footwork Grand Prix International	G	3.5 Footwork FA13-Mugen Honda V10	spin/2 laps behind	7/31
ret	BELGIAN GP	Spa	9	Footwork Grand Prix International	G	3.5 Footwork FA13-Mugen Honda V10	gearbox	14/30
7	ITALIAN GP	Monza	9	Footwork Grand Prix International	G	3.5 Footwork FA13-Mugen Honda V10	1 lap behind	16/28
6	PORTUGUESE GP	Estoril	9	Footwork Grand Prix International	G	3.5 Footwork FA13-Mugen Honda V10	1 lap behind	8/26
15	JAPANESE GP	Suzuka	9	Footwork Grand Prix International	G	3.5 Footwork FA13-Mugen Honda V10	2 laps behind	24/26
ret	AUSTRALIAN GP	Adelaide	9	Footwork Grand Prix International	G	3.5 Footwork FA13-Mugen Honda V10	accident on lap 1	11/26

1993 Championship position: Unplaced

ret	SOUTH AFRICAN GP	Kyalami	21	BMS Scuderia Italia SpA	G	3.5 LolaT93/30 BMS-Ferrari V12	engine	25/26
11	BRAZILIAN GP	Interlagos	21	BMS Scuderia Italia SpA	G	3.5 LolaT93/30 BMS-Ferrari V12	3 laps behind	25/26
11	EUROPEAN GP	Donington	21	BMS Scuderia Italia SpA	G	3.5 LolaT93/30 BMS-Ferrari V12	6 laps behind	24/26
dnq	SAN MARINO GP	Imola	21	BMS Scuderia Italia SpA	G	3.5 LolaT93/30 BMS-Ferrari V12		26/26
dnq	SPANISH GP	Barcelona	21	BMS Scuderia Italia SpA	G	3.5 LolaT93/30 BMS-Ferrari V12		26/26
ret	MONACO GP	Monte Carlo	21	BMS Scuderia Italia SpA	G	3.5 LolaT93/30 BMS-Ferrari V12	gearbox	24/26
dnq	CANADIAN GP	Montreal	21	BMS Scuderia Italia SpA	G	3.5 LolaT93/30 BMS-Ferrari V12		26/26
dnq	FRENCH GP	Magny Cours	21	BMS Scuderia Italia SpA	G	3.5 LolaT93/30 BMS-Ferrari V12		26/26
dnq	BRITISH GP	Silverstone	21	BMS Scuderia Italia SpA	G	3.5 LolaT93/30 BMS-Ferrari V12		26/26
16	GERMAN GP	Hockenheim	21	BMS Scuderia Italia SpA	G	3.5 LolaT93/30 BMS-Ferrari V12	no clutch/2 laps behind	26/26
ret	HUNGARIAN GP	Hungaroring	21	BMS Scuderia Italia SpA	G	3.5 LolaT93/30 BMS-Ferrari V12	engine overheating	25/26
14	BELGIAN GP	Spa	21	BMS Scuderia Italia SpA	G	3.5 LolaT93/30 BMS-Ferrari V12	car handling 'appalling'/-3 laps	25/25
ret	ITALIAN GP	Monza	21	BMS Scuderia Italia SpA	G	3.5 LolaT93/30 BMS-Ferrari V12	suspension failure	21/26
ret	PORTUGUESE GP	Estoril	21	BMS Scuderia Italia SpA	G	3.5 LolaT93/30 BMS-Ferrari V12	gearbox/accident	25/26

1994 Championship position: 24th   Wins: 0   Pole positions: 0   Fastest laps: 0   Points scored: 1

ret	BRAZILIAN GP	Interlagos	24	Minardi Scuderia Italia	G	3.5 Minardi M193B-Ford HB V8	electrics	22/28
ret	PACIFIC GP	T.I. Circuit	24	Minardi Scuderia Italia	G	3.5 Minardi M193B-Ford HB V8	collision with Wendlinger	15/28
ret	SAN MARINO GP	Imola	24	Minardi Scuderia Italia	G	3.5 Minardi M193B-Ford HB V8	lost wheel while exiting pits	15/28
6	MONACO GP	Monte Carlo	24	Minardi Scuderia Italia	G	3.5 Minardi M193B-Ford HB V8	1 lap behind	12/24
ret	SPANISH GP	Barcelona	24	Minardi Scuderia Italia	G	3.5 Minardi M193B-Ford HB V8	engine	14/27
11	CANADIAN GP	Montreal	24	Minardi Scuderia Italia	G	3.5 Minardi M194-Ford HB V8	2 laps behind	18/27
ret	FRENCH GP	Magny Cours	24	Minardi Scuderia Italia	G	3.5 Minardi M194-Ford HB V8	engine	21/28
ret	BRITISH GP	Silverstone	24	Minardi Scuderia Italia	G	3.5 Minardi M194-Ford HB V8	engine	17/28
ret	GERMAN GP	Hockenheim	24	Minardi Scuderia Italia	G	3.5 Minardi M194-Ford HB V8	multiple accident at start	23/28
7	HUNGARIAN GP	Hungaroring	24	Minardi Scuderia Italia	G	3.5 Minardi M194-Ford HB V8	2 laps behind	20/28
9*	BELGIAN GP	Spa	24	Minardi Scuderia Italia	G	3.5 Minardi M194-Ford HB V8	*1st place car dsq/-1 lap	18/28
ret	ITALIAN GP	Monza	24	Minardi Scuderia Italia	G	3.5 Minardi M194-Ford HB V8	gearbox	22/28
13	PORTUGUESE GP	Estoril	24	Minardi Scuderia Italia	G	3.5 Minardi M194-Ford HB V8	2 laps behind	19/28
14	EUROPEAN GP	Jerez	24	Minardi Scuderia Italia	G	3.5 Minardi M194-Ford HB V8	2 laps behind	20/28
ret	JAPANESE GP	Suzuka	24	Minardi Scuderia Italia	G	3.5 Minardi M194-Ford HB V8	spun off	21/28
ret	AUSTRALIAN GP	Adelaide	24	Minardi Scuderia Italia	G	3.5 Minardi M194-Ford HB V8	accident	16/28

GP Starts: 194   GP Wins: 5   Pole positions: 2   Fastest laps: 5 (1 shared)   Points: 186.50

JEAN ALESI

What if Jean Alesi had taken up his Williams contract instead of joining Ferrari in 1991? Almost certainly the popular French driver would now be able to look back on more than just a single Grand Prix victory in what must be seen as a career that has failed to achieve anything like the success his natural talent demanded.

Jean, who was born in Avignon of Sicilian descent, demonstrated his ability early in his career when in 1986 he shook the established order in French F3. Running his own Dallara-Alfa, Alesi scored two race wins, three second places and three other top-three finishes to claim the runner-up spot behind champion Yannick Dalmas. That this was achieved without the benefit of major-sponsor backing – so prevalent in the series – was not lost on the ORECA squad, who signed Jean to race for them in 1987. He duly took the team's fifth consecutive French F3 title, but only after a disastrous early season which eventually saw the troublesome Martini chassis replaced – at Jean's insistence – by a new Dallara 387, the switch allowing him to take six successive wins on his way to the crown.

Naturally Alesi moved into the ORECA F3000 team for the following season but the campaign proved to be a huge disappointment for all concerned, Jean being particularly unhappy at the lack of rapport on the engineering side. Marlboro's decision to back Lehto and Irvine for 1989 led to a switch to Eddie Jordan's team and the pair got on famously. Not only was the F3000 championship won – albeit narrowly from Érik Comas – but Alesi stepped into the Tyrrell vacated by Michele Alboreto to score a sensational fourth place in the French Grand Prix on his F1 debut. An 18-month contract was quickly signed and Alesi set about building a reputation as a fast and fearless racer intimidated by nobody – as Senna would find at Phoenix and Berger at Monaco in 1990 – but one sometimes running at the ragged edge or beyond, as at Monza, where he spun out in a fruitless attempt to match the pace of the McLarens.

Frank Williams decided he liked Jean's style and a contract was signed for him to race the Williams-Renault in 1991. However, after protracted nego-tiations it was announced he would be driving for Ferrari instead.

Initially he found the going tough, his relative lack of experience proving a handicap in a difficult team environment. There were drives of brilliance in 1992 – at Barcelona and Magny Cours, for example – but even more frustration in terms of solid results was to follow in 1993. Despite Ferrari's relative lack of success, Alesi signed for a further two years at Maranello, hoping the restructuring programme would bring him the success he craved. In the event 1994 turned out to be a desperately disappointing year. His early season was disrupted by a back injury sustained in a testing accident. This caused him to miss two races, and his return to the wheel was punctuated by driver errors and engine failures. The Latin blood within him reached boiling point at Monza as that elusive first Grand Prix win disappeared when the gearbox was damaged at a refuelling stop.

Jean's final year with the Prancing Horse brought – after 91 races – an emotional and hugely popular win in Canada. Brilliant drives in Brazil and at the Nürburgring once again highlighted his mesmerising car control, but his volatility, surely such a factor in these performances, finally saw him fall out with Jean Todt. Finding himself surplus to requirements, he lost little time in negotiating a seat at Benetton for 1996.

On paper his chances of success were good, and a serious World Championship bid lay in prospect. In the event it was the usual cocktail of brilliance (at Monaco, where he could have won) mixed with an equal measure of stupidity (needless shunts in Australia and Japan). The 1997 season saw much the same story and, despite some excellent drives (most notably at Monza), Alesi was left to contemplate a slide further down the grid after signing a two-year deal with Sauber. Predictably, perhaps, the first season brought optimism and some sparkling perfor-mances, but the second yielded only mounting frustration at midfield obscurity followed by discord when the team failed to progress. The now-veteran Alesi joins forces with Alain Prost for 2000. It will be interesting indeed to see if this potentially volatile partnership stays the course.

ALESI, Jean (F) b 11/6/1964, Avignon

1989

Championship position: 9th   Wins: 0   Pole positions: 0   Fastest laps: 0   Points scored: 8

	Race	Circuit	No	Entrant	Tyres	Car/Engine	Comment	Q Pos/Entries
4	FRENCH GP	Paul Ricard	4	Tyrrell Racing Organisation	G	3.5 Tyrrell 018-Cosworth V8		16/39
ret	BRITISH GP	Silverstone	4	Tyrrell Racing Organisation	G	3.5 Tyrrell 018-Cosworth V8	spun off	22/39
10	GERMAN GP	Hockenheim	4	Tyrrell Racing Organisation	G	3.5 Tyrrell 018-Cosworth V8	spin-pit stop-tyres/-2 laps	10/39
9	HUNGARIAN GP	Hungaroring	4	Tyrrell Racing Organisation	G	3.5 Tyrrell 018-Cosworth V8	pit stop-tyres/1 lap behind	11/39
5	ITALIAN GP	Monza	4	Tyrrell Racing Organisation	G	3.5 Tyrrell 018-Cosworth V8	1 lap behind	10/39
4	SPANISH GP	Jerez	4	Tyrrell Racing Organisation	G	3.5 Tyrrell 018-Cosworth V8	pit stop-tyres/1 lap behind	9/38
ret	JAPANESE GP	Suzuka	4	Tyrrell Racing Organisation	G	3.5 Tyrrell 018-Cosworth V8	gearbox	18/39
ret	AUSTRALIAN GP	Adelaide	4	Tyrrell Racing Organisation	G	3.5 Tyrrell 018-Cosworth V8	electrics	15/39

1990

Championship position: 9th   Wins: 0   Pole positions: 0   Fastest laps: 0   Points scored: 13

	Race	Circuit	No	Entrant	Tyres	Car/Engine	Comment	Q Pos/Entries
2	US GP (PHOENIX)	Phoenix	4	Tyrrell Racing Organisation	P	3.5 Tyrrell 018-Cosworth V8		4/35
7	BRAZILIAN GP	Interlagos	4	Tyrrell Racing Organisation	P	3.5 Tyrrell 018-Cosworth V8	collision, de Cesaris/-1 lap	7/35
6	SAN MARINO GP	Imola	4	Tyrrell Racing Organisation	P	3.5 Tyrrell 019-Cosworth V8	incident with Piquet/-1 lap	7/34
2	MONACO GP	Monte Carlo	4	Tyrrell Racing Organisation	P	3.5 Tyrrell 019-Cosworth V8		3/35
dns	"	"	4	Tyrrell Racing Organisation	P	3.5 Tyrrell 018-Cosworth V8	practice only	– / –
ret	CANADIAN GP	Montreal	4	Tyrrell Racing Organisation	P	3.5 Tyrrell 019-Cosworth V8	spun off	8/35
7	MEXICAN GP	Mexico City	4	Tyrrell Racing Organisation	P	3.5 Tyrrell 019-Cosworth V8	misfire	6/35
ret	FRENCH GP	Paul Ricard	4	Tyrrell Racing Organisation	P	3.5 Tyrrell 019-Cosworth V8	differential	13/35
8	BRITISH GP	Silverstone	4	Tyrrell Racing Organisation	P	3.5 Tyrrell 019-Cosworth V8	pit stop-tyres/1 lap behind	6/35
11/ret	GERMAN GP	Hockenheim	4	Tyrrell Racing Organisation	P	3.5 Tyrrell 019-Cosworth V8	c.v. joint/5 laps behind	8/35
ret	HUNGARIAN GP	Hungaroring	4	Tyrrell Racing Organisation	P	3.5 Tyrrell 019-Cosworth V8	collision with Martini	6/35
8	BELGIAN GP	Spa	4	Tyrrell Racing Organisation	P	3.5 Tyrrell 019-Cosworth V8	pit stop-tyres/1 lap behind	9/33
ret	ITALIAN GP	Monza	4	Tyrrell Racing Organisation	P	3.5 Tyrrell 019-Cosworth V8	spun off	5/33
8	PORTUGUESE GP	Estoril	4	Tyrrell Racing Organisation	P	3.5 Tyrrell 019-Cosworth V8	1 lap behind	8/33
ret	SPANISH GP	Jerez	4	Tyrrell Racing Organisation	P	3.5 Tyrrell 019-Cosworth V8	bumped by Berger-puncture	4/33
dns	JAPANESE GP	Suzuka	4	Tyrrell Racing Organisation	P	3.5 Tyrrell 019-Cosworth V8	neck injury in practice	(7)/30
8	AUSTRALIAN GP	Adelaide	4	Tyrrell Racing Organisation	P	3.5 Tyrrell 019-Cosworth V8	1 lap behind	5/30

1991

Championship position: 7th   Wins: 0   Pole positions: 0   Fastest laps: 1   Points scored: 21

	Race	Circuit	No	Entrant	Tyres	Car/Engine	Comment	Q Pos/Entries
12/ret	US GP (PHOENIX)	Phoenix	28	Scuderia Ferrari SpA	G	3.5 Fiat Ferrari 642/2 V12	gearbox/9 laps behind/FL	6/34
6	BRAZILIAN GP	Interlagos	28	Scuderia Ferrari SpA	G	3.5 Fiat Ferrari 642/2 V12		5/34
ret	SAN MARINO GP	Imola	28	Scuderia Ferrari SpA	G	3.5 Fiat Ferrari 642/2 V12	spun off	7/34
3	MONACO GP	Monte Carlo	28	Scuderia Ferrari SpA	G	3.5 Fiat Ferrari 642/2 V12		9/34
ret	CANADIAN GP	Montreal	28	Scuderia Ferrari SpA	G	3.5 Fiat Ferrari 642/2 V12	engine	7/34
ret	MEXICAN GP	Mexico City	28	Scuderia Ferrari SpA	G	3.5 Fiat Ferrari 642/2 V12	clutch	4/34
4	FRENCH GP	Magny Cours	28	Scuderia Ferrari SpA	G	3.5 Fiat Ferrari 643 V12		6/34
ret	BRITISH GP	Silverstone	28	Scuderia Ferrari SpA	G	3.5 Fiat Ferrari 643 V12	collision with Suzuki	6/34
3	GERMAN GP	Hockenheim	28	Scuderia Ferrari SpA	G	3.5 Fiat Ferrari 643 V12	ran without tyre change	6/34
5	HUNGARIAN GP	Hungaroring	28	Scuderia Ferrari SpA	G	3.5 Fiat Ferrari 643 V12		6/34
ret	BELGIAN GP	Spa	28	Scuderia Ferrari SpA	G	3.5 Fiat Ferrari 643 V12	engine	5/34
ret	ITALIAN GP	Monza	28	Scuderia Ferrari SpA	G	3.5 Fiat Ferrari 643 V12	engine	6/34
3	PORTUGUESE GP	Estoril	28	Scuderia Ferrari SpA	G	3.5 Fiat Ferrari 643 V12		6/34
4	SPANISH GP	Barcelona	28	Scuderia Ferrari SpA	G	3.5 Fiat Ferrari 643 V12		7/33
ret	JAPANESE GP	Suzuka	28	Scuderia Ferrari SpA	G	3.5 Fiat Ferrari 643 V12	engine	6/31
ret	AUSTRALIAN GP	Adelaide	28	Scuderia Ferrari SpA	G	3.5 Fiat Ferrari 643 V12	collision with Larini	7/31

1992

Championship position: 7th   Wins: 0   Pole positions: 0   Fastest laps: 0   Points scored: 18

	Race	Circuit	No	Entrant	Tyres	Car/Engine	Comment	Q Pos/Entries
ret	SOUTH AFRICAN GP	Kyalami	27	Scuderia Ferrari SpA	G	3.5 Fiat Ferrari F92A V12	engine	5/30
ret	MEXICAN GP	Mexico City	27	Scuderia Ferrari SpA	G	3.5 Fiat Ferrari F92A V12	engine	10/30
4	BRAZILIAN GP	Interlagos	27	Scuderia Ferrari SpA	G	3.5 Fiat Ferrari F92A V12	1 lap behind	6/31
3	SPANISH GP	Barcelona	27	Scuderia Ferrari SpA	G	3.5 Fiat Ferrari F92A V12		8/32
ret	SAN MARINO GP	Imola	27	Scuderia Ferrari SpA	G	3.5 Fiat Ferrari F92A V12	collision with Berger	7/32
ret	MONACO GP	Monte Carlo	27	Scuderia Ferrari SpA	G	3.5 Fiat Ferrari F92A V12	gearbox	4/32
3	CANADIAN GP	Montreal	27	Scuderia Ferrari SpA	G	3.5 Fiat Ferrari F92A V12		8/32
ret	FRENCH GP	Magny Cours	27	Scuderia Ferrari SpA	G	3.5 Fiat Ferrari F92A V12	engine	6/30
ret	BRITISH GP	Silverstone	27	Scuderia Ferrari SpA	G	3.5 Fiat Ferrari F92A V12	fire extinguisher discharged	8/32
5	GERMAN GP	Hockenheim	27	Scuderia Ferrari SpA	G	3.5 Fiat Ferrari F92A V12		5/32
ret	HUNGARIAN GP	Hungaroring	27	Scuderia Ferrari SpA	G	3.5 Fiat Ferrari F92A V12	spun off	9/31
ret	BELGIAN GP	Spa	27	Scuderia Ferrari SpA	G	3.5 Fiat Ferrari F92AT V12	spun off	5/30
ret	ITALIAN GP	Monza	27	Scuderia Ferrari SpA	G	3.5 Fiat Ferrari F92AT V12	fuel pressure	3/28
ret	PORTUGUESE GP	Estoril	27	Scuderia Ferrari SpA	G	3.5 Fiat Ferrari F92AT V12	spun off	10/26
5	JAPANESE GP	Suzuka	27	Scuderia Ferrari SpA	G	3.5 Fiat Ferrari F92A V12	1 lap behind	15/26
4	AUSTRALIAN GP	Adelaide	27	Scuderia Ferrari SpA	G	3.5 Fiat Ferrari F92AT V12	1 lap behind	6/26

1993

Championship position: 6th   Wins: 0   Pole positions: 0   Fastest laps: 0   Points scored: 16

	Race	Circuit	No	Entrant	Tyres	Car/Engine	Comment	Q Pos/Entries
ret	SOUTH AFRICAN GP	Kyalami	27	Scuderia Ferrari SpA	G	3.5 Fiat Ferrari F93A V12	hydraulics	5/26
8	BRAZILIAN GP	Interlagos	27	Scuderia Ferrari SpA	G	3.5 Fiat Ferrari F93A V12	2 stop & go penalties/1 lap behind	9/26
ret	EUROPEAN GP	Donington	27	Scuderia Ferrari SpA	G	3.5 Fiat Ferrari F93A V12	active suspension system	9/26
ret	SAN MARINO GP	Imola	27	Scuderia Ferrari SpA	G	3.5 Fiat Ferrari F93A V12	clutch	9/26
ret	SPANISH GP	Barcelona	27	Scuderia Ferrari SpA	G	3.5 Fiat Ferrari F93A V12	engine	8/26
3	MONACO GP	Monte Carlo	27	Scuderia Ferrari SpA	G	3.5 Fiat Ferrari F93A V12	despite collision with Berger	5/26
ret	CANADIAN GP	Montreal	27	Scuderia Ferrari SpA	G	3.5 Fiat Ferrari F93A V12	engine	6/26
ret	FRENCH GP	Magny Cours	27	Scuderia Ferrari SpA	G	3.5 Fiat Ferrari F93A V12	engine	6/26
9	BRITISH GP	Silverstone	27	Scuderia Ferrari SpA	G	3.5 Fiat Ferrari F93A V12	1 lap behind	12/26
7	GERMAN GP	Hockenheim	27	Scuderia Ferrari SpA	G	3.5 Fiat Ferrari F93A V12	pit stop-loose bodywork	10/26
ret	HUNGARIAN GP	Hungaroring	27	Scuderia Ferrari SpA	G	3.5 Fiat Ferrari F93A V12	collision with Fittipaldi	8/26
ret	BELGIAN GP	Spa	27	Scuderia Ferrari SpA	G	3.5 Fiat Ferrari F93A V12	suspension	4/25
2	ITALIAN GP	Monza	27	Scuderia Ferrari SpA	G	3.5 Fiat Ferrari F93A V12		3/26
4	PORTUGUESE GP	Estoril	27	Scuderia Ferrari SpA	G	3.5 Fiat Ferrari F93A V12		5/26
ret	JAPANESE GP	Suzuka	27	Scuderia Ferrari SpA	G	3.5 Fiat Ferrari F93A V12	electrics	14/24
4	AUSTRALIAN GP	Adelaide	27	Scuderia Ferrari SpA	G	3.5 Fiat Ferrari F93A V12	1 lap behind	7/24

	1994	Championship position: 5th		Wins: 0	Pole positions: 1		Fastest laps: 0	Points scored: 24	
3	BRAZILIAN GP	Interlagos	27	Scuderia Ferrari SpA	G	3.5 Fiat Ferrari 412T1 V12		1 lap behind	3/28
5	MONACO GP	Monte Carlo	27	Scuderia Ferrari SpA	G	3.5 Fiat Ferrari 412T1 V12		collision-Brabham/-1 lap	5/24
4	SPANISH GP	Barcelona	27	Scuderia Ferrari SpA	G	3.5 Fiat Ferrari 412T1 V12		1 lap behind	6/27
3	CANADIAN GP	Montreal	27	Scuderia Ferrari SpA	G	3.5 Fiat Ferrari 412T1 V12			2/27
ret	FRENCH GP	Magny Cours	27	Scuderia Ferrari SpA	G	3.5 Fiat Ferrari 412T1B V12		spun-then hit Barrichello	4/28
2*	BRITISH GP	Silverstone	27	Scuderia Ferrari SpA	G	3.5 Fiat Ferrari 412T1B V12		*2nd place car disqualified	4/28
ret	GERMAN GP	Hockenheim	27	Scuderia Ferrari SpA	G	3.5 Fiat Ferrari 412T1B V12		electrics on lap 1	2/28
ret	HUNGARIAN GP	Hungaroring	27	Scuderia Ferrari SpA	G	3.5 Fiat Ferrari 412T1B V12		gearbox	13/28
ret	BELGIAN GP	Spa	27	Scuderia Ferrari SpA	G	3.5 Fiat Ferrari 412T1B V12		engine	5/28
ret	ITALIAN GP	Monza	27	Scuderia Ferrari SpA	G	3.5 Fiat Ferrari 412T1B V12		gearbox	1/28
ret	PORTUGUESE GP	Estoril	27	Scuderia Ferrari SpA	G	3.5 Fiat Ferrari 412T1B V12		collision with Brabham	5/28
10	EUROPEAN GP	Jerez	27	Scuderia Ferrari SpA	G	3.5 Fiat Ferrari 412T1B V12		1 lap behind	16/28
3	JAPANESE GP	Suzuka	27	Scuderia Ferrari SpA	G	3.5 Fiat Ferrari 412T1B V12			7/28
6	AUSTRALIAN GP	Adelaide	27	Scuderia Ferrari SpA	G	3.5 Fiat Ferrari 412T1B V12		1 lap behind	8/28
	1995	Championship position: 5th		Wins: 1	Pole positions: 0		Fastest laps: 1	Points scored: 42	
5	BRAZILIAN GP	Interlagos	27	Scuderia Ferrari SpA	G	3.0 Fiat Ferrari 412T2 V12		1 lap behind	6/26
2	ARGENTINE GP	Buenos Aires	27	Scuderia Ferrari SpA	G	3.0 Fiat Ferrari 412T2 V12			6/26
2	SAN MARINO GP	Imola	27	Scuderia Ferrari SpA	G	3.0 Fiat Ferrari 412T2 V12			5/26
ret	SPANISH GP	Barcelona	27	Scuderia Ferrari SpA	G	3.0 Fiat Ferrari 412T2 V12		engine	2/26
ret	MONACO GP	Monte Carlo	27	Scuderia Ferrari SpA	G	3.0 Fiat Ferrari 412T2 V12		accident/FL	5/26
1	CANADIAN GP	Montreal	27	Scuderia Ferrari SpA	G	3.0 Fiat Ferrari 412T2 V12			5/24
5	FRENCH GP	Magny Cours	27	Scuderia Ferrari SpA	G	3.0 Fiat Ferrari 412T2 V12			4/24
2	BRITISH GP	Silverstone	27	Scuderia Ferrari SpA	G	3.0 Fiat Ferrari 412T2 V12			6/24
ret	GERMAN GP	Hockenheim	27	Scuderia Ferrari SpA	G	3.0 Fiat Ferrari 412T2 V12		engine	10/24
ret	HUNGARIAN GP	Hungaroring	27	Scuderia Ferrari SpA	G	3.0 Fiat Ferrari 412T2 V12		engine	6/24
ret	BELGIAN GP	Spa	27	Scuderia Ferrari SpA	G	3.0 Fiat Ferrari 412T2 V12		suspension	2/24
ret	ITALIAN GP	Monza	27	Scuderia Ferrari SpA	G	3.0 Fiat Ferrari 412T2 V12		wheel bearing	5/24
5	PORTUGUESE GP	Estoril	27	Scuderia Ferrari SpA	G	3.0 Fiat Ferrari 412T2 V12			7/24
2	EUROPEAN GP	Nürburgring	27	Scuderia Ferrari SpA	G	3.0 Fiat Ferrari 412T2 V12			6/24
5	PACIFIC GP	T I. Circuit	27	Scuderia Ferrari SpA	G	3.0 Fiat Ferrari 412T2 V12		1 lap behind	4/24
ret	JAPANESE GP	Suzuka	27	Scuderia Ferrari SpA	G	3.0 Fiat Ferrari 412T2 V12		differential	2/24
ret	AUSTRALIAN GP	Adelaide	27	Scuderia Ferrari SpA	G	3.0 Fiat Ferrari 412T2 V12		collision with Schumacher	5/24
	1996	Championship position: 4th		Wins: 0	Pole positions: 0		Fastest laps: 2	Points scored: 47	
ret	AUSTRALIAN GP	Melbourne	3	Mild Seven Benetton Renault	G	3.0 Benetton 196-Renault V10		collision with Irvine	6/22
2	BRAZILIAN GP	Interlagos	3	Mild Seven Benetton Renault	G	3.0 Benetton 196-Renault V10			5/22
3	ARGENTINE GP	Buenos Aires	3	Mild Seven Benetton Renault	G	3.0 Benetton 196-Renault V10		FL	4/22
ret	EUROPEAN GP	Nürburgring	3	Mild Seven Benetton Renault	G	3.0 Benetton 196-Renault V10		collision with Salo, lap 1	4/22
6	SAN MARINO GP	Imola	3	Mild Seven Benetton Renault	G	3.0 Benetton 196-Renault V10		stop & go penalty-1 lap behind	5/22
ret	MONACO GP	Monte Carlo	3	Mild Seven Benetton Renault	G	3.0 Benetton 196-Renault V10		rear suspension-led race/FL	3/22
2	SPANISH GP	Barcelona	3	Mild Seven Benetton Renault	G	3.0 Benetton 196-Renault V10			4/22
3	CANADIAN GP	Montreal	3	Mild Seven Benetton Renault	G	3.0 Benetton 196-Renault V10			4/22
3	FRENCH GP	Magny Cours	3	Mild Seven Benetton Renault	G	3.0 Benetton 196-Renault V10			3/22
ret	BRITISH GP	Silverstone	3	Mild Seven Benetton Renault	G	3.0 Benetton 196-Renault V10		rear wheel bearing	5/22
2	GERMAN GP	Hockenheim	3	Mild Seven Benetton Renault	G	3.0 Benetton 196-Renault V10			5/20
3	HUNGARIAN GP	Hungaroring	3	Mild Seven Benetton Renault	G	3.0 Benetton 196-Renault V10			5/20
4	BELGIAN GP	Spa	3	Mild Seven Benetton Renault	G	3.0 Benetton 196-Renault V10			7/20
2	ITALIAN GP	Monza	3	Mild Seven Benetton Renault	G	3.0 Benetton 196-Renault V10			6/20
4	PORTUGUESE GP	Estoril	3	Mild Seven Benetton Renault	G	3.0 Benetton 196-Renault V10			3/20
ret	JAPANESE GP	Suzuka	3	Mild Seven Benetton Renault	G	3.0 Benetton 196-Renault V10		crashed on lap 1	9/20

The high point of Alesi's long Grand Prix career to date was at the 1995 Canadian Grand Prix when, at last, the likeable French-Sicilian took a Grand Prix victory.

Alesi shares the podium with the Williams pair of Jacques Villeneuve and Damon Hill after the 1996 French Grand Prix. His two-year stint with Benetton failed to bring the success both parties had expected.

1997
Championship position: 3rd= Wins: 0 Pole positions: 1 Fastest laps: 0 Points scored: 36

ret	AUSTRALIAN GP	Melbourne	7	Mild Seven Benetton Renault	G	3.0 Benetton 197-Renault V10	ran out of fuel	8/24
6	BRAZILIAN GP	Interlagos	7	Mild Seven Benetton Renault	G	3.0 Benetton 197-Renault V10		6/22
7	ARGENTINE GP	Buenos Aires	7	Mild Seven Benetton Renault	G	3.0 Benetton 197-Renault V10		11/22
5	SAN MARINO GP	Imola	7	Mild Seven Benetton Renault	G	3.0 Benetton 197-Renault V10	1 lap behind	14/22
ret	MONACO GP	Monte Carlo	7	Mild Seven Benetton Renault	G	3.0 Benetton 197-Renault V10	spun and stalled	9/22
3	SPANISH GP	Barcelona	7	Mild Seven Benetton Renault	G	3.0 Benetton 197-Renault V10		4/22
2	CANADIAN GP	Montreal	7	Mild Seven Benetton Renault	G	3.0 Benetton 197-Renault V10		8/22
5	FRENCH GP	Magny Cours	7	Mild Seven Benetton Renault	G	3.0 Benetton 197-Renault V10		8/22
2	BRITISH GP	Silverstone	7	Mild Seven Benetton Renault	G	3.0 Benetton 197-Renault V10		11/22
6	GERMAN GP	Hockenheim	7	Mild Seven Benetton Renault	G	3.0 Benetton 197-Renault V10		6/22
11	HUNGARIAN GP	Hungaroring	7	Mild Seven Benetton Renault	G	3.0 Benetton 197-Renault V10	2 laps behind	9/22
8*	BELGIAN GP	Spa	7	Mild Seven Benetton Renault	G	3.0 Benetton 197-Renault V10	*3rd place car dsq	2/22
2	ITALIAN GP	Monza	7	Mild Seven Benetton Renault	G	3.0 Benetton 197-Renault V10		1/22
ret	AUSTRIAN GP	A1-Ring	7	Mild Seven Benetton Renault	G	3.0 Benetton 197-Renault V10		15/22
2	LUXEMBOURG GP	Nürburgring	7	Mild Seven Benetton Renault	G	3.0 Benetton 197-Renault V10	collision with Irvine	10/22
5*	JAPANESE GP	Suzuka	7	Mild Seven Benetton Renault	G	3.0 Benetton 197-Renault V10	*4th place car dsq	7/22
13	EUROPEAN GP	Jerez	7	Mild Seven Benetton Renault	G	3.0 Benetton 197-Renault V10	spin-1 lap behind	10/22

1998
Championship position: 11th Wins: 0 Pole positions: 0 Fastest laps: 0 Points scored: 9

ret	AUSTRALIAN GP	Melbourne	14	Red Bull Sauber Petronas	G	3.0 Sauber C17-Petronas V10	engine	12/22
9	BRAZILIAN GP	Interlagos	14	Red Bull Sauber Petronas	G	3.0 Sauber C17-Petronas V10	1 lap behind	15/22
5	ARGENTINE GP	Buenos Aires	14	Red Bull Sauber Petronas	G	3.0 Sauber C17-Petronas V10	lost side winglet at pit stop	11/22
6	SAN MARINO GP	Imola	14	Red Bull Sauber Petronas	G	3.0 Sauber C17-Petronas V10	1 lap behind	12/22
10	SPANISH GP	Barcelona	14	Red Bull Sauber Petronas	G	3.0 Sauber C17-Petronas V10	2 laps behind	14/22
ret/12	MONACO GP	Monte Carlo	14	Red Bull Sauber Petronas	G	3.0 Sauber C17-Petronas V10	gearbox/6 laps behind	11/22
ret	CANADIAN GP	Montreal	14	Red Bull Sauber Petronas	G	3.0 Sauber C17-Petronas V10	collision on lap 1	9/22
7th	FRENCH GP	Magny Cours	14	Red Bull Sauber Petronas	G	3.0 Sauber C17-Petronas V10	minor collisions/1 lap behind	11/22
ret	BRITISH GP	Silverstone	14	Red Bull Sauber Petronas	G	3.0 Sauber C17-Petronas V10	electrics	8/22
ret	AUSTRIAN GP	A1-Ring	14	Red Bull Sauber Petronas	G	3.0 Sauber C17-Petronas V10	collision with Fisichella	2/22
10	GERMAN GP	Hockenheim	14	Red Bull Sauber Petronas	G	3.0 Sauber C17-Petronas V10		11/22
7th	HUNGARIAN GP	Hungaroring	14	Red Bull Sauber Petronas	G	3.0 Sauber C17-Petronas V10	1 lap behind	11/22
3	BELGIAN GP	Spa	14	Red Bull Sauber Petronas	G	3.0 Sauber C17-Petronas V10		10/22
5	ITALIAN GP	Monza	14	Red Bull Sauber Petronas	G	3.0 Sauber C17-Petronas V10		8/22
10	LUXEMBOURG GP	Nürburgring	14	Red Bull Sauber Petronas	G	3.0 Sauber C17-Petronas V10	1 lap behind	11/22
7	JAPANESE GP	Suzuka	14	Red Bull Sauber Petronas	G	3.0 Sauber C17-Petronas V10		12/22

1999
Championship position: 15th= Wins: 0 Pole positions: 0 Fastest laps: 0 Points scored: 2

ret	AUSTRALIAN GP	Melbourne	11	Red Bull Sauber Petronas	B	3.0 Sauber C18-Petronas V10	gearbox on startline	16/22
ret	BRAZILIAN GP	Interlagos	11	Red Bull Sauber Petronas	B	3.0 Sauber C18-Petronas V10	gearbox	14/22
6	SAN MARINO GP	Imola	11	Red Bull Sauber Petronas	B	3.0 Sauber C18-Petronas V10	1 lap behind	13/22
ret	MONACO GP	Monte Carlo	11	Red Bull Sauber Petronas	B	3.0 Sauber C18-Petronas V10	hit wall	14/22
ret	SPANISH GP	Barcelona	11	Red Bull Sauber Petronas	B	3.0 Sauber C18-Petronas V10	transmission	5/22
ret	CANADIAN GP	Montreal	11	Red Bull Sauber Petronas	B	3.0 Sauber C18-Petronas V10	collision with Trulli	8/22
ret	FRENCH GP	Magny Cours	11	Red Bull Sauber Petronas	B	3.0 Sauber C18-Petronas V10	spun off	2/22
14	BRITISH GP	Silverstone	11	Red Bull Sauber Petronas	B	3.0 Sauber C18-Petronas V10	1 lap behind	10/22
ret	AUSTRIAN GP	A1-Ring	11	Red Bull Sauber Petronas	B	3.0 Sauber C18-Petronas V10	out of fuel	17/22
8	GERMAN GP	Hockenheim	11	Red Bull Sauber Petronas	B	3.0 Sauber C18-Petronas V10		21/22
16	HUNGARIAN GP	Hungaroring	11	Red Bull Sauber Petronas	B	3.0 Sauber C18-Petronas V10	fuel pressure/3 laps behind	11/22
9	BELGIAN GP	Spa	11	Red Bull Sauber Petronas	B	3.0 Sauber C18-Petronas V10		16/22
9	ITALIAN GP	Monza	11	Red Bull Sauber Petronas	B	3.0 Sauber C18-Petronas V10		13/22
ret	EUROPEAN GP	Nürburgring	11	Red Bull Sauber Petronas	B	3.0 Sauber C18-Petronas V10	driveshaft	16/22
ret	MALAYSIAN GP	Sepang	11	Red Bull Sauber Petronas	B	3.0 Sauber C18-Petronas V10		15/22
6	JAPANESE GP	Suzuka	11	Red Bull Sauber Petronas	B	3.0 Sauber C18-Petronas V10	1 lap behind	10/22

GP Starts: 167 GP Wins: 1 Pole positions: 2 Fastest laps: 4 Points: 236

PHILIPPE ALLIOT

A late starter in racing, Philippe tried his hand at the Motul racing school in 1975 and did well enough to embark on a season in Formule Renault in 1976, abandoning his studies in political science in the process.

Alliot spent two seasons in the shadow of one Alain Prost before clinching the Formule Renault title in 1978. The next four seasons were devoted to climbing the ladder in F3. He was third in the French championship in 1979 and spent three seasons contesting the European championship (finishing fifth, third, then fifth again) before a season in F2 in 1983, where he was always quick but prone to error in the ORECA Martini. The highlight of his season came with his third place at Le Mans, sharing the Kremer Porsche with Mario and Michael Andretti.

Alliot moved up into the big league with the underpowered, underfinanced RAM-Hart but his two seasons with the team were littered with shunts and no points were scored. So it was back to ORECA and F3000 for 1986, Alliot taking his March to victory in the round at Spa, but then an opportunity to drive for Ligier arose after Laffite's accident at Brands Hatch. Philippe caused a stir by keeping pace with Arnoux and scored a point in Mexico – which was enough to interest Larrousse, for whom he raced for the next three seasons. He then returned to Ligier, where chassis of various appellations (JS33, JS33B and JS33C) were all subjected to a comprehensive crash-testing programme.

It was therefore surprising that he should have been invited to join Jean Todt's Peugeot sports car team for 1991-92. Paired with Mauro Baldi, he won three times (Suzuka '91, Donington and Magny Cours '92) as the French manufacturer trampled all over meagre opposition and the sports car championship headed for extinction. Far from being an endangered species, a more self-confident Alliot then bounced back into Formula 1 for the third time at the age of 39 with Larrousse. At the behest of his former sports car entrant, Philippe was brought into the McLaren-Peugeot squad for 1994, but his role was largely confined to testing, Ron Dennis preferring the talents of Martin Brundle. Eventually he did get one race – deputising for the suspended Häkkinen in Hungary – before reappearing for Larrousse, just once, at Spa. Realising that his days in Grands Prix were over, Alliot hit the French Supertourisme trail in 1995 with a works Peugeot.

In 1996 Philippe raced in the Le Mans 24 Hours for Courage Competition, but the car he was sharing was eliminated after a stuck throttle pitched it into the wall (with Alliot at the wheel) when holding fourth place.

ALLIOT, Philippe (F) b 27/7/1954, Voves Eure et Loir, nr Chartres

	1984			Championship position: Unplaced					
	Race	Circuit	No	Entrant	Tyres	Car/Engine		Comment	Q Pos/Entries
ret	BRAZILIAN GP	Rio	9	Skoal Bandit Formula 1 Team	P	1.5 t/c RAM 02-Hart 4		battery mounting	26/27
ret	SOUTH AFRICAN GP	Kyalami	9	Skoal Bandit Formula 1 Team	P	1.5 t/c RAM 02-Hart 4		water leak-engine	22/27
dnq	BELGIAN GP	Zolder	9	Skoal Bandit Formula 1 Team	P	1.5 t/c RAM 02-Hart 4			27/27
ret	SAN MARINO GP	Imola	9	Skoal Bandit Formula 1 Team	P	1.5 t/c RAM 02-Hart 4		engine	23/28
ret	FRENCH GP	Dijon	9	Skoal Bandit Formula 1 Team	P	1.5 t/c RAM 02-Hart 4		electrics	23/27
dnq	MONACO GP	Monte Carlo	9	Skoal Bandit Formula 1 Team	P	1.5 t/c RAM 02-Hart 4			27/27
10*	CANADIAN GP	Montreal	9	Skoal Bandit Formula 1 Team	P	1.5 t/c RAM 02-Hart 4		* 10th place car dsq/-5 laps	26/26
ret	US GP (DETROIT)	Detroit	9	Skoal Bandit Formula 1 Team	P	1.5 t/c RAM 02-Hart 4		brakes-hit wall	20/27
dns	US GP (DALLAS)	Dallas	9	Skoal Bandit Formula 1 Team	P	1.5 t/c RAM 02-Hart 4		car damaged in practice	(24)/26
ret	BRITISH GP	Brands Hatch	9	Skoal Bandit Formula 1 Team	P	1.5 t/c RAM 02-Hart 4		accident-Johansson & Cheever	24/27
ret	GERMAN GP	Hockenheim	9	Skoal Bandit Formula 1 Team	P	1.5 t/c RAM 02-Hart 4		overheating	22/27
11	AUSTRIAN GP	Österreichring	9	Skoal Bandit Formula 1 Team	P	1.5 t/c RAM 02-Hart 4		3 laps behind	25/28
10*	DUTCH GP	Zandvoort	9	Skoal Bandit Formula 1 Team	P	1.5 t/c RAM 02-Hart 4		* 8th & 9th cars dsqd/-4 laps	26/27
ret	ITALIAN GP	Monza	9	Skoal Bandit Formula 1 Team	P	1.5 t/c RAM 02-Hart 4		electrics	23/27
ret	EUROPEAN GP	Nürburgring	9	Skoal Bandit Formula 1 Team	P	1.5 t/c RAM 02-Hart 4		turbo	25/26
ret	PORTUGUESE GP	Estoril	9	Skoal Bandit Formula 1 Team	P	1.5 t/c RAM 02-Hart 4		engine	27/27
	1985			Championship position: Unplaced					
9	BRAZILIAN GP	Rio	10	Skoal Bandit Formula 1 Team	P	1.5 t/c RAM 03-Hart 4		3 laps behind	20/25
ret	PORTUGUESE GP	Estoril	10	Skoal Bandit Formula 1 Team	P	1.5 t/c RAM 03-Hart 4		spun off	20/26
ret	SAN MARINO GP	Imola	10	Skoal Bandit Formula 1 Team	P	1.5 t/c RAM 03-Hart 4		engine	21/26
dnq	MONACO GP	Monte Carlo	10	Skoal Bandit Formula 1 Team	P	1.5 t/c RAM 03-Hart 4			23/26
ret	CANADIAN GP	Montreal	10	Skoal Bandit Formula 1 Team	P	1.5 t/c RAM 03-Hart 4		accident	21/25
ret	US GP (DETROIT)	Detroit	10	Skoal Bandit Formula 1 Team	P	1.5 t/c RAM 03-Hart 4		accident with Brundle	23/25
ret	FRENCH GP	Paul Ricard	10	Skoal Bandit Formula 1 Team	P	1.5 t/c RAM 03-Hart 4		fuel pressure	23/26
ret	BRITISH GP	Silverstone	10	Skoal Bandit Formula 1 Team	P	1.5 t/c RAM 03-Hart 4		accident with Ghinzani	21/26
ret	GERMAN GP	Nürburgring	10	Skoal Bandit Formula 1 Team	P	1.5 t/c RAM 03-Hart 4		oil pressure	21/27
ret	AUSTRIAN GP	Österreichring	9	Skoal Bandit Formula 1 Team	P	1.5 t/c RAM 03-Hart 4		turbo	21/27
ret	DUTCH GP	Zandvoort	9	Skoal Bandit Formula 1 Team	P	1.5 t/c RAM 03-Hart 4		engine	25/27
ret	ITALIAN GP	Monza	9	Skoal Bandit Formula 1 Team	P	1.5 t/c RAM 03-Hart 4		turbo	26/26
ret	BELGIAN GP	Spa	9	Skoal Bandit Formula 1 Team	P	1.5 t/c RAM 03-Hart 4		accident	20/24
ret	EUROPEAN GP	Brands Hatch	9	Skoal Bandit Formula 1 Team	P	1.5 t/c RAM 03-Hart 4		engine	23/27

1986

Championship position: 18th= Wins: 0 Pole positions: 0 Fastest laps: 0 Points scored: 1

ret	GERMAN GP	Hockenheim	26	Equipe Ligier	P	1.5 t/c Ligier JS27-Renault V6	engine	14/26
9	HUNGARIAN GP	Hungaroring	26	Equipe Ligier	P	1.5 t/c Ligier JS27-Renault V6	3 laps behind	12/26
ret	AUSTRIAN GP	Österreichring	26	Equipe Ligier	P	1.5 t/c Ligier JS27-Renault V6	engine	11/26
ret	ITALIAN GP	Monza	26	Equipe Ligier	P	1.5 t/c Ligier JS27-Renault V6	engine	14/27
ret	PORTUGUESE GP	Estoril	26	Equipe Ligier	P	1.5 t/c Ligier JS27-Renault V6	engine	11/27
6	MEXICAN GP	Mexico City	26	Equipe Ligier	P	1.5 t/c Ligier JS27-Renault V6	1 lap behind	10/26
8	AUSTRALIAN GP	Adelaide	26	Equipe Ligier	P	1.5 t/c Ligier JS27-Renault V6	3 laps behind	8/26

1987

Championship position: 16th= Wins: 0 Pole positions: 0 Fastest laps: 0 Points scored: 3

10	SAN MARINO GP	Imola	30	Larrousse Calmels	G	3.5 Lola LC87-Cosworth V8	2nd non-turbo/3 laps behind	23/27
8	BELGIAN GP	Spa	30	Larrousse Calmels	G	3.5 Lola LC87-Cosworth V8	1st non-turbo/3 laps behind	22/26
ret	MONACO GP	Monte Carlo	30	Larrousse Calmels	G	3.5 Lola LC87-Cosworth V8	engine	18/26
ret	US GP (DETROIT)	Detroit	30	Larrousse Calmels	G	3.5 Lola LC87-Cosworth V8	collision with Arnoux	20/26
ret	FRENCH GP	Paul Ricard	30	Larrousse Calmels	G	3.5 Lola LC87-Cosworth V8	transmission	23/26
ret	BRITISH GP	Silverstone	30	Larrousse Calmels	G	3.5 Lola LC87-Cosworth V8	gearbox	22/26
6	GERMAN GP	Hockenheim	30	Larrousse Calmels	G	3.5 Lola LC87-Cosworth V8	3rd non-turbo/2 laps behind	21/26
ret	HUNGARIAN GP	Hungaroring	30	Larrousse Calmels	G	3.5 Lola LC87-Cosworth V8	spun off	15/26
12	AUSTRIAN GP	Österreichring	30	Larrousse Calmels	G	3.5 Lola LC87-Cosworth V8	2nd non-turbo/3 laps behind	22/26
ret	ITALIAN GP	Monza	30	Larrousse Calmels	G	3.5 Lola LC87-Cosworth V8	spun off	23/28
ret	PORTUGUESE GP	Estoril	30	Larrousse Calmels	G	3.5 Lola LC87-Cosworth V8	fuel pump	19/27
6	SPANISH GP	Jerez	30	Larrousse Calmels	G	3.5 Lola LC87-Cosworth V8	1st non-turbo/1 lap behind	17/28
6	MEXICAN GP	Mexico City	30	Larrousse Calmels	G	3.5 Lola LC87-Cosworth V8	1st non-turbo/3 laps behind	24/27
ret	JAPANESE GP	Suzuka	30	Larrousse Calmels	G	3.5 Lola LC87-Cosworth V8	startline accident	19/27
ret	AUSTRALIAN GP	Adelaide	30	Larrousse Calmels	G	3.5 Lola LC87-Cosworth V8	electrics	17/27

1988

Championship position: Unplaced

ret	BRAZILIAN GP	Rio	30	Larrousse Calmels	G	3.5 Lola LC88-Cosworth V8	broken suspension-spun off	16/31
17	SAN MARINO GP	Imola	30	Larrousse Calmels	G	3.5 Lola LC88-Cosworth V8	pit stop-puncture/-3 laps	15/31
ret	MONACO GP	Monte Carlo	30	Larrousse Calmels	G	3.5 Lola LC88-Cosworth V8	collision with Patrese	13/30
ret	MEXICAN GP	Mexico City	30	Larrousse Calmels	G	3.5 Lola LC88-Cosworth V8	started from back/rear upright	13/30
10/ret	CANADIAN GP	Montreal	30	Larrousse Calmels	G	3.5 Lola LC88-Cosworth V8	engine cut out/3laps behind	17/31
ret	US GP (DETROIT)	Detroit	30	Larrousse Calmels	G	3.5 Lola LC88-Cosworth V8	gearbox	14/31
ret	FRENCH GP	Paul Ricard	30	Larrousse Calmels	G	3.5 Lola LC88-Cosworth V8	electrics	18/31
14	BRITISH GP	Silverstone	30	Larrousse Calmels	G	3.5 Lola LC88-Cosworth V8	2 laps behind	22/31
ret	GERMAN GP	Hockenheim	30	Larrousse Calmels	G	3.5 Lola LC88-Cosworth V8	spun off	20/31
12	HUNGARIAN GP	Hungaroring	30	Larrousse Calmels	G	3.5 Lola LC88-Cosworth V8	misfire/4 laps behind	20/31
9*	BELGIAN GP	Spa	30	Larrousse Calmels	G	3.5 Lola LC88-Cosworth V8	* 3rd & 4th cars dsq/-1 lap	16/31
ret	ITALIAN GP	Monza	30	Larrousse Calmels	G	3.5 Lola LC88-Cosworth V8	engine	20/31
ret	PORTUGUESE GP	Estoril	30	Larrousse Calmels	G	3.5 Lola LC88-Cosworth V8	engine	20/31
14	SPANISH GP	Jerez	30	Larrousse Calmels	G	3.5 Lola LC88-Cosworth V8	wheel problem/3 laps behind	12/31
9	JAPANESE GP	Suzuka	30	Larrousse Calmels	G	3.5 Lola LC88-Cosworth V8	1 lap behind	19/31
10/ret	AUSTRALIAN GP	Adelaide	30	Larrousse Calmels	G	3.5 Lola LC88-Cosworth V8	out of fuel/7 laps behind	24/31

1989

Championship position: 26th= Wins: 0 Pole positions: 0 Fastest laps: 0 Points scored: 1

12	BRAZILIAN GP	Rio	30	Larrousse Calmels	G	3.5 Lola LC88B-Lamborghini V12	3 laps behind	26/38
ret	SAN MARINO GP	Imola	30	Equipe Larrousse	G	3.5 Lola LC89-Lamborghini V12	engine-fuel injection	20/39
ret	MONACO GP	Monte Carlo	30	Equipe Larrousse	G	3.5 Lola LC89-Lamborghini V12	engine	17/38
nc	MEXICAN GP	Mexico City	30	Equipe Larrousse	G	3.5 Lola LC89-Lamborghini V12	accident damage-misfire/-41 laps	16/39
ret	US GP (PHOENIX)	Phoenix	30	Equipe Larrousse	G	3.5 Lola LC89-Lamborghini V12	spun off	12/39
ret	CANADIAN GP	Montreal	30	Equipe Larrousse	G	3.5 Lola LC89-Lamborghini V12	crashed	10/39
ret	FRENCH GP	Paul Ricard	30	Equipe Larrousse	G	3.5 Lola LC89-Lamborghini V12	engine	7/39
ret	BRITISH GP	Silverstone	30	Equipe Larrousse	G	3.5 Lola LC89-Lamborghini V12	engine	12/39
ret	GERMAN GP	Hockenheim	30	Equipe Larrousse	G	3.5 Lola LC89-Lamborghini V12	oil leak	15/39
dnpq	HUNGARIAN GP	Hungaroring	30	Equipe Larrousse	G	3.5 Lola LC89-Lamborghini V12		32/39
16/ret	BELGIAN GP	Spa	30	Equipe Larrousse	G	3.5 Lola LC89-Lamborghini V12	engine-oil pressure/-5 laps	11/39
ret	ITALIAN GP	Monza	30	Equipe Larrousse	G	3.5 Lola LC89-Lamborghini V12	throttle stuck-spun off	7/39
9	PORTUGUESE GP	Estoril	30	Equipe Larrousse	G	3.5 Lola LC89-Lamborghini V12	pit stop-tyres/1 lap behind	17/39
6	SPANISH GP	Jerez	30	Equipe Larrousse	G	3.5 Lola LC89-Lamborghini V12	pit stop-tyres/1 lap behind	5/38
ret	JAPANESE GP	Suzuka	30	Equipe Larrousse	G	3.5 Lola LC89-Lamborghini V12	engine	8/39
ret	AUSTRALIAN GP	Adelaide	30	Equipe Larrousse	G	3.5 Lola LC89-Lamborghini V12	collision with Berger	19/39

1990

Championship position: Unplaced

excl	US GP (PHOENIX)	Phoenix	26	Ligier Gitanes	G	3.5 Ligier JS33B-Cosworth V8	dsq in practice-outside assist	(26)/35
12	BRAZILIAN GP	Interlagos	26	Ligier Gitanes	G	3.5 Ligier JS33B-Cosworth V8	3 laps behind	10/35
9	SAN MARINO GP	Imola	26	Ligier Gitanes	G	3.5 Ligier JS33B-Cosworth V8	pit stop-tyres/1 lap behind	17/34
dns	" "	"	26	Ligier Gitanes	G	3.5 Ligier JS33-Cosworth V8	practice only	–/–
ret	MONACO GP	Monte Carlo	26	Ligier Gitanes	G	3.5 Ligier JS33B-Cosworth V8	gearbox	18/35
dns	" "	"	26	Ligier Gitanes	G	3.5 Ligier JS33-Cosworth V8	practice only	–/–
ret	CANADIAN GP	Montreal	26	Ligier Gitanes	G	3.5 Ligier JS33B-Cosworth V8	engine	17/35
18	MEXICAN GP	Mexico City	26	Ligier Gitanes	G	3.5 Ligier JS33B-Cosworth V8	pit stop-tyres/3 laps behind	22/35
dns	" "	" "	26	Ligier Gitanes	G	3.5 Ligier JS33-Cosworth V8	practice only	–/–
9	FRENCH GP	Paul Ricard	26	Ligier Gitanes	G	3.5 Ligier JS33B-Cosworth V8	pit stop-tyres/1 lap behind	12/35
dns	" "	"	26	Ligier Gitanes	G	3.5 Ligier JS33-Cosworth V8	practice only	–/–
13	BRITISH GP	Silverstone	26	Ligier Gitanes	G	3.5 Ligier JS33B-Cosworth V8	3 laps behind	22/35
dns	" "	"	26	Ligier Gitanes	G	3.5 Ligier JS33C-Cosworth V8	practice only	–/–
dsq	GERMAN GP	Hockenheim	26	Ligier Gitanes	G	3.5 Ligier JS33C-Cosworth V8	push start after startline accident	24/25
dns	" "	"	26	Ligier Gitanes	G	3.5 Ligier JS33C-Cosworth V8	practice only	–/–
14	HUNGARIAN GP	Hungaroring	26	Ligier Gitanes	G	3.5 Ligier JS33B-Cosworth V8	pit stop/spin/3 laps behind	21/35
dnq	BELGIAN GP	Spa	26	Ligier Gitanes	G	3.5 Ligier JS33B-Cosworth V8		27/33
13	ITALIAN GP	Monza	26	Ligier Gitanes	G	3.5 Ligier JS33B-Cosworth V8	3 laps behind	20/33
ret	PORTUGUESE GP	Estoril	26	Ligier Gitanes	G	3.5 Ligier JS33B-Cosworth V8	collision with Mansell	21/33
ret	SPANISH GP	Jerez	26	Ligier Gitanes	G	3.5 Ligier JS33B-Cosworth V8	spun off	13/33
10	JAPANESE GP	Suzuka	26	Ligier Gitanes	G	3.5 Ligier JS33B-Cosworth V8	1 lap behind	21/30
11	AUSTRALIAN GP	Adelaide	26	Ligier Gitanes	G	3.5 Ligier JS33B-Cosworth V8	3 laps behind	19/30

	1993	Championship position: 17th=	Wins: 0	Pole positions: 0	Fastest laps: 0	Points scored: 2		
ret	SOUTH AFRICAN GP	Kyalami	19	Equipe Larrousse	G	3.5 Larrousse LH93-Lamborghini V12	*spun off*	11/26
7	BRAZILIAN GP	Interlagos	19	Equipe Larrousse	G	3.5 Larrousse LH93-Lamborghini V12	*1 lap behind*	11/26
ret	EUROPEAN GP	Donington	19	Equipe Larrousse	G	3.5 Larrousse LH93-Lamborghini V12	*accident-hit by de Cesaris*	15/26
5	SAN MARINO GP	Imola	19	Equipe Larrousse	G	3.5 Larrousse LH93-Lamborghini V12	*2 laps behind*	14/26
ret	SPANISH GP	Barcelona	19	Equipe Larrousse	G	3.5 Larrousse LH93-Lamborghini V12	*gearbox*	13/26
12	MONACO GP	Monte Carlo	19	Equipe Larrousse	G	3.5 Larrousse LH93-Lamborghini V12	*3 laps behind*	15/26
ret	CANADIAN GP	Montreal	19	Equipe Larrousse	G	3.5 Larrousse LH93-Lamborghini V12	*gearbox*	15/26
9	FRENCH GP	Magny Cours	19	Equipe Larrousse	G	3.5 Larrousse LH93-Lamborghini V12	*2 laps behind*	10/26
11	BRITISH GP	Silverstone	19	Equipe Larrousse	G	3.5 Larrousse LH93-Lamborghini V12	*2 laps behind*	24/26
12	GERMAN GP	Hockenheim	19	Equipe Larrousse	G	3.5 Larrousse LH93-Lamborghini V12	*lost clutch/1 lap behind*	23/26
8	HUNGARIAN GP	Hungaroring	19	Equipe Larrousse	G	3.5 Larrousse LH93-Lamborghini V12	*early spin/2 laps behind*	19/26
12	BELGIAN GP	Spa	19	Equipe Larrousse	G	3.5 Larrousse LH93-Lamborghini V12	*2 laps behind*	18/25
9	ITALIAN GP	Monza	19	Equipe Larrousse	G	3.5 Larrousse LH93-Lamborghini V12	*collision at start/2 laps behind*	16/26
10	PORTUGUESE GP	Estoril	19	Equipe Larrousse	G	3.5 Larrousse LH93-Lamborghini V12	*lost clutch/2 laps behind*	20/26
	1994	Championship position: Unplaced						
ret	HUNGARIAN GP *	Hungaroring	7	Marlboro McLaren Peugeot	G	3.5 McLaren MP4/9-Peugeot V10	*engine*	14/28
ret	BELGIAN GP	Spa	19	Tourtel Larrousse F1	G	3.5 Larrousse LH94-Ford HB V8	*engine*	19/28

GP Starts: 109   GP Wins: 0   Pole positions: 0   Fastest laps: 0   Points: 7

CLIFF ALLISON

The son of a garage owner from Brough, Westmoreland, Allison entered racing in 1952 with the little F3 Cooper-JAP and progressed steadily in the formula, finishing fourth in the 1955 championship. That year he also began racing the works Lotus Eleven sports cars for Colin Chapman, culminating in an Index of Performance win with the little 750 cc Lotus at Le Mans in 1957 – a season which also saw the Hornsey team move into single-seaters with their Lotus 12.

Ambitious plans were made for 1958 and Cliff led the team in their World Championship assault. He scored a fine fourth at Spa, finishing behind three cars which it transpired would not have survived a further lap, and put up a tremendous performance in the German Grand Prix when a burst radiator cost him a possible sensational win in the Lotus 16. His efforts did not go unnoticed, though, and on the recommendation of Mike Hawthorn Cliff was invited by Ferrari for tests at Modena and offered a works drive for 1959.

After a solid first season at Maranello his fortunes were to be mixed; 1960 began with success in Argentina, Cliff winning the 1000 Km for sports cars with Phil Hill and taking second place in the Grand Prix, but a practice crash at Monaco in which he was flung from the car and badly broke his arm curtailed his season. When fully recovered, he signed for the UDT Laystall team to race their Lotus 18 in 1961 and played himself back to form in the many non-championship races held that year, his results including a second place in the International Trophy, run to the 2.5 litre Inter-Continental Formula. For the Belgian Grand Prix, Cliff had to set a quicker practice time than team-mate Henry Taylor in order to claim the car for the race. Disaster struck when he crashed heavily and was thrown from the Lotus, sustaining serious leg injuries which prompted his retirement from racing.

ALLISON, Cliff (GB) b 8/2/1932, Brough, Westmoreland

	1958	Championship position: 14th=		Wins: 0	Pole positions: 0	Fastest laps: 0	Points scored: 3	
	Race	Circuit	No	Entrant	Tyres	Car/Engine	Comment	Q Pos/Entries
6	MONACO GP	Monte Carlo	24	Team Lotus	D	2.0 Lotus 12-Climax 4	*13 laps behind*	13/28
6	DUTCH GP	Zandvoort	17	Team Lotus	D	2.2 Lotus 12-Climax 4	*2 laps behind*	11/17
4	BELGIAN GP	Spa	40	Team Lotus	D	2.2 Lotus 12-Climax 4	*broken suspension on last lap*	12/20
ret	FRENCH GP	Reims	26	Team Lotus	D	2.2 Lotus 12-Climax 4	*engine*	20/21
ret	BRITISH GP	Silverstone	17	Team Lotus	D	2.2 Lotus 12-Climax 4	*oil pressure*	5/21
dns	"	"	17	Team Lotus	D	2.2 Lotus 16-Climax 4	*practice only*	–/–
5/ret	GERMAN GP	Nürburgring	12	Team Lotus	D	2.0 Lotus 16-Climax 4	*radiator/10th after 5 F2 cars/-2 laps*	11/26
dns	PORTUGUESE GP	Oporto	18	Team Lotus	D	2.0 Lotus 16-Climax 4	*practice accident*	13/15
ret	"	"	18	Scuderia Centro Sud/Team Lotus	D	2.5 Maserati 250F 6	*borrowed car/engine*	–/–
7	ITALIAN GP	Monza	36	Team Lotus	D	1.5 Lotus 12-Climax 4	*F2 car/9 laps behind*	16/21
10	MOROCCAN GP	Casablanca	34	Team Lotus	D	2.0 Lotus 12-Climax 4	*4 laps behind*	16/25
	1959	Championship position: 13th=		Wins: 0	Pole positions: 0	Fastest laps: 0	Points scored: 2	
ret	MONACO GP	Monte Carlo	52	Scuderia Ferrari	D	1.5 Ferrari Dino 156 V6	*collision-von Trips & Halford*	15/24
9	DUTCH GP	Zandvoort	16	Scuderia Ferrari	D	2.4 Ferrari Dino 246 V6	*4 laps behind*	15/15
ret	GERMAN GP	AVUS	17	Scuderia Ferrari	D	2.4 Ferrari Dino 246 V6	*clutch in first heat*	14/16
5	ITALIAN GP	Monza	34	Scuderia Ferrari	D	2.4 Ferrari Dino 246 V6	*1 lap behind*	8/21
ret	US GP	Sebring	3	Scuderia Ferrari	D	2.4 Ferrari Dino 246 V6	*clutch*	7/19
	1960	Championship position: 12th=		Wins: 0	Pole positions: 0	Fastest laps: 0	Points scored: 6	
2	ARGENTINE GP	Buenos Aires	24	Scuderia Ferrari	D	2.4 Ferrari Dino 246 V6		7/22
dns	MONACO GP	Monte Carlo	32	Scuderia Ferrari	D	2.4 Ferrari Dino 246 V6	*accident at chicane*	18/24
	1961	Championship position: Unplaced						
8	MONACO GP	Monte Carlo	32	UDT-Laystall Racing Team	D	1.5 Lotus 18-Climax 4	*7 laps behind*	15/21
dnq	BELGIAN GP	Spa	16	UDT-Laystall Racing Team	D	1.5 Lotus 18-Climax 4	*injured in practice crash*	–/25

GP Starts: 16   GP Wins: 0   Pole positions: 0   Fastest laps: 0   Points: 11

CHRIS AMON

Chris Amon will always be best remembered as a notoriously unlucky driver who never managed to win a World Championship Grand Prix, for whenever he seemed poised to triumph dame fortune frowned and poor Chrissie was left to rue his unkind fate.

A New Zealand sheep farmer's son, Chris was racing a Maserati 250F by the age of 18, and he so impressed Reg Parnell in the

1962-63 winter series that he was invited to join the Parnell Grand Prix line-up at the tender age of 19. Amon learned quickly with the team, but the patron's untimely death was a big blow, and by 1965 Chris was spending most of his time with Bruce McLaren and his fledgling organisation, racing his big Elva sports cars. A proposed 1966 Grand Prix season with McLaren failed to get off the ground due to a lack of engines, so it was more sports car racing in Britain and in the Can-Am series, topped by a wonderful win for Ford at Le Mans with Bruce.

Amon's successful season was closely watched by Ferrari, who signed him for 1967. He got off to an encouraging start with wins in the Daytona 24 Hours and Monza 1000 Km, but then came turmoil. With Bandini killed, Parkes injured and Scarfiotti quitting, a huge burden fell on Chris's shoulders and he responded brilliantly with a string of great drives which continued into the following season, coming closest to a win in the 1968 British GP where he had a classic battle with Jo Siffert. The 1969 season started brightly, Chris taking a Dino 166 to the Tasman series and winning the championship, but the strain of the factory's huge racing programme was beginning to show, and F1 suffered most. Frustrated, Chris jumped ship to drive the new works March in 1970, winning the International Trophy and taking a superb second to Rodriguez at Spa, but the team's limitations were soon apparent and, despite an excellent run of placings, he signed a big two-year deal with Matra for 1971-72. A splendid aggregate win in the non-title Argentine GP boded well only for luck to desert him at crucial times, most cruelly at Monza when he lost his visor, and then at Clermont Ferrand when nobody could live with him until a puncture intervened.

With Matra's withdrawal, Chris agreed a return to March for 1973 but a disagreement saw him sensationally sacked at the start of the year. It was to be the start of a downward Formula 1 spiral for the Kiwi, who became progressively dispirited as he saw his efforts go to waste, first at Tecno and then disastrously in 1974 with his own Amon project. Even guest drives for Tyrrell and BRM failed to ignite the latent spark until, seemingly washed up, Chris accepted a drive in Mo Nunn's Ensign late in 1975. Suddenly there was a sense of purpose and in 1976 the old Amon was back, with a superb drive at Kyalami until a fuel problem halted his progress. The new MN176 was a cracking little chassis and

Chris really flew, but unfortunately it was fragile and after a couple of very lucky escapes when things broke he decided to get out in one piece, finally quitting F1 for good after being T-boned in a practice collision at Mosport driving for Wolf. Although he raced briefly in Can-Am in 1977, Chris then married for the second time and returned to New Zealand to tend the family farm.

AMON, Chris (NZ) b 20/7/1943, Bulls

1963 — Championship position: Unplaced

	Race	Circuit	No	Entrant	Tyres	Car/Engine	Comment	Q Pos/Entries
dns	MONACO GP	Monte Carlo	15	Reg Parnell (Racing)	D	1.5 Lola 4A-Climax V8	car driven by Trintignant	(15)/17
ret	BELGIAN GP	Spa	21	Reg Parnell (Racing)	D	1.5 Lola 4A-Climax V8	oil leak	15/20
ret	DUTCH GP	Zandvoort	10	Reg Parnell (Racing)	D	1.5 Lola 4A-Climax V8	water pump	12/19
dns	"	"	10T		D	1.5 Lotus 24-Climax V8	practice only	–/–
7	FRENCH GP	Reims	30	Reg Parnell (Racing)	D	1.5 Lola 4A-Climax V8	2 laps behind	17/21
7	BRITISH GP	Silverstone	19	Reg Parnell (Racing)	D	1.5 Lola 4A-Climax V8	2 laps behind	14/23
ret	GERMAN GP	Nürburgring	21	Reg Parnell (Racing)	D	1.5 Lola 4A-Climax V8	crashed-broken steering	14/26
dns	ITALIAN GP	Monza	38	Reg Parnell (Racing)	D	1.5 Lola 4A-Climax V8	practice accident	(15)/28
ret	MEXICAN GP	Mexico City	18	Reg Parnell (Racing)	D	1.5 Lotus 24-BRM V8	gearbox	19/21

1964 — Championship position: 16th= Wins: 0 Pole positions: 0 Fastest laps: 0 Points scored: 2

	Race	Circuit	No	Entrant	Tyres	Car/Engine	Comment	Q Pos/Entries
dnq	MONACO GP	Monte Carlo	17	Reg Parnell (Racing)	D	1.5 Lotus 25-BRM V8		18/20
5	DUTCH GP	Zandvoort	10	Reg Parnell (Racing)	D	1.5 Lotus 25-BRM V8	1 lap behind	13/18
ret	BELGIAN GP	Spa	27	Reg Parnell (Racing)	D	1.5 Lotus 25-BRM V8	con-rod	11/20
10	FRENCH GP	Rouen	34	Reg Parnell (Racing)	D	1.5 Lotus 25-BRM V8	4 laps behind	14/17
ret	BRITISH GP	Brands Hatch	15	Reg Parnell (Racing)	D	1.5 Lotus 25-BRM V8	clutch	11/25
11/ret	GERMAN GP	Nürburgring	14	Reg Parnell (Racing)	D	1.5 Lotus 25-BRM V8	suspension/3laps behind	9/24
ret	AUSTRIAN GP	Zeltweg	16	Reg Parnell (Racing)	D	1.5 Lotus 25-Climax V8	engine	17/20
ret	US GP	Watkins Glen	15	Reg Parnell (Racing)	D	1.5 Lotus 25-BRM V8	starter motor bolt	11/19
ret	MEXICAN GP	Mexico City	15	Reg Parnell (Racing)	D	1.5 Lotus 25-BRM V8	gearbox	12/19

1965 — Championship position: Unplaced

	Race	Circuit	No	Entrant	Tyres	Car/Engine	Comment	Q Pos/Entries
ret	FRENCH GP	Clermont Ferrand	24	Reg Parnell (Racing)	D	1.5 Lotus 25-BRM V8	fuel feed	8/17
dns	BRITISH GP	Silverstone	24	Ian Raby Racing	D	1.5 Brabham BT3-BRM V8	Raby drove car	–/–
ret	GERMAN GP	Nürburgring	19	Reg Parnell (Racing)	D	1.5 Lotus 25-BRM V8	electrics-ignition	16/22

1966 — Championship position: Unplaced

	Race	Circuit	No	Entrant	Tyres	Car/Engine	Comment	Q Pos/Entries
8	FRENCH GP	Reims	8	Cooper Car Co	D	3.0 Cooper T81-Maserati V12	loose hub nut/4 laps behind	7/17
dnq	ITALIAN GP	Monza	32	Chris Amon	–	2.0 Brabham BT11-BRM V8		22/22

1967 — Championship position: 4th= Wins: 0 Pole positions: 0 Fastest laps: 0 Points scored: 20

	Race	Circuit	No	Entrant	Tyres	Car/Engine	Comment	Q Pos/Entries
3	MONACO GP	Monte Carlo	20	Scuderia Ferrari SpA SEFAC	F	3.0 Ferrari 312/67 V12	2 laps behind	15/18
4	DUTCH GP	Zandvoort	3	Scuderia Ferrari SpA SEFAC	F	3.0 Ferrari 312/67 V12		9/17
3	BELGIAN GP	Spa	1	Scuderia Ferrari SpA SEFAC	F	3.0 Ferrari 312/67 V12		=4/18
ret	FRENCH GP	Le Mans	2	Scuderia Ferrari SpA SEFAC	F	3.0 Ferrari 312/67 V12	throttle cable	7/15
3	BRITISH GP	Silverstone	8	Scuderia Ferrari SpA SEFAC	F	3.0 Ferrari 312/67 V12		6/21
3	GERMAN GP	Nürburgring	8	Scuderia Ferrari SpA SEFAC	F	3.0 Ferrari 312/67 V12		9/25
6	CANADIAN GP	Mosport Park	20	Scuderia Ferrari SpA SEFAC	F	3.0 Ferrari 312/67 V12	3 laps behind	4/19
7	ITALIAN GP	Monza	2	Scuderia Ferrari SpA SEFAC	F	3.0 Ferrari 312/67 V12	pit stop-handling/-4 laps	4/18
ret	US GP	Watkins Glen	9	Scuderia Ferrari SpA SEFAC	F	3.0 Ferrari 312/67 V12	engine	4/18
9	MEXICAN GP	Mexico City	9	Scuderia Ferrari SpA SEFAC	F	3.0 Ferrari 312/67 V12	fuel feed problem/-3 laps	2/19

1968 — Championship position: 10 Wins: 0 Pole positions: 4 Fastest laps: 0 Points scored: 10

	Race	Circuit	No	Entrant	Tyres	Car/Engine	Comment	Q Pos/Entries
4	SOUTH AFRICAN GP	Kyalami	8	Scuderia Ferrari SpA SEFAC	F	3.0 Ferrari 312/67 V12	pit stop-fuel/2 laps behind	8/23
ret	SPANISH GP	Jarama	19	Scuderia Ferrari SpA SEFAC	F	3.0 Ferrari 312/67/68 V12	fuel pump	1/14
ret	BELGIAN GP	Spa	22	Scuderia Ferrari SpA SEFAC	F	3.0 Ferrari 312/67/68 V12	stone holed radiator	1/18
6	DUTCH GP	Zandvoort	9	Scuderia Ferrari SpA SEFAC	F	3.0 Ferrari 312/68 V12	pit stop-tyres/-5 laps	1/19
10	FRENCH GP	Rouen	24	Scuderia Ferrari SpA SEFAC	F	3.0 Ferrari 312/68 V12	engine/tyres/5 laps behind	5/18
2	BRITISH GP	Brands Hatch	5	Scuderia Ferrari SpA SEFAC	F	3.0 Ferrari 312/68 V12		3/20
ret	GERMAN GP	Nürburgring	8	Scuderia Ferrari SpA SEFAC	F	3.0 Ferrari 312/68 V12	spun off	2/20
ret	ITALIAN GP	Monza	9	Scuderia Ferrari SpA SEFAC	F	3.0 Ferrari 312/68 V12	spun off on oil	3/24
ret	CANADIAN GP	St Jovite	9	Scuderia Ferrari SpA SEFAC	F	3.0 Ferrari 312/68 V12	transmission	1/22
ret	US GP	Watkins Glen	6	Scuderia Ferrari SpA SEFAC	F	3.0 Ferrari 312/68 V12	water pipe	4/21
ret	MEXICAN GP	Mexico City	6	Scuderia Ferrari SpA SEFAC	F	3.0 Ferrari 312/68 V12	water pump drive-overheating	2/21

Chris rounds the Station hairpin at Monaco in 1969. Amon retired the Ferrari from second place early in the race, and the car was never a competitive proposition again that year.
The Kiwi driver soon became disillusioned with life at Maranello and quit the team in mid-season.

1969
Championship position: 12th Wins: 0 Pole positions: 0 Fastest laps: 0 Points scored: 4

Pos	GP	Circuit	No	Team	T	Car	Notes	Grid/Laps
ret	SOUTH AFRICAN GP	Kyalami	9	Scuderia Ferrari SpA SEFAC	F	3.0 Ferrari 312/69 V12	*engine*	5/18
ret	SPANISH GP	Montjuich Park	15	Scuderia Ferrari SpA SEFAC	F	3.0 Ferrari 312/69 V12	*engine while leading*	2/14
ret	MONACO GP	Monte Carlo	11	Scuderia Ferrari SpA SEFAC	F	3.0 Ferrari 312/69 V12	*differential*	2/16
3	DUTCH GP	Zandvoort	8	Scuderia Ferrari SpA SEFAC	F	3.0 Ferrari 312/69 V12		4/15
ret	FRENCH GP	Clermont Ferrand	6	Scuderia Ferrari SpA SEFAC	F	3.0 Ferrari 312/69 V12	*engine*	6/13
ret	BRITISH GP	Silverstone	11	Scuderia Ferrari SpA SEFAC	F	3.0 Ferrari 312/69 V12	*gearbox*	5/17

1970
Championship position: 7th= Wins: 0 Pole positions: 0 Fastest laps: 0 Points scored: 23

Pos	GP	Circuit	No	Team	T	Car	Notes	Grid/Laps
ret	SOUTH AFRICAN GP	Kyalami	15	March Engineering	F	3.0 March 701-Cosworth V8	*overheating*	=1/24
ret	SPANISH GP	Jarama	9	March Engineering	F	3.0 March 701-Cosworth V8	*engine/clutch*	6/22
ret	MONACO GP	Monte Carlo	28	March Engineering	F	3.0 March 701-Cosworth V8	*rear suspension bolt*	2/21
2	BELGIAN GP	Spa	10	March Engineering	F	3.0 March 701-Cosworth V8	*FL*	3/18
ret	DUTCH GP	Zandvoort	8	March Engineering	F	3.0 March 701-Cosworth V8	*clutch*	4/24
2	FRENCH GP	Clermont Ferrand	14	March Engineering	F	3.0 March 701-Cosworth V8		3/23
5	BRITISH GP	Brands Hatch	16	March Engineering	F	3.0 March 701-Cosworth V8	*1 lap behind*	18/25
ret	GERMAN GP	Hockenheim	5	March Engineering	F	3.0 March 701-Cosworth V8	*engine*	6/25
8	AUSTRIAN GP	Österreichring	4	March Engineering	F	3.0 March 701-Cosworth V8	*1 lap behind*	6/24
7	ITALIAN GP	Monza	48	March Engineering	F	3.0 March 701-Cosworth V8	*1 lap behind*	21/27
3	CANADIAN GP	St Jovite	20	March Engineering	F	3.0 March 701-Cosworth V8		=5/20
5	US GP	Watkins Glen	12	March Engineering	F	3.0 March 701-Cosworth V8	*pit stop-tyres/1 lap behind*	5/27
4	MEXICAN GP	Mexico City	12	March Engineering	F	3.0 March 701-Cosworth V8		5/18

1971
Championship position: 9th= Wins: 0 Pole positions: 1 Fastest laps: 0 Points scored: 9

Pos	GP	Circuit	No	Team	T	Car	Notes	Grid/Laps
5	SOUTH AFRICAN GP	Kyalami	19	Equipe Matra Sports	G	3.0 Matra-Simca MS120B V12	*1 lap behind*	2/25
3	SPANISH GP	Montjuich Park	20	Equipe Matra Sports	G	3.0 Matra-Simca MS120B V12		=2/22
ret	MONACO GP	Monte Carlo	20	Equipe Matra Sports	G	3.0 Matra-Simca MS120B V12	*cwp*	=3/23
ret	DUTCH GP	Zandvoort	20	Equipe Matra Sports	G	3.0 Matra-Simca MS120B V12	*spun off-damaged radiator*	5/24
5	FRENCH GP	Paul Ricard	20	Equipe Matra Sports	G	3.0 Matra-Simca MS120B V12		9/24
ret	BRITISH GP	Silverstone	21	Equipe Matra Sports	G	3.0 Matra-Simca MS120B V12	*dropped valve*	9/24
ret	GERMAN GP	Nürburgring	10	Equipe Matra Sports	G	3.0 Matra-Simca MS120B V12	*spun, damaged suspension*	16/23
6	ITALIAN GP	Monza	12	Equipe Matra Sports	G	3.0 Matra-Simca MS120B V12	*lost visor while leading race*	1/24
10	CANADIAN GP	Mosport Park	20	Equipe Matra Sports	G	3.0 Matra-Simca MS120B V12	*3 laps behind*	=4/27
12	US GP	Watkins Glen	11	Equipe Matra Sports	G	3.0 Matra-Simca MS120B V12	*pit stop-tyres/2 laps behind*	9/32

1972
Championship position: 9th= Wins: 0 Pole positions: 1 Fastest laps: 2 Points scored: 12

Pos	GP	Circuit	No	Team	T	Car	Notes	Grid/Laps
dns	ARGENTINE GP	Buenos Aires	16	Equipe Matra	G	3.0 Matra-Simca MS120C V12	*gearbox on warm-up lap*	(12)/22
15	SOUTH AFRICAN GP	Kyalami	15	Equipe Matra	G	3.0 Matra-Simca MS120C V12	*2 pit stops-vibration/-3 laps*	13/27
ret	SPANISH GP	Jarama	9	Equipe Matra	G	3.0 Matra-Simca MS120C V12	*gearbox*	6/26
6	MONACO GP	Monte Carlo	16	Equipe Matra	G	3.0 Matra-Simca MS120C V12	*4 pit stops-goggles/-3 laps*	=5/25
6	BELGIAN GP	Nivelles	5	Equipe Matra	G	3.0 Matra-Simca MS120D V12	*fuel stop lay 3rd/FL/-1 lap*	13/26
3	FRENCH GP	Clermont Ferrand	9	Equipe Matra	G	3.0 Matra-Simca MS120D V12	*pit stop-puncture/FL*	1/29
4	BRITISH GP	Brands Hatch	17	Equipe Matra	G	3.0 Matra-Simca MS120D V12	*1 lap behind*	17/27
dns	"	"	17	Equipe Matra	G	3.0 Matra-Simca MS120D V12	*practice only*	– / –
15	GERMAN GP	Nürburgring	8	Equipe Matra	G	3.0 Matra-Simca MS120D V12	*started late from pits/-1 lap*	8/27
5	AUSTRIAN GP	Österreichring	10	Equipe Matra	G	3.0 Matra-Simca MS120D V12		6/26
dns	"	"	30T	Equipe Matra	G	3.0 Matra-Simca MS120D V12	*practice only*	– / –
ret	ITALIAN GP	Monza	20	Equipe Matra	G	3.0 Matra-Simca MS120C V12	*brakes-worn pads*	2/27
dns	"	"	20T	Equipe Matra	G	3.0 Matra-Simca MS120C V12	*practice only*	– / –
6	CANADIAN GP	Mosport Park	4	Equipe Matra	G	3.0 Matra-Simca MS120D V12	*1 lap behind*	10/25
15	US GP	Watkins Glen	18	Equipe Matra	G	3.0 Matra-Simca MS120D V12	*started from back /-2 laps*	7/32

1973
Championship position: 19th= Wins: 0 Pole positions: 0 Fastest laps: 0 Points scored: 1

Pos	GP	Circuit	No	Team	T	Car	Notes	Grid/Laps
6	BELGIAN GP	Zolder	22	Martini Racing Team	F	3.0 Tecno PA123 F12	*3 laps behind*	15/23
ret	MONACO GP	Monte Carlo	22	Martini Racing Team	F	3.0 Tecno PA123 F12	*overheating*	12/26
ret	BRITISH GP	Silverstone	22	Martini Racing Team	F	3.0 Tecno PA123 F12	*fuel pressure*	29/29
ret	DUTCH GP	Zandvoort	22	Martini Racing Team	F	3.0 Tecno PA123 F12	*fuel pressure*	19/24
dns	"	"	22T	Martini Racing Team	F	3.0 Tecno E731 F12	*practice only*	– / –
dns	AUSTRIAN GP	Österreichring	22	Martini Racing Team	F	3.0 Tecno PA123 F12	*no race engine available*	(23)/25
dns	"	"	22T	Martini Racing Team	F	3.0 Tecno E731 F12	*no race engine available*	– / –
10	CANADIAN GP	Mosport Park	29	Elf Team Tyrrell	G	3.0 Tyrrell 005-Cosworth V8	*pit stop-tyres/3 laps behind*	11/26
dns	US GP	Watkins Glen	29	Elf Team Tyrrell	G	3.0 Tyrrell 005-Cosworth V8	*withdrawn after Cevert's death*	(13)/28

1974
Championship position: Unplaced

Pos	GP	Circuit	No	Team	T	Car	Notes	Grid/Laps
ret	SPANISH GP	Jarama	30	Chris Amon Racing	F	3.0 Amon AF101-Cosworth V8	*brakeshaft*	24/28
dns	MONACO GP	Monte Carlo	30	Chris Amon Racing	F	3.0 Amon AF101-Cosworth V8	*withdrawn-hub failure*	(20)/28
dnq	GERMAN GP	Nürburgring	30	Chris Amon Racing	F	3.0 Amon AF101-Cosworth V8	*driver unwell*	31/32
dnq	ITALIAN GP	Monza	22	Chris Amon Racing	F	3.0 Amon AF101-Cosworth V8		30/31
nc	CANADIAN GP	Mosport Park	15	Team Motul BRM	F	3.0 BRM P201 V12	*pit stop-misfire/-10 laps*	25/30
9	US GP	Watkins Glen	15	Team Motul BRM	F	3.0 BRM P201 V12	*2 laps behind*	12/30

1975
Championship position: Unplaced

Pos	GP	Circuit	No	Team	T	Car	Notes	Grid/Laps
12	AUSTRIAN GP	Österreichring	31	HB Bewaking Team Ensign	G	3.0 Ensign N175-Cosworth V8	*1 lap behind*	24/30
12	ITALIAN GP	Monza	32	HB Bewaking Team Ensign	G	3.0 Ensign N175-Cosworth V8	*misfire/4 laps behind*	19/28

1976
Championship position: 18th Wins: 0 Pole positions: 0 Fastest laps: 0 Points scored: 2

Pos	GP	Circuit	No	Team	T	Car	Notes	Grid/Laps
14	SOUTH AFRICAN GP	Kyalami	22	Team Ensign	G	3.0 Ensign N174-Cosworth V8	*pit stop-fuel/2 laps behind*	18/25
8	US GP WEST	Long Beach	22	Team Ensign	G	3.0 Ensign N174-Cosworth V8	*pit stop-brakes/2 laps behind*	17/27
5	SPANISH GP	Jarama	22	Team Ensign	G	3.0 Ensign N176-Cosworth V8	*1 lap behind*	10/30
ret	BELGIAN GP	Zolder	22	Team Ensign	G	3.0 Ensign N176-Cosworth V8	*lost wheel-crashed*	8/29
13	MONACO GP	Monte Carlo	22	Team Ensign	G	3.0 Ensign N176-Cosworth V8	*painful wrist/4 laps behind*	12/25
ret	SWEDISH GP	Anderstorp	22	Team Ensign	G	3.0 Ensign N176-Cosworth V8	*suspension failure-crashed*	3/27
ret	BRITISH GP	Brands Hatch	22	Team Ensign	G	3.0 Ensign N176-Cosworth V8	*water leak*	6/30
ret/dns	GERMAN GP	Nürburgring	22	Team Ensign	G	3.0 Ensign N176-Cosworth V8	*driver withdrew after first start*	17/28
dns	CANADIAN GP	Mosport Park	21	Walter Wolf Racing	G	3.0 Williams FW05-Cosworth V8	*practice accident*	(26)/27

GP Starts: 95 (97) GP Wins: 0 Pole positions: 5 Fastest laps: 3 Points: 83

BOB ANDERSON

This tough ex-motor cycle racer had tasted success before a damaged back ended his two-wheel career and he switched to four-wheel competition at the relatively late age of 29 in 1961. A season was spent learning the ropes in Formula Junior for Lotus before he bought the ex-Bowmaker Lola to have a crack at Formula 1 in 1963, competing in the many non-title races that abounded at the time. After a third place at Imola and a fourth at Syracuse, he won the Rome GP against fairly thin local opposition, quickly garnering the experience to compete full-time in the World Championship in 1964.

Making the absolute most of a minute budget, he frequently outdrove more vaunted competitors with his Brabham and was deservedly awarded the Wolfgang von Trips Trophy for the best private entrant. The days of the independent were already numbered but Bob – loyally supported by his French wife Marie-Edmée – ploughed on. His 1965 season was cut short after he wrote off his car in a practice accident at the Nürburgring, but this setback merely strengthened Anderson's resolve and he equipped his Brabham with an old Climax four-cylinder engine for the new 1966 3-litre formula.

Once again heroic performances gained placings which reflected the driver's skill and tenacity but as the Cosworth era dawned even Bob was facing the stark reality that time was up for the impecunious privateer. Testing his ancient Brabham on a wet track at Silverstone in preparation for the 1967 Canadian GP, he aquaplaned into a marshals' post, receiving severe throat and chest injuries. Poor Anderson had no chance of survival, and eventually succumbed four hours later in Northampton hospital.

Seen as a lone wolf, Anderson would have loved to be considered for a works drive but, while the Grand Prix circus wined and dined at the plushest of hotels on their travels, Bob was to be found resting his head in less expensive establishments – if there was time for sleep at all, given his other duties as team manager, mechanic and public relations man.

Today, the sometimes abrasive Anderson is a forgotten figure, but those who knew him remember a man of remarkable integrity and indomitable spirit who lived – and died – for his passion.

CONNY ANDERSSON

The likeable and humorous Andersson spent his younger days as a top motocross rider in his native Sweden while helping run his father's garage dealership and at the same time raising a family which comprised four daughters. There was little time to contemplate a racing career until he was bitten by the bug after a visit to a racing school and a drive in a Formula Vee car at the Nürburgring.

By wheeling and dealing in second-hand cars he scraped together enough cash to buy a Brabham BT21 and, at the relatively late age of 29, began his racing career.

Conny became trapped in F3 from 1970 to 1976 by his lack of the finance to move into higher spheres. But in his travels he acquitted himself well against the likes of Hunt, Scheckter, Jabouille and Laffite, who were all carving out top-line careers for themselves. In 1974, armed with a March-Toyota, he took six wins, four seconds and four thirds from twenty starts and began to be considered a serious prospect.

More success followed in 1975, despite the disappointment of a 'win' in the Monaco F3 race which was taken away when he was penalised for jumping the start. This drive caught the eye of John Surtees, who gave him an end-of-season test in one of his F1 cars, but he failed to land a full-time ride for 1976, so it was back to the European championship, where he was particularly unlucky to be pipped by Riccardo Patrese for the title.

His efforts finally brought him a one-off chance to drive a Surtees in the Dutch Grand Prix that season and, unwilling to face a further year in Formula 3, Conny then opted for another shot at F1 with the uncompetitive Stanley-BRM before calling it a day.

Anderson in his
immaculate Brabham
BT11-Climax in 1966.

ANDERSON, Bob (GB) b 19/5/1931, Hendon, London – d 14/8/1967, Northampton

	1963	Championship position: Unplaced						
	Race	Circuit	No	Entrant	Tyres	Car/Engine	Comment	Q Pos/Entries
12	BRITISH GP	Silverstone	22	DW Racing Enterprises	D	1.5 Lola 4-Climax V8	*7 laps behind*	16/23
12	ITALIAN GP	Monza	48	DW Racing Enterprises	D	1.5 Lola 4-Climax V8	*7 laps behind*	19/28
	1964	Championship position: 11th Wins: 0 Pole positions: 0 Fastest laps: 0 Points scored: 5						
7/ret	MONACO GP	Monte Carlo	16	DW Racing Enterprises	D	1.5 Brabham BT11-Climax V8	*gearbox mounting/-14 laps*	12/20
6	DUTCH GP	Zandvoort	34	DW Racing Enterprises	D	1.5 Brabham BT11-Climax V8	*2 laps behind*	11/18
dns	BELGIAN GP	Spa	18	DW Racing Enterprises	D	1.5 Brabham BT11-Climax V8	*ignition problems*	(19)/20
12	FRENCH GP	Rouen	32	DW Racing Enterprises	D	1.5 Brabham BT11-Climax V8	*7 laps behind*	15/17
7	BRITISH GP	Brands Hatch	19	DW Racing Enterprises	D	1.5 Brabham BT11-Climax V8	*2 laps behind*	7/25
ret	GERMAN GP	Nürburgring	16	DW Racing Enterprises	D	1.5 Brabham BT11-Climax V8	*suspension*	15/24
3	AUSTRIAN GP	Zeltweg	22	DW Racing Enterprises	D	1.5 Brabham BT11-Climax V8	*3 laps behind*	14/20
11	ITALIAN GP	Monza	22	DW Racing Enterprises	D	1.5 Brabham BT11-Climax V8	*3 laps behind*	14/25
	1965	Championship position: Unplaced						
nc	SOUTH AFRICAN GP	East London	14	DW Racing Enterprises	D	1.5 Brabham BT11-Climax V8	*pit stops-brakes/-35 laps*	12/25
9	MONACO GP	Monte Carlo	9	DW Racing Enterprises	D	1.5 Brabham BT11-Climax V8	*pit stops/15 laps behind*	9/17
dns	BELGIAN GP	Spa	24	DW Racing Enterprises	D	1.5 Brabham BT11-Climax V8	*withdrawn after practice*	(19)/21
9/ret	FRENCH GP	Clermont Ferrand	30	DW Racing Enterprises	D	1.5 Brabham BT11-Climax V8	*spun off/6 laps behind*	15/17
ret	BRITISH GP	Silverstone	18	DW Racing Enterprises	D	1.5 Brabham BT11-Climax V8	*gearbox*	17/23
ret	DUTCH GP	Zandvoort	36	DW Racing Enterprises	D	1.5 Brabham BT11-Climax V8	*engine-overheating*	16/17
dns	GERMAN GP	Nürburgring	18	DW Racing Enterprises	D	1.5 Brabham BT11-Climax V8	*practice accident*	(15)/22
	1966	Championship position: 17th= Wins: 0 Pole positions: 0 Fastest laps: 0 Points scored: 1						
ret	MONACO GP	Monte Carlo	15	DW Racing Enterprises	F	2.7 Brabham BT11-Climax 4	*engine*	8/16
7/ret	FRENCH GP	Reims	36	DW Racing Enterprises	F	2.7 Brabham BT11-Climax 4	*engine/4 laps behind*	=12/17
nc	BRITISH GP	Brands Hatch	21	DW Racing Enterprises	F	2.7 Brabham BT11-Climax 4	*pit stops-battery/-10 laps*	10/20
ret	DUTCH GP	Zandvoort	34	DW Racing Enterprises	F	2.7 Brabham BT11-Climax 4	*suspension*	=15/18
ret	GERMAN GP	Nürburgring	19	DW Racing Enterprises	F	2.7 Brabham BT11-Climax 4	*transmission*	15/30
6	ITALIAN GP	Monza	40	DW Racing Enterprises	F	2.7 Brabham BT11-Climax 4	*2 laps behind*	15/22
	1967	Championship position: 16th= Wins: 0 Pole positions: 0 Fastest laps: 0 Points scored: 2						
5	SOUTH AFRICAN GP	Kyalami	14	DW Racing Enterprises	F	2.7 Brabham BT11-Climax 4	*2 laps behind*	10/18
dnq	MONACO GP	Monte Carlo	15	DW Racing Enterprises	F	2.7 Brabham BT11-Climax 4		14/18
9	DUTCH GP	Zandvoort	21	DW Racing Enterprises	F	2.7 Brabham BT11-Climax 4	*4 laps behind*	17/17
8	BELGIAN GP	Spa	19	DW Racing Enterprises	F	2.7 Brabham BT11-Climax 4	*2 laps behind*	17/18
ret	FRENCH GP	Le Mans	17	DW Racing Enterprises	D	2.7 Brabham BT11-Climax 4	*ignition*	14/15
ret	BRITISH GP	Silverstone	19	DW Racing Enterprises	F	2.7 Brabham BT11-Climax 4	*engine*	17/21

GP Starts: 25   GP Wins: 0   Pole positions: 0   Fastest laps: 0   Points: 8

ANDERSSON, Conny (S) b 28/12/1939, Alingås

	1976	Championship position: Unplaced						
	Race	Circuit	No	Entrant	Tyres	Car/Engine	Comment	Q Pos/Entries
ret	DUTCH GP	Zandvoort	18	Team Surtees	G	3.0 Surtees TS19-Cosworth V8	*engine*	26/27
	1977	Championship position: Unplaced						
dnq	SPANISH GP	Jarama	35	Rotary Watches Stanley BRM	G	3.0 BRM P207 V12		31/31
dnq	BELGIAN GP	Zolder	35	Rotary Watches Stanley BRM	G	3.0 BRM P207 V12		29/32
dnq	SWEDISH GP	Anderstorp	35	Rotary Watches Stanley BRM	G	3.0 BRM P207 V12		30/31
dnq	FRENCH GP	Dijon	35	Rotary Watches Stanley BRM	G	3.0 BRM P207 V12		30/30

GP Starts: 1   GP Wins: 0   Pole positions: 0   Fastest laps: 0   Points: 0

MARIO ANDRETTI

WORLD CHAMPION: 1978

MARIO ANDRETTI

Having arrived in the United States as the teenage son of poor Italian immigrants, Andretti has gone on to become one of America's greatest motor racing stars in a career which has spanned over thirty years – all of them spent racing competitively at the top level.

His interest in motor sport was kindled as a boy in his native Italy, and as soon as Mario was old enough to race seriously he set out with his twin brother Aldo on the US sprint and midget racing trail, finally winning the championship in 1964, the season which also saw his USAC debut. The following year he not only won the first of his four USAC/Indy Car titles but also took third place on his Indy 500 debut. He was champion again in 1966 and through until 1969 – when he won his only Indy 500 – Mario was the man to beat, even if luck was not always with him in terms of results.

Andretti had idolised Ascari in his youth and gladly accepted the chance to go Grand Prix racing with Lotus, causing a sensation by putting his car on pole at Watkins Glen. His clashing USAC commitments limited his F1 appearances – and chances of success – with both Lotus and March, but he shone in sports cars, winning at Sebring and Watkins Glen for Ferrari in 1970, before achieving a dream by signing to race for the Scuderia in F1 in 1971. His start could not have been better, Mario winning the South African GP followed by the non-championship Questor GP, but at this stage he was still splitting his season between USAC racing and his Ferrari F1 and sports car programme, the latter proving most successful in 1972, when he took four wins in the 312P with Ickx.

Mario concentrated on American racing in 1973-74, racing for Vel's Parnelli in F5000 and USAC events, and in late 1974 he debuted the team's Grand Prix contender. He campaigned the VPJ4 throughout 1975 (and briefly in 1976) before Parnelli withdrew from F1, and then returned to a Lotus team in the doldrums. Together with Colin Chapman, he set about reviving the famous marque's fortunes and by the end of the 1976 season they were back in the winner's circle. Soon the team's 'ground-effect' type 78 and 79 cars were in the ascendancy, Mario magnificently winning the 1978 World Championship title after scoring six wins.

It was a different story in 1979 and 1980 as Lotus got it badly wrong, bogged down in a technical mire. Lured perhaps by sentiment as much as anything, Andretti joined Alfa Romeo in 1981, for what was to become another disappointing season, largely due to the inadequacies of the car. Mario drove as well as ever, comfortably outclassing his young team-mate Bruno Giacomelli, but decided to return to the States in 1982 to undertake a full Indy Car schedule, his first for some years, before a brief Formula 1 swansong with Ferrari.

Thereafter Mario concentrated on Indy Car racing full-time, and soon took what was to be his last Indy Car crown in 1984. But for another decade, revelling in the comforting surroundings of the Newman-Haas team, he remained capable of giving anyone a race on his day. By the end of his 'Arrivederci Mario' 1994 season, Andretti's Indy Car record was staggering. A record total of 407 starts, 52 wins and 66 pole positions are testimony to the enduring talent of this legendary figure.

Of course the hunger to drive remained unsatiated, and the chance of winning the Le Mans 24 Hours (and thereby matching Graham Hill's unique achievement of winning the World Championship, the Indy 500 and the Sarthe classic) was too much for Mario to pass up. He very nearly triumphed in 1995, but his minor shunt left the frustrated driver to make do with second place. After further unsuccessful attempts in the following two seasons it seemed that Andretti had finally had to admit defeat and leave this particular quest undone, but it has been reported that he intends to make another bid for victory in 2000.

He now regularly attends the CART races as part of the Newman-Haas team, supporting the efforts of his son Michael, who carries on the family tradition so superbly behind the wheel.

Mario fulfilled a childhood dream when he won the 1971 South African Grand Prix at the wheel of a Ferrari.

ANDRETTI, Mario (USA) b 28/2/1940, Montona, Italy

	1968			Championship position: Unplaced	Wins: 0	Pole positions: 1	Fastest laps: 0	Points scored: 0		
	Race	Circuit	No	Entrant	Tyres	Car/Engine		Comment		Q Pos/Entries
dns	ITALIAN GP	Monza	18	Gold Leaf Team Lotus	F	3.0 Lotus 49B-Cosworth V8		also aced in USA within 24 hours		(11)/24
ret	US GP	Watkins Glen	12	Gold Leaf Team Lotus	F	3.0 Lotus 49B-Cosworth V8		clutch		1/21
	1969			Championship position: Unplaced						
ret	SOUTH AFRICAN GP	Kyalami	3	Gold Leaf Team Lotus	F	3.0 Lotus 49B-Cosworth V8		transmission		6/18
ret	GERMAN GP	Nürburgring	3	Gold Leaf Team Lotus	F	3.0 Lotus 63-Cosworth V8 (4WD)		accident-lost control		15/26
ret	US GP	Watkins Glen	9	Gold Leaf Team Lotus	F	3.0 Lotus 63-Cosworth V8 (4WD)		rear suspension damage		13/18
	1970			Championship position: 15th=	Wins: 0	Pole positions: 0	Fastest laps: 0	Points scored: 4		
ret	SOUTH AFRICAN GP	Kyalami	8	STP Corporation	F	3.0 March 701-Cosworth V8		overheating		11/24
3	SPANISH GP	Jarama	18	STP Corporation	F	3.0 March 701-Cosworth V8		1 lap behind		19/22
ret	BRITISH GP	Brands Hatch	26	STP Corporation	F	3.0 March 701-Cosworth V8		rear suspension		9/25
ret	GERMAN GP	Hockenheim	11	STP Corporation	F	3.0 March 701-Cosworth V8		gear selection		9/25
ret	AUSTRIAN GP	Österreichring	5	STP Corporation	F	3.0 March 701-Cosworth V8		accident-jammed throttle		17/24
	1971			Championship position: 8th	Wins: 0	Pole positions: 0	Fastest laps: 1	Points scored: 12		
1	SOUTH AFRICAN GP	Kyalami	6	Scuderai Ferrari SpA SEFAC	F	3.0 Ferrari 312B F12		FL		4/25
ret	SPANISH GP	Montjuich Park	6	Scuderia Ferrari SpA SEFAC	F	3.0 Ferrari 312B F12		fuel pump		8/22
dnq	MONACO GP	Monte Carlo	6	Scuderia Ferrari SpA SEFAC	F	3.0 Ferrari 312B F12		missed the only dry session		20/23
ret	DUTCH GP	Zandvoort	4	Scuderia Ferrari SpA SEFAC	F	3.0 Ferrari 312B F12		fuel pump		18/24
4	GERMAN GP	Nürburgring	5	Scuderia Ferrari SpA SEFAC	F	3.0 Ferrari 312B2 F12				11/23
13	CANADIAN GP	Mosport Park	6	Scuderia Ferrari SpA SEFAC	F	3.0 Ferrari 312B2 F12		pit stop-engine/4 laps behind		13/27
dns	US GP	Watkins Glen	6	Scuderia Ferrari SpA SEFAC	F	3.0 Ferrari 312B2 F12		practised-but went to USAC race		(6)/32
	1972			Championship position: 12th=	Wins: 0	Pole positions: 0	Fastest laps: 0	Points scored: 4		
ret	ARGENTINE GP	Buenos Aires	10	Scuderia Ferrari SpA SEFAC	F	3.0 Ferrari 312B2 F12		engine misfire		9/22
4	SOUTH AFRICAN GP	Kyalami	7	Scuderia Ferrari SpA SEFAC	F	3.0 Ferrari 312B2 F12				6/27
ret	SPANISH GP	Jarama	7	Scuderia Ferrari SpA SEFAC	F	3.0 Ferrari 312B2 F12		engine		5/26
7	ITALIAN GP	Monza	3	Scuderia Ferrari SpA SEFAC	F	3.0 Ferrari 312B2 F12		pit stop-wheel/1 lap behind		7/27
6	US GP	Watkins Glen	9	Scuderia Ferrari SpA SEFAC	F	3.0 Ferrari 312B2 F12		handling problems/-1 lap		10/32
	1974			Championship position: Unplaced						
7	CANADIAN GP	Mosport Park	55	Vel's Parnelli Jones Racing	F	3.0 Parnelli VPJ4-Cosworth V8		stalled at start/1 lap behind		16/30
dsq	US GP	Watkins Glen	55	Vel's Parnelli Jones Racing	F	3.0 Parnelli VPJ4-Cosworth V8		push start on grid		3/30
	1975			Championship position: 14th	Wins: 0	Pole positions: 0	Fastest laps: 1	Points scored: 5		
ret	ARGENTINE GP	Buenos Aires	27	Vel's Parnelli Jones Racing	F	3.0 Parneiil VPJ4-Cosworth V8		driveshaft-c.v. joint		10/23
7	BRAZILIAN GP	Interlagos	27	Vel's Parnelli Jones Racing	G	3.0 Parnelli VPJ4-Cosworth V8				18/23
17/ret	SOUTH AFRICAN GP	Kyalami	27	Vel's Parnelli Jones Racing	G	3.0 Parnelli VPJ4-Cosworth V8		driveshaft-c.v. joint/-8 laps		6/28
ret	SPANISH GP	Montjuich Park	27	Vel's Parnelli Jones Racing	G	3.0 Parnelli VPJ4-Cosworth V8		broken suspension -accident/FL		4/26
ret	MONACO GP	Monte Carlo	27	Vel's Parnelli Jones Racing	G	3.0 Parnelli VPJ4-Cosworth V8		broken oil line-fire		13/26
4	SWEDISH GP	Anderstorp	27	Vel's Parnelli Jones Racing	G	3.0 Parnelli VPJ4-Cosworth V8				15/26
5	FRENCH GP	Paul Ricard	27	Vel's Parnelli Jones Racing	G	3.0 Parnelli VPJ4-Cosworth V8				=15/26
12	BRITISH GP	Silverstone	27	Vel's Parnelli Jones Racing	G	3.0 Parnelli VPJ4-Cosworth V8		collision-Jarier-pit stop/-2 laps		12/28
10/ret	GERMAN GP	Nürburgring	27	Vel's Parnelli Jones Racing	G	3.0 Parnelli VPJ4-Cosworth V8		broken wheel/fuel leak/-2 laps		13/26
ret	AUSTRIAN GP	Österreichring	27	Vel's Parnelli Jones Racing	G	3.0 Parnelli VPJ4-Cosworth V8		spun off		19/30
ret	ITALIAN GP	Monza	27	Vel's Parnelli Jones Racing	G	3.0 Parnelli VPJ4-Cosworth V8		multiple accident at chicane		15/28
ret	US GP	Watkins Glen	27	Vel's Parnelli Jones Racing	G	3.0 Parnelli VPJ4-Cosworth V8		suspension		5/24

Mario driving the Parnelli VPJ4-Cosworth in the 1975 French Grand Prix. This ambitious attempt to conquer Formula 1 by an American team eventually folded without notable success.

Mario winning the 1977 Spanish Grand Prix in the Lotus 78.

1976
Championship position: 6th Wins: 1 Pole positions: 1 Fastest laps: 1 Points scored: 22

ret	BRAZILIAN GP	Interlagos	6	John Player Team Lotus	G	3.0 Lotus 77-Cosworth V8	collision with Peterson	16/22
6	SOUTH AFRICAN GP	Kyalami	27	Vel's Parnelli Jones Racing	G	3.0 Parnelli VPJ4B-Cosworth V8	1 lap behind	13/25
ret	US GP WEST	Long Beach	27	Vel's Parnelli Jones Racing	G	3.0 Parnelli VPJ4B-Cosworth V8	water leak	15/27
ret	SPANISH GP	Jarama	5	John Player Team Lotus	G	3.0 Lotus 77-Cosworth V8	gear selection	9/30
ret	BELGIAN GP	Zolder	5	John Player Team Lotus	G	3.0 Lotus 77-Cosworth V8	driveshaft	11/29
ret	SWEDISH GP	Anderstorp	5	John Player Team Lotus	G	3.0 Lotus 77-Cosworth V8	engine/FL	2/27
5	FRENCH GP	Paul Ricard	5	John Player Team Lotus	G	3.0 Lotus 77-Cosworth V8		7/30
ret	BRITISH GP	Brands Hatch	5	John Player Team Lotus	G	3.0 Lotus 77-Cosworth V8	engine	3/30
12	GERMAN GP	Nürburgring	5	John Player Team Lotus	G	3.0 Lotus 77-Cosworth V8	pit stop-battery	12/28
5	AUSTRIAN GP	Österreichring	5	John Player Team Lotus	G	3.0 Lotus 77-Cosworth V8		9/25
3	DUTCH GP	Zandvoort	5	John Player Team Lotus	G	3.0 Lotus 77-Cosworth V8		6/27
ret	ITALIAN GP	Monza	5	John Player Team Lotus	G	3.0 Lotus 77-Cosworth V8	collision with Stuck	14/29
3	CANADIAN GP	Mosport Park	5	John Player Team Lotus	G	3.0 Lotus 77-Cosworth V8		5/27
ret	US GP EAST	Watkins Glen	5	John Player Team Lotus	G	3.0 Lotus 77-Cosworth V8	hit kerb-damaged suspension	11/27
1	JAPANESE GP	Mount Fuji	5	John Player Team Lotus	G	3.0 Lotus 77-Cosworth V8		1/27

1977
Championship position: 3rd Wins: 4 Pole positions: 7 Fastest laps: 4 Points scored: 47

5/ret	ARGENTINE GP	Buenos Aires	5	John Player Team Lotus	G	3.0 Lotus 78-Cosworth V8	rear wheel bearing/-2 laps	8/21
ret	BRAZILIAN GP	Interlagos	5	John Player Team Lotus	G	3.0 Lotus 78-Cosworth V8	ignition	3/22
ret	SOUTH AFRICAN GP	Kyalami	5	John Player Team Lotus	G	3.0 Lotus 78-Cosworth V8	collision Reutemann-suspension	6/23
1	US GP WEST	Long Beach	5	John Player Team Lotus	G	3.0 Lotus 78-Cosworth V8		2/22
1	SPANISH GP	Jarama	5	John Player Team Lotus	G	3.0 Lotus 78-Cosworth V8		1/31
5	MONACO GP	Monte Carlo	5	John Player Team Lotus	G	3.0 Lotus 78-Cosworth V8		10/26
ret	BELGIAN GP	Zolder	5	John Player Team Lotus	G	3.0 Lotus 78-Cosworth V8	hit Watson	1/32
6	SWEDISH GP	Anderstorp	5	John Player Team Lotus	G	3.0 Lotus 78-Cosworth V8	pit stop-fuel/FL	1/31
1	FRENCH GP	Dijon	5	John Player Team Lotus	G	3.0 Lotus 78-Cosworth V8	FL	1/30
14/ret	BRITISH GP	Silverstone	5	John Player Team Lotus	G	3.0 Lotus 78-Cosworth V8	engine/6 laps behind	6/36
ret	GERMAN GP	Hockenheim	5	John Player Team Lotus	G	3.0 Lotus 78-Cosworth V8	engine	7/30
ret	AUSTRIAN GP	Österreichring	5	John Player Team Lotus	G	3.0 Lotus 78-Cosworth V8	engine	3/30
ret	DUTCH GP	Zandvoort	5	John Player Team Lotus	G	3.0 Lotus 78-Cosworth V8	engine	1/34
1	ITALIAN GP	Monza	5	John Player Team Lotus	G	3.0 Lotus 78-Cosworth V8	FL	4/34
2	US GP EAST	Watkins Glen	5	John Player Team Lotus	G	3.0 Lotus 78-Cosworth V8		4/27
9/ret	CANADIAN GP	Mosport Park	5	John Player Team Lotus	G	3.0 Lotus 78-Cosworth V8	engine/FL/3 laps behind	1/27
ret	JAPANESE GP	Mount Fuji	5	John Player Team Lotus	G	3.0 Lotus 78-Cosworth V8	collision with Laffite	1/23

1978
Championship position: World Champion Wins: 6 Pole positions: 8 Fastest laps: 3 Points scored: 64

1	ARGENTINE GP	Buenos Aires	5	John Player Team Lotus	G	3.0 Lotus 78-Cosworth V8		1/27
4	BRAZILIAN GP	Rio	5	John Player Team Lotus	G	3.0 Lotus 78-Cosworth V8		3/28
7	SOUTH AFRICAN GP	Kyalami	5	John Player Team Lotus	G	3.0 Lotus 78-Cosworth V8	pit stop-fuel/FL/1 lap behind	2/30
2	US GP WEST	Long Beach	5	John Player Team Lotus	G	3.0 Lotus 78-Cosworth V8		4/30
11	MONACO GP	Monte Carlo	5	John Player Team Lotus	G	3.0 Lotus 78-Cosworth V8	pit stop-fuel gauge/-6 laps	4/30
1	BELGIAN GP	Zolder	5	John Player Team Lotus	G	3.0 Lotus 79-Cosworth V8		1/30
1	SPANISH GP	Jarama	5	John Player Team Lotus	G	3.0 Lotus 79-Cosworth V8	FL	1/29
ret	SWEDISH GP	Anderstorp	5	John Player Team Lotus	G	3.0 Lotus 79-Cosworth V8	engine	1/27
1	FRENCH GP	Paul Ricard	5	John Player Team Lotus	G	3.0 Lotus 79-Cosworth V8		2/29
ret	BRITISH GP	Brands Hatch	5	John Player Team Lotus	G	3.0 Lotus 79-Cosworth V8	engine	2/30
1	GERMAN GP	Hockenheim	5	John Player Team Lotus	G	3.0 Lotus 79-Cosworth V8		1/30
ret	AUSTRIAN GP	Österreichring	5	John Player Team Lotus	G	3.0 Lotus 79-Cosworth V8	crashed-on lap 1	2/31
1	DUTCH GP	Zandvoort	5	John Player Team Lotus	G	3.0 Lotus 79-Cosworth V8		1/33
6*	ITALIAN GP	Monza	5	John Player Team Lotus	G	3.0 Lotus 79-Cosworth V8	* 1st -1 min pen jump start//FL	1/32
ret	US GP EAST	Watkins Glen	5	John Player Team Lotus	G	3.0 Lotus 79-Cosworth V8	engine	1/27
10	CANADIAN GP	Montreal	5	John Player Team Lotus	G	3.0 Lotus 79-Cosworth V8	spin/1 lap behind	9/28

1979
Championship position: 10th= Wins: 0 Pole positions: 0 Fastest laps: 0 Points scored: 14

	Race	Circuit	No	Entrant	Tyres	Car/Engine	Comment	Q Pos/Entries
5	ARGENTINE GP	Buenos Aires	1	Martini Racing Team Lotus	G	3.0 Lotus 79-Cosworth V8	1 lap behind	7/26
ret	BRAZILIAN GP	Interlagos	1	Martini Racing Team Lotus	G	3.0 Lotus 79-Cosworth V8	fuel leak-fire	4/26
4	SOUTH AFRICAN GP	Kyalami	1	Martini Racing Team Lotus	G	3.0 Lotus 79-Cosworth V8		8/26
4	US GP WEST	Long Beach	1	Martini Racing Team Lotus	G	3.0 Lotus 79-Cosworth V8		6/26
3	SPANISH GP	Jarama	1	Martini Racing Team Lotus	G	3.0 Lotus 80-Cosworth V8		4/27
ret	BELGIAN GP	Zolder	1	Martini Racing Team Lotus	G	3.0 Lotus 80-Cosworth V8	brakes	5/28
dns	"	"	1	Martini Racing Team Lotus	G	3.0 Lotus 80-Cosworth V8	practice only	–/–
ret	MONACO GP	Monte Carlo	1	Martini Racing Team Lotus	G	3.0 Lotus 80-Cosworth V8	rear suspension	=13/25
ret	FRENCH GP	Dijon	1	Martini Racing Team Lotus	G	3.0 Lotus 80-Cosworth V8	brakes/suspension/flat tyre	12/27
ret	BRITISH GP	Silverstone	1	Martini Racing Team Lotus	G	3.0 Lotus 80-Cosworth V8	wheel bearing	9/26
ret	GERMAN GP	Hockenheim	1	Martini Racing Team Lotus	G	3.0 Lotus 79-Cosworth V8	driveshaft	11/26
ret	AUSTRIAN GP	Österreichring	1	Martini Racing Team Lotus	G	3.0 Lotus 79-Cosworth V8	clutch	15/26
ret	DUTCH GP	Zandvoort	1	Martini Racing Team Lotus	G	3.0 Lotus 79-Cosworth V8	rear suspension	17/26
5	ITALIAN GP	Monza	1	Martini Racing Team Lotus	G	3.0 Lotus 79-Cosworth V8		10/28
10/ret	CANADIAN GP	Montreal	1	Martini Racing Team Lotus	G	3.0 Lotus 79-Cosworth V8	out of fuel/6 laps behind	10/29
ret	US GP EAST	Watkins Glen	1	Martini Racing Team Lotus	G	3.0 Lotus 79-Cosworth V8	gearbox	17/30

1980
Championship position: 20th= Wins: 0 Pole positions: 0 Fastest laps: 0 Points scored: 1

	Race	Circuit	No	Entrant	Tyres	Car/Engine	Comment	Q Pos/Entries
ret	ARGENTINE GP	Buenos Aires	11	Team Essex Lotus	G	3.0 Lotus 81-Cosworth V8	fuel metering unit	6/28
ret	BRAZILIAN GP	Interlagos	11	Team Essex Lotus	G	3.0 Lotus 81-Cosworth V8	spun off	11/28
12	SOUTH AFRICAN GP	Kyalami	11	Team Essex Lotus	G	3.0 Lotus 81-Cosworth V8	broken exhaust/2 laps behind	15/28
ret	US GP WEST	Long Beach	11	Team Essex Lotus	G	3.0 Lotus 81-Cosworth V8	collision with Jarier	15/27
ret	BELGIAN GP	Zolder	11	Team Essex Lotus	G	3.0 Lotus 81-Cosworth V8	gear linkage	17/27
7	MONACO GP	Monte Carlo	11	Team Essex Lotus	G	3.0 Lotus 81-Cosworth V8	pit stop-gear linkage/-3 laps	19/27
ret	FRENCH GP	Paul Ricard	11	Team Essex Lotus	G	3.0 Lotus 81-Cosworth V8	gearbox	12/27
ret	BRITISH GP	Brands Hatch	11	Team Essex Lotus	G	3.0 Lotus 81-Cosworth V8	gearbox	9/27
7	GERMAN GP	Hockenheim	11	Team Essex Lotus	G	3.0 Lotus 81-Cosworth V8		9/26
ret	AUSTRIAN GP	Österreichring	11	Team Essex Lotus	G	3.0 Lotus 81-Cosworth V8	engine	17/25
8/ret	DUTCH GP	Zandvoort	11	Team Essex Lotus	G	3.0 Lotus 81-Cosworth V8	out of fuel/2 laps behind	10/28
ret	ITALIAN GP	Imola	11	Team Essex Lotus	G	3.0 Lotus 81-Cosworth V8	engine	10/28
ret	CANADIAN GP	Montreal	11	Team Essex Lotus	G	3.0 Lotus 81-Cosworth V8	engine	18/28
6	US GP EAST	Watkins Glen	11	Team Essex Lotus	G	3.0 Lotus 81-Cosworth V8	1 lap behind	11/27

1981
Championship position: 17th Wins: 0 Pole positions: 0 Fastest laps: 0 Points scored: 3

	Race	Circuit	No	Entrant	Tyres	Car/Engine	Comment	Q Pos/Entries
4	US GP WEST	Long Beach	22	Marlboro Team Alfa Romeo	M	3.0 Alfa Romeo 179C V12		6/29
ret	BRAZILIAN GP	Rio	22	Marlboro Team Alfa Romeo	M	3.0 Alfa Romeo 179C V12	collision at start	9/30
8	ARGENTINE GP	Buenos Aires	22	Marlboro Team Alfa Romeo	M	3.0 Alfa Romeo 179C V12	1 lap behind	17/29
ret	SAN MARINO GP	Imola	22	Marlboro Team Alfa Romeo	M	3.0 Alfa Romeo 179C V12	gearbox	12/30
10	BELGIAN GP	Zolder	22	Marlboro Team Alfa Romeo	M	3.0 Alfa Romeo 179C V12	misfire/1 lap behind	18/31
ret	MONACO GP	Monte Carlo	22	Marlboro Team Alfa Romeo	M	3.0 Alfa Romeo 179C V12	hit by de Cesaris	12/31
8	SPANISH GP	Jarama	22	Marlboro Team Alfa Romeo	M	3.0 Alfa Romeo 179C V12	hit by Piquet	8/30
8	FRENCH GP	Dijon	22	Marlboro Team Alfa Romeo	M	3.0 Alfa Romeo 179C V12	1 lap behind	10/29
ret	BRITISH GP	Silverstone	22	Marlboro Team Alfa Romeo	M	3.0 Alfa Romeo 179C V12	throttle linkage	11/30
9	GERMAN GP	Hockenheim	22	Marlboro Team Alfa Romeo	M	3.0 Alfa Romeo 179C V12	1 lap behind	12/30
ret	AUSTRIAN GP	Österreichring	22	Marlboro Team Alfa Romeo	M	3.0 Alfa Romeo 179C V12	engine	13/28
ret	DUTCH GP	Zandvoort	22	Marlboro Team Alfa Romeo	M	3.0 Alfa Romeo 179C V12	tyre failure-crashed	7/30
ret	ITALIAN GP	Monza	22	Marlboro Team Alfa Romeo	M	3.0 Alfa Romeo 179C V12	engine	13/30
7	CANADIAN GP	Montreal	22	Marlboro Team Alfa Romeo	M	3.0 Alfa Romeo 179C V12	1 lap behind	16/30
ret	CAESARS PALACE GP	Las Vegas	22	Marlboro Team Alfa Romeo	M	3.0 Alfa Romeo 179C V12	rear suspension	10/30

1982
Championship position: 19th Wins: 0 Pole positions: 0 Fastest laps: 0 Points scored: 4

	Race	Circuit	No	Entrant	Tyres	Car/Engine	Comment	Q Pos/Entries
ret	US GP WEST	Long Beach	5	TAG Williams Team	G	3.0 Williams FW07C-Cosworth V8	accident damage	14/31
3	ITALIAN GP	Monza	28	Scuderia Ferrari SpA SEFAC	G	1.5 t/c Ferrari 126C2 V6		1/30
ret	CAESARS PALACE GP	Las Vegas	28	Scuderia Ferrari SpA SEFAC	G	1.5 t/c Ferrari 126C2 V6	rear suspension	7/30

GP Starts: 128 GP Wins: 12 Pole positions: 18 Fastest laps: 10 Points: 180

ANDRETTI, Michael (USA) b 5/10/1962, Bethlehem, Pennsylvania

	Race	Circuit	No	Entrant	Tyres	Car/Engine	Comment	Q Pos/Entries

1993
Championship position: 11th= Wins: 0 Pole positions: 0 Fastest laps: 0 Points scored: 7

	Race	Circuit	No	Entrant	Tyres	Car/Engine	Comment	Q Pos/Entries
ret	SOUTH AFRICAN GP	Kyalami	7	Marlboro McLaren	G	3.5 McLaren MP4/8-Ford HB V8	accident-ran into Warwick	9/26
ret	BRAZILIAN GP	Interlagos	7	Marlboro McLaren	G	3.5 McLaren MP4/8-Ford HB V8	accident with Berger at start	5/26
ret	EUROPEAN GP	Donington	7	Marlboro McLaren	G	3.5 McLaren MP4/8-Ford HB V8	collision Wendlinger-spun off	6/26
ret	SAN MARINO GP	Imola	7	Marlboro McLaren	G	3.5 McLaren MP4/8-Ford HB V8	spun off-brake trouble	6/26
5	SPANISH GP	Barcelona	7	Marlboro McLaren	G	3.5 McLaren MP4/8-Ford HB V8	1 lap behind	7/26
8	MONACO GP	Monte Carlo	7	Marlboro McLaren	G	3.5 McLaren MP4/8-Ford HB V8	early pit stop new nose/-2 laps	9/26
14	CANADIAN GP	Montreal	7	Marlboro McLaren	G	3.5 McLaren MP4/8-Ford HB V8	started late from pits/-3 laps	12/26
6	FRENCH GP	Magny Cours	7	Marlboro McLaren	G	3.5 McLaren MP4/8-Ford HB V8	1 lap behind	16/26
ret	BRITISH GP	Silverstone	7	Marlboro McLaren	G	3.5 McLaren MP4/8-Ford HB V8	spun off first corner	11/26
ret	GERMAN GP	Hockenheim	7	Marlboro McLaren	G	3.5 McLaren MP4/8-Ford HB V8	collision, Berger- bent steering	12/26
ret	HUNGARIAN GP	Hungaroring	7	Marlboro McLaren	G	3.5 McLaren MP4/8-Ford HB V8	throttle failure	11/26
8	BELGIAN GP	Spa	7	Marlboro McLaren	G	3.5 McLaren MP4/8-Ford HB V8	stalled at pit stop/-1 lap	14/25
3	ITALIAN GP	Monza	7	Marlboro McLaren	G	3.5 McLaren MP4/8-Ford HB V8	despite early spin/-1 lap	9/26

GP Starts: 13 GP Wins: 0 Pole positions: 0 Fastest laps: 0 Points: 7

APICELLA, Marco (I) b 7/10/1965, Bologna

1993
Championship position: Unplaced Wins: 0 Pole positions: 0 Fastest laps: 0 Points scored: 0

	Race	Circuit	No	Entrant	Tyres	Car/Engine	Comment	Q Pos/Entries
ret	ITALIAN GP	Monza	15	Sasol Jordan	G	3.5 Jordan 193-Hart V10	collision-suspension damage	23/26

GP Starts: 1 GP Wins: 0 Pole positions: 0 Fastest laps: 0 Points: 0

MICHAEL ANDRETTI

The son of the legendary Mario, Michael followed his father into racing in 1980, first in Formula Ford and then in Super Vee (winning the 1982 championship). He broke into Indy cars the following season, which also saw him partner his father at Le Mans, where the pair finished third in a Porsche with Philippe Alliot.

Michael was soon making a big impact on the Indy Car scene, scoring the first of 37 wins to date in 1986. From that year through to 1992 – aside from a lean year in 1988, when he was sixth overall – he always finished in the top three places in the points standings, and 1991 proved to be a record-breaking season, with Andretti's Newman-Haas Lola taking eight wins, accumulating a record 234 points and posting single-season earnings of $2,461,734.

With this pedigree, the former Indy Car champion arrived in the high-profile world of Formula 1 with McLaren in 1993 with great expectations, only to be embroiled in a catalogue of collisions, spins and mechanical gremlins which seemed to sap his confidence visibly race by race. A lack of testing mileage, the FIA's rationing of practice laps and his unfamiliarity with the circuits all told against the pleasant American, who was under pressure to produce results.

Just as crucial, perhaps, was the difficulty he and his first wife Sandy experienced in coming to terms with the way of life in Europe, preferring to fly back to the States whenever possible. By September he had had enough. Having attained a little credibility by finishing third in the Italian GP, the younger Andretti ended his unhappy sojourn in F1 and headed back home buoyed by the prospect of returning to the familiarity of the Indy Car circuit for 1994 with a new challenger from Reynard.

Michael lost no time in resuming his winning ways at the season-opener at Surfers Paradise, but (despite another win in Toronto) he seemed ill at ease at Ganassi Racing and it was no surprise when he returned to his spiritual home at Newman-Haas for 1995.

In the increasingly competitive world of CART racing, Michael has remained one of the series' outstanding drivers. Now happily remarried, he has become the sport's elder statesman following the departure of his great rival Al Unser Jnr.

However, he still has the speed, courage and commitment to show younger pretenders that he cannot yet be discounted as a contender for honours.

MARCO APICELLA

This diminutive Italian was a contemporary of Caffi, Tarquini, Larini and Barbazza in the national F3 series in 1984-85. He was certainly quick but also somewhat erratic, sampling three different chassis in 1985 and taking a couple of wins at Misano. In 1986 he was teamed with Larini in Enzo Coloni's Dallaras and the young hot-shots dominated proceedings, with Apicella taking the runner-up slot.

If he felt something of a bridesmaid in that formula, it was as nothing to his experiences in the FIA F3000 championship, where he spent five seasons (1987-91) as 'the man most likely to', searching in vain for a win before he joined the wave of Europeans invading the Japanese F3000 series in a bid to revive his career. Marco was a surprise choice for a one-off Jordan ride in the 1993 Italian GP, and his race was short lived, Apicella being eliminated in a first-lap mêlée.

Tangible success came at last for the Italian when he was crowned 1994 All-Japan F3000 champion driving for the Dome team. Although the following year, when he raced the 5-Zigen team's Reynard, proved less successful, Apicella continued competing in Formula Nippon, turning in some solid performances, while testing the Dome F1 challenger which ultimately failed to make the grid.

In 1999 he reappeared in Europe to take occasional drives in a Riley & Scott sports car, bagging a fourth place at Brno. His vast experience was also put to good use in the newly inaugurated Italian F3000 series, Marco winning rounds at both Vallelunga and Misano for Monaco Motorsport.

RENÉ ARNOUX

Arnoux's early career was rich with promise. Winning the Shell Volant award set him on his way in Formule Renault, but René switched to Elf in 1974 when an opportunity arose to race their Formula 2 car, taking fourth place at Nogaro on his debut. In 1975 he competed in Formule Super Renault, winning the championship, before undertaking a full season of Formula 2 with an Elf-backed works Martini-Renault.

He was the fastest man around and came agonisingly close to taking the championship, scoring three wins (at Pau, Enna and Estoril) and six fastest laps but eventually lost out to Jabouille. Resolved to iron out the errors which had cost him so dear in 1976, Arnoux was back the following season and again won three races (at Silverstone, Pau and Nogaro), deservedly taking the coveted title.

The little Martini team, which had enjoyed enviable success in the junior formulae for many years, ambitiously moved into Formula 1 for 1978 and Arnoux was naturally entrusted with their neat Cosworth-powered car, but the underfinanced project was doomed from the start, leaving the GP novice to scratch around for drives from mid-season. He did a couple of races for Surtees, who would dearly have loved to have got his hands on him earlier, for after running a string of second-raters here at last he could see gold. However, René was destined for greater things, joining Renault for 1979.

Teamed with his old rival Jabouille, the still shy newcomer began to assert himself from mid-season onwards, and looked a serious championship prospect at the start of 1980. Consecutive wins in Brazil and South Africa proved sadly illusory, but the game little Frenchman never gave up the struggle although his car repeatedly let him down.

Unfortunately for Arnoux, his nemesis in the shape of Alain Prost joined the team for 1981,

immediately pushing the unhappy incumbent to the margins. He bounced back in 1982 to something like his best, all but matching Prost's speed, but not his measured performances. When he won the French GP in defiance of team orders it seemed that a split was inevitable, and sure enough he moved to Ferrari for 1983. Driving in typically forceful style, Arnoux mounted a serious championship bid on the back of three mid-season wins, but eventually fell just short.

In 1984 his performances became increasingly inconsistent and, despite an absolutely brilliant drive at Dallas, there were times when he seemed totally uninterested. It was a situation that could not last and early in 1985 an 'amicable' separation was agreed. Joining Ligier for 1986, Arnoux showed brief flashes of his old form in the Renault-powered car but, when he voiced criticism in the press of the Alfa engine the team had arranged to use the following season, the Italian concern immediately terminated the project. The team was then obliged to adapt their new design to accept the Megatron engine, and suffered the inevitable consequences. Things got even worse in 1988 with the totally disastrous JS31, which was perhaps one of the most evil-handling machines of recent times.

Although no longer a contender, Arnoux blithely drove on as if he were, but by now the summit of his ambitions was a desperate search for the championship point or two that would keep his team out of the pre-qualifying trap. His ever-increasing lack of track manners and general cussedness caused mounting consternation among his fellow drivers, and by the time he retired at the end of 1989 the halcyon days of the early eighties were all but forgotten.

The Frenchman finally made a return to the track in 1994, finishing 12th at Le Mans in a Dodge Viper. He was back in 1995 with a Ferrari 333SP, but much of his time has been spent acting as a driver coach and adviser to wealthy Brazilian hopeful Pedro Diniz in his attempt to carve out a top-flight Grand Prix career, and acting as a Grand Prix summariser on Italian TV.

ARNOUX, René (F) b 4/7/1948, Pontcharra, nr Grenoble

1978   Championship position: Unplaced

	Race	Circuit	No	Entrant		Tyres	Car/Engine	Comment	Q Pos/Entries
dnq	SOUTH AFRICAN GP	Kyalami	31	Automobiles Martini		G	3.0 Martini MK23-Cosworth V8		27/30
dnpq	MONACO GP	Monte Carlo	31	Automobiles Martini		G	3.0 Martini MK23-Cosworth V8		27/30
9	BELGIAN GP	Zolder	31	Automobiles Martini		G	3.0 Martini MK23-Cosworth V8	2 laps behind	19/30
14	FRENCH GP	Paul Ricard	31	Automobiles Martini		G	3.0 Martini MK23-Cosworth V8	1 lap behind	18/29
dnp	BRITISH GP	Brands Hatch	31	Automobiles Martini		G	3.0 Martini MK23-Cosworth V8	on reserve list-no practice allowed	–/–
dnpq	GERMAN GP	Hockenheim	31	Automobiles Martini		G	3.0 Martini MK23-Cosworth V8		=29/30
9	AUSTRIAN GP	Österreichring	31	Automobiles Martini		G	3.0 Martini MK23-Cosworth V8	2 laps behind	26/31
ret	DUTCH GP	Zandvoort	31	Automobiles Martini		G	3.0 Martini MK23-Cosworth V8	rear wing mounting	23/33
9	US GP EAST	Watkins Glen	18	Team Surtees		6	3.0 Surtees TS20-Cosworth V8	1 lap behind	21/27
ret	CANADIAN GP	Montreal	18	Team Surtees		6	3.0 Surtees TS20-Cosworth V8	oil pressure	16/28

1979   Championship position: 8th   Wins: 0   Pole positions: 2   Fastest laps: 2   Points scored: 17

	Race	Circuit	No	Entrant		Tyres	Car/Engine	Comment	Q Pos/Entries
dnq/ret	ARGENTINE GP	Buenos Aires	16	Equipe Renault Elf		M	.5 t/c Renault RS01 V6	dnq-started as 1st reserve/engine	25/26
ret	BRAZILIAN GP	Interlagos	16	Equipe Renault Elf		M	1.5 t/c Renault RS01 V6	spun off-could not restart	11/26
ret	SOUTH AFRICAN GP	Kyalami	16	Equipe Renault Elf		M	1.5 t/c Renault RS01 V6	burst tyre	10/26
dns	US GP WEST	Long Beach	16	Equipe Renault Elf		M	1.5 t/c Renault RS01 V6	c.v joint on race morning	(22)/26
9	SPANISH GP	Jarama	16	Equipe Renault Elf		M	1.5 t/c Renault RS01 V6	1 lap behind	11/27
ret	BELGIAN GP	Zolder	16	Equipe Renault Elf		M	1.5 t/c Renault RS01 V6	no turbo boost	18/28
ret	MONACO GP	Monte Carlo	16	Equipe Renault Elf		M	1.5 t/c Renault RS10 V6	accident-damaged suspension	19/25
3	FRENCH GP	Dijon	16	Equipe Renault Elf		M	1.5 t/c Renault RS12 V6	FL	2/27
2	BRITISH GP	Silverstone	16	Equipe Renault Elf		M	1.5 t/c Renault RS12 V6		5/26
ret	GERMAN GP	Hockenheim	16	Equipe Renault Elf		M	1.5 t/c Renault RS12 V6	puncture	10/26
6	AUSTRIAN GP	Österreichring	16	Equipe Renault Elf		M	1.5 t/c Renault RS12 V6	pit stop-fuel/FL/-1 lap	1/26
ret	DUTCH GP	Zandvoort	16	Equipe Renault Elf		M	1.5 t/c Renault RS12 V6	collision with Regazzoni	1/26
ret	ITALIAN GP	Monza	16	Equipe Renault Elf		M	1.5 t/c Renault RS12 V6	misfire	2/28
ret	CANADIAN GP	Montreal	16	Equipe Renault Elf		M	1.5 t/c Renault RS12 V6	accident with Stuck	8/29
2	US GP EAST	Watkins Glen	16	Equipe Renault Elf		M	1.5 t/c Renault RS12 V6		7/30

1980   Championship position: 6th   Wins: 2   Pole positions: 3   Fastest laps: 4   Points scored: 29

	Race	Circuit	No	Entrant		Tyres	Car/Engine	Comment	Q Pos/Entries
ret	ARGENTINE GP	Buenos Aires	16	Equipe Renault Elf		M	1.5 t/c Renault RE21 V6	suspension	19/28
1	BRAZILIAN GP	Interlagos	16	Equipe Renault Elf		M	1.5 t/c Renault RE21 V6	FL	6/28
1	SOUTH AFRICAN GP	Kyalami	16	Equipe Renault Elf		M	1.5 t/c Renault RE21 V6	FL	2/28
9	US GP WEST	Long Beach	16	Equipe Renault Elf		M	1.5 t/c Renault RE24 V6	brake problems/2 laps behind	2/27
4	BELGIAN GP	Zolder	16	Equipe Renault Elf		M	1.5 t/c Renault RE24 V6	1 lap behind	=5/27
ret	MONACO GP	Monte Carlo	16	Equipe Renault Elf		M	1.5 t/c Renault RE24 V6	accident with Patrese	20/27
5	FRENCH GP	Paul Ricard	16	Equipe Renault Elf		M	1.5 t/c Renault RE24 V6		=2/27
nc	BRITISH GP	Brands Hatch	16	Equipe Renault Elf		M	1.5 t/c Renault RE24 V6	pit stop-brakes/9 laps behind	16/27
ret	GERMAN GP	Hockenheim	16	Equipe Renault Elf		M	1.5 t/c Renault RE25 V6	valve spring	3/26
9	AUSTRIAN GP	Österreichring	16	Equipe Renault Elf		M	1.5 t/c Renault RE25 V6	pit stops-tyres/FL/1 lap behind	1/25
2	DUTCH GP	Zandvoort	16	Equipe Renault Elf		M	1.5 t/c Renault RE25 V6	FL	1/28
10	ITALIAN GP	Imola	16	Equipe Renault Elf		M	1.5 t/c Renault RE25 V6	shock absorber/2 laps behind	1/28
ret	CANADIAN GP	Montreal	16	Equipe Renault Elf		M	1.5 t/c Renault RE25 V6	brakes/gearbox	23/28
7	US GP EAST	Watkins Glen	16	Equipe Renault Elf		M	1.5 t/c Renault RE25 V6	pit stop-tyres/1 lap behind	6/27

1981   Championship position: 9th=   Wins: 0   Pole positions: 4   Fastest laps: 1   Points scored: 11

	Race	Circuit	No	Entrant		Tyres	Car/Engine	Comment	Q Pos/Entries
8	US GP WEST	Long Beach	16	Equipe Renault Elf		M	1.5 t/c Renault RE27B V6	3 laps behind	20/29
ret	BRAZILIAN GP	Rio	16	Equipe Renault Elf		M	1.5 t/c Renault RE27B V6	start line collision	8/30
5	ARGENTINE GP	Buenos Aires	16	Equipe Renault Elf		M	1.5 t/c Renault RE27B V6		5/29
8	SAN MARINO GP	Imola	16	Equipe Renault Elf		M	1.5 t/c Renault RE27B V6	1 lap behind	3/30
dnq	BELGIAN GP	Zolder	16	Equipe Renault Elf		M	1.5 t/c Renault RE30 V6		25/31
ret	MONACO GP	Monte Carlo	16	Equipe Renault Elf		M	1.5 t/c Renault RE30 V6	spun off	13/31
9	SPANISH GP	Jarama	16	Equipe Renault Elf		M	1.5 t/c Renault RE30 V6		17/30
4	FRENCH GP	Dijon	16	Equipe Renault Elf		M	1.5 t/c Renault RE30 V6		1/29
9/ret	BRITISH GP	Silverstone	16	Equipe Renault Elf		M	1.5 t/c Renault RE30 V6	engine/FL/4 laps behind	1/30
13	GERMAN GP	Hockenheim	16	Equipe Renault Elf		M	1.5 t/c Renault RE30 V6	pit stop-split tyre/1 lap behind	2/30
2	AUSTRIAN GP	Österreichring	16	Equipe Renault Elf		M	1.5 t/c Renault RE30 V6		1/28
ret	DUTCH GP	Zandvoort	16	Equipe Renault Elf		M	1.5 t/c Renault RE30 V6	accident	2/30
ret	ITALIAN GP	Monza	16	Equipe Renault Elf		M	1.5 t/c Renault RE30 V6	crashed	1/30
ret	CANADIAN GP	Montreal	16	Equipe Renault Elf		M	1.5 t/c Renault RE30 V6	startline collision	8/30
ret	CAESARS PALACE GP	Las Vegas	16	Equipe Renault Elf		M	1.5 t/c Renault RE30 V6	electrics	13/30

1982   Championship position: 6th   Wins: 2   Pole positions: 5   Fastest laps: 1   Points scored: 28

	Race	Circuit	No	Entrant		Tyres	Car/Engine	Comment	Q Pos/Entries
3	SOUTH AFRICAN GP	Kyalami	16	Equipe Renault Elf		M	1.5 t/c Renault RE30B V6		1/30
ret	BRAZILIAN GP	Rio	16	Equipe Renault Elf		M	1.5 t/c Renault RE30B V6	accident with Reutemann	4/31
ret	US GP WEST	Long Beach	16	Equipe Renault Elf		M	1.5 t/c Renault RE30B V6	hit by Giacomelli	3/31
ret	SAN MARINO GP	Imola	16	Equipe Renault Elf		M	1.5 t/c Renault RE30B V6	engine	1/14
ret	BELGIAN GP	Zolder	16	Equipe Renault Elf		M	1.5 t/c Renault RE30B V6	turbo compressor	2/32
ret	MONACO GP	Monte Carlo	16	Equipe Renault Elf		M	1.5 t/c Renault RE30B V6	spun off	1/31
10	US GP (DETROIT)	Detroit	16	Equipe Renault Elf		M	1.5 t/c Renault RE30B V6	3 laps behind	15/28
ret	CANADIAN GP	Montreal	16	Equipe Renault Elf		M	1.5 t/c Renault RE30B V6	spun off	2/29
ret	DUTCH GP	Zandvoort	16	Equipe Renault Elf		M	1.5 t/c Renault RE30B V6	suspension failure-crashed	1/31
ret	BRITISH GP	Brands Hatch	16	Equipe Renault Elf		M	1.5 t/c Renault RE30B V6	startline accident-hit by Patrese	6/30
1	FRENCH GP	Paul Ricard	16	Equipe Renault Elf		M	1.5 t/c Renault RE30B V6		1/30
2	GERMAN GP	Hockenheim	16	Equipe Renault Elf		M	1.5 t/c Renault RE30B V6		3/30
ret	AUSTRIAN GP	Österreichring	16	Equipe Renault Elf		M	1.5 t/c Renault RE30B V6	turbo	5/29
ret	SWISS GP	Dijon	16	Equipe Renault Elf		M	1.5 t/c Renault RE30B V6	fuel injection/5 laps behind	2/29
1	ITALIAN GP	Monza	16	Equipe Renault Elf		M	1.5 t/c Renault RE30B V6	FL	6/30
ret	CAESARS PALACE GP	Las Vegas	16	Equipe Renault Elf		M	1.5 t/c Renault RE30B V6	engine	2/30

1983 — Championship position: 3rd   Wins: 3   Pole positions: 4   Fastest laps: 2   Points scored: 49

Pos	GP	Circuit	No	Team	Tyre	Engine	Notes	Grid
10*	BRAZILIAN GP	Rio	28	Scuderia Ferrari SpA SEFAC	G	1.5 t/c Ferrari 126C2/B V6	*2nd place car dsq/-1 lap	6/27
3	US GP WEST	Long Beach	28	Scuderia Ferrari SpA SEFAC	G	1.5 t/c Ferrari 126C2/B V6		2/28
7	FRENCH GP	Paul Ricard	28	Scuderia Ferrari SpA SEFAC	G	1.5 t/c Ferrari 126C2/B V6	1 lap behind	4/29
3	SAN MARINO GP	Imola	28	Scuderia Ferrari SpA SEFAC	G	1.5 t/c Ferrari 126C2/B V6	1 lap behind	1/28
ret	MONACO GP	Monte Carlo	28	Scuderia Ferrari SpA SEFAC	G	1.5 t/c Ferrari 126C2/B V6	hit barrier	2/28
ret	BELGIAN GP	Spa	28	Scuderia Ferrari SpA SEFAC	G	1.5 t/c Ferrari 126C2/B V6	engine	5/28
ret	US GP (DETROIT)	Detroit	28	Scuderia Ferrari SpA SEFAC	G	1.5 t/c Ferrari 126C2/B V6	electrics	1/27
1	CANADIAN GP	Montreal	28	Scuderia Ferrari SpA SEFAC	G	1.5 t/c Ferrari 126C2/B V6		1/28
5	BRITISH GP	Silverstone	28	Scuderia Ferrari SpA SEFAC	G	1.5 t/c Ferrari 126C3 V6		1/29
1	GERMAN GP	Hockenheim	28	Scuderia Ferrari SpA SEFAC	G	1.5 t/c Ferrari 126C3 V6	FL	2/29
2	AUSTRIAN GP	Österreichring	28	Scuderia Ferrari SpA SEFAC	G	1.5 t/c Ferrari 126C3 V6		2/29
1	DUTCH GP	Zandvoort	28	Scuderia Ferrari SpA SEFAC	G	1.5 t/c Ferrari 126C3 V6	FL	10/29
2	ITALIAN GP	Monza	28	Scuderia Ferrari SpA SEFAC	G	1.5 t/c Ferrari 126C3 V6		3/29
9	EUROPEAN GP	Brands Hatch	28	Scuderia Ferrari SpA SEFAC	G	1.5 t/c Ferrari 126C3 V6	spin/1 lap behind	5/29
ret	SOUTH AFRICAN GP	Kyalami	28	Scuderia Ferrari SpA SEFAC	G	1.5 t/c Ferrari 126C3 V6	engine	4/26

1984 — Championship position: 6th   Wins: 0   Pole positions: 0   Fastest laps: 2   Points scored: 27

Pos	GP	Circuit	No	Team	Tyre	Engine	Notes	Grid
ret	BRAZILIAN GP	Rio	28	Scuderia Ferrari SpA SEFAC	G	1.5 t/c Ferrari 126C4 V6	battery	10/27
ret	SOUTH AFRICAN GP	Kyalami	28	Scuderia Ferrari SpA SEFAC	G	1.5 t/c Ferrari 126C4 V6	fuel injection	15/27
3	BELGIAN GP	Zolder	28	Scuderia Ferrari SpA SEFAC	G	1.5 t/c Ferrari 126C4 V6	FL	2/27
2	SAN MARINO GP	Imola	28	Scuderia Ferrari SpA SEFAC	G	1.5 t/c Ferrari 126C4 V6		6/28
4	FRENCH GP	Dijon	28	Scuderia Ferrari SpA SEFAC	G	1.5 t/c Ferrari 126C4 V6		11/27
3*	MONACO GP	Monte Carlo	28	Scuderia Ferrari SpA SEFAC	G	1.5 t/c Ferrari 126C4 V6	*3rd place car dsq/half points	3/27
5	CANADIAN GP	Montreal	28	Scuderia Ferrari SpA SEFAC	G	1.5 t/c Ferrari 126C4 V6	pit stop-tyres/2 laps behind	5/26
ret	US GP (DETROIT)	Detroit	28	Scuderia Ferrari SpA SEFAC	G	1.5 t/c Ferrari 126C4 V6	spun off	15/27
2	US GP (DALLAS)	Dallas	28	Scuderia Ferrari SpA SEFAC	G	1.5 t/c Ferrari 126C4 V6	started from back of grid	4/27
6	BRITISH GP	Brands Hatch	28	Scuderia Ferrari SpA SEFAC	G	1.5 t/c Ferrari 126C4 V6	collision with de Cesaris/-1 lap	13/27
6	GERMAN GP	Hockenheim	28	Scuderia Ferrari SpA SEFAC	G	1.5 t/c Ferrari 126C4 V6	pit stop-tyres/1 lap behind	10/27
7	AUSTRIAN GP	Österreichring	28	Scuderia Ferrari SpA SEFAC	G	1.5 t/c Ferrari 126C4 V6	pit stop-tyres/1 lap behind	15/28
11*/ret	DUTCH GP	Zandvoort	28	Scuderia Ferrari SpA SEFAC	G	1.5 t/c Ferrari 126C4 V6	electrics/FL/*8th & 9th cars dsq	15/27
ret	ITALIAN GP	Monza	28	Scuderia Ferrari SpA SEFAC	G	1.5 t/c Ferrari 126C4 V6	gearbox	14/27
5	EUROPEAN GP	Nürburgring	28	Scuderia Ferrari SpA SEFAC	G	1.5 t/c Ferrari 126C4 V6		6/26
9	PORTUGUESE GP	Estoril	28	Scuderia Ferrari SpA SEFAC	G	1.5 t/c Ferrari 126C4 V6	1 lap behind	17/27

1985 — Championship position: 17th=   Wins: 0   Pole positions: 0   Fastest laps: 0   Points scored: 3

Pos	GP	Circuit	No	Team	Tyre	Engine	Notes	Grid
4	BRAZILIAN GP	Rio	28	Scuderia Ferrari SpA SEFAC	G	1.5 t/c Ferrari 156/85	1 lap behind	7/25

1986 — Championship position: 8th=   Wins: 0   Pole positions: 0   Fastest laps: 0   Points scored: 14

Pos	GP	Circuit	No	Team	Tyre	Engine	Notes	Grid
4	BRAZILIAN GP	Rio	25	Equipe Ligier	P	1.5 t/c Ligier JS27-Renault V6		4/25
ret	SPANISH GP	Jerez	25	Equipe Ligier	P	1.5 t/c Ligier JS27-Renault V6	driveshaft	6/25
ret	SAN MARINO GP	Imola	25	Equipe Ligier	P	1.5 t/c Ligier JS27-Renault V6	lost wheel	8/26
5	MONACO GP	Monte Carlo	25	Equipe Ligier	P	1.5 t/c Ligier JS27-Renault V6	1 lap behind	12/26
ret	BELGIAN GP	Spa	25	Equipe Ligier	P	1.5 t/c Ligier JS27-Renault V6	engine	7/25
6	CANADIAN GP	Montreal	25	Equipe Ligier	P	1.5 t/c Ligier JS27-Renault V6	1 lap behind	5/25
ret	US GP (DETROIT)	Detroit	25	Equipe Ligier	P	1.5 t/c Ligier JS27-Renault V6	hit wall & Boutsen-suspension	4/26
5	FRENCH GP	Paul Ricard	25	Equipe Ligier	P	1.5 t/c Ligier JS27-Renault V6	1 lap behind	4/26
4	BRITISH GP	Brands Hatch	25	Equipe Ligier	P	1.5 t/c Ligier JS27-Renault V6	2 laps behind	8/26
4	GERMAN GP	Hockenheim	25	Equipe Ligier	P	1.5 t/c Ligier JS27-Renault V6		8/26
ret	HUNGARIAN GP	Hungaroring	25	Equipe Ligier	P	1.5 t/c Ligier JS27-Renault V6	engine	9/26
10	AUSTRIAN GP	Österreichring	25	Equipe Ligier	P	1.5 t/c Ligier JS27-Renault V6	pit stop-misfire/5 laps behind	12/26
ret	ITALIAN GP	Monza	25	Equipe Ligie	P	1.5 t/c Ligier JS27-Renault V6	gearbox	11/27
7	PORTUGUESE GP	Estoril	25	Equipe Ligier	P	1.5 t/c Ligier JS27-Renault V6	1 lap behind	10/27
15/ret	MEXICAN GP	Mexico City	25	Equipe Ligier	P	1.5 t/c Ligier JS27-Renault V6	engine/5 laps behind	13/26
7	AUSTRALIAN GP	Adelaide	25	Equipe Ligier	P	1.5 t/c Ligier JS27-Renault V6	pit stop-puncture/-3 laps	5/26

René's victory in the 1982 French Grand Prix at Paul Ricard caused a split with team mate Alain Prost after Arnoux failed to heed team orders.

Arnoux switched to Ferrari for 1983, mounting a serious championship bid. His win in the German Grand Prix was one of three victories that year for the Frenchman.

1987
Championship position: 19th=   Wins: 0   Pole positions: 0   Fastest laps: 0   Points scored: 1

	Race	Circuit	No	Team	Tyre	Car	Notes	Grid
dns	SAN MARINO GP	Imola	25	Ligier Loto	G	1.5 t/c Ligier JS29B-Megatron 4	suspension in a.m. warm-up	(14)/27
6	BELGIAN GP	Spa	25	Ligier Loto	G	1.5 t/c Ligier JS29B-Megatron 4	2 laps behind	16/26
11	MONACO GP	Monte Carlo	25	Ligier Loto	G	1.5 t/c Ligier JS29B-Megatron 4	4 laps behind	22/26
10	US GP (DETROIT)	Detroit	25	Ligier Loto	G	1.5 t/c Ligier JS29B-Megatron 4	3 laps behind	21/26
ret	FRENCH GP	Paul Ricard	25	Ligier Loto	G	1.5 t/c Ligier JS29C-Megatron 4	broken exhaust	13/26
ret	BRITISH GP	Silverstone	25	Ligier Loto	G	1.5 t/c Ligier JS29C-Megatron 4	electrics	16/26
ret	GERMAN GP	Hockenheim	25	Ligier Loto	G	1.5 t/c Ligier JS29C-Megatron 4	electrics	12/26
ret	HUNGARIAN GP	Hungaroring	25	Ligier Loto	G	1.5 t/c Ligier JS29C-Megatron 4	electrics	19/26
10	AUSTRIAN GP	Österreichring	25	Ligier Loto	G	1.5 t/c Ligier JS29C-Megatron 4	3 laps behind	16/26
10	ITALIAN GP	Monza	25	Ligier Loto	G	1.5 t/c Ligier JS29C-Megatron 4	2 laps behind	15/28
ret	PORTUGUESE GP	Estoril	25	Ligier Loto	G	1.5 t/c Ligier JS29C-Megatron 4	holed intercooler	18/27
ret	SPANISH GP	Jerez	25	Ligier Loto	G	1.5 t/c Ligier JS29C-Megatron 4	engine	14/28
ret	MEXICAN GP	Mexico City	25	Ligier Loto	G	1.5 t/c Ligier JS29C-Megatron 4	ignition	18/27
ret	JAPANESE GP	Suzuka	25	Ligier Loto	G	1.5 t/c Ligier JS29C-Megatron 4	out of fuel	18/27
ret	AUSTRALIAN GP	Adelaide	25	Ligier Loto	G	1.5 t/c Ligier JS29C-Megatron 4	electrics	20/27

1988
Championship position: Unplaced

	Race	Circuit	No	Team	Tyre	Car	Notes	Grid
ret	BRAZILIAN GP	Rio	25	Ligier Loto	G	3.5 Ligier JS31-Judd V8	clutch	18/31
dnq	SAN MARINO GP	Imola	25	Ligier Loto	G	3.5 Ligier JS31-Judd V8		29/31
ret	MONACO GP	Monte Carlo	25	Ligier Loto	G	3.5 Ligier JS31-Judd V8	started from pit lane/electrics	20/30
ret	MEXICAN GP	Mexico City	25	Ligier Loto	G	3.5 Ligier JS31-Judd V8	accident with Caffi	20/30
ret	CANADIAN GP	Montreal	25	Ligier Loto	G	3.5 Ligier JS31-Judd V8	gearbox	20/31
ret	US GP (DETROIT)	Detroit	25	Ligier Loto	G	3.5 Ligier JS31-Judd V8	engine	20/31
dnq	FRENCH GP	Paul Ricard	25	Ligier Loto	G	3.5 Ligier JS31-Judd V8		28/31
18	BRITISH GP	Silverstone	25	Ligier Loto	G	3.5 Ligier JS31-Judd V8	3 laps behind	25/31
17	GERMAN GP	Hockenheim	25	Ligier Loto	G	3.5 Ligier JS31-Judd V8	3 laps behind	17/31
ret	HUNGARIAN GP	Hungaroring	25	Ligier Loto	G	3.5 Ligier JS31-Judd V8	engine	25/31
ret	BELGIAN GP	Spa	25	Ligier Loto	G	3.5 Ligier JS31-Judd V8	accident with de Cesaris	17/31
13	ITALIAN GP	Monza	25	Ligier Loto	G	3.5 Ligier JS31-Judd V8	2 laps behind	24/31
10	PORTUGUESE GP	Estoril	25	Ligier Loto	G	3.5 Ligier JS31-Judd V8	2 laps behind	23/31
ret	SPANISH GP	Jerez	25	Ligier Loto	G	3.5 Ligier JS31-Judd V8	throttle jammed closed	19/31
17	JAPANESE GP	Suzuka	25	Ligier Loto	G	3.5 Ligier JS31-Judd V8	pit stop-tyres/3 laps behind	23/31
ret	AUSTRALIAN GP	Adelaide	25	Ligier Loto	G	3.5 Ligier JS31-Judd V8	accident with Berger	23/31

1989
Championship position: 23rd   Wins: 0   Pole positions: 0   Fastest laps: 0   Points scored: 2

	Race	Circuit	No	Team	Tyre	Car	Notes	Grid
dnq	BRAZILIAN GP	Rio	25	Ligier Loto	G	3.5 Ligier JS33-Cosworth V8		28/38
dnq	SAN MARINO GP	Imola	25	Ligier Loto	G	3.5 Ligier JS33-Cosworth V8		28/39
12	MONACO GP	Monte Carlo	25	Ligier Loto	G	3.5 Ligier JS33-Cosworth V8	4 laps behind	21/38
14	MEXICAN GP	Mexico City	25	Ligier Loto	G	3.5 Ligier JS33-Cosworth V8	lost use of clutch/-3 laps	25/39
dnq	US GP (PHOENIX)	Phoenix	25	Ligier Loto	G	3.5 Ligier JS33-Cosworth V8		29/39
5	CANADIAN GP	Montreal	25	Ligier Loto	G	3.5 Ligier JS33-Cosworth V8	1 lap behind	22/39
ret	FRENCH GP	Paul Ricard	25	Ligier Loto	G	3.5 Ligier JS33-Cosworth V8	gearbox	18/39
dnq	BRITISH GP	Silverstone	25	Ligier Loto	G	3.5 Ligier JS33-Cosworth V8		27/39
11	GERMAN GP	Hockenheim	25	Ligier Loto	G	3.5 Ligier JS33-Cosworth V8	gearbox problems/-3 laps	23/39
dnq	HUNGARIAN GP	Hungaroring	25	Ligier Loto	G	3.5 Ligier JS33-Cosworth V8		27/39
ret	BELGIAN GP	Spa	25	Ligier Loto	G	3.5 Ligier JS33-Cosworth V8	collision with Alliot	17/39
9	ITALIAN GP	Monza	25	Ligier Loto	G	3.5 Ligier JS33-Cosworth V8	2 laps behind	23/39
13	PORTUGUESE GP	Estoril	25	Ligier Loto	G	3.5 Ligier JS33-Cosworth V8	2 laps behind	23/39
dnq	SPANISH GP	Jerez	25	Ligier Loto	G	3.5 Ligier JS33-Cosworth V8		27/38
dnq	JAPANESE GP	Suzuka	25	Ligier Loto	G	3.5 Ligier JS33-Cosworth V8		27/39
ret	AUSTRALIAN GP	Adelaide	25	Ligier Loto	G	3.5 Ligier JS33-Cosworth V8	collision with Cheever	26/39

GP Starts: 149   GP Wins: 7   Pole positions: 18   Fastest laps: 12   Points: 181

PETER ARUNDELL

The sight of his vermilion-red helmet at the front of an F1 grid should have been a regular one during the mid-sixties, but sadly Grand Prix racing was to see the true Peter Arundell on only four occasions before a massive accident in a Formula 2 race at Reims effectively ended his aspirations to emulate his team-mate Jim Clark.

Arundell began his career with an MG TC in 1957 before racing a Lotus XI, and then a Lola sports car, soon becoming the fastest private practitioner behind the works entries. When Peter then won an end-of-season Junior race in the front-engined Elva-DKW, Colin Chapman was not slow to recognise the Essex man's potential and signed him for his Junior team in 1960, a season which saw him beat both his team-mates – Trevor Taylor and Jim Clark – on occasion. As number two to Taylor during 1961, Peter maintained his progress, highlighted by winning the Monaco Junior race, and for 1962 he rightfully assumed the team leadership, dominating proceedings with some brilliant displays, taking 18 wins from 25 starts, and easily claiming the BARC Junior championship.

In truth he should have been promoted to Formula 1 at this stage, and there would certainly have been a drive for him elsewhere had he chosen to seek it. Instead Peter waited patiently for his opportunity, knowing that a better prospect than a Lotus would be hard to find. So it was more Formula Junior in 1963, with occasional F1 outings merely confirming his talent. A superb drive into second place at the Solitude GP was matched in the Mediterranean GP at Enna.

Arundell's fully deserved promotion finally came in 1964, and the season began in tremendous style, his Grand Prix performances being backed by some equally impressive results in non-championship Formula 1 races. He was second in the News of the World Trophy at Goodwood and third at both the Aintree 200 and the Syracuse GP (shared with Spence). In the newly inaugurated Formula 2, Peter was just as impressive, taking third place at Pau, second in the Grovewood Trophy at Mallory Park and fourth in the London Trophy before the fateful Reims race, when his spinning Lotus was hit broadside by Ginther. The car was smashed into an earth bank and Arundell was hurled from the cockpit, suffering a broken arm, thigh and collarbone and severe concussion.

His rehabilitation was long and slow, but Chapman promised him a place in the team when fit, and he reappeared at the South African GP on New Year's Day in 1966, to take third place in the Lotus 33. Once the season got under way, Peter seemed a shadow of his former self, though, to be fair, the machinery at his disposal hardly gave him a chance to shine. Racing the works Formula 2 car brought only a second place at the Eifelrennen, so when Graham Hill was signed for 1967 Arundell was released.

Really that was the end for Peter, though in 1968 he briefly raced Alan Mann's Escort before a short spell with the McNamara F3 and Formula Vee projects in 1969.

ARUNDELL, Peter (GB) b 8/11/1933, Ilford, Essex

	1963	Championship position: Unplaced							
	Race	Circuit	No	Entrant	Tyres	Car/Engine		Comment	Q Pos/Entries
dns	FRENCH GP	Reims	22	Team Lotus	D	1.5 Lotus 25-Climax V8		*practised but drove in FJ event*	(16)/21
	1964	Championship position: 8th=	Wins: 0	Pole positions: 0		Fastest laps: 0	Points scored: 11		
3	MONACO GP	Monte Carlo	11	Team Lotus	D	1.5 Lotus 25-Climax V8		*3 laps behind*	6/20
3	DUTCH GP	Zandvoort	20	Team Lotus	D	1.5 Lotus 25-Climax V8		*1 lap behind*	6/18
9	BELGIAN GP	Spa	24	Team Lotus	D	1.5 Lotus 25-Climax V8		*pit stop-water/4 laps behind*	4/20
4	FRENCH GP	Rouen	4	Team Lotus	D	1.5 Lotus 25-Climax V8			4/17
	1966	Championship position: 17th=	Wins: 0	Pole positions: 0		Fastest laps: 0	Points scored: 1		
dns	BELGIAN GP	Spa	11	Team Lotus	F	3.0 Lotus 43-BRM H16		*engine in practice*	(18)/18
ret	FRENCH GP	Reims	4	Team Lotus	F	3.0 Lotus 43-BRM H16		*gearbox*	16/17
ret	BRITISH GP	Brands Hatch	2	Team Lotus	F	2.0 Lotus 33-BRM V8		*gear linkage*	20/20
dns	"	" "	1	Team Lotus	F	2.0 Lotus 33-Climax V8		*practice only*	– / –
ret	DUTCH GP	Zandvoort	8	Team Lotus	F	2.0 Lotus 33-BRM V8		*ignition*	=15/18
8*	GERMAN GP	Nürburgring	2	Team Lotus	F	2.0 Lotus 33-BRM V8		** 12th after 4 F2 cars/-1 lap*	18/30
8/ret	ITALIAN GP	Monza	24	Team Lotus	F	2.0 Lotus 33-BRM V8		*engine/5 laps behind*	13/22
6	US GP	Watkins Glen	2	Team Lotus	F	2.0 Lotus 33-Climax V8		*no practice/spin-pit stop/-7 laps*	– /19
dns	"	" "	2	Team Lotus	F	3.0 Lotus 43-BRM H16		*no practice time recorded*	– / –
7	MEXICAN GP	Mexico City	2	Team Lotus	F	2.0 Lotus 33-BRM V8		*4 laps behind*	18/19

GP Starts: 11   GP Wins: 0   Pole positions: 0   Fastest laps: 0   Points: 12

ALBERTO ASCARI

WORLD CHAMPION: 1952 & 1953

ALBERTO ASCARI

The son of a famous racing driver – his father, Antonio, was killed at Montlhéry when the young Ascari was just seven years old – it was perhaps inevitable that Alberto should also follow a career in the sport. After racing Bianchi motor cycles from 1937, he drove the very first Ferrari T815 sports car in the 1940 Mille Miglia with his cousin Minozzi, the pair leading their class before retirement.

The war soon brought racing to a halt in Italy, and it was 1947 before he was back in action. Second place in a little Cisitalia in a one-make race at Gezereh Island behind Cortese brought him to the fore, and he was soon impressing with his speed behind the wheel of a Maserati 4CLT. His first major success was in a sports car race at Modena that year, and he benefited greatly from the tutelage of team-mate Villoresi, whom he beat to win the 1948 San Remo GP. He was second to his mentor in the British GP and even drove once for rivals Alfa Romeo, finishing third in the French GP at Reims.

After winning the 1949 Buenos Aires GP for Maserati, both Ascari and Villoresi left for Ferrari, where Alberto was to enjoy spectacular success. In his first season he won the Swiss, Italian and Peron GPs in the T125. In 1950, Alfa were back in competition with their 158s and Ferrari concentrated mainly on Formula 2, winning a succession of races at Modena, Mons, Rome, Reims, Garda and the Nürburgring, while their T375 F1 car was being developed. He did, however, take a second at Monaco, and at season's end won the Penya Rhin GP at Barcelona in the new 4.5-litre car.

In 1951 Ascari won two Grands Prix as at last the might of Alfa was beaten, but the championship went to Fangio. With the change of formula restricting GP racing to 2-litre cars for 1952 and the Alfa team disbanded, Alberto was sitting pretty. His task in taking the championship was further eased by the absence of the injured Fangio, and missing the Swiss GP to compete at Indianapolis merely denied him the opportunity of a clean sweep, as the brilliant Italian surged to six championship victories, in addition to wins at Syracuse, Pau, Marseilles, Comminges and La Baule.

It was much the same in 1953 when he trampled on the opposition to take five more championship wins, adding victories at Pau and Bordeaux to his burgeoning tally. The run of success came to a halt with a move to Lancia for 1954 which left Ascari frustrated as the car was delayed until the end of that year. He did win the Mille Miglia in a Lancia sports car and was allowed to appear as a guest driver for both Maserati and Ferrari, putting in a brilliant drive at Monza against the works Mercedes.

With the Lancias 'au point' at the start of 1955, Ascari led the Argentine GP until he lost control of the car on melting tar, won the non-championship Turin GP and Naples GP at Posillipo, and led at Pau before finishing fifth. At the Monaco GP Alberto famously crashed his car into the harbour, emerging with facial injuries, but four days later he turned up unexpectedly at Monza to test a Ferrari sports car in preparation for the forthcoming Supercortemaggiore race. For some inexplicable reason Ascari crashed the car, and he was thrown onto the track and killed instantly. While the Italian nation mourned the loss of its finest driver, Fangio is reported to have said: 'I have lost my greatest opponent.' Clearly this was true, but close scrutiny of their careers reveals that only rarely did they have the opportunity to race against each other in equally matched machinery.

Ascari again! The Italian in the Ferrari T500 wins the 1953 Belgian GP his ninth successive Grand Prix win.

ASCARI, Alberto (I) b 13/7/1918, Milan – d 26/5/1955, Monza Circuit

	1950	Championship position: 5th		Wins: 0	Pole positions: 0	Fastest laps: 0	Points scored: 11		
	Race	Circuit	No	Entrant	Tyres	Car/Engine		Comment	Q Pos/Entries
2	MONACO GP	Monte Carlo	40	Scuderia Ferrari	P	1.5 s/c Ferrari 125F1 V12		1 lap behind	7/21
ret	SWISS GP	Bremgarten	18	Scuderia Ferrari	P	1.5 s/c Ferrari 125F1 V12		scavenger pump	5/18
5	BELGIAN GP	Spa	4	Scuderia Ferrari	P	3.3 Ferrari 125/275F1 V12		1 lap behind	=7/14
dns	FRENCH GP	Reims	10	Scuderia Ferrari	P	1.5 s/c Ferrari 125F1 V12		car quick enough-raced in F2 support	–/–
ret	ITALIAN GP	Monza	16	Scuderia Ferrari	P	4.5 Ferrari 375F1 V12		engine	2/27
2*	"	"	48	Scuderia Ferrari	P	4.5 Ferrari 375F1 V12		* took over Serafini's car	–/–
	1951	Championship position: 2nd		Wins: 2	Pole positions: 2	Fastest laps: 0	Points scored: 28		
6	SWISS GP	Bremgarten	20	Scuderia Ferrari	P	4.5 Ferrari 375F1 V12		2 laps behind	7/21
2	BELGIAN GP	Spa	8	Scuderia Ferrari	P	4.5 Ferrari 375F1 V12			4/13
ret	FRENCH GP	Reims	12	Scuderia Ferrari	E	4.5 Ferrari 375F1 V12		gearbox	3/23
2*	"	"	14	Scuderia Ferrari	E/P	4.5 Ferrari 375F1 V12		* took over González's car	–/–
ret	BRITISH GP	Silverstone	11	Scuderia Ferrari	P	4.5 Ferrari 375F1 V12		gearbox	4/20
1	GERMAN GP	Nürburgring	71	Scuderia Ferrari	P	4.5 Ferrari 375F1 V12			1/23
1	ITALIAN GP	Monza	2	Scuderia Ferrari	P	4.5 Ferrari 375F1 V12			3/22
4	SPANISH GP	Pedralbes	2	Scuderia Ferrari	P	4.5 Ferrari 375F1 V12		tyre problems/-2 laps	1/20
	1952	Championship position: World Champion		Wins: 6	Pole positions: 5	Fastest laps: 6 (1 shared)	Points scored: 53.5		
1	BELGIAN GP	Spa	4	Scuderia Ferrari	P	2.0 Ferrari 500 4		FL	1/22
1	FRENCH GP	Rouen	8	Scuderia Ferrari	P	2.0 Ferrari 500 4		FL	1/20
1	BRITISH GP	Silverstone	15	Scuderia Ferrari	P	2.0 Ferrari 500 4		FL	2/32
1	GERMAN GP	Nürburgring	101	Scuderia Ferrari	E	2.0 Ferrari 500 4		FL	1/32
1	DUTCH GP	Zandvoort	2	Scuderia Ferrari	P	2.0 Ferrari 500 4		FL	1/18
1	ITALIAN GP	Monza	12	Scuderia Ferrari	P	2.0 Ferrari 500 4		FL (shared with González)	1/35
	1953	Championship position: World Champion		Wins: 5	Pole positions: 6	Fastest laps: 5 (2 shared)	Points scored: 47		
1	ARGENTINE GP	Buenos Aires	10	Scuderia Ferrari	P	2.0 Ferrari 500 4		FL	1/16
1	DUTCH GP	Zandvoort	2	Scuderia Ferrari	P	2.0 Ferrari 500 4			1/20
1	BELGIAN GP	Spa	10	Scuderia Ferrari	P	2.0 Ferrari 500 4			2/22
4	FRENCH GP	Reims	10	Scuderia Ferrari	P	2.0 Ferrari 500 4		FL(shared with Fangio)	1/25
1	BRITISH GP	Silverstone	5	Scuderia Ferrari	P	2.0 Ferrari 500 4		FL(shared with González)	1/29
8*	GERMAN GP	Nürburgring	1	Scuderia Ferrari	P	2.0 Ferrari 500 4		lost wheel/*Villoresi took car/-1 lap	1/35
ret	"	"	4	Scuderia Ferrari	P	2.0 Ferrari 500 4		engine/took Villoresi's car/FL	–/–
1	SWISS GP	Bremgarten	46	Scuderia Ferrari	P	2.0 Ferrari 500 4		FL	2/23
ret	ITALIAN GP	Monza	4	Scuderia Ferrari	P	2.0 Ferrari 500 4		collision with Marimón	1/30
	1954	Championship position: 25th		Wins: 0	Pole positions: 0	Fastest laps: 2 (1 shared)	Points scored: 1.14		
ret	FRENCH GP	Reims	10	Officine Alfieri Maserati	P	2.5 Maserati 250F 6		engine	3/22
ret	BRITISH GP	Silverstone	31	Officine Alfieri Maserati	P	2.5 Maserati 250F 6		con rod/FL (shared)	29/31
ret	"	"	32	Officine Alfieri Maserati	P	2.5 Maserati 250F 6		took Villoresi's car/con rod	–/–
ret	ITALIAN GP	Monza	34	Scuderia Ferrari	E	2.5 Ferrari 625 4		engine	2/21
ret	SPANISH GP	Pedralbes	34	Scuderia Lancia	P	2.5 Lancia D50 V8		clutch/FL	1/22
	1955	Championship position: Unplaced							
ret	ARGENTINE GP	Buenos Aires	32	Scuderia Lancia	P	2.5 Lancia D50 V8		spun off on melting tar	3/22
ret	MONACO GP	Monte Carlo	26	Scuderia Lancia	P	2.5 Lancia D50 V8		crashed into harbour	2/22

GP Starts: 31   GP Wins: 13   Pole positions: 14   Fastest laps: 13   Points: 140.64

PETER ASHDOWN

Although his sole Grand Prix appearance was in a Cooper, Peter's reputation was built as a Lotus man. Consistently high placings in the marque's early sports cars between 1955 and 1957 brought him a works drive, but a broken collar-bone sustained in a crash at Rouen ended his season. On his return in 1959 Peter drove some sparkling races, the best of which saw him win the Auvernge Trophy in a Lotus XI at Clermont Ferrand, beating Behra's RS Porsche.

Though there were no further opportunities to compete in Grands Prix, Ashdown raced on until 1962, driving a Lola in Formula Junior, and his gift for handling small-capacity sports cars was underlined by class wins in the Nürburgring 1000 Km in both 1960 and 1962.

ASHDOWN, Peter (GB) b 16/10/1934, Danbury, nr Chelmsford, Essex

	1959	Championship position: Unplaced							
	Race	Circuit	No	Entrant	Tyres	Car/Engine		Comment	Q Pos/Entries
12	BRITISH GP (F2)	Aintree	52	Alan Brown Equipe	D	1.5 Cooper T45-Climax 4		3rd F2 car/6 laps behind	23/30

GP Starts: 1   GP Wins: 0   Pole positions: 0   Fastest laps: 0   Points: 0

IAN ASHLEY

Ashley raced extensively in Formula Ford, F3 and F5000 from 1967 to 1975, often showing great speed but not always the ability to keep the car on the road.

His forays into Grand Prix racing with some of the formula's lesser lights ranged between the undistinguished and, on one occasion, when he was very fortunate to escape a lurid 170 mph practice crash in Canada in 1977 with no worse than broken ankles, the disastrous.

After a slow recovery Ian took up the same career as his father and became a pilot. The itch to go racing remained, however, and in 1993 he returned to the tracks, looking trim and fit, to contest the fiercely competitive BTCC series in a Vauxhall Cavalier. The thrill of danger and speed had obviously not yet deserted Ashley, who subsequently tried his hand at racing motor-cycle sidecars!

GERRY ASHMORE

From a motor racing family – his father Fred was a prominent post-war driver – Gerry cut his teeth on Jaguars before taking the bold step of racing a Lotus 18 in Formula 1 in 1961. By far his best result was second place in the Naples GP, though he finished well behind Baghetti's Ferrari. Gerry courted disaster on his next visit to Italy, however, crashing, luckily without serious injury, on the first lap of the Italian GP in an accident independent from the von Trips tragedy.

After a handful of races with the Lotus in 1962, he continued to make occasional appearances, such as in 1965 with the ex-David Prophet Lotus 30 and in 1970 driving a Lotus Elan 2+2.

ASHLEY, Ian (GB) b 26/10/1947, Wuppertal, Germany

	1974		Championship position: Unplaced					
	Race	Circuit	No	Entrant	Tyres	Car/Engine	Comment	Q Pos/Entries
14	GERMAN GP	Nürburgring	32	Token Racing	F	3.0 Token RJ02-Cosworth V8	*1 lap behind*	26/32
nc	AUSTRIAN GP	Österreichring	35	Token Racing	F	3.0 Token RJ02-Cosworth V8	*2 stops-wheel problems/-8 laps*	25/31
dnq	CANADIAN GP	Mosport Park	42	Chequered Flag/Richard Oaten	G	3.0 Brabham BT42-Cosworth V8		30/30
dnq	US GP	Watkins Glen	42	Chequered Flag/Richard Oaten	G	3.0 Brabham BT42-Cosworth V8		29/30
	1975		Championship position: Unplaced					
dns	GERMAN GP	Nürburgring	20	Frank Williams Racing Cars	G	3.0 Williams FW03-Cosworth V8	*practice accident-leg injuries*	(20)/26
	1976		Championship position: Unplaced					
ret	BRAZILIAN GP	Interlagos	14	Stanley BRM	G	3.0 BRM P201B V12	*oil pump*	21/22
	1977		Championship position: Unplaced					
dnq	AUSTRIAN GP	Österreichring	39	Hesketh Racing	G	3.0 Hesketh 308E-Cosworth V8		28/30
dnq	DUTCH GP	Zandvoort	39	Hesketh Racing	G	3.0 Hesketh 308E-Cosworth V8		30/34
dnq	ITALIAN GP	Monza	25	Hesketh Racing	G	3.0 Hesketh 308E-Cosworth V8		30/34
17	US GP EAST	Watkins Glen	25	Hesketh Racing	G	3.0 Hesketh 308E-Cosworth V8	*pit stop-wheel bearing/-4 laps*	22/27
dns	CANADIAN GP	Mosport Park	25	Hesketh Racing	G	3.0 Hesketh 308E-Cosworth V8	*injured in practice accident*	(26)/27

GP Starts: 4   GP Wins: 0   Pole positions: 0   Fastest laps: 0   Points: 0

ASHMORE, Gerry (GB) b 25/7/1936, West Bromwich, Staffordshire

	1961		Championship position: Unplaced Wins: 0 Pole positions: 0 Fastest laps: 0 Points scored: 0					
	Race	Circuit	No	Entrant	Tyres	Car/Engine	Comment	Q Pos/Entries
ret	BRITISH GP	Aintree	40	Gerry Ashmore	D	1.5 Lotus 18-Climax 4	*ignition-misfire*	26/30
16	GERMAN GP	Nürburgring	27	Gerry Ashmore	D	1.5 Lotus 18-Climax 4	*2 laps behind*	25/27
ret	ITALIAN GP	Monza	18	Gerry Ashmore	D	1.5 Lotus 18-Climax 4	*accident on lap 1*	25/33
	1962		Championship position: Unplaced Wins: 0 Pole positions: 0 Fastest laps: 0 Points scored: 0					
dnq	ITALIAN GP	Monza	52	Gerry Ashmore	D	1.5 Lotus 18/21-Climax 4		24/30

GP Starts: 3   GP Wins: 0   Pole positions: 0   Fastest laps: 0   Points: 0

ASTON, Bill (GB) b 29/3/1900, Stafford – d 4/3/1974, Lingfield, Surrey

	1952		Championship position: Unplaced Wins: 0 Pole positions: 0 Fastest laps: 0 Points scored: 0					
	Race	Circuit	No	Entrant	Tyres	Car/Engine	Comment	Q Pos/Entries
dns	BRITISH GP	Silverstone	2	W S Aston	D	2.0 Aston NB 41-Butterworth F4	*too slow*	30/32
ret	GERMAN GP	Nürburgring	114	W S Aston	D	2.0 Aston NB 41-Butterworth F4	*oil pressure*	21/32
dnq	ITALIAN GP	Monza	64	W S Aston	D	2.0 Aston NB 41-Butterworth F4		31/35

GP Starts: 1   GP Wins: 0   Pole positions: 0   Fastest laps: 0   Points: 0

BILL ASTON

This amateur racing enthusiast served in the Great War and began his career on motor cycles before swiching to four-wheel competition. In the late forties Bill was a front-runner with a 500 cc Cooper-JAP in the extremely competitive Formula 3 class. As well as wins at home, he took a prestigious Continental victory at Brussels and placed second at Zandvoort in 1949. In 1951 his Cooper – now with an 1100 cc engine – led the GP des Frontières at Chimay before the engine seized, but he did take a third place at Goodwood in the Lavant Cup, then a five-lap sprint race.

His business dealings as both civil engineer and fruit farmer no doubt helped finance his Aston-Butterworth Formula 2 single-seaters which he ran with Robin Montgomerie-Charrington. Unfortunately, these small and beautifully bodied machines saw little success, being constantly afflicted by fuel system problems. Aston sensibly withdrew from the giddy heights of the Grand Prix world after this unsuccessful foray, but continued to enjoy racing at club events. In the late fifties he raced a Jaguar D-Type and Aston Martin DBR1, often winning his class. Even when he was well past sixty years of age, Bill continued to race (and win) with a Mini and the ex-Equipe Endeavour Jaguar 3.8 saloon.

RICHARD ATTWOOD

A trade apprentice at Jaguar, Attwood made his competition debut in the 1960 season with a Triumph TR3, before joining the Midland Racing Partnership to race in Formula Junior, spending most of 1961 and 1962 at club level. In 1963, driving a Mk 5A Lola-Ford, Dickie shot to international prominence by winning the Monaco Formula Junior race, and his performances won him the first Grovewood Award and the princely sum of £500.

In 1964 Attwood was given a couple of chances in the works BRM, taking fourth in the News of the World Trophy at Goodwood, but non-starting the 4WD P67 at the British GP. Racing in Formula 2 for MRP, he produced some excellent performances, most notably a win at Aspern in the Vienna GP, and second place – behind Clark – at Pau, plus further runner-up spots in the Eifelrennen and at Albi. His ability was being recognised more widely, and he became a founder member of the Ford sports-prototype team.

Joining Parnell Racing, Richard drove the team's none-too-quick Lotus 25-BRM sensibly to two points-scoring finishes, while in F2 he was again second at Pau, and won the Rome GP at Vallelunga. His sports car career was now taking off, and he began what was to be a long and successful partnership with David Piper, ending the season with a fantastic drive to win the Rand 9 Hours in Piper's Ferrari 365 P2.

Driving for BRM in the 1966 Tasman series, Attwood won the Gold Leaf Trophy race at Levin before another season of F2 and sports car events, which once again ended with a win at Kyalami in the Rand 9 Hours. Despite another successful Tasman interlude in New Zealand, where he took two second places and two thirds in four starts, Richard's only other single-seater drive in 1967 was a works Cooper outing at Mosport.

When Mike Spence was so tragically killed at Indianapolis, early in 1968, Attwood was signed to replace him at BRM. His debut for the team at Monaco was stunning, Dickie taking second place and fastest lap. Unfortunately subsequent performances were not so impressive and after the German GP he was released from his contract, returning to sports car racing.

In 1969 he was called back to F1 to try and reprise his Monaco performance for Lotus when Rindt was recovering from injury, scoring a fine fourth place, while later in the season he took Frank Williams' F2 Brabham to sixth (and second in class) at the Nürburgring. It was also the season in which he raced a factory Porsche for the first time, sharing a 908 Spyder with Elford to take second place in the BOAC 500. In 1970 he scored his greatest triumph, winning Le Mans in a Porsche 917 with Hans Herrmann, and took second place with the German at the Nürburgring 1000 Km. In 1971, Attwood's final racing year, he drove the John Wyer/Gulf Porsche, winning the Österreichring 1000 Km with Rodriguez, and finishing second at Le Mans with Müller.

Retiring at the end of the season for business reasons, Attwood was occasionally tempted back to the circuits in the eighties, mainly in historic sports car events, but also at Le Mans in 1984 when he raced a Nimrod.

ATTWOOD, Richard (GB) b 4/4/1940, Wolverhampton, Staffordshire

	1964			Championship position: Unplaced				
	Race	Circuit	No	Entrant	Tyres	Car/Engine	Comment	Q Pos/Entries
dns	BRITISH GP	Brands Hatch	21	Owen Racing Organisation	D	1.5 BRM P67 V8 4WD	car withdrawn	(24)/25

	1965			Championship position: 14th= Wins: 0 Pole positions: 0 Fastest laps: 0 Points scored: 2				
ret	MONACO GP	Monte Carlo	15	Reg Parnell (Racing)	D	1.5 Lotus 25-BRM V8	lost wheel	6/17
14/ret	BELGIAN GP	Spa	23	Reg Parnell (Racing)	D	1.5 Lotus 25-BRM V8	spun off in rain/-6 laps	13/21
13	BRITISH GP	Silverstone	22	Reg Parnell (Racing)	D	1.5 Lotus 25-BRM V8	pit stops/17 laps behind	16/23
12	DUTCH GP	Zandvoort	34	Reg Parnell (Racing)	D	1.5 Lotus 25-BRM V8	3 laps behind	17/17
ret	GERMAN GP	Nürburgring	20	Reg Parnell (Racing)	D	1.5 Lotus 25-BRM V8	water hose leak	17/22
6	ITALIAN GP	Monza	40	Reg Parnell (Racing)	D	1.5 Lotus 25-BRM V8	1 lap behind	13/23
10	US GP	Watkins Glen	21	Reg Parnell (Racing)	D	1.5 Lotus 25-BRM V8	pit stop/9 laps behind	=16/18
6	MEXICAN GP	Mexico City	21	Reg Parnell (Racing)	D	1.5 Lotus 25-BRM V8	1 lap behind	17/18

	1967			Championship position: Unplaced				
10	CANADIAN GP	Mosport Park	8	Cooper Car Co	F	3.0 Cooper T81B-Maserati V12	6 laps behind	14/19

	1968			Championship position: 13th= Wins: 0 Pole positions: 0 Fastest laps: 1 Points scored: 6				
2	MONACO GP	Monte Carlo	15	Owen Racing Organisation	D	3.0 BRM P126 V12	FL	6/18
ret	BELGIAN GP	Spa	12	Owen Racing Organisation	D	3.0 BRM P126 V12	broken oil pipe	11/18
7	DUTCH GP	Zandvoort	16	Owen Racing Organisation	D	3.0 BRM P126 V12	5 laps behind	15/19
7	FRENCH GP	Rouen	22	Owen Racing Organisation	D	3.0 BRM P126 V12	pit stop-tyres/3 laps behind	=13/18
ret	BRITISH GP	Brands Hatch	11	Owen Racing Organisation	D	3.0 BRM P126 V12	radiator holed by stone	15/20
14	GERMAN GP	Nürburgring	11	Owen Racing Organisation	D	3.0 BRM P126 V12	1 lap behind	20/20

	1969			Championship position: 13th= Wins: 0 Pole positions: 0 Fastest laps: 0 Points scored: 3				
4	MONACO GP	Monte Carlo	2	Gold Leaf Team Lotus	F	3.0 Lotus 49B-Cosworth V8		10/16
6*	GERMAN GP (F2)	Nürburgring	29	Frank Williams Racing Cars	D	1.6 Brabham BT30-Cosworth 4	*2nd-F2 class/no points scored	20/26

GP Starts: 17   GP Wins: 0   Pole positions: 0   Fastest laps: 1   Points: 11

BADOER, Luca (I) b 25/1/1971, Montebelluna, Treviso

	1993			Championship position: Unplaced				
	Race	Circuit	No	Entrant	Tyres	Car/Engine	Comment	Q Pos/Entries
ret	SOUTH AFRICAN GP	Kyalami	22	BMS Scuderia Italia SpA	G	3.5 Lola T93/30 BMS-Ferrari V12	gearbox	26/26
12	BRAZILIAN GP	Interlagos	22	BMS Scuderia Italia SpA	G	3.5 Lola T93/30 BMS-Ferrari V12	pit stop-new nose/-3 laps	21/26
dnq	EUROPEAN GP	Donington	22	BMS Scuderia Italia SpA	G	3.5 Lola T93/30 BMS-Ferrari V12		26/26
7	SAN MARINO GP	Imola	22	BMS Scuderia Italia SpA	G	3.5 Lola T93/30 BMS-Ferrari V12	3 laps behind	24/26
ret	SPANISH GP	Barcelona	22	BMS Scuderia Italia SpA	G	3.5 Lola T93/30 BMS-Ferrari V12	clutch	22/26
dnq	MONACO GP	Monte Carlo	22	BMS Scuderia Italia SpA	G	3.5 Lola T93/30 BMS-Ferrari V12		26/26
15	CANADIAN GP	Montreal	22	BMS Scuderia Italia SpA	G	3.5 Lola T93/30 BMS-Ferrari V12	4 laps behind	25/26
ret	FRENCH GP	Magny Cours	22	BMS Scuderia Italia SpA	G	3.5 Lola T93/30 BMS-Ferrari V12	suspension	22/26
ret	BRITISH GP	Silverstone	22	BMS Scuderia Italia SpA	G	3.5 Lola T93/30 BMS-Ferrari V12	engine-electrics	25/26
ret	GERMAN GP	Hockenheim	22	BMS Scuderia Italia SpA	G	3.5 Lola T93/30 BMS-Ferrari V12	suspension	25/26
ret	HUNGARIAN GP	Hungaroring	22	BMS Scuderia Italia SpA	G	3.5 Lola T93/30 BMS-Ferrari V12	spun off	26/26
13	BELGIAN GP	Spa	22	BMS Scuderia Italia SpA	G	3.5 Lola T93/30 BMS-Ferrari V12	2 laps behind	24/25
10	ITALIAN GP	Monza	22	BMS Scuderia Italia SpA	G	3.5 Lola T93/30 BMS-Ferrari V12	2 laps behind	25/26
14	PORTUGUESE GP	Estoril	22	BMS Scuderia Italia SpA	G	3.5 Lola T93/30 BMS-Ferrari V12	3 laps behind	26/26

	1995			Championship position: Unplaced				
ret	BRAZILIAN GP	Interlagos	24	Minardi Scuderia Italia	G	3.0 Minardi M195-Ford EDM V8	gearbox	18/26
ret/dns	ARGENTINE GP	Buenos Aires	24	Minardi Scuderia Italia	G	3.0 Minardi M195-Ford EDM V8	accident at first start	(13)/26
14	SAN MARINO GP	Imola	24	Minardi Scuderia Italia	G	3.0 Minardi M195-Ford EDM V8	4 laps behind	20/26
ret	SPANISH GP	Barcelona	24	Minardi Scuderia Italia	G	3.0 Minardi M195-Ford EDM V8	gearbox	21/26
ret	MONACO GP	Monte Carlo	24	Minardi Scuderia Italia	G	3.0 Minardi M195-Ford EDM V8	suspension	16/26
8	CANADIAN GP	Montreal	24	Minardi Scuderia Italia	G	3.0 Minardi M195-Ford EDM V8	1 lap behind	19/24
13	FRENCH GP	Magny Cours	24	Minardi Scuderia Italia	G	3.0 Minardi M195-Ford EDM V8	3 laps behind	17/24
10	BRITISH GP	Silverstone	24	Minardi Scuderia Italia	G	3.0 Minardi M195-Ford EDM V8	1 lap behind	18/24
ret	GERMAN GP	Hockenheim	24	Minardi Scuderia Italia	G	3.0 Minardi M195-Ford EDM V8	gearbox	16/24
8	HUNGARIAN GP	Hungaroring	24	Minardi Scuderia Italia	G	3.0 Minardi M195-Ford EDM V8	2 laps behind	12/24
ret	BELGIAN GP	Spa	24	Minardi Scuderia Italia	G	3.0 Minardi M195-Ford EDM V8	spun off	19/24
ret	ITALIAN GP	Monza	24	Minardi Scuderia Italia	G	3.0 Minardi M195-Ford EDM V8	accident	18/24
14	PORTUGUESE GP	Estoril	24	Minardi Scuderia Italia	G	3.0 Minardi M195-Ford EDM V8	3 laps behind	18/24
11	EUROPEAN GP	Nürburgring	24	Minardi Scuderia Italia	G	3.0 Minardi M195-Ford EDM V8	3 laps behind	18/24
15	PACIFIC GP	T.I. Circuit	24	Minardi Scuderia Italia	G	3.0 Minardi M195-Ford EDM V8	3 laps behind	16/24
9	JAPANESE GP	Suzuka	24	Minardi Scuderia Italia	G	3.0 Minardi M195-Ford EDM V8	2 laps behind	18/24
dns	AUSTRALIAN GP	Adelaide	24	Minardi Scuderia Italia	G	3.0 Minardi M195-Ford EDM V8	electrics before start	(15)/24

	1996			Championship position: Unplaced				
dnq	AUSTRALIAN GP	Melbourne	22	Forti Grand Prix	G	3.0 Forti FG01 95B-Ford Zetec R V8	not within 107% of pole	21/22
11	BRAZILIAN GP	Interlagos	22	Forti Grand Prix	G	3.0 Forti FG01 95B-Ford Zetec R V8	4 laps behind	19/22
ret	ARGENTINE GP	Buenos Aires	22	Forti Grand Prix	G	3.0 Forti FG01 95B-Ford Zetec R V8	accident-car overturned	21/22
dnq	EUROPEAN GP	Nürburgring	22	Forti Grand Prix	G	3.0 Forti FG01 95B-Ford Zetec R V8	not within 107% of pole	22/22
10	SAN MARINO GP	Imola	22	Forti Grand Prix	G	3.0 Forti FG03 97-Ford Zetec R V8	4 laps behind	21/22
ret	MONACO GP	Monte Carlo	22	Forti Grand Prix	G	3.0 Forti FG03 97-Ford Zetec R V8	collision with Villeneuve	21/22
dnq	SPANISH GP	Barcelona	22	Forti Grand Prix	G	3.0 Forti FG03-97 Ford Zetec R V8	not within 107% of pole	21/22
ret	CANADIAN GP	Montreal	22	Forti Grand Prix	G	3.0 Forti FG03 97-Ford Zetec R V8	gearbox	20/22
ret	FRENCH GP	Magny Cours	22	Forti Grand Prix	G	3.0 Forti FG03 97-Ford Zetec R V8	fuel pump	21/22
dnq	BRITISH GP	Silverstone	22	Forti Grand Prix	G	3.0 Forti FG03 97-Ford Zetec R V8	not within 107% of pole	22/22
dnp	GERMAN GP	Hockenheim	22	Forti Grand Prix	G	3.0 Forti FG03 97-Ford Zetec R V8	cars did not practice	–/–

	1999			Championship position: Unplaced						
ret	AUSTRALIAN GP	Melbourne	20	Fondmetal Minardi Ford	B	3.0 Minardi MO1-Ford Zetec R V10	*gearbox*	21/22
8	SAN MARINO GP	Imola	20	Fondmetal Minardi Ford	B	3.0 Minardi MO1-Ford Zetec R V10	*3 laps behind*	22/22
ret	MONACO GP	Monte Carlo	20	Fondmetal Minardi Ford	B	3.0 Minardi MO1-Ford Zetec R V10	*gearbox*	20/22
ret	SPANISH GP	Barcelona	20	Fondmetal Minardi Ford	B	3.0 Minardi MO1-Ford Zetec R V10	*spun off*	22/22
10	CANADIAN GP	Montreal	20	Fondmetal Minardi Ford	B	3.0 Minardi MO1-Ford Zetec R V10	*1 lap behind*	21/22
10	FRENCH GP	Magny Cours	20	Fondmetal Minardi Ford	B	3.0 Minardi MO1-Ford Zetec R V10	*1 lap behind*	20/22
ret	BRITISH GP	Silverstone	20	Fondmetal Minardi Ford	B	3.0 Minardi MO1-Ford Zetec R V10	*gearbox*	21/22
13	AUSTRIAN GP	A1-Ring	20	Fondmetal Minardi Ford	B	3.0 Minardi MO1-Ford Zetec R V10	*3 laps behind*	19/22
10	GERMAN GP	Hockenheim	20	Fondmetal Minardi Ford	B	3.0 Minardi MO1-Ford Zetec R V10	*1 lap behind*	19/22
14	HUNGARIAN GP	Hungaroring	20	Fondmetal Minardi Ford	B	3.0 Minardi MO1-Ford Zetec R V10	*2 laps behind*	19/22
ret	BELGIAN GP	Spa	20	Fondmetal Minardi Ford	B	3.0 Minardi MO1-Ford Zetec R V10	*suspension*	20/22
ret	ITALIAN GP	Monza	20	Fondmetal Minardi Ford	B	3.0 Minardi MO1-Ford Zetec R V10	*hit by Takagi*	19/22
ret	EUROPEAN GP	Nürburgring	20	Fondmetal Minardi Ford	B	3.0 Minardi MO1-Ford Zetec R V10	*gearbox when fourth*	19/22
ret	MALAYSIAN GP	Sepang	20	Fondmetal Minardi Ford	B	3.0 Minardi MO1-Ford Zetec R V10	*overheating*	21/22
ret	JAPANESE GP	Suzuka	20	Fondmetal Minardi Ford	B	3.0 Minardi MO1-Ford Zetec R V10	*engine*	22/22

GP Starts: 48 (49)　GP Wins: 0　Pole positions: 0　Fastest laps: 0　Points: 0

LUCA BADOER

Badoer was regarded as something of a prodigy when, aged only 19, he made his mark in Italian Formula 3 by winning the final round of the 1990 season ahead of championship contenders Colciago and Zanardi.

Naturally all eyes were on the former Italian karting champion from Montebelluna the following season and, after a quiet start in the early rounds, Luca reeled off four wins in a row amid growing acrimony as rival teams questioned the legality of his car. In fact the last of these victories was wiped out due to the team running a non-scrutineered tyre and Badoer's season never recovered thereafter.

He had done enough, however, to move up to F3000 for 1992 and, at the wheel of the superbly engineered Team Crypton Reynard, Luca was a convincing champion, winning three of the early rounds and overcoming the effects of a nasty shunt at Spa to clinch the title with another victory at Nogaro.

The slightly built Badoer then found himself pitched into the big time with the newly formed Lola Scuderia Italia team for 1993. The season was a fiasco with the car floundering at the back of the grid and the only question to be answered at most of the early Grands Prix was which of the two unfortunate drivers – Luca or Michele Alboreto – would fail to qualify. With the team folding after the Portuguese GP, Badoer was left looking for a drive for 1994 and an unimpressive winter test for Benetton left him out in the cold.

Despite this setback Badoer was back in business with Minardi the following season, the little Faenza team pluckily picking up the pieces in spite of their devastating loss to Ligier of a projected works Mugen engine deal. Running customer Ford V8s meant the drivers were consigned to the grid's lower reaches and the pursuit of the occasional point, but Luca managed to stay on board while the veteran Martini was dropped in mid-season. With his replacement, the well-sponsored Pedro Lamy, proving evenly matched with the shy and quiet Milanese driver, Badoer was forced to take his chances with back-markers Forti Corse in 1996.

It was a gamble which failed to pay off when the struggling team collapsed in financial ruin by mid-season, leaving Badoer largely unemployed (with the exception of a couple of sports car outings in a GT Lotus) over the next eighteen months.

In 1998 he won the role of Ferrari test driver, which precluded any chance of a return to Grand Prix racing, but a year later he was allowed to rejoin the Minardi family to resurrect his Grand Prix career.

It was to be a season of huge disappointments for Luca, who suffered a broken wrist in a testing accident at Fiorano and was then devastated to be passed over by Ferrari after Michael Schumacher had broken his leg at Silverstone. To add to the driver's woes, a fourth place and three World Championship points slipped away at the European Grand Prix when his Minardi's gearbox failed. Badoer was left in tears beside his stricken car, one of the saddest sights of the 1999 season.

GIANCARLO BAGHETTI

Baghetti will for ever be known for his extraordinary feat of winning the very first championship Grand Prix that he entered. In searing heat at Reims in 1961, the young Italian showed remarkable racecraft and composure as he took the sole surviving Ferrari to victory over the works Porsche driven by Dan Gurney. It was no fluke, for some weeks earlier Baghetti had done exactly the same thing in his first Formula 1 race at Syracuse and he had then followed that up with another victory, though the field at the Naples GP was weak and Giancarlo had an easy win. No other driver has ever won his first three Formula 1 races and probably none ever will, so Baghetti's place in motor racing folklore is secure.

His racing career started with an Alfa Romeo in 1956 and, after a second place in the Mille Miglia Rally in 1958, driving an Alfa 1900TI, Baghetti turned to sports car and Formula Junior racing over the next two years. He took three wins in the FJ Dragada-Lancia, and was invited to join the Scuderia Sant Ambroeus team who were in turn members of FISA (Federazione Italiane Scuderie Automobilistiche), a body helping to promote young Italian racing talent, the ultimate aim being a place in the Ferrari Formula 1 team. Eventually Baghetti was chosen and, as related above, the early results were sensational, but his subsequent career never matched those dizzy heights. His next race, in the rain at Aintree, ended in a shunt, and Monza brought an engine failure, though he did set fastest lap. In 1962 the Ferrari team were left behind by the V8 opposition and, although Baghetti scored a few decent finishes in Grands Prix and a second place in the Mediterranean GP, he was now being overshadowed by his old Junior rival Bandini, though the pair shared a Ferrari 196 to take second place in the Targa Florio.

With Ferrari in a state of disarray by the end of the year, Baghetti made a disastrous move (with Phil Hill) to Carlo Chiti's breakaway ATS organisation for 1963, and there was to be no Grand Prix salvation when he joined the Centro Sud team with their elderly BRMs. His reputation got him the occasional Grand Prix ride thereafter, but he could still be found in sports cars. He finished second, with Guichet, in the 1966 Targa Florio in a works Ferrari, and was a regular in the European touring car championship with a Fiat Abarth. Surprisingly for one so famous, he was quite happy to drop down into the Italian F3 championship between 1967 and 1968, and he also took a Lancia Fulvia on the London-Sydney marathon but was forced to abandon the trip when his passport and all his documents were stolen in Bombay.

Subsequently Giancarlo became a photo-journalist, enjoying his little slice of fame and living life to the full, until his recent death from cancer at the age of 60.

BAGHETTI, Giancarlo (I) b 25/12/1934, Milan – d 27/11/1995, Milan

	1961			Championship position: 9th Wins: 0 Pole positions: 0 Fastest laps: 1 Points scored: 9					
	Race	*Circuit*	*No*	*Entrant*	*Tyres*	*Car/Engine*		*Comment*	*Q Pos/Entries*
1	FRENCH GP	Reims	50	FISA	D	1.5 Ferrari 156 V6		*only driver to win first ever GP*	=12/26
ret	BRITISH GP	Aintree	58	Scuderia Sant Ambroeus	D	1.5 Ferrari 156 V6		*crashed in rain*	=18/30
ret	ITALIAN GP	Monza	32	Scuderia Sant Ambroeus	D	1.5 Ferrari 156 V6		*engine/FL*	6/33
	1962			Championship position: 11th Wins: 0 Pole positions: 0 Fastest laps: 0 Points scored: 5					
4	DUTCH GP	Zandvoort	2	Scuderia Ferrari SpA SEFAC	D	1.5 Ferrari 156 V6		*1 lap behind*	12/20
ret	BELGIAN GP	Spa	11	Scuderia Ferrari SpA SEFAC	D	1.5 Ferrari 156 V6		*ignition*	14/20
10	GERMAN GP	Nürburgring	2	Scuderia Ferrari SpA SEFAC	D	1.5 Ferrari 156 V6			13/30
5	ITALIAN GP	Monza	2	Scuderia Ferrari SpA SEFAC	D	1.5 Ferrari 156 V6			18/30
	1963			Championship position: Unplaced					
ret	BELGIAN GP	Spa	27	Automobili Tourismo Sport	D	1.5 ATS 100 V8		*gearbox*	20/20
ret	DUTCH GP	Zandvoort	26	Automobili Tourismo Sport	D	1.5 ATS 100 V8		*ignition*	15/19
15	ITALIAN GP	Monza	14	Automobili Tourismo Sport	D	1.5 ATS 100 V8		*pit stops/23 laps behind*	25/28
ret	US GP	Watkins Glen	26	Automobili Tourismo Sport	D	1.5 ATS 100 V8		*oil pump*	20/21
ret	MEXICAN GP	Mexico City	26	Automobili Tourismo Sport	D	1.5 ATS 100 V8		*carburation*	21/21
	1964			Championship position: Unplaced					
10	DUTCH GP	Zandvoort	32	Scuderia Centro Sud	D	1.5 BRM P57 V8		*6 laps behind*	16/18
8	BELGIAN GP	Spa	6	Scuderia Centro Sud	D	1.5 BRM P57 V8		*1 lap behind*	17/20
12	BRITISH GP	Brands Hatch	18	Scuderia Centro Sud	D	1.5 BRM P57 V8		*4 laps behind*	=21/25
ret	GERMAN GP	Nürburgring	18	Scuderia Centro Sud	D	1.5 BRM P57 V8		*throttle linkage*	21/24
7	AUSTRIAN GP	Zeltweg	18	Scuderia Centro Sud	D	1.5 BRM P57 V8		*7 laps behind*	15/20
8	ITALIAN GP	Monza	30	Scuderia Centro Sud	D	1.5 BRM P57 V8		*1 lap behind*	15/25
	1965			Championship position: Unplaced					
ret	ITALIAN GP	Monza	10	Brabham Racing Organisation	D	1.5 Brabham BT7-Climax V8		*cod rod*	19/23
	1966			Championship position: Unplaced					
nc	ITALIAN GP	Monza	44	Reg Parnell Racing Ltd	F	2.4 Ferrari Dino 246 V6		*car loaned by works/p-stop/-9 laps*	16/22
dns	"	"	44	Reg Parnell Racing Ltd	F	2.0 Lotus 25-BRM V8		*engine in practice*	– / –
	1967			Championship position: Unplaced					
ret	ITALIAN GP	Monza	24	Team Lotus	F	3.0 Lotus 49-Cosworth V8		*engine*	17/18

GP Starts: 21   GP Wins: 1   Pole positions: 0   Fastest laps: 1   Points: 14

First time winner. Giancarlo Baghetti leads the 1961 French Grand Prix at Reims. The young Italian withstood tremendous pressure from the Porsche's of Gurney (12) and Bonnier (10) and Jim Clark's Lotus (8).

BAILEY, Julian (GB) b 9/10/1961, Woolwich, London

1988 — Championship position: Unplaced

	Race	Circuit	No	Entrant	Tyres	Car/Engine	Comment	Q Pos/Entries
dnq	BRAZILIAN GP	Rio	4	Tyrrell Racing Organisation	G	3.5 Tyrrell 017-Cosworth V8		27/31
ret	SAN MARINO GP	Imola	4	Tyrrell Racing Organisation	G	3.5 Tyrrell 017-Cosworth V8	gearbox	21/31
dnq	MONACO GP	Monte Carlo	4	Tyrrell Racing Organisation	G	3.5 Tyrrell 017-Cosworth V8		30/30
dnq	MEXICAN GP	Mexico City	4	Tyrrell Racing Organisation	G	3.5 Tyrrell 017-Cosworth V8		29/30
ret	CANADIAN GP	Montreal	4	Tyrrell Racing Organisation	G	3.5 Tyrrell 017-Cosworth V8	collision with Sala on lap 1	23/31
9/ret	US GP (DETROIT)	Detroit	4	Tyrrell Racing Organisation	G	3.5 Tyrrell 017-Cosworth V8	hit wall/4 laps behind	23/31
dnq	FRENCH GP	Paul Ricard	4	Tyrrell Racing Organisation	G	3.5 Tyrrell 017-Cosworth V8		29/31
16	BRITISH GP	Silverstone	4	Tyrrell Racing Organisation	G	3.5 Tyrrell 017-Cosworth V8	2 laps behind	24/31
dnq	GERMAN GP	Hockenheim	4	Tyrrell Racing Organisation	G	3.5 Tyrrell 017-Cosworth V8		29/31
dnq	HUNGARIAN GP	Hungaroring	4	Tyrrell Racing Organisation	G	3.5 Tyrrell 017-Cosworth V8		29/31
dnq	BELGIAN GP	Spa	4	Tyrrell Racing Organisation	G	3.5 Tyrrell 017-Cosworth V8		30/31
12	ITALIAN GP	Monza	4	Tyrrell Racing Organisation	G	3.5 Tyrrell 017-Cosworth V8	2 laps behind	26/31
dnq	PORTUGUESE GP	Estoril	4	Tyrrell Racing Organisation	G	3.5 Tyrrell 017-Cosworth V8		27/31
dnq	SPANISH GP	Jerez	4	Tyrrell Racing Organisation	G	3.5 Tyrrell 017-Cosworth V8		29/31
14	JAPANESE GP	Suzuka	4	Tyrrell Racing Organisation	G	3.5 Tyrrell 017-Cosworth V8	2 laps behind	26/31
dnq	AUSTRALIAN GP	Adelaide	4	Tyrrell Racing Organisation	G	3.5 Tyrrell 017-Cosworth V8		28/31

1991 — Championship position: 18th=   Wins: 0   Pole positions: 0   Fastest laps: 0   Points scored: 1

	Race	Circuit	No	Entrant	Tyres	Car/Engine	Comment	Q Pos/Entries
dnq	US GP (PHOENIX)	Phoenix	12	Team Lotus	G	3.5 Lotus 102B-Judd V8		30/34
dnq	BRAZILIAN GP	Interlagos	12	Team Lotus	G	3.5 Lotus 102B-Judd V8		30/34
6	SAN MARINO GP	Imola	12	Team Lotus	G	3.5 Lotus 102B-Judd V8	3 laps behind	26/34
dnq	MONACO GP	Monte Carlo	12	Team Lotus	G	3.5 Lotus 102B-Judd V8		28/34

GP Starts: 7   GP Wins: 0   Pole positions: 0   Fastest laps: 0   Points: 1

BALDI, Mauro (I) b 31/1/1954, Reggio-Emilia

1982 — Championship position: 22nd=   Wins: 0   Pole positions: 0   Fastest laps: 0   Points scored: 2

	Race	Circuit	No	Entrant	Tyres	Car/Engine	Comment	Q Pos/Entries
dnq	SOUTH AFRICAN GP	Kyalami	30	Arrows Racing Team	P	3.0 Arrows A4-Cosworth V8		27/30
10*	BRAZILIAN GP	Rio	30	Arrows Racing Team	P	3.0 Arrows A4-Cosworth V8	* 1st & 2nd cars dsq/-6 laps	19/31
dnq	US GP WEST	Long Beach	30	Arrows Racing Team	P	3.0 Arrows A4-Cosworth V8		30/31
nc	BELGIAN GP	Zolder	30	Arrows Racing Team	P	3.0 Arrows A4-Cosworth V8	long pit stop-throttle/-19 laps	28/32
dnq	MONACO GP	Monte Carlo	30	Arrows Racing Team	P	3.0 Arrows A4-Cosworth V8		21/31
ret	US GP (DETROIT)	Detroit	30	Arrows Racing Team	P	3.0 Arrows A4-Cosworth V8	hit Boesel on lap 1	24/28
8	CANADIAN GP	Montreal	30	Arrows Racing Team	P	3.0 Arrows A4-Cosworth V8	2 laps behind	17/29
6	DUTCH GP	Zandvoort	30	Arrows Racing Team	P	3.0 Arrows A4-Cosworth V8	1 lap behind	16/31
9	BRITISH GP	Brands Hatch	30	Arrows Racing Team	P	3.0 Arrows A4-Cosworth V8	2 laps behind	26/30
ret	FRENCH GP	Paul Ricard	30	Arrows Racing Team	P	3.0 Arrows A4-Cosworth V8	accident with Mass	25/30
ret	GERMAN GP	Hockenheim	30	Arrows Racing Team	P	3.0 Arrows A4-Cosworth V8	misfire	24/30
6	AUSTRIAN GP	Österreichring	30	Arrows Racing Team	P	3.0 Arrows A4-Cosworth V8	1 lap behind	23/29
dnq	SWISS GP	Dijon	30	Arrows Racing Team	P	3.0 Arrows A4-Cosworth V8		29/29
12	ITALIAN GP	Monza	30	Arrows Racing Team	P	3.0 Arrows A5-Cosworth V8	3 laps behind	24/30
11	CAESARS PALACE GP	Las Vegas	30	Arrows Racing Team	P	3.0 Arrows A4-Cosworth V8	3 laps behind	23/30

1983 — Championship position: 16th   Wins: 0   Pole positions: 0   Fastest laps: 0   Points scored: 3

	Race	Circuit	No	Entrant	Tyres	Car/Engine	Comment	Q Pos/Entries
ret	BRAZILIAN GP	Rio	23	Marlboro Team Alfa Romeo	M	1.5 t/c Alfa Romeo 183T V8	collision damage	10/27
ret	US GP WEST	Long Beach	23	Marlboro Team Alfa Romeo	M	1.5 t/c Alfa Romeo 183T V8	accident	21/28
ret	FRENCH GP	Paul Ricard	23	Marlboro Team Alfa Romeo	M	1.5 t/c Alfa Romeo 183T V8	accident with Winkelhock	8/29
10/ret	SAN MARINO	Imola	23	Marlboro Team Alfa Romeo	M	1.5 t/c Alfa Romeo 183T V8	engine/3 laps behind	10/28
6	MONACO GP	Monte Carlo	23	Marlboro Team Alfa Romeo	M	1.5 t/c Alfa Romeo 183T V8	2 laps behind	13/28
ret	BELGIAN GP	Spa	23	Marlboro Team Alfa Romeo	M	1.5 t/c Alfa Romeo 183T V8	throttle linkage	12/28
12	US GP (DETROIT)	Detroit	23	Marlboro Team Alfa Romeo	M	1.5 t/c Alfa Romeo 183T V8	4 laps behind	25/27
10*	CANADIAN GP	Montreal	23	Marlboro Team Alfa Romeo	M	1.5 t/c Alfa Romeo 183T V8	* 9th place car dsq/-3 laps	26/28
7	BRITISH GP	Silverstone	23	Marlboro Team Alfa Romeo	M	1.5 t/c Alfa Romeo 183T V8	1 lap behind	11/29
ret	GERMAN GP	Hockenheim	23	Marlboro Team Alfa Romeo	M	1.5 t/c Alfa Romeo 183T V8	engine	7/29
ret	AUSTRIAN GP	Österreichring	23	Marlboro Team Alfa Romeo	M	1.5 t/c Alfa Romeo 183T V8	engine	9/29
5	DUTCH GP	Zandvoort	23	Marlboro Team Alfa Romeo	M	1.5 t/c Alfa Romeo 183T V8		12/29
ret	ITALIAN GP	Monza	23	Marlboro Team Alfa Romeo	M	1.5 t/c Alfa Romeo 183T V8	turbo	10/29
ret	EUROPEAN GP	Brands Hatch	23	Marlboro Team Alfa Romeo	M	1.5 t/c Alfa Romeo 183T V8	clutch	15/29
ret	SOUTH AFRICAN GP	Kyalami	23	Marlboro Team Alfa Romeo	M	1.5 t/c Alfa Romeo 183T V8	engine	17/26

1984 — Championship position: Unplaced

	Race	Circuit	No	Entrant	Tyres	Car/Engine	Comment	Q Pos/Entries
ret	BRAZILIAN GP	Rio	21	Spirit Racing	P	1.5 t/c Spirit 101-Hart 4	distributor	24/27
8	SOUTH AFRICAN GP	Kyalami	21	Spirit Racing	P	1.5 t/c Spirit 101-Hart 4	tyre vibration/4 laps behind	20/27
ret	BELGIAN GP	Zolder	21	Spirit Racing	P	1.5 t/c Spirit 101-Hart 4	suspension	25/27
8*	SAN MARINO GP	Imola	21	Spirit Racing	P	1.5 t/c Spirit 101-Hart 4	* 5th place car dsq/-2 laps	24/28
ret	FRENCH GP	Dijon	21	Spirit Racing	P	1.5 t/c Spirit 101-Hart 4	engine	27/27
dnq	MONACO GP	Monte Carlo	21	Spirit Racing	P	1.5 t/c Spirit 101-Hart 4		26/27
8	EUROPEAN GP	Nürburgring	21	Spirit Racing	P	1.5 t/c Spirit 101-Hart 4	2 laps behind	24/26
15	PORTUGUESE GP	Estoril	21	Spirit Racing	P	1.5 t/c Spirit 101-Hart 4	4 laps behind	25/27

1985 — Championship position: Unplaced

	Race	Circuit	No	Entrant	Tyres	Car/Engine	Comment	Q Pos/Entries
ret	BRAZILIAN GP	Rio	21	Spirit Enterprises Ltd	P	1.5 t/c Spirit 101D-Hart 4	turbo/misfire	24/25
ret	PORTUGUESE GP	Estoril	21	Spirit Enterprises Ltd	P	1.5 t/c Spirit 101D-Hart 4	spun off	24/26
ret	SAN MARINO GP	Imola	21	Spirit Enterprises Ltd	P	1.5 t/c Spirit 101D-Hart 4	electrics	26/26

GP Starts: 36   GP Wins: 0   Pole positions: 0   Fastest laps: 0   Points: 5

BALSA, Marcel (F) b 1/1/1909, Saint Frion – d 11/8/1984

1952 — Championship position: Unplaced

	Race	Circuit	No	Entrant	Tyres	Car/Engine	Comment	Q Pos/Entries
ret	GERMAN GP	Nürburgring	110	Marcel Balsa	–	2.0 BMW Special 6		25/32

GP Starts: 1   GP Wins: 0   Pole positions: 0   Fastest laps: 0   Points: 0

JULIAN BAILEY

The determination with which Julian Bailey has pursued his career has enabled him to ride out innumerable financial crises as well as serious injuries sustained when a huge crash at Snetterton in 1980 left him with multiple fractures of his arm and leg. By the end of 1981 he was back in business and quicker than ever. Racing in FF1600 in 1982, Julian was involved in a season-long battle with Mauricio Gugelmin which saw him lose out in the RAC championship but gain some recompense by winning the prestigious Formula Ford Festival at Brands Hatch.

Julian's career then got bogged down with a number of seasons spent scratching around in less than competitive cars – notably in F3. But he plugged away waiting for the break which finally came his way with an end-of-season deal to race a Lola in Formula 3000. Bailey took to the category and, with backing from Cavendish Finance, embarked on a full F3000 season in 1987. A superb win at Brands Hatch, his favourite circuit, provided the year's highlight, and the credibility which this win brought him led to a seat at Tyrrell for 1988, but as luck would have it the 017 car fielded by the team that year was a poor one and his season was a complete wash-out.

After some excellent drives for the Nissan sports car team (including a third place at Donington in 1989), Julian scraped up enough cash to buy a ride with Lotus at the start of the 1991 season but, despite picking up a sixth place at Imola, he was dropped in favour of Johnny Herbert. Accepting that Formula 1 would for ever be out of his reach, he concentrated on forging a career in the British touring car championship, enjoying the chance to race a works Toyota in 1993 alongside Will Hoy.

Unlike some other notable Grand Prix refugees, Julian became a convincing performer in this type of racing, but rarely had the machinery to challenge for the top BTCC honours.

Bailey found greater success with Toyota down in South Africa during 1996 and 1997, but it failed to gain him the planned return to the BTCC and he has since been spearheading the Lister-Storm challenge in GT racing at home and abroad.

MAURO BALDI

This Italian driver began racing in 1975 with a Renault 5, winning the Italian and European one-make championships and earning an F3 Ralt into the bargain. After finding his feet in 1978, Baldi was soon making his mark, finishing fourth in the 1979 European championship and third in the Italian series.

Victory in the Monaco F3 race in 1980 by the huge margin of 47 seconds was the platform from which Mauro began his domination of the formula. Armed with a March for the 1981 season, he trounced the opposition, recording eight wins and four second places in the 15-race European series.

By-passing Formula 2, he secured a drive with Arrows for 1982 and did well enough in a difficult car, but when the opportunity arose to rejoin his former boss Paolo Pavanello in the reconstructed Alfa Romeo team Mauro switched camps. However, the year disintegrated after political frictions had prompted the mid-season departure of designer Gérard Ducarouge. Unable to continue with the team for 1984 as a result of sponsor Benetton's preference for Patrese and Cheever, Mauro was left with no alternative but to race for the underfinanced Spirit outfit.

Meanwhile Baldi had taken the opportunity to race sports cars for Martini Lancia, winning at Spa in 1985, and he quickly became one of prototype racing's most successful exponents, forging his reputation with privateer Porsches before becoming a key member of the Sauber-Mercedes and Peugeot factory teams. Despite the recent decline of sports car racing, Baldi has remained active. In 1994 his major triumph came at Le Mans, where he shared the winning Porsche 962LM with Haywood and Dalmas. Mauro also reappeared in single-seater competition, driving for Dale Coyne in an Indy Car race at Mid-Ohio.

In 1995 he was part of the Ferrari 333SP sports car attack in IMSA, taking fourth place at Sebring with Alboreto and van de Poele, but he suffered three indifferent seasons before enjoying welcome success with Gianpiero Moretti's Ferrari in 1998, when he shared in victories at Daytona, Sebring and Watkins Glen.

In 1999 Baldi joined Jean-Pierre Jabouille's team to race in the World Sports Car Cup, taking a win at Spa, a second place at Monza and a third at Barcelona. He also drove for Dyson Racing in the States, sharing the second-placed Ferrari 333SP with Didier Theys at Road Atlanta.

MARCEL BALSA

An enthusiastic amateur, Balsa plugged away throughout the late forties and early fifties with a BMW special, restricting himself in the main to events on home soil. He was a distant fourth in the Luxembourg GP in 1949 and third at Cadours the following year, an event overshadowed by the death of Raymond Sommer.

His machine was neither particularly speedy nor for that matter reliable, though he did scrape a sixth place at Cadours in 1952. On paper his finest moment was in winning the 1953 Coupe de Printemps at Montlhéry, but the quality of the opposition was meagre to say the least.

LORENZO BANDINI

With such a name, he just had to be an Italian racing driver, though as a personality he didn't fit the stereotype, being calm and possessed of an even temperament and a pleasant disposition. Bandini worked as a garage mechanic for a Signor Freedi, who was later to become his father-in-law, before setting up on his own in Milan.

Dreaming of nothing but racing, he worked assiduously, until beginning his racing career tentatively with Fiats and later a Lancia Appia Zagato, in which he won his class in the 1958 Mille Miglia Rally. Later that year he bought a Volpini Formula Junior and finished third on aggregate on his debut in the Sicilian Gold Cup at Syracuse.

Bandini began the 1959 season with his own machine, but was quickly taken into the works Stanguellini team where he was soon a leading runner, winning the Liberty GP in Cuba at the beginning of 1960, and later taking the Pescara GP ahead of Denny Hulme. Already yearning for more powerful machinery, Lorenzo was fortunate to come under the wing of Signor Mimmo Dei, of the Scuderia Centro Sud, who put him into his Formula 1 Cooper for 1961. An early-season third place at the Pau GP was a splendid start, but Bandini was soon in the shadow of Giancarlo Baghetti, who had been given the FISA-backed Ferrari in preference to Lorenzo, and was about to enjoy his brief spell of fame. Much was made in the press of the rivalry between the two young Italians, but in fact there was no friction, as they were good friends. Bandini raced on in the Cooper without much success, but took a superb win in the sports car Pescara GP before the season was out.

In 1962 Bandini was invited to join the Ferrari team at last, but it was a season of disarray at Maranello, with drivers chosen for races on a seemingly ad hoc basis. Nevertheless he finished a cool third at the Monaco GP, and in non-title races he took fifth place at Pau and second at Naples and won the Mediterranean GP at Enna. Amazingly he was dropped from the F1 team in favour of Mairesse for 1963, so it was back to Centro Sud to race their newly acquired BRM, while continuing in the Ferrari sports car squad. After a second place in the Targa Florio, Bandini then shared a Ferrari 250P with Scarfiotti to win Le Mans and later took second in the Reims 12 Hours with Surtees. This success stood him in good stead, and after Mairesse was injured Lorenzo returned to the fold.

Largely due to the efforts of Surtees, the team were on their way back, and in 1964 Bandini was the Englishman's number two, accepting his position stoically and scoring his first, and only, Grand Prix victory at the bumpy Zeltweg airfield circuit, when more fancied runners failed. The final 1.5-litre season in 1965 was relatively uneventful and, though Bandini's position in the team remained the same, he was increasingly unhappy with the status quo and relations with Surtees were becoming a little strained. In sports cars, Ferrari's programme was limited, but Lorenzo won the Targa Florio with Vaccarella. The friction in the team continued into 1966, and Bandini drove the 2.4-litre Dino into second place at Monaco, even though Surtees wanted to race the car. The situation could not last and when Surtees quit Maranello, Bandini suddenly found himself leading the team. A certain win in the French GP was lost when a throttle cable snapped, and Scarfiotti and Parkes took the honours at Monza when he encountered fuel feed problems.

The 1967 season started well with victories in the Daytona 24 Hours and Monza 1000 Km in a Ferrari 330P4 shared with newcomer Chris Amon, and then second place in the Race of Champions behind Gurney's Eagle. The next race in which he competed was his favourite, the Monaco Grand Prix. Qualifying second on the grid, Bandini led in the early stages before dropping behind Denny Hulme's Brabham. Late in the race, however, he made a charge in a bid for victory. On the 82nd lap he clipped the chicane entering the harbour front, rolling the Ferrari, which burst into flames upside down in the middle of the track. The rescue crew were terribly slow to react and the ill-fated driver, dreadfully burnt and injured, lay trapped for what seemed an eternity. Broken and charred, he was eventually dragged from the foam-covered wreck and rushed to hospital. There was no prospect of recovery for poor Bandini and, mercifully perhaps, he passed away after clinging on to life for three days.

BANDINI, Lorenzo (I)   b 21/12/1935, Barce, Cyrenaica, Libya – d 10/5/1967, Monte Carlo

	1961	Championship position: Unplaced							
	Race	Circuit	No	Entrant	Tyres	Car/Engine	Comment		Q Pos/Entries
ret	BELGIAN GP	Spa	46	Scuderia Centro Sud	D	1.5 Cooper T53-Maserati 4	engine-oil pressure		17/25
12	BRITISH GP	Aintree	60	Scuderia Centro Sud	D	1.5 Cooper T53-Maserati 4	4 laps behind		21/30
ret	GERMAN GP	Nürburgring	32	Scuderia Centro Sud	D	1.5 Cooper T53-Maserati 4	engine		19/27
8	ITALIAN GP	Monza	62	Scuderia Centro Sud	D	1.5 Cooper T53-Maserati 4	2 laps behind		21/33

	1962	Championship position: 12th= Wins: 0 Pole positions: 0 Fastest laps: 0 Points scored: 4							
3	MONACO GP	Monte Carlo	38	Scuderia Ferrari SpA SEFAC	D	1.5 Ferrari 156 V6			10/21
ret	GERMAN GP	Nürburgring	4	Scuderia Ferrari SpA SEFAC	D	1.5 Ferrari 156 V6	accident		18/30
8	ITALIAN GP	Monza	6	Scuderia Ferrari SpA SEFAC	D	1.5 Ferrari 156 V6	2 laps behind		17/30

	1963	Championship position: 9th= Wins: 0 Pole positions: 0 Fastest laps: 0 Points scored: 6							
10	FRENCH GP	Reims	46	Scuderia Centro Sud	D	1.5 BRM P57 V8	8 laps behind		21/21
5	BRITISH GP	Silverstone	3	Scuderia Centro Sud	D	1.5 BRM P57 V8	1 lap behind		=7/23
ret	GERMAN GP	Nürburgring	15	Scuderia Centro Sud	D	1.5 BRM P57 V8	collision with Ireland		3/26
ret	ITALIAN GP	Monza	2	Scuderia Ferrari SpA SEFAC	D	1.5 Ferrari 156 V6	gearbox		6/28
5	US GP	Watkins Glen	24	Scuderia Ferrari SpA SEFAC	D	1.5 Ferrari 156 V6	4 laps behind		9/21
ret	MEXICAN GP	Mexico City	24	Scuderia Ferrari SpA SEFAC	D	1.5 Ferrari 156 V6	ignition		7/21
5	SOUTH AFRICAN GP	East London	4	Scuderia Ferrari SpA SEFAC	D	1.5 Ferrari 156 V6	1 lap behind		5/21

	1964	Championship position: 4th= Wins: 1 Pole positions: 0 Fastest laps: 0 Points scored: 23							
10/ret	MONACO GP	Monte Carlo	20	Scuderia Ferrari SpA SEFAC	D	1.5 Ferrari 156 V6	gearbox/33 laps behind		7/20
ret	DUTCH GP	Zandvoort	4	Scuderia Ferrari SpA SEFAC	D	1.5 Ferrari 158 V8	fuel injection pump		10/18
dns	"	"	4	Scuderia Ferrari SpA SEFAC	D	1.5 Ferrari 156 V6	practice only		– / –
ret	BELGIAN GP	Spa	11	Scuderia Ferrari SpA SEFAC	D	1.5 Ferrari 158 V8	no oil		9/20
9	FRENCH GP	Rouen	26	Scuderia Ferrari SpA SEFAC	D	1.5 Ferrari 158 V8	2 laps behind		8/17
5	BRITISH GP	Brands Hatch	8	Scuderia Ferrari SpA SEFAC	D	1.5 Ferrari 156 V6	2 laps behind		=8/25
3	GERMAN GP	Nürburgring	8	Scuderia Ferrari SpA SEFAC	D	1.5 Ferrari 156 V6			4/24
1	AUSTRIAN GP	Zeltweg	8	Scuderia Ferrari SpA SEFAC	D	1.5 Ferrari 156 V6			7/20
3	ITALIAN GP	Monza	4	Scuderia Ferrari SpA SEFAC	D	1.5 Ferrari 158 V8	1 lap behind		7/25
dns	"	"	4	Scuderia Ferrari SpA SEFAC	D	1.5 Ferrari 156 V6	practice only		– / –
dns	"	"	4	Scuderia Ferrari Spa SEFAC	D	1.5 Ferrari 1512 F12	practice only		– / –
ret	US GP	Watkins Glen	8	North American Racing Team	D	1.5 Ferrari 1512 F12	engine		8/19
dns	"	" "	8	North American Racing Team	D	1.5 Ferrari 156 V6	practice only		– / –
3	MEXICAN GP	Mexico City	8	North American Racing Team	D	1.5 Ferrari 1512 F12			3/19

	1965	Championship position: 6th Wins: 0 Pole positions: 0 Fastest laps: 0 Points scored: 13							
15/ret	SOUTH AFRICAN GP	East London	2	Scuderia Ferrari SpA SEFAC	D	1.5 Ferrari 1512 F12	ignition/19 laps behind		=6/25
2	MONACO GP	Monte Carlo	17	Scuderia Ferrari SpA SEFAC	D	1.5 Ferrari 1512 F12			4/17
9	BELGIAN GP	Spa	2	Scuderia Ferrari SpA SEFAC	D	1.5 Ferrari 1512 F12	2 laps behind		15/21
8/ret	FRENCH GP	Clermont Ferrand	4	Scuderia Ferrari SpA SEFAC	D	1.5 Ferrari 1512 F12	lost wheel spun off/-3 laps		=3/17
ret	BRITISH GP	Silverstone	2	Scuderia Ferrari SpA SEFAC	D	1.5 Ferrari 158 V8	piston		=9/23
9	DUTCH GP	Zandvoort	4	Scuderia Ferrari SpA SEFAC	D	1.5 Ferrari 158 V8	1 lap behind		12/17
6	GERMAN GP	Nürburgring	8	Scuderia Ferrari SpA SEFAC	D	1.5 Ferrari 158 V8			7/22
4	ITALIAN GP	Monza	4	Scuderia Ferrari SpA SEFAC	D	1.5 Ferrari 1512 F12			5/23
4	US GP	Watkins Glen	2	Scuderia Ferrari SpA SEFAC	D	1.5 Ferrari 1512 F12	1 lap behind		5/18
8	MEXICAN GP	Mexico City	2	Scuderia Ferrari SpA SEFAC	D	1.5 Ferrari 1512 F12	3 laps behind		7/18

	1966	Championship position: 8th= Wins: 0 Pole positions: 1 Fastest laps:2 Points scored: 12							
2	MONACO GP	Monte Carlo	16	Scuderia Ferrari SpA SEFAC	F	2.4 Ferrari Dino 246 V6	FL		5/16
dns	"	" "	16T	Scuderia Ferrari SpA SEFAC	F	3.0 Ferrari 312/66 V12	practice only		– / –
3	BELGIAN GP	Spa	7	Scuderia Ferrari SpA SEFAC	D	2.4 Ferrari Dino 246 V6	1 lap behind		5/18
nc	FRENCH GP	Reims	20	Scuderia Ferrari SpA SEFAC	F	3.0 Ferrari 312/66 V12	broken-throttle cable//FL/-11 laps		1/17
6	DUTCH GP	Zandvoort	2	Scuderia Ferrari SpA SEFAC	F	3.0 Ferrari 312/66 V12	spin/3 laps behind		9/18
6	GERMAN GP	Nürburgring	9	Scuderia Ferrari SpA SEFAC	D	3.0 Ferrari 312/66 V12			6/30
ret	ITALIAN GP	Monza	2	Scuderia Ferrari SpA SEFAC	F	3.0 Ferrari 312/66 V12	ignition		5/22
ret	US GP	Watkins Glen	9	Scuderia Ferrari SpA SEFAC	F	3.0 Ferrari 312/66 V12	engine		3/19

	1967	Championship position: Unplaced							
ret	MONACO GP	Monte Carlo	18	Scuderia Ferrari SpA SEFAC	F	3.0 Ferrari 312/67 V12	fatal accident-hit chicane exit		2/18

GP Starts: 42   GP Wins: 1   Pole positions: 1   Fastest laps: 2   Points: 58

In a race littered with retirements, Bandini, in his Ferrari 156 V6, took his only Grand Prix win in the 1964 Austrian GP.
The race was held at the Zeltweg airfield circuit, where the bumpy concrete surface took its toll on the machinery.

FABRIZIO BARBAZZA

Barbazza earned a reputation as a wild but fast driver in Italian F3, finishing third in the series with a Dallara-Alfa in 1985. Frustrated at the lack of opportunities in Europe, he then took the unusual step of moving across the Atlantic to contest the newly created American Racing Series, which he won. More succces was to follow in 1987. Filling a vacancy in Frank Arciero's Indy Car team, Fabrizio took a splendid third place at Indianapolis, earning the accolade of top rookie, and finished twelfth in the final points standings to claim the PPG Rookie of the Year Award.

Still intent on breaking into Grand Prix racing, Barbazza returned to Europe and scraped around in F3000 before finally securing an F1 drive in 1991, only to endure a dismal time fruitlessly attempting to qualify the AGS. Finding the finance to buy a seat in the Minardi team for 1993, Fabrizio confirmed that he has ability, gaining two valuable sixth places for the team before making way for Pierluigi Martini at mid-season.

In 1995 Barbazza once again headed Stateside to race, but after finishing eighth in the Daytona 24 Hours, he was very seriously injured in a horrendous multiple accident at Road Atlanta, which destroyed his Ferrari 333SP. Fabrizio spent a year recuperating before announcing to retire from racing. He has subsequently been involved in the design and development of safety features for racing circuits.

JOHN BARBER

Barber, a Billingsgate fish merchant, went racing with a Cooper-JAP before purchasing a Formula 2 Cooper-Bristol Mk1 for the 1952 season. He won a minor Libre race at Snetterton, but crashed the car badly at season's end.

He ventured to Argentina at the start of 1953 and drove steadily to eighth in the championship Grand Prix followed by a 12th place in the Buenos Aires Libre race. On his return to home shores he briefly raced the flying saucer-shaped Golding-Cooper, which is believed to have been built on the frame of his damaged Mk1. It was racing this car in the British Empire Trophy at the Isle of Man that he was innocently involved in the aftermath of a fatal accident which befell James Neilson. Barber soon dispensed with the car and was not seen in action again until a brief return to racing in 1955 with a Jaguar C-Type at national level.

BARBAZZA, Fabrizio (I) b 2/4/1963, Monza

	Race	Circuit	No	Entrant	Tyres	Car/Engine	Comment	Q Pos/Entries
	1991	Championship position: Unplaced						
dnq	SAN MARINO GP	Imola	18	Automobiles Gonfaronaise Sportive	G	3.5 AGS JH25-Cosworth DFR V8		28/34
dnq	MONACO GP	Monaco	18	Automobiles Gonfaronaise Sportive	G	3.5 AGS JH25-Cosworth DFR V8		29/34
dnq	CANADIAN GP	Montreal	18	Automobiles Gonfaronaise Sportive	G	3.5 AGS JH25-Cosworth DFR V8		27/34
dnq	MEXICAN GP	Mexico City	18	Automobiles Gonfaronaise Sportive	G	3.5 AGS JH25-Cosworth DFR V8		30/34
dnq	FRENCH GP	Magny Cours	18	Automobiles Gonfaronaise Sportive	G	3.5 AGS JH25B-Cosworth DFR V8		28/34
dnq	BRITISH GP	Silverstone	18	Automobiles Gonfaronaise Sportive	G	3.5 AGS JH25B-Cosworth DFR V8		29/34
dnpq	GERMAN GP	Hockenheim	18	Automobiles Gonfaronaise Sportive	G	3.5 AGS JH25B-Cosworth DFR V8		33/34
dnpq	HUNGARIAN GP	Hungaroring	18	Automobiles Gonfaronaise Sportive	G	3.5 AGS JH25B-Cosworth DFR V8		33/34
dnpq	BELGIAN GP	Spa	18	Automobiles Gonfaronaise Sportive	G	3.5 AGS JH25B-Cosworth DFR V8		34/34
dnpq	ITALIAN GP	Monza	18	Automobiles Gonfaronaise Sportive	G	3.5 AGS JH25B-Cosworth DFR V8		31/34
dnpq	PORTUGUESE GP	Estoril	18	Automobiles Gonfaronaise Sportive	G	3.5 AGS JH27-Cosworth DFR V8		31/34
dnpq	SPANISH GP	Barcelona	18	Automobiles Gonfaronaise Sportive	G	3.5 AGS JH27-Cosworth DFR V8		32/33
	1993	Championship position: 17th= Wins: 0 Pole positions: 0 Fastest laps: 0 Points scored: 2						
ret	SOUTH AFRICAN GP	Kyalami	24	Minardi Team	G	3.5 Minardi M193-Ford HB V8	accident-hit by Suzuki	24/26
ret	BRAZILIAN GP	Interlagos	24	Minardi Team	G	3.5 Minardi M193-Ford HB V8	collision, Brundle on lap 1	24/26
6	EUROPEAN GP	Donington	24	Minardi Team	G	3.5 Minardi M193-Ford HB V8	2 laps behind	20/26
6	SAN MARINO GP	Imola	24	Minardi Team	G	3.5 Minardi M193-Ford HB V8	2 laps behind	25/26
ret	SPANISH GP	Barcelona	24	Minardi Team	G	3.5 Minardi M193-Ford HB V8	spun off	25/26
11	MONACO GP	Monte Carlo	24	Minardi Team	G	3.5 Minardi M193-Ford HB V8	steering after collision/-3 laps	25/26
ret	CANADIAN GP	Montreal	24	Minardi Team	G	3.5 Minardi M193-Ford HB V8	gearbox	23/26
ret	FRENCH GP	Magny Cours	24	Minardi Team	G	3.5 Minardi M193-Ford HB V8	gearbox	24/26

GP Starts: 8   GP Wins: 0   Pole positions: 0   Fastest laps: 0   Points: 2

BARBER, John (GB) b *circa* 1929

	Race	Circuit	No	Entrant	Tyres	Car/Engine	Comment	Q Pos/Entries
	1953	Championship position: Unplaced						
8	ARGENTINE GP	Buenos Aires	22	Cooper Car Co/Frazer-Hartwell Syndicate	D	2.0 Cooper T23-Bristol 6	7 laps behind	16/16

GP Starts: 1   GP Wins: 0   Pole positions: 0   Fastest laps: 0   Points: 0

BARBER, Skip (USA) b 16/11/1936, Philadelphia, Pennsylvania

	1971				Championship position: Unplaced				
	Race	Circuit	No	Entrant	Tyres	Car/Engine		Comment	Q Pos/Entries
dnq	MONACO GP	Monte Carlo	28	Gene Mason Racing	F	3.0 March 711-Cosworth V8			23/23
nc	DUTCH GP	Zandvoort	22	Gene Mason Racing	F	3.0 March 711-Cosworth V8		10 laps behind	24/24
ret	CANADIAN GP	Mosport Park	33	Gene Mason Racing	F	3.0 March 711-Cosworth V8		oil pressure	24/27
nc	US GP	Watkins Glen	33	Gene Mason Racing	F	3.0 March 711-Cosworth V8		pit stop-gearbox/-7 laps	27/32
	1972				Championship position: Unplaced				
nc	CANADIAN GP	Mosport Park	33	Gene Mason Racing	G	3.0 March 711-Cosworth V8		pit stops-dirt in throttle/-56 laps	22/25
16	US GP	Watkins Glen	33	Gene Mason Racing	G	3.0 March 711-Cosworth V8		2 laps behind	20/32

GP Starts: 5   GP Wins: 0   Pole positions: 0   Fastest laps: 0   Points: 0

BARILLA, Paolo (I) b 20/4/1961, Milan

	1989				Championship position: Unplaced				
	Race	Circuit	No	Entrant	Tyres	Car/Engine		Comment	Q Pos/Entries
ret	JAPANESE GP	Suzuka	23	Minardi SpA	P	3.5 Minardi M189-Cosworth V8		clutch at start	19/39
	1990				Championship position: Unplaced				
ret	US GP (PHOENIX)	Phoenix	24	SCM Minardi Team	P	3.5 Minardi M189-Cosworth V8		driver cramp	14/35
ret	BRAZILIAN GP	Interlagos	24	SCM Minardi Team	P	3.5 Minardi M189-Cosworth V8		engine-valve	17/35
11	SAN MARINO GP	Imola	24	SCM Minardi Team	P	3.5 Minardi M190-Cosworth V8		spin/2 laps behind	27/34
dns	"	"	24	SCM Minardi Team	P	3.5 Minardi M189-Cosworth V8		practice only	– / –
ret	MONACO GP	Monte Carlo	24	SCM Minardi Team	P	3.5 Minardi M190-Cosworth V8		gearbox	19/35
dnq	CANADIAN GP	Montreal	24	SCM Minardi Team	P	3.5 Minardi M190-Cosworth V8			29/35
14	MEXICAN GP	Mexico City	24	SCM Minardi Team	P	3.5 Minardi M190-Cosworth V8		2 laps behind	16/35
dnq	FRENCH GP	Paul Ricard	24	SCM Minardi Team	P	3.5 Minardi M190-Cosworth V8			27/35
12	BRITISH GP	Silverstone	24	SCM Minardi Team	P	3.5 Minardi M190-Cosworth V8		2 laps behind	24/35
dnq	GERMAN GP	Hockenheim	24	SCM Minardi Team	P	3.5 Minardi M190-Cosworth V8			28/35
15	HUNGARIAN GP	Hungaroring	24	SCM Minardi Team	P	3.5 Minardi M190-Cosworth V8		3 laps behind	23/35
ret/dns	BELGIAN GP	Spa	24	SCM Minardi Team	P	3.5 Minardi M190-Cosworth V8		crashed at 2nd aborted start	25/33
dnq	ITALIAN GP	Monza	24	SCM Minardi Team	P	3.5 Minardi M190-Cosworth V8			28/33
dnq	PORTUGUESE GP	Estoril	24	SCM Minardi Team	P	3.5 Minardi M190-Cosworth V8			28/33
dnq	SPANISH GP	Jerez	24	SCM Minardi Team	P	3.5 Minardi M190-Cosworth V8			28/33

GP Starts: (8)9   GP Wins: 0   Pole positions: 0   Fastest laps: 0   Points: 0

SKIP BARBER

A late starter in racing, having competed in Formula Ford and FB in 1969-70 and become national champion, Barber was still relatively inexperienced when he headed to Europe in 1971 to buy a March 711 (to replace his 701, which had been written off in an early-season crash) which he intended to race in the US L & M F5000 series.

Before shipping the new car back, however, he tackled a few Grands Prix – 'keeping out of the way' – as well as the non-championship Jochen Rindt Memorial Trophy at Hockenheim, in which he managed a worthy sixth place.

Back in America, Barber enjoyed some success in Formula A with the car in 1972 before switching to GT machinery. Since his retirement from racing he has built up one of the world's leading racing schools and, in conjunction with Saab, instigated the very successful single-seater 'Pro Series' – now known as the Barber-Dodge Pro Series in deference to its engine supplier.

PAOLO BARILLA

The wealthy scion of a family owning a famous Italian pasta company, Barilla first came to international prominence in 1983 with a privately entered Lancia LC2. After some excellent performances he was invited to join the works team the following season, taking second place at Kyalami, third at Monza and the Nürburgring and fourth at Silverstone.

Switching to the Joest Porsche team, he drove immaculately to win the 1985 Le Mans 24 Hours (with Ludwig and Winter) and the 1986 Mount Fuji 1000 Km (with Ghinzani). However, Paolo still yearned for success in single-seaters and spent two largely unproductive seasons in F3000 switching from team to team in search of a winning formula.

His friendship with Giancarlo Minardi provided him with the long-sought opportunity to race in Formula 1 but his performances in the Minardi were disappointing and he was replaced by Gianni Morbidelli before the 1990 season was out.

RUBENS BARRICHELLO

Five times the Brazilian karting champion, Barrichello arrived in Europe as a shy 17-year-old at the beginning of 1990, having contested only 11 Formula Ford races in his native country. He came to compete in the GM Lotus Euroseries – one of the first rungs on the ladder to Formula 1 – with backing from Arisco (a Brazilian food conglomerate), which intended to take him all the way to the top. In the comfortable environment provided by Scuderia Salvati Draco, Rubens quickly became the season's front-runner, winning five rounds and the title.

This triumph earned him a seat in Dick Bennetts' West Surrey Racing F3 team for 1991. It was success again as Rubens came through late in the season to win the title when his main rival, David Coulthard, stumbled.

Already the subject of interest from Formula 1 teams, Barrichello took the next step up into F3000 and, despite the political and financial pressures that beset the Il Barone Rampante team, Rubens was a consistent finisher, achieving third place in the final standings. His seemingly inexorable climb to Grand Prix racing was complete when that great talent-spotter Eddie Jordan placed his faith in the 21-year-old to help wipe away the memories of a disastrous 1992 season.

He soon proved Eddie's wisdom with a stunning drive in the rain-soaked European GP at Donington which saw him run as high as second place until fuel-pressure problems ended his race, though this performance no doubt reflected the benefit of having traction control in slippery conditions. However, as the season developed he comfortably outpaced his more vaunted (if demotivated) team-mates Capelli and Boutsen, before the uncertainty regarding Rubens' real ability was increased by a succession of partners towards the end of the year. The arrival of Eddie Irvine at Suzuka helped lift the team – and Barrichello – to a new level of performance, and it was felt by many that he needed this sort of competition.

Certainly he started the 1994 season with real intent, before miraculously escaping serious injury in practice for the San Marino Grand Prix. The

horrendous events of that weekend must have left Rubens more traumatised than most as he struggled to come to terms with the loss of his friend and mentor Ayrton Senna. Understandably he took a little while to return to his best, and the joy of taking pole position at a rain-soaked Spa was probably the high point of his, and Jordan's, year.

Rumours abounded that Barrichello was a target for McLaren, but in the event he remained with Jordan for 1995, buoyed by the prospect of a works engine deal with Peugeot. Numerous excellent qualifying performances and second place in Canada showed what could be achieved, but a catalogue of mechanical failures were to cost Rubens and his team dear. The 1996 season soon produced the false dawn of a front-row start in Brazil, but after Barrichello slithered off the wet track in the race his year slipped into a downward spiral in which he never really regained his confidence.

Despite his tender years, Jordan felt they could coax no more from the personable young Brazilian, who they felt needed to raise his game to a more consistent level if he was to progress beyond the 'promising' category. An amicable parting led to Rubens' joining the newly formed Stewart Grand Prix team for 1997. The partnership proved a productive one, and his superb second place in the rain at Monaco gave credibility to both team and driver. While the following year was largely wasted in midfield obscurity, Barrichello emerged in 1999 as a much more mature performer. He ran at the front in a number of races and was rightly disappointed not to have been the man to give Stewart their first Grand Prix win when Johnny Herbert posted an unlikely victory at the Nürburgring.

Seven seasons in Formula 1 have yet to see the gentle Brazilian take a Grand Prix win, but a dream move to Ferrari in 2000 to partner Schumacher should see that ambition realised at last. Still aged only 27, Rubens can afford to be patient at Maranello and, provided he can cope with the politics and the pressure, he has every chance of inheriting the throne when 'King Michael' decides to step down.

BARRICHELLO, Rubens (BR) b 23/5/1972, São Paulo

1993
Championship position: 17th=　Wins: 0　Pole positions: 0　Fastest laps: 0　Points scored: 2

	Race	Circuit	No	Entrant		Tyres	Car/Engine	Comment	Q Pos/Entries
ret	SOUTH AFRICAN GP	Kyalami	14	Sasol Jordan		G	3.5 Jordan 193-Hart V10	gearbox	14/26
ret	BRAZILIAN GP	Interlagos	14	Sasol Jordan		G	3.5 Jordan 193-Hart V10	gearbox hydraulics	14/26
10/ret	EUROPEAN GP	Donington	14	Sasol Jordan		G	3.5 Jordan 193-Hart V10	fuel pressure/5 laps behind	12/26
ret	SAN MARINO GP	Imola	14	Sasol Jordan		G	3.5 Jordan 193-Hart V10	spun off	13/26
12	SPANISH GP	Barcelona	14	Sasol Jordan		G	3.5 Jordan 193-Hart V10	pit stop-front wing flap/-3 laps	17/26
9	MONACO GP	Monte Carlo	14	Sasol Jordan		G	3.5 Jordan 193-Hart V10	2 laps behind	16/26
ret	CANADIAN GP	Montreal	14	Sasol Jordan		G	3.5 Jordan 193-Hart V10	electrical	14/26
7	FRENCH GP	Magny Cours	14	Sasol Jordan		G	3.5 Jordan 193-Hart V10	fading brakes/1 lap behind	8/26
10	BRITISH GP	Silverstone	14	Sasol Jordan		G	3.5 Jordan 193-Hart V10	1 lap behind	15/26
ret	GERMAN GP	Hockenheim	14	Sasol Jordan		G	3.5 Jordan 193-Hart V10	wheel bearing failure	17/26
ret	HUNGARIAN GP	Hungaroring	14	Sasol Jordan		G	3.5 Jordan 193-Hart V10	collision-Suzuki/lost wheel	16/26
ret	BELGIAN GP	Spa	14	Sasol Jordan		G	3.5 Jordan 193-Hart V10	wheel bearing failure	13/25
ret	ITALIAN GP	Monza	14	Sasol Jordan		G	3.5 Jordan 193-Hart V10	collision-Lehto on lap 1	19/26
13	PORTUGUESE GP	Estoril	14	Sasol Jordan		G	3.5 Jordan 193-Hart V10	pit stop-puncture/3 laps behind	15/26
5	JAPANESE GP	Suzuka	14	Sasol Jordan		G	3.5 Jordan 193-Hart V10		12/24
11	AUSTRALIAN GP	Adelaide	14	Sasol Jordan		G	3.5 Jordan 193-Hart V10	3 laps behind	13/24

1994
Championship position: 6th　Wins: 0　Pole positions: 1　Fastest laps: 0　Points scored: 19

	Race	Circuit	No	Entrant		Tyres	Car/Engine	Comment	Q Pos/Entries
4	BRAZILIAN GP	Interlagos	14	Sasol Jordan		G	3.5 Jordan 194-Hart V10	1 lap behind	14/28
3	PACIFIC GP	T.I. Circuit	14	Sasol Jordan		G	3.5 Jordan 194-Hart V10	1 lap behind	8/28
dnq	SAN MARINO GP	Imola	14	Sasol Jordan		G	3.5 Jordan 194-Hart V10	unfit – accident in practice	28/28
ret	MONACO GP	Monte Carlo	14	Sasol Jordan		G	3.5 Jordan 194-Hart V10	electrics	15/24
ret	SPANISH GP	Barcelona	14	Sasol Jordan		G	3.5 Jordan 194-Hart V10	gearbox	5/27
7	CANADIAN GP	Montreal	14	Sasol Jordan		G	3.5 Jordan 194-Hart V10	1 lap behind	6/27
ret	FRENCH GP	Magny Cours	14	Sasol Jordan		G	3.5 Jordan 194-Hart V10	taken off by Alesi	7/28
4*	BRITISH GP	Silverstone	14	Sasol Jordan		G	3.5 Jordan 194-Hart V10	*2nd car dsq/collision Häkkinen	6/28
ret	GERMAN GP	Hockenheim	14	Sasol Jordan		G	3.5 Jordan 194-Hart V10	multiple accident on lap 1	11/28
ret	HUNGARIAN GP	Hungaroring	14	Sasol Jordan		G	3.5 Jordan 194-Hart V10	accident-Irvine & Katayama	10/28
ret	BELGIAN GP	Spa	14	Sasol Jordan		G	3.5 Jordan 194-Hart V10	spun off	1/28
4	ITALIAN GP	Monza	14	Sasol Jordan		G	3.5 Jordan 194-Hart V10		16/28
4	PORTUGUESE GP	Estoril	14	Sasol Jordan		G	3.5 Jordan 194-Hart V10		8/28
12	EUROPEAN GP	Jerez	14	Sasol Jordan		G	3.5 Jordan 194-Hart V10	pit stop-puncture/-1 lap	5/28
ret	JAPANESE GP	Suzuka	14	Sasol Jordan		G	3.5 Jordan 194-Hart V10	electrics	10/28
4	AUSTRALIAN GP	Adelaide	14	Sasol Jordan		G	3.5 Jordan 194-Hart V10		5/28

1995
Championship position: 11th　Wins: 0　Pole positions: 0　Fastest laps: 0　Points scored: 11

	Race	Circuit	No	Entrant		Tyres	Car/Engine	Comment	Q Pos/Entries
ret	BRAZILIAN GP	Interlagos	14	Total Jordan Peugeot		G	3.0 Jordan 195-Peugeot V10	gearbox	16/26
ret	ARGENTINE GP	Buenos Aires	14	Total Jordan Peugeot		G	3.0 Jordan 195-Peugeot V10	started from pitlane/oil leak	10/26
ret	SAN MARINO GP	Imola	14	Total Jordan Peugeot		G	3.0 Jordan 195-Peugeot V10	gearbox	10/26
7	SPANISH GP	Barcelona	14	Total Jordan Peugeot		G	3.0 Jordan 195-Peugeot V10	1 lap behind	8/26
ret	MONACO GP	Monte Carlo	14	Total Jordan Peugeot		G	3.0 Jordan 195-Peugeot V10	throttle	11/26
2	CANADIAN GP	Montreal	14	Total Jordan Peugeot		G	3.0 Jordan 195-Peugeot V10		9/24
6	FRENCH GP	Magny Cours	14	Total Jordan Peugeot		G	3.0 Jordan 195-Peugeot V10	1 lap behind	5/24
11/ret	BRITISH GP	Silverstone	14	Total Jordan Peugeot		G	3.0 Jordan 195-Peugeot V10	collision with Blundell/-2 laps	9/24
ret	GERMAN GP	Hockenheim	14	Total Jordan Peugeot		G	3.0 Jordan 195-Peugeot V10	engine	5/24
7	HUNGARIAN GP	Hungaroring	14	Total Jordan Peugeot		G	3.0 Jordan 195-Peugeot V10	1 lap behind	14/24
6	BELGIAN GP	Spa	14	Total Jordan Peugeot		G	3.0 Jordan 195-Peugeot V10		12/24
ret	ITALIAN GP	Monza	14	Total Jordan Peugeot		G	3.0 Jordan 195-Peugeot V10	hydraulics	6/24
11	PORTUGUESE GP	Estoril	14	Total Jordan Peugeot		G	3.0 Jordan 195-Peugeot V10	1 lap behind	8/24
4	EUROPEAN GP	Nürburgring	14	Total Jordan Peugeot		G	3.0 Jordan 195-Peugeot V10	1 lap behind	11/24
ret	PACIFIC GP	T.I. Circuit	14	Total Jordan Peugeot		G	3.0 Jordan 195-Peugeot V10	engine	11/24
ret	JAPANESE GP	Suzuka	14	Total Jordan Peugeot		G	3.0 Jordan 195-Peugeot V10	spun off	10/24
ret	AUSTRALIAN GP	Adelaide	14	Total Jordan Peugeot		G	3.0 Jordan 195-Peugeot V10	understeer-accident	7/24

1996
Championship position: 8th　Wins: 0　Pole positions: 0　Fastest laps: 0　Points scored: 14

	Race	Circuit	No	Entrant		Tyres	Car/Engine	Comment	Q Pos/Entries
ret	AUSTRALIAN GP	Melbourne	11	B & H Total Jordan Peugeot		G	3.0 Jordan 196-Peugeot V10	engine	8/22
ret	BRAZILIAN GP	Interlagos	11	B & H Total Jordan Peugeot		G	3.0 Jordan 196-Peugeot V10	spun off	2/22
4	ARGENTINE GP	Buenos Aires	11	B & H Total Jordan Peugeot		G	3.0 Jordan 196-Peugeot V10		6/22
5	EUROPEAN GP	Nürburgring	11	B & H Total Jordan Peugeot		G	3.0 Jordan 196-Peugeot V10		5/22
5	SAN MARINO GP	Imola	11	B & H Total Jordan Peugeot		G	3.0 Jordan 196-Peugeot V10	1 lap behind	9/22
ret	MONACO GP	Monte Carlo	11	B & H Total Jordan Peugeot		G	3.0 Jordan 196-Peugeot V10	spun off on lap 1	6/22
ret	SPANISH GP	Barcelona	11	B & H Total Jordan Peugeot		G	3.0 Jordan 196-Peugeot V10	clutch	7/22
ret	CANADIAN GP	Montreal	11	B & H Total Jordan Peugeot		G	3.0 Jordan 196-Peugeot V10	clutch	8/22
9	FRENCH GP	Magny Cours	11	B & H Total Jordan Peugeot		G	3.0 Jordan 196-Peugeot V10	1 lap behind	11/22
4	BRITISH GP	Silverstone	11	B & H Total Jordan Peugeot		G	3.0 Jordan 196-Peugeot V10		6/22
6	GERMAN GP	Hockenheim	11	B & H Total Jordan Peugeot		G	3.0 Jordan 196-Peugeot V10		9/20
6	HUNGARIAN GP	Hungaroring	11	B & H Total Jordan Peugeot		G	3.0 Jordan 196-Peugeot V10	1 lap behind	13/20
ret	BELGIAN GP	Spa	11	B & H Total Jordan Peugeot		G	3.0 Jordan 196-Peugeot V10	collision damage	10/20
5	ITALIAN GP	Monza	11	B & H Total Jordan Peugeot		G	3.0 Jordan 196-Peugeot V10		10/20
ret	PORTUGUESE GP	Estoril	11	B & H Total Jordan Peugeot		G	3.0 Jordan 196-Peugeot V10	spun off	9/20
9	JAPANESE GP	Suzuka	11	B & H Total Jordan Peugeot		G	3.0 Jordan 196-Peugeot V10		11/20

1997
Championship position: 13th　Wins: 0　Pole positions: 0　Fastest laps: 0　Points scored: 6

	Race	Circuit	No	Entrant		Tyres	Car/Engine	Comment	Q Pos/Entries
ret	AUSTRALIAN GP	Melbourne	22	Stewart Ford		B	3.0 Stewart SF1-Ford Zetec-R V10	engine	11/22
ret	BRAZILIAN GP	Interlagos	22	Stewart Ford		B	3.0 Stewart SF1-Ford Zetec-R V10	broken suspension link	11/22
ret	ARGENTINE GP	Buenos Aires	22	Stewart Ford		B	3.0 Stewart SF1-Ford Zetec-R V10	hydraulics	5/22
ret	SAN MARINO GP	Imola	22	Stewart Ford		B	3.0 Stewart SF1-Ford Zetec-R V10	engine	13/22
2	MONACO GP	Monte Carlo	22	Stewart Ford		B	3.0 Stewart SF1-Ford Zetec-R V10		10/22
ret	SPANISH GP	Barcelona	22	Stewart Ford		B	3.0 Stewart SF1-Ford Zetec-R V10	engine	17/22
ret	CANADIAN GP	Montreal	22	Stewart Ford		B	3.0 Stewart SF1-Ford Zetec-R V10	gearbox	3/22

ret	FRENCH GP	Magny Cours	22	Stewart Ford	B	3.0 Stewart SF1-Ford Zetec-R V10	engine	13/22
ret	BRITISH GP	Silverstone	22	Stewart Ford	B	3.0 Stewart SF1-Ford Zetec-R V10	engine	22/22
ret	GERMAN GP	Hockenheim	22	Stewart Ford	B	3.0 Stewart SF1-Ford Zetec-R V10	engine	12/22
ret	HUNGARIAN GP	Hungaroring	22	Stewart Ford	B	3.0 Stewart SF1-Ford Zetec-R V10	engine	11/22
ret	BELGIAN GP	Spa	22	Stewart Ford	B	3.0 Stewart SF1-Ford Zetec-R V10	spun off	12/22
13	ITALIAN GP	Monza	22	Stewart Ford	B	3.0 Stewart SF1-Ford Zetec-R V10	poor handling/1 lap behind	11/22
ret	AUSTRIAN GP	A1-Ring	22	Stewart Ford	B	3.0 Stewart SF1-Ford Zetec-R V10	crashed out	5/22
ret	LUXEMBOURG GP	Nürburgring	22	Stewart Ford	B	3.0 Stewart SF1-Ford Zetec-R V10	hydraulics	9/22
ret	JAPANESE GP	Suzuka	22	Stewart Ford	B	3.0 Stewart SF1-Ford Zetec-R V10	spun off	12/22
ret	EUROPEAN GP	Jerez	22	Stewart Ford	B	3.0 Stewart SF1-Ford Zetec-R V10	gearbox	12/22

1998 Championship position: 12th Wins: 0 Pole positions: 0 Fastest laps: 0 Points scored: 4

ret	AUSTRALIAN GP	Melbourne	10	Stewart Ford	B	3.0 Stewart SF2-Ford Zetec R V10	gearbox failure on grid	14/22
ret	BRAZILIAN GP	Interlagos	10	Stewart Ford	B	3.0 Stewart SF2-Ford Zetec R V10	gearbox	13/22
10	ARGENTINE GP	Buenos Aires	10	Stewart Ford	B	3.0 Stewart SF2-Ford Zetec R V10	loose bodywork/2 laps behind	14/22
ret	SAN MARINO GP	Imola	10	Stewart Ford	B	3.0 Stewart SF2-Ford Zetec R V10	spun off after collision on lap 1	17/22
5	SPANISH GP	Barcelona	10	Stewart Ford	B	3.0 Stewart SF2-Ford Zetec R V10	1 lap behind	9/22
ret	MONACO GP	Monte Carlo	10	Stewart Ford	B	3.0 Stewart SF2-Ford Zetec R V10	suspension failure	14/22
5	CANADIAN GP	Montreal	10	Stewart Ford	B	3.0 Stewart SF2-Ford Zetec R V10	1 lap behind	13/22
10	FRENCH GP	Magny Cours	10	Stewart Ford	B	3.0 Stewart SF2-Ford Zetec R V10	handling problems/2 laps behind	14/22
ret	BRITISH GP	Silverstone	10	Stewart Ford	B	3.0 Stewart SF2-Ford Zetec R V10	spun off	18/22
ret	AUSTRIAN GP	A1-Ring	10	Stewart Ford	B	3.0 Stewart SF2-Ford Zetec R V10	brakes	5/22
ret	GERMAN GP	Hockenheim	10	Stewart Ford	B	3.0 Stewart SF2-Ford Zetec R V10	gearbox	13/22
ret	HUNGARIAN GP	Hungaroring	10	Stewart Ford	B	3.0 Stewart SF2-Ford Zetec R V10	gearbox	14/22
ret/dns	BELGIAN GP	Spa	10	Stewart Ford	B	3.0 Stewart SF2-Ford Zetec R V10	accident at first start	14/22
10	ITALIAN GP	Monza	10	Stewart Ford	B	3.0 Stewart SF2-Ford Zetec R V10	1 lap behind	13/22
11	LUXEMBOURG GP	Nürburgring	10	Stewart Ford	B	3.0 Stewart SF2-Ford Zetec R V10	2 laps behind	12/22
ret	JAPANESE GP	Suzuka	10	Stewart Ford	B	3.0 Stewart SF2-Ford Zetec R V10	differential	16/22

1999 Championship position: 7th Wins: 0 Pole positions: 1 Fastest laps: 0 Points scored: 21

5	AUSTRALIAN GP	Melbourne	16	Stewart Ford	B	3.0 Stewart SF3-Ford CR1 V10		4/22
ret	BRAZILIAN GP	Interlagos	16	Stewart Ford	B	3.0 Stewart SF3-Ford CR1 V100	engine/lead race	3/22
3	SAN MARINO GP	Imola	16	Stewart Ford	B	3.0 Stewart SF3-Ford CR1 V10	1 lap behind	6/22
ret	MONACO GP	Monte Carlo	16	Stewart Ford	B	3.0 Stewart SF3-Ford CR1 V10	suspension failure-accident	5/22
dsq*	SPANISH GP	Barcelona	16	Stewart Ford	B	3.0 Stewart SF3-Ford CR1 V10	*illegal undertray/7th on road	7/22
ret	CANADIAN GP	Montreal	16	Stewart Ford	B	3.0 Stewart SF3-Ford CR1 V10	collision damage	5/22
3	FRENCH GP	Magny Cours	16	Stewart Ford	B	3.0 Stewart SF3-Ford CR1 V10		1/22
8	BRITISH GP	Silverstone	16	Stewart Ford	B	3.0 Stewart SF3-Ford CR1 V10	puncture	7/22
ret	AUSTRIAN GP	A1-Ring	16	Stewart Ford	B	3.0 Stewart SF3-Ford CR1 V10	engine	5/22
ret	GERMAN GP	Hockenheim	16	Stewart Ford	B	3.0 Stewart SF3-Ford CR1 V10	hydraulics	6/22
5	HUNGARIAN GP	Hungaroring	16	Stewart Ford	B	3.0 Stewart SF3-Ford CR1 V10		8/22
10	BELGIAN GP	Spa	16	Stewart Ford	B	3.0 Stewart SF3-Ford CR1 V10	lack of grip	7/22
4	ITALIAN GP	Monza	16	Stewart Ford	B	3.0 Stewart SF3-Ford CR1 V10		7/22
3	EUROPEAN GP	Nürburgring	16	Stewart Ford	B	3.0 Stewart SF3-Ford CR1 V10		15/22
5	MALAYSIAN GP	Sepang	16	Stewart Ford	B	3.0 Stewart SF3-Ford CR1 V10		6/22
8	JAPANESE GP	Suzuka	16	Stewart Ford	B	3.0 Stewart SF3-Ford CR1 V10	1 lap behind	13/22

GP Starts: 112 (113) GP Wins: 0 Pole positions: 2 Fastest laps: 0 Points: 77

BARTH, Edgar (D) b 26/1/1917, Herold-Erzegeberge – d 20/5/1965, Ludwigsburg, nr Stuttgart

1953 Championship position: Unplaced

	Race	Circuit	No	Entrant	Tyres	Car/Engine	Comment	Q Pos/Entries
ret	GERMAN GP	Nürburgring	35	Rennkollektiv EMW	–	2.0 EMW 6	exhaust	24/35

1957 Championship position: Unplaced

12*	GERMAN GP (F2)	Nürburgring	21	Dr Ing F Porsche KG	–	1.5 Porsche 550RS F4 sports car	*1st in F2 class/1 lap behind	12/24

1958 Championship position: Unplaced

6*	GERMAN GP (F2)	Nürburgring	21	Dr Ing F Porsche KG	–	1.5 Porsche RSK F4 sports car	*2nd in F2 class	16/26

1960 Championship position: Unplaced

7	ITALIAN GP (F2)	Monza	24	Dr Ing F Porsche KG	D	1.5 Porsche 718 F4	3 laps behind	12/16

1964 Championship position: Unplaced

ret	GERMAN GP	Nürburgring	12	Rob Walker Racing Team	D	1.5 Cooper T66-Climax V8	clutch	20/24

GP Starts: 5 GP Wins: 0 Pole positions: 0 Fastest laps: 0 Points: 0

BASSI, Giorgio (I) b 20/1/1934, Milan

1965 Championship position: Unplaced

	Race	Circuit	No	Entrant	Tyres	Car/Engine	Comment	Q Pos/Entries
ret	ITALIAN GP	Monza	52	Scuderia Centro Sud	D	1.5 BRM P57 V8	engine	22/23

GP Starts: 1 GP Wins: 0 Pole positions: 0 Fastest laps: 0 Points: 0

BAUER, Erwin (D) b 17/7/1912 – d 3/6/1958, Cologne

1953 Championship position: Unplaced

	Race	Circuit	No	Entrant	Tyres	Car/Engine	Comment	Q Pos/Entries
ret	GERMAN GP	Nürburgring	32	Erwin Bauer	–	2.0 Veritas RS 6		33/35

GP Starts: 1 GP Wins: 0 Pole positions: 0 Fastest laps: 0 Points: 0

EDGAR BARTH

A distinguished pre-war motor cycle racer, Barth drove the EMW sports cars between 1953 and 1956 and, by winning his class in the 1956 Coupe de Paris at Montlhéry, he attracted the attention of the Porsche team.

After a successful class-winning debut for Porsche at the 1957 Nürburgring 1000 Km, Edgar and his family defected from East Germany. He then became a mainstay of the company's Formula 2, sports and hill-climb programme. He won the Targa Florio outright in 1959 (with Seidel) and was European mountain champion in 1959, 1963 and 1964, by which time he was already suffering from the cancer to which he succumbed, at the age of 48, in May 1965.

His son, Jurgen, also represented the Porsche factory team, winning the Le Mans 24-hour race in 1977.

GIORGIO BASSI

His outing in Scuderia Centro Sud's elderly BRM was Bassi's only single-seater appearance at top level, but this Milanese driver was a regular on his national scene.

In Formula 3 he drove a de Tomaso-Ford, his best finish being third at the closing race of the 1964 season at Monza, while the following year he shared the 1000 cc ASA prototype with Pianta to take a class win in the Targa Florio after finishing 17th overall.

ERWIN BAUER

Although Bauer's inclusion in this book is due to a single outing in the German GP, he is nevertheless of interest in that he provided one of Lotus's earliest Continental successes. When Colin Chapman was deemed too inexperienced by the organisers to tackle the Nürburgring 1000 Km in 1954, Erwin was brought in as a last-minute substitute for the Lotus creator and claimed fourth in the 1500 cc class ahead of some much more vaunted machinery such as Porsches and Borgwards.

Bauer raced sports cars and saloons and also rallied throughout the fifties, sharing a Mercedes 220SE with Willi Heeks in 1956. In 1957 he teamed up with Gottfried Kochert in the Austrian's 2-litre Ferrari. Their partnership was to have a tragic ending at the 1958 Nürburgring 1000 Km when Bauer, having claimed tenth place at the end of the race, failed to appreciate that he had finished. Racing on for one more lap, he slid wide while passing a slower car and crashed fatally into the trees which lined the mountain circuit.

ÉLIE BAYOL

Bayol built a reputation as a very quick driver in René Bonnet's 750 cc Panhard during the 1951 season. For 1952 he ordered one of the latest OSCA F2 cars but, as this was not delivered until August, he was forced to make do in the meantime with a stripped sports model which he drove to good effect, finishing fourth at Pau, fifth at Marseille and sixth at Modena. He then raced the F2 car during the 1953 season, the undoubted highlight of which was an aggregate win in the Circuit du Lac at Aix-les-Bains.

Accepting an invitation to join the Gordini team for 1954, Bayol made a fine debut, taking fifth place in the Argentine GP, and followed this with fourth at Pau and fifth at Bordeaux, where he blotted his copybook by ignoring repeated signals to pit and hand his car over to team leader Jean Behra. Gordini sacked him, but he was later forgiven and rejoined the team for 1955, only for his season to be curtailed after he sustained serious head injuries when he crashed the latest 3-litre Gordini in practice at Le Mans.

Thankfully he made a full recovery and briefly reappeared on the circuits the following year, finishing sixth (with Pilette) at Monaco and in the Reims 12 Hours sports car race (with de Silva Ramos).

BAYOL, Élie (F) b 28/2/1914, Marseille – d 1995

	1952	Championship position: Unplaced							
	Race	Circuit	No	Entrant	Tyres	Car/Engine		Comment	Q Pos/Entries
ret	ITALIAN GP	Monza	34	Elie Bayol	–	2.0 OSCA 20 6		gearbox	10/35
	1953	Championship position: Unplaced							
ret	FRENCH GP	Reims	34	Elie Bayol	–	2.0 OSCA 20 6		mechanical	15/25
dns	SWISS GP	Berne	22	Elie Bayol	–	2.0 OSCA 20 6			– /23
ret	ITALIAN GP	Monza	34	OSCA Automobili	–	2.0 OSCA 20 6		mechanical	13/30
	1954	Championship position: 18th= Wins: 0 Pole positions: 0 Fastest laps: 0 Points scored: 2							
5	ARGENTINE GP	Buenos Aires	20	Equipe Gordini	E	2.5 Gordini Type 16 6		2 laps behind	15/18
	1955	Championship position: Unplaced							
ret	ARGENTINE GP	Buenos Aires	38	Equipe Gordini	E	2.5 Gordini Type 16 6		transmission	15/22
ret	MONACO GP	Monte Carlo	12	Equipe Gordini	E	2.5 Gordini Type 16 6		rear axle	16/22
	1956	Championship position: Unplaced							
6*	MONACO GP	Monte Carlo	4	Equipe Gordini	E	2.5 Gordini Type 32 8		* Pilette took over/-12 laps	11/19

GP Starts: 7   GP Wins: 0   Pole positions: 0   Fastest laps: 0   Points: 2

BEAUMAN, Don (GB) b 26/7/1928 – d 9/7/1955, Rathnew, County Wicklow, Republic of Ireland

	1954	Championship position: Unplaced							
	Race	Circuit	No	Entrant	Tyres	Car/Engine		Comment	Q Pos/Entries
11	BRITISH GP	Silverstone	25	Sir Jeremy Boles	D	2.0 Connaught A-Lea Francis 4		6 laps behind	17/31

GP Starts: 1   GP Wins: 0   Pole positions: 0   Fastest laps: 0   Points: 0

BECHEM, Karl-Günther (D) b 21/12/1921

	1952	Championship position: Unplaced							
	Race	Circuit	No	Entrant	Tyres	Car/Engine		Comment	Q Pos/Entries
ret	GERMAN GP	Nürburgring	130	'Bernhard Nacke'	–	2.0 BMW-Eigenbau 6		raced under pseudonym	30/32
	1953	Championship position: Unplaced							
ret	GERMAN GP	Nürburgring	41	Gunther Bechem	–	2.0 AFM U8-BMW 6			30/35

GP Starts: 2   GP Wins: 0   Pole positions: 0   Fastest laps: 0   Points: 0

DON BEAUMAN

A popular figure on the national scene, Beauman entered racing in 1950 with 500 cc Coopers before spending the 1953 season with the coveted pre-war TT Riley previously campaigned by his great chum Mike Hawthorn.

Supported by Sir Jeremy Boles, Beauman intensified his racing activities in 1954 with an F2 Connaught, winning Formula Libre events at Oulton Park and Brands Hatch as well as taking a class win in an Aston Martin at Zandvoort.

The 1955 season saw the London hotelier claim third place in the Glover Trophy at Goodwood and compete in the Le Mans 24-hour race in a works Jaguar. This shy and retiring figure, who had hopes of one day moving into Grand Prix racing, lost his life when he crashed his Connaught in the 1955 Leinster Trophy sports car race in Wicklow, Republic of Ireland.

KARL-GÜNTHER BECHEM

Bechem raced a BMW sports car in 1950, but it seems his family were none too keen on him taking part in sporting competition. So, apparently, he entered the 1952 German Grand Prix under the pseudonym of 'Bernhard Nacke' in order to conceal his racing activities. Quite how he could have kept his secret should he have had any success it is hard to imagine!

By 1953, however, Günther, using his real name, had become heavily involved with the Borgward team and their neat 1500 cc Rennsports. The season's highlight was a third place and class win in the Nürburgring 1000 Km shared with Theo Helfrich.

This potent machine was certainly a match for the rival Porsche 550 sports, especially when fuel injection was installed. Bechem won the Eifel mountain meeting at the Nürburgring in May 1954. At the end of that season, the team headed for Mexico to compete in the gruelling Carrera Panamericana road race. Early on prospects for outright success looked bright when Günther led initially. But, after surviving one off-road excursion, he crashed heavily at the end of the fourth leg of this 2000-mile marathon. The car was destroyed and poor Bechem seriously injured. Happily he made a complete recovery, but he never raced again.

JEAN BEHRA

How can a driver who never won a World Championship Grand Prix have left such a legacy? Even today those old enough to recall Behra remember the tiger, and those like me, too young to have seen him, are inspired by his mighty reputation and heroic deeds when, in the early fifties, he was cast as the perpetual underdog, battling for Gordini against the mighty works teams.

Behra took up the four-wheeled discipline after an immensely successful motor cycling career in which he was French champion three years running. Switching from his red bike to the French blue of Talbot, he placed sixth in the 1949 Coupe du Salon at Montlhéry, and then took part in the 1950 Monte Carlo Rally driving a Simca with Roger Loyer, another ex-motor cyclist who was later to race Gordinis. A month later Jean won a hill-climb in a borrowed Maserati four-cylinder, bringing him to the attention of Amédée Gordini. A drive in the 1950 Bol d'Or at St Germain convinced le patron that here was a nugget that could be polished, and Behra was signed for the 1951 season, beginning his serious motor racing career at the age of 30. He finished third in his first race at Les Sables d'Olonne, and then did the same at Cadours.

It was 1952, however, when Behra became a national hero for his deeds not in championship Grands Prix, though he did superbly well to finish third at Bremgarten and fifth at the Nürburgring – circuits for the skilled and brave – but at the non-championship Reims GP. With Ascari hitherto virtually unbeatable, there was some surprise when Behra shot into an early lead, and this became mild consternation as the light-blue car held off the Ferrari challenge for lap after lap. Then came frenzied hysteria as the T500 suffered an engine failure, leaving Jean to cruise to a historic victory, much to the delight of the delirious French public. There were post-race mutterings about an oversize engine, but the result stood and Behra was for ever taken to the hearts of his countrymen.

He stayed with Gordini to the end of the 1954 season, suffering the heartbreaking succession of maladies that inevitably struck at the little underfinanced équipe, but when results were achieved the success was all the sweeter, as at Pau in 1954 when, after more than three hours' racing, Behra defeated the works Ferrari of Trintignant by a mere 60 yards.

After a test in a Maserati at Monza, where Ascari no less could only equal his time, Behra signed for the 1955 season and was immediately rewarded with non-championship wins at Pau and Bordeaux. Although he was out of luck in championship Grands Prix, Behra took sports car wins at Bari, Monza, the Nürburgring and Oporto in the 300TS, before a crash in the Tourist Trophy resulted in his ear being sliced off – Jean sub-sequently receiving a plastic replacement. For 1956 he was relegated to the number two slot with the arrival of Stirling Moss, but this did not dampen his spirit; he merely raised his game to enjoy his best-ever championship year, even if that much sought first Grand Prix win still eluded him.

In 1957 he was cast as number two to Fangio, but still had his moments, none more memorable than the British GP when he left them all – Fangio, Hawthorn, Moss and Collins – in his wake until his Maserati's clutch failed. Perversely in non-title events his luck would hold, and he won the Pau, Modena and Moroccan GPs for Maserati, and the Caen GP and the International Trophy for BRM.

The following season, driving for BRM in F1 and for Porsche in sports cars and Formula 2, Behra had little luck with the cars from Bourne but won sports car races at AVUS and Rouen and took the Formula 2 honours at AVUS and in the Coupe de Vitesse at Reims. An offer to drive for a Ferrari team now bereft of Hawthorn, Collins and Musso in 1959 was too good to turn down, and the signs were encouraging when he won the Aintree 200 and finished second in the Syracuse GP after a spirited battle with Moss ended in a spin. Two sports car races for the Scuderia yielded a second place at Sebring with Allison and a third in the Nürburgring 1000 Km with Brooks, while he finished second in the Auvergne Trophy at Clermont Ferrand in his own Porsche. In championship Grands Prix, a great drive at Reims ended with engine failure. On pulling his stricken Ferrari into the pits, the frustration was too much for the little Frenchman, who was involved in a scuffle with team manager Tavoni which ended with Behra being shown the door. Running his own Porsches, he was entered for both the Grand Prix and the sports car race at AVUS, but in the rain-soaked support race he was killed instantly when he lost control on the slippery banking, crashed and was flung out of the car into a flag pole.

BEHRA, Jean (F) b 16/2/1921, Nice – d 1/8/1959, AVUS, Berlin, Germany

1951 — Championship position: Unplaced

	Race	Circuit	No	Entrant	Tyres	Car/Engine	Comment	Q Pos/Entries
ret	ITALIAN GP	Monza	50	Equipe Gordini	E	2.0 Gordini Type 15/i6 4	raced Trintignant's car - no practice	–/35

1952 — Championship position: 10th Wins: 0 Pole positions: 0 Fastest laps: 0 Points scored: 6

	Race	Circuit	No	Entrant	Tyres	Car/Engine	Comment	Q Pos/Entries
3	SWISS GP	Bremgarten	6	Equipe Gordini	E	2.0 Gordini Type 16 6	1 lap behind	7/21
ret	BELGIAN GP	Spa	16	Equipe Gordini	E	2.0 Gordini Type 16 6	hit Taruffi's spinning car	5/22
7	FRENCH GP	Rouen	4	Equipe Gordini	E	2.0 Gordini Type 16 6	6 laps behind	4/20
5	GERMAN GP	Nürburgring	108	Equipe Gordini	E	2.0 Gordini Type 16 6	1 lap behind	11/32
ret	DUTCH GP	Zandvoort	8	Equipe Gordini	E	2.0 Gordini Type 16 6	carburettor	6/18
ret	ITALIAN GP	Monza	6	Equipe Gordini	E	2.0 Gordini Type 16 6	valve	11/35

1953 — Championship position: Unplaced

	Race	Circuit	No	Entrant	Tyres	Car/Engine	Comment	Q Pos/Entries
6	ARGENTINE GP	Buenos Aires	30	Equipe Gordini	E	2.0 Gordini Type 16 6	3 laps behind	11/16
ret	BELGIAN GP	Spa	16	Equipe Gordini	E	2.0 Gordini Type 16 6	cylinder head gasket	14/22
10	FRENCH GP	Reims	2	Equipe Gordini	E	2.0 Gordini Type 16 6	5 laps behind	22/25
ret	BRITISH GP	Silverstone	30	Equipe Gordini	E	2.0 Gordini Type 16 6	fuel pump	22/29
ret	GERMAN GP	Nürburgring	9	Equipe Gordini	E	2.0 Gordini Type 16 6	gearbox	9/35
ret	SWISS GP	Bremgarten	6	Equipe Gordini	E	2.0 Gordini Type 16 6	oil pressure	12/23

1954 — Championship position: 21st Wins: 0 Pole positions: 0 Fastest laps: 1 (shared) Points scored: 0.14

	Race	Circuit	No	Entrant	Tyres	Car/Engine	Comment	Q Pos/Entries
dsq	ARGENTINE GP	Buenos Aires	18	Equipe Gordini	E	2.5 Gordini Type 16 6	outside assistance after spin	17/18
ret	BELGIAN GP	Spa	12	Equipe Gordini	E	2.5 Gordini Type 16 6	rear suspension	7/15
6	FRENCH GP	Reims	24	Equipe Gordini	E	2.5 Gordini Type 16 6	5 laps behind	17/22
ret	BRITISH GP	Silverstone	17	Equipe Gordini	E	2.5 Gordini Type 16 6	rear suspension/FL (shared)	5/31
10	GERMAN GP	Nürburgring	9	Equipe Gordini	E	2.5 Gordini Type 16 6	2 laps behind	9/23
ret	SWISS GP	Bremgarten	10	Equipe Gordini	E	2.5 Gordini Type 16 6	clutch	14/16
ret	ITALIAN GP	Monza	44	Equipe Gordini	E	2.5 Gordini Type 16 6	engine	12/21
ret	SPANISH GP	Pedralbes	46	Equipe Gordini	E	2.5 Gordini Type 16 6	brakes	18/22

1955 — Championship position: 8th= Wins: 0 Pole positions: 0 Fastest laps: 0 Points scored: 6

	Race	Circuit	No	Entrant	Tyres	Car/Engine	Comment	Q Pos/Entries
ret	ARGENTINE GP	Buenos Aires	16	Officine Alfieri Maserati	E	2.5 Maserati 250F 6	accident	4/22
ret	"	" "	20	Officine Alfieri Maserati	E	2.5 Maserati 250F 6	engine/Mantovani/Musso co-drove	–/–
6*		" "	28	Officine Alfieri Maserati	E	2.5 Maserati 250F 6	* took over Schell's car/-8 laps	–/–
3*	MONACO GP	Monte Carlo	34	Officine Alfieri Maserati	E	2.5 Maserati 250F 6	* Perdisa took over/-1 lap	5/22
ret		" "	40	Officine Alfieri Maserati	E	2.5 Maserati 250F 6	took Perdisa's car/spun off	–/–
ret	BELGIAN GP	Spa	20	Officine Alfieri Maserati	E	2.5 Maserati 250F 6	spun off	5/14
5*	"	"	24	Officine Alfieri Maserati	E	2.5 Maserati 250F 6	* took over Mieres' car/-1 lap	–/–
6	DUTCH GP	Zandvoort	14	Officine Alfieri Maserati	E	2.5 Maserati 250F 6	3 laps behind	6/16
ret	BRITISH GP	Aintree	2	Officine Alfieri Maserati	E	2.5 Maserati 250F 6	oil pipe	3/25
4	ITALIAN GP	Monza	36	Officine Alfieri Maserati	E	2.5 Maserati 250F 6		6/22

1956 — Championship position: 4th Wins: 0 Pole positions: 0 Fastest laps: 0 Points scored: 22

	Race	Circuit	No	Entrant	Tyres	Car/Engine	Comment	Q Pos/Entries
2	ARGENTINE GP	Buenos Aires	4	Officine Alfieri Maserati	P	2.5 Maserati 250F 6		4/15
3	MONACO GP	Monte Carlo	30	Officine Alfieri Maserati	P	2.5 Maserati 250F 6	1 lap behind	4/19
7	BELGIAN GP	Spa	32	Officine Alfieri Maserati	P	2.5 Maserati 250F 6	engine problems/-3 laps	4/16
3	FRENCH GP	Reims	4	Officine Alfieri Maserati	P	2.5 Maserati 250F 6		7/20
3	BRITISH GP	Silverstone	8	Officine Alfieri Maserati	P	2.5 Maserati 250F 6	2 laps behind	13/28
3	GERMAN GP	Nürburgring	6	Officine Alfieri Maserati	P	2.5 Maserati 250F 6		8/21
ret	ITALIAN GP	Monza	32	Officine Alfieri Maserati	P	2.5 Maserati 250F 6	magneto	5/26
ret	"	"	46	Officine Alfieri Maserati	P	2.5 Maserati 250F 6	took Maglioli's car/steering	–/–

1957 — Championship position: 7th= Wins: 0 Pole positions: 0 Fastest laps: 0 Points scored: 8

	Race	Circuit	No	Entrant	Tyres	Car/Engine	Comment	Q Pos/Entries
2	ARGENTINE GP	Buenos Aires	6	Officine Alfieri Maserati	P	2.5 Maserati 250F 6		3/16
6	FRENCH GP	Rouen	4	Officine Alfieri Maserati	P	2.5 Maserati 250F 6	pit stop-engine/8 laps behind	2/15
ret	BRITISH GP	Aintree	4	Officine Alfieri Maserati	P	2.5 Maserati 250F 6	clutch when leading	2/19
6	GERMAN GP	Nürburgring	2	Officine Alfieri Maserati	P	2.5 Maserati 250F 6		3/24
ret	PESCARA GP	Pescara	4	Officine Alfieri Maserati	P	2.5 Maserati 250F 6	oil pipe	4/16
ret	ITALIAN GP	Monza	6	Officine Alfieri Maserati	P	2.5 Maserati 250F V12	engine-overheating	5/19

1958 — Championship position: 10th= Wins: 0 Pole positions: 0 Fastest laps: 0 Points scored: 9

	Race	Circuit	No	Entrant	Tyres	Car/Engine	Comment	Q Pos/Entries
5	ARGENTINE GP	Buenos Aires	4	Ken Kavanagh	P	2.5 Maserati 250F 6	2 laps behind	4/10
ret	MONACO GP	Monte Carlo	6	Owen Racing Organisation	D	2.5 BRM P25 4	brakes	2/28
3	DUTCH GP	Zandvoort	14	Owen Racing Organisation	D	2.5 BRM P25 4		4/17
ret	BELGIAN GP	Spa	8	Owen Racing Organisation	D	2.5 BRM P25 4	oil pressure	10/20
ret	FRENCH GP	Reims	14	Owen Racing Organisation	D	2.5 BRM P25 4	fuel pump	9/21
ret	BRITISH GP	Silverstone	19	Owen Racing Organisation	D	2.5 BRM P25 4	puncture-hit hare	8/21
ret	GERMAN GP	Nürburgring	5	Owen Racing Organisation	D	2.5 BRM P25 4	suspension	12/26
4	PORTUGUESE GP	Oporto	8	Owen Racing Organisation	D	2.5 BRM P25 4	1 lap behind	4/15
ret	ITALIAN GP	Monza	8	Owen Racing Organisation	D	2.5 BRM P25 4	brakes/clutch	8/21
ret	MOROCCAN GP	Casablanca	14	Owen Racing Organisation	D	2.5 BRM P25 4	engine	4/25

1959 — Championship position: 13th= Wins: 0 Pole positions: 0 Fastest laps: 0 Points scored: 2

	Race	Circuit	No	Entrant	Tyres	Car/Engine	Comment	Q Pos/Entries
ret	MONACO GP	Monte Carlo	46	Scuderia Ferrari	D	2.4 Ferrari Dino 246 V6	engine	2/24
5	DUTCH GP	Zandvoort	1	Scuderia Ferrari	D	2.4 Ferrari Dino 246 V6	1 lap behind	4/15
ret	FRENCH GP	Reims	30	Scuderia Ferrari	D	2.4 Ferrari Dino 246 V6	engine	5/22
dns	GERMAN GP	AVUS	12	Jean Behra	D	1.5 Behra-Porsche F4	fatal accident in support race	–/16

GP Starts: 53 GP Wins: 0 Pole positions: 0 Fastest laps: 1 (shared) Points: 53.14

DEREK BELL

It seems incomprehensible that a driver as talented as Derek Bell has only started in nine World Championship Grands Prix. He seemed to be jinxed when it came to Formula 1 – always in the wrong car at the wrong time – and eventually he was passed over in favour of younger talent.

Tentatively entering the sport with a Lotus Seven in 1964, Bell soon moved into Formula 3, initially with a Lotus which was run – with the support of his step-father 'Colonel Hender' – under the Church Farm Racing banner. It proved to be a character-building couple of years for Bell, who realised that he needed the help of wiser and more experienced heads if his career was to progress. He therefore decided to team up with Peter Westbury, which got his career onto a stable footing and brought results as well.

Despite a lack of funds, Bell and his step-father financed a season of Formula 2 in 1968 with a Brabham BT23, which brought him to the attention of Ferrari, who offered him a drive midway through the season. His debut for the Scuderia started badly with Derek in the midst of a huge pile-up in the F2 Monza Lottery GP. Fortunately he was exonerated from blame and looked set to win at Zandvoort until his gearbox failed. Bell tasted Grand Prix racing in the scarlet cars and enjoyed a trip down-under to contest the Tasman championship. Unfortunately for Derek, Ferrari withdrew from the bulk of their programme in mid-1969, leaving him without a drive apart from a one-off outing in the 4WD McLaren.

To the rescue came Tom Wheatcroft, who, after financing a disastrous foray to the Tasman series, sponsored Derek for a full Formula 2 season in 1970, Clay Regazzoni just pipping him to the title. He was also invited by Jacques Swaters to drive a Ferrari 512 in the Spa 1000 Km – a race which was to lay the foundations of his future sports car success – and scored his only World Championship point with an appearance for Team Surtees at Watkins Glen. For 1971 Derek was paired with Jo Siffert in the Gulf/John Wyer Porsche as the team took the sports car championship. Derek stayed with Gulf/Wyer through the next three years, proving his worth as a top-drawer sports car driver while his miscellaneous Grand Prix appearances with Tecno and Surtees proved forgettable.

The 1975 season brought the first of his five Le Mans victories with Jacky Ickx in the Gulf and a successful championship campaign for Alfa Romeo – winning three times with Pescarolo – in the T33. The next few seasons saw a globe-trotting Derek competing in F5000, G8, touring cars, Formula Atlantic, World Championship of Makes events, etc. before joining the Rothmans Porsche factory squad which was to dominate sports car racing in the eighties (Derek taking the drivers' championship – with Hans Stuck – in 1985 and 1986). In recognition of his many fine performances Bell was awarded the MBE in 1986. The nineties found Derek enjoying the cut and thrust of racing in IMSA. With a Nissan GTP he took a splendid second place in the 1993 Sebring 12 Hours and finished fourth in the GTP championship standings.

After finishing sixth in the 1994 Le Mans 24 Hours, Derek announced he had driven in the French classic for the last time. But as he began his 32nd year in motor sport, the urge to race was still there. At Sebring he shared the second-place Spice-Chevrolet with Andy Wallace and Jan Lammers and, contrary to his earlier intentions, he was persuaded back to the Sarthe circuit once again, tempted by the chance of sharing a McLaren GTR with his son Justin and Wallace, the trio finishing a fine third overall.

Although an advanced age for a racing driver, Derek has continued to race selectively for sports car teams around the globe, confirming that his experience and reliability are still highly regarded commodities.

BELL, Derek (GB) b 31/10/1941, Pinner, Middlesex

	1968	Championship position: Unplaced						
	Race	Circuit	No	Entrant	Tyres	Car/Engine	Comment	Q Pos/Entries
ret	ITALIAN GP	Monza	7	Scuderia Ferrari SpA SEFAC	F	3.0 Ferrari 312/68 V12	fuel metering unit	8/24
ret	US GP	Watkins Glen	7	Scuderia Ferrari Spa SEFAC	F	3.0 Ferrari 312/68 V12	engine	15/21
	1969	Championship position: Unplaced						
ret	BRITISH GP	Silverstone	20	Bruce McLaren Motor Racing	G	3.0 McLaren M9A-Cosworth V8	rear suspension	15/17
	1970	Championship position: 22nd= Wins: 0 Pole positions: 0 Fastest laps: 0 Points scored: 1						
ret	BELGIAN GP	Spa	8	Tom Wheatcroft Racing	G	3.0 Brabham BT26A-Cosworth V8	gear linkage	15/18
6	US GP	Watkins Glen	18	Team Surtees	F	3.0 Surtees TS7-Cosworth V8	1 lap behind	13/27
	1971	Championship position: Unplaced						
ret	BRITISH GP	Silverstone	25	Team Surtees	F	3.0 Surtees TS9-Cosworth V8	radius rod	–/–
dns	"	"	25	Team Surtees	F	3.0 Surtees TS7-Cosworth V8	qualified in this car	23/24
	1972	Championship position: Unplaced						
dnq	FRENCH GP	Clermont Ferrand	21	Martini Racing Team	F	3.0 Tecno PA123 F12	chassis cracked	(28)/29
ret	GERMAN GP	Nürburgring	27	Martini Racing Team	F	3.0 Tecno PA123 F12	engine	25/27
dnq	ITALIAN GP	Monza	12	Martini Racing Team	F	3.0 Tecno PA123 F12		27/27
dns	CANADIAN GP	Mosport Park	31	Martini Racing Team	F	3.0 Tecno PA123 F12	accident in a.m. warm-up	(25)/25
ret	US GP	Watkins Glen	31	Martini Racing Team	F	3.0 Tecno PA123 F12	engine	30/32
	1974	Championship position: Unplaced						
dnq	BRITISH GP	Brands Hatch	*18	Bang & Olufsen Team Surtees	F	3.0 Surtees TS16-Cosworth V8	*also ran as 39 in 3rd session	27/34
11	GERMAN GP	Nürburgring	18	Bang & Olufsen Team Surtees	F	3.0 Surtees TS16-Cosworth V8		25/32
dnq	AUSTRIAN GP	Österreichring	18	Team Surtees	F	3.0 Surtees TS16-Cosworth V8		28/31
dnq	ITALIAN GP	Monza	18	Team Surtees	F	3.0 Surtees TS16-Cosworth V8		28/31
dnq	CANADIAN GP	Mosport Park	18	Team Surtees	F	3.0 Surtees TS16-Cosworth V8		27/30

GP Starts: 9 GP Wins: 0 Pole positions: 0 Fastest laps: 0 Points: 1

STEFAN BELLOF

Thought by many to be the great lost talent of the eighties, Bellof's progress in motor sport was indeed sensational.

Already a karting champion many times in his native Germany, Stefan took the national Formula Ford title at the first attempt in 1980, adding the international German FF title the following year, which saw his winning debut in Formula 3. Aboard a Ralt RT3 entered by ex-racer Bertram Schafer, Stefan won three races from just seven starts to finish third in the championship.

These exploits brought him to the attention of Willy Maurer, who, with help in the form of an engine deal from BMW's Dieter Stappert, made a place available for Stefan in his Formula 2 team for 1982. He won first time out at Silverstone in the rain after a battle with Frank Jelinski, following this up with a dominant win from pole position in round two at Hockenheim. Although he could not sustain this success, as various troubles blunted his challenge, he did record five fastest laps during the season.

He chose to continue in F2 with Maurer in 1983, but the focus of his attention shifted with the offer of a works Porsche drive. Paired with both the experienced Derek Bell and Jochen Mass, Stefan took the car by the scruff of the neck and, with his aggressive point-and-squirt driving style, began to demolish lap records (and on occasion the car itself). Championship wins were chalked up at Silverstone, Mount Fuji and Kyalami. Bellof continued this success with Rothmans Porsche in 1984, winning six rounds (Monza, the Nürburgring, Spa, Imola, Mount Fuji and Sandown Park) and the endurance drivers' championship. He also found time to win the six-round German endurance championship in a Brun-entered Porsche.

Having reportedly turned down an offer from ATS to enter Grands Prix in 1983, Stefan had no qualms about joining the Tyrrell team for the following season. Despite the lack of a turbo engine he was soon extracting the maximum from his car, and could well have won the rain-shortened Monaco GP if the race had been allowed to run longer. However, the punitive treatment meted out to the Tyrrell team after the Dutch GP brought an early end to his Formula 1 season and all his efforts were declared null and void.

His last season dawned with the prospect of waiting until mid-term for Renault turbo power, and a one-race suspension (Brazil) after a dispute with the team. Despite this Bellof still gave his all. It was such commitment, which some would say bordered on recklessness, which was to prove his undoing. He had switched to Walter Brun's team for sports car racing and at the Spa 1000 Km he attempted an audacious overtaking manoeuvre on former team-mate Jacky Ickx at Eau Rouge. Their Porsches collided and poor Stefan perished as his car was destroyed against the barriers.

BELLOF, Stefan (D) b 20/11/1957, Giessen – d 1/9/1985, Spa-Francorchamps Circuit, Belgium

1984		Championship position: Unplaced		(7 points scored disallowed by FIA)				
Race	Circuit	No	Entrant	Tyres	Car/Engine		Comment	Q Pos/Entries
ret/dsq BRAZILIAN GP	Rio	4	Tyrrell Racing Organisation	G	3.0 Tyrrell 012-Cosworth V8		throttle cable/dsq after appeal	23/27
ret/dsq SOUTH AFRICAN GP	Kyalami	4	Tyrrell Racing Organisation	G	3.0 Tyrrell 012-Cosworth V8		broken hub/dsq after appeal	24/27
6/dsq BELGIAN GP	Zolder	4	Tyrrell Racing Organisation	G	3.0 Tyrrell 012-Cosworth V8		6th on road/dsq after appeal	21/27
5/dsq SAN MARINO GP	Imola	4	Tyrrell Racing Organisation	G	3.0 Tyrrell 012-Cosworth V8		5th on road/dsq after appeal	21/28
ret/dsq FRENCH GP	Dijon	4	Tyrrell Racing Organisation	G	3.0 Tyrrell 012-Cosworth V8		engine /dsq after appeal	21/27
3/dsq MONACO GP	Monte Carlo	4	Tyrrell Racing Organisation	G	3.0 Tyrrell 012-Cosworth V8		3rd on road/dsq after appeal	20/27
ret/dsq CANADIAN GP	Montreal	4	Tyrrell Racing Organisation	G	3.0 Tyrrell 012-Cosworth V8		driveshaft/dsq after appeal	22/26
ret/dsq US GP (DETROIT)	Detroit	4	Tyrrell Racing Organisation	G	3.0 Tyrrell 012-Cosworth V8		accident/dsq after appeal	16/27
ret/dsq US GP (DALLAS)	Dallas	4	Tyrrell Racing Organisation	G	3.0 Tyrrell 012-Cosworth V8		hit wall/dsq after appeal	17/26
11/dsq BRITISH GP	Brands Hatch	4	Tyrrell Racing Organisation	G	3.0 Tyrrell 012-Cosworth V8		11th on road/dsq after appeal	26/28
dsq AUSTRIAN GP	Österreichring	4	Tyrrell Racing Organisation	G	3.0 Tyrrell 012-Cosworth V8		excl in practice/car underweight	28/28
9/dsq DUTCH GP	Zandvoort	4	Tyrrell Racing Organisation	G	3.0 Tyrrell 012-Cosworth V8		9th on road/dsq after appeal	24/27

	1985	Championship position: 15th=		Wins: 0	Pole positions: 0	Fastest laps: 0	Points scored: 4			
6	PORTUGUESE GP	Estoril	4	Tyrrell Racing Organisation		G	3.0 Tyrrell 012-Cosworth V8	2 laps behind	21/26
ret	SAN MARINO GP	Imola	4	Tyrrell Racing Organisation		G	3.0 Tyrrell 012-Cosworth V8	engine	24/26
dnq	MONACO GP	Monte Carlo	4	Tyrrell Racing Organisation		G	3.0 Tyrrell 012-Cosworth V8		22/26
11	CANADIAN GP	Montreal	4	Tyrrell Racing Organisation		G	3.0 Tyrrell 012-Cosworth V8	2 laps behind	23/25
4	US GP (DETROIT)	Detroit	4	Tyrrell Racing Organisation		G	3.0 Tyrrell 012-Cosworth V8		19/25
13	FRENCH GP	Paul Ricard	4	Tyrrell Racing Organisation		G	3.0 Tyrrell 012-Cosworth V8	3 laps behind	26/26
11	BRITISH GP	Silverstone	4	Tyrrell Racing Organisation		G	3.0 Tyrrell 012-Cosworth V8	6 laps behind	26/26
8	GERMAN GP	Nürburgring	3	Tyrrell Racing Organisation		G	1.5 t/c Tyrrell 014-Renault V6	1 lap behind	19/27
7/ret	AUSTRIAN GP	Österreichring	3	Tyrrell Racing Organisation		G	1.5 t/c Tyrrell 014-Renault V6	out of fuel/3 laps behind	22/27
ret	DUTCH GP	Zandvoort	4	Tyrrell Racing Organisation		G	1.5 t/c Tyrrell 014-Renault V6	engine	22/27

GP Starts: 20   GP Wins: 0   Pole positions: 0   Fastest laps: 0   Points: 4

BELMONDO Paul (F) b 23/4/1963, Boulogne-Billancourt, nr Paris

	1992	Championship position: Unplaced							
	Race	Circuit	No	Entrant	Tyres	Car/Engine		Comment	Q Pos/Entries
dnq	SOUTH AFRICAN GP	Kyalami	17	March F1		G	3.5 March CG911-Ilmor V10		27/30
dnq	MEXICAN GP	Mexico City	17	March F1		G	3.5 March CG911-Ilmor V10		28/30
dnq	BRAZILIAN GP	Interlagos	17	March F1		G	3.5 March CG911-Ilmor V10		28/31
12	SPANISH GP	Barcelona	17	March F1		G	3.5 March CG911-Ilmor V10	4 laps behind	23/32
13	SAN MARINO GP	Imola	17	March F1		G	3.5 March CG911-Ilmor V10	3 laps behind	24/32
dnq	MONACO GP	Monte Carlo	17	March F1		G	3.5 March CG911-Ilmor V10		30/32
14	CANADIAN GP	Montreal	17	March F1		G	3.5 March CG911-Ilmor V10	5 laps behind	20/32
dnq	FRENCH GP	Magny Cours	17	March F1		G	3.5 March CG911-Ilmor V10		27/30
dnq	BRITISH GP	Silverstone	17	March F1		G	3.5 March CG911-Ilmor V10		28/32
13	GERMAN GP	Hockenheim	17	March F1		G	3.5 March CG911-Ilmor V10	1 lap behind	22/32
9	HUNGARIAN GP	Hungaroring	17	March F1		G	3.5 March CG911-Ilmor V10	3 laps behind	17/31
	1994	Championship position: Unplaced							
dnq	BRAZILIAN GP	Interlagos	33	Pacific Grand Prix		G	3.5 Pacific PR01-Ilmor V10	no time set	28/28
dnq	PACIFIC GP	T.I. Circuit	33	Pacific Grand Prix		G	3.5 Pacific PR01-Ilmor V10		27/28
dnq	SAN MARINO GP	Imola	33	Pacific Grand Prix		G	3.5 Pacific PR01-Ilmor V10		27/28
ret	MONACO GP	Monte Carlo	33	Pacific Grand Prix		G	3.5 Pacific PR01-Ilmor V10	driver fatigue	24/24
ret	SPANISH GP	Barcelona	33	Pacific Grand Prix		G	3.5 Pacific PR01-Ilmor V10	spun off on lap 2	26/27
dnq	CANADIAN GP	Montreal	33	Pacific Grand Prix		G	3.5 Pacific PR01-Ilmor V10		27/27
dnq	FRENCH GP	Magny Cours	33	Pacific Grand Prix		G	3.5 Pacific PR01-Ilmor V10		28/28
dnq	BRITISH GP	Silverstone	33	Pacific Grand Prix		G	3.5 Pacific PR01-Ilmor V10		28/28
dnq	GERMAN GP	Hockenheim	33	Pacific Grand Prix		G	3.5 Pacific PR01-Ilmor V10		27/28
dnq	HUNGARIAN GP	Hungaroring	33	Pacific Grand Prix		G	3.5 Pacific PR01-Ilmor V10		28/28
dnq	BELGIAN GP	Spa	33	Pacific Grand Prix		G	3.5 Pacific PR01-Ilmor V10		28/28
dnq	ITALIAN GP	Monza	33	Pacific Grand Prix		G	3.5 Pacific PR01-Ilmor V10		28/28
dnq	PORTUGUESE GP	Estoril	33	Pacific Grand Prix		G	3.5 Pacific PR01-Ilmor V10		28/28
dnq	EUROPEAN GP	Jerez	33	Pacific Grand Prix		G	3.5 Pacific PR01-Ilmor V10		28/28
dnq	JAPANESE GP	Suzuka	33	Pacific Grand Prix		G	3.5 Pacific PR01-Ilmor V10		28/28
dnq	AUSTRALIAN GP	Adelaide	33	Pacific Grand Prix		G	3.5 Pacific PR01-Ilmor V10		27/28

GP Starts: 7   GP Wins: 0   Pole positions: 0   Fastest laps: 0   Points: 0

PAUL BELMONDO

Being the son of one of France's most famous actors has probably done Belmondo no favours, but he has steadily plugged away at his chosen career, shrugging aside the jealous accusations that he is no more than a 'playboy racer'.

Certainly the winner of the 1982 Pilote Elf was something of an enigma during his years in French Formula 3 between 1983 and 1986, the young Belmondo putting in some useful performances without being quite on the pace of each new batch of hot-shots as they leap-frogged over him on their way up.

Eventually, in 1987, he followed more stellar talents into F3000 and scored a fifth place at Pau with a GBDA Lola, but nothing concrete was achieved during the next three seasons save a single sixth place in the Le Mans round in 1990. A disastrous 1991 season with the Apomatox team's Reynard was hardly ideal preparation for his unexpected elevation to the Grand Prix ranks, but he settled into the second March in the first half of 1992 surprisingly well – ironically his best performances for the team were at Hockenheim and the Hungaroring, his last two races before his money ran out. Charged with bringing the car home in one piece at all costs, Paul's sensible approach helped to keep the team afloat financially, and even his greatest detractors would admit that he had done a sound job in difficult circumstances. Just as it seemed that Paul would join the ranks of ex-Formula 1 drivers, he became part of the new Pacific Grand Prix team for 1994. Unfortunately, the car was never remotely competitive and his frustrating second spell in F1 was largely spent accumulating a string of non-qualifications along with team-mate Gachot.

Following his stab at F1, Belmondo turned his attentions to GT racing; initially he drove a Ferrari GT40 in 1996, before setting up his own team running Chrysler Vipers. The high point to date came late in 1999, when Paul won the FIA GT round at Homestead, beating the works cars.

TOM BELSO

Forever being fatuously described as 'The smiling Dane' ill served this hard-working driver. After many years of endeavour he eventually became Denmark's first racing driver to compete in a World Championship Grand Prix and, more importantly, proved himself a formidable competitor in the early seventies in Formula 5000.

Originally a mechanic, his meticulous preparation was rewarded by the chance to race the Volvo on which he had worked. Tom was a winner first time out and by 1969, driving a Ford Escort, he was the Scandinavian saloon car champion. This success led to a test and subsequent drive in Formula Ford with Hawke in 1970.

Encouraged by his progress, Belso sold his business interests and moved his family to England to compete in Formula Atlantic in 1971. He finished third in the championship with an old Brabham and then took the leap into Formula 2 for 1972. A fourth place at Albi was the best result in a season strewn with engine problems, but he caught the eye of Jackie Epstein, who signed him for his Shellsport F5000 team – for which he drove splendidly for three seasons. It was during this period that Frank Williams gave Tom his Grand Prix opportunities. Lack of finance curtailed his racing activities for 1976 but, irrepressible as ever, he was back for one more tilt at F5000 in 1977 with John Jordan's Lola.

BELSO, Tom (DK) b 27/8/1942, Copenhagen

	1973	Championship position: Unplaced						
	Race	Circuit	No	Entrant	Tyres	Car/Engine	Comment	Q Pos/Entries
dns	SWEDISH GP	Anderstorp	26	Frank Williams Racing Cars	F	3.0 Iso Williams 1R-Cosworth V8	*practice only-Ganley raced car*	(22)/22
	1974	Championship position: Unplaced						
ret	SOUTH AFRICAN GP	Kyalami	21	Frank Williams Racing Cars	F	3.0 Williams FW01-Cosworth V8	*clutch slip*	27/27
dnq	SPANISH GP	Jarama	21	Frank Williams Racing Cars	F	3.0 Williams FW02-Cosworth V8		28/28
8	SWEDISH GP	Anderstorp	21	Frank Williams Racing Cars	F	3.0 Williams FW02-Cosworth V8	*1 lap behind*	21/28
dnq	BRITISH GP	Brands Hatch	21	Frank Williams Racing Cars	F	3.0 Williams FW01-Cosworth V8		=28/34

GP Starts: 2   GP Wins: 0   Pole positions: 0   Fastest laps: 0   Points: 0

BELTOISE, Jean-Pierre (F) b 26/4/1937, Paris

	1966	Championship position: Unplaced						
	Race	Circuit	No	Entrant	Tyres	Car/Engine	Comment	Q Pos/Entries
8*	GERMAN GP (F2)	Nürburgring	34	Matra Sports	D	1.0 Matra MS5-Cosworth 4	** 1st in F2 class/1 lap behind*	19/30
	1967	Championship position: Unplaced						
dnq	MONACO GP	Monte Carlo	1	Matra Sports	D	1.6 Matra MS7-Cosworth 4 F2		17/18
7	US GP	Watkins Glen	22	Matra Sports	G	1.6 Matra MS7-Cosworth 4 F2	*7 laps behind*	18/18
7	MEXICAN GP	Mexico City	22	Matra Sports	G	1.6 Matra MS7-Cosworth 4 F2	*2 laps behind*	14/19
	1968	Championship position: 9th Wins: 0 Pole positions: 0 Fastest laps: 2 Points scored: 11						
6	SOUTH AFRICAN GP	Kyalami	21	Matra Sports	D	1.6 Matra MS7-Cosworth 4 F2	*ballasted car/3 laps behind*	18/23
5	SPANISH GP	Jarama	6	Matra International	D	3.0 Matra MS10-Cosworth V8	*2 pit stops-oil leak/FL/-9 laps*	=4/14
ret	MONACO GP	Monte Carlo	1	Matra Sports	D	3.0 Matra MS11 V12	*hit chicane-damaged suspension*	8/18
8	BELGIAN GP	Spa	10	Matra Sports	D	3.0 Matra MS11 V12	*pit stop-fuel/3 laps behind*	13/18
2	DUTCH GP	Zandvoort	17	Matra Sports	D	3.0 Matra MS11 V12	*pit stop-sand in throttle slides/FL*	16/19
9	FRENCH GP	Rouen	6	Matra Sports	D	3.0 Matra MS11 V12	*pit stop-tyres/4 laps behind*	8/18
ret	BRITISH GP	Brands Hatch	18	Matra Sports	D	3.0 Matra MS11 V12	*oil pressure*	=13/18
ret	GERMAN GP	Nürburgring	12	Matra Sports	D	3.0 Matra MS11 V12	*crashed*	12/20
5	ITALIAN GP	Monza	6	Matra Sports	D	3.0 Matra MS11 V12	*2 laps behind*	19/24
ret	CANADIAN GP	St Jovite	18	Matra Sports	D	3.0 Matra MS11 V12	*transmission*	16/22
ret	US GP	Watkins Glen	21	Matra Sports	D	3.0 Matra MS11 V12	*driveshaft*	13/21
ret	MEXICAN GP	Mexico City	21	Matra Sports	D	3.0 Matra MS11 V12	*rear suspension*	13/21
	1969	Championship position: 5th Wins: 0 Pole positions: 0 Fastest laps: 1 Points scored: 21						
6	SOUTH AFRICAN GP	Kyalami	8	Matra International	D	3.0 Matra MS10-Cosworth V8	*2 laps behind*	=12/18
3	SPANISH GP	Montjuich Park	8	Matra International	D	3.0 Matra MS80-Cosworth V8	*2 pit stops-gear linkage/-3 laps*	12/14
ret	MONACO GP	Monte Carlo	8	Matra International	D	3.0 Matra MS80-Cosworth V8	*universal joint*	3/16
8	DUTCH GP	Zandvoort	5	Matra International	D	3.0 Matra MS80-Cosworth V8	*3 laps behind*	11/15
2	FRENCH GP	Clermont Ferrand	7	Matra International	D	3.0 Matra MS80-Cosworth V8		5/13
9	BRITISH GP	Silverstone (30)	4	Matra International	D	3.0 Matra MS84-Cosworth V8 4WD	*6 laps behind*	17/17
dns	"	"	4	Matra International	D	3.0 Matra MS80-Cosworth V8	*practice only/Stewart in race*	– / –
12/ret	GERMAN GP	Nürburgring	8	Matra International	D	3.0 Matra MS80-Cosworth V8	*front upright/6th F1 car/-2 laps*	10/26
3	ITALIAN GP	Monza	22	Matra International	D	3.0 Matra MS80-Cosworth V8	*FL*	6/15
4	CANADIAN GP	Mosport Park	18	Matra International	D	3.0 Matra MS80-Cosworth V8	*1 lap behind*	=2/20
ret	US GP	Watkins Glen	4	Matra International	D	3.0 Matra MS80-Cosworth V8	*engine*	7/18
5	MEXICAN GP	Mexico City	4	Matra International	D	3.0 Matra MS80-Cosworth V8		8/17
	1970	Championship position: 9th Wins: 0 Pole positions: 0 Fastest laps: 0 Points scored: 16						
4	SOUTH AFRICAN GP	Kyalami	3	Equipe Matra Elf	G	3.0 Matra-Simca MS120 V12		=7/24
ret	SPANISH GP	Jarama	4	Equipe Matra Elf	G	3.0 Matra-Simca MS120 V12	*engine*	4/22
ret	MONACO GP	Monte Carlo	8	Equipe Matra Elf	G	3.0 Matra-Simca MS120 V12	*cwp*	6/21
3	BELGIAN GP	Spa	25	Equipe Matra Elf	G	3.0 Matra-Simca MS120 V12		11/18
5	DUTCH GP	Zandvoort	23	Equipe Matra Elf	G	3.0 Matra-Simca MS120 V12	*1 lap behind*	10/24
13/ret	FRENCH GP	Clermont Ferrand	21	Equipe Matra Elf	G	3.0 Matra-Simca MS120 V12	*fuel pressure/3 laps behind*	2/23
ret	BRITISH GP	Brands Hatch	7	Equipe Matra Elf	G	3.0 Matra-Simca MS120 V12	*wheel bearing problem*	11/25

JEAN-PIERRE BELTOISE

Like Behra, Beltoise was a French motor cycle champion, winning 11 championships between 1961 and 1964 while working for the René Bonnet team as a mechanic. He made his four-wheel debut at Le Mans in 1963, winning the Index of Performance, but a year later his career was nearly ended when a horrendous accident at Reims left him with burns and multiple injuries, the most serious of which was a left arm so badly broken that its movement was permanently restricted. Nevertheless he was back in 1965 racing the F3 Matra (the

aerospace company having taken over the René Bonnet concern) and scored a great first win for the marque at Reims. His pre-eminence in this formula was later to be confirmed when he won the 1966 Monaco F3 race, and all four rounds of the Argentine Temporada series early in 1967. This success encouraged Matra to continue with their racing activities, and Beltoise was the spearhead of the team's Formula 2 programme from 1966, winning the F2 class of the German GP and later the European F2 championship for non-graded drivers in 1968 when he won rounds at Hockenheim, Jarama and Zandvoort.

Although he contested a number of Grands Prix in a ballasted F2 Matra, Beltoise had to wait until early 1968 to get his hands on the team's raucous V12-engined F1 car but was soon showing its potential with a brilliant second place and fastest lap at Zandvoort. In 1969 Beltoise was placed in Ken Tyrrell's team as number two to Stewart while development work was undertaken on the V12 project and scored seven point-scoring finishes, but the following season he raced the new Matra MS120-V12 and was unlucky not to win the French GP when a puncture robbed him of the lead. Athough Jean-Pierre had done well enough on occasion, Matra signed Amon for 1971, frustrating the Frenchman's F1 aspirations, and it was not a happy season for Beltoise, who received a suspension when he was blamed for his involvement in the fatal accident that befell Giunti in the Buenos Aires 1000 Km.

In 1972 he moved to BRM, where he was soon to enjoy his day of days, winning the Monaco GP with a scintillating performance in pouring rain. A second place in the International Trophy and a win in the John Player Victory race at Brands Hatch merely disguised the team's imminent decline, but Beltoise was to stay on until 1974, with a fantastic drive into second place at Kyalami in the P201 the only highlight of his final season with the team. An established member of the Matra squad, Jean-Pierre enjoyed a tremendous year in sports car racing, winning four championship rounds (the Nürburgring, Watkins Glen, Paul Ricard and Brands Hatch) but at season's end he was looking for work on two fronts. With Matra out of endurance racing, Beltoise was forced to scratch around for drives and the prospect of an F1 return with Ligier in 1976 evaporated when the seat went to Laffite. Jean-Pierre was involved with both the Ligier and Inaltera sports car projects before successfully switching to the French touring car scene, where he was to drive and gain much enjoyment for many years.

As seems to be becoming more prevalent nowadays, Beltoise now has the pleasure of charting the progress of his sons, Julien and Anthony, as they climb the racing ladder.

ret	GERMAN GP	Hockenheim	8	Equipe Matra Elf	G	3.0 Matra-Simca MS120 V12	front suspension	23/25
6	AUSTRIAN GP	Österreichring	19	Equipe Matra Elf	G	3.0 Matra-Simca MS120 V12	pit stop-fuel/1 lap behind	=7/24
3	ITALIAN GP	Monza	40	Equipe Matra Elf	G	3.0 Matra-Simca MS120 V12		15/27
8	CANADIAN GP	St Jovite	23	Equipe Matra Elf	G	3.0 Matra-Simca MS120 V12	5 laps behind	13/20
ret	US GP	Watkins Glen	6	Equipe Matra Elf	G	3.0 Matra-Simca MS120 V12	handling	18/27
5	MEXICAN GP	Mexico City	6	Equipe Matra Elf	G	3.0 Matra-Simca MS120 V12		6/18

1971 Championship position: 22nd Wins: 0 Pole positions: 0 Fastest laps: 0 Points scored: 1

6	SPANISH GP	Montjuich Park	21	Equipe Matra Sports	G	3.0 Matra-Simca MS120B V12	1 lap behind	6/22
ret	MONACO GP	Monte Carlo	21	Equipe Matra Sports	G	3.0 Matra-Simca MS120B V12	cwp	7/23
9	DUTCH GP	Zandvoort	21	Equipe Matra Sports	G	3.0 Matra-Simca MS120B V12	5 laps behind	11/24
7	FRENCH GP	Paul Ricard	21	Equipe Matra Sports	G	3.0 Matra-Simca MS120B V12		8/24
7	BRITISH GP	Silverstone	22	Equipe Matra Sports	G	3.0 Matra-Simca MS120B V12	2 laps behind	15/24
ret	CANADIAN GP	Mosport Park	21	Equipe Matra Sports	G	3.0 Matra-Simca MS120B V12	hit guard rail	=11/27
8	US GP	Watkins Glen	12	Equipe Matra Sports	G	3.0 Matra-Simca MS120B V12	1 lap behind	11/32

1972 Championship position: 11th Wins: 1 Pole positions: 0 Fastest laps: 1 Points scored: 9

ret	SOUTH AFRICAN GP	Kyalami	10	Marlboro BRM	F	3.0 BRM P160B V12	engine	11/27
ret	SPANISH GP	Jarama	19	Marlboro BRM	F	3.0 BRM P160B V12	gear selection	7/26
dns	"	"	19T	Marlboro BRM	F	3.0 BRM P180 V12	practice only	– / –
1	MONACO GP	Monte Carlo	17	Marlboro BRM	F	3.0 BRM P160B V12	FL	4/25
ret	BELGIAN GP	Nivelles	23	Marlboro BRM	F	3.0 BRM P160B V12	overheating	6/26
15	FRENCH GP	Clermont Ferrand	5T	Marlboro BRM	F	3.0 BRM P160B V12	started from back/spin/-1 lap	– / –
dns	"	" "	5	Marlboro BRM	F	3.0 BRM P160C V12	practice only	(14)/29
11	BRITISH GP	Brands Hatch	11	Marlboro BRM	F	3.0 BRM P160C V12	pit stop-puncture/-6 laps	6/27
dns	"	" "	43	Marlboro BRM	F	3.0 BRM P160C V12	practice only	– / –
9	GERMAN GP	Nürburgring	6	Marlboro BRM	F	3.0 BRM P160C V12	black flagged when 5th	13/27
8	AUSTRIAN GP	Österreichring	7	Marlboro BRM	F	3.0 BRM P160C V12		21/26
8	ITALIAN GP	Monza	21	Marlboro BRM	F	3.0 BRM P180 V12	1 lap behind	16/27
ret	CANADIAN GP	Mosport Park	14	Marlboro BRM	F	3.0 BRM P180 V12	oil cooler leak	=19/25
ret	US GP	Watkins Glen	17	Marlboro BRM	F	3.0 BRM P180 V12	ignition rotor	18/32

1973 Championship position: 10th Wins: 0 Pole positions: 0 Fastest laps: 0 Points scored: 9

ret	ARGENTINE GP	Buenos Aires	30	Marlboro BRM	F	3.0 BRM P160D V12	engine	7/19
ret	BRAZILIAN GP	Interlagos	15	Marlboro BRM	F	3.0 BRM P160D V12	electrics-damaged by stone	10/20
ret	SOUTH AFRICAN GP	Kyalami	16	Marlboro BRM	F	3.0 BRM P160D V12	clutch slip	7/25
5	SPANISH GP	Montjuich Park	15	Marlboro BRM	F	3.0 BRM P160E V12	1 lap behind	=9/22
ret	BELGIAN GP	Zolder	20	Marlboro BRM	F	3.0 BRM P160E V12	engine	5/23
ret	MONACO GP	Monte Carlo	20	Marlboro BRM	F	3.0 BRM P160E V12	hit kerb and armco	11/26
ret	SWEDISH GP	Anderstorp	20	Marlboro BRM	F	3.0 BRM P160E V12	engine	9/22
11	FRENCH GP	Paul Ricard	20	Marlboro BRM	F	3.0 BRM P160E V12	1 lap behind	15/25
ret/dns	BRITISH GP	Silverstone	20	Marlboro BRM	F	3.0 BRM P160E V12	accident 1st start/did not restart	=16/29
5	DUTCH GP	Zandvoort	20	Marlboro BRM	F	3.0 BRM P160E V12		9/24
ret	GERMAN GP	Nürburgring	20	Marlboro BRM	F	3.0 BRM P160E V12	puncture/gearbox	9/23
5	AUSTRIAN GP	Österreichring	20	Marlboro BRM	F	3.0 BRM P160E V12		13/25
13	ITALIAN GP	Monza	20	Marlboro BRM	F	3.0 BRM P160E V12	pit stop-puncture/1 lap behind	13/25
4	CANADIAN GP	Mosport Park	20	Marlboro BRM	F	3.0 BRM P160E V12		16/26
9	US GP	Watkins Glen	20	Marlboro BRM	F	3.0 BRM P160E V12	pit stop/1 lap behind	15/28

1974 Championship position: 13th Wins: 0 Pole positions: 0 Fastest laps: 0 Points scored: 10

5	ARGENTINE GP	Buenos Aires	14	Team Motul BRM	F	3.0 BRM P160E V12		14/26
10	BRAZILIAN GP	Interlagos	14	Team Motul BRM	F	3.0 BRM P160E V12	1 lap behind	17/25
2	SOUTH AFRICAN GP	Kyalami	14	Team Motul BRM	F	3.0 BRM P201 V12		=11/27
ret	SPANISH GP	Jarama	14	Team Motul BRM	F	3.0 BRM P201 V12		12/28
5	BELGIAN GP	Nivelles	14	Team Motul BRM	F	3.0 BRM P201 V12		7/32
ret	MONACO GP	Monte Carlo	14	Team Motul BRM	F	3.0 BRM P201 V12	collision with Hulme	=10/28
ret	SWEDISH GP	Anderstorp	14	Team Motul BRM	F	3.0 BRM P201 V12	engine	13/28
ret	DUTCH GP	Zandvoort	14	Team Motul BRM	F	3.0 BRM P201 V12	gearbox	16/27
10	FRENCH GP	Dijon	14	Team Motul BRM	F	3.0 BRM P201 V12	1 lap behind	17/30
12	BRITISH GP	Brands Hatch	14	Team Motul BRM	F	3.0 BRM P201 V12	pit stop-tyres/3 laps behind	23/34
ret	GERMAN GP	Nürburgring	14	Team Motul BRM	F	3.0 BRM P201 V12	accessory drive belt	15/32
ret	AUSTRIAN GP	Österreichring	14	Team Motul BRM	F	3.0 BRM P201 V12	engine	18/31
ret	ITALIAN GP	Monza	14	Team Motul BRM	F	3.0 BRM P201 V12	electrics	11/31
nc	CANADIAN GP	Mosport Park	14	Team Motul BRM	F	3.0 BRM P201 V12	pit stops-handling/-20 laps	17/30
dns	US GP	Watkins Glen	14	Team Motul BRM	F	3.0 BRM P201 V12	accident-broken bone in foot	30/30

GP Starts: 85 (86) GP Wins: 1 Pole positions: 0 Fastest laps: 4 Points: 77

BERETTA, Olivier (MC) b 23/11/1969, Monte Carlo

1994 Championship position: Unplaced

	Race	Circuit	No	Entrant	Tyres	Car/Engine	Comment	Q Pos/Entries
ret	BRAZILIAN GP	Interlagos	19	Tourtel Larrousse F1	G	3.5 Larrousse LH94-Ford HB V8	spun-collision with Gachot	23/28
ret	PACIFIC GP	T.I. Circuit	19	Tourtel Larrousse F1	G	3.5 Larrousse LH94-Ford HB V8	electrics	21/28
ret	SAN MARINO GP	Imola	19	Tourtel Larrousse F1	G	3.5 Larrousse LH94-Ford HB V8	engine	23/28
8	MONACO GP	Monte Carlo	19	Tourtel Larrousse F1	G	3.5 Larrousse LH94-Ford HB V8	2 laps behind	18/24
dns	SPANISH GP	Barcelona	19	Tourtel Larrousse F1	G	3.5 Larrousse LH94-Ford HB V8	engine failure on parade lap	(17)/27
ret	CANADIAN GP	Montreal	19	Tourtel Larrousse F1	G	3.5 Larrousse LH94-Ford HB V8	engine	22/27
ret*	FRENCH GP	Magny Cours	19	Tourtel Larrousse F1	G	3.5 Larrousse LH94-Ford HB V8	engine	25/28
14*	BRITISH GP	Silverstone	19	Tourtel Larrousse F1	G	3.5 Larrousse LH94-Ford HB V8	* 2nd place car dsq/-2 laps	24/28
7	GERMAN GP	Hockenheim	19	Tourtel Larrousse F1	G	3.5 Larrousse LH94-Ford HB V8	1 lap behind	24/28
9	HUNGARIAN GP	Hungaroring	19	Tourtel Larrousse F1	G	3.5 Larrousse LH94-Ford HB V8	2 laps behind	25/28

GP Starts: 9 GP Wins: 0 Pole positions: 0 Fastest laps: 0 Points: 0

OLIVIER BERETTA

This Monégasque began karting in 1983, scoring many wins before graduating to French F3 in 1989. It was the following year when he began to cause a stir. Armed with a Dallara-Alfa, he took third place in the Monaco F3 race and then won at Pau before his season tailed off, though he still took third in the overall standings. His 1991 campaign was less successful: a broken wrist in the Monaco F3 race hindered his progress, and he also attempted to race his Ralt in both the French and British series.

A move into F3000 in 1992 with Nelson Piquet's well-funded team saw disappointment for all concerned with Beretta making too many mistakes for comfort. But a move to Forti Corse brought immediate reward as he won the 1993 season-opener from pole at Donington. Thereafter he failed to make the podium and slipped down to finish sixth in the championship.

Olivier brought much-needed funds to Larrousse for 1994, and he was certainly not outclassed by his team leader Comas. At Hockenheim he came tantalisingly close to scoring a precious championship point, but one race

on his money ran out and a succession of rent-a-drivers were taken on to help the team see out the season.

Since 1996 Beretta has campaigned an ORECA Chrysler Viper with spectacular success. After the heartbreak of losing the GT2 title at the final round in 1997, he made no mistake the following year paired with Pedro Lamy.

The 1999 season saw Olivier and Karl Wendlinger crowned FIA GT champions as the Viper crushed the opposition.

GEORGES BERGER

Early in his long career Berger raced a little Jicey-BMW, his best finish being third at Chimay in 1950. In 1953 he got his hands on a private Gordini, and then briefly became part of the works team early the following year, taking a Type 16 car to fourth in the non-championship race at Rouen.

Thereafter, Georges was a stalwart racer in sports and GT racing, with machines such as a Maserati sports, an AC Bristol and a Ferrari 250GT. He often raced the latter car with another ex-Grand Prix driver, André Simon. But his greatest success was winning the Tour de France rally with Willy Mairesse in 1960, again in a Ferrari.

In 1967 Berger was killed while taking part in the Marathon de la Route, an 84-hour endurance race at the Nürburgring, when he crashed his Porsche 911.

ALLEN BERG

A stocky little Canadian driver, Berg emerged from the 1982 North American Formula Atlantic series by way of the winter Pacific championship (which he won for New Zealand ex-racer Graeme Lawrence in a Ralt) to contest the 1983 British F3 championship. With no experience of F3 cars or, naturally, the circuits, he did a good job in this formative season, especially after switching to the Eddie Jordan Racing team. This was the year in which the Senna–Brundle axis dominated proceedings, but Allen was regularly leading the rest in pursuit of the star duo.

Staying with EJR, hopes for success in 1984 were high, but a season of mishaps and frustrations saw him finish second in the standings to Johnny Dumfries. This left Berg's career in something of a vacuum, and it was a surprise when he scraped together sufficient finance to take over the unwieldy Osella in mid-1986 after Christian Danner had moved over to

Arrows. This was a year without the pressures of having to qualify, so Allen was at least able get some experience and racing mileage under his belt.

Berg subsequently tried his hand at the German touring car championship with his own car in 1991, but in subsequent seasons he found a happy hunting ground down Mexico way. He was Formula 2 champion in 1993 and took third place overall in the well-funded 1995 Formula 3 series.

BERG, Allen (CDN) b 1/8/1961, Calgary, Alberta

	1986	Championship position: Unplaced						
	Race	Circuit	No	Entrant	Tyres	Car/Engine	Comment	Q Pos/Entries
ret	US GP (DETROIT)	Detroit	22	Osella Squadra Corse	P	1.5 t/c Osella FA1F-Alfa Romeo V8	electrics	25/26
ret	FRENCH GP	Dijon	22	Osella Squadra Corse	P	1.5 t/c Osella FA1G-Alfa Romeo V8	turbo	26/26
ret/dns	BRITISH GP	Brands Hatch	22	Osella Squadra Corse	P	1.5 t/c Osella FA1H-Alfa Romeo V8	accident in first start	26/26
12	GERMAN GP	Hockenheim	22	Osella Squadra Corse	P	1.5 t/c Osella FA1F-Alfa Romeo V8	4 laps behind	26/26
ret	HUNGARIAN GP	Hungaroring	22	Osella Squadra Corse	P	1.5 t/c Osella FA1F-Alfa Romeo V8	turbo	26/26
ret	AUSTRIAN GP	Österreichring	22	Osella Squadra Corse	P	1.5 t/c Osella FA1F-Alfa Romeo V8	electrics	26/26
13	PORTUGUESE GP	Estoril	22	Osella Squadra Corse	P	1.5 t/c Osella FA1F-Alfa Romeo V8	7 laps behind	27/27
16	MEXICAN GP	Mexico City	22	Osella Squadra Corse	P	1.5 t/c Osella FA1F-Alfa Romeo V8	7 laps behind	26/26
nc	AUSTRALIAN GP	Adelaide	22	Osella Squadra Corse	P	1.5 t/c Osella FA1F-Alfa Romeo V8	started from pits/-21 laps	26/26

GP Starts: 8 (9) GP Wins: 0 Pole positions: 0 Fastest laps: 0 Points: 0

BERGER, Georges (B) b 14/9/1918, Brussels – d 23/8/1967, Nürburgring, Germany

	1953	Championship position: Unplaced						
	Race	Circuit	No	Entrant	Tyres	Car/Engine	Comment	Q Pos/Entries
ret	BELGIAN GP	Spa	34	Georges Berger	E	1.5 Gordini Type 15 4	engine	20/22
	1954	Championship position: Unplaced						
ret	FRENCH GP	Reims	30	Georges Berger	E	1.5 Gordini Type 16 6	engine-valve	20/22

GP Starts: 2 GP Wins: 0 Pole positions: 0 Fastest laps: 0 Points: 0

GERHARD BERGER

When Gerhard Berger finally hung up his helmet at the end of the 1997 season, he was really the last of the generation of superstars whose F1 careers dated back to the turbo era of the mid-eighties. Indeed he was slightly unfortunate to have had to pit himself against such giants of the sport as Senna, Prost, Piquet and Mansell over an eight-season spell between 1986 and 1993, otherwise his tally of ten wins could easily have been doubled.

With a limited racing background firstly in Alfas and then in the German and European Formula 3 series, Berger had gained a reputation as a fast and safe driver who, above all, brought his car home to the finish when he breezed into the ATS team towards the end of 1984. His sixth place at Monza was sufficient indication that here was a rough diamond waiting to be polished, and a close-season accident which left him with broken vertebrae in his neck was not enough to prevent him from lining up at the start of the 1985 season in the Arrows-BMW team. At first Gerhard struggled somewhat alongside the quiet and talented Thierry Boutsen, but his aggressive driving style began to pay dividends in the second half of the season.

Benetton were running BMW engines in 1986 and Berger's connections with the German company helped him to a place in the team, but he was soon to prove the wisdom of his selection with some eye-catching drives, especially when the Pirelli tyres were working well. After disappointment in Austria came his first Grand Prix win in Mexico and, on the not-too-distant horizon, a contract with Ferrari for 1987.

Despite a hesitant beginning, Gerhard's natural ebullience was quickly apparent and, after throwing away a victory in the Portuguese GP, he won the end-of-season Japanese and Australian races. In 1988 McLaren-Honda were utterly dominant, but Berger never gave up and a lucky win at Monza was just reward for perhaps his best-ever year. However, his final season at Maranello was distinctly low-key. Psychologically outgunned by Nigel Mansell, and striving to shake off the effects of a horrendous crash at Imola, he picked up a win at Estoril almost unnoticed before joining McLaren on a three-year contract to partner Ayrton Senna.

Initially it was a morale-sapping experience, as he struggled in his stellar team-mate's trail. He had difficulty fitting into the cockpit and was sometimes guilty of over-taxing his tyres, but gradually he got to grips with the situation at McLaren to become a perfect foil for Senna both on and off the track. Grand Prix wins came here and there; some were lucky and others well earned, with his final race for the team being perhaps his best, when his finely judged tactics brought him victory in Adelaide.

Enticed by a reputedly massive retainer, Gerhard rejoined Ferrari for 1993, but endured a pretty torrid year adapting to 'active' suspension, which he obviously disliked. Worryingly, he was involved in a number of alarming on-track incidents and claimed but a single podium finish. If he thought he could write it off as just a bad dream, then the start of the following year was to become a nightmare. Second place in the Pacific GP showed that Ferrari were at last back on course towards winning again, but then came the deaths of his close friends Ratzenberger and Senna at Imola. It must have been utterly devastating for Gerhard, who could easily have decided not to continue racing. However, after a week of soul-searching, he carried on with the sport he loves so much. His subsequent win at Hockenheim ended a dry spell of nearly four years for Ferrari, and was welcomed by all followers of the sport.

As Ferrari continued their restructuring in search of the holy grail of the World Championship, Gerhard forged a good relationship with new team boss Jean Todt. He worked diligently and selflessly in Maranello's cause, and certainly the results achieved in 1995 did not reflect his true level of performance throughout the year. He could have won at Imola and Monza, but in the end had to be content with six third-place finishes. Gerhard has always been a team player, but could be excused for feeling unhappy at being pushed to the margins with the arrival of Michael Schumacher in 1996. Understandably the chance to partner Jean Alesi once more, this time at Benetton, seemed like his best option.

Berger was to face a testing start to his Benetton career as he adapted to the nervous-handling car, but typically he worked away tirelessly and was rewarded by a second place at Silverstone. It could have been even better at Hockenheim a fortnight later, when a blown engine robbed him of victory with only a couple of laps remaining. What proved to be Gerhard's final season was then blighted by a sinus problem which caused him to miss three races, followed by the death of his father in an air accident. That he came back to deliver a superb performance in winning the German Grand Prix showed his doubters that he could not yet be written off. However, at season's end he decided to call time on a career which had spanned 210 races to take up a position as head of motor sport with BMW as they prepared for a Grand Prix return in 2000.

BERGER, Gerhard (A) b 27/8/1959, Wörgl, nr Innsbruck

1984 — Championship position: Unplaced

	Race	Circuit	No	Entrant	Tyres	Car/Engine	Comment	Q Pos/Entries
12/ret	AUSTRIAN GP	Österreichring	31	Team ATS	P	1.5 t/c ATS D7-BMW 4	*gearbox/3 laps behind*	20/28
6*	ITALIAN GP	Monza	31	Team ATS	P	1.5 t/c ATS D7-BMW 4	** not eligible for points/-2 laps*	20/27
ret	EUROPEAN GP	Nürburgring	31	Team ATS	P	1.5 t/c ATS D7-BMW 4	*accident with Surer*	18/26
13	PORTUGUESE GP	Estoril	31	Team ATS	P	1.5 t/c ATS D7-BMW 4	*2 laps behind*	23/27

1985 — Championship position: 17th= Wins: 0 Pole positions: 0 Fastest laps: 0 Points scored: 3

	Race	Circuit	No	Entrant	Tyres	Car/Engine	Comment	Q Pos/Entries
ret	BRAZILIAN GP	Rio	17	Barclay Arrows BMW	G	1.5 t/c Arrows A8-BMW 4	*suspension*	19/25
ret	PORTUGUESE GP	Estoril	17	Barclay Arrows BMW	G	1.5 t/c Arrows A8-BMW 4	*spun off*	17/26
ret	SAN MARINO GP	Imola	17	Barclay Arrows BMW	G	1.5 t/c Arrows A8-BMW 4	*electrics/engine*	10/26
ret	MONACO GP	Monte Carlo	17	Barclay Arrows BMW	G	1.5 t/c Arrows A8-BMW 4	*accident damage*	11/26
13	CANADIAN GP	Montreal	17	Barclay Arrows BMW	G	1.5 t/c Arrows A8-BMW 4	*3 laps behind*	12/25
11	US GP (DETROIT)	Detroit	17	Barclay Arrows BMW	G	1.5 t/c Arrows A8-BMW 4	*3 laps behind*	24/25
ret	FRENCH GP	Paul Ricard	17	Barclay Arrows BMW	G	1.5 t/c Arrows A8-BMW 4	*accident with Martini*	9/26
8	BRITISH GP	Silverstone	17	Barclay Arrows BMW	G	1.5 t/c Arrows A8-BMW 4	*2 laps behind*	17/26
7	GERMAN GP	Nürburgring	17	Barclay Arrows BMW	G	1.5 t/c Arrows A8-BMW 4	*1 lap behind*	17/27
ret	AUSTRIAN GP	Österreichring	17	Barclay Arrows BMW	G	1.5 t/c Arrows A8-BMW 4	*turbo*	17/27
9	DUTCH GP	Zandvoort	17	Barcaly Arrows BMW	G	1.5 t/c Arrows A8-BMW 4	*2 laps behind*	14/27
ret	ITALIAN GP	Monza	17	Barclay Arrows BMW	G	1.5 t/c Arrows A8-BMW 4	*engine*	11/26
7	BELGIAN GP	Spa	17	Barclay Arrows BMW	G	1.5 t/c Arrows A8-BMW 4	*1 lap behind*	8/24
10	EUROPEAN GP	Brands Hatch	17	Barclay Arrows BMW	G	1.5 t/c Arrows A8-BMW 4	*2 laps behind*	19/27
5	SOUTH AFRICAN GP	Kyalami	17	Barclay Arrows BMW	G	1.5 t/c Arrows A8-BMW 4	*1 lap behind*	11/21
6	AUSTRALIAN GP	Adelaide	17	Barclay Arrows BMW	G	1.5 t/c Arrows A8-BMW 4	*1 lap behind*	7/25

1986 — Championship position: 7th Wins: 1 Pole positions: 0 Fastest laps: 2 Points scored: 17

	Race	Circuit	No	Entrant	Tyres	Car/Engine	Comment	Q Pos/Entries
6	BRAZILIAN GP	Rio	20	Benetton Formula Ltd	P	1.5 t/c Benetton B186-BMW 4	*electrical problem/-2 laps*	16/25
6	SPANISH GP	Jerez	20	Benetton Formula Ltd	P	1.5 t/c Benetton B186-BMW 4	*1 lap behind*	7/25
3	SAN MARINO GP	Imola	20	Benetton Formula Ltd	P	1.5 t/c Benetton B186-BMW 4	*1 lap behind*	9/26
ret	MONACO GP	Monte Carlo	20	Benetton Formula Ltd	P	1.5 t/c Benetton B186-BMW 4	*wheel drive pegs*	5/26
10	BELGIAN GP	Spa	20	Benetton Formula Ltd	P	1.5 t/c Benetton B186-BMW 4	*lost clutch/2 laps behind*	2/25
ret	CANADIAN GP	Montreal	20	Benetton Formula Ltd	P	1.5 t/c Benetton B186-BMW 4	*turbo boost*	7/25
ret	US GP (DETROIT)	Detroit	20	Benetton Formula Ltd	P	1.5 t/c Benetton B186-BMW 4	*engine cut out*	12/26
ret	FRENCH GP	Paul Ricard	20	Benetton Formula Ltd	P	1.5 t/c Benetton B186-BMW 4	*gearbox*	8/26
ret	BRITISH GP	Brands Hatch	20	Benetton Formula Ltd	P	1.5 t/c Benetton B186-BMW 4	*electrics*	4/26
10	GERMAN GP	Hockenheim	20	Benetton Formula Ltd	P	1.5 t/c Benetton B186-BMW 4	*2 laps behind/FL*	4/26
ret	HUNGARIAN GP	Hungaroring	20	Benetton Formula Ltd	P	1.5 t/c Benetton B186-BMW 4	*fuel leak/transmission*	11/26
7	AUSTRIAN GP	Österreichring	20	Benetton Formula Ltd	P	1.5 t/c Benetton B186-BMW 4	*pit stop-battery/FL/-3 laps*	2/26
5	ITALIAN GP	Monza	20	Benetton Formula Ltd	P	1.5 t/c Benetton B186-BMW 4	*1 lap behind*	4/27
ret	PORTUGUESE GP	Estoril	20	Benetton Formula Ltd	P	1.5 t/c Benetton B186-BMW 4	*collision-Johansson-spun off*	4/27
1	MEXICAN GP	Mexico City	20	Benetton Formula Ltd	P	1.5 t/c Benetton B186-BMW 4		4/26
ret	AUSTRALIAN GP	Adelaide	20	Benetton Formula Ltd	P	1.5 t/c Benetton B186-BMW 4	*clutch/engine*	6/26

1987 — Championship position: 5th Wins: 2 Pole positions: 3 Fastest laps: 3 Points scored: 36

	Race	Circuit	No	Entrant	Tyres	Car/Engine	Comment	Q Pos/Entries
4	BRAZILIAN GP	Rio	28	Scuderia Ferrari SpA SEFAC	G	1.5 t/c Ferrari F1/87 V6		7/23
ret	SAN MARINO GP	Imola	28	Scuderia Ferrari SpA SEFAC	G	1.5 t/c Ferrari F1/87 V6	*electrics*	6/27
ret	BELGIAN GP	Spa	28	Scuderia Ferrari SpA SEFAC	G	1.5 t/c Ferrari F1/87 V6	*turbo*	4/26
4	MONACO GP	Monte Carlo	28	Scuderia Ferrari SpA SEFAC	G	1.5 t/c Ferrari F1/87 V6	*1 lap behind*	8/26
4	US GP (DETROIT)	Detroit	28	Scuderia Ferrari SpA SEFAC	G	1.5 t/c Ferrari F1/87 V6		12/26
ret	FRENCH GP	Paul Ricard	28	Scuderia Ferrari SpA SEFAC	G	1.5 t/c Ferrari F1/87 V6	*spun off-suspension*	6/26
ret	BRITISH GP	Silverstone	28	Scuderia Ferrari SpA SEFAC	G	1.5 t/c Ferrari F1/87 V6	*spun off*	8/26
ret	GERMAN GP	Hockenheim	28	Scuderia Ferrari SpA SEFAC	G	1.5 t/c Ferrari F1/87 V6	*turbo*	10/26
ret	HUNGARIAN GP	Hungaroring	28	Scuderia Ferrari SpA SEFAC	G	1.5 t/c Ferrari F1/87 V6	*differential*	2/26
ret	AUSTRIAN GP	Österreichring	28	Scuderia Ferrari SpA SEFAC	G	1.5 t/c Ferrari F1/87 V6	*turbo*	3/26
4	ITALIAN GP	Monza	28	Scuderia Ferrari SpA SEFAC	G	1.5 t/c Ferrari F1/87 V6		3/28
2	PORTUGUESE GP	Estoril	28	Scuderia Ferrari SpA SEFAC	G	1.5 t/c Ferrari F1/87 V6	*spin when leading/FL*	1/27
ret	SPANISH GP	Jerez	28	Scuderia Ferrari SpA SEFAC	G	1.5 t/c Ferrari F1/87 V6	*smashed oil cooler/engine/FL*	3/28
ret	MEXICAN GP	Mexico City	28	Scuderia Ferrari SpA SEFAC	G	1.5 t/c Ferrari F1/87 V6	*engine*	2/27
1	JAPANESE GP	Suzuka	28	Scuderia Ferrari SpA SEFAC	G	1.5 t/c Ferrari F1/87 V6		1/27
1	AUSTRALIAN GP	Adelaide	28	Scuderia Ferrari SpA SEFAC	G	1.5 t/c Ferrari F1/87 V6	*FL*	1/27

1988 — Championship position: 3rd Wins: 1 Pole positions: 1 Fastest laps: 2 Points scored: 41

	Race	Circuit	No	Entrant	Tyres	Car/Engine	Comment	Q Pos/Entries
2	BRAZILIAN GP	Rio	28	Scuderia Ferrari SpA SEFAC	G	1.5 t/c Ferrari F1/87/88C V6	*FL*	4/31
5	SAN MARINO GP	Imola	28	Scuderia Ferrari SpA SEFAC	G	1.5 t/c Ferrari F1/87/88C V6	*power loss-engine/-1 lap*	5/31
2	MONACO GP	Monte Carlo	28	Scuderia Ferrari SpA SEFAC	G	1.5 t/c Ferrari F1/87/88C V6		3/30
3	MEXICAN GP	Mexico City	28	Scuderia Ferrari SpA SEFAC	G	1.5 t/c Ferrari F1/87/88C V6		3/30
ret	CANADIAN GP	Montreal	28	Scuderia Ferrari SpA SEFAC	G	1.5 t/c Ferrari F1/87/88C V6	*electrics/engine*	3/31
ret	US GP (DETROIT)	Detroit	28	Scuderia Ferrari SpA SEFAC	G	1.5 t/c Ferrari F1/87/88C V6	*puncture*	2/31
4	FRENCH GP	Paul Ricard	28	Scuderia Ferrari SpA SEFAC	G	1.5 t/c Ferrari F1/87/88C V6	*1 lap behind*	3/31
9	BRITISH GP	Silverstone	28	Scuderia Ferrari SpA SEFAC	G	1.5 t/c Ferrari F1/87/88C V6	*low on fuel/1 lap behind*	1/31
3	GERMAN GP	Hockenheim	28	Scuderia Ferrari SpA SEFAC	G	1.5 t/c Ferrari F1/87/88C V6		3/31
4	HUNGARIAN GP	Hungaroring	28	Scuderia Ferrari SpA SEFAC	G	1.5 t/c Ferrari F1/87/88C V6		9/31
ret	BELGIAN GP	Spa	28	Scuderia Ferrari SpA SEFAC	G	1.5 t/c Ferrari F1/87/88C V6	*electrics/FL*	3/31
1	ITALIAN GP	Monza	28	Scuderia Ferrari SpA SEFAC	G	1.5 t/c Ferrari F1/87/88C V6		3/31
ret	PORTUGUESE GP	Estoril	28	Scuderia Ferrari SpA SEFAC	G	1.5 t/c Ferrari F1/87/88C V6	*spun off-fire extinguisher/FL*	4/31
6	SPANISH GP	Jerez	28	Scuderia Ferrari SpA SEFAC	G	1.5 t/c Ferrari F1/87/88C V6	*pit stop-tyres/low on fuel*	8/31
4	JAPANESE GP	Suzuka	28	Scuderia Ferrari SpA SEFAC	G	1.5 t/c Ferrari F1/87/88C V6		3/31
ret	AUSTRALIAN GP	Adelaide	28	Scuderia Ferrari SpA SEFAC	G	1.5 t/c Ferrari F1/87/88C V6	*accident with Arnoux*	4/31

1989
Championship position: 7th   Wins: 1   Pole positions: 0   Fastest laps: 1   Points scored: 21

ret	BRAZILIAN GP	Rio	28	Scuderia Ferrari SpA SEFAC	G	3.5 Ferrari 640 V12	collision with Senna	3/38
ret	SAN MARINO GP	Imola	28	Scuderia Ferrari SpA SEFAC	G	3.5 Ferrari 640 V12	crashed at Tamburello	5/39
ret	MEXICAN GP	Mexico City	28	Scuderia Ferrari SpA SEFAC	G	3.5 Ferrari 640 V12	transmission	6/39
ret	US GP (PHOENIX)	Phoenix	28	Scuderia Ferrari SpA SEFAC	G	3.5 Ferrari 640 V12	alternator	8/39
ret	CANADIAN GP	Montreal	28	Scuderia Ferrari SpA SEFAC	G	3.5 Ferrari 640 V12	alternator belt	4/39
ret	FRENCH GP	Paul Ricard	28	Scuderia Ferrari SpA SEFAC	G	3.5 Ferrari 640 V12	gearbox oil leak	6/39
ret	BRITISH GP	Silverstone	28	Scuderia Ferrari SpA SEFAC	G	3.5 Ferrari 640 V12	gearbox	4/39
ret	GERMAN GP	Hockenheim	28	Scuderia Ferrari SpA SEFAC	G	3.5 Ferrari 640 V12	puncture-crashed	4/39
ret	HUNGARIAN GP	Hungaroring	28	Scuderia Ferrari SpA SEFAC	G	3.5 Ferrari 640 V12	gearbox	6/39
ret	BELGIAN GP	Spa	28	Scuderia Ferrari SpA SEFAC	G	3.5 Ferrari 640 V12	spun off	3/39
2	ITALIAN GP	Monza	28	Scuderia Ferrari SpA SEFAC	G	3.5 Ferrari 640 V12		2/39
1	PORTUGUESE GP	Estoril	28	Scuderia Ferrari SpA SEFAC	G	3.5 Ferrari 640 V12	FL	2/39
2	SPANISH GP	Jerez	28	Scuderia Ferrari SpA SEFAC	G	3.5 Ferrari 640 V12		2/38
ret	JAPANESE GP	Suzuka	28	Scuderia Ferrari SpA SEFAC	G	3.5 Ferrari 640 V12	gearbox electrics	3/39
ret	AUSTRALIAN GP	Adelaide	28	Scuderia Ferrari SpA SEFAC	G	3.5 Ferrari 640 V12	collision with Alliot	14/39

1990
Championship position: 3rd=   Wins: 0   Pole positions: 2   Fastest laps: 3   Points scored: 43

ret	US GP (PHOENIX)	Phoenix	28	Honda Marlboro McLaren	G	3.5 McLaren MP4/5B-Honda V10	led-spun-pit stop/clutch//FL	1/35
2	BRAZILIAN GP	Interlagos	28	Honda Marlboro McLaren	G	3.5 McLaren MP4/5B-Honda V10	pit stop-tyres/FL	2/35
2	SAN MARINO GP	Imola	28	Honda Marlboro McLaren	G	3.5 McLaren MP4/5B-Honda V10		2/34
3	MONACO GP	Monte Carlo	28	Honda Marlboro McLaren	G	3.5 McLaren MP4/5B-Honda V10		5/35
4	CANADIAN GP	Montreal	28	Honda Marlboro McLaren	G	3.5 McLaren MP4/5B-Honda V10	1 min penalty-jumped start/FL	2/35
3	MEXICAN GP	Mexico City	28	Honda Marlboro McLaren	G	3.5 McLaren MP4/5B-Honda V10	pit stop-tyres	1/35
5	FRENCH GP	Paul Ricard	28	Honda Marlboro McLaren	G	3.5 McLaren MP4/5B-Honda V10	pit stop-tyres/lost 1st gear	2/35
14/ret	BRITISH GP	Silverstone	28	Honda Marlboro McLaren	G	3.5 McLaren MP4/5B-Honda V10	throttle cable/4 laps behind	3/35
3	GERMAN GP	Hockenheim	28	Honda Marlboro McLaren	G	3.5 McLaren MP4/5B-Honda V10		2/35
16/ret	HUNGARIAN GP	Hungaroring	28	Honda Marlboro McLaren	G	3.5 McLaren MP4/5B-Honda V10	collision with Mansell/-5 laps	3/35
3	BELGIAN GP	Spa	28	Honda Marlboro McLaren	G	3.5 McLaren MP4/5B-Honda V10	pit stop-tyres	2/33
3	ITALIAN GP	Monza	28	Honda Marlboro McLaren	G	3.5 McLaren MP4/5B-Honda V10	pit stop-tyres/brake problems	3/33
4	PORTUGUESE GP	Estoril	28	Honda Marlboro McLaren	G	3.5 McLaren MP4/5B-Honda V10	pit stop-tyres	4/33
ret	SPANISH GP	Jerez	28	Honda Marlboro McLaren	G	3.5 McLaren MP4/5B-Honda V10	collision with Boutsen	5/33
ret	JAPANESE GP	Suzuka	28	Honda Marlboro McLaren	G	3.5 McLaren MP4/5B-Honda V10	spun off	4/30
4	AUSTRALIAN GP	Adelaide	28	Honda Marlboro McLaren	G	3.5 McLaren MP4/5B-Honda V10	pit stop-tyres/cramp problems	2/30

1991
Championship position: 4th   Wins: 1   Pole positions: 2   Fastest laps: 2   Points scored: 43

ret	US GP (PHOENIX)	Phoenix	2	Honda Marlboro McLaren	G	3.5 McLaren MP4/6-Honda V12	fuel pump	7/34
3	BRAZILIAN GP	Interlagos	2	Honda Marlboro McLaren	G	3.5 McLaren MP4/6-Honda V12		4/34
2	SAN MARINO GP	Imola	2	Honda Marlboro McLaren	G	3.5 McLaren MP4/6-Honda V12	FL	5/34
ret	MONACO GP	Monte Carlo	2	Honda Marlboro McLaren	G	3.5 McLaren MP4/6-Honda V12	crashed	6/34
ret	CANADIAN GP	Montreal	2	Honda Marlboro McLaren	G	3.5 McLaren MP4/6-Honda V12	electrics	6/34
ret	MEXICAN GP	Mexico City	2	Honda Marlboro McLaren	G	3.5 McLaren MP4/6-Honda V12	engine-overheating	5/34
ret	FRENCH GP	Magny Cours	2	Honda Marlboro McLaren	G	3.5 McLaren MP4/6-Honda V12	engine	5/34
2	BRITISH GP	Silverstone	2	Honda Marlboro McLaren	G	3.5 McLaren MP4/6-Honda V12	wheel vibration/pit stop-tyres	4/34
4	GERMAN GP	Hockenheim	2	Honda Marlboro McLaren	G	3.5 McLaren MP4/6-Honda V12		3/34
4	HUNGARIAN GP	Hungaroring	2	Honda Marlboro McLaren	G	3.5 McLaren MP4/6-Honda V12		5/34
2	BELGIAN GP	Spa	2	Honda Marlboro McLaren	G	3.5 McLaren MP4/6-Honda V12		4/34
4	ITALIAN GP	Monza	2	Honda Marlboro McLaren	G	3.5 McLaren MP4/6-Honda V12		3/34
ret	PORTUGUESE GP	Estoril	2	Honda Marlboro McLaren	G	3.5 McLaren MP4/6-Honda V12	engine	2/34
ret	SPANISH GP	Jerez	2	Honda Marlboro McLaren	G	3.5 McLaren MP4/6-Honda V12	engine-valve	1/33
1	JAPANESE GP	Suzuka	2	Honda Marlboro McLaren	G	3.5 McLaren MP4/6-Honda V12		1/31
3	AUSTRALIAN GP	Adelaide	2	Honda Marlboro McLaren	G	3.5 McLaren MP4/6-Honda V12	race abandoned-half points/FL	2/32

1992
Championship position: 5th   Wins: 2   Pole positions: 0   Fastest laps: 2   Points scored: 49

5	SOUTH AFRICAN GP	Kyalami	2	Honda Marlboro McLaren	G	3.5 McLaren MP4/6B-Honda V12		3/30
4	MEXICAN GP	Mexico City	2	Honda Marlboro McLaren	G	3.5 McLaren MP4/6B-Honda V12	FL	5/30
ret	BRAZILIAN GP	Interlagos	2	Honda Marlboro McLaren	G	3.5 McLaren MP4/7A-Honda V12	started from pit lane/overheating	4/31
dns	"	"	2	Honda Marlboro McLaren	G	3.5 McLaren MP4/6B-Honda V12	practice only	–/–
4	SPANISH GP	Barcelona	2	Honda Marlboro McLaren	G	3.5 McLaren MP4/7A-Honda V12		7/32
ret	SAN MARINO GP	Imola	2	Honda Marlboro McLaren	G	3.5 McLaren MP4/7A-Honda V12	collision Alesi	4/32
ret	MONACO GP	Monte Carlo	2	Honda Marlboro McLaren	G	3.5 McLaren MP4/7A-Honda V12	gearbox	5/32
1	CANADIAN GP	Montreal	2	Honda Marlboro McLaren	G	3.5 McLaren MP4/7A-Honda V12	despite gearbox problems/FL	4/32
ret	FRENCH GP	Magny Cours	2	Honda Marlboro McLaren	G	3.5 McLaren MP4/7A-Honda V12	engine	4/30
5	BRITISH GP	Silverstone	2	Honda Marlboro McLaren	G	3.5 McLaren MP4/7A-Honda V12		5/32
ret	GERMAN GP	Hockenheim	2	Honda Marlboro McLaren	G	3.5 McLaren MP4/7A-Honda V12	2 pit stops/misfire	4/32
3	HUNGARIAN GP	Hungaroring	2	Honda Marlboro McLaren	G	3.5 McLaren MP4/7A-Honda V12		5/31
ret	BELGIAN GP	Spa	2	Honda Marlboro McLaren	G	3.5 McLaren MP4/7A-Honda V12	transmission failure at start	6/30
4	ITALIAN GP	Monza	2	Honda Marlboro McLaren	G	3.5 McLaren MP4/7A-Honda V12	started from pitlane/pit stop-tyres	5/28
2	PORTUGUESE GP	Estoril	2	Honda Marlboro McLaren	G	3.5 McLaren MP4/7A-Honda V12		4/26
2	JAPANESE GP	Suzuka	2	Honda Marlboro McLaren	G	3.5 McLaren MP4/7A-Honda V12		4/26
1	AUSTRALIAN GP	Adelaide	2	Honda Marlboro McLaren	G	3.5 McLaren MP4/7A-Honda V12	early tactical pit stop-tyres	4/26

1993
Championship position: 8th   Wins: 0   Pole positions: 0   Fastest laps: 0   Points scored: 12

6/ret	SOUTH AFRICAN GP	Kyalami	28	Scuderia Ferrari SpA	G	3.5 Fiat Ferrari F93A V12	engine/3 laps behind	15/26
ret	BRAZILIAN GP	Interlagos	28	Scuderia Ferrari SpA	G	3.5 Fiat Ferrari F93A V12	taken off by Andretti on l lap 1	13/26
ret	EUROPEAN GP	Donington	28	Scuderia Ferrari SpA	G	3.5 Fiat Ferrari F93A V12	active system leakage	8/26
ret	SAN MARINO GP	Imola	28	Scuderia Ferrari SpA	G	3.5 Fiat Ferrari F93A V12	gearbox	8/26
6	SPANISH GP	Barcelona	28	Scuderia Ferrari SpA	G	3.5 Fiat Ferrari F93A V12	2 laps behind	11/26
14/ret	MONACO GP	Monte Carlo	28	Scuderia Ferrari SpA	G	3.5 Fiat Ferrari F93A V12	collision-Hill/8 laps behind	7/26
4	CANADIAN GP	Montreal	28	Scuderia Ferrari SpA	G	3.5 Fiat Ferrari F93A V12	1 lap behind	5/26

14	FRENCH GP	Magny Cours	28	Scuderia Ferrari SpA	G	3.5 Fiat Ferrari F93A V12	*active system trouble/-2 laps*	14/26
ret	BRITISH GP	Silverstone	28	Scuderia Ferrari SpA	G	3.5 Fiat Ferrari F93A V12	*active system*	13/26
6	GERMAN GP	Hockenheim	28	Scuderia Ferrari SpA	G	3.5 Fiat Ferrari F93A V12		9/26
3	HUNGARIAN GP	Hungaroring	28	Scuderia Ferrari SpA	G	3.5 Fiat Ferrari F93A V12		6/26
10/ret	BELGIAN GP	Spa	28	Scuderia Ferrari SpA	G	3.5 Fiat Ferrari F93A V12	*collision-Brundle/-2 laps*	16/25
ret	ITALIAN GP	Monza	28	Scuderia Ferrari SpA	G	3.5 Fiat Ferrari F93A V12	*active system*	6/26
ret	PORTUGUESE GP	Estoril	28	Scuderia Ferrari SpA	G	3.5 Fiat Ferrari F93A V12	*active system-spun exiting pit lane*	8/26
ret	JAPANESE GP	Suzuka	28	Scuderia Ferrari SpA	G	3.5 Fiat Ferrari F93A V12	*engine*	5/24
5	AUSTRALIAN GP	Adelaide	28	Scuderia Ferrari SpA	G	3.5 Fiat Ferrari F93A V12	*1 lap behind*	6/24

1994 Championship position: 3rd Wins: 1 Pole positions: 2 Fastest laps: 0 Points scored: 41

ret	BRAZILIAN GP	Interlagos	28	Scuderia Ferrari SpA	G	3.5 Fiat Ferrari 412T1 V12	*engine-air valve leak*	17/28
2	PACIFIC GP	T.I. Circuit	28	Scuderia Ferrari SpA	G	3.5 Fiat Ferrari 412T1 V12		5/28
ret	SAN MARINO GP	Imola	28	Scuderia Ferrari SpA	G	3.5 Fiat Ferrari 412T1 V12	*led restart-later withdrew*	3/28
3	MONACO GP	Monte Carlo	28	Scuderia Ferrari SpA	G	3.5 Fiat Ferrari 412T1 V12		3/24
ret	SPANISH GP	Barcelona	28	Scuderia Ferrari SpA	G	3.5 Fiat Ferrari 412T1 V12	*gearbox*	7/27
4	CANADIAN GP	Montreal	28	Scuderia Ferrari SpA	G	3.5 Fiat Ferrari 412T1 V12		3/27
3	FRENCH GP	Magny Cours	28	Scuderia Ferrari SpA	G	3.5 Fiat Ferrari 412T1B V12		5/28
ret	BRITISH GP	Silverstone	28	Scuderia Ferrari SpA	G	3.5 Fiat Ferrari 412T1B V12	*engine*	3/28
1	GERMAN GP	Hockenheim	28	Scuderia Ferrari SpA	G	3.5 Fiat Ferrari 412T1B V12		1/28
12/ret	HUNGARIAN GP	Hungaroring	28	Scuderia Ferrari SpA	G	3.5 Fiat Ferrari 412T1B V12	*5 laps behind/engine*	4/28
ret	BELGIAN GP	Spa	28	Scuderia Ferrari SpA	G	3.5 Fiat Ferrari 412T1B V12	*engine*	11/28
2	ITALIAN GP	Monza	28	Scuderia Ferrari SpA	G	3.5 Fiat Ferrari 412T1B V12		2/28
ret	PORTUGUESE GP	Estoril	28	Scuderia Ferrari SpA	G	3.5 Fiat Ferrari 412T1B V12	*transmission*	1/28
5	EUROPEAN GP	Jerez	28	Scuderia Ferrari SpA	G	3.5 Fiat Ferrari 412T1B V12	*1 lap behind*	6/28
ret	JAPANESE GP	Suzuka	28	Scuderia Ferrari SpA	G	3.5 Fiat Ferrari 412T1B V12	*electrics*	11/28
2	AUSTRALIAN GP	Adelaide	28	Scuderia Ferrari SpA	G	3.5 Fiat Ferrari 412T1B V12		11/28

1995 Championship position: 6 Wins: 0 Pole positions: 1 Fastest laps: 2 Points scored: 31

3	BRAZILIAN GP	Interlagos	28	Scuderia Ferrari SpA	G	3.0 Fiat Ferrari 412T2 V12	*1 lap behind*	5/26
6	ARGENTINE GP	Buenos Aires	28	Scuderia Ferrari SpA	G	3.0 Fiat Ferrari 412T2 V12	*long tyre stop/2 laps behind*	8/26
3	SAN MARINO GP	Imola	28	Scuderia Ferrari SpA	G	3.0 Fiat Ferrari 412T2 V12	*FL*	2/26
3	SPANISH GP	Barcelona	28	Scuderia Ferrari SpA	G	3.0 Fiat Ferrari 412T2 V12		3/26
3	MONACO GP	Monte Carlo	28	Scuderia Ferrari SpA	G	3.0 Fiat Ferrari 412T2 V12		4/26
ret	CANADIAN GP	Montreal	28	Scuderia Ferrari SpA	G	3.0 Fiat Ferrari 412T2 V12	*collision with Brundle*	4/24
12	FRENCH GP	Magny Cours	28	Scuderia Ferrari SpA	G	3.0 Fiat Ferrari 412T2 V12	*long fuel stop/2 laps behind*	7/24
ret	BRITISH GP	Silverstone	28	Scuderia Ferrari SpA	G	3.0 Fiat Ferrari 412T2 V12	*loose wheel*	4/24
3	GERMAN GP	Hockenheim	28	Scuderia Ferrari SpA	G	3.0 Fiat Ferrari 412T2 V12		4/24
3	HUNGARIAN GP	Hungaroring	28	Scuderia Ferrari SpA	G	3.0 Fiat Ferrari 412T2 V12	*1 lap behind*	4/24
ret	BELGIAN GP	Spa	28	Scuderia Ferrari SpA	G	3.0 Fiat Ferrari 412T2 V12	*electrics*	1/24
ret	ITALIAN GP	Monza	28	Scuderia Ferrari SpA	G	3.0 Fiat Ferrari 412T2 V12	*suspension damage/FL*	3/24
4	PORTUGUESE GP	Estoril	28	Scuderia Ferrari SpA	G	3.0 Fiat Ferrari 412T2 V12		4/24
ret	EUROPEAN GP	Nürburgring	28	Scuderia Ferrari SpA	G	3.0 Fiat Ferrari 412T2 V12	*electrics*	4/24
4	PACIFIC GP	T.I. Circuit	28	Scuderia Ferrari SpA	G	3.0 Fiat Ferrari 412T2 V12	*1 lap behind*	5/24
ret	JAPANESE GP	Suzuka	28	Scuderia Ferrari SpA	G	3.0 Fiat Ferrari 412T2 V12	*electronic sensor*	5/24
ret	AUSTRALIAN GP	Adelaide	28	Scuderia Ferrari SpA	G	3.0 Fiat Ferrari 412T2 V12	*engine*	4/24

1996 Championship position: 6th Wins: 0 Pole positions: 0 Fastest laps: 1 Points scored: 21

4	AUSTRALIAN GP	Melbourne	4	Mild Seven Benetton Renault	G	3.0 Benetton 196-Renault V10		7/22
ret	BRAZILIAN GP	Interlagos	4	Mild Seven Benetton Renault	G	3.0 Benetton 196-Renault V10	*gearbox hydraulics*	8/22
ret	ARGENTINE GP	Buenos Aires	4	Mild Seven Benetton Renault	G	3.0 Benetton 196-Renault V10	*rear suspension*	5/22
9	EUROPEAN GP	Nürburgring	4	Mild Seven Benetton Renault	G	3.0 Benetton 196-Renault V10	*brake problems at start*	8/22
3	SAN MARINO GP	Imola	4	Mild Seven Benetton Renault	G	3.0 Benetton 196-Renault V10		7/22
ret	MONACO GP	Monte Carlo	4	Mild Seven Benetton Renault	G	3.0 Benetton 196-Renault V10	*gearbox sensor*	4/22
ret	SPANISH GP	Barcelona	4	Mild Seven Benetton Renault	G	3.0 Benetton 196-Renault V10	*spun off*	5/22
ret	CANADIAN GP	Montreal	4	Mild Seven Benetton Renault	G	3.0 Benetton 196-Renault V10	*spun off*	7/22
4	FRENCH GP	Magny Cours	4	Mild Seven Benetton Renault	G	3.0 Benetton 196-Renault V10		4/22
2	BRITISH GP	Silverstone	4	Mild Seven Benetton Renault	G	3.0 Benetton 196-Renault V10		7/22
ret/13	GERMAN GP	Hockenheim	4	Mild Seven Benetton Renault	G	3.0 Benetton 196-Renault V10	*engine /led race*	2/20
ret	HUNGARIAN GP	Hungaroring	4	Mild Seven Benetton Renault	G	3.0 Benetton 196-Renault V10	*engine*	6/20
6	BELGIAN GP	Spa	4	Mild Seven Benetton Renault	G	3.0 Benetton 196-Renault V10	*spin/FL*	5/20
ret	ITALIAN GP	Monza	4	Mild Seven Benetton Renault	G	3.0 Benetton 196-Renault V10	*hydraulics*	8/20
6	PORTUGUESE GP	Estoril	4	Mild Seven Benetton Renault	G	3.0 Benetton 196-Renault V10	*collision with Irvine at finish*	5/20
4	JAPANESE GP	Suzuka	4	Mild Seven Benetton Renault	G	3.0 Benetton 196-Renault V10	*collision with Irvine*	4/20

1997 Championship position: 6th Wins: 1 Pole positions: 1 Fastest laps: 2 Points scored: 27

4	AUSTRALIAN GP	Melbourne	8	Mild Seven Benetton Renault	G	3.0 Benetton B197--Renault V10		10/24
2	BRAZILIAN GP	Interlagos	8	Mild Seven Benetton Renault	G	3.0 Benetton B197--Renault V10		3/22
6	ARGENTINE GP	Buenos Aires	8	Mild Seven Benetton Renault	G	3.0 Benetton B197--Renault V10	*FL*	12/22
ret	SAN MARINO GP	Imola	8	Mild Seven Benetton Renault	G	3.0 Benetton B197--Renault V10	*spun off*	11/22
9	MONACO GP	Monte Carlo	8	Mild Seven Benetton Renault	G	3.0 Benetton B197--Renault V10	*pit stop-crash damage/-2 laps*	17/22
10	SPANISH GP	Barcelona	8	Mild Seven Benetton Renault	G	3.0 Benetton B197--Renault V10	*blistered tyres*	6/22
1	GERMAN GP	Hockenheim	8	Mild Seven Benetton Renault	G	3.0 Benetton B197--Renault V10	*FL*	1/22
8	HUNGARIAN GP	Hungaroring	8	Mild Seven Benetton Renault	G	3.0 Benetton B197--Renault V10		7/22
6*	BELGIAN GP	Spa	8	Mild Seven Benetton Renault	G	3.0 Benetton B197--Renault V10	*3rd place car dsq*	15/22
7	ITALIAN GP	Monza	8	Mild Seven Benetton Renault	G	3.0 Benetton B197--Renault V10		7/22
10	AUSTRIAN GP	A1-Ring	8	Mild Seven Benetton Renault	G	3.0 Benetton B197--Renault V10	*started from pits/-1 lap*	18/22
4	LUXEMBOURG GP	Nürburgring	8	Mild Seven Benetton Renault	G	3.0 Benetton B197--Renault V10		7/22
8	JAPANESE GP	Suzuka	8	Mild Seven Benetton Renault	G	3.0 Benetton B197--Renault V10		5/22
4*	EUROPEAN GP	Jerez	8	Mild Seven Benetton Renault	G	3.0 Benetton B197--Renault V10	*5th place car dsq*	8/22

GP Starts: 210   GP Wins: 10   Pole positions: 12   Fastest laps: 21   Points: 385

ÉRIC BERNARD

A four-times French karting champion, Bernard showed immediate ability in a Winfield School competition (in which he beat Jean Alesi) and his prize was a season in Formule Renault. Fifth place in the 1984 championship formed the platform for a successful title bid the following season.

He had little money but decided to tackle the French F3 series. Running his own Martini-Alfa, Éric finished a creditable fifth, and armed with a Ralt for 1987 ran old rival Alesi and his mighty ORECA team very close as the pair dominated proceedings.

The backing of Winfield and Elf facilitated the step up into F3000 and after a false start with a works Ralt Bernard switched to Bromley Motorsport to kick-start his season. A fine second place in the final round at Dijon led to a place in the DAMS Lola team for 1989. He won at Jerez, but was out of luck elsewhere and, compounding this with some unforced errors, could only finish a disappointed third in the championship. The year had its compensations, though, a couple of drives for Larrousse in mid-season paving the way for a full-time ride in 1990, with a magnificent fourth place in the British Grand Prix the highlight of his first full season. The Larrousse team lost the use of Lamborghini engines in 1991, putting Éric into the also-ran category, and his season ended disastrously when he sustained a broken leg in a practice crash at the Japanese GP.

With the injury proving slow to heal, Bernard was sidelined for the following season, but he was not forgotten by his long-time sponsors Elf and became the Ligier team's test driver in 1993. The oil giant then placed their faith in him for 1994, and Ligier gave him a contract for the season alongside newcomer Olivier Panis. Once the Briatore/Walkinshaw axis took control, however, the student remained in situ while the tutor, despite his third-place finish in the crash-decimated German GP, was dumped after the Portuguese race and replaced by Johnny Herbert. As some recompense it was arranged for him to take the Englishman's place at Team Lotus for the European GP at Jerez but after he finished in 18th place, three laps behind, his departure from the Grand Prix stage was barely noticed.

Éric has since followed many other erstwhile unemployed Grand Prix drivers into the world of sports car racing. After contesting the Global GT series in a Ferrari, he moved to DAMS to help develop their front-engined Panoz-Ford. The 1997 season brought little but a spate of retirements, but the following term he began an excellent partnership with David Brabham as the car became a contender for honours.

Outright victories finally came in 1999, the Frenchman sharing wins at Portland, Road Atlanta, Donington, the Nürburgring and Kyalami with Brabham, Wallace and Gounon. When DAMS were chosen to run Cadillac's sports challenger in 2000, the team lost little time in ensuring that they had Bernard's signature on a three-year contract.

BERNARD, Éric (F) b 26/8/1964, Istres

	1989	Championship position: Unplaced						
	Race	Circuit	No	Entrant	Tyres	Car/Engine	Comment	Q Pos/Entries
11/ret	FRENCH GP	Paul Ricard	29	Equipe Larrousse	G	3.5 Lola LC89-Lamborghini V12	engine/3 laps behind	15/39
ret	BRITISH GP	Silverstone	29	Equipe Larrousse	G	3.5 Lola LC89-Lamborghini V12	gearbox	13/39
	1990	Championship position: 13th Wins: 0 Pole positions: 0 Fastest laps: 0 Points scored: 5						
8	US GP (PHOENIX)	Phoenix	29	Espo Larrousse F1	G	3.5 Lola LC89-Lamborghini V12	spin/1 lap behind	15/35
ret	BRAZILIAN GP	Interlagos	29	Espo Larrousse F1	G	3.5 Lola LC89-Lamborghini V12	gearbox	11/35
13/ret	SAN MARINO GP	Imola	29	Espo Larrousse F1	G	3.5 Lola 90-Lamborghini V12	gearbox/5 laps behind	14/34
6	MONACO GP	Monte Carlo	29	Espo Larrousse F1	G	3.5 Lola 90-Lamborghini V12	2 laps behind	24/35
9	CANADIAN GP	Montreal	29	Espo Larrousse F1	G	3.5 Lola 90-Lamborghini V12	3 laps behind	23/35
ret	MEXICAN GP	Mexico City	29	Espo Larrousse F1	G	3.5 Lola 90-Lamborghini V12	brakes-spun off	26/35
8	FRENCH GP	Paul Ricard	29	Espo Larrousse F1	G	3.5 Lola 90-Lamborghini V12	pit stop-tyres/1 lap behind	11/35
4	BRITISH GP	Silverstone	29	Espo Larrousse F1	G	3.5 Lola 90-Lamborghini V12		8/35
ret	GERMAN GP	Hockenheim	29	Espo Larrousse F1	G	3.5 Lola 90-Lamborghini V12	fuel pressure	12/35

6	HUNGARIAN GP	Hungaroring	29	Espo Larrousse F1	G	3.5 Lola 90-Lamborghini V12	brake problems	12/35
9	BELGIAN GP	Spa	29	Espo Larrousse F1	G	3.5 Lola 90-Lamborghini V12	long pit stop-tyres/-1 lap	15/33
ret	ITALIAN GP	Monza	29	Espo Larrousse F1	G	3.5 Lola 90-Lamborghini V12	clutch	13/33
ret	PORTUGUESE GP	Estoril	29	Espo Larrousse F1	G	3.5 Lola 90-Lamborghini V12	gearbox	10/33
ret	SPANISH GP	Jerez	29	Espo Larrousse F1	G	3.5 Lola 90-Lamborghini V12	gearbox	18/33
ret	JAPANESE GP	Suzuka	29	Espo Larrousse F1	G	3.5 Lola 90-Lamborghini V12	engine oil leak and fire	17/30
ret	AUSTRALIAN GP	Adelaide	29	Espo Larrousse F1	G	3.5 Lola 90-Lamborghini V12	gear selection	23/30

1991   Championship position: 18th=   Wins: 0   Pole positions: 0   Fastest laps: 0   Points scored: 1

ret	US GP (PHOENIX)	Phoenix	29	Larrousse F1	G	3.5 Larrousse Lola L91-Cosworth V8	engine	19/34
ret	BRAZILIAN GP	Interlagos	29	Larrousse F1	G	3.5 Larrousse Lola L91-Cosworth V8	clutch	11/34
ret	SAN MARINO GP	Imola	29	Larrousse F1	G	3.5 Larrousse Lola L91-Cosworth V8	engine-water leak	17/34
9	MONACO GP	Monte Carlo	29	Larrousse F1	G	3.5 Larrousse Lola L91-Cosworth V8	2 laps behind	21/34
ret	CANADIAN GP	Montreal	29	Larrousse F1	G	3.5 Larrousse Lola L91-Cosworth V8	gearbox	19/34
6	MEXICAN GP	Mexico City	29	Larrousse F1	G	3.5 Larrousse Lola L91-Cosworth V8	1 lap behind	18/34
ret	FRENCH GP	Magny Cours	29	Larrousse F1	G	3.5 Larrousse Lola L91-Cosworth V8	puncture	23/34
ret	BRITISH GP	Silverstone	29	Larrousse F1	G	3.5 Larrousse Lola L91-Cosworth V8	gearbox	21/34
ret	GERMAN GP	Hockenheim	29	Larrousse F1	G	3.5 Larrousse Lola L91-Cosworth V8	transmission	25/34
ret	HUNGARIAN GP	Hungaroring	29	Larrousse F1	G	3.5 Larrousse Lola L91-Cosworth V8	engine	21/34
ret	BELGIAN GP	Spa	29	Larrousse F1	G	3.5 Larrousse Lola L91-Cosworth V8	gearbox	20/34
ret	ITALIAN GP	Monza	29	Larrousse F1	G	3.5 Larrousse Lola L91-Cosworth V8	engine	24/34
dnq	PORTUGUESE GP	Estoril	29	Larrousse F1	G	3.5 Larrousse Lola L91-Cosworth V8	gearbox	27/34
ret	SPANISH GP	Barcelona	29	Larrousse F1	G	3.5 Larrousse Lola L91-Cosworth V8	collision with Boutsen-lap 1	23/33
dnp	JAPANESE GP	Suzuka	29	Larrousse F1	G	3.5 Larrousse Lola L91-Cosworth V8	free practice accident-broken leg	–/–

1994   Championship position: 18th=   Wins: 0   Pole positions: 0   Fastest laps: 0   Points scored: 4

ret	BRAZILIAN GP	Interlagos	25	Ligier Gitanes Blondes	G	3.5 Ligier JS39B-Renault V10	multiple accident	20/28
10	PACIFIC GP	T.I. Circuit	25	Ligier Gitanes Blondes	G	3.5 Ligier JS39B-Renault V10	delayed fuel stop/-5 laps	18/28
12	SAN MARINO GP	Imola	25	Ligier Gitanes Blondes	G	3.5 Ligier JS39B-Renault V10	3 laps behind	17/28
ret	MONACO GP	Monte Carlo	25	Ligier Gitanes Blondes	G	3.5 Ligier JS39B-Renault V10	spun off	21/24
8	SPANISH GP	Barcelona	25	Ligier Gitanes Blondes	G	3.5 Ligier JS39B-Renault V10	3 laps behind	20/27
13	CANADIAN GP	Montreal	25	Ligier Gitanes Blondes	G	3.5 Ligier JS39B-Renault V10	3 laps behind	24/27
ret	FRENCH GP	Magny Cours	25	Ligier Gitanes Blondes	G	3.5 Ligier JS39B-Renault V10	gearbox	15/28
13*	BRITISH GP	Silverstone	25	Ligier Gitanes Blondes	G	3.5 Ligier JS39B-Renault V10	*2nd place car dsq/-2 laps	23/28
3	GERMAN GP	Hockenheim	25	Ligier Gitanes Blondes	G	3.5 Ligier JS39B-Renault V10		14/28
10	HUNGARIAN GP	Hungaroring	25	Ligier Gitanes Blondes	G	3.5 Ligier JS39B-Renault V10	2 laps behind	18/28
10*	BELGIAN GP	Spa	25	Ligier Gitanes Blondes	G	3.5 Ligier JS39B-Renault V10	*1st place car dsq/-2 laps	16/28
7	ITALIAN GP	Monza	25	Ligier Gitanes Blondes	G	3.5 Ligier JS39B-Renault V10	1 lap behind	12/28
10	PORTUGUESE GP	Estoril	25	Ligier Gitanes Blondes	G	3.5 Ligier JS39B-Renault V10	1 lap behind	21/28
18	EUROPEAN GP	Jerez	11	Team Lotus	G	3.5 Lotus 109-Mugen Honda V10	3 laps behind	22/28

GP Starts: 45   GP Wins: 0   Pole positions: 0   Fastest laps: 0   Points: 10

MIKE BEUTTLER

Born in Cairo in 1940 of English parents while his father was serving in the Army, Mike became involved in the motor racing world immediately upon leaving school at the age of 16, assuming administrative duties with the Chequered Flag team. He had occasional chances to drive their front-engined Gemini car, but only when he struck out on his own – at the comparatively late age of 24 – with a Brabham F3 in club and Libre events did his racing career start in earnest.

With the backing of stockbroker colleagues Ralph Clarke and David Mordaunt – which was to be so vital to his progress to Formula 1 – Beuttler moved into F3 for 1969 with encouraging results given the calibre of opposition. Staying with the class for another season, Mike won three high-profile events, at Silverstone, Brands Hatch and Montlhéry, gaining third place in the Shellsport F3 championship and second place in that year's Grovewood Awards for his efforts.

For 1971 ambitious plans were laid to race a March 712. Alistair Guthrie joined the roster of backers and with the factory 'overseeing' his efforts, Mike undertook a full European F2 series. However, it was to prove a bitter disappointment, with the car beset by sundry maladies until the last round when he won the Madunina GP at Vallelunga. March had also helped him into Formula 1, without any great success.

It was the same recipe for 1972, with the addition of another backer – Jack Durlacher – to help pay the bills but no worthwhile results in Grands Prix. The most interesting aspect of the season, in fact, was the team's decision to adapt their 722 F2 car to accept the Cosworth engine. So much better was this machine's handling than that of the notorious 721X that the full-works cars were quickly consigned to history and Peterson and Lauda found themseves the beneficiaries.

Beuttler and his partners gave it one more shot in 1973, starting the season with the old car, but he was no more competitive when the new March 731 finally arrived. Mike called it quits and, after a single outing in the Brands Hatch 1000 Km in 1974, turned his back on racing and went into business. He later moved to San Francisco, where he died at the tragically young age of 45.

BEUTTLER, Mike (GB) b 13/8/1940, Cairo, Egypt – d 29/12/1988, San Francisco, California, USA

1971 Championship position: Unplaced

	Race	Circuit	No	Entrant	Tyres	Car/Engine	Comment	Q Pos/Entries
ret	BRITISH GP	Silverstone	6	Clarke-Mordaunt-Guthrie Racing	F	3.0 March 711-Cosworth V8	oil pressure	20/24
dsq	GERMAN GP	Nürburgring	28	Clarke-Mordaunt-Guthrie Racing	F	3.0 March 711-Cosworth V8	puncture-wrong entry to pits	22/23
nc	AUSTRIAN GP	Österreichring	27	Clarke-Mordaunt-Guthrie Racing	F	3.0 March 711-Cosworth V8	pit stop-engine/7 laps behind	20/22
ret	ITALIAN GP	Monza	24	Clarke-Mordaunt-Guthrie Racing	F	3.0 March 711-Cosworth V8	engine	16/24
nc	CANADIAN GP	Mosport Park	19	STP March	F	3.0 March 711-Cosworth V8	pit stop/8 laps behind	22/27

1972 Championship position: Unplaced

	Race	Circuit	No	Entrant	Tyres	Car/Engine	Comment	Q Pos/Entries
dnq	SPANISH GP	Jarama	23	Clarke-Mordaunt-Guthrie Racing	F	3.0 March 721G-Cosworth V8		26/26
13	MONACO GP	Monte Carlo	5	Clarke-Mordaunt-Guthrie Racing	F	3.0 March 721G-Cosworth V8	4 laps behind	=22/25
ret	BELGIAN GP	Nivelles	14	Clarke-Mordaunt-Guthrie Racing	F	3.0 March 721G-Cosworth V8	driveshaft	22/26
ret	FRENCH GP	Clermont Ferrand	15	Clarke-Mordaunt-Guthrie Racing	F	3.0 March 721G-Cosworth V8	out of fuel	27/29
13	BRITISH GP	Brands Hatch	31	Clarke-Mordaunt-Guthrie Racing	F	3.0 March 721G-Cosworth V8	7 laps behind	23/27
8	GERMAN GP	Nürburgring	28	Clarke-Mordaunt-Guthrie Racing	F	3.0 March 721G-Cosworth V8		27/27
ret	AUSTRIAN GP	Österreichring	3	Clarke-Mordaunt-Guthrie Racing	F	3.0 March 721G-Cosworth V8	fuel metering unit	25/26
10	ITALIAN GP	Monza	16	Clarke-Mordaunt-Guthrie Racing	F	3.0 March 721G-Cosworth V8	1 lap behind	25/27
nc	CANADIAN GP	Mosport Park	27	Clarke-Mordaunt-Guthrie Racing	F	3.0 March 721G-Cosworth V8	spin-pit stop/21 laps behind	24/25
13	US GP	Watkins Glen	6	Clarke-Mordaunt-Guthrie Racing	F	3.0 March 721G-Cosworth V8	incident with Lauda/-2 laps	21/32

1973 Championship position: Unplaced

	Race	Circuit	No	Entrant	Tyres	Car/Engine	Comment	Q Pos/Entries
10/ret	ARGENTINE GP	Buenos Aires	22	Clarke-Mordaunt-Guthrie-Durlacher	G	3.0 March 721G-Cosworth V8	radius rod/6 laps behind	18/19
ret	BRAZILIAN GP	Interlagos	12	Clarke-Mordaunt-Guthrie-Durlacher	G	3.0 March 721G-Cosworth V8	overheating	19/20
nc	SOUTH AFRICAN GP	Kyalami	24	Clarke-Mordaunt-Guthrie-Durlacher	G	3.0 March 721G-Cosworth V8	pit stops/14 laps behind	23/25
7	SPANISH GP	Montjuich Park	12	Clarke-Mordaunt-Guthrie-Durlacher	G	3.0 March 721G/731-Cosworth V8	1 lap behind	19/22
11/ret	BELGIAN GP	Zolder	15	Clarke-Mordaunt-Guthrie-Durlacher	G	3.0 March 721G/731-Cosworth V8	spun off/7 laps behind	20/23
ret	MONACO GP	Monte Carlo	15	Clarke-Mordaunt-Guthrie-Durlacher	G	3.0 March 721G/731-Cosworth V8	engine	21/26
8	SWEDISH GP	Anderstorp	15	Clarke-Mordaunt-Guthrie-Durlacher	G	3.0 March 721G/731-Cosworth V8	3 laps behind	21/22
11	BRITISH GP	Silverstone	15	Clarke-Mordaunt-Guthrie-Durlacher	G	3.0 March 721G/731-Cosworth V8	2 laps behind	=23/29
ret	DUTCH GP	Zandvoort	15	Clarke-Mordaunt-Guthrie-Durlacher	F	3.0 March 721G/731-Cosworth V8	electrics	23/24
16	GERMAN GP	Nürburgring	15	Clarke-Mordaunt-Guthrie-Durlacher	F	3.0 March 721G/731-Cosworth V8	1 lap behind	21/23
ret	AUSTRIAN GP	Österreichring	15	Clarke-Mordaunt-Guthrie-Durlacher	F	3.0 March 721G/731-Cosworth V8	hit by Hailwood-broken oil cooler	11/25
ret	ITALIAN GP	Monza	15	Clarke-Mordaunt-Guthrie-Durlacher	F	3.0 March 721G/731-Cosworth V8	broken gear lever	12/25
ret	CANADIAN GP	Mosport Park	15	Clarke-Mordaunt-Guthrie-Durlacher	F	3.0 March 721G/731-Cosworth V8	engine	21/26
10	US GP	Watkins Glen	15	Clarke-Mordaunt-Guthrie-Durlacher	F	3.0 March 721G/731-Cosworth V8	1 lap behind	27/28

GP Starts: 28   GP Wins: 0   Pole positions: 0   Fastest laps: 0   Points: 0

BIANCHI, Lucien (B) b 10/11/1934, Milan, Italy – d. 30/3/1969, Le Mans Circuit, France

1959 Championship position: Unplaced

	Race	Circuit	No	Entrant	Tyres	Car/Engine	Comment	Q Pos/Entries
dnq	MONACO GP	Monte Carlo	10	Equipe Nationale Belge	D	1.5 Cooper T51-Climax 4 F2		19/24

1960 Championship position: 19th=   Wins: 0   Pole positions: 0   Fastest laps: 0   Points scored: 1

	Race	Circuit	No	Entrant	Tyres	Car/Engine	Comment	Q Pos/Entries
6	BELGIAN GP	Spa	32	Equipe Nationale Belge	D	2.5 Cooper T51-Climax 4	pit stop-drive shaft/-8 laps	15/18
ret	FRENCH GP	Reims	36	Fred Tuck Cars	D	2.5 Cooper T51-Climax 4	transmission	15/23
ret	BRITISH GP	Silverstone	24	Fred Tuck Cars	D	2.5 Cooper T51-Climax 4	engine	17/25

1961 Championship position: Unplaced

	Race	Circuit	No	Entrant	Tyres	Car/Engine	Comment	Q Pos/Entries
dnq	MONACO GP	Monte Carlo	10	Equipe Nationale Belge	D	1.5 Emeryson 1001-Maserati 4		19/21
ret	BELGIAN GP	Spa	12	Equipe Nationale Belge	D	1.5 Lotus 18-Climax 4	hired Seidel's car/oil pipe	– /25
dns	"	"	12	Equipe Nationale Belge	D	1.5 Emeryson 1001-Maserati 4	car uncompetitive	– / –
ret	FRENCH GP	Reims	28	UDT Laystall Racing Team	D	1.5 Lotus 18/21-Climax 4	overheating/clutch	19/26
ret	BRITISH GP	Aintree	32	UDT Laystall Racing Team	D	1.5 Lotus 18/21-Climax 4	gearbox	30/30

1962 Championship position: Unplaced

	Race	Circuit	No	Entrant	Tyres	Car/Engine	Comment	Q Pos/Entries
9	BELGIAN GP	Spa	19	Equipe Nationale Belge	D	1.5 Lotus 18/21-Climax 4	3 laps behind	18/20
16	GERMAN GP	Nürburgring	21	Equipe Nationale Belge	D	1.5 ENB-Maserati 4	1 lap behind	25/30

1963 Championship position: Unplaced

	Race	Circuit	No	Entrant	Tyres	Car/Engine	Comment	Q Pos/Entries
ret	BELGIAN GP	Spa	22	Reg Parnell (Racing)	D	1.5 Lola 4-Climax V8	accident in rain	16/20

1965 Championship position: Unplaced

	Race	Circuit	No	Entrant	Tyres	Car/Engine	Comment	Q Pos/Entries
12	BELGIAN GP	Spa	27	Scuderia Centro Sud	D	1.5 BRM P57 V8	3 laps behind	17/21

1968 Championship position: 17th=   Wins: 0   Pole positions: 0   Fastest laps: 0   Points scored: 5

	Race	Circuit	No	Entrant	Tyres	Car/Engine	Comment	Q Pos/Entries
3	MONACO GP	Monte Carlo	7	Cooper Car Co	F	3.0 Cooper T86B-BRM V12	4 laps behind	14/18
6	BELGIAN GP	Spa	15	Cooper Car Co	F	3.0 Cooper T86B-BRM V12	2 laps behind	12/18
ret	DUTCH GP	Zandvoort	14	Cooper Car Co	F	3.0 Cooper T86B-BRM V12	accident	18/19
ret	GERMAN GP	Nürburgring	19	Cooper Car Co	F	3.0 Cooper T86B-BRM V12	fuel leak	19/20
nc	CANADIAN GP	St Jovite	20	Cooper Car Co	F	3.0 Cooper T86B-BRM V12	pit stop-misfire/-34 laps	19/22
ret	US GP	Watkins Glen	19	Cooper Car Co	F	3.0 Cooper T86B-BRM V12	clutch	20/21
ret	MEXICAN GP	Mexico City	19	Cooper Car Co	F	3.0 Cooper T86B-BRM V12	engine	21/21

GP Starts: 17   GP Wins: 0   Pole positions: 0   Fastest laps: 0   Points: 6

BIANCO, Gino (I) b 22/7/1916, Milan, Italy – d circa 1980,

1952 Championship position: Unplaced

	Race	Circuit	No	Entrant	Tyres	Car/Engine	Comment	Q Pos/Entries
18	BRITISH GP	Silverstone	34	Escuderia Bandeirantes	P	2.0 Maserati A6GCM 6	8 laps behind	28/32
ret	GERMAN GP	Nürburgring	115	Escuderia Bandeirantes	P	2.0 Maserati A6GCM 6		16/32
ret	DUTCH GP	Zandvoort	18	Escuderia Bandeirantes	P	2.0 Maserati A6GCM 6	rear axle	12/18
ret	ITALIAN GP	Monza	46	Escuderia Bandeirantes	P	2.0 Maserati A6GCM 6	mechanical	24/35

GP Starts: 4   GP Wins: 0   Pole positions: 0   Fastest laps: 0   Points: 0

LUCIEN BIANCHI

Born in Italy, Lucien moved to Belgium as a child, when his father went to work as a racing mechanic for Johnny Claes. The young Bianchi nurtured hopes of a competition career, and in fact shared a Lancia with Claes in the 1955 Liège-Rome-Liège Rally, taking third place in what proved to be the terminally ill Claes' last event. Gradually Bianchi began to build his career in both sports cars and rallying, taking a class win with a Ferrari at Le Mans in 1957, and the first of three Tour de France rally wins (1957, 1958 and 1964).

Joining Equipe Nationale Belge, Lucien scored a third place at Pau in 1959, and a fourth the following year in the non-title South African GP, but the Belgian team was hardly front rank, and most of his success during this period was in sports cars, Bianchi winning the 1960 Paris 1000 Km with Gendebien in ENB's Ferrari, and the Sebring 12 Hours and the Angola GP in 1962.

Between 1963 and 1967, Formula 1 opportunities practically dried up, but Lucien busied himself in virtually every other form of competition – sports car and GT racing, Formula 2 (taking second on aggregate at Zolder in 1964) and Formula 3 as well as selected rallies. A reliable endurance racer, Bianchi became much in demand, driving works Porsches and Fords on occasion in addition to his regular seat in the Equipe Nationale Belge,

while the 1967 season saw him try his hand at the Indianapolis 500. Having comfortably posted a good qualifying time, he flew back to race in the Nürburgring 1000 Km for Porsche, where an electrical failure on the last lap cost him the race win and dropped him to fourth place. Afterwards he was given the news that he had been 'bumped' from the grid at Indy.

Bianchi found a regular Grand Prix drive at last in 1968, albeit in the fading Cooper team, and scored points in his first two races. However, he enjoyed his best-ever sports car season, winning the Le Mans 24 Hours with Rodriguez and the Watkins Glen 6 Hours with Ickx for John Wyer, and taking the Circuit of Mugello in a works Alfa Romeo. At the end of the year Bianchi took part in the London-Sydney Marathon, and his Citroën was in a seemingly unassailable lead, less than 100 miles from the finish, when the car was involved in an accident with a non-competing vehicle while his co-driver Ogier was at the wheel, leaving Lucien with a broken ankle and shock.

Recovered from this crushing disappointment, Bianchi signed for Autodelta to race their Alfa T33s, but while practising at the Le Mans test weekend he lost control on the Mulsanne Straight. The car veered across the track into a telegraph pole, disintegrated and burst into flames, and the luckless Bianchi was killed instantly.

GINO BIANCO

Bianco was born in Milan and moved to Brazil when still a child, aged 12. He gained a foothold in motor sport as a mechanic, but soon began driving in local hill-climbs, where one of his best successes came in the Gavea event of 1951 in a Maserati. With the patronage of Eitel Cantoni he was one of the Escuderia Bandeirantes squad who ventured to Europe in 1952, but no finishes were recorded in any of the races in which he competed.

He returned to Brazil and raced in 1953 at national level, but little is known about his subsequent whereabouts or activities, even in his country of adoption.

BINDER, Hans (A) b 12/6/1948, Zell am Ziller, nr Innsbruck

	1976	Championship position: Unplaced							
	Race	*Circuit*	*No*	*Entrant*	*Tyres*	*Car/Engine*	*Comment*		*Q Pos/Entries*
ret	AUSTRIAN GP	Österreichring	22	Team Ensign	G	3.0 Ensign N176-Cosworth V8	*throttle cable*		19/25
ret	JAPANESE GP	Mount Fuji	21	Walter Wolf Racing	G	3.0 Williams FW05-Cosworth V8	*wheel bearing*		25/27
	1977	Championship position: Unplaced							
ret	ARGENTINE GP	Buenos Aires	18	Durex Team Surtees	G	3.0 Surtees TS19-Cosworth V8	*damaged nose section*		18/21
ret	BRAZILIAN GP	Interlagos	18	Durex Team Surtees	G	3.0 Surtees TS19-Cosworth V8	*hit kerb-suspension damage*		20/22
11	SOUTH AFRICAN GP	Kyalami	18	Durex Team Surtees	G	3.0 Surtees TS19-Cosworth V8	*1 lap behind*		19/23
11	US GP WEST	Long Beach	18	Durex Team Surtees	G	3.0 Surtees TS19-Cosworth V8	*3 laps behind*		19/22
9	SPANISH GP	Jarama	18	Durex Team Surtees	G	3.0 Surtees TS19-Cosworth V8	*2 laps behind*		20/31
ret	MONACO GP	Monte Carlo	18	Durex Team Surtees	G	3.0 Surtees TS19-Cosworth V8	*fuel injection*		19/26
12	AUSTRIAN GP	Österreichring	33	ATS Racing Team	G	3.0 Penske PC4-Cosworth V8	*1 lap behind*		19/30
8	DUTCH GP	Zandvoort	35	ATS Racing Team	G	3.0 Penske PC4-Cosworth V8	*2 laps behind*		18/34
dnq	ITALIAN GP	Monza	33	ATS Racing Team	G	3.0 Penske PC4-Cosworth V8			32/34
11	US GP EAST	Watkins Glen	18	Durex Team Surtees	G	3.0 Surtees TS19-Cosworth V8	*2 laps behind*		25/27
ret	CANADIAN GP	Mosport Park	18	Durex Team Surtees	G	3.0 Surtees TS19-Cosworth V8	*collision with Keegan*		24/27
ret	JAPANESE GP	Mount Fuji	18	Durex Team Surtees	G	3.0 Surtees TS19-Cosworth V8	*collision with Takahara*		21/23
	1978	Championship position: Unplaced							
dnq	AUSTRIAN GP	Österreichring	10	ATS Racing Team	G	3.0 ATS HS1-Cosworth V8			30/31

GP Starts: 13   GP Wins: 0   Pole positions: 0   Fastest laps: 0   Points: 0

HANS BINDER

With promising performances in Formula Ford and the Polifac German F3 championship behind him, this protégé of Dr Helmut Marko entered Formula 2 in 1975 with a privately run March 752. He found the car a handful to drive and, although he finished second at the Salzburgring, an accident at Enna saw him switch to a works-loaned Chevron for the last four races.

Binder found himself in the same position the following season; after the first five races of the F2 campaign with the troubled Osella team brought no reward, a deal was struck with Fred Opert and Hans was back in a Chevron. Things improved rapidly, the Austrian claiming fourth place in the final three races at Estoril, Nogaro and Hockenheim.

One-off drives for Ensign in Austria (replacing a disaffected Amon) and for Wolf in Japan (the injured Ickx and local driver Kuwashima) whetted his appetite for 1977. With Team Surtees providing the bread and ATS-Penske the jam in his season, it would be charitable to say his performances were somewhat lacklustre, and in Grand Prix terms he was redundant.

CLEMENTE BIONDETTI

Biondetti's racing career began in 1923 on motor cycles, the Italian turning to cars in 1927. After early success in a Talbot, he joined the Maserati factory team in 1931, finishing third in both the Rome and French GPs.

His reputation really grew with Alfa Romeo, Biondetti valiantly hanging on to a trio of Mercedes in the Tripoli GP of 1937 as the rest of the field surrendered, before the engine blew. The 1938 season saw the first of his wins in the Mille Miglia and he was at his peak as a driver as war broke out. Despite being 49 when racing resumed, Biondetti took a hat-trick of wins (1947-49) in his beloved Mille Miglia as well as emerging triumphant in the Tour of Sicily in both 1948 and 1949. His win in the rain-soaked 1947 race was quite brilliant. Minus two gears and suffering fuel-feed problems with his Alfa Romeo, the veteran Italian beat the legendary Nuvolari into second place. Eschewing the pure Ferrari sports cars which had brought him his other recent successes, Biondetti built a Ferrari-Jaguar hybrid which failed at the Italian GP in 1950 and disappointed elsewhere.

Not surprisingly he then returned to the trusty steeds of the Prancing Horse, sharing Stagnoli's car to take third place in the 1952 Monaco Grand Prix, run that year for sports cars. The same year he was second in the Acerbo Cup, a 12-hour race at Pescara. For 1953 he raced the rival Lancia cars but returned to the fold in 1954 – his final season – marking his last appearance in the Mille Miglia with a fourth place. Clemente had known that he had been suffering from cancer for several years and felt that to continue racing any longer could endanger others. A year later he was dead.

BIONDETTI, Clemente (I) b 18/8/1898, Buddusó, Sardinia – d 24/2/1955, Florence

	1950	Championship position: Unplaced							
	Race	*Circuit*	*No*	*Entrant*	*Tyres*	*Car/Engine*	*Comment*		*Q Pos/Entries*
ret	ITALIAN GP	Monza	22	Clemente Biondetti	–	3.4 Ferrari 166S-Jaguar 6 sports	*engine*		25/27

GP Starts: 1   GP Wins: 0   Pole positions: 0   Fastest laps: 0   Points: 0

'B BIRA'

Prince Birabongse Bhanuban of Siam (now Thailand) was the true title of this aristocrat, who was educated at Eton and Cambridge before studying sculpture. In the mid-thirties he lived in London under the care of his cousin Prince Chula and, after 'Bira' had tried his hand with a Riley Imp and an MG Magnette, Chula gave him an ERA for his 21st birthday. Establishing the endearingly titled 'White Mouse Stable', 'Bira' won many races in a trio of ERAs in the immediate pre-war years, becoming one of the marque's most famous exponents. He also raced the ex-Whitney Straight Maserati and, less successfully, the ex-Seaman Delage, and his outstanding performances were rewarded with the BRDC Road Racing Gold Star in 1936, 1937 and 1938.

After the war 'Bira' was back in his ERA but soon switched to Maserati, winning the 1947 GP des Frontières at Chimay. He was to continue to race in partnership with Chula until the end of the 1948 season, but had meanwhile ventured out in an F2 Simca Gordini, winning a race at Skarpnack, Sweden.

Taking his Maserati San Remo into the Enrico Platé stable, 'Bira' had a busy year in 1949, which started with two fifths at Buenos Aires and a second to Fangio at Mar del Plata. He then returned to Europe and produced a run of excellent performances which brought second places at the Albi, French, San Remo and Rousillon Grands Prix, and third places in the Italian and Zandvoort GPs.

When the World Championship was inaugurated in 1950, 'Bira' managed a fourth place at Bremgarten but little else, as the cars were really outclassed. The following year he put an OSCA V12 engine into the Maserati, winning only the five-lap Libre Richmond Trophy race at Goodwood. He continued to race the OSCA in Formula 1 races into 1952, but also handled the fast but fragile works Gordini. It was a frustrating time for the little prince, who seemed to lose interest after a long run of bad luck. Nevertheless he returned to the track occasionally in 1953 with the Connaught team until his own Maserati A6GCM was delivered late in the year. The acquisition of a true Maserati 250F early in 1954 seemed to whet 'Bira's's appetite for racing and, in non-championship races, he won at Chimay and took second places at Rouen and Pescara, while in the French GP at Reims he took his best championship placing for some years. Early in 1955 he scored his last win in the New Zealand GP at Ardmore, before returning to Europe to finish sixth at the Bordeaux GP and third in the International Trophy – his final race before his sudden decision to retire.

'BIRA, B' (Prince Birabongse) (T) b 15/7/1914, Bangkok – d 23/12/1985, Baron's Court, London, England

	1950	Championship position: 6th		Wins: 0	Pole positions: 0	Fastest laps: 0	Points scored: 5			
	Race	Circuit	No	Entrant		Tyres	Car/Engine		Comment	Q Pos/Entries
ret	BRITISH GP	Silverstone	21	Enrico Platé		P	1.5 s/c Maserati 4CLT/48 4		fuel feed	5/21
5	MONACO GP	Monte Carlo	50	Enrico Platé		P	1.5 s/c Maserati 4CLT/48 4		5 laps behind	15/21
4	SWISS GP	Bremgarten	30	Enrico Platé		P	1.5 s/c Maserati 4CLT/48 4		2 laps behind	8/18
ret	ITALIAN GP	Monza	30	Enrico Platé		P	1.5 s/c Maserati 4CLT/48 4		engine	15/27
	1951	Championship position: Unplaced								
ret	SPANISH GP	Pedralbes	18	'B Bira'		P	4.5 Maserati 4CLT/48-OSCA V12		engine on lap 1	19/20
	1952	Championship position: Unplaced								
ret	SWISS GP	Bremgarten	10	Equipe Gordini		E	1.5 Gordini Type 15 4		engine	11/21
10	BELGIAN GP	Spa	20	Equipe Gordini		E	1.5 Gordini Type 15 4		4 laps behind	18/22
ret	FRENCH GP	Rouen	6	Equipe Gordini		E	2.0 Gordini Type 16 6		rear axle	8/20
11	BRITISH GP	Silverstone	26	Equipe Gordini		E	2.0 Gordini Type 16 6		4 laps behind	10/32
	1953	Championship position: Unplaced								
ret	FRENCH GP	Reims	42	Connaught Engineering		D	2.0 Connaught A-Lea Francis 4		transmission	11/25
7	BRITISH GP	Silverstone	10	Connaught Engineering		D	2.0 Connaught A-Lea Francis 4		8 laps behind	19/29
ret	GERMAN GP	Nürburgring	14	Connaught Engineering		D	2.0 Connaught A-Lea Francis 4		engine	15/35
11	ITALIAN GP	Monza	44	Scuderia Milan		P	2.0 Maserati A6GCM 6		8 laps behind	23/30
	1954	Championship position: 14th		Wins: 0	Pole positions: 0	Fastest laps: 0	Points scored: 3			
7	ARGENTINE GP	Buenos Aires	8	Officine Alfieri Maserati		P	2.5 Maserati A6GCM/250F 6		4 laps behind	10/18
6	BELGIAN GP	Spa	20	'B Bira'		P	2.5 Maserati 250F 6		1 lap behind	13/15
4	FRENCH GP	Reims	46	'B Bira'		P	2.5 Maserati 250F 6		1 lap behind	6/22
ret*	BRITISH GP	Silverstone	6	'B Bira'		P	2.5 Maserati 250F 6		* Flockhart took over-crashed	10/31
ret	GERMAN GP	Nürburgring	14	'B Bira'		P	2.5 Maserati 250F 6		steering	19/23
9	SPANISH GP	Pedralbes	18	'B Bira'		P	2.5 Maserati 250F 6		12 laps behind	15/22

GP Starts: 19   GP Wins: 0   Pole positions: 0   Fastest laps: 0   Points: 8

BIRGER, Pablo (RA) b 6/1/1924, Buenos Aires – d 9/3/1966, Buenos Aires

	1953	Championship position: Unplaced								
	Race	Circuit	No	Entrant		Tyres	Car/Engine		Comment	Q Pos/Entries
ret	ARGENTINE GP	Buenos Aires	34	Equipe Gordini		E	1.5 Gordini Type 15 4		cwp	14/16
	1955	Championship position: Unplaced								
ret	ARGENTINE GP	Buenos Aires	40	Equipe Gordini		E	2.0 Gordini Type 16 6		spun, hit by Menditéguy	9/22

GP Starts: 2   GP Wins: 0   Pole positions: 0   Fastest laps: 0   Points: 0

BLANCHARD, Harry (USA) b – d 31/1/1960, Buenos Aires, Argentina

	1959			Championship position: Unplaced					
	Race	Circuit	No	Entrant	Tyres	Car/Engine		Comment	Q Pos/Entries
7	US GP	Sebring	17	Blanchard Automobile Co	–	1.5 Porsche RSK F4 sports car		4 laps behind	16/19

GP Starts: 1   GP Wins: 0   Pole positions: 0   Fastest laps: 0   Points: 0

BLEEKEMOLEN, Michael (NL) b 2/10/1949

	1977			Championship position: Unplaced					
	Race	Circuit	No	Entrant	Tyres	Car/Engine		Comment	Q Pos/Entries
dnq	DUTCH GP	Zandvoort	32	RAM Racing/F & S Properties	G	3.0 March 761-Cosworth V8			34/34
	1978			Championship position: Unplaced					
dnq	DUTCH GP	Zandvoort	10	F & S Properties/ATS Racing Team	G	3.0 ATS HS1-Cosworth V8			29/33
dnq	ITALIAN GP	Monza	9	F & S Properties/ATS Racing Team	G	3.0 ATS HS1-Cosworth V8			27/32
ret	US GP EAST	Watkins Glen	9	F & S Properties/ATS Racing Team	G	3.0 ATS HS1-Cosworth V8		oil pump leak	25/27
dnq	CANADIAN GP	Montreal	9	F & S Properties/ATS Racing Team	G	3.0 ATS HS1-Cosworth V8			28/28

GP Starts: 1   GP Wins: 0   Pole positions: 0   Fastest laps: 0   Points: 0

BLOKDYK, Trevor (ZA) b 30/11/1935, Krugersdorp, Transvaal – d 19/03/1995, Hekpoort, nr Krugersdorp

	1963			Championship position: Unplaced					
	Race	Circuit	No	Entrant	Tyres	Car/Engine		Comment	Q Pos/Entries
12	SOUTH AFRICAN GP	East London	23	Scuderia Lupini	D	1.5 Cooper T51-Maserati 4		8 laps behind	19/21
	1965			Championship position: Unplaced					
dnq	SOUTH AFRICAN GP	East London	28	Trevor Blokdyk	D	1.5 Cooper T59-Ford 4			=21/25

GP Starts: 1   GP Wins: 0   Pole positions: 0   Fastest laps: 0   Points: 0

HARRY BLANCHARD

Blanchard was invited to race his Porsche RSK sports car in the inaugural US GP at Sebring in order to make up the numbers. He was a regular on the late-fifties American road racing scene, his best result being third place in the 1959 Watkins Glen GP, and was a class champion that year. However, Blanchard was fatally injured in the 1960 Buenos Aires 1000 Km when his Porsche crashed and overturned.

MICHAEL BLEEKEMOLEN

Bleekemolen was a Dutch Formula Super Vee and later Formula Ford driver who, due to his access to sponsorship money, found himself placed in a Grand Prix car in 1977 before he was really ready for the task. He was undeniably a quick driver in these lower formulae, but he needed much more experience to compete at Grand Prix level.

To this end Bleekemolen embarked on a full season of European Formula 3 in 1978, finishing fifth in the series, and then, again with the help of his F & S Properties backing, he joined ATS for another unsuccessful sortie into the world of Grands Prix. After that it was back to a diet of Formula 3, Michael plugging away for another three seasons with some good finishes but outright victory proving elusive. The racer in him still remained, however, and for many seasons he was a competitor in various Renault one-make series. He still enjoys occasional outings (such as at Monza in 1999 in a Kremer K8-Porsche), and can take pride in the burgeoning single-seater career of his son Sebastian.

TREVOR BLOKDYK

A former South African speedway champion, Trevor rode in Europe before returning home to compete on four wheels with a Ford-engined Type 52 Cooper in 1961. He proved to be an extremely fast and fearless competitor and itched to return to Europe, which he did in 1962, to race in Formula Junior. Trevor did well (second at Nogaro and Caserta) until the money ran out, so he then returned home to contest the South African championships – and his only Grand Prix – in the ex-Love Cooper.

Blokdyk was back in Europe once more in 1965 to race in F3, when he was one of that season's star performers until a massive crash at Albi hospitalised him for three months with pelvic and leg injuries. He made his comeback at Rouen in 1966, finishing sixth, and continued to race in F3 in 1968 and early 1969, before returning to compete in South Africa. Extremely popular, and always ready with a smile, Trevor took up farming upon retirement, but died suddenly of a heart attack, aged just 59.

MARK BLUNDELL

Mark Blundell is typical of a generation of British drivers who have worked so hard to get into Formula 1 – a lot of talent, but not a lot of money. This former motocross rider had a quite remarkable first season in Formula Ford, winning 25 of his 70 races and receiving the 1984 Grovewood Award in recognition of this achievement.

The next two seasons were spent in FF1600 and FF2000, before Mark plunged straight into the F3000 championship for 1987 with an elderly Lola. Cracking drives in early-season races at Spa and Vallelunga brought him points-scoring finishes and seemed to vindicate his decision to miss out on the traditional stepping-stone of Formula 3, especially when he was offered the works Lola for the 1988 F3000 season. Second place in the opening round at Jerez showed promise, but the season then slid away in a mire of development tweaks that saw the car engineered out of competitiveness.

In some ways 1989 was a make-or-break year for Blundell in F3000. He moved to the Middlebridge team and all the ingredients for success seemed to be there, but his season was ragged and he failed to make the top ten in the final points standings. Nevertheless he must have shown something, because Nissan paired him with Julian Bailey in their rapid car to contest the endurance championship and Williams signed him as a test driver for 1990.

It was a year well spent as Mark familiarised himself with the intricacies of a Formula 1 car, but with no prospect of racing for the team in the immediate future he understandably accepted an offer to join Brabham-Yamaha for 1991. Paired with the experienced Martin Brundle, he was certainly not overshadowed, and scored his first championship point at Spa in the Belgian GP. However, the finances of the team were already parlous and Blundell was reluctantly shown the door in favour of 'paying guests' at season's end.

The 1992 season was again spent on the F1 bench, Mark acting as test driver for McLaren, but brought an unexpected highlight when, in a one-off appearance for Peugeot, he won the Le Mans 24 Hours with Derek Warwick and Yannick Dalmas. The well-funded but under-achieving Ligier team had changed hands and, despite much criticism in the French press, new owner Cyril de Rouvre hired both Blundell and Brundle to revive their fortunes in 1993. Mark's superb third place in the opening race, followed by a fifth next time out in Brazil, boded well, but as the season wore on question marks were raised as the number of spins and incidents mounted, and suddenly he was facing an anxious winter, hoping to land a drive in 1994. In the event he found a berth at Tyrrell and Mark's third place in Spain was a fillip for a team struggling to restore their lost credibility. Surprisingly, it was the hitherto unregarded Katayama who took the eye as the year progressed and once more Mark was seeking employment at season's end. Luckily for him, Nigel Mansell's highly touted return to F1 with McLaren ended in farce, and the no-nonsense racer stepped up from the role of test driver, impressing everyone once more with his commitment. Though not far behind team-mate Häkkinen in terms of points, Blundell was perhaps always seen as a stop-gap until the arrival of David Coulthard, and he grabbed the opportunity to continue his racing career in Indy cars at PacWest after impressing in testing sessions which included fellow aspirants Allan McNish and JJ Lehto.

It was to be a frightening baptism for Blundell, who survived a monumental crash in only his second outing at Rio which sidelined him with a foot injury. Naturally it took some while for his confidence to return, but in 1997 success came in the form of three race wins (at Portland, Toronto and the 500-miler at Fontana). So outstanding were his performances that it seemed that Mark was a serious championship contender for 1998, but the PacWest bubble had burst, and the hapless driver ended up a lowly equal 17th in the final points standings. His 1999 season was no better, interrupted as it was by a neck injury incurred in a testing accident which caused him to miss eight races.

However, PacWest and sponsor Motorola still have great faith in their man, handing him a new two-year contract. Mercedes are focusing their efforts on Bruce McCaw's outfit in 2000, so Mark can look forward to an upturn in his fortunes and is confident of a return to the winner's circle.

BLUNDELL, Mark (GB) b 8/4/1966, Barnet, Hertfordshire

	1991	Championship position: 18th=		Wins: 0	Pole positions: 0		Fastest laps: 0	Points scored: 1		
	Race	Circuit	No	Entrant	Tyres	Car/Engine			Comment	Q Pos/Entries
ret	US GP (PHOENIX)	Phoenix	8	Motor Racing Developments Ltd	P	3.5 Brabham BT59Y-Yamaha V12			spun off	24/34
ret	BRAZILIAN GP	Interlagos	8	Motor Racing Developments Ltd	P	3.5 Brabham BT59Y-Yamaha V12			engine	25/34
8	SAN MARINO GP	Imola	8	Motor Racing Developments Ltd	P	3.5 Brabham BT60Y-Yamaha V12			3 laps behind	23/34
ret	MONACO GP	Monte Carlo	8	Motor Racing Developments Ltd	P	3.5 Brabham BT60Y-Yamaha V12			crashed on Modena's oil	22/34
dnq	CANADIAN GP	Montreal	8	Motor Racing Developments Ltd	P	3.5 Brabham BT60Y-Yamaha V12				29/34
ret	MEXICAN GP	Mexico City	8	Motor Racing Developments Ltd	P	3.5 Brabham BT60Y-Yamaha V12			engine	12/34
ret	FRENCH GP	Magny Cours	8	Motor Racing Developments Ltd	P	3.5 Brabham BT60Y-Yamaha V12			accident-slid into pit wall	17/34
ret	BRITISH GP	Silverstone	8	Motor Racing Developments Ltd	P	3.5 Brabham BT60Y-Yamaha V12			engine	12/34
12	GERMAN GP	Hockenheim	8	Motor Racing Developments Ltd	P	3.5 Brabham BT60Y-Yamaha V12			2 laps behind	21/34
ret	HUNGARIAN GP	Hungaroring	8	Motor Racing Developments Ltd	P	3.5 Brabham BT60Y-Yamaha V12			spun off-stalled	20/34
6	BELGIAN GP	Spa	8	Motor Racing Developments Ltd	P	3.5 Brabham BT60Y-Yamaha V12				13/34
12	ITALIAN GP	Monza	8	Motor Racing Developments Ltd	P	3.5 Brabham BT60Y-Yamaha V12			1 lap behind	11/34
ret	PORTUGUESE GP	Estoril	8	Motor Racing Developments Ltd	P	3.5 Brabham BT60Y-Yamaha V12			rear suspension collapsed-spun	15/34
ret	SPANISH GP	Barcelona	8	Motor Racing Developments Ltd	P	3.5 Brabham BT60Y-Yamaha V12			engine	12/33
dnpq	JAPANESE GP	Suzuka	8	Motor Racing Developments Ltd	P	3.5 Brabham BT60Y-Yamaha V12				30/31
17	AUSTRALIAN GP	Adelaide	8	Motor Racing Developments Ltd	P	3.5 Brabham BT60Y-Yamaha V12			abandoned after 14 laps/-1 lap	17/32

1993
Championship position: 10th Wins: 0 Pole positions: 0 Fastest laps: 0 Points scored: 10

	Race	Circuit	No	Entrant	Tyres	Car/Engine	Comment	Q Pos/Entries
3	SOUTH AFRICAN GP	Kyalami	26	Ligier Gitanes Blondes	G	3.5 Ligier JS39-Renault V10	1 lap behind	8/26
5	BRAZILIAN GP	Interlagos	26	Ligier Gitanes Blondes	G	3.5 Ligier JS39-Renault V10		10/26
ret	EUROPEAN GP	Donington	26	Ligier Gitanes Blondes	G	3.5 Ligier JS39-Renault V10	spun off	21/26
ret	SAN MARINO GP	Imola	26	Ligier Gitanes Blondes	G	3.5 Ligier JS39-Renault V10	spun off at first corner	7/26
7	SPANISH GP	Barcelona	26	Ligier Gitanes Blondes	G	3.5 Ligier JS39-Renault V10	2 laps behind	12/26
ret	MONACO GP	Monte Carlo	26	Ligier Gitanes Blondes	G	3.5 Ligier JS39-Renault V10	suspension	21/26
ret	CANADIAN GP	Montreal	26	Ligier Gitanes Blondes	G	3.5 Ligier JS39-Renault V10	spun off	10/26
ret	FRENCH GP	Magny Cours	26	Ligier Gitanes Blondes	G	3.5 Ligier JS39-Renault V10	collision-de Cesaris-spun off	4/26
7	BRITISH GP	Silverstone	26	Ligier Gitanes Blondes	G	3.5 Ligier JS39-Renault V10	spun/1 lap behind	9/26
3	GERMAN GP	Hockenheim	26	Ligier Gitanes Blondes	G	3.5 Ligier JS39-Renault V10		5/26
7	HUNGARIAN GP	Hungaroring	26	Ligier Gitanes Blondes	G	3.5 Ligier JS39-Renault V10	gear selection problems/-1 lap	12/26
11/ret	BELGIAN GP	Spa	26	Ligier Gitanes Blondes	G	3.5 Ligier JS39-Renault V10	taken off by Berger/-2 laps	15/25
ret	ITALIAN GP	Monza	26	Ligier Gitanes Blondes	G	3.5 Ligier JS39-Renault V10	hit barrier-tyre damage	14/26
ret	PORTUGUESE GP	Estoril	26	Ligier Gitanes Blondes	G	3.5 Ligier JS39-Renault V10	collision-Wendlinger	10/26
7	JAPANESE GP	Suzuka	26	Ligier Gitanes Blondes	G	3.5 Ligier JS39-Renault V10	brake and gearbox troubles	17/24
9	AUSTRALIAN GP	Adelaide	26	Ligier Gitanes Blondes	G	3.5 Ligier JS39-Renault V10	2 laps behind	14/24

1994
Championship position: 12 Wins: 0 Pole positions: 0 Fastest laps: 0 Points scored: 8

	Race	Circuit	No	Entrant	Tyres	Car/Engine	Comment	Q Pos/Entries
ret	BRAZILIAN GP	Interlagos	4	Tyrrell	G	3.5 Tyrrell 022-Yamaha V10	accident-wheel failure	12/28
ret	PACIFIC GP	T.I. Circuit	4	Tyrrell	G	3.5 Tyrrell 022-Yamaha V10	hit by Comas-spun and stalled	12/28
9	SAN MARINO GP	Imola	4	Tyrrell	G	3.5 Tyrrell 022-Yamaha V10	2 laps behind	12/28
ret	MONACO GP	Monte Carlo	4	Tyrrell	G	3.5 Tyrrell 022-Yamaha V10	engine	10/24
3	SPANISH GP	Barcelona	4	Tyrrell	G	3.5 Tyrrell 022-Yamaha V10		11/27
10	CANADIAN GP	Montreal	4	Tyrrell	G	3.5 Tyrrell 022-Yamaha V10	2 laps behind	13/27
10	FRENCH GP	Magny Cours	4	Tyrrell	G	3.5 Tyrrell 022-Yamaha V10	gearbox trouble/-5 laps	17/28
ret	BRITISH GP	Silverstone	4	Tyrrell	G	3.5 Tyrrell 022-Yamaha V10	gearbox	11/28
ret	GERMAN GP	Hockenheim	4	Tyrrell	G	3.5 Tyrrell 022-Yamaha V10	multiple accident on lap 1	7/28
5	HUNGARIAN GP	Hungaroring	4	Tyrrell	G	3.5 Tyrrell 022-Yamaha V10	1 lap behind	11/28
5*	BELGIAN GP	Spa	4	Tyrrell	G	3.5 Tyrrell 022-Yamaha V10	*1st place car dsq/-1 lap	12/28
ret	ITALIAN GP	Monza	4	Tyrrell	G	3.5 Tyrrell 022-Yamaha V10	brake trouble-spun out	21/28
ret	PORTUGUESE GP	Estoril	4	Tyrrell	G	3.5 Tyrrell 022-Yamaha V10	engine	12/28
13	EUROPEAN GP	Jerez	4	Tyrrell	G	3.5 Tyrrell 022-Yamaha V10	1 lap behind	14/28
ret	JAPANESE GP	Suzuka	4	Tyrrell	G	3.5 Tyrrell 022-Yamaha V10	electrics	13/28
ret	AUSTRALIAN GP	Adelaide	4	Tyrrell	G	3.5 Tyrrell 022-Yamaha V10	accident	13/28

1995
Championship position: 10th Wins: 0 Pole positions: 0 Fastest laps: 0 Points scored: 13

	Race	Circuit	No	Entrant	Tyres	Car/Engine	Comment	Q Pos/Entries
6	BRAZILIAN GP	Interlagos	7	Marlboro McLaren Mercedes	G	3.0 McLaren MP4/10-Mercedes V10	1 lap behind	9/26
ret	ARGENTINE GP	Buenos Aires	7	Marlboro McLaren Mercedes	G	3.0 McLaren MP4/10-Mercedes V10	engine	17/26
5	MONACO GP	Monte Carlo	7	Marlboro McLaren Mercedes	G	3.0 McLaren MP4/10B-Mercedes V10	1 lap behind	10/26
ret	CANADIAN GP	Montreal	7	Marlboro McLaren Mercedes	G	3.0 McLaren MP4/10B-Mercedes V10	engine	10/24
11	FRENCH GP	Magny Cours	7	Marlboro McLaren Mercedes	G	3.0 McLaren MP4/10B-Mercedes V10	2 laps behind	13/24
5	BRITISH GP	Silverstone	7	Marlboro McLaren Mercedes	G	3.0 McLaren MP4/10B-Mercedes V10	hit by Barrichello last lap	10/24
ret	GERMAN GP	Hockenheim	7	Marlboro McLaren Mercedes	G	3.0 McLaren MP4/10B-Mercedes V10	engine	8/24
ret	HUNGARIAN GP	Hungaroring	7	Marlboro McLaren Mercedes	G	3.0 McLaren MP4/10B-Mercedes V10	engine	13/24
5	BELGIAN GP	Spa	7	Marlboro McLaren Mercedes	G	3.0 McLaren MP4/10B-Mercedes V10		6/24
4	ITALIAN GP	Monza	7	Marlboro McLaren Mercedes	G	3.0 McLaren MP4/10B-Mercedes V10		9/24
9	PORTUGUESE GP	Estoril	7	Marlboro McLaren Mercedes	G	3.0 McLaren MP4/10B/C-Mercedes V10	1 lap behind	–/–
dns	"	"	7	Marlboro McLaren Mercedes	G	3.0 McLaren MP4/10C-Mercedes V10	set grid time in this car	12/24
ret	EUROPEAN GP	Nürburgring	7	Marlboro McLaren Mercedes	G	3.0 McLaren MP4/10C-Mercedes V10	spun off	10/24
9	PACIFIC GP	T.I. Circuit	7	Marlboro McLaren Mercedes	G	3.0 McLaren MP4/10B-Mercedes V10	2 laps behind	10/24
7	JAPANESE GP	Suzuka	7	Marlboro McLaren Mercedes	G	3.0 McLaren MP4/10B-Mercedes V10	1 lap behind	24/24
4	AUSTRALIAN GP	Adelaide	7	Marlboro McLaren Mercedes	G	3.0 McLaren MP4/10B-Mercedes V10	2 laps behind	10/24

GP Starts: 61 GP Wins: 0 Pole positions: 0 Fastest laps: 0 Points: 32

BOESEL, Raul (BR) b 4/12/1957, Curitiba

1982
Championship position: Unplaced

	Race	Circuit	No	Entrant	Tyres	Car/Engine	Comment	Q Pos/Entries
15	SOUTH AFRICAN GP	Kyalami	18	March Grand Prix Team	P	3.0 March 821-Cosworth V8	5 laps behind	21/30
ret	BRAZILIAN GP	Rio	18	Rothmans March Grand Prix Team	P	3.0 March 821-Cosworth V8	puncture-spun off	17/31
9*	US GP WEST	Long Beach	18	Rothmans March Grand Prix Team	P	3.0 March 821-Cosworth V8	* 10th car dsq/5 laps behind	23/31
8	BELGIAN GP	Zolder	18	Rothmans March Grand Prix Team	P	3.0 March 821-Cosworth V8	4 laps behind	26/32
dnpq	MONACO GP	Monte Carlo	18	Rothmans March Grand Prix Team	A	3.0 March 821-Cosworth V8		29/31
ret	US GP (DETROIT)	Detroit	18	Rothmans March Grand Prix Team	A	3.0 March 821-Cosworth V8	hit by Baldi	21/28
ret	CANADIAN GP	Montreal	18	Rothmans March Grand Prix Team	A	3.0 March 821-Cosworth V8	engine	21/29
ret	DUTCH GP	Zandvoort	18	Rothmans March Grand Prix Team	A	3.0 March 821-Cosworth V8	engine	22/31
dnq	BRITISH GP	Brands Hatch	18	Rothmans March Grand Prix Team	A	3.0 March 821-Cosworth V8		30/30
dnq	FRENCH GP	Paul Ricard	18	Rothmans March Grand Prix Team	A	3.0 March 821-Cosworth V8		30/30
ret	GERMAN GP	Hockenheim	18	Rothmans March Grand Prix Team	A	3.0 March 821-Cosworth V8	puncture	25/30
dnq	AUSTRIAN GP	Österreichring	18	Rothmans March Grand Prix Team	A	3.0 March 821-Cosworth V8		27/29
ret	SWISS GP	Dijon	18	Rothmans March Grand Prix Team	A	3.0 March 821-Cosworth V8	gearbox oil leak	24/29
dnq	ITALIAN GP	Monza	18	Rothmans March Grand Prix Team	M	3.0 March 821-Cosworth V8		29/30
13	CAESARS PALACE GP	Las Vegas	18	Rothmans March Grand Prix Team	M	3.0 March 821-Cosworth V8	6 laps behind	24/30

1983
Championship position: Unplaced

	Race	Circuit	No	Entrant	Tyres	Car/Engine	Comment	Q Pos/Entries
ret	BRAZILIAN GP	Rio	26	Equipe Ligier Gitanes	M	3.0 Ligier JS21-Cosworth V8	electrics	17/27
7	US GP WEST	Long Beach	26	Equipe Ligier Gitanes	M	3.0 Ligier JS21-Cosworth V8	2 laps behind	26/28
ret	FRENCH GP	Paul Ricard	26	Equipe Ligier Gitanes	M	3.0 Ligier JS21-Cosworth V8	engine	25/29
9	SAN MARINO GP	Imola	26	Equipe Ligier Gitanes	M	3.0 Ligier JS21-Cosworth V8	2 laps behind	25/28
ret	MONACO GP	Monte Carlo	26	Equipe Ligier Gitanes	M	3.0 Ligier JS21-Cosworth V8	accident with Winkelhock	18/28
13	BELGIAN GP	Spa	26	Equipe Ligier Gitanes	M	3.0 Ligier JS21-Cosworth V8	1 lap behind	26/28
10	US GP (DETROIT)	Detroit	26	Equipe Ligier Gitanes	M	3.0 Ligier JS21-Cosworth V8	2 laps behind	23/27

ret	CANADIAN GP	Montreal	26	Equipe Ligier Gitanes	M	3.0 Ligier JS21-Cosworth V8	wheel bearing	24/28
ret	BRITISH GP	Silverstone	26	Equipe Ligier Gitanes	M	3.0 Ligier JS21-Cosworth V8	hydraulic suspension leak	22/29
ret	GERMAN GP	Hockenheim	26	Equipe Ligier Gitanes	M	3.0 Ligier JS21-Cosworth V8	engine	25/29
dnq	AUSTRIAN GP	Österreichring	26	Equipe Ligier Gitanes	M	3.0 Ligier JS21-Cosworth V8		27/29
10	DUTCH GP	Zandvoort	26	Equipe Ligier Gitanes	M	3.0 Ligier JS21-Cosworth V8	2 laps behind	24/29
dnq	ITALIAN GP	Monza	26	Equipe Ligier Gitanes	M	3.0 Ligier JS21-Cosworth V8		27/29
15	EUROPEAN GP	Brands Hatch	26	Equipe Ligier Gitanes	M	3.0 Ligier JS21-Cosworth V8	3 laps behind	23/29
nc	SOUTH AFRICAN GP	Kyalami	26	Equipe Ligier Gitanes	M	3.0 Ligier JS21-Cosworth V8	11 laps behind	23/26

GP Starts: 23   GP Wins: 0   Pole positions: 0   Fastest laps: 0   Points: 0

RAUL BOESEL

After karting and saloon car success, Boesel followed the well-trodden path of Brazilian hopefuls bound for Europe with the aim of becoming the next Fittipaldi.

Never having driven a single-seater and with no English, Raul sensibly bought himself a drive with Van Diemen. Quickly learning from team-mates Moreno and Byrne, he finished runner-up in both Formula Ford championships in 1980, winning eight races. Opting for F3 for 1981, Boesel enjoyed a remarkably consistent season, finishing in the points in 16 of the 20 rounds and winning three of them to take third place in the Marlboro championship.

Well funded after his success, Raul took his sponsorship money into F1 with the RAM March team but it was to be a disastrous season. Things were not much better the following year, his F1 career effectively torpedoed as he struggled in a Ligier team then in decline.

Deciding to change course, he headed off to the States and found a ride with Dick Simon's Indy Car team in 1985 and '86. Just missing out on a couple of good seats for 1987, Boesel found himself a berth in the TWR Jaguar sports car team and enjoyed a highly successful season, the Brazilian winning the drivers' sports car title to raise his stature immensely.

Returning to Indy cars, Raul made little impression until 1993, when he enjoyed an excellent season with Simon. He posed a consistent threat to the élite, and was distinctly unlucky not to notch up a win. Unfortunately he was not so competitive the following year, and a beautiful partnership ended in litigation as the Brazilian took his Duracell sponsorship to Rahal-Hogan. His new team, running a Lola-Mercedes combination, struggled, however, and it was often Boesel's car which hit problems.

For 1996, Raul opted to join forces with Barry Green's team – the reigning champions – with hopes high for an upturn in his fortunes. Sadly for the Brazilian, only fleeting glimpses of competitiveness were seen in a season plagued with engine and electrical maladies and he took his substantial Brahma beer sponsorship to Patrick Racing for 1998. A late switch to Reynard chassis at the start of the season put the team on the pace and Raul posted some convincing performances, peaking with a pole position at Gateway. Unfortunately the second half of the year saw a slump in the team's fortunes and Boesel was left without a CART ride at season's end.

The Brazilian decided to switch to the Indy Racing League for 1998, and the past two seasons have brought only modest success. He briefly returned to the CART ranks in 1999 with Team KOOL Green at Miami (substituting for Paul Tracy), and with All American Racers at Chicago (where he scored a single point) and Laguna Seca. Raul also enjoyed a couple of sports car appearances in the DAMS Panoz, sharing third place at Mid Ohio (with Bernard) and fifth at Watkins Glen (with Bernard and Wallace).

BOB BONDURANT

Originally from Illinois, Bob later moved to the West Coast where he raced Triumphs and Corvettes with some success, though his big break came with the chance to race Carroll Shelby's hairy AC Cobra at Denver in 1963. A class win on his debut saw Bob signed full-time for 1964 as the Shelby team headed for Europe to contest the classic long-distance events. His best result was a fourth place at Le Mans (with Gurney) to win the GT class.

Bob had a hectic season in 1965, racing the Cobra and Ford GTs, in addition to a number of Formula 2 and Formula 3 outings. This led to an invitation to race the works Ferrari in place of the injured John Surtees at season's end.

Back in Europe for 1966 Bob raced for Bernard White's private team – picking up a fourth place at Monaco – in tandem with a freelance season of sports car rides, sharing Ferraris with Rindt, Parkes and Gregory and bringing a works Porsche into fourth place in the Nürburgring 1000 Km.

His career seemed to be over after a huge accident at Watkins Glen in 1967 prevented him from racing but he made a successsful comeback in Can-Am in 1970 and '71. Thereafter he concentrated on his racing driver schools, but was occasionally tempted back behind the wheel in SCCA and NASCAR races.

BONDURANT, Bob (USA) b 27/4/1933, Evanston, Illinois

	1965	Championship position: Unplaced							
	Race	Circuit	No	Entrant	Tyres	Car/Engine		Comment	Q Pos/Entries
9	US GP	Watkins Glen	24	North American Racing Team	D	1.5 Ferrari 158 V8		4 laps behind	=13/18
ret	MEXICAN GP	Mexico City	22	Reg Parnell (Racing)	D	1.5 Lotus 33-Climax V8		rear suspension bolt	18/18
	1966	Championship position: 14th=	Wins: 0	Pole positions: 0	Fastest laps: 0	Points scored: 3			
4	MONACO GP	Monte Carlo	19	Team Chamaco Collect	G	2.0 BRM P261 V8		5 laps behind	16/16
ret	BELGIAN GP	Spa	(8) 24	Team Chamaco Collect	G	2.0 BRM P261 V8		ran no 8 in practice/spun off	11/18
9	BRITISH GP	Brands Hatch	25	Team Chamaco Collect	G	2.0 BRM P261 V8		4 laps behind	14/20
ret	GERMAN GP	Nürburgring	14	Team Chamaco Collect	G	2.0 BRM P261 V8		engine	12/30
7	ITALIAN GP	Monza	48	Team Chamaco Collect	G	2.0 BRM P261 V8		3 laps behind	18/22
dsq	US GP	Watkins Glen	16	Anglo American Racers	G	2.7 Eagle T1G-Climax 4		push start	16/19
ret	MEXICAN GP	Mexico City	16	Anglo American Racers	G	3.0 Eagle T1G-Weslake V12		fuel feed	19/19
dns	"	" "	15	Anglo American Racers	G	2.7 Eagle T1G-Climax 4		practice only	– / –

GP Starts: 9   GP Wins: 0   Pole positions: 0   Fastest laps: 0   Points: 3

FELICE BONETTO

Known as 'Il Pirata' (the pirate), Bonetto was a fearless competitor who took no prisoners and was possessed of so much courage that some of his racing exploits placed him in the category of the foolhardy.

He was already well known in Italy in the late thirties by his performances in his privately entered Alfa Romeo in the Mille Miglia, but did not come to the fore internationally until the late forties, first with Cisitalia and then with Ferrari, for whom he scored second places in the Mille Miglia and the Monza and Naples GPs in 1949.

The independently minded Felice campaigned the Maserati Milano and his own Alfa sports car to such effect that after winning the 1950 Oporto GP and leading the Mille Miglia in the Alfa, he was offered a works drive in 1951. He was very much the number three in the team, however, which did not go down too well, and he took the offer of a contract with Lancia to race their sports cars in 1952. This brought him perhaps his greatest triumph, in the Targa Florio.

Despite his age Bonetto was more active than ever in 1953. Undertaking a full season of Grands Prix for the first time with the Maserati works team and racing sports cars again for Lancia, he won the Portuguese GP in Lisbon and placed third in the Mille Miglia before competing in the gruelling Carrera Panamericana. He lay in second place to Taruffi when he was killed after skidding off the road and crashing into a lamp standard in the village of Silao.

BONETTO, Felice (I) b 9/6/1903, Brescia – d 21/11/1953, Silao, Mexico

	1950	Championship position: 15th	Wins: 0	Pole positions: 0	Fastest laps: 0	Points scored: 2			
	Race	Circuit	No	Entrant	Tyres	Car/Engine		Comment	Q Pos/Entries
5	SWISS GP	Bremgarten	34	Scuderia Milano	P	1.5 s/c Maserati 4CLT/50 Milano 4		2 laps behind	12/18
ret	FRENCH GP	Reims	40	Scuderia Milano	P	1.5 s/c Maserati 4CLT/50 Milano 4		engine	11/20
dns	ITALIAN GP	Monza	52	Scuderia Milano	P	1.5 s/c Milano/Milano 'Speluzzi' 4		withdrawn	(23)/27
	1951	Championship position: 7th	Wins: 0	Pole positions: 0	Fastest laps: 0	Points scored: 7			
4	BRITISH GP	Silverstone	4	Alfa Romeo SpA	P	1.5 s/c Alfa Romeo 159A 8		3 laps behind	7/20
ret	GERMAN GP	Nürburgring	77	Alfa Romeo SpA	P	1.5 s/c Alfa Romeo 159A 8		supercharger	10/23
3*	ITALIAN GP	Monza	40	Alfa Romeo SpA	P	1.5 s/c Alfa Romeo 159A 8		* Farina took over/-1 lap	7/22
5	SPANISH GP	Pedralbes	24	Alfa Romeo SpA	P	1.5 s/c Alfa Romeo 159M 8		2 laps behind	8/20
	1952	Championship position: 11th=	Wins: 0	Pole positions: 0	Fastest laps: 0	Points scored: 2			
dsq	GERMAN GP	Nürburgring	105	Officine Alfieri Maserati	P	2.0 Maserati A6GCM 6		push start after spin	10/32
5	ITALIAN GP	Monza	22	Officine Alfieri Maserati	P	2.0 Maserati A6GCM 6		1 lap behind	13/32
	1953	Championship position: 8th	Wins: 0	Pole positions: 0	Fastest laps: 0	Points scored: 6.5			
ret	ARGENTINE GP	Buenos Aires	6	Officine Alfieri Maserati	P	2.0 Maserati A6GCM 6		transmission	15/16
3*	DUTCH GP	Zandvoort	16	Officine Alfieri Maserati	P	2.0 Maserati A6GCM 6		* Gonzalez took over/-1 lap	13/20
ret	FRENCH GP	Reims	24	Officine Alfieri Maserati	P	2.0 Maserati A6GCM 6		engine	2/25
6	BRITISH GP	Silverstone	25	Officine Alfieri Maserati	P	2.0 Maserati A6GCM 6		8 laps behind	16/29
4	GERMAN GP	Nürburgring	7	Officine Alfieri Maserati	P	2.0 Maserati A6GCM 6			7/35
ret*	SWISS GP	Bremgarten	30	Officine Alfieri Maserati	P	2.0 Maserati A6GCM 6		* Fangio took over/engine	10/23
4*	"	"	32	Officine Alfieri Maserati	P	2.0 Maserati A6GCM 6		* took Fangio's car/-1 lap	– / –
ret	ITALIAN GP	Monza	52	Officine Alfieri Maserati	P	2.0 Maserati A6GCM 6		out of fuel	7/30

GP Starts: 15   GP Wins: 0   Pole positions: 0   Fastest laps: 0   Points: 17.5

JOAKIM BONNIER

From a comfortable background, this Swedish driver had built a mighty reputation as an ice-racer in the early fifties with an Alfa Romeo Disco Volante, which led to him being appointed a distributor for that marque in 1954. Moving into circuit racing the following year, Bonnier soon proved to be a front-runner in Scandinavia before venturing further afield in 1956 to race the GT Alfa, winning events at Aintree, AVUS and Castelfusano, and taking a class win at the Nürburgring 1000 Km with Mackay-Fraser. By now he had started to run Maserati sports cars, and in 1957 became involved with the works team, finishing third in the Swedish GP in a 300TS.

Although he had not really reached the front rank of drivers, Jo bought a Maserati 250F which he raced in the 1957-58 seasons

with only moderate results, the best being second places at Syracuse and Caen against meagre opposition. At the tail-end of 1958 he joined BRM and soon became the first driver to win a championship Grand Prix for Bourne when he won the 1959 Dutch GP. He was to stay with BRM until the end of the 1960 season, but never came close to repeating his Zandvoort triumph, although he comfortably led the 1960 Argentine GP until the engine failed.

Having begun a successful association with Porsche in 1959, Bonnier took every opportunity to race for them again the following year, winning the Modena GP and taking a superb victory in the rain in the non-championship German GP in F2, and sharing the victorious RSK sports car with Herrmann in the Targa Florio. With the Porsche team planning a Grand Prix assault in 1961, Bonnier – feeling his talents were being overlooked at BRM – joined Dan Gurney to race the silver cars. After a winter interlude which included taking a Yeoman Credit Cooper to victory in New Zealand at the Teretonga international and at Levin, the 1961 season started with a second place in Seidel's Lotus at Pau before Bonnier concentrated on his Porsche commitments. He made a promising beginning, with some good results in non-championship races, including second places at Solitude, Karlskoga and Modena and thirds at Syracuse and Zeltweg, but in Grands Prix things were much tougher, and he was increasingly overshadowed by Gurney, especially in 1962 when he endured a fairly depressing time with the new Porsche 804 flat-eight, with a second place at Solitude and a third at the Karlskoga GP his only worthwhile results.

With Porsche withdrawing from Formula 1, Bonnier joined Rob Walker in 1963 and raced his privately entered cars for the next three seasons. When the mood took him he could still be extremely quick, but by now he seemed more interested in his pivotal role as leader of the newly formed Grand Prix Drivers' Association. When Walker released him for 1966, Jo formed his own team, picking up occasional points racing a Cooper-Maserati and then a McLaren, as well as scrounging a few works drives, but he was really a shadow of his former self, especially in 1971, when he was very slow indeed.

If nothing else Bonnier still enjoyed the life of a racing driver, and while the best days of his Grand Prix career had long been in the past, he raced sports cars with great gusto. He shared a Chaparral with Phil Hill to win the Nürburgring 1000 Km in 1966 and raced his own and the Ecurie Filipinetti's Lola T70s with some minor success, but it was the acquisition of a 2-litre Lola in 1970 that seemingly re-awakened the racer that had for so long lain dormant. He won G5/6 races at both Silverstone and Jyllandsring and took the European 2-litre championship with some terrific drives.

Although just past 40, Bonnier's racing activities showed no sign of slackening in 1971, and his lacklustre Grand Prix perform-ances were thrown into sharp relief by some more good results in the sports car categories, including a third in the Targa Florio with Attwood, second place in the Auvergne Trophy and an outright win in the Barcelona 1000 Km with Peterson. Retiring from Formula 1 at the end of the season, Bonnier raced on in a new Lola T280. However, at Le Mans in 1972 he was involved in a collision with a privateer Ferrari, and Jo's yellow Lola was launched over the barriers into the trees. The man who had spent so much time crusading for circuit safety over the years had become another victim among a whole generation of racers who paid the ultimate price.

BONNIER, Joakim (S) b 31/1/1930, Stockholm – d 11/6/1972, Le Mans Circuit, France

1956 — Championship position: Unplaced

	Race	Circuit	No	Entrant	Tyres	Car/Engine	Comment	Q Pos/Entries
ret	ITALIAN GP	Monza	34	Officine Alfieri Maserati	P	2.5 Maserati 250F 6	*took over Villoresi's car/engine*	– /26

1957 — Championship position: Unplaced

	Race	Circuit	No	Entrant	Tyres	Car/Engine	Comment	Q Pos/Entries
7	ARGENTINE GP	Buenos Aires	24	Scuderia Centro Sud	P	2.5 Maserati 250F 6	*5 laps behind*	13/16
ret	BRITISH GP	Aintree	28	Jo Bonnier	P	2.5 Maserati 250F 6	*transmission*	17/19
ret	PESCARA GP	Pescara	16	Scuderia Centro Sud	P	2.5 Maserati 250F 6	*overheating*	9/16
ret	ITALIAN GP	Monza	24	Scuderia Centro Sud	P	2.5 Maserati 250F 6	*overheating*	13/19

1958 — Championship position: 14th= Wins: 0 Pole positions: 0 Fastest laps: 0 Points scored: 3

	Race	Circuit	No	Entrant	Tyres	Car/Engine	Comment	Q Pos/Entries
ret	MONACO GP	Monte Carlo	58	Jo Bonnier	P	2.5 Maserati 250F 6	*accident*	16/28
10	DUTCH GP	Zandvoort	11	Jo Bonnier	P	2.5 Maserati 250F 6	*4 laps behind*	15/17
9	BELGIAN GP	Spa	36	Jo Bonnier	P	2.5 Maserati 250F 6	*2 laps behind*	14/20
8	FRENCH GP	Reims	38	Giorgio Scarlatti	P	2.5 Maserati 250F 6	*2 laps behind*	16/21
ret	BRITISH GP	Silverstone	22	Jo Bonnier	P	2.5 Maserati 250F 6	*gearbox*	13/21
ret	GERMAN GP	Nürburgring	16	Scuderia Centro Sud	P	2.5 Maserati 250F 6	*collision damage with Brabham*	9/26
ret	PORTUGUESE GP	Oporto	32	Jo Bonnier	P	2.5 Maserati 250F 6	*driver unwell*	14/15
ret	ITALIAN GP	Monza	12	Owen Racing Organisation	D	2.5 BRM P25 4	*transmission/fire*	10/21
4	MOROCCAN GP	Casablanca	18	Owen Racing Organisation	D	2.5 BRM P25 4		8/25

1959 — Championship position: 8th= Wins: 1 Pole positions: 1 Fastest laps: 0 Points scored: 10

	Race	Circuit	No	Entrant	Tyres	Car/Engine	Comment	Q Pos/Entries
ret	MONACO GP	Monte Carlo	18	Owen Racing Organisation	D	2.5 BRM P25 4	*brakes/accident*	7/24
1	DUTCH GP	Zandvoort	7	Owen Racing Organisation	D	2.5 BRM P25 4		1/15
ret	FRENCH GP	Reims	4	Owen Racing Organisation	D	2.5 BRM P25 4	*engine-head gasket*	6/22
ret	BRITISH GP	Aintree	10	Owen Racing Organisation	D	2.5 BRM P25 4	*throttle linkage*	10/30
5 agg	GERMAN GP	AVUS	9	Owen Racing Organisation	D	2.5 BRM P25 4	*7th heat 1/5th heat 2/-2 laps*	7/16
ret	PORTUGUESE GP	Monsanto	7	Owen Racing Organisation	D	2.5 BRM P25 4	*engine-fuel feed*	5/16
8	ITALIAN GP	Monza	6	Owen Racing Organisation	D	2.5 BRM P25 4	*2 laps behind*	11/21
dns	"	"	6	Owen Racing Organisation	D	2.5 BRM P48 4	*practice only*	– / –

1960 — Championship position: 13th= Wins: 0 Pole positions: 0 Fastest laps: 0 Points scored: 4

	Race	Circuit	No	Entrant	Tyres	Car/Engine	Comment	Q Pos/Entries
7	ARGENTINE GP	Buenos Aires	40	Owen Racing Organisation	D	2.5 BRM P25 4	*1 lap behind*	5/22
5	MONACO GP	Monte Carlo	2	Owen Racing Organisation	D	2.5 BRM P48 4	*pit stop-suspension/-17 laps*	3/24
ret	DUTCH GP	Zandvoort	14	Owen Racing Organisation	D	2.5 BRM P48 4	*engine-spun off on own oil*	4/21
ret	BELGIAN GP	Spa	6	Owen Racing Organisation	D	2.5 BRM P48 4	*engine*	7/18
ret	FRENCH GP	Reims	8	Owen Racing Organisation	D	2.5 BRM P48 4	*engine*	8/23
ret	BRITISH GP	Silverstone	6	Owen Racing Organisation	D	2.5 BRM P48 4	*rear suspension*	4/25
ret	PORTUGUESE GP	Oporto	20	Owen Racing Organisation	D	2.5 BRM P48 4	*engine*	13/16
5	US GP	Riverside	15	Owen Racing Organisation	D	2.5 BRM P48 4	*1 lap behind*	4/23

1961 — Championship position: 13th= Wins: 0 Pole positions: 0 Fastest laps: 0 Points scored: 3

	Race	Circuit	No	Entrant	Tyres	Car/Engine	Comment	Q Pos/Entries
ret	MONACO GP	Monte Carlo	2	Porsche System Engineering	D	1.5 Porsche 787 F4	*fuel injection*	9/21
dns	"	"	2	Porsche System Engineering	D	1.5 Porsche 718 F4	*practice only*	– / –
11	DUTCH GP	Zandvoort	6	Porsche System Engineering	D	1.5 Porsche 787 F4	*2 laps behind*	12/17
7	BELGIAN GP	Spa	18	Porsche System Engineering	D	1.5 Porsche 718 F4		9/25
7	FRENCH GP	Reims	10	Porsche System Engineering	D	1.5 Porsche 718 F4		=12/26
5	BRITISH GP	Aintree	8	Porsche System Engineering	D	1.5 Porsche 718 F4		=1/30
ret	GERMAN GP	Nürburgring	8	Porsche System Engineering	D	1.5 Porsche 718 F4	*engine*	4/27
ret	ITALIAN GP	Monza	44	Porsche System Engineering	D	1.5 Porsche 718 F4	*suspension*	8/33
dns	"	"	44	Porsche System Engineering	D	1.5 Porsche 787 F4	*practice only*	– / –
6	US GP	Watkins Glen	11	Porsche System Engineering	D	1.5 Porsche 718 F4	*2 laps behind*	=9/19

BRM's long-awaited maiden World Championship Grand Prix victory was finally achieved by Bonnier in the Dutch Grand Prix at Zandvoort in 1959. It was to be the only win for the Swedish driver at this level.

1962
Championship position: 14th Wins: 0 Pole positions: 0 Fastest laps: 0 Points scored: 3

7	DUTCH GP	Zandvoort	11	Porsche System Engineering	D	1.5 Porsche 804 F8	5 laps behind	13/20
5	MONACO GP	Monte Carlo	2	Porsche System Engineering	D	1.5 Porsche 718 F4	7 laps behind	18/21
10/ret	FRENCH GP	Rouen	32	Porsche System Engineering	D	1.5 Porsche 804 F8	gearbox/-12 laps	9/17
ret	BRITISH GP	Aintree	10	Porsche System Engineering	D	1.5 Porsche 804 F8	cwp	=7/21
7	GERMAN GP	Nürburgring	8	Porsche System Engineering	D	1.5 Porsche 804 F8		6/30
6	ITALIAN GP	Monza	18	Porsche System Engineering	D	1.5 Porsche 804 F8	1 lap behind	9/30
13	US GP	Watkins Glen	11	Porsche System Engineering	D	1.5 Porsche 804 F8	pit stops/21 laps behind	9/20

1963
Championship position: 9th= Wins: 0 Pole positions: 0 Fastest laps: 0 Points scored: 6

7	MONACO GP	Monte Carlo	11	R R C Walker Racing Team	D	1.5 Cooper T60-Climax V8	6 laps behind	11/17
5	BELGIAN GP	Spa	12	R R C Walker Racing Team	D	1.5 Cooper T60-Climax V8	2 laps behind	=12/20
dns	"	"	12	R R C Walker Racing Team	D	1.5 Cooper T66-Climax V8	practice only-oil leak engine	-/-
11	DUTCH GP	Zandvoort	28	R R C Walker Racing Team	D	1.5 Cooper T66-Climax V8	pit stop-gearbox/-24 laps	-/-
dns	"	"	28	R R C Walker Racing Team	D	1.5 Cooper T66-Climax V8	practice only-set grid time	8/19
nc	FRENCH GP	Reims	44	R R C Walker Racing Team	D	1.5 Cooper T60-Climax V8	ignition trouble/-21 laps	11/21
dns	"	"	44	R R C Walker Racing Team	D	1.5 Cooper T66-Climax V8	practice only-engine problems	-/-
ret	BRITISH GP	Silverstone	14	R R C Walker Racing Team	D	1.5 Cooper T66-Climax V8	oil pressure	=10/23
6	GERMAN GP	Nürburgring	16	R R C Walker Racing Team	D	1.5 Cooper T66-Climax V8	1 lap behind	12/26
7	ITALIAN GP	Monza	58	R R C Walker Racing Team	D	1.5 Cooper T66-Climax V8	pit stop-fuel/2 laps behind	11/28
dns	"	"	58	R R C Walker Racing Team	D	1.5 Cooper T66-Climax V8	practice only	-/-
8	US GP	Watkins Glen	11	R R C Walker Racing Team	D	1.5 Cooper T66-Climax V8	pit stops/25 laps behind	12/21
5	MEXICAN GP	Mexico City	11	R R C Walker Racing Team	D	1.5 Cooper T66-Climax V8	3 laps behind	8/21
6	SOUTH AFRICAN GP	East London	12	R R C Walker Racing Team	D	1.5 Cooper T66-Climax V8	2 laps behind	11/21

1964
Championship position: 15th Wins: 0 Pole positions: 0 Fastest laps: 0 Points scored: 3

5	MONACO GP	Monte Carlo	19	R R C Walker Racing Team	D	1.5 Cooper T66-Climax V8	4 laps behind	11/20
9	DUTCH GP	Zandvoort	26	R R C Walker Racing Team	D	1.5 Brabham BT11-BRM V8	4 laps behind	12/18
dns	"	"	26T	R R C Walker Racing Team	D	1.5 Cooper T66-Climax V8	practice only	-/-
ret	BELGIAN GP	Spa	16	R R C Walker Racing Team	D	1.5 Brabham BT11-BRM V8	unwell after practice crash	14/20
dns	"	"	16	R R C Walker Racing Team	D	1.5 Cooper T66-Climax V8	practice only-crashed car	-/-
ret	BRITISH GP	Brands Hatch	16	R R C Walker Racing Team	D	1.5 Brabham BT11-BRM V8	brake pipe	=8/25
dns	"	"	16	R R C Walker Racing Team	D	1.5 Cooper T66-Climax V8	practice only	-/-
ret	GERMAN GP	Nürburgring	11	R R C Walker Racing Team	D	1.5 Brabham BT11-BRM V8	electrics	12/24
6	AUSTRIAN GP	Zeltweg	11	R R C Walker Racing Team	D	1.5 Brabham BT7-Climax V8	4 laps behind	10/20
12	ITALIAN GP	Monza	34	R R C Walker Racing Team	D	1.5 Brabham BT7-Climax V8	alternator problems/-4 laps	=12/25
ret	US GP	Watkins Glen	16	R R C Walker Racing Team	D	1.5 Brabham BT7-Climax V8	stub axle	9/19
ret	MEXICAN GP	Mexico City	16	R R C Walker Racing Team	D	1.5 Brabham BT7-Climax V8	wishbone	8/19

1965
Championship position: Unplaced

ret	SOUTH AFRICAN GP	East London	11	R R C Walker Racing Team	D	1.5 Brabham BT7-Climax V8	clutch	=6/25
7	MONACO GP	Monte Carlo	12	R R C Walker Racing Team	D	1.5 Brabham BT7-Climax V8	3 laps behind	=12/17
ret	BELGIAN GP	Spa	20	R R C Walker Racing Team	D	1.5 Brabham BT7-Climax V8	ignition	7/21
ret	FRENCH GP	Clermont Ferrand	34	R R C Walker Racing Team	D	1.5 Brabham BT7-Climax V8	alternator drive	=10/17
7	BRITISH GP	Silverstone	15	R R C Walker Racing Team	D	1.5 Brabham BT7-Climax V8	1 lap behind	14/23
ret	DUTCH GP	Zandvoort	26	R R C Walker Racing Team	D	1.5 Brabham BT7-Climax V8	valve spring	15/17
7	GERMAN GP	Nürburgring	16	R R C Walker Racing Team	D	1.5 Brabham BT7-Climax V8		9/22
7	ITALIAN GP	Monza	42	R R C Walker Racing Team	D	1.5 Brabham BT7-Climax V8	2 laps behind	14/23
8	US GP	Watkins Glen	15	R R C Walker Racing Team	D	1.5 Brabham BT7-Climax V8	3 laps behind	10/18
ret	MEXICAN GP	Mexico City	15	R R C Walker Racing Team	D	1.5 Brabham BT7-Climax V8	broken wishbone	12/18

1966
Championship position: 17th= Wins: 0 Pole positions: 0 Fastest laps: 0 Points scored: 1

nc	MONACO GP	Monte Carlo	18	Anglo-Suisse Racing Team	F	3.0 Cooper T81-Maserati V12	pit stops/27 laps behind	14/16
dns	"	" "	18T	Reg Parnell Racing Ltd	F	2.7 Lotus 25-Climax 4	practice only	-/-
ret	BELGIAN GP	Spa	20	Anglo-Suisse Racing Team	F	3.0 Cooper T81-Maserati V12	spun off in rain	6/18
nc	FRENCH GP	Reims	30	Brabham Racing Organisation	F	2.5 Brabham BT22-Climax 4	16 laps behind	17/17
dns	"	"	30		D	3.0 Cooper T77-ATS V8	practice only/blown engine	-/-
ret	BRITISH GP	Brands Hatch	18	Anglo-Suisse Racing Team	F	1.5 Brabham BT7-Climax V8	car painted as a Ferrari/engine	15/20
7	DUTCH GP	Zandvoort	30	Anglo-Suisse Racing Team	F	3.0 Cooper T81-Maserati V12	6 laps behind	13/18
ret	GERMAN GP	Nürburgring	17	Anglo-Suisse Racing Team	F	3.0 Cooper T81-Maserati V12	clutch	13/30
ret	ITALIAN GP	Monza	38	Anglo-Suisse Racing Team	F	3.0 Cooper T81-Maserati V12	throttle linkage	12/22
nc	US GP	Watkins Glen	22	Anglo-Suisse Racing Team	F	3.0 Cooper T81-Maserati V12	pit stops/51 laps behind	15/19
6	MEXICAN GP	Mexico City	22	Anglo-Suisse Racing Team	F	3.0 Cooper T81-Maserati V12	2 laps behind	13/19

1967
Championship position: 14th= Wins: 0 Pole positions: 0 Fastest laps: 0 Points scored: 3

ret	SOUTH AFRICAN GP	Kyalami	15	Joakim Bonnier Racing Team	F	3.0 Cooper T81-Maserati V12	engine	12/18
ret	BELGIAN GP	Spa	39	Joakim Bonnier Racing Team	F	3.0 Cooper T81-Maserati V12	fuel feed	12/18
ret	BRITISH GP	Silverstone	23	Joakim Bonnier Racing Team	F	3.0 Cooper T81-Maserati V12	engine	19/21
5*	GERMAN GP	Nürburgring	16	Joakim Bonnier Racing Team	F	3.0 Cooper T81-Maserati V12	* 6th on road behind F2 car	=21/25
8	CANADIAN GP	Mosport Park	9	Joakim Bonnier Racing Team	F	3.0 Cooper T81-Maserati V12	5 laps behind	15/19
ret	ITALIAN GP	Monza	26	Joakim Bonnier Racing Team	F	3.0 Cooper T81-Maserati V12	overheating	14/18
6	US GP	Watkins Glen	16	Joakim Bonnier Racing Team	F	3.0 Cooper T81-Maserati V12	pit stop-wheel/7 laps behind	15/18
10	MEXICAN GP	Mexico City	16	Joakim Bonnier Racing Team	F	3.0 Cooper T81-Maserati V12	4 laps behind	17/19

1968
Championship position: 21st= Wins: 0 Pole positions: 0 Fastest laps: 0 Points scored: 3

ret	SOUTH AFRICAN GP	Kyalami	20	Joakim Bonnier Racing Team	F	3.0 Cooper T81-Maserati V12	lost rear wheel	19/23
dnq	MONACO GP	Monte Carlo	18	Joakim Bonnier Racing Team	G	3.0 McLaren M5A-BRM V12	not seeded	15/18
ret	BELGIAN GP	Spa	17	Joakim Bonnier Racing Team	G	3.0 McLaren M5A-BRM V12	wheel stud	16/18
8	DUTCH GP	Zandvoort	19	Joakim Bonnier Racing Team	G	3.0 McLaren M5A-BRM V12	8 laps behind	19/19
ret	BRITISH GP	Brands Hatch	23	Joakim Bonnier Racing Team	G	3.0 McLaren M5A-BRM V12	engine	20/20
6	ITALIAN GP	Monza	3	Joakim Bonnier Racing Team	G	3.0 McLaren M5A-BRM V12	4 laps behind	21/24
ret/dns	CANADIAN GP	St Jovite	22	Joakim Bonnier Racing Team	G	3.0 McLaren M5A-BRM V12	car would not start on grid	18/22
ret	US GP	Watkins Glen	17	Joakim Bonnier Racing Team	G	3.0 McLaren M5A-BRM V12	ignition trouble/4 laps behind	18/21
5	MEXICAN GP	Mexico City	17	Joakim Bonnier Racing Team	F	3.0 Honda RA301 V12	drove works spare/-1 lap	18/21
dns	"	" "	17	Joakim Bonnier Racing Team	G	3.0 McLaren M5A-BRM V12	engine in practice	-/-

	1969	Championship position: Unplaced							
ret	BRITISH GP	Silverstone	18	Ecurie Bonnier/Gold Leaf Team Lotus	F	3.0 Lotus 63-Cosworth V8		engine	16/17
ret	GERMAN GP	Nürburgring	16	Ecurie Bonnier	F	3.0 Lotus 49B-Cosworth V8		fuel leak	23/26
	1970	Championship position: Unplaced							
dnq	ITALIAN GP	Monza	38	Ecurie Bonnier	G	3.0 McLaren M7C-Cosworth V8			24/27
ret	US GP	Watkins Glen	27	Ecurie Bonnier	G	3.0 McLaren M7C-Cosworth V8		water pipe	24/27
	1971	Championship position: Unplaced							
ret	SOUTH AFRICAN GP	Kyalami	23	Ecurie Bonnier	G	3.0 McLaren M7C-Cosworth V8		suspension	23/25
dnq	GERMAN GP	Nürburgring	27	Ecurie Bonnier	G	3.0 McLaren M7C-Cosworth V8			23/23
dns	AUSTRIAN GP	Österreichring	28	Ecurie Bonnier	G	3.0 McLaren M7C-Cosworth V8		fuel leak before start	(19)/22
10	ITALIAN GP	Monza	28	Ecurie Bonnier	G	3.0 McLaren M7C-Cosworth V8		4 laps behind	21/24
16/ret	US GP	Watkins Glen	29	Ecurie Bonnier	G	3.0 McLaren M7C-Cosworth V8		out of fuel/5 laps behind	31/32

GP Starts: 103 (104)   GP Wins: 1   Pole positions: 1   Fastest laps: 0   Points: 39

ROBERTO BONOMI

Bonomi was a wealthy land-owner who was the Argentine sports car champion of 1952 and 1953, racing Ferraris. His success continued into 1954 with a Ferrari 250MM Vignale, Roberto scoring wins in the Argentine 500-mile race, and events at Primavera, Costa Nera Lealtad and Mendoza. He was therefore regularly chosen to supplement the works teams in the annual Buenos Aires 1000 Km sports car race, placing fifth in 1957 in a Maserati 350S V12 with Piotti.

Roberto then purchased a Maserati 300S which he raced in sports car and Libre events between 1958 and 1961.

He hired a Cooper for his only Grand Prix appearance in 1960, also racing the same car in the Formule Libre Cordoba GP before it was taken over by team-mate Menditéguy.

TOMMY 'SLIM' BORGUDD

Tommy Borgudd began racing in Formula Ford and sports cars in his native Sweden between 1969 and 1973, but lack of finance forced him to fall back on his career as a drummer (most famously in studio sessions with Abba). It was when he was working in New Orleans that he gained his nickname. After stepping in for a drummer called 'Memphis Slim', Borgudd was dubbed 'Little Slim'. Subsequently this was shortened to 'Slim' and it stuck, mainly because his subsequent pay-cheques were made out in this name and he had problems cashing them as his ID card showed his real name, Tommy!

After a few drives in 1976, Slim returned to the tracks on a more permanent basis the following year, and was soon performing heroics in both the Swedish and European F3 series with an outdated Ralt. Particularly impressive were his efforts in the European championship in 1979 when he finished third overall behind the dazzling Prost and experienced Bleekemolen despite having to miss races due to lack of money as the year wore on.

A planned season in Formula 2 in 1980 was aborted when the finance was not forthcoming, but Slim occasionally competed in a March in F3 while working on a deal that saw him join the ATS team in Grands Prix for 1981.

Sixth place – and a championship point – in the British Grand Prix was the high spot in a difficult season. Borgudd then began the next campaign with the Tyrrell team, but his money soon ran out and he was replaced by Brian Henton. That there is more to life than struggling at the back of the grid in Formula 1 has surely been proved by Slim, who went on to carve out a hugely successful, enjoyable – and profitable! – career as truck racing European Champion as well as briefly racing a Mazda Xedos touring car in the Nordic Cup.

LUKI BOTHA

Botha showed well on his single-seater debut in the 1966 end-of-season Rhodesian Grand Prix, bringing his Brabham BT11 into second place behind the visiting Bob Anderson's similar car. Less than three weeks later he made his only appearance in a Grand Prix at Kyalami but spent many laps in the pits after a collision at the start.

Botha took a step up in competitiveness after adding a Repco engine to his BT11, and finished third behind Charlton and Love in the Rand Autumn Trophy at Kyalami. However, his inexperience was soon apparent and, though showing a fair turn of speed, he had a number of 'offs' in the next few events. Sadly, he crashed again in a race in Mozambique, his car killing eight spectators. Botha escaped personal injury but never raced again.

BONOMI, Roberto (RA) b 30/9/1919, Buenos Aires

	1960			Championship position: Unplaced					
	Race	Circuit	No	Entrant	Tyres	Car/Engine		Comment	Q Pos/Entries
11	ARGENTINE GP	Buenos Aires	4	Scuderia Centro Sud	D	2.5 Cooper T51-Maserati 4		4 laps behind	17/22

GP Starts: 1   GP Wins: 0   Pole positions: 0   Fastest laps: 0   Points: 0

BORGUDD, Slim (Tommy) (S) b 25/11/1946, Borgholm, nr Kalmar

	1981			Championship position: 18= Wins: 0 Pole positions: 0 Fastest laps: 0 Points scored: 1					
	Race	Circuit	No	Entrant	Tyres	Car/Engine		Comment	Q Pos/Entries
13	SAN MARINO GP	Imola	10	Team ATS	M	3.0 ATS D4-Cosworth V8		pit stop-tyres/3 laps behind	24/30
dnq	BELGIAN GP	Zolder	10	Team ATS	M	3.0 ATS HGS1-Cosworth V8			27/31
dnpq	MONACO GP	Monte Carlo	10	Team ATS	M	3.0 ATS D4-Cosworth V8			27/31
dnq	SPANISH GP	Jarama	10	Team ATS	M	3.0 ATS HGS1-Cosworth V8			27/30
dnq	FRENCH GP	Dijon	10	Team ATS	M	3.0 ATS HGS1-Cosworth V8			27/29
6	BRITISH GP	Silverstone	10	Team ATS	A	3.0 ATS HGS1-Cosworth V8		1 lap behind	21/30
ret	GERMAN GP	Hockenheim	10	Team ATS	A	3.0 ATS HGS1-Cosworth V8		engine	20/30
ret	AUSTRIAN GP	Österreichring	10	Team ATS	A	3.0 ATS HGS1-Cosworth V8		brakes	21/28
10	DUTCH GP	Zandvoort	10	Team ATS	A	3.0 ATS HGS1-Cosworth V8		pit stop-tyres/4 laps behind	23/30
ret	ITALIAN GP	Monza	10	Team ATS	A	3.0 ATS HGS1-Cosworth V8		spun off	21/30
ret	CANADIAN GP	Montreal	10	Team ATS	A	3.0 ATS HGS1-Cosworth V8		spun off	21/30
dnq	CAESARS PALACE GP	Las Vegas	10	Team ATS	A	3.0 ATS HGS1-Cosworth V8			25/30
	1982			Championship position: Unplaced					
16	SOUTH AFRICAN GP	Kyalami	4	Team Tyrrell	G	3.0 Tyrrell 011-Cosworth V8		pit stop-tyres/5 laps behind	23/30
7*	BRAZILIAN GP	Rio	4	Team Tyrrell	G	3.0 Tyrrell 011-Cosworth V8		* 1st & 2nd cars dsq/-2 laps	21/31
10*	US GP WEST	Long Beach	4	Team Tyrrell	G	3.0 Tyrrell 011-Cosworth V8		* 3rd car dsq/collision/-7 laps	24/31

GP Starts: 10   GP Wins: 0   Pole positions: 0   Fastest laps: 0   Points: 1

BOTHA, Luki (ZA) b 16/1/1930

	1967			Championship position: Unplaced					
	Race	Circuit	No	Entrant	Tyres	Car/Engine		Comment	Q Pos/Entries
nc	SOUTH AFRICAN GP	Kyalami	20	Luki Botha	–	2.7 Brabham BT7-Climax 4		pit stop/20 laps behind	17/18

GP Starts: 1   GP Wins: 0   Pole positions: 0   Fastest laps: 0   Points: 0

BOULLION, Jean-Christophe b 27/12/1969, Saint Brieuc, nr Cote d'Amor

	1995			Championship position: 16th Wins: 0 Pole positions: 0 Fastest laps: 0 Points scored: 3					
	Race	Circuit	No	Entrant	Tyres	Car/Engine		Comment	Q Pos/Entries
8	MONACO GP	Monte Carlo	29	Red Bull Sauber Ford	G	3.0 Sauber C14-Ford Zetec-R V8		collision-Morbidelli/-4 laps	19/26
ret	CANADIAN GP	Montreal	29	Red Bull Sauber Ford	G	3.0 Sauber C14-Ford Zetec-R V8		spun off	18/24
ret	FRENCH GP	Magny Cours	29	Red Bull Sauber Ford	G	3.0 Sauber C14-Ford Zetec-R V8		gearbox	15/24
9	BRITISH GP	Silverstone	29	Red Bull Sauber Ford	G	3.0 Sauber C14-Ford Zetec-R V8		1 lap behind	16/24
5	GERMAN GP	Hockenheim	29	Red Bull Sauber Ford	G	3.0 Sauber C14-Ford Zetec-R V8		1 lap behind	14/24
10	HUNGARIAN GP	Hungaroring	29	Red Bull Sauber Ford	G	3.0 Sauber C14-Ford Zetec-R V8		3 laps behind	19/24
11	BELGIAN GP	Spa	29	Red Bull Sauber Ford	G	3.0 Sauber C14-Ford Zetec-R V8		1 lap behind	14/24
6	ITALIAN GP	Monza	29	Red Bull Sauber Ford	G	3.0 Sauber C14-Ford Zetec-R V8		started from pit lane/-1 lap	14/24
12	PORTUGUESE GP	Estoril	29	Red Bull Sauber Ford	G	3.0 Sauber C14-Ford Zetec-R V8		1 lap behind	14/24
ret	EUROPEAN GP	Nürburgring	29	Red Bull Sauber Ford	G	3.0 Sauber C14-Ford Zetec-R V8		spun off	13/24
ret	PACIFIC GP	T.I. Circuit	29	Red Bull Sauber Ford	G	3.0 Sauber C14-Ford Zetec-R V8		spun off	15/24

GP Starts: 11   GP Wins: 0   Pole positions: 0   Fastest laps: 0   Points: 3

JEAN-CHRISTOPHE BOULLION

'Jules', as he is universally known, was always a man to watch. The 1990 French FF1600 champion was soon impressing all in the French F3 championship with his style and speed. Fourth place in the 1992 series was a disappointment and reflected the major chink in his armour, inconsistency. Nevertheless he moved up to F3000 with Apomatox and endured a character-building year which yielded two second-place finishes. The shy and hitherto uncommunicative Frenchman really came of age in 1994 when a switch to DAMS saw him mount a late-season charge, Boullion winning the last three races to snatch the title at the final round.

Given a testing contract with Williams for 1995, he was soon setting some impressive times and jumped at the chance to race for Sauber in place of the disappointing Wendlinger. In view of his inexperience, Boullion did well to record two points-scoring finishes. However, on the debit side, perhaps he was pushing too hard, for there were too many spins.

His testing expertise was never in doubt, as he was capable of matching the times of Damon Hill. But questions still lingered over his qualities as a racer. Apart from the Renault Spyder series in 1997, Boullion had little opportunity to compete, accepting the task of shaking down the BAR team's first Grand Prix challenger in 1998 before returning to the Williams fold in 1999 to race their Laguna in the BTCC series. Sadly, a single podium finish and tenth place overall were all the little Frenchman had to show for his efforts.

THIERRY BOUTSEN

With no family racing background, Thierry went to the Pilette racing school where he soon became a star pupil and set out on a Formula Ford career. In 1978 the young Belgian raced a Crosslé in the Benelux countries, winning 15 of his 18 races, which brought him to the attention of his boyhood idol Jacky Ickx. With his help, Boutsen found a Formula 3 ride in 1979, but the season was fraught with troubles until a spectacular performance in the final round at Jarama, where he matched European champion Alain Prost. This one drive was enough to persuade the works Martini team to sign him in place of the little Frenchman, who was off to McLaren, and the new season began well, with three wins in the first four races, but when March launched their new wing car, a depressed Boutsen was powerless to prevent himself being overhauled by the determined Michele Alboreto.

Stepping up into Formula 2 with a works March in 1981, Boutsen was the surprise of the championship, winning races at the Nürburgring and Enna, and finishing runner-up once more, this time to Geoff Lees. Opting to race for Spirit in 1982 was something of a gamble which didn't quite come off, but his brilliant wins at the Nürburgring, Enna and especially Spa marked him down as an immediate Grand Prix prospect. Thierry's hopes of racing the Spirit F1 car in 1983 were dashed when Johansson got the nod but he managed to finance a ride with Arrows, with whom he was to stay for three more seasons, quietly but impressively getting on with the job in hand. The car was never really competitive, but Boutsen was always a contender for points, and when Benetton signed him it was a long-overdue promotion.

Results in his first season with Benetton, 1987, were a mite disappointing, with niggling mechanical problems restricting the team's progress, while in 1988 his position was somewhat eroded by the arrival of the gregarious Nannini, but Boutsen still finished third behind the dominant McLarens on four occasions.

Joining Williams with Renault power for 1989 offered Thierry his big chance, but though he did little wrong – indeed he took two brilliant wins in torrential rain at Montreal and Adelaide – it seemed that he didn't quite fit the bill at Didcot, rather unfairly being compared with Mansell. In 1990, already feeling under-appreciated at Williams, he scored an absolutely superb win in the Hungarian GP, proving he had nerves of steel by fending off Senna's late challenge, before he took the only feasible option open to him and signed a two-year deal with Ligier. Despite a massive budget, Ligier made a hash of things as usual, particularly in 1991 when Thierry just kept his head down hoping things would improve. In fact they did somewhat the following season, when Renault engines became available, but such was the strained atmosphere within the team that at the end of the year the Belgian was probably glad to be out of it. Without a drive for 1993, Thierry was soon called into the Jordan line-up, replacing the crestfallen Capelli. However, it was to be an undistinguished swansong, which came to a sad end when Boutsen retired from his farewell Formula 1 race at Spa on the first lap.

In 1994 and 1995, Thierry competed in the German Super Touring championship, but his Ford Mondeo was unable to challenge the dominance of Audi and BMW. On a wider stage, at Le Mans in 1995, he shared the sixth-place Kremer K8-Porsche with Hans Stuck and Christophe Bouchut. A return to sports cars and the sharp end of competition came in 1996 when Thierry was again paired with Stuck, in a works Porsche 911 GT1. After a second place at Le Mans, the experienced duo took end-of-season wins at Brands Hatch and Spa. Although eight top-six finishes were achieved the following year, no victories were forthcoming, and the seasoned campaigners were both dropped from the works squad.

Boutsen therefore headed over to the States to race a Porsche 911 GT1 in selected US GT championship events, also driving Toyota's latest Le Mans challenger, the GT-One. He returned in 1999 for another outing in one of the potent Japanese machines, but the race ended in near-disaster for the Belgian when his car was nudged into the barriers by a back-marker. Suffering from cracked vertebrae in his back, he decided it was time to call it a day and retired to spend more time with his second wife and young family, and concentrate on his aviation business.

BOUTSEN, Thierry (B) b 13/7/1957, Brussels

	1983	Championship position: Unplaced							
	Race	Circuit	No	Entrant	Tyres	Car/Engine		Comment	Q Pos/Entries
ret	BELGIAN GP	Spa	30	Arrows Racing Team	G	3.0 Arrows A6-Cosworth V8		rear suspension	18/28
7	US GP (DETROIT)	Detroit	30	Arrows Racing Team	G	3.0 Arrows A6-Cosworth V8		1 lap behind	10/27
7	CANADIAN GP	Montreal	30	Arrows Racing Team	G	3.0 Arrows A6-Cosworth V8		1 lap behind	15/28
15	BRITISH GP	Silverstone	30	Arrows Racing Team	G	3.0 Arrows A6-Cosworth V8		2 laps behind	17/29
9*	GERMAN GP	Hockenheim	30	Arrows Racing Team	G	3.0 Arrows A6-Cosworth V8		* 5th place car dsq/-1 lap	14/29
13	AUSTRIAN GP	Österreichring	30	Arrows Racing Team	G	3.0 Arrows A6-Cosworth V8		pit stop-plugs/-5 laps	19/29
14/ret	DUTCH GP	Zandvoort	30	Arrows Racing Team	G	3.0 Arrows A6-Cosworth V8		engine/ 4 laps behind	21/29
ret	ITALIAN GP	Monza	30	Arrows Racing Team	G	3.0 Arrows A6-Cosworth V8		engine	18/29
11	EUROPEAN GP	Brands Hatch	30	Arrows Racing Team	G	3.0 Arrows A6-Cosworth V8		1 lap behind	18/29
9	SOUTH AFRICAN GP	Kyalami	30	Arrows Racing Team	G	3.0 Arrows A6-Cosworth V8		3 laps behind	20/26

1984
Championship position: 14th=   Wins: 0   Pole positions: 0   Fastest laps: 0   Points scored: 5

6*	BRAZILIAN GP	Rio	18	Barclay Nordica Arrows BMW	G	3.0 Arrows A6-Cosworth V8	*5th place car dsq/-1 lap	21/27
12*	SOUTH AFRICAN GP	Kyalami	18	Barclay Nordica Arrows BMW	G	3.0 Arrows A6-Cosworth V8	*11th place car dsq/-5 laps	26/27
ret	BELGIAN GP	Zolder	18	Barclay Nordica Arrows BMW	G	1.5 t/c Arrows A7-BMW 4	misfire	17/27
5*	SAN MARINO GP	Imola	18	Barclay Nordica Arrows BMW	G	3.0 Arrows A6-Cosworth V8	*5th place car dsq/-1 lap	20/28
11	FRENCH GP	Dijon	18	Barclay Nordica Arrows BMW	G	1.5 t/c Arrows A7-BMW 4	2 laps behind	14/27
dnq	MONACO GP	Monte Carlo	18	Barclay Nordica Arrows BMW	G	1.5 t/c Arrows A7-BMW 4		24/27
ret	CANADIAN GP	Montreal	18	Barclay Nordica Arrows BMW	G	1.5 t/c Arrows A7-BMW 4	engine	18/26
ret	US GP (DETROIT)	Detroit	18	Barclay Nordica Arrows BMW	G	1.5 t/c Arrows A7-BMW 4	engine	13/27
ret	US GP (DALLAS)	Dallas	18	Barclay Nordica Arrows BMW	G	1.5 t/c Arrows A7-BMW 4	hit wall	20/27
ret	BRITISH GP	Brands Hatch	18	Barclay Nordica Arrows BMW	G	1.5 t/c Arrows A7-BMW 4	electrics	12/27
ret	GERMAN GP	Hockenheim	18	Barclay Nordica Arrows BMW	G	1.5 t/c Arrows A7-BMW 4	oil pressure	15/27
5	AUSTRIAN GP	Österreichring	18	Barclay Nordica Arrows BMW	G	1.5 t/c Arrows A7-BMW 4	1 lap behind	17/28
ret	DUTCH GP	Zandvoort	18	Barclay Nordica Arrows BMW	G	1.5 t/c Arrows A7-BMW 4	accident with Arnoux	11/27
10	ITALIAN GP	Monza	18	Barclay Nordica Arrows BMW	G	1.5 t/c Arrows A7-BMW 4	2 pit stops/6 laps behind	19/27
9/ret	EUROPEAN GP	Nürburgring	18	Barclay Nordica Arrows BMW	G	1.5 t/c Arrows A7-BMW 4	electrics/3 laps behind	11/26
ret	PORTUGUESE GP	Estoril	18	Barclay Nordica Arrows BMW	G	1.5 t/c Arrows A7-BMW 4	driveshaft	18/27

1985
Championship position: 11th=   Wins: 0   Pole positions: 0   Fastest laps: 0   Points scored: 11

11	BRAZILIAN GP	Rio	18	Barclay Arrows BMW	G	1.5 t/c Arrows A8-BMW 4	late start-fuel pressure/-4 laps	12/25
ret	PORTUGUESE GP	Estoril	18	Barclay Arrows BMW	G	1.5 t/c Arrows A8-BMW 4	electrics	16/26
2*	SAN MARINO GP	Imola	18	Barclay Arrows BMW	G	1.5 t/c Arrows A8-BMW 4	*1st place car dsq/1 lap behind	5/26
9	MONACO GP	Monte Carlo	18	Barclay Arrows BMW	G	1.5 t/c Arrows A8-BMW 4	2 laps behind	6/26
9	CANADIAN GP	Montreal	18	Barclay Arrows BMW	G	1.5 t/c Arrows A8-BMW 4	2 laps behind	7/25
7	US GP (DETROIT)	Detroit	18	Barclay Arrows BMW	G	1.5 t/c Arrows A8-BMW 4	1 lap behind	21/25
9	FRENCH GP	Paul Ricard	18	Barclay Arrows BMW	G	1.5 t/c Arrows A8-BMW 4	1 lap behind	12/26
ret	BRITISH GP	Silverstone	18	Barclay Arrows BMW	G	1.5 t/c Arrows A8-BMW 4	spun off	19/26
4	GERMAN GP	Nürburgring	18	Barclay Arrows BMW	G	1.5 t/c Arrows A8-BMW 4		15/27
8	AUSTRIAN GP	Österreichring	18	Barclay Arrows BMW	G	1.5 t/c Arrows A8-BMW 4	turbo boost problems/-3 laps	16/27
ret	DUTCH GP	Zandvoort	18	Barclay Arrows BMW	G	1.5 t/c Arrows A8-BMW 4	suspension	8/27
9	ITALIAN GP	Monza	18	Barclay Arrows BMW	G	1.5 t/c Arrows A8-BMW 4	1 lap behind	14/26
10/ret	BELGIAN GP	Spa	18	Barclay Arrows BMW	G	1.5 t/c Arrows A8-BMW 4	gearbox/3 laps behind	6/24
6	EUROPEAN GP	Brands Hatch	18	Barclay Arrows BMW	G	1.5 t/c Arrows A8-BMW 4	2 laps behind	12/27
6	SOUTH AFRICAN GP	Kyalami	18	Barclay Arrows BMW	G	1.5 t/c Arrows A8-BMW 4	1 lap behind	10/21
ret	AUSTRALIAN GP	Adelaide	18	Barclay Arrows BMW	G	1.5 t/c Arrows A8-BMW 4	oil leak	11/25

1986
Championship position: Unplaced

ret	BRAZILIAN GP	Rio	18	Barclay Arrows BMW	G	1.5 t/c Arrows A8-BMW 4	broken exhaust	15/25
7	SPANISH GP	Jerez	18	Barclay Arrows BMW	G	1.5 t/c Arrows A8-BMW 4	4 laps behind	19/25
7	SAN MARINO GP	Imola	18	Barclay Arrows BMW	G	1.5 t/c Arrows A8-BMW 4	2 laps behind	12/26
8	MONACO GP	Monte Carlo	18	Barclay Arrows BMW	G	1.5 t/c Arrows A8-BMW 4	3 laps behind	14/26
ret	BELGIAN GP	Spa	18	Barclay Arrows BMW	G	1.5 t/c Arrows A8-BMW 4	electrics	14/25
ret	CANADIAN GP	Montreal	18	Barclay Arrows BMW	G	1.5 t/c Arrows A8-BMW 4	electrics	12/25
ret	US GP (DETROIT)	Detroit	18	Barclay Arrows BMW	G	1.5 t/c Arrows A8-BMW 4	accident-hit by Arnoux	13/26
nc	FRENCH GP	Paul Ricard	18	Barclay Arrows BMW	G	1.5 t/c Arrows A8-BMW 4	stops-bodywork/-13 laps	21/26
nc	BRITISH GP	Brands Hatch	18	Barclay Arrows BMW	G	1.5 t/c Arrows A8-BMW 4	pit stop-electrics/-13 laps	13/26
ret	GERMAN GP	Hockenheim	18	Barclay Arrows BMW	G	1.5 t/c Arrows A9-BMW 4	turbo	21/26
ret	HUNGARIAN GP	Hungaroring	18	Barclay Arrows BMW	G	1.5 t/c Arrows A8-BMW 4	electrics	22/26
dns	"	"	18	Barclay Arrows BMW	G	1.5 t/c Arrows A9-BMW 4	practice only	–/–
ret	AUSTRIAN GP	Österreichring	18	Barclay Arrows BMW	G	1.5 t/c Arrows A9-BMW 4	turbo	18/26
dns	"	"	18	Barclay Arrows BMW	G	1.5 t/c Arrows A8-BMW 4	practice only	–/–
7	ITALIAN GP	Monza	18	Barclay Arrows BMW	G	1.5 t/c Arrows A8-BMW 4	2 laps behind	13/27
10	PORTUGUESE GP	Estoril	18	Barclay Arrows BMW	G	1.5 t/c Arrows A8-BMW 4	3 laps behind	21/27
7	MEXICAN GP	Mexico City	18	Barclay Arrows BMW	G	1.5 t/c Arrows A8-BMW 4	2 laps behind	21/26
ret	AUSTRALIAN GP	Adelaide	18	Barclay Arrows BMW	G	1.5 t/c Arrows A8-BMW 4	throttle spring	22/26

1987
Championship position: 8th   Wins: 0   Pole positions: 0   Fastest laps: 0   Points scored: 16

5	BRAZILIAN GP	Rio	20	Benetton Formula Ltd	G	1.5 t/c Benetton B187-Cosworth V6	1 lap behind	6/23
ret	SAN MARINO GP	Imola	20	Benetton Formula Ltd	G	1.5 t/c Benetton B187-Cosworth V6	engine	12/27
ret	BELGIAN GP	Spa	20	Benetton Formula Ltd	G	1.5 t/c Benetton B187-Cosworth V6	driveshaft	7/26
ret	MONACO GP	Monte Carlo	20	Benetton Formula Ltd	G	1.5 t/c Benetton B187-Cosworth V6	driveshaft	9/26
ret	US GP (DETROIT)	Detroit	20	Benetton Formula Ltd	G	1.5 t/c Benetton B187-Cosworth V6	brake disc	4/26
ret	FRENCH GP	Paul Ricard	20	Benetton Formula Ltd	G	1.5 t/c Benetton B187-Cosworth V6	distributor drive	5/26
7	BRITISH GP	Silverstone	20	Benetton Formula Ltd	G	1.5 t/c Benetton B187-Cosworth V6	3 laps behind	5/26
ret	GERMAN GP	Hockenheim	20	Benetton Formula Ltd	G	1.5 t/c Benetton B187-Cosworth V6	engine	6/26
4	HUNGARIAN GP	Hungaroring	20	Benetton Formula Ltd	G	1.5 t/c Benetton B187-Cosworth V6	1 lap behind	7/26
4	AUSTRIAN GP	Österreichring	20	Benetton Formula Ltd	G	1.5 t/c Benetton B187-Cosworth V6	1 lap behind	4/26
5	ITALIAN GP	Monza	20	Benetton Formula Ltd	G	1.5 t/c Benetton B187-Cosworth V6		6/28
14	PORTUGUESE GP	Estoril	20	Benetton Formula Ltd	G	1.5 t/c Benetton B187-Cosworth V6	pit stop-engine/6 laps behind	9/27
16/ret	SPANISH GP	Jerez	20	Benetton Formula Ltd	G	1.5 t/c Benetton B187-Cosworth V6	spun off-brakes	8/28
ret	MEXICAN GP	Mexico City	20	Benetton Formula Ltd	G	1.5 t/c Benetton B187-Cosworth V6	electrics	4/27
5	JAPANESE GP	Suzuka	20	Benetton Formula Ltd	G	1.5 t/c Benetton B187-Cosworth V6		3/27
3*	AUSTRALIAN GP	Adelaide	20	Benetton Formula Ltd	G	1.5 t/c Benetton B187-Cosworth V6	*2nd place car dsq/-1 lap	5/27

1988
Championship position: 4th   Wins: 0   Pole positions: 0   Fastest laps: 0   Points scored: 27

7	BRAZILIAN GP	Rio	20	Benetton Formula Ltd	G	3.5 Benetton B188-Cosworth V8	1 lap behind	7/31
4	SAN MARINO GP	Imola	20	Benetton Formula Ltd	G	3.5 Benetton B188-Cosworth V8	fractured exhaust/1 lap behind	8/31
8	MONACO GP	Monte Carlo	20	Benetton Formula Ltd	G	3.5 Benetton B188-Cosworth V8	2 laps behind	16/30
8	MEXICAN GP	Mexico City	20	Benetton Formula Ltd	G	3.5 Benetton B188-Cosworth V8	handling problems/-3 laps	11/30
3	CANADIAN GP	Montreal	20	Benetton Formula Ltd	G	3.5 Benetton B188-Cosworth V8		7/31
3	US GP (DETROIT)	Detroit	20	Benetton Formula Ltd	G	3.5 Benetton B188-Cosworth V8	1 lap behind	5/31
ret	FRENCH GP	Paul Ricard	20	Benetton Formula Ltd	G	3.5 Benetton B188-Cosworth V8	electrics	5/31
ret	BRITISH GP	Silverstone	20	Benetton Formula Ltd	G	3.5 Benetton B188-Cosworth V8	driveshaft-c.v. joint	12/31
6	GERMAN GP	Hockenheim	20	Benetton Formula Ltd	G	3.5 Benetton B188-Cosworth V8	dry set up-wet race/-1 lap	9/31
3	HUNGARIAN GP	Hungaroring	20	Benetton Formula Ltd	G	3.5 Benetton B188-Cosworth V8		3/31
dsq*	BELGIAN GP	Spa	20	Benetton Formula Ltd	G	3.5 Benetton B188-Cosworth V8	*3rd on the road/illegal fuel	6/31
6	ITALIAN GP	Monza	20	Benetton Formula Ltd	G	3.5 Benetton B188-Cosworth V8	misfire	8/31
3	PORTUGUESE GP	Estoril	20	Benetton Formula Ltd	G	3.5 Benetton B188-Cosworth V8		13/31

9	SPANISH GP	Jerez	20	Benetton Formula Ltd	G	3.5 Benetton B188-Cosworth V8	pit stop-nose cone	4/31
3	JAPANESE GP	Suzuka	20	Benetton Formula Ltd	G	3.5 Benetton B188-Cosworth V8		10/31
5	AUSTRALIAN GP	Adelaide	20	Benetton Formula Ltd	G	3.5 Benetton B188-Cosworth V8	misfire/broken exhaust/-1 lap	10/31

1989 Championship position: 5th   Wins: 0   Pole positions: 0   Fastest laps: 0   Points scored: 37

ret	BRAZILIAN GP	Rio	5	Canon Williams Team	G	3.5 Williams FW12C-Renault V10	engine	4/38
4	SAN MARINO GP	Imola	5	Canon Williams Team	G	3.5 Williams FW12C-Renault V10	understeer/clutch/-1 lap	6/39
10	MONACO GP	Monte Carlo	5	Canon Williams Team	G	3.5 Williams FW12C-Renault V10	pit stop-rear wing/-3 laps	3/38
ret	MEXICAN GP	Mexico City	5	Canon Williams Team	G	3.5 Williams FW12C-Renault V10	electrics	8/39
6	US GP (PHOENIX)	Phoenix	5	Canon Williams Team	G	3.5 Williams FW12C-Renault V10	pit stop-puncture/-1 lap	16/39
1	CANADIAN GP	Montreal	5	Canon Williams Team	G	3.5 Williams FW12C-Renault V10		6/39
ret	FRENCH GP	Paul Ricard	5	Canon Williams Team	G	3.5 Williams FW12C-Renault V10	gearbox	5/39
10	BRITISH GP	Silverstone	5	Canon Williams Team	G	3.5 Williams FW12C-Renault V10	clutch problems/-2 laps	7/39
ret	GERMAN GP	Hockenheim	5	Canon Williams Team	G	3.5 Williams FW12C-Renault V10	collision with Pirro-spun off	6/39
3	HUNGARIAN GP	Hungaroring	5	Canon Williams Team	G	3.5 Williams FW12C-Renault V10		4/39
4	BELGIAN GP	Spa	5	Canon Williams Team	G	3.5 Williams FW12C-Renault V10		4/39
3	ITALIAN GP	Monza	5	Canon Williams Team	G	3.5 Williams FW12C-Renault V10		6/39
ret	PORTUGUESE GP	Estoril	5	Canon Williams Team	G	3.5 Williams FW13-Renault V10	overheating	8/39
ret	SPANISH GP	Jerez	5	Canon Williams Team	G	3.5 Williams FW13-Renault V10	fuel pressure-pump	22/38
3*	JAPANESE GP	Suzuka	5	Canon Williams Team	G	3.5 Williams FW13-Renault V10	* 1st place car disqualified	7/39
1	AUSTRALIAN GP	Adelaide	5	Canon Williams Team	G	3.5 Williams FW13-Renault V10		5/39

1990 Championship position: 6th   Wins: 0   Pole positions: 1   Fastest laps: 1   Points scored: 34

3	US GP (PHOENIX)	Phoenix	5	Canon Williams Renault	G	3.5 Williams FW13B-Renault V10	engine cutting out	9/35
5	BRAZILIAN GP	Interlagos	5	Canon Williams Renault	G	3.5 Williams FW13B-Renault V10	long stop-tyres-nose/-1 lap	3/35
ret	SAN MARINO GP	Imola	5	Canon Williams Renault	G	3.5 Williams FW13B-Renault V10	missed gear-engine	4/34
4	MONACO GP	Monte Carlo	5	Canon Williams Renault	G	3.5 Williams FW13B-Renault V10	throttle problems/1 lap behind	6/35
ret	CANADIAN GP	Montreal	5	Canon Williams Renault	G	3.5 Williams FW13B-Renault V10	spun and collided with Larini	6/35
5	MEXICAN GP	Mexico City	5	Canon Williams Renault	G	3.5 Williams FW13B-Renault V10	brake problems	5/35
ret	FRENCH GP	Paul Ricard	5	Canon Williams Renault	G	3.5 Williams FW13B-Renault V10	engine	8/35
2	BRITISH GP	Silverstone	5	Canon Williams Renault	G	3.5 Williams FW13B-Renault V10	blistered tyres	4/35
6	GERMAN GP	Hockenheim	5	Canon Williams Renault	G	3.5 Williams FW13B-Renault V10	FL	6/35
1	HUNGARIAN GP	Hungaroring	5	Canon Williams Renault	G	3.5 Williams FW13B-Renault V10		1/35
ret	BELGIAN GP	Spa	5	Canon Williams Renault	G	3.5 Williams FW13B-Renault V10	transmission	4/33
ret	ITALIAN GP	Monza	5	Canon Williams Renault	G	3.5 Williams FW13B-Renault V10	suspension	6/33
ret	PORTUGUESE GP	Estoril	5	Canon Williams Renault	G	3.5 Williams FW13B-Renault V10	gearbox	7/33
4	SPANISH GP	Jerez	5	Canon Williams Renault	G	3.5 Williams FW13B-Renault V10	collision with Berger	7/33
5	JAPANESE GP	Suzuka	5	Canon Williams Renault	G	3.5 Williams FW13B-Renault V10	long pit stop-tyres	5/30
5	AUSTRALIAN GP	Adelaide	5	Canon Williams Renault	G	3.5 Williams FW13B-Renault V10	pit stop-tyres	9/30

1991 Championship position: Unplaced

ret	US GP (PHOENIX)	Phoenix	25	Ligier Gitanes	G	3.5 Ligier JS35-Lamborghini V12	electrics	20/34
10	BRAZILIAN GP	Interlagos	25	Ligier Gitanes	G	3.5 Ligier JS35-Lamborghini V12	3 laps behind	18/34
7	SAN MARINO GP	Imola	25	Ligier Gitanes	G	3.5 Ligier JS35-Lamborghini V12	cracked exhaust/-3 laps	24/34
7	MONACO GP	Monte Carlo	25	Ligier Gitanes	G	3.5 Ligier JS35-Lamborghini V12	2 laps behind	16/34
ret	CANADIAN GP	Montreal	25	Ligier Gitanes	G	3.5 Ligier JS35-Lamborghini V12	engine	16/34
8	MEXICAN GP	Mexico City	25	Ligier Gitanes	G	3.5 Ligier JS35-Lamborghini V12	2 laps behind	14/34
12	FRENCH GP	Magny Cours	25	Ligier Gitanes	G	3.5 Ligier JS35B-Lamborghini V12	3 laps behind	16/34
ret	BRITISH GP	Silverstone	25	Ligier Gitanes	G	3.5 Ligier JS35B-Lamborghini V12	engine	19/34
9	GERMAN GP	Hockenheim	25	Ligier Gitanes	G	3.5 Ligier JS35B-Lamborghini V12	1 lap behind	17/34
17/ret	HUNGARIAN GP	Hungaroring	25	Ligier Gitanes	G	3.5 Ligier JS35B-Lamborghini V12	engine/6 laps behind	19/34
11	BELGIAN GP	Spa	25	Ligier Gitanes	G	3.5 Ligier JS35B-Lamborghini V12	1 lap behind	18/34
ret	ITALIAN GP	Monza	25	Ligier Gitanes	G	3.5 Ligier JS35B-Lamborghini V12	spun off on lap 1	21/34
16	PORTUGUESE GP	Estoril	25	Ligier Gitanes	G	3.5 Ligier JS35B-Lamborghini V12	3 laps behind	20/34
ret	SPANISH GP	Barcelona	25	Ligier Gitanes	G	3.5 Ligier JS35B-Lamborghini V12	spun off on lap 1	26/33
9	JAPANESE GP	Suzuka	25	Ligier Gitanes	G	3.5 Ligier JS35B-Lamborghini V12	1 lap behind	17/31
ret	AUSTRALIAN GP	Adelaide	25	Ligier Gitanes	G	3.5 Ligier JS35B-Lamborghini V12	collision with Nakajima	20/32

1992 Championship position: 14th=   Wins: 0   Pole positions: 0   Fastest laps: 0   Points scored: 2

ret	SOUTH AFRICAN GP	Kyalami	25	Ligier Gitanes Blondes	G	3.5 Ligier JS37-Renault V10	engine	14/30
10	MEXICAN GP	Mexico City	25	Ligier Gitanes Blondes	G	3.5 Ligier JS37-Renault V10	2 laps behind	22/30
ret	BRAZILIAN GP	Interlagos	25	Ligier Gitanes Blondes	G	3.5 Ligier JS37-Renault V10	collision with Comas	10/31
ret	SPANISH GP	Barcelona	25	Ligier Gitanes Blondes	G	3.5 Ligier JS37-Renault V10	engine	14/32
ret	SAN MARINO GP	Imola	25	Ligier Gitanes Blondes	G	3.5 Ligier JS37-Renault V10	fuel pump	10/32
12	MONACO GP	Monte Carlo	25	Ligier Gitanes Blondes	G	3.5 Ligier JS37-Renault V10	3 laps behind	22/32
10	CANADIAN GP	Montreal	25	Ligier Gitanes Blondes	G	3.5 Ligier JS37-Renault V10	2 laps behind	21/32
ret	FRENCH GP	Magny Cours	25	Ligier Gitanes Blondes	G	3.5 Ligier JS37-Renault V10	spun off	9/30
10	BRITISH GP	Silverstone	25	Ligier Gitanes Blondes	G	3.5 Ligier JS37-Renault V10	2 laps behind	13/32
7	GERMAN GP	Hockenheim	25	Ligier Gitanes Blondes	G	3.5 Ligier JS37-Renault V10		8/32
ret	HUNGARIAN GP	Hungaroring	25	Ligier Gitanes Blondes	G	3.5 Ligier JS37-Renault V10	collision with Comas on lap 1	8/31
ret	BELGIAN GP	Spa	25	Ligier Gitanes Blondes	G	3.5 Ligier JS37-Renault V10	crashed at Blanchimont	7/30
ret	ITALIAN GP	Monza	25	Ligier Gitanes Blondes	G	3.5 Ligier JS37-Renault V10	electrics	8/28
8	PORTUGUESE GP	Estoril	25	Ligier Gitanes Blondes	G	3.5 Ligier JS37-Renault V10	2 laps behind	11/26
ret	JAPANESE GP	Suzuka	25	Ligier Gitanes Blondes	G	3.5 Ligier JS37-Renault V10	gearbox	10/26
5	AUSTRALIAN GP	Adelaide	25	Ligier Gitanes Blondes	G	3.5 Ligier JS37-Renault V10	1 lap behind	22/26

1993 Championship position: Unplaced

ret	EUROPEAN GP	Donington	15	Sasol Jordan	G	3.5 Jordan 193-Hart V10	throttle problems	19/26
ret	SAN MARINO GP	Imola	15	Sasol Jordan	G	3.5 Jordan 193-Hart V10	gearbox hydraulic failure	19/26
11	SPANISH GP	Barcelona	15	Sasol Jordan	G	3.5 Jordan 193-Hart V10	throttle/fuel pressure/-3 laps	21/26
ret	MONACO GP	Monte Carlo	15	Sasol Jordan	G	3.5 Jordan 193-Hart V10	suspension	23/26
12	CANADIAN GP	Montreal	15	Sasol Jordan	G	3.5 Jordan 193-Hart V10	2 laps behind	24/26
11	FRENCH GP	Magny Cours	15	Sasol Jordan	G	3.5 Jordan 193-Hart V10	2 laps behind	20/26
ret	BRITISH GP	Silverstone	15	Sasol Jordan	G	3.5 Jordan 193-Hart V10	wheel bearing	23/26
13	GERMAN GP	Hockenheim	15	Sasol Jordan	G	3.5 Jordan 193-Hart V10	ran without tyre change	24/26
9	HUNGARIAN GP	Hungaroring	15	Sasol Jordan	G	3.5 Jordan 193-Hart V10	2 laps behind	24/26
ret	BELGIAN GP	Spa	15	Sasol Jordan	G	3.5 Jordan 193-Hart V10	gearbox on lap 1	20/25

GP Starts: 163   GP Wins: 3   Pole positions: 1   Fastest laps: 1   Points: 132

DAVID BRABHAM

The youngest of the Brabham dynasty, David is the only one of the three brothers to have emulated his father in having started a World Championship Grand Prix. He will never be able to match the feats achieved by the legendary Sir Jack, but that should not reflect badly on David, who has thus far managed a worthy career without the aid of the massive finances needed for ultimate success.

A quick learner, David soon outgrew the Australian and New Zealand single-seater scene and headed first to the States to race in Formula Atlantic, then to England in 1988, initially to contest the Formula Vauxhall Lotus championship. This proved a backward step but a switch to Class B of the Formula 3 series was an instant success, Brabham winning five times from just nine starts. Moving up to Class A with the Jewson-backed Bowman Ralt the following season, he had a season-long battle for the F3 championship with Allan McNish in 1989, which was only resolved in David's favour on appeal the following February. With a win in the prestigious Macau F3 race, Brabham seemed set for a year in F3000 with Middlebridge Racing, but this was suddenly to become a Grand Prix chance when they acquired the Brabham team and Gregor Foitek quit his seat after just two races of the 1990 season. He applied himself sensibly and did as much as a novice could in an uncompetitive car, but was not retained at season's end.

Turning to sports cars, David drove for TWR Jaguar in 1991 (winning at the Nürburgring with Warwick) and Toyota in 1992 while waiting for the opportunity to return to Grand Prix racing, which finally presented itself with the ambitious but unproven Simtek team hiring him to lead their assault in 1994. It was a character-building year in which David was the team's mainstay. Following the tragic death of Roland Ratzenberger, he was partnered by no fewer than four other drivers and his determination and dedication in the face of adversity (which included a huge testing accident at Silverstone) were exemplary.

With Nick Wirth's fledgling outfit facing an uncertain future at the beginning of 1995, David amicably took his leave for the chance of a paid seat with BMW in the ever-growing BTCC. The aerodynamic regulations and rear-wheel drive configuration of the 318i left him at a great disadvantage, but typically Brabham got on with the job and was certainly not overshadowed by his much more experienced team-mate, multiple saloon champion Johnny Cecotto.

David understandably grabbed the chance to contest the 1996 All-Japan GT championship in a McLaren F1 GTR and had the satisfaction of snatching the title from main rival Ralf Schumacher. His success in this form of racing brought the opportunity to race a Panoz in 1997, and he has since been a standard-bearer for the marque, putting in a succession of excellent performances over the past three seasons which have seen him become a regular contender for honours. His disappointment must then have been immense when he found himself pipped at the last in the 1999 American Le Mans series by a team which failed to register a single win, but benefited from the idiosyncratic points scoring system. A true gentleman, however, and one of motor racing's most sporting competitors, David was the first to congratulate the victors.

BRABHAM, David (AUS) b 5/9/1965, Wimbledon, London, England

	1990			Championship position: Unplaced					Q Pos/Entries
	Race	Circuit	No	Entrant	Tyres	Car/Engine	Comment		
dnq	SAN MARINO GP	Imola	7	Motor Racing Developments	P	3.5 Brabham BT59-Judd V8			30/34
ret	MONACO GP	Monte Carlo	7	Motor Racing Developments	P	3.5 Brabham BT59-Judd V8	driveshaft-c.v. joint		25/35
dnq	CANADIAN GP	Montreal	7	Motor Racing Developments	P	3.5 Brabham BT59-Judd V8			30/35
ret	MEXICAN GP	Mexico City	7	Motor Racing Developments	P	3.5 Brabham BT59-Judd V8	electrics		21/35
15*	FRENCH GP	Paul Ricard	7	Motor Racing Developments	P	3.5 Brabham BT59-Judd V8	* 15th place car dsq/-3 laps		25/35
dnq	BRITISH GP	Silverstone	7	Motor Racing Developments	P	3.5 Brabham BT59-Judd V8			28/35
ret	GERMAN GP	Hockenheim	7	Motor Racing Developments	P	3.5 Brabham BT59-Judd V8	engine		21/35
dnq	HUNGARIAN GP	Hungaroring	7	Motor Racing Developments	P	3.5 Brabham BT59-Judd V8			28/35
ret	BELGIAN GP	Spa	7	Motor Racing Developments	P	3.5 Brabham BT59-Judd V8	electrics		24/33
dnq	ITALIAN GP	Monza	7	Motor Racing Developments	P	3.5 Brabham BT59-Judd V8			29/33
ret	PORTUGUESE GP	Estoril	7	Motor Racing Developments	P	3.5 Brabham BT59-Judd V8	gearbox		26/33
dnq	SPANISH GP	Jerez	7	Motor Racing Developments	P	3.5 Brabham BT59-Judd V8			27/33
ret	JAPANESE GP	Suzuka	7	Motor Racing Developments	P	3.5 Brabham BT59-Judd V8	clutch		23/30
ret	AUSTRALIAN GP	Adelaide	7	Motor Racing Developments	P	3.5 Brabham BT59-Judd V8	spun off		25/30
	1994			Championship position: Unplaced					
12	BRAZILIAN GP	Interlagos	31	MTV Simtek Ford	G	3.5 Simtek S941-Ford HB V8	4 laps behind		26/28
ret	PACIFIC GP	T.I. Circuit	31	MTV Simtek Ford	G	3.5 Simtek S941-Ford HB V8	electrics		25/26
ret	SAN MARINO GP	Imola	31	MTV Simtek Ford	G	3.5 Simtek S941-Ford HB V8	accident after steering failure		24/28
ret	MONACO GP	Monte Carlo	31	MTV Simtek Ford	G	3.5 Simtek S941-Ford HB V8	broken suspension		22/24
10	SPANISH GP	Barcelona	31	MTV Simtek Ford	G	3.5 Simtek S941-Ford HB V8	4 laps behind		24/27
14	CANADIAN GP	Montreal	31	MTV Simtek Ford	G	3.5 Simtek S941-Ford HB V8	4 laps behind		25/27
ret	FRENCH GP	Magny Cours	31	MTV Simtek Ford	G	3.5 Simtek S941-Ford HB V8	gearbox		24/28
15*	BRITISH GP	Silverstone	31	MTV Simtek Ford	G	3.5 Simtek S941-Ford HB V8	* 2nd place car dsq/-3 laps		25/28
ret	GERMAN GP	Hockenheim	31	MTV Simtek Ford	G	3.5 Simtek S941-Ford HB V8	clutch		25/28
11	HUNGARIAN GP	Hungaroring	31	MTV Simtek Ford	G	3.5 Simtek S941-Ford HB V8	3 laps behind		23/28
ret	BELGIAN GP	Spa	31	MTV Simtek Ford	G	3.5 Simtek S941-Ford HB V8	lost wheel after pit stop		21/28
ret	ITALIAN GP	Monza	31	MTV Simtek Ford	G	3.5 Simtek S941-Ford HB V8	brakes		26/28
ret	PORTUGUESE GP	Estoril	31	MTV Simtek Ford	G	3.5 Simtek S941-Ford HB V8	collision with Alesi		24/28
ret	EUROPEAN GP	Jerez	31	MTV Simtek Ford	G	3.5 Simtek S941-Ford HB V8	engine		25/28
12	JAPANESE GP	Suzuka	31	MTV Simtek Ford	G	3.5 Simtek S941-Ford HB V8	2 laps behind		24/28
ret	AUSTRALIAN GP	Adelaide	31	MTV Simtek Ford	G	3.5 Simtek S941-Ford HB V8	engine		24/28

GP Starts: 24   GP Wins: 0   Pole positions: 0   Fastest laps: 0   Points: 0

Sir JACK BRABHAM

Much has been made of Sir Jack's achievement in becoming the only driver to win the World Championship in a car of his own make. But that is only part of the story, for he was also the man who was largely responsible for developing the rear-engined Cooper which was to change the face of Formula 1 for ever; went to Indianapolis in 1961 and shook the establishment; built not only his own Grand Prix challenger but also a succession of superb Formula 2 cars which allowed so many drivers to shine; and was competitive to the end of his long career. Bowing out at the age of 44 in 1970, he could still show the youngsters a trick or two!

Jack had spent a number of years in the cut and thrust of midget racing on the cinder tracks of his native Australia, winning four successive titles between 1948 and 1951, before switching to hill-climbs, taking the championship in 1953. That season Jack was bought a Cooper-Bristol which was christened the RedeX Special and began to clean up with it but, eager to progress, he came to England in 1955 and soon joined up with the Cooper team, making an early Grand Prix debut in the 'Bobtail' special. Although he drove a Maserati 250F in 1956, taking third places in the Aintree 200 and the Vanwall Trophy at Snetterton, Jack spent most of the season racing Cooper's 1500 cc sports car, while developing the Formula 2 car which he was to use to such great effect in 1957.

In 1958 Moss won the Argentine GP with Rob Walker's little Cooper, proving that the car could be a serious contender, and Jack persevered with the works machine, steadily honing the ground-breaking design on a race-by-race basis. He took occasional national wins, for example in the London Trophy and the Gold Cup, before the start of two golden years in 1959-60 when the Cooper proved, if not always unbeatable, at least very reliable, and Brabham won his first two championship titles, taking seven Grand Prix wins in the process. Other victories included the Brussels and Pau GPs in 1960, and the International Trophy in 1961, the year the team's fortunes began to slip.

In 1962 Jack branched out on his own, using a Lotus as a stop-gap while his first Brabham was completed. It was late in the season before the BT3 appeared but this simple spaceframe car was very effective, soon taking World Championship points and a second place in the non-title Mexican GP. For 1963, Jack signed Dan Gurney to drive for the team and with such a fine driver on board he sometimes took a back seat, but his delight on the occasions when he beat the lanky Californian was obvious. Although Jack did not manage a championship win with his Brabham in the 1.5-litre formula, he scored a number of non-title victories, including races at Solitude and Zeltweg in 1963, and the International Trophy and Aintree 200 in 1964. In addition, he was very successful during the winter trips down-under for the Tasman series and in the newly introduced Formula 2, where he took four first places and two seconds in seven 1964 starts.

Brabham's finest season was 1966, when he won four championship Grands Prix with the ultra-reliable Repco-engined car to secure his third title, in addition to the F1 International Trophy and Gold Cup races, and no fewer than ten Formula 2 events in the Brabham-Honda. For 1967 reliability paid dividends once more; Jack took a couple of wins but Denny Hulme won the title for Brabham before heading off to McLaren. The Repco success was a minor miracle which couldn't last, and it didn't, with the four-cam 1968 engine a disastrous failure that blighted the season. Brabham switched to Ford power for 1969 and signed Jacky Ickx, but still won the International Trophy and had another crack at Indianapolis which ended in retirement with ignition troubles. In 1970, Jack's final year, he was quickly out of the traps with a runaway victory in South Africa, before enduring the heartache of losing a win at Monaco on the last corner when pressured into a mistake by Rindt. He also led the British GP until running out of fuel on the last lap, with Rindt once again the beneficiary.

Upon his retirement Brabham sold up and walked away from racing to spend more time on his other business interests, but the sport would not let him go. His three sons, Geoff, Gary and David, all became successful drivers in their own right, and the 'old man' is often seen at the circuits, proffering his advice, no doubt, in his own inimitable and economical way.

Despite his two World Championships with Cooper, perhaps Jack's finest season was in 1966 when he took the drivers' title for the third time at the age of 40. Uniquely, he did so in a car bearing his own name.
Right: Brabham holds off a stern challenge from Jim Clark's Lotus in the Dutch Grand Prix, the third in a run of four successive victories.

Sir JACK BRABHAM

WORLD CHAMPION: 1959, 1960 & 1966

BRABHAM, Jack (AUS) b 2/4/1926, Hurstville, nr Sydney

	1955	Championship position: Unplaced						
	Race	*Circuit*	*No*	*Entrant*	*Tyres*	*Car/Engine*	*Comment*	*Q Pos/Entries*
ret	BRITISH GP	Aintree	40	Cooper Car Co	D	2.0 Cooper T40-Bristol 6	*valve*	25/25
	1956	Championship position: Unplaced						
ret	BRITISH GP	Silverstone	30	Jack Brabham	D	2.5 Maserati 250F 6	*engine*	28/28
	1957	Championship position: Unplaced						
6	MONACO GP	Monte Carlo	14	Cooper Car Co/R R C Walker	D	2.0 Cooper T43-Climax 4	*out of fuel-pushed car home/-5 laps*	15/21
ret	FRENCH GP	Rouen	22	Cooper Car Co	D	2.0 Cooper T43-Climax 4	*hit straw bales*	13/15
7	"	"	24	Cooper Car Co	D	1.5 Cooper T43-Climax 4	*took MacDowel's car/-9 laps*	– / –
ret	BRITISH GP	Aintree	34	R R C Walker	D	2.0 Cooper T43-Climax 4	*clutch*	13/19
ret	GERMAN GP (F2)	Nürburgring	24	Cooper Car Co	D	1.5 Cooper T43-Climax 4	*transmission*	18/24
7	PESCARA GP	Pescara	24	Cooper Car Co	D	1.5 Cooper T43-Climax 4	*pit stop-fuel/3 laps behind*	16/16
	1958	Championship position: 14th=	Wins: 0	Pole positions: 0	Fastest laps: 0	Points scored: 3		
4	MONACO GP	Monte Carlo	16	Cooper Car Co	D	2.2 Cooper T45-Climax 4	*3 laps behind*	3/28
8	DUTCH GP	Zandvoort	8	Cooper Car Co	D	2.0 Cooper T45-Climax 4	*2 laps behind*	5/17
ret	BELGIAN GP	Spa	22	Cooper Car Co	D	2.2 Cooper T45-Climax 4	*overheating*	8/20
6	FRENCH GP	Reims	22	Cooper Car Co	D	2.2 Cooper T45-Climax 4	*1 lap behind*	12/21
6	BRITISH GP	Silverstone	11	Cooper Car Co	D	2.0 Cooper T45-Climax 4		10/21
ret	GERMAN GP (F2)	Nürburgring	24	Cooper Car Co	D	1.5 Cooper T45-Climax 4	*accident*	10/26
7	PORTUGUESE GP	Oporto	14	Cooper Car Co	D	2.2 Cooper T45-Climax 4	*2 laps behind*	8/15
ret	ITALIAN GP	Monza	4	Cooper Car Co	D	2.0 Cooper T45-Climax 4	*collision with Gendebien-lap 1*	15/21
11*	MOROCCAN GP (F2)	Casablanca	50	Cooper Car Co	D	1.5 Cooper T45-Climax 4	** 1st in F2 class/4 laps behind*	19/25
	1959	Championship position: WORLD CHAMPION		Wins: 2	Pole positions: 1	Fastest laps: 1	Points scored: 34	
1	MONACO GP	Monte Carlo	24	Cooper Car Co	D	2.5 Cooper T51-Climax 4	*FL*	3/24
2	DUTCH GP	Zandvoort	8	Cooper Car Co	D	2.5 Cooper T51-Climax 4		2/15
3	FRENCH GP	Reims	8	Cooper Car Co	D	2.5 Cooper T51-Climax 4		2/22
1	BRITISH GP	Aintree	12	Cooper Car Co	D	2.5 Cooper T51-Climax 4		1/30
ret	GERMAN GP	AVUS	1	Cooper Car Co	D	2.5 Cooper T51-Climax 4	*clutch-heat 1*	4/16
ret	PORTUGUESE GP	Monsanto	1	Cooper Car Co	D	2.5 Cooper T51-Climax 4	*accident-Cabral/hit straw bales*	2/16
3	ITALIAN GP	Monza	12	Cooper Car Co	D	2.5 Cooper T51-Climax 4		3/21
4	US GP	Sebring	8	Cooper Car Co	D	2.5 Cooper T51-Climax 4	*out of fuel/pushed over line*	2/19
dns	"	"	8	Cooper Car Co	D	2.5 Cooper T45-Climax 4	*practice only*	– / –
	1960	Championship position: WORLD CHAMPION		Wins: 5	Pole positions: 3	Fastest laps: 3 (1 shared)	Points scored: 43	
ret	ARGENTINE GP	Buenos Aires	18	Cooper Car Co	D	2.5 Cooper T51-Climax 4	*engine*	10/22
dsq	MONACO GP	Monte Carlo	8	Cooper Car Co	D	2.5 Cooper T53-Climax 4	*outside assistance after spin*	2/24
1	DUTCH GP	Zandvoort	11	Cooper Car Co	D	2.5 Cooper T53-Climax 4		2/21
1	BELGIAN GP	Spa	2	Cooper Car Co	D	2.5 Cooper T53-Climax 4	*FL (shared with Ireland & G Hill)*	1/18
1	FRENCH GP	Reims	16	Cooper Car Co	D	2.5 Cooper T53-Climax 4	*FL*	1/23
1	BRITISH GP	Silverstone	1	Cooper Car Co	D	2.5 Cooper T53-Climax 4		1/25
1	PORTUGUESE GP	Oporto	2	Cooper Car Co	D	2.5 Cooper T53-Climax 4		3/16
4	US GP	Riverside	2	Cooper Car Co	D	2.5 Cooper T53-Climax 4	*FL/1 lap behind*	2/23
	1961	Championship position: 11th=	Wins: 0	Pole positions: 1	Fastest laps: 1	Points scored: 4		
ret	MONACO GP	Monte Carlo	24	Cooper Car Co	D	1.5 Cooper T55-Climax 4	*ignition*	21/21
6	DUTCH GP	Zandvoort	10	Cooper Car Co	D	1.5 Cooper T55-Climax 4		7/17
ret	BELGIAN GP	Spa	28	Cooper Car Co	D	1.5 Cooper T55-Climax 4	*engine*	11/25
ret	FRENCH GP	Reims	2	Cooper Car Co	D	1.5 Cooper T55-Climax 4	*oil pressure*	14/26
4	BRITISH GP	Aintree	12	Cooper Car Co	D	1.5 Cooper T55-Climax 4		9/30
ret	GERMAN GP	Nürburgring	1	Cooper Car Co	D	1.5 Cooper T58-Climax V8	*accident-throttle jammed*	2/27
dns	"	"	1	Cooper Car Co	D	1.5 Cooper T55-Climax 4	*practice only*	– / –
ret	ITALIAN GP	Monza	10	Cooper Car Co	D	1.5 Cooper T58-Climax V8	*overheating*	10/33
dns	"	"	10	Cooper Car Co	D	1.5 Cooper T55-Climax 4	*practice only*	– / –
ret	US GP	Watkins Glen	1	Cooper Car Co	D	1.5 Cooper T58-Climax V8	*overheating/FL*	1/19
dns	"	"	1	Cooper Car Co	D	1.5 Cooper T55-Climax 4	*practice only*	– / –
	1962	Championship position: 9th	Wins: 0	Pole positions: 0	Fastest laps: 0	Points scored: 9		
ret	DUTCH GP	Zandvoort	8	Brabham Racing Organisation	D	1.5 Lotus 24-Climax V8	*accident*	4/20
8/ret	MONACO GP	Monte Carlo	22	Brabham Racing Organisation	D	1.5 Lotus 24-Climax V8	*spin-suspension*	6/21
6	BELGIAN GP	Spa	15	Brabham Racing Organisation	D	1.5 Lotus 24-Climax V8	*2 laps behind*	15/20
ret	FRENCH GP	Rouen	26	Brabham Racing Organisation	D	1.5 Lotus 24-Climax V8	*rear suspension*	4/17
5	BRITISH GP	Aintree	30	Brabham Racing Organisation	D	1.5 Lotus 24-Climax V8	*1 lap behind*	9/21
ret	GERMAN GP	Nürburgring	16	Brabham Racing Organisation	D	1.5 Brabham BT3-Climax V8	*throttle linkage*	24/30
4	US GP	Watkins Glen	17	Brabham Racing Organisation	D	1.5 Brabham BT3-Climax V8	*1 lap behind*	=4/20
4	SOUTH AFRICAN GP	East London	10	Brabham Racing Organisation	D	1.5 Brabham BT3-Climax V8		3/17
	1963	Championship position: 7th	Wins: 0	Pole positions: 0	Fastest laps: 0	Points scored: 14		
9	MONACO GP	Monte Carlo	3	Brabham Racing Organisation	D	1.5 Lotus 25-Climax V8	*borrowed car/pit stops/-23 laps*	16/17
dns	"	"	3	Brabham Racing Organisation	D	1.5 Brabham BT3-Climax V8	*engine in practice*	– / –
ret	BELGIAN GP	Spa	17	Brabham Racing Organisation	D	1.5 Brabham BT3-Climax V8	*fuel injection pump*	6/20
ret	DUTCH GP	Zandvoort	16	Brabham Racing Organisation	D	1.5 Brabham BT7-Climax V8	*spin-chassis damage*	4/19
4	FRENCH GP	Reims	6	Brabham Racing Organisation	D	1.5 Brabham BT7-Climax V8		=4/21
ret	BRITISH GP	Silverstone	8	Brabham Racing Organisation	D	1.5 Brabham BT7-Climax V8	*engine*	4/23
7	GERMAN GP	Nürburgring	9	Brabham Racing Organisation	D	1.5 Brabham BT7-Climax V8	*pit stop/1 lap behind*	8/26
5	ITALIAN GP	Monza	22	Brabham Racing Organisation	D	1.5 Brabham BT3-Climax V8	*pit stop-fuel/2 laps behind*	7/28
4	US GP	Watkins Glen	5	Brabham Racing Organisation	D	1.5 Brabham BT3-Climax V8	*2 laps behind*	5/21
2	MEXICAN GP	Mexico City	5	Brabham Racing Organisation	D	1.5 Brabham BT7-Climax V8		10/21
13/ret	SOUTH AFRICAN GP	East London	8	Brabham Racing Organisation	D	1.5 Brabham BT7-Climax V8	*spin-split fuel tank/-15 laps*	2/21

	1964		Championship position: 8th= Wins: 0 Pole positions: 0 Fastest laps: 1 Points scored: 11						
ret	MONACO GP	Monte Carlo	5	Brabham Racing Organisation	D	1.5 Brabham BT7-Climax V8	fuel injection		2/20
ret	DUTCH GP	Zandvoort	14	Brabham Racing Organisation	D	1.5 Brabham BT7-Climax V8	ignition		7/18
3	BELGIAN GP	Spa	14	Brabham Racing Organisation	D	1.5 Brabham BT7-Climax V8			3/20
3	FRENCH GP	Rouen	20	Brabham Racing Organisation	D	1.5 Brabham BT7-Climax V8	FL		5/17
4	BRITISH GP	Brands Hatch	5	Brabham Racing Organisation	D	1.5 Brabham BT7-Climax V8	1 lap behind		4/25
12/ret	GERMAN GP	Nürburgring	6	Brabham Racing Organisation	D	1.5 Brabham BT11-Climax V8	cwp		6/24
9	AUSTRIAN GP	Zeltweg	6	Brabham Racing Organisation	D	1.5 Brabham BT11-Climax V8	pit stop-fuel feed /29 laps behind		6/20
ret	ITALIAN GP	Monza	14	Brabham Racing Organisation	D	1.5 Brabham BT11-Climax V8	engine-con rod		11/25
ret	US GP	Watkins Glen	5	Brabham Racing Organisation	D	1.5 Brabham BT11-Climax V8	engine		7/19
ret	MEXICAN GP	Mexico City	5	Brabham Racing Organisation	D	1.5 Brabham BT11-Climax V8	electrics		7/19
	1965		Championship position: 10 Wins: 0 Pole positions: 0 Fastest laps: 0 Points scored: 9						
8	SOUTH AFRICAN GP	East London	7	Brabham Racing Organisation	G	1.5 Brabham BT11-Climax V8	pit stop-battery/4 laps behind		=3/25
ret	MONACO GP	Monte Carlo	1	Brabham Racing Organisation	G	1.5 Brabham BT11-Climax V8	engine		2/17
4	BELGIAN GP	Spa	14	Brabham Racing Organisation	G	1.5 Brabham BT11-Climax V8	1 lap behind		10/21
dns	BRITISH GP	Silverstone	7 (8)	Brabham Racing Organisation	G	1.5 Brabham BT11-Climax V8	Gurney took over car for race		(8)/23
5	GERMAN GP	Nürburgring	4	Brabham Racing Organisation	G	1.5 Brabham BT11-Climax V8			14/22
3	US GP	Watkins Glen	7	Brabham Racing Organisation	G	1.5 Brabham BT11-Climax V8			7/18
ret	MEXICAN GP	Mexico City	7	Brabham Racing Organisation	G	1.5 Brabham BT11-Climax V8	oil leak		4/18
	1966		Championship position: WORLD CHAMPION Wins: 4 Pole positions: 3 Fastest laps: 1 Points scored: 45						
ret	MONACO GP	Monte Carlo	7	Brabham Racing Organisation	G	3.0 Brabham BT19-Repco V8	gearbox		=10/16
4	BELGIAN GP	Spa	3	Brabham Racing Organisation	G	3.0 Brabham BT19-Repco V8	2 laps behind		4/18
1	FRENCH GP	Reims	12	Brabham Racing Organisation	G	3.0 Brabham BT19-Repco V8			4/17
1	BRITISH GP	Brands Hatch	5	Brabham Racing Organisation	G	3.0 Brabham BT19-Repco V8	FL		1/20
1	DUTCH GP	Zandvoort	16	Brabham Racing Organisation	G	3.0 Brabham BT19-Repco V8			1/18
1	GERMAN GP	Nürburgring	3	Brabham Racing Organisation	G	3.0 Brabham BT19-Repco V8			5/30
ret	ITALIAN GP	Monza	10	Brabham Racing Organisation	G	3.0 Brabham BT19-Repco V8	oil leak		6/22
dns	"	"	10T	Brabham Racing Organisation	G	3.0 Brabham BT20-Repco V8	practice only		–/–
ret	US GP	Watkins Glen	5	Brabham Racing Organisation	G	3.0 Brabham BT19-Repco V8	engine		1/19
dns	"	"	6	Brabham Racing Organisation	G	3.0 Brabham BT20-Repco V8	practice only		– /–
2	MEXICAN GP	Mexico City	5	Brabham Racing Organisation	G	3.0 Brabham BT20-Repco V8			4/19
	1967		Championship position: 2nd Wins: 2 Pole positions: 2 Fastest laps: 0 Points scored: 48						
6	SOUTH AFRICAN GP	Kyalami	1	Brabham Racing Organisation	G	3.0 Brabham BT20-Repco V8	pit stop-misfire/-4 laps		1/18
ret	MONACO GP	Monte Carlo	8	Brabham Racing Organisation	G	3.0 Brabham BT19-Repco V8	engine		1/18
2	DUTCH GP	Zandvoort	1	Brabham Racing Organisation	G	3.0 Brabham BT19-Repco V8			3/17
dns	"	"	1	Brabham Racing Organisation	G	3.0 Brabham BT24-Repco V8	practice only		– /–
ret	BELGIAN GP	Spa	25	Brabham Racing Organisation	G	3.0 Brabham BT24-Repco V8	engine		7/18
1	FRENCH GP	Le Mans	3	Brabham Racing Organisation	G	3.0 Brabham BT24-Repco V8			2/15
4	BRITISH GP	Silverstone	1	Brabham Racing Organisation	G	3.0 Brabham BT24-Repco V8	wing mirrors fell off!		3/21
2	GERMAN GP	Nürburgring	1	Brabham Racing Organisation	G	3.0 Brabham BT24-Repco V8			8/25
1	CANADIAN GP	Mosport Park	1	Brabham Racing Organisation	G	3.0 Brabham BT24-Repco V8			7/19
2	ITALIAN GP	Monza	16	Brabham Racing Organisation	G	3.0 Brabham BT24-Repco V8			2/18
5	US GP	Watkins Glen	1	Brabham Racing Organisation	G	3.0 Brabham BT24-Repco V8	pit stop-puncture/-4 laps		5/18
2	MEXICAN GP	Mexico City	1	Brabham Racing Organisation	G	3.0 Brabham BT24-Repco V8			5/19
	1968		Championship position: 23rd= Wins: 0 Pole positions: 0 Fastest laps: 0 Points scored: 2						
ret	SOUTH AFRICAN GP	Kyalami	2	Brabham Racing Organisation	G	3.0 Brabham BT24-Repco V8	valve spring		5/23
dns	SPANISH GP	Jarama	8	Brabham Racing Organisation	G	3.0 Brabham BT26-Repco V8	engine trouble in practice		(14)/14
ret	MONACO GP	Monte Carlo	2	Brabham Racing Organisation	G	3.0 Brabham BT26-Repco V8	rear radius arm		12/18
ret	BELGIAN GP	Spa	18	Brabham Racing Organisation	G	3.0 Brabham BT26-Repco V8	sticking throttle		18/18
ret	DUTCH GP	Zandvoort	5	Brabham Racing Organisation	G	3.0 Brabham BT26-Repco V8	spun off-could not restart		4/19
ret	FRENCH GP	Rouen	4	Brabham Racing Organisation	G	3.0 Brabham BT26-Repco V8	fuel pump		=13/18
ret	BRITISH GP	Brands Hatch	3	Brabham Racing Organisation	G	3.0 Brabham BT26-Repco V8	camshaft		8/20
5	GERMAN GP	Nürburgring	4	Brabham Racing Organisation	G	3.0 Brabham BT26-Repco V8			15/20
ret	ITALIAN GP	Monza	10	Brabham Racing Organisation	G	3.0 Brabham BT26-Repco V8	oil pressure		17/24
ret	CANADIAN GP	St Jovite	5	Brabham Racing Organisation	G	3.0 Brabham BT26-Repco V8	wishbone mounting		=10/22
ret	US GP	Watkins Glen	3	Brabham Racing Organisation	G	3.0 Brabham BT26-Repco V8	cam follower		8/21
10/ret	MEXICAN GP	Mexico City	3	Brabham Racing Organisation	G	3.0 Brabham BT26-Repco V8	oil pressure/6 laps behind		8/21
	1969		Championship position: 10th Wins: 0 Pole positions: 2 Fastest laps: 1 (shared) Points scored: 14						
ret	SOUTH AFRICAN GP	Kyalami	14	Motor Racing Developments	G	3.0 Brabham BT26A-Cosworth V8	lost rear wing		1/18
ret	SPANISH GP	Montjuich Park	3	Motor Racing Developments	G	3.0 Brabham BT26A-Cosworth V8	engine		5/14
ret	MONACO GP	Monte Carlo	5	Motor Racing Developments	G	3.0 Brabham BT26A-Cosworth V8	accident with Surtees		=8/16
6	DUTCH GP	Zandvoort	11	Motor Racing Developments	G	3.0 Brabham BT26A-Cosworth V8			8/15
ret	ITALIAN GP	Monza	28	Motor Racing Developments	G	3.0 Brabham BT26A-Cosworth V8	oil leak-loose fuel pump		7/15
2	CANADIAN GP	Mosport Park	12	Motor Racing Developments	G	3.0 Brabham BT26A-Cosworth V8	FL (shared with Ickx)		=5/20
4	US GP	Watkins Glen	8	Motor Racing Developments	G	3.0 Brabham BT26A-Cosworth V8	pit stop-fuel/2 laps behind		10/18
3	MEXICAN GP	Mexico City	8	Motor Racing Developments	G	3.0 Brabham BT26A-Cosworth V8	engine problems		1/17
	1970		Championship position: 5th= Wins: 1 Pole positions: 1 Fastest laps: 4 (1 shared) Points scored: 25						
1	SOUTH AFRICAN GP	Kyalami	12	Motor Racing Developments	G	3.0 Brabham BT33-Cosworth V8	FL (shared with Surtees)		3/24
ret	SPANISH GP	Jarama	7	Motor Racing Developments	G	3.0 Brabham BT33-Cosworth V8	engine/FL		1/22
2	MONACO GP	Monte Carlo	5	Motor Racing Developments	G	3.0 Brabham BT33-Cosworth V8	lost lead in last corner accident		4/21
ret	BELGIAN GP	Spa	18	Motor Racing Developments	G	3.0 Brabham BT33-Cosworth V8	flywheel and clutch		5/18
11	DUTCH GP	Zandvoort	18	Motor Racing Developments	G	3.0 Brabham BT33-Cosworth V8	2 pit stops-punctures/-4 laps		12/24
3	FRENCH GP	Clermont Ferrand	23	Motor Racing Developments	G	3.0 Brabham BT33-Cosworth V8	FL		5/23
2	BRITISH GP	Brands Hatch	17	Motor Racing Developments	G	3.0 Brabham BT33-Cosworth V8	out of fuel on last lap/FL		=1/25
ret	GERMAN GP	Hockenheim	3	Motor Racing Developments	G	3.0 Brabham BT33-Cosworth V8	split oil union		12/25
13	AUSTRIAN GP	Österreichring	10	Motor Racing Developments	G	3.0 Brabham BT33-Cosworth V8	pit stop-holed radiator/-4 laps		=7/24
ret	ITALIAN GP	Monza	44	Motor Racing Developments	G	3.0 Brabham BT33-Cosworth V8	accident when engine cut out		8/27
ret	CANADIAN GP	St Jovite	11	Motor Racing Developments	G	3.0 Brabham BT33-Cosworth V8	oil leak		19/20
10	US GP	Watkins Glen	15	Motor Racing Developments	G	3.0 Brabham BT33-Cosworth V8	3 laps behind		16/27
ret	MEXICAN GP	Mexico City	15	Motor Racing Developments	G	3.0 Brabham BT33-Cosworth V8	engine low oil pressure		4/18

GP Starts: 126   GP Wins: 14   Pole positions: 13   Fastest laps: 12   Points: 261

BILL BRACK

Brack was a leading light on the Canadian motor racing scene from the late sixties through to the late seventies, and also made occasional racing forays abroad.

Initially concentrating on the Formula A and B series which were popular at the time, Brack raced mainly in Lotus cars, later switching to Chevron and March (with major STP backing) to contest Formula Atlantic events before stepping aside for the younger Jacques Villeneuve in 1979.

His Grand Prix appearances at the wheel of 'third' works cars yielded little in terms of results but added local interest for the spectators nevertheless.

VITTORIO BRAMBILLA

Vittorio began racing motor cycles as early as 1957, winning the 125 cc Italian championship before turning to karting. He temporarily forsook his racing activities to tend the cars of his elder brother Ernesto, before returning to two-wheel competition in 1968. The following year he burst upon the Italian national scene in his F3 Birel, and his forceful driving style soon found him dubbed 'the Monza Gorilla', partly due to his burly physique.

Still relatively unknown, he moved into Formula 2 in 1970 with a Brabham BT23, taking a second place at the Salzburgring, and he was to spend another two years jumping between F2 and F3, gaining numerous successes in the latter category. It was the 1973 season which provided his big breakthrough. Vittorio had calmed his frenetic driving approach somewhat and, at the wheel of a well-sponsored March, he became a serious challenger for honours, looking particularly impressive as the season wore on and taking wins at the Salzburgring and Albi.

Brambilla's sponsors, Beta Tools, were so delighted that they helped him secure a place in the March Grand Prix line-up for 1974. Joining the team two races into the season, he soon proved to be as quick as team-mate Stuck, but the propensity to crash was still there. The following year was to be his best; he was much more consistent, qualified well and raced his heart out. In Sweden he was stunningly fast in practice, and simply drove away from the field at the start until tyre trouble intervened, a driveshaft then failing. His moment came in Austria, however, when he scored the March factory team's first-ever championship Grand Prix win in pouring rain at the Österreichring. It made no difference to the exuberant Italian that he managed to dismantle the front of the car on the slowing-down lap – or that half-points were awarded as the race had been ended prematurely with the chequered flag rather than being stopped and then restarted as should have been the case. Max Mosley had read the rule book and nobody could argue against him!

Unfortunately 1976 saw a return to the bad habits of old as in an effort to stay on the pace Brambilla indulged in a spate of chassis-crunching which must have driven the factory to distraction, such was the replacement tally. He scored only one points finish, but claimed a second in the International Trophy and fourth in the Race of Champions. However, the situation was redressed in 1977 when Brambilla took his Beta money to Surtees as number one driver. He had a pretty good working relationship with his demanding employer, and an excellent reliabilty record, though the car was just not quick enough for anything like outright success.

Nevertheless the partnership continued into 1978, with the new TS20 a no more effective challenger than its predecessor. At Monza Vittorio was involved in the start crash which claimed the life of Peterson, suffering severe concussion which kept him out of the cockpit for almost a year, before Alfa Romeo (for whom he had won four rounds of the World Sports Car Championship in 1977 with their T33) brought him back for the last three races of the season. He made two more appearances for them in 1980, but it was painfully obvious that his days as a Grand Prix driver were over, though he did race the Osella sports car in a few rounds of the World Championship of Makes, before phasing himself out completely in 1981.

BRACK, Bill (CDN) b 26/12/1935, Toronto

	1968	Championship position: Unplaced							
	Race	Circuit	No	Entrant	Tyres	Car/Engine		Comment	Q Pos/Entries
ret	CANADIAN GP	St Jovite	27	Gold Leaf Team Lotus	F	3.0 Lotus 49B-Cosworth V8		driveshaft	=20/22
	1969	Championship position: Unplaced							
nc	CANADIAN GP	Mosport Park	16	Owen Racing Organisation	D	3.0 BRM P138 V12		10 laps behind	18/20
	1972	Championship position: Unplaced							
ret	CANADIAN GP	Mosport Park	17	Marlboro BRM	F	3.0 BRM P180 V12		spun and stalled	23/25

GP Starts: 3   GP Wins: 0   Pole positions: 0   Fastest laps: 0   Points: 0

BRAMBILLA, Vittorio (I) b 11/11/1937, Monza

	1974	Championship position: 18th	Wins: 0	Pole positions: 0	Fastest laps: 0	Points scored: 1			
	Race	Circuit	No	Entrant	Tyres	Car/Engine		Comment	Q Pos/Entries
10	SOUTH AFRICAN GP	Kyalami	10	Beta Tools/March Engineering	G	3.0 March 741-Cosworth V8		1 lap behind	19/27
dns	SPANISH GP	Jarama	10	Beta Tools/March Engineering	G	3.0 March 741-Cosworth V8		accident in practice	(10)/28
9	BELGIAN GP	Nivelles	10	Beta Tools/March Engineering	G	3.0 March 741-Cosworth V8		2 laps behind	31/32
ret	MONACO GP	Monte Carlo	10	Beta Tools/March Engineering	G	3.0 March 741-Cosworth V8		multiple accident lap 1	15/28
10/ret	SWEDISH GP	Anderstorp	10	Beta Tools/March Engineering	G	3.0 March 741-Cosworth V8		engine/2 laps behind	17/28
10	DUTCH GP	Zandvoort	10	Beta Tools/March Engineering	G	3.0 March 741-Cosworth V8		3 laps behind	15/27
11	FRENCH GP	Dijon	10	Beta Tools/March Engineering	G	3.0 March 741-Cosworth V8		1 lap behind	16/30
ret	BRITISH GP	Brands Hatch	10	Beta Tools/March Engineering	G	3.0 March 741-Cosworth V8		fuel pressure	=15/34
13	GERMAN GP	Nürburgring	10	Beta Tools/March Engineering	G	3.0 March 741-Cosworth V8			23/32
6	AUSTRIAN GP	Österreichring	10	Beta Tools/March Engineering	G	3.0 March 741-Cosworth V8			20/31
ret	ITALIAN GP	Monza	10	Beta Tools/March Engineering	G	3.0 March 741-Cosworth V8		crashed at chicane	13/31
dns	CANADIAN GP	Mosport Park	10	Beta Tools/March Engineering	G	3.0 March 741-Cosworth V8		accident in practice	29/30
ret	US GP	Watkins Glen	10	Beta Tools/March Engineering	G	3.0 March 741-Cosworth V8		fuel metering unit	25/30
	1975	Championship position: 11th	Wins: 0	Pole positions: 1	Fastest laps: 1	Points scored: 6.5			
9	ARGENTINE GP	Buenos Aires	9	Beta Team March	G	3.0 March 741-Cosworth V8		1 lap behind	12/23
ret	BRAZILIAN GP	Interlagos	9	Beta Team March	G	3.0 March 741-Cosworth V8		engine	17/23
ret	SOUTH AFRICAN GP	Kyalami	9	Beta Team March	G	3.0 March 751-Cosworth V8		oil cooler leak	7/28
5*	SPANISH GP	Montjuich Park	9	Beta Team March	G	3.0 March 751-Cosworth V8		shortened race - *half points/-1 lap	5/26
ret	MONACO GP	Monte Carlo	9	Beta Team March	G	3.0 March 751-Cosworth V8		accident with Pryce	5/26
ret	BELGIAN GP	Zolder	9	Beta Team March	G	3.0 March 751-Cosworth V8		brakes	3/24
ret	SWEDISH GP	Anderstorp	9	Beta Team March	G	3.0 March 751-Cosworth V8		driveshaft	1/26
ret	DUTCH GP	Zandvoort	9	Beta Team March	G	3.0 March 751-Cosworth V8		collision with Depailler at start	11/25
ret	FRENCH GP	Paul Ricard	9	Beta Team March	G	3.0 March 751-Cosworth V8		rear damper	8/26
6	BRITISH GP	Silverstone	9	Beta Team March	G	3.0 March 751-Cosworth V8		1 lap behind	5/28
ret	GERMAN GP	Nürburgring	9	Beta Team March	G	3.0 March 751-Cosworth V8		puncture-suspension damage	11/26
1*	AUSTRIAN GP	Österreichring	9	Beta Team March	G	3.0 March 751-Cosworth V8		rain shortened race-*half points/FL	8/30
ret	ITALIAN GP	Monza	9	Beta Team March	G	3.0 March 751-Cosworth V8		clutch	9/28
7	US GP	Watkins Glen	9	Beta Team March	G	3.0 March 751-Cosworth V8			6/24
	1976	Championship position: 19th=	Wins: 0	Pole positions: 0	Fastest laps: 0	Points scored: 1			
ret	BRAZILIAN GP	Interlagos	9	Beta Team March	G	3.0 March 761-Cosworth V8		oil leak	7/22
8	SOUTH AFRICAN GP	Kyalami	9	Beta Team March	G	3.0 March 761-Cosworth V8		1 lap behind	5/25
ret	US GP WEST	Long Beach	9	Beta Team March	G	3.0 March 761-Cosworth V8		collision with Reutemann	8/27
ret	SPANISH GP	Jarama	9	Beta Team March	G	3.0 March 761-Cosworth V8		accident-damaged suspension	6/30
ret	BELGIAN GP	Zolder	9	Beta Team March	G	3.0 March 761-Cosworth V8		drive shaft	5/29
ret	MONACO GP	Monte Carlo	9	Beta Team March	G	3.0 March 761-Cosworth V8		suspension	9/25
10	SWEDISH GP	Anderstorp	9	Beta Team March	G	3.0 March 761-Cosworth V8		spin/1 lap behind	15/27
ret	FRENCH GP	Paul Ricard	9	Beta Team March	G	3.0 March 761-Cosworth V8		engine-oil pressure	11/30
ret	BRITISH GP	Brands Hatch	9	Beta Team March	G	3.0 March 761-Cosworth V8		collision with Peterson	10/30
ret	GERMAN GP	Nürburgring	9	Beta Team March	G	3.0 March 761-Cosworth V8		brake failure	13/28
ret	AUSTRIAN GP	Österreichring	9	Beta Team March	G	3.0 March 761-Cosworth V8		collision with Fittipaldi	7/25
6	DUTCH GP	Zandvoort	9	Beta Team March	G	3.0 March 761-Cosworth V8			7/27
7	ITALIAN GP	Monza	9	Beta Team March	G	3.0 March 761-Cosworth V8			16/29
14	CANADIAN GP	Mosport Park	9	Beta Team March	G	3.0 March 761-Cosworth V8		1 lap behind	3/27
ret	US GP EAST	Watkins Glen	9	Beta Team March	G	3.0 March 761-Cosworth V8		burst tyre	4/27
ret	JAPANESE GP	Mount Fuji	9	Beta Team March	G	3.0 March 761-Cosworth V8		engine	8/27
	1977	Championship position: 15th=	Wins: 0	Pole positions: 0	Fastest laps: 0	Points scored: 6			
7/ret	ARGENTINE GP	Buenos Aires	19	Beta Team Surtees	G	3.0 Surtees TS19-Cosworth V8		fuel feed/5 laps behind	13/21
ret	BRAZILIAN GP	Interlagos	19	Beta Team Surtees	G	3.0 Surtees TS19-Cosworth V8		damaged radiator on kerb	11/22
7	SOUTH AFRICAN GP	Kyalami	19	Beta Team Surtees	G	3.0 Surtees TS19-Cosworth V8			14/23
ret	US GP WEST	Long Beach	19	Beta Team Surtees	G	3.0 Surtees TS19-Cosworth V8		collision with Mass	11/22
ret	SPANISH GP	Jarama	19	Beta Team Surtees	G	3.0 Surtees TS19-Cosworth V8		collision with Regazzoni	11/31
8	MONACO GP	Monte Carlo	19	Beta Team Surtees	G	3.0 Surtees TS19-Cosworth V8			14/26
4	BELGIAN GP	Zolder	19	Beta Team Surtees	G	3.0 Surtees TS19-Cosworth V8			12/32
ret	SWEDISH GP	Anderstorp	19	Beta Team Surtees	G	3.0 Surtees TS19-Cosworth V8		engine	13/31
13	FRENCH GP	Dijon	19	Beta Team Surtees	G	3.0 Surtees TS19-Cosworth V8		pit stop-tyres/3 laps behind	11/30
8	BRITISH GP	Silverstone	19	Beta Team Surtees	G	3.0 Surtees TS19-Cosworth V8		pit stop-puncture/1 lap behind	8/36
5	GERMAN GP	Hockenheim	19	Beta Team Surtees	G	3.0 Surtees TS19-Cosworth V8			10/30
15	AUSTRIAN GP	Österreichring	19	Beta Team Surtees	G	3.0 Surtees TS19-Cosworth V8		spin/2 laps behind	13/30
12/ret	DUTCH GP	Zandvoort	19	Beta Team Surtees	G	3.0 Surtees TS19-Cosworth V8		spun off	22/34
ret	ITALIAN GP	Monza	19	Beta Team Surtees	G	3.0 Surtees TS19-Cosworth V8		hit by Watson-radiator	10/34
19	US GP EAST	Watkins Glen	19	Beta Team Surtees	G	3.0 Surtees TS19-Cosworth V8		pit stop-collision damage/-5 laps	11/27
6/ret	CANADIAN GP	Mosport Park	19	Beta Team Surtees	G	3.0 Surtees TS19-Cosworth V8		crashed on oil/2 laps behind	15/27
8	JAPANESE GP	Mount Fuji	19	Beta Team Surtees	G	3.0 Surtees TS19-Cosworth V8		2 pit stops-plug leads/-2 laps	=8/23

	1978	Championship position: 19th=		Wins: 0	Pole positions: 0		Fastest laps: 0	Points scored: 1		
18	ARGENTINE GP	Buenos Aires	19	Beta Team Surtees	G	3.0 Surtees TS19-Cosworth V8		*2 laps behind*	12/27
dnq	BRAZILIAN GP	Rio	19	Beta Team Surtees	G	3.0 Surtees TS19-Cosworth V8			27/28
12	SOUTH AFRICAN GP	Kyalami	19	Beta Team Surtees	G	3.0 Surtees TS19-Cosworth V8		*2 laps behind*	19/30
ret	US GP WEST	Long Beach	19	Beta Team Surtees	G	3.0 Surtees TS19-Cosworth V8		*cwp*	17/30
dnq	MONACO GP	Monte Carlo	19	Beta Team Surtees	G	3.0 Surtees TS20-Cosworth V8			24/30
dnq	"	" "	19	Beta Team Surtees	G	3.0 Surtees TS19-Cosworth V8			– / –
13/ret	BELGIAN GP	Zolder	19	Beta Team Surtees	G	3.0 Surtees TS20-Cosworth V8		*engine*	12/30
7	SPANISH GP	Jarama	19	Beta Team Surtees	G	3.0 Surtees TS20-Cosworth V8		*1 lap behind*	16/29
ret	SWEDISH GP	Anderstorp	19	Beta Team Surtees	G	3.0 Surtees TS20-Cosworth V8		*collision- Pironi-hit barrier*	18/27
17	FRENCH GP	Paul Ricard	19	Beta Team Surtees	G	3.0 Surtees TS20-Cosworth V8		*spin/2 laps behind*	19/29
9	BRITISH GP	Brands Hatch	19	Beta Team Surtees	G	3.0 Surtees TS20-Cosworth V8		*1 lap behind*	25/30
ret	GERMAN GP	Hockenheim	19	Beta Team Surtees	G	3.0 Surtees TS20-Cosworth V8		*fuel vaporisation*	20/30
6	AUSTRIAN GP	Österreichring	19	Beta Team Surtees	G	3.0 Surtees TS20-Cosworth V8		*1 lap behind*	21/31
dsq	DUTCH GP	Zandvoort	19	Beta Team Surtees	G	3.0 Surtees TS20-Cosworth V8		*push start after spin*	22/33
ret/dns	ITALIAN GP	Monza	19	Beta Team Surtees	G	3.0 Surtees TS20-Cosworth V8		*accident in first start*	23/32
	1979	Championship position: Unplaced							
12	ITALIAN GP	Monza	36	Autodelta	G	3.0 Alfa Romeo 177 F12		*1 lap behind*	22/28
ret	CANADIAN GP	Montreal	36	Autodelta	G	3.0 Alfa Romeo 179 F12		*fuel metering unit*	18/29
dnq	US GP EAST	Watkins Glen	36	Autodelta	G	3.0 Alfa Romeo 179 F12			25/30
	1980	Championship position: Unplaced							
ret	DUTCH GP	Zandvoort	22	Marlboro Team Alfa Romeo	G	3.0 Alfa Romeo 179 V12		*accident with Lees*	22/28
ret	ITALIAN GP	Imola	22	Marlboro Team Alfa Romeo	G	3.0 Alfa Romeo 179 V12		*spun off*	19/28

GP Starts: 73 (74)   GP Wins: 1   Pole positions: 1   Fastest laps: 1   Points: 15.5

TONI BRANCA

Branca raced internationally for just a couple of seasons, usually at events in his native Switzerland, but sometimes further afield. The Formula 1 events were contested with a Maserati 4CLT and Formula 2 races with a Type 15 Gordini.

Only occasionally did he mix it with the quick men – a front row start at Geneva in 1950 saw him lead briefly – but he did get the occasional top-six finish in lesser races: third at Aix-les-Bains, fifth at Erlen in 1950, and another fifth at Naples in '51 with the Gordini. His best finish with the Maserati was sixth in the 1951 Pescara GP.

Thereafter, Toni continued to compete, usually in hill-climbs, through to the mid-fifties with his Maser and later a Moretti.

ERIC BRANDON

Brandon was a boyhood friend of John Cooper, who not unnaturally became involved in racing from the early days of the little Cooper 500 cc

cars. By 1951 he was rightly regarded as one of the top drivers in the class, recording wins at home and abroad.

With Alan Brown he formed the Ecurie Richmond team, the pair running front-engined Cooper-Bristol cars to the Formula 2 rules in Grands Prix during 1952 and '53. Eric's best placing was a very distant fourth at a retirement-hit Syracuse GP in 1953.

Undaunted, Eric continued in his beloved F3, where he was always a front-runner, before moving into sports cars with the 1100 cc Halseylec-Climax which he raced in 1955 and early 1956.

BRANCA, 'Toni' (Antonio) (CH) b 15/9/1916 – d 10/5/1985, Sierre

	1950	Championship position: Unplaced						
	Race	Circuit	No	Entrant	Tyres	Car/Engine	Comment	Q Pos/Entries
11	SWISS GP	Bremgarten	40	Antonio Branca	P	1.5 s/c Maserati 4CLT 4	*7 laps behind*	17/18
10	BELGIAN GP	Spa	30	Antonio Branca	P	1.5 s/c Maserati 4CLT 4	*6 laps behind*	13/14
	1951	Championship position: Unplaced						
ret	GERMAN GP	Nürburgring	92	Antonio Branca	P	1.5 s/c Maserati 4CLT 4	*engine*	17/23

GP Starts: 3   GP Wins: 0   Pole positions: 0   Fastest laps: 0   Points: 0

BRANDON, Eric (GB) b 18/7/1920, East London – d 8/8/1982, Hampshire

	1952	Championship position: Unplaced						
	Race	Circuit	No	Entrant	Tyres	Car/Engine	Comment	Q Pos/Entries
8	SWISS GP	Bremgarten	24	Ecurie Richmond	D	2.0 Cooper T20-Bristol 6	*7 laps behind*	17/21
9	BELGIAN GP	Spa	12	Ecurie Richmond	D	2.0 Cooper T20-Bristol 6	*3 laps behind*	12/22
20	BRITISH GP	Silverstone	10	Ecurie Richmond	D	2.0 Cooper T20-Bristol 6	*9 laps behind*	18/32
13	ITALIAN GP	Monza	36	Ecurie Richmond	D	2.0 Cooper T20-Bristol 6	*7 laps behind*	20/35
	1954	Championship position: Unplaced						
ret	BRITISH GP	Silverstone	30	Ecurie Richmond	D	2.0 Cooper T23-Bristol 6		25/31

GP Starts: 5   GP Wins: 0   Pole positions: 0   Fastest laps: 0   Points: 0

BRIDGER, Tommy (GB) b 24/6/1934, Welwyn, Hertfordshire – d 3/7/1991, Aboyne, Aberdeenshire, Scotland

	1958	Championship position: Unplaced							
	Race	Circuit	No	Entrant	Tyres	Car/Engine		Comment	Q Pos/Entries
ret	MOROCCAN GP (F2)	Casablanca	56	British Racing Partnership	D	1.5 Cooper T45-Climax 4		accident	22/25

GP Starts: 1   GP Wins: 0   Pole positions: 0   Fastest laps: 0   Points: 0

TOMMY BRIDGER

Bridger first entered racing with a Cooper-JAP in 1953 and, once bitten by the bug, was back the following season, contesting minor events with a Kieft-Norton which he continued to race through 1955. Armed with a Cooper, he undertook a full season of F3 in both 1956 and 1957, enjoying some fantastic dices with 'the master', Jim Russell, usually emerging second best but dogging his rival's footsteps race in and race out.

For 1958 Tommy tried his hand at Formula 2, finishing second on aggregate in the minor Crystal Palace Trophy race, and eighth in the Coupe de Vitesse at Reims. His only Grand Prix appearance, in Morocco, ended in a crash from which he luckily emerged shaken but otherwise unharmed.

He returned to the circuits the following year, back in F3, winning four races in his faithful Cooper-Norton. In 1960 Bridger raced a third works Lotus Formula Junior at the British Grand Prix meeting.

TONY BRISE

After Tony Brise had made his Grand Prix debut for Frank Williams and then been snapped up by Graham Hill to race for the Embassy Hill team, he was suddenly very hot property. Yet at the beginning of 1974, no one had been interested in securing the talents of the man who had just won the John Player F3 championship outright and, with Richard Robarts, was joint Lombard North Central champion. He lacked the necessary finance to secure a seat in the March team for a season of Formula 2 and, despite a second place in the F3 Monaco support race, was thus consigned to a season of racing in Formula Atlantic.

Having come from a motor sport family – his father John was a 500 cc and stock car racer – it was natural that young Tony would involve himself in some way. He started racing karts from the age of 8, eventually becoming joint British karting champion in 1969. By now keen to try his hand at Formula Ford, but without the resources, Brise contented himself with karting until, late in 1970, the opportunity finally arose to drive an Elden – not the best of chassis but at least it was a start. He raced the car in 1971 before replacing it with a more competitive Merlyn to finish his first full season as runner-up in the BOC Formula Ford championship.

Bernie Ecclestone had spotted Tony's talent and offered him a Brabham BT28 for 1972, but this car turned out to be uncompetitive and only when he switched to a GRD did his fortunes improve. Mike Warner of GRD was another who wasn't slow to see Brise's talent and he signed him for 1973 to replace poor Roger Williamson who was bound for F1 where he was destined to meet his terrible fate at Zandvoort. As described earlier Brise did the business, but only Teddy Savory was there to back him in 1974 with the Modus Atlantic drive.

Of Brise the Grand Prix driver, sadly, we were to see precious little, but at each of the ten Grands Prix Tony contested, be it in practice or the race itself, his brilliance was evident. His loss in the plane crash that also claimed the life of Graham Hill and four members of the Hill team was a devastating blow for all followers of British motor racing, who felt they had lost a future World Champion.

BRISE, Tony (GB) b 28/3/1952, Dartford, Kent – d 29/11/1975, Arkley, nr Barnet, Hertfordshire

	1975	Championship position: 19th=		Wins: 0	Pole positions: 0		Fastest laps: 0	Points scored: 1	
	Race	Circuit	No	Entrant	Tyres	Car/Engine		Comment	Q Pos/Entries
7	SPANISH GP	Montjuich Park	21	Frank Williams Racing Cars	G	3.0 Williams FW03-Cosworth V8		hit by Pryce/2 laps behind	18/26
ret	BELGIAN GP	Zolder	23	Embassy Racing with Graham Hill	G	3.0 Hill GH1-Cosworth V8		engine	7/24
6	SWEDISH GP	Anderstorp	23	Embassy Racing with Graham Hill	G	3.0 Hill GH1-Cosworth V8		1 lap behind	17/26
7	DUTCH GP	Zandvoort	23	Embassy Racing with Graham Hill	G	3.0 Hill GH1-Cosworth V8		pit stop/1 lap behind	7/25
7	FRENCH GP	Paul Ricard	23	Embassy Racing with Graham Hill	G	3.0 Hill GH1-Cosworth V8			12/26
15/ret	BRITISH GP	Silverstone	23	Embassy Racing with Graham Hill	G	3.0 Hill GH1-Cosworth V8		crashed in rainstorm/-3 laps	13/28
ret	GERMAN GP	Nürburgring	23	Embassy Racing with Graham Hill	G	3.0 Hill GH1-Cosworth V8		crashed-suspension failure	17/26
15	AUSTRIAN GP	Österreichring	23	Embassy Racing with Graham Hill	G	3.0 Hill GH1-Cosworth V8		1 lap behind	16/30
ret	ITALIAN GP	Monza	23	Embassy Racing with Graham Hill	G	3.0 Hill GH1-Cosworth V8		multiple collision at chicane	6/28
ret	US GP	Watkins Glen	23	Embassy Racing with Graham Hill	G	3.0 Hill GH1-Cosworth V8		collision with Henton	17/24

GP Starts: 10   GP Wins: 0   Pole positions: 0   Fastest laps: 0   Points: 1

CHRIS BRISTOW

Many felt that Bristow had the ability to be a World Champion, while in the other camp his detractors maintained that he was too wild. Certainly he was very, very quick but sadly we would never find out just how much he could have achieved.

With the support of his father, Chris entered racing in 1956 at the wheel of an MG Special with which he scored an early win at Crystal Palace. Realising that he needed more competitive machinery than the special, he acquired an 1100 cc Cooper sports car for 1957 and won more than a dozen minor scratch and handicap events with it in a highly satisfying year.

For 1958 the Cooper was no longer eligible, so he purchased a very fast – but not so reliable – Elva, with which he traded places regularly with the more fashionable Lotus. His efforts brought him to the attention of the British Racing Partnership, who invited him to join them for 1959 to race their Formula 2 Cooper-Borgwards and Cooper-Monaco sports cars.

It was the John Davy Trophy at Brands Hatch that really brought him to the attention of the public, Bristow taking an aggregate win from Brabham, Salvadori and McLaren with an impressive display of speed coupled with a maturity that belied his inexperience.

For 1960 BRP – under the Yeoman Credit Racing Team banner – pinned their hopes on young Bristow and the experienced Harry Schell. When Schell was killed in practice for the International Trophy, Chris, something of loner, found himself paired with Tony Brooks. It would have been fascinating to measure his stature against a proven world-class pilot, but in the Belgian Grand Prix at Spa, while dicing with the Ferrari of the equally combative Willy Mairesse, he lost control of his Cooper, slid into some trackside fencing and was killed instantly in a gruesome accident.

PETE BROEKER

Broeker was something of a mystery when he turned up at the 1963 US Grand Prix with his odd-looking little Stebro, powered by a pushrod Ford motor. Qualifying some 15 seconds off the pole-position time, the Canadian circulated at the best pace he could manage to finish 22 laps adrift.

He brought an updated car over to Europe in 1964 to attempt to compete in a trio of Formula 2 races, where it proved to be hopelessly uncompetitive, although he did manage to finish 12th on aggregate in the Berlin GP at AVUS (but too many laps adrift to be classified).

Pete continued to race his Stebro on home soil over the next few seasons before switching in 1969 to a Chevron which brought him a number of top-six finishes in the Formula B category. He won a race in 1970 at Westwood and remained loyal to the marque as he graduated into Formula Atlantic in the mid-seventies.

BRISTOW, Chris (GB) b 2/12/1937, South London – d 19/6/1960, Spa-Francorchamps Circuit, Belgium

	1959	Championship position: Unplaced						
	Race	Circuit	No	Entrant	Tyres	Car/Engine	Comment	Q Pos/Entries
10*	BRITISH GP (F2)	Aintree	48	British Racing Partnership	D	1.5 Cooper T51-Borgward 4	* 1st in F2 class/5 laps behind	16/30
	1960	Championship position: Unplaced						
ret	MONACO GP	Monte Carlo	16	Yeoman Credit Racing Team	D	2.5 Cooper T51-Climax 4	gearbox	4/24
ret	DUTCH GP	Zandvoort	8	Yeoman Credit Racing Team	D	2.5 Cooper T51-Climax 4	engine	7/21
ret	BELGIAN GP	Spa	36	Yeoman Credit Racing Team	D	2.5 Cooper T51-Climax 4	fatal accident at Burnenville	9/18

GP Starts: 4   GP Wins: 0   Pole positions: 0   Fastest laps: 0   Points: 0

BROEKER, Peter (CDN) b 15/5/1929

	1963	Championship position: Unplaced						
	Race	Circuit	No	Entrant	Tyres	Car/Engine	Comment	Q Pos/Entries
7	US GP	Watkins Glen	21	Canadian Stebro Racing	D	1.5 Stebro 4-Ford 4	22 laps behind	21/21

GP Starts: 1   GP Wins: 0   Pole positions: 0   Fastest laps: 0   Points: 0

TONY BROOKS

TONY BROOKS

Tony Brooks was still a dental student with little front-line experience when he shot to international prominence on the back of an absolutely stunning win at the Syracuse GP in the works Connaught in 1955. In only his second-ever race abroad, the slightly built and reserved youngster trounced the works Maserati and Gordini cars, three times breaking the lap record, and setting a best race lap some five seconds faster than his qualifying time. It had all seemed so easy, yet this was the first Continental win by a British car and driver since Henry Segrave won at San Sebastian in 1924, so the excitement it generated was naturally immense. Few guessed that the floodgates were soon to be opened, and that for British teams and drivers this was just the start.

After racing a Healey in 1952, Tony switched to a Frazer Nash, competing mainly in club events during the next two seasons – successfully, but largely unnoticed. It was the middle of the 1955 season that really saw Brooks' career take a step forward. Having raced Aston Martin's DB3S at Le Mans and Goodwood (where he shared third place with Peter Collins), he drove Riseley-Prichard's F2 Connaught in the Daily Telegraph Trophy at Aintree, finishing fourth behind the Formula 1 cars of Hawthorn, Schell and Salvadori. A win in the F2 class of the Avon Trophy at Castle Combe immediately preceded his momentous Syracuse victory, which of course made Brooks a very hot property indeed.

Signed by BRM for the 1956 season, he took second place in the Aintree 200 after being hampered by brake trouble, and then – the team having withdrawn after practice at Monaco – he prepared for his first championship Grand Prix start at Silverstone. It was nearly his last; when the throttle stuck at Abbey Curve, the car somersaulted, throwing out the driver, who was lucky to escape with a fractured jaw.

Joining Vanwall for 1957, Brooks soon displayed the smooth style and masterful car control that was to bring him so much success in the next three seasons. After finishing second to Fangio, no less, at Monaco, his season was hampered by the effects of a crash at Le Mans, which accounted for his handing his car to Moss at Aintree, where the British pair shared a momentous victory in their home Grand Prix. The following season saw Vanwall and Ferrari wage a ferocious battle for supremacy, and although Hawthorn took the drivers' championship Moss, Brooks and Lewis-Evans ensured the constructors' title came to Britain. Tony's three victories at the classic circuits of Spa, the Nürburgring and Monza spoke for themselves. Here was a driver of true championship pedigree.

Unfortunately Tony Vandervell withdrew from racing at the end of the year, and Brooks joined Ferrari to drive their front-engined 246 Dino. He again put in some superb performances, finishing second at Monaco despite physical sickness due to cockpit fumes, and giving wonderful demonstrations of high-speed artistry at Reims and AVUS. Ferrari did not enter his cars at Aintree, so Vandervell brought out one of his Vanwalls especially for Brooks, but he retired with ignition trouble. If it were not for a clutch failure at the start of the Italian GP, Tony may have been able to take the championship from Brabham's fleet little Cooper, but it was not to be.

With increasing business interests and recently married to an Italian girl, Pina, Tony stayed in England during 1960 and, after a Vanwall previously promised by Vandervell failed to materialise, took in a limited programme of events in the Yeoman Credit Cooper. The 1959 Type 51 car was certainly not particularly competitive, especially when Colin Chapman's Lotus 18 and then Cooper's works T53 'lowline' designs appeared and swamped the opposition. Nevertheless Tony continued to give of his best, driving harder than ever in a fruitless attempt to make up for the car's lack of performance.

In 1961 he joined BRM alongside Graham Hill and once again endured the frustration of having to campaign with an under-powered four-cylinder Climax engine against the might of Ferrari and their V6 'sharknose' cars. There were still glimpses of the Brooks of old (at Aintree, where he set the fastest lap in the rain, and a superb drive into third place in the US GP), after which he quietly retired to successfully develop his Weybridge garage business.

Having recently retired from the day-to-day running of this concern, Tony now has more time to give to the sport and he has been a welcome and popular celebrity guest at some of the many popular historic car events around the world.

Driving the Vanwall, Tony sweeps through Eau Rouge on his way to winning the 1958 Belgian Grand Prix at Spa-Francorchamps.

Following Vanwall's withdrawal from racing at the end of 1958, Tony joined Ferrari and lost no time in assuming the leadership of the team. His win in the broiling heat of the French Grand Prix was typical of his unflustered style.

BROOKS, Tony (GB) b 25/2/1932, Dukinfield, Cheshire

	1956			Championship position: Unplaced					
	Race	*Circuit*	*No*	*Entrant*	*Tyres*	*Car/Engine*		*Comment*	*Q Pos/Entries*
dns	MONACO GP	Monte Carlo	12	Owen Racing Organisation	D	2.5 BRM P25 4		*valve problems in practice*	13/19
ret	BRITISH GP	Silverstone	24	Owen Racing Organisation	D	2.5 BRM P25 4		*crashed-throttle stuck open*	9/28
	1957			Championship position: 5th Wins: 0 Pole positions: 0 Fastest laps: 1 Points scored: 11					
2	MONACO GP	Monte Carlo	20	Vandervell Products	P	2.5 Vanwall 4			4/21
1*	BRITISH GP	Aintree	20	Vandervell Products	P	2.5 Vanwall 4		** Moss took over*	3/19
ret	"	"	18	Vandervell Products	P	2.5 Vanwall 4		*took over Moss car/engine*	–/–
9	GERMAN GP	Nürburgring	11	Vandervell Products	P	2.5 Vanwall 4		*road holding problems/-1 lap*	5/24
ret	PESCARA GP	Pescara	28	Vandervell Products	P	2.5 Vanwall 4		*engine*	6/16
7	ITALIAN GP	Monza	22	Vandervell Products	P	2.5 Vanwall 4		*pit stop-throttle/FL/-5 laps*	3/19
	1958			Championship position: 3rd Wins: 3 Pole positions: 1 Fastest laps: 0 Points scored: 24					
ret	MONACO GP	Monte Carlo	30	Vandervell Products	D	2.5 Vanwall 4		*spark plug*	1/28
ret	DUTCH GP	Zandvoort	2	Vandervell Products	D	2.5 Vanwall 4		*rear axle*	3/17
1	BELGIAN GP	Spa	4	Vandervell Products	D	2.5 Vanwall 4			5/20
ret	FRENCH GP	Reims	10	Vandervell Products	D	2.5 Vanwall 4		*gearbox*	5/21
ret	"	"	12	Vandervell Products	D	2.5 Vanwall 4		*engine/took over Lewis-Evans car*	–/–
7	BRITISH GP	Silverstone	8	Vandervell Products	D	2.5 Vanwall 4		*1 lap behind*	9/21
1	GERMAN GP	Nürburgring	8	Vandervell Products	D	2.5 Vanwall 4			2/26
ret	PORTUGUESE GP	Oporto	4	Vandervell Products	D	2.5 Vanwall 4		*spun off*	5/15
1	ITALIAN GP	Monza	28	Vandervell Products	D	2.5 Vanwall 4			2/21
ret	MOROCCAN GP	Casablanca	10	Vandervell Products	D	2.5 Vanwall 4		*engine*	7/25
	1959			Championship position: 2nd Wins: 2 Pole positions: 2 Fastest laps: 1 Points scored: 27					
2	MONACO GP	Monte Carlo	50	Scuderia Ferrari	D	2.4 Ferrari Dino 246 V6		*physically sick during race*	4/24
ret	DUTCH GP	Zandvoort	2	Scuderia Ferrari	D	2.4 Ferrari Dino 246 V6		*oil leak*	8/15
1	FRENCH GP	Reims	24	Scuderia Ferrari	D	2.4 Ferrari Dino 246 V6			1/22
ret	BRITISH GP	Aintree	20	Vandervell Products	D	2.5 Vanwall 4		*misfire*	17/30
1	GERMAN GP	AVUS	4	Scuderia Ferrari	D	2.4 Ferrari Dino 246 V6		*1st both heats/FL (heat 1)*	1/16
9	PORTUGUESE GP	Monsanto	14	Scuderia Ferrari	D	2.4 Ferrari Dino 246 V6		*5 laps behind*	10/16
ret	ITALIAN GP	Monza	30	Scuderia Ferrari	D	2.4 Ferrari Dino 246 V6		*clutch at start*	2/21
3	US GP	Sebring	2	Scuderia Ferrari	D	2.4 Ferrari Dino 246 V6		*hit by von Trips-pit stop*	4/19
	1960			Championship position: 10th Wins: 0 Pole positions: 0 Fastest laps: 0 Points scored: 7					
4	MONACO GP	Monte Carlo	18	Yeoman Credit Racing Team	D	2.5 Cooper T51-Climax 4		*1 lap behind*	3/24
ret	DUTCH GP	Zandvoort	9	Yeoman Credit Racing Team	D	2.5 Cooper T51-Climax 4		*gearbox*	10/21
ret	BELGIAN GP	Spa	38	Yeoman Credit Racing Team	D	2.5 Cooper T51-Climax 4		*gearbox*	2/18
ret	FRENCH GP	Reims	14	Vandervell Products	D	2.5 Vanwall VW11 4		*transmission vibration*	13/23
5	BRITISH GP	Silverstone	12	Yeoman Credit Racing Team	D	2.5 Cooper T51-Climax 4		*1 lap behind*	9/25
5	PORTUGUESE GP	Oporto	6	Yeoman Credit Racing Team	D	2.5 Cooper T51-Climax 4		*6 laps behind*	12/16
ret	US GP	Riverside	6	Yeoman Credit Racing Team	D	2.5 Cooper T51-Climax 4		*spun off*	9/23
	1961			Championship position: 10th Wins: 0 Pole positions: 0 Fastest laps: 1 Points scored: 6					
ret	MONACO GP	Monte Carlo	16	Owen Racing Organisation	D	1.5 BRM P48/57-Climax 4		*valve*	8/21
9	DUTCH GP	Zandvoort	5	Owen Racing Organisation	D	1.5 BRM P48/57-Climax 4		*1 lap behind*	8/17
13	BELGIAN GP	Spa	38	Owen Racing Organisation	D	1.5 BRM P48/57-Climax 4		*pit stop-6 laps behind*	7/25
ret	FRENCH GP	Reims	24	Owen Racing Organisation	D	1.5 BRM P48/57-Climax 4		*engine-overheating*	11/26
9	BRITISH GP	Aintree	22	Owen Racing Organisation	D	1.5 BRM P48/57-Climax 4		*FL*	6/30
ret	GERMAN GP	Nürburgring	16	Owen Racing Organisation	D	1.5 BRM P48/57-Climax 4		*engine*	9/27
5	ITALIAN GP	Monza	26	Owen Racing Organisation	D	1.5 BRM P48/57-Climax 4			13/33
3	US GP	Watkins Glen	5	Owen Racing Organisation	D	1.5 BRM P48/57-Climax 4			=5/19

GP Starts: 38   GP Wins: 6 (1 shared)   Pole positions: 3   Fastest laps: 3   Points: 75

ALAN BROWN

Along with his friend and team-mate, Eric Brandon, Brown was a star of the 500 cc championships with his F3 Cooper, his personal highlight in this category being a win in the 1951 Luxembourg GP.

For 1952 he teamed up with Brandon to race the new F2 Cooper-Bristols under the Ecurie Richmond banner, but they were effectively works machines. Things started well when Brown scored two points on the car's Continental debut at Bremgarten and followed this with two sixths, at the Monza Autodrome GP and the Belgian GP at Spa, but it was steadily overtaken by more sophisticated machinery, encouraging Alan to look elsewhere for racing success. He gave the prototype Vanwall its debut at the 1954 International Trophy, and raced a Connaught at the same event a year later, but he concentrated on sports cars – Coopers and Connaughts from 1953 to 1955 and then a Jaguar D-Type in 1956, his last season of racing.

He then went on to enter Formula 2 Coopers, giving rides to many aspiring racers, including Innes Ireland, Ken Tyrrell, Peter Ashdown and Mike Taylor.

WARWICK BROWN

A real tough nut – even by the standards of the Aussie school of hard knocks – Warwick had plenty of guts and not a little ability, but apart from a single Grand

Prix appearance he had to content himself with a career outside top-flight racing.

Early promise in 1972 with an elderly McLaren encouraged Brown to buy a Lola T300 for the 1973 Tasman series, which ended in disaster with a massive crash at Surfers Paradise hospitalising him for three months with both legs broken. Unbowed, he limped back to compete in 1974, winning the final Tasman round at Adelaide and setting his sights on US F5000 later in the year. During a successful trip he competed in three races and took third place at Riverside.

He won the 1975 Tasman title before heading Stateside again where he was to compete very successfully, especially for the VDS team, in both F5000 and Can-Am until 1979.

ADOLF BRUDES

Brudes began his racing career on motor cycles before turning to four wheels. Just before Italy entered the Second World War in 1940, he took third place in the Coppa Brescia in a BMW.

After the cessation of hostilities he resumed his racing activities, occasionally taking the wheel of a Veritas – as in his appearance in the 1952 German GP – but mainly competing in a Borgward in events as diverse as the long-distance Buenos Aires 1000 Km, Le Mans 24 Hours and Carrera Panamericana and speed record attempts at AVUS.

BROWN, Alan (GB) b 20/11/1919, Malton, Yorkshire

	1952	Championship position: 11th=		Wins: 0	Pole positions: 0	Fastest laps: 0	Points scored: 2		
	Race	Circuit	No	Entrant	Tyres	Car/Engine		Comment	Q Pos/Entries
5	SWISS GP	Bremgarten	26	Ecurie Richmond	D	2.0 Cooper T20-Bristol 6		*3 laps behind*	15/21
6	BELGIAN GP	Spa	10	Ecurie Richmond	D	2.0 Cooper T20-Bristol 6		*2 laps behind*	9/22
nc	BRITISH GP	Silverstone	11	Ecurie Richmond	D	2.0 Cooper T20-Bristol 6		*16 laps behind*	13/32
nc	ITALIAN GP	Monza	38	Ecurie Richmond	D	2.0 Cooper T20-Bristol 6		*12 laps behind*	21/35
	1953	Championship position: Unplaced							
9	ARGENTINE GP	Buenos Aires	20	Cooper Car Co	D	2.0 Cooper T20-Bristol 6		*hit spectator/10 laps behind*	12/16
ret	BRITISH GP	Silverstone	19	R J Chase	D	2.0 Cooper T23-Bristol 6		*fan belt*	21/29
ret	GERMAN GP	Nürburgring	38	Equipe Anglaise	D	2.0 Cooper T23-Bristol 6		*misfire-crashed*	17/35
12	ITALIAN GP	Monza	46	Equipe Anglaise	D	2.0 Cooper T23-Bristol 6		*10 laps behind*	24/30
	1954	Championship position: Unplaced							
dns	BRITISH GP	Silverstone	27	Equipe Anglaise	D	2.0 Cooper T23-Bristol 6			26/31

GP Starts: 8   GP Wins: 0   Pole positions: 0   Fastest laps: 0   Points: 2

BROWN, Warwick (AUS) b 24/12/1949, Sydney, New South Wales

	1976	Championship position: Unplaced							
	Race	Circuit	No	Entrant	Tyres	Car/Engine		Comment	Q Pos/Entries
14	US GP EAST	Watkins Glen	21	Walter Wolf Racing	G	3.0 Williams FW05-Cosworth V8		*5 laps behind*	23/27

GP Starts: 1   GP Wins: 0   Pole positions: 0   Fastest laps: 0   Points: 0

BRUDES von BRESLAU, Adolf (D) b 15/10/1899 – d 5/11/1986

	1952	Championship position: Unplaced							
	Race	Circuit	No	Entrant	Tyres	Car/Engine		Comment	Q Pos/Entries
ret	GERMAN GP	Nürburgring	126	Adolf Brudes	–	2.0 Veritas RS-BMW 6		*engine*	19/32

GP Starts: 1   GP Wins: 0   Pole positions: 0   Fastest laps: 0   Points: 0

MARTIN BRUNDLE

It must have been more than a little galling for Brundle to see Ayrton Senna sweeping all before him in Grand Prix racing, for they were once very evenly matched in Formula 3. Martin may not have the innate talent of the sadly deceased World Champion but, in a truly competitive F1 car, he would surely have been a Grand Prix winner at the very least.

Back in 1983, Brundle started the F3 season buoyed by a strong finish to his first year in the series and ready to pit himself against Senna, the latest Formula Ford/FF2000 hot-shot. Watching the Brazilian simply disappear into the distance to win no fewer than nine races would have broken the resolve of a lesser man, but in the second half of the season Martin staged a comeback. Winning six races, he fell just short in the chase for the Marlboro F3 title, but had given his career prospects a massive boost.

Joining Tyrrell in 1984, he finished fifth in his first race, and the nimble Cosworth-powered car was later in its element at Detroit, where Martin took a brilliant second place. Then came two blows to his progress. A practice crash at Dallas left him with broken ankles, ending his season, and, to add insult to injury, Tyrrell's points were later expunged due to the team's technical misdemeanours. Starting from scratch in 1985, Brundle waited patiently for the Renault turbo engine which by now was a long-overdue necessity for the team. Driving sensibly and displaying great car control, Brundle did what he could with the equipment at his disposal, showing the odd flash of naked aggression, no doubt due to the frustration of being so far off the pace.

Reasoning that any move would be beneficial, Brundle opted to join Zakspeed in 1987 but, a gutsy fifth at Imola notwithstanding, it turned out to be a big mistake. Now four seasons into his Grand Prix career and seemingly no further forward than when he came into Formula 1, Martin took the brave decision to join Jaguar for a season of sports car racing rather than just trail round at the tail-end of the Grand Prix pack. His courage was rewarded, the Norfolk man winning the World Sports Car drivers' title with victories at Jarama, Monza, Silverstone, Brands Hatch and Fuji. In tandem with this programme, he jetted back and forth across the Atlantic to compete for Jaguar in IMSA, sharing the winning car in the Daytona 24 Hours.

A one-off drive for Williams at Spa kept Brundle in the picture, and for 1989 he joined the Brabham team as a much more confident and purposeful performer, bringing the Judd-powered car into the points on three occasions. Unfortunately the team was already suffering from financial strictures and, tiring of the uncertainty over Brabham's plans, Martin went back to Jaguar for the 1990 season, the highlight of which was, of course, the team's Le Mans victory when Brundle shared the winning car with John Nielsen and Price Cobb. Tempted by a package which included a Yamaha engine, he rejoined Brabham for 1991, but spent a generally frustrating season watching the stop-start development of a quite promising car gradually tail away.

By the end of the year he was glad to be able to look forward to a really good drive at last. Joining his old Jaguar boss Tom Walkinshaw at Benetton, Brundle made a pretty disastrous start in the first four races, which in retrospect fatally damaged his long-term prospects with the team. From Imola onwards Martin scored points in every round bar Canada (a race which he could well have won), and it was very hard on him indeed when he was dropped in favour of Patrese. He moved to Ligier for 1993 and, after another tardy start to the season, helped bring about a welcome improvement in the team's fortunes, showing an application that had been sorely lacking there. His reward should have been the chance to carry on the good work in 1994, but in the end Martin successfully bided his time before grabbing the drive at McLaren vacated by Senna.

Brundle's second place at Monaco was the high spot in a fraught season at Woking, with the newly forged alliance with Peugeot doomed to last just 16 races. Honest, open and diligent, Martin would have loved to stay with the team for 1995, but in the end his seat went to Nigel Mansell. Brundle made a swift return to Ligier to work with Tom Walkinshaw once again, though the Mugen-Honda engine deal meant that Martin would only compete in 11 of the 17 races. Brundle shone on the team's home track of Magny Cours, hounding Coulthard's Williams to the finish line to claim fourth, and he picked up a place on the podium at Spa, but could achieve little else with a car that just wasn't quick enough.

The 1996 season saw Martin on the move once more, joining up again with Eddie Jordan (his old boss from the far-off F3 days of 1983). With Jordan needing to deliver the goods, it was to be a tough year for the once happy-go-lucky team who had by now become serious heavyweight under-achievers. After miraculously emerging unscathed from a first-corner crash in the opening Grand Prix at Melbourne, Brundle struggled to come to terms with the car's set-up. By mid-season things had improved but, crucially, he and team-mate Barrichello had already lost the confidence of the team management and both were bundled out at season's end to make way for Fisichella and Ralf Schumacher.

With no further Formula 1 prospects, Martin has since forged a brilliantly successful career as a TV commentator and taken on the role of adviser to David Coulthard. He kept his reflexes sharp by racing for Toyota at Le Mans for three successive years between 1997 and 1999 but, after coming so close to victory on two occasions, seems unlikely to return for a fourth time in 2000.

BRUNDLE, Martin (GB) b 1/6/1959, King's Lynn, Norfolk

1984   Championship position: Unplaced   (2 points scored disallowed by FIA)

	Race	Circuit	No	Entrant	Tyres	Car/Engine	Comment	Q Pos/Entries
5/dsq	BRAZILIAN GP	Rio	3	Tyrrell Racing Organisation	G	3.0 Tyrrell 012-Cosworth V8	5th but dsq after Dutch GP	19/27
11/dsq	SOUTH AFRICAN GP	Kyalami	3	Tyrrell Racing Organisation	G	3.0 Tyrrell 012-Cosworth V8	11th but dsq after Dutch GP	25/27
ret/dsq	BELGIAN GP	Zolder	3	Tyrrell Racing Organisation	G	3.0 Tyrrell 012-Cosworth V8	lost wheel/dsq after Dutch GP	22/27
11/dsq	SAN MARINO GP	Imola	3	Tyrrell Racing Organisation	G	3.0 Tyrrell 012-Cosworth V8	11th but dsq after Dutch GP	22/28
12/dsq	FRENCH GP	Dijon	3	Tyrrell Racing Organisation	G	3.0 Tyrrell 012-Cosworth V8	12th but dsq after Dutch GP	24/27
dnq	MONACO GP	Monte Carlo	3	Tyrrell Racing Organisation	G	3.0 Tyrrell 012-Cosworth V8	accident in practice	22/27
dsq	CANADIAN GP	Montreal	3	Tyrrell Racing Organisation	G	3.0 Tyrrell 012-Cosworth V8	10th but dsq after Dutch GP	21/26
dsq	US GP (DETROIT)	Detroit	3	Tyrrell Racing Organisation	G	3.0 Tyrrell 012-Cosworth V8	2nd but dsq after Dutch GP	11/27
dnq	US GP (DALLAS)	Dallas	3	Tyrrell Racing Organisation	G	3.0 Tyrrell 012-Cosworth V8	injured in practice accident	27/27

1985   Championship position: Unplaced

	Race	Circuit	No	Entrant	Tyres	Car/Engine	Comment	Q Pos/Entries
8	BRAZILIAN GP	Rio	3	Tyrrell Racing Organisation	G	3.0 Tyrrell 012-Cosworth V8	3 laps behind	21/25
ret	PORTUGUESE GP	Estoril	3	Tyrrell Racing Organisation	G	3.0 Tyrrell 012-Cosworth V8	gear linkage	22/26
9	SAN MARINO GP	Imola	3	Tyrrell Racing Organisation	G	3.0 Tyrrell 012-Cosworth V8	4 laps behind	25/26
10	MONACO GP	Monte Carlo	3	Tyrrell Racing Organisation	G	3.0 Tyrrell 012-Cosworth V8	4 laps behind	18/26
12	CANADIAN GP	Montreal	3	Tyrrell Racing Organisation	G	3.0 Tyrrell 012-Cosworth V8	2 laps behind	24/25
ret	US GP (DETROIT)	Detroit	3	Tyrrell Racing Organisation	G	3.0 Tyrrell 012-Cosworth V8	accident with Alliot	18/25
ret	FRENCH GP	Paul Ricard	3	Tyrrell Racing Organisation	G	1.5 t/c Tyrrell 014-Renault V6	gearbox	21/26
7	BRITISH GP	Silverstone	3	Tyrrell Racing Organisation	G	1.5 t/c Tyrrell 014-Renault V6	started fom back of grid/-2 laps	20/26
10	GERMAN GP	Nürburgring	4	Tyrrell Racing Organisation	G	3.0 Tyrrell 012-Cosworth V8	4 laps behind	26/27
dnq	AUSTRIAN GP	Österreichring	4	Tyrrell Racing Organisation	G	3.0 Tyrrell 012-Cosworth V8		27/27
7	DUTCH GP	Zandvoort	3	Tyrrell Racing Organisation	G	1.5 t/c Tyrrell 014-Renault V6	1 lap behind	21/27
8	ITALIAN GP	Monza	3	Tyrrell Racing Organisation	G	1.5 t/c Tyrrell 014-Renault V6	1 lap behind	18/26
13	BELGIAN GP	Spa	3	Tyrrell Racing Organisation	G	1.5 t/c Tyrrell 014-Renault V6	5 laps behind	21/24
ret	EUROPEAN GP	Brands Hatch	3	Tyrrell Racing Organisation	G	1.5 t/c Tyrrell 014-Renault V6	water pipe	16/27
7	SOUTH AFRICAN GP	Kyalami	3	Tyrrell Racing Organisation	G	1.5 t/c Tyrrell 014-Renault V6	2 laps behind	17/21
nc	AUSTRALIAN GP	Adelaide	3	Tyrrell Racing Organisation	G	1.5 t/c Tyrrell 014-Renault V6	pit stop-electrics/-33 laps	17/25

1986   Championship position: 11th   Wins: 0   Pole positions: 0   Fastest laps: 0   Points scored: 8

	Race	Circuit	No	Entrant	Tyres	Car/Engine	Comment	Q Pos/Entries
5	BRAZILIAN GP	Rio	3	Data General Team Tyrrell	G	1.5 t/c Tyrrell 014-Renault V6	1 lap behind	17/25
dns	"	"	3	Data General Team Tyrrell	G	1.5 t/c Tyrrell 015-Renault V6	crashed in practice	–/–
ret	SPANISH GP	Jerez	3	Data General Team Tyrrell	G	1.5 t/c Tyrrell 014-Renault V6	engine-lost lubricant	12/25
8	SAN MARINO GP	Imola	3	Data General Team Tyrrell	G	1.5 t/c Tyrrell 014-Renault V6	race car/2 laps behind	–/–
dns	"	"	3	Data General Team Tyrrell	G	1.5 t/c Tyrrell 015-Renault V6	crashed car in warm up	13/26
ret	MONACO GP	Monte Carlo	3	Data General Team Tyrrell	G	1.5 t/c Tyrrell 015-Renault V6	accident with Tambay	10/26
ret	BELGIAN GP	Spa	3	Data General Team Tyrrell	G	1.5 t/c Tyrrell 015-Renault V6	gearbox	12/25
9	CANADIAN GP	Montreal	3	Data General Team Tyrrell	G	1.5 t/c Tyrrell 015-Renault V6	2 laps behind	19/25
ret	US GP (DETROIT)	Detroit	3	Data General Team Tyrrell	G	1.5 t/c Tyrrell 015-Renault V6	electrics	16/26
10	FRENCH GP	Paul Ricard	3	Data General Team Tyrrell	G	1.5 t/c Tyrrell 015-Renault V6	lost 4th gear/3 laps behind	15/26
5	BRITISH GP	Brands Hatch	3	Data General Team Tyrrell	G	1.5 t/c Tyrrell 015-Renault V6	3 laps behind	11/26
ret	GERMAN GP	Hockenheim	3	Data General Team Tyrrell	G	1.5 t/c Tyrrell 015-Renault V6	electrics	15/26
6	HUNGARIAN GP	Hungaroring	3	Data General Team Tyrrell	G	1.5 t/c Tyrrell 015-Renault V6	lost 4th gear/2 laps behind	16/26
ret	AUSTRIAN GP	Österreichring	3	Data General Team Tyrrell	G	1.5 t/c Tyrrell 015-Renault V6	turbo	17/26
10	ITALIAN GP	Monza	3	Data General Team Tyrrell	G	1.5 t/c Tyrrell 015-Renault V6	misfire/2 laps behind	20/27
ret	PORTUGUESE GP	Estoril	3	Data General Team Tyrrell	G	1.5 t/c Tyrrell 015-Renault V6	engine	19/27
11	MEXICAN GP	Mexico City	3	Data General Team Tyrrell	G	1.5 t/c Tyrrell 015-Renault V6	2 pit stops-tyres/-3 laps	16/26
4	AUSTRALIAN GP	Adelaide	3	Data General Team Tyrrell	G	1.5 t/c Tyrrell 015-Renault V6	1 lap behind	16/26

1987   Championship position: 18th   Wins: 0   Pole positions: 0   Fastest laps: 0   Points scored: 2

	Race	Circuit	No	Entrant	Tyres	Car/Engine	Comment	Q Pos/Entries
ret	BRAZILIAN GP	Rio	9	West Zakspeed Racing	G	1.5 t/c Zakspeed 861 4	turbo	19/23
5	SAN MARINO GP	Imola	9	West Zakspeed Racing	G	1.5 t/c Zakspeed 871 4	2 laps behind	16/27
ret	BELGIAN GP	Spa	9	West Zakspeed Racing	G	1.5 t/c Zakspeed 871 4	engine	18/26
7	MONACO GP	Monte Carlo	9	West Zakspeed Racing	G	1.5 t/c Zakspeed 871 4	2 laps behind	14/26
ret	US GP (DETROIT)	Detroit	9	West Zakspeed Racing	G	1.5 t/c Zakspeed 871 4	turbo	15/26
ret	FRENCH GP	Paul Ricard	9	West Zakspeed Racing	G	1.5 t/c Zakspeed 871 4	lost rear wheel	18/26
nc	BRITISH GP	Silverstone	9	West Zakspeed Racing	G	1.5 t/c Zakspeed 871 4	pit stop-electrics/-11 laps	17/26
nc	GERMAN GP	Hockenheim	9	West Zakspeed Racing	G	1.5 t/c Zakspeed 871 4	pit stops-electrics/-10 laps	19/26
ret	HUNGARIAN GP	Hungaroring	9	West Zakspeed Racing	G	1.5 t/c Zakspeed 871 4	turbo	22/26
dsq*	AUSTRIAN GP	Österreichring	9	West Zakspeed Racing	G	1.5 t/c Zakspeed 871 4	14th/*bodywork infringement	17/26
ret	ITALIAN GP	Monza	9	West Zakspeed Racing	G	1.5 t/c Zakspeed 871 4	gearbox	17/28
ret	PORTUGUESE GP	Estoril	9	West Zakspeed Racing	G	1.5 t/c Zakspeed 871 4	gearbox	17/27
11	SPANISH GP	Jerez	9	West Zakspeed Racing	G	1.5 t/c Zakspeed 871 4	2 laps behind	20/28
ret	MEXICAN GP	Mexico City	9	West Zakspeed Racing	G	1.5 t/c Zakspeed 871 4	turbo	13/27
ret	JAPANESE GP	Suzuka	9	West Zakspeed Racing	G	1.5 t/c Zakspeed 871 4	engine overheating	16/27
ret	AUSTRALIAN GP	Adelaide	9	West Zakspeed Racing	G	1.5 t/c Zakspeed 871 4	turbo and gear selection	16/27

1988   Championship position: Unplaced

	Race	Circuit	No	Entrant	Tyres	Car/Engine	Comment	Q Pos/Entries
7*	BELGIAN GP	Spa	5	Canon Williams Team	G	3.5 Williams FW12-Judd V8	*3rd & 4th cars dsq/1- lap	12/31

1989   Championship position: 16th=   Wins: 0   Pole positions: 0   Fastest laps: 0   Points scored: 4

	Race	Circuit	No	Entrant	Tyres	Car/Engine	Comment	Q Pos/Entries
ret	BRAZILIAN GP	Rio	7	Motor Racing Developments	P	3.5 Brabham BT58-Judd V8	engine-wiring loom	13/38
ret	SAN MARINO GP	Imola	7	Motor Racing Developments	P	3.5 Brabham BT58-Judd V8	fuel pump	22/39
6	MONACO GP	Monte Carlo	7	Motor Racing Developments	P	3.5 Brabham BT58-Judd V8	pit stop when 3rd-battery/-2 laps	4/38
9	MEXICAN GP	Mexico City	7	Motor Racing Developments	P	3.5 Brabham BT58-Judd V8	1 lap behind	20/39
ret	US GP (PHOENIX)	Phoenix	7	Motor Racing Developments	P	3.5 Brabham BT58-Judd V8	brakes	5/39
dnpq	CANADIAN GP	Montreal	7	Motor Racing Developments	P	3.5 Brabham BT58-Judd V8		31/39
dnpq	FRENCH GP	Paul Ricard	7	Motor Racing Developments	P	3.5 Brabham BT58-Judd V8		32/39
ret	BRITISH GP	Silverstone	7	Motor Racing Developments	P	3.5 Brabham BT58-Judd V8	engine	20/39
8	GERMAN GP	Hockenheim	7	Motor Racing Developments	P	3.5 Brabham BT58-Judd V8	pit stop-slow puncture/-1 lap	12/39
12	HUNGARIAN GP	Hungaroring	7	Motor Racing Developments	P	3.5 Brabham BT58-Judd V8	hit Alesi and spun/-2 laps	15/39
ret	BELGIAN GP	Spa	7	Motor Racing Developments	P	3.5 Brabham BT58-Judd V8	brakes	20/39

6	ITALIAN GP	Monza	7	Motor Racing Developments	P	3.5 Brabham BT58-Judd V8	*1 lap behind*	12/39
8	PORTUGUESE GP	Estoril	7	Motor Racing Developments	P	3.5 Brabham BT58-Judd V8	*2 pit stops-tyres/1 lap behind*	10/39
ret	SPANISH GP	Jerez	7	Motor Racing Developments	P	3.5 Brabham BT58-Judd V8	*rear suspension-spun off*	8/38
5*	JAPANESE GP	Suzuka	7	Motor Racing Developments	P	3.5 Brabham BT58-Judd V8	**1st place car dsq/-1 lap*	13/39
ret	AUSTRALIAN GP	Adelaide	7	Motor Racing Developments	P	3.5 Brabham BT58-Judd V8	*hit by Senna in rain*	12/39

1991   Championship position: 15th=   Wins: 0   Pole positions: 0   Fastest laps: 0   Points scored: 2

11	US GP (PHOENIX)	Phoenix	7	Motor Racing Developments Ltd	P	3.5 Brabham BT59Y-Yamaha V12	*8 laps behind*	12/34
12	BRAZILIAN GP	Interlagos	7	Motor Racing Developments Ltd	P	3.5 Brabham BT59Y-Yamaha V12	*4 laps behind*	26/34
11	SAN MARINO GP	Imola	7	Motor Racing Developments Ltd	P	3.5 Brabham BT60Y-Yamaha V12	*4 laps behind*	18/34
dsq	MONACO GP	Monte Carlo	7	Motor Racing Developments Ltd	P	3.5 Brabham BT60Y-Yamaha V12	*missed weight check in practice*	27/34
ret	CANADIAN GP	Montreal	7	Motor Racing Developments Ltd	P	3.5 Brabham BT60Y-Yamaha V12	*engine*	20/34
ret	MEXICAN GP	Mexico City	7	Motor Racing Developments Ltd	P	3.5 Brabham BT60Y-Yamaha V12	*lost rear wheel*	17/34
ret	FRENCH GP	Magny Cours	7	Motor Racing Developments Ltd	P	3.5 Brabham BT60Y-Yamaha V12	*gearbox*	24/34
ret	BRITISH GP	Silverstone	7	Motor Racing Developments Ltd	P	3.5 Brabham BT60Y-Yamaha V12	*throttle cable*	14/34
11	GERMAN GP	Hockenheim	7	Motor Racing Developments Ltd	P	3.5 Brabham BT60Y-Yamaha V12	*2 laps behind*	15/34
ret	HUNGARIAN GP	Hungaroring	7	Motor Racing Developments Ltd	P	3.5 Brabham BT60Y-Yamaha V12	*foot cramp*	10/34
9	BELGIAN GP	Spa	7	Motor Racing Developments Ltd	P	3.5 Brabham BT60Y-Yamaha V12	*2 laps behind*	16/34
13	ITALIAN GP	Monza	7	Motor Racing Developments Ltd	P	3.5 Brabham BT60Y-Yamaha V12	*1 lap behind*	19/34
12	PORTUGUESE GP	Estoril	7	Motor Racing Developments Ltd	P	3.5 Brabham BT60Y-Yamaha V12	*2 laps behind*	19/34
10	SPANISH GP	Barcelona	7	Motor Racing Developments Ltd	P	3.5 Brabham BT60Y-Yamaha V12	*2 laps behind*	11/33
5	JAPANESE GP	Suzuka	7	Motor Racing Developments Ltd	P	3.5 Brabham BT60Y-Yamaha V12	*1 lap behind*	19/32
dnq	AUSTRALIAN GP	Adelaide	7	Motor Racing Developments Ltd	P	3.5 Brabham BT60Y-Yamaha V12		28/32

1992   Championship position: 6yj   Wins: 0   Pole positions: 0   Fastest laps: 0   Points scored: 38

ret	SOUTH AFRICAN GP	Kyalami	20	Camel Benetton Ford	G	3.5 Benetton B191B-Ford HB V8	*spun-broke clutch restarting*	8/30
ret	MEXICAN GP	Mexico City	20	Camel Benetton Ford	G	3.5 Benetton B191B-Ford HB V8	*overheating*	4/30
ret	BRAZILIAN GP	Interlagos	20	Camel Benetton Ford	G	3.5 Benetton B191B-Ford HB V8	*collision with Alesi*	7/31
ret	SPANISH GP	Barcelona	20	Camel Benetton Ford	G	3.5 Benetton B192-Ford HB V8	*spun off*	6/32
4	SAN MARINO GP	Imola	20	Camel Benetton Ford	G	3.5 Benetton B192-Ford HB V8		6/32
5	MONACO GP	Monte Carlo	20	Camel Benetton Ford	G	3.5 Benetton B192-Ford HB V8		7/32
ret	CANADIAN GP	Montreal	20	Camel Benetton Ford	G	3.5 Benetton B192-Ford HB V8	*final drive*	7/32
3	FRENCH GP	Magny Cours	20	Camel Benetton Ford	G	3.5 Benetton B192-Ford HB V8		7/30
3	BRITISH GP	Silverstone	20	Camel Benetton Ford	G	3.5 Benetton B192-Ford HB V8		6/32
4	GERMAN GP	Hockenheim	20	Camel Benetton Ford	G	3.5 Benetton B192-Ford HB V8		9/32
5	HUNGARIAN GP	Hungaroring	20	Camel Benetton Ford	G	3.5 Benetton B192-Ford HB V8		6/31
4	BELGIAN GP	Spa	20	Camel Benetton Ford	G	3.5 Benetton B192-Ford HB V8		9/30
2	ITALIAN GP	Monza	20	Camel Benetton Ford	G	3.5 Benetton B192-Ford HB V8		9/28
4	PORTUGUESE GP	Estoril	20	Camel Benetton Ford	G	3.5 Benetton B192-Ford HB V8	*1 lap behind*	6/26
3	JAPANESE GP	Suzuka	20	Camel Benetton Ford	G	3.5 Benetton B192-Ford HB V8		13/26
3	AUSTRALIAN GP	Adelaide	20	Camel Benetton Ford	G	3.5 Benetton B192-Ford HB V8		8/26

1993   Championship position: 7th   Wins: 0   Pole positions: 0   Fastest laps: 0   Points scored: 13

ret	SOUTH AFRICAN GP	Kyalami	25	Ligier Gitanes Blondes	G	3.5 Ligier JS39-Renault V10	*spun off on oil*	12/26
ret	BRAZILIAN GP	Interlagos	25	Ligier Gitanes Blondes	G	3.5 Ligier JS39-Renault V10	*collision, Barbazza -spun off*	16/26
ret	EUROPEAN GP	Donington	25	Ligier Gitanes Blondes	G	3.5 Ligier JS39-Renault V10	*spun off and stalled*	22/26
3	SAN MARINO GP	Imola	25	Ligier Gitanes Blondes	G	3.5 Ligier JS39-Renault V10	*1 lap behind*	10/26
ret	SPANISH GP	Barcelona	25	Ligier Gitanes Blondes	G	3.5 Ligier JS39-Renault V10	*puncture-spun off*	18/26
6	MONACO GP	Monte Carlo	25	Ligier Gitanes Blondes	G	3.5 Ligier JS39-Renault V10	*collision-pit stop/2 laps behind*	13/26
5	CANADIAN GP	Montreal	25	Ligier Gitanes Blondes	G	3.5 Ligier JS39-Renault V10	*1 lap behind*	7/26
5	FRENCH GP	Magny Cours	25	Ligier Gitanes Blondes	G	3.5 Ligier JS39-Renault V10		3/26
14/ret	BRITISH GP	Silverstone	25	Ligier Gitanes Blondes	G	3.5 Ligier JS39-Renault V10	*gearbox/6 laps behind*	6/26
8	GERMAN GP	Hockenheim	25	Ligier Gitanes Blondes	G	3.5 Ligier JS39-Renault V10	*stop & go penalty/1 lap behind*	6/26
5	HUNGARIAN GP	Hungaroring	25	Ligier Gitanes Blondes	G	3.5 Ligier JS39-Renault V10	*collision-Berger/1 lap behind*	13/26
7	BELGIAN GP	Spa	25	Ligier Gitanes Blondes	G	3.5 Ligier JS39-Renault V10	*1 lap behind*	11/25
ret	ITALIAN GP	Monza	25	Ligier Gitanes Blondes	G	3.5 Ligier JS39-Renault V10	*taken off by Senna*	12/26
6	PORTUGUESE GP	Estoril	25	Ligier Gitanes Blondes	G	3.5 Ligier JS39-Renault V10	*1 lap behind*	11/26
9/ret	JAPANESE GP	Suzuka	25	Ligier Gitanes Blondes	G	3.5 Ligier JS39-Renault V10	*collision-Lehto-spun off/-2 laps*	15/24
6	AUSTRALIAN GP	Adelaide	25	Ligier Gitanes Blondes	G	3.5 Ligier JS39-Renault V10	*1 lap behind*	8/24

1994   Championship position: 7th   Wins: 0   Pole positions: 0   Fastest laps: 0   Points scored: 16

ret	BRAZILIAN GP	Interlagos	8	Marlboro McLaren Peugeot	G	3.5 McLaren MP4/9-Peugeot V10	*multiple accident*	18/28
ret	PACIFIC GP	T.I. Circuit	8	Marlboro McLaren Peugeot	G	3.5 McLaren MP4/9-Peugeot V10	*overheating*	6/28
8	SAN MARINO GP	Imola	8	Marlboro McLaren Peugeot	G	3.5 McLaren MP4/9-Peugeot V10	*1 lap behind*	13/28
2	MONACO GP	Monte Carlo	8	Marlboro McLaren Peugeot	G	3.5 McLaren MP4/9-Peugeot V10		8/24
11/ret	SPANISH GP	Barcelona	8	Marlboro McLaren Peugeot	G	3.5 McLaren MP4/9-Peugeot V10	*6 laps behind/transmission*	8/27
ret	CANADIAN GP	Montreal	8	Marlboro McLaren Peugeot	G	3.5 McLaren MP4/9-Peugeot V10	*electrics*	12//27
ret	FRENCH GP	Magny Cours	8	Marlboro McLaren Peugeot	G	3.5 McLaren MP4/9-Peugeot V10	*engine*	12/28
ret	BRITISH GP	Silverstone	8	Marlboro McLaren Peugeot	G	3.5 McLaren MP4/9-Peugeot V10	*engine at start*	9/28
ret	GERMAN GP	Hockenheim	8	Marlboro McLaren Peugeot	G	3.5 McLaren MP4/9-Peugeot V10	*engine*	13/28
4/ret	HUNGARIAN GP	Hungaroring	8	Marlboro McLaren Peugeot	G	3.5 McLaren MP4/9-Peugeot V10	*engine failure on last lap*	6/28
ret	BELGIAN GP	Spa	8	Marlboro McLaren Peugeot	G	3.5 McLaren MP4/9-Peugeot V10	*spun off*	13/28
5	ITALIAN GP	Monza	8	Marlboro McLaren Peugeot	G	3.5 McLaren MP4/9-Peugeot V10		15/28
6	PORTUGUESE GP	Estoril	8	Marlboro McLaren Peugeot	G	3.5 McLaren MP4/9-Peugeot V10		7/28
ret	EUROPEAN GP	Jerez	8	Marlboro McLaren Peugeot	G	3.5 McLaren MP4/9-Peugeot V10	*engine*	15/28
ret	JAPANESE GP	Suzuka	8	Marlboro McLaren Peugeot	G	3.5 McLaren MP4/9-Peugeot V10	*spun off and hit marshal*	9/28
3	AUSTRALIAN GP	Adelaide	8	Marlboro McLaren Peugeot	G	3.5 McLaren MP4/9-Peugeot V10		9/28

1995   Championship position: 13th   Wins: 0   Pole positions: 0   Fastest laps: 0   Points scored: 7

9	SPANISH GP	Barcelona	25	Ligier Gitanes Blondes	G	3.0 Ligier JS41-Mugen Honda V10	*1 lap behind*	11/26
ret	MONACO GP	Monte Carlo	25	Ligier Gitanes Blondes	G	3.0 Ligier JS41-Mugen Honda V10	*spun off*	8/26
ret	CANADIAN GP	Montreal	25	Ligier Gitanes Blondes	G	3.0 Ligier JS41-Mugen Honda V10	*taken off by Berger*	14/24
4	FRENCH GP	Magny Cours	25	Ligier Gitanes Blondes	G	3.0 Ligier JS41-Mugen Honda V10		9/24
ret	BRITISH GP	Silverstone	25	Ligier Gitanes Blondes	G	3.0 Ligier JS41-Mugen Honda V10	*spun off*	11/24
ret	HUNGARIAN GP	Hungaroring	25	Ligier Gitanes Blondes	G	3.0 Ligier JS41-Mugen Honda V10	*engine*	8/24
3	BELGIAN GP	Spa	25	Ligier Gitanes Blondes	G	3.0 Ligier JS41-Mugen Honda V10		13/24

ret	ITALIAN GP	Monza	25	Ligier Gitanes Blondes	G	3.0 Ligier JS41-Mugen Honda V10	puncture-suspension damage	11/24
8	PORTUGUESE GP	Estoril	25	Ligier Gitanes Blondes	G	3.0 Ligier JS41-Mugen Honda V10	1 lap behind	9/24
7	EUROPEAN GP	Nürburgring	25	Ligier Gitanes Blondes	G	3.0 Ligier JS41-Mugen Honda V10	2 laps behind	12/24
ret	AUSTRALIAN GP	Adelaide	25	Ligier Gitanes Blondes	G	3.0 Ligier JS41-Mugen Honda V10	spun off	11/24
	1996	Championship position: 11th Wins: 0 Pole positions: 0 Fastest laps: 0 Points scored: 8						
ret	AUSTRALIAN GP	Melbourne	12	B & H Total Jordan Peugeot	G	3.0 Jordan 196-Peugeot V10	started from pits, collision-Diniz	19/22
ret/12	BRAZILIAN GP	Interlagos	12	B & H Total Jordan Peugeot	G	3.0 Jordan 196-Peugeot V10	spun off/7 laps behind	6/22
ret	ARGENTINE GP	Buenos Aires	12	B & H Total Jordan Peugeot	G	3.0 Jordan 196-Peugeot V10	collision with Marques	15/22
6	EUROPEAN GP	Nürburgring	12	B & H Total Jordan Peugeot	G	3.0 Jordan 196-Peugeot V10		11/22
ret	SAN MARINO GP	Imola	12	B & H Total Jordan Peugeot	G	3.0 Jordan 196-Peugeot V10	spun off	12/22
ret	MONACO GP	Monte Carlo	12	B & H Total Jordan Peugeot	G	3.0 Jordan 196-Peugeot V10	spun off	16/22
ret	SPANISH GP	Barcelona	12	B & H Total Jordan Peugeot	G	3.0 Jordan 196-Peugeot V10	gearbox	15/22
6	CANADIAN GP	Montreal	12	B & H Total Jordan Peugeot	G	3.0 Jordan 196-Peugeot V10	collision Lamy/1 lap behind	9/22
8	FRENCH GP	Magny Cours	12	B & H Total Jordan Peugeot	G	3.0 Jordan 196-Peugeot V10	excess understeer/1 lap behind	8/22
6	BRITISH GP	Silverstone	12	B & H Total Jordan Peugeot	G	3.0 Jordan 196-Peugeot V10	puncture/1 lap behind	8/22
10	GERMAN GP	Hockenheim	12	B & H Total Jordan Peugeot	G	3.0 Jordan 196-Peugeot V10	slow puncture/1 lap behind	10/20
ret	HUNGARIAN GP	Hungaroring	12	B & H Total Jordan Peugeot	G	3.0 Jordan 196-Peugeot V10	spun off-broken suspension	12/20
ret	BELGIAN GP	Spa	12	B & H Total Jordan Peugeot	G	3.0 Jordan 196-Peugeot V10	engine	8/20
4	ITALIAN GP	Monza	12	B & H Total Jordan Peugeot	G	3.0 Jordan 196-Peugeot V10		9/20
9	PORTUGUESE GP	Estoril	12	B & H Total Jordan Peugeot	G	3.0 Jordan 196-Peugeot V10	excess tyre wear/1 lap behind	10/20
5	JAPANESE GP	Suzuka	12	B & H Total Jordan Peugeot	G	3.0 Jordan 196-Peugeot V10		10/20

GP Starts: 158 GP Wins: 0 Pole positions: 0 Fastest laps: 0 Points: 98

CLEMAR BUCCI

Bucci forged his reputation in his native Argentina with a 4.5-litre Alfa Romeo, finishing third in the major Eva Peron Cup race in 1950. He continued to run this car in the early fifties, but was also involved in trying to race the ill-fated Cisitalia-based Autoar. Bucci took this futuristic rear-engined machine, developed with help from the Peronist government, to some fairly meaningless speed records in July 1953, but it proved completely unraceworthy when it was briefly practised at the 1954 Buenos Aires City GP. Bucci raced his trusty Alfa instead, but was apparently disqualified for not wearing a crash helmet!

He came to Europe in mid-1954 to race for Gordini, but had little luck in his four championship races and fared no better in the three non-title events he contested, posting retirements at Pescara, Rouen and Caen.

Clemar joined the works Maserati team for the 1955 Argentine GP, run in broiling heat, and then finished ninth in a 2.5-litre Ferrari sports car in the Formula Libre GP of Buenos Aires. This event held more interest for the locals than the championship race and drew a crowd estimated at 400,000. He was also invited to share a works Ferrari with Maglioli in that year's Buenos Aires 1000 Km, but the pair were disqualified after receiving outside assistance.

BUCCI, Clemar (RA) b 4/9/1920, Zenon Pereyra, Sante Fé

	1954	Championship position: Unplaced						
	Race	Circuit	No	Entrant	Tyres	Car/Engine	Comment	Q Pos/Entries
ret	BRITISH GP	Silverstone	18	Equipe Gordini	E	2.5 Gordini Type 16 6	crashed	13/31
ret	GERMAN GP	Nürburgring	11	Equipe Gordini	E	2.5 Gordini Type 16 6	lost wheel	16/23
ret	SWISS GP	Bremgarten	12	Equipe Gordini	E	2.5 Gordini Type 16 6	fuel pump on grid	10/15
ret	ITALIAN GP	Monza	46	Equipe Gordini	E	2.5 Gordini Type 16 6	transmission	17/21
	1955	Championship position: Unplaced						
ret	ARGENTINE GP	Buenos Aires	26	Officine Alfieri Maserati	P	2.5 Maserati 250F 6	fuel starvation/Schell/Menditéguy	20/22

GP Starts: 5 GP Wins: 0 Pole positions: 0 Fastest laps: 0 Points: 0

BUCKNUM, Ronnie (USA) b 5/4/1936, Alhambra, California – d 14/4/1992

	1964	Championship position: Unplaced						
	Race	Circuit	No	Entrant	Tyres	Car/Engine	Comment	Q Pos/Entries
ret	GERMAN GP	Nürburgring	20	Honda R & D Co	D	1.5 Honda RA271 V12	spun off	22/24
ret	ITALIAN GP	Monza	28	Honda R & D Co	D	1.5 Honda RA271 V12	brakes/oil leaks/overheating	=9/25
ret	US GP	Watkins Glen	28	Honda R & D Co	D	1.5 Honda RA271 V12	engine-head gasket	14/19
	1965	Championship position: 14th= Wins: 0 Pole positions: 0 Fastest laps: 0 Points scored: 2						
ret	MONACO GP	Monte Carlo	19	Honda R & D Co	G	1.5 Honda RA272 V12	gear linkage	=14/17
ret	BELGIAN GP	Spa	11	Honda R & D Co	G	1.5 Honda RA272 V12	transmission	11/21
ret	FRENCH GP	Clermont Ferrand	28	Honda R & D Co	G	1.5 Honda RA272 V12	ignition	16/17
ret	ITALIAN GP	Monza	22	Honda R & D Co	G	1.5 Honda RA272 V12	engine	6/23
13	US GP	Watkins Glen	12	Honda R & D Co	G	1.5 Honda RA272 V12	pit stop/18 laps behind	12/18
5	MEXICAN GP	Mexico City	12	Honda R & D Co	G	1.5 Honda RA272 V12	1 lap behind	10/18
	1966	Championship position: Unplaced						
ret	US GP	Watkins Glen	14	Honda R & D Co	G	3.0 Honda RA273 V12	transmission	18/19
8	MEXICAN GP	Mexico City	14	Honda R & D Co	G	3.0 Honda RA273 V12	pit stop-fire/5 laps behind	14/19

GP Starts: 11 GP Wins: 0 Pole positions: 0 Fastest laps: 0 Points: 2

RONNIE BUCKNUM

Although Bucknum had been competing in sports cars in America since 1957, his selection by Honda to spearhead their 1964 Grand Prix challenge was strange indeed. His lack of international racing pedigree had its attractions for the secretive Japanese, since Ronnie could test and race the car without raising undue attention or expectations, and the opposition would never really know just how well it was progressing in that first season. However, the novice did well just to survive a daunting debut at the Nürburgring which ended when the car suffered a steering failure.

Two more races were safely completed before the team signed the vastly more experienced Richie Ginther to head their 1965 challenge and embarked on a winter of testing at Suzuka, during which the unlucky Bucknum again suffered a steering failure, crashed and this time broke his leg. This set him back when the season began and he predictably played second fiddle to his team-mate, although he did score points with a fifth place in Mexico as Ginther swept aside the opposition to record Honda's first Grand Prix win.

If nothing else, everybody now knew who Ronnie Bucknum was and he was invited to join the Ford team for 1966, finishing third at Le Mans with Hutcherson. Honda still thought well of their man and once two of their 3-litre cars were available he returned for the end-of-season American races. Although this was his final bow in Grands Prix, in many ways Bucknum's career as a racing driver was really just beginning. After more sports cars in 1967, Ronnie went racing in Can-Am and USAC the following year, sensationally winning at Michigan in only his second oval race with an Eagle. Subsequently he raced sports and Trans-Am cars for Roger Penske and teamed up with Sam Posey in the NART Ferrari in long-distance events in the early seventies, by which time the Marine crewcut had been replaced by collar-length hair and a beard! Bucknum, who was later to suffer from diabetes, died at the comparatively young age of 57 in April 1992.

IVOR BUEB

Bueb began his career in 1952 in 500 cc racing, though he did not taste success until he got his hands on a Cooper for the 1954 season. Ivor did so well that he was invited to join the works team the following year, racing the 1100 cc sports car in adddition to his F3 commitments. The high point of his season, though, was his win at Le Mans with Hawthorn in the D-Type Jaguar.

Bueb cheerfully continued to race anything and everything that came his way in the next few seasons, winning the Reims 12 Hours for Jaguar (with Hamilton) in 1956 and repeating his Le Mans triumph with Hawthorn in 1957, a year which saw his Formula 1 debut for Connaught, Bueb claiming fifth at Syracuse and third at Pau in the ageing car.

Although opportunities at Grand Prix level were limited, Ivor maintained his busy racing schedule in 1958, campaigning his own Lotus 12 in F2 and driving for Ecurie Ecosse and Lister in sports cars. Teaming up with the ambitious BRP stable for 1959, Ivor was as competitive as ever with the team's Formula 2 Cooper-Borgward but disaster struck when he crashed fatally during the Auvergne Trophy race at Clermont Ferrand.

BUEB, Ivor (GB) b 6/6/1923, Dulwich, London – d 1/8/1959, Clermont-Ferrand, France

	1957	Championship position: Unplaced						
	Race	Circuit	No	Entrant	Tyres	Car/Engine	Comment	Q Pos/Entries
ret	MONACO GP	Monte Carlo	12	Connaught Engineering	D	2.5 Connaught B-Alta 4	*pit stop exhaust/fuel tank*	16/21
nc	BRITISH GP	Aintree	32	Gilby Engineering	D	2.5 Maserati 250F 6	*19 laps behind*	19/19
	1958	Championship position: Unplaced						
ret	BRITISH GP	Silverstone	15	B C Ecclestone	D	2.5 Connaught B-Alta 4	*gearbox oil pump*	17/21
11*/ret	GERMAN GP (F2)	Nürburgring	12	Ecurie Demi Litre	D	1.5 Lotus 12-Climax 4	*oil pipe/*6th-F2 class/-21 laps*	19/26
	1959	Championship position: Unplaced						
dnq	MONACO GP	Monte Carlo	34	British Racing Partnership	D	1.5 Cooper T51-Climax 4		17/24
13*	BRITISH GP (F2)	Aintree	46	British Racing Partnership	D	1.5 Cooper T51-Borgward 4	**4th in F2 class/6 laps behind*	18/30

GP Starts: 5   GP Wins: 0   Pole positions: 0   Fastest laps: 0   Points: 0

LUIZ-PEREIRA BUENO

Twice the Brazilian touring car champion, Bueno was a very talented driver who came to Britain in 1969 to race in Formula Ford courtesy of a Brazilian government scheme. He won five races and was well placed elsewhere with a Merlyn, but opted to return to Brazil and continue in domestic racing in 1970.

Regarded as highly as Emerson Fittipaldi, Bueno was keen to take up the offer of a full-time return to Europe in 1971, but could not afford to do so.

He did compete in the inaugural non-championship Brazilian GP in a works March 721 in 1972, finishing sixth, and the World Championship race for Team Surtees a year later.

IAN BURGESS

Burgess caused quite stir when in 1951 he won the Eifelrennen 500 cc race in the pouring rain at the Nürburgring ahead of more seasoned practitioners Wharton and Whitehead. Unfortunately he could not build on this triumph, and the next few seasons brought only moderate success.

It was only when he began working for the Cooper team at their Surbiton factory that his career started to prosper. Although employed in part to help run the Cooper's racing drivers school from Brands Hatch, Ian was cajoling the management into letting him race their new Formula 2 cars.

Fourth place in the 1957 Gold Cup at Oulton Park led to a season in Tommy Atkins' similar car for 1958. A brilliant start to the year saw Ian win at Crystal Palace and Snetterton and take fourth at both Montlhéry and Reims, until a broken leg sustained in a crash at AVUS curtailed his season.

He was back in 1959, driving for Atkins in F2 and also handling the Italian Scuderia Centro Sud team's Maserati-engined F1 Cooper, while a trip to New Zealand at the start of 1960 saw Ian win the Teretonga Trophy in Atkins' Cooper. For 1961 Burgess became involved with the American Camoradi Team, racing their Lotus 18 with only moderate success at minor events.

He concentrated on the plethora of non-championship races in 1962, driving a Cooper under the Anglo American Equipe banner. The season's highlight was an excellent drive to fourth at Solitude. For the 1963 season, his last in racing, Burgess joined the Scirocco team, bankrolled by wealthy American businessman Hugh Powell, but it proved to be a dismal and costly exercise for all concerned.

BUENO, Luiz Pereira (BR) b *circa* 1939

	1973	Championship position: Unplaced						
	Race	Circuit	No	Entrant	Tyres	Car/Engine	Comment	Q Pos/Entries
12	BRAZILIAN GP	Interlagos	23	Team Surtees	F	3.0 Surtees TS9B-Cosworth V8	pit stop-electrics/-4 laps	20/20

GP Starts: 1   GP Wins: 0   Pole positions: 0   Fastest laps: 0   Points: 0

BURGESS, Ian (GB) b 6/7/1930, London

	1958	Championship position: Unplaced						
	Race	Circuit	No	Entrant	Tyres	Car/Engine	Comment	Qual Pos/Entries
ret	BRITISH GP	Silverstone	12	Cooper Car Co	D	2.0 Cooper T45-Climax 4	clutch	16/21
7*	GERMAN GP (F2)	Nürburgring	26	High Efficiency Motors	D	1.5 Cooper T43-Climax 4 F2	* 3rd in F2 class	14/26
	1959	Championship position: Unplaced						
ret	FRENCH GP	Reims	18	Scuderia Centro Sud	D	2.5 Cooper T51-Maserati 4	engine	19/22
ret	BRITISH GP	Aintree	22	Scuderia Centro Sud	D	2.5 Cooper T51-Maserati 4	gearbox	13/30
6	GERMAN GP	AVUS	18	Scuderia Centro Sud	D	2.5 Cooper T51-Maserati 4	9th heat 1/6th heat 2/-4 laps	15/16
14	ITALIAN GP	Monza	42	Scuderia Centro Sud	D	2.5 Cooper T51-Maserati 4	5 laps behind	16/21
	1960	Championship position: Unplaced						
dnq	MONACO GP	Monte Carlo	42	Scuderia Centro Sud	D	2.5 Cooper T51-Maserati 4		24/24
10	FRENCH GP	Reims	42	Scuderia Centro Sud	D	2.5 Cooper T51-Maserati 4	pit stop/14 laps behind	22/23
ret	BRITISH GP	Silverstone	17	Scuderia Centro Sud	D	2.5 Cooper T51-Maserati 4	engine	20/25
ret	US GP	Riverside	19	Scuderia Centro Sud	D	2.5 Cooper T51-Maserati 4	ignition	23/23

	1961			Championship position: Unplaced					
dns	DUTCH GP	Zandvoort	18	Camoradi International	D	1.5 Lotus 18-Climax 4	qualified but reserve entry	(15)/17
dns	BELGIAN GP	Spa	50	Camoradi International	D	1.5 Lotus 18-Climax 4	no starting money offered	22/25
14	FRENCH GP	Reims	38	Camoradi International	D	1.5 Lotus 18-Climax 4	pit stop/10 laps behind	24/26
14	BRITISH GP	Aintree	44	Camoradi International	D	1.5 Lotus 18-Climax 4	6 laps behind	25/30
12	GERMAN GP	Nürburgring	30	Camoradi International	D	1.5 Cooper T53-Climax 4	1 lap behind	24/27
	1962			Championship position: Unplaced					
12	BRITISH GP	Aintree	36	Anglo American Equipe	D	1.5 Cooper T53-Climax 4	4 laps behind	16/21
11	GERMAN GP	Nürburgring	25	Anglo American Equipe	D	1.5 Cooper T53-Climax 4		16/30
dnq	ITALIAN GP	Monza	62	Anglo American Equipe	D	1.5 Cooper T53-Climax 4		25/30
	1963			Championship position: Unplaced					
ret	BRITISH GP	Silverstone	16	Scirocco-Powell (Racing Cars)	D	1.5 Scirocco 02-BRM V8	ignition	20/23
ret	GERMAN GP	Nürburgring	24	Scirocco-Powell (Racing Cars)	D	1.5 Scirocco 02-BRM V8	steering arm	19/26

GP Starts: 16   GP Wins: 0   Pole positions: 0   Fastest laps: 0   Points: 0

BUSSINELLO, Roberto (I) b 4/10/1927, Pistola

	1961			Championship position: Unplaced					
	Race	Circuit	No	Entrant	Tyres	Car/Engine	Comment	Qual Pos/Entries
ret	ITALIAN GP	Monza	54	Isobele de Tomaso	D	1.5 de Tomaso F1 004-Alfa Romeo 4	engine	24/33
	1965			Championship position: Unplaced					
dnq	GERMAN GP	Nürburgring	25	Scuderia Centro Sud	D	1.5 BRM P57 V8		21/22
13/ret	ITALIAN GP	Monza	50	Scuderia Centro Sud	D	1.5 BRM P57 V8	oil pressure/16 laps behind	21/23

GP Starts: 2   GP Wins: 0   Pole positions: 0   Fastest laps: 0   Points: 0

BYRNE, Tommy (IRL) b 6/5/1958, Drogheda, Co Louth

	1982			Championship position: Unplaced					
	Race	Circuit	No	Entrant	Tyres	Car/Engine	Comment	Qual Pos/Entries
dnq	GERMAN GP	Hockenheim	33	Theodore Racing Team	G	3.0 Theodore TY02-Cosworth V8		28/30
ret	AUSTRIAN GP	Österreichring	33	Theodore Racing Team	G	3.0 Theodore TY02-Cosworth V8	spun off	26/29
dnq	SWISS GP	Dijon	33	Theodore Racing Team	G	3.0 Theodore TY02-Cosworth V8		28/29
dnq	ITALIAN GP	Monza	33	Theodore Racing Team	G	3.0 Theodore TY02-Cosworth V8		30/30
ret	CAESARS PALACE GP	Las Vegas	33	Theodore Racing Team	G	3.0 Theodore TY02-Cosworth V8	spun off	26/30

GP Starts: 2   GP Wins: 0   Pole positions: 0   Fastest laps: 0   Points: 0

ROBERTO BUSSINELLO

Bussinello was an engineering graduate who began racing in 1958, also working as a development engineer and test driver for the de Tomaso team. He drove their F1 car on occasion, mainly in Italian events, taking fifth place in the Naples GP and fourth in the Coppa Italia of 1961.

In 1963 Bussinello moved to Alfa Romeo, again initially in a development role, but he was soon racing their lovely Giulietta GT car, finishing third in the 1964 Targa Florio and winning the Sandown Park 6-hour race at season's end. His handful of F1 sorties in the ageing Centro Sud BRM in 1965 yielded little, so it was back to Alfas and familiar territory for Roberto, who later acted as engineer to Muller's de Tomaso-Ford sports car in the early seventies.

TOMMY BYRNE

Tommy Byrne's rise to the top was so rapid he was pitched into Formula 1 before he had completed his first season in Formula 3. He felt the opportunity of racing the Theodore was too good to miss, but the car was uncompetitive and he was never given a second chance at the top level.

A sparkling Formula Ford debut in 1981 brought Byrne into the top Murray Taylor F3 team knowing he had to get results or else . . . And he did just that, taking seven wins and the Marlboro F3 title despite missing rounds while pursuing his Grand Prix adventure. Third place in the 1983 European F3 series led nowhere so Byrne headed off to America, where he was successful for more than a decade, but remained marooned in the junior single-seater classes.

GIULIO CABIANCA

A very experienced and reliable sports car driver, Cabianca spent most of the fifties pitting the works OSCA sports cars against more powerful opposition, regularly picking up class wins in classic events. He was seventh overall and first in class in the 1955 Targa Florio and after a superb drive repeated the feat in the 1957 Mille Miglia with Chiron (ninth overall). These performances led to his inclusion in the Ferrari sports car team for 1959 and 1960, when his best placing was fourth in the Targa Florio. He also took second place in the 1961 Mille Miglia in a Flammini Zagato.

With the F2 OSCA he finished third to Trintignant after taking an early lead in the 1958 Pau GP. Though his Grand Prix outings were few, he lay fifth in Bonnier's Maserati in the 1958 Italian GP before engine trouble, and scored points in the boycotted 1960 Italian GP for Scuderia Castellotti.

He lost his life testing one of Castellotti's Coopers at Modena in June 1961 when the throttle stuck open; the car ran through an open gateway into the street and crashed into a passing taxi, killing not only Cabianca but also the three unfortunate occupants of the cab.

ALEX CAFFI

Always the bridesmaid in Italian F3, Caffi was runner-up in both 1984 and 1985, when the lack of a Dallara chassis probably cost him the title, and third behind Coloni stars Larini and Apicella in 1986. Given a chance to race the unwieldy Osella at the Italian GP that season, Alex drove sensibly, kept out of the way and impressed everyone with his approach.

This led to a full season with the team in 1987. The car was totally uncompetitive, but Caffi plugged away uncomplainingly, quietly learning his trade. A move to the new Dallara team for 1988 brought some good performances in their neat little car, and the following season he seemed to be a star in the making, finishing fourth at Monaco and losing a potential good result at Phoenix when team-mate de Cesaris elbowed him into the wall.

In retrospect his move to the Arrows/Footwork operation proved to be a complete disaster. The 1990 season was spent marking time and when the Porsche-engined car arrived it was hopelessly overweight and underpowered. Things took a further dive when Alex was involved in a road accident which resulted in a broken jaw, and the atmosphere in the team was not helped when he threatened legal action to reclaim his seat at Hockenheim. A hot property barely two seasons earlier, Caffi's career was now on the skids, and after a brief flirtation with Andrea Moda he found himself languishing in the relative obscurity of the Italian and Spanish touring car championships with a works-backed Opel Vectra.

In 1998 Caffi joined forces with Andrea Chiesa to successfully race a Riley & Scott sports car in the International Sports Racing Series, and he continued to impress in this discipline in 1999 both in Europe and in the USA with his best placings being thirds in the FIA World Sports Car Cup at Spa (with de Lorenzi) and Kyalami (with Larini). In addition he took a fine sixth place at Le Mans in a Courage C52-Nissan prototype, sharing the driving duties with Montermini and Schiattarella.

CABIANCA, Giulio (I) b 19/2/1923, Verona – d 15/6/1961, Modena Autodrome

1958 Championship position: Unplaced

	Race	Circuit	No	Entrant	Tyres	Car/Engine	Comment	Qual Pos/Entries
dnq	MONACO GP	Monte Carlo	52	OSCA Automobili	–	1.5 Osca 4 F2		25/28
ret	ITALIAN GP	Monza	22	Jo Bonnier	–	2.5 Maserati 250F 6	engine	20/21

1959 Championship position: Unplaced

15	ITALIAN GP	Monza	28	Ottorino Volonterio	D	2.5 Maserati 250F 6	pit stop/8 laps behind	21/21

1960 Championship position: 16th= Wins: 0 Pole positions: 0 Fastest laps: 0 Points scored: 3

4	ITALIAN GP	Monza	2	Scuderia Castellotti	D	2.5 Cooper T51-Ferrari 4	2 laps behind	4/16

GP Starts: 3 GP Wins: 0 Pole positions: 0 Fastest laps: 0 Points: 3

CAFFI, Alex (I) b 18/3/1964, Rovato, Brescia

1986 Championship position: Unplaced

	Race	Circuit	No	Entrant	Tyres	Car/Engine	Comment	Qual Pos/Entries
11	ITALIAN GP	Monza	22	Osella Squadra Corse	P	1.5 t/c Osella FA1F-Alfa Romeo V8	6 laps behind	25/25

1987 Championship position: Unplaced

ret	BRAZILIAN GP	Rio	21	Osella Squadra Corse	G	1.5 t/c Osella FA1I-Alfa Romeo V8	driver exhaustion	21/23
12/ret	SAN MARINO GP	Imola	21	Osella Squadra Corse	G	1.5 t/c Osella FA1I-Alfa Romeo V8	out of fuel/5 laps behind	21/27
ret	BELGIAN GP	Spa	21	Osella Squadra Corse	G	1.5 t/c Osella FA1I-Alfa Romeo V8	engine	26/26
ret	MONACO GP	Monte Carlo	21	Osella Squadra Corse	G	1.5 t/c Osella FA1I-Alfa Romeo V8	electrics	16/26
ret	US GP (DETROIT)	Detroit	21	Osella Squadra Corse	G	1.5 t/c Osella FA1I-Alfa Romeo V8	gearbox	19/26
ret	FRENCH GP	Paul Ricard	21	Osella Squadra Corse	G	1.5 t/c Osella FA1I-Alfa Romeo V8	gearbox	20/26
ret	BRITISH GP	Silverstone	21	Osella Squadra Corse	G	1.5 t/c Osella FA1I-Alfa Romeo V8	engine	21/26
ret	GERMAN GP	Hockenheim	21	Osella Squadra Corse	G	1.5 t/c Osella FA1I-Alfa Romeo V8	engine	26/26
ret	HUNGARIAN GP	Hungaroring	21	Osella Squadra Corse	G	1.5 t/c Osella FA1I-Alfa Romeo V8	out of fuel	21/26
ret/dns	AUSTRIAN GP	Österreichring	21	Osella Squadra Corse	G	1.5 t/c Osella FA1I-Alfa Romeo V8	accident at 2nd start/electrics	21/26
ret	ITALIAN GP	Monza	21	Osella Squadra Corse	G	1.5 t/c Osella FA1I-Alfa Romeo V8	suspension	21/28
ret	PORTUGUESE GP	Estoril	21	Osella Squadra Corse	G	1.5 t/c Osella FA1I-Alfa Romeo V8	turbo	25/27
dnq	SPANISH GP	Jerez	21	Osella Squadra Corse	G	1.5 t/c Osella FA1I-Alfa Romeo V8		27/28
ret	MEXICAN GP	Mexico City	21	Osella Squadra Corse	G	1.5 t/c Osella FA1I-Alfa Romeo V8	engine	26/27
ret	JAPANESE GP	Suzuka	21	Osella Squadra Corse	G	1.5 t/c Osella FA1I-Alfa Romeo V8	out of fuel	24/27
dnq	AUSTRALIAN GP	Adelaide	21	Osella Squadra Corse	G	1.5 t/c Osella FA1I-Alfa Romeo V8		27/27

1988 Championship position: Unplaced

dnpq	BRAZILIAN GP	Rio	36	Scuderia Italia	G	3.5 Dallara 3087-Cosworth V8	F3000 car	31/31
ret	SAN MARINO GP	Imola	36	Scuderia Italia	G	3.5 Dallara 188-Cosworth V8	gearbox	24/31
ret	MONACO GP	Monte Carlo	36	Scuderia Italia	G	3.5 Dallara 188-Cosworth V8	hit by Capelli-spun off	17/30
ret	MEXICAN GP	Mexico City	36	Scuderia Italia	G	3.5 Dallara 188-Cosworth V8	brakes-accident	23/30
dnpq	CANADIAN GP	Montreal	36	Scuderia Italia	G	3.5 Dallara 188-Cosworth V8		31/31
8	US GP (DETROIT)	Detroit	36	Scuderia Italia	G	3.5 Dallara 188-Cosworth V8	cracked exhaust/-2 laps	22/31
12	FRENCH GP	Paul Ricard	36	Scuderia Italia	G	3.5 Dallara 188-Cosworth V8	puncture/fuel problems/-2 laps	14/31
11	BRITISH GP	Silverstone	36	Scuderia Italia	G	3.5 Dallara 188-Cosworth V8	1 lap behind	21/31
15	GERMAN GP	Hockenheim	36	Scuderia Italia	G	3.5 Dallara 188-Cosworth V8	pit stop-puncture/-2 laps	19/31
ret	HUNGARIAN GP	Hungaroring	36	Scuderia Italia	G	3.5 Dallara 188-Cosworth V8	engine	10/31
8*	BELGIAN GP	Spa	36	Scuderia Italia	G	3.5 Dallara 188-Cosworth V8	*3rd & 4th cars disqualified/-1 lap	15/31
ret	ITALIAN GP	Monza	36	Scuderia Italia	G	3.5 Dallara 188-Cosworth V8	electrics	21/31
7	PORTUGUESE GP	Estoril	36	Scuderia Italia	G	3.5 Dallara 188-Cosworth V8	broken exhaust/1 lap behind	17/31
10	SPANISH GP	Jerez	36	Scuderia Italia	G	3.5 Dallara 188-Cosworth V8	broken exhaust/1 lap behind	18/31
ret	JAPANESE GP	Suzuka	36	Scuderia Italia	G	3.5 Dallara 188-Cosworth V8	spun off	21/31
ret	AUSTRALIAN GP	Adelaide	36	Scuderia Italia	G	3.5 Dallara 188-Cosworth V8	clutch	11/31

1989 Championship position: 16th= Wins: 0 Pole positions: 0 Fastest laps: 0 Points scored: 4

dnpq	BRAZILIAN GP	Rio	21	Scuderia Italia	P	3.5 Dallara 189-Cosworth V8		31/38
7	SAN MARINO GP	Imola	21	Scuderia Italia	P	3.5 Dallara 189-Cosworth V8	pit stop-puncture1 lap behind	9/39
4	MONACO GP	Monte Carlo	21	Scuderia Italia	P	3.5 Dallara 189-Cosworth V8	2 laps behind	9/38
13	MEXICAN GP	Mexico City	21	Scuderia Italia	P	3.5 Dallara 189-Cosworth V8	spun/tyre wear/2 laps behind	19/39
ret	US GP (PHOENIX)	Phoenix	21	Scuderia Italia	P	3.5 Dallara 189-Cosworth V8	hit by de Cesaris	6/39
6	CANADIAN GP	Montreal	21	Scuderia Italia	P	3.5 Dallara 189-Cosworth V8	2 pit stops-tyres/2 spins/-2 laps	8/39
ret	FRENCH GP	Paul Ricard	21	Scuderia Italia	P	3.5 Dallara 189-Cosworth V8	clutch	26/39
dnpq	BRITISH GP	Silverstone	21	Scuderia Italia	P	3.5 Dallara 189-Cosworth V8		32/39
ret	GERMAN GP	Hockenheim	21	Scuderia Italia	P	3.5 Dallara 189-Cosworth V8	electrics	20/39
7	HUNGARIAN GP	Hungaroring	21	Scuderia Italia	P	3.5 Dallara 189-Cosworth V8		3/39
ret	BELGIAN GP	Spa	21	Scuderia Italia	P	3.5 Dallara 189-Cosworth V8	spun off	12/39
11/ret	ITALIAN GP	Monza	21	Scuderia Italia	P	3.5 Dallara 189-Cosworth V8	engine/6 laps behind	20/39
ret	PORTUGUESE GP	Estoril	21	Scuderia Italia	P	3.5 Dallara 189-Cosworth V8	collision with Piquet	7/39
ret	SPANISH GP	Jerez	21	Scuderia Italia	P	3.5 Dallara 189-Cosworth V8	engine	20/38
9*	JAPANESE GP	Suzuka	21	Scuderia Italia	P	3.5 Dallara 189-Cosworth V8	* 1st place car dsq/-1 lap	15/39
ret	AUSTRALIAN GP	Adelaide	21	Scuderia Italia	P	3.5 Dallara 189-Cosworth V8	spun off in rain	10/39

1990 Championship position: 16th= Wins: 0 Pole positions: 0 Fastest laps: 0 Points scored: 2

ret	BRAZILIAN GP	Interlagos	10	Footwork Arrows Racing	G	3.5 Arrows A11B-Cosworth V8	driver exhaustion	25/35
dnq	SAN MARINO GP	Imola	10	Footwork Arrows Racing	G	3.5 Arrows A11B-Cosworth V8		28/34
5	MONACO GP	Monte Carlo	10	Footwork Arrows Racing	G	3.5 Arrows A11B-Cosworth V8	tyre problems/2 laps behind	22/35
8	CANADIAN GP	Montreal	10	Footwork Arrows Racing	G	3.5 Arrows A11B-Cosworth V8	2 laps behind	26/35
dnq	MEXICAN GP	Mexico City	10	Footwork Arrows Racing	G	3.5 Arrows A11B-Cosworth V8		30/35
ret	FRENCH GP	Paul Ricard	10	Footwork Arrows Racing	G	3.5 Arrows A11B-Cosworth V8	rear suspension	22/35
7	BRITISH GP	Silverstone	10	Footwork Arrows Racing	G	3.5 Arrows A11B-Cosworth V8	1 lap behind	17/35
9	GERMAN GP	Hockenheim	10	Footwork Arrows Racing	G	3.5 Arrows A11B-Cosworth V8	1 lap behind	18/35
9	HUNGARIAN GP	Hungaroring	10	Footwork Arrows Racing	G	3.5 Arrows A11B-Cosworth V8	rev limiter problems/-1 lap	26/35

10	BELGIAN GP	Spa	10	Footwork Arrows Racing	G	3.5 Arrows A11B-Cosworth V8	oversteer problems/-1 lap	19/33
9	ITALIAN GP	Monza	10	Footwork Arrows Racing	G	3.5 Arrows A11B-Cosworth V8	pit stop-tyres/2 laps behind	21/33
13/ret	PORTUGUESE GP	Estoril	10	Footwork Arrows Racing	G	3.5 Arrows A11B-Cosworth V8	collision with Suzuki/-3 laps	17/33
9	JAPANESE GP	Suzuka	10	Footwork Arrows Racing	G	3.5 Arrows A11B-Cosworth V8	pit stop-tyres/1 lap behind	24/30
dnq	AUSTRALIAN GP	Adelaide	10	Footwork Arrows Racing	G	3.5 Arrows A11B-Cosworth V8		29/30

1991 Championship position: Unplaced

dnq	US GP (PHOENIX)	Phoenix	10	Footwork Grand Prix International	G	3.5 Footwork A11C-Porsche V12		28/34
dnq	BRAZILIAN GP	Interlagos	10	Footwork Grand Prix International	G	3.5 Footwork A11C-Porsche V12		27/34
dnq	SAN MARINO GP	Imola	10	Footwork Grand Prix International	G	3.5 Footwork FA12-Porsche V12		29/34
dnq	MONACO GP	Monte Carlo	10	Footwork Grand Prix International	G	3.5 Footwork FA12-Porsche V12	accident in practice	30/34
dnpq	GERMAN GP	Hockenheim	10	Footwork Grand Prix International	G	3.5 Footwork FA12-Cosworth V8		32/34
dnpq	HUNGARIAN GP	Hungaroring	10	Footwork Grand Prix International	G	3.5 Footwork FA12-Cosworth V8		32/34
dnq	BELGIAN GP	Spa	10	Footwork Grand Prix International	G	3.5 Footwork FA12-Cosworth V8		29/34
dnpq	ITALIAN GP	Monza	10	Footwork Grand Prix International	G	3.5 Footwork FA12-Cosworth V8		33/34
dnpq	PORTUGUESE GP	Estoril	10	Footwork Grand Prix International	G	3.5 Footwork FA12-Cosworth V8		33/34
dnpq	SPANISH GP	Barcelona	10	Footwork Grand Prix International	G	3.5 Footwork FA12-Cosworth V8		31/33
10	JAPANESE GP	Suzuka	10	Footwork Grand Prix International	G	3.5 Footwork FA12-Cosworth V8	2 laps behind	26/31
15	AUSTRALIAN GP	Adelaide	10	Footwork Grand Prix International	G	3.5 Footwork FA12-Cosworth V8	rain shortened race/-1 lap	23/32

1992 Championship position: Unplaced

dnp	SOUTH AFRICAN GP	Kyalami	34	Andrea Moda Formula	G	3.5 Coloni C4B-Judd V10	car ineligible-team excluded	– / –
dnp	MEXICAN GP	Mexico City	34	Andrea Moda Formula	G	3.5 Moda S921-Judd V10	cars arrived late-withdrawn	– / –

GP Starts: 56   GP Wins: 0   Pole positions: 0   Fastest laps: 0   Points: 6

CAMPBELL-JONES, John (GB) b 21/1/1930, Epsom, Surrey

1962 Championship position: 0   Wins: 0   Pole positions: 0   Fastest laps: 0   Points scored: 0

	Race	Circuit	No	Entrant	Tyres	Car/Engine	Comment	Qual Pos/Entries
11/ret	BELGIAN GP	Spa	4	Emeryson Cars	D	1.5 Lotus 18-Climax 4	borrowed car/gearbox/-16 laps	19/20
dns		"	4	Emeryson Cars	D	1.5 Emeryson 1006-Climax 4	practice only-broken gearbox	– / –

1963 Championship position: 0   Wins: 0   Pole positions: 0   Fastest laps: 0   Points scored: 0

13	BRITISH GP	Silverstone	24	Tim Parnell	D	1.5 Lola 4-Climax V8	pit stop/8 laps behind	23/23

GP Starts: 2   GP Wins: 0   Pole positions: 0   Fastest laps: 0   Points: 0

JOHN CAMPBELL-JONES

Campbell-Jones achieved some success in sports cars in 1958 before buying a Formula 2 Cooper to race at home and abroad. Usually to be found scratching around in minor F1 events, his 1961 season was cut short after a crash at Modena. His 1962 campaign in the Emeryson brought little but a distant fifth place on aggregate in the Brussels GP and sixth in the Aintree 200, but that was better than his team-mate Tony Settember could achieve.

Under the wing of the Parnell stable in 1963, he still could not make much headway despite having a much better car, and was not seen on the circuits again except for a surprise appearance in the 1966 Gold Cup at Oulton Park in an old BRP-Climax.

ADRIAN CAMPOS

Without much of a track record to speak of (half a dozen F3000 races) during the previous season, Campos was a surprise choice for the second seat in the Minardi team for 1987. Though naturally overshadowed by team-mate Nannini, he did better than many would have expected given his relative lack of experience.

The Spaniard was joined by fellow countryman Luis Perez Sala for 1988, but lost his seat to Pierluigi Martini after failing to qualify for three races in a row. Initially he had thoughts of retirement but was soon back in action in the Spanish touring car championship. As this series grew in prominence and competitiveness, Campos became a leading player, winning the championship in 1994 with an Alfa 155.

Adrian, now running a two-car team in the Spanish Open Fortuna by Nissan series, had the satisfaction in 1998 of helping the promising Marc Gené not only to the title, but also to a Grand Prix seat at Minardi.

CAMPOS, Adrian (E) b 17/6/1960, Alcira, nr Valencia

	1987	Championship position: Unplaced							
	Race	Circuit	No	Entrant	Tyres	Car/Engine		Comment	Qual Pos/Entries
dsq	BRAZILIAN GP	Rio	23	Minardi Team	G	1.5 t/c Minardi M187-MM V6		*incorrect starting procedure*	16/23
ret	SAN MARINO GP	Imola	23	Minardi Team	G	1.5 t/c Minardi M187-MM V6		*gearbox*	18/27
ret/dns	BELGIAN GP	Spa	23	Minardi Team	G	1.5 t/c Minardi M187-MM V6		*clutch at 1st start*	19/26
dns	MONACO GP	Monte Carlo	23	Minardi Team	G	1.5 t/c Minardi M187-MM V6		*accident in practice*	(25)/26
ret	US GP (DETROIT)	Detroit	23	Minardi Team	G	1.5 t/c Minardi M187-MM V6		*hit by Nakajima*	25/26
ret	FRENCH GP	Paul Ricard	23	Minardi Team	G	1.5 t/c Minardi M187-MM V6		*turbo*	21/26
ret	BRITISH GP	Silverstone	23	Minardi Team	G	1.5 t/c Minardi M187-MM V6		*fuel pump*	20/26
ret	GERMAN GP	Hockenheim	23	Minardi Team	G	1.5 t/c Minardi M187-MM V6		*engine*	18/26
ret	HUNGARIAN GP	Hungaroring	23	Minardi Team	G	1.5 t/c Minardi M187-MM V6		*spun off*	24/26
ret	AUSTRIAN GP	Österreichring	23	Minardi Team	G	1.5 t/c Minardi M187-MM V6		*electrics*	19/26
ret	ITALIAN GP	Monza	23	Minardi Team	G	1.5 t/c Minardi M187-MM V6		*engine fuel filter fire*	20/28
ret	PORTUGUESE GP	Estoril	23	Minardi Team	G	1.5 t/c Minardi M187-MM V6		*started from pits/holed intercooler*	20/27
14	SPANISH GP	Jerez	23	Minardi Team	G	1.5 t/c Minardi M187-MM V6		*4 laps behind*	24/28
ret	MEXICAN GP	Mexico City	23	Minardi Team	G	1.5 t/c Minardi M187-MM V6		*gear linkage*	19/27
ret	JAPANESE GP	Suzuka	23	Minardi Team	G	1.5 t/c Minardi M187-MM V6		*engine*	22/27
ret	AUSTRALIAN GP	Adelaide	23	Minardi Team	G	1.5 t/c Minardi M187-MM V6		*gearbox*	26/27
	1988	Championship position: Unplaced							
ret	BRAZILIAN GP	Rio	23	Lois Minardi Team	G	3.5 Minardi M188-Cosworth V8		*rear wing mounting*	23/31
16	SAN MARINO GP	Imola	23	Lois Minardi Team	G	3.5 Minardi M188-Cosworth V8		*3 laps behind*	22/31
dnq	MONACO GP	Monte Carlo	23	Lois Minardi Team	G	3.5 Minardi M188-Cosworth V8			29/30
dnq	MEXICAN GP	Mexico City	23	Lois Minardi Team	G	3.5 Minardi M188-Cosworth V8			30/30
dnq	CANADIAN GP	Montreal	23	Lois Minardi Team	G	3.5 Minardi M188-Cosworth V8			27/31

GP Starts: 16 (17) GP Wins: 0 Pole positions: 0 Fastest laps: 0 Points: 0

CANNON, John (CDN) b 21/6/1937, London, England

	1971	Championship position: Unplaced							
	Race	Circuit	No	Entrant	Tyres	Car/Engine		Comment	Q Pos/Entries
14	US GP	Watkins Glen	28	Yardley BRM	F	3.0 BRM P153 V12		*3 laps behind*	26/32

GP Starts: 1 GP Wins: 0 Pole positions: 0 Fastest laps: 0 Points: 0

CANTONI, Eitel (U) b 1896

	1952	Championship position: Unplaced							
	Race	Circuit	No	Entrant	Tyres	Car/Engine		Comment	Q Pos/Entries
ret	BRITISH GP	Silverstone	35	Escuderia Bandeirantes	P	2.0 Maserati A6GCM 6		*brakes on lap 1*	27/32
ret	GERMAN GP	Nürburgring	116	Escuderia Bandeirantes	P	2.0 Maserati A6GCM 6		*rear axle*	26/32
11	ITALIAN GP	Monza	50	Escuderia Bandeirantes	P	2.0 Maserati A6GCM 6		*5 laps behind*	23/35

GP Starts: 3 GP Wins: 0 Pole positions: 0 Fastest laps: 0 Points: 0

JOHN CANNON

A Canadian who had been born in Britain, Cannon in fact spent the early part of his career in California, where he began racing an Elva Courier in 1960. He drove a

variety of powerful sports machines in the early 1960s before concentrating on the popular Can-Am series.

Though his car was somewhat outdated, he put up a number of fine performances, none better than in the wet at Laguna Seca in 1968 when he lapped the field to score an amazing win. This success led to a drive in Formula A in 1969 and an opportunity to drive single-seaters at last. John won three rounds and finished fourth in the championship. The next year he took the SCCA Formula A title and then set about a completely new challenge, tackling the US GP in a BRM and the Questor GP in a March 701, as well as a full season in European F2, achieving moderate success.

It was back to the USA and the L & M F5000 series for 1972, although he also drove in some British F5000 rounds and was right on the pace. Thereafter Cannon continued racing in the formula which had brought him so much success, spiced with occasional drives in USAC and Can-Am.

EITEL CANTONI

Another of the contingent of South Americans who came to Europe in the late forties and early fifties. In 1952, after a fifth place in the Buenos Aires GP, Eitel joined the Brazilians Gino Bianco, Chico Landi and Alberto Crespo to race three of the new 2-litre Maserati A6GCMs. These cars were resplendent in buff paintwork, and entered under the Escuderia Bandeirantes banner.

As well as the three championship Grands Prix, Cantoni contested four other races in his brief Continental sojourn, yielding two finishes, seventh in the Modena GP and ninth in the AVUSrennen.

IVAN CAPELLI

The dividing line between success and failure in Grand Prix racing can be very narrow indeed, as the charming and popular Capelli has found to his cost. Having been generally perceived as being held back from the winner's circle only by the want of a top-flight car, the Italian's stock crashed with alarming rapidity when a golden opportunity with Ferrari turned sour.

Yet another ex-karting ace, Ivan went single-seater racing in 1982, taking sixth place in the Italian F3 championship. This brought him to the attention of Enzo Coloni, who quickly signed the Milanese to race his Ralt-Alfa. It was a stunning year for the team, with Capelli winning all but four of the series' 13 races to take the title by the staggering margin of 58 points. With Italy well and truly conquered, Coloni took his charge into the European arena, and once again Capelli triumphed, though much less decisively. His European F3 championship was tainted with allegations regarding the car's legality, and, as he acknowledged, he inherited a couple of lucky wins, including the prestigious Monaco race.

National Service then interrupted Ivan's racing progress, and when he entered the 1985 F3000 series at Vallelunga with a March, he immediately rolled it almost to the point of destruction. Despite the most meagre of budgets, Capelli and his team did an outstanding job and he won the Österreichring round to earn a couple of Grand Prix drives with Ken Tyrrell late in the season. Somewhat surprisingly, he was not on the F1 shopping list for 1986 and settled into another year of F3000 with the Genoa team, the mid-season arrival of Leyton House sponsorship giving the privateer outfit the boost it needed in its successsful championship quest. Capelli made another brief foray into Formula 1 with AGS, but long-term his future was to lie wrapped in the comforting folds of the turquoise-blue Leyton House March Racing Team. In a sense the team was Ivan's family; they believed in him and he reciprocated. Growing in stature, he had taken the car right to the front of the grid by the end of the 1988 season, and briefly led the Portuguese GP before taking a superb second place. This progress was temporarily halted in a disappointing year plagued by unreliability and the almost bewildering array of handling problems associated with the March CG891, but Capelli bounced back the following year, finishing second to Prost at Paul Ricard and looking a potential winner at Silverstone until retirement. Ivan's final year with the team was spent embroiled in development of the new Ilmor V10, and it has to be said that some of his performances were less than convincing. With the team's owner having been arrested over financial irregularities in Japan, the future looked bleak, and Capelli stood down for the two end-of-season races happy in the knowledge that he had a Ferrari contract in his pocket for 1992. However, it was to be a season of almost unmitigated misery for poor Ivan, who failed to come to grips with the Ferrari F92A, a car which missed the boat on just about every count.

Before the season was out, Capelli found himself cast aside in favour of test driver Nicola Larini and his options appeared limited. To everyone's surprise he was back on the grid at Kyalami with the Jordan team, reunited with his old boss from Leyton House/March, Ian Phillips. It was to be a brief and unhappy sojourn for the Italian, who crashed very heavily in South Africa and then failed to qualify at Interlagos before an amicable parting of the ways left a crushingly disappointed Capelli to come to the conclusion that he had no Formula 1 future at all when he had not yet reached the age of thirty.

Capelli picked up the pieces of his shattered career, and joined the Nissan works team to race the 2-litre Primera in the German Super Touring championship in 1995 and 1996, but since then he has been an infrequent competitor, picking up occasional sports car drives to keep his hand in.

Ivan still maintains his involvement in Grand Prix racing in a commentary role for Bernie Ecclestone's Italian digital broadcasts.

CAPELLI, Ivan (I) b 24/5/1963, Milan

1985
Championship position: 17th= Wins: 0 Pole positions: 0 Fastest laps: 0 Points scored: 3

	Race	Circuit	No	Entrant	Tyres	Car/Engine	Comment	Q Pos/Entries
ret	EUROPEAN GP	Brands Hatch	4	Tyrrell Racing Organisation	G	1.5 t/c Tyrrell 014-Renault V6	accident	24/27
4	AUSTRALIAN GP	Adelaide	4	Tyrrell Racing Organisation	G	1.5 t/c Tyrrell 014-Renault V6	1 lap behind	22/25

1986
Championship position: Unplaced

ret	ITALIAN GP	Monza	31	Jolly Club SpA	P	1.5 t/c AGS JH21C-MM V6	puncture	25/27
ret	PORTUGUESE GP	Estoril	31	Jolly Club SpA	P	1.5 t/c AGS JH21C-MM V6	transmission	25/27

1987
Championship position: 19th= Wins: 0 Pole positions: 0 Fastest laps: 0 Points scored: 1

dns	BRAZILIAN GP	Rio	16	Leyton House March Racing Team	G	3.5 March 87P-Cosworth V8	shortage of engine/ran F3000 car	23/23
ret	SAN MARINO GP	Imola	16	Leyton House March Racing Team	G	3.5 March 871-Cosworth V8	ignition	24/27
ret	BELGIAN GP	Spa	16	Leyton House March Racing Team	G	3.5 March 871-Cosworth V8	oil pressure	21/26
6*	MONACO GP	Monte Carlo	16	Leyton House March Racing Team	G	3.5 March 871-Cosworth V8	* 2nd non-turbo/2 laps behind	19/26
ret	US GP (DETROIT)	Detroit	16	Leyton House March Racing Team	G	3.5 March 871-Cosworth V8	battery	22/26
ret	FRENCH GP	Paul Ricard	16	Leyton House March Racing Team	G	3.5 March 871-Cosworth V8	engine	22/26
ret	BRITISH GP	Silverstone	16	Leyton House March Racing Team	G	3.5 March 871-Cosworth V8	gearbox	25/26
ret	GERMAN GP	Hockenheim	16	Leyton House March Racing Team	G	3.5 March 871-Cosworth V8	started from pit lane/distributor	24/26
10*	HUNGARIAN GP	Hungaroring	16	Leyton House March Racing Team	G	3.5 March 871-Cosworth V8	* 3rd non-turbo/-2 laps	18/26
11*	AUSTRIAN GP	Österreichring	16	Leyton House March Racing Team	G	3.5 March 871-Cosworth V8	* 1st non-turbo/-3 laps	23/26
13*	ITALIAN GP	Monza	16	Leyton House March Racing Team	G	3.5 March 871-Cosworth V8	* 2nd non-turbo/-3 laps	25/28
9*	PORTUGUESE GP	Estoril	16	Leyton House March Racing Team	G	3.5 March 871-Cosworth V8	* 1st non-turbo/-3 laps	22/27
12*	SPANISH GP	Jerez	16	Leyton House March Racing Team	G	3.5 March 871-Cosworth V8	* 3rd non-turbo/-2 laps	19/28
ret	MEXICAN GP	Mexico City	16	Leyton House March Racing Team	G	3.5 March 871-Cosworth V8	engine	20/27
ret	JAPANESE GP	Suzuka	16	Leyton House March Racing Team	G	3.5 March 871-Cosworth V8	accident with Arnoux	21/27
ret	AUSTRALIAN GP	Adelaide	16	Leyton House March Racing Team	G	3.5 March 871-Cosworth V8	spun off	23/27

1988
Championship position: 7th= Wins: 0 Pole positions: 0 Fastest laps: 0 Points scored: 17

ret	BRAZILIAN GP	Rio	16	Leyton House March Racing Team	G	3.5 March 881-Judd V8	started from pit lane/engine	9/31
ret	SAN MARINO GP	Imola	16	Leyton House March Racing Team	G	3.5 March 881-Judd V8	gearbox	9/31
10	MONACO GP	Monte Carlo	16	Leyton House March Racing Team	G	3.5 March 881-Judd V8	collision-Caffi-pit stop/-6 laps	22/30
16	MEXICAN GP	Mexico City	16	Leyton House March Racing Team	G	3.5 March 881-Judd V8	pit stop-gearbox/-6 laps	10/30
5	CANADIAN GP	Montreal	16	Leyton House March Racing Team	G	3.5 March 881-Judd V8	severe understeer/-1 lap	14/31
dns	US GP (DETROIT)	Detroit	16	Leyton House March Racing Team	G	3.5 March 881-Judd V8	accident in practice	(21)/31
9	FRENCH GP	Paul Ricard	16	Leyton House March Racing Team	G	3.5 March 881-Judd V8	1 lap behind	10/31
ret	BRITISH GP	Silverstone	16	Leyton House March Racing Team	G	3.5 March 881-Judd V8	electrics	6/31
5	GERMAN GP	Hockenheim	16	Leyton House March Racing Team	G	3.5 March 881-Judd V8		7/31
ret	HUNGARIAN GP	Hungaroring	16	Leyton House March Racing Team	G	3.5 March 881-Judd V8	misfire	4/31
3*	BELGIAN GP	Spa	16	Leyton House March Racing Team	G	3.5 March 881-Judd V8	*3rd & 4th place cars dsq	14/31
5	ITALIAN GP	Monza	16	Leyton House March Racing Team	G	3.5 March 881-Judd V8		11/31
2	PORTUGUESE GP	Estoril	16	Leyton House March Racing Team	G	3.5 March 881-Judd V8		3/31
ret	SPANISH GP	Jerez	16	Leyton House March Racing Team	G	3.5 March 881-Judd V8	engine	6/31
ret	JAPANESE GP	Suzuka	16	Leyton House March Racing Team	G	3.5 March 881-Judd V8	electrics	4/31
6	AUSTRALIAN GP	Adelaide	16	Leyton House March Racing Team	G	3.5 March 881-Judd V8	pit stop-puncture/gearbox/-1 lap	9/31

1989
Championship position: Unplaced

ret	BRAZILIAN GP	Rio	16	Leyton House March Racing Team	G	3.5 March 881-Judd V8	rear suspension	7/38
ret	SAN MARINO GP	Imola	16	Leyton House March Racing Team	G	3.5 March 881-Judd V8	spun off	13/39
11/ret	MONACO GP	Monte Carlo	16	Leyton House March Racing Team	G	3.5 March CG891-Judd V8	engine/4 laps behind	– / –
dns	"	"	16	Leyton House March Racing Team	G	3.5 March 881-Judd V8	practice only-qualifying car	22/38
ret	MEXICAN GP	Mexico City	16	Leyton House March Racing Team	G	3.5 March CG891-Judd V8	driveshaft-c.v. joint	4/39
dns	"	"	16	Leyton House March Racing Team	G	3.5 March 881-Judd V8	practice only	– / –
ret	US GP (PHOENIX)	Phoenix	16	Leyton House March Racing Team	G	3.5 March CG891-Judd V8	transmission	11/39
dns	"	"	16	Leyton House March Racing Team	G	3.5 March 881-Judd V8	practice only	– / –
ret	CANADIAN GP	Montreal	16	Leyton House March Racing Team	G	3.5 March CG891-Judd V8	spun off	21/39
dns	"	"	16	Leyton House March Racing Team	G	3.5 March 881-Judd V8	practice only	– / –
ret	FRENCH GP	Paul Ricard	16	Leyton House March Racing Team	G	3.5 March CG891-Judd V8	electrics-engine	12/39
ret	BRITISH GP	Silverstone	16	Leyton House March Racing Team	G	3.5 March CG891-Judd V8	transmission	8/39
ret	GERMAN GP	Hockenheim	16	Leyton House March Racing Team	G	3.5 March CG891-Judd V8	engine	22/39
ret	HUNGARIAN GP	Hungaroring	16	Leyton House March Racing Team	G	3.5 March CG891-Judd V8	transmission	14/39
12	BELGIAN GP	Spa	16	Leyton House March Racing Team	G	3.5 March CG891-Judd V8	1 lap behind	19/39
ret	ITALIAN GP	Monza	16	Leyton House March Racing Team	G	3.5 March CG891-Judd V8	engine	18/39
ret	PORTUGUESE GP	Estoril	16	Leyton House March Racing Team	G	3.5 March CG891-Judd V8	misfire	24/39
ret	SPANISH GP	Jerez	16	Leyton House March Racing Team	G	3.5 March CG891-Judd V8	transmission	19/38
ret	JAPANESE GP	Suzuka	16	Leyton House March Racing Team	G	3.5 March CG891-Judd V8	suspension	17/39
ret	AUSTRALIAN GP	Adelaide	16	Leyton House March Racing Team	G	3.5 March CG891-Judd V8	holed radiator	16/39

1990
Championship position: 10th= Wins: 0 Pole positions: 0 Fastest laps: 0 Points scored: 6

ret	US GP (PHOENIX)	Phoenix	16	Leyton House Racing	G	3.5 Leyton House CG901-Judd V8	electrics	– / –
dns	"	"	16	Leyton House Racing	G	3.5 March CG891-Judd V8	practice only-qualifying car	27/35
dnq	BRAZILIAN GP	Interlagos	16	Leyton House Racing	G	3.5 Leyton House CG901-Judd V8		29/35
dnq	"	"	16	Leyton House Racing	G	3.5 March CG891-Judd V8		– / –
ret	SAN MARINO GP	Imola	16	Leyton House Racing	G	3.5 Leyton House CG901-Judd V8	hit by Nakajima	19/34
ret	MONACO GP	Monte Carlo	16	Leyton House Racing	G	3.5 Leyton House CG901-Judd V8	brakes	23/35
10	CANADIAN GP	Montreal	16	Leyton House Racing	G	3.5 Leyton House CG901-Judd V8	handling problems/-3 laps	24/35
dnq	MEXICAN GP	Mexico City	16	Leyton House Racing	G	3.5 Leyton House CG901-Judd V8		28/35
2	FRENCH GP	Paul Ricard	16	Leyton House Racing	G	3.5 Leyton House CG901-Judd V8		7/35
ret	BRITISH GP	Silverstone	16	Leyton House Racing	G	3.5 Leyton House CG901-Judd V8	fuel line when 3rd	10/35
7	GERMAN GP	Hockenheim	16	Leyton House Racing	G	3.5 Leyton House CG901-Judd V8	lost 4th gear/1 lap behind	10/35
ret	HUNGARIAN GP	Hungaroring	16	Leyton House Racing	G	3.5 Leyton House CG901-Judd V8	gearbox	16/35
7	BELGIAN GP	Spa	16	Leyton House Racing	G	3.5 Leyton House CG901-Judd V8	broken exhaust/1 lap behind	12/33
ret	ITALIAN GP	Monza	16	Leyton House Racing	G	3.5 Leyton House CG901-Judd V8	engine cut out-fuel pump	16/33
ret	PORTUGUESE GP	Estoril	16	Leyton House Racing	G	3.5 Leyton House CG901-Judd V8	engine	12/33

ret	SPANISH GP	Jerez	16	Leyton House Racing	G	3.5 Leyton House CG901-Judd V8	leg cramp	19/33
ret	JAPANESE GP	Suzuka	16	Leyton House Racing	G	3.5 Leyton House CG901-Judd V8	misfire-electrics	13/30
ret	AUSTRALIAN GP	Adelaide	16	Leyton House Racing	G	3.5 Leyton House CG901-Judd V8	sticking throttle	14/30

1991		Championship position: 18th=	Wins: 0	Pole positions: 0	Fastest laps: 0	Points scored: 1		
ret	US GP (PHOENIX)	Phoenix	16	Leyton House Racing	G	3.5 Leyton House CG911-Ilmor V10	gearbox oil pump	18/34
ret	BRAZILIAN GP	Interlagos	16	Leyton House Racing	G	3.5 Leyton House CG911-Ilmor V10	engine	15/34
ret	SAN MARINO GP	Imola	16	Leyton House Racing	G	3.5 Leyton House CG911-Ilmor V10	spun off	22/34
ret	MONACO GP	Monte Carlo	16	Leyton House Racing	G	3.5 Leyton House CG911-Ilmor V10	leaking brake fluid	18/34
ret	CANADIAN GP	Montreal	16	Leyton House Racing	G	3.5 Leyton House CG911-Ilmor V10	engine	13/34
ret	MEXICAN GP	Mexico City	16	Leyton House Racing	G	3.5 Leyton House CG911-Ilmor V10	over-revved engine	22/34
ret	FRENCH GP	Magny Cours	16	Leyton House Racing	G	3.5 Leyton House CG911-Ilmor V10	spun avoiding Morbidelli	15/34
ret	BRITISH GP	Silverstone	16	Leyton House Racing	G	3.5 Leyton House CG911-Ilmor V10	selected wrong gear-spun off	16/34
ret	GERMAN GP	Hockenheim	16	Leyton House Racing	G	3.5 Leyton House CG911-Ilmor V10	engine-misfire	12/34
6	HUNGARIAN GP	Hungaroring	16	Leyton House Racing	G	3.5 Leyton House CG911-Ilmor V10	1 lap behind	9/34
ret	BELGIAN GP	Spa	16	Leyton House Racing	G	3.5 Leyton House CG911-Ilmor V10	engine	12/34
8	ITALIAN GP	Monza	16	Leyton House Racing	G	3.5 Leyton House CG911-Ilmor V10		12/34
17/ret	PORTUGUESE GP	Estoril	16	Leyton House Racing	G	3.5 Leyton House CG911-Ilmor V10	broken nose cone when 5th	9/34
ret	SPANISH GP	Barcelona	16	Leyton House Racing	G	3.5 Leyton House CG911-Ilmor V10	collision with Pirro	8/33

1992		Championship position: 12th=	Wins: 0	Pole positions: 0	Fastest laps: 0	Points scored: 3		
ret	SOUTH AFRICAN GP	Kyalami	28	Scuderia Ferrari SpA	G	3.5 Fiat Ferrari F92A V12	engine	9/30
ret	MEXICAN GP	Mexico City	28	Scuderia Ferrari SpA	G	3.5 Fiat Ferrari F92A V12	startline collision	20/30
5	BRAZILIAN GP	Interlagos	28	Scuderia Ferrari SpA	G	3.5 Fiat Ferrari F92A V12	pit stop-tyres/1 lap behind	11/31
10/ret	SPANISH GP	Barcelona	28	Scuderia Ferrari SpA	G	3.5 Fiat Ferrari F92A V12	spun off	5/32
ret	SAN MARINO GP	Imola	28	Scuderia Ferrari SpA	G	3.5 Fiat Ferrari F92A V12	spun off	8/32
ret	MONACO GP	Monte Carlo	28	Scuderia Ferrari SpA	G	3.5 Fiat Ferrari F92A V12	spun off-wedged car on Armco	8/32
ret	CANADIAN GP	Montreal	28	Scuderia Ferrari SpA	G	3.5 Fiat Ferrari F92A V12	crashed	9/32
ret	FRENCH GP	Magny Cours	28	Scuderia Ferrari SpA	G	3.5 Fiat Ferrari F92A V12	engine-electrics	8/30
9	BRITISH GP	Silverstone	28	Scuderia Ferrari SpA	G	3.5 Fiat Ferrari F92A V12	1 lap behind	14/32
ret	GERMAN GP	Hockenheim	28	Scuderia Ferrari SpA	G	3.5 Fiat Ferrari F92A V12	engine	12/32
6	HUNGARIAN GP	Hungaroring	28	Scuderia Ferrari SpA	G	3.5 Fiat Ferrari F92A V12	1 lap behind	10/31
ret	BELGIAN GP	Spa	28	Scuderia Ferrari SpA	G	3.5 Fiat Ferrari F92A V12	engine	12/30
ret	ITALIAN GP	Monza	28	Scuderia Ferrari SpA	G	3.5 Fiat Ferrari F92AT V12	spun off	7/28
ret	PORTUGUESE GP	Estoril	28	Scuderia Ferrari SpA	G	3.5 Fiat Ferrari F92AT V12	engine	16/26

1993		Championshjp position: Unplaced						
ret	SOUTH AFRICAN GP	Kyalami	15	Sasol Jordan	G	3.5 Jordan 193-Hart V10	crashed	18/26
dnq	BRAZILIAN GP	Interlagos	15	Sasol Jordan	G	3.5 Jordan 193-Hart V10		26/26

GP Starts: 93   GP Wins: 0   Pole positions: 0   Fastest laps: 0   Points: 31

PIERO CARINI

Carini came to prominence in 1950 when he finished third in the F2 Modena GP with a sports OSCA. This car proved fast but fragile in 1951, but he was invited to join Scuderia Marzotto for 1952 to race their Ferrari Grand Prix and sports cars. He did well enough to be signed by the works for 1953 as in effect a 'junior team' driver, along with Umberto Maglioli. Carini was used only occasionally and therefore decided to move to Alfa Romeo to race their very successful touring cars, scoring class wins in the 1954 Mille Miglia, Tour of Sicily and Dolomite Cup.

In 1955 he ventured abroad to score sports car wins in a Ferrari at Dakar and Caracas, Venezuela, as well as taking a class win in the Targa Florio in an OSCA with Cabianca.

He was competing in a 1500 cc sports car race near St Etienne in 1957 when his Ferrari Testa Rossa inexplicably crossed the central barrier and ploughed head on into a similar competing car. Carini was killed instantly.

CARINI, Piero (I) b 6/3/1921, Genova – d 30/5/1957, St Etienne, France

1952		Championship position: Unplaced						
	Race	Circuit	No	Entrant	Tyres	Car/Engine	Comment	Q Pos/Entries
ret	FRENCH GP	Rouen	40	Scuderia Marzotto	P	2.0 Ferrari 166 V12	head gasket	20/20
ret	GERMAN GP	Nürburgring	104	Scuderia Marzotto	P	2.0 Ferrari 166 V12	brakes	27/32
1953		Championship position: Unplaced						
ret	ITALIAN GP	Monza	12	Scuderia Ferrari		P	2.0 Ferrari 553 4	engine	20/30

GP Starts: 3   GP Wins: 0   Pole positions: 0   Fastest laps: 0   Points: 0

EUGENIO CASTELLOTTI

Castellotti was the archetypal Italian racing driver of the fifties: dashing, handsome, very fast, but wild and erratic. He often charged into the lead at the start of a race, only to be overhauled as his tyres gave out or the car cried enough in response to the punishing treatment to which it had been subjected.

Having been presented with a Ferrari sports car by a local benefactor in 1950 when aged only 20, Eugenio entered the spotlight in 1952 with a win in the Portuguese GP, third place in the Bari GP and second in the Monaco GP (held for sports cars that year), as well as a class win in the Circuit of Sicily. The following season saw him claim the first of his three Italian mountain championships, win the Messina 10 Hours in a Ferrari and finish third in the Carrera Panamericana in a Lancia.

Castellotti signed for Lancia for 1954, racing sports cars while waiting patiently for the chance to drive one of their much anticipated Grand Prix cars. In fact it was 1955 before he got his wish, making his Grand Prix debut at the Argentine GP, where he suffered from sun-stroke in the intense heat and finally crashed the car. Back in Europe, however, he made amends, finishing fourth in the Turin GP and second at Pau and – after Ascari had crashed his car into the harbour – Monaco. Days later Ascari was killed in a testing accident, and Castellotti led the team for one race, at Spa, before it was amalgamated with the Scuderia Ferrari, for whom he finished the season, taking third in the drivers' championship.

The 1956 season saw the Ferrari squad almost embarrassed by an over-supply of cars and drivers, which led to some friction within the team. This was particularly acute between Musso and Castellotti, the two Italians waging their own private duel in the Italian GP at Monza. Eugenio was by now at his peak, particularly in sports cars. A stunning win in atrocious conditions in the Mille Miglia made up in part for his disappointment the previous year when he destroyed his tyres racing too hard too early. Added to this was a victory in the Sebring 12 Hours and second in the Nürburgring 1000 Km (both with Fangio).

More sports car success lay ahead in 1957, Eugenio sharing the first and third cars in the Buenos Aires 1000 Km. On his return to Europe, he was recalled from a holiday to test the latest GP Ferrari at Modena. In wet conditions, the car crashed into a concrete barrier; 27-year-old Castellotti was hurled from the car and killed instantly.

CASTELLOTTI, Eugenio (I) b 10/10/1930, Lodi, Milan – d 14/3/1957, Modena Autodrome

	1955			Championship position: 3rd	Wins: 0	Pole positions: 1	Fastest laps: 0	Points scored: 12		
	Race	Circuit	No	Entrant	Tyres	Car/Engine		Comment		Q Pos/Entries
ret	ARGENTINE GP	Buenos Aires	36	Scuderia Lancia	P	2.5 Lancia D50 V8		Villoresi also drove/crashed		12/22
2	MONACO GP	Monte Carlo	30	Scuderia Lancia	P	2.5 Lancia D50 V8		pit stop-brakes		4/22
ret	BELGIAN GP	Spa	30	Scuderia Lancia	P	2.5 Lancia D50 V8		gearbox		1/14
5	DUTCH GP	Zandvoort	6	Scuderia Ferrari	E	2.5 Ferrari 555 4		3 laps behind		9/16
dns		"	6	Scuderia Ferrari	E	2.5 Ferrari 625 4		practice only		– / –
ret	BRITISH GP	Aintree	20	Scuderia Ferrari	E	2.5 Ferrari 625 4		transmission		10/25
6*	"	"	16	Scuderia Ferrari	E	2.5 Ferrari 625 4		* took Hawthorn's car/-3 laps		– / –
3	ITALIAN GP	Monza	4	Scuderia Ferrari	E	2.5 Ferrari 555 4				4/22
	1956			Championship position: 5th	Wins: 0	Pole positions: 0	Fastest laps: 0	Points scored: 7.5		
ret	ARGENTINE GP	Buenos Aires	32	Scuderia Ferrari	E	2.5 Lancia-Ferrari D50 V8		gearbox		2/15
ret	MONACO GP	Monte Carlo	22	Scuderia Ferrari	E	2.5 Lancia-Ferrari D50 V8		clutch		3/19
4*	"	"	20	Scuderia Ferrari	E	2.5 Lancia-Ferrari D50 V8		* took Fangio's car/-6 laps		– / –
ret	BELGIAN GP	Spa	4	Scuderia Ferrari	E	2.5 Lancia-Ferrari D50 V8		transmission		5/16
2	FRENCH GP	Reims	12	Scuderia Ferrari	E	2.5 Lancia-Ferrari D50 V8				2/20
10*	BRITISH GP	Silverstone	3	Scuderia Ferrari	E	2.5 Lancia-Ferrari D50 V8		*de Portago took over car		8/28
ret	GERMAN GP	Nürburgring	3	Scuderia Ferrari	E	2.5 Lancia-Ferrari D50 V8		magneto		3/21
ret	"	"	4	Scuderia Ferrari	E	2.5 Lancia-Ferrari D50 V8		accident-took Musso's car		– / –
ret	ITALIAN GP	Monza	24	Scuderia Ferrari	E	2.5 Lancia-Ferrari D50 V8		tyres-accident		2/26
8*	"	"	22	Scuderia Ferrari	E	2.5 Lancia-Ferrari D50 V8		*took Fangio's car/-4 laps		– / –
	1957			Championship position: Unplaced						
ret	ARGENTINE GP	Buenos Aires	14	Scuderia Ferrari	E	2.5 Lancia-Ferrari D50A V8		hub shaft-lost wheel		4/16

GP Starts: 14   GP Wins: 0   Pole positions: 1   Fastest laps: 0   Points: 19.5

JOHNNY CECOTTO

The son of an Italian immigrant, Cecotto began racing a 750 cc Honda motor cycle in his native Venezuela in 1972. Soon outgrowing domestic competition, he made a dramatic European debut, scoring a 250/350 cc double, and went on to take the 350 cc title in his first season, becoming the youngest-ever World Champion. More bike successes followed – at 20 he was the youngest winner of the famous Daytona 200 – but a crash early in 1977 put him out of contention for the season. He came back to win the F750 title in 1978, but as Kenny Roberts' star rose, Cecotto's appetite for bike racing waned.

He made an inconclusive F2 debut in 1980, taking part in just three races, but finally abandoned his bike career at the beginning of 1981. After a torrid first half of the season with Martini, Johnny changed teams and under the guiding influence of Markus Hotz knuckled down to the job, swiftly becoming a top-six regular and scoring points in the last four races of the season. A hoped-for Grand Prix opportunity for 1982 failed to materialise so Johnny remained in F2 with a works March. He lost the championship to his team-mate, Corrado Fabi, after the pair had finished the season level on points and Cecotto was forced to drop his worst score from his total. Nevertheless he had made the transition from two wheels to four brilliantly, and this time there was a seat for him in Formula 1.

His first Grand Prix season in the Theodore produced little save a welcome sixth place at Long Beach, so Cecotto moved to Toleman to partner F1 newcomer Ayrton Senna in 1984. He spent the first half of the season somewhat in the Brazilian's shadow, until a very heavy crash in practice for the British Grand Prix left him hospitalised with serious leg and ankle injuries. It was to be the end of his Formula 1 ambitions.

Upon recovery he forged a successful new career in the flourishing touring car scene. Driving for BMW, he won the 1989 Italian championship, and quickly became one of the Munich concern's favoured sons. Johnny has competed in the German, British and Italian series during the nineties and has been one of the undoubted stars of this class of racing. Even at the age of 42, he proved a match for Laurent Aïello and his Peugeot when his Schnizter BMW 320i snatched the 1998 German Super Touring title at the last gasp.

Cecotto has also made several appearances in Team Bigazzi's McLaren F1 GTR, including a couple of wins in Brazil in 1996, sharing the car with Nelson Piquet.

CECOTTO, Johnny (YV) b 25/1/1956, Caracas

	1983	Championship position: 19th=	Wins: 0	Pole positions: 0	Fastest laps: 0	Points scored: 1		
	Race	Circuit	No	Entrant	Tyres	Car/Engine	Comment	Q Pos/Entries
14	BRAZILIAN GP	Rio	34	Theodore Racing Team	G	3.0 Theodore N183-Cosworth V8	3 laps behind	19/27
6	US GP WEST	Long Beach	34	Theodore Racing Team	G	3.0 Theodore N183-Cosworth V8	1 lap behind	17/28
11	FRENCH GP	Paul Ricard	34	Theodore Racing Team	G	3.0 Theodore N183-Cosworth V8	2 laps behind	17/29
ret	SAN MARINO GP	Imola	34	Theodore Racing Team	G	3.0 Theodore N183-Cosworth V8	accident damage	23/28
dnpq	MONACO GP	Monte Carlo	34	Theodore Racing Team	G	3.0 Theodore N183-Cosworth V8		26/28
10	BELGIAN GP	Spa	34	Theodore Racing Team	G	3.0 Theodore N183-Cosworth V8	1 lap behind	25/28
ret	US GP (DETROIT)	Detroit	34	Theodore Racing Team	G	3.0 Theodore N183-Cosworth V8	gear linkage	26/27
ret	CANADIAN GP	Montreal	34	Theodore Racing Team	G	3.0 Theodore N183-Cosworth V8	cwp	23/28
dnq	BRITISH GP	Silverstone	34	Theodore Racing Team	G	3.0 Theodore N183-Cosworth V8		27/29
11	GERMAN GP	Hockenheim	34	Theodore Racing Team	G	3.0 Theodore N183-Cosworth V8	1 lap behind	22/29
dnq	AUSTRIAN GP	Österreichring	34	Theodore Racing Team	G	3.0 Theodore N183-Cosworth V8		28/29
dnq	DUTCH GP	Zandvoort	34	Theodore Racing Team	G	3.0 Theodore N183-Cosworth V8		28/29
12	ITALIAN GP	Monza	34	Theodore Racing Team	G	3.0 Theodore N183-Cosworth V8	2 laps behind	26/29
	1984	Championship position: Unplaced						
ret	BRAZILIAN GP	Rio	20	Toleman Group Motorsport	P	1.5 t/c Toleman TG183B-Hart 4	turbo boost pressure	18/27
ret	SOUTH AFRICAN GP	Kyalami	20	Toleman Group Motorsport	P	1.5 t/c Toleman TG183B-Hart 4	tyre failure	19/27
ret	BELGIAN GP	Zolder	20	Toleman Group Motorsport	P	1.5 t/c Toleman TG183B-Hart 4	clutch	16/27
nc	SAN MARINO GP	Imola	20	Toleman Group Motorsport	P	1.5 t/c Toleman TG183B-Hart 4	pit stop/8 laps behind	19/28
ret	FRENCH GP	Dijon	20	Toleman Group Motorsport	P	1.5 t/c Toleman TG183B-Hart 4	turbo	19/27
ret	MONACO GP	Monte Carlo	20	Toleman Group Motorsport	M	1.5 t/c Toleman TG184-Hart 4	spun off	18/27
9	CANADIAN GP	Montreal	20	Toleman Group Motorsport	M	1.5 t/c Toleman TG184-Hart 4	2 laps behind	20/26
ret	US GP (DETROIT)	Detroit	20	Toleman Group Motorsport	M	1.5 t/c Toleman TG184-Hart 4	clutch	17/27
ret	US GP (DALLAS)	Dallas	20	Toleman Group Motorsport	M	1.5 t/c Toleman TG184-Hart 4	hit wall	15/27
dnq	BRITISH GP	Brands Hatch	20	Toleman Group Motorsport	M	1.5 t/c Toleman TG184-Hart 4	crashed in practice-hurt legs	– / –

GP Starts: 18   GP Wins: 0   Pole positions: 0   Fastest laps: 0   Points: 1

FRANÇOIS CEVERT

Cevert's immense natural talent had been nurtured and developed over a four-year period in the Tyrrell team. He had been given what amounted to a personal master-class in the art of Grand Prix racing by Jackie Stewart and learned so well that at the time of his shocking death at Watkins Glen in 1973 he was the finished article, ready to assume the mantle of a champion after his team leader's impending retirement.

A Volant Shell award had seen François begin his racing career in 1967 at the wheel of his prize, an F3 Alpine. The season was something of a disaster, with the old car proving very unreliable. Undismayed by this, he bought a Tecno for the following year and, after getting to grips with its inherent understeer, went on to take the French F3 championship. So impressed were the Italian manufacturers that they offered Cevert a place in their Formula 2 team for 1969, and despite his lack of experience he took third place in the championship and a win in the Tropheés de France meeting at Reims. François also made his Grand Prix debut in the car in the Formula 2 class of the German GP.

For 1970 he planned another season with Tecno as well as finally accepting an offer to drive for Matra in sports cars, which came via his brother-in-law Jean-Pierre Beltoise. But when Johnny Servoz-Gavin suddenly retired in mid-season, Cevert took over the Tyrrell drive and his perspective had suddenly changed. Playing himself in sensibly with the March 701, the Frenchman scored a satisfying sixth place at Monza, but he really blossomed in 1971 with the superb Tyrrell, taking two excellent second places behind his leader at Paul Ricard and the Nürburgring before posting his first (and only) Grand Prix win in the US GP.

The 1972 Formula 1 season was more difficult, perhaps not helped by Stewart's illness, and Cevert finished in the points on only three occasions. He also drove quite regularly in other formulae, dovetailing appearances in John Coombs' Elf-backed March in F2 with a full Can-Am programme (which saw a win at Donnybrooke) and a one-off drive at Le Mans, where he took a splendid second place for Matra with Howden Ganley. Tyrrell were back at their best in 1973. Stewart, already intending to retire after one last season, used all his considerable gifts to take a third World Championship with François right behind him, the apprentice having matured to the point that he could now be the faster man on occasion. Certainly it was felt that Cevert could

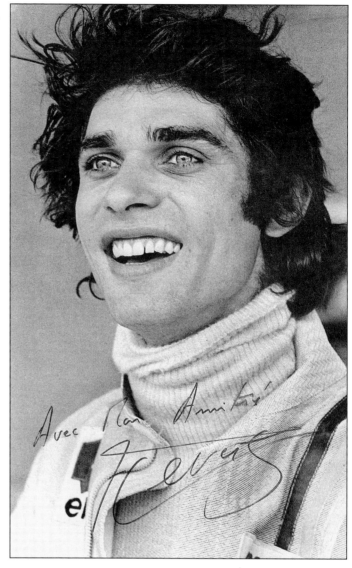

have taken the German GP if he had so chosen, but in the event he had to be content with no fewer than five second-place finishes before that fateful day at Watkins Glen in October when, attempting to take pole position, he lost control of his car on a bumpy part of the track, the Tyrrell being hurled into the barriers with such ferocity that François stood no chance of survival. France's most likely World Champion was gone, and Ken Tyrrell had lost the man who could perhaps have kept his team at the pinnacle in the post-Stewart era.

CEVERT, François (F) b 25/2/1944, Paris – d 6/10/1973, Watkins Glen Circuit, New York State, USA

	1969	Championship position: Unplaced							
	Race	Circuit	No	Entrant	Tyres	Car/Engine		Comment	Q Pos/Entries
ret	GERMAN GP (F2)	Nürburgring	28	Tecno Racing	D	1.6 Tecno F2/69-Cosworth 4 F2		gearbox	13/26
	1970	Championship position: 22nd= Wins: 0 Pole positions: 0 Fastest laps: 0 Points scored: 1							
ret	DUTCH GP	Zandvoort	6	Tyrrell Racing Organisation	D	3.0 March 701-Cosworth V8		engine	15/24
11	FRENCH GP	Clermont Ferrand	2	Tyrrell Racing Organisation	D	3.0 March 701-Cosworth V8		1 lap behind	13/23
7	BRITISH GP	Brands Hatch	2	Tyrrell Racing Organisation	D	3.0 March 701-Cosworth V8		1 lap behind	15/25
7	GERMAN GP	Hockenheim	23	Tyrrell Racing Organisation	D	3.0 March 701-Cosworth V8		1 lap behind	14/25
ret	AUSTRIAN GP	Österreichring	2	Tyrrell Racing Organisation	D	3.0 March 701-Cosworth V8		engine	9/24
6	ITALIAN GP	Monza	20	Tyrrell Racing Organisation	D	3.0 March 701-Cosworth V8			=10/27
9	CANADIAN GP	St Jovite	2	Tyrrell Racing Organisation	D	3.0 March 701-Cosworth V8		pit stop-shock absorber/-5 laps	4/20
ret	US GP	Watkins Glen	2	Tyrrell Racing Organisation	D	3.0 March 701-Cosworth V8		lost wheel	17/27
ret	MEXICAN GP	Mexico City	2	Tyrrell Racing Organisation	D	3.0 March 701-Cosworth V8		engine	9/18
	1971	Championship position: 3rd Wins: 1 Pole positions: 0 Fastest laps: 1 Points scored: 26							
ret	SOUTH AFRICAN GP	Kyalami	10	Elf Team Tyrrell	G	3.0 Tyrrell 002-Cosworth V8		accident	=8/25
7	SPANISH GP	Montjuich Park	12	Elf Team Tyrrell	G	3.0 Tyrrell 002-Cosworth V8		1 lap behind	12/22
ret	MONACO GP	Monte Carlo	12	Elf Team Tyrrell	G	3.0 Tyrrell 002-Cosworth V8		hit barrier/suspension-wheel	=15/23
ret	DUTCH GP	Zandvoort	6	Elf Team Tyrrell	G	3.0 Tyrrell 002-Cosworth V8		spun off/collision with Galli	12/24

			No	Entrant		Car/Engine	Comment	Q Pos/Entries
2	FRENCH GP	Paul Ricard	12	Elf Team Tyrrell	G	3.0 Tyrrell 002-Cosworth V8		7/24
10	BRITISH GP	Silverstone	14	Elf Team Tyrrell	G	3.0 Tyrrell 002-Cosworth V8	pit stop-fuel pipe/-3 laps	10/24
2	GERMAN GP	Nürburgring	3	Elf Team Tyrrell	G	3.0 Tyrrell 002-Cosworth V8	FL	5/23
ret	AUSTRIAN GP	Österreichring	12	Elf Team Tyrrell	G	3.0 Tyrrell 002-Cosworth V8	engine	3/22
3	ITALIAN GP	Monza	2	Elf Team Tyrrell	G	3.0 Tyrrell 002-Cosworth V8		5/24
6	CANADIAN GP	Mosport Park	12	Elf Team Tyrrell	G	3.0 Tyrrell 002-Cosworth V8	2 laps behind	3/27
1	US GP	Watkins Glen	9	Elf Team Tyrrell	G	3.0 Tyrrell 002-Cosworth V8		5/32

1972 Championship position: 6th= Wins: 0 Pole positions: 0 Fastest laps: 0 Points scored: 15

			No	Entrant		Car/Engine	Comment	Q Pos/Entries
ret	ARGENTINE GP	Buenos Aires	22	Elf Team Tyrrell	G	3.0 Tyrrell 002-Cosworth V8	gearbox	7/22
9	SOUTH AFRICAN GP	Kyalami	2	Elf Team Tyrrell	G	3.0 Tyrrell 002-Cosworth V8	pit stop-ignition/1 lap behind	=8/27
ret	SPANISH GP	Jarama	3	Elf Team Tyrrell	G	3.0 Tyrrell 002-Cosworth V8	ignition	12/26
18/ret	MONACO GP	Monte Carlo	2	Elf Team Tyrrell	G	3.0 Tyrrell 002-Cosworth V8	electrics/10 laps behind	12/25
2	BELGIAN GP	Nivelles	8	Elf Team Tyrrell	G	3.0 Tyrrell 002-Cosworth V8		5/26
4	FRENCH GP	Clermont Ferrand	7	Elf Team Tyrrell	G	3.0 Tyrrell 002-Cosworth V8		=7/29
dns	"	" "	7T/7	Elf Team Tyrrell	G	3.0 Tyrrell 005-Cosworth V8	practice only	–/–
ret	BRITISH GP	Brands Hatch	2	Elf Team Tyrrell	G	3.0 Tyrrell 002-Cosworth V8	spun off	=11/27
10	GERMAN GP	Nürburgring	7	Elf Team Tyrrell	G	3.0 Tyrrell 002-Cosworth V8	pit stop-tyre	5/27
dns	"	"	7T	Elf Team Tyrrell	G	3.0 Tyrrell 004-Cosworth V8	practice only	–/–
9	AUSTRIAN GP	Österreichring	2	Elf Team Tyrrell	G	3.0 Tyrrell 002-Cosworth V8	1 lap behind	20/26
ret	ITALIAN GP	Monza	2	Elf Team Tyrrell	G	3.0 Tyrrell 002-Cosworth V8	engine	14/27
dns	"	"	1T	Elf Team Tyrrell	G	3.0 Tyrrell 004-Cosworth V8	practice only	–/–
ret	CANADIAN GP	Mosport Park	2	Elf Team Tyrrell	G	3.0 Tyrrell 006-Cosworth V8	gearbox	=6/25
2	US GP	Watkins Glen	2	Elf Team Tyrrell	G	3.0 Tyrrell 006-Cosworth V8		4/32

1973 Championship position: 4th Wins: 0 Pole positions: 0 Fastest laps: 1 Points scored: 47

			No	Entrant		Car/Engine	Comment	Q Pos/Entries
2	ARGENTINE GP	Buenos Aires	8	Elf Team Tyrrell	G	3.0 Tyrrell 006-Cosworth V8		6/19
10	BRAZILIAN GP	Interlagos	4	Elf Team Tyrrell	G	3.0 Tyrrell 006-Cosworth V8	pit stop-puncture/-2 laps	5/20
nc	SOUTH AFRICAN GP	Kyalami	4	Elf Team Tyrrell	G	3.0 Tyrrell 005-Cosworth V8	3 pit stops-tyre-timing/-13 laps	–/–
dns	"	"	3	Elf Team Tyrrell	G	3.0 Tyrrell 006-Cosworth V8	practice only-Stewart drove	(9)/25
2	SPANISH GP	Montjuich Park	4	Elf Team Tyrrell	G	3.0 Tyrrell 006-Cosworth V8		3/22
2	BELGIAN GP	Zolder	6	Elf Team Tyrrell	G	3.0 Tyrrell 006-Cosworth V8	FL	4/23
4	MONACO GP	Monte Carlo	6	Elf Team Tyrrell	G	3.0 Tyrrell 006-Cosworth V8	1 lap behind	4/26
3	SWEDISH GP	Anderstorp	6	Elf Team Tyrrell	G	3.0 Tyrrell 006-Cosworth V8		2/22
dns	"	"	6T	Elf Team Tyrrell	G	3.0 Tyrrell 005-Cosworth V8	practice only	–/–
2	FRENCH GP	Paul Ricard	6	Elf Team Tyrrell	G	3.0 Tyrrell 006-Cosworth V8		4/25
5	BRITISH GP	Silverstone	6	Elf Team Tyrrell	G	3.0 Tyrrell 006-Cosworth V8		7/29
dns	"	"	43	Elf Team Tyrrell	G	3.0 Tyrrell 005-Cosworth V8	practice only	–/–
2	DUTCH GP	Zandvoort	6	Elf Team Tyrrell	G	3.0 Tyrrell 006-Cosworth V8		3/24
2	GERMAN GP	Nürburgring	6	Elf Team Tyrrell	G	3.0 Tyrrell 006-Cosworth V8		3/23
ret	AUSTRIAN GP	Österreichring	6	Elf Team Tyrrell	G	3.0 Tyrrell 006-Cosworth V8	collision with Merzario	10/25
dns	"	"	6T	Elf Team Tyrrell	G	3.0 Tyrrell 005-Cosworth V8	practice only	–/–
5	ITALIAN GP	Monza	6	Elf Team Tyrrell	G	3.0 Tyrrell 006-Cosworth V8		11/25
dns	"	"	6T	Elf Team Tyrrell	G	3.0 Tyrrell 005-Cosworth V8	practice only	–/–
ret	CANADIAN GP	Mosport Park	6	Elf Team Tyrrell	G	3.0 Tyrrell 006-Cosworth V8	collision with Scheckter	6/26
dns	US GP	Watkins Glen	6	Elf Team Tyrrell	G	3.0 Tyrrell 006-Cosworth V8	fatal practice accident	(4)/28

GP Starts: 47 GP Wins: 1 Pole positions: 0 Fastest laps: 2 Points: 89

EUGÈNE CHABOUD

With his friend Jean Trémoulet, Chaboud began racing late in 1936 with a Delahaye. The pair competed together until 1938 when, after winning the Le Mans 24-hour race, they went their separate ways.

Following the war, Chaboud was soon back racing, involved with Paul Vallée's Ecurie France team as sporting director and lead driver with his Delahaye 135S. In 1947 the team acquired a 1939 Talbot monoplace with which Eugène lost no time in winning races at Marseilles and Perpignan. The drive was then given to Louis Chiron, so Chaboud and Charles Pozzi left in disgust and set up their own team. Eugène emerged as French champion, and for 1948 they created Ecurie Leutitia, with Chaboud still racing his Delahaye. He took sixth place in the 1949 French GP, and was very unlucky at Le Mans when the car caught fire while leading the race by some nine miles and eventually had to be abandoned.

Chaboud's chance to race in more competitive machinery than the Delahaye came in 1950, when he was invited to drive a Lago-Talbot in place of the injured Martin. Sharing the car with Étancelin, he finished fifth in the French GP.

In the Le Mans 24 Hours of 1952, Chaboud lay sixth until, after the 22-hour mark, he crashed the Talbot. While lying under the overturned car waiting to be extricated, he had leisure to decide it was a good time to call it a day!

CHABOUD, Eugène (F) b 12/4/1907, Lyon – d 28/12/1983, Montfermeil

1950 Championship position: 15th= Wins: 0 Pole positions: 0 Fastest laps: 0 Points scored: 1

	Race	Circuit	No	Entrant		Car/Engine	Comment	Q Pos/Entries
ret	BELGIAN GP	Spa	20	Ecurie Leutitia	D	4.5 Lago-Talbot T26C 6	engine	11/14
dns	FRENCH GP	Reims	24	Ecurie Leutitia	D	4.5 Lago-Talbot T26C 6		(10)/20Δ
5*	"	"	16	Philippe Étancelin	D	4.5 Lago-Talbot T26C-DA 6	* took Étancelin's car/-5 laps	–/–

1951 Championship position: Unplaced

			No	Entrant		Car/Engine	Comment	Q Pos/Entries
8	FRENCH GP	Reims	44	Eugène Chaboud	D	4.5 Lago-Talbot T26C-GS 6	8 laps behind	14/23

GP Starts: 3 GP Wins: 0 Pole positions: 0 Fastest laps: 0 Points: 1

CHAMBERLAIN, Jay (USA)

	1962			Championship position: Unplaced					
	Race	Circuit	No	Entrant	Tyres	Car/Engine		Comment	Q Pos/Entries
15	BRITISH GP	Aintree	46	Ecurie Excelsior	D	1.5 Lotus 18-Climax 4		11 laps behind	20/21
dnq	GERMAN GP	Nürburgring	30	Ecurie Excelsior	D	1.5 Lotus 18-Climax 4			29/30
dnq	ITALIAN GP	Monza	26	Ecurie Excelsior	D	1.5 Lotus 18-Climax 4			29/30

GP Starts: 1   GP Wins: 0   Pole positions: 0   Fastest laps: 0   Points: 0

JAY CHAMBERLAIN

This SCCA sports car racer competed almost exclusively in Lotus cars, for which he was an early US distributor in the late fifties. He came to Europe in 1957 and finished ninth at Le Mans (with Mackay Fraser), winning the 750 cc class, and second in a sports car race at Rouen, before being seriously injured in a crash in practice for the Reims 12 Hours.

He recovered in time to return to Le Mans in 1958 but crashed at Mulsanne without harm. After racing a Formula Junior Lotus back in the States, Jay tried his hand at a Formula 1 season in Europe with a Lotus 18, his only result of any note being fifth in the minor Lavant Cup (for four-cylinder cars only) at Goodwood. He also ventured to Chimay and took a fourth place in the GP des Frontières in a Formula Junior Cooper.

DAVE CHARLTON

After club racing, Charlton moved into South Africa's major league in 1962, racing under the intriguingly titled Ecurie Tomahawk banner. Driving a four-cylinder-powered Lotus 20, he fared reasonably well on the local scene, but the car was not even good enough to qualify for practice in the 1965 Grand Prix.

The purchase of a Brabham BT11 brought him to the forefront in South Africa's national series, and helped ensure that he would be on the grid for the country's feature race as well. Building his reputation with Scuderia Scribante, Charlton was invited to England in early 1968 to test a works Cooper, also taking in the BOAC 500 in Sid Taylor's Lola T70.

In 1970 Dave purchased the ex-Bonnier Lotus 49C, which he used to devastating effect, cleaning up in the F1/FA series. This led to a deal to drive a works-run Brabham in the following year's Grand Prix, but more importantly secured lucrative sponsorship from Lucky Strike which allowed him to buy a Lotus 72 after his 49 was severely damaged in the 1971 Natal Winter Trophy. He raced the new car with great success, winning the 1972 series by a country mile to the chagrin of his great rival, John Love. Charlton blotted his copybook by spinning out of the 1973 Grand Prix and causing a multiple shunt, but success was to continue unabated when the Lotus was replaced by a McLaren M23. He comfortably won the 1974 series, but was extremely lucky to prevail over his new young challenger Ian Scheckter the following season – his consistency paid off and his six second places and one win were enough. The 1976 season was to see the beginning of the end of Charlton's domination. The championship was now run to Formula Atlantic rules and his Modus did not inspire quite the same awe among his competitors. By mid-1978 he had lost his long-time sponsorship deal and eventually forsook single-seaters for saloons, which he raced into the early eighties.

CHARLTON, Dave (ZA) b 27/10/1936, Brotton, nr Redcar, Yorkshire, England

	1965			Championship position: Unplaced					
	Race	Circuit	No	Entrant	Tyres	Car/Engine		Comment	Q Pos/Entries
dnpq	SOUTH AFRICAN GP	East London	32	Ecurie Tomahawk	D	1.5 Lotus 20-Ford 4		dnq for official practice	– / –
	1967			Championship position: Unplaced					
nc	SOUTH AFRICAN GP	Kyalami	19	Scuderia Scribante	–	2.7 Brabham BT11-Climax 4		17 laps behind	=7/18
	1968			Championship position: Unplaced					
ret	SOUTH AFRICAN GP	Kyalami	22	Scuderia Scribante	F	3.0 Brabham BT11-Repco V8		crown wheel and pinion	=14/23
	1970			Championship position: Unplaced					
12/ret	SOUTH AFRICAN GP	Kyalami	25	Scuderia Scribante	F	3.0 Lotus 49C-Cosworth V8		puncture/7 laps behind	13/24
	1971			Championship position: Unplaced					
ret	SOUTH AFRICAN GP	Kyalami	15	Motor Racing Developments	G	3.0 Brabham BT33-Cosworth V8		valve spring	12/25
dns	DUTCH GP	Zandvoort	12	Gold Leaf Team Lotus	F	3.0 Lotus 72D-Cosworth V8		Walker crashed car in practice	– / –
ret	BRITISH GP	Silverstone	2	Gold Leaf Team Lotus	F	3.0 Lotus 72D-Cosworth V8		engine	13/24
	1972			Championship position: Unplaced					
ret	SOUTH AFRICAN GP	Kyalami	26	Scuderia Scribante-Lucky Strike	F	3.0 Lotus 72D-Cosworth V8		fuel pressure-seized fuel pump	17/27
dnq	FRENCH GP	Clermont Ferrand	29	Scuderia Scribante-Lucky Strike	F	3.0 Lotus 72D-Cosworth V8			29/29
ret	BRITISH GP	Brands Hatch	29	Scuderia Scribante-Lucky Strike	F	3.0 Lotus 72D-Cosworth V8		gearbox	24/27
ret	GERMAN GP	Nürburgring	29	Scuderia Scribante-Lucky Strike	F	3.0 Lotus 72D-Cosworth V8		driver unwell	26/27

	1973	Championship position: Unplaced					
ret	SOUTH AFRICAN GP	Kyalami	25	Scuderia Scribante-Lucky Strike	F 3.0 Lotus 72D-Cosworth V8	*spun, caused multiple accident*	13/25
	1974	Championship position: Unplaced					
19	SOUTH AFRICAN GP	Kyalami	23	Scuderia Scribante-Lucky Strike	G 3.0 McLaren M23-Cosworth V8	*pit stop-collision-Robarts/-7 laps*	20/27
	1975	Championship position: Unplaced					
14	SOUTH AFRICAN GP	Kyalami	31	Lucky Strike Racing	G 3.0 McLaren M23-Cosworth V8	*2 laps behind*	20/28

GP Starts: 11   GP Wins: 0   Pole positions: 0   Fastest laps: 0   Points: 0

EDDIE CHEEVER

Eddie Cheever has enjoyed such a long innings in motor racing that it is perhaps easy to forget the startling impact he made on Formula 3 in 1975 when barely 18 years old, or the fact that two years later he had raced successfully for the Project Four team in Formula 2 (taking a superb win at Rouen in 1977) and the BMW Junior touring car team with their 320i in the German national series. The world was his oyster, or so it seemed, especially when a satisfactory test for Ferrari saw him lined up for a works F1 drive in 1978. But the best-laid plans don't always work out, and when Gilles Villeneuve was signed Eddie could see his chances of a regular ride were slim and backed away from the deal.

Cheever had his first stab at Grands Prix in 1978 when, after failing to qualify the hapless Theodore for the first two races, he switched to the Hesketh team, which at least enabled him to make the grid but had little else to recommend it. Then it was back to Formula 2 for the rest of the year and a series of morale-sapping incidents which seriously undermined his reputation, despite second-place finishes at Rouen and Enna.

Now no longer quite the hot property of just 12 months earlier, Eddie threw in his lot with Osella for another season of Formula 2 in 1979, and was to enjoy a happy year with the little Italian outfit, taking three wins (Silverstone, Pau and Zandvoort). When the team took the bold decision to enter Grand Prix racing the following year, naturally Cheever went with them. To say it was a character-building season would be an understatement, and Cheever certainly found out about life at the back of the grid. There was a little success to savour, however, for he joined the Lancia sports car team, winning a round of the World Championship of Makes at Mugello with Patrese, and taking second places at Brands Hatch and Watkins Glen with Alboreto.

A move to Tyrrell in 1981 found his career moving in the right direction, the American picking up points on no fewer than five occasions before being tempted to the Ligier team for 1982, where, when he managed to finish, it was usually in the points, including a second place at Detroit. Eddie was chosen to partner Alain Prost at Renault in 1983, a season which was to be his big opportunity to make the jump into the very front rank of driver talent. Although there were flashes of brilliance, he could not sustain them, and while he performed more than respectably, especially in qualifying, his performances were always judged against Prost's – a no-win situation. In the event, a switch to the Benetton Alfa team meant two seasons of disappointment and mechanical unreliability, but never did he ease his forceful driving style, or pay much attention to the subtle art of fuel economy. If the turbo engine lasted, all well and good; if not, then it was going out in a big way – and it usually did.

Out in the cold in 1986, save for a race for Lola at Detroit in place of the indisposed Tambay, Eddie drove the TWR Jaguar in endurance racing, winning at Silverstone and finishing well elsewhere, but the lure of Formula 1 was still great and he joined Arrows for three seasons during which his incredible enthusiasm sustained him through the frustrations of usually being no more than a midfield runner. There were occasional gems, such as his drives into third place at Monza in 1988 and Phoenix in 1989, where he hounded Patrese to the finish. But the down side was his increasing irritation with the team, which manifested itself on the track, particularly at Spa, where he was reprimanded for obstructive driving tactics.

Seeing no future in hanging on in Formula 1, Cheever joined the Indy Car trail in 1990, where in truth his form was something of a disappointment considering the abundant skill he possessed. A chance to build a solid platform for success with Chip Ganassi's team came and went, despite a second place at Phoenix and a fourth at Indianapolis in 1992. Subsequently Eddie teamed up with A J Foyt in a combustible partnership which came close to a win at Nazareth in 1995 but, predictably perhaps, failed to last out the season.

The ever-uncompromising Eddie then set his sights on the IRL with a win in the Indy 500 as his ultimate goal. After finishing 11th with John Menard's car in 1996, he decided to form his own team in 1997 and had the immediate bonus of a lucky win in the season opener at Walt Disney World. Mission was accomplished in 1998 when, starting from an unpromising 17th on the grid, Eddie sped to a superbly judged Indy 500 win. Driving beautifully, he led 76 of the 200 laps and even survived a collision with a back-marker.

Cheever has since been a mainstay of the IRL, but is apparently now setting his sights on NASCAR, planning to take in a few races in 2000 with a view to running his own team in the future.

CHEEVER, Eddie (USA) b 10/1/1958, Phoenix, Arizona

1978 — Championship position: Unplaced

	Race	Circuit	No	Entrant	Tyres	Car/Engine	Comment	Q Pos/Entries
dnq	ARGENTINE GP	Buenos Aires	32	Theodore Racing	G	3.0 Theodore TR1-Cosworth V8		26/27
dnq	BRAZILIAN GP	Rio	32	Theodore Racing	G	3.0 Theodore TR1-Cosworth V8		26/28
ret	SOUTH AFRICAN GP	Kyalami	24	Olympus Cameras/Hesketh Racing	G	3.0 Hesketh 308E-Cosworth V8	engine-oil line	25/30

1980 — Championship position: Unplaced

	Race	Circuit	No	Entrant	Tyres	Car/Engine	Comment	Q Pos/Entries
dnq	ARGENTINE GP	Buenos Aires	31	Osella Squadra Corse	G	3.0 Osella FA1-Cosworth V8		28/28
dnq	BRAZILIAN GP	Interlagos	31	Osella Squarda Corse	G	3.0 Osella FA1-Cosworth V8		28/28
ret	SOUTH AFRICAN GP	Kyalami	31	Osella Squadra Corse	G	3.0 Osella FA1-Cosworth V8	accident	23/28
ret	US GP WEST	Long Beach	31	Osella Squadra Corse	G	3.0 Osella FA1-Cosworth V8	driveshaft	19/27
dnq	BELGIAN GP	Zolder	31	Osella Squadra Corse	G	3.0 Osella FA1-Cosworth V8		27/27
dnq	MONACO GP	Monte Carlo	31	Osella Squadra Corse	G	3.0 Osella FA1-Cosworth V8		22/27
ret	FRENCH GP	Paul Ricard	31	Osella Squadra Corse	G	3.0 Osella FA1-Cosworth V8	engine	21/27
ret	BRITISH GP	Brands Hatch	31	Osella Squadra Corse	G	3.0 Osella FA1-Cosworth V8	rear suspension	20/27
ret	GERMAN GP	Hockenheim	31	Osella Squadra Corse	G	3.0 Osella FA1-Cosworth V8	gearbox	18/26
ret	AUSTRIAN GP	Österreichring	31	Osella Squadra Corse	G	3.0 Osella FA1-Cosworth V8	wheel bearing	19/25
ret	DUTCH GP	Zandvoort	31	Osella Squadra Corse	G	3.0 Osella FA1-Cosworth V8	engine	19/28
12	ITALIAN GP	Imola	31	Osella Squadra Corse	G	3.0 Osella FA1-Cosworth V8	3 laps behind	17/28
ret	CANADIAN GP	Montreal	31	Osella Squadra Corse	G	3.0 Osella FA1-Cosworth V8	fuel pressure	14/28
ret	US GP EAST	Watkins Glen	31	Osella Squadra Corse	G	3.0 Osella FA1-Cosworth V8	suspension	16/27

1981 — Championship position: 11th= Wins: 0 Pole positions: 0 Fastest laps: 0 Points scored: 10

	Race	Circuit	No	Entrant	Tyres	Car/Engine	Comment	Q Pos/Entries
5	US GP WEST	Long Beach	3	Tyrrell Racing	M	3.0 Tyrrell 010-Cosworth V8		8/29
nc	BRAZILIAN GP	Rio	3	Tyrrell Racing	M	3.0 Tyrrell 010-Cosworth V8	pit stops-collision damage/-13 laps	14/30
ret	ARGENTINE GP	Buenos Aires	3	Tyrrell Racing	M	3.0 Tyrrell 010-Cosworth V8	clutch	13/29
ret	SAN MARINO GP	Imola	3	Tyrrell Racing	M	3.0 Tyrrell 010-Cosworth V8	collision with Giacomelli	19/30
6	BELGIAN GP	Zolder	3	Tyrrell Racing	M	3.0 Tyrrell 010-Cosworth V8		8/31
5	MONACO GP	Monte Carlo	3	Tyrrell Racing	M	3.0 Tyrrell 010-Cosworth V8	2 laps behind	15/31
nc	SPANISH GP	Jarama	3	Tyrrell Racing	M	3.0 Tyrrell 010-Cosworth V8	long pit stop/19 laps behind	20/30
13	FRENCH GP	Dijon	3	Tyrrell Racing	M	3.0 Tyrrell 010-Cosworth V8	3 laps behind	19/29
4	BRITISH GP	Silverstone	3	Tyrrell Racing	M	3.0 Tyrrell 010-Cosworth V8	1 lap behind	23/30
5	GERMAN GP	Hockenheim	3	Tyrrell Racing	A	3.0 Tyrrell 011-Cosworth V8		18/30
dnq	AUSTRIAN GP	Österreichring	3	Tyrrell Racing	G	3.0 Tyrrell 011-Cosworth V8		25/28
dnq	"	"	3	Tyrrell Racing	G	3.0 Tyrrell 010-Cosworth V8		–/–
ret	DUTCH GP	Zandvoort	3	Tyrrell Racing	G	3.0 Tyrrell 011-Cosworth V8	suspension failure-accident	22/30
ret	ITALIAN GP	Monza	3	Tyrrell Racing	G	3.0 Tyrrell 011-Cosworth V8	spun off	17/30
12/ret	CANADIAN GP	Montreal	3	Tyrrell Racing	G	3.0 Tyrrell 011-Cosworth V8	engine/7 laps behind	14/30
ret	CAESARS PALACE GP	Las Vegas	3	Tyrrell Racing	G	3.0 Tyrrell 011-Cosworth V8	engine	19/30

1982 — Championship position: 12th Wins: 0 Pole positions: 0 Fastest laps: 0 Points scored: 15

	Race	Circuit	No	Entrant	Tyres	Car/Engine	Comment	Q Pos/Entries
ret	SOUTH AFRICAN GP	Kyalami	25	Equipe Talbot Gitanes	M	3.0 Ligier JS17-Matra V12	misfire	17/30
ret	BRAZILIAN GP	Rio	25	Equipe Talbot Gitanes	M	3.0 Ligier JS17-Matra V12	water leak	26/31
ret	US GP WEST	Long Beach	25	Equipe Talbot Gitanes	M	3.0 Ligier JS17B-Matra V12	gearbox	13/31
3	BELGIAN GP	Zolder	25	Equipe Talbot Gitanes	M	3.0 Ligier JS17B-Matra V12	3rd place car disqualified/-1 lap	16/32
ret	MONACO GP	Monte Carlo	25	Equipe Talbot Gitanes	M	3.0 Ligier JS19-Matra V12	engine	16/31
2	US GP (DETROIT)	Detroit	25	Equipe Talbot Gitanes	M	3.0 Ligier JS17B-Matra V12		9/28
10/ret	CANADIAN GP	Montreal	25	Equipe Talbot Gitanes	M	3.0 Ligier JS17B-Matra V12	out of fuel	12/29
dnq	DUTCH GP	Zandvoort	25	Equipe Talbot Gitanes	M	3.0 Ligier JS19-Matra V12		29/31
ret	BRITISH GP	Brands Hatch	25	Equipe Talbot Gitanes	M	3.0 Ligier JS19-Matra V12	engine	24/30
16	FRENCH GP	Paul Ricard	25	Equipe Talbot Gitanes	M	3.0 Ligier JS19-Matra V12	3 pit stops-tyres-skirts/-5 laps	19/30
ret	GERMAN GP	Hockenheim	25	Equipe Talbot Gitanes	M	3.0 Ligier JS19-Matra V12	handling	13/30
ret	AUSTRIAN GP	Österreichring	25	Equipe Talbot Gitanes	M	3.0 Ligier JS19-Matra V12	engine	22/29
nc	SWISS GP	Dijon	25	Equipe Talbot Gitanes	M	3.0 Ligier JS19-Matra V12	2 pit stops-tyres/-10 laps	16/29
6	ITALIAN GP	Monza	25	Equipe Talbot Gitanes	M	3.0 Ligier JS19-Matra V12	1 lap behind	14/30
3	CAESARS PALACE GP	Las Vegas	25	Equipe Talbot Gitanes	M	3.0 Ligier JS19-Matra V12		4/30

Cheever had his most competitive F1 drive in 1983, when he was number two to Alain Prost at Renault.
Left: Eddie leads Warwick, Jarier and Lauda in the Brazilian Grand Prix.

1983
Championship position: 6th= Wins: 0 Pole positions: 0 Fastest laps: 0 Points scored: 22

Result	Race	Circuit	No	Team		Engine	Notes	Grid
ret	BRAZILIAN GP	Rio	16	Equipe Renault Elf	M	1.5 t/c Renault RE30C V6	turbo	8/27
13/ret	US GP WEST	Long Beach	16	Equipe Renault Elf	M	1.5 t/c Renault RE30C V6	gearbox/8 laps behind	15/28
3	FRENCH GP	Paul Ricard	16	Equipe Renault Elf	M	1.5 t/c Renault RE40 V6		2/29
ret	SAN MARINO GP	Imola	16	Equipe Renault Elf	M	1.5 t/c Renault RE40 V6	turbo	6/28
ret	MONACO GP	Monte Carlo	16	Equipe Renault Elf	M	1.5 t/c Renault RE40 V6	engine cut out	3/28
3	BELGIAN GP	Spa	16	Equipe Renault Elf	M	1.5 t/c Renault RE40 V6		8/28
ret	US GP (DETROIT)	Detroit	16	Equipe Renault Elf	M	1.5 t/c Renault RE40 V6	distributor	7/27
2	CANADIAN GP	Montreal	16	Equipe Renault Elf	M	1.5 t/c Renault RE40 V6		6/28
ret	BRITISH GP	Silverstone	16	Equipe Renault Elf	M	1.5 t/c Renault RE40 V6	engine-head gasket	7/29
ret	GERMAN GP	Hockenheim	16	Equipe Renault Elf	M	1.5 t/c Renault RE40 V6	fuel injection pump	6/29
4	AUSTRIAN GP	Österreichring	16	Equipe Renault Elf	M	1.5 t/c Renault RE40 V6		8/29
ret	DUTCH GP	Zandvoort	16	Equipe Renault Elf	M	1.5 t/c Renault RE40 V6	electrics	11/29
3	ITALIAN GP	Monza	16	Equipe Renault Elf	M	1.5 t/c Renault RE40 V6		7/29
10	EUROPEAN GP	Brands Hatch	16	Equipe Renault Elf	M	1.5 t/c Renault RE40 V6	2 pit stops-tyres-visor/-1 lap	7/29
6	SOUTH AFRICAN GP	Kyalami	16	Equipe Renault Elf	M	1.5 t/c Renault RE40 V6	1 lap behind	14/26

1984
Championship position: 16th= Wins: 0 Pole positions: 0 Fastest laps: 0 Points scored: 3

Result	Race	Circuit	No	Team		Engine	Notes	Grid
4	BRAZILIAN GP	Rio	23	Benetton Team Alfa Romeo	G	1.5 t/c Alfa Romeo 184T V8	1 lap behind	12/27
ret	SOUTH AFRICAN GP	Kyalami	23	Benetton Team Alfa Romeo	G	1.5 t/c Alfa Romeo 184T V8	radiator	16/27
ret	BELGIAN GP	Zolder	23	Benetton Team Alfa Romeo	G	1.5 t/c Alfa Romeo 184T V8	engine	11/27
7*/ret	SAN MARINO GP	Imola	23	Benetton Team Alfa Romeo	G	1.5 t/c Alfa Romeo 184T V8	* 5th car dsq/out of fuel/-2 laps	8/28
ret	FRENCH GP	Dijon	23	Benetton Team Alfa Romeo	G	1.5 t/c Alfa Romeo 184T V8	engine	17/27
dnq	MONACO GP	Monte Carlo	23	Benetton Team Alfa Romeo	G	1.5 t/c Alfa Romeo 184T V8		23/27
11*/ret	CANADIAN GP	Montreal	23	Benetton Team Alfa Romeo	G	1.5 t/c Alfa Romeo 184T V8	* 10th car dsq/out of fuel/-7 laps	11/26
ret	US GP (DETROIT)	Detroit	23	Benetton Team Alfa Romeo	G	1.5 t/c Alfa Romeo 184T V8	engine	8/27
ret	US GP (DALLAS)	Dallas	23	Benetton Team Alfa Romeo	G	1.5 t/c Alfa Romeo 184T V8	hit wall	14/27
ret	BRITISH GP	Brands Hatch	23	Benetton Team Alfa Romeo	G	1.5 t/c Alfa Romeo 184T V8	accident damage	18/27
ret	GERMAN GP	Hockenheim	23	Benetton Team Alfa Romeo	G	1.5 t/c Alfa Romeo 184T V8	engine	18/27
ret	AUSTRIAN GP	Österreichring	23	Benetton Team Alfa Romeo	G	1.5 t/c Alfa Romeo 184T V8	engine	16/28
13*/ret	DUTCH GP	Zandvoort	23	Benetton Team Alfa Romeo	G	1.5 t/c Alfa Romeo 184T V8	* 8th/9th dsq/out of fuel/-6 laps	17/27
9*/ret	ITALIAN GP	Monza	23	Benetton Team Alfa Romeo	G	1.5 t/c Alfa Romeo 184T V8	out of fuel/6 laps behind	10/27
ret	EUROPEAN GP	Nürburgring	23	Benetton Team Alfa Romeo	G	1.5 t/c Alfa Romeo 184T V8	fuel pump	13/26
17	PORTUGUESE GP	Estoril	23	Benetton Team Alfa Romeo	G	1.5 t/c Alfa Romeo 184T V8	pit stop/6 laps behind	14/27

1985
Championship position: Unplaced

Result	Race	Circuit	No	Team		Engine	Notes	Grid
ret	BRAZILIAN GP	Rio	23	Benetton Team Alfa Romeo	G	1.5 t/c Alfa Romeo 185T V8	engine	18/25
ret	PORTUGUESE GP	Estoril	23	Benetton Team Alfa Romeo	G	1.5 t/c Alfa Romeo 185T V8	started from pit lane/engine	14/26
ret	SAN MARINO GP	Imola	23	Benetton Team Alfa Romeo	G	1.5 t/c Alfa Romeo 185T V8	engine	12/26
ret	MONACO GP	Monte Carlo	23	Benetton Team Alfa Romeo	G	1.5 t/c Alfa Romeo 185T V8	alternator	4/26
17	CANADIAN GP	Montreal	23	Benetton Team Alfa Romeo	G	1.5 t/c Alfa Romeo 185T V8	pit stop-electrics/-6 laps	11/25
9	US GP (DETROIT)	Detroit	23	Benetton Team Alfa Romeo	G	1.5 t/c Alfa Romeo 185T V8	pit stop-puncture/-2 laps	7/25
10	FRENCH GP	Paul Ricard	23	Benetton Team Alfa Romeo	G	1.5 t/c Alfa Romeo 185T V8	1 lap behind	18/26
ret	BRITISH GP	Silverstone	23	Benetton Team Alfa Romeo	G	1.5 t/c Alfa Romeo 185T V8	turbo	22/26
ret	GERMAN GP	Nürburgring	23	Benetton Team Alfa Romeo	G	1.5 t/c Alfa Romeo 184T V8	turbo	18/27
ret	AUSTRIAN GP	Österreichring	23	Benetton Team Alfa Romeo	G	1.5 t/c Alfa Romeo 184T V8	turbo	20/27
ret	DUTCH GP	Zandvoort	23	Benetton Team Alfa Romeo	G	1.5 t/c Alfa Romeo 184T V8	turbo	20/27
ret	ITALIAN GP	Monza	23	Benetton Team Alfa Romeo	G	1.5 t/c Alfa Romeo 184T V8	engine	17/26
ret	BELGIAN GP	Spa	23	Benetton Team Alfa Romeo	G	1.5 t/c Alfa Romeo 184T V8	gearbox	19/24
11	EUROPEAN GP	Brands Hatch	23	Benetton Team Alfa Romeo	G	1.5 t/c Alfa Romeo 184T V8	2 laps behind	18/27
ret	SOUTH AFRICAN GP	Kyalami	23	Benetton Team Alfa Romeo	G	1.5 t/c Alfa Romeo 184T V8	collision-Ghinzani & Patrese	14/21
ret	AUSTRALIAN GP	Adelaide	23	Benetton Team Alfa Romeo	G	1.5 t/c Alfa Romeo 184T V8	engine	13/25

1986
Championship position: Unplaced

Result	Race	Circuit	No	Team		Engine	Notes	Grid
ret	US GP (DETROIT)	Detroit	16	Team Haas (USA) Ltd	G	1.5 t/c Lola THL2-Cosworth V6	drive pegs	10/26

1987
Championship position: 10th Wins: 0 Pole positions: 0 Fastest laps: 0 Points scored: 8

Result	Race	Circuit	No	Team		Engine	Notes	Grid
ret	BRAZILIAN GP	Rio	18	USF&G Arrows Megatron	G	1.5 t/c Arrows A10-Megatron 4	engine	14/23
ret	SAN MARINO GP	Imola	18	USF&G Arrows Megatron	G	1.5 t/c Arrows A10-Megatron 4	engine	10/27
4	BELGIAN GP	Spa	18	USF&G Arrows Megatron	G	1.5 t/c Arrows A10-Megatron 4	1 lap behind	11/26
ret	MONACO GP	Monte Carlo	18	USF&G Arrows Megatron	G	1.5 t/c Arrows A10-Megatron 4	head gasket	6/26
6/ret	US GP (DETROIT)	Detroit	18	USF&G Arrows Megatron	G	1.5 t/c Arrows A10-Megatron 4	out of fuel/3 laps behind	6/26
ret	FRENCH GP	Paul Ricard	18	USF&G Arrows Megatron	G	1.5 t/c Arrows A10-Megatron 4	knocked off ignition switch	14/26
ret	BRITISH GP	Silverstone	18	USF&G Arrows Megatron	G	1.5 t/c Arrows A10-Megatron 4	engine	14/26
ret	GERMAN GP	Hockenheim	18	USF&G Arrows Megatron	G	1.5 t/c Arrows A10-Megatron 4	throttle cable	15/26
8	HUNGARIAN GP	Hungaroring	18	USF&G Arrows Megatron	G	1.5 t/c Arrows A10-Megatron 4	hit Warwick-pit stops/-2 laps	11/26
ret	AUSTRIAN GP	Österreichring	18	USF&G Arrows Megatron	G	1.5 t/c Arrows A10-Megatron 4	puncture	12/26
ret	ITALIAN GP	Monza	18	USF&G Arrows Megatron	G	1.5 t/c Arrows A10-Megatron 4	driveshaft	13/28
6	PORTUGUESE GP	Estoril	18	USF&G Arrows Megatron	G	1.5 t/c Arrows A10-Megatron 4	2 laps behind	11/27
8/ret	SPANISH GP	Jerez	18	USF&G Arrows Megatron	G	1.5 t/c Arrows A10-Megatron 4	out of fuel	13/28
4	MEXICAN GP	Mexico City	18	USF&G Arrows Megatron	G	1.5 t/c Arrows A10-Megatron 4		12/27
9	JAPANESE GP	Suzuka	18	USF&G Arrows Megatron	G	1.5 t/c Arrows A10-Megatron 4	1 lap behind	13/27
ret	AUSTRALIAN GP	Adelaide	18	USF&G Arrows Megatron	G	1.5 t/c Arrows A10-Megatron 4	engine	11/27

1988
Championship position: 12th Wins: 0 Pole positions: 0 Fastest laps: 0 Points scored: 6

Result	Race	Circuit	No	Team		Engine	Notes	Grid
8	BRAZILIAN GP	Rio	18	USF&G Arrows Megatron	G	1.5 t/c Arrows A10B-Megatron 4	1 lap behind	15/31
7	SAN MARINO GP	Imola	18	USF&G Arrows Megatron	G	1.5 t/c Arrows A10B-Megatron 4	1 lap behind	7/31
ret	MONACO GP	Monte Carlo	18	USF&G Arrows Megatron	G	1.5 t/c Arrows A10B-Megatron 4	electrics	9/30
6	MEXICAN GP	Mexico City	18	USF&G Arrows Megatron	G	1.5 t/c Arrows A10B-Megatron 4	1 lap behind	7/30
ret	CANADIAN GP	Montreal	18	USF&G Arrows Megatron	G	1.5 t/c Arrows A10B-Megatron 4	throttle return spring	8/31
ret	US GP (DETROIT)	Detroit	18	USF&G Arrows Megatron	G	1.5 t/c Arrows A10B-Megatron 4	engine	15/31
11	FRENCH GP	Paul Ricard	18	USF&G Arrows Megatron	G	1.5 t/c Arrows A10B-Megatron 4	handling/fuel problems/-2 laps	13/31
7	BRITISH GP	Silverstone	18	USF&G Arrows Megatron	G	1.5 t/c Arrows A10B-Megatron 4	1 lap behind	13/31
10	GERMAN GP	Hockenheim	18	USF&G Arrows Megatron	G	1.5 t/c Arrows A10B-Megatron 4	engine problems/1 lap behind	15/31
ret	HUNGARIAN GP	Hungaroring	18	USF&G Arrows Megatron	G	1.5 t/c Arrows A10B-Megatron 4	brakes	14/31

6*	BELGIAN GP	Spa	18	USF&G Arrows Megatron	G	1.5 t/c Arrows A10B-Megatron 4		* 3rd & 4th cars dsq/-1 lap	11/31
3	ITALIAN GP	Monza	18	USF&G Arrows Megatron	G	1.5 t/c Arrows A10B-Megatron 4			5/31
ret	PORTUGUESE GP	Estoril	18	USF&G Arrows Megatron	G	1.5 t/c Arrows A10B-Megatron 4		turbo	18/31
ret	SPANISH GP	Jerez	18	USF&G Arrows Megatron	G	1.5 t/c Arrows A10B-Megatron 4		handling	25/31
ret	JAPANESE GP	Suzuka	18	USF&G Arrows Megatron	G	1.5 t/c Arrows A10B-Megatron 4		turbo	15/31
ret	AUSTRALIAN GP	Adelaide	18	USF&G Arrows Megatron	G	1.5 t/c Arrows A10B-Megatron 4		engine	18/31

1989 Championship position: 11th= Wins: 0 Pole positions: 0 Fastest laps: 0 Points scored: 6

ret	BRAZILIAN GP	Rio	10	USF&G Arrows	G	3.5 Arrows A11-Cosworth V8		hit by Schneider	24/38
9	SAN MARINO GP	Imola	10	USF&G Arrows	G	3.5 Arrows A11-Cosworth V8		broken exhaust/2 laps behind	21/39
7	MONACO GP	Monte Carlo	10	USF&G Arrows	G	3.5 Arrows A11-Cosworth V8		spun-collision-Arnoux/-2 laps	20/38
7	MEXICAN GP	Mexico City	10	USF&G Arrows	G	3.5 Arrows A11-Cosworth V8		1 lap behind	24/39
3	US GP (PHOENIX)	Phoenix	10	USF&G Arrows	G	3.5 Arrows A11-Cosworth V8		brakes fading at finish	17/39
ret	CANADIAN GP	Montreal	10	USF&G Arrows	G	3.5 Arrows A11-Cosworth V8		electrics-engine	16/39
7	FRENCH GP	Paul Ricard	10	USF&G Arrows	G	3.5 Arrows A11-Cosworth V8		1 lap behind	25/39
dnq	BRITISH GP	Silverstone	10	USF&G Arrows	G	3.5 Arrows A11-Cosworth V8			28/39
12/ret	GERMAN GP	Hockenheim	10	USF&G Arrows	G	3.5 Arrows A11-Cosworth V8		fuel pick-up/5 laps behind	25/39
5	HUNGARIAN GP	Hungaroring	10	USF&G Arrows	G	3.5 Arrows A11-Cosworth V8		lost 4th place on last lap	16/39
ret	BELGIAN GP	Spa	10	USF&G Arrows	G	3.5 Arrows A11-Cosworth V8		lost wheel/warned for baulking	24/39
dnq	ITALIAN GP	Monza	10	USF&G Arrows	G	3.5 Arrows A11-Cosworth V8			27/39
ret	PORTUGUESE GP	Estoril	10	USF&G Arrows	G	3.5 Arrows A11-Cosworth V8		engine cut out-crashed	26/39
ret	SPANISH GP	Jerez	10	USF&G Arrows	G	3.5 Arrows A11-Cosworth V8		engine	23/38
8*	JAPANESE GP	Suzuka	10	USF&G Arrows	G	3.5 Arrows A11-Cosworth V8		* 1st place car dsq/-1 lap	24/39
ret	AUSTRALIAN GP	Adelaide	10	USF&G Arrows	G	3.5 Arrows A11-Cosworth V8		spun off in rain	22/39

GP Starts: 132 GP Wins: 0 Pole positions: 0 Fastest laps: 0 Points: 70

ANDREA CHIESA

A Swiss national born in Milan, Chiesa made a solid start in Italian F3 in 1986, but was hampered by problems with his VW engine. For 1987 he was well prepared, surging out of the blocks with three wins in the first four races, but his season then tailed off and Enrico Bertaggia pipped him to the title. Stepping up to F3000, Chiesa struggled in 1988, notching just a single point, but things improved the following year, Andrea winning at Enna and finishing second at Vallelunga to claim sixth place in the final points standings.

His third season in the formula, with Paul Stewart Racing, was much the same and he managed seventh in the final table, but his fourth, in 1991, was an utter disaster, Chiesa failing to score even a point with a competitive Reynard. But such are the vagaries of motor racing that when the Formula 1 team line-ups were confirmed for 1992, Andrea was confirmed at Fondmetal. He was out of his depth and his record of three starts (two spins, one collision) and seven DNQs tells the sorry tale. For Chiesa the F1 dream was over, but he briefly reappeared in 1993, racing in the opening round of the Indy Car series in Surfers Paradise, Australia.

After three years away from the sport Chiesa briefly returned to the track in a Riley & Scott with Alex Caffi at Laguna Seca in 1996. The partnership was successfully renewed in 1998 when the pair scored a couple of third places in the ISRS series at the Paul Ricard and Le Mans (Bugatti) rounds.

ETTORE CHIMERI

Chimeri was one of the local drivers who bolstered the grids for the two-race 'Temporada' series when top-flight motor sport returned briefly to the Argentine in 1960. He failed to finish the championship race, but took the outdated Maserati 250F to fourth place in the Formula Libre Buenos Aires GP in an event of huge attrition.

Tragically, two weeks later, he was killed in practice for a sports car race in Cuba.

CHIESA, Andrea (CH) b 6/5/1964, Milan

1992 Championship position: Unplaced

	Race	Circuit	No	Entrant	Tyres	Car/Engine	Comment	Q Pos/Entries
dnq	SOUTH AFRICAN GP	Kyalami	14	Fondmetal	G	3.5 Fondmetal GR01-Ford HB V8		28/30
ret	MEXICAN GP	Mexico City	14	Fondmetal	G	3.5 Fondmetal GR01-Ford HB V8	spun off	23/30
dnq	BRAZILIAN GP	Interlagos	14	Fondmetal	G	3.5 Fondmetal GR01-Ford HB V8		27/31
ret	SPANISH GP	Barcelona	14	Fondmetal	G	3.5 Fondmetal GR01-Ford HB V8	spun off	20/32
dnq	SAN MARINO GP	Imola	14	Fondmetal	G	3.5 Fondmetal GR01-Ford HB V8		28/32
dnq	MONACO GP	Monte Carlo	14	Fondmetal	G	3.5 Fondmetal GR01-Ford HB V8		29/32
dnq	CANADIAN GP	Montreal	14	Fondmetal	G	3.5 Fondmetal GR01-Ford HB V8		29/32
ret	FRENCH GP	Magny Cours	14	Fondmetal	G	3.5 Fondmetal GR02-Ford HB V8	collision with Gugelmin-lap 1	26/30
dnq	BRITISH GP	Silverstone	14	Fondmetal	G	3.5 Fondmetal GR02-Ford HB V8		29/32
dnq	GERMAN GP	Hockenheim	14	Fondmetal	G	3.5 Fondmetal GR01-Ford HB V8		29/32

GP Starts: 3 GP Wins: 0 Pole positions: 0 Fastest laps: 0 Points: 0

CHIMERI, Ettore (YV) b 1924 – d 27/2/1960, Cuba

1960 Championship position: Unplaced

	Race	Circuit	No	Entrant	Tyres	Car/Engine	Comment	Q Pos/Entries
ret	ARGENTINE GP	Buenos Aires	44	Ettore Chimeri	D	2.5 Maserati 250F 6	electrics/driver exhaustion	21/22

GP Starts: 1 GP Wins: 0 Pole positions: 0 Fastest laps: 0 Points: 0

LOUIS CHIRON

The bulk of Chiron's long motor racing story falls outside the scope of this book, but it is worthwhile outlining his pre-World Championship exploits, which began in the mid-twenties with a Bugatti, the make that was to be synonymous with the first part of his career. The 1928 season saw him victorious in the Rome, Marne, Spanish and Italian GPs, with victories in the German and Spanish GPs following in 1929. He also took a Delage to compete at Indianapolis, finishing a creditable seventh after a long tyre stop. More success came in 1930 as he added the European and Lyons GPs to his tally, and in 1931, still with the Bugatti, he took a brilliant win in the Monaco GP and shared a French GP triumph with Varzi.

Chiron was tempted away to Scuderia Ferrari for the 1933 season to race their Alfa Romeos, and remained with them until 1936, when the might of Mercedes and Auto Union had become virtually irresistible. He cut down his racing almost to the point of retirement in the immediate pre-war years, though he did find time to win the 1937 French GP in a sports Talbot.

As soon as was practicable after the war, Chiron was out in his Talbot once more. Outright success eluded him in 1946, but he won the 1947 French GP at Montlhéry, a victory he was to repeat at Reims two years later. In 1950 – the first season of the newly created World Championship – Chiron campaigned a 4CLT Maserati without success, except for a fine third place in his native Monte Carlo. After just one Grand Prix the following season, he abandoned the Maserati in favour of the trusty old Lago-Talbot, but the car was generally unreliable. The 1952 season started with near-disaster when he sustained serious burns when his Maserati-Platé caught fire at Syracuse. He did not compete for the rest of the season, but returned in 1953 at the wheel of the latest F2 OSCA which, though attractive, failed to live up to his expectations.

At the start of the 1954 season, Chiron was 54 years old, but he still had not had enough of winning, and he finally triumphed in the Monte Carlo Rally in a Lancia. Invited to handle a works Lancia in the 1955 Monaco GP, Chiron obliged with sixth place. When he finally retired, Prince Rainier asked him to run the Principality's two great events, which he did up until the 1979 Monaco GP, just a month before his death.

CHIRON, Louis (MC) b 3/8/1899, Monte Carlo – d 22/6/1979, Monte Carlo

	1950	Championship position: 0		Wins: 0	Pole positions: 0		Fastest laps: 0	Points scored: 0		
	Race	Circuit	No	Entrant	Tyres	Car/Engine			Comment	Q Pos/Entries
ret	BRITISH GP	Silverstone	19	Officine Alfieri Maserati	P	1.5 s/c Maserati 4CLT/48 4			oil leak/clutch	11/21
3	MONACO GP	Monte Carlo	48	Officine Alfieri Maserati	P	1.5 s/c Maserati 4CLT/48 4			2 laps behind	8/21
9	SWISS GP	Bremgarten	26	Officine Alfieri Maserati	P	1.5 s/c Maserati 4CLT/48 4			3 laps behind	16/18
ret	FRENCH GP	Reims	30	Officine Alfieri Maserati	P	1.5 s/c Maserati 4CLT/48 4			engine	14/20
ret	ITALIAN GP	Monza	6	Officine Alfieri Msaerati	P	1.5 s/c Maserati 4CLT/48 4			oil pressure	19/27
	1951	Championship position: Unplaced								
7	SWISS GP	Bremgarten	30	Enrico Platé	P	1.5 s/c Maserati 4CLT/48 4			2 laps behind	19/21
ret	BELGIAN GP	Spa	18	Ecurie Rosier	D	4.5 Lago-Talbot T26C 6			engine	9/13
6	FRENCH GP	Reims	42	Ecurie Rosier	D	4.5 Lago-Talbot T26C 6			6 laps behind	8/23
ret	BRITISH GP	Silverstone	23	Ecurie Rosier	D	4.5 Lago-Talbot T26C 6			brakes	13/20
ret	GERMAN GP	Nürburgring	85	Ecurie Rosier	D	4.5 Lago-Talbot T26C 6			ignition/engine	13/23
ret	ITALIAN GP	Monza	20	Ecurie Rosier	D	4.5 Lago-Talbot T26C 6			ignition	17/22
ret	SPANISH GP	Pedralbes	30	Ecurie Rosier	D	4.5 Lago-Talbot T26C 6			engine	12/20
	1953	Championship position: Unplaced								
nc	FRENCH GP	Reims	32	Louis Chiron	P	2.0 OSCA 20 6			17 laps behind	25/25
dns	BRITISH GP	Silverstone	27	Louis Chiron	P	2.0 OSCA 20 6				– /29
dns	SWISS GP	Bremgarten	12	Louis Chiron	P	2.0 OSCA 20 6				– /23
10	ITALIAN GP	Monza	32	Louis Chiron	P	2.0 OSCA 20 6			8 laps behind	25/30
	1955	Championship position: Unplaced								
6	MONACO GP	Monte Carlo	32	Scuderia Lancia	P	2.5 Lancia D50 V8			5 laps behind	19/22
	1956	Championship position: Unplaced								
dns	MONACO GP	Monte Carlo	34	Scuderia Centro Sud	P	2.5 Maserati 250F 6			two blown engines in practice	– /19
	1958	Championship position: Unplaced								
dnq	MONACO GP	Monte Carlo	56	André Testut	P	2.5 Maserati 250F 6			practiced Testut's car	– / –

GP Starts: 15   GP Wins: 0   Pole positions: 0   Fastest laps: 0   Points: 4

JOHNNY CLAES

A Belgian born in Fulham, London, whose mother was Scottish, Claes' first passion was jazz, but he became involved in motor racing after a chance visit to the 1947 French GP where his bilingualism allowed him to act as an interpreter to the English drivers. His Belgian father was wealthy, and when Johnny tried his hand at racing in 1948, a Talbot was duly ordered for him which saw much service in both 1949 and 1950. However, his first real success came at the wheel of an HWM in the 1950 GP des Frontières at Chimay, a race he was to win again the following season, this time in a Simca-Gordini.

With his Talbot effectively redundant following the adoption of Formula 2 regulations for Grands Prix, Claes secured drives with the Gordini, HWM and Connaught teams during the 1952 and 1953 seasons. Finding the competition tough at World Championship level, he tasted real success in the 1953 Liège-Rome-Liège Rally, which he won despite having to drive the car single-handed for 52 hours after his co-driver was taken ill.

By 1954 Johnny was a sick man and he raced little, though a visit to Le Mans with a Porsche saw him finish 12th overall and take the 1500 cc class. He was more active in 1955, the highlight of his season being third place at Le Mans in the Ecurie Belgique Jaguar with Jacques Swaters. His last competitive event was to be the Liège-Rome-Liège Rally of that year, in which he took third place partnered by Lucien Bianchi. His health then deteriorated rapidly and, laid low by tuberculosis, he died in February 1956, aged just 39.

CLAES, Johnny (B) b 11/8/1916, London, England – d 3/2/1956, Brussels

	Race	Circuit	No	Entrant	Tyres	Car/Engine	Comment	Q Pos/Entries
	1950	Championship position: Unplaced						
11	BRITISH GP	Silverstone	18	Ecurie Belge	D	4.5 Lago-Talbot T26C 6	6 laps behind	21/21
7	MONACO GP	Monte Carlo	6	Ecurie Belge	D	4.5 Lago-Talbot T26C 6	6 laps behind	19/21
10	SWISS GP	Bremgarten	4	Ecurie Belge	D	4.5 Lago-Talbot T26C 6	3 laps behind	14/18
8	BELGIAN GP	Spa	24	Ecurie Belge	D	4.5 Lago-Talbot T26C 6	3 laps behind	14/14
ret	FRENCH GP	Reims	42	Ecurie Belge	D	4.5 Lago-Talbot T26C 6	overheating	15/20
ret	ITALIAN GP	Monza	2	Ecurie Belge	D	4.5 Lago-Talbot T26C 6	overheating	22/27
	1951	Championship position: Unplaced						
13	SWISS GP	Bremgarten	2	Ecurie Belge	D	4.5 Lago-Talbot T26C-DA 6	7 laps behind	18/21
7	BELGIAN GP	Spa	16	Ecurie Belge	D	4.5 Lago-Talbot T26C-DA 6	3 laps behind	11/13
ret	FRENCH GP	Reims	28	Ecurie Belge	D	4.5 Lago-Talbot T26C-DA 6	crashed into house by circuit	12/23
13	BRITISH GP	Silverstone	25	Ecurie Belge	D	4.5 Lago-Talbot T26C-DA 6	10 laps behind	14/20
11	GERMAN GP	Nürburgring	94	Ecurie Belge	D	4.5 Lago-Talbot T26C-DA 6	3 laps behind	18/23
ret	ITALIAN GP	Monza	26	Ecurie Belge	D	4.5 Lago-Talbot T26C-DA 6	oil pump	21/22
ret	SPANISH GP	Pedralbes	36	Ecurie Belge	D	4.5 Lago-Talbot T26C-DA 6	hit straw bales	15/20
	1952	Championship position: Unplaced						
8	BELGIAN GP	Spa	18	Equipe Gordini	E	2.0 Gordini Type 16S 6 sports	F2 engine/3 laps behind	19/22
ret	FRENCH GP	Rouen	32	Ecurie Belge	E	1.5 Gordini Type 15 4	engine	19/20
14	BRITISH GP	Silverstone	27	Ecurie Belge	E	1.5 Gordini Type 15 4	6 laps behind	23/32
nc	GERMAN GP	Nürburgring	113	HW Motors Ltd	D	2.0 HWM-Alta 4	rear axle bearing/-3 laps	32/32
dnq	ITALIAN GP	Monza	66	Vickomtesse de Walckiers	E	1.5 Gordini Type 15 4	no time set	– /35
	1953	Championship position: Unplaced						
nc	DUTCH GP	Zandvoort	30	Ecurie Belge	E	2.0 Connaught A-Lea Francis 4	38 laps behind	17/20
ret	BELGIAN GP	Spa	6	Officine Alfieri Maserati	P	2.0 Maserati A6GCM 6	Fangio took over & crashed	10/22
nc	FRENCH GP	Reims	48	Ecurie Belge	E	2.0 Connaught A-Lea Francis 4	7 laps behind	21/25
ret	GERMAN GP	Nürburgring	12	Ecurie Belge	E	2.0 Connaught A-Lea Francis 4		25/35
ret	ITALIAN GP	Monza	26	Ecurie Belge	E	2.0 Connaught A-Lea Francis 4	loose fuel line	30/30
	1955	Championship position: Unplaced						
dns	BELGIAN GP	Spa	38	Stirling Moss Ltd	D	2.5 Maserati 250F 6	engine trouble in practice	14/14
nc	DUTCH GP	Zandvoort	50	Equipe Nationale Belge	E	2.5 Ferrari 500/625 4	22 laps behind	16/16

GP Starts: 23   GP Wins: 0   Pole positions: 0   Fastest laps: 0   Points: 0

JIM CLARK

WORLD CHAMPION: 1963 & 1965

JIM CLARK

It really was a different era, the mid-sixties. There was no hype, the Grand Prix world was just a small close-knit community of rivals who were still friends, and the 'mega-buck' world of sponsorship was only just looming around the corner. Jim Clark's tragic death in a relatively meaningless Formula 2 race at Hockenheim on 7 April 1968 was a savage blow to everyone connected with the sport, which from that day seemed to change; suddenly it was more of a business. That Clark was not part of the new commercial order perversely seemed somehow fitting, yet in reality Clark was the supreme modern professional racing driver of his day, becoming a tax-exile to maximise his earnings, and employing a manager to run his farming affairs back home in Scotland.

It was this well-off agricultural environment that provided the background to his early motor racing activities – just minor rallies and trials to start with, before he graduated to the Porsche with which he began to make his name in 1958. Despite strong parental opposition, young Jimmy was soon racing for the Border Reivers in their Jaguar D-Type, a little Lotus Elite and the rather more potent Lister Jaguar with which he took 12 wins in the 1959 season. Clark agreed to drive for Aston Martin's Grand Prix team in 1960, but the project was delayed and he was released to Lotus for Formula 2 and Junior racing. However, once Colin Chapman had him under contract he lost no time in promoting him to the Grand Prix team, although the priority was the Junior championship, in which he tied for the title with Trevor Taylor. He was also committed to the Reivers sports car team, sharing the third-placed Aston Martin DBR 1 with Salvadori in the Le Mans 24 Hours, a race he disliked so much that he refused to participate in it after the Lotus 23 failed to pass scrutineering in 1962.

The 1961 season saw the introduction of the new 1.5-litre formula and Clark could concentrate fully on the championship Grands Prix and the proliferation of lesser meetings which were organised. He took his first F1 win at Pau, but the year saw little luck come the Scotsman's way, culminating in the tragic collision with von Trips' Ferrari at Monza in September, from which he was fortunate indeed to emerge shocked but unscathed. However, the end-of-season sunshine races in South Africa provided instant and welcome rehabilitation, with Jimmy winning the non-championship Rand, Natal and South African GPs.

For 1962 Chapman built the magnificent monocoque Lotus 25, which, propelled by the Climax V8 engine and driven by Jimmy, simply became the standard-setter for the next three years. Much is made of the heartbreaking failure at East London which cost Clark the championship, but that is harsh indeed on Graham Hill, who suffered equal bad luck earlier in the season, and fully deserved the crown. There were no hiccoughs in 1963, though, as Jimmy scorched to the title, winning no fewer than seven championship Grands Prix and non-title races at Pau, Imola, Silverstone, Kalskoga and Oulton Park. Lotus also made their first assault on USAC racing, with Clark shaking Indianapolis to its roots with the funny little rear-engined car and taking second place on its first appearance. To prove it was no fluke, later in the season he won the Milwaukee 200. The revolution had truly begun.

Jimmy was still indisputably the man to beat in 1964, but unreliability, particularly with the new Lotus 33, saw the title pass to Surtees at the very last gasp in Mexico. However, Clark had thrilled the fans as never before, particularly those in Britain who were also lucky enough to watch him three-wheeling the Lotus Ford Cortina with such abandon. Having seen the championship lost, Clark and Chapman were in no mood to face a repeat of their misfortunes in 1965 and after a highly successful winter Tasman series, which yielded five wins, their World Championship rivals were subjected to the full onslaught of the car's performance and Jimmy's brilliance. Leaving aside Monaco (which Clark skipped in order to win the Indy 500), he won the first six Grands Prix of the season to put the outcome of the championship beyond doubt by August.

The new 3-litre formula for once found Chapman without a ready answer, Team Lotus having to make do with 2-litre Climax engines until the BRM H16s became available. Clark was now in the unusual position of an underdog, which made for a fascinating year, illuminated by superb drives at Zandvoort, where he used all his powers to bring a sick car into third place, and at Watkins Glen, where he took the BRM H16 engine to its only championship victory. But, untypically, there were rare moments when he let his frustrations show, such as when he slid off in the wet at the Nürburgring.

The following year saw the advent of the Lotus 49-Cosworth V8 and Clark gave us the full repertoire of his bounteous gifts. That Denny Hulme won the championship seemed almost unimportant (yes, it really was different in those days!), for all eyes were on Clark. A crushing win on the car's debut in the Dutch GP, one of Grand Prix racing's greatest-ever drives at Monza when he made up almost a whole lap on the opposition only to run short of fuel on the last lap having regained the lead, and his skill in bringing the car home at Watkins Glen with the rear suspension broken and the wheel angled drunkenly as he crossed the finish line live fresh in the memory to this day. The 1968 season began in typical Clark fashion, with an unruffled win in the South African GP to take his tally of World Championship Grand Prix victories to 25, overhauling the legendary Fangio's then record total. Little did the world suspect that he would never compete in a Grand Prix again. For after another enjoyable trip down-under during which he won four Tasman races from seven starts, and a Formula 2 race at Barcelona, came Hockenheim . . .

More than 25 years have passed since Clark's death, but he stands as one of the truly great drivers of any era. On the track only Ayrton Senna in modern-day racing could compare, for both drivers set the benchmark for their peers with performances that were often truly extraordinary. It is a shame that, while the brilliance of the Brazilian in the eighties and nineties has been captured for posterity, such were the times that the magnificence of Jimmy's career went largely unrecorded on moving film. Indeed interviews are also exceedingly rare, and thus those too young to have seen him race will sadly have to make do with very much second best by way of the written word.

CLARK, Jim (GB) b 4/3/1936, Kilmany, Fifeshire, Scotland – d 7/4/1968, Hockenheim Circuit, Germany

	1960							
		Championship position: 8th= Wins: 0 Pole positions: 0 Fastest laps: 0 Points scored: 8						
	Race	Circuit	No	Entrant	Tyres	Car/Engine	Comment	Q Pos/Entries
ret	DUTCH GP	Zandvoort	6	Team Lotus	D	2.5 Lotus 18-Climax 4	transmission	11/21
5	BELGIAN GP	Spa	18	Team Lotus	D	2.5 Lotus 18-Climax 4	2 laps behind	10/18
5	FRENCH GP	Reims	24	Team Lotus	D	2.5 Lotus 18-Climax 4	1 lap behind	10/23
16	BRITISH GP	Silverstone	8	Team Lotus	D	2.5 Lotus 18-Climax 4	pit stop-suspension/9 laps behind	8/25
3	PORTUGUESE GP	Oporto	14	Team Lotus	D	2.5 Lotus 18-Climax 4		8/16
16	US GP	Riverside	12	Team Lotus	D	2.5 Lotus 18-Climax 4	hit Surtees-pit stop/14 laps behind	5/23

	1961							
		Championship position: 7th= Wins: 0 Pole positions: 0 Fastest laps: 1 Points scored: 11						
10	MONACO GP	Monte Carlo	28	Team Lotus	D	1.5 Lotus 21-Climax 4	2 pit stops-plugs/-11 laps	3/21
3	DUTCH GP	Zandvoort	15	Team Lotus	D	1.5 Lotus 21-Climax 4	FL	11/17
12	BELGIAN GP	Spa	34	Team Lotus	D	1.5 Lotus 21-Climax 4	2 pit stops-gear change/-6 laps	16/25
3	FRENCH GP	Reims	8	Team Lotus	D	1.5 Lotus 21-Climax 4		5/26
ret	BRITISH GP	Aintree	18	Team Lotus	D	1.5 Lotus 21-Climax 4	oil leak	8/30
4	GERMAN GP	Nürburgring	14	Team Lotus	D	1.5 Lotus 21-Climax 4		8/27
ret	ITALIAN GP	Monza	36	Team Lotus	D	1.5 Lotus 21-Climax 4	collision with von Trips	7/33
7	US GP	Watkins Glen	14	Team Lotus	D	1.5 Lotus 21-Climax 4	pit stop-clutch/14 laps behind	=5/19

	1962							
		Championship position: 2nd Wins: 3 Pole positions: 6 Fastest laps: 5 Points scored: 30						
9	DUTCH GP	Zandvoort	4	Team Lotus	D	1.5 Lotus 25-Climax V8	pit stop-clutch/-10 laps	3/20
dns	"	"	4	Team Lotus	D	1.5 Lotus 24-Climax V8	practice only	– / –
ret	MONACO GP	Monte Carlo	18	Team Lotus	D	1.5 Lotus 25-Climax V8	clutch/FL	1/21
dns	"	"	18	Team Lotus	D	1.5 Lotus 24-Climax V8	practice only	– / –
1	BELGIAN GP	Spa	16	Team Lotus	D	1.5 Lotus 25-Climax V8	FL	12/20
dns	"	"	16	Team Lotus	D	1.5 Lotus 24-Climax V8	practice only	– / –
ret	FRENCH GP	Rouen	12	Team Lotus	D	1.5 Lotus 25-Climax V8	suspension	1/17
dns	"	"	12	Team Lotus	D	1.5 Lotus 24-Climax V8	practice only	– / –
1	BRITISH GP	Aintree	20	Team Lotus	D	1.5 Lotus 25-Climax V8	FL	1/21
dns	"	"	20	Team Lotus	D	1.5 Lotus 24-Climax V8	practice only	– / –
4	GERMAN GP	Nürburgring	5	Team Lotus	D	1.5 Lotus 25-Climax V8	stalled on grid-last away	3/30
ret	ITALIAN GP	Monza	20	Team Lotus	D	1.5 Lotus 25-Climax V8	transmission	1/30
1	US GP	Watkins Glen	8	Team Lotus	D	1.5 Lotus 25-Climax V8	FL	1/20
ret	SOUTH AFRICAN GP	East London	1	Team Lotus	D	1.5 Lotus 25-Climax V8	oil leak/FL	1/17

	1963							
		Championship position: WORLD CHAMPION Wins: 7 Pole positions: 7 Fastest laps: 6 Points scored: 73						
8/ret	MONACO GP	Monte Carlo	9	Team Lotus	D	1.5 Lotus 25-Climax V8	gear selection/22 laps behind	1/17
1	BELGIAN GP	Spa	1	Team Lotus	D	1.5 Lotus 25-Climax V8	FL	8/20
1	DUTCH GP	Zandvoort	6	Team Lotus	D	1.5 Lotus 25-Climax V8	FL	1/19
1	FRENCH GP	Reims	18	Team Lotus	D	1.5 Lotus 25-Climax V8	FL	1/21
dns	"	"	22	Team Lotus	D	1.5 Lotus 24-Climax V8	practice only	– / –
1	BRITISH GP	Silverstone	4	Team Lotus	D	1.5 Lotus 25-Climax V8		1/23
2	GERMAN GP	Nürburgring	3	Team Lotus	D	1.5 Lotus 25-Climax V8	engine on 7 cylinders/	1/26
1	ITALIAN GP	Monza	8	Team Lotus	D	1.5 Lotus 25-Climax V8	FL	3/28
3	US GP	Watkins Glen	8	Team Lotus	D	1.5 Lotus 25-Climax V8	left on the grid-battery/-1 lap /FL	2/21
1	MEXICAN GP	Mexico City	8	Team Lotus	D	1.5 Lotus 25-Climax V8	FL	1/21
1	SOUTH AFRICAN GP	East London	1	Team Lotus	D	1.5 Lotus 25-Climax V8		1/21

	1964							
		Championship position: 3rd Wins: 3 Pole positions: 5 Fastest laps: 4 Points scored: 32						
4/ret	MONACO GP	Monte Carlo	12	Team Lotus	D	1.5 Lotus 25-Climax V8	engine/4 laps behind	1/20
1	DUTCH GP	Zandvoort	18	Team Lotus	D	1.5 Lotus 25-Climax V8	FL	2/18
1	BELGIAN GP	Spa	23	Team Lotus	D	1.5 Lotus 25-Climax V8		=6/20
dns	"	"	2	Team Lotus	D	1.5 Lotus 33-Climax V8	practice only	– / –
ret	FRENCH GP	Rouen	2	Team Lotus	D	1.5 Lotus 25-Climax V8	engine/	1/17
dns	"	"	2	Team Lotus	D	1.5 Lotus 33-Climax V8	practice only	– / –

Silverstone, 1963. Clark on his way to his first World Championship, driving the Lotus 25-Climax V8 to victory in the British Grand Prix.

The dawn of a new era in Grand Prix racing at Zandvoort in 1967 as Jim Clark wins the Dutch Grand Prix with the new Ford-Cosworth-powered Lotus 49.
Battling for position behind him are Dan Gurney in the Eagle (*left*) and Chris Amon in the Ferrari.

1	BRITISH GP	Brands Hatch	1	Team Lotus	D	1.5 Lotus 25-Climax V8	*FL*	1/25
dns	"	"	1	Team Lotus	D	1.5 Lotus 33-Climax V8	*practice only*	– / –
ret	GERMAN GP	Nürburgring	1	Team Lotus	D	1.5 Lotus 33-Climax V8	*engine*	2/24
ret	AUSTRIAN GP	Zeltweg	1	Team Lotus	D	1.5 Lotus 33-Climax V8	*driveshaft*	3/20
ret	ITALIAN GP	Monza	8	Team Lotus	D	1.5 Lotus 25-Climax V8	*engine*	4/25
dns	"	"	8	Team Lotus	D	1.5 Lotus 33-Climax V8	*practice only*	– / –
ret	US GP	Watkins Glen	1	Team Lotus	D	1.5 Lotus 25-Climax V8	*fuel injection/Spence took car*	1/19
7/ret	"	"	2	Team Lotus	D	1.5 Lotus 33-Climax V8	*fuel starvation/Spence's car/FL*	– / –
5/ret	MEXICAN GP	Mexico City	1	Team Lotus	D	1.5 Lotus 33-Climax V8	*engine-oil leak//FL/-1 lap*	1/19
dns	"	"	1	Team Lotus	D	1.5 Lotus 25-Climax V8	*practice only*	– / –

1965   Championship position: WORLD CHAMPION   Wins: 6   Pole positions: 6   Fastest laps: 6   Points scored: 54

1	SOUTH AFRICAN GP	East London	5	Team Lotus	D	1.5 Lotus 33-Climax V8	*FL*	1/25
1	BELGIAN GP	Spa	17	Team Lotus	D	1.5 Lotus 33-Climax V8	*FL*	2/21
dns	"	"	17	Team Lotus	D	1.5 Lotus 33-Climax V8	*practice only*	– / –
1	FRENCH GP	Clermont Ferrand	6	Team Lotus	D	1.5 Lotus 25-Climax V8	*FL*	1/17
dns	"	"	6	Team Lotus	D	1.5 Lotus 33-Climax V8	*practice only*	– / –
1	BRITISH GP	Silverstone	5	Team Lotus	D	1.5 Lotus 33-Climax V8		1/23
dns	"	"	77	Team Lotus	D	1.5 Lotus 25-Climax V8	*practice only*	– / –
1	DUTCH GP	Zandvoort	6	Team Lotus	D	1.5 Lotus 33-Climax V8	*FL*	=2/17
1	GERMAN GP	Nürburgring	1	Team Lotus	D	1.5 Lotus 33-Climax V8	*FL*	1/22
10/ret	ITALIAN GP	Monza	24	Team Lotus	D	1.5 Lotus 33-Climax V8	*fuel pump/FL/12 laps behind*	1/23
dns	"	"	28	Team Lotus	D	1.5 Lotus 33-Climax V8	*practice only*	– / –
ret	US GP	Watkins Glen	5	Team Lotus	D	1.5 Lotus 33-Climax V8	*engine*	2/18
dns	"	"	6	Team Lotus	D	1.5 Lotus 25-Climax V8	*practice only*	– / –
ret	MEXICAN GP	Mexico City	5	Team Lotus	D	1.5 Lotus 33-Climax V8	*engine*	1/18

1966   Championship position: 6th   Wins: 0   Pole positions: 2   Fastest laps: 0   Points scored: 16

ret	MONACO GP	Monte Carlo	4	Team Lotus	F	2.0 Lotus 33-Climax V8	*suspension*	1/16
ret	BELGIAN GP	Spa	10	Team Lotus	F	2.1 Lotus 33-Climax V8	*engine*	10/18
dns	FRENCH GP	Reims	2	Team Lotus	F	2.0 Lotus 33-Climax V8	*hit in face by bird in practice*	– / –
4	BRITISH GP	Brands Hatch	1	Team Lotus	F	2.0 Lotus 33-Climax V8	*pit stop-brakes/1 lap behind*	5/20
3	DUTCH GP	Zandvoort	6	Team Lotus	F	2.0 Lotus 33-Climax V8	*2 pit stops-water/-2 laps*	=2/18
dns	"	"	8	Team Lotus	F	2.0 Lotus 33-BRM V8	*practice only*	– / –
ret	GERMAN GP	Nürburgring	1	Team Lotus	F	2.0 Lotus 33-Climax V8	*slid off road*	1/30
ret	ITALIAN GP	Monza	22	Team Lotus	F	3.0 Lotus 43-BRM H16	*gearbox*	3/22
1	US GP	Watkins Glen	1	Team Lotus	F	3.0 Lotus 43-BRM H16		2/19
dns	"	"	1/2	Team Lotus	F	2.0 Lotus 33-Climax V8	*practice only*	– / –
ret	MEXICAN GP	Mexico City	1	Team Lotus	F	3.0 Lotus 43-BRM H16	*gearbox*	2/19

1967   Championship position: 3rd   Wins: 4   Pole positions: 6   Fastest laps: 5   Points scored: 41

ret	SOUTH AFRICAN GP	Kyalami	7	Team Lotus	F	3.0 Lotus 43-BRM H16	*engine*	3/18
ret	MONACO GP	Monte Carlo	12	Team Lotus	F	2.0 Lotus 33-Climax V8	*shock absorber/FL*	=4/18
1	DUTCH GP	Zandvoort	5	Team Lotus	F	3.0 Lotus 49-Cosworth V8	*FL*	8/17
6	BELGIAN GP	Spa	21	Team Lotus	F	3.0 Lotus 49-Cosworth V8	*pit stop-plugs/1 lap behind*	1/18
ret	FRENCH GP	Le Mans	6	Team Lotus	F	3.0 Lotus 49-Cosworth V8	*cwp*	4/15
1	BRITISH GP	Silverstone	5	Team Lotus	F	3.0 Lotus 49-Cosworth V8		1/21
ret	GERMAN GP	Nürburgring	3	Team Lotus	F	3.0 Lotus 49-Cosworth V8	*suspension*	1/25
ret	CANADIAN GP	Mosport Park	3	Team Lotus	F	3.0 Lotus 49-Cosworth V8	*wet ignition/FL*	1/19
3	ITALIAN GP	Monza	20	Team Lotus	F	3.0 Lotus 49-Cosworth V8	*out of fuel last lap when 1st/FL*	1/18
1	US GP	Watkins Glen	5	Team Lotus	F	3.0 Lotus 49-Cosworth V8	*despite rear suspension failure*	2/18
1	MEXICAN GP	Mexico City	5	Team Lotus	F	3.0 Lotus 49-Cosworth V8	*FL*	1/19

1968   Championship position: 11th   Wins: 1   Pole positions: 1   Fastest laps: 1   Points scored: 9

1	SOUTH AFRICAN GP	Kyalami	4	Team Lotus	F	3.0 Lotus 49-Cosworth V8	*FL*	1/23

GP Starts: 72   GP Wins: 25   Pole positions: 33   Fastest laps: 28   Points: 274

PETER COLLINS

Peter Collins' death at the Nürburgring in August 1958, just two weeks after his wonderful performance at the British Grand Prix at Silverstone, left the racing world shocked. For although he was indisputably one of the fastest men around, he was also regarded as being one of the safest.

Handsome and congenial, the young Collins graduated from the 500 cc school, driving Coopers and then the JBS-Norton in 1951, both on the circuits and in hill-climbs, winning his class with BTD at Prescott and Shelsley Walsh.

With Formula 2 effectively becoming the premier racing class in 1952, John Heath of HWM signed the promising Collins to partner Moss and Macklin in a three-car team which roamed the Continent over the next two seasons. Peter proved to be extremely quick, but the cars were fragile and decent finishes were few and far between, though he managed a second place at Les Sables d'Olonne in 1952 and a third at the Eifelrennen the following year.

Collins' potential had been spotted by Aston Martin, who took him into their sports car squad with immediate results. Sharing a DB3 with Pat Griffiths, he won the 1952 BARC Goodwood 9 Hours and the 1953 Tourist Trophy, and he achieved many other good results (including second places at Le Mans in 1955 with Frère and in 1956 with Moss) in what was to be a very happy association with the team.

In 1954 Peter was recruited by Tony Vandervell to drive his Ferrari 'Thinwall Special', with which he was to delight British crowds in the popular Libre events of the day, winning at Snetterton and Goodwood. He was also one of the first to handle the new Vanwall Special, but at this stage it was still very much in its infancy. Having found him a constant thorn in their flesh in Libre racing, BRM signed him for a full season in 1955, but in the event their programme was behind schedule, and he mainly raced the Owen team's Maserati 250F until the P25 was ready. Late in the year Collins ran the new car in the Gold Cup at Oulton Park where it proved staggeringly quick before he retired it, erroneously as it turned out, due to a lack of oil pressure.

Peter accepted the chance to join Ferrari in 1956 alongside the great Fangio with glee, and 'the Maestro' was to have a big influence on his racing. From then on he began to take a much more serious attitude to his craft, though thankfully he never lost his fun-loving, light-hearted spirit off the track. For a new boy at the Scuderia, he settled in very quickly. After handing his machine to Fangio at Monaco, Collins took Grand Prix wins in Belgium and France and then shared second place at Silverstone. Although he drew a blank at the Nürburgring, come the Italian GP at Monza he still had an outside chance of the championship. When Fangio was forced to retire his car early in the race, Peter was asked to hand his car over to the Argentinian at a pit stop and did so without hesitation, even though it meant the end of his own title bid. His actions were particularly appreciated by Enzo Ferrari, who had a special affection for the loyal Englishman from that moment on. However, the 1957 season was not one of the Scuderia's better ones, and Peter scored Formula 1 wins only in the relatively minor Syracuse and Naples Grands Prix, and third places in France and Germany, where Fangio put on such an unforgettable display.

The following season began promisingly for Collins with sports car victories in the Buenos Aires 1000 Km and the Sebring 12 Hours, driving with Phil Hill. Peter had already raced the new Ferrari Dino 246 at the tail-end of the previous year, finishing fourth in the Modena GP, and a win in the International Trophy race at Silverstone boded well for a Ferrari revival. Arriving at the Nürburgring for the German Grand Prix, Peter lay third in the championship standings behind Mike Hawthorn and Stirling Moss, but in the race, with Tony Brooks leading in the Vanwall and Peter in hot pursuit, it seems he made a simple but costly error of judgement, clipping a bank, which somersaulted the car at over 100 mph over a hedge and down into a field. The luckless Collins was hurled from his machine, suffering severe head injuries from which he died soon after in hospital in Bonn, without regaining consciousness.

COLLINS, Peter (GB) b 6/11/1931, Kidderminster, Worcestershire – d 3/8/1958, Bonn, Germany

	Race	Circuit	No	Entrant	Tyres	Car/Engine	Comment	Q Pos/Entries
1952		Championship position: Unplaced						
ret	SWISS GP	Bremgarten	18	HW Motors Ltd	D	2.0 HWM-Alta 4	broken halfshaft-spun off	6/21
ret	BELGIAN GP	Spa	26	HW Motors Ltd	D	2.0 HWM-Alta 4	driveshaft	11/22
6	FRENCH GP	Rouen	22	HW Motors Ltd	D	2.0 HWM-Alta 4	7 laps behind	7/20
ret	BRITISH GP	Silverstone	29	HW Motors Ltd	D	2.0 HWM-Alta 4	ignition/crankshaft	14/32
dnq	GERMAN GP	Nürburgring	111	HW Motors Ltd	D	2.0 HWM-Alta 4	crankshaft insufficient practice	-/32
dnq	ITALIAN GP	Monza	54	HW Motors Ltd	D	2.0 HWM-Alta 4		28/35
1953		Championship position: Unplaced						
8	DUTCH GP	Zandvoort	36	HW Motors Ltd	D	2.0 HWM-Alta 4	6 laps behind	16/20
ret	BELGIAN GP	Spa	26	HW Motors Ltd	D	2.0 HWM-Alta 4	clutch	16/22
13	FRENCH GP	Reims	28	HW Motors Ltd	D	2.0 HWM-Alta 4	8 laps behind	17/25
ret	BRITISH GP	Silverstone	2	HW Motors Ltd	D	2.0 HWM-Alta 4	spun off	23/29
1954		Championship position: Unplaced						
ret	BRITISH GP	Silverstone	20	G A Vandervell	P	2.3 Vanwall 4	cylinder head gasket	11/31
7	ITALIAN GP	Monza	10	G A Vandervell	P	2.4 Vanwall 4	5 laps behind	16/21
dns	SPANISH GP	Pedralbes	42	G A Vandervell	P	2.4 Vanwall 4	practice accident	-/-
1955		Championship position: Unplaced						
ret	BRITISH GP	Aintree	42	Owen Racing Organisation	D	2.5 Maserati 250F 6	clutch	24/25
ret	ITALIAN GP	Monza	32	Officine Alfieri Maserati	P	2.5 Maserati 250F 6	rear suspension	11/22
1956		Championship position: 3rd Wins: 2 Pole positions: 0 Fastest laps: 0 Points scored: 25						
ret	ARGENTINE GP	Buenos Aires	36	Scuderia Ferrari	E	2.5 Ferrari 555 V8	collision with Piotti	9/15
2*	MONACO GP	Monte Carlo	26	Scuderia Ferrari	E	2.5 Lancia-Ferrari D50 V8	* Fangio took over	9/19
1	BELGIAN GP	Spa	8	Scuderia Ferrari	E	2.5 Lancia-Ferrari D50 V8		3/16
1	FRENCH GP	Reims	14	Scuderia Ferrari	E	2.5 Lancia-Ferrari D50 V8		3/20
ret	BRITISH GP	Silverstone	2	Scuderia Ferrari	E	2.5 Lancia-Ferrari D50 V8	oil pressure	4/28
2*	"	"	4	Scuderia Ferrari	E	2.5 Lancia-Ferrari D50 V8	* took de Portago's car/-1 lap	-/-
ret	GERMAN GP	Nürburgring	2	Scuderia Ferrari	E	2.5 Lancia-Ferrari D50 V8	split fuel pipe	2/21
ret*	"	"	5	Scuderia Ferrari	E	2.5 Lancia-Ferrari D50 V8	* took de Portago's car/accident	-/-
2*	ITALIAN GP	Monza	26	Scuderia Ferrari	E	2.5 Lancia-Ferrari D50 V8	* Fangio took over	7/26
1957		Championship position: 7th= Wins: 0 Pole positions: 0 Fastest laps: 0 Points scored: 8						
ret	ARGENTINE GP	Buenos Aires	10	Scuderia Ferrari	E	2.5 Lancia-Ferrari D50 V8	clutch	5/16
6*	"	"	18	Scuderia Ferrari	E	2.5 Lancia-Ferrari D50 V8	* Perdisa & von Trips/-2 laps	-/-
ret	MONACO GP	Monte Carlo	26	Scuderia Ferrari	E	2.5 Lancia-Ferrari 801 V8	accident with Moss & Hawthorn	2/21
dns	"	"	26	Scuderia Ferrari	E	2.5 Lancia-Ferrari D50 V8	practice only	-/-
3	FRENCH GP	Rouen	12	Scuderia Ferrari	E	2.5 Lancia-Ferrari 801 V8		5/15
ret	BRITISH GP	Aintree	12	Scuderia Ferrari	E	2.5 Lancia-Ferrari 801 V8	water leak/took Trintignant's car	8/19
4*	"	"	16	Scuderia Ferrari	E	2.5 Lancia-Ferrari 801 V8	*only 4 laps-no points awarded	-/-
3	GERMAN GP	Nürburgring	7	Scuderia Ferrari	E	2.5 Lancia-Ferrari 801 V8		4/24
ret	ITALIAN GP	Monza	30	Scuderia Ferrari	E	2.5 Lancia-Ferrari 801 V8	engine	7/19
1958		Championship position: 5th= Wins: 1 Pole positions: 0 Fastest laps: 0 Points scored: 14						
ret	ARGENTINE GP	Buenos Aires	18	Scuderia Ferrari	E	2.4 Ferrari Dino 246 V6	rear axle on grid	3/10
3	MONACO GP	Monte Carlo	36	Scuderia Ferrari	E	2.4 Ferrari Dino 246 V6		9/28
ret	DUTCH GP	Zandvoort	4	Scuderia Ferrari	E	2.4 Ferrari Dino 246 V6	gearbox seized-spun off	10/17
ret	BELGIAN GP	Spa	14	Scuderia Ferrari	E	2.4 Ferrari Dino 246 V6	engine-overheating	4/20
5	FRENCH GP	Reims	42	Scuderia Ferrari	E	2.4 Ferrari Dino 246 V6	out of fuel last lap	4/21
1	BRITISH GP	Silverstone	1	Scuderia Ferrari	E	2.4 Ferrari Dino 246 V6		6/21
ret	GERMAN GP	Nürburgring	2	Scuderia Ferrari	E	2.4 Ferrari Dino 246 V6	fatal accident	4/26

GP Starts: 32   GP Wins: 3   Pole positions: 0   Fastest laps: 0   Points: 47

Peter put in a flawless display to win the 1958 British Grand Prix at Silverstone in the Ferrari 246 Dino V6. Two weeks later he was killed in the German Grand Prix.

BERNARD COLLOMB

A former motor cycle racer from Nice, Collomb acquired a Cooper-Climax Formula 2 car which he raced briefly in 1960, embarking on a more ambitious programme of F1 races the following year. Fourth at Vienna and sixth at Naples were his best results in the car, which was replaced in mid-season by a new Cooper T53 with no discernible improvement in his results. Unfortunately this car was burnt out in practice for the 1962 Brussels GP, but Bernard reappeared in mid-1962 with another Cooper, achieving fifth place in the Mediterranean GP at Enna.

Collomb then bought himself a Lotus 24-Climax V8 for 1963, but he was ill-equipped to drive it to its full potential. It was given occasional unsuccessful outings in 1964 before being destroyed by fire on the way back to France from the 1965 Syracuse GP, where he had finished seventh. A Lotus 35 F2 car was then purchased which again saw little action after Collomb crashed it in the 1966 Barcelona F2 race. By the 1968 season he had wisely given up thoughts of success in single-seaters and could be found racing the little Alpine GT car.

COLLOMB, Bernard (F) b 7/10/1930

	1961			Championship position: Unplaced					
	Race	Circuit	No	Entrant	Tyres	Car/Engine	Comment	Q Pos/Entries
ret	FRENCH GP	Reims	52	Bernard Collomb	D	1.5 Cooper T53-Climax 4	valve	21/26
ret	GERMAN GP	Nürburgring	38	Bernard Collomb	D	1.5 Cooper T53-Climax 4	engine	26/27
	1962			Championship position: Unplaced					
ret	GERMAN GP	Nürburgring	31	Bernard Collomb	D	1.5 Cooper T53-Climax 4	gearbox	22/30
	1963			Championship position: Unplaced					
dnq	MONACO GP	Monte Carlo	24	Bernard Collomb	D	1.5 Lotus 24-Climax V8		17/17
10	GERMAN GP	Nürburgring	28	Bernard Collomb	D	1.5 Lotus 24-Climax V8	5 laps behind	21/26
	1964			Championship position: Unplaced					
dnq	MONACO GP	Monte Carlo	3	Bernard Collomb	D	1.5 Lotus 24-Climax V8		20/20

GP Starts: 4   GP Wins: 0   Pole positions: 0   Fastest laps: 0   Points: 0

COMAS, Érik (F) b 28/9/1963, Romans, nr Valence

	1991			Championship position: Unplaced					
	Race	Circuit	No	Entrant	Tyres	Car/Engine	Comment	Q Pos/Entries
dnq	US GP (PHOENIX)	Phoenix	26	Ligier Gitanes	G	3.5 Ligier JS35-Lamborghini V12		27/34
ret	BRAZILIAN GP	Interlagos	26	Ligier Gitanes	G	3.5 Ligier JS35-Lamborghini V12	spun off	23/34
10	SAN MARINO GP	Imola	26	Ligier Gitanes	G	3.5 Ligier JS35-Lamborghini V12	4 laps behind	19/34
10	MONACO GP	Monte Carlo	26	Ligier Gitanes	G	3.5 Ligier JS35-Lamborghini V12	2 laps behind	23/34
8	CANADIAN GP	Montreal	26	Ligier Gitanes	G	3.5 Ligier JS35-Lamborghini V12	1 lap behind	26/34
dnq	MEXICAN GP	Mexico City	26	Ligier Gitanes	G	3.5 Ligier JS35-Lamborghini V12		27/34
11	FRENCH GP	Magny Cours	26	Ligier Gitanes	G	3.5 Ligier JS35B-Lamborghini V12	2 laps behind	14/34
dnq	BRITISH GP	Silverstone	26	Ligier Gitanes	G	3.5 Ligier JS35B-Lamborghini V12		27/34
ret	GERMAN GP	Hockenheim	26	Ligier Gitanes	G	3.5 Ligier JS35B-Lamborghini V12	engine-oil pressure	26/34
10	HUNGARIAN GP	Hungaroring	26	Ligier Gitanes	G	3.5 Ligier JS35B-Lamborghini V12	2 laps behind	25/34
ret	BELGIAN GP	Spa	26	Ligier Gitanes	G	3.5 Ligier JS35B-Lamborghini V12	engine	26/34
11	ITALIAN GP	Monza	26	Ligier Gitanes	G	3.5 Ligier JS35B-Lamborghini V12	1 lap behind	22/34
11	PORTUGUESE GP	Estoril	26	Ligier Gitanes	G	3.5 Ligier JS35B-Lamborghini V12	1 lap behind	23/34
ret	SPANISH GP	Barcelona	26	Ligier Gitanes	G	3.5 Ligier JS35B-Lamborghini V12	electrics	25/33
ret	JAPANESE GP	Suzuka	26	Ligier Gitanes	G	3.5 Ligier JS35B-Lamborghini V12	alternator	20/31
18	AUSTRALIAN GP	Adelaide	26	Ligier Gitanes	G	3.5 Ligier JS35B-Lamborghini V12	rain shortened race/-1 lap	22/32
	1992			Championship position: 11th Wins: 0 Pole positions: 0 Fastest laps: 0 Points scored: 4					
7	SOUTH AFRICAN GP	Kyalami	26	Ligier Gitanes Blondes	G	3.5 Ligier JS37-Renault V10	lack of downforce/-2 laps	13/30
9	MEXICAN GP	Mexico City	26	Ligier Gitanes Blondes	G	3.5 Ligier JS37-Renault V10	2 laps behind	26/30
ret	BRAZILIAN GP	Interlagos	26	Ligier Gitanes Blondes	G	3.5 Ligier JS37-Renault V10	engine	15/31
ret	SPANISH GP	Barcelona	26	Ligier Gitanes Blondes	G	3.5 Ligier JS37-Renault V10	spun off	10/32
9	SAN MARINO GP	Imola	26	Ligier Gitanes Blondes	G	3.5 Ligier JS37-Renault V10	2 laps behind	13/32
10	MONACO GP	Monte Carlo	26	Ligier Gitanes Blondes	G	3.5 Ligier JS37-Renault V10	2 laps behind	23/32
6	CANADIAN GP	Montreal	26	Ligier Gitanes Blondes	G	3.5 Ligier JS37-Renault V10	1 lap behind	22/32
5	FRENCH GP	Magny Cours	26	Ligier Gitanes Blondes	G	3.5 Ligier JS37-Renault V10	1 lap behind	10/30
8	BRITISH GP	Silverstone	26	Ligier Gitanes Blondes	G	3.5 Ligier JS37-Renault V10	1 lap behind	10/32
6	GERMAN GP	Hockenheim	26	Ligier Gitanes Blondes	G	3.5 Ligier JS37-Renault V10		7/32
ret	HUNGARIAN GP	Hungaroring	26	Ligier Gitanes Blondes	G	3.5 Ligier JS37-Renault V10	collision with Boutsen lap 1	11/31
dnp	BELGIAN GP	Spa	26	Ligier Gitanes Blondes	G	3.5 Ligier JS37-Renault V10	accident in untimed practice	– /30
ret	ITALIAN GP	Monza	26	Ligier Gitanes Blondes	G	3.5 Ligier JS37-Renault V10	spun off	15/28
ret	PORTUGUESE GP	Estoril	26	Ligier Gitanes Blondes	G	3.5 Ligier JS37-Renault V10	over-revved engine	14/26
ret	JAPANESE GP	Suzuka	26	Ligier Gitanes Blondes	G	3.5 Ligier JS37-Renault V10	engine-oil pressure	8/26
ret	AUSTRALIAN GP	Adelaide	26	Ligier Gitanes Blondes	G	3.5 Ligier JS37-Renault V10	over-revved engine	9/26
	1993			Championship position: 20th= Wins: 0 Pole positions: 0 Fastest laps: 0 Points scored: 1					
ret	SOUTH AFRICAN GP	Kyalami	20	Larrousse F1	G	3.5 Larrousse LH93-Lamborghini V12	engine	19/26
10	BRAZILIAN GP	Interlagos	20	Larrousse F1	G	3.5 Larrousse LH93-Lamborghini V12	stop & go penalty/-2 laps	17/26
9	EUROPEAN GP	Donington	20	Larrousse F1	G	3.5 Larrousse LH93-Lamborghini V12	4 laps behind	17/26
ret	SAN MARINO GP	Imola	20	Larrousse F1	G	3.5 Larrousse LH93-Lamborghini V12	no oil pressure	17/26
9	SPANISH GP	Barcelona	20	Larrousse F1	G	3.5 Larrousse LH93-Lamborghini V12	2 laps behind	14/26
ret	MONACO GP	Monte Carlo	20	Larrousse F1	G	3.5 Larrousse LH93-Lamborghini V12	collision with Brundle	10/26

8	CANADIAN GP	Montreal	20	Larrousse F1		G	3.5 Larrousse LH93-Lamborghini V12	1 lap behind	13/26
16/ret	FRENCH GP	Magny Cours	20	Larrousse F1		G	3.5 Larrousse LH93-Lamborghini V12	gearbox/6 laps behind	9/26
ret	BRITISH GP	Silverstone	20	Larrousse F1		G	3.5 Larrousse LH93-Lamborghini V12	driveshaft at start	17/26
ret	GERMAN GP	Hockenheim	20	Larrousse F1		G	3.5 Larrousse LH93-Lamborghini V12	clutch at start	16/26
ret	HUNGARIAN GP	Hungaroring	20	Larrousse F1		G	3.5 Larrousse LH93-Lamborghini V12	oil leak	18/26
ret	BELGIAN GP	Spa	20	Larrousse F1		G	3.5 Larrousse LH93-Lamborghini V12	fuel pump/oil pressure	19/25
6	ITALIAN GP	Monza	20	Larrousse F1		G	3.5 Larrousse LH93-Lamborghini V12	2 laps behind	20/26
11	PORTUGUESE GP	Estoril	20	Larrousse F1		G	3.5 Larrousse LH93-Lamborghini V12	3 laps behind	22/26
ret	JAPANESE GP	Suzuka	20	Larrousse F1		G	3.5 Larrousse LH93-Lamborghini V12	engine	21/24
12	AUSTRALIAN GP	Adelaide	20	Larrousse F1		G	3.5 Larrousse LH93-Lamborghini V12	3 laps behind	21/24
1994		Championship position: 23rd		Wins: 0	Pole positions: 0	Fastest laps: 0	Points scored: 2		
9	BRAZILIAN GP	Interlagos	20	Tourtel Larrousse F1		G	3.5 Larrousse LH94-Ford HB V8	3 laps behind	13/28
6	PACIFIC GP	T.I. Circuit	20	Tourtel Larrousse F1		G	3.5 Larrousse LH94-Ford HB V8	collision-pit stop/-2 laps	16/28
ret	SAN MARINO GP	Imola	20	Tourtel Larrousse F1		G	3.5 Larrousse LH94-Ford HB V8	did not take part in restart	18/28
10	MONACO GP	Monte Carlo	20	Tourtel Larrousse F1		G	3.5 Larrousse LH94-Ford HB V8	lost clutch/3 laps behind	13/24
ret	SPANISH GP	Barcelona	20	Tourtel Larrousse F1		G	3.5 Larrousse LH94-Ford HB V8	water leak	16/27
ret	CANADIAN GP	Montreal	20	Tourtel Larrousse F1		G	3.5 Larrousse LH94-Ford HB V8	clutch	21/27
ret	FRENCH GP	Magny Cours	20	Tourtel Larrousse F1		G	3.5 Larrousse LH94-Ford HB V8	engine	20/28
ret	BRITISH GP	Silverstone	20	Tourtel Larrousse F1		G	3.5 Larrousse LH94-Ford HB V8	engine	22/28
6	GERMAN GP	Hockenheim	20	Tourtel Larrousse F1		G	3.5 Larrousse LH94-Ford HB V8		22/28
8	HUNGARIAN GP	Hungaroring	20	Tourtel Larrousse F1		G	3.5 Larrousse LH94-Ford HB V8	2 laps behind	21/28
ret	BELGIAN GP	Spa	20	Tourtel Larrousse F1		G	3.5 Larrousse LH94-Ford HB V8	engine	22/28
8	ITALIAN GP	Monza	20	Tourtel Larrousse F1		G	3.5 Larrousse LH94-Ford HB V8	1 lap behind	24/28
ret	PORTUGUESE GP	Estoril	20	Tourtel Larrousse F1		G	3.5 Larrousse LH94-Ford HB V8	accident	22/28
ret	EUROPEAN GP	Jerez	20	Tourtel Larrousse F1		G	3.5 Larrousse LH94-Ford HB V8	electrics	23/28
9	JAPANESE GP	Suzuka	20	Tourtel Larrousse F1		G	3.5 Larrousse LH94-Ford HB V8	1 lap behind	22/28

GP Starts: 59　GP Wins: 0　Pole positions: 0　Fastest laps: 0　Points: 7

ÉRIK COMAS

With Jean Alesi and Éric Bernard, Comas is one of a trio of French drivers whose careers were closely intertwined as they made inexorable progress into Formula 1 along the French motor racing conveyor-belt, but ultimately only Alesi stayed the course.

A French karting champion in 1983, Érik was soon sampling cars, racing a Renault 5 previously driven by Alesi, with which he won the Volant Elf at Paul Ricard, then moving up to Formule Renault as number two to Bernard in 1985. Scoring consistently, he finished second on points to his team-mate but only fourth overall after his lowest scores had been discounted, but he made no mistake a year later.

This led to a seat in the Winfield team in the national Formula 3 series in 1987, but Comas found himself as number two to Bernard once more and was somewhat overshadowed, though he did finish sixth in the final placings. Érik also took the chance to compete in the French Superproduction category, and immensely enjoyed pitting himself against old hands such as Jabouille and Jarier in the powerful 400 bhp machines.

For 1988, he was chosen to lead the ORECA team, normally an absolute guarantee of success in French F3. Comas delivered, but only just, pipping Éric Cheli to the title after a fraught season spent developing the team's Dallara. However, the job was done and once again he followed Bernard on the upward path, joining him in the DAMS F3000 team for the 1989 season. After a slow start, Comas soon shone and by the season's end it was his turn to outshine his team-mate. Two wins at Le Mans and Dijon brought him level with Alesi at the top of the points standings, but Jean was champion by virtue of an extra win. Érik finished the job in 1990; still with DAMS, but now number one driver, he won four of the 11 rounds, and now he was ready for Formula 1.

On paper, a two-year contract with Ligier alongside the experienced Thierry Boutsen seemed to be ideal. The first season with the Lamborghini-engined car would allow Érik a chance to learn the ropes and the second, 1992, with Renault power, would put him in the front rank. The best-laid plans do not always work out, however, and with the team already split into factions, any potential assets it held had been dissipated, while Érik's working relationship with Boutsen was such that they were barely on speaking terms.

For the 1993 and 1994 seasons he found refuge in the Larrousse team, making the best of a car run on very meagre resources. His sixth place at Monza in '93 was a fine achievement, but with the shortage of top seats in Formula 1 and a whole new generation of chargers knocking on the door, Comas had missed his big chance to make it to the very top. Personally he felt that Elf, who do so much for French drivers in the junior formulae, should have insisted that at least one of his compatriots be given an opportunity in a front-running team.

Érik subsequently found employment (and immediate success) driving in the All-Japan GT championship in a Toyota Supra in 1996, which led to an offer by Nissan to race their Skyline GT model alongside Aguri Suzuki in 1997. Comas rapidly became a key member of the NISMO team and was crowned All-Japan GT champion in 1998 and 1999. He has also been involved with the TWR-run Nissan prototype challenge, finishing sixth at Le Mans in 1998 with the R390 and winning the Fuji 1000 Km (with Motoyama and Kagayama) in 1999 with the R391.

GIANFRANCO COMOTTI

Franco's best days were pre-war, when he raced an Alfa Romeo and a Lago-Talbot with some success. He won the 1933 Naples GP in the former, and came close to winning the 1937 French GP at Reims in the latter. After leading he had to settle for second place behind Chiron.

After hostilities ceased he made a return to competition, moving to France to join the Ecurie France team to race their Lago-Talbots. These trusty machines were certainly not the fleetest, but they were reliable, and Comotti brought the car into fourth place in the 1948 French GP, some nine miles adrift of the winner. He also finished seventh in the Italian GP in Turin.

Back in Italy he linked up with the Ruggeri brothers to race their latest Maserati-based Milano car in 1950, but due to lack of funds these machines were never properly developed and Comotti left to join Scuderia Marzotto. In 1951, he finished second at Grenzlandring in a Ferrari 166 F2, and the following year he raced even more regularly for the team, with third in the Naples GP and sixth at Syracuse his best finishes. Franco also made a one-off Maserati appearance for the Escuderia Bandeirantes at AVUS before bringing his career, which had stretched back for more than two decades, to a close. Subsequently Comotti worked on the Continent with the oil and petroleum giant BP.

GEORGE CONSTANTINE

A very successful driver in SCCA events, Constantine drove his production  Jaguar XK120 in east coast races in the early 1950s. He then progressed to more powerful machinery, winning the 1956 Watkins Glen GP in a Jaguar D-Type. The 1959 season was his most successful, Constantine scoring many wins in an Aston Martin DBR2, including the Nassau Trophy, to earn the USSC Driver of the Year award with Walt Hansgen. It was not surprising, therefore, that he was one of the local attractions in the inaugural US Grand Prix at Sebring in a rented Cooper. His career continued into the early sixties, the veteran finishing fifth (and winning his class) in the 1962 Daytona 3 Hours.

JOHN CORDTS

Cordts enjoyed some success in the mid-sixties racing sports cars in his native Canada. He took a fifth place in the 1966 Player's 200 at Mosport and once he got his hands on a McLaren M2B results in the USRRC championship improved. A couple of outings in Can-Am in 1968 encouraged Cordts to become a regular in this series between 1969 and 1974, driving a succession of Chevrolet-powered McLarens. By far his best result was a second place in the Road America round at Elkhart Lake in 1974, but by this time the once vibrant series had lost much of its credibility.

COMOTTI, Gianfranco (I) b 24/7/1906, Brescia – d 10/5/1963, Bergamo

	1950	Championship position: Unplaced						
	Race	Circuit	No	Entrant	Tyres	Car/Engine	Comment	Q Pos/Entries
ret	ITALIAN GP	Monza	62	Scuderia Milano	P	1.5 s/c Milano 01-Speluzzi 4	engine	26/27
	1952	Championship position: Unplaced						
12	FRENCH GP	Rouen	38	Scuderia Marzotto	P	2.0 Ferrari 166 V12	14 laps behind	18/20

GP Starts: 2   GP Wins: 0   Pole positions: 0   Fastest laps: 0   Points: 0

CONSTANTINE, George (USA) b 22/2/1918

	1959	Championship position: Unplaced						
	Race	Circuit	No	Entrant	Tyres	Car/Engine	Comment	Q Pos/Entries
ret	US GP	Sebring	16	Mike Taylor	D	2.5 Cooper T45-Climax 4	head gasket	15/19

GP Starts: 1   GP Wins: 0   Pole positions: 0   Fastest laps: 0   Points: 0

CORDTS, John (CDN) b 23/7/1935

	1969	Championship position: Unplaced						
	Race	Circuit	No	Entrant	Tyres	Car/Engine	Comment	Q Pos/Entries
ret	CANADIAN GP	Mosport Park	26	Paul Seitz	D	2.7 Brabham BT23B-Climax 4	oil leak	19/20

GP Starts: 1   GP Wins: 0   Pole positions: 0   Fastest laps: 0   Points: 0

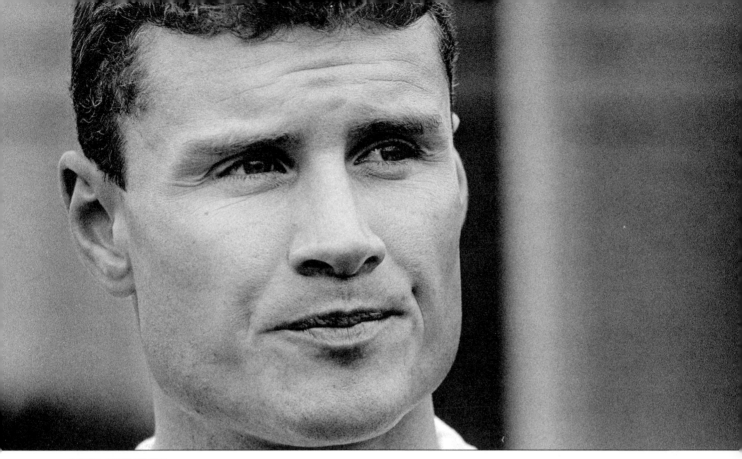

DAVID COULTHARD

With great parental encouragement, David was driving karts by the age of eight and was such a natural that it was inevitable that he would go racing. His breakthrough came in 1989, with his move into junior Formula Ford 1600. He dominated both championships, and joined Paul Stewart Racing in 1990 to contest the British Vauxhall Lotus Challenge and GM Lotus Euroseries. He could possibly have won the former, but a broken leg sustained in an accident at Spa stymied the young Scot's chances, and he ended up a disappointed fourth overall.

Staying with PSR in 1991, Coulthard moved up to Formula 3, and waged a season-long battle with Rubens Barrichello. Despite winning five rounds (one more than the Brazilian), he had to be content with the runner-up spot. There was, however, the satisfaction of winning the prestigious European Marlboro Masters of Formula 3 race at Zandvoort and he followed this up with a stunning drive to win the end-of-season race at Macau – proof indeed that David was truly a star in the making.

Perhaps expectations were too high as he took the step up to F3000 for 1992 and for a while the Scot struggled to find his feet, but by the end of the year he was on the podium and looking a good bet for honours in 1993 with a switch to the Pacific team. A first win was duly delivered at Enna, but his season tailed off somewhat thereafter. By this time David had had a number of outings as a test driver for the Williams-Renault team and he quickly impressed all at Didcot with his positive feedback.

He was appointed the team's official test driver for 1994 and was contemplating a third year in F3000 at the season-opener at Silverstone when the dreadful news of Senna's death came from Imola. David overcame his shock to take second place in that race before stepping into the Grand Prix arena and, in the inevitable turmoil that followed, displayed remarkable maturity for one so inexperienced.

Relaxed and easy off track, he showed tremendous poise behind the wheel. Always aware of the need for him to back Damon Hill's title bid, David was the perfect team-mate and, given his performances, must have been disappointed to have to surrender his seat to Nigel Mansell for the last three races of the year. The uncertainty regarding his immediate future was clearly unsettling for Coulthard, who hedged his bets and signed a contract with McLaren for 1995. In the event a tribunal confirmed that he would remain at Williams but his early-season form was decidedly patchy. He was constantly troubled by tonsillitis and it was only after his tonsils were removed that his real ability became apparent. David would have won the British Grand Prix but for a stop–go penalty incurred through no fault of his own, but his dream of a Grand Prix win was finally realised with a truly dominant performance at Estoril. On the debit side, though, he tended to make a number of elementary mistakes which cost him dear, culminating in the embarrassment of sliding into the wall on the pit lane entry in Adelaide.

David was free to move to McLaren for 1996, but all his innate self-assurance was needed during a difficult first full season with the team. Uncomfortable with the handling of the car, he was often a tad slower than team-mate Mika Häkkinen and, apart from being unlucky not to win in Monaco, generally delivered less than he promised.

The 1997 season began in the best possible fashion with a win in Australia which signified that McLaren were back after three lean years, and it was generally a much more convincing campaign for the Scot, who was evenly matched with Häkkinen and, having scored another victory at Monza, stepped aside to allow his team-mate to win the season's finale at Jerez.

He did the same in the 1998 Australian Grand Prix after a pre-race agreement and in some ways it proved to be his undoing. Häkkinen upped his game as the season progressed to mount his successful championship bid and David was left to play the subordinate role in the team. This pattern was to continue in 1999, with the often unlucky Coulthard too rarely making the absolute most of his equipment. On his day he had the legs of everybody, and no one could catch him at Spa, Magny Cours or Sepang, but only the first of these races brought him the win he deserved.

For David, the reality appears to be that he is not quite on the same level as Häkkinen or Michael Schumacher, but there should be no shame in that, for he is still a very talented driver with much to offer. His fifth season with McLaren could be crucial to the Scot's future. Whether he remains among the elite group contesting the championship, or ultimately slips down the grid to join the also-rans, is very much in his own hands.

David's first Formula 1 win came in the 1995 Portuguese Grand Prix at Estoril.
Right: He leads Williams team-mate Damon Hill and the Benetton of Michael Schumacher in the early stages of the race.

COULTHARD, David (GB) b 27/3/71, Twynholm, Kirkcudbright, Scotland

	1994	Championship position: 8th	Wins: 0	Pole positions: 0	Fastest laps: 2	Points scored: 14		
	Race	Circuit	No	Entrant	Tyres	Car/Engine	Comment	Q Pos/Entries
ret	SPANISH GP	Barcelona	2	Rothmans Williams Renault	G	3.5 Williams FW16-Renault V10	electrics	9/27
5	CANADIAN GP	Montreal	2	Rothmans Williams Renault	G	3.5 Williams FW16-Renault V10	1 lap behind	5/27
5*	BRITISH GP	Silverstone	2	Rothmans Williams Renault	G	3.5 Williams FW16-Renault V10	*2nd place car dsq/-1 lap	7/28
ret	GERMAN GP	Hockenheim	2	Rothmans Williams Renault	G	3.5 Williams FW16B-Renault V10	electrics/FL	6/28
ret	HUNGARIAN GP	Hungaroring	2	Rothmans Williams Renault	G	3.5 Williams FW16B-Renault V10	spun off	3/28
4*	BELGIAN GP	Spa	2	Rothmans Williams Renault	G	3.5 Williams FW16B-Renault V10	* 1st place car dsq	7/28
6/ret	ITALIAN GP	Monza	2	Rothmans Williams Renault	G	3.5 Williams FW16B-Renault V10	out of fuel when 2nd/-1 lap	5/28
2	PORTUGUESE GP	Estoril	2	Rothmans Williams Renault	G	3.5 Williams FW16B-Renault V10	FL	3/28

	1995	Championship position: 3rd	Wins: 1	Pole positions: 5	Fastest laps: 2	Points scored: 49		
2	BRAZILIAN GP	Interlagos	6	Rothmans Williams Renault	G	3.0 Williams FW17-Renault V10		3/26
ret	ARGENTINE GP	Buenos Aires	6	Rothmans Williams Renault	G	3.0 Williams FW17-Renault V10	clutch	1/26
4	SAN MARINO GP	Imola	6	Rothmans Williams Renault	G	3.0 Williams FW17-Renault V10		3/26
ret	SPANISH GP	Barcelona	6	Rothmans Williams Renault	G	3.0 Williams FW17-Renault V10	gearbox	4/26
ret	MONACO GP	Monte Carlo	6	Rothmans Williams Renault	G	3.0 Williams FW17-Renault V10	gearbox	3/26
ret	CANADIAN GP	Montreal	6	Rothmans Williams Renault	G	3.0 Williams FW17-Renault V10	spun off on lap 1	3/24
3	FRENCH GP	Magny Cours	6	Rothmans Williams Renault	G	3.0 Williams FW17-Renault V10		3/24
3	BRITISH GP	Silverstone	6	Rothmans Williams Renault	G	3.0 Williams FW17-Renault V10	stop & go penalty/speeding in pits	3/24
2	GERMAN GP	Hockenheim	6	Rothmans Williams Renault	G	3.0 Williams FW17-Renault V10		3/24
2	HUNGARIAN GP	Hungaroring	6	Rothmans Williams Renault	G	3.0 Williams FW17-Renault V10		2/24
ret	BELGIAN GP	Spa	6	Rothmans Williams Renault	G	3.0 Williams FW17-Renault V10	gearbox/FL	5/24
ret	ITALIAN GP	Monza	6	Rothmans Williams Renault	G	3.0 Williams FW17-Renault V10	wheel bearing	1/24
1	PORTUGUESE GP	Estoril	6	Rothmans Williams Renault	G	3.0 Williams FW17-Renault V10	FL	1/24
3	EUROPEAN GP	Nürburgring	6	Rothmans Williams Renault	G	3.0 Williams FW17B-Renault V10		1/24
2	PACIFIC GP	T.I. Circuit	6	Rothmans Williams Renault	G	3.0 Williams FW17B-Renault V10		1/24
ret	JAPANESE GP	Suzuka	6	Rothmans Williams Renault	G	3.0 Williams FW17B-Renault V10	spun off	6/24
ret	AUSTRALIAN GP	Adelaide	6	Rothmans Williams Renault	G	3.0 Williams FW17B-Renault V10	hit barrier on pit-lane entry	2/24

	1996	Championship position: 7th	Wins: 0	Pole positions: 0	Fastest laps: 0	Points scored: 18		
ret	AUSTRALIAN GP	Melbourne	8	Marlboro McLaren Mercedes	G	3.0 McLaren MP4/11-Mercedes V10	started from pits/stuck throttle	13/22
ret	BRAZILIAN GP	Interlagos	8	Marlboro McLaren Mercedes	G	3.0 McLaren MP4/11-Mercedes V10	spun off	14/22
7	ARGENTINE GP	Buenos Aires	8	Marlboro McLaren Mercedes	G	3.0 McLaren MP4/11-Mercedes V10		9/22
3	EUROPEAN GP	Nürburgring	8	Marlboro McLaren Mercedes	G	3.0 McLaren MP4/11-Mercedes V10		6/22
ret	SAN MARINO GP	Imola	8	Marlboro McLaren Mercedes	G	3.0 McLaren MP4/11-Mercedes V10	led early race/hydraulic failure	4/22
2	MONACO GP	Monte Carlo	8	Marlboro McLaren Mercedes	G	3.0 McLaren MP4/11-Mercedes V10		5/22
ret	SPANISH GP	Barcelona	8	Marlboro McLaren Mercedes	G	3.0 McLaren MP4/11-Mercedes V10	collision with Lamy at start	14/22
4	CANADIAN GP	Montreal	8	Marlboro McLaren Mercedes	G	3.0 McLaren MP4/11-Mercedes V10		10/22
6	FRENCH GP	Magny Cours	8	Marlboro McLaren Mercedes	G	3.0 McLaren MP4/11-Mercedes V10	1 lap behind	7/22
5	BRITISH GP	Silverstone	8	Marlboro McLaren Mercedes	G	3.0 McLaren MP4/11-Mercedes V10		9/22
5	GERMAN GP	Hockenheim	8	Marlboro McLaren Mercedes	G	3.0 McLaren MP4/11-Mercedes V10		7/20
ret	HUNGARIAN GP	Hungaroring	8	Marlboro McLaren Mercedes	G	3.0 McLaren MP4/11-Mercedes V10	engine	9/20
ret	BELGIAN GP	Spa	8	Marlboro McLaren Mercedes	G	3.0 McLaren MP4/11-Mercedes V10	spun off	4/20
ret	ITALIAN GP	Monza	8	Marlboro McLaren Mercedes	G	3.0 McLaren MP4/11-Mercedes V10	suspension damage-spun off	5/20
13	PORTUGUESE GP	Estoril	8	Marlboro McLaren Mercedes	G	3.0 McLaren MP4/11-Mercedes V10	collision-Häkkinen/-2 laps	8/20
8	JAPANESE GP	Suzuka	8	Marlboro McLaren Mercedes	G	3.0 McLaren MP4/11-Mercedes V10	collision with Diniz	8/20

1997
Championship position: 3rd=   Wins: 2   Pole positions: 0   Fastest laps: 1   Points scored: 36

Pos	Race	Circuit	No	Team		Car/Engine	Notes	Grid
1	AUSTRALIAN GP	Melbourne	10	West McLaren Mercedes	G	3.0 McLaren MP4/12-Mercedes V10		4/24
10	BRAZILIAN GP	Interlagos	10	West McLaren Mercedes	G	3.0 McLaren MP4/12-Mercedes V10	1 lap behind	12/22
ret	ARGENTINE GP	Buenos Aires	10	West McLaren Mercedes	G	3.0 McLaren MP4/12-Mercedes V10	collision with Ralf Schumacher	10/22
ret	SAN MARINO GP	Imola	10	West McLaren Mercedes	G	3.0 McLaren MP4/12-Mercedes V10	engine	10/22
ret	MONACO GP	Monte Carlo	10	West McLaren Mercedes	G	3.0 McLaren MP4/12-Mercedes V10	spun off on lap 1	6/22
6	SPANISH GP	Barcelona	10	West McLaren Mercedes	G	3.0 McLaren MP4/12-Mercedes V10	tyre problems	3/22
7	CANADIAN GP	Montreal	10	West McLaren Mercedes	G	3.0 McLaren MP4/12-Mercedes V10	led race-gear problems at stop/FL	5/22
7/ret	FRENCH GP	Magny Cours	10	West McLaren Mercedes	G	3.0 McLaren MP4/12-Mercedes V10	rammed off by Alesi/-1 lap	9/22
4	BRITISH GP	Silverstone	10	West McLaren Mercedes	G	3.0 McLaren MP4/12-Mercedes V10		6/22
ret	GERMAN GP	Hockenheim	10	West McLaren Mercedes	G	3.0 McLaren MP4/12-Mercedes V10	transmission	8/22
ret	HUNGARIAN GP	Hungaroring	10	West McLaren Mercedes	G	3.0 McLaren MP4/12-Mercedes V10	alternator	8/22
ret	BELGIAN GP	Spa	10	West McLaren Mercedes	G	3.0 McLaren MP4/12-Mercedes V10	spun off in wet on slicks	10/22
1	ITALIAN GP	Monza	10	West McLaren Mercedes	G	3.0 McLaren MP4/12-Mercedes V10		6/22
2	AUSTRIAN GP	A1-Ring	10	West McLaren Mercedes	G	3.0 McLaren MP4/12-Mercedes V10		10/22
ret	LUXEMBOURG GP	Nürburgring	10	West McLaren Mercedes	G	3.0 McLaren MP4/12-Mercedes V10	engine	6/22
10*/ret	JAPANESE GP	Suzuka	10	West McLaren Mercedes	G	3.0 McLaren MP4/12-Mercedes V10	* 5th car dsq/engine/-1 lap	6/22
2	EUROPEAN GP	Jerez	10	West McLaren Mercedes	G	3.0 McLaren MP4/12-Mercedes V10	let Häkkinen by to take win	11/22

1998
Championship position: 3rd   Wins: 1   Pole positions: 3   Fastest laps: 3   Points scored: 56

Pos	Race	Circuit	No	Team		Car/Engine	Notes	Grid
2	AUSTRALIAN GP	Melbourne	7	West McLaren Mercedes	B	3.0 McLaren MP4/13-Mercedes V10	allowed Häkkinen past to win	2/22
2	BRAZILIAN GP	Interlagos	7	West McLaren Mercedes	B	3.0 McLaren MP4/13-Mercedes V10		2/22
6	ARGENTINE GP	Buenos Aires	7	West McLaren Mercedes	B	3.0 McLaren MP4/13-Mercedes V10	collision with M Schumacher	1/22
1	SAN MARINO GP	Imola	7	West McLaren Mercedes	B	3.0 McLaren MP4/13-Mercedes V10		1/22
2	SPANISH GP	Barcelona	7	West McLaren Mercedes	B	3.0 McLaren MP4/13-Mercedes V10		2/22
ret	MONACO GP	Monte Carlo	7	West McLaren Mercedes	B	3.0 McLaren MP4/13-Mercedes V10	engine	2/22
ret	CANADIAN GP	Montreal	7	West McLaren Mercedes	B	3.0 McLaren MP4/13-Mercedes V10	throttle mechanism	1/22
6	FRENCH GP	Magny Cours	7	West McLaren Mercedes	B	3.0 McLaren MP4/13-Mercedes V10	refuelling problems/-1 lap/FL	3/22
ret	BRITISH GP	Silverstone	7	West McLaren Mercedes	B	3.0 McLaren MP4/13-Mercedes V10	spun off	4/22
2	AUSTRIAN GP	A1-Ring	7	West McLaren Mercedes	B	3.0 McLaren MP4/13-Mercedes V10	hit by Salo on lap 1/FL	14/22
2	GERMAN GP	Hockenheim	7	West McLaren Mercedes	B	3.0 McLaren MP4/13-Mercedes V10	FL	2/22
2	HUNGARIAN GP	Hungaroring	7	West McLaren Mercedes	B	3.0 McLaren MP4/13-Mercedes V10		2/22
7	BELGIAN GP	Spa	7	West McLaren Mercedes	B	3.0 McLaren MP4/13-Mercedes V10	hit by M Schumacher/-5 laps	2/22
ret	ITALIAN GP	Monza	7	West McLaren Mercedes	B	3.0 McLaren MP4/13-Mercedes V10	engine	4/22
3	LUXEMBOURG GP	Nürburgring	7	West McLaren Mercedes	B	3.0 McLaren MP4/13-Mercedes V10		5/22
3	JAPANESE GP	Suzuka	7	West McLaren Mercedes	B	3.0 McLaren MP4/13-Mercedes V10		3/22

1999
Championship position: 4th   Wins: 2   Pole positions: 0   Fastest laps: 3   Points scored: 48

Pos	Race	Circuit	No	Team		Car/Engine	Notes	Grid
ret	AUSTRALIAN GP	Melbourne	2	West McLaren Mercedes	B	3.0 McLaren MP4/14-Mercedes V10	hydraulics	2/22
ret	BRAZILIAN GP	Interlagos	2	West McLaren Mercedes	B	3.0 McLaren MP4/14-Mercedes V10	gearbox	2/22
2	SAN MARINO GP	Imola	2	West McLaren Mercedes	B	3.0 McLaren MP4/14-Mercedes V10		2/22
ret	MONACO GP	Monte Carlo	2	West McLaren Mercedes	B	3.0 McLaren MP4/14-Mercedes V10	oil leak	3/22
2	SPANISH GP	Barcelona	2	West McLaren Mercedes	B	3.0 McLaren MP4/14-Mercedes V10		3/22
7	CANADIAN GP	Montreal	2	West McLaren Mercedes	B	3.0 McLaren MP4/14-Mercedes V10	stop & go penalty	4/22
ret	FRENCH GP	Magny Cours	2	West McLaren Mercedes	B	3.0 McLaren MP4/14-Mercedes V10	led early in the race/FL	4/22
1	BRITISH GP	Silverstone	2	West McLaren Mercedes	B	3.0 McLaren MP4/14-Mercedes V10		3/22
2	AUSTRIAN GP	A1-Ring	2	West McLaren Mercedes	B	3.0 McLaren MP4/14-Mercedes V10	collision-Häkkinen at start	2/22
5	GERMAN GP	Hockenheim	2	West McLaren Mercedes	B	3.0 McLaren MP4/14-Mercedes V10	collision-Irvine new nose wing/FL	3/22
2	HUNGARIAN GP	Hungaroring	2	West McLaren Mercedes	B	3.0 McLaren MP4/14-Mercedes V10	FL	3/22
1	BELGIAN GP	Spa	2	West McLaren Mercedes	B	3.0 McLaren MP4/14-Mercedes V10	nudged Häkkinen at first corner	2/22
5	ITALIAN GP	Monza	2	West McLaren Mercedes	B	3.0 McLaren MP4/14-Mercedes V10		3/22
ret	EUROPEAN GP	Nürburgring	2	West McLaren Mercedes	B	3.0 McLaren MP4/14-Mercedes V10	spun off when in lead	2/22
ret	MALAYSIAN GP	Sepang	2	West McLaren Mercedes	B	3.0 McLaren MP4/14-Mercedes V10	fuel pressure	3/22
ret	JAPANESE GP	Suzuka	2	West McLaren Mercedes	B	3.0 McLaren MP4/14-Mercedes V10	gearbox	3/22

GP Starts: 90   GP Wins: 6   Pole positions: 8   Fastest laps: 11   Points: 221

Coulthard did not have the happiest of seasons in 1999, but he at least had the satisfaction of two Grand Prix victories.
Left: After strongly disputing the first corner with team-mate Häkkinen, David posted a commanding performance to win the Belgian Grand Prix.

PIERS COURAGE

Piers was the eldest son of the chairman of the Courage brewery group, but any thoughts that these connections were an asset to his motor racing aspirations were mistaken. His initial racing experience was gained regularly gyrating the Lotus Seven funded by his father, but after that Piers was on his own as far as finance was concerned. He teamed up with old pal Jonathan Williams in 1964 and the pair terrorised the circuits of Europe, initially with a Lotus 22. Entered under the grandiose Anglo-Swiss Racing Team banner, in reality Courage and Williams lived the sort of hand-to-mouth existence that most privateers had to endure, but third place at Reims and second at Zandvoort in a Brabham encouraged Piers to contest a full F3 season in 1965.

Charles Lucas entered a pair of Brabhams for Piers and Frank Williams, and it proved to be a very successful campaign for Courage, with four wins in major events at Silverstone, Goodwood, Caserta and Reims. This led to an invitation to race the Lotus 41 F3 car for 1966, and although it was inferior to the rival Brabhams Piers still managed a string of wins, earning a ride in Ron Harris' works F2 Lotus in the German GP, where he blotted his copybook by crashing.

BRM signed both Courage and Chris Irwin for 1967, the idea being to run them under the Tim Parnell banner, grooming them for a drive in the works team in the future. It all went sour for Piers very quickly, however, all his good work being repeatedly undone by silly spins. After the Monaco GP, Parnell stuck with Irwin, but Piers had to content himself with a season of Formula 2 in John Coombs' McLaren. His speed was not in doubt and some excellent drives netted him fourth place in the non-graded drivers' championship, but – and it was a big but – the disturbing tendency to crash remained, with major shunts at Pau, Enna and Brands Hatch. Coombs advised him to quit, but Piers was determined to continue.

Early in 1968 he bought the McLaren from Coombs and took it down-under to contest the Tasman series. Pitted against the Lotuses of Clark and Hill, Amon's Ferrari and McLaren's BRM in the seven-race series, Piers was second, fourth, fifth, third, third and fifth before the final round at Longford. In pouring rain Courage simply outdrove the opposition – Clark included – to win the race, but more importantly finally established his credibility.

Turning down an offer to replace the late Jim Clark at Lotus, Piers instead chose to race for Tim Parnell in Grands Prix while teaming up with his old pal Frank Williams in Formula 2, and so successful was their partnership that it was decided to enter F1 with a Brabham in 1969. Aside from a shunt at the Nürburgring, things could hardly have gone better, Courage driving superbly for the fledgling outfit to take second place at Monaco and Watkins Glen. He was also still racing in Formula 2, scoring a win at Enna and five third places, while an invitation to join the Matra team for Le Mans saw Piers take fourth place with Beltoise.

For 1970 Williams took the brave and possibly foolhardy step of running the newly constructed de Tomaso-Ford in place of the proven Brabham. The early part of the season was inconclusive with only a third place in the International Trophy to show for their efforts. Meanwhile Piers busied himself in a hectic schedule of endurance events for Alfa Romeo, highlighted by a win with de Adamich in the Buenos Aires 1000 Km. By the time of the Dutch GP at Zandvoort in June, progress seemed to have been made with the de Tomaso, which was placed ninth on the grid, but in the race tragedy struck when Courage slid wide, ran up a bank and crashed. The red car rolled over and burst into flames, and the unfortunate Piers stood no chance.

COURAGE, Piers (GB) b 27/5/1942, Colchester, Essex – d 21/6/1970, Zandvoort Circuit, Netherlands

	Race	Circuit	No	Entrant	Tyres	Car/Engine	Comment	Q Pos/Entries
	1966	Championship position: Unplaced						
ret	GERMAN GP (F2)	Nürburgring	32	Ron Harris-Team Lotus	D	1.0 Lotus 44-Cosworth 4	crashed	24/30
	1967	Championship position: Unplaced						
ret	SOUTH AFRICAN GP	Kyalami	16	Reg Parnell Racing Ltd	D	2.0 Lotus 25-BRM V8	oil pipe-engine	18/18
ret	MONACO GP	Monte Carlo	6	Reg Parnell Racing Ltd	D	2.1 BRM P261 V8	spun off-stalled	=12/18
dns	BRITISH GP	Silverstone	16	Reg Parnell Racing Ltd	D	2.1 BRM P261 V8	Irwin drove car in race	(16)/21
	1968	Championship position: 19th= Wins: 0 Pole positions: 0 Fastest laps: 0 Points scored: 4						
ret	SPANISH GP	Jarama	5	Reg Parnell Racing Ltd	D	3.0 BRM P126 V12	fuel metering unit	11/14
ret	MONACO GP	Monte Carlo	16	Reg Parnell Racing Ltd	D	3.0 BRM P126 V12	rear sub-frame fracture	11/18
ret	BELGIAN GP	Spa	14	Reg Parnell Racing Ltd	D	3.0 BRM P126 V12	engine	7/18
ret	DUTCH GP	Zandvoort	20	Reg Parnell Racing Ltd	D	3.0 BRM P126 V12	accident	14/19
6	FRENCH GP	Rouen	36	Reg Parnell Racing Ltd	D	3.0 BRM P126 V12	pit stop-tyres/3 laps behind	15/18
8	BRITISH GP	Brands Hatch	20	Reg Parnell Racing Ltd	D	3.0 BRM P126 V12	pit stops-misfire/-8 laps	16/20
8	GERMAN GP	Nürburgring	22	Reg Parnell Racing Ltd	D	3.0 BRM P126 V12		8/20
4	ITALIAN GP	Monza	27	Reg Parnell Racing Ltd	D	3.0 BRM P126 V12	1 lap behind	18/24
ret	CANADIAN GP	St Jovite	24	Reg Parnell Racing Ltd	D	3.0 BRM P126 V12	transmission	15/22
7/ret	US GP	Watkins Glen	22	Reg Parnell Racing Ltd	D	3.0 BRM P126 V12	broken suspension bolt/-10 laps	14/21
ret	MEXICAN GP	Mexico City	22	Reg Parnell Racing Ltd	D	3.0 BRM P126 V12	overheating	19/21
	1969	Championship position: 8th Wins: 0 Pole positions: 0 Fastest laps: 0 Points scored: 16						
ret	SPANISH GP	Montjuich Park	11	Frank Williams Racing Cars	D	3.0 Brabham BT26A-Cosworth V8	engine-valve spring	11/14
2	MONACO GP	Monte Carlo	16	Frank Williams Racing Cars	D	3.0 Brabham BT26A-Cosworth V8		=8/16
ret	DUTCH GP	Zandvoort	16	Frank Williams Racing Cars	D	3.0 Brabham BT26A-Cosworth V8	clutch	9/15
ret	FRENCH GP	Clermont Ferrand	9	Frank Williams Racing Cars	D	3.0 Brabham BT26A-Cosworth V8	nose-cone mounting	11/13
5	BRITISH GP	Silverstone	16	Frank Williams Racing Cars	D	3.0 Brabham BT26A-Cosworth V8	1 lap behind	10/17
ret	GERMAN GP	Nürburgring	17	Frank Williams Racing Cars	D	3.0 Brabham BT26A-Cosworth V8	accident	7/26
5	ITALIAN GP	Monza	32	Frank Williams Racing Cars	D	3.0 Brabham BT26A-Cosworth V8	low fuel pressure	4/15
ret	CANADIAN GP	Mosport Park	21	Frank Williams Racing Cars	D	3.0 Brabham BT26A-Cosworth V8	fuel leak	10/20
2	US GP	Watkins Glen	18	Frank Williams Racing Cars	D	3.0 Brabham BT26A-Cosworth V8		9/18
10	MEXICAN GP	Mexico City	18	Frank Williams Racing Cars	D	3.0 Brabham BT26A-Cosworth V8	spin-pit stop/4 laps behind	9/17
	1970	Championship position: Unplaced						
ret	SOUTH AFRICAN GP	Kyalami	22	Frank Williams Racing Cars	D	3.0 de Tomaso 505-Cosworth V8	suspension	20/24
dns	SPANISH GP	Jarama	12	Frank Williams Racing Cars	D	3.0 de Tomaso 505-Cosworth V8	accident in practice	(8)/22
nc	MONACO GP	Monte Carlo	24	Frank Williams Racing Cars	D	3.0 de Tomaso 505-Cosworth V8	pit stop-steering box/-22 laps	9/21
ret	BELGIAN GP	Spa	7	Frank Williams Racing Cars	D	3.0 de Tomaso 505-Cosworth V8	low oil pressure	12/18
ret	DUTCH GP	Zandvoort	4	Frank Williams Racing Cars	D	3.0 de Tomaso 505-Cosworth V8	fatal accident	9/24

GP Starts: 28 GP Wins: 0 Pole positions: 0 Fastest laps: 0 Points: 20

Piers established himself as a front-rank Grand Prix driver in 1969 when he teamed up with Frank Williams.
Left: **Courage takes his Brabham BT26A into fifth place at the British Grand Prix.**

CHRIS CRAFT

Chris began racing in a Ford Anglia in 1962 and soon built a reputation as one of Britain's foremost saloon car drivers, particularly with the Team Broadspeed Escort (1968-70). After F3 with a Tecno, he moved into sports cars, driving a Chevron in 1968, then teaming up with Alain de Cadenet to race his Porsche 908 and McLaren M8C. It was this association that led to Craft's brief flirtation with Formula 1.

It was to be merely a punctuation mark in a massive volume, for Chris continued to race sports and F5000 machines in the early seventies, then returned successfully to saloons (1976-79) with a Ford Capri. His career, which ran into hundreds of races, stretched into the eighties with the Dome sports car project. More recently Craft has been involved in the marketing of Gordon Murray's open-wheeled Rocket roadster, a fun machine which evokes the spirit of an earlier age.

JIM CRAWFORD

Crawford began his racing career as a mechanic who proved to be quicker in the car than his young charge, and this led to an offer from Derek Bennett to drive a works Chevron late in 1973. Jim built up his own car for 1974, just losing the Formula Atlantic title to John Nicholson. His performances earned him a testing contract with Lotus and a couple of Grand Prix outings in 1975, when he was again runner-up in the Atlantic series.

An expected Formula 2 drive in 1976 did not materialise and Crawford's career stalled. He spent 1978 in F3 and '79 back in Atlantic, before finding a ride in the Aurora AFX F1/F2 series in 1980, winning the F2 class in a Chevron. After putting together a full season in F2 in 1981 without much success, Jim decided to try his luck in the USA. It was a wise move, which was to revive and extend his career firstly into Can-Am in 1983 and '84 and then into Indy Car racing. He finished sixth at Indianapolis in 1988 and, but for an accident in which he sustained serious leg and foot injuries, he may have found a full-time ride, rather than employment just in the month of May.

CRAFT, Chris (GB) b 17/11/1939, Porthleven, nr Helston, Cornwall

	1971	Championship position: Unplaced							
	Race	*Circuit*	*No*	*Entrant*	*Tyres*	*Car/Engine*		*Comment*	*Q Pos/Entries*
dns	CANADIAN GP	Mosport Park	26	Ecurie Evergreen	G	3.0 Brabham BT33-Cosworth V8		*engine*	(25)/27
ret	US GP	Watkins Glen	24	Ecurie Evergreen	G	3.0 Brabham BT33-Cosworth V8		*chunking tyres/suspension*	30/32

GP Starts: 1   GP Wins: 0   Pole positions: 0   Fastest laps: 0   Points: 0

CRAWFORD, Jim (GB) b 13/2/1948, Dunfermline, Fifeshire, Scotland

	1975	Championship position: Unplaced							
	Race	*Circuit*	*No*	*Entrant*	*Tyres*	*Car/Engine*		*Comment*	*Q Pos/Entries*
ret	BRITISH GP	Silverstone	6	John Player Team Lotus	G	3.0 Lotus 72E-Cosworth V8		*spun off in rain*	25/28
13	ITALIAN GP	Monza	6	John Player Team Lotus	G	3.0 Lotus 72E-Cosworth V8		*6 laps behind*	25/28

GP Starts: 2   GP Wins: 0   Pole positions: 0   Fastest laps: 0   Points: 0

CREUS, Antonio (E) b 1924, Madrid – d 19/2/1966, Madrid

	1960	Championship position: Unplaced							
	Race	*Circuit*	*No*	*Entrant*	*Tyres*	*Car/Engine*		*Comment*	*Q Pos/Entries*
ret	ARGENTINE GP	Buenos Aires	12	Antonio Creus	D	2.5 Maserati 250F 6		*electrics/sunstroke*	22/22

GP Starts: 1   GP Wins: 0   Pole positions: 0   Fastest laps: 0   Points: 0

CROOK, Anthony (GB) b 16/2/1920, Manchester

	1952	Championship position: Unplaced							
	Race	*Circuit*	*No*	*Entrant*	*Tyres*	*Car/Engine*		*Comment*	*Q Pos/Entries*
nc	BRITISH GP	Silverstone	23	T A D Crook	D	2.0 Frazer Nash 421-Bristol 6		*10 laps behind*	25/32
	1953	Championship position: Unplaced							
ret	BRITISH GP	Silverstone	22	T A D Crook	D	2.0 Cooper T20-Bristol 6		*fuel feed on start line*	25/29

GP Starts: 2   GP Wins: 0   Pole positions: 0   Fastest laps: 0   Points: 0

TONY CROOK

Tony may have competed in only a couple of World Championship Grands Prix, but between 1946 and 1955 he was one of Britain's most active racers, mainly on home soil, in single-seaters and sports categories. He actually won the first post-war circuit race at Gransden Lodge in Raymond Mays' 328 Fraser Nash BMW, and raced this and a 2.9-litre Alfa Romeo with huge success in the late forties.

In 1950 Tony began racing the Bristol-engined cars for the first time, and with his Frazer Nash he racked up countless wins and places over the next three years. He finished second to Mike Hawthorn in the 1951 Goodwood racing season, and his mecurial presence enlivened many a national meeting. A highlight in this period was a fine third place with the Frazer Nash in the 1952 sports car-only Monaco GP.

In 1953 Crook purchased a pukka single-seater Cooper-Bristol Mk II and he enjoyed many spirited battles with his friend and rival Roy Salvadori. He also had a Mk I Cooper modified to compete in sports events and raced both cars in tandem. For 1954 Tony had the Mk II car rebuilt as an all-purpose 1½-seater and took great delight in seeing off the challenges of Salvadori in his Maserati and Archie Scott-Brown in his Lister Bristol. He went on to compete in more than 400 races, sprints and hill-climbs, setting countless lap records and BTDs. His last race was the Goodwood 12 Hours in which, during the night, he had the misfortune to spin on oil and be rammed by Stirling Moss. Tony was hospitalised for two weeks and decided upon retirement. He then acquired Bristol Cars Limited and remains chairman and managing director to this day.

GEOFFREY CROSSLEY

Racing enthusiast Crossley ordered the second Alta (GP2) from Geoffrey Taylor and upon delivery took it to compete in the 1949 Belgian Grand Prix at Spa. This may have seemed an ambitious step for someone with only a little pre-war experience in a Riley, but wisely he took things easily and finished seventh.

He made occasional appearances with the car over the next couple of years, picking up sixth place in the Jersey Road Race in 1950. It seems he was unhappy with the costs of running and maintaining this machine, and dropped out of the racing scene, apart from a brief reappearance in 1955, when his home-made Berkshire Special appeared at the Goodwood Easter meeting. The car performed so poorly it was immediately withdrawn and never raced again.

FRITZ d'OREY

D'Orey's parents were from Portugal and his grandfather was German, which probably accounts for his forename. The family were wealthy Packard car importers, and the young Fritz was soon behind the wheel of a Porsche Spyder.

In 1958 he acquired an ex-Chico Landi F1 Ferrari and raced it extensively in Brazil, Uruguay and Argentina, and his successes led to an invitation to race in Europe.

Having safely negotiated the French Grand Prix, Fritz crashed and wrote off the Maserati at Silverstone, which cut short his F1 plans for the season, but he later drove the TecMec at Sebring, although he was glad to retire the machine, which he felt was too dangerous. However, wins in Formula Junior at the GP de Messina and in sports cars in the Austrian GP with a Ferrari Testa Rossa led to the 22-year-old d'Orey signing a contract with Ferrari to race their sports cars in 1960.

Describing himself as 'a child and very crazy', Fritz escaped a huge crash at Monza when trying to keep pace with Phil Hill before having a much more serious accident at Le Mans when he slammed his Ferrari into a tree. Sustaining serious head injuries, d'Orey spent eight months in hospital making a full recovery, but never raced thereafter.

CROSSLEY, Geoffrey (GB) b 11/5/1921

1950 Championship position: Unplaced

	Race	Circuit	No	Entrant	Tyres	Car/Engine	Comment	Q Pos/Entries
ret	BRITISH GP	Silverstone	24	Geoffrey Crossley	D	1.5 s/c Alta GP 2 4	transmission	17/21
9	BELGIAN GP	Spa	26	Geoffrey Crossley	D	1.5 s/c Alta GP 2 4	5 laps behind	12/14

GP Starts: 2   GP Wins: 0   Pole positions: 0   Fastest laps: 0   Points: 0

d'OREY, Fritz (BR) b 25/3/1938 Sao Paulo

1959 Championship position: Unplaced

	Race	Circuit	No	Entrant	Tyres	Car/Engine	Comment	Q Pos/Entries
nc	FRENCH GP	Reims	38	Scuderia Centro Sud	D	2.5 Maserati 250F 6	10 laps behind	18/22
ret	BRITISH GP	Aintree	40	Scuderia Centro Sud	D	2.5 Maserati 250F 6	out of brakes-crashed	20/30
ret	US GP	Sebring	15	Camoradi USA	D	2.5 Tec Mec Maserati 250F 6	oil leak	17/19

GP Starts: 3   GP Wins: 0   Pole positions: 0   Fastest laps: 0   Points: 0

NANO da SILVA RAMOS

Holding dual French-Brazilian nationality, Ramos took part in his first races in Rio with an MG but wasn't really interested in the sport until he returned to France and purchased an Aston Martin DB2, with which he won the Rallye de Sable in 1953.

After more success in the car the following year, Ramos joined the Gordini team for 1955 and 1956, racing their Grand Prix and sports cars, and suffering the usual mixture of speed and unreliability associated with that marque. In single-seaters he finished fifth in the 1956 International Trophy and did well to claim points at Monaco, but achieved little else, while in sports car racing he scored a win for the team at Montlhéry against very poor opposition.

Equipe Gordini were on their last legs early in 1957, but Ramos took sixth place at Pau in the streamliner before their demise, and returned in an Alan Brown Cooper the following year to finish second.

In 1959 he raced briefly for Scuderia Centro Sud, claiming a very distant fourth in their outdated Maserati 250F in the Aintree 200.

CHUCK DAIGH

Having started racing in the mid-fifties, Daigh campaigned a modified Mercury-Kurtis special until 1958, when he became involved with Lance Reventlow's plans to build the powerful Chevrolet-engined Scarab sports car. This proved to be very successful, with Daigh winning the Governor's Cup (beating Hansgen's Lister) and the Nassau Trophy, and defeating Phil Hill's Ferrari at Riverside.

Ambitiously, a front-engined F1 car was then commissioned by Reventlow, but by the time it appeared in 1960 it had been rendered almost obsolete by the rear-engined Cooper and Lotus cars. Chuck struggled manfully against the odds but the car was withdrawn after just three races, reappearing only on home soil at season's end. Daigh meanwhile had the chance to try a proper F1 car at the British GP when he drove a third works Cooper. Amazingly the Scarab raced again, being wheeled out for the Inter-Continental Formula in 1961. Chuck finished seventh in the International Trophy race, but after he crashed in practice for the British Empire Trophy – suffering a cracked pelvis – the car was seen no more.

Fortunately Daigh was seen again, racing one of Jim Hall's early Chaparrals at Sebring in 1962, and tasted victory at Mosport in 1963 when he won the Player's 200 sports car race in a Lotus 19.

da SILVA RAMOS, 'Nano' Hernano (F/BR) b 7/12/1925, Paris

	1955	Championship position: Unplaced							
	Race	Circuit	No	Entrant	Tyres	Car/engine	Comment	Q Pos/Entries
8	DUTCH GP	Zandvoort	22	Equipe Gordini	E	2.5 Gordini Type 16 6	8 laps behind	14/16
ret	BRITISH GP	Aintree	24	Equipe Gordini	E	2.5 Gordini Type 16 6	engine	18/25
ret	ITALIAN GP	Monza	22	Equipe Gordini	E	2.5 Gordini Type 16 6	fuel pump	18/22
dns	"	"	24	Equipe Gordini	E	2.5 Gordini Type 32 8	practice only	– / –
	1956	Championship position: 15th= Wins: 0 Pole positions: 0 Fastest laps: 0 Points scored: 2							
5	MONACO GP	Monte Carlo	6	Equipe Gordini	E	2.5 Gordini Type 32 8	7 laps behind	14/19
8	FRENCH GP	Reims	32	Equipe Gordini	E	2.5 Gordini Type 32 8	4 laps behind	14/20
ret	BRITISH GP	Silverstone	14	Equipe Gordini	E	2.5 Gordini Type 32 8	rear axle	26/28
ret	ITALIAN GP	Monza	8	Equipe Gordini	E	2.5 Gordini Type 32 8	engine	21/26

GP Starts: 7   GP Wins: 0   Pole positions: 0   Fastest laps: 0   Points: 2

DAIGH, Chuck (USA) b 29/11/1923, Long Beach, California

	1960	Championship position: Unplaced							
	Race	Circuit	No	Entrant	Tyres	Car/Engine	Comment	Q Pos/Entries
dnq	MONACO GP	Monte Carlo	46	Reventlow Automobiles Inc	(G) D	2.4 Scarab 4	ran Goodyear tyres in practice	21/24
dns	DUTCH GP	Zandvoort	22	Reventlow Automobiles Inc	D	2.4 Scarab 4	dispute over start money	(19)/21
ret	BELGIAN GP	Spa	30	Reventlow Automobiles Inc	D	2.4 Scarab 4	engine	18/18
dns	FRENCH GP	Reims	26	Reventlow Automobiles Inc	D	2.4 Scarab 4	engine failure in practice	(23)/23
ret	BRITISH GP	Silverstone	3	Cooper Car Co	D	2.5 Cooper T51-Climax 4	engine-overheating	19/25
10	US GP	Riverside	23	Reventlow Automobiles Inc	D	2.4 Scarab 4	3 laps behind	18/23

GP Starts: 3   GP Wins: 0   Pole positions: 0   Fastest laps: 0   Points: 0

YANNICK DALMAS

French F3 in the mid-eighties must have been bewildering. Potential World Champions were two a penny, as the conveyor-belt churned out hot-shots one after another: the Ferté brothers, Grouillard, Raphanel, Alesi, Bernard, Trollé, Comas – and Dalmas.

The reigning French Formule Renault champion, Yannick took the number two seat to Raphanel in the all-conquering ORECA F3 team for 1985 and duly finished second in the championship. Next year it was his turn to lead the team and he won six of the 11 races, impressing all watchers with his flair and speed.

Moving up to F3000 for 1987, his machinery did not always work as well as one would expect, but when things were right he flew. Victories at Pau and in the final round at Jarama brought him into a slightly disappointing fifth place in the championship, but for Dalmas it mattered little. He had already been given his Grand Prix chance by Larrousse in Mexico, and a fifth place (no points scored being a non-regular driver) in Australia at season's end made his place in the F1 team for 1988 a formality.

The year was a personal disaster. Early-season shunts blunted his confidence and then what appeared to be an ear problem that sidelined him towards the end of the season turned out to be a life-threatening bout of Legionnaires' disease.

He returned to the Larrousse équipe for 1989, but a string of non-qualifications led to his leaving the team in mid-season in favour of Alboreto. Taking up a seat at AGS merely hastened his depressing slide and, while he did manage to qualify the car on occasion in 1990, it must have been a great relief when Peugeot offered him the chance to re-establish his career with a place in their sports car team. Paired with Rosberg, he won two races (Magny Cours and Mexico City) and in 1992 he shared the World Sports Car Drivers' title with Derek Warwick after winning at Le Mans, Silverstone and Fuji, also finishing second at Monza and Donington.

With Peugeot competing only at Le Mans in 1993 (where Yannick finished second with Boutsen and Fabi), he drove a Peugeot 405 in the French Supertourisme series, and he continued in 1994, taking fourth overall in the final standings. Undoubtedly the highlight of his year was a second Le Mans win (with Baldi and Haywood for Porsche), for his subsequent brief Grand Prix reappearance for Larrousse passed almost unnoticed.

Yannick scored a third Le Mans win in 1995 with a McLaren F1 GTR, but concentrated on his drive in the DTM/ITC series with the Opel Joest team. His two seasons in this category brought little reward, however, the frustrated driver dissatisfied with his equipment.

The 1997 season started with a win in a Ferrari 333SP at Sebring and Dalmas was then delighted to sign for Porsche to race their 911 GT1 prototype. He quickly became the cornerstone of the team's efforts, with his serious and professional approach much admired by all his co-drivers. He formed a particularly strong driver pairing with Allan McNish in 1998 when the Porsche was bettered only by the works Mercedes CLKs. The company's withdrawal from competition in 1999 left Dalmas without a regular drive but he was quickly snapped up by BMW Motorsport, enabling him to notch up a fourth Le Mans win with Pierluigi Martini and Jo Winkelhock in the BMW V12 LMR.

DALMAS, Yannick (F) b 28/7/1961, Le Beausset, nr Toulon

	1987			Championship position: Unplaced				
	Race	Circuit	No	Entrant	Tyres	Car/Engine	Comment	Q Pos/Entries
9	MEXICAN GP	Mexico City	29	Larrousse Calmels	G	3.5 Lola LC87-Cosworth V8	4th non-turbo/4 laps behind	23/27
14/ret*	JAPANESE GP	Suzuka	29	Larrousse Calmels	G	3.5 Lola LC87-Cosworth V8	electrics/*3rd non-turbo/-4 laps	23/27
5*	AUSTRALIAN GP	Adelaide	29	Larrousse Calmels	G	3.5 Lola LC87-Cosworth V8	* 2nd non-turbo-no points	21/27
	1988			Championship position: Unplaced				
ret	BRAZILIAN GP	Rio	29	Larrousse Calmels	G	3.5 Lola LC88-Cosworth V8	engine cut out	17/31
12	SAN MARINO GP	Imola	29	Larrousse Calmels	G	3.5 Lola LC88-Cosworth V8	broken front wing/-2 laps	19/31
7	MONACO GP	Monte Carlo	29	Larrousse Calmels	G	3.5 Lola LC88-Cosworth V8	spin/1 lap behind	21/30
9	MEXICAN GP	Mexico City	29	Larrousse Calmels	G	3.5 Lola LC88-Cosworth V8	3 laps behind	22/30
dnq	CANADIAN GP	Montreal	29	Larrousse Calmels	G	3.5 Lola LC88-Cosworth V8		29/31
7	US GP (DETROIT)	Detroit	29	Larrousse Calmels	G	3.5 Lola LC88-Cosworth V8	2 laps behind	25/31
13	FRENCH GP	Paul Ricard	29	Larrousse Calmels	G	3.5 Lola LC88-Cosworth V8	pit stop-loose seat belts/-2 laps	19/31
13	BRITISH GP	Silverstone	29	Larrousse Calmels	G	3.5 Lola LC88-Cosworth V8	2 laps behind	23/31
ret	GERMAN GP	Hockenheim	29	Larrousse Calmels	G	3.5 Lola LC88-Cosworth V8	clutch	21/31
9	HUNGARIAN GP	Hungaroring	29	Larrousse Calmels	G	3.5 Lola LC88-Cosworth V8	collision-Sala/misfire/-3 laps	17/31
ret	BELGIAN GP	Spa	29	Larrousse Calmels	G	3.5 Lola LC88-Cosworth V8	engine	23/31
ret	ITALIAN GP	Monza	29	Larrousse Calmels	G	3.5 Lola LC88-Cosworth V8	spun-holed oil tank	25/31
ret	PORTUGUESE GP	Estoril	29	Larrousse Calmels	G	3.5 Lola LC88-Cosworth V8	alternator belt	15/31
11	SPANISH GP	Jerez	29	Larrousse Calmels	G	3.5 Lola LC88-Cosworth V8	1 lap behind	16/31
	1989			Championship position: Unplaced				
dnq	BRAZILIAN GP	Rio	29	Larrousse Calmels Lola	G	3.5 Lola LC88B-Lamborghini V12		27/38
ret/dns	SAN MARINO GP	Imola	29	Equipe Larrousse	G	3.5 Lola LC89-Lamborghini V12	engine on dummy grid	(26)/39
dnq	MONACO GP	Monte Carlo	29	Equipe Larrousse	G	3.5 Lola LC89-Lamborghini V12		28/39
dnq	MEXICAN GP	Mexico City	29	Equipe Larrousse	G	3.5 Lola LC89-Lamborghini V12		29/39
dnq	US GP (PHOENIX)	Phoenix	29	Equipe Larrousse	G	3.5 Lola LC89-Lamborghini V12		30/39
dnq	CANADIAN GP	Montreal	29	Equipe Larrousse	G	3.5 Lola LC89-Lamborghini V12		28/39

dnpq	BRITISH GP	Silverstone	41	Automobiles Gonfaronaise Sportive	G	3.5 AGS JH23B-Cosworth V8			35/39
dnpq	GERMAN GP	Hockenheim	41	Automobiles Gonfaronaise Sportive	G	3.5 AGS JH23B-Cosworth V8			31/39
dnpq	"	"	41	Automobiles Gonfaronaise Sportive	G	3.5 AGS JH24-Cosworth V8			– / –
dnpq	HUNGARIAN GP	Hungaroring	41	Automobiles Gonfaronaise Sportive	G	3.5 AGS JH23B-Cosworth V8			33/39
dnpq	BELGIAN GP	Spa	41	Automobiles Gonfaronaise Sportive	G	3.5 AGS JH24-Cosworth V8			37/39
dnpq	ITALIAN GP	Monza	41	Automobiles Gonfaronaise Sportive	G	3.5 AGS JH24-Cosworth V8			37/39
excl	PORTUGUESE GP	Estoril	41	Automobiles Gonfaronaise Sportive	G	3.5 AGS JH24-Cosworth V8		*practised on wrong tyres*	38/38
dnpq	SPANISH GP	Jerez	41	Automobiles Gonfaronaise Sportive	G	3.5 AGS JH24-Cosworth V8			35/39
dnpq	JAPANESE GP	Suzuka	41	Automobiles Gonfaronaise Sportive	G	3.5 AGS JH24-Cosworth V8			38/39
dnpq	AUSTRALIAN GP	Adelaide	41	Automobiles Gonfaronaise Sportive	G	3.5 AGS JH24-Cosworth V8			37/39

1990 Championship position: Unplaced

dnpq	US GP (PHOENIX)	Phoenix	18	Automobiles Gonfaronaise Sportive	G	3.5 AGS JH24-Cosworth V8			32/35
ret	BRAZILIAN GP	Interlagos	18	Automobiles Gonfaronaise Sportive	G	3.5 AGS JH24-Cosworth V8		*front suspension*	26/35
dnpq	MONACO GP	Monte Carlo	18	Automobiles Gonfaranaise Sportive	G	3.5 AGS JH25-Cosworth V8			32/35
dnpq	CANADIAN GP	Montreal	18	Automobiles Gonfaronaise Sportive	G	3.5 AGS JH25-Cosworth V8			32/35
dnpq	MEXICAN GP	Mexico City	18	Automobiles Gonfaronaise Sportive	G	3.5 AGS JH25-Cosworth V8			31/35
17	FRENCH GP	Paul Ricard	18	Automobiles Gonfaronaise Sportive	G	3.5 AGS JH25-Cosworth V8		*5 laps behind*	26/35
dnpq	BRITISH GP	Silverstone	18	Automobiles Gonfaronaise Sportive	G	3.5 AGS JH25-Cosworth V8			32/35
dnq	GERMAN GP	Hockenheim	18	Automobiles Gonfaronaise Sportive	G	3.5 AGS JH25-Cosworth V8			29/35
dnq	HUNGARIAN GP	Hungaroring	18	Automobiles Gonfaronaise Sportive	G	3.5 AGS JH25-Cosworth V8			27/35
dnq	BELGIAN GP	Spa	18	Automobiles Gonfaronaise Sportive	G	3.5 AGS JH25-Cosworth V8			29/33
nc	ITALIAN GP	Monza	18	Automobiles Gonfaronaise Sportive	G	3.5 AGS JH25-Cosworth V8		*pit stops/8 laps behind*	24/33
ret	PORTUGUESE GP	Estoril	18	Automobiles Gonfaronaise Sportive	G	3.5 AGS JH25-Cosworth V8		*driveshaft*	25/33
9	SPANISH GP	Jerez	18	Automobiles Gonfaronaise Sportive	G	3.5 AGS JH25-Cosworth V8		*1 lap behind*	24/33
dnq	JAPANESE GP	Suzuka	18	Automobiles Gonfaronaise Sportive	G	3.5 AGS JH25-Cosworth V8			29/30
dnq	AUSTRALIAN GP	Adelaide	18	Automobiles Gonfaronaise Sportive	G	3.5 AGS JH25-Cosworth V8			28/30

1994 Championship position: Unplaced

ret	ITALIAN GP	Monza	19	Tourtel Larrousse F1	G	3.5 Larrousse LH94-Ford HB V8		*accident*	23/28
14	PORTUGUESE GP	Estoril	19	Tourtel Larrousse F1	G	3.5 Larrousse LH94-Ford HB V8		*2 laps behind*	23/28

GP Starts: 23 (24)   GP Wins: 0   Pole positions: 0   Fastest laps: 0   Points: 2

DALY, Derek (IRL) b 11/3/1953, Dundrum, Dublin

1978 Championship position: 19th=   Wins: 0   Pole positions: 0   Fastest laps: 0   Points scored: 1

	Race	Circuit	No	Entrant	Tyres	Car/Engine		Comment	Q Pos/Entries
dnpq	US GP WEST	Long Beach	24	Olympus Cameras with Hesketh	G	3.0 Hesketh 308E-Cosworth V8			30/30
dnpq	MONACO GP	Monte Carlo	24	Olympus Cameras with Hesketh	G	3.0 Hesketh 308E-Cosworth V8			26/30
dnq	BELGIAN GP	Zolder	24	Olympus Cameras with Hesketh	G	3.0 Hesketh 308E-Cosworth V8			26/30
dnq	FRENCH GP	Paul Ricard	22	Team Tissot Ensign	G	3.0 Ensign N177-Cosworth V8			28/29
ret	BRITISH GP	Brands Hatch	22	Team Tissot Ensign	G	3.0 Ensign N177-Cosworth V8		*lost wheel-crashed*	15/30
dsq	AUSTRIAN GP	Österreichring	22	Team Tissot Ensign	G	3.0 Ensign N177-Cosworth V8		*outside assistance after spin*	19/31
ret	DUTCH GP	Zandvoort	22	Team Tissot Ensign	G	3.0 Ensign N177-Cosworth V8		*driveshaft*	16/33
10	ITALIAN GP	Monza	22	Team Tissot Ensign	G	3.0 Ensign N177-Cosworth V8			18/32
8	US GP EAST	Watkins Glen	22	Team Tissot Ensign	G	3.0 Ensign N177-Cosworth V8		*1 lap behind*	19/27
6	CANADIAN GP	Montreal	22	Team Tissot Ensign	G	3.0 Ensign N177-Cosworth V8			15/28

1979 Championship position: Unplaced

11	ARGENTINE GP	Buenos Aires	22	Team Ensign	G	3.0 Ensign N177-Cosworth V8		*2 laps behind*	24/26
13	BRAZILIAN GP	Interlagos	22	Team Ensign	G	3.0 Ensign N177-Cosworth V8		*1 lap behind*	23/26
dnq	SOUTH AFRICAN GP	Kyalami	22	Team Ensign	G	3.0 Ensign N179-Cosworth V8			26/26
ret	US GP WEST	Long Beach	22	Team Ensign	G	3.0 Ensign N179-Cosworth V8		*collision with Rebaque*	26/26
dnq	SPANISH GP	Jarama	22	Team Ensign	G	3.0 Ensign N177-Cosworth V8			25/27
dnq	BELGIAN GP	Zolder	22	Team Ensign	G	3.0 Ensign N177-Cosworth V8			27/28
dnq	MONACO GP	Monte Carlo	22	Team Ensign	G	3.0 Ensign N179-Cosworth V8			24/25
8	AUSTRIAN GP	Österreichring	4	Candy Tyrrell Team	G	3.0 Tyrrell 009-Cosworth V8		*1 lap behind*	11/26
ret	CANADIAN GP	Montreal	33	Candy Tyrrell Team	G	3.0 Tyrrell 009-Cosworth V8		*engine*	24/29
ret	US GP EAST	Watkins Glen	33	Candy Tyrrell Team	G	3.0 Tyrrell 009-Cosworth V8		*spun off*	15/30

1980 Championship position: 10th=   Wins: 0   Pole positions: 0   Fastest laps: 0   Points scored: 6

4	ARGENTINE GP	Buenos Aires	4	Candy Tyrrell Team	G	3.0 Tyrrell 009-Cosworth V8			22/28
14	BRAZILIAN GP	Interlagos	4	Candy Tyrrell Team	G	3.0 Tyrrell 009-Cosworth V8		*2 laps behind*	24/28
ret	SOUTH AFRICAN GP	Kyalami	4	Candy Tyrrell Team	G	3.0 Tyrrell 010-Cosworth V8		*puncture*	16/28
8	US GP WEST	Long Beach	4	Candy Tyrrell Team	G	3.0 Tyrrell 010-Cosworth V8		*1 lap behind*	14/27
9	BELGIAN GP	Zolder	4	Candy Tyrrell Team	G	3.0 Tyrrell 010-Cosworth V8		*2 laps behind*	11/27
ret	MONACO GP	Monte Carlo	4	Candy Tyrrell Team	G	3.0 Tyrrell 010-Cosworth V8		*multiple accident on lap 1*	12/27
11	FRENCH GP	Paul Ricard	4	Candy Tyrrell Team	G	3.0 Tyrrell 010-Cosworth V8		*2 laps behind*	20/27
4	BRITISH GP	Brands Hatch	4	Candy Tyrrell Team	G	3.0 Tyrrell 010-Cosworth V8		*1 lap behind*	10/27
10	GERMAN GP	Hockenheim	4	Candy Tyrrell Team	G	3.0 Tyrrell 010-Cosworth V8		*1 lap behind*	22/26
ret	AUSTRIAN GP	Österreichring	4	Candy Tyrrell Team	G	3.0 Tyrrell 010-Cosworth V8		*sheared brake disc-crashed*	10/25
ret	DUTCH GP	Zandvoort	4	Candy Tyrrell Team	G	3.0 Tyrrell 010-Cosworth V8		*broken disc brake-crashed*	23/28
ret	ITALIAN GP	Imola	4	Candy Tyrrell Team	G	3.0 Tyrrell 010-Cosworth V8		*spun off*	22/28
ret/dns	CANADIAN GP	Montreal	4	Candy Tyrrell Team	G	3.0 Tyrrell 010-Cosworth V8		*startline crash-did not restart*	20/28
ret	US GP EAST	Watkins Glen	4	Candy Tyrrell Team	G	3.0 Tyrrell 010-Cosworth V8		*hit by de Cesaris*	21/27

1981 Championship position: Unplaced

dnq	US GP WEST	Long Beach	17	March Grand Prix Team	M	3.0 March 811-Cosworth V8			26/29
dnq	BRAZILIAN GP	Rio	17	March Grand Prix Team	M	3.0 March 811-Cosworth V8			30/30
dnq	ARGENTINE GP	Buenos Aires	17	March Grand Prix Team	M	3.0 March 811-Cosworth V8			27/29
dnq	SAN MARINO GP	Imola	18	March Grand Prix Team	M	3.0 March 811-Cosworth V8			26/30
dnq	BELGIAN GP	Zolder	18	March Grand Prix Team	M	3.0 March 811-Cosworth V8		*practice times disallowed*	– /31

dnpq	MONACO GP	Monte Carlo	18	March Grand Prix Team	M	3.0 March 811-Cosworth V8			28/31
16	SPANISH GP	Jarama	17	March Grand Prix Team	M	3.0 March 811-Cosworth V8	5 laps behind		22/30
ret	FRENCH GP	Dijon	17	March Grand Prix Team	A	3.0 March 811-Cosworth V8	engine		20/29
7	BRITISH GP	Silverstone	17	March Grand Prix Team	A	3.0 March 811-Cosworth V8	2 laps behind		17/30
ret	GERMAN GP	Hockenheim	17	March Grand Prix Team	A	3.0 March 811-Cosworth V8	steering tie rod		21/30
11	AUSTRIAN GP	Österreichring	17	March Grand Prix Team	A	3.0 March 811-Cosworth V8	6 laps behind		19/28
ret	DUTCH GP	Zandvoort	17	March Grand Prix Team	A	3.0 March 811-Cosworth V8	suspension		19/30
ret	ITALIAN GP	Monza	17	March Grand Prix Team	A	3.0 March 811-Cosworth V8	gearbox		19/30
8	CANADIAN GP	Montreal	17	March Grand Prix Team	A	3.0 March 811-Cosworth V8	2 laps behind		20/30
dnq	CAESARS PALACE GP	Las Vegas	17	March Grand Prix Team	A	3.0 March 811-Cosworth V8			27/30

1982   Championship position: 13th   Wins: 0   Pole positions: 0   Fastest laps: 0   Points scored: 8

14	SOUTH AFRICAN GP	Kyalami	33	Theodore Racing Team	A	3.0 Theodore TY01-Cosworth V8	clutch/brake problems/-4 laps		24/30
ret	BRAZILIAN GP	Rio	33	Theodore Racing Team	A	3.0 Theodore TY02-Cosworth V8	puncture-spun off		20/31
ret	US GP WEST	Long Beach	33	Theodore Racing Team	A	3.0 Theodore TY02-Cosworth V8	ran off track-stalled		22/31
ret	BELGIAN GP	Zolder	5	TAG Williams Team	G	3.0 Williams FW08-Cosworth V8	ran off road		15/32
6/ret	MONACO GP	Monte Carlo	5	TAG Williams Team	G	3.0 Williams FW08-Cosworth V8	gearbox/accident/-2 laps		8/31
5	US GP (DETROIT)	Detroit	5	TAG Williams Team	G	3.0 Williams FW08-Cosworth V8			12/28
7/ret	CANADIAN GP	Montreal	5	TAG Williams Team	G	3.0 Williams FW08-Cosworth V8	out of fuel/2 laps behind		13/29
5	DUTCH GP	Zandvoort	5	TAG Williams Team	G	3.0 Williams FW08-Cosworth V8	1 lap behind		12/31
5	BRITISH GP	Brands Hatch	5	TAG Williams Team	G	3.0 Williams FW08-Cosworth V8			10/30
7	FRENCH GP	Paul Ricard	5	TAG Williams Team	G	3.0 Williams FW08-Cosworth V8	1 lap behind		11/30
ret	GERMAN GP	Hockenheim	5	TAG Williams Team	G	3.0 Williams FW08-Cosworth V8	engine		20/30
ret	AUSTRIAN GP	Österreichring	5	TAG Williams Team	G	3.0 Williams FW08-Cosworth V8	hit by de Cesaris		9/29
9	SWISS GP	Dijon	5	TAG Williams Team	G	3.0 Williams FW08-Cosworth V8	1 lap behind		7/29
ret	ITALIAN GP	Monza	5	TAG Williams Team	G	3.0 Williams FW08-Cosworth V8	hit by Guerrero-suspension		13/30
6	CAESARS PALACE GP	Las Vegas	5	TAG Williams Team	G	3.0 Williams FW08-Cosworth V8	1 lap behind		14/30

GP Starts: 48 (49)   GP Wins: 0   Pole positions: 0   Fastest laps: 0   Points: 15

DEREK DALY

'Quick but accident prone' may be an unfair judgement on Derek Daly, but the likeable Irishman certainly had to endure more than his fair share of incidents during his Grand Prix career.

Early experience in the harum-scarum world of stock cars led Derek into Formula Ford in his native Ireland. In order to finance his efforts he went to Australia to work in the tin mines with his friend and fellow aspiring racer, David Kennedy, and earned enough to finance his season, winning the 1975 national championship. Then it was across the Irish Sea to try his luck in Formula Ford for 1976. It was a tough year for Daly, who was living out of a converted coach and perpetually strapped for cash, but it was all made worthwhile when he won the Formula Ford Festival at the end of the season.

Derek stepped up to Formula 3 for 1977 and, driving a Chevron, won the BP championship ahead of Nelson Piquet, while a one-off drive saw him finishing fifth on his Formula 2 debut at Estoril. So impressive was this performance that he got the seat for 1978, and offers also came in for Formula 1. He did a deal with Hesketh and made a sensational debut in the rain at the International Trophy race, leading all the big names until he spun off. Reality soon dawned, however, as he failed to qualify for the first three races and quit in disgust. Luckily Ensign needed a replacement for Ickx and Daly was back, scoring his first point in Canada. He was persuaded to stay on for 1979, but the revamped car was outclassed, and after Monaco Daly returned to his successful ICI Formula 2 ride. This left him available to step into the Tyrrell team, initially in place of the indisposed Jarier. A superb drive at Watkins Glen ended in Daly spinning out, but Tyrrell had seen enough to offer him a drive for 1980. It was again a story of hit and miss, the season yielding a pair of fourth places and a couple of huge shunts.

For 1981 he was forced to take a step backwards. The RAM March was not competitive, and the atmosphere in the team was tense, but he never gave up. Theodore then threw him a lifeline which put him back on the grid again in 1982, and with Reutemann's sudden decision to retire he found himself catapulted into the Williams team. It was a difficult season for Derek; he supported Rosberg with some classy drives, but found himself dumped at the end of the year.

Daly then took the decision to turn his back on F1 and try his luck in Indy cars. After a handful of rides in '83, and some promising per-formances early in 1984, his career was nearly ended by a huge crash at Michigan which badly smashed both his legs. After a long and painful recovery Derek made a tentative comeback to Indy cars late in 1986 and then raced in endurance events for Jaguar and in IMSA for Nissan before announcing his retirement in 1992.

Derek has since slipped effortlessly into the role of TV commentator on Grand Prix and Indy Car racing on Speedvision, as well as opening a racing school at Las Vegas Motor Speedway in 1996.

CRISTIAN DANNER

Christian got involved in motor sport by racing (and regularly crashing) a Renault 5 in Germany, and soon came to the attention of Manfred Cassani, who was looking for a young driver to promote. Danner was given a BMW M1 to race in the German G4 championship and a couple of ProCar GP support races, and did so well in these that BMW signed him on a three-year contract to race in the works March F2 team. With no single-seater experience, Christian struggled in 1981 – his first season – and he was usually overshadowed by the team's lead drivers, Boutsen, Corrado Fabi, Cecotto and Gabbiani, but by the end of 1983 he was not far off the pace, as witnessed by his pole position at the Nürburgring.

Unfortunately for Christian, BMW then pulled the plug on their F2 programme and at first he was left without a drive for 1984, eventually joining the Bob Sparshott team. That season was dominated by the Ralt-Hondas, but Danner was up there with the rest, and with a minimal budget he tackled the inaugural F3000 season in 1985 with the same team. This was to be the breakthrough year for Christian. Not the quickest driver but certainly the most consistent, he became the formula's first champion. This brought him a Grand Prix chance at Zakspeed, and then a contract with Osella for 1986, which was bought out in mid-season when Arrows needed a replacement for the badly injured Marc Surer.

Christian rejoined Zakspeed in 1987 and, paired with Martin Brundle, performed quite well given the equipment available. He was on the sidelines in 1988, but could have had the dubious privilege of a EuroBrun drive from mid-season had he not been too tall to fit into the car. The following season saw his final shot at F1, driving the Rial for Gunther Schmid. He scored a distant fourth at Phoenix, but finally quit as the team slid into oblivion.

Christian then spent the next few years as a real globe-trotter, competing in Japanese F3000, Indy cars and the GTCC, driving a BMW in 1991. Landing a works-backed Alfa in the DTM/ITC run by Schübel, Danner put in some very strong performances, and was rewarded with outright wins in 1995 at Helsinki and Norisring.

Christian is a co-owner with Andreas Leberle of the Project Indy CART team, which has always competed on very limited resources. Danner managed to drive in a couple of Indy Car races himself in 1995, the first of which, in Miami, brought the team a remarkable seventh place, despite his having to resort to an elderly '93 Lola. It is a testament to his racing abilities that, in 1997, even two years away from CART proved to be no barrier to Christian. At short notice, he hopped into the Payton/Coyne Lola at Detroit and picked up the team's first point of the year with a solid 12th-place finish.

Lack of finance has since kept Project Indy's plans on the back burner and therefore his racing activities have been centred on the German Super Touring series with an Alfa Romeo. Looking to the future, however, the charismatic Danner is exploring the possibilities of starting up a low-tech touring car series in Germany.

DANNER, Christian (D) b 4/4/1958, Munich

	1985			Championship position: Unplaced				
	Race	Circuit	No	Entrant	Tyres	Car/Engine	Comment	Q Pos/Entries
ret	BELGIAN GP	Spa	30	West Zakspeed Racing	G	1.5 t/c Zakspeed 841 4	gearbox	22/24
ret	EUROPEAN GP	Brands Hatch	30	West Zakspeed Racing	G	1.5 t/c Zakspeed 841 4	engine	25/27
	1986			Championship position: 18th= Wins: 0 Pole positions: 0 Fastest laps: 0 Points scored: 1				
ret	BRAZILIAN GP	Rio	22	Osella Squadra Corse	P	1.5 t/c Osella FA1F-Alfa Romeo V8	engine	24/25
ret	SPANISH GP	Jerez	22	Osella Squadra Corse	P	1.5 t/c Osella FA1F-Alfa Romeo V8	engine	23/25
ret	SAN MARINO GP	Imola	22	Osella Squadra Corse	P	1.5 t/c Osella FA1F-Alfa Romeo V8	electrics	25/26
dnq	MONACO GP	Monte Carlo	22	Osella Squadra Corse	P	1.5 t/c Osella FA1F-Alfa Romeo V8		24/26
ret	BELGIAN GP	Spa	22	Osella Squadra Corse	P	1.5 t/c Osella FA1F-Alfa Romeo V8	started from pit lane/engine	25/25
ret	CANADIAN GP	Montreal	22	Osella Squadra Corse	P	1.5 t/c Osella FA1F-Alfa Romeo V8	turbo	25/25
dnp	"	"	17	Barclay Arrows BMW	G	1.5 t/c Arrows A8-BMW 4	contractual problems	– / –

ret	US GP (DETROIT)	Detroit	17	Barclay Arrows BMW	G	1.5 t/c Arrows A8-BMW 4	electrics-fuel metering unit	19/26
11	FRENCH GP	Paul Ricard	17	Barclay Arrows BMW	G	1.5 t/c Arrows A8-BMW 4	stalled on grid/4 laps behind	18/26
ret/dns	BRITISH GP	Brands Hatch	17	Barclay Arrows BMW	G	1.5 t/c Arrows A8-BMW 4	accident-first start/did not restart	23/26
ret	GERMAN GP	Hockenheim	17	Barclay Arrows BMW	G	1.5 t/c Arrows A8-BMW 4	turbo	17/26
ret	HUNGARIAN GP	Hungaroring	17	Barclay Arrows BMW	G	1.5 t/c Arrows A9-BMW 4	rear suspension	21/26
dns	"	"	17	Barclay Arrows BMW	G	1.5 t/c Arrows A8-BMW 4	practice only	– / –
6	AUSTRIAN GP	Österreichring	17	Barclay Arrows BMW	G	1.5 t/c Arrows A8-BMW 4	3 laps behind	22/26
8	ITALIAN GP	Monza	17	Barclay Arrows BMW	G	1.5 t/c Arrows A8-BMW 4	2 laps behind	16/27
11	PORTUGUESE GP	Estoril	17	Barclay Arrows BMW	G	1.5 t/c Arrows A8-BMW 4	3 laps behind	22/27
9	MEXICAN GP	Mexico City	17	Barclay Arrows BMW	G	1.5 t/c Arrows A8-BMW 4	2 laps behind	20/26
ret	AUSTRALIAN GP	Adelaide	17	Barclay Arrows BMW	G	1.5 t/c Arrows A8-BMW 4	engine	24/26

1987   Championship position: Unplaced

9	BRAZILIAN GP	Rio	10	West Zakspeed Racing	G	1.5 t/c Zakspeed 861 4	3 laps behind	17/23
7	SAN MARINO GP	Imola	10	West Zakspeed Racing	G	1.5 t/c Zakspeed 861 4	2 laps behind	19/27
ret	BELGIAN GP	Spa	10	West Zakspeed Racing	G	1.5 t/c Zakspeed 871 4	brakes/spun off	20/26
excl	MONACO GP	Monte Carlo	10	West Zakspeed Racing	G	1.5 t/c Zakspeed 871 4	practice incident with Alboreto	– /26
8	US GP (DETROIT)	Detroit	10	West Zakspeed Racing	G	1.5 t/c Zakspeed 871 4	3 laps behind	16/26
ret	FRENCH GP	Paul Ricard	10	West Zakspeed Racing	G	1.5 t/c Zakspeed 871 4	engine	19/26
ret	BRITISH GP	Silverstone	10	West Zakspeed Racing	G	1.5 t/c Zakspeed 871 4	gearbox	18/26
ret	GERMAN GP	Hockenheim	10	West Zakspeed Racing	G	1.5 t/c Zakspeed 871 4	drive shaft	20/26
ret	HUNGARIAN GP	Hungaroring	10	West Zakspeed Racing	G	1.5 t/c Zakspeed 871 4	engine cut out	23/26
9	AUSTRIAN GP	Österreichring	10	West Zakspeed Racing	G	1.5 t/c Zakspeed 871 4	started from pit lane/-3 laps	20/26
9	ITALIAN GP	Monza	10	West Zakspeed Racing	G	1.5 t/c Zakspeed 871 4	2 laps behind	16/28
ret/dns	PORTUGUESE GP	Estoril	10	West Zakspeed Racing	G	1.5 t/c Zakspeed 871 4	accident in first start	16/27
ret	SPANISH GP	Jerez	10	West Zakspeed Racing	G	1.5 t/c Zakspeed 871 4	gearbox	22/28
ret	MEXICAN GP	Mexico City	10	West Zakspeed Racing	G	1.5 t/c Zakspeed 871 4	hit Johansson	17/27
ret	JAPANESE GP	Suzuka	10	West Zakspeed Racing	G	1.5 t/c Zakspeed 871 4	accident	17/27
7*	AUSTRALIAN GP	Adelaide	10	West Zakspeed Racing	G	1.5 t/c Zakspeed 871 4	* 2nd place car dsq/-3 laps	24/27

1989   Championship position: 21st=   Wins: 0   Pole positions: 0   Fastest laps: 0   Points scored: 3

14/ret	BRAZILIAN GP	Rio	38	Rial Racing	G	3.5 Rial ARC2-Cosworth V8	gearbox/5 laps behind	17/38
dnq	SAN MARINO GP	Imola	38	Rial Racing	G	3.5 Rial ARC2-Cosworth V8		29/38
dnq	MONACO GP	Monte Carlo	38	Rial Racing	G	3.5 Rial ARC2-Cosworth V8		27/38
12	MEXICAN GP	Mexico City	38	Rial Racing	G	3.5 Rial ARC2-Cosworth V8	2 laps behind	23/39
4	US GP (PHOENIX)	Phoenix	38	Rial Racing	G	3.5 Rial ARC2-Cosworth V8	1 lap behind	26/39
8	CANADIAN GP	Montreal	38	Rial Racing	G	3.5 Rial ARC2-Cosworth V8	3 laps behind	23/39
dnq	FRENCH GP	Paul Ricard	38	Rial Racing	G	3.5 Rial ARC2-Cosworth V8		29/39
dnq	BRITISH GP	Silverstone	38	Rial Racing	G	3.5 Rial ARC2-Cosworth V8		30/39
dnq	GERMAN GP	Hockenheim	38	Rial Racing	G	3.5 Rial ARC2-Cosworth V8		29/39
dnq	HUNGARIAN GP	Hungaroring	38	Rial Racing	G	3.5 Rial ARC2-Cosworth V8		29/39
dnq	BELGIAN GP	Spa	38	Rial Racing	G	3.5 Rial ARC2-Cosworth V8		29/39
dnq	ITALIAN GP	Monza	38	Rial Racing	G	3.5 Rial ARC2-Cosworth V8		28/39
dnq	PORTUGUESE GP	Estoril	38	Rial Racing	G	3.5 Rial ARC2-Cosworth V8		31/39

GP Starts: 34 (36)   GP Wins: 0   Pole positions: 0   Fastest laps: 0   Points: 4

DAPONTE, Jorge (RA) b 5/6/1923, Buenos Aires – d 3/1963

1954   Championship position: Unplaced

	Race	Circuit	No	Entrant	Tyres	Car/Engine	Comment	Q Pos/Entries
ret	ARGENTINE GP	Buenos Aires	34	Jorge Daponte	P	2.5 Maserati A6GCM/250F 6	transmission	18/18
nc	ITALIAN GP	Monza	8	Jorge Daponte	P	2.5 Maserati A6GCM/250F 6	10 laps behind	19/21

GP Starts: 2   GP Wins: 0   Pole positions: 0   Fastest laps: 0   Points: 0

DAVIS, Colin (GB) b 29/7/1932, London

1959   Championship position: Unplaced

	Race	Circuit	No	Entrant	Tyres	Car/Engine	Comment	Q Pos/Entries
ret	FRENCH GP	Reims	20	Scuderia Centro Sud	D	2.5 Cooper T51-Maserati 4	oil pipe	17/22
11	ITALIAN GP	Monza	40	Scuderia Centro Sud	D	2.5 Cooper T51-Maserati 4	4 laps behind	18/21

GP Starts: 2   GP Wins: 0   Pole positions: 0   Fastest laps: 0   Points: 0

COLIN DAVIS

Son of the legendary S C H 'Sammy' Davis, Colin began his career in 1954 with a Cooper Norton, using F3 as a good learning vehicle before switching to sports cars to pursue his intended aim of racing in long-distance events. Unusually for an Englishman with so much racing available in his homeland, Davis soon made Italy the centre of his activities, driving for de Tomaso, for Scuderia Centro Sud in Grands Prix and sports car races, and, from 1960, for Scuderia Serenissima. He was also a leading runner in Formula Junior, winning at Albi in 1959 and at Pau in 1960 with a Taraschi.

His greatest success still lay ahead, though, Colin winning the 1964 Targa Florio in a works Porsche 904 GT with Pucci. This led to other races for the Stuttgart team, and he finished second in the 1965 Targa with Mitter and fourth at Le Mans in 1966 with Siffert.

ANDREA de ADAMICH

With success in the 1965 Italian F3 championship and the 1966 European touring car series in an Alfa Romeo Giulia GTA behind him, de Adamich was given a works debut for Ferrari in the non-championship F1 Spanish GP at Jarama late in 1967 – finishing ninth after a puncture – but his Grand Prix career as a Ferrari driver faltered at the first hurdle with an accident at Kyalami in 1968 and came undone shortly afterwards when a crash in practice for the Race of Champions at Brands Hatch inflicted neck injuries which sidelined him for much of the season. Despite a victorious comeback with the works Ferrari Dino T166 which saw him win two races and the championship in the South American Formula 2 Temporada series, the Italian's big chance had gone.

Undaunted, he busied himself in the newly inaugurated F5000/FA series for Team Surtees on both sides of the Atlantic before returning to F1 in 1970, initially with backing from Alfa Romeo, racing their engine in a variety of 'third' works cars. A switch to Ford power made possible occasional good placings, but leg injuries sustained in the multiple accident caused by Jody Scheckter in the 1973 British Grand Prix brought his Formula 1 career to a premature end.

In parallel to his activities in Grand Prix racing, de Adamich was a works driver for Alfa Romeo in their successful T33 sports cars from 1970 to 1974, winning the Brands Hatch 1000 Km and the Watkins Glen 6 Hours in 1971. When his hectic racing schedule allowed, he also competed in Can-Am, touring cars and hill-climbs. After his retirement in 1974 Andrea returned to the Grand Prix scene as a respected motor sport journalist and TV commentator, and in recent seasons has overseen the racing exploits of his son Gordon.

de ADAMICH, Andrea (I) b 3/10/1941, Trieste

	Race	Circuit	No	Entrant	Tyres	Car/Engine	Comment	Q Pos/Entries
1968				Championship position: Unplaced				
ret	SOUTH AFRICAN GP	Kyalami	10	Scuderia Ferrari SpA SEFAC	F	3.0 Ferrari 312/67 V12	spun off on oil-crashed	7/23
1970				Championship position: Unplaced				
dnq	SPANISH GP	Jarama	20	Bruce McLaren Motor Racing	G	3.0 McLaren M7D-Alfa Romeo V8	not seeded	13/22
dnq	MONACO GP	Monte Carlo	10	Bruce McLaren Motor Racing	G	3.0 McLaren M7D-Alfa Romeo V8		18/21
dnq	DUTCH GP	Zandvoort	21	Bruce McLaren Motor Racing	G	3.0 McLaren M14D-Alfa Romeo V8	not seeded	19/24
nc	FRENCH GP	Clermont Ferrand	16	Bruce McLaren Motor Racing	G	3.0 McLaren M7D-Alfa Romeo V8	pit stops-water pipe/-9 laps	15/23
dns	BRITISH GP	Brands Hatch	11	Bruce McLaren Motor Racing	G	3.0 McLaren M7D-Alfa Romeo V8	leaking fuel tank	(19)/25
dnq	GERMAN GP	Hockenheim	20	Bruce McLaren Motor Racing	G	3.0 McLaren M14D-Alfa Romeo V8		22/25
12	AUSTRIAN GP	Österreichring	22	Bruce McLaren Motor Racing	G	3.0 McLaren M14D-Alfa Romeo V8	engine off song/-3 laps	14/24
8	ITALIAN GP	Monza	34	Bruce McLaren Motor Racing	G	3.0 McLaren M14D-Alfa Romeo V8	pit stop-tyres/fuel/-7 laps	13/27
ret	CANADIAN GP	St Jovite	8	Bruce McLaren Motor Racing	G	3.0 McLaren M14D-Alfa Romeo V8	engine	=11/20
dnq	US GP	Watkins Glen	10	Bruce McLaren Motor Racing	G	3.0 McLaren M14D-Alfa Romeo V8		27/27
1971				Championship position: Unplaced				
13	SOUTH AFRICAN GP	Kyalami	8	STP-March	F	3.0 March 711-Alfa Romeo V8	4 laps behind	22/25
ret	SPANISH GP	Montjuich Park	17	STP-March	F	3.0 March 711-Alfa Romeo V8	transmission	18/22
ret	FRENCH GP	Paul Ricard	19	STP-March	F	3.0 March 711-Alfa Romeo V8	engine	21/24
nc	BRITISH GP	Silverstone	19	STP-March	F	3.0 March 711-Alfa Romeo V8	pit stops-electrics/-12 laps	24/24
ret	GERMAN GP	Nürburgring	16	STP-March	F	3.0 March 711-Alfa Romeo V8	fuel injection	20/23
ret	ITALIAN GP	Monza	23	STP-March	F	3.0 March 711-Alfa Romeo V8	engine	20/24
11	US GP	Watkins Glen	27	STP-March	F	3.0 March 711-Alfa Romeo V8	2 laps behind	28/32
1972				Championship position: 16th= Wins: 0 Pole positions: 0 Fastest laps: 0 Points scored: 3				
ret	ARGENTINE GP	Buenos Aires	20	Ceramica Pagnossin Team Surtees	F	3.0 Surtees TS9B-Cosworth V8	fuel line	14/22
nc	SOUTH AFRICAN GP	Kyalami	18	Ceramica Pagnossin Team Surtees	F	3.0 Surtees TS9B-Cosworth V8	pit stop-brakes/-10 laps	=20/27
4	SPANISH GP	Jarama	26	Ceramica Pagnossin Team Surtees	F	3.0 Surtees TS9B-Cosworth V8	1 lap behind	13/26
7	MONACO GP	Monte Carlo	12	Ceramica Pagnossin Team Surtees	F	3.0 Surtees TS9B-Cosworth V8	3 laps behind	=18/25
ret	BELGIAN GP	Nivelles	36	Ceramica Pagnossin Team Surtees	F	3.0 Surtees TS9B-Cosworth V8	engine	10/26
14	FRENCH GP	Clermont Ferrand	28	Ceramica Pagnossin Team Surtees	F	3.0 Surtees TS9B-Cosworth V8	pit stop-puncture/-1 lap	13/29
ret	BRITISH GP	Brands Hatch	23	Ceramica Pagnossin Team Surtees	F	3.0 Surtees TS9B-Cosworth V8	spun off	=20/27
13	GERMAN GP	Nürburgring	16	Ceramica Pagnossin Team Surtees	F	3.0 Surtees TS9B-Cosworth V8	pit stop-handling/-1 lap	20/27
14	AUSTRIAN GP	Österreichring	11	Ceramica Pagnossin Team Surtees	F	3.0 Surtees TS9B-Cosworth V8	pit stops-engine/-3 laps	13/26
ret	ITALIAN GP	Monza	9	Ceramica Pagnossin Team Surtees	F	3.0 Surtees TS9B-Cosworth V8	brake calliper	21/27
ret	CANADIAN GP	Mosport Park	23	Ceramica Pagnossin Team Surtees	F	3.0 Surtees TS9B-Cosworth V8	gearbox	15/25
ret	US GP	Watkins Glen	25	Ceramica Pagnossin Team Surtees	F	3.0 Surtees TS9B-Cosworth V8	collision with Ganley	19/32
1973				Championship position: 15th= Wins: 0 Pole positions: 0 Fastest laps: 0 Points scored: 3				
8	SOUTH AFRICAN GP	Kyalami	12	Ceramica Pagnossin Team Surtees	F	3.0 Surtees TS9B-Cosworth V8	2 laps behind	20/25
ret	SPANISH GP	Montjuich Park	21	Ceramica Pagnossin MRD	G	3.0 Brabham BT37-Cosworth V8	hub failure-accident	17/22
4	BELGIAN GP	Zolder	9	Ceramica Pagnossin MRD	G	3.0 Brabham BT37-Cosworth V8	1 lap behind	18/23
7	MONACO GP	Monte Carlo	9	Ceramica Pagnossin MRD	G	3.0 Brabham BT37-Cosworth V8	3 laps behind	26/26
ret	FRENCH GP	Paul Ricard	9	Ceramica Pagnossin MRD	G	3.0 Brabham BT37-Cosworth V8	driveshaft	13/25
ret/dns	BRITISH GP	Silverstone	9	Ceramica Pagnossin MRD	G	3.0 Brabham BT42-Cosworth V8	accident at first start	20/29

GP Starts: 29 (30) GP Wins: 0 Pole positions: 0 Fastest laps: 0 Points: 6

ELIO de ANGELIS

From a wealthy background, Elio had a reputation as something of a cocky rich-kid when he stepped from karting into Italian F3 at the beginning of 1977. Winning his third-ever F3 race, de Angelis snatched the championship at the very last gasp from Piercarlo Ghinzani, and took an impressive seventh in the European series. After taking a controversial win in the 1978 Monaco F3 race, Elio moved up to Formula 2 but he endured a fairly barren year and, since he was not slow to show his feelings, was seen as something of a spoilt prima donna.

It may have been a considerable gamble, but at the age of just 20 the inexperienced de Angelis joined a Shadow team which was in steep decline. With the exuberance of youth and not a little skill, the young Roman extracted the very best from a poor car and his performances were not lost on Colin Chapman, who signed him for 1980. He made a great start for Lotus, taking a brilliant second place in Brazil, and – one or two silly incidents apart – soon settled down to become a most consistent points finisher over the next couple of seasons, the highlight of which was a hair's-breadth win over Keke Rosberg in the 1982 Austrian GP.

The following year was a transitional period for the team as they struggled to gain reliability from their Renault turbo-engined car, and results were thin on the ground. It was the reverse in 1984, though, as a string of excellent placings saw Elio leading the World Championship by mid-season, but in the end he had to settle for third place in the points table behind Lauda and Prost.

De Angelis had spent four seasons vying somewhat inconclusively for number one status with Nigel Mansell, but the arrival of Ayrton Senna in 1985 soon put the Roman in the shade, a lucky win at Imola following Prost's disqualification notwithstanding. Accepting the situation would not change in his favour, Elio joined Brabham in 1986 to race their radical but complicated 'lowline' BT55, but he managed just one finish, and that after losing a wheel, before a routine testing session at Paul Ricard in mid-May ended in catastrophe when the Brabham was thought to have suffered a component failure, crashing heavily at 180 mph. Elio's injuries were so severe he stood no chance of survival, dying in hospital a few hours later, and the entire motor racing world mourned the loss of a popular driver who had long since earned the respect of his peers.

ANGELIS, Elio de (I) b 26/3/1958, Rome – d 15/5/1986, Marseille, France

1979 Championship position: 15th= Wins: 0 Pole positions: 0 Fastest laps: 0 Points scored: 3

	Race	Circuit	No	Entrant	Tyres	Car/Engine	Comment	Q Pos/Entries
7	ARGENTINE GP	Buenos Aires	18	Interscope Shadow Racing Team	G	3.0 Shadow DN9-Cosworth V8	1 lap behind	16/26
12	BRAZILIAN GP	Interlagos	18	Interscope Shadow Racing Team	G	3.0 Shadow DN9-Cosworth V8	1 lap behind	20/26
ret	SOUTH AFRICAN GP	Kyalami	18	Interscope Shadow Racing Team	G	3.0 Shadow DN9-Cosworth V8	spun off	=14/26
7	US GP WEST	Long Beach	18	Interscope Shadow Racing Team	G	3.0 Shadow DN9-Cosworth V8	2 laps behind	21/26
ret	SPANISH GP	Jarama	18	Interscope Shadow Racing Team	G	3.0 Shadow DN9-Cosworth V8	engine	22/27
ret	BELGIAN GP	Zolder	18	Interscope Shadow Racing Team	G	3.0 Shadow DN9-Cosworth V8	hit Giacomelli	24/28
dnq	MONACO GP	Monte Carlo	18	Interscope Shadow Racing Team	G	3.0 Shadow DN9-Cosworth V8		21/25
dnq/16	FRENCH GP	Dijon	18	Interscope Shadow Racing Team	G	3.0 Shadow DN9-Cosworth V8	started as 1st reserve/-5 laps	25/27
12*	BRITISH GP	Silverstone	18	Interscope Shadow Racing Team	G	3.0 Shadow DN9-Cosworth V8	* 1min penalty-jump start/-3 laps	12/26
11	GERMAN GP	Hockenheim	18	Interscope Shadow Racing Team	G	3.0 Shadow DN9-Cosworth V8	2 laps behind	21/26
ret	AUSTRIAN GP	Österreichring	18	Interscope Shadow Racing Team	G	3.0 Shadow DN9-Cosworth V8	engine	22/26
ret	DUTCH GP	Zandvoort	18	Interscope Shadow Racing Team	G	3.0 Shadow DN9-Cosworth V8	driveshaft	22/26
ret	ITALIAN GP	Monza	18	Interscope Shadow Racing Team	G	3.0 Shadow DN9-Cosworth V8	distributor rotor arm	24/28
ret	CANADIAN GP	Montreal	18	Interscope Shadow Racing Team	G	3.0 Shadow DN9-Cosworth V8	broken rotor arm	23/29
4	US GP EAST	Long Beach	18	Interscope Shadow Racing Team	G	3.0 Shadow DN9-Cosworth V8		20/30

1980 Championship position: 7th Wins: 0 Pole positions: 0 Fastest laps: 0 Points scored: 13

	Race	Circuit	No	Entrant	Tyres	Car/Engine	Comment	Q Pos/Entries
ret	ARGENTINE GP	Buenos Aires	12	Team Essex Lotus	G	3.0 Lotus 81-Cosworth V8	suspension	5/28
2	BRAZILIAN GP	Interlagos	12	Team Essex Lotus	G	3.0 Lotus 81-Cosworth V8		7/28
ret	SOUTH AFRICAN GP	Kyalami	12	Team Essex Lotus	G	3.0 Lotus 81-Cosworth V8	spun off	14/28
ret	US GP WEST	Long Beach	12	Team Essex Lotus	G	3.0 Lotus 81-Cosworth V8	multiple accident-broken foot	20/27
10/ret	BELGIAN GP	Zolder	12	Team Essex Lotus	G	3.0 Lotus 81-Cosworth V8	spun off/3 laps behind	8/27
9/ret	MONACO GP	Monte Carlo	12	Team Essex Lotus	G	3.0 Lotus 81-Cosworth V8	spun off into wall/-8 laps	14/27
ret	FRENCH GP	Paul Ricard	12	Team Essex Lotus	G	3.0 Lotus 81-Cosworth V8	clutch	14/27
ret	BRITISH GP	Brands Hatch	12	Team Essex Lotus	G	3.0 Lotus 81-Cosworth V8	rear suspension	14/27
16/ret	GERMAN GP	Hockenheim	12	Team Essex Lotus	G	3.0 Lotus 81-Cosworth V8	wheel bearing/2 laps behind	11/26
6	AUSTRIAN GP	Österreichring	12	Team Essex Lotus	G	3.0 Lotus 81-Cosworth V8		9/25
ret	DUTCH GP	Zandvoort	12	Team Essex Lotus	G	3.0 Lotus 81-Cosworth V8	collision with Pironi	11/28
4	ITALIAN GP	Imola	12	Team Essex Lotus	G	3.0 Lotus 81-Cosworth V8	1 lap behind	18/28
10	CANADIAN GP	Montreal	12	Team Essex Lotus	G	3.0 Lotus 81-Cosworth V8	damaged skirt/2 laps behind	17/28
4	US GP EAST	Watkins Glen	12	Team Essex Lotus	G	3.0 Lotus 81-Cosworth V8		4/27

1981 Championship position: 8 Wins: 0 Pole positions: 0 Fastest laps: 0 Points scored: 14

	Race	Circuit	No	Entrant	Tyres	Car/Engine	Comment	Q Pos/Entries
ret	US GP WEST	Long Beach	11	Team Essex Lotus	M	3.0 Lotus 81-Cosworth V8	hit wall	13/29
dns	"		11T	Team Essex Lotus	M	3.0 Lotus 88-Cosworth V8	car banned by scrutineers	– / –
5	BRAZILIAN GP	Rio	11	Team Essex Lotus	M	3.0 Lotus 81-Cosworth V8		10/30
6	ARGENTINE GP	Buenos Aires	11	Team Essex Lotus	M	3.0 Lotus 81-Cosworth V8	1 lap behind	10/29
5	BELGIAN GP	Zolder	11	Team Essex Lotus	M	3.0 Lotus 81-Cosworth V8		14/31
ret	MONACO GP	Monte Carlo	11	Team Essex Lotus	M	3.0 Lotus 87-Cosworth V8	engine	6/31
5	SPANISH GP	Jarama	11	John Player Team Lotus	M	3.0 Lotus 87-Cosworth V8		10/30
6	FRENCH GP	Dijon	11	John Player Team Lotus	M	3.0 Lotus 87-Cosworth V8	1 lap behind	8/29
ret	BRITISH GP	Silverstone	11	John Player Team Lotus	G	3.0 Lotus 87-Cosworth V8	retired after being black-flagged	22/30
dns	"	"	11	John Player Team Lotus	G	3.0 Lotus 88B-Cosworth V8	practice only	– / –
7	GERMAN GP	Hockenheim	11	John Player Team Lotus	G	3.0 Lotus 87-Cosworth V8	1 lap behind	14/30
7	AUSTRIAN GP	Österreichring	11	John Player Team Lotus	G	3.0 Lotus 87-Cosworth V8	1 lap behind	9/28
5	DUTCH GP	Zandvoort	11	John Player Team Lotus	G	3.0 Lotus 87-Cosworth V8	1 lap behind	9/30
4	ITALIAN GP	Monza	11	John Player Team Lotus	G	3.0 Lotus 87-Cosworth V8		11/30
6	CANADIAN GP	Montreal	11	John Player Team Lotus	G	3.0 Lotus 87-Cosworth V8	1 lap behind	7/30
ret	CAESARS PALACE GP	Las Vegas	11	John Player Team Lotus	G	3.0 Lotus 87-Cosworth V8	water leak	15/30

1982 Championship position: 9h Wins: 1 Pole positions: 0 Fastest laps: 0 Points scored: 23

	Race	Circuit	No	Entrant	Tyres	Car/Engine	Comment	Q Pos/Entries
8	SOUTH AFRICAN GP	Kyalami	11	John Player Team Lotus	G	3.0 Lotus 87B-Cosworth V8	1 lap behind	15/30
ret	BRAZILIAN GP	Rio	11	John Player Team Lotus	G	3.0 Lotus 91-Cosworth V8	hit by Baldi	11/31
5*	US GP WEST	Long Beach	11	John Player Team Lotus	G	3.0 Lotus 91-Cosworth V8	* 3rd place car dsq/-1 lap	16/31
4*	BELGIAN GP	Zolder	11	John Player Team Lotus	G	3.0 Lotus 91-Cosworth V8	* 3rd place car dsq/-2 laps	13/32
5	MONACO GP	Monte Carlo	11	John Player Team Lotus	G	3.0 Lotus 91-Cosworth V8	1 lap behind	15/31
ret	US GP (DETROIT)	Detroit	11	John Player Team Lotus	G	3.0 Lotus 91-Cosworth V8	gearbox	8/28
4	CANADIAN GP	Montreal	11	John Player Team Lotus	G	3.0 Lotus 91-Cosworth V8	1 lap behind	10/29
ret	DUTCH GP	Zandvoort	11	John Player Team Lotus	G	3.0 Lotus 91-Cosworth V8	handling	15/31
4	BRITISH GP	Brands Hatch	11	John Player Team Lotus	G	3.0 Lotus 91-Cosworth V8		7/30
ret	FRENCH GP	Paul Ricard	11	John Player Team Lotus	G	3.0 Lotus 91-Cosworth V8	fuel pressure	13/30
ret	GERMAN GP	Hockenheim	11	John Player Team Lotus	G	3.0 Lotus 91-Cosworth V8	transmission	14/30
1	AUSTRIAN GP	Österreichring	11	John Player Team Lotus	G	3.0 Lotus 91-Cosworth V8	won by 0.050s from Rosberg	7/29
6	SWISS GP	Dijon	11	John Player Team Lotus	G	3.0 Lotus 91-Cosworth V8	1 lap behind	15/29
ret	ITALIAN GP	Monza	11	John Player Team Lotus	G	3.0 Lotus 91-Cosworth V8	handling/sticking throttle	17/30
ret	CAESARS PALACE GP	Las Vegas	11	John Player Team Lotus	G	3.0 Lotus 91-Cosworth V8	engine	20/30

1983 Championship position: 17th= Wins: 0 Pole positions: 1 Fastest laps: 0 Points scored: 2

	Race	Circuit	No	Entrant	Tyres	Car/Engine	Comment	Q Pos/Entries
13/dsq	BRAZILIAN GP	Rio	11	John Player Team Lotus	P	3.0 Lotus 91-Cosworth V8	dsq-did not practise in this car	– / –
dns	"	"	1	John Player Team Lotus	P	1.5 t/c Lotus 93T-Renault V6	turbo-warm-up lap-changed cars	13/27
ret	US GP WEST	Long Beach	11	John Player Team Lotus	P	1.5 t/c Lotus 93T-Renault V6	tyres	5/28
ret	FRENCH GP	Paul Ricard	11	John Player Team Lotus	P	1.5 t/c Lotus 93T-Renault V6	electrics	5/29
ret	SAN MARINO GP	Imola	11	John Player Team Lotus	P	1.5 t/c Lotus 93T-Renault V6	poor handling/driver gave up	9/28
ret	MONACO GP	Monte Carlo	11	John Player Team Lotus	P	1.5 t/c Lotus 93T-Renault V6	driveshaft	19/28
9	BELGIAN GP	Spa	11	John Player Team Lotus	P	1.5 t/c Lotus 93T-Renault V6	1 lap behind	13/28
ret	US GP (DETROIT)	Detroit	11	John Player Team Lotus	P	1.5 t/c Lotus 93T-Renault V6	transmission	4/27
ret	CANADIAN GP	Montreal	11	John Player Team Lotus	P	1.5 t/c Lotus 93T-Renault V6	throttle linkage	11/28
ret	BRITISH GP	Silverstone	11	John Player Team Lotus	P	1.5 t/c Lotus 94T-Renault V6	engine-turbo fire	4/29
ret	GERMAN GP	Hockenheim	11	John Player Team Lotus	P	1.5 t/c Lotus 94T-Renault V6	overheating	11/29
ret	AUSTRIAN GP	Österreichring	11	John Player Team Lotus	P	1.5 t/c Lotus 94T-Renault V6	spun, hit Giacomelli	– / –
dns	"	"	11	John Player Team Lotus	P	1.5 t/c Lotus 93T-Renault V6	practice only-qualifying car	12/29

ret	DUTCH GP	Zandvoort	11	John Player Team Lotus	P	1.5 t/c Lotus 94T-Renault V6	*fuel metering unit*	3/29
5	ITALIAN GP	Monza	11	John Player Team Lotus	P	1.5 t/c Lotus 94T-Renault V6		8/29
ret	EUROPEAN GP	Brands Hatch	11	John Player Team Lotus	P	1.5 t/c Lotus 94T-Renault V6	*engine*	1/29
ret	SOUTH AFRICAN GP	Kyalami	11	John Player Team Lotus	P	1.5 t/c Lotus 94T-Renault V6	*engine misfire*	11/26

1984   Championship position: 3rd   Wins: 0   Pole positions: 1   Fastest laps: 0   Points scored: 34

3	BRAZILIAN GP	Rio	11	John Player Team Lotus	G	1.5 t/c Lotus 95T-Renault V6		1/27
7	SOUTH AFRICAN GP	Kyalami	11	John Player Team Lotus	G	1.5 t/c Lotus 95T-Renault V6	*pit stop-throttle cable/-4 laps*	7/27
5	BELGIAN GP	Zolder	11	John Player Team Lotus	G	1.5 t/c Lotus 95T-Renault V6	*1 lap behind*	5/27
3/ret	SAN MARINO GP	Imola	11	John Player Team Lotus	G	1.5 t/c Lotus 95T-Renault V6	*out of fuel/1 lap behind*	11/28
5	FRENCH GP	Dijon	11	John Player Team Lotus	G	1.5 t/c Lotus 95T-Renault V6		2/27
5*	MONACO GP	Monte Carlo	11	John Player Team Lotus	G	1.5 t/c Lotus 95T-Renault V6	** 3rd place car dsq/half points*	11/27
4	CANADIAN GP	Montreal	11	John Player Team Lotus	G	1.5 t/c Lotus 95T-Renault V6	*1 lap behind*	3/26
2*	US GP (DETROIT)	Detroit	11	John Player Team Lotus	G	1.5 t/c Lotus 95T-Renault V6	** 2nd place car disqualified*	5/27
3	US GP (DALLAS)	Dallas	11	John Player Team Lotus	G	1.5 t/c Lotus 95T-Renault V6	*1 lap behind*	2/27
4	BRITISH GP	Brands Hatch	11	John Player Team Lotus	G	1.5 t/c Lotus 95T-Renault V6	*1 lap behind*	4/27
ret	GERMAN GP	Hockenheim	11	John Player Team Lotus	G	1.5 t/c Lotus 95T-Renault V6	*turbo*	2/27
ret	AUSTRIAN GP	Österreichring	11	John Player Team Lotus	G	1.5 t/c Lotus 95T-Renault V6	*engine*	3/28
4	DUTCH GP	Zandvoort	11	John Player Team Lotus	G	1.5 t/c Lotus 95T-Renault V6	*1 lap behind*	3/27
ret	ITALIAN GP	Monza	11	John Player Team Lotus	G	1.5 t/c Lotus 95T-Renault V6	*gearbox*	3/27
ret	EUROPEAN GP	Nürburgring	11	John Player Team Lotus	G	1.5 t/c Lotus 95T-Renault V6	*turbo*	23/26
5	PORTUGUESE GP	Estoril	11	John Player Team Lotus	G	1.5 t/c Lotus 95T-Renault V6		5/27

1985   Championship position: 5th   Wins: 1   Pole positions: 1   Fastest laps: 0   Points scored: 33

3	BRAZILIAN GP	Rio	11	John Player Special Team Lotus	G	1.5 t/c Lotus 97T-Renault V6	*1 lap behind*	3/25
4	PORTUGUESE GP	Estoril	11	John Player Special Team Lotus	G	1.5 t/c Lotus 97T-Renault V6	*1 lap behind*	4/26
1*	SAN MARINO GP	Imola	11	John Player Special Team Lotus	G	1.5 t/c Lotus 97T-Renault V6	**1st place car disqualified*	3/26
3	MONACO GP	Monte Carlo	11	John Player Special Team Lotus	G	1.5 t/c Lotus 97T-Renault V6		9/26
5	CANADIAN GP	Montreal	11	John Player Special Team Lotus	G	1.5 t/c Lotus 97T-Renault V6		1/25
5	US GP (DETROIT)	Detroit	11	John Player Special Team Lotus	G	1.5 t/c Lotus 97T-Renault V6		8/25
5	FRENCH GP	Paul Ricard	11	John Player Special Team Lotus	G	1.5 t/c Lotus 97T-Renault V6		7/26
nc	BRITISH GP	Silverstone	11	John Player Special Team Lotus	G	1.5 t/c Lotus 97T-Renault V6	*pit stop-engine/28 laps behind*	8/26
ret	GERMAN GP	Hockenheim	11	John Player Special Team Lotus	G	1.5 t/c Lotus 97T-Renault V6	*engine*	7/27
5	AUSTRIAN GP	Österreichring	11	John Player Special Team Lotus	G	1.5 t/c Lotus 97T-Renault V6		7/27
5	DUTCH GP	Zandvoort	11	John Player Special Team Lotus	G	1.5 t/c Lotus 97T-Renault V6	*1 lap behind*	11/27
6	ITALIAN GP	Monza	11	John Player Special Team Lotus	G	1.5 t/c Lotus 97T-Renault V6	*1 lap behind*	6/26
ret	BELGIAN GP	Spa	11	John Player Special Team Lotus	G	1.5 t/c Lotus 97T-Renault V6	*turbo*	9/24
5	EUROPEAN GP	Brands Hatch	11	John Player Special Team Lotus	G	1.5 t/c Lotus 97T-Renault V6	*1 lap behind*	9/27
ret	SOUTH AFRICAN GP	Kyalami	11	John Player Special Team Lotus	G	1.5 t/c Lotus 97T-Renault V6	*engine*	6/21
dsq*	AUSTRALIAN GP	Adelaide	11	John Player Special Team Lotus	G	1.5 t/c Lotus 97T-Renault V6	** excluded-changed grid position*	10/25

1986   Championship position: Unplaced

8	BRAZILIAN GP	Rio	8	Motor Racing Developments	P	1.5 t/c Brabham BT55-BMW 4	*lost wheel/3 laps behind*	14/25
ret	SPANISH GP	Jerez	8	Motor Racing Developments	P	1.5 t/c Brabham BT55-BMW 4	*gearbox*	15/25
ret	SAN MARINO GP	Imola	8	Motor Racing Developments	P	1.5 t/c Brabham BT55-BMW 4	*engine*	19/26
ret	MONACO GP	Monte Carlo	8	Motor Racing Developments	P	1.5 t/c Brabham BT55-BMW 4	*engine intercooler*	20/26

GP Starts: 108   GP Wins: 2   Pole positions: 3   Fastest laps: 0   Points: 122

His arm raised in victory, Elio in the Lotus just beats Keke Rosberg's Williams across the line to win the 1982 Austrian Grand Prix.

CAREL DE BEAUFORT

The last truly amateur driver to compete in Grand Prix racing on a regular basis, de Beaufort metamorphosed from the roly-poly dilettante of his early racing career into a much more serious and competent performer– without losing his perenially sunny disposition – to earn the respect of his peers.

De Beaufort began his racing career with production Porsche spyders in 1956 and was soon itching to pit himself against the stars of the day, racing his Porsche RSK sports car in the Formula 2 category of the 1957 German Grand Prix. He had to content himself, however, with occasional Grand Prix outings until the 1961 season, when he acquired the ex-Moss Rob Walker Porsche 718.

This car, with its four-cylinder engine, then saw extensive service over the next four seasons, the broad-shouldered Count – invariably driving in stockinged feet – battling nobly against more powerful fuel-injected cars. His orange-painted machine was entered in non-championship races the length and breadth of Europe, enjoying its greatest successes in 1963 with second place in both the Syracuse and Rome GPs and third in the Austrian GP at Zeltweg.

De Beaufort plugged away into the 1964 season with the by now veteran Porsche, but in practice for the German Grand Prix he crashed heavily, sustaining injuries from which there was no recovery and dying three days later in hospital in Düsseldorf.

de BEAUFORT, Count Carel Godin (NL) b 10/4/1934, Maarsbergen – d 3/8/1964, Düsseldorf

	1957	Championship position: Unplaced						
	Race	Circuit	No	Entrant	Tyres	Car/Engine	Comment	Q Pos/Entries
14	GERMAN GP (F2)	Nürburgring	27	Ecurie Maarsbergen	D	1.5 Porsche 550RS F4 sports car	3rd in F2 class/2 laps behind	20/24
	1958	Championship position: Unplaced						
11	DUTCH GP	Zandvoort	18	Ecurie Maarsbergen	D	1.5 Porsche RSK F4 sports car	6 laps behind	17/17
ret	GERMAN GP (F2)	Nürburgring	18	Ecurie Maarsbergen	D	1.5 Porsche RSK F4 sports car	mechanical	18/26
	1959	Championship position: Unplaced						
10	DUTCH GP	Zandvoort	15	Ecurie Maarsbergen	D	1.5 Porsche RSK F4 sports car	7 laps behind	14/25
9*	FRENCH GP	Reims	42	Scuderia Ugolini	D	2.5 Maserati 250F 6	* 8th place car dsq/-10 laps	20/22
	1960	Championship position: Unplaced						
8	DUTCH GP	Zandvoort	20	Ecurie Maarsbergen	D	1.5 Cooper T51-Climax 4 F2	6 laps behind	18/21

1961 — Championship position: Unplaced

	Race	Circuit	No	Entrant	Tyres	Car/Engine	Comment	Qual Pos/Entries
14	DUTCH GP	Zandvoort	8	Ecurie Maarsbergen	D	1.5 Porsche 718 F4	3 laps behind	17/17
11	BELGIAN GP	Spa	22	Ecurie Maarsbergen	D	1.5 Porsche 718 F4	2 laps behind	14/25
ret	FRENCH GP	Reims	14	Ecurie Maarsbergen	D	1.5 Porsche 718 F4	engine overheating	17/26
16	BRITISH GP	Aintree	56	Ecurie Maarsbergen	D	1.5 Porsche 718 F4	6 laps behind	=18/30
14	GERMAN GP	Nürburgring	31	Ecurie Maarsbergen	D	1.5 Porsche 718 F4	1 lap behind	17/27
7	ITALIAN GP	Monza	74	Ecurie Maarsbergen	D	1.5 Porsche 718 F4	2 laps behind	15/33

1962 — Championship position: 16th= Wins: 0 Pole positions: 0 Fastest laps: 0 Points scored: 2

	Race	Circuit	No	Entrant	Tyres	Car/Engine	Comment	Qual Pos/Entries
6	DUTCH GP	Zandvoort	14	Ecurie Maarsbergen	D	1.5 Porsche 718 F4	4 laps behind	14/20
dnq	MONACO GP	Monte Carlo	44	Ecurie Maarsbergen	D	1.5 Porsche 718 F4		20/21
7	BELGIAN GP	Spa	7	Ecurie Maarsbergen	D	1.5 Porsche 718 F4		13/20
6	FRENCH GP	Rouen	38	Ecurie Maarsbergen	D	1.5 Porsche 718 F4	2 laps behind	17/17
14	BRITISH GP	Aintree	54	Ecurie Maarsbergen	D	1.5 Porsche 718 F4	3 laps behind	17/21
13	GERMAN GP	Nürburgring	18	Ecurie Maarsbergen	D	1.5 Porsche 718 F4	6 laps behind	8/30
10	ITALIAN GP	Monza	32	Ecurie Maarsbergen	D	1.5 Porsche 718 F4		20/30
ret	US GP	Watkins Glen	12	Ecurie Maarsbergen	D	1.5 Porsche 718 F4	5 laps behind	14/20
11/ret	SOUTH AFRICAN GP	East London	15	Ecurie Maarsbergen	D	1.5 Porsche 718 F4	hit guard rail	16/17
							fuel pump/12 laps behind	

1963 — Championship position: 14th= Wins: 0 Pole positions: 0 Fastest laps: 0 Points scored: 2

	Race	Circuit	No	Entrant	Tyres	Car/Engine	Comment	Qual Pos/Entries
6	BELGIAN GP	Spa	29	Ecurie Maarsbergen	D	1.5 Porsche 718 F4	2 laps behind	18/20
9	DUTCH GP	Zandvoort	32	Ecurie Maarsbergen	D	1.5 Porsche 718 F4	5 laps behind	19/19
10	BRITISH GP	Silverstone	23	Ecurie Maarsbergen	D	1.5 Porsche 718 F4	6 laps behind	21/23
ret	GERMAN GP	Nürburgring	17	Ecurie Maarsbergen	D	1.5 Porsche 718 F4	lost wheel	17/26
dnq	ITALIAN GP	Monza	28	Ecurie Maarsbergen	D	1.5 Porsche 718 F4		24/28
6	US GP	Watkins Glen	12	Ecurie Maarsbergen	D	1.5 Porsche 718 F4	11 laps behind	19/21
10	MEXICAN GP	Mexico City	12	Ecurie Maarsbergen	D	1.5 Porsche 718 F4	7 laps behind	18/21
10	SOUTH AFRICAN GP	East London	14	Ecurie Maarsbergen	D	1.5 Porsche 718 F4	6 laps behind	20/21

1964 — Championship position: Unplaced

	Race	Circuit	No	Entrant	Tyres	Car/Engine	Comment	Qual Pos/Entries
ret	DUTCH GP	Zandvoort	28	Ecurie Maarsbergen	D	1.5 Porsche 718 F4	valve	17/18
dns	GERMAN GP	Nürburgring	29	Ecurie Maarsbergen	D	1.5 Porsche 718 F4	fatal practice accident	(23)/24

GP Starts: 28 GP Wins: 0 Pole positions: 0 Fastest laps: 0 Points: 4

de CABRAL, Mario Araujo (P) b 15/1/1934

1959 — Championship position: Unplaced

	Race	Circuit	No	Entrant	Tyres	Car/Engine	Comment	Qual Pos/Entries
10	PORTUGUESE GP	Monsanto	18	Scuderia Centro Sud	D	2.5 Cooper T51-Maserati 4	6 laps behind	14/16

1960 — Championship position: Unplaced

	Race	Circuit	No	Entrant	Tyres	Car/Engine	Comment	Qual Pos/Entries
ret	PORTUGUESE GP	Oporto	32	Scuderia Centro Sud	D	2.5 Cooper T51-Maserati 4	clutch/gearbox	15/16

1963 — Championship position: Unplaced

	Race	Circuit	No	Entrant	Tyres	Car/Engine	Comment	Qual Pos/Entries
ret	GERMAN GP	Nürburgring	22	Scuderia Centro Sud	D	1.5 Cooper T60-Climax V8	gearbox	20/26
dnq	ITALIAN GP	Monza	64	Scuderia Centro Sud	D	1.5 Cooper T60-Climax V8		21/28

1964 — Championship position: Unplaced

	Race	Circuit	No	Entrant	Tyres	Car/Engine	Comment	Qual Pos/Entries
ret	ITALIAN GP	Monza	50	Derrington-Francis Racing Team	D	1.5 D.F. ATS 100 V8	ignition	19/25

GP Starts: 4 GP Wins: 0 Pole positions: 0 Fastest laps: 0 Points: 0

MARIO de CABRAL

de Cabral was Portugal's outstanding driver of the late fifties, and acquitted himself well in his first two Grand Prix outings. He did not pursue a full-time racing career but appeared in the 1961 Pau GP, finishing in fourth place for Centro Sud, before National Service (as a paratrooper in Angola) took priority.

He managed to return to Formula 1 in 1963 with Centro Sud and made the grid for the 1964 Italian GP in the reworked but no less unsuccessful Derrington-Francis ATS. However, Mario was seriously injured when he crashed in the 1965 F2 Rouen GP, resulting in a three-year absence from the circuits.

On his return in 1968 de Cabral raced a variety of sports cars through to 1975, including David Piper's Porsche 917, in which he finished second at Villa Real in 1971. In 1973 he hired a works March for the F2 Estoril GP and performed very creditably to finish eighth on aggregate.

ANDREA de CESARIS

De Cesaris spent more than a decade trying to live down a reputation as a wild and erratic performer, who was only competing in the top echelon by virtue of his powerful sponsorship connections. As is usually the case, there was certainly more than a grain of truth in the snipings, though by the early nineties the enfant terrible had matured into a very professional performer.

A former world karting champion, Andrea was campaigning a Ralt run by Tiga's Tim Schenken in the 1978 British BP F3 championship at the age of 18. He continued in the formula the following year with Team Tiga's March, and though he won six rounds of

the Vandervell series the silly mistakes which were to become a feature of his Formula 1 career were already apparent, spoiling his championship chances, and he finished second to Chico Serra at the season's end.

Joining Ron Dennis's Project Four outfit for the 1980 season, de Cesaris enjoyed a successful debut in the New Zealand Pacific series, winning both races at Pukekohe, before racing a March 802 in Formula 2. Though paired with Serra, it was the Italian who soon gained the upper hand and number one treatment in the team. His vast potential was there to be seen, and once a problematical tyre situation was eradicated Andrea looked a real prospect, winning the final race at Misano and a well-earned promotion to the McLaren team newly acquired by Dennis for 1981.

The season began badly when he crashed into Prost on the first lap at Long Beach, and rollercoastered downhill as the number of accidents mounted alarmingly. In most cases it would have been 'goodbye and thank you very much', but luckily for Andrea he was welcomed back by Alfa Romeo, for whom he had made his Grand Prix debut at the end of 1980. Although there were still many moments of desperation, in his two seasons with the team de Cesaris came up with some excellent performances, including a great drive at Spa in 1983, when he comfortably led the first half of the race before trouble hit. With the Alfa operation siphoned off to Pavanello's Euroracing in 1984, Andrea was found a place in the Ligier team, where all the bad traits and indiscipline which had been largely eradicated the previous year were soon to return. He was extremely lucky to emerge unharmed from a huge barrel-rolling crash in Austria in 1985, and after one more race Guy Ligier replaced him with Philippe Streiff.

Nothing if not a survivor, de Cesaris was back once more in 1986, this time leading the Minardi team, but it was to be an uncomfortable year in which he was overshadowed by team-mate

Nannini despite first call on equipment. Team-hopping was an art at which de Cesaris was to become well-practised. Fetching up at Brabham in 1987, he proved the talent was still there, with excellent performances at Spa, Estoril, Jerez and Mexico, but so were the equally lacklustre displays. It was the same sweet and sour cocktail at Rial in 1988, with an impressive drive at Detroit, where he showed remarkable restraint to finish fourth. Andrea then had a two-year tenure at Dallara, where the Jekyll and Hyde character was ever more in evidence, with Mr Hyde playing the dominant role.

Just when it seemed that the game was up and de Cesaris' chequered Grand Prix career could go no further, he was a shock choice for Jordan for 1991. If the new team was a revelation then so was Andrea, who drove better than ever before, coming very close to a second place at Spa before his engine failed at the death. Though not retained by Jordan, his performances brought him to Tyrrell for 1992, where his racecraft and new-found maturity helped bring the team much-needed points on four occasions. Sadly, 1993 found Tyrrell in deep trouble despite the promise shown by a new Yamaha engine, and there was little sign of the de Cesaris we had seen in the previous two years.

After 14 seasons and close on 200 starts he began the 1994 season without a drive but, with Jordan's Eddie Irvine suspended, Andrea was soon back in business, albeit for just two races. At Monaco he drove sensibly to take fourth place, which must have helped his cause no end as Sauber searched for a replacement for the injured Wendlinger. Apart from a sixth place in France, however, it was hardly an auspicious Grand Prix swansong, for there were to be no more Formula 1 comebacks.

CESARIS, Andrea de (I) b 31/5/1959, Rome

1980 — Championship position: Unplaced

	Race	Circuit	No	Entrant	Tyres	Car/Engine	Comment	Q Pos/Entries
ret	CANADIAN GP	Montreal	22	Marlboro Team Alfa Romeo	G	3.0 Alfa Romeo 179 V12	engine	8/28
ret	US GP EAST	Watkins Glen	22	Marlboro Team Alfa Romeo	G	3.0 Alfa Romeo 179 V12	collision with Daly	10/27

1981 — Championship position: 18th= Wins: 0 Pole positions: 0 Fastest laps: 0 Points scored: 1

	Race	Circuit	No	Entrant	Tyres	Car/Engine	Comment	Q Pos/Entries
ret	US GP WEST	Long Beach	8	McLaren International	M	3.0 McLaren M29F-Cosworth V8	hit Prost	22/29
ret	BRAZILIAN GP	Rio	8	McLaren International	M	3.0 McLaren M29F-Cosworth V8	electrics	20/30
11	ARGENTINE GP	Buenos Aires	8	McLaren International	M	3.0 McLaren M29F-Cosworth V8	2 laps behind	18/29
6	SAN MARINO GP	Imola	8	McLaren International	M	3.0 McLaren M29F-Cosworth V8		14/30
ret	BELGIAN GP	Zolder	8	McLaren International	M	3.0 McLaren M29F-Cosworth V8	gearbox	23/31
ret	MONACO GP	Monte Carlo	8	McLaren International	M	3.0 McLaren MP4-Cosworth V8	collision with Prost	11/31
ret	SPANISH GP	Jarama	8	McLaren International	M	3.0 McLaren MP4-Cosworth V8	accident	14/30
11	FRENCH GP	Dijon	8	McLaren International	M	3.0 McLaren MP4-Cosworth V8	2 laps behind	5/29
ret	BRITISH GP	Silverstone	8	McLaren International	M	3.0 McLaren MP4-Cosworth V8	accident with Villeneuve	6/30
ret	GERMAN GP	Hockenheim	8	McLaren International	M	3.0 McLaren MP4-Cosworth V8	spun off	10/30
8	AUSTRIAN GP	Österreichring	8	McLaren International	M	3.0 McLaren MP4-Cosworth V8	1 lap behind	18/28
dns	DUTCH GP	Zandvoort	8	McLaren International	M	3.0 McLaren MP4-Cosworth V8	withdrawn-practice accidents	(13)/30
7/ret	ITALIAN GP	Monza	8	McLaren International	M	3.0 McLaren MP4-Cosworth V8	puncture-accident	16/30
ret	CANADIAN GP	Montreal	8	McLaren International	M	3.0 McLaren MP4-Cosworth V8	spun off	13/30
12	CAESARS PALACE GP	Las Vegas	8	McLaren International	M	3.0 McLaren MP4-Cosworth V8	p stops-tyres-handling/-6 laps	14/30

1982 — Championship position: 17th= Wins: 0 Pole positions: 1 Fastest laps: 0 Points scored: 5

	Race	Circuit	No	Entrant	Tyres	Car/Engine	Comment	Q Pos/Entries
13	SOUTH AFRICAN GP	Kyalami	22	Marlboro Team Alfa Romeo	M	3.0 Alfa Romeo 179D V12	4 laps behind	16/30
ret	BRAZILIAN GP	Rio	22	Marlboro Team Alfa Romeo	M	3.0 Alfa Romeo 182 V12	loose undertray	10/31
ret	US GP WEST	Long Beach	22	Marlboro Team Alfa Romeo	M	3.0 Alfa Romeo 182 V12	hit wall when 2nd	1/31
ret	SAN MARINO GP	Imola	22	Marlboro Team Alfa Romeo	M	3.0 Alfa Romeo 182 V12	fuel pump	7/14
ret	BELGIAN GP	Zolder	22	Marlboro Team Alfa Romeo	M	3.0 Alfa Romeo 182 V12	gear linkage	7/32
3/ret	MONACO GP	Monte Carlo	22	Marlboro Team Alfa Romeo	M	3.0 Alfa Romeo 182 V12	out of fuel on last lap	7/31
ret	US GP (DETROIT)	Detroit	22	Marlboro Team Alfa Romeo	M	3.0 Alfa Romeo 182 V12	transmission	2/28
6/ret	CANADIAN GP	Montreal	22	Marlboro Team Alfa Romeo	M	3.0 Alfa Romeo 182 V12	out of fuel when 3rd/-2 laps	9/29
ret	DUTCH GP	Zandvoort	22	Marlboro Team Alfa Romeo	M	3.0 Alfa Romeo 182 V12	electrics	9/31
ret	BRITISH GP	Brands Hatch	22	Marlboro Team Alfa Romeo	M	3.0 Alfa Romeo 182 V12	electrics	11/30
ret	FRENCH GP	Paul Ricard	22	Marlboro Team Alfa Romeo	M	3.0 Alfa Romeo 182 V12	puncture-accident	7/30
ret	GERMAN GP	Hockenheim	22	Marlboro Team Alfa Romeo	M	3.0 Alfa Romeo 182 V12	collision-broken oil radiator	9/30
ret	AUSTRIAN GP	Österreichring	22	Marlboro Team Alfa Romeo	M	3.0 Alfa Romeo 182 V12	collision at start-Giacomelli & Daly	11/29
10	SWISS GP	Dijon	22	Marlboro Team Alfa Romeo	M	3.0 Alfa Romeo 182 V12	2 laps behind	5/29
10	ITALIAN GP	Monza	22	Marlboro Team Alfa Romeo	M	3.0 Alfa Romeo 182 V12	pit stop-ignition/2 laps behind	9/30
dns		"	22	Marlboro Team Alfa Romeo	M	1.5 t/c Alfa Romeo 182T V8	practice only	– / –
9	CAESARS PALACE GP	Las Vegas	22	Marlboro Team Alfa Romeo	M	3.0 Alfa Romeo 182 V12	3 laps behind	18/30

1983 — Championship position: 8th Wins: 0 Pole positions: 0 Fastest laps: 1 Points scored: 15

	Race	Circuit	No	Entrant	Tyres	Car/Engine	Comment	Q Pos/Entries
excl	BRAZILIAN GP	Rio	22	Marlboro Team Alfa Romeo	M	1.5 t/c Alfa Romeo 183T V8	missed weight check-excluded	– / –
ret	US GP WEST	Long Beach	22	Marlboro Team Alfa Romeo	M	1.5 t/c Alfa Romeo 183T V8	gearbox	19/28
12	FRENCH GP	Paul Ricard	22	Marlboro Team Alfa Romeo	M	1.5 t/c Alfa Romeo 183T V8	pit stop-fuel-tyres/-4 laps	7/29
ret	SAN MARINO GP	Imola	22	Marlboro Team Alfa Romeo	M	1.5 t/c Alfa Romeo 183T V8	distributor	8/29
ret	MONACO GP	Monte Carlo	22	Marlboro Team Alfa Romeo	M	1.5 t/c Alfa Romeo 183T V8	gearbox	7/28
ret	BELGIAN GP	Spa	22	Marlboro Team Alfa Romeo	M	1.5 t/c Alfa Romeo 183T V8	engine when 2nd/led race/FL	3/28
ret	US GP (DETROIT)	Detroit	22	Marlboro Team Alfa Romeo	M	1.5 t/c Alfa Romeo 183T V8	turbo	8/27
ret	CANADIAN GP	Montreal	22	Marlboro Team Alfa Romeo	M	1.5 t/c Alfa Romeo 183T V8	engine	8/28
8	BRITISH GP	Silverstone	22	Marlboro Team Alfa Romeo	M	1.5 t/c Alfa Romeo 183T V8	1 lap behind	9/29
2	GERMAN GP	Hockenheim	22	Marlboro Team Alfa Romeo	M	1.5 t/c Alfa Romeo 183T V8		3/29
ret	AUSTRIAN GP	Österreichring	22	Marlboro Team Alfa Romeo	M	1.5 t/c Alfa Romeo 183T V8	out of fuel	11/29
ret	DUTCH GP	Zandvoort	22	Marlboro Team Alfa Romeo	M	1.5 t/c Alfa Romeo 183T V8	engine	8/29
ret	ITALIAN GP	Monza	22	Marlboro Team Alfa Romeo	M	1.5 t/c Alfa Romeo 183T V8	spun off	6/29
4	EUROPEAN GP	Brands Hatch	22	Marlboro Team Alfa Romeo	M	1.5 t/c Alfa Romeo 183T V8		14/29
2	SOUTH AFRICAN GP	Kyalami	22	Marlboro Team Alfa Romeo	M	1.5 t/c Alfa Romeo 183T V8		9/26

1984 — Championship position: 16th= Wins: 0 Pole positions: 0 Fastest laps: 0 Points scored: 3

	Race	Circuit	No	Entrant	Tyres	Car/Engine	Comment	Q Pos/Entries
ret	BRAZILIAN GP	Rio	26	Ligier Loto	M	1.5 t/c Ligier JS23-Renault V6	started spare from pits/gearbox	14/27
5	SOUTH AFRICAN GP	Kyalami	26	Ligier Loto	M	1.5 t/c Ligier JS23-Renault V6	2 laps behind	14/27
ret	BELGIAN GP	Zolder	26	Ligier Loto	M	1.5 t/c Ligier JS23-Renault V6	spun off	12/27
6*/ret	SAN MARINO GP	Imola	26	Ligier Loto	M	1.5 t/c Ligier JS23-Renault V6	* 5th place car dsq/out of fuel	12/28
10	FRENCH GP	Dijon	26	Ligier Loto	M	1.5 t/c Ligier JS23-Renault V6	started as 1st reserve/-2 laps	27/27
ret	MONACO GP	Monte Carlo	26	Ligier Loto	M	1.5 t/c Ligier JS23-Renault V6	accident damage	7/27
ret	CANADIAN GP	Montreal	26	Ligier Loto	M	1.5 t/c Ligier JS23-Renault V6	brakes	10/26
ret	US GP (DETROIT)	Detroit	26	Ligier Loto	M	1.5 t/c Ligier JS23-Renault V6	overheating	12/27
ret	US GP (DALLAS)	Dallas	26	Ligier Loto	M	1.5 t/c Ligier JS23-Renault V6	hit wall	16/27
10	BRITISH GP	Brands Hatch	26	Ligier Loto	M	1.5 t/c Ligier JS23-Renault V6	3 laps behind	19/27
7	GERMAN GP	Hockenheim	26	Ligier Loto	M	1.5 t/c Ligier JS23-Renault V6	1 lap behind	11/27
ret	AUSTRIAN GP	Österreichring	26	Ligier Loto	M	1.5 t/c Ligier JS23-Renault V6	fuel injection	18/28
ret	DUTCH GP	Zandvoort	26	Ligier Loto	M	1.5 t/c Ligier JS23-Renault V6	engine	14/27
ret	ITALIAN GP	Monza	26	Ligier Loto	M	1.5 t/c Ligier JS23-Renault V6	engine	16/27
7	EUROPEAN GP	Nürburgring	26	Ligier Loto	M	1.5 t/c Ligier JS23-Renault V6	2 laps behind	17/26
12	PORTUGUESE GP	Estoril	26	Ligier Loto	M	1.5 t/c Ligier JS23-Renault V6	1 lap behind	20/27

1985 — Championship position: 17th= Wins: 0 Pole positions: 0 Fastest laps: 0 Points scored: 3

	Race	Circuit	No	Entrant	Tyres	Car/Engine	Comment	Q Pos/Entries
ret	BRAZILIAN GP	Rio	25	Equipe Ligier	P	1.5 t/c Ligier JS25-Renault V6	hit Arnoux	13/25
ret	PORTUGUESE GP	Estoril	25	Equipe Ligier	P	1.5 t/c Ligier JS25-Renault V6	tyres/handling	8/26
ret	SAN MARINO GP	Imola	25	Equipe Ligier	P	1.5 t/c Ligier JS25-Renault V6	spun off	13/26
4	MONACO GP	Monte Carlo	25	Equipe Ligier	P	1.5 t/c Ligier JS25-Renault V6	1 lap behind	8/26

14	CANADIAN GP	Montreal	25	Equipe Ligier Gitanes	P	1.5 t/c Ligier JS25-Renault V6	spin-hit Winkelhock-p stop/-3 laps	15/25
10	US GP (DETROIT)	Detroit	25	Equipe Ligier Gitanes	P	1.5 t/c Ligier JS25-Renault V6	2 laps behind	17/25
ret	FRENCH GP	Paul Ricard	25	Equipe Ligier Gitanes	P	1.5 t/c Ligier JS25-Renault V6	driveshaft	13/26
ret	BRITISH GP	Silverstone	25	Equipe Ligier Gitanes	P	1.5 t/c Ligier JS25-Renault V6	clutch	7/26
ret	GERMAN GP	Nürburgring	25	Equipe Ligier Gitanes	P	1.5 t/c Ligier JS25-Renault V6	collision-broken steering arm	14/27
ret	AUSTRIAN GP	Österreichring	25	Equipe Ligier Gitanes	P	1.5 t/c Ligier JS25-Renault V6	accident-rolled car	18/27
ret	DUTCH GP	Zandvoort	25	Equipe Ligier Gitanes	P	1.5 t/c Ligier JS25-Renault V6	turbo	18/27

1986 Championship position: Unplaced

ret	BRAZILIAN GP	Rio	23	Minardi Team	P	1.5 t/c Minardi M185B-MM V6	turbo	22/25
ret	SPANISH GP	Jerez	23	Minardi Team	P	1.5 t/c Minardi M185B-MM V6	differential	24/25
ret	SAN MARINO GP	Imola	23	Minardi Team	P	1.5 t/c Minardi M185B-MM V6	engine	23/26
dnq	MONACO GP	Monte Carlo	23	Minardi Team	P	1.5 t/c Minardi M185B-MM V6		25/26
ret	BELGIAN GP	Spa	23	Minardi Team	P	1.5 t/c Minardi M185B-MM V6	out of fuel	19/25
ret	CANADIAN GP	Montreal	23	Minardi Team	P	1.5 t/c Minardi M185B-MM V6	gearbox	21/25
ret	US GP (DETROIT)	Detroit	23	Minardi Team	P	1.5 t/c Minardi M185B-MM V6	gearbox	23/26
ret	FRENCH GP	Paul Ricard	23	Minardi Team	P	1.5 t/c Minardi M185B-MM V6	turbo	23/26
ret	BRITISH GP	Brands Hatch	23	Minardi Team	P	1.5 t/c Minardi M185B-MM V6	electrics	21/26
ret	GERMAN GP	Hockenheim	23	Minardi Team	P	1.5 t/c Minardi M185B-MM V6	gearbox	23/26
ret	HUNGARIAN GP	Hungaroring	23	Minardi Team	P	1.5 t/c Minardi M186-MM V6	engine	20/26
ret	AUSTRIAN GP	Österreichring	23	Minardi Team	P	1.5 t/c Minardi M185B-MM V6	clutch	23/26
dns	"	"	23	Minardi Team	P	1.5 t/c Minardi M185B-MM V6	practice only	– / –
ret	ITALIAN GP	Monza	23	Minardi Team	P	1.5 t/c Minardi M186-MM V6	engine	21/27
ret	PORTUGUESE GP	Estoril	23	Minardi Team	P	1.5 t/c Minardi M186-MM V6	spun off	16/27
8	MEXICAN GP	Mexico City	23	Minardi Team	P	1.5 t/c Minardi M186-MM V6	2 laps behind	22/26
ret	AUSTRALIAN GP	Adelaide	23	Minardi Team	P	1.5 t/c Minardi M186-MM V6	fire extinguisher set off	11/26

1987 Championship position: 14th= Wins: 0 Pole positions: 0 Fastest laps: 0 Points scored: 4

ret	BRAZILIAN GP	Rio	8	Motor Racing Developments Ltd	G	1.5 t/c Brabham BT56-BMW 4	gearbox	13/23
ret	SAN MARINO GP	Imola	8	Motor Racing Developments Ltd	G	1.5 t/c Brabham BT56-BMW 4	spun off	15/27
3/ret	BELGIAN GP	Spa	8	Motor Racing Developments Ltd	G	1.5 t/c Brabham BT56-BMW 4	out of fuel/1 lap behind	13/26
ret	MONACO GP	Monte Carlo	8	Motor Racing Developments Ltd	G	1.5 t/c Brabham BT56-BMW 4	suspension	21/26
ret	US GP (DETROIT)	Detroit	8	Motor Racing Developments Ltd	G	1.5 t/c Brabham BT56-BMW 4	gearbox	17/26
ret	FRENCH GP	Paul Ricard	8	Motor Racing Developments Ltd	G	1.5 t/c Brabham BT56-BMW 4	turbo	11/26
ret	BRITISH GP	Silverstone	8	Motor Racing Developments Ltd	G	1.5 t/c Brabham BT56-BMW 4	broken fuel line-fire	9/26
ret	GERMAN GP	Hockenheim	8	Motor Racing Developments Ltd	G	1.5 t/c Brabham BT56-BMW 4	engine	7/26
ret	HUNGARIAN GP	Hungaroring	8	Motor Racing Developments Ltd	G	1.5 t/c Brabham BT56-BMW 4	gearbox	13/26
ret	AUSTRIAN GP	Österreichring	8	Motor Racing Developments Ltd	G	1.5 t/c Brabham BT56-BMW 4	turbo	10/26
ret	ITALIAN GP	Monza	8	Motor Racing Developments Ltd	G	1.5 t/c Brabham BT56-BMW 4	suspension	10/28
ret	PORTUGUESE GP	Estoril	8	Motor Racing Developments Ltd	G	1.5 t/c Brabham BT56-BMW 4	engine	13/27
ret	SPANISH GP	Jerez	8	Motor Racing Developments Ltd	G	1.5 t/c Brabham BT56-BMW 4	gearbox	10/28
ret	MEXICAN GP	Mexico City	8	Motor Racing Developments Ltd	G	1.5 t/c Brabham BT56-BMW 4	incident with Senna	10/27
ret	JAPANESE GP	Suzuka	8	Motor Racing Developments Ltd	G	1.5 t/c Brabham BT56-BMW 4	turbo	11/27
8*/ret	AUSTRALIAN GP	Adelaide	8	Motor Racing Developments Ltd	G	1.5 t/c Brabham BT56-BMW 4	* 2nd car dsq/spun off/-4 laps	10/27

1988 Championship position: 15th Wins: 0 Pole positions: 0 Fastest laps: 0 Points scored: 3

ret	BRAZILIAN GP	Rio	22	Rial Racing	G	3.5 Rial ARC1-Cosworth V8	engine	14/31
ret	SAN MARINO GP	Imola	22	Rial Racing	G	3.5 Rial ARC1-Cosworth V8	started from pits/suspension	16/31
ret	MONACO GP	Monte Carlo	22	Rial Racing	G	3.5 Rial ARC1-Cosworth V8	oil pressure	19/30
ret	MEXICAN GP	Mexico City	22	Rial Racing	G	3.5 Rial ARC1-Cosworth V8	gearbox	12/30
9/ret	CANADIAN GP	Montreal	22	Rial Racing	G	3.5 Rial ARC1-Cosworth V8	out of fuel/3 laps behind	12/31
4	US GP (DETROIT)	Detroit	22	Rial Racing	G	3.5 Rial ARC1-Cosworth V8	1 lap behind	12/31
10	FRENCH GP	Paul Ricard	22	Rial Racing	G	3.5 Rial ARC1-Cosworth V8	wheel stuck at pit stop/-2 laps	12/31
ret	BRITISH GP	Silverstone	22	Rial Racing	G	3.5 Rial ARC1-Cosworth V8	clutch	14/31
13	GERMAN GP	Hockenheim	22	Rial Racing	G	3.5 Rial ARC1-Cosworth V8	pit stop-tyres/2 spins/-2 laps	14/31
ret	HUNGARIAN GP	Hungaroring	22	Rial Racing	G	3.5 Rial ARC1-Cosworth V8	driveshaft-c.v. joint	18/31
ret	BELGIAN GP	Spa	22	Rial Racing	G	3.5 Rial ARC1-Cosworth V8	accident with Arnoux	19/31
ret	ITALIAN GP	Monza	22	Rial Racing	G	3.5 Rial ARC1-Cosworth V8	collision-Martini/suspension	18/31
ret	PORTUGUESE GP	Estoril	22	Rial Racing	G	3.5 Rial ARC1-Cosworth V8	driveshaft	12/31
ret	SPANISH GP	Jerez	22	Rial Racing	G	3.5 Rial ARC1-Cosworth V8	engine	23/31
ret	JAPANESE GP	Suzuka	22	Rial Racing	G	3.5 Rial ARC1-Cosworth V8	overheating	14/31
8/ret	AUSTRALIAN GP	Adelaide	22	Rial Racing	G	3.5 Rial ARC1-Cosworth V8	out of fuel/5 laps behind	15/31

1989 Championship position: 16th Wins: 0 Pole positions: 0 Fastest laps: 0 Points scored: 4

13/ret	BRAZILIAN GP	Rio	22	Scuderia Italia	P	3.5 Dallara 189-Cosworth V8	engine/4 laps behind	15/38
10	SAN MARINO GP	Imola	22	Scuderia Italia	P	3.5 Dallara 189-Cosworth V8	spin/2 laps behind	16/39
13	MONACO GP	Monte Carlo	22	Scuderia Italia	P	3.5 Dallara 189-Cosworth V8	collision-Piquet-pit stop/-4 laps	10/38
ret	MEXICAN GP	Mexico City	22	Scuderia Italia	P	3.5 Dallara 189-Cosworth V8	fuel pump	12/39
ret	US GP (PHOENIX)	Phoenix	22	Scuderia Italia	P	3.5 Dallara 189-Cosworth V8	fuel pump/5 laps behind	13/39
3	CANADIAN GP	Montreal	22	Scuderia Italia	P	3.5 Dallara 189-Cosworth V8		9/39
dnq	FRENCH GP	Paul Ricard	22	Scuderia Italia	P	3.5 Dallara 189-Cosworth V8		27/39
ret	BRITISH GP	Silverstone	22	Scuderia Italia	P	3.5 Dallara 189-Cosworth V8	gearbox	25/39
7	GERMAN GP	Hockenheim	22	Scuderia Italia	P	3.5 Dallara 189-Cosworth V8	1 lap behind	21/39
ret	HUNGARIAN GP	Hungaroring	22	Scuderia Italia	P	3.5 Dallara 189-Cosworth V8	clutch	18/39
11	BELGIAN GP	Spa	22	Scuderia Italia	P	3.5 Dallara 189-Cosworth V8	3 spins/1 lap behind	18/39
ret	ITALIAN GP	Monza	22	Scuderia Italia	P	3.5 Dallara 189-Cosworth V8	engine-electrics	17/39
ret	PORTUGUESE GP	Estoril	22	Scuderia Italia	P	3.5 Dallara 189-Cosworth V8	engine	19/39
7	SPANISH GP	Jerez	22	Scuderia Italia	P	3.5 Dallara 189-Cosworth V8	pit stop-tyres/1 lap behind	15/38
10	JAPANESE GP	Suzuka	22	Scuderia Italia	P	3.5 Dallara 189-Cosworth V8	collision-Pirro-pit stop/-2 laps	16/39
ret	AUSTRALIAN GP	Adelaide	22	Scuderia Italia	P	3.5 Dallara 189-Cosworth V8	spun off in rain	9/39

1990 Championship position: Unplaced

ret	US GP (PHOENIX)	Phoenix	22	Scuderia Italia	P	3.5 BMS Dallara 190-Cosworth V8	engine	3/35
ret	BRAZILIAN GP	Interlagos	22	Scuderia Italia	P	3.5 BMS Dallara 190-Cosworth V8	collision with Alesi	9/35

ret	SAN MARINO GP	Imola	22	Scuderia Italia	P	3.5 BMS Dallara 190-Cosworth V8	wheel hub	18/34
ret	MONACO GP	Monte Carlo	22	Scuderia Italia	P	3.5 BMS Dallara 190-Cosworth V8	throttle linkage	12/35
ret	CANADIAN GP	Montreal	22	Scuderia Italia	P	3.5 BMS Dallara 190-Cosworth V8	transmission	25/35
13	MEXICAN GP	Mexico City	22	Scuderia Italia	P	3.5 BMS Dallara 190-Cosworth V8	1 lap behind	15/35
15/dsq*	FRENCH GP	Paul Ricard	22	Scuderia Italia	P	3.5 BMS Dallara 190-Cosworth V8	*car underweight/-2 laps	21/35
ret	BRITISH GP	Silverstone	22	Scuderia Italia	P	3.5 BMS Dallara 190-Cosworth V8	gearbox	23/35
dnq	GERMAN GP	Hockenheim	22	Scuderia Italia	P	3.5 BMS Dallara 190-Cosworth V8		30/35
ret	HUNGARIAN GP	Hungaroring	22	Scuderia Italia	P	3.5 BMS Dallara 190-Cosworth V8	engine-oil leak	10/35
ret	BELGIAN GP	Spa	22	Scuderia Italia	P	3.5 BMS Dallara 190-Cosworth V8	engine	20/33
10	ITALIAN GP	Monza	22	Scuderia Italia	P	3.5 BMS Dallara 190-Cosworth V8	pit stop-tyres/2 laps behind	25/33
ret	PORTUGUESE GP	Estoril	22	Scuderia Italia	P	3.5 BMS Dallara 190-Cosworth V8	sticking throttle	18/33
ret	SPANISH GP	Jerez	22	Scuderia Italia	P	3.5 BMS Dallara 190-Cosworth V8	engine-dropped valve	17/33
ret	JAPANESE GP	Suzuka	22	Scuderia Italia	P	3.5 BMS Dallara 190-Cosworth V8	spun off	26/30
ret	AUSTRALIAN GP	Adelaide	22	Scuderia Italia	P	3.5 BMS Dallara 190-Cosworth V8	electrics	15/30

1991   Championship position: 9   Wins: 0   Pole positions: 0   Fastest laps: 0   Points scored: 9

dnpq	US GP (PHOENIX)	Phoenix	33	Team 7UP Jordan	G	3.5 Jordan 191-Ford HB V8		31/34
ret	BRAZILIAN GP	Interlagos	33	Team 7UP Jordan	G	3.5 Jordan 191-Ford HB V8	engine cut out-spun off	13/34
ret	SAN MARINO GP	Imola	33	Team 7UP Jordan	G	3.5 Jordan 191-Ford HB V8	gear linkage	11/34
ret	MONACO GP	Monte Carlo	33	Team 7UP Jordan	G	3.5 Jordan 191-Ford HB V8	throttle cable	10/34
4	CANADIAN GP	Montreal	33	Team 7UP Jordan	G	3.5 Jordan 191-Ford HB V8		11/34
4/ret	MEXICAN GP	Mexico City	33	Team 7UP Jordan	G	3.5 Jordan 191-Ford HB V8	throttle potentiometer/-1 lap	11/34
6	FRENCH GP	Magny Cours	33	Team 7UP Jordan	G	3.5 Jordan 191-Ford HB V8	1 lap behind	13/34
ret	BRITISH GP	Silverstone	33	Team 7UP Jordan	G	3.5 Jordan 191-Ford HB V8	accident-suspension failure	13/34
5	GERMAN GP	Hockenheim	33	Team 7UP Jordan	G	3.5 Jordan 191-Ford HB V8		7/34
7	HUNGARIAN GP	Hungaroring	33	Team 7UP Jordan	G	3.5 Jordan 191-Ford HB V8	1 lap behind	17/34
13/ret	BELGIAN GP	Spa	33	Team 7UP Jordan	G	3.5 Jordan 191-Ford HB V8	engine-overheating when 2nd	11/34
7	ITALIAN GP	Monza	33	Team 7UP Jordan	G	3.5 Jordan 191-Ford HB V8		14/34
8	PORTUGUESE GP	Estoril	33	Team 7UP Jordan	G	3.5 Jordan 191-Ford HB V8	1 lap behind	14/34
ret	SPANISH GP	Barcelona	33	Team 7UP Jordan	G	3.5 Jordan 191-Ford HB V8	electrics	17/33
ret	JAPANESE GP	Suzuka	33	Team 7UP Jordan	G	3.5 Jordan 191-Ford HB V8	spun off	11/31
8	AUSTRALIAN GP	Adelaide	33	Team 7UP Jordan	G	3.5 Jordan 191-Ford HB V8	rain-shortened race	12/32

1992   Championship position: 9th   Wins: 0   Pole positions: 0   Fastest laps: 0   Points scored: 8

ret	SOUTH AFRICAN GP	Kyalami	4	Tyrrell Racing Organisation	G	3.5 Tyrrell 020B-Ilmor V10	engine	10/30
5	MEXICAN GP	Mexico City	4	Tyrrell Racing Organisation	G	3.5 Tyrrell 020B-Ilmor V10	1 lap behind	11/30
ret	BRAZILIAN GP	Interlagos	4	Tyrrell Racing Organisation	G	3.5 Tyrrell 020B-Ilmor V10	electrics	13/31
ret	SPANISH GP	Barcelona	4	Tyrrell Racing Organisation	G	3.5 Tyrrell 020B-Ilmor V10	oil pressure	11/32
14/ret	SAN MARINO GP	Imola	4	Tyrrell Racing Organisation	G	3.5 Tyrrell 020B-Ilmor V10	fuel pressure/5 laps behind	14/32
ret	MONACO GP	Monte Carlo	4	Tyrrell Racing Organisation	G	3.5 Tyrrell 020B-Ilmor V10	gearbox	10/32
5	CANADIAN GP	Montreal	4	Tyrrell Racing Organisation	G	3.5 Tyrrell 020B-Ilmor V10	1 lap behind	14/32
ret	FRENCH GP	Magny Cours	4	Tyrrell Racing Organisation	G	3.5 Tyrrell 020B-Ilmor V10	spun off	19/30
ret	BRITISH GP	Silverstone	4	Tyrrell Racing Organisation	G	3.5 Tyrrell 020B-Ilmor V10	suspension-spun off	18/32
ret	GERMAN GP	Hockenheim	4	Tyrrell Racing Organisation	G	3.5 Tyrrell 020B-Ilmor V10	engine	20/32
8	HUNGARIAN GP	Hungaroring	4	Tyrrell Racing Organisation	G	3.5 Tyrrell 020B-Ilmor V10	2 laps behind	19/31
8	BELGIAN GP	Spa	4	Tyrrell Racing Organisation	G	3.5 Tyrrell 020B-Ilmor V10	1 lap behind	13/30
6	ITALIAN GP	Monza	4	Tyrrell Racing Organisation	G	3.5 Tyrrell 020B-Ilmor V10	1 lap behind	21/28
9	PORTUGUESE GP	Estoril	4	Tyrrell Racing Organisation	G	3.5 Tyrrell 020B-Ilmor V10	2 laps behind	12/26
4	JAPANESE GP	Suzuka	4	Tyrrell Racing Organisation	G	3.5 Tyrrell 020B-Ilmor V10	1 lap behind	9/26
ret	AUSTRALIAN GP	Adelaide	4	Tyrrell Racing Organisation	G	3.5 Tyrrell 020B-Ilmor V10	fuel pressure-fire	7/26

1993   Championship position: Unplaced

ret	SOUTH AFRICAN GP	Kyalami	4	Tyrrell Racing Organisation	G	3.5 Tyrrell 020C-Yamaha V10	transmission on grid at start	23/26
ret	BRAZILIAN GP	Interlagos	4	Tyrrell Racing Organisation	G	3.5 Tyrrell 020C-Yamaha V10	engine-electrics	23/26
ret	EUROPEAN GP	Donington	4	Tyrrell Racing Organisation	G	3.5 Tyrrell 020C-Yamaha V10	gearbox	25/26
ret	SAN MARINO GP	Imola	4	Tyrrell Racing Organisation	G	3.5 Tyrrell 020C-Yamaha V10	gearbox	18/26
dsq	SPANISH GP	Barcelona	4	Tyrrell Racing Organisation	G	3.5 Tyrrell 020C-Yamaha V10	black-flagged-push start	24/26
10	MONACO GP	Monte Carlo	4	Tyrrell Racing Organisation	G	3.5 Tyrrell 020C-Yamaha V10	2 laps behind	19/26
ret	CANADIAN GP	Montreal	4	Tyrrell Racing Organisation	G	3.5 Tyrrell 020C-Yamaha V10	active problems/spun off	19/26
15	FRENCH GP	Magny Cours	4	Tyrrell Racing Organisation	G	3.5 Tyrrell 020C-Yamaha V10	4 laps behind	25/26
nc	BRITISH GP	Silverstone	4	Tyrrell Racing Organisation	G	3.5 Tyrrell 021-Yamaha V10	pit stops after collision/-16 laps	21/26
ret	GERMAN GP	Hockenheim	4	Tyrrell Racing Organisation	G	3.5 Tyrrell 021-Yamaha V10	gearbox	19/26
11	HUNGARIAN GP	Hungaroring	4	Tyrrell Racing Organisation	G	3.5 Tyrrell 021-Yamaha V10	pit stop-transmission/-5 laps	22/26
ret	BELGIAN GP	Spa	4	Tyrrell Racing Organisation	G	3.5 Tyrrell 021-Yamaha V10	engine	17/25
ret	ITALIAN GP	Monza	4	Tyrrell Racing Organisation	G	3.5 Tyrrell 021-Yamaha V10	oil pressure	18/26
12	PORTUGUESE GP	Estoril	4	Tyrrell Racing Organisation	G	3.5 Tyrrell 021-Yamaha V10	spin/water leak/3 laps behind	17/26
ret	JAPANESE GP	Suzuka	4	Tyrrell Racing Organisation	G	3.5 Tyrrell 021-Yamaha V10	collision-Gounon-puncture	18/24
13	AUSTRALIAN GP	Adelaide	4	Tyrrell Racing Organisation	G	3.5 Tyrrell 021-Yamaha V10	4 laps behind	15/24

1994   Championship position: 18th=   Wins: 0   Pole positions: 0   Fastest laps: 0   Points scored: 4

ret	SAN MARINO GP	Imola	15	Sasol Jordan	G	3.5 Jordan 194-Hart V10	driver fatigue-spun off	21/28
4	MONACO GP	Monte Carlo	15	Sasol Jordan	G	3.5 Jordan 194-Hart V10	1 lap behind	14/24
ret	CANADIAN GP	Montreal	29	Sauber AG	G	3.5 Sauber C13-Mercedes Benz V10	engine	14/27
6	FRENCH GP	Magny Cours	29	Sauber AG	G	3.5 Sauber C13-Mercedes Benz V10	2 laps behind	11/28
ret	BRITISH GP	Silverstone	29	Sauber AG	G	3.5 Sauber C13-Mercedes Benz V10	engine	18/28
ret	GERMAN GP	Hockenheim	29	Sauber AG	G	3.5 Sauber C13-Mercedes Benz V10	multiple accident at start	18/28
ret	HUNGARIAN GP	Hungaroring	29	Sauber AG	G	3.5 Sauber C13-Mercedes Benz V10	collision with Morbidelli	17/28
ret	BELGIAN GP	Spa	29	Sauber AG	G	3.5 Sauber C13-Mercedes Benz V10	sticking throttle	15/28
ret	ITALIAN GP	Monza	29	Sauber AG	G	3.5 Sauber C13-Mercedes Benz V10	engine	8/28
ret	PORTUGUESE GP	Estoril	29	Sauber AG	G	3.5 Sauber C13-Mercedes Benz V10	spun off	17/28
ret	EUROPEAN GP	Jerez	29	Sauber AG	G	3.5 Sauber C13-Mercedes Benz V10	accelerator	18/28

GP Starts: 208   GP Wins: 0   Pole positions: 1   Fastest laps: 1   Points: 59

MARIA-TERESA de FILIPPIS

Maria-Teresa made a little bit of Grand Prix history when she became the first woman to start a World Championship Grand Prix, having competed successfully for a number of years in Italian national sports car racing, first with a little OSCA and then, from 1955, with a more powerful Maserati.

With the help, initially, of Luigi Musso, she broke into Formula 1 in 1958, scoring a fifth place at Syracuse in a rather thin field, before tackling four Grands Prix in her Maserati 250F.

She was taken under the wing of Jean Behra for 1959, but after his death at AVUS she retired from racing. Today she retains a link with the sport through her involvement in the Société des Anciens Pilotes.

de FILIPPIS, Maria-Teresa (I) b 11/11/1926

	1958	Championship position: Unplaced							
	Race	Circuit	No	Entrant	Tyres	Car/Engine		Comment	Q Pos/Entries
dnq	MONACO GP	Monte Carlo	44	Maria-Teresa de Filippis	P	2.5 Maserati 250F 6			=22/28
10	BELGIAN GP	Spa	26	Maria-Teresa de Filippis	P	2.5 Maserati 250F 6		2 laps behind	19/20
ret	PORTUGUESE GP	Oporto	30	Scuderia Centro Sud	P	2.5 Maserati 250F 6		mechanical	15/15
ret	ITALIAN GP	Monza	42	Maria-Teresa de Filippis	P	2.5 Maserati 250F 6		engine	21/21
	1959	Championship position: Unplaced							
dnq	MONACO GP	Monte Carlo	4	Dr Ing F Porsche KG	D	1.5 Behra-Porsche F4 F2			21/24

GP Starts: 3   GP Wins: 0   Pole positions: 0   Fastest laps: 0   Points: 0

de GRAFFENRIED, Baron Emmanuel (CH) b 18/5/1914, Paris, France

	1950	Championship position: Unplaced							
	Race	Circuit	No	Entrant	Tyres	Car/Engine		Comment	Q Pos/Entries
ret	BRITISH GP	Silverstone	20	Emmanuel de Graffenried	P	1.5 s/c Maserati 4CLT/50 4		engine	8/21
ret	MONACO GP	Monte Carlo	52	Emmanuel de Graffenried	P	1.5 s/c Maserati 4CLT/50 4		multiple accident	12/21
6	SWISS GP	Bremgarten	32	Emmanuel de Graffenried	P	1.5 s/c Maserati 4CLT/50 4		2 laps behind	11/18
6	ITALIAN GP	Monza	38	Emmanuel de Graffenried	P	1.5 s/c Maserati 4CLT/50 4		8 laps behind	17/27
	1951	Championship position: 12th= Wins: 0 Pole positions: 0 Fastest laps: 0 Points scored: 2							
5	SWISS GP	Bremgarten	26	Alfa Romeo SpA	P	1.5 s/c Alfa Romeo 159A 8		2 laps behind	5/21
ret	FRENCH GP	Reims	18	Enrico Platé	P	1.5 s/c Maserati 4CLT/50 4		transmission	16/23
ret	GERMAN GP	Nürburgring	79	Enrico Platé	P	1.5 s/c Maserati 4CLT/50 4		engine	16/23
ret	ITALIAN GP	Monza	36	Alfa Romeo SpA	P	1.5 s/c Alfa Romeo 159M 8		supercharger drive	9/22
6	SPANISH GP	Pedralbes	26	Alfa Romeo SpA	P	1.5 s/c Alfa Romeo 159M 8		4 laps behind	6/20
	1952	Championship position: Unplaced							
6	SWISS GP	Bremgarten	38	Enrico Platé	P	2.0 Maserati 4CLT/Platé 4		4 laps behind	8/21
ret*	FRENCH GP	Rouen	16	Enrico Platé	P	2.0 Maserati 4CLT/Platé 4		*Schell took over/brakes	11/20
19	BRITISH GP	Silverstone	32	Enrico Platé	P	2.0 Maserati 4CLT/Platé 4		no practice/9 laps behind	– /32
dnq	ITALIAN GP	Monza	60	Enrico Platé	P	2.0 Maserati 4CLT/Platé 4		engine	27/35
	1953	Championship position: 7th Wins: 0 Pole positions: 0 Fastest laps: 0 Points scored: 7							
5	DUTCH GP	Zandvoort	18	Emmanuel de Graffenried	P	2.0 Maserati A6GCM 6		2 laps behind	7/20
4	BELGIAN GP	Spa	30	Emmanuel de Graffenried	P	2.0 Maserati A6GCM 6		1 lap behind	9/22
7	FRENCH GP	Reims	46	Emmanuel de Graffenried	P	2.0 Maserati A6GCM 6		2 laps behind	9/25
ret	BRITISH GP	Silverstone	31	Emmanuel de Graffenried	P	2.0 Maserati A6GCM 6		clutch	26/29
5	GERMAN GP	Nürburgring	17	Emmanuel de Graffenried	P	2.0 Maserati A6GCM 6		1 lap behind	11/35
ret	SWISS GP	Bremgarten	42	Emmanuel de Graffenried	P	2.0 Maserati A6GCM 6		transmission	8/23
ret	ITALIAN GP	Monza	58	Emmanuel de Graffenried	P	2.0 Maserati A6GCM 6		engine	9/30
	1954	Championship position: Unplaced							
8	ARGENTINE GP	Buenos Aires	30	Emmanuel de Graffenried	P	2.5 Maserati A6GCM/250F 6		4 laps behind	13/18
ret*	BELGIAN GP	Spa	50	Emmanuel de Graffenried	P	2.5 Maserati A6GCM/250F 6		* camera car only-not 'racing'	– / –
ret*	SPANISH GP	Pedralbes	22	Emmanuel de Graffenried	P	2.5 Maserati A6GCM/250F 6		* Volonterio also drove/engine	21/22
	1956	Championship position: Unplaced							
7	ITALIAN GP	Monza	14	Scuderia Centro Sud	P	2.5 Maserati 250F 6		4 laps behind	19/26

GP Starts: 22   GP Wins: 0   Pole positions: 0   Fastest laps: 0   Points: 9

EMMANUEL de GRAFFENRIED

Although his racing activities began well before the Second World War in his native Switzerland, with both a 3-litre Alfa Romeo and a Type 6C Maserati, it was the immediate post-war years that saw 'Toulo '– as he was popularly known – at his zenith.

In 1946 he formed Team Autosport with former Mercedes driver Christian Kautz, the pair acquiring a new four-cylinder Maserati which de Graffenried brought into fifth place in the Prix de Geneva. He finished third in the car at Lausanne the following year, and drove splendidly to finish second to Farina in Geneva, and third in the Monaco GP behind Farina and Chiron in 1948, before his season was overshadowed by the death of Kautz in the Grand Prix de l'Europe at Bremgarten.

'Toulo' enjoyed his greatest triumph in 1949, winning the British Grand Prix in his latest San Remo-type 4CLT/48 Maserati, backing this up with second places in the Pau, Zandvoort and Swedish GPs and the Jersey Road Race in St Helier, as well as many other placings. He continued to race the car into the 1950 season but it was now a little long in the tooth. However, his performances were such that Alfa Romeo invited him to race for the team in the Grand Prix des Nations at Geneva, where he performed creditably to finish second to Fangio but only two seconds ahead of Taruffi after more than two hours' racing on this demanding street circuit.

Although de Graffenried was forced to continue racing his faithful Maserati in 1951, Alfa invited him to join their all-conquering team for three Grands Prix that year, where he again acquitted himself more than respectably. With the new Formula 2 rules in force for 1952, he drove Enrico Platé's Maseratis without achieving much success in the championship races, but picked up third places at Cadours and Aix-les-Bains.

Things were very different in 1953, however. Now at the wheel of the latest Maserati A6GCM model, he enjoyed some memorable races, winning the Syracuse GP, the Eifelrennen F2 race and the Lavant Cup at Goodwood. Installing a 2.5-litre engine in the car, de Graffenried raced it briefly in 1954, as well as competing in a Maserati sports car which he took to South America early in the season, winning the Circuit of Gavea race at Rio and the São Paulo GP. He raced little after this, having a few sports car outings in Ferraris and Maseratis before making a final Grand Prix appearance at Monza in 1956.

'Toulo' was not lost to the Grand Prix world, however, for he was closely involved with the sport and seen regularly at the circuits over the next three decades.

de KLERK, Peter (ZA) b 16/3/1935, Pilgrim's Rest, Transvaal

	1963			Championship position: Unplaced				
	Race	Circuit	No	Entrant	Tyres	Car/Engine	Comment	Q Pos/Entries
ret	SOUTH AFRICAN GP East London		18	Otelle Nucci	D	1.5 Alfa Romeo Special 4	gearbox	16/21
	1965			Championship position: Unplaced				
10	SOUTH AFRICAN GP East London		20	Otelle Nucci	D	1.5 Alfa Romeo Special 4	6 laps behind	17/25
	1969			Championship position: Unplaced				
nc	SOUTH AFRICAN GP Kyalami		19	Jack Holme	D	3.0 Brabham BT20-Repco V8	pit stop-clutch/13 laps behind	17/18
	1970			Championship position: Unplaced				
11	SOUTH AFRICAN GP Kyalami		24	Team Gunston	F	3.0 Brabham BT26A-Cosworth V8	pit stop/5 laps behind	21/24

GP Starts: 4   GP Wins: 0   Pole positions: 0   Fastest laps: 0   Points: 0

PIET (PETER) de KLERK

Piet got his first foothold in motor racing as a mechanic, indeed he workied his pasage from Durban to London in order to learn about racing cars and spent a short spell working for Colin Chapman. On his return to his homeland he found employment with Syd van der Vyver who also gave him the chance to his first chance to race. Moving to Johannesburg, he helped Doug Serrurier and Ernest Pieterse in building the Alfa special in 1960, but it was 1962 before the eager de Klerk was to get behind the wheel.

de Klerk quickly began to gain good placings with the car and was subsequently entrusted with a Brabham-Climax with which he was able to challenge more strongly the local maestro John Love. Piet, however, always seemed to be bridesmaid, finishing second on numerous occasions before temporarily abandoning single-seaters at the end of 1965 when Mike de Udy offered hi the chance to race abroad in his Porsche Carrera 6 sports cars.

In 1967 he drove a Lola-Aston Martin at Le Mans, before resuming his South African career in late 1968 with Love's old Brabham BT20. before once more concentrating on sports cars into the early seventies.

PEDRO de la ROSA

It was the end of a long and winding road for Pedro when he finally found his way onto the Grand Prix grid in 1999. After karting from an early age, the Spaniard was the national Fiat Uno champion way back in 1989 and took the Formula Ford title the following year, which led to a move into Formula Renault in Britain.

This championship was duly added to the list in 1992 and when de la Rosa graduated to Formula 3 in 1993 his upward career curve seemed untroubled. However, a satisfactory sixth place in that learning year was followed by a nightmare season when, saddled with an uncompetitive Renault engine, he could only watch as Jan Magnussen blitzed the rest of the field. Fortunately a late-season engine change proved there was nothing wrong with the driver, who then decided to progress his career in Japanese Formula 3.

Driving for TOM'S, he trounced the opposition with eight pole positions and eight wins from the nine rounds of the series, ensuring a move up to Formula Nippon for 1996. In his first year at this level Pedro was always quick but was let down by his lack of experience, which denied him better finishes. He was a good learner, though, and the following season took his Nova Engineering Lola to the championship with six wins from the ten rounds. As if his cup was not overflowing, de la Rosa also clinched the All-Japan GT championship in a Toyota Supra.

Seeing no purpose in racing in the European F3000 series, Pedro secured backing from Repsol and negotiated a place for himself as the Jordan test driver for 1998, impressing all concerned with his technical feedback.

His ability to make a healthy contribution to the Arrows sponsorship budget was no doubt a huge factor in Tom Walkinshaw's decision to sign the Spaniard the following season, but he soon proved his worth by scoring a priceless point for the team on his Grand Prix debut in Melbourne. Thereafter, lack of development saw Arrows treading water but Pedro was held in high esteem by the team, who regard him as a good find with excellent future prospects in Formula 1.

de la ROSA, Pedro (ESP) b 24/2/1971, Barcelona

	1999	Championship position: 17th=		Wins: 0	Pole positions: 0	Fastest laps: 0	Points scored: 1		
	Race	Circuit	No	Entrant	Tyres	Car/Engine	Comment		
6	AUSTRALIAN GP	Melbourne	14	Arrows	B	3.0 Arrows A20 V10	scored a point in first Grand Prix	18/22
ret	BRAZILIAN GP	Interlagos	14	Arrows	B	3.0 Arrows A20 V10	hydraulics	18/22
ret	SAN MARINO GP	Imola	14	Arrows	B	3.0 Arrows A20 V10	collision with Wurz	17/22
ret	MONACO GP	Monte Carlo	14	Arrows	B	3.0 Arrows A20 V10	gearbox	21/22
11	SPANISH GP	Barcelona	14	Arrows	B	3.0 Arrows A20 V10	2 laps behind	19/22
ret	CANADIAN GP	Montreal	14	Arrows	B	3.0 Arrows A20 V10	transmission	20/22
11	FRENCH GP	Magny Cours	14	Arrows	B	3.0 Arrows A20 V10	1 lap behind	21/22
ret	BRITISH GP	Silverstone	14	Arrows	B	3.0 Arrows A20 V10	gearbox at restart	20/22
ret	AUSTRIAN GP	A1-Ring	14	Arrows	B	3.0 Arrows A20 V10	spun off	21/22
ret	GERMAN GP	Hockenheim	14	Arrows	B	3.0 Arrows A20 V10	brakes-spun off	20/22
15	HUNGARIAN GP	Hungaroring	14	Arrows	B	3.0 Arrows A20 V10	2 laps behind	20/22
ret	BELGIAN GP	Spa	14	Arrows	B	3.0 Arrows A20 V10	transmission	22/22
ret	ITALIAN GP	Monza	14	Arrows	B	3.0 Arrows A20 V10r	accident damage	21/22
ret	EUROPEAN GP	Nürburgring	14	Arrows	B	3.0 Arrows A20 V10	gearbox	22/22
ret	MALAYSIAN GP	Sepang	14	Arrows	B	3.0 Arrows A20 V10	engine	20/22
13	JAPANESE GP	Suzuka	14	Arrows	B	3.0 Arrows A20 V10	2 laps behind	21/22

GP Starts: 16   GP Wins: 0   Pole positions: 0   Fastest laps: 0   Points: 1

ALFONSO de PORTAGO

One of the most colourful characters ever to have been seen in motor racing, 'Fon' was a fantastic all-round sportsman. A Spanish nobleman, he was three times French amateur champion jockey, and appeared twice at Aintree – where he never raced cars – in the Grand National steeplechase; he was an international-class swimmer; and in addition he created the Spanish bobsleigh team to take part in the 1956 Winter Olympics.

He took up motor racing in 1954, briefly sharing Schell's big 4.5-litre Ferrari on its way to second place in the Buenos Aires 1000 Km, but usually handled less potent machinery to begin with, his Maserati 2-litre winning a race at Metz.

In 1955 de Portago joined the Scuderia Ferrari and while his F1 outings were restricted to non-championship races his sports car programme saw him take second in the Venezuelan GP and win the Governor's Cup at Nassau. He was included in Ferrari's large Grand Prix squad during 1956, sharing the second-place car in the British GP with Collins, while in sports cars the highlight of his season was a win in the Tour de France in his Ferrari GT.

The 1957 season started well with a shared fifth place in the Argentine GP and success in sports car events, de Portago taking a win at Montlhéry and third places in both the Buenos Aires 1000 Km and the Cuban GP, the latter after a brilliant drive when time was lost at a long pit stop. He was unhappy at taking part in the Mille Miglia, which he considered unnecessarily dangerous, but he competed nevertheless, only for disaster to strike less than 120 km before the finish. It is thought that a tyre burst, hurling the Ferrari of de Portago and his long-time friend and co-driver Ed Nelson into the crowd. Ten unfortunate spectators were killed, along with the car's occupants, and the famous road race was banned forthwith by the Italian government.

de PORTAGO, Alfonso (E) b 11/10/1928, London, England – d 12/5/1957, Mille Miglia, between Goito and Guidizzolo, Italy

	1956	Championship position: 12th=		Wins: 0	Pole positions: 0	Fastest laps: 0	Points scored: 3		
	Race	Circuit	No	Entrant	Tyres	Car/Engine	Comment		Q Pos/Entries
ret	FRENCH GP	Reims	16	Scuderia Ferrari	E	2.5 Lancia-Ferrari D50 V8	gearbox		9/20
2*	BRITISH GP	Silverstone	4	Scuderia Ferrari	E	2.5 Lancia-Ferrari D50 V8	* Collins took over car/-1 lap		12/28
10*	"	"	3	Scuderia Ferrari	E	2.5 Lancia-Ferrari D50 V8	* took Castellotti's car/-9 laps		– / –
ret*	GERMAN GP	Nürburgring	5	Scuderia Ferrari	E	2.5 Lancia-Ferrari D50 V8	* Collins took over/crashed		10/21
ret	ITALIAN GP	Monza	30	Scuderia Ferrari	E	2.5 Lancia-Ferrari D50 V8	puncture		9/26
	1957	Championship position: 16th=		Wins: 0	Pole positions: 0	Fastest laps: 0	Points scored: 1		
5*	ARGENTINE GP	Buenos Aires	20	Scuderia Ferrari	E	2.5 Lancia-Ferrari D50A V8	* took González's car/-2 laps		– /16

GP Starts: 5   GP Wins: 0   Pole positions: 0   Fastest laps: 0   Points: 4

MAX de TERRA

Another Swiss 'gentleman racer' who competed in the late forties and early fifties, de Terra was usually seen in minor events and hill-climbs. He made up the numbers at a handful of major races in his native country and drove at a sedate pace throughout.

Having raced a Cisitalia D46 in the 1950 Prix de Berne, finishing tenth (and last), he arranged to drive Alfred Dattner's Simca in the 1952 Swiss GP and the following year he appeared at the wheel of an old Ferrari 166 entered by Rudi Fischer's Espadon team, plodding round to finish eighth, some 14 laps in arrears.

ALESSANDRO de TOMASO

A useful sports car driver in his native Argentina, first with a Maserati T200S and then the little OSCA, de Tomaso made his GP

debut in an old Ferrari in his home event in 1957, before coming to Europe to drive the small-capacity OSCA, winning the Index of Performance at Le Mans in 1958. After racing his Cooper-OSCA hybrid at Sebring in 1959, he retired from racing and based himself in Modena. He helped to develop the ISIS-Fiat Formula Junior car in 1960 and subsequently went on to build an unsuccessful Formula 1 car on two occasions (1962 and 1970). However, he did make money from a road car project, which was taken up by Ford in the late sixties.

CHARLES de TORNACO

The wealthy son of twenties racer Baron de Tornaco, the young Charles, encouraged by his long-time friend Jacques Swaters, took part in the 1949 Spa 24 Hours with a BMW, and then drove a Veritas in the 1950 event, before helping found Ecurie Belgique.

In truth, he was not a talented driver, but his enthusiasm was such that when the team regrouped as Ecurie Francorchamps in 1952, he remained, racing their Ferrari T500, though his best result that year was a fourth place at Chimay in an HWM. De Tornaco raced less regularly in 1953, but in practice for the Modena GP he rolled the team's Ferrari, fracturing his skull and breaking his neck. Scandalously, there was no proper medical assistance present, and he died on the way to hospital in an ordinary saloon car.

de TERRA, Max (CH) b 6/10/1918 – d 29/12/1982

	1952	Championship position: Unplaced							
	Race	Circuit	No	Entrant	Tyres	Car/Engine		Comment	Q Pos/Entries
ret	SWISS GP	Bremgarten	50	Alfred Daettner	E	1.5 Simca Gordini Type 11 4		magneto	21/21
	1953	Championship position: Unplaced							
nc	SWISS GP	Bremgarten	40	Ecurie Espadon	P	2.0 Ferrari 166C V12		14 laps behind	19/23

GP Starts: 2 GP Wins: 0 Pole positions: 0 Fastest laps: 0 Points: 0

de TOMASO, Alessandro (RA) b 10/7/1928, Buenos Aires

	1957	Championship position: Unplaced							
	Race	Circuit	No	Entrant	Tyres	Car/Engine		Comment	Q Pos/Entries
9	ARGENTINE GP	Buenos Aires	26	Scuderia Centro Sud	P	2.5 Ferrari 500/625 4		9 laps behind	12/16
	1959	Championship position: Unplaced							
ret	US GP	Sebring	14	Automobili OSCA	D	2.0 Cooper T43-OSCA 4		brakes	14/19

GP Starts: 2 GP Wins: 0 Pole positions: 0 Fastest laps: 0 Points: 0

de TORNACO, Baron Charles (B) b 7/6/1927, Brussels – d 18/9/1953, Modena Autodrome, Italy

	1952	Championship position: Unplaced							
	Race	Circuit	No	Entrant	Tyres	Car/Engine		Comment	Q Pos/Entries
7	BELGIAN GP	Spa	34	Ecurie Francorchamps	E	2.0 Ferrari 500 4		3 laps behind	13/22
ret	DUTCH GP	Zandvoort	24	Ecurie Francorchamps	E	2.0 Ferrari 500 4		engine	17/18
dnq	ITALIAN GP	Monza	70	Ecurie Francorchamps	E	2.0 Ferrari 500 4			25/35
	1953	Championship position: Unplaced							
dns	BELGIAN GP	Spa	44	Ecurie Francorchamps	E	2.0 Ferrari 500 4		practice only	– /22

GP Starts: 2 GP Wins: 0 Pole positions: 0 Fastest laps: 0 Points: 0

EMILIO de VILLOTA

After contesting the Shellsport championship in 1976 with a Lyncar, de Villota, a bank manager with Banco Iberico, gave up his day job and, with support from his former employers, went Grand Prix racing the following year with a McLaren M23. However, he was out of his depth and settled for a return to the G8 series, where he could shine in a competitive car. In 1978 the Aurora AFX F1 series was inaugurated, and de Villota became a staunch supporter of the championship during its short life. Racing a Lotus 78, he took third place overall in 1979, before clinching the title in 1980 with his RAM Racing Williams FW07.

After the series folded, de Villota – having failed to gain an entry for his home Grand Prix in 1981 – turned briefly to sports cars, winning the Enna 6 Hours and the Flying Tigers 1000 at Brands in a Lola T600 with Guy Edwards, before returning to Formula 1 in 1982 for a completely fruitless spell in the works March run by his old colleagues at RAM.

JEAN-DENIS DELÉTRAZ

With the cost of competing in Formula 1 escalating out of sight in the mid-nineties, the more impoverished teams towards the back of the grid increasingly looked to drivers who could bring a healthy budget to make ends meet. Thus began the worrying trend of pilots of modest pedigree making up the numbers. Certainly Deletraz's qualifications to compete at the highest level looked questionable, especially given his lack of recent top-flight competition, when he turned up to drive for Larrousse in Adelaide in 1994.

The wealthy Swiss had made a promising start to his career in French FF1600 back in 1985, but achieved little in two seasons of Formula 3 thereafter. His F3000 credentials were bolstered by a couple of third places for the GDBA team in 1988, but otherwise his record was unimpressive. Given Pacific's desperate financial state at the end of 1995, they could be excused for taking any lifeline thrown when he bought his rides, but the deal merely delayed the team's inevitable demise.

Deletraz has since continued his racing activities quite competitively in sports car racing, campaigning a McLaren F1 GTR, the factory Lotus GT and a Ferrari 333SP in partnership with Fabien Giroix.

de VILLOTA, Emilio (E) b 26/7/1946, Madrid

	1976	Championship position: Unplaced							
	Race	Circuit	No	Entrant	Tyres	Car/Engine		Comment	Q Pos/Entries
dnq	SPANISH GP	Jarama	33	RAM Racing	G	3.0 Brabham BT44B-Cosworth V8			28/30
	1977	Championship position: Unplaced							
13	SPANISH GP	Jarama	36	Iberia Airlines	G	3.0 McLaren M23-Cosworth V8		5 laps behind	23/31
dnq	BELGIAN GP	Zolder	36	Iberia Airlines	G	3.0 McLaren M23-Cosworth V8			28/32
dnq	SWEDISH GP	Anderstorp	36	Iberia Airlines	G	3.0 McLaren M23-Cosworth V8			26/31
dnq	BRITISH GP	Silverstone	36	Iberia Airlines	G	3.0 McLaren M23-Cosworth V8			30/36
dnq	GERMAN GP	Hockenheim	36	Iberia Airlines	G	3.0 McLaren M23-Cosworth V8			26/30
17/ret	AUSTRIAN GP	Österreichring	36	Iberia Airlines	G	3.0 McLaren M23-Cosworth V8		collision with course car/-4 laps	26/30
dnq	ITALIAN GP	Monza	36	Iberia Airlines	G	3.0 McLaren M23-Cosworth V8			29/34
	1978	Championship position: Unplaced							
dnq	SPANISH GP	Jarama	28	Centro Aseguredor F1	G	3.0 McLaren M23-Cosworth V8			27/28
	1981	Championship position: Unplaced							
dns	SPANISH GP	Jarama	37	Equipe Banco Occidental	M	3.0 Williams FW07-Cosworth V8		in breach of Concorde Agreement	– / –
	1982	Championship position: Unplaced							
dnpq	BELGIAN GP	Zolder	19	LBT Team March	A	3.0 March 821-Cosworth V8			32/32
dnpq	MONACO GP	Monte Carlo	19	LBT Team March	A	3.0 March 821-Cosworth V8			31/31
dnq	US GP (DETROIT)	Detroit	19	LBT Team March	A	3.0 March 821-Cosworth V8			27/28
dnq	CANADIAN GP	Montreal	19	LBT Team March	A	3.0 March 821-Cosworth V8			28/29
dnpq	DUTCH GP	Zandvoort	19	LBT Team March	A	3.0 March 821-Cosworth V8			31/31

GP Starts: 2   GP Wins: 0   Pole positions: 0   Fastest laps: 0   Points: 0

DELÉTRAZ, Jean-Denis (CH) b 1/10/1963, Geneva

	1994	Championship position: Unplaced							
	Race	Circuit	No	Entrant	Tyres	Car/Engine		Comment	Q Pos/Entries
ret	AUSTRALIAN GP	Adelaide	20	Tourtel Larrousse	G	3.5 Larrousse LH94-Ford HB V8		gearbox	25/26
	1995	Championship position: Unplaced							
ret	PORTUGUESE GP	Estoril	16	Pacific Grand Prix Ltd	G	3.0 Pacific PR02-Ford ED V8		driver suffering cramp	24/24
nc	EUROPEAN GP	Nürburgring	16	Pacific Grand Prix Ltd	G	3.0 Pacific PR02-Ford ED V8		7 laps behind	24/24

GP Starts: 3   GP Wins: 0   Pole positions: 0   Fastest laps: 0   Points: 0

PATRICK DEPAILLER

The archetypal wiry little Frenchman, a cigarette perpetually hanging from the corner of his mouth, Depailler was something of a free spirit – a throwback to an earlier age, who lived for the moment and raced accordingly.

Schooled in the French F3 championship, Patrick spent three seasons between 1967 and 1969 driving a works Alpine-Renault, but also had occasional races in the Alpine sports-prototype, taking a third place in the Monza 1000 Km of 1968. A switch to Formula 2 with the Elf-Pygmée team for 1970 proved something of a disaster, the final straw being a practice crash at the Salzburgring from which he was lucky to escape with slight burns. Luckily he still had the faith of Elf, who backed him again the following year but this time in a Tecno. Apart from a sixth place at Pau little went right for Depailler at this level, but he was more than happy to race the works Alpine-Renault once more, becoming the 1971 French F3 champion.

By 1972 he was already 28 years of age and had left it quite late in motor racing terms if he was going to make the leap up into the big time. After winning the Monaco F3 race, it was third time lucky in his attempts to crack Formula 2, Patrick taking second places in the races at Pau, Enna and Albi. His performances in the Elf/John Coombs March 722 put him in the frame for a couple of rides with his old chum Ken Tyrrell. It was more of the same in 1973, when once again a win in F2 just seemed to elude him, poor Patrick having to settle for no fewer than four second places this time around, and even worse was to follow. A motor cycle accident left him with a broken leg and he was forced to miss the two drives in North America that Tyrrell had lined up for him.

Fortunately his leg was soon to mend, and he was in the Tyrrell team full-time in 1974 with Jody Scheckter as his team-mate. In a highly competitive year, he brought the Tyrrell home in the points on six occasions and took a pole in Sweden, the first time a Frenchman had achieved this feat in a World Championship race, while in Formula 2 he finally broke his long dry spell, winning four rounds, at Pau, Mugello, Hockenheim and Vallelunga.

Patrick stuck with Tyrrell to become Formula 1 racing's 'nearly-man' over the next three seasons, taking seven second places in Grands Prix (and another in the 1975 non-title Swiss GP) before an emotional triumph at Monaco in 1978. Lured to Ligier for the 1979 season, when the team were at their zenith, if only for a short spell, Patrick won the Spanish GP and lay equal third in the championship when a mid-season hang-gliding accident sidelined him with serious leg injuries.

Struggling back to fitness, he joined Alfa Romeo in 1980, shrugging aside the frustrations of developing the unreliable car. He was beginning to make real progress when, in a solitary test session at Hockenheim, something went wrong with the car, probably a suspension breakage, depositing the helpless driver into the Armco at massive speed. He stood no chance of survival. Depailler had lived life to the full, and even in darker moments, as he fought the pain of his injuries, it would not be long before a broad smile would emerge, crinkling his face with laughter lines. A fitting way to remember him.

DEPAILLER, Patrick (F) b 9/8/1944, Clermont-Ferrand – d 1/8/1980, Hockenheim, Germany

	1972	Championship position: Unplaced						
	Race	Circuit	No	Entrant	Tyres	Car/Engine	Comment	Q Pos/Entries
nc	FRENCH GP	Clermont Ferrand	8	Elf Team Tyrrell	G	3.0 Tyrrell 004-Cosworth V8	*pit stops-suspension/-5 laps*	=17/29
7	US GP	Watkins Glen	3	Elf Team Tyrrell	G	3.0 Tyrrell 004-Cosworth V8	*1 lap behind*	11/32
	1974	Championship position: 9th Wins: 0 Pole positions: 1 Fastest laps: 1 Points scored: 14						
6	ARGENTINE GP	Buenos Aires	4	Elf Team Tyrrell	G	3.0 Tyrrell 005-Cosworth V8		15/26
8	BRAZILIAN GP	Interlagos	4	Elf Team Tyrrell	G	3.0 Tyrrell 005-Cosworth V8	*1 lap behind*	16/25
4	SOUTH AFRICAN GP	Kyalami	4	Elf Team Tyrrell	G	3.0 Tyrrell 005-Cosworth V8		15/27
8	SPANISH GP	Jarama	4	Elf Team Tyrrell	G	3.0 Tyrrell 006-Cosworth V8	*3 laps behind*	=17/28

ret	BELGIAN GP	Nivelles	4	Elf Team Tyrrell	G	3.0 Tyrrell 007-Cosworth V8	brake strap	11/32
9	MONACO GP	Monte Carlo	4	Elf Team Tyrrell	G	3.0 Tyrrell 006-Cosworth V8	started from back/-4 laps	– / –
dns	"	" "	4	Elf Team Tyrrell	G	3.0 Tyrrell 007-Cosworth V8	practised in this car	=4/28
2	SWEDISH GP	Anderstorp	4	Elf Team Tyrrell	G	3.0 Tyrrell 007-Cosworth V8	FL	1/28
6	DUTCH GP	Zandvoort	4	Elf Team Tyrrell	G	3.0 Tyrrell 007-Cosworth V8		8/27
8	FRENCH GP	Dijon	4	Elf Team Tyrrell	G	3.0 Tyrrell 006-Cosworth V8	1 lap behind	– / –
dns	" " "	"	4	Elf Team Tyrrell	G	3.0 Tyrrell 007-Cosworth V8	accident in practice	9/30
ret	BRITISH GP	Brands Hatch	4	Elf Team Tyrrell	G	3.0 Tyrrell 007-Cosworth V8	engine	10/34
ret	GERMAN GP	Nürburgring	4	Elf Team Tyrrell	G	3.0 Tyrrell 007-Cosworth V8	hit guard rail	5/32
ret	AUSTRIAN GP	Österreichring	4	Elf Team Tyrrell	G	3.0 Tyrrell 007-Cosworth V8	collision with Ickx	14/31
11	ITALIAN GP	Monza	4	Elf Team Tyrrell	G	3.0 Tyrrell 007-Cosworth V8	2 laps behind	=9/31
5	CANADIAN GP	Mosport Park	4	Elf Team Tyrrell	G	3.0 Tyrrell 007-Cosworth V8		7/30
6	US GP	Watkins Glen	4	Elf Team Tyrrell	G	3.0 Tyrrell 007-Cosworth V8		13/30

1975 Championship position: 9th Wins: 0 Pole positions: 0 Fastest laps: 1 Points scored: 12

5	ARGENTINE GP	Buenos Aires	4	Elf Team Tyrrell	G	3.0 Tyrrell 007-Cosworth V8		8/23
ret	BRAZILIAN GP	Interlagos	4	Elf Team Tyrrell	G	3.0 Tyrrell 007-Cosworth V8	front suspension-crashed	9/23
3	SOUTH AFRICAN GP	Kyalami	4	Elf Team Tyrrell	G	3.0 Tyrrell 007-Cosworth V8		5/28
ret	SPANISH GP	Montjuich Park	4	Elf Team Tyrrell	G	3.0 Tyrrell 007-Cosworth V8	multiple accident-lost wheel	7/26
5	MONACO GP	Monte Carlo	4	Elf Team Tyrrell	G	3.0 Tyrrell 007-Cosworth V8	FL	12/26
4	BELGIAN GP	Zolder	4	Elf Team Tyrrell	G	3.0 Tyrrell 007-Cosworth V8		12/24
12	SWEDISH GP	Anderstorp	4	Elf Team Tyrrell	G	3.0 Tyrrell 007-Cosworth V8	2 laps behind	2/26
9	DUTCH GP	Zandvoort	4	Elf Team Tyrrell	G	3.0 Tyrrell 007-Cosworth V8	2 laps behind	13/25
6	FRENCH GP	Paul Ricard	4	Elf Team Tyrrell	G	3.0 Tyrrell 007-Cosworth V8		13/26
9/ret	BRITISH GP	Silverstone	4	Elf Team Tyrrell	G	3.0 Tyrrell 007-Cosworth V8	spun off in rain/2 laps behind	17/28
9	GERMAN GP	Nürburgring	4	Elf Team Tyrrell	G	3.0 Tyrrell 007-Cosworth V8	pit stop-suspension/-1 lap	4/26
11	AUSTRIAN GP	Österreichring	4	Elf Team Tyrrell	G	3.0 Tyrrell 007-Cosworth V8	1 lap behind	7/30
7	ITALIAN GP	Monza	4	Elf Team Tyrrell	G	3.0 Tyrrell 007-Cosworth V8	1 lap behind	12/28
ret	US GP	Watkins Glen	4	Elf Team Tyrrell	G	3.0 Tyrrell 007-Cosworth V8	collision with Pace	8/24

1976 Championship position: 4 Wins: 0 Pole positions: 0 Fastest laps: 1 Points scored: 39

2	BRAZILIAN GP	Interlagos	4	Elf Team Tyrrell	G	3.0 Tyrrell 007-Cosworth V8		9/22
9	SOUTH AFRICAN GP	Kyalami	4	Elf Team Tyrrell	G	3.0 Tyrrell 007-Cosworth V8	1 lap behind	6/25
3	US GP WEST	Long Beach	4	Elf Team Tyrrell	G	3.0 Tyrrell 007-Cosworth V8		2/27
ret	SPANISH GP	Jarama	4	Elf Team Tyrrell	G	3.0 Tyrrell P34-Cosworth V8	brake failure-crashed	3/30
ret	BELGIAN GP	Zolder	4	Elf Team Tyrrell	G	3.0 Tyrrell P34-Cosworth V8	engine	4/29
3	MONACO GP	Monte Carlo	4	Elf Team Tyrrell	G	3.0 Tyrrell P34-Cosworth V8		4/25
2	SWEDISH GP	Anderstorp	4	Elf Team Tyrrell	G	3.0 Tyrrell P34-Cosworth V8		4/27
2	FRENCH GP	Paul Ricard	4	Elf Team Tyrrell	G	3.0 Tyrrell P34-Cosworth V8		3/30
ret	BRITISH GP	Brands Hatch	4	Elf Team Tyrrell	G	3.0 Tyrrell P34-Cosworth V8	engine	5/30
ret	GERMAN GP	Nürburgring	4	Elf Team Tyrrell	G	3.0 Tyrrell P34-Cosworth V8	collision with Regazzoni	3/28
ret	AUSTRIAN GP	Österreichring	4	Elf Team Tyrrell	G	3.0 Tyrrell P34-Cosworth V8	suspension	13/25
7	DUTCH GP	Zandvoort	4	Elf Team Tyrrell	G	3.0 Tyrrell P34-Cosworth V8		14/27
6	ITALIAN GP	Monza	4	Elf Team Tyrrell	G	3.0 Tyrrell P34-Cosworth V8		4/29
2	CANADIAN GP	Mosport Park	4	Elf Team Tyrrell	G	3.0 Tyrrell P34-Cosworth V8	FL	4/27
ret	US GP EAST	Watkins Glen	4	Elf Team Tyrrell	G	3.0 Tyrrell P34-Cosworth V8	detached fuel line	7/27
2	JAPANESE GP	Mount Fuji	4	Elf Team Tyrrell	G	3.0 Tyrrell P34-Cosworth V8	1 lap behind	13/27

1977 Championship position: 8th= Wins: 0 Pole positions: 0 Fastest laps: 0 Points scored: 20

ret	ARGENTINE GP	Buenos Aires	4	Elf Team Tyrrell	G	3.0 Tyrrell P34-Cosworth V8	engine-overheating	3/21
ret	BRAZILIAN GP	Interlagos	4	Elf Team Tyrrell	G	3.0 Tyrrell P34-Cosworth V8	spun off	6/22
3	SOUTH AFRICAN GP	Kyalami	4	Elf Team Tyrrell	G	3.0 Tyrrell P34-Cosworth V8		4/23
4	US GP WEST	Long Beach	4	Elf Team Tyrrell	G	3.0 Tyrrell P34-Cosworth V8		12/22
ret	SPANISH GP	Jarama	4	Elf Team Tyrrell	G	3.0 Tyrrell P34-Cosworth V8	engine	10/31
ret	MONACO GP	Monte Carlo	4	Elf Team Tyrrell	G	3.0 Tyrrell P34-Cosworth V8	brakes/gearbox	8/26
dns	"	" "	4	Elf Team Tyrrell	G	3.0 Tyrrell 007-Cosworth V8	practice only	– / –
8	BELGIAN GP	Zolder	4	Elf Team Tyrrell	G	3.0 Tyrrell P34-Cosworth V8	1 lap behind	5/32
4	SWEDISH GP	Anderstorp	4	Elf Team Tyrrell	G	3.0 Tyrrell P34-Cosworth V8		6/31
ret	FRENCH GP	Dijon	4	Elf Team Tyrrell	G	3.0 Tyrrell P34-Cosworth V8	collision with Stuck	12/30
ret	BRITISH GP	Silverstone	4	Elf Team Tyrrell	G	3.0 Tyrrell P34-Cosworth V8	brake failure-crashed	18/36
ret	GERMAN GP	Hockenheim	4	Elf Team Tyrrell	G	3.0 Tyrrell P34-Cosworth V8	engine	15/30
13	AUSTRIAN GP	Österreichring	4	Elf Team Tyrrell	G	3.0 Tyrrell P34-Cosworth V8	1 lap behind	10/30
ret	DUTCH GP	Zandvoort	4	Elf Team Tyrrell	G	3.0 Tyrrell P34-Cosworth V8	engine	11/34
ret	ITALIAN GP	Monza	4	Elf Team Tyrrell	G	3.0 Tyrrell P34-Cosworth V8	engine	13/34
14	US GP EAST	Watkins Glen	4	Elf Team Tyrrell	G	3.0 Tyrrell P34-Cosworth V8	3 laps behind	8/27
2	CANADIAN GP	Mosport Park	4	Elf Team Tyrrell	G	3.0 Tyrrell P34-Cosworth V8		6/27
3	JAPANESE GP	Mount Fuji	4	Elf Team Tyrrell	G	3.0 Tyrrell P34-Cosworth V8		15/23

1978 Championship position: 5th Wins: 1 Pole positions: 0 Fastest laps: 0 Points scored: 34

3	ARGENTINE GP	Buenos Aires	4	Elf Team Tyrrell	G	3.0 Tyrrell 008-Cosworth V8		10/26
ret	BRAZILIAN GP	Rio	4	Elf Team Tyrrell	G	3.0 Tyrrell 008-Cosworth V8	damaged brake cylinder	11/28
2	SOUTH AFRICAN GP	Kyalami	4	Elf Team Tyrrell	G	3.0 Tyrrell 008-Cosworth V8	lost lead on last lap-fuel pick up	11/30
3	US GP WEST	Long Beach	4	Elf Team Tyrrell	G	3.0 Tyrrell 008-Cosworth V8		12/30
1	MONACO GP	Monte Carlo	4	Elf Team Tyrrell	G	3.0 Tyrrell 008-Cosworth V8		5/30
ret	BELGIAN GP	Zolder	4	Elf Team Tyrrell	G	3.0 Tyrrell 008-Cosworth V8	gearbox	13/30
ret	SPANISH GP	Jarama	4	Elf Team Tyrrell	G	3.0 Tyrrell 008-Cosworth V8	engine	12/29
ret	SWEDISH GP	Anderstorp	4	Elf Team Tyrrell	G	3.0 Tyrrell 008-Cosworth V8	suspension-broken upright	12/27
ret	FRENCH GP	Paul Ricard	4	Elf Team Tyrrell	G	3.0 Tyrrell 008-Cosworth V8	engine	13/29
4	BRITISH GP	Brands Hatch	4	Elf Team Tyrrell	G	3.0 Tyrrell 008-Cosworth V8		10/30
ret	GERMAN GP	Hockenheim	4	Elf Team Tyrrell	G	3.0 Tyrrell 008-Cosworth V8	accident with Tambay at start	13/30
2	AUSTRIAN GP	Österreichring	4	Elf Team Tyrrell	G	3.0 Tyrrell 008-Cosworth V8		13/31
ret	DUTCH GP	Zandvoort	4	Elf Team Tyrrell	G	3.0 Tyrrell 008-Cosworth V8	engine	12/33
11	ITALIAN GP	Monza	4	Elf Team Tyrrell	G	3.0 Tyrrell 008-Cosworth V8		16/32
ret	US GP EAST	Watkins Glen	4	Elf Team Tyrrell	G	3.0 Tyrrell 008-Cosworth V8	loose hub	12/27
5	CANADIAN GP	Montreal	4	Elf Team Tyrrell	G	3.0 Tyrrell 008-Cosworth V8		13/28

1979		Championship position: 6th=		Wins: 0	Pole positions: 0	Fastest laps: 1	Points scored: 22		
4	ARGENTINE GP	Buenos Aires	25	Gitanes Ligier	G	3.0 Ligier JS11-Cosworth V8		*pit stop-misfire*	2/26
2	BRAZILIAN GP	Interlagos	25	Gitanes Ligier	G	3.0 Ligier JS11-Cosworth V8			2/26
ret	SOUTH AFRICAN GP	Kyalami	25	Gitanes Ligier	G	3.0 Ligier JS11-Cosworth V8		*spun off*	5/26
5	US GP WEST	Long Beach	25	Gitanes Ligier	G	3.0 Ligier JS11-Cosworth V8		*lost 4th gear*	4/26
1	SPANISH GP	Jarama	25	Gitanes Ligier	G	3.0 Ligier JS11-Cosworth V8			2/27
ret	BELGIAN GP	Zolder	25	Gitanes Ligier	G	3.0 Ligier JS11-Cosworth V8		*hit barrier*	2/28
5/ret	MONACO GP	Monte Carlo	25	Gitanes Ligier	G	3.0 Ligier JS11-Cosworth V8		*engine/FL/2 laps behind*	3/25
1980		Championship position: Unplaced							
ret	ARGENTINE GP	Buenos Aires	22	Marlboro Team Alfa Romeo	G	3.0 Alfa Romeo 179 V12		*engine*	23/28
ret	BRAZILIAN GP	Interlagos	22	Marlboro Team Alfa Romeo	G	3.0 Alfa Romeo 179 V12		*electrics*	21/28
nc	SOUTH AFRICAN GP	Kyalami	22	Marlboro Team Alfa Romeo	G	3.0 Alfa Romeo 179 V12		*pit stops-engine/25 laps behind*	7/28
ret	US GP WEST	Long Beach	22	Marlboro Team Alfa Romeo	G	3.0 Alfa Romeo 179 V12		*suspension*	3/27
ret	BELGIAN GP	Zolder	22	Marlboro Team Alfa Romeo	G	3.0 Alfa Romeo 179 V12		*exhaust*	10/27
ret	MONACO GP	Monte Carlo	22	Marlboro Team Alfa Romeo	G	3.0 Alfa Romeo 179 V12		*engine*	7/27
ret	FRENCH GP	Paul Ricard	22	Marlboro Team Alfa Romeo	G	3.0 Alfa Romeo 179 V12		*handling*	10/27
ret	BRITISH GP	Brands Hatch	22	Marlboro Team Alfa Romeo	G	3.0 Alfa Romeo 179 V12		*engine*	8/27

GP Starts: 95   GP Wins: 2   Pole positions: 1   Fastest laps: 4   Points: 141

PEDRO DINIZ

Diniz's father was a racer in his day, and now runs a huge chain of supermarkets in Brazil, so young Pedro was well placed to have a stab at racing. He completed a year in the Sud-Am F3 series before heading to Europe in 1991, where he secured a seat in the crack West Surrey Racing team. A season spent alongside the very quick Rubens Barrichello and Jordi Gené highlighted his shortcomings, but a move to Edenbridge Racing in 1992 showed he had learned much.

For 1993, Diniz jumped up to compete in F3000 with Forti Corse but was out of his depth. Staying on for 1994, he conjured up one fourth-place finish at Estoril, but the Brazilian's performances, while showing some promise, failed to convince.

Eyebrows were therefore raised when his name appeared on the 1995 F1 entry list paired with fellow countryman Roberto Moreno at Forti. In the event he was neat and tidy and proved evenly matched with his experienced colleague. However, the car was clearly uncompetitive and, with a massive personal sponsorship budget, Diniz lost no time in obtaining a drive for 1996 at Ligier, where his goal was to secure a championship point, which he achieved on two occasions.

For 1997 Diniz (accompanied by his wedge of cash) was tempted away by Tom Walkinshaw to join his newly reconstructed Arrows team as number two to Damon Hill. Again he silenced the doubters with a number of more-than-respectable performances. He even managed to out-qualify and out-race the reigning World Champion at Spa, of all places, and took a career-best fifth place in the Luxembourg Grand Prix. For 1998 the Brazilian found himself paired with Mika Salo and again had his moments, interestingly scoring points at the two classic circuits of Monaco and Spa.

It was patently obvious to Diniz that to climb further up the grid he needed a better car than Arrows had thus far provided, so he was on the move once more. Brushing aside threats of litigation for breach of contract, Pedro prepared to test himself against Jean Alesi at Sauber. Amazingly he outscored his team leader by three points to two, which proved nothing more than that, on this occasion, modest consistency paid more dividends than blinkered audacity.

For 2000 Diniz remains a Formula 1 fixture, trying once more to convince the sceptics that he is worthy of a place on the grid on merit, rather than by dint of the vast millions which ease his way into the cockpit.

DINIZ, Pedro Paulo (BR) b 22/5/1970, São Paulo

	Race	Circuit	No	Entrant	Tyres	Car/Engine	Comment	Q Pos/Entries
	1995	Championship position: Unplaced						
10	BRAZILIAN GP	Interlagos	21	Parmalat Forti Ford	G	3.0 Forti FG01-Ford ED V8	*7 laps behind*	25/26
nc	ARGENTINE GP	Buenos Aires	21	Parmalat Forti Ford	G	3.0 Forti FG01-Ford ED V8	*9 laps behind*	25/26
nc	SAN MARINO GP	Imola	21	Parmalat Forti Ford	G	3.0 Forti FG01-Ford ED V8	*7 laps behind*	26/26
ret	SPANISH GP	Barcelona	21	Parmalat Forti Ford	G	3.0 Forti FG01-Ford ED V8	*gearbox*	26/26
10	MONACO GP	Monte Carlo	21	Parmalat Forti Ford	G	3.0 Forti FG01-Ford ED V8	*6 laps behind*	22/26
ret	CANADIAN GP	Montreal	21	Parmalat Forti Ford	G	3.0 Forti FG01-Ford ED V8	*gearbox*	24/24

ret	FRENCH GP	Magny Cours	21	Parmalat Forti Ford	G	3.0 Forti FG01-Ford ED V8		collision with Martini on lap 1	23/24
ret	BRITISH GP	Silverstone	21	Parmalat Forti Ford	G	3.0 Forti FG01-Ford ED V8		gearbox	20/24
ret	GERMAN GP	Hockenheim	21	Parmalat Forti Ford	G	3.0 Forti FG01-Ford ED V8		started from pit lane/brakes	21/24
ret	HUNGARIAN GP	Hungaroring	21	Parmalat Forti Ford	G	3.0 Forti FG01-Ford ED V8		engine	23/24
13	BELGIAN GP	Spa	21	Parmalat Forti Ford	G	3.0 Forti FG01-Ford ED V8		2 laps behind	24/24
9	ITALIAN GP	Monza	21	Parmalat Forti Ford	G	3.0 Forti FG01-Ford ED V8		3 laps behind	23/24
16	PORTUGUESE GP	Estoril	21	Parmalat Forti Ford	G	3.0 Forti FG01-Ford ED V8		5 laps behind	22/24
13	EUROPEAN GP	Nürburgring	21	Parmalat Forti Ford	G	3.0 Forti FG01-Ford ED V8		5 laps behind	22/24
17	PACIFIC GP	T.I. Circuit	21	Parmalat Forti Ford	G	3.0 Forti FG01-Ford ED V8		6 laps behind	21/24
ret	JAPANESE GP	Suzuka	21	Parmalat Forti Ford	G	3.0 Forti FG01-Ford ED V8		spun off	21/24
7	AUSTRALIAN GP	Adelaide	21	Parmalat Forti Ford	G	3.0 Forti FG01-Ford ED V8		4 laps behind	21/24

1996 Championship position: 15th Wins: 0 Pole positions: 0 Fastest laps: 0 Points scored: 2

10	AUSTRALIAN GP	Melbourne	10	Ligier Gauloises-Blondes	G	3.0 Ligier JS43-Mugen Honda V10		collision-Brundle/-2 laps	20/22
8	BRAZILIAN GP	Interlagos	10	Ligier Gauloises-Blondes	G	3.0 Ligier JS43-Mugen Honda V10		* practice time disallowed/-2 laps	–*/22
ret	ARGENTINE GP	Buenos Aires	10	Ligier Gauloises-Blondes	G	3.0 Ligier JS43-Mugen Honda V10		car caught fire after refuelling	18/22
10	EUROPEAN GP	Nürburgring	10	Ligier Gauloises-Blondes	G	3.0 Ligier JS43-Mugen Honda V10		1 lap behind	17/22
7	SAN MARINO GP	Imola	10	Ligier Gauloises-Blondes	G	3.0 Ligier JS43-Mugen Honda V10		1 lap behind	17/22
ret	MONACO GP	Monte Carlo	10	Ligier Gauloises-Blondes	G	3.0 Ligier JS43-Mugen Honda V10		transmission	17/22
6	SPANISH GP	Barcelona	10	Ligier Gauloises-Blondes	G	3.0 Ligier JS43-Mugen Honda V10		spin/2 laps behind	17/22
ret	CANADIAN GP	Montreal	10	Ligier Gauloises-Blondes	G	3.0 Ligier JS43-Mugen Honda V10		engine	18/22
ret	FRENCH GP	Magny Cours	10	Ligier Gauloises-Blondes	G	3.0 Ligier JS43-Mugen Honda V10		engine	12/22
ret	BRITISH GP	Silverstone	10	Ligier Gauloises-Blondes	G	3.0 Ligier JS43-Mugen Honda V10		engine	18/22
ret	GERMAN GP	Hockenheim	10	Ligier Gauloises-Blondes	G	3.0 Ligier JS43-Mugen Honda V10		engine	11/20
ret	HUNGARIAN GP	Hungaroring	10	Ligier Gauloises-Blondes	G	3.0 Ligier JS43-Mugen Honda V10		collision with Salo on lap 1	15/20
ret	BELGIAN GP	Spa	10	Ligier Gauloises-Blondes	G	3.0 Ligier JS43-Mugen Honda V10		engine	15/20
6	ITALIAN GP	Monza	10	Ligier Gauloises-Blondes	G	3.0 Ligier JS43-Mugen Honda V10		1 lap behind	14/20
ret	PORTUGUESE GP	Estoril	10	Ligier Gauloises-Blondes	G	3.0 Ligier JS43-Mugen Honda V10		spun off	18/20
ret	JAPANESE GP	Suzuka	10	Ligier Gauloises-Blondes	G	3.0 Ligier JS43-Mugen Honda V10		spun off	16/20

1997 Championship position: 16th= Wins: 0 Pole positions: 0 Fastest laps: 0 Points scored: 2

10	AUSTRALIAN GP	Melbourne	2	Danka Arrows Yamaha	B	3.0 Arrows A18-Yamaha V10		4 laps behind	22/24
ret	BRAZILIAN GP	Interlagos	2	Danka Arrows Yamaha	B	3.0 Arrows A18-Yamaha V10		spun off	16/22
ret	ARGENTINE GP	Buenos Aires	2	Danka Arrows Yamaha	B	3.0 Arrows A18-Yamaha V10		engine	22/22
ret	SAN MARINO GP	Imola	2	Danka Arrows Yamaha	B	3.0 Arrows A18-Yamaha V10		hydraulics	17/22
ret	MONACO GP	Monte Carlo	2	Danka Arrows Yamaha	B	3.0 Arrows A18-Yamaha V10		spun off on lap 1	16/22
ret	SPANISH GP	Barcelona	2	Danka Arrows Yamaha	B	3.0 Arrows A18-Yamaha V10		engine	21/22
8	CANADIAN GP	Montreal	2	Danka Arrows Yamaha	B	3.0 Arrows A18-Yamaha V10		1 lap behind	16/22
ret	FRENCH GP	Magny Cours	2	Danka Arrows Yamaha	B	3.0 Arrows A18-Yamaha V10		spun off	16/22
ret	BRITISH GP	Silverstone	2	Danka Arrows Yamaha	B	3.0 Arrows A18-Yamaha V10		engine	17/22
ret	GERMAN GP	Hockenheim	2	Danka Arrows Yamaha	B	3.0 Arrows A18-Yamaha V10		collision with Herbert	16/22
ret	HUNGARIAN GP	Hungaroring	2	Danka Arrows Yamaha	B	3.0 Arrows A18-Yamaha V10		alternator	19/22
7*	BELGIAN GP	Spa	2	Danka Arrows Yamaha	B	3.0 Arrows A18-Yamaha V10		*5th car disqualified	8/22
ret	ITALIAN GP	Monza	2	Danka Arrows Yamaha	B	3.0 Arrows A18-Yamaha V10		broken suspension-spun off	17/22
13/ret	AUSTRIAN GP	A1-Ring	2	Danka Arrows Yamaha	B	3.0 Arrows A18-Yamaha V10		shock absorber/4 laps behind	17/22
5	LUXEMBOURG GP	Nürburgring	2	Danka Arrows Yamaha	B	3.0 Arrows A18-Yamaha V10			15/22
12	JAPANESE GP	Suzuka	2	Danka Arrows Yamaha	B	3.0 Arrows A18-Yamaha V10		1 lap behind	16/22
ret	EUROPEAN GP	Jerez	2	Danka Arrows Yamaha	B	3.0 Arrows A18-Yamaha V10		spun off	13/22

1998 Championship position: 13= Wins: 0 Pole positions: 0 Fastest laps: 0 Points scored: 3

ret	AUSTRALIAN GP	Melbourne	16	Danka Zepter Arrows	B	3.0 Arrows A19-V10		gearbox	20/22
ret	BRAZILIAN GP	Interlagos	16	Danka Zepter Arrows	B	3.0 Arrows A19-V10		transmission	22/22
ret	ARGENTINE GP	Buenos Aires	16	Danka Zepter Arrows	B	3.0 Arrows A19-V10		gearbox	18/22
ret	SAN MARINO GP	Imola	16	Danka Zepter Arrows	B	3.0 Arrows A19-V10		engine	18/22
ret	SPANISH GP	Barcelona	16	Danka Zepter Arrows	B	3.0 Arrows A19-V10		engine	15/22
6	MONACO GP	Monte Carlo	16	Danka Zepter Arrows	B	3.0 Arrows A19-V10		1 lap behind	12/22
9	CANADIAN GP	Montreal	16	Danka Zepter Arrows	G	3.0 Arrows A19-V10		1 lap behind	19/22
14	FRENCH GP	Magny Cours	16	Danka Zepter Arrows	B	3.0 Arrows A19-V10		2 laps behind	17/22
ret	BRITISH GP	Silverstone	16	Danka Zepter Arrows	B	3.0 Arrows A19-V10		spun off	13/22
ret	AUSTRIAN GP	A1-Ring	16	Danka Zepter Arrows	B	3.0 Arrows A19-V10		collision damage	13/22
ret	GERMAN GP	Hockenheim	16	Danka Zepter Arrows	B	3.0 Arrows A19-V10		throttle	18/22
11	HUNGARIAN GP	Hungaroring	16	Danka Zepter Arrows	B	3.0 Arrows A19-V10		3 laps behind	12/22
5	BELGIAN GP	Spa	16	Danka Zepter Arrows	B	3.0 Arrows A19-V10			16/22
ret	ITALIAN GP	Monza	16	Danka Zepter Arrows	B	3.0 Arrows A19-V10		spun off	20/22
ret	LUXEMBOURG GP	Nürburgring	16	Danka Zepter Arrows	B	3.0 Arrows A19-V10		hydraulics	17/22
ret	JAPANESE GP	Suzuka	16	Danka Zepter Arrows	B	3.0 Arrows A19-V10		spun off	18/22

1999 Championship position: 13th= Wins: 0 Pole positions: 0 Fastest laps: 0 Points scored: 3

ret	AUSTRALIAN GP	Melbourne	12	Red Bull Sauber Petronas	B	3.0 Sauber C18-Petronas V10		transmission	14/22
ret	BRAZILIAN GP	Interlagos	12	Red Bull Sauber Petronas	B	3.0 Sauber C18-Petronas V10		spun off	15/22
ret	SAN MARINO GP	Imola	12	Red Bull Sauber Petronas	B	3.0 Sauber C18-Petronas V10		spun off	15/22
ret	MONACO GP	Monte Carlo	12	Red Bull Sauber Petronas	B	3.0 Sauber C18-Petronas V10		brakes-crashed	15/22
ret	SPANISH GP	Barcelona	12	Red Bull Sauber Petronas	B	3.0 Sauber C18-Petronas V10		gearbox	12/22
6	CANADIAN GP	Montreal	12	Red Bull Sauber Petronas	B	3.0 Sauber C18-Petronas V10			18/22
ret	FRENCH GP	Magny Cours	12	Red Bull Sauber Petronas	B	3.0 Sauber C18-Petronas V10		transmission	11/22
6	BRITISH GP	Silverstone	12	Red Bull Sauber Petronas	B	3.0 Sauber C18-Petronas V10			12/22
6	AUSTRIAN GP	A1-Ring	12	Red Bull Sauber Petronas	B	3.0 Sauber C18-Petronas V10			16/22
ret	GERMAN GP	Hockenheim	12	Red Bull Sauber Petronas	B	3.0 Sauber C18-Petronas V10		hit by Villeneuve on lap 1	16/22
ret	HUNGARIAN GP	Hungaroring	12	Red Bull Sauber Petronas	B	3.0 Sauber C18-Petronas V10		spun off	12/22
ret	BELGIAN GP	Spa	12	Red Bull Sauber Petronas	B	3.0 Sauber C18-Petronas V10		spun off	18/22
ret	ITALIAN GP	Monza	12	Red Bull Sauber Petronas	B	3.0 Sauber C18-Petronas V10		spun off	16/22
ret	EUROPEAN GP	Nürburgring	12	Red Bull Sauber Petronas	B	3.0 Sauber C18-Petronas V10		collision with Wurz-rolled car	13/22
ret	MALAYSIAN GP	Sepang	12	Red Bull Sauber Petronas	B	3.0 Sauber C18-Petronas V10		spun off	17/22
11	JAPANESE GP	Suzuka	12	Red Bull Sauber Petronas	B	3.0 Sauber C18-Petronas V10		1 lap behind	17/22

GP Starts: 82 GP Wins: 0 Pole positions: 0 Fastest laps: 0 Points: 10

JOSÉ DOLHEM

Dolhem dabbled with racing in 1964 at the wheel of a Lotus Seven, but it was not until he had completed his university studies in engineering and economics in 1969 that he returned to the sport, having won the prized Volant Shell award.

He was regarded as something of a playboy racer in his early days. Certainly his 1972 Formula 2 season with a March was undistinguished and in his only F2 race the following year, the Rouen GP, where he drove for Team Surtees, he crashed on the warm-up lap after finishing third in his qualifying heat.

No doubt bringing much-needed finance, he raced for Surtees in both Grands Prix and Formula 2 in 1974, but his career was then interrupted by a neck injury sustained while skiing early in 1975. José continued to race in F2 – firstly with Fred Opert's Chevron in 1976 and later with Kauhsen and AGS cars – on and off without success until 1979. The half-brother of the late Didier Pironi, Dolhem lost his life in a private plane crash in April 1988.

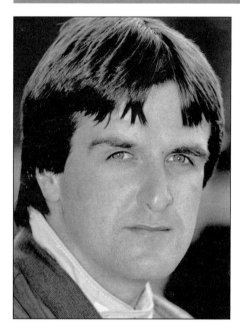

MARTIN DONNELLY

A graduate of FF2000, Donnelly made an immediate impact on the Marlboro Formula 3 series in his first season in 1986, winning four races and finishing third overall in the rankings. A favourite for the title the following year, his chances were ruined by a disastrous early-season run, and only when he switched to the Cellnet Intersport team did things improve and Martin return to the winner's circle.

He remained in F3 for a third year in 1988, but in mid-season he jumped ship, much to Intersport's chagrin, to join Eddie Jordan's Q8 F3000 team. In just four races, the Ulsterman took two wins and two second places. Things seemed set fair for a championship challenge in 1989, but after a win at Vallelunga had been wiped out he lost the initiative to new team-mate Jean Alesi, despite a victory at Brands Hatch.

Meanwhile Donnelly had made a steady GP debut for Arrows, and signed to drive for Lotus in 1990. The car was not one of the best, but Martin impressed nevertheless, until disaster struck in practice for the Spanish GP. He was very fortunate to survive when his car disintegrated after impact with the barriers, the helpless driver being tossed onto the track still strapped to the seat and the remnants of the car, and only first-class medical help at trackside saved his life.

Donnelly's rehabilitation was long and painful, but he was to make a miraculous recovery, although, sadly, it would not allow a return to the Grand Prix arena.

In 1992 he set up a Vauxhall Junior team and Martin Donnelly Racing has since been very successful in the junior single-seater formulae, helping guide and shape the careers of a new generation of young chargers with their sights set on Formula 1.

DOLHEM, José (F) b 26/4/1944, Paris – d 16/4/1988, nr St Etienne

	1974	Championship position: Unplaced						
	Race	Circuit	No	Entrant	Tyres	Car/Engine	Comment	Q Pos/Entries
dnq	FRENCH GP	Dijon	18	Bang & Olufsen Team Surtees	F	3.0 Surtees TS16-Cosworth V8		27/30
dnq	ITALIAN GP	Monza	19	Team Surtees	F	3.0 Surtees TS16-Cosworth V8		26/31
ret	US GP	Watkins Glen	18	Team Surtees	F	3.0 Surtees TS16-Cosworth V8	withdrawn after Koinigg's accident	26/30

GP Starts: 1   GP Wins: 0   Pole positions: 0   Fastest laps: 0   Points: 0

DONNELLY, Martin (GB) b 26/3/1964, Belfast, Northern Ireland

	1989	Championship position: 0 Wins: 0 Pole positions: 0 Fastest laps: 0 Points scored: 0						
	Race	Circuit	No	Entrant	Tyres	Car/Engine	Comment	Q Pos/Entries
12	FRENCH GP	Paul Ricard	9	USF&G Arrows Team	G	3.5 Arrows A11-Cosworth V8	started from pit lane/-3 laps	14/39
	1990	Championship position: 0 Wins: 0 Pole positions: 0 Fastest laps: 0 Points scored: 0						
dns	US GP (PHOENIX)	Phoenix	12	Camel Team Lotus	G	3.5 Lotus 102-Lamborghini V12	ignition failure on dummy grid	(19)/35
ret	BRAZILIAN GP	Interlagos	12	Camel Team Lotus	G	3.5 Lotus 102-Lamborghini V12	leg cramps-spun off	14/35
8	SAN MARINO GP	Imola	12	Camel Team Lotus	G	3.5 Lotus 102-Lamborghini V12	1 lap behind	12/34
ret	MONACO GP	Monte Carlo	12	Camel Team Lotus	G	3.5 Lotus 102-Lamborghini V12	gearbox	11/35
ret	CANADIAN GP	Montreal	12	Camel Team Lotus	G	3.5 Lotus 102-Lamborghini V12	engine	12/35
8	MEXICAN GP	Mexico City	12	Camel Team Lotus	G	3.5 Lotus 102-Lamborghini V12	tyre problems	12/35
12	FRENCH GP	Paul Ricard	12	Camel Team Lotus	G	3.5 Lotus 102-Lamborghini V12	handling problems/-1 lap	17/35
ret	BRITISH GP	Silverstone	12	Camel Team Lotus	G	3.5 Lotus 102-Lamborghini V12	engine	14/35
ret	GERMAN GP	Hockenheim	12	Camel Team Lotus	G	3.5 Lotus 102-Lamborghini V12	clutch	20/35
7	HUNGARIAN GP	Hungaroring	12	Camel Team Lotus	G	3.5 Lotus 102-Lamborghini V12	1 lap behind	18/35
12	BELGIAN GP	Spa	12	Camel Team Lotus	G	3.5 Lotus 102-Lamborghini V12	understeer/exhaust/-1 lap	22/23
ret	ITALIAN GP	Monza	12	Camel Team Lotus	G	3.5 Lotus 102-Lamborghini V12	engine	11/33
ret	PORTUGUESE GP	Estoril	12	Camel Team Lotus	G	3.5 Lotus 102-Lamborghini V12	alternator	15/33
dns	SPANISH GP	Jerez	12	Camel Team Lotus	G	3.5 Lotus 102-Lamborghini V12	injured in practice accident	(23)/33

GP Starts: 13   GP Wins: 0   Pole positions: 0   Fastest laps: 0   Points: 0

MARK DONOHUE

A graduate engineer, Mark merely dabbled with racing at first, but he was good enough to take a class of the SCCA production sports car championship in 1961 in an Elva Courier, then racing a Formula Junior Elva and a TVR before taking a championship double in 1965 with a Lotus 23 in SCCA class C and a Mustang in class B. By this time Donohue had been taken under the wing of Walt Hansgen, who was leading the works Ford Mk II sports car challenge in 1966. The pair shared second place at Sebring that year, Donohue's first major placing, but his mentor was tragically killed at the Le Mans testing in April, and Mark renewed an old association with Roger Penske, taking his Group 7 Lola-Chevrolet to a victory at Mosport in Can-Am before winning the 1967 and 1968 US Road Racing Championships.

Penske also entered Donohue in the Trans-Am championship in 1968, and Mark won ten of the 13 events to win the title easily, repeating the trick the following year with six wins from 12 starts. The 1969 season also saw Penske's first appearance at the Indy 500 as an entrant, Donohue qualifying fourth and finishing seventh to earn the 'Rookie of the Year' title. He was to finish second in the race in 1970 driving a Lola-Ford, and later on that season raced in Formula A, winning two of the three rounds he entered. Penske expanded his racing activities in 1971 and Mark faced a hectic schedule of Trans-Am (taking his third title), USAC (winning the Pocono 500 and the Michigan 200 in a McLaren) and sports car events, sharing a blue-painted Ferrari 512M with David Hobbs. However, his performance of the year was undoubtedly his Grand Prix debut at Mosport, Donohue taking a superb third place in Penske's McLaren M19A.

Grand Prix racing was just a diversion at this stage, for in 1972 Mark continued to race in USAC, duly winning the Indianapolis 500 in a Penske McLaren, and returned to Can-Am, where his title chances were ruined by a testing accident which saw him sidelined for a couple of months. He was back in 1973, however, and made no mistake this time round, taking six race victories and the championship in a Porsche 917. Mark announced his retirement at the end of the year, but was tempted back behind the wheel late in 1974 to apply his superb development expertise to the Penske Grand Prix challenger.

He was persuaded to race the car in 1975, but it was a disappointment to all concerned and Penske replaced it in mid-season with an 'off-the-shelf' March. Donohue was practising the car for the Austrian GP when a tyre is thought to have deflated, sending the March into catch fencing and over the Armco barrier. One marshal was killed and another seriously injured, but at first Mark, though dazed, was sitting up and talking. He seemed to have escaped relatively unharmed, but it was soon apparent that all was not well as he lapsed into unconsciousness and, despite brain surgery, he died three days later in Graz hospital.

DONOHUE, Mark (USA) b 18/3/1937, Summit, New Jersey – d 19/8/1975, Graz, Austria

	1971	Championship position: 16th= Wins: 0 Pole positions: 0 Fastest laps: 0 Points scored: 4							
	Race	Circuit	No	Entrant	Tyres	Car/Engine		Comment	Q Pos/Entries
3	CANADIAN GP	Mosport Park	10	Penske-White Racing	G	3.0 McLaren M19A-Cosworth V8			=7/27
dns	US GP	Watkins Glen	31	Penske-White Racing	G	3.0 McLaren M19A-Cosworth V8		practised-but raced USAC event	(19)/32
	1974	Championship position: Unplaced							
12	CANADIAN GP	Mosport Park	66	Penske Cars	G	3.0 Penske PC1-Cosworth V8		2 laps behind	24/30
ret	US GP	Watkins Glen	66	Penske Cars	G	3.0 Penske PC1-Cosworth V8		rear suspension bracket	14/30
	1975	Championship position: 15th Wins: 0 Pole positions: 0 Fastest laps: 0 Points scored: 4							
7	ARGENTINE GP	Buenos Aires	28	Penske Cars	G	3.0 Penske PC1-Cosworth V8		1 lap behind	16/23
ret	BRAZILIAN GP	Interlagos	28	Penske Cars	G	3.0 Penske PC1-Cosworth V8		handling	15/23
8	SOUTH AFRICAN GP	Kyalami	28	Penske Cars	G	3.0 Penske PC1-Cosworth V8		1 lap behind	18/28
ret	SPANISH GP	Montjuich Park	28	Penske Cars	G	3.0 Penske PC1-Cosworth V8		spun off on Scheckter's oil	17/26
ret	MONACO GP	Monte Carlo	28	Penske Cars	G	3.0 Penske PC1-Cosworth V8		hit guard rail	16/26
11	BELGIAN GP	Zolder	28	Penske Cars	G	3.0 Penske PC1-Cosworth V8		handling problems/-3 laps	21/24
5	SWEDISH GP	Anderstorp	28	Penske Cars	G	3.0 Penske PC1-Cosworth V8			16/26
8	DUTCH GP	Zandvoort	28	Penske Cars	G	3.0 Penske PC1-Cosworth V8		1 lap behind	18/25
ret	FRENCH GP	Paul Ricard	28	Penske Cars	G	3.0 Penske PC1-Cosworth V8		driveshaft	18/26
5/ret	BRITISH GP	Silverstone	28	Penske Cars	G	3.0 March 751-Cosworth V8		spun off in rainstorm/-1 lap	15/28
ret	GERMAN GP	Nürburgring	28	Penske Cars	G	3.0 March 751-Cosworth V8		puncture	19/26
dns	AUSTRIAN GP	Österreichring	28	Penske Cars	G	3.0 March 751-Cosworth V8		fatal accident in practice	(21)/30

GP Starts: 14 GP Wins: 0 Pole positions: 0 Fastest laps: 0 Points: 8

KEN DOWNING

A director of numerous companies, Downing was a supporter of the Connaught marque who also raced briefly in the early 1950s. He scored 17 wins in club events with his sports Connaught in 1951, before racing the A-Type model in 1953. Apart from a couple of Grand Prix appearances, he was seen little in major races, but did finish second in the GP of Chimay, being caught at the last gasp by Paul Frère's HWM in a thrilling finish.

After briefly racing an Aston Martin DB3S in 1953, Downing retired from the track, later emigrating to South Africa in 1955.

PADDY DRIVER

Driver was still a top-notch motor cycle rider, having made his name on Nortons, when he flirted briefly with car racing in 1963. Driving a Lotus 24, he finished seventh on aggregate in the Rand Grand Prix at Kyalami, but an end-over-end shunt in practice for the South African GP a fortnight later saw the car destroyed. Miraculously Paddy emerged shaken but unscathed and returned to motor cycle competition with an AJS/Matchless, on which he finished third in the 1965 500 cc World Championship.

His career on four wheels really began to take off in 1969 and from then on he enjoyed success in sports cars and single-seaters including a McLaren M10B-Chevrolet and a Team Gunston Lotus 72. Switching to saloon cars with a Mazda, Paddy continued racing into the eighties.

BOB DRAKE

A Los Angeles restaurateur, Bob was an SCCA racer in the mid-fifties who returned from a three-year sabbatical in 1960 to run up a number of West Coast successes in his Birdcage Maserati.

His only Grand Prix appearance was most notable for being the last hurrah at championship level for the wonderful, but aged, Maserati 250F, one of Formula 1 racing's greatest creations.

PIERO DROGO

Drogo raced extensively on the South American continent in sports cars and saloons. He took seventh in the 1956 Venezuelan GP at Caracas, and in 1957 won his class with a Ferrari Testa Rossa in the Buenos Aires 1000 Km. Fourth place overall in the same event a year later encouraged Piero to head for Europe to try his luck, but his first visit to Le Mans ended in disappointment when the car was eliminated in an accident.

Basing himself in Italy, he ran out of money in 1959 and found employment as a mechanic for Stanguellini to keep body and soul together. His chance to race in a Grand Prix came when he was invited to help fill the grid for the 1960 Italian event which was subject to a boycott by the British teams. Subsequently he formed Carrozzeria Sportscars in the early sixties which produced a number of re-bodied Ferraris known because of their square backs as 'breadvans', as well as producing the bodies for the lovely P-type Ferrari's.

Drogo lost his life in a road accident in 1972 when his car ploughed into the back of an unlit truck which had broken down in a tunnel.

DOWNING, Ken (GB) b 5/12/1917, Chesterton, Staffordshire

	1952			Championship position: Unplaced				
	Race	Circuit	No	Entrant	Tyres	Car/Engine	Comment	Q Pos/Entries
9	BRITISH GP	Silverstone	4	Connaught Engineering	D	2.0 Connaught A-Lea Francis 4	3 laps behind	5/32
ret	DUTCH GP	Zandvoort	22	Kenneth Downing	D	2.0 Connaught A-Lea Francis 4	oil pressure	13/18

GP Starts: 2 GP Wins: 0 Pole positions: 0 Fastest laps: 0 Points: 0

DRAKE, Bob (USA) b 14/12/1919 – d 18/4/1990

	1960			Championship position: Unplaced				
	Race	Circuit	No	Entrant	Tyres	Car/Engine	Comment	Q Pos/Entries
13	US GP	Riverside	20	Joe Lubin	D	2.5 Maserati 250F 6	7 laps behind	22/23

GP Starts: 1 GP Wins: 0 Pole positions: 0 Fastest laps: 0 Points: 0

DRIVER, Paddy (ZA) b 19/5/1934, Johannesburg

	1963			Championship position: Unplaced				
	Race	Circuit	No	Entrant	Tyres	Car/Engine	Comment	Q Pos/Entries
dns	SOUTH AFRICAN GP	East London	15	Selby Auto Spares	D	1.5 Lotus 24-BRM V8	practice accident	(22)/22
	1974			Championship position: Unplaced				
ret	SOUTH AFRICAN GP	Kyalami	30	Team Gunston	G	3.0 Lotus 72E-Cosworth V8	clutch slip	26/27

GP Starts: 1 GP Wins: 0 Pole positions: 0 Fastest laps: 0 Points: 0

DROGO, Piero (I) b 8/8/1926, Vignale, Monteferrato – d 28/4/1973, Bologna

	1960			Championship position: Unplaced					
	Race	Circuit	No	Entrant	Tyres	Car/Engine		Comment	Q Pos/Entries
8	ITALIAN GP	Monza	12	Scuderia Colonia	D	1.5 Cooper T43-Climax 4 F2		5 laps behind	15/16

GP Starts: 1   GP Wins: 0   Pole positions: 0   Fastest laps: 0   Points: 0

DUMFRIES, Johnny (GB) b 26/4/1958, Rothesay, Isle of Bute, Scotland

	1986			Championship position: 13th= Wins: 0 Pole positions: 0 Fastest laps: 0 Points scored: 3					
	Race	Circuit	No	Entrant	Tyres	Car/Engine		Comment	Q Pos/Entries
9	BRAZILIAN GP	Rio	11	John Player Special Team Lotus	G	1.5 t/c Lotus 98T-Renault V6		2 pit stops-misfire/-3 laps	11/25
ret	SPANISH GP	Jerez	11	John Player Special Team Lotus	G	1.5 t/c Lotus 98T-Renault V6		gearbox	10/25
ret	SAN MARINO GP	Imola	11	John Player Special Team Lotus	G	1.5 t/c Lotus 98T-Renault V6		wheel bearing	17/26
dnq	MONACO GP	Monte Carlo	11	John Player Special Team Lotus	G	1.5 t/c Lotus 98T-Renault V6			22/26
ret	BELGIAN GP	Spa	11	John Player Special Team Lotus	G	1.5 t/c Lotus 98T-Renault V6		spun off-holed radiator	13/25
ret	CANADIAN GP	Montreal	11	John Player Special Team Lotus	G	1.5 t/c Lotus 98T-Renault V6		accident with Johansson	16/25
7	US GP (DETROIT)	Detroit	11	John Player Special Team Lotus	G	1.5 t/c Lotus 98T-Renault V6		2 laps behind	14/26
ret	FRENCH GP	Paul Ricard	11	John Player Special Team Lotus	G	1.5 t/c Lotus 98T-Renault V6		engine	12/26
7	BRITISH GP	Brands Hatch	11	John Player Special Team Lotus	G	1.5 t/c Lotus 98T-Renault V6		3 laps behind	10/26
ret	GERMAN GP	Hockenheim	11	John Player Special Team Lotus	G	1.5 t/c Lotus 98T-Renault V6		holed water radiator	12/26
5	HUNGARIAN GP	Hungaroring	11	John Player Special Team Lotus	G	1.5 t/c Lotus 98T-Renault V6		2 laps behind	8/26
ret	AUSTRIAN GP	Österreichring	11	John Player Special Team Lotus	G	1.5 t/c Lotus 98T-Renault V6		engine	15/26
ret	ITALIAN GP	Monza	11	John Player Special Team Lotus	G	1.5 t/c Lotus 98T-Renault V6		gearbox	17/27
9	PORTUGUESE GP	Estoril	11	John Player Special Team Lotus	G	1.5 t/c Lotus 98T-Renault V6		2 laps behind	15/27
ret	MEXICAN GP	Mexico City	11	John Player Special Team Lotus	G	1.5 t/c Lotus 98T-Renault V6		electrics	17/26
6	AUSTRALIAN GP	Adelaide	11	John Player Special Team Lotus	G	1.5 t/c Lotus 98T-Renault V6		2 laps behind	14/26

GP Starts: 15   GP Wins: 0   Pole positions: 0   Fastest laps: 0   Points: 3

JOHNNY DUMFRIES

Looking at his record, it is clear Johnny Dumfries did little wrong and plenty right, yet his career petered out while those of many drivers with less ability have endured.

More formally known as the Earl of Dumfries, Johnny was determined to make it in his own right as a racing driver, and showed some promise and not a little speed when taken under the wing of Dave Morgan to race in Formula 3 in 1983. He landed a plum drive in the BP-backed Dave Price Racing team for 1984, and the season exceeded even his wildest expectations, Johnny winning the Marlboro F3 championship at home and nearly repeating the feat in the European series, achieving a magnificent total of 15 wins. His stock was justifiably high, and for 1985 he joined Onyx for a season in F3000, but a bright start soon faded and by mid-season he was out of work.

Luckily for Johnny, help was at hand in the form of Ayrton Senna, who declined to accept Derek Warwick as his new team-mate at Lotus, as he was entitled to under the terms of his contract. This gave Dumfries his big chance, but while he let no one down he was naturally very much the number two to Senna in all things. He did, however, score three points and handled himself pretty well. Politics of one sort had helped him into the team, and unfortunately the revolving door took him straight back out when an engine deal with Honda meant Satoru Nakajima would be Senna's partner in 1987. Johnny did some testing for Benetton and then went into endurance racing, with drives in both Porsches and Toyotas, but the unquestioned highlight was his win at Le Mans (with Lammers and Wallace) in 1988 in the TWR Jaguar.

GEORGE EATON

The affluent scion of a Canadian family involved with a merchandising concern, George had the wherewithal to go racing, graduating to a McLaren M1C via a fearsome Cobra. After a few races late in 1967, Eaton ran the car in Can-Am the following season, his best finish being a very impressive third at Laguna Seca in the wet.

Ordering a new McLaren M12 for Can-Am and a McLaren M10 for Formula A, he was a front-runner in both series, which brought an invitation to race the works BRM in the final two Grands Prix of 1969. This contact led to a deal for Eaton to drive for BRM in F1 for the full season in 1970, as well as racing their P54 prototype in Can-Am. All in all, it proved to be a great disappointment for both parties, leaving George somewhat disillusioned.

He raced for BRM once more in 1971, and also handled Ferrari sports cars at Sebring, Le Mans and Watkins Glen. But with success proving elusive, the wealthy Eaton gradually lost interest, and after taking part in the 1972 Daytona 6-hour race he left the racing scene to pursue other interests.

EATON, George (CDN) b 12/11/1945, Toronto, Ontario

	1969	Championship position: Unplaced							
	Race	Circuit	No	Entrant	Tyres	Car/Engine		Comment	Q Pos/Entries
ret	US GP	Watkins Glen	22	Owen Racing Organisation	D	3.0 BRM P138 V12		engine	18/18
ret	MEXICAN GP	Mexico City	22	Owen Racing Organisation	D	3.0 BRM P138 V12		gearbox	17/17
	1970	Championship position: Unplaced							
ret	SOUTH AFRICAN GP	Kyalami	21	Owen Racing Organisation	F	3.0 BRM P139 V12		engine	23/24
dnq	SPANISH GP	Jarama	21	Owen Racing Organisation	F	3.0 BRM P153 V12			22/22
dnq	MONACO GP	Monte Carlo	15	Yardley Team BRM	F	3.0 BRM P153 V12			21/21
ret	DUTCH GP	Zandvoort	3	Yardley Team BRM	F	3.0 BRM P153 V12		loose oil tank	18/24
12	FRENCH GP	Clermont Ferrand	4	Yardley Team BRM	F	3.0 BRM P153 V12		pit stop-plug lead/-2 laps	19/23
ret	BRITISH GP	Brands Hatch	24	Yardley Team BRM	F	3.0 BRM P153 V12		oil pressure	=16/25
11	AUSTRIAN GP	Österreichring	18	Yardley Team BRM	F	3.0 BRM P153 V12		2 laps behind	23/24
ret	ITALIAN GP	Monza	12	Yardley Team BRM	F	3.0 BRM P153 V12		overheating	23/27
10	CANADIAN GP	St Jovite	16	Yardley Team BRM	F	3.0 BRM P153 V12		pit stop/5 laps behind	=8/20
ret	US GP	Watkins Glen	21	Yardley Team BRM	F	3.0 BRM P153 V12		engine	14/27
	1971	Championship position: Unplaced							
15	CANADIAN GP	Mosport Park	28	Yardley Team BRM	F	3.0 BRM P160 V12		collision-Peterson/-5 laps	21/27

GP Starts: 11 GP Wins: 0 Pole positions: 0 Fastest laps: 0 Points: 0

GUY EDWARDS

Though not a front-rank driver, Edwards, intelligent and personable, had a talent for securing funding from sponsorship sources previously unconnected with motor sport, and with this backing he was able to rise from 2-litre sports cars via F5000 into Formula 1.

His first taste of Grands Prix ended bitterly, Guy losing his drive after a wrist injury had sidelined him from the Embassy Hill team. He then arranged substantial sponsorship to drive for Hesketh in 1976, but the team was in decline, and results were poor, while one last stab in the hopeless Stanley-BRM is best forgotten.

Perhaps realising his limitations, Edwards settled for a satisfying few seasons competing at national level and occasionally beyond, mainly racing Grand Prix machinery in the popular Aurora F1 series, before retiring from driving to become a successful sponsorship consultant, a role which has made him a millionaire.

In the austere financial climate of the early nineties, Edwards was employed by Team Lotus to find a major sponsor for the once great marque, but despite his best efforts none was forthcoming and their relationship ended somewhat acrimoniously in 1994.

EDWARDS, Guy (GB) b 30/12/1942, Macclesfield, Cheshire

	1974	Championship position: Unplaced							
	Race	Circuit	No	Entrant	Tyres	Car/Engine		Comment	Q Pos/Entries
11	ARGENTINE GP	Buenos Aires	27	Embassy Racing with Graham Hill	F	3.0 Lola T370-Cosworth V8		2 laps behind	25/26
ret	BRAZILIAN GP	Interlagos	27	Embassy Racing with Graham Hill	F	3.0 Lola T370-Cosworth V8		engine	25/25
dnq	SPANISH GP	Jarama	27	Embassy Racing with Graham Hill	F	3.0 Lola T370-Cosworth V8			27/28
12	BELGIAN GP	Nivelles	27	Embassy Racing with Graham Hill	F	3.0 Lola T370-Cosworth V8		3 laps behind	21/32
8	MONACO GP	Monte Carlo	27	Embassy Racing with Graham Hill	F	3.0 Lola T370-Cosworth V8		2 laps behind	26/28
7	SWEDISH GP	Anderstorp	27	Embassy Racing with Graham Hill	F	3.0 Lola T370-Cosworth V8		1 lap behind	18/28
ret	DUTCH GP	Zandvoort	27	Embassy Racing with Graham Hill	F	3.0 Lola T370-Cosworth V8		fuel system	14/27
15	FRENCH GP	Dijon	27	Embassy Racing with Graham Hill	F	3.0 Lola T370-Cosworth V8		3 laps behind	20/30
dns	BRITISH GP	Brands Hatch	27	Embassy Racing with Graham Hill	F	3.0 Lola T370-Cosworth V8		injury from previous race	– / –
dnq	GERMAN GP	Nürburgring	27	Embassy Racing with Graham Hill	F	3.0 Lola T370-Cosworth V8			29/32
	1976	Championship position: Unplaced							
dnq	BELGIAN GP	Zolder	25	Penthouse Rizla Racing with Hesketh	G	3.0 Hesketh 308D-Cosworth V8			29/29
17	FRENCH GP	Paul Ricard	25	Penthouse Rizla Racing with Hesketh	G	3.0 Hesketh 308D-Cosworth V8		1 lap behind	25/30
ret	BRITISH GP	Brands Hatch	25	Penthouse Rizla Racing with Hesketh	G	3.0 Hesketh 308D-Cosworth V8		accident	25/30
15	GERMAN GP	Nürburgring	25	Penthouse Rizla Racing with Hesketh	G	3.0 Hesketh 308D-Cosworth V8		1 lap behind	25/28
dns	ITALIAN GP	Monza	25	Penthouse Rizla Racing with Hesketh	G	3.0 Hesketh 308D-Cosworth V8		withdrew-allowed Watson to race	(23)/29
20	CANADIAN GP	Mosport Park	25	Penthouse Rizla Racing with Hesketh	G	3.0 Hesketh 308D-Cosworth V8		5 laps behind	24/27
	1977	Championship position: Unplaced							
dnpq	BRITISH GP	Silverstone	35	Rotary Watches-Stanley BRM	G	3.0 BRM P207 V12			33/36

GP Starts: 11 GP Wins: 0 Pole positions: 0 Fastest laps: 0 Points: 0

VIC ELFORD

Vic was something of a star performer in every type of racing to which he turned his hand, and it is a great shame he was not seen in a competitive Grand Prix car earlier in his career, which was largely spent rallying, sprinkled with whatever circuit racing his limited finances would allow.

He was a Ford works driver from 1964 until he switched to Porsche, Vic then winning the Group 3 title in 1967 and the Monte Carlo Rally in 1968. By now he had become an established member of the Porsche sports car team and produced some dazzling performances, winning the Daytona 24 Hours (after doing the lion's share of the driving), the Targa Florio – a truly epic performance – and the Nürburgring 1000 Km. Cooper, searching for a driver, offered Vic a chance at the French GP and he duly finished fourth first time out in the rain. He completed the season with them, but then the team folded.

For 1969 Elford continued with Porsche in sports car racing – taking time out to finish 11th in the Daytona 500 in a Dodge! – and drove for privateer Colin Crabbe in F1. Things looked promising until he was involved in Mario Andretti's accident at the German GP, his McLaren hitting debris from the American's car. Vic crashed badly and was lucky to escape with no worse than a broken arm and collar-bone.

The crash effectively spelt the end of his Grand Prix career, but he was soon back in the Porsche and driving as well as ever, winning the 1970 Nürburgring 1000 Km with Ahrens. Elford drove for BRM in the German GP of 1971, but was not really given a fair crack of the whip.

He raced on, driving for Porsche and Alfa Romeo in endurance events, handling Chaparrals, McLarens and Shadows in Can-Am, and a Chevron in F2, and even won a Trans-Am race in a Camaro at Watkins Glen before finally retiring in 1974. He was briefly team manager of the ATS F1 team in the second half of 1977, but now lives in Florida, involved with the Porsche marque once more, offering his considerable expertise to those lucky enough to be able to purchase the fabulous Stuttgart sports machines.

ELFORD, Vic (GB) b 10/6/1935, Peckham, London

	1968	Championship position: 17th=	Wins: 0	Pole positions: 0	Fastest laps: 0	Points scored: 5		
	Race	Circuit	No	Entrant	Tyres	Car/Engine	Comment	Q Pos/Entries
4	FRENCH GP	Rouen	30	Cooper Car Co	F	3.0 Cooper T86B-BRM V12	pit stop-tyres/-2 laps	18/18
ret	BRITISH GP	Brands Hatch	15	Cooper Car Co	F	3.0 Cooper T86B-BRM V12	engine	17/20
ret	GERMAN GP	Nürburgring	20	Cooper Car Co	F	3.0 Cooper T86B-BRM V12	accident	5/20
ret	ITALIAN GP	Monza	23	Cooper Car Co	F	3.0 Cooper T86B-BRM V12	lost brakes-spun off	22/24
5	CANADIAN GP	St Jovite	21	Cooper Car Co	F	3.0 Cooper T86B-BRM V12	4 laps behind	17/22
ret	US GP	Watkins Glen	18	Cooper Car Co	F	3.0 Cooper T86B-BRM V12	camshaft	17/21
8	MEXICAN GP	Mexico City	18	Cooper Car Co	F	3.0 Cooper T86B-BRM V12	2 laps behind	17/21
	1969	Championship position: 13th=	Wins: 0	Pole positions: 0	Fastest laps: 0	Points scored: 3		
7	MONACO GP	Monte Carlo	12	Colin Crabbe-Antique Automobiles	G	3.0 Cooper T86B-Maserati V12	6 laps behind	16/16
10	DUTCH GP	Zandvoort	18	Colin Crabbe-Antique Automobiles	G	3.0 McLaren M7A-Cosworth V8	6 laps behind	15/15
5	FRENCH GP	Clermont Ferrand	10	Colin Crabbe-Antique Automobiles	G	3.0 McLaren M7A-Cosworth V8	1 lap behind	10/13
6	BRITISH GP	Silverstone	19	Colin Crabbe-Antique Automobiles	G	3.0 McLaren M7A-Cosworth V8	2 laps behind	11/17
ret	GERMAN GP	Nürburgring	12	Colin Crabbe-Antique Automobiles	G	3.0 McLaren M7AB-Cosworth V8	hit debris from Andretti's crash	6/25
	1971	Championship position: Unplaced						
11	GERMAN GP	Nürburgring	22	Yardley Team BRM	F	3.0 BRM P160 V12	pit stop-coil/1 lap behind	18/23

GP Starts: 13   GP Wins: 0   Pole positions: 0   Fastest laps: 0   Points: 8

EMERY, Paul (GB) b 12/11/1916, Chiswick, London – d 3/2/1992, Epsom, Surrey

	1956	Championship position: Unplaced						
	Race	Circuit	No	Entrant	Tyres	Car/Engine	Comment	Q Pos/Entries
ret	BRITISH GP	Silverstone	32	Emeryson Cars	D	2.5 Emeryson-Alta 4	ignition	23/28
	1958	Championship position: Unplaced						
dnq	MONACO GP	Monte Carlo	14	B C Ecclestone	A	2.5 Connaught B-Alta 4		22/28

GP Starts: 1   GP Wins: 0   Pole positions: 0   Fastest laps: 0   Points: 0

ENGLAND, Paul (AUS) b 28/3/1929

	1957	Championship position: Unplaced						
	Race	Circuit	No	Entrant	Tyres	Car/Engine	Comment	Q Pos/Entries
ret	GERMAN GP (F2)	Nürburgring	26	Ridgeway Managements	D	1.5 Cooper T41-Climax 4	distributor	23/24

GP Starts: 1   GP Wins: 0   Pole positions: 0   Fastest laps: 0   Points: 0

PAUL EMERY

Paul Emery was one of those characters in life who was always chasing success, rarely found it, but had a hell of a good time along the way.

He and his father were indefatigable builders of specials, based around whatever components were available at the time. Given the name Emeryson, these machines were always technically interesting in some respect, but the finance essential to their development was always lacking.

Paul, a 500 cc racer of some note, developed an Emeryson-Alta in 1956, in which he finished second, to Moss no less, at Crystal Palace before racing it in the British Grand Prix. He was later to build the Emeryson F1 cars for ENB and Scirocco-Powell before jumping from project to project, most of which remained unrealised, eventually finding a niche building and driving oval-track midget racers.

HARALD ERTL

Ertl was a journalist/racer who competed in Formula Vee, Super Vee and F3 in Germany in the early seventies before moving on to the European touring car series, with victory in the 1973 Tourist Trophy with Derek Bell in a BMW the highlight.

He raised the finance to race in Formula 1 on and off for Hesketh between 1975 and 1977 and Ensign in 1978 but was never quite able to make the points – although he was desperately unlucky to lose sixth place at Hockenheim in 1978 when his engine failed – and was rarely more than a midfield runner in F2 during the same period. He had one more GP drive for ATS in 1980, but by then he was established as a leading light in the German G5 championship in BMW and Ford Capri turbos. A charming and popular figure around the circuits, Harald was killed in a light aeroplane crash in 1982 in which his wife and son were seriously injured.

ERTL, Harald (A) b 31/8/1948, Zell am See – d 7/4/1982, nr Glessen, Germany

1975
Championship position: Unplaced

	Race	Circuit	No	Entrant	Tyres	Car/Engine	Comment	Q Pos/Entries
8	GERMAN GP	Nürburgring	25	Warsteiner Brewery	G	3.0 Hesketh 308-Cosworth V8		23/26
ret	AUSTRIAN GP	Österreichring	32	Warsteiner Brewery	G	3.0 Hesketh 308-Cosworth V8	electrics	27/30
9	ITALIAN GP	Monza	34	Warsteiner Brewery	G	3.0 Hesketh 308-Cosworth V8	1 lap behind	17/28

1976
Championship position: Unplaced

	Race	Circuit	No	Entrant	Tyres	Car/Engine	Comment	Q Pos/Entries
15	SOUTH AFRICAN GP	Kyalami	24	Hesketh Racing	G	3.0 Hesketh 308D-Cosworth V8	4 laps behind	24/25
dnq	US GP WEST	Long Beach	24	Hesketh Racing	G	3.0 Hesketh 308D-Cosworth V8		26/27
dnq	SPANISH GP	Jarama	24	Hesketh Racing	G	3.0 Hesketh 308D-Cosworth V8		29/30
ret	BELGIAN GP	Zolder	24	Hesketh Racing	G	3.0 Hesketh 308D-Cosworth V8	engine	24/29
dnq	MONACO GP	Monte Carlo	24	Hesketh Racing	G	3.0 Hesketh 308D-Cosworth V8		24/25
ret	SWEDISH GP	Anderstorp	24	Hesketh Racing	G	3.0 Hesketh 308D-Cosworth V8	spun off-could not restart	23/27
dnq/ret	FRENCH GP	Paul Ricard	24	Hesketh Racing	G	3.0 Hesketh 308D-Cosworth V8	started illegally/driveshaft	29/30
7*	BRITISH GP	Brands Hatch	24	Hesketh Racing	G	3.0 Hesketh 308D-Cosworth V8	* 1st place car dsq/-3 laps	24/30
ret/dns	GERMAN GP	Nürburgring	24	Hesketh Racing	G	3.0 Hesketh 308D-Cosworth V8	crashed 1st start-did not restart	22/28
8	AUSTRIAN GP	Österreichring	24	Hesketh Racing	G	3.0 Hesketh 308D-Cosworth V8	1 lap behind	20/25
ret	DUTCH GP	Zandvoort	24	Hesketh Racing	G	3.0 Hesketh 308D-Cosworth V8	spun off-could not restart	24/27
16/ret	ITALIAN GP	Monza	24	Hesketh Racing	G	3.0 Hesketh 308D-Cosworth V8	driveshaft/3 laps behind	19/29
dns	CANADIAN GP	Mosport Park	24	Hesketh Racing	G	3.0 Hesketh 308D-Cosworth V8	practice accident with Amon	(23)/27
13	US GP EAST	Watkins Glen	24	Hesketh Racing	G	3.0 Hesketh 308D-Cosworth V8	hit Merzario-pit stop/-5 laps	21/27
8	JAPANESE GP	Mount Fuji	24	Hesketh Racing	G	3.0 Hesketh 308D-Cosworth V8	1 lap behind	22/27

1977
Championship position: Unplaced

	Race	Circuit	No	Entrant	Tyres	Car/Engine	Comment	Q Pos/Entries
ret	SPANISH GP	Jarama	25	Hesketh Racing	G	3.0 Hesketh 308E-Cosworth V8	radiator	18/31
dnq	MONACO GP	Monte Carlo	25	Hesketh Racing	G	3.0 Hesketh 308E-Cosworth V8		23/26
9	BELGIAN GP	Zolder	25	Hesketh Racing	G	3.0 Hesketh 308E-Cosworth V8	1 lap behind	25/32
16	SWEDISH GP	Anderstorp	25	Hesketh Racing	G	3.0 Hesketh 308E-Cosworth V8	4 laps behind	23/31
dnq	FRENCH GP	Dijon	25	Hesketh Racing	G	3.0 Hesketh 308E-Cosworth V8		25/30

1978
Championship position: Unplaced

	Race	Circuit	No	Entrant	Tyres	Car/Engine	Comment	Q Pos/Entries
11/ret	GERMAN GP	Hockenheim	23	Sachs Racing	G	3.0 Ensign N177-Cosworth V8	engine/4 laps behind	23/30
ret	AUSTRIAN GP	Österreichring	23	Sachs Racing	G	3.0 Ensign N177-Cosworth V8	collision-Patrese at restart	24/31
dnpq	DUTCH GP	Zandvoort	23	Sachs Racing	G	3.0 Ensign N177-Cosworth V8		31/33
dnpq	ITALIAN GP	Monza	23	Sachs Racing	G	3.0 Ensign N177-Cosworth V8		29/32
dnq	"	"	10	ATS Engineering	G	3.0 ATS HS1-Cosworth V8		26/32

1980
Championship position: 0   Wins: 0   Pole positions: 0   Fastest laps: 0   Points scored: 0

	Race	Circuit	No	Entrant	Tyres	Car/Engine	Comment	Q Pos/Entries
dnq	GERMAN GP	Hockenheim	10	Team ATS	G	3.0 ATS D4-Cosworth V8		26/26

GP Starts: 18 (19)   GP Wins: 0   Pole positions: 0   Fastest laps: 0   Points: 0

ESTÉFANO, Nasif (RA) b 18/11/1932, Concepción, Tucumán – d 21/10/1973

1960
Championship position: Unplaced

	Race	Circuit	No	Entrant	Tyres	Car/Engine	Comment	Q Pos/Entries
14	ARGENTINE GP	Buenos Aires	10	Nasif Estéfano/Scuderia Centro Sud	D	2.5 Maserati 250F 6	10 laps behind	20/22

1962
Championship position: Unplaced

	Race	Circuit	No	Entrant	Tyres	Car/Engine	Comment	Q Pos/Entries
dnq	ITALIAN GP	Monza	34	Scuderia de Tomaso	D	1.5 de Tomaso 801 F8		30/30

GP Starts: 1   GP Wins: 0   Pole positions: 0   Fastest laps: 0   Points: 0

NASIF ESTÉFANO

An Argentinian who was highly regarded on his own shores, Estéfano was tempted to Europe to drive fellow countryman Alessandro de Tomaso's car in 1962, and he raced this singularly unsuccessful machine briefly in a few non-championship events the following season. Before heading home for good, Nasif shared a Porsche 904GTS with compatriot Andrea Vianini, in the Reims 12-hour race, taking fifth place overall and class victory.

On his return to South America, Estéfano quickly asserted his skills to become 1965 and 1966 Argentine F3 champion, and was rightly regarded as one of the best local talents when the visiting teams from Europe contested the F3 Temporada series.

Subsequently he concentrated on racing touring cars and the 'Turismo Carretara' long-distance events. It was in one of these that he lost his life in October 1973.

PHILIPPE ÉTANCELIN

Easily recognisable by the famous reversed cap that was to become his trademark, 'Phi Phi', as he was known to his friends, began racing in 1927, scoring a big win at Reims with his Bugatti in his first season. In 1929 he won at Reims once more, and claimed further victories at Antibes, Comminges and La Baule, while success continued into 1930 with wins at Pau and in the Algerian GP.

Late in 1931, Étancelin took the decision to order an Alfa Romeo, which he ran relatively successfully until rule changes for 1934 forced him to switch to a Maserati. He often finished second or third with this car over the next few seasons, outright successes mainly eluding him, though he did win at Pau in 1936, and had previously shared the 1934 Le Mans-winning car with Chinetti.

After the war, Étancelin took an Alfa Romeo to the first race in Paris, but it was 1948 before he could compete regularly after taking delivery of a Lago-Talbot. The car was raced to good effect in 1949, 'Phi Phi' winning the Paris GP and finishing second at Marseilles, Monza and Brno. In 1950 – the first season of the World Championship – Étancelin picked up a couple of fifth places, racing his now elderly Talbot on through the 1951 season and into the following year in the few F1 and Libre events for which it was still eligible.

By 1953 this hard trier had virtually retired from racing after finishing third with 'Levegh' in the Casablanca 3 Hours, but the Rouen GP of that year was a non-championship event, so the organisers, hoping to bolster the grid, invited Formula 1 cars to compete as well. 'Phi Phi' was a local man and could not resist the temptation to dust off his trusty Talbot and take up the challenge to the works Ferraris. To the immense delight of a partisan crowd he brought the car home in third place, thus finishing a wonderful career in splendid fashion.

ÉTANCELIN, Philippe (F) b 28/12/1896, Rouen – d 13/10/1981, Neuilly sur Seine, nr Paris

	1950	Championship position: 10th=		Wins: 0	Pole positions: 0	Fastest laps: 0	Points scored: 3		
	Race	Circuit	No	Entrant	Tyres	Car/Engine		Comment	Q Pos/Entries
8	BRITISH GP	Silverstone	16	Philippe Étancelin	D	4.5 Lago-Talbot T26C 6		5 laps behind	14/21
ret	MONACO GP	Monte Carlo	14	Philippe Étancelin	D	4.5 Lago-Talbot T26C 6		oil pipe	4/21
ret	SWISS GP	Bremgarten	42	Philippe Étancelin	D	4.5 Lago-Talbot T26C 6		gearbox	6/18
ret	BELGIAN GP	Spa	16	Automobiles Talbot-Darracq	D	4.5 Lago-Talbot T26C-DA 6		overheating	6/14
5*	FRENCH GP	Reims	16	Philippe Étancelin	D	4.5 Lago-Talbot T26C-DA 6		*Chaboud took over/-5 laps	4/20
5	ITALIAN GP	Monza	24	Philippe Étancelin	D	4.5 Lago-Talbot T26C 6		5 laps behind	16/27
	1951	Championship position: Unplaced							
10	SWISS GP	Bremgarten	4	Philippe Étancelin	D	4.5 Lago-Talbot T26C-DA 6		3 laps behind	12/21
ret	BELGIAN GP	Spa	20	Philippe Étancelin	D	4.5 Lago-Talbot T26C-DA 6		transmission	10/13
ret	FRENCH GP	Reims	38	Philippe Étancelin	D	4.5 Lago-Talbot T26C-DA 6		engine	10/23
ret	GERMAN GP	Nürburgring	86	Philippe Étancelin	D	4.5 Lago-Talbot T26C-DA 6		gearbox	21/23
8	SPANISH GP	Pedralbes	34	Philippe Étancelin	D	4.5 Lago-Talbot T26C-DA 6		7 laps behind	13/20
	1952	Championship position: Unplaced							
8	FRENCH GP	Rouen	28	Escuderia Bandeirantes	P	2.0 Maserati A6GCM 6		7 laps behind	16/20

GP Starts: 12   GP Wins: 0   Pole positions: 0   Fastest laps: 0   Points: 3

EVANS, Bob (GB) b 11/6/1947, Waddington, Lincolnshire

	1975	Championship position: Unplaced							
	Race	Circuit	No	Entrant	Tyres	Car/Engine		Comment	Q Pos/Entries
15	SOUTH AFRICAN GP	Kyalami	14	Stanley BRM	G	3.0 BRM P201 V12		2 laps behind	24/28
ret	SPANISH GP	Montjuich Park	14	Stanley BRM	G	3.0 BRM P201 V12		fuel metering unit	23/26
dnq	MONACO GP	Monte Carlo	14	Stanley BRM	G	3.0 BRM P201 V12			22/26
9	BELGIAN GP	Zolder	14	Stanley BRM	G	3.0 BRM P201 V12		2 laps behind	20/24
13	SWEDISH GP	Anderstorp	14	Stanley BRM	G	3.0 BRM P201 V12		2 laps behind	23/26
ret	DUTCH GP	Zandvoort	14	Stanley BRM	G	3.0 BRM P201 V12		gearbox	20/25
17	FRENCH GP	Paul Ricard	14	Stanley BRM	G	3.0 BRM P201 V12		2 laps behind	25/26
ret	AUSTRIAN GP	Österreichring	14	Stanley BRM	G	3.0 BRM P201 V12		engine	25/30
ret	ITALIAN GP	Monza	14	Stanley BRM	G	3.0 BRM P201 V12		engine-electrics	20/28
	1976	Championship position: Unplaced							
10	SOUTH AFRICAN GP	Kyalami	5	John Player Team Lotus	G	3.0 Lotus 77-Cosworth V8		1 lap behind	23/25
dnq	US GP WEST	Long Beach	5	John Player Team Lotus	G	3.0 Lotus 77-Cosworth V8			24/27
ret	BRITISH GP	Brands Hatch	32	RAM Racing	G	3.0 Brabham BT44B-Cosworth V8		gearbox	22/30

GP Starts: 10   GP Wins: 0   Pole positions: 0   Fastest laps: 0   Points: 0

BOB EVANS

Evans was one of many British drivers of the period who, having worked tremendously hard to reach Formula 1, had neither the machinery nor the opportunity to show what they could really do. He had begun his racing career in a Sprite before moving into Formula Ford and then F3 in 1971, but only after he had fortunately recovered from a broken neck sustained when he crashed while testing at Castle Combe.

It was F5000 that was to provide Bob with his big breakthrough. With a solid season in a Trojan under his belt, long-time supporter Alan McKechnie bought him a Lola T332 for 1974 and he duly swept to the Rothmans championship, picking up the first-place Grovewood Award in the process.

This led to an offer to drive for BRM in 1975. The car was well past its best and it was to Evans' credit that he plugged away so valiantly in the face of adversity. Things looked better for 1976 when Colin Chapman, impressed with his performances, gave Bob a testing contract – and three races, the best of which was the Race of Champions, when the car ran out fuel and fourth place was lost.

Apart from a RAM drive in the British GP later that year, and a one-off outing to 11th place in the Hexagon Penske in the 1977 Race of Champions, that was that for Evans, who returned to the relative obscurity of the Aurora championship in a Surtees TS19 in 1978.

CORRADO FABI

Having started his racing career at the age of 12, raced a Formula 3 car before he was 18, and become a convincing European Formula 2 champion by the age of 21, Corrado Fabi was clearly a young man in a hurry – but where was he headed? Towards a brief Formula 1 career and racing oblivion, as it turned out, for today who remembers Teo's younger brother who promised so much a decade ago?

So swift was his rise to prominence (1979 – half a season in Italian F3; 1980 – third in the European F3 championship; 1981 – third in the European Formula 2 championship; 1982 – European Formula 2 champion) that it seemed certain he was a World Champion in the making.

Then it was into Grands Prix, and a cold shower of reality, with the back-of-the-grid Osella team in 1983. Struggling to qualify must have been a culture shock for the easy-going Corrado, and after three races in a competitive car standing in for Teo at Brabham in 1984 no more was seen of the younger Fabi in Formula 1. Surely a great talent had been allowed to slip away.

FABI, Corrado (I) b 12/4/1961, Milan

	1983			Championship position: Unplaced					
	Race	Circuit	No	Entrant	Tyres	Car/Engine		Comment	Q Pos/Entries
ret	BRAZILIAN GP	Rio	31	Osella Squadra Corse	M	3.0 Osella FA1D-Cosworth V8		engine	24/27
dnq	US GP WEST	Long Beach	31	Osella Squadra Corse	M	3.0 Osella FA1D-Cosworth V8			27/28
ret	FRENCH GP	Paul Ricard	31	Osella Squadra Corse	M	3.0 Osella FA1D-Cosworth V8		engine	23/29
ret	SAN MARINO GP	Imola	31	Osella Squadra Corse	M	3.0 Osella FA1D-Cosworth V8		spun off	26/28
dnq	MONACO GP	Monte Carlo	31	Osella Squadra Corse	M	3.0 Osella FA1D-Cosworth V8			24/28
ret	BELGIAN GP	Spa	31	Osella Squadra Corse	M	3.0 Osella FA1D-Cosworth V8		rear suspension	24/28
dnq	US GP (DETROIT)	Detroit	31	Osella Squadra Corse	M	3.0 Osella FA1D-Cosworth V8			27/27
ret	CANADIAN GP	Montreal	31	Osella Squadra Corse	M	3.0 Osella FA1D-Cosworth V8		engine	25/28
dnq	BRITISH GP	Silverstone	31	Osella Squadra Corse	M	3.0 Osella FA1E-Alfa Romeo V12			28/29
dnq	GERMAN GP	Hockenheim	31	Osella Squadra Corse	M	3.0 Osella FA1E-Alfa Romeo V12			28/29
10	AUSTRIAN GP	Österreichring	31	Osella Squadra Corse	M	3.0 Osella FA1E-Alfa Romeo V12		3 laps behind	26/29
11/ret	DUTCH GP	Zandvoort	31	Osella Squadra Corse	M	3.0 Osella FA1E-Alfa Romeo V12		engine	25/29
ret	ITALIAN GP	Monza	31	Osella Squadra Corse	M	3.0 Osella FA1E-Alfa Romeo V12		oil union	25/29
dnq	EUROPEAN GP	Brands Hatch	31	Osella Squadra Corse	M	3.0 Osella FA1E-Alfa Romeo V12			28/29
ret	SOUTH AFRICAN GP	Kyalami	31	Osella Squadra Corse	M	3.0 Osella FA1E-Alfa Romeo V12		engine	25/26
	1984			Championship position: Unplaced					
ret	MONACO GP	Monte Carlo	2	MRD International	M	1.5 t/c Brabham BT53-BMW 4		water in electrics/spun off	15/27
ret	CANADIAN GP	Montreal	2	MRD International	M	1.5 t/c Brabham BT53-BMW 4		lost turbo boost	16/26
7	US GP (DALLAS)	Dallas	2	MRD International	M	1.5 t/c Brabham BT53-BMW 4		3 laps behind	11/27

GP Starts: 12   GP Wins: 0   Pole positions: 0   Fastest laps: 0   Points: 0

TEO FABI

Teo Fabi was fortunate enough to have a foot in both the Formula 1 and Indy Car camps. However, sadly for the Italian, he was unable to make the most of either opportunity.

The European karting champion of 1975, Teo began his rise to prominence with fourth place in the 1978 European F3 championship, followed by a trip down-under to win the New Zealand Formula Pacific series. This set up a season in Formula 2 for 1979 with a semi-works March, but Fabi took a while to find his feet and finished a disappointed tenth in the final standings.

With the backing of Robin Herd, who rated him very highly, Teo led the works March Formula 2 effort in 1980. The season was dominated by the Toleman pair of Henton and Warwick, but Fabi was third, and seemed certain to join the March F1 team for 1981 until the drive went to Derek Daly at the eleventh hour. Instead Teo opted for a season in Can-Am with the Paul Newman team's March 817 and won four races, but the more consistent Geoff Brabham took the title.

In 1982 the Toleman team gave Teo a Grand Prix opportunity that he was soon to regret taking. The year was a disaster and Fabi's stock in Europe was low, but help was at hand and, with Herd's backing, Teo got himself a ride in Indy cars for 1983. He put the Forsythe March on pole for the Indy 500 – only his second outing for the team – and led the race. He went on to score four wins that season and was undisputed Rookie of the Year. Teo then took on a punishing schedule for 1984, accepting an offer to continue in Indy cars while racing in F1 for Brabham whenever commitments allowed, and in the end he gave up the Indy ride to concentrate full-time on F1. Rejoining Toleman for 1985, he earned pole position at the Nürburgring, which indicated the car's potential, but reliability was elusive. After the take-over by Benetton, Fabi stayed on, and the 1986 BMW-powered car proved very fast, Teo taking two pole positions, but he was over-shadowed by his team-mate Berger and then, in 1987, by Boutsen.

Realising his chances of finding a top seat in F1 were slim, Fabi opted for a return to Indy cars in 1988 with the ambitious Porsche project but this was to prove fraught with many problems over its three-year span and yielded but a single win, in 1989. Teo then successfully turned to endurance racing with TWR Jaguar, winning the 1991 drivers' championship, mainly by dint of his consistent finishes.

He had to be content with a place in the Toyota team at Le Mans the following year, but set up yet another return to Indy cars for 1993, although his tenure with the Pennzoil Hall/VDS team was to prove largely undistinguished. The 1995 season saw a real return to form, however, as Teo joined forces once more with Jerry Forsythe and Robin Herd. Often a front-runner, the little Italian was distinctly unlucky not to pick up a win, but his performances were not deemed sufficient for him to retain his seat and he was passed over in favour of Indy Lights sensation Greg Moore.

Teo made a brief return to CART action in 1996, substituting for the injured Mark Blundell with PacWest. His races at Long Beach and Nazareth were as low key as the Italian himself, who then slipped quietly away from the racing scene.

FABI, Teo (I) b 9/3/1955, Milan

1982 — Championship position: Unplaced

	Race	Circuit	No	Entrant	Tyres	Car/Engine	Comment	Q Pos/Entries
dnq	SOUTH AFRICAN GP	Kyalami	36	Candy Toleman Motorsport	P	1.5 t/c Toleman TG181B-Hart 4	no time recorded	–/–
dnq	BRAZILIAN GP	Rio	36	Candy Toleman Motorsport	P	1.5 t/c Toleman TG181B-Hart 4		27/31
dnq	US GP WEST	Long Beach	36	Candy Toleman Motorsport	P	1.5 t/c Toleman TG181C-Hart 4		27/31
nc	SAN MARINO GP	Imola	36	Toleman Group Motorsport	P	1.5 t/c Toleman TG181C-Hart 4	pit stop/8 laps behind	10/14
ret	BELGIAN GP	Zolder	36	Toleman Group Motorsport	P	1.5 t/c Toleman TG181C-Hart 4	brakes	23/32
dnpq	MONACO GP	Monte Carlo	36	Toleman Group Motorsport	P	1.5 t/c Toleman TG181C-Hart 4		27/31
dnq	DUTCH GP	Zandvoort	36	Toleman Group Motorsport	P	1.5 t/c Toleman TG181C-Hart 4		28/31
ret	BRITISH GP	Brands Hatch	36	Toleman Group Motorsport	P	1.5 t/c Toleman TG181C-Hart 4	startline accident	15/30
ret	FRENCH GP	Paul Ricard	36	Toleman Group Motorsport	P	1.5 t/c Toleman TG181C-Hart 4	oil pump drive	21/30
dnq	GERMAN GP	Hockenheim	36	Toleman Group Motorsport	P	1.5 t/c Toleman TG181C-Hart 4	no time recorded	–/–
ret	AUSTRIAN GP	Österreichring	36	Toleman Group Motorsport	P	1.5 t/c Toleman TG181C-Hart 4	driveshaft	17/29
ret	SWISS GP	Dijon	36	Toleman Group Motorsport	P	1.5 t/c Toleman TG181C-Hart 4	misfire	23/29
ret	ITALIAN GP	Monza	36	Toleman Group Motorsport	P	1.5 t/c Toleman TG181C-Hart 4	engine cut out	22/30
dnq	CAESARS PALACE GP	Las Vegas	36	Toleman Group Motorsport	P	1.5 t/c Toleman TG181C-Hart 4		28/30

1984 — Championship position: 12th Wins: 0 Pole positions: 0 Fastest laps: 0 Points scored: 9

	Race	Circuit	No	Entrant	Tyres	Car/Engine	Comment	Q Pos/Entries
ret	BRAZILIAN GP	Rio	2	MRD International	M	1.5 t/c Brabham BT53-BMW 4	turbo	16/27
ret	SOUTH AFRICAN GP	Kyalami	2	MRD International	M	1.5 t/c Brabham BT53-BMW 4	turbo compressor	6/27
ret	BELGIAN GP	Zolder	2	MRD International	M	1.5 t/c Brabham BT53-BMW 4	spun off	18/27
ret	SAN MARINO GP	Imola	2	MRD International	M	1.5 t/c Brabham BT53-BMW 4	turbo	9/28
9	FRENCH GP	Dijon	2	MRD International	M	1.5 t/c Brabham BT53-BMW 4	1 lap behind	18/27
3*	US GP (DETROIT)	Detroit	2	MRD International	M	1.5 t/c Brabham BT53-BMW 4	* 2nd place car disqualified	23/27
ret	BRITISH GP	Brands Hatch	2	MRD International	M	1.5 t/c Brabham BT53-BMW 4	electrics	14/27
ret	GERMAN GP	Hockenheim	2	MRD International	M	1.5 t/c Brabham BT53-BMW 4	lost turbo boost	8/27
4	AUSTRIAN GP	Österreichring	2	MRD International	M	1.5 t/c Brabham BT53-BMW 4		7/28
5	DUTCH GP	Zandvoort	2	MRD International	M	1.5 t/c Brabham BT53-BMW 4	1 lap behind	10/27
ret	ITALIAN GP	Monza	2	MRD International	M	1.5 t/c Brabham BT53-BMW 4	engine/broken oil line	5/27
ret	EUROPEAN GP	Nürburgring	2	MRD International	M	1.5 t/c Brabham BT53-BMW 4	gearbox	10/26

1985 — Championship position: Unplaced Wins: 0 Pole positions: 1 Fastest laps: 0 Points scored: 0

	Race	Circuit	No	Entrant	Tyres	Car/Engine	Comment	Q Pos/Entries
ret	MONACO GP	Monte Carlo	19	Toleman Group Motorsport	P	1.5 t/c Toleman TG185-Hart 4	turbo	20/26
ret	CANADIAN GP	Montreal	19	Toleman Group Motorsport	P	1.5 t/c Toleman TG185-Hart 4	started from pit lane/turbo	18/25
ret	US GP (DETROIT)	Detroit	19	Toleman Group Motorsport	P	1.5 t/c Toleman TG185-Hart 4	clutch	13/25
14/ret	FRENCH GP	Paul Ricard	19	Toleman Group Motorsport	P	1.5 t/c Toleman TG185-Hart 4	fuel pressure/4 laps behind	19/26
ret	BRITISH GP	Silverstone	19	Toleman Group Motorsport	P	1.5 t/c Toleman TG185-Hart 4	cwp	9/26
ret	GERMAN GP	Nürburgring	19	Toleman Group Motorsport	P	1.5 t/c Toleman TG185-Hart 4	clutch	1/27
ret	AUSTRIAN GP	Österreichring	19	Toleman Group Motorsport	P	1.5 t/c Toleman TG185-Hart 4	electrics	6/27
ret	DUTCH GP	Zandvoort	19	Toleman Group Motorsport	P	1.5 t/c Toleman TG185-Hart 4	wheel bearing	5/27
12	ITALIAN GP	Monza	19	Toleman Group Motorsport	P	1.5 t/c Toleman TG185-Hart 4	2 pit stops-handling/-4 laps	15/26
ret	BELGIAN GP	Spa	19	Toleman Group Motorsport	P	1.5 t/c Toleman TG185-Hart 4	throttle linkage	11/24
ret	EUROPEAN GP	Brands Hatch	19	Toleman Group Motorsport	P	1.5 t/c Toleman TG185-Hart 4	engine	20/27
ret	SOUTH AFRICAN GP	Kyalami	19	Toleman Group Motorsport	P	1.5 t/c Toleman TG185-Hart 4	engine	7/21
ret	AUSTRALIAN GP	Adelaide	19	Toleman Group Motorsport	P	1.5 t/c Toleman TG185-Hart 4	engine	24/25

1986 — Championship position: 15th Wins: 0 Pole positions: 2 Fastest laps: 1 Points scored: 2

	Race	Circuit	No	Entrant	Tyres	Car/Engine	Comment	Q Pos/Entries
10	BRAZILIAN GP	Rio	19	Benetton Formula Ltd	P	1.5 t/c Benetton B186-BMW 4	pit stop-electrics/-5 laps	12/25
5	SPANISH GP	Jerez	19	Benetton Formula Ltd	P	1.5 t/c Benetton B186-BMW 4	hit Laffite-pit stop/-1 lap	9/25
ret	SAN MARINO GP	Imola	19	Benetton Formula Ltd	P	1.5 t/c Benetton B186-BMW 4	engine	10/26
ret	MONACO GP	Monte Carlo	19	Benetton Formula Ltd	P	1.5 t/c Benetton B186-BMW 4	brakes	16/26
7	BELGIAN GP	Spa	19	Benetton Formula Ltd	P	1.5 t/c Benetton B186-BMW 4	collision with Tambay/-1 lap	6/25
ret	CANADIAN GP	Montreal	19	Benetton Formula Ltd	P	1.5 t/c Benetton B186-BMW 4	battery	15/25
ret	US GP (DETROIT)	Detroit	19	Benetton Formula Ltd	P	1.5 t/c Benetton B186-BMW 4	gearbox	17/26
ret	FRENCH GP	Paul Ricard	19	Benetton Formula Ltd	P	1.5 t/c Benetton B186-BMW 4	engine misfire	9/26
ret	BRITISH GP	Brands Hatch	19	Benetton Formula Ltd	P	1.5 t/c Benetton B186-BMW 4	fuel system	7/26
ret	GERMAN GP	Hockenheim	19	Benetton Formula Ltd	P	1.5 t/c Benetton B186-BMW 4	accident at start	9/26
ret	HUNGARIAN GP	Hungaroring	19	Benetton Formula Ltd	P	1.5 t/c Benetton B186-BMW 4	transmission-spun off	13/26
ret	AUSTRIAN GP	Österreichring	19	Benetton Formula Ltd	P	1.5 t/c Benetton B186-BMW 4	engine	1/26
ret	ITALIAN GP	Monza	19	Benetton Formula Ltd	P	1.5 t/c Benetton B186-BMW 4	started from back/puncture/FL	1/27
8	PORTUGUESE GP	Estoril	19	Benetton Formula Ltd	P	1.5 t/c Benetton B186-BMW 4	2 laps behind	5/27
ret	MEXICAN GP	Mexico City	19	Benetton Formula Ltd	P	1.5 t/c Benetton B186-BMW 4	engine	9/26
10	AUSTRALIAN GP	Adelaide	19	Benetton Formula Ltd	P	1.5 t/c Benetton B186-BMW 4	2 pit stops-tyres/-5 laps	13/26

1987 — Championship position: 9th Wins: 0 Pole positions: 0 Fastest laps: 1 Points scored: 12

	Race	Circuit	No	Entrant	Tyres	Car/Engine	Comment	Q Pos/Entries
ret	BRAZILIAN GP	Rio	19	Benetton Formula Ltd	G	1.5 t/c Benetton B187-Cosworth V6	turbo	4/23
ret	SAN MARINO GP	Imola	19	Benetton Formula Ltd	G	1.5 t/c Benetton B187-Cosworth V6	turbo/FL	5/27
ret	BELGIAN GP	Spa	19	Benetton Formula Ltd	G	1.5 t/c Benetton B187-Cosworth V6	engine/oil pump drive belt	9/26
8	MONACO GP	Monte Carlo	19	Benetton Formula Ltd	G	1.5 t/c Benetton B187-Cosworth V6	2 laps behind	12/26
ret	US GP (DETROIT)	Detroit	19	Benetton Formula Ltd	G	1.5 t/c Benetton B187-Cosworth V6	accident with Cheever	8/26
5/ret	FRENCH GP	Paul Ricard	19	Benetton Formula Ltd	G	1.5 t/c Benetton B187-Cosworth V6	driveshaft/3 laps behind	7/26
6	BRITISH GP	Silverstone	19	Benetton Formula Ltd	G	1.5 t/c Benetton B187-Cosworth V6	2 laps behind	6/26
ret	GERMAN GP	Hockenheim	19	Benetton Formula Ltd	G	1.5 t/c Benetton B187-Cosworth V6	engine	9/26
ret	HUNGARIAN GP	Hungaroring	19	Benetton Formula Ltd	G	1.5 t/c Benetton B187-Cosworth V6	gearbox	12/26
3	AUSTRIAN GP	Österreichring	19	Benetton Formula Ltd	G	1.5 t/c Benetton B187-Cosworth V6	1 lap behind	5/26
7	ITALIAN GP	Monza	19	Benetton Formula Ltd	G	1.5 t/c Benetton B187-Cosworth V6	1 lap behind	7/28
4/ret	PORTUGUESE GP	Estoril	19	Benetton Formula Ltd	G	1.5 t/c Benetton B187-Cosworth V6	out of fuel/1 lap behind	10/27
ret	SPANISH GP	Jerez	19	Benetton Formula Ltd	G	1.5 t/c Benetton B187-Cosworth V6	engine	6/28
5	MEXICAN GP	Mexico City	19	Benetton Formula Ltd	G	1.5 t/c Benetton B187-Cosworth V6	2 laps behind	6/27
ret	JAPANESE GP	Suzuka	19	Benetton Formula Ltd	G	1.5 t/c Benetton B187-Cosworth V6	engine	6/27
ret	AUSTRALIAN GP	Adelaide	19	Benetton Formula Ltd	G	1.5 t/c Benetton B187-Cosworth V6	brakes	9/27

GP Starts: 64 GP Wins: 0 Pole positions: 3 Fastest laps: 2 Points: 23

FABRE, Pascal (F) b 9/1/1960, Lyon

	1987			Championship position: Unplaced					
	Race	Circuit	No	Entrant	Tyres	Car/Engine	Comment		Q Pos/Entries
12*	BRAZILIAN GP	Rio	14	Team El Charro AGS	G	3.5 AGS JH22-Cosworth V8	* 3rd non-turbo/-6 laps		22/23
13*	SAN MARINO GP	Imola	14	Team El Charro AGS	G	3.5 AGS JH22-Cosworth V8	* 3rd non-turbo/-6 laps		26/27
10/ret	BELGIAN GP	Spa	14	Team El Charro AGS	G	3.5 AGS JH22-Cosworth V8	* 3rd non-turbo/electrics/-5 laps		25/26
13	MONACO GP	Monte Carlo	14	Team El Charro AGS	G	3.5 AGS JH22-Cosworth V8	*3rd non-turbo/-7 laps		24/26
12	US GP (DETROIT)	Detroit	14	Team El Charro AGS	G	3.5 AGS JH22-Cosworth V8	* 3rd non-turbo/-5 laps		26/26
9	FRENCH GP	Paul Ricard	14	Team El Charro AGS	G	3.5 AGS JH22-Cosworth V8	* 3rd non-turbo/-6 laps		26/26
9	BRITISH GP	Silverstone	14	Team El Charro AGS	G	3.5 AGS JH22-Cosworth V8	* 2nd non-turbo/-6 laps		26/26
ret	GERMAN GP	Hockenheim	14	Team El Charro AGS	G	3.5 AGS JH22-Cosworth V8	engine		25/26
13	HUNGARIAN GP	Hungaroring	14	Team El Charro AGS	G	3.5 AGS JH22-Cosworth V8	* 4th non-turbo/-5 laps		26/26
nc	AUSTRIAN GP	Österreichring	14	Team El Charro AGS	G	3.5 AGS JH22-Cosworth V8	started from pit lane/-7 laps		26/26
dnq	ITALIAN GP	Monza	14	Team El Charro AGS	G	3.5 AGS JH22-Cosworth V8			28/28
dnq	PORTUGUESE GP	Estoril	14	Team El Charro AGS	G	3.5 AGS JH22-Cosworth V8			27/27
ret	SPANISH GP	Jerez	14	Team El Charro AGS	G	3.5 AGS JH22-Cosworth V8	clutch		25/28
dnq	MEXICAN GP	Mexico City	14	Team El Charro AGS	G	3.5 AGS JH22-Cosworth V8			27/27

GP Starts: 11   GP Wins: 0   Pole positions: 0   Fastest laps: 0   Points: 0

PASCAL FABRE

Fabre seemed quite promising in his first season of Formula 2 in 1982 when paired with the very quick Philippe Streiff in the little AGS team, but he was forced to drop back into European F3 the following year and, despite a bright start, lack of finance forced his Martini off the grid before the season was out. Back in F2, he surprised many in 1984 with his speed in a March-BMW, winning at Hockenheim in mid-season only to depart from his team abruptly due to financial differences.

His plans for a Formula 3000 drive in 1985 fell through, and he had to settle for a single race at the end of the year before arranging a full season with a minimal budget in 1986. A winning start at Silverstone, followed by a second at Vallelunga, gave him an early-season lead which he was unable to maintain, Pascal finishing seventh in the championship table.

Prompted no doubt by his past links with the team, AGS chose Fabre to drive their F1 challenger in 1987. The car was slow, but he flogged away, usually bringing it to the finish, until he lost his ride to Roberto Moreno, who lost little time in scoring the team's first championship point.

Pascal then moved on to sports cars, most notably with the Cougar-Porsche project, but more recently he has been racing a Ferrari 333SP with Michel Ferté.

LUIGI FAGIOLI

'The old Abruzzi robber', as he became affectionately known, Fagioli was one of Italy's greatest drivers and a true individualist, who often found himself at odds with those in authority. His career started in 1926, but he really shot to fame upon joining the Maserati team in 1930. Over the next three seasons he won occasionally but was often out of luck, which prompted him to join Ferrari's Alfa Romeo team in the second half of the 1933 season. Soon he had won the GPs of Pescara, Comminges, Marseilles and Italy, which brought an invitation to drive for Mercedes-Benz as number two driver in 1934.

In his first race, the Eifelrennen, irked at being told to stay behind the sister entry of von Brauchitsch, Fagioli showed his displeasure by parking his car out on the circuit and returning to the pits on foot. It was not to be the last time he would find himself in conflict with the team, but that did not stop him winning the Italian and Spanish GPs that year, and those at Monaco, AVUS and Barcelona the following season. He continued with the team for 1936 before moving to their great rivals Auto Union, but was forced to miss much of the season through illness, although he was fifth at Tripoli.

In fact Fagioli did not return to the Grand Prix arena until 1950, with the all-conquering Alfa Romeo team. His experience stood him in good stead and some cold and calculating performances brought him third place in the World Championship. He was retained for 1951 but at the French GP he was hauled from the car at a pit stop as he recovered from an early spin to allow Fangio to take over and complete the race, the Argentinian going on to win. This was the last straw for the proud Fagioli, and he never raced a GP car again.

Turning to his own OSCA, he won his class in the Mille Miglia, a feat which he repeated in 1952 at the wheel of a Lancia Aurelia tourer. More remarkable was the fact that he was third overall ahead of many pure sports racers. That year the Monaco GP was held for sports cars only, and during practice Fagioli lost control of his car in the tunnel and broadsided out into a stone balustrade. Thrown out, he was taken to hospital unconscious, with a broken arm and leg. Four days later he regained consciousness and seemed to be out of danger, but three weeks after the crash he relapsed – with a complete failure of the nervous system – and died, aged 54.

FAGIOLI, Luigi (I) b 9/6/1898, Osimo, nr Ancona – d 20/6/1952, Monte Carlo, Monaco

	1950	Championship position: 3rd		Wins: 0	Pole positions: 0		Fastest laps: 0	Points scored: 28		
	Race	Circuit	No	Entrant		Tyres	Car/Engine		Comment	Q Pos/Entries
2	BRITISH GP	Silverstone	3	Alfa Romeo SpA		P	1.5 s/c Alfa Romeo 158/50 8			2/21
ret	MONACO GP	Monte Carlo	36	Alfa Romeo SpA		P	1.5 s/c Alfa Romeo 158/50 8		*multiple accident on lap 1*	5/21
2	SWISS GP	Bremgarten	12	Alfa Romeo SpA		P	1.5 s/c Alfa Romeo 158/50 8			3/18
2	BELGIAN GP	Spa	12	Alfa Romeo SpA		P	1.5 s/c Alfa Romeo 158/50 8			3/14
2	FRENCH GP	Reims	4	Alfa Romao SpA		P	1.5 s/c Alfa Romeo 158/50 8			3/20
3	ITALIAN GP	Monza	36	Alfa Romeo SpA		P	1.5 s/c Alfa Romeo 158/50 8			5/27
	1951	Championship position: 9th		Wins: 1 (shared)	Pole positions: 0		Fastest laps: 0	Points scored: 4		
1*	FRENCH GP	Reims	8	Alfa Romeo SpA		P	1.5 s/c Alfa Romeo 159B 8		** Fangio took over car*	7/23
11*	"	"	4	Alfa Romeo SpA		P	1.5 s/c Alfa Romeo 159B 8		** took Fangio's car/-22 laps*	– / –

GP Starts: 7   GP Wins: 1* *(shared)*   Pole positions: 0   Fastest laps: 0   Points: 32

JACK FAIRMAN

Fairman was an engineer who began competing in 1934 with a 12/50 Alvis in trials, soon moving on to hill-climbs and events at Brooklands. These remained his staple diet until the war intervened, during which he saw service in the Tank Corps.

Jack's career moved onto a wider stage in the late forties as he raced at Le Mans and Spa for the first time. Strong as an ox, and an extremely safe and reliable driver, Fairman was ideally suited to long-distance sports car racing, in which he raced with distinction for Bristol, Jaguar, Ecurie Ecosse and Aston Martin during the fifties. His greatest successes came in 1959 when, driving the Aston, he won the Nürburgring 1000 Km (with Moss at his brilliant best) and the Tourist Trophy at Goodwood (with Moss and Shelby).

With his engineering background Fairman was also in great demand as a test driver and was instrumental in the development of the Connaught GP car, being rewarded with points finishes in each of his two Grand Prix appearances in 1956.

Jack seemed to thrive on picking up irregular rides here and there and raced a bewildering succession of machines in different categories (including on occasion works cars from Cooper and BRM and the Rob Walker 4WD Ferguson) during an extremely long career which lasted into the early sixties. His final Formula 1 race was in 1963 at the City of Imola GP when he took over one of de Beaufort's Ecurie Maarsbergen Porsches at short notice, finishing a distant seventh.

FAIRMAN, Jack (GB) b 15/3/1913, Smallfield, nr Horley, Surrey

	1953	Championship position: Unplaced								
	Race	Circuit	No	Entrant		Tyres	Car/Engine		Comment	Q Pos/Entries
ret	BRITISH GP	Silverstone	4	John Heath		D	2.0 HWM-Alta 4		*clutch*	27/29
nc	ITALIAN GP	Monza	20	Connaught Engineering		D	2.0 Connaught A-Lea Francis 4		*19 laps behind*	22/30
	1955	Championship position: Unplaced								
dns	BRITISH GP	Aintree	34	Connaught Engineering		D	2.5 Connaught B-Alta 4		*engine problems*	(21)/25
	1956	Championship position: 8th		Wins: 0	Pole positions: 0		Fastest laps: 0	Points scored: 5		
4	BRITISH GP	Silverstone	21	Connaught Engineering		P	2.5 Connaught B-Alta 4		*3 laps behind*	21/28
5	ITALIAN GP	Monza	6	Connaught Engineering		P/A	2.5 Connaught B-Alta 4		*3 laps behind*	16/26
	1957	Championship position: Unplaced								
ret	BRITISH GP	Aintree	24	Owen Racing Organisation		D	2.5 BRM P25 4		*engine*	16/19
	1958	Championship position: Unplaced								
ret	BRITISH GP	Silverstone	14	B C Ecclestone		D	2.5 Connaught B-Alta 4		*ignition*	19/21
8	MOROCCAN GP	Casablanca	32	Cooper Car Co		D	2.0 Cooper T45-Climax 4		*3 laps behind*	11/25
	1959	Championship position: Unplaced								
ret	BRITISH GP	Aintree	38	High Efficiency Motors		D	2.5 Cooper T45-Climax 4		*gearbox*	15/30
ret	ITALIAN GP	Monza	22	High Efficiency Motors		D	2.5 Cooper T45-Maserati 4		*engine*	20/21
	1960	Championship position: Unplaced								
ret	BRITISH GP	Silverstone	23	C T Atkins		D	2.5 Cooper T51-Climax 4		*fuel pump*	15/25
	1961	Championship position: Unplaced								
dsq*	BRITISH GP	Aintree	26	R R C Walker Racing Team		D	1.5 Ferguson P99-Climax 4		*Moss took car/*earlier push start*	20/30
ret	ITALIAN GP	Monza	30	Fred Tuck		D	1.5 Cooper T45-Climax 4		*engine*	26/33

GP Starts: 12   GP Wins: 0   Pole positions: 0   Fastest laps: 0   Points: 5

JUAN MANUEL FANGIO

WORLD CHAMPION: 1951, 1954, 1955, 1956 & 1957

JUAN MANUEL FANGIO

Fangio will always be 'the Maestro' and justifiably so. For all his phenomenal achievements in Grand Prix racing – five World Championships and 24 wins from just 51 starts – it was as much the way he conducted himself outside the cockpit which has created an aura that exists to this day.

His origins were humble. The son of an Italian immigrant family, he grew up in Argentina in a motoring environment, working in a garage from the age of 11 to supplement the family income. He saved everything he could towards the purchase of à Model T Ford, which he raced secretly before switching to a Ford V8 special and the real beginnings of his competition career. Supported by the people of his home town, Balcarce, he acquired a Chevrolet and won the 1940 Gran Premio del Norte, a 5,900 mile road race, scoring his first major success. Throughout the next seven years he raced in these marathons with a Chevrolet, often competing with 'Los Galvez' for the top honours.

When Varzi, Villoresi, Farina and Wimille were invited to appear in Libre events in 1948, Fangio was among their local opposition, and performed so well that he was sponsored for a brief trip to Europe in 1948 with Galvez, driving a Simca-Gordini at Reims before returning home with a Maserati 4CLT.

For 1949 he was back in Europe and, at the age of 38, enjoyed a staggering debut season, winning his first race at San Remo, and following it up with wins at Perpignan, Marseilles, Pau, Albi and Monza. This led to an invitation to join the Alfa Romeo team in 1950 and he eventually finished second in the World Championship to Farina, despite winning three of the six races. He also won at Pescara, Geneva and San Remo in the Alfa, and at Pau and Angoulême in a Maserati. After handling the pre-war Mercedes in the early-season Libre events back in Argentina, Fangio then took the first of his five titles in 1951, before Alfa withdrew from competition.

In 1952, the newly crowned champion started the year in imperious form on his home continent, winning six Libre events in Argentina, Brazil and Uruguay, before returning to Europe to drive for Maserati. However, he crashed at the Monza GP and was lucky to escape with his life, suffering concussion and a broken vertebra in his neck when he was thrown from the car. He convalesced in Balcarce for the rest of the season and had leisure to ponder the thin dividing line between glory and disaster, but it did not prevent him from undertaking an even bigger racing schedule in 1953. He drove Maserati's A6GCM to victory in the Italian and Modena GPs and also took the opportunity to return to his roots by winning the Carrera Panamericana road race in a works Lancia.

His stature was unrivalled and Mercedes-Benz made it their top priority to sign him when they re-entered racing in 1954. While the cars were being prepared, he continued to drive for Maserati, winning the first two races of the season before scoring another four wins in the silver machine. The combination of Fangio's sublime talent and German technology was over-whelming, and if the car lasted he generally won. Such was his mastery that it is thought he allowed team-mates Kling and Moss to takes victories at AVUS and Aintree respectively, though he never admitted it. Despite being a relatively old man in Grand Prix terms by this stage, he had all the resources necessary to maintain his dominant position, his seemingly inexhaustible talents equal to the demands of any situation. If there was a corner that needed to be taken flat out, then Fangio would do it; his physical strength and stamina allowed him to cope with broiling heat or pouring rain; and his powers of concentration enabled him to annihilate the opposition when his car ran well, or nurse a sick machine to the chequered flag when lesser mortals would have given up.

Fangio also had the acumen to choose the best machinery available and then make the best possible use of it. Even an uncom-fortable year at Scuderia Ferrari in 1956, where he could have been undermined by the young Italian pretenders, did not prevent him taking a fourth World Championship, but he moved back to Maserati for 1957 and, with the 250F in the final stages of its useful development, took his fifth and perhaps finest championship win, highlighted by one of Grand Prix racing's greatest-ever performances at the Nürburgring, where he overhauled Hawthorn and Collins to win a sensational German GP, having gambled that a pit stop for fresh tyres would pay off rather than run non-stop as did the Ferraris. His personal standards were such that at each track he set out to better his previous performances there. He was the World Champion and it was expected, but at the Italian GP even he could not defeat Stirling Moss, by now nearly his equal as a driver. With the advantage of driving one of the emerging Vanwalls, Moss repeated the win at Pescara, and the writing was on the wall for Fangio. With no wish to return to Ferrari and with Maserati winding down their operation, his thoughts were perhaps turning to retirement, but in the event he was to race on into 1958 as an independent, selecting his races. After a fourth place in the Argentine GP he took his final win in the Libre Buenos Aires GP. He was then tempted to Indianapolis to take part in the famous 500 and, despite being given a car which was far from new, duly passed his qualification tests, but he was unhappy with the machine. Perhaps fortuitously, he was forced to return home to deal with an urgent matter relating to his garage business and thus missed the race, which was marred by tragedy after a multiple crash on the first lap.

For Fangio there was to be just one more Grand Prix, and it was perhaps one of his best. Coming home fourth, he could have been lapped right at the finish by the winner Hawthorn, who chose to spare him this indignity. However, the spectators were unaware that Fangio had raced without the benefit of a clutch from early on. With the engine turning at 8,000 rpm, 'the Maestro' relied on his ears to judge when to change gear throughout the race in a remarkable display which showed his legendary empathy with his machinery. He went home to Balcarce never to return as a driver, deciding that the time was right for him to stop. Of course his presence graced the circuits on many further occasions, and he held a magnetic attraction for young and old alike, who recognised they were rubbing shoulders not only with a legendary racing driver, but also with a man of great sincerity and generosity of heart to whom the sport owes a great debt.

Driving for the *Alfa Corse* team Fangio took his first title in 1951. He is pictured sharing the win in the French Grand Prix at Reims, having taken over Fagioli's car number 8 in mid race after his own car encountered mechanical problems.

FANGIO, Juan Manuel (RA) b 24/6/1911, Balcarce, Buenos Aires – d 17/7/1995, Balcarce, Buenos Aires

	1950	Championship position: 2nd	Wins: 3	Pole positions: 4	Fastest laps: 3	Points scored: 27			
	Race	Circuit	No	Entrant	Tyres	Car/Engine		Comment	Q Pos/Entries
ret	BRITISH GP	Silverstone	1	Alfa Romeo SpA	P	1.5 s/c Alfa Romeo 158/50 8		*oil pipe*	3/21
1	MONACO GP	Monte Carlo	34	Alfa Romeo SpA	P	1.5 s/c Alfa Romeo 158/50 8		*FL*	1/21
ret	SWISS GP	Bremgarten	14	Alfa Romeo SpA	P	1.5 s/c Alfa Romeo 158/50 8		*valve*	1/18
1	BELGIAN GP	Spa	10	Alfa Romeo SpA	P	1.5 s/c Alfa Romeo 158/50 8			2/14
1	FRENCH GP	Reims	6	Alfa Romeo SpA	P	1.5 s/c Alfa Romeo 158/50 8		*FL*	1/20
ret	ITALIAN GP	Monza	18	Alfa Romeo SpA	P	1.5 s/c Alfa Romeo 158/50 8		*gearbox/FL*	1/27
ret	"	"	60	Alfa Romeo SpA	P	1.5 s/c Alfa Romeo 158/50 8		*took Taruffi's car/engine*	– / –

	1951	Championship position: WORLD CHAMPION	Wins: 3 (1 shared)	Pole positions: 4	Fastest laps: 5	Points scored: 37			
1	SWISS GP	Bremgarten	24	Alfa Romeo SpA	P	1.5 s/c Alfa Romeo 159A 8		*FL*	1/21
9	BELGIAN GP	Spa	2	Alfa Romeo SpA	P	1.5 s/c Alfa Romeo 159B 8		*jammed rear wheel in pits/FL*	1/13
11*	FRENCH GP	Reims	4	Alfa Romeo SpA	P	1.5 s/c Alfa Romeo 159A 8		* Fagioli took over	1/23
1*	"	"	8	Alfa Romeo SpA	P	1.5 s/c Alfa Romeo 159A 8		*took over Fagioli's car/FL*	– / –
2	BRITISH GP	Silverstone	2	Alfa Romeo SpA	P	1.5 s/c Alfa Romeo 159B 8			2/20
2	GERMAN GP	Nürburgring	75	Alfa Romeo SpA	P	1.5 s/c Alfa Romeo 159B 8		*FL*	3/23
ret	ITALIAN GP	Monza	38	Alfa Romeo SpA	P	1.5 s/c Alfa Romeo 159M 8		*engine*	1/22
1	SPANISH GP	Pedralbes	22	Alfa Romeo SpA	P	1.5 s/c Alfa Romeo 159M 8		*FL*	2/20

	1953	Championship position: 2nd	Wins: 1	Pole positions: 2	Fastest laps: 2 (1 shared)	Points scored: 29			
ret	ARGENTINE GP	Buenos Aires	2	Officine Alfieri Maserati	P	2.0 Maserati A6GCM 6		*universal joint*	2/16
ret	DUTCH GP	Zandvoort	12	Officine Alfieri Maserati	P	2.0 Maserati A6GCM 6		*rear axle*	2/20
ret	BELGIAN GP	Spa	4	Officine Alfieri Maserati	P	2.0 Maserati A6GCM 6		*engine*	1/22
ret	"	"	6	Officine Alfieri Maserati	P	2.0 Maserati A6GCM 6		*took Claes' car/steering-accident*	– / –
2	FRENCH GP	Reims	18	Officine Alfieri Maserati	P	2.0 Maserati A6GCM 6		*FL (shared)*	4/25
2	BRITISH GP	Silverstone	23	Officine Alfieri Maserati	P	2.0 Maserati A6GCM 6			4/29
2	GERMAN GP	Nürburgring	5	Officine Alfieri Maserati	P	2.0 Maserati A6GCM 6			2/35
4*	SWISS GP	Bremgarten	32	Officine Alfieri Maserati	P	2.0 Maserati A6GCM 6		*Bonetto took over/-1 lap	1/23
ret	"	"	30	Officine Alfieri Maserati	P	2.0 Maserati A6GCM 6		* took Bonetto's car/engine	– / –
1	ITALIAN GP	Monza	50	Officine Alfieri Maserati	P	2.0 Maserati A6GCM 6		*FL*	2/30

	1954	Championship position: WORLD CHAMPION	Wins: 6	Pole positions: 5	Fastest laps: 3 (1 shared)	Points scored: 57.14			
1	ARGENTINE GP	Buenos Aires	2	Officine Alfieri Maserati	P	2.5 Maserati 250F 6			3/18
1	BELGIAN GP	Spa	26	Officine Alfieri Maserati	P	2.5 Maserati 250F 6		*FL*	1/15
1	FRENCH GP	Reims	18	Daimler Benz AG	C	2.5 Mercedes-Benz W196 8 str			1/22
4	BRITISH GP	Silverstone	1	Daimler Benz AG	C	2.5 Mercedes-Benz W196 8 str		*FL (shared)/1 lap behind*	1/31
1	GERMAN GP	Nürburgring	18	Daimler Benz AG	C	2.5 Mercedes-Benz W196 8			1/23
1	SWISS GP	Bremgarten	4	Daimler Benz AG	C	2.5 Mercedes-Benz W196 8		*FL*	2/15
1	ITALIAN GP	Monza	16	Daimler Benz AG	C	2.5 Mercedes-Benz W196 8 str			1/21
3	SPANISH GP	Pedralbes	2	Daimler Benz AG	C	2.5 Mercedes-Benz W196 8		*1 lap behind*	2/22

	1955	Championship position: WORLD CHAMPION	Wins: 4	Pole positions: 3	Fastest laps: 3	Points scored: 41			
1	ARGENTINE GP	Buenos Aires	2	Daimler Benz AG	C	2.5 Mercedes-Benz W196 8		*FL*	2/22
ret	MONACO GP	Monte Carlo	2	Daimler Benz AG	C	2.5 Mercedes-Benz W196 8		*rear axle/FL*	1/22
1	BELGIAN GP	Spa	10	Daimler Benz AG	C	2.5 Mercedes-Benz W196 8		*FL*	2/14
1	DUTCH GP	Zandvoort	8	Daimler Benz AG	C	2.5 Mercedes-Benz W196 8			1/16
2	BRITISH GP	Aintree	10	Daimler Benz AG	C	2.5 Mercedes-Benz W196 8			2/25
1	ITALIAN GP	Monza	18	Daimler Benz AG	C	2.5 Mercedes-Benz W196 8			1/22

	1956	Championship position: WORLD CHAMPION	Wins: 2 (1 shared)	Pole positions: 6	Fastest laps: 4	Points scored: 33			
ret	ARGENTINE GP	Buenos Aires	30	Scuderia Ferrari	E	2.5 Lancia-Ferrari D50 V8		*fuel pump*	1/15
1*	"	"	34	Scuderia Ferrari	E	2.5 Lancia-Ferrari D50 V8		*took over Musso's car/FL*	– / –
4*	MONACO GP	Monte Carlo	20	Scuderia Ferrari	E	2.5 Lancia-Ferrari D50 V8		*Castellotti took over car/-6 laps	1/19
2*	"	"	26	Scuderia Ferrari	E	2.5 Lancia-Ferrari D50 V8		* took Collins' car/FL no points	– / –
ret	BELGIAN GP	Spa	2	Scuderia Ferrari	E	2.5 Lancia-Ferrari D50 V8		*transmission*	1/16
4	FRENCH GP	Reims	10	Scuderia Ferrari	E	2.5 Lancia-Ferrari D50 V8		*pit stop-split fuel pipe/FL*	1/20
1	BRITISH GP	Silverstone	1	Scuderia Ferrari	E	2.5 Lancia-Ferrari D50 V8			2/28
1	GERMAN GP	Nürburgring	1	Scuderia Ferrari	E	2.5 Lancia-Ferrari D50 V8		*FL*	1/21
8*	ITALIAN GP	Monza	22	Scuderia Ferrari	E	2.5 Lancia-Ferrari D50 V8		*Castellotti took over car/-4 laps	1/26
2*	"	"	26	Scuderia Ferrari	E	2.5 Lancia-Ferrari D50 V8		* took over Collins' car	– / –

1957			Championship position: WORLD CHAMPION	Wins: 4	Pole positions: 4	Fastest laps: 2	Points scored: 46	
1	ARGENTINE GP	Buenos Aires	2	Officine Alfieri Maserati	P	2.5 Maserati 250F 6		2/16
1	MONACO GP	Monte Carlo	32	Officine Alfieri Maserati	P	2.5 Maserati 250F 6	*FL*	1/21
dns	"	"	32	Officine Alfieri Maserati	P	2.5 Maserati 250F V12	*practice only*	–/–
1	FRENCH GP	Rouen	2	Officine Alfieri Maserati	P	2.5 Maserati 250F 6		1/15
ret	BRITISH GP	Aintree	2	Officine Alfieri Maserati	P	2.5 Maserati 250F 6	*engine*	4/19
1	GERMAN GP	Nürburgring	1	Officine Alfieri Maserati	P	2.5 Maserati 250F 6	*FL*	1/24
2	PESCARA GP	Pescara	2	Officine Alfieri Maserati	P	2.5 Maserati 250F 6		1/16
dns			2	Officine Alfieri Maserati	P	2.5 Maserati 250F V12	*practice only*	–/–
2	ITALIAN GP	Monza	2	Officine Alfieri Maserati	P	2.5 Maserati 250F 6		4/19
dns	"	"	2	Officine Alfieri Maserati	P	2.5 Maserati 250F V12	*practice only*	–/–
1958			Championship position: 14th	Wins: 0	Pole positions: 1	Fastest laps: 1	Points scored: 7	
4	ARGENTINE GP	Buenos Aires	2	Scuderia Sud Americana	P	2.5 Maserati 250F 6	*FL*	1/10
4	FRENCH GP	Reims	34	Juan Manuel Fangio	P	2.5 Maserati 250F 6	*lost clutch*	8/21

GP Starts: 51   GP Wins: 24   Pole positions: 29   Fastest laps: 23   Points: 277.14

Master and pupil. Fangio and Moss were able to demonstrate the superiority of their Mercedes W196s at the 1955 Dutch Grand Prix.

The 1957 German Grand Prix was by general consensus Fangio's greatest race. In a scintillating drive with the Maserati 250F the Argentine humbled the works Ferraris of Hawthorn and Collins.

GIUSEPPE FARINA

Giuseppe 'Nino' Farina was very much his own man, a private person, who did not make any great attempts to mix and guarded his private life jealously. He even played down his achievement in becoming World Champion in 1950, refusing to get involved in the razzmatazz which followed.

By the time he won the title, he was one of the most senior campaigners still regularly active, having made his competition debut in the Aosta-St Bernard hill-climb as far back as 1932. It was a chastening experience for he crashed and ended up in hospital, but it was to be only the first of many accidents sustained in a long career by this tough, aristocratic Italian who seemed totally indestructible.

After driving a Maserati with little success, his first break came when he raced an Alfa Romeo under the tutelage of the great Nuvolari. At that time the red cars were outclassed by the mighty German machines and the young Farina often ran out of road in his desperate attempts to keep pace. He did, however, win the Naples GP in 1937 and was Italian champion in the years 1937-39, with further successes in the Alfa Romeo 158 at the Antwerp GP, Coppa Ciano and Prix de Berne. He also gave a fantastic display at the 1939 Swiss GP with the underpowered Alfa, leading many faster cars before giving way. Having won the Tripoli GP, Farina was probably reaching his peak when the war suspended all racing activity, but in 1946 he returned to immediate effect, winning the GP des Nations at Geneva. Enzo Ferrari had great regard for his ability, Farina excelling on fast courses with his imperious, upright, arms-at-length driving style.

In 1948 he drove an independent Maserati, winning at Monaco, Geneva and Mar del Plata, and he continued with the car into the following season, when he won the Lausanne GP and finished second in the International Trophy, but also drove for Ferrari, winning the Rosario GP in a Tipo 166.

When Alfa Romeo returned to action in 1950 Farina joined Fangio and Fagioli in the classic 158s and, keeping a cool head and showing tremendous courage, took the first-ever World Championship for drivers. In 1951 he remained with Alfa and won the Belgian GP, but was outshone by Fangio, and he was to find the same problem when he joined Ferrari the following year. With Ascari sweeping all before him, 'Nino' was left in his wake, picking up wins only in the minor GPs at Naples and Monza. He was none too happy to play second fiddle , but was generally unable to match the searing pace set by his team-mate, although he did take a brilliant win in the German GP after losing a wheel. When Ascari moved to Lancia for 1954, Farina sniffed another title chance after a bright start to the season which included a win in the Syracuse GP, but after crashing in the Mille Miglia he recovered only to be involved in a very nasty incident at Monza when his car caught fire, leaving the driver with badly burned legs.

He bravely returned in 1955, needing morphine to complete the Argentine GP, in which he shared two cars, and also took points at Monaco and Spa. His injuries caused him to announce his retirement at the end of the season, but he was soon back in a half-hearted attempt to qualify at Indianapolis, before yet another accident in practice at the Monza Supercortemaggiore race, which left him with a broken collar-bone. Recovered once more, he returned to Indy, but after his car was crashed with fatal results by a young American, Keith Andrews, he lost interest and retired for good. It was ironic that after surviving so many racing accidents, Farina should lose his life in a road crash in 1966.

Farina in classic straight-arm pose, driving the Alfa Romeo 158 to victory in the 1950 British Grand Prix.

GIUSEPPE FARINA

WORLD CHAMPION: 1950

FARINA, Giuseppe (I) b 30/10/1906, Turin – d 30/6/1966, Aiguebelle, nr Chambéry, France

1950 Championship position: WORLD CHAMPION Wins: 3 Pole positions: 2 Fastest laps: 4 Points scored: 30

	Race	Car	No	Entrant	Tyres	Car/Engine	Comment	Q Pos/Entries
1	BRITISH GP	Silverstone	2	Alfa Romeo SpA	P	1.5 s/c Alfa Romeo 158/50 8	FL	1/21
ret	MONACO GP	Monte Carlo	32	Alfa Romeo SpA	P	1.5 s/c Alfa Romeo 158/50 8	multiple accident-lap 1	2/21
1	SWISS GP	Bremgarten	16	Alfa Romeo SpA	P	1.5 s/c Alfa Romeo 158/50 8	FL	2/18
4	BELGIAN GP	Spa	8	Alfa Romeo SpA	P	1.5 s/c Alfa Romeo 158/50 8	long pit stop/FL	1/14
ret	FRENCH GP	Reims	2	Alfa Romeo SpA	P	1.5 s/c Alfa Romeo 158/50 8	fuel pump	2/20
1	ITALIAN GP	Monza	10	Alfa Romeo SpA	P	1.5 s/c Alfa Romeo 158/50 8		3/27

1951 Championship position: 4th Wins: 1 Pole positions: 0 Fastest laps: 1 Points scored: 22

	Race	Car	No	Entrant	Tyres	Car/Engine	Comment	Q Pos/Entries
3	SWISS GP	Bremgarten	22	Alfa Romeo SpA	P	1.5 s/c Alfa Romeo 159A 8		2/21
1	BELGIAN GP	Spa	4	Alfa Romeo SpA	P	1.5 s/c Alfa Romeo 159A 8		2/13
5	FRENCH GP	Reims	2	Alfa Romeo SpA	P	1.5 s/c Alfa Romeo 159A 8	4 laps behind	2/23
ret	BRITISH GP	Silverstone	1	Alfa Romeo SpA	P	1.5 s/c Alfa Romeo 159B 8	slipping clutch/FL	3/20
ret	GERMAN GP	Nürburgring	76	Alfa Romeo SpA	P	1.5 s/c Alfa Romeo 159B 8	overheating engine	4/23
ret	ITALIAN GP	Monza	34	Alfa Romeo SpA	P	1.5 s/c Alfa Romeo 159M 8	engine	2/22
3*	"	"	40	Alfa Romeo SpA	P	1.5 s/c Alfa Romeo 159A 8	* took Bonetto's car/FL/-1 lap	– / –
3	SPANISH GP	Pedralbes	20	Alfa Romeo SpA	P	1.5 s/c Alfa Romeo 159M 8		4/20

1952 Championship position: 2nd Wins: 0 Pole positions: 2 Fastest laps: 0 Points scored: 27

	Race	Car	No	Entrant	Tyres	Car/Engine	Comment	Q Pos/Entries
ret	SWISS GP	Bremgarten	28	Scuderia Ferrari	P	2.0 Ferrari 500 4	magneto	1/21
ret	"	"	32	Scuderia Ferrari	P	2.0 Ferrari 500 4	took Simon's car/magneto	– / –
2	BELGIAN GP	Spa	2	Scuderia Ferrari	P	2.0 Ferrari 500 4		2/22
2	FRENCH GP	Rouen	10	Scuderia Ferrari	P	2.0 Ferrari 500 4	1 lap behind	2/20
6	BRITISH GP	Silverstone	16	Scuderia Ferrari	P	2.0 Ferrari 500 4	pit stop-plugs/3 laps behind	1/32
2	GERMAN GP	Nürburgring	102	Scuderia Ferrari	E	2.0 Ferrari 500 4		2/32
2	DUTCH GP	Zandvoort	4	Scuderia Ferrari	P	2.0 Ferrari 500 4		2/18
4	ITALIAN GP	Monza	10	Scuderia Ferrari	P	2.0 Ferrari 500 4		3/35

1953 Championship position: 3rd Wins: 1 Pole positions: 0 Fastest laps: 0 Points scored: 32

	Race	Car	No	Entrant	Tyres	Car/Engine	Comment	Q Pos/Entries
ret	ARGENTINE GP	Buenos Aires	12	Scuderia Ferrari	P	2.0 Ferrari 500 4	boy killed running into car's path	4/16
2	DUTCH GP	Zandvoort	6	Scuderia Ferrari	P	2.0 Ferrari 500 4		3/20
ret	BELGIAN GP	Spa	12	Scuderia Ferrari	P	2.0 Ferrari 500 4	engine	4/22
5	FRENCH GP	Reims	14	Scuderia Ferrari	P	2.0 Ferrari 500 4		6/25
3	BRITISH GP	Silverstone	6	Scuderia Ferrari	P	2.0 Ferrari 500 4	2 laps behind	5/29
1	GERMAN GP	Nürburgring	2	Scuderia Ferrari	P	2.0 Ferrari 500 4		3/35
2	SWISS GP	Bremgarten	24	Scuderia Ferrari	P	2.0 Ferrari 500 4		3/23
2	ITALIAN GP	Monza	6	Scuderia Ferrari	P	2.0 Ferrari 500 4		3/30

1954 Championship position: 7th= Wins: 0 Pole positions: 1 Fastest laps: 0 Points scored: 6

	Race	Car	No	Entrant	Tyres	Car/Engine	Comment	Q Pos/Entries
2	ARGENTINE GP	Buenos Aires	10	Scuderia Ferrari	P	2.5 Ferrari 625 4		1/18
ret	BELGIAN GP	Spa	4	Scuderia Ferrari	P	2.5 Ferrari 553 4	ignition	3/15
dns	"	"	4	Scuderia Ferrari	P	2.5 Ferrari 625 4	practice only	– / –

1955 Championship position: 5th Wins: 0 Pole positions: 0 Fastest laps: 0 Points scored: 10.33

	Race	Car	No	Entrant	Tyres	Car/Engine	Comment	Q Pos/Entries
3	ARGENTINE GP	Buenos Aires	10	Scuderia Ferrari	E	2.5 Ferrari 625/555 4	Magliolio/Trintignant drove/-2 laps	5/22
2	"	"	12	Scuderia Ferrari	E	2.5 Ferrari 625/555 4	Gonzalez's car/Trintignant also	– / –
4	MONACO GP	Monte Carlo	42	Scuderia Ferrari	E	2.5 Ferrari 625 4	1 lap behind	14/22
3	BELGIAN GP	Spa	2	Scuderia Ferrari	E	2.5 Ferrari 555 4		4/14
dns	ITALIAN GP	Monza	2	Scuderia Ferrari	E	2.5 Lancia D50 V8	withdrawn-tyre trouble in practice	5/22

GP Starts: 33 GP Wins: 5 Pole positions: 5 Fastest laps: 5 Points: 127.33

Farina in the Ferrari T500 at the 1953 German Grand Prix. It was his only World Championship win for the Scuderia, the former Alfa Romeo star being largely overshadowed by the brilliance of his team-mate Alberto Ascari.

RUDI FISCHER

A restaurateur and highly proficient amateur racer and hill-climb expert, Fischer enjoyed great success with his own single-seater Ferraris in the early fifties, run under the Ecurie Espadon banner.

Encouraged by his form in a Simca in 1949, and a sixth place in the Prix de Berne, sharing an HWM with Moss, he acquired a V12 Ferrari for the 1951 season, which he drove to great effect, particularly in non-championship events, finishing second at Bordeaux, third at San Remo and Syracuse and fourth in the Dutch GP. That season he also won F2 events at AVUS, Aix-les-Bains and Angoulême and enjoyed success in hill-climbs.

For 1952 Rudi managed to buy one of the latest T500 Ferraris, and did justice to it by finishing second in the Swiss GP and third in the German GP at World Championship level, while victories at AVUS and in the Eifelrennen were the highlights of a productive programme of lesser races.

It was some surprise when this excellent and most underrated driver quit international racing at the end of the season, although he continued to make occasional appearances, mostly in hill-climbs, into the late fifties.

MIKE FISHER

Fisher raced a variety of machinery including a Lotus 18 and Porsche 906 and 910 sports cars, but was something of mystery when he entered the 1967 Canadian Grand Prix with the ex-Jim Clark Lotus 33 which had been bought that summer by Earl Chiles. In fact this car was the famous 'R11' with which the great Scotsman had utterly dominated the 1965 World Championship. The car was fitted with a 2-litre BRM unit for Fisher, who performed quite respectably both in Canada and in practice for the Mexican GP, where he was unfortunate not to start when a diaphragm 'worth five cents' on his fuel metering unit ruptured.

His racing career was then interrupted by the Vietnam war as Mike entered pilot training in 1968 and flew fighters (including the F-102, F-101, F-4 and F-15) until he was assigned to the Pentagon in 1994.

In 1997 Fisher briefly held the role of CART's executive vice-president of racing, but after only three races of the season quit his role by mutual consent.

FISCHER, Rudi (CH) b 19/5/1912, Stuttgart, Germany – d 30/12/1976, Luzern

	1951	Championship position: Unplaced							
	Race	Circuit	No	Entrant		Tyres	Car/Engine	Comment	Q Pos/Entries
11	SWISS GP	Bremgarten	38	Ecurie Espadon		P	2.5 Ferrari 212 V12	3 laps behind	10/21
6	GERMAN GP	Nürburgring	91	Ecurie Espadon		P	2.5 Ferrari 212 V12	1 lap behind	8/23
dns	ITALIAN GP	Monza	14	Ecurie Espadon		P	2.5 Ferrari 212 V12	practice crash	–/–
	1952	Championship position: 4th=	Wins: 0	Pole positions: 0	Fastest laps: 0	Points scored: 10			
2	SWISS GP	Bremgarten	42	Ecurie Espadon		P	2.0 Ferrari 500 4		5/21
11*	FRENCH GP	Rouen	36	Ecurie Espadon		P	2.0 Ferrari 212 V12	* Hirt took over/13 laps behind	17/20
dns	"	"	34	Ecurie Espadon		P	2.0 Ferrari 500 4	con-rod failure in practice	–/–
13	BRITISH GP	Silverstone	19	Ecurie Espadon		P	2.0 Ferrari 500 4	5 laps behind	15/32
3	GERMAN GP	Nürburgring	117	Ecurie Espadon		P	2.0 Ferrari 500 4		6/32
ret	ITALIAN GP	Monza	18	Ecurie Espadon		P	2.0 Ferrari 500 4	engine	14/35

GP Starts: 7   GP Wins: 0   Pole positions: 0   Fastest laps: 0   Points: 10

FISHER, Mike (US) b 13/3/1943, Hollywood, California

	1967	Championship position: Unplaced							
	Race	Circuit	No	Entrant		Tyres	Car/Engine	Q Pos/Entries	
11	CANADIAN GP	Mosport Park	6	Mike Fisher		F	2.0 Lotus 33-BRM V8	pit stops-electrics/-9 laps	18/19
ret/dns	MEXICAN GP	Mexico City	10	Mike Fisher		F	2.0 Lotus 33-BRM V8	fuel metering unit on grid	(18)/19

GP Starts: 1 (2)   GP Wins: 0   Pole positions: 0   Fastest laps: 0   Points: 0

GIANCARLO FISICHELLA

A quiet and open-minded Italian, Fisichella was surrounded by cars from an early age when he played among the machines in his father's garage workshop. By the time he was ten he was competing in the national Minikart series and he soon progressed through the karting ranks, becoming runner-up in both the World and Intercontinental Championship series, only misfortune denying him the ultimate prize.

Moving up to Italian F3 in 1992, Fisichella spent two seasons learning his trade before switching to the official RC Motorsport team. Giancarlo then simply scorched away from the opposition, winning ten of the twenty rounds of the series and adding the prestigious one-off Monaco and Macau races to his impressive CV.

Obviously a talent to watch, Fisichella was snapped up by Minardi on a long-term contract and given the test driver role for 1995 while he gained experience and polished his racecraft in the ITC with an Alfa Romeo 156. Another full season in the high-tech category was successfully completed in 1996, but of greater significance was his Grand Prix baptism with Minardi. Joining the rather more seasoned Pedro Lamy in the Faenza squad, Fisichella immediately showed the speed to eclipse his team-mate, but the young lions blotted their copybooks by colliding on the opening

lap at Monaco when points were there for the taking. Fisichella was obliged to make way for Giovanni Lavaggi after the British GP, but his stock was high enough for him to be placed in the Jordan team for 1997 alongside rookie Ralf Schumacher. Certainly it was Giancarlo who looked the brighter prospect with some mature and accomplished performances and the fact that his season tailed off somewhat was no barrier to the young Italian's transfer to Benetton after a contract wrangle between Jordan and Flavio Briatore was settled in court.

Fisichella undoubtedly brought a new sense of purpose to Benetton in 1998 and his two second places in Monaco and Montreal showed that here was a potential Grand Prix winner of the future. His second term presented a similar picture: occasional outstanding performances mixed with lacklustre showings when he failed to cut the mustard.

Ironically his long-term contract could be a double-edged sword. Already comfortably ensconced in a multi-million-dollar lifestyle, the pleasant, easy-going Roman has yet to produce the goods on a consistent basis. When everything is right he shows the skills to deliver, but such is the pace of Formula 1 that he could rapidly find himself surplus to requirements if he fails to progress.

FISICHELLA, Giancarlo (I)

	1996	Championship position: Unplaced							
	Race	Circuit	No	Entrant	Tyres	Car/Engine		Comment	Q Pos/Entries
ret	AUSTRALIAN GP	Melbourne	21	Minardi Team	G	3.0 Minardi 195B-Ford EDM V8		clutch	16/22
13	EUROPEAN GP	Nürburgring	21	Minardi Team	G	3.0 Minardi 195B-Ford EDM V8		2 laps behind	18/22
ret	SAN MARINO GP	Imola	21	Minardi Team	G	3.0 Minardi 195B-Ford EDM V8		engine	19/22
ret	MONACO GP	Monte Carlo	21	Minardi Team	G	3.0 Minardi 195B-Ford EDM V8		collision with Lamy on lap 1	18/22
ret	SPANISH GP	Barcelona	21	Minardi Team	G	3.0 Minardi 195B-Ford EDM V8		collision damage at start	19/22
8	CANADIAN GP	Montreal	21	Minardi Team	G	3.0 Minardi 195B-Ford EDM V8		2 laps behind	16/22
ret	FRENCH GP	Magny Cours	21	Minardi Team	G	3.0 Minardi 195B-Ford EDM V8		fuel pressure	18/22
11	BRITISH GP	Silverstone	21	Minardi Team	G	3.0 Minardi 195B-Ford EDM V8		2 laps behind	19/22

1997
Championship position: 8th Wins: 0 Pole positions: 0 Fastest laps: 1 Points scored: 20

ret	AUSTRALIAN GP	Melbourne	12	B & H Total Jordan Peugeot	G	3.0 Jordan 197-Peugeot V10	spun off	14/24
8	BRAZILIAN GP	Interlagos	12	B & H Total Jordan Peugeot	G	3.0 Jordan 197-Peugeot V10		7/22
ret	ARGENTINE GP	Buenos Aires	12	B & H Total Jordan Peugeot	G	3.0 Jordan 197-Peugeot V10	collision with Ralf Schumacher	9/22
4	SAN MARINO GP	Imola	12	B & H Total Jordan Peugeot	G	3.0 Jordan 197-Peugeot V10		6/22
6	MONACO GP	Monte Carlo	12	B & H Total Jordan Peugeot	G	3.0 Jordan 197-Peugeot V10	1 lap behind	4/22
9	SPANISH GP	Barcelona	12	B & H Total Jordan Peugeot	G	3.0 Jordan 197-Peugeot V10	FL	8/22
3	CANADIAN GP	Montreal	12	B & H Total Jordan Peugeot	G	3.0 Jordan 197-Peugeot V10		6/22
9	FRENCH GP	Magny Cours	12	B & H Total Jordan Peugeot	G	3.0 Jordan 197-Peugeot V10	drove spare car/1 lap behind	11/22
7	BRITISH GP	Silverstone	12	B & H Total Jordan Peugeot	G	3.0 Jordan 197-Peugeot V10	1 lap behind	10/22
11	GERMAN GP	Hockenheim	12	B & H Total Jordan Peugeot	G	3.0 Jordan 197-Peugeot V10	puncture then oil cooler/-5 laps	2/22
ret	HUNGARIAN GP	Hungaroring	12	B & H Total Jordan Peugeot	G	3.0 Jordan 197-Peugeot V10	spun off	13/22
2	BELGIAN GP	Spa	12	B & H Total Jordan Peugeot	G	3.0 Jordan 197-Peugeot V10		4/22
4	ITALIAN GP	Monza	12	B & H Total Jordan Peugeot	G	3.0 Jordan 197-Peugeot V10		3/22
4	AUSTRIAN GP	A1-Ring	12	B & H Total Jordan Peugeot	G	3.0 Jordan 197-Peugeot V10		14/22
ret	LUXEMBOURG GP	Nürburgring	12	B & H Total Jordan Peugeot	G	3.0 Jordan 197-Peugeot V10	collision with Ralf Schumacher	4/22
7*	JAPANESE GP	Suzuka	12	B & H Total Jordan Peugeot	G	3.0 Jordan 197-Peugeot V10	*5th place car dsq	9/22
11	EUROPEAN GP	Jerez	12	B & H Total Jordan Peugeot	G	3.0 Jordan 197-Peugeot V10		17/22

1998
Championship position: 9th Wins: 0 Pole positions: 1 Fastest laps: 0 Points scored: 16

ret	AUSTRALIAN GP	Melbourne	5	Mild Seven Benetton Playlife	B	3.0 Benetton B198-Playlife V10	broken rear wing support	7/22
6	BRAZILIAN GP	Interlagos	5	Mild Seven Benetton Playlife	B	3.0 Benetton B198-Playlife V10	1 lap behind	7/22
7	ARGENTINE GP	Buenos Aires	5	Mild Seven Benetton Playlife	B	3.0 Benetton B198-Playlife V10		10/22
ret	SAN MARINO GP	Imola	5	Mild Seven Benetton Playlife	B	3.0 Benetton B198-Playlife V10	spun off into wall	10/22
ret	SPANISH GP	Barcelona	5	Mild Seven Benetton Playlife	B	3.0 Benetton B198-Playlife V10	collision with Irvine	4/22
2	MONACO GP	Monte Carlo	5	Mild Seven Benetton Playlife	B	3.0 Benetton B198-Playlife V10		3/22
2	CANADIAN GP	Montreal	5	Mild Seven Benetton Playlife	B	3.0 Benetton B198-Playlife V10		4/22
9	FRENCH GP	Magny Cours	5	Mild Seven Benetton Playlife	B	3.0 Benetton B198-Playlife V10	1 lap behind	9/22
5	BRITISH GP	Silverstone	5	Mild Seven Benetton Playlife	B	3.0 Benetton B198-Playlife V10	1 lap behind	11/22
ret	AUSTRIAN GP	A1-Ring	5	Mild Seven Benetton Playlife	B	3.0 Benetton B198-Playlife V10	collision with Alesi	1/22
7	GERMAN GP	Hockenheim	5	Mild Seven Benetton Playlife	B	3.0 Benetton B198-Playlife V10		8/22
8	HUNGARIAN GP	Hungaroring	5	Mild Seven Benetton Playlife	B	3.0 Benetton B198-Playlife V10	1 lap behind	8/22
ret	BELGIAN GP	Spa	5	Mild Seven Benetton Playlife	B	3.0 Benetton B198-Playlife V10	ran into back of Nakano	7/22
8	ITALIAN GP	Monza	5	Mild Seven Benetton Playlife	B	3.0 Benetton B198-Playlife V10	1 lap behind	11/22
6	LUXEMBOURG GP	Nürburgring	5	Mild Seven Benetton Playlife	B	3.0 Benetton B198-Playlife V10		4/22
8	JAPANESE GP	Suzuka	5	Mild Seven Benetton Playlife	B	3.0 Benetton B198-Playlife V10		10/22

1999
Championship position: 9th Wins: 0 Pole positions: 0 Fastest laps: 0 Points scored: 13

4	AUSTRALIAN GP	Melbourne	9	Mild Seven Benetton Playlife	B	3.0 Benetton B199-Playlife V10	collided with Trulli-new nose cone	7/22
ret	BRAZILIAN GP	Interlagos	9	Mild Seven Benetton Playlife	B	3.0 Benetton B199-Playlife V10	clutch	5/22
5	SAN MARINO GP	Imola	9	Mild Seven Benetton Playlife	B	3.0 Benetton B199-Playlife V10	1 lap behind	16/22
5	MONACO GP	Monte Carlo	9	Mild Seven Benetton Playlife	B	3.0 Benetton B199-Playlife V10	1 lap behind	9/22
9	SPANISH GP	Barcelona	9	Mild Seven Benetton Playlife	B	3.0 Benetton B199-Playlife V10	lack of grip/1 lap behind	13/22
2	CANADIAN GP	Montreal	9	Mild Seven Benetton Playlife	B	3.0 Benetton B199-Playlife V10		7/22
ret	FRENCH GP	Magny Cours	9	Mild Seven Benetton Playlife	B	3.0 Benetton B199-Playlife V10	spun off	7/22
7	BRITISH GP	Silverstone	9	Mild Seven Benetton Playlife	B	3.0 Benetton B199-Playlife V10		17/22
12/ret	AUSTRIAN GP	A1-Ring	9	Mild Seven Benetton Playlife	B	3.0 Benetton B199-Playlife V10	engine/3 laps behind	12/22
ret	GERMAN GP	Hockenheim	9	Mild Seven Benetton Playlife	B	3.0 Benetton B199-Playlife V10	suspension failure after spin	10/22
ret	HUNGARIAN GP	Hungaroring	9	Mild Seven Benetton Playlife	B	3.0 Benetton B199-Playlife V10	fuel pressure	4/22
11	BELGIAN GP	Spa	9	Mild Seven Benetton Playlife	B	3.0 Benetton B199-Playlife V10	lack of grip	13/22
ret	ITALIAN GP	Monza	9	Mild Seven Benetton Playlife	B	3.0 Benetton B199-Playlife V10	nudged into spin	17/22
ret	EUROPEAN GP	Nürburgring	9	Mild Seven Benetton Playlife	B	3.0 Benetton B199-Playlife V10r	spun off when leading	6/22
11	MALAYSIAN GP	Sepang	9	Mild Seven Benetton Playlife	B	3.0 Benetton B199-Playlife V10	collision damage/4 laps behind	11/22
14/ret	JAPANESE GP	Suzuka	9	Mild Seven Benetton Playlife	B	3.0 Benetton B199-Playlife V10	engine/5 laps behind	14/22

GP Starts: 57 GP Wins: 0 Pole positions: 1 Fastest laps: 1 Points: 49

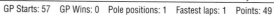

Giancarlo took the Benetton to second place in the 1999 Canadian Grand Prix.

JOHN FITCH

With just two Grand Prix races recorded against his name, the uninitiated may be given the false impression that John Fitch was just another insignificant run-of-the-mill driver – far from it.

Born into a wealthy family, and with a motoring background courtesy of his step-father, Fitch served as a fighter pilot during World War II, and was held as a POW after being shot down. In poor physical condition upon his release, he did not turn to motor racing until 1949, but was soon a major name in SCCA circles. In March 1951, on his first racing trip overseas, he won the Peron Grand Prix, a sports car race in Buenos Aires, driving an Allard-Cadillac. This victory brought him to the attention of millionaire racer and entrant Briggs Cunningham, who took him into his sports car team, which was attempting to win Le Mans and other long-distance events. John won the Sebring 12 Hours, and finished third in the Cunningham at Le Mans in 1953, a season which also saw him dip his toe into single-seater racing with HWM in the Italian GP and finish fourth at Aix-les-Bains in a Cooper-Bristol, attempt to qualify for Indianapolis, and take part in the Monte Carlo and Alpine Rallies . . .

Having impressed Neubauer during a test in a 300SL Mercedes in 1952, Fitch finally got the call from the great man and found himself in the factory sports car team for 1955, and reserve driver (not used) at a couple of Grands Prix. Unfortunately this was the year of the Le Mans disaster, and Fitch's co-driver 'Levegh' was a central figure in the tragedy. John did, however, have the satisfaction of sharing the winning Mercedes with Moss at Dundrod later in the year before the Stuttgart team withdrew from racing.

Fitch then returned to the States, initially to help Chevrolet's sports car effort, which limited his racing somewhat, but nothing was allowed to get in the way of his annual pilgrimage to Sebring which lasted until 1964 – by which time he was fully involved in the management of the Lime Rock circuit, which was used for both racing and the testing of road cars.

FITCH, John (USA) b 4/8/1917, Indianapolis, Indiana

	1953	Championship position: Unplaced							
	Race	Circuit	No	Entrant	Tyres	Car/Engine		Comment	Q Pos/Entries
ret	ITALIAN GP	Monza	18	HW Motors Ltd	D	2.0 HWM-Alta 4		engine	26/30
	1955	Championship position: Unplaced							
9	ITALIAN GP	Monza	40	Stirling Moss Ltd	D	2.5 Maserati 250F 6		4 laps behind	20/22

GP Starts: 2   GP Wins: 0   Pole positions: 0   Fastest laps: 0   Points: 0

FITTIPALDI, Christian (BR) b 18/1/1971, São Paulo

	1992	Championship position: 17th=		Wins: 0	Pole positions: 0	Fastest laps: 0	Points scored: 1		
	Race	Circuit	No	Entrant	Tyres	Car/Engine		Comment	Q Pos/Entries
ret	SOUTH AFRICAN GP	Kyalami	23	Minardi Team	G	3.5 Minardi M191B-Lamborghini V12		electrics	20/30
ret	MEXICAN GP	Mexico City	23	Minardi Team	G	3.5 Minardi M191B-Lamborghini V12		spun off	17/30
ret	BRAZILIAN GP	Interlagos	23	Minardi Team	G	3.5 Minardi M191B-Lamborghini V12		gearbox	20/31
11	SPANISH GP	Barcelona	23	Minardi Team	G	3.5 Minardi M191B-Lamborghini V12		4 laps behind	22/32
ret	SAN MARINO GP	Imola	23	Minardi Team	G	3.5 Minardi M192-Lamborghini V12		transmission	25/32
8	MONACO GP	Monte Carlo	23	Minardi Team	G	3.5 Minardi M192-Lamborghini V12		1 lap behind	17/32
13/ret	CANADIAN GP	Montreal	23	Minardi Team	G	3.5 Minardi M192-Lamborghini V12		gearbox oil fire 4 laps behind	25/32
dnq	FRENCH GP	Magny Cours	23	Minardi Team	G	3.5 Minardi M192-Lamborghini V12		practice crash-injured back	28/30
dnq	BELGIAN GP	Spa	23	Minardi Team	G	3.5 Minardi M192-Lamborghini V12			27/30
dnq	ITALIAN GP	Monza	23	Minardi Team	G	3.5 Minardi M192-Lamborghini V12			27/28
12	PORTUGUESE GP	Estoril	23	Minardi Team	G	3.5 Minardi M192-Lamborghini V12		3 laps behind	26/26
6	JAPANESE GP	Suzuka	23	Minardi Team	G	3.5 Minardi M192-Lamborghini V12		1 lap behind	12/26
9	AUSTRALIAN GP	Adelaide	23	Minardi Team	G	3.5 Minardi M192-Lamborghini V12		2 laps behind	17/26
	1993	Championship position: 13th=		Wins: 0	Pole positions: 0	Fastest laps: 0	Points scored: 5		
4	SOUTH AFRICAN GP	Kyalami	23	Minardi Team	G	3.5 Minardi M193-Ford HB V8		1 lap behind	13/26
ret	BRAZILIAN GP	Interlagos	23	Minardi Team	G	3.5 Minardi M193-Ford HB V8		spun off in rainstorm	20/26
7	EUROPEAN GP	Donington	23	Minardi Team	G	3.5 Minardi M193-Ford HB V8		3 laps behind	16/26
ret	SAN MARINO GP	Imola	23	Minardi Team	G	3.5 Minardi M193-Ford HB V8		damaged steering	23/26
8	SPANISH GP	Barcelona	23	Minardi Team	G	3.5 Minardi M193-Ford HB V8		2 laps behind	20/26
5	MONACO GP	Monte Carlo	23	Minardi Team	G	3.5 Minardi M193-Ford HB V8		2 laps behind	17/26
9	CANADIAN GP	Montreal	23	Minardi Team	G	3.5 Minardi M193-Ford HB V8		gearbox trouble/2 laps behind	17/26
8	FRENCH GP	Magny Cours	23	Minardi Team	G	3.5 Minardi M193-Ford HB V8		ran without stop/1 lap behind	23/26
12/ret	BRITISH GP	Silverstone	23	Minardi Team	G	3.5 Minardi M193-Ford HB V8		gearbox/2 laps behind	19/26
11	GERMAN GP	Hockenheim	23	Minardi Team	G	3.5 Minardi M193-Ford HB V8		ran without stop/1 lap behind	20/26
ret	HUNGARIAN GP	Hungaroring	23	Minardi Team	G	3.5 Minardi M193-Ford HB V8		collision-Alesi-suspension	14/26
ret	BELGIAN GP	Spa	23	Minardi Team	G	3.5 Minardi M193-Ford HB V8		accident	22/25
8	ITALIAN GP	Monza	23	Minardi Team	G	3.5 Minardi M193-Ford HB V8		ran into Martini at finish/-2 laps	24/26
9	PORTUGUESE GP	Estoril	23	Minardi Team	G	3.5 Minardi M193-Ford HB V8		ran without stop/2 laps behind	24/26

	1994	Championship position: 14th		Wins: 0	Pole positions: 0	Fastest laps: 0	Points scored: 6		
ret	BRAZILIAN GP	Interlagos	9	Footwork Ford	G	3.5 Footwork FA15-Ford HB V8		gearbox	11/28
4	PACIFIC GP	T.I. Circuit	9	Footwork Ford	G	3.5 Footwork FA15-Ford HB V8		1 lap behind	9/28
13/ret	SAN MARINO GP	Imola	9	Footwork Ford	G	3.5 Footwork FA15-Ford HB V8		brakes/4 laps behind	16/28
ret	MONACO GP	Monte Carlo	9	Footwork Ford	G	3.5 Footwork FA15-Ford HB V8		gearbox	6/24
ret	SPANISH GP	Barcelona	9	Footwork Ford	G	3.5 Footwork FA15-Ford HB V8		engine	21/27
dsq	CANADIAN GP	Montreal	9	Footwork Ford	G	3.5 Footwork FA15-Ford HB V8		6th on road-car underweight	16/27
8	FRENCH GP	Magny Cours	9	Footwork Ford	G	3.5 Footwork FA15-Ford HB V8			18/28
9*	BRITISH GP	Silverstone	9	Footwork Ford	G	3.5 Footwork FA15-Ford HB V8		*2nd place car dsq/-2 laps	20/28
4	GERMAN GP	Hockenheim	9	Footwork Ford	G	3.5 Footwork FA15-Ford HB V8			17/28
14/ret	HUNGARIAN GP	Hungaroring	9	Footwork Ford	G	3.5 Footwork FA15-Ford HB V8		8 laps behind/gearbox	16/28
ret	BELGIAN GP	Spa	9	Footwork Ford	G	3.5 Footwork FA15-Ford HB V8		engine	24/28
ret	ITALIAN GP	Monza	9	Footwork Ford	G	3.5 Footwork FA15-Ford HB V8		engine	19/28
8	PORTUGUESE GP	Estoril	9	Footwork Ford	G	3.5 Footwork FA15-Ford HB V8		1 lap behind	11/28
17	EUROPEAN GP	Jerez	9	Footwork Ford	G	3.5 Footwork FA15-Ford HB V8		long p stop-nose/3-laps	19/28
8	JAPANESE GP	Suzuka	9	Footwork Ford	G	3.5 Footwork FA15-Ford HB V8		1 lap behind	18/28
8	AUSTRALIAN GP	Adelaide	9	Footwork Ford	G	3.5 Footwork FA15-Ford HB V8		1 lap behind	19/28

GP Starts: 40   GP Wins: 0   Pole positions: 0   Fastest laps: 0   Points: 12

CHRISTIAN FITTIPALDI

With excellent backing from his Brazilian sponsors, and the guidance of his father Wilson, himself a former Grand Prix driver, Christian earned himself the right to become a Formula 1 driver on talent alone. Sadly, his Grand Prix career was spent driving mediocre machinery, and he was unable to impress sufficiently to attract an offer from a front-line team and decided to pursue a career in CART.

With a single season in South American F3 behind him, he came to Britain to race in the 1990 F3 championship. Taking the number two seat to Häkkinen in the crack West Surrey Racing team, Fittipaldi finished fourth in the final standings with just one win at Donington. Moving up to F3000 for 1991 with Pacific Racing, young Christian was certainly fortunate to be in a Reynard chassis, but he held to his conviction that consistency would count and, when he had to, could show the pack a clean pair of heels, as he proved at Jerez and Nogaro. The championship was his, and he thus became the third Grand Prix driver to emerge from this remarkable family.

His first season with Minardi was interrupted when a practice crash at Magny Cours inflicted back injuries that put him out for a spell, but after a shaky return he bounced back in Japan to score his first championship point. Continuing with the underfinanced Minardi team in 1993, Fittipaldi started well but, with the car less and less competitive as the season progressed, the young Brazilian was stood down for the final two races to make room for the well-financed Gounon. Meanwhile Christian, his sponsors and advisers were busy trying to arrange a move to a bigger team for 1994. He moved a further rung up the Grand Prix ladder with Footwork, but was disappointed not to have made it into a better-funded team with more chance of success. The season started brightly and Christian was superb at Monaco with the neat Ford HB-engined car, qualifying sixth and running in fourth place, but things went downhill when the team became bogged down trying to implement the mid-season rule changes without the necessary resources.

Frustrated by his lack of progress and impatient for success, Fittipaldi abandoned his Formula 1 career to join the Indy Car circuit in 1995. His season with Derrick Walker was naturally a learning one, and the high point was undoubtedly lasting the distance to claim second place in the Indianapolis 500. For 1996 Christian obtained a seat alongside Michael Andretti at Newman-Haas, and at last he had the opportunity to shine, looking particularly impressive in the wet at Detroit and Portland. His prospects were bright for 1997, but only two races into the season Christian suffered a badly broken leg in an accident at Surfers Paradise and did extremely well upon his return to pick up his previous pace.

If Fittipaldi, who fitted comfortably into the Newman-Haas camp, thought a breakthrough was imminent he was to be disappointed in 1998, when minor problems often blunted the team's challenge. Christian has shown in the past that patience is a virtue and the 1999 season saw a much more complete driver. Not only did he win a CART race (at the 71st attempt, at Road America), but he looked a possible PPG Cup champion, having finished among the top ten in each of the first seven races. Unfortunately he suffered a nasty accident in testing and was forced to sit on the sidelines for five races, which scuppered his chances.

Now just as at home on the oval tracks as on road courses, Christian, not yet thirty years of age, has the ammunition to go gunning for glory in the new millennium.

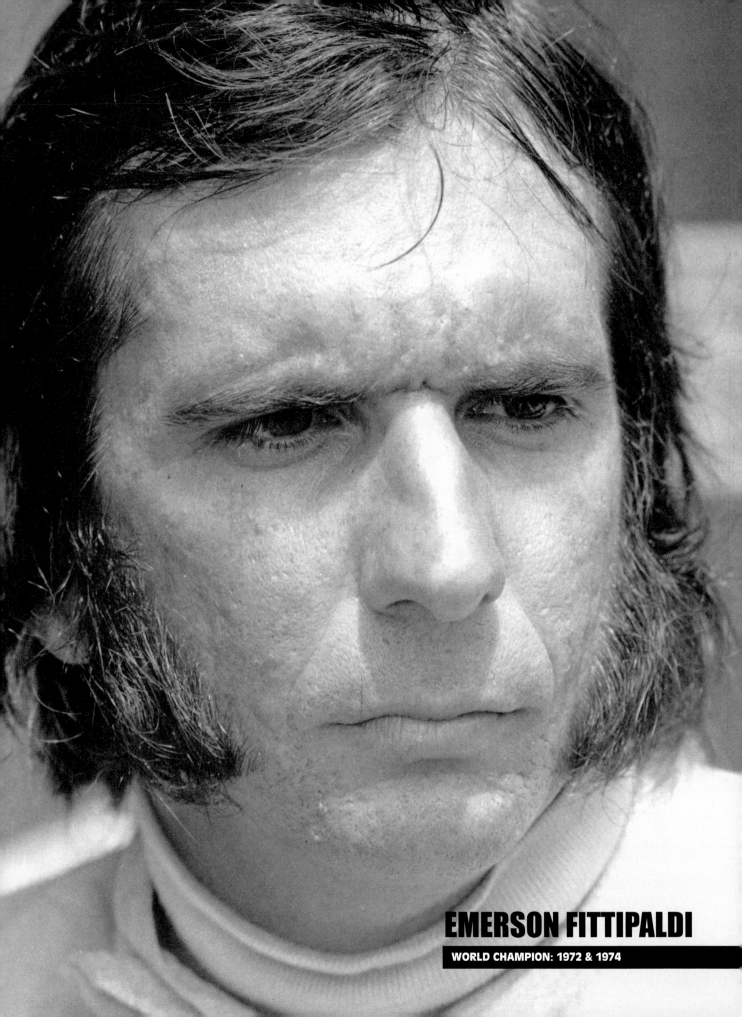

EMERSON FITTIPALDI

WORLD CHAMPION: 1972 & 1974

EMERSON FITTIPALDI

Crowned the youngest-ever World Champion at 25 in 1972, Emerson Fittipaldi was one of the outstanding drivers of the seventies, but a spectacularly ill-judged career move at the end of 1975 turned him into a Grand Prix racing also-ran, before he came back from retirement to forge a second magnificent career and conquer the world of Indy Car racing.

Success in Brazil led Fittipaldi to turn his sights to Europe. The sale of his Formula Vee car financed a three-month trip to England in 1969 and he quickly made his mark in a Formula Ford Merlyn. Emerson's talent was obvious and a move up to F3 in a Jim Russell Lotus 59 paid immediate dividends, the Brazilian winning a string of races, which gave him the confidence to move into Formula 2 with Mike Warner in 1970. An outright win eluded him, but he finished virtually every race in the top six, and Colin Chapman soon had his signature on a Lotus F1 contract.

Fittipaldi was eased onto the Grand Prix scene with a Lotus 49C, but tragedy soon befell the team with the death of Jochen Rindt at Monza. Emerson was suddenly thrust into the spotlight upon the team's return at Watkins Glen, and he provided a great morale booster for Chapman by winning the race, albeit only after Rodriguez hit trouble late on. For 1971 Fittipaldi was given the number one seat, but lost momentum after a mid-season road accident. Nevertheless he did remarkably well in his first full Formula 1 season and, with the Lotus 72 finely honed, he became the man to beat the following year. Victories in the Race of Champions and International Trophy provided the springboard for a mid-season burst of scintillating form which saw him claim the World Championship.

Joined in the team by Ronnie Peterson for 1973, Emerson was quick straight out of the blocks with three wins in the first six Grands Prix, and a second title looked a formality, but his year then turned sour, particularly after a practice crash at Zandvoort left him with a niggling ankle injury. By the end of the season he was somewhat overshadowed by Peterson and accepted a big-money offer from McLaren for 1974. It proved to be a wise decision, his smooth, unruffled driving and great tactical acumen bringing him his second World Championship in an evenly contested season. The following year yielded just one Grand Prix win at Silverstone, Emerson keeping his head in a rainstorm while those all around were spinning out. In the end Lauda's Ferrari had the legs of his McLaren, and he had to settle for second place in the championship.

Then came the bombshell. He was to join the Copersucar-Fittipaldi team established by his brother Wilson for 1976 to drive the outfit's well-funded but uncompetitive Brazilian-built challenger. From Olympian heights, Emerson soon found himself in a valley of despair as the project struggled on, occasionally

On his way to the championship for the first time. Emerson in the JPS Lotus winning the 1972 Spanish Grand Prix, at Jarama. It was one of five victories that year.

breaking into the top six but achieving little else. A magnificent race at Rio in 1978, when he finished a brilliant second to Reutemann's Ferrari, and an excellent third place at Long Beach in 1980 were but isolated reminders of former glories. At the end of that season Emerson switched from driving to management duties but the Fittipaldi team was finally forced to close its doors at the end of 1982.

Returning home to Brazil, he concentrated on the family orange-growing and automobile accessory businesses, not missing racing in the slightest. A few races in super karts for fun in 1983 led to an invitation to take part in an IMSA race at Miami early in 1984 and he enjoyed himself so much that he was soon tempted to accept an Indy Car drive at Long Beach, finishing a remarkable fifth. The wheel-to-wheel racing ignited Emerson's lost passion for driving and he was soon to get a big break, joining the Patrick Racing team to replace the severely injured Chip Ganassi. With Fittipaldi as the focal point, the team steadily grew in stature, ultimate success arriving in 1989 when he not only won the PPG Indy Car World Series title but also took a famous last-gasp win in the Indy 500 after a coming-together with Al Unser Jnr on the penultimate lap.

'Emmo' joined Roger Penske's three-car team in 1990, and was one of the undoubted top guns in the Indy Car championship. In 1993 he won the Indy 500 for the second time with a beautifully judged performance and finished second to Nigel Mansell in the points standings. Joined by Al Unser Jnr in an all-conquering three-car Penske squad for 1994, Fittipaldi proved that he still had plenty of racing mileage left. Despite recording only one win (at Phoenix), he was runner-up to the utterly dominant Unser in the PPG Cup ranking. His major disappointment came at Indianapolis where he threw the car into the wall with the race all but won. After this season of plenty for Team Penske 1995 came as a shock to the system, with Emmo and Unser struggling with the recalcitrant PC24. The nadir was the pair's failure to qualify at Indy, but there were some high spots too and Fittipaldi took a well-judged win at Nazareth.

Although the inevitable rumours of his retirement abounded, Fittipaldi had no intention of giving up competition and he was back in 1996, running a Penske under the guidance of Carl Hogan. The Brazilian put in some spirited performances, but his season – and ultimately his career – came to an abrupt end when he crashed heavily in the Marlboro 500 at Michigan.

Suffering from a crushed vertebra in his neck, the 49-year-old spent five hours in surgery and was fortunate not to have sustained permanent injury. While recovering, Emmo still hankered after a return to action, but another accident – a light aircraft crash in his native Brazil – in 1997 left him with serious back injuries. Wisely all thoughts of racing again were abandoned, but he is still a regular on the CART scene, guiding the career of the highly promising Brazilian Helio Castro-Neves.

FITTIPALDI, Emerson (BR) b 12/12/1946, São Paulo

1970 — Championship position: 10th   Wins: 1   Pole positions: 0   Fastest laps: 0   Points scored: 12

	Race	Circuit	No	Entrant	Tyres	Car/Engine	Comment	Q Pos/Entries
8	BRITISH GP	Brands Hatch	28	Gold Leaf Team Lotus	F	3.0 Lotus 49C-Cosworth V8	2 laps behind	22/25
4	GERMAN GP	Hockenheim	17	Gold Leaf Team Lotus	F	3.0 Lotus 49C-Cosworth V8		13/25
15	AUSTRIAN GP	Österreichring	8	Gold Leaf Team Lotus	F	3.0 Lotus 49C-Cosworth V8	pit stop-fuel/5 laps behind	15/24
dns	ITALIAN GP	Monza	26	Gold Leaf Team Lotus	F	3.0 Lotus 72C-Cosworth V8	withdrawn after Rindt's accident	25/27
1	US GP	Watkins Glen	24	Gold Leaf Team Lotus	F	3.0 Lotus 72C-Cosworth V8		3/27
ret	MEXICAN GP	Mexico City	24	Gold Leaf Team Lotus	F	3.0 Lotus 72C-Cosworth V8	engine	18/18

1971 — Championship position: 6th   Wins: 0   Pole positions: 0   Fastest laps: 0   Points scored: 16

	Race	Circuit	No	Entrant	Tyres	Car/Engine	Comment	Q Pos/Entries
ret	SOUTH AFRICAN GP	Kyalami	2	Gold Leaf Team Lotus	F	3.0 Lotus 72C-Cosworth V8	engine	=5/25
ret	SPANISH GP	Montjuich Park	2	Gold Leaf Team Lotus	F	3.0 Lotus 72C-Cosworth V8	rear suspension	14/22
5	MONACO GP	Monte Carlo	1	Gold Leaf Team Lotus	F	3.0 Lotus 72D-Cosworth V8	1 lap behind	17/23
3	FRENCH GP	Paul Ricard	1	Gold Leaf Team Lotus	F	3.0 Lotus 72D-Cosworth V8		17/24
3	BRITISH GP	Silverstone	1	Gold Leaf Team Lotus	F	3.0 Lotus 72D-Cosworth V8		3/24
ret	GERMAN GP	Nürburgring	8	Gold Leaf Team Lotus	F	3.0 Lotus 72D-Cosworth V8	oil leak	8/23
2	AUSTRIAN GP	Österreichring	2	Gold Leaf Team Lotus	F	3.0 Lotus 72D-Cosworth V8		5/22
8	ITALIAN GP	Monza	5	World Wide Racing	F	Turbine Lotus 56B-Pratt & Whitney	1 lap behind	18/24
7	CANADIAN GP	Mosport Park	2	Gold Leaf Team Lotus	F	3.0 Lotus 72D-Cosworth V8	2 laps behind	=4/27
nc	US GP	Watkins Glen	2	Gold Leaf Team Lotus	F	3.0 Lotus 72D-Cosworth V8	pit stops-throttle/-10 laps	2/32

1972 — Championship position: WORLD CHAMPION   Wins: 5   Pole positions: 3   Fastest laps: 0   Points scored: 61

	Race	Circuit	No	Entrant	Tyres	Car/Engine	Comment	Q Pos/Entries
ret	ARGENTINE GP	Buenos Aires	11	John Player Team Lotus	F	3.0 Lotus 72D-Cosworth V8	broken rear suspension	=5/22
2	SOUTH AFRICAN GP	Kyalami	8	John Player Team Lotus	F	3.0 Lotus 72D-Cosworth V8		=3/27
1	SPANISH GP	Jarama	5	John Player Team Lotus	F	3.0 Lotus 72D-Cosworth V8		3/26
3	MONACO GP	Monte Carlo	5	John Player Team Lotus	F	3.0 Lotus 72D-Cosworth V8	1 lap behind	1/25
1	BELGIAN GP	Nivelles	32	John Player Team Lotus	F	3.0 Lotus 72D-Cosworth V8		1/26
2	FRENCH GP	Clermont Ferrand	1	John Player Team Lotus	F	3.0 Lotus 72D-Cosworth V8		=7/29
1	BRITISH GP	Brands Hatch	8	John Player Team Lotus	F	3.0 Lotus 72D-Cosworth V8		2/27
ret	GERMAN GP	Nürburgring	2	John Player Team Lotus	F	3.0 Lotus 72D-Cosworth V8	gearbox casing-oil fire	3/27
1	AUSTRIAN GP	Österreichring	31	John Player Team Lotus	F	3.0 Lotus 72D-Cosworth V8		1/26
1	ITALIAN GP	Monza	6	World Wide Racing	F	3.0 Lotus 72D-Cosworth V8		6/27
11	CANADIAN GP	Mosport Park	5	John Player Team Lotus	F	3.0 Lotus 72D-Cosworth V8	pit stop-nose cone/gearbox/-2 laps	=4/25
ret	US GP	Watkins Glen	10	John Player Team Lotus	F	3.0 Lotus 72D-Cosworth V8	shock absorber	9/32

1973 — Championship position: 2nd   Wins: 3   Pole positions: 1   Fastest laps: 5 (1 shared)   Points scored: 55

	Race	Circuit	No	Entrant	Tyres	Car/Engine	Comment	Q Pos/Entries
1	ARGENTINE GP	Buenos Aires	2	John Player Team Lotus	G	3.0 Lotus 72D-Cosworth V8	FL	2/19
1	BRAZILIAN GP	Interlagos	1	John Player Team Lotus	G	3.0 Lotus 72D-Cosworth V8	FL (shared with Hulme)	2/20
3	SOUTH AFRICAN GP	Kyalami	1	John Player Team Lotus	G	3.0 Lotus 72D-Cosworth V8	FL	2/25
1	SPANISH GP	Montjuich Park	1	John Player Team Lotus	G	3.0 Lotus 72E-Cosworth V8		=7/22
3	BELGIAN GP	Zolder	1	John Player Team Lotus	G	3.0 Lotus 72E-Cosworth V8		9/23
2	MONACO GP	Monte Carlo	1	John Player Team Lotus	G	3.0 Lotus 72E-Cosworth V8	FL	5/26
12/ret	SWEDISH GP	Anderstorp	1	John Player Team Lotus	G	3.0 Lotus 72E-Cosworth V8	transmission/4 laps behind	4/22

Fittipaldi moved to McLaren in 1974 and took his second World Championship at the wheel of the M23 after a close-fought battle with the Ferraris of Lauda and Regazzoni.

	Race	Circuit	No	Team	G	Engine	Notes	Grid
ret	FRENCH GP	Paul Ricard	1	John Player Team Lotus	G	3.0 Lotus 72E-Cosworth V8	*accident with Scheckter*	3/25
ret	BRITISH GP	Silverstone	1	John Player Team Lotus	G	3.0 Lotus 72E-Cosworth V8	*transmission-c.v. joint*	=4/29
ret	DUTCH GP	Zandvoort	1	John Player Team Lotus	G	3.0 Lotus 72E-Cosworth V8	*in pain after practice accident*	16/24
6	GERMAN GP	Nürburgring	1	John Player Team Lotus	G	3.0 Lotus 72E-Cosworth V8		14/23
11/ret	AUSTRIAN GP	Österreichring	1	John Player Team Lotus	G	3.0 Lotus 72E-Cosworth V8	*fuel pipe/6 laps behind*	1/25
2	ITALIAN GP	Monza	1	John Player Team Lotus	G	3.0 Lotus 72E-Cosworth V8		4/25
2	CANADIAN GP	Mosport Park	1	John Player Team Lotus	G	3.0 Lotus 72E-Cosworth V8	*FL*	5/26
6	US GP	Watkins Glen	1	John Player Team Lotus	G	3.0 Lotus 72E-Cosworth V8		3/28

1974   Championship position: WORLD CHAMPION   Wins: 3   Pole positions: 2   Fastest laps: 0   Points scored: 55

	Race	Circuit	No	Team	G	Engine	Notes	Grid
10	ARGENTINE GP	Buenos Aires	5	Marlboro Team Texaco	G	3.0 McLaren M23-Cosworth V8	*knocked off ignition/-2 laps*	3/26
1	BRAZILIAN GP	Interlagos	5	Marlboro Team Texaco	G	3.0 McLaren M23-Cosworth V8		1/25
7	SOUTH AFRICAN GP	Kyalami	5	Marlboro Team Texaco	G	3.0 McLaren M23-Cosworth V8		5/27
3	SPANISH GP	Jarama	5	Marlboro Team Texaco	G	3.0 McLaren M23-Cosworth V8		4/28
1	BELGIAN GP	Nivelles	5	Marlboro Team Texaco	G	3.0 McLaren M23-Cosworth V8	*1 lap behind*	4/32
5	MONACO GP	Monte Carlo	5	Marlboro Team Texaco	G	3.0 McLaren M23-Cosworth V8		=12/28
4	SWEDISH GP	Anderstorp	5	Marlboro Team Texaco	G	3.0 McLaren M23-Cosworth V8	*1 lap behind*	9/28
3	DUTCH GP	Zandvoort	5	Marlboro Team Texaco	G	3.0 McLaren M23-Cosworth V8		3/27
ret	FRENCH GP	Dijon	5	Marlboro Team Texaco	G	3.0 McLaren M23-Cosworth V8	*engine*	5/30
2	BRITISH GP	Brands Hatch	5	Marlboro Team Texaco	G	3.0 McLaren M23-Cosworth V8		8/34
ret	GERMAN GP	Nürburgring	5	Marlboro Team Texaco	G	3.0 McLaren M23-Cosworth V8	*accident damage/collision-Hulme*	3/32
ret	AUSTRIAN GP	Österreichring	5	Marlboro Team Texaco	G	3.0 McLaren M23-Cosworth V8	*engine*	3/31
2	ITALIAN GP	Monza	5	Marlboro Team Texaco	G	3.0 McLaren M23-Cosworth V8		6/31
1	CANADIAN GP	Mosport Park	5	Marlboro Team Texaco	G	3.0 McLaren M23-Cosworth V8		1/30
4	US GP	Watkins Glen	5	Marlboro Team Texaco	G	3.0 McLaren M23-Cosworth V8		8/30

1975   Championship position: 2nd   Wins: 2   Pole positions: 0   Fastest laps: 1   Points scored: 45

	Race	Circuit	No	Team	G	Engine	Notes	Grid
1	ARGENTINE GP	Buenos Aires	1	Marlboro Team Texaco	G	3.0 McLaren M23-Cosworth V8		5/23
2	BRAZILIAN GP	Interlagos	1	Marlboro Team Texaco	G	3.0 McLaren M23-Cosworth V8		2/23
nc	SOUTH AFRICAN GP	Kyalami	1	Marlboro Team Texaco	G	3.0 McLaren M23-Cosworth V8	*pit stop-misfire/-13 laps*	11/28
dns	SPANISH GP	Montjuich Park	1	Marlboro Team Texaco	G	3.0 McLaren M23-Cosworth V8	*protest at poor safety of track*	(26)/26
2	MONACO GP	Monte Carlo	1	Marlboro Team Texaco	G	3.0 McLaren M23-Cosworth V8		9/26
7	BELGIAN GP	Zolder	1	Marlboro Team Texaco	G	3.0 McLaren M23-Cosworth V8	*brake problems/1 lap behind*	8/24
8	SWEDISH GP	Anderstorp	1	Marlboro Team Texaco	G	3.0 McLaren M23-Cosworth V8	*handling problems/-1 lap*	11/26
ret	DUTCH GP	Zandvoort	1	Marlboro Team Texaco	G	3.0 McLaren M23-Cosworth V8	*engine*	6/25
4	FRENCH GP	Paul Ricard	1	Marlboro Team Texaco	G	3.0 McLaren M23-Cosworth V8		10/26
1	BRITISH GP	Silverstone	1	Marlboro Team Texaco	G	3.0 McLaren M23-Cosworth V8		7/28
ret	GERMAN GP	Nürburgring	1	Marlboro Team Texaco	G	3.0 McLaren M23-Cosworth V8	*puncture suspension damage*	=8/26
9	AUSTRIAN GP	Österreichring	1	Marlboro Team Texaco	G	3.0 McLaren M23-Cosworth V8	*1 lap behind*	3/30
2	ITALIAN GP	Monza	1	Marlboro Team Texaco	G	3.0 McLaren M23-Cosworth V8		3/28
2	US GP	Watkins Glen	1	Marlboro Team Texaco	G	3.0 McLaren M23-Cosworth V8	*FL*	2/24

1976   Championship position: 16th=   Wins: 0   Pole positions: 0   Fastest laps: 0   Points scored: 3

	Race	Circuit	No	Team	G	Engine	Notes	Grid
13	BRAZILIAN GP	Interlagos	30	Copersucar-Fittipaldi	G	3.0 Fittipaldi FD04-Cosworth V8	*misfire/3 laps behind*	5/22
17/ret	SOUTH AFRICAN GP	Kyalami	30	Copersucar-Fittipaldi	G	3.0 Fittipaldi FD04-Cosworth V8	*engine/4 laps behind*	21/25
6	US GP WEST	Long Beach	30	Copersucar-Fittipaldi	G	3.0 Fittipaldi FD04-Cosworth V8	*1 lap behind*	16/27
ret	SPANISH GP	Jarama	30	Copersucar-Fittipaldi	G	3.0 Fittipaldi FD04-Cosworth V8	*gear linkage*	19/30
dnq	BELGIAN GP	Zolder	30	Copersucar-Fittipaldi	G	3.0 Fittipaldi FD04-Cosworth V8		27/29
6	MONACO GP	Monte Carlo	30	Copersucar-Fittipaldi	G	3.0 Fittipaldi FD04-Cosworth V8	*1 lap behind*	7/25
ret	SWEDISH GP	Anderstorp	30	Copersucar-Fittipaldi	G	3.0 Fittipaldi FD04-Cosworth V8	*handling*	21/27
ret	FRENCH GP	Paul Ricard	30	Copersucar-Fittipaldi	G	3.0 Fittipaldi FD04-Cosworth V8	*engine/oil pressure*	21/30
6*	BRITISH GP	Brands Hatch	30	Copersucar-Fittipaldi	G	3.0 Fittipaldi FD04-Cosworth V8	** 1st place car dsq/-2 laps*	21/30
13	GERMAN GP	Nürburgring	30	Copersucar-Fittipaldi	G	3.0 Fittipaldi FD04-Cosworth V8		20/28
ret	AUSTRIAN GP	Österreichring	30	Copersucar-Fittipaldi	G	3.0 Fittipaldi FD04-Cosworth V8	*collision with Brambilla*	17/25
ret	DUTCH GP	Zandvoort	30	Copersucar-Fittipaldi	G	3.0 Fittipaldi FD04-Cosworth V8	*electrics*	17/27
15	ITALIAN GP	Monza	30	Copersucar-Fittipaldi	G	3.0 Fittipaldi FD04-Cosworth V8	*2 laps behind*	20/29
ret	CANADIAN GP	Mosport Park	30	Copersucar-Fittipaldi	G	3.0 Fittipaldi FD04-Cosworth V8	*exhaust and rear wing bracket*	17/27
9	US GP EAST	Watkins Glen	30	Copersucar-Fittipaldi	G	3.0 Fittipaldi FD04-Cosworth V8	*2 laps behind*	15/27
ret	JAPANESE GP	Mount Fuji	30	Copersucar-Fittipaldi	G	3.0 Fittipaldi FD04-Cosworth V8	*withdrew-bad weather conditions*	23/27

1977   Championship position: 12th   Wins: 0   Pole positions: 0   Fastest laps: 0   Points scored: 11

	Race	Circuit	No	Team	G	Engine	Notes	Grid
4	ARGENTINE GP	Buenos Aires	28	Copersucar-Fittipaldi	G	3.0 Fittipaldi FD04-Cosworth V8		16/21
4	BRAZILIAN GP	Interlagos	28	Copersucar-Fittipaldi	G	3.0 Fittipaldi FD04-Cosworth V8		16/22
10	SOUTH AFRICAN GP	Kyalami	28	Copersucar-Fittipaldi	G	3.0 Fittipaldi FD04-Cosworth V8	*1 lap behind*	9/23
5	US GP WEST	Long Beach	28	Copersucar-Fittipaldi	G	3.0 Fittipaldi FD04-Cosworth V8		7/22
14	SPANISH GP	Jarama	28	Copersucar-Fittipaldi	G	3.0 Fittipaldi FD04-Cosworth V8	*vibration/overheating/-5 laps*	19/31
ret	MONACO GP	Monte Carlo	28	Copersucar-Fittipaldi	G	3.0 Fittipaldi FD04-Cosworth V8	*engine*	18/26
ret	BELGIAN GP	Zolder	28	Copersucar-Fittipaldi	G	3.0 Fittipaldi F5-Cosworth V8	*water in electrics*	16/32
18	SWEDISH GP	Anderstorp	28	Copersucar-Fittipaldi	G	3.0 Fittipaldi FD04-Cosworth V8	*handling/6 laps behind*	18/31
dns	"	"	28	Copersucar-Fittipaldi	G	3.0 Fittipaldi F5-Cosworth V8	*accident in practice*	– / –
11	FRENCH GP	Dijon	28	Copersucar-Fittipaldi	G	3.0 Fittipaldi F5-Cosworth V8	*3 laps behind*	22/30
ret	BRITISH GP	Silverstone	28	Copersucar-Fittipaldi	G	3.0 Fittipaldi F5-Cosworth V8	*engine*	22/36
dnq	GERMAN GP	Hockenheim	28	Copersucar-Fittipaldi	G	3.0 Fittipaldi F5-Cosworth V8		28/30
11	AUSTRIAN GP	Österreichring	28	Copersucar-Fittipaldi	G	3.0 Fittipaldi F5-Cosworth V8	*1 lap behind*	23/30
4	DUTCH GP	Zandvoort	28	Copersucar-Fittipaldi	G	3.0 Fittipaldi F5-Cosworth V8	*1 lap behind*	17/34
dnq	ITALIAN GP	Monza	28	Copersucar-Fittipaldi	G	3.0 Fittipaldi F5-Cosworth V8		26/34
13	US GP EAST	Watkins Glen	28	Copersucar-Fittipaldi	G	3.0 Fittipaldi F5-Cosworth V8	*2 laps behind*	18/27
ret	CANADIAN GP	Mosport Park	28	Copersucar-Fittipaldi	G	3.0 Fittipaldi F5-Cosworth V8	*engine*	19/27

1978   Championship position: 19th=   Wins: 0   Pole positions: 0   Fastest laps: 0   Points scored: 17

	Race	Circuit	No	Team	G	Engine	Notes	Grid
9	ARGENTINE GP	Buenos Aires	14	Fittipaldi Automotive	G	3.0 Fittipaldi F5A-Cosworth V8		17/27
2	BRAZILIAN GP	Rio	14	Fittipaldi Automotive	G	3.0 Fittipaldi F5A-Cosworth V8		7/28
ret	SOUTH AFRICAN GP	Kyalami	14	Fittipaldi Automotive	G	3.0 Fittipaldi F5A-Cosworth V8	*driveshaft*	16/30

Emerson's attempt to achieve glory with his own team was to end in failure.
The closest he came to a Grand Prix win was in Brazil in 1978 with the Fittipaldi F5A, which is seen (right) leading Niki Lauda's Brabham-Alfa.

8	US GP WEST	Long Beach	14	Fittipaldi Automotive	G	3.0 Fittipaldi F5A-Cosworth V8	1 lap behind	15/30
9	MONACO GP	Monte Carlo	14	Fittipaldi Automotive	G	3.0 Fittipaldi F5A-Cosworth V8	1 lap behind	20/30
ret	BELGIAN GP	Zolder	14	Fittipaldi Automotive	G	3.0 Fittipaldi F5A-Cosworth V8	collision with Ickx at start	15/30
ret	SPANISH GP	Jarama	14	Fittipaldi Automotive	G	3.0 Fittipaldi F5A-Cosworth V8	thottle linkage	15/29
6	SWEDISH GP	Anderstorp	14	Fittipaldi Automotive	G	3.0 Fittipaldi F5A-Cosworth V8	1 lap behind	13/27
ret	FRENCH GP	Paul Ricard	14	Fittipaldi Automotive	G	3.0 Fittipaldi F5A-Cosworth V8	rear suspension	15/29
ret	BRITISH GP	Brands Hatch	14	Fittipaldi Automotive	G	3.0 Fittipaldi F5A-Cosworth V8	engine	11/30
4	GERMAN GP	Hockenheim	14	Fittipaldi Automotive	G	3.0 Fittipaldi F5A-Cosworth V8		10/30
4	AUSTRIAN GP	Österreichring	14	Fittipaldi Automotive	G	3.0 Fittipaldi F5A-Cosworth V8	1 lap behind	6/31
5	DUTCH GP	Zandvoort	14	Fittipaldi Automotive	G	3.0 Fittipaldi F5A-Cosworth V8		10/33
8	ITALIAN GP	Monza	14	Fittipaldi Automotive	G	3.0 Fittipaldi F5A-Cosworth V8		13/32
5	US GP EAST	Watkins Glen	14	Fittipaldi Automotive	G	3.0 Fittipaldi F5A-Cosworth V8		13/27
ret	CANADIAN GP	Montreal	14	Fittipaldi Automotive	G	3.0 Fittipaldi F5A-Cosworth V8	collision with Stuck	6/28

1979 — Championship position: 21st   Wins: 0   Pole positions: 0   Fastest laps: 0   Points scored: 1

6	ARGENTINE GP	Buenos Aires	14	Fittipaldi Automotive	G	3.0 Fittipaldi F5A-Cosworth V8	1 lap behind	11/26
11	BRAZILIAN GP	Interlagos	14	Fittipaldi Automotive	G	3.0 Fittipaldi F5A-Cosworth V8	1 lap behind	9/26
dns	"	"	14	Fittipaldi Automotive	G	3.0 Fittipaldi F6-Cosworth V8	practice only	–/–
13	SOUTH AFRICAN GP	Kyalami	14	Fittipaldi Automotive	G	3.0 Fittipaldi F6-Cosworth V8	4 laps behind	18/26
dns	" "	"	14	Fittipaldi Automotive	G	3.0 Fittipaldi F5A-Cosworth V8	practice only	–/–
ret	US GP WEST	Long Beach	14	Fittipaldi Automotive	G	3.0 Fittipaldi F5A-Cosworth V8	driveshaft	16/26
dns	" "	"	14	Fittipaldi Automotive	G	3.0 Fittipaldi F6-Cosworth V8	practice only	–/–
11	SPANISH GP	Jarama	14	Fittipaldi Automotive	G	3.0 Fittipaldi F5A-Cosworth V8	1 lap behind	19/27
dns	"	"	14	Fittipaldi Automotive	G	3.0 Fittipaldi F6-Cosworth V8	practice only	–/–
9	BELGIAN GP	Zolder	14	Fittipaldi Automotive	G	3.0 Fittipaldi F5A-Cosworth V8	2 laps behind	23/28
ret	MONACO GP	Monte Carlo	14	Fittipaldi Automotive	G	3.0 Fittipaldi F5A-Cosworth V8	engine	17/25
ret	FRENCH GP	Paul Ricard	14	Fittipaldi Automotive	G	3.0 Fittipaldi F5A-Cosworth V8	engine-oil loss	18/27
ret	BRITISH GP	Silverstone	14	Fittipaldi Automotive	G	3.0 Fittipaldi F5A-Cosworth V8	engine	22/26
ret	GERMAN GP	Hockenheim	14	Fittipaldi Automotive	G	3.0 Fittipaldi F5A-Cosworth V8	electrics	22/26
ret	AUSTRIAN GP	Österreichring	14	Fittipaldi Automotive	G	3.0 Fittipaldi F6A-Cosworth V8	brakes	19/26
dns	"	"	14	Fittipaldi Automotive	G	3.0 Fittipaldi F5A-Cosworth V8	practice only	–/–
ret	DUTCH GP	Zandvoort	14	Fittipaldi Automotive	G	3.0 Fittipaldi F6A-Cosworth V8	electrics	21/26
dns	"	"	14	Fittipaldi Automotive	G	3.0 Fittipaldi F5A-Cosworth V8	practice only	–/–
8	ITALIAN GP	Monza	14	Fittipaldi Automotive	G	3.0 Fittipaldi F6A-Cosworth V8	1 lap behind	20/28
8	CANADIAN GP	Montreal	14	Fittipaldi Automotive	G	3.0 Fittipaldi F6A-Cosworth V8	wheel bearing problem/-5 laps	15/29
7	US GP EAST	Watkins Glen	14	Fittipaldi Automotive	G	3.0 Fittipaldi F6A-Cosworth V8	5 laps behind	23/30

1980 — Championship position: 15th=   Wins: 0   Pole positions: 0   Fastest laps: 0   Points scored: 5

nc	ARGENTINE GP	Buenos Aires	20	Skol Fittipaldi Team	G	3.0 Fittipaldi F7-Cosworth V8	pit stops/16 laps behind	24/28
15	BRAZILIAN GP	Interlagos	20	Skol Fittipaldi Team	G	3.0 Fittipaldi F7-Cosworth V8	2 laps behind	19/28
8	SOUTH AFRICAN GP	Kyalami	20	Skol Fittipaldi Team	G	3.0 Fittipaldi F7-Cosworth V8	1 lap behind	18/28
3	US GP WEST	Long Beach	20	Skol Fittipaldi Team	G	3.0 Fittipaldi F7-Cosworth V8		24/27
ret	BELGIAN GP	Zolder	20	Skol Fittipaldi Team	G	3.0 Fittipaldi F7-Cosworth V8	electrics	24/27
6	MONACO GP	Monte Carlo	20	Skol Fittipaldi Team	G	3.0 Fittipaldi F7-Cosworth V8	2 laps behind	18/27
13/ret	FRENCH GP	Paul Ricard	20	Skol Fittipaldi Team	G	3.0 Fittipaldi F7-Cosworth V8	engine	24/27
12	BRITISH GP	Brands Hatch	20	Skol Fittipaldi Team	G	3.0 Fittipaldi F8-Cosworth V8	4 laps behind	22/27
ret	GERMAN GP	Hockenheim	20	Skol Fittipaldi Team	G	3.0 Fittipaldi F8-Cosworth V8	broken skirt	12/26
11	AUSTRIAN GP	Österreichring	20	Skol Fittipaldi Team	G	3.0 Fittipaldi F8-Cosworth V8	1 lap behind	23/25
ret	DUTCH GP	Zandvoort	20	Skol Fittipaldi Team	G	3.0 Fittipaldi F8-Cosworth V8	brakes	21/28
ret	ITALIAN GP	Imola	20	Skol Fittipaldi Team	G	3.0 Fittipaldi F8-Cosworth V8	hit guard rail	15/28
ret	CANADIAN GP	Montreal	20	Skol Fittipaldi Team	G	3.0 Fittipaldi F8-Cosworth V8	gearbox	16/28
ret	US GP EAST	Watkins Glen	20	Skol Fittipaldi Team	G	3.0 Fittipaldi F8-Cosworth V8	rear suspension	19/27

GP Starts: 144   GP Wins: 14   Pole positions: 6   Fastest laps: 6   Points: 281

WILSON FITTIPALDI

Wilson had to content himself with life as a racing driver for ever in the shadow of his brilliant younger brother, but that should not disguise the fact that he was a more than useful performer in his own right.

He made a brief and dispiriting trip to Europe in 1966 before returning home to Brazil, where he raced saloons, sports cars and Formula Fords, as well as acting as engineer for Emerson's Super Vee efforts. Wilson was back in Europe in 1970 to race in F3, and a good showing was enough to see him joining his brother in Formula 2 in 1971, driving first a Lotus 69, then a March. Given his lack of experience, he fared well, taking fourth on his debut at Hockenheim, second at Vallelunga and third again at Hockenheim at season's end. A deal was struck with Bernie Ecclestone to race a Brabham in Formula 1 in 1972, as effectively the third driver to Reutemann and Hill, but he did not enjoy the best of luck after a sixth place on his debut in the non-championship Brazilian GP. Things were better the following year, and his drive at Monaco was particularly impressive, Wilson holding third place in the BT42 when the fuel system failed. But at least he scored some points in Argentina and Germany, and took an aggregate win in Formula 2 at Misano.

Wilson was now set on developing a Grand Prix car of his own and much of 1974 was spent setting up the Copersucar-Fittipaldi team which made its debut in 1975. The car was not a success, and Wilson was a perpetual backmarker. At the end of the year came the shock announcement that Emerson would drive for the team in 1976, so the elder Fittipaldi happily retired to fill a management position in a project which was doomed to eventual failure.

Over the past decade Wilson has been much in evidence at the circuits, helping guide the racing career of his son Christian, but he has still found time to race himself occasionally. In 1995 he won the 24th Brazilian 1000-mile race in a Porsche 993 turbo.

FITTIPALDI, Wilson (BR) b 25/12/1943, São Paulo

1972	Championship position: Unplaced							
	Race	Circuit	No	Entrant	Tyres	Car/Engine	Comment	Q Pos/Entries
7	SPANISH GP	Jarama	22	Motor Racing Developments	G	3.0 Brabham BT33-Cosworth V8	2 laps behind	14/26
9	MONACO GP	Monte Carlo	21	Motor Racing Developments	G	3.0 Brabham BT33-Cosworth V8	3 laps behind	21/25
ret	BELGIAN GP	Nivelles	18	Motor Racing Developments	G	3.0 Brabham BT34-Cosworth V8	gearbox	18/26
8	FRENCH GP	Clermont Ferrand	19	Motor Racing Developments	G	3.0 Brabham BT34-Cosworth V8		16/29
12/ret	BRITISH GP	Brands Hatch	28	Motor Racing Developments	G	3.0 Brabham BT34-Cosworth V8	suspension/2 laps behind	22/27
7	GERMAN GP	Nürburgring	26	Motor Racing Developments	G	3.0 Brabham BT34-Cosworth V8		21/27
ret	AUSTRIAN GP	Österreichring	28	Motor Racing Developments	G	3.0 Brabham BT34-Cosworth V8	brake pipe	15/26
ret	ITALIAN GP	Monza	29	Motor Racing Developments	G	3.0 Brabham BT34-Cosworth V8	broken rear suspension	15/27
ret	CANADIAN GP	Mosport Park	9	Motor Racing Developments	G	3.0 Brabham BT34-Cosworth V8	gearbox	11/25
ret	US GP	Watkins Glen	30	Motor Racing Developments	G	3.0 Brabham BT34-Cosworth V8	engine	13/32
1973	Championship position: 15th=	Wins: 0	Pole positions: 0	Fastest laps: 0	Points scored: 3			
6	ARGENTINE GP	Buenos Aires	12	Motor Racing Developments	G	3.0 Brabham BT37-Cosworth V8	1 lap behind	12/19
ret	BRAZILIAN GP	Interlagos	18	Motor Racing Developments	G	3.0 Brabham BT37-Cosworth V8	engine	=11/20
ret	SOUTH AFRICAN GP	Kyalami	19	Motor Racing Developments	G	3.0 Brabham BT37-Cosworth V8	gear selection	17/25
10	SPANISH GP	Montjuich Park	17	Motor Racing Developments	G	3.0 Brabham BT42-Cosworth V8	pit stop-throttle cable/-6 laps	12/22
ret	BELGIAN GP	Zolder	11	Motor Racing Developments	G	3.0 Brabham BT42-Cosworth V8	engine/brakes	19/23
11/ret	MONACO GP	Monte Carlo	11	Motor Racing Developments	G	3.0 Brabham BT42-Cosworth V8	split collector pot/-7 laps	9/26
ret	SWEDISH GP	Anderstorp	11	Motor Racing Developments	G	3.0 Brabham BT42-Cosworth V8	accident on lap 1	13/22
16/ret	FRENCH GP	Paul Ricard	11	Motor Racing Developments	G	3.0 Brabham BT42-Cosworth V8	throttle linkage/-4 laps	19/25
ret	BRITISH GP	Silverstone	11	Motor Racing Developments	G	3.0 Brabham BT42-Cosworth V8	oil pipe	13/29
ret	DUTCH GP	Zandvoort	11	Motor Racing Developments	G	3.0 Brabham BT42-Cosworth V8	spun off	13/24
5	GERMAN GP	Nürburgring	11	Motor Racing Developments	G	3.0 Brabham BT42-Cosworth V8		13/23
ret	AUSTRIAN GP	Österreichring	11	Motor Racing Developments	G	3.0 Brabham BT42-Cosworth V8	fuel metering unit	16/25
ret	ITALIAN GP	Monza	11	Motor Racing Developments	G	3.0 Brabham BT42-Cosworth V8	brakes	16/25
11	CANADIAN GP	Mosport Park	11	Motor Racing Developments	G	3.0 Brabham BT42-Cosworth V8	3 laps behind	10/26
nc	US GP	Watkins Glen	11	Motor Racing Developments	G	3.0 Brabham BT42-Cosworth V8	pit stops-various/-7 laps	26/28

	1975			Championship position: Unplaced						
ret	ARGENTINE GP	Buenos Aires	30	Copersucar-Fittipaldi	G	3.0 Fittipaldi FD01-Cosworth V8	crashed	23/23
13	BRAZILIAN GP	Interlagos	30	Copersucar-Fittipaldi	G	3.0 Fittipaldi FD02-Cosworth V8	1 lap behind	21/23
dnq	SOUTH AFRICAN GP	Kyalami	30	Copersucar-Fittipaldi	G	3.0 Fittipaldi FD02-Cosworth V8		27/28
ret	SPANISH GP	Montjuich Park	30	Copersucar-Fittipaldi	G	3.0 Fittipaldi FD02-Cosworth V8	protest at lack of safety of track	26/26
dnq	MONACO GP	Monte Carlo	30	Copersucar-Fittipaldi	G	3.0 Fittipaldi FD02-Cosworth V8		26/26
12	BELGIAN GP	Zolder	30	Copersucar-Fittipaldi	G	3.0 Fittipaldi FD02-Cosworth V8	3 laps behind	24/24
17	SWEDISH GP	Anderstorp	30	Copersucar-Fittipaldi	G	3.0 Fittipaldi FD02-Cosworth V8	pit stop/6 laps behind	25/26
11	DUTCH GP	Zandvoort	30	Copersucar-Fittipaldi	G	3.0 Fittipaldi FD03-Cosworth V8	4 laps behind	24/25
dns	"	"	30T	Copersucar-Fittipaldi	G	3.0 Fittipaldi FD03-Cosworth V8	practice only	– / –
ret	FRENCH GP	Paul Ricard	30	Copersucar-Fittipaldi	G	3.0 Fittipaldi FD03-Cosworth V8	engine	23/26
19/ret	BRITISH GP	Silverstone	30	Copersucar-Fittipaldi	G	3.0 Fittipaldi FD03-Cosworth V8	crashed in rain/6 laps behind	24/28
ret	GERMAN GP	Nürburgring	30	Copersucar-Fittipaldi	G	3.0 Fittipaldi FD03-Cosworth V8	engine	22/26
dns	AUSTRIAN GP	Österreichring	30	Copersucar-Fittipaldi	G	3.0 Fittipaldi FD03-Cosworth V8	practice accident-injured hand	(20)/30
10	US GP	Watkins Glen	30	Copersucar-Fittipaldi	G	3.0 Fittipaldi FD03-Cosworth V8	4 laps behind	23/24

GP Starts: 35   GP Wins: 0   Pole positions: 0   Fastest laps: 0   Points: 3

RON FLOCKHART

Flockhart began by racing motor cycles, but in 1948 he switched to MG and JP-Vincent cars, before taking a serious step up with the purchase of an ERA D-Type in 1952. He enjoyed a fabulous 1953 season with the ex-Mays car, embarrassing many a newer machine in Formula Libre races. Naturally this brought him to the attention of BRM, who signed him up in 1954, initially to race in national Formula Libre events with the supercharged car. He also made his GP debut that season, taking over Bira's Maserati in the British GP before crashing.

In 1956 Ron was invited to race in sports cars for Ecurie Ecosse and won at Le Mans (with Sanderson) with their Jaguar E-Type, while he took full advantage of a last-minute opportunity to race for Connaught, finishing third in the Italian GP. The 1957 season saw him repeat his Le Mans success for Ecosse (this time with Bueb), but his luck with BRM was still out, an accident in the French GP leaving him with burns to arm and legs. The following year was marred by further injury after a crash at Rouen in a sports car race, but he was back in action for 1959 and won the Lady Wigram Trophy in New Zealand and the minor Silver City Trophy at Snetterton for BRM. Easily his best effort that year was to finish sixth in the French GP when a stone smashed his goggles and he drove on gamely to the finish with the use of virtually only one eye and a badly cut face.

After parting company with the Bourne concern, Flockhart raced for Alan Brown in Formula 2 in 1960, and finished second in the GP of Chimay behind Jack Lewis and fourth at Pau. Ron also drove a single Grand Prix for both Lotus and Cooper, but already his thoughts were turning towards his other passion, aviation. He had gained a pilot's licence back in 1948, and now set about breaking flying records. He raced less frequently in 1961, and after taking part in three races in New Zealand and Australia with his Lotus 18 early in 1962, Flockhart was killed when his aeroplane broke up in turbulence while he was in Australia practising for a London-to-Sydney record attempt.

GREGOR FOITEK

Winning that curious anomaly, the Swiss F3 championship, in 1986 in a Dallara meant little, and the wealthy Foitek's first season in F3000 the following year was to be a more searching test. A poor start and a string of DNQs were to some extent overcome by switching teams to GA Motorsport in mid-season, though it was 1988 before he tasted success with a superb win at Vallelunga. But then came a worrying number of incidents, culminating in the Johnny Herbert crash at Brands Hatch, when Gregor's Lola was launched into a terrifying series of barrel-rolls from which he was fortunate to escape with no more than a fractured wrist.

Moving into Grands Prix in 1989, he spent a fruitless time trying in vain to qualify the EuroBrun, and decided to quit while ahead when the rear wing fell off on his debut for Rial. Foitek took his money to Brabham at the start of 1990 and at least made a couple starts, but then he moved to the Onyx team, which was on the way to oblivion as a Swiss gentleman by the name of Monteverdi took control. All in all, it was a sorry mess and before long Foitek had disappeared from view.

FITZAU, Theo (D) b 10/2/1923 – d 18/3/1982

	1953	Championship position: Unplaced						
	Race	*Circuit*	*No*	*Entrant*	*Tyres*	*Car/Engine*	*Comment*	*Q Pos/Entries*
ret	GERMAN GP	Nürburgring	28	Helmut Niedermeyer	–	2.0 AFM U8-BMW 6		21/35

GP Starts: 1 GP Wins: 0 Pole positions: 0 Fastest laps: 0 Points: 0

FLINTERMAN, Jan (NL) b 2/10/1919 – d 26/12/1992, Leiden

	1952	Championship position: Unplaced						
	Race	*Circuit*	*No*	*Entrant*	*Tyres*	*Car/Engine*	*Comment*	*Q Pos/Entries*
ret	DUTCH GP	Zandvoort	20	Escuderia Bandeirantes	P	2.0 Maserati A6GCM 6	*rear axle*	15/18
9*	"	"	16	Escuderia Bandeirantes	P	2.0 Maserati A6GCM 6	*took Landi's car/-7 laps	– / –

GP Starts: 1 GP Wins: 0 Pole positions: 0 Fastest laps: 0 Points: 0

FLOCKHART, Ron (GB) b 16/6/1923, Edinburgh, Scotland – d 12/4/1962, Dandenong Ranges, nr Melbourne, Australia

	1954	Championship position: Unplaced						
	Race	*Circuit*	*No*	*Entrant*	*Tyres*	*Car/Engine*	*Comment*	*Q Pos/Entries*
ret	BRITISH GP	Silverstone	6	Prince Bira	P	2.5 Maserati 250F 6	*took over Bira's car/crashed*	– /33
	1956	Championship position: 9th= Wins: 0 Pole positions: 0 Fastest laps: 0 Points scored: 4						
ret	BRITISH GP	Silverstone	25	Owen Racing Organisation	D	2.5 BRM P25 4	*engine*	17/28
3	ITALIAN GP	Monza	4	Connaught Engineering	P/A	2.5 Connaught B-Alta 4	*1 lap behind*	24/26
	1957	Championship position: Unplaced						
ret	MONACO GP	Monte Carlo	6	Owen Racing Organisation	D	2.5 BRM P25 4	*timing gear*	11/21
ret	FRENCH GP	Rouen	26	Owen Racing Organisation	D	2.5 BRM P25 4	*accident-suffered burns*	11/15
	1958	Championship position: Unplaced						
dnq	MONACO GP	Monte Carlo	22	R R C Walker Racing Team	D	2.0 Cooper T43-Climax 4		17/28
ret	MOROCCAN GP	Casablanca	20	Owen Racing Organisation	D	2.5 BRM P25 4	*camshaft*	15/25
	1959	Championship position: Unplaced						
ret	MONACO GP	Monte Carlo	20	Owen Racing Organisation	D	2.5 BRM P25 4	*brake failure-spun off*	10/24
6	FRENCH GP	Reims	44	Owen Racing Organisation	D	2.5 BRM P25 4		13/22
ret	BRITISH GP	Aintree	42	Owen Racing Organisation	D	2.5 BRM P25 4	*spun off*	11/30
7	PORTUGUESE GP	Oporto	8	Owen Racing Organisation	D	2.5 BRM P25 4	*3 laps behind*	11/16
13	ITALIAN GP	Monza	4	Owen Racing Organisation	D	2.5 BRM P25 4	*5 laps behind*	15/21
	1960	Championship position: =19th Wins: 0 Pole positions: 0 Fastest laps: 0 Points scored: 1						
6	FRENCH GP	Reims	22	Team Lotus	D	2.5 Lotus 18-Climax 4	*1 lap behind*	14/23
ret	US GP	Riverside	4	Cooper Car Co	D	2.5 Cooper T51-Climax 4	*transmission*	21/23

GP Starts: 13 GP Wins: 0 Pole positions: 0 Fastest laps: 0 Points: 5

FOITEK, Gregor (CH) b 27/3/1965, Zurich

	1989	Championship position: Unplaced						
	Race	*Circuit*	*No*	*Entrant*	*Tyres*	*Car/Engine*	*Comment*	*Q Pos/Entries*
dnq	BRAZILIAN GP	Rio	33	EuroBrun Racing	P	3.5 EuroBrun ER188B-Judd V8		29/38
dnpq	SAN MARINO GP	Imola	33	EuroBrun Racing	P	3.5 EuroBrun ER188B-Judd V8		32/39
dnpq	MONACO GP	Monte Carlo	33	EuroBrun Racing	P	3.5 EuroBrun ER188B-Judd V8		35/38
dnpq	MEXICAN GP	Mexico City	33	EuroBrun Racing	P	3.5 EuroBrun ER188B-Judd V8		32/39
dnpq	US GP (PHOENIX)	Phoenix	33	EuroBrun Racing	P	3.5 EuroBrun ER188B-Judd V8		33/39
dnpq	CANADIAN GP	Montreal	33	EuroBrun Racing	P	3.5 EuroBrun ER188B-Judd V8		33/39
dnpq	FRENCH GP	Paul Ricard	33	EuroBrun Racing	P	3.5 EuroBrun ER188B-Judd V8		38/39
dnpq	BRITISH GP	Silverstone	33	EuroBrun Racing	P	3.5 EuroBrun ER188B-Judd V8		33/39
dnpq	GERMAN GP	Hockenheim	33	EuroBrun Racing	P	3.5 EuroBrun ER189-Judd V8		37/39
dnpq	"	"	33	EuroBrun Racing	P	3.5 EuroBrun ER188B-Judd V8		– / –
dnpq	HUNGARIAN GP	Hungaroring	33	EuroBrun Racing	P	3.5 EuroBrun ER189-Judd V8		37/39
dnpq	"	"	33	EuroBrun Racing	P	3.5 EuroBrun ER188B-Judd V8		– / –
dnpq	BELGIAN GP	Spa	33	EuroBrun Racing	P	3.5 EuroBrun ER188B-Judd V8		38/39
dnq	SPANISH GP	Jerez	38	Rial Racing	G	3.5 Rial ARC2-Cosworth V8	*accident-rear wing collapsed*	29/38
	1990	Championship position: Unplaced						
ret	US GP (PHOENIX)	Phoenix	7	Motor Racing Developments	P	3.5 Brabham BT58-Judd V8	*collision with Grouillard*	23/35
ret	BRAZILIAN GP	Interlagos	7	Motor Racing Developments	P	3.5 Brabham BT58-Judd V8	*gear selection*	22/35
ret	SAN MARINO GP	Imola	35	Moneytron Onyx	G	3.5 Onyx ORE 1B-Cosworth V8	*engine*	24/34
7/ret	MONACO GP	Monte Carlo	35	Moneytron Onyx	G	3.5 Onyx ORE 1B-Cosworth V8	*collision-Bernard/-6 laps*	20/35
ret	CANADIAN GP	Montreal	35	Moneytron Onyx	G	3.5 Onyx ORE 1B-Cosworth V8	*over-revved engine*	21/35
15	MEXICAN GP	Mexico City	35	Moneytron Onyx	G	3.5 Onyx ORE 1B-Cosworth V8	*brake problems/2 laps behind*	23/35
dnq	FRENCH GP	Paul Ricard	35	Moneytron Onyx	G	3.5 Onyx ORE 1B-Cosworth V8		29/35
dnq	BRITISH GP	Silverstone	35	Monteverdi Onyx Formula One	G	3.5 Onyx ORE 1B-Cosworth V8		30/35
ret	GERMAN GP	Hockenheim	35	Monteverdi Onyx Formula One	G	3.5 Monteverdi ORE 1B-Cosworth V8	*spun off*	26/35
dnq	HUNGARIAN GP	Hungaroring	35	Monteverdi Onyx Formula One	G	3.5 Monteverdi ORE 1B-Cosworth V8		30/35

GP Starts: 7 GP Wins: 0 Pole positions: 0 Fastest laps: 0 Points: 0

GEORGE FOLLMER

Follmer was 39 when he first sampled life in Formula 1, thrown in at the deep end with the newly formed UOP Shadow team in 1973. At first things went well, but as the season wore on he slipped further down the grid, and by the end of the year his Grand Prix tenure was over.

He started racing in 1960, but it was 1964-65 before he began competing seriously, becoming USRRC champion in the under-2-litre class with six wins in nine races in a Lotus-Porsche sports car. This led to an invitation to race a works Porsche 904 in the 1966 Sebring 12-hour race, in which Follmer finished seventh with Kolb, winning the under-2-litre class.

Still a part-time racer and full-time insurance broker, George financed his own Lola-Chevrolet for 1967 to race in USRRC events, but the car repeatedly broke down, and when Roger Penske offered him a Can-Am ride late in the season Follmer accepted, taking two third places and a sixth in his three races. The die was cast. Seeing how a serious team was run, George then embarked upon a professional racing career, competing successfully in USAC, Can-Am, Trans-Am and Formula A before his 1973 season with Shadow.

Following his sojourn in Formula 1, Follmer initially took a ride in NASCAR, but was soon tempted back into Can-Am by Shadow's Don Nichols. The next few seasons saw George on a regular diet of Can-Am, Trans-Am (winning the 1976 championship) and sports cars until his career was interrupted by a terrible practice crash at Laguna Seca in 1978 which left him with a broken leg and internal injuries. But despite still being in some pain from his leg injuries, he made a comeback in 1979 and continued racing into the early eighties in Trans-Am with a Chevrolet Camaro.

FOLLMER, George (USA) b 27/1/1934, Phoenix, Arizona

	1973	Championship position: 13th		Wins: 0	Pole positions: 0	Fastest laps: 0	Points scored: 5		
	Race	Circuit	No	Entrant	Tyres	Car/Engine		Comment	Q Pos/Entries
6	SOUTH AFRICAN GP	Kyalami	23	UOP Shadow Racing Team	G	3.0 Shadow DN1-Cosworth V8		2 laps behind	21/25
3	SPANISH GP	Montjuich Park	20	UOP Shadow Racing Team	G	3.0 Shadow DN1-Cosworth V8			=14/22
ret	BELGIAN GP	Zolder	16	UOP Shadow Racing Team	G	3.0 Shadow DN1-Cosworth V8		stuck throttle slides	11/23
dns	MONACO GP	Monte Carlo	16	UOP Shadow Racing Team	G	3.0 Shadow DN1-Cosworth V8		practice collision with Merzario	(20)/26
14	SWEDISH GP	Anderstorp	16	UOP Shadow Racing Team	G	3.0 Shadow DN1-Cosworth V8		6 laps behind	19/22
ret	FRENCH GP	Paul Ricard	16	UOP Shadow Racing Team	G	3.0 Shadow DN1-Cosworth V8		vapour lock	20/25
ret/dns	BRITISH GP	Silverstone	16	UOP Shadow Racing Team	G	3.0 Shadow DN1-Cosworth V8		accident-first start	=25/29
10	DUTCH GP	Zandvoort	16	UOP Shadow Racing Team	G	3.0 Shadow DN1-Cosworth V8		5 laps behind	22/24
ret	GERMAN GP	Nürburgring	16	UOP Shadow Racing Team	G	3.0 Shadow DN1-Cosworth V8		accident	22/23
ret	AUSTRIAN GP	Österreichring	16	UOP Shadow Racing Team	G	3.0 Shadow DN1-Cosworth V8		cwp	20/25
10	ITALIAN GP	Monza	16	UOP Shadow Racing Team	G	3.0 Shadow DN1-Cosworth V8		1 lap behind	21/25
17	CANADIAN GP	Mosport Park	16	UOP Shadow Racing Team	G	3.0 Shadow DN1-Cosworth V8		pit stop/7 laps behind	13/26
14	US GP	Watkins Glen	16	UOP Shadow Racing Team	G	3.0 Shadow DN1-Cosworth V8		2 laps behind	21/28

GP Starts: 11 (12)   GP Wins: 0   Pole positions: 0   Fastest laps: 0   Points: 5

FONTANA, Norberto (RA) b 20/1/1975

	1997	Championship position: Unplaced						
	Race	Circuit	No	Entrant	Tyres	Car/Engine	Comment	Q Pos/Entries
ret	FRENCH GP	Magny Cours	17	Red Bull Sauber Petronas	G	3.0 Sauber C16-Petronas V10	spun off	20/22
9	BRITISH GP	Silverstone	17	Red Bull Sauber Petronas	G	3.0 Sauber C16-Petronas V10	* times disallowed/-1 lap	14*/22
9	GERMAN GP	Hockenheim	17	Red Bull Sauber Petronas	G	3.0 Sauber C16-Petronas V10	1 lap behind	18/22
14	EUROPEAN GP	Jerez	17	Red Bull Sauber Petronas	G	3.0 Sauber C16-Petronas V10	1 lap behind	18/22

GP Starts: 4   GP Wins: 0   Pole positions: 0   Fastest laps: 0   Points: 0

NORBERTO FONTANA

Fontana was a highly impressive German F3 champion in 1995 with ten wins from sixteen starts and the Marlboro Masters title to boot. The diminutive Argentinian defeated rivals such as Ralf Schumacher, Jarno Trulli and Alexander Wurz but, while these drivers have since established themselves as Grand Prix stars, Norberto has spent the last two and a half seasons trying to regain ground lost after an unimpressive four-race stint at Sauber in 1997 deputising for the injured Gianni Morbidelli.

Norberto could well have grabbed a seat at Sauber at the beginning of 1996 had it not been for a neck injury sustained in an accident at the end-of-year F3 Macau GP in 1995. Instead, he had to be content with the test-driver role with the Swiss team and headed out to Japan to compete in Formula Nippon.

During his three seasons in the Far East Fontana was, predictably, a front-runner. He won four times, but the championship itself was to prove elusive and, with his ultimate goal a place on the Formula 1 grid, Norberto opted to return to Europe in 1999 to contest the FIA F3000 series.

It was not a move which brought much success, the well-funded Red Bull Sauber Junior Team star scoring a meagre four points to finish 13th in the final standings.

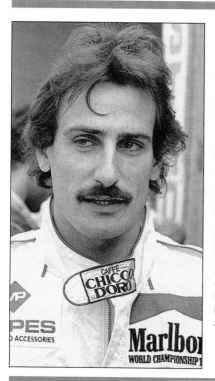

FRANCO FORINI

Forini raced in European F3 before finding success in the Italian F3 series. Having finished third and fifth with his Dallara-Alfa in 1983 and '84, the Swiss driver switched to a VW-powered car in 1985 and emerged as a worthy champion ahead of Barbazza and Caffi.

A largely moribund F3000 season in 1986 left Forini out of the picture, until a surprise call from Osella brought him briefly into the Grand Prix arena in 1987.

PHILIP FOTHERINGHAM-PARKER

A company director who raced intermittently in the immediate post-war years, Fotheringham-Parker's greatest success was second place with a Maserati in the 1949 Wakefield Trophy race at the Curragh.

He raced the 4CLT in the 1951 British GP and also used it to win a very minor Formula 1 race at Winfield that year.

In 1953 he raced with Sydney Allard at Le Mans, and took part in the 1954 Monte Carlo Rally in a Ford Zephyr.

FORINI, Franco (CH) b 22/9/1958, Muralto, nr Locarno

	1987			Championship position: Unplaced					
	Race	Circuit	No	Entrant	Tyres	Car/Engine		Comment	Q Pos/Entries
ret	ITALIAN GP	Monza	22	Osella Squadra Corse	G	1.5 t/c Osella FA1I-Alfa Romeo V8		turbo	26/28
ret	PORTUGUESE GP	Estoril	22	Osella Squadra Corse	G	1.5 t/c Osella FA1I-Alfa Romeo V8		rear wheel bearing	26/27
dnq	SPANISH GP	Jerez	22	Osella Squadra Corse	G	1.5 t/c Osella FA1I-Alfa Romeo V8			28/28

GP Starts: 2　GP Wins: 0　Pole positions: 0　Fastest laps: 0　Points: 0

FOTHERINGHAM-PARKER, Philip (GB) b 22/9/1907, Beckenham, Kent – d 15/10/1981, Beckley, nr Rye, East Sussex

	1951			Championship position: Unplaced					
	Race	Circuit	No	Entrant	Tyres	Car/Engine		Comment	Q Pos/Entries
ret	BRITISH GP	Silverstone	17	Philip Fotheringham-Parker	D	1.5 s/c Maserati 4CL 4		oil pipe	16/20

GP Starts: 1　GP Wins: 0　Pole positions: 0　Fastest laps: 0　Points: 0

HEINZ-HARALD FRENTZEN

For Heinz-Harald it has been a long and sometimes frustrating road to the top, and even when he seemed to have finally climbed to the summit of Formula 1 with the chance of a lifetime at Williams in 1997, the likeable German had to prove himself all over again at Jordan after his dream move had turned sour.

He raced karts from 1980 to 1985, taking a German junior championship, before three seasons in German FF2000, where he finished runner-up in 1987. This set up a move into the German Opel Lotus Challenge the following year, and Heinz-Harald not only took the title but also scored a couple of wins in the GM Lotus Euroseries.

It was in 1989 that motor racing aficianados worldwide really started to take an interest in the trio of talented youngsters, Wendlinger, Michael Schumacher and Frentzen, who were battling for the German F3 title. Eventually, the last two shared second place just one point adrift of Wendlinger, but their performances were such that all three were earmarked to join the Mercedes Benz Group C programme for 1990. In addition Heinz-Harald found long-term backing from Camel to join Eddie Jordan in F3000.

It was now that his career began to stall; left in the third car at EJR and with no real experience, he struggled all year, and with the troublesome Lola in '91 things hardly improved. Worse was to follow . . . Camel took their budget to Benetton with Schumacher for 1992, and Heinz-Harald was left high and dry without a drive of any sort. He agreed to race for March in '93, but wisely backed away and plumped instead to go to Japan to compete in F3000 for Super Nova, in place of the indisposed Volker Weidler. The time he spent there did a great deal to build his confidence, and when the chance of a test for Sauber came in the autumn of 1993 Frentzen was equipped to make the most of it.

His first year in F1 saw Heinz-Harald assume the team leadership after Wendlinger's accident and quickly become a top-six contender, despite the Sauber's obvious limitations, and this quiet and unassuming man took

another giant stride forward in 1995, working ceaselessly to push the Ford-engined car towards the front of the grid. In the second half of the season Frentzen put in some superb drives to enhance his rising reputation. That he had come to be so highly regarded in just two seasons of Formula 1 in a car not good enough to challenge the leaders showed the reservoir of talent which he possessed.

Despite the introduction of the new Ford Zetec-R V10, the German's 1996 season was something of an anti-climax, with Frentzen seeming less than fully committed when the Sauber C15 failed to come up to scratch. Williams, of course, had already made their move and controversially signed Frentzen to replace Damon Hill for the 1997 season.

Life at Williams is never a bed of roses and it was to prove less than fertile ground for Frentzen, who failed to bloom in the harsh environment. A win at Imola and a string of podium finishes brought the runner-up position in the championship behind team-mate Jacques Villeneuve, but lurking in the background was the feeling that his contribution could, and should, have been much greater. Worse was to follow for 1998, which turned into something of a nightmare for the mild-mannered Frentzen. The new narrow-track and grooved-tyre regulations found the Williams FW20 wanting and Heinz-Harald seemed resigned to his number two status behind Villeneuve.

He was prematurely written off by many, but not by Eddie Jordan, who swiftly moved to bring the German on board for the 1999 season. A superb second place at the opening race in Australia provided Heinz-Harald with an immediate and much-needed boost to his confidence and he simply never looked back. Team-mate Damon Hill was left floundering by Frentzen's pace, and his smooth style and calmness under pressure brought two well-judged wins which, together with a further ten top-six finishes, earned an impressive third place in the championship table. More importantly, perhaps, Frentzen had regained his credibility as a top-rank driver.

FRENTZEN, Heinz-Harald (D) b 18/5/1967, Mönchengladbach

1994

Championship position: 13th Wins: 0 Pole positions: 0 Fastest laps: 0 Points scored: 7

	Race	Circuit	No	Entrant		Tyres	Car/Engine	Comment	Q Pos/Entries
ret	BRAZILIAN GP	Interlagos	30	Sauber Mercedes		G	3.5 Sauber C13-Mercedes Benz V10	spun off	5/28
5	PACIFIC GP	T.I. Circuit	30	Sauber Mercedes		G	3.5 Sauber C13-Mercedes Benz V10	1 lap behind	11/28
7	SAN MARINO GP	Imola	30	Sauber Mercedes		G	3.5 Sauber C13-Mercedes Benz V10	1 lap behind	7/28
dns	MONACO GP	Monte Carlo	30	Sauber Mercedes		G	3.5 Sauber C13-Mercedes Benz V10	withdrawn-Wendlinger crash	–/–
ret	SPANISH GP	Barcelona	30	Sauber Mercedes		G	3.5 Sauber C13-Mercedes Benz V10	gearbox	12/27
ret	CANADIAN GP	Montreal	30	Sauber Mercedes		G	3.5 Sauber C13-Mercedes Benz V10	spun off	10/27
4	FRENCH GP	Magny Cours	30	Sauber Mercedes		G	3.5 Sauber C13-Mercedes Benz V10		10/28
7*	BRITISH GP	Silverstone	30	Sauber Mercedes		G	3.5 Sauber C13-Mercedes Benz V10	*2nd place car dsq/-1 lap	13/28
ret	GERMAN GP	Hockenheim	30	Sauber Mercedes		G	3.5 Sauber C13-Mercedes Benz V10	multiple accident at start	9/28
ret	HUNGARIAN GP	Hungaroring	30	Sauber Mercedes		G	3.5 Sauber C13-Mercedes Benz V10	gearbox	8/28
ret	BELGIAN GP	Spa	30	Sauber Mercedes		G	3.5 Sauber C13-Mercedes Benz V10	spun off	9/28
ret	ITALIAN GP	Monza	30	Sauber Mercedes		G	3.5 Sauber C13-Mercedes Benz V10	engine	11/28
ret	PORTUGUESE GP	Estoril	30	Sauber Mercedes		G	3.5 Sauber C13-Mercedes Benz V10	engine	9/28
6	EUROPEAN GP	Jerez	30	Sauber Mercedes		G	3.5 Sauber C13-Mercedes Benz V10	1 lap behind	4/28
6	JAPANESE GP	Suzuka	30	Sauber Mercedes		G	3.5 Sauber C13-Mercedes Benz V10		3/28
7	AUSTRALIAN GP	Adelaide	30	Sauber Mercedes		G	3.5 Sauber C13-Mercedes Benz V10	1 lap behind	10/28

1995

Championship position: 9th Wins: 0 Pole positions: 0 Fastest laps: 0 Points scored: 15

	Race	Circuit	No	Entrant	Tyres	Car/Engine	Comment	Q Pos/Entries
ret	BRAZILIAN GP	Interlagos	30	Red Bull Sauber Ford	G	3.0 Sauber C14-Ford Zetec-R V8	electrics	14/26
5	ARGENTINE GP	Buenos Aires	30	Red Bull Sauber Ford	G	3.0 Sauber C14-Ford Zetec-R V8	2 laps behind	9/26
6	SAN MARINO GP	Imola	30	Red Bull Sauber Ford	G	3.0 Sauber C14-Ford Zetec-R V8	1 lap behind	14/26
8	SPANISH GP	Barcelona	30	Red Bull Sauber Ford	G	3.0 Sauber C14-Ford Zetec-R V8	1 lap behind	12/26
6	MONACO GP	Monte Carlo	30	Red Bull Sauber Ford	G	3.0 Sauber C14-Ford Zetec-R V8	2 laps behind	14/26
ret	CANADIAN GP	Montreal	30	Red Bull Sauber Ford	G	3.0 Sauber C14-Ford Zetec-R V8	engine	12/24
10	FRENCH GP	Magny Cours	30	Red Bull Sauber Ford	G	3.0 Sauber C14-Ford Zetec-R V8	1 lap behind	12/24
6	BRITISH GP	Silverstone	30	Red Bull Sauber Ford	G	3.0 Sauber C14-Ford Zetec-R V8	1 lap behind	12/24
ret	GERMAN GP	Hockenheim	30	Red Bull Sauber Ford	G	3.0 Sauber C14-Ford Zetec-R V8	engine	11/24
5	HUNGARIAN GP	Hungaroring	30	Red Bull Sauber Ford	G	3.0 Sauber C14-Ford Zetec-R V8	1 lap behind	11/24
4	BELGIAN GP	Spa	30	Red Bull Sauber Ford	G	3.0 Sauber C14-Ford Zetec-R V8		10/24
3	ITALIAN GP	Monza	30	Red Bull Sauber Ford	G	3.0 Sauber C14-Ford Zetec-R V8		10/24
6	PORTUGUESE GP	Estoril	30	Red Bull Sauber Ford	G	3.0 Sauber C14-Ford Zetec-R V8	started from back/-1 lap	5/24
ret	EUROPEAN GP	Nürburgring	30	Red Bull Sauber Ford	G	3.0 Sauber C14-Ford Zetec-R V8	collision with Diniz	8/24
7	PACIFIC GP	T.I. Circuit	30	Red Bull Sauber Ford	G	3.0 Sauber C14-Ford Zetec-R V8	1 lap behind	8/24
8	JAPANESE GP	Suzuka	30	Red Bull Sauber Ford	G	3.0 Sauber C14-Ford Zetec-R V8	1 lap behind	8/24
ret	AUSTRALIAN GP	Adelaide	30	Red Bull Sauber Ford	G	3.0 Sauber C14-Ford Zetec-R V8	gearbox	6/24

1996

Championship position: 12th Wins: 0 Pole positions: 0 Fastest laps: 0 Points scored: 7

	Race	Circuit	No	Entrant	Tyres	Car/Engine	Comment	Q Pos/Entries
8	AUSTRALIAN GP	Melbourne	15	Red Bull Sauber Ford	G	3.0 Sauber C15-Ford Zetec R V10	1 lap behind	9/22
ret	BRAZILIAN GP	Interlagos	15	Red Bull Sauber Ford	G	3.0 Sauber C15-Ford Zetec R V10	engine	14/22
ret	ARGENTINE GP	Buenos Aires	15	Red Bull Sauber Ford	G	3.0 Sauber C15-Ford Zetec R V10	spun off	11/22
ret	EUROPEAN GP	Nürburgring	15	Red Bull Sauber Ford	G	3.0 Sauber C15-Ford Zetec R V10	spun off-damaged front wing	10/22
ret	SAN MARINO GP	Imola	15	Red Bull Sauber Ford	G	3.0 Sauber C15-Ford Zetec R V10	brakes	10/22
4	MONACO GP	Monte Carlo	15	Red Bull Sauber Ford	G	3.0 Sauber C15-Ford Zetec R V10	collision/1 lap behind	9/22
4	SPANISH GP	Barcelona	15	Red Bull Sauber Ford	G	3.0 Sauber C15-Ford Zetec R V10	1 laps behind	11/22
ret	CANADIAN GP	Montreal	15	Red Bull Sauber Ford	G	3.0 Sauber C15-Ford Zetec R V10	gearbox	12/22
ret	FRENCH GP	Magny Cours	15	Red Bull Sauber Ford	G	3.0 Sauber C15-Ford Zetec R V10	throttle-spun off	13/22
8	BRITISH GP	Silverstone	15	Red Bull Sauber Ford	G	3.0 Sauber C15-Ford Zetec R V10	1 lap behind	11/22
8	GERMAN GP	Hockenheim	15	Red Bull Sauber Ford	G	3.0 Sauber C15-Ford Zetec R V10	1 lap behind	13/20
ret	HUNGARIAN GP	Hungaroring	15	Red Bull Sauber Ford	G	3.0 Sauber C15-Ford Zetec R V10	engine	10/20
ret	BELGIAN GP	Spa	15	Red Bull Sauber Ford	G	3.0 Sauber C15-Ford Zetec R V10	collision - Herbert & Panis	11/20
ret	ITALIAN GP	Monza	15	Red Bull Sauber Ford	G	3.0 Sauber C15-Ford Zetec R V10	spun off	13/20
7	PORTUGUESE GP	Estoril	15	Red Bull Sauber Ford	G	3.0 Sauber C15-Ford Zetec R V10	1 lap behind	11/20
6	JAPANESE GP	Suzuka	15	Red Bull Sauber Ford	G	3.0 Sauber C15-Ford Zetec R V10		7/20

1997

Championship position: 2nd Wins: 1 Pole positions: 1 Fastest laps: 6 Points scored: 42

	Race	Circuit	No	Entrant	Tyres	Car/Engine	Comment	Q Pos/Entries
8/ret	AUSTRALIAN GP	Melbourne	4	Rothmans Williams Renault	G	3.0 Williams FW19-Renault V10	brake disc failure-spun off/FL	2/24
9	BRAZILIAN GP	Interlagos	4	Rothmans Williams Renault	G	3.0 Williams FW19-Renault V10		8/22
ret	ARGENTINE GP	Buenos Aires	4	Rothmans Williams Renault	G	3.0 Williams FW19-Renault V10	clutch	2/22
1	SAN MARINO GP	Imola	4	Rothmans Williams Renault	G	3.0 Williams FW19-Renault V10	FL	2/22
ret	MONACO GP	Monte Carlo	4	Rothmans Williams Renault	G	3.0 Williams FW19-Renault V10	hit barriers	1/22
8	SPANISH GP	Barcelona	4	Rothmans Williams Renault	G	3.0 Williams FW19-Renault V10		2/22
4	CANADIAN GP	Montreal	4	Rothmans Williams Renault	G	3.0 Williams FW19-Renault V10		4/22
2	FRENCH GP	Magny Cours	4	Rothmans Williams Renault	G	3.0 Williams FW19-Renault V10		2/22
ret	BRITISH GP	Silverstone	4	Rothmans Williams Renault	G	3.0 Williams FW19-Renault V10	collision with Verstappen	2/22
ret	GERMAN GP	Hockenheim	4	Rothmans Williams Renault	G	3.0 Williams FW19-Renault V10	collision with Irvine	5/22
ret	HUNGARIAN GP	Hungaroring	4	Rothmans Williams Renault	G	3.0 Williams FW19-Renault V10	fuel valve/FL	6/22
3*	BELGIAN GP	Spa	4	Rothmans Williams Renault	G	3.0 Williams FW19-Renault V10	*5th place car dsq	7/22
3	ITALIAN GP	Monza	4	Rothmans Williams Renault	G	3.0 Williams FW19-Renault V10		2/22
3	AUSTRIAN GP	A1-Ring	4	Rothmans Williams Renault	G	3.0 Williams FW19-Renault V10		4/22
3	LUXEMBOURG GP	Nürburgring	4	Rothmans Williams Renault	G	3.0 Williams FW19-Renault V10	FL	3/22
2	JAPANESE GP	Suzuka	4	Rothmans Williams Renault	G	3.0 Williams FW19-Renault V10	FL	6/22
6	EUROPEAN GP	Jerez	4	Rothmans Williams Renault	G	3.0 Williams FW19-Renault V10	FL	3/22

1998

Championship position: 7th= Wins: 0 Pole positions: 0 Fastest laps: 0 Points scored: 17

	Race	Circuit	No	Entrant	Tyres	Car/Engine	Comment	Q Pos/Entries
3	AUSTRALIAN GP	Melbourne	2	Winfield Williams	G	3.0 Williams FW20-Mechachrome V10	1 lap behind	6/22
5	BRAZILIAN GP	Interlagos	2	Winfield Williams	G	3.0 Williams FW20-Mechachrome V10	1 lap behind	3/22
9	ARGENTINE GP	Buenos Aires	2	Winfield Williams	G	3.0 Williams FW20-Mechachrome V10	1 lap behind	6/22
5	SAN MARINO GP	Imola	2	Winfield Williams	G	3.0 Williams FW20-Mechachrome V10		8/22
8	SPANISH GP	Barcelona	2	Winfield Williams	G	3.0 Williams FW20-Mechachrome V10	2 laps behind	13/22
ret	MONACO GP	Monte Carlo	2	Winfield Williams	G	3.0 Williams FW20-Mechachrome V10	pushed off by Irvine	5/22
ret	CANADIAN GP	Montreal	2	Winfield Williams	G	3.0 Williams FW20-Mechachrome V10	pushed off by M Schumacher	7/22

15/ret	FRENCH GP	Magny Cours	2	Winfield Williams	G	3.0 Williams FW20-Mechachrome V10	collision-bent track rod/-3 laps	8/22
ret	BRITISH GP	Silverstone	2	Winfield Williams	G	3.0 Williams FW20-Mechachrome V10	spun off	6/22
ret	AUSTRIAN GP	A1-Ring	2	Winfield Williams	G	3.0 Williams FW20-Mechachrome V10	engine	7/22
9	GERMAN GP	Hockenheim	2	Winfield Williams	G	3.0 Williams FW20-Mechachrome V10		10/22
5	HUNGARIAN GP	Hungaroring	2	Winfield Williams	G	3.0 Williams FW20-Mechachrome V10	raced with intestinal bug	7/22
4	BELGIAN GP	Spa	2	Winfield Williams	G	3.0 Williams FW20-Mechachrome V10		9/22
7	ITALIAN GP	Monza	2	Winfield Williams	G	3.0 Williams FW20-Mechachrome V10	1 lap behind	12/22
5	LUXEMBOURG GP	Nürburgring	2	Winfield Williams	G	3.0 Williams FW20-Mechachrome V10		7/22
5	JAPANESE GP	Suzuka	2	Winfield Williams	G	3.0 Williams FW20-Mechachrome V10		5/22

1999	Championship position: 3rd	Wins: 2	Pole positions: 1	Fastest laps: 0	Points scored: 54

2	AUSTRALIAN GP	Melbourne	8	Benson & Hedges Jordan	B	3.0 Jordan 199-Mugen Honda V10		5/22
3/ret	BRAZILIAN GP	Interlagos	8	Benson & Hedges Jordan	B	3.0 Jordan 199-Mugen Honda V10	stopped on last lap-low fuel	8/22
ret	SAN MARINO GP	Imola	8	Benson & Hedges Jordan	B	3.0 Jordan 199-Mugen Honda V10	slid off on Irvine's oi;	7/22
4	MONACO GP	Monte Carlo	8	Benson & Hedges Jordan	B	3.0 Jordan 199-Mugen Honda V10		6/22
ret	SPANISH GP	Barcelona	8	Benson & Hedges Jordan	B	3.0 Jordan 199-Mugen Honda V10	differential	8/22
11/ret	CANADIAN GP	Montreal	8	Benson & Hedges Jordan	B	3.0 Jordan 199-Mugen Honda V10	brake disc exploded-crashed	6/22
1	FRENCH GP	Magny Cours	8	Benson & Hedges Jordan	B	3.0 Jordan 199-Mugen Honda V10		5/22
4	BRITISH GP	Silverstone	8	Benson & Hedges Jordan	B	3.0 Jordan 199-Mugen Honda V10		5/22
4	AUSTRIAN GP	A1-Ring	8	Benson & Hedges Jordan	B	3.0 Jordan 199-Mugen Honda V10		4/22
3	GERMAN GP	Hockenheim	8	Benson & Hedges Jordan	B	3.0 Jordan 199-Mugen Honda V10		2/22
4	HUNGARIAN GP	Hungaroring	8	Benson & Hedges Jordan	B	3.0 Jordan 199-Mugen Honda V10		5/22
3	BELGIAN GP	Spa	8	Benson & Hedges Jordan	B	3.0 Jordan 199-Mugen Honda V10		3/22
1	ITALIAN GP	Monza	8	Benson & Hedges Jordan	B	3.0 Jordan 199-Mugen Honda V10		2/22
ret	EUROPEAN GP	Nürburgring	8	Benson & Hedges Jordan	B	3.0 Jordan 199-Mugen Honda V10	electrics when leading	1/22
6	MALAYSIAN GP	Sepang	8	Benson & Hedges Jordan	B	3.0 Jordan 199-Mugen Honda V10	fine drive from low grid position	14/22
4	JAPANESE GP	Suzuka	8	Benson & Hedges Jordan	B	3.0 Jordan 199-Mugen Honda V10		4/22

GP Starts: 97   GP Wins: 0   Pole positions: 2   Fastest laps: 6   Points: 142

PAUL FRÈRE

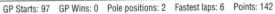

Paul Frère was a rarity in that he was not a full-time driver, preferring to maintain his profession as an international motoring journalist throughout a long and successful racing career.

He made his debut in the Spa 24 Hours, sharing an MG with Jacques Swaters, the pair finishing fourth in class, but it was not until 1952 that he raced in earnest. After winning a big production car race in an Oldsmobile at Spa, Frère picked up a last-minute drive with HWM in the GP des Frontières at Chimay. Left at the start, he overhauled Downing's Connaught right at the death to score a surprise win. HWM's John Heath immediately offered Paul a drive in the forthcoming Belgian GP and he delighted his entrant by bringing the car home in fifth place in pouring rain.

Frère raced for HWM again in 1953; his luck was out this time in Grands Prix, but he did finish a brilliant second in the rain in the Eifelrennen. For 1954 he accepted a few rides with Gordini in F1, and drove at Le Mans for the first time in an Aston Martin sports car.

The Sarthe classic was to become an important race in Frère's career. Second in the tragic 1955 race in an Aston, he was involved in a first-lap crash in a works Jaguar in 1956, finished fourth in 1957 and '58, second again in an Aston in 1959, and finally won in 1960 sharing a works Ferrari with Gendebien. This partnership incidentally was also victorious in the Reims 12 Hours of 1957.

Ferrari also gave Paul an opportunity to drive his Formula 1 cars, and he did not disappoint, taking fourth place in the 1955 Belgian GP and a quite magnificent second behind Peter Collins at Spa again in 1956. He made a return to single-seaters in 1960, his final season, winning the South African GP in an Equipe Nationale Belge Cooper, then showing his consistency and reliable driving skills on his return to Europe to take fifth places at Syracuse and Brussels and sixth at Pau.

JOE FRY

A man of a quiet and retiring disposition, J G 'Joe' Fry was a sprint and hill-climb specialist who developed his own lightweight specials. In 1949 he broke Raymond Mays' record at Shelsley Walsh, and his sprint machine was one of the fastest in the country regardless of engine capacity. In its 1950 guise, the rear-engined 'Freikaiserwagen' was fitted with a potent twin-cylinder Blackburn air-cooled engine with two-stage supercharging, but in a minor meeting at Blandford Camp, in Dorset, Fry lost control of the machine on a fast bend and crashed with fatal results. Just a few weeks earlier he had shared a Maserati with Shawe-Taylor in the British Grand Prix.

FRÈRE, Paul (B) b 30/1/1917, Le Havre, France

	1952	Championship position: 11th=		Wins: 0	Pole positions: 0	Fastest laps: 0	Points scored: 2			
	Race	Circuit	No	Entrant		Tyres	Car/Engine		Comment	Q Pos/Entries
5	BELGIAN GP	Spa	28	HW Motors Ltd		D	2.0 HWM-Alta 4		*2 laps behind*	8/22
ret	GERMAN GP	Nürburgring	112	HW Motors Ltd		D	2.0 HWM-Alta 4		*transmission*	13/32
ret	DUTCH GP	Zandvoort	14	Ecurie Belge		E	1.5 Simca Gordini Type 15 4		*clutch/gearbox*	11/18
	1953	Championship position: Unplaced								
10	BELGIAN GP	Spa	24	HW Motors Ltd		D	2.0 HWM-Alta 4		*6 laps behind*	11/22
ret	SWISS GP	Bremgarten	14	HW Motors Ltd		D	2.0 HWM-Alta 4		*engine*	16/23
	1954	Championship position: Unplaced								
ret	BELGIAN GP	Spa	16	Equipe Gordini		E	2.0 Gordini Type 16 6		*engine*	10/15
ret	FRENCH GP	Reims	28	Equipe Gordini		E	2.0 Gordini Type 16 6		*rear axle*	19/22
ret	GERMAN GP	Nürburgring	10	Equipe Gordini		E	2.0 Gordini Type 16 6		*lost wheel*	6/23
	1955	Championship position: 11th		Wins: 0	Pole positions: 0	Fastest laps: 0	Points scored: 3			
8*	MONACO GP	Monte Carlo	48	Scuderia Ferrari		E	2.5 Ferrari 555 4		**took Taruffi's car/-14 laps*	– /22
4	BELGIAN GP	Spa	6	Scuderia Ferrari		E	2.5 Ferrari 555 4			8/14
	1956	Championship position: 6th=		Wins: 0	Pole positions: 0	Fastest laps: 0	Points scored: 6			
2	BELGIAN GP	Spa	6	Scuderia Ferrari		E	2.5 Lancia-Ferrari D50 V8			8/16

GP Starts: 11 GP Wins: 0 Pole positions: 0 Fastest laps: 0 Points: 11

FRY, Joe (GB) b 1915, Chipping Sodbury, Gloucestershire – d 29/7/1950, Blandford Camp, Dorset

	1950	Championship position: Unplaced								
	Race	Circuit	No	Entrant		Tyres	Car/Engine		Comment	Q Pos/Entries
10*	BRITISH GP	Silverstone	10	Joe Fry		D	1.5 s/c Maserati 4CL 4		** Shawe-Taylor also drove*	20/21

GP Starts: 1 GP Wins: 0 Pole positions: 0 Fastest laps: 0 Points: 0

GABBIANI, Beppe (I) b 2/1/1957, Piacenza

	1978	Championship position: Unplaced								
	Race	Circuit	No	Entrant		Tyres	Car/Engine		Comment	Q Pos/Entries
dnq	US GP EAST	Watkins Glen	19	Team Surtees		G	3.0 Surtees TS20-Cosworth V8			27/27
dnq	CANADIAN GP	Montreal	19	Team Surtees		G	3.0 Surtees TS20-Cosworth V8			24/28
	1981	Championship position: Unplaced								
ret	US GP WEST	Long Beach	32	Osella Squadra Corse		M	3.0 Osella FA1B-Cosworth V8		*accident-broken suspension*	24/29
dnq	BRAZILIAN GP	Rio	32	Osella Squadra Corse		M	3.0 Osella FA1B-Cosworth V8			27/30
dnq	ARGENTINE GP	Buenos Aires	32	Osella Squadra Corse		M	3.0 Osella FA1B-Cosworth V8			26/29
ret	SAN MARINO GP	Imola	32	Osella Squadra Corse		M	3.0 Osella FA1B-Cosworth V8		*collision with Alboreto*	20/30
ret	BELGIAN GP	Zolder	32	Osella Squadra Corse		M	3.0 Osella FA1B-Cosworth V8		*engine*	22/31
dnq	MONACO GP	Monte Carlo	31	Osella Squadra Corse		M	3.0 Osella FA1B-Cosworth V8			26/31
dnq	SPANISH GP	Jarama	31	Osella Squadra Corse		M	3.0 Osella FA1B-Cosworth V8			26/30
dnq	FRENCH GP	Dijon	31	Osella Squadra Corse		M	3.0 Osella FA1B-Cosworth V8			28/29
dnq	BRITISH GP	Silverstone	31	Osella Squadra Corse		M	3.0 Osella FA1B-Cosworth V8			30/30
dnq	GERMAN GP	Hockenheim	31	Osella Squadra Corse		M	3.0 Osella FA1B-Cosworth V8			27/30
dnq	AUSTRIAN GP	Österreichring	31	Osella Squadra Corse		M	3.0 Osella FA1B-Cosworth V8			28/28
dnq	DUTCH GP	Zandvoort	31	Osella Squadra Corse		M	3.0 Osella FA1B-Cosworth V8			29/30
dnq	ITALIAN GP	Monza	31	Osella Squadra Corse		M	3.0 Osella FA1B-Cosworth V8			26/30
dnq	CANADIAN GP	Montreal	31	Osella Squadra Corse		M	3.0 Osella FA1B-Cosworth V8			30/30
dnq	CAESARS PALACE GP	Las Vegas	31	Osella Squadra Corse		M	3.0 Osella FA1B-Cosworth V8			30/30

GP Starts: 3 GP Wins: 0 Pole positions: 0 Fastest laps: 0 Points: 0

BEPPE GABBIANI

After seven years in karting, this Italian rich kid decided to try his hand at F3 in 1977, immediately winning his first big race at Paul Ricard. Flushed with his success, Beppe was soon in Formula 2 and by the end of the 1978 season he had had a couple of GP drives with Surtees in place of the injured Vittorio Brambilla.

Gabbiani's fortunes dipped in the first part of 1979, when he seemed to crash regularly in Formula 2 and a 'rent-a-drive' in a Shadow in a non-championship F1 race at Imola saw him non-start after an embarrassing practice period. But to be fair he was a quick driver, and he buckled down to rescue his season with second places in F2 at Mugello and Misano.

His next season in F2 with Maurer brought little success after a late start, and for 1981 he joined Osella for a tilt at Grands Prix which found him out of his depth. The Italian's Formula 1 opportunities had undoubtedly come too soon, and he retrenched in 1982, returning to F2 with Maurer, where he faced a stern challenge from gifted team-mate Stefan Bellof. Given a real chance to demonstrate his class in 1983 with the top Onyx March team, Gabbiani started brilliantly, with four wins in the first five races, but the title eventually slipped from his grasp as the Ralt-Hondas of Palmer and Thackwell overwhelmed him. After this disappointment Gabbiani's front-line career dribbled away, a few outings in F2 and F3000 offering little encouragement. In the nineties he continued to make occasional forays onto the circuits, most recently in 1999 at Monza where he raced a Riley & Scott in the International Sports Racing Series.

BERTRAND GACHOT

A very confident and determined driver, Gachot assiduously built his career to reach his goal of racing in a front-running Formula 1 team, only to throw it away with a moment of madness when an assault on a London taxi-driver after a traffic altercation left him facing imprisonment.

Brilliantly successful in Formula Ford, winning the major British 1600 title in 1985 and the 2000 crown the following year after a torrid battle with Mark Blundell, Bertrand graduated to the British F3 championship with West Surrey Racing for 1987 and emerged as runner-up after another no-holds-barred battle, this time with Johnny Herbert.

A solid 1988 season in F3000 lacked only a win and he finished fifth overall, quickly tying up a deal to race for the newly formed Onyx Grand Prix team in 1989. It was not a happy season for Gachot who, having been overshadowed by the experienced Johansson, found himself replaced by J J Lehto. Taking his sponsorship money to Rial for a couple more unproductive outings, Gachot then plunged into a disastrous 1990 season with the Coloni-Subaru. Then came the big break with Eddie Jordan's fledgling F1 team, whose new Gary Anderson-designed car was a revelation. Suddenly Gachot was really racing and showing his undoubted talent – until his shock incarceration. His drive with Jordan was lost but, undaunted, he bounced back with the struggling Larrousse team. Bertrand's F1 career was on hold in 1993 – although he made a good Indy Car debut at Toronto – while he finalised plans to lead Pacific's Grand Prix challenge in 1994.

Bertrand had worked ceaselessly to help find sponsorship for the team and it must have been doubly hard for him to realise that the PR01 was a substandard car which had no prospects of improvement. Although the sparser grids in 1995 guaranteed that Pacific would at least be starting races, their second Grand Prix challenger proved no great step forward from the first, despite being a totally new design. As the team's financial situation worsened Gachot stood down to allow pay drivers Lavaggi and Deletraz to provide a cash lifeline, but he did return for the last three races to see out the season. Given Pacific's previous track record of excellence in other formulae, there was plenty of sympathy for their hapless plight, but there is no room for sentiment in F1 and the team followed Simtek into liquidation. For Keith Wiggins and Bertrand Gachot, a dream was over.

GACHOT, Bertrand (F) b 23/12/1962, Luxembourg

	1989			Championship position: Unplaced				
	Race	Circuit	No	Entrant	Tyres	Car/Engine	Comment	Q Pos/Entries
dnpq	BRAZILIAN GP	Rio	37	Moneytron Onyx	G	3.5 Onyx ORE 1-Cosworth V8		38/38
dnpq	SAN MARINO GP	Imola	37	Moneytron Onyx	G	3.5 Onyx ORE 1-Cosworth V8		31/39
dnpq	MONACO GP	Monte Carlo	37	Moneytron Onyx	G	3.5 Onyx ORE 1-Cosworth V8		34/39
dnpq	MEXICAN GP	Mexico City	37	Moneytron Onyx	G	3.5 Onyx ORE 1-Cosworth V8		31/39
dnpq	US GP (PHOENIX)	Phoenix	37	Moneytron Onyx	G	3.5 Onyx ORE 1-Cosworth V8		39/39
dnpq	CANADIAN GP	Montreal	37	Moneytron Onyx	G	3.5 Onyx ORE 1-Cosworth V8		32/39
13	FRENCH GP	Paul Ricard	37	Moneytron Onyx	G	3.5 Onyx ORE 1-Cosworth V8	pit stop-overheating battery/-4 laps	11/39
12	BRITISH GP	Silverstone	37	Moneytron Onyx	G	3.5 Onyx ORE 1-Cosworth V8	raced spare car/2 laps behind	21/39
dnq	GERMAN GP	Hockenheim	37	Moneytron Onyx	G	3.5 Onyx ORE 1-Cosworth V8		28/39
ret	HUNGARIAN GP	Hungaroring	37	Moneytron Onyx	G	3.5 Onyx ORE 1-Cosworth V8	differential	21/39

ret	BELGIAN GP	Spa	37	Moneytron Onyx	G	3.5 Onyx ORE 1-Cosworth V8	wheel bearing-crashed	23/39
ret	ITALIAN GP	Monza	37	Moneytron Onyx	G	3.5 Onyx ORE 1-Cosworth V8	accident-holed radiator	22/39
dnq	JAPANESE GP	Suzuka	39	Rial Racing	G	3.5 Rial ARC2-Cosworth V8		30/39
dnq	AUSTRALIAN GP	Adelaide	39	Rial Racing	G	3.5 Rial ARC2-Cosworth V8		29/39

1990 Championship position: Unplaced

dnpq	US GP (PHOENIX)	Phoenix	31	Subaru Coloni Racing	G	3.5 Coloni C3B-Subaru F12	no time set	– /35
dnpq	BRAZILIAN GP	Interlagos	31	Subaru Coloni Racing	G	3.5 Coloni C3B-Subaru F12		33/35
dnpq	SAN MARINO GP	Imola	31	Subaru Coloni Racing	G	3.5 Coloni C3B-Subaru F12		31/34
dnpq	MONACO GP	Monte Carlo	31	Subaru Coloni Racing	G	3.5 Coloni C3B-Subaru F12		34/33
dnpq	CANADIAN GP	Montreal	31	Subaru Coloni Racing	G	3.5 Coloni C3B-Subaru F12		33/35
dnpq	MEXICAN GP	Mexico City	31	Subaru Coloni Racing	G	3.5 Coloni C3B-Subaru F12		33/35
dnpq	FRENCH GP	Paul Ricard	31	Subaru Coloni Racing	G	3.5 Coloni C3B-Subaru F12		34/35
dnpq	BRITISH GP	Silverstone	31	Subaru Coloni Racing	G	3.5 Coloni C3B-Subaru F12		34/35
dnpq	GERMAN GP	Hockenheim	31	Subaru Coloni Racing	G	3.5 Coloni C3C-Cosworth V8		33/35
dnpq	HUNGARIAN GP	Hungaroring	31	Subaru Coloni Racing	G	3.5 Coloni C3C-Cosworth V8		32/35
dnq	BELGIAN GP	Spa	31	Subaru Coloni Racing	G	3.5 Coloni C3C-Cosworth V8		30/33
dnq	ITALIAN GP	Monza	31	Subaru Coloni Racing	G	3.5 Coloni C3C-Cosworth V8		30/33
dnq	PORTUGUESE GP	Estoril	31	Subaru Coloni Racing	G	3.5 Coloni C3C-Cosworth V8		30/33
dnq	SPANISH GP	Jerez	31	Subaru Coloni Racing	G	3.5 Coloni C3C-Cosworth V8		30/33
dnq	JAPANESE GP	Suzuka	31	Subaru Coloni Racing	G	3.5 Coloni C3C-Cosworth V8		30/30
dnq	AUSTRALIAN GP	Adelaide	31	Subaru Coloni Racing	G	3.5 Coloni C3C-Cosworth V8		30/30

1991 Championship position: 12= Wins: 0 Pole positions: 0 Fastest laps: 0 Points scored: 4

10/ret	US GP (PHOENIX)	Phoenix	32	Team 7UP Jordan	G	3.5 Jordan 191-Ford HB V8	engine/6 laps behind	14/34
13/ret	BRAZILIAN GP	Interlagos	32	Team 7UP Jordan	G	3.5 Jordan 191-Ford HB V8	fuel pick-up/8 laps behind	10/34
ret	SAN MARINO GP	Imola	32	Team 7UP Jordan	G	3.5 Jordan 191-Ford HB V8	damage after earlier spin	12/34
8	MONACO GP	Monte Carlo	32	Team 7UP Jordan	G	3.5 Jordan 191-Ford HB V8	2 laps behind	24/34
5	CANADIAN GP	Montreal	32	Team 7UP Jordan	G	3.5 Jordan 191-Ford HB V8		14/34
ret	MEXICAN GP	Mexico City	32	Team 7UP Jordan	G	3.5 Jordan 191-Ford HB V8	spun off	20/34
ret	FRENCH GP	Magny Cours	32	Team 7UP Jordan	G	3.5 Jordan 191-Ford HB V8	spun off on first lap	19/34
6	BRITISH GP	Silverstone	32	Team 7UP Jordan	G	3.5 Jordan 191-Ford HB V8	1 lap behind	17/34
6	GERMAN GP	Hockenheim	32	Team 7UP Jordan	G	3.5 Jordan 191-Ford HB V8		11/34
9	HUNGARIAN GP	Hungaroring	32	Team 7UP Jordan	G	3.5 Jordan 191-Ford HB V8	spin/FL/1 lap behind	16/34
dnq	AUSTRALIAN GP	Adelaide	29	Larrousse F1	G	3.5 Larrousse Lola L91-Cosworth V8		30/32

1992 Championship position: 17th= Wins: 0 Pole positions: 0 Fastest laps: 0 Points scored: 1

ret	SOUTH AFRICAN GP	Kyalami	29	Central Park Venturi Larrousse	G	3.5 Venturi LC92-Lamborghini V12	suspension damage	22/30
11	MEXICAN GP	Mexico City	29	Central Park Venturi Larrousse	G	3.5 Venturi LC92-Lamborghini V12	engine misfire/3 laps behind	13/30
ret	BRAZILIAN GP	Interlagos	29	Central Park Venturi Larrousse	G	3.5 Venturi LC92-Lamborghini V12	rear suspension	18/31
ret	SPANISH GP	Barcelona	29	Central Park Venturi Larrousse	G	3.5 Venturi LC92-Lamborghini V12	engine	24/32
ret	SAN MARINO GP	Imola	29	Central Park Venturi Larrousse	G	3.5 Venturi LC92-Lamborghini V12	spun off	19/32
6	MONACO GP	Monte Carlo	29	Central Park Venturi Larrousse	G	3.5 Venturi LC92-Lamborghini V12	1 lap behind	15/32
dsq*	CANADIAN GP	Montreal	29	Central Park Venturi Larrousse	G	3.5 Venturi LC92-Lamborghini V12	shunted by Grouillard-*push start	19/32
ret	FRENCH GP	Magny Cours	29	Central Park Venturi Larrousse	G	3.5 Venturi LC92-Lamborghini V12	collision with Suzuki lap 1	13/30
ret	BRITISH GP	Silverstone	29	Central Park Venturi Larrousse	G	3.5 Venturi LC92-Lamborghini V12	rear wheel bearing	11/32
14	GERMAN GP	Hockenheim	29	Central Park Venturi Larrousse	G	3.5 Venturi LC92-Lamborghini V12	1 lap behind	25/32
ret	HUNGARIAN GP	Hungaroring	29	Central Park Venturi Larrousse	G	3.5 Venturi LC92-Lamborghini V12	collision with Suzuki	15/31
18/ret	BELGIAN GP	Spa	29	Central Park Venturi Larrousse	G	3.5 Venturi LC92-Lamborghini V12	spun off/4 laps behind	20/30
ret	ITALIAN GP	Monza	29	Central Park Venturi Larrousse	G	3.5 Venturi LC92-Lamborghini V12	engine	10/28
ret	PORTUGUESE GP	Estoril	29	Central Park Venturi Larrousse	G	3.5 Venturi LC92-Lamborghini V12	fuel pressure	13/26
ret	JAPANESE GP	Suzuka	29	Central Park Venturi Larrousse	G	3.5 Venturi LC92-Lamborghini V12	collision with Katayama	18/26
ret	AUSTRALIAN GP	Adelaide	29	Central Park Venturi Larrousse	G	3.5 Venturi LC92-Lamborghini V12	engine	21/26

1994 Championship position: Unplaced

ret	BRAZILIAN GP	Interlagos	34	Pacific Grand Prix Ltd	G	3.5 Pacific PR01-Ilmor V10	hit by Beretta-spun off	25/28
dnq	PACIFIC GP	T.I. Circuit	34	Pacific Grand Prix Ltd	G	3.5 Pacific PR01-Ilmor V10		28/28
ret	SAN MARINO GP	Imola	34	Pacific Grand Prix Ltd	G	3.5 Pacific PR01-Ilmor V10	engine	25/28
ret	MONACO GP	Monte Carlo	34	Pacific Grand Prix Ltd	G	3.5 Pacific PR01-Ilmor V10	gearbox	23/24
ret	SPANISH GP	Barcelona	34	Pacific Grand Prix Ltd	G	3.5 Pacific PR01-Ilmor V10	wing damage	25/27
ret	CANADIAN GP	Montreal	34	Pacific Grand Prix Ltd	G	3.5 Pacific PR01-Ilmor V10	engine	26/27
dnq	FRENCH GP	Magny Cours	34	Pacific Grand Prix Ltd	G	3.5 Pacific PR01-Ilmor V10		27/28
dnq	BRITISH GP	Silverstone	34	Pacific Grand Prix Ltd	G	3.5 Pacific PR01-Ilmor V10		27/28
dnq	GERMAN GP	Hockenheim	34	Pacific Grand Prix Ltd	G	3.5 Pacific PR01-Ilmor V10		28/28
dnq	HUNGARIAN GP	Hungaroring	34	Pacific Grand Prix Ltd	G	3.5 Pacific PR01-Ilmor V10		27/28
dnq	BELGIAN GP	Spa	34	Pacific Grand Prix Ltd	G	3.5 Pacific PR01-Ilmor V10		27/28
dnq	ITALIAN GP	Monza	34	Pacific Grand Prix Ltd	G	3.5 Pacific PR01-Ilmor V10		27/28
dnq	PORTUGUESE GP	Estoril	34	Pacific Grand Prix Ltd	G	3.5 Pacific PR01-Ilmor V10		27/28
dnq	EUROPEAN GP	Jerez	34	Pacific Grand Prix Ltd	G	3.5 Pacific PR01-Ilmor V10		27/28
dnq	JAPANESE GP	Suzuka	34	Pacific Grand Prix Ltd	G	3.5 Pacific PR01-Ilmor V10		27/28
dnq	AUSTRALIAN GP	Adelaide	34	Pacific Grand Prix Ltd	G	3.5 Pacific PR01-Ilmor V10		28/28

1995 Championship position: Unplaced

ret	BRAZILIAN GP	Interlagos	16	Pacific Grand Prix Ltd	G	3.0 Pacific PR02-Ford ED V8	gearbox	20/26
ret	ARGENTINE GP	Buenos Aires	16	Pacific Grand Prix Ltd	G	3.0 Pacific PR02-Ford ED V8	collision with Wendlinger	23/26
ret	SAN MARINO GP	Imola	16	Pacific Grand Prix Ltd	G	3.0 Pacific PR02-Ford ED V8	gearbox	22/26
ret	SPANISH GP	Barcelona	16	Pacific Grand Prix Ltd	G	3.0 Pacific PR02-Ford ED V8	fire	24/26
ret	MONACO GP	Monte Carlo	16	Pacific Grand Prix Ltd	G	3.0 Pacific PR02-Ford ED V8	gearbox	21/26
ret	CANADIAN GP	Montreal	16	Pacific Grand Prix Ltd	G	3.0 Pacific PR02-Ford ED V8	battery	20/24
ret	FRENCH GP	Magny Cours	16	Pacific Grand Prix Ltd	G	3.0 Pacific PR02-Ford ED V8	gearbox	22/24
12	BRITISH GP	Silverstone	16	Pacific Grand Prix Ltd	G	3.0 Pacific PR02-Ford ED V8	3 laps behind	21/24
ret	PACIFIC GP	T.I. Circuit	16	Pacific Grand Prix Ltd	G	3.0 Pacific PR02-Ford ED V8	hydraulics	24/24
ret	JAPANESE GP	Suzuka	16	Pacific Grand Prix Ltd	G	3.0 Pacific PR02-Ford ED V8	driveshaft bearing	23/24
8	AUSTRALIAN GP	Adelaide	16	Pacific Grand Prix Ltd	G	3.0 Pacific PR02-Ford ED V8	5 laps behind	23/24

GP Starts: 47 GP Wins: 0 Pole positions: 0 Fastest laps: 1 Points: 5

PATRICK GAILLARD

A graduate of Formule Super Renault, Gaillard made his reputation in Formula 3 with a Chevron, finishing third in the 1978 European championship in a works B43 and winning rounds at Imola and the Nürburgring. He moved into Formula 2 for the 1979 season, but stepped into the Ensign seat vacated by Derek Daly at the French GP. The car was extremely difficult to handle, and Patrick, though very brave, qualified only twice in five races before he in turn was replaced by Marc Surer.

Gaillard made a brief return the following season to finish sixth in the infamous Spanish GP which was subsequently downgraded from championship status. He then picked up the odd Formula 2 ride before slipping from the limelight.

GIOVANNI 'NANNI' GALLI

Giovanni Galli was the son of a wealthy textile merchant, who began racing at the comparatively late age of 24. He had sensed that his family would be opposed to his early racing activities, and ran under the pseudonym 'Nanni', which stuck. He bought a Mini-Cooper with which he entered the 1965 Italian touring car championship and proceeded to take ten class wins in ten starts, before moving on to an Alfa Romeo GTA.

Galli began to forge a reputation in sports car racing in the factory Alfa Romeo T33 in 1967, though he had to wait until the following season for success, winning the Circuit of Mugello (with Bianchi and Vaccarella), and finishing second in both the Targa Florio and the Imola 500 Km (both with Giunti). He was to be a mainstay of the Autodelta sports car programme right through until 1972, with many placings in the top six.

In tandem with his long-distance activities, Galli moved into single-seaters, initially with Tecno in Formula 2. He then graduated to Grand Prix racing via an Alfa Romeo engine-supply deal, first at Monza in 1970 with McLaren, and then with March in 1971. For 1972, he became involved in the well-funded but unsuccessful Tecno F1 project, his best result being a third place in the poorly supported GP of the Italian Republic at Vallelunga. With Clay Regazzoni indisposed, Galli was invited to represent Ferrari in the French GP, but could finish no better than 13th.

For 1973, 'Nanni' joined Frank Williams to race his new Iso car, but after a handful of disappointing outings, he quit the team and announced his retirement, athough he was to return briefly in 1974 at the wheel of a works Abarth sports car.

OSCAR GÁLVEZ

A great hidden talent, Gálvez was the early rival and inspiration to Fangio back in their native Argentina both before and after the war. Oscar and his younger brother Juan set new standards of preparation and performance in the gruelling road races so popular there and they were usually seriously threatened only by 'the Maestro'.

Gálvez was equally skilled at the art of circuit racing. Driving an Alfa Romeo, he won the Formula Libre Eva Peron Cup in 1949, beating Fangio, and was highly placed in the same event on a number of other occasions. Invited to drive a works Maserati in 1953 (his only Grand Prix), Oscar finished fifth.

In the absence of Fangio, 'Los Gálvez' continued to dominate South American road racing in their Fords through the fifties and into the early sixties until disaster struck when Juan was killed in a crash early in 1963. Oscar raced on, but retired following a serious accident in 1964 to concentrate on managing the works-supported Ford team.

GAILLARD, Patrick (F) b 12/2/1952, Paris

	1979	Championship position: Unplaced						
	Race	Circuit	No	Entrant	Tyres	Car/Engine	Comment	Q Pos/Entries
dnq	FRENCH GP	Dijon	22	Team Ensign	G	3.0 Ensign N179-Cosworth V8		26/27
13	BRITISH GP	Silverstone	22	Team Ensign	G	3.0 Ensign N179-Cosworth V8	3 laps behind	23/26
dnq	GERMAN GP	Hockenheim	22	Team Ensign	G	3.0 Ensign N179-Cosworth V8		25/26
ret	AUSTRIAN GP	Österreichring	22	Team Ensign	G	3.0 Ensign N179-Cosworth V8	front suspension	24/26
dnq	DUTCH GP	Zandvoort	22	Team Ensign	G	3.0 Ensign N179-Cosworth V8		25/26

GP Starts: 2   GP Wins: 0   Pole positions: 0   Fastest laps: 0   Points: 0

GALLI, Nanni (Giovanni) (I) b 2/10/1940, Bologna

	1970	Championship position: Unplaced						
	Race	Circuit	No	Entrant	Tyres	Car/Engine	Comment	Q Pos/Entries
dnq	ITALIAN GP	Monza	36	Bruce McLaren Motor Racing	G	3.0 McLaren M7D-Alfa Romeo V8		27/27
	1971	Championship position: Unplaced						
dnq	MONACO GP	Monte Carlo	19	STP March	F	3.0 March 711-Alfa Romeo V8		21/23
ret	DUTCH GP	Zandvoort	18	STP March	F	3.0 March 711-Alfa Romeo V8	incident with Cevert-spun off	20/24
dns	FRENCH GP	Paul Ricard	33	STP March	F	3.0 March 711-Cosworth V8	Soler-Roig drove car in race	(20)/24
11	BRITISH GP	Silverstone	20	STP March	F	3.0 March 711-Cosworth V8	3 laps behind	21/24
12	GERMAN GP	Nürburgring	17	STP March	F	3.0 March 711-Alfa Romeo V8	broken engine mounting/-2 laps	21/23
12	AUSTRIAN GP	Österreichring	19	STP March	F	3.0 March 711-Alfa Romeo V8	pit stop/3 laps behind	15/22
ret	ITALIAN GP	Monza	22	STP March	F	3.0 March 711-Cosworth V8	electrics	19/24
16	CANADIAN GP	Mosport Park	18	STP March	F	3.0 March 711-Cosworth V8	7 laps behind	20/27
ret	US GP	Watkins Glen	26	STP March	F	3.0 March 711-Cosworth V8	steering and suspension	25/32
	1972	Championship position: Unplaced						
ret	BELGIAN GP	Nivelles	22	Martini Racing Team	F	3.0 Tecno PA123 F12	spun-hit by Regazzoni-suspension	24/26
13	FRENCH GP	Clermont Ferrand	30	Scuderia Ferrari SpA SEFAC	F	3.0 Ferrari 312B2 F12	1 lap behind	21/29
ret	BRITISH GP	Brands Hatch	30	Martini Racing Team	F	3.0 Tecno PA123 F12	spun off	=18/27
nc	AUSTRIAN GP	Österreichring	15	Martini Racing Team	F	3.0 Tecno PA123 F12	pit stops/9 laps behind	24/26
ret	ITALIAN GP	Monza	11	Martini Racing Team	F	3.0 Tecno PA123 F12	engine	23/27
	1973	Championship position: Unplaced						
ret	ARGENTINE GP	Buenos Aires	36	Frank Williams Racing Cars	F	3.0 Iso Williams FX3B-Cosworth V8	accessory belt to pumps	16/19
9	BRAZILIAN GP	Interlagos	20	Frank Williams Racing Cars	F	3.0 Iso Williams FX3B-Cosworth V8	2 laps behind	18/20
11	SPANISH GP	Montjuich Park	24	Frank Williams Racing Cars	F	3.0 Iso Williams 1R-Cosworth V8	pit stop/6 laps behind	20/22
ret	BELGIAN GP	Zolder	26	Frank Williams Racing Cars	F	3.0 Iso Williams 1R-Cosworth V8	engine	17/23
ret	MONACO GP	Monte Carlo	26	Frank Williams Racing Cars	F	3.0 Iso Williams 1R-Cosworth V8	driveshaft	22/26

GP Starts: 17   GP Wins: 0   Pole positions: 0   Fastest laps: 0   Points: 0

GÁLVEZ, Oscar (RA) b 17/8/1913, Buenos Aires – d 16/12/1989, Buenos Aires

	1953	Championship position: 11th= Wins: 0 Pole positions: 0 Fastest laps: 0 Points scored: 2						
	Race	Circuit	No	Entrant	Tyres	Car/Engine	Comment	Q Pos/Entries
5	ARGENTINE GP	Buenos Aires	8	Officine Alfieri Maserati	P	2.0 Maserati A6GCM 6	1 lap behind	9/16

GP Starts: 1   GP Wins: 0   Pole positions: 0   Fastest laps: 0   Points: 2

GAMBLE, Fred (USA) b 17/3/1932, Pittsburgh, Pennsylvania

	1960	Championship position: 0 Wins: 0 Pole positions: 0 Fastest laps: 0 Points scored: 0						
	Race	Circuit	No	Entrant	Tyres	Car/Engine	Comment	Q Pos/Entries
10	ITALIAN GP	Monza	28	Camoradi International	D	1.5 Behra-Porsche F4 F2	9 laps behind	14/16

GP Starts: 1   GP Wins: 0   Pole positions: 0   Fastest laps: 0   Points: 0

FRED GAMBLE

Gamble was never a serious racer – he never pretended to be – but, like all race fans, he dreamed that one day he might drive in a Grand Prix. In his case, though, the dream was to come true! After gaining experience with Triumph and MGA cars in the US, Fred stumbled into 'Lucky' Casner, a colourful personality and real wheeler-dealer. In 1960 they formed Scuderia Camoradi with the aim of tackling some of Europe's famous sports car races with a Maserati Birdcage and a Corvette. Fred was only allowed to race the latter car and drove within his limits to finish tenth at Le Mans.

By coincidence the Camoradi base in Modena housed the ex-Behra Porsche F2 car and, knowing that the organisers of the Italian GP were anxious to fill the grid boycotted by the British teams, Fred contacted them and was amazed to be offered $1000 starting money. In the race he ran out of fuel out on the track, and was forced to run half a mile back to his pit. Armed with a 5-gallon can, he refilled the car and eventually finished tenth and last! Gamble returned to the States at the end of the year, and later worked with Shelby's Cobra project, before accepting an offer to join Goodyear in 1963. He was the cutting edge of the tyre giant's move into Grand Prix racing and had the immense satisfaction of seeing two championships won in 1966 and 1967, before handing over the reins to Leo Mehl.

HOWDEN GANLEY

It took a long time for Ganley to realise his ambition to become a Grand Prix driver – which was fired by a visit as a youngster in his native New Zealand to the Grand Prix at Ardmore in 1955. He sailed for England in 1961 with just $50 in his pocket, and found employment as a mechanic preparing cars at a racing school. The urge to drive was occasionally satisfied over the next few years, but his engineering talent kept him well occupied (and paid), so his racing career was on hold.

It was 1967 before Howden embarked on a serious season of Formula 3 in his own shiny-new Brabham which had been financed by his engagement as crew chief for Skip Scott and Peter Revson in the 1966 Can-Am series. Howden plugged away in the formula for another two seasons, mixing it with the best, hoping for the big break which was to come in 1970.

Given the opportunity to compete in F5000, he finished runner-up to Peter Gethin in the championship with a private McLaren M10B, and this success brought an offer to join the BRM team for 1971 as a junior driver. It was a mixed first season, but Howden scored some points at Monza and Watkins Glen, and in non-championship races finished second in the Oulton Park Gold Cup, fourth in the Jochen Rindt Memorial at Hockenheim and fifth in the Race of Champions. Continuing with BRM for 1972, he did not enjoy the best of seasons, again being restricted in the main from using the latest chassis. The high spot of his year came in a different arena, with second place at Le Mans sharing a works Matra with Cevert.

For 1973 Howden threw in his lot with Frank Williams and the Iso-FX3, which was to be a severe disappointment for all concerned, with only a sixth place in Canada salvaging some pride. The season was redeemed a little by his inclusion in the Gulf/John Wyer sports car team,

for whom Ganley's best result was second in the Spa 1000 Km in the Mirage with Schuppan. At the beginning of 1974, Ganley was scratching for a drive, and after racing for March in the first two GPs, and taking fifth in the GP Presidente Medici – a Brazilian non-championship race – he unwisely accepted an offer to drive the mysterious F1 Maki, a Japanese dog with no pedigree. The car suffered a suspension failure in practice for the German GP and Ganley was left with serious foot and ankle injuries which ended his Grand Prix career. Howden, who later ran Tiga Cars with Tim Schenken, is currently a board member of the BRDC at Silverstone.

GANLEY, Howden (NZ) b 24/12/1941, Hamilton

1971 — Championship position: 14th= Wins: 0 Pole positions: 0 Fastest laps: 0 Points scored: 5

	Race	Circuit	No	Entrant	Tyres	Car/Engine	Comment	Q Pos/Entries
ret	SOUTH AFRICAN GP	Kyalami	27	Yardley BRM	F	3.0 BRM P153 V12	driver unwell	24/25
10	SPANISH GP	Montjuich Park	16	Yardley BRM	F	3.0 BRM P153 V12	4 laps behind	=16/22
dnq	MONACO GP	Monte Carlo	16	Yardley BRM	F	3.0 BRM P153 V12		19/23
7	DUTCH GP	Zandvoort	10	Yardley BRM	F	3.0 BRM P153 V12	4 laps behind	9/24
10	FRENCH GP	Paul Ricard	16	Yardley BRM	F	3.0 BRM P153 V12	1 lap behind	16/24
8	BRITISH GP	Silverstone	17	Yardley BRM	F	3.0 BRM P153 V12	pit stop-puncture/-2 laps	11/24
ret	GERMAN GP	Nürburgring	23	Yardley BRM	F	3.0 BRM P153 V12	engine	14/23
ret	AUSTRIAN GP	Österreichring	15	Yardley BRM	F	3.0 BRM P160 V12	ignition	14/22
5	ITALIAN GP	Monza	19	Yardley BRM	F	3.0 BRM P160 V12		4/24
dns	CANADIAN GP	Mosport Park	16	Yardley BRM	F	3.0 BRM P160 V12	accident on warm-up lap	=(7)/27
4	US GP	Watkins Glen	16	Yardley BRM	F	3.0 BRM P160 V12		13/32

1972 — Championship position: 12= Wins: 0 Pole positions: 0 Fastest laps: 0 Points scored: 4

	Race	Circuit	No	Entrant	Tyres	Car/Engine	Comment	Q Pos/Entries
9	ARGENTINE GP	Buenos Aires	3	Marlboro BRM	F	3.0 BRM P160B V12	2 laps behind	13/22
nc	SOUTH AFRICAN GP	Kyalami	23	Marlboro BRM	F	3.0 BRM P160B V12	pit stop/9 laps behind	16/27
ret	SPANISH GP	Jarama	25	Marlboro BRM	F	3.0 BRM P160B V12	engine	20/26
ret	MONACO GP	Monte Carlo	19	Marlboro BRM	F	3.0 BRM P180 V12	collision-Hailwood-suspension	=18/25
8	BELGIAN GP	Nivelles	25	Marlboro BRM	F	3.0 BRM P160B V12	2 laps behind	15/26
dns	FRENCH GP	Clermont Ferrand	23	Marlboro BRM	F	3.0 BRM P160B V12	car driven by Beltoise	(22)/29
4	GERMAN GP	Nürburgring	17	Marlboro BRM	F	3.0 BRM P160C V12		18/27
6	AUSTRIAN GP	Österreichring	9	Marlboro BRM	F	3.0 BRM P160C V12		10/26
11	ITALIAN GP	Monza	22	Marlboro BRM	F	3.0 BRM P160C V12	pit stop/3 laps behind	17/27
10	CANADIAN GP	Mosport Park	15	Marlboro BRM	F	3.0 BRM P160C V12	2 laps behind	14/25
ret	US GP	Watkins Glen	16	Marlboro BRM	F	3.0 BRM P160C V12	engine	17/32

	1973	Championship position: 19th=			Wins: 0	Pole positions: 0	Fastest laps: 0	Points scored: 1		
nc	ARGENTINE GP	Buenos Aires	38	Frank Williams Racing Cars	F	3.0 Iso Williams FX3B-Cosworth V8		pit stop/17 laps behind		19/19
7	BRAZILIAN GP	Interlagos	19	Frank Williams Racing Cars	F	3.0 Iso Williams FX3B-Cosworth V8		1 lap behind		16/20
10	SOUTH AFRICAN GP	Kyalami	21	Frank Williams Racing Cars	F	3.0 Iso Williams FX3B-Cosworth V8		pit stop-puncture/-6 laps		19/25
ret	SPANISH GP	Montjuich Park	23	Frank Williams Racing Cars	F	3.0 Iso Williams 1R-Cosworth V8		out of fuel		21/22
ret	BELGIAN GP	Zolder	25	Frank Williams Racing Cars	F	3.0 Iso Williams 1R-Cosworth V8		throttle stuck/accident		21/23
ret	MONACO GP	Monte Carlo	25	Frank Williams Racing Cars	F	3.0 Iso Williams 1R-Cosworth V8		driveshaft		10/26
11	SWEDISH GP	Anderstorp	25	Frank Williams Racing Cars	F	3.0 Iso Williams 1R-Cosworth V8		4 laps behind		11/22
14	FRENCH GP	Paul Ricard	25	Frank Williams Racing Cars	F	3.0 Iso Williams 1R-Cosworth V8		3 laps behind		24/25
9	BRITISH GP	Silverstone	25	Frank Williams Racing Cars	F	3.0 Iso Williams 1R-Cosworth V8		1 lap behind		18/29
9	DUTCH GP	Zandvoort	25	Frank Williams Racing Cars	F	3.0 Iso Williams 1R-Cosworth V8		collision-Lauda-pit stop/-4 laps		15/24
dns	GERMAN GP	Nürburgring	25	Frank Williams Racing Cars	F	3.0 Iso Williams 1R-Cosworth V8		practice accident		(19)/23
nc	AUSTRIAN GP	Österreichring	25	Frank Williams Racing Cars	F	3.0 Iso Williams 1R-Cosworth V8		pit stop/10 laps behind		21/25
nc	ITALIAN GP	Monza	25	Frank Williams Racing Cars	F	3.0 Iso Williams 1R-Cosworth V8		pit stops/11 laps behind		20/25
6	CANADIAN GP	Mosport Park	25	Frank Williams Racing Cars	F	3.0 Iso Williams 1R-Cosworth V8		1 lap behind		22/26
12	US GP	Watkins Glen	25	Frank Williams Racing Cars	F	3.0 Iso Williams 1R-Cosworth V8		pit stop/2 laps behind		20/28
	1974	Championship position: Unplaced								
8/ret	ARGENTINE GP	Buenos Aires	10	March Engineering	G	3.0 March 741-Cosworth V8		out of fuel/1 lap behind		19/26
ret	BRAZILIAN GP	Interlagos	10	March Engineering	F	3.0 March 741-Cosworth V8		ignition		20/25
dnq	BRITISH GP	Brands Hatch	25	Maki Engineering	F	3.0 Maki F101-Cosworth V8				32/34
dnq	GERMAN GP	Nürburgring	25	Maki Engineering	F	3.0 Maki F101-Cosworth V8		injured in practice accident		32/32

GP Starts: 35   GP Wins: 0   Pole positions: 0   Fastest laps: 0   Points: 10

FRANK GARDNER

Frank is another driver whose brief Grand Prix career did no justice to his talent, for here was one of the world's toughest, most determined and professional drivers, who was destined to enjoy an immensely long and successful career outside the sphere of Formula 1.

A typical Australian all-round sportsman, boxer, swimmer and motor cycle ace, Frank took up car racing in 1956-57 when he won 23 out of 24 races in a C-Type Jaguar to become NSW sports car champion. Inevitably he headed for England and found employment not as a driver but as a mechanic, for Aston Martin, Jim Russell and, in 1962, Jack Brabham's newly formed team, working on the Formula Junior cars. He drove the Brabham a few times that year but turned down Jack's offer of a full-time ride for 1963 (taken instead by Denny Hulme), opting to join Ian Walker for a massively successful sports and Formula Junior programme.

This had established Gardner as a serious proposition, and he moved to John Willment's team in 1964 to drive in Formula 2, also handling his stable of powerful sports and saloon cars. Ambitiously, the team went into Formula 1 in 1965, but were just not up to it, though they did take an aggregate fourth place in the Race of Champions. Frank felt he had made a bit of a fool of himself, and gave Grand Prix racing a wide berth except for a couple of drives in 1968. He contested the Tasman series in a Brabham during this period, giving a good account of himself against the likes of Clark, Hill and Stewart, and did more Formula 2 in the MRP Lola and a works Brabham, but really established a niche in saloon cars, taking a string of championships from 1968 with Alan Mann's Escort into the seventies with both the Ford Mustang and Chevrolet Camaro. In fact Gardner seemed to be racing virtually every weekend, as he was also contesting F5000 in the works Lola, taking the championship in both 1971 and '72, before suddenly quitting single-seaters after the Tasman series early in 1973 ('I drove like an old woman' was Frank's over-critical assessment, having won one round and taken three second places).

He continued to thunder on in the Camaro, until returning to his native land to race in the sports sedan championships, inevitably winning the title in 1976 and '77. Frank Gardner was truly a 'racing' driver in the very best sense of the word.

GARDNER, Frank (AUS) b 1/10/1930, Sydney, New South Wales

	1964	Championship position: Unplaced							
	Race	Circuit	No	Entrant	Tyres	Car/Engine		Comment	Q Pos/Entries
ret	BRITISH GP	Brands Hatch	26	John Willment Automobiles	D	1.5 Brabham BT10-Ford 4		startline accident	19/25
	1965	Championship position: Unplaced							
12	SOUTH AFRICAN GP	East London	16	John Willment Automobiles	D	1.5 Brabham BT11-BRM V8		pit stop/10 laps behind	15/25
ret	MONACO GP	Monte Carlo	11	John Willment Automobiles	D	1.5 Brabham BT11-BRM V8		engine mounting	=10/17
ret	BELGIAN GP	Spa	26	John Willment Automobiles	D	1.5 Brabham BT11-BRM V8		ignition	18/21
8	BRITISH GP	Silverstone	17	John Willment Automobiles	D	1.5 Brabham BT11-BRM V8		2 laps behind	13/23
11	DUTCH GP	Zandvoort	30	John Willment Automobiles	D	1.5 Brabham BT11-BRM V8		3 laps behind	=10/17
ret	GERMAN GP	Nürburgring	21	John Willment Automobiles	D	1.5 Brabham BT11-BRM V8		gearbox	18/22
ret	ITALIAN GP	Monza	46	John Willment Automobiles	D	1.5 Brabham BT11-BRM V8		engine	16/23
	1968	Championship position: Unplaced							
dnq	ITALIAN GP	Monza	28	Bernard White Racing Ltd	G	3.0 BRM P261 V12			23/24

GP Starts: 8   GP Wins: 0   Pole positions: 0   Fastest laps: 0   Points: 0

GARTNER, Jo (A) b 4/1/1954, Vienna – d 1/6/1986, Le Mans Circuit, France

	Race	Circuit	No	Entrant		Tyres	Car/Engine	Comment	Q Pos/Entries
	1984			Championship position: Unplaced					
ret	SAN MARINO GP	Imola	30	Osella Squadra Corse		P	3.0 Osella FA1E-Alfa Romeo V12	*engine*	26/28
ret	BRITISH GP	Brands Hatch	30	Osella Squadra Corse		P	1.5 t/c Osella FA1F-Alfa Romeo V8	*accident at start*	27/27
ret	GERMAN GP	Nürburgring	30	Osella Squadra Corse		P	1.5 t/c Osella FA1F-Alfa Romeo V8	*turbo*	23/27
ret	AUSTRIAN GP	Österreichring	30	Osella Squadra Corse		P	1.5 t/c Osella FA1F-Alfa Romeo V8	*engine*	22/28
12*	DUTCH GP	Zandvoort	30	Osella Squadra Corse		P	1.5 t/c Osella FA1F-Alfa Romeo V8	** 8th & 9th cars dsq/-5 laps*	23/27
5*	ITALIAN GP	Monza	30	Osella Squadra Corse		P	1.5 t/c Osella FA1F-Alfa Romeo V8	** not eligible for points/-2 laps*	24/27
12/ret	EUROPEAN GP	Nürburgring	30	Osella Squadra Corse		P	1.5 t/c Osella FA1F-Alfa Romeo V8	*fuel feed/7 laps behind*	22/26
16/ret	PORTUGUESE GP	Estoril	30	Osella Squadra Corse		P	1.5 t/c Osella FA1F-Alfa Romeo V8	*out of fuel/5 laps behind*	24/27

GP Starts: 8   GP Wins: 0   Pole positions: 0   Fastest laps: 0   Points: 0

JO GARTNER

Much self-sacrifice and an iron determination to succeed against seemingly overwhelming odds kept Jo Gartner in motor racing when many drivers with lesser fibre would have fallen by the wayside.

From his early Formula 3 days (he was third in the 1978 European championship), Jo proved he had talent, but he was lacking finance and had to act as his own mechanic, running second-rate machinery for much of his Formula 2 career – though he did have his day, winning the Pau GP in 1983. Finding some backing, he got himself briefly into the Osella Grand Prix team in 1984, and even scored a fifth place for them at Monza but, against his expectations and much to his dismay, he was not retained for the following year.

Gartner then switched to sports car and IMSA racing, which he enjoyed but saw as a means to get back into Formula 1. Sadly it was not to be, for he was killed instantly during the 1986 Le Mans 24 Hours when his Porsche crashed on the Mulsanne Straight in the middle of the night.

TONY GAZE

An ex-RAF pilot, Gaze was successful in his native Australia in the immediate post-war years with a 1936 Alta before coming to Britain to try his hand. He initially raced one of Geoffrey Taylor's Altas, before buying one of John Heath's HWMs to race in Grands Prix during 1952. He was soon to turn his attention to sports car racing, an arena where he had more chance of success, racing his Maserati, HWM-Jaguar and Ferrari over the next few seasons both at home and abroad.

Gaze was something of a pioneering figure with his regular racing trips 'down-under' between 1954 and 1956, and was a prime mover in the development of Australian motor sport, helping to bring European-style circuit racing to that continent, thus encouraging greater international competition in the years that followed.

'GEKI' (Giacomo Russo)

Racing under the pseudonym 'Geki', this talented driver from Milan was a multiple Formula Junior champion in Italy during the early 1960s, graduating from the relatively primitive Stanguellini to a Lotus. He was always difficult to beat at Monza, and thus a local attraction come Grand Prix time each year; after hiring Rob Walker's car and failing to qualify in 1964, he was subsequently seen in a works Lotus.

After an abortive time with the Abarth F2 car in 1964, 'Geki' raced occasionally for the Alfa Romeo works team in sports cars and GTs during 1965-66, and was still competing successfully in Italian F3 with a Matra when he met his death at Caserta in 1967. Having been involved in a multiple pile-up, the Swiss driver, Fehr Beat, jumped from his stricken car and ran back along the track to warn the leading bunch – which included 'Geki', who was tragically unable to avoid striking and killing his unfortunate rival. The Italian's Matra then ploughed into a concrete wall and he perished when the car burst into flames.

GAZE, Tony (AUS) b 3/3/1920, Melbourne, Australia

	1952	Championship position: Unplaced						
	Race	Circuit	No	Entrant	Tyres	Car/Engine	Comment	Q Pos/Entries
15	BELGIAN GP	Spa	42	Tony Gaze	D	2.0 HWM-Alta 4	6 laps behind	16/22
ret	BRITISH GP	Silverstone	28	Tony Gaze	D	2.0 HWM-Alta 4	cylinder head gasket	26/32
ret	GERMAN GP	Nürburgring	120	Tony Gaze	D	2.0 HWM-Alta 4	suspension	14/32
dnq	ITALIAN GP	Monza	56	Tony Gaze	D	2.0 HWM-Alta 4		30/35

GP Starts: 3   GP Wins: 0   Pole positions: 0   Fastest laps: 0   Points: 0

'GEKI' (RUSSO, Giacomo) (I) b 23/10/1937, Milan – d 18/6/1967, Caserta, nr Naples

	1964	Championship position: Unplaced						
	Race	Circuit	No	Entrant	Tyres	Car/Engine	Comment	Q Pos/Entries
dnq	ITALIAN GP	Monza	36	R R C Walker Racing Team	D	1.5 Brabham BT11-BRM V8		23/25
	1965	Championship position: Unplaced						
ret	ITALIAN GP	Monza	28	Team Lotus	D	1.5 Lotus 25-Climax V8	gearbox oil seal	20/23
	1966	Championship position: Unplaced						
9	ITALIAN GP	Monza	(22)20	Team Lotus	F	2.0 Lotus 33-Climax V8	5 laps behind	20/22

GP Starts: 2   GP Wins: 0   Pole positions: 0   Fastest laps: 0   Points: 0

OLIVIER GENDEBIEN

A Belgian aristocrat, and former World War II paratrooper, Gendebien spent some four years in forestry in the Congo, where he met rally driver Charles Fraikin, who was lamenting the lack of a co-driver with whom to compete back in Europe.

Gendebien then returned and raced a Veritas in the GP des Frontières at Chimay, finishing sixth, before joining Fraikin, initially to rally a Jaguar, the pair staying together until 1955. By the time they split they had become known as 'the eternal bridesmaids' due to the number of times they had to be content with second place. Twice they just missed winning the Liège-Rome-Liège Rally but in 1955 it was third time lucky with a Mercedes 300SL. Without his partner, Olivier had great success, winning his class with a Plymouth in the Round Italy Rally, the Tulip Rally and the Northern Roads Rally in a Porsche, all in 1954.

Such was the impression made that he was offered a contract to drive a works Ferrari in sports car events and selected Grands Prix. His first race for the team nearly ended in disaster, when in late 1955 he crashed heavily in practice for the Tourist Trophy at Dundrod, suffering concussion. He was fit for the start of 1956 and, with virtually no single-seater experience behind him, finished fifth on his Grand Prix debut at the Argentine GP, followed by sixth in the Mendoza GP. The season also saw a splendid run of finishes in sports car races, including second places at Buenos Aires and in the Supercortemaggiore at Monza and thirds in the Nürburgring 1000 Km, Targa Florio and Le Mans.

That was to be the first of seven wonderful seasons that Gendebien spent in Ferrari's sports car team. He subsequently won the Reims 12 Hours in 1957 and '58, the Targa Florio in 1958, '61 and '62, Sebring in 1959, '60 and '61 and the Nürburgring 1000 Km in 1962, not forgetting his splendid achievement of four wins at Le Mans in 1958, '60, '61 and '62, after the last of which he retired.

He was no slouch in a Grand Prix car either. His outings were generally infrequent, but whenever he raced a competitive machine he invariably brought it into the points, as a check on the statistics overleaf will show. But it is inevitably as one of the greatest sports car drivers of any era that he will be best remembered.

GENDEBIEN, Olivier (B) b 12/1/1924, Brussels – d. 10/1998

	1956	Championship position: 15th=		Wins: 0	Pole positions: 0		Fastest laps: 0	Points scored: 2		
	Race	Circuit	No	Entrant		Tyres	Car/Engine		Comment	Q Pos/Entries
5	ARGENTINE GP	Buenos Aires	38	Scuderia Ferrari		E	2.5 Ferrari-Lancia 555/D50 V8		7 laps behind	10/15
ret	FRENCH GP	Reims	44	Scuderia Ferrari		E	2.5 Lancia-Ferrari D50 V8		clutch	11/20
	1958	Championship position: Unplaced								
6	BELGIAN GP	Spa	20	Scuderia Ferrari		E	2.4 Ferrari-Dino 246 V6		1 lap behind	6/20
ret	ITALIAN GP	Monza	20	Scuderia Ferrari		E	2.4 Ferrari-Dino 246 V6		suspension	5/21
ret	MOROCCAN GP	Casablanca	2	Scuderia Ferrari		E	2.4 Ferrari-Dino 246 V6		spun, hit by Picard	6/25
	1959	Championship position: 11th		Wins: 0	Pole positions: 0		Fastest laps: 0	Points scored: 3		
4	FRENCH GP	Reims	22	Scuderia Ferrari		D	2.4 Ferrari-Dino 246 V6			11/22
6	ITALIAN GP	Monza	38	Scuderia Ferrari		D	2.4 Ferrari-Dino 246 V6		1 lap behind	6/21
	1960	Championship position: 6th		Wins: 0	Pole positions: 0		Fastest laps: 0	Points scored: 10		
3	BELGIAN GP	Spa	34	Yeoman Credit Racing Team		D	2.5 Cooper T51-Climax 4		1 lap behind	5/18
2	FRENCH GP	Reims	44	Yeoman Credit Racing Team		D	2.5 Cooper T51-Climax 4			9/23
9	BRITISH GP	Silverstone	14	Yeoman Credit Racing Team		D	2.5 Cooper T51-Climax 4		3 laps behind	12/25
7	PORTUGUESE GP	Oporto	8	Yeoman Credit Racing Team		D	2.5 Cooper T51-Climax 4		stuck in top gear/-9 laps	14/16
12	US GP	Riverside	7	Yeoman Credit Racing Team		D	2.5 Cooper T51-Climax 4		pit stop/6 laps behind	8/23
	1961	Championship position: 13th=		Wins: 0	Pole positions: 0		Fastest laps: 0	Points scored: 3		
dnq	MONACO GP	Monte Carlo	12	Equipe Nationale Belge		D	1.5 Emeryson 1003-Maserati 4			20/21
4	BELGIAN GP	Spa	8	Scuderia Ferrari SpA SEFAC		D	1.5 Ferrari 156 V6			3/25
11*	US GP	Watkins Glen	21	UDT Laystall Racing Team		D	1.5 Lotus 18/21-Climax 4		*unwell-Gregory took over/-8 laps	15/19

GP Starts: 14   GP Wins: 0   Pole positions: 0   Fastest laps: 0   Points: 18

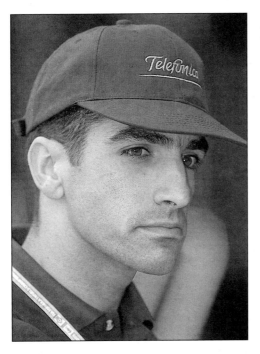

MARC GENÉ

The Spaniard had taken the Italian Superformula championship in 1994, but his step up to British Formula 3 the following year proved somewhat disappointing when he struggled in the wake of his team-mate Helio Castro-Neves. In mitigation, Marc was at this stage still studying at university, which naturally curtailed the amount of time he could devote to his racing career.

Budget problems kept him out of action for much of 1996, but he managed to gain a place in the Pacific F3000 team at the start of 1997. Unfortunately an accident in the second round at Pau left Gené with a cracked vertebra, which sidelined him for a month, and when he was fit to return his place in the team had gone. Although he was able to find another berth with Nordic for a couple of races his season lay in tatters.

So it was back to his day job as an accountant in Spain and competition in the less pressurised atmosphere of the Open Fortuna by Nissan single-seater series. Driving for Adrian Campos, Marc swept to a convincing championship win, chalking up six victories from twelve races. In truth there wasn't a huge amount of competition for him to beat, but it was to give his career a massive boost.

With the Spanish communications giant Telefonica backing Minardi in 1999, Marc was suddenly a shock candidate for a place with the Faenza team and immediately impressed the Minardi hierarchy with his hard work and willingness to learn.

Certainly he was not outclassed by his more experienced team-mate Badoer, and he had the great satisfaction of bringing his car into sixth place at the European Grand Prix. This single point pushed the little Italian team above the mega-rich British American Racing to ensure that, for one season at least, they were not bottom of the pile.

GENÉ, Marc (ESP) b 29/3/1974, Sabadell

	1999	Championship position: 17th=		Wins: 0	Pole positions: 0		Fastest laps: 0	Points scored: 1		
ret	AUSTRALIAN GP	Melbourne	21	Fondmetal Minardi Ford		B	3.0 Minardi M01-Ford Zetec R V10		colision with Trulli	22/22
9	BRAZILIAN GP	Interlagos	21	Fondmetal Minardi Ford		B	3.0 Minardi M01-Ford Zetec R V10		3 laps behind	20/22
9	SAN MARINO GP	Imola	21	Fondmetal Minardi Ford		B	3.0 Minardi M01-Ford Zetec R V10		3 laps behind	21/22
ret	MONACO GP	Monte Carlo	21	Fondmetal Minardi Ford		B	3.0 Minardi M01-Ford Zetec R V10		accident	22/22
ret	SPANISH GP	Barcelona	21	Fondmetal Minardi Ford		B	3.0 Minardi M01-Ford Zetec R V10		clutch on lap 1	21/22
8	CANADIAN GP	Montreal	21	Fondmetal Minardi Ford		B	3.0 Minardi M01-Ford Zetec R V10		1 lap behind	22/22
ret	FRENCH GP	Magny Cours	21	Fondmetal Minardi Ford		B	3.0 Minardi M01-Ford Zetec R V10		spun off in rain	19/22
15	BRITISH GP	Silverstone	21	Fondmetal Minardi Ford		B	3.0 Minardi M01-Ford Zetec R V10		2 laps behind	22/22
11	AUSTRIAN GP	A1-Ring	21	Fondmetal Minardi Ford		B	3.0 Minardi M01-Ford Zetec R V10		1 lap behind	22/22
9	GERMAN GP	Hockenheim	21	Fondmetal Minardi Ford		B	3.0 Minardi M01-Ford Zetec R V10		1 lap behind	15/22
17	HUNGARIAN GP	Hungaroring	21	Fondmetal Minardi Ford		B	3.0 Minardi M01-Ford Zetec R V10		3 laps behind	22/22
16	BELGIAN GP	Spa	21	Fondmetal Minardi Ford		B	3.0 Minardi M01-Ford Zetec R V10		1 lap behind	21/22
ret	ITALIAN GP	Monza	21	Fondmetal Minardi Ford		B	3.0 Minardi M01-Ford Zetec R V10		collision on lap 1	17/22
6	EUROPEAN GP	Nürburgring	21	Fondmetal Minardi Ford		B	3.0 Minardi M01-Ford Zetec R V10			20/22
9	MALAYSIAN GP	Sepang	21	Fondmetal Minardi Ford		B	3.0 Minardi M01-Ford Zetec R V10		1 lap behind	19/22
ret	JAPANESE GP	Suzuka	21	Fondmetal Minardi Ford		B	3.0 Minardi M01-Ford Zetec R V10		gearbox	20/22

GP Starts: 16   GP Wins: 0   Pole positions: 0   Fastest laps: 0   Points: 1

BOB GERARD

Gerard enjoyed an extremely long and active career in motor racing, from his early days as a trialist with a Riley in 1933 through to the early 1970s as an entrant.

At first he was identified with the family Riley, but it was after the war that he really came into his own, with an ERA, winning the British Empire Trophy in 1947, '48 and '49, in addition to the 1949 Jersey Road Race. Bob also came close to winning that year's British Grand Prix, finishing second to de Graffenried.

As the fifties dawned, the old ERA was placed sixth in a couple of Grands Prix, but it was only really suitable for national races, so Gerard had to wait until 1953, when he acquired a Cooper-Bristol, to prove his worth. He drove it doggedly, frequently putting more powerful cars to shame and regularly scoring respectable placings in minor Formula 2 and Libre events until 1956.

Gerard made his final GP appearance in 1957 at the wheel of the unsuccessful rear-engined Cooper-BG-Bristol, just missing the points. From 1959 to 1961 he happily drove a Turner in club events, before retiring from active service to enter a Cooper for John Taylor, mainly in non-championship races, later running Formula 2 cars for Alan Rollinson, Mike Beckwith and Peter Gethin among others.

GERARD, Bob (GB) b 19/1/1914, Leicester – d 26/1/1990, South Croxton, Leicester

	1950	Championship position: Unplaced							
	Race	*Circuit*	*No*	*Entrant*	*Tyres*	*Car/Engine*		*Comment*	*Q Pos/Entries*
6	BRITISH GP	Silverstone	12	Bob Gerard	D	1.5 s/c ERA B Type 6		*3 laps behind*	13/21
6	MONACO GP	Monte Carlo	26	Bob Gerard	D	1.5 s/c ERA B Type 6		*6 laps behind*	16/21
	1951	Championship position: Unplaced							
11	BRITISH GP	Silverstone	8	Bob Gerard	D	1.5 s/c ERA B Type 6		*8 laps behind*	10/20
	1953	Championship position: Unplaced							
11	FRENCH GP	Reims	38	Bob Gerard	D	2.0 Cooper T23-Bristol 6		*5 laps behind*	12/25
ret	BRITISH GP	Silverstone	17	Bob Gerard	D	2.0 Cooper T23-Bristol 6		*front suspension*	18/29
	1954	Championship position: Unplaced							
10	BRITISH GP	Silverstone	29	Bob Gerard	D	2.0 Cooper T23-Bristol 6		*5 laps behind*	18/31
	1956	Championship position: Unplaced							
11	BRITISH GP	Silverstone	26	Bob Gerard	D	2.2 Cooper T23-Bristol 6		*13 laps behind*	22/28
	1957	Championship position: Unplaced							
6	BRITISH GP	Aintree	38	Bob Gerard	D	2.2 Cooper BG43-Bristol 6		*8 laps behind*	18/19

GP Starts: 8   GP Wins: 0   Pole positions: 0   Fastest laps: 0   Points: 0

GERINI, Gerino (I) 10/8/1928, Rome

	1956			Championship position: 20= Wins: 0 Pole positions: 0 Fastest laps: 0 Points scored: 1.5					
	Race	Circuit	No	Entrant	Tyres	Car/Engine		Comment	Q Pos/Entries
4*	ARGENTINE GP	Buenos Aires	10	Officine Alfieri Maserati	P	2.5 Maserati 250F 6		*shared with Landi/-6 laps	– /15
10	ITALIAN GP	Monza	42	Scuderia Guastalla	P	2.5 Maserati 250F 6		8 laps behind	17/26
	1958			Championship position: Unplaced					
dnq	MONACO GP	Monte Carlo	48	Scuderia Centro Sud	P	2.5 Maserati 250F 6			20/28
9	FRENCH GP	Reims	32	Scuderia Centro Sud	P	2.5 Maserati 250F 6		3 laps behind	15/21
ret	BRITISH GP	Silverstone	6	Scuderia Centro Sud	P	2.5 Maserati 250F 6		gearbox	18/21
ret	ITALIAN GP	Monza	40	Scuderia Centro Sud	P	2.5 Maserati 250F 6		mechanical	19/21
12*	MOROCCAN GP	Casablanca	28	Scuderia Centro Sud	P	2.5 Maserati 250F 6		*12th behind one F2 car/-5 laps	17/25

GP Starts: 6   GP Wins: 0   Pole positions: 0   Fastest laps: 0   Points: 1.5

GERINO GERINI

This Italian driver raced Ferrari sports cars in the mid-fifties, before switching to rivals Maserati.

The 1956 season started promisingly, with a shared fourth place (with Landi) in the Argentine GP, plus a third at Naples and a fifth at Syracuse, but then nothing of note was achieved except a class win in the Maserati sports car at the Coppa Inter Europa at Monza.

In fact Gerini was not to reappear in Grands Prix until 1958, when, apart from a distant sixth place at Caen, he struggled to make an impression in the by now elderly 250F. He briefly reappeared in sports cars in 1960, when his Ferrari crashed out of the Nürburgring 1000 Km.

PETER GETHIN

It is perhaps unfair that Gethin should be best remembered for his sensational Grand Prix win at Monza in 1971, when he took his BRM to a wonderful victory by the margin of one-hundredth of a second in a four-car dash to the line, for in fact he enjoyed a splendid career which spanned some 15 years and encompassed almost every category of the sport.

After an early start in a Lotus Seven in 1962, Peter soon became one of the country's top club sports car drivers in his Lotus 23. He then moved into Formula 3 in 1965 with Charles Lucas, but his career really stood still until 1968 when he ran a full Formula 2 season with Frank Lythgoe, finishing strongly with a brilliant second at Albi and a third at Vallelunga after a Brabham had been acquired to replace a disappointing Chevron.

It was the introduction of F5000 in 1969 that really put Peter's career on the map. In a semi-works McLaren, he dominated the early part of the season with four straight wins and then defended his advantage grimly as his championship lead was whittled away. The final round ended in anti-climax with a collision but the title went to Gethin, and he proved himself a more than worthy champion by retaining the crown convincingly the following year. By this time he was closely involved with the McLaren Grand Prix effort; having made a promising debut to finish sixth in the Race of Champions, he was brought into the team after the sad loss of Bruce McLaren in a testing accident at Goodwood and also took over the vacant Can-Am drive, winning a round at Elkhart Lake.

Staying with the team for 1971, Peter inexplicably continued to struggle in Grands Prix, though he did finish second on aggregate in the International Trophy, but it was something of a surprise when he moved to BRM. Almost immediately he won at Monza and then repeated that triumph in the tragically shortened Victory Race at Brands Hatch, in which team-mate Jo Siffert perished.

Hopes were high for 1972, but Peter endured a thin time of it with BRM, though an equally low-key season in Formula 2 with Chevron did bring an unexpected win in the Pau GP. So it was back to F5000 at home and abroad, which yielded a shock win in the Race of Champions. Gethin made a couple more Grand Prix appearances, but concentrated on F5000 with Chevron and VDS, and also raced in the newly revived Can-Am series before retiring at the end of 1977. He later became involved with the March F2 team, looking after Beppe Gabbiani, and had a brief spell with Toleman in F1 in 1984. Peter currently runs a racing driver's school at Goodwood.

GETHIN, Peter (GB) b 21/2/1940, Epsom, Surrey

	1970	Championship position: 22nd=		Wins: 0		Pole positions: 0	Fastest laps: 0	Points scored: 1	
	Race	Circuit	No	Entrant	Tyres	Car/Engine		Comment	Q Pos/Entries
ret	DUTCH GP	Zandvoort	20	Bruce McLaren Motor Racing	G	3.0 McLaren M14A-Cosworth V8		spun off	11/24
ret	GERMAN GP	Hockenheim	24	Bruce McLaren Motor Racing	G	3.0 McLaren M14A-Cosworth V8		engine-throttle slides	17/25
10	AUSTRIAN GP	Österreichring	23	Bruce McLaren Motor Racing	G	3.0 McLaren M14A-Cosworth V8		1 lap behind	20/24
nc	ITALIAN GP	Monza	32	Bruce McLaren Motor Racing	G	3.0 McLaren M14A-Cosworth V8		pit stops-various/-8 laps	18/27
6	CANADIAN GP	St Jovite	6	Bruce McLaren Motor Racing	G	3.0 McLaren M14A-Cosworth V8		2 laps behind	=11/20
14	US GP	Watkins Glen	9	Bruce McLaren Motor Racing	G	3.0 McLaren M14A-Cosworth V8		pit stop-tyres/8 laps behind	21/27
ret	MEXICAN GP	Mexico City	9	Bruce McLaren Motor Racing	G	3.0 McLaren M14A-Cosworth V8		engine	10/18
	1971	Championship position: 9th		Wins: 1		Pole positions: 0	Fastest laps: 0	Points scored: 9	
ret	SOUTH AFRICAN GP	Kyalami	12	Bruce McLaren Motor Racing	G	3.0 McLaren M14A-Cosworth V8		loose fuel line	11/25
8	SPANISH GP	Montjuich Park	10	Bruce McLaren Motor Racing	G	3.0 McLaren M14A-Cosworth V8		2 laps behind	7/22
ret	MONACO GP	Monte Carlo	10	Bruce McLaren Motor Racing	G	3.0 McLaren M14A-Cosworth V8		hit chicane	14/23
nc	DUTCH GP	Zandvoort	28	Bruce McLaren Motor Racing	G	3.0 McLaren M19A-Cosworth V8		spin-pit stop/10 laps behind	23/24
9	FRENCH GP	Paul Ricard	10	Bruce McLaren Motor Racing	G	3.0 McLaren M19A-Cosworth V8		1 lap behind	19/24
ret	BRITISH GP	Silverstone	10	Bruce McLaren Motor Racing	G	3.0 McLaren M19A-Cosworth V8		oil pressure	14/24
ret	GERMAN GP	Nürburgring	20	Bruce McLaren Motor Racing	G	3.0 McLaren M19A-Cosworth V8		accident-damaged suspension	19/23
10	AUSTRIAN GP	Österreichring	23	Yardley BRM	F	3.0 BRM P160 V12		misfire/2 laps behind	16/22
1	ITALIAN GP	Monza	18	Yardley BRM	F	3.0 BRM P160 V12			11/24
14	CANADIAN GP	Mosport Park	15	Yardley BRM	F	3.0 BRM P160 V12		5 laps behind	=15/27
9	US GP	Watkins Glen	15	Yardley BRM	F	3.0 BRM P160 V12		broken valve spring/-1 lap	23/32
	1972	Championship position: 20		Wins: 0		Pole positions: 0	Fastest laps: 0	Points scored: 1	
ret	ARGENTINE GP	Buenos Aires	5	Marlboro BRM	F	3.0 BRM P160B V12		accident-broken fuel line	18/22
nc	SOUTH AFRICAN GP	Kyalami	11	Marlboro BRM	F	3.0 BRM P160B V12		pit stops/14 laps behind	=18/27
ret	SPANISH GP	Jarama	8	Marlboro BRM	F	3.0 BRM P180 V12		engine	21/26
ret/dsq	*MONACO GP	Monte Carlo	18	Marlboro BRM	F	3.0 BRM P160B V12		hit chicane/*reversed into pits	=5/25
ret	BELGIAN GP	Nivelles	24	Marlboro BRM	F	3.0 BRM P160B V12		fuel pump-engine misfire	17/26
dns	FRENCH GP	Clermont Ferrand	22	Marlboro BRM	F	3.0 BRM P160B V12		crashed in practice	(23)/29
ret	BRITISH GP	Brands Hatch	12	Marlboro BRM	F	3.0 BRM P160B V12		engine	16/27
13	AUSTRIAN GP	Österreichring	6	Marlboro BRM	F	3.0 BRM P160C V12		pit stops/3 laps behind	16/26
6	ITALIAN GP	Monza	23	Marlboro BRM	F	3.0 BRM P160C V12			12/27
ret	CANADIAN GP	Mosport Park	16	Marlboro BRM	F	3.0 BRM P160C V12		rear suspension mounting	=12/25
ret	US GP	Watkins Glen	14	Marlboro BRM	F	3.0 BRM P160C V12		engine	29/32
	1973	Championship position: Unplaced							
ret	CANADIAN GP	Mosport Park	19	Marlboro BRM	F	3.0 BRM P160E V12		oil pump belt	25/26
	1974	Championship position: Unplaced							
ret	BRITISH GP	Brands Hatch	27	Embassy Racing with Graham Hill	F	3.0 Lola T370-Cosworth V8		did not fit car/deflating tyre	=19/34

GP Starts: 30   GP Wins: 1   Pole positions: 0   Fastest laps: 0   Points: 11

Monza 1971, and Peter Gethin scores his only Grand Prix victory in a BRM P160. He still holds the distinction of winning the Grand Prix with the fastest average speed, some 150.755 mph.

PIERCARLO GHINZANI

'Better to be at the back in Formula 1 than not to be in Formula 1 at all,' said Piercarlo Ghinzani, and that's pretty well where he stayed in a Grand Prix career that was to span eight seasons, mostly at the tail-end of the grid.

It was all a long way from the start of his career when, after his 1970 debut in Italian Formula Ford, he began the slow climb up the motor racing ladder through Formula Italia to Formula 3 in 1973. His early days in Italian F3 were underfinanced, but he did finish second to Riccardo Patrese in 1976. Moving up to the European series in 1977, Piercarlo did extremely well to take the title, his phlegmatic approach being vital in a team that was beset by upheaval. The next step into Formula 2 with a March was a big disappointment, and this appeared to be a major blow to his aspirations.

Salvation was nigh. In 1981 he was called in as a last-minute replacement for Osella after Giorgio Francia's credentials failed to satisfy FISA, and he qualified for the Belgian GP. This was the start of what was to be a long association with the little team, his best result being a much-needed fifth place at Dallas in 1984. He did take a brief sabbatical in mid-1985 when a second Toleman was entered, but returned to the fold for 1986. In Grands Prix, results were understandably hard to find, but he had been successful in endurance events, winning the Fuji 1000 Km in a Porsche with Barilla.

In 1987, Ghinzani tried his luck in a Ligier team suddenly shorn of potential when an Alfa Romeo engine deal foundered as the season dawned, and then it was on to an equally fruitless sojourn at Zakspeed, before just one more season back in the Osella camp.

Ghinzani certainly had staying power; he started 96 Grands Prix, but more pointedly failed to qualify for another 31 – a real glutton for punishment!

Subsequently Piercarlo has formed his own Formula 3 team which is a leading light in the Italian championship, and he is reportedly eyeing up a move to the newly inaugurated Italian F3000 championship for the year 2000.

GHINZANI, Piercarlo (I) b 16/1/1952, Riviera d'Adda, Bergamo

1981 — Championship position: Unplaced

	Race	Circuit	No	Entrant	Tyres	Car/Engine	Comment	Q Pos/Entries
13	BELGIAN GP	Zolder	31	Osella Squadra Corse	M	3.0 Osella FA1B-Cosworth V8	spin-pit stop/4 laps behind	24/31
dnq	MONACO GP	Monte Carlo	32	Osella Squadra Corse	M	3.0 Osella FA1B-Cosworth V8		25/31

1983 — Championship position: Unplaced

	Race	Circuit	No	Entrant	Tyres	Car/Engine	Comment	Q Pos/Entries
dnq	BRAZILIAN GP	Rio	32	Osella Squadra Corse	M	3.0 Osella FA1D-Cosworth V8		27/27
dnq	US GP WEST	Long Beach	32	Osella Squadra Corse	M	3.0 Osella FA1D-Cosworth V8		28/28
dnq	FRENCH GP	Paul Ricard	32	Osella Squadra Corse	M	3.0 Osella FA1D-Cosworth V8		28/29
dnq	SAN MARINO GP	Imola	32	Osella Squadra Corse	M	3.0 Osella FA1E-Alfa Romeo V12		28/28
dnq	MONACO GP	Monte Carlo	32	Osella Squadra Corse	M	3.0 Osella FA1E-Alfa Romeo V12		27/28
dnq	BELGIAN GP	Spa	32	Osella Squadra Corse	M	3.0 Osella FA1E-Alfa Romeo V12		27/28
ret	US GP (DETROIT)	Detroit	32	Osella Squadra Corse	M	3.0 Osella FA1E-Alfa Romeo V12	overheating	24/27
dnq	CANADIAN GP	Montreal	32	Osella Squadra Corse	M	3.0 Osella FA1E-Alfa Romeo V12		28/28
ret	BRITISH GP	Silverstone	32	Osella Squadra Corse	M	3.0 Osella FA1E-Alfa Romeo V12	started from pits-fuel pressure	26/29
ret	GERMAN GP	Hockenheim	32	Osella Squadra Corse	M	3.0 Osella FA1E-Alfa Romeo V12	engine	26/29
11	AUSTRIAN GP	Österreichring	32	Osella Squadra Corse	M	3.0 Osella FA1E-Alfa Romeo V12	4 laps behind	25/29
dnq	DUTCH GP	Zandvoort	32	Osella Squadra Corse	M	3.0 Osella FA1E-Alfa Romeo V12		27/29
ret	ITALIAN GP	Monza	32	Osella Squadra Corse	M	3.0 Osella FA1E-Alfa Romeo V12	gearbox	23/29
nc	EUROPEAN GP	Brands Hatch	32	Osella Squadra Corse	M	3.0 Osella FA1E-Alfa Romeo V12	3 pit stops-throttle/-13 laps	24/29
ret	SOUTH AFRICAN GP	Kyalami	32	Osella Squadra Corse	M	3.0 Osella FA1E-Alfa Romeo V12	engine	26/26

1984 — Championship position: 19th   Wins: 0   Pole positions: 0   Fastest laps: 0   Points scored: 2

	Race	Circuit	No	Entrant	Tyres	Car/Engine	Comment	Q Pos/Entries
ret	BRAZILIAN GP	Rio	24	Osella Squadra Corse	P	1.5 t/c Osella FA1F-Alfa Romeo V8	gearbox	22/27
dns	SOUTH AFRICAN GP	Kyalami	24	Osella Squadra Corse	P	1.5 t/c Osella FA1F-Alfa Romeo V8	accident in a.m. warm up	27/27
ret	BELGIAN GP	Zolder	24	Osella Squadra Corse	P	1.5 t/c Osella FA1F-Alfa Romeo V8	transmission	20/27
dnq	SAN MARINO GP	Imola	24	Osella Squadra Corse	P	1.5 t/c Osella FA1F-Alfa Romeo V8		27/28
12*	FRENCH GP	Dijon	24	Osella Squadra Corse	P	1.5 t/c Osella FA1F-Alfa Romeo V8	* 12th place car dsq/-5 laps	26/27
7*	MONACO GP	Monte Carlo	24	Osella Squadra Corse	P	1.5 t/c Osella FA1F-Alfa Romeo V8	* 3rd place car dsq/-1 lap	19/27
ret	CANADIAN GP	Montreal	24	Osella Squadra Corse	P	1.5 t/c Osella FA1F-Alfa Romeo V8	gearbox	19/26
ret	US GP (DETROIT)	Detroit	24	Osella Squadra Corse	P	1.5 t/c Osella FA1F-Alfa Romeo V8	accident with Hesnault	26/27
5	US GP (DALLAS)	Dallas	24	Osella Squadra Corse	P	1.5 t/c Osella FA1F-Alfa Romeo V8	2 laps behind	18/27
9	BRITISH GP	Brands Hatch	24	Osella Squadra Corse	P	1.5 t/c Osella FA1F-Alfa Romeo V8	3 laps behind	21/27
ret	GERMAN GP	Hockenheim	24	Osella Squadra Corse	P	1.5 t/c Osella FA1F-Alfa Romeo V8	electrics	21/27
ret	AUSTRIAN GP	Österreichring	24	Osella Squadra Corse	P	1.5 t/c Osella FA1F-Alfa Romeo V8	gearbox	23/28
ret	DUTCH GP	Zandvoort	24	Osella Squadra Corse	P	1.5 t/c Osella FA1F-Alfa Romeo V8	fuel pump	21/27
7/ret	ITALIAN GP	Monza	24	Osella Squadra Corse	P	1.5 t/c Osella FA1F-Alfa Romeo V8	out of fuel/2 laps behind	22/27
ret	EUROPEAN GP	Nürburgring	24	Osella Squadra Corse	P	1.5 t/c Osella FA1F-Alfa Romeo V8	accident	20/26
ret	PORTUGUESE GP	Estoril	24	Osella Squadra Corse	P	1.5 t/c Osella FA1F-Alfa Romeo V8	engine	22/27

1985 — Championship position: Unplaced

	Race	Circuit	No	Entrant	Tyres	Car/Engine	Comment	Q Pos/Entries
12	BRAZILIAN GP	Rio	24	Osella Squadra Corse	P	1.5 t/c Osella FA1F-Alfa Romeo V8	4 laps behind	22/25
9	PORTUGUESE GP	Estoril	24	Osella Squadra Corse	P	1.5 t/c Osella FA1F-Alfa Romeo V8	6 laps behind	26/26

nc	SAN MARINO GP	Imola	24	Osella Squadra Corse	P	1.5 t/c Osella FA1G-Alfa Romeo V8	*pit stop-gearbox/-14 laps*	22/26
dnq	MONACO GP	Monte Carlo	24	Osella Squadra Corse	P	1.5 t/c Osella FA1G-Alfa Romeo V8		21/26
ret	CANADIAN GP	Montreal	24	Osella Squadra Corse	P	1.5 t/c Osella FA1G-Alfa Romeo V8	*engine*	22/25
ret	US GP (DETROIT)	Detroit	24	Osella Squadra Corse	P	1.5 t/c Osella FA1G-Alfa Romeo V8	*accident*	22/25
15	FRENCH GP	Paul Ricard	24	Osella Squadra Corse	P	1.5 t/c Osella FA1G-Alfa Romeo V8	*4 laps behind*	24/26
ret	BRITISH GP	Silverstone	24	Osella Squadra Corse	P	1.5 t/c Osella FA1G-Alfa Romeo V8	*accident damage on lap 1*	25/26
ret/dns	AUSTRIAN GP	Österreichring	20	Toleman Group Motorsport	P	1.5 t/c Toleman TG185-Hart 4	*engine-first start/did not restart*	(19)/27
ret	DUTCH GP	Zandvoort	20	Toleman Group Motorsport	P	1.5 t/c Toleman TG185-Hart 4		15/27
ret	ITALIAN GP	Monza	20	Toleman Group Motorsport	P	1.5 t/c Toleman TG185-Hart 4	*stalled at start*	21/26
ret	BELGIAN GP	Spa	20	Toleman Group Motorsport	P	1.5 t/c Toleman TG185-Hart 4	*accident*	16/24
ret	EUROPEAN GP	Brands Hatch	20	Toleman Group Motorsport	P	1.5 t/c Toleman TG185-Hart 4	*engine*	14/27
ret	SOUTH AFRICAN GP	Kyalami	20	Toleman Group Motorsport	P	1.5 t/c Toleman TG185-Hart 4	*engine*	13/21
ret	AUSTRALIAN GP	Adelaide	20	Toleman Group Motorsport	P	1.5 t/c Toleman TG185-Hart 4	*clutch*	21/25
1986			Championship position: Unplaced					
ret	BRAZILIAN GP	Rio	21	Osella Squadra Corse	P	1.5 t/c Osella FA1G-Alfa Romeo V8	*engine*	23/25
ret	SPANISH GP	Jerez	21	Osella Squadra Corse	P	1.5 t/c Osella FA1G-Alfa Romeo V8	*engine*	21/25
ret	SAN MARINO GP	Imola	21	Osella Squadra Corse	P	1.5 t/c Osella FA1G-Alfa Romeo V8	*out of fuel*	26/26
dnq	MONACO GP	Monte Carlo	21	Osella Squadra Corse	P	1.5 t/c Osella FA1G-Alfa Romeo V8		21/26
ret	BELGIAN GP	Spa	21	Osella Squadra Corse	P	1.5 t/c Osella FA1G-Alfa Romeo V8	*engine*	24/25
ret	CANADIAN GP	Montreal	21	Osella Squadra Corse	P	1.5 t/c Osella FA1G-Alfa Romeo V8	*gearbox*	23/25
ret	US GP (DETROIT)	Detroit	21	Osella Squadra Corse	P	1.5 t/c Osella FA1G-Alfa Romeo V8	*turbo*	22/26
ret	FRENCH GP	Paul Ricard	21	Osella Squadra Corse	P	1.5 t/c Osella FA1H-Alfa Romeo V8	*accident with Nannini*	25/26
ret/dns	BRITISH GP	Brands Hatch	21	Osella Squadra Corse	P	1.5 t/c Osella FA1G-Alfa Romeo V8	*accident in first start*	24/26
ret	GERMAN GP	Hockenheim	21	Osella Squadra Corse	P	1.5 t/c Osella FA1G-Alfa Romeo V8	*clutch*	25/26
ret	HUNGARIAN GP	Hungaroring	21	Osella Squadra Corse	P	1.5 t/c Osella FA1G-Alfa Romeo V8	*rear suspension*	23/26
11	AUSTRIAN GP	Österreichring	21	Osella Squadra Corse	P	1.5 t/c Osella FA1G-Alfa Romeo V8	*6 laps behind*	25/26
ret	ITALIAN GP	Monza	21	Osella Squadra Corse	P	1.5 t/c Osella FA1G-Alfa Romeo V8	*spun off-broken suspension*	26/27
ret	PORTUGUESE GP	Estoril	21	Osella Squadra Corse	P	1.5 t/c Osella FA1G-Alfa Romeo V8	*engine*	24/27
ret	MEXICAN GP	Mexico City	21	Osella Squadra Corse	P	1.5 t/c Osella FA1G-Alfa Romeo V8	*turbo*	25/26
ret	AUSTRALIAN GP	Adelaide	21	Osella Squadra Corse	P	1.5 t/c Osella FA1G-Alfa Romeo V8	*transmission*	25/26
1987			Championship position: Unplaced					
ret	SAN MARINO GP	Imola	26	Ligier Loto	G	1.5 t/c Ligier JS29B-Megatron 4	*withdrawn-handling problems*	20/27
7/ret	BELGIAN GP	Spa	26	Ligier Loto	G	1.5 t/c Ligier JS29B-Megatron 4	*out of fuel/3 laps behind*	17/26
12	MONACO GP	Monte Carlo	26	Ligier Loto	G	1.5 t/c Ligier JS29B-Megatron 4	*4 laps behind*	20/26
nc	US GP (DETROIT)	Detroit	26	Ligier Loto	G	1.5 t/c Ligier JS29B-Megatron 4	*pit stop- clutch/12 laps behind*	23/26
ret	FRENCH GP	Paul Ricard	26	Ligier Loto	G	1.5 t/c Ligier JS29C-Megatron 4	*engine*	17/26
excl	BRITISH GP	Silverstone	26	Ligier Loto	G	1.5 t/c Ligier JS29C-Megatron 4	*disqualified in practice*	19/26
ret	GERMAN GP	Hockenheim	26	Ligier Loto	G	1.5 t/c Ligier JS29C-Megatron 4	*engine*	17/26
12	HUNGARIAN GP	Hungaroring	26	Ligier Loto	G	1.5 t/c Ligier JS29C-Megatron 4	*bad oversteer/3 laps behind*	25/26
8	AUSTRIAN GP	Österreichring	26	Ligier Loto	G	1.5 t/c Ligier JS29C-Megatron 4	*2 laps behind*	18/26
8	ITALIAN GP	Monza	26	Ligier Loto	G	1.5 t/c Ligier JS29C-Megatron 4	*2 laps behind*	19/28
ret	PORTUGUESE GP	Estoril	26	Ligier Loto	G	1.5 t/c Ligier JS29C-Megatron 4	*clutch*	23/27
ret	SPANISH GP	Jerez	26	Ligier Loto	G	1.5 t/c Ligier JS29C-Megatron 4	*ignition*	23/28
ret	MEXICAN GP	Mexico City	26	Ligier Loto	G	1.5 t/c Ligier JS29C-Megatron 4	*overheating*	21/27
13/ret	JAPANESE GP	Suzuka	26	Ligier Loto	G	1.5 t/c Ligier JS29C-Megatron 4	*out of fuel*	25/27
ret	AUSTRALIAN GP	Adelaide	26	Ligier Loto	G	1.5 t/c Ligier JS29C-Megatron 4	*engine*	22/27
1988			Championship position: Unplaced					
dnq	BRAZILIAN GP	Rio	9	West Zakspeed Racing	G	1.5 t/c Zakspeed 881 4		28/31
ret	SAN MARINO GP	Imola	9	West Zakspeed Racing	G	1.5 t/c Zakspeed 881 4	*electrics*	25/31
ret	MONACO GP	Monte Carlo	9	West Zakspeed Racing	G	1.5 t/c Zakspeed 881 4	*gearbox*	23/30
15	MEXICAN GP	Mexico City	9	West Zakspeed Racing	G	1.5 t/c Zakspeed 881 4	*broken nose wing-p stop/-6 laps*	18/30
14/ret	CANADIAN GP	Montreal	9	West Zakspeed Racing	G	1.5 t/c Zakspeed 881 4	*engine*	22/31
dnq	US GP (DETROIT)	Detroit	9	West Zakspeed Racing	G	1.5 t/c Zakspeed 881 4		30/31
excl	FRENCH GP	Paul Ricard	9	West Zakspeed Racing	G	1.5 t/c Zakspeed 881 4	*dsq for missing weight check*	(24)/31
dnq	BRITISH GP	Silverstone	9	West Zakspeed Racing	G	1.5 t/c Zakspeed 881 4		28/31
14	GERMAN GP	Hockenheim	9	West Zakspeed Racing	G	1.5 t/c Zakspeed 881 4	*lost clutch/2 laps behind*	23/31
dnq	HUNGARIAN GP	Hungaroring	9	West Zakspeed Racing	G	1.5 t/c Zakspeed 881 4		30/31
ret	BELGIAN GP	Spa	9	West Zakspeed Racing	G	1.5 t/c Zakspeed 881 4	*engine oil leak*	24/31
ret	ITALIAN GP	Monza	9	West Zakspeed Racing	G	1.5 t/c Zakspeed 881 4	*engine*	16/31
dnq	PORTUGUESE GP	Estoril	9	West Zakspeed Racing	G	1.5 t/c Zakspeed 881 4		28/31
dnq	SPANISH GP	Jerez	9	West Zakspeed Racing	G	1.5 t/c Zakspeed 881 4		30/31
dnq	JAPANESE GP	Suzuka	9	West Zakspeed Racing	G	1.5 t/c Zakspeed 881 4		29/31
ret	AUSTRALIAN GP	Adelaide	9	West Zakspeed Racing	G	1.5 t/c Zakspeed 881 4	*fuel pump*	26/31
1989			Championship position: Unplaced					
dnpq	BRAZILIAN GP	Rio	18	Osella Squadra Corse	P	3.5 Osella FA1M-Cosworth V8		32/38
dnpq	SAN MARINO GP	Imola	18	Osella Squadra Corse	P	3.5 Osella FA1M-Cosworth V8		33/39
dnpq	MONACO GP	Monte Carlo	18	Osella Squadra Corse	P	3.5 Osella FA1M-Cosworth V8		30/38
excl	MEXICAN GP	Mexico City	18	Osella Squadra Corse	P	3.5 Osella FA1M-Cosworth V8	*dsq for missed weight check*	37/39
dnpq	US GP (PHOENIX)	Phoenix	18	Osella Squadra Corse	P	3.5 Osella FA1M-Cosworth V8		31/39
dnpq	CANADIAN GP	Montreal	18	Osella Squadra Corse	P	3.5 Osella FA1M-Cosworth V8		34/39
dnpq	FRENCH GP	Paul Ricard	18	Osella Squadra Corse	P	3.5 Osella FA1M-Cosworth V8		35/39
dnpq	BRITISH GP	Silverstone	18	Osella Squadra Corse	P	3.5 Osella FA1M-Cosworth V8		34/39
dnpq	GERMAN GP	Hockenheim	18	Osella Squadra Corse	P	3.5 Osella FA1M-Cosworth V8		34/39
ret	HUNGARIAN GP	Hungaroring	18	Osella Squadra Corse	P	3.5 Osella FA1M-Cosworth V8	*electrics*	22/39
dnpq	BELGIAN GP	Spa	18	Osella Squadra Corse	P	3.5 Osella FA1M-Cosworth V8		32/39
dnpq	ITALIAN GP	Monza	18	Osella Squadra Corse	P	3.5 Osella FA1M-Cosworth V8		33/39
dnpq	PORTUGUESE GP	Estoril	18	Osella Squadra Corse	P	3.5 Osella FA1M-Cosworth V8		33/39
ret	SPANISH GP	Jerez	18	Osella Squadra Corse	P	3.5 Osella FA1M-Cosworth V8	*gearbox*	25/38
dnpq	JAPANESE GP	Suzuka	18	Osella Squadra Corse	P	3.5 Osella FA1M-Cosworth V8		31/39
ret	AUSTRALIAN GP	Adelaide	18	Osella Squadra Corse	P	3.5 Osella FA1M-Cosworth V8	*car hit by Piquet in rain*	21/39

GP Starts: 74 (76)   GP Wins: 0   Pole positions: 0   Fastest laps: 0   Points: 2

BRUNO GIACOMELLI

Bruno, who sees himself as 'cool but enthusiastic', seemed to be well set for a successful Grand Prix career, but after he had been given some excellent early opportunities his star waned and was eventually reduced to a distant flicker.

Bruno came through Formula Italia to contest the 1976 BP Formula 3 championship in a March, and he did very well to run a close second to Rupert Keegan in his first season in the category. Benefiting from the close attentions of Robin Herd and the March factory, Giacomelli graduated to Formula 2 in 1977 and took three wins, but suffered through poor reliability. Enjoying substantial backing, he made his Grand Prix debut in a third works McLaren in selected races, but at this point he was still focusing on Formula 2. In 1978 he blitzed the opposition, winning eight of the 12 rounds in the works March to become the first Italian ever to win the title.

In 1979, Bruno joined the Alfa Romeo team for what was to be very much a learning year. The gloves were off in 1980 and at first he floundered, prone to silly errors which undid much good work. Then, after Depailler's death in a mid-season testing accident, he found himself leading the team, and rose to the challenge magnificently.

Maybe he lacked motivation, for while there were occasions during the next three seasons when his undoubted ability shone, too often he seemed uninterested and at odds with his machinery. Out of a Grand Prix drive from 1984, Giacomelli surfaced occasionally in Indy Car and sports car racing over the next few seasons to no great effect, so it was a considerable surprise when he was brought into the Life team in 1990 to replace the disenchanted Gary Brabham. The exercise was something of a joke, however, as Bruno rarely seemed to venture beyond the pit lane.

In 1995 Giacomelli was keeping his hand in racing a Porsche in the Monza four-hour race, and after two seasons away from the tracks he garnered enough sponsorship in 1998 to contest the highly competitive Porsche Supercup series, where he performed more than respectably on occasion.

GIACOMELLI, Bruno (I) b 10/9/1952, Borgo Poncarale, Brescia

	1977	Championship position: Unplaced						
	Race	Circuit	No	Entrant	Tyres	Car/Engine	Comment	Q Pos/Entries
ret	ITALIAN GP	Monza	14	Marlboro Team McLaren	G	3.0 McLaren M23-Cosworth V8	engine/spun off	15/34
	1978	Championship position: Unplaced						
8	BELGIAN GP	Zolder	33	Marlboro Team McLaren	G	3.0 McLaren M26-Cosworth V8	1 lap behind	21/30
ret	FRENCH GP	Paul Ricard	33	Marlboro Team McLaren	G	3.0 McLaren M26-Cosworth V8	engine	22/29
7	BRITISH GP	Brands Hatch	33	Marlboro Team McLaren	G	3.0 McLaren M26-Cosworth V8	1 lap behind	16/30
ret	DUTCH GP	Zandvoort	33	Marlboro Team McLaren	G	3.0 McLaren M26-Cosworth V8	spun off-stalled	19/33
14	ITALIAN GP	Monza	33	Marlboro Team McLaren	G	3.0 McLaren M26-Cosworth V8	1 lap behind	20/32
	1979	Championship position: Unplaced						
ret	BELGIAN GP	Zolder	35	Autodelta	G	3.0 Alfa Romeo 177 F12	hit by de Angelis	14/28
17	FRENCH GP	Dijon	35	Autodelta	G	3.0 Alfa Romeo 177 F12	pit stop/5 laps behind	17/27
ret	ITALIAN GP	Monza	35	Autodelta	G	3.0 Alfa Romeo 179 V12	spun off	18/28
dnp	CANADIAN GP	Montreal	35	Autodelta	G	3.0 Alfa Romeo 179 V12	had to pre qualify-withdrawn	– / –
ret	US GP EAST	Watkins Glen	35	Autodelta	G	3.0 Alfa Romeo 179 V12	spun avoiding Rosberg	18/30
	1980	Championship position: 17th= Wins: 0 Pole positions: 1 Fastest laps: 0 Points scored: 4						
5	ARGENTINE GP	Buenos Aires	23	Marlboro Team Alfa Romeo	G	3.0 Alfa Romeo 179 V12	1 lap behind	20/28
13	BRAZILIAN GP	Interlagos	23	Marlboro Team Alfa Romeo	G	3.0 Alfa Romeo 179 V12	1 lap behind	17/28
ret	SOUTH AFRICAN GP	Kyalami	23	Marlboro Team Alfa Romeo	G	3.0 Alfa Romeo 179 V12	engine	12/28
ret	US GP WEST	Long Beach	23	Marlboro Team Alfa Romeo	G	3.0 Alfa Romeo 179 V12	collison with Jones	6/27
ret	BELGIAN GP	Zolder	23	Marlboro Team Alfa Romeo	G	3.0 Alfa Romeo 179 V12	suspension	18/27
ret	MONACO GP	Monte Carlo	23	Marlboro Team Alfa Romeo	G	3.0 Alfa Romeo 179 V12	multiple accident	8/27
ret	FRENCH GP	Paul Ricard	23	Marlboro Team Alfa Romeo	G	3.0 Alfa Romeo 179 V12	handling	9/27
ret	BRITISH GP	Brands Hatch	23	Marlboro Team Alfa Romeo	G	3.0 Alfa Romeo 179 V12	spun off	6/27
5	GERMAN GP	Hockenheim	23	Marlboro Team Alfa Romeo	G	3.0 Alfa Romeo 179 V12		19/26
ret	AUSTRIAN GP	Österreichring	23	Marlboro Team Alfa Romeo	G	3.0 Alfa Romeo 179 V12	rear suspension	8/25
ret	DUTCH GP	Zandvoort	23	Marlboro Team Alfa Romeo	G	3.0 Alfa Romeo 179 V12	damaged skirt	8/28
ret	ITALIAN GP	Imola	23	Marlboro Team Alfa Romeo	G	3.0 Alfa Romeo 179 V12	puncture-spun off	4/28
ret	CANADIAN GP	Montreal	23	Marlboro Team Alfa Romeo	G	3.0 Alfa Romeo 179 V12	damaged skirt	4/28
ret	US GP EAST	Watkins Glen	23	Marlboro Team Alfa Romeo	G	3.0 Alfa Romeo 179 V12	electrics	1/27
	1981	Championship position: 15th Wins: 0 Pole positions: 0 Fastest laps: 0 Points scored: 7						
ret	US GP WEST	Long Beach	23	Marlboro Team Alfa Romeo	M	3.0 Alfa Romeo 179C V12	collision with Lammers	9/29
nc	BRAZILIAN GP	Rio	23	Marlboro Team Alfa Romeo	M	3.0 Alfa Romeo 179C V12	4 pit stops-electrics/22 laps behind	6/30
10/ret	ARGENTINE GP	Buenos Aires	23	Marlboro Team Alfa Romeo	M	3.0 Alfa Romeo 179C V12	out of fuel/2 laps behind	22/29

ret	SAN MARINO GP	Imola	23	Marlboro Team Alfa Romeo	M	3.0 Alfa Romeo 179C V12	collision with Cheever	11/30
9	BELGIAN GP	Zolder	23	Marlboro Team Alfa Romeo	M	3.0 Alfa Romeo 179C V12		17/31
ret	MONACO GP	Monte Carlo	23	Marlboro Team Alfa Romeo	M	3.0 Alfa Romeo 179C V12	accident with Alboreto	18/31
10	SPANISH GP	Jarama	23	Marlboro Team Alfa Romeo	M	3.0 Alfa Romeo 179C V12		6/30
15	FRENCH GP	Dijon	23	Marlboro Team Alfa Romeo	M	3.0 Alfa Romeo 179C V12	3 laps behind	12/29
ret	BRITISH GP	Silverstone	23	Marlboro Team Alfa Romeo	M	3.0 Alfa Romeo 179C V12	gearbox	12/30
15	GERMAN GP	Hockenheim	23	Marlboro Team Alfa Romeo	M	3.0 Alfa Romeo 179C V12	2 laps behind	19/30
ret	AUSTRIAN GP	Österreichring	23	Marlboro Team Alfa Romeo	M	3.0 Alfa Romeo 179C V12	engine fire	16/28
ret	DUTCH GP	Zandvoort	23	Marlboro Team Alfa Romeo	M	3.0 Alfa Romeo 179C V12	suspension-crashed	14/30
8	ITALIAN GP	Monza	23	Marlboro Team Alfa Romeo	M	3.0 Alfa Romeo 179C V12	2 laps behind	10/30
4	CANADIAN GP	Montreal	23	Marlboro Team Alfa Romeo	M	3.0 Alfa Romeo 179C V12	1 lap behind	15/30
3	CAESARS PALACE GP	Las Vegas	23	Marlboro Team Alfa Romeo	M	3.0 Alfa Romeo 179C V12		8/30

1982   Championship position: 22=   Wins: 0   Pole positions: 0   Fastest laps: 0   Points scored: 2

11	SOUTH AFRICAN GP	Kyalami	23	Marlboro Team Alfa Romeo	M	3.0 Alfa Romeo 179D V12	3 laps behind	19/30
ret	BRAZILIAN GP	Rio	23	Marlboro Team Alfa Romeo	M	3.0 Alfa Romeo 182 V12	engine	16/31
ret	US GP WEST	Long Beach	23	Marlboro Team Alfa Romeo	M	3.0 Alfa Romeo 182 V12	accident with Arnoux	5/31
ret	SAN MARINO GP	Imola	23	Marlboro Team Alfa Romeo	M	3.0 Alfa Romeo 182 V12	engine	6/14
ret	BELGIAN GP	Zolder	23	Marlboro Team Alfa Romeo	M	3.0 Alfa Romeo 182 V12	startline accident	17/32
ret	MONACO GP	Monte Carlo	23	Marlboro Team Alfa Romeo	M	3.0 Alfa Romeo 182 V12	transmission	3/31
ret	US GP (DETROIT)	Detroit	23	Marlboro Team Alfa Romeo	M	3.0 Alfa Romeo 182 V12	collision-Watson-hit barrier	6/28
ret	CANADIAN GP	Montreal	23	Marlboro Team Alfa Romeo	M	3.0 Alfa Romeo 182 V12	accident with Mansell	5/29
11	DUTCH GP	Zandvoort	23	Marlboro Team Alfa Romeo	M	3.0 Alfa Romeo 182 V12	2 laps behind	8/31
7	BRITISH GP	Brands Hatch	23	Marlboro Team Alfa Romeo	M	3.0 Alfa Romeo 182 V12	1 lap behind	14/30
9	FRENCH GP	Paul Ricard	23	Marlboro Team Alfa Romeo	M	3.0 Alfa Romeo 182 V12	1 lap behind	8/30
5	GERMAN GP	Hockenheim	23	Marlboro Team Alfa Romeo	M	3.0 Alfa Romeo 182 V12	1 lap behind	12/30
ret	AUSTRIAN GP	Österreichring	23	Marlboro Team Alfa Romeo	M	3.0 Alfa Romeo 182 V12	hit by de Cesaris	13/29
12	SWISS GP	Dijon	23	Marlboro Team Alfa Romeo	M	3.0 Alfa Romeo 182 V12	2 laps behind	9/29
ret	ITALIAN GP	Monza	23	Marlboro Team Alfa Romeo	M	3.0 Alfa Romeo 182 V12	broken side pod	8/30
10	CAESARS PALACE GP	Las Vegas	23	Marlboro Team Alfa Romeo	M	3.0 Alfa Romeo 182 V12	2 laps behind	16/30

1983   Championship position: 19th=   Wins: 0   Pole positions: 0   Fastest laps: 0   Points scored: 1

ret	BRAZILIAN GP	Rio	36	Candy Toleman Motorsport	P	1.5 t/c Toleman TG183B-Hart 4	spun off	15/27
ret	US GP WEST	Long Beach	36	Candy Toleman Motorsport	P	1.5 t/c Toleman TG183B-Hart 4	battery-could not restart at p stop	14/28
13/ret	FRENCH GP	Paul Ricard	36	Candy Toleman Motorsport	P	1.5 t/c Toleman TG183B-Hart 4	gearbox/5 laps behind	13/29
ret	SAN MARINO GP	Imola	36	Candy Toleman Motorsport	P	1.5 t/c Toleman TG183B-Hart 4	rear suspension	17/28
dnq	MONACO GP	Monte Carlo	36	Candy Toleman Motorsport	P	1.5 t/c Toleman TG183B-Hart 4		21/28
8	BELGIAN GP	Spa	36	Candy Toleman Motorsport	P	1.5 t/c Toleman TG183B-Hart 4		16/28
9	US GP (DETROIT)	Detroit	36	Candy Toleman Motorsport	P	1.5 t/c Toleman TG183B-Hart 4	1 lap behind	17/27
nc	CANADIAN GP	Montreal	36	Candy Toleman Motorsport	P	1.5 t/c Toleman TG183B-Hart 4	2 pit stops-engine/-27 laps	10/28
ret	BRITISH GP	Silverstone	36	Candy Toleman Motorsport	P	1.5 t/c Toleman TG183B-Hart 4	turbo	12/29
ret	GERMAN GP	Hockenheim	36	Candy Toleman Motorsport	P	1.5 t/c Toleman TG183B-Hart 4	turbo	10/29
ret	AUSTRIAN GP	Österreichring	36	Candy Toleman Motorsport	P	1.5 t/c Toleman TG183B-Hart 4	accident damage	7/29
13	DUTCH GP	Zandvoort	36	Candy Toleman Motorsport	P	1.5 t/c Toleman TG183B-Hart 4	pit stop/4 laps behind	13/29
7	ITALIAN GP	Monza	36	Candy Toleman Motorsport	P	1.5 t/c Toleman TG183B-Hart 4		14/29
6	EUROPEAN GP	Brands Hatch	36	Candy Toleman Motorsport	P	1.5 t/c Toleman TG183B-Hart 4		12/29
ret	SOUTH AFRICAN GP	Kyalami	36	Candy Toleman Motorsport	P	1.5 t/c Toleman TG183B-Hart 4	turbo fire	16/26

1990   Championship position: Unplaced

dnpq	SAN MARINO GP	Imola	39	Life Racing Engines	P	3.5 Life L190 W12		33/34
dnpq	MONACO GP	Monte Carlo	39	Life Racing Engines	P	3.5 Life L190 W12		35/35
dnpq	CANADIAN GP	Montreal	39	Life Racing Engines	P	3.5 Life L190 W12		35/35
dnpq	MEXICAN GP	Mexico City	39	Life Racing Engines	P	3.5 Life L190 W12		35/35
dnpq	FRENCH GP	Paul Ricard	39	Life Racing Engines	P	3.5 Life L190 W12	no time recorded	– / –
dnpq	BRITISH GP	Silverstone	39	Life Racing Engines	P	3.5 Life L190 W12		35/35
dnpq	GERMAN GP	Hockenheim	39	Life Racing Engines	P	3.5 Life L190 W12		35/35
dnpq	HUNGARIAN GP	Hungaroring	39	Life Racing Engines	P	3.5 Life L190 W12		35/35
dnpq	BELGIAN GP	Spa	39	Life Racing Engines	P	3.5 Life L190 W12		33/33
dnpq	ITALIAN GP	Monza	39	Life Racing Engines	P	3.5 Life L190 W12		33/33
dnpq	PORTUGUESE GP	Estoril	39	Life Racing Engines	P	3.5 Life-Judd V8	no time recorded	– /33
dnpq	SPANISH GP	Jerez	39	Life Racing Engines	P	3.5 Life-Judd V8		33/33

GP Starts: 69   GP Wins: 0   Pole positions: 1   Fastest laps: 0   Points: 14

DICK GIBSON

Dick, then a director of a motor company in Barnstaple, bought Tony Crook's modified Cooper-Bristol to embark on competition, but soon switched to an A-Type Connaught which he raced in 1955 and through 1956 with modest success. But it was with the acquisition of a rear-engined Formula 2 Cooper that he began to make a mark, sixth place in the International Coupe de Vitesse at Reims and seventh in the International Trophy at Silverstone being his best major placings in 1957.

Dick ran the Cooper again the following year, and after competing in New Zealand returned for the European season before venturing to South Africa early in 1959. It was a worthwhile trip, for he won three (Natal, Cape Town and Pietermaritzburg) of the four races and claimed the RAC South African International Championship. Naturally he returned the following year but, after finishing seventh in the South African Grand Prix, he was involved in a nasty shunt at another meeting which left him hospitalised. The damaged car was brought back to England and restored, with Dick preferring to allow Keith Ballisat, George Pfaff and Vic Wilson to drive it under the Equipe Prideaux banner.

GIBSON, Dick (GB) b 16/4/1918, Bourne

1957   Championship position: Unplaced

	Race	Circuit	No	Entrant	Tyres	Car/Engine	Comment	Q Pos/Entries
ret	GERMAN GP (F2)	Nürburgring	29	R Gibson	D	1.5 Cooper T43-Climax 4 F2	steering	24/24

1958   Championship position: Unplaced

ret	GERMAN GP (F2)	Nürburgring	19	R Gibson	D	1.5 Cooper T43-Climax 4 F2	mechanical	23/26

GP Starts: 2   GP Wins: 0   Pole positions: 0   Fastest laps: 0   Points: 0

GINTHER, Richie (USA) b 5/8/1930, Hollywood, California – d 20/9/1989, France

1960   Championship position: 8th=   Wins: 0   Pole positions: 0   Fastest laps: 0   Points scored: 8

	Race	Circuit	No	Entrant	Tyres	Car/Engine	Comment	Q Pos/Entries
6	MONACO GP	Monte Carlo	34	Scuderia Ferrari	D	2.4 Ferrari-Dino 246P V6	rear-engined prototype/-30 laps	9/24
6	DUTCH GP	Zandvoort	3	Scuderia Ferrari	D	2.4 Ferrari-Dino 246 V6	1 lap behind	12/21
dns	FRENCH GP	Reims	28	Reventlow Automobiles Inc	D	2.4 Scarab 4	engine problems	(20)/23
2	ITALIAN GP	Monza	18	Scuderia Ferrari	D	2.4 Ferrari-Dino 246 V6		2/16

1961   Championship position: 5   Wins: 0   Pole positions: 0   Fastest laps: 2 (1 shared)   Points scored: 16

2	MONACO GP	Monte Carlo	36	Scuderia Ferrari SpA SEFAC	D	1.5 Ferrari 156 V6	FL (shared with Moss)	2/21
5	DUTCH GP	Zandvoort	2	Scuderia Ferrari SpA SEFAC	D	1.5 Ferrari 156 V6		3/17
3	BELGIAN GP	Spa	6	Scuderia Ferrari SpA SEFAC	D	1.5 Ferrari 156 V6	FL	5/25
15/ret	FRENCH GP	Reims	18	Scuderia Ferrari SpA SEFAC	D	1.5 Ferrari 156 V6	oil pressure/12 laps behind	3/26
3	BRITISH GP	Aintree	6	Scuderia Ferrari SpA SEFAC	D	1.5 Ferrari 156 V6		=1/30
8	GERMAN GP	Nürburgring	5	Scuderia Ferrari SpA SEFAC	D	1.5 Ferrari 156 V6		14/27
ret	ITALIAN GP	Monza	6	Scuderia Ferrari SpA SEFAC	D	1.5 Ferrari 156 V6	engine	4/33

1962   Championship position: 8th   Wins: 0   Pole positions: 0   Fastest laps: 0   Points scored: 10

ret	DUTCH GP	Monza	18	Owen Racing Organisation	D	1.5 BRM P48/57 V8	pushed off by Trevor Taylor	7/20
ret	MONACO GP	Monte Carlo	8	Owen Racing Organisation	D	1.5 BRM P48/57 V8	throttle stuck-accident	=14/21
dns	"	" "	8	Owen Racing Organisation	D	1.5 BRM P57 V8	practice only	– / –
ret	BELGIAN GP	Spa	2	Owen Racing Organisation	D	1.5 BRM P57 V8	gearbox	9/20
3	FRENCH GP	Rouen	10	Owen Racing Organisation	D	1.5 BRM P57 V8	would not start on grid/-2 laps	10/17
13	BRITISH GP	Aintree	14	Owen Racing Organisation	D	1.5 BRM P57 V8	5 laps behind	=7/21
8	GERMAN GP	Nürburgring	12	Owen Racing Organisation	D	1.5 BRM P57 V8		7/30
2	ITALIAN GP	Monza	12	Owen Racing Organisation	D	1.5 BRM P57 V8		3/30
ret	US GP	Watkins Glen	5	Owen Racing Organisation	D	1.5 BRM P57 V8	engine/gearbox	2/20
7	SOUTH AFRICAN GP	East London	4	Owen Racing Organisation	D	1.5 BRM P57 V8	4 laps behind	=6/17

1963   Championship position: 2nd=   Wins: 0   Pole positions: 0   Fastest laps: 0   Points scored: 34

2	MONACO GP	Monte Carlo	5	Owen Racing Organisation	D	1.5 BRM P57 V8		=3/17
4	BELGIAN GP	Spa	8	Owen Racing Organisation	D	1.5 BRM P57 V8	1 lap behind	9/20
5	DUTCH GP	Zandvoort	14	Owen Racing Organisation	D	1.5 BRM P57 V8	1 lap behind	=6/19
ret	FRENCH GP	Reims	4	Owen Racing Organisation	D	1.5 BRM P57 V8	holed radiator	12/21
4	BRITISH GP	Silverstone	2	Owen Racing Organisation	D	1.5 BRM P57 V8	1 lap behind	=7/23
3	GERMAN GP	Nürburgring	2	Owen Racing Organisation	D	1.5 BRM P57 V8		6/26
2	ITALIAN GP	Monza	10	Owen Racing Organisation	D	1.5 BRM P57 V8		4/28
2	US GP	Watkins Glen	2	Owen Racing Organisation	D	1.5 BRM P57 V8		4/21
3	MEXICAN GP	Mexico City	2	Owen Racing Organisation	D	1.5 BRM P57 V8		5/21
ret	SOUTH AFRICAN GP	East London	6	Owen Racing Organisation	D	1.5 BRM P57 V8	driveshaft	=7/21

1964   Championship position: 4th=   Wins: 0   Pole positions: 0   Fastest laps: 0   Points scored: 23

2	MONACO GP	Monte Carlo	7	Owen Racing Organisation	D	1.5 BRM P261 V8	1 lap behind	=8/20
11	DUTCH GP	Zandvoort	8	Owen Racing Organisation	D	1.5 BRM P261 V8	p stop-fuel vaporisation/-16 laps	8/18
4	BELGIAN GP	Spa	2	Owen Racing Organisation	D	1.5 BRM P261 V8		8/20
5	FRENCH GP	Rouen	10	Owen Racing Organisation	D	1.5 BRM P261 V8		9/17
8	BRITISH GP	Brands Hatch	4	Owen Racing Organisation	D	1.5 BRM P261 V8	3 laps behind	14/25
7	GERMAN GP	Nürburgring	4	Owen Racing Organisation	D	1.5 BRM P261 V8	1 lap behind	11/24
2	AUSTRIAN GP	Zeltweg	4	Owen Racing Organisation	D	1.5 BRM P261 V8		=4/20
4	ITALIAN GP	Monza	20	Owen Racing Organisation	D	1.5 BRM P261 V8	1 lap behind	=9/25
4	US GP	Watkins Glen	4	Owen Racing Organisation	D	1.5 BRM P261 V8	3 laps behind	13/19
8	MEXICAN GP	Mexico City	4	Owen Racing Organisation	D	1.5 BRM P261 V8	1 lap behind	11/19

1965   Championship position: 7th=   Wins: 1   Pole positions: 0   Fastest laps: 0   Points scored: 11

ret	MONACO GP	Monte Carlo	20	Honda R & D Co	G	1.5 Honda RA272 V12	driveshaft	17/17
6	BELGIAN GP	Spa	10	Honda R & D Co	G	1.5 Honda RA272 V12	1 lap behind	4/21
ret	FRENCH GP	Clermont Ferrand	26	Honda R & D Co	G	1.5 Honda RA272 V12	ignition	7/17
ret	BRITISH GP	Silverstone	11	Honda R & D Co	G	1.5 Honda RA272 V12	fuel injection	=3/23
6	DUTCH GP	Zandvoort	22	Honda R & D Co	G	1.5 Honda RA272 V12	led race/1 lap behind	=2/17
14/ret	ITALIAN GP	Monza	20	Honda R & D Co	G	1.5 Honda RA272 V12	ignition/19 laps behind	17/23
7	US GP	Watkins Glen	11	Honda R & D Co	G	1.5 Honda RA272 V12	2 laps behind	3/18
1	MEXICAN GP	Mexico City (12)	11	Honda R & D Co	G	1.5 Honda RA272 V12		3/18

1966   Championship position: 11th   Wins: 0   Pole positions: 0   Fastest laps: 0   Points scored: 5

ret	MONACO GP	Monte Carlo	9	Cooper Car Co	D	3.0 Cooper T81-Maserati V12	driveshaft	9/16
5	BELGIAN GP	Spa	18	Cooper Car Co	D	3.0 Cooper T81-Maserati V12	3 laps behind	8/18
ret	ITALIAN GP	Monza	18	Honda Racing Team	G	3.0 Honda RA273 V12	tyre threw tread-accident	7/22
nc	US GP	Watkins Glen	12	Honda Racing Team	G	3.0 Honda RA273 V12	pit stops-gearbox/-27 laps	8/19
4	MEXICAN GP	Mexico City	12	Honda Racing Team	G	3.0 Honda RA273 V12	FL/1 lap behind	3/19

1967   Championship position: Unplaced

dnq	MONACO GP	Monte Carlo	22	Anglo American Racers	G	3.0 Eagle T1G-Weslake V12		18/18

GP Starts: 52   GP Wins: 1   Pole positions: 0   Fastest laps: 3   Points: 107

RICHIE GINTHER

Small and freckle-faced, Richie Ginther was always just outside the top echelon of Grand Prix talent but on his day he was more than capable of delivering the goods. In many ways he was the pefect number two driver, being conscientious, reliable and an extremely fine tester, with a rare mechanical sympathy born of his early days as a mechanic on both cars and aeroplanes during his National Service.

Although he had run an MG in 1951, it was two years later that he really became involved in serious competition when he shared Phil Hill's Ferrari in the Carrera Panamericana. The pair were lucky to emerge unscathed from a crash which wrote off the car, but returned the following year to take second place behind Maglioli's works entry.

Richie then found employment with Ferrari importer Johnnie von Neumann, who gave him plenty of drives over the next few seasons, Ginther making a big name for himself in West Coast racing and coming to the attention of Luigi Chinetti, who in turn entered him in his Ferraris, Richie's programme including a visit to Le Mans in 1957. Combining his job running the car agency with a racing career was becoming something of a strain, but after he shared a Ferrari sports car with von Trips to take second place in the Buenos Aires 1000 Km, Ginther was offered a four-race contract by the Scuderia. He quit his job and took the opportunity, moving to Italy with his wife. Although the sports car races yielded no success, his single-seater rides were a revelation. He was second in the Modena GP in the front-engined F2 car and made three Grand Prix starts, finishing an impressive sixth at Monaco in the rear-engined prototype, and second at Monza in the boycotted Italian GP. Quickly realising his tremendous engineering expertise, Ferrari gave Richie the role of chief development driver in addition to his racing duties. In 1961 the team virtually swept the board with their 'sharknose' 156 V6 car and Ginther really impressed with his spirited pursuit of Stirling Moss at Monaco. Surprisingly he found himself surplus to requirements at the end of the year but BRM were more than willing to bring him into the fold.

He made an ideal partner to Graham Hill, putting in much hard work as the Bourne team came good at last and won the World Championship. The 1963 season was his most successful and consistent, Ginther scoring points in every Grand Prix bar one to finish equal second with his team-mate in the championship behind runaway winner Jim Clark. Ginther stayed on for a third year in 1964, again proving his mechanical sympathy by finishing every Grand Prix.

It was all-change for 1965 as Ginther was hired to bring some much-needed experience to the still-fledgling Honda project. As the season wore on the car became a real threat, until Richie had his greatest moment when he won the Mexican Grand Prix at the last race of the year. It must have been galling for all concerned that it marked the end of the 1.5-litre formula, for Honda would have been a very tough act to beat in 1966 under the old rules. As it was they had to start again, and after filling in with a Cooper until the new car was ready towards the end of the season, Ginther was fortunate to escape a huge accident at Monza when a tyre failed. For 1967 Honda went with John Surtees and Richie joined up with Dan Gurney at Eagle. He lay second in the Race of Champions before retiring, but then surprisingly failed to qualify at Monaco. While practising for the Indianapolis 500 he suddenly decided that it was time to quit. Richie became involved in team management roles, for example running a Porsche 911 with Elliot Forbes-Robinson in 1971, before cutting his links with the sport and dropping out of the rat race to live in a camper in the desert. He returned to the circuits in 1977, invited to the German GP at Hockenheim by Goodyear to present the winner, Niki Lauda, with a prize to mark the tyre company's 100th win, though many would not have recognised him with his moustache and long hair replacing the once familiar crew-cut.

It was a frail and sick Ginther who arrived at Donington in 1989 to attend BRM's 40th anniversary celebrations, and it was with much sadness but little surprise that the racing world learned of his death after a heart attack just days later while holidaying in France.

YVES GIRAUD-CABANTOUS

Giraud-Cabantous began his long career back in 1925, and by 1927 he had won his first race, the GP des Frontières at Chimay in a Salmson. He was soon developing his own cars and in 1930 won the Bol d'Or 24-hour race in his own Caban, later successfully racing a Bugatti and a Delahaye, in which he finished second at Le Mans. After the war, Yves joined the Ecurie France team, emerging victorious at Chimay, Montlhéry and San Remo in 1947, and winning the GP de Paris in 1948. He was also involved with the infamous CTA Arsenal project, before purchasing a Talbot which he was to race extensively over the next five seasons.

In 1950 he joined the official Talbot team and by finishing fourth in the British Grand Prix became the first French driver to score World Championship points. Financial difficulties saw the team disbanded, but Giraud-Cabantous continued on his own with the Talbot, finishing third at Albi in 1952, then joined the HWM team for a number of races in 1952-53. His 'steady-as-she-goes' approach by this time was perhaps understandable, but he did bring the car home to the finish regularly. In sports cars he was second sharing Rosier's Talbot in the Reims 12 Hours in 1953, his last full season. Yves made occasional appearances over the next few years, in the little VP and Giaur sports cars, before retiring in 1957 to concentrate fully on his transport business.

IGNAZIO GIUNTI

From a well-to-do Rome family, Giunti was racing from his teens, driving Alfas in hill-climbs and club events. He progressed to the works Alfa team in 1966, winning the touring car section of the European mountain-climb championship the following year. Giunti was a regular member of the Autodelta sports car team in 1968, taking second in the Targa Florio and fourth (and class win) at Le Mans with Galli, who was his regular partner through into 1969.

For 1970, Ignazio was signed by Ferrari for their successful sports car programme, sharing the winning 512S in the Sebring 12 Hours, Targa Florio and Rand 9 Hours, also taking second place in the Monza 1000 Km and third in the Watkins Glen 6 Hours. Meanwhile Giunti made a very impressive Grand Prix debut to finish fourth at Spa, earning three more drives. Though Regazzoni had laid claim to the number two seat in F1, Giunti stayed with the team for 1971. In the season's first sports car race, the Buenos Aires 1000 Km, Ignazio, unsighted by another car, ploughed into the back of the Matra of Beltoise which had run out of fuel and was being pushed along the track by its driver. The Ferrari somersaulted some 200 yards down the track, exploding into flames, leaving poor Giunti no chance of survival. Sustaining 70 per cent burns and multiple injuries, he died in hospital some two hours later.

GIRAUD-CABANTOUS, Yves (F) b 8/10/1904, St Gaudens – d 30/3/1973

	1950	Championship position: 10= Wins: 0 Pole positions: 0 Fastest laps: 0 Points scored: 3							
	Race	Circuit	No	Entrant	Tyres	Car/Engine	Comment	Q Pos/Entries
4	BRITISH GP	Silverstone	14	Automobiles Talbot-Darracq SA	D	4.5 Lago-Talbot T26C-DA 6	2 laps behind	6/21
ret	SWISS GP	Bremgarten	6	Automobiles Talbot-Darracq SA	D	4.5 Lago-Talbot T26C-DA 6	crashed	7/18
ret	BELGIAN GP	Spa	18	Automobiles Talbot-Darracq SA	D	4.5 Lago-Talbot T26C-DA 6	engine	9/14
8	FRENCH GP	Reims	18	Automobiles Talbot-Darracq SA	D	4.5 Lago-Talbot T26C-DA 6	12 laps behind	5/20
	1951	Championship position: 12= Wins: 0 Pole positions: 0 Fastest laps: 0 Points scored: 2							
ret	SWISS GP	Bremgarten	6	Yves Giraud-Cabantous	D	4.5 Lago-Talbot T26C 6	ignition	15/21
5	BELGIAN GP	Spa	22	Yves Giraud-Cabantous	D	4.5 Lago-Talbot T26C 6	2 laps behind	8/13
7	FRENCH GP	Reims	46	Yves Giraud-Cabantous	D	4.5 Lago-Talbot T26C 6	6 laps behind	11/23
ret	GERMAN GP	Nürburgring	87	Yves Giraud-Cabantous	D	4.5 Lago-Talbot T26C 6	crashed	11/23
8	ITALIAN GP	Monza	24	Yves Giraud-Cabantous	D	4.5 Lago-Talbot T26C 6	8 laps behind	14/22
ret	SPANISH GP	Pedralbes	32	Yves Giraud-Cabantous	D	4.5 Lago-Talbot T26C 6	hit dog on track/overheating	14/20
	1952	Championship position: Unplaced							
10	FRENCH GP	Rouen	24	HW Motors Ltd	D	2.0 HWM-Alta 4	9 laps behind	10/20
	1953	Championship position: Unplaced							
14	FRENCH GP	Reims	30	HW Motors Ltd	D	2.0 HWM-Alta 4	10 laps behind	18/25
15	ITALIAN GP	Monza	16	HW Motors Ltd	D	2.0 HWM-Alta 4	13 laps behind	28/30

GP Starts: 13 GP Wins: 0 Pole positions: 0 Fastest laps: 0 Points: 5

GIUNTI, Ignazio (I) b 30/8/1941, Rome – d 10/1/1971, Buenos Aires, Argentina

	1970	Championship position: 17th= Wins: 0 Pole positions: 0 Fastest laps: 0 Points scored: 3							
	Race	Circuit	No	Entrant	Tyres	Car/Engine	Comment	Q Pos/Entries
4	BELGIAN GP	Spa	28	Scuderia Ferrari SpA SEFAC	F	3.0 Ferrari 312B F12	pit stop-oil leak	8/18
14	FRENCH GP	Clermont Ferrand	11	Scuderia Ferrari SpA SEFAC	F	3.0 Ferrari 312B F12	pit stop-throttle/3 laps behind	11/23
7	AUSTRIAN GP	Österreichring	14	Scuderia Ferrari SpA SEFAC	F	3.0 Ferrari 312B F12	pit stop-wheel change/-1 lap	5/24
ret	ITALIAN GP	Monza	6	Scuderia Ferrari SpA SEFAC	F	3.0 Ferrari 312B F12	overheating	5/27

GP Starts: 4 GP Wins: 0 Pole positions: 0 Fastest laps: 0 Points: 3

GODIA, Francesco (E) b 21/3/1921, Barcelona – d 28/11/1990, Barcelona

	1951	Championship position: Unplaced							
	Race	Circuit	No	Entrant	Tyres	Car/Engine	Comment	Q Pos/Entries
10	SPANISH GP	Pedralbes	44	Scuderia Milano	P	1.5 s/c Maserati 4CLT/48 4	10 laps behind	17/20
	1954	Championship position: Unplaced							
6	SPANISH GP	Pedralbes	16	Officine Alfieri Maserati	P	2.5 Maserati 250F 6	4 laps behind	13/22
	1956	Championship position: 6th= Wins: 0 Pole positions: 0 Fastest laps: 0 Points scored: 6							
ret	BELGIAN GP	Spa	36	Officine Alfieri Maserati	P	2.5 Maserati 250F 6	crashed	14/16
7	FRENCH GP	Reims	40	Officine Alfieri Maserati	P	2.5 Maserati 250F 6	4 laps behind	17/20
8	BRITISH GP	Silverstone	10	Officine Alfieri Maserati	P	2.5 Maserati 250F 6	7 laps behind	25/28
4	GERMAN GP	Nürburgring	20	Officine Alfieri Maserati	P	2.5 Maserati 250F 6	2 laps behind	16/21
4	ITALIAN GP	Monza	38	Officine Alfieri Maserati	P	2.5 Maserati 250F 6	1 lap behind	18/26
	1957	Championship position: Unplaced							
ret	GERMAN GP	Nürburgring	18	Francesco Godia-Sales	P	2.5 Maserati 250F 6	steering	21/24
ret	PESCARA GP	Pescara	10	Francesco Godia-Sales	P	2.5 Maserati 250F 6	engine	12/16
9	ITALIAN GP	Monza	10	Francesco Godia-Sales	P	2.5 Maserati 250F 6	6 laps behind	15/19
	1958	Championship position: Unplaced							
8	ARGENTINE GP	Buenos Aires	10	Francesco Godia-Sales	P	2.5 Maserati 250F 6	5 laps behind	9/10
dnq	MONACO GP	Monte Carlo	4	Francesco Godia-Sales	P	2.5 Maserati 250F 6		18/28
ret	BELGIAN GP	Spa	38	Francesco Godia-Sales	P	2.5 Maserati 250F 6	engine	18/20
ret	FRENCH GP	Reims	40	Francesco Godia-Sales	P	2.5 Maserati 250F 6	Fangio set qual time/crashed	11/21

GP Starts: 13 GP Wins: 0 Pole positions: 0 Fastest laps: 0 Points: 6

GOETHALS, Christian (B) b 4/8/1928

	1958	Championship position: Unplaced							
	Race	Circuit	No	Entrant	Tyres	Car/Engine	Comment	Q Pos/Entries
ret	GERMAN GP (F2)	Nürburgring	27	Ecurie Eperon d'Or	D	1.5 Cooper T43-Climax 4	fuel pump	24/26

GP Starts: 1 GP Wins: 0 Pole positions: 0 Fastest laps: 0 Points: 0

FRANCESCO GODIA

This wealthy Spanish businessman could afford to indulge his passion whenever he pleased, though he was really only competing regularly between 1956 – when he initially became part of the Maserati works team on the understanding that his car could be taken if needed by a more senior driver – and 1958, when he entered the car himself after the factory's closure. Not one to risk his neck unduly, he gained placings in races of high attrition, as when he finished fourth in the German and Italian GPs of 1956.

Perhaps the most fascinating feature of his long but intermittent career – which spanned more than twenty years – was its variety: in 1949 he raced a vintage Delage to fourth place at Le Mans; he made his GP debut in a Maserati 4CLT in 1951; and by the time his racing days were drawing to a close in 1969, he was handling machines such as the Ford GT40 and Porsche 908 Spyder.

CHRISTIAN GOETHALS

This amateur Belgian driver raced a Porsche Spyder in minor Continental events from the mid-fifties. With his brother, he took second place at Reims in 1956 in the up-to-1500 cc sports car race and won the same class at Forez the following year.

Goethals acquired an F2 Cooper for 1958, but gained little success, and soon returned to a Porsche RSK. In 1960 he finished fifth in the Buenos Aires 1000 Km and second in the GP de Spa, but after he crashed out of the Angola GP in Luanda later in the season, no more was seen of Goethals and his Porsche on the circuits.

JOSÉ FROILAN GONZÁLEZ

González was invariably tagged 'the Bull of the Pampas' by the press and the name perfectly described the vast bulk of this unlikely looking racing driver. However, he was called Pepe by his friends, who knew him as a kind-hearted, good-natured soul, despite his sometimes fearsome façade.

A surprisingly keen sportsman for one of his physique, González was a fair soccer player, swimmer and cyclist before he was old enough to begin a competition career racing motor cycles and then production cars. He caught the eye in 1949 at the wheel of a Maserati four-cylinder found for him by Fangio and joined his compatriot in Europe in 1950, driving a Maserati without luck in the championship races but taking a second place in the Albi GP.

His breakthrough came in 1951 when he defeated the visiting Mercedes-Benz team in both the Libre races at Buenos Aires in a Ferrari 166, and he began his proper Grand Prix career as a works driver for Ferrari. His style, hunched over the wheel, hard on the throttle, sliding the car to the limits of the track – and beyond on many occasions – was far from pretty, but no one could argue with his speed, and he soon gained immortality by defeating the works Alfa Romeos in the 1951 British GP, becoming the first driver to win a World Championship Grand Prix for the Scuderia. González also won the non-title Pescara GP before signing for Maserati for 1952, a season which saw him race in only one Grand Prix, although he also handled the brutish BRM V16, winning the Goodwood Trophy, and Vandervell's Thinwall Ferrari, in which he took the Richmond Trophy. He continued with Maserati as Fangio's team-mate in 1953, but was in the shadow of his great friend and rival before a crash in practice for a sports car race at Lisbon sidelined him for three months with a fractured vertebra.

Signed by Ferrari for 1954, Gonzalez enjoyed his finest season, taking his 625 to another glorious win for the team over the for once hapless Mercedes, as well as claiming wins in the non-title International Trophy and Bari and Bordeaux GPs. His year also saw four wins in sports cars, including Le Mans, where he shared the winning Ferrari with Trintignant, before a practice crash in the Tourist Trophy left him with an injured arm. He returned home to Argentina and, apart from a visit to his beloved Silverstone to race the Vanwall in 1956 which ended with driveshaft failure at the start, mainly restricted his racing to home territory. His guest appearances in his home Grands Prix showed there was still considerable fire in his belly and he duelled with Ascari's Lancia for the lead in 1955 before finishing second, but after the 1957 race he was content just to take part in his Chevrolet-engined Ferrari, turning his attention more to his motor business.

GONZÁLEZ, José Froilan (RA) b 5/10/1922, Arrecifes

	1950			Championship position: Unplaced					
	Race	*Circuit*	*No*	*Entrant*	*Tyres*	*Car/Engine*		*Comment*	*Q Pos/Entries*
ret	MONACO GP	Monte Carlo	2	Scuderia Achille Varzi	P	1.5 s/c Maserati 4CLT/50 4		*multiple accident/car on fire*	3/21
ret	FRENCH GP	Reims	36	Scuderia Achille Varzi	P	1.5 s/c Maserati 4CLT/50 4		*engine*	8/20
	1951			Championship position: 3rd Wins: 1 Pole positions: 1 Fastest laps: 0 Points scored: 27					
ret	SWISS GP	Bremgarten	42	José Froilan González	D	4.5 Lago-Talbot T26-GS 6		*oil pump*	13/21
2*	FRENCH GP	Reims	14	Scuderia Ferrari	E	4.5 Ferrari 375F1 V12		** Ascari took over car*	6/23
1	BRITISH GP	Silverstone	16	Scuderia Ferrari	P	4.5 Ferrari 375F1 V12			1/20
3	GERMAN GP	Nürburgring	2	Scuderia Ferrari	P	4.5 Ferrari 375F1 V12			2/23
2	ITALIAN GP	Monza	6	Scuderia Ferrari	P	4.5 Ferrari 375F1 V12			4/22
2	SPANISH GP	Pedralbes	6	Scuderia Ferrari	P	4.5 Ferrari 375F1 V12			3/20
	1952			Championship position: 8th Wins: 0 Pole positions: 0 Fastest laps: 1 (shared) Points scored: 6.5					
2	ITALIAN GP	Monza	26	Officine Alfieri Maserati	P	2.0 Maserati A6GCM 6		*FL (shared with Ascari)*	5/35
	1953			Championship position: 0 Wins: 0 Pole positions: 0 Fastest laps: 2 (1 shared) Points scored: 14.5					
3	ARGENTINE GP	Buenos Aires	4	Officine Alfieri Maserati	P	2.0 Maserati A6GCM 6		*1 lap behind*	5/16
ret	DUTCH GP	Zandvoort	14	Officine Alfieri Maserati	P	2.0 Maserati A6GCM 6		*rear axle*	5/20
3*	"	"	16	Officine Alfieri Maserati	P	2.0 Maserati A6GCM 6		** took Bonetto's car/-1 lap*	– / –
ret	BELGIAN GP	Spa	2	Officine Alfieri Maserati	P	2.0 Maserati A6GCM 6		*throttle/FL*	3/22
3	FRENCH GP	Reims	20	Officine Alfieri Maserati	P	2.0 Maserati A6GCM 6			5/25
4	BRITISH GP	Silverstone	24	Officine Alfieri Maserati	P	2.0 Maserati A6GCM 6		*FL(shared)/oil leak/-2 laps*	2/29
	1954			Championship position: 2nd Wins: 1 Pole positions: 1 Fastest laps: 3 (1 shared) Points scored: 26.64					
3	ARGENTINE GP	Buenos Aires	12	Scuderia Ferrari	P	2.5 Ferrari 625 4		*FL*	2/18
ret	BELGIAN GP	Spa	6	Scuderia Ferrari	P	2.5 Ferrari 553/555 4		*engine-oil pipe*	2/15
4*	"	"	10	Scuderia Ferrari	P	2.5 Ferrari 625 4		** took Hawthorn's car/-1 lap*	– / –
ret	FRENCH GP	Reims	2	Scuderia Ferrari	P	2.5 Ferrari 553/555 4		*engine*	4/22
1	BRITISH GP	Silverstone	9	Scuderia Ferrari	P	2.5 Ferrari 625 4		*FL (shared)*	2/31
2*	GERMAN GP	Nürburgring	1	Scuderia Ferrari	P	2.5 Ferrari 625 4		** Hawthorn took over car*	5/23
2	SWISS GP	Bremgarten	20	Scuderia Ferrari	P	2.5 Ferrari 625 4			1/16
ret	ITALIAN GP	Monza	32	Scuderia Ferrari	P	2.5 Ferrari 553 4		*gearbox/FL*	5/21
3*	"	"	38	Scuderia Ferrari	P	2.5 Ferrari 625 4		** shared Magliolis's car/-2 laps*	– / –
	1955			Championship position: 12= Wins: 0 Pole positions: 1 Fastest laps: 0 Points scored: 2					
2*	ARGENTINE GP	Buenos Aires	12	Scuderia Ferrari	E	2.5 Ferrari 625 4		** Farina/Trintignant also drove/*	1/22
	1956			Championship position: Unplaced					
ret	ARGENTINE GP	Buenos Aires	12	Officine Alfieri Maserati	P	2.5 Maserati 250F 6		*valve*	5/15
ret	BRITISH GP	Silverstone	18	Vandervell Products Ltd	P	2.5 Vanwall 4		*driveshaft on grid*	6/28
	1957			Championship position: 14th= Wins: 0 Pole positions: 0 Fastest laps: 0 Points scored: 1					
5*	ARGENTINE GP	Buenos Aires	20	Scuderia Ferrari	E	2.5 Lancia-Ferrari D50 V8		** shared with de Portago/-2 laps*	10/16
	1960			Championship position: Unplaced					
10	ARGENTINE GP	Buenos Aires	32	Scuderia Ferrari	D	2.4 Ferrari-Dino 246 V6		*3 laps behind*	11/22

GP Starts: 26   GP Wins: 2   Pole positions: 3   Fastest laps: 6   Points: 77.64

History in the making as Gonzalez in his Ferrari 375F1 defeats the Alfas to win the 1951 British Grand Prix.
At the end of the season Alfa Romeo withdrew from racing and Ferrari were about to take over as the team to beat.

GONZÁLEZ, Oscar (U)

	1956			Championship position: Unplaced					
	Race	Circuit	No	Entrant	Tyres	Car/Engine		Comment	Q Pos/Entries
6*	ARGENTINE GP	Buenos Aires	16	Alberto Uria	–	2.5 Maserati A6GCM/250F 6		*shared with Uria/-10 laps	-/15

GP Starts: 1   GP Wins: 0   Pole positions: 0   Fastest laps: 0   Points: 0

GORDINI, Aldo (F) b 20/5/1921, Bologna, Italy – d 28/1/1995

	1951			Championship position: Unplaced					
	Race	Circuit	No	Entrant	Tyres	Car/Engine		Comment	Q Pos/Entries
ret	FRENCH GP	Reims	36	Equipe Gordini	E	1.5 s/c Gordini Type 15 4		valve gear	17/23

GP Starts: 1   GP Wins: 0   Pole positions: 0   Fastest laps: 0   Points: 0

OSCAR GONZÁLEZ

The less-well-known González joined his Uruguayan compatriot Uria to share the latter's Maserati in the 1956 Argentine Grand Prix. After taking over the car he circulated steadily round the circuit, and by all accounts displayed impeccable track manners and 'did not interfere with the leaders' as he was lapped with great regularity.

ALDO GORDINI

The son of 'Le Sorcier', Aldo's name and Latin looks betrayed his Italian heritage, for father Amédée – né Amadeo – Gordini had settled in France after the Great War.

As the young Gordini grew up he of course became imbued with the racing activities of his father, who raced in the inter-war years and then began to build his own machines before hostilities not only put paid to sporting competition once again, but also destroyed the Gordini factory.

So it was 1946 before Aldo went to work as a mechanic as Gordini reconstructed his team. The youngster had the urge to race, and was allowed occasional outings. taking class honours in the Coupe du Salon at Montlhéry in both 1948 and 1949.

In 1950 he drove the Type 11 car in selected Formula 2 races, taking second place at Cadours and fifth at Aix-les-Bains, and sharing fifth with Trintignant at Roubaix. The following year, which was his last as a racer, he drove in his only championship event at Reims, and once again took fifth place at Aix-les Bains.

HORACE GOULD

In a period when fat Italians regularly occupied the cockpits of Formula 1 cars, to Horace Gould it seemed quite reasonable that a fat Bristolian should do the same. After all, he had spent a couple of seasons competing in a Cooper-Bristol – albeit usually in second-division races, with the notable exception of the 1954 British GP. So for 1955 he took himself off to Modena and bought a Maserati 250F, living a hand-to-mouth existence and scrounging parts from the factory to keep his machine on the grid.

Horace enjoyed a nomadic three seasons on the Continent, entering selected Grands Prix (his best result was fifth at Silverstone in 1956) and cannily entering his 'Maser' in non-championship races where starting money was good and the chances of decent placings were high. Horace finished third at Albi and fourth at Syracuse in 1955, second at Naples in 1956 and fourth, behind the three works Ferraris of Hawthorn, Collins and Musso, in the same race in 1957. Once the factory withdrew, it was really the end for Gould, who could no longer gain the assistance he needed to keep running the car. His last hurrah was a fourth place at Syracuse in 1958, though he was tempted back just one more time – to the boycotted 1960 Italian GP – where the old Maserati failed even to turn a wheel in practice due to crossed fuel-lines. Horace, who later helped his son in his racing activities, died of a sudden heart attack in 1968.

GOULD, Horace (GB) b 20/9/1921, Southmead, Bristol – d 4/11/1968, Southmead, Bristol

	1954			Championship position: Unplaced					
	Race	*Circuit*	*No*	*Entrant*	*Tyres*	*Car/Engine*		*Comment*	*Q Pos/Entries*
nc	BRITISH GP	Silverstone	28	Goulds' Garage (Bristol)	D	2.0 Cooper T23-Bristol 6		*pit stops/46 laps behind*	20/31
	1955			Championship position: Unplaced					
ret	DUTCH GP	Zandvoort	32	Goulds' Garage (Bristol)	D	2.5 Maserati 250F 6		*crashed*	15/16
ret	BRITISH GP	Aintree	48	Goulds' Garage (Bristol)	D	2.5 Maserati 250F 6		*brakes*	22/25
ret	ITALIAN GP	Monza	38	Officine Alfieri Maserati	D	2.5 Maserati 250F 6		*suspension*	21/22
	1956			Championship position: 15th= Wins: 0 Pole positions: 0 Fastest laps: 0 Points scored: 2					
8	MONACO GP	Monte Carlo	18	Goulds' Garage (Bristol)	D	2.5 Maserati 250F 6		*15 laps behind*	18/19
ret	BELGIAN GP	Spa	26	Goulds' Garage (Bristol)	D	2.5 Maserati 250F 6		*gearbox*	15/16
5	BRITISH GP	Silverstone	31	Goulds' Garage (Bristol)	D	2.5 Maserati 250F 6		*4 laps behind*	14/28
ret	GERMAN GP	Nürburgring	19	Goulds' Garage (Bristol)	D	2.5 Maserati 250F 6		*oil pressure*	13/21
	1957			Championship position: Unplaced					
ret	MONACO GP	Monte Carlo	22	H H Gould	D	2.5 Maserati 250F 6		*crashed*	12/21
ret	FRENCH GP	Rouen	30	H H Gould	D	2.5 Maserati 250F 6		*rear axle*	14/15
dns	BRITISH GP	Aintree	30	H H Gould	D	2.5 Maserati 250F 6		*injured in practice accident*	(15)/19
ret	GERMAN GP	Nürburgring	19	H H Gould	D	2.5 Maserati 250F 6		*rear axle*	19/24
ret	PESCARA GP	Pescara	18	H H Gould	D	2.5 Maserati 250F 6		*crashed*	11/16
10	ITALIAN GP	Monza	14	H H Gould	D	2.5 Maserati 250F 6		*9 laps behind*	18/19
	1958			Championship position: Unplaced					
9	ARGENTINE GP	Buenos Aires	12	H H Gould	D	2.5 Maserati 250F 6		*9 laps behind*	10/10
dnq	MONACO GP	Monte Carlo	42	Scuderia Centro Sud	D	2.5 Maserati 250F 6		*loan car*	27/28
dns	DUTCH GP	Zandvoort	12	H H Gould	D	2.5 Maserati 250F 6		*Gregory drove in race*	–/–

GP Starts: 14   GP Wins: 0   Pole positions: 0   Fastest laps: 0   Points: 2

GOUNON, Jean-Marc (F) b 1/1/1963, Aubenas

	1993			Championship position: Unplaced					
	Race	*Circuit*	*No*	*Entrant*	*Tyres*	*Car/Engine*		*Comment*	*Q Pos/Entries*
ret	JAPANESE GP	Suzuka	23	Minardi Team	G	3.5 Minardi 193-Ford HB V8		*collision-ater called in by team*	24/24
ret	AUSTRALIAN GP	Adelaide	23	Minardi Team	G	3.5 Minardi 193-Ford HB V8		*spun off*	22/24
	1994			Championship position: Unplaced					
9	FRENCH GP	Magny Cours	32	MTV Simtek Ford	G	3.5 Simtek S941-Ford HB V8		*4 laps behind*	26/28
16*	BRITISH GP	Silverstone	32	MTV Simtek Ford	G	3.5 Simtek S941-Ford HB V8		*2nd car dsq/3 laps behind*	26/28
ret	GERMAN GP	Hockenheim	32	MTV Simtek Ford	G	3.5 Simtek S941-Ford HB V8		*gearbox*	26/28
ret	HUNGARIAN GP	Hungaroroing	32	MTV Simtek Ford	G	3.5 Simtek S941-Ford HB V8		*handling*	26/28
11*	BELGIAN GP	Spa	32	MTV Simtek Ford	G	3.5 Simtek S941-Ford HB V8		*1st place car dsq/-2 laps*	25/28
ret	ITALIAN GP	Monza	32	MTV Simtek Ford	G	3.5 Simtek S941-Ford HB V8		*transmission*	25/28
15	PORTUGUESE GP	Estoril	32	MTV Simtek Ford	G	3.5 Simtek S941-Ford HB V8		*4 laps behind*	26/28

GP Starts: 9   GP Wins: 0   Pole positions: 0   Fastest laps: 0   Points: 0

JEAN-MARC GOUNON

After making an excellent debut to finish fourth overall in the 1988 French F3 championship, Gounon convincingly took the title a year later in the ORECA Reynard. He then became a stalwart on the F3000 scene from 1990 to 1992, making the best of things when he was in the right team but maybe the wrong chassis (a Ralt in 1991 and a Lola in 1992). Jean-Marc proved he was capable of being blindingly quick when circumstances allowed and his wins at Pau and Vallelunga were just reward for his efforts.

At the end of 1993, at the relatively late age of 30, this amiable Frenchman finally realised his ambition to race a Formula 1 car, buying a ride for the year's last two Grands Prix, having been patiently waiting for another opportunity following the March team's collapse before the start of the season.

Though he had hoped that his two drives for Minardi would lead to a full Grand Prix season in 1994, for he had access to the government fund set up in the wake of the ban on tobacco sponsorship introduced in France, Jean-Marc was forced to bide his time racing a BMW 318 in the French Supertourisme series, finishing a creditable fifth in the points standings. His chance to return to the Grand Prix stage came with Simtek, when he filled the seat tragically vacated by Roland Ratzenberger, and then by Andrea Montermini, who had crashed on his debut in Spain. Never able to do better than qualify on the last row of the grid, Jean-Marc nevertheless plugged away with great enthusiasm, his ninth place on his debut in France actually being the team's best result all year. However, when his sponsorship money eventually ran out, he was replaced by Mimmo Schiattarella.

Gounon has since forged a rewarding career in sports car racing, excellent performances in 1996 with a Ferrari and the following season in a McLaren F1 GTR leading to a seat in the semi-works Persson Motorsport Mercedes CLK. In 1999 he raced a DAMS Lola and, variously paired with Éric Bernard and Christophe Tinseau, scored wins at Donington, Brno, the Nürburgring and Kyalami.

KEITH GREENE

Growing up in the environment of his father Syd's Gilby Engineering concern, it was natural for young Keith to want to try his hand. Entered by his father in handicaps and similar events soon after his 18th birthday, Keith soon got to grips with a Cooper-Climax sports car, replacing this with a Lotus XI for the 1958 season.

It was 1959 which saw the start of his single-seater career and a splendid second place in the F2 Aintree 200. Greene continued with the Cooper until the 1961 season, when Gilby ambitiously built their own chassis for the 1.5-litre formula. It found no success at the very highest level, but did gain modest placings when fitted with a BRM V8 engine in 1962, Keith taking the car to third place in the Naples GP behind the works Ferraris of Mairesse and Bandini, and a trio of fourths at Brussels, Snetterton and Goodwood.

When the Formula 1 project was abandoned, Keith turned to sports and GT racing for the rest of the sixties, before taking on management roles with a whole roster of teams through the seventies and right into the nineties.

MASTEN GREGORY

Although his father died when he was very young, Masten was born into a wealthy Kansas family, and much later, when his mother sold the family business, he came into a great deal of money, some of which he immediately invested in some potent sports cars to further his fledgling racing career.

In the early days he was 'hairy' but very fast, particularly when he received his Allard J2X and then the even more powerful C-Type Jaguar. His US exploits in this car led to an offer to drive in the 1954 Buenos Aires 1000 Km, and although his outing ended in retirement the trip was still worthwhile, for he purchased the race-winning 4.5-litre Ferrari, which he then brought over to Europe. In his first race, paired with the veteran Biondetti, Gregory finished fourth in the Reims 12 Hours, and the season was to be a fruitful one, with third place in the Portuguese GP, second in class at the Tourist Trophy and a win in the Nassau Trophy. More success followed in the next two seasons, before Masten took the plunge into Grand Prix racing with Scuderia Centro Sud in 1957. Having already shared the winning works Ferrari in the Argentine 1000 Km, Gregory took a brilliant third place on his Grand Prix debut at Monaco and later scored points at both Monza and Pescara. He stayed with the Maserati for 1958, but the car was past its best.

Masten then negotiated a works drive with Cooper as number three to Jack Brabham and Bruce McLaren for 1959, and despite his position in the team he gave some excellent performances, finishing third at Zandvoort and second at Monsanto, as well as producing a great drive at AVUS. However, after bailing out of his Tojeiro-Jaguar in the Tourist Trophy at Goodwood when the steering failed, Gregory sustained rib and shoulder injuries which caused him to miss the season's remaining Grands Prix and he found his services were not retained by Cooper for 1960. He was irked at this, to say the least, and returned to Scuderia Centro Sud to race their Maserati-engined Coopers, but enjoyed little luck.

In 1961 Masten became involved with the American Camoradi outfit, running a Cooper in F1 and a Maserati in sports car

racing. He won the Nürburgring 1000 Km in the 'Birdcage' Maserati with Casner, but in mid-season moved over to the UDT-Laystall team to race the more competitive Lotus 18. He continued with the team in 1962, partnered by Innes Ireland, and gained a victory in the minor Kanonloppet F1 race at Karlskoga in the Lotus, and a win in the Player's 200 at Mosport with a Lotus 19 sports car, but achieved little else.

The next few seasons saw his Grand Prix career draw to a close with less and less competitive machinery, but there were compensations, including an unexpected triumph at Le Mans with Rindt in the NART Ferrari, which suddenly opened up a whole new career for Masten back in sports cars. Over the next five years (1966-71) he raced Ford GT40s, Ferrari P3s, Porsche 910s, Lola T70s and Alfa Romeo T33s among others before retiring after the 1972 Le Mans 24 Hours. A chain-smoker, he died suddenly after a heart attack in 1985, aged just 53.

GREENE, Keith (GB) b 5/1/1938, Leytonstone, London

1959 Championship position: Unplaced

	Race	Circuit	No	Entrant	Tyres	Car/Engine	Comment	Q Pos/Entries
dnq	BRITISH GP	Aintree	54	Gilby Engineering Co Ltd	D	2.5 Cooper T45-Climax 4 F2		– /30

1960 Championship position: Unplaced

	Race	Circuit	No	Entrant	Tyres	Car/Engine	Comment	Q Pos/Entries
ret	BRITISH GP	Silverstone	22	Gilby Engineering Co Ltd	D	2.5 Cooper T45-Maserati 4	overheating	22/25

1961 Championship position: Unplaced

	Race	Circuit	No	Entrant	Tyres	Car/Engine	Comment	Q Pos/Entries
15	BRITISH GP	Aintree	54	Gilby Engineering Co Ltd	D	1.5 Gilby-Climax 4	6 laps behind	23/30

1962 Championship position: Unplaced

	Race	Circuit	No	Entrant	Tyres	Car/Engine	Comment	Q Pos/Entries
dns	BRITISH GP	Aintree	48	John Dalton	D	1.5 Lotus 18/21-Climax 4	practiced only - drove Shelly's car	– / –
ret	GERMAN GP	Nürburgring	27	Gilby Engineering Co Ltd	D	1.5 Gilby-BRM V8	front suspension	19/30
dnq	ITALIAN GP	Monza	56	Gilby Engineering Co Ltd	D	1.5 Gilby-BRM V8		23/30

GP Starts: 3 GP Wins: 0 Pole positions: 0 Fastest laps: 0 Points: 0

GREGORY, Masten (USA) b 29/2/1932, Kansas City, Missouri – d 8/11/1985, Porto Ecole, nr Rome, Italy

1957 Championship position: 6th Wins: 0 Pole positions: 0 Fastest laps: 0 Points scored: 10

	Race	Circuit	No	Entrant	Tyres	Car/Engine	Comment	Q Pos/Entries
3	MONACO GP	Monte Carlo	2	Scuderia Centro Sud	P	2.5 Maserati 250F 6	2 laps behind	10/21
8	GERMAN GP	Nürburgring	16	Scuderia Centro Sud	P	2.5 Maserati 250F 6	1 lap behind	10/24
4	PESCARA GP	Pescara	14	Scuderia Centro Sud	P	2.5 Maserati 250F 6		7/16
4	ITALIAN GP	Monza	26	Scuderia Centro Sud	P	2.5 Maserati 250F 6	3 laps behind	11/19

1958 Championship position: Unplaced

	Race	Circuit	No	Entrant	Tyres	Car/Engine	Comment	Q Pos/Entries
ret	DUTCH GP	Zandvoort	12	H H Gould	D	2.5 Maserati 250F 6	fuel pump	14/17
ret	BELGIAN GP	Spa	30	Scuderia Centro Sud	D	2.5 Maserati 250F 6	engine	9/20
4*	ITALIAN GP	Monza	32	Temple Buell	D	2.5 Maserati 250F 6	Shelby co-drove-no points allowed	11/21
6	MOROCCAN GP	Casablanca	22	Temple Buell	D	2.5 Maserati 250F 6	1 lap behind	13/25

1959 Championship position: 8th= Wins: 0 Pole positions: 0 Fastest laps: 0 Points scored: 10

	Race	Circuit	No	Entrant	Tyres	Car/Engine	Comment	Q Pos/Entries
ret	MONACO GP	Monte Carlo	26	Cooper Car Co	D	2.5 Cooper T51-Climax 4	gearbox	11/24
3	DUTCH GP	Zandvoort	9	Cooper Car Co	D	2.5 Cooper T51-Climax 4		7/15
ret	FRENCH GP	Reims	10	Cooper Car Co	D	2.5 Cooper T51-Climax 4	exhaustion	7/22
7	BRITISH GP	Aintree	14	Cooper Car Co	D	2.5 Cooper T51-Climax 4	overheating/2 laps behind	5/30
ret	GERMAN GP	AVUS	3	Cooper Car Co	D	2.5 Cooper T51-Climax 4	engine-heat 1	5/16
2	PORTUGUESE GP	Monsanto	2	Cooper Car Co	D	2.5 Cooper T51-Climax 4	1 lap behind	3/16

1960 Championship position: Unplaced

	Race	Circuit	No	Entrant	Tyres	Car/Engine	Comment	Q Pos/Entries
12	ARGENTINE GP	Buenos Aires	2	Camoradi International	D	1.5 Behra-Porsche F4	4 laps behind	16/22
dnq	MONACO GP	Monte Carlo	40	Scuderia Centro Sud	D	2.5 Cooper T51-Maserati 4		20/24
dns	DUTCH GP	Zandvoort	19	Scuderia Centro Sud	D	2.5 Cooper T51-Maserati 4	starting money dispute	(16)/21
9	FRENCH GP	Reims	40	Scuderia Centro Sud	D	2.5 Cooper T51-Maserati 4	pit stop/13 laps behind	17/23
14	BRITISH GP	Silverstone	16	Scuderia Centro Sud	D	2.5 Cooper T51-Maserati 4	6 laps behind	14/25
ret	PORTUGUESE GP	Oporto	30	Scuderia Centro Sud	D	2.5 Cooper T51-Maserati 4	gearbox	11/16

1961 Championship position: Unplaced

	Race	Circuit	No	Entrant	Tyres	Car/Engine	Comment	Q Pos/Entries
dnq	MONACO GP	Monte Carlo	14	Camoradi International	D	1.5 Cooper T53-Climax 4		18/21
dnq	DUTCH GP	Zandvoort	17	Camoradi International	D	1.5 Cooper T53-Climax 4	'qualified-but on reserve list'	(10)/17
10	BELGIAN GP	Spa	44	Camoradi International	D	1.5 Cooper T53-Climax 4	1 lap behind	12/25
12	FRENCH GP	Reims	36	Camoradi International	D	1.5 Cooper T53-Climax 4	pit stop/9 laps behind	16/26
11	BRITISH GP	Aintree	42	Camoradi International	D	1.5 Cooper T53-Climax 4	4 laps behind	16/30
ret	ITALIAN GP	Monza	22	UDT Laystall Racing Team	D	1.5 Lotus 18/21-Climax 4	rear suspension	=17/33
ret	US GP	Watkins Glen	22	UDT Laystall Racing Team	D	1.5 Lotus 18/21-Climax 4	gear selection	11/19
11*	" "	" "	21	UDT Laystall Racing Team	D	1.5 Lotus 18/21-Climax 4	* took Gendebien's car/-8 laps	– / –

1962 Championship position: 18th Wins: 0 Pole positions: 0 Fastest laps: 0 Points scored: 1

	Race	Circuit	No	Entrant	Tyres	Car/Engine	Comment	Q Pos/Entries
ret	DUTCH GP	Zandvoort	10	UDT Laystall Racing Team	D	1.5 Lotus 18/21-Climax 4	driveshaft	16/20
dnq	MONACO GP	Monte Carlo	32	UDT Laystall Racing Team	D	1.5 Lotus 24-BRM V8	faster than 3 other starters	16/21
ret	BELGIAN GP	Spa	21	UDT Laystall Racing Team	D	1.5 Lotus 24-BRM V8	withdrawn after Ireland's accident	+7/20
dns	"	"	20	UDT Laystall Racing Team	D	1.5 Lotus 24-Climax V8	practised in Ireland's car	– / –
ret	FRENCH GP	Rouen	34	UDT Laystall Racing Team	D	1.5 Lotus 24-Climax V8	ignition	7/17
7	BRITISH GP	Aintree	34	UDT Laystall Racing Team	D	1.5 Lotus 24-Climax V8	1 lap behind	14/21
12	ITALIAN GP	Monza	38	UDT Laystall Racing Team	D	1.5 Lotus 24-BRM V8	overheating & gearbox stops/-9 laps	6/30
6	US GP	Watkins Glen	16	UDT Laystall Racing Team	D	1.5 Lotus 24-BRM V8	1 lap behind	7/20

1963 Championship position: Unplaced

	Race	Circuit	No	Entrant	Tyres	Car/Engine	Comment	Q Pos/Entries
ret	FRENCH GP	Reims	48	Tim Parnell	D	1.5 Lotus 24-BRM V8	gearbox housing	19/21
11	BRITISH GP	Silverstone	21	Reg Parnell (Racing)	D	1.5 Lotus 24-BRM V8	7 laps behind	22/21
ret	ITALIAN GP	Monza	42	Tim Parnell	D	1.5 Lotus 24-BRM V8	engine	12/28
ret	US GP	Watkins Glen	17	Reg Parnell (Racing)	D	1.5 Lola 4A-Climax V8	engine	=7/21
ret	MEXICAN GP	Mexico City	17	Reg Parnell (Racing)	D	1.5 Lola 4A-Climax V8	radius arm bolt	14/21

1965 Championship position: Unplaced

	Race	Circuit	No	Entrant	Tyres	Car/Engine	Comment	Q Pos/Entries
ret	BELGIAN GP	Spa	29	Scuderia Centro Sud	D	1.5 BRM P57 V8	fuel pump	20/21
12	BRITISH GP	Silverstone	12	Scuderia Centro Sud	D	1.5 BRM P57 V8	pit stop/10 laps behind	19/23
8	GERMAN GP	Nürburgring	24	Scuderia Centro Sud	D	1.5 BRM P57 V8	1 lap behind	19/22
ret	ITALIAN GP	Monza	48	Scuderia Centro Sud	D	1.5 BRM P57 V8	gearbox	23/23

GP Starts: 38 GP Wins: 0 Pole positions: 0 Fastest laps: 0 Points: 21

GEORGES GRIGNARD

Grignard began his career in rallying in the twenties, taking part in the Monte Carlo Rallies of 1928 and '29, and raced intermittently during the following decade while building up his garage business. After the war he reappeared in a Delahaye which he raced for much of 1946. Georges then joined the Ecurie Vallée team for 1947 but, having disposed of the Delahaye, found himself virtually sidelined until late 1948, when he finally took delivery of a long-awaited Talbot. Once wedded to his beloved car, Grignard raced it extensively over the next few seasons, his best placings being third at Pau in 1949 and sixth at Rouen in 1953.

Not a particularly quick driver, he nevertheless possessed mechanical sympathy and continued to compete, mainly in sports cars, until 1955, after which he retired to his garage business. He was still not finished with the Talbot marque, however, for in 1959 he took the opportunity to buy up all the liquidated stock, subsequently acting as a supplier to collectors around the world.

OLIVIER GROUILLARD

Even from his earliest days in French Formula 3 Grouillard developed something of a reputation as a wild and uncompromising performer. After finishing fourth in the 1983 series, he graduated to the all-conquering Marlboro-backed ORECA team the following year and swept to the title as was the established custom for the chosen incumbent, though it was a close-run thing, Grouillard edging out his rival Frédéric Delavallade by just two points, 108 to 106.

Rustling up enough budget for half a season in F3000 with ORECA in 1985, Grouillard made a good impression, coming close to a win at Enna. It was much the same the following year, when he was able to take part in only four races; he could have won at Mugello but made a mistake and ended up in fourth place. Back with ORECA again in 1987 he showed speed, but was rather overshadowed by team-mate Dalmas, who was on a somewhat quicker path to Formula 1. But Olivier was nothing if not persistent, and for 1988 he got himself into the well-funded GDBA team, running works-backed Lolas. He finished runner-up to Roberto Moreno, winning two races and putting in some superb performances.

At last Grouillard found himself in Formula 1 with Ligier, but after a bright start relations between the tempestuous youngster and his volcanic proprietor broke down and the driver was forced to seek alternative employment with Osella. The next two seasons were spent trying to qualify for races above all else, and after the briefest of flirtations with the almost extinct AGS team the future looked bleak.

Once again Grouillard dug himself out of a corner, finding the cash to join the underfinanced Tyrrell team. Freed from the perils of qualifying, he had a car that at the very least he could go racing with, but Olivier was overwhelmingly outperformed by team-mate Andrea de Cesaris and succeeded only in attracting criticism for his bad track manners when being lapped.

For 1993 Grouillard took himself off to the States for a full season of Indy Car racing but failed completely to make a worthwhile impression, finishing 28th in the points standings.

The Frenchman returned to Europe in 1994 and scratched around for a suitable ride. He competed at Le Mans in a Venturi 600LM and saw a huge upturn in his fortunes in GT racing. Having split with Giroix Racing in mid-1995 to join Dave Price, he finished the year with three straight wins at Silverstone, Nogaro and Zhuhai in China, sharing a Harrods-backed McLaren F1 GTR with Andy Wallace. The team stayed together for 1996 and more good top-six finishes were achieved, although there was only one outright win (at Silverstone).

In 1997 Grouillard took the opportunity to race a works Toyota Supra in the All-Japan GT championship, and partnered the Andrettis, father and son, in their unsuccessful attempt to win the Le Mans 24-hour race with the Courage C36-Porsche.

GRIGNARD, Georges (F) b 25/7/1905, Villeneuve-Saint-Georges – d 7/12/1977

1951 — Championship position: Unplaced

	Race	Circuit	No	Entrant	Tyres	Car/Engine	Comment	Q Pos/Entries
ret	SPANISH GP	Pedralbes	38	Georges Grignard	D	4.5 Lago-Talbot T26C-DA 6	overheating-engine	16/20

GP Starts: 1   GP Wins: 0   Pole positions: 0   Fastest laps: 0   Points: 0

GROUILLARD, Olivier (F) b 2/9/1958, Fenouillet,Toulouse

1989 — Championship position: 26th=   Wins: 0   Pole positions: 0   Fastest laps: 0   Points scored: 1

	Race	Circuit	No	Entrant	Tyres	Car/Engine	Comment	Q Pos/Entries
9	BRAZILIAN GP	Rio	26	Ligier Loto	G	3.5 Ligier JS33-Cosworth V8	oil leak/1 lap behind	22/38
dsq	SAN MARINO GP	Imola	26	Ligier Loto	G	3.5 Ligier JS33-Cosworth V8	car worked on between starts	10/39
ret	MONACO GP	Monte Carlo	26	Ligier Loto	G	3.5 Ligier JS33-Cosworth V8	gearbox	16/38
8	MEXICAN GP	Mexico City	26	Ligier Loto	G	3.5 Ligier JS33-Cosworth V8	lost clutch/1 lap behind	11/39
dnq	US GP (PHOENIX)	Phoenix	26	Ligier Loto	G	3.5 Ligier JS33-Cosworth V8		27/39
dnq	CANADIAN GP	Montreal	26	Ligier Loto	G	3.5 Ligier JS33-Cosworth V8		30/39
6	FRENCH GP	Paul Ricard	26	Ligier Loto	G	3.5 Ligier JS33-Cosworth V8	tyre & gearbox problems/-1 lap	17/39
7	BRITISH GP	Silverstone	26	Ligier Loto	G	3.5 Ligier JS33-Cosworth V8	1 lap behind	24/39
ret	GERMAN GP	Hockenheim	26	Ligier Loto	G	3.5 Ligier JS33-Cosworth V8	input shaft	11/39
dnq	HUNGARIAN GP	Hungaroring	26	Ligier Loto	G	3.5 Ligier JS33-Cosworth V8		28/39
13	BELGIAN GP	Spa	26	Ligier Loto	G	3.5 Ligier JS33-Cosworth V8	1 lap behind	26/39
ret	ITALIAN GP	Monza	26	Ligier Loto	G	3.5 Ligier JS33-Cosworth V8	pit stop gearbox/ret-exhaust	21/39
dnq	PORTUGUESE GP	Estoril	26	Ligier Loto	G	3.5 Ligier JS33-Cosworth V8		28/39
ret	SPANISH GP	Jerez	26	Ligier Loto	G	3.5 Ligier JS33-Cosworth V8	engine trumpet	24/38
ret	JAPANESE GP	Suzuka	26	Ligier Loto	G	3.5 Ligier JS33-Cosworth V8	engine	23/39
ret	AUSTRALIAN GP	Adelaide	26	Ligier Loto	G	3.5 Ligier JS33-Cosworth V8	hit wall in rain	24/39

1990 — Championship position: Unplaced

	Race	Circuit	No	Entrant	Tyres	Car/Engine	Comment	Q Pos/Entries
ret	US GP (PHOENIX)	Phoenix	14	Osella Squadra Corse	P	3.5 Osella FA1M-Cosworth V8	collision with Foitek	8/35
ret	BRAZILIAN GP	Interlagos	14	Osella Squadra Corse	P	3.5 Osella FA1M-Cosworth V8	collision with Alboreto	21/35
ret	SAN MARINO GP	Imola	14	Osella Squadra Corse	P	3.5 Osella FA1ME-Cosworth V8	wheel bearing	23/34
dnq	MONACO GP	Monte Carlo	14	Osella Squadra Corse	P	3.5 Osella FA1ME-Cosworth V8		28/35
13	CANADIAN GP	Montreal	14	Osella Squadra Corse	P	3.5 Osella FA1ME-Cosworth V8	handling problems/5 laps behind	15/35
19	MEXICAN GP	Mexico City	14	Osella Squadra Corse	P	3.5 Osella FA1ME-Cosworth V8	gear selection problems/-4 laps	20/35
dnpq	FRENCH GP	Paul Ricard	14	Osella Squadra Corse	P	3.5 Osella FA1ME-Cosworth V8		31/35
dnq	BRITISH GP	Silverstone	14	Osella Squadra Corse	P	3.5 Osella FA1ME-Cosworth V8		27/35
dnq	GERMAN GP	Hockenheim	14	Osella Squadra Corse	P	3.5 Osella FA1ME-Cosworth V8		27/35
dnpq	HUNGARIAN GP	Hungaroring	14	Osella Squadra Corse	P	3.5 Osella FA1ME-Cosworth V8		31/35
16	BELGIAN GP	Spa	14	Osella Squadra Corse	P	3.5 Osella FA1ME-Cosworth V8	pit stop-tyres/2 laps behind	23/33
ret	ITALIAN GP	Monza	14	Osella Squadra Corse	P	3.5 Osella FA1ME-Cosworth V8	wheel bearing	23/33
dnq	PORTUGUESE GP	Estoril	14	Osella Squadra Corse	P	3.5 Osella FA1ME-Cosworth V8		27/33
ret	SPANISH GP	Jerez	14	Osella Squadra Corse	P	3.5 Osella FA1ME-Cosworth V8	wheel bearing	21/33
dnq	JAPANESE GP	Suzuka	14	Osella Squadra Corse	P	3.5 Osella FA1ME-Cosworth V8		27/30
13	AUSTRALIAN GP	Adelaide	14	Osella Squadra Corse	P	3.5 Osella FA1ME-Cosworth V8	2 stops-tyres/handling/-7 laps	22/30

1991 — Championship position: Unplaced

	Race	Circuit	No	Entrant	Tyres	Car/Engine	Comment	Q Pos/Entries
dnpq	US GP (PHOENIX)	Phoenix	14	Fondmetal F1 SpA	G	3.5 Fomet FA1M-E90-Cosworth V8		33/34
dnpq	BRAZILIAN GP	Interlagos	14	Fondmetal F1 SpA	G	3.5 Fomet FA1M-E90-Cosworth V8		34/34
dnpq	SAN MARINO GP	Imola	14	Fondmetal F1 SpA	G	3.5 Fomet F1-Cosworth V8		32/34
dnpq	MONACO GP	Monte Carlo	14	Fondmetal F1 SpA	G	3.5 Fomet F1-Cosworth V8		34/34
dnpq	CANADIAN GP	Montreal	14	Fondmetal F1 SpA	G	3.5 Fomet F1-Cosworth V8		31/34
ret	MEXICAN GP	Mexico City	14	Fondmetal F1 SpA	G	3.5 Fomet F1-Cosworth V8	started from back/oil line	10/34
ret	FRENCH GP	Magny Cours	14	Fondmetal F1 SpA	G	3.5 Fomet F1-Cosworth V8	oil leak	21/34
dnpq	BRITISH GP	Silverstone	14	Fondmetal F1 SpA	G	3.5 Fomet F1-Cosworth V8		31/34
dnpq	GERMAN GP	Nürburgring	14	Fondmetal F1 SpA	G	3.5 Fomet F1-Cosworth V8		31/34
dnq	HUNGARIAN GP	Hungaroring	14	Fondmetal F1 SpA	G	3.5 Fomet F1-Cosworth V8		27/34
10	BELGIAN GP	Spa	14	Fondmetal F1 SpA	G	3.5 Fomet F1-Cosworth V8	1 lap behind	23/24
ret	ITALIAN GP	Monza	14	Fondmetal F1 SpA	G	3.5 Fomet F1-Cosworth V8	engine	26/34
dnpq	PORTUGUESE GP	Estoril	14	Fondmetal F1 SpA	G	3.5 Fomet F1-Cosworth V8		32/34
dnpq	SPANISH GP	Barcelona	17	Automobiles Gonfaronaise Sportive	G	3.5 AGS JH27-Cosworth V8		33/33

1992 — Championship position: Unplaced

	Race	Circuit	No	Entrant	Tyres	Car/Engine	Comment	Q Pos/Entries
ret	SOUTH AFRICAN GP	Kyalami	3	Tyrrell Racing Organisation	G	Tyrrell 020B-Ilmor V10	clutch	12/30
ret	MEXICAN GP	Mexico City	3	Tyrrell Racing Organisation	G	Tyrrell 020B-Ilmor V10	engine	16/30
ret	BRAZILIAN GP	Interlagos	3	Tyrrell Racing Organisation	G	Tyrrell 020B-Ilmor V10	engine	17/31
ret	SPANISH GP	Barcelona	3	Tyrrell Racing Organisation	G	Tyrrell 020B-Ilmor V10	spun off	15/32
8	SAN MARINO GP	Imola	3	Tyrrell Racing Organisation	G	Tyrrell 020B-Ilmor V10	2 laps behind	20/32
ret	MONACO GP	Monte Carlo	3	Tyrrell Racing Organisation	G	Tyrrell 020B-Ilmor V10	gearbox	24/32
12	CANADIAN GP	Montreal	3	Tyrrell Racing Organisation	G	Tyrrell 020B-Ilmor V10	2 laps behind	26/32
11	FRENCH GP	Magny Cours	3	Tyrrell Racing Organisation	G	Tyrrell 020B-Ilmor V10	3 laps behind	22/30
11	BRITISH GP	Kyalami	3	Tyrrell Racing Organisation	G	Tyrrell 020B-Ilmor V10	2 laps behind	20/32
ret	GERMAN GP	Hockenheim	3	Tyrrell Racing Organisation	G	Tyrrell 020B-Ilmor V10	overheating	14/32
ret	HUNGARIAN GP	Hungaroring	3	Tyrrell Racing Organisation	G	Tyrrell 020B-Ilmor V10	collision with Wendlinger	22/31
ret	BELGIAN GP	Spa	3	Tyrrell Racing Organisation	G	Tyrrell 020B-Ilmor V10	spun off lap 1	22/30
ret	ITALIAN GP	Monza	3	Tyrrell Racing Organisation	G	Tyrrell 020B-Ilmor V10	engine	18/28
ret	PORTUGUESE GP	Estoril	3	Tyrrell Racing Organisation	G	Tyrrell 020B-Ilmor V10	gearbox	15/26
ret	JAPANESE GP	Suzuka	3	Tyrrell Racing Organisation	G	Tyrrell 020B-Ilmor V10	spun off	21/26
ret	AUSTRALIAN GP	Adelaide	3	Tyrrell Racing Organisation	G	Tyrrell 020B-Ilmor V10	collision with Martini lap 1	13/26

GP Starts: 41   GP Wins: 0   Pole positions: 0   Fastest laps: 0   Points: 1

ANDRÉ GUELFI

A very useful performer, Guelfi confined himself to racing in North Africa and France during a long competition career that stretched back to 1950 when he raced a Delahaye. After driving a Jaguar, he came to prominence in 1953 racing a Gordini sports car, taking it to class and outright wins at Agadir. He shared a works car with Behra in the 12-hour race at Casablanca that year, but it was retired with a broken shock absorber.

Joining the ever-changing roster of pilots at Gordini, Guelfi was given a single appearance at Pescara in 1954, but his race ended on the first lap when the car caught fire. His true métier was sports cars, however, and, with Jacky Pollet, he drove a works Gordini into sixth place at Le Mans, taking the 2000 cc–3000 cc class win. Though still racing mainly in Morocco – he was champion in 1955 – André continued to make regular sorties to France. In 1957 he finished a distant seventh in the Pau GP as the pale-blue machines were reaching imminent extinction. The new rear-engined Coopers were now the way forward and Guelfi made a good impression when he took second place in the Prix de Paris at Montlhéry in June 1958, only three seconds behind Henry Taylor in a similar car. With a Formula 2 class being added to bolster the field for the first (and only) Grand Prix of Morocco at season's end, Guelfi entered a car, but in truth was not as quick as could have been expected, though he stayed the distance to finish last.

He subsequently raced on in Morocco through the sixties, and as late as 1968 his name still appeared in the results when he took second place in a race in Rabat in a Porsche 911R.

MIGUEL ANGEL GUERRA

Until the first-corner accident which eliminated Marco Apicella at Monza in 1993, the unfortunate Argentinian had the unwanted tag of having just about the shortest Grand Prix career on record, for he was barely a third of a lap into his debut, the 1981 San Marino Grand Prix, when he was pushed off the track and into the wall, sustaining a broken ankle and wrist in the process.

He had three seasons in Formula 2 behind him: the first, in 1978, saw a few outings in a Chevron; the next, in a March, yielded his best finish (third place at Hockenheim); and he then endured a disappointing year with the troublesome Minardi.

Guerra recovered from his Imola crash to reappear briefly in Formula 2 at the end of the 1981 season in the Adriatic GP at Misano, finishing a distant 13th. However, his racing career was far from over, and on his return to Argentina Guerra was a front-runner in the Formula 2/3 CoDaSur series until 1987 when he made the switch to touring cars, in which he has been a regular competitor throughout the nineties.

Along with fellow ex-Grand Prix drivers Larrauri and Hoffmann, Miguel is currently one of the stars of the SudAm Super Touring championship.

GUELFI, André (F/MA) b 6/5/1919

	1958	Championship position: Unplaced							
	Race	Circuit	No	Entrant	Tyres	Car/Engine	Comment	Q Pos/Entries
15*	MOROCCAN GP (F2)	Casablanca	60	André Guelfi	D	1.5 Cooper T45-Climax 4 F2	* 4th in F2 class/-5 laps	25/25

GP Starts: 1   GP Wins: 0   Pole positions: 0   Fastest laps: 0   Points: 0

GUERRA, Miguel Angel (RA) b 31/8/1953, Buenos Aires

	1981	Championship position: Unplaced							
	Race	Circuit	No	Entrant	Tyres	Car/Engine	Comment	Q Pos/Entries
dnq	US GP WEST	Long Beach	31	Osella Squadra Corse	M	3.0 Osella FA1B-Cosworth V8		27/29
dnq	BRAZILIAN GP	Rio	31	Osella Squadra Corse	M	3.0 Osella FA1B-Cosworth V8		28/30
dnq	ARGENTINE GP	Buenos Aires	31	Osella Squadra Corse	M	3.0 Osella FA1B-Cosworth V8		25/29
ret	SAN MARINO GP	Imola	31	Osella Squadra Corse	M	3.0 Osella FA1B-Cosworth V8	spun/collision-Salazar/hit wall	22/30

GP Starts: 1   GP Wins: 0   Pole positions: 0   Fastest laps: 0   Points: 0

GUERRERO, Roberto (COL/USA) b 16/11/1958, Medellin, Colombia

	1982	Championship position: Unplaced							
	Race	Circuit	No	Entrant	Tyres	Car/Entrant	Comment	Q Pos/Entries
dnp	SOUTH AFRICAN GP	Kyalami	14	Ensign Racing	A	3.0 Ensign N180B-Cosworth V8	withdrawn, injunction by Maurer	– / –
dnq	BRAZILIAN GP	Rio	14	Ensign Racing	A	3.0 Ensign N181-Cosworth V8		28/31
ret	US GP WEST	Long Beach	14	Ensign Racing	A	3.0 Ensign N181-Cosworth V8	hit wall	19/31
dnq	BELGIAN GP	Zolder	14	Ensign Racing	A	3.0 Ensign N181-Cosworth V8		29/32
dnq	MONACO GP	Monte Carlo	14	Ensign Racing	A	3.0 Ensign N181-Cosworth V8		26/31
ret	US GP (DETROIT)	Detroit	14	Ensign Racing	M	3.0 Ensign N181-Cosworth V8	accident with de Angelis	11/28
ret	CANADIAN GP	Montreal	14	Ensign Racing	M	3.0 Ensign N181-Cosworth V8	clutch	20/29
dnq	DUTCH GP	Zandvoort	14	Ensign Racing	M	3.0 Ensign N181-Cosworth V8		27/31
ret	BRITISH GP	Brands Hatch	14	Ensign Racing	M	3.0 Ensign N181-Cosworth V8	engine	19/30

dnq	FRENCH GP	Paul Ricard	14	Ensign Racing	M	3.0 Ensign N181-Cosworth V8		28/30
8	GERMAN GP	Hockenheim	14	Ensign Racing	M	3.0 Ensign N181-Cosworth V8	*1 lap behind*	22/30
ret	AUSTRIAN GP	Österreichring	14	Ensign Racing	M	3.0 Ensign N181-Cosworth V8	*driveshaft*	16/29
ret	SWISS GP	Dijon	14	Ensign Racing	M	3.0 Ensign N181-Cosworth V8	*engine*	19/29
nc	ITALIAN GP	Monza	14	Ensign Racing	M	3.0 Ensign N181-Cosworth V8	*hit Daly-pit stop/-12 laps*	18/30
dns	CAESARS PALACE GP	Las Vegas	14	Ensign Racing	M	3.0 Ensign N181-Cosworth V8	*engine in warm-up*	(15)/30
1983		Championship position: Unplaced						
nc	BRAZILIAN GP	Rio	33	Theodore Racing Team	G	3.0 Theodore N183-Cosworth V8	*pit stop/10 laps behind*	14/27
ret	US GP WEST	Long Beach	33	Theodore Racing Team	G	3.0 Theodore N183-Cosworth V8	*gearbox*	18/28
ret	FRENCH GP	Paul Ricard	33	Theodore Racing Team	G	3.0 Theodore N183-Cosworth V8	*engine*	22/29
ret	SAN MARINO GP	Imola	33	Theodore Racing Team	G	3.0 Theodore N183-Cosworth V8	*incident with Sullivan*	21/28
dnpq	MONACO GP	Monte Carlo	33	Theodore Racing Team	G	3.0 Theodore N183-Cosworth V8	*no tyres*	28/28
ret	BELGIAN GP	Spa	33	Theodore Racing Team	G	3.0 Theodore N183-Cosworth V8	*engine*	14/28
nc	US GP (DETROIT)	Detroit	33	Theodore Racing Team	G	3.0 Theodore N183-Cosworth V8	*pit stop/22 laps behind*	11/27
ret	CANADIAN GP	Montreal	33	Theodore Racing Team	G	3.0 Theodore N183-Cosworth V8	*engine*	21/28
16	BRITISH GP	Silverstone	33	Theodore Racing Team	G	3.0 Theodore N183-Cosworth V8	*3 laps behind*	21/29
ret	GERMAN GP	Hockenheim	33	Theodore Racing Team	G	3.0 Theodore N183-Cosworth V8	*engine*	24/29
ret	AUSTRIAN GP	Österreichring	33	Theodore Racing Team	G	3.0 Theodore N183-Cosworth V8	*gearbox*	21/29
12	DUTCH GP	Zandvoort	33	Theodore Racing Team	G	3.0 Theodore N183-Cosworth V8	*incident-Jarier-pit stop/-4 laps*	20/29
13	ITALIAN GP	Monza	33	Theodore Racing Team	G	3.0 Theodore N183-Cosworth V8	*2 laps behind*	21/29
12	EUROPEAN GP	Brands Hatch	33	Theodore Racing Team	G	3.0 Theodore N183-Cosworth V8	*1 lap behind*	21/29

GP Starts: 21   GP Wins: 0   Pole positions: 0   Fastest laps: 0   Points: 0

ROBERTO GUERRERO

This personable Colombian driver could have made a good career for himself in Formula 1 had he not chosen to move into Indy Car racing at the end of 1983 when no suitable F1 drive was available, for, on his speedy passage to the top, Roberto had already displayed genuine talent. Joint second in the British F3 series in the unfashionable Argo, and an immediate winner at Thruxton in his first Formula 2 season, Guerrero's fine performances caught the eye of Mo Nunn, who gave him the Ensign drive for 1982. Roberto did extremely well in difficult circumstances, as he did in his second season following the team's merger with Theodore.

So it was off to the States, and stardom, Guerrero finishing second in the 1984 Indy 500, and winning two races in 1987, at Phoenix and Mid-Ohio, before a crash while testing at Indy left him in a coma for 17 days. He made a full recovery but his career never quite regained its earlier momentum, and he became bogged down in the largely disappointing Alfa Romeo Indy programme until he joined Kenny Bernstein's team in mid-1991. Roberto took pole at Indy in 1992 but crashed on the warm-up lap and spent the rest of the campaign on the sidelines. He then signed with Bernstein for a full season in 1993, but after a generally lacklustre year he lost his ride with three races remaining.

No longer capable of getting a full-time drive, Roberto joined forces with Pagan Racing in 1994 and did well to scrape into the Indy 500 as 33rd and final qualifier with a two-year-old Lola-Buick. Unfortunately Guerrero, now a US citizen, was posted as first retirement again when he spun into the wall. He remained with the little team for 1995, targeting the Brickyard once more (though he raced at Phoenix as a shakedown for the month of May), and this time things went much better. He finished a creditable 12th, having lost time under caution early on.

When the Indy Racing League was formed in 1996 it must have come as 'manna from heaven' to the likes of Guerrero. Not only did it give him a racing lifeline, but it also represented a tantalising opportunity to have his image engraved on the magnificent Borg Warner Trophy, something that he came agonisingly close to achieving back in 1987 when, after a totally dominant performance, the race was snatched from his grasp by Al Unser Snr when clutch problems at a pit stop slowed him near the finish.

Roberto has been a regular competitor in this much-maligned series but, thus far, victory in the Indy 500 still eludes him.

MAURICIO GUGELMIN

Presentable, articulate and displaying a mature approach to racing from his early days, Mauricio had a great deal of skill as well. A Formula Ford champion in 1981 in his native Brazil, Gugelmin followed his friend and ex-karting rival Ayrton Senna to Europe, initially taking the same route to the top – FF1600 and FF2000, then Formula 3 with West Surrey Racing in 1985. Fast, safe and above all consistent, Mauricio took the title, and rounded off the season, and his F3 career, with a win in the prestigious Macau GP.

Gugelmin moved into F3000 with West Surrey Racing for 1986, enduring a frustrating year fraught with problems, but his fortunes improved the following season. Now running a works Ralt-Honda with fellow Brazilian Roberto Moreno, he won the opening round at Silverstone, but a spate of mid-season non-finishes left him fourth in the points at season's end.

Mauricio then joined the Leyton House March team and was happy to remain with them for four seasons in which he experienced the highs (third place in Brazil in 1989) and lows (a run of non-qualifications in 1990 when the car's sensitive chassis proved nearly impossible to set up) of F1. By the end of 1991 the whole organisation was crumbling after 18 months of internal dissent and personnel changes, and Gugelmin took his leave to join his old mentor Ian Phillips at Jordan. The year was a debacle for the team as they struggled with the Yamaha engine, but Mauricio earned their respect by never giving less than his best.

Without a drive for 1993, Gugelmin made his Indy Car debut in the last three races of the season, and while he enjoyed little success he showed enough promise to decide that this was where his racing future now lay.

Despite a minimal budget, he joined Ganassi Racing in a team run quite separately from that of star driver Michael Andretti. The lack of a helping hand from an experienced team-mate and the absence of shared technical feedback (though there was some cross-fertilisation by mid-season) no doubt frustrated the Brazilian, who must have been pleased to out-qualify his illustrious peer on more than one occasion.

In 1995 Mauricio moved to the small but promising PacWest Racing Group and really got moving with a career-best second place in the season-opener in Miami. Crucially this cemented his sponsorship for the year, and allowed him to face the season with renewed confidence. At Indianapolis Mauricio showed just how well he had adapted to oval racing, leading the most laps in the race before handling problems caused him to fade to sixth at the finish. Thereafter his form was patchy, but he bounced back at Laguna Seca with a strong third place.

Without doubt one of the most popular drivers in the series, Gugelmin has since remained a fixture with Bruce McCaw's Californian-based team. Thus far his best season Stateside was in 1997, when the Brazilian posted his only CART victory to date at Vancouver and finished fourth in the championship.

GUGELMIN, Mauricio (BR) b 20/4/1963, Joinville

1988		Championship position: 13th=		Wins: 0	Pole positions: 0	Fastest laps: 0	Points scored: 5		
	Race	Circuit	No	Entrant	Tyres	Car/Engine		Comment	Q Pos/Entries
ret	BRAZILIAN GP	Rio	15	Leyton House March Racing Team	G	3.5 March 881-Judd V8		transmission on lap 1	13/31
15	SAN MARINO GP	Imola	15	Leyton House March Racing Team	G	3.5 March 881-Judd V8		fuel pick-up problems/-2 laps	20/31
ret	MONACO GP	Monte Carlo	15	Leyton House March Racing Team	G	3.5 March 881-Judd V8		started from pits/electrics-engine	14/30
ret	MEXICAN GP	Mexico City	15	Leyton House March Racing Team	G	3.5 March 881-Judd V8		electrical short-circuit	16/30
ret	CANADIAN GP	Montreal	15	Leyton House March Racing Team	G	3.5 March 881-Judd V8		gearbox	18/31

ret	US GP (DETROIT)	Detroit	15	Leyton House March Racing Team	G	3.5 March 881-Judd V8	*engine*	13/31
8	FRENCH GP	Paul Ricard	15	Leyton House March Racing Team	G	3.5 March 881-Judd V8	*lost clutch/1 lap behind*	16/31
4	BRITISH GP	Silverstone	15	Leyton House March Racing Team	G	3.5 March 881-Judd V8		5/31
8	GERMAN GP	Hockenheim	15	Leyton House March Racing Team	G	3.5 March 881-Judd V8	*1 lap behind*	10/31
5	HUNGARIAN GP	Hungaroring	15	Leyton House March Racing Team	G	3.5 March 881-Judd V8	*1 lap behind*	8/31
ret	BELGIAN GP	Spa	15	Leyton House March Racing Team	G	3.5 March 881-Judd V8	*clutch-spun off*	13/31
8	ITALIAN GP	Monza	15	Leyton House March Racing Team	G	3.5 March 881-Judd V8	*engine down on power*	13/31
ret	PORTUGUESE GP	Estoril	15	Leyton House March Racing Team	G	3.5 March 881-Judd V8	*engine*	5/31
7	SPANISH GP	Jerez	15	Leyton House March Racing Team	G	3.5 March 881-Judd V8		11/31
10	JAPANESE GP	Suzuka	15	Leyton House March Racing Team	G	3.5 March 881-Judd V8	*clutch problems/1 lap behind*	13/31
ret	AUSTRALIAN GP	Adelaide	15	Leyton House March Racing Team	G	3.5 March 881-Judd V8	*hit by Nakajima*	19/31

1989   Championship position: 16th=   Wins: 0   Pole positions: 0   Fastest laps: 1   Points scored: 4

3	BRAZILIAN GP	Rio	15	Leyton House March Racing Team	G	3.5 March 881-Judd V8	*2 pit stops-tyres*	12/38
ret	SAN MARINO GP	Imola	15	Leyton House March Racing Team	G	3.5 March 881-Judd V8	*clutch/puncture/ret gearbox*	19/39
ret	MONACO GP	Monte Carlo	15	Leyton House March Racing Team	G	3.5 March CG891-Judd V8	*started from pit lane/engine*	14/38
dnq	MEXICAN GP	Mexico City	15	Leyton House March Racing Team	G	3.5 March CG891-Judd V8		28/39
dsq	US GP (PHOENIX)	Phoenix	15	Leyton House March Racing Team	G	3.5 March CG891-Judd V8	*topped up brake fluid in race*	18/39
ret	CANADIAN GP	Montreal	15	Leyton House March Racing Team	G	3.5 March CG891-Judd V8	*electrics*	17/39
nc	FRENCH GP	Paul Ricard	15	Leyton House March Racing Team	G	3.5 March CG891-Judd V8	*pit stop-misfire/FL*	10/39
ret	BRITISH GP	Silverstone	15	Leyton House March Racing Team	G	3.5 March CG891-Judd V8	*started from pit lane/gearbox*	6/39
ret	GERMAN GP	Hockenheim	15	Leyton House March Racing Team	G	3.5 March CG891-Judd V8	*gearbox*	14/39
ret	HUNGARIAN GP	Hungaroring	15	Leyton House March Racing Team	G	3.5 March CG891-Judd V8	*electrics*	13/39
7	BELGIAN GP	Spa	15	Leyton House March Racing Team	G	3.5 March CG891-Judd V8	*1 lap behind*	9/39
ret	ITALIAN GP	Monza	15	Leyton House March Racing Team	G	3.5 March CG891-Judd V8	*throttle problems*	25/39
10	PORTUGUESE GP	Estoril	15	Leyton House March Racing Team	G	3.5 March CG891-Judd V8	*pit stop-tyres-stalled/-2 laps*	14/39
ret	SPANISH GP	Jerez	15	Leyton House March Racing Team	G	3.5 March CG891-Judd V8	*hit by Sala*	26/38
7*	JAPANESE GP	Suzuka	15	Leyton House March Racing Team	G	3.5 March CG891-Judd V8	** 1st place car dsq/-1 lap*	20/39
7	AUSTRALIAN GP	Adelaide	15	Leyton House March Racing Team	G	3.5 March CG891-Judd V8	*4 laps behind*	25/39

1990   Championship position: 18th   Wins: 0   Pole positions: 0   Fastest laps: 0   Points scored: 1

14	US GP (PHOENIX)	Phoenix	15	Leyton House March Racing Team	G	3.5 Leyton House CG901-Judd V8	*pit stop-tyres/vibration/-6 laps*	25/35
dns	"	"	15	Leyton House March Racing Team	G	3.5 March CG891-Judd V8	*practice only*	– / –
dnq	BRAZILIAN GP	Interlagos	15	Leyton House March Racing Team	G	3.5 Leyton House CG901-Judd V8		30/35
ret	SAN MARINO GP	Imola	15	Leyton House March Racing Team	G	3.5 Leyton House CG901-Judd V8	*misfire-electrics*	13/34
dnq	MONACO GP	Monte Carlo	15	Leyton House March Racing Team	G	3.5 Leyton House CG901-Judd V8		29/35
dnq	CANADIAN GP	Montreal	15	Leyton House March Racing Team	G	3.5 Leyton House CG901-Judd V8		28/35
dnq	MEXICAN GP	Mexico City	15	Leyton House March Racing Team	G	3.5 Leyton House CG901-Judd V8		29/25
ret	FRENCH GP	Paul Ricard	15	Leyton House March Racing Team	G	3.5 Leyton House CG901-Judd V8	*engine when 4th*	10/35
dns	BRITISH GP	Silverstone	15	Leyton House March Racing Team	G	3.5 Leyton House CG901-Judd V8	*fuel pump on dummy grid*	15/35
ret	GERMAN GP	Hockenheim	15	Leyton House March Racing Team	G	3.5 Leyton House CG901-Judd V8	*engine*	14/35
8	HUNGARIAN GP	Hungaroring	15	Leyton House March Racing Team	G	3.5 Leyton House CG901-Judd V8	*brake problems-spin/-1 lap*	17/35
6	BELGIAN GP	Spa	15	Leyton House March Racing Team	G	3.5 Leyton House CG901-Judd V8	*clutch problems*	14/33
ret	ITALIAN GP	Monza	15	Leyton House March Racing Team	G	3.5 Leyton House CG901-Judd V8	*engine*	10/33
12	PORTUGUESE GP	Estoril	15	Leyton House March Racing Team	G	3.5 Leyton House CG901-Judd V8	*feeling unwell/2 laps behind*	14/33
8	SPANISH GP	Jerez	15	Leyton House March Racing Team	G	3.5 Leyton House CG901-Judd V8	*tyres & clutch problems/-1 lap*	12/33
ret	JAPANESE GP	Suzuka	15	Leyton House March Racing Team	G	3.5 Leyton House CG901-Judd V8	*engine cut out*	16/30
ret	AUSTRALIAN GP	Adelaide	15	Leyton House March Racing Team	G	3.5 Leyton House CG901-Judd V8	*rear brakes*	16/30

1991   Championship position: Unplaced

ret	US GP (PHOENIX)	Phoenix	15	Leyton House Racing	G	3.5 Leyton House CG911-Ilmor V10	*gearbox*	23/34
ret	BRAZILIAN GP	Interlagos	15	Leyton House Racing	G	3.5 Leyton House CG911-Ilmor V10	*driver unwell, withdrew*	8/34
12/ret	SAN MARINO	Phoenix	15	Leyton House Racing	G	3.5 Leyton House CG911-Ilmor V10	*engine/6 laps behind*	15/34
ret	MONACO GP	Monte Carlo	15	Leyton House Racing	G	3.5 Leyton House CG911-Ilmor V10	*throttle cable*	15/34
ret	CANADIAN GP	Montreal	15	Leyton House Racing	G	3.5 Leyton House CG911-Ilmor V10	*engine*	23/34
ret	MEXICAN GP	Mexico City	15	Leyton House Racing	G	3.5 Leyton House CG911-Ilmor V10	*engine*	21/34
7	FRENCH GP	Magny Cours	15	Leyton House Racing	G	3.5 Leyton House CG911-Ilmor V10	*2 laps behind*	9/34
ret	BRITISH GP	Silverstone	15	Leyton House Racing	G	3.5 Leyton House CG911-Ilmor V10	*chassis vibration numbed leg*	9/34
ret	GERMAN GP	Phoenix	15	Leyton House Racing	G	3.5 Leyton House CG911-Ilmor V10	*gearbox*	16/34
11	HUNGARIAN GP	Hungaroring	15	Leyton House Racing	G	3.5 Leyton House CG911-Ilmor V10	*2 laps behind*	13/34
ret	BELGIAN GP	Spa	15	Leyton House Racing	G	3.5 Leyton House CG911-Ilmor V10	*engine*	15/34
15	ITALIAN GP	Monza	15	Leyton House Racing	G	3.5 Leyton House CG911-Ilmor V10	*no clutch/foot injury/-4 laps*	18/34
7	PORTUGUESE GP	Estoril	15	Leyton House Racing	G	3.5 Leyton House CG911-Ilmor V10	*1 lap behind*	7/34
7	SPANISH GP	Barcelona	15	Leyton House Racing	G	3.5 Leyton House CG911-Ilmor V10	*1 lap behind*	13/33
8	JAPANESE GP	Suzuka	15	Leyton House Racing	G	3.5 Leyton House CG911-Ilmor V10	*1 lap behind*	18/31
14/ret	AUSTRALIAN GP	Adelaide	15	Leyton House Racing	G	3.5 Leyton House CG911-Ilmor V10	*crashed into pit lane entrance*	14/32

1992   Championship position: Unplaced

11	SOUTH AFRICAN GP	Kyalami	33	Sasol Jordan Yamaha	G	3.5 Jordan 192-Yamaha V12	*2 laps behind*	23/30
ret	MEXICAN GP	Mexico City	33	Sasol Jordan Yamaha	G	3.5 Jordan 192-Yamaha V12	*engine lap 1*	8/30
ret	BRAZILIAN GP	Interlagos	33	Sasol Jordan Yamaha	G	3.5 Jordan 192-Yamaha V12	*gearbox*	21/31
ret	SPANISH GP	Barcelona	33	Sasol Jordan Yamaha	G	3.5 Jordan 192-Yamaha V12	*spun off*	17/32
7	SAN MARINO GP	Imola	33	Sasol Jordan Yamaha	G	3.5 Jordan 192-Yamaha V12	*2 laps behind*	18/32
ret	MONACO GP	Monte Carlo	33	Sasol Jordan Yamaha	G	3.5 Jordan 192-Yamaha V12	*transmission*	13/32
ret	CANADIAN GP	Montreal	33	Sasol Jordan Yamaha	G	3.5 Jordan 192-Yamaha V12	*transmission*	24/32
ret	FRENCH GP	Magny Cours	33	Sasol Jordan Yamaha	G	3.5 Jordan 192-Yamaha V12	*multiple collision-lap 1*	24/30
ret	BRITISH GP	Silverstone	33	Sasol Jordan Yamaha	G	3.5 Jordan 192-Yamaha V12	*engine*	24/32
15	GERMAN GP	Nürburgring	33	Sasol Jordan Yamaha	G	3.5 Jordan 192-Yamaha V12	*2 laps behind*	23/32
10	HUNGARIAN GP	Hungaroring	33	Sasol Jordan Yamaha	G	3.5 Jordan 192-Yamaha V12	*4 laps behind*	21/31
14	BELGIAN GP	Spa	33	Sasol Jordan Yamaha	G	3.5 Jordan 192-Yamaha V12	*2 laps behind*	24/30
ret	ITALIAN GP	Monza	33	Sasol Jordan Yamaha	G	3.5 Jordan 192-Yamaha V12	*transmission*	26/28
ret	PORTUGUESE GP	Estoril	33	Sasol Jordan Yamaha	G	3.5 Jordan 192-Yamaha V12	*electrics*	20/26
ret	JAPANESE GP	Suzuka	33	Sasol Jordan Yamaha	G	3.5 Jordan 192-Yamaha V12	*crashed*	25/26
ret	AUSTRALIAN GP	Adelaide	33	Sasol Jordan Yamaha	G	3.5 Jordan 192-Yamaha V12	*brake problem-crashed*	20/26

GP Starts: 74   GP Wins: 0   Pole positions: 0   Fastest laps: 1   Points: 10

DAN GURNEY

DAN GURNEY

Some drivers seem to exude a natural warmth, and by their demeanour both on and off the track firmly entrench themselves in the hearts of motor racing fans across the globe. Dan Gurney comes into this category. Standing at Paddock Bend at the start of the 1968 British Grand Prix, I remember spontaneously cheering loudly with the rest as he set off in grim but hopeless pursuit of the field, Lady Luck having left him stranded on the line. This minor moment serves to underline how universally popular the tall American was and still is to this day, not only for his many fine achievements but also for his stature as one of the sport's least affected and most enthusiastic participants.

The son of an opera singer, Gurney revelled in the environment of his Riverside youth, taking little interest in his studies, but enjoying the illicit drag racing around the local strips. After National Service he began his competition career in 1955 with a Triumph TR2, before building his reputation with a Porsche. By 1957 Dan was running a Ferrari entered by Frank Arciero, and was so successful that Luigi Chinetti arranged for him to race at Le Mans and Reims in 1958. In both races his co-driver crashed the car, but Dan had shown sufficient promise to be offered a test with Ferrari late that year.

Signing a contract with the wily Commendatore for the 1959 season which bound him tightly, Gurney soon proved to be a major asset, particularly after the acrimonious departure of Behra, scoring points in three of his four Grands Prix. The strictures of Maranello were such that Dan decided to join BRM for 1960, but it was an unhappy year with the car woefully unreliable – made even worse by a freak accident at Zandvoort in which a small boy was killed when Dan's brakes failed and the car crashed. Joining Porsche for 1961, Gurney found that the four-cylinder car was reliable (he finished all but one of his 14 Formula 1 races) but not quite capable of winning. He stayed on for 1962 and gained some reward with the flat-eight car, winning his first Grand Prix at Rouen and then the non-title race at Solitude. This was to be the pinnacle of Porsche's achievements as a manufacturer in Formula 1, as they withdrew at season's end, leaving Dan to join Jack Brabham as the team's number one driver for Formula 1, but free to continue his sports and USAC programme which had begun so promisingly in 1962. Again it was so near yet so far in Grands Prix as Gurney repeatedly challenged Jim Clark et al. over the next three seasons but was almost invariably frustrated by niggling problems which restricted him to just two victories. It seems ironic that after his departure to build his own Eagle racers the Brabham should have come good and won the World Championship for the next two seasons.

Gurney's Anglo American Racers car looked superb in its dark-blue livery, but stood no chance of success until its punchless four-cylinder Climax engine was replaced by the complex but potent Weslake unit. By 1967 this was a truly competitive proposition and Dan took victories in the Race of Champions and the Belgian GP before the onslaught of Cosworth power eventually overwhelmed the project. June of that year was kind to Dan, who also shared a Ford GT40 with A J Foyt to win the Le Mans 24 Hours. By now Gurney was extending his efforts to Can-Am and USAC, and after winning the Rex Mays 100 at Riverside in 1967 he finished second in the Indianapolis 500 the following season as well as winning at Mosport and Riverside again.

In a long and glittering career, perhaps Gurney's greatest moment came in 1967 when his Eagle-Weslake won the 1967 Belgian Grand Prix.

Formula 1 seemed a thing of the past in 1969 as Dan developed his USAC programme, finishing second at Indy yet again but winning at Donnybrooke. The following year he won at Sears Point and was third at Indy, before stepping into the breach at McLaren following Bruce's tragic death in a testing accident at Goodwood. After being away Dan never really found the pace in Formula 1, but he won two of the three Can-Am rounds he contested before problems over conflicting oil contracts precipitated his departure from the team. Realising that perhaps his best days were now behind him, he retired from racing, his place in the USAC team being filled by Bobby Unser, who was to bring Eagle so much success in the seventies. Happily Dan was not tempted to return full-time, but he couldn't resist a one-off NASCAR outing in 1980 at his home track of Riverside, where he lay a superb third before gearbox trouble.

Gurney continued to enter his Eagles in USAC and had the satisfaction of winning Indy at last, as a constructor if not as a driver, with Gordon Johncock and Bobby Unser scoring victories in 1973 and 1975 respectively. Dan eventually withdrew from single-seater racing, concentrating successfully on IMSA with the backing of Toyota throughout the early nineties.

In 1996 he re-entered the CART arena in partnership with the Japanese car giant, but the four-year alliance has brought little but disappointment for Gurney and his hard-working team at Santa Anna. The slow development of the Toyota powerplant, increasingly uncompetitive Goodyear tyres and the lack of a front-line driver are just some of the reasons that the Eagle has failed to soar to the heights that the partners were expecting.

GURNEY, Dan (USA) b 13/4/1931, Port Jefferson, New York

1959 — Championship position: 7th Wins: 0 Pole positions: 0 Fastest laps: Points scored: 13

	Race	Circuit	No	Entrant	Tyres	Car/Engine	Comment	Q Pos/Entries
ret	FRENCH GP	Reims	28	Scuderia Ferrari	D	2.4 Ferrari Dino 246 V6	radiator	12/22
2	GERMAN GP	AVUS	6	Scuderia Ferrari	D	2.4 Ferrari Dino 246 V6	2nd heat 1/3rd heat 2	3/16
3	PORTUGUESE GP	Monsanto	16	Scuderia Ferrari	D	2.4 Ferrari Dino 246 V6	1 lap behind	6/16
4	ITALIAN GP	Monza	36	Scuderia Ferrari	D	2.4 Ferrari Dino 246 V6		4/21

1960 — Championship position: Unplaced

	Race	Circuit	No	Entrant	Tyres	Car/Engine	Comment	Q Pos/Entries
10/ret	MONACO GP	Monte Carlo	4	Owen Racing Organisation	D	2.5 BRM P48 4	suspension/52 laps behind	14/24
ret	DUTCH GP	Zandvoort	15	Owen Racing Organisation	D	2.5 BRM P48 4	brake failure-accident	6/21
ret	BELGIAN GP	Spa	8	Owen Racing Organisation	D	2.5 BRM P48 4	engine	12/21
ret	FRENCH GP	Reims	10	Owen Racing Organisation	D	2.5 BRM P48 4	engine	6/23
10	BRITISH GP	Silverstone	5	Owen Racing Organisation	D	2.5 BRM P48 4	pit stop/3 laps behind	6/25
ret	PORTUGUESE GP	Oporto	24	Owen Racing Organisation	D	2.5 BRM P48 4	engine	2/16
ret	US GP	Riverside	16	Owen Racing Organisation	D	2.5 BRM P48 4	overheating	3/23

1961 — Championship position: 3rd= Wins: 0 Pole positions: 0 Fastest laps: 0 Points scored: 21

	Race	Circuit	No	Entrant	Tyres	Car/Engine	Comment	Q Pos/Entries
5	MONACO GP	Monte Carlo	4	Porsche System Engineering	D	1.5 Porsche 718 F4	2 laps behind	11/21
10	DUTCH GP	Zandvoort	7	Porsche System Engineering	D	1.5 Porsche 787 F4	1 lap behind	6/17
6	BELGIAN GP	Spa	20	Porsche System Engineering	D	1.5 Porsche 718 F4		10/25
2	FRENCH GP	Reims	12	Porsche System Engineering	D	1.5 Porsche 718 F4		9/26
7	BRITISH GP	Aintree	10	Porsche System Engineering	D	1.5 Porsche 718 F4	1 lap behind	12/30
7	GERMAN GP	Nürburgring	9	Porsche System Engineering	D	1.5 Porsche 718 F4		7/27
2	ITALIAN GP	Monza	46	Porsche System Engineering	D	1.5 Porsche 718 F4		=12/33
dns	"	"	46	Porsche System Engineering	D	1.5 Porsche 787 F4	practice only	– / –
2	US GP	Watkins Glen	12	Porsche System Engineering	D	1.5 Porsche 718 F4		7/19

1962 — Championship position: 5th Wins: 1 Pole positions: 1 Fastest laps: 0 Points scored: 15

	Race	Circuit	No	Entrant	Tyres	Car/Engine	Comment	Q Pos/Entries
ret	DUTCH GP	Zandvoort	12	Porsche System Engineering	D	1.5 Porsche 804 F8	gearbox	8/20
ret	MONACO GP	Monte Carlo	4	Porsche System Engineering	D	1.5 Porsche 804 F8	first corner accident	=3/21
dns	BELGIAN GP	Spa	23	Autosport Team Wolfgang Seidel	D	1.5 Lotus 24-BRM V8	car unraceworthy	20/20
1	FRENCH GP	Rouen	30	Porsche System Engineering	D	1.5 Porsche 804 F8		6/17
9	BRITISH GP	Aintree	8	Porsche System Engineering	D	1.5 Porsche 804 F8	2 laps behind	6/21
3	GERMAN GP	Nürburgring	7	Porsche System Engineering	D	1.5 Porsche 804 F8		1/30
13/ret	ITALIAN GP	Monza	16	Porsche System Engineering	D	1.5 Porsche 804 F8	cwp/20 laps behind	=6/30
5	US GP	Watkins Glen	10	Porsche System Engineering	D	1.5 Porsche 804 F8	1 lap behind	=4/20

1963 — Championship position: 5th Wins: 0 Pole positions: 0 Fastest laps: 1 Points scored: 19

	Race	Circuit	No	Entrant	Tyres	Car/Engine	Comment	Q Pos/Entries
ret	MONACO GP	Monte Carlo	4	Brabham Racing Organisation	D	1.5 Brabham BT7-Climax V8	cwp	6/17
3	BELGIAN GP	Spa	18	Brabham Racing Organisation	D	1.5 Brabham BT7-Climax V8	1 lap behind	2/20
2	DUTCH GP	Zandvoort	18	Brabham Racing Organisation	D	1.5 Brabham BT7-Climax V8	1 lap behind	14/19
5	FRENCH GP	Reims	8	Brabham Racing Organisation	D	1.5 Brabham BT7-Climax V8		3/21
ret	BRITISH GP	Silverstone	9	Brabham Racing Organisation	D	1.5 Brabham BT7-Climax V8	engine	2/23
ret	GERMAN GP	Nürburgring	10	Brabham Racing Organisation	D	1.5 Brabham BT7-Climax V8	gearbox	13/26
14/ret	ITALIAN GP	Monza	24	Brabham Racing Organisation	D	1.5 Brabham BT7-Climax V8	fuel feed	5/28
ret	US GP	Watkins Glen	6	Brabham Racing Organisation	D	1.5 Brabham BT7-Climax V8	cracked chassis	6/21
6	MEXICAN GP	Mexico City	6	Brabham Racing Organisation	D	1.5 Brabham BT7-Climax V8	fuel starvation/3 laps behind	4/21
2	SOUTH AFRICAN GP	East London	9	Brabham Racing Organisation	D	1.5 Brabham BT7-Climax V8	FL	3/21

1964 — Championship position: 6th Wins: 2 Pole positions: 2 Fastest laps: 2 Points scored: 19

	Race	Circuit	No	Entrant	Tyres	Car/Engine	Comment	Q Pos/Entries
ret	MONACO GP	Monte Carlo	6	Brabham Racing Organisation	D	1.5 Brabham BT7-Climax V8	gearbox	5/20
ret	DUTCH GP	Zandvoort	16	Brabham Racing Organisation	D	1.5 Brabham BT7-Climax V8	steering wheel	1/18
6/ret	BELGIAN GP	Spa	15	Brabham Racing Organisation	D	1.5 Brabham BT7-Climax V8	out of fuel last lap/FL	1/20
1	FRENCH GP	Rouen	22	Brabham Racing Organisation	D	1.5 Brabham BT7-Climax V8		2/17
13	BRITISH GP	Brands Hatch	6	Brabham Racing Organisation	D	1.5 Brabham BT7-Climax V8	pit stop-ignition/5 laps behind	3/25
10	GERMAN GP	Nürburgring	5	Brabham Racing Organisation	D	1.5 Brabham BT7-Climax V8	2 pit stops-overheating/-1 lap	3/24
ret	AUSTRIAN GP	Zeltweg	5	Brabham Racing Organisation	D	1.5 Brabham BT7-Climax V8	front suspension/FL	=4/20
10	ITALIAN GP	Monza	16	Brabham Racing Organisation	D	1.5 Brabham BT7-Climax V8	pit stop-alternator/-3 laps	2/25
ret	US GP	Watkins Glen	6	Brabham Racing Organisation	D	1.5 Brabham BT7-Climax V8	oil pressure-engine	3/19
1	MEXICAN GP	Mexico City	6	Brabham Racing Organisation	D	1.5 Brabham BT7-Climax V8		2/19

1965 — Championship position: 4th Wins: 0 Pole positions: 0 Fastest laps: 1 Points scored: 25

	Race	Circuit	No	Entrant	Tyres	Car/Engine	Comment	Q Pos/Entries
ret	SOUTH AFRICAN GP	East London	8	Brabham Racing Organisation	G	1.5 Brabham BT11-Climax V8	ignition	9/25
10	BELGIAN GP	Spa	15	Brabham Racing Organisation	G	1.5 Brabham BT11-Climax V8	pit stop-wet ignition/-2 laps	5/21
ret	FRENCH GP	Clermont Ferrand	14	Brabham Racing Organisation	G	1.5 Brabham BT11-Climax V8	engine	5/17
6	BRITISH GP	Silverstone	7	Brabham Racing Organisation	G	1.5 Brabham BT11-Climax V8	drove Brabham's car/-1 lap	7/23
3	DUTCH GP	Zandvoort	16	Brabham Racing Organisation	G	1.5 Brabham BT11-Climax V8		5/17
3	GERMAN GP	Nürburgring	5	Brabham Racing Organisation	G	1.5 Brabham BT11-Climax V8		5/22
3	ITALIAN GP	Monza	12	Brabham Racing Organisation	G	1.5 Brabham BT11-Climax V8		9/23
2	US GP	Watkins Glen	8	Brabham Racing Organisation	G	1.5 Brabham BT11-Climax V8		8/18
2	MEXICAN GP	Mexico City	8	Brabham Racing Organisation	G	1.5 Brabham BT11-Climax V8	FL	2/18

1966 — Championship position: 12th Wins: 0 Pole positions: 0 Fastest laps: 0 Points scored: 4

	Race	Circuit	No	Entrant	Tyres	Car/Engine	Comment	Q Pos/Entries
nc	BELGIAN GP	Spa	27	Anglo American Racers	G	2.7 Eagle T1G-Climax 4	pit stop-tyres/5 laps behind	15/19
5	FRENCH GP	Reims	26	Anglo American Racers	G	2.7 Eagle T1G-Climax 4	3 laps behind	14/17
ret	BRITISH GP	Brands Hatch	16	Anglo American Racers	G	2.7 Eagle T1G-Climax 4	engine	3/20
ret	DUTCH GP	Zandvoort	10	Anglo American Racers	G	2.7 Eagle T1G-Climax 4	engine-oil line	4/18
7	GERMAN GP	Nürburgring	12	Anglo American Racers	G	2.7 Eagle T1G-Climax 4	1 lap behind	8/30
ret	ITALIAN GP	Monza	30	Anglo American Racers	G	3.0 Eagle T1G-Weslake V12	oil temperature	19/22
dns	"	"	34	Anglo American Racers	G	2.7 Eagle T1G-Climax 4	practice only	– / –
ret	US GP	Watkins Glen	15	Anglo American Racers	G	3.0 Eagle T1G-Weslake V12	clutch slip	14/19
5	MEXICAN GP	Mexico City	(16)15	Anglo American Racers	G	2.7 Eagle T1G-Climax 4	1 lap behind	9/19
dns	"	" "	15	Anglo American Racers	G	3.0 Eagle T1G-Weslake V12	practice only	– / –

	1967	Championship position: 8th		Wins: 1	Pole positions: 0		Fastest laps: 2	Points scored: 13		
ret	SOUTH AFRICAN GP	Kyalami	9	Anglo American Racers	G	2.7 Eagle T1G-Climax 4		wishbone mounting	11/18
ret	MONACO GP	Monte Carlo	23	Anglo American Racers	G	3.0 Eagle T1G-Weslake V12		fuel pump drive	7/18
ret	DUTCH GP	Zandvoort	15	Anglo American Racers	G	3.0 Eagle T1G-Weslake V12		fuel injection	2/17
1	BELGIAN GP	Spa	36	Anglo American Racers	G	3.0 Eagle T1G-Weslake V12		FL	2/18
ret	FRENCH GP	Le Mans	9	Anglo American Racers	G	3.0 Eagle T1G-Weslake V12		fuel line	3/15
ret	BRITISH GP	Silverstone	9	Anglo American Racers	G	3.0 Eagle T1G-Weslake V12		clutch	5/21
ret	GERMAN GP	Nürburgring	9	Anglo American Racers	G	3.0 Eagle T1G-Weslake V12		driveshaft when 1st/FL	5/25
3	CANADIAN GP	Mosport Park	10	Anglo American Racers	G	3.0 Eagle T1G-Weslake V12		1 lap behind	5/19
ret	ITALIAN GP	Monza	8	Anglo American Racers	G	3.0 Eagle T1G-Weslake V12		engine	5/18
ret	US GP	Watkins Glen	11	Anglo American Racers	G	3.0 Eagle T1G-Weslake V12		rear uspension	3/18
ret	MEXICAN GP	Mexico City	11	Anglo American Racers	G	3.0 Eagle T1G-Weslake V12		damaged radiator	3/19
	1968	Championship position: 21st		Wins: 0	Pole positions: 0		Fastest laps: 0	Points scored: 3		
ret	SOUTH AFRICAN GP	Kyalami	6	Anglo American Racers	G	3.0 Eagle T1G-Weslake V12		oil leak/overheating	12/23
ret	MONACO GP	Monte Carlo	19	Anglo American Racers	G	3.0 Eagle T1G-Weslake V12		ignition	=17/18
ret	DUTCH GP	Zandvoort	18	Motor Racing Developments	G	3.0 Brabham BT24-Repco V8		sand in throttle slides	12/19
ret	BRITISH GP	Brands Hatch	24	Anglo American Racers	G	3.0 Eagle T1G-Weslake V12		fuel pump	=6/20
9	GERMAN GP	Nürburgring	14	Anglo American Racers	G	3.0 Eagle T1G-Weslake V12		pit stop-cut tyre	10/20
ret	ITALIAN GP	Monza	21	Anglo American Racers	G	3.0 Eagle T1G-Weslake V12		oil pressure	13/24
ret	CANADIAN GP	St Jovite	11	Anglo American Racers	G	3.0 McLaren M7A-Cosworth V8		overheating-oil pressure	=3/22
4	US GP	Watkins Glen	14	Anglo American Racers	G	3.0 McLaren M7A-Cosworth V8		1 lap behind	7/21
ret	MEXICAN GP	Mexico City	14	Anglo American Racers	G	3.0 McLaren M7A-Cosworth V8		rear suspension	5/21
	1970	Championship position: 22nd =		Wins: 0	Pole positions: 0		Fastest laps: 0	Points scored: 1		
ret	DUTCH GP	Zandvoort	32	Bruce McLaren Motor Racing	G	3.0 McLaren M14A-Cosworth V8		timing gear	20/24
6	FRENCH GP	Clermont Ferrand	17	Bruce McLaren Motor Racing	G	3.0 McLaren M14A-Cosworth V8			17/23
ret	BRITISH GP	Brands Hatch	10	Bruce McLaren Motor Racing	G	3.0 McLaren M14A-Cosworth V8		engine-overheating	12/25

GP Starts: 86   GP Wins: 4   Pole positions: 3   Fastest laps: 6   Points: 133

HUBERT HAHNE

With only a very few exceptions Hahne's racing career was spent racing cars made or powered by BMW. He built his reputation in 1964-66, racing the works BMW 1800Ti touring cars in the European championship. A fine second place in the F2 class in the 1966 German GP in a Matra then pointed Hahne in the direction of single-seaters and he became the non-graded works driver in the Lola-BMW for 1967 and a couple of races in 1968, when he returned to BMW tourers and also had the occasional Ford ride.

For 1969, Hubert was back with BMW's own F2 car, taking two second places at Hockenheim and a fourth in the Eifelrennen, although the season was marred by the death of Gerhard Mitter in practice for the German Grand Prix. He continued in F2 with BMW in 1970, winning the Rhine Cup race at Hockenheim, but had little other success. Taking delivery of a March 701 for the German Grand Prix at Hockenheim, he naturally expected to do well at his favourite circuit and there was much consternation when he failed to qualify the car. A disgruntled Hahne threatened legal action, contending that the car was delivered in an unraceworthy condition, but after this had been disproved by Ronnie Peterson in a subsequent test Hahne announced his retirement from racing.

HAHNE, Hubert (D) b 28/3/1935, Moers

	1966	Championship position: Unplaced							
	Race	Circuit	No	Entrant	Tyres	Car/Engine		Comment	Q Pos/Entries
9*	GERMAN GP (F2)	Nürburgring	26	Tyrrell Racing Organisation	D	1.0 Matra MS5-BRM 4 F2		*2nd in F2 class/-1 lap	28/30
	1967	Championship position: Unplaced							
ret	GERMAN GP	Nürburgring	17	Bayerische Motoren Werke	D	2.0 Lola T100-BMW 4 F2		front suspension	15/25
	1968	Championship position: Unplaced							
10	GERMAN GP	Nürburgring	18	Bayerische Motoren Werke	D	2.0 Lola T102-BMW 4 F2			18/20
	1969	Championship position: Unplaced							
dns	GERMAN GP (F2)	Nürburgring	23	Bayerische Motoren Werke	D	1.6 BMW T269-BMW 4 F2		withdrawn after Mitter's accident	(17)/26
	1970	Championship position: Unplaced							
dnq	GERMAN GP	Hockenheim	26	Hubert Hahne	F	3.0 March 701-Cosworth V8			25/25

GP Starts: 3   GP Wins: 0   Pole positions: 0   Fastest laps: 0   Points: 0

MIKE HAILWOOD

Despite being the son of a brash millionaire, Mike Hailwood was totally without affectation and truly one of racing's 'nice guys'. He lived life to the full, but was nevertheless a dedicated sportsman who was undoubtedly one of motor cycle racing's greatest-ever exponents – many consider him the greatest of them all – and a fine all-round racing driver who missed out on ultimate success but still left a not inconsiderable mark on the four-wheeled sport.

By the age of 18 he was already a British motor cycle champion in four classes, winning his first World Championship in 1961. During the next six seasons Mike took a further eight World Championships in the 500 cc, 350 cc and 250 cc classes. His first taste of four-wheeled competition came in 1963, and with a couple of Junior races satisfactorily completed he joined the Reg Parnell team briefly in preparation for a full season the following year. He scored a World Championship point at Monaco in 1964 but felt uncomfortable in the Formula 1 environment, perhaps frustrated at being an also-ran in one category and the top dog in the other. He did a few more races for Parnell in 1965 before concentrating almost exclusively on bikes once more, though he did enjoy some winter sunshine racing sports cars, winning the 1966 Dickie Dale 3 Hours with David Hobbs in Bernard White's GT40.

With Honda having pulled out of Grand Prix motor cycle racing at the end of 1967, the sport was heading for a period of essentially privateer participation, so Mike turned to cars once again from the beginning of 1969. The newly inaugurated F5000 series provided an ideal base to rebuild his career, and in tandem he began a successful sports car programme, mainly for John Wyer, finishing third at Le Mans in 1969. In 1971 he joined forces with John Surtees to race his F5000 car, and benefited greatly from his guidance, taking second place in the series behind Frank Gardner. Late in the year, Surtees put Mike into his Formula 1 team for the Italian GP with startling results. In a great drive, Hailwood jousted for the lead in the four-car bunch which slipstreamed around the Monza circuit before finishing fourth.

Full of confidence, he lined up a massive programme with Surtees for 1972, undertaking the F2 Brazilian Torneio and F5000 Tasman series before the season proper had even started. A second place in the Race of Champions boded well for Formula 1, but Mike's luck was definitely out. In South Africa he put in an astounding drive to pressure Stewart before his suspension broke and at Monza he knew he had the opposition covered before the airbox blew off his Surtees. No one deserved a Grand Prix win more that year, but it was not to be. There was, however, the compensation of taking the European Formula 2 championship for Surtees with some excellent performances.

Unfortunately the progress made was not built upon in 1973, when unreliability beset the team to the extent that Mike failed to finish a single race in the points. In fact his season was best remembered for a typical act of bravery when he rescued Clay Regazzoni from his blazing car in South Africa to earn the George Medal. His only success came in endurance racing, when he shared the John Wyer Mirage with Derek Bell to win the Spa 1000 Km.

Frustrated at his lack of success at Surtees, Hailwood switched to McLaren in 1974, running a third works car in Yardley livery. Suddenly he was back in the frame, always running competitively until an accident at the German Grand Prix left him with such a badly broken leg that it was to spell the end of his Grand Prix career.

He announced his retirement in 1975, but after a couple of years kicking his heels 'Mike the Bike' was back. In a sensational return to the Isle of Man TT races in 1978, he won the Formula 1 event on a Ducati and in 1979 he was back again to smash the lap record and take the Senior TT on his Suzuki. There were no more comebacks, however, for in 1981 Mike lost his life in a tragic road accident when his car ran into a lorry executing an illegal U-turn across a dual carriageway after he had nipped out for a fish and chip family supper. The entire world of racing, on both two wheels and four, were united in their grief at the loss of one of motor sport's most popular and genuine sons.

HAILWOOD, Mike (GB) b 2/4/1940, Great Milton Birmingham – d 23/3/1981, Birmingham

	1963	Championship position: Unplaced							
	Race	Circuit	No	Entrant	Tyres	Car/Engine		Comment	Q Pos/Entries
8	BRITISH GP	Silverstone	20	Reg Parnell (Racing)	D	1.5 Lotus 24-Climax V8		4 laps behind	17/23
10	ITALIAN GP	Monza	40	Reg Parnell (Racing)	D	1.5 Lola 4-Climax V8		4 laps behind	18/28

1964
Championship position: 19th= Wins: 0 Pole positions: 0 Fastest laps: 0 Points scored: 1

6	MONACO GP	Monte Carlo	18	Reg Parnell (Racing)	D	1.5 Lotus 25-BRM V8	4 laps behind	15/20
12/ret	DUTCH GP	Zandvoort	12	Reg Parnell (Racing)	D	1.5 Lotus 25-BRM V8	cwp	14/18
8	FRENCH GP	Rouen	6	Reg Parnell (Racing)	D	1.5 Lotus 25-BRM V8	1 lap behind	13/17
ret	BRITISH GP	Brands Hatch	14	Reg Parnell (Racing)	D	1.5 Lotus 25-BRM V8	oil pipe	=12/25
ret	GERMAN GP	Nürburgring	15	Reg Parnell (Racing)	D	1.5 Lotus 25-BRM V8	engine	13/24
8	AUSTRIAN GP	Zeltweg	17	Reg Parnell (Racing)	D	1.5 Lotus 25-BRM V8	pit stop-suspension/-10 laps	=18/20
ret	ITALIAN GP	Monza	40	Reg Parnell (Racing)	D	1.5 Lotus 25-BRM V8	engine	=16/25
8/ret	US GP	Watkins Glen	14	Reg Parnell (Racing)	D	1.5 Lotus 25-BRM V8	oil pipe/9 laps behind	16/19
ret	MEXICAN GP	Mexico City	14	Reg Parnell (Racing)	D	1.5 Lotus 25-BRM V8	overheating	17/19

1965
Championship position: Unplaced

ret	MONACO GP	Monte Carlo	16	Reg Parnell (Racing)	D	1.5 Lotus 25-BRM V8	gearbox	=12/17

1971
Championship position: 18th= Wins: 0 Pole positions: 0 Fastest laps: 0 Points scored: 3

4	ITALIAN GP	Monza	9	Team Surtees	F	3.0 Surtees TS9-Cosworth V8	0.18 sec behind winner Gethin	17/24
15/ret	US GP	Watkins Glen	20	Team Surtees	F	3.0 Surtees TS9-Cosworth V8	spun on oil-hit barrier	15/32

1972
Championship position: 8th Wins: 0 Pole positions: 0 Fastest laps: 1 Points scored: 13

ret	SOUTH AFRICAN GP	Kyalami	17	Brooke Bond Oxo/R. Walker/Team Surtees	F	3.0 Surtees TS9B-Cosworth V8	suspension when 2nd/FL	=3/27
ret	SPANISH GP	Jarama	15	Brooke Bond Oxo/R. Walker/Team Surtees	F	3.0 Surtees TS9B-Cosworth V8	master switch solenoid	15/26
ret	MONACO GP	Monte Carlo	11	Brooke Bond Oxo/R. Walker/Team Surtees	F	3.0 Surtees TS9B-Cosworth V8	hit by Ganley	11/25
4	BELGIAN GP	Nivelles	34	Brooke Bond Oxo/R. Walker/Team Surtees	F	3.0 Surtees TS9B-Cosworth V8		8/26
6	FRENCH GP	Clermont Ferrand	26	Brooke Bond Oxo/R. Walker/Team Surtees	F	3.0 Surtees TS9B-Cosworth V8		10/29
ret	BRITISH GP	Brands Hatch	21	Brooke Bond Oxo/R. Walker/Team Surtees	F	3.0 Surtees TS9B-Cosworth V8	gearbox	7/27
ret	GERMAN GP	Nürburgring	14	Brooke Bond Oxo/R. Walker/Team Surtees	F	3.0 Surtees TS9B-Cosworth V8	suspension	16/27
4	AUSTRIAN GP	Österreichring	25	Brooke Bond Oxo/R. Walker/Team Surtees	F	3.0 Surtees TS9B-Cosworth V8		12/26
2	ITALIAN GP	Monza	10	Brooke Bond Oxo/R. Walker/Team Surtees	F	3.0 Surtees TS9B-Cosworth V8		9/27
17/ret	US GP	Watkins Glen	23	Brooke Bond Oxo/R. Walker/Team Surtees	F	3.0 Surtees TS9B-Cosworth V8	collision with Beuttler/-3 laps	14/32
dns	"	" " "	24T	Brooke Bond Oxo/R. Walker/Team Surtees	F	3.0 Surtees TS14-Cosworth V8	practice only	–/–

1973
Championship position: Unplaced

ret	ARGENTINE GP	Buenos Aires	26	Brooke Bond Oxo/R. Walker/Team Surtees	F	3.0 Surtees TS14A-Cosworth V8	driveshaft	10/19
ret	BRAZILIAN GP	Interlagos	5	Brooke Bond Oxo/R. Walker/Team Surtees	F	3.0 Surtees TS14A-Cosworth V8	gearbox	14/20
ret	SOUTH AFRICAN GP	Kyalami	10	Brooke Bond Oxo/R. Walker/Team Surtees	F	3.0 Surtees TS14A-Cosworth V8	accident/saved Regazzoni	12/25
ret	SPANISH GP	Montjuich Park	9	Brooke Bond Oxo/R. Walker/Team Surtees	F	3.0 Surtees TS14A-Cosworth V8	started from pit lane/oil pipe	=9/22
ret	BELGIAN GP	Zolder	23	Brooke Bond Oxo/R. Walker/Team Surtees	F	3.0 Surtees TS14A-Cosworth V8	spun off	13/23
8	MONACO GP	Monte Carlo	23	Brooke Bond Oxo/R. Walker/Team Surtees	F	3.0 Surtees TS14A-Cosworth V8	pit stop-puncture/-3 laps	=13/26
ret	SWEDISH GP	Anderstorp	23	Brooke Bond Oxo/R. Walker/Team Surtees	F	3.0 Surtees TS14A-Cosworth V8	vibration caused by tyres	10/22
ret	FRENCH GP	Paul Ricard	23	Brooke Bond Oxo/R. Walker/Team Surtees	F	3.0 Surtees TS14A-Cosworth V8	engine-oil leak	11/25
ret/dns	BRITISH GP	Silverstone	23	Brooke Bond Oxo/R. Walker/Team Surtees	F	3.0 Surtees TS14A-Cosworth V8	accident-1st start/did not restart	12/29
ret	DUTCH GP	Zandvoort	23	Brooke Bond Oxo/R. Walker/Team Surtees	F	3.0 Surtees TS14A-Cosworth V8	electrics	24/24
14	GERMAN GP	Nürburgring	23	Brooke Bond Oxo/R. Walker/Team Surtees	F	3.0 Surtees TS14A-Cosworth V8	1 lap behind	=17/23
10	AUSTRIAN GP	Österreichring	23	Brooke Bond Oxo/R. Walker/Team Surtees	F	3.0 Surtees TS14A-Cosworth V8	pit stop-puncture/-5 laps	15/25
7	ITALIAN GP	Monza	23	Brooke Bond Oxo/R. Walker/Team Surtees	F	3.0 Surtees TS14A-Cosworth V8		8/25
9	CANADIAN GP	Mosport Park	23	Brooke Bond Oxo/R. Walker/Team Surtees	F	3.0 Surtees TS14A-Cosworth V8	2 laps behind	12/26
ret	US GP	Watkins Glen	23	Brooke Bond Oxo/R. Walker/Team Surtees	F	3.0 Surtees TS14A-Cosworth V8	broken suspension	7/28

1974
Championship position: 10= Wins: 0 Pole positions: 0 Fastest laps: 0 Points scored: 12

4	ARGENTINE GP	Buenos Aires	33	Yardley Team McLaren	G	3.0 McLaren M23-Cosworth V8		9/26
5	BRAZILIAN GP	Interlagos	33	Yardley Team McLaren	G	3.0 McLaren M23-Cosworth V8	1 lap behind	7/25
3	SOUTH AFRICAN GP	Kyalami	33	Yardley Team McLaren	G	3.0 McLaren M23-Cosworth V8		=11/27
9	SPANISH GP	Jarama	33	Yardley Team McLaren	G	3.0 McLaren M23-Cosworth V8	3 laps behind	=17/28
7	BELGIAN GP	Nivelles	33	Yardley Team McLaren	G	3.0 McLaren M23-Cosworth V8	fuel starvation/1 lap behind	13/32
ret	MONACO GP	Monte Carlo	33	Yardley Team McLaren	G	3.0 McLaren M23-Cosworth V8	accident	=10/28
ret	SWEDISH GP	Anderstorp	33	Yardley Team McLaren	G	3.0 McLaren M23-Cosworth V8	fuel line	11/28
4	DUTCH GP	Zandvoort	33	Yardley Team McLaren	G	3.0 McLaren M23-Cosworth V8		4/27
7	FRENCH GP	Dijon	33	Yardley Team McLaren	G	3.0 McLaren M23-Cosworth V8	1 lap behind	6/30
ret	BRITISH GP	Brands Hatch	33	Yardley Team McLaren	G	3.0 McLaren M23-Cosworth V8	spun off-could not restart	=11/34
15/ret	GERMAN GP	Nürburgring	33	Yardley Team McLaren	G	3.0 McLaren M23-Cosworth V8	accident-leg injuries/-2 laps	12/32

GP Starts: 49 (50) GP Wins: 0 Pole positions: 0 Fastest laps: 1 Points: 29

Mike Hailwood in the Yardley McLaren leads Emerson Fittipaldi's Marlboro McLaren and Jody Scheckter's Tyrrell in the 1974 Dutch GP.

MIKA HÄKKINEN

Mika has always seemed bound for great things. With the benefit of long-term sponsorship and the guiding hand of Keke Rosberg, he negotiated the slippery slope to the top in very short order and still showed the patience to bide his time when necessary. After sustaining very serious head injuries in practice for the Australian GP at the end of 1995, Häkkinen came back with his appetite undiminished and eventually fulfilled his early promise by taking successive World Championships with McLaren-Mercedes in 1998 and 1999.

A multiple karting champion in his native Finland, winner of three FF1600 titles in 1987, and GM Lotus Euroseries champion in 1988, Häkkinen had a pretty impressive CV to take into the 1989 Formula 3 season. Initially things went wrong. Having opted to stay with the Dragon team that had served him so well in 1988, he found himself way off the pace, but he persevered and when he switched to the WSR squad for the prestigious Cellnet F3 race at the end of the season he promptly won it.

A deal was then concluded for 1990 and Mika never looked back, winning a total of 12 races at home and abroad. He took the British F3 championship, and before the year was out had a Formula 1 seat with Lotus. In his first season in Grand Prix racing, the confident young Finn impressed everyone with his car control in a chassis that was never a match for the best, scoring points in only his third race. The following season, with a much better car, the team on the up and Ford HB engines, Mika firmly established himself in the top echelon, extracting the very maximum from the sleek Lotus 107.

Now came an unexpected chance that Häkkinen wisely grabbed. With Senna prevaricating over his contract at McLaren, Ron Dennis lost little time in signing Mika as cover in case the Brazilian should carry out his threat not to race. In the end Senna contested the full season, and Mika was left sitting on the sidelines, waiting patiently for his opportunity, which finally came when Michael Andretti headed back home. In his first race, in Portugal, Mika out-qualified his master, and lay third until he ran wide and into the barrier. In his next race, in Japan, he was more circumspect, settling for a career-best third place in wildly fluctuating weather and track conditions.

For 1994, Häkkinen assumed the McLaren team leadership in the wake of Senna's departure for Williams. However, the optimism engendered by a new liaison with Peugeot soon evaporated and his year was spent in frustration which sometimes turned into desperation, such was his desire to succeed. Ill-advised first-corner moves at Monaco and Hockenheim saw him eliminated, the latter indiscretion earning him a one-race ban. A much-heralded partnership with Mercedes Benz for 1995 brought promise of a new dawn for McLaren's sagging fortunes, but once more the team were never really on the pace, although Mika drove superbly in a handful of races, taking second places at Monza and Suzuka. His performance in Japan was all the more admirable since he had undergone an appendectomy only ten days earlier, missing the previous weekend's Pacific GP.

Mika was handed the perfect start to his 1998 World Championship quest when he won the Australian Grand Prix after team-mate David Coulthard moved over to allow the Finn to take the chequered flag first.

Less than a fortnight after that sparkling performance came disaster in Adelaide: Mika was very close to losing his life and only prompt action saved him. The fun-loving Finn made a miraculously swift return, and after a shaky start soon proved he had lost none of the blinding speed he had always shown in the past. Indeed the 1996 season was the one in which Mika established himself as a bona fide number one driver; all that was missing was the breakthrough Grand Prix victory that the driver and team had been working so hard to achieve over the past three years.

That win came in the opening race of the 1997 season at Melbourne, but unfortunately for the Finn it was David Coulthard's name that went into the record books. Undeterred, Mika continued to knock on the door, shrugging aside the heartbreak of a late, late retirement when leading the British Grand Prix to bounce back with more determination than ever. He had to wait until the season's finale at Jerez before taking the top step of the podium, and in the event the victory was somewhat hollow in that both Jacques Villeneuve and David Coulthard allowed Häkkinen through to the chequered flag.

By 1998, however, his time had come. After Coulthard had stood by a pre-race agreement to allow the Finn to take first place in the Australian Grand Prix, Mika then scorched away from his team-mate to begin a thrilling championship battle with Michael Schumacher. Wins in Brazil, Spain, Monaco, Austria and Germany were topped by perhaps his greatest triumph, at the Luxembourg Grand Prix, when he pulled out a top-drawer performance to defeat his Ferrari rival. His championship clincher in Japan was to be a much easier win after Schumacher had stalled his car at the start.

Back-to-back titles are notoriously hard to achieve and being the hot favourite for a repeat championship seemed to take its toll on both McLaren and Häkkinen. Brilliant performances were interspersed with inexplicable lapses by both driver and team, who, it seemed, were going to lose the championship despite Schumacher's enforced absence after his Silverstone shunt.

In the end, Mika's fluctuating title battle with Eddie Irvine and Ferrari was won with a truly dominant performance in Japan. And, while there was some sympathy for the underdog Irishman who had run the Finn so close, the general consensus was that the right man had claimed the World Championship crown.

MIKA HÄKKINEN

WORLD CHAMPION: 1998 & 1999

HÄKKINEN, Mika (SF) b 28/9/1968, Helsinki

1991 Championship position: 15th Wins: 0 Pole positions: 0 Fastest laps: 0 Points scored: 2

	Race	Circuit	No	Entrant	Tyres	Car/Engine	Comment	Q Pos/Entries
ret	US GP (PHOENIX)	Phoenix	11	Team Lotus	G	3.5 Lotus 102B-Judd V8	engine-oil union fire	13/34
9	BRAZILIAN GP	Interlagos	11	Team Lotus	G	3.5 Lotus 102B-Judd V8	3 laps behind	22/34
5	SAN MARINO GP	Imola	11	Team Lotus	G	3.5 Lotus 102B-Judd V8	3 laps behind	25/34
ret	MONACO GP	Monte Carlo	11	Team Lotus	G	3.5 Lotus 102B-Judd V8	oil leak/caught fire	26/34
ret	CANADIAN GP	Montreal	11	Team Lotus	G	3.5 Lotus 102B-Judd V8	spun off	24/34
9	MEXICAN GP	Mexico City	11	Team Lotus	G	3.5 Lotus 102B-Judd V8	2 laps behind	24/34
dnq	FRENCH GP	Magny Cours	11	Team Lotus	G	3.5 Lotus 102B-Judd V8		27/34
12	BRITISH GP	Silverstone	11	Team Lotus	G	3.5 Lotus 102B-Judd V8	2 laps behind	25/34
ret	GERMAN GP	Hockenheim	11	Team Lotus	G	3.5 Lotus 102B-Judd V8	engine	23/34
14	HUNGARIAN GP	Hungaroring	11	Team Lotus	G	3.5 Lotus 102B-Judd V8	3 laps behind	26/34
ret	BELGIAN GP	Spa	11	Team Lotus	G	3.5 Lotus 102B-Judd V8	engine	24/34
14	ITALIAN GP	Monza	11	Team Lotus	G	3.5 Lotus 102B-Judd V8	4 laps behind	25/34
14	PORTUGUESE GP	Estoril	11	Team Lotus	G	3.5 Lotus 102B-Judd V8	3 laps behind	26/34
ret	SPANISH GP	Barcelona	11	Team Lotus	G	3.5 Lotus 102B-Judd V8	spun off	21/33
ret	JAPANESE GP	Suzuka	11	Team Lotus	G	3.5 Lotus 102B-Judd V8	spun off	21/31
19	AUSTRALIAN GP	Adelaide	11	Team Lotus	G	3.5 Lotus 102B-Judd V8	race stopped 14 laps/-1 lap	25/32

1992 Championship position: 8 Wins: 0 Pole positions: 0 Fastest laps: 0 Points scored: 11

	Race	Circuit	No	Entrant	Tyres	Car/Engine	Comment	Q Pos/Entries
9	SOUTH AFRICAN GP	Kyalami	11	Team Lotus	G	3.5 Lotus102D-Ford HB V8	2 laps behind	21/30
6	MEXICAN GP	Mexico City	11	Team Lotus	G	3.5 Lotus102D-Ford HB V8	1 lap behind	18/30
10	BRAZILIAN GP	Interlagos	11	Team Lotus	G	3.5 Lotus102D-Ford HB V8	4 laps behind	24/31
ret	SPANISH GP	Barcelona	11	Team Lotus	G	3.5 Lotus102D-Ford HB V8	spun off	21/32
dnq	SAN MARINO GP	Imola	11	Team Lotus	G	3.5 Lotus102D-Ford HB V8		27/32
ret	MONACO GP	Monte Carlo	11	Team Lotus	G	3.5 Lotus107-Ford HB V8	clutch	14/32
dns	"	"	11	Team Lotus	G	3.5 Lotus102D-Ford HB V8	practice only	– / –
ret	CANADIAN GP	Montreal	11	Team Lotus	G	3.5 Lotus107-Ford HB V8	gearbox	10/32
4*	FRENCH GP	Magny Cours	11	Team Lotus	G	3.5 Lotus107-Ford HB V8	*aggregate of two parts/-1 lap	11/30
6	BRITISH GP	Silverstone	11	Team Lotus	G	3.5 Lotus107-Ford HB V8		9/32
ret	GERMAN GP	Hockenheim	11	Team Lotus	G	3.5 Lotus107-Ford HB V8	engine	13/32
4	HUNGARIAN GP	Hungaroring	11	Team Lotus	G	3.5 Lotus107-Ford HB V8		16/31
6	BELGIAN GP	Spa	11	Team Lotus	G	3.5 Lotus107-Ford HB V8		8/30
ret	ITALIAN GP	Monza	11	Team Lotus	G	3.5 Lotus107-Ford HB V8	electrics	11/28
5	PORTUGUESE GP	Estoril	11	Team Lotus	G	3.5 Lotus107-Ford HB V8	1 lap behind	7/26
ret	JAPANESE GP	Suzuka	11	Team Lotus	G	3.5 Lotus107-Ford HB V8	engine	7/26
7	AUSTRALIAN GP	Adelaide	11	Team Lotus	G	3.5 Lotus107-Ford HB V8	1 lap behind	10/26

1993 Championship position: 15th= Wins: 0 Pole positions: 0 Fastest laps: 0 Points scored: 4

	Race	Circuit	No	Entrant	Tyres	Car/Engine	Comment	Q Pos/Entries
ret	PORTUGUESE GP	Estoril	7	Marlboro McLaren	G	3.5 McLaren MP4/8-Ford HB V8	accident-crashed into barrier	3/26
3	JAPANESE GP	Suzuka	7	Marlboro McLaren	G	3.5 McLaren MP4/8-Ford HB V8		3/24
ret	AUSTRALIAN GP	Adelaide	7	Marlboro McLaren	G	3.5 McLaren MP4/8-Ford HB V8	brakes	5/24

1994 Championship position: 4th Wins: 0 Pole positions: 0 Fastest laps: 0 Points scored: 26

	Race	Circuit	No	Entrant	Tyres	Car/Engine	Comment	Q Pos/Entries
ret	BRAZILIAN GP	Interlagos	7	Marlboro McLaren Peugeot	G	3.5 McLaren MP4/9-Peugeot V10	engine-electrics	8/28
ret	PACIFIC GP	T.I. Circuit	7	Marlboro McLaren Peugeot	G	3.5 McLaren MP4/9-Peugeot V10	hydraulics	4/28
3	SAN MARINO GP	Imola	7	Marlboro McLaren Peugeot	G	3.5 McLaren MP4/9-Peugeot V10		8/28
ret	MONACO GP	Monte Carlo	7	Marlboro McLaren Peugeot	G	3.5 McLaren MP4/9-Peugeot V10	first corner collision with Hill	2/24
ret	SPANISH GP	Barcelona	7	Marlboro McLaren Peugeot	G	3.5 McLaren MP4/9-Peugeot V10	engine	3/27
ret	CANADIAN GP	Montreal	7	Marlboro McLaren Peugeot	G	3.5 McLaren MP4/9-Peugeot V10	engine	7/27
ret	FRENCH GP	Magny Cours	7	Marlboro McLaren Peugeot	G	3.5 McLaren MP4/9-Peugeot V10	engine	9/28
3*	BRITISH GP	Silverstone	7	Marlboro McLaren Peugeot	G	3.5 McLaren MP4/9-Peugeot V10	*2nd place car dsq	5/28
ret	GERMAN GP	Hockenheim	7	Marlboro McLaren Peugeot	G	3.5 McLaren MP4/9-Peugeot V10	instigated first corner accident	8/28
2*	BELGIAN GP	Spa	7	Marlboro McLaren Peugeot	G	3.5 McLaren MP4/9-Peugeot V10	*1st place car dsq	8/28
3	ITALIAN GP	Monza	7	Marlboro McLaren Peugeot	G	3.5 McLaren MP4/9-Peugeot V10		7/28
3	PORTUGUESE GP	Estoril	7	Marlboro McLaren Peugeot	G	3.5 McLaren MP4/9-Peugeot V10		4/28
3	EUROPEAN GP	Jerez	7	Marlboro McLaren Peugeot	G	3.5 McLaren MP4/9-Peugeot V10		9/28
7	JAPANESE GP	Suzuka	7	Marlboro McLaren Peugeot	G	3.5 McLaren MP4/9-Peugeot V10		8/28
12/ret	AUSTRALIAN GP	Adelaide	7	Marlboro McLaren Peugeot	G	3.5 McLaren MP4/9-Peugeot V10	brakes-accident/5 laps behind	4/28

1995 Championship position: 7th Wins: 0 Pole positions: 0 Fastest laps: 0 Points scored: 17

	Race	Circuit	No	Entrant	Tyres	Car/Engine	Comment	Q Pos/Entries
4	BRAZILIAN GP	Interlagos	8	Marlboro McLaren Mercedes	G	3.0 McLaren MP4/10-Mercedes V10	1 lap behind	7/26
ret	ARGENTINE GP	Buenos Aires	8	Marlboro McLaren Mercedes	G	3.0 McLaren MP4/10-Mercedes V10	collision with Irvine on lap 1	5/26
5	SAN MARINO GP	Imola	8	Marlboro McLaren Mercedes	G	3.0 McLaren MP4/10-Mercedes V10	1 lap behind	6/26
ret	SPANISH GP	Barcelona	8	Marlboro McLaren Mercedes	G	3.0 McLaren MP4/10-Mercedes V10	fuel pressure	9/26
ret	MONACO GP	Monte Carlo	8	Marlboro McLaren Mercedes	G	3.0 McLaren MP4/10B-Mercedes V10	engine	6/26
ret	CANADIAN GP	Montreal	8	Marlboro McLaren Mercedes	G	3.0 McLaren MP4/10B-Mercedes V10	collision with Herbert-lap 1	7/24
7	FRENCH GP	Magny Cours	8	Marlboro McLaren Mercedes	G	3.0 McLaren MP4/10B-Mercedes V10	1 lap behind	8/24
ret	BRITISH GP	Silverstone	8	Marlboro McLaren Mercedes	G	3.0 McLaren MP4/10B-Mercedes V10	electrics	8/24
ret	GERMAN GP	Hockenheim	8	Marlboro McLaren Mercedes	G	3.0 McLaren MP4/10B-Mercedes V10	engine	7/24
ret	HUNGARIAN GP	Hungaroring	8	Marlboro McLaren Mercedes	G	3.0 McLaren MP4/10B-Mercedes V10	engine	5/24
ret	BELGIAN GP	Spa	8	Marlboro McLaren Mercedes	G	3.0 McLaren MP4/10B-Mercedes V10	spun off	3/24
2	ITALIAN GP	Monza	8	Marlboro McLaren Mercedes	G	3.0 McLaren MP4/10B-Mercedes V10		7/24
ret	PORTUGUESE GP	Estoril	8	Marlboro McLaren Mercedes	G	3.0 McLaren MP4/10B-Mercedes V10	engine	– / –
dns	" "	"	8	Marlboro McLaren Mercedes	G	3.0 McLaren MP4/10C-Mercedes V10	set grid time in this car	13/24
8	EUROPEAN GP	Nürburgring	8	Marlboro McLaren Mercedes	G	3.0 McLaren MP4/10C-Mercedes V10	2 laps behind	9/24
2	JAPANESE GP	Suzuka	8	Marlboro McLaren Mercedes	G	3.0 McLaren MP4/10B-Mercedes V10		3/24
dns	AUSTRALIAN GP	Adelaide	8	Marlboro McLaren Mercedes	G	3.0 McLaren MP4/10B-Mercedes V10	accident in practice	(24)/24

1996 Championship position: 5th Wins: 0 Pole positions: 0 Fastest laps: 0 Points scored: 31

	Race	Circuit	No	Entrant	Tyres	Car/Engine	Comment	Q Pos/Entries
5	AUSTRALIAN GP	Melbourne	7	Marlboro McLaren Mercedes	G	3.0 McLaren MP4/11-Mercedes V10		5/22
4	BRAZILIAN GP	Interlagos	7	Marlboro McLaren Mercedes	G	3.0 McLaren MP4/11-Mercedes V10	spun off	7/22
ret	ARGENTINE GP	Buenos Aires	7	Marlboro McLaren Mercedes	G	3.0 McLaren MP4/11-Mercedes V10	throttle mechanism	8/22
8	EUROPEAN GP	Nürburgring	7	Marlboro McLaren Mercedes	G	3.0 McLaren MP4/11-Mercedes V10	speeding in pits-stop & go pen	9/22
8	SAN MARINO GP	Imola	7	Marlboro McLaren Mercedes	G	3.0 McLaren MP4/11-Mercedes V10	engine	11/22
6/ret	MONACO GP	Monte Carlo	7	Marlboro McLaren Mercedes	G	3.0 McLaren MP4/11-Mercedes V10	collision Salo & Irvine /-5 laps	8/22

5	SPANISH GP	Barcelona	7	Marlboro McLaren Mercedes	G	3.0 McLaren MP4/11-Mercedes V10	1 lap behind	10/22
5	CANADIAN GP	Montreal	7	Marlboro McLaren Mercedes	G	3.0 McLaren MP4/11-Mercedes V10	spin/1 lap behind	6/22
5	FRENCH GP	Magny Cours	7	Marlboro McLaren Mercedes	G	3.0 McLaren MP4/11-Mercedes V10	lost 2nd and 3rd gears	5/22
3	BRITISH GP	Silverstone	7	Marlboro McLaren Mercedes	G	3.0 McLaren MP4/11-Mercedes V10		4/22
ret	GERMAN GP	Hockenheim	7	Marlboro McLaren Mercedes	G	3.0 McLaren MP4/11-Mercedes V10	gearbox	4/20
4	HUNGARIAN GP	Hungaroring	7	Marlboro McLaren Mercedes	G	3.0 McLaren MP4/11-Mercedes V10	1 lap behind	7/20
3	BELGIAN GP	Spa	7	Marlboro McLaren Mercedes	G	3.0 McLaren MP4/11-Mercedes V10		6/20
3	ITALIAN GP	Monza	7	Marlboro McLaren Mercedes	G	3.0 McLaren MP4/11-Mercedes V10		4/20
ret	PORTUGUESE GP	Estoril	7	Marlboro McLaren Mercedes	G	3.0 McLaren MP4/11-Mercedes V10	handling after collision damage	7/20
3	JAPANESE GP	Suzuka	7	Marlboro McLaren Mercedes	G	3.0 McLaren MP4/11-Mercedes V10		5/20

1997 Championship position: 5th= Wins: 1 Pole positions: 1 Fastest laps: 1 Points scored: 27

3	AUSTRALIAN GP	Melbourne	9	West McLaren Mercedes	G	3.0 McLaren MP4/12-Mercedes V10		6/24
4	BRAZILIAN GP	Interlagos	9	West McLaren Mercedes	G	3.0 McLaren MP4/12-Mercedes V10		4/22
5	ARGENTINE GP	Buenos Aires	9	West McLaren Mercedes	G	3.0 McLaren MP4/12-Mercedes V10		17/22
6	SAN MARINO GP	Imola	9	West McLaren Mercedes	G	3.0 McLaren MP4/12-Mercedes V10	1 lap behind	8/22
ret	MONACO GP	Monte Carlo	9	West McLaren Mercedes	G	3.0 McLaren MP4/12-Mercedes V10	collision with Alesi	8/22
7	SPANISH GP	Barcelona	9	West McLaren Mercedes	G	3.0 McLaren MP4/12-Mercedes V10		5/22
ret	CANADIAN GP	Montreal	9	West McLaren Mercedes	G	3.0 McLaren MP4/12-Mercedes V10	lap 1 collision-lost rear wing	9/22
ret	FRENCH GP	Magny Cours	9	West McLaren Mercedes	G	3.0 McLaren MP4/12-Mercedes V10	engine	10/22
ret	BRITISH GP	Silverstone	9	West McLaren Mercedes	G	3.0 McLaren MP4/12-Mercedes V10	engine/led race	3/22
3	GERMAN GP	Hockenheim	9	West McLaren Mercedes	G	3.0 McLaren MP4/12-Mercedes V10		3/22
ret	HUNGARIAN GP	Hungaroring	9	West McLaren Mercedes	G	3.0 McLaren MP4/12-Mercedes V10	hydraulics	4/22
dsq*	BELGIAN GP	Spa	9	West McLaren Mercedes	G	3.0 McLaren MP4/12-Mercedes V10	3rd on road/* fuel irregularities	5/22
9	ITALIAN GP	Monza	9	West McLaren Mercedes	G	3.0 McLaren MP4/12-Mercedes V10	delayed by tyre problems/FL	5/22
ret	AUSTRIAN GP	A1-Ring	9	West McLaren Mercedes	G	3.0 McLaren MP4/12-Mercedes V10	engine	2/22
ret	LUXEMBOURG GP	Nürburgring	9	West McLaren Mercedes	G	3.0 McLaren MP4/12-Mercedes V10	engine	1/22
4	JAPANESE GP	Suzuka	9	West McLaren Mercedes	G	3.0 McLaren MP4/12-Mercedes V10		4/22
1	EUROPEAN GP	Jerez	9	West McLaren Mercedes	G	3.0 McLaren MP4/12-Mercedes V10	Coulthard gave up position	5/22

1998 Championship position: WORLD CHAMPION Wins: 8 Pole positions: 9 Fastest laps: 6 Points scored: 100

1	AUSTRALIAN GP	Melbourne	8	West McLaren Mercedes	B	3.0 McLaren MP4/13-Mercedes V10	Coulthard gave up lead/FL	1/22
1	BRAZILIAN GP	Interlagos	8	West McLaren Mercedes	B	3.0 McLaren MP4/13-Mercedes V10	FL	1/22
2	ARGENTINE GP	Buenos Aires	8	West McLaren Mercedes	B	3.0 McLaren MP4/13-Mercedes V10		3/22
ret	SAN MARINO GP	Imola	8	West McLaren Mercedes	B	3.0 McLaren MP4/13-Mercedes V10	gearbox	2/22
1	SPANISH GP	Barcelona	8	West McLaren Mercedes	B	3.0 McLaren MP4/13-Mercedes V10	FL	1/22
1	MONACO GP	Monte Carlo	8	West McLaren Mercedes	B	3.0 McLaren MP4/13-Mercedes V10	FL	1/22
ret	CANADIAN GP	Montreal	8	West McLaren Mercedes	B	3.0 McLaren MP4/13-Mercedes V10	gearbox on lap 1	2/22
3	FRENCH GP	Magny Cours	8	West McLaren Mercedes	B	3.0 McLaren MP4/13-Mercedes V10		1/22
2	BRITISH GP	Silverstone	8	West McLaren Mercedes	B	3.0 McLaren MP4/13-Mercedes V10	survived mid-race spin in rain	1/22
1	AUSTRIAN GP	A1-Ring	8	West McLaren Mercedes	B	3.0 McLaren MP4/13-Mercedes V10		3/22
1	GERMAN GP	Hockenheim	8	West McLaren Mercedes	B	3.0 McLaren MP4/13-Mercedes V10		1/22
6	HUNGARIAN GP	Hungaroring	8	West McLaren Mercedes	B	3.0 McLaren MP4/13-Mercedes V10	handling problems/1 lap behind	1/22
ret	BELGIAN GP	Spa	8	West McLaren Mercedes	B	3.0 McLaren MP4/13-Mercedes V10	collision with Herbert	1/22
4	ITALIAN GP	Monza	8	West McLaren Mercedes	B	3.0 McLaren MP4/13-Mercedes V10	FL	3/22
1	LUXEMBOURG GP	Nürburgring	8	West McLaren Mercedes	B	3.0 McLaren MP4/13-Mercedes V10	FL	3/22
1	JAPANESE GP	Suzuka	8	West McLaren Mercedes	B	3.0 McLaren MP4/13-Mercedes V10		2/22

1999 Championship position: WORLD CHAMPION Wins: 5 Pole positions: 11 Fastest laps: 6 Points scored: 76

ret	AUSTRALIAN GP	Melbourne	1	West McLaren Mercedes	B	3.0 McLaren MP4/14-Mercedes V10	throttle	1/22
1	BRAZILIAN GP	Interlagos	1	West McLaren Mercedes	B	3.0 McLaren MP4/14-Mercedes V10	FL	1/22
ret	SAN MARINO GP	Imola	1	West McLaren Mercedes	B	3.0 McLaren MP4/14-Mercedes V10	spun off when leading	1/22
3	MONACO GP	Monte Carlo	1	West McLaren Mercedes	B	3.0 McLaren MP4/14-Mercedes V10	FL	1/22
1	SPANISH GP	Barcelona	1	West McLaren Mercedes	B	3.0 McLaren MP4/14-Mercedes V10		1/22
1	CANADIAN GP	Montreal	1	West McLaren Mercedes	B	3.0 McLaren MP4/14-Mercedes V10		2/22
2	FRENCH GP	Magny Cours	1	West McLaren Mercedes	B	3.0 McLaren MP4/14-Mercedes V10		14/22
ret	BRITISH GP	Silverstone	1	West McLaren Mercedes	B	3.0 McLaren MP4/14-Mercedes V10	precautionary after lost wheel/FL	1/22
3	AUSTRIAN GP	A1-Ring	1	West McLaren Mercedes	B	3.0 McLaren MP4/14-Mercedes V10	recovered from lap 1 spin/FL	1/22
ret	GERMAN GP	Hockenheim	1	West McLaren Mercedes	B	3.0 McLaren MP4/14-Mercedes V10	tyre failure-crashed	1/22
1	HUNGARIAN GP	Hungaroring	1	West McLaren Mercedes	B	3.0 McLaren MP4/14-Mercedes V10		1/22
2	BELGIAN GP	Spa	1	West McLaren Mercedes	B	3.0 McLaren MP4/14-Mercedes V10	FL	1/22
ret	ITALIAN GP	Monza	1	West McLaren Mercedes	B	3.0 McLaren MP4/14-Mercedes V10	spun off when leading	1/22
5	EUROPEAN GP	Nürburgring	1	West McLaren Mercedes	B	3.0 McLaren MP4/14-Mercedes V10	delayed by wet/dry tyre changes/FL	3/22
3	MALAYSIAN GP	Sepang	1	West McLaren Mercedes	B	3.0 McLaren MP4/14-Mercedes V10		4/22
1	JAPANESE GP	Suzuka	1	West McLaren Mercedes	B	3.0 McLaren MP4/14-Mercedes V10		2/22

GP Starts: 128   GP Wins: 14   Pole positions: 21   Fastest laps: 13   Points: 294

Mika winning the 1999 Brazilian Grand Prix, the first of his five victories during the course of his unsteady progress towards his second drivers' title.

BRUCE HALFORD

Despite possessing only limited experience gained with a Cooper-Bristol, Halford purchased the ex-Bira Maserati 250F in 1956 but tasted success only in minor F1 races, his best placing being third at Caen in both 1957 and '58. By then, however, the car was showing its age and he turned to a Lister-Jaguar and a year of national sports car racing – which must certainly have sharpened up his driving, for he was a much improved performer when he returned to single-seaters in 1959 with a new Lotus 16, though his best result was a third in the Silver City Trophy race at Snetterton, guesting for the BRM team.

In 1960 Halford handled a Cooper with only moderate success, thereafter scaling down his racing activities.

With the new-found popularity of historic racing in the late seventies, Bruce returned to the circuits at the wheel of an immaculate Lotus 16 and enjoyed himself immensely in the friendly but fiercely competitive atmosphere.

HALFORD, Bruce (GB) b 18/5/1931, Hampton-in-Arden, nr Birmingham, Warwickshire

	1956	Championship position: Unplaced							
	Race	Circuit	No	Entrant	Tyres	Car/Engine		Comment	Q Pos/Entries
ret	BRITISH GP	Silverstone	29	Bruce Halford	D	2.5 Maserati 250F 6		engine	20/28
dsq	GERMAN GP	Nürburgring	21	Bruce Halford	D	2.5 Maserati 250F 6		push start after a spin	11/21
ret	ITALIAN GP	Monza	48	Bruce Halford	D	2.5 Maserati 250F 6		engine	22/26
	1957	Championship position: Unplaced							
11	GERMAN GP	Nürburgring	15	Bruce Halford	D	2.5 Maserati 250F 6		1 lap behind	16/24
ret	PESCARA GP	Pescara	20	Bruce Halford	D	2.5 Maserati 250F 6		differential	14/16
ret	ITALIAN GP	Monza	16	Bruce Halford	D	2.5 Maserati 250F 6		engine	14/19
	1959	Championship position: Unplaced							
ret	MONACO GP	Monte Carlo	44	John Fisher	D	1.5 Lotus 16-Climax 4		accident with Allison and von Trips	16/24
	1960	Championship position: Unplaced							
dnq	MONACO GP	Monte Carlo	12	Fred Tuck Cars	D	2.5 Cooper T51-Climax 4			17/24
8/ret	FRENCH GP	Reims	48	Yeoman Credit Racing Team	D	2.5 Cooper T51-Climax 4		engine	16/23

GP Starts: 8   GP Wins: 0   Pole positions: 0   Fastest laps: 0   Points: 0

HALL, Jim (USA) b 23/7/1935, Abilene, Texas

	1960	Championship position: Unplaced							
	Race	Circuit	No	Entrant	Tyres	Car/Engine		Comment	Q Pos/Entries
7	US GP	Riverside	24	Jim Hall	D	2.5 Lotus 18-Climax 4		2 laps behind	12/23
	1961	Championship position: Unplaced							
ret	US GP	Watkins Glen	17	Jim Hall	D	1.5 Lotus 18/21-Climax 4		fuel leak	=18/19
	1962	Championship position: Unplaced							
dns	US GP	Watkins Glen	25	Jim Hall	D	1.5 Lotus 21-Climax 4		engine-dropped valve	(18)/20
	1963	Championship position: 12th Wins: 0 Pole positions: 0 Fastest laps: 0 Points scored: 3							
ret	MONACO GP	Monte Carlo	12	British Racing Partnership	D	1.5 Lotus 24-BRM V8		gearbox	13/17
ret	BELGIAN GP	Spa	5	British Racing Partnership	D	1.5 Lotus 24-BRM V8		accident in rain	=12/20
8	DUTCH GP	Zandvoort	42	British Racing Partnership	D	1.5 Lotus 24-BRM V8		3 laps behind	=17/19
11	FRENCH GP	Reims	34	British Racing Partnership	D	1.5 Lotus 24-BRM V8		pit stop/8 laps behind	18/21
6	BRITISH GP	Silverstone	12	British Racing Partnership	D	1.5 Lotus 24-BRM V8		2 laps behind	13/23
5	GERMAN GP	Nürburgring	20	British Racing Partnership	D	1.5 Lotus 24-BRM V8		1 lap behind	16/26
8	ITALIAN GP	Monza	30	British Racing Partnership	D	1.5 Lotus 24-BRM V8		2 laps behind	17/28
10/ret	US GP	Watkins Glen	16	British Racing Partnership	D	1.5 Lotus 24-BRM V8		gearbox	16/21
8	MEXICAN GP	Mexico City	16	British Racing Partnership	D	1.5 Lotus 24-BRM V8		5 laps behind	15/21

GP Starts: 11   GP Wins: 0   Pole positions: 0   Fastest laps: 0   Points: 3

HAMILTON, Duncan (GB) b 30/4/1920, Cork, Ireland – d 13/5/1994, Sherbourne, Dorset

	1951	Championship position: Unplaced							
	Race	Circuit	No	Entrant	Tyres	Car/Engine		Comment	Q Pos/Entries
12	BRITISH GP	Silverstone	18	Duncan Hamilton	D	4.5 Lago-Talbot T26C 6		9 laps behind	11/20
ret	GERMAN GP	Nürburgring	88	Duncan Hamilton	D	4.5 Lago-Talbot T26C 6		oil pressure	20/23
	1952	Championship position: Unplaced							
ret	BRITISH GP	Silverstone	30	HW Motors Ltd	D	2.0 HWM-Alta 4		engine	11/32
7	DUTCH GP	Zandvoort	28	HW Motors Ltd	D	2.0 HWM-Alta 4		5 laps behind	10/18
	1953	Championship position: Unplaced							
ret	BRITISH GP	Silverstone	3	HW Motors Ltd	D	2.0 HWM-Alta 4		clutch	17/29

GP Starts: 5   GP Wins: 0   Pole positions: 0   Fastest laps: 0   Points: 0

JIM HALL

It is a pity that Jim Hall decided not to extend his season-long Grand Prix career and returned to the States, for he was undoubtedly a talented driver and could have gone much further in this sphere had he chosen to. As it was, Formula 1's loss was sports car racing's gain, for he would then set about building and racing a succession of just about the most exciting sports cars ever seen.

A multi-millionaire teenager after the death of his parents in an air crash, Hall soon became involved with racing and exotic cars, teaming up with Carroll Shelby to run a Texas Maserati dealership until he went into the oil business in 1958, continuing to race in SCCA events.

Hall made an impressive GP debut at Riverside in 1960, lying fifth until last-lap gremlins intervened. This encouraged him to race a Lotus in 1961 and '62 – without success, although he finished fourth in the non-championship 1962 Mexican GP. His 1963 season with BRP was quite encouraging, Jim twice finishing in the points in GPs and taking fourth place in the Glover Trophy and sixth in the Lombank Trophy and at Solitude.

With the Formula 1 bug out of his system, Hall set about completing the task he and Hap Sharp had first undertaken in 1962, namely building an advanced automatic-transmission sports car. Immersed in the Chaparral's innovative design, Jim continued to drive, regularly clocking up wins and placings, and in 1965 the car dominated USRRC sports car racing in North America. From 1966, he concentrated his driving activities on Can-Am, leaving the long-distance programme to Hill, Bonnier and Spence until rule changes forced his Chaparral 2F out.

However, in the 1968 Stardust GP at Las Vegas, his Can-Am car ran into the back of a McLaren driven by Lothar Motschenbacher. The Chaparral flipped and was demolished, and Hall lay in hospital for nine weeks with multiple injuries. Apart from a couple of Trans-Am races in 1970, his racing career was over, but he continued to be involved with the sport throughout the seventies, collaborating with Carl Haas in F5000 before

making a successful move to Indy Car racing with his own chassis. Hall pulled out at the end of the 1982 season and did not return until 1991. A fairy-tale first-time victory by John Andretti proved to be illusory, for the next three seasons saw the Pennzoil entry consistently underperforming.

In 1995, bolstered by the talents of Rookie of the Year Gil de Ferran, the team were back in business, taking a win in the season's finale at Laguna Seca. More success was anticipated in 1996 but, despite another win in Cleveland, Jim, after much thought, decided the time was right for him to call it a day.

'It's been my life. It's been a lot of fun.' Certainly, the long, tall Texan took his leave having made an indelible mark on motor racing history.

DUNCAN HAMILTON

A larger-than-life character, this former Fleet Air Arm pilot drove a Maserati before managing to get hold of a Lago-Talbot which he raced during the 1951 season, taking second place in the International Trophy and fifth in the non-championship Dutch GP. With Formula 2 becoming the premier category for 1952, his car was redundant except for Libre events, so Duncan thereafter had a handful of outings in John Heath's HWMs. His best placings were fourth in the 1952 Eifelrennen, and sixth in the Ulster Trophy at Dundrod and the Crystal Palace Trophy in '53.

However, his greatest moments came in sports car racing. Having finished sixth at Le Mans with a Nash-Healey in 1951, Hamilton won the race two years later in a works Jaguar D-Type shared with Tony Rolt. The pair returned the following season, this time in Duncan's own D-Type, and finished second after a thrilling chase of González's Ferrari in the wet. Hamilton scored further major wins in the Coupe de Paris at Montlhéry in '54 and '56 and the 1956 Reims 12 Hours with Ivor Bueb. There were numerous excellent placings elsewhere, including a third in the 1956 Swedish GP when Duncan shared a works Ferrari with de Portago and Mike Hawthorn. It was after the death of his close friend early in 1959 that Duncan retired from racing to concentrate on his successful garage business.

HAMPSHIRE, David (GB) b 29/12/1917, Mickleover, nr Derby – d 25/8/1990, Newton-Soleney, nr Burton-on-Trent, Derbyshire

	1950			Championship position: Unplaced					
	Race	Circuit	No	Entrant	Tyres	Car/Engine		Comment	Q Pos/Entries
9	BRITISH GP	Silverstone	6	Scuderia Ambrosiana	D	1.5 s/c Maserati 4CLT/48 4		6 laps behind	16/21
ret	FRENCH GP	Reims	34	Scuderia Ambrosiana	D	1.5 s/c Maserati 4CLT/48 4		engine	18/20

GP Starts: 2   GP Wins: 0   Pole positions: 0   Fastest laps: 0   Points: 0

HANSGEN, Walt (USA) b 28/10/1919, Westfield, New Jersey – d 7/4/1966, Orléans, France

	1961			Championship position: Unplaced					
	Race	Circuit	No	Entrant	Tyres	Car/Engine		Comment	Q Pos/Entries
ret	US GP	Watkins Glen	60	Momo Corporation	D	1.5 Cooper T53-Climax 4		accident	14/19
	1964			Championship position: 16th= Wins: 0 Pole positions: 0 Fastest laps: 0 Points scored: 2					
5	US GP	Watkins Glen	17	Team Lotus	D	1.5 Lotus 33-Climax V8		3 laps behind	17/19

GP Starts: 2   GP Wins: 0   Pole positions: 0   Fastest laps: 0   Points: 2

DAVID HAMPSHIRE

A company director who began racing a Maserati before the war, Hampshire found his principal successes between 1947 and 1949 driving an ERA. He finished second in the British Empire Trophy on the Isle of Man in 1948, and shared the car with band leader Billy Cotton to take fourth place in the British GP in 1949.

The ERA was getting long in the tooth, and Hampshire was glad to take the opportunity to drive Reg Parnell's Scuderia Ambrosiana semi-works Maserati at a couple of Grands Prix.

He raced the car again in 1951, as well as wheeling out his venerable ERA for few minor outings. Also that year he shared a works Aston Martin DB2 with Reg Parnell, the pair finishing seventh. Hampshire raced little thereafter.

He reappeared in 1955 for a couple of outings in a Lister-Bristol, taking ninth (and class win) with Scott-Russell in the BARC 9-hour race at Goodwood.

WALT HANSGEN

One of the greatest American sports car drivers of the 1950s, Hansgen built a mighty reputation with his own Jaguar XK120, before racing a D-Type for Briggs Cunningham from 1956. In 1958 he visited Britain to take delivery of a Lister-Jaguar, which he raced briefly before returning home to campaign the car with great success.

In the early 1960s Walt undertook occasional single-seater drives, earning fifth place at Watkins Glen in 1964 in a Lotus with a steady drive, and finishing 12th at Indianapolis the same year.

But it was in sports cars that Hansgen really shone, taking victories in a wide variety of machines including a Cooper-Monaco, before racing John Mecom's stable of cars which boasted a Ferrari 250LM, a Lotus 19, a Scarab Chevrolet and a Lola T70.

Hansgen began 1966 sharing the Ford MkII with his protégé Mark Donohue, taking third at Daytona and second at Sebring, but he was killed when he crashed the car in the Le Mans 24 Hours test weekend in April 1966.

MIKE HARRIS

With third place in the 1962 Rhodesian Grand Prix and that country's championship to his name, Harris entered the series of races staged around the end-of-year South African Grand Prix with an ex-Reg Parnell Cooper fitted with an Alfa engine.

Unfortunately for Mike, his luck was out, and he retired from all three events. A puncture ended his Natal Grand Prix, and he also failed to finish his qualifying heat of the Rand Grand Prix, thus missing the final.

The championship race at East London appears to have been Harris' last major single-seater outing for he did not race at national level thereafter.

CUTH HARRISON

T C (Cuth) Harrison was an extremely enthusiastic amateur driver who raced an ERA C-Type – mainly in national events, where his duels with Bob Gerard were lively indeed, but also occasionally on the Continent, finishing sixth in the 1949 Italian Grand Prix.

The 1950 season, his last with the car, brought no success in Grands Prix, but he did finish second in the British Empire Trophy in the Isle of Man, before concentrating on his thriving garage business in Sheffield and returning to trials with an 1172 cc Harford, with which he was the 1952 RAC champion.

His name is still widely seen today, particularly in the north of England, due to that now ultra-successful car dealership he began developing in the 1950s.

BRIAN HART

For the past twenty-five years, Brian has been designing and building racing engines for Formula 2 and then Formula 1, with the Toleman, RAM, Jordan, Footwork and Arrows teams among his customers, but long before that he enjoyed a worthy career as a driver.

Between 1958 and 1963, Hart scored numerous wins in Formula Junior and sports car events with Lotus and Terrier chassis, taking third place in the Grovewood Awards for 1963.

Moving up to Formula 2, Brian gained an almost immediate victory in the Pergusa GP, driving a Ron Harris-entered Lotus, and although he stepped back into Formula 3 in 1966 he was to become an F2 mainstay, mostly racing for Bob Gerard, for whom he won the 1969 Rhine Cup race at Hockenheim after a great drive.

As his flourishing engine business grew, Hart inevitably found less time to go racing and he eventually retired at the end of 1971.

HARRIS, Mike (ZA) b 25/5/1939, Mulfulira, Zambia

	1962	Championship position: Unplaced						
	Race	Circuit	No	Entrant	Tyres	Car/Engine	Comment	Q Pos/Entries
ret	SOUTH AFRICAN GP	East London	22	Mike Harris	D	1.5 Cooper T53-Alfa Romeo 4	big end bearings	14/17

GP Starts: 1 GP Wins: 0 Pole positions: 0 Fastest laps: 0 Points: 0

HARRISON, Cuth (GB) b 6/7/1906, Ecclesall, Sheffield – d 21/1/1981, Sheffield

	1950	Championship position: Unplaced						
	Race	Circuit	No	Entrant	Tyres	Car/Engine	Comment	Q Pos/Entries
7	BRITISH GP	Silverstone	11	Cuth Harrison	D	1.5 s/c ERA B Type 6	3 laps behind	15/21
ret	MONACO GP	Monte Carlo	24	Cuth Harrison	D	1.5 s/c ERA B Type 6	multiple accident	14/21
ret	ITALIAN GP	Monza	32	Cuth Harrison	D	1.5 s/c ERA B Type 6	engine	21/27

GP Starts: 3 GP Wins: 0 Pole positions: 0 Fastest laps: 0 Points: 0

HART, Brian (GB) b 7/9/1936, Enfield, Middlesex

	1967	Championship position: Unplaced						
	Race	Circuit	No	Entrant	Tyres	Car/Engine	Comment	Q Pos/Entries
12*	GERMAN GP (F2)	Nürburgring	25	Ron Harris	F	1.6 Protos-Cosworth 4 F2	4th in F2 class/-3 laps	24/25

GP Starts: 1 GP Wins: 0 Pole positions: 0 Fastest laps: 0 Points: 0

MASAHIRO HASEMI

A former motocross rider, Hasemi turned to cars with a Nissan Bluebird, and rightly earned a reputation as one of Japan's finest drivers, having been a champion in Formula 2 (1980), sports cars (1990 with Anders Olofsson) and touring cars (1989, 1991 and 1992).

He caused a stir with the locally built Kojima on his only Grand Prix appearance in 1976. Benefiting from special Dunlop wet-weather tyres, Hasemi set fastest lap in the pouring rain before they – and his challenge – faded.

He has often been seen outside Japan as a member of the Nissan sports-prototype team, competing regularly at Le Mans, but enjoyed his greatest success in winning the 1992 Daytona 24 Hours with his compatriots Kazuyoshi Hoshino and Toshio Suzuki.

During the nineties Masahiro has been running his own Nissan Skyline in the All-Japan GT championship, as well as racing an Opel Vectra in the touring car championship.

PAUL HAWKINS

'Hawkeye' was another of those tough Aussies who came to Britain in the early sixties with no money, but plenty of determination to further their racing careers and the willingness to graft ceaselessly to achieve their goal.

He found employment in the Healey factory in 1960, with an opportunity to race their Sprites. This led to two happy seasons with Ian Walker's sports car and Formula Junior team, before he was tempted to join John Willment in 1964 to race all sorts of cars, taking an aggregate second place in the Rand GP and winning the Rhodesian GP in an F2 Brabham, the same car that he used to make his GP debut in South Africa in 1965.

Back in Europe, Paul had an unproductive time in Dickie Stoop's Lotus 33, which he spectacularly crashed into the harbour at Monaco, but he won the F2 Eifelrennen in an Alexis. Apart from a few F1 races with Tim Parnell early in 1966, Hawkins turned his attention to sports cars, which offered him a better opportunity to show his talent. Racing his own Ford GT40, he achieved numerous excellent wins and countless placings during 1967 and '68, with his trips to South Africa proving particularly fruitful, and was also in demand by the top sports car teams of the period as a freelance, winning the 1967 Targa Florio for Porsche and the 1967 Paris 1000 Km and the 1968 Monza 1000 Km for John Wyer.

With his Lola T70 run from the factory, 'Hawkeye' embarked on a season of sports car racing in 1969 and it was a terrible blow for the sport when this no-nonsense character lost his life after crashing into a tree during the Tourist Trophy race at Oulton Park.

HASEMI, Masahiro (J) b 13/11/1945, Tokyo

	1976	Championship position: Unplaced						
	Race	Circuit	No	Entrant	Tyres	Car/Engine	Comment	Q Pos/Entries
11	JAPANESE GP	Mount Fuji	51	Kojima Engineering	D	3.0 Kojima KE007-Cosworth V8	pit stop-tyres/FL/7 laps behind	10/27

GP Starts: 1 GP Wins: 0 Pole positions: 0 Fastest laps: 1 Points: 0

HAWKINS, Paul (AUS) b 12/10/1937, Melbourne, Victoria – d 26/5/1969, Oulton Park, Cheshire, England

	1965	Championship position: Unplaced						
	Race	Circuit	No	Entrant	Tyres	Car/Engine	Comment	Q Pos/Entries
9	SOUTH AFRICAN GP	East London	18	John Willment Automobiles	D	1.5 Brabham BT10-Ford 4 F2	4 laps behind	16/25
10/ret	MONACO GP	Monte Carlo	10	DW Racing Enterprises	D	1.5 Lotus 33-Climax V8	crashed into harbour/-21 laps	=14/17
ret	GERMAN GP	Nürburgring	22	DW Racing Enterprises	D	1.5 Lotus 33-Climax V8	oil pipe	20/22

GP Starts: 3 GP Wins: 0 Pole positions: 0 Fastest laps: 0 Points: 0

MIKE HAWTHORN

WORLD CHAMPION: 1958

MIKE HAWTHORN

Blond and debonair, Hawthorn was in the vanguard of the new wave of English talent which came to the fore in Grand Prix racing in the early fifties, and to him fell the signal honour of becoming Great Britain's first-ever World Champion driver.

His rise was meteoric, Mike winning a championship Grand Prix barely two years after his circuit racing debut in a Riley in 1951. During that first full season he won the Leinster Trophy and the Ulster Handicap as well as the Brooklands Memorial Trophy for his consistent successes throughout the year at Goodwood, and for 1952 he took delivery of one of the new Cooper-Bristols, which had been purchased for him by a family friend, Bob Chase. The team would be run by his father Leslie. The season started well with F2 and Libre wins at the Goodwood Easter meeting before he headed for the Continent and fourth place on his Grand Prix debut at Spa. Certainly the car was quite useful, but Mike coaxed far, far more from it than anyone else with his uninhibited driving.

A minor meeting at Boreham saw a fantastic display of his ability. In pouring rain he left the great Villoresi floundering in his 4.5-litre Ferrari until the track dried and the little Cooper was overhauled. The Italian went back to Italy to report to Ferrari that he had unearthed a new British star. Arriving at Modena for the late-season Grand Prix, Mike was invited to drive for the Scuderia in 1953, and had plenty of time to consider the offer as he crashed the Cooper in practice and found himself hospitalised. He duly joined Ferrari's star-studded line-up and wisely took things easy to begin with, watching and learning from his more experienced team-mates.

It was to be a magnificent first season for the Englishman abroad, and he finished every championship Grand Prix bar one in the points, the highlight being a glorious victory, over Fangio no less, in the French GP at Reims after a wheel-to-wheel battle to the flag. Beyond the World Championship, Hawthorn won the International Trophy and the Ulster Trophy at Dundrod, while in sports cars he took the Spa 24 Hours with Farina, his achievements earning him a BRDC Gold Star. The 1954 season began badly when he crashed at Syracuse and received serious burns to his arms and legs, and there was then a furore over his exemption from National Service due to a kidney ailment, followed by the death of his father in a road accident. Mike decided that it would be impossible to run the family garage business if he stayed at Maranello so, after signing off with a win at Pedralbes, he looked forward to racing for Vanwall in 1955, but the new car needed development and Mike was seriously unimpressed with the disarray of Vandervell's organisation. Even in victory he was followed by controversy, for when he won the Le Mans 24 Hours for Jaguar with Ivor Bueb he found the finger of blame pointed towards him as the unwitting instigator of the tragedy which killed more than eighty people. Some semblance of order was restored with an end-of-season return to Ferrari by way of the Lancia team which they had just taken over, and a splendid drive for Jaguar in the Tourist Trophy.

His desire to honour his contract with the sports car team for 1956 meant Mike had to join BRM for Formula 1, and the cars' unreliability restricted him to just a handful of outings. Hawthorn decided that for success he must drive for an Italian team, and he was welcomed back to Ferrari to drive alongside his great mate Peter Collins. The atmosphere, so strained in 1956, was completely changed with Mike's return and soon he was back to his consistent best. The magnificent Fangio bestrode the 1957 season in his Maserati, but when the Argentinian retired early in 1958 the title was there to be taken. Ironically the threat to Ferrari came from Vanwall, who had been so shambolic during Mike's brief tenure as a driver. He paced himself brilliantly, taking risks when necessary but making sure that he finished at all costs. The death of Collins in the German GP hit him very hard and, with Musso and Lewis-Evans also having lost their lives that year, Hawthorn, newly crowned as World Champion, announced his retirement.

Mike was planning both marriage and an expansion of his garage business when, on a rainy January morning in 1959, he lost control of his potent Jaguar near Guildford and was killed instantly when it wrapped itself around a tree.

Mike's championship year was a model of consistency. Though he managed only one Grand Prix win in 1958, Hawthorn took the Ferrari Dino 246 to five second-place finishes, including one in the season's finale *(right)* in Morocco.

Mike hard at work rounding Spa's La Source hairpin in the Ferrari 625 during the 1954 Belgian Grand Prix.

HAWTHORN, Mike (GB) b 10/4/1929, Mexborough, Yorkshire – d 22/1/1959, Guildford-by-pass, Surrey

	1952			Championship position: 4th= Wins: 0 Pole positions: 0 Fastest laps: 0 Points scored: 10				
	Race	Circuit	No	Entrant	Tyres	Car/Engine	Comment	Q Pos/Entries
4	BELGIAN GP	Spa	8	L D Hawthorn	D	2.0 Cooper T20-Bristol 6	2 pit stops-fuel leak/-1 lap	6/22
ret	FRENCH GP	Rouen	42	A H M Bryde	D	2.0 Cooper T20-Bristol 6	ignition	15/20
3	BRITISH GP	Silverstone	9	L D Hawthorn	D	2.0 Cooper T20-Bristol 6	2 laps behind	7/32
4	DUTCH GP	Zandvoort	32	L D Hawthorn	D	2.0 Cooper T20-Bristol 6	2 laps behind	3/18
nc	ITALIAN GP	Monza	42	L D Hawthorn	D	2.0 Cooper T20-Bristol 6	long pit stop-magneto/-38 laps	12/35
	1953			Championship position: 4 Wins: 1 Pole positions: 0 Fastest laps: 0 Points scored: 27				
4	ARGENTINE GP	Buenos Aires	16	Scuderia Ferrari	P	2.0 Ferrari 500 4		6/16
4	DUTCH GP	Zandvoort	8	Scuderia Ferrari	P	2.0 Ferrari 500 4	1 lap behind	6/20
6	BELGIAN GP	Spa	14	Scuderia Ferrari	P	2.0 Ferrari 500 4	1 lap behind	7/22
1	FRENCH GP	Reims	16	Scuderia Ferrari	P	2.0 Ferrari 500 4	1 lap behind	7/25
5	BRITISH GP	Silverstone	8	Scuderia Ferrari	P	2.0 Ferrari 500 4		3/29
3	GERMAN GP	Nürburgring	3	Scuderia Ferrari	P	2.0 Ferrari 500 4	spin-pit stop/3 laps behind	4/35
3	SWISS GP	Bremgarten	26	Scuderia Ferrari	P	2.0 Ferrari 500 4		7/23
4	ITALIAN GP	Monza	8	Scuderia Ferrari	P	2.0 Ferrari 500 4	1 lap behind	6/30
	1954			Championship position: 3 Wins: 1 Pole positions: 0 Fastest laps: 1 (shared) Points scored: 24.64				
dsq	ARGENTINE GP	Buenos Aires	14	Scuderia Ferrari	P	2.5 Ferrari 625 4	push start after spin	4/18
4*	BELGIAN GP	Spa	10	Scuderia Ferrari	P	2.5 Ferrari 625 4	exhaust fumes/*Gonzalez took over	5/15
ret	FRENCH GP	Reims	6	Scuderia Ferrari	P	2.5 Ferrari 553/555 4	engine	8/22
2	BRITISH GP	Silverstone	11	Scuderia Ferrari	P	2.5 Ferrari 625/555 4	FL (shared)	3/31
ret	GERMAN GP	Nürburgring	3	Scuderia Ferrari	P	2.5 Ferrari 625/555 4	rear axle	2/23
2*	"	"	1	Scuderia Ferrari	P	2.5 Ferrari 625/555 4	* took over Gonzalez's car	– / –
ret	SWISS GP	Bremgarten	22	Scuderia Ferrari	P	2.5 Ferrari 625/555 4	fuel pump	6/16
2	ITALIAN GP	Monza	40	Scuderia Ferrari	P	2.5 Ferrari 625/555 4	1 lap behind	7/21
1	SPANISH GP	Pedralbes	38	Scuderia Ferrari	P	2.5 Ferrari 553 4		3/22

	1955			Championship position: Unplaced					
ret	MONACO GP	Monte Carlo	18	Vandervell Products Ltd	P	2.5 Vanwall 4		*throttle linkage*	12/22
ret	BELGIAN GP	Spa	40	Vandervell Products Ltd	P	2.5 Vanwall 4		*gearbox*	9/14
7	DUTCH GP	Zandvoort	2	Scuderia Ferrari	E	2.5 Ferrari 555 4		*pit stop/3 laps behind*	5/16
dns	"		2	Scuderia Ferrari	E	2.5 Ferrari 625 4		*practice only*	–/–
6*	BRITISH GP	Aintree	16	Scuderia Ferrari	E	2.5 Ferrari 625/555 4		** unwell-Castellotti took car/-3 laps*	12/25
ret	ITALIAN GP	Monza	6	Scuderia Ferrari	E	2.5 Ferrari 555 4		*gearbox mounting*	14/22
dns	"	"	T	Scuderia Ferrari	E	2.5 Lancia D50 V8		*practice only-did not fit well in car*	–/–

	1956			Championship position: 9th=	Wins: 0	Pole positions: 0	Fastest laps: 0	Points scored: 4	
3	ARGENTINE GP	Buenos Aires	14	Owen Racing Organisation	D	2.5 Maserati 250F 6		*2 laps behind*	8/15
dns	MONACO GP	Monte Carlo	10	Owen Racing Organisation	D	2.5 BRM P25 4		*engine problems in practice*	10/19
dns	BELGIAN GP	Spa	38	Officine Alfieri Maserati	P	2.5 Maserati 250F 6		*ill-feeling at MH driving works car*	(13)/16
10*	FRENCH GP	Reims	24	Vandervell Products Ltd	P	2.5 Vanwall 4		** Schell took over/-5 laps*	6/20
ret	BRITISH GP	Silverstone	23	Owen Racing Organisation	D	2.5 BRM P25 4		*oil leak-universal joint*	3/28

	1957			Championship position: 4th	Wins: 0	Pole positions: 0	Fastest laps: 0	Points scored: 13	
ret	ARGENTINE GP	Buenos Aires	16	Scuderia Ferrari	E	2.5 Lancia-Ferrari D50A V8		*clutch*	7/16
ret	MONACO GP	Monte Carlo	28	Scuderia Ferrari	E	2.5 Lancia-Ferrari D50A V8		*accident with Moss and Collins*	5/21
7/ret	"	"	24	Scuderia Ferrari	E	2.5 Lancia-Ferrari 801 V8		*shared with von Trips/engine/-5 laps*	–/–
4	FRENCH GP	Rouen	14	Scuderia Ferrari	E	2.5 Lancia-Ferrari 801 V8		*1 lap behind*	7/15
3	BRITISH GP	Aintree	10	Scuderia Ferrari	E	2.5 Lancia-Ferrari 801 V8			5/19
2	GERMAN GP	Nürburgring	8	Scuderia Ferrari	E	2.5 Lancia-Ferrari 801 V8			2/24
6	ITALIAN GP	Monza	34	Scuderia Ferrari	E	2.5 Lancia-Ferrari 801 V8		*pit stop-oil pipe/4 laps behind*	10/19

	1958			Championship position: WORLD CHAMPION	Wins: 1	Pole positions: 3	Fastest laps: 5	Points scored: 49	
3	ARGENTINE GP	Buenos Aires	20	Scuderia Ferrari	E	2.4 Ferrari Dino 246 V6			2/10
ret	MONACO GP	Monte Carlo	38	Scuderia Ferrari	E	2.4 Ferrari Dino 246 V6		*fuel pump/FL*	6/28
5	DUTCH GP	Zandvoort	5	Scuderia Ferrari	E	2.4 Ferrari Dino 246 V6		*1 lap behind*	6/17
2	BELGIAN GP	Spa	16	Scuderia Ferrari	E	2.4 Ferrari Dino 246 V6		*FL*	1/20
1	FRENCH GP	Reims	4	Scuderia Ferrari	E	2.4 Ferrari Dino 246 V6		*FL*	1/21
2	BRITISH GP	Silverstone	2	Scuderia Ferrari	E	2.4 Ferrari Dino 246 V6		*FL*	4/21
ret	GERMAN GP	Nürburgring	3	Scuderia Ferrari	E	2.4 Ferrari Dino 246 V6		*clutch*	1/26
2	PORTUGUESE GP	Oporto	22	Scuderia Ferrari	E	2.4 Ferrari Dino 246 V6		*FL*	2/15
2	ITALIAN GP	Monza	14	Scuderia Ferrari	E	2.4 Ferrari Dino 246 V6			3/21
2	MOROCCAN GP	Casablanca	6	Scuderia Ferrari	E	2.4 Ferrari Dino 246 V6			1/25

GP Starts: 45   GP Wins: 3   Pole positions: 4   Fastest laps: 6 (1 shared)   Points: 127.64

BOY HAYJE

A former saloon car racer and Dutch Formula Ford champion, and a protégé of Toine Hezemans, Boy raced the ex-James Hunt March 731 in F5000 in 1975 without realising much by way of results, and thus switched to Formula 3 in 1976, a year which saw him make a promising GP debut at Zandvoort.

With backing from his loyal sponsors, Hayje secured a seat in the RAM March team for 1977, a move which was to prove disastrous for all concerned, the Dutchman departing abruptly following his non-qualification at his home Grand Prix. He then took his backing to Fred Opert in Formula 2 for 1978, again with little reward.

Thereafter Hayje perhaps found his true level and success came his way at last, racing in the European Renault 5 turbo championship.

HAYJE, Boy (NL) b 3/5/1949, Amsterdam

	1976			Championship position: Unplaced					
	Race	*Circuit*	*No*	*Entrant*	*Tyres*	*Car/Engine*		*Comment*	*Q Pos/Entries*
ret	DUTCH GP	Zandvoort	39	F & S Properties	G	3.0 Penske PC3-Cosworth V8		*driveshaft*	21/27
	1977			Championship position: Unplaced					
ret	SOUTH AFRICAN GP	Kyalami	33	RAM Racing/F & S Properties	G	3.0 March 761-Cosworth V8		*gearbox*	21/23
dnq	SPANISH GP	Jarama	33	RAM Racing/F & S Properties	G	3.0 March 761-Cosworth V8			28/31
dnq	MONACO GP	Monte Carlo	33	RAM Racing/F & S Properties	G	3.0 March 761-Cosworth V8			22/26
nc	BELGIAN GP	Zolder	33	RAM Racing/F & S Properties	G	3.0 March 761-Cosworth V8		*7 laps behind*	27/32
dnq	SWEDISH GP	Anderstorp	33	RAM Racing/F & S Properties	G	3.0 March 761-Cosworth V8			28/31
dnq	DUTCH GP	Zandvoort	33	RAM Racing/F & S Properties	G	3.0 March 761-Cosworth V8			31/34

GP Starts: 3   GP Wins: 0   Pole positions: 0   Fastest laps: 0   Points: 0

WILLI HEEKS

A skilled pilot who drove the BMW-engined Formula 2 AFM cars with great verve, Heeks scored wins in 1950 in the Maipokalrennen at Hockenheim and at Dessau. The following year saw him carry the challenge to the Veritas marque once more, but his best placing was third at the Nürburgring in the Eifelrennen. Competition in Germany at this time was vibrant and there were plenty of excellent drivers such as Heeks who were rarely seen racing outside their own country. By 1953, the AFM was no longer competitive and Willi joined the ranks of the Veritas runners, although most of his major races ended in retirement. He did cause something of a stir in the German GP when his car led the Ferrari of Rosier before eventually breaking down.

He subsequently drove a Mercedes 220S with Erwin Bauer in a number of races during 1956, including the Nürburgring 1000 Km.

THEO HELFRICH

A manager in the motoring trade in Mannheim, the balding Helfrich enjoyed considerable success in the early fifties and was one of Germany's best 'lesser-known' pilots. Driving a Veritas he won at Hockenheim in 1950, and over the next year or so scored some excellent placings with the car, bringing an invitation from Mercedes-Benz to race one of their three 300SLs at Le Mans. Paired with Niedermayr, Theo took a fine second place behind the Riess/Lang car.

In 1953 he raced a single-seater Veritas and won the German Formula 2 championship as well as helping to develop the little Borgward sports car. Theo and Günther Bechem brought the potent little machine into third place overall, and easily won the 750–1500 cc class. Although Helfrich handled Klenk's car in the 1954 German Grand Prix, the rule changes had swept away Formula 2 in favour of the new 2.5-litre F1. Thus Theo purchased an F3 Cooper and proceeded to win in hill-climbs and minor races, taking seven wins in ten outings that year. Perhaps his most notable performance, though, was second to Moss in that year's Eifelrennen.

Purchasing a 1500 cc Porsche Spyder, Helfrich raced on for a couple more years, taking fifth place at Rouen in 1956.

HEEKS, Willi (D) b 13/2/1922, Moorlage – d 8/1996

	1952	Championship position: Unplaced						
	Race	*Circuit*	*No*	*Entrant*	*Tyres*	*Car/Engine*	*Comment*	*Q Pos/Entries*
ret	GERMAN GP	Nürburgring	123	Willi Heeks	–	2.0 AFM U8-BMW 6		9/32
	1953	Championship position: Unplaced						
ret	GERMAN GP	Nürburgring	23	Willi Heeks	–	2.0 Veritas Meteor 6		18/35

GP Starts: 2   GP Wins: 0   Pole positions: 0   Fastest laps: 0   Points: 0

HELFRICH, Theo (D) b 13/5/1913, Frankfurt-am-Main – d 29/4/1978

	1952	Championship position: Unplaced						
	Race	*Circuit*	*No*	*Entrant*	*Tyres*	*Car/Engine*	*Comment*	*Q Pos/Entries*
ret	GERMAN GP	Nürburgring	122	Theo Helfrich	–	2.0 Veritas RS 6		18/32
	1953	Championship position: Unplaced						
12	GERMAN GP	Nürburgring	24	Theo Helfrich	–	2.0 Veritas RS 6	*2 laps behind*	28/35
	1954	Championship position: Unplaced						
ret	GERMAN GP	Nürburgring	22	Hans Klenk	–	2.0 Klenk Meteor-BMW 6	*engine*	21/23

GP Starts: 3   GP Wins: 0   Pole positions: 0   Fastest laps: 0   Points: 0

BRIAN HENTON

Career setbacks that would have seen a less determined character throw in the towel only seemed to encourage this tough, no-nonsense driver to get stuck in once more and prove his critics wrong. With three seasons of Formula Vee and Super Vee racing behind him, Brian took the plunge into F3 – initially with his own GRD before a move into the works March F3 team for 1974 really put him on the map. Easily winning the Lombard and Forward Trust championships, he graduated to Formula 2 and a brief and salutary stint with Lotus. This was followed by an abortive 1976 season after a planned drive with Tom Wheatcroft foundered after just one race, and Henton had to start all over again.

His patriotic private British Formula One March got him back on the F1 grid, but he soon ran out of funds, so it was back to Formula 2 for 1978, Brian enjoying some success in his own car, and 1979, when he finished a close second to Marc Surer in the championship, winning at Mugello and Misano. With BP and Toleman behind him, Henton made no mistake the following year, taking the title and re-establishing himself as a serious proposition once more.

Brian had certainly earned his move back into Grands Prix with Toleman, but the season was another major disappointment, the underdeveloped car beset by turbo problems. Henton could have been sunk without trace, but he managed to find a seat for 1982, first with Arrows, deputising for the injured Surer, and then at Tyrrell in place of Slim Borgudd. He did a solid job, nearly making the points, and was credited with fastest lap at Brands Hatch, but it was not enough for Tyrrell to retain him. A one-off drive into fourth place for Theodore in the 1983 Race of Champions rounded off a career which eventually failed to meet Henton's expectations, but it wasn't for want of trying.

HENTON, Brian (GB) b 19/9/1946, Derby

	1975	Championship position: Unplaced							
	Race	Circuit	No	Entrant	Tyres	Car/Engine		Comment	Q Pos/Entries
16/ret	BRITISH GP	Silverstone	15	John Player Team Lotus	G	3.0 Lotus 72E-Cosworth V8		crashed in rainstorm/-3 laps	21/28
dns	AUSTRIAN GP	Österreichring	6	John Player Team Lotus	G	3.0 Lotus 72E-Cosworth V8		accident in practice	(23)/30
nc	US GP	Watkins Glen	6	John Player Team Lotus	G	3.0 Lotus 72F-Cosworth V8		pit stop/10 laps behind	19/24
	1977	Championship position: Unplaced							
10	US GP WEST	Long Beach	10	Team Rothmans International	G	3.0 March 761B-Cosworth V8		3 laps behind	18/22
dnq	SPANISH GP	Jarama	38	British Formula One Racing Team	G	3.0 March 761B-Cosworth V8			29/31
dnq	BRITISH GP	Silverstone	38	British Formula One Racing Team	G	3.0 March 761B-Cosworth V8			29/36
dnq	AUSTRIAN GP	Österreichring	38	British Formula One Racing Team	G	3.0 March 761B-Cosworth V8			27/30
dsq	DUTCH GP	Zandvoort	38	HB Bewaking Alarm Systems	G	3.0 Boro/Ensign N175-Cosworth V8		push start after spin	23/34
dnq	ITALIAN GP	Monza	38	HB Bewaking Alarm Systems	G	3.0 Boro/Ensign N175-Cosworth V8			28/34
	1978	Championship position: Unplaced							
dns	AUSTRIAN GP	Österreichring	18	Team Surtees	G	3.0 Surtees TS20-Cosworth V8		tried Keegan's car in practice	– / –
	1981	Championship position: Unplaced							
dnq	SAN MARINO GP	Imola	35	Candy Toleman Motorsport	M	1.5 t/c Toleman TG181-Hart 4			30/30
dnq	BELGIAN GP	Zolder	35	Candy Toleman Motorsport	P	1.5 t/c Toleman TG181-Hart 4			30/31
dnpq	MONACO GP	Monte Carlo	35	Candy Toleman Motorsport	P	1.5 t/c Toleman TG181-Hart 4			30/31
dnq	SPANISH GP	Jarama	35	Candy Toleman Motorsport	P	1.5 t/c Toleman TG181-Hart 4			28/30
dnq	FRENCH GP	Dijon	35	Candy Toleman Motorsport	P	1.5 t/c Toleman TG181-Hart 4			26/29
dnq	BRITISH GP	Silverstone	35	Candy Toleman Motorsport	P	1.5 t/c Toleman TG181-Hart 4			26/30
dnq	GERMAN GP	Hockenheim	35	Candy Toleman Motorsport	P	1.5 t/c Toleman TG181-Hart 4			26/30
dnq	AUSTRIAN GP	Österreichring	35	Candy Toleman Motorsport	P	1.5 t/c Toleman TG181-Hart 4			27/28
dnq	DUTCH GP	Zandvoort	35	Candy Toleman Motorsport	P	1.5 t/c Toleman TG181-Hart 4			26/30
10	ITALIAN GP	Monza	35	Candy Toleman Motorsport	P	1.5 t/c Toleman TG181-Hart 4		3 laps behind	23/30
dnq	CANADIAN GP	Montreal	35	Candy Toleman Motorsport	P	1.5 t/c Toleman TG181-Hart 4			27/30
dnq	CAESARS PALACE GP	Las Vegas	35	Candy Toleman Motorsport	P	1.5 t/c Toleman TG181-Hart 4			29/30
	1982	Championship position: Unplaced	Fastest laps: 1						
dnq	SOUTH AFRICAN GP	Kyalami	29	Arrows Racing Team	P	3.0 Arrows A4-Cosworth V8			29/30
dnq	BRAZILIAN GP	Rio	29	Arrows Racing Team	P	3.0 Arrows A4-Cosworth V8			29/31
ret	US GP WEST	Long Beach	29	Arrows Racing Team	P	3.0 Arrows A4-Cosworth V8		accident	20/31
ret	SAN MARINO GP	Imola	4	Team Tyrrell	G	3.0 Tyrrell 011-Cosworth V8		clutch	11/14
ret	BELGIAN GP	Zolder	4	Team Tyrrell	G	3.0 Tyrrell 011-Cosworth V8		engine	22/32
8	MONACO GP	Monte Carlo	4	Team Tyrrell	G	3.0 Tyrrell 011-Cosworth V8		pit stop-puncture/-4 laps	17/31
9	US GP (DETROIT)	Detroit	4	Team Tyrrell	G	3.0 Tyrrell 011-Cosworth V8		pit stop/2 laps behind	20/28
nc	CANADIAN GP	Montreal	4	Team Tyrrell	G	3.0 Tyrrell 011-Cosworth V8		hit barrier-pit stop/-11 laps	26/29
ret	DUTCH GP	Zandvoort	4	Team Tyrrell	G	3.0 Tyrrell 011-Cosworth V8		throttle linkage	20/31
8	BRITISH GP	Brands Hatch	4	Team Tyrrell	G	3.0 Tyrrell 011-Cosworth V8		pit stop-tyres/FL/1 lap behind	17/30
10	FRENCH GP	Paul Ricard	4	Team Tyrrell	G	3.0 Tyrrell 011-Cosworth V8		1 lap behind	23/30
7	GERMAN GP	Hockenheim	4	Team Tyrrell	G	3.0 Tyrrell 011-Cosworth V8		1 lap behind	18/30
ret	AUSTRIAN GP	Österreichring	4	Team Tyrrell	G	3.0 Tyrrell 011-Cosworth V8		engine	19/29
11	SWISS GP	Dijon	4	Team Tyrrell	G	3.0 Tyrrell 011-Cosworth V8		2 laps behind	18/29
ret	ITALIAN GP	Monza	4	Team Tyrrell	G	3.0 Tyrrell 011-Cosworth V8		spun off-collision with Daly	20/30
8	CAESARS PALACE GP	Las Vegas	4	Team Tyrrell	G	3.0 Tyrrell 011-Cosworth V8		1 lap behind	19/30

GP Starts: 19   GP Wins: 0   Pole positions: 0   Fastest laps: 1   Points: 0

JOHNNY HERBERT

Perhaps Britain's most talented young prospect of the eighties, Johnny Herbert has built a successful career for himself in the world of Grand Prix racing – indeed 1999 has just seen him take an unlikely but well-deserved win in the European Grand Prix to add to his emotional and hugely popular victories at Silverstone and Monza in 1995 – yet one wonders if the horrific crash at Brands Hatch in 1988 which interrupted his meteoric rise somehow robbed his career of an impetus which might have seen him be a true contender for the World Championship itself.

Racing in karts from the age of ten, Herbert worked his way through the classes, taking numerous championships on the way, before graduating to FF1600 and winning the prestigious Brands Hatch Formula Ford Festival in 1985. Johnny's path then crossed that of Eddie Jordan, who took him into Formula 3 in 1987. Herbert won the title and a Benetton test, which led to an option to drive for the team in 1989, so it was a season of F3000 next, which started brilliantly with a win at Jerez, followed by a number of highly competitive drives before that fateful Brands accident.

Johnny had the goal of reaching the grid in Brazil to make his debut for Benetton, and after months of painful rehabilitation he not only drove in Rio, but brought the car into fourth place. But as the year progressed it became clear that he was still handicapped by his injuries, and he was summarily replaced by the less talented Pirro. Now came a period when Johnny had to step down into Japanese F3000, take the occasional F1 ride and wait for another chance (an unexpected victory at Le Mans with Mazda in 1991 providing a highlight).

Luckily his old mentor at Benetton, Peter Collins, was now busy reviving the fortunes of Lotus, and Herbert was very much the man he wanted for the job. Brought back into the team full-time early in 1991, Herbert repeatedly showed he had the talent to win but, unfortunately, not the car. Locked into a contract at Lotus, Herbert was left trapped and frustrated as the team struggled on against overwhelming odds during the 1994 season. Johnny lost heart and, despite a morale-boosting fourth place on the grid at Monza, his relationship with team boss and father figure Peter Collins soured to the point that a split was inevitable.

Both parties must have been relieved when Flavio Briatore bought out his contract in September that year, for not only did Collins have some much-needed finance to stagger on at Lotus, but Johnny had a contract which saw him through to the end of 1995. Initially he was placed at Ligier, but after a fine performance at Jerez he was whisked into the Benetton team in the hope that he might assist Schumacher's title bid.

As mentioned before, 1995 was the year that Johnny found tangible success; indeed, apart from his two wins, his consistency brought him within a whisker of taking third place in the World Championship. Unfortunately his status at Benetton was very much that of the number two to Schumacher, and his gripes to the press after a disappointing showing in the Belgian GP could not have helped his cause.

Not retained at season's end, Herbert found a ride at Sauber and, after a somewhat frosty start when his experience was underutilised in testing, he gradually won the team's confidence, especially after team-mate Frentzen seemed to lose his motivation. Third place at Monaco was the best result in a year littered with retirements, but despite the loss of the Ford engine deal to Stewart Herbert had done enough to earn a new two-year contract with the Swiss constructor. Johnny was now the team's mainstay and was charged with the task of developing the new Sauber C16 with its Petronas (née Ferrari) engine largely on his own.

The car was a capable points scorer but never a likely winner, and the ever-jovial Herbert made the best of his situation. Things changed for the worse in 1998 with the arrival of Jean Alesi. Simply, the two drivers failed to gel and Herbert appeared to be worn down as much by the Frenchman's hystrionics as by his undeniable edge in speed on the track.

He was considered a touch fortunate to secure a two-year deal with Stewart Gand Prix beginning in 1999, but after a quiet first half to the season Johnny picked up the pace and duly supplied the team's afore-mentioned maiden Grand Prix win. Another superb drive in Malaysia gave Herbert a further boost to his confidence as he prepared to welcome Eddie Irvine on board as his new team-mate in the restructured Jaguar team for 2000.

HERBERT, Johnny (GB) b 25/6/1964, Brentwood, Essex

1989

Championship position: 14th= Wins: 0 Pole positions: 0 Fastest laps: 0 Points scored: 5

	Race	Circuit	No	Entrant		Tyres	Car/Engine	Comment	Q Pos/Entries
4	BRAZILIAN GP	Rio	20	Benetton Formula		G	3.5 Benetton B188-Cosworth V8		10/38
11	SAN MARINO GP	Imola	20	Benetton Formula		G	3.5 Benetton B188-Cosworth V8	spin/2 laps behind	23/39
14	MONACO GP	Monte Carlo	20	Benetton Formula		G	3.5 Benetton B188-Cosworth V8	hit Arnoux/stop-new wing/-4 laps	24/38
15	MEXICAN GP	Mexico City	20	Benetton Formula		G	3.5 Benetton B188-Cosworth V8	pit stops-gearbox-tyres/-3 laps	18/39
5	US GP (PHOENIX)	Phoenix	20	Benetton Formula		G	3.5 Benetton B188-Cosworth V8	lost 4th gear/1 lap behind	25/39
dnq	CANADIAN GP	Montreal	20	Benetton Formula		G	3.5 Benetton B188-Cosworth V8		29/39
ret	BELGIAN GP	Spa	4	Tyrrell Racing Organisation		G	3.5 Tyrrell 018-Cosworth V8	spun off-hit barrier	16/39
dnq	PORTUGUESE GP	Estoril	4	Tyrrell Racing Organisation		G	3.5 Tyrrell 018-Cosworth V8		27/39

1990

Championship position: Unplaced

	Race	Circuit	No	Entrant		Tyres	Car/Engine	Comment	Q Pos/Entries
ret	JAPANESE GP	Suzuka	12	Camel Team Lotus		G	3.5 Lotus 102-Lamborghini V12	engine	15/30
ret	AUSTRALIAN GP	Adelaide	12	Camel Team Lotus		G	3.5 Lotus 102-Lamborghini V12	clutch	18/30

1991

Championship position: Unplaced

	Race	Circuit	No	Entrant		Tyres	Car/Engine	Comment	Q Pos/Entries
dnq	CANADIAN GP	Montreal	12	Team Lotus		G	3.5 Lotus 102B-Judd V8		30/34
10	MEXICAN GP	Mexico City	12	Team Lotus		G	3.5 Lotus 102B-Judd V8	2 laps behind	25/34
10	FRENCH GP	Magny Cours	12	Team Lotus		G	3.5 Lotus 102B-Judd V8	left at start-gears/-2 laps	20/34
14/ret	BRITISH GP	Silverstone	12	Team Lotus		G	3.5 Lotus 102B-Judd V8	engine/4 laps behind	24/34
7	BELGIAN GP	Spa	12	Team Lotus		G	3.5 Lotus 102B-Judd V8		21/34
ret	PORTUGUESE GP	Estoril	12	Team Lotus		G	3.5 Lotus 102B-Judd V8	engine/gearbox	22/34
ret	JAPANESE GP	Suzuka	12	Team Lotus		G	3.5 Lotus 102B-Judd V8	engine cut out	23/31
11	AUSTRALIAN GP	Adelaide	12	Team Lotus		G	3.5 Lotus 102B-Judd V8	race stopped at 14 laps	21/32

1992

Championship position: 14th= Wins: 0 Pole positions: 0 Fastest laps: 0 Points scored: 2

	Race	Circuit	No	Entrant		Tyres	Car/Engine	Comment	Q Pos/Entries
6	SOUTH AFRICAN GP	Kyalami	12	Team Lotus		G	3.5 Lotus 102D-Ford HB V8	1 lap behind	11/30
7	MEXICAN GP	Mexico City	12	Team Lotus		G	3.5 Lotus 102D-Ford HB V8	1 lap behind	12/30
ret	BRAZILIAN GP	Interlagos	12	Team Lotus		G	3.5 Lotus 102D-Ford HB V8	taken off by Boutsen and Comas	26/31
ret	SPANISH GP	Barcelona	12	Team Lotus		G	3.5 Lotus 102D-Ford HB V8	spun off	26/32
ret	SAN MARINO GP	Imola	12	Team Lotus		G	3.5 Lotus 107-Ford HB V8	gearbox	26/32
ret	MONACO GP	Monte Carlo	12	Team Lotus		G	3.5 Lotus 107-Ford HB V8	handling-slid into barriers	9/32
ret	CANADIAN GP	Montreal	12	Team Lotus		G	3.5 Lotus 107-Ford HB V8	clutch	6/32
6*	FRENCH GP	Magny Cours	12	Team Lotus		G	3.5 Lotus 107-Ford HB V8	* aggregate of two parts/-1 lap	12/30
ret	BRITISH GP	Silverstone	12	Team Lotus		G	3.5 Lotus 107-Ford HB V8	gearbox	7/32
ret	GERMAN GP	Hockenheim	12	Team Lotus		G	3.5 Lotus 107-Ford HB V8	engine cut out	11/32
ret	HUNGARIAN GP	Hungaroring	12	Team Lotus		G	3.5 Lotus 107-Ford HB V8	spun avoiding Comas/Boutsen	13/31
13/ret	BELGIAN GP	Spa	12	Team Lotus		G	3.5 Lotus 107-Ford HB V8	engine/2 laps behind	10/30
ret	ITALIAN GP	Monza	12	Team Lotus		G	3.5 Lotus 107-Ford HB V8	engine	13/28
ret	PORTUGUESE GP	Estoril	12	Team Lotus		G	3.5 Lotus 107-Ford HB V8	collision-bent steering arm	9/26
ret	JAPANESE GP	Suzuka	12	Team Lotus		G	3.5 Lotus 107-Ford HB V8	gearbox	6/26
13	AUSTRALIAN GP	Adelaide	12	Team Lotus		G	3.5 Lotus 107-Ford HB V8	pit stop-nose & track rod/-4 laps	12/26

1993

Championship position: 9th Wins: 0 Pole positions: 0 Fastest laps: 0 Points scored: 11

	Race	Circuit	No	Entrant		Tyres	Car/Engine	Comment	Q Pos/Entries
ret	SOUTH AFRICAN GP	Kyalami	12	Team Lotus		G	3.5 Lotus 107B-Ford HB V8	fuel pressure	17/26
4	BRAZILIAN GP	Interlagos	12	Team Lotus		G	3.5 Lotus 107B-Ford HB V8		12/26
4	EUROPEAN GP	Donington	12	Team Lotus		G	3.5 Lotus 107B-Ford HB V8	1 lap behind	11/26
8/ret	SAN MARINO GP	Imola	12	Team Lotus		G	3.5 Lotus 107B-Ford HB V8	engine	12/26
ret	SPANISH GP	Barcelona	12	Team Lotus		G	3.5 Lotus 107B-Ford HB V8	started from back/active failure	10/26
ret	MONACO GP	Monte Carlo	12	Team Lotus		G	3.5 Lotus 107B-Ford HB V8	gearbox failed-crashed	14/26
10	CANADIAN GP	Montreal	12	Team Lotus		G	3.5 Lotus 107B-Ford HB V8	lack of grip/2 laps behind	20/26
ret	FRENCH GP	Magny Cours	12	Team Lotus		G	3.5 Lotus 107B-Ford HB V8	spun off	19/26
4	BRITISH GP	Silverstone	12	Team Lotus		G	3.5 Lotus 107B-Ford HB V8		7/26
10	GERMAN GP	Hockenheim	12	Team Lotus		G	3.5 Lotus 107B-Ford HB V8	actuator problem/1 lap behind	13/26
ret	HUNGARIAN GP	Hungaroring	12	Team Lotus		G	3.5 Lotus 107B-Ford HB V8	spun and stalled	20/26
5	BELGIAN GP	Spa	12	Team Lotus		G	3.5 Lotus 107B-Ford HB V8	1 lap behind	10/25
ret	ITALIAN GP	Monza	12	Team Lotus		G	3.5 Lotus 107B-Ford HB V8	crashed at Parabolica	7/26
ret	PORTUGUESE GP	Estoril	12	Team Lotus		G	3.5 Lotus 107B-Ford HB V8	crashed	14/26
11	JAPANESE GP	Suzuka	12	Team Lotus		G	3.5 Lotus 107B-Ford HB V8	2 laps behind	19/24
ret	AUSTRALIAN GP	Adelaide	12	Team Lotus		G	3.5 Lotus 107B-Ford HB V8	hydraulics	20/24

1994

Championship position: Unplaced

	Race	Circuit	No	Entrant		Tyres	Car/Engine	Comment	Q Pos/Entries
7	BRAZILIAN GP	Interlagos	12	Team Lotus		G	3.5 Lotus 107C-Mugen Honda V10	2 laps behind	21/28
7	PACIFIC GP	T.I. Circuit	12	Team Lotus		G	3.5 Lotus 107C-Mugen Honda V10	3 laps behind	23/28
10	SAN MARINO GP	Imola	12	Team Lotus		G	3.5 Lotus 107C-Mugen Honda V10	2 laps behind	20/28
ret	MONACO GP	Monte Carlo	12	Team Lotus		G	3.5 Lotus 107C-Mugen Honda V10	gearbox	16/24
ret	SPANISH GP	Barcelona	12	Team Lotus		G	3.5 Lotus 109-Mugen Honda V10	spun off	22/27
8	CANADIAN GP	Montreal	12	Team Lotus		G	3.5 Lotus 109-Mugen Honda V10	1 lap behind	17/27
7	FRENCH GP	Magny Cours	12	Team Lotus		G	3.5 Lotus 109-Mugen Honda V10	2 laps behind	19/28
11*	BRITISH GP	Silverstone	12	Team Lotus		G	3.5 Lotus 109-Mugen Honda V10	*2nd place car dsq/-2 laps	21/28
ret	GERMAN GP	Hockenheim	12	Team Lotus		G	3.5 Lotus 109-Mugen Honda V10	collision with Brundle-lap 1	15/28
ret	HUNGARIAN GP	Hungaroring	12	Team Lotus		G	3.5 Lotus 109-Mugen Honda V10	electrics	24/28
12*	BELGIAN GP	Spa	12	Team Lotus		G	3.5 Lotus 109-Mugen Honda V10	*1st place car dsq/-3 laps	20/28
ret	ITALIAN GP	Monza	12	Team Lotus		G	3.5 Lotus 109-Mugen Honda V10	engine	4/28
11	PORTUGUESE GP	Estoril	12	Team Lotus		G	3.5 Lotus 109-Mugen Honda V10	1 lap behind	20/28
8	EUROPEAN GP	Jerez	25	Ligier Gitanes Blondes		G	3.5 Ligier JS39B-Renault V10	1 lap behind	7/28
ret	JAPANESE GP	Suzuka	6	Mild Seven Benetton Ford		G	3.5 Benetton B194-Ford Zetec-R V8	accident	5/28
ret	AUSTRALIAN GP	Adelaide	6	Mild Seven Benetton Ford		G	3.5 Benetton B194-Ford Zetec-R V8	gearbox	7/28

1995

Championship position: 4th Wins: 2 Pole positions: 0 Fastest laps: 0 Points scored: 45

	Race	Circuit	No	Entrant		Tyres	Car/Engine	Comment	Q Pos/Entries
ret	BRAZILIAN GP	Interlagos	2	Mild Seven Benetton Renault		G	3.0 Benetton B195-Renault V10	collision with Suzuki	4/26
4	ARGENTINE GP	Buenos Aires	2	Mild Seven Benetton Renault		G	3.0 Benetton B195-Renault V10	1 lap behind	11/26
7	SAN MARINO GP	Imola	2	Mild Seven Benetton Renault		G	3.0 Benetton B195-Renault V10	2 laps behind	8/26
2	SPANISH GP	Barcelona	2	Mild Seven Benetton Renault		G	3.0 Benetton B195-Renault V10		7/26
4	MONACO GP	Monte Carlo	2	Mild Seven Benetton Renault		G	3.0 Benetton B195-Renault V10	1 lap behind	7/26

ret	CANADIAN GP	Montreal	2	Mild Seven Benetton Renault	G	3.0 Benetton B195-Renault V10	collision with Häkkinen	6/24
ret	FRENCH GP	Magny Cours	2	Mild Seven Benetton Renault	G	3.0 Benetton B195-Renault V10	collision with Alesi	10/24
1	BRITISH GP	Silverstone	2	Mild Seven Benetton Renault	G	3.0 Benetton B195-Renault V10		5/24
4	GERMAN GP	Hockenheim	2	Mild Seven Benetton Renault	G	3.0 Benetton B195-Renault V10		9/24
4	HUNGARIAN GP	Hungaroring	2	Mild Seven Benetton Renault	G	3.0 Benetton B195-Renault V10	1 lap behind	9/24
7	BELGIAN GP	Spa	2	Mild Seven Benetton Renault	G	3.0 Benetton B195-Renault V10		4/24
1	ITALIAN GP	Monza	2	Mild Seven Benetton Renault	G	3.0 Benetton B195-Renault V10		8/24
7	PORTUGUESE GP	Estoril	2	Mild Seven Benetton Renault	G	3.0 Benetton B195-Renault V10	1 lap behind	6/24
5	EUROPEAN GP	Nürburgring	2	Mild Seven Benetton Renault	G	3.0 Benetton B195-Renault V10	1 lap behind	7/24
6	PACIFIC GP	T.I. Circuit	2	Mild Seven Benetton Renault	G	3.0 Benetton B195-Renault V10	1 lap behind	7/24
3	JAPANESE GP	Suzuka	2	Mild Seven Benetton Renault	G	3.0 Benetton B195-Renault V10		9/24
ret	AUSTRALIAN GP	Adelaide	2	Mild Seven Benetton Renault	G	3.0 Benetton B195-Renault V10	driveshaft	8/24

1996   Championship position: 14th   Wins: 0   Pole positions: 0   Fastest laps: 0   Points scored: 4

ret/dns*	AUSTRALIAN GP	Melbourne	14	Red Bull Sauber Ford	G	3.0 Sauber C15-Ford Zetec R V10	*car damaged in first start	14/22
ret	BRAZILIAN GP	Interlagos	14	Red Bull Sauber Ford	G	3.0 Sauber C15-Ford Zetec R V10	engine	12/22
9	ARGENTINE GP	Buenos Aires	14	Red Bull Sauber Ford	G	3.0 Sauber C15-Ford Zetec R V10	1 lap behind	17/22
7	EUROPEAN GP	Nürburgring	14	Red Bull Sauber Ford	G	3.0 Sauber C15-Ford Zetec R V10		12/22
ret	SAN MARINO GP	Imola	14	Red Bull Sauber Ford	G	3.0 Sauber C15-Ford Zetec R V10	engine	15/22
3	MONACO GP	Monte Carlo	14	Red Bull Sauber Ford	G	3.0 Sauber C15-Ford Zetec R V10		13/22
ret	SPANISH GP	Barcelona	14	Red Bull Sauber Ford	G	3.0 Sauber C15-Ford Zetec R V10	spun off	9/22
7	CANADIAN GP	Montreal	14	Red Bull Sauber Ford	G	3.0 Sauber C15-Ford Zetec R V10	1 lap behind	15/22
dsq*/11	FRENCH GP	Magny Cours	14	Red Bull Sauber Ford	G	3.0 Sauber C15-Ford Zetec R V10	* front deflector dimensions	17/22
ret	BRITISH GP	Silverstone	14	Red Bull Sauber Ford	G	3.0 Sauber C15-Ford Zetec R V10	1 lap behind	13/22
ret	GERMAN GP	Hockenheim	14	Red Bull Sauber Ford	G	3.0 Sauber C15-Ford Zetec R V10	gearbox sensor	14/20
ret	HUNGARIAN GP	Hungaroring	14	Red Bull Sauber Ford	G	3.0 Sauber C15-Ford Zetec R V10	engine	8/20
ret	BELGIAN GP	Spa	14	Red Bull Sauber Ford	G	3.0 Sauber C15-Ford Zetec R V10	collision-Frentzen & Panis	12/20
9/ret	ITALIAN GP	Monza	14	Red Bull Sauber Ford	G	3.0 Sauber C15-Ford Zetec R V10	engine/2 laps behind	12/20
8	PORTUGUESE GP	Estoril	14	Red Bull Sauber Ford	G	3.0 Sauber C15-Ford Zetec R V10	1 lap behind	12/20
10	JAPANESE GP	Suzuka	14	Red Bull Sauber Ford	G	3.0 Sauber C15-Ford Zetec R V10		13/20

1997   Championship position: 10th   Wins: 0   Pole positions: 0   Fastest laps: 0   Points scored: 15

ret	AUSTRALIAN GP	Melbourne	16	Red Bull Sauber Petronas	G	3.0 Sauber C16-Petronas V10	collision at first corner	7/24
7	BRAZILIAN GP	Interlagos	16	Red Bull Sauber Petronas	G	3.0 Sauber C16-Petronas V10		13/22
4	ARGENTINE GP	Buenos Aires	16	Red Bull Sauber Petronas	G	3.0 Sauber C16-Petronas V10		8/22
ret	SAN MARINO GP	Imola	16	Red Bull Sauber Petronas	G	3.0 Sauber C16-Petronas V10	electrics	7/22
ret	MONACO GP	Monte Carlo	16	Red Bull Sauber Petronas	G	3.0 Sauber C16-Petronas V10	crashed into barrier	7/22
5	SPANISH GP	Barcelona	16	Red Bull Sauber Petronas	G	3.0 Sauber C16-Petronas V10		10/22
5	CANADIAN GP	Montreal	16	Red Bull Sauber Petronas	G	3.0 Sauber C16-Petronas V10		13/22
8	FRENCH GP	Magny Cours	16	Red Bull Sauber Petronas	G	3.0 Sauber C16-Petronas V10	1 lap behind	14/22
ret	BRITISH GP	Silverstone	16	Red Bull Sauber Petronas	G	3.0 Sauber C16-Petronas V10	transmission	9/22
ret	GERMAN GP	Hockenheim	16	Red Bull Sauber Petronas	G	3.0 Sauber C16-Petronas V10	collision with Diniz	14/22
3	HUNGARIAN GP	Hungaroring	16	Red Bull Sauber Petronas	G	3.0 Sauber C16-Petronas V10		10/22
4*	BELGIAN GP	Spa	16	Red Bull Sauber Petronas	G	3.0 Sauber C16-Petronas V10	*3rd place car dsq	11/22
ret	ITALIAN GP	Monza	16	Red Bull Sauber Petronas	G	3.0 Sauber C16-Petronas V10	hit by Ralf Schumacher	12/22
8	AUSTRIAN GP	A1-Ring	16	Red Bull Sauber Petronas	G	3.0 Sauber C16-Petronas V10		12/22
7	LUXEMBOURG GP	Nürburgring	16	Red Bull Sauber Petronas	G	3.0 Sauber C16-Petronas V10		16/22
6*	JAPANESE GP	Suzuka	16	Red Bull Sauber Petronas	G	3.0 Sauber C16-Petronas V10	*5th place car dsq	8/22
8	EUROPEAN GP	Jerez	16	Red Bull Sauber Petronas	G	3.0 Sauber C16-Petronas V10		14/22

1998   Championship position: 15th=   Wins: 0   Pole positions: 0   Fastest laps: 0   Points scored: 1

6	AUSTRALIAN GP	Melbourne	15	Red Bull Sauber Petronas	G	3.0 Sauber C17-Petronas V10	1 lap behind	6/22
11/ret	BRAZILIAN GP	Interlagos	15	Red Bull Sauber Petronas	G	3.0 Sauber C17-Petronas V10	neck strain/5 laps behind	14/22
ret	ARGENTINE GP	Buenos Aires	15	Red Bull Sauber Petronas	G	3.0 Sauber C17-Petronas V10	collision with Hill-puncture	12/22
ret	SAN MARINO GP	Imola	15	Red Bull Sauber Petronas	G	3.0 Sauber C17-Petronas V10	puncture	11/22
7	SPANISH GP	Barcelona	15	Red Bull Sauber Petronas	G	3.0 Sauber C17-Petronas V10	1 lap behind	7/22
7	MONACO GP	Monte Carlo	15	Red Bull Sauber Petronas	G	3.0 Sauber C17-Petronas V10	1 lap behind	9/22
ret	CANADIAN GP	Montreal	15	Red Bull Sauber Petronas	G	3.0 Sauber C17-Petronas V100	spun off	12/22
8	FRENCH GP	Magny Cours	15	Red Bull Sauber Petronas	G	3.0 Sauber C17-Petronas V10	1 lap behind	13/22
ret	BRITISH GP	Silverstone	15	Red Bull Sauber Petronas	G	3.0 Sauber C17-Petronas V10	spun off	9/22
8	AUSTRIAN GP	A1-Ring	15	Red Bull Sauber Petronas	G	3.0 Sauber C17-Petronas V10	1 lap behind	18/22
ret	GERMAN GP	Hockenheim	15	Red Bull Sauber Petronas	G	3.0 Sauber C17-Petronas V10	gearbox	12/22
10	HUNGARIAN GP	Hungaroring	15	Red Bull Sauber Petronas	G	3.0 Sauber C17-Petronas V10	1 lap behind	15/22
ret	BELGIAN GP	Spa	15	Red Bull Sauber Petronas	G	3.0 Sauber C17-Petronas V10	collision with Häkkinen on lap 1	12/22
ret	ITALIAN GP	Monza	15	Red Bull Sauber Petronas	G	3.0 Sauber C17-Petronas V10	spun off	15/22
ret	LUXEMBOURG GP	Nürburgring	15	Red Bull Sauber Petronas	G	3.0 Sauber C17-Petronas V10	engine	13/22
10	JAPANESE GP	Suzuka	15	Red Bull Sauber Petronas	G	3.0 Sauber C17-Petronas V10	1 lap behind	11/22

1999   Championship position: 8   Wins: 1   Pole positions: 0   Fastest laps: 0   Points scored: 15

dns	AUSTRALIAN GP	Melbourne	17	Stewart Ford	B	3.0 Stewart SF3 Ford CR1 V10	oil leak before start	(13)/22
ret	BRAZILIAN GP	Interlagos	17	Stewart Ford	B	3.0 Stewart SF3 Ford CR1 V10	hydraulics	10/22
10/ret	SAN MARINO GP	Imola	17	Stewart Ford	B	3.0 Stewart SF3 Ford CR1 V10	engine/4 laps behind	12/22
ret	MONACO GP	Monte Carlo	17	Stewart Ford	B	3.0 Stewart SF3 Ford CR1 V10	suspension failure	13/22
ret	SPANISH GP	Barcelona	17	Stewart Ford	B	3.0 Stewart SF3 Ford CR1 V10	transmission	14/22
5	CANADIAN GP	Montreal	17	Stewart Ford	B	3.0 Stewart SF3 Ford CR1 V10		10/22
ret	FRENCH GP	Magny Cours	17	Stewart Ford	B	3.0 Stewart SF3 Ford CR1 V10	gearbox	9/22
12	BRITISH GP	Silverstone	17	Stewart Ford	B	3.0 Stewart SF3 Ford CR1 V10		11/22
14	AUSTRIAN GP	A1-Ring	17	Stewart Ford	B	3.0 Stewart SF3 Ford CR1 V10	collision damage new wing/-4 laps	6/22
11/ret	GERMAN GP	Hockenheim	17	Stewart Ford	B	3.0 Stewart SF3 Ford CR1 V10	gearbox/5 laps behind	17/22
11	HUNGARIAN GP	Hungaroring	17	Stewart Ford	B	3.0 Stewart SF3 Ford CR1 V10	1 lap behind	10/22
ret	BELGIAN GP	Spa	17	Stewart Ford	B	3.0 Stewart SF3 Ford CR1 V10	wheel bearing/brakes	10/22
ret	ITALIAN GP	Monza	17	Stewart Ford	B	3.0 Stewart SF3 Ford CR1 V10	clutch	15/22
1	EUROPEAN GP	Nürburgring	17	Stewart Ford	B	3.0 Stewart SF3 Ford CR1 V10		14/22
4	MALAYSIAN GP	Sepang	17	Stewart Ford	B	3.0 Stewart SF3 Ford CR1 V10		5/22
7	JAPANESE GP	Suzuka	17	Stewart Ford	B	3.0 Stewart SF3 Ford CR1 V10	1 lap behind	8/22

GP Starts: 144 (145)   GP Wins: 3   Pole positions: 0   Fastest laps: 0   Points: 98

HANS HERRMANN

Young Herrmann displayed considerable promise both in a Veritas (ninth in the German GP and fourth at the AVUSrennen) and a Porsche sports car in 1953, which earned him a golden opportunity to race for Mercedes-Benz on their return to Grand Prix and sports car racing in 1954. Although naturally somewhat overshadowed by his more experienced peers, he scored good championship finishes at Bremgarten and Monza, and took third behind Kling and Fangio in what amounted to a Mercedes demonstration race against meagre opposition at AVUS. He still drove for Porsche in sports cars, and won the support race at AVUS and another at the Nürburgring. Better still he took sixth in the Mille Miglia, again taking the up-to-1500 cc class, before venturing across to Mexico to compete in the Carrera Panamericana. In another superb drive, Hans took his Porsche 550 Spyder to third overall and naturally won his class.

Prospects were promising indeed for the young German in 1955, but after sharing fourth place with Moss and Kling in the searing heat of Argentina, a practice accident for the next Grand Prix at Monte Carlo left him in hospital with cracked vertebrae and broken ribs.

With Mercedes' withdrawal from racing after the Le Mans tragedy, Herrmann, now fully recovered, joined Porsche for 1956 and with von Trips he took sixth (and a class win) at Sebring. Sharing a Ferrari with Gendebien he was third in the Targa Florio that year, but would then become a mainstay of the Porsche team. He was third at Le Mans with Behra in 1958 and fourth in the Nürburgring 1000 Km the following year with Maglioli. Sadly his subsequent Grand Prix appearances were generally restricted to less-than-competitive machinery, and he caused a stir only with his spectacular crash in the 1959 German GP at AVUS, when he was thrown from his BRM, fortunately without serious injury.

Hans enjoyed some excellent drives in Formula 2 for Porsche in 1960, taking second at Solitude, fourth at Modena and fifth in the non-championship German Grand Prix, but found real success throughout the decade in sports cars, winning the Sebring 12 Hours (1960 and 1968), the Daytona 24 Hours (1968), the Targa Florio (1960) and the Paris 1000 Km (1968). He was of course involved in the incredible finish at Le Mans in 1969 when his Porsche was pipped by Jacky Ickx's Ford, but he made amends a year later to bow out on a high note, retiring from racing after winning the Sarthe classic in a Porsche 917 with Richard Attwood.

FRANÇOIS HESNAULT

It was some surprise when Hesnault was drafted into the Ligier team in 1984, for his credentials showed only a single second-place finish in a round of the previous year's European F3 championship. However, the Frenchman acquitted himself respectably enough, sometimes proving more than a match for his team-mate Andrea de Cesaris, particularly at Dijon.

A move to Brabham in 1985 proved a big let-down, with a shaken Hesnault leaving the team after being lucky to escape injury in a massive testing accident at Paul Ricard. He did, however, reappear later in the season, at the wheel of a Renault which was acting as a camera car in the German Grand Prix.

HANS HEYER

With a natty Tyrolean hat as his trademark, Hans Heyer was a popular figure in seventies touring car racing. He was European touring car champion in 1974 driving a Ford Escort RS2000, and among his wins that year was the prestigious round at the Nürburgring where, after 38 laps and 531.18 miles of racing, Hans and Klaus Ludwig defeated the 3-litre Capri of Niki Lauda/Toine Hezemans/Dieter Glemser.

In subsequent seasons he raced a Porsche 934 turbo, taking second at Imola in 1976, produced another superb drive to claim third place and a class win at the Nürburgring in 1977 in an RS 1800 Escort, and then drove a Mercedes 450SLC to third places at Monza and the Salzburgring the following year.

His appearance in this section of the book is rather made under false pretences for he failed to qualify the ATS-entered Penske and was placed as third reserve. Somehow he managed to get onto the grid for his only Grand Prix start. He was subsequently disqualified, but his race had already ended with a gear linkage failure.

HERRMANN, Hans (D) b 23/2/1928, Stuttgart

1953 Championship position: Unplaced

	Race	Circuit	No	Entrant	Tyres	Car/Engine	Comment	Q Pos/Entries
9	GERMAN GP	Nürburgring	31	Hans Herrmann	–	2.0 Veritas Meteor 6	1 lap behind	14/35

1954 Championship position: 6th Wins: 0 Pole positions: 0 Fastest laps: 1 Points scored: 8

	Race	Circuit	No	Entrant	Tyres	Car/Engine	Comment	Q Pos/Entries
ret	FRENCH GP	Reims	22	Daimler Benz AG	C	2.5 Mercedes Benz W196 8 str	engine/FL	7/22
ret	GERMAN GP	Nürburgring	20	Daimler Benz AG	C	2.5 Mercedes Benz W196 8 str	fuel pipe	4/23
3	SWISS GP	Bremgarten	6	Daimler Benz AG	C	2.5 Mercedes Benz W196 8	1 lap behind	7/16
4	ITALIAN GP	Monza	12	Daimler Benz AG	C	2.5 Mercedes Benz W196 8	pit stop-plugs/3 laps behind	8/21
ret	SPANISH GP	Pedralbes	6	Daimler Benz AG	C	2.5 Mercedes Benz W196 8	fuel injection pump	9/22

1955 Championship position: 17th= Wins: 0 Pole positions: 0 Fastest laps: 0 Points scored: 1

	Race	Circuit	No	Entrant	Tyres	Car/Engine	Comment	Q Pos/Entries
4*	ARGENTINE GP	Buenos Aires	8	Daimler Benz AG	C	2.5 Mercedes Benz W196 8	* Moss & Kling co-drove/-2 laps	10/22
dns	MONACO GP	Monte Carlo	4	Daimler Benz AG	C	2.5 Mercedes Benz W196 8	accident-internal injuries	– / –

1957 Championship position: Unplaced

	Race	Circuit	No	Entrant	Tyres	Car/Engine	Comment	Q Pos/Entries
dnq	MONACO GP	Monte Carlo	40	Officine Alfieri Maserati	P	2.5 Maserati 250F 6		18/21
ret	GERMAN GP	Nürburgring	17	Scuderia Centro Sud	P	2.5 Maserati 250F 6	broken chassis	11/24

1958 Championship position: Unplaced

	Race	Circuit	No	Entrant	Tyres	Car/Engine	Comment	Q Pos/Entries
ret	GERMAN GP	Nürburgring	17	Scuderia Centro Sud	P	2.5 Maserati 250F 6	engine	20/26
ret	ITALIAN GP	Monza	24	Jo Bonnier	P	2.5 Maserati 250F 6	engine	18/21
9	MOROCCAN GP	Casablanca	24	Jo Bonnier	P	2.5 Maserati 250F 6	3 laps behind	18/25

1959 Championship position: Unplaced

	Race	Circuit	No	Entrant	Tyres	Car/Engine	Comment	Q Pos/Entries
ret	BRITISH GP	Aintree	24	Scuderia Centro Sud	D	2.5 Cooper T51-Maserati 4	clutch	19/30
ret	GERMAN GP	AVUS	11	British Racing Partnership	D	2.5 BRM P25 4	8 heat 1/crashed heat 2	11/16

1960 Championship position: 19th= Wins: 0 Pole positions: 0 Fastest laps: 0 Points scored: 1

	Race	Circuit	No	Entrant	Tyres	Car/Engine	Comment	Q Pos/Entries
6	ITALIAN GP	Monza	26	Porsche System Engineering	D	1.5 Porsche 718 F4	F2 car/3 laps behind	10/16

1961 Championship position: Unplaced

	Race	Circuit	No	Entrant	Tyres	Car/Engine	Comment	Q Pos/Entries
9	MONACO GP	Monte Carlo	6	Porsche System Engineering	D	1.5 Porsche 718 F4	pit stop/9 laps behind	12/21
15	DUTCH GP	Zandvoort	9	Ecurie Maarsbergen	D	1.5 Porsche 718 F4	3 laps behind	13/17
13	GERMAN GP	Nürburgring	11	Porsche System Engineering	D	1.5 Porsche 718 F4	1 lap behind	11/27

1966 Championship position: Unplaced

	Race	Circuit	No	Entrant	Tyres	Car/Engine	Comment	Q Pos/Entries
11*	GERMAN GP (F2)	Nürburgring	28	Roy Winkelmann Racing	–	1.0 Brabham BT18-Cosworth 4 F2	* 4th in F2 class/1 lap behind	23/30

1969 Championship position: Unplaced

	Race	Circuit	No	Entrant	Tyres	Car/Engine	Comment	Q Pos/Entries
dns	GERMAN GP (F2)	Nürburgring	21	Roy Winkelmann Racing	F	1.6 Lotus 59B-Cosworth 4	withdrawn after Mitter's accident	(26)/26

GP Starts: 18 GP Wins: 0 Pole positions: 0 Fastest laps: 1 Points: 10

HESNAULT, François (F) b 30/12/1956, Neuilly-sur-Seine, nr Paris

1984 Championship position: Unplaced

	Race	Circuit	No	Entrant	Tyres	Car/Engine	Comment	Q Pos/Entries
ret	BRAZILIAN GP	Rio	25	Ligier Loto	M	1.5 t/c Ligier JS23-Renault V6	overheating	20/27
10	SOUTH AFRICAN GP	Kyalami	25	Ligier Loto	M	1.5 t/c Ligier JS23-Renault V6	hit by Brundle/4 laps behind	17/27
ret	BELGIAN GP	Zolder	25	Ligier Loto	M	1.5 t/c Ligier JS23-Renault V6	radiator	23/27
ret	SAN MARINO GP	Imola	25	Ligier Loto	M	1.5 t/c Ligier JS23-Renault V6	hit by Laffite	17/28
dns	FRENCH GP	Dijon	25	Ligier Loto	M	1.5 t/c Ligier JS23-Renault V6	withdrawn to allow de Cesaris in	(15)/27
ret	MONACO GP	Monte Carlo	25	Ligier Loto	M	1.5 t/c Ligier JS23-Renault V6	water in the electrics	17/27
ret	CANADIAN GP	Montreal	25	Ligier Loto	M	1.5 t/c Ligier JS23-Renault V6	turbo	13/26
ret	US GP (DETROIT)	Detroit	25	Ligier Loto	M	1.5 t/c Ligier JS23-Renault V6	accident with Ghinzani	18/27
ret	US GP (DALLAS)	Dallas	25	Ligier Loto	M	1.5 t/c Ligier JS23-Renault V6	hit wall-lap 1	19/27
ret	BRITISH GP	Brands Hatch	25	Ligier Loto	M	1.5 t/c Ligier JS23-Renault V6	electrics	20/27
8	GERMAN GP	Hockenheim	25	Ligier Loto	M	1.5 t/c Ligier JS23-Renault V6	1 lap behind	17/27
8	AUSTRIAN GP	Österreichring	25	Ligier Loto	M	1.5 t/c Ligier JS23-Renault V6	2 laps behind	21/28
7	DUTCH GP	Zandvoort	25	Ligier Loto	M	1.5 t/c Ligier JS23-Renault V6	2 laps behind	20/27
ret	ITALIAN GP	Monza	25	Ligier Loto	M	1.5 t/c Ligier JS23-Renault V6	spun off	18/27
10	EUROPEAN GP	Nürburgring	25	Ligier Loto	M	1.5 t/c Ligier JS23-Renault V6	3 laps behind	19/26
ret	PORTUGUESE GP	Estoril	25	Ligier Loto	M	1.5 t/c Ligier JS23-Renault V6	electrics	21/27

1985 Championship position: Unplaced

	Race	Circuit	No	Entrant	Tyres	Car/Engine	Comment	Q Pos/Entries
ret	BRAZILIAN GP	Rio	8	Motor Racing Developments	P	1.5 t/c Brabham BT54-BMW 4	accident	17/25
ret	PORTUGUESE GP	Estoril	8	Motor Racing Developments	P	1.5 t/c Brabham BT54-BMW 4	electrics	19/26
ret	SAN MARINO GP	Imola	8	Motor Racing Developments	P	1.5 t/c Brabham BT54-BMW 4	engine	20/26
dnq	MONACO GP	Monte Carlo	8	Motor Racing Developments	P	1.5 t/c Brabham BT54-BMW 4		25/26
ret	GERMAN GP	Nürburgring	14	Equipe Renault Elf	G	1.5 t/c Renault RE60 V6	clutch	23/27

GP Starts: 19 GP Wins: 0 Pole positions: 0 Fastest laps: 0 Points: 0

HEYER, Hans (D) b 16/3/1943, Mönchengladbach

1977 Championship position: Unplaced

	Race	Circuit	No	Entrant	Tyres	Car/Engine	Comment	Q Pos/Entries
dnq/ret	GERMAN GP	Hockenheim	35	ATS Racing Team	G	3.0 Penske PC4-Cosworth V8	dnq-started illegally/gear linkage	27/30

GP Starts: 1 GP Wins: 0 Pole positions: 0 Fastest laps: 0 Points: 0

DAMON HILL

Damon has earned his success the hard way for, just like his father Graham, he has had to work his way up to the top with plenty of determination but little in the way of the financial help which is such a crucial element in modern-day racing. Sadly, of course, his illustrious father has not been able to offer him the benefit of his experience, but it is to Damon's great credit that, once he had decided on a career in motor sport, he progressed entirely on his own merits. There can have been no one in the F1 paddock who begrudged him his success when, in 1996, he emulated his father in winning the World Championship.

In fact, at first he was more interested in bikes than cars and made his competition debut on two wheels, which led him into a job as a despatch rider while he worked on his fledgling career. After a brief taste of Formula Ford at the end of 1983, Hill found himself drawn into the world of motor racing and, with the help of Brands Hatch supremo John Webb in the form of free tuition and a little promotion, he went racing seriously in 1985, enjoying a very competitive year of Formula Ford. His elevation to F3 for 1986 with Murray Taylor Racing may have been a little premature, but he finished ninth in the championship and then proved himself in the formula during a two-year spell at Intersport, winning splendidly at Zandvoort and Spa in 1987 and taking two more victories in 1988, including the prestigious Grand Prix support race at Silverstone.

Damon then moved up to F3000 for 1989 and gave a good account of himself in the troubled Footwork before switching to Middlebridge the following year, when luck was not on his side in terms of results but more importantly he established himself as a genuine racer, capable of beating anyone in the field. A third year of F3000 in 1991 should have brought some real success at last but his Lola was no match for the Reynards and his first win remained elusive. There was, however, the consolation of a Williams testing contract, and the following year his work for the team helped ensure that the damage to his reputation arising from a calamitous half-season with Brabham, when he managed to qualify only twice, was merely superficial. So impressed was Patrick Head with his contribution that he was to be Damon's strongest advocate when the chance of a Grand Prix drive with the team in 1993 arose.

The way he handled his first year in a top team was exemplary in every respect. Unfazed by a couple of early gaffes at Kyalami and Imola, Hill pushed team leader Alain Prost harder and harder as the season wore on, while remaining acutely aware of the delicate political situation within the team. The fact that he won three Grands Prix was a bonus, his drive at Spa when he withstood severe pressure from Schumacher demonstrating that he had the stuff of which real winners are made. In 1994 he faced his biggest test with the arrival of Ayrton Senna. Tragically, within three races, Damon was facing the task of rebuilding shattered morale at Williams in the way his father had done at Lotus in 1968. In Damon's case, he still had comparatively little experience and rose to the challenge magnificently. Nigel Mansell's return in France prompted Hill to raise his game and push back the veteran's claim to a full-time seat alongside him, then at Silverstone came a win in the British Grand Prix, a triumph made so special because it is a race Graham never won.

In a season of drama and controversy, Damon took advantage of Schumacher's disqualifications and enforced absence through suspension to close the gap enough to enable him to still win the championship. A superb drive in the wet at Suzuka was worthy of the German at his best, and it was all to play for in Adelaide. The manner in which the title was decided when Schumacher bounced back off the wall into Hill's path was unsatisfactory to say the least, and his critics thought Hill should have avoided the situation. In any event, the title was lost, but Damon's exemplary reaction in the aftermath spoke volumes for him as a person.

The slate was wiped clean for 1995 and with the latest Williams FW17 in formidable form Hill set out on the championship trail with renewed vigour. A potential victory in Brazil was lost with suspension failure, but two consecutive wins seemed to indicate that the Englishman was on course for the title. Unfortunately Schumacher and Benetton had other ideas and Damon soon found himself on the ropes as the German ruthlessly exploited every weakness in the Williams armour. It was not until Hungary that the tide was stemmed, but, just as in boxing, winning occasional rounds does not win the fight and, despite his dominant performance in the final race at Adelaide, this World Championship bout went to Schumacher on points by a comfortable margin.

When you have a multi-million-dollar contract and you drive for one of the world's leading Grand Prix teams, then expectations are naturally high, as Hill had found during the two seasons he had been leading the Williams challenge. For such a polite and genuinely decent individual it must have been hurtful to have been thrown more brickbats than bouquets by a despicable element of the press, who lay waiting to pounce on any error with glee. It goes with the territory, they would say, but the treatment meted out to him at times during this period was disgraceful.

Undoubtedly the 1996 season was Damon's best-ever chance of taking the championship and with the advantage of his major rivals bedding down in new teams, and a rookie partner in Jacques Villeneuve, he could have no excuses if he failed. In the event, of course, mission was accomplished, with the popular Englishman winning eight of the sixteen races to pip his team-mate to the crown. The only shadow across his season was the decision by Frank Williams to dispense with his services in favour of Heinz-Harald Frentzen, leaving Damon with no chance to secure a top ride in 1997.

So, after protracted negotiations with Jordan, Hill threw in his lot with Tom Walkinshaw at Arrows amid much brave talk of winning races. In the event he very nearly did, a superb drive in Hungary bringing second place when the car hit trouble on the penultimate lap. Otherwise it was a different story as the unfancied team struggled to make an impact, with Damon and his ambitious employer failing to see eye to eye. After negotiations with both McLaren and Prost, Hill joined up with Eddie Jordan for '98, tempted by a healthy retainer and the prospect of Mugen Honda-powered cars. At first it seemed like a huge mistake for all concerned, Hill struggling to make any impact in a poorly developed car, and it wasn't until the air was cleared in mid-season that things moved in the right direction. Fourth places at Hockenheim and the Hungaroring preceded the now famous wet-race win at Spa with which Damon was finally able to realise Eddie Jordan's dreams of victory.

Grand Prix racing has little room for sentiment, however, as Hill was soon to find in 1999 when he was comprehensively overshadowed by his new team-mate Heinz-Harald Frentzen. So unhappy was Damon with his performances in the new generation of Formula 1 car that he contemplated immediate retirement after a miserable showing in the French Grand Prix. As it transpired, he continued in tentative fashion until the season's end. Physically, Damon had emerged unscathed but, sadly, his reputation had received a severe bruising.

HILL, Damon (GB) b 17/9/1960, Hampstead, London

1992 — Championship position: Unplaced

	Race	Circuit	No	Entrant	Tyres	Car/Engine	Comment	Q Pos/Entries
dnq	SPANISH GP	Barcelona	8	Motor Racing Developments Ltd	G	3.5 Brabham BT60B-Judd V10		30/32
dnq	SAN MARINO GP	Imola	8	Motor Racing Developments Ltd	G	3.5 Brabham BT60B-Judd V10		29/32
dnq	MONACO GP	Monte Carlo	8	Motor Racing Developments Ltd	G	3.5 Brabham BT60B-Judd V10		28/32
dnq	CANADIAN GP	Montreal	8	Motor Racing Developments Ltd	G	3.5 Brabham BT60B-Judd V10		30/32
dnq	FRENCH GP	Magny Cours	8	Motor Racing Developments Ltd	G	3.5 Brabham BT60B-Judd V10		30/30
16	BRITISH GP	Silverstone	8	Motor Racing Developments Ltd	G	3.5 Brabham BT60B-Judd V10	4 laps behind	26/32
dnq	GERMAN GP	Hockenheim	8	Motor Racing Developments Ltd	G	3.5 Brabham BT60B-Judd V10		30/32
11	HUNGARIAN GP	Hungaroring	8	Motor Racing Developments Ltd	G	3.5 Brabham BT60B-Judd V10	4 laps behind	25/31

1993 — Championship position: 3rd Wins: 3 Pole positions: 2 Fastest laps: 4 Points scored: 69

	Race	Circuit	No	Entrant	Tyres	Car/Engine	Comment	Q Pos/Entries
ret	SOUTH AFRICAN GP	Kyalami	0	Canon Williams Team	G	3.5 Williams FW15C-Renault V10	accident with Zanardi	4/26
2	BRAZILIAN GP	Interlagos	0	Canon Williams Team	G	3.5 Williams FW15C-Renault V10		2/26
2	EUROPEAN GP	Donington	0	Canon Williams Team	G	3.5 Williams FW15C-Renault V10		2/26
ret	SAN MARINO GP	Imola	0	Canon Williams Team	G	3.5 Williams FW15C-Renault V10	spun off	2/26
ret	SPANISH GP	Barcelona	0	Canon Williams Team	G	3.5 Williams FW15C-Renault V10	engine	2/26
2	MONACO GP	Monte Carlo	0	Canon Williams Team	G	3.5 Williams FW15C-Renault V10	despite collision with Berger	4/26
3	CANADIAN GP	Montreal	0	Canon Williams Team	G	3.5 Williams FW15C-Renault V10		2/26
2	FRENCH GP	Magny Cours	0	Canon Williams Team	G	3.5 Williams FW15C-Renault V10		1/26
ret	BRITISH GP	Silverstone	0	Canon Williams Team	G	3.5 Williams FW15C-Renault V10	engine/FL	2/26
15/ret	GERMAN GP	Hockenheim	0	Canon Williams Team	G	3.5 Williams FW15C-Renault V10	blown tyre when leading/-2 laps	2/26
1	HUNGARIAN GP	Hungaroring	0	Canon Williams Team	G	3.5 Williams FW15C-Renault V10		2/26
1	BELGIAN GP	Spa	0	Canon Williams Team	G	3.5 Williams FW15C-Renault V10		2/25
1	ITALIAN GP	Monza	0	Canon Williams Team	G	3.5 Williams FW15C-Renault V10	FL	2/26
3	PORTUGUESE GP	Estoril	0	Canon Williams Team	G	3.5 Williams FW15C-Renault V10	started from back of grid/FL	1/26
4	JAPANESE GP	Suzuka	0	Canon Williams Team	G	3.5 Williams FW15C-Renault V10	pit stop-puncture	6/24
3	AUSTRALIAN GP	Adelaide	0	Canon Williams Team	G	3.5 Williams FW15C-Renault V10	FL	3/24

1994 — Championship position: 2nd Wins: 6 Pole positions: 2 Fastest laps: 6 Points scored: 91

	Race	Circuit	No	Entrant	Tyres	Car/Engine	Comment	Q Pos/Entries
2	BRAZILIAN GP	Interlagos	0	Rothmans Williams Renault	G	3.5 Williams FW16-Renault V10	1 lap behind	4/28
ret	PACIFIC GP	T.I. Circuit	0	Rothmans Williams Renault	G	3.5 Williams FW16-Renault V10	transmission	3/28
6	SAN MARINO GP	Imola	0	Rothmans Williams Renault	G	3.5 Williams FW16-Renault V10	pit stop-collision damage/FL	4/28
ret	MONACO GP	Monte Carlo	0	Rothmans Williams Renault	G	3.5 Williams FW16-Renault V10	first corner collision-Häkkinen	4/24
1	SPANISH GP	Barcelona	0	Rothmans Williams Renault	G	3.5 Williams FW16-Renault V10		2/27
2	CANADIAN GP	Montreal	0	Rothmans Williams Renault	G	3.5 Williams FW16-Renault V10		4/27
2	FRENCH GP	Magny Cours	0	Rothmans Williams Renault	G	3.5 Williams FW16-Renault V10	FL	1/28
1	BRITISH GP	Silverstone	0	Rothmans Williams Renault	G	3.5 Williams FW16-Renault V10	FL	1/28
8	GERMAN GP	Hockenheim	0	Rothmans Williams Renault	G	3.5 Williams FW16B-Renault V10	collision-Katayama/-1 lap	3/28
2	HUNGARIAN GP	Hungaroring	0	Rothmans Williams Renault	G	3.5 Williams FW16B-Renault V10		2/28
1*	BELGIAN GP	Spa	0	Rothmans Williams Renault	G	3.5 Williams FW16B-Renault V10	*1st place car dsq/FL	3/28
1	ITALIAN GP	Monza	0	Rothmans Williams Renault	G	3.5 Williams FW16B-Renault V10	FL	3/28
1	PORTUGUESE GP	Estoril	0	Rothmans Williams Renault	G	3.5 Williams FW16B-Renault V10		2/28
2	EUROPEAN GP	Jerez	0	Rothmans Williams Renault	G	3.5 Williams FW16B-Renault V10		2/28
1	JAPANESE GP	Suzuka	0	Rothmans Williams Renault	G	3.5 Williams FW16B-Renault V10	FL	2/28
ret	AUSTRALIAN GP	Adelaide	0	Rothmans Williams Renault	G	3.5 Williams FW16B-Renault V10	collision with Schumacher	3/28

1995 — Championship position: 2nd Wins: 4 Pole positions: 7 Fastest laps: 4 Points scored: 69

	Race	Circuit	No	Entrant	Tyres	Car/Engine	Comment	Q Pos/Entries
ret	BRAZILIAN GP	Interlagos	5	Rothmans Williams Renault	G	3.0 Williams FW17-Renault V10	suspension	1/26
1	ARGENTINE GP	Buenos Aires	5	Rothmans Williams Renault	G	3.0 Williams FW17-Renault V10		2/26
1	SAN MARINO GP	Imola	5	Rothmans Williams Renault	G	3.0 Williams FW17-Renault V10		4/26
4	SPANISH GP	Barcelona	5	Rothmans Williams Renault	G	3.0 Williams FW17-Renault V10	FL	5/26
2	MONACO GP	Monte Carlo	5	Rothmans Williams Renault	G	3.0 Williams FW17-Renault V10		1/26
ret	CANADIAN GP	Montreal	5	Rothmans Williams Renault	G	3.0 Williams FW17-Renault V10	gearbox	2/24
2	FRENCH GP	Magny Cours	5	Rothmans Williams Renault	G	3.0 Williams FW17-Renault V10		1/24
ret	BRITISH GP	Silverstone	5	Rothmans Williams Renault	G	3.0 Williams FW17-Renault V10	collision with Schumacher/FL	1/24
ret	GERMAN GP	Hockenheim	5	Rothmans Williams Renault	G	3.0 Williams FW17-Renault V10	spun off	1/24
1	HUNGARIAN GP	Hungaroring	5	Rothmans Williams Renault	G	3.0 Williams FW17-Renault V10	FL	1/24
2	BELGIAN GP	Spa	5	Rothmans Williams Renault	G	3.0 Williams FW17-Renault V10	stop & go pen/speeding in pits	8/24
ret	ITALIAN GP	Monza	5	Rothmans Williams Renault	G	3.0 Williams FW17-Renault V10	ran into back of Schumacher	4/24
3	PORTUGUESE GP	Estoril	5	Rothmans Williams Renault	G	3.0 Williams FW17-Renault V10		2/24
ret	EUROPEAN GP	Nürburgring	5	Rothmans Williams Renault	G	3.0 Williams FW17B-Renault V10	collision-Alesi/later spun off	2/24
3	PACIFIC GP	T.I. Circuit	5	Rothmans Williams Renault	G	3.0 Williams FW17B-Renault V10		2/24
ret	JAPANESE GP	Suzuka	5	Rothmans Williams Renault	G	3.0 Williams FW17B-Renault V10	stop & go penalty/later spun off	4/24
1	AUSTRALIAN GP	Adelaide	5	Rothmans Williams Renault	G	3.0 Williams FW17B-Renault V10	FL	1/24

1996 — Championship position: WORLD CHAMPION Wins: 8 Pole positions: 9 Fastest laps: 5 Points scored: 97

	Race	Circuit	No	Entrant	Tyres	Car/Engine	Comment	Q Pos/Entries
1	AUSTRALIAN GP	Melbourne	5	Rothmans Williams Renault	G	3.0 Williams FW18-Renault V10		2/22
1	BRAZILIAN GP	Interlagos	5	Rothmans Williams Renault	G	3.0 Williams FW18-Renault V10	FL	1/22
1	ARGENTINE GP	Buenos Aires	5	Rothmans Williams Renault	G	3.0 Williams FW18-Renault V10		1/22
4	EUROPEAN GP	Nürburgring	5	Rothmans Williams Renault	G	3.0 Williams FW18-Renault V10	poor start/slow pitstop/FL	1/22
1	SAN MARINO GP	Imola	5	Rothmans Williams Renault	G	3.0 Williams FW18-Renault V10	FL	2/22
ret	MONACO GP	Monte Carlo	5	Rothmans Williams Renault	G	3.0 Williams FW18-Renault V10	engine/led race	2/22
ret	SPANISH GP	Barcelona	5	Rothmans Williams Renault	G	3.0 Williams FW18-Renault V10	spun off	1/22
1	CANADIAN GP	Montreal	5	Rothmans Williams Renault	G	3.0 Williams FW18-Renault V10		1/22
1	FRENCH GP	Magny Cours	5	Rothmans Williams Renault	G	3.0 Williams FW18-Renault V10		2/22
ret	BRITISH GP	Silverstone	5	Rothmans Williams Renault	G	3.0 Williams FW18-Renault V10	wheel bearing failure-spun off	1/22
1	GERMAN GP	Hockenheim	5	Rothmans Williams Renault	G	3.0 Williams FW18-Renault V10	FL	1/20
2	HUNGARIAN GP	Hungaroring	5	Rothmans Williams Renault	G	3.0 Williams FW18-Renault V10	FL	2/20
5	BELGIAN GP	Spa	5	Rothmans Williams Renault	G	3.0 Williams FW18-Renault V10	long pit stop	2/20
ret	ITALIAN GP	Monza	5	Rothmans Williams Renault	G	3.0 Williams FW18-Renault V10	clipped tyre stack-spun off	1/20
2	PORTUGUESE GP	Estoril	5	Rothmans Williams Renault	G	3.0 Williams FW18-Renault V10		1/20
1	JAPANESE GP	Suzuka	5	Rothmans Williams Renault	G	3.0 Williams FW18-Renault V10		2/20

On top of the world. Damon in his title-winning season for Williams, 1996, heading for his fifth victory of the year in the Canadian Grand Prix in Montreal.

1997
Championship position: 12th   Wins: 0   Pole positions: 0   Fastest laps: 0   Points scored: 7

dns	AUSTRALIAN GP	Melbourne	1	Danka Arrows Yamaha	B	3.0 Arrows A18-Yamaha V10	throttle sensor on parade lap	20/24
17/ret	BRAZILIAN GP	Interlagos	1	Danka Arrows Yamaha	B	3.0 Arrows A18-Yamaha V10	engine fire	9/22
ret	ARGENTINE GP	Buenos Aires	1	Danka Arrows Yamaha	B	3.0 Arrows A18-Yamaha V10	engine	13/22
ret	SAN MARINO GP	Imola	1	Danka Arrows Yamaha	B	3.0 Arrows A18-Yamaha V10	ran into back of Nakano	15/22
ret	MONACO GP	Monte Carlo	1	Danka Arrows Yamaha	B	3.0 Arrows A18-Yamaha V10	collision with Irvine	13/22
ret	SPANISH GP	Barcelona	1	Danka Arrows Yamaha	B	3.0 Arrows A18-Yamaha V10	engine	15/22
9	CANADIAN GP	Montreal	1	Danka Arrows Yamaha	B	3.0 Arrows A18-Yamaha V10	1 lap behind	15/22
12	FRENCH GP	Magny Cours	1	Danka Arrows Yamaha	B	3.0 Arrows A18-Yamaha V10	3 laps behind	17/22
6	BRITISH GP	Silverstone	1	Danka Arrows Yamaha	B	3.0 Arrows A18-Yamaha V10		12/22
8	GERMAN GP	Hockenheim	1	Danka Arrows Yamaha	B	3.0 Arrows A18-Yamaha V10	1 lap behind	13/22
2	HUNGARIAN GP	Hungaroring	1	Danka Arrows Yamaha	B	3.0 Arrows A18-Yamaha V10	led race until hydraulic problem	3/22
13*/ret	BELGIAN GP	Spa	1	Danka Arrows Yamaha	B	3.0 Arrows A18-Yamaha V10	wheel nut/*3rd place car dsq	9/22
ret	ITALIAN GP	Monza	1	Danka Arrows Yamaha	B	3.0 Arrows A18-Yamaha V10	engine	14/22
7	AUSTRIAN GP	A1-Ring	1	Danka Arrows Yamaha	B	3.0 Arrows A18-Yamaha V10		7/22
8	LUXEMBOURG GP	Nürburgring	1	Danka Arrows Yamaha	B	3.0 Arrows A18-Yamaha V10		13/22
11*	JAPANESE GP	Suzuka	1	Danka Arrows Yamaha	B	3.0 Arrows A18-Yamaha V10	*5th place car dsq/-1 lap	17/22
ret	EUROPEAN GP	Jerez	1	Danka Arrows Yamaha	B	3.0 Arrows A18-Yamaha V10	hydraulics	4/22

1998
Championship position: 6   Wins: 1   Pole positions: 0   Fastest laps: 0   Points scored: 20

8	AUSTRALIAN GP	Melbourne	9	B & H Jordan Mugen Honda	G	3.0 Jordan 198-Mugen Honda V10	1 lap behind	10/22
dsq*	BRAZILIAN GP	Interlagos	9	B & H Jordan Mugen Honda	G	3.0 Jordan 198-Mugen Honda V10	* car under weight/10th on road	11/22
8	ARGENTINE GP	Buenos Aires	9	B & H Jordan Mugen Honda	G	3.0 Jordan 198-Mugen Honda V10	1 lap behind	9/22
10/ret	SAN MARINO GP	Imola	9	B & H Jordan Mugen Honda	G	3.0 Jordan 198-Mugen Honda V10	engine/5 laps behind	7/22
ret	SPANISH GP	Barcelona	9	B & H Jordan Mugen Honda	G	3.0 Jordan 198-Mugen Honda V10	engine	8/22
8	MONACO GP	Monte Carlo	9	B & H Jordan Mugen Honda	G	3.0 Jordan 198-Mugen Honda V10	2 laps behind	15/22
ret	CANADIAN GP	Montreal	9	B & H Jordan Mugen Honda	G	3.0 Jordan 198-Mugen Honda V10	electrics	10/22
ret	FRENCH GP	Magny Cours	9	B & H Jordan Mugen Honda	G	3.0 Jordan 198-Mugen Honda V10	hydraulics	7/22
ret	BRITISH GP	Silverstone	9	B & H Jordan Mugen Honda	G	3.0 Jordan 198-Mugen Honda V10	spun off	7/22
7	AUSTRIAN GP	A1-Ring	9	B & H Jordan Mugen Honda	G	3.0 Jordan 198-Mugen Honda V10		15/22
4	GERMAN GP	Hockenheim	9	B & H Jordan Mugen Honda	G	3.0 Jordan 198-Mugen Honda V10		5/22
4	HUNGARIAN GP	Hungaroring	9	B & H Jordan Mugen Honda	G	3.0 Jordan 198-Mugen Honda V10		4/22
1	BELGIAN GP	Spa	9	B & H Jordan Mugen Honda	G	3.0 Jordan 198-Mugen Honda V10	first win for Jordan	3/22
6	ITALIAN GP	Monza	9	B & H Jordan Mugen Honda	G	3.0 Jordan 198-Mugen Honda V10		14/22
9	LUXEMBOURG GP	Nürburgring	9	B & H Jordan Mugen Honda	G	3.0 Jordan 198-Mugen Honda V10	1 lap behind	10/22
4	JAPANESE GP	Suzuka	9	B & H Jordan Mugen Honda	G	3.0 Jordan 198-Mugen Honda V10		8/22

1999
Championship position: 11=-   Wins: 0   Pole positions: 0   Fastest laps: 0   Points scored: 7

ret	AUSTRALIAN GP	Melbourne	7	Benson & Hedges Jordan	B	3.0 Jordan 199-Mugen Honda V10	lap 1 collision-Trulli spun off	9/22
ret	BRAZILIAN GP	Interlagos	7	Benson & Hedges Jordan	B	3.0 Jordan 199-Mugen Honda V10	collision with Wurz	7/22
4	SAN MARINO GP	Imola	7	Benson & Hedges Jordan	B	3.0 Jordan 199-Mugen Honda V10	1 lap behind	8/22
ret	MONACO GP	Monte Carlo	7	Benson & Hedges Jordan	B	3.0 Jordan 199-Mugen Honda V10	collision with Ralf Schumacher	17/22
7	SPANISH GP	Barcelona	7	Benson & Hedges Jordan	B	3.0 Jordan 199-Mugen Honda V10	1 lap behind	11/22
ret	CANADIAN GP	Montreal	7	Benson & Hedges Jordan	B	3.0 Jordan 199-Mugen Honda V10	crashed	14/22
ret	FRENCH GP	Magny Cours	7	Benson & Hedges Jordan	B	3.0 Jordan 199-Mugen Honda V10	engine	18/22
5	BRITISH GP	Silverstone	7	Benson & Hedges Jordan	B	3.0 Jordan 199-Mugen Honda V10		6/22
8	AUSTRIAN GP	A1-Ring	7	Benson & Hedges Jordan	B	3.0 Jordan 199-Mugen Honda V10	1 lap behind	11/22
ret	GERMAN GP	Hockenheim	7	Benson & Hedges Jordan	B	3.0 Jordan 199-Mugen Honda V10	unhappy with brakes	8/22
6	HUNGARIAN GP	Hungaroring	7	Benson & Hedges Jordan	B	3.0 Jordan 199-Mugen Honda V10		6/22
6	BELGIAN GP	Spa	7	Benson & Hedges Jordan	B	3.0 Jordan 199-Mugen Honda V10		4/22
10	ITALIAN GP	Monza	7	Benson & Hedges Jordan	B	3.0 Jordan 199-Mugen Honda V10	lost time in pitstop	9/22
ret	EUROPEAN GP	Nürburgring	7	Benson & Hedges Jordan	B	3.0 Jordan 199-Mugen Honda V10	electrics	7/22
ret	MALAYSIAN GP	Sepang	7	Benson & Hedges Jordan	B	3.0 Jordan 199-Mugen Honda V10	collision with Fisichella	9/22
ret	JAPANESE GP	Suzuka	7	Benson & Hedges Jordan	B	3.0 Jordan 199-Mugen Honda V10	driver retired car	12/22

GP Starts: 116   GP Wins: 22   Pole positions: 20   Fastest laps: 19   Points: 360

GRAHAM HILL
WORLD CHAMPION: 1962 & 1968

GRAHAM HILL

Universally popular, Graham captured the public's imagination like no other racing driver of the period. Ordinary people, particularly those who had only a passing interest in the sport, took to this suave but somehow homely character, who could charm and amuse in a way which, say, the reserved Clark, opinionated Surtees or rather earnest Stewart could not – due in part, perhaps, to the fact that he had started his career from nothing and shown unbelievable single-mindedness and much courage, not to mention an appetite for hard work, to reach the very top of his profession.

The early days were spent scrounging drives in return for his services as a mechanic, before he began racing regularly in 1956 in Lotus and Cooper sports cars. In fact, he was working as a mechanic for Colin Chapman, who didn't consider him that seriously as a driver until he had proved himself elsewhere. When Lotus entered Grand Prix racing in 1958, Graham was back as a driver, making his debut at Monaco, where a wheel fell off. His two seasons with the fragile Lotus 16 were largely unsuccessful, the cars suffering all sorts of failures.

For 1960 he joined BRM, who had won a Grand Prix and were theoretically better placed to further his career. He missed the chance of his first Grand Prix win at Silverstone that year when, having taken the lead from Jack Brabham, a slight error brought a heavy penalty when he spun into retirement. If outright victory was still elusive, then at least he was now finishing races, and consolidating his position as a fine all-rounder by driving for Porsche in Formula 2 and sports cars, taking third and a class win in the Buenos Aires 1000 Km with Bonnier. After another barren year in 1961 when the British four-cylinder cars were outclassed by Ferrari, it was win or bust for the BRM team with the threat of closure if success was not achieved in 1962.

Armed with the new V8-engined car, Graham responded brilliantly by winning the Dutch GP, and then, after losing seemingly certain triumphs in both the Monaco and French GPs, he took the BRM to three more victories to claim a thoroughly deserved first World Championship.

The next three seasons saw some magnificent racing with Hill battling it out for supremacy with Clark, Surtees, Gurney et al., and coming very close to a second title in Mexico City in 1964, where an accidental collision with Bandini cost him his chance. However, the championship seemed to be of less importance in those days, each race carrying more weight in its own right. Memorably he took a hat-trick of wins in both the Monaco and US GPs, but there were many great drives which brought only podium finishes, such was the level of competition.

Graham was certainly one of the most active drivers of the period, and every weekend he seemed to be flying somewhere to race, handling a bewildering array of machinery from Seattle to Kyalami, or Karlskoga to Pukekohe. Driving Ferrari sports and GT cars for Maranello Concessionaires, he won the 1963 and 1964 Tourist Trophy races and the 1964 Reims 12 Hours and Paris 1000 Km, as well as taking second place at Le Mans the same year – all co-driving with Bonnier. Graham was unable to add to his tally of Grand Prix wins during the first year of the 3-litre formula in 1966, but he scored a contentious victory after a confused finish at the Indianapolis 500.

It was a great surprise when Hill moved camps in 1967, joining Jim Clark at Lotus, to race the new Ford-Cosworth-engined Lotus 49. Its potential was

Graham's first win came in the 1962 Dutch Grand Prix. It was the perfect springboard for the BRM driver to take his first world title.

enormous, and Graham was back in the hunt, but he had to endure a string of disappointments as his car fell prey to niggling maladies. Everything changed on 7 April 1968, when the team was devastated by the death of Jim Clark at Hockenheim. Graham helped restore morale by immediately winning the next two races in Spain and Monaco, and as the season wore on he resisted the challenges of Stewart and Hulme to take his second championship. Joined by Jochen Rindt in 1969, Hill won his fifth Monaco GP, but was soon overshadowed by the Austrian and the season ended in near-disaster when he was thrown from his Lotus at Watkins Glen when a tyre deflated, suffering badly broken legs.

Now aged 40, many believed it was time for him to retire, but Graham was no quitter and sheer bloody-mindedness saw him back in the cockpit of Rob Walker's Lotus at Kyalami despite still being almost unable to walk. Surprisingly he managed some points finishes early on and drove superbly in the Race of Champions to take fourth place despite gearbox trouble, but with Walker's Lotus 72 late in arriving the season petered out. Moving to Brabham for 1971, Graham won the International Trophy in the new 'lobster-claw' BT34, but had a thin time of it elsewhere. In Formula 2 he led the smart Rondel team, winning a thrilling race at Thruxton from Ronnie Peterson to show there was life in the old dog yet, but in truth a slow decline had already set in. His second season at Brabham was thoroughly lacklustre, and the year was illuminated only by his victory in the Le Mans 24 Hours for Matra with Pescarolo, Graham thus completing the unique achievement of winning the World Championship, the Indy 500 and the Sarthe classic.

With no prospect of a decent works drive in Grands Prix, Hill took the logical step of setting up his own team, showing some spirit with the difficult-to-handle Shadow in 1973 but getting nowhere fast in the reliable but heavy Lola the following year. In 1975 Graham took the decision to build his own car, but after failing to qualify at Monaco he remained out of the cockpit until announcing his retirement at the British GP meeting. Of course, by this time Graham had taken on Tony Brise, and felt he had in his charge a future champion. However, returning from a test session with the team's latest car at Paul Ricard in late November, Hill, piloting his own plane, clipped the tree tops in dense fog over Arkley golf course while approaching Elstree airfield and crashed. Not only did one of motor racing's great figures perish, so too did poor Brise and four other team members.

HILL, Graham (GB) b 15/2/1929, Hampstead, London – d 29/11/1975, Arkley, nr Barnet, Hertfordshire

	1958			Championship position: Unplaced					Q Pos/Entries
	Race	Circuit	No	Entrant	Tyres	Car/Engine		Comment	
ret	MONACO GP	Monte Carlo	26	Team Lotus	D	2.0 Lotus 12-Climax 4		half shaft-lost wheel	15/28
ret	DUTCH GP	Zandvoort	16	Team Lotus	D	2.0 Lotus 12-Climax 4		overheating	13/17
ret	BELGIAN GP	Spa	42	Team Lotus	D	2.0 Lotus 12-Climax 4		engine	15/20
ret	FRENCH GP	Reims	24	Team Lotus	D	2.0 Lotus 16-Climax 4		overheating	19/21
ret	BRITISH GP	Silverstone	16	Team Lotus	D	2.0 Lotus 16-Climax 4		overheating-oil pressure	14/21
ret	GERMAN GP (F2)	Nürburgring	25	Team Lotus	D	1.5 Lotus 16-Climax 4		oil pipe	25/26
ret	PORTUGUESE GP	Oporto	20	Team Lotus	D	2.2 Lotus 16-Climax 4		spun off	12/15
6	ITALIAN GP	Monza	38	Team Lotus	D	2.2 Lotus 16-Climax 4		pit stop-misfire/-8 laps	12/21
16	MOROCCAN GP	Casablanca	36	Team Lotus	D	2.0 Lotus 16-Climax 4		behind four F2 cars/-7 laps	12/25
	1959			Championship position: Unplaced					
ret	MONACO GP	Monte Carlo	40	Team Lotus	D	2.5 Lotus 16-Climax 4		fire	14/24
7	DUTCH GP	Zandvoort	14	Team Lotus	D	2.5 Lotus 16-Climax 4		pit stop-smoke in car/-2 laps	5/15
ret	FRENCH GP	Reims	32	Team Lotus	D	2.5 Lotus 16-Climax 4		radiator	14/22
9	BRITISH GP	Aintree	28	Team Lotus	D	2.5 Lotus 16-Climax 4		spin/5 laps behind	9/30
ret	GERMAN GP	AVUS	16	Team Lotus	D	2.5 Lotus 16-Climax 4		gearbox-heat 1	10/16
ret	PORTUGUESE GP	Monsanto	11	Team Lotus	D	2.5 Lotus 16-Climax 4		split fuel tank-spun-hit by Phil Hill	15/16
ret	ITALIAN GP	Monza	18	Team Lotus	D	2.5 Lotus 16-Climax 4		clutch	10/21
	1960			Championship position: 13th=	Wins: 0	Pole positions: 0	Fastest laps: 1	Points scored: 4	
ret	ARGENTINE GP	Buenos Aires	42	Owen Racing Organisation	D	2.5 BRM P25 4		overheating	3/22
7/ret	MONACO GP	Monte Carlo	6	Owen Racing Organisation	D	2.5 BRM P48 4		spun off	6/24
3	DUTCH GP	Zandvoort	16	Owen Racing Organisation	D	2.5 BRM P48 4			5/21
ret	BELGIAN GP	Spa	10	Owen Racing Organisation	D	2.5 BRM P48 4		engine	=6/18
ret	FRENCH GP	Reims	12	Owen Racing Organisation	D	2.5 BRM P48 4		stalled on grid-hit by Trintignant	3/23
ret	BRITISH GP	Silverstone	4	Owen Racing Organisation	D	2.5 BRM P48 4		spun off when leading/FL	2/25
ret	PORTUGUESE GP	Oporto	22	Owen Racing Organisation	D	2.5 BRM P48 4		gearbox	5/16
ret	US GP	Riverside	17	Owen Racing Organisation	D	2.5 BRM P48 4		gearbox	11/23
	1961			Championship position: 13th=	Wins: 0	Pole positions: 0	Fastest laps: 0	Points scored: 3	
ret	MONACO GP	Monte Carlo	18	Owen Racing Organisation	D	1.5 BRM P48/57-Climax 4		fuel pump	4/21
8	DUTCH GP	Zandvoort	4	Owen Racing Organisation	D	1.5 BRM P48/57-Climax 4			5/17
ret	BELGIAN GP	Spa	36	Owen Racing Organisation	D	1.5 BRM P48/57-Climax 4		oil leak	6/25
6	FRENCH GP	Reims	22	Owen Racing Organisation	D	1.5 BRM P48/57-Climax 4			6/26
ret	BRITISH GP	Aintree	20	Owen Racing Organisation	D	1.5 BRM P48/57-Climax 4		engine	11/30
ret	GERMAN GP	Nürburgring	17	Owen Racing Organisation	D	1.5 BRM P48/57-Climax 4		accident	6/27
ret	ITALIAN GP	Monza	24	Owen Racing Organisation	D	1.5 BRM P48/57-Climax 4		engine	5/33
dns	"	"	24	Owen Racing Organisation	D	1.5 BRM P57 V8		practice only	– / –
5	US GP	Watkins Glen	4	Owen Racing Organisation	D	1.5 BRM P48/57-Climax 4		1 lap behind	2/19
	1962			Championship position: WORLD CHAMPION	Wins: 4	Pole positions: 1	Fastest laps: 3	Points scored: 52	
1	DUTCH GP	Zandvoort	17	Owen Racing Organisation	D	1.5 BRM P57 V8			2/20
6/ret	MONACO GP	Monte Carlo	10	Owen Racing Organisation	D	1.5 BRM P57 V8		engine/8 laps behind	2/21
2	BELGIAN GP	Spa	1	Owen Racing Organisation	D	1.5 BRM P57 V8			1/20
9	FRENCH GP	Rouen	8	Owen Racing Organisation	D	1.5 BRM P57 V8		pit stop-fuel injection/FL/-10 laps	2/17
4	BRITISH GP	Aintree	12	Owen Racing Organisation	D	1.5 BRM P57 V8			=4/21
1	GERMAN GP	Nürburgring	11	Owen Racing Organisation	D	1.5 BRM P57 V8		FL	2/30
1	ITALIAN GP	Monza	14	Owen Racing Organisation	D	1.5 BRM P57 V8		FL	2/30
2	US GP	Watkins Glen	4	Owen Racing Organisation	D	1.5 BRM P57 V8			3/20
1	SOUTH AFRICAN GP	East London	3	Owen Racing Organisation	D	1.5 BRM P57 V8			2/17

In the 1960s Hill was the master of Monaco, winning the race five times.
Right: Driving a Lotus 49B in the 1969 race, he leads the Matra of Beltoise.

1963

Championship position: 2nd= Wins: 2 Pole positions: 2 Fastest laps: 0 Points scored: 29

Pos	Race	Circuit	Grid	Entrant		Car	Notes	Q
1	MONACO GP	Monte Carlo	6	Owen Racing Organisation	D	1.5 BRM P57 V8		2/17
ret	BELGIAN GP	Spa	7	Owen Racing Organisation	D	1.5 BRM P57 V8	gearbox	1/20
ret	DUTCH GP	Zandvoort	12	Owen Racing Organisation	D	1.5 BRM P57 V8	overheating	2/19
dns	"	"	12	Owen Racing Organisation	D	1.5 BRM P61 V8	practice only	–/–
dsq/3*	FRENCH GP	Reims	2	Owen Racing Organisation	D	1.5 BRM P61 V8	* dsq for push start	2/21
dns	"	"	2	Owen Racing Organisation	D	1.5 BRM P57 V8	practice only	–/–
3	BRITISH GP	Silverstone	1	Owen Racing Organisation	D	1.5 BRM P57 V8	out of fuel last lap when 2nd	3/23
ret	GERMAN GP	Nürburgring	1	Owen Racing Organisation	D	1.5 BRM P57 V8	gearbox	4/26
dns	"	"	1	Owen Racing Organisation	D	1.5 BRM P61 V8	practice only	–/–
ret	ITALIAN GP	Monza	12	Owen Racing Organisation	D	1.5 BRM P61 V8	clutch	2/28
dns	"	"	12	Owen Racing Organisation	D	1.5 BRM P57 V8	practice only	–/–
1	US GP	Watkins Glen	1	Owen Racing Organisation	D	1.5 BRM P57 V8		1/21
4	MEXICAN GP	Mexico City	1	Owen Racing Organisation	D	1.5 BRM P57 V8	1 lap behind	3/21
3	SOUTH AFRICAN GP	East London	5	Owen Racing Organisation	D	1.5 BRM P57 V8	1 lap behind	6/21

1964

Championship position: 2nd Wins: 2 Pole positions: 1 Fastest laps: 1 Points scored: 41

Pos	Race	Circuit	Grid	Entrant		Car	Notes	Q
1	MONACO GP	Monte Carlo	8	Owen Racing Organisation	D	1.5 BRM P261 V8	FL	=3/20
4	DUTCH GP	Zandvoort	6	Owen Racing Organisation	D	1.5 BRM P261 V8	1 lap behind	3/18
5/ret	BELGIAN GP	Spa	1	Owen Racing Organisation	D	1.5 BRM P261 V8	out of fuel last lap	2/20
2	FRENCH GP	Rouen	8	Owen Racing Organisation	D	1.5 BRM P261 V8		6/17
2	BRITISH GP	Brands Hatch	3	Owen Racing Organisation	D	1.5 BRM P261 V8		2/25
2	GERMAN GP	Nürburgring	3	Owen Racing Organisation	D	1.5 BRM P261 V8		5/24
ret	AUSTRIAN GP	Zeltweg	3	Owen Racing Organisation	D	1.5 BRM P261 V8	distributor drive	1/20
ret	ITALIAN GP	Monza	18	Owen Racing Organisation	D	1.5 BRM P261 V8	clutch on startline	3/25
1	US GP	Watkins Glen	3	Owen Racing Organisation	D	1.5 BRM P261 V8		4/19
11	MEXICAN GP	Mexico City	3	Owen Racing Organisation	D	1.5 BRM P261 V8	hit by Bandini when 2nd/-2 laps	6/19

1965

Championship position: 2nd Wins: 2 Pole positions: 4 Fastest laps: 3 Points scored: 47

Pos	Race	Circuit	Grid	Entrant		Car	Notes	Q
3	SOUTH AFRICAN GP	East London	3	Owen Racing Organisation	D	1.5 BRM P261 V8		5/25
1	MONACO GP	Monte Carlo	3	Owen Racing Organisation	D	1.5 BRM P261 V8	FL	1/17
5	BELGIAN GP	Spa	7	Owen Racing Organisation	D	1.5 BRM P261 V8	1 lap behind	1/21
5	FRENCH GP	Clermont Ferrand	10	Owen Racing Organisation	D	1.5 BRM P261 V8	1 lap behind	13/17
2	BRITISH GP	Silverstone	3	Owen Racing Organisation	D	1.5 BRM P261 V8	FL	2/23
4	DUTCH GP	Zandvoort	10	Owen Racing Organisation	D	1.5 BRM P261 V8		1/17
2	GERMAN GP	Nürburgring	9	Owen Racing Organisation	D	1.5 BRM P261 V8		3/22
2	ITALIAN GP	Monza	30	Owen Racing Organisation	D	1.5 BRM P261 V8		4/23
1	US GP	Watkins Glen	3	Owen Racing Organisation	D	1.5 BRM P261 V8	FL	1/18
ret	MEXICAN GP	Mexico City	3	Owen Racing Organisation	D	1.5 BRM P261 V8	engine	5/18

1966

Championship position: 5th Wins: 0 Pole positions: 0 Fastest laps: 0 Points scored: 17

Pos	Race	Circuit	Grid	Entrant		Car	Notes	Q
3	MONACO GP	Monte Carlo	11	Owen Racing Organisation	D	2.0 BRM P261 V8	1 lap behind	4/16
dns	"	" "	11T	Owen Racing Organisation	G	3.0 BRM P83 H16	practice only	–/–
ret	BELGIAN GP	Spa	14	Owen Racing Organisation	D	2.0 BRM P261 V8	spun off in rainstorm	9/18
ret	FRENCH GP	Reims	16	Owen Racing Organisation	D	2.0 BRM P261 V8	engine	8/17
dns	"	"	T2	Owen Racing Organisation	G	3.0 BRM P83 H16	practice only	–/–
3	BRITISH GP	Brands Hatch	3	Owen Racing Organisation	G	2.0 BRM P261 V8	1 lap behind	4/20
2	DUTCH GP	Zandvoort	12	Owen Racing Organisation	G	2.0 BRM P261 V8	1 lap behind	7/18
4	GERMAN GP	Nürburgring	5	Owen Racing Organisation	G	2.0 BRM P261 V8		10/30
ret	ITALIAN GP	Monza	26	Owen Racing Organisation	G	3.0 BRM P83 H16	engine-camshaft	11/22
dns	"	"	26	Owen Racing Organisation	G	2.0 BRM P261 V8	practice only	–/–
ret	US GP	Watkins Glen	3	Owen Racing Organisation	G	3.0 BRM P83 H16	cwp	5/19
ret	MEXICAN GP	Mexico City	3	Owen Racing Organisation	G	3.0 BRM P83 H16	engine	7/19

1967

Championship position: 6th= Wins: 0 Pole positions: 3 Fastest laps: 2 Points scored: 15

Pos	Race	Circuit	Grid	Entrant		Car	Notes	Q
ret	SOUTH AFRICAN GP	Kyalami	8	Team Lotus	F	2.1 Lotus 43-BRM H16	hit kerb	15/18
2	MONACO GP	Monte Carlo	14	Team Lotus	F	2.1 Lotus 33-BRM V8	1 lap behind	8/18
ret	DUTCH GP	Zandvoort	6	Team Lotus	F	3.0 Lotus 49-Cosworth V8	timing gears	1/17
ret	BELGIAN GP	Spa	22	Team Lotus	F	3.0 Lotus 49-Cosworth V8	gearbox	3/18
ret	FRENCH GP	Le Mans	7	Team Lotus	F	3.0 Lotus 49-Cosworth V8	gearbox/FL	1/15
ret	BRITISH GP	Silverstone	6	Team Lotus	F	3.0 Lotus 49-Cosworth V8	engine	2/21
ret	GERMAN GP	Nürburgring	4	Team Lotus	F	3.0 Lotus 49-Cosworth V8	rear suspension mounting	14/25
4	CANADIAN GP	Mosport Park	4	Team Lotus	F	3.0 Lotus 49-Cosworth V8	2 laps behind	2/19
ret	ITALIAN GP	Monza	22	Team Lotus	F	3.0 Lotus 49-Cosworth V8	engine	8/18
2	US GP	Watkins Glen	6	Team Lotus	F	3.0 Lotus 49-Cosworth V8	gearbox problems/FL	1/18
ret	MEXICAN GP	Mexico City	6	Team Lotus	F	3.0 Lotus 49-Cosworth V8	driveshaft-u-joint	4/19

1968

Championship position: WORLD CHAMPION Wins: 3 Pole positions: 2 Fastest laps: 0 Points scored: 48

Pos	Race	Circuit	Grid	Entrant		Car	Notes	Q
2	SOUTH AFRICAN GP	Kyalami	5	Team Lotus	F	3.0 Lotus 49-Cosworth V8		2/23
1	SPANISH GP	Jarama	10	Gold Leaf Team Lotus	F	3.0 Lotus 49-Cosworth V8		6/14
1	MONACO GP	Monte Carlo	9	Gold Leaf Team Lotus	F	3.0 Lotus 49B-Cosworth V8		1/18
ret	BELGIAN GP	Spa	1	Gold Leaf Team Lotus	F	3.0 Lotus 49B-Cosworth V8	driveshaft-u-joint	14/18
9/ret	DUTCH GP	Zandvoort	3	Gold Leaf Team Lotus	F	3.0 Lotus 49B-Cosworth V8	spun off/9 laps behind	3/19
ret	FRENCH GP	Rouen	12	Gold Leaf Team Lotus	F	3.0 Lotus 49B-Cosworth V8	driveshaft	9/18
ret	BRITISH GP	Brands Hatch	8	Gold Leaf Team Lotus	F	3.0 Lotus 49B-Cosworth V8	driveshaft-u-joint	1/20
2	GERMAN GP	Nürburgring	3	Gold Leaf Team Lotus	F	3.0 Lotus 49B-Cosworth V8		4/20
ret	ITALIAN GP	Monza	16	Gold Leaf Team Lotus	F	3.0 Lotus 49B-Cosworth V8	lost wheel	5/24
4	CANADIAN GP	St Jovite	3	Gold Leaf Team Lotus	F	3.0 Lotus 49B-Cosworth V8	pit stop-vibration/-4 laps	5/22
2	US GP	Watkins Glen	10	Gold Leaf Team Lotus	F	3.0 Lotus 49B-Cosworth V8		3/21
1	MEXICAN GP	Mexico City	3	Gold Leaf Team Lotus	F	3.0 Lotus 49B-Cosworth V8		3/21

1969

Championship position: 7th Wins: 1 Pole positions: 0 Fastest laps: 0 Points scored: 19

Pos	Race	Circuit	Grid	Entrant		Car	Notes	Q
2	SOUTH AFRICAN GP	Kyalami	1	Gold Leaf Team Lotus	F	3.0 Lotus 49B-Cosworth V8		=7/18
ret	SPANISH GP	Montjuich Park	1	Gold Leaf Team Lotus	F	3.0 Lotus 49B-Cosworth V8	rear wing collapsed-crashed	3/14
1	MONACO GP	Monte Carlo	1	Gold Leaf Team Lotus	F	3.0 Lotus 49B-Cosworth V8		4/16
7	DUTCH GP	Zandvoort	1	Gold Leaf Team Lotus	F	3.0 Lotus 49B-Cosworth V8	pit stop-handling/2 laps behind	3/15

dns	"	"	1T	Gold Leaf Team Lotus	F	3.0 Lotus 63-Cosworth V8	practice only	–/–
6	FRENCH GP	Clermont Ferrand	1	Gold Leaf Team Lotus	F	3.0 Lotus 49B-Cosworth V8	1 lap behind	8/13
7	BRITISH GP	Silverstone	1	Gold Leaf Team Lotus	F	3.0 Lotus 49B-Cosworth V8	pit stop-fuel/2 laps behind	12/17
dns	"	"	1	Gold Leaf Team Lotus	F	3.0 Lotus 63-Cosworth V8	practice only	–/–
dns	"	"	9	Motor Racing Developments	G	3.0 Brabham BT26A-Cosworth V8	waiting for his Lotus to arrive	–/–
4	GERMAN GP	Nürburgring	1	Gold Leaf Team Lotus	F	3.0 Lotus 49B-Cosworth V8		9/26
9/ret	ITALIAN GP	Monza	2	Gold Leaf Team Lotus	F	3.0 Lotus 49B-Cosworth V8	driveshaft/5 laps behind	9/15
ret	CANADIAN GP	Mosport Park	1	Gold Leaf Team Lotus	F	3.0 Lotus 49B-Cosworth V8	engine	7/20
ret	US GP	Watkins Glen	1	Gold Leaf Team Lotus	F	3.0 Lotus 49B-Cosworth V8	puncture-thrown out-broken legs	4/18

1970 — Championship position: 13th   Wins: 0   Pole positions: 0   Fastest laps: 0   Points scored: 7

6	SOUTH AFRICAN GP	Kyalami	11	Rob Walker Racing Team	F	3.0 Lotus 49C-Cosworth V8	1 lap behind	19/24
4	SPANISH GP	Jarama	6	Rob Walker Racing Team	F	3.0 Lotus 49C-Cosworth V8	1 lap behind	18/22
5	MONACO GP	Monte Carlo	1	Brooke Bond Oxo Racing/Rob Walker	F	3.0 Lotus 49C-Cosworth V8	raced borrowed GLTL car/-1 lap	12/21
ret	BELGIAN GP	Spa	23	Brooke Bond Oxo Racing/Rob Walker	F	3.0 Lotus 49C-Cosworth V8	engine	16/18
nc	DUTCH GP	Zandvoort	15	Brooke Bond Oxo Racing/Rob Walker	F	3.0 Lotus 49C-Cosworth V8	pit stop-handling/-9 laps	21/24
10	FRENCH GP	Clermont Ferrand	8	Brooke Bond Oxo Racing/Rob Walker	F	3.0 Lotus 49C-Cosworth V8	1 lap behind	20/23
6	BRITISH GP	Brands Hatch	14	Brooke Bond Oxo Racing/Rob Walker	F	3.0 Lotus 49C-Cosworth V8	1 lap behind	23/25
ret	GERMAN GP	Hockenheim	9	Brooke Bond Oxo Racing/Rob Walker	F	3.0 Lotus 49C-Cosworth V8	engine	21/25
dns	ITALIAN GP	Monza	28	Brooke Bond Oxo Racing/Rob Walker	F	3.0 Lotus 72C-Cosworth V8	withdrawn after Rindt's accident	(16)/27
nc	CANADIAN GP	St Jovite	9	Brooke Bond Oxo Racing/Rob Walker	F	3.0 Lotus 72C-Cosworth V8	pit stop-gearbox/-13 laps	20/20
ret	US GP	Watkins Glen	14	Brooke Bond Oxo Racing/Rob Walker	F	3.0 Lotus 72C-Cosworth V8	clutch	10/27
ret	MEXICAN GP	Mexico City	14	Brooke Bond Oxo Racing/Rob Walker	F	3.0 Lotus 72C-Cosworth V8	overheating	8/18

1971 — Championship position: 21st   Wins: 0   Pole positions: 0   Fastest laps: 0   Points scored: 2

9	SOUTH AFRICAN GP	Kyalami	14	Motor Racing Developments	G	3.0 Brabham BT33-Cosworth V8	pit stop-rear wing/-2 laps	19/25
ret	SPANISH GP	Montjuich Park	7	Motor Racing Developments	G	3.0 Brabham BT34-Cosworth V8	steering	15/22
ret	MONACO GP	Monte Carlo	7	Motor Racing Developments	G	3.0 Brabham BT34-Cosworth V8	hit wall at Tabac	=9/23
10	DUTCH GP	Zandvoort	24	Motor Racing Developments	G	3.0 Brabham BT34-Cosworth V8	5 laps behind	16/24
ret	FRENCH GP	Paul Ricard	7	Motor Racing Developments	G	3.0 Brabham BT34-Cosworth V8	oil pressure	4/24
ret	BRITISH GP	Silverstone	7	Motor Racing Developments	G	3.0 Brabham BT34-Cosworth V8	hit by Oliver on grid	16/24
9	GERMAN GP	Nürburgring	24	Motor Racing Developments	G	3.0 Brabham BT34-Cosworth V8	left on grid	13/23
5	AUSTRIAN GP	Österreichring	7	Motor Racing Developments	G	3.0 Brabham BT34-Cosworth V8		8/22
11/ret	ITALIAN GP	Monza	10	Motor Racing Developments	G	3.0 Brabham BT34-Cosworth V8	gearbox/7 laps behind	14/24
ret	CANADIAN GP	Mosport Park	37	Motor Racing Developments	G	3.0 Brabham BT34-Cosworth V8	spun off	=15/27
7	US GP	Watkins Glen	22	Motor Racing Developments	G	3.0 Brabham BT34-Cosworth V8	1 lap behind	20/32

1972 — Championship position: 12th   Wins: 0   Pole positions: 0   Fastest laps: 0   Points scored: 4

ret	ARGENTINE GP	Buenos Aires	1	Motor Racing Developments	G	3.0 Brabham BT33-Cosworth V8	fuel pump/tyre problems	=16/22
6	SOUTH AFRICAN GP	Kyalami	19	Motor Racing Developments	G	3.0 Brabham BT33-Cosworth V8	1 lap behind	14/27
10	SPANISH GP	Jarama	18	Motor Racing Developments	G	3.0 Brabham BT37-Cosworth V8	spin/4 laps behind	23/26
12	MONACO GP	Monte Carlo	20	Motor Racing Developments	G	3.0 Brabham BT37-Cosworth V8	4 laps behind	=18/25
ret	BELGIAN GP	Nivelles	17	Motor Racing Developments	G	3.0 Brabham BT37-Cosworth V8	rear upright	16/26
10	FRENCH GP	Clermont Ferrand	18	Motor Racing Developments	G	3.0 Brabham BT37-Cosworth V8	hit by Beltoise	24/29
ret	BRITISH GP	Brands Hatch	26	Motor Racing Developments	G	3.0 Brabham BT37-Cosworth V8	spun off	=20/27
6	GERMAN GP	Nürburgring	11	Motor Racing Developments	G	3.0 Brabham BT37-Cosworth V8		15/27
ret	AUSTRIAN GP	Österreichring	16	Motor Racing Developments	G	3.0 Brabham BT37-Cosworth V8	fuel metering unit	14/26
5	ITALIAN GP	Monza	28	Motor Racing Developments	G	3.0 Brabham BT37-Cosworth V8	brake problems	13/27
8	CANADIAN GP	Mosport Park	7	Motor Racing Developments	G	3.0 Brabham BT37-Cosworth V8	1 lap behind	17/25
11	US GP	Watkins Glen	28	Motor Racing Developments	G	3.0 Brabham BT37-Cosworth V8	spin/2 laps behind	28/32

1973 — Championship position: Unplaced

ret	SPANISH GP	Montjuich Park	25	Embassy Racing	G	3.0 Shadow DN1-Cosworth V8	brakes	22/22
9	BELGIAN GP	Zolder	12	Embassy Racing	G	3.0 Shadow DN1-Cosworth V8	pit stop-plug lead/-5 laps	23/23
ret	MONACO GP	Monte Carlo	12	Embassy Racing	G	3.0 Shadow DN1-Cosworth V8	rear suspension	25/26
ret	SWEDISH GP	Anderstorp	12	Embassy Racing	G	3.0 Shadow DN1-Cosworth V8	ignition	18/22
10	FRENCH GP	Paul Ricard	12	Embassy Racing	G	3.0 Shadow DN1-Cosworth V8	1 lap behind	16/25
ret	BRITISH GP	Silverstone	12	Embassy Racing	G	3.0 Shadow DN1-Cosworth V8	steering rack/front subframe	27/29
nc	DUTCH GP	Zandvoort	12	Embassy Racing	G	3.0 Shadow DN1-Cosworth V8	4 pit stops-water/-16 laps	17/24
13	GERMAN GP	Nürburgring	12	Embassy Racing	G	3.0 Shadow DN1-Cosworth V8		20/23
ret	AUSTRIAN GP	Österreichring	12	Embassy Racing	G	3.0 Shadow DN1-Cosworth V8	rear suspension mounting	22/25
14	ITALIAN GP	Monza	12	Embassy Racing	G	3.0 Shadow DN1-Cosworth V8	1 lap behind	22/25
16	CANADIAN GP	Mosport Park	12	Embassy Racing	G	3.0 Shadow DN1-Cosworth V8	4 pit stops-various/-7 laps	17/26
13	US GP	Watkins Glen	12	Embassy Racing	G	3.0 Shadow DN1-Cosworth V8	pit stop-puncture/-2 laps	19/28

1974 — Championship position: 18th   Wins: 0   Pole positions: 0   Fastest laps: 0   Points scored: 1

ret	ARGENTINE GP	Buenos Aires	26	Embassy Racing with Graham Hill	F	3.0 Lola T370-Cosworth V8	engine	=17/26
11	BRAZILIAN GP	Interlagos	26	Embassy Racing with Graham Hill	F	3.0 Lola T370-Cosworth V8	1 lap behind	21/25
12	SOUTH AFRICAN GP	Kyalami	26	Embassy Racing with Graham Hill	F	3.0 Lola T370-Cosworth V8	1 lap behind	18/27
ret	SPANISH GP	Jarama	26	Embassy Racing with Graham Hill	F	3.0 Lola T370-Cosworth V8	engine	20/28
8	BELGIAN GP	Nivelles	26	Embassy Racing with Graham Hill	F	3.0 Lola T370-Cosworth V8	2 laps behind	29/32
7	MONACO GP	Monte Carlo	26	Embassy Racing with Graham Hill	F	3.0 Lola T370-Cosworth V8	2 laps behind	=21/28
6	SWEDISH GP	Anderstorp	26	Embassy Racing with Graham Hill	F	3.0 Lola T370-Cosworth V8	1 lap behind	15/28
ret	DUTCH GP	Zandvoort	26	Embassy Racing with Graham Hill	F	3.0 Lola T370-Cosworth V8	loose clutch housing bolts	19/27
13	FRENCH GP	Dijon	26	Embassy Racing with Graham Hill	F	3.0 Lola T370-Cosworth V8	2 laps behind	21/30
13	BRITISH GP	Brands Hatch	26	Embassy Racing with Graham Hill	F	3.0 Lola T370-Cosworth V8	2 pit stops-punctures/-6 laps	22/34
9	GERMAN GP	Nürburgring	26	Embassy Racing with Graham Hill	F	3.0 Lola T370-Cosworth V8		19/32
12	AUSTRIAN GP	Österreichring	26	Embassy Racing with Graham Hill	F	3.0 Lola T370-Cosworth V8	pit stop-tyres/6 laps behind	21/31
8	ITALIAN GP	Monza	26	Embassy Racing with Graham Hill	F	3.0 Lola T370-Cosworth V8	1 lap behind	21/31
14	CANADIAN GP	Mosport Park	26	Embassy Racing with Graham Hill	F	3.0 Lola T370-Cosworth V8	3 laps behind	20/30
8	US GP	Watkins Glen	26	Embassy Racing with Graham Hill	F	3.0 Lola T370-Cosworth V8	1 lap behind	24/30

1975 — Championship position: Unplaced

10	ARGENTINE GP	Buenos Aires	22	Embassy Racing with Graham Hill	G	3.0 Lola T370-Cosworth V8	1 lap behind	21/23
12	BRAZILIAN GP	Interlagos	22	Embassy Racing with Graham Hill	G	3.0 Lola T370-Cosworth V8	1 lap behind	20/23
dns	SOUTH AFRICAN GP	Kyalami	22	Embassy Racing with Graham Hill	G	3.0 Lola T370-Cosworth V8	practice accident-car damaged	(28)/28
dnq	MONACO GP	Monte Carlo	23	Embassy Racing with Graham Hill	G	3.0 Hill GH1-Cosworth V8		21/26
dnq	"	"	23T	Embassy Racing with Graham Hill	G	3.0 Lola T370-Cosworth V8		–/–

GP Starts: 176   GP Wins: 14   Pole positions: 13   Fastest laps: 10   Points: 289

PHIL HILL

PHIL HILL

Phil Hill is always remembered as the man who became America's first World Champion when he took the crown driving a Ferrari in 1961, yet that season he won only two Grands Prix and they were his only victories in small-capacity racing cars. In a long career he was overwhelmingly more effective and successful in big, powerful sports machines.

After business studies on the west coast, Phil decided he preferred working on cars to the office life and by 1950 he was racing an MG TC, which was duly replaced by a succession of machines all of which were hard-earned by the sweat of his brow. In 1952 he got a big break with a drive in Alan Guiberson's Ferrari, taking sixth place in the Carrera Panamericana, but the following year he fared badly and briefly considered retirement. He was persuaded to continue, however, and second place in the 1954 Carrera was a marvellous morale-booster. His career then took off in a big way Stateside, Phil winning the 1955 SCCA championship, and after he had finished second in the 1956 Buenos Aires 1000 Km he was given a contract to drive sports cars for the Scuderia. He won the Swedish GP and the Messina 5 Hours that season in works cars, and added more good results the following year, including a win in the Venezuelan GP at Caracas with Peter Collins.

By 1958 Phil was itching to get his hands on a Grand Prix car, but Ferrari seemed unwilling to give him the opportunity he craved, save for a little practice at the Libre Buenos Aires GP. Enzo felt he was best suited to sports cars, and Hill proved as much when he won at Buenos Aires and Sebring and then put in a brilliant drive in the wet to win Le Mans with Gendebien. However, by now his need to race in Formula 1 bordered on the obsessional and he hired Bonnier's Maserati to give himself a debut at the French GP. Perhaps Ferrari took the hint because come the German GP Hill was handed the team's F2 car, and then at Monza he was entrusted with the real thing – a Ferrari 246 – taking third and fastest lap. By backing off at the finish of the Moroccan GP to allow Hawthorn to move into second place and thus take the championship, Phil did his standing no harm and he became a full-time Grand Prix team member thereafter. He spent 1959 learning the art of Grand Prix driving, sometimes proving a little ragged in his approach and indulging in some hairy moments, but taking fourth place in the championship nevertheless. By 1960 the big front-engined cars were almost on the point of obsolescence, but Hill gave the dinosaurs one last hurrah by winning the rather hollow Italian GP held on Monza's banked circuit which was boycotted by the British teams.

The following season was to be his finest. In addition to winning the Sebring 12 Hours and Le Mans for the second time with Gendebien, he took the little 'shark-nose' Ferrari to victory at Spa and Monza to be crowned as World Champion in the saddest of circumstances following the terrible death of his team-mate and championship rival Wolfgang von Trips. Things progress quickly in Formula 1, however, and in 1962 Ferrari were totally eclipsed, leaving Phil with a few placings but no hope of defending his title. He was still regarded as one of the finest exponents of sports car racing, however, and confirmed it by winning Le Mans for the third time with Gendebien, as well as the Nürburgring 1000 Km.

Such was the disharmony at Maranello that year that Phil joined what was effectively a breakaway group to race the ATS in 1963. To say it was a disastrous move would be an understatement, and it effectively destroyed his Grand Prix career. Initially left without a drive, he was called into the Cooper team following the tragic loss of Tim Mayer at Longford, but it was an unhappy liaison, with Phil's confidence hitting rock bottom at Zeltweg where he wrote off two cars. This resulted in the ignominy of his being dropped for Monza, but he was reinstated for the final two races.

Save for a drive in Gurney's Eagle at Monza in 1966, his Grand Prix career was done, but he still had something left. He had been a key member of the Ford works sports car effort in 1964-65, but a move to Jim Hall's Chaparral team gave the twilight of his career a final glow. In 1966 he won the Nürburgring 1000 Km with Bonnier, and a Can-Am round at Laguna Seca, and in his final season he took a memorable victory at Brands Hatch sharing the Chaparral 2F with Mike Spence.

After this last win he drifted into contented retirement, restoring vintage cars and keeping in touch with the sport in a commentary role. Currently he is a regular participant in historic events and no doubt watches with satisfaction the promising progress of his son Derek in the junior formulae.

Belgian Grand Prix, 1962. Phil Hill leads his young team-mate Ricardo Rodriguez. Faced with the challenge of the fuel-injected V8-powered cars from Lotus, BRM and Cooper, the reigning World Champion was already struggling in the defence of his title.

HILL, Phil (USA) b 20/4/1927, Miami, Florida

1958 — Championship position: 10 Wins: 0 Pole positions: 0 Fastest laps: 1 Points scored: 9

	Race	Circuit	No	Entrant	Tyres	Car/Engine	Comment	Q Pos/Entries
7	FRENCH GP	Reims	36	Joakim Bonnier	P	2.5 Maserati 250F 6	1 lap behind	13/21
9*	GERMAN GP (F2)	Nürburgring	23	Scuderia Ferrari	E	1.5 Ferrari Dino 156 V6 F2	*5th in F2 class	13/26
3	ITALIAN GP	Monza	18	Scuderia Ferrari	E	2.4 Ferrari Dino 246 V6	FL	7/21
3	MOROCCAN GP	Casablanca	4	Scuderia Ferrari	E	2.4 Ferrari Dino 246 V6		5/25

1959 — Championship position: 4th Wins: 0 Pole positions: 0 Fastest laps: 1 Points scored: 20

	Race	Circuit	No	Entrant	Tyres	Car/Engine	Comment	Q Pos/Entries
4	MONACO GP	Monte Carlo	48	Scuderia Ferrari	D	2.4 Ferrari Dino 246 V6	3 spins-pit stop-wheels/-3 laps	5/24
6	DUTCH GP	Zandvoort	3	Scuderia Ferrari	D	2.4 Ferrari Dino 246 V6	2 laps behind	12/15
2	FRENCH GP	Reims	26	Scuderia Ferrari	D	2.4 Ferrari Dino 246 V6		3/22
3	GERMAN GP	AVUS	5	Scuderia Ferrari	D	2.4 Ferrari Dino 246 V6	3rd heat 1/2nd heat 2	6/16
ret	PORTUGUESE GP	Monsanto	15	Scuderia Ferrari	D	2.4 Ferrari Dino 246 V6	hit a spinning Graham Hill	7/16
2	ITALIAN GP	Monza	32	Scuderia Ferrari	D	2.4 Ferrari Dino 246 V6	FL	5/21
ret	US GP	Sebring	5	Scuderia Ferrari	D	2.4 Ferrari Dino 246 V6	clutch	8/19

1960 — Championship position: 5th Wins: 1 Pole positions: 1 Fastest laps: 2 (1 shared) Points scored: 16

	Race	Circuit	No	Entrant	Tyres	Car/Engine	Comment	Q Pos/Entries
8	ARGENTINE GP	Buenos Aires	26	Scuderia Ferrari	D	2.4 Ferrari Dino 246 V6	3 laps behind	6/22
3	MONACO GP	Monte Carlo	36	Scuderia Ferrari	D	2.4 Ferrari Dino 246 V6		10/24
ret	DUTCH GP	Zandvoort	1	Scuderia Ferrari	D	2.4 Ferrari Dino 246 V6	engine	13/21
4	BELGIAN GP	Spa	24	Scuderia Ferrari	D	2.4 Ferrari Dino 246 V6	pit stop-fuel leak/FL (shared)/-1 lap	4/18
12/ret	FRENCH GP	Reims	2	Scuderia Ferrari	D	2.4 Ferrari Dino 246 V6	transmission	2/23
7	BRITISH GP	Silverstone	10	Scuderia Ferrari	D	2.4 Ferrari Dino 246 V6	2 laps behind	10/25
ret	PORTUGUESE GP	Oporto	26	Scuderia Ferrari	D	2.4 Ferrari Dino 246 V6	hit straw bales	10/16
1	ITALIAN GP	Monza	20	Scuderia Ferrari	D	2.4 Ferrari Dino 246 V6	FL	1/16
6	US GP	Riverside	9	Yeoman Credit Racing Team	D	2.5 Cooper T51-Climax 4	1 lap behind	13/23

1961 — Championship position: WORLD CHAMPION Wins: 2 Pole positions: 5 Fastest laps: 2 Points scored: 38

	Race	Circuit	No	Entrant	Tyres	Car/Engine	Comment	Q Pos/Entries
3	MONACO GP	Monte Carlo	38	Scuderia Ferrari SpA SEFAC	D	1.5 Ferrari 156 V6		5/21
2	DUTCH GP	Zandvoort	1	Scuderia Ferrari SpA SEFAC	D	1.5 Ferrari 156 V6		1/17
1	BELGIAN GP	Spa	4	Scuderia Ferrari SpA SEFAC	D	1.5 Ferrari 156 V6		1/25
9	FRENCH GP	Reims	16	Scuderia Ferrari SpA SEFAC	D	1.5 Ferrari 156 V6	spin/FL/2 laps behind	1/26
2	BRITISH GP	Aintree	2	Scuderia Ferrari SpA SEFAC	D	1.5 Ferrari 156 V6		1/30
3	GERMAN GP	Nürburgring	4	Scuderia Ferrari SpA SEFAC	D	1.5 Ferrari 156 V6	FL	1/26
1	ITALIAN GP	Monza	2	Scuderia Ferrari SpA SEFAC	D	1.5 Ferrari 156 V6		3/33

1962 — Championship position: 6th Wins: 0 Pole positions: 0 Fastest laps: 0 Points scored: 14

	Race	Circuit	No	Entrant	Tyres	Car/Engine	Comment	Q Pos/Entries
3	DUTCH GP	Zandvoort	1	Scuderia Ferrari SpA SEFAC	D	1.5 Ferrari 156 V6		9/20
2	MONACO GP	Monte Carlo	36	Scuderia Ferrari SpA SEFAC	D	1.5 Ferrari 156 V6		9/21
3	BELGIAN GP	Spa	9	Scuderia Ferrari SpA SEFAC	D	1.5 Ferrari 156 V6		4/20
ret	BRITISH GP	Aintree	2	Scuderia Ferrari SpA SEFAC	D	1.5 Ferrari 156 V6	ignition	=11/21
ret	GERMAN GP	Nürburgring	1	Scuderia Ferrari SpA SEFAC	D	1.5 Ferrari 156 V6	shock absorbers	12/30
11	ITALIAN GP	Monza	10	Scuderia Ferrari SpA SEFAC	D	1.5 Ferrari 156 V6	pit stop-tyres/5 laps behind	15/30
dns	US GP	Watkins Glen	11	Porsche System Engineering	D	1.5 Porsche 804 F8	practice only-Bonnier unwell	–/–

1963 — Championship position: Unplaced

	Race	Circuit	No	Entrant	Tyres	Car/Engine	Comment	Q Pos/Entries
ret	BELGIAN GP	Spa	26	Automobili Tourisimo Sport	D	1.5 ATS 100 V8	gearbox	17/20
ret	DUTCH GP	Zandvoort	24	Automobili Tourisimo Sport	D	1.5 ATS 100 V8	rear hub	13/19
nc	FRENCH GP	Reims	42	Ecurie Filipinetti	D	1.5 Lotus 24-BRM V8	pit stops-fuel pump/-19 laps	13/21
11	ITALIAN GP	Monza	16	Automobili Tourisimo Sport	D	1.5 ATS 100 V8	pit stops-various/7 laps behind	14/28
ret	US GP	Watkins Glen	25	Automobili Tourisimo Sport	D	1.5 ATS 100 V8	oil pump	15/21
ret	MEXICAN GP	Mexico City	25	Automobili Tourisimo Sport	D	1.5 ATS 100 V8	rear suspension	17/21

1964 — Championship position: 19th= Wins: 0 Pole positions: 0 Fastest laps: 0 Points scored: 1

	Race	Circuit	No	Entrant	Tyres	Car/Engine	Comment	Q Pos/Entries
9/ret	MONACO GP	Monte Carlo	9	Cooper Car Co	D	1.5 Cooper T73-Climax V8	rear suspension	=8/20
8	DUTCH GP	Zandvoort	22	Cooper Car Co	D	1.5 Cooper T73-Climax V8	4 laps behind	9/18
ret	BELGIAN GP	Spa	21	Cooper Car Co	D	1.5 Cooper T73-Climax V8	engine	15/20
7	FRENCH GP	Rouen	14	Cooper Car Co	D	1.5 Cooper T73-Climax V8	1 lap behind	10/17
6	BRITISH GP	Brands Hatch	10	Cooper Car Co	D	1.5 Cooper T73-Climax V8	2 laps behind	15/25
ret	GERMAN GP	Nürburgring	10	Cooper Car Co	D	1.5 Cooper T73-Climax V8	engine	8/24
ret	AUSTRIAN GP	Zeltweg	10	Cooper Car Co	D	1.5 Cooper T66-Climax V8	accident-car written off	20/20
dns	"	"	10	Cooper Car Co	D	1.5 Cooper T73-Climax V8	accident in practice	–/–
ret	US GP	Watkins Glen	10	Cooper Car Co	D	1.5 Cooper T73-Climax V8	ignition	19/19
9/ret	MEXICAN GP	Mexico City	10	Cooper Car Co	D	1.5 Cooper T73-Climax V8	engine/2 laps behind	15/19

1966 — Championship position: Unplaced

	Race	Circuit	No	Entrant	Tyres	Car/Engine	Comment	Q Pos/Entries
dns	MONACO GP	Monte Carlo	20	Phil Hill	F	1.5 Lotus 33-Climax V8	camera car-not competing	–/–
dns	BELGIAN GP	Spa	28	Phil Hill	F	4.7 McLaren-Ford V8	camera car-not competing	–/–
dnq	ITALIAN GP	Monza	34	Anglo American Racers	G	2.7 Eagle TG101-Climax 4		21/22

GP Starts: 48 GP Wins: 3 Pole positions: 6 Fastest laps: 6 Points: 98

PETER HIRT

Hirt, along with de Terra, was a gentleman Swiss driver who occasionally took part in major races and never remotely troubled the leaders.

He purchased one of Loof's Veritas-Meteors with fellow countryman Paul Glauser, and ran it during the 1950 and 1951 seasons, but it proved very unreliable in his hands, regularly posting early retirements. He was glad to join forces with Rudi Fischer in 1952 when the Swiss pair ran Formula 2 Ferraris under the Ecurie Espadon (swordfish) banner. Peter ran the old T212 car with no great success, and after having a bash in the team's T500 at Bremgarten late in 1953 he was seen no more on the circuits at major level.

DAVID HOBBS

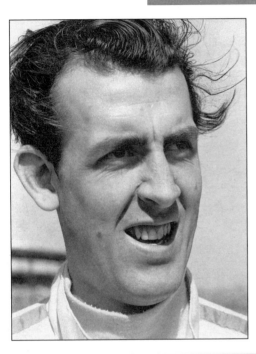

With only the occasional foray into Grand Prix racing, Hobbs forged a very satisfying career for himself over three decades, starting in the early 1960s with Lotus and Jaguar sports cars before graduating to Formula Junior, Formula 2 and then 'big-banger' sports cars with the Lola T70 in 1965.

His first Formula 1 break came with Bernard White's BRM, in which he finished third in the 1966 Syracuse GP, and this led to a season of F2 with Team Surtees in 1967, before he fully established himself in the top league of sports car racing with the John Wyer team in 1968 by winning the Monza 1000 Km in a Ford GT40.

The advent of F5000/Formula A in 1969 was to provide a profitable furrow for David to plough over the next few seasons, particularly with Carl Hogan's Lola in the States, where he was to base himself more and more. In 1974 he finished fifth in the Indianapolis 500 with a McLaren, and later in the season he deputised for the injured Mike Hailwood in a couple of Grands Prix. The sheer variety of cars that Hobbs drove throughout a career that encompassed F1, F2, endurance, Can-Am, F5000, touring cars, IMSA and much more is simply bewildering. Into the nineties David still raced occasionally, before concentrating on his role as a TV commentator for Speedvision in America, which he performed with all the characteristic professionalism one would expect from this seasoned racer.

HIRT, Peter (CH) b 30/3/1910 – d 26/6/1992

	1951	Championship position: Unplaced						
	Race	Circuit	No	Entrant	Tyres	Car/Engine	Comment	Q Pos/Entries
ret	SWISS GP	Bremgarten	52	Peter Hirt	–	2.0 Veritas Meteor 6	fuel pump-lap 1	16/21
	1952	Championship position: Unplaced						
7	SWISS GP	Bremgarten	44	Ecurie Espadon	P	2.0 Ferrari 212 V12	6 laps behind	19/21
11*	FRENCH GP	Rouen	34	Ecurie Espadon	P	2.0 Ferrari 212 V12	*took over Fischer's car/-13 laps	– / –
ret	BRITISH GP	Silverstone	20	Ecurie Espadon	P	2.0 Ferrari 212 V12	brakes	24/32
	1953	Championship position: Unplaced						
ret	SWISS GP	Bremgarten	38	Ecurie Espadon	P	2.0 Ferrari 500 4	water pump	17/23

GP Starts: 5   GP Wins: 0   Pole positions: 0   Fastest laps: 0   Points: 0

HOBBS, David (GB) b 9/6/1939, Leamington Spa, Warwickshire

	1967	Championship position: Unplaced						
	Race	Circuit	No	Entrant	Tyres	Car/Engine	Comment	Q Pos/Entries
8	BRITISH GP	Silverstone	20	Bernard White Racing	G	2.0 BRM P261 V8	3 laps behind	14/21
10*	GERMAN GP (F2)	Nürburgring	27	Lola Cars Ltd	F	1.6 Lola T100-BMW 4 F2	*3rd in F2 class/-2 laps	20/25
9	CANADIAN GP	Mosport Park	12	Bernard White Racing	G	2.0 BRM P261 V8	5 laps behind	12/19
	1968	Championship position: Unplaced						
ret	ITALIAN GP	Monza	15	Honda Racing	F	3.0 Honda RA301 V12	engine	15/24
	1971	Championship position: Unplaced						
10	US GP	Watkins Glen	31	Penske White Racing	G	3.0 McLaren M19A-Cosworth V8	stood in for Donohue/-1 lap	24/32
	1974	Championship position: Unplaced						
7	AUSTRIAN GP	Österreichring	33	Yardley Team McLaren	G	3.0 McLaren M23-Cosworth V8	1 lap behind	17/31
9	ITALIAN GP	Monza	33	Yardley Team McLaren	G	3.0 McLaren M23-Cosworth V8	1 lap behind	23/31

GP Starts: 7   GP Wins: 0   Pole positions: 0   Fastest laps: 0   Points: 0

HOFFMANN, Ingo (BR) b 18/2/1953, São Paulo

	1976	Championship position: Unplaced							
	Race	Circuit	No	Entrant	Tyres	Car/Engine	Comment		Q Pos/Entries
11	BRAZILIAN GP	Interlagos	31	Copersucar-Fittipaldi	G	3.0 Fittipaldi FD03-Cosworth V8	1 lap behind		20/22
dnq	US GP WEST	Long Beach	31	Copersucar-Fittipaldi	G	3.0 Fittipaldi FD04-Cosworth V8			22/27
dnq	SPANISH GP	Jarama	31	Copersucar-Fittipaldi	G	3.0 Fittipaldi FD04-Cosworth V8			30/30
dnq	FRENCH GP	Paul Ricard	31	Copersucar-Fittipaldi	G	3.0 Fittipaldi FD04-Cosworth V8			28/30
	1977	Championship position: Unplaced							
ret	ARGENTINE GP	Buenos Aires	29	Copersucar-Fittipaldi	G	3.0 Fittipaldi FD04-Cosworth V8	engine		19/21
7	BRAZILIAN GP	Interlagos	29	Copersucar-Fittipaldi	G	3.0 Fittipaldi FD04-Cosworth V8	2 laps behind		19/22

GP Starts: 3   GP Wins: 0   Pole positions: 0   Fastest laps: 0   Points: 0

HOSHINO, Kazuyoshi (J) b 1/7/1947, Shizuoka Prefecture

	1976	Championship position: Unplaced							
	Race	Circuit	No	Entrant	Tyres	Car/Engine	Comment		Q Pos/Entries
ret	JAPANESE GP	Mount Fuji	52	Heros Racing	B	3.0 Tyrrell 007-Cosworth V8	used up tyres-no more available		21/27
	1977	Championship position: Unplaced							
11	JAPANESE GP	Mount Fuji	52	Heros Racing	B	3.0 Kojima KE009-Cosworth V8	2 laps behind		11/23

GP Starts: 2   GP Wins: 0   Pole positions: 0   Fastest laps: 0   Points: 0

INGO HOFFMANN

Hoffmann was a talented driver whose career was laid waste by a disastrous spell in the Fittipaldi brothers' Copersucar team.

A top Super Vee and saloon car driver in his native Brazil, Ingo came to Britain in 1975 and contested the Formula 3 series in a March, before his move into Grands Prix with Fittipaldi. With the team beset by all sorts of problems, Hoffmann's difficulties were inevitably very much secondary to those of the team leader and after just two races of the 1977 season the second car was withdrawn, leaving the unhappy Ingo to concentrate on a programme of Formula 2 for Project Four with a Ralt.

Although outright success eluded him in this class, he proved to be a very quick and tough competitor, and produced some great performances – particularly in 1978, his last season in Europe, in the Project Four March. It is a shame that a second Grand Prix chance did not come the Brazilian's way, but since his return home he has become an eight-times winner in the Brazilian stock car championship with more than forty wins to his name.

In recent years he has successfully shared a BMW with Nelson Piquet in long-distance touring car events and still competes in the SudAm Super Touring championship with a BMW 320i, finishing third overall in the 1998 series.

KAZUYOSHI HOSHINO

His remarkable performance in the rain-sodden 1976 Japanese GP with a private Tyrrell on Bridgestone tyres confirmed Hoshino as one of Japan's leading drivers – indeed many believe he is Japan's greatest-ever racer.

Kazuyoshi was a works Nissan driver as far back as 1969, and since then he has swept the board in many forms of domestic racing, being a four-times Formula 2/F3000 champion as well as a multiple Grand Champion.

The 1993 season saw the veteran snatch the Japanese F3000 title for the third time at the wheel of a Lola from the grasp of a clutch of young and hungry European drivers. Typically he continued to be ultra-competitive in Formula Nippon right up to the end of 1996, his final year in single-seaters.

Hoshino has also been a regular member of the Nissan sports car team, winning the Daytona 24 Hours in 1992 with his compatriots Masahiro Hasemi and Toshio Suzuki. More recently he finished third at Le Mans in 1998 in the Nissan R390 with Aguri Suzuki and Masahiro Kageyama.

In 1994 he took the All-Japan touring car title outright, having previously shared the crown with Toshio Suzuki in 1990.

Since 1997 Hoshino has concentrated racing Nissan on the Japanese GT and Touring Car championships as well as running his own Formula Nippon team.

DENNY HULME

If there can be such a thing as an unfashionable World Champion, then that is what Denny Hulme was. Self-effacing to the point of anonymity in his public persona, he eschewed the glamorous trappings that Grand Prix racing had to offer, but in fact he was no shrinking violet and his inner determination was second to none, born of many years working as a humble mechanic.

After making an impact on the local scene, he came to Europe in 1960 with George Lawton on the 'New Zealand Driver to Europe' scheme, racing a Cooper in Formula 2 and Formula Junior around the Continent. Unfortunately poor Lawton was soon killed at Roskilde Ring but Hulme carried on before returning home to contest his local series early in 1961. He was soon back in Europe, carving out a reputation for himself in Ken Tyrrell's Cooper and the works Brabham, replacing the retired Gavin Youl.

While still working as a mechanic at Brabham, Hulme took over the leadership of the Junior team in 1963, winning seven of the 14 races he entered. Although top-flight chances were limited, Jack was shrewd enough to realise the young New Zealander's potential and took him down to the 1964 Tasman series, where he won at Levin and finished second in the New Zealand GP. Supporting his boss in the Formula 2 championship that year, Denny won two races, at Clermont Ferrand and Zolder, with plenty of other good placings besides. In 1965 Brabham had the problem of running himself, Gurney and Hulme, so he shuffled the pack to ensure that Hulme was well prepared for the 3-litre formula, and Denny backed 'Black Jack' superbly in 1966 as his mentor enjoyed an Indian summer and took the championship. As well as having another successful Formula 2 season, Denny also raced sports cars, taking second place at Le Mans with Ken Miles in a Ford GT40, and winning the Tourist Trophy and Martini International in Sid Taylor's Lola.

In 1967 it was Hulme's turn to take the spotlight. His wins in the Monaco and German GPs were the outstanding performances, but he scored points in all but two races to edge out his boss and claim the drivers' crown for himself. Typically thinking ahead, Denny had already decided to join forces with fellow 'Kiwi' Bruce McLaren in 1968, and he started the year in the team's new bright-orange livery. An early-season win in the International Trophy and then third to Bruce in the Race of Champions indicated things were on the right track, and sure enough Hulme's consistent approach put him in with an outside title chance after wins at Monza and Mont Tremblant. In the end his efforts fell short, but as a team McLaren had established themselves as a front-line outfit in both Formula 1 and Can-Am, which proved a lucrative sideline for both driver and constructor. Hulme took the Can-Am title that year, but this success could have been a double-edged sword, for the 1969 Grand Prix season only provided Denny with an end-of-season win in Mexico.

The following season should have been a real breakthrough year for the team, but instead it saw catastrophe as McLaren was killed in a testing accident, and Hulme was involved in a practice crash at Indy which left him with nasty burns to hands and feet. That the team recovered so well from Bruce's loss was a great credit to Denny, who hid his own devastation and gave the team a new sense of purpose by winning the Can-Am championship for the second time. From then on the tough New Zealander's approach became more circumspect. If he could sniff the scent of victory then he would really get stuck in, as we saw at Kyalami in 1972 and Sweden in 1973, but generally he drove within his limits. He was always a factor, even in his final season in 1974 when he pounced to claim a win in Argentina after a patient race. But after he had been on the scene of Peter Revson's fatal accident at Kyalami, he was generally content to let younger lions risk their necks before unobtrusively easing himself into a retirement of sorts.

Though Formula 1 was in the past, the lure of competition was too strong, and from 1978 he raced touring cars and trucks as and when the fancy took him with all the grit and determination he showed in his heyday. He was competing in the Bathurst 1000 Km in October 1992 when suddenly he pulled his BMW M3 over and parked neatly on the grass alongside the Armco barrier. For a while nothing happened, and when marshals arrived they found Denny dead, still strapped into the car, having apparently suffered a heart attack at the early age of 56.

Denny Hulme's victory in the 1967 Monaco Grand Prix at the wheel of the Brabham BT20-Repco V8 paved the way for his World Championship triumph.

DENNY HULME

WORLD CHAMPION: 1967

HULME, Denny (Clive Denis) (NZ) b 18/6/1936, Nelson – d 4/10/1992, Bathurst Circuit, NSW, Australia

1965 — Championship position: 11th   Wins: 0   Pole positions: 0   Fastest laps: 0   Points scored: 5

	Race	Circuit	No	Entrant	Tyres	Car/Engine	Comment	Q Pos/Entries
8	MONACO GP	Monte Carlo	2	Brabham Racing Organisation	G	1.5 Brabham BT7-Climax V8	pit stop/8 laps behind	8/17
4	FRENCH GP	Clermont Ferrand	16	Brabham Racing Organisation	G	1.5 Brabham BT11-Climax V8		6/17
ret	BRITISH GP	Silverstone	14	Brabham Racing Organisation	G	1.5 Brabham BT7-Climax V8	alternator belt	=9/23
5	DUTCH GP	Zandvoort	14	Brabham Racing Organisation	G	1.5 Brabham BT11-Climax V8	1 lap behind	7/17
ret	GERMAN GP	Nürburgring	6	Brabham Racing Organisation	G	1.5 Brabham BT7-Climax V8	fuel leak	13/22
ret	ITALIAN GP	Monza	14	Brabham Racing Organisation	G	1.5 Brabham BT11-Climax V8	suspension	12/23

1966 — Championship position: 4th   Wins: 0   Pole positions: 0   Fastest laps: 1   Points scored: 18

	Race	Circuit	No	Entrant	Tyres	Car/Engine	Comment	Q Pos/Entries
ret	MONACO GP	Monte Carlo	8	Brabham Racing Organisation	G	2.5 Brabham BT11-Climax 4	driveshaft	6/16
ret	BELGIAN GP	Spa	4	Brabham Racing Organisation	G	2.5 Brabham BT11-Climax 4	collision with Siffert	13/18
3	FRENCH GP	Reims	14	Brabham Racing Organisation	G	3.0 Brabham BT20-Repco V8	out of fuel last lap/-2 laps	9/17
dns	"	"	12	Brabham Racing Organisation	G	3.0 Brabham BT19-Repco V8	practice only	– / –
2	BRITISH GP	Brands Hatch	6	Brabham Racing Organisation	G	3.0 Brabham BT20-Repco V8		2/20
ret	DUTCH GP	Zandvoort	18	Brabham Racing Organisation	G	3.0 Brabham BT20-Repco V8	ignition/FL	=2/18
ret	GERMAN GP	Nürburgring	4	Brabham Racing Organisation	G	3.0 Brabham BT20-Repco V8	ignition	16/30
3	ITALIAN GP	Monza	12	Brabham Racing Organisation	G	3.0 Brabham BT20-Repco V8		10/22
ret	US GP	Watkins Glen	6	Brabham Racing Organisation	G	3.0 Brabham BT20-Repco V8	oil pressure	7/19
3	MEXICAN GP	Mexico City	6	Brabham Racing Organisation	G	3.0 Brabham BT20-Repco V8	1 lap behind	6/19

1967 — Championship position: WORLD CHAMPION   Wins: 2   Pole positions: 0   Fastest laps: 2   Points scored: 51

	Race	Circuit	No	Entrant	Tyres	Car/Engine	Comment	Q Pos/Entries
4	SOUTH AFRICAN GP	Kyalami	2	Brabham Racing Organisation	G	3.0 Brabham BT20-Repco V8	2 pit stops-brakes/FL/-2 laps	2/18
1	MONACO GP	Monte Carlo	9	Brabham Racing Organisation	G	3.0 Brabham BT20-Repco V8		=4/18
3	DUTCH GP	Zandvoort	2	Brabham Racing Organisation	G	3.0 Brabham BT20-Repco V8		=6/17
ret	BELGIAN GP	Spa	26	Brabham Racing Organisation	G	3.0 Brabham BT19-Repco V8	engine	14/18
2	FRENCH GP	Le Mans	4	Brabham Racing Organisation	G	3.0 Brabham BT24-Repco V8		6/15
2	BRITISH GP	Silverstone	2	Brabham Racing Organisation	G	3.0 Brabham BT24-Repco V8	FL	4/21
1	GERMAN GP	Nürburgring	2	Brabham Racing Organisation	G	3.0 Brabham BT24-Repco V8		2/25
2	CANADIAN GP	Mosport Park	2	Brabham Racing Organisation	G	3.0 Brabham BT24-Repco V8		3/19
ret	ITALIAN GP	Monza	18	Brabham Racing Organisation	G	3.0 Brabham BT24-Repco V8	overheating engine	6/18
3	US GP	Watkins Glen	2	Brabham Racing Organisation	G	3.0 Brabham BT24-Repco V8	1 lap behind	6/18
3	MEXICAN GP	Mexico City	2	Brabham Racing Organisation	G	3.0 Brabham BT24-Repco V8	1 lap behind	6/19

1968 — Championship position: 3rd   Wins: 2   Pole positions: 0   Fastest laps: 0   Points scored: 33

	Race	Circuit	No	Entrant	Tyres	Car/Engine	Comment	Q Pos/Entries
5	SOUTH AFRICAN GP	Kyalami	1	Bruce McLaren Motor Racing	G	3.0 McLaren M5A-BRM V12	2 laps behind	9/23
2	SPANISH GP	Jarama	1	Bruce McLaren Motor Racing	G	3.0 McLaren M7A-Cosworth V8		3/14
5	MONACO GP	Monte Carlo	12	Bruce McLaren Motor Racing	G	3.0 McLaren M7A-Cosworth V8	long pit stop-driveshaft/-7 laps	=9/18
ret	BELGIAN GP	Spa	6	Bruce McLaren Motor Racing	G	3.0 McLaren M7A-Cosworth V8	driveshaft	5/18
ret	DUTCH GP	Zandvoort	1	Bruce McLaren Motor Racing	G	3.0 McLaren M7A-Cosworth V8	damp ignition	7/19
5	FRENCH GP	Rouen	8	Bruce McLaren Motor Racing	G	3.0 McLaren M7A-Cosworth V8	2 laps behind	4/18
4	BRITISH GP	Brands Hatch	1	Bruce McLaren Motor Racing	G	3.0 McLaren M7A-Cosworth V8	1 lap behind	=10/20
7	GERMAN GP	Nürburgring	1	Bruce McLaren Motor Racing	G	3.0 McLaren M7A-Cosworth V8		11/20
1	ITALIAN GP	Monza	1	Bruce McLaren Motor Racing	G	3.0 McLaren M7A-Cosworth V8		7/24
1	CANADIAN GP	St Jovite	1	Bruce McLaren Motor Racing	G	3.0 McLaren M7A-Cosworth V8		=6/22
ret	US GP	Watkins Glen	1	Bruce McLaren Motor Racing	G	3.0 McLaren M7A-Cosworth V8	spun off	5/21
ret	MEXICAN GP	Mexico City	1	Bruce McLaren Motor Racing	G	3.0 McLaren M7A-Cosworth V8	suspension collapsed-crashed	4/21

1969 — Championship position: 6th   Wins: 1   Pole positions: 0   Fastest laps: 0   Points scored: 20

	Race	Circuit	No	Entrant	Tyres	Car/Engine	Comment	Q Pos/Entries
3	SOUTH AFRICAN GP	Kyalami	5	Bruce McLaren Motor Racing	G	3.0 McLaren M7A-Cosworth V8		3/18
4	SPANISH GP	Montjuich Park	5	Bruce McLaren Motor Racing	G	3.0 McLaren M7A-Cosworth V8	pit stop-handling/-3 laps	8/14
6	MONACO GP	Monte Carlo	3	Bruce McLaren Motor Racing	G	3.0 McLaren M7A-Cosworth V8	unwell/2 laps behind	12/16
4	DUTCH GP	Zandvoort	7	Bruce McLaren Motor Racing	G	3.0 McLaren M7A-Cosworth V8		7/15
8	FRENCH GP	Clermont Ferrand	4	Bruce McLaren Motor Racing	G	3.0 McLaren M7A-Cosworth V8	brake problems/3 laps behind	2/13
ret	BRITISH GP	Silverstone	5	Bruce McLaren Motor Racing	G	3.0 McLaren M7A-Cosworth V8	engine	3/17
ret	GERMAN GP	Nürburgring	9	Bruce McLaren Motor Racing	G	3.0 McLaren M7A-Cosworth V8	transmission	5/26
7	ITALIAN GP	Monza	16	Bruce McLaren Motor Racing	G	3.0 McLaren M7A-Cosworth V8	brake problems/2 laps behind	2/15

Denny's last win came at the 1974 Argentine Grand Prix. Crowd safety didn't seem to be much of an issue at the Buenos Aires circuit if this photo is anything to go by!

ret	CANADIAN GP	Mosport Park	5	Bruce McLaren Motor Racing	G	3.0 McLaren M7A-Cosworth V8	distributor	=5/20
ret	US GP	Watkins Glen	5	Bruce McLaren Motor Racing	G	3.0 McLaren M7A-Cosworth V8	gear selection	2/18
1	MEXICAN GP	Mexico City	5	Bruce McLaren Motor Racing	G	3.0 McLaren M7A-Cosworth V8		4/17

1970 — Championship position: 4th   Wins: 0   Pole positions: 0   Fastest laps: 0   Points scored: 27

2	SOUTH AFRICAN GP	Kyalami	6	Bruce McLaren Motor Racing	G	3.0 McLaren M14A-Cosworth V8		6/24
ret	SPANISH GP	Jarama	9	Bruce McLaren Motor Racing	G	3.0 McLaren M14A-Cosworth V8	rotor arm shaft	2/22
4	MONACO GP	Monte Carlo	11	Bruce McLaren Motor Racing	G	3.0 McLaren M14A-Cosworth V8		3/21
4	FRENCH GP	Clermont Ferrand	19	Bruce McLaren Motor Racing	G	3.0 McLaren M14D-Cosworth V8		7/23
3	BRITISH GP	Brands Hatch	9	Bruce McLaren Motor Racing	G	3.0 McLaren M14D-Cosworth V8		=4/25
3	GERMAN GP	Hockenheim	4	Bruce McLaren Motor Racing	G	3.0 McLaren M14A-Cosworth V8		16/25
ret	AUSTRIAN GP	Österreichring	21	Bruce McLaren Motor Racing	G	3.0 McLaren M14A-Cosworth V8	engine	=11/24
4	ITALIAN GP	Monza	30	Bruce McLaren Motor Racing	G	3.0 McLaren M14A-Cosworth V8		9/27
ret	CANADIAN GP	St Jovite	5	Bruce McLaren Motor Racing	G	3.0 McLaren M14A-Cosworth V8	flywheel	15/20
7	US GP	Watkins Glen	8	Bruce McLaren Motor Racing	G	3.0 McLaren M14A-Cosworth V8	2 laps behind	11/27
3	MEXICAN GP	Mexico City	8	Bruce McLaren Motor Racing	G	3.0 McLaren M14A-Cosworth V8		14/18

1971 — Championship position: 9   Wins: 0   Pole positions: 0   Fastest laps: 1   Points scored: 9

6	SOUTH AFRICAN GP	Kyalami	11	Bruce McLaren Motor Racing	G	3.0 McLaren M19A-Cosworth V8	suspension problems/-1 lap	=5/25
5	SPANISH GP	Montjuich Park	9	Bruce McLaren Motor Racing	G	3.0 McLaren M19A-Cosworth V8		9/22
4	MONACO GP	Monte Carlo	9	Bruce McLaren Motor Racing	G	3.0 McLaren M19A-Cosworth V8		6/23
12	DUTCH GP	Zandvoort	26	Bruce McLaren Motor Racing	G	3.0 McLaren M19A-Cosworth V8	7 laps behind	14/24
ret	FRENCH GP	Paul Ricard	9	Bruce McLaren Motor Racing	G	3.0 McLaren M19A-Cosworth V8	ignition	11/24
ret	BRITISH GP	Silverstone	9	Bruce McLaren Motor Racing	G	3.0 McLaren M19A-Cosworth V8	engine	8/24
ret	GERMAN GP	Nürburgring	18	Bruce McLaren Motor Racing	G	3.0 McLaren M19A-Cosworth V8	fuel leak	6/23
ret	AUSTRIAN GP	Österreichring	9	Bruce McLaren Motor Racing	G	3.0 McLaren M19A-Cosworth V8	engine	9/22
4	CANADIAN GP	Mosport Park	9	Bruce McLaren Motor Racing	G	3.0 McLaren M19A-Cosworth V8	FL/1 lap behind	10/27
ret	US GP	Watkins Glen	7	Bruce McLaren Motor Racing	G	3.0 McLaren M19A-Cosworth V8	spun off on oil	3/32

1972 — Championship position: 3rd   Wins: 1   Pole positions: 0   Fastest laps: 1   Points scored: 39

2	ARGENTINE GP	Buenos Aires	17	Yardley Team McLaren	G	3.0 McLaren M19A-Cosworth V8		4/22
1	SOUTH AFRICAN GP	Kyalami	12	Yardley Team McLaren	G	3.0 McLaren M19A-Cosworth V8		=3/27
ret	SPANISH GP	Jarama	11	Yardley Team McLaren	G	3.0 McLaren M19A-Cosworth V8	gearbox	2/26
dns	"	"	11	Yardley Team McLaren	G	3.0 McLaren M19C-Cosworth V8	practice only	–/–
15	MONACO GP	Monte Carlo	14	Yardley Team McLaren	G	3.0 McLaren M19C-Cosworth V8	hit guard rail/6 laps behind	7/25
dns	"	" "	14T	Yardley Team McLaren	G	3.0 McLaren M19C-Cosworth V8	practice only	–/–
3	BELGIAN GP	Nivelles	9	Yardley Team McLaren	G	3.0 McLaren M19C-Cosworth V8		3/26
dns			9T	Yardley Team McLaren	G	3.0 McLaren M19A-Cosworth V8	practice only-not timed	–/–
7	FRENCH GP	Clermont Ferrand	2	Yardley Team McLaren	G	3.0 McLaren M19C-Cosworth V8	pit stop-puncture	2/29
dns	"	" "	2T	Yardley Team McLaren	G	3.0 McLaren M19C-Cosworth V8	practice only	–/–
5	BRITISH GP	Brands Hatch	18	Yardley Team McLaren	G	3.0 McLaren M19C-Cosworth V8	1 lap behind	=11/27
ret	GERMAN GP	Nürburgring	3	Yardley Team McLaren	G	3.0 McLaren M19C-Cosworth V8	engine	10/27
2	AUSTRIAN GP	Österreichring	12	Yardley Team McLaren	G	3.0 McLaren M19C-Cosworth V8	FL	7/26
dns			12T	Yardley Team McLaren	G	3.0 McLaren M19C-Cosworth V8	practice only	–/–
3	ITALIAN GP	Monza	14	Yardley Team McLaren	G	3.0 McLaren M19C-Cosworth V8		5/27
dns		"	14T	Yardley Team McLaren	G	3.0 McLaren M19A-Cosworth V8	practice only	–/–
3	CANADIAN GP	Mosport Park	18	Yardley Team McLaren	G	3.0 McLaren M19C-Cosworth V8		2/25
dns	"	" "	18T	Yardley Team McLaren	G	3.0 McLaren M19C-Cosworth V8	practice only	–/–
3	US GP	Watkins Glen	19	Yardley Team McLaren	G	3.0 McLaren M19C-Cosworth V8		3/22

1973 — Championship position: 6th   Wins: 1   Pole positions: 1   Fastest laps: 3 (1 shared)   Points scored: 26

5	ARGENTINE GP	Buenos Aires	14	Yardley Team McLaren	G	3.0 McLaren M19C-Cosworth V8	1 lap behind	8/19
3	BRAZILIAN GP	Interlagos	7	Yardley Team McLaren	G	3.0 McLaren M19C-Cosworth V8	FL(shared with Fittipaldi)	5/20
5	SOUTH AFRICAN GP	Kyalami	5	Yardley Team McLaren	G	3.0 McLaren M23-Cosworth V8	p stop-puncture/2 laps behind	1/25
6	SPANISH GP	Montjuich Park	5	Yardley Team McLaren	G	3.0 McLaren M23-Cosworth V8	pit stop-wheel/1 lap behind	2/22
7	BELGIAN GP	Zolder	7	Yardley Team McLaren	G	3.0 McLaren M23-Cosworth V8	spin-pit stop/3 laps behind	2/23
6	MONACO GP	Monte Carlo	7	Yardley Team McLaren	G	3.0 McLaren M23-Cosworth V8	pit stop-gear linkage/-2 laps	3/26
1	SWEDISH GP	Anderstorp	7	Yardley Team McLaren	G	3.0 McLaren M23-Cosworth V8	FL	6/22
8	FRENCH GP	Paul Ricard	7	Yardley Team McLaren	G	3.0 McLaren M23-Cosworth V8	pit stop-tyre/FL	6/25
3	BRITISH GP	Silverstone	7	Yardley Team McLaren	G	3.0 McLaren M23-Cosworth V8		=2/29
ret	DUTCH GP	Zandvoort	7	Yardley Team McLaren	G	3.0 McLaren M23-Cosworth V8	engine	4/24
12	GERMAN GP	Nürburgring	7	Yardley Team McLaren	G	3.0 McLaren M23-Cosworth V8	pit stop-exhaust	8/23
8	AUSTRIAN GP	Österreichring	7	Yardley Team McLaren	G	3.0 McLaren M23-Cosworth V8	3 pit stops-plugs/-1 lap	3/25
15	ITALIAN GP	Monza	7	Yardley Team McLaren	G	3.0 McLaren M23-Cosworth V8	spin-pit stop/2 laps behind	3/25
13	CANADIAN GP	Mosport Park	7	Yardley Team McLaren	G	3.0 McLaren M23-Cosworth V8	pit stop-puncture/-5 laps	7/26
4	US GP	Watkins Glen	7	Yardley Team McLaren	G	3.0 McLaren M23-Cosworth V8		9/28

1974 — Championship position: 7th   Wins: 1   Pole positions: 0   Fastest laps: 1   Points scored: 20

1	ARGENTINE GP	Buenos Aires	6	Marlboro Team Texaco	G	3.0 McLaren M23-Cosworth V8		10/26
12	BRAZILIAN GP	Interlagos	6	Marlboro Team Texaco	G	3.0 McLaren M23-Cosworth V8	pit stop-front tyres/-1 lap	11/25
9	SOUTH AFRICAN GP	Kyalami	6	Marlboro Team Texaco	G	3.0 McLaren M23-Cosworth V8	1 lap behind	9/27
6	SPANISH GP	Jarama	56	Marlboro Team Texaco	G	3.0 McLaren M23-Cosworth V8	pit stop-suspension/-2 laps	8/28
6	BELGIAN GP	Nivelles	6	Marlboro Team Texaco	G	3.0 McLaren M23-Cosworth V8	FL	12/32
ret	MONACO GP	Monte Carlo	6	Marlboro Team Texaco	G	3.0 McLaren M23-Cosworth V8	collision with Beltoise	=12/28
ret	SWEDISH GP	Anderstorp	6	Marlboro Team Texaco	G	3.0 McLaren M23-Cosworth V8	suspension	12/28
ret	DUTCH GP	Zandvoort	6	Marlboro Team Texaco	G	3.0 McLaren M23-Cosworth V8	ignition	9/27
6	FRENCH GP	Dijon	6	Marlboro Team Texaco	G	3.0 McLaren M23-Cosworth V8		11/30
7	BRITISH GP	Brands Hatch	6	Marlboro Team Texaco	G	3.0 McLaren M23-Cosworth V8	1 lap behind	=19/34
ret	GERMAN GP	Nürburgring	6	Marlboro Team Texaco	G	3.0 McLaren M23-Cosworth V8	accident on starting grid	7/32
dsq	"	"	5T	Marlboro Team Texaco	G	3.0 McLaren M23-Cosworth V8	restarted from pits in spare car	–/–
2	AUSTRIAN GP	Österreichring	6	Marlboro Team Texaco	G	3.0 McLaren M23-Cosworth V8		10/31
6	ITALIAN GP	Monza	6	Marlboro Team Texaco	G	3.0 McLaren M23-Cosworth V8	1 lap behind	19/31
6	CANADIAN GP	Mosport Park	6	Marlboro Team Texaco	G	3.0 McLaren M23-Cosworth V8	1 lap behind	14/30
ret	US GP	Watkins Glen	6	Marlboro Team Texaco	G	3.0 McLaren M23-Cosworth V8	engine	17/30

GP Starts: 112   GP Wins: 8   Pole positions: 1   Fastest laps: 9 (1 shared)   Points: 248

JAMES HUNT

WORLD CHAMPION: 1976

JAMES HUNT

Some drivers are cut out for the big stage, and undoubtedly James Hunt was a prime example. Here was a man who, having been quick but not at all convincing in his early career, took to Grand Prix racing like the proverbial 'duck to water', confounding his critics who had given him the unkind but not entirely inappropriate nickname of 'Hunt the Shunt'.

Though the son of a Surrey stockbroker, James had to finance his early racing career largely from his own pocket, stacking the shelves in his local Sainsbury's in order to race his Mini before moving into Formula Ford in 1968 with an Alexis and then a Merlyn Mk 11A in 1969. Midway through the season James moved up to F3 with a Brabham BT21B, but found the competition hot, gaining success only in Libre events at Brands Hatch.

It was during the 1970 season, when he was equipped with a Lotus 59, that people began to sit up and take notice, and not only because of his wins at Rouen and Zolder, for late in the season he was involved in a last-corner collision with Dave Morgan which saw the irate James exact pugilistic retribution on the spot. His penchant for attracting controversy followed him into the 1971 season, which was littered with accidents and mechanical gremlins, but once again he proved beyond doubt that when trouble stayed away he was a serious contender. March certainly thought so as they signed him for their STP-backed works car in 1972, but the team fell apart and as luck would have it James joined forces with Lord Hesketh's Dastle F3 team. Almost immediately Hesketh took the plunge into Formula 2 and Hunt placed the team's car on the front row at the Salzburgring in his first race. After a really good drive he was forced to pull out with engine trouble, but crucially James had proved to himself that he was good enough. In the next race he gave a superb display at Oulton Park to finish third and there was now no stopping the upward momentum of 'young Master James'.

Third place in the 1973 Race of Champions with a hired Surtees convinced Lord Hesketh that Hunt had the talent for the big time, and James proved his faith was not misplaced, putting in some sensational performances once the team had acquired a March 731, with his drives at Zandvoort and Watkins Glen, where he dogged the Lotus of Ronnie Peterson, standing out. The Hesketh bandwagon was really gathering pace by now, and in 1974 the team launched their own car, which proved an immediate success, with Hunt winning the International Trophy before embarking on an up-and-down Grand Prix season which was marred by trivial mechanical failures and some misjudgements on the part of the driver, but contained some race-performance gems, such as in Austria where he drove from 18th after a pit stop to third at the finish. His reputation was such that Dan Gurney invited him over to the States to drive his Eagle in US F5000 for three races, his best result being a second at the Monterey GP. He also sampled sports cars, taking fourth at the Nürburgring 750 Km with Schuppan and Bell in John Wyer's Gulf-Ford.

That Hunt was a top-drawer racer was finally confirmed in 1975 when he drove the Hesketh to a magnificent win in the Dutch GP, defeating Lauda's Ferrari. To prove it was no fluke, Hunt took three second places that year before the financial burden of running the team independently became

Hesketh's great day as Hunt wins the 1975 Dutch Grand Prix for the privateer team.

too great for its aristocratic patron. Briefly James looked to be without a drive for 1976, but with Fittipaldi's sudden defection to his family's Copersucar-backed project, Hunt found himself installed alongside Jochen Mass at McLaren. It was to be a season of high drama, controversy and courage, which saw James and his great pal Niki Lauda fight it out for the championship in a fashion which captured the imagination of the world at large and was surely instrumental in increasing the sport's popularity during subsequent years. James soon asserted his number one status in the team by claiming pole in Brazil and then winning the Race of Champions and International Trophy. His first Grand Prix win for McLaren was contentious, Hunt being re-instated after a post-race disqualification in Spain, but a victory in France kept him in touch, and then came the famous British GP at Brands. Hunt, having been taken out by Regazzoni in a first-corner mêlée, won the restarted race but was then disqualified. His championship chances seemed over, but after Lauda's fiery accident at the Nürburgring James had an outside chance. By the time the Austrian had bravely returned to the cockpit, Hunt had made inroads into his points lead, and once on a roll he proved difficult to resist with two brilliant wins in Canada and the US. The showdown in Japan was hyped more intensely than anything ever seen before, and while his rival withdrew Hunt stayed out on a flooded track to take third place and the coveted championship.

James was now a public figure way beyond the confines of the sport, and perhaps this began to affect his racing. In 1977 he still put in some superb performances to win at Silverstone, Watkins Glen and Fuji, but his refusal to appear on the rostrum at the final race showed the more petulant side to his nature. The ground-effect Lotus was by this time in the ascendancy and McLaren were slow to follow this route, which left Hunt struggling in 1978, though it has to be said the driver's apparent lack of motivation certainly didn't help matters. Feeling a move would be beneficial for all concerned, Hunt switched to Walter Wolf for one final season in 1979, but the car proved difficult to handle and James seemed generally disinclined to give his all when there was little chance of outright success. Abruptly, and with no regrets, he quit the cockpit after the Monaco GP.

Another career was soon to open up for the extremely articulate and self-opinionated Hunt. He joined Murray Walker in the BBC's commentary booth to form a wonderful partnership and would enliven many a dreary race with his astute and pithy comments. By the early nineties, despite well-publicised money worries, Hunt's roller-coaster personal life had at last become settled, and it was a great shock when he died in 1993 after a massive heart attack at the age of 45.

HUNT, James (GB) b 29/8/1947, Belmont, nr Sutton, Surrey – d 15/6/1993, Wimbledon, London

1973   Championship position: 8th   Wins: 0   Pole positions: 0   Fastest laps: 2   Points scored: 14

	Race	Circuit	No	Entrant	Tyres	Car/Engine	Comment	Q Pos/Entries
9/ret	MONACO GP	Monte Carlo	27	Hesketh Racing	F	3.0 March 731-Cosworth V8	engine/5 laps behind	18/26
6	FRENCH GP	Paul Ricard	27	Hesketh Racing	F	3.0 March 731-Cosworth V8		14/25
4	BRITISH GP	Silverstone	27	Hesketh Racing	F	3.0 March 731-Cosworth V8	FL	11/29
3	DUTCH GP	Zandvoort	27	Hesketh Racing	F	3.0 March 731-Cosworth V8		7/24
ret	AUSTRIAN GP	Österreichring	27	Hesketh Racing	F	3.0 March 731-Cosworth V8	fuel metering unit	9/25
dns	ITALIAN GP	Monza	27	Hesketh Racing	F	3.0 March 731-Cosworth V8	car damaged in practice	(25)/25
7	CANADIAN GP	Mosport Park	27	Hesketh Racing	F	3.0 March 731-Cosworth V8	pit stop-tyres/2 laps behind	15/26
2	US GP	Watkins Glen	27	Hesketh Racing	F	3.0 March 731-Cosworth V8	FL	5/28

1974   Championship position: 8th   Wins: 0   Pole positions: 0   Fastest laps: 0   Points scored: 15

	Race	Circuit	No	Entrant	Tyres	Car/Engine	Comment	Q Pos/Entries
ret	ARGENTINE GP	Buenos Aires	24	Hesketh Racing	F	3.0 March 731-Cosworth V8	overheating	5/26
9	BRAZILIAN GP	Interlagos	24	Hesketh Racing	F	3.0 March 731-Cosworth V8	1 lap behind	18/25
ret	SOUTH AFRICAN GP	Kyalami	24	Hesketh Racing	F	3.0 Hesketh 308-Cosworth V8	c.v. joint	14/27
10	SPANISH GP	Jarama	24	Hesketh Racing	F	3.0 Hesketh 308-Cosworth V8	pit stop-tyres/brakes/-3 laps	11/28
ret	BELGIAN GP	Nivelles	24	Hesketh Racing	F	3.0 Hesketh 308-Cosworth V8	rear suspension	9/32
ret	MONACO GP	Monte Carlo	24	Hesketh Racing	F	3.0 Hesketh 308-Cosworth V8	driveshaft	=7/28
3	SWEDISH GP	Anderstorp	24	Hesketh Racing	F	3.0 Hesketh 308-Cosworth V8		6/27
ret	DUTCH GP	Zandvoort	24	Hesketh Racing	F	3.0 Hesketh 308-Cosworth V8	collision with Pryce	6/27
ret	FRENCH GP	Dijon	24	Hesketh Racing	F	3.0 Hesketh 308-Cosworth V8	collision with Pryce	10/30
ret	BRITISH GP	Brands Hatch	24	Hesketh Racing	F	3.0 Hesketh 308-Cosworth V8	rear suspension-spun off	=5/34
ret	GERMAN GP	Nürburgring	24	Hesketh Racing	F	3.0 Hesketh 308-Cosworth V8	transmission	13/32
3	AUSTRIAN GP	Österreichring	24	Hesketh Racing	F	3.0 Hesketh 308-Cosworth V8	pit stop-tyre	7/31
ret	ITALIAN GP	Monza	24	Hesketh Racing	F	3.0 Hesketh 308-Cosworth V8	engine	8/31
4	CANADIAN GP	Mosport Park	24	Hesketh Racing	F	3.0 Hesketh 308-Cosworth V8		8/30
3	US GP	Watkins Glen	24	Hesketh Racing	F	3.0 Hesketh 308-Cosworth V8	fuel problems	2/30

1975   Championship position: 4th   Wins: 1   Pole positions: 0   Fastest laps: 1   Points scored: 33

	Race	Circuit	No	Entrant	Tyres	Car/Engine	Comment	Q Pos/Entries
2	ARGENTINE GP	Buenos Aires	24	Hesketh Racing	G	3.0 Hesketh 308-Cosworth V8	FL	6/23
6	BRAZILIAN GP	Interlagos	24	Hesketh Racing	G	3.0 Hesketh 308-Cosworth V8		7/23
ret	SOUTH AFRICAN GP	Kyalami	24	Hesketh Racing	G	3.0 Hesketh 308-Cosworth V8	fuel metering unit	12/28
ret	SPANISH GP	Montjuich Park	24	Hesketh Racing	G	3.0 Hesketh 308-Cosworth V8	spun off	3/26
ret	MONACO GP	Monte Carlo	24	Hesketh Racing	G	3.0 Hesketh 308-Cosworth V8	hit guard rail	11/26
ret	BELGIAN GP	Zolder	24	Hesketh Racing	G	3.0 Hesketh 308-Cosworth V8	gear linkage	11/24
ret	SWEDISH GP	Anderstorp	24	Hesketh Racing	G	3.0 Hesketh 308-Cosworth V8	brake pipe leakage	13/26
1	DUTCH GP	Zandvoort	24	Hesketh Racing	G	3.0 Hesketh 308-Cosworth V8	pit stop-tyres	3/25
2	FRENCH GP	Paul Ricard	24	Hesketh Racing	G	3.0 Hesketh 308-Cosworth V8		3/26
4/ret	BRITISH GP	Silverstone	24	Hesketh Racing	G	3.0 Hesketh 308-Cosworth V8	spun off in rainstorm/1 lap behind	9/28
ret	GERMAN GP	Nürburgring	24	Hesketh Racing	G	3.0 Hesketh 308-Cosworth V8	rear hub	=8/26
2*	AUSTRIAN GP	Österreichring	24	Hesketh Racing	G	3.0 Hesketh 308-Cosworth V8	*rain shortened race half points	2/30
5	ITALIAN GP	Monza	24	Hesketh Racing	G	3.0 Hesketh 308C-Cosworth V8		8/28
4	US GP	Watkins Glen	24	Hesketh Racing	G	3.0 Hesketh 308C-Cosworth V8		15/24
dns	"	" "	24	Hesketh Racing	G	3.0 Hesketh 308-Cosworth V8	practice only	–/–

1976   Championship position: WORLD CHAMPION   Wins: 5   Pole positions: 8   Fastest laps: 2   Points scored: 69

	Race	Circuit	No	Entrant	Tyres	Car/Engine	Comment	Q Pos/Entries
ret	BRAZILIAN GP	Interlagos	11	Marlboro Team McLaren	G	3.0 McLaren M23-Cosworth V8	stuck throttle-crashed	1/22
2	SOUTH AFRICAN GP	Kyalami	11	Marlboro Team McLaren	G	3.0 McLaren M23-Cosworth V8		1/25
ret	US GP WEST	Long Beach	11	Marlboro Team McLaren	G	3.0 McLaren M23-Cosworth V8	collision with Depailler	3/27
1	SPANISH GP	Jarama	11	Marlboro Team McLaren	G	3.0 McLaren M23-Cosworth V8	disqualified but later reinstated/	1/30
ret	BELGIAN GP	Zolder	11	Marlboro Team McLaren	G	3.0 McLaren M23-Cosworth V8	transmission	3/29
ret	MONACO GP	Monte Carlo	11	Marlboro Team McLaren	G	3.0 McLaren M23-Cosworth V8	engine	14/25
5	SWEDISH GP	Anderstorp	11	Marlboro Team McLaren	G	3.0 McLaren M23-Cosworth V8		8/27
1	FRENCH GP	Paul Ricard	11	Marlboro Team McLaren	G	3.0 McLaren M23-Cosworth V8		1/30
dsq	BRITISH GP	Brands Hatch	11	Marlboro Team McLaren	G	3.0 McLaren M23-Cosworth V8	used spare car in restart/1st on road	2/30
1	GERMAN GP	Nürburgring	11	Marlboro Team McLaren	G	3.0 McLaren M23-Cosworth V8	race restarted	1/28
4	AUSTRIAN GP	Österreichring	11	Marlboro Team McLaren	G	3.0 McLaren M23-Cosworth V8	FL	1/25
1	DUTCH GP	Zandvoort	11	Marlboro Team McLaren	G	3.0 McLaren M23-Cosworth V8		2/27

Japanese Grand Prix, 1976.
Hunt brings his McLaren
home in third place to win
the World Championship at
the last gasp.

	Race	Circuit	No	Entrant	Tyres	Car/Engine	Comment	Q Pos/Entries
ret	ITALIAN GP	Monza	11	Marlboro Team McLaren	G	3.0 McLaren M23-Cosworth V8	ran off circuit-stuck in sand	27/29
1	CANADIAN GP	Mosport Park	11	Marlboro Team McLaren	G	3.0 McLaren M23-Cosworth V8		1/27
1	US GP EAST	Watkins Glen	11	Marlboro Team McLaren	G	3.0 McLaren M23-Cosworth V8	FL	1/27
3	JAPANESE GP	Mount Fuji	11	Marlboro Team McLaren	G	3.0 McLaren M23-Cosworth V8	pit stop-tyre/1 lap behind	2/27

1977 Championship position: 5th Wins: 3 Pole positions: 6 Fastest laps: 3 Points scored: 40

	Race	Circuit	No	Entrant	Tyres	Car/Engine	Comment	Q Pos/Entries
ret	ARGENTINE GP	Buenos Aires	1	Marlboro Team McLaren	G	3.0 McLaren M23-Cosworth V8	suspension mounting/FL	1/21
2	BRAZILIAN GP	Interlagos	1	Marlboro Team McLaren	G	3.0 McLaren M23-Cosworth V8	FL	1/22
4	SOUTH AFRICAN GP	Kyalami	1	Marlboro Team McLaren	G	3.0 McLaren M23-Cosworth V8		1/23
7	US GP WEST	Long Beach	1	Marlboro Team McLaren	G	3.0 McLaren M23-Cosworth V8	hit Watson-pit stop/-1 lap	8/22
ret	SPANISH GP	Jarama	1	Marlboro Team McLaren	G	3.0 McLaren M26-Cosworth V8	engine	7/31
ret	MONACO GP	Monte Carlo	1	Marlboro Team McLaren	G	3.0 McLaren M26-Cosworth V8	engine	7/26
7	BELGIAN GP	Zolder	1	Marlboro Team McLaren	G	3.0 McLaren M26-Cosworth V8	1 lap behind	– / –
dns	"	"	1	Marlboro Team McLaren	G	3.0 McLaren M23-Cosworth V8	set grid time in this car	9/32
12	SWEDISH GP	Anderstorp	1	Marlboro Team McLaren	G	3.0 McLaren M26-Cosworth V8	1 lap behind	3/31
3	FRENCH GP	Dijon	1	Marlboro Team McLaren	G	3.0 McLaren M26-Cosworth V8		2/30
1	BRITISH GP	Silverstone	1	Marlboro Team McLaren	G	3.0 McLaren M26-Cosworth V8	FL	1/36
ret	GERMAN GP	Hockenheim	1	Marlboro Team McLaren	G	3.0 McLaren M26-Cosworth V8	fuel pump	4/30
ret	AUSTRIAN GP	Österreichring	1	Marlboro Team McLaren	G	3.0 McLaren M26-Cosworth V8	engine	2/30
ret	DUTCH GP	Zandvoort	1	Marlboro Team McLaren	G	3.0 McLaren M26-Cosworth V8	collision with Andretti	3/34
ret	ITALIAN GP	Monza	1	Marlboro Team McLaren	G	3.0 McLaren M26-Cosworth V8	spun off	1/34
1	US GP EAST	Watkins Glen	1	Marlboro Team McLaren	G	3.0 McLaren M26-Cosworth V8		1/27
ret	CANADIAN GP	Mosport Park	1	Marlboro Team McLaren	G	3.0 McLaren M26-Cosworth V8	hit Mass	2/27
1	JAPANESE GP	Mount Fuji	1	Marlboro Team McLaren	G	3.0 McLaren M26-Cosworth V8		2/23

1978 Championship position: 13 Wins: 0 Pole positions: 0 Fastest laps: 0 Points scored: 8

	Race	Circuit	No	Entrant	Tyres	Car/Engine	Comment	Q Pos/Entries
4	ARGENTINE GP	Buenos Aires	7	Marlboro Team McLaren	G	3.0 McLaren M26-Cosworth V8		6/27
ret	BRAZILIAN GP	Rio	7	Marlboro Team McLaren	G	3.0 McLaren M26-Cosworth V8	spun off	2/28
ret	SOUTH AFRICAN GP	Kyalami	7	Marlboro Team McLaren	G	3.0 McLaren M26-Cosworth V8	engine	3/30
ret	US GP WEST	Long Beach	7	Marlboro Team McLaren	G	3.0 McLaren M26-Cosworth V8	spun off-damaged suspension	7/30
ret	MONACO GP	Monte Carlo	7	Marlboro Team McLaren	G	3.0 McLaren M26-Cosworth V8	anti-roll bar	6/30
ret	BELGIAN GP	Zolder	7	Marlboro Team McLaren	G	3.0 McLaren M26-Cosworth V8	startline collision with Patrese	6/30
6	SPANISH GP	Jarama	7	Marlboro Team McLaren	G	3.0 McLaren M26-Cosworth V8	pit stop-tyres/1 lap behind	4/29
8	SWEDISH GP	Anderstorp	7	Marlboro Team McLaren	G	3.0 McLaren M26-Cosworth V8	1 lap behind	14/27
3	FRENCH GP	Paul Ricard	7	Marlboro Team McLaren	G	3.0 McLaren M26-Cosworth V8	driver unwell	4/29
ret	BRITISH GP	Brands Hatch	7	Marlboro Team McLaren	G	3.0 McLaren M26-Cosworth V8	spun off	14/30
dns	"	"	7	Marlboro Team McLaren	G	3.0 McLaren M26E-Cosworth V8	practice only	– / –
dsq	GERMAN GP	Hockenheim	7	Marlboro Team McLaren	G	3.0 McLaren M26-Cosworth V8	took short cut to pits	8/30
ret	AUSTRIAN GP	Österreichring	7	Marlboro Team McLaren	G	3.0 McLaren M26-Cosworth V8	collision with Daly	8/31
10	DUTCH GP	Zandvoort	7	Marlboro Team McLaren	G	3.0 McLaren M26-Cosworth V8	handling problems/-1 lap	7/33
ret	ITALIAN GP	Monza	7	Marlboro Team McLaren	G	3.0 McLaren M26-Cosworth V8	distributor	10/32
7	US GP EAST	Watkins Glen	7	Marlboro Team McLaren	G	3.0 McLaren M26-Cosworth V8	1 lap behind	6/27
ret	CANADIAN GP	Montreal	7	Marlboro Team McLaren	G	3.0 McLaren M26-Cosworth V8	spun off	19/28

1979 Championship position: Unplaced

	Race	Circuit	No	Entrant	Tyres	Car/Engine	Comment	Q Pos/Entries
ret	ARGENTINE GP	Buenos Aires	20	Olympus Cameras Wolf Racing	G	3.0 Wolf WR7-Cosworth V8	electrics	18/26
ret	BRAZILIAN GP	Interlagos	20	Olympus Cameras Wolf Racing	G	3.0 Wolf WR7-Cosworth V8	loose steering rack	10/26
8	SOUTH AFRICAN GP	Kyalami	20	Olympus Cameras Wolf Racing	G	3.0 Wolf WR7-Cosworth V8	1 lap behind	13/26
ret	US GP WEST	Long Beach	20	Olympus Cameras Wolf Racing	G	3.0 Wolf WR8-Cosworth V8	driveshaft	8/26
ret	SPANISH GP	Jarama	20	Olympus Cameras Wolf Racing	G	3.0 Wolf WR7-Cosworth V8	brakes	15/27
dns	"	"	20	Olympus Cameras Wolf Racing	G	3.0 Wolf WR8-Cosworth V8	practice only	– / –
ret	BELGIAN GP	Zolder	20	Olympus Cameras Wolf Racing	G	3.0 Wolf WR7-Cosworth V8	spun off	9/28
dns	"	"	20	Olympus Cameras Wolf Racing	G	3.0 Wolf WR7-Cosworth V8	practice only	– / –
ret	MONACO GP	Monte Carlo	20	Olympus Cameras Wolf Racing	G	3.0 Wolf WR7-Cosworth V8	c.v. joint	10/25

GP Starts: 92 GP Wins: 10 Pole positions: 14 Fastest laps: 8 Points: 179

GUS HUTCHISON

An amateur racer from Dallas, Hutchison was the US Formula B champion in 1967, with a Lotus 41B, winning each of the first seven races he entered. Late in 1969, he bought the ex-Jacky Ickx Brabham BT26 for a successful 1970 season of SCCA Continental racing and also took the car to Watkins Glen for that year's US GP.

Gus was then a regular competitor in the early seventies in the L & M F5000 series with both Lola and March chassis.

HUTCHISON, Gus (USA) b 26/4/1937, Atlanta, Georgia

1970 Championship position: Unplaced

	Race	Circuit	No	Entrant	Tyres	Car/Engine	Comment	Q Pos/Entries
ret	US GP	Watkins Glen	31	Gus Hutchison	G	3.0 Brabham BT26A-Cosworth V8	loose supplementary fuel tank	22/27

GP Starts: 1 GP Wins: 0 Pole positions: 0 Fastest laps: 0 Points: 0

JACKY ICKX

JACKY ICKX

Here was a prodigy with the brio of Rindt and the controlled circumspection of Stewart, absolutely brilliant in the wet and endowed with such natural driving gifts that surely the World Championship would be a formality. In the end it was not to be, as his mercurial powers became diluted in a succession of less and less competitive cars.

The son of a famous motor racing journalist, Jacky was three times Belgium's motor cycle trials champion before moving to cars, and quickly became the man to beat in his Lotus Cortina, taking his national saloon car championship in 1965. Though only 21, Ickx was pitched straight into a season of Formula 2 in 1966 under the guidance of Ken Tyrrell, who could see his vast potential. It was at the following year's German GP that the young Jacky caused a sensation by qualifying the little Matra third fastest in practice, and though he had to start with the other Formula 2 cars at the back of the grid, he soon carved his way through the field to fourth place before his suspension broke. Now a hot property, he guested for Cooper at Monza to score his first championship point, before signing for Ferrari in 1968.

His first great win was not long in coming, Ickx showing sublime control in the wet to win at Rouen, and his consistent placings left him with an outside championship chance until a practice crash in Canada scuppered his hopes. By this time he was already regarded as one of the world's very best sports car drivers; racing for John Wyer, he had already won the Spa 1000 Km twice in addition to victories at Brands Hatch, Watkins Glen and Kyalami, and so anxious were Gulf to keep their prize asset that they arranged for Jacky to join Brabham for 1969. In the light of Ferrari's plight that year, it was a smart move with Ickx reaching the heights of his considerable brilliance by defeating Jackie Stewart in the German GP. Another win followed in Canada, but Ickx had to be content with the runner-up spot in the championship that year. Meanwhile the wisdom of Gulf's decision was demonstrated when Jacky took a sensational last-gasp victory at Le Mans over Herrmann's Porsche.

In 1970 he rejoined Ferrari to race in both Formula 1 and sports car events, but once again he was the nearly-man, just failing to overhaul the late Jochen Rindt's points total after winning three Grands Prix. Apart from a non-title win in the Rindt Memorial race at Hockenheim, and yet another masterful display in the wet at Zandvoort, the following Grand Prix season was not as competitive as Ickx would have hoped, while in 1972 Ferrari were still a potent force, but not consistent enough. Jacky predictably took another superb win at the Nürburgring, as well as chalking up brilliant victories in the team's sports cars, races at Daytona, Sebring, Brands Hatch, the Österreichring and Watkins Glen all surrendering to the Belgian that year alone.

With Ferrari falling into one of their periodical troughs in 1973, Ickx's patience ran out by mid-season and he quit the team, freelancing for McLaren and Williams before joining Ronnie Peterson at Lotus for 1974. Apart from a memorable win in the Race of Champions, it was a disastrous move, the bewildered Belgian switching back and forth between the almost undriveable new Lotus 76 and the by now venerable 72E. Things got even worse in 1975, with Ickx and Lotus parting company in mid-season. By now his Formula 1 career was in the balance and a move to the Wolf-Williams team at the beginning of 1976 tipped him into the also-ran category. A brief spell at Ensign, ironically replacing Chris Amon, showed the spark was there, but a nasty crash at Watkins Glen convinced him his highly successful sports car career was a better bet.

Jacky completed a remarkable hat-trick of Le Mans wins between 1975 and 1977, and won a string of rounds of the World Championship of Makes in the Martini Porsche partnered by Jochen Mass. In 1979 Ickx was back in the Grand Prix world, replacing the injured Depailler at Ligier, but sadly it was not a successful return, the finesse of his driving style not suited to the ground-effect cars of the time. Racing in Can-Am for Jim Hall, Ickx took the 1979 title, before concentrating almost exclusively on endurance racing in the eighties. After taking a fifth Le Mans win in 1981, he became a key member of the Rothmans Porsche team the following season and won the drivers' World Championship, scoring a record sixth win at Le Mans in addition to victories at Spa, Fuji and Brands Hatch. Jacky continued to race successfully through to the end of the 1985 season, when he took honourable retirement, hailed not only as one of the all-time greats of sports car racing but also, by those who remembered his halcyon days, as one of Grand Prix racing's most brilliant talents.

On the way to a Ferrari 1-2 finish, Jacky Ickx leads team-mate Clay Regazzoni in the 1970 Austrian Grand Prix at the Österreichring.

ICKX, Jacky (B) b 1/1/1945, Ixelles, Brussels

	1966	Championship position: Unplaced							
	Race	Circuit	No	Entrant	Tyres	Car/Engine		Comment	Q Pos/Entries
ret	GERMAN GP (F2)	Nürburgring	27	Ken Tyrrell Racing	D	1.0 Matra MS5-Cosworth 4		*transmission*	17/30

	1967	Championship position: 19th= Wins: 0 Pole positions: 0 Fastest laps: 0 Points scored: 1							
ret	GERMAN GP (F2)	Nürburgring	29	Ken Tyrrell Racing	D	1.6 Matra MS7-Cosworth 4 F2	*suspension (FL in F2 class)*	3/25
6	ITALIAN GP	Monza	32	Cooper Car Co	F	3.0 Cooper T81B-Maserati V12	*puncture on last lap/-2 laps*	15/18
ret	US GP	Watkins Glen	21	Cooper Car Co	F	3.0 Cooper T86-Maserati V12	*overheating*	16/18

	1968	Championship position: 4th Wins: 1 Pole positions: 1 Fastest laps: 1 Points scored: 27							
ret	SOUTH AFRICAN GP	Kyalami	9	Scuderia Ferrari SpA SEFAC	F	3.0 Ferrari 312/67 V12	*oil tank/driver exhausted*	=10/23
ret	SPANISH GP	Jarama	21	Scuderia Ferrari SpA SEFAC	F	3.0 Ferrari 312/67/68 V12	*ignition*	8/14
3	BELGIAN GP	Spa	23	Scuderia Ferrari SpA SEFAC	F	3.0 Ferrari 312/67/68 V12		3/18
4	DUTCH GP	Zandvoort	10	Scuderia Ferrari SpA SEFAC	F	3.0 Ferrari 312/68 V12	*2 laps behind*	6/19
1	FRENCH GP	Rouen	26	Scuderia Ferrari SpA SEFAC	F	3.0 Ferrari 312/68 V12		3/18
3	BRITISH GP	Brands Hatch	6	Scuderia Ferrari SpA SEFAC	F	3.0 Ferrari 312/68 V12	*1 lap behind*	12/20
4	GERMAN GP	Nürburgring	9	Scuderia Ferrari SpA SEFAC	F	3.0 Ferrari 312/68 V12	*pit stops-visor*	1/20
3	ITALIAN GP	Monza	8	Scuderia Ferrari SpA SEFAC	F	3.0 Ferrari 312/68 V12		4/24
dns	CANADIAN GP	St Jovite	10	Scuderia Ferrari SpA SEFAC	F	3.0 Ferrari 312/68 V12	*practice accident-broken leg*	(=13)/22
ret	MEXICAN GP	Mexico City	7	Scuderia Ferrari SpA SEFAC	F	3.0 Ferrari 312/68 V12	*ignition*	15/21

	1969	Championship position: 2 Wins: 2 Pole positions: 2 Fastest laps: 3 (1 shared) Points scored: 37							
ret	SOUTH AFRICAN GP	Kyalami	15	Motor Racing Developments	G	3.0 Brabham BT26A-Cosworth V8	*starter solenoid after pit stop*	14/18
6/ret	SPANISH GP	Montjuich Park	4	Motor Racing Developments	G	3.0 Brabham BT26A-Cosworth V8	*rear suspension/7 laps behind*	7/14
ret	MONACO GP	Monte Carlo	6	Motor Racing Developments	G	3.0 Brabham BT26A-Cosworth V8	*rear suspension*	7/16
5	DUTCH GP	Zandvoort	12	Motor Racing Developments	G	3.0 Brabham BT26A-Cosworth V8		5/15
3	FRENCH GP	Clermont Ferrand	11	Motor Racing Developments	G	3.0 Brabham BT26A-Cosworth V8		4/13
2	BRITISH GP	Silverstone	7	Motor Racing Developments	G	3.0 Brabham BT26A-Cosworth V8	*out of fuel last lap/1 lap behind*	4/17
1	GERMAN GP	Nürburgring	6	Motor Racing Developments	G	3.0 Brabham BT26A-Cosworth V8	*FL*	1/26
10/ret	ITALIAN GP	Monza	26	Motor Racing Developments	G	3.0 Brabham BT26A-Cosworth V8	*oil pressure/6 laps behind*	15/15
1	CANADIAN GP	Mosport Park	11	Motor Racing Developments	G	3.0 Brabham BT26A-Cosworth V8	*FL (shared with Brabham)*	1/20
ret	US GP	Watkins Glen	7	Motor Racing Developments	G	3.0 Brabham BT26A-Cosworth V8	*engine*	8/18
2	MEXICAN GP	Mexico City	7	Motor Racing Developments	G	3.0 Brabham BT26A-Cosworth V8	*FL*	2/17

	1970	Championship position: 2nd Wins: 3 Pole positions: 4 Fastest laps: 4 (1 shared) Points scored: 40							
ret	SOUTH AFRICAN GP	Kyalami	17	Scuderia Ferrari SpA SEFAC	F	3.0 Ferrari 312B F12	*engine*	5/24
ret	SPANISH GP	Jarama	2	Scuderia Ferrari SpA SEFAC	F	3.0 Ferrari 312B F12	*collision with Oliver-burns*	7/22
ret	MONACO GP	Monte Carlo	26	Scuderia Ferrari SpA SEFAC	F	3.0 Ferrari 312B F12	*driveshaft*	5/21
8	BELGIAN GP	Spa	27	Scuderia Ferrari SpA SEFAC	F	3.0 Ferrari 312B F12	*pit stop-fuel leak/-2 laps*	4/18
3	DUTCH GP	Zandvoort	25	Scuderia Ferrari SpA SEFAC	F	3.0 Ferrari 312B F12	*pit stop-puncture/FL/-1 lap*	3/24
ret	FRENCH GP	Clermont Ferrand	10	Scuderia Ferrari SpA SEFAC	F	3.0 Ferrari 312B F12	*engine*	1/23
ret	BRITISH GP	Brands Hatch	3	Scuderia Ferrari SpA SEFAC	F	3.0 Ferrari 312B F12	*differential*	3/25
2	GERMAN GP	Hockenheim	10	Scuderia Ferrari SpA SEFAC	F	3.0 Ferrari 312B F12	*FL*	1/25
1	AUSTRIAN GP	Österreichring	12	Scuderia Ferrari SpA SEFAC	F	3.0 Ferrari 312B F12	*FL (shared with Regazzoni)*	3/24
ret	ITALIAN GP	Monza	2	Scuderia Ferrari SpA SEFAC	F	3.0 Ferrari 312B F12	*clutch*	1/27
1	CANADIAN GP	St Jovite	18	Scuderia Ferrari SpA SEFAC	F	3.0 Ferrari 312B F12		2/20
4	US GP	Watkins Glen	3	Scuderia Ferrari SpA SEFAC	F	3.0 Ferrari 312B F12	*pit stop-fuel leak/FL/-1 lap*	1/27
1	MEXICAN GP	Mexico City	3	Scuderia Ferrari SpA SEFAC	F	3.0 Ferrari 312B F12	*FL*	3/18

	1971	Championship position: 4th= Wins: 1 Pole positions: 2 Fastest laps: 3 Points scored: 19							
8	SOUTH AFRICAN GP	Kyalami	4	Scuderia Ferrari SpA SEFAC	F	3.0 Ferrari 312B F12	*1 lap behind*	=8/25
2	SPANISH GP	Montjuich Park	4	Scuderia Ferrari SpA SEFAC	F	3.0 Ferrari 312B F12	*FL*	1/22
3	MONACO GP	Monte Carlo	4	Scuderia Ferrari SpA SEFAC	F	3.0 Ferrari 312B2 F12		2/23
1	DUTCH GP	Zandvoort	2	Scuderia Ferrari SpA SEFAC	F	3.0 Ferrari 312B2 F12	*wet race/FL*	1/24
ret	FRENCH GP	Paul Ricard	4	Scuderia Ferrari SpA SEFAC	F	3.0 Ferrari 312B2 F12	*engine*	3/24
ret	BRITISH GP	Silverstone	4	Scuderia Ferrari SpA SEFAC	F	3.0 Ferrari 312B2 F12	*engine*	6/24
ret	GERMAN GP	Nürburgring	4	Scuderia Ferrari SpA SEFAC	D	3.0 Ferrari 312B2 F12	*spun off*	2/23
ret	AUSTRIAN GP	Österreichring	4	Scuderia Ferrari SpA SEFAC	F	3.0 Ferrari 312B2 F12	*electrics-plug leads*	6/22
ret	ITALIAN GP	Monza	3	Scuderia Ferrari SpA SEFAC	F	3.0 Ferrari 312B F12	*engine damper*	2/24
dns	"	"	3	Scuderia Ferrari SpA SEFAC	F	3.0 Ferrari 312B2 F12	*practice only*	– / –
8	CANADIAN GP	Mosport Park	4	Scuderia Ferrari SpA SEFAC	F	3.0 Ferrari 312B2 F12	*2 laps behind*	=11/27
ret	US GP	Watkins Glen	32	Scuderia Ferrari SpA SEFAC	F	3.0 Ferrari 312B F12	*alternator fell off/FL*	8/32
dns	"	"	4	Scuderia Ferrari SpA SEFAC	F	3.0 Ferrari 312B2 F12	*practice only*	– / –

	1972	Championship position: 4th Wins: 1 Pole positions: 4 Fastest laps: 3 Points scored: 27							
3	ARGENTINE GP	Buenos Aires	8	Scuderia Ferrari SpA SEFAC	F	3.0 Ferrari 312B2 F12		8/22
8	SOUTH AFRICAN GP	Kyalami	5	Scuderia Ferrari SpA SEFAC	F	3.0 Ferrari 312B2 F12	*1 lap behind*	7/27
2	SPANISH GP	Jarama	4	Scuderia Ferrari SpA SEFAC	F	3.0 Ferrari 312B2 F12	*FL*	1/26
2	MONACO GP	Monte Carlo	6	Scuderia Ferrari SpA SEFAC	F	3.0 Ferrari 312B2 F12		2/25
ret	BELGIAN GP	Nivelles	29	Scuderia Ferrari SpA SEFAC	F	3.0 Ferrari 312B2 F12	*fuel injection*	4/26
11	FRENCH GP	Clermont Ferrand	3	Scuderia Ferrari SpA SEFAC	F	3.0 Ferrari 312B2 F12	*1 lap behind*	4/29
ret	BRITISH GP	Brands Hatch	5	Scuderia Ferrari SpA SEFAC	F	3.0 Ferrari 312B2 F12	*oil pressure/led race*	1/27
1	GERMAN GP	Nürburgring	4	Scuderia Ferrari SpA SEFAC	F	3.0 Ferrari 312B2 F12	*FL*	1/27
ret	AUSTRIAN GP	Österreichring	18	Scuderia Ferrari SpA SEFAC	F	3.0 Ferrari 312B2 F12	*fuel pressure*	9/26
ret	ITALIAN GP	Monza	4	Scuderia Ferrari SpA SEFAC	F	3.0 Ferrari 312B2 F12	*electrics/FL*	1/27
12	CANADIAN GP	Mosport Park	10	Scuderia Ferrari SpA SEFAC	F	3.0 Ferrari 312B2 F12	*pit stop-puncture/-3 laps*	8/25
5	US GP	Watkins Glen	7	Scuderia Ferrari SpA SEFAC	F	3.0 Ferrari 312B2 F12		12/32

1973
Championship position: 9th Wins: 0 Pole positions: 0 Fastest laps: 0 Points scored: 12

4	ARGENTINE GP	Buenos Aires	18	Scuderia Ferrari SpA SEFAC	G	3.0 Ferrari 312B2 F12		3/19
5	BRAZILIAN GP	Interlagos	9	Scuderia Ferrari SpA SEFAC	G	3.0 Ferrari 312B2 F12	pit stop-puncture/1 lap behind	3/20
ret	SOUTH AFRICAN GP	Kyalami	8	Scuderia Ferrari SpA SEFAC	G	3.0 Ferrari 312B2 F12	accident -Regazzoni & Hailwood	11/25
12	SPANISH GP	Montjuich Park	7	Scuderia Ferrari SpA SEFAC	G	3.0 Ferrari 312B3 F12	pit stop-brakes/6 laps behind	6/22
ret	BELGIAN GP	Zolder	3	Scuderia Ferrari SpA SEFAC	G	3.0 Ferrari 312B3 F12	oil pump	3/23
ret	MONACO GP	Monte Carlo	3	Scuderia Ferrari SpA SEFAC	G	3.0 Ferrari 312B3 F12	driveshaft	7/26
6	SWEDISH GP	Anderstorp	3	Scuderia Ferrari SpA SEFAC	G	3.0 Ferrari 312B3 F12	1 lap behind	8/22
5	FRENCH GP	Paul Ricard	3	Scuderia Ferrari SpA SEFAC	G	3.0 Ferrari 312B3 F12		12/25G
8	BRITISH GP	Silverstone	3	Scuderia Ferrari SpA SEFAC	G	3.0 Ferrari 312B3 F12		19/29
3	GERMAN GP	Nürburgring	30	Yardley Team McLaren	G	3.0 McLaren M23-Cosworth V8		4/23
8	ITALIAN GP	Monza	3	Scuderia Ferrari SpA SEFAC	G	3.0 Ferrari 312B3 F12	clipped chicane/1 lap behind	14/25
7	US GP	Watkins Glen	26	Frank Williams Racing Cars	F	3.0 Iso Williams IR-Cosworth V8	1 lap behind	24/28

1974
Championship position: 10th Wins: 0 Pole positions: 0 Fastest laps: 0 Points scored: 12

ret	ARGENTINE GP	Buenos Aires	2	John Player Team Lotus	G	3.0 Lotus 72E-Cosworth V8	transmission	7/26
3	BRAZILIAN GP	Interlagos	2	John Player Team Lotus	G	3.0 Lotus 72E-Cosworth V8	1 lap behind	5/25
ret	SOUTH AFRICAN GP	Kyalami	2	John Player Team Lotus	G	3.0 Lotus 76-Cosworth V8	brake balance/hit by Peterson	10/27
ret	SPANISH GP	Jarama	2	John Player Team Lotus	G	3.0 Lotus 76-Cosworth V8	leaking brake fluid	5/28
ret	BELGIAN GP	Nivelles	2	John Player Team Lotus	G	3.0 Lotus 76-Cosworth V8	brakes	16/32
ret	MONACO GP	Monte Carlo	2	John Player Team Lotus	G	3.0 Lotus 72E-Cosworth V8	gearbox	19/28
dns	"	"	2T	John Player Team Lotus	G	3.0 Lotus 76-Cosworth V8	practice only	– / –
ret	SWEDISH GP	Anderstorp	2	John Player Team Lotus	G	3.0 Lotus 72E-Cosworth V8	oil pressure	7/28
11	DUTCH GP	Zandvoort	2	John Player Team Lotus	G	3.0 Lotus 72E-Cosworth V8	pit stop-loose wheel/-4 laps	18/27
dns	"	"	2T	John Player Team Lotus	G	3.0 Lotus 76-Cosworth V8	practice only	– / –
5	FRENCH GP	Dijon	2	John Player Team Lotus	G	3.0 Lotus 72E-Cosworth V8		13/30
3	BRITISH GP	Brands Hatch	2	John Player Team Lotus	G	3.0 Lotus 72E-Cosworth V8		=11/34
5	GERMAN GP	Nürburgring	2	John Player Team Lotus	G	3.0 Lotus 72E-Cosworth V8		9/32
ret	AUSTRIAN GP	Österreichring	2	John Player Team Lotus	G	3.0 Lotus 76-Cosworth V8	collision with Depailler	– / –
dns	"	"	2T	John Player Team Lotus	G	3.0 Lotus 76-Cosworth V8	used to set grid time	22/31
ret	ITALIAN GP	Monza	2	John Player Team Lotus	G	3.0 Lotus 76-Cosworth V8	throttle linkage	16/31
13	CANADIAN GP	Mosport Park	2	John Player Team Lotus	G	3.0 Lotus 72E-Cosworth V8	2 laps behind	21/30
dns	"	" "	2T	John Player Team Lotus	G	3.0 Lotus 76-Cosworth V8	practice only	– / –
ret	US GP	Watkins Glen	2	John Player Team Lotus	G	3.0 Lotus 72E-Cosworth V8	hit guard rail	16/30

1975
Championship position: 16th Wins: 0 Pole positions: 0 Fastest laps: 0 Points scored: 3

8	ARGENTINE GP	Buenos Aires	6	John Player Team Lotus	G	3.0 Lotus 72E-Cosworth V8	1 lap behind	18/23
9	BRAZILIAN GP	Interlagos	6	John Player Team Lotus	G	3.0 Lotus 72E-Cosworth V8		12/23
12	SOUTH AFRICAN GP	Kyalami	6	John Player Team Lotus	G	3.0 Lotus 72E-Cosworth V8	2 laps behind	21/28
2*	SPANISH GP	Montjuich Park	6	John Player Team Lotus	G	3.0 Lotus 72E-Cosworth V8	* shortened race/half points only	16/26
8	MONACO GP	Monte Carlo	6	John Player Team Lotus	G	3.0 Lotus 72E-Cosworth V8	1 lap behind	14/26
ret	BELGIAN GP	Zolder	6	John Player Team Lotus	G	3.0 Lotus 72E-Cosworth V8	front brake shaft	16/24
15	SWEDISH GP	Anderstorp	6	John Player Team Lotus	G	3.0 Lotus 72E-Cosworth V8	3 laps behind	18/26
ret	DUTCH GP	Zandvoort	6	John Player Team Lotus	G	3.0 Lotus 72E-Cosworth V8	engine	21/25
ret	FRENCH GP	Paul Ricard	6	John Player Team Lotus	G	3.0 Lotus 72E-Cosworth V8	brake shaft	19/26

1976
Championship position: Unplaced

8	BRAZILIAN GP	Interlagos	20	Frank Williams Racing Cars	G	3.0 Williams FW05-Cosworth V8	1 lap behind	19/22
16	SOUTH AFRICAN GP	Kyalami	20	Frank Williams Racing Cars	G	3.0 Williams FW05-Cosworth V8	pit stop/5 laps behind	19/25
dnq	US GP WEST	Long Beach	20	Frank Williams Racing Cars	G	3.0 Williams FW05-Cosworth V8		25/27
7	SPANISH GP	Jarama	20	Walter Wolf Racing	G	3.0 Williams FW05-Cosworth V8	1 lap behind	21/30
dnq	BELGIAN GP	Zolder	20	Walter Wolf Racing	G	3.0 Williams FW05-Cosworth V8		28/29
dnq	MONACO GP	Monte Carlo	20	Walter Wolf Racing	G	3.0 Williams FW05-Cosworth V8		21/25
10	FRENCH GP	Paul Ricard	20	Walter Wolf Racing	G	3.0 Williams FW05-Cosworth V8	1 lap behind	19/30
dnq	BRITISH GP	Silverstone	20	Walter Wolf Racing	G	3.0 Williams FW05-Cosworth V8		27/30
ret	DUTCH GP	Zandvoort	22	Team Ensign	G	3.0 Ensign N176-Cosworth V8	electrics	11/27
10	ITALIAN GP	Monza	22	Team Ensign	G	3.0 Ensign N176-Cosworth V8		10/29
13	CANADIAN GP	Mosport Park	22	Team Ensign	G	3.0 Ensign N176-Cosworth V8	1 lap behind	16/27
ret	US GP EAST	Watkins Glen	22	Team Ensign	G	3.0 Ensign N176-Cosworth V8	accident-broken ankle/burns	19/27

1977
Championship position: Unplaced

10	MONACO GP	Monte Carlo	22	Team Tissot Ensign with Castrol	G	3.0 Ensign N177-Cosworth V8	1 lap behind	17/26

1978
Championship position: Unplaced

ret	MONACO GP	Monte Carlo	22	Team Tissot Ensign	G	3.0 Ensign N177-Cosworth V8	brakes	16/30
12	BELGIAN GP	Zolder	22	Team Tissot Ensign	G	3.0 Ensign N177-Cosworth V8	multiple accident-pit stop/-6 laps	22/30
ret	SPANISH GP	Jarama	22	Team Tissot Ensign	G	3.0 Ensign N177-Cosworth V8	engine	21/29
dnq	SWEDISH GP	Anderstorp	22	Team Tissot Ensign	G	3.0 Ensign N177-Cosworth V8		27/27

1979
Championship position: 15th= Wins: 0 Pole positions: 0 Fastest laps: 0 Points scored: 3

ret	FRENCH GP	Dijon	25	Ligier Gitanes	G	3.0 Ligier JS11-Cosworth V8	engine	14/27
6	BRITISH GP	Silverstone	25	Ligier Gitanes	G	3.0 Ligier JS11-Cosworth V8	1 lap behind	=16/26
ret	GERMAN GP	Hockenheim	25	Ligier Gitanes	G	3.0 Ligier JS11-Cosworth V8	burst tyre	14/26
ret	AUSTRIAN GP	Österreichring	25	Ligier Gitanes	G	3.0 Ligier JS11-Cosworth V8	engine	21/26
5	DUTCH GP	Zandvoort	25	Ligier Gitanes	G	3.0 Ligier JS11-Cosworth V8	1 lap behind	20/26
ret	ITALIAN GP	Monza	25	Ligier Gitanes	G	3.0 Ligier JS11-Cosworth V8	engine	11/28
ret	CANADIAN GP	Montreal	25	Ligier Gitanes	G	3.0 Ligier JS11-Cosworth V8	gearbox	16/29
ret	US GP EAST	Watkins Glen	25	Ligier Gitanes	G	3.0 Ligier JS11-Cosworth V8	spun off	24/30

GP Starts: 116 GP Wins: 8 Pole positions: 13 Fastest laps: 14 Points: 181

JÉSUS IGLESIAS

This Argentinan driver was very fast indeed in his Chevrolet special and was invited to handle one of the works Gordinis in the 1955 Argentine GP. Even though he was more used to the conditions than most of the visiting drivers, he too it seems succumbed to the broiling heat, though he did last some 38 of the 96 laps.

He appears to have driven a Maserati into 16th place in the well-supported Buenos Aires City GP, a Libre event held a couple of weeks after his outing in the French car.

Thereafter it was back to his Chevrolet special, in which he earned some glory by taking second place in the 500-mile race at Rafaelo in 1956. Two years later he achieved fame of a kind by contriving to collide with Stirling Moss on the opening lap of the Buenos Aires Libre GP. The first heat of the race was started in wet conditions and Iglesias powered from the back of the grid, braking far too late for the first corner. He ran at unabated speed into Moss's Cooper, sending the little machine some three to four feet into the air before it shot off the circuit towards a crowd of photographers. Both cars were hors de combat, but fortunately no one was hurt, though had this unpleasant incident had more serious results Iglesias may have gained worldwide notoriety.

TAKI INOUE

Press handouts from Formula 1 teams tell you little you really want to know about a driver. You know the sort of thing: residence, hobbies, favourite music, favourite singers, favourite food, etc. How about Monte Carlo, shopping, jazz and rock, Eric Clapton and Globe fish! Well, it's a hell of a lot more interesting than Taki's racing exploits, which date back to 1985 and the Fuji Freshman championship. He came to England to compete in FF1600 in 1987 before returning home to tackle Japanese F3 through until 1993, the sum total of his achievements being a few fourth places. A move into Japanese F3000 with a top team, Super Nova, still brought little by way of results, but that didn't prevent him gaining a superlicence to race for Simtek in the Japanese GP. Result – spun into pit wall along the straight.

Far from that being the end of Inoue's Grand Prix curriculum vitae, he found the necessary to buy a seat at Footwork for the whole 1995 season; Jack Oliver must have needed the dosh. 'His learning curve has been steep, but his performance very flat,' Oliver is quoted as saying in Autocourse. Indeed it was two bizarre incidents that he was involved in (happily without serious injury) which left the most impression, the first when his Footwork was overturned by the course car in Monaco while being towed back to the pits, the second in Hungary when he was knocked flying by a rescue vehicle sent to attend after his car had broken down. Back to the press handout. Learned profession: racing driver. Mmm . . .

IGLESIAS, Jésus Ricardo (RA) b 22/2/1922, Pergamino, nr Buenos Aires

	1955	Championship position: Unplaced						
	Race	Circuit	No	Entrant	Tyres	Car/Engine	Comment	Q Pos/Entries
ret	ARGENTINE GP	Buenos Aires	42	Equipe Gordini	E	2.5 Gordini Type 16 6	transmission/exhaustion	17/22

GP Starts: 1   GP Wins: 0   Pole positions: 0   Fastest laps: 0   Points: 0

INOUE, Taki (J) b 5/9/1963, Kobe

	1994	Championship position: Unplaced						
	Race	Circuit	No	Entrant	Tyres	Car/Engine	Comment	Q Pos/Entries
ret	JAPANESE GP	Suzuka	32	MTV Simtek Ford	G	3.5 Simtek S941-Ford HB V8	crashed into pit wall in rain	26/28
	1995	Championship position: 0 Wins: 0 Pole positions: 0 Fastest laps: 0 Points scored: 0						
ret	BRAZILIAN GP	Interlagos	10	Footwork Hart	G	3.0 Footwork FA16-Hart V8	fire	21/26
ret	ARGENTINE GP	Buenos Aires	10	Footwork Hart	G	3.0 Footwork FA16-Hart V8	spun off	26/26
ret	SAN MARINO GP	Imola	10	Footwork Hart	G	3.0 Footwork FA16-Hart V8	spun off	19/26
ret	SPANISH GP	Barcelona	10	Footwork Hart	G	3.0 Footwork FA16-Hart V8	engine fire	18/26
ret	MONACO GP	Monte Carlo	10	Footwork Hart	G	3.0 Footwork FA16-Hart V8	gearbox	26/26
9	CANADIAN GP	Montreal	10	Footwork Hart	G	3.0 Footwork FA16-Hart V8	2 laps behind	22/24
ret	FRENCH GP	Magny Cours	10	Footwork Hart	G	3.0 Footwork FA16-Hart V8	collision with Katayama-lap 1	18/24
ret	BRITISH GP	Silverstone	10	Footwork Hart	G	3.0 Footwork FA16-Hart V8	spun off	19/24
ret	GERMAN GP	Hockenheim	10	Footwork Hart	G	3.0 Footwork FA16-Hart V8	gearbox	19/24
ret	HUNGARIAN GP	Hungaroring	10	Footwork Hart	G	3.0 Footwork FA16-Hart V8	engine	18/24
12	BELGIAN GP	Spa	10	Footwork Hart	G	3.0 Footwork FA16-Hart V8	1 lap behind	18/24
8	ITALIAN GP	Monza	10	Footwork Hart	G	3.0 Footwork FA16-Hart V8	1 lap behind	20/24
15	PORTUGUESE GP	Estoril	10	Footwork Hart	G	3.0 Footwork FA16-Hart V8	3 laps behind	19/24
dns	EUROPEAN GP	Nürburgring	10	Footwork Hart	G	3.0 Footwork FA16-Hart V8	electrics before start	(21)/24
ret	PACIFIC GP	T.I. Circuit	10	Footwork Hart	G	3.0 Footwork FA16-Hart V8	engine	20/24
12	JAPANESE GP	Suzuka	10	Footwork Hart	G	3.0 Footwork FA16-Hart V8	2 laps behind	19/24
ret	AUSTRALIAN GP	Adelaide	10	Footwork Hart	G	3.0 Footwork FA16-Hart V8	accident	19/24

GP Starts: 17 (18)   GP Wins: 0   Pole positions: 0   Fastest laps: 0   Points: 0

INNES IRELAND

It was all-change; the front-engined cars were out, as was the casual racing attire and devil-may-care attitude, but Innes carried the spirit of a fast-disappearing age into the sixties and in career terms it was to cost him dear.

The son of a veterinary surgeon, he showed no inclination to follow the same path and instead took up an engineering apprentice-ship. After dabbling in racing between 1952 and 1955, a period which saw him complete his National Service as a paratrooper, Innes really got his racing career into gear with a Lotus XI in 1956. He began to build his reputation in 1957 and 1958, racing both his own car and the Ecurie Ecosse Jaguar D-Type. A class win in the Lotus at the Reims 12 Hours impressed Colin Chapman sufficiently for him to sign Innes for the 1959 season, and he took a fourth place in the International Trophy before making an impressive Grand Prix debut at Zandvoort. The cars were very unreliable, and little else was achieved until the 1960 season when the new rear-engined Lotus 18 proved sensationally quick. On its debut in Argentina, Ireland led comfortably until the gear linkage broke, and then at home he stormed to victory in the Glover Trophy at Goodwood, ahead of Moss, and the International Trophy, putting Brabham in his place. Although a Grand Prix victory was not to be his that season, Innes enjoyed a fabulous year, for in addition to the wins previously mentioned he took the Lombank Trophy and recorded some excellent placings as well as Formula 2 wins at Goodwood and Oulton Park.

The 1961 season started badly for Innes with a heavy crash at Monaco when he selected the wrong gear, but despite a fractured kneecap he was soon back in his stride, producing a splendid performance to win the Solitude GP, followed by a win in the Flugplatzrennen at Zeltweg. His great moment arrived at the end of the season when he won the US GP after a text book drive. Much to his chagrin, Ireland was then released from his contract by Chapman, who had decided that youngsters Jim Clark and Trevor Taylor would race for him in 1962. It was effectively the end of Innes' front-line career. Joining the UDT-Laystall team, he found success in sports cars, winning the Tourist Trophy in a 250 GTO, but endured a largely frustrating time in single-seaters. He won the Crystal Palace Trophy in 1962 and the following season (the team having been renamed BRP) he enjoyed a respectable early-season run in non-championship events with both a Lotus 24 and the team's own BRP chassis, winning the Glover Trophy and finishing third at Snetterton, second at Aintree, fourth at Silverstone and third at Solitude, before an accident at Seattle left him with a dislocated hip.

In 1964 Innes plugged away with the disappointing BRP, claiming a victory in the Daily Mirror Trophy at Snetterton, but the team closed its doors at the end of the year, leaving Ireland to find a berth in the Parnell Racing team for 1965. His off-track popularity was as high as ever, but sadly he was by then less than reliable as a driver. Appearing late for a practice session in Mexico saw him dismissed on the spot, but Tim Parnell must have forgiven him as he raced for the team again in the 1966 South African GP! Innes then found employment racing sports cars, sharing a Ford GT40 with Amon to take fifth place in the Spa 1000 Km. He drew down the curtain on his single-seater career late in 1966 when he joined Bernard White's suitably 'happy-go-lucky' équipe and took fourth place in the Gold Cup at Oulton Park, before his last two Grand Prix appearances in the US and Mexico. His hell-raising lifestyle had not fitted in with the new professionalism of the age, but this unique character, who could both charm and outrage in short order, continued to be happily associated with the sport in both journalistic and organisational capacities on and off until his death from cancer in 1993.

IRELAND, Innes (GB) b 12/6/1930, Mytholroyd, nr Todmorden, Yorkshire – d 22/10/1993, Reading, Berkshire

1959   Championship position: 10th=   Wins: 0   Pole positions: 0   Fastest laps: 0   Points scored: 5

	Race	Circuit	No	Entrant	Tyres	Car/Engine	Comment	Q Pos/Entries
4	DUTCH GP	Zandvoort	12	Team Lotus	D	2.5 Lotus 16-Climax 4	1 lap behind	9/15
ret	FRENCH GP	Reims	34	Team Lotus	D	2.5 Lotus 16-Climax 4	front hub bearing	15/22
ret	GERMAN GP	AVUS	15	Team Lotus	D	2.5 Lotus 16-Climax 4	gear selection/cwp-heat 1	13/16
ret	PORTUGUESE GP	Monsanto	12	Team Lotus	D	2.5 Lotus 16-Climax 4	gearbox	16/16
ret	ITALIAN GP	Monza	20	Team Lotus	D	2.5 Lotus 16-Climax 4	brakes	14/21
5	US GP	Sebring	10	Team Lotus	D	2.5 Lotus 16-Climax 4	3 laps behind	9/19

1960   Championship position: 4th   Wins: 0   Pole positions: 0   Fastest laps: 1 (shared)   Points scored: 18

	Race	Circuit	No	Entrant	Tyres	Car/Engine	Comment	Q Pos/Entries
6	ARGENTINE GP	Buenos Aires	20	Team Lotus	D	2.5 Lotus 18-Climax 4	gear linkage-spin/-1 lap	2/22
9	MONACO GP	Monte Carlo	22	Team Lotus	D	2.5 Lotus 18-Climax 4	long pit stop-engine/-44 laps	7/24
2	DUTCH GP	Zandvoort	4	Team Lotus	D	2.5 Lotus 18-Climax 4		3/21
ret	BELGIAN GP	Spa	14	Team Lotus	D	2.5 Lotus 18-Climax 4	spun off/FL(shared)	8/18
7	FRENCH GP	Reims	20	Team Lotus	D	2.5 Lotus 18-Climax 4	pit stop-suspension/-7 laps	4/23
3	BRITISH GP	Silverstone	7	Team Lotus	D	2.5 Lotus 18-Climax 4		5/25
6	PORTUGUESE GP	Oporto	16	Team Lotus	D	2.5 Lotus 18-Climax 4	pit stop-fuel feed problems/-7 laps	7/16
2	US GP	Riverside	10	Team Lotus	D	2.5 Lotus 18-Climax 4		7/23

1961   Championship position: 6th   Wins: 1   Pole positions: 0   Fastest laps: 0   Points scored: 12

	Race	Circuit	No	Entrant	Tyres	Car/Engine	Comment	Q Pos/Entries
dns	MONACO GP	Monte Carlo	30	Team Lotus	D	1.5 Lotus 21-Climax 4	accident in practice	(10)/21
ret	BELGIAN GP	Spa	32	Team Lotus	D	1.5 Lotus 21-Climax 4	engine	18/25
4	FRENCH GP	Reims	6	Team Lotus	D	1.5 Lotus 21-Climax 4		10/26
10	BRITISH GP	Aintree	16	Team Lotus	D	1.5 Lotus 21-Climax 4	despite spin/3 laps behind	7/30
ret	GERMAN GP	Nürburgring	15	Team Lotus	D	1.5 Lotus 21-Climax 4	fire	16/27
ret	ITALIAN GP	Monza	38	Team Lotus	D	1.5 Lotus 18/21-Climax 4	chassis frame	– / –
dns	"	"	38	Team Lotus	D	1.5 Lotus 21-Climax 4	practice only/car to Moss for race	9/33
1	US GP	Watkins Glen	15	Team Lotus	D	1.5 Lotus 21-Climax 4		8/19

1962   Championship position: 16   Wins: 0   Pole positions: 0   Fastest laps: 0   Points scored: 3

	Race	Circuit	No	Entrant	Tyres	Car/Engine	Comment	Q Pos/Entries
ret	DUTCH GP	Zandvoort	9	UDT Laystall Racing Team	D	1.5 Lotus 24-Climax V8	locked brake overturned	6/20
ret	MONACO GP	Monte Carlo	34	UDT Laystall Racing Team	D	1.5 Lotus 24-Climax V8	fuel pump	8/21
dns	"	" "	34	UDT Laystall Racing Team	D	1.5 Lotus 18-Climax V8	practice only	– / –
ret	BELGIAN GP	Spa	20	UDT Laystall Racing Team	D	1.5 Lotus 24-Climax V8	rear suspension	=5/20
dns	"	"	21	UDT Laystall Racing Team	D	1.5 Lotus 24-BRM V8	practice only	– / –
ret	FRENCH GP	Rouen	36	UDT Laystall Racing Team	D	1.5 Lotus 24-Climax V8	puncture	8/17
16	BRITISH GP	Aintree	32	UDT Laystall Racing Team	D	1.5 Lotus 24-Climax V8	gear selection on grid/-14 laps	3/21
ret	ITALIAN GP	Monza	40	UDT Laystall Racing Team	D	1.5 Lotus 24-Climax V8	front suspension	=4/30
8	US GP	Watkins Glen	15	UDT Laystall Racing Team	D	1.5 Lotus 24-Climax V8	pit stop/4 laps behind	16/20
5	SOUTH AFRICAN GP	East London	11	UDT Laystall Racing Team	D	1.5 Lotus 24-Climax V8	1 lap behind	4/17

1963   Championship position: 9th=   Wins: 0   Pole positions: 0   Fastest laps: 0   Points scored: 6

	Race	Circuit	No	Entrant	Tyres	Car/Engine	Comment	Q Pos/Entries
ret	MONACO GP	Monte Carlo	14	British Racing Partnership	D	1.5 Lotus 24-BRM V8	wrong gear selection- accident	5/17
ret	BELGIAN GP	Spa	4	British Racing Partnership	D	1.5 BRP 1-BRM V8	gear selection	7/20
dns	"	"	4	British Racing Partnership	D	1.5 Lotus 24-BRM V8	practice only	– / –
4	DUTCH GP	Zandvoort	30	British Racing Partnership	D	1.5 BRP 1-BRM V8	1 lap behind	=6/19
dns	"	"	30	British Racing Partnership	D	1.5 Lotus 24-BRM V8	practice only	– / –
9	FRENCH GP	Reims	32	British Racing Partnership	D	1.5 BRP 1-BRM V8	pit stop-gearbox/4 laps behind	3/21
dsq	BRITISH GP	Silverstone	11	British Racing Partnership	D	1.5 BRP 1-BRM V8	ignition at pit stop-push start	=10/23
dns	"	"	11	British Racing Partnership	D	1.5 Lotus 24-BRM V8	practice only	– / –
ret	GERMAN GP	Nürburgring	14	British Racing Partnership	D	1.5 Lotus 24-BRM V8	collision with Bandini	11/26
dns	"	"	14	British Racing Partnership	D	1.5 BRP 1-BRM V8	accident in practice	– / –
4/ret	ITALIAN GP	Monza	32	British Racing Partnership	D	1.5 BRP 1-BRM V8	engine	10/28

1964   Championship position: 12th   Wins: 0   Pole positions: 0   Fastest laps: 0   Points scored: 4

	Race	Circuit	No	Entrant	Tyres	Car/Engine	Comment	Q Pos/Entries
dns	MONACO GP	Monte Carlo	14	British Racing Partnership	D	1.5 Lotus 24-BRM V8	practice accident	(17)/20
10	BELGIAN GP	Spa	3	British Racing Partnership	D	1.5 BRP 1-BRM V8	pit stop/4 laps behind	16/20
ret	FRENCH GP	Rouen	16	British Racing Partnership	D	1.5 BRP 1-BRM V8	accident	11/17
10	BRITISH GP	Brands Hatch	11	British Racing Partnership	D	1.5 BRP 2-BRM V8	engine problems/-3 laps	10/25
5	AUSTRIAN GP	Zeltweg	14	British Racing Partnership	D	1.5 BRP 2-BRM V8	pit stop-engine/3 laps behind	11/20
5	ITALIAN GP	Monza	46	British Racing Partnership	D	1.5 BRP 2-BRM V8	fuel feed problems/-1 lap	=12/25
ret	US GP	Watkins Glen	11	British Racing Partnership	D	1.5 BRP 2-BRM V8	gear lever	10/19
12	MEXICAN GP	Mexico City	11	British Racing Partnership	D	1.5 BRP 2-BRM V8	pit stop/4 laps behind	16/19

1965   Championship position: Unplaced

	Race	Circuit	No	Entrant	Tyres	Car/Engine	Comment	Q Pos/Entries
13	BELGIAN GP	Spa	22	Reg Parnell (Racing)	D	1.5 Lotus 25-BRM V8	pit stop/5 laps behind	16/21
ret	FRENCH GP	Clermont Ferrand	22	Reg Parnell (Racing)	D	1.5 Lotus 25-BRM V8	gearbox	17/17
ret	BRITISH GP	Silverstone	23	Reg Parnell (Racing)	D	1.5 Lotus 25-BRM V8	engine	15/23
10	DUTCH GP	Zandvoort	38	Reg Parnell (Racing)	D	1.5 Lotus 25-BRM V8	2 laps behind	13/17
9	ITALIAN GP	Monza	38	Reg Parnell (Racing)	D	1.5 Lotus 25-BRM V8	2 laps behind	18/23
ret	US GP	Watkins Glen	22	Reg Parnell (Racing)	D	1.5 Lotus 25-BRM V8	unwell with flu	18/18
dns	MEXICAN GP	Mexico City	22	Reg Parnell (Racing)	D	1.5 Lotus 25-BRM V8	dropped by team-late for practice	(13)/18

1966   Championship position: Unplaced

	Race	Circuit	No	Entrant	Tyres	Car/Engine	Comment	Q Pos/Entries
ret	US GP	Watkins Glen	10	Bernard White Racing	D	2.0 BRM P261 V8	flat battery	17/19
ret	MEXICAN GP	Mexico City	10	Bernard White Racing	D	2.0 BRM P261 V8	gearbox	17/19

GP Starts: 50   GP Wins: 1   Pole positions: 0   Fastest laps: 1 (shared)   Points: 47

EDDIE IRVINE

Eddie Irvine's bold, but ultimately unsuccessful, attempt to wrest the drivers' championship from Mika Häkkinen not only saved the 1999 season from McLaren domination but also gave the Ulsterman the platform to show the talents that had for so long been subjugated to the needs of Michael Schumacher.

Many onlookers were surprised at his emergence, but Eddie's early career had promised a great deal, from his beginnings in the British and Irish FF1600 series. Driving a works Van Diemen, he won both the RAC British and Esso FF1600 championships in 1987, amassing 14 victories, and to crown his year Irvine also took the Brands Hatch Formula Ford Festival in convincing style. Moving up to Formula 3 in 1988, Eddie found winning a tougher proposition; he managed eight top-three placings but just could not break the dominance of JJ Lehto and Gary Brabham.

His graduation to F3000 the following season with Pacific found the team struggling, but Irvine got stuck in and never gave up. His reward was a move to Eddie Jordan's team in 1990 and he rapidly developed into a front-runner, winning at Hockenheim and finishing third in the championship. Subsequently opting to continue his career in the Japanese F3000 series, he finished sixth in the final table in 1991 and 1992, and was very unfortunate to lose the 1993 championship to Kazuyoshi Hoshino after scoring more points than the veteran. Highly thought of by Toyota, Irvine drove for the company in Japan in 1992 and also at Le Mans, both in 1993, when he was fourth and set fastest lap, and 1994, when he came second.

Eddie was given his F1 chance by Jordan at Suzuka in 1993, and rarely can a Grand Prix debut have brought so much controversy. As, revelling in the tricky conditions, he battled with Damon Hill for sixth place, he first balked and then had the temerity to repass the race leader, Ayrton Senna, who was attempting to lap him; in the closing stages he punted Derek Warwick off to claim his first championship point; and then he suffered a physical and verbal assault from the irate Brazilian after the race. It certainly moved the self-assured Ulsterman to centre stage, if only for a weekend.

Signed for a full season of Grand Prix racing with Jordan in 1994, Irvine

was soon embroiled in further controversy. Blamed for a four-car pile-up in Brazil, he harshly received a one-race ban. Quite reasonably, Eddie appealed and was sent away with his punishment increased three-fold! A less resilient character than the Ulsterman may have suffered a loss of confidence, but he bounced back all the stronger, a late-season drive to fourth place at Jerez being the best of a number of fine displays.

In 1995 Irvine matured even further to outshine team-mate Barrichello more often than not. His performances in qualifying were particularly impressive but it still came as a mild shock when it was announced that Eddie would be joining Michael Schumacher at Ferrari in 1996.

This was to prove the chance of a lifetime for Irvine, who was astute enough to accept his subordinate role to the German in the team on the sound basis that a spell at Maranello could only improve his own standing as a driver. His first season brought little in terms of worthwhile finishes nor was he given sufficient testing to enable him to back his team leader as effectively as he would have wished, but he carved a comfortable and profitable niche for himself, wearing an air of casual indifference or open defiance depending upon his mood.

The 1998 season saw an even more confident Eddie raise his game, and he not only became a reliably consistent points scorer but also had the look of a genuine contender for victory should the opportunity arise. However, few people anticipated that the opening race of 1999 at Melbourne would bring that first Grand Prix win and that he would then be sucked into the vortex of a thrilling championship battle with the McLarens of Häkkinen and Coulthard. Picking up Ferrari's challenge after Schumacher's unfortunate Silverstone accident, Irvine realistically assessed his situation and took the fight to the McLaren pair with great tenacity, and was predictably consummate in waging a war of mind-games.

In the end, of course, Eddie came up just short and had to give best to Häkkinen in Japan. There was, by way of consolation, a multi-million-pound move to Jaguar for 2000 and the chance to emerge from Schumacher's shadow and prove he has what it takes as a team leader in his own right.

IRVINE, Eddie (GB) b 10/11/1965, Conlig, Co Down, Northern Ireland

1993
Championship position: 20th= Wins: 0 Pole positions: 0 Fastest laps: 0 Points scored: 1

	Race	Circuit	No	Entrant	Tyres	Car/Engine	Comment	Q Pos/Entries
6	JAPANESE GP	Suzuka	15	Team Sasol Jordan	G	3.5 Jordan 193-Hart V10		8/24
ret	AUSTRALIAN GP	Adelaide	15	Team Sasol Jordan	G	3.5 Jordan 193-Hart V10	suspension damage after spin	19/24

1994
Championship position: 14th= Wins: 0 Pole positions: 0 Fastest laps: 0 Points scored: 6

	Race	Circuit	No	Entrant	Tyres	Car/Engine	Comment	Q Pos/Entries
ret	BRAZILIAN GP	Interlagos	15	Sasol Jordan	G	3.5 Jordan 194-Hart V10	hit Verstappen-multiple crash	16/28
6	SPANISH GP	Barcelona	15	Sasol Jordan	G	3.5 Jordan 194-Hart V10	1 lap behind	13/27
ret	CANADIAN GP	Montreal	15	Sasol Jordan	G	3.5 Jordan 194-Hart V10	spun off	8/27
ret	FRENCH GP	Magny Cours	15	Sasol Jordan	G	3.5 Jordan 194-Hart V10	gearbox	6/28
ret/dns	BRITISH GP	Silverstone	15	Sasol Jordan	G	3.5 Jordan 194-Hart V10	engine failure on parade lap	12/28
ret	GERMAN GP	Hockenheim	15	Sasol Jordan	G	3.5 Jordan 194-Hart V10	multiple accident at start	10/28
ret	HUNGARIAN GP	Hungaroring	15	Sasol Jordan	G	3.5 Jordan 194-Hart V10	collision-Barrichello & Katayama	7/28
13*/ret	BELGIAN GP	Spa	15	Sasol Jordan	G	3.5 Jordan 194-Hart V10	*1st car dsq/alternator/-4 laps	4/28
ret	ITALIAN GP	Monza	15	Sasol Jordan	G	3.5 Jordan 194-Hart V10	engine	9/28
7	PORTUGUESE GP	Estoril	15	Sasol Jordan	G	3.5 Jordan 194-Hart V10	1 lap behind	13/28
4	EUROPEAN GP	Jerez	15	Sasol Jordan	G	3.5 Jordan 194-Hart V10		10/28
5	JAPANESE GP	Suzuka	15	Sasol Jordan	G	3.5 Jordan 194-Hart V10		6/28
ret	AUSTRALIAN GP	Adelaide	15	Sasol Jordan	G	3.5 Jordan 194-Hart V10	spun off	6/28

1995
Championship position: 12th Wins: 0 Pole positions: 0 Fastest laps: 0 Points scored: 10

	Race	Circuit	No	Entrant	Tyres	Car/Engine	Comment	Q Pos/Entries
ret	ARGENTINE GP	Buenos Aires	15	Total Jordan Peugeot	G	3.0 Jordan 195-Peugeot V10	gearbox	8/26
ret	BRAZILIAN GP	Interlagos	15	Total Jordan Peugeot	G	3.0 Jordan 195-Peugeot V10	engine	4/26
8	SAN MARINO GP	Imola	15	Total Jordan Peugeot	G	3.0 Jordan 195-Peugeot V10	2 laps behind	7/26
5	SPANISH GP	Barcelona	15	Total Jordan Peugeot	G	3.0 Jordan 195-Peugeot V10	1 lap behind	6/26
ret	MONACO GP	Monte Carlo	15	Total Jordan Peugeot	G	3.0 Jordan 195-Peugeot V10	broken wheel rim	9/26
3	CANADIAN GP	Montreal	15	Total Jordan Peugeot	G	3.0 Jordan 195-Peugeot V10		8/24
9	FRENCH GP	Magny Cours	15	Total Jordan Peugeot	G	3.0 Jordan 195-Peugeot V10	1 lap behind	11/24
ret	BRITISH GP	Silverstone	15	Total Jordan Peugeot	G	3.0 Jordan 195-Peugeot V10	electrics	7/24
9	GERMAN GP	Hockenheim	15	Total Jordan Peugeot	G	3.0 Jordan 195-Peugeot V10	engine	6/24
13/ret	HUNGARIAN GP	Hungaroring	15	Total Jordan Peugeot	G	3.0 Jordan 195-Peugeot V10	clutch/7 laps behind	7/24
ret	BELGIAN GP	Spa	15	Total Jordan Peugeot	G	3.0 Jordan 195-Peugeot V10	car caught fire in refuelling	7/24
ret	ITALIAN GP	Monza	15	Total Jordan Peugeot	G	3.0 Jordan 195-Peugeot V10	engine	12/24
10	PORTUGUESE GP	Estoril	15	Total Jordan Peugeot	G	3.0 Jordan 195-Peugeot V10	1 lap behind	10/24
6	EUROPEAN GP	Nürburgring	15	Total Jordan Peugeot	G	3.0 Jordan 195-Peugeot V10	1 lap behind	5/24
11	PACIFIC GP	T.I. Circuit	15	Total Jordan Peugeot	G	3.0 Jordan 195-Peugeot V10	2 laps behind	6/24
4	JAPANESE GP	Suzuka	15	Total Jordan Peugeot	G	3.0 Jordan 195-Peugeot V10		7/24
ret	AUSTRALIAN GP	Adelaide	15	Total Jordan Peugeot	G	3.0 Jordan 195-Peugeot V10	engine	9/24

1996
Championship position: 10 Wins: 0 Pole positions: 0 Fastest laps: 0 Points scored: 11

	Race	Circuit	No	Entrant	Tyres	Car/Engine	Comment	Q Pos/Entries
3	AUSTRALIAN GP	Melbourne	2	Scuderia Ferrari	G	3.0 Ferrari F310-V10		3/22
7	BRAZILIAN GP	Interlagos	2	Scuderia Ferrari	G	3.0 Ferrari F310-V10	misfire/handling/1 lap behind	10/22
5	ARGENTINE GP	Buenos Aires	2	Scuderia Ferrari	G	3.0 Ferrari F310-V10		10/22
ret	EUROPEAN GP	Nürburgring	2	Scuderia Ferrari	G	3.0 Ferrari F310-V10	collision with Panis	7/22
4	SAN MARINO GP	Imola	2	Scuderia Ferrari	G	3.0 Ferrari F310-V10		6/22
7/ret	MONACO GP	Monte Carlo	2	Scuderia Ferrari	G	3.0 Ferrari F310-V10	collision-Salo & Häkkinen/-7 laps	7/22
ret	SPANISH GP	Barcelona	2	Scuderia Ferrari	G	3.0 Ferrari F310-V10	spun off on lap 1	6/22
ret	CANADIAN GP	Montreal	2	Scuderia Ferrari	G	3.0 Ferrari F310-V10	spun-broken suspension	5/22
ret	FRENCH GP	Magny Cours	2	Scuderia Ferrari	G	3.0 Ferrari F310-V10	gearbox	10/22
ret	BRITISH GP	Silverstone	2	Scuderia Ferrari	G	3.0 Ferrari F310-V10	gearbox bearing	10/22
ret	GERMAN GP	Hockenheim	2	Scuderia Ferrari	G	3.0 Ferrari F310-V10	gearbox	8/20
ret	HUNGARIAN GP	Hungaroring	2	Scuderia Ferrari	G	3.0 Ferrari F310-V10	gearbox	4/20
ret	BELGIAN GP	Spa	2	Scuderia Ferrari	G	3.0 Ferrari F310-V10	gearbox	9/20
ret	ITALIAN GP	Monza	2	Scuderia Ferrari	G	3.0 Ferrari F310-V10	hit tyre stack - suspension	7/20
5	PORTUGUESE GP	Estoril	2	Scuderia Ferrari	G	3.0 Ferrari F310-V10	hit by Berger on last lap	6/20
ret	JAPANESE GP	Suzuka	2	Scuderia Ferrari	G	3.0 Ferrari F310-V10	collision with Berger	6/20

1997
Championship position: 7th Wins: 0 Pole positions: 0 Fastest laps: 0 Points scored: 24

	Race	Circuit	No	Entrant	Tyres	Car/Engine	Comment	Q Pos/Entries
ret	AUSTRALIAN GP	Melbourne	6	Scuderia Ferrari Marlboro	G	3.0 Ferrari F310B-V10	first corner ollision	5/24
16	BRAZILIAN GP	Interlagos	6	Scuderia Ferrari Marlboro	G	3.0 Ferrari F310B-V10	ill-fitting belts in spare/-2 laps	14/22
2	ARGENTINE GP	Buenos Aires	6	Scuderia Ferrari Marlboro	G	3.0 Ferrari F310B-V10		7/22
3	SAN MARINO GP	Imola	6	Scuderia Ferrari Marlboro	G	3.0 Ferrari F310B-V10		9/22
3	MONACO GP	Monte Carlo	6	Scuderia Ferrari Marlboro	G	3.0 Ferrari F310B-V10		13/22
12	SPANISH GP	Barcelona	6	Scuderia Ferrari Marlboro	G	3.0 Ferrari F310B-V10	stop & go pen-blocking/- 1 lap	11/22
ret	CANADIAN GP	Montreal	6	Scuderia Ferrari Marlboro	G	3.0 Ferrari F310B-V10	spun off on lap 1	12/22
3	FRENCH GP	Magny Cours	6	Scuderia Ferrari Marlboro	G	3.0 Ferrari F310B-V10		5/22
ret	BRITISH GP	Silverstone	6	Scuderia Ferrari Marlboro	G	3.0 Ferrari F310B-V10	driveshaft	7/22
ret	GERMAN GP	Hockenheim	6	Scuderia Ferrari Marlboro	G	3.0 Ferrari F310B-V10	collision with Frentzen	10/22
9/ret	HUNGARIAN GP	Hungaroring	6	Scuderia Ferrari Marlboro	G	3.0 Ferrari F310B-V10	collision with Nakano/-1 lap	5/22
10*/ret	BELGIAN GP	Spa	6	Scuderia Ferrari Marlboro	G	3.0 Ferrari F310B-V10	* 3rd car dsq/collision-Diniz/- 1 lap	17/22
8	ITALIAN GP	Monza	6	Scuderia Ferrari Marlboro	G	3.0 Ferrari F310B-V10		10/22
ret	AUSTRIAN GP	A1-Ring	6	Scuderia Ferrari Marlboro	G	3.0 Ferrari F310B-V10	hit Alesi-collision damage	8/22
ret	LUXEMBOURG GP	Nürburgring	6	Scuderia Ferrari Marlboro	G	3.0 Ferrari F310B-V10	engine	14/22
3	JAPANESE GP	Suzuka	6	Scuderia Ferrari Marlboro	G	3.0 Ferrari F310B-V10		3/22
5	EUROPEAN GP	Jerez	6	Scuderia Ferrari Marlboro	G	3.0 Ferrari F310B-V10		7/22

1998
Championship position: 4th Wins: 0 Pole positions: 0 Fastest laps: 0 Points scored: 48

	Race	Circuit	No	Entrant	Tyres	Car/Engine	Comment	Q Pos/Entries
4	AUSTRALIAN GP	Melbourne	4	Scuderia Ferrari Marlboro	G	3.0 Ferrari F300-V10	1 lap behind	8/22
8	BRAZILIAN GP	Interlagos	4	Scuderia Ferrari Marlboro	G	3.0 Ferrari F300-V10	1 lap behind	6/22
3	ARGENTINE GP	Buenos Aires	4	Scuderia Ferrari Marlboro	G	3.0 Ferrari F300-V10		4/22
3	SAN MARINO GP	Imola	4	Scuderia Ferrari Marlboro	G	3.0 Ferrari F300-V10		6/22
ret	SPANISH GP	Barcelona	4	Scuderia Ferrari Marlboro	G	3.0 Ferrari F300-V10	collision with Fisichella	10/22
3	MONACO GP	Monte Carlo	4	Scuderia Ferrari Marlboro	G	3.0 Ferrari F300-V10		7/22

	Race	Circuit	No	Entrant	Tyres	Car/Engine	Comment	Q Pos/Entries
3	CANADIAN GP	Montreal	4	Scuderia Ferrari Marlboro	G	3.0 Ferrari F300-V10		8/22
2	FRENCH GP	Magny Cours	4	Scuderia Ferrari Marlboro	G	3.0 Ferrari F300-V10		4/22
3	BRITISH GP	Silverstone	4	Scuderia Ferrari Marlboro	G	3.0 Ferrari F300-V10		5/22
4	AUSTRIAN GP	A1-Ring	4	Scuderia Ferrari Marlboro	G	3.0 Ferrari F300-V10		8/22
8	GERMAN GP	Hockenheim	4	Scuderia Ferrari Marlboro	G	3.0 Ferrari F300-V10		6/22
ret	HUNGARIAN GP	Hungaroring	4	Scuderia Ferrari Marlboro	G	3.0 Ferrari F300-V10	gearbox	5/22
ret	BELGIAN GP	Spa	4	Scuderia Ferrari Marlboro	G	3.0 Ferrari F300-V10	spun off	5/22
2	ITALIAN GP	Monza	4	Scuderia Ferrari Marlboro	G	3.0 Ferrari F300-V10		5/22
4	LUXEMBOURG GP	Nürburgring	4	Scuderia Ferrari Marlboro	G	3.0 Ferrari F300-V10		2/22
2	JAPANESE GP	Suzuka	4	Scuderia Ferrari Marlboro	G	3.0 Ferrari F300-V10		4/22

1999   Championship position: 2nd   Wins: 4   Pole positions: 0   Fastest laps: 1   Points scored: 74

	Race	Circuit	No	Entrant	Tyres	Car/Engine	Comment	Q Pos/Entries
1	AUSTRALIAN GP	Melbourne	4	Scuderia Ferrari Marlboro	B	3.0 Ferrari F399-V10		6/22
5	BRAZILIAN GP	Interlagos	4	Scuderia Ferrari Marlboro	B	3.0 Ferrari F399-V10	pit stop-air resevoir/1 lap behind	6/22
ret	SAN MARINO GP	Imola	4	Scuderia Ferrari Marlboro	B	3.0 Ferrari F399-V10	engine	4/22
2	MONACO GP	Monte Carlo	4	Scuderia Ferrari Marlboro	B	3.0 Ferrari F399-V10		4/22
4	SPANISH GP	Barcelona	4	Scuderia Ferrari Marlboro	B	3.0 Ferrari F399-V10		2/22
3	CANADIAN GP	Montreal	4	Scuderia Ferrari Marlboro	B	3.0 Ferrari F399-V10	FL	3/22
6	FRENCH GP	Magny Cours	4	Scuderia Ferrari Marlboro	B	3.0 Ferrari F399-V10		17/22
2	BRITISH GP	Silverstone	4	Scuderia Ferrari Marlboro	B	3.0 Ferrari F399-V10		4/22
1	AUSTRIAN GP	A1-Ring	4	Scuderia Ferrari Marlboro	B	3.0 Ferrari F399-V10		3/22
1	GERMAN GP	Hockenheim	4	Scuderia Ferrari Marlboro	B	3.0 Ferrari F399-V10	team mate Salo gave up lead	5/22
3	HUNGARIAN GP	Hungaroring	4	Scuderia Ferrari Marlboro	B	3.0 Ferrari F399-V10		2/22
4	BELGIAN GP	Spa	4	Scuderia Ferrari Marlboro	B	3.0 Ferrari F399-V10	wrong set-up on car	6/22
6	ITALIAN GP	Monza	4	Scuderia Ferrari Marlboro	B	3.0 Ferrari F399-V10		8/22
7	EUROPEAN GP	Nürburgring	4	Scuderia Ferrari Marlboro	B	3.0 Ferrari F399-V10		9/22
1	MALAYSIAN GP	Sepang	4	Scuderia Ferrari Marlboro	B	3.0 Ferrari F399-V10		2/22
3	JAPANESE GP	Suzuka	4	Scuderia Ferrari Marlboro	B	3.0 Ferrari F399-V10		5/22

GP Starts: 96 (97)   GP Wins: 4   Pole positions: 0   Fastest laps: 1   Points: 173

CHRIS IRWIN

An outstanding prospect, Irwin made an immediate impression in his first full Formula 3 season in 1964, taking third in the Grovewood Awards. Further success in F3 with the Chequered Flag Merlyn brought him a works Formula 2 drive for that marque in 1965. He then gained a works drive for Brabham in 1966, concentrating on F3 but occasionally racing in F2, and scoring a fine third place in the Albi GP. Given an old four-cylinder-engined Brabham, Chris finished seventh on his GP debut at Brands Hatch, impressing Tim Parnell, who signed him along with Piers Courage to share the semi-works BRM for 1967.

In fact, Courage made a tardy start to the season, while Irwin, after scoring a fourth at Sandown Park and a third at Longford in the Tasman series, followed by sixth place in the Race of Champions and fourth at Syracuse in Parnell's old Lotus 25-BRM, took his chance with some solid and sensible drives in both the 2-litre car and the heavy and unreliable H16, which he took to fifth in the French GP.

Chris had also joined up with John Surtees to race the works Lola in Formula 2, winning the 1968 Eifelrennen race at the Nürburgring and finishing third at Zolder, before a return to the 'Ring in Alan Mann's Ford PL3 sports car ended in a catastrophic practice crash. Poor Chris received very serious head injuries, from which he eventually made a recovery, but he never raced again.

IRWIN, Chris (GB)   b 27/6/1942, Wandsworth, London

1966   Championship position: Unplaced

	Race	Circuit	No	Entrant	Tyres	Car/Engine	Comment	Q Pos/Entries
7	BRITISH GP	Brands Hatch	7	Brabham Racing Organisation	G	2.7 Brabham BT11-Climax 4	2 laps behind	12/20

1967   Championship position: 16th=   Wins: 0   Pole positions: 0   Fastest laps: 0   Points scored: 2

	Race	Circuit	No	Entrant	Tyres	Car/Engine	Comment	Q Pos/Entries
7	DUTCH GP	Zandvoort	18	Reg Parnell Motor Racing	F	2.0 Lotus 25-BRM V8	2 laps behind	13/17
ret	BELGIAN GP	Spa	17	Reg Parnell Motor Racing	D	2.0 BRM P261 V8	engine	15/18
5/ret	FRENCH GP	Le Mans	15	Reg Parnell Motor Racing	G	3.0 BRM P83 H16	engine/4 laps behind	9/15
dns	"	"	15	Reg Parnell Motor Racing	D/G	2.0 BRM P261 V8	practice only/Stewart in race	–/–
7	BRITISH GP	Silverstone	15	Reg Parnell Motor Racing	D	2.0 BRM P261 V8	3 laps behind	13/21
dns	"	"	15	Reg Parnell Motor Racing	G	3.0 BRM P83 H16	practice only/Stewart in race	–/–
7*	GERMAN GP	Nürburgring	18	Reg Parnell Motor Racing	G	3.0 BRM P83 H16	stop-gearbox/*9th on road/-2 laps	19/25
ret	CANADIAN GP	Mosport Park	17	Reg Parnell Motor Racing	G	3.0 BRM P83 H16	spun off	11/19
ret	ITALIAN GP	Monza	38	Reg Parnell Motor Racing	G	3.0 BRM P83 H16	injection pump drive	16/18
ret	US GP	Watkins Glen	17	Reg Parnell Motor Racing	G	3.0 BRM P83 H16	engine	14/18
ret	MEXICAN GP	Mexico City	17	Reg Parnell Motor Racing	G	3.0 BRM P83 H16	low oil pressure	15/19

GP Starts: 10   GP Wins: 1   Pole positions: 0   Fastest laps: 0   Points: 2

JEAN-PIERRE JABOUILLE

Success was a long time coming for this popular Frenchman who, while never one to take the eye, certainly knew how to put the machinery at his disposal to the best use.

With no previous experience, Jean-Pierre competed in the R8 Renault Gordini series in 1966 and won a few races, earning an invitation to drive in French F3 in a team with the more seasoned Philippe Vidal. The F3 scene was very competitive, but Jabouille made his mark in 1968 when he ran and maintained his own car, keeping out of trouble and earning enough prize money from one race to make it to the next. The series that year was dominated by Cevert, but Jean-Pierre won five races to finish runner-up and gain an end-of-year Formula 2 ride with Matra at Hockenheim.

Alpine offered him a contract for 1969 as number two to Depailler, and he stayed with the team as a test and development driver over the next few seasons, his rather fragmented racing programme doing little to further his ambitions. Threre were outings for Pygmée in F2 in 1970 and for Elf-Tecno the following season, when he finished second at Pau, and Jabouille also tried his hand at sports cars, taking a splendid second place in the Paris 1000 Km in a Ferrari 512S. The Frenchman's career seemed to be stuck in something of a rut in 1972 when he received decidedly 'second best' treatment in the Elf/John Coombs team, and made his feelings known. When he was given a March 722, things improved and he took second place at Mantorp Park. His lot was much the same in 1973, when much of his time was given over to the development of the Alpine A440 sports car, but he was loaned to Matra for Le Mans, sharing the third-placed car with Jaussaud.

In 1974 Jabouille made a couple of unsuccessful attempts to qualify for a Grand Prix with Williams and Surtees, but concentrated on the same mix as the year before, only this time with more success. In Formula 2 he won his first race at Hockenheim and, racing the Alpine, he finished runner-up in the European 2-litre series. Seconded to Matra for Le Mans again, he finished third once more, this time with Migault. Determined to improve upon his somewhat patchy record of success in Formula 2, Jabouille took the brave step of constructing his own chassis for 1975 with the support of Elf. He lost out to his great chum Laffite in the championship but, thanks to his connections with Elf, he at least had the consolation of a decent Grand Prix opportunity, qualifying the Tyrrell for the French GP. It was a popular triumph when Jean-Pierre finally clinched the Formula 2 title in 1976 with three wins, and no one begrudged the Parisian his hard-earned triumph.

This goal achieved, Jabouille then undertook the development work on the F1 Renault turbo project, accepting the early disappointments with equanimity as failure heaped upon failure over the first two seasons until the glorious moment for France and Renault when the car finally came good – fittingly at Dijon – in 1979. Although overshadowed by the sparkling Arnoux in 1980, Jean-Pierre took a shrewd and well-judged win at the Österreichring before a crash in Montreal after a suspension failure left him with badly broken legs. Having already agreed to join Ligier for 1981, he made it back into the cockpit for the start of the season, but it soon became painfully obvious that he was far from fit and, with his leg injuries slow to heal, he decided to retire in mid-season.

Missing the thrill of competition, Jean-Pierre was soon back on the circuits, racing in the French Supertourisme series. His vast engineering and development experience later made a valuable contribution to Peugeot's successful sports car racing programme, and in 1993 he shared the third-placed car at Le Mans, before succeeding Jean Todt at the head of the French company's motor sport division as they prepared to enter Grand Prix racing as engine supplier to McLaren in 1994. It was to prove a torrid baptism for Peugeot, the newcomers perhaps underestimating the level of technology required to compete at the highest level. Certainly partnering McLaren, themselves in a trough after so many seasons of greatness, made the task even harder, although a parting of the ways less than twelve months later can have benefited neither concern. Eddie Jordan was delighted to step in and embrace the French giant but, after another troubled and inconclusive year in 1995, it was Jabouille's head that rolled when victory seemed no nearer.

In 1997 he formed his own very successful sports car team, initially running a Porsche 911 GT1 for Mauro Baldi and Emmanuel Collard, and latterly a Ferrari 333SP, with which Baldi and Laurent Redon took an outright win at Spa in 1999 in the International Sports Racing Series.

JOHN JAMES

John, an engineer by profession, had his first race in a Lea Francis at Brooklands immediately before the war, and when competition resumed he competed in hill-climbs and sprints with a Monza-type 2.3 Alfa Romeo. This was replaced by a Type 54 Bugatti for similar events in 1948 before one of two Sunbeams which he had stored away throughout the war was completely rebuilt. It was this car that brought James a fourth place in the 1949 Wakefield Trophy at the Curragh in Eire.

In 1951 John purchased a Maserati 4CLT from Reg Parnell and, apart from his appearance in the British Grand Prix, piloted it to eighth places in both the Woodcote Cup and the Daily Graphic Trophy races at Goodwood. With the change in regulations rendering the 4CLT suitable only for Formula Libre events in 1952, John used it mainly for fun in sprints until his retirement from the sport the following year.

JABOUILLE, Jean-Pierre (F) b 1/10/1942, Paris

1974 — Championship position: Unplaced

	Race	Circuit	No	Entrant	Tyres	Car/Engine	Comment	Q Pos/Entries
dnq	FRENCH GP	Dijon	21	Frank Williams Racing Cars	F	3.0 Williams FW01-Cosworth V8		25/30
dnq	AUSTRIAN GP	Österreichring	19	Team Surtees	F	3.0 Surtees TS16-Cosworth V8		30/31

1975 — Championship position: Unplaced

12	FRENCH GP	Paul Ricard	15	Elf Team Tyrrell	G	3.0 Tyrrell 007-Cosworth V8		21/26

1977 — Championship position: Unplaced

ret	BRITISH GP	Silverstone	15	Equipe Renault Elf	M	1.5 t/c Renault RS01 V6	turbo	21/36
ret	DUTCH GP	Zandvoort	15	Equipe Renault Elf	M	1.5 t/c Renault RS01 V6	rear suspension	10/34
ret	ITALIAN GP	Monza	15	Equipe Renault Elf	M	1.5 t/c Renault RS01 V6	engine	20/34
ret	US GP EAST	Watkins Glen	15	Equipe Renault Elf	M	1.5 t/c Renault RS01 V6	alternator	14/27
dnq	CANADIAN GP	Mosport Park	15	Equipe Renault Elf	M	1.5 t/c Renault RS01 V6		27/27

1978 — Championship position: 17th Wins: 0 Pole positions: 0 Fastest laps: 0 Points scored: 3

ret	SOUTH AFRICAN GP	Kyalami	15	Equipe Renault Elf	M	1.5 t/c Renault RS01 V6	engine-misfire	6/30
ret	US GP WEST	Long Beach	15	Equipe Renault Elf	M	1.5 t/c Renault RS01 V6	turbo	13/30
10	MONACO GP	Monte Carlo	15	Equipe Renault Elf	M	1.5 t/c Renault RS01 V6	brake problem/4 laps behind	12/30
nc	BELGIAN GP	Zolder	15	Equipe Renault Elf	M	1.5 t/c Renault RS01 V6	3 pit stops-brakes/-14 laps	10/30
13	SPANISH GP	Jarama	15	Equipe Renault Elf	M	1.5 t/c Renault RS01 V6	4 laps behind	11/29
ret	SWEDISH GP	Anderstorp	15	Equipe Renault Elf	M	1.5 t/c Renault RS01 V6	engine	10/27
ret	FRENCH GP	Paul Ricard	15	Equipe Renault Elf	M	1.5 t/c Renault RS01 V6	engine	11/29
ret	BRITISH GP	Brands Hatch	15	Equipe Renault Elf	M	1.5 t/c Renault RS01 V6	engine	12/30
ret	GERMAN GP	Hockenheim	15	Equipe Renault Elf	M	1.5 t/c Renault RS01 V6	engine	9/30
ret	AUSTRIAN GP	Österreichring	15	Equipe Renault Elf	M	1.5 t/c Renault RS01 V6	gearbox	3/31
ret	DUTCH GP	Zandvoort	15	Equipe Renault Elf	M	1.5 t/c Renault RS01 V6	engine	9/33
ret	ITALIAN GP	Monza	15	Equipe Renault Elf	M	1.5 t/c Renault RS01 V6	engine	3/32
4	US GP EAST	Watkins Glen	15	Equipe Renault Elf	M	1.5 t/c Renault RS01 V6		9/27
12	CANADIAN GP	Montreal	15	Equipe Renault Elf	M	1.5 t/c Renault RS01 V6	pit stop/5 laps behind	22/28

1979 — Championship position: 13th Wins: 1 Pole positions: 4 Fastest laps: 0 Points scored: 9

ret	ARGENTINE GP	Buenos Aires	15	Equipe Renault Elf	M	1.5 t/c Renault RS01 V6	engine	12/26
10	BRAZILIAN GP	Interlagos	15	Equipe Renault Elf	M	1.5 t/c Renault RS01 V6	stalled on grid/1 lap behind	7/26
ret	SOUTH AFRICAN GP	Kyalami	15	Equipe Renault Elf	M	1.5 t/c Renault RS01 V6	engine	1/26
dns	US GP WEST	Long Beach	15	Equipe Renault Elf	M	1.5 t/c Renault RS01 V6	practice accident-injured arm	(20)/26
ret	SPANISH GP	Jarama	15	Equipe Renault Elf	M	1.5 t/c Renault RS10 V6	turbo	9/27
ret	BELGIAN GP	Zolder	15	Equipe Renault Elf	M	1.5 t/c Renault RS10 V6	turbo	17/28
nc	MONACO GP	Monte Carlo	15	Equipe Renault Elf	M	1.5 t/c Renault RS10 V6	pit stops-engine/8 laps behind	20/25
1	FRENCH GP	Dijon	15	Equipe Renault Elf	M	1.5 t/c Renault RS11 V6		1/27
ret	BRITISH GP	Silverstone	15	Equipe Renault Elf	M	1.5 t/c Renault RS11 V6	engine	2/26
ret	GERMAN GP	Hockenheim	15	Equipe Renault Elf	M	1.5 t/c Renault RS11 V6	spun off	1/26
ret	AUSTRIAN GP	Österreichring	15	Equipe Renault Elf	M	1.5 t/c Renault RS11 V6	clutch/gearbox	3/26
ret	DUTCH GP	Zandvoort	15	Equipe Renault Elf	M	1.5 t/c Renault RS11 V6	clutch	4/26
14/ret	ITALIAN GP	Monza	15	Equipe Renault Elf	M	1.5 t/c Renault RS11 V6	engine	1/28
ret	CANADIAN GP	Montreal	15	Equipe Renault Elf	M	1.5 t/c Renault RS14 V6	brakes	7/29
ret	US GP EAST	Watkins Glen	15	Equipe Renault Elf	M	1.5 t/c Renault RS14 V6	camshaft belt	8/30

1980 — Championship position: 8th Wins: 1 Pole positions: 2 Fastest laps: 0 Points scored: 9

ret	ARGENTINE GP	Buenos Aires	15	Equipe Renault Elf	M	1.5 t/c Renault RS22 V6	gearbox	9/28
ret	BRAZILIAN GP	Interlagos	15	Equipe Renault Elf	M	1.5 t/c Renault RS22 V6	turbo	1/28
ret	SOUTH AFRICAN GP	Kyalami	15	Equipe Renault Elf	M	1.5 t/c Renault RS23 V6	puncture	1/28
10	US GP WEST	Long Beach	15	Equipe Renault Elf	M	1.5 t/c Renault RS23 V6	pit stop-brakes/9 laps behind	11/27
ret	BELGIAN GP	Zolder	15	Equipe Renault Elf	M	1.5 t/c Renault RS23 V6	clutch	=5/27
ret	MONACO GP	Monte Carlo	15	Equipe Renault Elf	M	1.5 t/c Renault RS23 V6	gearbox	16/27
ret	FRENCH GP	Paul Ricard	15	Equipe Renault Elf	M	1.5 t/c Renault RS23 V6	transmission	6/27
ret	BRITISH GP	Brands Hatch	15	Equipe Renault Elf	M	1.5 t/c Renault RS23 V6	engine	13/27
ret	GERMAN GP	Hockenheim	15	Equipe Renault Elf	M	1.5 t/c Renault RS23 V6	engine	2/26
1	AUSTRIAN GP	Österreichring	15	Equipe Renault Elf	M	1.5 t/c Renault RS23 V6		2/25
ret	DUTCH GP	Zandvoort	15	Equipe Renault Elf	M	1.5 t/c Renault RS23 V6	handling/differential	2/28
ret	ITALIAN GP	Imola	15	Equipe Renault Elf	M	1.5 t/c Renault RS23 V6	gearbox	2/28
ret	CANADIAN GP	Montreal	15	Equipe Renault Elf	M	1.5 t/c Renault RS23 V6	suspension failure-accident	13/28

1981 — Championship position: Unplaced

dns	BRAZILIAN GP	Rio	25	Equipe Talbot Gitanes	M	3.0 Ligier JS17-Matra V12	w/drawn in practice/Jarier drove	(26)/30
dnq	ARGENTINE GP	Buenos Aires	25	Equipe Talbot Gitanes	M	3.0 Ligier JS17-Matra V12		28/29
nc	SAN MARINO GP	Imola	25	Equipe Talbot Gitanes	M	3.0 Ligier JS17-Matra V12	pit stops-engine/-15 laps	18/30
ret	BELGIAN GP	Zolder	25	Equipe Talbot Gitanes	M	3.0 Ligier JS17-Matra V12	transmission	16/31
dnq	MONACO GP	Monte Carlo	25	Equipe Talbot Gitanes	M	3.0 Ligier JS17-Matra V12		22/31
ret	SPANISH GP	Jarama	25	Equipe Talbot Gitanes	M	3.0 Ligier JS17-Matra V12	brakes	19/30

GP Starts: 49 GP Wins: 2 Pole positions: 6 Fastest laps: 0 Points: 21

JAMES, John (GB) b 10/5/1914, Packwood, nr Hockley Heath, Warwickshire

1951 — Championship position: Unplaced

	Race	Circuit	No	Entrant	Tyres	Car/Engine	Comment	Q Pos/Entries
ret	BRITISH GP	Silverstone	16	John James	D	1.5 s/c Maserati 4CLT/48 4	radiator	17/20

GP Starts: 1 GP Wins: 0 Pole positions: 0 Fastest laps: 0 Points: 0

JEAN-PIERRE JARIER

Jarier had his few fleeting moments in Grand Prix racing when nobody could live with him, but this inconsistent Frenchman ultimately flattered to deceive and the once bright promise soon faded.

After impressing in saloons and Formula France, Jean-Pierre graduated to the highly competitive French F3 series, finishing third in the championship in 1970 with a Tecno before making an assault on the European Formula 2 championship in 1971. He took the Shell Arnold team's March to a couple of third-place finishes at Albi and Vallelunga, and had his first taste of Grand Prix racing when the team hired the ex-Hubert Hahne March 701 for the Italian GP, bringing the car home in a steady 12th place.

Unfortunately his career took a step backwards the following year when the Shell Arnold team ran out of funds just after Jarier had taken third place at Monza in the Lottery GP. The wealthy José Dolhem took over the ride, so it was back to the harum-scarum world of Formula 3, but then came his big break. Signed to lead the March Formula 2 team, Jean-Pierre also found himself promoted to Formula 1 after Chris Amon was sensationally dismissed before the start of the 1973 season. In Grands Prix he was not surprisingly a little overwhelmed but was nevertheless unlucky not to score the occasional point here and there, but in Formula 2 it was a different story as he stormed to the European championship with eight victories in 13 rounds.

Now in demand, Jarier signed for Shadow in 1974 as number two to Peter Revson, but the American was soon tragically killed at Kyalami, leaving the burden of leading the team on the young Frenchman's shoulders. He responded with much courage, taking third place in the International Trophy and then the Monaco GP. He was also a key member of the Matra sports car team that year, sharing the winning car at Spa (with Ickx), the Nürburgring, Watkins Glen, Paul Ricard and Brands Hatch (all with Beltoise).

The following season started sensationally for Jarier. On pole in Argentina, he was unlucky to strip his clutch, and was then leading in Brazil by the proverbial country mile until a metering unit failed. This dominance was not to last, however, and his season disintegrated in a series of spins and crashes while team-mate Tom Pryce was busy asserting himself. Jarier gathered his resources for 1976. In the Brazilian GP, he lay a splendid second and was closing on the leader, Lauda, when he unluckily crashed out on James Hunt's oil. Things were never the same after that as the moody Frenchman became increasingly disenchanted with life at Shadow, who dropped him at the end of the season.

He hoped for a drive at Ligier in 1977, but in the event found himself in the ATS team running the Penske. A sixth place on his debut boded well, but the car was never really more than a midfield runner and Jarier failed to score any further points. By the end of the season he was briefly back at Shadow, and then had a one-off outing with Ligier. Meanwhile Alfa Romeo, remembering his superb sports car displays with Matra, had invited Jean-Pierre to drive their T33 cars at Dijon and Paul Ricard, and he won both races with Merzario, while he also raced a Mirage-Renault at Le Mans that year, taking second place with Vern Schuppan.

Jarier was back with ATS in 1978, but achieved little, quitting the team in mid-season. However, his whole career was suddenly revived at the end of the year when he took over the Lotus seat left vacant by the death of Ronnie Peterson. At Watkins Glen he set fastest lap and was in third place until he ran out of fuel near the end, and then in Montreal 'Jumper' put the Lotus on pole and fairly streaked away from the field until a small oil leak in a brake pipe ended his dominance. Ken Tyrrell, looking for a replacement for the Ligier-bound Depailler, gave Jarier the chance to build on his swiftly restored credibility. His two seasons with the team yielded ten points-scoring finishes, but the cars were not world beaters nor did Jarier seem totally involved once he realised there was nothing to aim for.

Early in 1981 he deputised for the still injury-troubled Jabouille at Ligier, before taking the only drive available at Osella. He stayed on for 1982, but apart from a splendid fourth place for the little team at Imola he lost interest badly as the year wore on. He was in the last-chance saloon the following season; he had finally secured a place in the Ligier line-up, but unfortunately the car was not quite the competitive proposition he had dreamed of racing in previous years. On the one occasion a victory was possible, Jarier made a hash of things, running into the back of Rosberg at Long Beach when well placed.

After a decade as a Grand Prix driver, he faced the fact that he was no longer in demand and quietly slipped out of single-seater racing, contenting himself in the French Supertourisme series for many years. In the early nineties 'Jumper' – now somewhat plumper – acquitted himself nobly in the Global GT series: driving a Porsche 911SR, he won rounds at Paul Ricard and Suzuka (with Wollek and Pareja) in 1994, and in 1995 he took second place in a Porsche GTZ at both Jerez and Paul Ricard.

Despite his 'advancing' years, Jarier still has few peers in his class of GT racing. He was French GT champion for the first time in 1998 and, again driving one of his beloved Porsche 911s, repeated the feat in 1999.

JARIER, Jean-Pierre (F) b 10/7/1946, Charenton, nr Paris

1971 — Championship position: Unplaced

	Race	Circuit	No	Entrant	Tyres	Car/Engine	Comment	Q Pos/Entries
12	ITALIAN GP	Monza	26	Shell Arnold	G	3.0 March 701-Cosworth V8	pit stops-brakes/-8 laps	24/24

1973 — Championship position: Unplaced

ret	ARGENTINE GP	Buenos Aires	24	STP March Racing Team	G	3.0 March 721G-Cosworth V8	gear linkage	17/19
ret	BRAZILIAN GP	Interlagos	11	STP March Racing Team	G	3.0 March 721G-Cosworth V8	gearbox	15/20
nc	SOUTH AFRICAN GP	Kyalami	14	STP March Racing Team	G	3.0 March 721G-Cosworth V8	13 laps behind	18/25
ret	BELGIAN GP	Zolder	14	STP March Racing Team	G	3.0 March 721G/731-Cosworth V8	accident	16/23
ret	MONACO GP	Monte Carlo	14	STP March Racing Team	G	3.0 March 721G/731-Cosworth V8	gearbox	=13/26
ret	SWEDISH GP	Anderstorp	14	STP March Racing Team	G	3.0 March 721G/731-Cosworth V8	throttle cable	20/22
ret	FRENCH GP	Paul Ricard	14	STP March Racing Team	G	3.0 March 721G/731-Cosworth V8	driveshaft	7/25
ret	AUSTRIAN GP	Österreichring	18	March Racing Team	G	3.0 March 731-Cosworth V8	engine	12/25
nc	CANADIAN GP	Mosport Park	18	March Racing Team	G	3.0 March 731-Cosworth V8	spun off/gearbox/-9 laps	23/25
11/ret	US GP	Watkins Glen	18	March Racing Team	G	3.0 March 731-Cosworth V8	accident/2 laps behind	18/28

1974 — Championship position: 14th   Wins: 0   Pole positions: 0   Fastest laps: 0   Points scored: 6

ret	ARGENTINE GP	Buenos Aires	17	UOP Shadow Racing Team	G	3.0 Shadow DN1-Cosworth V8	collision with Revson	16/26
ret	BRAZILIAN GP	Interlagos	17	UOP Shadow Racing Team	G	3.0 Shadow DN1-Cosworth V8	brakes	19/25
nc	SPANISH GP	Jarama	17	UOP Shadow Racing Team	G	3.0 Shadow DN3-Cosworth V8	hit by Merzario-pit stop/-11 laps	13/28
13	BELGIAN GP	Nivelles	17	UOP Shadow Racing Team	G	3.0 Shadow DN3-Cosworth V8	3 laps behind	17/32
3	MONACO GP	Monte Carlo	17	UOP Shadow Racing Team	G	3.0 Shadow DN3-Cosworth V8		6/28
5	SWEDISH GP	Anderstorp	17	UOP Shadow Racing Team	G	3.0 Shadow DN3-Cosworth V8		8/28
ret	DUTCH GP	Zandvoort	17	UOP Shadow Racing Team	G	3.0 Shadow DN3-Cosworth V8	clutch	7/27
12	FRENCH GP	Dijon	17	UOP Shadow Racing Team	G	3.0 Shadow DN3-Cosworth V8	1 lap behind	12/30
ret	BRITISH GP	Brands Hatch	17	UOP Shadow Racing Team	G	3.0 Shadow DN3-Cosworth V8	suspension	=15/34
8	GERMAN GP	Nürburgring	17	UOP Shadow Racing Team	G	3.0 Shadow DN3-Cosworth V8		18/32
8	AUSTRIAN GP	Österreichring	17	UOP Shadow Racing Team	G	3.0 Shadow DN3-Cosworth V8	fuel problems-pit stop/-2 laps	24/31
ret	ITALIAN GP	Monza	17	UOP Shadow Racing Team	G	3.0 Shadow DN3-Cosworth V8	engine	=9/31
ret	CANADIAN GP	Mosport Park	17	UOP Shadow Racing Team	G	3.0 Shadow DN3-Cosworth V8	driveshaft	5/30
10	US GP	Watkins Glen	17	UOP Shadow Racing Team	G	3.0 Shadow DN3-Cosworth V8	2 laps behind	10/30

1975 — Championship position: 18th   Wins: 0   Pole positions: 2   Fastest laps: 1   Points scored: 1.5

dns	ARGENTINE GP	Buenos Aires	17	UOP Shadow Racing Team	G	3.0 Shadow DN5-Cosworth V8	cwp in warm-up	(1)/23
ret	BRAZILIAN GP	Interlagos	17	UOP Shadow Racing Team	G	3.0 Shadow DN5-Cosworth V8	fuel metering unit/FL	1/23
ret	SOUTH AFRICAN GP	Kyalami	17	UOP Shadow Racing Team	G	3.0 Shadow DN5-Cosworth V8	engine	13/28
4*	SPANISH GP	Montjuich Park	17	UOP Shadow Racing Team	G	3.0 Shadow DN5-Cosworth V8	* shortened race-half points/-1 lap	10/26
ret	MONACO GP	Monte Carlo	17	UOP Shadow Racing Team	G	3.0 Shadow DN5-Cosworth V8	spun-hit barrier on lap 1	3/26
ret	BELGIAN GP	Zolder	17	UOP Shadow Racing Team	G	3.0 Shadow DN5-Cosworth V8	spun off	10/24
ret	SWEDISH GP	Anderstorp	17	UOP Shadow Racing Team	G	3.0 Shadow DN5-Cosworth V8	engine	3/26
ret	DUTCH GP	Zandvoort	17	UOP Shadow Racing Team	G	3.0 Shadow DN5-Cosworth V8	puncture-spun off	10/25
8	FRENCH GP	Paul Ricard	17	UOP Shadow Racing Team	G	3.0 Shadow DN5-Cosworth V8		4/26
14/ret	BRITISH GP	Silverstone	17	UOP Shadow Racing Team	G	3.0 Shadow DN5-Cosworth V8	spun off/3 laps behind	11/28
ret	GERMAN GP	Nürburgring	17	UOP Shadow Racing Team	G	3.0 Shadow DN5-Cosworth V8	puncture	12/26
ret	AUSTRIAN GP	Österreichring	17	UOP Shadow Racing Team	G	3.0 Shadow DN7-Matra V12	fuel injection	14/30
ret	ITALIAN GP	Monza	17	UOP Shadow Racing Team	G	3.0 Shadow DN7-Matra V12	fuel pump	13/28
ret	US GP	Watkins Glen	17	UOP Shadow Racing Team	G	3.0 Shadow DN5-Cosworth V8	wheel bearing	4/24
dns	"	" " "	17	UOP Shadow Racing Team	G	3.0 Shadow DN7-Matra V12	practice only	–/–

1976 — Championship position: Unplaced

ret	BRAZILIAN GP	Interlagos	17	Shadow Racing Team	G	3.0 Shadow DN5-Cosworth V8	spun off on Hunt's oil/FL	3/22
ret	SOUTH AFRICAN GP	Kyalami	17	Shadow Racing Team	G	3.0 Shadow DN5-Cosworth V8	radiator/engine	15/25
7	US GP WEST	Long Beach	17	Shadow Racing Team	G	3.0 Shadow DN5-Cosworth V8	1 lap behind	7/27
ret	SPANISH GP	Jarama	17	Shadow Racing Team	G	3.0 Shadow DN5-Cosworth V8	electrics	15/30
9	BELGIAN GP	Zolder	17	Shadow Racing Team	G	3.0 Shadow DN5-Cosworth V8	1 lap behind	14/29
8	MONACO GP	Monte Carlo	17	Shadow Racing Team	G	3.0 Shadow DN5-Cosworth V8	2 laps behind	10/25
12	SWEDISH GP	Anderstorp	17	Shadow Racing Team	G	3.0 Shadow DN5-Cosworth V8	1 lap behind	14/27
12	FRENCH GP	Paul Ricard	17	Shadow Racing Team	G	3.0 Shadow DN5-Cosworth V8	1 lap behind	15/30
9	BRITISH GP	Brands Hatch	17	Shadow Racing Team	G	3.0 Shadow DN5-Cosworth V8	pit stop/6 laps behind	23/30
11	GERMAN GP	Nürburgring	17	Shadow Racing with Tabatip	G	3.0 Shadow DN5-Cosworth V8		23/28
ret	AUSTRIAN GP	Österreichring	17	Shadow Racing with Tabatip	G	3.0 Shadow DN5-Cosworth V8	fuel pump	18/25
10	DUTCH GP	Zandvoort	17	Shadow Racing Team	G	3.0 Shadow DN5-Cosworth V8	1 lap behind	20/27
19	ITALIAN GP	Monza	17	Shadow Racing Team	G	3.0 Shadow DN5-Cosworth V8	pit stop/5 laps behind	17/29
18	CANADIAN GP	Mosport Park	17	Shadow Racing Team	G	3.0 Shadow DN5-Cosworth V8	3 laps behind	18/27
10	US GP EAST	Watkins Glen	17	Shadow Racing Team	G	3.0 Shadow DN5-Cosworth V8	2 laps behind	16/27
10	JAPANESE GP	Mount Fuji	17	Shadow Racing Team	G	3.0 Shadow DN5-Cosworth V8	4 laps behind	15/27

1977 — Championship position: 19th   Wins: 0   Pole positions: 0   Fastest laps: 0   Points scored: 1

6	US GP WEST	Long Beach	34	ATS Racing Team	G	3.0 Penske PC4-Cosworth V8	1 lap behind	9/22
dnq	SPANISH GP	Jarama	34	ATS Racing Team	G	3.0 Penske PC4-Cosworth V8	driver unwell	26/31
11	MONACO GP	Monte Carlo	34	ATS Racing Team	G	3.0 Penske PC4-Cosworth V8	pit stop/2 laps behind	12/26
11	BELGIAN GP	Zolder	34	ATS Racing Team	G	3.0 Penske PC4-Cosworth V8	2 laps behind	26/32
8	SWEDISH GP	Anderstorp	34	ATS Racing Team	G	3.0 Penske PC4-Cosworth V8		17/31
ret	FRENCH GP	Dijon	34	ATS Racing Team	G	3.0 Penske PC4-Cosworth V8	gearbox problem-spun off	19/30
9	BRITISH GP	Silverstone	34	ATS Racing Team	G	3.0 Penske PC4-Cosworth V8	1 lap behind	20/36
ret	GERMAN GP	Hockenheim	34	ATS Racing Team	G	3.0 Penske PC4-Cosworth V8	damage from startline accident	12/30
14	AUSTRIAN GP	Österreichring	34	ATS Racing Team	G	3.0 Penske PC4-Cosworth V8	pit stop/2 laps behind	18/30
ret	DUTCH GP	Zandvoort	34	ATS Racing Team	G	3.0 Penske PC4-Cosworth V8	engine	21/34
ret	ITALIAN GP	Monza	34	ATS Racing Team	G	3.0 Penske PC4-Cosworth V8	engine	18/34
9	US GP EAST	Watkins Glen	16	Shadow Racing Team	G	3.0 Shadow DN8-Cosworth V8	1 lap behind	16/27
ret	JAPANESE GP	Mount Fuji	27	Ligier Gitanes	G	3.0 Ligier JS7-Matra V12	engine	17/23

1978 — Championship position: Unplaced   Pole positions: 1   Fastest laps: 1

12	ARGENTINE GP	Buenos Aires	10	ATS Racing Team	G	3.0 ATS HS1-Cosworth V8	1 lap behind	11/26
dns	BRAZILIAN GP	Rio	10	ATS Racing Team	G	3.0 ATS HS1-Cosworth V8	car driven by Mass	(16)/28
8	SOUTH AFRICAN GP	Kyalami	10	ATS Racing Team	G	3.0 ATS HS1-Cosworth V8	1 lap behind	17/30
11	US GP WEST	Long Beach	10	ATS Racing Team	G	3.0 ATS HS1-Cosworth V8	pit stop-hit Brambilla/-5 laps	19/30
dnq	MONACO GP	Monte Carlo	10	ATS Racing Team	G	3.0 ATS HS1-Cosworth V8		23/30
dnq	GERMAN GP	Hockenheim	10	ATS Racing Team	G	3.0 ATS HS1-Cosworth V8		26/30
15/ret	US GP EAST	Watkins Glen	55	John Player Team Lotus	G	3.0 Lotus 79-Cosworth V8	out of fuel/FL/4 laps behind	8/27
ret	CANADIAN GP	Montreal	55	John Player Team Lotus	G	3.0 Lotus 79-Cosworth V8	oil leak	1/28

1979 — Championship position: 10=   Wins: 0   Pole positions: 0   Fastest laps: 0   Points scored: 14

ret	ARGENTINE GP	Buenos Aires	4	Team Tyrrell	G	3.0 Tyrrell 009-Cosworth V8	engine	4/26
ret/dns	BRAZILIAN GP	Interlagos	4	Team Tyrrell	G	3.0 Tyrrell 009-Cosworth V8	electrics on warm-up lap	(15)/26
3	SOUTH AFRICAN GP	Kyalami	4	Team Tyrrell	G	3.0 Tyrrell 009-Cosworth V8		9/26
6	US GP WEST	Long Beach	4	Team Tyrrell	G	3.0 Tyrrell 009-Cosworth V8	pit stop-tyres/1 lap behind	7/26
5	SPANISH GP	Jarama	4	Team Tyrrell	G	3.0 Tyrrell 009-Cosworth V8		12/27
11	BELGIAN GP	Zolder	4	Candy Team Tyrrell	G	3.0 Tyrrell 009-Cosworth V8	pit stops-skirts/3 laps behind	11/28
ret	MONACO GP	Monte Carlo	4	Candy Team Tyrrell	G	3.0 Tyrrell 009-Cosworth V8	broken rear upright	6/25
5	FRENCH GP	Dijon	4	Candy Team Tyrrell	G	3.0 Tyrrell 009-Cosworth V8		10/27
3	BRITISH GP	Silverstone	4	Candy Team Tyrrell	G	3.0 Tyrrell 009-Cosworth V8	1 lap behind	=16/26
ret	DUTCH GP	Zandvoort	4	Candy Team Tyrrell	G	3.0 Tyrrell 009-Cosworth V8	jammed throttle-spun off	16/26
6	ITALIAN GP	Monza	4	Candy Team Tyrrell	G	3.0 Tyrrell 009-Cosworth V8		16/28
ret	CANADIAN GP	Montreal	4	Candy Team Tyrrell	G	3.0 Tyrrell 009-Cosworth V8	engine	13/29
ret	US GP EAST	Watkins Glen	4	Candy Team Tyrrell	G	3.0 Tyrrell 009-Cosworth V8	collision with Daly-spun off	11/30

1980 — Championship position: 10=   Wins: 0   Pole positions: 0   Fastest laps: 0   Points scored: 6

ret	ARGENTINE GP	Buenos Aires	3	Candy Team Tyrrell	G	3.0 Tyrrell 009-Cosworth V8	accident damage	18/28
12	BRAZILIAN GP	Interlagos	3	Candy Team Tyrrell	G	3.0 Tyrrell 009-Cosworth V8	1 lap behind	22/28
7	SOUTH AFRICAN GP	Kyalami	3	Candy Team Tyrrell	G	3.0 Tyrrell 010-Cosworth V8	1 lap behind	13/28
ret	US GP WEST	Long Beach	3	Candy Team Tyrrell	G	3.0 Tyrrell 010-Cosworth V8	multiple collision	12/27
5	BELGIAN GP	Zolder	3	Candy Team Tyrrell	G	3.0 Tyrrell 010-Cosworth V8	1 lap behind	9/27
ret	MONACO GP	Monte Carlo	3	Candy Team Tyrrell	G	3.0 Tyrrell 010-Cosworth V8	multiple collision lap 1	9/27
14	FRENCH GP	Paul Ricard	3	Candy Team Tyrrell	G	3.0 Tyrrell 010-Cosworth V8	2 pit stops-side pod/-4 laps	16/27
5	BRITISH GP	Brands Hatch	3	Candy Team Tyrrell	G	3.0 Tyrrell 010-Cosworth V8	1 lap behind	11/27
15	GERMAN GP	Hockenheim	3	Candy Team Tyrrell	G	3.0 Tyrrell 010-Cosworth V8	1 lap behind	23/26
ret	AUSTRIAN GP	Österreichring	3	Candy Team Tyrrell	G	3.0 Tyrrell 010-Cosworth V8	engine	13/25
5	DUTCH GP	Zandvoort	3	Candy Team Tyrrell	G	3.0 Tyrrell 010-Cosworth V8		17/28
ret	ITALIAN GP	Imola	3	Candy Team Tyrrell	G	3.0 Tyrrell 010-Cosworth V8	brakes	12/28
7	CANADIAN GP	Montreal	3	Candy Team Tyrrell	G	3.0 Tyrrell 010-Cosworth V8	1 lap behind	15/28
nc	US GP EAST	Watkins Glen	3	Candy Team Tyrrell	G	3.0 Tyrrell 010-Cosworth V8	pit stops/19 laps behind	22/27

1981 — Championship position: Unplaced

ret	US GP WEST	Long Beach	25	Equipe Talbot Gitanes	M	3.0 Ligier JS17-Matra V12	fuel pump	10/29
7	BRAZILIAN GP	Rio	25	Equipe Talbot Gitanes	M	3.0 Ligier JS17-Matra V12		23/30
8	BRITISH GP	Silverstone	32	Osella Squadra Corse	M	3.0 Osella FA1B-Cosworth V8	pit stop/3 laps behind	20/30
8	GERMAN GP	Hockenheim	32	Osella Squadra Corse	M	3.0 Osella FA1B-Cosworth V8	1 lap behind	17/30
10	AUSTRIAN GP	Österreichring	32	Osella Squadra Corse	M	3.0 Osella FA1B-Cosworth V8	2 laps behind	14/28
ret	DUTCH GP	Zandvoort	32	Osella Squadra Corse	M	3.0 Osella FA1B-Cosworth V8	gearbox	18/30
9	ITALIAN GP	Monza	32	Osella Squadra Corse	M	3.0 Osella FA1C-Cosworth V8	2 laps behind	18/30
ret	CANADIAN GP	Montreal	32	Osella Squadra Corse	M	3.0 Osella FA1C-Cosworth V8	collision with Rebaque	23/30
ret	CAESARS PALACE GP	Las Vegas	32	Osella Squadra Corse	M	3.0 Osella FA1C-Cosworth V8	transmission	21/30

1982 — Championship position: 20th   Wins: 0   Pole positions: 0   Fastest laps: 0   Points scored: 3

ret	SOUTH AFRICAN GP	Kyalami	31	Osella Squadra Corse	P	3.0 Osella FA1C-Cosworth V8	spun avoiding Mansell-lap 1	26/30
9*	BRAZILIAN GP	Rio	31	Osella Squadra Corse	P	3.0 Osella FA1C-Cosworth V8	* 1st & 2nd place dsq/-3 laps	23/31
ret	US GP WEST	Long Beach	31	Osella Squadra Corse	P	3.0 Osella FA1C-Cosworth V8	engine	10/31
4	SAN MARINO GP	Imola	31	Osella Squadra Corse	P	3.0 Osella FA1C-Cosworth V8	1 lap behind	9/14
ret	BELGIAN GP	Zolder	31	Osella Squadra Corse	P	3.0 Osella FA1C-Cosworth V8	broken rear wing	18/32
dnq	MONACO GP	Monte Carlo	31	Osella Squadra Corse	P	3.0 Osella FA1C-Cosworth V8		25/31
ret	US GP (DETROIT)	Detroit	31	Osella Squadra Corse	P	3.0 Osella FA1C-Cosworth V8	electrics	22/28
dns	CANADIAN GP	Montreal	31	Osella Squadra Corse	P	3.0 Osella FA1C-Cosworth V8	w/drawn after Paletti's accident	(18)/29
14	DUTCH GP	Zandvoort	31	Osella Squadra Corse	P	3.0 Osella FA1C-Cosworth V8	pit stop/3 laps behind	23/31
ret	BRITISH GP	Brands Hatch	31	Osella Squadra Corse	P	3.0 Osella FA1C-Cosworth V8	accident with Serra	18/30
ret	FRENCH GP	Paul Ricard	31	Osella Squadra Corse	P	3.0 Osella FA1C-Cosworth V8	driveshaft	17/30
ret	GERMAN GP	Hockenheim	31	Osella Squadra Corse	P	3.0 Osella FA1C-Cosworth V8	steering	21/30
dnq	AUSTRIAN GP	Österreichring	31	Osella Squadra Corse	P	3.0 Osella FA1C-Cosworth V8		28/29
ret	SWISS GP	Dijon	31	Osella Squadra Corse	P	3.0 Osella FA1C-Cosworth V8	engine	17/29
ret	ITALIAN GP	Monza	31	Osella Squadra Corse	P	3.0 Osella FA1C-Cosworth V8	lost rear wheel-accident	15/30
dnq	CAESARS PALACE GP	Las Vegas	31	Osella Squadra Corse	P	3.0 Osella FA1C-Cosworth V8	accident in practice	27/30

1983 — Championship position: Unplaced

ret	BRAZILIAN GP	Rio	25	Equipe Ligier Gitanes	M	3.0 Ligier JS21-Cosworth V8	rear suspension	12/27
ret	US GP WEST	Long Beach	25	Equipe Ligier Gitanes	M	3.0 Ligier JS21-Cosworth V8	accident with Rosberg	10/28
9	FRENCH GP	Paul Ricard	25	Equipe Ligier Gitanes	M	3.0 Ligier JS21-Cosworth V8	1 lap behind	20/29
ret	SAN MARINO GP	Imola	25	Equipe Ligier Gitanes	M	3.0 Ligier JS21-Cosworth V8	holed radiator	19/28
ret	MONACO GP	Monte Carlo	25	Equipe Ligier Gitanes	M	3.0 Ligier JS21-Cosworth V8	hydraulic suspension pump	9/28
ret	BELGIAN GP	Spa	25	Equipe Ligier Gitanes	M	3.0 Ligier JS21-Cosworth V8	accident with Watson	21/28
ret	US GP (DETROIT)	Detroit	25	Equipe Ligier Gitanes	M	3.0 Ligier JS21-Cosworth V8	seized wheel nut	19/27
ret	CANADIAN GP	Montreal	25	Equipe Ligier Gitanes	M	3.0 Ligier JS21-Cosworth V8	gearbox	16/28
10	BRITISH GP	Silverstone	25	Equipe Ligier Gitanes	M	3.0 Ligier JS21-Cosworth V8	pit stop-tyres/2 laps behind	25/29
8	GERMAN GP	Hockenheim	25	Equipe Ligier Gitanes	M	3.0 Ligier JS21-Cosworth V8	pit stop-tyres/1 lap behind	19/29
7	AUSTRIAN GP	Österreichring	25	Equipe Ligier Gitanes	M	3.0 Ligier JS21-Cosworth V8	pit stop-tyres/2 laps behind	20/29
ret	DUTCH GP	Zandvoort	25	Equipe Ligier Gitanes	M	3.0 Ligier JS21-Cosworth V8	suspension	22/29
9	ITALIAN GP	Monza	25	Equipe Ligier Gitanes	M	3.0 Ligier JS21-Cosworth V8	1 lap behind	19/29
dns	EUROPEAN GP	Brands Hatch	25	Equipe Ligier Gitanes	M	3.0 Ligier JS21-Cosworth V8	transmission on warm up	(22)/29
10	SOUTH AFRICAN GP	Kyalami	25	Equipe Ligier Gitanes	M	3.0 Ligier JS21-Cosworth V8	4 laps behind	21/26

GP Starts: 132 (135)   GP Wins: 0   Pole positions: 3   Fastest laps: 3   Points: 31.5

STEFAN JOHANSSON

Bright, bubbly and immensely likeable, Stefan Johansson had gathered together all the credentials required to take him to the top of Grand Prix racing. Somehow, though, it never quite happened for him despite golden opportunities with two front-running teams.

Stefan's father raced Mini-Coopers, and the youngster was soon competing in karts before moving up the Swedish racing ladder in various third-hand single-seaters which he frequently had to drive above and beyond their limit to gain a modicum of success. He first hit the headlines in 1976 when still a complete novice by managing to shunt current Formula 3 big-shot Riccardo Patrese out of a European championship round. Stefan's F3 progress stuttered on over the next few seasons, with eyebrows raised over his wild and sometimes not so wonderful driving, but he eventually began to make some solid progress before having to return home when his money ran out.

It was in 1979 that things started to fall into place, for after a poor start to his British F3 championship campaign with a Chevron, a switch to March chassis seemed to work wonders and Stefan was on the pace thereafter. Then came a quite unexpected chance with the Shadow team at the beginning of 1980. In retrospect Stefan shouldn't have taken up the offer for his reputation inevitably suffered when he failed to qualify in Argentina and Brazil, but at least he was able to come back to a seat in the top Project Four F3 team and went on to win the Vandervell championship after a great tussle with Kenneth Acheson. Understandably on a high, he moved into Formula 2 with a Toleman and finished fourth in the final standings, gaining victories at Hockenheim and Mantorp Park. Joining the Spirit-Honda team for 1982, Johansson looked a good bet for championship honours, but it wasn't to be his year as bad luck seemed to dog his heels throughout the season.

Stefan moved into Formula 1 with Spirit and Honda in 1983, and by general consensus the Swede did a fine job with a far from sorted machine, but he found himself out of work when Honda abandoned the project to move to Williams. Johansson decided to drive anything and everything in 1984, travelling the globe to race in an effort to prove his worth, and it worked. Tyrrell called him in to replace the injured Brundle before political problems forced the team's withdrawal, and then Toleman gave him an opportunity and were sufficiently impressed to make plans to run him in 1985. In the event the team were unable to obtain tyres, which in truth worked in Stefan's favour, for he was available to take over from Arnoux at Ferrari just one race into the 1985 season. This was his main chance and he grabbed it with some gutsy race performances, bringing the car home regularly to earn a contract for 1986.

His second season was fraught with endless technical problems, but the ever-smiling Swede plugged away, and he was lucky enough to be given a second top-line chance with McLaren in 1987. Again some of his races were excellent, but too often he qualified poorly, leaving himself much to do to retrieve the situation once the racing started. The decision to bring Ayrton Senna in to partner Alain Prost for 1988 saw Johansson seeking employment elsewhere and he could hardly have found a worse berth than Ligier. The season was a write-off and things looked little better in 1989 with the new Onyx outfit, but to Stefan's credit he helped to establish the team's credibility with a terrific third place in Portugal. Just to show there is no such thing as loyalty in Grand Prix racing, poor Johansson was dumped just two races into the 1990 season in favour of the well-financed Foitek.

Desperate to stay in Formula 1, Stefan signed to drive for AGS in 1991, but when the team changed hands he found himself redundant once more, and a few outings for Footwork in place of the injured Caffi did him no favours as the team were in the midst of a crisis not of their own making with the ill-fated Porsche engine.

For 1992, Johansson found a niche for himself in Indy Car racing with Tony Bettenhausen's small team. Over the next four seasons he was generally a midfield runner, but the acquisition of an up-to-date Reynard for 1996 at last gave Stefan a realistic chance of success. In the event it was a largely disappointing year for the Swede and at the end of it he was so disillusioned that he didn't even bother to look for another ride. Johansson soon found enjoyment in his racing again, however, when he won the 1997 Sebring 12 Hours in Team Scandia's Ferrari 333SP, and things got even better when he shared Joest Racing's Le Mans-winning Porsche WSC95 with Alboreto and Kristensen.

Although he continues to race in selected sports car events, of late most of Stefan's time has been spent setting up and running an ever-improving Indy Lights team. Plans are already in place for Johansson Motorsports to graduate to the CART series, possibly as early as 2000.

JOHANSSON, Stefan (S) b 8/9/1956, Växjö

	1980	Championship position: Unplaced							
	Race	Circuit	No	Entrant	Tyres	Car/Engine		Comment	Q Pos/Entries
dnq	ARGENTINE GP	Buenos Aires	17	Shadow Cars	G	3.0 Shadow DN11-Cosworth V8			26/28
dnq	BRAZILIAN GP	Interlagos	17	Shadow Cars	G	3.0 Shadow DN11-Cosworth V8			27/28
	1983	Championship position: Unplaced							
ret	BRITISH GP	Silverstone	40	Spirit Racing	G	1.5 t/c Spirit 201-Honda V6		fuel pump belt	14/29
ret	GERMAN GP	Hockenheim	40	Spirit Racing	G	1.5 t/c Spirit 201-Honda V6		engine	13/29

12	AUSTRIAN GP	Österreichring	40	Spirit Racing	G	1.5 t/c Spirit 201-Honda V6	2 pit stops-hit by Alboreto/-5 laps	16/29
7	DUTCH GP	Zandvoort	40	Spirit Racing	G	1.5 t/c Spirit 201-Honda V6	pit stop-tyres/2 laps behind	16/29
ret	ITALIAN GP	Monza	40	Spirit Racing	G	1.5 t/c Spirit 201-Honda V6	distributor	17/29
14	EUROPEAN GP	Brands Hatch	40	Spirit Racing	G	1.5 t/c Spirit 201-Honda V6	pit stop-tyres/2 laps behind	19/29

1984 Championship position: 16th= Wins: 0 Pole positions: 0 Fastest laps: 0 Points scored: 3

ret/dsq*	BRITISH GP	Brands Hatch	3	Tyrrell Racing Organisation	G	3.0 Tyrrell 012-Cosworth V8	accident damage/*after Dutch GP	25/27
9/dsq*	GERMAN GP	Hockenheim	3	Tyrrell Racing Organisation	G	3.0 Tyrrell 012-Cosworth V8	9th on road/*after Dutch GP	26/27
dnq	AUSTRIAN GP	Österreichring	3	Tyrrell Racing Organisation	G	3.0 Tyrrell 012-Cosworth V8		27/28
8/dsq*	DUTCH GP	Zandvoort	3	Tyrrell Racing Organisation	G	3.0 Tyrrell 012-Cosworth V8	8th on road/*after Dutch GP	25/27
4	ITALIAN GP	Monza	19	Toleman Group Motorsport	M	1.5 t/c Toleman TG184-Hart 4	2 laps behind	17/27
ret	EUROPEAN GP	Nürburgring	20	Toleman Group Motorsport	M	1.5 t/c Toleman TG184-Hart 4	overheating	26/26
11	PORTUGESE GP	Estoril	20	Toleman Group Motorsport	M	1.5 t/c Toleman TG184-Hart 4	1 lap behind	10/27

1985 Championship position: 7th Wins: 0 Pole positions: 0 Fastest laps: 0 Points scored: 26

7	BRAZILIAN GP	Rio	4	Tyrrell Racing Organisation	G	3.0 Tyrrell 012-Cosworth V8	pit stop-tyres/3 laps behind	23/25
8	PORTUGESE GP	Estoril	28	Scuderia Ferrari SpA SEFAC	G	1.5 t/c Ferrari 156/85 V6	pit stop-brakes/5 laps behind	11/26
6/ret	SAN MARINO GP	Imola	28	Scuderia Ferrari SpA SEFAC	G	1.5 t/c Ferrari 156/85 V6	out of fuel/3 laps behind	15/26
ret	MONACO GP	Monte Carlo	28	Scuderia Ferrari SpA SEFAC	G	1.5 t/c Ferrari 156/85 V6	accident damage	15/26
2	CANADIAN GP	Montreal	28	Scuderia Ferrari SpA SEFAC	G	1.5 t/c Ferrari 156/85 V6		4/25
2	US GP (DETROIT)	Detroit	28	Scuderia Ferrari SpA SEFAC	G	1.5 t/c Ferrari 156/85 V6		9/25
4	FRENCH GP	Paul Ricard	28	Scuderia Ferrari SpA SEFAC	G	1.5 t/c Ferrari 156/85 V6		16/26
ret	BRITISH GP	Silverstone	28	Scuderia Ferrari SpA SEFAC	G	1.5 t/c Ferrari 156/85 V6	hit spinning Tambay	11/26
9	GERMAN GP	Nürburgring	28	Scuderia Ferrari SpA SEFAC	G	1.5 t/c Ferrari 156/85 V6	pit stop-tyre-hit by Alboreto/-1 lap	2/27
4	AUSTRIAN GP	Österreichring	28	Scuderia Ferrari SpA SEFAC	G	1.5 t/c Ferrari 156/85 V6		12/27
ret	DUTCH GP	Zandvoort	28	Scuderia Ferrari SpA SEFAC	G	1.5 t/c Ferrari 156/85 V6	engine	17/27
5/ret	ITALIAN GP	Monza	28	Scuderia Ferrari SpA SEFAC	G	1.5 t/c Ferrari 156/85 V6	out of fuel/1 lap behind	10/26
ret	BELGIAN GP	Spa	28	Scuderia Ferrari SpA SEFAC	G	1.5 t/c Ferrari 156/85 V6	engine-spun off	5/24
ret	EUROPEAN GP	Brands Hatch	28	Scuderia Ferrari SpA SEFAC	G	1.5 t/c Ferrari 156/85 V6	electrics	13/27
4	SOUTH AFRICAN GP	Kyalami	28	Scuderia Ferrari SpA SEFAC	G	1.5 t/c Ferrari 156/85 V6	pit stop-tyres/1 lap behind	16/21
5	AUSTRALIAN GP	Adelaide	28	Scuderia Ferrari SpA SEFAC	G	1.5 t/c Ferrari 156/85 V6	pit stop-tyres/1 lap behind	15/25

1986 Championship position: 5th Wins: 0 Pole positions: 0 Fastest laps: 0 Points scored: 23

ret	BRAZILIAN GP	Rio	28	Scuderia Ferrari SpA SEFAC	G	1.5 t/c Ferrari F1/86 V6	brakes-spun off	8/25
ret	SPANISH GP	Jerez	28	Scuderia Ferrari SpA SEFAC	G	1.5 t/c Ferrari F1/86 V6	brakes-accident	11/25
4	SAN MARINO GP	Imola	28	Scuderia Ferrari SpA SEFAC	G	1.5 t/c Ferrari F1/86 V6	pit stop-brakes/1 lap behind	7/26
10	MONACO GP	Monte Carlo	28	Scuderia Ferrari SpA SEFAC	G	1.5 t/c Ferrari F1/86 V6	handling problems/-3 laps	15/26
3	BELGIAN GP	Spa	28	Scuderia Ferrari SpA SEFAC	G	1.5 t/c Ferrari F1/86 V6		11/25
ret	CANADIAN GP	Montreal	28	Scuderia Ferrari SpA SEFAC	G	1.5 t/c Ferrari F1/86 V6	accident with Dumfries	18/25
ret	US GP (DETROIT)	Detroit	28	Scuderia Ferrari SpA SEFAC	G	1.5 t/c Ferrari F1/86 V6	electrics	5/26
ret	FRENCH GP	Paul Ricard	28	Scuderia Ferrari SpA SEFAC	G	1.5 t/c Ferrari F1/86 V6	turbo	10/26
ret	BRITISH GP	Brands Hatch	28	Scuderia Ferrari SpA SEFAC	G	1.5 t/c Ferrari F1/86 V6	engine	18/26
11/ret	GERMAN GP	Hockenheim	28	Scuderia Ferrari SpA SEFAC	G	1.5 t/c Ferrari F1/86 V6	broken rear wing/-3 laps	11/26
4	HUNGARIAN GP	Hungaroring	28	Scuderia Ferrari SpA SEFAC	G	1.5 t/c Ferrari F1/86 V6	2 pit stops-tyres/1 lap behind	7/26
3	AUSTRIAN GP	Österreichring	28	Scuderia Ferrari SpA SEFAC	G	1.5 t/c Ferrari F1/86 V6	2 pit stops-tyres/wing/-2 laps	14/26
3	ITALIAN GP	Monza	28	Scuderia Ferrari SpA SEFAC	G	1.5 t/c Ferrari F1/86 V6		12/27
6	PORTUGESE GP	Estoril	28	Scuderia Ferrari SpA SEFAC	G	1.5 t/c Ferrari F1/86 V6	hit by Berger/1 lap behind	8/27
12/ret	MEXICAN GP	Mexico City	28	Scuderia Ferrari SpA SEFAC	G	1.5 t/c Ferrari F1/86 V6	turbo/4 laps behind	14/26
3	AUSTRALIAN GP	Adelaide	28	Scuderia Ferrari SpA SEFAC	G	1.5 t/c Ferrari F1/86 V6	1 lap behind	12/26

1987 Championship position: 6th Wins: 0 Pole positions: 0 Fastest laps: 0 Points scored: 30

3	BRAZILIAN GP	Rio	2	Marlboro McLaren International	G	1.5 t/c McLaren MP4/3-TAG V6		10/23
4	SAN MARINO GP	Imola	2	Marlboro McLaren International	G	1.5 t/c McLaren MP4/3-TAG V6		9/27
2	BELGIAN GP	Spa	2	Marlboro McLaren International	G	1.5 t/c McLaren MP4/3-TAG V6		10/26
ret	MONACO GP	Monte Carlo	2	Marlboro McLaren International	G	1.5 t/c McLaren MP4/3-TAG V6	engine	7/26
7	US GP (DETROIT)	Detroit	2	Marlboro McLaren International	G	1.5 t/c McLaren MP4/3-TAG V6	pit stop-electrics/-3 laps	11/26
8/ret	FRENCH GP	Paul Ricard	2	Marlboro McLaren International	G	1.5 t/c McLaren MP4/3-TAG V6	alternator belt/-6 laps	9/26
ret	BRITISH GP	Silverstone	2	Marlboro McLaren International	G	1.5 t/c McLaren MP4/3-TAG V6	engine	10/26
2	GERMAN GP	Hockenheim	2	Marlboro McLaren International	G	1.5 t/c McLaren MP4/3-TAG V6	finished on 3 wheels	8/26
ret	HUNGARIAN GP	Hungaroring	2	Marlboro McLaren International	G	1.5 t/c McLaren MP4/3-TAG V6	transmission	8/26
7	AUSTRIAN GP	Österreichring	2	Marlboro McLaren International	G	1.5 t/c McLaren MP4/3-TAG V6	stop-puncture-loose wheel/-2 laps	14/26
6	ITALIAN GP	Monza	2	Marlboro McLaren International	G	1.5 t/c McLaren MP4/3-TAG V6		11/28
5	PORTUGUESE GP	Estoril	2	Marlboro McLaren International	G	1.5 t/c McLaren MP4/3-TAG V6	1 lap behind	8/27
3	SPANISH GP	Jerez	2	Marlboro McLaren International	G	1.5 t/c McLaren MP4/3-TAG V6		11/28
ret	MEXICAN GP	Mexico City	2	Marlboro McLaren International	G	1.5 t/c McLaren MP4/3-TAG V6	spun off	15/27
3	JAPANESE GP	Suzuka	2	Marlboro McLaren International	G	1.5 t/c McLaren MP4/3-TAG V6		10/27
ret	AUSTRALIAN GP	Adelaide	2	Marlboro McLaren International	G	1.5 t/c McLaren MP4/3-TAG V6	brakes	8/27

1988 Championship position: Unplaced

9	BRAZILIAN GP	Rio	26	Ligier Loto	G	3.5 Ligier JS31-Judd V8	3 laps behind	21/31
dnq	SAN MARINO GP	Imola	26	Ligier Loto	G	3.5 Ligier JS31-Judd V8		28/31
ret	MONACO GP	Monte Carlo	26	Ligier Loto	G	3.5 Ligier JS31-Judd V8	electrics	26/30
10	MEXICAN GP	Mexico City	26	Ligier Loto	G	3.5 Ligier JS31-Judd V8	4 laps behind	24/30
ret	CANADIAN GP	Montreal	26	Ligier Loto	G	3.5 Ligier JS31-Judd V8	engine	25/31
ret	US GP (DETROIT)	Detroit	26	Ligier Loto	G	3.5 Ligier JS31-Judd V8	engine	18/31
dnq	FRENCH GP	Paul Ricard	26	Ligier Loto	G	3.5 Ligier JS31-Judd V8		30/31
dnq	BRITISH GP	Silverstone	26	Ligier Loto	G	3.5 Ligier JS31-Judd V8		29/31
dnq	GERMAN GP	Hockenheim	26	Ligier Loto	G	3.5 Ligier JS31-Judd V8		28/31
ret	HUNGARIAN GP	Hungaroring	26	Ligier Loto	G	3.5 Ligier JS31-Judd V8	stuck throttle	24/31
11*/ret	BELGIAN GP	Spa	26	Ligier Loto	G	3.5 Ligier JS31-Judd V8	cwp/*3rd & 4th dsq/-4 laps	20/31
dnq	ITALIAN GP	Monza	26	Ligier Loto	G	3.5 Ligier JS31-Judd V8		28/31
ret	PORTUGUESE GP	Estoril	26	Ligier Loto	G	3.5 Ligier JS31-Judd V8	engine	24/31
ret	SPANISH GP	Jerez	26	Ligier Loto	G	3.5 Ligier JS31-Judd V8	lost wheel	21/31
dnq	JAPANESE GP	Suzuka	26	Ligier Loto	G	3.5 Ligier JS31-Judd V8		27/31
9/ret	AUSTRALIAN GP	Adelaide	26	Ligier Loto	G	3.5 Ligier JS31-Judd V8	out of fuel/6 laps behind	22/31

	1989			Championship position: 11th=	Wins: 0	Pole positions: 0	Fastest laps: 0	Points scored: 6		
dnpq	BRAZILIAN GP	Rio	36	Moneytron Onyx	G	3.5 Onyx ORE 1-Cosworth V8				37/38
dnpq	SAN MARINO GP	Imola	36	Moneytron Onyx	G	3.5 Onyx ORE 1-Cosworth V8				34/39
dnpq	MONACO GP	Monte Carlo	36	Moneytron Onyx	G	3.5 Onyx ORE 1-Cosworth V8				31/38
ret	MEXICAN GP	Mexico City	36	Moneytron Onyx	G	3.5 Onyx ORE 1-Cosworth V8		transmission		21/39
ret	US GP (PHOENIX)	Phoenix	36	Moneytron Onyx	G	3.5 Onyx ORE 1-Cosworth V8		puncture-suspension damage		19/39
dsq	CANADIAN GP	Montreal	36	Moneytron Onyx	G	3.5 Onyx ORE 1-Cosworth V8		trailing air gun/black flagged		18/39
5	FRENCH GP	Paul Ricard	36	Moneytron Onyx	G	3.5 Onyx ORE 1-Cosworth V8		throttle linkage problems/-1 lap		13/39
dnpq	BRITISH GP	Silverstone	36	Moneytron Onyx	G	3.5 Onyx ORE 1-Cosworth V8				31/39
ret	GERMAN GP	Hockenheim	36	Moneytron Onyx	G	3.5 Onyx ORE 1-Cosworth V8		rear wheel bearing		24/39
ret	HUNGARIAN GP	Hungaroring	36	Moneytron Onyx	G	3.5 Onyx ORE 1-Cosworth V8		gear selection		24/39
8	BELGIAN GP	Spa	36	Moneytron Onyx	G	3.5 Onyx ORE 1-Cosworth V8		1 lap behind		15/39
dnpq	ITALIAN GP	Monza	36	Moneytron Onyx	G	3.5 Onyx ORE 1-Cosworth V8				30/39
3	PORTUGUESE GP	Estoril	36	Moneytron Onyx	G	3.5 Onyx ORE 1-Cosworth V8				12/39
dnpq	SPANISH GP	Jerez	36	Moneytron Onyx	G	3.5 Onyx ORE 1-Cosworth V8				31/38
dnpq	JAPANESE GP	Suzuka	36	Moneytron Onyx	G	3.5 Onyx ORE 1-Cosworth V8				33/39
dnpq	AUSTRALIAN GP	Adelaide	36	Moneytron Onyx	G	3.5 Onyx ORE 1-Cosworth V8				31/39
	1990			Championship position: Unplaced						
dnq	US GP (PHOENIX)	Phoenix	35	Moneytron Onyx Formula One	G	3.5 Onyx ORE 1-Cosworth V8				28/35
dnq	BRAZILIAN GP	Interlagos	35	Moneytron Onyx Formula One	G	3.5 Onyx ORE 1-Cosworth V8				27/35
	1991			Championship position: Unplaced						
dnq	US GP (PHOENIX)	Phoenix	18	Automobiles Gonfaronaise Sportive	G	3.5 AGS JH25-Cosworth V8				29/34
dnq	BRAZILIAN GP	Interlagos	18	Automobiles Gonfaronaise Sportive	G	3.5 AGS JH25-Cosworth V8				28/34
ret	CANADIAN GP	Montreal	10	Footwork Grand Prix International	G	3.5 Footwork FA12-Porsche V12		engine		25/34
dnq	MEXICAN GP	Mexico City	10	Footwork Grand Prix International	G	3.5 Footwork FA12-Porsche V12				29/34
dnq	FRENCH GP	Magny Cours	10	Footwork Grand Prix International	G	3.5 Footwork FA12-Cosworth V8				30/34
dnq	BRITISH GP	Silverstone	10	Footwork Grand Prix International	G	3.5 Footwork FA12-Cosworth V8				28/34

GP Starts: 79   GP Wins: 0   Pole positions: 0   Fastest laps: 0   Points: 88

LESLIE JOHNSON

Johnson raced an ERA E-Type in the immediate post-war years, taking part in the 1950 British GP, the very first round of the World Championship, and later became the chairman of this once illustrious marque. His major driving successes, however, were often achieved at the wheel of rival cars. In 1948 he won the Spa 24 Hours sports car race in an Aston Martin shared with St John Horsfall and he was second at Spa again the following year, also in an Aston, this time with Brackenbury. In

1950, now driving a Jaguar XK120, Johnson was third in the Tourist Trophy and fifth in the Mille Miglia, and a year later came fourth in the Jaguar with Tony Rolt. Driving a Nash-Healey, Leslie finished third at Le Mans with Tommy Wisdom in 1952, and was also fourth in class (despite shock absorber problems) in that year's Mille Miglia in the same machine. Johnson collapsed with serious heart problems during the 1954 Monte Carlo Rally and it was partly as a result of this condition that he died in 1959.

BRUCE JOHNSTONE

Bruce enhanced his reputation with a Volvo before entering single-seater competition, and he really came to prominence nationally in 1960, when he finished sixth in the Formula Libre South African Grand Prix won by Paul Frère. Less than a year later he finished runner-up to Syd van der Vyver in the 1961 South African championship with his Cooper-Alfa, and was invited to drive for the Yeoman Credit team, under the stewardship of Reg Parnell. It was not a happy partnership, however, as Johnstone crashed the car both in the Natal GP and then in practice for the South African GP, rendering him a non-starter.

Bruce came to Europe briefly in 1962 and drove for Ian Walker, winning the up-to-1.5 litre class in the Nürburgring 1000 Km with Peter Ashdown in a Lotus 23, and taking fifth in the Vanwall Trophy at Snetterton with Walker's Formula Junior Lotus. He also drove a works BRM in the Gold Cup race at Oulton Park, finishing fourth, and took the same car to ninth place in his only championship Grand Prix appearance later that year. Undeniably Johnstone was a talented and versatile driver, for he won the Rand 9 Hours at Kyalami sharing David Piper's Ferrari 250 GTO that year, before slipping out of competition prematurely.

JOHNSON, Leslie (GB) b 1911 – d 8/6/1959, Withington, nr Andoversford, Gloucestershire

	1950			Championship position: Unplaced				
	Race	Circuit	No	Entrant	Tyres	Car/Engine	Comment	Q Pos/Entries
ret	BRITISH GP	Silverstone	8	T A S O Mathieson	D	1.5 s/c ERA E type 6	supercharger	12/21

GP Starts: 1   GP Wins: 0   Pole positions: 0   Fastest laps: 0   Points: 0

JOHNSTONE, Bruce (ZA) b 30/1/1937, Durban

	1962			Championship position: Unplaced				
	Race	Circuit	No	Entrant	Tyres	Car/engine	Comment	Q Pos/Entries
9	SOUTH AFRICAN GP	East London	5	Owen Racing Organisation	D	1.5 BRM P48/57 V8	6 laps behind	17/17

GP Starts: 1   GP Wins: 0   Pole positions: 0   Fastest laps: 0   Points: 0

ALAN JONES

WORLD CHAMPION: 1980

ALAN JONES

Tough and downright bloody-minded Alan Jones may have been, but once he had established himself in the Williams team there were few to argue with the Australian's methods. Endowed with immense physical strength and bucket loads of bravery, he became perhaps the 'ground-effect' era's most skilled practitioner with a driving style that appeared brutal at times, but certainly brought results.

The son of Stan Jones, a famous fifties Australian racer, young Alan left school to work in his father's Holden dealership, racing a Mini and then an old Cooper before coming to England in 1967 only to find that even a Formula Ford drive was out of his reach. Undaunted, he was back in 1970 with fellow racing aspirant Brian McGuire and the Aussie pair set about running a couple of F3 Brabhams financed by buying and selling second-hand cars. Money was tight, with Alan and his wife Beverley living a hand-to-mouth existence to pay for the racing programme, but by 1973 Jones had a foot on the ladder to the top with a DART-entered GRD, taking second place in the John Player championship. Then came a setback as the team folded, leaving Alan with no drive for 1974 until one Harry Stiller came to the rescue. He ran the Australian in Formula Atlantic, and then at the end of the year Jones made a big impression in a one-off F5000 drive for John MacDonald.

Alan stepped up to Formula 1 in 1975 with Stiller's Hesketh, but the team managed only three Grands Prix before its owner packed his bags and went abroad for tax reasons, leaving Alan high and dry. Graham Hill then invited him to join the Embassy team in place of the injured Rolf Stommelen, and he brought the car into fifth place at the Nürburgring before the German was fit to resume. Fortunately, MacDonald found Jones a seat in his RAM F5000 car while he continued to look for a Formula 1 ride. After a sensational drive to second place in the 1976 Race of Champions at the wheel of a Surtees Alan was placed under contract for the season, but relations soon became strained between team boss and driver, with Jones more interested in his US F5000 programme with Theodore, which brought wins at Mosport and Watkins Glen. He ended the F1 season with fourth place at Mount Fuji, but without the prospect of a Grand Prix ride after a complete breakdown of communications with Surtees.

Then in 1977 tragedy worked in his favour. When Tom Pryce was killed in South Africa Alan took over the vacant seat at Shadow and seized the opportunity brilliantly, winning in Austria and scoring points finishes with some aggressive drives. Frank Williams, rebuilding his team in the wake of the Walter Wolf fiasco, saw Jones as just the sort of pragmatic charger he needed for 1978 and, at the wheel of Patrick Head's no-nonsense machine, the Aussie regularly put himself among the leaders, often dogging the omnipotent Lotus 79s. Eleventh place in the championship was in no way a reflection of the team's competitiveness that year, but Alan had the satisfaction of also making his mark in Can-Am, taking the title in the Haas/Hall Lola T333.

The following season marked the true blossoming of Alan Jones the racing driver. The new ground-effect Williams FW07 proved that the imitator had leapfrogged the innovator, and in Alan's hands the car was simply stunning. A spate of retirements in the first half of the year torpedoed his title hopes, but four wins from five starts gave a fair indication of his late-season dominance. Nothing was left to chance in 1980 as Jones squeezed every ounce of potential from the car. He never once eased up, and certainly took no prisoners, but the title was won with crushing dominance. There was no let-up in 1981 either, as he headed towards self-imposed retirement; he still raced as if that first Grand Prix win had not yet been achieved, finishing on a high note with a lights-to-flag win at Caesars Palace.

Jones and the Williams FW08 were an almost unbeatable combination in 1980. The tough Australian scored five wins and three second places on his way to the World Championship.

Perhaps the story should have ended there. But after racing Porsches back in Australia, and despite a broken leg sustained in a riding accident, Jones was tempted back in 1983. In his all-too-brief spell with Arrows, he took third in the Race of Champions, and then raced at Long Beach, before pulling out when he was unable to agree a contract.

The terms offered by Haas Lola proved sufficiently tempting to bring him back to the Grand Prix arena late in 1985. Both technically and administratively, the project was something of a fiasco, leaving Alan to pick his way through the 1986 season with no more than occasional glimpses of his racing past. Wisely there were no further attempts to extend his Grand Prix career, Jones preferring to keep his hand in 'down-under' in touring cars.

In 1995 he was still winning occasional races in a Holden Commodore, and as the profile of this form of racing in Australia rose enormously Alan found major sponsorship from Marlboro. He formed his own team in 1996, running Ford Falcons, but by mid-season he had lost this substantial backing and took the decision to race only in selected events thereafter.

JONES, Alan (AUS) b 2/11/1946, Melbourne, Victoria

1975

Championship position: 17th   Wins: 0   Pole positions: 0   Fastest laps: 0   Points scored: 2

	Race	Circuit	No	Entrant	Tyres	Car/Engine	Comment	Q Pos/Entries
ret	SPANISH GP	Montjuich Park	25	Custom Made Harry Stiller Racing	G	3.0 Hesketh 308-Cosworth V8	hit by Donohue	20/26
ret	MONACO GP	Monte Carlo	26	Custom Made Harry Stiller Racing	G	3.0 Hesketh 308-Cosworth V8	lost wheel	18/26
ret	BELGIAN GP	Zolder	26	Custom Made Harry Stiller Racing	G	3.0 Hesketh 308-Cosworth V8	hit by Laffite	13/24
11	SWEDISH GP	Anderstorp	26	Custom Made Harry Stiller Racing	G	3.0 Hesketh 308-Cosworth V8	1 lap behind	19/26
13	DUTCH GP	Zandvoort	22	Embassy Racing with Graham Hill	G	3.0 Hill GH1-Cosworth V8	pit stop-tyres/5 laps behind	17/25
16	FRENCH GP	Paul Ricard	22	Embassy Racing with Graham Hill	G	3.0 Hill GH1-Cosworth V8	spin-pit stop/1 lap behind	20/26
10	BRITISH GP	Silverstone	22	Embassy Racing with Graham Hill	G	3.0 Hill GH1-Cosworth V8	2 pit stops-tyres/2 laps behind	20/28
5	GERMAN GP	Nürburgring	22	Embassy Racing with Graham Hill	G	3.0 Hill GH1-Cosworth V8		21/26

1976

Championship position: 14th=   Wins: 0   Pole positions: 0   Fastest laps: 0   Points scored: 7

	Race	Circuit	No	Entrant	Tyres	Car/Engine	Comment	Q Pos/Entries
nc	US GP WEST	Long Beach	19	Durex Team Surtees	G	3.0 Surtees TS19-Cosworth V8	2 pit stops/10 laps behind	19/27
9	SPANISH GP	Jarama	19	Durex Team Surtees	G	3.0 Surtees TS19-Cosworth V8	1 lap behind	20/30
5	BELGIAN GP	Zolder	19	Durex Team Surtees	G	3.0 Surtees TS19-Cosworth V8	1 lap behind	16/29
ret	MONACO GP	Monte Carlo	19	Durex Team Surtees	G	3.0 Surtees TS19-Cosworth V8	collision with Reutemann	19/25
13	SWEDISH GP	Anderstorp	19	Durex Team Surtees	G	3.0 Surtees TS19-Cosworth V8	1 lap behind	18/27
ret	FRENCH GP	Paul Ricard	19	Durex Team Surtees	G	3.0 Surtees TS19-Cosworth V8	rear anti-roll bar	18/30
5	BRITISH GP	Brands Hatch	19	Durex Team Surtees	G	3.0 Surtees TS19-Cosworth V8	1 lap behind	19/30
10	GERMAN GP	Nürburgring	19	Durex Team Surtees	G	3.0 Surtees TS19-Cosworth V8		14/28
ret	AUSTRIAN GP	Österreichring	19	Durex Team Surtees	G	3.0 Surtees TS19-Cosworth V8	engine cut out-crashed	15/25
8	DUTCH GP	Zandvoort	19	Durex Team Surtees	G	3.0 Surtees TS19-Cosworth V8	1 lap behind	16/27
12	ITALIAN GP	Monza	19	Durex Team Surtees	G	3.0 Surtees TS19-Cosworth V8	pit stop-thought race stopped/-1 lap	18/29
16	CANADIAN GP	Mosport Park	19	Durex Team Surtees	G	3.0 Surtees TS19-Cosworth V8	pit stop/2 laps behind	20/27
8	US GP EAST	Watkins Glen	19	Durex Team Surtees	G	3.0 Surtees TS19-Cosworth V8	1 lap behind	18/27
4	JAPANESE GP	Mount Fuji	19	Durex/Theodore Team Surtees	G	3.0 Surtees TS19-Cosworth V8	1 lap behind	20/27

1977

Championship position: 7th   Wins: 1   Pole positions: 0   Fastest laps: 0   Points scored: 22

	Race	Circuit	No	Entrant	Tyres	Car/Engine	Comment	Q Pos/Entries
ret	US GP WEST	Long Beach	17	Shadow Racing Team	G	3.0 Shadow DN8-Cosworth V8	gearbox	14/22
ret	SPANISH GP	Jarama	17	Shadow Racing Team	G	3.0 Shadow DN8-Cosworth V8	collision with Peterson	14/31
6	MONACO GP	Monte Carlo	17	Shadow Racing Team	G	3.0 Shadow DN8-Cosworth V8		11/26
5	BELGIAN GP	Zolder	17	Shadow Racing Team	G	3.0 Shadow DN8-Cosworth V8		17/32
17	SWEDISH GP	Anderstorp	17	Shadow Racing Team	G	3.0 Shadow DN8-Cosworth V8	2 pit stops-ignition/-5 laps	11/31
ret	FRENCH GP	Dijon	17	Shadow Racing Team	G	3.0 Shadow DN8-Cosworth V8	driveshaft	10/30
7	BRITISH GP	Silverstone	17	Shadow Racing Team	G	3.0 Shadow DN8-Cosworth V8	1 lap behind	12/36
ret	GERMAN GP	Hockenheim	17	Shadow Racing Team	G	3.0 Shadow DN8-Cosworth V8	startline accident	17/30
1	AUSTRIAN GP	Österreichring	17	Shadow Racing Team	G	3.0 Shadow DN8-Cosworth V8		14/30
ret	DUTCH GP	Zandvoort	17	Shadow Racing Team	G	3.0 Shadow DN8-Cosworth V8	engine	=13/34
3	ITALIAN GP	Monza	17	Shadow Racing Team	G	3.0 Shadow DN8-Cosworth V8		16/34
ret	US GP EAST	Watkins Glen	17	Shadow Racing Team	G	3.0 Shadow DN8-Cosworth V8	accident with Peterson	13/27
4	CANADIAN GP	Mosport Park	17	Shadow Racing Team	G	3.0 Shadow DN8-Cosworth V8		7/27
4	JAPANESE GP	Mount Fuji	17	Shadow Racing Team	G	3.0 Shadow DN8-Cosworth V8		12/23

1978

Championship position: 11th   Wins: 0   Pole positions: 0   Fastest laps: 2   Points scored: 11

	Race	Circuit	No	Entrant	Tyres	Car/Engine	Comment	Q Pos/Entries
ret	ARGENTINE GP	Buenos Aires	27	Williams Grand Prix Engineering	G	3.0 Williams FW06-Cosworth V8	fuel vapour lock	14/27
11	BRAZILIAN GP	Rio	27	Williams Grand Prix Engineering	G	3.0 Williams FW06-Cosworth V8	3 pit stops-tyres/-5 laps	8/28
4	SOUTH AFRICAN GP	Kyalami	27	Williams Grand Prix Engineering	G	3.0 Williams FW06-Cosworth V8		18/30
7	US GP WEST	Long Beach	27	Williams Grand Prix Engineering	G	3.0 Williams FW06-Cosworth V8	broken front wings/-1 lap/FL	8/30
ret	MONACO GP	Monte Carlo	27	Williams Grand Prix Engineering	G	3.0 Williams FW06-Cosworth V8	gearbox oil leak	10/30
10	BELGIAN GP	Zolder	27	Williams Grand Prix Engineering	G	3.0 Williams FW06-Cosworth V8	2 pit stops-tyres/-2 laps	11/30
8	SPANISH GP	Jarama	27	Williams Grand Prix Engineering	G	3.0 Williams FW06-Cosworth V8	1 lap behind	18/29
ret	SWEDISH GP	Anderstorp	27	Williams Grand Prix Engineering	G	3.0 Williams FW06-Cosworth V8	front wheel bearing seized	9/27
5	FRENCH GP	Paul Ricard	27	Williams Grand Prix Engineering	G	3.0 Williams FW06-Cosworth V8		14/29
ret	BRITISH GP	Brands Hatch	27	Williams Grand Prix Engineering	G	3.0 Williams FW06-Cosworth V8	driveshaft	6/30
ret	GERMAN GP	Hockenheim	27	Williams Grand Prix Engineering	G	3.0 Williams FW06-Cosworth V8	fuel vaporisation	6/30
ret	AUSTRIAN GP	Österreichring	27	Williams Grand Prix Engineering	G	3.0 Williams FW06-Cosworth V8	accident	15/31
ret	DUTCH GP	Zandvoort	27	Williams Grand Prix Engineering	G	3.0 Williams FW06-Cosworth V8	broken throttle cable	11/33
13	ITALIAN GP	Monza	27	Williams Grand Prix Engineering	G	3.0 Williams FW06-Cosworth V8	pit stop-tyre/1 lap behind	6/32
2	US GP EAST	Watkins Glen	27	Williams Grand Prix Engineering	G	3.0 Williams FW06-Cosworth V8		3/27
9	CANADIAN GP	Montreal	27	Williams Grand Prix Engineering	G	3.0 Williams FW06-Cosworth V8	handling problems/FL	5/28

1979

Championship position: 3   Wins: 4   Pole positions: 3   Fastest laps: 1   Points scored: 43

	Race	Circuit	No	Entrant	Tyres	Car/Engine	Comment	Q Pos/Entries
9	ARGENTINE GP	Buenos Aires	27	Albilad-Saudia Racing Team	G	3.0 Williams FW06-Cosworth V8	pit stop-tyres/2 laps behind	15/26
ret	BRAZILIAN GP	Interlagos	27	Albilad-Saudia Racing Team	G	3.0 Williams FW06-Cosworth V8	fuel pressure	13/26
ret	SOUTH AFRICAN GP	Kyalami	27	Albilad-Saudia Racing Team	G	3.0 Williams FW06-Cosworth V8	rear suspension	19/26
3	US GP WEST	Long Beach	27	Albilad-Saudia Racing Team	G	3.0 Williams FW06-Cosworth V8		10/26
ret	SPANISH GP	Jarama	27	Albilad-Saudia Racing Team	G	3.0 Williams FW07-Cosworth V8	gear selection	13/27
ret	BELGIAN GP	Zolder	27	Albilad-Saudia Racing Team	G	3.0 Williams FW07-Cosworth V8	electrics	4/28
ret	MONACO GP	Monte Carlo	27	Albilad-Saudia Racing Team	G	3.0 Williams FW07-Cosworth V8	hit guard rail	9/25
4	FRENCH GP	Dijon	27	Albilad-Saudia Racing Team	G	3.0 Williams FW07-Cosworth V8		7/27
ret	BRITISH GP	Silverstone	27	Albilad-Saudia Racing Team	G	3.0 Williams FW07-Cosworth V8	water pump when 1st	1/26
1	GERMAN GP	Hockenheim	27	Albilad-Saudia Racing Team	G	3.0 Williams FW07-Cosworth V8		2/26
1	AUSTRIAN GP	Österreichring	27	Albilad-Saudia Racing Team	G	3.0 Williams FW07-Cosworth V8		2/26
1	DUTCH GP	Zandvoort	27	Albilad-Saudia Racing Team	G	3.0 Williams FW07-Cosworth V8		2/26
9	ITALIAN GP	Monza	27	Albilad-Saudia Racing Team	G	3.0 Williams FW07-Cosworth V8	pit stop-battery/1 lap behind	4/28
1	CANADIAN GP	Montreal	27	Albilad-Saudia Racing Team	G	3.0 Williams FW07-Cosworth V8	FL	1/29
ret	US GP EAST	Watkins Glen	27	Albilad-Saudia Racing Team	G	3.0 Williams FW07-Cosworth V8	lost rear wheel	1/30

1980

Championship position: WORLD CHAMPION   Wins: 5   Pole positions: 3   Fastest laps: 5   Points scored: 71

	Race	Circuit	No	Entrant	Tyres	Car/Engine	Comment	Q Pos/Entries
1	ARGENTINE GP	Buenos Aires	27	Albilad-Williams Racing Team	G	3.0 Williams FW07-Cosworth V8	FL	1/28
3	BRAZILIAN GP	Interlagos	27	Albilad-Williams Racing Team	G	3.0 Williams FW07B-Cosworth V8		10/28
ret	SOUTH AFRICAN GP	Kyalami	27	Albilad-Williams Racing Team	G	3.0 Williams FW07B-Cosworth V8	gearbox oil cooler	8/28
ret	US GP WEST	Long Beach	27	Albilad-Williams Racing Team	G	3.0 Williams FW07B-Cosworth V8	collision with Giacomelli	5/27

2	BELGIAN GP	Zolder	27	Albilad-Williams Racing Team	G	3.0 Williams FW07B-Cosworth V8			1/27
ret	MONACO GP	Monte Carlo	27	Albilad-Williams Racing Team	G	3.0 Williams FW07B-Cosworth V8	differential		3/27
1	FRENCH GP	Paul Ricard	27	Albilad-Williams Racing Team	G	3.0 Williams FW07B-Cosworth V8	FL		4/27
1	BRITISH GP	Brands Hatch	27	Albilad-Williams Racing Team	G	3.0 Williams FW07B-Cosworth V8			3/27
3	GERMAN GP	Hockenheim	27	Albilad-Williams Racing Team	G	3.0 Williams FW07B-Cosworth V8	pit stop-puncture/FL		1/26
2	AUSTRIAN GP	Österreichring	27	Albilad-Williams Racing Team	G	3.0 Williams FW07B-Cosworth V8			3/25
11	DUTCH GP	Zandvoort	27	Albilad-Williams Racing Team	G	3.0 Williams FW07B-Cosworth V8	ran off road-pit stop/-3 laps		4/28
2	ITALIAN GP	Imola	27	Albilad-Williams Racing Team	G	3.0 Williams FW07B-Cosworth V8	FL		6/28
1	CANADIAN GP	Montreal	27	Albilad-Williams Racing Team	G	3.0 Williams FW07B-Cosworth V8			2/28
1	US GP EAST	Watkins Glen	27	Albilad-Williams Racing Team	G	3.0 Williams FW07B-Cosworth V8	FL		5/27

1981		Championship position: 3rd	Wins: 2	Pole positions: 0	Fastest laps: 5	Points scored: 46		

1	US GP WEST	Long Beach	1	Albilad-Williams Racing Team	M	3.0 Williams FW07C-Cosworth V8	FL	2/29
2	BRAZILIAN GP	Rio	1	Albilad-Williams Racing Team	M	3.0 Williams FW07C-Cosworth V8		3/30
4	ARGENTINE GP	Buenos Aires	1	Albilad-Williams Racing Team	M	3.0 Williams FW07C-Cosworth V8	down on power engine	3/29
12	SAN MARINO GP	Imola	1	Albilad-Williams Racing Team	M	3.0 Williams FW07C-Cosworth V8	pit stop-front wing/-2 laps	8/30
ret	BELGIAN GP	Zolder	1	Albilad-Williams Racing Team	M	3.0 Williams FW07C-Cosworth V8	accident	6/31
2	MONACO GP	Monte Carlo	1	Albilad-Williams Racing Team	M	3.0 Williams FW07C-Cosworth V8	pit stop -fuel starvation/FL	7/31
7	SPANISH GP	Jarama	1	TAG Williams Team	M	3.0 Williams FW07C-Cosworth V8	went off when leading/FL	9/29
17	FRENCH GP	Dijon	1	TAG Williams Team	G	3.0 Williams FW07C-Cosworth V8	3 pit stops-steering/tyres/-4 laps	7/30
ret	BRITISH GP	Silverstone	1	TAG Williams Team	G	3.0 Williams FW07C-Cosworth V8	went off avoiding Villeneuve	4/30
11	GERMAN GP	Hockenheim	1	TAG Williams Team	G	3.0 Williams FW07C-Cosworth V8	pit stop-fuel starvation/-1 lap /FL	6/28
4	AUSTRIAN GP	Österreichring	1	TAG Williams Team	G	3.0 Williams FW07C-Cosworth V8		4/30
3	DUTCH GP	Zandvoort	1	TAG Williams Team	G	3.0 Williams FW07C-Cosworth V8	FL	5/30
2	ITALIAN GP	Monza	1	TAG Williams Team	G	3.0 Williams FW07C-Cosworth V8		3/30
ret	CANADIAN GP	Montreal	1	TAG Williams Team	G	3.0 Williams FW07C-Cosworth V8	handling	2/30
1	CAESARS PALACE GP	Las Vegas	1	TAG Williams Team	G	3.0 Williams FW07C-Cosworth V8		

1983		Championship position: Unplaced					

ret	US GP WEST	Long Beach	30	Arrows Racing Team	G	3.0 Arrows A6-Cosworth V8	driver discomfort	12/28

1985		Championship position: Unplaced					

ret	ITALIAN GP	Monza	33	Team Haas (USA) Ltd	G	1.5 t/c Lola THL1-Hart 4	distributor	25/26
ret	EUROPEAN GP	Brands Hatch	33	Team Haas (USA) Ltd	G	1.5 t/c Lola THL1-Hart 4	holed water radiator	22/27
dns	SOUTH AFRICAN GP	Kyalami	33	Team Haas (USA) Ltd	G	1.5 t/c Lola THL1-Hart 4	driver unwell	(18)/21
ret	AUSTRALIAN GP	Adelaide	33	Team Haas (USA) Ltd	G	1.5 t/c Lola THL1-Hart 4	electrics	19/25

1986		Championship position: 12th	Wins: 0	Pole positions: 0	Fastest laps: 0	Points scored: 4		

ret	BRAZILIAN GP	Rio	15	Team Haas (USA) Ltd	G	1.5 t/c Lola THL1-Hart 4	distributor rotor arm	19/25
ret	SPANISH GP	Jerez	15	Team Haas (USA) Ltd	G	1.5 t/c Lola THL1-Hart 4	accident with Palmer-lap 1	17/25
ret	SAN MARINO GP	Imola	15	Team Haas (USA) Ltd	G	1.5 t/c Lola THL2-Cosworth V6	radiator-overheating engine	21/26
ret	MONACO GP	Monte Carlo	15	Team Haas (USA) Ltd	G	1.5 t/c Lola THL2-Cosworth V6	incident with Streiff	18/26
11/ret	BELGIAN GP	Spa	15	Team Haas (USA) Ltd	G	1.5 t/c Lola THL2-Cosworth V6	out of fuel/3 laps behind	16/25
10	CANADIAN GP	Montreal	15	Team Haas (USA) Ltd	G	1.5 t/c Lola THL2-Cosworth V6	2 pit stops-tyres/-3 laps	13/25
ret	US GP (DETROIT)	Detroit	15	Team Haas (USA) Ltd	G	1.5 t/c Lola THL2-Cosworth V6	drive pegs	21/26
ret	FRENCH GP	Paul Ricard	15	Team Haas (USA) Ltd	G	1.5 t/c Lola THL2-Cosworth V6	accident	20/26
ret	BRITISH GP	Brands Hatch	15	Team Haas (USA) Ltd	G	1.5 t/c Lola THL2-Cosworth V6	throttle linkage	14/26
9	GERMAN GP	Hockenheim	15	Team Haas (USA) Ltd	G	1.5 t/c Lola THL2-Cosworth V6	started from back of grid/-2 laps	19/26
ret	HUNGARIAN GP	Hungaroring	15	Team Haas (USA) Ltd	G	1.5 t/c Lola THL2-Cosworth V6	differential	10/26
4	AUSTRIAN GP	Österreichring	15	Team Haas (USA) Ltd	G	1.5 t/c Lola THL2-Cosworth V6	slipping clutch/2 laps behind	16/26
6	ITALIAN GP	Monza	15	Team Haas (USA) Ltd	G	1.5 t/c Lola THL2-Cosworth V6	2 stops-tyre-balance weight/-2 laps	18/27
ret	PORTUGESE GP	Estoril	15	Team Haas (USA) Ltd	G	1.5 t/c Lola THL2-Cosworth V6	brakes-spun off	17/27
ret	MEXICAN GP	Mexico City	15	Team Haas (USA) Ltd	G	1.5 t/c Lola THL2-Cosworth V6	gearbox/engine overheating	15/26
ret	AUSTRALIAN GP	Adelaide	15	Team Haas (USA) Ltd	G	1.5 t/c Lola THL2-Cosworth V6	engine	15/26

GP Starts: 116   GP Wins: 12   Pole positions: 6   Fastest laps: 13   Points: 206

OSWALD KARCH

Karch raced on both sides of the German border in the early fifties, and, in common with many other competitors at the time, he drove a BMW-Eigenbau during the 1950 season, but this was replaced with the almost equally ubiquitous Veritas RS two-seater sports.

Apart from appearing in the German Grand Prix in 1953, he enjoyed quite a successful national racing season in 1954, with the elderly sports, and he also took the machine to Morocco to race in the Casablanca 12-hour race, taking sixth place in the hotly contested 751–2000 cc class, sharing the driving duties with one Herr Sterzebecker.

KARCH, Oswald (D) b 6/3/1917, Ludwigshafen

	1953			Championship position: Unplaced				
	Race	Circuit	No	Entrant	Tyres	Car/Engine	Comment	Q Pos/Entries
ret	GERMAN GP	Nürburgring	26	Oswald Karch	–	2.0 Veritas RS 6		34/35

GP Starts: 1   GP Wins: 0   Pole positions: 0   Fastest laps: 0   Points: 0

UKYO KATAYAMA

This diminutive Japanese driver first ventured to Europe some time before he entered Grand Prix racing with Larrousse in 1992, for he tried his hand at Formule Renault in France in 1986 and the French Formula 3 series in 1987 after winning junior 1600 single-seater championships at home, taking the Tsukuba class B title in 1983 and the Suzuka FFJ 1600 crown in 1984.

From 1988 he concentrated on racing in his national F3000 series, finally becoming champion in 1991, though he did come over to drive the uncompetitive Footwork briefly at the beginning of 1989.

Given his F1 opportunity, Katayama was certainly committed. A possible first World Championship point was lost in Canada when he buzzed the engine, but his lack of strength and stamina seemed to count against him. With the faith of his sponsor Cabin intact, Ukyo moved to Tyrrell with Yamaha engines for 1993. Sadly the season was not a happy one, with the promise of the new V10 being compromised by the short-comings of the chassis, and poor Katayama was involved in a seemingly endless catalogue of spins in a desperate attempt to make up for its failings.

Just about everyone was writing off the little Japanese in terms of a Grand Prix career, but he blossomed in 1994. The new Tyrrell 022 was a much better chassis and taking fifth place in the season's opening race at Interlagos can have done his confidence no harm. Despite the fact that he scored points on only two more occasions that year, his performances deserved more. He qualified fifth and ran in third at Hockenheim before throttle trouble, and then put in two storming drives at Monza and Jerez which went unrewarded.

Katayama's standing in the Grand Prix fraternity had risen immensely after his splendid season so it must have been crushingly disappointing for Ukyo to be cast back into the role of also-ran once more in 1995, when Tyrrell failed to make the progress they expected. It must also be said that the arrival of Mika Salo certainly placed him under pressure.

Ukyo stayed with the team for a fourth season in 1996, largely, it is thought, because of the substantial backing of Mild Seven. His form was more competitive, but health problems eventually blunted his motivation, especially after a dispiriting run of retirements in mid-season. It was surprising, therefore, when he decided to continue in F1 with Minardi in 1997, but given the need to adapt to the different language and culture he performed respectably. Tellingly, though, Ukyo was outshone by his novice team-mate Jarno Trulli and he came to the conclusion that it was time to step down and let a younger Japanese driver carry the hopes of his nation.

Katayama has since spent more of his time on his other passion of mountain-climbing, but he still races for Toyota, taking second place in both the Le Mans 24 Hours and the Fuji 1000 Km in 1999 with their potent GT-One prototype.

KATAYAMA, Ukyo (J) b 29/5/1963, Tokyo

	1992			Championship position: Unplaced					
	Race	Circuit	No	Entrant	Tyres	Car/Engine		Comment	Q Pos/Entries
12	SOUTH AFRICAN GP	Kyalami	30	Central Park Venturi Larrousse	G	3.5 Venturi LC92-Lamborghini V12		4 laps behind	18/30
12	MEXICAN GP	Mexico City	30	Central Park Venturi Larrousse	G	3.5 Venturi LC92-Lamborghini V12		3 laps behind	24/30
9	BRAZILIAN GP	Interlagos	30	Central Park Venturi Larrousse	G	3.5 Venturi LC92-Lamborghini V12		3 laps behind	25/31
dnq	SPANISH GP	Barcelona	30	Central Park Venturi Larrousse	G	3.5 Venturi LC92-Lamborghini V12			27/32
ret	SAN MARINO GP	Imola	30	Central Park Venturi Larrousse	G	3.5 Venturi LC92-Lamborghini V12		spun off	17/32
dnpq	MONACO GP	Monte Carlo	30	Central Park Venturi Larrousse	G	3.5 Venturi LC92-Lamborghini V12			31/32
ret	CANADIAN GP	Montreal	30	Central Park Venturi Larrousse	G	3.5 Venturi LC92-Lamborghini V12		engine	11/32
ret	FRENCH GP	Magny Cours	30	Central Park Venturi Larrousse	G	3.5 Venturi LC92-Lamborghini V12		engine	18/30
ret	BRITISH GP	Silverstone	30	Central Park Venturi Larrousse	G	3.5 Venturi LC92-Lamborghini V12		gear linkage	16/32
ret	GERMAN GP	Hockenheim	30	Central Park Venturi Larrousse	G	3.5 Venturi LC92-Lamborghini V12		accident	16/32
ret	HUNGARIAN GP	Hungaroring	30	Central Park Venturi Larrousse	G	3.5 Venturi LC92-Lamborghini V12		engine	20/31
17	BELGIAN GP	Spa	30	Central Park Venturi Larrousse	G	3.5 Venturi LC92-Lamborghini V12		2 laps behind	26/30
9/ret	ITALIAN GP	Monza	30	Central Park Venturi Larrousse	G	3.5 Venturi LC92-Lamborghini V12		transmission-spun off/-3 laps	23/28
ret	PORTUGUESE GP	Estoril	30	Central Park Venturi Larrousse	G	3.5 Venturi LC92-Lamborghini V12		spun off	25/26
11	JAPANESE GP	Suzuka	30	Central Park Venturi Larrousse	G	3.5 Venturi LC92-Lamborghini V12		1 lap behind	20/26
ret	AUSTRALIAN GP	Adelaide	30	Central Park Venturi Larrousse	G	3.5 Venturi LC92-Lamborghini V12		differential	26/26
	1993			Championship position: Unplaced					
ret	SOUTH AFRICAN GP	Kyalami	3	Tyrrell Racing Organisation	G	3.5 Tyrrell 020C-Yamaha V10		transmission	21/26
ret	BRAZILIAN GP	Interlagos	3	Tyrrell Racing Organisation	G	3.5 Tyrrell 020C-Yamaha V10		crashed in rainstorm	22/26
ret	EUROPEAN GP	Donington	3	Tyrrell Racing Organisation	G	3.5 Tyrrell 020C-Yamaha V10		clutch failure	18/26
ret	SAN MARINO GP	Imola	3	Tyrrell Racing Organisation	G	3.5 Tyrrell 020C-Yamaha V10		engine-water leak	22/26
ret	SPANISH GP	Barcelona	3	Tyrrell Racing Organisation	G	3.5 Tyrrell 020C-Yamaha V10		spun off	23/26
ret	MONACO GP	Monte Carlo	3	Tyrrell Racing Organisation	G	3.5 Tyrrell 020C-Yamaha V10		oil leak	22/26
17	CANADIAN GP	Montreal	3	Tyrrell Racing Organisation	G	3.5 Tyrrell 020C-Yamaha V10		spin-pit stop/suspension/-5 laps	22/26

ret	FRENCH GP	Magny Cours	3	Tyrrell Racing Organisation	G	3.5 Tyrrell 020C-Yamaha V10	*engine*	21/26
13	BRITISH GP	Silverstone	3	Tyrrell Racing Organisation	G	3.5 Tyrrell 020C-Yamaha V10	*4 laps behind*	22/26
dns	"	"	3	Tyrrell Racing Organisation	G	3.5 Tyrrell 021-Yamaha V10	*practice only*	– / –
ret	GERMAN GP	Hockenheim	3	Tyrrell Racing Organisation	G	3.5 Tyrrell 021-Yamaha V10	*spun off*	21/26
10	HUNGARIAN GP	Hungaroring	3	Tyrrell Racing Organisation	G	3.5 Tyrrell 021-Yamaha V10	*4 laps behind*	23/26
15	BELGIAN GP	Spa	3	Tyrrell Racing Organisation	G	3.5 Tyrrell 021-Yamaha V10	*4 laps behind*	23/25
14	ITALIAN GP	Monza	3	Tyrrell Racing Organisation	G	3.5 Tyrrell 021-Yamaha V10	*suspension/puncture/-6 laps*	17/26
dns	"	"	3	Tyrrell Racing Organisation	G	3.5 Tyrrell 020C-Yamaha V10	*practice only*	– / –
ret	PORTUGUESE GP	Estoril	3	Tyrrell Racing Organisation	G	3.5 Tyrrell 021-Yamaha V10	*crashed*	21/26
ret	JAPANESE GP	Suzuka	3	Tyrrell Racing Organisation	G	3.5 Tyrrell 021-Yamaha V10	*engine*	13/24
ret	AUSTRALIAN GP	Adelaide	3	Tyrrell Racing Organisation	G	3.5 Tyrrell 021-Yamaha V10	*started from back/crashed*	18/24

1994   Championship position: 17th   Wins: 0   Pole positions: 0   Fastest laps: 0   Points scored: 5

5	BRAZILIAN GP	Interlagos	3	Tyrrell	G	3.5 Tyrrell 022-Yamaha V10	*2 laps behind*	10/28
ret	PACIFIC GP	T.I. Circuit	3	Tyrrell	G	3.5 Tyrrell 022-Yamaha V10	*engine*	14/28
5	SAN MARINO GP	Imola	3	Tyrrell	G	3.5 Tyrrell 022-Yamaha V10	*1 lap behind*	9/28
ret	MONACO GP	Monte Carlo	3	Tyrrell	G	3.5 Tyrrell 022-Yamaha V10	*gearbox*	11/24
ret	SPANISH GP	Barcelona	3	Tyrrell	G	3.5 Tyrrell 022-Yamaha V10	*engine*	10/27
ret	CANADIAN GP	Montreal	3	Tyrrell	G	3.5 Tyrrell 022-Yamaha V10	*spun off*	9/27
ret	FRENCH GP	Magny Cours	3	Tyrrell	G	3.5 Tyrrell 022-Yamaha V10	*spun and stalled*	14/28
6*	BRITISH GP	Silverstone	3	Tyrrell	G	3.5 Tyrrell 022-Yamaha V10	**2nd place car dsq/-1 lap*	8/28
ret	GERMAN GP	Hockenheim	3	Tyrrell	G	3.5 Tyrrell 022-Yamaha V10	*sticking throttle*	5/28
ret	HUNGARIAN GP	Hungaroring	3	Tyrrell	G	3.5 Tyrrell 022-Yamaha V10	*collision with Barrichello & Irvine*	5/28
ret	BELGIAN GP	Spa	3	Tyrrell	G	3.5 Tyrrell 022-Yamaha V10	*engine*	23/28
ret	ITALIAN GP	Monza	3	Tyrrell	G	3.5 Tyrrell 022-Yamaha V10	*brake disc failure/accident*	14/28
ret	PORTUGUESE GP	Estoril	3	Tyrrell	G	3.5 Tyrrell 022-Yamaha V10	*started from pit lane/gearbox*	6/28
7	EUROPEAN GP	Jerez	3	Tyrrell	G	3.5 Tyrrell 022-Yamaha V10	*stalled at start/1 lap behind*	13/28
ret	JAPANESE GP	Suzuka	3	Tyrrell	G	3.5 Tyrrell 022-Yamaha V10	*spun off in rain*	14/28
ret	AUSTRALIAN GP	Adelaide	3	Tyrrell	G	3.5 Tyrrell 022-Yamaha V10	*spun off*	15/28

1995   Championship position: Unplaced

ret	BRAZILIAN GP	Interlagos	3	Nokia Tyrrell Yamaha	G	3.0 Tyrrell 023-Yamaha V10	*spun off*	11/26
8	ARGENTINE GP	Buenos Aires	3	Nokia Tyrrell Yamaha	G	3.0 Tyrrell 023-Yamaha V10	*3 laps behind*	15/26
ret	SAN MARINO GP	Imola	3	Nokia Tyrrell Yamaha	G	3.0 Tyrrell 023-Yamaha V10	*spun off*	15/26
ret	SPANISH GP	Barcelona	3	Nokia Tyrrell Yamaha	G	3.0 Tyrrell 023-Yamaha V10	*engine*	17/26
ret	MONACO GP	Monte Carlo	3	Nokia Tyrrell Yamaha	G	3.0 Tyrrell 023-Yamaha V10	*accident*	15/26
ret	CANADIAN GP	Montreal	3	Nokia Tyrrell Yamaha	G	3.0 Tyrrell 023-Yamaha V10	*engine*	16/24
ret	FRENCH GP	Magny Cours	3	Nokia Tyrrell Yamaha	G	3.0 Tyrrell 023-Yamaha V10	*collision with Inoue*	19/24
ret	BRITISH GP	Silverstone	3	Nokia Tyrrell Yamaha	G	3.0 Tyrrell 023-Yamaha V10	*fuel pressure*	14/24
7	GERMAN GP	Hockenheim	3	Nokia Tyrrell Yamaha	G	3.0 Tyrrell 023-Yamaha V10	*1 lap behind*	17/24
ret	HUNGARIAN GP	Hungaroring	3	Nokia Tyrrell Yamaha	G	3.0 Tyrrell 023-Yamaha V10	*accident*	17/24
ret	BELGIAN GP	Spa	3	Nokia Tyrrell Yamaha	G	3.0 Tyrrell 023-Yamaha V10	*spun off*	15/24
nc	ITALIAN GP	Monza	3	Nokia Tyrrell Yamaha	G	3.0 Tyrrell 023-Yamaha V10	*pit stop-sensor problem/-6 laps*	17/24
ret/dns	PORTUGUESE GP	Estoril	3	Nokia Tyrrell Yamaha	G	3.0 Tyrrell 023-Yamaha V10	*accident at first start*	(16)/24
14	PACIFIC GP	T.I. Circuit	3	Nokia Tyrrell Yamaha	G	3.0 Tyrrell 023-Yamaha V10	*3 laps behind*	17/24
ret	JAPANESE GP	Suzuka	3	Nokia Tyrrell Yamaha	G	3.0 Tyrrell 023-Yamaha V10	*spun off*	14/24
ret	AUSTRALIAN GP	Adelaide	3	Nokia Tyrrell Yamaha	G	3.0 Tyrrell 023-Yamaha V10	*engine*	16/24

1996   Championship position: Unplaced

11	AUSTRALIAN GP	Melbourne	18	Tyrrell Yamaha	G	3.0 Tyrrell 024-Yamaha V10	*3 laps behind*	15/22
9	BRAZILIAN GP	Interlagos	18	Tyrrell Yamaha	G	3.0 Tyrrell 024-Yamaha V10	*2 laps behind*	16/22
ret	ARGENTINE GP	Buenos Aires	18	Tyrrell Yamaha	G	3.0 Tyrrell 024-Yamaha V10	*tranmission*	13/22
dsq*	EUROPEAN GP	Nürburgring	18	Tyrrell Yamaha	G	3.0 Tyrrell 024-Yamaha V10	**push start /12th on road*	16/22
ret	SAN MARINO GP	Imola	18	Tyrrell Yamaha	G	3.0 Tyrrell 024-Yamaha V10	*transmission*	16/22
ret	MONACO GP	Monte Carlo	18	Tyrrell Yamaha	G	3.0 Tyrrell 024-Yamaha V10	*stuck throttle - hit barrier*	15/22
ret	SPANISH GP	Barcelona	18	Tyrrell Yamaha	G	3.0 Tyrrell 024-Yamaha V10	*electrics*	16/22
ret	CANADIAN GP	Montreal	18	Tyrrell Yamaha	G	3.0 Tyrrell 024-Yamaha V10	*collision with Rosset*	17/22
ret	FRENCH GP	Magny Cours	18	Tyrrell Yamaha	G	3.0 Tyrrell 024-Yamaha V10	*engine*	15/22
ret	BRITISH GP	Silverstone	18	Tyrrell Yamaha	G	3.0 Tyrrell 024-Yamaha V10	*engine*	12/22
ret	GERMAN GP	Hockenheim	18	Tyrrell Yamaha	G	3.0 Tyrrell 024-Yamaha V10	*spun off*	16/20
7	HUNGARIAN GP	Hungaroring	18	Tyrrell Yamaha	G	3.0 Tyrrell 024-Yamaha V10	*3 laps behind*	14/20
8	BELGIAN GP	Spa	18	Tyrrell Yamaha	G	3.0 Tyrrell 024-Yamaha V10		17/20
10	ITALIAN GP	Monza	18	Tyrrell Yamaha	G	3.0 Tyrrell 024-Yamaha V10	*2 laps behind*	16/20
12	PORTUGUESE GP	Estoril	18	Tyrrell Yamaha	G	3.0 Tyrrell 024-Yamaha V10	*2 laps behind*	14/20
ret	JAPANESE GP	Suzuka	18	Tyrrell Yamaha	G	3.0 Tyrrell 024-Yamaha V10	*engine*	14/20

1997   Championship position: Unplaced

ret	AUSTRALIAN GP	Melbourne	20	Minardi Team	B	3.0 Minardi M197-Hart V8	*engine*	15/24
18	BRAZILIAN GP	Interlagos	20	Minardi Team	B	3.0 Minardi M197-Hart V8	*5 laps behind*	18/22
ret	ARGENTINE GP	Buenos Aires	20	Minardi Team	B	3.0 Minardi M197-Hart V8	*spun off*	21/22
11	SAN MARINO GP	Imola	20	Minardi Team	B	3.0 Minardi M197-Hart V8	*3 laps behind*	22/22
10	MONACO GP	Monte Carlo	20	Minardi Team	B	3.0 Minardi M197-Hart V8	*2 laps behind*	20/22
ret	SPANISH GP	Barcelona	20	Minardi Team	B	3.0 Minardi M197-Hart V8	*hydraulic pump*	20/22
ret	CANADIAN GP	Montreal	20	Minardi Team	B	3.0 Minardi M197-Hart V8	*stuck throttle-crashed*	22/22
11	FRENCH GP	Magny Cours	20	Minardi Team	B	3.0 Minardi M197-Hart V8	*2 laps behind*	21/22
ret	BRITISH GP	Silverstone	20	Minardi Team	B	3.0 Minardi M197-Hart V8	*spun into pit wall at start*	19/22
ret	GERMAN GP	Hockenheim	20	Minardi Team	B	3.0 Minardi M197-Hart V8	*out of fuel*	22/22
10	HUNGARIAN GP	Hungaroring	20	Minardi Team	B	3.0 Minardi M197-Hart V8	*1 lap behind*	20/22
14*	BELGIAN GP	Spa	20	Minardi Team	B	3.0 Minardi M197-Hart V8	**3rd place car dsq/-2 laps*	20/22
ret	ITALIAN GP	Monza	20	Minardi Team	B	3.0 Minardi M197-Hart V8	*puncture-hit barrier-retired in pits*	21/22
11	AUSTRIAN GP	A1-Ring	20	Minardi Team	B	3.0 Minardi M197-Hart V8	*2 laps behind*	19/22
ret	LUXEMBOURG GP	Nürburgring	20	Minardi Team	B	3.0 Minardi M197-Hart V8	*collision-suspension damage*	22/22
ret	JAPANESE GP	Suzuka	20	Minardi Team	B	3.0 Minardi M197-Hart V8	*engine*	19/22
17	EUROPEAN GP	Jerez	20	Minardi Team	B	3.0 Minardi M197-Hart V8	*1 lap behind*	19/22

GP Starts: 00   GP Wins: 0   Pole positions: 0   Fastest laps: 0   Points: 5

RUPERT KEEGAN

The much hyped Keegan did possess talent, but perhaps not quite as much as he and his father, backer and number-one fan Mike believed.

Starting his career with a win first time out in a Ford Escort Mexico, Keegan soon moved into Formula Ford, where he was quick but erratic. A successful end to the 1974 season encouraged him to move into Formula 3 the following year with the ex-Henton March 743, but the season was punctuated with crashes, including a very nasty one at Thruxton.

Things changed dramatically in 1976, with a more consistent Rupert winning nine rounds of the BP championship and the title to line up a seat in the Hesketh Grand Prix team for 1977. The car was awful but Keegan emerged with great credit, qualifying for every race in which he was entered, only to jump out of the frying pan and into the fire by joining the ailing Surtees team in 1978.

Left with no alternatives, Rupert drove an Arrows in the 1979 Aurora F1 series, winning five rounds and the championship, but his return to the Grand Prix arena in 1980 with the RAM Williams brought little reward, and the same could be said of his final shot in the Rothmans March at the end of 1982. After a spell in endurance racing and a brief flirtation with Indy cars, Keegan quit to pursue an entrepreneurial business career.

In 1995, at the age of forty, he made a surprise reappearance on the track, driving a Lister Storm at Le Mans with Geoff Lees and Dominic Chappell.

KEEGAN, Rupert (GB) b 26/2/1955, Westcliff-on-Sea, Essex

1977 — Championship position: Unplaced

	Race	Circuit	No	Entrant	Tyres	Car/Engine	Comment	Q Pos/Entries
ret	SPANISH GP	Jarama	24	Penthouse Rizla Racing	G	3.0 Hesketh 308E-Cosworth V8	missed gearchange-accident	16/31
12	MONACO GP	Monte Carlo	24	Penthouse Rizla Racing	G	3.0 Hesketh 308E-Cosworth V8	broken anti-roll bar/-3 laps	20/26
ret	BELGIAN GP	Zolder	24	Penthouse Rizla Racing	G	3.0 Hesketh 308E-Cosworth V8	spun off	19/32
13	SWEDISH GP	Anderstorp	24	Penthouse Rizla Racing	G	3.0 Hesketh 308E-Cosworth V8	handling problems/-1 lap	24/31
10	FRENCH GP	Dijon	24	Penthouse Rizla Racing	G	3.0 Hesketh 308E-Cosworth V8	2 laps behind	14/30
ret	BRITISH GP	Silverstone	24	Penthouse Rizla Racing	G	3.0 Hesketh 308E-Cosworth V8	collision-Merzario-lost wheel	=13/36
ret	GERMAN GP	Hockenheim	24	Penthouse Rizla Racing	G	3.0 Hesketh 308E-Cosworth V8	accident-hit Ribeiro	23/30
7	AUSTRIAN GP	Österreichring	24	Penthouse Rizla Racing	G	3.0 Hesketh 308E-Cosworth V8	2 spins/1 lap behind	=20/30
ret	DUTCH GP	Zandvoort	24	Penthouse Rizla Racing	G	3.0 Hesketh 308E-Cosworth V8	accident	26/34
9	ITALIAN GP	Monza	24	Penthouse Rizla Racing	G	3.0 Hesketh 308E-Cosworth V8	pit stop/4 laps behind	23/34
8	US GP EAST	Watkins Glen	24	Penthouse Rizla Racing	G	3.0 Hesketh 308E-Cosworth V8	1 lap behind	20/27
ret	CANADIAN GP	Mosport Park	24	Penthouse Rizla Racing	G	3.0 Hesketh 308E-Cosworth V8	hit Binder	25/27

1978 — Championship position: Unplaced

	Race	Circuit	No	Entrant	Tyres	Car/Engine	Comment	Q Pos/Entries
ret	ARGENTINE GP	Buenos Aires	18	Durex Team Surtees	G	3.0 Surtees TS19-Cosworth V8	overheating	19/27
ret	BRAZILIAN GP	Rio	18	Durex Team Surtees	G	3.0 Surtees TS19-Cosworth V8	accident	=24/28
ret	SOUTH AFRICAN GP	Kyalami	18	Durex Team Surtees	G	3.0 Surtees TS19-Cosworth V8	oil line-engine	23/30
dns	US GP WEST	Long Beach	18	Durex Team Surtees	G	3.0 Surtees TS19-Cosworth V8	practice accident	(22)/30
ret	MONACO GP	Monte Carlo	18	Durex Team Surtees	G	3.0 Surtees TS19-Cosworth V8	transmission	– / –
dns	"	" "	18	Durex Team Surtees	G	3.0 Surtees TS20-Cosworth V8	practice only-set grid time	=18/30
dnq	BELGIAN GP	Zolder	18	Durex Team Surtees	G	3.0 Surtees TS20-Cosworth V8		25/30
11	SPANISH GP	Jarama	18	Durex Team Surtees	G	3.0 Surtees TS20-Cosworth V8	2 laps behind	23/29
dnq	SWEDISH GP	Anderstorp	18	Durex Team Surtees	G	3.0 Surtees TS20-Cosworth V8		25/27
ret	FRENCH GP	Paul Ricard	18	Durex Team Surtees	G	3.0 Surtees TS20-Cosworth V8	engine	23/29
dnq	BRITISH GP	Brands Hatch	18	Durex Team Surtees	G	3.0 Surtees TS20-Cosworth V8		28/30
dnq	"	" "	18	Durex Team Surtees	G	3.0 Surtees TS19-Cosworth V8		– / –
dnq	GERMAN GP	Hockenheim	18	Durex Team Surtees	G	3.0 Surtees TS20-Cosworth V8		27/30
dnq	AUSTRIAN GP	Österreichring	18	Durex Team Surtees	G	3.0 Surtees TS20-Cosworth V8		29/31
dns	DUTCH GP	Zandvoort	18	Durex Team Surtees	G	3.0 Surtees TS20-Cosworth V8	injured in pre-race warm-up	(25)/33

1980 — Championship position: Unplaced

	Race	Circuit	No	Entrant	Tyres	Car/Engine	Comment	Q Pos/Entries
11	BRITISH GP	Brands Hatch	50	RAM/Williams Grand Prix Engineering	G	3.0 Williams FW07-Cosworth V8	pit stop/3 laps behind	18/27
dnq	GERMAN GP	Hockenheim	50	RAM/Penthouse Rizla Racing	G	3.0 Williams FW07B-Cosworth V8		25/26
15	AUSTRIAN GP	Österreichring	50	RAM/Penthouse Rizla Racing	G	3.0 Williams FW07B-Cosworth V8	2 laps behind	20/25
dnq	DUTCH GP	Zandvoort	50	RAM/Penthouse Rizla Racing	G	3.0 Williams FW07B-Cosworth V8		25/28
11	ITALIAN GP	Imola	50	RAM/Penthouse Rizla Racing	G	3.0 Williams FW07B-Cosworth V8	2 laps behind	21/28
dnq	CANADIAN GP	Montreal	50	RAM/Penthouse Rizla Racing	G	3.0 Williams FW07B-Cosworth V8		27/28
9	US GP EAST	Watkins Glen	50	RAM/Penthouse Rizla Racing	G	3.0 Williams FW07B-Cosworth V8	2 laps behind	15/27

1982 — Championship position: Unplaced

	Race	Circuit	No	Entrant	Tyres	Car/Engine	Comment	Q Pos/Entries
dnq	GERMAN GP	Hockenheim	17	Rothmans March Grand Prix Team	A	3.0 March 821-Cosworth V8		29/30
ret	AUSTRIAN GP	Österreichring	17	Rothmans March Grand Prix Team	A	3.0 March 821-Cosworth V8	accident-bent steering arm	24/29
ret	SWISS GP	Dijon	17	Rothmans March Grand Prix Team	A	3.0 March 821-Cosworth V8	spun off	22/29
dnq	ITALIAN GP	Monza	17	Rothmans March Grand Prix Team	M	3.0 March 821-Cosworth V8		27/30
12	CAESARS PALACE GP	Las Vegas	17	Rothmans March Grand Prix Team	M	3.0 March 821-Cosworth V8	2 laps behind	25/30

GP Starts: 25　GP Wins: 0　Pole positions: 0　Fastest laps: 0　Points: 0

KEIZAN, Eddie (ZA) b 12/9/1944, Johannesburg

	1973	Championship position: Unplaced						
	Race	Circuit	No	Entrant	Tyres	Car/Engine	Comment	Q Pos/Entries
nc	SOUTH AFRICAN GP	Kyalami	26	Blignaut-Lucky Strike Racing	F	3.0 Tyrrell 004-Cosworth V8	2 pit stops/12 laps behind	22/25
	1974	Championship position: Unplaced						
14	SOUTH AFRICAN GP	Kyalami	32	Blignaut-Embassy Racing SA	G	3.0 Tyrrell 004-Cosworth V8	2 laps behind	24/27
	1975	Championship position: Unplaced						
13	SOUTH AFRICAN GP	Kyalami	33	Team Gunston	G	3.0 Lotus 72-Cosworth V8	2 laps behind	22/28

GP Starts: 3   GP Wins: 0   Pole positions: 0   Fastest laps: 0   Points: 0

KELLY, Joe (IRL) b 13/3/1913, South America – d 12/1993, Chester, England

	1950	Championship position: Unplaced						
	Race	Circuit	No	Entrant	Tyres	Car/Engine	Comment	Q Pos/Entries
nc	BRITISH GP	Silverstone	23	Joe Kelly	D	1.5 s/c Alta GP 4	pit stops/23 laps behind	19/21
	1951	Championship position: Unplaced						
nc	BRITISH GP	Silverstone	5	Joe Kelly	D	1.5 s/c Alta GP 4	pit stops/15 laps behind	18/20

GP Starts: 2   GP Wins: 0   Pole positions: 0   Fastest laps: 0   Points: 0

EDDIE KEIZAN

Eddie raced saloons in his native South Africa from the late sixties, winning the championship twice, before switching to a mixed diet of Formula Ford and sports car racing with a Lola T212 in 1971. It was the purchase of an F5000 Surtees in 1972 which put him on the map as Gold Star champion in that class.

He then raced a Tyrrell 004 and then an ex-Fittipaldi Lotus 72 in the domestic series, and naturally the local Grands Prix as well. Eddie loved the Lotus, setting his fastest-ever lap time at Kyalami with it, but it was to prove unreliable and he endured a terrible run of mechanical failures with the car.

At the end of 1975 it was decided that the South African championship was no longer able to sustain 'pukka' Formula 1 machinery for financial reasons and the premier class was henceforth to be for Formula Atlantic cars. These relatively underpowered machines held little appeal for Eddie, who moved into the South African touring car championship with his own team, running a BMW 535, and won the title twice more in 1977 and 1978.

He crowned his career by scoring a great victory in the Wynn's 1000 at Kyalami in 1979, when he was forced to drive for most of the race after his co-driver, Helmut Kelleners, was taken ill, defeating such luminaries as Watson, Mass, Surer and Stuck. When Ian Scheckter suffered a neck injury, Keizan was back in the BMW in the Wynn's in 1980 but this time an almost certain victory was lost when a driveshaft broke.

With his thriving business interests taking up more of his time, Eddie did not race again for ten years, but thereafter he occasionally donned his overalls to drive a BMW in South African endurance events.

JOE KELLY

Although born in South America, Joe was a larger-than-life motor dealer from Dublin, who had a tilt at Grands Prix with the last of Geoffrey Taylor's three GP Altas. This attractive machine never achieved any real success, but Kelly did manage to take a second place in the Wakefield Trophy handicap race behind Hamilton's Maserati at the Curragh in 1950 and third place in the Ulster Trophy at Dundrod in 1952 against much better opposition.

With the introduction of rule changes favouring Formula 2, Kelly had his Alta extensively modified to take a Bristol engine. He raced this machine, renamed the IRA (Irish Racing Automobile), sporadically through 1952 and '53, but was far more interested in enjoying himself at the wheel of his Jaguar C-Type (particularly at the Curragh), which he raced in his inimitable hard-charging style through until 1955, when his career was brought to an end after a three-car accident at Oulton Park.

Kelly, who sustained serious injuries and narrowly escaped the amputation of a badly damaged leg, then concentrated on his extensive business interests which included the Ferrari dealership for Ireland and property development in the United Kingdom.

LORIS KESSEL

A Swiss garage owner and former Alfa saloon racer, Kessel graduated from Formula 3 with no great record of success outside his native championship. A season of Formula 2 with a March in 1975 saw him briefly lead the opening race at Estoril and score a couple of fourth places at Hockenheim, but little else.

His undistinguished spell in the RAM F1 team in 1976 ended in legal acrimony, then followed a brief flirtation with the Apollon. Thereafter he made occasional appearances in F3 until 1981, when he returned to Formula 2 without success. However, in 1993, after many years out of the spotlight, he was to be found in the Porsche 962C that finished seventh in the Le Mans 24 Hours.

LEO KINNUNEN

Kinnunen raced successfully for a number of seasons in his native Finland with Volvos, Porsches and an F3 Titan before being plucked from this relative obscurity to partner Pedro Rodriguez in the Gulf/Wyer sports car team for 1970, the pair winning at Daytona, Brands Hatch, Monza and Watkins Glen.

Between 1971 and '73, Leo swept the board in Interserie racing with a Porsche 917 Spyder entered by AAW-Finland, who also backed his unhappy Grand Prix season in 1974. After this debacle, Kinnunen returned to sports car and GT racing, competing in Porsches for the rest of the decade.

HANS KLENK

This ex-Messerschmitt pilot built specials in Stuttgart from 1950, but soon moved onto competing with the Veritas previously used by his friend Karl Kling. In 1952 he was second at both AVUS, behind Fischer's Ferrari, and Grenzlandring. But the highlight of his competition career was undoubtedly joining Mercedes that year to take second in the Mille Miglia and then win the Carrera Panamericana with Kling in the 300SLR.

In 1953 he was second to a Ferrari at AVUS once more, this time Swaters', but a serious accident when testing a Mercedes brought his racing career to a premature end. In 1954 he built his own Klenk-Meteor, based on the Veritas, which was driven briefly by Helfrich.

KESSEL, Loris (CH) b 1/4/1950, Lugano

	1976	Championship position: Unplaced							
	Race	Circuit	No	Entrant	Tyres	Car/Engine	Comment		Q Pos/Entries
dnq	SPANISH GP	Jarama	32	RAM Racing	G	3.0 Brabham BT44B-Cosworth V8			26/30
12	BELGIAN GP	Zolder	32	RAM Racing	G	3.0 Brabham BT44B-Cosworth V8	pit stop/7 laps behind		23/29
ret	SWEDISH GP	Anderstorp	32	RAM Racing	G	3.0 Brabham BT44B-Cosworth V8	accident		26/27
dnq	FRENCH GP	Paul Ricard	32	RAM Racing	G	3.0 Brabham BT44B-Cosworth V8			30/30
nc	AUSTRIAN GP	Österreichring	32	RAM Racing	G	3.0 Brabham BT44B-Cosworth V8	pit stop-fuel union/-10 laps		25/25
	1977	Championship position: Unplaced							
dnq	ITALIAN GP	Monza	41	Jolly Club of Switzerland	G	3.0 Apollon-Williams FW03-Cosworth V8	crashed in practice		33/34

GP Starts: 3 GP Wins: 0 Pole positions: 0 Fastest laps: 0 Points: 0

KINNUNEN, Leo (SF) b 5/8/1943, Tampere

	1974	Championship position: Unplaced							
	Race	Circuit	No	Entrant	Tyres	Car/Engine	Comment		Q Pos/Entries
dnq	BELGIAN GP	Nivelles	44	AAW Racing Team	F	3.0 Surtees TS16-Cosworth V8			32/32
ret	SWEDISH GP	Anderstorp	23	AAW Racing Team	F	3.0 Surtees TS16-Cosworth V8	electrics		26/28
dnq	FRENCH GP	Dijon	23	AAW Racing Team	F	3.0 Surtees TS16-Cosworth V8			29/30
dnq	BRITISH GP	Brands Hatch	43	AAW Racing Team	F	3.0 Surtees TS16-Cosworth V8			34/34
dnq	AUSTRIAN GP	Österreichring	43	AAW Racing Team	F	3.0 Surtees TS16-Cosworth V8			27/31
dnq	ITALIAN GP	Monza	23	AAW Racing Team	F	3.0 Surtees TS16-Cosworth V8			31/31

GP Starts: 1 GP Wins: 0 Pole positions: 0 Fastest laps: 0 Points: 0

KLENK, Hans (D) b 18/10/1919, Künzelsau

	1952	Championship position: Unplaced							
	Race	Circuit	No	Entrant	Tyres	Car/Engine	Comment		Q Pos/Entries
nc	GERMAN GP	Nürburgring	128	Hans Klenk	–	2.0 Veritas Meteor 6	4 laps behind		8/32

GP Starts: 1 GP Wins: 0 Pole positions: 0 Fastest laps: 0 Points: 0

KARL KLING

Kling drove production cars in hill-climbs and trials as an amateur before the war but his racing career did not really start in earnest until 1947, when he scored a victory at Hockenheim with a BMW.

The next two seasons saw him crowned German sports car champion in the 2-litre class with the potent Veritas. In 1950, he raced the Veritas-Meteor in Formula 2, winning races at Grenzlandring and Solitude, and the Eifelrennen at the Nürburgring, which led to an invitation to help develop the pre-war Mercedes, which raced again at the start of 1951 in South America, taking second place in the Eva Peron Cup.

Leading the Mercedes 300SL sports car attack in 1952, Kling missed out at Le Mans, but made up for it elsewhere, winning the Carrera Panamericana and the Prix de Berne, and taking second in the Mille Miglia. After a short stay with Alfa Romeo in 1953, Kling was back in the silver cars the following season, but very much in the shadow of Fangio – although the Argentinian, allegedly, allowed him to take the Berlin GP at AVUS.

Relegated in the pecking order in 1955 by the arrival of Stirling Moss, Karl did not enjoy much success in Grands Prix, but took third place at Aintree, behind the star duo, and shared the second-placed Mercedes sports car with Fangio in both the Tourist Trophy and the Targa Florio, before retiring to take up a management position within the company following their withdrawal from racing at the end of the 1955 season.

ERNST KLODWIG

If not quite the fastest of the drivers who competed in the East German national races which ran from 1950 through to 1954, Klodwig was certainly one of the most consistent.

He was a regular top-three finisher – racing against the likes of Rudi Krause, Paul Geifzu and Edgar Barth – with his neat little 'Eigenbau' (self-built) BMW. The car was also often referred to as a 'Heck' (tail) on account of its rear-mounted engine following the Auto Union philosophy.

In his two German Grand Prix appearances in the West, the car made it to the chequered flag, but was so far off the pace that it was not officially classified as a finisher.

KLING, Karl (D) b 16/9/1910, Giessen

	1954	Championship position: 0	Wins: 0	Pole positions: 0		Fastest laps: 0	Points scored: 0		
	Race	Circuit	No	Entrant	Tyres	Car/Engine		Comment	Q Pos/Entries
2	FRENCH GP	Reims	20	Daimler Benz AG	C	2.5 Mercedes-Benz W196 8 str			2/22
7	BRITISH GP	Silverstone	2	Daimler Benz AG	C	2.5 Mercedes-Benz W196 8 str		3 laps behind	6/31
4	GERMAN GP	Nürburgring	19	Daimler Benz AG	C	2.5 Mercedes-Benz W196 8		led race-suspension problems/FL	– /23
ret	SWISS GP	Bremgarten	8	Daimler Benz AG	C	2.5 Mercedes-Benz W196 8		injector pump drive	5/16
ret	ITALIAN GP	Monza	14	Daimler Benz AG	C	2.5 Mercedes-Benz W196 8 str		radius rod-crashed	4/21
5	SPANISH GP	Pedralbes	4	Daimler Benz AG	C	2.5 Mercedes-Benz W196 8		1 lap behind	12/22
	1955	Championship position: 0	Wins: 0	Pole positions: 0		Fastest laps: 0	Points scored: 0		
ret	ARGENTINE GP	Buenos Aires	4	Daimler Benz AG	C	2.5 Mercedes-Benz W196 8		crashed	6/22
4*	"	" "	8	Daimler Benz AG	C	2.5 Mercedes-Benz W196 8		* Moss & Herrmann drove/-2 laps	– / –
ret	BELGIAN GP	Spa	12	Daimler Benz AG	C	2.5 Mercedes-Benz W196 8		oil pipe	6/14
ret	DUTCH GP	Zandvoort	12	Daimler Benz AG	C	2.5 Mercedes-Benz W196 8		spun off	3/16
3	BRITISH GP	Aintree	14	Daimler Benz AG	C	2.5 Mercedes-Benz W196 8			4/25
ret	ITALIAN GP	Monza	20	Daimler Benz AG	C	2.5 Mercedes-Benz W196 8		gearbox	3/22

GP Starts: 11   GP Wins: 0   Pole positions: 0   Fastest laps: 1   Points: 17

KLODWIG, Ernst (D) b 23/5/1903 – d 15/4/1973

	1952	Championship position: 0	Wins: 0	Pole positions: 0		Fastest laps: 0	Points scored: 0		
	Race	Circuit	No	Entrant	Tyres	Car/Engine		Comment	Q Pos/Entries
nc	GERMAN GP	Nürburgring	135	Ernst Klodwig	–	2.0 BMW-Heck Eigenbau 6		4 laps behind	29/32
	1953	Championship position: 0	Wins: 0	Pole positions: 0		Fastest laps: 0	Points scored: 0		
nc	GERMAN GP	Nürburgring	37	Ernst Klodwig	–	2.0 BMW-Heck Eigenbau 6		3 laps behind	32/35

GP Starts: 2   GP Wins: 0   Pole positions: 0   Fastest laps: 0   Points: 0

HELMUTH KOINIGG

Although he came from a relatively affluent background, Helmuth found his lack of sufficient funds a great hindrance in his attempts to break through to the sport's higher echelons.

Koinigg started competing in the ex-Lauda Mini Cooper S, and soon attracted the attention of Helmut Marko, becoming involved in his McNamara project in Formula Vee. He was to spend the bulk of his short career trapped, albeit tremendously successfully, in Formula Vee and Super Vee, with only occasional outings in Formula Ford offering a glimpse of his natural talent on a wider stage.

Without the backing to race in Formula 2, Koinigg nonetheless found himself in demand by the Ford Cologne team, and he also handled Martini Racing's G5 Porsche before raising the finance to hire a private Brabham for the 1974 Austrian GP.

Although he failed to qualify the car, Helmuth did well enough to interest Surtees, who signed him up, but in only his second race for the team, at Watkins Glen, the young Austrian inexplicably failed to brake for a corner, crashing at huge speed through three layers of catch fencing and the steel barriers. He was killed instantly.

RUDI KRAUSE

With post-war Germany divided into to countries. The communist Deutsch Democratic Republic ran their own hotly-contested series from 1950-53, mainly on ad-hoc courses often conjured up by dint of closing sections of autobahn. Krause was a leading runner throughout, mainly in BMW based specials. He took many top three finishes and was well-placed to win when faster drivers such as Barth hit trouble.

Rudi drove a Veritas sports at Avus in 1951, but retired on lap 1. He later ventured into the west proper to participate in two Grands Prix. When the DDR championship ceased, Krause turned to rallying with a BMW.

ROBERT LA CAZE

Although a French native, La Caze was domiciled in Morocco, and throughout the 1950s was a leading figure on the motor sport scene in North Africa, where he raced and rallied various Renaults, a Lancia and a Delahaye to great effect in the early part of the decade.

In 1954 Robert won the Moroccan International Rally in a Simca, and he subsequently raced a Mercedes 300SL in 1956 and appeared at Le Mans in a works Gordini the following year.

With Morocco given the honour of hosting a round of the F1 World Championship in 1958, La Caze was invited to take part. Running a Formula 2 Cooper, he circulated steadily to take third in class behind the works cars of Brabham and McLaren.

KOINIGG, Helmuth (A) b 3/11/1948, Vienna – d 6/10/1974, Watkins Glen Circuit, New York State, USA

	1974			Championship position: Unplaced					
	Race	Circuit	No	Entrant	Tyres	Car/Engine	Comment		Q Pos/Entries
dnq	AUSTRIAN GP	Österreichring	32	Scuderia Finotto	G	3.0 Brabham BT42-Cosworth V8			31/31
10	CANADIAN GP	Mosport Park	19	Team Surtees	F	3.0 Surtees TS16-Cosworth V8	2 laps behind		22/30
ret	US GP	Watkins Glen	19	Team Surtees	F	3.0 Surtees TS16-Cosworth V8	fatal accident		23/30

GP Starts: 2   GP Wins: 0   Pole positions: 0   Fastest laps: 0   Points: 0

KRAUSE, Rudolf (D) b 30/3/1907 – d 11/4/1987

	1952			Championship position: Unplaced					
	Race	Circuit	No	Entrant	Tyres	Car/Engine	Comment		Q Pos/Entries
ret	GERMAN GP	Nürburgring	136	Rudolf Krause	–	2.0 BMW-Reif 6			23/32
	1953			Championship position: 0 Wins: 0 Pole positions: 0		Fastest laps: 0 Points scored: 0			
14	GERMAN GP	Nürburgring	36	Dora Greifzu	–	2.0 BMW-Greifzu 6	2 laps behind		26/35

GP Starts: 2   GP Wins: 0   Pole positions: 0   Fastest laps: 0   Points: 0

La CAZE, Robert (MA) b 26/2/1917, Paris, France

	1958			Championship position: Unplaced					
	Race	Circuit	No	Entrant	Tyres	Car/Engine	Comment		Q Pos/Entries
14*	MOROCCAN GP	Casablanca	58	Robert la Caze	D	1.5 Cooper T45-Climax 4 F2	* 3rd in F2 class/5 laps behind	23/25

GP Starts: 1   GP Wins: 0   Pole positions: 0   Fastest laps: 0   Points: 0

JACQUES LAFFITE

The smiling countenance of Jacques Laffite brightened the Grand Prix scene for more than a decade, during which he was a consistent performer who really excelled only when his car was absolutely on the pace – but then he simply flew.

His introduction to the sport was as a mechanic to Jean-Pierre Jabouille during his 1968 F3 season. Jacques resolved to race himself and started in Formula France before hitting the French F3 trail in the early seventies. In 1973 he won the French F3 championship in his Martini, and came close to taking the British John Player title as well, his splendid season including big wins in the prestigious Monaco and Pau GPs. With backing from BP France, Laffite moved into Formula 2 in 1974 with a March-BMW, soon establishing himself among the front-runners and winning a round at the Salzburgring. Having tried a number of drivers during the first half of

the season, Frank Williams decided on Jacques for the German GP, and although his race ended in a shunt he had impressed more than the previous incumbents and settled in for the next season and a half. In 1975 Williams were very much in the doldrums, but Laffite profited from others' misfortune to provide the team with a much-needed second place in Germany. In Formula 2 meanwhile, racing an Elf-backed Martini, Jacques clocked up six victories, edging out Jabouille to secure the European title, and he also took the Kauhsen/Autodelta Alfa T33 to victory at Dijon, Monza and the Nürburgring.

Ousting the originally nominated driver, Jean-Pierre Beltoise, Laffite joined Guy Ligier's debutant Ligier-Matra team for 1976 and quickly became a favourite son at Vichy, working hard to bring the car to a competitive pitch. He was rewarded with a win at Anderstorp in 1977, but it soon became clear that Cosworth power was a necessity for sustained success. At the beginning of 1979, now partnered by Depailler, Jacques flashed to victory in the opening two Grands Prix, but the dominance could not be sustained, as development brought more questions than answers. He took another win at Hockenheim the following season, but plans were already afoot to return to Matra power in 1981 under the Talbot banner. The team enjoyed a remarkably consistent season, and a strong run saw Laffite take two wins and make a late bid for the title before finishing fourth just behind Piquet, Reutemann and Jones. The promise evaporated in 1982, however, and Jacques managed only two points-scoring finishes all year, prompting his return to Williams on a two-year deal to drive alongside Keke Rosberg.

His year began soundly, but the Cosworth car became less and less competitive and Laffite suffered the late-season embarrassment of non-qualification at Monza and Brands Hatch. Things picked up in 1984, but with Rosberg extracting the very maximum from the car, the Frenchman's efforts seemed pedestrian by comparison.

Despite rumours of retirement, Jacques returned to Ligier and rediscovered some of his form of old, enough at least to ensure that his beaming smile appeared on the rostrum from time to time. Perhaps spurred by the arrival of Arnoux, Laffite produced some sparkling displays in 1986, even leading the Detroit race briefly. Then came a multiple shunt at the start at Brands Hatch which left the unlucky Jacques trapped in his car with both legs broken. His Grand Prix career was over.

Jacques was to return to the circuits, enjoying the cut and thrust of the French touring car series over the ensuing seasons. In 1995 he was still a regular in the Supertourisme series driving an Opel Vectra, but now races mainly for fun in selected events. He also made a welcome return to the Grand Prix paddock working for Ligier in a PR capacity.

LAFFITE, Jacques (F) b 21/11/1943, Paris

1974
Championship position: Unplaced

	Race	Circuit	No	Entrant	Tyres	Car/Engine	Comment	Q Pos/Entries
ret	GERMAN GP	Nürburgring	21	Frank Williams Racing Cars	F	3.0 Williams FW02-Cosworth V8	accident-suspension damage	21/32
nc	AUSTRIAN GP	Österreichring	21	Frank Williams Racing Cars	F	3.0 Williams FW02-Cosworth V8	wheel damage on grid/-17 laps	12/31
ret	ITALIAN GP	Monza	21	Frank Williams Racing Cars	F	3.0 Williams FW02-Cosworth V8	engine	17/31
15/ret	CANADIAN GP	Mosport Park	21	Frank Williams Racing Cars	F	3.0 Williams FW02-Cosworth V8	puncture/6 laps behind	18/30
ret	US GP	Watkins Glen	21	Frank Williams Racing Cars	F	3.0 Williams FW02-Cosworth V8	rear wheel	11/30

1975
Championship position: 12th   Wins: 0   Pole positions: 0   Fastest laps: 0   Points scored: 6

	Race	Circuit	No	Entrant	Tyres	Car/Engine	Comment	Q Pos/Entries
ret	ARGENTINE GP	Buenos Aires	21	Frank Williams Racing Cars	G	3.0 Williams FW02-Cosworth V8	gearbox	17/23
11	BRAZILIAN GP	Interlagos	21	Frank Williams Racing Cars	G	3.0 Williams FW02-Cosworth V8	1 lap behind	19/23
nc	SOUTH AFRICAN GP	Kyalami	21	Frank Williams Racing Cars	G	3.0 Williams FW02-Cosworth V8	pit stop/9 laps behind	23/28
dnq	MONACO GP	Monte Carlo	21	Frank Williams Racing Cars	G	3.0 Williams FW04-Cosworth V8		19/26
ret	BELGIAN GP	Zolder	21	Frank Williams Racing Cars	G	3.0 Williams FW04-Cosworth V8	gearbox	17/24
ret	DUTCH GP	Zandvoort	21	Frank Williams Racing Cars	G	3.0 Williams FW04-Cosworth V8	engine	15/25
11	FRENCH GP	Paul Ricard	21	Frank Williams Racing Cars	G	3.0 Williams FW04-Cosworth V8		=15/26
ret	BRITISH GP	Silverstone	21	Frank Williams Racing Cars	G	3.0 Williams FW04-Cosworth V8	gearbox	19/28
2	GERMAN GP	Nürburgring	21	Frank Williams Racing Cars	G	3.0 Williams FW04-Cosworth V8		15/26
ret	AUSTRIAN GP	Österreichring	21	Frank Williams Racing Cars	G	3.0 Williams FW04-Cosworth V8	handling	12/30
ret	ITALIAN GP	Monza	21	Frank Williams Racing Cars	G	3.0 Williams FW04-Cosworth V8	gearbox	18/28
dns	US GP	Watkins Glen	21	Frank Williams Racing Cars	G	3.0 Williams FW04-Cosworth V8	visor cleaner fluid in eyes	(21)/24

1976
Championship position: 7th=   Wins: 0   Pole positions: 1   Fastest laps: 0   Points scored: 20

	Race	Circuit	No	Entrant	Tyres	Car/Engine	Comment	Q Pos/Entries
ret	BRAZILIAN GP	Interlagos	26	Ligier Gitanes	G	3.0 Ligier JS5-Matra V12	gear linkage	11/22
ret	SOUTH AFRICAN GP	Kyalami	26	Ligier Gitanes	G	3.0 Ligier JS5-Matra V12	engine	8/25
4	US GP WEST	Long Beach	26	Ligier Gitanes	G	3.0 Ligier JS5-Matra V12		12/27
12	SPANISH GP	Jarama	26	Ligier Gitanes	G	3.0 Ligier JS5-Matra V12	reinstated after dsq/-3 laps	8/30
3	BELGIAN GP	Zolder	26	Ligier Gitanes	G	3.0 Ligier JS5-Matra V12		6/29
12/ret	MONACO GP	Monte Carlo	26	Ligier Gitanes	G	3.0 Ligier JS5-Matra V12	collision with Mass/-3 laps	8/25
4	SWEDISH GP	Anderstorp	26	Ligier Gitanes	G	3.0 Ligier JS5-Matra V12		7/27
14	FRENCH GP	Paul Ricard	26	Ligier Gitanes	G	3.0 Ligier JS5-Matra V12	1 lap behind	13/30
ret/dsq*	BRITISH GP	Brands Hatch	26	Ligier Gitanes	G	3.0 Ligier JS5-Matra V12	suspension/*spare car in restart	13/30
ret/dns	GERMAN GP	Nürburgring	26	Ligier Gitanes	G	3.0 Ligier JS5-Matra V12	gearbox at 1st start	6/28
2	AUSTRIAN GP	Österreichring	26	Ligier Gitanes	G	3.0 Ligier JS5-Matra V12		5/25
ret	DUTCH GP	Zandvoort	26	Ligier Gitanes	G	3.0 Ligier JS5-Matra V12	oil pressure	10/27
3	ITALIAN GP	Monza	26	Ligier Gitanes	G	3.0 Ligier JS5-Matra V12		1/29
ret	CANADIAN GP	Mosport Park	26	Ligier Gitanes	G	3.0 Ligier JS5-Matra V12	oil pressure	9/27
ret	US GP EAST	Watkins Glen	26	Ligier Gitanes	G	3.0 Ligier JS5-Matra V12	burst tyre-suspension damage	12/27
7	JAPANESE GP	Mount Fuji	26	Ligier Gitanes	G	3.0 Ligier JS5-Matra V12	1 lap behind	11/27

1977
Championship position: 10   Wins: 1   Pole positions: 0   Fastest laps: 1   Points scored: 18

	Race	Circuit	No	Entrant	Tyres	Car/Engine	Comment	Q Pos/Entries
nc	ARGENTINE GP	Buenos Aires	26	Ligier Gitanes	G	3.0 Ligier JS7-Matra V12	3 pit stops-misfire/-16 laps	15/21
ret	BRAZILIAN GP	Interlagos	26	Ligier Gitanes	G	3.0 Ligier JS7-Matra V12	accident	14/22
ret	SOUTH AFRICAN GP	Kyalami	26	Ligier Gitanes	G	3.0 Ligier JS7-Matra V12	hit by Pryce's crashing car	12/23
9/ret	US GP WEST	Long Beach	26	Ligier Gitanes	G	3.0 Ligier JS7-Matra V12	electrics/2 laps behind	5/22
7	SPANISH GP	Jarama	26	Ligier Gitanes	G	3.0 Ligier JS7-Matra V12	pit stop-loose wheel/1 lap behind/FL	2/31
7	MONACO GP	Monte Carlo	26	Ligier Gitanes	G	3.0 Ligier JS7-Matra V12		16/26
ret	BELGIAN GP	Zolder	26	Ligier Gitanes	G	3.0 Ligier JS7-Matra V12	engine	10/32
1	SWEDISH GP	Anderstorp	26	Ligier Gitanes	G	3.0 Ligier JS7-Matra V12		8/31
8	FRENCH GP	Dijon	26	Ligier Gitanes	G	3.0 Ligier JS7-Matra V12	collision-Stuck-pit stop/-2 laps	5/30
6	BRITISH GP	Silverstone	26	Ligier Gitanes	G	3.0 Ligier JS7-Matra V12	1 lap behind	15/36
ret	GERMAN GP	Hockenheim	26	Ligier Gitanes	G	3.0 Ligier JS7-Matra V12	engine	6/30
ret	AUSTRIAN GP	Österreichring	26	Ligier Gitanes	G	3.0 Ligier JS7-Matra V12	oil leak onto tyres	6/30
2	DUTCH GP	Zandvoort	26	Ligier Gitanes	G	3.0 Ligier JS7-Matra V12		2/34
8	ITALIAN GP	Monza	26	Ligier Gitanes	G	3.0 Ligier JS7-Matra V12	pit stop-overheating/-2 laps	8/34
7	US GP EAST	Watkins Glen	26	Ligier Gitanes	G	3.0 Ligier JS7-Matra V12	1 lap behind	10/27
ret	CANADIAN GP	Mosport Park	26	Ligier Gitanes	G	3.0 Ligier JS7-Matra V12	driveshaft	11/27
5/ret	JAPANESE GP	Mount Fuji	26	Ligier Gitanes	G	3.0 Ligier JS7-Matra V12	out of fuel/1 lap behind	5/23

1978
Championship position: 8th   Wins: 0   Pole positions: 0   Fastest laps: 0   Points scored: 19

	Race	Circuit	No	Entrant	Tyres	Car/Engine	Comment	Q Pos/Entries
16/ret	ARGENTINE GP	Buenos Aires	26	Ligier Gitanes	G	3.0 Ligier JS7-Matra V12	engine/2 laps behind	8/27
9	BRAZILIAN GP	Rio	26	Ligier Gitanes	G	3.0 Ligier JS7-Matra V12	pit stop-tyres/2 laps behind	14/28
5	SOUTH AFRICAN GP	Kyalami	26	Ligier Gitanes	G	3.0 Ligier JS7/9-Matra V12		13/30
dns	"	"	26	Ligier Gitanes	G	3.0 Ligier JS7-Matra V12	practice only	– / –
5	US GP WEST	Long Beach	26	Ligier Gitanes	G	3.0 Ligier JS7/9-Matra V12		14/30
dns	"	"	26	Ligier Gitanes	G	3.0 Ligier JS7-Matra V12	practice only-set grid time	– / –
ret	MONACO GP	Monte Carlo	26	Ligier Gitanes	G	3.0 Ligier JS9-Matra V12	gearbox	15/30
dns	"	"	26	Ligier Gitanes	G	3.0 Ligier JS7-Matra V12	practice only	– / –
5/ret	BELGIAN GP	Zolder	26	Ligier Gitanes	G	3.0 Ligier JS7/9-Matra V12	hit by Reutemann/-1 lap	14/30
3	SPANISH GP	Jarama	26	Ligier Gitanes	G	3.0 Ligier JS9-Matra V12		=9/29
dns	"	"	26	Ligier Gitanes	G	3.0 Ligier JS7/9-Matra V12	practice only	– / –
7	SWEDISH GP	Anderstorp	26	Ligier Gitanes	G	3.0 Ligier JS9-Matra V12	1 lap behind	11/27
dns	"	"	26	Ligier Gitanes	G	3.0 Ligier JS7/9-Matra V12	practice only	– / –
7	FRENCH GP	Paul Ricard	26	Ligier Gitanes	G	3.0 Ligier JS7/9-Matra V12		10/29
10	BRITISH GP	Brands Hatch	26	Ligier Gitanes	G	3.0 Ligier JS7/9-Matra V12	2 pit stops-tyres/-3 laps	7/30
3	GERMAN GP	Hockenheim	26	Ligier Gitanes	G	3.0 Ligier JS9-Matra V12		7/30
5	AUSTRIAN GP	Österreichring	26	Ligier Gitanes	G	3.0 Ligier JS9-Matra V12	1 lap behind	5/31
8	DUTCH GP	Zandvoort	26	Ligier Gitanes	G	3.0 Ligier JS9-Matra V12	1 lap behind	6/33
4	ITALIAN GP	Monza	26	Ligier Gitanes	G	3.0 Ligier JS9-Matra V12		8/32
11	US GP EAST	Watkins Glen	26	Ligier Gitanes	G	3.0 Ligier JS9-Matra V12	pit stop-tyre/1 lap behind	10/27
ret	CANADIAN GP	Montreal	26	Ligier Gitanes	G	3.0 Ligier JS9-Matra V12	transmission	10/28

1979
Championship position: 4th   Wins: 2   Pole positions: 4   Fastest laps: 2   Points scored: 36

1	ARGENTINE GP	Buenos Aires	26	Ligier Gitanes	G	3.0 Ligier JS11-Cosworth V8	*FL*	1/26
1	BRAZILIAN GP	Rio	26	Ligier Gitanes	G	3.0 Ligier JS11-Cosworth V8	*FL*	1/26
ret	SOUTH AFRICAN GP	Kyalami	26	Ligier Gitanes	G	3.0 Ligier JS11-Cosworth V8	*puncture-spun off*	6/26
ret	US GP WEST	Long Beach	26	Ligier Gitanes	G	3.0 Ligier JS11-Cosworth V8	*started from pit lane/brakes*	5/26
ret	SPANISH GP	Jarama	26	Ligier Gitanes	G	3.0 Ligier JS11-Cosworth V8	*engine*	1/27
2	BELGIAN GP	Zolder	26	Ligier Gitanes	G	3.0 Ligier JS11-Cosworth V8		1/28
ret	MONACO GP	Monte Carlo	26	Ligier Gitanes	G	3.0 Ligier JS11-Cosworth V8	*gearbox*	5/25
8	FRENCH GP	Dijon	26	Ligier Gitanes	G	3.0 Ligier JS11-Cosworth V8	*1 lap behind*	8/27
ret	BRITISH GP	Silverstone	26	Ligier Gitanes	G	3.0 Ligier JS11-Cosworth V8	*engine-plugs*	10/26
3	GERMAN GP	Hockenheim	26	Ligier Gitanes	G	3.0 Ligier JS11-Cosworth V8		3/26
3	AUSTRIAN GP	Österreichring	26	Ligier Gitanes	G	3.0 Ligier JS11-Cosworth V8		8/26
3	DUTCH GP	Zandvoort	26	Ligier Gitanes	G	3.0 Ligier JS11-Cosworth V8		7/26
ret	ITALIAN GP	Monza	26	Ligier Gitanes	G	3.0 Ligier JS11-Cosworth V8	*engine*	7/28
ret	CANADIAN GP	Montreal	26	Ligier Gitanes	G	3.0 Ligier JS11-Cosworth V8	*engine*	5/29
ret	US GP EAST	Watkins Glen	26	Ligier Gitanes	G	3.0 Ligier JS11-Cosworth V8	*spun off*	4/30

1980
Championship position: 4th   Wins: 1   Pole positions: 1   Fastest laps: 1   Points scored: 34

ret	ARGENTINE GP	Buenos Aires	26	Equipe Ligier Gitanes	G	3.0 Ligier JS11/15-Cosworth V8	*engine*	2/28
ret	BRAZILIAN GP	Interlagos	26	Equipe Ligier Gitanes	G	3.0 Ligier JS11/15-Cosworth V8	*electrics*	5/28
2	SOUTH AFRICAN GP	Kyalami	26	Equipe Ligier Gitanes	G	3.0 Ligier JS11/15-Cosworth V8		4/28
ret	US GP WEST	Long Beach	26	Equipe Ligier Gitanes	G	3.0 Ligier JS11/15-Cosworth V8	*puncture-suspension*	13/27
11	BELGIAN GP	Zolder	26	Equipe Ligier Gitanes	G	3.0 Ligier JS11/15-Cosworth V8	*pit stop-engine/-4 laps/FL*	3/27
2	MONACO GP	Monte Carlo	26	Equipe Ligier Gitanes	G	3.0 Ligier JS11/15-Cosworth V8		5/27
3	FRENCH GP	Paul Ricard	26	Equipe Ligier Gitanes	G	3.0 Ligier JS11/15-Cosworth V8		1/27
ret	BRITISH GP	Brands Hatch	26	Equipe Ligier Gitanes	G	3.0 Ligier JS11/15-Cosworth V8	*wheel/tyre failure-crashed*	2/27
1	GERMAN GP	Hockenheim	26	Equipe Ligier Gitanes	G	3.0 Ligier JS11/15-Cosworth V8		5/26
4	AUSTRIAN GP	Österreichring	26	Equipe Ligier Gitanes	G	3.0 Ligier JS11/15-Cosworth V8		5/25
3	DUTCH GP	Zandvoort	26	Equipe Ligier Gitanes	G	3.0 Ligier JS11/15-Cosworth V8		6/28
9	ITALIAN GP	Imola	26	Equipe Ligier Gitanes	G	3.0 Ligier JS11/15-Cosworth V8	*1 lap behind*	20/28
8/ret	CANADIAN GP	Montreal	26	Equipe Ligier Gitanes	G	3.0 Ligier JS11/15-Cosworth V8	*out of fuel/2 laps behind*	9/28
5	US GP EAST	Watkins Glen	26	Equipe Ligier Gitanes	G	3.0 Ligier JS11/15-Cosworth V8	*1 lap behind*	12/27

1981
Championship position: 4th   Wins: 2   Pole positions: 1   Fastest laps: 1   Points scored: 44

ret	US GP WEST	Long Beach	26	Equipe Talbot Gitanes	M	3.0 Ligier JS17-Matra V12	*collision with Cheever*	12/29
6	BRAZILIAN GP	Rio	26	Equipe Talbot Gitanes	M	3.0 Ligier JS17-Matra V12		16/30
ret	ARGENTINE GP	Buenos Aires	26	Equipe Talbot Gitanes	M	3.0 Ligier JS17-Matra V12	*vibration/handling*	21/29
ret	SAN MARINO GP	Imola	26	Equipe Talbot Gitanes	M	3.0 Ligier JS17-Matra V12	*accident with Arnoux*	10/30
2	BELGIAN GP	Zolder	26	Equipe Talbot Gitanes	M	3.0 Ligier JS17-Matra V12		9/31
3	MONACO GP	Monte Carlo	26	Equipe Talbot Gitanes	M	3.0 Ligier JS17-Matra V12		8/31
2	SPANISH GP	Jarama	26	Equipe Talbot Gitanes	M	3.0 Ligier JS17-Matra V12		1/30
ret	FRENCH GP	Dijon	26	Equipe Talbot Gitanes	M	3.0 Ligier JS17-Matra V12	*front suspension*	6/29
3	BRITISH GP	Silverstone	26	Equipe Talbot Gitanes	M	3.0 Ligier JS17-Matra V12	*1 lap behind*	14/30
3	GERMAN GP	Hockenheim	26	Equipe Talbot Gitanes	M	3.0 Ligier JS17-Matra V12		7/30
1	AUSTRIAN GP	Österreichring	26	Equipe Talbot Gitanes	M	3.0 Ligier JS17-Matra V12	*FL*	4/28
ret	DUTCH GP	Zandvoort	26	Equipe Talbot Gitanes	M	3.0 Ligier JS17-Matra V12	*collision with Reutemann*	6/30
ret	ITALIAN GP	Monza	26	Equipe Talbot Gitanes	M	3.0 Ligier JS17-Matra V12	*puncture*	4/30
1	CANADIAN GP	Montreal	26	Equipe Talbot Gitanes	M	3.0 Ligier JS17-Matra V12		10/30
6	CAESARS PALACE GP	Las Vegas	26	Equipe Talbot Gitanes	M	3.0 Ligier JS17-Matra V12	*pit stop-tyres*	12/30

1982
Championship position: 17th=   Wins: 0   Pole positions: 0   Fastest laps: 0   Points scored: 5

ret	SOUTH AFRICAN GP	Kyalami	26	Equipe Talbot Gitanes	M	3.0 Ligier JS17-Matra V12	*fuel vaporisation-misfire*	11/30
ret	BRAZILIAN GP	Rio	26	Equipe Talbot Gitanes	M	3.0 Ligier JS17-Matra V12	*handling/misfire*	24/31
ret	US GP WEST	Long Beach	26	Equipe Talbot Gitanes	M	3.0 Ligier JS17B-Matra V12	*ran off track and stalled*	15/31
9	BELGIAN GP	Zolder	26	Equipe Talbot Gitanes	M	3.0 Ligier JS17-Matra V12	*pit stop-tyres/4 laps behind*	19/32
ret	MONACO GP	Monte Carlo	26	Equipe Talbot Gitanes	M	3.0 Ligier JS19-Matra V12	*handling*	18/31
6	US GP (DETROIT)	Detroit	26	Equipe Talbot Gitanes	M	3.0 Ligier JS17-Matra V12	*1 lap behind*	13/28
ret	CANADIAN GP	Montreal	26	Equipe Talbot Gitanes	M	3.0 Ligier JS17-Matra V12	*handling*	19/29
ret	DUTCH GP	Zandvoort	26	Equipe Talbot Gitanes	M	3.0 Ligier JS19-Matra V12	*handling*	21/31
ret	BRITISH GP	Brands Hatch	26	Equipe Talbot Gitanes	M	3.0 Ligier JS19-Matra V12	*gearbox*	20/30
14	FRENCH GP	Paul Ricard	26	Equipe Talbot Gitanes	M	3.0 Ligier JS19-Matra V12	*3 pit stops-handling-tyres/-3 laps*	16/30
ret	GERMAN GP	Hockenheim	26	Equipe Talbot Gitanes	M	3.0 Ligier JS19-Matra V12	*handling*	16/30
3	AUSTRIAN GP	Österreichring	26	Equipe Talbot Gitanes	M	3.0 Ligier JS19-Matra V12	*1 lap behind*	14/29
ret	SWISS GP	Dijon	26	Equipe Talbot Gitanes	M	3.0 Ligier JS19-Matra V12	*skirts/handling*	13/29
ret	ITALIAN GP	Monza	26	Equipe Talbot Gitanes	M	3.0 Ligier JS19-Matra V12	*gearbox*	21/30
ret	CAESARS PALACE GP	Las Vegas	26	Equipe Talbot Gitanes	M	3.0 Ligier JS19-Matra V12	*ignition*	11/30

1983
Championship position: 11th   Wins: 0   Pole positions: 0   Fastest laps: 0   Points scored: 11

4	BRAZILIAN GP	Rio	2	TAG Williams Team	G	3.0 Williams FW08C-Cosworth V8		18/27
4	US GP WEST	Long Beach	2	TAG Williams Team	G	3.0 Williams FW08C-Cosworth V8	*1 lap behind*	4/28
6	FRENCH GP	Paul Ricard	2	TAG Williams Team	G	3.0 Williams FW08C-Cosworth V8	*pit stop-fuel/1 lap behind*	19/29
7	SAN MARINO GP	Imola	2	TAG Williams Team	G	3.0 Williams FW08C-Cosworth V8	*pit stop-fuel/1 lap behind*	16/28
ret	MONACO GP	Monte Carlo	2	TAG Williams Team	G	3.0 Williams FW08C-Cosworth V8	*gearbox*	8/28
6	BELGIAN GP	Spa	2	TAG Williams Team	G	3.0 Williams FW08C-Cosworth V8		11/28
5	US GP (DETROIT)	Detroit	2	TAG Williams Team	G	3.0 Williams FW08C-Cosworth V8		20/27
ret	CANADIAN GP	Montreal	2	TAG Williams Team	G	3.0 Williams FW08C-Cosworth V8	*gearbox*	13/28
12	BRITISH GP	Silverstone	2	TAG Williams Team	G	3.0 Williams FW08C-Cosworth V8	*pit stop-fuel/2 laps behind*	20/29
6	GERMAN GP	Hockenheim	2	TAG Williams Team	G	3.0 Williams FW08C-Cosworth V8	*1 lap behind*	15/29
ret	AUSTRIAN GP	Österreichring	2	TAG Williams Team	G	3.0 Williams FW08C-Cosworth V8	*collision-Ghinzani and Surer*	24/29
ret	DUTCH GP	Zandvoort	2	TAG Williams Team	G	3.0 Williams FW08C-Cosworth V8	*tyres*	17/29
dnq	ITALIAN GP	Monza	2	TAG Williams Team	G	3.0 Williams FW08C-Cosworth V8		28/29
dnq	EUROPEAN GP	Brands Hatch	2	TAG Williams Team	G	3.0 Williams FW08C-Cosworth V8		29/29
ret	SOUTH AFRICAN GP	Kyalami	2	TAG Williams Team	G	1.5 t/c Williams FW09-Honda V6	*spun off on lap 1*	10/26

	1984			Championship position: 14th=	Wins: 0	Pole positions: 0	Fastest laps: 0	Points scored: 5		
ret	BRAZILIAN GP	Rio	5	Williams Grand Prix Engineering	G	1.5 t/c Williams FW09-Honda V6		electrics	13/27
ret	SOUTH AFRICAN GP	Kyalami	5	Williams Grand Prix Engineering	G	1.5 t/c Williams FW09-Honda V6		c.v. joint	11/27
ret	BELGIAN GP	Zolder	5	Williams Grand Prix Engineering	G	1.5 t/c Williams FW09-Honda V6		electrics	15/27
ret	SAN MARINO GP	Imola	5	Williams Grand Prix Engineering	G	1.5 t/c Williams FW09-Honda V6		engine	15/28
8	FRENCH GP	Dijon	5	Williams Grand Prix Engineering	G	1.5 t/c Williams FW09-Honda V6		1 lap behind	12/27
8*	MONACO GP	Monte Carlo	5	Williams Grand Prix Engineering	G	1.5 t/c Williams FW09-Honda V6		* 3rd place car dsq/-1 lap	16/27
ret	CANADIAN GP	Montreal	5	Williams Grand Prix Engineering	G	1.5 t/c Williams FW09-Honda V6		lost turbo boost	17/26
5*	US GP (DETROIT)	Detroit	5	Williams Grand Prix Engineering	G	1.5 t/c Williams FW09-Honda V6		* 2nd place car dsq/-1 lap	19/27
4	US GP (DALLAS)	Dallas	5	Williams Grand Prix Engineering	G	1.5 t/c Williams FW09-Honda V6		2 laps behind	24/27
ret	BRITISH GP	Brands Hatch	5	Williams Grand Prix Engineering	G	1.5 t/c Williams FW09B-Honda V6		water pump	16/27
ret	GERMAN GP	Hockenheim	5	Williams Grand Prix Engineering	G	1.5 t/c Williams FW09B-Honda V6		engine	12/27
ret	AUSTRIAN GP	Österreichring	5	Williams Grand Prix Engineering	G	1.5 t/c Williams FW09B-Honda V6		engine	11/28
ret	DUTCH GP	Zandvoort	5	Williams Grand Prix Engineering	G	1.5 t/c Williams FW09B-Honda V6		engine	8/27
ret	ITALIAN GP	Monza	5	Williams Grand Prix Engineering	G	1.5 t/c Williams FW09B-Honda V6		turbo	13/27
ret	EUROPEAN GP	Nürburgring	5	Williams Grand Prix Engineering	G	1.5 t/c Williams FW09B-Honda V6		engine	14/26
14	PORTUGUESE GP	Estoril	5	Williams Grand Prix Engineering	G	1.5 t/c Williams FW09B-Honda V6		2 pit stops-bodywork/-3 laps	15/27
	1985			Championship position: 9	Wins: 0	Pole positions: 0	Fastest laps: 1	Points scored: 16		
6	BRAZILIAN GP	Rio	26	Equipe Ligier	P	1.5 t/c Ligier JS25-Renault V6		hit de Cesaris-pit stop/-2 laps	15/25
ret	PORTUGUESE GP	Estoril	26	Equipe Ligier	P	1.5 t/c Ligier JS25-Renault V6		tyres/handling	18/26
ret	SAN MARINO GP	Imola	26	Equipe Ligier	P	1.5 t/c Ligier JS25-Renault V6		turbo	16/26
6	MONACO GP	Monte Carlo	26	Equipe Ligier	P	1.5 t/c Ligier JS25-Renault V6		spin/1 lap behind	16/26
8	CANADIAN GP	Montreal	26	Equipe Ligier Gitanes	P	1.5 t/c Ligier JS25-Renault V6		1 min pen-jumped start/-1 lap	19/25
12	US GP (DETROIT)	Detroit	26	Equipe Ligier Gitanes	P	1.5 t/c Ligier JS25-Renault V6		pit stop/5 laps behind	16/25
ret	FRENCH GP	Paul Ricard	26	Equipe Ligier Gitanes	P	1.5 t/c Ligier JS25-Renault V6		turbo	15/26
3	BRITISH GP	Silverstone	26	Equipe Ligier Gitanes	P	1.5 t/c Ligier JS25-Renault V6		1 lap behind	16/26
3	GERMAN GP	Nürburgring	26	Equipe Ligier Gitanes	P	1.5 t/c Ligier JS25-Renault V6			13/27
ret	AUSTRIAN GP	Österreichring	26	Equipe Ligier Gitanes	P	1.5 t/c Ligier JS25-Renault V6		lost wheel-crashed	15/27
ret	DUTCH GP	Zandvoort	26	Equipe Ligier Gitanes	P	1.5 t/c Ligier JS25-Renault V6		electrics	13/27
ret	ITALIAN GP	Monza	26	Equipe Ligier Gitanes	P	1.5 t/c Ligier JS25-Renault V6		engine	20/26
11/ret	BELGIAN GP	Spa	26	Equipe Ligier Gitanes	P	1.5 t/c Ligier JS25-Renault V6		hit barrier/5 laps behind	17/24
ret	EUROPEAN GP	Brands Hatch	26	Equipe Ligier Gitanes	P	1.5 t/c Ligier JS25-Renault V6		engine/FL	10/27
2	AUSTRALIAN GP	Adelaide	26	Equipe Ligier Gitanes	P	1.5 t/c Ligier JS25-Renault V6			20/25
	1986			Championship position: 8	Wins: 0	Pole positions: 0	Fastest laps: 0	Points scored: 14		
3	BRAZILIAN GP	Rio	26	Equipe Ligier	P	1.5 t/c Ligier JS27-Renault V6			5/25
ret	SPANISH GP	Jerez	26	Equipe Ligier	P	1.5 t/c Ligier JS27-Renault V6		driveshaft	8/25
ret	SAN MARINO GP	Imola	26	Equipe Ligier	P	1.5 t/c Ligier JS27-Renault V6		transmission	14/26
6	MONACO GP	Monte Carlo	26	Equipe Ligier	P	1.5 t/c Ligier JS27-Renault V6		started from back/-1 lap	7/26
5	BELGIAN GP	Spa	26	Equipe Ligier	P	1.5 t/c Ligier JS27-Renault V6			17/25
7	CANADIAN GP	Montreal	26	Equipe Ligier	P	1.5 t/c Ligier JS27-Renault V6		1 lap behind	8/25
2	US GP (DETROIT)	Detroit	26	Equipe Ligier	P	1.5 t/c Ligier JS27-Renault V6			6/26
6	FRENCH GP	Paul Ricard	26	Equipe Ligier	P	1.5 t/c Ligier JS27-Renault V6		2 pit stops-tyres/1 lap behind	11/26
ret/dns	BRITISH GP	Brands Hatch	26	Equipe Ligier	P	1.5 t/c Ligier JS27-Renault V6		accident-1st start/did not restart	19/26

GP Starts: 174 (176)   GP Wins: 6   Pole positions: 7   Fastest laps: 6   Points: 228

FRANCK LAGORCE

This quiet Frenchman is just another in the ever-lengthening queue of Grand Prix aspirants to have graduated with honours from F3000, only to find no outlet for their talent, for he has shown in the junior formulae that he is a fine prospect. After six seasons of karting, Franck's car racing career was given a flying start in 1987 with second place in the Volant Ekron and the opportunity to move into FF1600. In 1990 he stepped into Formule Renault and finished second in the championship, before two seasons in French F3 with a Dallara-Opel which culminated in his being crowned champion in 1992.

Joining DAMS in 1993, Lagorce was number two to Panis, and though Olivier was to take the crown Franck's role was not entirely subordinate, for he won the final two rounds at Magny Cours and Nogaro to take equal fourth in the series with Gil de Ferran. He switched to the rival Apomatox team in 1994, scoring two fine wins, but in truth he let the championship slip through his fingers after looking a good bet throughout the year. Already the official reserve and test driver with Ligier, Franck was given a tantalising glimpse of Grand Prix racing with a couple of end-of-season drives, but spent 1995 consigned to his Ligier testing role.

After returning to racing competition in the Renault Spyder series, Franck joined Pescarolo and Collard in the Courage at Le Mans in 1996, taking seventh place. Deciding that he would rather be in a factory-backed sports car than struggling with a back-of-the-grid Formula 1 team, Lagorce abandoned his efforts to find a place on the Grand Prix stage and opted to join Éric Bernard in the DAMS-run Panoz for 1997.

Franck has since been part of both the Nissan and Mercedes squads for the Le Mans 24 Hours.

LAGORCE, Franck (F) b 1/9/1968, L'Hay-Les-Roses, nr Paris

	1994			Championship position: Unplaced					
	Race	Circuit	No	Entrant	Tyres	Car/Engine		Comment	Q Pos/Entries
ret	JAPANESE GP	Suzuka	25	Ligier Gitanes Blondes	G	3.5 Ligier JS39B-Renault V10		touched by Martini-spun off	20/28
11	AUSTRALIAN GP	Adelaide	25	Ligier Gitanes Blondes	G	3.5 Ligier JS39B-Renault V10		2 laps behind	20/28

GP Starts: 2   GP Wins: 0   Pole positions: 0   Fastest laps: 0   Points: 0

JAN LAMMERS

In a career stretching back more than twenty-five years, Lammers has tried his hand at most forms of racing since his early success as the Dutch Group 1 saloon car champion. Progressing through the single-seater formulae, the pint-sized Dutchman took the 1978 European F3 championship by the narrowest of margins with a Ralt, earning a chance with the restructured Shadow team alongside Elio de Angelis for 1979. The cars were not competitive, and Lammers found little more joy during his associations with ATS, Ensign and Theodore over the next two seasons, although he startled the Formula 1 fraternity at Long Beach in 1980 by qualifying his car fourth on the grid.

After his Grand Prix career had fizzled out, Jan enjoyed a productive spell in the Richard Lloyd Porsche sports car team before having a crack at Indy Car racing late in 1985. However, he found his greatest success in the TWR Jaguar team, partnering John Watson to three wins (Jarama, Monza and Mount Fuji) in 1987, and winning Le Mans in 1988 with Dumfries and Wallace. He also won the Daytona 24-hour race for Jaguar twice (1988 and '90). After racing in Japanese F3000 in 1991, Lammers joined the Toyota sports car team for 1992, and made an unexpected return to F1 at the end of the year with March. But plans for a full Grand Prix season in 1993 came to nought when the financially bereft Bicester team was finally forced to close its doors, leaving him to take in a limited programme of European F3000.

Jan was a somewhat surprising choice to race the TWR Volvo estate alongside Rickard Rydell in the 1994 BTCC, and though excellent progress was made in the car's debut year Lammers still hankered after a single-seater career. The Dutchman kicked off 1995 with a win in the F3000/F2 invitation race at Kyalami, and then took second place in the Sebring 12 Hours in a Ferrari with Bell and Wallace before he lined up with Vortex for a projected full season in F3000. Unfortunately, Jan rarely rose above the midfield positions and quit in frustration after just three races.

Since 1996 Lammers has concentrated on sports car and GT racing, initially with the factory Lotus team and latterly with the Konrad Motorsports Lola.

LAMMERS, Jan (NL) b 2/6/1956, Zandvoort

	1979	Championship position: Unplaced							
	Race	Circuit	No	Entrant	Tyres	Car/Engine	Comment	Q Pos/Entries
ret	ARGENTINE GP	Buenos Aires	17	Samson Shadow Racing Team	G	3.0 Shadow DN9-Cosworth V8	transmission	21/26
14	BRAZILIAN GP	Interlagos	17	Samson Shadow Racing Team	G	3.0 Shadow DN9-Cosworth V8	1 lap behind	21/26
ret	SOUTH AFRICAN GP	Kyalami	17	Samson Shadow Racing Team	G	3.0 Shadow DN9-Cosworth V8	collision with Rebaque	21/26
ret	US GP WEST	Long Beach	17	Samson Shadow Racing Team	G	3.0 Shadow DN9-Cosworth V8	collision-Pironi-bent suspension	14/26
12	SPANISH GP	Jarama	17	Samson Shadow Racing Team	G	3.0 Shadow DN9-Cosworth V8	2 laps behind	24/27
10	BELGIAN GP	Zolder	17	Samson Shadow Racing Team	G	3.0 Shadow DN9-Cosworth V8	2 laps behind	21/28
dnq	MONACO GP	Monte Carlo	17	Samson Shadow Racing Team	G	3.0 Shadow DN9-Cosworth V8		23/25
18	FRENCH GP	Dijon	17	Samson Shadow Racing Team	G	3.0 Shadow DN9-Cosworth V8	pit stop/7 laps behind	21/27
11	BRITISH GP	Silverstone	17	Samson Shadow Racing Team	G	3.0 Shadow DN9-Cosworth V8	3 laps behind	21/26
10	GERMAN GP	Hockenheim	17	Samson Shadow Racing Team	G	3.0 Shadow DN9-Cosworth V8	1 lap behind	20/26
ret	AUSTRIAN GP	Österreichring	17	Samson Shadow Racing Team	G	3.0 Shadow DN9-Cosworth V8	crashed	23/26
ret	DUTCH GP	Zandvoort	17	Samson Shadow Racing Team	G	3.0 Shadow DN9-Cosworth V8	gearbox	23/26
dnq	ITALIAN GP	Monza	17	Samson Shadow Racing Team	G	3.0 Shadow DN9-Cosworth V8		25/28
9	CANADIAN GP	Montreal	17	Samson Shadow Racing Team	G	3.0 Shadow DN9-Cosworth V8	5 laps behind	21/29
dnq	US GP EAST	Watkins Glen	17	Samson Shadow Racing Team	G	3.0 Shadow DN9-Cosworth V8		27/30
	1980	Championship position: Unplaced							
dnq	ARGENTINE GP	Buenos Aires	10	Team ATS	G	3.0 ATS D3-Cosworth V8		27/28
dnq	BRAZILIAN GP	Interlagos	10	Team ATS	G	3.0 ATS D3-Cosworth V8		25/28
dnq	SOUTH AFRICAN GP	Kyalami	9	Team ATS	G	3.0 ATS D3-Cosworth V8	replaced injured Surer	28/28
ret	US GP WEST	Long Beach	9	Team ATS	G	3.0 ATS D4-Cosworth V8	driveshaft-lap 1	4/27
12/ret	BELGIAN GP	Zolder	9	Team ATS	G	3.0 ATS D4-Cosworth V8	engine/8 laps behind	15/27
nc	MONACO GP	Monte Carlo	9	Team ATS	G	3.0 ATS D4-Cosworth V8	hit Patrese-pit stop/-12 laps	13/27
dnq	FRENCH GP	Paul Ricard	14	Unipart Racing Team	G	3.0 Ensign N180-Cosworth V8		26/27
dnq	BRITISH GP	Brands Hatch	14	Unipart Racing Team	G	3.0 Ensign N180-Cosworth V8		25/27
14	GERMAN GP	Hockenheim	14	Unipart Racing Team	G	3.0 Ensign N180-Cosworth V8	1 lap behind	24/26
dnq	AUSTRIAN GP	Österreichring	14	Unipart Racing Team	G	3.0 Ensign N180-Cosworth V8		25/25
dnq	DUTCH GP	Zandvoort	14	Unipart Racing Team	G	3.0 Ensign N180-Cosworth V8		26/28
dnq	ITALIAN GP	Imola	14	Unipart Racing Team	G	3.0 Ensign N180-Cosworth V8		27/28
12	CANADIAN GP	Montreal	14	Unipart Racing Team	G	3.0 Ensign N180-Cosworth V8	4 laps behind	19/28
dnq/ret	US GP EAST	Watkins Glen	14	Unipart Racing Team	G	3.0 Ensign N180-Cosworth V8	1st reserve/steering mounting	25/27
	1981	Championship position: Unplaced							
ret	US GP WEST	Long Beach	9	Team ATS	M	3.0 ATS D4-Cosworth V8	collision with Giacomelli	21/29
dnq	BRAZILIAN GP	Rio	9	Team ATS	M	3.0 ATS D4-Cosworth V8		25/30
12	ARGENTINE GP	Buenos Aires	9	Team ATS	M	3.0 ATS D4-Cosworth V8	pit stop/2 laps behind	23/29
dnq	SAN MARINO GP	Imola	9	Team ATS	M	3.0 ATS D4-Cosworth V8		27/30
	1982	Championship position: Unplaced							
dnq	BELGIAN GP	Zolder	33	Theodore Racing Team	A	3.0 Theodore TY02-Cosworth V8		30/32

dnq	MONACO GP	Monte Carlo	33	Theodore Racing Team	G	3.0 Theodore TY02-Cosworth V8			22/31
dns	US GP (DETROIT)	Detroit	33	Theodore Racing Team	G	3.0 Theodore TY02-Cosworth V8	*injured in unofficial practice*		– / –
ret	DUTCH GP	Zandvoort	33	Theodore Racing Team	G	3.0 Theodore TY02-Cosworth V8	*engine*		26/31
dnq	BRITISH GP	Brands Hatch	33	Theodore Racing Team	G	3.0 Theodore TY02-Cosworth V8			28/30
dnq	FRENCH GP	Paul Ricard	33	Theodore Racing Team	G	3.0 Theodore TY02-Cosworth V8			27/30
	1992	Championship position: Unplaced							
ret	JAPANESE GP	Suzuka	16	March F1	G	3.5 March CG911-Ilmor V10	*clutch*		23/26
12	AUSTRALIAN GP	Adelaide	16	March F1	G	3.5 March CG911-Ilmor V10	*3 laps behind*		25/26

GP Starts: 23   GP Wins: 0   Pole positions: 0   Fastest laps: 0   Points: 0

LAMY, Pedro (P) b 20/3/1972, Aldeia Galega

	1993	Championship position: Unplaced							
	Race	*Circuit*	*No*	*Entrant*	*Tyres*	*Car/Engine*	*Comment*		*Q Pos/Entries*
11/ret	ITALIAN GP	Monza	11	Team Lotus	G	3.5 Lotus 107B-Ford HB V8	*engine/4 laps behind*		26/26
ret	PORTUGUESE GP	Estoril	11	Team Lotus	G	3.5 Lotus 107B-Ford HB V8	*accident*		18/26
13/ret	JAPANESE GP	Suzuka	11	Team Lotus	G	3.5 Lotus 107B-Ford HB V8	*accident*		20/24
ret	AUSTRALIAN GP	Adelaide	11	Team Lotus	G	3.5 Lotus 107B-Ford HB V8	*collision-Katayama on lap 1*		23/24
	1994	Championship position: Unplaced							
10	BRAZILIAN GP	Interlagos	11	Team Lotus	G	3.5 Lotus 107C-Mugen Honda V10	*3 laps behind*		24/28
8	PACIFIC GP	T.I. Circuit	11	Team Lotus	G	3.5 Lotus 107C-Mugen Honda V10	*4 laps behind*		24/28
ret	SAN MARINO GP	Imola	11	Team Lotus	G	3.5 Lotus 107C-Mugen Honda V10	*hit Lehto at first start-*		22/28
11	MONACO GP	Monte Carlo	11	Team Lotus	G	3.5 Lotus 107C-Mugen Honda V10	*5 laps behind*		19/24
	1995	Championship position: 17th= Wins: 0 Pole positions: 0 Fastest laps: 0 Points scored: 1							
9	HUNGARIAN GP	Hungaroring	23	Minardi Scuderia Italia	G	3.0 Minardi M195-Ford EDM V8	*3 laps behind*		15/24
10	BELGIAN GP	Spa	23	Minardi Scuderia Italia	G	3.0 Minardi M195-Ford EDM V8			17/24
ret	ITALIAN GP	Monza	23	Minardi Scuderia Italia	G	3.0 Minardi M195-Ford EDM V8	*differential on lap 1*		19/24
ret	PORTUGUESE GP	Estoril	23	Minardi Scuderia Italia	G	3.0 Minardi M195-Ford EDM V8	*gearbox*		17/24
9	EUROPEAN GP	Nürburgring	23	Minardi Scuderia Italia	G	3.0 Minardi M195-Ford EDM V8	*3 laps behind*		16/24
13	PACIFIC GP	T.I. Circuit	23	Minardi Scuderia Italia	G	3.0 Minardi M195-Ford EDM V8	*3 laps behind*		14/24
11	JAPANESE GP	Suzuka	23	Minardi Scuderia Italia	G	3.0 Minardi M195-Ford EDM V8	*2 laps behind*		17/24
6	AUSTRALIAN GP	Adelaide	23	Minardi Scuderia Italia	G	3.0 Minardi M195-Ford EDM V8	*3 laps behind*		17/24
	1996	Championship position: Unplaced							
ret	AUSTRALIAN GP	Melbourne	20	Minardi Team	G	3.0 Minardi 195B-Ford EDM V8	*seat belts*		17/22
10	BRAZILIAN GP	Interlagos	20	Minardi Team	G	3.0 Minardi 195B-Ford EDM V8	*3 laps behind*		18/22
ret	ARGENTINE GP	Buenos Aires	20	Minardi Team	G	3.0 Minardi 195B-Ford EDM V8	*differential*		19/22
12	EUROPEAN GP	Nürburgring	20	Minardi Team	G	3.0 Minardi 195B-Ford EDM V8	*2 laps behind*		19/22
9	SAN MARINO GP	Imola	20	Minardi Team	G	3.0 Minardi 195B-Ford EDM V8	*2 laps behind*		18/22
ret	MONACO GP	Monte Carlo	20	Minardi Team	G	3.0 Minardi 195B-Ford EDM V8	*collision with Fisichella*		19/22
ret	SPANISH GP	Barcelona	20	Minardi Team	G	3.0 Minardi 195B-Ford EDM V8	*collision damage at start*		18/22
ret	CANADIAN GP	Montreal	20	Minardi Team	G	3.0 Minardi 195B-Ford EDM V8	*hit by Brundle*		19/22
12	FRENCH GP	Magny Cours	20	Minardi Team	G	3.0 Minardi 195B-Ford EDM V8	*3 laps behind*		19/22
ret	BRITISH GP	Silverstone	20	Minardi Team	G	3.0 Minardi 195B-Ford EDM V8	*hydraulic pressue*		20/22
12	GERMAN GP	Hockenheim	20	Minardi Team	G	3.0 Minardi 195B-Ford EDM V8	*2 laps behind*		18/20
ret	HUNGARIAN GP	Hungaroring	20	Minardi Team	G	3.0 Minardi 195B-Ford EDM V8	*suspension*		19/20
10	BELGIAN GP	Spa	20	Minardi Team	G	3.0 Minardi 195B-Ford EDM V8	*1 lap behind*		19/20
ret	ITALIAN GP	Monza	20	Minardi Team	G	3.0 Minardi 195B-Ford EDM V8	*engine*		18/20
16	PORTUGUESE GP	Estoril	20	Minardi Team	G	3.0 Minardi 195B-Ford EDM V8	*5 laps behind*		19/20
12	JAPANESE GP	Suzuka	20	Minardi Team	G	3.0 Minardi 195B-Ford EDM V8	*2 laps behind*		18/20

GP Starts: 32   GP Wins: 0   Pole positions: 0   Fastest laps: 0   Points: 1

LANDI, Chico (Francisco) (BR) b 14/7/1907 – d 7/6/1989, São Paulo

	1951	Championship position: Unplaced						
	Race	*Circuit*	*No*	*Entrant*	*Tyres*	*Q Pos/Entries*		
ret	ITALIAN GP	Monza	12	Francisco Landi	P	4.5 Ferrari 375F1/50 V12	*transmission-lap 1*	16/22
	1952	Championship position: Unplaced						
9*	DUTCH GP	Zandvoort	16	Escuderia Bandeirantes	P	2.0 Maserati A6GCM 6	** Flinterman took over/-7 laps*	16/18
8	ITALIAN GP	Monza	48	Escuderia Bandeirantes	P	2.0 Maserati A6GCM 6	*4 laps behind*	18/35
	1953	Championship position: Unplaced						
ret	SWISS GP	Bremgarten	4	Escuderia Bandeirantes	P	2.0 Maserati A6GCM 6	*gearbox*	20/23
ret	ITALIAN GP	Monza	42	Scuderia Milano	P	2.0 Maserati A6GCM 6	*engine-piston*	21/30
	1956	Championship position: 20th= Wins: 0 Pole positions: 0 Fastest laps: 0 Points scored: 1.5						
4*	ARGENTINE GP	Buenos Aires	10	Officine Alfieri Maserati	P	2.5 Maserati 250F 6	** Gerini took over/-6 laps*	11/15

GP Starts: 6   GP Wins: 0   Pole positions: 0   Fastest laps: 0   Points: 1.5

LANG, Hermann (D) b 6/4/1909, Bad Cannstatt, nr Stuttgart – d 19/10/1987, Bad Cannstatt, nr Stuttgart

	1953	Championship position: 11th= Wins: 0 Pole positions: 0 Fastest laps: 0 Points scored: 2						
	Race	*Circuit*	*No*	*Entrant*	*Tyres*	*Car/Engine*	*Comment*	*Q Pos/Entries*
5	SWISS GP	Bremgarten	34	Officine Alfieri Maserati	P	2.0 Maserati A6GCM 6	*stood in for González/-3 laps*	11/23
	1954	Championship position: Unplaced						
ret	GERMAN GP	Nürburgring	21	Daimler Benz AG	C	2.5 Mercedes-Benz W196 8	*spun off*	11/23

GP Starts: 2   GP Wins: 0   Pole positions: 0   Fastest laps: 0   Points: 2

PEDRO LAMY

A former motocrosser and karting champion, Lamy won the Portuguese FF1600 title in 1989 to quickly graduate to the GM Lotus Euroseries. Blindingly fast in pre-season testing, Pedro suffered a shock when the racing began and he struggled to qualify, but a switch of teams soon helped restore his confidence and he ended the season strongly by winning the final round of the German series, thus ensuring a move to replace champion Barrichello in the Draco Racing team for 1991. He was out of the traps with a succession of wins to build up such a healthy points cushion that he could even afford to have a couple of shunts at Spa and Imola on his way to the championship.

With sound backing and shrewd management, Pedro opted for a season of German Formula 3 for 1992 and this was the year that he really came to prominence. Totally dominating proceedings in his WTS Reynard-Opel, he won 11 races in the 26-round series and underlined his mastery when he also won the big Marlboro Zandvoort meeting.

A year in F3000 furthered his reputation as a very quick – but sometimes erratic – driver and some of his track manners were dubious to say the least. He won one race, at Pau, and remained in contention for the title until the final round when a collision cost him his chance. By now he had been called into the Lotus line-up at Monza to replace the unfit Zanardi. Lamy had a tough baptism but, with the backing of Portuguese sponsors, secured a full-time ride with the team for 1994.

His season suffered a setback at Imola where he was fortunate to escpape unscathed when his Lotus ran into the back of Lehto's stalled Benetton and was soon shattered when he was involved in a massive testing accident at Silverstone. Lamy's car ended up over the barriers with Pedro suffering fractured and dislocated knees and a broken wrist, but it could have been much, much worse. Happily, he made an amazingly swift recovery, and was soon back in the paddock looking to get back into competition at the earliest opportunity. In the event he had to wait until the middle of 1995 when Minardi finally decided to dispense with the services of Pierluigi Martini, but he was quickly back in the groove, matching the performances of team-mate Luca Badoer. Sixth place at the season's finale in Adelaide brought the softly spoken Lamy his first World Championship point, and a seat with the team in 1996.

With the demise of Simtek, Pacific and Forti, Minardi were once again consigned to the back of the field, and Lamy's main challenge came from his team-mates, Fisichella, Marques and later Lavaggi. The former in particular proved a stern test, and when the pair took each other out on the first lap at Monaco Giancarlo Minardi not unnaturally castigated his young chargers. Unfortunately Pedro was out of the GP frame for 1997 and he successfully chased a GT ride with Porsche, taking fifth at Le Mans.

He joined Olivier Beretta to race the works Chrysler Viper in 1998, and the pair stormed to the GT2 title, scoring eight wins in their class. The ambitious Lamy, however, was keen to move up to prototypes and, after winning a place in the ill-fated works Mercedes squad for Le Mans alongside Schneider and Lagorce, the Portuguese driver sampled life in the American Le Mans Series with a BMW V12 LM in the hope of running the full season in 2000.

CHICO LANDI

Landi was the first Brazilian ace to try his luck in Europe, making the move in the late forties after building up a fine record with his Alfa Romeo. He won the Bari GP in a Ferrari in 1948, and raced spasmodically in Grands Prix and other events over the next few seasons.

His best single-seater result was a second place in the Albi GP with a Ferrari T375 in 1952, a season which also saw him gain a string of fine placings at home. Landi raced on into the late fifties, before retiring to become a leading figure in the administration of Brazilian motor sport.

HERMANN LANG

One of the true stars of pre-war racing, Lang had been a motor cycling champion in 1930 and 1931 before he joined Mercedes in 1933, initially working in the experimental department and then, in 1934, as Fagioli's mechanic. Given his chance to race the following season, young Lang immediately tamed the fearsome silver beasts and became a full team member in 1937, celebrating with wins at Tripoli and AVUS. He was to add six more major victories to his tally before the war interrupted his career when he was undoubtedly at his peak.

Hermann was immediately back in action when peace returned, and rejoined the Mercedes team for their South American trip in February 1951, finishing second in the Peron Cup and third in the Eva Peron Cup. He then raced the team's 300SL cars in 1952, winning Le Mans (with Fritz Riess) and the Nürburgring sports car race, and scoring second places in the Prix de Berne and the Carrera Panamericana. In 1953 Lang made a surprise return to Grands Prix, replacing the injured Gonzalez in the Maserati team at Spa and taking fifth place.

When Mercedes returned to GP racing in 1954, he was invited to drive in the German Grand Prix, but his race ended in disappointment when he spun off while challenging team-mate Kling for second place. He retired from competition immediately after this race, but for many years continued to demonstrate the famous cars which had brought him so much success early in his racing days.

NICOLA LARINI

The talented little Italian is yet another example of a driver who, having achieved success in the junior formulae, reached Formula 1, only to endure the frustration of making up the numbers at the back of the grid. However, Nicola has at least had the satisfaction of an opportunity to show his prowess at Ferrari when, standing in for the indisposed Jean Alesi, he took a splendid second place behind Schumacher in the San Marino GP at Imola in 1994.

Larini's first win in a racing car came in a Fiat Abarth in 1984, and later that season he switched to Italian F3, qualifying fourth fastest for his first race. Driving a Martini-Alfa Romeo the following year he won two races and finished sixth in the championship. Taken under the wing of Enzo Coloni, Nicola upstaged his team leader Marco Apicella to win the 1986 Italian F3 championship in a Dallara before briefly moving into Formula 3000 with the rival Forti Corse team.

Coloni then gave him his Grand Prix debut at the end of 1987, before he joined Osella for a couple of character-building seasons where he never gave less than 100 per cent. After an unhappy season with Ligier in 1990, Nicola threw in his lot with the ambitious but ill-starred Modena team, which soon foundered. Given a testing contract by Ferrari to develop their active suspension system, Larini re-established his reputation as a class driver by winning the 1992 Italian touring car championship for Alfa Romeo. His stock was to rise even higher in 1993 when he moved with Alfa into the high-profile German series, regularly destroying the opposition with some brilliant drives to take the DTM title as well. The next three seasons saw Mercedes and Opel break Alfa's dominance and winning became a much tougher proposition, but Larini remained not only a popular and formidable competitor, but also undoubtedly one of the category's star attractions.

His continuing role as Ferrari test driver led to a Grand Prix return in 1997 when he was given a seat at Sauber. But, after he had scored a point in his first race, Larini's dream opportunity turned into a nightmare and he was summarily dropped amidst some unsavoury mud-slinging by both sides. Relieved to be out of a team in which he claimed the ambience was 'terrible', Nicola has returned to Alfa Romeo to race their 156 in the Italian Super Touring championship.

LARINI, Nicola (I) b 19/3/1964, Lido di Camaiore

	1987	Championship position: Unplaced						
	Race	Circuit	No	Entrant	Tyres	Car/Engine	Comment	Q Pos/Entries
dnq	ITALIAN GP	Monza	32	Enzo Coloni Racing Car System	G	3.5 Coloni FC187-Cosworth V8		27/28
ret	SPANISH GP	Jerez	32	Enzo Coloni Racing Car System	G	3.5 Coloni FC187-Cosworth V8	suspension	26/28
	1988	Championship position: Unplaced						
dnq	BRAZILIAN GP	Rio	21	Osella Squadra Corse	G	1.5 t/c Osella FA1I-Alfa Romeo V8		29/31
excl	SAN MARINO GP	Imola	21	Osella Squadra Corse	G	1.5 t/c Osella FA1L-Alfa Romeo V8	failed to pass scrutineering	– /31
9	MONACO GP	Monte Carlo	21	Osella Squadra Corse	G	1.5 t/c Osella FA1L-Alfa Romeo V8	3 laps behind	25/30
dnq	MEXICAN GP	Mexico City	21	Osella Squadra Corse	G	1.5 t/c Osella FA1L-Alfa Romeo V8		28/30
dnq	CANADIAN GP	Montreal	21	Osella Squadra Corse	G	1.5 t/c Osella FA1L-Alfa Romeo V8		28/31
ret	US GP (DETROIT)	Detroit	21	Osella Squadra Corse	G	1.5 t/c Osella FA1L-Alfa Romeo V8	engine	27/31
ret	FRENCH GP	Paul Ricard	21	Osella Squadra Corse	G	1.5 t/c Osella FA1L-Alfa Romeo V8	driveshaft	25/31
19/ret	BRITISH GP	Silverstone	21	Osella Squadra Corse	G	1.5 t/c Osella FA1L-Alfa Romeo V8	out of fuel/5 laps behind	26/31
ret	GERMAN GP	Hockenheim	21	Osella Squadra Corse	G	1.5 t/c Osella FA1L-Alfa Romeo V8	started from pit lane/turbo pipe	18/31
dnpq	HUNGARIAN GP	Hungaroring	21	Osella Squadra Corse	G	1.5 t/c Osella FA1L-Alfa Romeo V8		31/31
ret	BELGIAN GP	Spa	21	Osella Squadra Corse	G	1.5 t/c Osella FA1L-Alfa Romeo V8	electrics	26/31
ret	ITALIAN GP	Monza	21	Osella Squadra Corse	G	1.5 t/c Osella FA1L-Alfa Romeo V8	engine	17/31
12	PORTUGUESE GP	Estoril	21	Osella Squadra Corse	G	1.5 t/c Osella FA1L-Alfa Romeo V8	pit stop-steering/fuel/-7 laps	25/31
ret	SPANISH GP	Jerez	21	Osella Squadra Corse	G	1.5 t/c Osella FA1L-Alfa Romeo V8	suspension	14/31
ret	JAPANESE GP	Suzuka	21	Osella Squadra Corse	G	1.5 t/c Osella FA1L-Alfa Romeo V8	lost wheel	24/31
dnpq	AUSTRALIAN GP	Adelaide	21	Osella Squadra Corse	G	1.5 t/c Osella FA1L-Alfa Romeo V8		31/31
	1989	Championship position: Unplaced						
dsq	BRAZILIAN GP	Rio	17	Osella Squadra Corse	P	3.5 Osella FA1M-Cosworth V8	started from wrong grid position	19/38
12/ret	SAN MARINO GP	Imola	17	Osella Squadra Corse	P	3.5 Osella FA1M-Cosworth V8	broken hub-crashed/-6 laps	14/39
dnpq	MONACO GP	Monte Carlo	17	Osella Squadra Corse	P	3.5 Osella FA1M-Cosworth V8		32/38
dnpq	MEXICAN GP	Mexico City	17	Osella Squadra Corse	P	3.5 Osella FA1M-Cosworth V8		33/39
dnpq	US GP (PHOENIX)	Phoenix	17	Osella Squadra Corse	P	3.5 Osella FA1M-Cosworth V8		34/39
ret	CANADIAN GP	Montreal	17	Osella Squadra Corse	P	3.5 Osella FA1M-Cosworth V8	electrics	15/39
dnpq	FRENCH GP	Paul Ricard	17	Osella Squadra Corse	P	3.5 Osella FA1M-Cosworth V8		31/39
ret	BRITISH GP	Silverstone	17	Osella Squadra Corse	P	3.5 Osella FA1M-Cosworth V8	started from pitlane/handling	17/39
dnpq	GERMAN GP	Hockenheim	17	Osella Squadra Corse	P	3.5 Osella FA1M-Cosworth V8		32/39
dnpq	HUNGARIAN GP	Hungaroring	17	Osella Squadra Corse	P	3.5 Osella FA1M-Cosworth V8		31/39
dnpq	BELGIAN GP	Spa	17	Osella Squadra Corse	P	3.5 Osella FA1M-Cosworth V8		31/39
ret	ITALIAN GP	Monza	17	Osella Squadra Corse	P	3.5 Osella FA1M-Cosworth V8	gearbox	24/39
excl	PORTUGUESE GP	Estoril	17	Osella Squadra Corse	P	3.5 Osella FA1M-Cosworth V8	excluded-missed weight check	35/39
ret	SPANISH GP	Jerez	17	Osella Squadra Corse	P	3.5 Osella FA1M-Cosworth V8	suspension-crashed	11/38
ret	JAPANESE GP	Suzuka	17	Osella Squadra Corse	P	3.5 Osella FA1M-Cosworth V8	brakes	10/39
ret/tdns	AUSTRALIAN GP	Adelaide	17	Osella Squadra Corse	P	3.5 Osella FA1M-Cosworth V8	electrics on the grid at 2nd start	11/39

1990		Championship position: Unplaced						
ret	US GP (PHOENIX)	Phoenix	25	Ligier Gitanes	G	3.5 Ligier JS33B-Cosworth V8	stuck throttle	13/35
11	BRAZILIAN GP	Interlagos	25	Ligier Gitanes	G	3.5 Ligier JS33B-Cosworth V8	pit stop-tyres/3 laps behind	20/35
10	SAN MARINO GP	Imola	25	Ligier Gitanes	G	3.5 Ligier JS33B-Cosworth V8	gearbox problems/-2 laps	21/34
ret	MONACO GP	Monte Carlo	25	Ligier Gitanes	G	3.5 Ligier JS33B-Cosworth V8	gearbox/differential	17/35
ret	CANADIAN GP	Montreal	25	Ligier Gitanes	G	3.5 Ligier JS33B-Cosworth V8	hit by Boutsen	20/35
16	MEXICAN GP	Mexico City	25	Ligier Gitanes	G	3.5 Ligier JS33B-Cosworth V8	2 laps behind	24/35
14	FRENCH GP	Paul Ricard	25	Ligier Gitanes	G	3.5 Ligier JS33B-Cosworth V8	brake problems/2 laps behind	19/35
10	BRITISH GP	Silverstone	25	Ligier Gitanes	G	3.5 Ligier JS33B-Cosworth V8	2 laps behind	21/35
10	GERMAN GP	Hockenheim	25	Ligier Gitanes	G	3.5 Ligier JS33B-Cosworth V8	2 pit stops-tyres/-2 laps	22/35
11	HUNGARIAN GP	Hungaroring	25	Ligier Gitanes	G	3.5 Ligier JS33B-Cosworth V8	1 lap behind	25/35
14	BELGIAN GP	Spa	25	Ligier Gitanes	G	3.5 Ligier JS33B-Cosworth V8	2 stops-handling-tyres/-2 laps	21/33
11	ITALIAN GP	Monza	25	Ligier Gitanes	G	3.5 Ligier JS33B-Cosworth V8	2 laps behind	26/33
10	PORTUGUESE GP	Estoril	25	Ligier Gitanes	G	3.5 Ligier JS33B-Cosworth V8	pit stop-tyres/2 laps behind	23/33
7	SPANISH GP	Jerez	25	Ligier Gitanes	G	3.5 Ligier JS33B-Cosworth V8	1 lap behind	20/33
7	JAPANESE GP	Suzuka	25	Ligier Gitanes	G	3.5 Ligier JS33B-Cosworth V8	pit stop-tyres/1 lap behind	18/30
10	AUSTRALIAN GP	Adelaide	25	Ligier Gitanes	G	3.5 Ligier JS33B-Cosworth V8	2 laps behind	12/30
1991		Championship position: Unplaced						
7	US GP (PHOENIX)	Phoenix	34	Modena Team SpA	G	3.5 Lambo 291-Lamborghini V12	3 laps behind	17/34
dnpq	BRAZILIAN GP	Interlagos	34	Modena Team SpA	G	3.5 Lambo 291-Lamborghini V12		32/34
dnpq	SAN MARINO GP	Imola	34	Modena Team SpA	G	3.5 Lambo 291-Lamborghini V12		33/34
dnpq	MONACO GP	Monte Carlo	34	Modena Team SpA	G	3.5 Lambo 291-Lamborghini V12		31/34
dnpq	CANADIAN GP	Montreal	34	Modena Team SpA	G	3.5 Lambo 291-Lamborghini V12		32/34
excl*	MEXICAN GP	Mexico City	34	Modena Team SpA	G	3.5 Lambo 291-Lamborghini V12	*rear wing height infringement	31/34
dnpq	FRENCH GP	Paul Ricard	34	Modena Team SpA	G	3.5 Lambo 291-Lamborghini V12		32/34
dnpq	BRITISH GP	Silverstone	34	Modena Team SpA	G	3.5 Lambo 291-Lamborghini V12		32/34
ret	GERMAN GP	Hockenheim	34	Modena Team SpA	G	3.5 Lambo 291-Lamborghini V12	spun avoiding Blundell on lap 1	24/34
16	HUNGARIAN GP	Hungaroring	34	Modena Team SpA	G	3.5 Lambo 291-Lamborghini V12	3 laps behind	24/34
dnq	BELGIAN GP	Spa	34	Modena Team SpA	G	3.5 Lambo 291-Lamborghini V12		28/34
16	ITALIAN GP	Monza	34	Modena Team SpA	G	3.5 Lambo 291-Lamborghini V12	5 laps behind	23/34
dnq	PORTUGUESE GP	Estoril	34	Modena Team SpA	G	3.5 Lambo 291-Lamborghini V12		29/34
dnq	SPANISH GP	Barcelona	34	Modena Team SpA	G	3.5 Lambo 291-Lamborghini V12		28/33
dnq	JAPANESE GP	Suzuka	34	Modena Team SpA	G	3.5 Lambo 291-Lamborghini V12		28/31
ret	AUSTRALIAN GP	Adelaide	34	Modena Team SpA	G	3.5 Lambo 291-Lamborghini V12	collision with Alesi	19/32
1992		Championship position: Unplaced						
12	JAPANESE GP	Suzuka	28	Scuderia Ferrari SpA	G	3.5 Fiat Ferrari F9200 V12	left at start/active car/-1 lap	11/26
11	AUSTRALIAN GP	Adelaide	28	Scuderia Ferrari SpA	G	3.5 Fiat Ferrari F9200 V12	again left at start-clutch/-2 laps	19/26
1994		Championship position: 14th= Wins: 0 Pole positions: 0 Fastest laps: 0 Points scored: 6						
ret	PACIFIC GP	T.I. Circuit	27	Scuderia Ferrari	G	3.5 Fiat Ferrari 412T1 V12	ran off track into Senna-lap 1	7/28
2	SAN MARINO GP	Imola	27	Scuderia Ferrari	G	3.5 Fiat Ferrari 412T1 V12		6/28
1997		Championship position: 19th Wins: 0 Pole positions: 0 Fastest laps: 0 Points scored: 1						
6	AUSTRALIAN GP	Melbourne	17	Red Bull Sauber Petronas	G	3.0 Sauber C16-Petronas V10		13/24
11	BRAZILIAN GP	Interlagos	17	Red Bull Sauber Petronas	G	3.0 Sauber C16-Petronas V10	1 lap behind	19/22
ret	ARGENTINE GP	Buenos Aires	17	Red Bull Sauber Petronas	G	3.0 Sauber C16-Petronas V10	spun off	14/22
7	SAN MARINO GP	Imola	17	Red Bull Sauber Petronas	G	3.0 Sauber C16-Petronas V10	1 lap behind	12/22
ret	MONACO GP	Monte Carlo	17	Red Bull Sauber Petronas	G	3.0 Sauber C16-Petronas V10	accident	11/22

GP Starts: 48 (49)   GP Wins: 0   Pole positions: 0   Fastest laps: 0   Points: 7

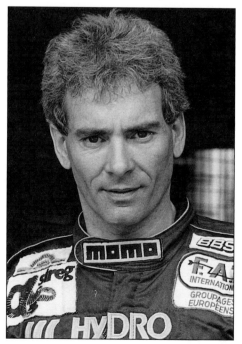

OSCAR LARRAURI

Having raced in Argentinian F3 from 1979, Oscar 'Poppy' Larrauri found the going tough when he made the move to Europe until he secured the top drive in the Pavanello Euroracing F3 team for 1982. He then showed his mettle, winning seven races and the European championship. Unfortunately his aspirations were soon blunted by an unhappy Formula 2 liaison with Minardi, which left him out in the cold as far as single-seaters were concerned. 'Poppy' then began a long and rewarding association with Walter Brun, racing the Swiss entrant's Group C Porsche sports cars through to the early nineties, the high spot being a win at Jerez in 1986.

However, Brun's over-ambitious move into Formula 1 was a different story which found 'Poppy' struggling to qualify uncompetitive machinery. He subsequently embarked on a busy racing career based in Italy, where he drove a Jolly Club Ferrari 348 in the GT Supercar championship in 1993 and '94. At the end of that season he took a Ferrari F40 to victory in the final round of the All-Japan GT championship, and success continued in 1995 when he shared the victorious Porsche 962 K8 at the Daytona 24 Hours. The bulk of the year was spent contesting the Italian Superturismo series in a Jolly Club Alfa T155.

In 1996 Larrauri returned to race for the first time in a decade in his native Argentina, and he has since taken consecutive Super Touring titles in 1997 and '98 with a BMW 320i.

LARRAURI, Oscar (RA) b 19/8/1954, Buenos Aires

	1988	Championship position: Unplaced							
	Race	Circuit	No	Entrant	Tyres	Car/Engine	Comment		Q Pos/Entries
ret/dns	BRAZILIAN GP	Rio	32	EuroBrun Racing	G	3.5 EuroBrun ER188-Cosworth V8	electrics on parade lap		(26)/31
dnq	SAN MARINO GP	Imola	32	EuroBrun Racing	G	3.5 EuroBrun ER188-Cosworth V8			27/31
ret	MONACO GP	Monte Carlo	32	EuroBrun Racing	G	3.5 EuroBrun ER188-Cosworth V8	accident		18/31
13	MEXICAN GP	Mexico City	32	EuroBrun Racing	G	3.5 EuroBrun ER188-Cosworth V8	handling/battery problems/-4 laps		26/30
ret	CANADIAN GP	Montreal	32	EuroBrun Racing	G	3.5 EuroBrun ER188-Cosworth V8	accident		24/31
ret	US GP (DETROIT)	Detroit	32	EuroBrun Racing	G	3.5 EuroBrun ER188-Cosworth V8	gearbox		24/31
ret	FRENCH GP	Paul Ricard	32	EuroBrun Racing	G	3.5 EuroBrun ER188-Cosworth V8	clutch		27/31
dnq	BRITISH GP	Silverstone	32	EuroBrun Racing	G	3.5 EuroBrun ER188-Cosworth V8			27/31
16	GERMAN GP	Hockenheim	32	EuroBrun Racing	G	3.5 EuroBrun ER188-Cosworth V8	2 laps behind		26/31
dnq	HUNGARIAN GP	Hungaroring	32	EuroBrun Racing	G	3.5 EuroBrun ER188-Cosworth V8			27/31
dnpq	BELGIAN GP	Spa	32	EuroBrun Racing	G	3.5 EuroBrun ER188-Cosworth V8			31/31
dnpq	ITALIAN GP	Monza	32	EuroBrun Racing	G	3.5 EuroBrun ER188-Cosworth V8			31/31
dnpq	PORTUGUESE GP	Estoril	32	EuroBrun Racing	G	3.5 EuroBrun ER188-Cosworth V8			31/31
dnq	SPANISH GP	Jerez	32	EuroBrun Racing	G	3.5 EuroBrun ER188-Cosworth V8			28/31
dnq	JAPANESE GP	Suzuka	32	EuroBrun Racing	G	3.5 EuroBrun ER188-Cosworth V8			28/31
ret	AUSTRALIAN GP	Adelaide	32	EuroBrun Racing	G	3.5 EuroBrun ER188-Cosworth V8	half shaft-spun off		25/31
	1989	Championship position: Unplaced							
dnpq	ITALIAN GP	Monza	33	EuroBrun Racing	P	3.5 EuroBrun ER189-Judd V8			36/39
dnpq	"	"	33	EuroBrun Racing	P	3.5 EuroBrun ER188B-Judd V8			– / –
dnpq	PORTUGUESE GP	Estoril	33	EuroBrun Racing	P	3.5 EuroBrun ER189-Judd V8			34/39
dnpq	"	"	33	EuroBrun Racing	P	3.5 EuroBrun ER188B-Judd V8			– / –
dnpq	SPANISH GP	Jerez	33	EuroBrun Racing	P	3.5 EuroBrun ER189-Judd V8			37/38
dnpq	"	"	33	EuroBrun Racing	P	3.5 EuroBrun ER188B-Judd V8			– / –
dnpq	JAPANESE GP	Suzuka	33	EuroBrun Racing	P	3.5 EuroBrun ER189-Judd V8			35/39
dnpq	AUSTRALIAN GP	Adelaide	33	EuroBrun Racing	P	3.5 EuroBrun ER189-Judd V8			35/39

GP Starts: 7 (8)   GP Wins: 0   Pole positions: 0   Fastest laps: 0   Points: 0

LARRETA, Alberto Rodriguez (RA) b 14/1/1934, Buenos Aires – d 11/3/1977

	1960	Championship position: Unplaced							
	Race	Circuit	No	Entrant	Tyres	Car/Engine	Comment		Q Pos/Entries
9	ARGENTINE GP	Buenos Aires	46	Team Lotus	D	2.5 Lotus 16-Climax 4	3rd works car/3 laps behind		15/22

GP Starts: 1   GP Wins: 0   Pole positions: 0   Fastest laps: 0   Points: 0

LARROUSSE, Gérard (F) b 23/5/1940, Lyon

	1974	Championship position: Unplaced							
	Race	Circuit	No	Entrant	Tyres	Car/Engine	Comment		Q Pos/Entries
ret	BELGIAN GP	Nivelles	43	Scuderia Finotto	G	3.0 Brabham BT42-Cosworth V8	chunking tyres		28/32
dnq	FRENCH GP	Dijon	43	Scuderia Finotto	G	3.0 Brabham BT42-Cosworth V8			30/30

GP Starts: 1   GP Wins: 0   Pole positions: 0   Fastest laps: 0   Points: 0

GÉRARD LARROUSSE

After a distinguished career in rallying in the sixties with Alpine and Porsche cars, Gérard made the transition to circuit racing with ease, sharing the second-place Porsche with Herrmann at Le Mans in 1969. Over the next few seasons, Larrousse built up a fine reputation in endurance racing, winning the 1971 Sebring 12 Hours and the Nürburgring 1000 Km for Porsche, before enjoying two fabulously successful years with Matra in 1973 and 1974 during which, partnered by Pescarolo, Gérard won Le Mans twice and added further victories at Vallelunga, Dijon, the Österreichring, Watkins Glen, Imola and Kyalami. In 1974, he was also the European 2-litre champion in an Alpine-Renault and briefly sampled the ambience of Formula 1, but had a miserable time with the poorly prepared rent-a-drive Finotto Brabham.

In 1975 he undertook a season of Formula 2 with the Elf, winning the Jim Clark Trophy at Hockenheim on aggregate, in addition to a sports car programme for Renault. At the end of the season he was appointed competitions manager at Renault, overseeing the development of their Formula 1 turbo car, and later moved to Ligier before establishing his own team, which competed on minimal budgets and was supported by a motley collection of sponsors from 1987 through to 1994, when the financial climate was such that Larrousse was finally forced to close its doors after a possible merger with French F3000 champions and Grand Prix aspirants DAMS came to nought.

NIKI LAUDA

WORLD CHAMPION: 1975, 1977 & 1984

NIKI LAUDA

There are some who try to buck the system but usually fail, and others who play the game and manipulate it to their own ends. Niki Lauda managed to do both, with the adroitness of his off-track political and business manoeuvrings being matched only by that of his driving and racecraft, which saw him win three world titles.

After a couple of seasons in which he struggled to make an impression in Formula 3 and sports cars, with a Porsche 908, Lauda took a bank loan to finance a season of Formula 2 in a semi-works March and a one-off drive in his home GP in 1971. Although his results were hardly inspiring there were fleeting glimpses of his talent. Already the quiet self-confidence was there, as was the inner determination to overcome every setback, and he effectively mortgaged himself to the hilt to buy a seat in the works March team alongside Ronnie Peterson for 1972. To say the F1 season was disastrous is almost an understatement, and the dreadful 721X proved absolutely hopeless. Fortunately the F2 March 722 was competitive, at least allowing Niki to compete with his peers. His win in the spring John Player F2 race at Oulton Park was one indication of his potential, his ability to closely match Peterson's testing times another, but March discarded him right at the end of the year, and he virtually saved his career by joining BRM for 1973 in a pay-as-you-race deal which he knew it would be difficult to honour.

When Lauda managed to overshadow his team-mates in the early races, took his first championship points at Zolder and held third place in the Monaco GP, he was able to put his contract problems behind him, but only by locking himself into a three-year deal. There were a few successful touring car races for BMW which proved quite lucrative, but most important was the fact that he had been targeted by Ferrari for 1974. Contract or not, there was no way Louis Stanley was going to stop Niki heading for Maranello, and the young Austrian wriggled his way out of the deal. Displaying typical pragmatism, he set about his new task at Ferrari with a huge programme of testing and constant development which paid immediate dividends. There were a couple of wins and four second places, but a mid-season dip in form cost him his title chance.

For a driver in his first year with a front-line team he had performed admirably, but Lauda was privately convinced that in 1975 the title would be his, and once the transverse-gearbox car was introduced there was no stopping him. Nine pole positions and five Grand Prix wins (complemented by victory in the International Trophy) saw the Austrian sweep to his first championship, and 1976 showed every sign of going the same way until the fiery crash at the Nürburgring which so nearly took his life. Though badly burned around the head, Niki returned to defend his title just weeks later and the fact that he

Champion performance. Lauda in the Ferrari 312T leads Emerson Fittipaldi and the rest of the field through the chicane at the 1975 United States Grand Prix at Watkins Glen. The Austrian rounded off his first championship-winning season with a dominant victory.

ultimately failed to retain his crown was largely irrelevant, despite the dreadful treatment the Italian press meted out to him after his decision to pull out of the Japanese GP. Even at Ferrari there were doubters who thought he had lost his bottle, however, and Reutemann was brought into the team, much to Lauda's annoyance.

Inwardly Niki must have relished the challenge, and with a perfect blend of aggression and circumspection he all but humiliated his new team-mate the following season to prove to the hierarchy that he was still the boss. A second title was duly won and, with a characteristic lack of sentiment, Lauda then announced that he was moving to Brabham. His two years with the team brought only limited success, Niki winning the Swedish GP in the notorious fan car and the Italian GP in 1978, and the non-title Dino Ferrari Trophy at Imola the following season. At Montreal that year, he tried the new Cosworth BT49 in practice and made the shock decision to retire then and there.

He stayed away for two years, during which he built up his airline business, before being tempted back in 1982. Perhaps it was his ego, the money, or maybe just the challenge of proving the inevitable doubters wrong. One thing was for sure: once he had demonstrated to himself that the speed was still there, he wasn't going to mess around. There was a job to be done in developing John Barnard's innovative McLaren MP4 and Niki was just the man to do it. True, there were occasional lapses and lacklustre performances in the Cosworth car, but once his attention turned to the TAG turbo-powered machine at the end of 1983 Lauda was fully focused. He needed to be for 1984, when he was joined by Alain Prost. Using all his experience, the wily Lauda hung on to the Frenchman's tail and eventually took his third World Championship by the narrowest of margins after a fabulous year. His final season perhaps went according to expectation, as the still hungry Prost forced the pace, while Niki was happy to adopt a more tactical approach. Unfortunately the season was blighted by unreliability, but at Zandvoort we saw Lauda the racer one last time, as he kept his number one McLaren in front of Prost's sister-car in a Formula 3-style battle to the finish.

This time Niki stayed retired, but in 1992 he was invited to act as a consultant to Ferrari as they attempted to recapture the glory days which had been gone for so many years. It has been a long and sometimes painful process of reconstruction for Maranello, with Michael Schumacher seen as the final piece of the jigsaw. Niki, however, is no longer part of the management structure but, after successfully receiving a kidney transplant, he regularly attends Grands Prix in a commentary role for Austrian television.

LAUDA, Niki (A) b 22/2/1949, Vienna

	Race	Circuit	No	Entrant	Tyres	Car/Engine	Comment	Q Pos/Entries
1971				Championship position: Unplaced				
ret	AUSTRIAN GP	Österreichring	26	STP March Racing Team	F	3.0 March 711-Cosworth V8	*handling*	21/22
1972				Championship position: Unplaced				
11	ARGENTINE GP	Buenos Aires	15	STP March Racing Team	G	3.0 March 721-Cosworth V8	*2 laps behind*	22/22
7	SOUTH AFRICAN GP	Kyalami	4	STP March Racing Team	G	3.0 March 721-Cosworth V8	*1 lap behind*	=20/27
ret	SPANISH GP	Jarama	24	STP March Racing Team	G	3.0 March 721X-Cosworth V8	*sticking throttle*	25/26
16	MONACO GP	Monte Carlo	4	STP March Racing Team	G	3.0 March 721X-Cosworth V8	*pit stop-wheel/fuel leak/-6 laps*	=22/25
12	BELGIAN GP	Nivelles	12	STP March Racing Team	G	3.0 March 721X-Cosworth V8	*handling problems/-3 laps*	25/26
dns	"	"	14	Clarke-Mordaunt-Guthrie Racing	G	3.0 March 721G-Cosworth V8	*practice only*	– / –
ret	FRENCH GP	Clermont Ferrand	14	STP March Racing Team	G	3.0 March 721G-Cosworth V8	*loose drive shaft*	25/29
9	BRITISH GP	Brands Hatch	4	STP March Racing Team	G	3.0 March 721G-Cosworth V8	*3 laps behind*	=18/27
ret	GERMAN GP	Nürburgring	23	STP March Racing Team	G	3.0 March 721G-Cosworth V8	*split oil tank*	24/27
10	AUSTRIAN GP	Österreichring	4	STP March Racing Team	G	3.0 March 721G-Cosworth V8	*1 lap behind*	22/26
13	ITALIAN GP	Monza	18	STP March Racing Team	G	3.0 March 721G-Cosworth V8	*pit stop-throttle slides/-5 laps*	20/27
dsq	CANADIAN GP	Mosport Park	26	STP March Racing Team	G	3.0 March 721G-Cosworth V8	*outside assistance on track*	=19/25
nc	US GP	Watkins Glen	5	STP March Racing Team	G	3.0 March 721G-Cosworth V8	*pit stop-fuel pressure/-10 laps*	26/32
1973				Championship position: 17th Wins: 0 Pole positions: 0 Fastest laps: 0 Points scored: 2				
ret	ARGENTINE GP	Buenos Aires	34	Marlboro BRM	F	3.0 BRM P160C V12	*oil pressure*	13/19
8	BRAZILIAN GP	Interlagos	16	Marlboro BRM	F	3.0 BRM P160C V12	*stopped-electrics/-2 laps*	13/20
ret	SOUTH AFRICAN GP	Kyalami	17	Marlboro BRM	F	3.0 BRM P160D V12	*engine*	10/25
ret	SPANISH GP	Montjuich Park	16	Marlboro BRM	F	3.0 BRM P160E V12	*tyres*	11/22
5	BELGIAN GP	Zolder	21	Marlboro BRM	F	3.0 BRM P160E V12	*pit stop-fuel/1 lap behind*	14/23
ret	MONACO GP	Monte Carlo	21	Marlboro BRM	F	3.0 BRM P160E V12	*gearbox*	6/26
13	SWEDISH GP	Anderstorp	21	Marlboro BRM	F	3.0 BRM P160E V12	*pit stop-engine/5 laps behind*	15/22
9	FRENCH GP	Paul Ricard	21	Marlboro BRM	F	3.0 BRM P160E V12		17/25
12	BRITISH GP	Silverstone	21	Marlboro BRM	F	3.0 BRM P160E V12	*pit stop-tyres/4 laps behind*	=8/29
ret	DUTCH GP	Zandvoort	21	Marlboro BRM	F	3.0 BRM P160E V12	*tyres/fuel pump*	11/24
ret	GERMAN GP	Nürburgring	21	Marlboro BRM	F	3.0 BRM P160E V12	*crashed-fractured wrist*	5/23
dns	AUSTRIAN GP	Österreichring	21	Marlboro BRM	F	3.0 BRM P160E V12	*pain from German GP injury*	(25)/25
ret	ITALIAN GP	Monza	21	Marlboro BRM	F	3.0 BRM P160E V12	*tyre failure-accident*	15/25
ret	CANADIAN GP	Mosport Park	21	Marlboro BRM	F	3.0 BRM P160E V12	*transmission*	8/26
ret	US GP	Watkins Glen	21	Marlboro BRM	F	3.0 BRM P160E V12	*fuel pump*	22/28
1974				Championship position: 4th Wins: 2 Pole positions: 9 Fastest laps: 3 Points scored: 38				
2	ARGENTINE GP	Buenos Aires	12	Scuderia Ferrari SpA SEFAC	G	3.0 Ferrari 312B3 F12		8/26
ret	BRAZILIAN GP	Interlagos	12	Scuderia Ferrari SpA SEFAC	G	3.0 Ferrari 312B3 F12	*broken wing stay*	3/25
16/ret	SOUTH AFRICAN GP	Kyalami	12	Scuderia Ferrari SpA SEFAC	G	3.0 Ferrari 312B3 F12	*ignition/4 laps behind*	1/27
1	SPANISH GP	Jarama	12	Scuderia Ferrari SpA SEFAC	G	3.0 Ferrari 312B3 F12	*FL*	1/28
2	BELGIAN GP	Nivelles	12	Scuderia Ferrari SpA SEFAC	G	3.0 Ferrari 312B3 F12		3/32
ret	MONACO GP	Monte Carlo	12	Scuderia Ferrari SpA SEFAC	G	3.0 Ferrari 312B3 F12	*ignition*	1/28
ret	SWEDISH GP	Anderstorp	12	Scuderia Ferrari SpA SEFAC	G	3.0 Ferrari 312B3 F12	*transmission*	3/28
1	DUTCH GP	Zandvoort	12	Scuderia Ferrari SpA SEFAC	G	3.0 Ferrari 312B3 F12		1/27
2	FRENCH GP	Dijon	12	Scuderia Ferrari SpA SEFAC	G	3.0 Ferrari 312B3 F12		1/30
5	BRITISH GP	Brands Hatch	12	Scuderia Ferrari SpA SEFAC	G	3.0 Ferrari 312B3 F12	*trapped in pits/-1 lap/FL*	=1/34
ret	GERMAN GP	Nürburgring	12	Scuderia Ferrari SpA SEFAC	G	3.0 Ferrari 312B3 F12	*hit Scheckter/*	1/32
ret	AUSTRIAN GP	Österreichring	12	Scuderia Ferrari SpA SEFAC	G	3.0 Ferrari 312B3 F12	*engine*	1/31
ret	ITALIAN GP	Monza	12	Scuderia Ferrari SpA SEFAC	G	3.0 Ferrari 312B3 F12	*engine*	1/31
ret	CANADIAN GP	Mosport Park	12	Scuderia Ferrari SpA SEFAC	G	3.0 Ferrari 312B3 F12	*hit barrier when 1st/FL*	2/30
ret	US GP	Watkins Glen	12	Scuderia Ferrari SpA SEFAC	G	3.0 Ferrari 312B3 F12	*front suspension*	5/30
1975				Championship position: WORLD CHAMPION Wins: 5 Pole positions: 9 Fastest laps: 2 Points scored: 64.5				
6	ARGENTINE GP	Buenos Aires	12	Scuderia Ferrari SpA SEFAC	G	3.0 Ferrari 312B3 F12		4/23
5	BRAZILIAN GP	Interlagos	12	Scuderia Ferrari SpA SEFAC	G	3.0 Ferrari 312B3 F12		4/23
5	SOUTH AFRICAN GP	Kyalami	12	Scuderia Ferrari SpA SEFAC	G	3.0 Ferrari 312T F12		4/28
dns	"	"	12		G	3.0 Ferrari 312B3 F12	*practice only*	– / –
ret	SPANISH GP	Montjuich Park	12	Scuderia Ferrari SpA SEFAC	G	3.0 Ferrari 312T F12	*hit by Andretti*	1/26
1	MONACO GP	Monte Carlo	12	Scuderia Ferrari SpA SEFAC	G	3.0 Ferrari 312T F12		1/26
1	BELGIAN GP	Zolder	12	Scuderia Ferrari SpA SEFAC	G	3.0 Ferrari 312T F12		1/24
1	SWEDISH GP	Anderstorp	12	Scuderia Ferrari SpA SEFAC	G	3.0 Ferrari 312T F12	*FL*	5/26
2	DUTCH GP	Zandvoort	12	Scuderia Ferrari SpA SEFAC	G	3.0 Ferrari 312T F12	*FL*	1/25
1	FRENCH GP	Paul Ricard	12	Scuderia Ferrari SpA SEFAC	G	3.0 Ferrari 312T F12		1/26
8	BRITISH GP	Silverstone	12	Scuderia Ferrari SpA SEFAC	G	3.0 Ferrari 312T F12	*2 laps behind*	3/28
3	GERMAN GP	Nürburgring	12	Scuderia Ferrari SpA SEFAC	G	3.0 Ferrari 312T F12	*pit stops-tyre problems*	1/26
6*	AUSTRIAN GP	Österreichring	12	Scuderia Ferrari SpA SEFAC	G	3.0 Ferrari 312T F12	**rain shortened race-half points*	1/30
3	ITALIAN GP	Monza	12	Scuderia Ferrari SpA SEFAC	G	3.0 Ferrari 312T F12		1/28
1	US GP	Watkins Glen	12	Scuderia Ferrari SpA SEFAC	G	3.0 Ferrari 312T F12		1/24
1976				Championship position: 2nd Wins: 4 Pole positions: 3 Fastest laps: 4 Points scored: 68				
1	BRAZILIAN GP	Interlagos	1	Scuderia Ferrari SpA SEFAC	G	3.0 Ferrari 312T F12		2/22
1	SOUTH AFRICAN GP	Kyalami	1	Scuderia Ferrari SpA SEFAC	G	3.0 Ferrari 312T F12	*FL*	2/25
2	US GP WEST	Long Beach	1	Scuderia Ferrari SpA SEFAC	G	3.0 Ferrari 312T F12		4/27
2	SPANISH GP	Jarama	1	Scuderia Ferrari SpA SEFAC	G	3.0 Ferrari 312T2 F12		2/30
1	BELGIAN GP	Zolder	1	Scuderia Ferrari SpA SEFAC	G	3.0 Ferrari 312T2 F12	*FL*	1/29
dns	"	"	1		G	3.0 Ferrari 312T F12	*practice only*	– / –
1	MONACO GP	Monte Carlo	1	Scuderia Ferrari SpA SEFAC	G	3.0 Ferrari 312T2 F12		1/25
3	SWEDISH GP	Anderstorp	1	Scuderia Ferrari SpA SEFAC	G	3.0 Ferrari 312T2 F12		5/27
ret	FRENCH GP	Paul Ricard	1	Scuderia Ferrari SpA SEFAC	G	3.0 Ferrari 312T2 F12	*engine/FL*	2/30
1*	BRITISH GP	Brands Hatch	1	Scuderia Ferrari SpA SEFAC	G	3.0 Ferrari 312T2 F12	** 1st place car dsq/FL*	1/30
ret/dns	GERMAN GP	Nürburgring	1	Scuderia Ferrari SpA SEFAC	G	3.0 Ferrari 312T2 F12	*accident-first start-badly burnt*	2/28
4	ITALIAN GP	Monza	1	Scuderia Ferrari SpA SEFAC	G	3.0 Ferrari 312T2 F12		5/29

8	CANADIAN GP	Mosport Park	1	Scuderia Ferrari SpA SEFAC	G	3.0 Ferrari 312T2 F12		6/27
3	US GP EAST	Watkins Glen	1	Scuderia Ferrari SpA SEFAC	G	3.0 Ferrari 312T2 F12		5/27
ret	JAPANESE GP	Mount Fuji	1	Scuderia Ferrari SpA SEFAC	G	3.0 Ferrari 312T2 F12	withdrew-due to conditions	3/27

1977 Championship position: WORLD CHAMPION Wins: 3 Pole positions: 2 Fastest laps: 3 Points scored: 72

ret	ARGENTINE GP	Buenos Aires	11	Scuderia Ferrari SpA SEFAC	G	3.0 Ferrari 312T2 F12	fuel metering unit	4/21
3	BRAZILIAN GP	Interlagos	11	Scuderia Ferrari SpA SEFAC	G	3.0 Ferrari 312T2 F12		13/22
1	SOUTH AFRICAN GP	Kyalami	11	Scuderia Ferrari SpA SEFAC	G	3.0 Ferrari 312T2 F12		3/23
2	US GP WEST	Long Beach	11	Scuderia Ferrari SpA SEFAC	G	3.0 Ferrari 312T2 F12	FL	1/22
dns	SPANISH GP	Jarama	11	Scuderia Ferrari SpA SEFAC	G	3.0 Ferrari 312T2 F12	broke rib in Sun a.m. warm-up	(3)/31
2	MONACO GP	Monte Carlo	11	Scuderia Ferrari SpA SEFAC	G	3.0 Ferrari 312T2 F12		6/26
2	BELGIAN GP	Zolder	11	Scuderia Ferrari SpA SEFAC	G	3.0 Ferrari 312T2 F12		11/32
ret	SWEDISH GP	Anderstorp	11	Scuderia Ferrari SpA SEFAC	G	3.0 Ferrari 312T2 F12	handling	15/31
5	FRENCH GP	Dijon	11	Scuderia Ferrari SpA SEFAC	G	3.0 Ferrari 312T2 F12		9/30
2	BRITISH GP	Silverstone	11	Scuderia Ferrari SpA SEFAC	G	3.0 Ferrari 312T2 F12		3/36
1	GERMAN GP	Hockenheim	11	Scuderia Ferrari SpA SEFAC	G	3.0 Ferrari 312T2 F12	FL	3/30
2	AUSTRIAN GP	Österreichring	11	Scuderia Ferrari SpA SEFAC	G	3.0 Ferrari 312T2 F12		1/30
1	DUTCH GP	Zandvoort	11	Scuderia Ferrari SpA SEFAC	G	3.0 Ferrari 312T2 F12	FL	4/34
2	ITALIAN GP	Monza	11	Scuderia Ferrari SpA SEFAC	G	3.0 Ferrari 312T2 F12		5/34
4	US GP EAST	Watkins Glen	11	Scuderia Ferrari SpA SEFAC	G	3.0 Ferrari 312T2 F12		7/27

1978 Championship position: 4th Wins: 2 Pole positions: 1 Fastest laps: 4 Points scored: 44

2	ARGENTINE GP	Buenos Aires	1	Parmalat Racing Team	G	3.0 Brabham BT45C-Alfa Romeo F12		5/27
3	BRAZILIAN GP	Rio	1	Parmalat Racing Team	G	3.0 Brabham BT45C-Alfa Romeo F12		10/28
ret	SOUTH AFRICAN GP	Kyalami	1	Parmalat Racing Team	G	3.0 Brabham BT46-Alfa Romeo F12	engine	1/30
ret	US GP WEST	Long Beach	1	Parmalat Racing Team	G	3.0 Brabham BT46-Alfa Romeo F12	ignition	3/30
2	MONACO GP	Monte Carlo	1	Parmalat Racing Team	G	3.0 Brabham BT46-Alfa Romeo F12	FL	3/30
ret	BELGIAN GP	Zolder	1	Parmalat Racing Team	G	3.0 Brabham BT46-Alfa Romeo F12	hit by Scheckter at start	3/30
ret	SPANISH GP	Jarama	1	Parmalat Racing Team	G	3.0 Brabham BT46-Alfa Romeo F12	engine	6/29
1	SWEDISH GP	Anderstorp	1	Parmalat Racing Team	G	3.0 Brabham BT46B-Alfa Romeo F12	fan car/FL	3/27
ret	FRENCH GP	Paul Ricard	1	Parmalat Racing Team	G	3.0 Brabham BT46-Alfa Romeo F12	engine	3/29
2	BRITISH GP	Brands Hatch	1	Parmalat Racing Team	G	3.0 Brabham BT46-Alfa Romeo F12	FL	4/30
ret	GERMAN GP	Hockenheim	1	Parmalat Racing Team	G	3.0 Brabham BT46-Alfa Romeo F12	engine	3/30
dns	"	"	1	Parmalat Racing Team	G	3.0 Brabham BT46C-Alfa Romeo F12	practice only	– / –
ret	AUSTRIAN GP	Österreichring	1	Parmalat Racing Team	G	3.0 Brabham BT46-Alfa Romeo F12	crashed	12/31
3	DUTCH GP	Zandvoort	1	Parmalat Racing Team	G	3.0 Brabham BT46-Alfa Romeo F12	FL	3/33
1*	ITALIAN GP	Monza	1	Parmalat Racing Team	G	3.0 Brabham BT46-Alfa Romeo F12	* 1st & 2nd cars penalised 1 min	4/32
ret	US GP EAST	Watkins Glen	1	Parmalat Racing Team	G	3.0 Brabham BT46-Alfa Romeo F12	engine	5/27
ret	CANADIAN GP	Montreal	1	Parmalat Racing Team	G	3.0 Brabham BT46-Alfa Romeo F12	brakes-accident	7/28

1979 Championship position: 0 Wins: 0 Pole positions: 0 Fastest laps: 0 Points scored: 0

ret	ARGENTINE GP	Buenos Aires	5	Parmalat Racing Team	G	3.0 Brabham BT48-Alfa Romeo V12	fuel pressure	– / –
dns	"	"	5	Parmalat Racing Team	G	3.0 Brabham BT46-Alfa Romeo F12	practice only-set grid time	23/26
ret	BRAZILIAN GP	Interlagos	5	Parmalat Racing Team	G	3.0 Brabham BT48-Alfa Romeo V12	gear linkage	12/26
6	SOUTH AFRICAN GP	Kyalami	5	Parmalat Racing Team	G	3.0 Brabham BT48-Alfa Romeo V12	pit stop-tyres/1 lap behind	4/26
ret	US GP WEST	Long Beach	5	Parmalat Racing Team	G	3.0 Brabham BT48-Alfa Romeo V12	collision with Tambay	11/26
ret	SPANISH GP	Jarama	5	Parmalat Racing Team	G	3.0 Brabham BT48-Alfa Romeo V12	water leak	6/27
ret	BELGIAN GP	Zolder	5	Parmalat Racing Team	G	3.0 Brabham BT48-Alfa Romeo V12	engine	13/28
ret	MONACO GP	Monte Carlo	5	Parmalat Racing Team	G	3.0 Brabham BT48-Alfa Romeo V12	accident with Pironi	4/25
ret	FRENCH GP	Dijon	5	Parmalat Racing Team	G	3.0 Brabham BT48-Alfa Romeo V12	spun off-could not restart	6/27
ret	BRITISH GP	Silverstone	5	Parmalat Racing Team	G	3.0 Brabham BT48-Alfa Romeo V12	brakes	6/26
ret	GERMAN GP	Hockenheim	5	Parmalat Racing Team	G	3.0 Brabham BT48-Alfa Romeo V12	engine	7/26
ret	AUSTRIAN GP	Österreichring	5	Parmalat Racing Team	G	3.0 Brabham BT48-Alfa Romeo V12	oil leak	4/26
ret	DUTCH GP	Zandvoort	5	Parmalat Racing Team	G	3.0 Brabham BT48-Alfa Romeo V12	withdrew-wrist injury	9/26
4	ITALIAN GP	Monza	5	Parmalat Racing Team	G	3.0 Brabham BT48-Alfa Romeo V12		9/28
dnp	CANADIAN GP	Montreal	5	Parmalat Racing Team	G	3.0 Brabham BT49-Cosworth V8	quit after Friday a.m. practice	– / –

1982 Championship position: 5th Wins: 2 Pole positions: 0 Fastest laps: 1 Points scored: 30

4	SOUTH AFRICAN GP	Kyalami	8	Marlboro McLaren International	M	3.0 McLaren MP4-Cosworth V8		13/30
ret	BRAZILIAN GP	Rio	8	Marlboro McLaren International	M	3.0 McLaren MP4B-Cosworth V8	hit by Reutemann	5/31
1	US GP WEST	Long Beach	8	Marlboro McLaren International	M	3.0 McLaren MP4B-Cosworth V8	FL	2/31
dsq*	BELGIAN GP	Zolder	8	Marlboro McLaren International	M	3.0 McLaren MP4B-Cosworth V8	3rd on road/*car underweight	4/32

Lauda and Ferrari were back on top in 1977, taking their second drivers' championship in three years before the Austrian made a shock exit at season's end.

Despite being outpaced by team-mate Alain Prost through much of the 1984 season, Lauda clinched his third world title by finishing second in the Portuguese Grand Prix.

ret	MONACO GP	Monte Carlo	8	Marlboro McLaren International	M	3.0 McLaren MP4B-Cosworth V8	engine	12/31
ret	US GP (DETROIT)	Detroit	8	Marlboro McLaren International	M	3.0 McLaren MP4B-Cosworth V8	hit Rosberg	10/28
ret	CANADIAN GP	Montreal	8	Marlboro McLaren International	M	3.0 McLaren MP4B-Cosworth V8	clutch	11/29
4	DUTCH GP	Zandvoort	8	Marlboro McLaren International	M	3.0 McLaren MP4B-Cosworth V8		5/31
1	BRITISH GP	Brands Hatch	8	Marlboro McLaren International	M	3.0 McLaren MP4B-Cosworth V8		5/30
8	FRENCH GP	Paul Ricard	8	Marlboro McLaren International	M	3.0 McLaren MP4B-Cosworth V8	pit stop-tyres/1 lap behind	9/30
dns	GERMAN GP	Hockenheim	8	Marlboro McLaren International	M	3.0 McLaren MP4B-Cosworth V8	hurt wrist in practice	(8)/30
5	AUSTRIAN GP	Österreichring	8	Marlboro McLaren International	M	3.0 McLaren MP4B-Cosworth V8	1 lap behind	10/29
3	SWISS GP	Dijon	8	Marlboro McLaren International	M	3.0 McLaren MP4B-Cosworth V8		4/29
ret	ITALIAN GP	Monza	8	Marlboro McLaren International	M	3.0 McLaren MP4B-Cosworth V8	handling/brakes	10/30
ret	CAESARS PALACE GP	Las Vegas	8	Marlboro McLaren International	M	3.0 McLaren MP4B-Cosworth V8	engine	13/30

1983   Championship position: 10th   Wins: 0   Pole positions: 0   Fastest laps: 1   Points scored: 12

3	BRAZILIAN GP	Rio	8	Marlboro McLaren International	M	3.0 McLaren MP4/1C-Cosworth V8		9/27
2	US GP WEST	Long Beach	8	Marlboro McLaren International	M	3.0 McLaren MP4/1C-Cosworth V8	FL	23/28
ret	FRENCH GP	Paul Ricard	8	Marlboro McLaren International	M	3.0 McLaren MP4/1C-Cosworth V8	wheel bearing	12/29
ret	SAN MARINO GP	Imola	8	Marlboro McLaren International	M	3.0 McLaren MP4/1C-Cosworth V8	hit barrier	18/28
dnq	MONACO GP	Monte Carlo	8	Marlboro McLaren International	M	3.0 McLaren MP4/1C-Cosworth V8		22/28
ret	BELGIAN GP	Spa	8	Marlboro McLaren International	M	3.0 McLaren MP4/1C-Cosworth V8	engine	15/28
ret	US GP (DETROIT)	Detroit	8	Marlboro McLaren International	M	3.0 McLaren MP4/1C-Cosworth V8	shock absorber	18/27
ret	CANADIAN GP	Montreal	8	Marlboro McLaren International	M	3.0 McLaren MP4/1C-Cosworth V8	spun off-could not restart	19/28
6	BRITISH GP	Silverstone	8	Marlboro McLaren International	M	3.0 McLaren MP4/1C-Cosworth V8	pit stop-tyres/1 lap behind	15/29
dsq*	GERMAN GP	Hockenheim	8	Marlboro McLaren International	M	3.0 McLaren MP4/1C-Cosworth V8	5th on road/*reversed into pits	18/29
6	AUSTRIAN GP	Österreichring	8	Marlboro McLaren International	M	3.0 McLaren MP4/1C-Cosworth V8	pit stop-tyres/2 laps behind	14/29
ret	DUTCH GP	Zandvoort	8	Marlboro McLaren International	M	1.5 t/c McLaren MP4/1E-TAG V6	brakes	19/29
ret	ITALIAN GP	Monza	8	Marlboro McLaren International	M	1.5 t/c McLaren MP4/1E-TAG V6	electrics	13/29
ret	EUROPEAN GP	Brands Hatch	8	Marlboro McLaren International	M	1.5 t/c McLaren MP4/1E-TAG V6	engine	13/29
11/ret	SOUTH AFRICAN GP	Kyalami	8	Marlboro McLaren International	M	1.5 t/c McLaren MP4/1E-TAG V6	electrics/6 laps behind	12/26

1984   Championship position: WORLD CHAMPION   Wins: 5   Pole positions: 0   Fastest laps: 5   Points scored: 72

ret	BRAZILIAN GP	Rio	8	Marlboro McLaren International	M	1.5 t/c McLaren MP4/2-TAG V6	electrics	6/27
1	SOUTH AFRICAN GP	Kyalami	8	Marlboro McLaren International	M	1.5 t/c McLaren MP4/2-TAG V6		8/27
ret	BELGIAN GP	Zolder	8	Marlboro McLaren International	M	1.5 t/c McLaren MP4/2-TAG V6	water pump	14/27
ret	SAN MARINO GP	Imola	8	Marlboro McLaren International	M	1.5 t/c McLaren MP4/2-TAG V6	engine	5/28
1	FRENCH GP	Dijon	8	Marlboro McLaren International	M	1.5 t/c McLaren MP4/2-TAG V6		9/27
ret	MONACO GP	Monte Carlo	8	Marlboro McLaren International	M	1.5 t/c McLaren MP4/2-TAG V6	spun off	8/27
2	CANADIAN GP	Montreal	8	Marlboro McLaren International	M	1.5 t/c McLaren MP4/2-TAG V6		8/26
ret	US GP (DETROIT)	Detroit	8	Marlboro McLaren International	M	1.5 t/c McLaren MP4/2-TAG V6	electrics	10/27
9/ret	US GP (DALLAS)	Dallas	8	Marlboro McLaren International	M	1.5 t/c McLaren MP4/2-TAG V6	hit wall/FL/7 laps behind	5/27
1	BRITISH GP	Brands Hatch	8	Marlboro McLaren International	M	1.5 t/c McLaren MP4/2-TAG V6	FL	3/27
2	GERMAN GP	Hockenheim	8	Marlboro McLaren International	M	1.5 t/c McLaren MP4/2-TAG V6		7/27
1	AUSTRIAN GP	Österreichring	8	Marlboro McLaren International	M	1.5 t/c McLaren MP4/2-TAG V6	FL	4/28
2	DUTCH GP	Zandvoort	8	Marlboro McLaren International	M	1.5 t/c McLaren MP4/2-TAG V6		6/27
1	ITALIAN GP	Monza	8	Marlboro McLaren International	M	1.5 t/c McLaren MP4/2-TAG V6	FL	4/27
4	EUROPEAN GP	Nürburgring	8	Marlboro McLaren International	M	1.5 t/c McLaren MP4/2-TAG V6		15/26
2	PORTUGESE GP	Estoril	8	Marlboro McLaren International	M	1.5 t/c McLaren MP4/2-TAG V6	FL	11/27

1985   Championship position: 10th   Wins: 1   Pole positions: 0   Fastest laps: 1   Points scored: 14

ret	BRAZILIAN GP	Rio	1	Marlboro McLaren International	G	1.5 t/c McLaren MP4/2B-TAG V6	fuel metering unit	9/25
ret	PORTUGESE GP	Estoril	1	Marlboro McLaren International	G	1.5 t/c McLaren MP4/2B-TAG V6	engine	7/26
4	SAN MARINO GP	Imola	1	Marlboro McLaren International	G	1.5 t/c McLaren MP4/2B-TAG V6	gearbox problems/-1 lap	8/26
ret	MONACO GP	Monte Carlo	1	Marlboro McLaren International	G	1.5 t/c McLaren MP4/2B-TAG V6	spun off-could not restart	14/26
ret	CANADIAN GP	Montreal	1	Marlboro McLaren International	G	1.5 t/c McLaren MP4/2B-TAG V6	engine	17/25
ret	US GP (DETROIT)	Detroit	1	Marlboro McLaren International	G	1.5 t/c McLaren MP4/2B-TAG V6	brakes	12/25
ret	FRENCH GP	Paul Ricard	1	Marlboro McLaren International	G	1.5 t/c McLaren MP4/2B-TAG V6	gearbox	6/26
ret	BRITISH GP	Silverstone	1	Marlboro McLaren International	G	1.5 t/c McLaren MP4/2B-TAG V6	electrics	10/26
5	GERMAN GP	Nürburgring	1	Marlboro McLaren International	G	1.5 t/c McLaren MP4/2B-TAG V6	pit stop-loose wheel/FL	12/27
ret	AUSTRIAN GP	Österreichring	1	Marlboro McLaren International	G	1.5 t/c McLaren MP4/2B-TAG V6	engine	3/27
1	DUTCH GP	Zandvoort	1	Marlboro McLaren International	G	1.5 t/c McLaren MP4/2B-TAG V6		10/27
ret	ITALIAN GP	Monza	1	Marlboro McLaren International	G	1.5 t/c McLaren MP4/2B-TAG V6	transmission	16/26
dns	BELGIAN GP	Spa	1	Marlboro McLaren International	G	1.5 t/c McLaren MP4/2B-TAG V6	injured wrist in practice accident	– / –
ret	SOUTH AFRICAN GP	Kyalami	1	Marlboro McLaren International	G	1.5 t/c McLaren MP4/2B-TAG V6	turbo	8/21
ret	AUSTRALIAN GP	Adelaide	1	Marlboro McLaren International	G	1.5 t/c McLaren MP4/2B-TAG V6	brake problem-hit wall	16/25

GP Starts: 170 (171)   GP Wins: 25   Pole positions: 24   Fastest laps: 24   Points: 420.5

ROGER LAURENT

A member of the famed Ecurie Belgique, Laurent raced the team's Veritas RS, before making occasional appearances in their newly acquired Lago-Talbot in 1951, taking seventh place at Albi. The following year he ventured to Helsinki to win an F1 race against entirely local opposition, without an F1 car among them!

Now renamed Ecurie Francorchamps, the team ran a Ferrari T500 in 1952, but with de Tornaco behind the wheel at Spa, Laurent hired an HWM for the Grand Prix. It was Roger's turn to try the T500 in the German GP and he finished a solid sixth. He coaxed a few other decent placings from the yellow-painted machine, most notably second at Chimay in 1953 and fourth at Syracuse in 1954.

Laurent also enjoyed quite a successful time in the team's sports car programme, particularly when the Jaguar XK120 was replaced by a C-Type in 1954. He was third in the Dutch GP for sports machines and, with Swaters, third at Reims and then fourth at Le Mans. A crash in practice for a race at Bari in 1955 left him with a broken leg, but he did return when fit.

His final racing season was in 1956, when he once again took fourth place at Le Mans in a Jaguar D-Type shared with Rousselle.

GIOVANNI LAVAGGI

A former consultant engineer, Lavaggi began competing in local rallies, but then got his kicks skiing and hang-gliding until a broken leg ended this dangerous pastime.

Returning to the track, Giovanni quickly found a niche, successfully handling a Kremer Porsche 962 sports car in 1989. But with Formula 1 his long-term aim, he cut down on his business commitments to spend a preparatory year in F3000. His 1992 season with Crypton was disappointing to say the least, with the Italian failing to qualify for eight of ten races.

Undaunted by the collapse of the March F1 team, for whom he had hoped to drive, the personable and friendly Lavaggi had a brief tilt at Indy Car racing in 1994 before he raised enough finance to buy his four-race stint at Pacific in 1995. Giovanni was briefly back on the Grand Prix stage the following season with cash-strapped Minardi, where, to his credit, he was not that far off the pace of team-mate Pedro Lamy.

Lavaggi found his true level in sports car racing, his victory in the 1995 Daytona 24-hour race, in which he shared a Kremer Porsche, being the undoubted highlight of his career.

LAURENT, Roger (B) b 21/2/1913, Liège

	1952	Championship position: Unplaced						
	Race	Circuit	No	Entrant	Tyres	Car/Engine	Comment	Q Pos/Entries
12	BELGIAN GP	Spa	30	HW Motors Ltd	D	2.0 HWM-Alta 4	4 laps behind	20/22
6	GERMAN GP	Nürburgring	119	Ecurie Francorchamps	E	2.0 Ferrari 500 4	2 laps behind	17/32

GP Starts: 2 GP Wins: 0 Pole positions: 0 Fastest laps: 0 Points: 0

LAVAGGI, Giovanni (I) b 18/2/1958, Sicily

	1995	Championship position: Unplaced						
	Race	Circuit	No	Entrant	Tyres	Car/Engine	Comment	Q Pos/Entries
ret	GERMAN GP	Hockenheim	16	Pacific Grand Prix Ltd	G	3.0 Pacific PR02-Ford ED V8	gearbox	24/24
ret	HUNGARIAN GP	Hungaroring	16	Pacific Grand Prix Ltd	G	3.0 Pacific PR02-Ford ED V8	spun off	24/24
ret	BELGIAN GP	Spa	16	Pacific Grand Prix Ltd	G	3.0 Pacific PR02-Ford ED V8	gearbox	23/24
ret	ITALIAN GP	Monza	16	Pacific Grand Prix Ltd	G	3.0 Pacific PR02-Ford ED V8	spun off	24/24
	1996	Championship position: Unplaced						
	Race	Circuit	No	Entrant	Tyres	Car/Engine	Comment	Q Pos/Entries
dnq	GERMAN GP	Hockenheim	21	Minardi Team	G	3.0 Minardi 195B-Ford EDM V8	not within 107% of pole	20/20
10/ret	HUNGARIAN GP	Hungaroring	21	Minardi Team	G	3.0 Minardi 195B-Ford EDM V8	spun off//8 laps behind	20/20
dnq	BELGIAN GP	Spa	21	Minardi Team	G	3.0 Minardi 195B-Ford EDM V8	not within 107% of pole	20/20
ret	ITALIAN GP	Monza	21	Minardi Team	G	3.0 Minardi 195B-Ford EDM V8	engine	20/20
15	PORTUGUESE GP	Estoril	21	Minardi Team	G	3.0 Minardi 195B-Ford EDM V8	5 laps behind	20/20
dnq	JAPANESE GP	Suzuka	21	Minardi Team	G	3.0 Minardi 195B-Ford EDM V8	not within 107% of pole	20/20

GP Starts: 7 GP Wins: 0 Pole positions: 0 Fastest laps: 0 Points: 0

LAWRENCE, Chris (GB) b 27/7/1933

	1966	Championship position: Unplaced						
	Race	Circuit	No	Entrant	Tyres	Car/Engine	Comment	Q Pos/Entries
11	BRITISH GP	Brands Hatch	24	J A Pearce Engineering Ltd	D	2.9 Cooper T73-Ferrari V12	7 laps behind	19/20
ret	GERMAN GP	Nürburgring	20	J A Pearce Engineering Ltd	D	2.9 Cooper T73-Ferrari V12	front suspension	27/30

GP Starts: 2 GP Wins: 0 Pole positions: 0 Fastest laps: 0 Points: 0

CHRIS LAWRENCE

A club driver from the late fifties in MGs and particularly Morgans, with which he clocked up some modest triumphs, Lawrence ran a London engine-tuning business, and became involved in the ill-fated Deep-Sanderson sports car project of 1963-64.

With the introduction of the 3-litre formula in 1966, Chris raced a shoestring Cooper-Ferrari special, which he took to fifth place in that year's Gold Cup race at Oulton Park. Following the project's demise in 1967, he resurfaced briefly in sports car racing, then worked in France designing road cars, before returning to his beloved Morgans in the early seventies, running a tuning company specialising in that marque.

Subsequently, Chris spent a number of years in America, but he is now back in Britain working on designs for the Morgan company once more.

MICHEL LECLÈRE

A runner-up in the 1972 Formule Renault series, Leclère won the French Formula 3 championship for Alpine the following year.

Michel's career seemed to be taking shape well during 1974-75 when he was a front-runner in Formula 2 and won races at Rouen, Zolder and Silverstone, earning an F1 chance with Tyrrell and a contract with Wolf-Williams for 1976. In the event, the car was awful and the team despondent, and poor Leclère was jettisoned in mid-season, returning to Formula 2 with Elf-Renault and finishing fourth in the championship.

His career never really recovered after a disastrous F2 season with Kauhsen in 1977 destroyed his chances of a Formula 1 comeback. Thereafter he scratched about with only occasional sports car and single-seater outings before quitting for good.

NEVILLE LEDERLE

Rightly regarded as one of his country's outstanding prospects, Lederle made an immediate impression on South African racing with his Lotus 18 late in 1961. This promise was confirmed the following year, when he finished sixth in the South African GP to score a point in what was to be his only Grand Prix start. This achievement proved to be a double-edged sword, however, for he was classed as a graded driver and was therefore not eligible to score points in Formula Junior or national races outside South Africa.

Neville stayed at home in 1963, dominating his domestic series with a string of wins in his Lotus 21, until a practice accident at the Rand 9 Hours sports car race left him sidelined with a broken leg. He missed that year's Grand Prix and also the 1964 Springbok series, after his injury proved very slow to heal. This, coupled with increasing business commitments, prompted Lederle's retirement, though he did bring the old Lotus out for the end-of-season Rand Grand Prix and the South African GP in January 1965, where, as fastest non-qualifier, he just failed to make the grid.

LECLÈRE, Michel (F) b 18/3/1946, Mantes la Jolie, nr Paris

	1975	Championship position: Unplaced							
	Race	Circuit	No	Entrant	Tyres	Car/Engine	Comment		Q Pos/Entries
ret	US GP	Watkins Glen	15	Elf Team Tyrrell	G	3.0 Tyrrell 007-Cosworth V8	engine		20/24
	1976	Championship position: Unplaced							
13	SOUTH AFRICAN GP	Kyalami	21	Frank Williams Racing Cars	G	3.0 Williams FW05-Cosworth V8	2 laps behind		22/25
dnq	US GP WEST	Long Beach	21	Frank Williams Racing Cars	G	3.0 Williams FW05-Cosworth V8			21/27
10	SPANISH GP	Jarama	21	Walter Wolf Racing	G	3.0 Williams FW05-Cosworth V8			23/30
11	BELGIAN GP	Zolder	21	Walter Wolf Racing	G	3.0 Williams FW05-Cosworth V8	2 laps behind		25/29
11	MONACO GP	Monte Carlo	21	Walter Wolf Racing	G	3.0 Williams FW05-Cosworth V8	2 laps behind		18/25
ret	SWEDISH GP	Anderstorp	21	Walter Wolf Racing	G	3.0 Williams FW05-Cosworth V8	engine		25/27
13	FRENCH GP	Paul Ricard	21	Walter Wolf Racing	G	3.0 Williams FW05-Cosworth V8	1 lap behind		22/30

GP Starts: 7   GP Wins: 0   Pole positions: 0   Fastest laps: 0   Points: 0

LEDERLE, Neville (ZA) b 25/9/1938, Theunisssen, Winburg, Orange Free State

	1962	Championship position: 18th=		Wins: 0	Pole positions: 0	Fastest laps: 0	Points scored: 1		
	Race	Circuit	No	Entrant	Tyres	Car/Engine	Comment		Q Pos/Entries
6	SOUTH AFRICAN GP	East London	20	Neville Lederle	D	1.5 Lotus 21-Climax 4	4 laps behind		10/17
	1965	Championship position: Unplaced							
dnq	SOUTH AFRICAN GP	East London	23	Scuderia Scribante	D	1.5 Lotus 21-Climax 4			=21/25

GP Starts: 1   GP Wins: 0   Pole positions: 0   Fastest laps: 0   Points: 1

GEOFF LEES

A professional racing driver in the truest sense of the word, Lees never really had the Formula 1 opportunities that his talent demanded, but he has nevertheless enjoyed continued success in virtually every other type of racing he has tried. A Formula Ford champion in the mid-seventies, Geoff soon moved into F3 with a works Chevron, then tackled the Aurora F1 series and Can-Am, and won the Macau GP twice, while taking the occasional Grand Prix chances that came his way.

In 1981 he won the European Formula 2 championship with the Ralt-Honda, but even this could not bring Lees the big chance he had hoped for, and he eventually turned his back on Europe. For many years he lived in Japan, marrying a local girl, and carved out a fine career, particularly as leader of the TOM'S Toyota sports car team.

Between 1995 and mid-1997 Geoff led the Lister Storm line-up, mainly partnering Tiff Needell, but continued lack of success blunted his enthusiasm and he found a more rewarding berth with the GTC team, racing their McLaren F1 GTRs.

In 1998 his great experience was still in demand by Toyota for their Le Mans challenge. The race brought heartbreak, however, for Lees (with co-drivers Boutsen and Kelleners) when a possible first victory at the Sarthe circuit was lost when their car failed just 80 minutes from the finish when leading.

ARTHUR LEGAT

If ever a driver was identified with just one circuit, then it must be dear old Arthur Legat, who first saw competition at the Chimay track in Belgium when it opened in 1926, for he was still in action there some thirty years later! This fast and very dangerous 6.754-mile temporary road course close to the French border hosted the annual Grand Prix des Fontières and was a magnet for semi-professional and amateur racers who came to test their skills. In his younger days, Legat won the race twice with his Bugatti T37A, in 1931 and 1932, and actually appeared there 25 times in total.

Having bought a Veritas-Meteor for the 1951 season he then wheeled out the machine almost unchanged for occasional outings during the next few seasons, venturing to Spa for the Belgian Grand Prix in 1952 and 1953, when the German machine conformed to the then current Formula 2 regulations.

LEES, Geoff (GB) b 1/5/1951, Atherstone, Warwickshire

	1978	Championship position: Unplaced						
	Race	*Circuit*	*No*	*Entrant*	*Tyres*	*Car/Engine*	*Comment*	*Q Pos/Entries*
dnq	BRITISH GP	Brands Hatch	23	Mario Deliotti Racing	G	3.0 Ensign N175-Cosworth V8		29/30
	1979	Championship position: Unplaced						
7	GERMAN GP	Hockenheim	4	Candy Tyrrell Team	G	3.0 Tyrrell 009-Cosworth V8	*1 lap behind*	16/26
	1980	Championship position: Unplaced						
13/ret	SOUTH AFRICAN GP	Kyalami	17	Shadow Cars	G	3.0 Shadow DN11-Cosworth V8	*suspension failure/-8 laps*	25/28
dnq	US GP WEST	Long Beach	17	Shadow Cars	G	3.0 Shadow DN11-Cosworth V8	*unwell w/drawn after 1st practice*	26/27
dnq	BELGIAN GP	Zolder	17	Shadow Cars	G	3.0 Shadow DN12-Cosworth V8		25/27
dnq	MONACO GP	Monte Carlo	17	Shadow Cars	G	3.0 Shadow DN12-Cosworth V8		23/27
dnq	FRENCH GP	Paul Ricard	17	Shadow Cars	G	3.0 Shadow DN12-Cosworth V8		25/27
ret	DUTCH GP	Zandvoort	41	Unipart Racing Team	G	3.0 Ensign N180-Cosworth V8	*accident with Brambilla*	24/28
dnq	ITALIAN GP	Imola	41	Unipart Racing Team	G	3.0 Ensign N180-Cosworth V8		28/28
dnq	US GP EAST	Watkins Glen	51	RAM/Theodore/Rainbow Jeans Racing	G	3.0 Williams FW07B-Cosworth V8	*no time recorded*	– /27
	1982	Championship position: Unplaced						
ret/dns	CANADIAN GP	Montreal	33	Theodore Racing Team	G	3.0 Theodore TY02-Cosworth V8	*1st start accident/did not restart*	25/29
12	FRENCH GP	Paul Ricard	12	John Player Team Lotus	G	3.0 Lotus 91-Cosworth V8	*pit stop-puncture/-2 laps*	24/30

GP Starts: 4 (5)   GP Wins: 0   Pole positions: 0   Fastest laps: 0   Points: 0

LEGAT, Arthur (B) b 1/11/1898, Haine-Saint-Paul – d 23/2/1960, Haine-Saint-Pierre

	1952	Championship position: Unplaced						
	Race	*Circuit*	*No*	*Entrant*	*Tyres*	*Car/Engine*	*Comment*	*Q Pos/Entries*
nc	BELGIAN GP	Spa	38	Arthur Legat	E	2.0 Veritas Meteor 6	*5 laps behind*	21/22
	1953	Championship position: 0 Wins: 0 Pole positions: 0 Fastest laps: 0 Points scored: 0						
ret	BELGIAN GP	Spa	36	Arthur Legat	E	2.0 Veritas Meteor 6	*transmission*	19/22

GP Starts: 2   GP Wins: 0   Pole positions: 0   Fastest laps: 0   Points: 0

JJ LEHTO

Involved in motor sport since taking up karting at the age of six, JJ built up a tremendous record in the junior formulae, winning the Scandinavian FF1600 championship in 1986 before coming to England in 1987 to take the British and European FF2000 titles.

His career carefully nurtured and guided by the shrewd hands of Keke Rosberg, Lehto moved into Fomula 3 in 1988 with the Pacific Racing team that had brought him his FF2000 success. After a devastating start to the season he cruised to yet another championship, with a total of eight wins and only a late-season charge from Gary Brabham by way of serious competition.

Lehto and Pacific found things tougher when they moved up to F3000 together, however, with the Finn finding only modest success (and being somewhat overshadowed by team-mate Eddie Irvine) before replacing the out-of-favour Bertrand Gachot at Onyx late in 1989. This was to prove his salvation, for a sparkling qualifying performance in the Spanish Grand Prix effectively cemented his place in the team. The following season was largely wasted as the once promising little team fell into the hands of Peter Monteverdi and then folded after the Hungarian GP.

Then followed a two-year deal with Scuderia Italia. The first season, with Judd engines, was generally encouraging, with the team making progress, and JJ scored his first podium finish at Imola, but the switch to Ferrari engines in 1992 was to prove dispiriting and Lehto's once sky-high reputation was starting to be questioned. Certainly his career had not yet produced the success widely expected, but he was still highly thought of, and joined the Sauber team for 1993. Early-season promise soon evaporated when internal politics divided the team into two camps, but perhaps more tellingly team-mate Karl Wendlinger was looking the better long-term prospect.

Given his F1 record, JJ was seen as fortunate to gain a chance at Benetton in 1994, and it seemed certain to be his best-ever opportunity to make the big breakthrough to the front rank. Unfortunately it all went horribly wrong when a testing crash left him with fractured neck vertebrae and his confidence never fully recovered. Inconsistent qualifying performances led to his being replaced by Jos Verstappen, and when he did get a return, due to Schumacher's enforced absence, he was slower than his inexperienced team-mate. Perhaps it might have been different for JJ if he had been put into a front-line team much earlier in his career, or maybe he just wasn't all he was cracked up to be in the first place . . .

In 1995 he took up the challenge of the DTM/ITC with Opel, but without doubt the season's high spot was his win at Le Mans with Yannick Dalmas and Masanori Sekiya in a McLaren F1 GTR. Indeed, sports car racing was to bring a welcome upturn in fortunes for Lehto. In 1997, driving a Schnitzer-run McLaren F1 GTR, the Finn won four rounds outright (at Hockenheim, Helsinki, Spa and Mugello) and was easily the best of the drivers challenging the might of the silver Mercedes.

Shrewd management brought Lehto a chance to take a crack at CART in 1998, JJ joining veteran team owner Carl Hogan to race a Reynard-Mercedes in which, surprisingly perhaps, he shone on the ovals but struggled somewhat on the road courses. All seemed set fair for a continuation of this partnership until he was unceremoniously dumped just before the start of the 1999 season. Poor Lehto's career seemed to lie in tatters, but once again sports cars proved to be his salvation. A win in the Sebring 12 Hours for BMW led to a contract to race Schnitzer's BMW V12 LM in the American Le Mans Series, where he formed a strong partnership once more with Steve Soper, winning at Sears Point, Laguna Seca and Las Vegas.

LEHTO JJ (Jyrki Jarvilehto) (SF) b 31/1/1966, Espoo

	1989	Championship position: Unplaced							
	Race	Circuit	No	Entrant	Tyres	Car/Engine		Comment	Q Pos/Entries
dnpq	PORTUGUESE GP	Estoril	37	Moneytron Onyx	G	3.5 Onyx ORE 1-Cosworth V8			32/39
ret	SPANISH GP	Jerez	37	Moneytron Onyx	G	3.5 Onyx ORE 1-Cosworth V8		gearbox	17/38
dnpq	JAPANESE GP	Suzuka	37	Moneytron Onyx	G	3.5 Onyx ORE 1-Cosworth V8			36/39
ret	AUSTRALIAN GP	Adelaide	37	Moneytron Onyx	G	3.5 Onyx ORE 1-Cosworth V8		engine-electrics	17/39
	1990	Championship position: Unplaced							
dnq	US GP (PHOENIX)	Phoenix	36	Moneytron Onyx Formula One	G	3.5 Onyx ORE 1-Cosworth V8		no time recorded	– /35
dnq	BRAZILIAN GP	Interlagos	36	Moneytron Onyx Formula One	G	3.5 Onyx ORE 1-Cosworth V8			28/35
12	SAN MARINO GP	Imola	36	Moneytron Onyx Formula One	G	3.5 Onyx ORE 1B-Cosworth V8		engine problems/-2 laps	26/35
ret	MONACO GP	Monte Carlo	36	Moneytron Onyx Formula One	G	3.5 Onyx ORE 1B-Cosworth V8		gearbox	26/35
ret	CANADIAN GP	Montreal	36	Moneytron Onyx Formula One	G	3.5 Onyx ORE 1B-Cosworth V8		engine	22/35
ret	MEXICAN GP	Mexico City	36	Moneytron Onyx Formula One	G	3.5 Onyx ORE 1B-Cosworth V8		engine	27/35
dnq	FRENCH GP	Paul Ricard	36	Moneytron Onyx Formula One	G	3.5 Onyx ORE 1B-Cosworth V8			30/35
dnq	BRITISH GP	Silverstone	36	Monteverdi Onyx Formula One	G	3.5 Onyx ORE 1B-Cosworth V8			29/35
nc	GERMAN GP	Hockenheim	36	Monteverdi Onyx Formula One	G	3.5 Monteverdi ORE 1B-Cosworth V8		misfire/bodywork /-6 laps	25/35
dnq	HUNGARIAN GP	Hungaroring	36	Monteverdi Onyx Formula One	G	3.5 Monteverdi ORE 1B-Cosworth V8			29/35
	1991	Championship position: 12th=	Wins: 0	Pole positions: 0		Fastest laps: 0	Points scored: 4		
ret	US GP (PHOENIX)	Phoenix	22	Scuderia Italia SpA	P	3.5 BMS Dallara 191-Judd V10		clutch	10/34
ret	BRAZILIAN GP	Interlagos	22	Scuderia Italia SpA	P	3.5 BMS Dallara 191-Judd V10		alternator	19/34
3	SAN MARINO GP	Imola	22	Scuderia Italia SpA	P	3.5 BMS Dallara 191-Judd V10		1 lap behind	16/34
11	MONACO GP	Monte Carlo	22	Scuderia Italia SpA	P	3.5 BMS Dallara 191-Judd V10		3 laps behind	13/34
ret	CANADIAN GP	Montreal	22	Scuderia Italia SpA	P	3.5 BMS Dallara 191-Judd V10		engine	17/34

ret	MEXICAN GP	Mexico City	22	Scuderia Italia SpA	P	3.5 BMS Dallara 191-Judd V10	engine	16/34
ret	FRENCH GP	Magny Cours	22	Scuderia Italia SpA	P	3.5 BMS Dallara 191-Judd V10	puncture	26/34
13	BRITISH GP	Silverstone	22	Scuderia Italia SpA	P	3.5 BMS Dallara 191-Judd V10	3 laps behind	11/34
ret	GERMAN GP	Hockenheim	22	Scuderia Italia SpA	P	3.5 BMS Dallara 191-Judd V10	engine	20/34
ret	HUNGARIAN GP	Hungaroring	22	Scuderia Italia SpA	P	3.5 BMS Dallara 191-Judd V10	engine	12/34
ret	BELGIAN GP	Spa	22	Scuderia Italia SpA	P	3.5 BMS Dallara 191-Judd V10	engine	14/34
ret	ITALIAN GP	Monza	22	Scuderia Italia SpA	P	3.5 BMS Dallara 191-Judd V10	puncture-suspension	20/24
ret	PORTUGUESE GP	Estoril	22	Scuderia Italia SpA	P	3.5 BMS Dallara 191-Judd V10	gear linkage	18/34
8	SPANISH GP	Barcelona	22	Scuderia Italia SpA	P	3.5 BMS Dallara 191-Judd V10	1 lap behind	15/33
ret	JAPANESE GP	Suzuka	22	Scuderia Italia SpA	P	3.5 BMS Dallara 191-Judd V10	spun avoiding de Cesaris	12/31
12	AUSTRALIAN GP	Phoenix	22	Scuderia Italia SpA	P	3.5 BMS Dallara 191-Judd V10	rain shortened race	11/32

1992 — Championship position: Unplaced

ret	SOUTH AFRICAN GP	Kyalami	21	Scuderia Italia SpA	G	3.5 BMS Dallara 192-Ferrari V12	final drive	24/30
8	MEXICAN GP	Mexico City	21	Scuderia Italia SpA	G	3.5 BMS Dallara 192-Ferrari V12	1 lap behind	7/30
8	BRAZILIAN GP	Interlagos	21	Scuderia Italia SpA	G	3.5 BMS Dallara 192-Ferrari V12	2 laps behind	16/31
ret	SPANISH GP	Barcelona	21	Scuderia Italia SpA	G	3.5 BMS Dallara 192-Ferrari V12	spun off	12/32
11/ret	SAN MARINO GP	Imola	21	Scuderia Italia SpA	G	3.5 BMS Dallara 192-Ferrari V12	engine cut out/3 laps behind	16/32
9	MONACO GP	Monte Carlo	21	Scuderia Italia SpA	G	3.5 BMS Dallara 192-Ferrari V12	2 laps behind	20/32
9	CANADIAN GP	Montreal	21	Scuderia Italia SpA	G	3.5 BMS Dallara 192-Ferrari V12	1 lap behind	23/32
9*	FRENCH GP	Magny Cours	21	Scuderia Italia SpA	G	3.5 BMS Dallara 192-Ferrari V12	*agg of 2 parts/2 laps behind	17/30
13	BRITISH GP	Silverstone	21	Scuderia Italia SpA	G	3.5 BMS Dallara 192-Ferrari V12	2 laps behind	19/32
10	GERMAN GP	Hockenheim	21	Scuderia Italia SpA	G	3.5 BMS Dallara 192-Ferrari V12	1 lap behind	21/32
dnq	HUNGARIAN GP	Hungaroring	21	Scuderia Italia SpA	G	3.5 BMS Dallara 192-Ferrari V12		28/31
7	BELGIAN GP	Spa	21	Scuderia Italia SpA	G	3.5 BMS Dallara 192-Ferrari V12	1 lap behind	16/30
11/ret	ITALIAN GP	Monza	21	Scuderia Italia SpA	G	3.5 BMS Dallara 192-Ferrari V12	electrics-engine/6 laps behind	14/28
ret	PORTUGUESE GP	Estoril	21	Scuderia Italia SpA	G	3.5 BMS Dallara 192-Ferrari V12	accident damage	19/26
9	JAPANESE GP	Suzuka	21	Scuderia Italia SpA	G	3.5 BMS Dallara 192-Ferrari V12	1 lap behind	22/26
ret	AUSTRALIAN GP	Phoenix	21	Scuderia Italia SpA	G	3.5 BMS Dallara 192-Ferrari V12	gearbox	24/26

1993 — Championship position: 13th=   Wins: 0   Pole positions: 0   Fastest laps: 0   Points scored: 5

5	SOUTH AFRICAN GP	Kyalami	30	Sauber	G	3.5 Sauber C12-Ilmor V10	2 laps behind	6/26
ret	BRAZILIAN GP	Interlagos	30	Sauber	G	3.5 Sauber C12-Ilmor V10	electrics	7/26
ret	EUROPEAN GP	Donington	30	Sauber	G	3.5 Sauber C12-Ilmor V10	started spare from pit lane/handling	7/26
4/ret	SAN MARINO GP	Imola	30	Sauber	G	3.5 Sauber C12-Ilmor V10	engine/2 laps behind	16/26
ret	SPANISH GP	Barcelona	30	Sauber	G	3.5 Sauber C12-Ilmor V10	engine	9/26
ret	MONACO GP	Monte Carlo	30	Sauber	G	3.5 Sauber C12-Ilmor V10	collision with Wendlinger	11/26
7	CANADIAN GP	Montreal	30	Sauber	G	3.5 Sauber C12-Ilmor V10	lost 2nd & 3rd gears/-1 lap	11/26
ret	FRENCH GP	Magny Cours	30	Sauber	G	3.5 Sauber C12-Ilmor V10	gearbox	18/26
8	BRITISH GP	Silverstone	30	Sauber	G	3.5 Sauber C12-Ilmor V10	1 lap behind	16/26
ret	GERMAN GP	Hockenheim	30	Sauber	G	3.5 Sauber C12-Ilmor V10	stuck throttle-spun out	18/26
ret	HUNGARIAN GP	Hungaroring	30	Sauber	G	3.5 Sauber C12-Ilmor V10	engine	15/26
9	BELGIAN GP	Spa	30	Sauber	G	3.5 Sauber C12-Ilmor V10	understeer/1 lap behind	9/25
ret	ITALIAN GP	Monza	30	Sauber	G	3.5 Sauber C12-Ilmor V10	started-back of grid/accident- lap 1	13/26
7	PORTUGUESE GP	Estoril	30	Sauber	G	3.5 Sauber C12-Ilmor V10	stop & go pen/2 laps behind	12/26
8	JAPANESE GP	Suzuka	30	Sauber	G	3.5 Sauber C12-Ilmor V10	collision Brundle/1 lap behind	11/24
ret	AUSTRALIAN GP	Phoenix	30	Sauber	G	3.5 Sauber C12-Ilmor V10	stuck throttle-accident	12/24

1994 — Championship position: 24th=   Wins: 0   Pole positions: 0   Fastest laps: 0   Points scored: 1

ret	SAN MARINO GP	Imola	6	Mild Seven Benetton Ford	G	3.5 Benetton B194-Ford Zetec-R V8	stalled on grid-hit by Lamy	5/28
7	MONACO GP	Monte Carlo	6	Mild Seven Benetton Ford	G	3.5 Benetton B194-Ford Zetec-R V8	1 lap behind	17/24
ret	SPANISH GP	Barcelona	6	Mild Seven Benetton Ford	G	3.5 Benetton B194-Ford Zetec-R V8	engine	4/27
6	CANADIAN GP	Montreal	6	Mild Seven Benetton Ford	G	3.5 Benetton B194-Ford Zetec-R V8	1 lap behind	20/27
9	ITALIAN GP	Monza	5	Mild Seven Benetton Ford	G	3.5 Benetton B194-Ford Zetec-R V8	1 lap behind	20/28
ret	PORTUGUESE GP	Estoril	5	Mild Seven Benetton Ford	G	3.5 Benetton B194-Ford Zetec-R V8	spun off	14/28
ret	JAPANESE GP	Suzuka	29	Sauber Mercedes	G	3.5 Sauber C13-Mercedes Benz V10	engine on lap 1	15/28
10	AUSTRALIAN GP	Adelaide	29	Sauber Mercedes	G	3.5 Sauber C13-Mercedes Benz V10	2 laps behind	17/28

GP Starts: 62   GP Wins: 0   Pole positions: 0   Fastest laps: 0   Points: 10

LEONI, Lamberto (I) b 24/5/1953, Argenta, Ferrara

1977 — Championship position: Unplaced

	Race	Circuit	No	Entrant	Tyres	Car/Engine	Comment	Q Pos/Entries
dnq	ITALIAN GP	Monza	18	Team Surtees	G	3.0 Surtees TS19-Cosworth V8		27/34

1978 — Championship position: Unplaced

ret	ARGENTINE GP	Buenos Aires	23	Team Tissot Ensign	G	3.0 Ensign N177-Cosworth V8	engine	22/27
dns	BRAZILIAN GP	Rio	23	Team Tissot Ensign	G	3.0 Ensign N177-Cosworth V8	driveshaft on warm-up	(17)/28
dnq	SOUTH AFRICAN GP	Kyalami	22	Team Tissot Ensign	G	3.0 Ensign N177-Cosworth V8		29/30
dnq	US GP WEST	Long Beach	22	Team Tissot Ensign	G	3.0 Ensign N177-Cosworth V8		26/30

GP Starts: 1   GP Wins: 0   Pole positions: 0   Fastest laps: 0   Points: 0

LESTON, Les (GB) b 16/12/1920, Nottingham

1956 — Championship position: Unplaced

	Race	Circuit	No	Entrant	Tyres	Car/Engine	Comment	Q Pos/Entries
ret	ITALIAN GP	Monza	2	Connaught Engineering	P/A	2.5 Connaught-Alta B Type 4	torsion bar	20/26

1957 — Championship position: Unplaced

dnq	MONACO GP	Monte Carlo	16	Cooper Car Co	D	1.5 Cooper T43-Climax 4		21/21
ret	BRITISH GP	Aintree	26	Owen Racing Organisation	D	2.5 BRM P25 4	engine	12/19

GP Starts: 2   GP Wins: 0   Pole positions: 0   Fastest laps: 0   Points: 0

LAMBERTO LEONI

A Fomula Italia champion, Leoni proved to be quick in Italian F3 without gaining the necessary solid results. Racing in Formula 2 in 1977, he unexpectedly won the Adriatic GP on aggregate in his Ferrari-engined Chevron after a dismal start to the season in a Ralt. After failing to qualify his rented works Surtees at Monza in '77, Leoni joined Ensign for the following year, but only made the grid once in four outings and swiftly departed the team.

From then on his career stuttered on with occasional outings in Formula 2, seemingly with the aim of keeping his licence intact, but he then tackled F3000 more seriously and enjoyed some success before being sidelined after a massive shunt at the Österreichring in 1986.

Forming his own FIRST F3000 team, Lamberto returned more determined than ever in 1987, enjoying a consistent final season before retiring to concentrate on management duties, initially guiding the fortunes of Marco Apicella.

LES LESTON

A star of the exciting 500 cc Formula 3 racing of the early fifties, Leston scored an early British win on the Continent in 1952, winning the Luxembourg GP. A runner-up in 1952 and '53, he finally claimed the crown in 1954 at the wheel of a works Cooper before concentrating on sports car racing, enjoying a successful 1955 season in Peter Bell's Connaught.

Les mainly raced John Willment's Cooper sports in 1956, but handled a Connaught in the Italian GP and took third place in the Richmond Trophy with the same car. In 1957 he raced a Formula 2 Cooper in national events, drove for BRM in the British GP and took sixth place in the Nürburgring 1000 Km for Aston Martin, but after escaping with a shaking from a massive crash at Caen in 1958 when his F2 Lotus seized, Les concentrated on his expanding racewear business. He did not desert the circuits, though, having great fun in the early sixties in his red Lotus Elite with the famous 'DAD 10' plate.

'LEVEGH'

Ultimately a tragic figure, 'Levegh' was given the name of his uncle, a racer in the early part of the century. From before the war, he became obsessed with the Le Mans 24-hour race, waiting patiently for an opportunity to take part in this classic and finally achieving his ambition as relief driver in the Talbot team in 1938. After the war he raced a Delage, taking second at Pau in 1947 before acquiring a Talbot in 1949, which he raced in Grands Prix in 1950 and '51.

He finished fourth at Le Mans in a works Talbot in 1951, but was dissatisfied with the car's performance, and resolved to return the following year in his own car, which was specially prepared at huge expense by 'Levegh' himself. His investment was very nearly rewarded when he drove the car single-handedly for more than 22 hours, only to lose a massive lead when he missed a gearchange and damaged the engine.

His dream of victory seemed over, but in 1955 Neubauer, remembering his exploits, offered him a drive in the works Mercedes. By some strange premonition, 'Levegh' had voiced his unease at the narrowness of the straight in front of the pits, and it was his misfortune to be involved in a collision at this point that catapulted his car into the crowd, killing the Frenchman and 80 others in the worst disaster in motor racing history.

'LEVEGH', (Bouillin, Pierre) (F) b 22/12/1905, Paris – d 11/6/1955, Le Mans Circuit

	1950	Championship position: Unplaced							
	Race	Circuit	No	Entrant	Tyres	Car/Engine		Comment	Q Pos/Entries
7	BELGIAN GP	Spa	22	'Pierre Levegh'	D	4.5 Lago-Talbot T26C 6		2 laps behind	10/14
ret	FRENCH GP	Reims	22	'Pierre Levegh'	D	4.5 Lago-Talbot T26C 6		engine	9/20
ret	ITALIAN GP	Monza	56	'Pierre Levegh'	D	4.5 Lago-Talbot T26C 6			20/27
	1951	Championship position: Unplaced							
8	BELGIAN GP	Spa	26	'Pierre Levegh'	D	4.5 Lago-Talbot T26C 6		4 laps behind	13/13
9	GERMAN GP	Nürburgring	90	'Pierre Levegh'	D	4.5 Lago-Talbot T26C 6		2 laps behind	19/23
ret	ITALIAN GP	Monza	22	'Pierre Levegh'	D	4.5 Lago-Talbot T26C 6		engine	20/22

GP Starts: 6   GP Wins: 0   Pole positions: 0   Fastest laps: 0   Points: 0

LEWIS, Jack (GB) b 1/11/1936

	1961	Championship position: Unplaced							
	Race	Circuit	No	Entrant	Tyres	Car/Engine	Comment		Q Pos/Entries
9	BELGIAN GP	Spa	40	H & L Motors	D	1.5 Cooper T53-Climax 4	1 lap behind		13/25
ret	FRENCH GP	Reims	44	H & L Motors	D	1.5 Cooper T53-Climax 4	overheating		18/26
ret	BRITISH GP	Aintree	46	H & L Motors	D	1.5 Cooper T53-Climax 4	steering		=14/30
9	GERMAN GP	Nürburgring	28	H & L Motors	D	1.5 Cooper T53-Climax 4			18/27
4	ITALIAN GP	Monza	60	H & L Motors	D	1.5 Cooper T53-Climax 4			16/33
	1962	Championship position: Unplaced							
8	DUTCH GP	Zandvoort	21	Ecurie Galloise	D	1.5 Cooper T53-Climax 4	pit stop/10 laps behind		19/20
dnq	MONACO GP	Monte Carlo	24	Ecurie Galloise	D	1.5 BRM P48/57 V8	faster than 3 starters		=14/21
ret	FRENCH GP	Rouen	42	Ecurie Galloise	D	1.5 Cooper T53-Climax 4	brakes-hit Graham Hill		16/17
10	BRITISH GP	Aintree	42	Ecurie Galloise	D	1.5 Cooper T53-Climax 4	3 laps behind		15/21
ret	GERMAN GP	Nürburgring	20	Ecurie Galloise	D	1.5 Cooper T53-Climax 4	front shock absober		21/30

GP Starts: 9   GP Wins: 0   Pole positions: 0   Fastest laps: 0   Points: 3

JACK LEWIS

Now an almost forgotten figure in motor racing, Jack Lewis showed plenty of natural talent but perhaps not the necessary resilience to overcome the setbacks that are a part of any sport.

In 1958 he purchased the ex-Bueb F3 Cooper and won three races in his first season, which encouraged him to move into Formula 2 in 1959 with a Cooper. Despite setting the fastest practice time for the Pau GP (ahead of Brabham and Trintignant) and taking third in the Aintree 200, Lewis was frustrated by organisers' general reluctance to accept his entry, and returned to the tracks in 1960 well prepared to prove himself a serious competitor. He did just that, winning the Autocar F2 British championship, as well as races at Chimay and Montlhéry.

For 1961 he set out on the Grand Prix trail with a Cooper, setting 12th-fastest practice time on his debut at Spa, and fighting off Tony Brooks' late challenge to take fourth place in the Italian GP. Given 'grade A driver' status, Lewis then bought a BRM 48/57 for 1962, which he took to third in the Pau GP, but he failed to qualify at Monaco and was so dissatisfied with the car that it was returned to the factory.

Back in his Cooper, Lewis seemed to lose heart, feeling his reputation had suffered after the BRM episode, and it was a despondent Welshman who slipped into retirement at the age of just 27.

STUART LEWIS-EVANS

With his father 'Pop' a noted Formula 3 racer in his own right, it was no surprise when Stuart followed in his footsteps, and from 1951 he was one of the formula's leading exponents. He spent five seasons in this cut-and-thrust environment before Connaught gave him a chance to race at the end of 1956.

Encouraging early-season performances in the Connaught, including victory in the Richmond Trophy at Goodwood and fourth place in the Monaco Grand Prix, then took Stuart into the Vanwall team for the rest of 1957. Some of his drives were brilliant, for example at Naples, where he led Hawthorn, and Reims, where he finished third. In World Championship races he displayed a rare blend of speed and finesse, but had only a fifth at Pescara to show for his efforts.

Although a slight, frail figure, Lewis-Evans embarked on a daunting racing programme in 1958, competing successfully in Formula 2 for BRP and in sports cars for Aston Martin, in addition to driving for Vanwall in Grands Prix. He played a crucial part in gaining the constructors' championship for the team but, in what should have been a glorious finale to the year in Morocco, Lewis-Evans' car crashed in flames after its transmission had locked. The poor driver was extricated from the wreckage suffering from terrible burns and, despite being flown back to England for expert attention, he succumbed some six days later.

LEWIS-EVANS, Stuart (GB) b 20/4/1930 – d 25/10/1958, East Grinstead, Sussex

	1957	Championship position: 10th=		Wins: 0	Pole positions: 0	Fastest laps: 0	Points scored: 5			
	Race	Circuit	No	Entrant	Tyres	Car/Engine		Comment		Q Pos/Entries
4	MONACO GP	Monte Carlo	10	Connaught Engineering	D	2.5 Connaught-Alta B Type 4		3 laps behind		13/21
ret	FRENCH GP	Rouen	18	Vandervell Products Ltd	P	2.5 Vanwall 4		steering		10/15
7	BRITISH GP	Aintree	22	Vandervell Products Ltd	P	2.5 Vanwall 4		pit stop-throttle/8 laps behind		6/19
ret	GERMAN GP	Nürburgring	12	Vandervell Products Ltd	P	2.5 Vanwall 4		gearbox		9/24
5	PESCARA GP	Pescara	30	Vandervell Products Ltd	P	2.5 Vanwall 4		pit stop-tyres/1 lap behind		8/16
ret	ITALIAN GP	Monza	20	Vandervall Products Ltd	P	2.5 Vanwall 4		cracked cylinder head		1/19
	1958	Championship position: 9th=		Wins: 0	Pole positions: 0	Fastest laps: 0	Points scored: 11			
ret	MONACO GP	Monte Carlo	32	Vandervell Products Ltd	D	2.5 Vanwall 4		overheating		7/28
ret	DUTCH GP	Zandvoort	3	Vandervell Products Ltd	D	2.5 Vanwall 4		engine		1/17
3	BELGIAN GP	Spa	6	Vandervell Products Ltd	D	2.5 Vanwall 4				11/20
ret*	FRENCH GP	Reims	12	Vandervell Products Ltd	D	2.5 Vanwall 4		engine/*Brooks took over car		10/21
4	BRITISH GP	Silverstone	9	Vandervell Products Ltd	D	2.5 Vanwall 4				7/21
3	PORTUGESE GP	Oporto	6	Vandervell Products Ltd	D	2.5 Vanwall 4		1 lap behind		3/15
ret	ITALIAN GP	Monza	30	Vandervell Products Ltd	D	2.5 Vanwall 4		overheating		4/21
ret	MOROCCAN GP	Casablanca	12	Vandervell Products Ltd	D	2.5 Vanwall 4		engine-crashed-fatal burns		3/25

GP Starts: 14   GP Wins: 0   Pole positions: 2   Fastest laps: 0   Points: 16

LIGIER, Guy (F) b 12/7/1930, Vichy

	1966	Championship position: Unplaced							
	Race	Circuit	No	Entrant	Tyres	Car/Engine	Comment		Q Pos/Entries
nc	MONACO GP	Monte Carlo	21	Guy Ligier	D	3.0 Cooper T81-Maserati V12	pit stop/25 laps behind		15/16
nc	BELGIAN GP	Spa	22	Guy Ligier	D	3.0 Cooper T81-Maserati V12	4 laps behind		12/18
nc	FRENCH GP	Reims	42	Guy Ligier	D	3.0 Cooper T81-Maserati V12	6 laps behind		11/17
10	BRITISH GP	Brands Hatch	19	Guy Ligier	D	3.0 Cooper T81-Maserati V12	5 laps behind		17/20
9	DUTCH GP	Zandvoort	36	Guy Ligier	D	3.0 Cooper T81-Maserati V12	6 laps behind		17/18
dns	GERMAN GP	Nürburgring	18	Guy Ligier	D	3.0 Cooper T81-Maserati V12	practice accident-broken knee		–./30
	1967	Championship position: 19th=		Wins: 0	Pole positions: 0	Fastest laps: 0	Points scored: 1		
10	BELGIAN GP	Spa	32	Guy Ligier	F	3.0 Cooper T81-Maserati V12	3 laps behind		18/18
nc	FRENCH GP	Le Mans	16	Guy Ligier	F	3.0 Cooper T81-Maserati V12	pit stop/12 laps behind		15/15
10	BRITISH GP	Silverstone	18	Guy Ligier	F	3.0 Brabham BT20-Repco V8	4 laps behind		21/21
6	GERMAN GP	Nürburgring	15	Guy Ligier	F	3.0 Brabham BT20-Repco V8	8th behind F2 cars/-1 lap		25/25
ret	ITALIAN GP	Monza	12	Guy Ligier	F	3.0 Brabham BT20-Repco V8	engine		18/18
ret	US GP	Watkins Glen	19	Guy Ligier	F	3.0 Brabham BT20-Repco V8	camshaft		17/18
11	MEXICAN GP	Mexico City	19	Guy Ligier	F	3.0 Brabham BT20-Repco V8	4 laps behind		19/19

GP Starts: 12   GP Wins: 0   Pole positions: 2   Fastest laps: 0   Points: 1

GUY LIGIER

This uncompromising character came late onto the motor racing scene after a distinguished rugby career. A close friend and business partner of Jo Schlesser, he began racing in 1963 with a Porsche Carrera, then moving into endurance racing with a Porsche 904GT. Ligier competed in Formula 2 in 1964 and gained some minor success in a Brabham BT10, with fifth in the Pergusa GP and sixth places at both Albi and Montlhéry. In 1965 he raced a Ford GT, winning the sports and GT race at Albi, but achieving little of note elsewhere.

Taking delivery of a Cooper-Maserati, he joined the Grand Prix circus in 1966, but his season ended early, Ligier sustaining a smashed knee-cap after crashing in practice for the German GP. Undaunted, he returned in 1967, eventually replacing the Cooper with a more competitive Brabham, and scoring his only championship point at the Nürburgring. He did record a major success in sports cars that year, however, winning the Reims 12 Hours in a Ford GT40 with Schlesser.

In 1968 Guy returned to Formula 2 but, disillusioned after Schlesser's death at Rouen, he quit in mid-season, only to return the following year with the ex-Alan Mann Escort, before building a prototype sports car which he successfully debuted in 1970. This sports car programme eventually led to a Formula 1 machine being built for 1976 and, though the Ligier team often failed to make the most of their resources, the blue cars were a constant presence on the grid until the end of 1996, even though Ligier himself had sold most of his shareholding in 1992-93.

In 1997 Ligier finally disposed of the remaining 18 per cent of his interest in the team to Flavio Briatore for what amounted to a knock-down price. When the Italian subsequently sold the team on for a handsome profit, the unhappy founder was left contemplating recourse to the courts in an attempt to gain fairer compensation.

LIPPI, Roberto (I) b 17/10/1926, Rome

	1961			Championship position: Unplaced					
	Race	*Circuit*	*No*	*Entrant*	*Tyres*	*Car/Engine*		*Comment*	*Q Pos/Entries*
ret	ITALIAN GP	Monza	52	Scuderia Settecolli	D	1.5 de Tomaso 002-Osca 4		*engine*	32/33
	1962			Championship position: Unplaced					
dnq	ITALIAN GP	Monza	50	Scuderia Settecolli	D	1.5 de Tomaso 002-Osca 4			28/30
	1963			Championship position: Unplaced					
dnq	ITALIAN GP	Monza	44	Scuderia Settecolli	D	1.5 de Tomaso 002-Ferrari V6			28/28

GP Starts: 1   GP Wins: 0   Pole positions: 0   Fastest laps: 0   Points: 0

ROBERTO LIPPI

Roberto was a highly rated Italian who had raced sports cars from the mid-fifties. In 1955 he shared a Maserati with Scarlatti to take eighth place in the Targa Florio, and he was Italian 750 cc Sports champion in 1957. He came to real prominence nationally with the introduction of Formula Junior in 1958 driving the Stanguellini-Fiat. He won the inaugural event of this series and subsequently went on to take the championship. He remained a leading runner in this class over the next couple of seasons, but was less successful in 1960 when he switched to a de Sanctis.

Lippi's Formula 1 experiences were less happy: plugging away in the uncompetitive de Tomaso-OSCA 4, his best results were scored at his favourite home track of Vallelunga in 1961 (fifth) and 1963 (fourth). He briefly returned to Formula Junior in 1963, racing a Cooper-Ford with his customary verve against much younger competitors.

LELLA LOMBARDI

In 1975 Lella became the first and thus far the only woman to have finished in the top six in a Grand Prix (albeit one which was shortened and thus only counted for half-points).

Always harbouring an ambition to go racing, she drove in Formula Monza and F3 with Lotus and Brabham cars, before winning the Italian Ford Mexico championship in 1973.

In 1974 she was signed to race the Shellsport-Luxembourg Lola in F5000 and silenced her critics by finishing fourth in the final standings. This led to a full F1 season with March in 1975, with the result in Spain the high point, although she did extremely well to finish seventh in the German GP. Her hopes of continuing with March in 1976 were dashed when she lost her backing after the first race of the season, and her brief flirtation with the RAM team was predictably fruitless.

Although squeezed out of Formula 1, Lella continued her career, mainly in sports cars, through into the early eighties. She was to enjoy some excellent results in the Osella prototype with Giorgio Francia, the pair winning the Ignazio Giunti Trophy at Vallelunga in 1979, and the Ore di Mugello in 1981, a year which also saw them finish second in the Monza 1000 Km.

It was with great sadness that the motor racing world learned of her tragically early death, at the age of 48, from cancer in March 1992.

LOMBARDI, Lella (I) b 26/3/1943, Frugarolo, nr Alessandria – d 3/3/1992, Milan

	1974			Championship position: Unplaced					
	Race	*Circuit*	*No*	*Entrant*	*Tyres*	*Car/Engine*		*Comment*	*Q Pos/Entries*
dnq	BRITISH GP	Brands Hatch	208	Allied Polymer Group	G	3.0 Brabham BT42-Cosworth V8			=28/34
	1975			Championship position: 21st Wins: 0 Pole positions: 0 Fastest laps: 0 Points scored: 0.5					
ret	SOUTH AFRICAN GP	Kyalami	10	March Engineering	G	3.0 March 741-Cosworth V8		*engine*	26/28
6*	SPANISH GP	Montjuich Park	10	Lavazza March	G	3.0 March 751-Cosworth V8		*half points-shortened race/-2 laps*	24/26
dnq	MONACO GO	Monte Carlo	10	Lavazza March	G	3.0 March 751-Cosworth V8			25/26

	Race	Circuit	No	Entrant	Tyres	Car/Engine	Comment	Q Pos/Entries
ret	BELGIAN GP	Zolder	10	Lavazza March	G	3.0 March 751-Cosworth V8	engine-oil leak	23/24
ret	SWEDISH GP	Anderstorp	10	Lavazza March	G	3.0 March 751-Cosworth V8	fuel metering unit	24/26
14	DUTCH GP	Zandvoort	10	Lavazza March	G	3.0 March 751-Cosworth V8	pit stop-tyres/5 laps behind	23/25
18	FRENCH GP	Paul Ricard	10	Lavazza March	G	3.0 March 751-Cosworth V8	pit stop-handling/-4 laps	26/26
ret	BRITISH GP	Silverstone	29	Lavazza March	G	3.0 March 751-Cosworth V8	ignition	22/28
7	GERMAN GP	Nürburgring	29	Lavazza March	G	3.0 March 751-Cosworth V8		25/26
17	AUSTRIAN GP	Österreichring	29	Lavazza March	G	3.0 March 751-Cosworth V8	3 laps behind	22/30
ret	ITALIAN GP	Monza	29	Lavazza March	G	3.0 March 751-Cosworth V8	brake failure-crashed	24/28
dns	US GP	Watkins Glen	20	Frank Williams Racing Cars	G	3.0 Williams FW04-Cosworth V8	ignition in warm up	(24)/24
	1976		Championship position: Unplaced					
14	BRAZILIAN GP	Interlagos	10	Lavazza March	G	3.0 March 761-Cosworth V8	pit stop-engine/4 laps behind	22/22
dnq	BRITISH GP	Brands Hatch	33	RAM Racing with Lavazza	G	3.0 Brabham BT44B-Cosworth V8		30/30
dnq	GERMAN GP	Nürburgring	33	RAM Racing with Lavazza	G	3.0 Brabham BT44B-Cosworth V8	legal wrangle-car impounded	27/28
12	AUSTRIAN GP	Österreichring	33	RAM Racing with Lavazza	G	3.0 Brabham BT44B-Cosworth V8	4 laps behind	24/25

GP Starts: 12 GP Wins: 0 Pole positions: 0 Fastest laps: 0 Points: 0.5

ERNST LOOF

Loof was eight times a German motor cycle champion between 1930 and 1938 and worked for BMW, building the sports car which von Hanstein used to win the 1000 Miles of Brescia before the war.

However, it is as designer and engineer of the splendid Veritas machines of the late forties and early fifties that he is best remembered. He seldom took the wheel, but did appear in the 1953 German GP, the marque's last season in top-flight competition.

Loof rallied a BMW in 1954, but by then he had begun to develop cancer and, suffering a brain tumour, died after a long illness in 1956.

HENRI LOUVEAU

Though not a driver of the first rank, Louveau was nevertheless a more than useful performer whose best days were in the immediate post-war years. In 1946 he drove a Maserati 4CL, winning at Lille, where he shared with Sommer, and gaining second places at Forez, Perpignan and Albi. The following year he was second at Lyon and third at Pau with the 'Maser' and also raced a recently purchased Delage with success, taking a second at Perpignan once more, third at Marseilles, fifth in the Jersey Road Race and sixth in the Italian GP.

The Delage was put to good use over the next three seasons, with seconds at Montlhéry and Chimay in 1948, third at Pescara in 1949 and fourth at Rouen in 1950. But the most thrilling of his races in the car must have been the 1949 Le Mans 24-hour race, when Henri was second having driven the Delage at Grand Prix pace over the last couple of hours and just failed to overhaul the sick car of Chinetti, which was touring to the finish.

Having handled Rosier's Talbot in the 1950 Italian GP, Henri planned to race the car regularly in the 1951 season, which began with a series of non-championship events. He began with fourth at Syracuse, crashed at Pau, where he was lucky to escape without injury after the car flipped, eighth at San Remo, sixth at Bordeaux, eleventh in the rain-halted International Trophy, and fourth in the Paris GP at Montlhéry. A week later came the championship race at the fearsome Bremgarten road circuit in Berne. With the track made even more treacherous by the wet conditions, Henri's Talbot skidded off the road, struck a barrier and overturned in a repeat of his Pau crash. This time he was not so fortunate, suffering concussion and a fractured leg, which prompted his retirement from racing.

LOOF, Ernst (D) b 4/7/1907, Neindorf – d 3/3/1956, Bonn

	1953		Championship position: Unplaced					
	Race	Circuit	No	Entrant	Tyres	Car/Engine	Comment	Q Pos/Entries
ret	GERMAN GP	Nürburgring	30	Ernst Loof	–	2.0 Veritas Meteor 6	fuel pump	31/35

GP Starts: 1 GP Wins: 0 Pole positions: 0 Fastest laps: 0 Points: 0

LOUVEAU, Henri (F) b 25/1/1910 – d 7/1/1991

	1950		Championship position: Unplaced					
	Race	Circuit	No	Entrant	Tyres	Car/Engine	Comment	Q Pos/Entries
ret	ITALIAN GP	Monza	64	Ecurie Louis Rosier	D	4.5 Lago-Talbot T26C-GS 6		14/27
	1951		Championship position: Unplaced					
ret	SWISS GP	Bremgarten	10	Ecurie Louis Rosier	D	4.5 Lago-Talbot T26C 6	hit telgraph pole/broken leg	11/21

GP Starts: 2 GP Wins: 0 Pole positions: 0 Fastest laps: 0 Points: 0

LOVE, John (RSR) b 7/12/1924, Bulawayo

	1962	Championship position: Unplaced						
	Race	Circuit	No	Entrant	Tyres	Car/Engine	Comment	Q Pos/Entries
8	SOUTH AFRICAN GP	East London	18	John Love	D	1.5 Cooper T55-Climax 4	4 laps behind	12/17
	1963	Championship position: Unplaced						
9	SOUTH AFRICAN GP	East London	19	John Love	D	1.5 Cooper T55-Climax 4	5 laps behind	13/21
	1964	Championship position: Unplaced						
dnq	ITALIAN GP	Monza	24	Cooper Car Co	D	1.5 Cooper T73-Climax V8	engine seized in practice	24/25
	1965	Championship position: Unplaced						
ret	SOUTH AFRICAN GP	East London	17	John Love	D	1.5 Cooper T55-Climax 4	driveshaft	18/25
	1967	Championship position: 11th= Wins: 0 Pole positions: 0 Fastest laps: 0 Points scored: 6						
2	SOUTH AFRICAN GP	Kyalami	17	John Love	F	2.7 Cooper T79-Climax 4	pit stop-fuel when in lead	5/18
	1968	Championship position: Unplaced						
9	SOUTH AFRICAN GP	Kyalami	17	Team Gunston	F	3.0 Brabham BT20-Repco V8	5 laps behind	17/23
	1969	Championship position: Unplaced						
ret	SOUTH AFRICAN GP	Kyalami	16	Team Gunston	D	3.0 Lotus 49-Cosworth V8	ignition	11/18
	1970	Championship position: Unplaced						
8	SOUTH AFRICAN GP	Kyalami	23	Team Gunston	D	3.0 Lotus 49-Cosworth V8	2 laps behind	22/24
	1971	Championship position: Unplaced						
ret	SOUTH AFRICAN GP	Kyalami	24	Team Peco/Gunston	F	3.0 March 701-Cosworth V8	differential	21/25
	1972	Championship position: Unplaced						
16/ret	SOUTH AFRICAN GP	Kyalami	27	Team Gunston	F	3.0 Surtees TS9-Cosworth V8	puncture-spun off/-6 laps	26/27

GP Starts: 9 GP Wins: 0 Pole positions: 0 Fastest laps: 0 Points: 6

JOHN LOVE

John Love was well known in Europe, having ventured to England in 1961 to race Ken Tyrrell's Formula Junior Cooper along with Tony Maggs. Although in his late thirties, Love was back for more in 1962, driving the works Mini-Cooper with spectacular success as well as competing in Formula Junior, but his season was cut short by an accident at Albi in which he sustained a badly broken arm. Business interests kept him at home from then onwards, apart from an abortive trip to the 1964 Italian GP, when his works Cooper was ill prepared.

The first of Love's six South African championships came in 1964, and it was a tally that was only halted by a determined rival in Dave Charlton, with whom he had some ding-dong battles over the years. Success generally eluded John in the local World Championship Grands Prix, though, with the exception of the 1967 event, when only a late pit stop for fuel prevented him taking what would have been a fairy-tale victory.

In addition to his single-seater exploits in South Africa, Love also regularly raced sports cars with distinction in the Springbok series of the late sixties and early seventies.

PETE LOVELY

An SCCA sports car champion of 1955, Lovely came to Europe in the late fifties to race briefly for Lotus. With Ireland, he took a class win in the 1958 Reims 12 Hours, but a hoped-for Grand Prix debut at Monaco in 1959 came to nought when he failed to qualify, Pete returning disenchanted to the States. He did make a Grand Prix start the following season with an elderly Cooper, however.

Throughout the sixties his racing took a back seat to his thriving VW garage business in Seattle but, itching to get back behind the wheel, he then bought a Lotus 49, competing at a sedate pace in selected World Championship Grands Prix between 1969 and 1971.

In recent years Pete has been a competitor at historic events with contemporary machinery from his racing days.

LOVELY, Pete (USA) b 11/4/1926, Livingston

	1959	Championship position: Unplaced							
	Race	Circuit	No	Entrant	Tyres	Car/Engine		Comment	Q Pos/Entries
dnq	MONACO GP	Monte Carlo	42	Team Lotus	D	2.5 Lotus 16-Climax 4			22/24
	1960	Championship position: Unplaced							
11	US GP	Riverside	25	Fred Armbruster	D	2.4 Cooper T45-Ferrari 4		6 laps behind	20/23
	1969	Championship position: 0	Wins: 0	Pole positions: 0	Fastest laps: 0	Points scored: 0			
7	CANADIAN GP	Mosport Park	25	Pete Lovely Volkswagen Inc	F	3.0 Lotus 49B-Cosworth V8		9 laps behind	16/20
ret	US GP	Watkins Glen	21	Pete Lovely Volkswagen Inc	F	3.0 Lotus 49B-Cosworth V8		driveshaft	16/18
9	MEXICAN GP	Mexico City	21	Pete Lovely Volkswagen Inc	F	3.0 Lotus 49B-Cosworth V8		3 laps behind	16/17
	1970	Championship position: Unplaced							
dnq	DUTCH GP	Zandvoort	31	Pete Lovely Volkswagen Inc	F	3.0 Lotus 49B-Cosworth V8			23/24
dnq	FRENCH GP	Clermont Ferrand	25	Pete Lovely Volkswagen Inc	F	3.0 Lotus 49B-Cosworth V8			22/23
nc	BRITISH GP	Brands Hatch	29	Pete Lovely Volkswagen Inc	F	3.0 Lotus 49B-Cosworth V8		pit stop-tyres/11 laps behind	24/25
dnq	US GP	Watkins Glen	28	Pete Lovely Volkswagen Inc	F	3.0 Lotus 49B-Cosworth V8			26/27
	1971	Championship position: Unplaced							
nc	CANADIAN GP	Mosport Park	35	Pete Lovely Volkswagen Inc	F	3.0 Lotus 49/69-Cosworth V8		pit stop-fuel/9 laps behind	26/27
nc	US GP	Watkins Glen	30	Pete Lovely Volkswagen Inc	F	3.0 Lotus 49/69-Cosworth V8		pit stop-fuel/10 laps behind	32/32

GP Starts: 7   GP Wins: 0   Pole positions: 0   Fastest laps: 0   Points: 0

LOYER, Roger (F) b 5/8/1907 – d 24/3/1988

	1954	Championship position: Unplaced							
	Race	Circuit	No	Entrant	Tyres	Car/Engine		Comment	Q Pos/Entries
ret	ARGENTINE GP	Buenos Aires	22	Equipe Gordini	E	2.5 Gordini Type 16 6		lack of oil	16/18

GP Starts: 1   GP Wins: 0   Pole positions: 0   Fastest laps: 0   Points: 0

LUCAS, Jean (F) b 25/4/1917, Le Mans

	1955	Championship position: Unplaced							
	Race	Circuit	No	Entrant	Tyres	Car/Engine		Comment	Q Pos/Entries
ret	ITALIAN GP	Monza	24	Equipe Gordini	E	2.5 Gordini Type 32 8		subbed for Manzon/engine	22/22
dns	"	"	22	Equipe Gordini	E	2.5 Gordini Type 16 6		practice only	– / –

GP Starts: 1   GP Wins: 0   Pole positions: 0   Fastest laps: 0   Points: 0

ROGER LOYER

A successful motor cycle rider, with a Velocette, Loyer continued to enjoy two-wheeled competition after he had taken up car racing. He drove the little Cisitalia D46 between 1947 and 1949, before joining the Equipe Gordini in 1950 to race their F2 Simca Gordini, the best result coming in the minor Circuit of Medoc race near Bordeaux.

Over the next few seasons, Roger appeared mainly in sports cars for the Gordini concern, winning the Coupe du Salon at Montlhéry, and at Agen in 1953.

His one opportunity at Grand Prix level came at the beginning of 1954 in the Argentine GP, and he also drove the same car in the Buenos Aires City Libre GP a couple of weeks later, retiring his own machine before sharing Bayol's to finish a distant tenth.

JEAN LUCAS

Turning to racing after beginning his career in rallies, Jean recorded his best results behind the wheel of sports cars, winning at Spa in 1949 and Montlhéry the following year in Luigi Chinetti's Ferrari. In 1953 Lucas joined Gordini as team manager and occasional driver, though he was still to be seen racing his own Ferrari under the Los Amigos banner in North African events such as those held at Agadir and Marrakesh which were popular at the time. It was only when urgent business matters called Manzon away from the Monza circuit that Lucas stood in to make his solitary World Championship appearance.

In 1956 he took an old Ferrari 625 to fifth place in the Caen GP, and in 1957 he finished second in the F2 Coupe de Vitesse at Reims in Alan Brown's Cooper. He also took third place in his Los Amigos Jaguar D-Type at Le Mans that year, but driving du Puy's Maserati 250F in the end-of-season Moroccan GP he overturned the car and was badly injured.

Realising that he would not be able to race again to his fullest abilities, he threw himself into administrative roles within the sport as well as co-founding the magazine Sport-Auto with Gérard Crombac in 1962, moving on to other publishing projects when his interest in motor sport had waned.

BRETT LUNGER

An heir to the DuPont family, Lunger began racing in 1965 with a Corvette, later graduating to Can-Am with a Caldwell-Chevrolet, but by his own admission he did not really know how to race properly, and it was more for fun than anything else.

His career then went on hold while he went to Vietnam with the Marines, only resuming in 1971 when he took part in the L & M F5000 series, finishing third in the championship. For 1972 Brett came to Europe to race in Formula 2 as well with a works-supported March 722, but could not match his Stateside success.

Lunger stayed in F5000 on both sides of the Atlantic until 1975, when he finally got a taste of Grand Prix racing with Hesketh, contesting three races in a second car alongside James Hunt. During the next three seasons the personable American, armed with a sizeable budget, plugged away without any real signs of making a breakthrough, even though he had decent cars at his disposal, including McLaren M23 and M26 machines run by B & S Fabrications.

Eventually falling out with his team at the end of 1978, Brett enjoyed a one-off ride with Ensign – his last Grand Prix appearance – after which he briefly drove in sports car events.

LUNGER, Brett (USA) b 14/11/1945, Wilmington, Delaware

	1975	Championship position: Unplaced						
	Race	Circuit	No	Entrant	Tyres	Car/Engine	Comment	Q Pos/Entries
13	AUSTRIAN GP	Österreichring	25	Hesketh Racing	G	3.0 Hesketh 308-Cosworth V8	1 lap behind	17/30
10	ITALIAN GP	Monza	25	Hesketh Racing	G	3.0 Hesketh 308-Cosworth V8	2 laps behind	21/28
ret	US GP	Watkins Glen	25	Hesketh Racing	G	3.0 Hesketh 308-Cosworth V8	missed gearchange-crashed	18/24
	1976	Championship position: Unplaced						
11	SOUTH AFRICAN GP	Kyalami	18	Team Surtees	G	3.0 Surtees TS19-Cosworth V8	1 lap behind	20/25
dnq	US GP WEST	Long Beach	18	Team Surtees	G	3.0 Surtees TS19-Cosworth V8		27/27
dnq	SPANISH GP	Jarama	18	Team Surtees	G	3.0 Surtees TS19-Cosworth V8		25/30
ret	BELGIAN GP	Zolder	18	Team Surtees	G	3.0 Surtees TS19-Cosworth V8	electrics	26/29
15	SWEDISH GP	Anderstorp	18	Team Surtees	G	3.0 Surtees TS19-Cosworth V8	2 laps behind	24/27
16	FRENCH GP	Paul Ricard	18	Team Surtees	G	3.0 Surtees TS19-Cosworth V8	1 lap behind	23/30
ret	BRITISH GP	Brands Hatch	18	Team Surtees	G	3.0 Surtees TS19-Cosworth V8	gearbox	18/30
ret/dns	GERMAN GP	Nürburgring	18	Team Surtees	G	3.0 Surtees TS19-Cosworth V8	in Lauda's crash/did not restart	24/28
10/ret	AUSTRIAN GP	Österreichring	18	Team Surtees	G	3.0 Surtees TS19-Cosworth V8	brake failure-crashed/-3 laps	16/25
14	ITALIAN GP	Monza	18	Team Surtees	G	3.0 Surtees TS19-Cosworth V8	stop-thought race stopped/-2 laps	25/29
15	CANADIAN GP	Mosport Park	18	Team Surtees	G	3.0 Surtees TS19-Cosworth V8	2 laps behind	22/27
11	US GP EAST	Watkins Glen	18	Team Surtees	G	3.0 Surtees TS19-Cosworth V8	2 laps behind	24/27
	1977	Championship position: Unplaced						
14	SOUTH AFRICAN GP	Kyalami	30	Chesterfield Racing	G	3.0 March 761-Cosworth V8	2 laps behind	23/23
ret	US GP WEST	Long Beach	30	Chesterfield Racing	G	3.0 March 761-Cosworth V8	collision with Reutemann	21/22
10	SPANISH GP	Jarama	30	Chesterfield Racing	G	3.0 March 761-Cosworth V8	3 laps behind	25/31
dns	BELGIAN GP	Zolder	30	Chesterfield Racing	G	3.0 McLaren M23-Cosworth V8	car unready after engine change	(22)/32
11	SWEDISH GP	Anderstorp	30	Chesterfield Racing	G	3.0 McLaren M23-Cosworth V8	1 lap behind	22/31
dnq	FRENCH GP	Dijon	30	Chesterfield Racing	G	3.0 McLaren M23-Cosworth V8		25/30
13	BRITISH GP	Silverstone	30	Chesterfield Racing	G	3.0 McLaren M23-Cosworth V8	pit stop/4 laps behind	19/36
ret	GERMAN GP	Hockenheim	30	Chesterfield Racing	G	3.0 McLaren M23-Cosworth V8	damage from startline accident	21/30
10	AUSTRIAN GP	Österreichring	30	Chesterfield Racing	G	3.0 McLaren M23-Cosworth V8	1 lap behind	17/30
9	DUTCH GP	Zandvoort	30	Chesterfield Racing	G	3.0 McLaren M23-Cosworth V8	2 laps behind	20/34
ret	ITALIAN GP	Monza	30	Chesterfield Racing	G	3.0 McLaren M23-Cosworth V8	engine	22/34
10	US GP EAST	Watkins Glen	30	Chesterfield Racing	G	3.0 McLaren M23-Cosworth V8	2 laps behind	17/27
11/ret	CANADIAN GP	Mosport Park	30	Chesterfield Racing	G	3.0 McLaren M23-Cosworth V8	engine/4 laps behind	20/27

	1978	Championship position: Unplaced							
13	ARGENTINE GP	Buenos Aires	30	Liggett Group/B & S Fabrications	G	3.0 McLaren M23-Cosworth V8	*1 lap behind*	24/27
ret	BRAZILIAN GP	Rio	30	Liggett Group/B & S Fabrications	G	3.0 McLaren M23-Cosworth V8	*overheating*	13/28
11	SOUTH AFRICAN GP	Kyalami	30	Liggett Group/B & S Fabrications	G	3.0 McLaren M23-Cosworth V8	*2 laps behind*	20/30
dnq	US GP WEST	Long Beach	30	Liggett Group/B & S Fabrications	G	3.0 McLaren M23-Cosworth V8		25/30
dnpq	MONACO GP	Monte Carlo	30	Liggett Group/B & S Fabrications	G	3.0 McLaren M26-Cosworth V8		29/30
7	BELGIAN GP	Zolder	30	Liggett Group/B & S Fabrications	G	3.0 McLaren M26-Cosworth V8	*1 lap behind*	24/30
dnq	SPANISH GP	Jarama	30	Liggett Group/B & S Fabrications	G	3.0 McLaren M26-Cosworth V8		26/29
dnq	"	"	30	Liggett Group/B & S Fabrications	G	3.0 McLaren M23-Cosworth V8		– / –
dnq	SWEDISH GP	Anderstorp	30	Liggett Group/B & S Fabrications	G	3.0 McLaren M26-Cosworth V8		26/27
dnq	"	"	30	Liggett Group/B & S Fabrications	G	3.0 McLaren M23-Cosworth V8		– / –
ret	FRENCH GP	Paul Ricard	30	Liggett Group/B & S Fabrications	G	3.0 McLaren M26-Cosworth V8	*engine*	24/29
dns	"	"	30	Liggett Group/B & S Fabrications	G	3.0 McLaren M23-Cosworth V8	*practice only*	– / –
8	BRITISH GP	Brands Hatch	30	Liggett Group/B & S Fabrications	G	3.0 McLaren M26-Cosworth V8	*1 lap behind*	24/30
dnpq	GERMAN GP	Hockenheim	30	Liggett Group/B & S Fabrications	G	3.0 McLaren M26-Cosworth V8		=29/30
8	AUSTRIAN GP	Österreichring	30	Liggett Group/B & S Fabrications	G	3.0 McLaren M26-Cosworth V8	*pit stop-tyres/2 laps behind*	17/31
ret	DUTCH GP	Zandvoort	30	Liggett Group/B & S Fabrications	G	3.0 McLaren M26-Cosworth V8	*engine*	21/33
ret/dns	ITALIAN GP	Monza	30	Liggett Group/B & S Fabrications	G	3.0 McLaren M26-Cosworth V8	*startline accident/did not restart*	21/32
13	US G P EAST	Watkins Glen	23	Team Tissot Ensign	G	3.0 Ensign N177-Cosworth V8	*1 lap behind*	24/27

GP Starts: 32 (34)   GP Wins: 0   Pole positions: 0   Fastest laps: 0   Points: 0

MIKE MacDOWEL

MacDowel was a keen amateur racer who made a name for himself in the 1172 cc Lotus sports car in 1955 with ten wins and five second places, and this success earned him a place in the Cooper works team for 1956 with their latest sports model.

His only Grand Prix appearance came in 1957 at Reims (a track he disliked due to the fact that the edges of the flat, fast bends were hard to see) when his car was taken over in mid-race by Jack Brabham, but later in the year he finished second in the Prix de Paris at Montlhéry.

After a lengthy period away from racing, he returned to action on the hill-climb scene in 1968, winning the RAC championships in 1973 and '74 in his potent 5-litre Repco-engined Brabham BT36X. Though past the age of 60, Mike, looking extremely fit and trim, was still competing in hill-climbs in the early 1990s and now enjoys appearances at the hugely popular historic racing festivals.

HERBERT MACKAY-FRASER

Originally from Connecticut, Mackay-Fraser tried his hand at ranching in Wyoming before moving to California, where his motor racing career took off, Herbert racing an XK120 Jaguar around the state. He then relocated again to Rio de Janeiro, where he competed in national events with a Ferrari 750 Monza, but it was always his ambition to race in Europe and in June 1955 he brought his Ferrari across to compete under the 'Kangaroo Stable' banner.

Settling in London, he soon integrated himself into the British motor racing scene, driving for Colin Chapman's fledgling sports car team at home and taking in a number of races on the Continent in his own Ferrari and Bonnier's Maserati during 1956. However, he really made a name for himself in the Reims 12-hour race, which he led superbly in Bueb's Lotus until engine troubles intervened.

In 1957 he continued his successful association with Lotus, and made an impressive debut for BRM in the French Grand Prix, which augured well for the future. But sadly a week later he was dead, after crashing his Lotus in the Coupe de Vitesse at Reims.

MacDOWEL, Mike (GB) b 13/9/1932, Great Yarmouth, Norfolk

	1957	Championship position: Unplaced						
	Race	Circuit	No	Entrant	Tyres	Car/Engine	Comment	Q Pos/Entries
7*	FRENCH GP	Rouen	24	Cooper Car Co	D	1.5 Cooper T43-Climax 4	*Brabham took over car/-9 laps	15/15

GP Starts: 1   GP Wins: 0   Pole positions: 0   Fastest laps: 0   Points: 0

MACKAY-FRASER, Herbert (USA) b 23/6/1927, Connecticut – d 14/7/1957, Reims-Gueux Circuit, France

	1957	Championship position: Unplaced						
	Race	Circuit	No	Entrant	Tyres	Car/Engine	Comment	Q Pos/Entries
ret	FRENCH GP	Rouen	28	Owen Racing Organisation	D	2.5 BRM P25 4	*rear pot joint near seized*	12/15

GP Starts: 1   GP Wins: 0   Pole positions: 0   Fastest laps: 0   Points: 0

LANCE MACKLIN

A polished and extremely stylish driver, Macklin spent the bulk of his career driving for John Heath's underfinanced HWM team, and his Grand Prix career suffered through the cars' lack of reliability.

Early experience with an Invicta, and then a Maserati, led to him joining HWM for 1950 and he immediately made his mark with a second place at Naples and a third at Mettet and Perigueux. The minor Continental races provided a happy hunting ground for the team at this time with good starting and prize money on offer. Macklin continued to pick up many good places over the next few seasons, highlighted by a superb win in the 1952 International Trophy at Silverstone.

Lance also raced occasionally for Aston Martin, finishing third at Le Mans in 1951, but four years later he became involved in the catastrophic accident at the Sarthe that claimed so many lives when 'Levegh's Mercedes was launched off the back of his Healey and wreckage flew into the crowd. Macklin survived unhurt and raced on, but after a narrow escape in the Tourist Trophy at Dundrod, when he crashed to avoid a multiple accident in which two drivers were killed and another seriously injured, he decided to call it a day.

DAMIEN MAGEE

An Ulsterman who showed potential in the junior formulae from his early days, Magee always seemed to be scratching round for a decent ride. With no substantial backing to speak of, he was forced to drive any sort of car he could get his hands on. Never less than 100 per cent committed, no sooner would poor Magee get a car going well than it seemed to be sold from under him.

Damien's only Grand Prix start came at very short notice in 1975 when he replaced Merzario in Sweden for Williams, though he did try to qualify the RAM-Brabham the following year at Paul Ricard. However, Magee had a regular drive at last for 1976 and 1977, in the Shellsport G8 series.

MACKLIN, Lance (GB) b 2/9/1919, Kensington, London

	1952	Championship position: Unplaced						
	Race	Circuit	No	Entrant	Tyres	Car/Engine	Comment	Q Pos/Entries
ret	SWISS GP	Bremgarten	20	HW Motors Ltd	D	2.0 HWM-Alta 4	withdrawn/suspension problems	12/21
11	BELGIAN GP	Spa	24	HW Motors Ltd	D	2.0 HWM-Alta 4	4 laps behind	14/22
9	FRENCH GP	Rouen	20	HW Motors Ltd	D	2.0 HWM-Alta 4	7 laps behind	14/20
15	BRITISH GP	Silverstone	31	HW Motors Ltd	D	2.0 HWM-Alta 4	6 laps behind	29/32
8	DUTCH GP	Zandvoort	26	HW Motors Ltd	D	2.0 HWM-Alta 4	6 laps behind	9/18
dnq	ITALIAN GP	Monza	52	HW Motors Ltd	D	2.0 HWM-Alta 4		32/35
	1953	Championship position: Unplaced						
ret	DUTCH GP	Zandvoort	38	HW Motors Ltd	D	2.0 HWM-Alta 4	throttle	15/20
ret	BELGIAN GP	Spa	22	HW Motors Ltd	D	2.0 HWM-Alta 4	engine	17/22
ret	FRENCH GP	Reims	26	HW Motors Ltd	D	2.0 HWM-Alta 4	clutch	16/25
ret	BRITISH GP	Silverstone	1	HW Motors Ltd	D	2.0 HWM-Alta 4	clutch housing	12/29
ret	SWISS GP	Bremgarten	16	HW Motors Ltd	D	2.0 HWM-Alta 4	engine-valve	15/23
ret	ITALIAN GP	Monza	14	HW Motors Ltd	D	2.0 HWM-Alta 4	engine	27/30
	1954	Championship position: Unplaced						
ret	FRENCH GP	Reims	32	HW Motors Ltd	D	2.0 HWM-Alta 4	engine	15/22
	1955	Championship position: Unplaced						
dnq	MONACO GP	Monte Carlo	22	Stirling Moss Ltd	D	2.5 Maserati 250F 6		21/22
8	BRITISH GP	Aintree	46	Stirling Moss Ltd	D	2.5 Maserati 250F 6	11 laps behind	16/25

GP Starts: 13   GP Wins: 0   Pole positions: 0   Fastest laps: 0   Points: 0

MAGEE, Damien (GB) b 17/11/1945, Belfast, Northern Ireland

	1975	Championship position: Unplaced						
	Race	Circuit	No	Entrant	Tyres	Car/Engine	Comment	Q Pos/Entries
14	SWEDISH GP	Anderstorp	20	Frank Williams Racing Cars	G	3.0 Williams FW03-Cosworth V8	2 laps behind	22/26
	1976	Championship position: Unplaced						
dnq	FRENCH GP	Paul Ricard	33	RAM Racing	G	3.0 Brabham BT44B-Cosworth V8		27/30

GP Starts: 1   GP Wins: 0   Pole positions: 0   Fastest laps: 0   Points: 0

TONY MAGGS

With only a handful of races in an Austin Healey in South Africa behind him, Maggs came to England in 1959 to gain experience and his talent was quickly recognised, Tony soon progressing to a Formula 2 Cooper. He returned in 1960 to race a variety of machines, finishing third in the Vanwall Trophy in a Cooper, and doing well in the Formula Junior Gemini.

His big break came in 1961, when Ken Tyrrell signed him for a season of Formula Junior with his Cooper, young Tony winning eight races and sharing the European FJ title with Jo Siffert. He also made a steady start in Grand Prix racing with Louise Bryden-Brown's Lotus 18, impressing the Cooper team, who signed him as number two to Bruce McLaren.

Always consistent, Maggs scored some fine placings over the next two seasons in a team that was slowly losing its competitive edge, but he was not retained for 1964 and joined up with Centro Sud to race their elderly BRM cars, even getting among the points on two occasions. With no real F1 prospects in sight, Maggs undertook a programme of Formula 2 in an MRP Lola and sports cars in David Piper's Ferrari GTO, the pair winning the Rand 9 Hours at Kyalami.

After handling Parnell's Lotus in the 1965 South African GP, Maggs raced abroad for the last time, taking second place in the Rome GP and fourth at both Oulton Park and Pau in MRP's F2 Lola, and third place in the Sebring 12 Hours with Piper in his Ferrari 250LM.

Tony had planned to race the Surtees Lola in Formula 2, but when he crashed his Brabham in a national race at Pietermaritzburg a small boy who was standing in a prohibited area was unfortunately hit and killed, and a distraught Maggs immediately retired from racing to concentrate on farming.

MAGGS, Tony (ZA) b 9/2/1937, Pretoria

	1961	Championship position: Unplaced							
	Race	Circuit	No	Entrant	Tyres	Car/Engine		Comment	Q Pos/Entries
13	BRITISH GP	Aintree	50	Louise Bryden-Brown	D	1.5 Lotus 18-Climax 4		6 laps behind	24/30
11	GERMAN GP	Nürburgring	33	Louise Bryden-Brown	D	1.5 Lotus 18-Climax 4		1 lap behind	22/27
	1962	Championship position: 7th Wins: 0 Pole positions: 0 Fastest laps: 0 Points scored: 13							
5	DUTCH GP	Zandvoort	7	Cooper Car Co	D	1.5 Cooper T55-Climax 4		2 laps behind	15/20
ret	MONACO GP	Monte Carlo	16	Cooper Car Co	D	1.5 Cooper T55-Climax 4		gearbox	19/21
ret	BELGIAN GP	Spa	26	Cooper Car Co	D	1.5 Cooper T60-Climax V8		gearbox	10/20
2	FRENCH GP	Rouen	24	Cooper Car Co	D	1.5 Cooper T60-Cliamx V8		1 lap behind	11/17
6	BRITISH GP	Aintree	18	Cooper Car Co	D	1.5 Cooper T60-Climax V8		1 lap behind	13/21
9	GERMAN GP	Nürburgring	10	Cooper Car Co	D	1.5 Cooper T55-Climax 4			23/30
dns	"	"	10	Cooper Car Co	D	1.5 Cooper T60-Climax V8		accident in practice	– / –
7	ITALIAN GP	Monza	30	Cooper Car Co	D	1.5 Cooper T60-Climax V8		1 lap behind	12/30
7	US GP	Watkins Glen	22	Cooper Car Co	D	1.5 Cooper T60-Climax V8		3 laps behind	10/20
3	SOUTH AFRCAN GP	East London	9	Cooper Car Co	D	1.5 Cooper T60-Climax V8			=6/17
	1963	Championship position: 8th Wins: 0 Pole positions: 0 Fastest laps: 0 Points scored: 9							
5	MONACO GP	Monte Carlo	8	Cooper Car Co	D	1.5 Cooper T66-Climax V8		2 laps behind	10/17
7/ret	BELGIAN GP	Spa	15	Cooper Car Co	D	1.5 Cooper T66-Climax V8		accident in rain/5 laps behind	4/20
ret	DUTCH GP	Zandvoort	22	Cooper Car Co	D	1.5 Cooper T66-Climax V8		overheating	9/19
2	FRENCH GP	Reims	12	Cooper Car Co	D	1.5 Cooper T66-Climax V8			8/21
9	BRITISH GP	Silverstone	7	Cooper Car Co	D	1.5 Cooper T66-Climax V8		4 laps behind	=7/23
ret	GERMAN GP	Nürburgring	6	Cooper Car Co	D	1.5 Cooper T66-Climax V8		camshaft	10/26
6	ITALIAN GP	Monza	20	Cooper Car Co	D	1.5 Cooper T66-Climax V8		2 laps behind	13/28
ret	US GP	Watkins Glen	4	Cooper Car Co	D	1.5 Cooper T66-Climax V8		ignition	9/21
ret	MEXICAN GP	Mexico City	4	Cooper Car Co	D	1.5 Cooper T66-Climax V8		engine	13/21
7	SOUTH AFRICAN GP	East London	11	Cooper Car Co	D	1.5 Cooper T66-Climax V8		3 laps behind	10/21
	1964	Championship position: 12th Wins: 0 Pole positions: 0 Fastest laps: 0 Points scored: 4							
dns	DUTCH GP	Zandvoort	30	Scuderia Centro Sud	D	1.5 BRM P57 V8		accident in practice	(15)/18
dns	BELGIAN GP	Spa	7	Scuderia Centro Sud	D	1.5 BRM P57 V8		engine failure in practice	(18)/20
ret	BRITISH GP	Brands Hatch	17	Scuderia Centro Sud	D	1.5 BRM P57 V8		gearbox	23/25
6	GERMAN GP	Nürburgring	26	Scuderia Centro Sud	D	1.5 BRM P57 V8		1 lap behind	16/24
4	AUSTRIAN GP	Zeltweg	19	Scuderia Centro Sud	D	1.5 BRM P57 V8		3 laps behind	=18/20
	1965	Championship position: Unplaced							
11	SOUTH AFRICAN GP	East London	15	Reg Parnell (Racing)	D	1.5 Lotus 25-BRM V8		8 laps behind	13/25

GP Starts: 25   GP Wins: 0   Pole positions: 0   Fastest laps: 0   Points: 26

MAGLIOLI, Umberto (I) b 5/6/1928, Bioglio, Vercelli – d 1999

	1953	Championship position: Unplaced						
	Race	Circuit	No	Entrant	Tyres	Car/Engine	Comment	Q Pos/Entries
8	ITALIAN GP	Monza	10	Scuderia Ferrari	P	2.0 Ferrari 553 4	5 laps behind	11/30
	1954	Championship position: 15th=	Wins: 0	Pole positions: 0	Fastest laps: 0	Points scored: 2		
9	ARGENTINE GP	Buenos Aires	16	Scuderia Ferrari	P	2.5 Ferrari 625 4	5 laps behind	12/18
7	SWISS GP	Bremgarten	24	Scuderia Ferrari	P	2.5 Ferrari 553 4	5 laps behind	11/16
3*	ITALIAN GP	Monza	38	Scuderia Ferrari	P	2.5 Ferrari 625 4	* Gonzalez took over/-2 laps	13/21
	1955	Championship position: 16th=	Wins: 0	Pole positions: 0	Fastest laps: 0	Points scored: 1.33		
3*	ARGENTINE GP	Buenos Aires	10	Scuderia Ferrari	E	2.5 Ferrari 625 4	*with Farina/Trintignant/-2 laps	(22)/22
6	ITALIAN GP	Monza	12	Scuderia Ferrari	E	2.5 Ferrari 555 4	1 lap behind	12/22
	1956	Championship position: Unplaced						
ret	BRITISH GP	Silverstone	12	Scuderia Guastalla	P	2.5 Maserati 250F 6	gearbox	24/28
ret	GERMAN GP	Nürburgring	8	Officine Alfieri Maserati	P	2.5 Maserati 250F 6	steering	7/21
ret*	ITALIAN GP	Monza	46	Officine Alfieri Maserati	P	2.5 Maserati 250F 6	* Behra took over/steering	13/26
	1957	Championship position: Unplaced						
ret	GERMAN GP (F2)	Nürburgring	20	Dr Ing F Porsche KG	–	1.5 Porsche 550RS F4	engine	15/24

GP Starts: 10   GP Wins: 0   Pole positions: 0   Fastest laps: 0   Points: 3.33

UMBERTO MAGLIOLI

A most accomplished sports car driver for nearly two decades, the pipe-smoking Maglioli found his Grand Prix opportunities severely limited, given his position as a junior Ferrari driver. He had made his reputation as national production car champion in 1952 with Lancia, then winning the 1953 Targa Florio and the Carrera Panamericana in 1954 in the marque's cars. Despite success at Maranello in hill-climbs and sports car races which included victories in the Pescara 12 Hours, Buenos Aires 1000 Km and Circuit of Mugello, Umberto joined Maserati for 1956, again racing only occasionally in Grands Prix, but he also began the start of a long and fruitful association with Porsche by winning the Targa Florio with von Trips.

A practice crash at Salzburg in 1957 sidelined him with leg injuries but he bounced back in 1959, winning the Sebring 12 Hours with Hans Herrmann. Little success came Maglioli's way in the early sixties, but a return to the Ferrari sports car team in 1963 saw him take third place at Le Mans and in the Nürburgring 1000 Km, followed by another win at Sebring in 1964.

Throughout the rest of the decade he continued to race a variety of potent machines, including a Ford GT40 and the works Porsche 907, with which, paired with Vic Elford, he won the Targa Florio in 1968, his last major victory.

MAGNUSSEN, Jan (DK) b 4/7/1973, Roskilde

	1995	Championship position: Unplaced						
	Race	Circuit	No	Entrant	Tyres	Car/Engine	Comment	Q Pos/Entries
10	PACIFIC GP	T.I. Circuit	8	Marlboro McLaren Mercedes	G	3.0 McLaren MP4/10B-Mercedes V10	2 laps behind	12/24
	1997	Championship position: Unplaced						
ret	AUSTRALIAN GP	Melbourne	23	Stewart Ford	B	3.0 Stewart SF1-Ford Zetec-R V10	suspension	19/24
ret/dns	BRAZILIAN GP	Interlagos	23	Stewart Ford	B	3.0 Stewart SF1-Ford Zetec-R V10	accident at first start	20/22
10/ret	ARGENTINE GP	Buenos Aires	23	Stewart Ford	B	3.0 Stewart SF1-Ford Zetec-R V10	engine/6 laps behind	15/22
ret	SAN MARINO GP	Imola	23	Stewart Ford	B	3.0 Stewart SF1-Ford Zetec-R V10	spun off	16/22
7	MONACO GP	Monte Carlo	23	Stewart Ford	B	3.0 Stewart SF1-Ford Zetec-R V10	1 lap behind	19/22
13	SPANISH GP	Barcelona	23	Stewart Ford	B	3.0 Stewart SF1-Ford Zetec-R V10	1 lap behind	22/22
ret	CANADIAN GP	Montreal	23	Stewart Ford	B	3.0 Stewart SF1-Ford Zetec-R V10	accident on lap 1	21/22
ret	FRENCH GP	Magny Cours	23	Stewart Ford	B	3.0 Stewart SF1-Ford Zetec-R V10	brakes	15/22
ret	BRITISH GP	Silverstone	23	Stewart Ford	B	3.0 Stewart SF1-Ford Zetec-R V10	engine	15/22
ret	GERMAN GP	Hockenheim	23	Stewart Ford	B	3.0 Stewart SF1-Ford Zetec-R V10	engine	12/22
ret	HUNGARIAN GP	Hungaroring	23	Stewart Ford	B	3.0 Stewart SF1-Ford Zetec-R V10	collision damage	17/22
12	BELGIAN GP	Spa	23	Stewart Ford	B	3.0 Stewart SF1-Ford Zetec-R V10	1 lap behind	18/22
ret	ITALIAN GP	Monza	23	Stewart Ford	B	3.0 Stewart SF1-Ford Zetec-R V10	transmission	13/22
ret	AUSTRIAN GP	A1-Ring	23	Stewart Ford	B	3.0 Stewart SF1-Ford Zetec-R V10	engine	6/22
ret	LUXEMBOURG GP	Nürburgring	23	Stewart Ford	B	3.0 Stewart SF1-Ford Zetec-R V10	driveshaft	12/22
ret	JAPANESE GP	Suzuka	23	Stewart Ford	B	3.0 Stewart SF1-Ford Zetec-R V10	spun off	14/22
9	EUROPEAN GP	Jerez	23	Stewart Ford	B	3.0 Stewart SF1-Ford Zetec-R V10		11/22
	1998	Championship position: 15th=	Wins: 0	Pole positions: 0	Fastest laps: 0	Points scored: 1		
ret	AUSTRALIAN GP	Melbourne	19	Stewart Ford	B	3.0 Stewart SF2-Ford Zetec R V10	collision with Ralf Schumacher	18/22
10	BRAZILIAN GP	Interlagos	19	Stewart Ford	B	3.0 Stewart SF2-Ford Zetec R V10	2 laps behind	16/22
ret	ARGENTINE GP	Buenos Aires	19	Stewart Ford	B	3.0 Stewart SF2-Ford Zetec R V10	transmission	22/22
ret	SAN MARINO GP	Imola	19	Stewart Ford	B	3.0 Stewart SF2-Ford Zetec R V10	gearbox	20/22
12	SPANISH GP	Barcelona	19	Stewart Ford	B	3.0 Stewart SF2-Ford Zetec R V10	2 laps behnd	20/22
ret	MONACO GP	Monte Carlo	19	Stewart Ford	B	3.0 Stewart SF2-Ford Zetec R V10	suspension failure	17/22
6	CANADIAN GP	Montreal	19	Stewart Ford	B	3.0 Stewart SF2-Ford Zetec R V10		20/22

GP Starts: 24 (25)   GP Wins: 0   Pole positions: 0   Fastest laps: 0   Points: 1

JAN MAGNUSSEN

When the 5 ft 5 in Dane decimated the opposition to win the British F3 championship with Paul Stewart Racing in 1994, taking an amazing 14 wins from 18 starts, comparisons with the late Ayrton Senna were perhaps inevitable. Certainly Jackie Stewart regarded him as a potential World Champion of the future. Sadly, thus far that dazzling promise has remained largely unfulfilled and Magnussen is no longer on the Formula 1 team managers' shortlists.

A hugely successful karting career which culminated in the senior world crown in 1990 set him on the path to the top of motor sport. Without any sponsorship to speak of, Jan drove in FF1600 in 1992 and not only took that title, but capped it with a stunning display to win the prestigious end-of-year Formula Ford Festival at Brands Hatch. A year in the Vauxhall Euroseries had its ups and downs, but still Magnussen's innate talent shone through, and two late-season F3 drives with PSR cemented his place for 1994, leading to the aforementioned success.

Signed by McLaren as a test driver, Jan also joined Mercedes for their DTM/ITC programme, which represented a great opportunity for the young Dane to work with a major manufacturer. Initially he hankered for single-seater action, but after his season was interrupted by a broken leg, sustained in a bizarre paddock accident when he fell off his scooter, Magnussen returned more fully focused, eventually taking second place to Bernd Schneider in the ITC series.

At the end of the season, he gave an assured performance on his Grand Prix debut at the Pacific GP, but he was forced to continue in the Mercedes ITC team in 1996. A chance of single-seater action came in the form of a few Indy Car outings, initially with Penske, replacing the injured Paul Tracy, and then with Hogan, filling in for Emerson Fittipaldi. The heavy Penske chassis did him no favours but, given his lack of testing, Jan did a solid enough job.

When Paul and Jackie Stewart made the transition to Formula 1 for 1997 Jan was given the second seat alongside Rubens Barrichello, but it was to be a traumatic debut season for the Dane, who failed to match the pace of his more experienced team-mate. Fortunately, as the year wore on he finally seemed to be getting to grips with the task and he was kept on for 1998 in the hope that he could make the big breakthrough. In the event Magnussen's confidence seemed to be eroded by the team's criticism of his perceived lack of performance, and after scoring his first-ever championship point in Montreal he was summarily dropped in favour of Jos Verstappen.

Looking to reinvigorate his flagging career, Magnussen has since taken his opportunity to shine with Panoz Racing's sports roadster in the American Le Mans Series, as well as reviving his CART prospects in 1999 with a seven-race stint for Pat Patrick.

GUY MAIRESSE

A tough and independent character with a big heart, Mairesse built up a long-distance haulage business from modest beginnings as a lorry driver before the war. He became interested in the sport after Paul Vallée invited him to the 1946 Coupe du Salon purely as a spectator. After winning the 1947 Lyons-Charbonnières Rally, Guy then bought a Delahaye from Vallée for 1948 which he took to victory at Chimay.

Joining his great friend's Ecurie France team for 1949 to race the Lago-Talbot, Mairesse took fourth at Pau and fifth at Albi, and in 1950, teamed with Meyrat, he finished second at Le Mans in a Talbot 'monoplace'. On the Vallée team's demise, he bought the Le Mans car and a Talbot T26C, prepared by Giraud Cabantous, which he raced in only a couple of Grands Prix in 1951 due to his increasing business commitments.

At the start of 1952, Mairesse sold his cars but still appeared occasionally in machines provided by others, and it was while practising for the Coupe de Paris at Montlhéry in 1954 that he lost his life, swerving to avoid a slower car and crashing into a concrete wall.

MAIRESSE, Guy (F) b 10/8/1910, La Capelle, l'Aisne – d 24/4/1954, Montlhéry Circuit, nr Paris

	1950	Championship position: 0	Wins: 0	Pole positions: 0	Fastest laps: 0	Points scored: 0		
	Race	Circuit	No	Entrant	Tyres	Car/Engine	Comment	Q Pos/Entries
ret	ITALIAN GP	Monza	40	Guy Mairesse	D	4.5 Lago-Talbot T26C 6		11/27
	1951	Championship position: 0	Wins: 0	Pole positions: 0	Fastest laps: 0	Points scored: 0		
nc	SWISS GP	Bremgarten	40	Guy Mairesse	D	4.5 Lago-Talbot T26C 6	11 laps behind	21/21
9	FRENCH GP	Reims	48	Guy Mairesse	D	4.5 Lago-Talbot T26C 6	11 laps behind	19/23

GP Starts: 3   GP Wins: 0   Pole positions: 0   Fastest laps: 0   Points: 0

WILLY MAIRESSE

Mairesse drove with a grim determination and frequently came unstuck, suffering a whole series of lurid accidents which burnt and battered his small frame but never dented his fearless approach.

He sprang to prominence in 1956 when he took his second-hand Mercedes 300SL to victory in the Liège-Rome-Liège Rally, beating the favourite, Olivier Gendebien, in the process, which sparked a bitter competition rivalry between the two Belgians. In 1957 Willy over-reached himself, wrecking a series of expensive cars, and he was lucky that Jacques Swaters rescued him from probable obscurity by furnishing him with a Ferrari Berlinetta for 1958 which he took to second place in the Reims 12 Hours. Mairesse clashed with Gendebien once more in the 1959 Tour de France, defeating his rival on a number of timed stages but missing out on overall victory. Ferrari took an interest in the little man, however, and offered him a drive in the 1960 Targa Florio. He finished fourth and was immediately taken into the works team for both F1 and sports cars. Late in the year he scored the first of two successive Tour de France victories in a Ferrari 250GT, but only after Gendebien of all people had helped to manhandle the Mairesse car from a ditch.

This gutsy display from Willy made him Ferrari's blue-eyed boy of the moment and he was retained in the sports car team for 1961, taking a number of GT victories and second place at Le Mans with Parkes. After buying a couple of GP rides at Spa and Reims, Mairesse blew another Ferrari F1 chance by crashing at the Nürburgring, but another win in the Tour de France may have kept him employed in 1962, Willy accepting the role of test driver vacated by Ginther, who had moved to BRM.

The season started with wins in the Brussels and Naples GPs, before more success with victory in theTarga Florio. At the Belgian GP, though, Mairesse was involved in a lurid high-speed accident with Trevor Taylor, receiving burns which kept him out until a comeback at Monza which netted fourth place. He survived the Ferrari clear-out to partner Surtees in 1963, but his erratic performances culminated in a needless accident at the German GP when he wrote off the car and put himself out of racing for the remainder of the season. His Ferrari career finally at an end, Mairesse was still a more than useful sports car driver, and joined the Equipe Nationale Belge, winning the 1964 Angola GP in their Ferrari GTO and the Spa 500 Km in 1965. His last major win came the following year when he shared a Filipinetti Porsche Carrera with Herbert Müller to win the Targa Florio. His accident-prone career finally came to an end at the 1968 Le Mans 24 Hours when a door flew open on his Ford GT40, causing him to crash heavily, Mairesse suffering severe head injuries which left him unconscious for two weeks. He never fully recovered and after a year spent in poor health, and with no prospect of a return to racing, he committed suicide in an Ostend hotel room.

MAIRESSE, Willy (B) b 1/10/1928 Momminges – d 2/9/1969 Ostend

	1960	Championship position: 13th=		Wins: 0	Pole positions: 0		Fastest laps: 0	Points scored: 4		
	Race	*Circuit*	*No*	*Entrant*		*Tyres*	*Car/Engine*		*Comment*	*Q Pos/Entries*
ret	BELGIAN GP	Spa	22	Scuderia Ferrari		D	2.4 Ferrari Dino 246 V6		*transmission*	13/18
ret	FRENCH GP	Reims	6	Scuderia Ferrari		D	2.4 Ferrari Dino 246 V6		*transmission*	11/23
3	ITALIAN GP	Monza	16	Scuderia Ferrari		D	2.4 Ferrari Dino 246 V6		*gearbox problems/-1 lap*	3/16
	1961	Championship position: Unplaced								
ret	BELGIAN GP	Spa	10	Equipe Nationale Belge		D	1.5 Lotus 18-Climax 4		*hired Tony Marsh's car/ignition*	– /25
dns	"	"	10	Equipe Nationale Belge		D	1.5 Emeryson 1003-Maserati 4		*car too slow*	– / –
ret	FRENCH GP	Reims	48	Team Lotus		D	1.5 Lotus 21-Climax 4		*hired 3rd works car/fuel system*	20/26
ret	GERMAN GP	Nürburgring	6	Scuderia Ferrari SpA SEFAC		D	1.5 Ferrari 156 V6		*crashed*	13/27
	1962	Championship position: 14th=		Wins: 0	Pole positions: 0		Fastest laps: 0	Points scored: 3		
7/ret	MONACO GP	Monte Carlo	40	Scuderia Ferrari SpA SEFAC		D	1.5 Ferrari 156 V6		*oil pressure/10 laps behind*	=3/21
ret	BELGIAN GP	Spa	10	Scuderia Ferrari SpA SEFAC		D	1.5 Ferrari 156 V6		*huge accident with T Taylor*	=5/20
4	ITALIAN GP	Monza	8	Scuderia Ferrari SpA SEFAC		D	1.5 Ferrari 156 V6			10/30
	1963	Championship position: Unplaced								
ret	MONACO GP	Monte Carlo	20	Scuderia Ferrari SpA SEFAC		D	1.5 Ferrari 156 V6		*transmission*	7/17
ret	BELGIAN GP	Spa	10	Scuderia Ferrari SpA SEFAC		D	1.5 Ferrari 156 V6		*engine*	3/20
ret	GERMAN GP	Nürburgring	8	Scuderia Ferrari SpA SEFAC		D	1.5 Ferrari 156 V6		*crashed*	7/26
	1965	Championship position: Unplaced								
dns	BELGIAN GP	Spa	28	Scuderia Centro Sud		D	1.5 BRM P57 V8		*did only one prctice lap*	21/21

GP Starts: 12   GP Wins: 0   Pole positions: 0   Fastest laps: 0   Points: 7

NIGEL MANSELL

WORLD CHAMPION: 1992

NIGEL MANSELL

If you look at it objectively, there were two Nigel Mansells. One belonged to sections of the motor racing press, who saw him as the whingeing, ungracious 'chip-on-the-shoulder Brit' who courted success and disaster in equal measure but was actually a brilliant racing driver, good for endless column inches and therefore a lucrative source of income. The second Mansell belonged to the 'man in the street', who didn't give a damn about the scribblings of the journalists, but was content merely to revel in the many scintillating displays served up by one of the most brave, committed and entertaining drivers of his age, a man who still retained the common touch even if he was a superstar. In truth, of course, Mansell was a mixture of all these things, it really just depends on your perspective. I prefer to concentrate on the latter persona, for his remarkable deeds in a racing car are of primary concern in a book of this nature.

Mansell's story is well chronicled, but his dogged refusal to give up when the early part of his career seemed to be leading nowhere marked him down as a potential champion, even if his results in Formula 3 at the time indicated otherwise. The man most responsible for helping Nigel's career over that crucial first hurdle was none other than Colin Chapman, who knew a 'good 'un' when he saw one and placed him in the Lotus team as a test driver. When given his Grand Prix debut in Austria, Mansell endured acute discomfort from petrol which leaked into his cockpit to tough it out until the engine failed, and this was the stuff that Lotus needed as they slipped from their pedestal in the early eighties.

Certainly there were still rough edges, and Mansell made plenty of mistakes, but there were virtues. He absolutely gave his all, in contrast to team-mate de Angelis who could lose heart when his car was not performing. When Chapman died of a sudden heart attack in December 1982, it was a crushing blow to Nigel, not least because he had lost his greatest believer. His level of competitiveness was raised when the team received their new Renault turbo-powered, Gérard Ducarouge-designed car midway through the following season, as he demonstrated in the European GP at Brands Hatch, but he endured a generally unhappy time in 1984. A probable win in the rain at Monaco was thrown away when he slithered into the Armco and there were many at that stage who doubted if he would ever win a Grand Prix.

His move to Williams in 1985 changed everything. Soon coming to terms with Keke Rosberg, Nigel broke his duck at last, and continued his new-found form into the 1986 season, putting new team-mate Nelson Piquet in the shade with a series of brilliant drives to take five Grand Prix wins. The championship seemed to be there for the taking but a gaffe in the penultimate round in Mexico when he failed to put the car into gear on the grid was to cost him dear. Now under pressure at the final race in Adelaide, poor Nigel had the race covered and the championship within his grasp until a tyre failure sent him crashing out. Undaunted, he predictably bounced back in 1987, this time clocking up six wins in the Williams-Honda, but a practice crash at Suzuka handed the title to team-mate Piquet. The Williams team then lost their Honda engines to McLaren, and Nigel was forced to spend a year in purgatory with the Judd-powered car, though in the rain at Silverstone he drove quite brilliantly into second place.

Accepting a massive offer from Maranello, Mansell entered Ferrari folklore with a first-time-out win in Brazil, and carried the fight to McLaren with captivating brio. His win in Hungary after a stunning bit of opportunism in traffic was the highlight of a brilliant season which was soured somewhat after a skirmish with Senna in Portugal led to his suspension from the Spanish GP a week later. Greater disenchantment was to follow in 1990, when Alain Prost joined the Ferrari payroll. The little Frenchman hi-jacked the team's attentions with four early-season wins, prompting Mansell to announce his retirement. An offer from Williams to return to Didcot in 1991 was enough to persuade him to continue, and it was a decision he was not to regret. Driving as well as ever before, Mansell's slow start to the season eventually counted against him, for despite a mid-season burst of five wins, punctuated by a heart-breaking pit-stop fiasco in Portugal, Nigel was unable to overhaul Senna in the race for the title.

In 1992 Nigel finally got the job done. With what was undeniably the best car, he fairly scorched away with the championship, taking five straight wins at the start of the season. Apart from an ill-judged clash with Senna in Canada, he hardly put a foot wrong and thoroughly earned his World Championship. Sadly relations with Williams had deteriorated to the point that an agreement could not be reached for Mansell to continue in 1993 and, with the parties seemingly unable (or unwilling) to find a compromise, he headed off to the States and a new life in Indy Car racing with the Newman-Haas Lola.

Proving all the doubters wrong, Nigel not only won the PPG Cup at his first attempt but – a crash at Phoenix apart – made light of the black art of racing on ovals to such effect that he was almost omnipotent. Mansell was very unlucky to miss out on a first-time win in the Indy 500 at the last gasp when a full-course yellow saw him outfumbled by the wily Fittipaldi. Perhaps more importantly, however, Nigel had found a new environment in which he felt appreciated, and this undoubtedly showed in his contented demeanour. Sadly it was not to last. Penske wheeled out a new car in 1994 which left everyone else trailing in its wake, and Nigel's motivation, such a crucial part of his success, appeared to be less than total. The chance to return to Grand Prix racing in the wake of Senna's death proved irresistible but, despite an end-of-season win at Adelaide, Williams decided to stick with Damon Hill and David Coulthard for 1995.

In hindsight, perhaps, a fully charged Mansell may have been a better choice to challenge Schumacher's dominance. Instead a multi-million-dollar marriage of convenience was forged with Marlboro McLaren Mercedes which ended in farce when he first failed to fit properly in the car, and then gave up when the expensively redesigned machine failed to meet his expectations. This rather sad postscript to Mansell's Grand Prix career was gleefully pounced upon by his detractors, while, apart from a handful of over-hyped touring car appearances for Ford in the BTCC during 1998, his legions of loyal fans have since been left to pin their hopes on ill-founded rumours of a comeback.

MANSELL, Nigel (GB) b 8/8/1953, Baughton, Upton on Severn, Worcestershire

1980 — Championship position: Unplaced

	Race	Circuit	No	Entrant	Tyres	Car/Engine	Comment	Q Pos/Entries
ret	AUSTRIAN GP	Österreichring	43	Team Essex Lotus	G	3.0 Lotus 81B-Cosworth V8	*engine*	24/25
ret	DUTCH GP	Zandvoort	43	Team Essex Lotus	G	3.0 Lotus 81B-Cosworth V8	*brake failure-spun off*	16/28
dnq	ITALIAN GP	Imola	43	Team Essex Lotus	G	3.0 Lotus 81B-Cosworth V8		25/28

1981 — Championship position: 14th= Wins: 0 Pole positions: 0 Fastest laps: 0 Points scored: 8

	Race	Circuit	No	Entrant	Tyres	Car/Engine	Comment	Q Pos/Entries
ret	US GP WEST	Long Beach	12	Team Essex Lotus	M	3.0 Lotus 81B-Cosworth V8	*hit wall*	7/29
11	BRAZILIAN GP	Rio	12	Team Essex Lotus	M	3.0 Lotus 81B-Cosworth V8	*1 lap behind*	13/30
ret	ARGENTINE GP	Buenos Aires	12	Team Essex Lotus	M	3.0 Lotus 81B-Cosworth V8	*engine*	15/29
3	BELGIAN GP	Zolder	12	Team Essex Lotus	M	3.0 Lotus 81B-Cosworth V8		10/31
ret	MONACO GP	Monte Carlo	12	Team Essex Lotus	M	3.0 Lotus 87-Cosworth V8	*rear suspension*	3/31
6	SPANISH GP	Jarama	12	John Player Team Lotus	M	3.0 Lotus 87-Cosworth V8		11/30
7	FRENCH GP	Dijon	12	John Player Team Lotus	M	3.0 Lotus 87-Cosworth V8	*1 lap behind*	13/29
dnq	BRITISH GP	Silverstone	12	John Player Team Lotus	G	3.0 Lotus 87-Cosworth V8		27/30
dns	"	"	12		G	3.0 Lotus 88B-Cosworth V8	*disqualified during practice*	– / –
ret	GERMAN GP	Hockenheim	12	John Player Team Lotus	G	3.0 Lotus 87-Cosworth V8	*fuel leak*	15/30
ret	AUSTRIAN GP	Österreichring	12	John Player Team Lotus	G	3.0 Lotus 87-Cosworth V8	*engine*	11/28
ret	DUTCH GP	Zandvoort	12	John Player Team Lotus	G	3.0 Lotus 87-Cosworth V8	*electrics*	17/30
ret	ITALIAN GP	Monza	12	John Player Team Lotus	G	3.0 Lotus 87-Cosworth V8	*handling*	12/30
ret	CANADIAN GP	Montreal	12	John Player Team Lotus	G	3.0 Lotus 87-Cosworth V8	*accident with Prost*	5/30
4	CAESARS PALACE GP	Las Vegas	12	John Player Team Lotus	G	3.0 Lotus 87-Cosworth V8		9/32

1982 — Championship position: 14th= Wins: 0 Pole positions: 0 Fastest laps: 0 Points scored: 7

	Race	Circuit	No	Entrant	Tyres	Car/Engine	Comment	Q Pos/Entries
ret	SOUTH AFRICAN GP	Kyalami	12	John Player Team Lotus	G	3.0 Lotus 87B-Cosworth V8	*electrics*	18/30
3*	BRAZILIAN GP	Rio	12	John Player Team Lotus	G	3.0 Lotus 91-Cosworth V8	** 1st and 2nd place cars dsq*	14/31
7	US GP WEST	Long Beach	12	John Player Team Lotus	G	3.0 Lotus 91-Cosworth V8	*2 laps behind*	17/31
ret	BELGIAN GP	Zolder	12	John Player Team Lotus	G	3.0 Lotus 91-Cosworth V8	*clutch*	9/32
4	MONACO GP	Monte Carlo	12	John Player Team Lotus	G	3.0 Lotus 91-Cosworth V8	*1 lap behind*	11/31
ret	US GP (DETROIT)	Detroit	12	John Player Team Lotus	G	3.0 Lotus 91-Cosworth V8	*engine*	7/28
ret	CANADIAN GP	Montreal	12	John Player Team Lotus	G	3.0 Lotus 91-Cosworth V8	*accident with Giacomelli*	14/29
ret	BRITISH GP	Brands Hatch	12	John Player Team Lotus	G	3.0 Lotus 91-Cosworth V8	*handling & driver discomfort*	23/30
9	GERMAN GP	Hockenheim	12	John Player Team Lotus	G	3.0 Lotus 91-Cosworth V8	*pit stop-in pain/2 laps behind*	19/30
ret	AUSTRIAN GP	Österreichring	12	John Player Team Lotus	G	3.0 Lotus 91-Cosworth V8	*engine*	12/29
8	SWISS GP	Dijon	12	John Player Team Lotus	G	3.0 Lotus 91-Cosworth V8	*1 lap behind*	26/29
7	ITALIAN GP	Monza	12	John Player Team Lotus	G	3.0 Lotus 91-Cosworth V8	*1 lap behind*	23/30
ret	CAESARS PALACE GP	Las Vegas	12	John Player Team Lotus	G	3.0 Lotus 91-Cosworth V8	*accident with Baldi*	21/30

1983 — Championship position: 0 Wins: 0 Pole positions: 0 Fastest laps: 1 Points scored: 0

	Race	Circuit	No	Entrant	Tyres	Car/Engine	Comment	Q Pos/Entries
12	BRAZILIAN GP	Rio	12	John Player Team Lotus	P	3.0 Lotus 92-Cosworth V8	*pit stop-tyres/2 laps behind*	22/27
12	US GP WEST	Long Beach	12	John Player Team Lotus	P	3.0 Lotus 92-Cosworth V8	*3 stops-tyres/handling/-3 laps*	13/28
ret	FRENCH GP	Paul Ricard	12	John Player Team Lotus	P	3.0 Lotus 92-Cosworth V8	*handling/driver discomfort*	18/29
12/ret	SAN MARINO GP	Imola	12	John Player Team Lotus	P	3.0 Lotus 92-Cosworth V8	*broken rear wing-spun/-4 laps*	15/28
ret	MONACO GP	Monte Carlo	12	John Player Team Lotus	P	3.0 Lotus 92-Cosworth V8	*accident with Alboreto*	14/28
ret	BELGIAN GP	Spa	12	John Player Team Lotus	P	3.0 Lotus 92-Cosworth V8	*gearbox*	19/28
6	US GP (DETROIT)	Detroit	12	John Player Team Lotus	P	3.0 Lotus 92-Cosworth V8	*1 lap behind*	14/27
ret	CANADIAN GP	Montreal	12	John Player Team Lotus	P	3.0 Lotus 92-Cosworth V8	*handling/tyres*	18/28
4	BRITISH GP	Silverstone	12	John Player Team Lotus	P	1.5 t/c Lotus 94T-Renault V6	*pit stop-fuel*	– / –
dns	"	"	12		P	1.5 t/c Lotus 93T-Renault V6	*practice only/set grid time*	18/29
ret	GERMAN GP	Hockenheim	12	John Player Team Lotus	P	1.5 t/c Lotus 93T-Renault V6	*engine*	– / –
dns	"	"	12		P	1.5 t/c Lotus 93T-Renault V6	*practice only/set grid time*	17/29
5	AUSTRIAN GP	Österreichring	12	John Player Team Lotus	P	1.5 t/c Lotus 94T-Renault V6	*pit stop-fuel/1 lap behind*	3/29
ret	DUTCH GP	Zandvoort	12	John Player Team Lotus	P	1.5 t/c Lotus 94T-Renault V6	*spun off*	5/29
8	ITALIAN GP	Monza	12	John Player Team Lotus	P	1.5 t/c Lotus 94T-Renault V6		11/29
3	EUROPEAN GP	Brands Hatch	12	John Player Team Lotus	P	1.5 t/c Lotus 94T-Renault V6	*FL*	3/29
nc	SOUTH AFRICAN GP	Kyalami	12	John Player Team Lotus	P	1.5 t/c Lotus 94T-Renault V6	*stops-gear linkage/tyres/-9 laps*	7/26

1984 — Championship position: 9th Wins: 0 Pole positions: 1 Fastest laps: 0 Points scored: 13

	Race	Circuit	No	Entrant	Tyres	Car/Engine	Comment	Q Pos/Entries
ret	BRAZILIAN GP	Rio	12	John Player Team Lotus	G	1.5 t/c Lotus 95T-Renault V6	*slid off track*	5/27
ret	SOUTH AFRICAN GP	Kyalami	12	John Player Team Lotus	G	1.5 t/c Lotus 95T-Renault V6	*turbo inlet duct*	3/27
ret	BELGIAN GP	Zolder	12	John Player Team Lotus	G	1.5 t/c Lotus 95T-Renault V6	*clutch*	10/27
ret	SAN MARINO GP	Imola	12	John Player Team Lotus	G	1.5 t/c Lotus 95T-Renault V6	*brake failure-crashed*	18/28
3	FRENCH GP	Dijon	12	John Player Team Lotus	G	1.5 t/c Lotus 95T-Renault V6		6/27
ret	MONACO GP	Monte Carlo	12	John Player Team Lotus	G	1.5 t/c Lotus 95T-Renault V6	*hit barrier when leading*	2/27
6	CANADIAN GP	Montreal	12	John Player Team Lotus	G	1.5 t/c Lotus 95T-Renault V6	*gearbox problems/-2 laps*	7/26
ret	US GP (DETROIT)	Detroit	12	John Player Team Lotus	G	1.5 t/c Lotus 95T-Renault V6	*gearbox*	3/27
6/ret	US GP (DALLAS)	Dallas	12	John Player Team Lotus	G	1.5 t/c Lotus 95T-Renault V6	*gearbox/3 laps behind*	1/27
ret	BRITISH GP	Brands Hatch	12	John Player Team Lotus	G	1.5 t/c Lotus 95T-Renault V6	*gearbox*	8/27
4	GERMAN GP	Hockenheim	12	John Player Team Lotus	G	1.5 t/c Lotus 95T-Renault V6		16/27
ret	AUSTRIAN GP	Österreichring	12	John Player Team Lotus	G	1.5 t/c Lotus 95T-Renault V6	*engine*	8/28
3	DUTCH GP	Zandvoort	12	John Player Team Lotus	G	1.5 t/c Lotus 95T-Renault V6		12/27
ret	ITALIAN GP	Monza	12	John Player Team Lotus	G	1.5 t/c Lotus 95T-Renault V6	*spun off*	7/27
ret	EUROPEAN GP	Nürburgring	12	John Player Team Lotus	G	1.5 t/c Lotus 95T-Renault V6	*engine*	8/26
ret	PORTUGUESE GP	Estoril	12	John Player Team Lotus	G	1.5 t/c Lotus 95T-Renault V6	*lost brake fluid-spun off*	6/27

1985 — Championship position: 6th Wins: 2 Pole positions: 1 Fastest laps: 1 Points scored: 31

	Race	Circuit	No	Entrant	Tyres	Car/Engine	Comment	Q Pos/Entries
ret	BRAZILIAN GP	Rio	5	Canon Williams Honda Team	G	1.5 t/c Williams FW10-Honda V6	*broken exhaust/accident damage*	5/25
5	PORTUGUESE GP	Estoril	5	Canon Williams Honda Team	G	1.5 t/c Williams FW10-Honda V6	*started from pit lane/-2 laps*	9/26
5	SAN MARINO GP	Imola	5	Canon Williams Honda Team	G	1.5 t/c Williams FW10-Honda V6	*gearbox problems/-2 laps*	7/26
7	MONACO GP	Monte Carlo	5	Canon Williams Honda Team	G	1.5 t/c Williams FW10-Honda V6	*brake problems/1 lap behind*	2/26
6	CANADIAN GP	Montreal	5	Canon Williams Honda Team	G	1.5 t/c Williams FW10-Honda V6		16/25
ret	US GP (DETROIT)	Detroit	5	Canon Williams Honda Team	G	1.5 t/c Williams FW10-Honda V6	*brake problems-crashed*	2/25
dns	FRENCH GP	Paul Ricard	5	Canon Williams Honda Team	G	1.5 t/c Williams FW10-Honda V6	*accident in practice*	(8)/26

ret	BRITISH GP	Silverstone	5	Canon Williams Honda Team	G	1.5 t/c Williams FW10-Honda V6	clutch	5/26
6	GERMAN GP	Nürburgring	5	Canon Williams Honda Team	G	1.5 t/c Williams FW10-Honda V6		10/27
ret	AUSTRIAN GP	Österreichring	5	Canon Williams Honda Team	G	1.5 t/c Williams FW10-Honda V6	engine	2/27
6	DUTCH GP	Zandvoort	5	Canon Williams Honda Team	G	1.5 t/c Williams FW10-Honda V6	pit stop-tyres/1 lap behind	7/27
11/ret	ITALIAN GP	Monza	5	Canon Williams Honda Team	G	1.5 t/c Williams FW10-Honda V6	engine/FL/4 laps behind	3/26
2	BELGIAN GP	Spa	5	Canon Williams Honda Team	G	1.5 t/c Williams FW10-Honda V6		7/24
1	EUROPEAN GP	Brands Hatch	5	Canon Williams Honda Team	G	1.5 t/c Williams FW10-Honda V6		3/27
1	SOUTH AFRICAN GP	Kyalami	5	Canon Williams Honda Team	G	1.5 t/c Williams FW10-Honda V6		1/21
ret	AUSTRALIAN GP	Adelaide	5	Canon Williams Honda Team	G	1.5 t/c Williams FW10-Honda V6	transmission	2/25

1986   Championship position: 2nd   Wins: 5   Pole positions: 2   Fastest laps: 4   Points scored: 72

ret	BRAZILIAN GP	Rio	5	Canon Williams Honda Team	G	1.5 t/c Williams FW11-Honda V6	accident with Senna-lap 1	3/25
2	SPANISH GP	Jerez	5	Canon Williams Honda Team	G	1.5 t/c Williams FW11-Honda V6	FL	3/25
ret	SAN MARINO	Imola	5	Canon Williams Honda Team	G	1.5 t/c Williams FW11-Honda V6	engine	3/26
4	MONACO GP	Monte Carlo	5	Canon Williams Honda Team	G	1.5 t/c Williams FW11-Honda V6		2/26
1	BELGIAN GP	Spa	5	Canon Williams Honda Team	G	1.5 t/c Williams FW11-Honda V6		5/25
1	CANADIAN GP	Montreal	5	Canon Williams Honda Team	G	1.5 t/c Williams FW11-Honda V6		1/25
5	US GP (DETROIT)	Detroit	5	Canon Williams Honda Team	G	1.5 t/c Williams FW11-Honda V6	pit stop-tyres/1 lap behind	2/26
1	FRENCH GP	Paul Ricard	5	Canon Williams Honda Team	G	1.5 t/c Williams FW11-Honda V6	FL	2/26
1	BRITISH GP	Brands Hatch	5	Canon Williams Honda Team	G	1.5 t/c Williams FW11-Honda V6	FL	2/26
3	GERMAN GP	Hockenheim	5	Canon Williams Honda Team	G	1.5 t/c Williams FW11-Honda V6		6/26
3	HUNGARIAN GP	Hungaroring	5	Canon Williams Honda Team	G	1.5 t/c Williams FW11-Honda V6	pit stop-tyres/handling/-1 lap	4/26
ret	AUSTRIAN GP	Österreichring	5	Canon Williams Honda Team	G	1.5 t/c Williams FW11-Honda V6	driveshaft-c.v.joint	6/26
2	ITALIAN GP	Monza	5	Canon Williams Honda Team	G	1.5 t/c Williams FW11-Honda V6		3/27
1	PORTUGUESE GP	Estoril	5	Canon Williams Honda Team	G	1.5 t/c Williams FW11-Honda V6	FL	2/27
5	MEXICAN GP	Mexico City	5	Canon Williams Honda Team	G	1.5 t/c Williams FW11-Honda V6	last away/pit stop-tyres/-1 lap	3/26
ret	AUSTRALIAN GP	Adelaide	5	Canon Williams Honda Team	G	1.5 t/c Williams FW11-Honda V6	tyre failure-crashed	1/26

1987   Championship position: 2nd   Wins: 6   Pole positions: 8   Fastest laps: 3   Points scored: 61

6	BRAZILIAN GP	Rio	5	Canon Williams Honda Team	G	1.5 t/c Williams FW11B-Honda V6	pit stop-paper in radiator/-1 lap	1/23
1	SAN MARINO GP	Imola	5	Canon Williams Honda Team	G	1.5 t/c Williams FW11B-Honda V6		2/27
ret	BELGIAN GP	Spa	5	Canon Williams Honda Team	G	1.5 t/c Williams FW11B-Honda V6	collision damage-Senna/	1/26
ret	MONACO GP	Monte Carlo	5	Canon Williams Honda Team	G	1.5 t/c Williams FW11B-Honda V6	wastegate pipe	1/26
5	US GP (DETROIT)	Detroit	5	Canon Williams Honda Team	G	1.5 t/c Williams FW11B-Honda V6	p stop-tyres-wheel stuck/-1 lap	1/26
1	FRENCH GP	Paul Ricard	5	Canon Williams Honda Team	G	1.5 t/c Williams FW11B-Honda V6		1/26
1	BRITISH GP	Silverstone	5	Canon Williams Honda Team	G	1.5 t/c Williams FW11B-Honda V6	FL	2/26
ret	GERMAN GP	Hockenheim	5	Canon Williams Honda Team	G	1.5 t/c Williams FW11B-Honda V6	engine/FL	1/26
14/ret	HUNGARIAN GP	Hungaroring	5	Canon Williams Honda Team	G	1.5 t/c Williams FW11B-Honda V6	lost wheel nut/6 laps behind	1/26
1	AUSTRIAN GP	Österreichring	5	Canon Williams Honda Team	G	1.5 t/c Williams FW11B-Honda V6	FL	2/26
3	ITALIAN GP	Monza	5	Canon Williams Honda Team	G	1.5 t/c Williams FW11B-Honda V6		2/28
ret	PORTUGUESE GP	Estoril	5	Canon Williams Honda Team	G	1.5 t/c Williams FW11B-Honda V6	electrics	2/27
1	SPANISH GP	Jerez	5	Canon Williams Honda Team	G	1.5 t/c Williams FW11B-Honda V6		2/28
1	MEXICAN GP	Mexico City	5	Canon Williams Honda Team	G	1.5 t/c Williams FW11B-Honda V6		1/27
dns	JAPANESE GP	Suzuka	5	Canon Williams Honda Team	G	1.5 t/c Williams FW11B-Honda V6	practice accident/injured back	(7)/27

1988   Championship position: 9th   Wins: 0   Pole positions: 0   Fastest laps: 1   Points scored: 12

ret	BRAZILIAN GP	Rio	5	Canon Williams Team	G	3.5 Williams FW12-Judd V8	overheating/electrics	2/31
ret	SAN MARINO GP	Imola	5	Canon Williams Team	G	3.5 Williams FW12-Judd V8	engine/electrics	11/31
ret	MONACO GP	Monte Carlo	5	Canon Williams Team	G	3.5 Williams FW12-Judd V8	accident with Alboreto	5/30
ret	MEXICAN GP	Mexico City	5	Canon Williams Team	G	3.5 Williams FW12-Judd V8	engine	14/30
ret	CANADIAN GP	Montreal	5	Canon Williams Team	G	3.5 Williams FW12-Judd V8	engine	9/31
ret	US GP (DETROIT)	Detroit	5	Canon Williams Team	G	3.5 Williams FW12-Judd V8	electrics	6/31
ret	FRENCH GP	Paul Ricard	5	Canon Williams Team	G	3.5 Williams FW12-Judd V8	suspension	9/31
2	BRITISH GP	Silverstone	5	Canon Williams Team	G	3.5 Williams FW12-Judd V8	FL	11/31
ret	GERMAN GP	Hockenheim	5	Canon Williams Team	G	3.5 Williams FW12-Judd V8	spun off	11/31
ret	HUNGARIAN GP	Hungaroring	5	Canon Williams Team	G	3.5 Williams FW12-Judd V8	driver exhaustion	2/31
ret	PORTUGUESE GP	Estoril	5	Canon Williams Team	G	3.5 Williams FW12-Judd V8	spun off	6/31

Mansell is magic!
The hero of the Silverstone crowd, seen winning the 1991 British Grand Prix at the wheel of the Williams FW14, finally achieved his championship dream the following season with an updated version of the same car.

2	SPANISH GP	Jerez	5	Canon Williams Team	G	3.5 Williams FW12-Judd V8		3/31
ret	JAPANESE GP	Suzuka	5	Canon Williams Team	G	3.5 Williams FW12-Judd V8	spun off-hit Piquet	8/31
ret	AUSTRALIAN GP	Adelaide	5	Canon Williams Team	G	3.5 Williams FW12-Judd V8	brakes-spun off	3/31

1989   Championship position: 4th   Wins: 2   Pole positions: 0   Fastest laps: 3   Points scored: 38

1	BRAZILIAN GP	Rio	27	Scuderia Ferrari SpA SEFAC	G	3.5 Ferrari 640 V12		6/38
ret	SAN MARINO GP	Imola	27	Scuderia Ferrari SpA SEFAC	G	3.5 Ferrari 640 V12	gearbox	3/39
ret	MONACO GP	Monte Carlo	27	Scuderia Ferrari SpA SEFAC	G	3.5 Ferrari 640 V12	gear selection	5/38
ret	MEXICAN GP	Mexico City	27	Scuderia Ferrari SpA SEFAC	G	3.5 Ferrari 640 V12	gearbox/FL	3/39
ret	US GP (PHOENIX)	Phoenix	27	Scuderia Ferrari SpA SEFAC	G	3.5 Ferrari 640 V12	alternator	4/39
dsq	CANADIAN GP	Montreal	27	Scuderia Ferrari SpA SEFAC	G	3.5 Ferrari 640 V12	started from pits before start	5/39
2	FRENCH GP	Paul Ricard	27	Scuderia Ferrari SpA SEFAC	G	3.5 Ferrari 640 V12	started from pit lane	3/39
2	BRITISH GP	Silverstone	27	Scuderia Ferrari SpA SEFAC	G	3.5 Ferrari 640 V12	FL	3/39
3	GERMAN GP	Hockenheim	27	Scuderia Ferrari SpA SEFAC	G	3.5 Ferrari 640 V12		3/39
1	HUNGARIAN GP	Hungaroring	27	Scuderia Ferrari SpA SEFAC	G	3.5 Ferrari 640 V12	FL	12/39
3	BELGIAN GP	Spa	27	Scuderia Ferrari SpA SEFAC	G	3.5 Ferrari 640 V12		6/39
ret	ITALIAN GP	Monza	27	Scuderia Ferrari SpA SEFAC	G	3.5 Ferrari 640 V12	gearbox	3/39
dsq*/ret	PORTUGUESE GP	Estoril	27	Scuderia Ferrari SpA SEFAC	G	3.5 Ferrari 640 V12	* reversed in pits/collision-Senna	3/39
ret	JAPANESE GP	Suzuka	27	Scuderia Ferrari SpA SEFAC	G	3.5 Ferrari 640 V12	engine	4/39
ret	AUSTRALIAN GP	Adelaide	27	Scuderia Ferrari SpA SEFAC	G	3.5 Ferrari 640 V12	spun off in rain	7/39

1990   Championship position: 5th   Wins: 1   Pole positions: 3   Fastest laps: 3   Points scored: 37

ret	US GP (PHOENIX)	Phoenix	2	Scuderia Ferrari SpA SEFAC	G	3.5 Ferrari 641 V12	gearbox/clutch-spun off	17/35
4	BRAZILIAN GP	Interlagos	2	Scuderia Ferrari SpA SEFAC	G	3.5 Ferrari 641 V12	pit stop-tyres-anti-roll bar	5/35
ret	SAN MARINO GP	Imola	2	Scuderia Ferrari SpA SEFAC	G	3.5 Ferrari 641/2 V12	engine	5/34
ret	MONACO GP	Monte Carlo	2	Scuderia Ferrari SpA SEFAC	G	3.5 Ferrari 641/2 V12	battery/electrics	7/35
3	CANADIAN GP	Montreal	2	Scuderia Ferrari SpA SEFAC	G	3.5 Ferrari 641/2 V12		7/35
2	MEXICAN GP	Mexico City	2	Scuderia Ferrari SpA SEFAC	G	3.5 Ferrari 641/2 V12		4/35
18/ret	FRENCH GP	Paul Ricard	2	Scuderia Ferrari SpA SEFAC	G	3.5 Ferrari 641/2 V12	engine/FL/8 laps behind	1/35
ret	BRITISH GP	Silverstone	2	Scuderia Ferrari SpA SEFAC	G	3.5 Ferrari 641/2 V12	gearbox/FL	1/35
ret	GERMAN GP	Hockenheim	2	Scuderia Ferrari SpA SEFAC	G	3.5 Ferrari 641/2 V12	undertray damage	4/35
17/ret	HUNGARIAN GP	Hungaroring	2	Scuderia Ferrari SpA SEFAC	G	3.5 Ferrari 641/2 V12	collision with Berger/-6 laps	5/35
ret	BELGIAN GP	Spa	2	Scuderia Ferrari SpA SEFAC	G	3.5 Ferrari 641/2 V12	handling problems	5/33
4	ITALIAN GP	Monza	2	Scuderia Ferrari SpA SEFAC	G	3.5 Ferrari 641/2 V12	throttle problems	4/33
1	PORTUGUESE GP	Estoril	2	Scuderia Ferrari SpA SEFAC	G	3.5 Ferrari 641/2 V12		1/33
2	SPANISH GP	Jerez	2	Scuderia Ferrari SpA SEFAC	G	3.5 Ferrari 641/2 V12		3/33
ret	JAPANESE GP	Suzuka	2	Scuderia Ferrari SpA SEFAC	G	3.5 Ferrari 641/2 V12	driveshaft	3/30
2	AUSTRALIAN GP	Adelaide	2	Scuderia Ferrari SpA SEFAC	G	3.5 Ferrari 641/2 V12	FL	3/30

1991   Championship position: 2nd   Wins: 5   Pole positions: 2   Fastest laps: 6   Points scored: 72

ret	US GP	Phoenix	5	Canon Williams Team	G	3.5 Williams FW14-Renault V10	gearbox	4/34
ret	BRAZILIAN GP	Interlagos	5	Canon Williams Team	G	3.5 Williams FW14-Renault V10	gearbox/FL	3/34
ret	SAN MARINO GP	Imola	5	Canon Williams Team	G	3.5 Williams FW14-Renault V10	collision with Brundle	4/34
2	MONACO GP	Monte Carlo	5	Canon Williams Team	G	3.5 Williams FW14-Renault V10		5/34
6/ret	CANADIAN GP	Montreal	5	Canon Williams Team	G	3.5 Williams FW14-Renault V10	leading-engine cut out last lap/FL	2/34
2	MEXICAN GP	Mexico City	5	Canon Williams Team	G	3.5 Williams FW14-Renault V10	FL	2/34
1	FRENCH GP	Magny Cours	5	Canon Williams Team	G	3.5 Williams FW14-Renault V10	FL	4/34
1	BRITISH GP	Silverstone	5	Canon Williams Team	G	3.5 Williams FW14-Renault V10	FL	1/34
1	GERMAN GP	Hockenheim	5	Canon Williams Team	G	3.5 Williams FW14-Renault V10		1/34
2	HUNGARIAN GP	Hungaroring	5	Canon Williams Team	G	3.5 Williams FW14-Renault V10		3/34
ret	BELGIAN GP	Spa	5	Canon Williams Team	G	3.5 Williams FW14-Renault V10	voltage regulator	3/34
1	ITALIAN GP	Monza	5	Canon Williams Team	G	3.5 Williams FW14-Renault V10		2/34
dsq*	PORTUGUESE GP	Estoril	5	Canon Williams Team	G	3.5 Williams FW14-Renault V10	*wheel change in pit lane/FL	4/34
1	SPANISH GP	Barcelona	5	Canon Williams Team	G	3.5 Williams FW14-Renault V10		2/33
ret	JAPANESE GP	Suzuka	5	Canon Williams Team	G	3.5 Williams FW14-Renault V10	spun off	3/31
2*	AUSTRALIAN GP	Adelaide	5	Canon Williams Team	G	3.5 Williams FW14-Renault V10	race stopped 14 laps/*half pts	3/32

1992   Championship position: WORLD CHAMPION   Wins: 9   Pole positions: 14   Fastest laps: 8   Points scored: 108

1	SOUTH AFRICAN GP	Kyalami	5	Canon Williams Team	G	3.5 Williams FW14B-Renault V10	FL	1/30
1	MEXICAN GP	Mexico City	5	Canon Williams Team	G	3.5 Williams FW14B-Renault V10		1/30
1	BRAZILIAN GP	Interlagos	5	Canon Williams Team	G	3.5 Williams FW14B-Renault V10		1/31
1	SPANISH GP	Barcelona	5	Canon Williams Team	G	3.5 Williams FW14B-Renault V10	FL	1/32
1	SAN MARINO GP	Imola	5	Canon Williams Team	G	3.5 Williams FW14B-Renault V10		1/32
2	MONACO GP	Monte Carlo	5	Canon Williams Team	G	3.5 Williams FW14B-Renault V10	pit stop for tyres when leading/FL	1/32
ret	CANADIAN GP	Montreal	5	Canon Williams Team	G	3.5 Williams FW14B-Renault V10	spun off trying to pass Senna	3/32
1	FRENCH GP	Magny Cours	5	Canon Williams Team	G	3.5 Williams FW14B-Renault V10	aggregate of 2 parts/FL	1/30
1	BRITISH GP	Silverstone	5	Canon Williams Team	G	3.5 Williams FW14B-Renault V10	FL	1/32
1	GERMAN GP	Hockenheim	5	Canon Williams Team	G	3.5 Williams FW14B-Renault V10		1/32
2	HUNGARIAN GP	Hungaroring	5	Canon Williams Team	G	3.5 Williams FW14B-Renault V10	FL	2/31
2	BELGIAN GP	Spa	5	Canon Williams Team	G	3.5 Williams FW14B-Renault V10		1/30
ret	ITALIAN GP	Monza	5	Canon Williams Team	G	3.5 Williams FW14B-Renault V10	hydraulics/gearbox/FL	1/28
1	PORTUGUESE GP	Estoril	5	Canon Williams Team	G	3.5 Williams FW14B-Renault V10		1/26
ret	JAPANESE GP	Suzuka	5	Canon Williams Team	G	3.5 Williams FW14B-Renault V10	engine/FL	1/26
ret	AUSTRALIAN GP	Adelaide	5	Canon Williams Team	G	3.5 Williams FW14B-Renault V10	hit by Senna	1/26

1994   Championship position: 9th   Wins: 1   Pole positions: 1   Fastest laps: 0   Points scored: 13

ret	FRENCH GP	Magny Cours	2	Rothmans Williams Renault	G	3.5 Williams FW16-Renault V10	transmission	2/28
ret	EUROPEAN GP	Jerez	2	Rothmans Williams Renault	G	3.5 Williams FW16B-Renault V10	spun off	3/28
4	JAPANESE GP	Suzuka	2	Rothmans Williams Renault	G	3.5 Williams FW16B-Renault V10		4/28
1	AUSTRALIAN GP	Adelaide	2	Rothmans Williams Renault	G	3.5 Williams FW16B-Renault V10		1/28

1995   Championship position: Unplaced

10	SAN MARINO GP	Imola	7	Marlboro McLaren Mercedes	G	3.0 McLaren MP4/10B-Mercedes V10	2 laps behind	9/26
ret	SPANISH GP	Barcelona	7	Marlboro McLaren Mercedes	G	3.0 McLaren MP4/10B-Mercedes V10	handling-driver gave up	10/26

GP Starts: 187   GP Wins: 31   Pole positions: 32   Fastest laps: 30   Points: 482

SERGIO MANTOVANI

A young Italian businessman, Mantovani made a good impression in both sports and touring cars in 1952, finishing sixth in the Bari GP (second in class) in a Ferrari, and second in the GT class of the Pescara 12 Hours in a Lancia Aurelia.

This led him to buy a Maserati, and he was soon assimilated into the works team, sharing a 2-litre sports car with Fangio to take third in the 1953 Targa Florio, and winning the Circuit of Caserta race. This led to a drive in that year's Italian GP, though he had to hand his car over to Musso in the race.

In 1954 he became a good, solid team member who could be relied upon to look after the car and bring it home, taking fifth places in the German and Swiss Grands Prix, and thirds in both the Syracuse and Rome non-championship events.

Retained in the squad for 1955, Sergio was involved in a practice crash at the Valentino GP in Turin in which he sustained serious leg injuries which resulted in the amputation of one limb above the knee.

His racing career was over, but he then became a member of the Italian Sporting Commission, thus retaining his links with the sport.

MANTOVANI, Sergio (I) b 22/5/1929, Cusano Milanino, nr Milan

	1953	Championship position: Unplaced							
	Race	Circuit	No	Entrant	Tyres	Car/Engine		Comment	Q Pos/Entries
7*	ITALIAN GP	Monza	56	Officine Alfieri Maserati	P	2.0 Maserati A6GCM 6		* Musso took over/-4 laps	12/30
	1954	Championship position: 12th= Wins: 0 Pole positions: 0 Fastest laps: 0 Points scored: 4							
7	BELGIAN GP	Spa	30	Officine Alfieri Maserati	P	2.5 Maserati 250F 6		2 laps behind	11/15
dns	FRENCH GP	Reims	40	Officine Alfieri Maserati	P	2.5 Maserati 250F 6		practice only	– /22
5	GERMAN GP	Nürburgring	7	Officine Alfieri Maserati	P	2.5 Maserati 250F 6			15/23
5	SWISS GP	Bremgarten	28	Officine Alfieri Maserati	P	2.5 Maserati 250F 6		2 laps behind	9/16
9	ITALIAN GP	Monza	18	Officine Alfieri Maserati	P	2.5 Maserati 250F 6		pit stop/6 laps behind	9/21
ret	SPANISH GP	Pedralbes	12	Officine Alfieri Maserati	P	2.5 Maserati 250F 6		brake problems-crashed	10/22
	1955	Championship position: Unplaced							
ret	ARGENTINE GP	Buenos Aires	20	Officine Alfieri Maserati	P	2.5 Maserati 250F 6		Musso/Behra co-drove fuel feed	19/22
7*	"	" "	22	Officine Alfieri Maserati	P	2.5 Maserati 250F 6		* Musso/Schell co-drove/-13 laps	– / -

GP Starts: 7   GP Wins: 0   Pole positions: 0   Fastest laps: 0   Points: 4

MANZON, Robert (F) b 12/4/1917, Marseille

	1950	Championship position: 10th= Wins: 0 Pole positions: 0 Fastest laps: 0 Points scored: 3							
	Race	Circuit	No	Entrant	Tyres	Car/Engine		Comment	Q Pos/Entries
ret	MONACO GP	Monte Carlo	10	Equipe Simca Gordini	E	1.5 s/c Simca-Gordini Type 15 4		multiple accident	11/21
4	FRENCH GP	Reims	44	Equipe Simca Gordini	E	1.5 s/c Simca-Gordini Type 15 4		3 laps behind	13/20
ret	ITALIAN GP	Monza	44	Equipe Simca Gordini	E	1.5 s/c Simca-Gordini Type 15 4		transmission	10/27
	1951	Championship position: Unplaced							
ret	FRENCH GP	Reims	30	Equipe Simca Gordini	E	1.5 s/c Simca-Gordini Type 15 4		engine	23/23
7	GERMAN GP	Nürburgring	82	Equipe Simca Gordini	E	1.5 s/c Simca-Gordini Type 15 4		1 lap behind	9/23
ret	ITALIAN GP	Monza	46	Equipe Simca Gordini	E	1.5 s/c Simca-Gordini Type 15 4		radiator	13/22
9	SPANISH GP	Pedralbes	14	Equipe Simca Gordini	E	1.5 s/c Simca-Gordini Type 15 4		7 laps behind	9/20
	1952	Championship position: 6th Wins: 0 Pole positions: 0 Fastest laps: 0 Points scored: 9							
ret	SWISS GP	Bremgarten	8	Equipe Gordini	E	2.0 Gordini Type 16 6		cooling damper	3/21
3	BELGIAN GP	Spa	14	Equipe Gordini	E	2.0 Gordini Type 16 6			4/22
4	FRENCH GP	Rouen	2	Equipe Gordini	E	2.0 Gordini Type 16 6		3 laps behind	5/20
ret	BRITISH GP	Silverstone	24	Equipe Gordini	E	2.0 Gordini Type 16 6		transmission	4/32
ret	GERMAN GP	Nürburgring	107	Equipe Gordini	E	2.0 Gordini Type 16 6		lost wheel	4/32
5	DUTCH GP	Zandvoort	10	Equipe Gordini	E	2.0 Gordini Type 16 6		3 laps behind	8/18
14	ITALIAN GP	Monza	2	Equipe Gordini	E	2.0 Gordini Type 16 6		9 laps behind	7/35
	1953	Championship position: Unplaced							
ret	ARGENTINE GP	Buenos Aires	26	Equipe Gordini	E	2.0 Gordini Type 16 6		lost wheel	8/16
	1954	Championship position: 12th= Wins: 0 Pole positions: 0 Fastest laps: 0 Points scored: 4							
3	FRENCH GP	Reims	34	Equipe Rosier	P	2.5 Ferrari 625 4		1 lap behind	12/22
ret	BRITISH GP	Silverstone	14	Equipe Rosier	P	2.5 Ferrari 625 4		cracked cylinder block	15/31
9	GERMAN GP	Nürburgring	24	Equipe Rosier	P	2.5 Ferrari 625 4		2 laps behind	12/23
dns	SWISS GP	Bremgarten	24	Scuderia Ferrari	P	2.5 Ferrari 553 4		practice accident	– / –
ret	ITALIAN GP	Monza	6	Equipe Rosier	P	2.5 Ferrari 625 4		engine	15/21
ret	SPANISH GP	Pedralbes	20	Equipe Rosier	P	2.5 Ferrari 625 4		engine	17/22

	1955			Championship position: Unplaced			
ret	MONACO GP	Monte Carlo	8	Equipe Gordini	E 2.5 Gordini Type 16 6	gearbox	13/22
dns	"	"	8	Equipe Gordini	E 2.5 Gordini Type 32 8	practice only	–/–
ret	DUTCH GP	Zandvoort	20	Equipe Gordini	E 2.5 Gordini Type 16 6	transmission	11/16
ret	BRITISH GP	Aintree	22	Equipe Gordini	E 2.5 Gordini Type 16 6	transmission	11/25
	1956			Championship position: Unplaced			
ret	MONACO GP	Monte Carlo	2	Equipe Gordini	E 2.5 Gordini Type 16 6	brakes crashed	12/19
dns	"	"	2	Equipe Gordini	E 2.5 Gordini Type 32 8	practice only	–/–
9	FRENCH GP	Reims	30	Equipe Gordini	E 2.5 Gordini Type 32 8	5 laps behind	15/20
9	BRITISH GP	Silverstone	15	Equipe Gordini	E 2.5 Gordini Type 32 8	7 laps behind	18/28
ret	GERMAN GP	Nürburgring	10	Equipe Gordini	E 2.5 Gordini Type 32 8	suspension	15/21
ret	ITALIAN GP	Monza	10	Equipe Gordini	E 2.5 Gordini Type 32 8	gearbox	23/26

GP Starts: 28   GP Wins: 0   Pole positions: 0   Fastest laps: 0   Points: 16

ROBERT MANZON

Manzon raced his own 1100 cc Cisitalia in 1947, taking wins at Angoulême and Comminges and chasing the Simca Gordinis sufficiently impressively in other events to persuade Amédée to sign him midway through the 1948 season. In his first race, at the Circuit des Ramparts in Angoulême (a circuit on which he always shone), he led the final and set fastest lap before retirement.

He was to become a mainstay of the team and in 1949 he was second to Trintignant at Angoulême, and runner-up to Sommer at Lausanne as well as winning the Bol d'Or at Montlhéry in a production Simca sports car with a special 1000 cc engine. The cars were gaining a reputation for unreliabilty because their engines were so highly stressed, but when they lasted good results often followed. In 1950 Manzon took fourth place in the World Championship French GP at Reims, while in the Formula 2 category he won the GP of Perigueux, the Circuit of Mettet in Belgium and was second at Roubaix and third in the Swiss GP at Bremgarten. The following season he triumphed only once, at Mettet again, but took second places at Les Sables d'Olonne, Rouen and Cadours.

Gordini introduced the new six-cylinder car for 1952, and this brought a much-needed boost in competitiveness. Robert put the extra performance to good use with some fine placings in the championship Grands Prix, including an excellent third at Spa behind the works Ferraris. His best non-title race finish was a second place shared with Bira at Marseilles, while in Gordini sports cars he won the Coupe du Salon at Montlhéry. One of his best-ever performances came at the beginning of 1953 in the Argentine GP when he lay second after a great drive before the car shed a wheel. He took fifth in the subsequent Libre race at Buenos Aires, but on his return to France he quit the team, racing a Lancia sports car for the remainder of the year before joining Louis Rosier's équipe in 1954. His best result was undoubtedly a third place behind two Mercedes-Benz making their stunning debut at Reims, although he did take a second at Bordeaux behind Gonzalez' works Ferrari.

In 1955 he was back in his spiritual home with 'Le Sorcier', but unhappily gained no real success, just a fifth place at Bordeaux. The following year saw heartbreak at Monaco, where he lay third until a gearbox failure just three laps from the finish. He did take a couple of wins – at the Naples GP, where he inherited the lead after the works Ferraris failed, and in the Pescara sports car race, where in the team's 2-litre sports car he defeated Taruffi's Ferrari after an outstanding drive. The much underrated Manzon decided to retire for both family and business reasons at the end of the season.

MARIMÓN, Onofre (RA) b 19/12/1923, Cordoba – d 31/7/1954, Nürburgring, Germany

	1951	Championship position: Unplaced							
	Race	Circuit	No	Entrant	Tyres	Car/Engine	Comment	Q Pos/Entries
ret	FRENCH GP	Reims	50	Scuderia Milano	P	1.5 s/c Maserati 4CLT/Milano 4	engine	15/23
	1953	Championship position: 9th=	Wins: 0	Pole positions: 0	Fastest laps: 0	Points scored: 4		
3	BELGIAN GP	Spa	28	Officine Alfieri Maserati	P	2.0 Maserati A6GCM 6	1 lap behind	6/22
9	FRENCH GP	Reims	22	Officine Alfieri Maserati	P	2.0 Maserati A6GCM 6	5 laps behind	8/25
ret	BRITISH GP	Silverstone	26	Officine Alfieri Maserati	P	2.0 Maserati A6GCM 6	engine	7/29
ret	GERMAN GP	Nürburgring	8	Officine Alfieri Maserati	P	2.0 Maserati A6GCM 6	suspension	8/35
ret	SWISS GP	Bremgarten	36	Officine Alfieri Maserati	P	2.0 Maserati A6GCM 6	oil pipe	5/23
ret	ITALIAN GP	Monza	54	Officine Alfieri Maserati	P	2.0 Maserati A6GCM 6	hit Ascari's spinning car	4/30
	1954	Championship position: 10th=	Wins: 0	Pole positions: 0	Fastest laps: 1 (shared)	Points scored: 4.14		
ret	ARGENTINE GP	Buenos Aires	4	Officine Alfieri Maserati	P	2.5 Maserati 250F 6	spun off	6/18
ret	BELGIAN GP	Spa	28	Officine Alfieri Maserati	P	2.5 Maserati 250F 6	engine	4/15
ret	FRENCH GP	Reims	12	Officine Alfieri Maserati	P	2.5 Maserati 250F 6	gearbox	5/22
3	BRITISH GP	Silverstone	33	Officine Alfieri Maserati	P	2.5 Maserati 250F 6	1 lap behind/FL(shared)	28/31
dns	GERMAN GP	Nürburgring	6	Officine Alfieri Maserati	P	2.5 Maserati 250F 6	fatal accident in practice	(8)/23

GP Starts: 11   GP Wins: 0   Pole positions: 0   Fastest laps: 1   Points: 8.14

ONOFRE MARIMÓN

A protégé of Fangio, who had frequently raced against his father, Domingo, in the long-distance South American road races, Onofre first made his mark in 1950 by winning the race at Mar del Plata in his 'Meccanica Nacional' special. The urge to race in Europe was overwhelming and Marimón came over briefly in 1951, racing for Scuderia Milano in the French GP and sharing a Talbot with Gonzalez at Le Mans.

He returned for a full season in 1953, making an immediate impression with third place in the Belgian GP, and second in the non-championship Modena GP. In 1954, with Fangio having been lured to Mercedes, and Gonzalez to Ferrari, Onofre found himself as effective Maserati team leader and he did well in the early-season races, winning the Rome GP at Castel Fusano and finishing third at Pau.

In Grands Prix he tried hard to emulate his peers, but in practice for the German Grand Prix he failed to negotiate a corner, and his Maserati plunged through a hedge and somersaulted down a slope, killing its driver instantly.

MARKO, Helmut (A) b 27/4/1943, Graz

	1971	Championship position: Unplaced							
	Race	Circuit	No	Entrant	Tyres	Car/Engine	Comment	Q Pos/Entries
dns	GERMAN GP	Nürburgring	27	Ecurie Bonnier	G	3.0 McLaren M7C-Cosworth V8	practice only-only did 1 lap	–/–
11	AUSTRIAN GP	Österreichring	16	Yardley-BRM	F	3.0 BRM P153 V12	2 laps behind	17/22
ret	ITALIAN GP	Monza	21	Yardley-BRM	F	3.0 BRM P153 V12	engine	12/24
dns	"	"	20T	Yardley-BRM	F	3.0 BRM P160 V12	practice only	–/–
12	CANADIAN GP	Mosport Park	31	Yardley-BRM	F	3.0 BRM P153 V12	pit stop-fuel/4 laps behind	19/27
13	US GP	Watkins Glen	17	Yardley-BRM	F	3.0 BRM P160 V12	pit stop-fuel/2 laps behind	17/32
	1972	Championship position: Unplaced							
10	ARGENTINE GP	Buenos Aires	7	Austria-Marlboro BRM	F	3.0 BRM P153 V12	2 laps behind	19/22
14	SOUTH AFRICAN GP	Kyalami	24	Austria-Marlboro BRM	F	3.0 BRM P153 V12	3 laps behind	23/27
8	MONACO GP	Monte Carlo	26	Austria-Marlboro BRM	F	3.0 BRM P153B V12	3 laps behind	17/25
10	BELGIAN GP	Nivelles	27	Austria-Marlboro BRM	F	3.0 BRM P153B V12	2 laps behind	23/26
ret	FRENCH GP	Clermont Ferrand	25	Austria-Marlboro BRM	F	3.0 BRM P160B V12	stone pierced visor/eye injury	6/29

GP Starts: 9   GP Wins: 0   Pole positions: 0   Fastest laps: 0   Points: 0

HELMUT MARKO

Like many Austrian drivers, Marko, whose racing career had been delayed while he gained a doctorate in law, cut his teeth on Super Vee racers. In 1969 he drove the works McNamara in F3, but he had already tried his hand in sports cars, on which he concentrated the following year.

Driving Martini Racing's Porsche, Marko soon made his mark, finishing third at Le Mans in 1970 and then winning the classic race with Gijs van Lennep a year later. Luck generally deserted Helmut in other major events, but he handled a little Lola T212 sports car entered by Karl von Wendt to devastating effect in 1971, winning the Auvergne Trophy, the Cape 3 Hours and three rounds of the European 2-litre championship. By this time he had made a solid start to his Grand Prix career, his initial hire-drive agreement with BRM proving so satisfactory that he soon became a full team member.

For the 1972 season Marko had a BRM contract for Formula 1, and a seat in the Alfa Romeo sports car team, for whom he scored second places in both the Targa Florio and the Österreichring 1000 Km and thirds at Daytona and in the Nürburgring 1000 Km. His F1 season started well with fourth place in the non-championship Brazilian GP, but in the French GP at Clermont Ferrand a freak accident saw a stone thrown up by another car shatter his visor and embed itself in the unfortunate driver's eye. Happily Marko was able to bring the car safely to a halt, but the sight of the eye could not be saved, and a potentially fine Grand Prix career was lost.

Marko subsequently stayed within the sport working for Renault Austria, and also guided the fledgling career of the ill-fated Helmuth Koinigg, while he later helped Karl Wendlinger to make such an impact on his entry to Formula 1. Over recent seasons Marko has run a successful Formula 3000 team, taking Jörg Müller to the title in 1996.

TARSO MARQUES

Following his apprenticeship in karting and Formula Opel Lotus, Marques made a good impression when he stepped up to the 1993 SudAm Formula 3 series with a Ralt-Mugen Honda. The ambitious Brazilian youngster headed to Europe to contest the F3000 championship the following season and garnered a fourth place at Magny Cours. A move to a seat in the crack DAMS team for 1995 put the fast but sometimes wayward Tarso in contention for F3000 championship honours, but he eventually had to settle for fifth in the standings with a win at Estoril to his credit.

A chance to shine in Grands Prix came early in 1996 when Marques was entrusted with the Minardi for the two South American races. Although he immediately impressed, the Brazilian was consigned to a testing role with Bridgestone until a recall to the ranks came in mid-1997 when Trulli left to drive for Prost. Unfortunately, nothing startling was achieved in the tail-end car and Marques was left without a drive of any sort for 1998.

However, a fabulous test for the Payton-Coyne team was to alert the CART community to the Brazilian's undoubted speed, and he was given six races by Penske in 1999. The car's uncompetitiveness hampered Tarso's chances of making a big impact and it remains to be seen where his stop–start career will lead him in the future.

MARQUES, Tarso (BR) b 19/1/1976, Curitiba

	1996	Championship position: Unplaced							
	Race	Circuit	No	Entrant	Tyres	Car/Engine		Comment	Q Pos/Entries
ret	BRAZILIAN GP	Interlagos	21	Minardi Team		G	3.0 Minardi 195B-Ford EDM V8	practice time disallowed/spun off	– /22
ret	ARGENTINE GP	Buenos Aires	21	Minardi Team		G	3.0 Minardi 195B-Ford EDM V8	collision with Brundle	14/22
	1997	Championship position: Unplaced							
ret	FRENCH GP	Magny Cours	21	Minardi Team		B	3.0 Minardi M197-Hart V8	engine	22/22
10	BRITISH GP	Silverstone	21	Minardi Team		B	3.0 Minardi M197-Hart V8	1 lap behind	21/22
ret	GERMAN GP	Hockenheim	21	Minardi Team		B	3.0 Minardi M197-Hart V8	transmission	21/22
12	HUNGARIAN GP	Hungaroring	21	Minardi Team		B	3.0 Minardi M197-Hart V8	2 laps behind	22/22
ret	BELGIAN GP	Spa	21	Minardi Team		B	3.0 Minardi M197-Hart V8	spun off	22/22
14	ITALIAN GP	Monza	21	Minardi Team		B	3.0 Minardi M197-Hart V8	2 laps behind	22/22
exc*	AUSTRIAN GP	A1-Ring	21	Minardi Team		B	3.0 Minardi M197-Hart V8	*car underweight–excluded–	–*/22
ret	LUXEMBOURG GP	Nürburgring	21	Minardi Team		B	3.0 Minardi M197-Hart V8	engine	22/22
ret	JAPANESE GP	Suzuka	21	Minardi Team		B	3.0 Minardi M197-Hart V8	gearbox	20/22
15	EUROPEAN GP	Jerez	21	Minardi Team		B	3.0 Minardi M197-Hart V8	1 lap behind	20/22

GP Starts: 11   GP Wins: 0   Pole positions: 0   Fastest laps: 0   Points: 0

MARR, Leslie (GB) b 14/8/1922, Durham

	1954			Championship position: Unplaced					
	Race	Circuit	No	Entrant	Tyres	Car/Engine		Comment	Q Pos/Entries
13	BRITISH GP	Silverstone	23	Leslie Marr	D	2.0 Connaught-Lea Francis A Type 4		8 laps behind	22/31
	1955			Championship position: Unplaced					
ret	BRITISH GP	Aintree	38	Leslie Marr	D	2.5 Connaught-Alta B Type 4 str		brake pipe-spun off	19/25

GP Starts: 2   GP Wins: 0   Pole positions: 0   Fastest laps: 0   Points: 0

MARSH, Tony (GB) b 20/7/1931, Stourbridge, Worcestershire

	1957			Championship position: Unplaced					
	Race	Circuit	No	Entrant	Tyres	Car/Engine		Comment	Q Pos/Entries
15*	GERMAN GP (F2)	Nürburgring	25	Ridgeway Managements	D	1.5 Cooper T43-Climax 4 F2		* 4th in F2 class/5 laps behind	22/24
	1958			Championship position: Unplaced					
8*	GERMAN GP (F2)	Nürburgring	30	Tony Marsh	D	1.5 Cooper T45-Climax 4 F2		* 4th in F2 class	17/26
	1961			Championship position: Unplaced					
dns	BELGIAN GP	Spa	42	Tony Marsh	D	1.5 Lotus 18-Climax 4		no starting money offered	(20)/25
ret	BRITISH GP	Aintree	48	Tony Marsh	D	1.5 Lotus 18-Climax 4		ignition	27/30
15	GERMAN GP	Nürburgring	37	Tony Marsh	D	1.5 Lotus 18-Climax 4		2 laps behind	20/27

GP Starts: 4   GP Wins: 0   Pole positions: 0   Fastest laps: 0   Points: 0

LESLIE MARR

Marr was a professional artist who mainly raced his Connaught in national events during 1952-53, before trying his hand against tougher opposition in 1954, when he gained his greatest success in Libre events, placing third in the Glover Trophy, and third in the F2 class in the Aintree 200.

By 1955 Marr had taken delivery of a B-Type model, but after the British GP he raced it little until early 1956, when he drove splendidly to finish fourth in the New Zealand GP, after starting from the back of the grid without benefit of practice, and then took third place in the Lady Wigram Trophy at Christchurch.

TONY MARSH

Hill-climbs, trials, sprints, rallies – in fact almost every type of four-wheeled competition was sampled by Tony Marsh in the early fifties, when, at the wheel of the ex-Collins Cooper, he won his first three RAC hill-climb championships.

In 1957 he bought a Formula 2 Cooper, which he used to dominate Libre events at home and also raced on the Continent, making his debut in the German GP, where he took fourth in the F2 class. Over the next three seasons Marsh sensibly raced the Cooper in events where success was a realistic proposition, his best result being a win in the 1960 Lewis-Evans Trophy at Brands Hatch.

For 1961 Tony obtained a Lotus 18, which he drove in Grands Prix and even hill-climbs, winning five of the six events he entered, but despite a third on aggregate in the Brussels GP he soon set it aside in favour of a BRM. Then in 1962 a planned season with a works-tended BRM ended in legal action as Marsh felt the machine was unraceworthy. From then on he concentrated fully on the hill-climb scene, eventually replacing the BRM with a fearsome 4.3-litre Marsh-Oldsmobile special, with which he took another three titles to add to those won back in the fifties.

EUGÈNE MARTIN

Martin had a broad engineering background and when he began racing a BMW/Frazer-Nash in the late forties he soon modified it extensively, subsequently winning races at Angoulême and the GP of Lyons in 1947.

The latter victory put him in demand, and he briefly tried the CTA Arsenal before racing the Jicey during 1948-49. Invited to join Talbot for 1950, Martin crashed in only his second race for the team at Berne and was seriously injured, prompting his temporary retirement. He was to reappear occasionally, having acquired the Jicey, and drove a works Gordini at the 1954 Pau GP, which was to be his final race and unfortunately ended in a crash. He then concentrated on his new role as technical director of the Salmson company, whose machines were to bear a marked resemblance to the Martin cars Eugène had briefly marketed in 1952-53.

MARTIN, Eugène (F) b 24/3/1915, Suresnes

	1950	Championship position: Unplaced						
	Race	Circuit	No	Entrant	Tyres	Car/Engine	Comment	Q Pos/Entries
ret	BRITISH GP	Silverstone	17	Automobiles Talbot-Darracq SA	D	4.5 Lago-Talbot T26C-DA 6	engine-oil pressure	7/21
ret	SWISS GP	Bremgarten	8	Automobiles Talbot-Darracq SA	D	4.5 Lago-Talbot T26C-DA 6	crashed-injured	9/18

GP Starts: 2   GP Wins: 0   Pole positions: 0   Fastest laps: 0   Points: 0

PIERLUIGI MARTINI

Little Martini had the resilience to shrug off a disastrous debut year in Grand Prix racing and sensibly return to shallower waters until he was truly ready to plunge back into the deep end. He then became a well-respected part of the Grand Prix community, albeit with only a tantalising glimpse of ultimate success.

The nephew of Italian seventies racer Giancarlo Martini, Pierluigi spent a couple of years hidden in Italian F3 driving the ubiquitous Dallara before emerging as something of a surprise European F3 champion in 1983. At the wheel of a Pavesi Ralt, he put together a late-season run to snatch the title at the very last from under the nose of John Nielsen, but a second place on his Formula 2 debut in a Minardi that season may have given him ideas above his station. After he had tested a Brabham but failed to land a drive, 1984 saw a hapless attempt to qualify a works Toleman at Monza and his lack of experience was merely amplified during the 1985 season. The task of leading the singleton Minardi challenge was beyond him and he dropped back to F3000 for the 1986 season with the Pavesi team. It proved to be a good decision for, freed from the pressure of Formula 1, he soon found his feet to put in a determined bid for the championship, winning rounds at Imola, Mugello and Birmingham. Any hopes of a title win were dashed when he was disqualified in the final round at Jarama after some illegal tinkering with the car between the two parts of the interrupted race. The team lost their way the following year, constantly switching Ralt chassis, and Pierluigi was largely wasting his time. A move to the FIRST team in 1988 bounced him back to the front despite being hampered by a difficult March chassis, and a victory at Enna kept his interest in the series alive even though he had made a surprise return to Grand Prix racing with Minardi.

Scoring their first-ever championship point on his comeback in Detroit, the Italian soon found himself the spearhead of the little Faenza outfit's upward progress. In 1989 he hauled the team from the brink of the pre-qualification abyss to a brief but brilliant moment at Estoril when for one glorious lap a Minardi led a Grand Prix. At the last race of the year in Adelaide, he qualified third on the grid but had to settle for a distant sixth place on unsuitable Pirelli race tyres, and the following season was to prove relatively uneventful while Minardi waited with eager anticipation for the Ferrari power which they hoped would provide the leg-up required to place them among the front-runners.

Sadly for Martini, the partnership was hardly a distinguished one, and at the end of the year he moved to Scuderia Italia along with the V12 engines. It was akin to being transferred from one First Division football team to another when the player was eyeing a move to the Premiership. Enduring a year of endless frustrations, Martini found himself without a drive when the team concluded a deal to race Lolas in 1993. He wasn't to know how lucky he was to miss out on that débâcle. He bided his time before keeping his Grand Prix career alive with a mid-season return to the homely confines of Minardi. After all this time, it was hard to see him breaking out of the ranks of the also-ran teams – no matter how much he may previously have deserved the chance. So it was to prove, Pierluigi running for the most part in midfield anonymity until the middle of the 1995 season when his drive was taken by the then up-and-coming Portuguese driver Pedro Lamy.

Although his Grand Prix sojourn had come to an end, Martini accepted the chance to race Scuderia Italia's Porsche 911 GT1 in 1997 and took a win in Joest's Porsche WSC95 at Donington with Stefan Johansson. The pinnacle of the little Italian's career finally arrived in 1999 when he partnered Yannick Dalmas and Jo Winkelhock to victory at Le Mans driving a works BMW V12 LMR. Having turned down the chance to race sports cars in the USA, Pierluigi is currently chasing a suitable touring car drive for 2000.

MARTINI, Pierluigi (I) b 23/4/1961, Lugo di Romagna, nr Ravenna

	1984	Championship position: Unplaced							
	Race	Circuit	No	Entrant	Tyres	Car/Engine		Comment	Q Pos/Entries
dnq	ITALIAN GP	Monza	20	Toleman Group Motorsport	M	1.5 t/c Toleman TG184-Hart 4			27/27

	1985	Championship position: Unplaced							
ret	BRAZILIAN GP	Rio	29	Minardi Team	P	3.0 Minardi M185-Cosworth V8		engine	25/25
ret	PORTUGUESE GP	Estoril	29	Minardi Team	P	3.0 Minardi M185-Cosworth V8		started from pit lane/spun off	25/26
ret	SAN MARINO GP	Imola	29	Minardi Team	P	1.5 t/c Minardi M185-MM V6		turbo	19/26
dnq	MONACO GP	Monte Carlo	29	Minardi Team	P	1.5 t/c Minardi M185-MM V6		no time-knee injury in practice	– /26
ret	CANADIAN GP	Montreal	29	Minardi Team	P	1.5 t/c Minardi M185-MM V6		accident	25/25
ret	US GP (DETROIT)	Detroit	29	Minardi Team	P	1.5 t/c Minardi M185-MM V6		engine	25/25
ret	FRENCH GP	Paul Ricard	29	Minardi Team	P	1.5 t/c Minardi M185-MM V6		accident with Berger	25/26
ret	BRITISH GP	Silverstone	29	Minardi Team	P	1.5 t/c Minardi M185-MM V6		transmission	23/26
11/ret	GERMAN GP	Nürburgring	29	Minardi Team	P	1.5 t/c Minardi M185-MM V6		engine/5 laps behind	27/27
ret	AUSTRIAN GP	Österreichring	29	Minardi Team	P	1.5 t/c Minardi M185-MM V6		suspension	26/27
ret	DUTCH GP	Zandvoort	29	Minardi Team	P	1.5 t/c Minardi M185-MM V6		accident	24/27
ret	ITALIAN GP	Monza	29	Minardi Team	P	1.5 t/c Minardi M185-MM V6		fuel pump	23/26
12	BELGIAN GP	Spa	29	Minardi Team	P	1.5 t/c Minardi M185-MM V6		5 laps behind	24/24
ret	EUROPEAN GP	Brands Hatch	29	Minardi Team	P	1.5 t/c Minardi M185-MM V6		accident	26/27
ret	SOUTH AFRICAN GP	Kyalami	29	Minardi Team	P	1.5 t/c Minardi M185-MM V6		radiator	19/21
8	AUSTRALIAN GP	Adelaide	29	Minardi Team	P	1.5 t/c Minardi M185-MM V6		4 laps behind	23/25

Championship position: 16th= Wins: 0 Pole positions: 0 Fastest laps: 0 Points scored: 1

	1988	Championship position: 16th= ...							
6	US GP (DETROIT)	Detroit	23	Lois Minardi Team	G	3.5 Minardi M188-Cosworth V8		1 lap behind	16/31
15	FRENCH GP	Paul Ricard	23	Lois Minardi Team	G	3.5 Minardi M188-Cosworth V8		3 laps behind	22/31
15	BRITISH GP	Silverstone	23	Lois Minardi Team	G	3.5 Minardi M188-Cosworth V8		2 laps behind	19/31
dnq	GERMAN GP	Hockenheim	23	Lois Minardi Team	G	3.5 Minardi M188-Cosworth V8			30/31
ret	HUNGARIAN GP	Hungaroring	23	Lois Minardi Team	G	3.5 Minardi M188-Cosworth V8		collision with Piquet	16/31
dnq	BELGIAN GP	Spa	23	Lois Minardi Team	G	3.5 Minardi M188-Cosworth V8			28/31
ret	ITALIAN GP	Monza	23	Lois Minardi Team	G	3.5 Minardi M188-Cosworth V8		engine	14/31
ret	PORTUGUESE GP	Estoril	23	Lois Minardi Team	G	3.5 Minardi M188-Cosworth V8		engine	14/31
ret	SPANISH GP	Jerez	23	Lois Minardi Team	G	3.5 Minardi M188-Cosworth V8		gearbox	20/31
13	JAPANESE GP	Suzuka	23	Lois Minardi Team	G	3.5 Minardi M188-Cosworth V8		2 laps behind	17/31
7	AUSTRALIAN GP	Adelaide	23	Lois Minardi Team	G	3.5 Minardi M188-Cosworth V8		2 laps behind	14/31

Championship position: 14th= Wins: 0 Pole positions: 0 Fastest laps: 0 Points scored: 5

	1989	Championship position: 14th= ...							
ret	BRAZILIAN GP	Rio	23	Minardi Team SpA	P	3.5 Minardi M188B-Cosworth V8		engine mounting	16/38
ret	SAN MARINO GP	Imola	23	Minardi Team SpA	P	3.5 Minardi M188B-Cosworth V8		gearbox	11/39
ret	MONACO GP	Monte Carlo	23	Minardi Team SpA	P	3.5 Minardi M188B-Cosworth V8		clutch	11/38
ret	MEXICAN GP	Mexico City	23	Minardi Team SpA	P	3.5 Minardi M189-Cosworth V8		engine	22/39
ret	US GP (PHOENIX)	Phoenix	23	Minardi Team SpA	P	3.5 Minardi M189-Cosworth V8		engine	15/39
ret	CANADIAN GP	Montreal	23	Minardi Team SpA	P	3.5 Minardi M189-Cosworth V8		collision with Modena	11/39
ret	FRENCH GP	Paul Ricard	23	Minardi Team SpA	P	3.5 Minardi M189-Cosworth V8		overheating	23/39
5	BRITISH GP	Silverstone	23	Minardi Team SpA	P	3.5 Minardi M189-Cosworth V8		pit stop-paper in radiator/-1 lap	11/39
9	GERMAN GP	Hockenheim	23	Minardi Team SpA	P	3.5 Minardi M189-Cosworth V8		chassis problems/-1 lap	13/39
ret	HUNGARIAN GP	Hungaroring	23	Minardi Team SpA	P	3.5 Minardi M189-Cosworth V8		wheel bearing	10/39
9	BELGIAN GP	Spa	23	Minardi Team SpA	P	3.5 Minardi M189-Cosworth V8		pit stop-tyres/1 lap behind	14/39
7	ITALIAN GP	Monza	23	Minardi Team SpA	P	3.5 Minardi M189-Cosworth V8		1 lap behind	15/39
5	PORTUGUESE GP	Estoril	23	Minardi Team SpA	P	3.5 Minardi M189-Cosworth V8		led race for 1 lap/-1 lap	5/39
ret	SPANISH GP	Jerez	23	Minardi Team SpA	P	3.5 Minardi M189-Cosworth V8		spun off	4/38
6	AUSTRALIAN GP	Adelaide	23	Minardi Team SpA	P	3.5 Minardi M189-Cosworth V8		3 laps behind	3/39

	1990	Championship position: Unplaced							
7	US GP (PHOENIX)	Phoenix	23	SCM Minardi Team	P	3.5 Minardi M189-Cosworth V8		pit stop-tyres/1 lap behind	2/35
9	BRAZILIAN GP	Interlagos	23	SCM Minardi Team	P	3.5 Minardi M190-Cosworth V8		pit stop-tyres-brakes/-2 laps	8/35
dns	SAN MARINO GP	Imola	23	SCM Minardi Team	P	3.5 Minardi M190-Cosworth V8		accident in practice	(10)/34
ret	MONACO GP	Monte Carlo	23	SCM Minardi Team	P	3.5 Minardi M190-Cosworth V8		electrics	8/35
ret	CANADIAN GP	Montreal	23	SCM Minardi Team	P	3.5 Minardi M190-Cosworth V8		hit by Suzuki	16/35
12	MEXICAN GP	Mexico City	23	SCM Minardi Team	P	3.5 Minardi M190-Cosworth V8		lack of power/1 lap behind	7/35
ret	FRENCH GP	Paul Ricard	23	SCM Minardi Team	P	3.5 Minardi M190-Cosworth V8		electrics	23/35

Portuguese Grand Prix, Estoril, 1989, and Minardi's great moment. For one lap Martini led the race before reality set in and he had to settle for fifth place.

ret	BRITISH GP	Silverstone	23	SCM Minardi Team	P	3.5 Minardi M190-Cosworth V8	alternator	18/35
ret	GERMAN GP	Hockenheim	23	SCM Minardi Team	P	3.5 Minardi M190-Cosworth V8	engine	15/35
ret	HUNGARIAN GP	Hungaroring	23	SCM Minardi Team	P	3.5 Minardi M190-Cosworth V8	collision with Alesi	14/35
15	BELGIAN GP	Spa	23	SCM Minardi Team	P	3.5 Minardi M190-Cosworth V8	understeer/2 laps behind	16/33
ret	ITALIAN GP	Monza	23	SCM Minardi Team	P	3.5 Minardi M190-Cosworth V8	suspension	15/33
11	PORTUGUESE GP	Estoril	23	SCM Minardi Team	P	3.5 Minardi M190-Cosworth V8	2 laps behind	16/33
ret	SPANISH GP	Jerez	23	SCM Minardi Team	P	3.5 Minardi M190-Cosworth V8	loose wheel	11/33
8	JAPANESE GP	Suzuka	23	SCM Minardi Team	P	3.5 Minardi M190-Cosworth V8	1 lap behind	11/30
9	AUSTRALIAN GP	Adelaide	23	SCM Minardi Team	P	3.5 Minardi M190-Cosworth V8	2 laps behind	10/30

1991 — Championship position: 11th   Wins: 0   Pole positions: 0   Fastest laps: 0   Points scored: 6

9/ret	US GP (PHOENIX)	Phoenix	23	SCM Minardi Team	G	3.5 Minardi M191-Ferrari V12	engine	15/34
ret	BRAZILIAN GP	Interlagos	23	SCM Minardi Team	G	3.5 Minardi M191-Ferrari V12	spun off	20/34
4	SAN MARINO GP	Imola	23	SCM Minardi Team	G	3.5 Minardi M191-Ferrari V12	2 laps behind	9/34
12	MONACO GP	Monte Carlo	23	SCM Minardi Team	G	3.5 Minardi M191-Ferrari V12	stop & go penalty/-6 laps	14/34
7	CANADIAN GP	Montreal	23	SCM Minardi Team	G	3.5 Minardi M191-Ferrari V12	started from pitlane -1 lap	18/34
ret	MEXICAN GP	Mexico City	23	SCM Minardi Team	G	3.5 Minardi M191-Ferrari V12	spun off on Berger's oil	15/34
9	FRENCH GP	Magny Cours	23	SCM Minardi Team	G	3.5 Minardi M191-Ferrari V12	2 laps behind	12/34
9	BRITISH GP	Silverstone	23	SCM Minardi Team	G	3.5 Minardi M191-Ferrari V12	1 lap behind	23/34
ret	GERMAN GP	Hockenheim	23	SCM Minardi Team	G	3.5 Minardi M191-Ferrari V12	spun off on own oil	10/34
ret	HUNGARIAN GP	Hungaroring	23	SCM Minardi Team	G	3.5 Minardi M191-Ferrari V12	engine	18/34
12	BELGIAN GP	Spa	23	SCM Minardi Team	G	3.5 Minardi M191-Ferrari V12	2 laps behind	9/34
ret	ITALIAN GP	Monza	23	SCM Minardi Team	G	3.5 Minardi M191-Ferrari V12	spun off/brakes	10/34
4	PORTUGUESE GP	Estoril	23	SCM Minardi Team	G	3.5 Minardi M191-Ferrari V12		8/34
13	SPANISH GP	Barcelona	23	SCM Minardi Team	G	3.5 Minardi M191-Ferrari V12	2 laps behind	19/33
ret	JAPANESE GP	Suzuka	23	SCM Minardi Team	G	3.5 Minardi M191-Ferrari V12	clutch	7/31
ret	AUSTRALIAN GP	Adelaide	23	SCM Minardi Team	G	3.5 Minardi M191-Ferrari V12	spun off in heavy rain	10/32

1992 — Championship position: 14th=   Wins: 0   Pole positions: 0   Fastest laps: 0   Points scored: 2

ret	SOUTH AFRICAN GP	Kyalami	22	Scuderia Italia SpA	G	3.5 BMS Dallara 192-Ferrari V12	clutch	25/30
ret	MEXICAN GP	Mexico City	22	Scuderia Italia SpA	G	3.5 BMS Dallara 192-Ferrari V12	handling	9/30
ret	BRAZILIAN GP	Interlagos	22	Scuderia Italia SpA	G	3.5 BMS Dallara 192-Ferrari V12	clutch	8/31
6	SPANISH GP	Barcelona	22	Scuderia Italia SpA	G	3.5 BMS Dallara 192-Ferrari V12	2 laps behind	13/32
6	SAN MARINO GP	Imola	22	Scuderia Italia SpA	G	3.5 BMS Dallara 192-Ferrari V12	1 lap behind	15/32
ret	MONACO GP	Monte Carlo	22	Scuderia Italia SpA	G	3.5 BMS Dallara 192-Ferrari V12	accident lap 1	18/32
8	CANADIAN GP	Montreal	22	Scuderia Italia SpA	G	3.5 BMS Dallara 192-Ferrari V12	1 lap behind	15/32
10	FRENCH GP	Magny Cours	22	Scuderia Italia SpA	G	3.5 BMS Dallara 192-Ferrari V12	agg of two parts/-2 laps	25/30
15	BRITISH GP	Silverstone	22	Scuderia Italia SpA	G	3.5 BMS Dallara 192-Ferrari V12	3 laps behind	22/32
11	GERMAN GP	Hockenheim	22	Scuderia Italia SpA	G	3.5 BMS Dallara 192-Ferrari V12	1 lap behind	18/32
ret	HUNGARIAN GP	Hungaroring	22	Scuderia Italia SpA	G	3.5 BMS Dallara 192-Ferrari V12	gearbox	26/31
ret	BELGIAN GP	Spa	22	Scuderia Italia SpA	G	3.5 BMS Dallara 192-Ferrari V12	spun off on lap 1	19/30
8	ITALIAN GP	Monza	22	Scuderia Italia SpA	G	3.5 BMS Dallara 192-Ferrari V12	1 lap behind	22/28
ret	PORTUGUESE GP	Estoril	22	Scuderia Italia SpA	G	3.5 BMS Dallara 192-Ferrari V12	puncture from Patrese's debris	21/26
10	JAPANESE GP	Suzuka	22	Scuderia Italia SpA	G	3.5 BMS Dallara 192-Ferrari V12	1 lap behind	19/26
ret	AUSTRALIAN GP	Adelaide	22	Scuderia Italia SpA	G	3.5 BMS Dallara 192-Ferrari V12	collision with Grouillard-lap 1	14/26

1993 — Championship position: Unplaced

ret	BRITISH GP	Silverstone	24	Minardi Team	G	3.5 Minardi M193-Ford HB V8	cramp in arm	20/26
14	GERMAN GP	Hockenheim	24	Minardi Team	G	3.5 Minardi M193-Ford HB V8	1 lap behind	22/26
ret	HUNGARIAN GP	Hungaroring	24	Minardi Team	G	3.5 Minardi M193-Ford HB V8	spun off	7/26
ret	BELGIAN GP	Spa	24	Minardi Team	G	3.5 Minardi M193-Ford HB V8	spun off	21/25
7	ITALIAN GP	Monza	24	Minardi Team	G	3.5 Minardi M193-Ford HB V8	hit by Fittipaldi at finish/-2 laps	22/26
8	PORTUGUESE GP	Estoril	24	Minardi Team	G	3.5 Minardi M193-Ford HB V8	2 laps behind	19/26
10	JAPANESE GP	Suzuka	24	Minardi Team	G	3.5 Minardi M193-Ford HB V8	2 laps behind	22/24
ret	AUSTRALIAN GP	Phoenix	24	Minardi Team	G	3.5 Minardi M193-Ford HB V8	gearbox	16/24

1994 — Championship position: 18th=   Wins: 0   Pole positions: 0   Fastest laps: 0   Points scored: 4

8	BRAZILIAN GP	Interlagos	23	Minardi Scuderia Italia	G	3.5 Minardi M193B-Ford HB V8	2 laps behind	15/28
ret	PACIFIC GP	T.I. Circuit	23	Minardi Scuderia Italia	G	3.5 Minardi M193B-Ford HB V8	electrics	17/28
ret	SAN MARINO GP	Imola	23	Minardi Scuderia Italia	G	3.5 Minardi M193B-Ford HB V8	spun off	14/28
ret	MONACO GP	Monte Carlo	23	Minardi Scuderia Italia	G	3.5 Minardi M193B-Ford HB V8	collision-Morbidelli on lap 1	9/24
5	SPANISH GP	Barcelona	23	Minardi Scuderia Italia	G	3.5 Minardi M193B-Ford HB V8	1 lap behind	18/27
9	CANADIAN GP	Montreal	23	Minardi Scuderia Italia	G	3.5 Minardi M194-Ford HB V8	1 lap behind	15/27
5	FRENCH GP	Magny Cours	23	Minardi Scuderia Italia	G	3.5 Minardi M194-Ford HB V8	2 laps behind	16/28
10*	BRITISH GP	Silverstone	23	Minardi Scuderia Italia	G	3.5 Minardi M194-Ford HB V8	*2nd place car dsq/-2 laps	14/28
ret	GERMAN GP	Hockenheim	23	Minardi Scuderia Italia	G	3.5 Minardi M194-Ford HB V8	multiple accident on lap 1	20/28
ret	HUNGARIAN GP	Hungaroring	23	Minardi Scuderia Italia	G	3.5 Minardi M194-Ford HB V8	spun off	15/28
8*	BELGIAN GP	Spa	23	Minardi Scuderia Italia	G	3.5 Minardi M194-Ford HB V8	*1st place car dsq/-1 lap	10/28
ret	ITALIAN GP	Monza	23	Minardi Scuderia Italia	G	3.5 Minardi M194-Ford HB V8	spun off	18/28
12	PORTUGUESE GP	Estoril	23	Minardi Scuderia Italia	G	3.5 Minardi M194-Ford HB V8	2 laps behind	18/28
15	EUROPEAN GP	Jerez	23	Minardi Scuderia Italia	G	3.5 Minardi M194-Ford HB V8	2 laps behind	17/28
ret	JAPANESE GP	Suzuka	23	Minardi Scuderia Italia	G	3.5 Minardi M194-Ford HB V8	touched Lagorce-spun off	16/28
9	AUSTRALIAN GP	Adelaide	23	Minardi Scuderia Italia	G	3.5 Minardi M194-Ford HB V8	2 laps behind	18/28

1995 — Championship position: Unplaced

dns	BRAZILIAN GP	Interlagos	23	Minardi Scuderia Italia	G	3.0 Minardi M195-Ford EDM V8	gearbox on formation lap	(17)/26
ret	ARGENTINE GP	Buenos Aires	23	Minardi Scuderia Italia	G	3.0 Minardi M195-Ford EDM V8	spun off	16/26
12	SAN MARINO GP	Imola	23	Minardi Scuderia Italia	G	3.0 Minardi M195-Ford EDM V8	4 laps behind	18/26
14	SPANISH GP	Barcelona	23	Minardi Scuderia Italia	G	3.0 Minardi M195-Ford EDM V8	3 laps behind	19/26
7	MONACO GP	Monte Carlo	23	Minardi Scuderia Italia	G	3.0 Minardi M195-Ford EDM V8	2 laps behind	18/26
ret	CANADIAN GP	Montreal	23	Minardi Scuderia Italia	G	3.0 Minardi M195-Ford EDM V8	throttle	17/24
ret	FRENCH GP	Magny Cours	23	Minardi Scuderia Italia	G	3.0 Minardi M195-Ford EDM V8	gearbox	20/24
7	BRITISH GP	Silverstone	23	Minardi Scuderia Italia	G	3.0 Minardi M195-Ford EDM V8	1 lap behind	15/24
ret	GERMAN GP	Hockenheim	23	Minardi Scuderia Italia	G	3.0 Minardi M195-Ford EDM V8	engine	20/24

GP Starts: 119   GP Wins: 0   Pole positions: 0   Fastest laps: 0   Points: 18

JOCHEN MASS

Maybe lacking the killer instinct which separates the winners from the rest, Jochen Mass was nevertheless a very talented racing driver who looked destined for the very top on the evidence of his early career, which began in 1970 with an Alfa saloon before he joined Ford Germany to race their Capri. He really shot to prominence in 1972 by winning the European touring car championship for drivers after major wins at Spa, Zandvoort, Silverstone and Jarama. In addition to a planned F3 programme, he also made his Formula 2 debut in the works March and scored a superb win in the Eifelrennen.

Retaining his Ford touring car links, Mass signed for the Surtees Formula 2 team in 1973, and won the rounds at Kinnekulle and Hockenheim. He finished a solid second in the championship standings and also earned his Grand Prix debut at Silverstone. Unfortunately his car was wiped out in the Jody Scheckter-instigated multiple shunt, but he was soon back in action, taking seventh place in the German GP. Promoted to the Surtees F1 team full-time in 1974, Jochen enjoyed a useful start to the year with a fourth place in the Medici GP in Brasilia and then second in the International Trophy race. Once the Grand Prix season proper got under way, however, things soon began to go wrong, with a succession of technical maladies afflicting the team. Things reached boiling point when a superb drive in the German GP was ended by engine failure, prompting him to follow Pace's example and quit in frustration. Picking up the vacant Yardley McLaren seat for the final two races of the season, Mass was offered a full works ride in place of the retired Denny Hulme for 1975 and emerged as an excellent number two to Fittipaldi, winning the shortened Spanish GP in Barcelona, and impressing mightily at both Paul Ricard and Watkins Glen.

The German's subordinate role in the team was to continue during the next two seasons as James Hunt breezed in to highlight the gulf that exists between champions and contenders. Jochen did have his moments, though, and was distinctly unlucky not to win the 1976 German GP, his gamble to run on slicks looking likely to pay off until Lauda's accident halted proceedings. He could, however, be relied upon to provide the team with plenty of top-six finishes and was happy to deliver. In 1977 a couple of Formula 2 races for March brought him victories at Hockenheim and the Nürburgring, and he began his long and tremendously successful sports car partnership with Jacky Ickx, winning three rounds of the World Championship of Makes in the Martini Racing Porsche.

Making the break from an increasingly down-trodden existence at McLaren, he joined the ATS team as number one driver in 1978, but the season was to be desperately disappointing and ended prematurely when Mass suffered a broken knee and thigh in a testing accident at Silverstone. It was to his credit that he made a strong comeback in 1979 with Arrows. Despite being in an outclassed car, he put in some spirited drives, none more stirring than at Monaco where he lay third until brake problems intervened. Continuing with the team for another season, he again proved a consistent performer. Ironically, his best placing was second in the Spanish GP, which was subsequently denied championship status, but he produced another excellent display at Monaco. Out of a drive for 1981, Jochen concentrated on sports car and G5 racing before an unhappy return to the Grand Prix arena with the RAM team in 1982.

Disillusioned after this final year of F1, Mass turned to sports car racing full-time. With Rothmans Porsche, he took eight wins between 1982 and 1985, before briefly switching to IMSA, and after racing a Brun Porsche in 1987 he joined Sauber, which eventually became the full works Mercedes-Benz team. He remained a very capable driver and his huge experience made him the ideal tutor to the German company's young lions, Schumacher, Wendlinger and Frentzen. Jochen scored three wins in 1988 and added five more in 1989, including a long-awaited and much-deserved victory at Le Mans. In 1990 he won another two rounds but there were no successes the following year, when the programme was running down as Sauber looked towards Formula 1. In 1992 Mass moved into a team management role in the German touring car championship, but continued to enjoy his racing, mainly in GT cars. Throughout the nineties Jochen was a regular in the Grand Prix paddock, where his irreverent sense of humour was a commodity often in short supply.

MASS, Jochen (D) b 30/9/1946, Dorfen, nr Munich

	1973			Championship position: Unplaced					
	Race	Circuit	No	Entrant	Tyres	Car/Engine		Comment	Q Pos/Entries
ret/dns	BRITISH GP	Silverstone	31	Team Surtees	F	3.0 Surtees TS14A-Cosworth V8		multiple accident at 1st start	=14/29
7	GERMAN GP	Nürburgring	31	Team Surtees	F	3.0 Surtees TS14A-Cosworth V8			15/23
ret	US GP	Watkins Glen	30	Team Surtees	F	3.0 Surtees TS14A-Cosworth V8		engine	17/28

1974 — Championship position: Unplaced

ret	ARGENTINE GP	Buenos Aires	19	Team Surtees	F	3.0 Surtees TS16-Cosworth V8	engine	=17/26
17	BRAZILIAN GP	Interlagos	19	Team Surtees	F	3.0 Surtees TS16-Cosworth V8	pit stop/2 laps behind	10/25
ret	SOUTH AFRICAN GP	Kyalami	19	Team Surtees	F	3.0 Surtees TS16-Cosworth V8	withdrawn after accident	17/27
ret	SPANISH GP	Jarama	19	Bang & Olufsen Team Surtees	F	3.0 Surtees TS16-Cosworth V8	gearbox	19/28
ret	BELGIAN GP	Nivelles	19	Bang & Olufsen Team Surtees	F	3.0 Surtees TS16-Cosworth V8	broken right rear upright	26/32
dns	MONACO GP	Monte Carlo	19	Bang & Olufsen Team Surtees	F	3.0 Surtees TS16-Cosworth V8	lack of suspension parts	(=16)/28
ret	SWEDISH GP	Anderstorp	19	Bang & Olufsen Team Surtees	F	3.0 Surtees TS16-Cosworth V8	suspension	22/28
ret	DUTCH GP	Zandvoort	19	Bang & Olufsen Team Surtees	F	3.0 Surtees TS16-Cosworth V8	c.v. joint	20/27
ret	FRENCH GP	Dijon	19	Bang & Olufsen Team Surtees	F	3.0 Surtees TS16-Cosworth V8	clutch	18/30
14	BRITISH GP	Brands Hatch	19	Bang & Olufsen Team Surtees	F	3.0 Surtees TS16-Cosworth V8	pit stop-puncture/-7 laps	=15/34
ret	GERMAN GP	Nürburgring	19	Bang & Olufsen Team Surtees	F	3.0 Surtees TS16-Cosworth V8	engine	10/32
16	CANADIAN GP	Mosport Park	33	Yardley Team McLaren	G	3.0 McLaren M23-Cosworth V8	pit stop after spin/-8 laps	12/30
7	US GP	Watkins Glen	33	Yardley Team McLaren	G	3.0 McLaren M23-Cosworth V8		20/30

1975 — Championship position: 7th   Wins: 1   Pole positions: 0   Fastest laps: 1   Points scored: 20

14	ARGENTINE GP	Buenos Aires	2	Marlboro Team Texaco	G	3.0 McLaren M23-Cosworth V8	hit Scheckter-pit stop/-3 laps	13/23
3	BRAZILIAN GP	Interlagos	2	Marlboro Team Texaco	G	3.0 McLaren M23-Cosworth V8		10/23
6	SOUTH AFRICAN GP	Kyalami	2	Marlboro Team Texaco	G	3.0 McLaren M23-Cosworth V8		16/28
1*	SPANISH GP	Montjuich Park	2	Marlboro Team Texaco	G	3.0 McLaren M23-Cosworth V8	race stopped/*half points	11/26
6	MONACO GP	Monte Carlo	2	Marlboro Team Texaco	G	3.0 McLaren M23-Cosworth V8		15/26
ret	BELGIAN GP	Zolder	2	Marlboro Team Texaco	G	3.0 McLaren M23-Cosworth V8	collision with Watson	15/24
ret	SWEDISH GP	Anderstorp	2	Marlboro Team Texaco	G	3.0 McLaren M23-Cosworth V8	water leak	14/26
ret	DUTCH GP	Zandvoort	2	Marlboro Team Texaco	G	3.0 McLaren M23-Cosworth V8	engine cut out-crashed	8/25
3	FRENCH GP	Paul Ricard	2	Marlboro Team Texaco	G	3.0 McLaren M23-Cosworth V8	FL	7/26
7/ret	BRITISH GP	Silverstone	2	Marlboro Team Texaco	G	3.0 McLaren M23-Cosworth V8	accident in rainstorm/-1 lap	10/28
ret	GERMAN GP	Nürburgring	2	Marlboro Team Texaco	G	3.0 McLaren M23-Cosworth V8	tyre failure-crashed-lap 1	6/26
4*	AUSTRIAN GP	Österreichring	2	Marlboro Team Texaco	G	3.0 McLaren M23-Cosworth V8	*rain shortened race-half points	9/30
ret	ITALIAN GP	Monza	2	Marlboro Team Texaco	G	3.0 McLaren M23-Cosworth V8	damaged suspension	5/28
3	US GP	Watkins Glen	2	Marlboro Team Texaco	G	3.0 McLaren M23-Cosworth V8		9/24

1976 — Championship position: 9th   Wins: 0   Pole positions: 0   Fastest laps: 1   Points scored: 19

6	BRAZILIAN GP	Interlagos	12	Marlboro Team McLaren	G	3.0 McLaren M23-Cosworth V8		6/22
3	SOUTH AFRICAN GP	Kyalami	12	Marlboro Team McLaren	G	3.0 McLaren M23-Cosworth V8		4/25
5	US GP WEST	Long Beach	12	Marlboro Team McLaren	G	3.0 McLaren M23-Cosworth V8		14/27
ret	SPANISH GP	Jarama	12	Marlboro Team McLaren	G	3.0 McLaren M23-Cosworth V8	engine/FL	4/30
6	BELGIAN GP	Zolder	12	Marlboro Team McLaren	G	3.0 McLaren M23-Cosworth V8	1 lap behind	18/29
5	MONACO GP	Monte Carlo	12	Marlboro Team McLaren	G	3.0 McLaren M23-Cosworth V8	1 lap behind	11/25
11	SWEDISH GP	Anderstorp	12	Marlboro Team McLaren	G	3.0 McLaren M23-Cosworth V8	1 lap behind	13/27
15	FRENCH GP	Paul Ricard	12	Marlboro Team McLaren	G	3.0 McLaren M23-Cosworth V8	hit by Reutemann-pit stop/-1 lap	14/30
ret	BRITISH GP	Brands Hatch	12	Marlboro Team McLaren	G	3.0 McLaren M23-Cosworth V8	clutch	12/30
3	GERMAN GP	Nürburgring	12	Marlboro Team McLaren	G	3.0 McLaren M23-Cosworth V8		9/28
7	AUSTRIAN GP	Österreichring	12	Marlboro Team McLaren	G	3.0 McLaren M23-Cosworth V8		12/25
9	DUTCH GP	Zandvoort	12	Marlboro Team McLaren	G	3.0 McLaren M26-Cosworth V8	1 lap behind	15/27
dns	"	"	12	Marlboro Team McLaren	G	3.0 McLaren M23-Cosworth V8	practice only	–/–
ret	ITALIAN GP	Monza	12	Marlboro Team McLaren	G	3.0 McLaren M23-Cosworth V8	ignition	–/–
dns	"	"	12	Marlboro Team McLaren	G	3.0 McLaren M26-Cosworth V8	practice only-set grid time	28/29
5	CANADIAN GP	Mosport Park	12	Marlboro Team McLaren	G	3.0 McLaren M23-Cosworth V8		11/27
4	US GP EAST	Watkins Glen	12	Marlboro Team McLaren	G	3.0 McLaren M23-Cosworth V8		17/27
ret	JAPANESE GP	Mount Fuji	12	Marlboro Team McLaren	G	3.0 McLaren M23-Cosworth V8	slid off track	12/27

1977 — Championship position: 6   Wins: 0   Pole positions: 0   Fastest laps: 0   Points scored: 25

ret	ARGENTINE GP	Buenos Aires	2	Marlboro Team McLaren	G	3.0 McLaren M23-Cosworth V8	engine cut out-spun off	5/21
ret	BRAZILIAN GP	Interlagos	2	Marlboro Team McLaren	G	3.0 McLaren M23-Cosworth V8	spun off	4/22
5	SOUTH AFRICAN GP	Kyalami	2	Marlboro Team McLaren	G	3.0 McLaren M23-Cosworth V8		13/23
ret	US GP WEST	Long Beach	2	Marlboro Team McLaren	G	3.0 McLaren M23-Cosworth V8	rear end vibration	15/22
4	SPANISH GP	Jarama	2	Marlboro Team McLaren	G	3.0 McLaren M23-Cosworth V8		9/31
4	MONACO GP	Monte Carlo	2	Marlboro Team McLaren	G	3.0 McLaren M23-Cosworth V8		9/26
ret	BELGIAN GP	Zolder	2	Marlboro Team McLaren	G	3.0 McLaren M23-Cosworth V8	spun off	6/32
2	SWEDISH GP	Anderstorp	2	Marlboro Team McLaren	G	3.0 McLaren M23-Cosworth V8		9/31
9	FRENCH GP	Dijon	2	Marlboro Team McLaren	G	3.0 McLaren M23-Cosworth V8	hit Reutemann-pit stop/-2 laps	7/30
4	BRITISH GP	Silverstone	2	Marlboro Team McLaren	G	3.0 McLaren M26-Cosworth V8		11/36
dns	"	"	2	Marlboro Team McLaren	G	3.0 McLaren M23-Cosworth V8	practice only	–/–
ret	GERMAN GP	Hockenheim	2	Marlboro Team McLaren	G	3.0 McLaren M23-Cosworth V8	gearbox	13/30
dns	"	"	2	Marlboro Team McLaren	G	3.0 McLaren M23-Cosworth V8	practice only	–/–
6	AUSTRIAN GP	Österreichring	2	Marlboro Team McLaren	G	3.0 McLaren M26-Cosworth V8	pit stop/1 lap behind	9/30
ret	DUTCH GP	Zandvoort	2	Marlboro Team McLaren	G	3.0 McLaren M26-Cosworth V8	hit by Jones	=13/34
4	ITALIAN GP	Monza	2	Marlboro Team McLaren	G	3.0 McLaren M26-Cosworth V8		9/34
ret	US GP EAST	Watkins Glen	2	Yardley Team McLaren	G	3.0 McLaren M26-Cosworth V8	fuel pump belt	15/27
3	CANADIAN GP	Mosport Park	2	Marlboro Team McLaren	G	3.0 McLaren M26-Cosworth V8	despite being hit by Hunt	5/27
ret	JAPANESE GP	Mount Fuji	2	Marlboro Team McLaren	G	3.0 McLaren M26-Cosworth V8	engine	=8/23

1978 — Championship position: Unplaced

11	ARGENTINE GP	Buenos Aires	9	ATS Racing Team	G	3.0 ATS HS1-Cosworth V8		13/27
7	BRAZILIAN GP	Rio	9	ATS Racing Team	G	3.0 ATS HS1-Cosworth V8		20/28
ret	SOUTH AFRICAN GP	Kyalami	9	ATS Racing Team	G	3.0 ATS HS1-Cosworth V8	1 lap behind	15/30
ret	US GP WEST	Long Beach	9	ATS Racing Team	G	3.0 ATS HS1-Cosworth V8	engine	16/30
dnq	MONACO GP	Monte Carlo	9	ATS Racing Team	G	3.0 ATS HS1-Cosworth V8	brake master cylinder	21/30
11	BELGIAN GP	Zolder	9	ATS Racing Team	G	3.0 ATS HS1-Cosworth V8		16/30
9	SPANISH GP	Jarama	9	ATS Racing Team	G	3.0 ATS HS1-Cosworth V8	pit stop-tyres/2 laps behind	17/29
13	SWEDISH GP	Anderstorp	9	ATS Racing Team	G	3.0 ATS HS1-Cosworth V8	pit stop-tyres/1 lap behind	19/27
13	FRENCH GP	Paul Ricard	9	ATS Racing Team	G	3.0 ATS HS1-Cosworth V8	2 laps behind	25/29
nc	BRITISH GP	Brands Hatch	9	ATS Racing Team	G	3.0 ATS HS1-Cosworth V8	1 lap behind	26/30
ret	GERMAN GP	Hockenheim	9	ATS Racing Team	G	3.0 ATS HS1-Cosworth V8	pit stop/10 laps behind	22/30
dnq	AUSTRIAN GP	Österreichring	9	ATS Racing Team	G	3.0 ATS HS1-Cosworth V8	suspension breakage	28/31
dnq	DUTCH GP	Zandvoort	9	ATS Racing Team	G	3.0 ATS HS1-Cosworth V8		30/33

	Race	Circuit	No	Entrant	Tyres	Car/Engine	Comment	Q Pos/Entries
1979		Championship position: 15th		Wins: 0	Pole positions: 0	Fastest laps: 0	Points scored: 3	
8	ARGENTINE GP	Buenos Aires	30	Warsteiner Arrows Racing Team	G	3.0 Arrows A1-Cosworth V8	*2 laps behind*	14/26
7	BRAZILIAN GP	Interlagos	30	Warsteiner Arrows Racing Team	G	3.0 Arrows A1-Cosworth V8	*1 lap behind*	19/26
12	SOUTH AFRICAN GP	Kyalami	30	Warsteiner Arrows Racing Team	G	3.0 Arrows A1-Cosworth V8	*pit stop-tyre/4 laps behind*	20/26
9	US GP WEST	Long Beach	30	Warsteiner Arrows Racing Team	G	3.0 Arrows A1-Cosworth V8	*2 laps behind*	13/26
8	SPANISH GP	Jarama	30	Warsteiner Arrows Racing Team	G	3.0 Arrows A1-Cosworth V8		17/27
ret	BELGIAN GP	Zolder	30	Warsteiner Arrows Racing Team	G	3.0 Arrows A1-Cosworth V8	*spun off-could not restart*	22/28
6	MONACO GP	Monte Carlo	30	Warsteiner Arrows Racing Team	G	3.0 Arrows A1-Cosworth V8	*pit stop-brake cooler/-7 laps*	8/25
15	FRENCH GP	Dijon	30	Warsteiner Arrows Racing Team	G	3.0 Arrows A2-Cosworth V8	*handling/5 laps behind*	22/27
ret	BRITISH GP	Silverstone	30	Warsteiner Arrows Racing Team	G	3.0 Arrows A2-Cosworth V8	*gearbox*	20/26
6	GERMAN GP	Hockenheim	30	Warsteiner Arrows Racing Team	G	3.0 Arrows A2-Cosworth V8	*1 lap behind*	18/26
ret	AUSTRIAN GP	Österreichring	30	Warsteiner Arrows Racing Team	G	3.0 Arrows A2-Cosworth V8	*engine*	20/26
6	DUTCH GP	Zandvoort	30	Warsteiner Arrows Racing Team	G	3.0 Arrows A2-Cosworth V8	*2 laps behind*	18/26
ret	ITALIAN GP	Monza	30	Warsteiner Arrows Racing Team	G	3.0 Arrows A2-Cosworth V8	*suspension*	21/28
dnq	CANADIAN GP	Montreal	30	Warsteiner Arrows Racing Team	G	3.0 Arrows A2-Cosworth V8		25/29
dnq	US GP EAST	Watkins Glen	30	Warsteiner Arrows Racing Team	G	3.0 Arrows A2-Cosworth V8		26/30
1980		Championship position: 17th		Wins: 0	Pole positions: 0	Fastest laps: 0	Points scored: 4	
ret	ARGENTINE GP	Buenos Aires	30	Warsteiner Arrows Racing Team	G	3.0 Arrows A3-Cosworth V8	*gearbox*	14/28
10	BRAZILIAN GP	Interlagos	30	Warsteiner Arrows Racing Team	G	3.0 Arrows A3-Cosworth V8	*1 lap behind*	16/28
6	SOUTH AFRICAN GP	Kyalami	30	Warsteiner Arrows Racing Team	G	3.0 Arrows A3-Cosworth V8	*1 lap behind*	=19/23
7	US GP WEST	Long Beach	30	Warsteiner Arrows Racing Team	G	3.0 Arrows A3-Cosworth V8	*pit stop-hit by Zunino/-1 lap*	17/27
ret	BELGIAN GP	Zolder	30	Warsteiner Arrows Racing Team	G	3.0 Arrows A3-Cosworth V8	*spun off*	13/27
4	MONACO GP	Monte Carlo	30	Warsteiner Arrows Racing Team	G	3.0 Arrows A3-Cosworth V8	*1 lap behind*	15/27
10	FRENCH GP	Paul Ricard	30	Warsteiner Arrows Racing Team	G	3.0 Arrows A3-Cosworth V8	*1 lap behind*	15/27
13	BRITISH GP	Brands Hatch	30	Warsteiner Arrows Racing Team	G	3.0 Arrows A3-Cosworth V8	*pit stop-steering wheel/-7 laps*	24/27
8	GERMAN GP	Hockenheim	30	Warsteiner Arrows Racing Team	G	3.0 Arrows A3-Cosworth V8		17/26
dnq	AUSTRIAN GP	Österreichring	30	Warsteiner Arrows Racing Team	G	3.0 Arrows A3-Cosworth V8	*practice crash-no time set*	– / –
11	CANADIAN GP	Montreal	30	Warsteiner Arrows Racing Team	G	3.0 Arrows A3-Cosworth V8	*3 laps behind*	21/28
ret	US GP EAST	Watkins Glen	30	Warsteiner Arrows Racing Team	G	3.0 Arrows A3-Cosworth V8	*driveshaft*	24/27
1982		Championship position: Unplaced						
12	SOUTH AFRICAN GP	Kyalami	17	March Grand Prix Team	P	3.0 March 821-Cosworth V8	*3 laps behind*	22/30
8*	BRAZILIAN GP	Rio	17	Rothmans March Grand Prix Team	P	3.0 March 821-Cosworth V8	*pit stop/1 & 2 cars dsq/-2 laps*	22/31
8	US GP WEST	Long Beach	17	Rothmans March Grand Prix Team	P	3.0 March 821-Cosworth V8	*2 laps behind*	21/31
ret	BELGIAN GP	Zolder	17	Rothmans March Grand Prix Team	P	3.0 March 821-Cosworth V8	*engine*	27/32
dnq	MONACO GP	Monte Carlo	17	Rothmans March Grand Prix Team	A	3.0 March 821-Cosworth V8		23/31
7	US GP (DETROIT)	Detroit	17	Rothmans March Grand Prix Team	A	3.0 March 821-Cosworth V8	*1 lap behind*	18/28
11	CANADIAN GP	Montreal	17	Rothmans March Grand Prix Team	A	3.0 March 821-Cosworth V8	*pit stop/4 laps behind*	22/29
ret	DUTCH GP	Zandvoort	17	Rothmans March Grand Prix Team	A	3.0 March 821-Cosworth V8	*engine*	24/31
10	BRITISH GP	Brands Hatch	17	Rothmans March Grand Prix Team	A	3.0 March 821-Cosworth V8	*pit stop/3 laps behind*	25/30
ret	FRENCH GP	Paul Ricard	17	Rothmans March Grand Prix Team	A	3.0 March 821-Cosworth V8	*accident with Baldi*	26/30

GP Starts: 104 (105)   GP Wins: 1   Pole positions: 0   Fastest laps: 2   Points: 71

JEAN MAX

Max spent much of his early career bound up in the Formula Ford and F3 GRAC projects, before switching to an F3 Tecno in 1970.

With Motul backing for 1971, he raced briefly in Formula 2 for Williams, handling the team's March 701 in that year's French GP. After a couple of unsuccessful outings for Rondel in Formula 2 the following year, Max returned to French F3 in 1973 with a Martini, again backed by the French oil giants.

MICHAEL MAY

Principally an engineer, May nevertheless raced successfully in Formula Junior with a Stanguellini, winning the first Monaco race in 1959 and taking second places in the Eifelrennen and at Pau.

He showed great promise at the wheel of Seidel's Lotus in 1961, particularly at Monaco, but a practice crash at the Nürburgring persuaded him to pursue his original vocation, working on fuel injection development with both Porsche, for whom he was also a test driver, and then Ferrari.

'MAX, Jean' (Max Jean) (F) b 27/7/1943, Marseille

	Race	Circuit	No	Entrant	Tyres	Car/Engine	Comment	Q Pos/Entries
1971		Championship position: Unplaced						
14	FRENCH GP	Paul Ricard	28	Frank Williams Racing Cars	G	3.0 March 701-Cosworth V8	*pit stops/9 laps behind*	23/24

GP Starts: 1   GP Wins: 0   Pole positions: 0   Fastest laps: 0   Points: 0

MAY, Michael (CH) b 18/8/1934, Stuttgart, Germany

	Race	Circuit	No	Entrant	Tyres	Car/Engine	Comment	Q Pos/Entries
1961		Championship position: Unplaced						
ret	MONACO GP	Monte Carlo	8	Scuderia Colonia	D	1.5 Lotus 18-Climax 4	*oil pipe*	14/21
11	FRENCH GP	Reims	46	Scuderia Colonia	D	1.5 Lotus 18-Climax 4	*4 laps behind*	22/26
dns	GERMAN GP	Nürburgring	25	Scuderia Colonia	D	1.5 Lotus 18-Climax 4	*accident in practice*	27/27

GP Starts: 2   GP Wins: 0   Pole positions: 0   Fastest laps: 0   Points: 0

TIM MAYER

An outstanding prospect, Tim began racing an Austin Healey in 1959, and competed in Formula Junior while he studied English Literature at Yale. After graduation he won the FJ championship with a Cooper in 1962 and more success followed in Penske's Cooper-Monaco. He was given a chance with an old works Cooper in the 1962 US GP and then joined Ken Tyrrell's FJ team for 1963. Mayer was set to race in Grands Prix for Cooper in 1964, but a hitherto successful Tasman series with mentor Bruce McLaren ended in disaster when the young American crashed fatally at Longford in Tasmania.

FRANÇOIS MAZET

Mazet did well in two seasons of French F3 with Winfield Racing's Tecno and gained a seat as number two to Tim Schenken in the Sports Motor Formula 2 team for 1970. It was generally a disappointing year so, with Shell backing, he raced Siffert's Chevron in F2 when the Swiss star was committed elsewhere, a fourth place at Pau being his best result. He also raced a March under the team's banner at Paul Ricard, and did some ETC races for Ford Germany. Mazet was later involved with the Essex Petroleum sponsorship of Lotus in the early 1980s.

KEN McALPINE

A former hill-climber and speed-triallist, the wealthy McAlpine, a member of the civil engineering family, became a major benefactor of the Connaught team, racing their Formula 2 A-Type car in selected Grands Prix between 1952 and 1955.

His best results were achieved in the less rarefied atmosphere of Libre events, Ken taking third place in the 1954 Glover Trophy. He enjoyed some success with the team's sports car during this period and finished second in the British Empire Trophy in 1955, his final racing season before retiring to concentrate on his business interests.

MAYER, Tim (USA) b 22/2/1938, Dalton, Pennsylvania – d 28/2/1964, Longford Circuit, Tasmania, Australia

	1962	Championship position: Unplaced							
	Race	Circuit	No	Entrant	Tyres	Car/Engine		Comment	Q Pos/Entries
ret	US GP	Watkins Glen	23	Cooper Car Co	D	1.5 Cooper T53-Climax 4		ignition	12/20

GP Starts: 1 GP Wins: 0 Pole positions: 0 Fastest laps: 0 Points: 0

MAZET, François (F) b 26/2/1943, Paris

	1971	Championship position: Unplaced							
	Race	Circuit	No	Entrant	Tyres	Car/Engine		Comment	Q Pos/Entries
13	FRENCH GP	Paul Ricard	34	Jo Siffert Automobiles	F	3.0 March 701-Cosworth V8		5 laps behind	24/24

GP Starts: 1 GP Wins: 0 Pole positions: 0 Fastest laps: 0 Points: 0

McALPINE, Ken (GB) b 21/9/1920, Chobham, Surrey

	1952	Championship position: Unplaced							
	Race	Circuit	No	Entrant	Tyres	Car/Engine		Comment	Q Pos/Entries
16	BRITISH GP	Silverstone	3	Connaught Engineering	D	2.0 Connaught-Lea Francis A Type 4		6 laps behind	17/32
ret	ITALIAN GP	Monza	28	Connaught Engineering	D	2.0 Connaught-Lea Francis A Type 4		rear suspension	22/35
	1953	Championship position: Unplaced							
ret	DUTCH GP	Zandvoort	28	Connaught Engineering	D	2.0 Connaught-Lea Francis A Type 4		engine	14/20
ret	BRITISH GP	Silverstone	11	Connaught Engineering	D	2.0 Connaught-Lea Francis A Type 4		split hose on startline	13/29
13	GERMAN GP	Nürburgring	16	Connaught Engineering	D	2.0 Connaught-Lea Francis A Type 4		2 laps behind	16/35
nc	ITALIAN GP	Monza	24	Connaught Engineering	D	2.0 Connaught-Lea Francis A Type 4		pit stops/24 laps behind	18/30
	1955	Championship position: Unplaced							
ret	BRITISH GP	Aintree	32	Connaught Engineering	D	2.5 Connaught-Alta B Type 4 str		oil pressure	17/25

GP Starts: 7 GP Wins: 0 Pole positions: 0 Fastest laps: 0 Points: 0

BRUCE McLAREN

Of all the many motor racing fatalities of the era, the death of Bruce McLaren was perhaps the most shocking. By general consensus the safest driver in the sport, his fatal accident while testing his Can-Am McLaren at Goodwood in 1970 was greeted at the time with utter disbelief.

Arriving in Europe virtually unknown, but with the endorsement of Jack Brabham, on a scholarship from the New Zealand Grand Prix Association in March 1958, McLaren's early career was sensational. In Formula 2 with a works Cooper, he took a class win and fifth overall in the German Grand Prix and, showing a maturity beyond his years, mixed it with seasoned competitors on unfamiliar tracks to such good effect that he finished runner-up in the Autocar F2 championship. Promoted to the F1 works team with Brabham in 1959, Bruce was completely unfazed in the top flight and at the end of the season became the youngest-ever GP winner (at 22) when he won the US GP at Sebring. The 1960 season opened with another triumph, this time in Argentina, but the rest of the year saw him content to understudy Brabham as he headed towards a second successive title. There is no doubt that Bruce learned much from his mentor, who moved on at the end of 1961 to build his own cars. Unfortunately, Cooper's fortunes now began to decline, although McLaren picked up a fortunate win at Monaco and also won the non-title Reims GP. During this period Bruce was happy to spend the winter months back home competing in the Tasman series which provided him with a number of wins. In 1964 he was forced to

McLaren at work in the Cooper at the 1963 Belgian GP. After more than seven years' unstinting and loyal service, the Kiwi set up his own team which has since gone on to rack up more than 100 Grand Prix victories.

enter his own cars down-under and thus Bruce McLaren Motor Racing was born. That year also saw a great ambition fulfilled when he won the New Zealand GP at his eighth attempt. Tragedy struck with the death of Tim Mayer, whom Bruce had taken under his wing, but the young American's elder brother Teddy stayed on to become a pillar of the new team which slowly took shape over the next two seasons. Initially the programme centred on the Cooper Zerex Special sports car, later developments of which were to lead towards the team's successful Can-Am cars, which formed the basis of McLaren's emergence as a constructor. Meanwhile Bruce plugged away faithfully at Cooper to the end of the 1965 season, but his various freelance activities, which included racing for Ford in endurance events, had grown to such an extent that the final break was inevitable.

He introduced the white Formula 1 McLaren in 1966, but his season was hampered by the lack of a suitable engine, and the demands of a sports car programme with the McLaren Elva Oldsmobile which by this time was really taking off in North America. However, the highlight of the year for Bruce was winning the Le Mans 24 Hours for Ford with Chris Amon. The pace of expansion continued in 1967, when McLaren was totally involved in F1, now with BRM power. However, this was still an interim unit – indeed, Bruce was glad to race Dan Gurney's second Eagle for a spell after Ginther's sudden retirement rather than use his own machine. A Formula 2 version of the car appeared for the first time which Bruce drove when sports car and F1 commitments permitted. In addition, he shared the victorious Ford Mk II with Andretti at the Sebring 12 Hours, and also won rounds of the growing Can-Am series at Monterey and Riverside on his way to the title.

Clearly the task of heading the team and developing and driving the cars was becoming too much for Bruce to handle on his own, and he tempted Denny Hulme from Brabham for 1968 to take some of the weight off his shoulders. It was a move that showed his wisdom, for he was quite prepared to play second fiddle to the new World Champion, though when the mood took him McLaren the racer, for so long closeted, was allowed to re-emerge, as at Brands Hatch where he unleashed a stunning performance to win the Race of Champions in the bright-tangerine M7A. Onlookers that day were tempted to wonder just what reservoirs of talent lay untapped. Shortly afterwards he took his final Grand Prix win at Spa, but it was Hulme who led the team's title challenge for the rest of the season. However, it was the ever-consistent Bruce who enjoyed the uper hand in 1969, finishing third in the championship behind Stewart and Ickx. He also took the Can-Am title for the second time, dominating the series with six outright victories and three second places.

Though there were hints of impending retirement, Bruce carried on racing into 1970, with plans afoot to tackle Indianapolis after the success of the Can-Am cars. In due course a McLaren would win the Indy 500, but sadly the team's founder and inspiration was not around to see the success. He perished on a sunny June afternoon when a piece of bodywork flew from the car, sending it out of control. Poor Bruce was killed instantly when the car careered into a disused marshals' post.

Mention the name McLaren in the 1990s and most people will immediately think of the wonderful red and white cars which have established so many records. But Ron Dennis can surely testify that all those lucky enough to have either met the remarkable New Zealander or seen him in action will also never forget the man with the silver helmet in the tangerine car who began it all some three decades ago.

BRUCE McLAREN

McLAREN, Bruce (NZ) b 30/8/1937, Auckland – d 2/6/1970, Goodwood Circuit, Sussex, England

1958 — Championship position: Unplaced

	Race	Circuit	No	Entrant	Tyres	Car/Engine	Comment	Q Pos/Entries
5*	GERMAN GP (F2)	Nürburgring	20	Cooper Car Co	D	1.5 Cooper T45-Climax 4 F2	* 1st in F2 class/no points	15/26
13*	MOROCCAN GP (F2)	Casablanca	52	Cooper Car Co	D	1.5 Cooper T45-Climax 4	* 2nd in F2 class	21/25

1959 — Championship position: 6th Wins: 1 Pole positions: 0 Fastest laps: 1 (shared) Points scored: 16.5

	Race	Circuit	No	Entrant	Tyres	Car/Engine	Comment	Q Pos/Entries
5*	MONACO GP	Monte Carlo	22	Cooper Car Co	D	1.5 Cooper T45-Climax 4	* 2nd in F2 class/no points/-4 laps	13/24
5	FRENCH GP	Reims	12	Cooper Car Co	D	2.2 Cooper T51-Climax 4		10/22
3	BRITISH GP	Aintree	16	Cooper Car Co	D	2.5 Cooper T51-Climax 4	FL (shared with Moss)	6/30
ret	GERMAN GP	AVUS	2	Cooper Car Co	D	2.5 Cooper T51-Climax 4	4th in heat 1/clutch heat 2	9/16
ret	PORTUGUESE GP	Monsanto	3	Cooper Car Co	D	2.5 Cooper T51-Climax 4	clutch	8/16
ret	ITALIAN GP	Monza	8	Cooper Car Co	D	2.5 Cooper T51-Climax 4	engine	9/21
1	US GP	Sebring	9	Cooper Car Co	D	2.5 Cooper T51-Climax 4		10/19

1960 — Championship position: 2nd Wins: 1 Pole positions: 0 Fastest laps: 1 Points scored: 37

	Race	Circuit	No	Entrant	Tyres	Car/Engine	Comment	Q Pos/Entries
1	ARGENTINE GP	Buenos Aires	16	Cooper Car Co	D	2.5 Cooper T51-Climax 4		12/22
2	MONACO GP	Monte Carlo	10	Cooper Car Co	D	2.5 Cooper T53-Climax 4	FL	11/24
ret	DUTCH GP	Zandvoort	12	Cooper Car Co	D	2.5 Cooper T53-Climax 4	drive shaft	9/21
2	BELGIAN GP	Spa	4	Cooper Car Co	D	2.5 Cooper T53-Climax 4		14/18
3	FRENCH GP	Reims	18	Cooper Car Co	D	2.5 Cooper T53-Climax 4		7/23
4	BRITISH GP	Silverstone	2	Cooper Car Co	D	2.5 Cooper T53-Climax 4	1 lap behind	3/25
2	PORTUGUESE GP	Oporto	4	Cooper Car Co	D	2.5 Cooper T53-Climax 4		6/16
3	US GP	Riverside	3	Cooper Car Co	D	2.5 Cooper T53-Climax 4		10/23

1961 — Championship position: 7th= Wins: 0 Pole positions: 0 Fastest laps: 0 Points scored: 11

	Race	Circuit	No	Entrant	Tyres	Car/Engine	Comment	Q Pos/Entries
6	MONACO GP	Monte Carlo	26	Cooper Car Co	D	1.5 Cooper T55-Climax 4	5 laps behind	7/21
12	DUTCH GP	Zandvoort	11	Cooper Car Co	D	1.5 Cooper T55-Climax 4	2 laps behind	14/17
ret	BELGIAN GP	Spa	30	Cooper Car Co	D	1.5 Cooper T55-Climax 4	ignition	15/25
5	FRENCH GP	Reims	4	Cooper Car Co	D	1.5 Cooper T55-Climax 4		8/26
8	BRITISH GP	Aintree	14	Cooper Car Co	D	1.5 Cooper T55-Climax 4	1 lap behind	=14/30
6	GERMAN GP	Nürburgring	2	Cooper Car Co	D	1.5 Cooper T55-Climax 4		12/27
3	ITALIAN GP	Monza	12	Cooper Car Co	D	1.5 Cooper T55-Climax 4		14/33
4	US GP	Watkins Glen	2	Cooper Car Co	D	1.5 Cooper T55-Climax 4		=3/19

1962 — Championship position: 3rd Wins: 1 Pole positions: 0 Fastest laps: 1 Points scored: 32

	Race	Circuit	No	Entrant	Tyres	Car/Engine	Comment	Q Pos/Entries
ret	DUTCH GP	Zandvoort	6	Cooper Car Co	D	1.5 Cooper T60-Climax V8	gearbox/FL	5/20
1	MONACO GP	Monte Carlo	14	Cooper Car Co	D	1.5 Cooper T60-Climax V8		=3/21
ret	BELGIAN GP	Spa	25	Cooper Car Co	D	1.5 Cooper T60-Climax V8	oil pressure	2/20
4	FRENCH GP	Rouen	22	Cooper Car Co	D	1.5 Cooper T60-Climax V8	pit stop/3 laps behind	3/17
3	BRITISH GP	Aintree	16	Cooper Car Co	D	1.5 Cooper T60-Climax V8		=4/21
5	GERMAN GP	Nürburgring	9	Cooper Car Co	D	1.5 Cooper T60-Climax V8		5/30
3	ITALIAN GP	Monza	28	Cooper Car Co	D	1.5 Cooper T60-Climax V8		=4/30
3	US GP	Watkins Glen	21	Cooper Car Co	D	1.5 Cooper T60-Climax V8	1 lap behind	6/20
2	SOUTH AFRICAN GP	East London	8	Cooper Car Co	D	1.5 Cooper T60-Climax V8		=6/17

1963 — Championship position: 6th Wins: 0 Pole positions: 0 Fastest laps: 0 Points scored: 17

	Race	Circuit	No	Entrant	Tyres	Car/Engine	Comment	Q Pos/Entries
3	MONACO GP	Monte Carlo	7	Cooper Car Co	D	1.5 Cooper T66-Climax V8		8/17
2	BELGIAN GP	Spa	14	Cooper Car Co	D	1.5 Cooper T66-Climax V8		5/20
ret	DUTCH GP	Zandvoort	20	Cooper Car Co	D	1.5 Cooper T66-Climax V8	gearbox	3/19
12/ret	FRENCH GP	Reims	10	Cooper Car Co	D	1.5 Cooper T66-Climax V8	ignition/11 laps behind	6/21
ret	BRITISH GP	Silverstone	6	Cooper Car Co	D	1.5 Cooper T66-Climax V8	engine	6/23
ret	GERMAN GP	Nürburgring	5	Cooper Car Co	D	1.5 Cooper T66-Climax V8	car failure-crashed	5/26
3	ITALIAN GP	Monza	18	Cooper Car Co	D	1.5 Cooper T66-Climax V8	1 lap behind	8/28
11/ret	US GP	Watkins Glen	3	Cooper Car Co	D	1.5 Cooper T66-Climax V8	fuel pump/36 laps behind	11/21
ret	MEXICAN GP	Mexico City	3	Cooper Car Co	D	1.5 Cooper T66-Climax V8	engine	6/21
4	SOUTH AFRICAN GP	East London	10	Cooper Car Co	D	1.5 Cooper T66-Climax V8	1 lap behind	9/21

1964 — Championship position: 7th Wins: 0 Pole positions: 0 Fastest laps: 0 Points scored: 13

	Race	Circuit	No	Entrant	Tyres	Car/Engine	Comment	Q Pos/Entries
ret	MONACO GP	Monte Carlo	10	Cooper Car Co	D	1.5 Cooper T66-Climax V8	oil leak-main bearing	10/20
dns	"	" "	10	Cooper Car Co	D	1.5 Cooper T73-Climax V8	practice only	– / –
7	DUTCH GP	Zandvoort	24	Cooper Car Co	D	1.5 Cooper T73-Climax V8	2 laps behind	5/18
2	BELGIAN GP	Spa	20	Cooper Car Co	D	1.5 Cooper T73-Climax V8		=6/20
6	FRENCH GP	Rouen	12	Cooper Car Co	D	1.5 Cooper T73-Climax V8	1 lap behind	7/17
ret	BRITISH GP	Brands Hatch	9	Cooper Car Co	D	1.5 Cooper T73-Climax V8	gearbox	6/25
ret	GERMAN GP	Nürburgring	9	Cooper Car Co	D	1.5 Cooper T73-Climax V8	engine	7/24
ret	AUSTRIAN GP	Zeltweg	9	Cooper Car Co	D	1.5 Cooper T73-Climax V8	engine	9/20
2	ITALIAN GP	Monza	26	Cooper Car Co	D	1.5 Cooper T73-Climax V8		5/25
ret	US GP	Watkins Glen	9	Cooper Car Co	D	1.5 Cooper T73-Climax V8	engine	5/19
7	MEXICAN GP	Mexico City	9	Cooper Car Co	D	1.5 Cooper T73-Climax V8	1 lap behind	10/19

1965 — Championship position: 8th= Wins: 0 Pole positions: 0 Fastest laps: 0 Points scored: 10

	Race	Circuit	No	Entrant	Tyres	Car/Engine	Comment	Q Pos/Entries
5	SOUTH AFRICAN GP	East London	9	Cooper Car Co	D	1.5 Cooper T77-Climax V8	1 lap behind	8/25
5	MONACO GP	Monte Carlo	7	Cooper Car Co	D	1.5 Cooper T77-Climax V8	2 laps behind	7/17
3	BELGIAN GP	Spa	4	Cooper Car Co	D	1.5 Cooper T77-Climax V8	1 lap behind	9/21
ret	FRENCH GP	Clermont Ferrand	18	Cooper Car Co	D	1.5 Cooper T77-Climax V8	steering	9/17
10	BRITISH GP	Silverstone	9	Cooper Car Co	D	1.5 Cooper T77-Climax V8	3 laps behind	11/23
ret	DUTCH GP	Zandvoort	18	Cooper Car Co	D	1.5 Cooper T77-Climax V8	transmission	9/17
ret	GERMAN GP	Nürburgring	11	Cooper Car Co	D	1.5 Cooper T77-Climax V8	gear selection	10/22
5	ITALIAN GP	Monza	16	Cooper Car Co	D	1.5 Cooper T77-Climax V8	1 lap behind	11/23
ret	US GP	Watkins Glen	9	Cooper Car Co	D	1.5 Cooper T77-Climax V8	no oil pressure	9/18
ret	MEXICAN GP	Mexico City	9	Cooper Car Co	D	1.5 Cooper T77-Climax V8	gear selection	15/18

1966 — Championship position: 14th= Wins: 0 Pole positions: 0 Fastest laps: 0 Points scored: 3

	Race	Circuit	No	Entrant	Tyres	Car/Engine	Comment	Q Pos/Entries
ret	MONACO GP	Monte Carlo	2	Bruce McLaren Motor Racing	F	3.0 McLaren M2B-Ford V8	oil leak	=10/16
dns	BELGIAN GP	Spa	24	Bruce McLaren Motor Racing	F	3.0 McLaren M2B-Serenissima V8	bearings in practice	(16)/19
6	BRITISH GP	Brands Hatch	14	Bruce McLaren Motor Racing	F	3.0 McLaren M2B-Serenissima V8	2 laps behind	13/20

dns	DUTCH GP	Zandvoort	20	Bruce McLaren Motor Racing	F	3.0 McLaren M2B-Serenissima V8	engine in practice	(14)/18
5	US GP	Watkins Glen	17	Bruce McLaren Motor Racing	F	3.0 McLaren M2B-Ford V8	3 laps behind	11/19
ret	MEXICAN GP	Mexico City	17	Bruce McLaren Motor Racing	F	3.0 McLaren M2B-Ford V8	engine	15/19

1967 Championship position: 14th Wins: 0 Pole positions: 0 Fastest laps: 0 Points scored: 3

4	MONACO GP	Monte Carlo	16	Bruce McLaren Motor Racing	G	2.1 McLaren M4B-BRM V8	pit stop-battery//-3 laps	=9/18
ret	DUTCH GP	Zandvoort	17	Bruce McLaren Motor Racing	G	2.1 McLaren M4B-BRM V8	spun off	14/17
ret	FRENCH GP	Le Mans	8	Anglo American Racers	G	3.0 Eagle T1G102-Weslake V12	ignition drive	5/15
ret	BRITISH GP	Silverstone	10	Anglo American Racers	G	3.0 Eagle T1G102-Weslake V12	engine	10/21
ret	GERMAN GP	Nürburgring	10	Anglo American Racers	G	3.0 Eagle T1G102-Weslake V12	oil pipe leak	6/25
7	CANADIAN GP	Mosport Park	19	Bruce McLaren Motor Racing	G	3.0 McLaren M5A-BRM V12	pit stop-battery/4 laps behind	6/19
ret	ITALIAN GP	Monza	4	Bruce McLaren Motor Racing	G	3.0 McLaren M5A-BRM V12	engine	3/18
ret	US GP	Watkins Glen	14	Bruce McLaren Motor Racing	G	3.0 McLaren M5A-BRM V12	water pipe	9/18
ret	MEXICAN GP	Mexico City	14	Bruce McLaren Motor Racing	G	3.0 McLaren M5A-BRM V12	oil pressure	8/19

1968 Championship position: 5th Wins: 1 Pole positions: 0 Fastest laps: 0 Points scored: 22

ret	SPANISH GP	Jarama	2	Bruce McLaren Motor Racing	G	3.0 McLaren M7A-Cosworth V8	oil loss	=4/14
ret	MONACO GP	Monte Carlo	14	Bruce McLaren Motor Racing	G	3.0 McLaren M7A-Cosworth V8	spun off	7/10
1	BELGIAN GP	Spa	5	Bruce McLaren Motor Racing	G	3.0 McLaren M7A-Cosworth V8		6/18
ret	DUTCH GP	Zandvoort	2	Bruce McLaren Motor Racing	G	3.0 McLaren M7A-Cosworth V8	crashed	8/19
8	FRENCH GP	Rouen	10	Bruce McLaren Motor Racing	G	3.0 McLaren M7A-Cosworth V8	pit stop-tyres/4 laps behind	6/18
7	BRITISH GP	Brands Hatch	7	Bruce McLaren Motor Racing	G	3.0 McLaren M7A-Cosworth V8	3 laps behind	=10/20
13	GERMAN GP	Nürburgring	2	Bruce McLaren Motor Racing	G	3.0 McLaren M7A-Cosworth V8	1 lap behind	16/20
ret	ITALIAN GP	Monza	2	Bruce McLaren Motor Racing	G	3.0 McLaren M7A-Cosworth V8	oil loss	2/24
2	CANADIAN GP	St Jovite	2	Bruce McLaren Motor Racing	G	3.0 McLaren M7A-Cosworth V8	1 lap behind	8/22
6	US GP	Watkins Glen	2	Bruce McLaren Motor Racing	G	3.0 McLaren M7A-Cosworth V8	pit stop-fuel/5 laps behind	10/21
2	MEXICAN GP	Mexico City	2	Bruce McLaren Motor Racing	G	3.0 McLaren M7A-Cosworth V8		9/21

1969 Championship position: 3rd Wins: 0 Pole positions: 0 Fastest laps: 0 Points scored: 26

5	SOUTH AFRICAN GP	Kyalami	6	Bruce McLaren Motor Racing	G	3.0 McLaren M7A-Cosworth V8	1 lap behind	=7/18
2	SPANISH GP	Montjuich Park	6	Bruce McLaren Motor Racing	G	3.0 McLaren M7C-Cosworth V8	2 laps behind	13/14
5	MONACO GP	Monte Carlo	4	Bruce McLaren Motor Racing	G	3.0 McLaren M7C-Cosworth V8	1 lap behind	11/16
ret	DUTCH GP	Zandvoort	6	Bruce McLaren Motor Racing	G	3.0 McLaren M7C-Cosworth V8	front stub axle	6/15
4	FRENCH GP	Clermont Ferrand	5	Bruce McLaren Motor Racing	G	3.0 McLaren M7C-Cosworth V8	1 lap behind	7/13
3	BRITISH GP	Silverstone	6	Bruce McLaren Motor Racing	G	3.0 McLaren M7C-Cosworth V8	1 lap behind	=7/17
3	GERMAN GP	Nürburgring	10	Bruce McLaren Motor Racing	G	3.0 McLaren M7C-Cosworth V8		8/24
4	ITALIAN GP	Monza	18	Bruce McLaren Motor Racing	G	3.0 McLaren M7C-Cosworth V8		5/15
5	CANADIAN GP	Mosport Park	4	Bruce McLaren Motor Racing	G	3.0 McLaren M7C-Cosworth V8	3 laps behind	=8/20
dns	US GP	Watkins Glen	6	Bruce McLaren Motor Racing	G	3.0 McLaren M7C-Cosworth V8	engine in warm up	(6)/18
ret	MEXICAN GP	Mexico City	6	Bruce McLaren Motor Racing	G	3.0 McLaren M7C-Cosworth V8	fuel system	7/17

1970 Championship position: 14th Wins: 0 Pole positions: 0 Fastest laps: 0 Points scored: 6

ret	SOUTH AFRICAN GP	Kyalami	5	Bruce McLaren Motor Racing	G	3.0 McLaren M14A-Cosworth V8	engine	10/24
2	SPANISH GP	Jarama	11	Bruce McLaren Motor Racing	G	3.0 McLaren M14A-Cosworth V8	1 lap behind	12/22
ret	MONACO GP	Monte Carlo	12	Bruce McLaren Motor Racing	G	3.0 McLaren M14A-Cosworth V8	hit chicane-suspension damage	10/21

GP Starts: 101 GP Wins: 4 Pole positions: 0 Fastest laps: 3 Points: 196.5

The last day of the high wings. McLaren took second place in the 1969 Spanish Grand Prix, but accidents to the Lotus cars of Hill and Rindt resulted in the huge rear aerofoils being immediately outlawed on safety grounds.

GRAHAM McRAE

Although the sum total of McRae's Grand Prix career was one lap in Frank Williams' Iso car in the 1973 British GP, 'Cassius', as he was popularly known, nevertheless enjoyed a long racing career, mainly in F5000 single-seaters, winning the 1972 US L & M series in his modified Leda.

McRae built his own chassis in the late sixties and came to Europe to race in Formula 2 in 1969 with the ex-Courage Brabham. He soon switched to F5000, with a McLaren M10-Chevrolet, which launched him on his path to success as both driver and constructor.

Although his form tailed off towards the mid-seventies, McRae continued to race in Can-Am up until the early eighties with a modified version of his GM3 F5000 car.

CARLOS MENDITÉGUY

A fine all-round sportsman and top-ranked polo player, Menditéguy made his mark at the 1951 Peron Cup races when his performances in an Alfa Romeo took the eye. From then on he was a regular local attraction when the big European teams visited for the Grands Prix and the Buenos Aires Libre races.

In 1956 Menditéguy led the Grand Prix until, missing a gear, he broke the car's half-shaft and slid the Maserati into a fence. Another fine drive in the Mendoza GP yielded only fourth place after low oil pressure had blunted his challenge, but he did share the winning Maserati sports car with Moss in the Buenos Aires 1000 Km.

Third place in the 1957 Grand Prix persuaded Maserati to give him an opportunity to race in Europe, but he had an unhappy sojourn, feeling his car was the least well prepared, while the team opined that he was too hard on the machinery. In mid-season he returned to Argentina in disgust. In 1958 he shared Godia's Maserati to take third place in the Buenos Aires City GP, and in 1960, in the last Argentine Grand Prix for more than a decade, showed his talent had not deserted him by taking a Centro Sud Cooper into fourth place.

McRAE, Graham (NZ) b 5/3/1940, Wellington

	1973	Championship position: Unplaced						
	Race	Circuit	No	Entrant	Tyres	Car/Engine	Comment	Q Pos/Entries
ret	BRITISH GP	Silverstone	26	Frank Williams Racing Cars	F	3.0 Iso Williams 1R-Cosworth V8	sticking throttle on lap 1	28/29

GP Starts: 1   GP Wins: 0   Pole positions: 0   Fastest laps: 0   Points: 0

MENDITÉGUY, Carlos (RA) b 10/8/1915, Buenos Aires – d 28/4/1973

	1953	Championship position: Unplaced						
	Race	Circuit	No	Entrant	Tyres	Car/Engine	Comment	Q Pos/Entries
ret	ARGENTINE GP	Buenos Aires	32	Equipe Gordini	E	2.0 Gordini Type 16 6	gearbox	10/16
	1954	Championship position: Unplaced						
dns	ARGENTINE GP	Buenos Aires	36	Onofre Marimon	P	2.5 Maserati A6GCM/250F 6	engine in practice	(9)/18
	1955	Championship position: 12= Wins: 0 Pole positions: 0 Fastest laps: 0 Points scored: 2						
ret	ARGENTINE GP	Buenos Aires	24	Officine Alfieri Maserati	P	2.5 Maserati 250F 6	crashed	13/22
ret	"	" "	26	Officine Alfieri Maserati	P	2.5 Maserati 250F 6	Bucci/Schell co-drove/fuel feed	– / –
5	ITALIAN GP	Monza	34	Officine Alfieri Maserati	P	2.5 Maserati 250F 6	1 lap behind	16/22
	1956	Championship position: Unplaced						
ret	ARGENTINE GP	Buenos Aires	6	Officine Alfieri Maserati	P	2.5 Maserati 250F 6	half-shaft/led race	6/15
	1957	Championship position: 12th= Wins: 0 Pole positions: 0 Fastest laps: 0 Points scored: 4						
3	ARGENTINE GP	Buenos Aires	8	Officine Alfieri Maserati	P	2.5 Maserati 250F 6	1 lap behind	8/16
ret	MONACO GP	Monte Carlo	36	Officine Alfieri Maserati	P	2.5 Maserati 250F 6	crashed at chicane-broken nose	7/21
ret	FRENCH GP	Rouen	8	Officine Alfieri Maserati	P	2.5 Maserati 250F 6	engine	9/15
ret	BRITISH GP	Aintree	8	Officine Alfieri Maserati	P	2.5 Maserati 250F 6	transmission	11/19
	1958	Championship position: Unplaced						
7	ARGENTINE GP	Buenos Aires	6	Scuderia Sud Americana	P	2.5 Maserati 250F 6	4 laps behind	6/10
	1960	Championship position: 16th= Wins: 0 Pole positions: 0 Fastest laps: 0 Points scored: 3						
4	ARGENTINE GP	Buenos Aires	6	Scuderia Centro Sud	D	2.5 Cooper T51-Maserati 4		12/22

GP Starts: 10   GP Wins: 0   Pole positions: 0   Fastest laps: 0   Points: 9

ARTURO MERZARIO

'Little Art' made his name in the late sixties with works Fiat Abarths in both GT and European mountain-climb events. If one race in particular advanced his career prospects, then it was the Mugello GP in 1969, which he won after a superb drive in the Abarth 2-litre, beating the likes of Vaccarella and de Adamich. This brought an invitation to join the Ferrari sports car team for 1970 and the start of a three-year association with the Scuderia.

His best season was probably 1972, Merzario making a sparkling Grand Prix debut at Brands Hatch, winning the Spa 1000 Km with Redman, the Targa Florio with Munari and the Rand 9 Hours with Regazzoni in the 312P. In addition, racing for Abarth, he was crowned European 2-litre champion. The following season saw Ferrari in something of a trough, but Merzario knuckled down to a hit-and-miss season of Formula 1 while team leader Ickx just gave up. His feisty spirit appealed to Frank Williams, who signed him for 1974. The season began with a third place in the Medici GP at Brasilia, but once the serious business began success was elusive. The pair ploughed on into the 1975 season but Merzario's fortunes in Formula 1 could hardly have been worse. By mid-season he had quit Williams to concentrate on his commitments with the Alfa sports car team, taking their T33 to wins at Dijon, Monza, Enna and the Nürburgring. After a brief liaison with Copersucar at Monza, Arturo lined up a works March drive for 1976, but the strain of running a four-car team showed and the Italian, unhappy with his lot, grabbed the chance to join Wolf-Williams in mid-season following the sudden departure of Ickx.

With no other options open to him, Merzario entered his own March in 1977 before the money ran out due to a lack of results. He had a good one-off drive for Shadow in Austria, but this was overlooked due to Alan Jones' splendid win in the sister car. While his Grand Prix career had been heading for the rocks for some time, Arturo managed to salvage his reputation somewhat by continuing his sports car success with Alfa Romeo, and in 1977 he won champi-

onship rounds at Dijon, Enna, Estoril and Paul Ricard in Autodelta's last fling. The following year Merzario took the brave and ultimately completely foolhardy step of fielding his own F1 chassis. Two versions of this appalling device were built during the next two seasons but the cars rarely looked capable of qualifying. Very much the poorer but seemingly no wiser, the little Italian persisted with his folly in 1980, making an equally fruitless attempt to mix it with the constructors in Formula 2 with his Merzario M1-BMW, which was just as embarrassing as his Grand Prix 'contender'.

Arturo has returned to the tracks once more in the nineties, winning the inaugural Maserati Bi-turbo Cup race at Imola in 1995, and after driving in the Porsche Supercup the jaunty Italian has been a competitive force in various sports car races at both national and international level.

MERZARIO, Arturo (I) b 11/3/1943, Civenna, Como

	1972	Championship position: 20th		Wins: 0	Pole positions: 0	Fastest laps: 0	Points scored: 1		
	Race	Circuit	No	Entrant	Tyres	Car/Engine		Comment	Q Pos/Entries
6	BRITISH GP	Brands Hatch	6	Scuderia Ferrari SpA SEFAC	F	3.0 Ferrari 312B2 F12		pit stop-tyre/1 lap behind	=8/27
12	GERMAN GP	Nürburgring	19	Scuderia Ferrari SpA SEFAC	F	3.0 Ferrari 312B2 F12		pit stop-oil pressure/-1 lap	22/27
	1973	Championship position: 12th		Wins: 0	Pole positions: 0	Fastest laps: 0	Points scored: 6		
9	ARGENTINE GP	Buenos Aires	20	Scuderia Ferrari SpA SEFAC	G	3.0 Ferrari 312B2 F12		gearbox problems/-4 laps	14/19
4	BRAZILIAN GP	Interlagos	10	Scuderia Ferrari SpA SEFAC	G	3.0 Ferrari 312B2 F12		1 lap behind	17/20
4	SOUTH AFRICAN GP	Kyalami	9	Scuderia Ferrari SpA SEFAC	G	3.0 Ferrari 312B2 F12		1 lap behind	15/25
ret	MONACO GP	Monte Carlo	4	Scuderia Ferrari SpA SEFAC	G	3.0 Ferrari 312B3 F12		oil pressure	16/26
7	FRENCH GP	Paul Ricard	4	Scuderia Ferrari SpA SEFAC	G	3.0 Ferrari 312B3 F12			10/25
7	AUSTRIAN GP	Österreichring	4	Scuderia Ferrari SpA SEFAC	G	3.0 Ferrari 312B3 F12		1 lap behind	6/25
ret	ITALIAN GP	Monza	4	Scuderia Ferrari SpA SEFAC	G	3.0 Ferrari 312B3 F12		hit chicane-suspension damage	7/25
15	CANADIAN GP	Mosport Park	4	Scuderia Ferrari SpA SEFAC	G	3.0 Ferrari 312B3 F12		pit stops-lost nose cone/-5 laps	20/26
16	US GP	Watkins Glen	4	Scuderia Ferrari SpA SEFAC	G	3.0 Ferrari 312B3 F12		pit stop-rear wing/-4 laps	12/28
	1974	Championship position: 17th		Wins: 0	Pole positions: 0	Fastest laps: 0	Points scored: 4		
ret	ARGENTINE GP	Buenos Aires	20	Frank Williams Racing Cars	G	3.0 Williams FW01-Cosworth V8		engine	13/26
ret	BRAZILIAN GP	Interlagos	20	Frank Williams Racing Cars	G	3.0 Williams FW01-Cosworth V8		dirt in throttle slides	9/25
6	SOUTH AFRICAN GP	Kyalami	20	Frank Williams Racing Cars	G	3.0 Williams FW02-Cosworth V8			3/27

Result	GP	Circuit	No.	Entrant	Tyre	Car/Engine	Notes	Pos
ret	SPANISH GP	Jarama	20	Frank Williams Racing Cars	G	3.0 Williams FW03-Cosworth V8	hit and vaulted barrier	7/28
ret	BELGIAN GP	Nivelles	20	Frank Williams Racing Cars	G	3.0 Williams FW03-Cosworth V8	driveshaft	6/32
ret	MONACO GP	Monte Carlo	20	Frank Williams Racing Cars	G	3.0 Williams FW03-Cosworth V8	multiple accident	14/28
dns	"	"	20T	Frank Williams Racing Cars	G	3.0 Williams FW03-Cosworth V8	practice only	–/–
dns	SWEDISH GP	Anderstorp	20	Frank Williams Racing Cars	G	3.0 Williams FW02-Cosworth V8	unwell	28/28
ret	DUTCH GP	Zandvoort	20	Frank Williams Racing Cars	G	3.0 Williams FW02-Cosworth V8	gearbox	21/27
9	FRENCH GP	Dijon	20	Frank Williams Racing Cars	G	3.0 Williams FW02-Cosworth V8	1 lap behind	15/30
ret	BRITISH GP	Brands Hatch	20	Frank Williams Racing Cars	G	3.0 Williams FW01-Cosworth V8	engine	=15/34
dns	"	"	20	Frank Williams Racing Cars	G	3.0 Williams FW03-Cosworth V8	practice only	–/–
ret	GERMAN GP	Nürburgring	20	Frank Williams Racing Cars	G	3.0 Williams FW03-Cosworth V8	throttle linkage	16/32
ret	AUSTRIAN GP	Österreichring	20	Frank Williams Racing Cars	G	3.0 Williams FW03-Cosworth V8	fuel pressure	9/31
4	ITALIAN GP	Monza	20	Frank Williams Racing Cars	G	3.0 Williams FW03-Cosworth V8		15/31
ret	CANADIAN GP	Mosport Park	20	Frank Williams Racing Cars	G	3.0 Williams FW03-Cosworth V8	handling	19/30
ret	US GP	Watkins Glen	20	Frank Williams Racing Cars	G	3.0 Williams FW03-Cosworth V8	extinguisher-electrical short	15/30

1975 — Championship position: Unplaced

Result	GP	Circuit	No.	Entrant	Tyre	Car/Engine	Notes	Pos
nc	ARGENTINE GP	Buenos Aires	20	Frank Williams Racing Cars	G	3.0 Williams FW03-Cosworth V8	2 stops-fuel metering unit/-9 laps	20/23
ret	BRAZILIAN GP	Interlagos	20	Frank Williams Racing Cars	G	3.0 Williams FW03-Cosworth V8	fuel metering unit	11/23
ret	SOUTH AFRICAN GP	Kyalami	20	Frank Williams Racing Cars	G	3.0 Williams FW03-Cosworth V8	engine	15/28
ret	SPANISH GP	Montjuich Park	20	Frank Williams Racing Cars	G	3.0 Williams FW04-Cosworth V8	withdrew in safety, protest	(25)/26
dnq	MONACO GP	Monte Carlo	20	Frank Williams Racing Cars	G	3.0 Williams FW03-Cosworth V8		20/26
ret	BELGIAN GP	Zolder	20	Frank Williams Racing Cars	G	3.0 Williams FW03-Cosworth V8	clutch	19/24
11	ITALIAN GP	Monza	30	Copersucar-Fittipaldi	G	3.0 Fittipaldi FD03-Cosworth V8	4 laps behind	26/28

1976 — Championship position: Unplaced

Result	GP	Circuit	No.	Entrant	Tyre	Car/Engine	Notes	Pos
dnq	US GP WEST	Long Beach	35	Ovoro Team March	G	3.0 March 761-Cosworth V8		23/27
ret	SPANISH GP	Jarama	35	Ovoro Team March	G	3.0 March 761-Cosworth V8	gear linkage	18/30
ret	BELGIAN GP	Zolder	35	Ovoro Team March	G	3.0 March 761-Cosworth V8	engine	21/29
dnq	MONACO GP	Monte Carlo	35	Ovoro Team March	G	3.0 March 761-Cosworth V8	accident in practice	25/25
14/ret	SWEDISH GP	Anderstorp	35	Ovoro Team March	G	3.0 March 761-Cosworth V8	engine/2 laps behind	19/27
9	FRENCH GP	Paul Ricard	35	Ovoro Team March	G	3.0 March 761-Cosworth V8		20/30
ret	BRITISH GP	Brands Hatch	35	Ovoro Team March	G	3.0 March 761-Cosworth V8	engine	9/30
ret	GERMAN GP	Nürburgring	20	Walter Wolf Racing	G	3.0 Williams FW05-Cosworth V8	brakes	21/28
ret	AUSTRIAN GP	Österreichring	20	Walter Wolf Racing	G	3.0 Williams FW05-Cosworth V8	spun off	21/25
ret	DUTCH GP	Zandvoort	20	Walter Wolf Racing	G	3.0 Williams FW05-Cosworth V8	spun off	23/27
dns	ITALIAN GP	Monza	20	Walter Wolf Racing	G	3.0 Williams FW05-Cosworth V8	withdrawn after practice	(24)/29
ret	CANADIAN GP	Mosport Park	20	Walter Wolf Racing	G	3.0 Williams FW05-Cosworth V8	spun off	25/27
ret	US GP EAST	Watkins Glen	20	Walter Wolf Racing	G	3.0 Williams FW05-Cosworth V8	spun, hit by Ertl	25/27
ret	JAPANESE GP	Mount Fuji	20	Walter Wolf Racing	G	3.0 Williams FW05-Cosworth V8	gearbox	19/27

1977 — Championship position: Unplaced

Result	GP	Circuit	No.	Entrant	Tyre	Car/Engine	Notes	Pos
ret	SPANISH GP	Jarama	37	Team Merzario	G	3.0 March 761B-Cosworth V8	suspension	21/31
dnq	MONACO GP	Monte Carlo	37	Team Merzario	G	3.0 March 761B-Cosworth V8		21/26
14	BELGIAN GP	Zolder	37	Team Merzario	G	3.0 March 761B-Cosworth V8	pit stop-tyres-fuel pump/-5 laps	14/32
ret	FRENCH GP	Dijon	37	Team Merzario	G	3.0 March 761B-Cosworth V8	gearbox	18/30
ret	BRITISH GP	Silverstone	37	Team Merzario	G	3.0 March 761B-Cosworth V8	driveshaft	17/36
dnq	GERMAN GP	Hockenheim	37	Team Merzario	G	3.0 March 761B-Cosworth V8		29/30
ret	AUSTRIAN GP	Österreichring	16	Shadow Racing Team	G	3.0 Shadow DN8-Cosworth V8	gear linkage	=20/30
dnq	DUTCH GP	Zandvoort	37	Team Merzario	G	3.0 March 761B-Cosworth V8		28/34

1978 — Championship position: Unplaced

Result	GP	Circuit	No.	Entrant	Tyre	Car/Engine	Notes	Pos
ret	ARGENTINE GP	Buenos Aires	37	Team Merzario	G	3.0 Merzario A1-Cosworth V8	differential	20/27
dnq	BRAZILIAN GP	Rio	37	Team Merzario	G	3.0 Merzario A1-Cosworth V8		=24/28
ret	SOUTH AFRICAN GP	Kyalami	37	Team Merzario	G	3.0 Merzario A1-Cosworth V8	radius rod mounting	26/30
ret	US GP WEST	Long Beach	37	Team Merzario	G	3.0 Merzario A1-Cosworth V8	gearbox	21/30
dnpq	MONACO GP	Monte Carlo	37	Team Merzario	G	3.0 Merzario A1-Cosworth V8		30/30
dnpq	BELGIAN GP	Zolder	37	Team Merzario	G	3.0 Merzario A1-Cosworth V8		30/30
dnq	SPANISH GP	Jarama	37	Team Merzario	G	3.0 Merzario A1-Cosworth V8		25/29
nc	SWEDISH GP	Anderstorp	37	Team Merzario	G	3.0 Merzario A1-Cosworth V8	pit stop/8 laps behind	22/27
dnq	FRENCH GP	Paul Ricard	37	Team Merzario	G	3.0 Merzario A1-Cosworth V8		27/29
ret	BRITISH GP	Brands Hatch	37	Team Merzario	G	3.0 Merzario A1-Cosworth V8	fuel pump	23/30
dnq	GERMAN GP	Hockenheim	37	Team Merzario	G	3.0 Merzario A1-Cosworth V8		28/30
dnq	AUSTRIAN GP	Österreichring	37	Team Merzario	G	3.0 Merzario A1-Cosworth V8		27/31
ret	DUTCH GP	Zandvoort	37	Team Merzario	G	3.0 Merzario A1-Cosworth V8	engine	27/33
ret	ITALIAN GP	Monza	37	Team Merzario	G	3.0 Merzario A1-Cosworth V8	engine	22/32
ret	US GP EAST	Watkins Glen	37	Team Merzario	G	3.0 Merzario A1-Cosworth V8	gearbox oil leak	26/27
dnq	CANADIAN GP	Montreal	37	Team Merzario	G	3.0 Merzario A1-Cosworth V8		25/28

1979 — Championship position: Unplaced

Result	GP	Circuit	No.	Entrant	Tyre	Car/Engine	Notes	Pos
ret/dns	ARGENTINE GP	Buenos Aires	24	Team Merzario	G	3.0 Merzario A1B-Cosworth V8	accident in first start	22/26
dnq	BRAZILIAN GP	Rio	24	Team Merzario	G	3.0 Merzario A1B-Cosworth V8		26/26
dnq	SOUTH AFRICAN GP	Kyalami	24	Team Merzario	G	3.0 Merzario A1B-Cosworth V8		25/26
ret	US GP WEST	Long Beach	24	Team Merzario	G	3.0 Merzario A1B-Cosworth V8	engine	24/26
dns	" "	" "	24	Team Merzario	G	3.0 Merzario A2-Cosworth V8	practice only	–/–
dnq	SPANISH GP	Jarama	24	Team Merzario	G	3.0 Merzario A2-Cosworth V8		26/27
dnq	BELGIAN GP	Zolder	24	Team Merzario	G	3.0 Merzario A2-Cosworth V8		26/28
dnq	FRENCH GP	Dijon	24	Team Merzario	G	3.0 Merzario A2-Cosworth V8		27/27
dnq	BRITISH GP	Silverstone	24	Team Merzario	G	3.0 Merzario A2-Cosworth V8		26/26
dnq	GERMAN GP	Hockenheim	24	Team Merzario	G	3.0 Merzario A2-Cosworth V8		26/26
dnq	AUSTRIAN GP	Österreichring	24	Team Merzario	G	3.0 Merzario A2-Cosworth V8		26/26
dnq	DUTCH GP	Zandvoort	24	Team Merzario	G	3.0 Merzario A2-Cosworth V8		27/28
dnq	ITALIAN GP	Monza	24	Team Merzario	G	3.0 Merzario A2-Cosworth V8		29/29
dnq	CANADIAN GP	Montreal	24	Team Merzario	G	3.0 Merzario A2-Cosworth V8		30/30
dnq	US GP EAST	Watkins Glen	24	Team Merzario	G	3.0 Merzario A2-Cosworth V8		

GP Starts: 56 (57)   GP Wins: 0   Pole positions: 0   Fastest laps: 0   Points: 11

ROBERTO MIÈRES

Mières was a natural athlete who excelled at rowing, yachting and rugby until a broken leg ended his interest in the oval-ball game. After reaching championship class at tennis, he turned to motor sport with an MG, which was soon replaced by a Mercedes SSK with which he won an important race at Rosario. Racing the ex-Varzi Bugatti, Mières won the Argentine sports car championship, and as a result was invited to accompany Fangio and Gonzalez on a short trip to Europe, during which he took a Ferrari to fourth in the Geneva GP of 1950.

Returning home he waited for an opportunity to race abroad once more, which finally came in 1953, when Gordini invited him to replace the injured Behra. Little came his way in terms of results, but he drove brilliantly to finish fourth in the F1 Albi GP with the F2 car. In 1954 Roberto ordered a Maserati 250F, but he started the season with the interim A6GCM/250 and scored a superb second place in the Buenos Aires City GP. He was frustrated by the non-appearance of his new car for most of the year, but made the best of it, taking third at Pau and fourth in the International Trophy at Silverstone. When the 250F eventually arrived, Mières immediately took fourth places in Swiss and Spanish GPs, so impressing the factory that he was taken on for 1955.

Ably supporting team leader Jean Behra, Mières enjoyed a consistent season, doing particularly well in non-championship races, taking second in the Turin GP and third at both Pau and Bordeaux. Political upheaval at home prompted Mières to retire from Grands Prix at the end of 1955 to tend his business intesests, and he returned to his earlier passion of yachting.

Roberto was tempted back behind the wheel, however. He finished fourth In the 1957 Buenos Aires 1000 Km in the Ecurie Ecosse Jaguar D-Type, while in 1958 he raced a Centro Sud Maserati 250 F in the Buenos Aires City GP, and shared a works Porsche with Barth and d'Orey in the 1000 Km, claiming a class win and fifth place overall.

Mières subsequently raced occasionally in the USA, and took part in single-seater and saloon car events at home until 1962-63, when he decided to concentrate on his considerable competition yachting skills.

MIÈRES, Roberto (RA) b 3/12/1924, Mar del Plata

	1953	Championship position: Unplaced							
	Race	Circuit	No	Entrant	Tyres	Car/Engine		Comment	Q Pos/Entries
ret	DUTCH GP	Zandvoort	22	Equipe Gordini	E	2.0 Gordini Type 16 6		transmission	19/20
ret	FRENCH GP	Reims	8	Equipe Gordini	E	2.0 Gordini Type 16 6		rear axle	24/25
6	ITALIAN GP	Monza	40	Equipe Gordini	E	2.0 Gordini Type 16 6		3 laps behind	16/30
	1954	Championship position: 7th=	Wins: 0	Pole positions: 0	Fastest laps: 0	Points scored: 6			
ret	ARGENTINE GP	Buenos Aires	32	Roberto Mières	P	2.5 Maserati A6GCM/250F 6		engine	8/18
ret	BELGIAN GP	Spa	24	Roberto Mières	P	2.5 Maserati A6GCM/250F 6		fire	12/15
ret	FRENCH GP	Reims	16	Roberto Mières	P	2.5 Maserati A6GCM/250F 6		engine	11/22
6	BRITISH GP	Silverstone	4	Roberto Mières	P	2.5 Maserati A6GCM/250F 6		3 laps behind	31/31
ret	GERMAN GP	Nürburgring	8	Roberto Mières	P	2.5 Maserati 250F 6		fuel tank leak	17/23
4	SWISS GP	Bremgarten	30	Officine Alfieri Maserati	P	2.5 Maserati 250F 6		2 laps behind	12/16
ret	ITALIAN GP	Monza	24	Officine Alfieri Maserati	P	2.5 Maserati 250F 6		suspension	10/21
4	SPANISH GP	Pedralbes	10	Officine Alfieri Maserati	P	2.5 Maserati 250F 6		1 lap behind	11/22
	1955	Championship position: 7th	Wins: 0	Pole positions: 0	Fastest laps: 0	Points scored: 7			
5	ARGENTINE GP	Buenos Aires	15	Officine Alfieri Maserati	P	2.5 Maserati 250F 6		5 laps behind	16/22
ret	MONACO GP	Monte Carlo	36	Officine Alfieri Maserati	P	2.5 Maserati 250F 6		rear axle	6/22
5*	BELGIAN GP	Spa	24	Officine Alfieri Maserati	P	2.5 Maserati 250F 6		* Behra took over/1 lap behind	11/14
4	DUTCH GP	Zandvoort	16	Officine Alfieri Maserati	P	2.5 Maserati 250F 6		FL/1 lap behind	7/16
ret	BRITISH GP	Aintree	6	Officine Alfieri Maserati	P	2.5 Maserati 250F 6		engine	6/25
7	ITALIAN GP	Monza	28	Officine Alfieri Maserati	P	2.5 Maserati 250F 6		2 laps behind	7/22

GP Starts: 17   GP Wins: 0   Pole positions: 0   Fastest laps: 1   Points: 13

FRANÇOIS MIGAULT

A former Volant Shell winner, Migault seemed to have a promising future when he shone in Formula 3 during the 1970 and '71 seasons with a Tecno. His first Formula 2 races brought fourth place at Albi and fifth at Rouen, before he made his first attempt at Grands Prix with the enthusiastic but naïve Connew project in 1972. François marked time somewhat in 1973 with the F2 Pygmée, before joining compatriots Beltoise and Pescarolo in the Motul-backed BRM team for 1974. Despite making do with the worst of machinery, as befitted the third driver, Migault did well to qualify the car for most of the races, his best result being a fifth place in the International Trophy. Subsequently he scraped a handful of rides in 1975 with Hill and Williams, but nothing of note was achieved before an equally moribund year in Formula 2 with the works Osella in 1976.

Already experienced in sports cars, François had shared a Matra with Jabouille to take third place at Le Mans in 1974, and went one better in 1976, finishing second in the Mirage GR8. Since then he has become a perennial at his local Sarthe circuit, although outright success has so far eluded him (he was still trying in 1998), and in the nineties he was active in the USA, racing a Kudzu-Buick in IMSA.

JOHN MILES

The son of the late thespian Sir Bernard Miles, John chose not to pursue a life in the theatre, gaining numerous victories at club level in his Diva-Ford in 1964. Under the wing of Willment he continued his winning ways in 1965 and received a third-place Grovewood Award.

Scoring nine consecutive wins with the Willment Lotus Elan at the start of 1966, John soon became involved with the works team, racing the GT Europa and F3 Lotus 41 in 1967 and 1968 with tremendous success. A planned season with Lotus in Formula 2 in 1969 never took off, but he did finish third in the Rome GP and fifth at Hockhenheim from three starts before Colin Chapman entrusted him with the task of developing the Lotus 63 4WD car in five Grands Prix.

His reward was a place alongside Jochen Rindt in the Lotus team for the 1970 season, which started well with a fifth place in the Lotus 49C in South Africa, but gradually declined as Miles' apprehension over the fragility of the new Lotus 72 steadily grew. After Rindt's fatal crash at Monza, John was summarily replaced by Reine Wisell and his Grand Prix career was done. He did make a brief appearance for BRM in the non-championship Jochen Rindt Memorial race at Hockenheim the following season, whilst racing for the DART sports car team, but soon retired to concentrate on his new occupation as a motoring journalist, road-testing cars, before returning to Lotus Cars in an engineering capacity.

ANDRÉ MILHOUX

A useful sports and production car driver, Milhoux, in what was his only single-seater appearance of note, took part in the 1956 German Grand Prix as a substitute for André Pilette, who had injured himself in practice.

Milhoux had successfully handled huge Plymouths and Fords in Belgian events and partnered compatriot Paul Frère to win the 2-litre touring car class in the 1953 Mille Miglia, the pair driving a Chrysler – highly unsuitable, one would think, for this event.

Subsequently André moved into pukka sports machines. He finished fifth overall with Seidel in the 1955 Le Mans 24 Hours (taking second place in the 1100–1500 cc class), and fourth in the Paris 1000 Km in 1956 sharing an Equipe National Belge Ferrari with Pilette. He crashed heavily in practice for the 1958 Spa GP driving one of the team's yellow Ferraris but, having been lucky to escape unhurt, quit while he was ahead.

GERHARD MITTER

An outstanding driver, Mitter was an infrequent Grand Prix competitor who surely deserved more opportunities at the highest level, as he showed with his fourth place in de Beaufort's old Porsche in the 1963 German GP. As it was, he had to be content with just the annual outing at the Nürburgring, mainly in the Formula 2 class.

Gerhard was a top Formula Junior driver in the early sixties with his DKW-engined Lotus before joining Porsche in 1964. He was to become a mainstay of the German company's endurance racing programme, winning the Austrian GP in 1966 and the Targa Florio in 1969 and gaining many other fine placings, also becoming three-times European mountain-climb champion between 1966 and 1968.

In 1969 Mitter was also involved in the development of the Dornier-built BMW F2 contender, but he crashed fatally during practice for that year's German GP when, it was thought, a wheel may have come off the car.

MIGAULT, François (F) b 4/12/1944, Le Mans

	1972	Championship position: Unplaced						
	Race	Circuit	No	Entrant	Tyres	Car/Engine	Comment	Q Pos/Entries
dns	BRITISH GP	Brands Hatch	34	Darnvall Connew Racing Team	F	3.0 Connew PC1-Cosworth V8	suspension in practice	(27)/27
ret	AUSTRIAN GP	Österreichring	29	Darnvall Connew Racing Team	F	3.0 Connew PC1-Cosworth V8	rear wishbone mounting point	26/26
	1974	Championship position: Unplaced						
ret	ARGENTINE GP	Buenos Aires	37	Team BRM	F	3.0 BRM P160E V12	water leak	24/26
16	BRAZILIAN GP	Interlagos	37	Team BRM	F	3.0 BRM P160E V12	2 laps behind	23/25
15	SOUTH AFRICAN GP	Kyalami	37	Team BRM	F	3.0 BRM P160E V12	3 laps behind	25/27
ret	SPANISH GP	Jarama	37	Team BRM	F	3.0 BRM P160E V12	engine	23/28
16	BELGIAN GP	Nivelles	37	Team BRM	F	3.0 BRM P160E V12	3 laps behind	25/32
ret	MONACO GP	Monte Carlo	37	Team BRM	F	3.0 BRM P160E V12	brake failure-crashed	=21/28
ret	DUTCH GP	Zandvoort	37	Team BRM	F	3.0 BRM P201 V12	gear linkage	– / –
dns	"		37	Team BRM	F	3.0 BRM P160E V12	practiced car-Pescarolo in race	25/27
14	FRENCH GP	Dijon	37	Team BRM	F	3.0 BRM P160E V12	2 laps behind	22/30
nc	BRITISH GP	Brands Hatch	37	Team BRM	F	3.0 BRM P160E V12	2 pit stops-rear wing/-13 laps	14/34
dnq	GERMAN GP	Nürburgring	37	Team BRM	F	3.0 BRM P160E V12		27/32
ret	ITALIAN GP	Monza	37	Team BRM	F	3.0 BRM P201 V12	gearbox	24/31
	1975	Championship position: Unplaced						
nc	SPANISH GP	Montjuich Park	23	Embassy Racing with Graham Hill	G	3.0 Hill GH1-Cosworth V8	hit Peterson-pit stop/-11 laps	22/26
ret	BELGIAN GP	Zolder	22	Embassy Racing with Graham Hill	G	3.0 Hill GH1-Cosworth V8	rear suspension sub-frame	22/24
dns	FRENCH GP	Paul Ricard	20	Frank Williams Racing Cars	G	3.0 Williams FW03-Cosworth V8	engine in practice	(24)/26

GP Starts: 13   GP Wins: 0   Pole positions: 0   Fastest laps: 0   Points: 0

MILES, John (GB) b 14/6/1943, Islington, London

	1969	Championship position: Unplaced						
	Race	Circuit	No	Entrant	Tyres	Car/Engine	Comment	Q Pos/Entries
ret	FRENCH GP	Clermont Ferrand	14	Gold Leaf Team Lotus	F	3.0 Lotus 63-Cosworth V8	fuel pump belt	12/13
10	BRITISH GP	Silverstone	9	Gold Leaf Team Lotus	F	3.0 Lotus 63-Cosworth V8	pit stop-gearbox/-9 laps	14/17
ret	ITALIAN GP	Monza	6	Gold Leaf Team Lotus	F	3.0 Lotus 63-Cosworth V8	engine	14/15
ret	CANADIAN GP	Mosport Park	3	Gold Leaf Team Lotus	F	3.0 Lotus 63-Cosworth V8	gearbox	11/20
ret	MEXICAN GP	Mexico City	9	Gold Leaf Team Lotus	F	3.0 Lotus 63-Cosworth V8	fuel pump	11/17
	1970	Championship position: 19th= Wins: 0 Pole positions: 0 Fastest laps: 0 Points scored: 2						
5	SOUTH AFRICAN GP	Kyalami	10	Gold Leaf Team Lotus	F	3.0 Lotus 49C-Cosworth V8	1 lap behind	14/24
dnq	SPANISH GP	Jarama	19	Gold Leaf Team Lotus	F	3.0 Lotus 72-Cosworth V8	not seeded	15/22
dnq	"	"	19	Gold Leaf Team Lotus	F	3.0 Lotus 49C-Cosworth V8		– / –
dnq	MONACO GP	Monte Carlo	2	Gold Leaf Team Lotus	F	3.0 Lotus 49C-Cosworth V8	practice only	19/21
dnq	"	"	2T	Gold Leaf Team Lotus	F	3.0 Lotus 72-Cosworth V8		– / –
ret	BELGIAN GP	Spa	21	Gold Leaf Team Lotus	F	3.0 Lotus 72-Cosworth V8	gear selection/tyres	13/18
dns	"		21	Gold Leaf Team Lotus	F	3.0 Lotus 49C-Cosworth V8	practice only-Rindt in race	– / –
7	DUTCH GP	Zandvoort	12	Gold Leaf Team Lotus	F	3.0 Lotus 72-Cosworth V8	2 laps behind	8/24
8	FRENCH GP	Clermont Ferrand	7	Gold Leaf Team Lotus	F	3.0 Lotus 72-Cosworth V8		18/23
ret	BRITISH GP	Brands Hatch	6	Gold Leaf Team Lotus	F	3.0 Lotus 72-Cosworth V8	engine	7/25
ret	GERMAN GP	Hockenheim	16	Gold Leaf Team Lotus	F	3.0 Lotus 72-Cosworth V8	engine	10/25
ret	AUSTRIAN GP	Österreichring	7	Gold Leaf Team Lotus	F	3.0 Lotus 72C-Cosworth V8	front brake shaft	10/24
dns	ITALIAN GP	Monza	24	Gold Leaf Team Lotus	F	3.0 Lotus 72C-Cosworth V8	w/drawn after Rindt's accident	(19)/27

GP Starts: 12   GP Wins: 0   Pole positions: 0   Fastest laps: 0   Points: 2

MILHOUX, André (B) 9/12/1928, Bressoux

	1956	Championship position: Unplaced						
	Race	Circuit	No	Entrant	Tyres	Car/Engine	Comment	Q Pos/Entries
ret	GERMAN GP	Nürburgring	11	Equipe Gordini	E	2.5 Gordini Type 32 8	engine misfire	21/21

GP Starts: 1   GP Wins: 0   Pole positions: 0   Fastest laps: 0   Points: 0

MITTER, Gerhard (D) b 30/8/1935, Schönlinde – d 1/8/1969, Nürburgring Circuit

	1963	Championship position: 12th Wins: 0 Pole positions: 0 Fastest laps: 0 Points scored: 3						
	Race	Circuit	No	Entrant	Tyres	Car/Engine	Comment	Q Pos/Entries
ret	DUTCH GP	Zandvoort	34	Ecurie Maarsbergen	D	1.5 Porsche 718 F4	clutch	16/19
4	GERMAN GP	Nürburgring	26	Ecurie Maarsbergen	D	1.5 Porsche 718 F4		15/25
	1964	Championship position: Unplaced						
9	GERMAN GP	Nürburgring	23	Team Lotus	D	1.5 Lotus 25-Climax V8	1 lap behind	19/24
	1965	Championship position: Unplaced						
ret	GERMAN GP	Nürburgring	3	Team Lotus	D	1.5 Lotus 25-Climax V8	water hose	12/22
	1966	Championship position: Unplaced						
dns	GERMAN GP	Nürburgring	30	Ron Harris Team Lotus	D	1.0 Lotus 44-Cosworth 4 F2	not fully fit after crash at Spa	(11)/30
	1967	Championship position: Unplaced						
ret	GERMAN GP (F2)	Nürburgring	20	Gerhard Mitter	D	1.6 Brabham BT23-Cosworth 4 F2	engine	23/25
	1969	Championship position: Unplaced						
dns	GERMAN GP (F2)	Nürburgring	24	Bayerische Motoren Werke	D	BMW 269-4 F2	lost wheel-fatal accident	(25)/25

GP Starts: 5   GP Wins: 0   Pole positions: 0   Fastest laps: 0   Points: 3

STEFANO MODENA

Modena had served notice in karting that he was a man to watch, and when he finally got into Formula 3 he was soon a front-runner, taking fourth place in the Italian championship in 1986, impressing the F1 fraternity with a superb second place in the Monaco Grand Prix support race, and earning the title of 'European Champion' after victory in the one-off meeting at Imola.

Now with substantial backing, Modena moved straight into F3000 with the Onyx team and he took the championship at the first attempt, winning three races (at Vallelunga, Birmingham and Imola), but it was the way he went about the whole business that marked him as a special talent.

Much was expected of the tousled-haired Italian when he entered Grand Prix racing but after an end-of-season ride with Brabham he was forced to endure a discouraging learning year in 1988 with the uncompetitive EuroBrun before being given a chance to really show what he could do with Brabham in 1989.

He finished in third place at Monaco, but the team lacked the financial resources to progress, and Stefano then marked time until 1991 when he moved to a Tyrrell team newly equipped with Honda power. Things started well with yet another superb display at Monaco, which ended with a broken engine when he lay second behind Senna, and then second place in the next race in Canada, but as the season wore on Modena seemed to lose heart too easily.

It was some surprise when he was signed to drive the Jordan-Yamaha in 1992, and it was to be a troubled season for the team which found the enigmatic Italian temperamentally unsuited to the situation. He scored a point in the last race of the year but was consigned to the wilderness for 1993, racing a BMW in the Italian touring car championship.

All was not lost for Modena, however, his excellent form in the Alfa Romeo T155 during the early part of 1994 gaining the Superturismo driver a passport to the higher-profile DTM late on in the season. He made a sensational debut at AVUS, qualifying third and winning both heats, thoroughly eclipsing the established Alfa aces. Naturally, in light of his drives in the series' final three rounds, Stefano was signed to race for a full DTM/ITC season with hopes high for even greater success. In reality 1995 saw Alfa lost in a technical mire, and in common with his colleagues Modena generally had to play second fiddle to both Mercedes and Opel.

Subsequently Modena, who had harboured hopes of gaining a ride in CART, has been a mainstay of the German Super Touring championship. The 1997 season with the ageing Alfa 155 was a disaster and the arrival of the 156 model the following year rarely allowed him to finish in the top ten, but 1999 saw an upturn in the Italian's fortunes as the 156 at last became a competitive proposition.

MODENA, Stefano (I) b 12/5/1963, Modena

	1987	Championship position: Unplaced						
	Race	Circuit	No	Entrant	Tyres	Car/Engine	Comment	Q Pos/Entries
ret	AUSTRALIAN GP	Adelaide	7	Motor Racing Developments	G	1.5 t/c Brabham BT56-BMW 4	driver exhaustion	15/27
	1988	Championship position: Unplaced						
ret	BRAZILIAN GP	Rio	33	EuroBrun Racing	G	3.5 EuroBrun ER188-Cosworth V8	engine cut out-fuel pump	24/31
nc	SAN MARINO GP	Imola	33	EuroBrun Racing	G	3.5 EuroBrun ER188-Cosworth V8	gearbox trouble/-8 laps	26/31
excl*	MONACO GP	Monte Carlo	33	EuroBrun Racing	G	3.5 EuroBrun ER188-Cosworth V8	*missed weight check	– /30
excl*	MEXICAN GP	Mexico City	33	EuroBrun Racing	G	3.5 EuroBrun ER188-Cosworth V8	*rear wing height infringement	– /30

12	CANADIAN GP	Montreal	33	EuroBrun Racing	G	3.5 EuroBrun ER188-Cosworth V8	3 laps behind	15/31
ret	US GP (DETROIT)	Detroit	33	EuroBrun Racing	G	3.5 EuroBrun ER188-Cosworth V8	spun off	19/31
14	FRENCH GP	Paul Ricard	33	EuroBrun Racing	G	3.5 EuroBrun ER188-Cosworth V8	3 laps behind	20/31
12	BRITISH GP	Silverstone	33	EuroBrun Racing	G	3.5 EuroBrun ER188-Cosworth V8	1 lap behind	20/31
ret	GERMAN GP	Hockenheim	33	EuroBrun Racing	G	3.5 EuroBrun ER188-Cosworth V8	engine	25/31
11	HUNGARIAN GP	Hungaroring	33	EuroBrun Racing	G	3.5 EuroBrun ER188-Cosworth V8	4 laps behind	26/31
dnq	BELGIAN GP	Spa	33	EuroBrun Racing	G	3.5 EuroBrun ER188-Cosworth V8		29/31
dnq	ITALIAN GP	Monza	33	EuroBrun Racing	G	3.5 EuroBrun ER188-Cosworth V8		30/31
dnq	PORTUGUESE GP	Estoril	33	EuroBrun Racing	G	3.5 EuroBrun ER188-Cosworth V8		29/31
13	SPANISH GP	Jerez	33	EuroBrun Racing	G	3.5 EuroBrun ER188-Cosworth V8	2 laps behind	26/31
dnq	JAPANESE GP	Suzuka	33	EuroBrun Racing	G	3.5 EuroBrun ER188-Cosworth V8		30/31
ret	AUSTRALIAN GP	Adelaide	33	EuroBrun Racing	G	3.5 EuroBrun ER188-Cosworth V8	driveshaft	20/31

1989   Championship position: 16th=   Wins: 0   Pole positions: 0   Fastest laps: 0   Points scored: 4

ret	BRAZILIAN GP	Rio	8	Motor Racing Developments	P	3.5 Brabham BT58-Judd V8	driveshaft-c.v.joint	14/38
ret	SAN MARINO GP	Imola	8	Motor Racing Developments	P	3.5 Brabham BT58-Judd V8	spun into barrier	17/39
3	MONACO GP	Monte Carlo	8	Motor Racing Developments	P	3.5 Brabham BT58-Judd V8	1 lap behind	8/38
10	MEXICAN GP	Mexico City	8	Motor Racing Developments	P	3.5 Brabham BT58-Judd V8	1 lap behind	9/39
ret	US GP (PHOENIX)	Phoenix	8	Motor Racing Developments	P	3.5 Brabham BT58-Judd V8	brakes	7/39
ret	CANADIAN GP	Montreal	8	Motor Racing Developments	P	3.5 Brabham BT58-Judd V8	collision with Martini	7/39
ret	FRENCH GP	Paul Ricard	8	Motor Racing Developments	P	3.5 Brabham BT58-Judd V8	engine	22/39
ret	BRITISH GP	Silverstone	8	Motor Racing Developments	P	3.5 Brabham BT58-Judd V8	engine	14/39
ret	GERMAN GP	Hockenheim	8	Motor Racing Developments	P	3.5 Brabham BT58-Judd V8	engine	16/39
11	HUNGARIAN GP	Hungaroring	8	Motor Racing Developments	P	3.5 Brabham BT58-Judd V8	damaged nose cone/-1 lap	8/39
ret	BELGIAN GP	Spa	8	Motor Racing Developments	P	3.5 Brabham BT58-Judd V8	started from pit lane/handling	8/39
excl*	ITALIAN GP	Monza	8	Motor Racing Developments	P	3.5 Brabham BT58-Judd V8	*missed weight check	–/39
14	PORTUGUESE GP	Estoril	8	Motor Racing Developments	P	3.5 Brabham BT58-Judd V8	shock absorber/misfire/-2 laps	11/39
ret	SPANISH GP	Jerez	8	Motor Racing Developments	P	3.5 Brabham BT58-Judd V8	engine cut out-electrics	12/38
8	AUSTRALIAN GP	Adelaide	8	Motor Racing Developments	P	3.5 Brabham BT58-Judd V8	6 laps behind	8/39

1990   Championship position: 16th=   Wins: 0   Pole positions: 0   Fastest laps: 0   Points scored: 2

5	US GP (PHOENIX)	Phoenix	8	Motor Racing Developments	P	3.5 Brabham BT58-Judd V8	went up escape road	10/35
ret	BRAZILIAN GP	Interlagos	8	Motor Racing Developments	P	3.5 Brabham BT58-Judd V8	spun off	12/35
ret	SAN MARINO GP	Imola	8	Motor Racing Developments	P	3.5 Brabham BT59-Judd V8	brakes	15/34
ret	MONACO GP	Monte Carlo	8	Motor Racing Developments	P	3.5 Brabham BT59-Judd V8	transmission	14/35
7	CANADIAN GP	Montreal	8	Motor Racing Developments	P	3.5 Brabham BT59-Judd V8	2 laps behind	10/35
11	MEXICAN GP	Mexico City	8	Motor Racing Developments	P	3.5 Brabham BT59-Judd V8	1 lap behind	10/35
13	FRENCH GP	Paul Ricard	8	Motor Racing Developments	P	3.5 Brabham BT59-Judd V8	2 laps behind	20/35
9	BRITISH GP	Silverstone	8	Motor Racing Developments	P	3.5 Brabham BT59-Judd V8	spin-pit stop/2 laps behind	20/35
ret	GERMAN GP	Hockenheim	8	Motor Racing Developments	P	3.5 Brabham BT59-Judd V8	clutch on startline	17/35
ret	HUNGARIAN GP	Hungaroring	8	Motor Racing Developments	P	3.5 Brabham BT59-Judd V8	engine	20/35
17/ret	BELGIAN GP	Spa	8	Motor Racing Developments	P	3.5 Brabham BT59-Judd V8	engine/5 laps behind	13/33
ret	ITALIAN GP	Monza	8	Motor Racing Developments	P	3.5 Brabham BT59-Judd V8	engine	17/33
ret	PORTUGUESE GP	Estoril	8	Motor Racing Developments	P	3.5 Brabham BT59-Judd V8	gearbox	24/33
ret	SPANISH GP	Jerez	8	Motor Racing Developments	P	3.5 Brabham BT59-Judd V8	collision with Tarquini	25/33
ret	JAPANESE GP	Suzuka	8	Motor Racing Developments	P	3.5 Brabham BT59-Judd V8	spun off	22/30
12	AUSTRALIAN GP	Adelaide	8	Motor Racing Developments	P	3.5 Brabham BT59-Judd V8	pit stop-tyres/4 laps behind	17/30

1991   Championship position: 8th   Wins: 0   Pole positions: 0   Fastest laps: 0   Points scored: 10

4	US GP (PHOENIX)	Phoenix	4	Braun Tyrrell Honda	P	3.5 Tyrrell 020-Honda V10		11/34
ret	BRAZILIAN GP	Interlagos	4	Braun Tyrrell Honda	P	3.5 Tyrrell 020-Honda V10	gearshift	9/34
ret	SAN MARINO GP	Imola	4	Braun Tyrrell Honda	P	3.5 Tyrrell 020-Honda V10	transmission	6/34
ret	MONACO GP	Monte Carlo	4	Braun Tyrrell Honda	P	3.5 Tyrrell 020-Honda V10	lay 2nd for 42 laps/engine	2/34
2	CANADIAN GP	Montreal	4	Braun Tyrrell Honda	P	3.5 Tyrrell 020-Honda V10		9/34
11	MEXICAN GP	Mexico City	4	Braun Tyrrell Honda	P	3.5 Tyrrell 020-Honda V10	3 tyre stops/2 laps behind	8/34
ret	FRENCH GP	Magny Cours	4	Braun Tyrrell Honda	P	3.5 Tyrrell 020-Honda V10	gearbox	11/34
7	BRITISH GP	Silverstone	4	Braun Tyrrell Honda	P	3.5 Tyrrell 020-Honda V10	1 lap behind	10/34
13	GERMAN GP	Hockenheim	4	Braun Tyrrell Honda	P	3.5 Tyrrell 020-Honda V10	3 tyre stops/4 laps behind	14/34
12	HUNGARIAN GP	Hungaroring	4	Braun Tyrrell Honda	P	3.5 Tyrrell 020-Honda V10	2 laps behind	8/34
ret	BELGIAN GP	Spa	4	Braun Tyrrell Honda	P	3.5 Tyrrell 020-Honda V10	oil leak/fire	10/34
ret	ITALIAN GP	Monza	4	Braun Tyrrell Honda	P	3.5 Tyrrell 020-Honda V10	engine	13/34
ret	PORTUGUESE GP	Estoril	4	Braun Tyrrell Honda	P	3.5 Tyrrell 020-Honda V10	engine	12/34
16	SPANISH GP	Jerez	4	Braun Tyrrell Honda	P	3.5 Tyrrell 020-Honda V10	3 laps behind	14/33
6	JAPANESE GP	Suzuka	4	Braun Tyrrell Honda	P	3.5 Tyrrell 020-Honda V10	1 lap behind	14/31
10	AUSTRALIAN GP	Adelaide	4	Braun Tyrrell Honda	P	3.5 Tyrrell 020-Honda V10	race stopped at 14 laps	9/32

1992   Championship position: 17th=   Wins: 0   Pole positions: 0   Fastest laps: 0   Points scored: 1

dnq	SOUTH AFRICAN GP	Kyalami	32	Sasol Jordan Yamaha	G	3.5 Jordan 192-Yamaha V12		29/30
ret	MEXICAN GP	Mexico City	32	Sasol Jordan Yamaha	G	3.5 Jordan 192-Yamaha V12	started from pitlane/gearbox	15/30
ret	BRAZILIAN GP	Interlagos	32	Sasol Jordan Yamaha	G	3.5 Jordan 192-Yamaha V12	gearbox	12/31
dnq	SPANISH GP	Barcelona	32	Sasol Jordan Yamaha	G	3.5 Jordan 192-Yamaha V12		29/32
ret	SAN MARINO GP	Imola	32	Sasol Jordan Yamaha	G	3.5 Jordan 192-Yamaha V12	started from pitlane/gearbox	23/32
ret	MONACO GP	Monte Carlo	32	Sasol Jordan Yamaha	G	3.5 Jordan 192-Yamaha V12	crashed at Casino square	21/32
ret	CANADIAN GP	Montreal	32	Sasol Jordan Yamaha	G	3.5 Jordan 192-Yamaha V12	started from back/ransmission	17/32
ret	FRENCH GP	Magny Cours	32	Sasol Jordan Yamaha	G	3.5 Jordan 192-Yamaha V12	engine	20/30
ret	BRITISH GP	Silverstone	32	Sasol Jordan Yamaha	G	3.5 Jordan 192-Yamaha V12	engine	23/32
dnq	GERMAN GP	Hockenheim	32	Sasol Jordan Yamaha	G	3.5 Jordan 192-Yamaha V12		27/32
ret	HUNGARIAN GP	Hungaroring	32	Sasol Jordan Yamaha	G	3.5 Jordan 192-Yamaha V12	hit by Grouillard	24/31
15	BELGIAN GP	Spa	32	Sasol Jordan Yamaha	G	3.5 Jordan 192-Yamaha V12	2 laps behind	17/30
dnq	ITALIAN GP	Monza	32	Sasol Jordan Yamaha	G	3.5 Jordan 192-Yamaha V12		28/28
13	PORTUGUESE GP	Estoril	32	Sasol Jordan Yamaha	G	3.5 Jordan 192-Yamaha V12	3 laps behind	24/26
7	JAPANESE GP	Suzuka	32	Sasol Jordan Yamaha	G	3.5 Jordan 192-Yamaha V12	1 lap behind	17/26
6	AUSTRALIAN GP	Adelaide	32	Sasol Jordan Yamaha	G	3.5 Jordan 192-Yamaha V12	1 lap behind	15/26

GP Starts: 70   GP Wins: 0   Pole positions: 0   Fastest laps: 0   Points: 17

ANDREA MONTERMINI

When Montermini crashed his Simtek heavily during practice for the 1994 Spanish GP and was taken to hospital with relatively minor ankle and foot injuries, a number of observers thought that might be the last Grand Prix racing would see of the little Italian, rather cruelly commenting that he was not good enough to take part at this exalted level. Of course he did return, albeit only with back-of-the-grid strugglers Pacific and Forti, and succeeded in winning the respect of the Formula 1 paddock at large, with his racer's appetite remaining undimmed despite overwhelming odds.

A closer look at Andrea's racing history reveals a good deal of success during the early stages of his career, which began in 1987 in Italian Formula Alfa Boxer. Fourth place in the 1988 Italian F3 standings was supplemented by second place in the Monaco F3 race the following year.

Montermini then spent three seasons in European F3000 between 1990 and 1992: his first year, with Madgwick, was promising, the second, in a difficult-to-tame Ralt, perhaps less so. However, the Italian's final season in the formula, though beset by financial problems which saw him swap teams, brought him second place in the championship with three wins.

In 1993 Andrea caused a stir in Indy Car circles when he arrived in Detroit to drive a year-old Lola for the Euromotorsports team. Sixth place in practice was impressive, and fourth at the finish an outstanding achievement. Since the collapse of Forti in mid-1996 Montermini has pursued a career in sports cars, initially impressing with Gianpiero Moretti's Ferrari in 1997. Wins in the Professional Racing Series at Lime Rock, Pikes Peak Raceway and Sebring led to a Nissan works drive at Le Mans in 1998, where, teamed with Lammers and Comas, he took sixth place, a feat which he repeated a year later at the wheel of a Courage-Nissan in company with fellow countrymen Caffi and Schiattarella.

The diminutive Italian joined Dan Gurney's underperforming CART team for a four-race spell towards the end of 1999, scoring a couple of points on his debut in Vancouver, while no doubt hoping to find a full-time drive in this increasingly competitive category.

MONTERMINI, Andrea (I) b 30/5/1964, Sassuolo

	1994	Championship position: Unplaced							
	Race	Circuit	No	Entrant	Tyres	Car/Engine	Comment		Q Pos/Entries
dnq	SPANISH GP	Barcelona	32	MTV Simtek Ford	G	3.5 Simtek S941-Ford HB V8	injured in practice accident		27/27
	1995	Championship position: Unplaced							
9	BRAZILIAN GP	Interlagos	17	Pacific Grand Prix Ltd	G	3.0 Pacific PR02-Ford ED V8	6 laps behind		22/26
ret	ARGENTINE GP	Buenos Aires	17	Pacific Grand Prix Ltd	G	3.0 Pacific PR02-Ford ED V8	suspension damage		22/26
ret	SAN MARINO GP	Imola	17	Pacific Grand Prix Ltd	G	3.0 Pacific PR02-Ford ED V8	gearbox		24/26
ret/dns	SPANISH GP	Barcelona	17	Pacific Grand Prix Ltd	G	3.0 Pacific PR02-Ford ED V8	gearbox before start		(23)/26
dsq	MONACO GP	Monte Carlo	17	Pacific Grand Prix Ltd	G	3.0 Pacific PR02-Ford ED V8	jump start-ignored black flag		25/26
ret	CANADIAN GP	Montreal	17	Pacific Grand Prix Ltd	G	3.0 Pacific PR02-Ford ED V8	gearbox		21/24
nc	FRENCH GP	Magny Cours	17	Pacific Grand Prix Ltd	G	3.0 Pacific PR02-Ford ED V8	10 laps behind		21/24
ret	BRITISH GP	Silverstone	17	Pacific Grand Prix Ltd	G	3.0 Pacific PR02-Ford ED V8	spun off		24/24
8	GERMAN GP	Hockenheim	17	Pacific Grand Prix Ltd	G	3.0 Pacific PR02-Ford ED V8	3 laps behind		23/24
12	HUNGARIAN GP	Hungaroring	17	Pacific Grand Prix Ltd	G	3.0 Pacific PR02-Ford ED V8	4 laps behind		22/24
ret	BELGIAN GP	Spa	17	Pacific Grand Prix Ltd	G	3.0 Pacific PR02-Ford ED V8	fuel pressure		21/24
ret/dns	ITALIAN GP	Monza	17	Pacific Grand Prix Ltd	G	3.0 Pacific PR02-Ford ED V8	accident at first start		(21)/24
ret	PORTUGUESE GP	Estoril	17	Pacific Grand Prix Ltd	G	3.0 Pacific PR02-Ford ED V8	gearbox		21/24
ret	EUROPEAN GP	Nürburgring	17	Pacific Grand Prix Ltd	G	3.0 Pacific PR02-Ford ED V8	out of fuel		20/24
ret	PACIFIC GP	T.I. Circuit	17	Pacific Grand Prix Ltd	G	3.0 Pacific PR02-Ford ED V8	gearbox		23/24
ret	JAPANESE GP	Suzuka	17	Pacific Grand Prix Ltd	G	3.0 Pacific PR02-Ford ED V8	spun off		20/24
ret	AUSTRALIAN GP	Adelaide	17	Pacific Grand Prix Ltd	G	3.0 Pacific PR02-Ford ED V8	gearbox		22/24
	1996	Championship position: Unplaced							
dnq	AUSTRALIAN GP	Melbourne	23	Forti Grand Prix	G	3.0 Forti FG01 95B-Ford Zetec R V8	not within 107% of pole		22/22
ret	BRAZILIAN GP	Interlagos	23	Forti Grand Prix	G	3.0 Forti FG01 95B-Ford Zetec R V8	4 laps behind		20/22
10	ARGENTINE GP	Buenos Aires	23	Forti Grand Prix	G	3.0 Forti FG01 95B-Ford Zetec R V8	3 laps behind		22/22
dnq	EUROPEAN GP	Nürburgring	23	Forti Grand Prix	G	3.0 Forti FG01 95B-Ford Zetec R V8	not within 107% of pole		21/22
dnq	SAN MARINO GP	Imola	23	Forti Grand Prix	G	3.0 Forti FG0-Ford Zetec R V8	not within 107% of pole		22/22
dns	MONACO GP	Monte Carlo	23	Forti Grand Prix	G	3.0 Forti FG03-Ford Zetec R V8	accident in warm up		22/22
dnq	SPANISH GP	Barcelona	23	Forti Grand Prix	G	3.0 Forti FG03-Ford Zetec R V8			22/22
ret	CANADIAN GP	Montreal	23	Forti Grand Prix	G	3.0 Forti FG03-Ford Zetec R V8	loose ballast		22/22
ret	FRENCH GP	Magny Cours	23	Forti Grand Prix	G	3.0 Forti FG03-Ford Zetec R V8	electrics		21/22
dnq	BRITISH GP	Silverstone	23	Forti Grand Prix	G	3.0 Forti FG03-Ford Zetec R V8			21/22
dnp	GERMAN GP	Hockenheim	23	Forti Grand Prix	G	3.0 Forti FG01 95B-Ford Zetec R V8	cars did not practice		–/–

GP Starts: 19 (21) GP Wins: 0 Pole positions: 0 Fastest laps: 0 Points: 0

MONTGOMERIE-CHARRINGTON, Robin (GB) b 22/6/1915, London

	1952	Championship position: Unplaced							
	Race	Circuit	No	Entrant	Tyres	Car/Engine	Comment		Q Pos/Entries
ret	BELGIAN GP	Spa	40	Robin Montgomerie-Charrington	D	2.0 Aston Butterworth F4	misfire		15/22

GP Starts: 1 GP Wins: 0 Pole positions: 0 Fastest laps: 0 Points: 0

ROBERT MONTGOMERIE-CHARRINGTON

Popularly known as 'Monty', this enthusiastic amateur raced an 1100 cc JAP-engined Cooper, but in truth was no match for the leading exponents such as Eric Brandon and Alan Brown, who could be relied upon to extract the maximum potential from these extremely rapid little rear-engined machines.

Another of his F3 competitors was Bill Aston, who set about building his Formula 2 contender, the Aston-Butterworth, for the 1952 season. 'Monty' became involved and duly purchased one of these machines, which was finished in pale blue livery. This was the national racing colour of the United States, and apparently reflected the financial input of an American benefactor.

Montgomerie-Charrington fared no better than Aston during the machines' short racing history, his only result of note being third place in the Grand Prix des Frontières at Chimay despite coasting to a halt when out of fuel on the last lap. Before the 1952 season was out, 'Monty' had abandoned his racing activities and emigrated to the USA.

GIANNI MORBIDELLI

When Gianni set foot on the podium for the first time in Adelaide at the end of 1995 having claimed a hugely popular third place in the Footwork-Hart, he could look back with satisfaction on a job well done, but faced the prospect of no further Grand Prix employment. It was a situation which the polite and personable Italian had known before, but it was galling for him nonetheless to have to settle for a testing contract with Jordan before a similar role with Ferrari led to another Grand Prix opportunity with Sauber.

With a racing background (his family produced World Championship-winning motor cycles), Morbidelli raced karts from 1981 to 1986 before moving into Italian F3. Although he was certainly quick he was prone to accidents, which spoiled his 1988 season, but the following year he deservedly claimed the crown with his Forti Corse Dallara, earning a testing contract with Ferrari.

The 1990 season saw him make a brief unscheduled Grand Prix debut for Dallara in place of the indisposed Pirro, before he concentrated on his planned F3000 campaign with Forti, which got off to a slow start. Once he got to grips with the Lola he scored a fine win at Enna and, with Paolo Barilla out of favour at Minardi, Gianni finished the season back in Formula 1 with the luxury of a contract in his pocket for a full season with the Faenza team (and Ferrari power) in 1991. The campaign failed to live up to expectations, but Gianni impressed enough for Ferrari to draft him in to replace the departed Prost in Australia, where he finished sixth in the rain-shortened race to earn a priceless half-point.

He returned to Minardi in 1992, but the season was spent in the mire once more as they struggled to develop their Lamborghini-powered car. Without the necessary sponsorship to retain his place, Morbidelli then found himself dumped and was left to race in the Italian touring car championship with an Alfa Romeo. Luckily Jack Oliver had faith in Morbidelli's abilities and drafted him into his Footwork team to renew his Grand Prix career in 1994. With customer Cosworth power the team were never in the hunt for major honours, but Gianni scored three priceless points to help keep his seat as pay-drivers hovered in the hope Oliver would take their money.

So highly did Oliver think of Morbidelli that he retained his services in 1995 as team leader, no doubt assisted by the arrival of Taki Inoue, who brought much-needed finance. Sixth place in Canada was a bonus, but within another race Morbidelli was forced onto the sidelines as Max Papis bought his way in. Fortunately for Oliver, he was able to recall Gianni for the final three races and was of course rewarded with that podium finish which was the team's best result since 1989.

Morbidelli's reinstatement to the Grand Prix ranks with Sauber in 1997 came after Nicola Larini's bust-up with the team and Gianni was to find out that the number two seat in the Swiss outfit was no easy berth. Any chance of making an impression was stymied when he broke his arm badly in a testing accident, which forced him out for three races, and the season ended with another injury after a practice crash in Japan.

Looking for a fresh challenge in 1998, Gianni turned to touring cars, driving for Volvo in the BTCC. By his own admission, he found it difficult to adapt to front-wheel drive but he was not the first ex-Grand Prix driver to fail to adjust to the demands of this specialised form of racing.

MORBIDELLI, Gianni (I) b 13/1/1968, Pesaro, nr Rimini

1990 — Championship position: Unplaced

	Race	Circuit	No	Entrant	Tyres	Car/Engine	Comment	Q Pos/Entries
dnq	US GP (PHOENIX)	Phoenix	21	Scuderia Italia	P	3.5 BMS Dallara F190-Cosworth V8		29/35
14	BRAZILIAN GP	Interlagos	21	Scuderia Italia	P	3.5 BMS Dallara F190-Cosworth V8	pit stop-jammed throttle/-7 laps	16/35
ret	JAPANESE GP	Suzuka	24	SCM Minardi Team	P	3.5 Minardi M190-Cosworth V8	spun off	20/30
ret	AUSTRALIAN GP	Adelaide	24	SCM Minardi Team	P	3.5 Minardi M190-Cosworth V8	gearbox	20/30

1991 — Championship position: 24th   Wins: 0   Pole positions: 0   Fastest laps: 0   Points scored: 0.5

	Race	Circuit	No	Entrant	Tyres	Car/Engine	Comment	Q Pos/Entries
ret	US GP (PHOENIX)	Phoenix	24	SCM Minardi Team	G	3.5 Minardi M191-Ferrari V12	gearbox	26/34
8	BRAZILIAN GP	Interlagos	24	SCM Minardi Team	G	3.5 Minardi M191-Ferrari V12	2 laps behind	21/34
ret	SAN MARINO GP	Imola	24	SCM Minardi Team	G	3.5 Minardi M191-Ferrari V12	gearbox	8/34
ret	MONACO GP	Monte Carlo	24	SCM Minardi Team	G	3.5 Minardi M191-Ferrari V12	gearbox	17/34
ret	CANADIAN GP	Montreal	24	SCM Minardi Team	G	3.5 Minardi M191-Ferrari V12	spun off	15/34
7	MEXICAN GP	Mexico City	24	SCM Minardi Team	G	3.5 Minardi M191-Ferrari V12	1 lap behind	23/34
ret	FRENCH GP	Magny Cours	24	SCM Minardi Team	G	3.5 Minardi M191-Ferrari V12	spun off	10/34
11	BRITISH GP	Silverstone	24	SCM Minardi Team	G	3.5 Minardi M191-Ferrari V12	2 laps behind	20/34
ret	GERMAN GP	Hockenheim	24	SCM Minardi Team	G	3.5 Minardi M191-Ferrari V12	differential	19/34
13	HUNGARIAN GP	Hungaroring	24	SCM Minardi Team	G	3.5 Minardi M191-Ferrari V12	2 laps behind	23/24
ret	BELGIAN GP	Spa	24	SCM Minardi Team	G	3.5 Minardi M191-Ferrari V12	clutch	19/34
9	ITALIAN GP	Monza	24	SCM Minardi Team	G	3.5 Minardi M191-Ferrari V12	1 lap behind	17/34
9	PORTUGUESE GP	Estoril	24	SCM Minardi Team	G	3.5 Minardi M191-Ferrari V12	1 lap behind	13/34
14/ret	SPANISH GP	Barcelona	24	SCM Minardi Team	G	3.5 Minardi M191-Ferrari V12	spun off	16/33
ret	JAPANESE GP	Suzuka	24	SCM Minardi Team	G	3.5 Minardi M191-Ferrari V12	wheel bearing	8/31
6*	AUSTRALIAN GP	Adelaide	27	Scuderia Ferrari SpA	G	3.5 Fiat Ferrari 643 V12	shortened race/*half points only	8/32

1992 — Championship position: Unplaced

	Race	Circuit	No	Entrant	Tyres	Car/Engine	Comment	Q Pos/Entries
ret	SOUTH AFRICAN GP	Kyalami	24	Minardi Team	G	3.5 Minardi M191B-Lamborghini V12	engine	19/30
ret	MEXICAN GP	Mexico City	24	Minardi Team	G	3.5 Minardi M191B-Lamborghini V12	spun off	21/30
7	BRAZILIAN GP	Interlagos	24	Minardi Team	G	3.5 Minardi M191B-Lamborghini V12	2 laps behind	23/31
ret	SPANISH GP	Barcelona	24	Minardi Team	G	3.5 Minardi M191B-Lamborghini V12	handling	25/32
ret	SAN MARINO GP	Imola	24	Minardi Team	G	3.5 Minardi M192-Lamborghini V12	transmission	21/32
ret	MONACO GP	Monte Carlo	24	Minardi Team	G	3.5 Minardi M192-Lamborghini V12	flat battery	12/32
11	CANADIAN GP	Montreal	24	Minardi Team	G	3.5 Minardi M192-Lamborghini V12	2 laps behind	13/32
8	FRENCH GP	Magny Cours	24	Minardi Team	G	3.5 Minardi M192-Lamborghini V12	agg of two parts/1 lap behind	16/30
17/ret	BRITISH GP	Silverstone	24	Minardi Team	G	3.5 Minardi M192-Lamborghini V12	engine/6 laps behind	25/32
12	GERMAN GP	Hockenheim	24	Minardi Team	G	3.5 Minardi M192-Lamborghini V12	1 lap behind	26/32
dnq	HUNGARIAN GP	Hungaroring	24	Minardi Team	G	3.5 Minardi M192-Lamborghini V12		27/31
16	BELGIAN GP	Spa	24	Minardi Team	G	3.5 Minardi M192-Lamborghini V12	2 laps behind	23/30
ret	ITALIAN GP	Monza	24	Minardi Team	G	3.5 Minardi M192-Lamborghini V12	engine	12/28
14	PORTUGUESE GP	Estoril	24	Minardi Team	G	3.5 Minardi M192-Lamborghini V12	3 laps behind	18/26
14	JAPANESE GP	Suzuka	24	Minardi Team	G	3.5 Minardi M192-Lamborghini V12	2 laps behind	14/26
10	AUSTRALIAN GP	Adelaide	24	Minardi Team	G	3.5 Minardi M192-Lamborghini V12	2 laps behind	16/26

1994 — Championship position: 22   Wins: 0   Pole positions: 0   Fastest laps: 0   Points scored: 3

	Race	Circuit	No	Entrant	Tyres	Car/Engine	Comment	Q Pos/Entries
ret	BRAZILIAN GP	Interlagos	10	Footwork Ford	G	3.5 Footwork FA15-Ford HB V8	gearbox	6/28
ret	PACIFIC GP	T.I. Circuit	10	Footwork Ford	G	3.5 Footwork FA15-Ford HB V8	engine	13/28
ret	SAN MARINO GP	Imola	10	Footwork Ford	G	3.5 Footwork FA15-Ford HB V8	engine	11/28
ret	MONACO GP	Monte Carlo	10	Footwork Ford	G	3.5 Footwork FA15-Ford HB V8	collision-Martini on lap 1	7/24
ret	SPANISH GP	Barcelona	10	Footwork Ford	G	3.5 Footwork FA15-Ford HB V8	fuel filter	15/27
ret	CANADIAN GP	Montreal	10	Footwork Ford	G	3.5 Footwork FA15-Ford HB V8	engine	11/27
ret	FRENCH GP	Magny Cours	10	Footwork Ford	G	3.5 Footwork FA15-Ford HB V8	collision with Panis	22/28
ret	BRITISH GP	Silverstone	10	Footwork Ford	G	3.5 Footwork FA15-Ford HB V8	split fuel pipe	16/28
5	GERMAN GP	Hockenheim	10	Footwork Ford	G	3.5 Footwork FA15-Ford HB V8		16/28
ret	HUNGARIAN GP	Hungaroring	10	Footwork Ford	G	3.5 Footwork FA15-Ford HB V8	collision with de Cesaris	19/28
6*	BELGIAN GP	Spa	10	Footwork Ford	G	3.5 Footwork FA15-Ford HB V8	1 lap behind	14/28
ret	ITALIAN GP	Monza	10	Footwork Ford	G	3.5 Footwork FA15-Ford HB V8	collision with Zanardi	17/28
9	PORTUGUESE GP	Estoril	10	Footwork Ford	G	3.5 Footwork FA15-Ford HB V8	1 lap behind	16/28
11	EUROPEAN GP	Jerez	10	Footwork Ford	G	3.5 Footwork FA15-Ford HB V8	1 lap behind	8/28
ret	JAPANESE GP	Suzuka	10	Footwork Ford	G	3.5 Footwork FA15-Ford HB V8	crashed in rainstorm	12/28
ret	AUSTRALIAN GP	Adelaide	10	Footwork Ford	G	3.5 Footwork FA15-Ford HB V8	oil leak	21/28

1995 — Championship position: 14th=   Wins: 0   Pole positions: 0   Fastest laps: 0   Points scored: 5

	Race	Circuit	No	Entrant	Tyres	Car/Engine	Comment	Q Pos/Entries
ret	BRAZILIAN GP	Interlagos	9	Footwork Hart	G	3.0 Footwork FA16-Hart V8	fuel pump	13/26
ret	ARGENTINE GP	Buenos Aires	9	Footwork Hart	G	3.0 Footwork FA16-Hart V8	electrics	12/26
13	SAN MARINO GP	Imola	9	Footwork Hart	G	3.0 Footwork FA16-Hart V8	4 laps behind	11/26
11	SPANISH GP	Barcelona	9	Footwork Hart	G	3.0 Footwork FA16-Hart V8	2 laps behind	14/26
9	MONACO GP	Monte Carlo	9	Footwork Hart	G	3.0 Footwork FA16-Hart V8	4 laps behind	13/26
6	CANADIAN GP	Montreal	9	Footwork Hart	G	3.0 Footwork FA16-Hart V8	1 lap behind	13/24
14	FRENCH GP	Magny Cours	9	Footwork Hart	G	3.0 Footwork FA16-Hart V8	3 laps behind	16/24
ret	PACIFIC GP	T.I. Circuit	9	Footwork Hart	G	3.0 Footwork FA16-Hart V8	engine	19/24
ret	JAPANESE GP	Suzuka	9	Footwork Hart	G	3.0 Footwork FA16-Hart V8	spun off	15/24
3	AUSTRALIAN GP	Adelaide	9	Footwork Hart	G	3.0 Footwork FA16-Hart V8	2 laps behind	13/24

1997 — Championship position: Unplaced

	Race	Circuit	No	Entrant	Tyres	Car/Engine	Comment	Q Pos/Entries
14	SPANISH GP	Barcelona	17	Red Bull Sauber Petronas	G	3.0 Sauber C16-Petronas V10	2 laps behind	13/22
10	CANADIAN GP	Montreal	17	Red Bull Sauber Petronas	G	3.0 Sauber C16-Petronas V10	1 lap behind	18/22
ret	HUNGARIAN GP	Hungaroring	17	Red Bull Sauber Petronas	G	3.0 Sauber C16-Petronas V10	engine	15/22
9*	BELGIAN GP	Spa	17	Red Bull Sauber Petronas	G	3.0 Sauber C16-Petronas V10	*3rd place car dsq	13/22
12	ITALIAN GP	Monza	17	Red Bull Sauber Petronas	G	3.0 Sauber C16-Petronas V10	1 lap behind	18/22
9	AUSTRIAN GP	A1-Ring	17	Red Bull Sauber Petronas	G	3.0 Sauber C16-Petronas V10		13/22
9	LUXEMBOURG GP	Nürburgring	17	Red Bull Sauber Petronas	G	3.0 Sauber C16-Petronas V10	1 lap behind	19/22
dns	JAPANESE GP	Suzuka	17	Red Bull Sauber Petronas	G	3.0 Sauber C16-Petronas V10	practice accident-hurt wrist	(18)/22

GP Starts: 67   GP Wins: 0   Pole positions: 0   Fastest laps: 0   Points: 8.5

ROBERTO MORENO

I doubt if there is a driver featured in this book with more resilience than Roberto Moreno. Over the past two decades plenty of talented drivers have, at best, seen their careers end up in racing cul-de-sacs or found themselves with no drives at all. The Brazilian has faced both these hurdles with seemingly endless regularity, but has still managed, by a combination of unquenchable optimism, huge application and no little ability, to remain much in demand.

A childhood friend and karting companion of Nelson Piquet, Roberto followed the future World Champion to Europe in 1979; he soon made a big impact in a Royale, and then in 1980 won 15 races and the British FF1600 championship in a Van Diemen. A testing contract with Lotus gave Moreno the lifeline to sustain a Formula 3 career, while a victory in the Australian GP with a Ralt (beating Piquet and Jones) at the end of 1981 raised his profile greatly. He started 1982 winning in Formula Atlantic in the USA before having a disastrous outing for Lotus at Zandvoort, where he failed to qualify, which handicapped his career for a number of years. In 1984 he finished second to team-mate Thackwell in the Formula 2 championship, but a chance of a Formula 1 return with Toleman foundered when the team failed to tie up a tyre deal. This led Roberto to try his hand at Indy Car racing with Rick Galles, and while results were disappointing the little Brazilian certainly impressed.

Returning to Europe in 1987, Moreno was back with Ralt in F3000, but his luck was out. Leading round after round, his car always seemed to hit trouble and he only managed to win one race, at Enna. Fortune did smile with a return to Grands Prix with the little AGS team which yielded a point in the Australian GP, but with no chance of racing with them in 1988 due to a lack of funds Moreno was forced to stay in F3000, and showed his talent by clinching the championship with a virtually unsponsored Reynard, winning four rounds.

Buoyed by a testing contract with Ferrari, Roberto took up a drive with Coloni, then joined EuroBrun, only for the team to fold. Dramatically, after a run of non-qualifications, he was then given the Benetton seat in place of the injured Nannini, and a sensational debut in Japan saw him finish second to team-mate Piquet and gain a well-earned contract for 1991. His big season was something of an anti-climax, however, and when Michael Schumacher was snatched from Jordan, Roberto found himself turfed out of the team, ironically after his best race of the year at Spa. After seeing out the season with Jordan and Minardi, Moreno was back at square one in 1992, with the hapless Andrea Moda outfit, though he did brilliantly to qualify the car at Monaco. When the team were finally thrown out of the championship Roberto was left with no option but to find a ride in Italian touring cars, but in 1993 he was enjoying his racing again with an Alfa in the French Supertourisme championship.

It was quite a surprise when it was announced that Roberto would partner Pedro Diniz in the new Forti Corse F1 team in 1995, but the all-Brazilian driver pairing were forced to spend most of their races looking in their mirrors as the leaders lapped them with monotonous regularity. In 1996, after a ten-year absence, Roberto returned to Indy Car racing with the underfinanced Payton-Coyne Racing. Predictably his professionalism brought its reward with a superb third place in the US 500 at Michigan, the team's best-ever finish. Initially without a ride for 1997, Roberto was soon in action as a replacement for the injured Christian Fittipaldi at Newman-Haas. The fact that he outqualified team-mate Michael Andretti three times in six races raised a few eyebrows, but no one else, it seemed, shared the Brazilian's innate self-confidence.

The following season began with two races for Project Indy before Moreno quit, and it seemed that his only future lay in the Indy Racing League. Indeed he started 1999 in that category with a sixth place at Phoenix before another call into CART action as a substitute for Mark Blundell at PacWest. Roberto immediately established a great rapport with the team and helped to refocus their efforts before taking on an even more rewarding stand-in role at Newman-Haas. Once again Moreno stepped in for the unfortunate Fittipaldi and drove splendidly, taking a career-best second place at Laguna Seca. It seems Roberto's efforts have been recognised at last, as 'Supersub' finally gets a full-time ride with Patrick Racing for 2000.

MORENO, Roberto 'Pupo' (BR) b 11/2/1959, Rio de Janeiro

	1982			Championship position: Unplaced					
	Race	Circuit	No	Entrant	Tyres	Car/Engine		Comment	Q Pos/Entries
dnq	DUTCH GP	Zandvoort	12	John Player Team Lotus	G	3.0 Lotus 91-Cosworth V8			30/31
	1987			Championship position: 19th= Wins: 0 Pole positions: 0 Fastest laps: 0 Points scored: 1					
ret	JAPANESE GP	Suzuka	14	Team El Charro AGS	G	3.5 AGS JH22-Cosworth V8		engine-fuel injection	27/27
6*	AUSTRALIAN GP	Adelaide	14	Team El Charro AGS	G	3.5 AGS JH22-Cosworth V8		* 3rd non-turbo/3 laps behind	25/27
	1989			Championship position: Unplaced					
dnq	BRAZILIAN GP	Rio	31	Coloni SpA	P	3.5 Coloni FC188B-Cosworth V8			30/38
dnq	SAN MARINO GP	Imola	31	Coloni SpA	P	3.5 Coloni FC188B-Cosworth V8			30/39
ret	MONACO GP	Monte Carlo	31	Coloni SpA	P	3.5 Coloni FC188B-Cosworth V8		gearbox	25/38
dnq	MEXICAN GP	Mexico City	31	Coloni SpA	P	3.5 Coloni FC188B-Cosworth V8			30/39
dnq	US GP (PHOENIX)	Phoenix	31	Coloni SpA	P	3.5 Coloni FC188B-Cosworth V8			28/39
ret	CANADIAN GP	Montreal	31	Coloni SpA	P	3.5 Coloni C3-Cosworth V8		transmission	26/39
dns	"	"	31	Coloni SpA	P	3.5 Coloni FC188B-Cosworth V8		practice only	– / –

	Race	Circuit	No	Entrant	Tyres	Car/Engine	Comment	Q Pos/Entries
dnq	FRENCH GP	Paul Ricard	31	Coloni SpA	P	3.5 Coloni C3-Cosworth V8		30/39
ret	BRITISH GP	Silverstone	31	Coloni SpA	P	3.5 Coloni C3-Cosworth V8	*gearbox*	23/39
dnpq	GERMAN GP	Hockenheim	31	Coloni SpA	P	3.5 Coloni C3-Cosworth V8		35/39
dnpq	HUNGARIAN GP	Hungaroring	31	Coloni SpA	P	3.5 Coloni C3-Cosworth V8		36/39
dnpq	BELGIAN GP	Spa	31	Coloni SpA	P	3.5 Coloni C3-Cosworth V8		33/39
dnpq	ITALIAN GP	Monza	31	Coloni SpA	P	3.5 Coloni C3-Cosworth V8		32/39
ret	PORTUGUESE GP	Estoril	31	Coloni SpA	P	3.5 Coloni C3-Cosworth V8	*electrics*	15/39
dnpq	SPANISH GP	Jerez	31	Coloni SpA	P	3.5 Coloni C3-Cosworth V8		32/38
dnpq	JAPANESE GP	Suzuka	31	Coloni SpA	P	3.5 Coloni C3-Cosworth V8		32/39
dnpq	AUSTRALIAN GP	Adelaide	31	Coloni SpA	P	3.5 Coloni C3-Cosworth V8		34/39

1990 Championship position: 10th Wins: 0 Pole positions: 0 Fastest laps: 0 Points scored: 6

	Race	Circuit	No	Entrant	Tyres	Car/Engine	Comment	Q Pos/Entries
13	US GP (PHOENIX)	Phoenix	33	EuroBrun Racing	P	3.5 EuroBrun ER189-Judd V8	*pit stop-flat battery/-5 laps*	16/35
dnpq	BRAZILIAN GP	Interlagos	33	EuroBrun Racing	P	3.5 EuroBrun ER189-Judd V8		32/35
ret	SAN MARINO GP	Imola	33	EuroBrun Racing	P	3.5 EuroBrun ER189-Judd V8	*sticking throttle-lap 1*	25/34
dnq	MONACO GP	Monte Carlo	33	EuroBrun Racing	P	3.5 EuroBrun ER189-Judd V8		30/35
dnq	CANADIAN GP	Montreal	33	EuroBrun Racing	P	3.5 EuroBrun ER189-Judd V8		27/35
excl	MEXICAN GP	Mexico City	33	EuroBrun Racing	P	3.5 EuroBrun ER189B-Judd V8	*push start after practice spin*	26/35
dnpq	FRENCH GP	Paul Ricard	33	EuroBrun Racing	P	3.5 EuroBrun ER189B-Judd V8		32/35
dnpq	BRITISH GP	Silverstone	33	EuroBrun Racing	P	3.5 EuroBrun ER189B-Judd V8		31/35
dnpq	GERMAN GP	Hockenheim	33	EuroBrun Racing	P	3.5 EuroBrun ER189B-Judd V8		32/35
dnpq	HUNGARIAN GP	Hungaroring	33	EuroBrun Racing	P	3.5 EuroBrun ER189B-Judd V8		33/35
dnpq	BELGIAN GP	Spa	33	EuroBrun Racing	P	3.5 EuroBrun ER189B-Judd V8		31/33
dnpq	ITALIAN GP	Monza	33	EuroBrun Racing	P	3.5 EuroBrun ER189B-Judd V8		31/33
dnpq	PORTUGUESE GP	Estoril	33	EuroBrun Racing	P	3.5 EuroBrun ER189B-Judd V8		31/33
dnpq	SPANISH GP	Jerez	33	EuroBrun Racing	P	3.5 EuroBrun ER189B-Judd V8		31/33
2	JAPANESE GP	Suzuka	19	Benetton Formula	G	3.5 Benetton B190-Ford HB V8		9/30
7	AUSTRALIAN GP	Adelaide	19	Benetton Formula	G	3.5 Benetton B190-Ford HB V8	*pit stop-tyres/1 lap behind*	8/30

1991 Championship position: 10th Wins: 0 Pole positions: 0 Fastest laps: 1 Points scored: 8

	Race	Circuit	No	Entrant	Tyres	Car/Engine	Comment	Q Pos/Entries
ret	US GP (PHOENIX)	Phoenix	19	Camel Benetton Ford	G	3.5 Benetton B190B-Ford HB V8	*hit Patrese's spun car*	8/34
7	BRAZILIAN GP	Interlagos	19	Camel Benetton Ford	G	3.5 Benetton B190B-Ford HB V8	*1 lap behind*	14/34
13/ret	SAN MARINO GP	Imola	19	Camel Benetton Ford	G	3.5 Benetton B190B-Ford HB V8	*gearbox/engine/-7 laps*	13/34
4	MONACO GP	Monte Carlo	19	Camel Benetton Ford	G	3.5 Benetton B190B-Ford HB V8	*1 lap behind*	8/34
ret	CANADIAN GP	Montreal	19	Camel Benetton Ford	G	3.5 Benetton B190B-Ford HB V8	*spun off-suspension damage*	5/34
5	MEXICAN GP	Mexico City	19	Camel Benetton Ford	G	3.5 Benetton B190B-Ford HB V8	*1 lap behind*	9/34
ret	FRENCH GP	Magny Cours	19	Camel Benetton Ford	G	3.5 Benetton B190B-Ford HB V8	*driver unwell*	8/34
ret	BRITISH GP	Silverstone	19	Camel Benetton Ford	G	3.5 Benetton B190B-Ford HB V8	*gearbox*	7/34
8	GERMAN GP	Hockenheim	19	Camel Benetton Ford	G	3.5 Benetton B190B-Ford HB V8	*1 lap behind*	9/34
8	HUNGARIAN GP	Hungaroring	19	Camel Benetton Ford	G	3.5 Benetton B190B-Ford HB V8	*1 lap behind*	15/34
4	BELGIAN GP	Spa	19	Camel Benetton Ford	G	3.5 Benetton B190B-Ford HB V8	*FL*	8/34
ret	ITALIAN GP	Monza	32	Team 7UP Jordan	G	3.5 Jordan 191-Ford HB V8	*spun off-brakes*	9/34
10	PORTUGUESE GP	Estoril	32	Team 7UP Jordan	G	3.5 Jordan 191-Ford HB V8	*1 lap behind*	16/34
16	AUSTRALIAN GP	Adelaide	24	Minardi Team	G	3.5 Minardi M191-Ferrari V12	*rain shortened race/-1 lap*	18/32

1992 Championship position: Unplaced

	Race	Circuit	No	Entrant	Tyres	Car/Engine	Comment	Q Pos/Entries
dnpq	BRAZILIAN GP	Interlagos	34	Andrea Moda Formula	G	3.5 Moda S921-Judd V10		31/31
dnpq	SPANISH GP	Barcelona	34	Andrea Moda Formula	G	3.5 Moda S921-Judd V10		31/32
dnpq	SAN MARINO GP	Imola	34	Andrea Moda Formula	G	3.5 Moda S921-Judd V10		31/32
ret	MONACO GP	Monte Carlo	34	Andrea Moda Formula	G	3.5 Moda S921-Judd V10	*engine*	26/32
dnpq	CANADIAN GP	Montreal	34	Andrea Moda Formula	G	3.5 Moda S921-Judd V10		31/32
dnp	FRENCH GP	Magny Cours	34	Andrea Moda Formula	G	3.5 Moda S921-Judd V10	*team failed to arrive*	– / –
dnpq	BRITISH GP	Silverstone	34	Andrea Moda Formula	G	3.5 Moda S921-Judd V10		31/32
dnpq	GERMAN GP	Hockenheim	34	Andrea Moda Formula	G	3.5 Moda S921-Judd V10		31/32
dnq	HUNGARIAN GP	Hungaroring	34	Andrea Moda Formula	G	3.5 Moda S921-Judd V10		30/31
dnq	BELGIAN GP	Spa	34	Andrea Moda Formula	G	3.5 Moda S921-Judd V10		28/30
dnp	ITALIAN GP	Monza	34	Andrea Moda Formula	G	3.5 Moda S921-Judd V10	*team excluded*	– / –

1995 Championship position: Unplaced

	Race	Circuit	No	Entrant	Tyres	Car/Engine	Comment	Q Pos/Entries
ret	BRAZILIAN GP	Interlagos	22	Parmalat Forti Ford	G	3.0 Forti FG01-Ford ED V8	*spun off*	23/26
nc	ARGENTINE GP	Buenos Aires	22	Parmalat Forti Ford	G	3.0 Forti FG01-Ford ED V8	*9 laps behind*	24/26
nc	SAN MARINO GP	Imola	22	Parmalat Forti Ford	G	3.0 Forti FG01-Ford ED V8	*7 laps behind*	25/26
ret	SPANISH GP	Barcelona	22	Parmalat Forti Ford	G	3.0 Forti FG01-Ford ED V8	*water pump*	25/26
ret	MONACO GP	Monte Carlo	22	Parmalat Forti Ford	G	3.0 Forti FG01-Ford ED V8	*brake pipe*	24/26
ret	CANADIAN GP	Montreal	22	Parmalat Forti Ford	G	3.0 Forti FG01-Ford ED V8	*blocked fuel line*	23/24
16	FRENCH GP	Magny Cours	22	Parmalat Forti Ford	G	3.0 Forti FG01-Ford ED V8	*6 laps behind*	24/24
ret	BRITISH GP	Silverstone	22	Parmalat Forti Ford	G	3.0 Forti FG01-Ford ED V8	*hydraulic pressure*	22/24
ret	GERMAN GP	Hockenheim	22	Parmalat Forti Ford	G	3.0 Forti FG01-Ford ED V8	*driveshaft*	22/24
ret	HUNGARIAN GP	Hungaroring	22	Parmalat Forti Ford	G	3.0 Forti FG01-Ford ED V8	*gearshift failure*	21/24
14	BELGIAN GP	Spa	22	Parmalat Forti Ford	G	3.0 Forti FG01-Ford ED V8	*2 laps behind*	22/24
ret/dns	ITALIAN GP	Monza	22	Parmalat Forti Ford	G	3.0 Forti FG01-Ford ED V8	*accident at first start*	(22)/24
17	PORTUGUESE GP	Estoril	22	Parmalat Forti Ford	G	3.0 Forti FG01-Ford ED V8	*7 laps behind*	23/24
ret	EUROPEAN GP	Nürburgring	22	Parmalat Forti Ford	G	3.0 Forti FG01-Ford ED V8	*driveshaft*	23/24
16	PACIFIC GP	T.I. Circuit	22	Parmalat Forti Ford	G	3.0 Forti FG01-Ford ED V8	*5 laps behind*	22/24
ret	JAPANESE GP	Suzuka	22	Parmalat Forti Ford	G	3.0 Forti FG01-Ford ED V8	*gearbox on lap 1*	22/24
ret	AUSTRALIAN GP	Adelaide	22	Parmalat Forti Ford	G	3.0 Forti FG01-Ford ED V8	*accident*	20/24

GP Starts: 41 (42) GP Wins: 0 Pole positions: 0 Fastest laps: 1 Points: 15

MORGAN, Dave (GB) b 7/8/1944, Shepton Mallet, Somerset

1975 Championship position: Unplaced

	Race	Circuit	No	Entrant	Tyres	Car/Engine	Comment	Q Pos/Entries
18/ret	BRITISH GP	Silverstone	19	National Organs-Team Surtees	G	3.0 Surtees TS16-Cosworth V8	*crashed in rainstorm/-6 laps*	23/28

GP Starts: 1 GP Wins: 0 Pole positions: 0 Fastest laps: 0 Points: 0

DAVE MORGAN

Having begun racing in 1965 with a Mini, Dave progressed to Formula 3 in 1970 with a March 703 and a highly competitive season ended in a controversial accident with James Hunt at Crystal Palace. Morgan was suspended for 12 months for 'dangerous driving', but happily he was subsequently allowed to continue his racing activities in Formula Atlantic in 1971.

The high point of his career came at the start of 1972 when his private Brabham took a surprise but well-earned win in the Formula 2 race at Mallory Park. Two seasons in the formula brought little more success, and Morgan returned to Formula Atlantic in 1974, but with the support of his sponsors Dave then organised his one Grand Prix drive with a Surtees in 1975. He then retired from the circuits, but returned in 1980-81, racing a Colt Lancer in the RAC Tricentrol series.

In the early nineties he acted as Eric van de Poele's engineer in F3000 and Formula 1, before heading to Mexico to work in the thriving junior single-seater series. Subsequently, Dave moved up to the CART series with Payton-Coyne Racing.

SILVIO MOSER

After racing Alfas in the early sixties this pleasant little Swiss driver switched to junior single-seaters in 1964 with huge success, both in European F3 and in the Temporada series, winning all four rounds in his Formula Junior Lotus.

Moser then moved into Formula 2 with his own team, but continued to race in F3 – where he was more competitive, winning races at Syracuse, La Chatre and Rosario. He then went into Formula 1 full-time , initially with an elderly Cooper-ATS, then with the ex-Ligier Brabham, scoring a fifth place at Zandvoort in 1968, and a sixth at Watkins Glen in 1969.

Silvio then embarked on a disastrous 1970 season with the hopeless Bellasi-Ford, which scuppered his immediate Grand Prix expectations. Returning to Formula 2, he drove a Brabham in 1971 and '72, taking second at the Monza Lottery GP, but had a thin time of it with a Surtees in 1973. Moser was planning to race a March in Formula 2 in 1974, as well as making a return to Grands Prix with a Bretscher Brabham, but he crashed a Lola sports car heavily in the Monza 1000 Km, sustaining serious internal and head injuries. Despite several operations, poor Moser died in hospital the following month without regaining consciousness.

MOSER, Silvio (CH) b 24/4/1941, Zurich – d 26/5/1974, Locarno

	1966	Championship position: Unplaced							
	Race	Circuit	No	Entrant	Tyres	Car/Engine		Comment	Q Pos/Entries
dns	GERMAN GP (F2)	Nürburgring	35	Silvio Moser	D	1.0 Brabham BT16-Cosworth 4 F2		engine in practice	(29)/30
	1967	Championship position: Unplaced							
ret	BRITISH GP	Silverstone	22	Charles Vögele	D	2.7 Cooper T77-ATS V8		no oil pressure	20/21
	1968	Championship position: 23rd Wins: 0 Pole positions: 0 Fastest laps: 0 Points scored: 2							
dnq	MONACO GP	Monte Carlo	21	Charles Vögele	G	3.0 Brabham BT20-Repco V8			16/18
5	DUTCH GP	Zandvoort	22	Charles Vögele	G	3.0 Brabham BT20-Repco V8		3 laps behind	17/19
nc	BRITISH GP	Brands Hatch	19	Charles Vögele	G	3.0 Brabham BT20-Repco V8		pit stops-gearbox/-28 laps	19/20
dnq	ITALIAN GP	Monza	12	Charles Vögele	G	3.0 Brabham BT20-Repco V8			24/24
	1969	Championship position: 16th= Wins: 0 Pole positions: 0 Fastest laps: 0 Points scored: 1							
ret	MONACO GP	Monte Carlo	17	Silvio Moser Racing Team	G	3.0 Brabham BT24-Cosworth V8		driveshaft	=14/16
ret	DUTCH GP	Zandvoort	17	Silvio Moser Racing Team	G	3.0 Brabham BT24-Cosworth V8		steering/electrics	14/15
7	FRENCH GP	Clermont Ferrand	12	Silvio Moser Racing Team	G	3.0 Brabham BT24-Cosworth V8		2 laps behind	13/13
ret	ITALIAN GP	Monza	36	Silvio Moser Racing Team	G	3.0 Brabham BT24-Cosworth V8		fuel leak	13/15
ret	CANADIAN GP	Mosport Park	20	Silvio Moser Racing Team	G	3.0 Brabham BT24-Cosworth V8		put off road by Pease	20/20
6	US GP	Watkins Glen	19	Silvio Moser Racing Team	G	3.0 Brabham BT24-Cosworth V8		pit stop/10 laps behind	17/18
11/ret	MEXICAN GP	Mexico City	19	Silvio Moser Racing Team	G	3.0 Brabham BT24-Cosworth V8		fuel leak/5 laps behind	13/17
	1970	Championship position: Unplaced							
dnq	DUTCH GP	Zandvoort	29	Silvio Moser Racing Team	G	3.0 Bellasi-Cosworth V8			24/24
dnq	FRENCH GP	Clermont Ferrand	24	Silvio Moser Racing Team	G	3.0 Bellasi-Cosworth V8			21/23
dnq	GERMAN GP	Nürburgring	27	Silvio Moser Racing Team	G	3.0 Bellasi-Cosworth V8			24/25
ret	AUSTRIAN GP	Österreichring	24	Silvio Moser Racing Team	G	3.0 Bellasi-Cosworth V8		radiator	24/24
dnq	ITALIAN GP	Monza	56	Silvio Moser Racing Team	G	3.0 Bellasi-Cosworth V8			26/27
	1971	Championship position: Unplaced							
ret	ITALIAN GP	Monza	27	Jolly Club Switzerland	G	3.0 Bellasi-Cosworth V8		shock absorber	22/24

GP Starts: 12   GP Wins: 0   Pole positions: 0   Fastest laps: 0   Points: 3

Sir STIRLING MOSS

Sir STIRLING MOSS

The long career and many brilliant deeds of Stirling Moss far outstrip the space available to describe them here, and his successes are also far too numerous to list. Thus a broad brush must be used to give an impression of this patriotic and ultra-professional driver, who had a clear idea of his own worth. Without vanity, he quite soundly reasoned that the World Championship which the British public were so desperate for him to win was utterly meaningless as a measure of a driver's abilities. Painstaking and thorough in his approach, in his prime Stirling's mastery of the skills of his profession was absolute. Capable of driving just about any machine with equal excellence, Moss never gave less than 100 per cent and, no matter what the situation, he simply never gave up.

His career began in 1947 with a BMW 328, but he was soon scrapping it out in the rough and tumble of 500 cc racing with a Cooper-JAP. In 1950 he scored his first major success, winning the Tourist Trophy in a Jaguar XK120, and during the next three seasons he drove a variety of cars – HWM, Formula 3 Kieft, Frazer-Nash and Jaguar – sampling success in all of them. Only the ERA G-Type was a complete failure, and by 1953 Stirling's talents were coveted by Ferrari. Actually Moss had his eyes fixed on a seat with Mercedes-Benz, but Neubauer was not yet convinced that the youngster was ready. So for the 1954 season Moss bought a Maserati 250F and promptly took third place at Spa. Later in the year, he accepted the offer of a works car, and duly led the Mercedes of Fangio at Monza until the oil tank split. He was then signed by Mercedes for the 1955 season alongside the Maestro. In Grands Prix he watched and learned much from his august partner, scoring a famous victory in the British GP in the July sunshine at Aintree, and he also won the Mille Miglia and the Targa Florio in the silver sports cars. Unfortunately the Le Mans disaster prompted Mercedes' withdrawal from the sport, and Stirling joined Maserati as number one driver in 1956. Despite wins at Monaco and Monza, retirements elsewhere cost him dear and the championship went to Fangio and Ferrari. It was a very productive year overall, however, with no fewer than 16 race wins in the 250F, the Maserati 300TS and the Vanwall among others.

His patriotism was at last rewarded when Vanwall offered him a machine worthy of his talents in 1957, and in the British GP Moss fulfilled a long-held ambition by giving a green car victory in a World Championship Grand Prix after taking over Brooks' sister entry. There were further wins at Pescara and Monza, and hopes were high for the championship in 1958. He started the season with a quite brilliant win in Rob Walker's little Cooper before resuming the fight in Vandervell's machines. Once again the unreliability of the car torpedoed Moss's personal title chances but, with Brooks and Lewis-Evans backing him up, the team took the constructors' title before withdrawing from Grand Prix racing at the season's end.

By now Moss had ceased to worry unduly about the championship. Certainly Ferrari would have given anything to sign him, but he preferred the comfortable ambience of Walker's little team, with Rob himself offering discreet guidance and Alf Francis fettling the cars. Stirling possibly hindered his chances by switching about a bit too often, surmising that the BRP BRM would be better suited to Reims and Aintree, but he won in Portugal and Italy in the Walker Cooper. In 1960 Stirling had the choice of a Cooper and the new Lotus 18, which he used to win the Monaco GP, but in practice for the Belgian GP his Lotus shed a wheel, leaving him suffering from serious back injuries. Characteristically, he set himself impossible targets for his comeback and returned in time to take another win at the end of the year at Riverside.

In 1961 we saw the true genius of Moss at Monaco and particularly the Nürburgring, where he defeated the shark-nose Ferrari 156 V6 cars of Phil Hill and Taffy von Trips. These victories were inevitably just outcrops of a seam of success that ran through the season, into the winter months at Nassau, and then across the world early in 1962 in Australia and New Zealand. On his return to Britain, Moss drove the pale-green UDT-entered Lotus to seventh in the Lombank Trophy before heading down to Goodwood for the Easter Monday meeting. Why he crashed is still not clear, but his car was wrecked and Stirling was hospitalised with serious head injuries. His recuperation was to be a slow one this time. Almost a year later he tried a car in a private test but his fears were realised. The sharp edge of his reflexes had gone, and wisely he decided he would not race again, thus leaving intact memories of a driver who always competed at the peak of his powers. Stirling then launched himself into myriad business ventures, many of which kept him in touch with the sport. In the late seventies he was tempted back to the track, mainly for fun, in historic cars and saloons.

With the new millennium approaching, Stirling, who had just celebrated his seventieth birthday, was given a knighthood in the 2000 New Year's Honours. It was a fitting confirmation of the high esteem in which this truly great driver is held.

Moss wins the 1958 Dutch Grand Prix in the Vanwall. Despite four wins that season, five non-finishes cost him the world title, which went to Mike Hawthorn.

MOSS, Stirling (GB) b 17/9/1929, West Kensington, London

1951 — Championship position: Unplaced

	Race	Circuit	No	Entrant	Tyres	Car/Engine	Comment	Q Pos/Entries
8	SWISS GP	Bremgarten	14	HW Motors Ltd	D	2.0 HWM-Alta 4	2 laps behind	14/21

1952 — Championship position: Unplaced

	Race	Circuit	No	Entrant	Tyres	Car/Engine	Comment	Q Pos/Entries
ret	SWISS GP	Bremgarten	46	HW Motors Ltd	D	2.0 HWM-Alta 4	withdrawn-hub failure of team-mate	9/21
ret	BELGIAN GP	Spa	32	ERA Ltd	D	2.0 ERA G Type-Bristol 6	engine	10/22
ret	BRITISH GP	Silverstone	12	ERA Ltd	D	2.0 ERA G Type-Bristol 6	engine	16/32
ret	DUTCH GP	Zandvoort	36	ERA Ltd	D	2.0 ERA G Type-Bristol 6	no practice time set/engine	–/18
ret	ITALIAN GP	Monza	32	Connaught Engineering	D	2.0 Connaught-Lea Francis A Type 4	engine-push rod	9/35

1953 — Championship position: Unplaced

	Race	Circuit	No	Entrant	Tyres	Car/Engine	Comment	Q Pos/Entries
9	DUTCH GP	Zandvoort	34	Connaught Engineering	D	2.0 Connaught-Lea Francis A Type 4	7 laps behind	9/20
ret	FRENCH GP	Reims	36	Cooper Car Co	D	2.0 Cooper Alta Special-4	clutch	13/25
6	GERMAN GP	Nürburgring	19	Cooper Car Co	D	2.0 Cooper Alta Special Mk 11-4	1 lap behind	12/35
13	ITALIAN GP	Monza	28	Cooper Car Co	D	2.0 Cooper Alta Special Mk 11-4	pit stop-fuel leak 10 laps behind	10/30

1954 — Championship position: 10th= Wins: 0 Pole positions: 0 Fastest laps: 1 (shared) Points scored: 4.14

	Race	Circuit	No	Entrant	Tyres	Car/Engine	Comment	Q Pos/Entries
3	BELGIAN GP	Spa	22	Equipe Moss	P	2.5 Maserati 250F 6	1 lap behind	9/15
ret	BRITISH GP	Silverstone	7	A E Moss	P	2.5 Maserati 250F 6	gearbox/FL (shared)	4/31
ret	GERMAN GP	Nürburgring	16	A E Moss	P	2.5 Maserati 250F 6	engine	3/23
ret	SWISS GP	Bremgarten	32	Officine Alfieri Maserati	P	2.5 Maserati 250F 6	oil pressure	3/16
nc	ITALIAN GP	Monza	28	Officine Alfieri Maserati	P	2.5 Maserati 250F 6	split oil tank/9 laps behind	3/21
ret	SPANISH GP	Pedralbes	8	Officine Alfieri Maserati	P	2.5 Maserati 250F 6	oil pump	6/22

1955 — Championship position: 2nd Wins: 1 Pole positions: 1 Fastest laps: 2 Points scored: 23

	Race	Circuit	No	Entrant	Tyres	Car/Engine	Comment	Q Pos/Entries
ret	ARGENTINE GP	Buenos Aires	6	Daimler Benz AG	C	2.5 Mercedes-Benz W196 8	fuel vapour lock	8/22
4*	"	"	8	Daimler Benz AG	C	2.5 Mercedes-Benz W196 8	*Herrmann/Kling also drove	–/–/–
9/ret	MONACO GP	Monte Carlo	6	Daimler Benz AG	C	2.5 Mercedes-Benz W196 8	engine/19 laps behind	3/22
2	BELGIAN GP	Spa	14	Daimler Benz AG	C	2.5 Mercedes-Benz W196 8		3/14
2	DUTCH GP	Zandvoort	10	Daimler Benz AG	C	2.5 Mercedes-Benz W196 8		2/16
1	BRITISH GP	Aintree	12	Daimler Benz AG	C	2.5 Mercedes-Benz W196 8	FL	1/25
ret	ITALIAN GP	Monza	16	Daimler Benz AG	C	2.5 Mercedes-Benz W196 8 str	engine/FL	2/22

1956 — Championship position: 2nd Wins: 2 Pole positions: 1 Fastest laps: 3 Points scored: 28

	Race	Circuit	No	Entrant	Tyres	Car/Engine	Comment	Q Pos/Entries
ret	ARGENTINE GP	Buenos Aires	2	Officine Alfieri Maserati	P	2.5 Maserati 250F 6	engine	7/15
1	MONACO GP	Monte Carlo	28	Officine Alfieri Maserati	P	2.5 Maserati 250F 6		2/19
ret	BELGIAN GP	Spa	30	Officine Alfieri Maserati	P	2.5 Maserati 250F 6	lost wheel	2/16
3*	"	"	34	Officine Alfieri Maserati	P	2.5 Maserati 250F 6	* took over Perdisa's car/FL	–/–/–
ret	FRENCH GP	Reims	2	Officine Alfieri Maserati	P	2.5 Maserati 250F 6	gear lever	8/20
5*	"	"	6	Officine Alfieri Maserati	P	2.5 Maserati 250F 6	*took Perdisa's car/-2 laps	–/–/–
ret	BRITISH GP	Silverstone	7	Officine Alfieri Maserati	P	2.5 Maserati 250F 6	gearbox/FL	1/28
2	GERMAN GP	Nürburgring	7	Officine Alfieri Maserati	P	2.5 Maserati 250F 6		4/21
1	ITALIAN GP	Monza	36	Officine Alfieri Maserati	P	2.5 Maserati 250F 6	FL	6/26

1957 — Championship position: 2nd Wins: 3 (1 shared) Pole positions: 2 Fastest laps: 3 Points scored: 25

	Race	Circuit	No	Entrant	Tyres	Car/Engine	Comment	Q Pos/Entries
8	ARGENTINE GP	Buenos Aires	4	Officine Alfieri Maserati	P	2.5 Maserati 250F 6	pit stop-throttle/-7 laps/FL	1/16
ret	MONACO GP	Monte Carlo	18	Vandervell Products Ltd	P	2.5 Vanwall 4	hit chicane	3/21
ret	BRITISH GP	Aintree	18	Vandervell Products Ltd	P	2.5 Vanwall 4	Brooks took over/engine	1/19
1*	"	"	20	Vandervell Products Ltd	P	2.5 Vanwall 4	* took over from Brooks/FL	–/–/–
5	GERMAN GP	Nürburgring	10	Vandervell Products Ltd	P	2.5 Vanwall 4	suspension problems	7/24
1	PESCARA GP	Pescara	26	Vandervell Products Ltd	P	2.5 Vanwall 4	FL	2/16
1	ITALIAN GP	Monza	18	Vandervell Products Ltd	P	2.5 Vanwall 4		2/19

1958 — Championship position: 2nd Wins: 4 Pole positions: 3 Fastest laps: 3 Points scored: 41

	Race	Circuit	No	Entrant	Tyres	Car/Engine	Comment	Q Pos/Entries
1	ARGENTINE GP	Buenos Aires	14	R R C Walker Racing Team	C	1.9 Cooper T43-Climax 4	tyres worn out at finish	7/10
ret	MONACO GP	Monte Carlo	28	Vandervell Products Ltd	D	2.5 Vanwall 4	engine	8/28
1	DUTCH GP	Zandvoort	1	Vandervell Products Ltd	D	2.5 Vanwall 4	FL	2/17
ret	BELGIAN GP	Spa	2	Vandervell Products Ltd	D	2.5 Vanwall 4	dropped valve	3/20
2	FRENCH GP	Reims	8	Vandervell Products Ltd	D	2.5 Vanwall 4		6/21
ret	BRITISH GP	Silverstone	7	Vandervell Products Ltd	D	2.5 Vanwall 4	engine	1/21
ret	GERMAN GP	Nürburgring	7	Vandervell Products Ltd	D	2.5 Vanwall 4	magneto/FL	3/26
1	PORTUGUESE GP	Oporto	2	Vandervell Products Ltd	D	2.5 Vanwall 4		1/15
ret	ITALIAN GP	Monza	26	Vandervell Products Ltd	D	2.5 Vanwall 4	gearbox	1/21
1	MOROCCAN GP	Casablanca	8	Vandervell Products Ltd	D	2.5 Vanwall 4	FL	2/25

1959 — Championship position: 3rd Wins: 2 Pole positions: 4 Fastest laps: 4 (1 shared) Points scored: 25.5

	Race	Circuit	No	Entrant	Tyres	Car/Engine	Comment	Q Pos/Entries
ret	MONACO GP	Monte Carlo	30	R R C Walker Racing Team	D	2.5 Cooper T51-Climax 4	transmission	1/24
dns	"	" "	30	R R C Walker Racing Team	D	2.5 Cooper T51-BRM 4	practice only	–/–
ret	DUTCH GP	Zandvoort	11	R R C Walker Racing Team	D	2.5 Cooper T51-Climax 4	gearbox/FL	3/15
dns	"	"	15	Ecurie Maarsbergen	D	1.5 Porsche-RSK F4 sports	practice only	–/–
dsq	FRENCH GP	Reims	2	British Racing Partnership	D	2.5 BRM P25 4	outside assistance after spin/FL	4/22
2	BRITISH GP	Aintree	6	British Racing Partnership	D	2.5 BRM P25 4	FL (shared with McLaren)	7/30
ret	GERMAN GP	AVUS	7	R R C Walker Racing Team	D	2.5 Cooper T51-Climax 4	transmission-heat 1	2/16
1	PORTUGUESE GP	Monsanto	4	R R C Walker Racing Team	D	2.5 Cooper T51-Climax 4	FL	1/16
1	ITALIAN GP	Monza	14	R R C Walker Racing Team	D	2.5 Cooper T51-Climax 4		1/21
ret	US GP	Sebring	7	R R C Walker Racing Team	D	2.5 Cooper T51-Climax 4	transmission	1/19

1960 — Championship position: 3rd Wins: 2 Pole positions: 4 Fastest laps: 2 Points scored: 19

	Race	Circuit	No	Entrant	Tyres	Car/Engine	Comment	Q Pos/Entries
ret	ARGENTINE GP	Buenos Aires	36	R R C Walker Racing Team	D	2.5 Cooper T51-Climax 4	suspension/FL	1/22
3*	"	"	38	R R C Walker Racing Team	D	2.5 Cooper T51-Climax 4	* took over from Trintignant/no pts	–/–
dns	"	" "		R R C Walker Racing Team	D	2.5 Cooper T43-Climax 4	practice only	–/–
1	MONACO GP	Monte Carlo	28	R R C Walker Racing Team	D	2.5 Lotus 18-Climax 4		1/24
dns	"	" "	T	Reventlow Automobiles Inc	G/D	2.5 Scarab 4	practice only	–/–
4	DUTCH GP	Zandvoort	7	R R C Walker Racing Team	D	2.5 Lotus 18-Climax 4	pit stop when 1st/FL	1/21
dns	BELGIAN GP	Spa	12	R R C Walker Racing Team	D	2.5 Lotus 18-Cliamx 4	injured in practice accident	(3)/18
dsq	PORTUGUESE GP	Oporto	12	R R C Walker Racing Team	D	2.5 Lotus 18-Climax 4	pushed car against traffic flow	4/16
dns	"	"	12	R R C Walker Racing Team	D	2.5 Cooper T51-Climax 4	practice only	–/–
1	US GP	Riverside	5	R R C Walker Racing Team	D	2.5 Lotus 18-Climax 4		1/23

1961		Championship position: 3rd Wins: 2 Pole positions: 1 Fastest laps: 1 (shared) Points scored: 21						
1	MONACO GP	Monte Carlo	20	R R C Walker Racing Team	D	1.5 Lotus 18-Climax 4	FL (shared with Ginther)	1/21
dns	"	"	20	R R C Walker Racing Team	D	1.5 Cooper T53-Climax 4	practice only	–/–
4	DUTCH GP	Zandvoort	14	R R C Walker Racing Team	D	1.5 Lotus 18-Climax 4		4/17
dns	"	"	14	R R C Walker Racing Team	D	1.5 Cooper T53-Climax 4	practice only	–/–
8	BELGIAN GP	Spa	14	R R C Walker Racing Team	D	1.5 Lotus 18/21-Climax 4		8/25
ret	FRENCH GP	Reims	26	R R C Walker Racing Team	D	1.5 Lotus 18/21-Climax 4	brake pipe	4/26
dns	"	"	26	UDT-Laystall Racing Team	D	1.5 Lotus 18-Climax 4	practice only	–/–
ret	BRITISH GP	Aintree	28	R R C Walker Racing Team	D	1.5 Lotus 18/21-Climax 4	brake pipe	5/30
dsq*	"	"	26	R R C Walker Racing Team	D	1.5 Ferguson P99-Climax 4	took Fairman's car/*push start	–/–
1	GERMAN GP	Nürburgring	7	R R C Walker Racing Team	D	1.5 Lotus 18/21-Climax 4		3/27
ret	ITALIAN GP	Monza	28	R R C Walker Racing Team	D	1.5 Lotus 21-Climax 4	drove Ireland's car/wheel bearing	–/–
dns	"	"	28	R R C Walker Racing Team	D	1.5 Lotus 18/21-Climax 4	practice only/set grid time	11/33
dns	"	"	28	R R C Walker Racing Team	D	1.5 Lotus 18/21-Climax V8	practice only	–/–
ret	US GP	Watkins Glen	7	R R C Walker Racing Team	D	1.5 Lotus 18/21-Climax 4	engine	=3/19
dns	"	" "	7	R R C Walker Racing Team	D	1.5 Lotus 18/21-Climax V8	practice only	–/–

GP Starts: 66   GP Wins: 16 (1 shared)   Pole positions: 16   Fastest laps: 19   Points: 186.64

GINO MUNARON

Though not of the top echelon Munaron was a very professional driver who raced a whole roster of sports and touring cars throughout the decade from 1955 to 1965. Apart from handling his own machines, Gino was a sometime works driver for Ferrari, Maserati and Osca during the fifties, and among his best placings were first at Hyeres in 1955 (Ferrari), third at Pescara and fourth at Bari (Maserati) in 1956, third (driving a Ferrari 250 GT single-handed) in the Reims 12 Hours in 1957, third in the Venezuelan GP at Caracas (Ferrari), and third once more in the Auvergne Trophy at Clermont Ferrand (Osca) in 1959.

In 1960 Munaron drove an elderly Maserati 250F in the Argentine GP and on his return to Europe he linked up with the Scuderia Castellotti, racing their Cooper-Ferrari without success in a handful of races. The following year he entered a Cooper T43-Alfa for the Syracuse Grand Prix, but failed to qualify, reappearing in the Castellotti Cooper in a couple of Inter-Continental races (for 2.5-litre machines) held in Britain later that season. Although his single-seater career petered out, Gino was to race GT cars for a few seasons to come. He drove the works Alfa Romeo Giulia TI in 1964, scoring a fifth place (with de Adamich) in the Spa 24 Hours and second in the Coppa Inter Europa 4 Hours at Monza.

DAVID MURRAY

A chartered accountant by profession, Murray enthusiastically raced an ERA and then a 4CLT Maserati in British and Continental events, as well as taking in occasional rallies and hill-climbs.

He is perhaps best known, however, as the man who formed the famous Ecurie Ecosse team in 1952. After taking part in the British GP with the organisation's Cooper-Bristol, Murray then took on the chief management role in the team, masterminding their hugely successful sports car programme which culminated in the dark blue cars' wonderful triumphs at Le Mans in 1956 and 1957.

MUNARON, Gino (I) b 2/4/1928, Turin

	1960			Championship position: Unplaced				
	Race	Circuit	No	Entrant	Tyres	Car/Engine	Comment	Q Pos/Entries
13	ARGENTINE GP	Buenos Aires	14	Gino Munaron	D	2.5 Maserati 250F 6	8 laps behind	19/22
dnq	MONACO GP	Monte Carlo	30	Scuderia Eugenio Castellotti	D	2.5 Cooper T51-Ferrari 4	shared car with Scarlatti	–/–
ret	FRENCH GP	Reims	30	Scuderia Eugenio Castellotti	D	2.5 Cooper T51-Ferrari 4	transmission	19/23
15	BRITISH GP	Silverstone	21	Scuderia Eugenio Castellotti	D	2.5 Cooper T51-Ferrari 4	7 laps behind	–/25
ret	ITALIAN GP	Monza	4	Scuderia Eugenio Castellotti	D	2.5 Cooper T51-Ferrari 4	oil pipe	8/16

GP Starts: 4   GP Wins: 0   Pole positions: 0   Fastest laps: 0   Points: 0

MURRAY, David (GB) b 28/12/1909, Edinburgh, Scotland – d 5/4/1973, Las Palmas, Canary Islands, Spain

	1950			Championship position: Unplaced				
	Race	Circuit	No	Entrant	Tyres	Car/Engine	Comment	Q Pos/Entries
ret	BRITISH GP	Silverstone	5	Scuderia Ambrosiana	D	1.5 s/c Maserati 4CLT/48 4	engine	18/21
dns	FRENCH GP	Reims	34	Scuderia Ambrosiana	D	1.5 s/c Maserati 4CLT/48 4	car raced by Hampshire	20/20
ret	ITALIAN GP	Monza	50	Scuderia Ambrosiana	D	1.5 s/c Maserati 4CLT/48 4	gearbox/valves	24/27
	1951			Championship position: Unplaced				
ret	BRITISH GP	Silverstone	15	Scuderia Ambrosiana	D	1.5 s/c Maserati 4CLT/48 4	valve springs	15/20
dns	GERMAN GP	Nürburgring	89	Scuderia Ambrosiana	D	1.5 s/c Maserati 4CLT/48 4	accident in practice	(23)/23
	1952			Championship position: Unplaced				
ret	BRITISH GP	Silverstone	7	Ecurie Ecosse	D	2.0 Cooper T20-Bristol 6	engine/spark plugs	22/32

GP Starts: 4   GP Wins: 0   Pole positions: 0   Fastest laps: 0   Points: 0

LUIGI MUSSO

The last of an ill-fated generation of Italian Grand Prix drivers, Musso followed one of his elder brothers into the sport with some less than earth-shattering performances, but he slowly gained experience and, armed with one of the latest Maserati sports cars for 1953, proved almost unbeatable as he sped to the Italian 2-litre championship.

So impressed were Maserati that he shared Mantovani's car at that year's Italian GP before racing works sports and Grand Prix machines the following season, when he was again sports car champion of Italy, winning the Circuit of Senigallia, and taking second in the Targa Florio and third in the Mille Miglia. In single-seaters he inherited a win in the Pescara GP, and took a fine second place in the Spanish GP at season's end. For 1955 Musso undertook another busy schedule of racing, scoring points only at Zandvoort, but taking second places in non-championship races at Syracuse, Bordeaux and Naples. Driving the Maserati T300S in sports car events, his only win came at the Monza Supercortemaggiore race with Behra.

In 1956 Luigi was invited to join the Scuderia Ferrari, and the association began on a high note when he shared the winning car with Fangio in the Argentine GP, following this with a second place in the Syracuse GP. Unfortunately a crash in the Nürburgring 1000 Km left him temporarily sidelined with a broken arm, though he made a contentious comeback at Monza, first refusing to hand his car to the waiting Fangio at a pit stop, then taking the lead of the Italian GP only for his steering to fail after a tyre threw a tread.

Something of a nearly-man, outright success seemed continually to elude the Italian in World Championship races in 1957. He was a runner-up in both France and Britain, as well as in the non-title Syracuse and Modena GPs, though he did at last take a victory at Reims in the GP de Marne. This sequence continued into 1958, when a succession of yet more second places (Argentine GP, Buenos Aires City GP, Buenos Aires 1000 Km and Monaco GP) was broken by victory in the Syracuse GP and the Targa Florio.

After crashing his Ferrari at Spa with tyre failure, Musso arrived at Reims for the French GP determined to make amends, but while he was chasing his team-mate Hawthorn he ran wide on the long Gueux curve at 150 mph. The car ran into a ditch and flipped, killing the driver instantly.

MUSSO, Luigi (I) b 28/7/1924, Rome – d 6/7/1958, Reims Circuit, France

	1953	Championship position: Unplaced							
	Race	Circuit	No	Entrant	Tyres	Car/Engine		Comment	Q Pos/Entries
7*	ITALIAN GP	Monza	56	Officine Alfieri Maserati	P	2.0 Maserati A6GCM 6		*took Mantovani's car/-4 laps	– /30
	1954	Championship position: 7th= Wins: 0 Pole positions: 0 Fastest laps: 0 Points scored: 6							
dns	ARGENTINE GP	Buenos Aires	6	Officine Alfieri Maserati	P	2.5 Maserati A6GCM/250F 6		engine in practice	7/18
ret	ITALIAN GP	Monza	20	Officine Alfieri Maserati	P	2.5 Maserati 250F 6		transmission	14/21
2	SPANISH GP	Pedralbes	14	Officine Alfieri Maserati	P	2.5 Maserati 250F 6			7/22
	1955	Championship position: 8th= Wins: 0 Pole positions: 0 Fastest laps: 0 Points scored: 6							
7*	ARGENTINE GP	Buenos Aires	22	Officine Alfieri Maserati	P	2.5 Maserati 250F 6		*Mantovani/Schell c/drove/-13 laps	18/22
ret	"	"	20	Officine Alfieri Maserati	P	2.5 Maserati 250F 6		fuel feed/Behra/Mantovani c/drove	– / –
ret	MONACO GP	Monte Carlo	38	Officine Alfieri Maserati	P	2.5 Maserati 250F 6		transmission	8/22
7	BELGIAN GP	Spa	22	Officine Alfieri Maserati	P	2.5 Maserati 250F 6		2 laps behind	7/14
3	DUTCH GP	Zandvoort	18	Officine Alfieri Maserati	P	2.5 Maserati 250F 6			4/16
5	BRITISH GP	Silverstone	4	Officine Alfieri Maserati	P	2.5 Maserati 250F 6		1 lap behind	9/25
ret	ITALIAN GP	Monza	30	Officine Alfieri Maserati	P	2.5 Maserati 250F 6		gearbox	10/22
	1956	Championship position: 9th= Wins: 0 Pole positions: 0 Fastest laps: 0 Points scored: 4							
1*	ARGENTINE GP	Buenos Aires	34	Scuderia Ferrari	E	2.5 Lancia-Ferrari D50 V8		* Fangio took over	3/15
ret	"	"	30	Scuderia Ferrari	E	2.5 Lancia-Ferrari D50 V8		switched to Fangio's car/fuel pump	– / –
ret	MONACO GP	Monte Carlo	24	Scuderia Ferrari	E	2.5 Lancia-Ferrari D50 V8		crashed avoiding Fangio	8/19
ret*	GERMAN GP	Nurburging	4	Scuderia Ferrari	E	2.5 Lancia-Ferrari D50 V8		* Castellotti took car-crashed	5/21
ret	ITALIAN GP	Monza	28	Scuderia Ferrari	E	2.5 Lancia-Ferrari D50 V8		steering arm-crashed	3/26

	1957	Championship position: 3rd		Wins: 0	Pole positions: 0	Fastest laps: 1	Points scored: 16			
ret	ARGENTINE GP	Buenos Aires	12	Scuderia Ferrari		E	2.5 Lancia-Ferrari D50A V8	clutch	6/16
2	FRENCH GP	Rouen	10	Scuderia Ferrari		E	2.5 Lancia-Ferrari 801 V8	FL	3/15
2	BRITISH GP	Aintree	14	Scuderia Ferrari		E	2.5 Lancia-Ferrari 801 V8		10/19
4	GERMAN GP	Nürburgring	6	Scuderia Ferrari		E	2.5 Lancia-Ferrari 801 V8		8/24
ret	PESCARA GP	Pescara	34	Scuderia Ferrari		E	2.5 Lancia-Ferrari 801 V8	split oil tank-seized engine	3/16
8	ITALIAN GP	Monza	32	Scuderia Ferrari		E	2.5 Lancia-Ferrari 801 V8	5 laps behind	9/19
	1958	Championship position: 7th=		Wins: 0	Pole positions: 0	Fastest laps: 0	Points scored: 12			
2	ARGENTINE GP	Buenos Aires	16	Scuderia Ferrari		E	2.4 Ferrari Dino 246 V6		5/10
2	MONACO GP	Monte Carlo	34	Scuderia Ferrari		E	2.4 Ferrari Dino 246 V6		10/28
7	DUTCH GP	Zandvoort	6	Scuderia Ferrari		E	2.4 Ferrari Dino 246 V6	pit stop/2 laps behind	12/17
ret	BELGIAN GP	Spa	18	Scuderia Ferrari		E	2.4 Ferrari Dino 246 V6	tyre-crashed at Stavelot	2/20
ret	FRENCH GP	Reims	2	Scuderia Ferrari		E	2.4 Ferrari Dino 246 V6	fatal accident	2/21

GP Starts: 24   GP Wins: 1(shared)   Pole positions: 0   Fastest laps: 1   Points: 44

'NACKE, Bernhard' (D) *see* BECHEM, Karl-Günther

	1952	Championship position: Unplaced							
	Race	Circuit	No	Entrant	Tyres	Car/Engine		Comment	Q Pos/Entries
ret	GERMAN GP	Nürburgring	130	'Bernhard Nacke'	–	2.0 BMW-Eigenbau 6		spark plugs	30/32

GP Starts: 1   GP Wins: 0   Pole positions: 0   Fastest laps: 0   Points: 0

SATORU NAKAJIMA

Nakajima was chosen by Honda to represent them on the Grand Prix stage after a glittering career in Japan which saw him win five Formula 2 titles, the last three consecutively between 1984 and '86.

Brought into the Lotus team alongside the brilliant Ayrton Senna, the Japanese driver inevitably appeared in an unfavourable light during his first season, and his number two status continued when Nelson Piquet took over as team leader in 1988-89, but Satoru quietly got on with the job as the fortunes of the Hethel outfit plummeted. His last race for the team was in the wet at Adelaide in 1989, and he astonished everyone as he made a mockery of the conditions to finish fourth and take fastest lap.

With help from long-time sponsors Honda and Epson, Satoru moved to Tyrrell in 1990, gaining the odd point with the nimble Cosworth car. He then endured a disappointing final year in F1, despite having V10 Honda power, and it was with some relief that he bowed out and retired from the sport, his head held high and no longer having to carry the burden of his fanatical countrymen's expectations.

Since his retirement Satoru, a huge name in Japan after his Grand Prix exploits, has earned millions from endorsements and advertising. He has also taken on the role of team owner, running a PIAA-backed Reynard in Formula Nippon, and has been a mentor to his driver, Toranosuke Takagi, Japan's most exciting prospect of the late nineties.

NAKAJIMA, Satoru (J) b 23/2/1953, Okazaki City

	1987	Championship position: 11th		Wins: 0	Pole positions: 0	Fastest laps: 0	Points scored: 7			
	Race	Circuit	No	Entrant	Tyres	Car/Engine		Comment	Q Pos/Entries
7	BRAZILIAN GP	Rio	11	Camel Team Lotus Honda	G	1.5 t/c Lotus 99T-Honda V6		pit stop-tyres/-2 laps	12/23
6	SAN MARINO GP	Imola	11	Camel Team Lotus Honda	G	1.5 t/c Lotus 99T-Honda V6		pit stop-tyres/-2 laps	13/27
5	BELGIAN GP	Spa	11	Camel Team Lotus Honda	G	1.5 t/c Lotus 99T-Honda V6		pit stop-tyres/-1 lap	15/26
10	MONACO GP	Monte Carlo	11	Camel Team Lotus Honda	G	1.5 t/c Lotus 99T-Honda V6		hit by Alliot/Capelli-p stop/-3 laps	17/26
ret	US GP (DETROIT)	Detroit	11	Camel Team Lotus Honda	G	1.5 t/c Lotus 99T-Honda V6		accident with Campos	24/26

	Event	Circuit	No	Team	Tyre	Car/Engine	Notes	Grid/Fin
nc	FRENCH GP	Paul Ricard	11	Camel Team Lotus Honda	G	1.5 t/c Lotus 99T-Honda V6	*stops-tyre-wheel problems/-9 laps*	16/26
4	BRITISH GP	Silverstone	11	Camel Team Lotus Honda	G	1.5 t/c Lotus 99T-Honda V6	*pit stop-tyres/2 laps behind*	12/26
ret	GERMAN GP	Hockenheim	11	Camel Team Lotus Honda	G	1.5 t/c Lotus 99T-Honda V6	*turbo*	14/26
ret	HUNGARIAN GP	Hungaroring	11	Camel Team Lotus Honda	G	1.5 t/c Lotus 99T-Honda V6	*driveshaft*	17/26
13	AUSTRIAN GP	Österreichring	11	Camel Team Lotus Honda	G	1.5 t/c Lotus 99T-Honda V6	*pit stop-puncture/-3 laps*	13/26
11	ITALIAN GP	Monza	11	Camel Team Lotus Honda	G	1.5 t/c Lotus 99T-Honda V6	*spin/pit stop-tyres/-3 laps*	14/28
8	PORTUGUESE GP	Estoril	11	Camel Team Lotus Honda	G	1.5 t/c Lotus 99T-Honda V6	*pit stop-tyres/2 laps behind*	15/27
9	SPANISH GP	Jerez	11	Camel Team Lotus Honda	G	1.5 t/c Lotus 99T-Honda V6	*pit stop-tyres/2 laps behind*	18/28
ret	MEXICAN GP	Mexico City	11	Camel Team Lotus Honda	G	1.5 t/c Lotus 99T-Honda V6	*hit Warwick*	16/27
6	JAPANESE GP	Suzuka	11	Camel Team Lotus Honda	G	1.5 t/c Lotus 99T-Honda V6		12/27
ret	AUSTRALIAN GP	Adelaide	11	Camel Team Lotus Honda	G	1.5 t/c Lotus 99T-Honda V6	*hydraulic leak*	14/27

1988   Championship position: 16th   Wins: 0   Pole positions: 0   Fastest laps: 0   Points scored: 1

	Event	Circuit	No	Team	Tyre	Car/Engine	Notes	Grid/Fin
6	BRAZILIAN GP	Rio	2	Camel Team Lotus Honda	G	1.5 t/c Lotus 100T-Honda V6	*pit stop-tyres/1 lap behind*	10/31
8	SAN MARINO GP	Imola	2	Camel Team Lotus Honda	G	1.5 t/c Lotus 100T-Honda V6	*1 lap behind*	12/31
dnq	MONACO GP	Monte Carlo	2	Camel Team Lotus Honda	G	1.5 t/c Lotus 100T-Honda V6		27/30
ret	MEXICAN GP	Mexico City	2	Camel Team Lotus Honda	G	1.5 t/c Lotus 100T-Honda V6	*turbo*	6/30
11	CANADIAN GP	Montreal	2	Camel Team Lotus Honda	G	1.5 t/c Lotus 100T-Honda V6	*pit stop-tyres/3 laps behind*	13/31
dnq	US GP (DETROIT)	Detroit	2	Camel Team Lotus Honda	G	1.5 t/c Lotus 100T-Honda V6		28/31
7	FRENCH GP	Paul Ricard	2	Camel Team Lotus Honda	G	1.5 t/c Lotus 100T-Honda V6	*pit stop-tyres/handling/-1 lap*	8/31
10	BRITISH GP	Silverstone	2	Camel Team Lotus Honda	G	1.5 t/c Lotus 100T-Honda V6	*lost 5th gear/1 lap behind*	10/31
9	GERMAN GP	Hockenheim	2	Camel Team Lotus Honda	G	1.5 t/c Lotus 100T-Honda V6	*1 lap behind*	8/31
7	HUNGARIAN GP	Hungaroring	2	Camel Team Lotus Honda	G	1.5 t/c Lotus 100T-Honda V6	*hit by Streiff/3 laps behind*	19/31
ret	BELGIAN GP	Spa	2	Camel Team Lotus Honda	G	1.5 t/c Lotus 100T-Honda V6	*engine*	8/31
ret	ITALIAN GP	Monza	2	Camel Team Lotus Honda	G	1.5 t/c Lotus 100T-Honda V6	*engine*	12/31
ret	PORTUGUESE GP	Estoril	2	Camel Team Lotus Honda	G	1.5 t/c Lotus 100T-Honda V6	*accident damage*	16/31
ret	SPANISH GP	Jerez	2	Camel Team Lotus Honda	G	1.5 t/c Lotus 100T-Honda V6	*spun off*	15/31
7	JAPANESE GP	Suzuka	2	Camel Team Lotus Honda	G	1.5 t/c Lotus 100T-Honda V6	*1 lap behind*	6/31
ret	AUSTRALIAN GP	Adelaide	2	Camel Team Lotus Honda	G	1.5 t/c Lotus 100T-Honda V6	*hit Gugelmin*	13/31

1989   Championship position: 21   Wins: 0   Pole positions: 0   Fastest laps: 1   Points scored: 3

	Event	Circuit	No	Team	Tyre	Car/Engine	Notes	Grid/Fin
8	BRAZILIAN GP	Rio	12	Camel Team Lotus	G	3.5 Lotus 101-Judd V8	*2 pit stops-tyres/clutch/-1 lap*	21/38
nc	SAN MARINO GP	Imola	12	Camel Team Lotus	G	3.5 Lotus 101-Judd V8	*pit stop-electrics/-12 laps*	24/39
dnq	MONACO GP	Monte Carlo	12	Camel Team Lotus	G	3.5 Lotus 101-Judd V8		29/38
ret	MEXICAN GP	Mexico City	12	Camel Team Lotus	G	3.5 Lotus 101-Judd V8	*gearbox-spun off*	15/39
ret	US GP (PHOENIX)	Phoenix	12	Camel Team Lotus	G	3.5 Lotus 101-Judd V8	*throttle cable bracket*	23/39
dnq	CANADIAN GP	Montreal	12	Camel Team Lotus	G	3.5 Lotus 101-Judd V8		27/39
ret	FRENCH GP	Paul Ricard	12	Camel Team Lotus	G	3.5 Lotus 101-Judd V8	*electrics-engine cut out*	19/39
8	BRITISH GP	Silverstone	12	Camel Team Lotus	G	3.5 Lotus 101-Judd V8	*1 lap behind*	16/39
ret	GERMAN GP	Hockenheim	12	Camel Team Lotus	G	3.5 Lotus 101-Judd V8	*spun off*	18/39
ret	HUNGARIAN GP	Hungaroring	12	Camel Team Lotus	G	3.5 Lotus 101-Judd V8	*collision with Warwick*	20/39
dnq	BELGIAN GP	Spa	12	Camel Team Lotus	G	3.5 Lotus 101-Judd V8		27/39
10	ITALIAN GP	Monza	12	Camel Team Lotus	G	3.5 Lotus 101-Judd V8	*2 pit stops-tyres/-2 laps*	19/39
7	PORTUGUESE GP	Estoril	12	Camel Team Lotus	G	3.5 Lotus 101-Judd V8	*1 lap behind*	25/39
ret	SPANISH GP	Jerez	12	Camel Team Lotus	G	3.5 Lotus 101-Judd V8	*hit by Capelli-spun off*	18/38
ret	JAPANESE GP	Suzuka	12	Camel Team Lotus	G	3.5 Lotus 101-Judd V8	*engine*	12/39
4	AUSTRALIAN GP	Adelaide	12	Camel Team Lotus	G	3.5 Lotus 101-Judd V8	*FL in the rain*	23/39

1990   Championship position: 14th   Wins: 0   Pole positions: 0   Fastest laps: 0   Points scored: 3

	Event	Circuit	No	Team	Tyre	Car/Engine	Notes	Grid/Fin
6	US GP (PHOENIX)	Phoenix	3	Tyrrell Racing Organisation	P	3.5 Tyrrell 018-Cosworth V8	*1 lap behind*	11/35
8	BRAZILIAN GP	Interlagos	3	Tyrrell Racing Organisation	P	3.5 Tyrrell 018-Cosworth V8	*collision with Senna/-1 lap*	19/35
ret	SAN MARINO GP	Imola	3	Tyrrell Racing Organisation	P	3.5 Tyrrell 019-Cosworth V8	*hit Capelli-lap 1*	20/34
ret	MONACO GP	Monte Carlo	3	Tyrrell Racing Organisation	P	3.5 Tyrrell 019-Cosworth V8	*suspension*	21/35
11	CANADIAN GP	Montreal	3	Tyrrell Racing Organisation	P	3.5 Tyrrell 019-Cosworth V8	*3 laps behind*	13/35
ret	MEXICAN GP	Mexico City	3	Tyrrell Racing Organisation	P	3.5 Tyrrell 019-Cosworth V8	*collision with Suzuki*	9/35
ret	FRENCH GP	Paul Ricard	3	Tyrrell Racing Organisation	P	3.5 Tyrrell 019-Cosworth V8	*transmission*	15/35
ret	BRITISH GP	Silverstone	3	Tyrrell Racing Organisation	P	3.5 Tyrrell 019-Cosworth V8	*electrics*	12/35
ret	GERMAN GP	Hockenheim	3	Tyrrell Racing Organisation	P	3.5 Tyrrell 019-Cosworth V8	*engine*	13/35
ret	HUNGARIAN GP	Hungaroring	3	Tyrrell Racing Organisation	P	3.5 Tyrrell 019-Cosworth V8	*spun off*	15/35
ret	BELGIAN GP	Spa	3	Tyrrell Racing Organisation	P	3.5 Tyrrell 019-Cosworth V8	*misfire*	10/33
6	ITALIAN GP	Monza	3	Tyrrell Racing Organisation	P	3.5 Tyrrell 019-Cosworth V8	*1 lap behind*	14/33
dns	PORTUGUESE GP	Estoril	3	Tyrrell Racing Organisation	P	3.5 Tyrrell 019-Cosworth V8	*withdrawn-driver unwell*	(20)/33
ret	SPANISH GP	Jerez	3	Tyrrell Racing Organisation	P	3.5 Tyrrell 019-Cosworth V8	*spun off*	14/33
6	JAPANESE GP	Suzuka	3	Tyrrell Racing Organisation	P	3.5 Tyrrell 019-Cosworth V8		14/30
ret	AUSTRALIAN GP	Adelaide	3	Tyrrell Racing Organisation	P	3.5 Tyrrell 019-Cosworth V8	*spun off*	13/30

1991   Championship position: 15th   Wins: 0   Pole positions: 0   Fastest laps: 0   Points scored: 2

	Event	Circuit	No	Team	Tyre	Car/Engine	Notes	Grid/Fin
5	US GP (PHOENIX)	Phoenix	3	Braun Tyrrell Honda	P	3.5 Tyrrell 020-Honda V10	*1 lap behind*	16/34
ret	BRAZILIAN GP	Interlagos	3	Braun Tyrrell Honda	P	3.5 Tyrrell 020-Honda V10	*spun off*	16/34
ret	SAN MARINO GP	Imola	3	Braun Tyrrell Honda	P	3.5 Tyrrell 020-Honda V10	*transmission*	10/34
ret	MONACO GP	Monte Carlo	3	Braun Tyrrell Honda	P	3.5 Tyrrell 020-Honda V10	*spun and stalled*	11/34
10	CANADIAN GP	Montreal	3	Braun Tyrrell Honda	P	3.5 Tyrrell 020-Honda V10	*2 laps behind*	12/34
12	MEXICAN GP	Mexico City	3	Braun Tyrrell Honda	P	3.5 Tyrrell 020-Honda V10	*3 laps behind*	13/34
ret	FRENCH GP	Magny Cours	3	Braun Tyrrell Honda	P	3.5 Tyrrell 020-Honda V10	*spun off*	18/34
8	BRITISH GP	Silverstone	3	Braun Tyrrell Honda	P	3.5 Tyrrell 020-Honda V10	*1 lap behind*	15/34
ret	GERMAN GP	Hockenheim	3	Braun Tyrrell Honda	P	3.5 Tyrrell 020-Honda V10	*gearbox*	13/34
15	HUNGARIAN GP	Hungaroring	3	Braun Tyrrell Honda	P	3.5 Tyrrell 020-Honda V10	*3 laps behind*	14/34
ret	BELGIAN GP	Spa	3	Braun Tyrrell Honda	P	3.5 Tyrrell 020-Honda V10	*slid off at Les Combes*	22/34
ret	ITALIAN GP	Monza	3	Braun Tyrrell Honda	P	3.5 Tyrrell 020-Honda V10	*sticking throttle*	15/34
13	PORTUGUESE GP	Estoril	3	Braun Tyrrell Honda	P	3.5 Tyrrell 020-Honda V10	*3 laps behind*	21/34
17	SPANISH GP	Barcelona	3	Braun Tyrrell Honda	P	3.5 Tyrrell 020-Honda V10	*3 laps behind*	18/33
ret	JAPANESE GP	Suzuka	3	Braun Tyrrell Honda	P	3.5 Tyrrell 020-Honda V10	*suspension*	15/31
ret	AUSTRALIAN GP	Adelaide	3	Braun Tyrrell Honda	P	3.5 Tyrrell 020-Honda V10	*collision with Boutsen*	24/32

GP Starts: 74   GP Wins: 0   Pole positions: 0   Fastest laps: 1   Points: 16

SHINJI NAKANO

Shinji began karting at the age of 13 way back in 1984 and spent a successful five years in this discipline until switching to Japanese Formula 3 in 1989. He then took the brave decision to chance his arm in the Formula Opel Lotus Euroseries for two seasons in 1990-91, but endured a thin time of it and returned to Japan for 1992 to race for Satoru Nakajima in both F3000 and Formula 3.

This over-ambitious schedule proved to be his undoing, and he decided to concentrate solely on Formula 3 in 1993 in a bid to restart his now flagging career. Helped greatly by Mugen Honda boss Hirotoshita Honda, he moved back up to the All-Japan F3000 championship the following year and gradually worked his way to the front end of the grid.

His connections were crucial in his placement in the Prost team for 1997 where at first he was all at sea. Certainly Alain Prost gave little time to his number two driver and was pushing hard to drop him from the team, but in the end Mr Honda stood firm and his protégé was safe. Accepting the situation, Alain then spent some time helping Shinji to come to terms with Formula 1, with the result that his performances improved no end in the second half of the season.

For 1998 Nakano was found a seat at Minardi and did a tidy job under difficult circumstances, but not unnaturally nothing in the way of startling results was achieved.

A few days' testing for the Jordan team was the only action that Nakano could find in 1999, but he has struck a deal to race in CART in 2000, driving a Honda-powered car for Walker Racing.

NAKANO, Shinji (J) b 1/4/1971, Oksaka

1997		Championship position: 16th=		Wins: 0		Pole positions: 0		Fastest laps: 0	Points scored: 2	
	Race	Circuit	No	Entrant	Tyres	Car/Engine			Comment	Q Pos/Entries
7	AUSTRALIAN GP	Melbourne	15	Prost Gauloise Blondes	B	3.0 Prost JS45-Mugen Honda V10			1 lap behind	16/24
14	BRAZILIAN GP	Interlagos	15	Prost Gauloise Blondes	B	3.0 Prost JS45-Mugen Honda V10			1 lap behind	15/22
ret	ARGENTINE GP	Buenos Aires	15	Prost Gauloise Blondes	B	3.0 Prost JS45-Mugen Honda V10			engine	20/22
ret	SAN MARINO GP	Imola	15	Prost Gauloise Blondes	B	3.0 Prost JS45-Mugen Honda V10			shunted off by Hill	18/22
ret	MONACO GP	Monte Carlo	15	Prost Gauloise Blondes	B	3.0 Prost JS45-Mugen Honda V10			spun off	21/22
ret	SPANISH GP	Barcelona	15	Prost Gauloise Blondes	B	3.0 Prost JS45-Mugen Honda V10			gearbox	16/22
6	CANADIAN GP	Montreal	15	Prost Gauloise Blondes	B	3.0 Prost JS45-Mugen Honda V10				19/22
ret	FRENCH GP	Magny Cours	15	Prost Gauloise Blondes	B	3.0 Prost JS45-Mugen Honda V10			spun off	12/22
11/ret	BRITISH GP	Silverstone	15	Prost Gauloise Blondes	B	3.0 Prost JS45-Mugen Honda V10			engine	15/22
7	GERMAN GP	Hockenheim	15	Prost Gauloise Blondes	B	3.0 Prost JS45-Mugen Honda V10				17/22
6	HUNGARIAN GP	Hungaroring	15	Prost Gauloise Blondes	B	3.0 Prost JS45-Mugen Honda V10				16/22
ret	BELGIAN GP	Spa	15	Prost Gauloise Blondes	B	3.0 Prost JS45-Mugen Honda V10			spun off	16/22
11	ITALIAN GP	Monza	15	Prost Gauloise Blondes	B	3.0 Prost JS45-Mugen Honda V10				15/22
ret	AUSTRIAN GP	A-1 Ring	15	Prost Gauloise Blondes	B	3.0 Prost JS45-Mugen Honda V10			engine	16/22
ret	LUXEMBOURG GP	Nürburgring	15	Prost Gauloise Blondes	B	3.0 Prost JS45-Mugen Honda V10			engine	17/22
ret	JAPANESE GP	Suzuka	15	Prost Gauloise Blondes	B	3.0 Prost JS45-Mugen Honda V10			wheel bearing	15/22
10	EUROPEAN GP	Jerez	15	Prost Gauloise Blondes	B	3.0 Prost JS45-Mugen Honda V10				15/22
1998		Championship position: Unplaced								
ret	AUSTRALIAN GP	Melbourne	22	Fondmetal Minardi Ford	B	3.0 Minardi M198-Ford Zetec r V10			driveshaft	22/22
ret	BRAZILIAN GP	Interlagos	22	Fondmetal Minardi Ford	B	3.0 Minardi M198-Ford Zetec r V10			spun off	18/22
13	ARGENTINE GP	Buenos Aires	22	Fondmetal Minardi Ford	B	3.0 Minardi M198-Ford Zetec r V10			3 laps behind	19/22
ret	SAN MARINO GP	Imola	22	Fondmetal Minardi Ford	B	3.0 Minardi M198-Ford Zetec r V10			engine	21/22
14	SPANISH GP	Barcelona	22	Fondmetal Minardi Ford	B	3.0 Minardi M198-Ford Zetec r V10			2 laps behind	20/22
9	MONACO GP	Monte Carlo	22	Fondmetal Minardi Ford	B	3.0 Minardi M198-Ford Zetec r V10			2 laps behind	19/22
7	CANADIAN GP	Montreal	22	Fondmetal Minardi Ford	B	3.0 Minardi M198-Ford Zetec r V10			1 lap behind	18/22
17/ret	FRENCH GP	Magny Cours	22	Fondmetal Minardi Ford	B	3.0 Minardi M198-Ford Zetec r V10			engine/6 laps behind	21/22
8	BRITISH GP	Silverstone	22	Fondmetal Minardi Ford	B	3.0 Minardi M198-Ford Zetec r V10			2 laps behind	21/22
11	AUSTRIAN GP	A-1 Ring	22	Fondmetal Minardi Ford	B	3.0 Minardi M198-Ford Zetec r V10			1 lap behind	21/22
ret	GERMAN GP	Hockenheim	22	Fondmetal Minardi Ford	B	3.0 Minardi M198-Ford Zetec r V10			gearbox	20/22
15	HUNGARIAN GP	Hungaroring	22	Fondmetal Minardi Ford	B	3.0 Minardi M198-Ford Zetec r V10			3 laps behind	19/22
8	BELGIAN GP	Spa	22	Fondmetal Minardi Ford	B	3.0 Minardi M198-Ford Zetec r V10			5 laps behind	21/22
ret	ITALIAN GP	Monza	22	Fondmetal Minardi Ford	B	3.0 Minardi M198-Ford Zetec r V10			engine	21/22
15	LUXEMBOURG GP	Nürburgring	22	Fondmetal Minardi Ford	B	3.0 Minardi M198-Ford Zetec r V10			2 laps behind	20/22
ret	JAPANESE GP	Suzuka	22	Fondmetal Minardi Ford	B	3.0 Minardi M198-Ford Zetec r V10			throttle	20/22

GP Starts: 33   GP Wins: 0   Pole positions: 0   Fastest laps: 0   Points: 2

ALESSANDRO NANNINI

The beaming countenance and charming manner of Alessandro Nannini were among the more pleasing aspects of life in the Formula 1 paddock in the late eighties. Certainly it was Grand Prix racing's loss when his career was so devastatingly wrecked by a helicopter accident in which his right arm was severed. Surgeons were able to re-attach the limb but controlling an F1 car was now beyond him and the popular Italian's misfortune seemed all the more cruel since his Grand Prix prospects had been at their zenith.

Sandro began his racing activities off road with a Lancia Stratos, before turning to circuit racing in 1981 in Formula Italia. He then took a big jump into Formula 2 with Minardi in 1982, replacing the team's previous star, Michele Alboreto, who had moved into F1 with Tyrrell. Nannini soon proved himself a worthy successor and by the end of the season he had taken a second place at Misano. In 1983 Minardi produced a promising but initially unworkable new car, and Nannini had to resort to the old chassis to take another second place, this time at the Nürburgring. By 1984, still loyal to the team, Sandro's F2 career was really treading water, but everyone had seen the talent and Lancia signed him to drive for their sports car team between 1984 and 1986.

Having dispensed with the services of Pierluigi Martini, Minardi entered two cars in 1986, with Sandro very much the number two (in theory at least) to the experienced Andrea de Cesaris. He was to spend two seasons with the little team, which in truth had little hope of success. However, Sandro made his mark and, unlike a number of other Grand Prix talents, managed to escape to a front-line team before too many seasons at the back of the field could dull his edge. Chosen to partner Thierry Boutsen at Benetton, he proved more than a match for the Belgian, making the rostrum on two occasions. Nannini was thrust into the position of team leader in 1989 and took some time to adjust to the new situation, but once the new Ford engine arrived his season began to take off. He won the Japanese GP on a technical knock-out after Senna was excluded following his tête-à-tête with Prost, and then took a fine second to Boutsen's Williams in the rain-soaked Australian GP.

In 1990 Sandro was joined by the experienced and cunning Nelson Piquet, who immediately established a rapport with John Barnard in developing the B190. Having been somewhat overshadowed, Nannini suddenly found his form again at Hockenheim, where he led until finally giving best to Senna. The battle with the Brazilian was rejoined in Hungary, where Ayrton crassly elbowed the Benetton out of second place, ending Sandro's chances of a win. Certainly the Italian's star was in the ascendant, and there was reportedly a Ferrari contract being bandied about, if not for 1991, then certainly for some time in the future.

It was all to prove academic after the helicopter accident, but Nannini bravely fought back, to the admiration and great pleasure of the motor racing world. In 1992 he raced an Alfa Romeo successfully in the Italian touring car championship, before proving that he was not in the Alfa team on sentiment alone with some fine displays in the 1993 German series, backing his team-mate Larini superbly as they defeated the Mercedes on home territory.

After a blindingly good start to 1994, the problems of developing the second evolution Alfa Romeo told on Nannini, whose performances became somewhat erratic, but he bounced back to form in 1996, winning seven rounds of the marathon 26-race ITC series to finish third in the championship.

With the collapse of the ITC, Nannini moved into the FIA GT series for 1997 with a works Mercedes CLK-GTR, but it was a mixed year in which only four second-place finishes were achieved. Although rumours linked him with BMW's Le Mans efforts, Sandro has not raced since.

NANNINI, Alessandro (I) b 7/7/1959, Siena

	1986	Championship position: Unplaced						
	Race	Circuit	No	Entrant	Tyres	Car/Engine	Comment	Q Pos/Entries
ret	BRAZILIAN GP	Rio	24	Minardi Team	P	1.5 t/c Minardi M185B-MM V6	clutch	25/25
dns	SPANISH GP	Jerez	24	Minardi Team	P	1.5 t/c Minardi M185B-MM V6	differential on parade lap	(25)/25
ret	SAN MARINO GP	Imola	24	Minardi Team	P	1.5 t/c Minardi M185B-MM V6	collision-suspension damage	18/26

dnq	MONACO GP	Monte Carlo	24	Minardi Team	P	1.5 t/c Minardi M185B-MM V6		26/26
ret	BELGIAN GP	Spa	24	Minardi Team	P	1.5 t/c Minardi M185B-MM V6	gearbox	22/25
ret	CANADIAN GP	Montreal	24	Minardi Team	P	1.5 t/c Minardi M185B-MM V6	turbo	20/25
ret	US GP (DETROIT)	Detroit	24	Minardi Team	P	1.5 t/c Minardi M185B-MM V6	turbo	24/26
ret	FRENCH GP	Paul Ricard	24	Minardi Team	P	1.5 t/c Minardi M185B-MM V6	accident with Ghinzani	19/26
ret	BRITISH GP	Brands Hatch	24	Minardi Team	P	1.5 t/c Minardi M185B-MM V6	started from pits/driveshaft	20/26
ret	GERMAN GP	Hockenheim	24	Minardi Team	P	1.5 t/c Minardi M185B-MM V6	overheating	22/26
ret	HUNGARIAN GP	Hungaroring	24	Minardi Team	P	1.5 t/c Minardi M185B-MM V6	engine	17/26
ret	AUSTRIAN GP	Österreichring	24	Minardi Team	P	1.5 t/c Minardi M185B-MM V6	suspension-spun off	19/26
dns	"		24		P	1.5 t/c Minardi M186-MM V6	practice only	– / –
ret	ITALIAN GP	Monza	24	Minardi Team	P	1.5 t/c Minardi M185B-MM V6	electrics	19/27
ret	PORTUGUESE GP	Estoril	24	Minardi Team	P	1.5 t/c Minardi M185B-MM V6	gearbox	18/27
14	MEXICAN GP	Mexico City	24	Minardi Team	P	1.5 t/c Minardi M185B-MM V6	pit stop-tyres/4 laps behind	24/26
ret	AUSTRALIAN GP	Adelaide	24	Minardi Team	P	1.5 t/c Minardi M185B-MM V6	crashed into barrier	18/26

1987   Championship position: Unplaced

ret	BRAZILIAN GP	Rio	24	Minardi Team	G	1.5 t/c Minardi M/187-MM V6	suspension	15/23
ret	SAN MARINO GP	Imola	24	Minardi Team	G	1.5 t/c Minardi M/187-MM V6	turbo	17/27
ret	BELGIAN GP	Spa	24	Minardi Team	G	1.5 t/c Minardi M/187-MM V6	turbo	14/26
ret	MONACO GP	Monte Carlo	24	Minardi Team	G	1.5 t/c Minardi M/187-MM V6	electrics	13/26
ret	US GP (DETROIT)	Detroit	24	Minardi Team	G	1.5 t/c Minardi M/187-MM V6	gearbox	18/26
ret	FRENCH GP	Paul Ricard	24	Minardi Team	G	1.5 t/c Minardi M/187-MM V6	turbo	15/26
ret	BRITISH GP	Silverstone	24	Minardi Team	G	1.5 t/c Minardi M/187-MM V6	engine	15/26
ret	GERMAN GP	Hockenheim	24	Minardi Team	G	1.5 t/c Minardi M/187-MM V6	engine	16/26
11	HUNGARIAN GP	Hungaroring	24	Minardi Team	G	1.5 t/c Minardi M/187-MM V6	3 laps behind	20/26
ret	AUSTRIAN GP	Österreichring	24	Minardi Team	G	1.5 t/c Minardi M/187-MM V6	engine	15/26
16/ret	ITALIAN GP	Monza	24	Minardi Team	G	1.5 t/c Minardi M/187-MM V6	out of fuel/5 laps behind	18/28
11/ret	PORTUGUESE GP	Estoril	24	Minardi Team	G	1.5 t/c Minardi M/187-MM V6	out of fuel/4 laps behind	14/27
ret	SPANISH GP	Jerez	24	Minardi Team	G	1.5 t/c Minardi M/187-MM V6	turbo	21/28
ret	MEXICAN GP	Mexico City	24	Minardi Team	G	1.5 t/c Minardi M/187-MM V6	turbo	14/27
ret	JAPANESE GP	Suzuka	24	Minardi Team	G	1.5 t/c Minardi M/187-MM V6	engine	15/27
ret	AUSTRALIAN GP	Adelaide	24	Minardi Team	G	1.5 t/c Minardi M/187-MM V6	hit wall	13/27

1988   Championship position: 9th   Wins: 0   Pole positions: 0   Fastest laps: 1   Points scored: 12

ret	BRAZILIAN GP	Rio	19	Benetton Formula	G	3.5 Benetton B188-Cosworth V8	overheating	12/31
6	SAN MARINO GP	Imola	19	Benetton Formula	G	3.5 Benetton B188-Cosworth V8	1 lap behind	4/31
ret	MONACO GP	Monte Carlo	19	Benetton Formula	G	3.5 Benetton B188-Cosworth V8	gearbox	6/30
7	MEXICAN GP	Mexico City	19	Benetton Formula	G	3.5 Benetton B188-Cosworth V8	2 laps behind	8/30
ret	CANADIAN GP	Montreal	19	Benetton Formula	G	3.5 Benetton B188-Cosworth V8	ignition/water leak	5/31
ret	US GP (DETROIT)	Detroit	19	Benetton Formula	G	3.5 Benetton B188-Cosworth V8	front suspension damage	7/31
6	FRENCH GP	Paul Ricard	19	Benetton Formula	G	3.5 Benetton B188-Cosworth V8	1 lap behind	6/31
3	BRITISH GP	Silverstone	19	Benetton Formula	G	3.5 Benetton B188-Cosworth V8	two spins	8/31
18	GERMAN GP	Hockenheim	19	Benetton Formula	G	3.5 Benetton B188-Cosworth V8	pit stop-throttle cable/-4 laps/FL	6/31
ret	HUNGARIAN GP	Hungaroring	19	Benetton Formula	G	3.5 Benetton B188-Cosworth V8	water pipe leak	5/31
dsq	BELGIAN GP	Spa	19	Benetton Formula	G	3.5 Benetton B188-Cosworth V8	4th on road/*illegal fuel	7/31
9	ITALIAN GP	Monza	19	Benetton Formula	G	3.5 Benetton B188-Cosworth V8	started lfrom pit lane/-1 lap	9/31
ret	PORTUGUESE GP	Estoril	19	Benetton Formula	G	3.5 Benetton B188-Cosworth V8	exhausted due to chassis vibration	9/31
3	SPANISH GP	Jerez	19	Benetton Formula	G	3.5 Benetton B188-Cosworth V8		5/31
5	JAPANESE GP	Suzuka	19	Benetton Formula	G	3.5 Benetton B188-Cosworth V8		12/31
ret	AUSTRALIAN GP	Adelaide	19	Benetton Formula	G	3.5 Benetton B188-Cosworth V8	spun off-could not restart	8/31

1989   Championship position: 6th   Wins: 1   Pole positions: 0   Fastest laps: 0   Points scored: 32

6	BRAZILIAN GP	Rio	19	Benetton Formula	G	3.5 Benetton B188-Cosworth V8	2 stops-tyres/broken wing stay	11/38
3	SAN MARINO GP	Imola	19	Benetton Formula	G	3.5 Benetton B188-Cosworth V8	vibration /-1 lap	7/39
8	MONACO GP	Monte Carlo	19	Benetton Formula	G	3.5 Benetton B188-Cosworth V8	brakes-clipped barrier/-3 laps	15/38
4	MEXICAN GP	Mexico City	19	Benetton Formula	G	3.5 Benetton B188-Cosworth V8		13/39
ret	US GP (PHOENIX)	Phoenix	19	Benetton Formula	G	3.5 Benetton B188-Cosworth V8	driver exhausted	3/39
dsq	CANADIAN GP	Montreal	19	Benetton Formula	G	3.5 Benetton B188-Cosworth V8	started from pits before green	13/39
ret	FRENCH GP	Paul Ricard	19	Benetton Formula	G	3.5 Benetton B189-Ford V8	suspension	4/39
3	BRITISH GP	Silverstone	19	Benetton Formula	G	3.5 Benetton B189-Ford V8	broken exhaust	9/39
ret	GERMAN GP	Hockenheim	19	Benetton Formula	G	3.5 Benetton B189-Ford V8	ignition	7/39
ret	HUNGARIAN GP	Hungaroring	19	Benetton Formula	G	3.5 Benetton B189-Ford V8	gearbox	7/39
5	BELGIAN GP	Spa	19	Benetton Formula	G	3.5 Benetton B189-Ford V8		7/39
ret	ITALIAN GP	Monza	19	Benetton Formula	G	3.5 Benetton B189-Ford V8	brakes	8/39
4	PORTUGUESE GP	Estoril	19	Benetton Formula	G	3.5 Benetton B189-Ford V8		13/39
ret	SPANISH GP	Jerez	19	Benetton Formula	G	3.5 Benetton B189-Ford V8	spun off	14/38
1*	JAPANESE GP	Suzuka	19	Benetton Formula	G	3.5 Benetton B189-Ford V8	*1st place car disqualified	6/39
2	AUSTRALIAN GP	Adelaide	19	Benetton Formula	G	3.5 Benetton B189-Ford V8	broken exhaust	4/39

1990   Championship position: 8th   Wins: 0   Pole positions: 0   Fastest laps: 1   Points scored: 21

11	US GP (PHOENIX)	Phoenix	19	Benetton Formula	G	3.5 Benetton B189B-Ford V8	2 stops-accident damage/-2 laps	22/35
10/ret	BRAZILIAN GP	Interlagos	19	Benetton Formula	G	3.5 Benetton B189B-Ford V8	collision-de Cesaris/-3 laps	15/35
3	SAN MARINO GP	Imola	19	Benetton Formula	G	3.5 Benetton B190-Ford V8	FL	9/34
ret	MONACO GP	Monte Carlo	19	Benetton Formula	G	3.5 Benetton B190-Ford V8	oil pressure	16/35
ret	CANADIAN GP	Montreal	19	Benetton Formula	G	3.5 Benetton B190-Ford V8	spun off	4/35
4	MEXICAN GP	Mexico City	19	Benetton Formula	G	3.5 Benetton B190-Ford V8		14/35
16*/ret	FRENCH GP	Paul Ricard	19	Benetton Formula	G	3.5 Benetton B190-Ford V8	15th car dsq/engine/-5 laps	5/35
ret	BRITISH GP	Silverstone	19	Benetton Formula	G	3.5 Benetton B190-Ford V8	hit Patrese-spun and stalled	13/35
2	GERMAN GP	Hockenheim	19	Benetton Formula	G	3.5 Benetton B190-Ford V8	led race	9/35
ret	HUNGARIAN GP	Hungaroring	19	Benetton Formula	G	3.5 Benetton B190-Ford V8	collision with Senna	7/35
4	BELGIAN GP	Spa	19	Benetton Formula	G	3.5 Benetton B190-Ford V8		6/33
8	ITALIAN GP	Monza	19	Benetton Formula	G	3.5 Benetton B190-Ford V8	long pit stop-tyres/-1 lap	8/33
6	PORTUGUESE GP	Estoril	19	Benetton Formula	G	3.5 Benetton B190-Ford V8		9/33
3	SPANISH GP	Jerez	19	Benetton Formula	G	3.5 Benetton B190-Ford V8		9/33

GP Starts: 76(77)   GP Wins: 1   Pole positions: 0   Fastest laps: 2   Points: 65

EMANUELE NASPETTI

Driving for the top-notch Forti team, Naspetti won a titanic struggle with Mauro Martini to clinch the 1988 Italian F3 championship in only his second year of racing cars, having been in karting between 1980 and '86.

Drawing a blank in his first season of F3000, Naspetti then came under the wing of Eddie Jordan in 1990 but again disapppointed, scoring but a single point. It was a different story in 1991 when, with the advantage of a Heini Mader-tended Cosworth engine in his Forti Corse Reynard, the Italian came out of his shell to string together a run of four victories at Enna, Hockenheim, Brands Hatch and Spa. Still with Forti, he stayed in the formula for a fourth year in 1992, winning at Pau, but then jumped at the chance to join the Formula 1 March team, replacing Paul Belmondo in mid-season. Emanuele proved surprisingly quick to adapt, clinging tenaciously to his team-mate Wendlinger for most of his debut race at Spa.

Naspetti spent much of 1993 frustrated at the lack of a Formula 1 drive, but did make a one-off appearance for Jordan in Portugal as a reward for his efforts as a test driver.

Since then he has carved out a niche for himself in the Italian Superturismo series with a BMW 320i. A controversial stop-and-go penalty in the final round cost him the chance of the title in 1996, but he made amends the following year as he dominated the championship. Emanuele subsequently hankered after a return to single-seaters and visited the States to sound out the possibility of a ride in CART but, thus far, he has continued to race in Italy, where his BMW has had to play second fiddle to Giovanardi's Alfa Romeo.

MASSIMO NATILI

One of a number of promising Italian Formula Junior drivers tested by Scuderia Centro Sud, Massimo was given a handful of outings in 1961, none of which brought any success.

In 1962 he was lucky to survive a crash in a Monza FJ race, when an anonymous spectator pulled him from his blazing car with burns to face and legs. He reappeared for Centro Sud in 1963, and took a fourth place in the 1964 Rome GP with a Brabham-Giannini. He continued to race competitively in Italian F3 with a Brabham and was the 1965 1-litre national sports car champion with a Lotus 23.

BRIAN NAYLOR

A motor-dealer from Stockport and a former merchant navy radio officer who won awards for gallantry in the war, Naylor began racing in 1954 with a Cooper-MG but soon switched to a Lotus chassis, regularly clocking up victories the length and breadth of Britain. In 1957 he bought a Formula 2 Cooper, which he was to race in selected events, including Grands Prix, over the next three years.

Naylor was never content to drive standard fare, and experimented with a Maserati-engined Lotus before developing his own Cooper-based JBW-Maserati, which he ran with great success in Libre events but was outclassed in Formula 1 and Inter-Continental racing. Ill-health brought about his retirement at the end of the 1961 season.

NASPETTI, Emanuele (I) b 24/2/1968, Ancona

	1992	Championship position: Unplaced						
	Race	Circuit	No	Entrant	Tyres	Car/Engine	Comment	Q Pos/Entries
12	BELGIAN GP	Spa	17	March F1	G	3.5 March CG911-Ilmor V10	1 lap behind	21/30
ret	ITALIAN GP	Monza	17	March F1	G	3.5 March CG911-Ilmor V10	collision-Wendlinger-spun off	24/28
11	PORTUGUESE GP	Estoril	17	March F1	G	3.5 March CG911-Ilmor V10	3 laps behind	23/26
13	JAPANESE GP	Suzuka	17	March F1	G	3.5 March CG911-Ilmor V10	2 laps behind	26/26
ret	AUSTRALIAN GP	Adelaide	17	March F1	G	3.5 March CG911-Ilmor V10	gearbox	23/26
	1993	Championship position: Unplaced						
ret	PORTUGUESE GP	Estoril	15	Sasol Jordan	G	3.5 Jordan 193-Hart V10	engine fire	23/26

GP Starts: 6   GP Wins: 0   Pole positions: 0   Fastest laps: 0   Points: 0

NATILI, Massimo (I) b 28/7/1935, Ronciglione, Viterbo

	1961	Championship position: Unplaced						
	Race	Circuit	No	Entrant	Tyres	Car/Engine	Comment	Q Pos/Entries
ret	BRITISH GP	Aintree	62	Scuderia Centro Sud	D	1.5 Cooper T51-Maserati 4	gearbox	28/30
dnq	ITALIAN GP	Monza	60	Scuderia Centro Sud	D	1.5 Cooper T51-Maserati 4	practised-but entry taken by Lewis	– / –

GP Starts: 1   GP Wins: 0   Pole positions: 0   Fastest laps: 0   Points: 0

NAYLOR, Brian (GB) b 24/3/1923, Salford, Manchester – d 8/8/1989, Marbella, Spain

	1957	Championship position: Unplaced						
	Race	Circuit	No	Entrant	Tyres	Car/Engine	Comment	Q Pos/Entries
13*	GERMAN GP (F2)	Nürburgring	28	J B Naylor	D	1.5 Cooper T43-Climax 4 F2	* 2nd in F2 class/-2 laps	17/24
	1958	Championship position: Unplaced						
ret	GERMAN GP (F2)	Nürburgring	29	J B Naylor	D	1.5 Cooper T45-Climax 4 F2	fuel pump	21/26
	1959	Championship position: Unplaced						
ret	BRITISH GP	Aintree	36	J B Naylor	D	2.5 JBW-Maserati 4	transmission	14/30
	1960	Championship position: Unplaced						
dnq	MONACO GP	Monte Carlo	20	J B Naylor	D	2.5 JBW-Maserati 4		19/24
13	BRITISH GP	Silverstone	25	J B Naylor	D	2.5 JBW-Maserati 4	pit stop/5 laps behind	18/25
ret	ITALIAN GP	Monza	6	J B Naylor	D	2.5 JBW-Maserati 4	gearbox	7/16
ret	US GP	Riverside	21	J B Naylor	D	2.5 JBW-Maserati 4	engine	17/23
	1961	Championship position: Unplaced						
ret	ITALIAN GP	Monza	14	J B Naylor	D	1.5 JBW-Climax 4	engine	31/33

GP Starts: 7   GP Wins: 0   Pole positions: 0   Fastest laps: 0   Points: 0

NEEDELL, Tiff (GB) b 29/10/1951, Havant, Hampshire

	1980	Championship position: Unplaced						
	Race	Circuit	No	Entrant	Tyres	Car/Engine	Comment	Q Pos/Entries
ret	BELGIAN GP	Zolder	14	Unipart Racing Team	G	3.0 Ensign N180-Cosworth V8	engine	23/27
dnq	MONACO GP	Monte Carlo	14	Unipart Racing Team	G	3.0 Ensign N180-Cosworth V8		26/27

GP Starts: 1   GP Wins: 0   Pole positions: 0   Fastest laps: 0   Points: 0

TIFF NEEDELL

Tiff spent the formative years of his racing career in Formula Ford, winning the FF16000 championship in 1975 and finishing as runner-up in the FF2000 series the following year, when he won the premier Grovewood Award.

After brief spells in Formula 3 and the Aurora F1/F2 championship, Needell's Grand Prix ambitions were thwarted in 1979, when he was refused a super-licence to drive the Ensign, although he was to get his opportunity in 1980.

By then, Tiff had extended his repertoire to encompass Japanese Formula 2, touring cars, the Procar series and sports car racing, where he was to remain active throughout the eighties and nineties, latterly with the Lister Storm.

It is his successful career as a journalist and broadcaster, however, for which he is now best known.

PATRICK NEVE

A one-time pupil at the Jim Russell driving school, Neve later worked as an instructor to finance his own racing activities, but gained enough success in the school's Merlyn to set himself up for a successful year in 1974, winning the STP Formula Ford championship in a Lola T340.

Moving up to Formula 3 in 1975, Patrick drove well enough in the Safir to gain a test with Brabham and a drive with the RAM team in '76. After a couple of non-championship races, he was bundled out of the car by de Villota's banknotes in Spain, but raced in Belgium before departing for a one-off drive with Ensign.

The following year could have seen him make his breakthrough; he led a Formula 2 race at Silverstone until suspension problems dropped him to third place and then spent an unhappy Grand Prix season with the post-Wolf Frank Williams team running a March. The relationship ended in acrimony after the Canadian GP, and Neve's career never really recovered.

After an abortive attempt to make the grid in Belgium in 1978, his planned season of Formula 2 with Kauhsen fell through when the German's sponsors pulled out, leaving the Belgian to race the unsuccessful Pilbeam. Thereafter he appeared only occasionally in BMW Procars and touring cars.

NEVE, Patrick (B) b 13/10/1949, Liège

	1976	Championship position: Unplaced							
	Race	Circuit	No	Entrant	Tyres	Car/Engine	Comment		Q Pos/Entries
ret	BELGIAN GP	Zolder	33	Tissot RAM Racing	G	3.0 Brabham BT44B-Cosworth V8	driveshaft cv joint		19/29
18	FRENCH GP	Paul Ricard	22	Team Ensign	G	3.0 Ensign N176-Cosworth V8	1 lap behind		26/30
	1977	Championship position: Unplaced							
12	SPANISH GP	Jarama	27	Williams Grand Prix Engineering	G	3.0 March 761-Cosworth V8	pit stop/4 laps behind		22/31
10	BELGIAN GP	Zolder	27	Williams Grand Prix Engineering	G	3.0 March 761-Cosworth V8	pit stop-tyres/2 laps behind		24/32
15	SWEDISH GP	Anderstorp	27	Williams Grand Prix Engineering	G	3.0 March 761-Cosworth V8	3 laps behind		20/31
dnq	FRENCH GP	Dijon	27	Williams Grand Prix Engineering	G	3.0 March 761-Cosworth V8			24/30
10	BRITISH GP	Silverstone	27	Williams Grand Prix Engineering	G	3.0 March 761-Cosworth V8	2 laps behind		26/36
dnq	GERMAN GP	Hockenheim	27	Williams Grand Prix Engineering	G	3.0 March 761-Cosworth V8			25/30
9	AUSTRIAN GP	Österreichring	27	Williams Grand Prix Engineering	G	3.0 March 761-Cosworth V8	1 lap behind		22/30
dnq	DUTCH GP	Zandvoort	27	Williams Grand Prix Engineering	G	3.0 March 761-Cosworth V8			27/34
7	ITALIAN GP	Monza	27	Williams Grand Prix Engineering	G	3.0 March 761-Cosworth V8	2 laps behind		24/34
18	US GP EAST	Watkins Glen	27	Williams Grand Prix Engineering	G	3.0 March 761-Cosworth V8	4 laps behind		24/27
ret	CANADIAN GP	Mosport Park	27	Williams Grand Prix Engineering	G	3.0 March 761-Cosworth V8	oil pressure		21/27
	1978	Championship position: Unplaced							
dnpq	BELGIAN GP	Zolder	–	Patrick Neve	G	3.0 March 781S-Cosworth V8	dnq for official practice sessions		– / –

GP Starts: 10   GP Wins: 0   Pole positions: 0   Fastest laps: 0   Points: 0

NICHOLSON, John (NZ) b 6/10/1941, Auckland

	1974	Championship position: Unplaced						
	Race	Circuit	No	Entrant	Tyres	Car/Engine	Comment	Q Pos/Entries
dnq	BRITISH GP	Brands Hatch	29	Pinch (Plant) Ltd	F	3.0 Lyncar 006-Cosworth V8		31/34
	1975	Championship position: Unplaced						
17/ret	BRITISH GP	Silverstone	32	Pinch (Plant) Ltd	G	3.0 Lyncar 006-Cosworth V8	crashed in rainstorm/-5 laps	26/28

GP Starts: 1   GP Wins: 0   Pole positions: 0   Fastest laps: 0   Points: 0

NIEDERMAYR, Helmut (D) b 29/11/1915 – d 3/4/1985

	1952	Championship position: Unplaced						
	Race	Circuit	No	Entrant	Tyres	Car/Engine	Comment	Q Pos/Entries
nc	GERMAN GP	Nürburgring	124	Helmut Niedermayr	–	2.0 AFM 6-BMW 6	3 laps behind	22/32

GP Starts: 1   GP Wins: 0   Pole positions: 0   Fastest laps: 0   Points: 0

JOHN NICHOLSON

John had already tasted success in his native New Zealand with a Brabham BT18 when he made his way to England and walked straight into a job at McLaren working on their racing engines. When his urge to compete resurfaced, he quickly became a leading figure in Formula Atlantic, initially with a March and then with his own Lyncar-Nicholson, in which he won the 1973 and 1974 championships.

By 1973 he had established his own thriving engine business servicing and preparing Cosworths for McLaren and many others, which prevented him from undertaking a major racing programme abroad, but he did dip into Formula 1 with the Lyncar in British events, his best result being a sixth at the 1974 Race of Champions. Plans to purchase a McLaren M23 and have a real go fell through, much to Nicholson's dismay, but he did race subsequently in both Formula 2 and F5000 in 1976, and then took in the Peter Stuyvesant New Zealand series early in 1978, before concentrating on his business commitments and indulging his passion for speed with a new-found interest in powerboat racing.

HELMUT NIEDERMAYR

Within a couple of months in the summer of 1952, Niedermayr surely experienced the high and low points of his career. At the end of June he shared the second-place Mercedes Benz 300SL with Helfrich at Le Mans, and at the beginning of August he crashed into the crowd at the Grenzlandring circuit, killing at least 13 spectators and injuring many others.

Helmut eventually returned to the track, appearing briefly in Hans Klenk's special in the 1954 AVUS GP, and thereafter was seen in a Porsche in rallies and sports car events.

BRAUSCH NIEMANN

Brausch achieved amazing feats in a wide-wheeled Lotus Seven seemingly held together with lashings of masking tape, and known as either the 'coffin on cotton reels' or 'masked marvel', often putting to shame far more potent machinery in national racing in the early sixties.

This led to his chance to race a FJ Lotus 22, in which he took numerous top-six places between 1963 and 1965. After driving Lotus 23 and 30 sports cars, then a Lotus Ford Cortina, Niemann turned to racing enduro motor cycles, winning the South African championship in 1979.

NIEMANN, Brausch (ZA) b 7/1/1939, Durban

	1963			Championship position: Unplaced				
	Race	Circuit	No	Entrant	Tyres	Car/Engine	Comment	Q Pos/Entries
14	SOUTH AFRICAN GP	East London	21	Ted Lanfear	D	1.5 Lotus 22-Ford 4	19 laps behind	15/21
	1965			Championship position: Unplaced				
dnq	SOUTH AFRICAN GP	East London	27	Ted Lanfear	D	1.5 Lotus 22-Ford 4		24/25

GP Starts: 1   GP Wins: 0   Pole positions: 0   Fastest laps: 0   Points: 0

GUNNAR NILSSON

This cheery and gregarious Swede was always his own man, and the courage and dignity he showed after the diagnosis of terminal cancer said as much for him as his all-too-brief motor racing career.

Having made a late start in the sport, Gunnar had his first full season of racing in Formula Super Vee in 1973, learning a great deal in a short time from the experienced Freddy Kottulinsky, who was instrumental in his early development. He also tried his hand at Formula 2 at Norisring and, given his novice status, did remarkably well to finish a lucky fourth on aggregate with a GRD. In 1974 he raced in the German Polifac F3 championship in a private March, and impressed sufficiently to bargain his way into the works team contesting the British series alongside Alex Ribeiro in 1975. Things could hardly have started better, as he won the first race at Thruxton to set up his year, which ended with him taking the BP championship. An end-of-season switch to Formula Atlantic merely underlined his talent as he won the last five rounds in succession in a Chevron B29.

Though tied to March and BMW for 1976, Nilsson got together with Ronnie Peterson to contrive a swap deal which saw Gunnar join the Lotus team at a time when it was at a low ebb. It was a gamble, but it soon paid off with Nilsson on the rostrum in his third race. The arrival of Mario Andretti only strengthened the team's hand as they sought to recapture past glories, and Gunnar benefited greatly from the American driver's guidance. Ken Tyrrell, no less, predicted that here was a future World Champion – praise indeed.

Happy to stay with Lotus for another year in 1977, Nilsson maintained his upward momentum during the first half of the season, culminating in his only Grand Prix win in the wet at Zolder when he memorably moved through the field before picking off the leader Niki Lauda with clinical precision. The second half of the year saw a sudden downturn in his fortunes as inconsistency set in. Of course no one knew it, but the cancer he had developed was already well advanced. With Peterson returning to the Lotus fold for 1978, Gunnar signed for the newly formed Arrows team, but in the event he was never well enough to drive the car. By the following autumn he was fighting to live just long enough to see his Gunnar Nilsson Cancer Treatment Campaign successfully launched, before passing away that October.

NILSSON, Gunnar (S) b 20/11/1948, Helsingborg – d 20/10/1978, Hammersmith, London

1976
Championship position: 10th   Wins: 0   Pole positions: 0   Fastest laps: 0   Points scored: 11

	Race	Circuit	No	Entrant	Tyres	Car/Engine	Comment	Q Pos/Entries
ret	SOUTH AFRICAN GP	Kyalami	6	John Player Team Lotus	G	3.0 Lotus 77-Cosworth V8	clutch	25/25
ret	US GP WEST	Long Beach	6	John Player Team Lotus	G	3.0 Lotus 77-Cosworth V8	suspension-crashed	20/27
3	SPANISH GP	Jarama	6	John Player Team Lotus	G	3.0 Lotus 77-Cosworth V8		7/30
ret	BELGIAN GP	Zolder	6	John Player Team Lotus	G	3.0 Lotus 77-Cosworth V8	crashed	22/29
ret	MONACO GP	Monte Carlo	6	John Player Team Lotus	G	3.0 Lotus 77-Cosworth V8	engine	16/25
ret	SWEDISH GP	Anderstorp	6	John Player Team Lotus	G	3.0 Lotus 77-Cosworth V8	spun into barrier	6/27
ret	FRENCH GP	Paul Ricard	6	John Player Team Lotus	G	3.0 Lotus 77-Cosworth V8	transmission	12/30
ret	BRITISH GP	Brands Hatch	6	John Player Team Lotus	G	3.0 Lotus 77-Cosworth V8	engine	14/30
5	GERMAN GP	Nürburgring	6	John Player Team Lotus	G	3.0 Lotus 77-Cosworth V8		16/28
3	AUSTRIAN GP	Österreichring	6	John Player Team Lotus	G	3.0 Lotus 77-Cosworth V8		4/25
ret	DUTCH GP	Zandvoort	6	John Player Team Lotus	G	3.0 Lotus 77-Cosworth V8	crashed on oil	13/27
13	ITALIAN GP	Monza	6	John Player Team Lotus	G	3.0 Lotus 77-Cosworth V8	pit stop-broken nose cone/-1 lap	12/29
12	CANADIAN GP	Mosport Park	6	John Player Team Lotus	G	3.0 Lotus 77-Cosworth V8	last away at start/1 lap behind	15/27
ret	US GP EAST	Watkins Glen	6	John Player Team Lotus	G	3.0 Lotus 77-Cosworth V8	engine	20/27
6	JAPANESE GP	Mount Fuji	6	John Player Team Lotus	G	3.0 Lotus 77-Cosworth V8	1 lap behind	16/27

1977
Championship position: 8th   Wins: 1   Pole positions: 0   Fastest laps: 1   Points scored: 20

	Race	Circuit	No	Entrant	Tyres	Car/Engine	Comment	Q Pos/Entries
dns	ARGENTINE GP	Buenos Aires	6	John Player Team Lotus	G	3.0 Lotus 78-Cosworth V8	Andretti drove car	(10)/21
5	BRAZILIAN GP	Interlagos	6	John Player Team Lotus	G	3.0 Lotus 78-Cosworth V8	2 pit stops-tyres/-1 lap	10/22
12	SOUTH AFRICAN GP	Kyalami	6	John Player Team Lotus	G	3.0 Lotus 78-Cosworth V8	pit stop-tyres-new nose/-1 lap	10/23
8	US GP WEST	Long Beach	6	John Player Team Lotus	G	3.0 Lotus 78-Cosworth V8	1 lap behind	16/22
5	SPANISH GP	Jarama	6	John Player Team Lotus	G	3.0 Lotus 78-Cosworth V8		12/31
ret	MONACO GP	Monte Carlo	6	John Player Team Lotus	G	3.0 Lotus 78-Cosworth V8	gearbox	13/26

1	BELGIAN GP	Zolder	6	John Player Team Lotus	G	3.0 Lotus 78-Cosworth V8		FL	3/32
19/ret	SWEDISH GP	Anderstorp	6	John Player Team Lotus	G	3.0 Lotus 78-Cosworth V8		wheel bearing/8 laps behind	7/31
4	FRENCH GP	Dijon	6	John Player Team Lotus	G	3.0 Lotus 78-Cosworth V8			3/30
3	BRITISH GP	Silverstone	6	John Player Team Lotus	G	3.0 Lotus 78-Cosworth V8			5/36
ret	GERMAN GP	Hockenheim	6	John Player Team Lotus	G	3.0 Lotus 78-Cosworth V8		engine	9/30
ret	AUSTRIAN GP	Österreichring	6	John Player Team Lotus	G	3.0 Lotus 78-Cosworth V8		engine	16/30
ret	DUTCH GP	Zandvoort	6	John Player Team Lotus	G	3.0 Lotus 78-Cosworth V8		hit Reutemann	5/34
ret	ITALIAN GP	Monza	6	John Player Team Lotus	G	3.0 Lotus 78-Cosworth V8		broken front upright	19/34
ret	US GP EAST	Watkins Glen	6	John Player Team Lotus	G	3.0 Lotus 78-Cosworth V8		hit by Peterson	12/27
ret	CANADIAN GP	Mosport Park	6	John Player Team Lotus	G	3.0 Lotus 78-Cosworth V8		throttle stuck-crashed	4/27
ret	JAPANESE GP	Mount Fuji	6	John Player Team Lotus	G	3.0 Lotus 78-Cosworth V8		gearbox	14/23

GP Starts: 31 GP Wins: 1 Pole positions: 0 Fastest laps: 1 Points: 31

HIDEKI NODA

The inscrutable Japanese are famed for their polite and formal manner, but the self-deprecating Noda goes against the stereotype. Perhaps it is because most of his racing career has been based in Europe that he has developed a Western sense of humour. He came from Japan to contest the 1989 Vauxhall and GM Lotus series, and then F3 with a Ralt, and the high point in this class came in 1991 when he won at Silverstone.

Three years in F3000 brought steady but hardly spectacular progress, though Hideki took a third at Enna in 1994. 'People think I'm useless,' said the ever-smiling Noda as eyebrows were raised when he found a seat at Larrousse at the end of 1994. He did a neat and tidy job in a poor car – a lot better than most people expected. Plans to join Simtek for a series of races in 1995 came to nought when the team folded, and to add insult to injury it appears they had taken his deposit.

Hideki then switched to the Indy Lights series, where he was quick but erratic. The highlight of his two years in the States came at Portland in 1997 when he became the first Japanese driver to win a CART-sanctioned event.

In 1998 Noda returned to Japan to race successfully in both Formula Nippon and the All-Japan GT championship, driving the Hoshino team's Ralt in the former and a Toyota Supra with co-driver Wayne Gardner in the latter.

RODNEY NUCKEY

After showing a great deal of skill in his own F3 Cooper-Norton during the 1952 season, his record including wins at Falkenberg and Skarpnack in Sweden, Nuckey was sufficiently encouraged to purchase a Formula 2 Cooper-Bristol which he put to good use in 1953, taking a third place in the Syracuse GP, fourth in the London Trophy at Crystal Palace and fifth in the Eifelrennen. He continued to race the car in 1954, mainly in Formula Libre events, along with the Ecurie Richmond F3 Cooper.

NODA, Hideki (J) b 7/3/1969, Osaka

	1994	Championship position: Unplaced							
	Race	Circuit	No	Entrant	Tyres	Car/Engine		Comment	Q Pos/Entries
ret	EUROPEAN GP	Jerez	19	Tourtel Larrousse F1	G	3.5 Larrousse LH94-Ford HB V8		gearbox	24/28
ret	JAPANESE GP	Suzuka	19	Tourtel Larrousse F1	G	3.5 Larrousse LH94-Ford HB V8		started from pits/injection	23/28
ret	AUSTRALIAN GP	Adelaide	19	Tourtel Larrousse F1	G	3.5 Larrousse LH94-Ford HB V8		oil leak	23/28

GP Starts: 3 GP Wins: 0 Pole positions: 0 Fastest laps: 0 Points: 0

NUCKEY, Rodney (GB) b 26/6/1929, Wood Green, London

	1953	Championship position: Unplaced							
	Race	Circuit	No	Entrant	Tyres	Car/Engine		Comment	Q Pos/Entries
11	GERMAN GP	Nürburgring	40	Rodney Nuckey	D	2.0 Cooper T23-Bristol 6		2 laps behind	20/35
	1954	Championship position: Unplaced							
dns	BRITISH GP	Silverstone	30	Ecurie Richmond	D	2.0 Cooper T23-Bristol 6		Brandon drove car	– / –

GP Starts: 1 GP Wins: 0 Pole positions: 0 Fastest laps: 0 Points: 0

O'BRIEN, Robert (USA)

	1952	Championship position: Unplaced							
	Race	Circuit	No	Entrant	Tyres	Car/Engine		Comment	Q Pos/Entries
nc	BELGIAN GP	Spa	44	Robert O'Brien	E	1.5 Simca-Gordini Type 15 4		6 laps behind	22/22

GP Starts: 1 GP Wins: 0 Pole positions: 0 Fastest laps: 0 Points: 0

JACK OLIVER

It's hard to believe that Oliver has been involved in motor sport for nearly forty years, having started with a Mini way back in 1961. He really came to prominence, however, driving a Lotus Elan, with which he embarrassed many a more powerful GT car in 1965, before moving into single-seaters the following year, when he showed much promise but achieved little success in Formula 3.

Jack's breakthrough year was 1967 when he drove the Lotus Components F2 car, doing himself a power of good in the eyes of Colin Chapman by taking fifth overall and the F2 class win in the German GP. With the death of Jim Clark at Hockenheim, Oliver was promoted into the Lotus team as number two to Graham Hill, but had something of a torrid baptism, crashing in both the Monaco and French GPs before redeeming himself with a splendid performance at Brands Hatch, where he led the British GP until engine failure. Seen as nothing more than a stop-gap by Chapman, who had set his heart on having Jochen Rindt in the team, Oliver bowed out with a fine third place in Mexico to take up a two-year contract with BRM.

The following season was a miserable one for BRM, but Oliver salvaged his year by racing for John Wyer's Gulf team. Paired with Ickx, he won at Sebring and they then scored a famous victory at Le Mans, Jack's contribution to which is often overlooked. The second year of his BRM deal brought scarcely more joy than the first, even though he had the excellent P153 to drive. Apart from a fifth place in Austria and a third in the Gold Cup at Oulton Park, the catalogue of retirements made depressing reading. Jack's sharp, young, Essex personality didn't sit well with Louis Stanley, who preferred drivers typical of a different era, so a parting of the ways was probably inevitable. The season was not completely lost, for Oliver ventured into Can-Am with the Autocast project and took three second places. Meanwhile he returned to sports cars once more with Wyer, winning the Daytona 24 Hours and Monza 1000 Km, but was released after he preferred to take up an invitation to race Don Nichols' Shadow in Can-Am. Keen to keep his Formula 1 career afloat, Oliver arranged some drives in a third McLaren, and his versatility was proven when he stood in for Mark Donohue in Penske's Trans-Am Javelin to take third place at Riverside.

With the 1972 British GP being held at Brands Hatch (one of Jack's favourite circuits), he drove for BRM, but he spent most of the season testing Shadow's latest Can-Am car. He got on well with Don Nichols, and when Shadow entered Grand Prix racing the following year Oliver had one of the drives. It was a perplexing season, with the DN1 chassis proving difficult to sort, but a wet race in Canada saw Jack take third place – although many insist that in fact he won, as the lap charts were thrown into confusion by the use of a pace car. Oliver concentrated on Can-Am alone in 1974 and it paid off handsomely with him winning the series at the fourth attempt in Nichols' machines. Although increasingly involved in the management side of things, Oliver contested the 1975 and 1976 US F5000 series, before a Formula 1 swansong as a driver in 1977. He took the Shadow DN8 into fifth place at the Race of Champions, and later in the year raced in his final Grand Prix in Sweden, finishing ninth.

Along with Alan Rees and Tony Southgate, Oliver quit Shadow at the end of the year and unveiled the 1978 Arrows Formula 1 car, which was subsequently the subject of legal action from Nichols over design copyright. Jack then spent the next decade keeping Arrows on the F1 grid but in 1990 he sold out to the Japanese Footwork concern, whose name the team took. Oliver remained at the helm as a director, and regained control of the team at the end of 1993 when the parent company hit financial difficulties in Japan. The Arrows name was back.

In 1996 Oliver sold a major portion of the team to Tom Walkinshaw and was content to take a back-seat role as the new incumbent set about trying to end Arrows' winless streak, which has now lasted for more than two decades. At the start of 1999 Jack finally disposed of his remaining interest in the team he founded, walking away an exceedingly wealthy man after the reportedly massive buyout.

OLIVER, Jackie (GB) b 14/8/1942, Chadwell Heath, nr Romford, Essex

	1967			Championship position: Unplaced					
	Race	Circuit	No	Entrant	Tyres	Car/Engine		Comment	Q Pos/Entries
5*	GERMAN GP (F2)	Nürburgring	24	Lotus Components Ltd	F	1.6 Lotus 48-Cosworth 4		* 1st in F2 class/no pts scored	16/25

	1968		Championship position: 13th=	Wins: 0	Pole positions: 0	Fastest laps: 1	Points scored: 6	
ret	MONACO GP	Monte Carlo	10	Gold Leaf Team Lotus	F	3.0 Lotus 49-Cosworth V8	*hit McLaren*	13/18
5/ret	BELGIAN GP	Spa	2	Gold Leaf Team Lotus	F	3.0 Lotus 49B-Cosworth V8	*driveshaft/2 laps behind*	15/18
nc	DUTCH GP	Zandvoort	4	Gold Leaf Team Lotus	F	3.0 Lotus 49B-Cosworth V8	*stops-water in electrics/-10 laps*	10/19
dns	FRENCH GP	Rouen	14	Gold Leaf Team Lotus	F	3.0 Lotus 49B-Cosworth V8	*car destroyed in accident*	(11)/19
ret	BRITISH GP	Brands Hatch	9	Gold Leaf Team Lotus	F	3.0 Lotus 49B-Cosworth V8	*transmission*	2/20
11	GERMAN GP	Nürburgring	21	Gold Leaf Team Lotus	F	3.0 Lotus 49B-Cosworth V8	*1 lap behind*	13/20
ret	ITALIAN GP	Monza	19	Gold Leaf Team Lotus	F	3.0 Lotus 49B-Cosworth V8	*transmission/FL (disputed)*	12/24
ret	CANADIAN GP	St Jovite	4	Gold Leaf Team Lotus	F	3.0 Lotus 49B-Cosworth V8	*transmission*	9/22
dns	US GP	Watkins Glen	11	Gold Leaf Team Lotus	F	3.0 Lotus 49B-Cosworth V8	*accident in practice*	(16)/21
3	MEXICAN GP	Mexico City	11	Gold Leaf Team Lotus	F	3.0 Lotus 49B-Cosworth V8		14/21
	1969		Championship position: 16th=	Wins: 0	Pole positions: 0	Fastest laps: 0	Points scored: 1	
7	SOUTH AFRICAN GP	Kyalami	11	Owen Racing Organisation	D	3.0 BRM P133 V12	*pit stop-3 laps behind*	15/18
ret	SPANISH GP	Montjuich Park	12	Owen Racing Organisation	D	3.0 BRM P133 V12	*burst oil pipe*	10/14
ret	MONACO GP	Monte Carlo	15	Owen Racing Organisation	D	3.0 BRM P133 V12	*hit Attwood-front wishbone*	13/16
ret	DUTCH GP	Zandvoort	15	Owen Racing Organisation	D	3.0 BRM P133 V12	*gear selection*	13/15
ret	BRITISH GP	Silverstone	15	Owen Racing Organisation	D	3.0 BRM P133 V12	*transmission*	13/17
ret	GERMAN GP	Nürburgring	15	Owen Racing Organisation	D	3.0 BRM P138 V12	*damaged sump*	16/26
ret	ITALIAN GP	Monza	15	Owen Racing Organisation	D	3.0 BRM P139 V12	*oil pressure*	11/15
dns	"	"	15	Owen Racing Organisation	D	3.0 BRM P138 V12	*practice only*	–/–
ret	CANADIAN GP	Mosport Park	15	Owen Racing Organisation	D	3.0 BRM P139 V12	*engine*	12/20
ret	US GP	Watkins Glen	15	Owen Racing Organisation	D	3.0 BRM P139 V12	*engine*	14/18
6	MEXICAN GP	Mexico City	15	Owen Racing Organisation	D	3.0 BRM P139 V12	*2 laps behind*	12/17
	1970		Championship position: 19th=	Wins: 0	Pole positions: 0	Fastest laps: 0	Points scored: 2	
ret	SOUTH AFRICAN GP	Kyalami	19	Owen Racing Organisation	D	3.0 BRM P153 V12	*gear selection*	12/24
ret	SPANISH GP	Jarama	15	Yardley Team BRM	D	3.0 BRM P153 V12	*broken stub axle-hit Ickx-fire*	11/22
ret	MONACO GP	Monte Carlo	16	Yardley Team BRM	D	3.0 BRM P153 V12	*engine-throttle cable*	17/21
ret	BELGIAN GP	Spa	2	Yardley Team BRM	D	3.0 BRM P153 V12	*engine*	14/18
ret	DUTCH GP	Zandvoort	2	Yardley Team BRM	D	3.0 BRM P153 V12	*engine*	5/24
ret	FRENCH GP	Clermont Ferrand	5	Yardley Team BRM	D	3.0 BRM P153 V12	*engine*	12/23
ret	BRITISH GP	Brands Hatch	23	Yardley Team BRM	D	3.0 BRM P153 V12	*engine*	=4/25
ret	GERMAN GP	Hockenheim	18	Yardley Team BRM	D	3.0 BRM P153 V12	*engine*	18/25
5	AUSTRIAN GP	Österreichring	16	Yardley Team BRM	D	3.0 BRM P153 V12	*1 lap behind*	13/24
ret	ITALIAN GP	Monza	8	Yardley Team BRM	D	3.0 BRM P153 V12	*engine*	6/27
nc	CANADIAN GP	St Jovite	15	Yardley Team BRM	D	3.0 BRM P153 V12	*pit stop-broken wishbone/-38 laps*	10/20
ret	US GP	Watkins Glen	20	Yardley Team BRM	D	3.0 BRM P153 V12	*engine*	7/27
7	MEXICAN GP	Mexico City	20	Yardley Team BRM	D	3.0 BRM P153 V12	*1 lap behind*	13/18
	1971		Championship position: Unplaced					
ret	BRITISH GP	Silverstone	11	Bruce McLaren Motor Racing	G	3.0 McLaren M14A-Cosworth V8	*hit Hill at start-broke radius rod*	22/24
9	AUSTRIAN GP	Österreichring	10	Bruce McLaren Motor Racing	G	3.0 McLaren M19A-Cosworth V8	*1 lap behind*	22/22
7	ITALIAN GP	Monza	14	Bruce McLaren Motor Racing	G	3.0 McLaren M14A-Cosworth V8		13/24
	1972		Championship position: Unplaced					
ret	BRITISH GP	Brands Hatch	14	Marlboro BRM	F	3.0 BRM P160B V12	*rear radius rod*	=14/27
	1973		Championship position: 14th	Wins: 0	Pole positions: 0	Fastest laps: 0	Points scored: 4	
ret	SOUTH AFRICAN GP	Kyalami	22	UOP Shadow Racing Team	G	3.0 Shadow DN1-Cosworth V8	*engine*	14/25
ret	SPANISH GP	Montjuich Park	19	UOP Shadow Racing Team	G	3.0 Shadow DN1-Cosworth V8	*oil leak*	13/22
ret	BELGIAN GP	Zolder	17	UOP Shadow Racing Team	G	3.0 Shadow DN1-Cosworth V8	*accident*	22/23
10	MONACO GP	Monte Carlo	17	UOP Shadow Racing Team	G	3.0 Shadow DN1-Cosworth V8	*6 laps behind*	23/26
ret	SWEDISH GP	Anderstorp	17	UOP Shadow Racing Team	G	3.0 Shadow DN1-Cosworth V8	*transmission*	17/22
ret	FRENCH GP	Paul Ricard	17	UOP Shadow Racing Team	G	3.0 Shadow DN1-Cosworth V8	*clutch*	21/25
ret/dns	BRITISH GP	Silverstone	17	UOP Shadow Racing Team	G	3.0 Shadow DN1-Cosworth V8	*hit Lauda in first start*	=25/29
ret	DUTCH GP	Zandvoort	17	UOP Shadow Racing Team	G	3.0 Shadow DN1-Cosworth V8	*stuck throttle-hit barrier*	10/24
8	GERMAN GP	Nürburgring	17	UOP Shadow Racing Team	G	3.0 Shadow DN1-Cosworth V8		=17/23
ret	AUSTRIAN GP	Österreichring	17	UOP Shadow Racing Team	G	3.0 Shadow DN1-Cosworth V8	*fuel leak*	18/25
11	ITALIAN GP	Monza	17	UOP Shadow Racing Team	G	3.0 Shadow DN1-Cosworth V8	*1 lap behind*	19/25
3	CANADIAN GP	Mosport Park	17	UOP Shadow Racing Team	G	3.0 Shadow DN1-Cosworth V8		14/26
15	US GP	Watkins Glen	17	UOP Shadow Racing Team	G	3.0 Shadow DN1-Cosworth V8	*pit stop-loose wheels/4- laps*	23/28
	1977		Championship position: Unplaced					
9	SWEDISH GP	Anderstorp	16	Shadow Racing Team	G	3.0 Shadow DN8-Cosworth V8		16/31

GP Starts: 49(50)   GP Wins: 0   Pole positions: 0   Fastest laps: 1   Points: 13

1968 British GP, Brands Hatch, and Oliver is already in trouble with the smoking Lotus 49B. He leads Siffert, Amon, Stewart and Surtees before his inevitable retirement after setting the pace at the start.

DANNY ONGAIS

This Hawaiian-born driver first found fame as a drag racer with the Vel's Parnelli team, before trying his hand in SCCA national racing in 1974. He then tackled US F5000 with Interscope Racing's Lola in 1975 and 1976, and although a win eluded him he was a regular contender. The following season Interscope ran him in USAC racing – where he shone, taking a win at Michigan – and in IMSA, where he won two rounds in a Porsche 935 turbo, and he made his Grand Prix debut at the end-of-year North American rounds in the team's Penske.

Danny's struggles in F1 in 1978 – he scraped onto the grid for the first two Grands Prix in the works Ensign, then floundered with the embarrassing Interscope Shadow – were in sharp contrast to his rapidly blossoming career in USAC, where he took five wins in the Parnelli VPJ6.

Although Danny enjoyed further success for Interscope in IMSA sports car events, winning the 1979 Daytona 24 Hours in a Porsche, and taking third place the following year, this was the high point of his Indy Car career, as he was to suffer appalling leg injuries in a crash at Indianapolis in 1981. Happily he recovered to make a return to the track but, although he raced on until 1987, he was never quite the same force again.

It came as a huge surprise when he came out of retirement in 1996 after Scott Brayton was killed in practice for the Indy 500. However, the veteran brought the Menard Lola home in a splendid seventh place, which encouraged him to race in the event the following May.

Unfortunately for Danny, it was not a happy return, for he crashed heavily when the engine on his car blew during his first lap of qualifying, resulting in an overnight stay in hospital.

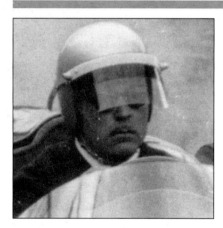

ARTHUR OWEN

Owen was a director of a jewellery business in St Helier, Jersey, who not unnaturally gained his early competition experience on the Bouley Bay hill-climb in the early fifties with a Skinner special. By the mid-fifties, Arthur and his friend Bill Knight had acquired a potent Cooper sports car and set about breaking speed records at Montlhéry and Monza.

Though he was only an occasional circuit racer, Owen was invited to take part in the 1960 Italian Grand Prix, which was boycotted by the major English teams because the organisers insisted on including the banked part of the circuit. Arthur then turned his attention to the hills, unleashing his 2.2-litre Type 53 Cooper 'Lowline' on the opposition. After coming close to winning the British hill-climb championship in 1961, he made no mistake the following year.

In 1963 and 1964 Owen raced a Lotus 23 sports car, and he was one of a select group of drivers invited to compete in the inaugural race held at the Suzuka circuit.

ONGAIS, Danny (USA) b 21/5/1942, Honolulu, Hawaii

	1977			Championship position: Unplaced				
	Race	Circuit	No	Entrant	Tyres	Car/Engine	Comment	Q Pos/Entries
ret	US GP EAST	Watkins Glen	14	Interscope Racing	G	3.0 Penske PC4-Cosworth V8	spun off	26/27
7	CANADIAN GP	Mosport Park	14	Interscope Racing	G	3.0 Penske PC4-Cosworth V8	2 laps behind	22/27
	1978			Championship position: Unplaced				
ret	ARGENTINE GP	Buenos Aires	22	Team Tissot Ensign	G	3.0 Ensign N177-Cosworth V8	rotor arm	21/27
ret	BRAZILIAN GP	Rio	22	Team Tissot Ensign	G	3.0 Ensign N177-Cosworth V8	brake disc mounting bolt	23/28
dnpq	US GP WEST	Long Beach	39	Interscope Racing	G	3.0 Shadow DN9-Cosworth V8		29/30
dnpq	DUTCH GP	Zandvoort	39	Interscope Racing	G	3.0 Shadow DN9-Cosworth V8		32/33

GP Starts: 4   GP Wins: 0   Pole positions: 0   Fastest laps: 0   Points: 0

OWEN, Arthur (GB) b 23/3/1915, London

	1960			Championship position: Unplaced				
	Race	Circuit	No	Entrant	Tyres	Car/Engine	Comment	Q Pos/Entries
ret	ITALIAN GP	Monza	8	Arthur Owen	D	2.2 Cooper T45-Climax 4	locked brakes-suspension damage	11/16

GP Starts: 1   GP Wins: 0   Pole positions: 0   Fastest laps: 0   Points: 0

CARLOS PACE

A long-time friend and rival of the Fittipaldi brothers – fellow Paulistas – Pace raced for most of the sixties in Brazil, beginning in karts where his opponents included Wilson Fittipaldi. Driving a variety of machines from Renault Gordinis to Formula Vee cars and a potent Alfa Romeo T33/2, Carlos took the Brazilian national championship three years in a row between 1967 and 1969.

Together with Wilson Fittipaldi, Carlos arrived in Europe in 1970 to contest a very competitive Formula 3 series with a Lotus 59 entered

by Jim Russell. Despite his lack of knowledge of the British circuits, Pace was soon very much one of the front-runners and by the end of the year he had collected the Forward Trust championship. After spending his winter at home, where he endured a disappointing Torneio series, Carlos returned with a healthy dose of sponsorship which was eagerly accepted by Frank Williams, who provided a March for the Formula 2 season. Just as in F3 the previous year, Pace became one of the men to beat, and soon won a round at Imola, though the entry for this race wasn't one of the best.

Frank was keen to run Pace in his second F1 car in 1972, and the pair went 50/50 on a deal. While the unfortunate number one driver, Pescarolo, had a dreadful time, Carlos made good progress in the old March, taking valuable championship points in two of his first four races. Broadening his horizons, he briefly raced in Formula 2 with Pygmée, and then joined Ferrari's sports car team to take second place in the Österreichring 1000 Km, which brought an invitation from Gulf to race their Mirage at Watkins Glen, where he took third place. Late in the 1972 season, Pace dropped a bombshell on Williams by announcing his intention to join Surtees in 1973, and by the end-of-year Victory Race he was already installed in one of 'Big John's cars, taking second place in the TS9B. In 1973 he raced regularly for Surtees in Formula 1 and was a revelation. The highlights were his performances in Germany and Austria, but too many mechanical problems left him lowly placed in the final championship table. In tandem with F1, he drove for Ferrari in sports car events and, teamed with Merzario, took a string of placings, including second at Le Mans and the Nürburgring.

Despite the poor reliability of the Surtees, Carlos stayed with the team for 1974, but after a fourth place in his home GP, a succession of niggling problems blighted his prospects, and in mid-season he quit in frustration. It didn't take long for Bernie Ecclestone to bring him into the Brabham team alongside Carlos Reutemann and he soon proved to be every bit as competitive as his team-mate. A great drive in Austria was halted by a broken fuel line when victory seemed possible and he posted fastest race laps at Monza and Watkins Glen, where he served due notice of his intentions for the 1975 season. At Interlagos came the highlight of his career, his first Grand Prix win recorded in front of his ecstatic home fans, but luck rarely went his way throughout the year. His competitiveness was severely blunted in 1976 when Brabham ran Alfa Romeo engines, but he got stuck in and never gave up in his efforts to develop the car.

By the end of the year he was enthusiastic about his prospects for 1977. Second place in the Argentine Grand Prix vindicated his optimism, but prior to the start of the European season came the terrible news of his death in a light plane crash back in Brazil.

PACE, Carlos (BR) b 6/10/1944, São Paulo – d 18/3/1977, nr São Paulo

1972	Championship position: 16th=	Wins: 0	Pole positions: 0	Fastest laps: 0	Points scored: 3			
	Race	Circuit	No	Entrant	Tyres	Car/Engine	Comment	Q Pos/Entries
17	SOUTH AFRICAN GP	Kyalami	22	Team Williams-Motul	G	3.0 March 711-Cosworth V8	delayed start-fuel pump/-6 laps	24/27

6	SPANISH GP	Jarama	29	Team Williams-Motul	G	3.0 March 711-Cosworth V8	*1 lap behind*	16/26
17	MONACO GP	Monte Carlo	23	Team Williams-Motul	G	3.0 March 711-Cosworth V8	*pit stop-electrics/-8 laps*	24/25
5	BELGIAN GP	Nivelles	16	Team Williams-Motul	G	3.0 March 711-Cosworth V8	*1 lap behind*	11/26
ret	FRENCH GP	Clermont Ferrand	17	Team Williams-Motul	G	3.0 March 711-Cosworth V8	*engine*	11/29
ret	BRITISH GP	Brands Hatch	25	Team Williams-Motul	G	3.0 March 711-Cosworth V8	*collision-Reutemann/differential*	13/27
nc	GERMAN GP	Nürburgring	21	Team Williams-Motul	G	3.0 March 711-Cosworth V8	*long pit stop-handling/-3 laps*	11/27
nc	AUSTRIAN GP	Österreichring	23	Team Williams-Motul	G	3.0 March 711-Cosworth V8	*pit stop-fuel leak/-8 laps*	=17/26
ret	ITALIAN GP	Monza	26	Team Williams-Motul	G	3.0 March 711-Cosworth V8	*hit by Regazzoni at chicane*	18/27
9/ret	CANADIAN GP	Mosport Park	29	Team Williams-Motul	G	3.0 March 711-Cosworth V8	*fuel pressure/2 laps behind*	18/25
ret	US GP	Watkins Glen	27	Team Williams-Motul	G	3.0 March 711-Cosworth V8	*fuel injection*	15/32

1973   Championship position: 11th   Wins: 0   Pole positions: 0   Fastest laps: 2   Points scored: 7

ret	ARGENTINE GP	Buenos Aires	28	Brooke Bond Oxo-Team Surtees	F	3.0 Surtees TS14A-Cosworth V8	*suspension*	15/19
ret	BRAZILIAN GP	Interlagos	6	Brooke Bond Oxo-Team Surtees	F	3.0 Surtees TS14A-Cosworth V8	*suspension*	6/20
ret	SOUTH AFRICAN GP	Kyalami	11	Brooke Bond Oxo-Team Surtees	F	3.0 Surtees TS14A-Cosworth V8	*burst tyre/crashed*	9/25
ret	SPANISH GP	Montjuich Park	10	Brooke Bond Oxo-Team Surtees	F	3.0 Surtees TS14A-Cosworth V8	*driveshaft*	16/22
8	BELGIAN GP	Zolder	24	Brooke Bond Oxo-Team Surtees	F	3.0 Surtees TS14A-Cosworth V8	*pit stop-rear wing/-4 laps*	=7/23
ret	MONACO GP	Monte Carlo	24	Brooke Bond Oxo-Team Surtees	F	3.0 Surtees TS14A-Cosworth V8	*driveshaft*	17/26
10	SWEDISH GP	Anderstorp	24	Brooke Bond Oxo-Team Surtees	F	3.0 Surtees TS14A-Cosworth V8	*pit stop-tyres-vibration/-3 laps*	16/22
13	FRENCH GP	Paul Ricard	24	Brooke Bond Oxo-Team Surtees	F	3.0 Surtees TS14A-Cosworth V8	*pit stop-tyres/3 laps behind*	18/25
ret/dns	BRITISH GP	Silverstone	24	Brooke Bond Oxo-Team Surtees	F	3.0 Surtees TS14A-Cosworth V8	*multiple accident in first start*	=14/29
7	DUTCH GP	Zandvoort	24	Brooke Bond Oxo-Team Surtees	F	3.0 Surtees TS14A-Cosworth V8	*pit stop-tyres/engine/-3 laps*	8/24
4	GERMAN GP	Nürburgring	24	Brooke Bond Oxo-Team Surtees	F	3.0 Surtees TS14A-Cosworth V8	*FL*	=11/23
3	AUSTRIAN GP	Österreichring	24	Brooke Bond Oxo-Team Surtees	F	3.0 Surtees TS14A-Cosworth V8	*FL*	8/25
ret	ITALIAN GP	Monza	24	Brooke Bond Oxo-Team Surtees	F	3.0 Surtees TS14A-Cosworth V8	*tyre failure*	5/25
ret	CANADIAN GP	Mosport Park	24	Brooke Bond Oxo-Team Surtees	F	3.0 Surtees TS14A-Cosworth V8	*broken wheel*	19/26
ret	US GP	Watkins Glen	24	Brooke Bond Oxo-Team Surtees	F	3.0 Surtees TS14A-Cosworth V8	*broken suspension*	10/28

1974   Championship position: 12th   Wins: 0   Pole positions: 0   Fastest laps: 2   Points scored: 11

ret	ARGENTINE GP	Buenos Aires	18	Team Surtees	F	3.0 Surtees TS16-Cosworth V8	*engine*	11/26
4	BRAZILIAN GP	Interlagos	18	Team Surtees	F	3.0 Surtees TS16-Cosworth V8	*1 lap behind*	12/25
11	SOUTH AFRICAN GP	Kyalami	18	Bang & Olufsen Team Surtees	F	3.0 Surtees TS16-Cosworth V8	*1 lap behind*	2/27
13	SPANISH GP	Jarama	18	Bang & Olufsen Team Surtees	F	3.0 Surtees TS16-Cosworth V8	*2 pit stops-tyres/-6 laps*	15/28
ret	BELGIAN GP	Nivelles	18	Bang & Olufsen Team Surtees	F	3.0 Surtees TS16-Cosworth V8	*tyre vibration*	8/32
ret	MONACO GP	Monte Carlo	18	Bang & Olufsen Team Surtees	F	3.0 Surtees TS16-Cosworth V8	*multiple accident*	18/28
ret	SWEDISH GP	Anderstorp	18	Bang & Olufsen Team Surtees	F	3.0 Surtees TS16-Cosworth V8	*poor handling-withdrawn*	24/28
dnq	FRENCH GP	Dijon	34	Hexagon Racing with John Goldie	F	3.0 Brabham BT42-Cosworth V8		24/30
9	BRITISH GP	Brands Hatch	8	Motor Racing Developments	G	3.0 Brabham BT44-Cosworth V8	*1 lap behind*	=19/34
12	GERMAN GP	Nürburgring	8	Motor Racing Developments	G	3.0 Brabham BT44-Cosworth V8	*pit stop-handling*	17/32
ret	AUSTRIAN GP	Österreichring	8	Motor Racing Developmants	G	3.0 Brabham BT44-Cosworth V8	*fuel line*	4/31
5	ITALIAN GP	Monza	8	Motor Racing Developments	G	3.0 Brabham BT44-Cosworth V8	*pit stop-tyre/1 lap behind/FL*	3/31
8	CANADIAN GP	Mosport Park	8	Motor Racing Developments	G	3.0 Brabham BT44-Cosworth V8	*pit stop-tyre/1 lap behind*	9/30
2	US GP	Watkins Glen	8	Motor Racing Developments	G	3.0 Brabham BT44-Cosworth V8	*FL*	4/30

1975   Championship position: 6th   Wins: 1   Pole positions: 1   Fastest laps: 1   Points scored: 24

ret	ARGENTINE GP	Buenos Aires	8	Martini Racing	G	3.0 Brabham BT44B-Cosworth V8	*engine*	2/23
1	BRAZILIAN GP	Interlagos	8	Martini Racing	G	3.0 Brabham BT44B-Cosworth V8		6/23
4	SOUTH AFRICAN GP	Kyalami	8	Martini Racing	G	3.0 Brabham BT44B-Cosworth V8	*FL*	1/28
ret	SPANISH GP	Montjuich Park	8	Martini Racing	G	3.0 Brabham BT44B-Cosworth V8	*accident avoiding Stommelen*	14/26
3	MONACO GP	Monte Carlo	8	Martini Racing	G	3.0 Brabham BT44B-Cosworth V8		8/26
8	BELGIAN GP	Zolder	8	Martini Racing	G	3.0 Brabham BT44B-Cosworth V8	*1 lap behind*	2/24
ret	SWEDISH GP	Anderstorp	8	Martini Racing	G	3.0 Brabham BT44B-Cosworth V8	*spun off*	6/26
5	DUTCH GP	Zandvoort	8	Martini Racing	G	3.0 Brabham BT44B-Cosworth V8	*pit stop-tyres/1 lap behind*	9/25
ret	FRENCH GP	Paul Ricard	8	Martini Racing	G	3.0 Brabham BT44B-Cosworth V8	*driveshaft*	=5/26
2/ret	BRITISH GP	Silverstone	8	Martini Racing	G	3.0 Brabham BT44B-Cosworth V8	*spun off in rainstorm/-1 lap*	2/28
ret	GERMAN GP	Nürburgring	8	Martini Racing	G	3.0 Brabham BT44B-Cosworth V8	*rear upright*	2/26
ret	AUSTRIAN GP	Österreichring	8	Martini Racing	G	3.0 Brabham BT44B-Cosworth V8	*engine*	6/30
ret	ITALIAN GP	Monza	8	Martini Racing	G	3.0 Brabham BT44B-Cosworth V8	*throttle linkage*	10/28
ret	US GP	Watkins Glen	8	Martini Racing	G	3.0 Brabham BT44B-Cosworth V8	*collision with Depailler*	16/24

1976   Championship position: 14th=   Wins: 0   Pole positions: 0   Fastest laps: 0   Points scored: 7

10	BRAZILIAN GP	Interlagos	8	Martini Racing	G	3.0 Brabham BT45-Alfa Romeo F12	*1 lap behind*	10/22
ret	SOUTH AFRICAN GP	Kyalami	8	Martini Racing	G	3.0 Brabham BT45-Alfa Romeo F12	*engine*	14/25
9	US GP WEST	Long Beach	8	Martini Racing	G	3.0 Brabham BT45-Alfa Romeo F12	*pit stop-handling/-3 laps*	13/27
6	SPANISH GP	Jarama	8	Martini Racing	G	3.0 Brabham BT45-Alfa Romeo F12	*1 lap behind*	11/30
ret	BELGIAN GP	Zolder	8	Martini Racing	G	3.0 Brabham BT45-Alfa Romeo F12	*electrics*	9/29
9	MONACO GP	Monte Carlo	8	Martini Racing	G	3.0 Brabham BT45-Alfa Romeo F12	*2 laps behind*	13/25
8	SWEDISH GP	Anderstorp	8	Martini Racing	G	3.0 Brabham BT45-Alfa Romeo F12		10/27
4	FRENCH GP	Paul Ricard	8	Martini Racing	G	3.0 Brabham BT45-Alfa Romeo F12		5/30
8	BRITISH GP	Brands Hatch	8	Martini Racing	G	3.0 Brabham BT45-Alfa Romeo F12	*pit stops-tyres/3 laps behind*	16/30
4	GERMAN GP	Nürburgring	8	Martini Racing	G	3.0 Brabham BT45-Alfa Romeo F12		7/28
ret	AUSTRIAN GP	Österreichring	8	Martini Racing	G	3.0 Brabham BT45-Alfa Romeo F12	*brake failure-hit barrier*	8/25
ret	DUTCH GP	Zandvoort	8	Martini Racing	G	3.0 Brabham BT45-Alfa Romeo F12	*oil leak*	9/27
ret	ITALIAN GP	Monza	8	Martini Racing	G	3.0 Brabham BT45-Alfa Romeo F12	*engine*	3/29
7	CANADIAN GP	Mosport Park	8	Martini Racing	G	3.0 Brabham BT45-Alfa Romeo F12		10/27
ret	US GP EAST	Watkins Glen	8	Martini Racing	G	3.0 Brabham BT45-Alfa Romeo F12	*collision with Mass*	10/27
ret	JAPANESE GP	Mount Fuji	8	Martini Racing	G	3.0 Brabham BT45-Alfa Romeo F12	*withdrew due to conditions*	6/27

1977   Championship position: 15th=   Wins: 0   Pole positions: 0   Fastest laps: 0   Points scored: 6

2	ARGENTINE GP	Buenos Aires	8	Martini Racing	G	3.0 Brabham BT45-Alfa Romeo F12		6/21
ret	BRAZILIAN GP	Interlagos	8	Martini Racing	G	3.0 Brabham BT45-Alfa Romeo F12	*accident damage*	5/22
13	SOUTH AFRICAN GP	Kyalami	8	Martini Racing	G	3.0 Brabham BT45B-Alfa Romeo F12	*pit stops-tyres/2 laps behind*	2/23
dns	"	"	8	Martini Racing	G	3.0 Brabham BT45B-Alfa Romeo F12	*practice only*	– / –

GP Starts: 71 (72)   GP Wins: 1   Pole positions: 1   Fastest laps: 5   Points: 58

NELLO PAGANI

This aristocratic Italian was first and foremost a motor cycle racer, winning the inaugural 125 cc World Championship in 1949 on a Mondial and finishing second in the 500 cc class on the MV Agusta.

He was a talented car racer too, as witnessed by his wins at Pau in 1947 and 1948 in a Maserati, though his appearances on four wheels were necessarily limited.

In 1950 he drove a Maserati to seventh in his only Grand Prix appearance, at Bremgarten, and took a fourth at the Modena GP in a Simca-Gordini. Although he was to appear occasionally thereafter, taking second in class in the Mille Miglia with an OSCA in 1952, Pagani was more involved with the bike world, later managing the legendary MV Agusta team.

RICCARDO PALETTI

Riccardo began racing at 19 in Italian SuperFord, but soon graduated to Formula 3 and then, after just 15 F3 races, made the big jump into Formula 2 – albeit briefly – at the end of 1979. Back for more at the end of 1980, Paletti drove sensibly within his limits and, with the benefit of winter testing, he joined the Onyx team full-time for 1981. The year started well with his March taking a second place at Silverstone and a third at Thruxton, but then his season tailed off disappointingly.

With the help of generous sponsorship, Paletti found himself a seat in the tiny Osella team for 1982, but the young Italian faced a steep learning curve. Sadly he never had the chance to progress, for in Montreal his Osella accelerated away from its place at the tail of the grid and hurtled into the back of the stalled Ferrari of Pironi at over 100 mph with devastating consequences. In a gruesome accident, Paletti suffered massive internal injuries and he died in hospital shortly afterwards.

TORSTEN PALM

After a little rallying in a Volvo, Torsten entered Scandinavian F3 with a Brabham in 1969, before teaming up with Picko Troberg for a programme that was successful at home but less so when they ventured abroad.

In 1973 Palm hired the second works Surtees for three Formula 2 races, taking a third place at Karlskoga, and he then had a handful of outings the following year, this time in a GRD, finishing sixth at the Salzburgring. Palm briefly surfaced in Grands Prix in 1975, hiring a Hesketh to contest two races before retiring to guide the career of the then promising Eje Elgh.

PAGANI, Nello (I) b 11/10/1911, Milan

	1950	Championship position: Unplaced							
	Race	Circuit	No	Entrant	Tyres	Car/Engine		Comment	Q Pos/Entries
7	SWISS GP	Bremgarten	2	Scuderia Achille Varzi	P	1.5 s/c Maserati 4CLT/48 4		3 laps behind	15/18

GP Starts: 1   GP Wins: 0   Pole positions: 0   Fastest laps: 0   Points: 0

PALETTI, Riccardo (I) b 15/6/1958, Milan – d 13/6/1982, Montreal, Canada

	1982	Championship position: Unplaced							
	Race	Circuit	No	Entrant	Tyres	Car/Engine		Comment	Q Pos/Entries
dnq	SOUTH AFRICAN GP	Kyalami	32	Osella Squadra Corse	P	3.0 Osella FA1C-Cosworth V8			28/30
dnpq	BRAZILIAN GP	Rio	32	Osella Squadra Corse	P	3.0 Osella FA1C-Cosworth V8			31/31
dnq	US GP WEST	Long Beach	32	Osella Squadra Corse	P	3.0 Osella FA1C-Cosworth V8			28/31
ret	SAN MARINO GP	Imola	32	Osella Squadra Corse	P	3.0 Osella FA1C-Cosworth V8		suspension	13/14
dnpq	BELGIAN GP	Zolder	32	Osella Sqaudra Corse	P	3.0 Osella FA1C-Cosworth V8			31/32
dnpq	MONACO GP	Monte Carlo	32	Osella Squadra Corse	P	3.0 Osella FA1C-Cosworth V8			28/31
dns	US GP (DETROIT)	Detroit	32	Osella Squadra Corse	P	3.0 Osella FA1C-Cosworth V8		crashed in a.m. warm-up	(23)/28
ret/dns	CANADIAN GP	Montreal	32	Osella Squadra Corse	P	3.0 Osella FA1C-Cosworth V8		fatal accident at first start	23/26

GP Starts: 1 (2)   GP Wins: 0   Pole positions: 0   Fastest laps: 0   Points: 0

PALM, Torsten (S) b 23/7/1947, Kristinehamn

	1975	Championship position: 0		Wins: 0	Pole positions: 0	Fastest laps: 0	Points scored: 0		
	Race	Circuit	No	Entrant	Tyres	Car/Engine		Comment	Q Pos/Entries
dnq	MONACO GP	Monte Carlo	25	Polar Caravans	G	3.0 Hesketh 308-Cosworth V8			24/26
10/ret	SWEDISH GP	Anderstorp	32	Polar Caravans	G	3.0 Hesketh 308-Cosworth V8		out of fuel/2 laps behind	21/26

GP Starts: 1   GP Wins: 0   Pole positions: 0   Fastest laps: 0   Points: 0

JONATHAN PALMER

A brilliant early career for Palmer failed to bring the fully competitive Grand Prix car his efforts had so obviously merited, and so another talent was never truly tested at the highest level.

Palmer's racing career took a back seat while he qualified as a doctor, but early races with a van Diemen in 1979 and 1980 brought him a drive with Dick Bennetts' crack Formula 3 team for 1981. In a superb year, Jonathan took seven pole positions and eight wins and set ten fastest laps to win the Marlboro F3 championship by a large margin from his rivals. A move into Formula 2 with the Ralt team brought him back down to earth with a jolt as they struggled to find a competitive set-up, but it was a different story in 1983 when, with the full attention of Honda, Jonathan and his team-mate Mike Thackwell dominated proceedings, Palmer winning six of the 12 rounds (five of them in a row at the end of the season) with a display of brilliant driving backed by much planning and hard work behind the scenes.

After a drive for Williams in the 1983 European GP, Palmer found himself first with the RAM team, then the ambitious but overstretched Zakspeed outfit, struggling even to gain sight of a top-six finish. Luckily he kept his competitive edge sharpened in sports cars; driving a Richard Lloyd Porsche, he won at Brands Hatch in 1984 with Jan Lammers and finished second at Le Mans in 1985, and in 1987 he won the Norisring race with Baldi in Brun's Porsche.

By now Palmer was at the start of a three-year association with Tyrrell. The first two years, spent struggling with a Cosworth against the turbo brigade, found him picking up the crumbs, but some excellent drives brought hard-earned points for the team and Jonathan won the Jim Clark Trophy for top non-turbo driver in 1987. A competitive new chassis allowed Palmer to take a splendid fifth at Imola in 1989, but his form sagged after the arrival of Jean Alesi, who stole the show. The season's finale saw a despondent Jonathan fail to qualify, and his Grand Prix career was over.

In 1990 he acted as a test driver for McLaren-Honda and returned to competition in sports cars with a Porsche 962, but after the sudden death of James Hunt the personable and ever-talkative Palmer moved into a commentary role for BBC TV.

Jonathan has recently set up his own ultra-professional junior single-seater series, Formula Palmer Audi. At a realistic cost the identically prepared cars offer up-and-coming young drivers the chance to show their skills as they seek to make their way in the sport.

PALMER, Jonathan (GB) b 7/11/1956, Lewisham, London

	1983	Championship position: Unplaced						
	Race	Circuit	No	Entrant	Tyres	Car/Engine	Comment	Q Pos/Entries
13	EUROPEAN GP	Brands Hatch	42	TAG Williams Team	G	3.0 Williams FW08C-Cosworth V8	*pit stop-tyres/2 laps behind*	25/29
	1984	Championship position: Unplaced						
8*	BRAZILIAN GP	Rio	10	Skoal Bandit Formula 1 Team	P	1.5 t/c RAM 01-Hart 4	* 5th place car dsq/-3 laps	27/27
ret	SOUTH AFRICAN GP	Kyalami	10	Skoal Bandit Formula 1 Team	P	1.5 t/c RAM 01-Hart 4	gearbox/electrics	21/27
10*	BELGIAN GP	Zolder	10	Skoal Bandit Formula 1 Team	P	1.5 t/c RAM 02-Hart 4	* 5th car dsq/pit stop/-6 laps	26/27
9*	SAN MARINO GP	Imola	10	Skoal Bandit Formula 1 Team	P	1.5 t/c RAM 02-Hart 4	* 5th place car dsq/-3 laps	25/28
13	FRENCH GP	Dijon	10	Skoal Bandit Formula 1 Team	P	1.5 t/c RAM 02-Hart 4	* 12th car dsq/-7 laps	22/27
dnq	MONACO GP	Monte Carlo	10	Skoal Bandit Formula 1 Team	P	1.5 t/c RAM 02-Hart 4		25/27
ret	US GP (DETROIT)	Detroit	10	Skoal Bandit Formula 1 Team	P	1.5 t/c RAM 02-Hart 4	tyre failure-accident	24/27
ret	US GP (DALLAS)	Dallas	10	Skoal Bandit Formula 1 Team	P	1.5 t/c RAM 02-Hart 4	electrics	25/27
ret	BRITISH GP	Brands Hatch	10	Skoal Bandit Formula 1 Team	P	1.5 t/c RAM 02-Hart 4	steering failure-accident	23/27
ret	GERMAN GP	Hockenheim	10	Skoal Bandit Formula 1 Team	P	1.5 t/c RAM 02-Hart 4	turbo	25/27
9	AUSTRIAN GP	Österreichring	10	Skoal Bandit Formula 1 Team	P	1.5 t/c RAM 02-Hart 4	2 laps behind	24/28
9*	DUTCH GP	Zandvoort	10	Skoal Bandit Formula 1 Team	P	1.5 t/c RAM 02-Hart 4	* 8th & 9th cars dsq/-4 laps	22/27
ret	ITALIAN GP	Monza	10	Skoal Bandit Formula 1 Team	P	1.5 t/c RAM 02-Hart 4	oil pressure	26/27
ret	EUROPEAN GP	Nürburgring	10	Skoal Bandit Formula 1 Team	P	1.5 t/c RAM 02-Hart 4	turbo	21/26
ret	PORTUGUESE GP	Estoril	10	Skoal Bandit Formula 1 Team	P	1.5 t/c RAM 02-Hart 4	gearbox	26/27

1985 — Championship position: Unplaced

Result	GP	Circuit	No	Team	Tyre	Engine	Comment	Pos
ret	PORTUGUESE GP	Estoril	30	West Zakspeed Racing	G	1.5 t/c Zakspeed 841 4	suspension damage	23/26
dns	SAN MARINO GP	Imola	30	West Zakspeed Racing	G	1.5 t/c Zakspeed 841 4	engine misfire on warm-up	(17)/26
11	MONACO GP	Monte Carlo	30	West Zakspeed Racing	G	1.5 t/c Zakspeed 841 4	spin/4 laps behind	19/26
ret	FRENCH GP	Paul Ricard	30	West Zakspeed Racing	G	1.5 t/c Zakspeed 841 4	engine	22/26
ret	BRITISH GP	Silverstone	30	West Zakspeed Racing	G	1.5 t/c Zakspeed 841 4	engine	24/26
ret	GERMAN GP	Nürburgring	30	West Zakspeed Racing	G	1.5 t/c Zakspeed 841 4	alternator belt	24/27
ret	AUSTRIAN GP	Österreichring	30	West Zakspeed Racing	G	1.5 t/c Zakspeed 841 4	engine	25/27
ret	DUTCH GP	Zandvoort	30	West Zakspeed Racing	G	1.5 t/c Zakspeed 841 4	engine-oil pressure	23/27

1986 — Championship position: Unplaced

Result	GP	Circuit	No	Team	Tyre	Engine	Comment	Pos
ret	BRAZILIAN GP	Rio	14	West Zakspeed Racing	G	1.5 t/c Zakspeed 861 4	cracked airbox	21/25
ret	SPANISH GP	Jerez	14	West Zakspeed Racing	G	1.5 t/c Zakspeed 861 4	accident with Jones	16/25
ret	SAN MARINO GP	Imola	14	West Zakspeed Racing	G	1.5 t/c Zakspeed 861 4	started from pit lane/brakes	20/26
12	MONACO GP	Monte Carlo	14	West Zakspeed Racing	G	1.5 t/c Zakspeed 861 4	pit stop/4 laps behind	19/26
nc	BELGIAN GP	Spa	14	West Zakspeed Racing	G	1.5 t/c Zakspeed 861 4	pit stops-alternator belt/-6 laps	20/25
ret	CANADIAN GP	Montreal	14	West Zakspeed Racing	G	1.5 t/c Zakspeed 861 4	started from pit lane/engine	22/25
8	US GP (DETROIT)	Detroit	14	West Zakspeed Racing	G	1.5 t/c Zakspeed 861 4	2 laps behind	20/26
ret	FRENCH GP	Paul Ricard	14	West Zakspeed Racing	G	1.5 t/c Zakspeed 861 4	engine	22/26
9	BRITISH GP	Brands Hatch	14	West Zakspeed Racing	G	1.5 t/c Zakspeed 861 4	pit stop/6 laps behind	22/26
ret	GERMAN GP	Hockenheim	14	West Zakspeed Racing	G	1.5 t/c Zakspeed 861 4	engine	16/26
10	HUNGARIAN GP	Hungaroring	14	West Zakspeed Racing	G	1.5 t/c Zakspeed 861 4	pit stop-brakes/6 laps behind	24/26
ret	AUSTRIAN GP	Österreichring	14	West Zakspeed Racing	G	1.5 t/c Zakspeed 861 4	engine	21/26
ret	ITALIAN GP	Monza	14	West Zakspeed Racing	G	1.5 t/c Zakspeed 861 4	engine	22/26
12	PORTUGUESE GP	Estoril	14	West Zakspeed Racing	G	1.5 t/c Zakspeed 861 4	3 laps behind	22/27
10/ret	MEXICAN GP	Mexico City	14	West Zakspeed Racing	G	1.5 t/c Zakspeed 861 4	out of fuel/3 laps behind	20/27
9/ret	AUSTRALIAN GP	Adelaide	14	West Zakspeed Racing	G	1.5 t/c Zakspeed 861 4	trailing bodywork/-5 laps	18/26
								21/26

1987 — Championship position: 11th (winner non-turbo Jim Clark Cup) Wins: 0 Pole positions: 0 Fastest laps: 0 Points scored: 7

Result	GP	Circuit	No	Team	Tyre	Engine	Comment	Pos
10*	BRAZILIAN GP	Rio	3	Data General Team Tyrrell	G	3.5 Tyrrell-DG016-Cosworth V8	* 1st non-turbo/3 laps behind	18/23
ret	SAN MARINO GP	Imola	3	Data General Team Tyrrell	G	3.5 Tyrrell-DG016-Cosworth V8	clutch	25/27
ret/dns	BELGIAN GP	Spa	3	Data General Team Tyrrell	G	3.5 Tyrrell-DG016-Cosworth V8	accident-Streiff/did not restart	24/26
5*	MONACO GP	Monte Carlo	3	Data General Team Tyrrell	G	3.5 Tyrrell-DG016-Cosworth V8	* 1st non-turbo/-2 laps	15/26
11*	US GP (DETROIT)	Detroit	3	Data General Team Tyrrell	G	3.5 Tyrrell-DG016-Cosworth V8	* 1st non-turbo/-3 laps	13/26
7*	FRENCH GP	Paul Ricard	3	Data General Team Tyrrell	G	3.5 Tyrrell-DG016-Cosworth V8	2nd non-turbo/-4 laps	24/26
8*	BRITISH GP	Silverstone	3	Data General Team Tyrrell	G	3.5 Tyrrell-DG016-Cosworth V8	* 1st non-turbo/-5 laps	24/26
5*	GERMAN GP	Hockenheim	3	Data General Team Tyrrell	G	3.5 Tyrrell-DG016-Cosworth V8	* 2nd non-turbo/-1 lap	23/26
7*	HUNGARIAN GP	Hungroring	3	Data General Team Tyrrell	G	3.5 Tyrrell-DG016-Cosworth V8	* 1st non-turbo/-2 laps	16/26
14*	AUSTRIAN GP	Österreichring	3	Data General Team Tyrrell	G	3.5 Tyrrell-DG016-Cosworth V8	* 3rd non-turbo/-5 laps	24/26
14*	ITALIAN GP	Monza	3	Data General Team Tyrrell	G	3.5 Tyrrell-DG016-Cosworth V8	* 3rd non-turbo/-3 laps	22/28
10*	PORTUGUESE GP	Estoril	3	Data General Team Tyrrell	G	3.5 Tyrrell-DG016-Cosworth V8	*2nd non-turbo/-3 laps	24/27
ret	SPANISH GP	Jerez	3	Data General Team Tyrrell	G	3.5 Tyrrell-DG016-Cosworth V8	hit by Arnoux	16/28
7*	MEXICAN GP	Mexico City	3	Data General Team Tyrrell	G	3.5 Tyrrell-DG016-Cosworth V8	* 2nd non-turbo/-3 laps	22/27
8*	JAPANESE GP	Suzuka	3	Data General Team Tyrrell	G	3.5 Tyrrell-DG016-Cosworth V8	* 1st non-turbo/-1 lap	20/27
4*	AUSTRALIAN GP	Adelaide	3	Data General Team Tyrrell	G	3.5 Tyrrell-DG016-Cosworth V8	* 1st non-turbo/-2 laps	19/27

1988 — Championship position: 13th Wins: 0 Pole positions: 0 Fastest laps: 0 Points scored: 5

Result	GP	Circuit	No	Team	Tyre	Engine	Comment	Pos
ret	BRAZILIAN GP	Rio	3	Tyrrell Racing Organisation	G	3.5 Tyrrell 017-Cosworth V8	transmission	22/31
14	SAN MARINO GP	Imola	3	Tyrrell Racing Organisation	G	3.5 Tyrrell 017-Cosworth V8	engine problem/2 laps behind	23/31
5	MONACO GP	Monte Carlo	3	Tyrrrel Racing Organisation	G	3.5 Tyrrell 017-Cosworth V8	1 lap behind	10/30
dnq	MEXICAN GP	Mexico City	3	Tyrrell Racing Organisation	G	3.5 Tyrrell 017-Cosworth V8		27/30
6	CANADIAN GP	Montreal	3	Tyrrell Racing Organisation	G	3.5 Tyrrell 017-Cosworth V8	cockpit problems/-2 laps	19/31
5	US GP (DETROIT)	Detroit	3	Tyrrell Racing Organisation	G	3.5 Tyrrell 017-Cosworth V8	1 lap behind	17/31
ret	FRENCH GP	Paul Ricard	3	Tyrrell Racing Organisation	G	3.5 Tyrrell 017-Cosworth V8	engine	23/31
ret	BRITISH GP	Silverstone	3	Tyrrell Racing Organisation	G	3.5 Tyrrell 017-Cosworth V8	transmission	17/31
11	GERMAN GP	Hockenheim	3	Tyrrell Racing Organisation	G	3.5 Tyrrell 017-Cosworth V8	1 lap behind	24/31
ret	HUNGARIAN GP	Hungaroring	3	Tyrrell Racing Organisation	G	3.5 Tyrrell 017-Cosworth V8	engine cut out	21/31
12*/ret	BELGIAN GP	Spa	3	Tyrrell Racing Organisation	G	3.5 Tyrrell 017-Cosworth V8	throttle/*3rd & 4th dsq/-4 laps	21/31
dnq	ITALIAN GP	Monza	3	Tyrrell Racing Organisation	G	3.5 Tyrrell 017-Cosworth V8		27/31
ret	PORTUGUESE GP	Estoril	3	Tyrrell Racing Organisation	G	3.5 Tyrrell 017-Cosworth V8	overheating	22/31
ret	SPANISH GP	Jerez	3	Tyrrell Racing Organisation	G	3.5 Tyrrell 017-Cosworth V8	accident-water radiator	22/31
12	JAPANESE GP	Suzuka	3	Tyrrell Racing Organisation	G	3.5 Tyrrell 017-Cosworth V8	1 lap behind	16/31
ret	AUSTRALIAN GP	Adelaide	3	Tyrrell Racing Organisation	G	3.5 Tyrrell 017-Cosworth V8	transmission	17/31

1989 — Championship position: 23rd= Wins: 0 Pole positions: 0 Fastest laps: 1 Points scored: 2

Result	GP	Circuit	No	Team	Tyre	Engine	Comment	Pos
7	BRAZILIAN GP	Rio	3	Tyrrell Racing Organisation	G	3.5 Tyrrell 017B-Cosworth V8	1 lap behind	18/38
6*	SAN MARINO GP	Imola	3	Tyrrell Racing Organisation	G	3.5 Tyrrell 018-Cosworth V8	spin/1 lap behind	– / –
dns	"	"	3	Tyrrell Racing Organisation	G	3.5 Tyrrell 017B-Cosworth V8	practice only-set grid time	25/39
9	MONACO GP	Monte Carlo	3	Tyrrell Racing Organisation	G	3.5 Tyrrell 018-Cosworth V8	3 laps behind	23/38
ret	MEXICAN GP	Mexico City	3	Tyrrell Racing Organisation	G	3.5 Tyrrell 018-Cosworth V8	throttle linkage	14/39
9/ret	US GP (PHOENIX)	Phoenix	3	Tyrrell Racing Organisation	G	3.5 Tyrrell 018-Cosworth V8	fuel shortage/6 laps behind	21/39
ret	CANADIAN GP	Montreal	3	Tyrrell Racing Organisation	G	3.5 Tyrrell 018-Cosworth V8	hit wall/FL	14/39
10	FRENCH GP	Paul Ricard	3	Tyrrell Racing Organisation	G	3.5 Tyrrell 018-Cosworth V8	5 stops-hit by Arnoux/-2 laps	9/39
ret	BRITISH GP	Silverstone	3	Tyrrell Racing Organisation	G	3.5 Tyrrell 018-Cosworth V8	spun off	18/39
ret	GERMAN GP	Hockenheim	3	Tyrrell Racing Organisation	G	3.5 Tyrrell 018-Cosworth V8	throttle cable	19/39
13	HUNGARIAN GP	Hungaroring	3	Tyrrell Racing Organisation	G	3.5 Tyrrell 018-Cosworth V8	pit stop-broken injector/-4 laps	19/39
14	BELGIAN GP	Spa	3	Tyrrell Racing Organisation	G	3.5 Tyrrell 018-Cosworth V8	misfire/2 laps behind	21/39
ret	ITALIAN GP	Monza	3	Tyrrell Racing Organisation	G	3.5 Tyrrell 018-Cosworth V8	started from back of grid/engine	14/39
6	PORTUGUESE GP	Estoril	3	Tyrrell Racing Organisation	G	3.5 Tyrrell 018-Cosworth V8	1 lap behind	18/39
10	SPANISH GP	Jerez	3	Tyrrell Racing Organisation	G	3.5 Tyrrell 018-Cosworth V8	misfire/2 laps behind	13/38
ret	JAPANESE GP	Suzuka	3	Tyrrell Racing Organisation	G	3.5 Tyrrell 018-Cosworth V8	fuel leak	26/39
dnq	AUSTRALIAN GP	Adelaide	3	Tyrrell Racing Organisation	G	3.5 Tyrrell 018-Cosworth V8		27/39

GP Starts: 82 (84)   GP Wins: 0   Pole positions: 0   Fastest laps: 1   Points: 14

OLIVIER PANIS

In the seventies and eighties the Grand Prix grids were full of French drivers, many of them at the top of their profession. By the late nineties only Panis and Jean Alesi represented 'La Belle France', and at the turn of the millennium Olivier, for the time being at least, can be removed from the list.

Following the traditional karting, Pilote Elf and Formule Renault junior route, the quiet and impeccably mannered Panis emerged as champion in 1989 to earn a move into French F3. His first year, in a Dallara, brought fourth place in the championship, while in the second, despite taking five wins and six poles in a Ralt, he was narrowly beaten to the title by Christophe Bouchut. Olivier then took the well-trodden path to F3000 with the Apomatox team. It was to be a tough year struggling with the Lola chassis, but Panis still impressed enough to land the plum drive with DAMS for 1993. True to its reputation, this amazingly hard-fought series yet again saw the points spread evenly among the leading contenders, but it was Panis who finished at the head of the table in front of fellow Grand Prix aspirants Lamy, Coulthard, de Ferran and Beretta.

Over the next two years, with the backing and confidence of Elf, Panis quietly established himself as a Grand Prix regular, shunting other hopefuls such as Comas, Bernard, Beretta and even younger chargers like Lagorce and Boullion into touch.

Given his chance at Ligier, Olivier made a remarkably assured start to his Formula 1 career, highlighted by his second place in a German GP decimated by accidents. Paired with the experienced Brundle and Suzuki in 1995, he handled the politics of being a Frenchman in an increasingly cosmopolitan team with aplomb and his second place in the end-of-season race at Adelaide no doubt helped him survive the winter reshuffles.

He was undisputed team leader in 1996, paired with the wealthy but inex-perienced Pedro Diniz as the financially pressured outfit faced up to life as one of Grand Prix racing's poorer relations. Despite the Ligier JS43 suffering from traction problems Panis got the best out of the car wherever he could, and was a shock winner of the rain-hit Monaco Grand Prix. Revelling in the slippery conditions, he drove quite superbly on the day and resisted the challenge of David Coulthard's McLaren for much of the latter part of the race.

With the takeover of Ligier by Alain Prost completed prior to the start of the 1997 season, Panis was the newly renamed Prost team's spearhead, and he kicked off the season in fine style, scoring the revamped organisa-tion's (and Bridgestone's) first-ever points with a fifth place in Australia.

Third in Brazil and second in Spain saw the Frenchman driving at the top of his form until disaster struck when he crashed violently in the Canadian Grand Prix in Montreal. Both of his legs were badly broken and he spent several months recuperating. Happily he was fit enough to return before the end of the season, but it was very much a case of 'what might have been'.

The promise of 1997 gave way to gloom in 1998 when the first true Prost challenger was compromised by an overweight gearbox and incurable handling problems, and only late in the year was there a glimmer of hope for the frustrated Panis and his team-mate Jarno Trulli.

Things did not improve much in 1999 and when Olivier's relationship with Alain Prost reached rock bottom by mid-year it became clear that his tenure with the team was finally over. Having put himself under the management of Keke Rosberg, the Frenchman was soon found alternative employment, signing a testing contract for McLaren, although plans for him to race in the revitalised German touring car series with Mercedes in 2000 have now been dropped.

PANIS, Olivier (F) b 2/9/1966, Lyon

1994

Championship position: 11th   Wins: 0   Pole positions: 0   Fastest laps: 0   Points scored: 9

	Race	Circuit	No	Entrant		Tyres	Car/Engine	Comment	Q Pos/Entries
11	BRAZILIAN GP	Interlagos	26	Ligier Gitanes Blondes		G	3.5 Ligier JS39B-Renault V10	3 laps behind	19/28
9	PACIFIC GP	T.I. Circuit	26	Ligier Gitanes Blondes		G	3.5 Ligier JS39B-Renault V10	5 laps behind	22/28
11	SAN MARINO GP	Imola	26	Ligier Gitanes Blondes		G	3.5 Ligier JS39B-Renault V10	2 laps behind	19/28
9	MONACO GP	Monte Carlo	26	Ligier Gitanes Blondes		G	3.5 Ligier JS39B-Renault V10	2 laps behind	20/24
7	SPANISH GP	Barcelona	26	Ligier Gitanes Blondes		G	3.5 Ligier JS39B-Renault V10	2 laps behind	19/27
12	CANADIAN GP	Montreal	26	Ligier Gitanes Blondes		G	3.5 Ligier JS39B-Renault V10	2 laps behind	19/27
ret	FRENCH GP	Magny Cours	26	Ligier Gitanes Blondes		G	3.5 Ligier JS39B-Renault V10	collision with Morbidelli	13/28
12*	BRITISH GP	Silverstone	26	Ligier Gitanes Blondes		G	3.5 Ligier JS39B-Renault V10	*2nd place car dsq/2 laps behind	15/28
2	GERMAN GP	Hockenheim	26	Ligier Gitanes Blondes		G	3.5 Ligier JS39B-Renault V10		12/28
6	HUNGARIAN GP	Hungaroring	26	Ligier Gitanes Blondes		G	3.5 Ligier JS39B-Renault V10	1 lap behind	9/28
7*	BELGIAN GP	Spa	26	Ligier Gitanes Blondes		G	3.5 Ligier JS39B-Renault V10	*1st place car dsq/1 lap behind	17/28
10	ITALIAN GP	Monza	26	Ligier Gitanes Blondes		G	3.5 Ligier JS39B-Renault V10	2 laps behind	6/28
9/dsq*	PORTUGUESE GP	Estoril	26	Ligier Gitanes Blondes		G	3.5 Ligier JS39B-Renault V10	* dsq excessive skidblock wear	15/28
9	EUROPEAN GP	Jerez	26	Ligier Gitanes Blondes		G	3.5 Ligier JS39B-Renault V10	1 lap behind	11/28
11	JAPANESE GP	Suzuka	26	Ligier Gitanes Blondes		G	3.5 Ligier JS39B-Renault V10	1 lap behind	19/28
5	AUSTRALIAN GP	Adelaide	26	Ligier Gitanes Blondes		G	3.5 Ligier JS39B-Renault V10	1 lap behind	12/28

1995

Championship position: 8th   Wins: 0   Pole positions: 0   Fastest laps: 0   Points scored: 16

	Race	Circuit	No	Entrant		Tyres	Car/Engine	Comment	Q Pos/Entries
ret	BRAZILIAN GP	Interlagos	26	Ligier Gitanes Blondes		G	3.0 Ligier JS41-Mugen Honda V10	spun off on lap 1	10/26
7	ARGENTINE GP	Buenos Aires	26	Ligier Gitanes Blondes		G	3.0 Ligier JS41-Mugen Honda V10	2 laps behind	18/26
9	SAN MARINO GP	Imola	26	Ligier Gitanes Blondes		G	3.0 Ligier JS41-Mugen Honda V10	2 laps behind	12/26
6	SPANISH GP	Barcelona	26	Ligier Gitanes Blondes		G	3.0 Ligier JS41-Mugen Honda V10	1 lap behind	15/26
ret	MONACO GP	Monte Carlo	26	Ligier Gitanes Blondes		G	3.0 Ligier JS41-Mugen Honda V10	accident	12/26
4	CANADIAN GP	Montreal	26	Ligier Gitanes Blondes		G	3.0 Ligier JS41-Mugen Honda V10		11/24
8	FRENCH GP	Magny Cours	26	Ligier Gitanes Blondes		G	3.0 Ligier JS41-Mugen Honda V10	1 lap behind	6/24
4	BRITISH GP	Silverstone	26	Ligier Gitanes Blondes		G	3.0 Ligier JS41-Mugen Honda V10		13/24
ret	GERMAN GP	Hockenheim	26	Ligier Gitanes Blondes		G	3.0 Ligier JS41-Mugen Honda V10	engine	12/24
6	HUNGARIAN GP	Hungaroring	26	Ligier Gitanes Blondes		G	3.0 Ligier JS41-Mugen Honda V10	1 lap behind	10/24
9	BELGIAN GP	Spa	26	Ligier Gitanes Blondes		G	3.0 Ligier JS41-Mugen Honda V10		9/24
ret	ITALIAN GP	Monza	26	Ligier Gitanes Blondes		G	3.0 Ligier JS41-Mugen Honda V10	spun off	13/24
ret	PORTUGUESE GP	Estoril	26	Ligier Gitanes Blondes		G	3.0 Ligier JS41-Mugen Honda V10	spun off	11/24
ret	EUROPEAN GP	Nürburgring	26	Ligier Gitanes Blondes		G	3.0 Ligier JS41-Mugen Honda V10	spun off	14/24
8	PACIFIC GP	T.I. Circuit	26	Ligier Gitanes Blondes		G	3.0 Ligier JS41-Mugen Honda V10	2 laps behind	9/24
5	JAPANESE GP	Suzuka	26	Ligier Gitanes Blondes		G	3.0 Ligier JS41-Mugen Honda V10	1 lap behind	11/24
2	AUSTRALIAN GP	Adelaide	26	Ligier Gitanes Blondes		G	3.0 Ligier JS41-Mugen Honda V10	2 laps behind	12/24

1996

Championship position: 9th   Wins: 1   Pole positions: 0   Fastest laps: 0   Points scored: 13

	Race	Circuit	No	Entrant		Tyres	Car/Engine	Comment	Q Pos/Entries
7	AUSTRALIAN GP	Melbourne	9	Ligier Gauloises-Blondes		G	3.0 Ligier JS43-Mugen Honda V10	1 lap behind	11/22
6	BRAZILIAN GP	Interlagos	9	Ligier Gauloises-Blondes		G	3.0 Ligier JS43-Mugen Honda V10	1 lap behind	15/22
8	ARGENTINE GP	Buenos Aires	9	Ligier Gauloises-Blondes		G	3.0 Ligier JS43-Mugen Honda V10		12/22
ret	EUROPEAN GP	Nürburgring	9	Ligier Gauloises-Blondes		G	3.0 Ligier JS43-Mugen Honda V10	collision with Irvine	15/22
ret	SAN MARINO GP	Imola	9	Ligier Gauloises-Blondes		G	3.0 Ligier JS43-Mugen Honda V10	gearbox	13/22
1	MONACO GP	Monte Carlo	9	Ligier Gauloises-Blondes		G	3.0 Ligier JS43-Mugen Honda V10		14/22
ret	SPANISH GP	Barcelona	9	Ligier Gauloises-Blondes		G	3.0 Ligier JS43-Mugen Honda V10	spun off	8/22
ret	CANADIAN GP	Montreal	9	Ligier Gauloises-Blondes		G	3.0 Ligier JS43-Mugen Honda V10	alternator	11/22
7	FRENCH GP	Magny Cours	9	Ligier Gauloises-Blondes		G	3.0 Ligier JS43-Mugen Honda V10	1 lap behind	9/22
ret	BRITISH GP	Silverstone	9	Ligier Gauloises-Blondes		G	3.0 Ligier JS43-Mugen Honda V10	handling	16/22
7	GERMAN GP	Hockenheim	9	Ligier Gauloises-Blondes		G	3.0 Ligier JS43-Mugen Honda V10		12/20
5	HUNGARIAN GP	Hungaroring	9	Ligier Gauloises-Blondes		G	3.0 Ligier JS43-Mugen Honda V10	1 lap behind	11/20
ret	BELGIAN GP	Spa	9	Ligier Gauloises-Blondes		G	3.0 Ligier JS43-Mugen Honda V10	collision-Frentzen & Herbert	12/20
ret	ITALIAN GP	Monza	9	Ligier Gauloises-Blondes		G	3.0 Ligier JS43-Mugen Honda V10	spun off	11/20
10	PORTUGUESE GP	Estoril	9	Ligier Gauloises-Blondes		G	3.0 Ligier JS43-Mugen Honda V10	1 lap behind	15/20
7	JAPANESE GP	Suzuka	9	Ligier Gauloises-Blondes		G	3.0 Ligier JS43-Mugen Honda V10		12/20

Panis had his day of days at Monaco in 1996, when he took his Ligier-Mugen Honda to a surprise win on a wet track.

	1997	Championship position: 9th		Wins: 0	Pole positions: 0		Fastest laps: 0	Points scored: 16		
5	AUSTRALIAN GP	Melbourne	14	Prost Gauloise Blondes	B	3.0 Prost JS45-Mugen Honda V10				9/24
3	BRAZILIAN GP	Interlagos	14	Prost Gauloise Blondes	B	3.0 Prost JS45-Mugen Honda V10				5/22
ret	ARGENTINE GP	Buenos Aires	14	Prost Gauloise Blondes	B	3.0 Prost JS45-Mugen Honda V10		hydraulic leak		3/22
8	SAN MARINO GP	Imola	14	Prost Gauloise Blondes	B	3.0 Prost JS45-Mugen Honda V10		failed damper/ 1 lap behind		4/22
4	MONACO GP	Monte Carlo	14	Prost Gauloise Blondes	B	3.0 Prost JS45-Mugen Honda V10				12/22
2	SPANISH GP	Barcelona	14	Prost Gauloise Blondes	B	3.0 Prost JS45-Mugen Honda V10				12/22
11/ret	CANADIAN GP	Montreal	14	Prost Gauloise Blondes	B	3.0 Prost JS45-Mugen Honda V10		accident/broken legs/-3 laps		10/22
6	LUXEMBOURG GP	Nürburgring	14	Prost Gauloise Blondes	B	3.0 Prost JS45-Mugen Honda V10				11/22
ret	JAPANESE GP	Suzuka	14	Prost Gauloise Blondes	B	3.0 Prost JS45-Mugen Honda V10		engine		10/22
7	EUROPEAN GP	Jerez	14	Prost Gauloise Blondes	B	3.0 Prost JS45-Mugen Honda V10				9/22
	1998	Championship position: Unplaced								
9	AUSTRALIAN GP	Melbourne	11	Gauloises Prost Peugeot	B	3.0 Prost AP01-Peugeot V10		1 lap behind		21/22
ret	BRAZILIAN GP	Interlagos	11	Gauloises Prost Peugeot	B	3.0 Prost AP01-Peugeot V10		engine		9/22
15/ret	ARGENTINE GP	Buenos Aires	11	Gauloises Prost Peugeot	B	3.0 Prost AP01-Peugeot V10		engine/7 laps behind		15/22
11/ret	SAN MARINO GP	Imola	11	Gauloises Prost Peugeot	B	3.0 Prost AP01-Peugeot V10		engine/6 laps behind		13/22
16/ret	SPANISH GP	Barcelona	11	Gauloises Prost Peugeot	B	3.0 Prost AP01-Peugeot V10		engine/5 laps behind		12/22
ret	MONACO GP	Monte Carlo	11	Gauloises Prost Peugeot	B	3.0 Prost AP01-Peugeot V10		suspension		18/22
ret	CANADIAN GP	Montreal	11	Gauloises Prost Peugeot	B	3.0 Prost AP01-Peugeot V10		engine		15/22
11	FRENCH GP	Magny Cours	11	Gauloises Prost Peugeot	B	3.0 Prost AP01-Peugeot V10		2 laps behind		16/22
ret	BRITISH GP	Silverstone	11	Gauloises Prost Peugeot	B	3.0 Prost AP01-Peugeot V10		spun off		16/22
ret	AUSTRIAN GP	A-1 Ring	11	Gauloises Prost Peugeot	B	3.0 Prost AP01-Peugeot V10		clutch		10/22
15	GERMAN GP	Hockenheim	11	Gauloises Prost Peugeot	B	3.0 Prost AP01-Peugeot V10		1 lap behind		16/22
12	HUNGARIAN GP	Hungaroring	11	Gauloises Prost Peugeot	B	3.0 Prost AP01-Peugeot V10		3 laps behind		20/22
ret/dns	BELGIAN GP	Spa	11	Gauloises Prost Peugeot	B	3.0 Prost AP01-Peugeot V10		accident at first start		15/22
ret	ITALIAN GP	Monza	11	Gauloises Prost Peugeot	B	3.0 Prost AP01-Peugeot V10		rear vibration		9/22
12	LUXEMBOURG GP	Nürburgring	11	Gauloises Prost Peugeot	B	3.0 Prost AP01-Peugeot V10		2 laps behind		15/22
11	JAPANESE GP	Suzuka	11	Gauloises Prost Peugeot	B	3.0 Prost AP01-Peugeot V10		1 lap behind		13/22
	1999	Championship position: 15th=		Wins: 0	Pole positions: 0		Fastest laps: 0	Points scored: 2		
ret	AUSTRALIAN GP	Melbourne	18	Gauloises Prost Peugeot	B	3.0 Prost AP02-Peugeot V10		stuck wheel nut		20/22
6	BRAZILIAN GP	Interlagos	18	Gauloises Prost Peugeot	B	3.0 Prost AP02-Peugeot V10		1 lap behind		12/22
ret	SAN MARINO GP	Imola	18	Gauloises Prost Peugeot	B	3.0 Prost AP02-Peugeot V10		throttle		11/22
ret	MONACO GP	Monte Carlo	18	Gauloises Prost Peugeot	B	3.0 Prost AP02-Peugeot V10		engine		18/22
ret	SPANISH GP	Barcelona	18	Gauloises Prost Peugeot	B	3.0 Prost AP02-Peugeot V10		gearbox hydraulics		15/22
9	CANADIAN GP	Montreal	18	Gauloises Prost Peugeot	B	3.0 Prost AP02-Peugeot V10		1 lap behind		15/22
8	FRENCH GP	Magny Cours	18	Gauloises Prost Peugeot	B	3.0 Prost AP02-Peugeot V10				3/22
13	BRITISH GP	Silverstone	18	Gauloises Prost Peugeot	B	3.0 Prost AP02-Peugeot V10				15/22
10	AUSTRIAN GP	A-1 Ring	18	Gauloises Prost Peugeot	B	3.0 Prost AP02-Peugeot V10		1 lap behind		18/22
6	GERMAN GP	Hockenheim	18	Gauloises Prost Peugeot	B	3.0 Prost AP02-Peugeot V10				7/22
10	HUNGARIAN GP	Hungaroring	18	Gauloises Prost Peugeot	B	3.0 Prost AP02-Peugeot V10		1 lap behind		14/22
13	BELGIAN GP	Spa	18	Gauloises Prost Peugeot	B	3.0 Prost AP02-Peugeot V10				17/22
11	ITALIAN GP	Monza	18	Gauloises Prost Peugeot	B	3.0 Prost AP02-Peugeot V10		1 lap behind		10/22
9	EUROPEAN GP	Nürburgring	18	Gauloises Prost Peugeot	B	3.0 Prost AP02-Peugeot V10		1 lap behind		5/22
ret	MALAYSIAN GP	Sepang	18	Gauloises Prost Peugeot	B	3.0 Prost AP02-Peugeot V10		engine		12/22
ret	JAPANESE GP	Suzuka	18	Gauloises Prost Peugeot	B	3.0 Prost AP02-Peugeot V10		gearbox		6/22

GP Starts: 91   GP Wins: 1   Pole positions: 0   Fastest laps: 0   Points: 56

MASSIMILIANO ('MAX') PAPIS

After karting and a few years in Italian F3, Papis stepped up to European F3000 in 1993 with the Vortex team and enjoyed a solid first season. He switched to Mythos for another crack the following year and jaws soon dropped when the Italian proved dominant at Barcelona with a performance he could not repeat.

Taken under the wing of former Lotus boss Peter Collins (who had given him a test in 1994), Papis proved that he had more to offer than many would have supposed once he got behind the wheel of a Footwork and Max certainly relished his chance to join the Grand Prix ranks. Only the late challenge of Boullion, who pipped him for sixth place, denied Papis a championship point at Monza.

The Italian raced Gianpiero Moretti's Ferrari 333SP sports car in America in 1996 and his impressive performances caught the eye of the Arciero-Wells team, who gave him his CART chance after the tragic death of Jeff Krosnoff. For much of 1997 and 1998 Max was handicapped by the lack of horsepower from the Toyota engine, but he comfortably eclipsed his team-mates Matsushita and Gordon. The big breakthrough came for Papis when Bobby Rahal put him into one of his cars for 1999. Only cruel luck robbed him of a deserved victory on the last lap of the US 500, but throughout the season he had consistently shown that his day will surely come.

PAPIS, Massimiliano (I) b 3/10/1969, Como

	1995	Championship position: Unplaced							
	Race	Circuit	No	Entrant	Tyres	Car/Engine		Comment	Q Pos/Entries
ret	BRITISH GP	Silverstone	9	Footwork Hart	G	3.0 Footwork FA16-Hart V8		accident-slid off	17/24
ret	GERMAN GP	Hockenheim	9	Footwork Hart	G	3.0 Footwork FA16-Hart V8		transmission on startline	15/24
ret	HUNGARIAN GP	Hungaroring	9	Footwork Hart	G	3.0 Footwork FA16-Hart V8		brakes	20/24
ret	BELGIAN GP	Spa	9	Footwork Hart	G	3.0 Footwork FA16-Hart V8		spun off	20/24
7	ITALIAN GP	Monza	9	Footwork Hart	G	3.0 Footwork FA16-Hart V8		1 lap behind	15/24
ret/dns	PORTUGUESE GP	Estoril	9	Footwork Hart	G	3.0 Footwork FA16-Hart V8		gearbox at first start	(20)/24
12	EUROPEAN GP	Nürburgring	9	Footwork Hart	G	3.0 Footwork FA16-Hart V8		3 laps behind	17/24

GP Starts: 6 (7)   GP Wins: 0   Pole positions: 0   Fastest laps: 0   Points: 0

MICHAEL PARKES

Born into a motoring family (his father was the chairman of Alvis cars), Mike first took to the circuits with an MG TD while working as an engineer with the Rootes group, and soon graduated to a Frazer Nash.

He started to race seriously in 1957 with a Lotus, bringing an invitation from Colin Chapman to act as reserve driver for the works

team at Le Mans, and then became involved with David Fry's Formula 2 project, which was intended for Stuart Lewis-Evans. Apart from the occasional Libre success in minor events during 1958-59, the car was not really competitive and Mike failed to qualify it for the F2 class of the British GP at Aintree.

A few outings in Sir Gawaine Baillie's Lotus Elite during 1960 showed his potential but brought little by way of results, but his breakthrough came in 1961 when he raced for Tommy Sopwith's Equipe Endeavour in GT and Formula Junior events, and also handled Maranello Concessionaires' Ferrari GT, winning races regularly in all classes. The high point of his season was undoubtedly the Le Mans 24 Hours, in which he shared a Ferrari 3-litre Testa Rossa with Willy Mairesse to take a superb second place.

Although he began 1962 with a rare Formula 1 outing at Mallory Park, taking fourth place in the 1000 Guineas race in a Bowmaker Cooper, Parkes' immediate future remained in the sports and GT category. His superb form of the previous year was repeated with much the same machinery, his tally including a hat-trick of wins in one day at Brands Hatch. Another fine outing brought second place in the Nürburgring 1000 Km in the works Ferrari, and it was no surprise when he joined the Scuderia for the 1963 season as development engineer and reserve driver.

Over the next three seasons, Mike became one the world's leading sports car drivers, winning the Sebring 12 Hours and Spa 500 Km in 1964 – a season cut short by a testing accident – and the Monza 1000 Km in 1965. After John Surtees' sudden departure from the team, Mike was elevated to Grand Prix status and, with a special long chassis to accommodate his 6 ft 4 in frame, he took second place on his debut in the French GP and repeated the feat at Monza. His success in sports cars continued, Parkes winning the Monza and Spa 1000 Km in 1966, and finishing second at Daytona, Monza and Le Mans in 1967, a season which started with much promise when he dead-heated with Scarfiotti to share a win at Syracuse and then demolished the opposition in the International Trophy at Silverstone. However, disaster struck in the Belgian GP when he crashed his Ferrari and suffered serious leg injuries.

Mike continued in a management role at Ferrari while he recovered from the accident, and made a tentative return in the Paris 1000 Km in 1969, returning to the track in 1970 and 1971 for NART and Scuderia Filipinetti. Though he could not repeat his previous triumphs, Parkes produced some useful performances, including a superb drive to fifth place in the 1972 Targa Florio with Peter Westbury in the little Lola T212. He was then involved in the Fiat 128 touring car programme before moving to Lancia to help develop the Stratos. Tragically, Parkes was killed in a road accident in 1977 when his car was involved in a collision with a lorry.

PARKES, Michael (GB) b 24/9/1931, Richmond, Surrey – d 28/8/1977, nr Turin, Italy

	1959	Championship position: Unplaced							
	Race	Circuit	No	Entrant	Tyres	Car/Engine		Comment	Q Pos/Entries
dnq	BRITISH GP (F2)	Aintree	60	David Fry	D	1.5 Fry-Climax 4 F2			– /30
	1966	Championship position: 8th= Wins: 0 Pole positions: 1 Fastest laps: 0 Points scored: 12							
2	FRENCH GP	Reims	22	Scuderia Ferrari SpA SEFAC	F	3.0 Ferrari 312/66-V12			3/17
ret	DUTCH GP	Zandvoort	4	Scuderia Ferrari SpA SEFAC	F	3.0 Ferrari 312/66-V12		*spun off*	5/18
ret	GERMAN GP	Nürburgring	10	Scuderia Ferrari SpA SEFAC	D	3.0 Ferrari 312/66-V12		*engine failure-crashed*	7/30
2	ITALIAN GP	Monza	4	Scuderia Ferrari SpA SEFAC	F	3.0 Ferrari 312/66-V12			1/22
	1967	Championship position: 16th= Wins: 0 Pole positions: 0 Fastest laps: 0 Points scored: 2							
5	DUTCH GP	Zandvoort	4	Scuderia Ferrari SpA SEFAC	F	3.0 Ferrari 312/66-V12		*1 lap behind*	10/17
ret	BELGIAN GP	Spa	3	Scuderia Ferrari SpA SEFAC	F	3.0 Ferrari 312/66-V12		*went off on oil/broken legs*	8/18

GP Starts: 6   GP Wins: 0   Pole positions: 1   Fastest laps: 0   Points: 14

REG PARNELL

Something of a wayward performer in his youth (his licence was withdrawn from 1937 to 1939 following a serious accident at Silverstone), Reg Parnell matured to become one of Britain's most seasoned professionals and later a respected elder statesman, guiding the fortunes of a new generation of Grand Prix talent.

The Derbyshire pig farmer began racing in 1935 with an MG Magnette, and found success immediately before the war with a 4.7-litre Bugatti. The war years took away a large part of what should have been the prime of his career, but he did not idle his time away, purchasing a vast array of temporarily redundant racing machinery in readiness for peace.

Racing a Maserati and an E-Type ERA bought from Peter Whitehead, he was soon tackling Continental races with great gusto, but eventually the Maserati 4CLT/48 brought more success, particularly at Goodwood, where he seemed to be able to win at will.

Such was the respect he commanded that Reg was invited to drive a works Alfa Romeo in the very first World Championship race at Silverstone in 1950, finishing an excellent third.

In 1951 he drove Tony Vandervell's 'Thinwall Special' Ferrari to points finishes in two Grands Prix, and won the International Trophy at Silverstone when the race was abandoned after a rainstorm. Less happy was his association with BRM and their problematic V16 car, which defeated even Reg's efforts.

He found the ready-made Ferrari T500 – no longer a Grand Prix challenger due to the change in formula – just the ticket for national events, and chalked up many successes during the 1954 season. He later drove Rob Walker's Connaught on occasion as well as a Ferrari Super Squalo, which he used to win the 1957 New Zealand GP and the South Island race at Dunedin, before retiring to take up the full-time team manager's job at Aston Martin, having been a key member of the team since the early fifties.

When David Brown pulled out of racing, Reg was immediately in demand and spent 1961 and 1962 overseeing the Yeoman Credit and Bowmaker Lola teams, before setting up his own Reg Parnell Racing team which was still in its infancy when the sturdy Parnell died unexpectedly of peritonitis after a routine appendix operation in January 1964 at the age of 52.

Reg driving Tony Vandervell's 'Thinwall Special' to fourth place in the 1951 French Grand Prix. Under contract to BRM, he was only driving the car because the Bourne team had failed to make the race.

PARNELL, Reg (GB) b 2/7/1911, Derby – d 7/1/1964, Derby

	1950	Championship position: 7th=	Wins: 0	Pole positions: 0	Fastest laps: 0	Points scored: 4		
	Race	Circuit	No	Entrant	Tyres	Car/Engine	Comment	Q Pos/Entries
3	BRITISH GP	Silverstone	4	Alfa Romeo SpA	P	1.5 s/c Alfa Romeo 158 8	guest driver	4/21
ret	FRENCH GP	Reims	32	Scuderia Ambrosiana	D	1.5 s/c Maserati 4CLT/48 4	engine	12/20
	1951	Championship position: 8th	Wins: 0	Pole positions: 0	Fastest laps: 0	Points scored: 5		
4	FRENCH GP	Reims	26	G A Vandervell	P	4.5 Ferrari 375/Thinwall Spl V12	4 laps behind	9/23
5	BRITISH GP	Silverstone	6	BRM Ltd	D	1.5 s/c BRM P15 V16	5 laps behind	20/20
dns	ITALIAN GP	Monza	30	BRM Ltd	D	1.5 s/c BRM P15 V16	engine in practice	(8)/22
	1952	Championship position: Unplaced						
7	BRITISH GP	Silverstone	8	A H M Bryde	D	2.0 Cooper T20-Bristol 6	3 laps behind	6/32
	1954	Championship position: Unplaced						
ret	BRITISH GP	Silverstone	12	Scuderia Ambrosiana	A	2.5 Ferrari 500/625 4	water jacket	14/31

GP Starts: 6   GP Wins: 0   Pole positions: 0   Fastest laps: 0   Points: 9

TIM PARNELL

Big, bluff and affable, Tim never managed to match the success of his father Reg on the circuits, but he had an enjoyable career in minor Formula 1 and F2 races in the late fifties and early sixties.

Suitably encouraged by a sound Formula Junior season in 1960, Tim purchased a Lotus 18 in 1961, which he hauled to the far corners of the Continent in search of limited success.

Illness curtailed his 1962 campaign, but he returned in 1963, only for the sudden death of his father the following January to thrust him into the role of running the Parnell team.

He remained a team manager for the rest of the decade, latterly with the BRM works team. He also ran his own outfit, working with drivers such as Mike Spence (1966) and Pedro Rodriguez (1969).

PARNELL, Tim (GB) b 25/6/1932, Derby

	1959	Championship position: Unplaced						
	Race	Circuit	No	Entrant	Tyres	Car/Engine	Comment	Q Pos/Entries
dnq	BRITISH GP (F2)	Aintree	66	R H H Parnell	D	1.5 Cooper T45-Climax 4		–/30
	1961	Championship position: Unplaced						
ret	BRITISH GP	Aintree	38	Tim Parnell	D	1.5 Lotus 18-Climax 4	clutch	29/30
10	ITALIAN GP	Monza	16	Tim Parnell	D	1.5 Lotus 18-Climax 4	3 laps behind	27/33
	1963	Championship position: Unplaced						
dnq	GERMAN GP	Nürburgring	30	Tim Parnell	D	1.5 Lotus 18/21-Climax 4		25/26

GP Starts: 2   GP Wins: 0   Pole positions: 0   Fastest laps: 0   Points: 0

RICCARDO PATRESE

RICCARDO PATRESE

At the end of the 1993 season, the curtain finally fell on the Formula 1 career of Riccardo Patrese, during which he had competed in a staggering total of 256 World Championship Grands Prix. During the 17 seasons that he had spent racing at the highest level, he had matured from a wild and cocksure enfant terrible into a contented and charming elder statesman, happy still to be part of the scene which had changed so much during his marathon innings.

A former karting whizz-kid who took the world title in 1974, Patrese moved into cars the following season in Formula Italia. He finished runner-up to Bruno Giacomelli and then embarked on a full season of Formula 3 in 1976. The ensuing fierce battle with Conny Andersson for the European championship went all the way to a bitter final round before the title fell to the Italian. Riccardo then enjoyed a successful year in Formula 2 with a Chevron but before long he had been propelled into the Shadow team to replace Zorzi. While his off-track demeanour ruffled a few feathers, there was certainly no doubting his talent behind the wheel. Patrese was part of the new breakaway Arrows team at the start of 1978 and he was sensationally quick, leading comfortably in South Africa until an engine failure robbed him of a deserved victory. Unfortunately his driving still had some rough edges, and in the emotional aftermath of Peterson's accident at Monza Riccardo was targeted for blame. The treatment he received would have broken a lesser man, but he simply got on with the job, although in retrospect staying loyal to Arrows could have been his biggest mistake. From 1979 through to 1981 he struggled to find sustained success with cars which showed occasional promise that remained unfulfilled, and secretly he must have regretted turning down the tempting opportunities he was offered in 1978.

A move to Brabham found him in a truly competitive environment, but a lucky win at Monaco was the highlight of an inconclusive year, disfigured by a rash of mistakes. It was a similar story in 1983, Riccardo tossing away victory at Imola early in the season yet signing off from the Brabham team with a perfect display at Kyalami to show what might have been. He certainly had time to ponder his wasted chances over the next few years as he became caught in a depressing downward spiral, struggling with the Benetton-sponsored Alfa for two seasons before returning to a Brabham team that was beginning its terminal decline. At least he had been able to savour the taste of success in his role as a works driver for Lancia Martini with wins at Silverstone and the Nürburgring in 1982, Kyalami in 1984 and Spa a year later.

When he was picked for the second Williams drive, most observers felt Patrese was extremely lucky to have been given such an opportunity, and he certainly failed to pull up any trees with the Judd-engined car in 1988. However, the following season, with Mansell off to Ferrari and Renault power at his disposal, a rejuvenated Riccardo appeared. Relaxed and confident, he forged an excellent working relationship with Patrick Head and was largely responsible for the development work which was to bring the Didcot team back to the top of the pile. Certainly he was unlucky not to win at least two races that year, but he put that to rights in 1990 with an emotional win at Imola, helping to erase his painful memories of 1983. Even the return of Mansell in 1991 – which Patrese took with great equanimity – failed to blunt his spirit, and he gave as good as he got, particularly in the first half of the season. Victories in Mexico and Portugal set the seal on what was probably his best-ever year. Statistically the following season, when he was runner-up to Mansell in the World Championship, was more successful, but his performances were less convincing, and he was very fortunate to escape unharmed after a horrifying coming-together with Berger at Estoril, but showed his steel by bouncing back with a win at Suzuka.

Accepting a lucrative contract with Benetton for 1993, Riccardo found it difficult to rediscover his recent sparkling form. A depressing early-season run was arrested by midsummer, but by then the Benetton management had already decided to dispense with the services of Grand Prix racing's most experienced campaigner.

Riccardo subsequently took a well-paid drive in German Super Touring with Ford, but the Mondeo was never more than a midfield runner. Apart from a one-off return to Le Mans with Nissan in 1997, Patrese has since eased himself into comfortable and well-deserved retirement.

Though he was largely overshadowed by Nelson Piquet during his time with the team, Riccardo signed off his Brabham career with a win in the 1983 South African Grand Prix.

PATRESE, Riccardo (I) b 17/4/1954, Padua

1977
Championship position: 19th= Wins: 0 Pole positions: 0 Fastest laps: 0 Points scored: 1

	Race	Circuit	No	Entrant	Tyres	Car/Engine	Comment	Q Pos/Entries
9	MONACO GP	Monte Carlo	16	Shadow Racing Team	G	3.0 Shadow DN8-Cosworth V8	1 lap behind	15/26
ret	BELGIAN GP	Zolder	16	Shadow Racing Team	G	3.0 Shadow DN8-Cosworth V8	crashed	15/32
ret	FRENCH GP	Dijon	16	Shadow Racing Team	G	3.0 Shadow DN8-Cosworth V8	clutch/engine	15/30
ret	BRITISH GP	Silverstone	16	Shadow Racing Team	G	3.0 Shadow DN8-Cosworth V8	fuel pressure	25/36
10/ret	GERMAN GP	Hockenheim	16	Shadow Racing Team	G	3.0 Shadow DN8-Cosworth V8	lost wheel/5 laps behind	16/30
13	DUTCH GP	Zandvoort	16	Shadow Racing Team	G	3.0 Shadow DN8-Cosworth V8	pit stop/8 laps behind	16/34
ret	ITALIAN GP	Monza	16	Shadow Racing Team	G	3.0 Shadow DN8-Cosworth V8	spun off on oil	=6/34
10/ret	CANADIAN GP	Mosport Park	16	Shadow Racing Team	G	3.0 Shadow DN8-Cosworth V8	spun off/4 laps behind	8/27
6	JAPANESE GP	Mount Fuji	16	Shadow Racing Team	G	3.0 Shadow DN8-Cosworth V8	1 lap behind	13/23

1978
Championship position: 11th= Wins: 0 Pole positions: 0 Fastest laps: 0 Points scored: 11

	Race	Circuit	No	Entrant	Tyres	Car/Engine	Comment	Q Pos/Entries
10	BRAZILIAN GP	Rio	36	Arrows Racing Team	G	3.0 Arrows FA1-Cosworth V8	2 pit stops-fuel/4 laps behind	18/28
ret	SOUTH AFRICAN GP	Kyalami	35	Arrows Racing Team	G	3.0 Arrows FA1-Cosworth V8	engine/led race	7/30
6	US GP WEST	Long Beach	35	Arrows Racing Team	G	3.0 Arrows FA1-Cosworth V8	pit stop-tyre/1 lap behind	9/30
6	MONACO GP	Monte Carlo	35	Arrows Racing Team	G	3.0 Arrows FA1-Cosworth V8		14/30
ret	BELGIUM GP	Zolder	35	Arrows Racing Team	G	3.0 Arrows FA1-Cosworth V8	rear suspension	8/30
ret	SPANISH GP	Jarama	35	Arrows Racing Team	G	3.0 Arrows FA1-Cosworth V8	engine	8/29
2	SWEDISH GP	Anderstorp	35	Arrows Racing Team	G	3.0 Arrows FA1-Cosworth V8		5/27
8	FRENCH GP	Paul Ricard	35	Arrows Racing Team	G	3.0 Arrows FA1-Cosworth V8		12/29
ret	BRITISH GP	Brands Hatch	35	Arrows Racing Team	G	3.0 Arrows FA1-Cosworth V8	rear suspension after puncture	5/30
9	GERMAN GP	Hockenheim	35	Arrows Racing Team	G	3.0 Arrows FA1-Cosworth V8	1 lap behind	14/30
ret	AUSTRIAN GP	Österreichring	35	Arrows Racing Team	G	3.0 Arrows A1-Cosworth V8	collision with Ertl at restart	16/31
ret	DUTCH GP	Zandvoort	35	Arrows Racing Team	G	3.0 Arrows A1-Cosworth V8	collision with Pironi	13/33
ret	ITALIAN GP	Monza	35	Arrows Racing Team	G	3.0 Arrows A1-Cosworth V8	engine	12/32
4	CANADIAN GP	Montreal	35	Arrows Racing Team	G	3.0 Arrows A1-Cosworth V8		12/28

1979
Championship position: 19th= Wins: 0 Pole positions: 0 Fastest laps: 0 Points scored: 2

	Race	Circuit	No	Entrant	Tyres	Car/Engine	Comment	Q Pos/Entries
dns	ARGENTINE GP	Buenos Aires	29	Warsteiner Arrows Racing Team	G	3.0 Arrows A1-Cosworth V8	accident in a.m. warm-up	(13)/26
9	BRAZILIAN GP	Interlagos	29	Warsteiner Arrows Racing Team	G	3.0 Arrows A1-Cosworth V8	1 lap behind	16/26
11	SOUTH AFRICAN GP	Kyalami	29	Warsteiner Arrows Racing Team	G	3.0 Arrows A1-Cosworth V8	3 laps behind	16/26
ret	US GP WEST	Long Beach	29	Warsteiner Arrows Racing Team	G	3.0 Arrows A1-Cosworth V8	brakes	9/26
10	SPANISH GP	Jarama	29	Warsteiner Arrows Racing Team	G	3.0 Arrows A1-Cosworth V8	1 lap behind	16/27
5	BELGIUM GP	Zolder	29	Warsteiner Arrows Racing Team	G	3.0 Arrows A1-Cosworth V8		16/28
ret	MONACO GP	Monte Carlo	29	Warsteiner Arrows Racing Team	G	3.0 Arrows A1-Cosworth V8	suspension	15/25
14	FRENCH GP	Dijon	29	Warsteiner Arrows Racing Team	G	3.0 Arrows A2-Cosworth V8	3 laps behind	19/27
ret	BRITISH GP	Silverstone	29	Warsteiner Arrows Racing Team	G	3.0 Arrows A2-Cosworth V8	gearbox	19/26
dns	"	"	29	Warsteiner Arrows Racing Team	G	3.0 Arrows A1-Cosworth V8	practice only	–/–
ret	GERMAN GP	Hockenheim	29	Warsteiner Arrows Racing Team	G	3.0 Arrows A2-Cosworth V8	puncture	19/26
ret	AUSTRIAN GP	Österreichring	29	Warsteiner Arrows Racing Team	G	3.0 Arrows A2-Cosworth V8	rear suspension	13/26
ret	DUTCH GP	Zandvoort	29	Warsteiner Arrows Racing Team	G	3.0 Arrows A2-Cosworth V8	brake failure-spun off	19/26
13	ITALIAN GP	Monza	29	Warsteiner Arrows Racing Team	G	3.0 Arrows A2-Cosworth V8	pit stop/3 laps behind	17/28
ret	CANADIAN GP	Montreal	29	Warsteiner Arrows Racing Team	G	3.0 Arrows A1-Cosworth V8	spun off-could not restart	14/29
dns	"	"	29	Warsteiner Arrows Racing Team	G	3.0 Arrows A1-Cosworth V8	practice only	–/–
ret	US GP EAST	Watkins Glen	29	Warsteiner Arrows Racing Team	G	3.0 Arrows A2-Cosworth V8	rear suspension	19/30

1980
Championship position: 9th Wins: 0 Pole positions: 0 Fastest laps: 1 Points scored: 7

	Race	Circuit	No	Entrant	Tyres	Car/Engine	Comment	Q Pos/Entries
ret	ARGENTINE GP	Buenos Aires	29	Warsteiner Arrows Racing Team	G	3.0 Arrows A3-Cosworth V8	engine	7/28
6	BRAZILIAN GP	Interlagos	29	Warsteiner Arrows Racing Team	G	3.0 Arrows A3-Cosworth V8	1 lap behind	14/28
ret	SOUTH AFRICAN GP	Kyalami	29	Warsteiner Arrows Racing Team	G	3.0 Arrows A3-Cosworth V8	locked brakes-accident	11/28
2	US GP WEST	Long Beach	29	Warsteiner Arrows Racing Team	G	3.0 Arrows A3-Cosworth V8		8/27
ret	BELGIUM GP	Zolder	29	Warsteiner Arrows Racing Team	G	3.0 Arrows A3-Cosworth V8	spun off	16/27
8	MONACO GP	Monte Carlo	29	Warsteiner Arrows Racing Team	G	3.0 Arrows A3-Cosworth V8	hit by Arnoux-pit stop/-3 laps/FL	11/27
9	FRENCH GP	Paul Ricard	29	Warsteiner Arrows Racing Team	G	3.0 Arrows A3-Cosworth V8	1 lap behind	18/27
9	BRITISH GP	Brands Hatch	29	Warsteiner Arrows Racing Team	G	3.0 Arrows A3-Cosworth V8	3 laps behind	21/27
9	GERMAN GP	Hockenheim	29	Warsteiner Arrows Racing Team	G	3.0 Arrows A3-Cosworth V8	1 lap behind	10/26
14	AUSTRIAN GP	Österreichring	29	Warsteiner Arrows Racing Team	G	3.0 Arrows A3-Cosworth V8	1 lap behind	18/25
ret	DUTCH GP	Zandvoort	29	Warsteiner Arrows Racing Team	G	3.0 Arrows A3-Cosworth V8	engine	14/28
ret	ITALIAN GP	Imola	29	Warsteiner Arrows Racing Team	G	3.0 Arrows A3-Cosworth V8	engine	7/28
ret	CANADIAN GP	Montreal	29	Warsteiner Arrows Racing Team	G	3.0 Arrows A3-Cosworth V8	collision with Prost	11/28
ret	US GP EAST	Watkins Glen	29	Warsteiner Arrows Racing Team	G	3.0 Arrows A3-Cosworth V8	spun off	20/27

1981
Championship position: 11th= Wins: 0 Pole positions: 0 Fastest laps: 0 Points scored: 10

	Race	Circuit	No	Entrant	Tyres	Car/Engine	Comment	Q Pos/Entries
ret	US GP WEST	Long Beach	29	Arrows Racing Team	M	3.0 Arrows A3-Cosworth V8	fuel filter/led race	1/29
3	BRAZILIAN GP	Rio	29	Arrows Racing Team	M	3.0 Arrows A3-Cosworth V8		4/30
7	ARGENTINE GP	Buenos Aires	29	Arrows Racing Team	M	3.0 Arrows A3-Cosworth V8	1 lap behind	9/29
2	SAN MARINO GP	Imola	29	Arrows Racing Team	M	3.0 Arrows A3-Cosworth V8		9/30
ret/dns	BELGIUM GP	Zolder	29	Arrows Racing Team	M	3.0 Arrows A3-Cosworth V8	hit by Stohr at start/did not restart	4/31
ret	MONACO GP	Monte Carlo	29	Arrows Racing Team	M	3.0 Arrows A3-Cosworth V8	gearbox	5/31
ret	SPANISH GP	Jarama	29	Arrows Racing Team	M	3.0 Arrows A3-Cosworth V8	engine	12/30
14	FRENCH GP	Dijon	29	Arrows Racing Team	M	3.0 Arrows A3-Cosworth V8	3 laps behind	18/29
10/ret	BRITISH GP	Silverstone	29	Arrows Racing Team	P	3.0 Arrows A3-Cosworth V8	engine/4 laps behind	10/30
ret	GERMAN GP	Hockenheim	29	Arrows Racing Team	P	3.0 Arrows A3-Cosworth V8	engine	13/30
ret	AUSTRIAN GP	Österreichring	29	Arrows Racing Team	P	3.0 Arrows A3-Cosworth V8	engine	10/28
ret	DUTCH GP	Zandvoort	29	Arrows Racing Team	P	3.0 Arrows A3-Cosworth V8	suspension	10/30
ret	ITALIAN GP	Monza	29	Arrows Racing Team	P	3.0 Arrows A3-Cosworth V8	gearbox	20/30
ret	CANADIAN GP	Montreal	29	Arrows Racing Team	P	3.0 Arrows A3-Cosworth V8	spun off	18/30
11	CAESARS PALACE GP	Las Vegas	29	Arrows Racing Team	P	3.0 Arrows A3-Cosworth V8	2 pit stops/4 laps behind	11/30

1982
Championship position: 10th Wins: 1 Pole positions: 0 Fastest laps: 2 Points scored: 21

	Race	Circuit	No	Entrant	Tyres	Car/Engine	Comment	Q Pos/Entries
ret	SOUTH AFRICAN GP	Kyalami	2	Parmalat Racing Team	G	1.5 t/c Brabham BT50-BMW 4	turbo bearing	4/30
ret	BRAZILIAN GP	Rio	2	Parmalat Racing Team	G	3.0 Brabham BT49D-Cosworth V8	driver fatigue	9/31

3*	US GP WEST	Long Beach	2	Parmalat Racing Team	G	3.0 Brabham BT49C-Cosworth V8	*3rd place car dsq	18/31
dns	" "	" "	2	Parmalat Racing Team	G	3.0 Brabham BT49D-Cosworth V8	practice only-accident damage	– / –
ret	BELGIUM GP	Zolder	2	Parmalat Racing Team	G	1.5 t/c Brabham BT50-BMW 4	spun off	11/32
1	MONACO GP	Monte Carlo	2	Parmalat Racing Team	G	3.0 Brabham BT49D-Cosworth V8	FL	2/31
ret	US GP (DETROIT)	Detroit	2	Parmalat Racing Team	G	3.0 Brabham BT49D-Cosworth V8	hit barrier	14/28
2	CANADIAN GP	Montreal	2	Parmalat Racing Team	G	3.0 Brabham BT49D-Cosworth V8		8/29
15	DUTCH GP	Zandvoort	2	Parmalat Racing Team	G	1.5 t/c Brabham BT50-BMW 4	pit stop-gear linkage/-3 laps	10/31
ret	BRITISH GP	Brands Hatch	2	Parmalat Racing Team	G	1.5 t/c Brabham BT50-BMW 4	stalled at start-hit by Arnoux	2/30
ret	FRENCH GP	Paul Ricard	2	Parmalat Racing Team	G	1.5 t/c Brabham BT50-BMW 4	engine/FL	4/30
ret	GERMAN GP	Hockenheim	2	Parmalat Racing Team	G	1.5 t/c Brabham BT50-BMW 4	engine	6/30
ret	AUSTRIAN GP	Österreichring	2	Parmalat Racing Team	G	1.5 t/c Brabham BT50-BMW 4	engine	2/29
5	SWISS GP	Dijon	2	Parmalat Racing Team	G	1.5 t/c Brabham BT50-BMW 4	1 lap behind	3/29
ret	ITALIAN GP	Monza	2	Parmalat Racing Team	G	1.5 t/c Brabham BT50-BMW 4	clutch	4/30
ret	CAESARS PALACE GP	Las Vegas	2	Parmalat Racing Team	G	1.5 t/c Brabham BT50-BMW 4	clutch	5/30

1983 Championship position: 9th= Wins: 1 Pole positions: 1 Fastest laps: 1 Points scored: 13

ret	BRAZILIAN GP	Rio	6	Fila Sport	M	1.5 t/c Brabham BT52-BMW 4	exhaust	7/27
10/ret	US GP WEST	Long Beach	6	Fila Sport	M	1.5 t/c Brabham BT52-BMW 4	distributor/3 laps behind	11/28
ret	FRENCH GP	Paul Ricard	6	Fila Sport	M	1.5 t/c Brabham BT52-BMW 4	overheating	3/29
ret	SAN MARINO GP	Imola	6	Fila Sport	M	1.5 t/c Brabham BT52-BMW 4	spun off when first/FL	5/28
ret	MONACO GP	Monte Carlo	6	Fila Sport	M	1.5 t/c Brabham BT52-BMW 4	electrics	17/28
ret	BELGIUM GP	Spa	6	Fila Sport	M	1.5 t/c Brabham BT52-BMW 4	engine	6/28
ret	US GP (DETROIT)	Detroit	6	Fila Sport	M	1.5 t/c Brabham BT52-BMW 4	brakes	15/27
ret	CANADIAN GP	Montreal	6	Fila Sport	M	1.5 t/c Brabham BT52-BMW 4	gearbox	5/28
ret	BRITISH GP	Silverstone	6	Fila Sport	M	1.5 t/c Brabham BT52B-BMW 4	turbo	5/29
3	GERMAN GP	Hockenheim	6	Fila Sport	M	1.5 t/c Brabham BT52B-BMW 4		8/29
ret	AUSTRIAN GP	Österreichring	6	Fila Sport	M	1.5 t/c Brabham BT52B-BMW 4	overheating	6/29
9	DUTCH GP	Zandvoort	6	Fila Sport	M	1.5 t/c Brabham BT52B-BMW 4	pit stop-fuel/2 laps behind	6/29
ret	ITALIAN GP	Monza	6	Fila Sport	M	1.5 t/c Brabham BT52B-BMW 4	electrics/engine	1/29
7	EUROPEAN GP	Brands Hatch	6	Fila Sport	M	1.5 t/c Brabham BT52B-BMW 4		2/29
1	SOUTH AFRICAN GP	Kyalami	6	Fila Sport	M	1.5 t/c Brabham BT52B-BMW 4		3/26

1984 Championship position: 13th Wins: 0 Pole positions: 0 Fastest laps: 0 Points scored: 8

ret	BRAZILIAN GP	Rio	22	Benetton Team Alfa Romeo	G	1.5 t/c Alfa Romeo 184T V8	gearbox	11/27
4	SOUTH AFRICAN GP	Kyalami	22	Benetton Team Alfa Romeo	G	1.5 t/c Alfa Romeo 184T V8	2 laps behind	18/27
ret	BELGIUM GP	Zolder	22	Benetton Team Alfa Romeo	G	1.5 t/c Alfa Romeo 184T V8	ignition	7/27
ret	SAN MARINO GP	Imola	22	Benetton Team Alfa Romeo	G	1.5 t/c Alfa Romeo 184T V8	electrics	10/28
ret	FRENCH GP	Dijon	22	Benetton Team Alfa Romeo	G	1.5 t/c Alfa Romeo 184T V8	engine	16/27
ret	MONACO GP	Monte Carlo	22	Benetton Team Alfa Romeo	G	1.5 t/c Alfa Romeo 184T V8	steering	14/27
ret	CANADIAN GP	Montreal	22	Benetton Team Alfa Romeo	G	1.5 t/c Alfa Romeo 184T V8	crashed	14/26
ret	US GP (DETROIT)	Detroit	22	Benetton Team Alfa Romeo	G	1.5 t/c Alfa Romeo 184T V8	spun off-suspension damage	25/27
ret	US GP (DALLAS)	Dallas	22	Benetton Team Alfa Romeo	G	1.5 t/c Alfa Romeo 184T V8	hit wall	21/27
12*/ret	BRITISH GP	Brands Hatch	22	Benetton Team Alfa Romeo	G	1.5 t/c Alfa Romeo 184T V8	out of fuel/*11th car dsq/-5 laps	17/27
ret	GERMAN GP	Hockenheim	22	Benetton Team Alfa Romeo	G	1.5 t/c Alfa Romeo 184T V8	fuel metering unit	20/27
10/ret	AUSTRIAN GP	Österreichring	22	Benetton Team Alfa Romeo	G	1.5 t/c Alfa Romeo 184T V8	out of fuel/3 laps behind	13/28
ret	DUTCH GP	Zandvoort	22	Benetton Team Alfa Romeo	G	1.5 t/c Alfa Romeo 184T V8	engine	18/27
3	ITALIAN GP	Monza	22	Benetton Team Alfa Romeo	G	1.5 t/c Alfa Romeo 184T V8	1 lap behind	9/27
6	EUROPEAN GP	Nürburgring	22	Benetton Team Alfa Romeo	G	1.5 t/c Alfa Romeo 184T V8	1 lap behind	9/26
8	PORTUGUESE GP	Estoril	22	Benetton Team Alfa Romeo	G	1.5 t/c Alfa Romeo 184T V8	1 lap behind	12/27

1985 Championship position: Unplaced

ret	BRAZILIAN GP	Rio	22	Benetton Team Alfa Romeo	G	1.5 t/c Alfa Romeo 185T V8	puncture	14/25
ret	PORTUGUESE GP	Estoril	22	Benetton Team Alfa Romeo	G	1.5 t/c Alfa Romeo 185T V8	spun off	13/26
ret	SAN MARINO GP	Imola	22	Benetton Team Alfa Romeo	G	1.5 t/c Alfa Romeo 185T V8	engine	18/26
ret	MONACO GP	Monte Carlo	22	Benetton Team Alfa Romeo	G	1.5 t/c Alfa Romeo 185T V8	accident with Piquet	12/26
10	CANADIAN GP	Montreal	22	Benetton Team Alfa Romeo	G	1.5 t/c Alfa Romeo 185T V8	2 laps behind	13/25
ret	US GP (DETROIT)	Detroit	22	Benetton Team Alfa Romeo	G	1.5 t/c Alfa Romeo 185T V8	electrics	14/25
11	FRENCH GP	Paul Ricard	22	Benetton Team Alfa Romeo	G	1.5 t/c Alfa Romeo 185T V8	1 lap behind	17/26
9	BRITISH GP	Silverstone	22	Benetton Team Alfa Romeo	G	1.5 t/c Alfa Romeo 185T V8	3 laps behind	14/26
ret	GERMAN GP	Nürburgring	22	Benetton Team Alfa Romeo	G	1.5 t/c Alfa Romeo 184T V8	gearbox	9/27
ret	AUSTRIAN GP	Österreichring	22	Benetton Team Alfa Romeo	G	1.5 t/c Alfa Romeo 184T V8	engine	10/27
ret	DUTCH GP	Zandvoort	22	Benetton Team Alfa Romeo	G	1.5 t/c Alfa Romeo 184T V8	turbo	19/27
ret	ITALIAN GP	Monza	22	Benetton Team Alfa Romeo	G	1.5 t/c Alfa Romeo 184T V8	exhaust	13/26
ret	BELGIUM GP	Spa	22	Benetton Team Alfa Romeo	G	1.5 t/c Alfa Romeo 184T V8	engine	15/24
9	EUROPEAN GP	Brands Hatch	22	Benetton Team Alfa Romeo	G	1.5 t/c Alfa Romeo 184T V8	2 laps behind	11/27
ret	SOUTH AFRICAN GP	Kyalami	22	Benetton Team Alfa Romeo	G	1.5 t/c Alfa Romeo 184T V8	hit by Cheever-lap 1	12/21
ret	AUSTRALIAN GP	Adelaide	22	Benetton Team Alfa Romeo	G	1.5 t/c Alfa Romeo 184T V8	exhaust	14/25

1986 Championship position: 15th= Wins: 0 Pole positions: 0 Fastest laps: 0 Points scored: 2

ret	BRAZILIAN GP	Rio	7	Motor Racing Developments Ltd	P	1.5 t/c Brabham BT55-BMW 4	split water pipe	10/25
ret	SPANISH GP	Jerez	7	Motor Racing Developments Ltd	P	1.5 t/c Brabham BT55-BMW 4	gearbox	14/25
6/ret	SAN MARINO GP	Imola	7	Motor Racing Developments Ltd	P	1.5 t/c Brabham BT55-BMW 4	out of fuel/2 laps behind	16/26
ret	MONACO GP	Monte Carlo	7	Motor Racing Developments Ltd	P	1.5 t/c Brabham BT55-BMW 4	fuel pump	6/26
8	BELGIUM GP	Spa	7	Motor Racing Developments Ltd	P	1.5 t/c Brabham BT55-BMW 4	started from pit lane/-1 lap	15/25
ret	CANADIAN GP	Montreal	7	Motor Racing Developments Ltd	P	1.5 t/c Brabham BT55-BMW 4	turbo	9/25
6	US GP (DETROIT)	Detroit	7	Motor Racing Developments Ltd	P	1.5 t/c Brabham BT55-BMW 4	1 lap behind	8/26
7	FRENCH GP	Paul Ricard	7	Motor Racing Developments Ltd	P	1.5 t/c Brabham BT55-BMW 4	2 laps behind	16/26
ret	BRITISH GP	Brands Hatch	7	Motor Racing Developments Ltd	P	1.5 t/c Brabham BT54-BMW 4	engine	15/26
ret	GERMAN GP	Hockenheim	7	Motor Racing Developments Ltd	P	1.5 t/c Brabham BT55-BMW 4	turbo	7/26
ret	HUNGARIAN GP	Hungaroring	7	Motor Racing Developments Ltd	P	1.5 t/c Brabham BT55-BMW 4	spun off	14/26
ret	AUSTRIAN GP	Österreichring	7	Motor Racing Developments Ltd	P	1.5 t/c Brabham BT55-BMW 4	engine	4/26
ret	ITALIAN GP	Monza	7	Motor Racing Developments Ltd	P	1.5 t/c Brabham BT55-BMW 4	accident with Tambay	10/27
ret	PORTUGUESE GP	Estoril	7	Motor Racing Developments Ltd	P	1.5 t/c Brabham BT55-BMW 4	engine	9/27
13/ret	MEXICAN GP	Mexico City	7	Motor Racing Developments Ltd	P	1.5 t/c Brabham BT55-BMW 4	spun off/4 laps behind	5/26
ret	AUSTRALIAN GP	Adelaide	7	Motor Racing Developments Ltd	P	1.5 t/c Brabham BT55-BMW 4	engine-electrics	19/26

	1987	Championship position: 13th		Wins: 0	Pole positions: 0		Fastest laps: 0	Points scored: 6	
ret	BRAZILIAN GP	Rio	7	Motor Racing Developments Ltd	G	1.5 t/c Brabham BT56-BMW 4	loose battery		11/23
9	SAN MARINO GP	Imola	7	Motor Racing Developments Ltd	G	1.5 t/c Brabham BT56-BMW 4	2 laps behind		8/27
ret	BELGIUM GP	Spa	7	Motor Racing Developments Ltd	G	1.5 t/c Brabham BT56-BMW 4	clutch		8/26
ret	MONACO GP	Monte Carlo	7	Motor Racing Developments Ltd	G	1.5 t/c Brabham BT56-BMW 4	electrics		10/26
9	US GP (DETROIT)	Detroit	7	Motor Racing Developments Ltd	G	1.5 t/c Brabham BT56-BMW 4	spun-hit Palmer/-3 laps		9/26
ret	FRENCH GP	Paul Ricard	7	Motor Racing Developments Ltd	G	1.5 t/c Brabham BT56-BMW 4	transmission		12/26
ret	BRITISH GP	Silverstone	7	Motor Racing Developments Ltd	G	1.5 t/c Brabham BT56-BMW 4	fuel metering unit		11/26
ret	GERMAN GP	Hockenheim	7	Motor Racing Developments Ltd	G	1.5 t/c Brabham BT56-BMW 4	turbo		11/26
5	HUNGARIAN GP	Hungaroring	7	Motor Racing Developments Ltd	G	1.5 t/c Brabham BT56-BMW 4	1 lap behind		10/26
ret	AUSTRIAN GP	Österreichring	7	Motor Racing Developments Ltd	G	1.5 t/c Brabham BT56-BMW 4	engine		8/26
ret	ITALIAN GP	Monza	7	Motor Racing Developments Ltd	G	1.5 t/c Brabham BT56-BMW 4	engine		9/28
ret	PORTUGUESE GP	Estoril	7	Motor Racing Developments Ltd	G	1.5 t/c Brabham BT56-BMW 4	engine		7/27
13	SPANISH GP	Jerez	7	Motor Racing Developments Ltd	G	1.5 t/c Brabham BT56-BMW 4	4 laps behind		9/28
3	MEXICAN GP	Mexico City	7	Motor Racing Developments Ltd	G	1.5 t/c Brabham BT56-BMW 4			8/27
11/ret	JAPANESE GP	Suzuka	7	Motor Racing Developments Ltd	G	1.5 t/c Brabham BT56-BMW 4	engine/2 laps behind		9/27
9/ret	AUSTRALIAN GP	Adelaide	5	Canon Williams Team	G	1.5 t/c Williams FW11B-Honda V6	engine/6 laps behind		7/27

	1988	Championship position: 11th		Wins: 0	Pole positions: 0		Fastest laps: 0	Points scored: 8	
ret	BRAZILIAN GP	Rio	6	Canon Williams Team	G	3.5 Williams FW12-Judd V8	overheating		8/31
13	SAN MARINO GP	Imola	6	Canon Williams Team	G	3.5 Williams FW12-Judd V8	precautionary stop-handling/-2 laps		6/31
6	MONACO GP	Monte Carlo	6	Canon Williams Team	G	3.5 Williams FW12-Judd V8	1 lap behind		8/30
ret	MEXICAN GP	Mexico City	6	Canon Williams Team	G	3.5 Williams FW12-Judd V8	engine		17/30
ret	CANADIAN GP	Montreal	6	Canon Williams Team	G	3.5 Williams FW12-Judd V8	engine		11/31
ret	US GP (DETROIT)	Detroit	6	Canon Williams Team	G	3.5 Williams FW12-Judd V8	electrics		10/31
ret	FRENCH GP	Paul Ricard	6	Canon Williams Team	G	3.5 Williams FW12-Judd V8	brakes		15/31
8	BRITISH GP	Silverstone	6	Canon Williams Team	G	3.5 Williams FW12-Judd V8	1 lap behind		15/31
ret	GERMAN GP	Hockenheim	6	Canon Williams Team	G	3.5 Williams FW12-Judd V8	slid off		13/31
6	HUNGARIAN GP	Hungaroring	6	Canon Williams Team	G	3.5 Williams FW12-Judd V8	1 lap behind		6/31
ret	BELGIUM GP	Spa	6	Canon Williams Team	G	3.5 Williams FW12-Judd V8	engine		5/31
7	ITALIAN GP	Monza	6	Canon Williams Team	G	3.5 Williams FW12-Judd V8			10/31
ret	PORTUGUESE GP	Estoril	6	Canon Williams Team	G	3.5 Williams FW12-Judd V8	radiator		11/31
5	SPANISH GP	Jerez	6	Canon Williams Team	G	3.5 Williams FW12-Judd V8	fined $10,000-practice incident		7/31
6	JAPANESE GP	Suzuka	6	Canon Williams Team	G	3.5 Williams FW12-Judd V8			11/31
4	AUSTRALIAN GP	Adelaide	6	Canon Williams Team	G	3.5 Williams FW12-Judd V8			6/31

	1989	Championship position: 3rd		Wins: 0	Pole positions: 1		Fastest laps: 1	Points scored: 40	
ret	BRAZILIAN GP	Rio	6	Canon Williams Team	G	3.5 Williams FW12C-Renault V10	engine/led race/FL		2/38
ret	SAN MARINO GP	Imola	6	Canon Williams Team	G	3.5 Williams FW12C-Renault V10	engine		4/39
15	MONACO GP	Monte Carlo	6	Canon Williams Team	G	3.5 Williams FW12C-Renault V10	pit stop-wing end/-4 laps		7/38
2	MEXICAN GP	Mexico City	6	Canon Williams Team	G	3.5 Williams FW12C-Renault V10			5/39
2	US GP (PHOENIX)	Phoenix	6	Canon Williams Team	G	3.5 Williams FW12C-Renault V10			14/39
2	CANADIAN GP	Montreal	6	Canon Williams Team	G	3.5 Williams FW12C-Renault V10	pit stop-tyres/led race		3/39
3	FRENCH GP	Paul Ricard	6	Canon Williams Team	G	3.5 Williams FW12C-Renault V10	spin		8/39
ret	BRITISH GP	Silverstone	6	Canon Williams Team	G	3.5 Williams FW12C-Renault V10	stone burst radiator-crashed		5/39
4	GERMAN GP	Hockenheim	6	Canon Williams Team	G	3.5 Williams FW12C-Renault V10	p stop-tyres/vibration/gearbox/-1 lap		5/39
ret	HUNGARIAN GP	Hungaroring	6	Canon Williams Team	G	3.5 Williams FW12C-Renault V10	engine/led race		1/39
ret	BELGIAN GP	Spa	6	Canon Williams Team	G	3.5 Williams FW12C-Renault V10	collision with Alboreto		5/39
4	ITALIAN GP	Monza	6	Canon Williams Team	G	3.5 Williams FW12C-Renault V10	handling problems		5/39
ret	PORTUGUESE GP	Estoril	6	Canon Williams Team	G	3.5 Williams FW13-Renault V10	overheating		6/39
dns	"	"	6	Canon Williams Team	G	3.5 Williams FW12C-Renault V10	practice only		–/–
5	SPANISH GP	Jerez	6	Canon Williams Team	G	3.5 Williams FW12C-Renault V10			6/38
dns	"	"	6	Canon Williams Team	G	3.5 Williams FW13-Renault V10	practice only		–/–
2*	JAPANESE GP	Suzuka	6	Canon Williams Team	G	3.5 Williams FW13-Renault V10	* 1st place car dsq		5/39
3	AUSTRALIAN GP	Adelaide	6	Canon Williams Team	G	3.5 Williams FW13-Renault V10			6/39

	1990	Championship position: 7th		Wins: 1	Pole positions: 0		Fastest laps: 4	Points scored: 23	
9	US GP (PHOENIX)	Phoenix	6	Canon Williams Renault	G	3.5 Williams FW13B-Renault V10	hit Grouillard-pit stop/-1 lap		12/35
13/ret	BRAZILIAN GP	Interlagos	6	Canon Williams Renault	G	3.5 Williams FW13B-Renault V10	oil cooler/6 laps behind		4/35
1	SAN MARINO GP	Imola	6	Canon Williams Renault	G	3.5 Williams FW13B-Renault V10			3/34
ret	MONACO GP	Monte Carlo	6	Canon Williams Renault	G	3.5 Williams FW13B-Renault V10	electrics-engine		4/35
ret	CANADIAN GP	Montreal	6	Canon Williams Renault	G	3.5 Williams FW13B-Renault V10	brakes		9/35
9	MEXICAN GP	Mexico City	6	Canon Williams Renault	G	3.5 Williams FW13B-Renault V10	spin-pit stop-tyres		2/35
6	FRENCH GP	Paul Ricard	6	Canon Williams Renault	G	3.5 Williams FW13B-Renault V10	pit stop-tyres/misfire		6/35
ret	BRITISH GP	Silverstone	6	Canon Williams Renault	G	3.5 Williams FW13B-Renault V10	collision damage-undertray		7/35
5	GERMAN GP	Hockenheim	6	Canon Williams Renault	G	3.5 Williams FW13B-Renault V10	pit stop-tyres		5/35
4	HUNGARIAN GP	Hungaroring	6	Canon Williams Renault	G	3.5 Williams FW13B-Renault V10	pit stop-tyres/FL		2/35
ret	BELGIAN GP	Spa	6	Canon Williams Renault	G	3.5 Williams FW13B-Renault V10	gearbox		7/33
5	ITALIAN GP	Monza	6	Canon Williams Renault	G	3.5 Williams FW13B-Renault V10	pit stop-tyres		5/33
7	PORTUGUESE GP	Estoril	6	Canon Williams Renault	G	3.5 Williams FW13B-Renault V10	long pit stop-tyres/FL/-1 lap		5/33
5	SPANISH GP	Jerez	6	Canon Williams Renault	G	3.5 Williams FW13B-Renault V10	2 pit stops-tyres/FL		6/33
4	JAPANESE GP	Suzuka	6	Canon Williams Renault	G	3.5 Williams FW13B-Renault V10	pit stop-tyres/FL		8/30
6	AUSTRALIAN GP	Adelaide	6	Canon Williams Renault	G	3.5 Williams FW13B-Renault V10	spin-pit stop-tyres/-1 lap		6/30

	1991	Championship position: 3rd		Wins: 2	Pole positions: 4		Fastest laps: 3	Points scored: 53	
ret	US GP (PHOENIX)	Phoenix	6	Canon Williams Team	G	3.5 Williams FW14-Renault V10	gearbox/spun		3/34
2	BRAZILIAN GP	Interlagos	6	Canon Williams Team	G	3.5 Williams FW14-Renault V10			2/34
ret	SAN MARINO GP	Imola	6	Canon Williams Team	G	3.5 Williams FW14-Renault V10	elctrics/engine		2/34
ret	MONACO GP	Monte Carlo	6	Canon Williams Team	G	3.5 Williams FW14-Renault V10	hit Modena's oil-crashed		3/34
3	CANADIAN GP	Montreal	6	Canon Williams Team	G	3.5 Williams FW14-Renault V10			1/34
1	MEXICAN GP	Mexico City	6	Canon Williams Team	G	3.5 Williams FW14-Renault V10			1/34
5	FRENCH GP	Magny Cours	6	Canon Williams Team	G	3.5 Williams FW14-Renault V10	1 lap behind		1/34
ret	BRITISH GP	Silverstone	6	Canon Williams Team	G	3.5 Williams FW14-Renault V10	collision with Berger-lap 1		3/34
2	GERMAN GP	Hockenheim	6	Canon Williams Team	G	3.5 Williams FW14-Renault V10	FL		4/34
3	HUNGARIAN GP	Hungaroring	6	Canon Williams Team	G	3.5 Williams FW14-Renault V10			2/34

	Race	Circuit	No	Entrant	Tyres	Car/Engine	Comment	Q Pos/Entries
5	BELGIAN GP	Spa	6	Canon Williams Team	G	3.5 Williams FW14-Renault V10		17/34
ret	ITALIAN GP	Monza	6	Canon Williams Team	G	3.5 Williams FW14-Renault V10	clutch	4/34
1	PORTUGUESE GP	Estoril	6	Canon Williams Team	G	3.5 Williams FW14-Renault V10		1/34
3	SPANISH GP	Barcelona	6	Canon Williams Team	G	3.5 Williams FW14-Renault V10	FL	4/33
3	JAPANESE GP	Suzuka	6	Canon Williams Team	G	3.5 Williams FW14-Renault V10		5/31
5	AUSTRALIAN GP	Adelaide	6	Canon Williams Team	G	3.5 Williams FW14-Renault V10	rain shortened race-14 laps	4/32
1992		Championship position: 2nd	Wins: 1	Pole positions: 0		Fastest laps: 2 Points scored: 56		
2	SOUTH AFRICAN GP	Kyalami	6	Canon Williams Team	G	3.5 Williams FW14B-Renault V10		4/30
2	MEXICAN GP	Mexico City	6	Canon Williams Team	G	3.5 Williams FW14B-Renault V10		2/30
2	BRAZILIAN GP	Interlagos	6	Canon Williams Team	G	3.5 Williams FW14B-Renault V10	FL	2/31
ret	SPANISH GP	Barcelona	6	Canon Williams Team	G	3.5 Williams FW14B-Renault V10	spun off	4/32
2	SAN MARINO GP	Imola	6	Canon Williams Team	G	3.5 Williams FW14B-Renault V10	FL	2/32
3	MONACO GP	Monte Carlo	6	Canon Williams Team	G	3.5 Williams FW14B-Renault V10		2/32
ret	CANADIAN GP	Montreal	6	Canon Williams Team	G	3.5 Williams FW14B-Renault V10	gearbox	2/32
2*	FRENCH GP	Magny Cours	6	Canon Williams Team	G	3.5 Williams FW14B-Renault V10	*aggregate of two parts	2/30
2	BRITISH GP	Silverstone	6	Canon Williams Team	G	3.5 Williams FW14B-Renault V10		2/32
8/ret	GERMAN GP	Hockenheim	6	Canon Williams Team	G	3.5 Williams FW14B-Renault V10	spun off-stalled/FL/-1 lap	2/32
ret	HUNGARIAN GP	Hungaroring	6	Canon Williams Team	G	3.5 Williams FW14B-Renault V10	engine	1/31
3	BELGIAN GP	Spa	6	Canon Williams Team	G	3.5 Williams FW14B-Renault V10		4/30
5	ITALIAN GP	Monza	6	Canon Williams Team	G	3.5 Williams FW14B-Renault V10	led until car stuck in 4th gear	4/28
ret	PORTUGUESE GP	Estoril	6	Canon Williams Team	G	3.5 Williams FW14B-Renault V10	crashed after hitting Berger	2/26
1	JAPANESE GP	Suzuka	6	Canon Williams Team	G	3.5 Williams FW14B-Renault V10		2/24
ret	AUSTRALIAN GP	Adelaide	6	Canon Williams Team	G	3.5 Williams FW14B-Renault V10	fuel pressure	3/26
1993		Championship position: 5th	Wins: 0	Pole positions: 0		Fastest laps: 0 Points scored: 20		
ret	SOUTH AFRICAN GP	Kyalami	6	Camel Benetton Ford	G	3.5 Benetton B192B-Ford HB V8	spun off	7/26
ret	BRAZILIAN GP	Interlagos	6	Camel Benetton Ford	G	3.5 Benetton B192B-Ford HB V8	active suspension	6/26
5	EUROPEAN GP	Donington	6	Camel Benetton Ford	G	3.5 Benetton B193-Ford HB V8	2 laps behind	10/26
ret	SAN MARINO GP	Imola	6	Camel Benetton Ford	G	3.5 Benetton B193B-Ford HB V8	spun off and stalled on lap 1	11/26
4	SPANISH GP	Barcelona	6	Camel Benetton Ford	G	3.5 Benetton B193B-Ford HB V8	1 lap behind	5/26
ret	MONACO GP	Monte Carlo	6	Camel Benetton Ford	G	3.5 Benetton B193B-Ford HB V8	engine	6/26
ret	CANADIAN GP	Montreal	6	Camel Benetton Ford	G	3.5 Benetton B193B-Ford HB V8	driver cramp	4/26
10	FRENCH GP	Magny Cours	6	Camel Benetton Ford	G	3.5 Benetton B193-Ford HB V8	pit stop-collision Fittipaldi/-2 laps	12/26
3	BRITISH GP	Silverstone	6	Camel Benetton Ford	G	3.5 Benetton B193-Ford HB V8		5/26
5	GERMAN GP	Hockenheim	6	Camel Benetton Ford	G	3.5 Benetton B193-Ford HB V8		7/26
2	HUNGARIAN GP	Hungaroring	6	Camel Benetton Ford	G	3.5 Benetton B193-Ford HB V8		5/26
6	BELGIAN GP	Spa	6	Camel Benetton Ford	G	3.5 Benetton B193-Ford HB V8	1 lap behind	8/25
5	ITALIAN GP	Monza	6	Camel Benetton Ford	G	3.5 Benetton B193-Ford HB V8	active suspension/-1 lap	10/26
16/ret	PORTUGUESE GP	Estoril	6	Camel Benetton Ford	G	3.5 Benetton B193-Ford HB V8	hit Warwick-spun off/-8 laps	7/26
ret	JAPANESE GP	Suzuka	6	Camel Benetton Ford	G	3.5 Benetton B193-Ford HB V8	oil on tyres-crashed	10/27
8/ret	AUSTRALIAN GP	Adelaide	6	Camel Benetton Ford	G	3.5 Benetton B193-Ford HB V8	engine/2 laps behind	9/24

GP Starts: 255 (256)   GP Wins: 6   Pole positions: 8   Fastest laps: 13   Points: 281

AL PEASE

An amateur racer who had been on the Canadian racing scene from the early fifties with a Riley, Pease returned to the circuits in the early sixties with a Lotus 23 sports car, taking eighth place in the 1963 Canadian GP.

He had the backing to enable him to enter the original Eagle – hopelessly, as it turned out – in three successive Canadian GPs (1967-69).

A sometime racer in Formula A, Pease handled a Lola T140-Chevrolet and a Brabham BT23B-Climax 4 with modest success during 1969 and 1970.

PEASE, Al (CDN) b 15/10/1921

	Race	Circuit	No	Entrant	Tyres	Car/Engine	Comment	Q Pos/Entries
	1967	Championship position: Unplaced						
nc	CANADIAN GP	Mosport Park	11	Castrol Oils Ltd	G	2.7 Eagle TG101-Climax 4	43 laps behind	16/19
	1968	Championship position: Unplaced						
dns	CANADIAN GP	St Jovite	25	Castrol Oils Ltd	G	2.7 Eagle TG101-Climax 4	engine failure in practice	(17)/20
	1969	Championship position: Unplaced						
ret	CANADIAN GP	Mosport Park	69	John Maryon	F	2.7 Eagle TG101-Climax 4	black flagged-too slow	17/20

GP Starts: 2   GP Wins: 0   Pole positions: 0   Fastest laps: 0   Points: 0

ROGER PENSKE

Roger Penske the racing driver has long since disappeared into the mists of time, to be replaced by the imposing figure who has built a business empire and progressively developed a small racing team, with Mark Donohue as driver, into the premier power in US single-seater racing, producing their own chassis for the Indy Car series.

However, Penske was a very good driver indeed. Racing a Porsche RSK, he won the SCCA 'F' category championship in 1960 before acquiring a Cooper-Monaco, which he modified and was later to rename the Zerex Special. Between 1961 and 1963 he gained many successes with this car and performed equally well in others, such as John Mecom's Ferrari GTO.

His drives in the US GPs of 1961 and 1962 offered him little but the chance to rub shoulders with the stars of the day, though he did bring his cars home to the finish. In 1964 he raced in future rival Jim Hall's Chaparral team, winning races at Monterey and Nassau and taking second place in the Riverside GP. At the end of the season Penske retired from driving to start his automobile business and the rest, as they say, is history.

CESARE PERDISA

From a wealthy publishing background, Perdisa first made his mark on the racing scene in 1954 with some excellent drives in his Maserati T200S sports car, finishing fourth at the Imola GP, fifth in the Portuguese GP and third at Syracuse. Proving this was no flash in the pan, the 1955 season saw wins at the Imola Shell GP and the Bari GP and second place at the Monza Supercortemaggiore in works machines, and his first Grand Prix, at Monaco, where Behra took over his car to share a third-place finish.

After missing the early-season Argentine races due to appendicitis, Perdisa was back in harness by Monaco, but again his points finishes were due in part to the efforts of another driver, this time Moss. Cesare was injured in a practice crash at the German Grand Prix and did not race for the Maserati team again. Lining up for rivals Ferrari in Argentina at the start of 1957, he took a shared sixth place in the Grand Prix, seventh in the Buenos Aires City GP, and won the 1000-km sports car race with co-drivers Gregory, Castellotti and Musso. However, on returning to Europe, perhaps due to pressure from his family, Cesare suddenly announced his retirement from racing.

PENSKE, Roger (USA) b 20/2/1937, Shaker Heights, Ohio

	1961	Championship position: Unplaced						
	Race	Circuit	No	Entrant	Tyres	Car/Engine	Comment	Q Pos/Entries
8	US GP	Watkins Glen	6	John M Wyatt III	D	1.5 Cooper T53-Climax 4	4 laps behind	16/19
	1962	Championship position: Unplaced						
9	US GP	Watkins Glen	14	Dupont Team Zerex	D	1.5 Lotus 24-Climax V8	4 laps behind	13/20

GP Starts: 2   GP Wins: 0   Pole positions: 0   Fastest laps: 0   Points: 0

PERDISA, Cesare (I) b 21/10/1932, Bologna – d 5/1998

	1955	Championship position: 12th=		Wins: 0	Pole positions: 0		Fastest laps: 0	Points scored: 2	
	Race	Circuit	No	Entrant	Tyres	Car/Engine		Comment	Q Pos/Entries
ret*	MONACO GP	Monte Carlo	40	Officine Alfieri Maserati	P	2.5 Maserati 250F 6		* Behra took over and spun off	11/22
3*	"	" "	34	Officine Alfieri Maserati	P	2.5 Maserati 250F 6		* took over Behra's car/-1 lap	–/–
8	BELGIAN GP	Spa	26	Officine Alfieri Maserati	P	2.5 Maserati 250F 6		3 laps behind	13/14
	1956	Championship position: 12th=		Wins: 0	Pole positions: 0		Fastest laps: 0	Points scored: 3	
7	MONACO GP	Monte Carlo	32	Officine Alfieri Maserati	P	2.5 Maserati 250F 6		pit stops/14 laps behind	7/19
3*	BELGIAN GP	Spa	34	Officine Alfieri Maserati	P	2.5 Maserati 250F 6		* Moss took over	9/16
5*	FRENCH GP	Reims	6	Officine Alfieri Maserati	P	2.5 Maserati 250F 6		* Moss took over/-2 laps	13/20
7	BRITISH GP	Silverstone	9	Officine Alfieri Maserati	P	2.5 Maserati 250F 6		6 laps behind	15/28
dns	GERMAN GP	Nürburgring	8	Officine Alfieri Maserati	P	2.5 Maserati 250F 6		injured-Maglioli drove car	(6)/21
	1957	Championship position: Unplaced							
6*	ARGENTINE GP	Buenos Aires	18	Scuderia Ferrari	E	2.5 Lancia-Ferrari D50 V8		*Collins/von Trips co-drove/-2 laps	11/16

GP Starts: 7   GP Wins: 0   Pole positions: 0   Fastest laps: 0   Points: 5

LARRY PERKINS

Affectionately known as the 'Cowangie Kid' because he was from the tiny village of that name in Victoria, Larry came to Britain on the heels of Tim Schenken, with just as big a reputation, having left a winning trail through Formula Vee, Formula Ford and Australian F2 in three successive seasons between 1970 and 1972.

Once in Europe, Perkins finished fifth in the 1972 Formula Ford Festival before taking a shot at Formula 3 in 1973, his season improving after he switched to a Brabham. In 1974 Larry was involved in the ill-fated Amon F1 project and an unhappy attempt to qualify at the Nürburgring, before re-establishing his career back in F3 in 1975 with the works Ralt, winning the European championship.

Perkins landed a deal to drive the Boro (née Ensign) for the first part of 1976, and then came his big chance with Brabham, replacing the Ferrari-bound Reutemann for the final three races. To be frank, he blew it and found himself signing a contract to race the truly awful Stanley-BRM in 1977. After two races he gratefully jumped from the sinking ship, subsequently appearing briefly and unsuccessfully with Surtees.

Returning to Australia, Larry – now something of a big fish in a small pond – regained some pride winning the 1979 Australian F5000 series, before concentrating on a long, hugely successful and rewarding career in touring car racing.

Larry has won the famous Bathurst race six times to date and his Holden Commodore team has consistently been a major force in the Australian national series.

XAVIER PERROT

Perrot was a Swiss garage owner who had been competing since the early sixties in strictly national racing and hill-climbs with machines such as an Abarth-Simca and then a Lotus 23.

In 1968 he purchased an ex-Winkelmann Racing Brabham to race in Formula 2, but found himself out of his depth. Not easily discouraged, Perrot was back for more in 1969, and by mid-season was looking more of a serious proposition, taking sixth in the F2 class in the German GP, and fourth in the Rhine Cup at Hockenheim. In 1970 he equipped himself with the latest March 702 and gained a somewhat lucky win in the Preis von Deutschland at the Nürburgring, which was the best result of the underrated Swiss driver's career. Perrot continued in Formula 2 in 1971 and into early 1972, gaining some useful results, and actually drove Siffert's March 701 in the Jochen Rindt Memorial Trophy F1 race at Hockenheim to finish 11th. Finding his F2 car ideally suited to hill-climbs, he successfully pursued this form of the sport thereafter.

PERKINS, Larry (AUS) b 18/3/1950, Murrayville, Victoria

	1974	Championship position: Unplaced						
	Race	Circuit	No	Entrant	Tyres	Car/Engine	Comment	Q Pos/Entries
dnq	GERMAN GP	Nürburgring	30	Dalton-Amon International	F	3.0 Amon AF101-Cosworth V8	practice crash-hit barrier	30/32
	1976	Championship position: Unplaced						
13	SPANISH GP	Jarama	37	HB Bewaking Alarm Systems	G	3.0 Boro Ensign N175-Cosworth V8	pit stop/3 laps behind	24/30
8	BELGIAN GP	Zolder	37	HB Bewaking Alarm Systems	G	3.0 Boro Ensign N175-Cosworth V8	1 lap behind	20/29
dnq	MONACO GP	Monte Carlo	37	HB Bewaking Alarm Systems	G	3.0 Boro Ensign N175-Cosworth V8		23/25
ret	SWEDISH GP	Anderstorp	37	HB Bewaking Alarm Systems	G	3.0 Boro Ensign N175-Cosworth V8	engine	22/27
ret	DUTCH GP	Zandvoort	37	HB Bewaking Alarm Systems	G	3.0 Boro Ensign N175-Cosworth V8	spun off	19/27
ret	ITALIAN GP	Monza	40	HB Bewaking Alarm Systems	G	3.0 Boro Ensign N175-Cosworth V8	engine	13/29
17	CANADIAN GP	Mosport Park	7	Martini Racing	G	3.0 Brabham BT45-Alfa Romeo F12	spin/2 laps behind	19/27
ret	US GP EAST	Watkins Glen	7	Martini Racing	G	3.0 Brabham BT45-Alfa Romeo F12	front suspension	13/27
ret	JAPANESE GP	Mount Fuji	7	Martini Racing	G	3.0 Brabham BT45-Alfa Romeo F12	withdrawn due to conditions	17/27
	1977	Championship position: Unplaced						
ret	BRAZILIAN GP	Interlagos	14	Rotary Watches Stanley BRM	G	3.0 BRM P207 V12	engine lost water	22/22
15	SOUTH AFRICAN GP	Kyalami	14	Rotary Watches Stanley BRM	G	3.0 BRM P201B/204 V12	engine on 10 cylinders/-5 laps	22/23
12	BELGIAN GP	Zolder	18	Team Surtees	G	3.0 Surtees TS19-Cosworth V8	2 pit stops-tyres/-3 laps	23/32
dnq	SWEDISH GP	Anderstorp	18	Team Surtees	G	3.0 Surtees TS19-Cosworth V8		27/31
dnq	FRENCH GP	Dijon	18	Team Surtees	G	3.0 Surtees TS19-Cosworth V8		27/30

GP Starts: 11   GP Wins: 0   Pole positions: 0   Fastest laps: 0   Points: 0

PERROT, Xavier (CH) b 1/2/1932, Zurich

	1969	Championship position: Unplaced						
	Race	Circuit	No	Entrant	Tyres	Car/Engine	Comment	Q Pos/Entries
10*	GERMAN GP (F2)	Nürburgring	30	Squadra Tartaruga	F	1.6 Brabham BT23C-Cosworth 4 F2	* 6th in F2 class/1 lap behind	24/26

GP Starts: 1   GP Wins: 0   Pole positions: 0   Fastest laps: 0   Points: 0

HENRI PESCAROLO

Pescarolo began his lengthy involvement with the sport in a minor way during 1965 when he raced a Lotus Seven, and was soon offered the third place in the Matra Formula 3 team for the following year. It proved to be something of a false start to his F3 career, as his car was not ready until mid-season. It was a different story in 1967, however, when he became the man to beat,

winning the European championship. His victories that year included the important events at Barcelona, Monaco, Rouen and Zandvoort, so his promotion to the Formula 2 team in 1968 was a formality. Supporting Beltoise, Henri put in some excellent drives, taking second places at Barcelona, Hockenheim, Zandvoort and Hockenheim again before finishing the year with his first win at Albi. Highly regarded by Matra, he was given a run in the second V12 car in the end-of-season Grands Prix.

Pescarolo's career then received a big setback when, while testing the Matra sports car at Le Mans, he crashed on the Mulsanne Straight and suffered serious burns which laid him low until mid-season. Henri did well to return at the German GP, where he took the F2 Matra into fifth place overall and won the small-capacity class, and the season ended on a bright note when he shared the MS630 sports car with Beltoise to win the Paris 1000 Km at Montlhéry. With Matra now committed to their own Grand Prix project once more, Beltoise returned from his year with Tyrrell and Pescarolo joined him in the Matra V12s. Henri put in some solid performances that year, with a third place at Monaco his best finish. He was also a member of the sports car squad, taking victory in the Buenos Aires 1000 Km with Beltoise.

Pescarolo was surplus to requirements at Matra in 1971 and took some backing from Motul to Frank Williams, which enabled the team to go racing in both F1 and F2. Henri started the season with the old March 701 and picked up a second place on aggregate in the non-title Argentine GP, but Frank Williams was soon over-extended both financially and logistically, which showed in the team's preparation and lack of competitiveness as the year wore on. Meanwhile Pescarolo pursued a parallel programme in sports cars with Alfa Romeo, winning the BOAC 1000 Km with de Adamich. Despite all the problems, Henri was back in the Williams fold in 1972. It turned out to be a miserable season for all concerned as his March 721 was involved in a succession of crashes which required extensive and expensive rebuilds and, to cap it all, the prototype Politoys was written off in the midst of all this on its Brands Hatch debut. Fortunately Pescarolo escaped the carnage largely unhurt, and was buoyed up by his Le

Mans win with Graham Hill in the Matra. Racing for the smart Rondel squad in Formula 2, Henri also won at Enna that year, and took another victory at Thruxton in 1973 after bringing Motul sponsorship to the team. With only the occasional Grand Prix ride that season, Pescarolo returned to Matra for a hugely successful programme of sports car racing, winning at Vallelunga, Dijon, Le Mans (for the second time), the Österreichring and Watkins Glen.

With Motul backing once more, Pescarolo made a full-time return to Grand Prix racing with BRM in 1974, but the team had lost their way, and his only decent finish came in the International Trophy where he was fourth. His partnership with Larrousse at Matra was still a potent one, however, and Henri completed a hat-trick of Le Mans victories and scored other wins at Monza and the Österreichring. By now, of course, he was widely recognised as one of sports car racing's best talents and in 1975 he returned to Alfa Romeo, winning rounds at Spa, the Österreichring and Watkins Glen, all with Derek Bell.

Henri made a last attempt to find success in Formula 1 with a privately entered Surtees in 1976, but neither he nor the car was remotely competitive. From then on Pescarolo concentrated on his sports car career, taking a fourth win at Le Mans in 1984, and raising his tally of World Championship victories to 21 by the end of 1986.

In 1991 he shared the winning Porsche at the Daytona 24-hour race and he subsequently continued his career Stateside in IMSA, before focusing his efforts on Le Mans with the Courage C36.

Henri has more recently looked after Elf's La Filière young driver scheme which has helped so many French drivers to the top echelons of the sport. In 1999 he entered his own Courage C36-Porsche to register a remarkable 33rd Le Mans 24 Hours start, finishing in ninth place.

PESCAROLO, Henri (F) b 25/9/1942, Paris

1968 — Championship position: Unplaced

	Race	Circuit	No	Entrant	Tyres	Car/Engine	Comment	Q Pos/Entries
ret	CANADIAN GP	St Jovite	19	Matra Sports	D	3.0 Matra MS11 V12	oil pressure	=20/22
dns	US GP	Watkins Glen	21T	Matra Sports	D	3.0 Matra MS11 V12	engine trouble in practice	(21)/21
9	MEXICAN GP	Mexico City	9	Matra Sports	D	3.0 Matra MS11 V12	3 laps behind	20/21

1969 — Championship position: Unplaced

	Race	Circuit	No	Entrant	Tyres	Car/Engine	Comment	Q Pos/Entries
5*	GERMAN GP (F2)	Nürburgring	26	Matra Sports	D	1.6 Matra MS7-Cosworth 4	* 1st in F2 class/no points scored	14/26

1970 — Championship position: 12th Wins: 0 Pole positions: 0 Fastest laps: 0 Points scored: 8

	Race	Circuit	No	Entrant	Tyres	Car/Engine	Comment	Q Pos/Entries
7	SOUTH AFRICAN GP	Kyalami	4	Equipe Matra Elf	G	3.0 Matra-Simca MS120 V12	2 laps behind	18/24
ret	SPANISH GP	Jarama	22	Equipe Matra Elf	G	3.0 Matra-Simca MS120 V12	engine-con rod	10/22
3	MONACO GP	Monte Carlo	9	Equipe Matra Elf	G	3.0 Matra-Simca MS120 V12		7/21
6/ret	BELGIAN GP	Spa	26	Equipe Matra Elf	G	3.0 Matra-Simca MS120 V12	out of fuel/1 lap behind	17/18
8	DUTCH GP	Zandvoort	24	Equipe Matra Elf	G	3.0 Matra-Simca MS120 V12	2 laps behind	13/24
5	FRENCH GP	Clermont Ferrand	20	Equipe Matra Elf	G	3.0 Matra-Simca MS120 V12		8/23
ret	BRITISH GP	Brands Hatch	8	Equipe Matra Elf	G	3.0 Matra-Simca MS120 V12	spun off	13/25
6	GERMAN GP	Hockenheim	14	Equipe Matra Elf	G	3.0 Matra-Simca MS120 V12	pit stop-gearbox/1 lap behind	5/25
14	AUSTRIAN GP	Österreichring	20	Equipe Matra Elf	G	3.0 Matra-Simca MS120 V12	pit stop-wheel change/-4 laps	12/24
ret	ITALIAN GP	Monza	42	Equipe Matra Elf	G	3.0 Matra-Simca MS120 V12	engine-valve spring	17/27
7	CANADIAN GP	St Jovite	24	Equipe Matra Elf	G	3.0 Matra-Simca MS120 V12	tyres shot/3 laps behind	=8/20
8	US GP	Watkins Glen	7	Equipe Matra Elf	G	3.0 Matra-Simca MS120 V12	pit stops/3 laps behind	12/27
9	MEXICAN GP	Mexico City	7	Equipe Matra Elf	G	3.0 Matra-Simca MS120 V12	pit stop-gearbox/-4 laps	11/18

1971 — Championship position: 16th= Wins: 0 Pole positions: 0 Fastest laps: 0 Points scored: 4

	Race	Circuit	No	Entrant	Tyres	Car/Engine	Comment	Q Pos/Entries
11	SOUTH AFRICAN GP	Kyalami	22	Frank Williams Racing Cars	G	3.0 March 701-Cosworth V8	2 laps behind	=16/25
ret	SPANISH GP	Montjuich Park	27	Frank Williams Racing Cars	G	3.0 March 711-Cosworth V8	pit stop-rear wing-could not restart	11/22
8	MONACO GP	Monte Carlo	27	Frank Williams Racing Cars	G	3.0 March 711-Cosworth V8	pit stop-puncture/-3 laps	13/23
13	DUTCH GP	Zandvoort	31	Frank Williams Racing Cars	G	3.0 March 711-Cosworth V8	spin-pit stop-nose cone/-8 laps	15/24
ret	FRENCH GP	Paul Ricard	27	Frank Williams Racing Cars	G	3.0 March 711-Cosworth V8	gearbox	18/24
4	BRITISH GP	Silverstone	26	Frank Williams Racing Cars	G	3.0 March 711-Cosworth V8	1 lap behind	17/24
ret	GERMAN GP	Nürburgring	14	Frank Williams Racing Cars	G	3.0 March 711-Cosworth V8	suspension	10/23
6	AUSTRIAN GP	Österreichring	25	Frank Williams Racing Cars	G	3.0 March 711-Cosworth V8		13/22
ret	ITALIAN GP	Monza	16	Frank Williams Racing Cars	G	3.0 March 711-Cosworth V8	suspension/FL	10/24
dns	CANADIAN GP	Mosport Park	27	Frank Williams Racing Cars	G	3.0 March 711-Cosworth V8	went off in warm-up	(27)/27
ret	US GP	Watkins Glen	21	Frank Williams Racing Cars	G	3.0 March 711-Cosworth V8	engine	22/32

1972 — Championship position: Unplaced

	Race	Circuit	No	Entrant	Tyres	Car/Engine	Comment	Q Pos/Entries
8	ARGENTINE GP	Buenos Aires	23	Team Williams-Motul	G	3.0 March 721-Cosworth V8	2 laps behind	15/22
11	SOUTH AFRICAN GP	Kyalami	21	Team Williams-Motul	G	3.0 March 721-Cosworth V8	2 laps behind	22/27
11	SPANISH GP	Jarama	14	Team Williams-Motul	G	3.0 March 721-Cosworth V8	4 laps behind	19/26
ret	MONACO GP	Monte Carlo	22	Team Williams-Motul	G	3.0 March 721-Cosworth V8	aquaplaned-hit barrier	=8/25
nc	BELGIAN GP	Nivelles	15	Team Williams-Motul	G	3.0 March 721-Cosworth V8	pit stop-throttle problems/-26 laps	19/26
dns	FRENCH GP	Clermont Ferrand	16	Team Williams-Motul	G	3.0 March 721-Cosworth V8	crashed in practice	(12)/29
ret	BRITISH GP	Brands Hatch	24	Team Williams-Motul	G	3.0 Politoys FX3-Cosworth V8	steering failure-accident	26/27
ret	GERMAN GP	Nürburgring	20	Team Williams-Motul	G	3.0 March 721-Cosworth V8	crashed while 6th	9/27
dns	AUSTRIAN GP	Österreichring	22	Team Williams-Motul	G	3.0 March 721-Cosworth V8	accident in practice	(23)/26
dnq	ITALIAN GP	Monza	25	Team Williams-Motul	G	3.0 March 721-Cosworth V8	accident in practice	26/27
13	CANADIAN GP	Mosport Park	28	Team Williams-Motul	G	3.0 March 721-Cosworth V8	pit stop-handling/-7 laps	21/25
14	US GP	Watkins Glen	26	Team Williams-Motul	G	3.0 March 721-Cosworth V8	2 laps behind	22/32

1973 — Championship position: Unplaced

	Race	Circuit	No	Entrant	Tyres	Car/Engine	Comment	Q Pos/Entries
8	SPANISH GP	Montjuich Park	11	STP March Racing Team	G	3.0 March 721G/731-Cosworth V8	2 laps behind	18/22
ret	FRENCH GP	Paul Ricard	26	Frank Williams Racing Cars	F	3.0 Iso Williams 1R-Cosworth V8	overheating	23/25
10	GERMAN GP	Nürburgring	26	Frank Williams Racing Cars	F	3.0 Iso Williams 1R-Cosworth V8		=11/23

Pescarolo's best-ever Grand Prix result came in Monaco in 1970 when, almost unnoticed, he took the Matra into third place behind the sensational finish provided by Rindt and Brabham.

	1974			Championship position: Unplaced					
9	ARGENTINE GP	Buenos Aires	15	Motul Team BRM	F	3.0 BRM P160E V12	*1 lap behind*	21/26
14	BRAZILIAN GP	Interlagos	15	Motul Team BRM	F	3.0 BRM P160E V12	*2 laps behind*	22/25
18	SOUTH AFRICAN GP	Kyalami	15	Motul Team BRM	F	3.0 BRM P160E V12	*2 pit stops-nose cone/-6 laps*	21/27
12	SPANISH GP	Jarama	15	Motul Team BRM	F	3.0 BRM P160E V12	*pit stop/4 laps behind*	21/28
ret	BELGIAN GP	Nivelles	15	Motul Team BRM	F	3.0 BRM P106E V12	*spun off*	15/32
ret	MONACO GP	Monte Carlo	15	Motul Team BRM	F	3.0 BRM P160E V12	*gearbox*	27/28
ret	SWEDISH GP	Anderstorp	15	Motul Team BRM	F	3.0 BRM P201 V12	*fire on lap 1*	19/28
ret	DUTCH GP	Zandvoort	15	Motul Team BRM	F	3.0 BRM P160E V12	*handling*	24/27
dns	"	"	15	Motul Team BRM	F	3.0 BRM P201 V12	*practice only*	– / –
ret	FRENCH GP	Dijon	15	Motul Team BRM	F	3.0 BRM P201 V12	*clutch on startline*	19/30
ret	BRITISH GP	Brands Hatch	15	Motul Team BRM	F	3.0 BRM P201 V12	*engine*	24/34
10	GERMAN GP	Nürburgring	15	Motul Team BRM	F	3.0 BRM P201 V12		24/32
ret	ITALIAN GP	Monza	15	Motul Team BRM	F	3.0 BRM P201 V12	*engine*	25/31
	1976			Championship position: Unplaced					
dnq	MONACO GP	Monte Carlo	38	Team Norev Racing/BS Fabrications	G	3.0 Surtees TS19-Cosworth V8		22/25
ret	FRENCH GP	Paul Ricard	38	Team Norev Racing/BS Fabrications	G	3.0 Surtees TS19-Cosworth V8	*rear hub*	24/30
ret	BRITISH GP	Brands Hatch	38	Team Norev Racing/BS Fabrications	G	3.0 Surtees TS19-Cosworth V8	*fuel pressure*	26/30
dnq	GERMAN GP	Nürburgring	38	Team Norev Racing/BS Fabrications	G	3.0 Surtees TS19-Cosworth V8	*fuel system problems*	28/28
9	AUSTRIAN GP	Österreichring	38	Team Norev Racing/BS Fabrications	G	3.0 Surtees TS19-Cosworth V8	*2 laps behind*	22/25
11	DUTCH GP	Zandvoort	38	Team Norev Racing/BS Fabrications	G	3.0 Surtees TS19-Cosworth V8	*1 lap behind*	22/27
17	ITALIAN GP	Monza	38	Team Norev Racing/BS Fabrications	G	3.0 Surtees TS19-Cosworth V8	*pit stop/3 laps behind*	22/29
19	CANADIAN GP	Mosport Park	38	Team Norev Racing/BS Fabrications	G	3.0 Surtees TS19-Cosworth V8	*3 laps behind*	21/27
nc	US GP EAST	Watkins Glen	38	Team Norev Racing/BS Fabrications	G	3.0 Surtees TS19-Cosworth V8	*hit chicane-pit stop/-11 laps*	26/27

GP Starts: 57   GP Wins: 0   Pole positions: 0   Fastest laps: 1   Points: 12

ALESSANDRO PESENTI-ROSSI

Pesenti-Rossi was regarded as an Italian national F3 racer of little pedigree until 1974, when he did well in his GRD at home and undertook a couple of Formula 2 races with a Beta-backed March. In 1975 Alessandro again achieved some success, including a second place on aggregate at Mugello.

Somewhat ambitiously he made a short-lived attempt to break into Grand Prix racing in mid-1976 with a privately entered Tyrrell. He and his backers sensibly decided to invest their money more wisely the following year when he returned to Formula 2 with a March 772, though three fourth places on home soil (at Vallelunga, Mugello and Misano) were the best he could muster. After he failed to qualify for the Preis von Württemberg at Hockenheim in a Chevron at the start of 1978, no more was seen of the wiry Italian at this level.

JOSEF PETERS

Peters was a stalwart of the buoyant German domestic series of the early fifties driving his trusty two-seater Veritas.

Mostly he just seemed to make up the numbers, but he finished third in the 1953 Formula 2 race at Grenzlandring – a well-supported meeting marred by the accident in which Niedermayr's car ran into the crowd with such devastating consequences.

The sports-bodied Veritas was put to good use in the 1953 Nürburgring 1000 Km, when Josef and Wolfgang Seidel took fifth place overall and won the 1500 cc–2000 cc class.

PESENTI-ROSSI, Alessandro (I) b 31/8/1942, Bergamo

	1976			Championship position: Unplaced				
	Race	Circuit	No	Entrant	Tyres	Car/Engine	Comment	Q Pos/Entries
14	GERMAN GP	Nürburgring	40	Scuderia Gulf Rondini	G	3.0 Tyrrell 007-Cosworth V8	*1 lap behind*	26/28
11	AUSTRIAN GP	Österreichring	39	Scuderia Gulf Rondini	G	3.0 Tyrrell 007-Cosworth V8	*3 laps behind*	23/25
dnq	DUTCH GP	Zandvoort	40	Scuderia Gulf Rondini	G	3.0 Tyrrell 007-Cosworth V8		27/27
18	ITALIAN GP	Monza	37	Scuderia Gulf Rondini	G	3.0 Tyrrell 007-Cosworth V8	*3 laps behind*	21/29

GP Starts: 3   GP Wins: 0   Pole positions: 0   Fastest laps: 0   Points: 0

PETERS, Josef (D) b 16/9/1914, Düsseldorf

	1952			Championship position: Unplaced				
	Race	Circuit	No	Entrant	Tyres	Car/Engine	Comment	Q Pos/Entries
ret	GERMAN GP	Nürburgring	129	Josef Peters		– 2.0 Veritas RS 6-BMW 6 (sports car)		20/32

GP Starts: 1   GP Wins: 0   Pole positions: 0   Fastest laps: 0   Points: 0

RONNIE PETERSON

RONNIE PETERSON

Everybody loved Ronnie. Whatever your allegiances, the big blond Swede was the entertainer of the early seventies, thrilling everyone with his astonishing car control. Just watching him drift a Lotus 72 through the old Woodcote Corner was worth the price of admission alone. With all that natural talent, he should surely have been a World Champion, but sadly luck decreed otherwise.

Ronnie was Swedish karting champion between 1963 and 1966 and then switched to Formula 3, at first in a home-brewed special before acquiring a Tecno for 1968. This proved to be a wise move as he took his national championship, and gained a place in the works F3 team for the following year. At this time his big rival was compatriot Reine Wisell, and he and Ronnie were to have many duels in the 1-litre F3 formula. Peterson won the prestigious Monaco race during a successful 1969 season which brought the offer of a three-year contract with March from 1970. He gained some valuable experience in his first year with the Colin Crabbe-entered F1 car and ran a full season of Formula 2 guided by Malcolm Guthrie.

Promoted to the full works teams the following season, he quickly established himself as one of the world's leading talents, scoring four second places in Grands Prix to finish as runner-up in the World Championship, while in Formula 2 he displayed Rindt-like qualities to take the European championship with five wins. Locked into the final year of his March deal, Peterson was lumbered with the hopeless 721X in 1972 and things improved only marginally when the hastily cobbled-together 721G was pressed into service. His racing in F2 was limited by a successful sports car programme for Ferrari; teamed with Schenken, he won at Buenos Aires and the Nürburgring and took four second places.

Ronnie joined Lotus for 1973 but his slow start to the season eventually counted against him when a late burst of four wins took him into third place in the championship. So dominant was his form that team-mate Emerson Fittipaldi opted for McLaren for 1974, allowing Jacky Ickx to partner Peterson. The season was desperately disappointing because of the difficulties experienced with the new Lotus 76, but the compensation for the Swede's army of admirers was the opportunity to savour his sublime driving talent a little longer at the wheel of the now aged Lotus 72E. Wins at Monaco, Dijon and Monza were the stuff of true genius. Peterson was forced to soldier on in the old faithful during 1975 while a new car was prepared, and he could no longer compensate for its deficiencies. Unfortunately, when the Type 77 was introduced at the opening race of 1976 it appeared to be another lemon, and then Ronnie contrived to collide with new team-mate Mario Andretti. This was the final straw for Peterson, who engineered a move back to March for the rest of the season. In the underfinanced little team's car he managed to score a brilliant win at Monza, before being tempted to Tyrrell for 1977. However, the six-wheeler was just not suited to Ronnie's style, and he was regularly outpaced by team-mate Depailler. By the end of the year his reputation had been seriously dented, but salvation was nigh. Colin Chapman took him back, albeit strictly as number two to Andretti, to race the superb Lotus 79.

Keeping his word, Peterson was content to play the support role in the team. Mario headed for his deserved championship win and Ronnie picked up the crumbs, in the shape of wins in South Africa and Austria. However, tragedy lay around the corner. At Monza he became embroiled in a first-lap multiple crash, which left him suffering from severe leg injuries. Worse was to come, for once in hospital complications set in. He slipped into a coma and within hours he was gone. The sense of disbelief was matched only by the grief felt throughout motor racing. For Lotus, what should have been a time of great joy became instead a period of hollow celebration.

Lotus boss Colin Chapman hurls his cap into the air as Peterson wins the 1974 French Grand Prix at Dijon in the venerable Lotus 72E.

PETERSON, Ronnie (S) b 14/2/1944, Orebro – d 11/9/1978, Milan, Italy

1970 — Championship position: Unplaced

	Race	Circuit	No	Entrant	Tyres	Car/Engine	Comment	Q Pos/Entries
7	MONACO GP	Monte Carlo	23	Antique Automobiles Racing Team	G	3.0 March 701-Cosworth V8	*2 laps behind*	13/21
nc	BELGIAN GP	Spa	14	Antique Automobiles Racing Team	G	3.0 March 701-Cosworth V8	*spin-pit stop/8 laps behind*	9/18
9	DUTCH GP	Zandvoort	22	Colin Crabbe Racing	G	3.0 March 701-Cosworth V8	*2 laps behind*	16/24
ret	FRENCH GP	Clermont Ferrand	18	Colin Crabbe Racing	G	3.0 March 701-Cosworth V8	*transmission*	9/23
9	BRITISH GP	Brands Hatch	27	Colin Crabbe Racing	G	3.0 March 701-Cosworth V8	*pit stop-clutch/8 laps behind*	14/25
ret	GERMAN GP	Hockenheim	22	Colin Crabbe Racing	G	3.0 March 701-Cosworth V8	*engine*	19/25
ret	ITALIAN GP	Monza	52	Colin Crabbe Racing	G	3.0 March 701-Cosworth V8	*engine*	14/27
nc	CANADIAN GP	St Jovite	26	Colin Crabbe Racing	G	3.0 March 701-Cosworth V8	*pit stops-fuel leak/-25 laps*	16/20
11	US GP	Watkins Glen	29	Colin Crabbe Racing	G	3.0 March 701-Cosworth V8	*2 pit stops-tyres/-4 laps*	15/27

1971 — Championship position: 2nd Wins: 0 Pole positions: 0 Fastest laps: 0 Points scored: 33

	Race	Circuit	No	Entrant	Tyres	Car/Engine	Comment	Q Pos/Entries
10	SOUTH AFRICAN GP	Kyalami	7	STP March Racing Team	F	3.0 March 711-Cosworth V8	*pit stop-plug lead/-2 laps*	=13/25
ret	SPANISH GP	Montjuich Park	18	STP March Racing Team	F	3.0 March 711-Cosworth V8	*ignition*	13/22
2	MONACO GP	Monte Carlo	17	STP March Racing Team	F	3.0 March 711-Cosworth V8		8/23
4	DUTCH GP	Zandvoort	16	STP March Racing Team	F	3.0 March 711-Cosworth V8	*2 laps behind*	–/–
dns	"	"	16T	STP March Racing Team	F	3.0 March 711-Alfa Romeo V8	*qualified in this car*	13/24
ret	FRENCH GP	Paul Ricard	17	STP March Racing Team	F	3.0 March 711-Alfa Romeo V8	*engine*	12/24
2	BRITISH GP	Silverstone	18	STP March Racing Team	F	3.0 March 711-Cosworth V8		5/24
5	GERMAN GP	Nürburgring	15	STP March Racing Team	F	3.0 March 711-Cosworth V8	*pit stop-radiator cover*	7/23
8	AUSTRIAN GP	Österreichring	17	STP March Racing Team	F	3.0 March 711-Cosworth V8	*handling problems/-1 lap*	11/22
2	ITALIAN GP	Monza	25	STP March Racing Team	F	3.0 March 711-Cosworth V8		6/24
2	CANADIAN GP	Mosport Park	17	STP March Racing Team	F	3.0 March 711-Cosworth V8		6/27
3	US GP	Watkins Glen	25	STP March Racing Team	F	3.0 March 711-Cosworth V8		12/32

1972 — Championship position: 9th Wins: 0 Pole positions: 0 Fastest laps: 0 Points scored: 12

	Race	Circuit	No	Entrant	Tyres	Car/Engine	Comment	Q Pos/Entries
6	ARGENTINE GP	Buenos Aires	14	STP March Racing Team	G	3.0 March 721-Cosworth V8	*spin/1 lap behind*	10/22
5	SOUTH AFRICAN GP	Kyalami	3	STP March Racing Team	G	3.0 March 721-Cosworth V8	*handling problems*	=8/27
ret	SPANISH GP	Jarama	2	STP March Racing Team	G	3.0 March 721X-Cosworth V8	*fuel leak/suspension/body damage*	9/26
11	MONACO GP	Monte Carlo	3	STP March Racing Team	G	3.0 March 721X-Cosworth V8	*hit Ickx-pit stop/4 laps behind*	15/25
dns	"	"	3T	STP March Racing Team	G	3.0 March 721-Cosworth V8	*practice only*	–/–
9	BELGIAN GP	Nivelles	11	STP March Racing Team	G	3.0 March 721X-Cosworth V8	*2 laps behind*	14/26
5	FRENCH GP	Clermont Ferrand	12	STP March Racing Team	G	3.0 March 721G-Cosworth V8	*broken roll bar*	9/29
7/ret	BRITISH GP	Brands Hatch	3	STP March Racing Team	G	3.0 March 721G-Cosworth V8	*out of fuel-spun off/-2 laps*	=8/27
3	GERMAN GP	Nürburgring	10	STP March Racing Team	G	3.0 March 721G-Cosworth V8	*spin*	4/27
12	AUSTRIAN GP	Österreichring	5	STP March Racing Team	G	3.0 March 721G-Cosworth V8	*pit stop-fuel/2 laps behind*	11/26
9	ITALIAN GP	Monza	19	STP March Racing Team	G	3.0 March 721G-Cosworth V8	*pit stop-handling/1 lap behind*	24/27
dsq	CANADIAN GP	Mosport Park	25	STP March Racing Team	G	3.0 March 721G-Cosworth V8	*push start after collision*	3/25
4	US GP	Watkins Glen	4	STP March Racing Team	G	3.0 March 721G-Cosworth V8	*accident in practice*	27/32

1973 — Championship position: 3rd Wins: 4 Pole positions: 9 Fastest laps: 2 Points scored: 52

	Race	Circuit	No	Entrant	Tyres	Car/Engine	Comment	Q Pos/Entries
ret	ARGENTINE GP	Buenos Aires	4	John Player Team Lotus	G	3.0 Lotus 72D-Cosworth V8	*oil pressure*	5/19
ret	BRAZILIAN GP	Interlagos	2	John Player Team Lotus	G	3.0 Lotus 72D-Cosworth V8	*rear wheel/*	1/20
11	SOUTH AFRICAN GP	Kyalami	2	John Player Team Lotus	G	3.0 Lotus 72D-Cosworth V8	*pit stop-throttle linkage/-6 laps*	4/25
ret	SPANISH GP	Montjuich Park	2	John Player Team Lotus	G	3.0 Lotus 72E-Cosworth V8	*gearbox//FL*	1/22
ret	BELGIAN GP	Zolder	2	John Player Team Lotus	G	3.0 Lotus 72E-Cosworth V8	*spun off*	1/23
3	MONACO GP	Monte Carlo	2	John Player Team Lotus	G	3.0 Lotus 72E-Cosworth V8	*engine problems/1 lap behind*	2/26
2	SWEDISH GP	Anderstorp	2	John Player Team Lotus	G	3.0 Lotus 72E-Cosworth V8	*puncture last lap when 1st*	1/22
1	FRENCH GP	Paul Ricard	2	John Player Team Lotus	G	3.0 Lotus 72E-Cosworth V8		5/25
2	BRITISH GP	Silverstone	2	John Player Team Lotus	G	3.0 Lotus 72E-Cosworth V8		1/29
11/ret	DUTCH GP	Zandvoort	2	John Player Team Lotus	G	3.0 Lotus 72E-Cosworth V8	*gearbox/FL/-6 laps*	1/24
ret	GERMAN GP	Nürburgring	2	John Player Team Lotus	G	3.0 Lotus 72E-Cosworth V8	*distributor*	2/23
1	AUSTRIAN GP	Österreichring	2	John Player Team Lotus	G	3.0 Lotus 72E-Cosworth V8		2/25
1	ITALIAN GP	Monza	2	John Player Team Lotus	G	3.0 Lotus 72E-Cosworth V8		1/25
ret	CANADIAN GP	Mosport Park	2	John Player Team Lotus	G	3.0 Lotus 72E-Cosworth V8	*puncture-spun off*	1/26
1	US GP	Watkins Glen	2	John Player Team Lotus	G	3.0 Lotus 72E-Cosworth V8		1/28

1974 — Championship position: 5th Wins: 3 Pole positions: 1 Fastest laps: 2 Points scored: 35

	Race	Circuit	No	Entrant	Tyres	Car/Engine	Comment	Q Pos/Entries
13	ARGENTINE GP	Buenos Aires	1	John Player Team Lotus	G	3.0 Lotus 72E-Cosworth V8	*pit stop-battery-tyres/-5 laps*	1/26
6	BRAZILIAN GP	Interlagos	1	John Player Team Lotus	G	3.0 Lotus 72E-Cosworth V8	*pit stop-tyre/1 lap behind*	4/25
ret	SOUTH AFRICAN GP	Kyalami	1	John Player Team Lotus	G	3.0 Lotus 76-Cosworth V8	*hit Ickx*	16/27
dns	"	"	1	John Player Team Lotus	G	3.0 Lotus 72E-Cosworth V8	*practice only*	–/–
ret	SPANISH GP	Jarama	1	John Player Team Lotus	G	3.0 Lotus 76-Cosworth V8	*engine*	2/28
ret	BELGIAN GP	Nivelles	1	John Player Team Lotus	G	3.0 Lotus 76-Cosworth V8	*fuel leak*	5/32
dns	"	"	1T	John Player Team Lotus	G	3.0 Lotus 72E-Cosworth V8	*practice only*	–/–
1	MONACO GP	Monte Carlo	1	John Player Team Lotus	G	3.0 Lotus 72E-Cosworth V8	*FL*	3/28
ret	SWEDISH GP	Anderstorp	1	John Player Team Lotus	G	3.0 Lotus 72E-Cosworth V8	*driveshaft*	5/28
dns	"	"	1T	John Player Team Lotus	G	3.0 Lotus 76-Cosworth V8	*practice only*	–/–
8	DUTCH GP	Zandvoort	1	John Player Team Lotus	G	3.0 Lotus 72E-Cosworth V8	*pit stop-tyres/FL/-2 laps*	10/27
1	FRENCH GP	Dijon	1	John Player Team Lotus	G	3.0 Lotus 72E-Cosworth V8		2/30
dns	"	"	1T	John Player Team Lotus	G	3.0 Lotus 76-Cosworth V8	*practice only*	–/–
10	BRITISH GP	Brands Hatch	1	John Player Team Lotus	G	3.0 Lotus 72E-Cosworth V8	*pit stops-tyres/2 laps behind*	=1/34
4	GERMAN GP	Nürburgring	1	John Player Team Lotus	G	3.0 Lotus 76-Cosworth V8	*cobbled together race car*	–/–
dns	"	"	1	John Player Team Lotus	G	3.0 Lotus 72E-Cosworth V8	*crashed car in practice*	8/32
ret	AUSTRIAN GP	Österreichring	1	John Player Team Lotus	G	3.0 Lotus 72E-Cosworth V8	*driveshaft*	5/31
dns	"	"	1T	John Player Team Lotus	G	3.0 Lotus 76-Cosworth V8	*practice only*	–/–
1	ITALIAN GP	Monza	1	John Player Team Lotus	G	3.0 Lotus 72E-Cosworth V8		7/31
dns	"	"	1	John Player Team Lotus	G	3.0 Lotus 76-Cosworth V8	*practice only*	–/–
3	CANADIAN GP	Mosport Park	1	John Player Team Lotus	G	3.0 Lotus 72E-Cosworth V8		10/30
ret	US GP	Watkins Glen	1	John Player Team Lotus	G	3.0 Lotus 72E-Cosworth V8	*fuel line*	19/30

1975 — Championship position: 12th=   Wins: 0   Pole positions: 0   Fastest laps: 0   Points scored: 6

	Race	Circuit	No	Entrant	Tyres	Car/Engine	Comment	Q Pos/Entries
ret	ARGENTINE GP	Buenos Aires	5	John Player Team Lotus	G	3.0 Lotus 72E-Cosworth V8	brakes/gearbox	11/23
15	BRAZILIAN GP	Interlagos	5	John Player Team Lotus	G	3.0 Lotus 72E-Cosworth V8	stalled on grid/-2 laps	16/23
10	SOUTH AFRICAN GP	Kyalami	5	John Player Team Lotus	G	3.0 Lotus 72E-Cosworth V8	pit stop-tyres/1 lap behind	8/28
ret	SPANISH GP	Montjuich Park	5	John Player Team Lotus	G	3.0 Lotus 72E-Cosworth V8	collision with Migault	12/26
4	MONACO GP	Monte Carlo	5	John Player Team Lotus	G	3.0 Lotus 72E-Cosworth V8		4/26
ret	BELGIAN GP	Zolder	5	John Player Team Lotus	G	3.0 Lotus 72E-Cosworth V8	brake failure-went off	14/24
9	SWEDISH GP	Anderstorp	5	John Player Team Lotus	G	3.0 Lotus 72E-Cosworth V8	1 lap behind	9/26
15/ret	DUTCH GP	Zandvoort	5	John Player Team Lotus	G	3.0 Lotus 72E-Cosworth V8	out of fuel/6 laps behind	16/25
10	FRENCH GP	Paul Ricard	5	John Player Team Lotus	G	3.0 Lotus 72E-Cosworth V8		17/26
ret	BRITISH GP	Silverstone	5	John Player Team Lotus	G	3.0 Lotus 72E-Cosworth V8	engine	16/28
ret	GERMAN GP	Nürburgring	5	John Player Team Lotus	G	3.0 Lotus 72E-Cosworth V8	clutch	18/26
5*	AUSTRIAN GP	Österreichring	5	John Player Team Lotus	G	3.0 Lotus 72E-Cosworth V8	* rain-shortened race-half points	13/30
ret	ITALIAN GP	Monza	5	John Player Team Lotus	G	3.0 Lotus 72E-Cosworth V8	engine	11/28
5	US GP	Watkins Glen	5	John Player Team Lotus	G	3.0 Lotus 72E-Cosworth V8		14/24

1976 — Championship position: 11th=   Wins: 1   Pole positions: 1   Fastest laps: 1   Points scored: 10

	Race	Circuit	No	Entrant	Tyres	Car/Engine	Comment	Q Pos/Entries
ret	BRAZILIAN GP	Interlagos	5	John Player Team Lotus	G	3.0 Lotus 77-Cosworth V8	collision with Andretti	18/22
ret	SOUTH AFRICAN GP	Kyalami	10	March Engineering	G	3.0 March 761-Cosworth V8	accident with Depailler	10/25
10	US GP WEST	Long Beach	10	Theodore Racing	G	3.0 March 761-Cosworth V8	pit stop-boiling brake fluid/-3 laps	6/27
ret	SPANISH GP	Jarama	10	March Engineering	G	3.0 March 761-Cosworth V8	transmission	16/30
ret	BELGIAN GP	Zolder	10	March Engineering	G	3.0 March 761-Cosworth V8	spun avoiding Reutemann	10/29
ret	MONACO GP	Monte Carlo	10	March Engineering	G	3.0 March 761-Cosworth V8	spun off	3/25
7	SWEDISH GP	Anderstorp	10	March Engineering	G	3.0 March 761-Cosworth V8		9/27
19/ret	FRENCH GP	Paul Ricard	10	March Engineering	G	3.0 March 761-Cosworth V8	fuel metering unit/-3 laps	6/30
ret	BRITISH GP	Brands Hatch	10	March Engineering	G	3.0 March 761-Cosworth V8	fuel pressure	7/30
ret	GERMAN GP	Nürburgring	10	March Engineering	G	3.0 March 761-Cosworth V8	went off at Flugplatz	11/28
6	AUSTRIAN GP	Österreichring	10	March Engineering	G	3.0 March 761-Cosworth V8		3/25
ret	DUTCH GP	Zandvoort	10	March Engineering	G	3.0 March 761-Cosworth V8	oil pressure	1/27
1	ITALIAN GP	Monza	10	March Engineering	G	3.0 March 761-Cosworth V8	FL	8/29
9	CANADIAN GP	Mosport Park	10	March Engineering	G	3.0 March 761-Cosworth V8	1 lap behind	2/27
ret	US GP EAST	Watkins Glen	10	March Engineering	G	3.0 March 761-Cosworth V8	front suspension bulkhead	3/27
ret	JAPANESE GP	Mount Fuji	10	March Engineering	G	3.0 March 761-Cosworth V8	engine cut out	9/27

1977 — Championship position: 14th   Wins: 0   Pole positions: 0   Fastest laps: 1   Points scored: 7

	Race	Circuit	No	Entrant	Tyres	Car/Engine	Comment	Q Pos/Entries
ret	ARGENTINE GP	Buenos Aires	3	Elf Team Tyrrell	G	3.0 Tyrrell P34-Cosworth V8	spun off	14/21
ret	BRAZILIAN GP	Interlagos	3	Elf Team Tyrrell	G	3.0 Tyrrell P34-Cosworth V8	accident avoiding Mass & Regazzoni	8/22
ret	SOUTH AFRICAN GP	Kyalami	3	Elf Team Tyrrell	G	3.0 Tyrrell P34-Cosworth V8	fuel pressure	7/23
ret	US GP WEST	Long Beach	3	Elf Team Tyrrell	G	3.0 Tyrrell P34-Cosworth V8	fuel line	10/22
8	SPANISH GP	Jarama	3	Elf Team Tyrrell	G	3.0 Tyrrell P34-Cosworth V8	1 lap behind	15/31
ret	MONACO GP	Monte Carlo	3	Elf Team Tyrrell	G	3.0 Tyrrell P34-Cosworth V8	brakes	4/26
3	BELGIAN GP	Zolder	3	Elf Team Tyrrell	G	3.0 Tyrrell P34-Cosworth V8		8/32
ret	SWEDISH GP	Anderstorp	3	Elf Team Tyrrell	G	3.0 Tyrrell P34-Cosworth V8	ignition	10/31
12	FRENCH GP	Dijon	3	Elf Team Tyrrell	G	3.0 Tyrrell P34-Cosworth V8	pit stop-tyres/3 laps behind	17/30
ret	BRITISH GP	Silverstone	3	Elf Team Tyrrell	G	3.0 Tyrrell P34-Cosworth V8	engine	10/36
9/ret	GERMAN GP	Hockenheim	3	Elf Team Tyrrell	G	3.0 Tyrrell P34-Cosworth V8	engine/5 laps behind	14/30
5	AUSTRIAN GP	Österreichring	3	Elf Team Tyrrell	G	3.0 Tyrrell P34-Cosworth V8		15/30
ret	DUTCH GP	Zandvoort	3	Elf Team Tyrrell	G	3.0 Tyrrell P34-Cosworth V8	ignition	7/34
6	ITALIAN GP	Monza	3	Elf Team Tyrrell	G	3.0 Tyrrell P34-Cosworth V8		12/34
16	US GP EAST	Watkins Glen	3	Elf Team Tyrrell	G	3.0 Tyrrell P34-Cosworth V8	pit stops-tyres/FL/-3 laps	5/27
ret	CANADIAN GP	Mosport Park	3	Elf Team Tyrrell	G	3.0 Tyrrell P34-Cosworth V8	fuel leak	3/27
ret	JAPANESE GP	Mount Fuji	3	Elf Team Tyrrell	G	3.0 Tyrrell P34-Cosworth V8	hit by Villeneuve	18/23

1978 — Championship position: 2nd   Wins: 2   Pole positions: 3   Fastest laps: 3   Points scored: 51

	Race	Circuit	No	Entrant	Tyres	Car/Engine	Comment	Q Pos/Entries
5	ARGENTINE GP	Buenos Aires	6	John Player Team Lotus	G	3.0 Lotus 78-Cosworth V8		3/27
ret	BRAZILIAN GP	Rio	6	John Player Team Lotus	G	3.0 Lotus 78-Cosworth V8	collision with Villeneuve	1/28
1	SOUTH AFRICAN GP	Kyalami	6	John Player Team Lotus	G	3.0 Lotus 78-Cosworth V8	took lead on last lap	12/30
4	US GP WEST	Long Beach	6	John Player Team Lotus	G	3.0 Lotus 78-Cosworth V8	pit stop-tyres	6/30
ret	MONACO GP	Monte Carlo	6	John Player Team Lotus	G	3.0 Lotus 78-Cosworth V8	gearbox	7/30
2	BELGIAN GP	Zolder	6	John Player Team Lotus	G	3.0 Lotus 78-Cosworth V8	pit stop-tyre/FL	7/30
2	SPANISH GP	Jarama	6	John Player Team Lotus	G	3.0 Lotus 79-Cosworth V8		2/29
3	SWEDISH GP	Anderstorp	6	John Player Team Lotus	G	3.0 Lotus 79-Cosworth V8	held up by Patrese	4/27
2	FRENCH GP	Paul Ricard	6	John Player Team Lotus	G	3.0 Lotus 79-Cosworth V8		5/29
ret	BRITISH GP	Brands Hatch	6	John Player Team Lotus	G	3.0 Lotus 79-Cosworth V8	fuel pump	1/30
ret	GERMAN GP	Hockenheim	6	John Player Team Lotus	G	3.0 Lotus 79-Cosworth V8	gearbox/FL	2/30
1	AUSTRIAN GP	Österreichring	6	John Player Team Lotus	G	3.0 Lotus 79-Cosworth V8	FL	1/31
2	DUTCH GP	Zandvoort	6	John Player Team Lotus	G	3.0 Lotus 79-Cosworth V8		2/33
ret/dns	ITALIAN GP	Monza	6	John Player Team Lotus	G	3.0 Lotus 78-Cosworth V8	fatal accident at 1st start	– / –
dns	"	"	6	John Player Team Lotus	G	3.0 Lotus 79-Cosworth V8	car damaged in practice	(5)/32

GP Starts: 122 (123)   GP Wins: 10   Pole positions: 14   Fastest laps: 9   Points: 206

PICARD, François (F) b 26/4/1921, Villefranche-sur-Saone – d 6/1996, Monte Carlo, Monaco

1958 — Championship position: 0   Wins: 0   Pole positions: 0   Fastest laps: 0   Points scored: 0

	Race	Circuit	No	Entrant	Tyres	Car/Engine	Comment	Q Pos/Entries
ret	MOROCCAN GP (F2)	Casablanca	54	R R C Walker Racing Team	D	1.5 Cooper T43-Climax 4 F2	hit Gendebien's spinning car	24/25

GP Starts: 1   GP Wins: 0   Pole positions: 0   Fastest laps: 0   Points: 0

FRANÇOIS PICARD

Picard began racing in 1949, initially with a Renault 4CV, before switching to a Porsche, with which he won the 1952 Circuit of Agadir. From 1953 on he became a well-known Ferrari privateer, racing mainly in France and North Africa. He gained some good results partnering Charles Pozzi, the pair winning their class at both the Reims and Hyères 12-hour races in 1954. Over the next two seasons, Picard ran a Ferrari 500 Monza, taking numerous placings including second at the 1955 Coupe de Paris, and third in the Agadir GP and Paris 1000 Km in 1956. He continued in sports cars until the Moroccan GP of 1958, when he drove in his first, and only, single-seater race in Rob Walker's Cooper. The unlucky Picard crashed into Gendebien's spinning car, sustaining serious injuries which left him incapacitated for six months. Happily he recovered, but he never raced again.

ERNIE PIETERSE

A leading figure on the South African stage, Ernie raced saloons and GTs, finishing third in an Alfa Giulietta GTI in the 1958 Rand 9 Hours, before eventually joining the burgeoning single-seater series in the early sixties.

Racing an Alfa-engined Heron Special in 1961, he scored his first single-seater victory at Kyalami and later that year won the Rhodesian GP at Belvedere.

He continued with this car into 1962, but soon replaced it with an ex-works Lotus 21-Climax 4, becoming national champion after a thrilling season-long battle with Syd van der Vyver. Joining the Lawson Organisation should have brought even more success in 1963 but, despite a whole clutch of top-three finishes through to the end of 1964, outright wins were to elude him.

Pieterse slipped from competition at this level after failing to qualify for the South African GP on New Year's Day 1965.

PAUL PIETSCH

Pietsch was a notable pre-war driver who, after success aplenty in hill-climbs from the early thirties with an Alfa Romeo 'Monza', was invited to join the Auto Union team in 1935. He did not get many opportunities to race, but shared the third-place car in the 1935 Italian GP with Rosemeyer, before branching out on his own with a Maserati, with which he led the 1939 German GP until plug trouble dropped him to third.

After the war Pietsch concentrated on building up his thriving publishing business, but he found time to race a Maserati and a Veritas, winning the Eifelrennen in the latter in 1951.

He was given a works Alfa Romeo for that year's German GP, but crashed heavily in the race when lying fifth, escaping injury, and after another serious accident at AVUS the following year Pietsch decided to quit for good.

PIETERSE, Ernest (ZA) b 4/7/1938, Parows-Belleville

	1962	Championship position: Unplaced							
	Race	Circuit	No	Entrant	Tyres	Car/Engine		Comment	Q Pos/Entries
10	SOUTH AFRICAN GP	East London	14	Ernest Pieterse	D	1.5 Lotus 21-Climax 4		11 laps behind	=13/27
	1963	Championship position: Unplaced							
ret	SOUTH AFRICAN GP	East London	7	Lawson Organisation	D	1.5 Lotus 21-Climax 4		engine	12/21
	1965	Championship position: Unplaced							
dnq	SOUTH AFRICAN GP	East London	22	Lawson Organisation	D	1.5 Lotus 21-Climax 4			25/25

GP Starts: 2   GP Wins: 0   Pole positions: 0   Fastest laps: 0   Points: 0

PIETSCH, Paul (D) b 20/6/1911, Freiburg im Breisgau

	1950	Championship position: Unplaced							
	Race	Circuit	No	Entrant	Tyres	Car/Engine		Comment	Q Pos/Entries
ret	ITALIAN GP	Monza	28	Paul Pietsch	P	1.5 s/c Maserati 4CLT/48		engine at start	27/27
	1951	Championship position: Unplaced							
ret	GERMAN GP	Nürburgring	78	Alfa Romeo SpA	P	1.5 s/c Alfa Romeo 159 8		spun off	7/23
	1952	Championship position: Unplaced							
ret	GERMAN GP	Nürburgring	127	Motor-Presse-Verlag	–	2.0 Veritas Meteor 6		gearbox	7/32

GP Starts: 3   GP Wins: 0   Pole positions: 0   Fastest laps: 0   Points: 0

ANDRÉ PILETTE

André's father, who had raced at Indianapolis in 1912, finishing fifth, and taken third place in the French GP the same year, died when he was only three. Nevertheless tales of his exploits were to set the youngster on course for a career in motor sport.

After gaining some experience in the late forties with his own machines, Pilette joined the Ecurie Belgique, finally taking their Talbot to sixth place in the 1951 Belgian GP. Then, at the Dutch GP, he had the first of two huge accidents in which he was seriously injured (the second at Albi in 1952 wrote off the Talbot). He reappeared in Claes' Connaught at the Grand Prix at Spa in 1953, and then aligned himself with Gordini for 1954. He competed in only three Grands Prix, but raced in a good number of non-title races, his best results being second places at Chimay and Cadours. Back with his countrymen to form Ecurie Nationale Belge in 1955, Pilette ironically only found success in the Coupe de Paris in a Gordini.

The 1956 season started well, but then he had another bad accident in practice for the German GP, which sidelined him for nearly two years. He finished fourth at Le Mans in 1959, and then second in 1960 with Ricardo Rodriguez in a NART Ferrari.

In 1961 André reappeared in single-seaters, with the ENB Emeryson-Climax, which proved a total flop, but, being a glutton for punishment, he was back in 1963 with an old Lotus 18/21 four-cylinder, before a final fling in the ex-Powell Scirocco in 1964. Subsequently he opened a racing school at Zolder which he ran until the late eighties.

PILETTE, André (B) b 6/10/1918, Paris, France – d 27/12/1993

	1951	Championship position: Unplaced						
	Race	Circuit	No	Entrant	Tyres	Car/Engine	Comment	Q Pos/Entries
6	BELGIAN GP	Spa	24	Ecurie Belgique	E	4.5 Lago-Talbot T26C 6	3 laps behind	12/13
	1953	Championship position: Unplaced						
nc	BELGIAN GP	Spa	40	Ecurie Belge	E	2.0 Connaught A Type-Lea Francis 4	7 laps behind	18/22
	1954	Championship position: 15th= Wins: 0 Pole positions: 0 Fastest laps: 0 Points scored: 2						
5	BELGIAN GP	Spa	18	Equipe Gordini	E	2.5 Gordini Type 16 6	1 lap behind	8/15
9	BRITISH GP	Silverstone	19	Equipe Gordini	E	2.5 Gordini Type 16 6	4 laps behind	12/31
ret	GERMAN GP	Nürburgring	12	Equipe Gordini	E	2.5 Gordini Type 16 6	suspension	20/23
	1956	Championship position: Unplaced						
6*	MONACO GP	Monte Carlo	4	Equipe Gordini	E	2.5 Gordini Type 32 8	* took Bayol's car/-12 laps	– /19
6	BELGIAN GP	Spa	20	Scuderia Ferrari	E	2.5 Lancia-Ferrari D50 V8	3 laps behind	16/16
11	FRENCH GP	Reims	34	Equipe Gordini	E	2.5 Gordini Type 16 6	6 laps behind	19/20
dns	GERMAN GP	Nürburgring	11	Equipe Gordini	E	2.5 Gordini Type 32 8	practice accident	(18)/21
	1961	Championship position: Unplaced						
dnq	ITALIAN GP	Monza	68	André Pilette	D	1.5 Emeryson P-Climax 4		33/33
	1963	Championship position: Unplaced						
dnq	GERMAN GP	Nürburgring	29	Tim Parnell	D	1.5 Lotus 18/21-Climax 4		23/26
dnq	ITALIAN GP	Monza	46	André Pilette	D	1.5 Lotus 18/21-Climax 4		27/28
	1964	Championship position: Unplaced						
ret	BELGIAN GP	Spa	28	Equipe Scirocco Belge	D	1.5 Scirocco 02-Climax V8	engine	20/20
dnq	GERMAN GP	Nürburgring	28	Equipe Scirocco Belge	D	1.5 Scirocco 02-Climax V8		24/24

GP Starts: 9 GP Wins: 0 Pole positions: 0 Fastest laps: 0 Points: 2

PILETTE, Teddy (B) b 26/7/1942, Brussels

	1974	Championship position: Unplaced						
	Race	Circuit	No	Entrant	Tyres	Car/Engine	Comment	Q Pos/Entries
17	BELGIAN GP	Nivelles	34	Motor Racing Developments	G	3.0 Brabham BT42-Cosworth V8	pit stop-tyres/4 laps behind	27/32
	1977	Championship position: Unplaced						
dnq	GERMAN GP	Hockenheim	40	Stanley BRM	G	3.0 BRM P207 V12		30/30
dnq	DUTCH GP	Zandvoort	29	Stanley BRM	G	3.0 BRM P207 V12		33/34
dnq	ITALIAN GP	Monza	29	Stanley BRM	G	3.0 BRM P207 V12		31/34

GP Starts: 1 GP Wins: 0 Pole positions: 0 Fastest laps: 0 Points: 0

PIOTTI, Luigi (I), 27/10/1913 – d 19/4/1971

	1955	Championship position: Unplaced						
	Race	Circuit	No	Entrant	Tyres	Car/Engine	Comment	Q Pos/Entries
dns	ITALIAN GP	Monza	46	Scuderia Volpini/Luigi Piotti	P	2.5 Arzani-Volpini 4	mechanical problems-no time	– / –
	1956	Championship position: Unplaced						
ret	ARGENTINE GP	Buenos Aires	8	Officine Alfieri Maserati	P	2.5 Maserati 250F 6	collision with Collins	12/15
6	ITALIAN GP	Monza	40	Luigi Piotti	P	2.5 Maserati 250F 6	3 laps behind	15/26
	1957	Championship position: Unplaced						
10	ARGENTINE GP	Buenos Aires	28	Luigi Piotti	P	2.5 Maserati 250F 6	10 laps behind	14/26

	Race	Circuit	No	Entrant	Tyres	Car/Engine	Comment	Q Pos/Entries
dnq	MONACO GP	Monte Carlo	42	Luigi Piotti	P	2.5 Maserati 250F 6		20/21
ret	PESCARA GP	Pescara	12	Luigi Piotti	P	2.5 Maserati 250F 6	engine	13/16
ret	ITALIAN GP	Monza	12	Luigi Piotti	P	2.5 Maserati 250F 6	engine	17/19
	1958			Championship position: Unplaced				
dnq	MONACO GP	Monte Carlos	54	Automobili OSCA	–	1.5 OSCA 4 sports car		26/28

GP Starts: 5   GP Wins: 0   Pole positions: 0   Fastest laps: 0   Points: 0

PIPER, David (GB) b 2/12/1930, Edgware, Middlesex

	Race	Circuit	No	Entrant	Tyres	Car/Engine	Comment	Q Pos/Entries
	1959			Championship position: Unplaced				
ret	BRITISH GP	Aintree	64	Dorchester Service Station	D	1.5 Lotus 16-Climax 4 F2	engine-head gasket	22/30
	1960			Championship position: Unplaced				
dns	FRENCH GP	Reims	34	Robert Bodle Ltd	D	2.5 Lotus 16-Climax 4	engine in practice	(21)/23
12	BRITISH GP	Silverstone	26	Robert Bodle Ltd	D	2.5 Lotus 16-Climax 4	5 laps behind	24/25

GP Starts: 2   GP Wins: 0   Pole positions: 0   Fastest laps: 0   Points: 0

TEDDY PILETTE

Teddy followed his father André into the sport but cleared his own path, setting out in Formula Junior in 1962, then having a spell with the Fiat-Abarth GT team.

In 1965 he used a Fiat-Abarth saloon to win his class in the Belgian championship, and he then became involved in what was to be a long-term association with Count van der Straten's VDS team, first driving an Alfa Romeo T33 and then a Lola T70.

In 1971 Pilette began racing in F5000, which is where he found his greatest success, winning the European championship with a Chevron B28 in 1973 and repeating the feat with a Lola T400 in 1975, before heading for a season in the United States.

Pilette finally emulated his father's achievement by starting a Grand Prix in 1974, in a rented Brabham, and later became another of the masochists who tried to qualify the lumbering Stanley-BRM in 1977, even campaigning the dreadful car in the British Aurora AFX series the following year.

In the mid-nineties Pilette returned briefly to the racing scene as a constructor with a Formula 3 car carrying his name. This ill-starred machine was hopelessly outclassed and was soon consigned to history.

LUIGI PIOTTI

A businessman and part-time racer, Piotti achieved minor success in sports cars, including a class win in the 1952 Tour of Sicily in an OSCA, third place in a rather weak Targa Florio with a Lancia in 1954 and a win in the Hyères 12 Hours the same year in a Ferrari with Trintignant.

He made his Formula 1 debut in 1955, taking seventh place in the Syracuse GP in a works Maserati 250F, before purchasing a car for the 1956 season, in which he proved hopelessly slow, especially in the Argentine GP where he continually balked faster cars, eventually colliding with Collins' Ferrari. Later he caused a furore at the Italian GP by using his car to push Moss' fuel-starved machine into the pits and thus give the Englishman a chance to win the race. Piotti plodded through the 1957 season with the Maserati, and after finding little success in an OSCA in 1958 wisely returned to a more sedate occupation.

DAVID PIPER

From farming stock, Piper began his career by competing in sprints and hill-climbs, but soon hit the circuits in a little Lotus XI before buying a Lotus 16 with which, by swapping engines, he raced in both F1 and F2 in 1959-60, perhaps his best result in the car being a second place in the 1960 Lady Wigram Trophy in New Zealand.

In 1961 he joined Jo Siffert on the Continent for a season of Formula Junior racing, before returning home to drive the F1 Gilby in the Gold Cup. Although he did a handful of national F1 races in 1962, he had become disillusioned with single-seaters and bought a Ferrari GTO, which gave his career a new lease of life. Between 1962 and 1970, Piper raced all over the world in his own Ferraris and later Porsches, occasionally winning races in places as far afield as South Africa, Angola, Sweden and Japan, but always proving a reliable driver and a consistent finisher.

In 1970 Piper crashed his Porsche 917 while working on the Steve McQueen film Le Mans, and had the lower part of a leg amputated. Later on, he returned to race in historic events and he has become a mainstay of these enjoyable festivals with his stable of racing thoroughbreds.

NELSON PIQUET

WORLD CHAMPION: 1981, 1983 & 1987

NELSON PIQUET

Three world titles testify to the standing of Nelson Piquet, yet many begrudge him his successes, feeling they were not earned in the manner of a true champion. Of course the Brazilian couldn't have cared less. Racing above all to please himself, he went about things in his own way and that approach generally paid dividends. Never happier than when he had some technical advantage to exploit, Nelson felt no embarrassment at using that edge to beat his hapless rivals.

Having raced karts and Super Vee cars in Brazil, Nelson came to Europe in 1977 to tackle the European F3 series, winning two rounds after switching to a Ralt chassis. The following year he concentrated on F3 once more, this time in Britain. His initial object was to beat his Brazilian rival Chico Serra, who was getting a good press back at home, but eventually it was Derek Warwick who was to be his sternest challenger for the two championships on offer that year. They ended up taking one apiece, but by now Nelson was interesting Formula 1 teams. Mo Nunn gave him a debut in his forgiving Ensign, before the heavy steering of the BS Fabrications McLaren posed more searching questions. However, his practice performance in the third Brabham-Alfa at Montreal prompted Bernie Ecclestone to offer him a contract for 1979.

A superb drive in the Race of Champions took him into second place, and though the Grand Prix season yielded little by way of hard results Nelson was clearly a driver destined for the very top. When Lauda quit towards the end of the season Brabham did not have far to look for a new team leader to handle the Cosworth-powered BT49 in 1980. Nelson took three Grand Prix wins and finished runner-up to Alan Jones that year, and was to go all the way in 1981. After a tense and closely fought season, Piquet typically did just enough to edge out Carlos Reutemann in the final race at Caesars Palace. Realising

that turbo power was now a necessity, Brabham spent the 1982 season bringing their new BMW-engined car to a competitive state – something achieved when Nelson won in Montreal – and then trying to make it reliable. The knowledge gained was then incorporated into the design of Gordon Murray's flat-bottomed 1983 contender which was tailored to the mid-race refuelling tactics the team had pioneered the previous year. At the wheel of the splendid little BT52, Piquet battled with Prost for the title, whittling away the Frenchman's lead before taking the crown at the last gasp at Kyalami. In 1984 the Brabham was no match for the McLarens and even Nelson was left in their wake but, digging deep, he conjured up back-to-back wins in Montreal and Detroit to salvage something from a disappointing year. The end of the superb Piquet–Brabham relationship came in 1985, with Nelson hamstrung by running uncompetitive Pirellis, but there was one last win, at Paul Ricard, when the hard-compound Italian tyres held sway.

Piquet was ready to better his financial position and signed for Williams for 1986. The season should have been a walk-over for the Didcot team, but the atmosphere soon became strained as Nigel Mansell

refused to play second fiddle and set about launching his own title bid. The upshot was that Alain Prost stole the championship at the death, leaving Nelson fuming over Williams' indecisive handling of team tactics. Honda were not pleased either, and would switch to McLaren at the end of the following season. Piquet knew the score in 1987, and set about winning the title despite Mansell. With a good deal of fortune and some help from his luckless team-mate, Nelson did just that. His third title may have been achieved more by stealth than by absolute speed, but the results justified the means in Piquet's book. A two-year spell at Lotus was a complete disaster for all concerned. The massive retainer Nelson picked up from Camel was out of all proportion to his on-track return, and while his bank balance may never have been higher than it was at the end of 1989, never was his stock so low. His subsequent inclusion in the Benetton team for 1990 was greeted with huge surprise, but as the season wore on the wisdom of the move became apparent. Nelson struck up a good working relationship with John Barnard and the pair brought the Benetton B190 to a very competitive pitch, Nelson exploiting others' misfortune to win both the Japanese and Australian GPs. Even his sternest critics were forced to admit that his drive in Adelaide was right out of the top drawer. He was to take one more very fortuitous (but highly satisfying) win at Mansell's expense in Canada the following year before being swept away amid the personnel changes that engulfed the team that season.

With no suitable F1 offers available, Piquet decided to try his hand at the Indianapolis 500 in 1992. Unfortunately a huge crash in practice left him with very badly crushed feet and legs, easily the most severe injuries he had suffered in his long career, and his rehabilitation was long and painful. Nelson vowed never to return to the cockpit but, once fit, he was back at the Brickyard in 1993, and by qualifying for the race he finished the job left uncompleted 12 months earlier.

Competing now mainly for fun, Nelson has since renewed his links with BMW and has raced a 320i tourer in long-distance events both at home and in Europe, usually with Ingo Hoffmann and Johnny Cecotto. Piquet has also made a couple of visits to Le Mans with the Bigazzi McLaren F1 GTR, finishing eighth in 1996 with Cecotto and Danny Sullivan.

Piquet's first World Championship was won in 1981. *Above:* **The Brazilian guides his sleek Brabham into second place in the Dutch Grand Prix at Zandvoort.**

PIQUET, Nelson (BR) b 17/8/1952, Rio de Janeiro

1978 — Championship position: Unplaced

	Race	Circuit	No	Entrant	Tyres	Car/Engine	Comment	Q Pos/Entries
ret	GERMAN GP	Hockenheim	22	Team Tissot Ensign	G	3.0 Ensign N177-Cosworth V8	*engine*	21/30
ret	AUSTRIAN GP	Österreichring	29	BS Fabrications	G	3.0 McLaren M23-Cosworth V8	*slid off in first part of two part race*	20/31
ret	DUTCH GP	Zandvoort	29	BS Fabrications	G	3.0 McLaren M23-Cosworth V8	*driveshaft*	26/33
9	ITALIAN GP	Monza	29	BS Fabrications	G	3.0 McLaren M23-Cosworth V8		24/32
11	CANADIAN GP	Montreal	66	Parmalat Racing Team	G	3.0 Brabham BT46-Alfa Romeo F12	*1 lap behind*	14/28

1979 — Championship position: 15th= Wins: 0 Pole positions: 0 Fastest laps: 1 Points scored: 3

	Race	Circuit	No	Entrant	Tyres	Car/Engine	Comment	Q Pos/Entries
ret/dns	ARGENTINE GP	Buenos Aires	6	Parmalat Racing Team	G	3.0 Brabham BT46-Alfa Romeo F12	*accident-first start-hurt foot*	20/26
ret	BRAZILIAN GP	Interlagos	6	Parmalat Racing Team	G	3.0 Brabham BT48-Alfa Romeo V12	*hit Reutemann*	22/26
7	SOUTH AFRICAN GP	Kyalami	6	Parmalat Racing Team	G	3.0 Brabham BT48-Alfa Romeo V12	*1 lap behind*	12/26
8	US GP WEST	Long Beach	6	Parmalat Racing Team	G	3.0 Brabham BT48-Alfa Romeo V12	*pit stop-tyres/2 laps behind*	12/26
ret	SPANISH GP	Jarama	6	Parmalat Racing Team	G	3.0 Brabham BT48-Alfa Romeo V12	*fuel metering unit*	7/27
ret	BELGIAN GP	Zolder	6	Parmalat Racing Team	G	3.0 Brabham BT48-Alfa Romeo V12	*engine*	3/28
7/ret	MONACO GP	Monte Carlo	6	Parmalat Racing Team	G	3.0 Brabham BT48-Alfa Romeo V12	*driveshaft/8 laps behind*	18/25
ret	FRENCH GP	Dijon	6	Parmalat Racing Team	G	3.0 Brabham BT48-Alfa Romeo V12	*spun off*	4/27
ret	BRITISH GP	Silverstone	6	Parmalat Racing Team	G	3.0 Brabham BT48-Alfa Romeo V12	*spun off-could not restart*	3/26
12/ret	GERMAN GP	Hockenheim	6	Parmalat Racing Team	G	3.0 Brabham BT48-Alfa Romeo V12	*engine/3 laps behind*	4/26
ret	AUSTRIAN GP	Österreichring	6	Parmalat Racing Team	G	3.0 Brabham BT48-Alfa Romeo V12	*engine*	7/26
4	DUTCH GP	Zandvoort	6	Parmalat Racing Team	G	3.0 Brabham BT48-Alfa Romeo V12	*1 lap behind*	11/26
ret	ITALIAN GP	Monza	6	Parmalat Racing Team	G	3.0 Brabham BT48-Alfa Romeo V12	*collision with Regazzoni*	8/28
ret	CANADIAN GP	Montreal	6	Parmalat Racing Team	G	3.0 Brabham BT49-Cosworth V8	*gearbox*	4/29
8/ret	US GP EAST	Watkins Glen	6	Parmalat Racing Team	G	3.0 Brabham BT49-Cosworth V8	*driveshaft/FL/-6 laps*	2/30

1980 — Championship position: 2nd Wins: 3 Pole positions: 2 Fastest laps: 1 Points scored: 54

	Race	Circuit	No	Entrant	Tyres	Car/Engine	Comment	Q Pos/Entries
2	ARGENTINE GP	Buenos Aires	5	Parmalat Racing Team	G	3.0 Brabham BT49-Cosworth V8		4/28
ret	BRAZILIAN GP	Interlagos	5	Parmalat Racing Team	G	3.0 Brabham BT49-Cosworth V8	*suspension failure-accident*	9/28
4	SOUTH AFRICAN GP	Kyalami	5	Parmalat Racing Team	G	3.0 Brabham BT49-Cosworth V8		3/28
1	US GP WEST	Long Beach	5	Parmalat Racing Team	G	3.0 Brabham BT49-Cosworth V8	*FL*	1/27
ret	BELGIAN GP	Zolder	5	Parmalat Racing Team	G	3.0 Brabham BT49-Cosworth V8	*crashed into catch fence*	7/27
3	MONACO GP	Monte Carlo	5	Parmalat Racing Team	G	3.0 Brabham BT49-Cosworth V8		4/27
4	FRENCH GP	Paul Ricard	5	Parmalat Racing Team	G	3.0 Brabham BT49-Cosworth V8		8/27
2	BRITISH GP	Brands Hatch	5	Parmalat Racing Team	G	3.0 Brabham BT49-Cosworth V8		5/27
4	GERMAN GP	Hockenheim	5	Parmalat Racing Team	G	3.0 Brabham BT49-Cosworth V8		6/26
5	AUSTRIAN GP	Österreichring	5	Parmalat Racing Team	G	3.0 Brabham BT49-Cosworth V8		7/25
1	DUTCH GP	Zandvoort	5	Parmalat Racing Team	G	3.0 Brabham BT49-Cosworth V8		5/28
1	ITALIAN GP	Imola	5	Parmalat Racing Team	G	3.0 Brabham BT49-Cosworth V8		5/28
ret	CANADIAN GP	Montreal	5	Parmalat Racing Team	G	3.0 Brabham BT49-Cosworth V8	*engine*	1/28
ret	US GP EAST	Watkins Glen	5	Parmalat Racing Team	G	3.0 Brabham BT49-Cosworth V8	*spun off-push started*	2/27

1981 — Championship position: WORLD CHAMPION Wins: 3 Pole positions: 4 Fastest laps: 1 Points scored: 50

	Race	Circuit	No	Entrant	Tyres	Car/Engine	Comment	Q Pos/Entries
3	US GP WEST	Long Beach	5	Parmalat Racing Team	M	3.0 Brabham BT49C-Cosworth V8		4/29
12	BRAZILIAN GP	Rio	5	Parmalat Racing Team	M	3.0 Brabham BT49C-Cosworth V8	*pit stop-tyres/2 laps behind*	1/30
1	ARGENTINE GP	Buenos Aires	5	Parmalat Racing Team	M	3.0 Brabham BT49C-Cosworth V8	*FL*	1/29
1	SAN MARINO GP	Imola	5	Parmalat Racing Team	M	3.0 Brabham BT49C-Cosworth V8		5/30
ret	BELGIAN GP	Zolder	5	Parmalat Racing Team	M	3.0 Brabham BT49C-Cosworth V8	*collision with Jones*	2/31
ret	MONACO GP	Monte Carlo	5	Parmalat Racing Team	M	3.0 Brabham BT49C-Cosworth V8	*spun off*	1/31
ret	SPANISH GP	Jarama	5	Parmalat Racing Team	M	3.0 Brabham BT49C-Cosworth V8	*collision with Andretti*	9/30
3	FRENCH GP	Dijon	5	Parmalat Racing Team	M	3.0 Brabham BT49C-Cosworth V8		4/29
ret	BRITISH GP	Silverstone	5	Parmalat Racing Team	G	3.0 Brabham BT49C-Cosworth V8	*tyre failure-accident*	3/30
dns	"	"	5	Parmalat Racing Team	G	1.5 t/c Brabham BT50-BMW 4	*practice only*	– / –
1	GERMAN GP	Hockenheim	5	Parmalat Racing Team	G	3.0 Brabham BT49C-Cosworth V8		6/30
3	AUSTRIAN GP	Österreichring	5	Parmalat Racing Team	G	3.0 Brabham BT49C-Cosworth V8		7/28
2	DUTCH GP	Zandvoort	5	Parmalat Racing Team	G	3.0 Brabham BT49C-Cosworth V8		3/30
6/ret	ITALIAN GP	Monza	5	Parmalat Racing Team	G	3.0 Brabham BT49C-Cosworth V8	*engine failed on last lap/-1 lap*	6/30
5	CANADIAN GP	Montreal	5	Parmalat Racing Team	G	3.0 Brabham BT49C-Cosworth V8	*1 lap behind*	1/30
5	CAESARS PALACE GP	Las Vegas	5	Parmalat Racing Team	G	3.0 Brabham BT49C-Cosworth V8		4/30

1982 — Championship position: 11th Wins: 1 Pole positions: 1 Fastest laps: 3 Points scored: 20

	Race	Circuit	No	Entrant	Tyres	Car/Engine	Comment	Q Pos/Entries
ret	SOUTH AFRICAN GP	Kyalami	1	Parmalat Racing Team	G	1.5 t/c Brabham BT50-BMW 4	*spun off*	2/30
dsq*	BRAZILIAN GP	Rio	1	Parmalat Racing Team	G	3.0 Brabham BT49D-Cosworth V8	*1st/* water cooled brakes/FL*	7/31
ret	US GP WEST	Long Beach	1	Parmalat Racing Team	G	3.0 Brabham BT49D-Cosworth V8	*hit wall*	6/31
5*	BELGIAN GP	Zolder	1	Parmalat Racing Team	G	1.5 t/c Brabham BT50-BMW 4	** 3rd car dsq/pit stop/-3 laps*	10/32
ret	MONACO GP	Monte Carlo	1	Parmalat Racing Team	G	1.5 t/c Brabham BT50-BMW 4	*gearbox*	13/31
dnq	US GP (DETROIT)	Detroit	1	Parmalat Racing Team	G	1.5 t/c Brabham BT50-BMW 4		28/28
1	CANADIAN GP	Montreal	1	Parmalat Racing Team	G	1.5 t/c Brabham BT50-BMW 4		4/29
2	DUTCH GP	Zandvoort	1	Parmalat Racing Team	G	1.5 t/c Brabham BT50-BMW 4		3/31
ret	BRITISH GP	Brands Hatch	1	Parmalat Racing Team	G	1.5 t/c Brabham BT50-BMW 4	*fuel metering unit*	3/30
ret	FRENCH GP	Paul Ricard	1	Parmalat Racing Team	G	1.5 t/c Brabham BT50-BMW 4	*engine*	6/30
ret	GERMAN GP	Hockenheim	1	Parmalat Racing Team	G	1.5 t/c Brabham BT50-BMW 4	*accident with Salazar/FL*	4/30
ret	AUSTRIAN GP	Österreichring	1	Parmalat Racing Team	G	1.5 t/c Brabham BT50-BMW 4	*engine/FL*	1/29
4	SWISS GP	Dijon	1	Parmalat Racing Team	G	1.5 t/c Brabham BT50-BMW 4	*pit stop-tyres/fuel/1 lap behind*	6/29
ret	ITALIAN GP	Monza	1	Parmalat Racing Team	G	1.5 t/c Brabham BT50-BMW 4	*clutch*	2/30
ret	CAESARS PALACE GP	Las Vegas	1	Parmalat Racing Team	G	1.5 t/c Brabham BT50-BMW 4	*spark plug electrode*	12/30

1983 — Championship position: WORLD CHAMPION Wins: 3 Pole positions: 1 Fastest laps: 4 Points scored: 59

	Race	Circuit	No	Entrant	Tyres	Car/Engine	Comment	Q Pos/Entries
1	BRAZILIAN GP	Rio	5	Fila Sport	M	1.5 t/c Brabham BT52-BMW 4	*FL*	4/27
ret	US GP WEST	Long Beach	5	Fila Sport	M	1.5 t/c Brabham BT52-BMW 4	*jammed throttle linkage*	20/28
2	FRENCH GP	Paul Ricard	5	Fila Sport	M	1.5 t/c Brabham BT52-BMW 4	*pit stop-fuel*	6/29
ret	SAN MARINO GP	Imola	5	Fila Sport	M	1.5 t/c Brabham BT52-BMW 4	*engine*	2/28

2	MONACO GP	Monte Carlo	5	Fila Sport	M	1.5 t/c Brabham BT52-BMW 4	FL	6/28
4	BELGIAN GP	Spa	5	Fila Sport	M	1.5 t/c Brabham BT52-BMW 4		4/28
4	US GP (DETROIT)	Detroit	5	Fila Sport	M	1.5 t/c Brabham BT52-BMW 4		2/27
ret	CANADIAN GP	Montreal	5	Fila Sport	M	1.5 t/c Brabham BT52-BMW 4	throttle cable	3/28
2	BRITISH GP	Silverstone	5	Fila Sport	M	1.5 t/c Brabham BT52B-BMW 4		6/29
13/ret	GERMAN GP	Hockenheim	5	Fila Sport	M	1.5 t/c Brabham BT52B-BMW 4	fire-leaking fuel/3 laps behind	4/29
3	AUSTRIAN GP	Österreichring	5	Fila Sport	M	1.5 t/c Brabham BT52B-BMW 4		4/29
ret	DUTCH GP	Zandvoort	5	Fila Sport	M	1.5 t/c Brabham BT52B-BMW 4	accident with Prost	1/29
1	ITALIAN GP	Monza	5	Fila Sport	M	1.5 t/c Brabham BT52B-BMW 4	FL	4/29
1	EUROPEAN GP	Brands Hatch	5	Fila Sport	M	1.5 t/c Brabham BT52B-BMW 4		4/29
3	SOUTH AFRICAN GP	Kyalami	5	Fila Sport	M	1.5 t/c Brabham BT52B-BMW 4	FL	2/26

1984   Championship position: 5th   Wins: 2   Pole positions: 9   Fastest laps: 3 (1 shared)   Points scored: 29

ret	BRAZILIAN GP	Rio	1	MRD International	M	1.5 t/c Brabham BT53-BMW 4	engine	7/27
ret	SOUTH AFRICAN GP	Kyalami	1	MRD International	M	1.5 t/c Brabham BT53-BMW 4	turbo	1/27
9*/ret	BELGIAN GP	Zolder	1	MRD International	M	1.5 t/c Brabham BT53-BMW 4	engine/*6th car dsq/-4 laps	9/27
ret	SAN MARINO GP	Imola	1	MRD International	M	1.5 t/c Brabham BT53-BMW 4	turbo/FL	1/28
ret	FRENCH GP	Dijon	1	MRD International	M	1.5 t/c Brabham BT53-BMW 4	turbo	3/27
ret	MONACO GP	Monte Carlo	1	MRD International	M	1.5 t/c Brabham BT53-BMW 4	wet electrics	9/27
1	CANADIAN GP	Montreal	1	MRD International	M	1.5 t/c Brabham BT53-BMW 4	FL	1/26
1	US GP (DETROIT)	Detroit	1	MRD International	M	1.5 t/c Brabham BT53-BMW 4		1/27
ret	US GP (DALLAS)	Dallas	1	MRD International	M	1.5 t/c Brabham BT53-BMW 4	jammed throttle hit wall	12/27
7	BRITISH GP	Brands Hatch	1	MRD International	M	1.5 t/c Brabham BT53-BMW 4	lost turbo boost/1 lap behind	1/27
ret	GERMAN GP	Hockenheim	1	MRD International	M	1.5 t/c Brabham BT53-BMW 4	gearbox	5/27
2	AUSTRIAN GP	Österreichring	1	MRD International	M	1.5 t/c Brabham BT53-BMW 4		1/28
ret	DUTCH GP	Zandvoort	1	MRD International	M	1.5 t/c Brabham BT53-BMW 4	oil pressure-loose oil union	2/27
ret	ITALIAN GP	Monza	1	MRD International	M	1.5 t/c Brabham BT53-BMW 4	engine	1/27
3	EUROPEAN GP	Nürburgring	1	MRD International	M	1.5 t/c Brabham BT53-BMW 4	FL (shared with Alboreto)	1/26
6	PORTUGUESE GP	Estoril	1	MRD International	M	1.5 t/c Brabham BT53-BMW 4	spin/1 lap behind	1/27

1985   Championship position: 8th   Wins: 1   Pole positions: 1   Fastest laps: 0   Points scored: 21

ret	BRAZILIAN GP	Rio	7	Motor Racing Developments Ltd	P	1.5 t/c Brabham BT54-BMW 4	transmission	8/25
ret	PORTUGUESE GP	Estoril	7	Motor Racing Developments Ltd	P	1.5 t/c Brabham BT54-BMW 4	tyres/handling	10/26
8	SAN MARINO GP	Imola	7	Motor Racing Developments Ltd	P	1.5 t/c Brabham BT54-BMW 4	pit stop-tyres/out of fuel-/3 laps	9/26
ret	MONACO GP	Monte Carlo	7	Motor Racing Developments Ltd	P	1.5 t/c Brabham BT54-BMW 4	accident with Patrese	13/26
ret	CANADIAN GP	Montreal	7	Motor Racing Developments Ltd	P	1.5 t/c Brabham BT54-BMW 4	transmission	9/25
6	US GP (DETROIT)	Detroit	7	Motor Racing Developments Ltd	P	1.5 t/c Brabham BT54-BMW 4	1 lap behind	10/25
1	FRENCH GP	Paul Ricard	7	Motor Racing Developments Ltd	P	1.5 t/c Brabham BT54-BMW 4		5/26
4	BRITISH GP	Silverstone	7	Motor Racing Developmants Ltd	P	1.5 t/c Brabham BT54-BMW 4	1 lap behind	2/26
ret	GERMAN GP	Nürburgring	7	Motor Racing Developments Ltd	P	1.5 t/c Brabham BT54-BMW 4	turbo	6/27
ret	AUSTRIAN GP	Österreichring	7	Motor Racing Developments Ltd	P	1.5 t/c Brabham BT54-BMW 4	exhaust	5/27
8	DUTCH GP	Zandvoort	7	Motor Racing Developments Ltd	P	1.5 t/c Brabham BT54-BMW 4	stalled on grid/1 lap behind/	1/27
2	ITALIAN GP	Monza	7	Motor Racing Developments Ltd	P	1.5 t/c Brabham BT54-BMW 4		4/26
5	BELGIAN GP	Spa	7	Motor Racing Developments Ltd	P	1.5 t/c Brabham BT54-BMW 4	1 lap behind	3/24
ret	EUROPEAN GP	Brands Hatch	7	Motor Racing Developments Ltd	P	1.5 t/c Brabham BT54-BMW 4	hit Rosberg's spinning car	2/27
ret	SOUTH AFRICAN GP	Kyalami	7	Motor Racing Developments Ltd	P	1.5 t/c Brabham BT54-BMW 4	engine	2/21
ret	AUSTRALIAN GP	Adelaide	7	Motor Racing Developments Ltd	P	1.5 t/c Brabham BT54-BMW 4	electrical fire	9/25

1986   Championship position: 3rd   Wins: 4   Pole positions: 2   Fastest laps: 7   Points scored: 69

1	BRAZILIAN GP	Rio	6	Canon Williams Team	G	1.5 t/c Williams FW11-Honda V6	FL	2/25
ret	SPANISH GP	Jerez	6	Canon Williams Team	G	1.5 t/c Williams FW11-Honda V6	overheating	2/25
2	SAN MARINO GP	Imola	6	Canon Williams Team	G	1.5 t/c Williams FW11-Honda V6	FL	2/26
7	MONACO GP	Monte Carlo	6	Canon Williams Team	G	1.5 t/c Williams FW11-Honda V6	1 lap behind	11/26
ret	BELGIAN GP	Spa	6	Canon Williams Team	G	1.5 t/c Williams FW11-Honda V6	turbo boost control	1/25
3	CANADIAN GP	Montreal	6	Canon Williams Team	G	1.5 t/c Williams FW11-Honda V6	FL	3/25
ret	US GP (DETROIT)	Detroit	6	Canon Williams Team	G	1.5 t/c Williams FW11-Honda V6	hit wall/FL	3/26
3	FRENCH GP	Paul Ricard	6	Canon Williams Team	G	1.5 t/c Williams FW11-Honda V6		3/26
2	BRITISH GP	Brands Hatch	6	Canon Williams Team	G	1.5 t/c Williams FW11-Honda V6		1/26
1	GERMAN GP	Hockenheim	6	Canon Williams Team	G	1.5 t/c Williams FW11-Honda V6		5/26
1	HUNGARIAN GP	Hungaroring	6	Canon Williams Team	G	1.5 t/c Williams FW11-Honda V6	FL	2/26
ret	AUSTRIAN GP	Österreichring	6	Canon Williams Team	G	1.5 t/c Williams FW11-Honda V6	engine	7/26
1	ITALIAN GP	Monza	6	Canon Williams Team	G	1.5 t/c Williams FW11-Honda V6		6/27
3	PORTUGUESE GP	Estoril	6	Canon Williams Team	G	1.5 t/c Williams FW11-Honda V6		6/27
4	MEXICAN GP	Mexico City	6	Canon Williams Team	G	1.5 t/c Williams FW11-Honda V6	1 lap behind/FL	2/26
2	AUSTRALIAN GP	Adelaide	6	Canon Williams Team	G	1.5 t/c Williams FW11-Honda V6	precautionary tyre stop/FL	2/26

1987   Championship position: WORLD CHAMPION   Wins: 3   Pole positions: 4   Fastest laps: 4   Points scored: 76

2	BRAZILIAN GP	Rio	6	Canon Williams Team	G	1.5 t/c Williams FW11B-Honda V6	FL	2/23
dns	SAN MARINO GP	Imola	6	Canon Williams Team	G	1.5 t/c Williams FW11B-Honda V6	accident/not allowed to start	(3)/27
ret	BELGIAN GP	Spa	6	Canon Williams Team	G	1.5 t/c Williams FW11B-Honda V6	turbo sensor	2/26
2	MONACO GP	Monte Carlo	6	Canon Williams Team	G	1.5 t/c Williams FW11B-Honda V6		3/26
2	US GP (DETROIT)	Detroit	6	Canon Williams Team	G	1.5 t/c Williams FW11B-Honda V6		3/26
2	FRENCH GP	Paul Ricard	6	Canon Williams Team	G	1.5 t/c Williams FW11B-Honda V6	FL	4/26
2	BRITISH GP	Silverstone	6	Canon Williams Team	G	1.5 t/c Williams FW11B-Honda V6		1/26
1	GERMAN GP	Hockenheim	6	Canon Williams Team	G	1.5 t/c Williams FW11B-Honda V6		4/26
1	HUNGARIAN GP	Hungaroring	6	Canon Williams Team	G	1.5 t/c Williams FW11B-Honda V6	FL	3/26
2	AUSTRIAN GP	Österreichring	6	Canon Williams Team	G	1.5 t/c Williams FW11B-Honda V6		1/26
1	ITALIAN GP	Monza	6	Canon Williams Team	G	1.5 t/c Williams FW11B-Honda V6		1/28
3	PORTUGUESE GP	Estoril	6	Canon Williams Team	G	1.5 t/c Williams FW11B-Honda V6		4/27
4	SPANISH GP	Jerez	6	Canon Williams Team	G	1.5 t/c Williams FW11B-Honda V6		1/28
2	MEXICAN GP	Mexico City	6	Canon Williams Team	G	1.5 t/c Williams FW11B-Honda V6	FL	3/27
15/ret	JAPANESE GP	Suzuka	6	Canon Williams Team	G	1.5 t/c Williams FW11B-Honda V6	engine/5 laps behind	5/27
ret	AUSTRALIAN GP	Adelaide	6	Canon Williams Team	G	1.5 t/c Williams FW11B-Honda V6	brakes/gear linkage	3/27

1988
Championship position: 6th=   Wins: 0   Pole positions: 0   Fastest laps: 0   Points scored: 22

Pos	Race	Circuit	No	Entrant	Tyres	Car/Engine	Comment	Q Pos/Entries
3	BRAZILIAN GP	Rio	1	Camel Team Lotus Honda	G	1.5 t/c Lotus 100T-Honda V6		5/31
3	SAN MARINO GP	Imola	1	Camel Team Lotus Honda	G	1.5 t/c Lotus 100T-Honda V6	1 lap behind	3/31
ret	MONACO GP	Monte Carlo	1	Camel Team Lotus Honda	G	1.5 t/c Lotus 100T-Honda V6	accident damage	11/30
ret	MEXICAN GP	Mexico City	1	Camel Team Lotus Honda	G	1.5 t/c Lotus 100T-Honda V6	engine	4/30
4	CANADIAN GP	Montreal	1	Camel Team Lotus Honda	G	1.5 t/c Lotus 100T-Honda V6	1 lap behind	6/31
ret	US GP (DETROIT)	Detroit	1	Camel Team Lotus Honda	G	1.5 t/c Lotus 100T-Honda V6	spun off	8/31
5	FRENCH GP	Paul Ricard	1	Camel Team Lotus Honda	G	1.5 t/c Lotus 100T-Honda V6	1 lap behind	7/31
5	BRITISH GP	Silverstone	1	Camel Team Lotus Honda	G	1.5 t/c Lotus 100T-Honda V6		7/31
ret	GERMAN GP	Hockenheim	1	Camel Team Lotus Honda	G	1.5 t/c Lotus 100T-Honda V6	dry tyres-wet race-spun off	5/31
8	HUNGARIAN GP	Hungaroring	1	Camel Team Lotus Honda	G	1.5 t/c Lotus 100T-Honda V6	hit Martini-pit stop/-3 laps	13/31
4*	BELGIAN GP	Spa	1	Camel Team Lotus Honda	G	1.5 t/c Lotus 100T-Honda V6	*3rd & 4th place cars dsq	9/31
ret	ITALIAN GP	Monza	1	Camel Team Lotus Honda	G	1.5 t/c Lotus 100T-Honda V6	clutch/spun off	7/31
ret	PORTUGUESE GP	Estoril	1	Camel Team Lotus Honda	G	1.5 t/c Lotus 100T-Honda V6	clutch	8/31
8	SPANISH GP	Jerez	1	Camel Team Lotus Honda	G	1.5 t/c Lotus 100T-Honda V6		9/31
ret	JAPANESE GP	Suzuka	1	Camel Team Lotus Honda	G	1.5 t/c Lotus 100T-Honda V6	driver unwell	5/31
3	AUSTRALIAN GP	Adelaide	1	Camel Team Lotus Honda	G	1.5 t/c Lotus 100T-Honda V6		5/31

1989
Championship position: 8th   Wins: 0   Pole positions: 0   Fastest laps: 0   Points scored: 12

Pos	Race	Circuit	No	Entrant	Tyres	Car/Engine	Comment	Q Pos/Entries
ret	BRAZILIAN GP	Rio	11	Camel Team Lotus	G	3.5 Lotus 101-Judd V8	fuel pump	9/38
ret	SAN MARINO GP	Imola	11	Camel Team Lotus	G	3.5 Lotus 101-Judd V8	engine	8/39
ret	MONACO GP	Monte Carlo	11	Camel Team Lotus	G	3.5 Lotus 101-Judd V8	collision with de Cesaris	19/38
11	MEXICAN GP	Mexico City	11	Camel Team Lotus	G	3.5 Lotus 101-Judd V8	understeer/1 lap behind	26/39
ret	US GP (PHOENIX)	Phoenix	11	Camel Team Lotus	G	3.5 Lotus 101-Judd V8	hit wall	22/39
4	CANADIAN GP	Montreal	11	Camel Team Lotus	G	3.5 Lotus 101-Judd V8	2 pit stops-tyres/low oil pressure	19/39
8	FRENCH GP	Paul Ricard	11	Camel Team Lotus	G	3.5 Lotus 101-Judd V8	2 pit stops-tyres/-2 laps	20/39
4	BRITISH GP	Silverstone	11	Camel Team Lotus	G	3.5 Lotus 101-Judd V8		10/39
5	GERMAN GP	Hockenheim	11	Camel Team Lotus	G	3.5 Lotus 101-Judd V8	pit stop-tyres/1 lap behind	8/39
6	HUNGARIAN GP	Hungaroring	11	Camel Team Lotus	G	3.5 Lotus 101-Judd V8	pit stop-tyres	17/39
dnq	BELGIAN GP	Spa	11	Camel Team Lotus	G	3.5 Lotus 101-Judd V8		28/39
ret	ITALIAN GP	Monza	11	Camel Team Lotus	G	3.5 Lotus 101-Judd V8	spun avoiding Gachot	11/39
ret	PORTUGUESE GP	Estoril	11	Camel Team Lotus	G	3.5 Lotus 101-Judd V8	collision with Caffi	20/39
8	SPANISH GP	Jerez	11	Camel Team Lotus	G	3.5 Lotus 101-Judd V8	2 stops-tyres-puncture/-2 laps	7/38
4*	JAPANESE GP	Suzuka	11	Camel Team Lotus	G	3.5 Lotus 101-Judd V8	* 1st place car dsq	11/39
ret	AUSTRALIAN GP	Adelaide	11	Camel Team Lotus	G	3.5 Lotus 101-Judd V8	hit Ghinzani in rain	18/39

1990
Championship position: 3rd   Wins: 2   Pole positions: 0   Fastest laps: 0   Points scored: 44

Pos	Race	Circuit	No	Entrant	Tyres	Car/Engine	Comment	Q Pos/Entries
4	US GP (PHOENIX)	Phoenix	20	Benetton Formula	G	3.5 Benetton B189B-Ford HB V8	pit stop-tyres	6/35
6	BRAZILIAN GP	Interlagos	20	Benetton Formula	G	3.5 Benetton B189B-Ford HB V8	1 lap behind	13/35
5	SAN MARINO GP	Imola	20	Benetton Formula	G	3.5 Benetton B190-Ford HB V8	collision-Alesi/pit stop-tyres	8/34
dsq	MONACO GP	Monte Carlo	20	Benetton Formula	G	3.5 Benetton B190-Ford HB V8	spin-push start-black flagged	10/35
2	CANADIAN GP	Montreal	20	Benetton Formula	G	3.5 Benetton B190-Ford HB V8		5/35
6	MEXICAN GP	Mexico City	20	Benetton Formula	G	3.5 Benetton B190-Ford HB V8	pit stop-tyres	8/35
4	FRENCH GP	Paul Ricard	20	Benetton Formula	G	3.5 Benetton B190-Ford HB V8	pit stop-tyres	9/35
5	BRITISH GP	Silverstone	20	Benetton Formula	G	3.5 Benetton B190-Ford HB V8	started from back/lost bodywork	11/35
ret	GERMAN GP	Hockenheim	20	Benetton Formula	G	3.5 Benetton B190-Ford HB V8	engine	7/35
3	HUNGARIAN GP	Hungaroring	20	Benetton Formula	G	3.5 Benetton B190-Ford HB V8	electrical problems	9/35
5	BELGIAN GP	Spa	20	Benetton Formula	G	3.5 Benetton B190-Ford HB V8	understeer/no clutch	8/33
7	ITALIAN GP	Monza	20	Benetton Formula	G	3.5 Benetton B190-Ford HB V8	pit stop-puncture/-1 lap	9/33
5	PORTUGUESE GP	Estoril	20	Benetton Formula	G	3.5 Benetton B190-Ford HB V8	pit stop-tyres	6/33
ret	SPANISH GP	Jerez	20	Benetton Formula	G	3.5 Benetton B190-Ford HB V8	electrics	8/33
1	JAPANESE GP	Suzuka	20	Benetton Formula	G	3.5 Benetton B190-Ford HB V8		6/30
1	AUSTRALIAN GP	Adelaide	20	Benetton Formula	G	3.5 Benetton B190-Ford HB V8		7/30

1991
Championship position: 6th   Wins: 1   Pole positions: 0   Fastest laps: 0   Points scored: 26.5

Pos	Race	Circuit	No	Entrant	Tyres	Car/Engine	Comment	Q Pos/Entries
3	US GP (PHOENIX)	Phoenix	20	Camel Benetton Ford	P	3.5 Benetton B190B-Ford HB V8		5/34
5	BRAZILIAN GP	Interlagos	20	Camel Benetton Ford	P	3.5 Benetton B190B-Ford HB V8		7/34
ret	SAN MARINO GP	Imola	20	Camel Benetton Ford	P	3.5 Benetton B191-Ford HB V8	spun off lap 1	14/34
ret	MONACO GP	Monte Carlo	20	Camel Benetton Ford	P	3.5 Benetton B191-Ford HB V8	hit by Berger-suspension	4/34
1	CANADIAN GP	Montreal	20	Camel Benetton Ford	P	3.5 Benetton B191-Ford HB V8		8/34
ret	MEXICAN GP	Mexico City	20	Camel Benetton Ford	P	3.5 Benetton B191-Ford HB V8	wheel bearing	6/34
8	FRENCH GP	Magny Cours	20	Camel Benetton Ford	P	3.5 Benetton B191-Ford HB V8	2 laps behind	7/34
5	BRITISH GP	Silverstone	20	Camel Benetton Ford	P	3.5 Benetton B191-Ford HB V8		8/34
ret	GERMAN GP	Hockenheim	20	Camel Benetton Ford	P	3.5 Benetton B191-Ford HB V8	engine	8/34
ret	HUNGARIAN GP	Hungaroring	20	Camel Benetton Ford	P	3.5 Benetton B191-Ford HB V8	gearbox	11/34
3	BELGIAN GP	Spa	20	Camel Benetton Ford	P	3.5 Benetton B191-Ford HB V8		6/34
6	ITALIAN GP	Monza	20	Camel Benetton Ford	P	3.5 Benetton B191-Ford HB V8		8/34
5	PORTUGUESE GP	Estoril	20	Camel Benetton Ford	P	3.5 Benetton B191-Ford HB V8		11/34
11	SPANISH GP	Barcelona	20	Camel Benetton Ford	P	3.5 Benetton B191-Ford HB V8	electrics/wet set up/-2 laps	10/33
7	JAPANESE GP	Suzuka	20	Camel Benetton Ford	P	3.5 Benetton B191-Ford HB V8	1 lap behind	10/30
4*	AUSTRALIAN GP	Adelaide	20	Camel Benetton Ford	P	3.5 Benetton B191-Ford HB V8	* rain shortened race half points	5/32

GP Starts: 203 (204)   GP Wins: 23   Pole positions: 24   Fastest laps: 23   Points: 485.5

PIROCCHI, Renato (I) b 26/6/1933, Notaresco, Teramo

1961
Championship position: Unplaced

Pos	Race	Circuit	No	Entrant	Tyres	Car/Engine	Comment	Q Pos/Entries
12	ITALIAN GP	Monza	58	Pescara Racing Club	D	1.5 Cooper T51-Maserati 4	5 laps behind	29/33

GP Starts: 1   GP Wins: 0   Pole positions: 0   Fastest laps: 0   Points: 0

RENATO PIROCCHI

After a promising start in small-capacity Stanguellini sports cars in the mid-fifties, Pirocchi was to become one of the stars of the Italian Formula Junior series, then in its infancy. In 1959 he raced a Taraschi and began a friendly rivalry with Bandini, the pair enjoying a spectacular dice at Syracuse in particular. For the following year, Renato switched to a Stanguellini chassis in common with most of his competitors and ended a marvellous season as Italian champion, although probably his most important win was in the prestigious Havana GP in Cuba.

Pirocchi's brief flirtation with Formula 1 machinery in 1961 was to be less successful. Driving a rather tired Cooper entered by the Pescara Racing Club, and on one occasion a Scuderia Centro Sud Cooper (as number two to his old sparring partner Bandini), he was, at best, a backmarker.

DIDIER PIRONI

Pironi's ambition to become France's first-ever World Champion driver was never realised. The crash at Hockenheim in 1982 which destroyed his career and almost cost him his legs would see to that, leaving the cool and unemotional Frenchman to fight the greater battle of learning to walk again, while Alain Prost was enjoying his nation's plaudits in 1985.

Didier's interest in motor racing was awakened by a visit to a meeting with his cousin José Dolhem, and as soon as he was old enough he attended the Winfield racing school, winning the prize of an Elf-sponsored Martini for 1973. It was a hard learning year for the young Pironi, who, rather than whingeing, clinically analysed all the ingredients that were lacking in his first season and set about putting them into place for his return in 1974. His attention to detail obviously paid dividends for Pironi became French Formule Renault champion at the wheel of a Martini MK14.

Moving into Formule Super Renault in 1975 as number two to René Arnoux, Didier dutifully supported his team-mate before taking over the number one seat a year later. His dominance was almost total and he ran away with the championship, gaining promotion to the Elf Martini Formula 2 squad in 1977, again as number two to Arnoux. While he was finding his feet in this category, Pironi gambled on dropping into Formula 3 for just one event, the Monaco Formula 3 race. His reasoning was sound, for a win here would be a valuable calling card in his future dealings. Naturally mission was accomplished and he resumed his Formula 2 racing with the air of a man who knew his destiny. Raising his game, by the end of the year he had taken his first win at Estoril, and earned a Grand Prix contract with Tyrrell for the 1978 season.

As one now expected of this coolest of customers, his first tilt at the big time was accomplished with all the aplomb of a seasoned veteran. Finishing four of his first six races in the points maybe raised expectations a little too high, as he ended the year with a few shunts. However, there was also the considerable kudos of a win at Le Mans in the Elf-backed Alpine-Renault to reinforce his burgeoning reputation. In fact Didier was top of the turbo team's shopping list for 1979, but Tyrrell kept him to his contract, and thus he spent the year looking for an escape route, which he found in the shape of a move to Ligier for 1980.

Overshadowing the incumbent, Jacques Laffite, with some stunning drives, Pironi took his first Grand Prix win at Zolder, and was unlucky not to win the British GP at Brands Hatch after a brilliant drive through the field. With Jody Scheckter heading for retirement, another door opened for Didier, who joined Villeneuve at Maranello for 1981. The new turbo cars were unrefined, but Gilles was at his brilliant best, leaving Pironi groping somewhat for the first time. Clearly a single fourth place was unacceptable to Ferrari, but it was doubly so to Pironi, who resolved not to be found wanting in 1982.

Four races into what was to prove a bitter and tragic season came a flashpoint at Imola when Pironi stole the win from Villeneuve on the last lap against team orders. All lines of communication between the two drivers were cut. Two weeks later at Zolder came Villeneuve's horrendous fatal accident, and previous feudings were now irrelevant. Didier, now centre stage at Ferrari, unleashed a superb run of impressive performances which came to an end when, unsighted in pouring rain, he ran into Prost's Renault in practice for the German GP. Pironi's season was over and his total of 39 points left him tantalisingly within touching distance of the title before Keke Rosberg edged him out by a mere five points.

Although, almost miraculously, Pironi's feet and ankles were saved, he would never regain the feel and movement necessary to allow him to return to the cockpit. For thrills he turned to the dangerous sport of powerboat racing, which became a lethal pastime when he crashed off the Isle of Wight in August 1987.

PIRONI, Didier (F) b 26/3/1952, Villecresnes, nr Paris – d 23/8/1987, off the Isle of Wight, England

1978
Championship position: 15th   Wins: 0   Pole positions: 0   Fastest laps: 0   Points scored: 7

	Race	Circuit	No	Entrant	Tyres	Car/Engine	Comment	Q Pos/Entries
14	ARGENTINE GP	Buenos Aires	3	Elf Team Tyrrell	G	3.0 Tyrrell 008-Cosworth V8	1 lap behind	23/27
6	BRAZILIAN GP	Rio	3	Elf Team Tyrrell	G	3.0 Tyrrell 008-Cosworth V8	1 lap behind	19/28
6	SOUTH AFRICAN GP	Kyalami	3	Elf Team Tyrrell	G	3.0 Tyrrell 008-Cosworth V8	1 lap behind	14/30
ret	US GP WEST	Long Beach	3	Elf Team Tyrrell	G	3.0 Tyrrell 008-Cosworth V8	gearbox	24/30
5	MONACO GP	Monte Carlo	3	Elf Team Tyrrell	G	3.0 Tyrrell 008-Cosworth V8		13/30
6	BELGIAN GP	Zolder	3	Elf Team Tyrrell	G	3.0 Tyrrell 008-Cosworth V8	1 lap behind	23/30
12	SPANISH GP	Jarama	3	Elf Team Tyrrell	G	3.0 Tyrrell 008-Cosworth V8	pit stop/distributor/4 laps behind	13/29
ret	SWEDISH GP	Anderstrop	3	Elf Team Tyrrell	G	3.0 Tyrrell 008-Cosworth V8	collision with Brambilla	17/27
10	FRENCH GP	Paul Ricard	3	Elf Team Tyrrell	G	3.0 Tyrrell 008-Cosworth V8		16/29
ret	BRITISH GP	Brands Hatch	3	Elf Team Tyrrell	G	3.0 Tyrrell 008-Cosworth V8	gearbox mounting bolts	19/30
5	GERMAN GP	Hockenheim	3	Elf Team Tyrrell	G	3.0 Tyrrell 008-Cosworth V8		16/30
ret	AUSTRIAN GP	Österreichring	3	Elf Team Tyrrell	G	3.0 Tyrrell 008-Cosworth V8	crashed	9/31
ret	DUTCH GP	Zandvoort	3	Elf Team Tyrrell	G	3.0 Tyrrell 008-Cosworth V8	accident with Patrese	17/33
ret/dns	ITALIAN GP	Monza	3	Elf Team Tyrrell	G	3.0 Tyrrell 008-Cosworth V8	accident-first start	(14)/32
10	US GP EAST	Watkins Glen	3	Elf Team Tyrrell	G	3.0 Tyrrell 008-Cosworth V8	1 lap behind	16/27
7	CANADIAN GP	Montreal	3	Elf Team Tyrrell	G	3.0 Tyrrell 008-Cosworth V8		18/28

1979
Championship position: 10th=   Wins: 0   Pole positions: 0   Fastest laps: 0   Points scored: 14

	Race	Circuit	No	Entrant	Tyres	Car/Engine	Comment	Q Pos/Entries
ret/dns	ARGENTINE GP	Buenos Aires	3	Team Tyrrell	G	3.0 Tyrrell 009-Cosworth V8	accident-first start	(8)/26
4	BRAZILIAN GP	Interlagos	3	Team Tyrrell	G	3.0 Tyrrell 009-Cosworth V8		8/26
ret	SOUTH AFRICAN GP	Kyalami	3	Team Tyrrell	G	3.0 Tyrrell 009-Cosworth V8	throttle linkage	7/26
dsq	US GP WEST	Long Beach	3	Team Tyrrell	G	3.0 Tyrrell 009-Cosworth V8	push start after spin	17/26
6	SPANISH GP	Jarama	3	Team Tyrrell	G	3.0 Tyrrell 009-Cosworth V8		10/27
3	BELGIAN GP	Zolder	3	Candy Tyrrell Team	G	3.0 Tyrrell 009-Cosworth V8		12/28
ret	MONACO GP	Monte Carlo	3	Candy Tyrrell Team	G	3.0 Tyrrell 009-Cosworth V8	accident with Lauda	7/25
ret	FRENCH GP	Dijon	3	Candy Tyrrell Team	G	3.0 Tyrrell 009-Cosworth V8	suspension	11/27
10	BRITISH GP	Silverstone	3	Candy Tyrrell Team	G	3.0 Tyrrell 009-Cosworth V8	pit stop/2 laps behind	15/26
9	GERMAN GP	Hockenheim	3	Candy Tyrrell Team	G	3.0 Tyrrell 009-Cosworth V8	pit stop/1 lap behind	8/26
7	AUSTRIAN GP	Österreichring	3	Candy Tyrrell Team	G	3.0 Tyrrell 009-Cosworth V8	1 lap behind	10/26
ret	DUTCH GP	Zandvoort	3	Candy Tyrrell Team	G	3.0 Tyrrell 009-Cosworth V8	rear suspension	10/26
10	ITALIAN GP	Monza	3	Candy Tyrrell Team	G	3.0 Tyrrell 009-Cosworth V8	pit stop-hit by Watson/-1 lap	12/28
5	CANADIAN GP	Montreal	3	Candy Tyrrell Team	G	3.0 Tyrrell 009-Cosworth V8	1 lap behind	6/29
3	US GP EAST	Watkins Glen	3	Candy Tyrrell Team	G	3.0 Tyrrell 009-Cosworth V8		10/30

1980
Championship position: 5th   Wins: 1   Pole positions: 2   Fastest laps: 2   Points scored: 32

	Race	Circuit	No	Entrant	Tyres	Car/Engine	Comment	Q Pos/Entries
ret	ARGENTINE GP	Buenos Aires	25	Equipe Ligier Gitanes	G	3.0 Ligier JS11/15-Cosworth V8	engine	3/28
4	BRAZILIAN GP	Interlagos	25	Equipe Ligier Gitanes	G	3.0 Ligier JS11/15-Cosworth V8		2/28
3	SOUTH AFRICAN GP	Kyalami	25	Equipe Ligier Gitanes	G	3.0 Ligier JS11/15-Cosworth V8		5/28
6	US GP WEST	Long Beach	25	Equipe Ligier Gitanes	G	3.0 Ligier JS11/15-Cosworth V8	1 lap behind	9/27
1	BELGIAN GP	Zolder	25	Equipe Ligier Gitanes	G	3.0 Ligier JS11/15-Cosworth V8		2/27
ret	MONACO GP	Monte Carlo	25	Equipe Ligier Gitanes	G	3.0 Ligier JS11/15-Cosworth V8	gearbox/hit barrier when 1st	1/27
2	FRENCH GP	Paul Ricard	25	Equipe Ligier Gitanes	G	3.0 Ligier JS11/15-Cosworth V8		=2/27
ret	BRITISH GP	Brands Hatch	25	Equipe Ligier Gitanes	G	3.0 Ligier JS11/15-Cosworth V8	rim/tyre failure/crashed/FL	1/27
ret	GERMAN GP	Hockenheim	25	Equipe Ligier Gitanes	G	3.0 Ligier JS11/15-Cosworth V8	driveshaft	7/26
ret	AUSTRIAN GP	Österreichring	25	Equipe Ligier Gitanes	G	3.0 Ligier JS11/15-Cosworth V8	handling	6/25
ret	DUTCH GP	Zandvoort	25	Equipe Ligier Gitanes	G	3.0 Ligier JS11/15-Cosworth V8	accident with de Angelis	15/28
6	ITALIAN GP	Imola	25	Equipe Ligier Gitanes	G	3.0 Ligier JS11/15-Cosworth V8	1 lap behind	13/28
3*	CANADIAN GP	Montreal	25	Equipe Ligier Gitanes	G	3.0 Ligier JS11/15-Cosworth V8	* 1st-but 1 min penalty/FL	3/28
3	US GP EAST	Watkins Glen	25	Equipe Ligier Gitanes	G	3.0 Ligier JS11/15-Cosworth V8		7/27

1981
Championship position: 13th   Wins: 0   Pole positions: 0   Fastest laps: 1   Points scored: 9

	Race	Circuit	No	Entrant	Tyres	Car/Engine	Comment	Q Pos/Entries
ret	US GP WEST	Long Beach	28	Scuderia Ferrari SpA SEFAC	M	1.5 t/c Ferrari 126CK V6	engine	11/29
ret	BRAZILIAN GP	Rio	28	Scuderia Ferrari SpA SEFAC	M	1.5 t/c Ferrari 126CK V6	collision with Prost	17/30
ret	ARGENTINE GP	Buenos Aires	28	Scuderia Ferrari SpA SEFAC	M	1.5 t/c Ferrari 126CK V6	engine	12/29
5	SAN MARINO GP	Imola	28	Scuderia Ferrari SpA SEFAC	M	1.5 t/c Ferrari 126CK V6		6/30
8	BELGIAN GP	Zolder	28	Scuderia Ferrari SpA SEFAC	M	1.5 t/c Ferrari 126CK V6	led race until brake problems	3/31
4	MONACO GP	Monte Carlo	28	Scuderia Ferrari SpA SEFAC	M	1.5 t/c Ferrari 126CK V6	1 lap behind	17/31
15	SPANISH GP	Jarama	28	Scuderia Ferrari SpA SEFAC	M	1.5 t/c Ferrari 126CK V6	p stop/new nose/tyres/-4 laps	13/30
5	FRENCH GP	Dijon	28	Scuderia Ferrari SpA SEFAC	M	1.5 t/c Ferrari 126CK V6	1 lap behind	14/29
ret	BRITISH GP	Silverstone	28	Scuderia Ferrari SpA SEFAC	M	1.5 t/c Ferrari 126CK V6	engine	4/31
ret	GERMAN GP	Hockenheim	28	Scuderia Ferrari SpA SEFAC	M	1.5 t/c Ferrari 126CK V6	engine	5/30
9	AUSTRIAN GP	Österreichring	28	Scuderia Ferrari SpA SEFAC	M	1.5 t/c Ferrari 126CK V6	1 lap behind	8/28
ret	DUTCH GP	Zandvoort	28	Scuderia Ferrari SpA SEFAC	M	1.5 t/c Ferrari 126CK V6	accident with Tambay	12/30
5	ITALIAN GP	Monza	28	Scuderia Ferrari SpA SEFAC	M	1.5 t/c Ferrari 126CK V6		8/30
ret	CANADIAN GP	Montreal	28	Scuderia Ferrari SpA SEFAC	M	1.5 t/c Ferrari 126CK V6	engine	12/30
9	CAESARS PALACE GP	Las Vegas	28	Scuderia Ferrari SpA SEFAC	M	1.5 t/c Ferrari 126CK V6	tyres/damage check/FL/-2 laps	18/30

1982
Championship position: 2nd   Wins: 2   Pole positions: 2   Fastest laps: 2   Points scored: 39

	Race	Circuit	No	Entrant	Tyres	Car/Engine	Comment	Q Pos/Entries
18	SOUTH AFRICAN GP	Kyalami	28	Scuderia Ferrari SpA SEFAC	G	1.5 t/c Ferrari 126C2 V6	pit stops/tyres/6 laps behind	6/30
6*	BRAZILIAN GP	Rio	28	Scuderia Ferrari SpA SEFAC	G	1.5 t/c Ferrari 126C2 V6	pit stop/tyres/*1st & 2nd dsq	8/31
ret	US GP WEST	Long Beach	28	Scuderia Ferrari SpA SEFAC	G	1.5 t/c Ferrari 126C2 V6	hit wall	9/31
1	SAN MARINO GP	Imola	28	Scuderia Ferrari SpA SEFAC	G	1.5 t/c Ferrari 126C2 V6	took Villeneuve on last lap/FL	4/14
dns	BELGIAN GP	Zolder	28	Scuderia Ferrari SpA SEFAC	G	1.5 t/c Ferrari 126C2 V6	withdrawn-Villeneuve's accident	(6)/32
2/ret	MONACO GP	Monte Carlo	28	Scuderia Ferrari SpA SEFAC	G	1.5 t/c Ferrari 126C2 V6	electrics/1 lap behind	5/31
3	US GP (DETROIT)	Detroit	28	Scuderia Ferrari SpA SEFAC	G	1.5 t/c Ferrari 126C2 V6		4/28
9	CANADIAN GP	Montreal	28	Scuderia Ferrari SpA SEFAC	G	1.5 t/c Ferrari 126C2 V6	pit stop/mechanical/FL/-3 laps	1/29
1	DUTCH GP	Zandvoort	28	Scuderia Ferrari SpA SEFAC	G	1.5 t/c Ferrari 126C2 V6		4/31
2	BRITISH GP	Brands Hatch	28	Scuderia Ferrari SpA SEFAC	G	1.5 t/c Ferrari 126C2 V6		4/30
3	FRENCH GP	Paul Ricard	28	Scuderia Ferrari SpA SEFAC	G	1.5 t/c Ferrari 126C2 V6		3/30
dns	GERMAN GP	Hockenheim	28	Scuderia Ferrari SpA SEFAC	G	1.5 t/c Ferrari 126C2 V6	badly injured in practice accident	(1)/30

GP Starts: 68 (70)   GP Wins: 3   Pole positions: 4   Fastest laps: 5   Points: 101

EMANUELE PIRRO

Something of a nearly-man, Pirro's career has been a tale of ups and downs, as the unlucky Italian always seemed to fall short of ultimate success in most of the categories he raced in. That was until he teamed up with Audi at the beginning of 1994 and took the Italian Superturismo championship by storm with his 80 Competition. Three successive titles represented a sweet success for the tall and lanky Roman, whose earlier career exploits had promised so much.

Moving from karts to Formula Fiat, he won the championship in 1980 before graduating to the European Formula 3 series, taking the runner-up slot behind Euroracing team-mate Larrauri in 1982. When the team went to F1 with Alfa Romeo in 1983, Pirro had to find an F3 ride elsewhere and after a bright start faded to third in the championship. Stepping up to Formula 2 for 1984 with Onyx, he established a good rapport with the team, and stayed with them for F3000 in 1985, victories at Thruxton and Vallelunga earning him a Brabham F1 test which came to nought. So it was back to F3000 in 1986, and second place in the championship behind Capelli, a mid-season slump costing Pirro his title chance.

Still seeking an F1 ride, Emanuele busied himself with some superb performances in BMW touring cars, and took on the role of test driver for McLaren before replacing Herbert at Benetton midway through 1989. His half-season was not productive enough, and he was dropped for 1990 when Nelson Piquet was signed up, leaving Emanuele to find a place in the Dallara squad for the next two seasons. With no worthwhile results to speak of and, crucially, precious few drives that caught the eye, Pirro found himself passed over in favour of fresher talent in 1992, switching to the Italian touring car championship with a Bigazzi BMW.

After being synonymous with the BMW marque on and off over the years, his switch to Audi was something of a surprise but it paid off in a big way for both parties, with his aforementioned hat-trick of Superturismo titles.

Recent seasons have not been as productive for the Italian; with the Audi variously handicapped by weight penalties and restricted to using two-wheel drive, he has endured a lean time of it in the German Super Touring series.

In 1999 Pirro and team-mate Frank Biela were drafted into the Audi Sport Team Joest sports car squad for Le Mans, where the touring car stars took third place with Didier Theys in the Audi R8R.

PIRRO Emanuele (I) b 12/1/1962, Rome

	1989	Championship position: 23rd=		Wins: 0	Pole positions: 0		Fastest laps: 0	Points scored: 2		
	Race	Circuit	No	Entrant		Tyres	Car/Engine		Comment	Q Pos/Entries
9	FRENCH GP	Paul Ricard	20	Benetton Formula Ltd		G	3.5 Benetton B188-Cosworth V8		2 laps behind	24/39
11	BRITISH GP	Silverstone	20	Benetton Formula Ltd		G	3.5 Benetton B188-Cosworth V8		2 laps behind	26/39
ret	GERMAN GP	Hockenheim	20	Benetton Formula Ltd		G	3.5 Benetton B189-Cosworth V8		accident	9/39
8	HUNGARIAN GP	Hungaroring	20	Benetton Formula Ltd		G	3.5 Benetton B189-Cosworth V8		1 lap behind	25/39
10	BELGIAN GP	Spa	20	Benetton Formula Ltd		G	3.5 Benetton B189-Cosworth V8		1 lap behind	13/39
ret	ITALIAN GP	Monza	20	Benetton Formula Ltd		G	3.5 Benetton B189-Cosworth V8		gearbox/clutch on lap 1	9/39
ret	PORTUGUESE GP	Estoril	20	Benetton Formula Ltd		G	3.5 Benetton B189-Cosworth V8		shock absorber	16/39
ret	SPANISH GP	Jerez	20	Benetton Formula Ltd		G	3.5 Benetton B189-Cosworth V8		leg cramp-spun off when 4th	10/38
ret	JAPANESE GP	Suzuka	20	Benetton Formula Ltd		G	3.5 Benetton B189-Cosworth V8		accident with de Cesaris	22/39
5	AUSTRALIAN GP	Adelaide	20	Benetton Formula Ltd		G	3.5 Benetton B189-Cosworth V8		2 laps behind	13/39
	1990	Championship position: Unplaced								
ret	SAN MARINO GP	Imola	21	Scuderia Italia SpA		P	3.5 BMS Dallara 190-Cosworth V8		started from back/engine	22/34
ret/dns	MONACO GP	Monte Carlo	21	Scuderia Italia SpA		P	3.5 BMS Dallara 190-Cosworth V8		stalled on dummy grid	(9)/35
ret	CANADIAN GP	Montreal	21	Scuderia Italia SpA		P	3.5 BMS Dallara 190-Cosworth V8		collided with Alboreto	19/35
ret	MEXICAN GP	Mexico City	21	Scuderia Italia SpA		P	3.5 BMS Dallara 190-Cosworth V8		engine	18/35
ret	FRENCH GP	Paul Ricard	21	Scuderia Italia SpA		P	3.5 BMS Dallara 190-Cosworth V8		brakes-spun off	24/35
11	BRITISH GP	Silverstone	21	Scuderia Italia SpA		P	3.5 BMS Dallara 190-Cosworth V8		2 laps behind	19/35

ret	GERMAN GP	Hockenheim	21	Scuderia Italia SpA	P	3.5 BMS Dallara 190-Cosworth V8	startline collision-Brabham	23/35
10	HUNGARIAN GP	Hungaroring	21	Scuderia Italia SpA	P	3.5 BMS Dallara 190-Cosworth V8	1 lap behind	13/35
ret	BELGIAN GP	Spa	21	Scuderia Italia SpA	P	3.5 BMS Dallara 190-Cosworth V8	cracked water pipe	17/33
ret	ITALIAN GP	Monza	21	Scuderia Italia SpA	P	3.5 BMS Dallara 190-Cosworth V8	gearbox-spun off	19/33
15	PORTUGUESE GP	Estoril	21	Scuderia Italia SpA	P	3.5 BMS Dallara 190-Cosworth V8	3 laps behind	13/33
ret	SPANISH GP	Jerez	21	Scuderia Italia SpA	P	3.5 BMS Dallara 190-Cosworth V8	throttle slides-spun off	16/33
ret	JAPANESE GP	Suzuka	21	Scuderia Italia SpA	P	3.5 BMS Dallara 190-Cosworth V8	alternator	19/30
ret	AUSTRALIAN GP	Adelaide	21	Scuderia Italia SpA	P	3.5 BMS Dallara 190-Cosworth V8	engine-electrics	21/30

1991 Championship position: 18th   Wins: 0   Pole positions: 0   Fastest laps: 0   Points scored: 1

ret	US GP (PHOENIX)	Phoenix	21	Scuderia Italia SpA	P	3.5 BMS Dallara 191-Judd V10	clutch	9/34
11	BRAZILIAN GP	Rio	21	Scuderia Italia SpA	P	3.5 BMS Dallara 191-Judd V10	3 laps behind	12/34
dnpq	SAN MARINO GP	Imola	21	Scuderia Italia SpA	P	3.5 BMS Dallara 191-Judd V10		31/34
6	MONACO GP	Monte Carlo	21	Scuderia Italia SpA	P	3.5 BMS Dallara 191-Judd V10	1 lap behind	12/34
9	CANADIAN GP	Montreal	21	Scuderia Italia SpA	P	3.5 BMS Dallara 191-Judd V10	1 lap behind	10/34
dnpq	MEXICAN GP	Mexico City	21	Scuderia Italia SpA	P	3.5 BMS Dallara 191-Judd V10		34/34
dnpq	FRENCH GP	Magny Cours	21	Scuderia Italia SpA	P	3.5 BMS Dallara 191-Judd V10		31/34
10	BRITISH GP	Silverstone	21	Scuderia Italia SpA	P	3.5 BMS Dallara 191-Judd V10	2 laps behind	18/34
10	GERMAN GP	Hockenheim	21	Scuderia Italia SpA	P	3.5 BMS Dallara 191-Judd V10	1 lap behind	18/34
ret	HUNGARIAN GP	Hungaroring	21	Scuderia Italia SpA	P	3.5 BMS Dallara 191-Judd V10	engine-oil pressure	7/34
8	BELGIAN GP	Spa	21	Scuderia Italia SpA	P	3.5 BMS Dallara 191-Judd V10	1 lap behind	25/34
10	ITALIAN GP	Monza	21	Scuderia Italia SpA	P	3.5 BMS Dallara 191-Judd V10	1 lap behind	16/34
ret	PORTUGUESE GP	Estoril	21	Scuderia Italia SpA	P	3.5 BMS Dallara 191-Judd V10	engine	17/34
15	SPANISH GP	Barcelona	21	Scuderia Italia SpA	P	3.5 BMS Dallara 191-Judd V10	3 laps behind	9/33
ret	JAPANESE GP	Suzuka	21	Scuderia Italia SpA	P	3.5 BMS Dallara 191-Judd V10	spun off avoiding de Cesaris	16/31
7	AUSTRALIAN GP	Adelaide	21	Scuderia Italia SpA	P	3.5 BMS Dallara 191-Judd V10	rain stopped race after 14 laps	13/32

GP Starts: 36 (37)   GP Wins: 0   Pole positions: 0   Fastest laps: 0   Points: 3

JACQUES POLLET

'Jacky' breezed into the Gordini squad for a single race at Chimay in 1953, and was taken on as a trainee works driver the following season. In single-seaters he took sixth in the Bordeaux GP and shared the third-placed car with Behra at Caen. Pollet led briefly at Chimay until a stone smashed his goggles, and he was moving back through the field until he crashed into the crowd, with two spectators being fatally injured.

In sports machines he won his class at Le Mans with Guelfi and also won the Tour de France Rally with Goulthier. His association with the team continued in 1955, but apart from fourth at Albi little was achieved. Thereafter Pollet competed in a Mercedes 300S, finishing eighth overall (fourth in class) in the 1956 Mille Miglia.

BEN PON

A class winner for Porsche at Le Mans in 1961, the popular Dutchman's only Grand Prix appearance ended in embarrassment as he spun out on oil in his works-loaned Porsche on lap 3 of the 1962 Dutch GP. It could easily have been tragic, for his car overturned and the driver was thrown out, only luckily escaping injury.

Over the next few seasons he was at the forefront of the Porsche challenge in sports and GT events, usually under the Racing Team Holland banner, but occasionally as a member of the full works team. He won races in his 904GT at Limbourg, Solitude and Zandvoort, and was third and a class winner in the 1965 Spa 1000 Km in a 914GTS. At the end of that year he retired to run the Dutch Racing Team.

POLLET, Jacques (F) b 28/7/1932

1954 Championship position: Unplaced

	Race	Circuit	No	Entrant	Tyres	Car/Engine	Comment	Q Pos/Entries
ret	FRENCH GP	Reims	26	Equipe Gordini	E	2.5 Gordini Type 16 6	engine	18/22
ret	SPANISH GP	Pedralbes	48	Equipe Gordini	E	2.5 Gordini Type 16 6	engine	16/22

1955 Championship position: Unplaced

7	MONACO GP	Monte Carlo	10	Equipe Gordini	E	2.5 Gordini Type 16 6	9 laps behind	20/22
10	DUTCH GP	Zandvoort	24	Equipe Gordini	E	2.5 Gordini Type 16 6	10 laps behind	12/16
ret	ITALIAN GP	Monza	26	Equipe Gordini	E	2.5 Gordini Type 16 6	engine	19/22

GP Starts: 5   GP Wins: 0   Pole positions: 0   Fastest laps: 0   Points: 0

PON, Ben (NL) b 9/12/1936, Leiden

1962 Championship position: Unplaced

	Race	Circuit	No	Entrant	Tyres	Car/Engine	Comment	Q Pos/Entries
ret	DUTCH GP	Zandvoort	15	Ecurie Maarsbergen	D	1.5 Porsche 787 F4	spun off	18/20

GP Starts: 1   GP Wins: 0   Pole positions: 0   Fastest laps: 0   Points: 0

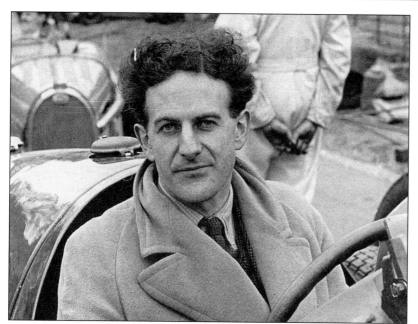

DENNIS POORE

A British hill-climb champion in 1950 with his Alfa Romeo 3.8S, Poore, a wealthy industrialist, briefly became a member of the Connaught Racing Syndicate in 1952, scoring a fine fourth place in the British GP. He then severed his connections with the Send concern and linked up with the Aston Martin sports car team for 1953.

His best result with the car came in 1955 winning the Goodwood International 9 Hours in a DB3S with Peter Walker.

He continued to race his old Alfa Romeo in numerous events during this period, winning the Dick Seaman Trophy race three times in a row between 1951 and 1953.

SAM POSEY

Posey was a versatile American driver who loved the ambience of Formula 1 and wanted to make a real impact on the Grand Prix scene, but never really had the chance to do so.

He performed capably in Can-Am, Trans-Am and sports cars in the late sixties, and finished fourth at Daytona and Le Mans in 1970, but his real success came in Formula A, Sam challenging David Hobbs and Graham McRae for the championships of 1971 and 1972.

After a brief tilt at USAC, during the course of which he finished fifth at both Indianapolis and Pocono with an Eagle-Offy in 1972, and sixth at Ontario in 1973, Sam raced the Norris Industries Talon in US F5000 in 1974 and briefly in 1976 until his sponsorship dried up.

Thereafter he focused his attentions on IMSA and was a Le Mans regular for many years. Racing a works 3.5-litre BMW CSL, he won the 1975 Sebring 12-hour race with Redman, Stuck and Moffat.

When Sam decided to wind down his racing career he effortlessly took up a TV commentary role which has kept him in touch with the sport.

POORE, Dennis (GB) b 19/8/1916, West London – d 12/2/1987, Kensington, London

	1952	Championship position:10th=		Wins: 0	Pole positions: 0	Fastest laps: 0	Points scored: 3		
	Race	Circuit	No	Entrant	Tyres	Car/Engine		Comment	Q Pos/Entries
4	BRITISH GP	Silverstone	6	Connaught Engineering	D	2.0 Connaught A Type 4		2 laps behind	8/32
12	ITALIAN GP	Monza	30	Connaught Racing Syndicate	D	2.0 Connaught A Type 4		6 laps behind	19/35

GP Starts: 2   GP Wins: 0   Pole positions: 0   Fastest laps: 0   Points: 3

POSEY, Sam (USA) b 26/5/1944, New York City, New York

	1971	Championship position: Unplaced							
	Race	Circuit	No	Entrant	Tyres	Car/Engine		Comment	Q Pos/Entries
ret	US GP	Watkins Glen	19	Team Surtees	F	3.0 Surtees TS9-Cosworth V8		engine	18/32
	1972	Championship position: Unplaced							
12	US GP	Watkins Glen	34	Champcarr Inc	G	3.0 Surtees TS9B-Cosworth V8		2 laps behind	23/32

GP Starts: 2   GP Wins: 0   Pole positions: 0   Fastest laps: 0   Points: 0

CHARLES POZZI

A shrewd motor dealer who traded in luxury cars after the war, Pozzi was briefly associated with Paul Vallée's Ecurie France before leaving together with Eugène Chaboud. The pair formed their own team, Ecurie Leutitia, usually fielding Delahayes, with one of which Pozzi won the 1949 Comminges GP at St Gaudens. In 1950 he shared Rosier's Talbot in the French GP, but for the most part he confined himself to sports cars, winning the Casablanca 12 Hours in a Talbot in 1952.

During 1953-54 he raced François Picard's Ferrari, before pressure of business forced his retirement, as he was by now the importer for both Chrysler and Rolls-Royce in France. He maintained his interest in the sport for many years and, having become the Ferrari importer, he entered Daytonas and 512Bs at Le Mans throughout the seventies.

JACKIE PRETORIOUS

A leading light on the thriving South African racing scene in the 1960s, Jackie handled the local Serrurier-built LDS-Climax in national events, but used a Lotus to finish ninth in the non-championship 1966 Grand Prix. Between 1968 and 1970 he was successful in Lola single-seaters and sports cars entered by Serrurier, but his best season was predictably when handling the Team Gunston Brabham BT26A in 1971, Pretorious winning championship races at Killarney and the Natal Roy Hesketh circuit.

At the 1973 South African Grand Prix, Jackie was called in by Williams to replace Nanni Galli, injured in an earlier testing accident, before returning to business in the local series with his ex-Motul Brabham BT38.

DAVID PROPHET

Never a driver likely to make an impression above national level, Prophet, a Midlands motor trader, raced enthusiastically in some serious machinery for more than a decade. While competing in Formula Junior, he took his Brabham to South Africa late in the 1963 season and raced in the national Grand Prix, also taking sixth place on aggregate in the Rand GP and finishing second in the Libre Rhodesian GP.

David raced in European F2 from 1964 to 1967 with little success, but found more joy in sports cars, particularly with the Lotus 30. In 1968-69, he raced his Ford GT40 and then a Lola T70, before becoming a regular competitor in Formula 5000 in 1970 with a McLaren 10B which he then took to the non-championship 1971 Argentine GP to claim a lucrative fourth place on aggregate after more fancied runners had fallen by the wayside. He was killed in 1981 when the helicopter in which he was leaving the Silverstone circuit crashed just after take-off.

POZZI, Charles (F) b 27/8/1909, Paris

	1950			Championship position: Unplaced					
	Race	Circuit	No	Entrant	Tyres	Car/Engine		Comment	Q Pos/Entries
6*	FRENCH GP	Reims	26	Charles Pozzi	D	4.5 Lago-Talbot T26C 6		* Rosier took over car/-8 laps	16/20

GP Starts: 1   GP Wins: 0   Pole positions: 0   Fastest laps: 0   Points: 0

PRETORIOUS, Jackie (ZA) b 22/11/1934, Potchefstroom, Transvaal

	1965			Championship position: Unplaced				
	Race	Circuit	No	Entrant	Tyres	Car/Engine	Comment	Q Pos/Entries
dnpq	SOUTH AFRICAN GP	East London	29	Jackie Pretorious	D	1.5 LDS Mk1-Alfa Romeo 4	dnq for official practice	– / –
	1968			Championship position: Unplaced				
nc	SOUTH AFRICAN GP	Kyalami	23	Team Pretoria	F	2.7 Brabham BT11-Climax 4	10 laps behind	23/23
	1971			Championship position: Unplaced				
ret	SOUTH AFRICAN GP	Kyalami	25	Team Gunston	F	3.0 Brabham BT26A-Cosworth V8	engine	20/25
	1973			Championship position: Unplaced				
ret	SOUTH AFRICAN GP	Kyalami	20	Frank Williams Racing Cars	F	3.0 Iso Williams FX3B-Cosworth V8	overheating	24/25

GP Starts: 3   GP Wins: 0   Pole positions: 0   Fastest laps: 0   Points: 0

PROPHET, David (GB) b 9/10/1937, Hong Kong – d 29/3/1981, Silverstone, Northamptonshire

	1963			Championship position: Unplaced				
	Race	Circuit	No	Entrant	Tyres	Car/Engine	Comment	Q Pos/Entries
ret	SOUTH AFRICAN GP	East London	22	David Prophet	D	1.5 Brabham BT6-Ford 4	oil pressure	14/21
	1965			Championship position: Unplaced				
14	SOUTH AFRICAN GP	East London	19	David Prophet Racing	D	1.5 Brabham BT10-Ford 4	14 laps behind	19/25

GP Starts: 2   GP Wins: 0   Pole positions: 0   Fastest laps: 0   Points: 0

ALAIN PROST

WORLD CHAMPION: 1985, 1986, 1989 & 1993

ALAIN PROST

When Alain Prost retired at the end of 1993, his record stood at four World Championships, a total of 51 Grand Prix wins and nearly 800 points from 199 starts. Simple mathematics tell the story: an average of four points from every Grand Prix. Yet despite these staggering statistics, there are plenty of fans who wouldn't give the Frenchman the time of day. Perhaps only Stewart can divide opinion so sharply, and the issues were much clearer in his case, being centred on safety. But as the years roll by, Alain will rightly be lauded as one of the sport's absolute greats. Certainly a decade or two hence there will be few, if any, followers of motor racing who will be able to understand the current dismissive attitude of an ill-informed minority towards his wonderful achievements.

Prost's car racing career had been set on a stellar path from the start. After racing karts in the company of Cheever and Patrese he turned to cars in 1975, enrolling at the Winfield school. He won the traditional Pilote Elf prize of a car for the following season's Formule Renault series and certainly put it to good use, winning 12 of 13 races. Promotion to Formule Super Renault duly followed, and eight wins later that trophy went on the Prost mantelpiece as well. He moved into Formula 3 in 1978, but the Martini MK21B-Renault was not truly competitive until a close-season revamp saw the car emerge as the MK27. Alain proved virtually unbeatable with it, taking the European and French titles and the all-important Monaco F3 race. He was ready for Formula 1, and McLaren were the first takers.

Australian Grand Prix, Adelaide, 1986. Alain Prost takes his second World Championship with the McLaren-TAG. Throughout the season the Frenchman used all his brilliant racecraft to stay on terms with the faster Williams-Hondas of Mansell and Piquet.

In 1980 the team were not in great shape and on the point of total transition, but Prost was unfazed and scored points in his first two Grands Prix. Even in that first season the traits that later served him so well were there: the smooth driving style, the willingness to speak his mind honestly and a genuine concern about the sport and its image. The chance to join Renault for 1981 was too good to turn down and Prost moved in to completely flummox partner Arnoux. Alain scored three wins that year and two more were added in 1982, but there could have been many others if the Renault had not let him down so often. It was largely thanks to Prost that the RE30B had reached such a competitive position, and he was just as formidable a force in 1983 with its successor. Apart from an error at Zandvoort he hardly put a foot wrong, yet still the championship slipped through his fingers at the very last. Renault and the French press pointed the finger of blame at a bemused Prost, who took the only course of action possible and high-tailed it to McLaren, who knew better than to look a gift horse in the mouth. While the Renault F1 effort slid into oblivion over the next two seasons, Alain was busy winning the small matter of 12 Grands Prix. In 1984 he lost out to Niki Lauda by just half a point, but finally cracked it to become the first French World Champion in 1985.

With Williams-Honda dominant in 1986, few gave Alain any hope of retaining his crown, but he hung in, picking up every point possible and coaxing four wins from the McLaren-TAG to steal the title in Adelaide. The following year even Prost's powers were unable to halt the Williams steamroller, but he did overtake Jackie Stewart's long-standing total of Grand Prix wins in Portugal. Then in 1988 Prost too had Honda power, but with the Japanese V6 came Ayrton Senna. That first season saw a McLaren carve-up, with the pair winning all but one of the 16 races. Senna had the edge and Prost, at times non-plussed, had to settle for second-best for once. It was a different story in 1989; Alain raised his game and the battle was on, especially after a steady deterioration in the drivers' relationship. The title was settled in the Frenchman's favour when he subtly chopped the Brazilian at Suzuka. It was truly an awful way to decide a championship, and yet history repeated itself in 1990, except that Alain was now on the receiving end as Senna drove into the back of his Ferrari at the start. This wiped out a season's truly brilliant endeavour by Prost, who had moved into his new environment and immediately given the Italian team a real sense of purpose. Unfortunately this was not to be maintained in 1991, when Maranello politics and intrigue reached new heights, with Prost locked in bitter off-track arguments. When it finally arrived, the new 643 was disappointing and by the season's end the Frenchman had been fired for his outspoken views.

Disillusioned, he took a year's sabbatical from the cockpit, despite massive pressure to join Ligier. This move left him plenty of time to weigh up his options and by mid-1992 he had tied up a deal to race for Williams in 1993, expecting to partner Nigel Mansell. Of course it is now history that Nigel chose to vacate his seat, leaving Prost in a very strong position to take his fourth World Championship. In a no-win situation, Alain got the job done in his usual undramatic style, his season yielding thirteen pole positions and another seven wins. With the prospect of Ayrton Senna joining the team in 1994, Prost concluded that he just didn't need the aggravation, and announced that he was going to retire at the end of the season.

There were tempting opportunities to reconsider. He tested a McLaren-Peugeot early in 1994, but eventually confirmed his decision to retire. In the aftermath of Senna's death he declared that he would not race again but in 1995 he tested for McLaren once more, subsequently joining the team in a test and advisory capacity. With a new era already dawning in Formula 1, Alain then took on a huge new challenge with his purchase of the Ligier team, which was renamed Prost Grand Prix prior to the start of the 1997 season. Alain immediately set about a major overhaul of the underperforming French constructor, moving its base from Magny Cours to the outskirts of Paris.

Like Jackie Stewart, he is an exacting taskmaster, expecting, perhaps unrealistically, his drivers to match his own standards, and three seasons as a team owner have already taught Prost that any success will have to be earned the hard way.

PROST, Alain (F) b 24/2/1955, Lorette, Saint-Chamond, nr St Etienne

1980
Championship position: 15th=   Wins: 0   Pole positions: 0   Fastest laps: 0   Points scored: 5

	Race	Circuit	No	Entrant	Tyres	Car/Engine	Comment	Q Pos/Entries
6	ARGENTINE GP	Buenos Aires	8	Marlboro Team McLaren	G	3.0 McLaren M29-Cosworth V8	1 lap behind	12/28
5	BRAZILIAN GP	Interlagos	8	Marlboro Team McLaren	G	3.0 McLaren M29-Cosworth V8		13/28
dns	SOUTH AFRICAN GP	Kyalami	8	Marlboro Team McLaren	G	3.0 McLaren M29-Cosworth V8	practice accident/hurt wrist	(22)/28
ret	BELGIAN GP	Zolder	8	Marlboro Team McLaren	G	3.0 McLaren M29-Cosworth V8	transmission	19/27
ret	MONACO GP	Monte Carlo	8	Marlboro Team McLaren	G	3.0 McLaren M29-Cosworth V8	multiple accident on first lap	10/27
ret	FRENCH GP	Paul Ricard	8	Marlboro Team McLaren	G	3.0 McLaren M29-Cosworth V8	transmission	7/27
6	BRITISH GP	Brands Hatch	8	Marlboro Team McLaren	G	3.0 McLaren M29-Cosworth V8	1 lap behind	7/27
11	GERMAN GP	Hockenheim	8	Marlboro Team McLaren	G	3.0 McLaren M29-Cosworth V8	pit stops/tyre/skirt problems	14/26
7	AUSTRIAN GP	Österreichring	8	Marlboro Team McLaren	G	3.0 McLaren M29-Cosworth V8		12/25
6	DUTCH GP	Zandvoort	8	Marlboro Team McLaren	G	3.0 McLaren M30-Cosworth V8		18/28
7	ITALIAN GP	Imola	8	Marlboro Team McLaren	G	3.0 McLaren M30-Cosworth V8	1 lap behind	24/28
ret	CANADIAN GP	Montreal	8	Marlboro Team McLaren	G	3.0 McLaren M30-Cosworth V8	suspension failure/accident	12/28
dns	US GP EAST	Watkins Glen	8	Marlboro Team McLaren	G	3.0 McLaren M30-Cosworth V8	practice accident	(13)/27

1981
Championship position: 5th   Wins: 3   Pole positions: 2   Fastest laps: 1   Points scored: 43

	Race	Circuit	No	Entrant	Tyres	Car/Engine	Comment	Q Pos/Entries
ret	US GP WEST	Long Beach	15	Equipe Renault Elf	M	1.5 t/c Renault RE22B V6	hit by de Cesaris	14/29
ret	BRAZILIAN GP	Rio	15	Equipe Renault Elf	M	1.5 t/c Renault RE22B V6	hit by Pironi	5/30
3	ARGENTINE GP	Buenos Aires	15	Equipe Renault Elf	M	1.5 t/c Renault RE22B V6		2/29
ret	SAN MARINO GP	Imola	15	Equipe Renault Elf	M	1.5 t/c Renault RE22B V6	gearbox	4/30
ret	BELGIAN GP	Zolder	15	Equipe Renault Elf	M	1.5 t/c Renault RE30 V6	clutch	12/31
ret	MONACO GP	Monte Carlo	15	Equipe Renault Elf	M	1.5 t/c Renault RE30 V6	engine	9/31
ret	SPANISH GP	Jarama	15	Equipe Renault Elf	M	1.5 t/c Renault RE30 V6	spun off	5/30
1*	FRENCH GP	Dijon	15	Equipe Renault Elf	M	1.5 t/c Renault RE30 V6	*aggregate of two parts/FL	3/29
ret	BRITISH GP	Silverstone	15	Equipe Renault Elf	M	1.5 t/c Renault RE30 V6	engine	2/30
2	GERMAN GP	Hockenheim	15	Equipe Renault Elf	M	1.5 t/c Renault RE30 V6		1/30
ret	AUSTRIAN GP	Österreichring	15	Equipe Renault Elf	M	1.5 t/c Renault RE30 V6	front suspension	2/28
1	DUTCH GP	Zandvoort	15	Equipe Renault Elf	M	1.5 t/c Renault RE30 V6		1/30
1	ITALIAN GP	Monza	15	Equipe Renault Elf	M	1.5 t/c Renault RE30 V6		3/30
ret	CANADIAN GP	Montreal	15	Equipe Renault Elf	M	1.5 t/c Renault RE30 V6	accident with Mansell	4/30
2	CAESARS PALACE GP	Las Vegas	15	Equipe Renault Elf	M	1.5 t/c Renault RE30 V6		5/30

1982
Championship position: 4th   Wins: 2   Pole positions: 5   Fastest laps: 4   Points scored: 34

	Race	Circuit	No	Entrant	Tyres	Car/Engine	Comment	Q Pos/Entries
1	SOUTH AFRICAN GP	Kyalami	15	Equipe Renault Elf	M	1.5 t/c Renault RE30B V6	FL	5/30
1*	BRAZILIAN GP	Rio	15	Equipe Renault Elf	M	1.5 t/c Renault RE30B V6	* 1st & 2nd place cars dsq/FL	1/31
ret	US GP WEST	Long Beach	15	Equipe Renault Elf	M	1.5 t/c Renault RE30B V6	brake problems/hit wall	4/31
ret	SAN MARINO GP	Imola	15	Equipe Renault Elf	M	1.5 t/c Renault RE30B V6	engine	2/14
ret	BELGIAN GP	Zolder	15	Equipe Renault Elf	M	1.5 t/c Renault RE30B V6	spun off	1/32
7/ret	MONACO GP	Monte Carlo	15	Equipe Renault Elf	M	1.5 t/c Renault RE30B V6	spun off/3 laps behind	4/31
nc	US GP (DETROIT)	Detroit	15	Equipe Renault Elf	M	1.5 t/c Renault RE30B V6	pit stop/fuel pump/FL/-8 laps	1/28
ret	CANADIAN GP	Montreal	15	Equipe Renault Elf	M	1.5 t/c Renault RE30B V6	engine	3/29
ret	DUTCH GP	Zandvoort	15	Equipe Renault Elf	M	1.5 t/c Renault RE30B V6	engine	2/31
6	BRITISH GP	Brands Hatch	15	Equipe Renault Elf	M	1.5 t/c Renault RE30B V6		8/30
2	FRENCH GP	Paul Ricard	15	Equipe Renault Elf	M	1.5 t/c Renault RE30B V6	Arnoux won against team orders	2/30
ret	GERMAN GP	Hockenheim	15	Equipe Renault Elf	M	1.5 t/c Renault RE30B V6	fuel injection	2/30
8/ret	AUSTRIAN GP	Österreichring	15	Equipe Renault Elf	M	1.5 t/c Renault RE30B V6	fuel injection/5 laps behind	3/29
2	SWISS GP	Dijon	15	Equipe Renault Elf	M	1.5 t/c Renault RE30B V6	FL	1/29
ret	ITALIAN GP	Monza	15	Equipe Renault Elf	M	1.5 t/c Renault RE30B V6	fuel injection	5/30
4	CAESARS PALACE GP	Las Vegas	15	Equipe Renault Elf	M	1.5 t/c Renault RE30B V6		1/30

1983
Championship position: 2nd   Wins: 4   Pole positions: 3   Fastest laps: 3   Points scored: 57

	Race	Circuit	No	Entrant	Tyres	Car/Engine	Comment	Q Pos/Entries
7	BRAZILIAN GP	Rio	15	Equipe Renault Elf	M	1.5 t/c Renault RE30C V6	1 lap behind	2/27
11	US GP WEST	Long Beach	15	Equipe Renault Elf	M	1.5 t/c Renault RE40 V6	pit stip/misfire/3 laps behind	8/28
1	FRENCH GP	Paul Ricard	15	Equipe Renault Elf	M	1.5 t/c Renault RE40 V6	FL	1/29
2	SAN MARINO GP	Imola	15	Equipe Renault Elf	M	1.5 t/c Renault RE40 V6		4/28
3	MONACO GP	Monte Carlo	15	Equipe Renault Elf	M	1.5 t/c Renault RE40 V6		1/28
1	BELGIAN GP	Spa	15	Equipe Renault Elf	M	1.5 t/c Renault RE40 V6		1/28
8	US GP (DETROIT)	Detroit	15	Equipe Renault Elf	M	1.5 t/c Renault RE40 V6	pit stop/fuel/1 lap behind	13/27
5	CANADIAN GP	Montreal	15	Equipe Renault Elf	M	1.5 t/c Renault RE40 V6	1 lap behind	2/28
1	BRITISH GP	Silverstone	15	Equipe Renault Elf	M	1.5 t/c Renault RE40 V6	FL	3/29
4	GERMAN GP	Hockenheim	15	Equipe Renault Elf	M	1.5 t/c Renault RE40 V6		5/29
1	AUSTRIAN GP	Österreichring	15	Equipe Renault Elf	M	1.5 t/c Renault RE40 V6	FL	5/29
ret	DUTCH GP	Zandvoort	15	Equipe Renault Elf	M	1.5 t/c Renault RE40 V6	collision with Piquet	4/29
ret	ITALIAN GP	Monza	15	Equipe Renault Elf	M	1.5 t/c Renault RE40 V6	turbo	5/29
2	EUROPEAN GP	Brands Hatch	15	Equipe Renault Elf	M	1.5 t/c Renault RE40 V6	turbo	8/29
ret	SOUTH AFRICAN GP	Kyalami	15	Equipe Renault Elf	M	1.5 t/c Renault RE40 V6	turbo	5/26

1984
Championship position: 2nd   Wins: 7   Pole positions: 3   Fastest laps: 3   Points scored: 71.5

	Race	Circuit	No	Entrant	Tyres	Car/Engine	Comment	Q Pos/Entries
1	BRAZILIAN GP	Rio	7	Marlboro McLaren International	M	1.5 t/c McLaren MP4/2-TAG V6	FL	4/27
2	SOUTH AFRICAN GP	Kyalami	7	Marlboro McLaren International	M	1.5 t/c McLaren MP4/2-TAG V6	started from pit lane	5/27
ret	BELGIAN GP	Zolder	7	Marlboro McLaren International	M	1.5 t/c McLaren MP4/2-TAG V6	distributor	8/27
1	SAN MARINO GP	Imola	7	Marlboro McLaren International	M	1.5 t/c McLaren MP4/2-TAG V6		2/28
7	FRENCH GP	Dijon	7	Marlboro McLaren International	M	1.5 t/c McLaren MP4/2-TAG V6		5/27
1*	MONACO GP	Monte Carlo	7	Marlboro McLaren International	M	1.5 t/c McLaren MP4/2-TAG V6	2 pit stops/loose wheel/FL *rain shortened race-half points	1/27
3	CANADIAN GP	Montreal	7	Marlboro McLaren International	M	1.5 t/c McLaren MP4/2-TAG V6		2/26
4*	US GP (DETROIT)	Detroit	7	Marlboro McLaren International	M	1.5 t/c McLaren MP4/2-TAG V6	* 2nd place car disqualified	2/27
ret	US GP (DALLAS)	Dallas	7	Marlboro McLaren International	M	1.5 t/c McLaren MP4/2-TAG V6	hit wall	7/27
ret	BRITISH GP	Brands Hatch	7	Marlboro McLaren International	M	1.5 t/c McLaren MP4/2-TAG V6	gearbox	2/27
1	GERMAN GP	Hockenheim	7	Marlboro McLaren International	M	1.5 t/c McLaren MP4/2-TAG V6	FL	1/27
ret	AUSTRIAN GP	Österreichring	7	Marlboro McLaren International	M	1.5 t/c McLaren MP4/2-TAG V6	spun off	2/28
1	DUTCH GP	Zandvoort	7	Marlboro McLaren International	M	1.5 t/c McLaren MP4/2-TAG V6		1/27
ret	ITALIAN GP	Monza	7	Marlboro McLaren International	M	1.5 t/c McLaren MP4/2-TAG V6	engine	2/27
1	EUROPEAN GP	Nürburgring	7	Marlboro McLaren International	M	1.5 t/c McLaren MP4/2-TAG V6		2/26
1	PORTUGUESE GP	Estoril	7	Marlboro McLaren International	M	1.5 t/c McLaren MP4/2-TAG V6		2/27

1985

Championship position: WORLD CHAMPION   Wins: 5   Pole positions: 2   Fastest laps: 6   Points scored: 76

Pos	Race	Circuit	No	Team		Car	Notes	Grid
1	BRAZILIAN GP	Rio	2	Marlboro McLaren International	G	1.5 t/c McLaren MP4/2B-TAG V6	FL	6/25
ret	PORTUGUESE GP	Estoril	2	Marlboro McLaren International	G	1.5 t/c McLaren MP4/2B-TAG V6	spun off	2/26
dsq*	SAN MARINO GP	Imola	2	Marlboro McLaren International	G	1.5 t/c McLaren MP4/2B-TAG V6	* 1st but car underweight	6/26
1	MONACO GP	Monte Carlo	2	Marlboro McLaren International	G	1.5 t/c McLaren MP4/2B-TAG V6		5/26
3	CANADIAN GP	Montreal	2	Marlboro McLaren International	G	1.5 t/c McLaren MP4/2B-TAG V6		5/25
ret	US GP (DETROIT)	Detroit	2	Marlboro McLaren International	G	1.5 t/c McLaren MP4/2B-TAG V6	brake failure/accident	4/25
3	FRENCH GP	Paul Ricard	2	Marlboro McLaren International	G	1.5 t/c McLaren MP4/2B-TAG V6		4/26
1	BRITISH GP	Silverstone	2	Marlboro McLaren International	G	1.5 t/c McLaren MP4/2B-TAG V6	FL	3/26
2	GERMAN GP	Nürburgring	2	Marlboro McLaren International	G	1.5 t/c McLaren MP4/2B-TAG V6		3/27
1	AUSTRIAN GP	Österreichring	2	Marlboro McLaren International	G	1.5 t/c McLaren MP4/2B-TAG V6	FL	1/27
2	DUTCH GP	Zandvoort	2	Marlboro McLaren International	G	1.5 t/c McLaren MP4/2B-TAG V6	FL	3/27
1	ITALIAN GP	Monza	2	Marlboro McLaren International	G	1.5 t/c McLaren MP4/2B-TAG V6		5/26
3	BELGIAN GP	Spa	2	Marlboro McLaren International	G	1.5 t/c McLaren MP4/2B-TAG V6	FL	1/24
4	EUROPEAN GP	Brands Hatch	2	Marlboro McLaren International	G	1.5 t/c McLaren MP4/2B-TAG V6		6/27
3	SOUTH AFRICAN GP	Kyalami	2	Marlboro McLaren International	G	1.5 t/c McLaren MP4/2B-TAG V6		9/21
ret	AUSTRALIAN GP	Adelaide	2	Marlboro McLaren International	G	1.5 t/c McLaren MP4/2B-TAG V6	engine	4/25

1986

Championship position: WORLD CHAMPION   Wins: 4   Pole positions: 1   Fastest laps: 2   Points scored: 74

Pos	Race	Circuit	No	Team		Car	Notes	Grid
ret	BRAZILIAN GP	Rio	1	Marlboro McLaren International	G	1.5 t/c McLaren MP4/2C-TAG V6	engine	9/25
3	SPANISH GP	Jerez	1	Marlboro McLaren International	G	1.5 t/c McLaren MP4/2C-TAG V6		4/25
1	SAN MARINO GP	Imola	1	Marlboro McLaren International	G	1.5 t/c McLaren MP4/2C-TAG V6		4/26
1	MONACO GP	Monte Carlo	1	Marlboro McLaren International	G	1.5 t/c McLaren MP4/2C-TAG V6	FL	1/26
6	BELGIAN GP	Spa	1	Marlboro McLaren International	G	1.5 t/c McLaren MP4/2C-TAG V6	first lap collision and spin/FL	3/25
2	CANADIAN GP	Montreal	1	Marlboro McLaren International	G	1.5 t/c McLaren MP4/2C-TAG V6		4/25
3	US GP (DETROIT)	Detroit	1	Marlboro McLaren International	G	1.5 t/c McLaren MP4/2C-TAG V6		7/26
2	FRENCH GP	Paul Ricard	1	Marlboro McLaren International	G	1.5 t/c McLaren MP4/2C-TAG V6		5/26
3	BRITISH GP	Brands Hatch	1	Marlboro McLaren International	G	1.5 t/c McLaren MP4/2C-TAG V6		6/26
6/ret	GERMAN GP	Hockenheim	1	Marlboro McLaren International	G	1.5 t/c McLaren MP4/2C-TAG V6	out of fuel	2/26
ret	HUNGARIAN GP	Hungaroring	1	Marlboro McLaren International	G	1.5 t/c McLaren MP4/2C-TAG V6	accident with Arnoux	3/26
1	AUSTRIAN GP	Österreichring	1	Marlboro McLaren International	G	1.5 t/c McLaren MP4/2C-TAG V6		5/26
dsq*/ret	ITALIAN GP	Monza	1	Marlboro McLaren International	G	1.5 t/c McLaren MP4/2C-TAG V6	* car change after green/engine	2/27
2	PORTUGUESE GP	Estoril	1	Marlboro McLaren International	G	1.5 t/c McLaren MP4/2C-TAG V6		3/27
2	MEXICAN GP	Mexico City	1	Marlboro McLaren International	G	1.5 t/c McLaren MP4/2C-TAG V6		6/26
1	AUSTRALIAN GP	Adelaide	1	Marlboro McLaren International	G	1.5 t/c McLaren MP4/2C-TAG V6		4/26

1987

Championship position: 4th   Wins: 3   Pole positions: 0   Fastest laps: 2   Points scored: 46

Pos	Race	Circuit	No	Team		Car	Notes	Grid
1	BRAZILIAN GP	Rio	1	Marlboro McLaren International	G	1.5 t/c McLaren MP4/3-TAG V6		5/23
ret	SAN MARINO GP	Imola	1	Marlboro McLaren International	G	1.5 t/c McLaren MP4/3-TAG V6	alternator	4/27
1	BELGIAN GP	Spa	1	Marlboro McLaren International	G	1.5 t/c McLaren MP4/3-TAG V6	FL	6/26
9/ret	MONACO GP	Monte Carlo	1	Marlboro McLaren International	G	1.5 t/c McLaren MP4/3-TAG V6	engine/3 laps behind	4/26
3	US GP (DETROIT)	Detroit	1	Marlboro McLaren International	G	1.5 t/c McLaren MP4/3-TAG V6		5/26
3	FRENCH GP	Paul Ricard	1	Marlboro McLaren International	G	1.5 t/c McLaren MP4/3-TAG V6		2/26
ret	BRITISH GP	Silverstone	1	Marlboro McLaren International	G	1.5 t/c McLaren MP4/3-TAG V6	clutch bearings/electrics	4/26
7/ret	GERMAN GP	Hockenheim	1	Marlboro McLaren International	G	1.5 t/c McLaren MP4/3-TAG V6	alternator belt/5 laps behind	3/26
3	HUNGARIAN GP	Hungaroring	1	Marlboro McLaren International	G	1.5 t/c McLaren MP4/3-TAG V6		4/26
6	AUSTRIAN GP	Österreichring	1	Marlboro McLaren International	G	1.5 t/c McLaren MP4/3-TAG V6	started from pit lane/-2 laps	9/26
15	ITALIAN GP	Monza	1	Marlboro McLaren International	G	1.5 t/c McLaren MP4/3-TAG V6	pit stop/misfire/4 laps behind	5/28
1	PORTUGUESE GP	Estoril	1	Marlboro McLaren International	G	1.5 t/c McLaren MP4/3-TAG V6		3/27
2	SPANISH GP	Jerez	1	Marlboro McLaren International	G	1.5 t/c McLaren MP4/3-TAG V6		7/28
ret	MEXICAN GP	Mexico City	1	Marlboro McLaren International	G	1.5 t/c McLaren MP4/3-TAG V6	accident with Piquet	5/27
7	JAPANESE GP	Suzuka	1	Marlboro McLaren International	G	1.5 t/c McLaren MP4/3-TAG V6	pit stop/puncture/FL/-1 lap	2/27
ret	AUSTRALIAN GP	Adelaide	1	Marlboro McLaren International	G	1.5 t/c McLaren MP4/3-TAG V6	brake problem/accident	2/27

1988

Championship position: 2nd   Wins: 7   Pole positions: 2   Fastest laps: 7   Points scored: 95

Pos	Race	Circuit	No	Team		Car	Notes	Grid
1	BRAZILIAN GP	Rio	11	Honda Marlboro McLaren	G	1.5 t/c McLaren MP4/4-Honda V6		3/31
2	SAN MARINO GP	Imola	11	Honda Marlboro McLaren	G	1.5 t/c McLaren MP4/4-Honda V6	FL	2/30
1	MONACO GP	Monte Carlo	11	Honda Marlboro McLaren	G	1.5 t/c McLaren MP4/4-Honda V6		2/30
1	MEXICAN GP	Mexico City	11	Honda Marlboro McLaren	G	1.5 t/c McLaren MP4/4-Honda V6	FL	2/30
2	CANADIAN GP	Montreal	11	Honda Marlboro McLaren	G	1.5 t/c McLaren MP4/4-Honda V6		2/31
2	US GP (DETROIT)	Detroit	11	Honda Marlboro McLaren	G	1.5 t/c McLaren MP4/4-Honda V6	FL	4/31
1	FRENCH GP	Paul Ricard	11	Honda Marlboro McLaren	G	1.5 t/c McLaren MP4/4-Honda V6	FL	1/31
ret	BRITISH GP	Silverstone	11	Honda Marlboro McLaren	G	1.5 t/c McLaren MP4/4-Honda V6	handling in wet conditions	4/31
2	GERMAN GP	Hockenheim	11	Honda Marlboro McLaren	G	1.5 t/c McLaren MP4/4-Honda V6		2/31
2	HUNGARIAN GP	Hungaroring	11	Honda Marlboro McLaren	G	1.5 t/c McLaren MP4/4-Honda V6	FL	7/31
2	BELGIAN GP	Spa	11	Honda Marlboro McLaren	G	1.5 t/c McLaren MP4/4-Honda V6		2/31
ret	ITALIAN GP	Monza	11	Honda Marlboro McLaren	G	1.5 t/c McLaren MP4/4-Honda V6	engine	2/31
1	PORTUGUESE GP	Estoril	11	Honda Marlboro McLaren	G	1.5 t/c McLaren MP4/4-Honda V6		1/31
1	SPANISH GP	Jerez	11	Honda Marlboro McLaren	G	1.5 t/c McLaren MP4/4-Honda V6	FL	2/31
2	JAPANESE GP	Suzuka	11	Honda Marlboro McLaren	G	1.5 t/c McLaren MP4/4-Honda V6		2/31
1	AUSTRALIAN GP	Adelaide	11	Honda Marlboro McLaren	G	1.5 t/c McLaren MP4/4-Honda V6	FL	2/31

1989

Championship position: WORLD CHAMPION   Wins: 4   Pole positions: 2   Fastest laps: 5   Points scored: 81

Pos	Race	Circuit	No	Team		Car	Notes	Grid
2	BRAZILIAN GP	Rio	2	Honda Marlboro McLaren	G	3.5 McLaren MP4/5-Honda V10		5/38
2	SAN MARINO GP	Imola	2	Honda Marlboro McLaren	G	3.5 McLaren MP4/5-Honda V10	aggregate of two parts/FL	2/39
2	MONACO GP	Monte Carlo	2	Honda Marlboro McLaren	G	3.5 McLaren MP4/5-Honda V10	FL	2/38
5	MEXICAN GP	Mexico City	2	Honda Marlboro McLaren	G	3.5 McLaren MP4/5-Honda V10	wrong choice of tyre type	2/39
1	US GP (PHOENIX)	Phoenix	2	Honda Marlboro McLaren	G	3.5 McLaren MP4/5-Honda V10		2/39
ret	CANADIAN GP	Montreal	2	Honda Marlboro McLaren	G	3.5 McLaren MP4/5-Honda V10	suspension failure	1/39
1	FRENCH GP	Paul Ricard	2	Honda Marlboro McLaren	G	3.5 McLaren MP4/5-Honda V10		1/39
1	BRITISH GP	Silverstone	2	Honda Marlboro McLaren	G	3.5 McLaren MP4/5-Honda V10		2/39
2	GERMAN GP	Hockenheim	2	Honda Marlboro McLaren	G	3.5 McLaren MP4/5-Honda V10		2/39
4	HUNGARIAN GP	Hungaroring	2	Honda Marlboro McLaren	G	3.5 McLaren MP4/5-Honda V10	late tyre stop	5/39
2	BELGIAN GP	Spa	2	Honda Marlboro McLaren	G	3.5 McLaren MP4/5-Honda V10	FL	2/39

1	ITALIAN GP	Monza	2	Honda Marlboro McLaren	G	3.5 McLaren MP4/5-Honda V10	*FL*	4/39
2	PORTUGUESE GP	Estoril	2	Honda Marlboro McLaren	G	3.5 McLaren MP4/5-Honda V10		4/39
3	SPANISH GP	Jerez	2	Honda Marlboro McLaren	G	3.5 McLaren MP4/5-Honda V10		3/38
ret	JAPANESE GP	Suzuka	2	Honda Marlboro McLaren	G	3.5 McLaren MP4/5-Honda V10	*accident with Senna/FL*	2/39
ret/dns	AUSTRALIAN GP	Adelaide	2	Honda Marlboro McLaren	G	3.5 McLaren MP4/5-Honda V10	*refused to restart-due to rain*	2/39

1990   Championship position: 2nd   Wins: 5   Pole positions: 0   Fastest laps: 2   Points scored: 73

ret	US GP (PHOENIX)	Phoenix	1	Scuderia Ferrari SpA	G	3.5 Fiat Ferrari 641 V12	*engine oil leak*	7/35
1	BRAZILIAN GP	Rio	1	Scuderia Ferrari SpA	G	3.5 Fiat Ferrari 641 V12		6/35
4	SAN MARINO GP	Imola	1	Scuderia Ferrari SpA	G	3.5 Fiat Ferrari 641 V12		6/34
ret	MONACO GP	Monte Carlo	1	Scuderia Ferrari SpA	G	3.5 Fiat Ferrari 641 V12	*electrics*	2/35
5	CANADIAN GP	Montreal	1	Scuderia Ferrari SpA	G	3.5 Fiat Ferrari 641 V12	*worn brakes*	3/35
1	MEXICAN GP	Mexico City	1	Scuderia Ferrari SpA	G	3.5 Fiat Ferrari 641 V12	*FL*	13/35
1	FRENCH GP	Paul Ricard	1	Scuderia Ferrari SpA	G	3.5 Fiat Ferrari 641 V12		4/35
1	BRITISH GP	Silverstone	1	Scuderia Ferrari SpA	G	3.5 Fiat Ferrari 641 V12		5/35
4	GERMAN GP	Hockenheim	1	Scuderia Ferrari SpA	G	3.5 Fiat Ferrari 641 V12		3/35
ret	HUNGARIAN GP	Hungaroring	1	Scuderia Ferrari SpA	G	3.5 Fiat Ferrari 641 V12	*clutch seized-spun off*	8/35
2	BELGIAN GP	Spa	1	Scuderia Ferrari SpA	G	3.5 Fiat Ferrari 641 V12	*FL*	3/33
2	ITALIAN GP	Monza	1	Scuderia Ferrari SpA	G	3.5 Fiat Ferrari 641 V12		2/33
3	PORTUGUESE GP	Estoril	1	Scuderia Ferrari SpA	G	3.5 Fiat Ferrari 641 V12		2/33
1	SPANISH GP	Jerez	1	Scuderia Ferrari SpA	G	3.5 Fiat Ferrari 641 V12		2/33
ret	JAPANESE GP	Suzuka	1	Scuderia Ferrari SpA	G	3.5 Fiat Ferrari 641 V12	*first corner crash with Senna*	2/30
3	AUSTRALIAN GP	Adelaide	1	Scuderia Ferrari SpA	G	3.5 Fiat Ferrari 641 V12		4/30

1991   Championship position: 5th   Wins: 0   Pole positions: 0   Fastest laps: 1   Points scored: 31

2	US GP (PHOENIX)	Phoenix	27	Scuderia Ferrari SpA	G	3.5 Fiat Ferrari 642 V12		2/34
4	BRAZILIAN GP	Interlagos	27	Scuderia Ferrari SpA	G	3.5 Fiat Ferrari 642 V12		6/34
dns	SAN MARINO GP	Imola	27	Scuderia Ferrari SpA	G	3.5 Fiat Ferrari 642 V12	*spun off on parade lap*	(3)/34
5	MONACO GP	Monte Carlo	27	Scuderia Ferrari SpA	G	3.5 Fiat Ferrari 642 V12	*late pit stop-tyres/FL/-1 lap*	7/34
ret	CANADIAN GP	Montreal	27	Scuderia Ferrari SpA	G	3.5 Fiat Ferrari 642 V12	*gearbox*	4/34
ret	MEXICAN GP	Mexico City	27	Scuderia Ferrari SpA	G	3.5 Fiat Ferrari 642 V12	*alternator*	7/34
2	FRENCH GP	Magny Cours	27	Scuderia Ferrari SpA	G	3.5 Fiat Ferrari 643 V12		2/34
3	BRITISH GP	Silverstone	27	Scuderia Ferrari SpA	G	3.5 Fiat Ferrari 643 V12		5/34
ret	GERMAN GP	Hockenheim	27	Scuderia Ferrari SpA	G	3.5 Fiat Ferrari 643 V12	*spun off unable to restart*	5/34
ret	HUNGARIAN GP	Hungaroring	27	Scuderia Ferrari SpA	G	3.5 Fiat Ferrari 643 V12	*engine*	4/34
ret	BELGIAN GP	Spa	27	Scuderia Ferrari SpA	G	3.5 Fiat Ferrari 643 V12	*engine*	2/34
3	ITALIAN GP	Monza	27	Scuderia Ferrari SpA	G	3.5 Fiat Ferrari 643 V12		5/34
ret	PORTUGUESE GP	Estoril	27	Scuderia Ferrari SpA	G	3.5 Fiat Ferrari 643 V12	*engine*	5/34
2	SPANISH GP	Barcelona	27	Scuderia Ferrari SpA	G	3.5 Fiat Ferrari 643 V12		6/33
4	JAPANESE GP	Suzuka	27	Scuderia Ferrari SpA	G	3.5 Fiat Ferrari 643 V12		4/31

1993   Championship position: WORLD CHAMPION   Wins: 7   Pole positions: 13   Fastest laps: 6   Points scored: 99

1	SOUTH AFRICAN GP	Kyalami	2	Canon Williams Team	G	3.5 Williams FW15C-Renault V10	*FL*	1/26
ret	BRAZILIAN GP	Interlagos	2	Canon Williams Team	G	3.5 Williams FW15C-Renault V10	*spun off in rainstorm*	1/26
3	EUROPEAN GP	Donington	2	Canon Williams Team	G	3.5 Williams FW15C-Renault V10		1/26
1	SAN MARINO GP	Imola	2	Canon Williams Team	G	3.5 Williams FW15C-Renault V10	*FL*	1/26
1	SPANISH GP	Barcelona	2	Canon Williams Team	G	3.5 Williams FW15C-Renault V10		1/26
4	MONACO GP	Monte Carlo	2	Canon Williams Team	G	3.5 Williams FW15C-Renault V10	*jump start-stop & go penalty/FL*	1/26
1	CANADIAN GP	Montreal	2	Canon Williams Team	G	3.5 Williams FW15C-Renault V10		1/26
1	FRENCH GP	Magny Cours	2	Canon Williams Team	G	3.5 Williams FW15C-Renault V10		2/26
1	BRITISH GP	Silverstone	2	Canon Williams Team	G	3.5 Williams FW15C-Renault V10	*50th Grand Prix win*	1/26
1	GERMAN GP	Hockenheim	2	Canon Williams Team	G	3.5 Williams FW15C-Renault V10	*stop & go penalty*	1/26
12	HUNGARIAN GP	Hungaroring	2	Canon Williams Team	G	3.5 Williams FW15C-Renault V10	*started at back/stop-wing//FL/-7 laps*	1/26
3	BELGIAN GP	Spa	2	Canon Williams Team	G	3.5 Williams FW15C-Renault V10	*FL*	1/25
12	ITALIAN GP	Monza	2	Canon Williams Team	G	3.5 Williams FW15C-Renault V10	*engine/5 laps behind*	1/26
2	PORTUGUESE GP	Estoril	2	Canon Williams Team	G	3.5 Williams FW15C-Renault V10		2/26
2	JAPANESE GP	Suzuka	2	Canon Williams Team	G	3.5 Williams FW15C-Renault V10	*FL*	1/24
2	AUSTRALIAN GP	Adelaide	2	Canon Williams Team	G	3.5 Williams FW15C-Renault V10		2/24

GP Starts: 199 (200)   GP Wins: 51   Pole positions: 33   Fastest laps: 41   Points: 798.5

Alain Prost's fourth title, won in 1993 with Williams-Renault, is now almost overlooked. The Frenchman did not enjoy the political climate in Grand Prix racing at the time and was happy to retire at season's end.

TOM PRYCE

Tom Pryce's death at Kyalami in 1977 robbed Britain of one of its great natural talents of the era who, had he survived, would surely have gone on to achieve much greater things. The quiet and reserved Welshman had got into motor racing in 1970 via a competition in the Daily Express in which he won a Lola T200 Formula Ford. He made a good start in the car before switching to the Formula Ford 100 series in 1971, where he dominated in his TAS Racing Royale. This success took him to the works Royale team to race in Formula Super Vee before embarking on a Formula 3 season with the team in 1972. Unfortunately this effort was hampered by a lack of finance, and Tom's season was interrupted by a broken leg sustained in a heat of the Monaco F3 race.

Royale ran Tom in Formula Atlantic in 1973 and he was enjoying a successful season when he was given an opportunity to drive the Motul Rondel F2 car in selected races. A second place at Norisring signified better things ahead, and sure enough in 1974 Tom joined the little Token team for the International Trophy and Belgian GP. When the team's entry for Monaco was refused due to the Welshman's lack of experience, he contested the F3 support race instead and, in an astonishing display of dominance, simply drove into the distance to win by the proverbial country mile.

With Shadow still looking for a suitable replacement for the late Peter Revson, Pryce was drafted into the team after Brian Redman had decided not to stay. In only his second race at Dijon he put the car onto the second row of the grid and that was enough for Don Nichols to decide he had found his man. The 1975 season started well with a win in the Race of Champions, but it was an up-and-down year, pole position for the British GP and superb drives in both Germany and Austria being the highlights. The team received a major setback when UOP, their main sponsor, pulled out at the end of the year and the subsequent cash shortage certainly hindered both the team's and Tom's progress in 1976, the Welshman loyally staying on when plenty of others would have been seeking to better their lot elsewhere. The 1977 season began with new sponsors and a fresh enthusiasm, but a bizarre and horrendous accident at Kyalami cruelly cut him down. Thankfully he was probably already dead as his car hurtled towards oblivion, having hit an errant marshal as he crossed the track carrying a fire extinguisher.

PRYCE, Tom (GB) b 11/6/1949, Ruthin, Denbighshire, North Wales – d 5/3/1977, Kyalami Circuit, South Africa

1974 Championship position: 18th=   Wins: 0   Pole positions: 0   Fastest laps: 0   Points scored: 1

	Race	Circuit	No	Entrant	Tyres	Car/Engine	Comment	Q Pos/Entries
ret	BELGIAN GP	Nivelles	42	Token Racing	F	3.0 Token RJ02-Cosworth V8	collision with Scheckter	20/32
ret	DUTCH GP	Zandvoort	16	UOP Shadow Racing Team	G	3.0 Shadow DN3-Cosworth V8	collision with Hunt	11/27
ret	FRENCH GP	Dijon	16	UOP Shadow Racing Team	G	3.0 Shadow DN3-Cosworth V8	collision with Hunt	3/30
8	BRITISH GP	Brands Hatch	16	UOP Shadow Racing Team	G	3.0 Shadow DN3-Cosworth V8	1 lap behind	=5/34
6	GERMAN GP	Nürburgring	16	UOP Shadow Racing Team	G	3.0 Shadow DN3-Cosworth V8		11/32
ret	AUSTRIAN GP	Österreichring	16	UOP Shadow Racing Team	G	3.0 Shadow DN3-Cosworth V8	spun off-could not restart	16/31
10	ITALIAN GP	Monza	16	UOP Shadow Racing Team	G	3.0 Shadow DN3-Cosworth V8	2 laps behind	22/31
ret	CANADIAN GP	Mosport Park	16	UOP Shadow Racing Team	G	3.0 Shadow DN3-Cosworth V8	engine	13/30
nc	US GP	Watkins Glen	16	UOP Shadow Racing Team	G	3.0 Shadow DN3-Cosworth V8	stops/nose cone/misfire/-12 laps	18/30

1975 Championship position: 10th   Wins: 0   Pole positions: 1   Fastest laps: 0   Points scored: 8

	Race	Circuit	No	Entrant	Tyres	Car/Engine	Comment	Q Pos/Entries
12/ret	ARGENTINE GP	Buenos Aires	16	UOP Shadow Racing Team	G	3.0 Shadow DN3B-Cosworth V8	transmission/2 laps behind	14/23
ret	BRAZILIAN GP	Interlagos	16	UOP Shadow Racing Team	G	3.0 Shadow DN3B-Cosworth V8	spun off	14/23
9	SOUTH AFRICAN GP	Kyalami	16	UOP Shadow Racing Team	G	3.0 Shadow DN5-Cosworth V8	1 lap behind	19/28
ret	SPANISH GP	Montjuich Park	16	UOP Shadow Racing Team	G	3.0 Shadow DN5-Cosworth V8	collision with Brise	8/26
ret	MONACO GP	Monte Carlo	16	UOP Shadow Racing Team	G	3.0 Shadow DN5-Cosworth V8	hit barrier-damaged rear wing	2/26
6	BELGIAN GP	Zolder	16	UOP Shadow Racing Team	G	3.0 Shadow DN5-Cosworth V8		5/24
ret	SWEDISH GP	Anderstorp	16	UOP Shadow Racing Team	G	3.0 Shadow DN5-Cosworth V8	spun off-could not restart	7/26
6	DUTCH GP	Zandvoort	16	UOP Shadow Racing Team	G	3.0 Shadow DN5-Cosworth V8	1 lap behind	12/25
ret	FRENCH GP	Paul Ricard	16	UOP Shadow Racing Team	G	3.0 Shadow DN5-Cosworth V8	transmission	=5/26
ret	BRITISH GP	Silverstone	16	UOP Shadow Racing Team	G	3.0 Shadow DN5-Cosworth V8	spun off	1/28
4	GERMAN GP	Nürburgring	16	UOP Shadow Racing Team	G	3.0 Shadow DN5-Cosworth V8		16/26
3*	AUSTRIAN GP	Österreichring	16	UOP Shadow Racing Team	G	3.0 Shadow DN5-Cosworth V8	*rain shortened race-half points	15/30
6	ITALIAN GP	Monza	16	UOP Shadow Racing Team	G	3.0 Shadow DN5-Cosworth V8		14/28
nc	US GP	Watkins Glen	16	UOP Shadow Racing Team	G	3.0 Shadow DN5-Cosworth V8	pit stops/misfire/-7 laps	7/24

1976 Championship position: 11th=   Wins: 0   Pole positions: 0   Fastest laps: 0   Points scored: 10

	Race	Circuit	No	Entrant	Tyres	Car/Engine	Comment	Q Pos/Entries
3	BRAZILIAN GP	Interlagos	16	Shadow Racing Team	G	3.0 Shadow DN5-Cosworth V8		12/22
7	SOUTH AFRICAN GP	Kyalami	16	Shadow Racing Team	G	3.0 Shadow DN5-Cosworth V8	1 lap behind	7/25
ret	US GP WEST	Long Beach	16	Shadow Racing Team	G	3.0 Shadow DN5-Cosworth V8	driveshaft	5/27
8	SPANISH GP	Jarama	16	Shadow Racing Team	G	3.0 Shadow DN5-Cosworth V8	1 lap behind	22/30
10	BELGIAN GP	Zolder	16	Shadow Racing Team	G	3.0 Shadow DN5-Cosworth V8	2 laps behind	13/29

7	MONACO GP	Monte Carlo	16	Shadow Racing Team	G	3.0 Shadow DN5-Cosworth V8	*1 lap behind*	15/25
9	SWEDISH GP	Anderstorp	16	Shadow Racing Team	G	3.0 Shadow DN5-Cosworth V8	*1 lap behind*	12/27
8	FRENCH GP	Paul Ricard	16	Shadow Racing Team	G	3.0 Shadow DN5-Cosworth V8		16/30
4	BRITISH GP	Brands Hatch	16	Shadow Racing Team	G	3.0 Shadow DN5-Cosworth V8	*1 lap behind*	20/30
8	GERMAN GP	Nürburgring	16	Shadow Racing with Tabatip	G	3.0 Shadow DN5-Cosworth V8		18/28
ret	AUSTRIAN GP	Österreichring	16	Shadow Racing with Tabatip	G	3.0 Shadow DN5-Cosworth V8	*brakes*	6/25
4	DUTCH GP	Zandvoort	16	Shadow Racing Team	G	3.0 Shadow DN8-Cosworth V8		3/27
8	ITALIAN GP	Monza	16	Shadow Racing Team	G	3.0 Shadow DN8-Cosworth V8		15/29
11	CANADIAN GP	Mosport Park	16	Shadow Racing Team	G	3.0 Shadow DN8-Cosworth V8	*1 lap behind*	13/27
ret	US GP EAST	Watkins Glen	16	Shadow Racing Team	G	3.0 Shadow DN8-Cosworth V8	*engine*	9/27
ret	JAPANESE GP	Mount Fuji	16	Shadow Racing Team	G	3.0 Shadow DN8-Cosworth V8	*engine-seized*	14/27
	1977	Championship position: 0	Wins: 0	Pole positions: 0	Fastest laps: 0	Points scored: 0			
nc	ARGENTINE GP	Buenos Aires	16	Shadow Racing Team	G	3.0 Shadow DN8-Cosworth V8	*pit stop/gear selection/-8 laps*	9/21
ret	BRAZILIAN GP	Interlagos	16	Shadow Racing Team	G	3.0 Shadow DN8-Cosworth V8	*engine*	12/22
ret	SOUTH AFRICAN GP	Kyalami	16	Shadow Racing Team	G	3.0 Shadow DN8-Cosworth V8	*fatal accident*	15/23

GP Starts: 42   GP Wins: 0   Pole positions: 1   Fastest laps: 0   Points: 19

DAVID PURLEY

Some drivers leave behind memories far greater than the sum of their deeds, and David Purley was undoubtedly such a man: a model of personal courage, a great sportsman, and a fine racing driver as well. He began racing with a big Cobra in 1968, then moved on to a Chevron GT, before taking a shot at Formula 3 in 1970 in his family-backed Lec Refrigeration Brabham. At this stage he was a little wild and wayward, and he certainly relished the dangerous challenge presented by events such as the GP of Chimay, taking a hat-trick of wins on this road circuit between 1970 and '72.

By 1972 Purley had progressed to Formula 2, taking a splendid third place at Pau, but in 1973 he dropped down for a season of Formula Atlantic, during the course of which he hired a March to go Grand Prix racing for the first time. Although his results were forgettable, his actions at the Dutch GP when he single-handedly tried in vain to save poor Roger Williamson were certainly not. David's bravery won him the George Medal, and the admiration of the Grand Prix world.

In 1974 Purley teamed up with Peter Harper to race in Formula 2 once more and enjoyed a successful season, taking second places at the Salzburgring, Rouen and Enna, and in the end-of-year Macau GP. Back under his own Lec banner, Purley then contested two seasons of F5000 with a Chevron, taking the Shellsport championship in 1976 with six victories.

Seeing Formula 1 as unfinished business, David commissioned his own Lec chassis to race in 1977, taking a sixth place in the Race of Champions, and then briefly leading the wet Belgian GP during a round of pit stops. Disaster struck in practice for the British GP when he crashed his car, sustaining horrendous multiple injuries that would have killed a man of lesser fortitude. Displaying incredible will to survive and then recover, Purley endured months of rehabilitation, racing his Porsche in club events in preparation for a serious return to the track in the Aurora series towards the end of 1979. He may have competed in only four rounds, but a fourth place at Snetterton was an amazing achievement.

Purley then restricted his racing to occasional club events, but his love for speed and danger remained unquenchable. He took up aerobatics with a Pitts Special biplane, until fate at last caught up with him in July 1985, when his plane crashed into the sea off Bognor Regis. One of Britain's greatest characters had finally run out of luck.

PURLEY, David (GB) b 26/1/1945, Bognor Regis, Sussex – d 2/7/1985, off coast nr Bognor Regis, Sussex

	1973	Championship position: Unplaced						
	Race	*Circuit*	*No*	*Entrant*	*Tyres*	*Car/Engine*	*Comment*	*Q Pos/Entries*
ret	MONACO GP	Monte Carlo	18	LEC Refrigeration Racing	F	3.0 March 731-Cosworth V8	*oil tank*	24/26
dns	BRITISH GP	Silverstone	18	LEC Refrigeration Racing	F	3.0 March 731-Cosworth V8	*practice accident*	(=16)/29
ret	DUTCH GP	Zandvoort	18	LEC Refrigeration Racing	F	3.0 March 731-Cosworth V8	*stopped-tried to aid Williamson*	21/24
15	GERMAN GP	Nürburgring	18	LEC Refrigeration Racing	F	3.0 March 731-Cosworth V8	*1 lap behind*	23/23
9	ITALIAN GP	Monza	29	LEC Refrigeration Racing	F	3.0 March 731-Cosworth V8	*1 lap behind*	24/25
	1974	Championship position: Unplaced						
dnq	BRITISH GP	Brands Hatch	42	Team Harper-Token Racing	F	3.0 Token RJ02-Cosworth V8		=25/34
	1977	Championship position: Unplaced						
dnq	SPANISH GP	Jarama	31	LEC Refrigeration Racing	G	3.0 LEC CRP1-Cosworth V8		30/31
13	BELGIAN GP	Zolder	31	LEC Refrigeration Racing	G	3.0 LEC CRP1-Cosworth V8	*3 laps behind*	20/32
14	SWEDISH GP	Anderstorp	31	LEC Refrigeration Racing	G	3.0 LEC CRP1-Cosworth V8	*2 laps behind*	19/31
ret	FRENCH GP	Dijon	31	LEC Refrigeration Racing	G	3.0 LEC CRP1-Cosworth V8	*brake failure/accident*	21/30
dnpq	BRITISH GP	Silverstone	31	LEC Refrigeration Racing	G	3.0 LEC CRP1-Cosworth V8	*accident in pre-qualifying*	31/36

GP Starts: 7   GP Wins: 0   Pole positions: 0   Fastest laps: 0   Points: 0

DIETER QUESTER

Since coming into motor racing in 1965, after many years competing in speedboats and motor cycling, Quester has been identified with the BMW marque for the bulk of his long career – not surprisingly, perhaps, since he had married Julianna, the daughter of Alexander von Falkenhausen.

Dieter really came to prominence by winning the Austrian touring car championship in a BMW 1800 in 1966, and his sideways driving style in the factory BMW then took him to two consecutive European touring car titles in 1968-69. He was also part of BMW's largely unsuccessful Formula 2 programme, though he did manage a victory at Hockenheim at the end of 1970. Quester switched to a March for a season of Formula 2 in 1971, and performed well, winning the Lottery GP and scoring five second places. It was around this period that, frustrated at being unable to get a Formula 1 ride, he more than once seriously considered retirement, but he carried on and eventually drove a rented Surtees in the 1974 Austrian GP.

Subsequently concentrating on sports cars and saloons, he was European G2 touring car champion in 1977 and a regular in the BMW Procar series of 1979-80, while throughout the nineties he has been a permanent fixture in BMW touring cars in the European, German and Austrian championships, as well as competing in a BMW M3 in the IMSA GT3 class in America in 1996 and 1997.

IAN RABY

A car dealer from Brighton, Raby began racing in the early fifties in Formula 3 with specials which he christened 'Puddle Jumper', but he wasn't really competitive until he raced a Cooper in 1956. After two years with Cooper and Elva sports cars, Raby returned to single-seaters in 1959-60 with both a Cooper and a Hume-Climax, gaining success only in modest Formula Libre races.

In 1961-62 he raced mainly in Formula Junior, before buying the Gilby-BRM from Syd Greene to race in Formula 1 in 1963. Ian gained a third place at Vallelunga in the Rome GP, but precious little else, and in 1964-65 he relied on a Brabham BT3, still no more than making up the numbers.

With the new 3-litre formula in operation for 1966, Raby stepped down into F2 with a Brabham BT14-Cosworth. He scored a good fourth place at the Eifelrennen, before a crash at Brands Hatch curtailed his season. Despite his relatively old age, Ian undertook a full season of Formula 2 in 1967, gaining the occasional top-six finish, before a serious crash at Zandvoort left him hospitalised with multiple injuries to which, he succumbed some weeks later.

QUESTER, Dieter (A) b 30/5/1939, Vienna

	1969	Championship position: Unplaced						
	Race	Circuit	No	Entrant	Tyres	Car/Engine	Comment	Q Pos/Entries
dns	GERMAN GP	Nürburgring	25	Bayerische Moteren Werke	D	1.6 BMW 269 4 F2	w/drawn after Mitter's accident	(21)/26
	1974	Championship position: Unplaced						
9	AUSTRIAN GP	Österreichring	30	Memphis International-Team Surtees	F	3.0 Surtees TS16-Cosworth V8	3 laps behind	23/31

GP Starts: 1   GP Wins: 0   Pole positions: 0   Fastest laps: 0   Points: 0

RABY, Ian (GB) b 22/9/1921 – d 7/11/1967

	1963	Championship position: Unplaced						
	Race	Circuit	No	Entrant	Tyres	Car/Engine	Comment	Q Pos/Entries
ret	BRITISH GP	Silverstone	26	Ian Raby (Racing)	D	1.5 Gilby-BRM V8	gearbox	19/23
dnq	GERMAN GP	Nürburgring	25	Ian Raby (Racing)	D	1.5 Gilby-BRM V8		24/26
dnq	ITALIAN GP	Monza	50	Ian Raby (Racing)	D	1.5 Gilby-BRM V8		22/28
	1964	Championship position: Unplaced						
ret	BRITISH GP	Brands Hatch	23	Ian Raby (Racing)	D	1.5 Brabham BT3-BRM V8	rear hub-accident	=16/25
dnq	ITALIAN GP	Monza	56	Ian Raby (Racing)	D	1.5 Brabham BT3-BRM V8		25/25
	1965	Championship position: Unplaced						
11	BRITISH GP	Silverstone	24	Ian Raby (Racing)	D	1.5 Brabham BT3-BRM V8	7 laps behind	20/23
dnq	GERMAN GP	Nürburgring	23	Ian Raby (Racing)	D	1.5 Brabham BT3-BRM V8		22/22

GP Starts: 3   GP Wins: 0   Pole positions: 0   Fastest laps: 0   Points: 0

RAHAL, Bobby (USA) b 10/1/1953, Medina, Ohio

	1978	Championship position: Unplaced						
	Race	Circuit	No	Entrant	Tyres	Car/Engine	Comment	Q Pos/Entries
12	US GP EAST	Watkins Glen	21	Walter Wolf Racing	G	3.0 Wolf WR5-Cosworth V8	1 lap behind	20/27
ret	CANADIAN GP	Montreal	21	Walter Wolf Racing	G	3.0 Wolf WR1-Cosworth V8	fuel system	20/28
dns	"	"	21	Walter Wolf Racing	G	3.0 Wolf WR5-Cosworth V8	practice accident	–/–

GP Starts: 2   GP Wins: 0   Pole positions: 0   Fastest laps: 0   Points: 0

BOBBY RAHAL

From the start, Rahal was refreshingly different from most American drivers in that he wanted to go road racing, and was prepared to come to Europe and measure himself against the best talent around. After three years (1975-77) in Canadian Formula Atlantic, where he was somewhat overshadowed by the exploits of Gilles Villeneuve, Bobby crossed the Atlantic for a selection of Formula 3 races with Walter Wolf Racing. He did well enough to be offered a drive with the team in the end-of-season United States and Canadian GPs, the latter in the old WR1 chassis, which had been dragged from a museum after he had pranged his WR5 in practice.

Determined to make the grade, he came back to Europe in 1979 for a full Formula 2 season with a works Chevron, scoring some good finishes in a car which was not the most competitive in the series. That was the end of Rahal's dreams of Formula 1, however, for in 1980 he went Can-Am racing, which was to be followed by a successful year in endurance events, Bobby winning the Daytona 24 Hours and taking second place at Brands Hatch in a Porsche 935 turbo.

In 1982 he moved into Indy Car racing, winning the Cleveland race and finishing second in the PPG Cup, and in 1986, racing for Truesports, Rahal won the championship and the Indy 500. He won the title again in 1992, having set up his own team in partnership with Carl Hogan.

After this third championship Bobby raced on to the end of the 1998 season, and although he failed to add to his 24 career wins Rahal remained a canny and robust racer who could never be discounted, given his still-burning desire to succeed. Having ended a fabulous CART career, Bobby continues to run his own highly professional outfit from the safer side of the pit wall.

PIERRE-HENRI RAPHANEL

After finishing third overall in the 1984 series, Raphanel was French Formula 3 champion in 1985, successfully defending his early-season lead from ORECA team-mate Yannick Dalmas as the season wore on.

Promoted into the ORECA F3000 team for 1986, Raphanel soon found his feet and ended the season looking a good bet for honours in 1987, but somehow he failed to spark thereafter, enduring two lacklustre seasons. At the end of 1988 he stood in for his former team-mate Dalmas at Larrousse, but gearbox problems stymied his chances of qualifying.

Signing to race for Coloni in 1989, he found himself among the early-risers attempting to pre-qualify, and did extremely well to get on the grid at Monaco. A mid-season move to Rial merely meant that he could turn up a little later for practice, but he was still to find his Sundays free.

Pierre-Henri subsequently drove in Japanese Group C and touring cars, and figured in Toyota's Le Mans challenge, finishing second in 1992 (with Sekiya and Acheson). Raphanel has since enjoyed a successful career in sports cars, and after racing a Courage-Porsche at the Sarthe circuit with Pascal Fabre in 1994 then switched to GT racing with a McLaren F1 GTR between 1995 and 1997.

In 1999 he competed in the All-Japan touring car championship with a Toyota Supra, but the Frenchman apparently plans to return to the FIA GT series in 2000 with the Belmondo team.

RAPHANEL, Pierre-Henri (F) b 27/5/1961, Algiers, Algeria

	1988	Championship position: Unplaced						
	Race	Circuit	No	Entrant	Tyres	Car/engine	Comment	Q Pos/Entries
dnq	AUSTRALIAN GP	Adelaide	29	Larrousse Calmels	G	3.5 Lola LC88-Cosworth V8		29/31
	1989	Championship position: Unplaced						
dnpq	BRAZILIAN GP	Rio	32	Coloni SpA	P	3.5 Coloni FC88-Cosworth V8		34/38
dnpq	SAN MARINO GP	Imola	32	Coloni SpA	P	3.5 Coloni FC88-Cosworth V8		36/39
ret	MONACO GP	Monte Carlo	32	Coloni SpA	P	3.5 Coloni FC88-Cosworth V8	gearbox	18/38
dnpq	MEXICAN GP	Mexico City	32	Coloni SpA	P	3.5 Coloni FC88-Cosworth V8		39/39
dnpq	US GP (PHOENIX)	Phoenix	32	Coloni SpA	P	3.5 Coloni FC88-Cosworth V8		32/39
dnpq	CANADIAN GP	Montreal	32	Coloni SpA	P	3.5 Coloni C3-Cosworth V8		39/39
dnpq	FRENCH GP	Paul Ricard	32	Coloni SpA	P	3.5 Coloni C3-Cosworth V8		36/39
dnpq	BRITISH GP	Silverstone	32	Coloni SpA	P	3.5 Coloni FC3-Cosworth V8		37/39
dnpq	GERMAN GP	Hockenheim	32	Coloni SpA	P	3.5 Coloni FC3-Cosworth V8		36/39
dnpq	HUNGARIAN GP	Hungaroring	32	Coloni SpA	P	3.5 Coloni FC88-Cosworth V8		39/39
dnq	BELGIAN GP	Spa	39	Rial Racing	G	3.5 Rial ARC2-Cosworth V8		30/39
dnq	ITALIAN GP	Monza	39	Rial Racing	G	3.5 Rial ARC2-Cosworth V8		29/39
dnq	PORTUGUESE GP	Estoril	39	Rial Racing	G	3.5 Rial ARC2-Cosworth V8		30/39
dnq	SPANISH GP	Jerez	39	Rial Racing	G	3.5 Rial ARC2-Cosworth V8		28/38
dnq	JAPANESE GP	Suzuka	38	Rial Racing	G	3.5 Rial ARC2-Cosworth V8		29/39
dnq	AUSTRALIAN GP	Adelaide	38	Rial Racing	G	3.5 Rial ARC2-Cosworth V8		29/39

GP Starts: 1   GP Wins: 0   Pole positions: 0   Fastest laps: 0   Points: 0

RATZENBERGER, Roland (A) b 4/7/1962, Salzburg – d 30/4/1994, Imola Circuit, Italy

	1994	Championship position: Unplaced							
	Race	Circuit	No	Entrant	Tyres	Car/Engine		Comment	Q Pos/Entries
dnq	BRAZILIAN GP	Interlagos	32	MTV Simtek Ford	G	3.5 Simtek S941-Ford HB V8			27/28
11	PACIFIC GP	T.I. Circuit	32	MTV Simtek Ford	G	3.5 Simtek S941-Ford HB V8		5 laps behind	26/28
dns	SAN MARINO GP	Imola	32	MTV Simtek Ford	G	3.5 Simtek S941-Ford HB V8		fatal accident in practice	(26)/28

GP Starts: 1   GP Wins: 0   Pole positions: 0   Fastest laps: 0   Points: 0

ROLAND RATZENBERGER

When Roland was a surprise choice for the second seat at Simtek Grand Prix at the beginning of 1994, he was something of a forgotten figure, having spent the previous four seasons making a very successful career for himself in Japan after his options in Europe had narrowed back in 1989.

Victory in the Formula Ford Festival at Brands Hatch way back in 1986 led to rides with BMW in the FIA world touring car championship, Formula 3 programmes in both Britain and Germany and British F3000. His record in all these disciplines was more than respectable but failed to unlock the doors to a higher echelon, so Roland headed east to continue his racing. He won in touring cars, F3000 and Group C with the SARD Toyota team, the latter category being a particular favourite.

Sadly Roland's part on the Grand Prix stage was truly tragic, for the chance to show his undoubted talent was cruelly cut short when his Simtek crashed during practice for the San Marino GP at nearly 200 mph following a suspected front-wing failure.

HECTOR REBAQUE

An ambitious young Mexican hot-shot, Rebaque came to England in 1974 as a raw 18-year-old to try his hand at Formula Atlantic as a protégé of Fred Opert in a Chevron. The following year, he moved into Formula 2 in Opert's Chevron, before returning across the pond to contest the Canadian Formula Atlantic series in 1975 and 1976.

Itching to get into Grand Prix racing, Hector joined the Hesketh team for a few outings in 1977, qualifying just once. Determined to succeed, he set up his own team the following season, fielding ex-works Lotus 78s, but managed only one top-six finish, in Germany. For 1979 he had Lotus 79s at his disposal but results remained discouraging, so he took the brave – if foolhardy – step of commissioning his own chassis, which only appeared for the last three Grands Prix of the year before the team folded.

In 1980 Hector kicked his heels until the opportunity arose to join Brabham in place of Zunino. Now in a top-notch car, it was up to the driver to prove himself, and on occasion he showed a good turn of speed. In Argentina in 1981, for example, he had the BT49C in a comfortable second place until a rotor arm broke.

Rebaque briefly tried his hand at Indy Car racing in 1982, luckily winning a race at Elkhart Lake when many of the leaders ran out of fuel, but after a mid-season crash at Michigan he developed a distinct aversion to ovals, and retired at season's end at the age of 29.

REBAQUE, Hector (MEX) b 5/2/1956, Mexico City

	1977	Championship position: Unplaced							
	Race	Circuit	No	Entrant	Tyres	Car/Engine		Comment	Q Pos/Entries
dnq	BELGIAN GP	Zolder	39	Hesketh Racing	G	3.0 Hesketh 308E-Cosworth V8			32/32
dnq	SWEDISH GP	Anderstorp	39	Hesketh Racing	G	3.0 Hesketh 308E-Cosworth V8			29/31
dnq	FRENCH GP	Dijon	39	Hesketh Racing	G	3.0 Hesketh 308E-Cosworth V8			28/30
ret	GERMAN GP	Hockenheim	25	Hesketh Racing	G	3.0 Hesketh 308E-Cosworth V8		battery	24/30
dnq	AUSTRIAN GP	Österreichring	25	Hesketh Racing	G	3.0 Hesketh 308E-Cosworth V8			29/30
dnq	DUTCH GP	Zandvoort	25	Hesketh Racing	G	3.0 Hesketh 308E-Cosworth V8			32/34
	1978	Championship position: Unplaced							
dnq	ARGENTINE GP	Buenos Aires	25	Team Rebaque	G	3.0 Lotus 78-Cosworth V8			25/27
ret	BRAZILIAN GP	Rio	25	Team Rebaque	G	3.0 Lotus 78-Cosworth V8		driver fatigue	22/28
10	SOUTH AFRICAN GP	Kyalami	25	Team Rebaque	G	3.0 Lotus 78-Cosworth V8		1 lap behind	21/30
dnpq	US GP WEST	Long Beach	25	Team Rebaque	G	3.0 Lotus 78-Cosworth V8			28/30
dnpq	MONACO GP	Monte Carlo	25	Team Rebaque	G	3.0 Lotus 78-Cosworth V8			28/30

			No	Entrant	Tyres	Car/Engine	Comment	Q Pos/Entries
dnpq	BELGIAN GP	Zolder	25	Team Rebaque	G	3.0 Lotus 78-Cosworth V8		29/30
ret	SPANISH GP	Jarama	25	Team Rebaque	G	3.0 Lotus 78-Cosworth V8	exhaust system	20/29
12	SWEDISH GP	Anderstorp	25	Team Rebaque	G	3.0 Lotus 78-Cosworth V8	2 laps behind	21/27
dnq	FRENCH GP	Paul Ricard	25	Team Rebaque	G	3.0 Lotus 78-Cosworth V8		29/29
ret	BRITISH GP	Brands Hatch	25	Team Rebaque	G	3.0 Lotus 78-Cosworth V8	gearbox	21/30
6	GERMAN GP	Hockenheim	25	Team Rebaque	G	3.0 Lotus 78-Cosworth V8		18/30
ret	AUSTRIAN GP	Österreichring	25	Team Rebaque	G	3.0 Lotus 78-Cosworth V8	clutch	18/31
11	DUTCH GP	Zandvoort	25	Team Rebaque	G	3.0 Lotus 78-Cosworth V8	1 lap behind	20/33
dnq	ITALIAN GP	Monza	25	Team Rebaque	G	3.0 Lotus 78-Cosworth V8		25/32
ret	US GP EAST	Watkins Glen	25	Team Rebaque	G	3.0 Lotus 78-Cosworth V8	clutch	23/27
dnq	CANADIAN GP	Montreal	25	Team Rebaque	G	3.0 Lotus 78-Cosworth V8		26/28

1979 Championship position: Unplaced

			No	Entrant	Tyres	Car/Engine	Comment	Q Pos/Entries
ret	ARGENTINE GP	Buenos Aires	31	Team Rebaque	G	3.0 Lotus 79-Cosworth V8	suspension	19/26
dnq	BRAZILIAN GP	Interlagos	31	Team Rebaque	G	3.0 Lotus 79-Cosworth V8		25/26
ret	SOUTH AFRICAN GP	Kyalami	31	Team Rebaque	G	3.0 Lotus 79-Cosworth V8	engine	23/26
ret	US GP WEST	Long Beach	31	Team Rebaque	G	3.0 Lotus 79-Cosworth V8	accident with Daly	25/26
ret	SPANISH GP	Jarama	31	Team Rebaque	G	3.0 Lotus 79-Cosworth V8	engine	23/27
ret	BELGIAN GP	Zolder	31	Team Rebaque	G	3.0 Lotus 79-Cosworth V8	driveshaft	15/28
12	FRENCH GP	Dijon	31	Team Rebaque	G	3.0 Lotus 79-Cosworth V8	2 laps behind	24/27
9	BRITISH GP	Silverstone	31	Team Rebaque	G	3.0 Lotus 79-Cosworth V8	2 laps behind	24/26
ret	GERMAN GP	Hockenheim	31	Team Rebaque	G	3.0 Lotus 79-Cosworth V8	handling	24/26
dnq	AUSTRIAN GP	Österreichring	31	Team Rebaque	G	3.0 Lotus 79-Cosworth V8		25/26
7	DUTCH GP	Zandvoort	31	Team Rebaque	G	3.0 Lotus 79-Cosworth V8	2 laps behind	24/26
dnq	ITALIAN GP	Monza	31	Team Rebaque	G	3.0 Rebaque HR100-Cosworth V8		28/28
ret	CANADIAN GP	Montreal	31	Team Rebaque	G	3.0 Rebaque HR100-Cosworth V8	engine mounting	22/29
dnq	US GP EAST	Watkins Glen	31	Team Rebaque	G	3.0 Rebaque HR100-Cosworth V8		28/30

1980 Championship position: Unplaced

			No	Entrant	Tyres	Car/Engine	Comment	Q Pos/Entries
7	BRITISH GP	Brands Hatch	6	Parmalat Racing Team	G	3.0 Brabham BT49-Cosworth V8	2 laps behind	17/27
ret	GERMAN GP	Hockenheim	6	Parmalat Racing Team	G	3.0 Brabham BT49-Cosworth V8	gearbox	15/26
10	AUSTRIAN GP	Österreichring	6	Parmalat Racing Team	G	3.0 Brabham BT49-Cosworth V8	1 lap behind	14/25
ret	DUTCH GP	Zandvoort	6	Parmalat Racing Team	G	3.0 Brabham BT49-Cosworth V8	gearbox	13/28
ret	ITALIAN GP	Imola	6	Parmalat Racing Team	G	3.0 Brabham BT49-Cosworth V8	broken rear suspension	9/28
6	CANADIAN GP	Montreal	6	Parmalat Racing Team	G	3.0 Brabham BT49-Cosworth V8	1 lap behind	10/28
ret	US GP EAST	Watkins Glen	6	Parmalat Racing Team	G	3.0 Brabham BT49-Cosworth V8	engine	8/27

1981 Championship position: Unplaced

			No	Entrant	Tyres	Car/Engine	Comment	Q Pos/Entries
ret	US GP WEST	Long Beach	6	Parmalat Racing Team	M	3.0 Brabham BT49C-Cosworth V8	accident	15/29
ret	BRAZILIAN GP	Rio	6	Parmalat Racing Team	M	3.0 Brabham BT49C-Cosworth V8	rear suspension damage	11/30
ret	ARGENTINE GP	Buenos Aires	6	Parmalat Racing Team	M	3.0 Brabham BT49C-Cosworth V8	distibutor rotor arm	6/29
4	SAN MARINO GP	Imola	6	Parmalat Racing Team	M	3.0 Brabham BT49C-Cosworth V8		13/30
ret	BELGIAN GP	Zolder	6	Parmalat Racing Team	M	3.0 Brabham BT49C-Cosworth V8	accident	21/31
dnq	MONACO GP	Monte Carlo	6	Parmalat Racing Team	M	3.0 Brabham BT49C-Cosworth V8		23/31
ret	SPANISH GP	Jarama	6	Parmalat Racing Team	M	3.0 Brabham BT49C-Cosworth V8	gearbox	18/30
9	FRENCH GP	Dijon	6	Parmalat Racing Team	M	3.0 Brabham BT49C-Cosworth V8	2 laps behind	15/29
5	BRITISH GP	Silverstone	6	Parmalat Racing Team	G	3.0 Brabham BT49C-Cosworth V8	1 lap behind	13/30
4	GERMAN GP	Hockenheim	6	Parmalat Racing Team	G	3.0 Brabham BT49C-Cosworth V8		16/30
ret	AUSTRIAN GP	Österreichring	6	Parmalat Racing Team	G	3.0 Brabham BT49C-Cosworth V8	clutch	15/28
4	DUTCH GP	Zandvoort	6	Parmalat Racing Team	G	3.0 Brabham BT49C-Cosworth V8	1 lap behind	15/30
ret	ITALIAN GP	Monza	6	Parmalat Racing Team	G	3.0 Brabham BT49C-Cosworth V8	electrics	14/30
ret	CANADIAN GP	Montreal	6	Parmalat Racing Team	G	3.0 Brabham BT49C-Cosworth V8	spun off	6/30
ret	CAESARS PALACE GP	Las Vegas	6	Parmalat Racing Team	G	3.0 Brabham BT49C-Cosworth V8	spun off	16/30

GP Starts: 41   GP Wins: 0   Pole positions: 0   Fastest laps: 0   Points: 13

REDMAN, Brian (GB) b 9/3/1937, Colne, Lancashire

1968 Championship position: 19th=   Wins: 0   Pole positions: 0   Fastest laps: 0   Points scored: 4

	Race	Circuit	No	Entrant	Tyres	Car/Engine	Comment	Q Pos/Entries
ret	SOUTH AFRICAN GP	Kyalami	14	Cooper Car Co	F	3.0 Cooper T81B-Maserati V12	overheating/oil leak	21/23
3	SPANISH GP	Jarama	14	Cooper Car Co	F	3.0 Cooper T86B-BRM V12	1 lap behind	13/14
ret	BELGIAN GP	Spa	16	Cooper Car Co	F	3.0 Cooper T86B-BRM V12	accident/broken suspension	10/18

1970 Championship position: Unplaced

			No	Entrant	Tyres	Car/Engine	Comment	Q Pos/Entries
dnp	SOUTH AFRICAN GP	Kyalami	11	Rob Walker Racing Team	F	3.0 Lotus 49C-Cosworth V8	reserve, stand-by for Hill	– / –
dns	BRITISH GP	Brands Hatch	25	Frank Williams Racing Cars	D	3.0 de Tomaso 505-Cosworth V8	hub failure in practice	25/25
dnq	GERMAN GP	Hockenheim	25	Frank Williams Racing Cars	D	3.0 de Tomaso 505-Cosworth V8	unseeded car	20/25

1971 Championship position: Unplaced

			No	Entrant	Tyres	Car/Engine	Comment	Q Pos/Entries
7	SOUTH AFRICAN GP	Kyalami	28	Team Surtees	F	3.0 Surtees TS7-Cosworth V8	1 lap behind	=16/25

1972 Championship position: 12th=   Wins: 0   Pole positions: 0   Fastest laps: 0   Points scored: 4

			No	Entrant	Tyres	Car/Engine	Comment	Q Pos/Entries
5	MONACO GP	Monte Carlo	15	Yardley Team McLaren	G	3.0 McLaren M19A-Cosworth V8	pit stop/puncture/-3 laps	10/25
9	FRENCH GP	Clermont Ferrand	11	Yardley Team McLaren	G	3.0 McLaren M19A-Cosworth V8		15/29
5	GERMAN GP	Nürburgring	5	Yardley Team McLaren	G	3.0 McLaren M19A-Cosworth V8		19/27
ret	US GP	Watkins Glen	15	Marlboro BRM	F	3.0 BRM P180 V12	engine	24/32

1973 Championship position: Unplaced

			No	Entrant	Tyres	Car/Engine	Comment	Q Pos/Entries
dsq	US GP	Watkins Glen	31	Shadow Racing Team	G	3.0 Shadow DN1-Cosworth V8	outside assistance-push start	13/28

1974 Championship position: Unplaced

			No	Entrant	Tyres	Car/Engine	Comment	Q Pos/Entries
7	SPANISH GP	Jarama	16	UOP Shadow Racing Team	G	3.0 Shadow DN3-Cosworth V8	3 laps behind	22/28
18/ret	BELGIAN GP	Nivelles	16	UOP Shadow Racing Team	G	3.0 Shadow DN3-Cosworth V8	engine/5 laps behind	18/32
ret	MONACO GP	Monte Carlo	16	UOP Shadow Racing Team	G	3.0 Shadow DN3-Cosworth V8	multiple accident	=16/28

GP Starts: 12   GP Wins: 0   Pole positions: 0   Fastest laps: 0   Points: 8

BRIAN REDMAN

The 1999 season saw the fortieth anniversary of the start of Brian's competition career, which began in the modest surroundings of Rufforth with a Morris 1000. Since those far-off days the Lancastrian has probably raced on more of the world's circuits than most of his peers, but he is hardly a household name. It could have been so different, for Redman had the talent to have become a Grand Prix winner, but his distaste for the high-pressure Formula 1 environment prompted him to turn his back on the GP paddock to enjoy an enormously successful and rewarding career in other forms of racing.

After early outings with a Mini, Redman made a name for himself in 1965 with a Jaguar E-Type before campaigning a Lola T70 in 1966. His career gradually gained momentum during 1967 in Formula 2 – with David Bridges' Lola – and sports car events, Brian winning the Rand 9 Hours in a Mirage with Ickx. In 1968 he had his first taste of Grand Prix racing with Cooper, which ended with a broken arm after a crash at Spa when his car's suspension failed. This came after a run of impressive performances, most notably victories in the BOAC 500 and Spa 1000 Km with Ickx in the GT40 and a brilliant drive in the F2 Eifelrennen with the Ferrari Dino that brought an offer of a works drive, which he declined.

Redman then began a long period in sports car racing (1969-73) with Porsche and Ferrari, winning virtually all the major classics with the striking exception of Le Mans, which has strangely eluded him. He made occasional returns to Grand Prix racing, usually as a replacement driver, but often without the benefit of testing and preparation. However, by this time Brian had established himself as the man to beat in US F5000, winning three successive titles between 1974 and 1976 in the Haas/Hall Lola. Overcoming serious injuries received at the start of 1977 when his Can-Am Lola flipped, Brian was soon back, winning at Sebring in 1978 and taking the IMSA title in 1981.

Based in Florida, Redman subsequently graced a wide variety of classes, racing as competitively as ever and revelling in the less-pressured atmosphere of motor sport in North America. He now also fronts the Redman-Bright F3000 team which successfully ran Gonzalo Rodriguez before the Uruguayan driver's tragic death in a CART accident at Laguna Seca in 1999.

ALAN REES

A very useful driver in Formula Junior, Rees drove for the works Lotus team in 1962, taking three wins before a crash in a Lotus 23 at the Nürburgring 1000 Km sports car race curtailed his season.

For 1963, he joined the Roy Winkelmann team and would become its mainstay as both driver and, later, team manager. Concentrating on Formula 2 between 1964 and 1968, Rees drove countless races in the team's Brabhams, often beating the stars of the day, such as Rindt, Stewart and Clark. However, his Grand Prix opportunities were limited to a couple of races in the Winkelmann F2 car and a single outing in a rather tired works Cooper at the 1967 British GP.

By the end of 1968, Rees had decided that he was not going to progress any further as a driver and he retired to the team manager's role, before becoming a founder member of March, later acting as team manager of Shadow and Arrows.

REES, Alan (GB) b 12/1/1938, Langstone, nr Newport, Monmouthshire, Wales

	1966			Championship position: Unplaced				
	Race	Circuit	No	Entrant	Tyres	Car/Engine	Comment	Q Pos/Entries
ret	GERMAN GP (F2)	Nürburgring	29	Roy Winkelmann Racing	–	1.0 Brabham BT18-Cosworth 4 F2	gearbox/engine	25/30
	1967			Championship position: Unplaced				
9	BRITISH GP	Silverstone	14	Cooper Car Co	F	3.0 Cooper T81-Maserati V12	4 laps behind	15/21
7*	GERMAN GP (F2)	Nürburgring	22	Roy Winkelmann Racing	–	1.6 Brabham BT23-Cosworth 4 F2	* 2nd in F2 class	17/25

GP Starts: 3   GP Wins: 0   Pole positions: 0   Fastest laps: 0   Points: 0

CLAY REGAZZONI

A driver right out of the old school, Regazzoni took no prisoners with his rough-and-ready approach to racing during his early days of Formula 3. And while he may have tempered his approach in the ensuing years, he was always liable to revert to type, leaving his competitors a little wary as they locked horns with the hard-racing Swiss.

After competing with a Healey Sprite, Clay joined forces with fellow countryman Silvio Moser to race F2 and F3 Brabhams in 1965-66 before switching to Tecnos. Regazzoni joined the works team in 1968 to compete in the European Formula 2 championship, where some of his driving tactics became a cause for concern. Things reached a low ebb in mid-season, when he was disqualified for overtaking

at the site of an accident at Monza and then, in the next race at Zandvoort, was involved in Chris Lambert's fatal accident. The fall-out from this incident was to last for some considerable time, and though Regazzoni was absolved from blame some mud would always stick. The 1969 season brought an invitation from Ferrari to race their 166 Dino, but little of note was achieved, and he soon returned to the Tecno ranks. This proved a wise decision, for the team's F2 car really came good in 1970. Up to this point Clay had been regarded as something of a neanderthal, but wins at Hockenheim, Paul Ricard, Enna and Imola helped dispel this image and he jumped into the Ferrari F1 team with no qualms at all. Fourth place on his debut was a great effort, but better was to come when, after a splendid second at the Österreichring, he took the ultimate prize for a Ferrari driver, winning the Italian GP at Monza. His place was now secure, but over the next two seasons, apart from the Race of Champions in 1971, there were to be no more wins – some good performances to be sure, but too many incidents for the Scuderia's liking. Thus at the end of 1972 he was released, but soon found a seat with the Marlboro BRM squad.

Regazzoni took his change of circumstances with equanimity and started the season with a great drive in the Argentine GP, taking pole and leading the race for 30 laps before troubles dropped him back. His year was largely spent in midfield anonymity, however, before a surprise recall to Ferrari, who were restructuring after a terrible year. The 1974 season was probably the Swiss driver's finest. There were off-track excursions but he was a remarkably consistent finisher and took a superb win at the Nürburgring to get within touching distance of the World Championship. His value to Ferrari at this period was immense, Clay proving the ideal foil for Niki Lauda, quite capable of picking up the pieces if necessary, as in the non-title Swiss GP and then the Italian GP at Monza the following season. Unfortunately there was still the occasional brainstorm, and his tactics at Watkins Glen, where he blatantly blocked Fittipaldi, were a disgrace. In 1976 we saw the same cocktail – a brilliant win at Long Beach, and a crass first-corner manoeuvre at Paddock Bend in the infamous British GP. Certainly his form began to tail off towards the end of that year, and his services were no longer required.

Joining the little Ensign squad for 1977 was akin to leaving the Ritz to dine at Wimpy, but Regazzoni was happy just to be part of the scene. There were, of course, the inevitable crashes, but a couple of fifth places near the end of the season kept Mo Nunn happy enough. Clay was tempted by the lure of Indianapolis that year, and qualified in a Theodore McLaren, but retired the car in the race with a water leak. His Swiss connections helped him into the Shadow team for 1978, but apart from Anderstorp it was a pretty dismal year. It was difficult to see much future for Regazzoni by this stage, but Frank Williams was to take Clay on board. He reasoned that in a good car he had been almost as quick as Lauda, and his experience would be an asset in the team's expanded two-car operation. Frank's hunch was to prove correct, as Clay won at Silverstone to score the Williams team's first-ever Grand Prix win, and a special place in their history. Sentiment didn't cloud Williams' judgement when it came to his 1980 line-up, however, and when Carlos Reutemann became available Regazzoni was out.

Unperturbed, Clay counted his blessings and headed back to Ensign. The team now had a healthier budget and a new car, but the season was only four races old when disaster struck. In the Grand Prix at Long Beach, the brake pedal snapped, leaving his red, white and blue machine hurtling down the escape road into a parked Brabham. Poor Regazzoni sustained serious spinal damage, which has since confined him to a wheelchair, but despite this crippling injury Clay lost none of his enthusiasm for the sport, working regularly as a commentator for Swiss TV for more than a decade.

Regazzoni even started competing again in specially adapted saloon cars, and he is was fully involved in developing the hand control systems for these cars.

REGAZZONI, 'Clay' (Gianclaudio) (CH) b 5/9/1939, Mendrisio, nr Lugano

1970
Championship position: 3rd   Wins: 1   Pole positions: 1   Fastest laps: 3 (1 shared)   Points scored: 33

	Race	Circuit	No	Entrant	Tyres	Car/Engine	Comment	Q Pos/Entries
4	DUTCH GP	Zandvoort	26	Scuderia Ferrari SpA SEFAC	F	3.0 Ferrari 312B F12	1 lap behind	6/24
4	BRITISH GP	Brands Hatch	4	Scuderia Ferrari SpA SEFAC	F	3.0 Ferrari 312B F12		6/25
ret	GERMAN GP	Hockenheim	15	Scuderia Ferrari SpA SEFAC	F	3.0 Ferrari 312B F12	gearbox problems/spun off	3/25
2	AUSTRIAN GP	Österreichring	27	Scuderia Ferrari SpA SEFAC	F	3.0 Ferrari 312B F12	FL (shared with Ickx)	2/24
1	ITALIAN GP	Monza	4	Scuderia Ferrari SpA SEFAC	F	3.0 Ferrari 312B F12	FL	3/27
2	CANADIAN GP	St Jovite	19	Scuderia Ferrari SpA SEFAC	F	3.0 Ferrari 312B F12	FL	3/20
13	US GP	Watkins Glen	4	Scuderia Ferrari SpA SEFAC	F	3.0 Ferrari 312B F12	pit stop/fuel pipe/-7 laps	6/27
2	MEXICAN GP	Mexico City	4	Scuderia Ferrari SpA SEFAC	F	3.0 Ferrari 312B F12		1/18

1971
Championship position: 7th   Wins: 0   Pole positions: 1   Fastest laps: 0   Points scored: 13

	Race	Circuit	No	Entrant	Tyres	Car/Engine	Comment	Q Pos/Entries
3	SOUTH AFRICAN GP	Kyalami	5	Scuderia Ferrari SpA SEFAC	F	3.0 Ferrari 312B F12		3/25
ret	SPANISH GP	Montjuich Park	5	Scuderia Ferrari SpA SEFAC	F	3.0 Ferrari 312B2 F12	engine	=2/25
dns	"	" "	5T	Scuderia Ferrari SpA SEFAC	F	3.0 Ferrari 312B2 F12	practice only	– / –
ret	MONACO GP	Monte Carlo	3	Scuderia Ferrari SpA SEFAC	F	3.0 Ferrari 312B2 F12	hit chicane-suspension	11/23
3	DUTCH GP	Zandvoort	3	Scuderia Ferrari SpA SEFAC	F	3.0 Ferrari 312B2 F12	late spin/1 lap behind	4/24
dns	"	" "	3T	Scuderia Ferrari SpA SEFAC	F	3.0 Ferrari 312B F12	practice only	– / –
ret	FRENCH GP	Paul Ricard	5	Scuderia Ferrari SpA SEFAC	F	3.0 Ferrari 312B2 F12	spun off-damaged wheel	2/24
ret	BRITISH GP	Silverstone	5	Scuderia Ferrari SpA SEFAC	F	3.0 Ferrari 312B2 F12	engine	1/24
3	GERMAN GP	Nürburgring	6	Scuderia Ferrari SpA SEFAC	F	3.0 Ferrari 312B2 F12		4/23
dns			31	Scuderia Ferrari SpA SEFAC	F	3.0 Ferrari 312B F12	practice only	– / –
ret	AUSTRIAN GP	Österreichring	5	Scuderia Ferrari SpA SEFAC	F	3.0 Ferrari 312B2 F12	engine	4/22
ret	ITALIAN GP	Monza	4	Scuderia Ferrari SpA SEFAC	F	3.0 Ferrari 312B2 F12	engine damper	8/24
ret	CANADIAN GP	Mosport Park	5	Scuderia Ferrari SpA SEFAC	F	3.0 Ferrari 312B2 F12	electrical fire/accident	18/27
dns	"	" "	25T	Scuderia Ferrari SpA SEFAC	F	3.0 Ferrari 312B F12	practice only	– / –
6	US GP	Watkins Glen	5	Scuderia Ferrari SpA SEFAC	F	3.0 Ferrari 312B2 F12	spin	4/32

1972
Championship position: 6th=   Wins: 0   Pole positions: 0   Fastest laps: 0   Points scored: 15

	Race	Circuit	No	Entrant	Tyres	Car/Engine	Comment	Q Pos/Entries
4	ARGENTINE GP	Buenos Aires	9	Scuderia Ferrari SpA SEFAC	F	3.0 Ferrari 312B2 F12		=5/22
12	SOUTH AFRICAN GP	Kyalami	6	Scuderia Ferrari SpA SEFAC	F	3.0 Ferrari 312B2 F12	pit stop/tyres/2 laps behind	2/27
3	SPANISH GP	Jarama	6	Scuderia Ferrari SpA SEFAC	F	3.0 Ferrari 312B2 F12	1 lap behind	8/26
ret	MONACO GP	Monte Carlo	7	Scuderia Ferrari SpA SEFAC	F	3.0 Ferrari 312B2 F12	hit barrier	3/25
ret	BELGIAN GP	Nivelles	30	Scuderia Ferrari SpA SEFAC	F	3.0 Ferrari 312B2 F12	hit Galli's spinning car	2/26
2	GERMAN GP	Nürburgring	9	Scuderia Ferrari SpA SEFAC	F	3.0 Ferrari 312B2 F12	hit Stewart on last lap	7/27
ret	AUSTRIAN GP	Österreichring	19	Scuderia Ferrari SpA SEFAC	F	3.0 Ferrari 312B2 F12	fuel pressure	2/26
ret	ITALIAN GP	Monza	5	Scuderia Ferrari SpA SEFAC	F	3.0 Ferrari 312B2 F12	hit Pace at chicane	4/27
5	CANADIAN GP	Mosport Park	11	Scuderia Ferrari SpA SEFAC	F	3.0 Ferrari 312B2 F12	handling problems	=6/25
8	US GP	Watkins Glen	8	Scuderia Ferrari SpA SEFAC	F	3.0 Ferrari 312B2 F12	exhaust fell off/1 lap behind	6/32

1973
Championship position: 17th=   Wins: 0   Pole positions: 1   Fastest laps: 0   Points scored: 2

	Race	Circuit	No	Entrant	Tyres	Car/Engine	Comment	Q Pos/Entries
7	ARGENTINE GP	Buenos Aires	32	Marlboro BRM	F	3.0 BRM P160D V12	3 laps behind	1/19
6	BRAZILIAN GP	Interlagos	14	Marlboro BRM	F	3.0 BRM P160D V12	1 lap behind	4/20
ret	SOUTH AFRICAN GP	Kyalami	15	Marlboro BRM	F	3.0 BRM P160D V12	accident/rescued by Hailwood	5/25
9	SPANISH GP	Montjuich Park	14	Marlboro BRM	F	3.0 BRM P160E V12	pit stops/tyres/6 laps behind	=7/22
10/ret	BELGIAN GP	Zolder	19	Marlboro BRM	F	3.0 BRM P160E V12	spun off	12/23
ret	MONACO GP	Monte Carlo	19	Marlboro BRM	F	3.0 BRM P160E V12	boiling brake fluid	8/26
9	SWEDISH GP	Anderstorp	19	Marlboro BRM	F	3.0 BRM P160E V12	3 laps behind	12/22
12	FRENCH GP	Paul Ricard	19	Marlboro BRM	F	3.0 BRM P160E V12	1 lap behind	9/25
7	BRITISH GP	Silverstone	19	Marlboro BRM	F	3.0 BRM P160E V12		10/29
8	DUTCH GP	Zandvoort	19	Marlboro BRM	F	3.0 BRM P160E V12	2 pit stops/tyre/fuel/-4 laps	12/24
ret	GERMAN GP	Nürburgring	19	Marlboro BRM	F	3.0 BRM P160E V12	engine	10/23
6	AUSTRIAN GP	Österreichring	19	Marlboro BRM	F	3.0 BRM P160E V12		14/25
ret	ITALIAN GP	Monza	19	Marlboro BRM	F	3.0 BRM P160E V12	coil	18/25
8	US GP	Watkins Glen	19	Marlboro BRM	F	3.0 BRM P160E V12	1 lap behind	16/28

1974
Championship position: 2nd   Wins: 1   Pole positions: 1   Fastest laps: 3   Points scored: 52

	Race	Circuit	No	Entrant	Tyres	Car/Engine	Comment	Q Pos/Entries
3	ARGENTINE GP	Buenos Aires	11	Scuderia Ferrari SpA SEFAC	G	3.0 Ferrari 312B3 F12	FL	2/26
2	BRAZILIAN GP	Interlagos	11	Scuderia Ferrari SpA SEFAC	G	3.0 Ferrari 312B3 F12	FL	8/25
ret	SOUTH AFRICAN GP	Kyalami	11	Scuderia Ferrari SpA SEFAC	G	3.0 Ferrari 312B3 F12	oil pressure	6/27
2	SPANISH GP	Jarama	11	Scuderia Ferrari SpA SEFAC	G	3.0 Ferrari 312B3 F12		3/28
4	BELGIAN GP	Nivelles	11	Scuderia Ferrari SpA SEFAC	G	3.0 Ferrari 312B3 F12		1/32
4	MONACO GP	Monte Carlo	11	Scuderia Ferrari SpA SEFAC	G	3.0 Ferrari 312B3 F12		2/28
ret	SWEDISH GP	Anderstorp	11	Scuderia Ferrari SpA SEFAC	G	3.0 Ferrari 312B3 F12	transmission	4/28
2	DUTCH GP	Zandvoort	11	Scuderia Ferrari SpA SEFAC	G	3.0 Ferrari 312B3 F12		2/27
3	FRENCH GP	Dijon	11	Scuderia Ferrari SpA SEFAC	G	3.0 Ferrari 312B3 F12		4/30
4	BRITISH GP	Brands Hatch	11	Scuderia Ferrari SpA SEFAC	G	3.0 Ferrari 312B3 F12		=5/34
1	GERMAN GP	Nürburgring	11	Scuderia Ferrari SpA SEFAC	G	3.0 Ferrari 312B3 F12		2/32
5	AUSTRIAN GP	Österreichring	11T	Scuderia Ferrari SpA SEFAC	G	3.0 Ferrari 312B3 F12	pit stop/tyre/FL	8/31
ret	ITALIAN GP	Monza	11	Scuderia Ferrari SpA SEFAC	G	3.0 Ferrari 312B3 F12	engine oil seal	5/31
2	CANADIAN GP	Mosport Park	11	Scuderia Ferrari SpA SEFAC	G	3.0 Ferrari 312B3 F12		6/30
11	US GP	Watkins Glen	11	Scuderia Ferrari SpA SEFAC	G	3.0 Ferrari 312B3 F12	3 pit stops/handling/-4 laps	9/30

1975
Championship position: 5th   Wins: 1   Pole positions: 0   Fastest laps: 4   Points scored: 25

	Race	Circuit	No	Entrant	Tyres	Car/Engine	Comment	Q Pos/Entries
4	ARGENTINE GP	Buenos Aires	11	Scuderia Ferrari SpA SEFAC	G	3.0 Ferrari 312B3 F12		7/23
4	BRAZILIAN GP	Interlagos	11	Scuderia Ferrari SpA SEFAC	G	3.0 Ferrari 312B3 F12		5/23
16/ret	SOUTH AFRICAN GP	Kyalami	11	Scuderia Ferrari SpA SEFAC	G	3.0 Ferrari 312T F12	throttle linkage/7 laps behind	9/28
nc	SPANISH GP	Montjuich Park	11	Scuderia Ferrari SpA SEFAC	G	3.0 Ferrari 312T F12	pit stop-collision/4 laps behind	2/26
ret	MONACO GP	Monte Carlo	11	Scuderia Ferrari SpA SEFAC	G	3.0 Ferrari 312T F12	spun off-damaged suspension	6/26
5	BELGIAN GP	Zolder	11	Scuderia Ferrari SpA SEFAC	G	3.0 Ferrari 312T F12	pit stop/tyre/FL	4/24
3	SWEDISH GP	Anderstorp	11	Scuderia Ferrari SpA SEFAC	G	3.0 Ferrari 312T F12		12/26
3	DUTCH GP	Zandvoort	11	Scuderia Ferrari SpA SEFAC	G	3.0 Ferrari 312T F12		2/25

ret	FRENCH GP	Paul Ricard	11	Scuderia Ferrari SpA SEFAC	G	3.0 Ferrari 312T F12	engine	9/26
13	BRITISH GP	Silverstone	11	Scuderia Ferrari SpA SEFAC	G	3.0 Ferrari 312T F12	pit stops/tyres/FL/-2 laps	4/28
ret	GERMAN GP	Nürburgring	11	Scuderia Ferrari SpA SEFAC	G	3.0 Ferrari 312T F12	engine/FL	5/26
7	AUSTRIAN GP	Österreichring	11	Scuderia Ferrari SpA SEFAC	G	3.0 Ferrari 312T F12		5/30
1	ITALIAN GP	Monza	11	Scuderia Ferrari SpA SEFAC	G	3.0 Ferrari 312T F12	FL	2/28
ret	US GP	Watkins Glen	11	Scuderia Ferrari SpA SEFAC	G	3.0 Ferrari 312T F12	w/drawn-protest over reprimand	11/24

1976   Championship position: 5th   Wins: 1   Pole positions: 1   Fastest laps: 3   Points scored: 31

7	BRAZILIAN GP	Interlagos	2	Scuderia Ferrari SpA SEFAC	G	3.0 Ferrari 312T F12	pit stop/tyre	4/22
ret	SOUTH AFRICAN GP	Kyalami	2	Scuderia Ferrari SpA SEFAC	G	3.0 Ferrari 312T F12	engine	9/25
1	US GP WEST	Long Beach	2	Scuderia Ferrari SpA SEFAC	G	3.0 Ferrari 312T F12	FL	1/27
11	SPANISH GP	Jarama	2	Scuderia Ferrari SpA SEFAC	G	3.0 Ferrari 312T2 F12	pit stop/gear selection/-3 laps	5/30
2	BELGIAN GP	Zolder	2	Scuderia Ferrari SpA SEFAC	G	3.0 Ferrari 312T2 F12		2/29
14/ret	MONACO GP	Monte Carlo	2	Scuderia Ferrari SpA SEFAC	G	3.0 Ferrari 312T2 F12	spun off/FL/5 laps behind	2/25
6	SWEDISH GP	Anderstorp	2	Scuderia Ferrari SpA SEFAC	G	3.0 Ferrari 312T2 F12		11/27
ret	FRENCH GP	Paul Ricard	2	Scuderia Ferrari SpA SEFAC	G	3.0 Ferrari 312T2 F12	engine-spun off	4/30
ret/dsq*	BRITISH GP	Brands Hatch	2	Scuderia Ferrari SpA SEFAC	G	3.0 Ferrari 312T2 F12	accident/*used T car in restart	4/30
9	GERMAN GP	Nürburgring	2	Scuderia Ferrari SpA SEFAC	G	3.0 Ferrari 312T2 F12	pit stop/nose cone	5/28
2	DUTCH GP	Zandvoort	2	Scuderia Ferrari SpA SEFAC	G	3.0 Ferrari 312T2 F12	FL	5/27
2	ITALIAN GP	Monza	2	Scuderia Ferrari SpA SEFAC	G	3.0 Ferrari 312T2 F12		9/29
6	CANADIAN GP	Mosport Park	2	Scuderia Ferrari SpA SEFAC	G	3.0 Ferrari 312T2 F12	1 lap behind	12/27
7	US GP EAST	Watkins Glen	2	Scuderia Ferrari SpA SEFAC	G	3.0 Ferrari 312T2 F12	1 lap behind	14/27
5	JAPANESE GP	Mount Fuji	2	Scuderia Ferrari SpA SEFAC	G	3.0 Ferrari 312T2 F12	pit stop/tyre	7/27

1977   Championship position: 17th=   Wins: 0   Pole positions: 0   Fastest laps: 0   Points scored: 5

6	ARGENTINE GP	Buenos Aires	22	Team Tissot Ensign with Castrol	G	3.0 Ensign N177-Cosworth V8	2 laps behind	12/21
ret	BRAZILIAN GP	Interlagos	22	Team Tissot Ensign with Castrol	G	3.0 Ensign N177-Cosworth V8	hit catch-fencing spun onto track	9/22
9	SOUTH AFRICAN GP	Kyalami	22	Team Tissot Ensign with Castrol	G	3.0 Ensign N177-Cosworth V8		16/23
ret	US GP WEST	Long Beach	22	Team Tissot Ensign with Castrol	G	3.0 Ensign N177-Cosworth V8	gearbox	13/22
ret	SPANISH GP	Jarama	22	Team Tissot Ensign with Castrol	G	3.0 Ensign N177-Cosworth V8	collision with Brambilla	8/31
dnq	MONACO GP	Monte Carlo	22	Team Tissot Ensign with Castrol	G	3.0 Ensign N177-Cosworth V8		24/26
ret	BELGIAN GP	Zolder	22	Team Tissot Ensign with Castrol	G	3.0 Ensign N177-Cosworth V8	engine	13/32
7	SWEDISH GP	Anderstorp	22	Team Tissot Ensign with Castrol	G	3.0 Ensign N177-Cosworth V8		14/31
7	FRENCH GP	Dijon	22	Team Tissot Ensign with Castrol	G	3.0 Ensign N177-Cosworth V8	1 lap behind	16/30
dnq	BRITISH GP	Silverstone	22	Team Tissot Ensign with Castrol	G	3.0 Ensign N177-Cosworth V8		28/36
ret	GERMAN GP	Hockenheim	22	Team Tissot Ensign with Castrol	G	3.0 Ensign N177-Cosworth V8	startline accident	22/30
ret	AUSTRIAN GP	Österreichring	22	Team Tissot Ensign with Castrol	G	3.0 Ensign N177-Cosworth V8	spun off	11/30
ret	DUTCH GP	Zandvoort	22	Team Tissot Ensign with Castrol	G	3.0 Ensign N177-Cosworth V8	throttle cable	9/34
5	ITALIAN GP	Monza	22	Team Tissot Ensign with Castrol	G	3.0 Ensign N177-Cosworth V8		=6/34
5	US GP EAST	Watkins Glen	22	Team Tissot Ensign with Castrol	G	3.0 Ensign N177-Cosworth V8		19/27
ret	CANADIAN GP	Mosport Park	22	Team Tissot Ensign with Castrol	G	3.0 Ensign N177-Cosworth V8	crashed on lap 1	14/27
ret	JAPANESE GP	Mount Fuji	22	Team Tissot Ensign with Castrol	G	3.0 Ensign N177-Cosworth V8	engine	10/23

1978   Championship position: 16th=   Wins: 0   Pole positions: 0   Fastest laps: 0   Points scored: 4

15	ARGENTINE GP	Buenos Aires	17	Shadow Racing Team	G	3.0 Shadow DN8-Cosworth V8	pit stop/tyre/1 lap behind	16/27
5	BRAZILIAN GP	Rio	17	Shadow Racing Team	G	3.0 Shadow DN8-Cosworth V8	1 lap behind	15/28
dnq	SOUTH AFRICAN GP	Kyalami	17	Shadow Racing Team	G	3.0 Shadow DN8-Cosworth V8		28/30
10	US GP WEST	Long Beach	17	Shadow Racing Team	G	3.0 Shadow DN8-Cosworth V8	1 lap behind	20/30
dnq	MONACO GP	Monte Carlo	17	Shadow Racing Team	G	3.0 Shadow DN9-Cosworth V8		22/30
ret	BELGIAN GP	Zolder	17	Shadow Racing Team	G	3.0 Shadow DN9-Cosworth V8	differential	18/30
15/ret	SPANISH GP	Jarama	17	Shadow Racing Team	G	3.0 Shadow DN9-Cosworth V8	fuel union/8 laps behind	22/29
5	SWEDISH GP	Anderstorp	17	Shadow Racing Team	G	3.0 Shadow DN9-Cosworth V8	1 lap behind	16/27
ret	FRENCH GP	Paul Ricard	17	Shadow Racing Team	G	3.0 Shadow DN9-Cosworth V8	electrics	17/29
ret	BRITISH GP	Brands Hatch	17	Shadow Racing Team	G	3.0 Shadow DN9-Cosworth V8	gearbox	17/30
dnq	GERMAN GP	Hockenheim	17	Shadow Racing Team	G	3.0 Shadow DN9-Cosworth V8		25/30
nc	AUSTRIAN GP	Österreichring	17	Shadow Racing Team	G	3.0 Shadow DN9-Cosworth V8	pit stop/tyres/4 laps behind	22/31
dnq	DUTCH GP	Zandvoort	17	Shadow Racing Team	G	3.0 Shadow DN9-Cosworth V8		28/33
nc	ITALIAN GP	Monza	17	Shadow Racing Team	G	3.0 Shadow DN9-Cosworth V8	pit stops/7 laps behind	15/32
14	US GP EAST	Watkins Glen	17	Shadow Racing Team	G	3.0 Shadow DN9-Cosworth V8	pit stop/tyres/3 laps behind	17/27
dnq	CANADIAN GP	Montreal	17	Shadow Racing Team	G	3.0 Shadow DN9-Cosworth V8		23/28

1979   Championship position: 5th   Wins: 1   Pole positions: 0   Fastest laps: 2   Points scored: 32

10	ARGENTINE GP	Buenos Aires	28	Albilad-Saudia Racing Team	G	3.0 Williams FW06-Cosworth V8	pit stop/tyres/2 laps behind	17/26
15	BRAZILIAN GP	Interlagos	28	Albilad-Saudia Racing Team	G	3.0 Williams FW06-Cosworth V8	pit stop/damage check/-2 laps	17/26
9	SOUTH AFRICAN GP	Kyalami	28	Albilad-Saudia Racing Team	G	3.0 Williams FW06-Cosworth V8	2 laps behind	22/26
ret	US GP WEST	Long Beach	28	Albilad-Saudia Racing Team	G	3.0 Williams FW06-Cosworth V8	engine	15/26
ret	SPANISH GP	Jarama	28	Albilad-Saudia Racing Team	G	3.0 Williams FW07-Cosworth V8	engine	14/27
ret	BELGIAN GP	Zolder	28	Albilad-Saudia Racing Team	G	3.0 Williams FW07-Cosworth V8	accident-Scheckter & Villeneuve	8/28
2	MONACO GP	Monte Carlo	28	Albilad-Saudia Racing Team	G	3.0 Williams FW07-Cosworth V8		16/25
6	FRENCH GP	Dijon	28	Albilad-Saudia Racing Team	G	3.0 Williams FW07-Cosworth V8		9/27
1	BRITISH GP	Silverstone	28	Albilad-Saudia Racing Team	G	3.0 Williams FW07-Cosworth V8	FL	4/26
2	GERMAN GP	Hockenheim	28	Albilad-Saudia Racing Team	G	3.0 Williams FW07-Cosworth V8		6/26
5	AUSTRIAN GP	Österreichring	28	Albilad-Saudia Racing Team	G	3.0 Williams FW07-Cosworth V8		6/26
ret	DUTCH GP	Zandvoort	28	Albilad-Saudia Racing Team	G	3.0 Williams FW07-Cosworth V8	accident with Arnoux at start	3/26
3	ITALIAN GP	Monza	28	Albilad-Saudia Racing Team	G	3.0 Williams FW07-Cosworth V8	FL	6/28
3	CANADIAN GP	Montreal	28	Albilad-Saudia Racing Team	G	3.0 Williams FW07-Cosworth V8		3/29
ret	US GP EAST	Watkins Glen	28	Albilad-Saudia Racing Team	G	3.0 Williams FW07-Cosworth V8	collision with Piquet	5/30

1980   Championship position: Unplaced

nc	ARGENTINE GP	Buenos Aires	14	Unipart Racing Team	G	3.0 Ensign N180-Cosworth V8	3 pit stops/throttle/-9 laps	15/28
ret	BRAZILIAN GP	Interlagos	14	Unipart Racing Team	G	3.0 Ensign N180-Cosworth V8	handling	12/28
9	SOUTH AFRICAN GP	Kyalami	14	Unipart Racing Team	G	3.0 Ensign N180-Cosworth V8	1 lap behind	=19/28
ret	US GP WEST	Long Beach	14	Unipart Racing Team	G	3.0 Ensign N180-Cosworth V8	brake failure-accident	23/27

GP Starts: 132   GP Wins: 5   Pole positions: 5   Fastest laps: 15   Points: 212

CARLOS REUTEMANN

Carlos Reutemann was certainly the enigma of his times. Picturing some of his majestic Grand Prix wins, it seems impossible to believe that here was anything other than a World Champion. Yet there were days when his performance was so lacklustre that you would cringe with embarrassment at his feeble showing. That was the contradiction of this deep-thinking perfectionist, who was ultimately unable to summon from within himself the consistency which must underpin any championship success.

Carlos was a cattle-rancher's son from Santa Fe, Argentina, who began racing in 1965. Competing mainly in saloons such as Ford Torinos, he soon became one of the country's top talents, gaining some valuable single-seater experience in the 1968 Temporada Formula 2 series. In 1970 he was chosen by the Automovil Club Argentino for a sponsored season in Europe racing a Brabham BT30. The year passed relatively uneventfully, with Carlos learning a great deal and taking the occasional top-six finish. Returning home, he served notice of his talent by taking an aggregate third place in the non-championship Argentine GP in an elderly McLaren M7C. Back in Europe for another season of Formula 2, Reutemann really came good in

Reutemann's winning Brabham BT44B on the banked Karussel curve at the old Nürburgring circuit in the 1975 German Grand Prix.

the latter stages of the year. Although he won only at Hockenheim, there were plenty of brilliant performances and he finished runner-up to Ronnie Peterson in the final standings.

Having newly acquired the Brabham team, Bernie Ecclestone signed Carlos for 1972 and the Argentinian was to make a sensational GP debut at Buenos Aires, putting the hitherto unloved Brabham BT34 on pole position before finishing seventh. Reutemann then won the non-title Brazilian GP at Interlagos to underline his vast promise, but his momentum was broken soon after his return to Europe when a nasty crash at Thruxton in the F2 Rondel Brabham left him with a crushed ankle. This injury proved troublesome and slow to mend, which knocked his confidence for the rest of that year.

The 1973 season saw him back in the groove, particularly once the new BT42 was introduced. There were flashes of brilliance and he soon became a regular top-six finisher. With the superb BT44 at his disposal at the start of 1974, Reutemann launched a ferocious opening onslaught, leading the first two Grands Prix before encountering problems, and then winning the third, at Kyalami. But, just as suddenly, his form then vanished before mysteriously reappearing when he won the Austrian GP with a stunning performance. There was another victory at Watkins Glen which prompted thoughts that a World Championship bid was on the cards for the following season, but once again he flattered to deceive. Winning the German GP was the high-point, but he seemed unsettled by the competitive presence of new team-mate Carlos Pace. Things took a turn for the worse in 1976, when Brabham became involved in the Alfa engine project. The powerplant was woefully unreliable, and Reutemann soon became fed up with the situation. He engineered his way out of his contract to join Ferrari, who were anxious to find a replacement for the recently injured Niki Lauda, but in the event Carlos raced only at Monza due to the Austrian's amazing recovery. Despite a win in the Brazilian GP at the beginning of 1977, Reutemann was completely overshadowed by Lauda, who with total disdain took great delight in heaping any little humiliation he could upon the Argentinian.

With the Rat's two-fingered departure at the end of the year, Carlos was promoted to lead the Ferrari challenge in 1978, and his form certainly improved, Reutemann taking four wins including a brilliantly judged performance to outwit Lauda at Brands Hatch. Despite this success, he found himself unwanted by Ferrari and joined Lotus in 1979, which was in hindsight the worst possible move. The new Lotus 80 was a technical nightmare and Reutemann stuck resolutely with the 79, with which, to be fair, he put in some brilliant performances which went largely unregarded. Frank Williams still had faith in him and for 1980 Carlos was included in the team alongside Alan Jones. It was a mystery that a driver of such experience should take such a long time to come to terms with his situation; a win at Monaco was achieved by caution and he seemed content to let Jones force the pace as the Australian charged towards his well-deserved championship. The following season saw a far more aggressive Reutemann. He took the FOCA-only South African GP and then embarked on an early-season run of brilliant performances to put himself in a seemingly impregnable position. Then, almost inevitably, came the slump. The title went down to the line at Las Vegas, and Carlos set himself for glory with an utterly brilliant lap to put the car on pole. But once the lights went green Reutemann, his confidence punctured by a mysterious handling problem encountered in the warm-up, just seemed to fade away. A season's work appeared to be tossed away without so much as a whimper as Nelson Piquet snatched the title by a point.

Reutemann was back in 1982, but perhaps the roll of the dice at Caesars Palace still weighed heavily on the mind of this introspective and complex man. Just two races into the season, he suddenly retired for reasons that have never really been explained. An enigma to the end.

CARLOS REUTEMANN

REUTEMANN, Carlos (RA) b 12/4/1942, Santa Fé

1972 — Championship position: 16th   Wins: 0   Pole positions: 1   Fastest laps: 0   Points scored: 3

	Race	Circuit	No	Entrant	Tyres	Car/Engine	Comment	Q Pos/Entries
7	ARGENTINE GP	Buenos Aires	2	Motor Racing Developments	G	3.0 Brabham BT34-Cosworth V8	pit stop/loose air box/-2 laps	1/22
ret	SOUTH AFRICAN GP	Kyalami	20	Motor Racing Developments	G	3.0 Brabham BT34-Cosworth V8	fuel line	15/27
13	BELGIAN GP	Nivelles	19	Motor Racing Developments	G	3.0 Brabham BT37-Cosworth V8	pit stops/clutch/gear lever/-4 laps	9/26
12	FRENCH GP	Clermont Ferrand	20	Motor Racing Developments	G	3.0 Brabham BT37-Cosworth V8	1 lap behind	=19/29
8	BRITISH GP	Brands Hatch	27	Motor Racing Developments	G	3.0 Brabham BT37-Cosworth V8	pit stop/wheels/3 laps behind	10/27
ret	GERMAN GP	Nürburgring	12	Motor Racing Developments	G	3.0 Brabham BT37-Cosworth V8	gearbox	6/27
ret	AUSTRIAN GP	Österreichring	17	Motor Racing Developments	G	3.0 Brabham BT37-Cosworth V8	fuel metering unit	5/26
ret	ITALIAN GP	Monza	30	Motor Racing Developments	G	3.0 Brabham BT37-Cosworth V8	hit chicane-suspension damage	11/27
4	CANADIAN GP	Mosport Park	8	Motor Racing Developments	G	3.0 Brabham BT37-Cosworth V8		9/25
ret	US GP	Watkins Glen	29	Motor Racing Developments	G	3.0 Brabham BT37-Cosworth V8	engine	5/32

1973 — Championship position: 7th   Wins: 0   Pole positions: 0   Fastest laps: 0   Points scored: 16

	Race	Circuit	No	Entrant	Tyres	Car/Engine	Comment	Q Pos/Entries
ret	ARGENTINE GP	Buenos Aires	10	Motor Racing Developments	G	3.0 Brabham BT37-Cosworth V8	gearbox	9/19
11	BRAZILIAN GP	Interlagos	17	Motor Racing Developments	G	3.0 Brabham BT37-Cosworth V8	stop/fuel metering unit/-2 laps	7/20
7	SOUTH AFRICAN GP	Kyalami	18	Motor Racing Developments	G	3.0 Brabham BT37-Cosworth V8	pit stop/tyre/2 laps behind	8/25
ret	SPANISH GP	Montjuich Park	18	Motor Racing Developments	G	3.0 Brabham BT42-Cosworth V8	driveshaft	=14/22
ret	BELGIAN GP	Zolder	10	Motor Racing Developments	G	3.0 Brabham BT42-Cosworth V8	oil leak	=7/23
ret	MONACO GP	Monte Carlo	10	Motor Racing Developments	G	3.0 Brabham BT42-Cosworth V8	gearbox	19/26
4	SWEDISH GP	Anderstorp	10	Motor Racing Developments	G	3.0 Brabham BT42-Cosworth V8		5/22
3	FRENCH GP	Paul Ricard	10	Motor Racing Developments	G	3.0 Brabham BT42-Cosworth V8		8/25
6	BRITISH GP	Silverstone	10	Motor Racing Developments	G	3.0 Brabham BT42-Cosworth V8		=8/29
ret	DUTCH GP	Zandvoort	10	Motor Racing Developments	G	3.0 Brabham BT42-Cosworth V8	burst tyre	5/24
ret	GERMAN GP	Nürburgring	10	Motor Racing Developments	G	3.0 Brabham BT42-Cosworth V8	engine	10/23
4	AUSTRIAN GP	Österreichring	10	Motor Racing Developments	G	3.0 Brabham BT42-Cosworth V8		5/25
6	ITALIAN GP	Monza	10	Motor Racing Developments	G	3.0 Brabham BT42-Cosworth V8		10/25
8	CANADIAN GP	Mosport Park	10	Motor Racing Developments	G	3.0 Brabham BT42-Cosworth V8	pit stop/tyres/2 laps behind	4/26
3	US GP	Watkins Glen	10	Motor Racing Developments	G	3.0 Brabham BT42-Cosworth V8		2/28

1974 — Championship position: 6th   Wins: 3   Pole positions: 1   Fastest laps: 1   Points scored: 32

	Race	Circuit	No	Entrant	Tyres	Car/Engine	Comment	Q Pos/Entries
7/ret	ARGENTINE GP	Buenos Aires	7	Motor Racing Developments	G	3.0 Brabham BT44-Cosworth V8	led race/out of fuel/-1 lap	6/26
7	BRAZILIAN GP	Interlagos	7	Motor Racing Developments	G	3.0 Brabham BT44-Cosworth V8	led race/tyre problems/-1 lap	2/25
1	SOUTH AFRICAN GP	Kyalami	7	Motor Racing Developments	G	3.0 Brabham BT44-Cosworth V8	FL	4/27
ret	SPANISH GP	Jarama	7	Motor Racing Developments	G	3.0 Brabham BT44-Cosworth V8	spun off	6/28
ret	BELGIAN GP	Nivelles	7	Motor Racing Developments	G	3.0 Brabham BT44-Cosworth V8	broken fuel line	24/32
ret	MONACO GP	Monte Carlo	7	Motor Racing Developments	G	3.0 Brabham BT44-Cosworth V8	hit Peterson	=7/28
ret	SWEDISH GP	Anderstorp	7	Motor Racing Developments	G	3.0 Brabham BT44-Cosworth V8	oil leak	10/28
12	DUTCH GP	Zandvoort	7	Motor Racing Developments	G	3.0 Brabham BT44-Cosworth V8	pit stop/tyres/4 laps behind	12/27
ret	FRENCH GP	Dijon	7	Motor Racing Developments	G	3.0 Brabham BT44-Cosworth V8	handling	8/30
6	BRITISH GP	Brands Hatch	7	Motor Racing Developments	G	3.0 Brabham BT44-Cosworth V8	spin/1 lap behind	4/34
3	GERMAN GP	Nürburgring	7	Motor Racing Developments	G	3.0 Brabham BT44-Cosworth V8		6/32
1	AUSTRIAN GP	Österreichring	7	Motor Racing Developments	G	3.0 Brabham BT44-Cosworth V8		2/31
ret	ITALIAN GP	Monza	7	Motor Racing Developments	G	3.0 Brabham BT44-Cosworth V8	gearbox bearing	2/31
9	CANADIAN GP	Mosport Park	7	Motor Racing Developments	G	3.0 Brabham BT44-Cosworth V8	pit stop/tyres/1 lap behind	4/30
1	US GP	Watkins Glen	7	Motor Racing Developments	G	3.0 Brabham BT44-Cosworth V8		1/30

1975 — Championship position: 3rd   Wins: 1   Pole positions: 0   Fastest laps: 0   Points scored: 37

	Race	Circuit	No	Entrant	Tyres	Car/Engine	Comment	Q Pos/Entries
3	ARGENTINE GP	Buenos Aires	7	Martini Racing	G	3.0 Brabham BT44B-Cosworth V8	led race	3/23
8	BRAZILIAN GP	Interlagos	7	Martini Racing	G	3.0 Brabham BT44B-Cosworth V8	pit stop-tyre/led race	3/23
2	SOUTH AFRICAN GP	Kyalami	7	Martini Racing	G	3.0 Brabham BT44B-Cosworth V8		2/28
3*	SPANISH GP	Montjuich Park	7	Martini Racing	G	3.0 Brabham BT44B-Cosworth V8	race stopped/*half points/-1 lap	15/26
9	MONACO GP	Monte Carlo	7	Martini Racing	G	3.0 Brabham BT44B-Cosworth V8	wrong tyre choice/-2 laps	10/26
3	BELGIAN GP	Zolder	7	Martini Racing	G	3.0 Brabham BT44B-Cosworth V8		6/24
2	SWEDISH GP	Anderstorp	7	Martini Racing	G	3.0 Brabham BT44B-Cosworth V8	led race	4/26
4	DUTCH GP	Zandvoort	7	Martini Racing	G	3.0 Brabham BT44B-Cosworth V8	pit stop-tyres/1 lap behind	5/25
14	FRENCH GP	Paul Ricard	7	Martini Racing	G	3.0 Brabham BT44B-Cosworth V8	pit stop-tyres/1 lap behind	11/26
ret	BRITISH GP	Silverstone	7	Martini Racing	G	3.0 Brabham BT44B-Cosworth V8	engine	8/28
1	GERMAN GP	Nürburgring	7	Martini Racing	G	3.0 Brabham BT44B-Cosworth V8		10/26
14	AUSTRIAN GP	Österreichring	7	Martini Racing	G	3.0 Brabham BT44B-Cosworth V8	1 lap behind	11/30
4	ITALIAN GP	Monza	7	Martini Racing	G	3.0 Brabham BT44B-Cosworth V8		7/28
ret	US GP	Watkins Glen	7	Martini Racing	G	3.0 Brabham BT44B-Cosworth V8	engine	3/24

1976 — Championship position: 16th   Wins: 0   Pole positions: 0   Fastest laps: 0   Points scored: 3

	Race	Circuit	No	Entrant	Tyres	Car/Engine	Comment	Q Pos/Entries
12/ret	BRAZILIAN GP	Interlagos	7	Martini Racing	G	3.0 Brabham BT45-Alfa Romeo F12	out of fuel/3 laps behind	15/22
ret	SOUTH AFRICAN GP	Kyalami	7	Martini Racing	G	3.0 Brabham BT45-Alfa Romeo F12	engine	11/25
ret	US GP WEST	Long Beach	7	Martini Racing	G	3.0 Brabham BT45-Alfa Romeo F12	collision with Brambilla	10/27
4	SPANISH GP	Jarama	7	Martini Racing	G	3.0 Brabham BT45-Alfa Romeo F12	1 lap behind	12/30
ret	BELGIAN GP	Zolder	7	Martini Racing	G	3.0 Brabham BT45-Alfa Romeo F12	engine	12/29
ret	MONACO GP	Monte Carlo	7	Martini Racing	G	3.0 Brabham BT45-Alfa Romeo F12	collision with Jones	20/25
ret	SWEDISH GP	Anderstorp	7	Martini Racing	G	3.0 Brabham BT45-Alfa Romeo F12	engine	16/27
11	FRENCH GP	Paul Ricard	7	Martini Racing	G	3.0 Brabham BT45-Alfa Romeo F12	1 lap behind	10/30
ret	BRITISH GP	Brands Hatch	7	Martini Racing	G	3.0 Brabham BT45-Alfa Romeo F12	oil pressure	15/30
ret	GERMAN GP	Nürburgring	7	Martini Racing	G	3.0 Brabham BT45-Alfa Romeo F12	engine	10/28
ret	AUSTRIAN GP	Österreichring	7	Martini Racing	G	3.0 Brabham BT45-Alfa Romeo F12	clutch	14/25
ret	DUTCH GP	Zandvoort	7	Martini Racing	G	3.0 Brabham BT45-Alfa Romeo F12	clutch-fluid loss	12/27
9	ITALIAN GP	Monza	35	Scuderia Ferrari SpA SEFAC	G	3.0 Ferrari 312T2 F12		7/29

1977 — Championship position: 4th   Wins: 1   Pole positions: 0   Fastest laps: 0   Points scored: 42

	Race	Circuit	No	Entrant	Tyres	Car/Engine	Comment	Q Pos/Entries
3	ARGENTINE GP	Buenos Aires	12	Scuderia Ferrari SpA SEFAC	G	3.0 Ferrari 312T2 F12		7/21
1	BRAZILIAN GP	Interlagos	12	Scuderia Ferrari SpA SEFAC	G	3.0 Ferrari 312T2 F12		2/22
8	SOUTH AFRICAN GP	Kyalami	12	Scuderia Ferrari SpA SEFAC	G	3.0 Ferrari 312T2 F12		8/23
ret	US GP WEST	Long Beach	12	Scuderia Ferrari SpA SEFAC	G	3.0 Ferrari 312T2 F12	collision with Lunger	4/22
2	SPANISH GP	Jarama	12	Scuderia Ferrari SpA SEFAC	G	3.0 Ferrari 312T2 F12		4/31

	Race	Circuit	No	Team	Tyre	Car	Notes	Grid/Fin
3	MONACO GP	Monte Carlo	12	Scuderia Ferrari SpA SEFAC	G	3.0 Ferrari 312T2 F12		3/26
ret	BELGIAN GP	Zolder	12	Scuderia Ferrari SpA SEFAC	G	3.0 Ferrari 312T2 F12	spun off	7/32
3	SWEDISH GP	Anderstorp	12	Scuderia Ferrari SpA SEFAC	G	3.0 Ferrari 312T2 F12		12/31
6	FRENCH GP	Dijon	12	Scuderia Ferrari SpA SEFAC	G	3.0 Ferrari 312T2 F12	1 lap behind	6/30
15	BRITISH GP	Silverstone	12	Scuderia Ferrari SpA SEFAC	G	3.0 Ferrari 312T2 F12	pit stop-brake problem/-6 laps	=13/36
4	GERMAN GP	Hockenheim	12	Scuderia Ferrari SpA SEFAC	G	3.0 Ferrari 312T2 F12		8/30
4	AUSTRIAN GP	Österreichring	12	Scuderia Ferrari SpA SEFAC	G	3.0 Ferrari 312T2 F12		5/30
6	DUTCH GP	Zandvoort	12	Scuderia Ferrari SpA SEFAC	G	3.0 Ferrari 312T2 F12	pit stop/wing damage/-2 laps	6/34
ret	ITALIAN GP	Monza	12	Scuderia Ferrari SpA SEFAC	G	3.0 Ferrari 312T2 F12	spun off on oil	2/34
6	US GP EAST	Watkins Glen	12	Scuderia Ferrari SpA SEFAC	G	3.0 Ferrari 312T2 F12	1 lap behind	6/27
ret	CANADIAN GP	Mosport Park	12	Scuderia Ferrari SpA SEFAC	G	3.0 Ferrari 312T2 F12	fuel pressure	12/27
2	JAPANESE GP	Mount Fuji	12	Scuderia Ferrari SpA SEFAC	G	3.0 Ferrari 312T2 F12		7/23

1978 Championship position: 3rd   Wins: 4   Pole positions: 2   Fastest laps: 2   Points scored: 48

	Race	Circuit	No	Team	Tyre	Car	Notes	Grid/Fin
7	ARGENTINE GP	Buenos Aires	11	Scuderia Ferrari SpA SEFAC	M	3.0 Ferrari 312T2 F12	pit stop/tyres	2/27
1	BRAZILIAN GP	Rio	11	Scuderia Ferrari SpA SEFAC	M	3.0 Ferrari 312T2 F12	FL	4/28
ret	SOUTH AFRICAN GP	Kyalami	11	Scuderia Ferrari SpA SEFAC	M	3.0 Ferrari 312T2 F12	spun off on oil	9/30
1	US GP WEST	Long Beach	11	Scuderia Ferrari SpA SEFAC	M	3.0 Ferrari 312T3 F12		1/30
8	MONACO GP	Monte Carlo	11	Scuderia Ferrari SpA SEFAC	M	3.0 Ferrari 312T3 F12	hit kerb/damaged tyres/-1 lap	1/30
3	BELGIAN GP	Zolder	11	Scuderia Ferrari SpA SEFAC	M	3.0 Ferrari 312T3 F12		2/30
ret	SPANISH GP	Jarama	11	Scuderia Ferrari SpA SEFAC	M	3.0 Ferrari 312T3 F12	driveshaft/accident	3/29
10	SWEDISH GP	Anderstorp	11	Scuderia Ferrari SpA SEFAC	M	3.0 Ferrari 312T3 F12	pit stops/tyres/1 lap behind	8/27
18	FRENCH GP	Paul Ricard	11	Scuderia Ferrari SpA SEFAC	M	3.0 Ferrari 312T3 F12	pit stops/tyres/FL/-5 laps	8/29
1	BRITISH GP	Brands Hatch	11	Scuderia Ferrari SpA SEFAC	M	3.0 Ferrari 312T3 F12		8/30
ret	GERMAN GP	Hockenheim	11	Scuderia Ferrari SpA SEFAC	M	3.0 Ferrari 312T3 F12	fuel vaporisation	12/30
dsq	AUSTRIAN GP	Österreichring	11	Scuderia Ferrari SpA SEFAC	M	3.0 Ferrari 312T3 F12	outside assistance after spin	4/31
7	DUTCH GP	Zandvoort	11	Scuderia Ferrari SpA SEFAC	M	3.0 Ferrari 312T3 F12		4/33
3	ITALIAN GP	Monza	11	Scuderia Ferrari SpA SEFAC	M	3.0 Ferrari 312T3 F12		11/32
1	US GP EAST	Watkins Glen	11	Scuderia Ferrari SpA SEFAC	M	3.0 Ferrari 312T3 F12		2/27
3	CANADIAN GP	Montreal	11	Scuderia Ferrari SpA SEFAC	M	3.0 Ferrari 312T3 F12		11/28

1979 Championship position: 6th=   Wins: 0   Pole positions: 0   Fastest laps: 0   Points scored: 25

	Race	Circuit	No	Team	Tyre	Car	Notes	Grid/Fin
2	ARGENTINE GP	Buenos Aires	2	Martini Racing Team Lotus	G	3.0 Lotus 79-Cosworth V8		3/26
3	BRAZILIAN GP	Interlagos	2	Martini Racing Team Lotus	G	3.0 Lotus 79-Cosworth V8		3/26
5	SOUTH AFRICAN GP	Kyalami	2	Martini Racing Team Lotus	G	3.0 Lotus 79-Cosworth V8		11/26
ret	US GP WEST	Long Beach	2	Martini Racing Team Lotus	G	3.0 Lotus 79-Cosworth V8	started from pit lane/driveshaft	2/26
2	SPANISH GP	Jarama	2	Martini Racing Team Lotus	G	3.0 Lotus 79-Cosworth V8		8/27
4	BELGIAN GP	Zolder	2	Martini Racing Team Lotus	G	3.0 Lotus 79-Cosworth V8		10/28
3	MONACO GP	Monte Carlo	2	Martini Racing Team Lotus	G	3.0 Lotus 79-Cosworth V8		11/25
13/ret	FRENCH GP	Dijon	2	Martini Racing Team Lotus	G	3.0 Lotus 79-Cosworth V8	accident with Rosberg/-3 laps	13/27
8	BRITISH GP	Silverstone	2	Martini Racing Team Lotus	G	3.0 Lotus 79-Cosworth V8	pit stop-tyre/2 laps behind	8/26
ret	GERMAN GP	Hockenheim	2	Martini Racing Team Lotus	G	3.0 Lotus 79-Cosworth V8	collision with Mass-spun off	13/26
ret	AUSTRIAN GP	Österreichring	2	Martini Racing Team Lotus	G	3.0 Lotus 79-Cosworth V8	handling	17/26
ret	DUTCH GP	Zandvoort	2	Martini Racing Team Lotus	G	3.0 Lotus 79-Cosworth V8	collision with Jarier	13/26
7	ITALIAN GP	Monza	2	Martini Racing Team Lotus	G	3.0 Lotus 79-Cosworth V8		13/28
ret	CANADIAN GP	Montreal	2	Martini Racing Team Lotus	G	3.0 Lotus 79-Cosworth V8	rear suspension	11/29
ret	US GP EAST	Watkins Glen	2	Martini Racing Team Lotus	G	3.0 Lotus 79-Cosworth V8	spun off	6/30

Reutemann's career took him from Brabham to Ferrari and then to Lotus before he joined Williams in 1980. Despite these top drives, the championship was always to elude the Argentine driver.
Right: His Williams FW07B leads Jody Scheckter's Ferrari in the 1980 Dutch Grand Prix at Zandvoort.

	1980	Championship position: 3rd	Wins: 1	Pole positions: 0	Fastest laps: 1	Points scored: 49			
ret	ARGENTINE GP	Buenos Aires	28	Albilad-Williams Racing Team	G	3.0 Williams FW07B-Cosworth V8		engine	10/28
ret	BRAZILIAN GP	Interlagos	28	Albilad-Williams Racing Team	G	3.0 Williams FW07B-Cosworth V8		driveshaft	4/28
5	SOUTH AFRICAN GP	Kyalami	28	Albilad-Williams Racing Team	G	3.0 Williams FW07B-Cosworth V8		1 lap behind	6/28
ret	US GP WEST	Long Beach	28	Albilad-Williams Racing Team	G	3.0 Williams FW07B-Cosworth V8		driveshaft	7/27
3	BELGIAN GP	Zolder	28	Albilad-Williams Racing Team	G	3.0 Williams FW07B-Cosworth V8			4/27
1	MONACO GP	Monte Carlo	28	Albilad-Williams Racing Team	G	3.0 Williams FW07B-Cosworth V8		FL	2/27
6	FRENCH GP	Paul Ricard	28	Albilad-Williams Racing Team	G	3.0 Williams FW07B-Cosworth V8			5/27
3	BRITISH GP	Brands Hatch	28	Albilad-Williams Racing Team	G	3.0 Williams FW07B-Cosworth V8			4/27
2	GERMAN GP	Hockenheim	28	Albilad-Williams Racing Team	G	3.0 Williams FW07B-Cosworth V8			4/26
3	AUSTRIAN GP	Österreichring	28	Albilad-Williams Racing Team	G	3.0 Williams FW07B-Cosworth V8			4/25
4	DUTCH GP	Zandvoort	28	Albilad-Williams Racing Team	G	3.0 Williams FW07B-Cosworth V8			3/28
3	ITALIAN GP	Imola	28	Albilad-Williams Racing Team	G	3.0 Williams FW07B-Cosworth V8			3/28
2	CANADIAN GP	Montreal	28	Albilad-Williams Racing Team	G	3.0 Williams FW07B-Cosworth V8			5/28
2	US GP EAST	Watkins Glen	28	Albilad-Williams Racing Team	G	3.0 Williams FW07B-Cosworth V8			3/27
	1981	Championship position: 2nd	Wins: 2	Pole positions: 2	Fastest laps: 2	Points scored: 49			
2	US GP WEST	Long Beach	2	Albilad-Williams Racing Team	M	3.0 Williams FW07C-Cosworth V8			3/29
1	BRAZILIAN GP	Rio	2	Albilad-Williams Racing Team	M	3.0 Williams FW07C-Cosworth V8			2/30
2	ARGENTINE GP	Buenos Aires	2	Albilad-Williams Racing Team	M	3.0 Williams FW07C-Cosworth V8			4/29
3	SAN MARINO GP	Imola	2	Albilad-Williams Racing Team	M	3.0 Williams FW07C-Cosworth V8			2/30
1	BELGIAN GP	Zolder	2	Albilad-Williams Racing Team	M	3.0 Williams FW07C-Cosworth V8		FL	1/31
ret	MONACO GP	Monte Carlo	2	Albilad-Williams Racing Team	M	3.0 Williams FW07C-Cosworth V8		gearbox	4/31
4	SPANISH GP	Jarama	2	TAG Williams Team	M	3.0 Williams FW07C-Cosworth V8			3/30
10	FRENCH GP	Dijon	2	TAG Williams Team	M	3.0 Williams FW07C-Cosworth V8		misfire/2 laps behind	7/29
2	BRITISH GP	Silverstone	2	TAG Williams Team	G	3.0 Williams FW07C-Cosworth V8			9/30
ret	GERMAN GP	Hockenheim	2	TAG Williams Team	G	3.0 Williams FW07C-Cosworth V8		engine	3/30
5	AUSTRIAN GP	Österreichring	2	TAG Williams Team	G	3.0 Williams FW07C-Cosworth V8			5/28
ret	DUTCH GP	Zandvoort	2	TAG Williams Team	G	3.0 Williams FW07C-Cosworth V8		accident with Laffite	5/30
3	ITALIAN GP	Monza	2	TAG Williams Team	G	3.0 Williams FW07C-Cosworth V8		FL	2/30
10	CANADIAN GP	Montreal	2	TAG Williams Team	G	3.0 Williams FW07C-Cosworth V8		wrong tyre choice in rain/-3 laps	2/30
8	CAESARS PALACE GP	Las Vegas	2	TAG Williams Team	G	3.0 Williams FW07C-Cosworth V8		handling problems/-1 lap	1/30
	1982	Championship position: 15th=	Wins: 0	Pole positions: 0	Fastest laps: 0	Points scored: 6			
2	SOUTH AFRICAN GP	Kyalami	5	TAG Williams Team	G	3.0 Williams FW07C-Cosworth V8			8/30
ret	BRAZILIAN GP	Rio	5	TAG Williams Team	G	3.0 Williams FW07C-Cosworth V8		accident with Arnoux	6/31

GP Starts: 146   GP Wins: 12   Pole positions: 6   Fastest laps: 6   Points: 310

LANCE REVENTLOW

The multi-millionaire son of Woolworth heiress Barbara Hutton, Reventlow began competing in the mid-fifties with a Mercedes before getting his hands on an 1100 cc Cooper to race in the US in 1956. The following year he came to Europe to buy a Maserati sports car, which he crashed badly at Snetterton, escaping unharmed. He also raced an F2 Cooper briefly, before returning home.

Reventlow then decided to build his own sports car, the Scarab, for 1958. It was a success and, with Chuck Daigh, Lance ambitiously planned a front-engined Grand Prix car which the pair would drive, but when it finally appeared in 1960 the outdated design was hopelessly outclassed. So frustrated were the drivers that, by the British GP, the car had been temporarily abandoned in favour of a third works Cooper. Both Lance and Daigh practised in it, but Chuck, being the faster, drove it in the race. The Scarab project struggled on in the hope of some success in the 1961 Inter-Continental Formula, but when that folded, so did the team.

Reventlow returned to the States to race a new Scarab rear-engined sports car briefly before losing interest in the sport completely. He was killed in 1972, when he was a passenger in a light aeroplane which crashed in bad weather over the Rocky Mountains.

REVENTLOW, Lance (USA) b 24/2/1936, London, England – d 24/7/1972, Colorado

	1960	Championship position: Unplaced						
	Race	Circuit	No	Entrant	Tyres	Car/Engine	Comment	Q Pos/Entries
dnq	MONACO GP	Monte Carlo	48	Reventlow Automobiles Inc	G/D	2.4 Scarab 4		23/24
dns	DUTCH GP	Zandvoort	21	Reventlow Automobiles Inc	D	2.4 Scarab 4	dispute over starting money	21/21
ret	BELGIAN GP	Spa	28	Reventlow Automobiles Inc	D	2.4 Scarab 4	engine	16/18
dns	BRITISH GP	Silverstone	3	Cooper Car Co	D	2.5 Cooper T51-Climax 4	car driven by Daigh in race	(23)/25

GP Starts: 1   GP Wins: 0   Pole positions: 0   Fastest laps: 0   Points: 0

PETER REVSON

Despite his family being a part of the Revlon cosmetics empire, Peter Revson made his way in motor racing very much under his own steam. He was initially regarded rather unfairly as just another American rich-kid playboy after his first unsuccessful attempts at Grand Prix racing, but eventually returned to fulfil his long-held ambition of winning a Grand Prix and, almost as importantly, win the respect and admiration of his peers.

Peter's career started in Hawaii with a Morgan which he shipped back to the States and raced there before trying his hand in a Formula Junior Taraschi. However, the lure of European racing, not to mention European culture, exerted a great pull on the young Revson, who cashed in everything he could to finance his expedition in 1963. Leading the nomadic existence that was so typical of the time, which often meant living out of the transporter, he raced a Formula Junior Cooper on the Continent and won the Copenhagen GP, but soon laid plans for a Formula 1 assault.

Reg Parnell's team had lost their sponsor and took Peter under their wing by way of a semi-works deal. His first tilt at Formula 1 in 1964 brought little cheer except a fourth place at Solitude, and he changed tack in 1965, joining the works Lotus F2 team run for the factory by Ron Harris. A win in the Eifelrennen was lost when he went off on the last lap but he finished second and, dropping into F3, also took the Monaco support race. Despite the season's progress, the gloss was wearing off Revson's European idyll and he headed back to the States to race a little Brabham BT8 sports car, winning his class at Seattle and Las Vegas.

For the 1966 season Revson joined Skip Scott in a Ford GT40 and over the next three seasons he began to build his career in big sports cars in Can-Am and Trans-Am before stepping back into single-seaters with a fine drive to fifth at Indianapolis in 1969. The following season he took second at Sebring with actor Steve McQueen in a Porsche 908 and then raced Carl Haas's Lola in Can-Am. In 1971 he joined the McLaren team to contest the money-spinning series, winning five rounds in the McLaren M8F, and his performance when taking second place in the Indy 500 for McLaren raised his profile greatly. He was invited to drive for Tyrrell at Watkins Glen in a one-off Grand Prix return before arranging a full season of both Formula 1 and Can-Am with McLaren in 1972.

The team's F1 M19 wasn't quite a winner, but Peter did a superb job with plenty of placings and few mistakes despite having to miss some races due to clashing USAC commitments. Revson stayed with the team in 1973 and once behind the wheel of the M23 proved a winner at last. His performance in the British GP was exemplary. On a damp track he first grabbed the initiative and then controlled the later stages to score a beautifully judged victory. There was one more win to follow in the rain-soaked confusion of Mosport, but by now internal pressures were afflicting the team, and Peter in particular.

Emerson Fittipaldi was moving in for 1974 with massive support from Marlboro and Texaco, and Teddy Mayer was willing to run Revson only as a third entry in Yardley colours. Not surprisingly Revson decided to seek better treatment elsewhere, joining the Shadow team. The season started with great promise as the new DN3 showed a fair turn of speed, but in testing for the South African GP at Kyalami tragedy struck when a suspension failure is thought to have caused the car to crash into a guard rail. The Shadow was totally destroyed in the massive impact and Revson had no chance of survival.

REVSON, Peter (USA) b 27/2/1939, New York City, New York – d 22/3/1974, Kyalami Circuit, South Africa

1964 Championship position: Unplaced

	Race	Circuit	No	Entrant	Tyres	Car/Engine	Comment	Q Pos/Entries
dnq	MONACO GP	Monte Carlo	2	Revson Racing (America)	D	1.5 Lotus 24-BRM V8		19/20
dsq	BELGIAN GP	Spa	29	Reg Parnell (Racing)	D	1.5 Lotus 24-BRM V8	engine cut out-push start	10/20
dns	FRENCH GP	Rouen	36	Reg Parnell (Racing)	D	1.5 Lotus 25-BRM V8	car driven by Hailwood	– / –
ret	BRITISH GP	Brands Hatch	24	Revson Racing (America)	D	1.5 Lotus 24-BRM V8	gear selectors	=21/25
14	GERMAN GP	Nürburgring	27	Revson Racing (America)	D	1.5 Lotus 24-BRM V8	accident/	18/24
13	ITALIAN GP	Monza	38	Revson Racing (America)	D	1.5 Lotus 24-BRM V8	6 laps behind	18/25

1971 Championship position: Unplaced

ret	US GP	Watkins Glen	10	Elf Team Tyrrell	G	3.0 Tyrrell 001-Cosworth V8	clutch	21/32

1972 Championship position: 5th Wins: 0 Pole positions: 1 Fastest laps: 0 Points scored: 23

ret	ARGENTINE GP	Buenos Aires	18	Team Yardley McLaren	G	3.0 McLaren M19A-Cosworth V8	engine	3/22
3	SOUTH AFRICAN GP	Kyalami	14	Team Yardley McLaren	G	3.0 McLaren M19A-Cosworth V8		12/27
5	SPANISH GP	Jarama	20	Team Yardley McLaren	G	3.0 McLaren M19A-Cosworth V8	1 lap behind	11/26
7	BELGIAN GP	Nivelles	10	Team Yardley McLaren	G	3.0 McLaren M19A-Cosworth V8	2 laps behind	7/26
3	BRITISH GP	Brands Hatch	19	Team Yardley McLaren	G	3.0 McLaren M19A-Cosworth V8		3/27
3	AUSTRIAN GP	Österreichring	14	Team Yardley McLaren	G	3.0 McLaren M19C-Cosworth V8		4/26
dns	"	"	14T	Team Yardley McLaren	G	3.0 McLaren M19A-Cosworth V8	practice only	– / –
4	ITALIAN GP	Monza	15	Team Yardley McLaren	G	3.0 McLaren M19C-Cosworth V8		8/27
dns	"	"	14T	Team Yardley McLaren	G	3.0 McLaren M19A-Cosworth V8	practice only	– / –
2	CANADIAN GP	Mosport Park	19	Team Yardley McLaren	G	3.0 McLaren M19A-Cosworth V8		1/25
dns	"	"	19T	Team Yardley McLaren	G	3.0 McLaren M19A-Cosworth V8	practice only	– / –
18/ret	US GP	Watkins Glen	20	Team Yardley McLaren	G	3.0 McLaren M19C-Cosworth V8	ignition/5 laps behind	2/32

1973 Championship position: 5th Wins: 2 Pole positions: 0 Fastest laps: 0 Points scored: 38

8	ARGENTINE GP	Buenos Aires	16	Yardley Team McLaren	G	3.0 McLaren M19C-Cosworth V8	tyre problems/4 laps behind	11/19
ret	BRAZILIAN GP	Interlagos	8	Yardley Team McLaren	G	3.0 McLaren M19C-Cosworth V8	gearbox	=11/20
2	SOUTH AFRICAN GP	Kyalami	6	Yardley Team McLaren	G	3.0 McLaren M19C-Cosworth V8		6/25
4	SPANISH GP	Montjuich Park	6	Yardley Team McLaren	G	3.0 McLaren M23-Cosworth V8	1 lap behind	5/22
ret	BELGIAN GP	Zolder	8	Yardley Team McLaren	G	3.0 McLaren M23-Cosworth V8	spun off	10/23
5	MONACO GP	Monte Carlo	8	Yardley Team McLaren	G	3.0 McLaren M23-Cosworth V8	2 laps behind	15/26
7	SWEDISH GP	Anderstorp	8	Yardley Team McLaren	G	3.0 McLaren M23-Cosworth V8	1 lap behind	7/22
1	BRITISH GP	Silverstone	8	Yardley Team McLaren	G	3.0 McLaren M23-Cosworth V8		=2/29
4	DUTCH GP	Zandvoort	8	Yardley Team McLaren	G	3.0 McLaren M23-Cosworth V8		6/24
9	GERMAN GP	Nürburgring	8	Yardley Team McLaren	G	3.0 McLaren M23-Cosworth V8		7/23
ret	AUSTRIAN GP	Österreichring	8	Yardley Team McLaren	G	3.0 McLaren M23-Cosworth V8	clutch	4/25
3	ITALIAN GP	Monza	8	Yardley Team McLaren	G	3.0 McLaren M23-Cosworth V8		2/25
1	CANADIAN GP	Mosport Park	8	Yardley Team McLaren	G	3.0 McLaren M23-Cosworth V8		2/26
5	US GP	Watkins Glen	8	Yardley Team McLaren	G	3.0 McLaren M23-Cosworth V8		8/28

1974 Championship position: Unplaced

ret	ARGENTINE GP	Buenos Aires	16	UOP Shadow Racing Team	G	3.0 Shadow DN3-Cosworth V8	collision-Hailwood & Regazzoni	4/26
ret	BRAZILIAN GP	Interlagos	16	UOP Shadow Racing Team	G	3.0 Shadow DN3-Cosworth V8	overheating	6/25
dnp	SOUTH AFRICAN GP	Kyalami	16	UOP Shadow Racing Team	G	3.0 Shadow DN3-Cosworth V8	fatal crash in pre-race practice	– / –

GP Starts: 30 GP Wins: 2 Pole positions: 1 Fastest laps: 0 Points: 61

RHODES, John (GB) b 18/8/1927, Wolverhampton, Staffordshire

1965 Championship position: Unplaced

	Race	Circuit	No	Entrant	Tyres	Car/Engine	Comment	Q Pos/Entries
ret	BRITISH GP	Silverstone	20	Gerard Racing	D	1.5 Cooper T60-Climax V8	ignition	21/23

GP Starts: 1 GP Wins: 0 Pole positions: 0 Fastest laps: 0 Points: 0

RIBEIRO, Alex-Dias (BR) b 7/11/1948, Belo Horizonte

1976 Championship position: Unplaced

	Race	Circuit	No	Entrant	Tyres	Car/Engine	Comment	Q Pos/Entries
12	US GP EAST	Watkins Glen	25	Hesketh Racing with Rizla/Penthouse	G	3.0 Hesketh 308D-Cosworth V8	2 laps behind	22/27

1977 Championship position: Unplaced

ret	ARGENTINE GP	Buenos Aires	9	Hollywood March Racing	G	3.0 March 761B-Cosworth V8	broken gear lever	20/21
ret	BRAZILIAN GP	Interlgos	9	Hollywood March Racing	G	3.0 March 761B-Cosworth V8	engine	21/22
ret	SOUTH AFRICAN GP	Kyalami	9	Hollywood March Racing	G	3.0 March 761B-Cosworth V8	engine	17/23
ret	US GP WEST	Long Beach	9	Hollywood March Racing	G	3.0 March 761B-Cosworth V8	gearbox oil leak	22/22
dnq	SPANISH GP	Jarama	9	Hollywood March Racing	G	3.0 March 761B-Cosworth V8		27/31
dnq	MONACO GP	Monte Carlo	9	Hollywood March Racing	G	3.0 March 761B-Cosworth V8	accident in practice	25/26
dnq	BELGIAN GP	Zolder	9	Hollywood March Racing	G	3.0 March 761B-Cosworth V8		30/32
dnq	SWEDISH GP	Anderstorp	9	Hollywood March Racing	G	3.0 March 761B-Cosworth V8		25/31
dnq	FRENCH GP	Dijon	9	Hollywood March Racing	G	3.0 March 761B-Cosworth V8		23/30
dnq	BRITISH GP	Silverstone	9	Hollywood March Racing	G	3.0 March 761B-Cosworth V8		27/36
8	GERMAN GP	Hockenheim	9	Hollywood March Racing	G	3.0 March 761B-Cosworth V8	1 lap behind	20/30
dnq	AUSTRIAN GP	Österreichring	9	Hollywood March Racing	G	3.0 March 761B-Cosworth V8	accident in practice	30/30
11	DUTCH GP	Zandvoort	9	Hollywood March Racing	G	3.0 March 761B-Cosworth V8	3 laps behind	24/34
dnq	ITALIAN GP	Monza	9	Hollywood March Racing	G	3.0 March 761B-Cosworth V8		25/34
15	US GP EAST	Watkins Glen	9	Hollywood March Racing	G	3.0 March 761B-Cosworth V8	3 laps behind	23/27
8	CANADIAN GP	Mosport Park	9	Hollywood March Racing	G	3.0 March 761B-Cosworth V8	2 laps behind	23/27
12	JAPANESE GP	Mount Fuji	9	Hollywood March Racing	G	3.0 March 761B-Cosworth V8	4 laps behind	23/23

	1979			Championship position: Unplaced				
dnq	CANADIAN GP	Montreal	19	Fittipaldi Automotive	G	3.0 Fittipaldi F6A-Cosworth V8		28/29
dnq	US GP EAST	Watkins Glen	19	Fittipaldi Automotive	G	3.0 Fittipaldi F6A-Cosworth V8		29/30

GP Starts: 10   GP Wins: 0   Pole positions: 0   Fastest laps: 0   Points: 0

RIESS, Fritz (D) b 11/7/1922, Nuremburg – d 5/1991

	1952			Championship position: Unplaced				
	Race	Circuit	No	Entrant	Tyres	Car/Engine	Comment	Q Pos/Entries
7	GERMAN GP	Nürburgring	121	Fritz Riess	–	2.0 Veritas RS 6 sports car	2 laps behind	12/32

GP Starts: 1   GP Wins: 0   Pole positions: 0   Fastest laps: 0   Points: 0

JOHN RHODES

A Formula Junior regular in the early sixties, Rhodes raced the Midland Racing Partnership Cooper in 1961, with victory in the minor Irish FJ championship providing the highlight of his season.

In 1962 he raced for Bob Gerard, taking 13th in the International Trophy in a Cooper and driving an Ausper-Ford in Formula Junior events. He signed to race for Ken Tyrrell in the formula the following year, but also began to drive the works Mini-Coopers with which he was to become synonymous throughout the sixties.

John's single-seater outings were then confined to a few races with Bob Gerard's faithful old Cooper in 1965, the car proving to be very slow in his only Grand Prix appearance at Silverstone.

ALEX RIBEIRO

The 1973 Brazilian Formula Ford champion with five wins from seven starts, Alex then headed for Europe and an excellent first season in F3 with a works GRD, winning three rounds. His career continued its upward trend with a factory F3 March in 1975, which led to a full season for the team in Formula 2 in 1976. Although a win eluded him, he was, with Arnoux, usually the fastest man around.

Hiring a Hesketh, Alex made a steady F1 debut in the US GP, before taking on his only full Grand Prix season with a works March in 1977. It was to be a disastrous campaign, with drivers and management blaming each other for the cars' disappointing performances.

Back in Formula 2 in 1978 with his own 'Jesus Saves Racing' March 782, Alex initially showed he had lost none of his talent with a brilliant win at the Nürburgring, but gradually his season tailed off and the little team lost heart. In 1979 Ribeiro reappeared with Fittipaldi at the non-championship Dino Ferrari GP, but retired early on. He was later invited to drive for the team in the end-of-season North American races, but failed to qualify the car on both occasions. Alex subsequently enjoyed a long career in touring cars (and occasionally Sud-Am single-seaters) back in his native Brazil.

In 1999 he returned to the Grand Prix scene, having been invited to drive the Mercedes CLK circuit safety car.

FRITZ RIESS

Having shown much promise in Hermann Holbein's beautifully constructed HH single-seater in 1948, Riess then switched to AFM and in 1950 he enjoyed some fine tussles with Ulmen's Veritas-Meteor, winning the Eifelrennen and finishing second to Ulmen at Sachsenring. He continued with the team the following year, winning at the Riem airfield circuit and then taking second place behind Pietsch in the Eifelrennen, before successfully joining the ranks of the Veritas runners in 1952 with his two-seater sports model.

Invited by Mercedes to join their team for Le Mans, Riess shared the winning 300SL with Lang and then finished third in the Prix de Berne at Bremgarten. He raced infrequently from 1953 onwards but was still active in 1957, when he took a class win in the Nürburgring 1000 Km, again in a Mercedes-Benz 300SL.

JOCHEN RINDT

You really needed to see Rindt in action to appreciate his genius. The little skittering Formula 2 cars were thrown to the limits of their adhesion as he almost danced them to win after win. Then his phenomenal skill took the huge overweight Cooper-Maserati into undreamed-of angles as the unwieldy beast was driven with such ferocity that, inevitably perhaps, finishes were few and far between.

Although Rindt had been around in Formula Junior and taken part in the non-championship 1963 Austrian GP, his potential remained hidden until he burst upon an unsuspecting British public at a big Formula 2 race at Crystal Palace in 1964. Sensationally he defeated the established aces of the day in the formula that was to become largely his personal domain in future years. With the Zeltweg race part of the championship calendar that year, Rindt hired Rob Walker's Brabham. Though he retired in the race, Jochen was keen to drive for Walker's équipe in 1965, but while Rob greatly admired the Austrian's talents he felt his career would be better nurtured at Cooper.

His first season with the team was spent learning the ropes under the tutelage of Bruce McLaren, and success was found more regularly in Formula 2, although his big win that year was at Le Mans where he took a NART-entered Ferrari 250LM to an unlikely victory with Masten Gregory. Cooper's competitiveness was restored in 1966 when Jochen emerged as a true front-runner, although he was pushed aside somewhat by the mid-season arrival of John Surtees. Signing a three-year deal with Cooper proved to have been a big mistake when Rindt was trapped in a poor car in 1967, but he spent his energies making up for it in Formula 2, taking Roy Winkelmann's Brabham to nine victories and four second places from 15 starts.

Joining a Brabham team fresh from two World Championships should have been the passport to well-deserved Grand Prix success for Rindt but, alas, it was not to be. The latest Repco engine proved to be hopelessly unreliable and Jochen was left with just a couple of third places at the end of the year. He also had a shot at Indianapolis in the team's BT25-Repco, but his race ended in retirement. Rindt's Formula 2 success continued unabated, but the lack of Grand Prix success led him to accept a drive at Lotus alongside Graham Hill for the 1969 season. Although he had equal status with the new World Champion, it soon became clear during the Tasman series that he had the edge, Jochen winning races at Christchurch and Warwick Farm.

The European season started badly for Rindt when he crashed in the Spanish GP

British Grand Prix, Silverstone, 1969. Rindt drifts the Lotus 49B-Ford through the fast bends of the Northamptonshire track.

after the massive rear aerofoil collapsed, putting him into hospital. He was back to his best by the British GP, where he fought a glorious duel with Stewart's Matra before minor problems dropped him from contention. He could not be denied much longer, however, taking his long-awaited maiden Grand Prix victory at Watkins Glen. Although Colin Chapman had supplied Rindt with a car worthy of his talents, theirs was an uneasy alliance. Jochen would dearly have liked to have returned to Brabham – now a competitive force again – but in the end lashings of money, the promise of total number-one status and a ground-breaking new car for 1970 held sway.

After starting the year in the old Lotus 49, taking second in the Race of Champions, Rindt gave the sensational-looking Lotus 72 its debut in Spain. However, it still needed some development and for Monaco Jochen was back in the old car. It was here he took perhaps his most famous victory, his incredible late-race charge forcing Jack Brabham into a final-corner error. The new 72 was finally considered fully raceworthy at Zandvoort and Jochen scored the first of four successive wins which put him within touching distance of the title. At Brands Hatch he was very lucky, as Brabham ran out of fuel on the last lap, but at Hockenheim he and Jacky Ickx gave a wonderful display of high-speed artistry. Having previously agreed places on the circuit where overtaking manoeuvres were acceptable, both drivers fought a great battle within those parameters. At the finish Chapman, who by now had grown much closer to Rindt than had seemed possible a year before, offered his congratulations. 'A monkey could have won in your car today,' was Jochen's retort. Then came Monza. There were rumours of retirement, for Jochen had lost close friends Bruce McLaren and Piers Courage in accidents in the preceding months. However, during practice 'something broke' on the car, which veered at enormous speed into the barrier. The front of the Lotus was totally destroyed and poor Rindt was pronounced dead on arrival at hospital in Milan. A month later at Watkins Glen, the inexperienced Emerson Fittipaldi took the Lotus 72 to a surprise victory, thus ensuring that Rindt became the sport's first and to date, thankfully, only posthumous World Champion.

JOCHEN RINDT

WORLD CHAMPION: 1970

RINDT, Jochen (A) b 18/4/1942, Mainz-am-Rhein, Germany – d 5/9/1970, Milan, Italy

1964 — Championship position: Unplaced

	Race	Circuit	No	Entrant	Tyres	Car/Engine	Comment	Q Pos/Entries
ret	AUSTRIAN GP	Zeltweg	12	Rob Walker Racing Team	D	1.5 Brabham BT11-BRM V8	steering	13/20

1965 — Championship position: 13th Wins: 0 Pole positions: 0 Fastest laps: 0 Points scored: 4

	Race	Circuit	No	Entrant	Tyres	Car/Engine	Comment	Q Pos/Entries
ret	SOUTH AFRICAN GP	East London	10	Cooper Car Co	D	1.5 Cooper T73-Climax V8	electrics	10/25
dnq	MONACO GP	Monte Carlo	8	Cooper Car Co	D	1.5 Cooper T77-Climax V8		16/17
11	BELGIAN GP	Spa	5	Cooper Car Co	D	1.5 Cooper T77-Climax V8	3 laps behind	14/21
ret	FRENCH GP	Clermont Ferrand	20	Cooper Car Co	D	1.5 Cooper T77-Climax V8	collision with Amon	12/17
14/ret	BRITISH GP	Silverstone	10	Cooper Car Co	D	1.5 Cooper T77-Climax V8	engine	12/23
ret	DUTCH GP	Zandvoort	20	Cooper Car Co	D	1.5 Cooper T77-Climax V8	no oil pressure	14/17
4	GERMAN GP	Nürburgring	12	Cooper Car Co	D	1.5 Cooper T77-Climax V8		8/22
8	ITALIAN GP	Monza	18	Cooper Car Co	D	1.5 Cooper T77-Climax V8	2 laps behind	7/23
6	US GP	Watkins Glen	10	Cooper Car Co	D	1.5 Cooper T77-Climax V8	2 laps behind	=13/18
ret	MEXICAN GP	Mexico City	10	Cooper Car Co	D	1.5 Cooper T77-Climax V8	ignition	16/18

1966 — Championship position: 3rd Wins: 0 Pole positions: 0 Fastest laps: 0 Points scored: 24

	Race	Circuit	No	Entrant	Tyres	Car/Engine	Comment	Q Pos/Entries
ret	MONACO GP	Monte Carlo	10	Cooper Car Co	D	3.0 Cooper T81-Maserati V12	engine	7/16
2	BELGIAN GP	Spa	19	Cooper Car Co	D	3.0 Cooper T81-Maserati V12		2/18
4	FRENCH GP	Reims	6	Cooper Car Co	D	3.0 Cooper T81-Maserati V12	2 laps behind	5/17
5	BRITISH GP	Brands Hatch	11	Cooper Car Co	D	3.0 Cooper T81-Maserati V12	1 lap behind	7/20
ret	DUTCH GP	Zandvoort	26	Cooper Car Co	D	3.0 Cooper T81-Maserati V12	crashed	6/18
3	GERMAN GP	Nürburgring	8	Cooper Car Co	D	3.0 Cooper T81-Maserati V12		9/30
4	ITALIAN GP	Monza	16	Cooper Car Co	F	3.0 Cooper T81-Maserati V12	flat tyre last lap/1 lap behind	8/22
2	US GP	Watkins Glen	8	Cooper Car Co	F	3.0 Cooper T81-Maserati V12	1 lap behind	9/19
ret	MEXICAN GP	Mexico City	8	Cooper Car Co	F	3.0 Cooper T81-Maserati V12	lost wheel-suspension bolt	5/19

1967 — Championship position: 11th= Wins: 0 Pole positions: 0 Fastest laps: 0 Points scored: 6

	Race	Circuit	No	Entrant	Tyres	Car/Engine	Comment	Q Pos/Entries
ret	SOUTH AFRICAN GP	Kyalami	3	Cooper Car Co	F	3.0 Cooper T81-Maserati V12	engine	=7/18
ret	MONACO GP	Monte Carlo	10	Cooper Car Co	F	3.0 Cooper T81-Maserati V12	gearbox	16/18
ret	DUTCH GP	Zandvoort	12	Cooper Car Co	F	3.0 Cooper T81B-Maserati V12	suspension	4/17
4	BELGIAN GP	Spa	29	Cooper Car Co	F	3.0 Cooper T81B-Maserati V12		=4/18
ret	FRENCH GP	Le Mans	12	Cooper Car Co	F	3.0 Cooper T81B-Maserati V12	engine	8/15
ret	BRITISH GP	Silverstone	11	Cooper Car Co	F	3.0 Cooper T86-Maserati V12	engine	8/21
dns	"	"	11	Cooper Car Co	F	3.0 Cooper T81B-Maserati V12	practice only	–/–
ret	GERMAN GP	Nürburgring	5	Cooper Car Co	F	3.0 Cooper T86-Maserati V12	engine-overheating	10/25
dns	"	"	5	Cooper Car Co	F	3.0 Cooper T81B-Maserati V12	practice only	–/–
ret	CANADIAN GP	Mosport Park	71	Cooper Car Co	F	3.0 Cooper T81-Maserati V12	ignition	8/19
dns	"	" "	7	Cooper Car Co	F	3.0 Cooper T86-Maserati V12	engine in practice	–/–
4	ITALIAN GP	Monza	30	Cooper Car Co	F	3.0 Cooper T86-Maserati V12		11/18
ret	US GP	Watkins Glen	4	Cooper Car Co	F	3.0 Cooper T81B-Maserati V12	engine	8/19
dns	"	" "	21	Cooper Car Co	F	3.0 Cooper T86-Maserati V12	Ickx drove car in race	–/–

1968 — Championship position: 12th Wins: 0 Pole positions: 2 Fastest laps: 0 Points scored: 8

	Race	Circuit	No	Entrant	Tyres	Car/Engine	Comment	Q Pos/Entries
3	SOUTH AFRICAN GP	Kyalami	3	Brabham Racing Organisation	G	3.0 Brabham BT24-Repco V8		4/23
ret	SPANISH GP	Jarama	4	Brabham Racing Organisation	G	3.0 Brabham BT24-Repco V8	low oil pressure	=9/14
ret	MONACO GP	Monte Carlo	3	Brabham Racing Organisation	G	3.0 Brabham BT24-Repco V8	spun off	5/18
ret	BELGIAN GP	Spa	19	Brabham Racing Organisation	G	3.0 Brabham BT26-Repco V8	engine	17/18
ret	DUTCH GP	Zandvoort	6	Brabham Racing Organisation	G	3.0 Brabham BT26-Repco V8	damp ignition	2/19
ret	FRENCH GP	Rouen	2	Brabham Racing Organisation	G	3.0 Brabham BT26-Repco V8	fuel leak	1/18
ret	BRITISH GP	Brands Hatch	4	Brabham Racing Organisation	G	3.0 Brabham BT26-Repco V8	fuel system	5/20
dns	"	" "	4	Brabham Racing Organisation	G	3.0 Brabham BT24-Repco V8	practice only	–/–
3	GERMAN GP	Nürburgring	5	Brabham Racing Organisation	G	3.0 Brabham BT26-Repco V8		3/20
ret	ITALIAN GP	Monza	11	Brabham Racing Organisation	G	3.0 Brabham BT26-Repco V8	engine	10/24
ret	CANADIAN GP	St Jovite	6	Brabham Racing Organisation	G	3.0 Brabham BT26-Repco V8	engine	1/22
ret	US GP	Watkins Glen	4	Brabham Racing Organisation	G	3.0 Brabham BT26-Repco V8	engine	6/21
ret	MEXICAN GP	Mexico City	4	Brabham Racing Organisation	G	3.0 Brabham BT26-Repco V8	ignition	10/21

Rindt in the Lotus 72 at the 1970 British Grand Prix. The Austrian won the race after Brabham ran out of fuel on the last lap.

	1969	Championship position: 4th	Wins: 1	Pole positions: 5	Fastest laps: 2	Points scored: 22			
ret	SOUTH AFRICAN GP	Kyalami	2	Gold Leaf Team Lotus	F	3.0 Lotus 49B-Cosworth V8		fuel pump	2/18
ret	SPANISH GP	Montjuich Park	2	Gold Leaf Team Lotus	F	3.0 Lotus 49B-Cosworth V8		broken rear wing/accident//FL	1/14
ret	DUTCH GP	Zandvoort	2	Gold Leaf Team Lotus	F	3.0 Lotus 49B-Cosworth V8		driveshaft	1/15
ret	FRENCH GP	Clermont Ferrand	15	Gold Leaf Team Lotus	F	3.0 Lotus 49B-Cosworth V8		driver unwell-double vision	3/13
4	BRITISH GP	Silverstone	2	Gold Leaf Team Lotus	F	3.0 Lotus 49B-Cosworth V8		pit stops/rear wing/fuel/	1/17
ret	GERMAN GP	Nürburgring	2	Gold Leaf Team Lotus	F	3.0 Lotus 49B-Cosworth V8		ignition	3/26
2	ITALIAN GP	Monza	4	Gold Leaf Team Lotus	F	3.0 Lotus 49B-Cosworth V8			1/15
3	CANADIAN GP	Mosport Park	2	Gold Leaf Team Lotus	F	3.0 Lotus 49B-Cosworth V8			=2/20
dns	"	" "	T	Gold Leaf Team Lotus	F	3.0 Lotus 63-Cosworth V8 4WD		practice only	–/–
1	US GP	Watkins Glen	2	Gold Leaf Team Lotus	F	3.0 Lotus 49B-Cosworth V8		FL	1/18
ret	MEXICAN GP	Mexico City	2	Gold Leaf Team Lotus	F	3.0 Lotus 49B-Cosworth V8		broken front suspension	6/17
	1970	Championship position: WORLD CHAMPION	Wins: 5	Pole positions: 3	Fastest laps: 1	Points scored: 45			
13/ret	SOUTH AFRICAN GP	Kyalami	9	Gold Leaf Team Lotus	F	3.0 Lotus 49C-Cosworth V8		engine/8 laps behind	4/24
ret	SPANISH GP	Jarama	3	Gold Leaf Team Lotus	F	3.0 Lotus 72-Cosworth V8		ignition	9/22
1	MONACO GP	Monte Carlo	3	Gold Leaf Team Lotus	F	3.0 Lotus 49C-Cosworth V8		FL	8/21
ret	BELGIAN GP	Spa	20	Gold Leaf Team Lotus	F	3.0 Lotus 49C-Cosworth V8		engine	2/18
dns	"	"	20	Gold Leaf Team Lotus	F	3.0 Lotus 72-Cosworth V8		practice only	–/–
1	DUTCH GP	Zandvoort	10	Gold Leaf Team Lotus	F	3.0 Lotus 72-Cosworth V8			1/24
1	FRENCH GP	Clermont Ferrand	6	Gold Leaf Team Lotus	F	3.0 Lotus 72-Cosworth V8			6/23
1	BRITISH GP	Brands Hatch	5	Gold Leaf Team Lotus	F	3.0 Lotus 72-Cosworth V8			1/25
1	GERMAN GP	Hockenheim	2	Gold Leaf Team Lotus	F	3.0 Lotus 72-Cosworth V8			2/25
ret	AUSTRIAN GP	Österreichring	6	Gold Leaf Team Lotus	F	3.0 Lotus 72-Cosworth V8		engine	1/24
dns	ITALIAN GP	Monza	22	Gold Leaf Team Lotus	F	3.0 Lotus 72-Cosworth V8		fatal accident in practice	(12)/27

GP Starts: 60   GP Wins: 6   Pole positions: 10   Fastest laps: 3   Points: 109

JOHN RISELEY-PRICHARD

Riseley-Prichard's competition career began modestly in 1952 and '53 at national level with a Riley, but in 1954 he bought Rob Walker's Connaught, which he drove mainly in minor races (winning an obscure Formula 1 event at Davidstow, Cornwall), but also in that year's British Grand Prix. John raced it for fun in Formula Libre events into the 1955 season, but when he let the young Tony Brooks take the wheel he soon realised his limitations as a driver.

He shared a works Aston Martin with Brooks in that year's Le Mans 24-hour race, but in the wake of Levegh's terrible accident his family is thought to have persuaded him to retire from the sport and concentrate on his profession as a Lloyd's insurance broker.

RICHARD ROBARTS

A Formula Ford club racer from 1969 to 1972, Robarts drove an F3 GRD in 1973, sharing the Lombard North Central championship with Tony Brise.

Richard bought the second seat in the Brabham team for 1974, but when his backing fell through, he lost his place to the well-funded Rikki von Opel.

A hoped-for second chance with Williams in Sweden later that year failed to materialise when Tom Belso took over the car at the last minute, which left Robarts pretty much in the wilderness until he found the necessary sponsorship to go racing in Formula 2 in 1976 with a year-old March. He found the level of competition a bit too hot, but enjoyed some success with occasional outings in the Shellsport G8 series.

RISELEY-PRICHARD, John (GB) b 17/1/1924, Hereford

	1954	Championship position: Unplaced							
	Race	Circuit	No	Entrant	Tyres	Car/Engine		Comment	Q Pos/Entries
ret	BRITISH GP	Silverstone	24	R R C Walker Racing Team	D	2.0 Connaught A Type 4		spun off	21/31

GP Starts: 1   GP Wins: 0   Pole positions: 0   Fastest laps: 0   Points: 0

ROBARTS, Richard (GB) b 22/9/1944, Bicknacre, nr Chelmsford, Essex

	1974	Championship position: Unplaced							
	Race	Circuit	No	Entrant	Tyres	Car/Engine		Comment	Q Pos/Entries
ret	ARGENTINE GP	Buenos Aires	8	Motor Racing Developments	G	3.0 Brabham BT44-Cosworth V8		gearbox	22/26
15	BRAZILIAN GP	Interlagos	8	Motor Racing Developments	G	3.0 Brabham BT44-Cosworth V8		2 laps behind	24/25
17	SOUTH AFRICAN GP	Kyalami	8	Motor Racing Developments	G	3.0 Brabham BT44-Cosworth V8		4 laps behind	23/27
dns	SWEDISH GP	Anderstorp	20	Frank Williams Racing Cars	G	3.0 Iso Williams FW02-Cosworth V8		car driven by Belso	(25)/28

GP Starts: 3   GP Wins: 0   Pole positions: 0   Fastest laps: 0   Points: 0

PEDRO RODRIGUEZ

Pedro Rodriguez looked just great in a late-sixties Grand Prix car. His head seemed perpetually laid right back, and you could clearly see his eyes staring through the big aviator goggles as he went about his work. Aesthetics aside, that his talent went largely unregarded in Formula 1 is something of a mystery, and it was only right at the end of his life that his legend was forged.

Two years older than his brother Ricardo, Pedro was racing bikes by the age of 12 and a Jaguar XK120 by the time he was 15. He was soon joined by his sibling and the pair became notorious for their daring exploits in the late fifties. Attracting the attention of Luigi Chinetti, Pedro began racing his NART Ferraris, taking second place in the 1958 Nassau Trophy. The brothers eventually came to Europe and set about building a brilliant reputation in Chinetti's Ferraris, winning both the Nürburgring and Paris 1000 Km in 1961.

The death of Ricardo in Mexico at the end of 1962 was a devasting blow for Pedro, who nevertheless carried on racing, but was largely restricted to North America during 1963 and 1964. There were wins at Daytona in the GT class in 1963, and outright in 1964, sharing a GTO with Phil Hill. There were also end-of-year F1 drives for Lotus and Ferrari, but no offers of permanent Grand Prix employment came his way, so the little Mexican stuck it out in sports car racing, taking the occasional single-seater opportunities he was given. For the 1967 South African GP, Pedro was offered a works Cooper drive, but no deal beyond that. In a race of high attrition, he drove steadily to score a surprise win, a feat which eluded even Rindt during his spell with the team. Rodriguez was naturally then taken on for the rest of the year, but the car was rapidly becoming uncompetitive, and he did well just to scrape the odd point thereafter. His season was also interrupted by injury when an accident at Enna in the F2 Protos left him with a broken foot.

Pedro joined BRM in 1968 and, after an unsuccessful Tasman series, started the season in fine form, taking a memorable second place in the Race of Champions when he sliced through the field after being left at the start. After a rather lucky second place at Spa, the season slid into mediocrity as the team lost their way, and it was Pedro who paid the price, making way for John Surtees in 1969. As luck would have it, that was to be a terrible year at Bourne, and Pedro was fortunate to be out of the firing line, racing Tim Parnell's semi-works machine until he accepted an offer to drive the equally disappointing Ferrari.

Rodriguez had become much in demand as a sports car driver following his 1968 Le Mans victory with Bianchi in John Wyer's Ford GT40. He drove for both Ferrari and Matra the following year, before returning to Wyer in 1970. He was also back at BRM, and this time they had come up with a really good car in the P153. There were two races that year which Pedro would leave as a legacy to the portfolio of great motor racing performances. At Brands Hatch, driving the fearsome Gulf Porsche 917, he produced an unforgettable display in the rain to win the 1000 Km by a five-lap margin, and then in the Belgian GP at Spa he drove a masterful race, almost to the point of perfection, to beat Amon's March. He would score no more Grand Prix victories, only a win in the 1971 Rothmans Trophy at Oulton Park, but he continued to drive the Porsche with a fearlessness that was frightening. In 1971 Rodriguez won the Daytona 24 Hours, Monza 1000 Km and Spa 1000 Km with Jack Oliver, and the Österreichring 1000 Km with Richard Attwood to confirm his position as sports car racing's leading exponent.

Pedro lived for racing, and could not refuse the offer of a drive in an Interserie round at Norisring. Driving Herbert Müller's Ferrari 512M, Rodriguez crashed heavily when a tyre was thought to have deflated. The car burst into flames and when the driver was finally released he was found to have succumbed to multiple injuries.

RODRIGUEZ, Pedro (MEX) b 18/1/1940, Mexico City – d 11/7/1971, Norisring Circuit, Germany

	1963	Championship position: Unplaced							
	Race	Circuit	No	Entrant	Tyres	Car/Engine		Comment	Q Pos/Entries
ret	US GP	Watkins Glen	10	Team Lotus	D	1.5 Lotus 25-Climax V8		engine	=13/21
ret	MEXICAN GP	Mexico City	10	Team Lotus	D	1.5 Lotus 25-Climax V8		rear suspension	20/21
	1964	Championship position: 19th= Wins: 0 Pole positions: 0 Fastest laps: 0 Points scored: 1							
6	MEXICAN GP	Mexico City	18	North American Racing Team	D	1.5 Ferrari 156 V6		1 lap behind	9/19
	1965	Championship position: 14th= Wins: 0 Pole positions: 0 Fastest laps: 0 Points scored: 2							
5	US GP	Watkins Glen	14	North American Racing Team	D	1.5 Ferrari 1512 F12		1 lap behind	15/18
7	MEXICAN GP	Mexico City	14	North American Racing Team	D	1.5 Ferrari 1512 F12		3 laps behind	14/18
	1966	Championship position: Unplaced							
ret	FRENCH GP	Reims	2	Team Lotus	F	2.0 Lotus 33-Climax V8		engine-broken oil pipe	=12/27
ret	GERMAN GP (F2)	Nürburgring	31	Ron Harris-Team Lotus	D	1.0 Lotus 44-Cosworth 4 F2		engine	21/30
ret	US GP	Watkins Glen	11	Team Lotus	F	2.0 Lotus 33-BRM V8		starter motor after pit stop	10/19
ret	MEXICAN GP	Mexico City	11	Team Lotus	F	2.0 Lotus 33-Climax V8		gearbox	8/19

1967 — Championship position: 6th= · Wins: 1 · Pole positions: 0 · Fastest laps: 0 · Points scored: 15

1	SOUTH AFRICAN GP	Kyalami	4	Cooper Car Co	F	3.0 Cooper T81-Maserati V12		4/18
5	MONACO GP	Monte Carlo	11	Cooper Car Co	F	3.0 Cooper T81-Maserati V12	4 laps behind	5/17
ret	DUTCH GP	Zandvoort	14	Cooper Car Co	F	3.0 Cooper T81-Maserati V12	gearbox	13/18
9/ret	BELGIAN GP	Spa	30	Cooper Car Co	F	3.0 Cooper T81-Maserati V12	engine/3 laps behind	13/18
6	FRENCH GP	Le Mans	14	Cooper Car Co	F	3.0 Cooper T81-Maserati V12	4 laps behind	13/15
5	BRITISH GP	Silverstone	12	Cooper Car Co	F	3.0 Cooper T81-Maserati V12	1 lap behind	9/21
8th	GERMAN GP	Nürburgring	6	Cooper Car Co	F	3.0 Cooper T81-Maserati V12	11 th behind 3 F2 cars/-2 laps	11/25
dns	"	"	6	Cooper Car Co	F	3.0 Cooper T86-Maserati V12	practice only	– / –
6	MEXICAN GP	Mexico City	21	Cooper Car Co	F	3.0 Cooper T81B-Maserati V12	2 laps behind	13/19

1968 — Championship position: 6th= · Wins: 0 · Pole positions: 0 · Fastest laps: 1 · Points scored: 18

ret	SOUTH AFRICAN GP	Kyalami	11	Owen Racing Organisation	G	3.0 BRM P126 V12	ignition/boiling fuel	=10/23
ret	SPANISH GP	Jarama	9	Owen Racing Organisation	G	3.0 BRM P133 V12	crashed	2/14
ret	MONACO GP	Monte Carlo	4	Owen Racing Organisation	G	3.0 BRM P133 V12	hit barrier	=9/18
2	BELGIAN GP	Spa	11	Owen Racing Organisation	G	3.0 BRM P133 V12		8/18
3	DUTCH GP	Zandvoort	15	Owen Racing Organisation	G	3.0 BRM P133 V12	1 lap behind	5/17
nc	FRENCH GP	Rouen	20	Owen Racing Organisation	G	3.0 BRM P133 V12	pit stops/gearbox/FL/-7 laps	10/18
ret	BRITISH GP	Brands Hatch	10	Owen Racing Organisation	G	3.0 BRM P133 V12	timing chain	=13/20
dns	"	"	10	Owen Racing Organisation	G	3.0 BRM P126 V12	practice only	– / –
6	GERMAN GP	Nürburgring	10	Owen Racing Organisation	G	3.0 BRM P133 V12		14/20
ret	ITALIAN GP	Monza	26	Owen Racing Organisation	G	3.0 BRM P138 V12	engine	16/24
3	CANADIAN GP	St Jovite	16	Owen Racing Organisation	G	3.0 BRM P133 V12		12/22
ret	US GP	Watkins Glen	8	Owen Racing Organisation	G	3.0 BRM P133 V12	broken rear suspension	11/21
dns	"	"	8	Owen Racing Organisation	G	3.0 BRM P138 V12	practice only	– / –
4	MEXICAN GP	Mexico City	8	Owen Racing Organisation	G	3.0 BRM P133 V12	2 laps behind	12/21

1969 — Championship position: 13th= · Wins: 0 · Pole positions: 0 · Fastest laps: 0 · Points scored: 3

ret	SOUTH AFRICAN GP	Kyalami	12	Reg Parnell (Racing) Ltd	D	3.0 BRM P126 V12	engine	16/18
ret	SPANISH GP	Montjuich Park	9	Reg Parnell (Racing) Ltd	D	3.0 BRM P126 V12	engine	14/14
ret	MONACO GP	Monte Carlo	10	Reg Parnell (Racing) Ltd	D	3.0 BRM P126 V12	engine	=14/16
ret	BRITISH GP	Silverstone	12	Scuderia Ferrari SpA SEFAC	F	3.0 Ferrari 312/68/69 V12	engine	=7/17
6	ITALIAN GP	Monza	10	Scuderia Ferrari SpA SEFAC	F	3.0 Ferrari 312/68/69 V12	2 laps behind	12/15
ret	CANADIAN GP	Mosport Park	6	North American Racing Team	F	3.0 Ferrari 312/68/69 V12	oil pressure	13/20
5	US GP	Watkins Glen	12	North American Racing Team	F	3.0 Ferrari 312/68/69 V12	7 laps behind	12/18
7	MEXICAN GP	Mexico City	12	North American Racing Team	F	3.0 Ferrari 312/68/69 V12	2 laps behind	15/17

1970 — Championship position: 7th= · Wins: 1 · Pole positions: 0 · Fastest laps: 0 · Points scored: 23

9	SOUTH AFRICAN GP	Kyalami	20	Owen Racing Organisation	D	3.0 BRM P153 V12	pit stop/misfire/4 laps behind	16/24
ret	SPANISH GP	Jarama	10	Yardley Team BRM	D	3.0 BRM P153 V12	withdrawn after Oliver's crash	5/22
6	MONACO GP	Monte Carlo	17	Yardley Team BRM	D	3.0 BRM P153 V12	sticking throttle/-2 laps	20/21
1	BELGIAN GP	Spa	1	Yardley Team BRM	D	3.0 BRM P153 V12		6/18
10	DUTCH GP	Zandvoort	1	Yardley Team BRM	D	3.0 BRM P153 V12	2 stops/loose nose cone/-3 laps	7/24
ret	FRENCH GP	Clermont Ferrand	3	Yardley Team BRM	D	3.0 BRM P153 V12	gearbox	10/23
ret	BRITISH GP	Brands Hatch	22	Yardley Team BRM	D	3.0 BRM P153 V12	spun off	=16/25
ret	GERMAN GP	Hockenheim	6	Yardley Team BRM	D	3.0 BRM P153 V12	ignition	8/25
4	AUSTRIAN GP	Österreichring	17	Yardley Team BRM	D	3.0 BRM P153 V12	1 lap behind	22/24
ret	ITALIAN GP	Monza	10	Yardley Team BRM	D	3.0 BRM P153 V12	engine	2/27
4	CANADIAN GP	St Jovite	14	Yardley Team BRM	D	3.0 BRM P153 V12	pit stop-fuel/1 lap behind	7/20
2	US GP	Watkins Glen	19	Yardley Team BRM	D	3.0 BRM P153 V12	pit stop when leading/fuel	4/27
6	MEXICAN GP	Mexico City	19	Yardley Team BRM	D	3.0 BRM P153 V12		7/18

1971 — Championship position: 9= · Wins: 0 · Pole positions: 0 · Fastest laps: 0 · Points scored: 9

ret	SOUTH AFRICAN GP	Kyalami	16	Yardley-BRM	F	3.0 BRM P160 V12	overheating	10/25
dns	"	"	16T	Yardley-BRM	F	3.0 BRM P153 V12	practice only	– / –
4	SPANISH GP	Montjuich Park	14	Yardley-BRM	F	3.0 BRM P160 V12		4/22
9	MONACO GP	Monte Carlo	15	Yardley-BRM	F	3.0 BRM P160 V12	pit stop/wheel change/-4 laps	5/23
dns	"	"	15T	Yardley-BRM	F	3.0 BRM P153 V12	practice only	– / –
2	DUTCH GP	Zandvoort	8	Yardley-BRM	F	3.0 BRM P160 V12	led race	2/24
ret	FRENCH GP	Paul Ricard	15	Yardley-BRM	F	3.0 BRM P160 V12	coil	5/24

GP Starts: 55 · GP Wins: 2 · Pole positions: 0 · Fastest laps: 1 · Points: 71

Pedro wins the 1970 Belgian Grand Prix at the daunting Spa-Francorchamps circuit. Shadowing the BRM is Amon's March, which hounded the Mexican for most of the race.

RICARDO RODRIGUEZ

The younger of the two racing Rodriguez brothers, Ricardo gave up bike racing at the age of 14, having won the Mexican championship, to race an Opel sedan. By 1957 he was already competing abroad, taking a class win in the Nassau Tourist Trophy with a Porsche Spyder.

The brothers Rodriguez came to Europe in 1960 with a NART Ferrari, though it was with André Pilette that Ricardo gained his best result, a second at Le Mans in a 250GT. Teamed with Pedro, he took third in the Sebring 12 Hours and second in the Nürburgring 1000 Km.

Invited by the Scuderia to join their Grand Prix line-up for the Italian GP, he sensationally put the car on the front row of the grid alongside the ill-fated championship favourite, von Trips. Not surprisingly he was signed by the team for a full season in 1962, but the car was far from the dominant machine of just a year earlier and young Ricardo, still a little wild and fearless, was used selectively. In a bright start, the Mexican took second place at the Pau GP, before confirming his outstanding potential in a number of World Championship rounds. In sports car racing he was out of luck, except for a win in the Targa Florio sharing a Ferrari 246 V6 with Gendebien and Mairesse.

When Ferrari decided not to enter their cars for the non-championship Mexican GP, Ricardo arranged to race one of Rob Walker's Lotus-Climax V8s. Striving for pole position, the young charger came unstuck, crashing on the banking and dying from multiple injuries.

FRANCO ROL

A wealthy Italian aristocrat, Rol was a gentleman racer who made more of a mark in sports cars than in single-seater competition. Equipped with a special short-chassis Alfa Romeo coupé, he tackled the classic road races in the late forties. In 1948 he led the Giro de Sicilia before retiring, but fared better the following season, finishing second in class. The same year Franco took a splendid third in the Mille Miglia.

In 1950 he joined up with Chiron to race in the Platé Maseratis, which were by then well past their best, but he did manage a fifth place in the San Marino GP at Ospedaletti. Rol's next chance to sample a monoposto came at the end of the next season at Monza with the newly built OSCA. It was hopelessly outclassed on its debut but, undaunted, he reappeared with the car at the beginning of 1952 in the Valentino GP, where it expired with a blown gasket.

Franco was included in an expanded works Maserati driver line-up for the 1952 Italian GP, but his car failed on the 24th lap. Rol's racing career was brought to an end after he suffered serious injuries while competing in the 1953 Tour of Sicily.

RODRIGUEZ, Ricardo (MEX) b 14/2/1942, Mexico City – d 1/11/1962, Mexico City

	1961	Championship position: Unplaced							
	Race	Circuit	No	Entrant	Tyres	Car/Engine		Comment	Q Pos/Entries
ret	ITALIAN GP	Monza	8	Scuderia Ferrari SpA SEFAC	D	1.5 Ferrari 156 V6		fuel pump	2/33
	1962	Championship position: 12= Wins: 0 Pole positions: 0 Fastest laps: 0 Points scored: 4							
ret	DUTCH GP	Zandvoort	3	Scuderia Ferrari SpA SEFAC	D	1.5 Ferrari 156 V6		crashed	11/20
dns	MONACO GP	Monte Carlo	40T	Scuderia Ferrari SpA SEFAC	D	1.5 Ferrari 156 V6		practised in Mairesse car	– / –
4	BELGIAN GP	Spa	12	Scuderia Ferrari SpA SEFAC	D	1.5 Ferrari 156 V6			=7/20
6	GERMAN GP	Nürburgring	3	Scuderia Ferrari SpA SEFAC	D	1.5 Ferrari 156 V6			10/30
14	ITALIAN GP	Monza	4	Scuderia Ferrari SpA SEFAC	D	1.5 Ferrari 156 V6		pit stops/ignition/-23 laps	11/30

GP Starts: 5   GP Wins: 0   Pole positions: 0   Fastest laps: 0   Points: 4

ROL, Franco (I) b 5/6/1908 – d 5/6/1977

	1950	Championship position: Unplaced							
	Race	Circuit	NO	Entrant	Tyres	Car/Engine		Comment	Q Pos/Entries
ret	MONACO GP	Monte Carlo	44	Officine Alfieri Maserati	P	1.5 s/c Maserati 4CLT/48 4		multiple accident	17/21
ret	FRENCH GP	Reims	28	Officine Alfieri Maserati	P	1.5 s/c Maserati 4CLT/48 4		engine	7/20
ret	ITALIAN GP	Monza	4	Officine Alfieri Maserati	P	1.5 s/c Maserati 4CLT/48 4			9/27
	1951	Championship position: Unplaced							
9	ITALIAN GP	Monza	44	OSCA Automobili	P	4.5 OSCA 4500G V12		13 laps behind	18/22
	1952	Championship position: Unplaced							
ret	ITALIAN GP	Monza	24	Officine Alfieri Maserati	P	2.0 Maserati A6GCM 6		engine	16/35

GP Starts: 5   GP Wins: 0   Pole positions: 0   Fastest laps: 0   Points: 0

TONY ROLT

Perhaps the brightest young talent of a generation of pre-war amateur drivers, Rolt, an Army officer who would become a celebrated resident of Colditz Castle, won the British Empire Trophy at Donington in an ERA as a 19-year-old before the outbreak of hostilities. When peace returned he was soon back in action with an Alfa Romeo, a Delage and a Nash-Healey. Although he shared Peter Walker's ERA at the 1950 British GP, in the main Rolt restricted himself to national racing, enjoying himself with Rob Walker's Delage in 1951 and, in his only HWM drive, taking second place in the 1952 International Trophy behind team-mate Lance Macklin.

Between 1953 and 1955, Rolt raced Walker's dark-blue Connaught with great succes in national events, winning numerous Formula 2, Libre and handicap races, and also drove for the works Jaguar sports car team, paired with the extrovert Duncan Hamilton. This larger-than-life duo won the Le Mans 24-hour race in 1953, and took second place the following year both at Le Mans and in the Reims 12 Hours.

BERTIL ROOS

A graduate of the Opert driving school, where he was later an instructor, the self-confident Roos looked to have a bright future after winning the 1973 US Super Vee title and doing well in both European Formula 2 and Canadian Formula Atlantic.

His big opportunity came when Shadow invited him to drive their car in the 1974 Swedish GP, but it was an unhappy and brief alliance, the Swede failing to impress the team and subsequently being passed over in favour of Tom Pryce.

Thereafter, Roos returned to Atlantic racing in the USA and Canada.

ROLT, Tony (GB) b 16/10/1918

	1950	Championship position: Unplaced						
	Race	Circuit	No	Entrant	Tyres	Car/Engine	Comment	Q Pos/Entries
ret	BRITISH GP	Silverstone	9	Peter Walker	D	1.5 s/c ERA E Type 6	shared Walker's car/gearbox	– / –
	1953	Championship position: Unplaced						
ret	BRITISH GP	Silverstone	14	R R C Walker Racing Team	D	2.0 Connaught A Type 4	half shaft	10/29
	1955	Championship position: Unplaced						
ret*	BRITISH GP	Aintree	36	R R C Walker Racing Team	D	2.5 Connaught B Type 4	*taken over by Walker/throttle	15/25

GP Starts: 3 GP Wins: 0 Pole positions: 0 Fastest laps: 0 Points: 0

ROOS, Bertil (S) b 12/10/1943, Gothenburg

	1974	Championship position: Unplaced						
	Race	Circuit	No	Entrant	Tyres	Car/Engine	Comment	Q Pos/Entries
ret	SWEDISH GP	Anderstorp	16	UOP Shadow Racing Team	G	3.0 Shadow DN3-Cosworth V8	transmission	23/28

GP Starts: 1 GP Wins: 0 Pole positions: 0 Fastest laps: 0 Points: 0

KEKE ROSBERG

WORLD CHAMPION: 1982

KEKE ROSBERG

The buccaneering Finn became a firm favourite in the mid-eighties after he had taken a surprise World Championship win in a season clouded by tragedy. His subsequent exuberant performances, stabbing the turbo-powered Williams around the world's circuits with frightening commitment, did much to supply the entertainment factor which was often missing from the sport.

Born in Sweden of Finnish parentage, Keijo Rosberg was three times his country's karting champion before moving with equal success into the rough-and-tumble world of Formula Vee and Super Vee, taking the Castrol GTX title in the latter category in 1975. He found a seat in the Toj Formula 2 team in 1976, but apart from a fourth place at Rouen this was not a successful alliance. By the end of the year Keke had linked up with Fred Opert, who satisfied the Finn's insatiable appetite for racing in 1977 by running him first in New Zealand, where he took the Stuyvesant title, and then in the European Formula 2 championship and the Labatt's Atlantic series in North America.

There was no let-up the following year when Rosberg undertook a mind-numbing schedule which totalled some forty races. In addition to repeating the previous season's marathon stint for Opert, Keke moved into Formula 1 and scored a shock win in a rain-drenched International Trophy race for the new Theodore team. Although this result was something of a fluke, there was no doubting the Finn's stunning car control, and his name was noted down as one to watch by Formula 1 team managers. In World Championship races, of course, it was a different story, as he struggled to make an impression in three different makes of car.

Resigned to a season of Can-Am in 1979, Rosberg was often quicker but, tellingly, also more erratic than champion Jacky Ickx, but a route back into Grand Prix racing was to re-open after James Hunt's sudden retirement. His half-season in a difficult car failed to provide any satisfactory results, but he was back in the frame to stay. When Wolf amalgamated with Fittipaldi for 1980 Keke was part of the package, and on his maiden outing at Buenos Aires he scored his first championship points. However, the team lacked the technical and financial resources to make a real impact and Rosberg was forced to make up the numbers until the end of 1981 when it closed its doors.

The cards suddenly began to fall for the Finn when he took over the Williams seat vacated by Alan Jones at the start of 1982. Within two races the team's other star driver, Carlos Reutemann, had also walked away from Grand Prix racing and suddenly Keke was leading the team. Showing incredible maturity for one not familiar with racing at the sharp end of the grid, Rosberg made the odd mistake but maximised every potential points-scoring opportunity and took a splendidly thought-out win in the Swiss GP at Dijon. By the end of the year he had overhauled the unfortunate Didier Pironi's points total and claimed a fairytale World Championship triumph. The following year saw Keke hampered by a lack of turbo

From also-ran to champion in the space of a year – that was the amazing turn-around in the career of Keke Rosberg, who left the Fittipaldi team for Williams and found glory with the FW08 *(above)* in 1982.

power, but this didn't prevent him taking a classic win, driving on slicks throughout, on a damp track at Monaco. He took the Cosworth car into battle with great ferocity elsewhere, never admitting defeat when many others would have been content merely to cruise round. When he finally got a turbo engine himself, Keke was to be frustrated by the poor handling of the Williams chassis, but nevertheless he scored perhaps the best win of his career in searing heat in Dallas in 1984 when most of his rivals failed to avoid a meeting with the concrete walls. Rosberg's relationship with Williams was never completely harmonious and he wanted away at the end of the season but, forced to see out his contract, he got on with the job without further complaint. Initially at least, he was unhappy with the arrival of Nigel Mansell for 1985 but soon established a rapport with his new team-mate. Having agreed a lucrative deal with McLaren, Rosberg signed off from Williams with a sparkling win in Adelaide to start the final short chapter of his Grand Prix career, but the partnership was to be something of disappointment for both sides, with Keke rather taken aback by his inability to come to terms with the talents of Alain Prost.

Rosberg quit without regrets, but stayed closely involved with the sport, making a return to the wheel in the World Sports Car Championship with Peugeot in 1991. With Dalmas, he took wins at both Magny Cours and Mexico, before switching to the German touring car championship the following year to race a Mercedes. Apart from his role in guiding young Finnish talent (the careers of both Mika Häkkinen and JJ Lehto are under his shrewd managership), Keke has formed his own DTM/ITC team, running works-backed Opels and led by the experienced Klaus Ludwig. In 1995 he announced another retirement, but it wouldn't be a massive surprise if we saw him behind the wheel again in selected events in the future.

ROSBERG, Keke (Keijo) (SF) b 6/12/1948, Stockholm, Sweden

1978 — Championship position: Unplaced

	Race	Circuit	No	Entrant	Tyres	Car/Engine	Comment	Q Pos/Entries
ret	SOUTH AFRICAN GP	Kyalami	32	Theodore Racing Hong Kong	G	3.0 Theodore TR1-Cosworth V8	clutch/engine/fuel leak	24/30
dnpq	US GP WEST	Long Beach	32	Theodore Racing Hong Kong	G	3.0 Theodore TR1-Cosworth V8		27/30
dnpq	MONACO GP	Monte Carlo	32	Theodore Racing Hong Kong	G	3.0 Theodore TR1-Cosworth V8		25/30
dnq	BELGIAN GP	Zolder	32	Theodore Racing Hong Kong	G	3.0 Theodore TR1-Cosworth V8		27/30
dnpq	SPANISH GP	Jarama	32	Theodore Racing Hong Kong	G	3.0 Theodore TR1-Cosworth V8		29/29
15	SWEDISH GP	Anderstorp	10	ATS Racing Team	G	3.0 ATS HS1-Cosworth V8	p stops/ignition/clutch/-7 laps	23/27
16	FRENCH GP	Paul Ricard	10	ATS Racing Team	G	3.0 ATS HS1-Cosworth V8	2 laps behind	26/29
ret	BRITISH GP	Brands Hatch	10	ATS Racing Team	G	3.0 ATS HS1-Cosworth V8	front suspension	22/30
10	GERMAN GP	Hockenheim	32	Theodore Racing Hong Kong	G	3.0 Wolf WR3-Cosworth V8	pit stop/nose cone/-3 laps	19/30
nc	AUSTRIAN GP	Österreichring	32	Theodore Racing Hong Kong	G	3.0 Wolf WR3-Cosworth V8	pit stop/tyres/5 laps behind	25/31
ret	DUTCH GP	Zandvoort	32	Theodore Racing Hong Kong	G	3.0 Wolf WR4-Cosworth V8	stuck throttle/accident	24/33
dns	"	"	32	Theodore Racing Hong Kong	G	3.0 Wolf WR3-Cosworth V8	practice only	– / –
dnpq	ITALIAN GP	Monza	32	Theodore Racing Hong Kong	G	3.0 Wolf WR4-Cosworth V8		30/32
ret	US GP EAST	Watkins Glen	32	ATS Racing Team	G	3.0 ATS D1-Cosworth V8	gear linkage	15/27
nc	CANADIAN GP	Montreal	32	ATS Racing Team	G	3.0 ATS D1-Cosworth V8	pit stops/misfire/-12 laps	21/28

1979 — Championship position: Unplaced

	Race	Circuit	No	Entrant	Tyres	Car/Engine	Comment	Q Pos/Entries
9	FRENCH GP	Dijon	20	Olympus Cameras Wolf Racing	G	3.0 Wolf WR8-Cosworth V8	gearbox problems/-1 lap	16/27
ret	BRITISH GP	Silverstone	20	Olympus Cameras Wolf Racing	G	3.0 Wolf WR7-Cosworth V8	fuel system	14/26
dns	"	"	20	Olympus Cameras Wolf Racing	G	3.0 Wolf WR9-Cosworth V8	practice only	– / –
ret	GERMAN GP	Hockenheim	20	Olympus Cameras Wolf Racing	G	3.0 Wolf WR8-Cosworth V8	engine	17/26
dns	"	"	20	Olympus Cameras Wolf Racing	G	3.0 Wolf WR9-Cosworth V8	practice only	– / –
ret	AUSTRIAN GP	Österreichring	20	Olympus Cameras Wolf Racing	G	3.0 Wolf WR9-Cosworth V8	electrics	12/26
dns	"	"	20	Olympus Cameras Wolf Racing	G	3.0 Wolf WR8-Cosworth V8	practice only	– / –
ret	DUTCH GP	Zandvoort	20	Olympus Cameras Wolf Racing	G	3.0 Wolf WR8-Cosworth V8	engine	8/26
ret	ITALIAN GP	Monza	20	Olympus Cameras Wolf Racing	G	3.0 Wolf WR8-Cosworth V8	engine	23/28
dns	"	"	20	Olympus Cameras Wolf Racing	G	3.0 Wolf WR9-Cosworth V8	practice only	– / –
dnq	CANADIAN GP	Montreal	20	Olympus Cameras Wolf Racing	G	3.0 Wolf WR9-Cosworth V8		27/29
ret	US GP EAST	Watkins Glen	20	Olympus Cameras Wolf Racing	G	3.0 Wolf WR8/9-Cosworth V8	collision with Pironi	12/30

1980 — Championship position: 10th=   Wins: 0   Pole positions: 0   Fastest laps: 0   Points scored: 6

	Race	Circuit	No	Entrant	Tyres	Car/Engine	Comment	Q Pos/Entries
3	ARGENTINE GP	Buenos Aires	21	Skol Fittipaldi Team	G	3.0 Fittipaldi F7-Cosworth V8		13/28
9	BRAZILIAN GP	Interlagos	21	Skol Fittipaldi Team	G	3.0 Fittipaldi F7-Cosworth V8	1 lap behind	15/28
ret	SOUTH AFRICAN GP	Kyalami	21	Skol Fittipaldi Team	G	3.0 Fittipaldi F7-Cosworth V8	brake failure/crashed	24/28
ret	US GP WEST	Long Beach	21	Skol Fittipaldi Team	G	3.0 Fittipaldi F7-Cosworth V8	overheating	22/27
7	BELGIAN GP	Zolder	21	Skol Fittipaldi Team	G	3.0 Fittipaldi F7-Cosworth V8	1 lap behind	21/27
dnq	MONACO GP	Monte Carlo	21	Skol Fittipaldi Team	G	3.0 Fittipaldi F7-Cosworth V8		24/27
ret	FRENCH GP	Paul Ricard	21	Skol Fittipaldi Team	G	3.0 Fittipaldi F7-Cosworth V8	crashed	23/27
dnq	BRITISH GP	Brands Hatch	21	Skol Fittipaldi Team	G	3.0 Fittipaldi F7-Cosworth V8		26/27
ret	GERMAN GP	Hockenheim	21	Skol Fittipaldi Team	G	3.0 Fittipaldi F8-Cosworth V8	wheel bearing	8/26
16	AUSTRIAN GP	Österreichring	21	Skol Fittipaldi Team	G	3.0 Fittipaldi F8-Cosworth V8	pit stop/2 laps behind	11/25
dnq	DUTCH GP	Zandvoort	21	Skol Fittipaldi Team	G	3.0 Fittipaldi F8-Cosworth V8		28/28
5	ITALIAN GP	Imola	21	Skol Fittipaldi Team	G	3.0 Fittipaldi F8-Cosworth V8	1 lap behind	11/28
9	CANADIAN GP	Montreal	21	Skol Fittipaldi Team	G	3.0 Fittipaldi F8-Cosworth V8	2 laps behind	6/28
10	US GP EAST	Watkins Glen	21	Skol Fittipaldi Team	G	3.0 Fittipaldi F8-Cosworth V8	2 laps behind	14/27

1981 — Championship position: Unplaced

	Race	Circuit	No	Entrant	Tyres	Car/Engine	Comment	Q Pos/Entries
ret	US GP WEST	Long Beach	20	Fittipaldi Automotive	M	3.0 Fittipaldi F8C-Cosworth V8	rotor arm	16/29
9	BRAZILIAN GP	Rio	20	Fittipaldi Automotive	M	3.0 Fittipaldi F8C-Cosworth V8	1 lap behind	12/30
ret	ARGENTINE GP	Buenos Aires	20	Fittipaldi Automotive	M	3.0 Fittipaldi F8C-Cosworth V8	fuel pump belt	8/29
ret	SAN MARINO GP	Imola	20	Fittipaldi Automotive	A	3.0 Fittipaldi F8C-Cosworth V8	engine	15/30
ret	BELGIAN GP	Zolder	20	Fittipaldi Automotive	A	3.0 Fittipaldi F8C-Cosworth V8	broken gear lever	11/31
dnq	MONACO GP	Monte Carlo	20	Fittipaldi Automotive	A/M	3.0 Fittipaldi F8C-Cosworth V8		21/31
12	SPANISH GP	Jarama	20	Fittipaldi Automotive	M	3.0 Fittipaldi F8C-Cosworth V8	2 laps behind	15/30
ret	FRENCH GP	Dijon	20	Fittipaldi Automotive	M	3.0 Fittipaldi F8C-Cosworth V8	broken rear cross beam	17/29
ret	BRITISH GP	Silverstone	20	Fittipaldi Automotive	M	3.0 Fittipaldi F8C-Cosworth V8	rear suspension	16/30
dnq	GERMAN GP	Hockenheim	20	Fittipaldi Automotive	M	3.0 Fittipaldi F8C-Cosworth V8		25/30
dnq	DUTCH GP	Zandvoort	20	Fittipaldi Automotive	P	3.0 Fittipaldi F8C-Cosworth V8		27/30
dnq	ITALIAN GP	Monza	20	Fittipaldi Automotive	P	3.0 Fittipaldi F8C-Cosworth V8		29/30
dnq	CANADIAN GP	Montreal	20	Fittipaldi Automotive	P	3.0 Fittipaldi F8C-Cosworth V8		25/30
10	CAESARS PALACE GP	Las Vegas	20	Fittipaldi Automotive	P	3.0 Fittipaldi F8C-Cosworth V8	2 laps behind	20/30

One of Rosberg's greatest drives came in Dallas in 1984 where, despite the searing heat, he drove the opposition into the ground with his Williams-Honda.

	1982	Championship position: WORLD CHAMPION	Wins: 1	Pole positions: 1	Fastest laps: 0	Points scored: 44		
5	SOUTH AFRICAN GP	Kyalami	6	TAG Williams Team	G	3.0 Williams FW07C-Cosworth V8		7/30
dsq*	BRAZILIAN GP	Rio	6	TAG Williams Team	G	3.0 Williams FW07C-Cosworth V8	*illegal brakes/2nd on road	3/31
2	US GP WEST	Long Beach	6	TAG Williams Team	G	3.0 Williams FW07C-Cosworth V8		8/31
2	BELGIAN GP	Zolder	6	TAG Williams Team	G	3.0 Williams FW08-Cosworth V8		3/32
ret	MONACO GP	Monte Carlo	6	TAG Williams Team	G	3.0 Williams FW08-Cosworth V8	front suspension	6/31
4	US GP (DETROIT)	Detroit	6	TAG Williams Team	G	3.0 Williams FW08-Cosworth V8		3/28
ret	CANADIAN GP	Montreal	6	TAG Williams Team	G	3.0 Williams FW08-Cosworth V8	gearbox	7/29
3	DUTCH GP	Zandvoort	6	TAG Williams Team	G	3.0 Williams FW08-Cosworth V8		7/31
ret	BRITISH GP	Brands Hatch	6	TAG Williams Team	G	3.0 Williams FW08-Cosworth V8	fuel pressure	1/30
5	FRENCH GP	Paul Ricard	6	TAG Williams Team	G	3.0 Williams FW08-Cosworth V8		10/30
3	GERMAN GP	Hockenheim	6	TAG Williams Team	G	3.0 Williams FW08-Cosworth V8	1 lap behind	10/30
2	AUSTRIAN GP	Österreichring	6	TAG Williams Team	G	3.0 Williams FW08-Cosworth V8		6/29
1	SWISS GP	Dijon	6	TAG Williams Team	G	3.0 Williams FW08-Cosworth V8		8/29
8	ITALIAN GP	Monza	6	TAG Williams Team	G	3.0 Williams FW08-Cosworth V8	pit stop/lost rear wing/-2 laps	7/30
5	CAESARS PALACE GP	Las Vegas	6	TAG Williams Team	G	3.0 Williams FW08-Cosworth V8		6/30

	1983	Championship position: 5th	Wins: 1	Pole positions: 1	Fastest laps: 0	Points scored: 27		
dsq	BRAZILIAN GP	Rio	1	TAG Williams Team	G	3.0 Williams FW08C-Cosworth V8	push start at pit stop/2nd on road	1/27
ret	US GP WEST	Long Beach	1	TAG Williams Team	G	3.0 Williams FW08C-Cosworth V8	accident with Jarier	3/28
5	FRENCH GP	Paul Ricard	1	TAG Williams Team	G	3.0 Williams FW08C-Cosworth V8	1 lap behind	16/29
4	SAN MARINO GP	Imola	1	TAG Williams Team	G	3.0 Williams FW08C-Cosworth V8	1 lap behind	11/28
1	MONACO GP	Monte Carlo	1	TAG Williams Team	G	3.0 Williams FW08C-Cosworth V8		5/28
5	BELGIAN GP	Spa	1	TAG Williams Team	G	3.0 Williams FW08C-Cosworth V8		9/28
2	US GP (DETROIT)	Detroit	1	TAG Williams Team	G	3.0 Williams FW08C-Cosworth V8		12/27
4	CANADIAN GP	Montreal	1	TAG Williams Team	G	3.0 Williams FW08C-Cosworth V8		9/28
11	BRITISH GP	Silverstone	1	TAG Williams Team	G	3.0 Williams FW08C-Cosworth V8	pit stop/tyres/2 laps behind	13/29
10	GERMAN GP	Hockenheim	1	TAG Williams Team	G	3.0 Williams FW08C-Cosworth V8	pit stop/tyres/1 lap behind	12/29
8	AUSTRIAN GP	Österreichring	1	TAG Williams Team	G	3.0 Williams FW08C-Cosworth V8	pit stop/tyres/2 laps behind	15/29
ret	DUTCH GP	Zandvoort	1	TAG Williams Team	G	3.0 Williams FW08C-Cosworth V8	misfire	23/29
11*	ITALIAN GP	Monza	1	TAG Williams Team	G	3.0 Williams FW08C-Cosworth V8	*9th on road/1 min pen/-1 lap	16/29
ret	EUROPEAN GP	Brands Hatch	1	TAG Williams Team	G	3.0 Williams FW08C-Cosworth V8	engine	16/29
5	SOUTH AFRICAN GP	Kyalami	1	TAG Williams Team	G	1.5 t/c Williams FW09-Honda V6	pit stop/tyres/1 lap behind	6/26

	1984	Championship position: 8th	Wins: 1	Pole positions: 0	Fastest laps: 0	Points scored: 20.5		
2	BRAZILIAN GP	Rio	6	Williams Grand Prix Engineering	G	1.5 t/c Williams FW09-Honda V6		9/27
ret	SOUTH AFRICAN GP	Kyalami	6	Williams Grand Prix Engineering	G	1.5 t/c Williams FW09-Honda V6	loose wheel nut-lost wheel	2/27
4/ret	BELGIAN GP	Zolder	6	Williams Grand Prix Engineering	G	1.5 t/c Williams FW09-Honda V6	out of fuel/1 lap behind	3/27
ret	SAN MARINO GP	Imola	6	Williams Grand Prix Engineering	G	1.5 t/c Williams FW09-Honda V6	electrics	3/28
6	FRENCH GP	Dijon	6	Williams Grand Prix Engineering	G	1.5 t/c Williams FW09-Honda V6	1 lap behind	4/27
4*	MONACO GP	Monte Carlo	6	Williams Grand Prix Engineering	G	1.5 t/c Williams FW09-Honda V6	*rain shortened race-half points	10/27
ret	CANADIAN GP	Montreal	6	Williams Grand Prix Engineering	G	1.5 t/c Williams FW09-Honda V6	fuel system	15/26
ret	US GP (DETROIT)	Detroit	6	Williams Grand Prix Engineering	G	1.5 t/c Williams FW09-Honda V6	exhaust/turbo	21/27
1	US GP (DALLAS)	Dallas	6	Williams Grand Prix Engineering	G	1.5 t/c Williams FW09-Honda V6		8/27
ret	BRITISH GP	Brands Hatch	6	Williams Grand Prix Engineering	G	1.5 t/c Williams FW09B-Honda V6	intercooler hose/engine	5/27
ret	GERMAN GP	Hockenheim	6	Williams Grand Prix Engineering	G	1.5 t/c Williams FW09B-Honda V6	electrics	19/27
ret	AUSTRIAN GP	Österreichring	6	Williams Grand Prix Engineering	G	1.5 t/c Williams FW09B-Honda V6	handling	9/28
8*/ret	DUTCH GP	Zandvoort	6	Williams Grand Prix Engineering	G	1.5 t/c Williams FW09B-Honda V6	*8th & 9th cars dsq/out of fuel	7/27
ret	ITALIAN GP	Monza	6	Williams Grand Prix Engineering	G	1.5 t/c Williams FW09B-Honda V6	engine	6/27
ret	EUROPEAN GP	Nürburgring	6	Williams Grand Prix Engineering	G	1.5 t/c Williams FW09B-Honda V6	hit by Senna	4/26
ret	PORTUGUESE GP	Estoril	6	Williams Grand Prix Engineering	G	1.5 t/c Williams FW09B-Honda V6	engine	4/27

	1985	Championship position: 3rd	Wins: 2	Pole positions: 2	Fastest laps: 3	Points scored: 40		
ret	BRAZILIAN GP	Rio	6	Canon Williams Team	G	1.5 t/c Williams FW10-Honda V6	turbo	2/25
ret	PORTUGUESE GP	Estoril	6	Canon Williams Team	G	1.5 t/c Williams FW10-Honda V6	spun off	3/26
ret	SAN MARINO GP	Imola	6	Canon Williams Team	G	1.5 t/c Williams FW10-Honda V6	throttle linkage/brakes	2/26
8	MONACO GP	Monte Carlo	6	Canon Williams Team	G	1.5 t/c Williams FW10-Honda V6	2 laps behind	7/26
4	CANADIAN GP	Montreal	6	Canon Williams Team	G	1.5 t/c Williams FW10-Honda V6		8/25
1	US GP (DETROIT)	Detroit	6	Canon Williams Team	G	1.5 t/c Williams FW10-Honda V6		5/25
2	FRENCH GP	Paul Ricard	6	Canon Williams Team	G	1.5 t/c Williams FW10-Honda V6	FL	1/26
ret	BRITISH GP	Silverstone	6	Canon Williams Team	G	1.5 t/c Williams FW10-Honda V6	exhaust	1/26
12/ret	GERMAN GP	Nürburgring	6	Canon Williams Team	G	1.5 t/c Williams FW10-Honda V6	brake caliper/6 laps behind	4/27
ret	AUSTRIAN GP	Österreichring	6	Canon Williams Team	G	1.5 t/c Williams FW10-Honda V6	engine	4/27
ret	DUTCH GP	Zandvoort	6	Canon Williams Team	G	1.5 t/c Williams FW10-Honda V6	engine	2/27
ret	ITALIAN GP	Monza	6	Canon Williams Team	G	1.5 t/c Williams FW10-Honda V6	engine	2/26
4	BELGIAN GP	Spa	6	Canon Williams Team	G	1.5 t/c Williams FW10-Honda V6		10/24
3	EUROPEAN GP	Brands Hatch	6	Canon Williams Team	G	1.5 t/c Williams FW10-Honda V6		4/27
2	SOUTH AFRICAN GP	Kyalami	6	Canon Williams Team	G	1.5 t/c Williams FW10-Honda V6	FL	3/21
1	AUSTRALIAN GP	Adelaide	6	Canon Williams Team	G	1.5 t/c Williams FW10-Honda V6	FL	3/25

	1986	Championship position: 6th	Wins: 0	Pole positions: 1	Fastest laps: 0	Points scored: 22		
ret	BRAZILIAN GP	Rio	2	Marlboro McLaren International	G	1.5 t/c McLaren MP4/2C-TAG V6	engine	7/25
4	SPANISH GP	Jerez	2	Marlboro McLaren International	G	1.5 t/c McLaren MP4/2C-TAG V6		5/25
5/ret	SAN MARINO GP	Imola	2	Marlboro McLaren International	G	1.5 t/c McLaren MP4/2C-TAG V6	out of fuel/2 laps behind	6/26
2	MONACO GP	Monte Carlo	2	Marlboro McLaren International	G	1.5 t/c McLaren MP4/2C-TAG V6		9/26
ret	BELGIAN GP	Spa	2	Marlboro McLaren International	G	1.5 t/c McLaren MP4/2C-TAG V6	engine	8/25
4	CANADIAN GP	Montreal	2	Marlboro McLaren International	G	1.5 t/c McLaren MP4/2C-TAG V6		6/25
ret	US GP (DETROIT)	Detroit	2	Marlboro McLaren International	G	1.5 t/c McLaren MP4/2C-TAG V6	transmission	9/26
4	FRENCH GP	Paul Ricard	2	Marlboro McLaren International	G	1.5 t/c McLaren MP4/2C-TAG V6		7/26
ret	BRITISH GP	Brands Hatch	2	Marlboro McLaren International	G	1.5 t/c McLaren MP4/2C-TAG V6	gearbox	5/26
5/ret	GERMAN GP	Hockenheim	2	Marlboro McLaren International	G	1.5 t/c McLaren MP4/2C-TAG V6	out of fuel/1 lap behind	1/26
ret	HUNGARIAN GP	Hungaroring	2	Marlboro McLaren International	G	1.5 t/c McLaren MP4/2C-TAG V6	rear suspension	5/26
9/ret	AUSTRIAN GP	Österreichring	2	Marlboro McLaren International	G	1.5 t/c McLaren MP4/2C-TAG V6	electrics/5 laps behind	3/26
4	ITALIAN GP	Monza	2	Marlboro McLaren International	G	1.5 t/c McLaren MP4/2C-TAG V6		8/27
ret	PORTUGUESE GP	Estoril	2	Marlboro McLaren International	G	1.5 t/c McLaren MP4/2C-TAG V6	engine	7/27
ret	MEXICAN GP	Mexico City	2	Marlboro McLaren International	G	1.5 t/c McLaren MP4/2C-TAG V6	puncture	11/26
ret	AUSTRALIAN GP	Adelaide	2	Marlboro McLaren International	G	1.5 t/c McLaren MP4/2C-TAG V6	tyre failure when leading	7/26

GP Starts: 114   GP Wins: 5   Pole positions: 5   Fastest laps: 3   Points: 159.5

LOUIS ROSIER

A former motor cycle racer and hill-climb specialist, Rosier had just started to develop his racing career when the war intervened, and it was 1947 before this garage owner from Clermont Ferrand could compete on a wider stage.

Equipped with his self-prepared Talbot, Rosier won the 1947 Albi GP after more speedy opponents had dropped out and this win obviously set the tone for the rest of his career, for he usually raced well within his limits and placed great store by strategy and reliability as a route to success. In 1948, as a member of the Ecurie France team, he took delivery of a single-seater Lago-Talbot, winning the Grand Prix du Salon and finishing fourth at the Comminges, Pau and British GPs. The following season, with the Talbot probably at its peak relative to the opposition, Rosier won the Belgian GP and, with a succession of steady finishes, was crowned champion of France, a title he was to hold for four years.

Alfa Romeo ruled the roost in 1950, the year of the inaugural World Championship, but the crafty Rosier was always well placed to pick up the pieces, and he took some good points-scoring finishes in championship Grands Prix, as well as winning the Albi and Dutch GPs. Adapting his Talbot to sports car specification, he also won that season's Le Mans 24-hour race with his son Jean-Louis, though it was the father who was the pillar of the achievement, driving for some 20 hours. By 1951 the Talbot was no longer a competitive proposition, but Louis still managed to coax the elderly car to the finish with astonishing consistency, winning the non-championship Dutch and Bordeaux GPs.

The 1952 season brought a change of regulations, and Rosier lost no time in getting his hands on a Ferrari T375 and a state-of-the-art Ferrari T500 F2 car. The Italian machines were naturally painted French blue, and Rosier quickly put one of them to good use, winning the Albi GP in the big-engined model. For 1953 he continued with the same equipment, taking yet another win in the Albi GP and a victory in the Sables d'Olonne GP with the T500, while his old Talbot was brought out for the Reims 12 Hours, in which he took second place with Giraud-Cabantous.

By now Rosier was well past his best as a driver, but he pushed ahead undaunted the following season, and after racing a Ferrari 625 he bought a Maserati 250F which he continued to campaign in Grands Prix and non-championship events in a steady and reliable fashion, as well as handling his own Ferrari 3-litre sports car. Ironically, Rosier shared a Maserati T300S with Behra to win the 1956 Paris 1000 Km, his last win, before returning to the Montlhéry circuit he knew so well in this Ferrari for the Coupe du Salon. In pouring rain, Rosier overturned his car and suffered severe head injuries from which he died three weeks later. He was posthumously awarded the French Order of the Nation.

ROSIER, Louis (F) b 5/11/1905, Chapdes-Beaufort, nr Clermont Ferrand – d 29/10/1956, Paris

	1950			Championship position: 4th Wins: 0 Pole positions: 0 Fastest laps: 0 Points scored: 13					
	Race	Circuit	No	Entrant	Tyres	Car/Engine	Comment		Q Pos/Entries
5	BRITISH GP	Silverstone	15	Ecurie Rosier	D	4.5 Lago-Talbot T26C 6	2 laps behind		9/21
ret	MONACO GP	Monte Carlo	16	Ecurie Rosier	D	4.5 Lago-Talbot T26C 6	multiple accident		10/21
3	SWISS GP	Bremgarten	10	Automobiles Talbot-Darracq SA	D	4.5 Lago-Talbot T26C-DA 6	1 lap behind		10/18
3	BELGIAN GP	Spa	14	Automobiles Talbot-Darracq SA	D	4.5 Lago-Talbot T26C-DA 6			=7/14
ret	FRENCH GP	Reims	20	Automobiles Talbot-Darracq SA	D	4.5 Lago-Talbot T26C-DA 6	overheating		6/20
6*	"	"	26	Charles Pozzi	D	4.5 Lago-Talbot T26C 6	* took Pozzi's car/8 laps behind		–/–
4	ITALIAN GP	Monza	58	Ecurie Rosier	D	4.5 Lago-Talbot T26C 6	5 laps behind		13/27
	1951			Championship position: 10= Wins: 0 Pole positions: 0 Fastest laps: 0 Points scored: 3					
9	SWISS GP	Bremgarten	8	Ecurie Rosier	D	4.5 Lago-Talbot T26C-DA 6	3 laps behind		8/21
4	BELGIAN GP	Spa	14	Ecurie Rosier	D	4.5 Lago-Talbot T26C-DA 6	2 laps behind		7/13
ret	FRENCH GP	Reims	40	Ecurie Rosier	D	4.5 Lago-Talbot T26C-DA 6	transmisssion-rear axle		13/23
10	BRITISH GP	Silverstone	22	Ecurie Rosier	D	4.5 Lago-Talbot T26C-DA 6	7 laps behind		9/20
8	GERMAN GP	Nürburgring	84	Ecurie Rosier	D	4.5 Lago-Talbot T26C-DA 6	1 lap behind		15/23
7	ITALIAN GP	Monza	18	Ecurie Rosier	D	4.5 Lago-Talbot T26C-DA 6	7 laps behind		15/22
7	SPANISH GP	Pedrlbes	28	Ecurie Rosier	D	4.5 Lago-Talbot T26C-DA 6	6 laps behind		20/20
	1952			Championship position: Unplaced					
ret	SWISS GP	Bremgarten	12	Ecurie Rosier	D	2.0 Ferrari 500 4	crashed		20/21
ret	BELGIAN GP	Spa	22	Ecurie Rosier	D	2.0 Ferrari 500 4	transmission		17/22
ret	FRENCH GP	Rouen	14	Ecurie Rosier	D	2.0 Ferrari 500 4	engine		9/20
10	ITALIAN GP	Monza	62	Ecurie Rosier	D	2.0 Ferrari 500 4	5 laps behind		17/35
	1953			Championship position: Unplaced					
7	DUTCH GP	Zandvoort	10	Ecurie Rosier	D	2.0 Ferrari 500 4	4 laps behind		8/20
8	BELGIAN GP	Spa	32	Ecurie Rosier	D	2.0 Ferrari 500 4	3 laps behind		13/22
8	FRENCH GP	Reims	44	Ecurie Rosier	D	2.0 Ferrari 500 4	4 laps behind		10/25
10	BRITISH GP	Silverstone	9	Ecurie Rosier	D	2.0 Ferrari 500 4	12 laps behind		24/29
10	GERMAN GP	Nürburgring	20	Ecurie Rosier	D	2.0 Ferrari 500 4	1 lap behind		22/35
ret	SWISS GP	Bremgarten	10	Ecurie Rosier	D	2.0 Ferrari 500 4	spun off		14/23
nc	ITALIAN GP	Monza	64	Ecurie Rosier	D	2.0 Ferrari 500 4	15 laps behind		17/30
	1954			Championship position: Unplaced					
ret	ARGENTINE GP	Buenos Aires	24	Ecurie Rosier	D	2.5 Ferrari 500/625 4	spun off		14/18
ret	FRENCH GP	Reims	36	Ecurie Rosier	D	2.5 Ferrari 500/625 4	engine		13/22

ret	BRITISH GP	Silverstone	15	Ecurie Rosier	D	2.5 Ferrari 500/625 4		engine	30/31
8	GERMAN GP	Nürburgring	25	Ecurie Rosier	D	2.5 Ferrari 500/625 4		1 lap behind	18/23
8	ITALIAN GP	Monza	26	Officine Alfieri Maserati	P	2.5 Maserati 250F 6		6 laps behind	20/21
7	SPANISH GP	Pedralbes	26	Ecurie Rosier	P	2.5 Maserati 250F 6		6 laps behind	20/22

1955		Championship position: Unplaced							
ret	MONACO GP	Monte Carlo	14	Ecurie Rosier	P	2.5 Maserati 250F 6		split oil tank	17/22
9	BELGIAN GP	Spa	28	Ecurie Rosier	P	2.5 Maserati 250F 6		3 laps behind	12/14
9	DUTCH GP	Zandvoort	28	Ecurie Rosier	P	2.5 Maserati 250F 6		8 laps behind	13/16

1956		Championship position: 15th= Wins: 0 Pole positions: 0 Fastest laps: 0 Points scored: 2							
ret	MONACO GP	Monte Carlo	8	Ecurie Rosier	P	2.5 Maserati 250F 6		engine	15/19
8	BELGIAN GP	Spa	24	Ecurie Rosier	P	2.5 Maserati 250F 6		3 laps behind	10/16
6	FRENCH GP	Reims	36	Ecurie Rosier	P	2.5 Maserati 250F 6		3 laps behind	12/20
ret	BRITISH GP	Silverstone	27	Ecurie Rosier	P	2.5 Maserati 250F 6		carburettor union	27/28
5	GERMAN GP	Nürburgring	15	Ecurie Rosier	P	2.5 Maserati 250F 6		3 laps behind	14/21

GP Starts: 38   GP Wins: 0   Pole positions: 0   Fastest laps: 0   Points: 18

RICARDO ROSSET

Rosset enjoyed a sound debut year in the 1993 British F3 championship, and hopes were therefore high for his second season in the class. In the end he had to be content with a single win and numerous placings as Jan Magnussen swept all before him. The Brazilian moved up to F3000 in 1995 with few expecting him to figure among the front-runners, especially as he was partnered in the Super Nova line-up by the highly experienced Vincenzo Sospiri. In the event he proved almost the equal of his team leader in terms of speed and eventually took the runner-up slot behind the Italian.

Ricardo's performances brought a drive at Arrows in 1996 where he was initially well off the pace of his team-mate Jos Verstappen, but he proved more impressive after a mid-season heart-to-heart with the team management. He then threw in his lot with Sospiri once more as Eric Broadley launched a brave but ultimately foolhardy attempt to return Lola to the Grand Prix grids in 1997. The débâcle left Rosset with nothing but a testing contract at Tyrrell to fill his time and the budget to negotiate a seat in the team for 1998.

With Tyrrell effectively in its death-throes Ricardo struggled to make an impact, blaming a lack of technical support from the team, who he claimed had 'ruined [his] career' and destroyed his credibility.

RICARDO ROSSET (B) b São Paulo 27/7/1968

	1996	Championship position: Unplaced							
	Race	Circuit	No	Entrant	Tyres	Car/Engine		Comment	Q Pos/Entries
9	AUSTRALIAN GP	Melbourne	16	TWR Arrows	G	3.0 Footwork FA17-Hart V8		2 laps behind	18/22
ret	BRAZILIAN GP	Interlagos	16	TWR Arrows	G	3.0 Footwork FA17-Hart V8		spun into pit wall	19/22
ret	ARGENTINE GP	Buenos Aires	16	TWR Arrows	G	3.0 Footwork FA17-Hart V8		fuel pump	20/22
11	EUROPEAN GP	Nürburgring	16	TWR Arrows	G	3.0 Footwork FA17-Hart V8		2 laps behind	20/22
ret	SAN MARINO GP	Imola	16	TWR Arrows	G	3.0 Footwork FA17-Hart V8		out of fuel	20/22
ret	MONACO GP	Monte Carlo	16	TWR Arrows	G	3.0 Footwork FA17-Hart V8		spun off	20/22
ret	SPANISH GP	Barcelona	16	TWR Arrows	G	3.0 Footwork FA17-Hart V8		multiple collision on lap 1	20/22
ret	CANADIAN GP	Montreal	16	TWR Arrows	G	3.0 Footwork FA17-Hart V8		collision with Katayama	21/22
11	FRENCH GP	Magny Cours	16	TWR Arrows	G	3.0 Footwork FA17-Hart V8		3 laps behind	20/22
ret	BRITISH GP	Silverstone	16	TWR Arrows	G	3.0 Footwork FA17-Hart V8		* time disallowed / electrics	17*/22
11	GERMAN GP	Hockenheim	16	TWR Arrows	G	3.0 Footwork FA17-Hart V8		1 lap behind	19/20
8	HUNGARIAN GP	Hungaroring	16	TWR Arrows	G	3.0 Footwork FA17-Hart V8		3 laps behind	18/20
9	BELGIAN GP	Spa	16	TWR Arrows	G	3.0 Footwork FA17-Hart V8		1 lap behind	18/20
ret	ITALIAN GP	Monza	16	TWR Arrows	G	3.0 Footwork FA17-Hart V8		spun off	19/20
14	PORTUGUESE GP	Estoril	16	TWR Arrows	G	3.0 Footwork FA17-Hart V8		3 laps behind	17/20
13	JAPANESE GP	Suzuka	16	TWR Arrows	G	3.0 Footwork FA17-Hart V8		2 laps behind	19/20
	1997	Championship position: Unplaced							
dnq	AUSTRALIAN GP	Melbourne	25	Mastercard Lola F1 Team	B	3.0 Lola T/97/30-Ford Zetec R V8		not within 107% of pole	24/24
dnp	BRAZILIAN GP	Interlagos	25	Mastercard Lola F1 Team	B	3.0 Lola T/97/30-Ford Zetec R V8		cars did not practice	– / –
	1998	Championship position: Unplaced							
ret	AUSTRALIAN GP	Melbourne	20	Tyrrell Ford	G	3.0 Tyrrell 026-Ford Zetec R V10		gearbox	19/22
ret	BRAZILIAN GP	Interlagos	20	Tyrrell Ford	G	3.0 Tyrrell 026-Ford Zetec R V10		gearbox	21/22
14	ARGENTINE GP	Buenos Aires	20	Tyrrell Ford	G	3.0 Tyrrell 026-Ford Zetec R V10		4 laps behind	21/22
ret	SAN MARINO GP	Imola	20	Tyrrell Ford	G	3.0 Tyrrell 026-Ford Zetec R V10		engine	22/22
dnq	SPANISH GP	Barcelona	20	Tyrrell Ford	G	3.0 Tyrrell 026-Ford Zetec R V10			22/22
dnq	MONACO GP	Monte Carlo	20	Tyrrell Ford	G	3.0 Tyrrell 026-Ford Zetec R V10			22/22
8	CANADIAN GP	Montreal	20	Tyrrell Ford	G	3.0 Tyrrell 026-Ford Zetec R V10		1 lap behind	22/22
ret	FRENCH GP	Magny Cours	20	Tyrrell Ford	G	3.0 Tyrrell 026-Ford Zetec R V10		engine	18/22
ret	BRITISH GP	Silverstone	20	Tyrrell Ford	G	3.0 Tyrrell 026-Ford Zetec R V10		engine	22/22
12	AUSTRIAN GP	A1-Ring	20	Tyrrell Ford	G	3.0 Tyrrell 026-Ford Zetec R V10		2 laps behind	22/22
ret	GERMAN GP	Hockenheim	20	Tyrrell Ford	G	3.0 Tyrrell 026-Ford Zetec R V10		injured wrist in free practice	–/22
dnq	HUNGARIAN GP	Hungaroring	20	Tyrrell Ford	G	3.0 Tyrrell 026-Ford Zetec R V10			22/22
ret/dns	BELGIAN GP	Spa	20	Tyrrell Ford	G	3.0 Tyrrell 026-Ford Zetec R V10		accident at first start	20/22
12	ITALIAN GP	Monza	20	Tyrrell Ford	G	3.0 Tyrrell 026-Ford Zetec R V10		2 laps behind	18/22
ret	LUXEMBOURG GP	Nürburgring	20	Tyrrell Ford	G	3.0 Tyrrell 026-Ford Zetec R V10		engine	22/22
dnq	JAPANESE GP	Suzuka	20	Tyrrell Ford	G	3.0 Tyrrell 026-Ford Zetec R V10			22/22

GP Starts: 27 (28)   GP Wins: 0   Pole positions: 0   Fastest laps: 0   Points: 0

ROTHENGATTER, Huub (NL) b 8/10/1954, Bussum, nr Hilversum

	1984			Championship position: Unplaced					
	Race	Circuit	No	Entrant	Tyres	Car/Engine	Comment		Q Pos/Entries
nc	CANADIAN GP	Montreal	21	Spirit Racing	P	1.5 t/c Spirit 101-Hart 4	engine problems/-14 laps		24/26
dnq	US GP (DETROIT)	Detroit	21	Spirit Racing	P	3.0 Spirit 101-Cosworth V8			27/27
ret	US GP (DALLAS)	Dallas	21	Spirit Racing	P	1.5 t/c Spirit 101-Hart 4	fuel leak in cockpit		23/27
nc	BRITISH GP	Brands Hatch	21	Spirit Racing	P	1.5 t/c Spirit 101-Hart 4	pit stop/nose cone/-9 laps		22/27
9*	GERMAN GP	Hockenheim	21	Spirit Racing	P	1.5 t/c Spirit 101-Hart 4	* 9th place car dsq/-4 laps		24/27
nc	AUSTRIAN GP	Österreichring	21	Spirit Racing	P	1.5 t/c Spirit 101-Hart 4	pit stop/exhaust/-28 laps		26/28
dnq/ret	DUTCH GP	Zandvoort	21	Spirit Racing	P	1.5 t/c Spirit 101-Hart 4	allowed to start/throttle cable		27/27
8	ITALIAN GP	Monza	21	Spirit Racing	P	1.5 t/c Spirit 101-Hart 4	3 laps behind		25/27
	1985			Championship position: Unplaced					
ret	GERMAN GP	Nürburgring	24	Osella Squadra Corse	P	1.5 t/c Osella FA1G-Alfa Romeo V8	gearbox		25/27
9	AUSTRIAN GP	Österreichring	24	Osella Squadra Corse	P	1.5 t/c Osella FA1G-Alfa Romeo V8	4 laps behind		24/27
nc	DUTCH GP	Zandvoort	24	Osella Squadra Corse	P	1.5 t/c Osella FA1G-Alfa Romeo V8	24 laps behind		26/27
ret	ITALIAN GP	Monza	24	Osella Squadra Corse	P	1.5 t/c Osella FA1G-Alfa Romeo V8	engine		22/26
nc	BELGIAN GP	Spa	24	Osella Squadra Corse	P	1.5 t/c Osella FA1G-Alfa Romeo V8	6 laps behind		23/24
dnq	EUROPEAN GP	Brands Hatch	24	Osella Squadra Corse	P	1.5 t/c Osella FA1G-Alfa Romeo V8			27/27
ret	SOUTH AFRICAN GP	Kyalami	24	Osella Squadra Corse	P	1.5 t/c Osella FA1G-Alfa Romeo V8	electrics		21/21
7	AUSTRALIAN GP	Adelaide	24	Osella Squadra Corse	P	1.5 t/c Osella FA1G-Alfa Romeo V8	4 laps behind		25/25
	1986			Championship position: Unplaced					
ret	SAN MARINO GP	Imola	29	West Zakspeed Racing	G	1.5 t/c Zakspeed 861 4	turbo		24/26
dnq	MONACO GP	Monte Carlo	29	West Zakspeed Racing	G	1.5 t/c Zakspeed 861 4			23/26
ret	BELGIAN GP	Spa	29	West Zakspeed Racing	G	1.5 t/c Zakspeed 861 4	alternator/battery		23/25
12	CANADIAN GP	Montreal	29	West Zakspeed Racing	G	1.5 t/c Zakspeed 861 4	6 laps behind		24/25
dns	US GP (DETROIT)	Detroit	29	West Zakspeed Racing	G	1.5 t/c Zakspeed 861 4	electrics on-warm-up lap		26/26
ret	FRENCH GP	Paul Ricard	29	West Zakspeed Racing	G	1.5 t/c Zakspeed 861 4	hit Dumfries		24/26
ret	BRITISH GP	Brands Hatch	29	West Zakspeed Racing	G	1.5 t/c Zakspeed 861 4	engine		25/26
ret	GERMAN GP	Hockenheim	29	West Zakspeed Racing	G	1.5 t/c Zakspeed 861 4	gearbox		24/26
ret	HUNGARIAN GP	Hungaroring	29	West Zakspeed Racing	G	1.5 t/c Zakspeed 861 4	oil radiator		25/26
8	AUSTRIAN GP	Österreichring	29	West Zakspeed Racing	G	1.5 t/c Zakspeed 861 4	4 laps behind		24/26
ret	ITALIAN GP	Monza	29	West Zakspeed Racing	G	1.5 t/c Zakspeed 861 4	engine		24/27
ret	PORTUGUESE GP	Estoril	29	West Zakspeed Racing	G	1.5 t/c Zakspeed 861 4	transmission		26/27
dns	MEXICAN GP	Mexico City	29	West Zakspeed Racing	G	1.5 t/c Zakspeed 861 4	practice accident/no spare car		23/26
ret	AUSTRALIAN GP	Adelaide	29	West Zakspeed Racing	G	1.5 t/c Zakspeed 861 4	rear suspension		23/26

GP Starts: 25 (26)   GP Wins: 0   Pole positions: 0   Fastest laps: 0   Points: 0

HUUB ROTHENGATTER

A tall, genial Dutchman, Rothengatter successfully financed a Grand Prix career after a fairly unspectacular climb through the ranks. Graduating to Formula 2 in 1979 with a Chevron, he looked a little rough round the edges, but the following season, equipped with a Toleman, he improved immensely and scored an excellent win at Zolder.

At this point Rothengatter harboured hopes of a Formula 1 ride, but in the event he missed the first half of 1981 completely before making a brief return to Formula 2, and it was not until 1984 that he finally realised his ambition with the Spirit team, now shorn of Honda power. Halfway through the following season he joined Osella in place of Ghinzani, who had moved to Toleman, and he then had a year with Zakspeed.

Huub had basically just been making up the numbers, but he remained remarkably cheerful nevertheless, clearly enjoying his bit part on the Grand Prix stage. He later successfully managed the budding career of fellow countryman Jos Verstappen.

LLOYD RUBY

This Indianapolis 500 perennial began racing midgets after the war, but it was more than a decade before he joined the USAC trail, soon developing a reputation as a shrewd tactician who looked after his cars. However, he never succeded in winning the '500' – third place in 1964 was his best finish – though he came heart-breakingly close on a number of occasions, notably in 1969, when a routine pit stop went disastrously wrong.

In the early sixties Ruby also went sports car racing with a Lotus Monte Carlo, and became a local attraction at the 1961 US GP in a guest appearance in a Lotus 18. His mechanical sympathy prompted Ford to take him into their sports car team to develop their prototype and he won the Daytona 24 Hours in 1965 and 1966 with Ken Miles. This experienced pairing also took a win at Sebring in 1966, but injury caused Lloyd to miss Le Mans and a chance of victory.

RUBY, Lloyd (USA) b 12/1/1928, Wichita Falls, Texas

	1961	Championship position: Unplaced						
	Race	Circuit	No	Entrant	Tyres	Car/Engine	Comment	Q Pos/Entries
ret	US GP	Watkins Glen	26	J Frank Harrison	D	1.5 Lotus 18-Climax 4	magneto	=18/19

GP Starts: 1   GP Wins: 0   Pole positions: 0   Fastest laps: 0   Points: 0

RUSSO, Giacomo see 'Geki'

RUTTMAN, Troy (USA) b 11/3/1930, Mooreland, Oklahoma – d 19/5/1997

	1958	Championship position: Unplaced						
	Race	Circuit	No	Entrant	Tyres	Car/Engine	Comment	Q Pos/Entries
10	FRENCH GP	Reims	30	Scuderia Centro Sud	P	2.5 Maserati 250F 6	5 laps behind	18/21
dns	GERMAN GP	Nürburgring	14	Scuderia Centro Sud	P	2.5 Maserati 250F 6	engine in practice	– /26

GP Starts: 1   GP Wins: 0   Pole positions: 0   Fastest laps: 0   Points: 0

RYAN, Peter (CDN) b 10/6/1940 – d 2/7/1962

	1961	Championship position: Unplaced						
	Race	Circuit	No	Entrant	Tyres	Car/Engine	Comment	Q Pos/Entries
9	US GP	Watkins Glen	16	J Wheeler Autosport	D	1.5 Lotus 18/21-Climax 4	4 laps behind	13/19

GP Starts: 1   GP Wins: 0   Pole positions: 0   Fastest laps: 0   Points: 0

SAID, 'Bob' (Boris) (USA) b 5/5/1932, New York City, New York

	1959	Championship position: Unplaced						
	Race	Circuit	No	Entrant	Tyres	Car/Engine	Comment	Q Pos/Entries
ret	US GP	Sebring	18	Connaught Cars-Paul Emery	D	2.5 Connaught C Type Alta 4	spun off on lap 1	13/19

GP Starts: 1   GP Wins: 0   Pole positions: 0   Fastest laps: 0   Points: 0

TROY RUTTMAN

While Lloyd Ruby tried in vain to win the Indy 500 for more than two decades, Troy Ruttman was only 22 when he triumphed at the Brickyard at only his fourth attempt in 1952, becoming the youngest driver to win the classic event. However, it could easily have been his last year in racing for he was later seriously injured in a sprint car race at Cedar Rapids, Iowa, and didn't return to action until 1954.

Thereafter he raced fairly infrequently, though he was invited to compete in the 1957 'Two Worlds Trophy' race at Monza, finishing second. He returned for the race in 1958, and stayed on in Europe to try his hand at Grand Prix racing with Scuderia Centro Sud. In conflict with the American racing authorities, allegedly over his love for gambling, Troy returned to Indianapolis in 1960, leading briefly. Then, in addition to his annual trips to the Speedway, Troy successfully took up stock-car racing with Mercury, before suddenly announcing his retirement from the sport immediately after completing his final Indy 500 in 1964.

PETER RYAN

This Canadian youngster built a fine reputation during his tragically short career, initially at the wheel of a Porsche RS60 with which he won a thrilling Sundown GP at Harewood in 1961. That triumph was followed by victory in the Canadian GP at Mosport in a Lotus 23, Ryan beating a similar car handled by no less a driver than Stirling Moss.

In 1962, Peter came to Europe for a planned season of Formula Junior in a works Lotus, but in the event he was loaned to the Ian Walker stable. Ryan immediately confirmed his promise by beating Peter Arundell in the works car at Mallory Park, but sadly, during a heat of the Coupe de Vitesse des Juniors at Reims, Peter's Lotus was involved in a collision with the Gemini of Bill Moss. The young Canadian was thrown from his machine and died from internal injuries.

'BOB' SAID

Born in New York of Syrian-Russian parents, Said holds the distinction of being the first American to win a post-war European race – at Rouen with

an OSCA in 1953 – having already made his mark at home in a Jaguar and his Cisitalia sports car, with which he won the Seneca Cup at Watkins Glen. His two seasons in Europe went pretty well; he won the Anerley Trophy in 1953 with the OSCA, then switched to a Ferrari for 1954, taking second place in the Bari GP and the Trullo d'Oro at Castellana.

Briefly dropping out of racing to lose a bundle in real-estate, Said returned to the tracks late in 1957, winning his class at Nassau with a Ferrari. He drove Paul Emery's ancient Connaught at Sebring in 1959 and continued to race in minor events until 1962, when, 'dead broke', he borrowed $2,600 to venture into property speculation once more. This time his gamble paid off and within two years he had made a million dollars.

LUIS PEREZ SALA

This talented and charming Spanish driver contested the 1985 Italian F3 championship with the Pavesi team's Ralt-Alfa, winning a round of the series, but didn't pull up any trees. However, he was a different proposition when he moved up to Formula 3000 with Pavesi the following season. Luis was well served by his team and, in his own quiet way, soon got to grips with the formula, winning two rounds (at Enna and Birmingham). Backing these victories up with a consistent finishing record, he took fifth place in the points table.

This excellent first season booked him a place in the works Lola team for 1987, and he again won two races (at Donington and Le Mans) but was unable to stop Stefano Modena's title charge, having to settle for the runner-up slot.

With Spanish backing, Sala joined his former rival Adrian Campos at Minardi for 1988 and looked quite promising in the early races, but once his countryman had been replaced by Pierluigi Martini the picture changed. Suddenly Luis was very much second-best within the team, particularly the following season when Minardi were quite capable of scoring points.

At the end of the year Sala was out, but he went on to enjoy an excellent career with Nissan in the Spanish touring car championship throughout the nineties.

SALA, Luis Perez (E) b 15/5/1959, Barcelona

1988 — Championship position: Unplaced

	Race	Circuit	No	Entrant	Tyres	Car/Engine	Comment	Q Pos/Entries
ret	BRAZILIAN GP	Rio	24	Lois Minardi Team	G	3.5 Minardi M188-Cosworth V8	*rear wing mounting*	20/31
11	SAN MARINO GP	Imola	24	Lois Minardi Team	G	3.5 Minardi M188-Cosworth V8	*2 laps behind*	18/31
ret	MONACO GP	Monte Carlo	24	Lois Minardi Team	G	3.5 Minardi M188-Cosworth V8	*suspension*	15/30
11	MEXICAN GP	Mexico City	24	Lois Minardi Team	G	3.5 Minardi M188-Cosworth V8	*4 laps behind*	25/30
13	CANADIAN GP	Montreal	24	Lois Minardi Team	G	3.5 Minardi M188-Cosworth V8	*5 laps behind*	21/31
ret	US GP (DETROIT)	Detroit	24	Lois Minardi Team	G	3.5 Minardi M188-Cosworth V8	*gearbox*	26/31
nc	FRENCH GP	Paul Ricard	24	Lois Minardi Team	G	3.5 Minardi M188-Cosworth V8	*4 pit stops-electrics/-10 laps*	26/31
ret	BRITISH GP	Silverstone	24	Lois Minardi Team	G	3.5 Minardi M188-Cosworth V8	*ran into back of Streiff*	18/31
dnq	GERMAN GP	Hockenheim	24	Lois Minardi Team	G	3.5 Minardi M188-Cosworth V8		27/31
10	HUNGARIAN GP	Hungaroring	24	Lois Minardi Team	G	3.5 Minardi M188-Cosworth V8	*4 laps behind*	11/31
dnq	BELGIAN GP	Spa	24	Lois Minardi Team	G	3.5 Minardi M188-Cosworth V8		27/31
ret	ITALIAN GP	Monza	24	Lois Minardi Team	G	3.5 Minardi M188-Cosworth V8	*gearbox*	19/31
8	PORTUGUESE GP	Estoril	24	Lois Minardi Team	G	3.5 Minardi M188-Cosworth V8	*2 laps behind*	19/31
12	SPANISH GP	Jerez	24	Lois Minardi Team	G	3.5 Minardi M188-Cosworth V8	*2 laps behind*	24/31
15	JAPANESE GP	Suzuka	24	Lois Minardi Team	G	3.5 Minardi M188-Cosworth V8	*2 laps behind*	22/31
ret	AUSTRALIAN GP	Adelaide	24	Lois Minardi Team	G	3.5 Minardi M188-Cosworth V8	*engine*	21/31

1989 — Championship position: 26th= Wins: 0 Pole positions: 0 Fastest laps: 0 Points scored: 1

	Race	Circuit	No	Entrant	Tyres	Car/Engine	Comment	Q Pos/Entries
ret	BRAZILIAN GP	Rio	24	Lois Minardi Team	P	3.5 Minardi M188B-Cosworth V8	*collision-Grouillard on lap 1*	23/38
ret	SAN MARINO GP	Imola	24	Lois Minardi Team	P	3.5 Minardi M188B-Cosworth V8	*spun off*	15/39
ret	MONACO GP	Monte Carlo	24	Lois Minardi Team	P	3.5 Minardi M188B-Cosworth V8	*engine/cockpit fire*	26/38
dnq	MEXICAN GP	Mexico City	24	Lois Minardi Team	P	3.5 Minardi M189-Cosworth V8		27/39
ret	US GP (PHOENIX)	Phoenix	24	Lois Minardi Team	P	3.5 Minardi M189-Cosworth V8	*overheating*	20/39
ret	CANADIAN GP	Montreal	24	Lois Minardi Team	P	3.5 Minardi M189-Cosworth V8	*started from pit lane/crashed*	24/39
dnq	FRENCH GP	Paul Ricard	24	Lois Minardi Team	P	3.5 Minardi M189-Cosworth V8		28/39
6	BRITISH GP	Silverstone	24	Lois Minardi Team	P	3.5 Minardi M189-Cosworth V8	*1 lap behind*	15/39
dnq	GERMAN GP	Hockenheim	24	Lois Minardi Team	P	3.5 Minardi M189-Cosworth V8		27/39
ret	HUNGARIAN GP	Hungaroring	24	Lois Minardi Team	P	3.5 Minardi M189-Cosworth V8	*accident with Modena*	23/39
15	BELGIAN GP	Spa	24	Lois Minardi Team	P	3.5 Minardi M189-Cosworth V8	*3 laps behind*	25/39
8	ITALIAN GP	Monza	24	Lois Minardi Team	P	3.5 Minardi M189-Cosworth V8	*2 laps behind*	26/39
12	PORTUGUESE GP	Estoril	24	Lois Minardi Team	P	3.5 Minardi M189-Cosworth V8	*2 laps behind*	9/39
ret	SPANISH GP	Jerez	24	Lois Minardi Team	P	3.5 Minardi M189-Cosworth V8	*collision with Gugelmin*	21/38
ret	JAPANESE GP	Suzuka	24	Lois Minardi Team	P	3.5 Minardi M189-Cosworth V8	*forced off by Nakajima-lap 1*	14/39
dnq	AUSTRALIAN GP	Adelaide	24	Lois Minardi Team	P	3.5 Minardi M189-Cosworth V8		28/39

GP Starts: 26   GP Wins: 0   Pole positions: 0   Fastest laps: 0   Points: 1

ELISEO SALAZAR

A virtual unknown when he came to Britain in 1979 to contest the Vandervell F3 championship, Salazar made a good impression with some gritty performances, despite being saddled with the initially temperamental 'ground-effect' Ralt RT3 while his rivals ran more proven machinery. For 1980 the Chilean switched to the Aurora British F1 series with the RAM Racing Williams FW07 and won three races (including the once prestigious International Trophy), but finished second to his team-mate, Emilio de Villota, in the championship.

With much-needed financial backing available, Salazar joined the revamped March team the following season but soon became disillusioned and took his cash to Ensign, where he put in some excellent performances, finishing in sixth place at Zandvoort. For 1982, Eliseo joined the autocratic Gunther Schmid's ATS team but, apart from a fifth place at Imola, he was largely in the shadow of Manfred Winkelhock. However, he was involved in a much-publicised incident at Hockenheim after being involved in a collision with Nelson Piquet, when he was assaulted by the irate Brazilian.

His options now limited if he wished to stay in Formula 1, Salazar went back to RAM for 1983 but, perhaps predictably, things rapidly disintegrated, and after a string of non-qualifications he found himself out of a drive.

The Chilean then spent many years racing in sports cars and, after a good 1994 season in IMSA, found the backing to join Dick Simon's Indy Car team for 1995. Salazar did surprisingly well in this highly competitive series, appearing particularly comfortable on the ovals. Fourth place in the Indianapolis 500 was the year's high point, and the veteran stayed with Simon in 1996 as he moved to the rival Indy Racing League.

Since then Salazar's grit and determination have certainly been tested, the Chilean returning on three separate occasions from huge accidents in which he suffered broken limbs. He has one IRL victory, at Las Vegas in 1997, to his credit and has continued a parallel career in sports car racing, in a Ferrari 333SP and latterly a Riley & Scott.

SALAZAR, Eliseo (RCH) b 14/11/1954, Santiago

	1981	Championship position: 18th=		Wins: 0	Pole positions: 0	Fastest laps: 0	Points scored: 1		
	Race	Circuit	No	Entrant	Tyres	Car/Engine		Comment	Q Pos/Entries
dnq	US GP WEST	Long Beach	18	March Grand Prix Team	M	3.0 March 811-Cosworth V8			29/29
dnq	BRAZILIAN GP	Rio	18	March Grand Prix Team	M	3.0 March 811-Cosworth V8			29/30
dnq	ARGENTINE GP	Buenos Aires	18	March Grand Prix Team	M	3.0 March 811-Cosworth V8			29/29
ret	SAN MARINO GP	Imola	17	March Grand Prix Team	M	3.0 March 811-Cosworth V8		oil pressure	23/30
dnq	BELGIAN GP	Zolder	17	March Grand Prix Team	M	3.0 March 811-Cosworth V8			26/31
dnpq	MONACO GP	Monte Carlo	17	March Grand Prix Team	M	3.0 March 811-Cosworth V8			29/31
14	SPANISH GP	Jarama	14	Ensign Racing	M	3.0 Ensign N180B-Cosworth V8		3 laps behind	24/30
ret	FRENCH GP	Dijon	14	Ensign Racing	A	3.0 Ensign N180B-Cosworth V8		rear suspension	22/29
dnq	BRITISH GP	Silverstone	14	Ensign Racing	A	3.0 Ensign N180B-Cosworth V8			28/30
nc	GERMAN GP	Hockenheim	14	Ensign Racing	A	3.0 Ensign N180B-Cosworth V8		pit stop-brakes/6 laps behind	23/30
ret	AUSTRIAN GP	Österreichring	14	Ensign Racing	A	3.0 Ensign N180B-Cosworth V8		engine	20/28
6	DUTCH GP	Zandvoort	14	Ensign Racing	A	3.0 Ensign N180B-Cosworth V8		2 laps behind	24/30
ret	ITALIAN GP	Monza	14	Ensign Racing	A	3.0 Ensign N180B-Cosworth V8		tyre failure	24/30
ret	CANADIAN GP	Montreal	14	Ensign Racing	A	3.0 Ensign N180B-Cosworth V8		spun off	24/30
nc	CAESARS PALACE GP	Las Vegas	14	Ensign Racing	A	3.0 Ensign N180B-Cosworth V8		brake problems/-14 laps	24/30
	1982	Championship position: 22nd=		Wins: 0	Pole positions: 0	Fastest laps: 0	Points scored: 2		
9	SOUTH AFRICAN GP	Kyalami	10	Team ATS	A	3.0 ATS D5-Cosworth V8		2 laps behind	12/30
ret	BRAZILIAN GP	Rio	10	Team ATS	A	3.0 ATS D5-Cosworth V8		engine	18/31
ret	US GP WEST	Long Beach	10	Team ATS	A	3.0 ATS D5-Cosworth V8		hit wall	26/31
5	SAN MARINO GP	Imola	10	Team ATS	A	3.0 ATS D5-Cosworth V8		3 laps behind	14/14
ret	BELGIAN GP	Zolder	10	Team ATS	A	3.0 ATS D5-Cosworth V8		startline accident	20/32
ret	MONACO GP	Monte Carlo	10	Team ATS	M	3.0 ATS D5-Cosworth V8		fire extinguisher went off	20/31
ret	US GP (DETROIT)	Detroit	10	Team ATS	M	3.0 ATS D5-Cosworth V8		crashed	25/28
ret	CANADIAN GP	Montreal	10	Team ATS	M	3.0 ATS D5-Cosworth V8		transmission	24/29
13	DUTCH GP	Zandvoort	10	Team ATS	M	3.0 ATS D5-Cosworth V8		2 laps behind	25/31
dnq	BRITISH GP	Brands Hatch	10	Team ATS	M	3.0 ATS D5-Cosworth V8			29/30
ret	FRENCH GP	Paul Ricard	10	Team ATS	M	3.0 ATS D5-Cosworth V8		crashed	22/30
ret	GERMAN GP	Hockenheim	10	Team ATS	M	3.0 ATS D5-Cosworth V8		accident with Piquet	23/30
dnq	AUSTRIAN GP	Österreichring	10	Team ATS	M	3.0 ATS D5-Cosworth V8			29/29
14	SWISS GP	Dijon	10	Team ATS	M	3.0 ATS D5-Cosworth V8		3 laps behind	25/29
9	ITALIAN GP	Monza	10	Team ATS	M	3.0 ATS D5-Cosworth V8		2 laps behind	25/30
dnq	CAESARS PALACE GP	Las Vegas	10	Team ATS	M	3.0 ATS D5-Cosworth V8			29/30
	1983	Championship position: Unplaced							
15	BRAZILIAN GP	Rio	17	RAM Automotive Team March	P	3.0 March RAM 01-Cosworth V8		4 laps behind	26/27
ret	US GP WEST	Long Beach	17	RAM Automotive Team March	P	3.0 March RAM 01-Cosworth V8		gear linkage	25/28
dnq	FRENCH GP	Paul Ricard	17	RAM Automotive Team March	P	3.0 March RAM 01-Cosworth V8			27/29
dnq	SAN MARINO GP	Imola	17	RAM Automotive Team March	P	3.0 March RAM 01-Cosworth V8			27/28
dnq	MONACO GP	Monte Carlo	17	RAM Automotive Team March	P	3.0 March RAM 01-Cosworth V8			25/28
dnq	BELGIAN GP	Spa	17	RAM Automotive Team March	P	3.0 March RAM 01-Cosworth V8			28/28

GP Starts: 24   GP Wins: 0   Pole positions: 0   Fastest laps: 0   Points: 3

MIKA SALO

Salo could so easily have become the forgotten one of the two Mikas following a hard-fought British Formula 3 championship in 1990 when the Finn from Helsinki pushed his rival Häkkinen all the way in a two-horse battle for the title. The champion was snapped up by Lotus, while Salo, despite six wins to his credit, was left without sufficient backing even to scrape up a ride in European F3000.

It must have been a choker for the uninhibited Salo, who had an almost unbroken list of successes in karts and FF1600 behind him in Scandinavia, but at least he had the lifeline of employment in Japan testing and racing on behalf of Yokohama. Running on these tyres in the All-Japan F3000 championship failed to produce the most spectacular of results, but in his four-year stay in the Far East Mika built up a massive amount of experience.

He was therefore ideally placed to step into a vacant seat at Lotus for the 1994 Japanese GP and took his big chance to shine in a poor car, finishing tenth in the appalling race conditions without once making an error. From forgotten man he was suddenly in demand, and when it was clear that Lotus had finally closed its doors Salo joined Tyrrell for the 1995 season.

A sensational debut in Brazil could have yielded points but for his suffering cramp, and he spent the rest of the season generally over-shadowing his team-mate Katayama. There were plenty of rough edges, and his driving tactics were sometimes a little questionable, but Mika plugged away in a disappointing car to take three points-scoring finishes in the last six races. The maturing Finn undoubtedly had the speed to go much further up the Grand Prix ladder, but after a bright start to the 1996 season he found himself wondering if he could even finish a race, let alone challenge for a worthwhile result, given the fragility of the Yamaha engine.

Locked into a three-year deal with Tyrrell, Salo was joined in 1997 by the equally hungry Jos Verstappen and the young lions had customer Ford power, which increased reliability but at the price of straightline speed. When circumstances presented him with a chance to score points with the Tyrrell at Monaco, Mika drove a brilliant non-stop race to take fifth place and emphasise that a talent was largely being wasted.

It was something of a sideways move for Salo when he switched to Arrows for 1998 to replace Damon Hill. For the Finn it was much the same scenario as at Tyrrell: tidy but none-too-quick machinery with questionable reliability. A fourth place was achieved at Monaco in the black car but no other top-six finishes were forthcoming. When Pedro Diniz defected to Sauber at season's end, he took his massive sponsorship package with him, and this had far-reaching consequences for Salo, who found himself pushed out by Pedro de la Rosa and Toranosuke Takagi, who both came with substantial backing.

This was to be a blessing in disguise if the Finn but knew it, for he was free to take over from Ricardo Zonta at BAR after the Brazilian had sustained a foot injury. Mika at least managed to bring the car to the finish in one of his three races before stepping down, and was then rapidly called back into action, this time with Ferrari. This was Salo's big chance, and he certainly made an impression in the German Grand Prix when he had total control of the race before moving aside to let team-mate Eddie Irvine take the ten points in his championship quest.

His selflessness no doubt played a big part in the Finn's being offered a seat at Sauber for 2000. Midfield mediocrity may be all Salo has in prospect, but now at least he has the regular ride which is the minimum this talented driver deserves.

SALO, Mika (SF) b 25/9/1967, Helsinki

	1994	Championship position: Unplaced						
	Race	Circuit	No	Entrant	Tyres	Car/Engine	Comment	Q Pos/Entries
10	JAPANESE GP	Suzuka	11	Team Lotus	G	3.5 Lotus 109-Mugen Honda V10	1 lap behind	25/28
ret	AUSTRALIAN GP	Adelaide	11	Team Lotus	G	3.5 Lotus 109-Mugen Honda V10	electrics	22/28

1995
Championship position: 14th= Wins: 0 Pole positions: 0 Fastest laps: 0 Points scored: 5

7	BRAZILIAN GP	Interlagos	4	Nokia Tyrrell Yamaha	G	3.0 Tyrrell 023-Yamaha V10	*2 laps behind*	12/26
ret	ARGENTINE GP	Buenos Aires	4	Nokia Tyrrell Yamaha	G	3.0 Tyrrell 023-Yamaha V10	*collision with Suzuki*	7/26
ret	SAN MARINO GP	Imola	4	Nokia Tyrrell Yamaha	G	3.0 Tyrrell 023-Yamaha V10	*engine*	13/26
10	SPANISH GP	Barcelona	4	Nokia Tyrrell Yamaha	G	3.0 Tyrrell 023-Yamaha V10	*1 lap behind*	13/26
ret	MONACO GP	Monte Carlo	4	Nokia Tyrrell Yamaha	G	3.0 Tyrrell 023-Yamaha V10	*started from pit lane/engine*	17/26
7	CANADIAN GP	Montreal	4	Nokia Tyrrell Yamaha	G	3.0 Tyrrell 023-Yamaha V10	*1 lap behind*	15/24
15	FRENCH GP	Magny Cours	4	Nokia Tyrrell Yamaha	G	3.0 Tyrrell 023-Yamaha V10	*3 laps behind*	14/24
8	BRITISH GP	Silverstone	4	Nokia Tyrrell Yamaha	G	3.0 Tyrrell 023-Yamaha V10	*1 lap behind*	23/24
ret	GERMAN GP	Hockenheim	4	Nokia Tyrrell Yamaha	G	3.0 Tyrrell 023-Yamaha V10	*clutch*	13/24
ret	HUNGARIAN GP	Hungaroring	4	Nokia Tyrrell Yamaha	G	3.0 Tyrrell 023-Yamaha V10	*throttle*	16/24
8	BELGIAN GP	Spa	4	Nokia Tyrrell Yamaha	G	3.0 Tyrrell 023-Yamaha V10		11/24
5	ITALIAN GP	Monza	4	Nokia Tyrrell Yamaha	G	3.0 Tyrrell 023-Yamaha V10	*1 lap behind*	16/24
13	PORTUGUESE GP	Estoril	4	Nokia Tyrrell Yamaha	G	3.0 Tyrrell 023-Yamaha V10	*2 laps behind*	15/24
10	EUROPEAN GP	Nürburgring	4	Nokia Tyrrell Yamaha	G	3.0 Tyrrell 023-Yamaha V10	*3 laps behind*	15/24
12	PACIFIC GP	T.I. Circuit	4	Nokia Tyrrell Yamaha	G	3.0 Tyrrell 023-Yamaha V10	*3 laps behind*	18/24
6	JAPANESE GP	Suzuka	4	Nokia Tyrrell Yamaha	G	3.0 Tyrrell 023-Yamaha V10	*1 lap behind*	12/24
5	AUSTRALIAN GP	Adelaide	4	Nokia Tyrrell Yamaha	G	3.0 Tyrrell 023-Yamaha V10	*3 laps behind*	14/24

1996
Championship position: 13th Wins: 0 Pole positions: 0 Fastest laps: 0 Points scored: 5

6	AUSTRALIAN GP	Melbourne	19	Tyrrell Yamaha	G	3.0 Tyrrell 024-Yamaha V10	*3 laps behind*	10/22
5	BRAZILIAN GP	Interlagos	19	Tyrrell Yamaha	G	3.0 Tyrrell 024-Yamaha V10	*1 lap behind*	11/22
ret	ARGENTINE GP	Buenos Aires	19	Tyrrell Yamaha	G	3.0 Tyrrell 024-Yamaha V10	*throttle*	16/22
dsq*	EUROPEAN GP	Nürburgring	19	Tyrrell Yamaha	G	3.0 Tyrrell 024-Yamaha V10	** 10th-dsq car underweight*	14/22
ret	SAN MARINO GP	Imola	19	Tyrrell Yamaha	G	3.0 Tyrrell 024-Yamaha V10	*engine*	8/22
5/ret	MONACO GP	Monte Carlo	19	Tyrrell Yamaha	G	3.0 Tyrrell 024-Yamaha V10	*collison-Irvine & Häkikinen/-5 laps*	11/22
dsq*	SPANISH GP	Barcelona	19	Tyrrell Yamaha	G	3.0 Tyrrell 024-Yamaha V10	** switched to spare car before start*	12/22
ret	CANADIAN GP	Montreal	19	Tyrrell Yamaha	G	3.0 Tyrrell 024-Yamaha V10	*engine*	14/22
10	FRENCH GP	Magny Cours	19	Tyrrell Yamaha	G	3.0 Tyrrell 024-Yamaha V10	*2 laps behind*	14/22
7	BRITISH GP	Silverstone	19	Tyrrell Yamaha	G	3.0 Tyrrell 024-Yamaha V10	*1 lap behind*	14/22
9	GERMAN GP	Hockenheim	19	Tyrrell Yamaha	G	3.0 Tyrrell 024-Yamaha V10	*1 laps behind*	15/20
ret	HUNGARIAN GP	Hungaroring	19	Tyrrell Yamaha	G	3.0 Tyrrell 024-Yamaha V10	*collision with Diniz*	16/20
7	BELGIAN GP	Spa	19	Tyrrell Yamaha	G	3.0 Tyrrell 024-Yamaha V10		13/20
ret	ITALIAN GP	Monza	19	Tyrrell Yamaha	G	3.0 Tyrrell 024-Yamaha V10	*engine*	17/20
11	PORTUGUESE GP	Estoril	19	Tyrrell Yamaha	G	3.0 Tyrrell 024-Yamaha V10	*1 lap behind*	13/20
ret	JAPANESE GP	Suzuka	19	Tyrrell Yamaha	G	3.0 Tyrrell 024-Yamaha V10	*engine*	15/20

1997
Championship position: 16th= Wins: 0 Pole positions: 0 Fastest laps: 0 Points scored: 2

ret	AUSTRALIAN GP	Melbourne	19	Tyrrell	G	3.0 Tyrrell 025-Ford ED4 V8	*engine*	18/24
13	BRAZILIAN GP	Interlagos	19	Tyrrell	G	3.0 Tyrrell 025-Ford ED4 V8	*1 lap behind*	22/22
8	ARGENTINE GP	Buenos Aires	19	Tyrrell	G	3.0 Tyrrell 025-Ford ED4 V8	*1 lap behind*	19/22
9	SAN MARINO GP	Imola	19	Tyrrell	G	3.0 Tyrrell 025-Ford ED4 V8	*2 laps behind*	19/22
5	MONACO GP	Monte Carlo	19	Tyrrell	G	3.0 Tyrrell 025-Ford ED4 V8	*ran without pit stop in rain*	14/22
ret	SPANISH GP	Barcelona	19	Tyrrell	G	3.0 Tyrrell 025-Ford ED4 V8	*puncture*	14/22
ret	CANADIAN GP	Montreal	19	Tyrrell	G	3.0 Tyrrell 025-Ford ED4 V8	*engine*	17/22
ret	FRENCH GP	Magny Cours	19	Tyrrell	G	3.0 Tyrrell 025-Ford ED4 V8	*engine*	19/22
ret	BRITISH GP	Silverstone	19	Tyrrell	G	3.0 Tyrrell 025-Ford ED4 V8	*engine*	18/22
ret	GERMAN GP	Hockenheim	19	Tyrrell	G	3.0 Tyrrell 025-Ford ED4 V8	*clutch*	19/22
13	HUNGARIAN GP	Hungaroring	19	Tyrrell	G	3.0 Tyrrell 025-Ford ED4 V8	*2 laps behind*	21/22
11*	BELGIAN GP	Spa	19	Tyrrell	G	3.0 Tyrrell 025-Ford ED4 V8	**3rd place car dsq/-1 lap*	19/22
ret	ITALIAN GP	Monza	19	Tyrrell	G	3.0 Tyrrell 025-Ford ED4 V8	*engine*	19/22
ret	AUSTRIAN GP	A1-Ring	19	Tyrrell	G	3.0 Tyrrell 025-Ford ED4 V8	*transmission*	21/22
10	LUXEMBOURG GP	Nürburgring	19	Tyrrell	G	3.0 Tyrrell 025-Ford ED4 V8	*1 lap behind*	20/22
ret	JAPANESE GP	Suzuka	19	Tyrrell	G	3.0 Tyrrell 025-Ford ED4 V8	*engine*	22/22
12	EUROPEAN GP	Jerez	19	Tyrrell	G	3.0 Tyrrell 025-Ford ED4 V8	*1 lap behind*	21/22

1998
Championship position: 13= Wins: 0 Pole positions: 0 Fastest laps: 0 Points scored: 3

ret	AUSTRALIAN GP	Melbourne	17	Danka Zepter Arrows	B	3.0 Arrows A19-V10	*electrics*	16/22
ret	BRAZILIAN GP	Interlagos	17	Danka Zepter Arrows	B	3.0 Arrows A19-V10	*engine*	20/22
ret	ARGENTINE GP	Buenos Aires	17	Danka Zepter Arrows	B	3.0 Arrows A19-V10	*gearbox*	17/22
9	SAN MARINO GP	Imola	17	Danka Zepter Arrows	B	3.0 Arrows A19-V10	*2 laps behind*	14/22
ret	SPANISH GP	Barcelona	17	Danka Zepter Arrows	B	3.0 Arrows A19-V10	*engine*	17/22
4	MONACO GP	Monte Carlo	17	Danka Zepter Arrows	B	3.0 Arrows A19-V10		8/22
ret	CANADIAN GP	Montreal	17	Danka Zepter Arrows	B	3.0 Arrows A19-V10	*crashed*	17/22
13	FRENCH GP	Magny Cours	17	Danka Zepter Arrows	B	3.0 Arrows A19-V10	*2 laps behind*	19/22
ret	BRITISH GP	Silverstone	17	Danka Zepter Arrows	B	3.0 Arrows A19-V10	*spun off*	14/22
ret	AUSTRIAN GP	A1-Ring	17	Danka Zepter Arrows	B	3.0 Arrows A19-V10	*collision damage*	6/22
14	GERMAN GP	Hockenheim	17	Danka Zepter Arrows	B	3.0 Arrows A19-V10	*1 lap behind*	17/22
ret	HUNGARIAN GP	Hungaroring	17	Danka Zepter Arrows	B	3.0 Arrows A19-V10	*hydraulic leak*	13/22
ret/dns	BELGIAN GP	Spa	17	Danka Zepter Arrows	B	3.0 Arrows A19-V10	*accident at first start*	18/22
ret	ITALIAN GP	Monza	17	Danka Zepter Arrows	B	3.0 Arrows A19-V10	*hydraulics*	16/22
14	LUXEMBOURG GP	Nürburgring	17	Danka Zepter Arrows	B	3.0 Arrows A19-V10	*2 laps behind*	16/22
ret	JAPANESE GP	Suzuka	17	Danka Zepter Arrows	B	3.0 Arrows A19-V10	*hydraulics*	15/22

1999
Championship position: 10th Wins: 0 Pole positions: 0 Fastest laps: 0 Points scored: 10

7/ret	SAN MARINO GP	Imola	23	British American Racing	B	3.0 BAR 01-Supertec V10	*electrics/2 laps behind*	19/22
ret	MONACO GP	Monte Carlo	23	British American Racing	B	3.0 BAR 01-Supertec V10	*brakes*	12/22
8	SPANISH GP	Barcelona	23	British American Racing	B	3.0 BAR 01-Supertec V10	*1 lap behind*	16/22
9	AUSTRIAN GP	A1-Ring	3	Scuderia Marlboro Ferrari	B	3.0 Ferrari F399-V10	*1 lap behind*	7/22
2	GERMAN GP	Hockenheim	3	Scuderia Marlboro Ferrari	B	3.0 Ferrari F399-V10	*lead race-allowed Irvine to win*	4/22
12	HUNGARIAN GP	Hungaroring	3	Scuderia Marlboro Ferrari	B	3.0 Ferrari F399-V10	*2 laps behind*	18/22
7	BELGIAN GP	Spa	3	Scuderia Marlboro Ferrari	B	3.0 Ferrari F399-V10		9/22
3	ITALIAN GP	Monza	3	Scuderia Marlboro Ferrari	B	3.0 Ferrari F399-V10		6/22
ret	EUROPEAN GP	Nürburgring	3	Scuderia Marlboro Ferrari	B	3.0 Ferrari F399-V10	*brakes*	12/22

GP Starts: 77 GP Wins: 0 Pole positions: 0 Fastest laps: 0 Points: 25

ROY SALVADORI

While not possessing the talent of his contemporaries Moss, Hawthorn, Collins and Brooks, Salvadori was a fine all-round driver, particularly in sports cars, who became a household name in Britain thanks to his many victories in races on home soil. Though born of Italian parentage, Salvadori was very much a Londoner at heart, and began racing for fun in 1946 before entering selected events the following year in an Alfa Romeo. Deciding to pursue a professional career, Roy sampled a variety of machines including a Healey, a Jaguar and a Frazer Nash on his way up the ladder.

In 1952 he campaigned a four-cylinder Ferrari in the British GP and a few other minor races in addition to racing Tony Crook's Frazer Nash, but his sights were by now set on Grand Prix racing and he joined Connaught for the 1953 season. While he drew a blank in the World Championship races, there were plenty of successful outings in national events. He was happy to compete in almost any type of machine and often took part in three or more races during a single race meeting.

Joining Syd Greene to race his potent Maserati 250F, Salvadori again concentrated on events at home during 1954-56, but by this time he was already a regular member of the Aston Martin sports car team, a role he was to fulfil right to the end of their programme, which finished on such a high note in 1959 when Roy shared the winning DBR1 at Le Mans with Carroll Shelby.

For 1957 Roy aligned himself with Cooper as they developed their rear-engined Formula 2 car in preparation for a full season of Grands Prix the following year. Fifth place in the British GP at Aintree put him among the championship points scorers for the first time, and in non-title races he took a second at Caen and a fourth at Reims. The 1958 season saw the Surbiton team's first sustained effort at the top level, and Brabham and Salvadori both scored some excellent results. Roy's second place to Brooks in the German GP may have been distant but it was a portent of even greater things to follow, but Roy was sadly not to be part of the great works Cooper triumph.

In 1959 Salvadori continued to drive Coopers in Formula 2, but for Tommy Atkins, his best result being a win in the London Trophy at Crystal Palace. Meanwhile Aston Martin had ambitiously decided to embark on a Grand Prix programme of their own and Roy was to be one of the drivers, but crucially they had opted to adopt the traditional front-engined layout which, of course, was soon doomed to oblivion. Their cars were superbly crafted and beautifully turned out, but after Salvadori had scored a totally misleading second place in the International Trophy early in 1959, they proved to be a major disappointment. The engine just didn't possess enough power and, depite major reworkings, the project was a hopeless failure which drifted on into 1960, by which time the writing was well and truly on the wall.

The following season Roy joined John Surtees in Reg Parnell's well-funded Yeoman Credit-backed team racing Coopers. However, the Surbiton-built cars had had their day, as Colin Chapman had devoured every lesson they had to offer and combined them with his own thinking to push his Lotus 18 and 21 models to the fore. Salvadori was as close as he ever would be to winning a Grand Prix at Watkins Glen that year when he was closing in on Innes Ireland's leading Lotus before the engine failed. The team had high hopes for 1962 with the new Lola chassis, but it was to be a desperately disappointing season for Salvadori, who was totally overshadowed by Surtees, almost being reduced to the role of hack driver. Wisely perhaps, he decided that Grand Prix success was now beyond his reach, and he returned to sports and touring car racing with Tommy Atkins' Cooper Monaco, Shelby Cobra and Jaguar E-Type cars. Although his front-line career was behind him, there was no easing up in his driving style, for Roy had never taken any prisoners and he wasn't going to change his approach in the twilight of his career!

By the time he retired early in 1965 Salvadori had driven on most of the world's circuits. He knew the risks attendant on them, for he had seen many of his peers perish over his long career, and indeed had come perilously close to joining them on more than one occasion. He also knew his own worth and the thought of racing without starting money was anathema to him. After his driving days were over, he became the team manager at Cooper in 1966-67, before retiring to Monaco in the late sixties, where he resides to this day. His apartment overlooking the Monte Carlo circuit still attracts many old friends from his racing days for a wonderful view of the Grand Prix each May.

SALVADORI, Roy (GB) b 12/5/1922, Dovercourt, Essex

1952 — Championship position: Unplaced

	Race	Circuit	No	Entrant	Tyres	Car/Engine	Comment	Q Pos/Entries
8	BRITISH GP	Silverstone	14	G Caprara	D	2.0 Ferrari 500 4	3 laps behind	19/32

1953 — Championship position: Unplaced

	Race	Circuit	No	Entrant	Tyres	Car/Engine	Comment	Q Pos/Entries
ret	DUTCH GP	Zandvoort	26	Connaught Engineering	D	2.0 Connaught-Lea Francis A Type 4	engine	11/20
ret	FRENCH GP	Reims	50	Connaught Engineering	D	2.0 Connaught-Lea Francis A Type 4	ignition	19/25
ret	BRITISH GP	Silverstone	12	Connaught Engineering	D	2.0 Connaught-Lea Francis A Type 4	radius rod	28/29
ret	GERMAN GP	Nürburgring	15	Connaught Engineering	D	2.0 Connaught-Lea Francis A Type 4	engine	13/35
ret	ITALIAN GP	Monza	22	Connaught Engineering	D	2.0 Connaught-Lea Francis A Type 4	throttle cable	14/30

1954 — Championship position: Unplaced

	Race	Circuit	No	Entrant	Tyres	Car/Engine	Comment	Q Pos/Entries
ret	FRENCH GP	Reims	44	Gilby Engineering Ltd	D	2.5 Maserati 250F 6	driveshaft	10/22
ret	BRITISH GP	Silverstone	5	Gilby Engineering Ltd	D	2.5 Maserati 250F 6	gearbox	7/31

1955 — Championship position: Unplaced

	Race	Circuit	No	Entrant	Tyres	Car/Engine	Comment	Q Pos/Entries
ret	BRITISH GP	Aintree	44	Gilby Engineering Ltd	D	2.5 Maserati 250F 6	gearbox	20/25

1956 — Championship position: Unplaced

	Race	Circuit	No	Entrant	Tyres	Car/Engine	Comment	Q Pos/Entries
ret	BRITISH GP	Silverstone	28	Gilby Engineering Ltd	D	2.5 Maserati 250F 6	fuel starvation	7/28
ret	GERMAN GP	Nürburgring	16	Gilby Engineering Ltd	D	2.5 Maserati 250F 6	rear suspension	9/21
nc	ITALIAN GP	Monza	44	Gilby Engineering Ltd	D	2.5 Maserati 250F 6	9 laps behind	14/26

1957 — Championship position: 14th= Wins: 0 Pole positions: 0 Fastest laps: 0 Points scored: 2

	Race	Circuit	No	Entrant	Tyres	Car/Engine	Comment	Q Pos/Entries
dnq	MONACO GP	Monte Carlo	8	Owen Racing Organisation	D	2.5 BRM P25 4		17/21
ret	FRENCH GP	Rouen	20	Vandervell Products Ltd	P	2.5 Vanwall 4	engine	6/15
5	BRITISH GP	Aintree	36	Cooper Car Co	D	2.0 Cooper T43-Climax 4	5 laps behind	14/19
ret	GERMAN GP (F2)	Nürburgring	23	Cooper Car Co	D	1.5 Cooper T43-Climax 4	suspension	14/24
ret	PESCARA GP	Pescara	22	Cooper Car Co	D	1.5 Cooper T43-Climax 4	suspension	15/16

1958 — Championship position: 4th Wins: 0 Pole positions: 0 Fastest laps: 0 Points scored: 15

	Race	Circuit	No	Entrant	Tyres	Car/Engine	Comment	Q Pos/Entries
ret	MONACO GP	Monte Carlo	18	Cooper Car Co	D	2.0 Cooper T45-Climax 4	gearbox	4/28
4	DUTCH GP	Zandvoort	7	Cooper Car Co	D	2.2 Cooper T45-Climax 4	1 lap behind	9/17
8	BELGIAN GP	Spa	24	Cooper Car Co	D	2.0 Cooper T45-Climax 4	1 lap behind	13/20
nc	FRENCH GP	Reims	20	Cooper Car Co	D	2.0 Cooper T45-Climax 4	clutch slip/13 laps behind	14/21
3	BRITISH GP	Silverstone	10	Cooper Car Co	D	2.2 Cooper T45-Climax 4		3/21
2	GERMAN GP	Nürburgring	10	Cooper Car Co	D	2.2 Cooper T45-Climax 4		6/26
9	PORTUGUESE GP	Oporto	16	Cooper Car Co	D	2.0 Cooper T45-Climax 4	4 laps behind	11/15
5	ITALIAN GP	Monza	6	Cooper Car Co	D	2.2 Cooper T45-Climax 4	8 laps behind	14/21
7	MOROCCAN GP	Casablanca	30	Cooper Car Co	D	2.2 Cooper T45-Climax 4	2 laps behind	14/25

1959 — Championship position: Unplaced

	Race	Circuit	No	Entrant	Tyres	Car/Engine	Comment	Q Pos/Entries
ret	MONACO GP	Monte Carlo	38	High Efficiency Motors	D	2.5 Cooper T45-Maserati 4	transmisssion/-17 laps	8/24
ret	DUTCH GP	Zandvoort	4	David Brown Corporation	A	2.5 Aston Martin DBR4/250 6	overheating	13/15
ret	FRENCH GP	Reims	16	High Efficiency Motors	D	2.5 Cooper T45-Maserati 4	engine	16/22
6	BRITISH GP	Aintree	2	David Brown Corporation	A	2.5 Aston Martin DBR4/250 6	1 lap behind	2/30
6	PORTUGUESE GP	Monsanto	10	David Brown Corporation	A	2.5 Aston Martin DBR4/250 6	3 laps behind	12/16
ret	ITALIAN GP	Monza	24	David Brown Corporation	A	2.5 Aston Martin DBR4/250 6	engine	17/21
ret	US GP	Sebring	12	High Efficiency Motors	D	2.5 Cooper T45-Maserati 4	transmission	11/19

1960 — Championship position: Unplaced

	Race	Circuit	No	Entrant	Tyres	Car/Engine	Comment	Q Pos/Entries
ret	MONACO GP	Monte Carlo	14	High Efficiency Motors	D	2.5 Cooper T51-Climax 4	overheating	12/24
dns	DUTCH GP	Zandvoort	17	David Brown Corporation	D	2.5 Aston Martin DBR4/250 6	starting money dispute	(20)/21
ret	BRITISH GP	Silverstone	18	David Brown Corporation	D	2.5 Aston Martin DBR4/250 6	steering	13/25
8	US GP	Riverside	14	High Efficiency Motors	D	2.5 Cooper T51-Climax 4	2 laps behind	15/23

1961 — Championship position: 17th Wins: 0 Pole positions: 0 Fastest laps: 0 Points scored: 2

	Race	Circuit	No	Entrant	Tyres	Car/Engine	Comment	Q Pos/Entries
8	FRENCH GP	Reims	42	Yeoman Credit Racing Team	D	1.5 Cooper T53-Climax 4	1 lap behind	15/26
6	BRITISH GP	Aintree	36	Yeoman Credit Racing Team	D	1.5 Cooper T53-Climax 4		13/30
10	GERMAN GP	Nürburgring	19	Yeoman Credit Racing Team	D	1.5 Cooper T53-Climax 4		15/27
6	ITALIAN GP	Monza	40	Yeoman Credit Racing Team	D	1.5 Cooper T53-Climax 4	1 lap behind	=17/33
ret	US GP	Watkins Glen	19	Yeoman Credit Racing Team	D	1.5 Cooper T53-Climax 4	engine when 2nd	12/19

1962 — Championship position: Unplaced

	Race	Circuit	No	Entrant	Tyres	Car/Engine	Comment	Q Pos/Entries
ret	DUTCH GP	Zandvoort	20	Bowmaker Racing Team	D	1.5 Lola 4-Climax V8	withdrawn after Surtees' crash	17/20
ret	MONACO GP	Monte Carlo	26	Bowmaker Racing Team	D	1.5 Lola 4-Climax V8	suspension	12/21
ret	FRENCH GP	Rouen	20	Bowmaker Racing Team	D	1.5 Lola 4-Climax V8	oil pressure	14/17
ret	BRITISH GP	Aintree	26	Bowmaker Racing Team	D	1.5 Lola 4-Climax V8	battery	=11/21
ret	GERMAN GP	Nürburgring	15	Bowmaker Racing Team	D	1.5 Lola 4-Climax V8	gearbox	9/30
ret	ITALIAN GP	Monza	44	Bowmaker Racing Team	D	1.5 Lola 4-Climax V8	engine	13/30
dns	US GP	Watkins Glen	19	Bowmaker Racing Team	D	1.5 Lola 4-Climax V8	Surtees drove car	(11)/20
ret	SOUTH AFRICAN GP	Kyalami	7	Bowmaker Racing Team	D	1.5 Lola 4-Climax V8	fuel leak-split tank	11/17

GP Starts: 47 GP Wins: 0 Pole positions: 0 Fastest laps: 0 Points: 19

SANESI, Consalvo (I) b 28/3/1911, Terranuova Bracciolini, Arezzo

1950 — Championship position: Championship position: 4th Wins: 0 Pole positions: 0 Fastest laps: 0 Points scored: 15

	Race	Circuit	No	Entrant	Tyres	Car/Engine	Comment	Q Pos/Entries
ret	ITALIAN GP	Monza	46	Scuderia Alfa Romeo SpA	P	1.5 s/c Alfa Romeo 158 8	engine	4/27

1951 — Championship position: 10th= Wins: 0 Pole positions: 0 Fastest laps: 0 Points scored: 3

	Race	Circuit	No	Entrant	Tyres	Car/Engine	Comment	Q Pos/Entries
4	SWISS GP	Bremgarten	28	Scuderia Alfa Romeo SpA	P	1.5 s/c Alfa Romeo 159 8	1 lap behind	4/21
ret	BELGIAN GP	Spa	6	Scuderia Alfa Romeo SpA	P	1.5 s/c Alfa Romeo 159 8	radiator	6/13
10	FRENCH GP	Reims	6	Scuderia Alfa Romeo SpA	P	1.5 s/c Alfa Romeo 159 8	pushed car to finish/-19 laps	5/23
6	BRITISH GP	Silverstone	3	Scuderia Alfa Romeo SpA	P	1.5 s/c Alfa Romeo 159 8	6 laps behind	6/20

GP Starts: 5 GP Wins: 0 Pole positions: 0 Fastest laps: 0 Points: 3

CONSALVO SANESI

Sanesi's main role at Alfa Romeo was as a test driver, but he was also given numerous opportunities to drive the superb Tipo 158/159 series cars in races. In 1946, he won his heat and finished third in the Milan GP, while in 1947 he was second to Varzi at Bari and third in the Italian GP held at Sempione Park after claiming pole position.

The following year saw Consalvo take second place in the French GP and third with fastest lap at the Monza Autodrome GP. In 1949 Alfa Corse did not compete in Formula 1, though Sanesi finished second in the touring car class in the Mille Miglia with an Alfa, and when the team returned in 1950 he drove in only one Grand Prix but won the Coppa Inter Europa sports car race at Monza.

Consalvo had his most active Grand Prix season in 1951, scoring points in two of his four starts, but after Alfa's withdrawal from Grand Prix racing at the end of the year, he concentrated fully on sports cars, winning his class in the 1954 Carrera Panamericana. A testing accident later that year with the Disco Volante left him with serious injuries, but he returned to competition in 1955, taking second place in the Verminico hill-climb with a 1.9 Alfa.

STÉPHANE SARRAZIN

Stéphane made his mark in French Formula 3 during 1996 and, in particular, 1997, when he finished second in the final standings behind Patrice Gay.

His performances earned him a seat in the Apomatox-run Prost Junior Team for 1998 and he kicked off his F3000 career with a superb win in the wet at Oschersleben. His season slid away somewhat after that, but he retained his place for 1999.

Before the series got under way Sarrazin found himself elevated to the Grand Prix ranks when Minardi called him up at short notice to deputise for the injured Luca Badoer. With no testing, the Frenchman acquitted himself extremely well on his Grand Prix debut, but his race ended dramatically when his car suffered a suspension failure.

Back in F3000, Stéphane again took a single win at the Hungaroring, but it was the series champion Nick Heidfeld who was chosen for the vacant Prost Grand Prix seat for 2000. It had been thought that the Frenchman was being groomed for this place, and a disappointed Sarrazin has elected to take over Heidfeld's prized West Competition drive to compete for a third year in the F3000 series.

SARRAZIN, Stéphane (F) b 2/11/1974, Ales

	1999	Championship position: Unplaced							
	Race	Circuit	No	Entrant	Tyres	Car/Engine	Comment	Q Pos/Entries
ret	BRAZILIAN GP	Interlagos	20	Fondmetal Minardi Ford	B	3.0 Minardi M01-Ford Zetec R V10	stuck throttle-accident	17/22

GP Starts: 1   GP Wins: 0   Pole positions: 0   Fastest laps: 0   Points: 0

SCARFIOTTI, Ludovico (I) b 18/10/1933, Turin – d 8/6/1968, Rossfeld, Germany

	1963	Championship position: 15th= Wins: 0 Pole positions: 0 Fastest laps: 0 Points scored: 1							
	Race	Circuit	No	Entrant	Tyres	Car/Engine	Comment	Q Pos/Entries
6	DUTCH GP	Zandvoort	4	Scuderia Ferrari SpA SEFAC	D	1.5 Ferrari 156 V6	2 laps behind	11/19
dns	FRENCH GP	Reims	14	Scuderia Ferrari SpA SEFAC	D	1.5 Ferrari 156 V6	practice accident	(14)/21
	1964	Championship position: Unplaced						
9	ITALIAN GP	Monza	6	Scuderia Ferrari SpA SEFAC	D	1.5 Ferrari 156 V6	1 lap behind	=16/25
	1965	Championship position: Unplaced						
dns	MEXICAN GP	Mexico City	24	Scuderia Ferrari SpA SEFAC	D	1.5 Ferrari 1512 F12	car driven by Rodriguez	–/–
	1966	Championship position: 10th Wins: 0 Pole positions: 0 Fastest laps: 1 Points scored: 9						
ret	GERMAN GP	Nürburgring	11	Scuderia Ferrari SpA SEFAC	D	2.4 Ferrari Dino 246 V6	electrics	4/30
1	ITALIAN GP	Monza	6	Scuderia Ferrari SpA SEFAC	F	3.0 Ferrari 312/66 V12	FL	2/22
	1967	Championship position: 19th= Wins: 0 Pole positions: 0 Fastest laps: 0 Points scored: 1						
6	DUTCH GP	Zandvoort	22	Scuderia Ferrari SpA SEFAC	F	3.0 Ferrari 312/67 V12	1 lap behind	15/17
nc	BELGIAN GP	Spa	2	Scuderia Ferrari SpA SEFAC	F	3.0 Ferrari 312/67 V12	pit stop-hydraulic pipe/-4 laps	9/18
ret	ITALIAN GP	Monza	10	Anglo American Racers	G	3.0 Eagle T1G-Weslake V12	engine	10/18
	1968	Championship position: 13th= Wins: 0 Pole positions: 0 Fastest laps: 0 Points scored: 6						
ret	SOUTH AFRICAN GP	Kyalami	15	Cooper Car Co	F	3.0 Cooper T86-Maserati V12	broken brake line-accident	15/23
4	SPANISH GP	Jarama	15	Cooper Car Co	F	3.0 Cooper T86B-BRM V12	1 lap behind	12/14
4	MONACO GP	Monte Carlo	6	Cooper Car Co	F	3.0 Cooper T86B-BRM V12	pit stop/wheel change/-4 laps	=17/18

GP Starts: 10   GP Wins: 1   Pole positions: 0   Fastest laps: 1   Points: 17

LUDOVICO SCARFIOTTI

A great all-rounder who wasn't out of the top drawer, Scarfiotti nevertheless had his moment of glory in 1966, taking the 3-litre Ferrari to a momentous victory in front of the rapturous 'tifosi' at Monza on a glorious September afternoon. It was the zenith of a career that had started a decade earlier in a far more modest Fiat 1100 saloon. Winning his class in the Mille Miglia in 1956 and 1957, Scarfiotti originally raced just for fun – as he could afford to, being related to the wealthy Agnelli family who, of course, controlled the FIAT empire. He tested a works Ferrari sports car as early as 1958, but had to be content with campaigning a little 2-litre OSCA, taking second place in the Naples GP at Posillipo.

Ludovico finally joined the Scuderia's sports car team in 1960, sharing the fourth-place car with Cabianca and Mairesse in the Targa Florio. His first real success came in 1962 when he took the European mountain-climb championship in Ferrari's 2-litre V6 car, and this confirmed his place in the works team for 1963 alongside Surtees and Mairesse, when the rest of the Scuderia's drivers were being shown the door. His early-season sports car outings were encouraging. Sharing the 250P with Surtees, he won at Sebring and he later won at Le Mans, this time with Bandini. Impressed with his efforts, Ferrari rewarded him with his Grand Prix debut at Zandvoort and after a steady drive he took sixth place, enough to earn another opportunity at Reims. Unfortunately a practice crash in which he hit a telegraph pole left him with leg injuries serious enough not only to keep him out for some while but also to prompt him to announce his retirement from F1.

Scarfiotti was back in action in 1964, winning the Nürburgring 1000 Km with Vaccarella in the works Ferrari 275P and finishing second at Mosport in the 330P. Contrary to his earlier intentions, he was back in a Ferrari single-seater at Monza, but was mostly used by the Scuderia in sports cars the following year. Driving the lovely 1.6-litre Ferrari Dino, Ludovico took his second mountain-climb championship, and he was also second in the Monza 1000 Km.

The 1966 season was his best, but only courtesy of his famous Italian GP victory, as little else was achieved bar a second place in the Nürburgring 1000 Km. Scarfiotti was one of four drivers (Bandini, Parkes and newcomer Amon were the others) representing Ferrari in 1967, and the season started well with second places with the Ferrari P4 sports car at Daytona and in the Monza 1000 Km. Then came a fifth place in the Race of Champions and a staged dead-heat with Parkes to win the Syracuse GP before the first disaster. Bandini was killed at Monaco and soon Parkes – with whom Scarfiotti had just taken a second place at Le Mans – was badly injured at Spa. 'Lulu' seemed to lose heart and after a dispute with the management took his leave, appearing in Dan Gurney's Eagle at Monza.

For 1968 Scarfiotti found himself a berth at Cooper. The cars were slow but reliable, and he managed to pick up a couple of fourth-place finishes. Although he had forsaken Ferrari, his sports car talents were not about to be allowed to go to waste, and he signed for Porsche to race their prototypes. A second place in the BOAC 500 at Brands was to be his best placing for the Stuttgart firm, for while practising for the Rossfeld hill-climb in June 1968 he inexplicably ran straight on at a corner and crashed into a clump of trees with fatal consequences.

GIORGIO SCARLATTI

A solid and dependable but not too quick Italian sports car driver, Scarlatti raced a Maserati T200S in 1954-55, his best finishes being a second in class in the Tour of Sicily, and third places at Bari and Caserta. At this time he bought a Ferrari 500 to race in Formula 1, but after a fourth place in the 1956 Naples GP he proved to be hopelessly slow in his efforts to qualify at Monaco.

For 1957, Giorgio aligned himself with the works Maserati team and shared a point with Schell for their fifth place in the Italian GP, taking another fifth at the Modena GP and sixth at the Pescara GP, although he was ten minutes behind the winner.

After the works team had closed their doors, Scarlatti soldiered on with the 250F, sharing fourth place in the Buenos Aires City GP after Behra took over the car, and earned third place (and a class win) in the Targa Florio when he partnered Behra in the Frenchman's Porsche.

In 1959, Giorgio again raced the outdated Maserati, but disappointed when entrusted with the third works Cooper at Monza in place of the injured Masten Gregory.

He continued to race various ill-prepared single-seaters without success until 1961, though he did a little better in sports cars, winning that year's Pescara 4 Hours with a young Lorenzo Bandini in a Ferrari 246 V6.

SCARLATTI, Giorgio (I) b 2/10/1921, Rome – d 1992

	1956	Championship position: Unplaced						
	Race	Circuit	No	Entrant	Tyres	Car/Engine	Comment	Q Pos/Entries
dnq	MONACO GP	Monte Carlo	36	Giorgio Scarlatti	P	2.0 Ferrari 500 4		17/19
ret	GERMAN GP	Nürburgring	14	Scuderia Centro Sud	P	2.0 Ferrari 500 4	engine	17/21
	1957	Championship position: 16th= Wins: 0 Pole positions: 0 Fastest laps: 0 Points scored: 1						
ret*	MONACO GP	Monte Carlo	34	Officine Alfieri Maserati	P	2.5 Maserati 250F 6	*Schell took over/oil pressure	14/21
10	GERMAN GP	Nürburgring	4	Officine Alfieri Maserati	P	2.5 Maserati 250F 6	1 lap behind	13/24
6	PESCARA GP	Pescara	8	Officine Alfieri Maserati	P	2.5 Maserati 250F 6	1 lap behind	10/16
5*	ITALIAN GP	Monza	8	Officine Alfieri Maserati	P	2.5 Maserati 250F 6	* Schell took over car/-3 laps	12/19
	1958	Championship position: Unplaced						
ret	MONACO GP	Monte Carlo	46	Giorgio Scarlatti	P	2.5 Maserati 250F 6	engine-con rod	14/28
ret	DUTCH GP	Zandvoort	10	Giorgio Scarlatti	P	2.5 Maserati 250F 6	rear axle	16/17
	1959	Championship position: Unplaced						
dnq	MONACO GP	Monte Carlo	54	Scuderia Ugolini	D	2.5 Maserati 250F 6		18/24
8*	FRENCH GP	Reims	40	Scuderia Ugolini	D	2.5 Maserati 250F 6	*8th car dsq/9 laps behind	21/22
12	ITALIAN GP	Monza	10	Cooper Car Co	D	2.5 Cooper T51-Climax 4	4 laps behind	12/21
	1960	Championship position: Unplaced						
ret	ARGENTINE GP	Buenos Aires	8	Giorgio Scarlatti	D	2.5 Maserati 250F 6	overheating	18/22
dnq	MONACO GP	Monte Carlo	30	Scuderia Castellotti	D	2.5 Cooper T51-Ferrari 4		22/24
ret	ITALIAN GP	Monza	36	Scuderia Castellotti	D	2.5 Cooper T51-Maserati 4	throttle cable	5/16
	1961	Championship position: Unplaced						
ret	FRENCH GP	Reims	34	Scuderia Serenissima	D	1.5 de Tomaso F1 001-OSCA 4	engine	– / –
dns	"	"	32	Scuderia Serenissima	D	1.5 Cooper T51-Maserati 4	car raced by Trintignant	26/26

GP Starts: 12   GP Wins: 0   Pole positions: 0   Fastest laps: 0   Points: 1

IAN SCHECKTER

Ian, the elder brother of World Champion Jody, followed his brother to Europe in mid-1972 after winning the domestic Formula Ford series with a Merlyn. After a brief stay, during which he proved his competitiveness, Scheckter returned to South Africa to contest the national championship in a Team Gunston Chevron and attempt to break Dave Charlton's long-held stranglehold on the title.

Ian made his Grand Prix debut at Kyalami in 1974 and had a handful of Formula 1 outings over the next couple of years, but it was only after he had finally clinched the South African championship (by now for Formula Atlantic cars) in 1976 that he took up the offer of a full-time Grand Prix drive with March in 1977.

The season was an utter shambles for the bewildered Scheckter, who managed just two finishes from 13 starts, and his Formula 1 career was buried. He returned home to renew his successful association with Lexington Racing, winning the Atlantic tiles in 1977-78 and 1978-79, before switching to saloon car racing with BMW South Africa's 535i. His son Jaki now follows in the family footsteps racing in junior single-seaters.

SCHECKTER, Ian (ZA) b 22/8/1947, East London

	1974	Championship position: Unplaced							
	Race	Circuit	No	Entrant	Tyres	Car/Engine		Comment	Q Pos/Entries
13	SOUTH AFRICAN GP	Kyalami	29	Team Gunston	G	3.0 Lotus 72E-Cosworth V8		2 laps behind	22/27
dnq	AUSTRIAN GP	Österreichring	31	Hesketh Racing	F	3.0 Hesketh 308-Cosworth V8			26/31
	1975	Championship position: Unplaced							
ret	SOUTH AFRICAN GP	Kyalami	32	Lexington Racing	G	3.0 Tyrrell 007-Cosworth V8		spun off	17/28
ret	SWEDISH GP	Anderstorp	21	Frank Williams Racing Cars	G	3.0 Williams FW04-Cosworth V8		burst tyre/spun off	20/26
12	DUTCH GP	Zandvoort	20	Frank Williams Racing Cars	G	3.0 Williams FW03-Cosworth V8		5 laps behind	19/25
	1976	Championship position: Unplaced							
ret	SOUTH AFRICAN GP	Kyalami	15	Lexington Racing	G	3.0 Tyrrell 007-Cosworth V8		collision with Leclère	16/25
	1977	Championship position: Unplaced							
ret	ARGENTINE GP	Buenos Aires	10	Team Rothmans International	G	3.0 March 761B-Cosworth V8		battery terminal	17/21
ret	BRAZILIAN GP	Interlagos	10	Team Rothmans International	G	3.0 March 761B-Cosworth V8		transmission	17/22
11	SPANISH GP	Jarama	10	Team Rothmans International	G	3.0 March 761B-Cosworth V8		3 laps behind	17/31
dnq	MONACO GP	Monte Carlo	10	Team Rothmans International	G	3.0 March 761B-Cosworth V8		injured in practice accident	26/26
ret	BELGIAN GP	Zolder	10	Team Rothmans International	G	3.0 March 761B-Cosworth V8		spun off	21/32
dns	"	"	10	Team Rothmans International	G	3.0 March 771-Cosworth V8		practice only	– / –
ret	SWEDISH GP	Anderstorp	10	Team Rothmans International	G	3.0 March 761B-Cosworth V8		driveshaft c.v. joint	21/31
nc	FRENCH GP	Dijon	10	Team Rothmans International	G	3.0 March 761B-Cosworth V8		11 laps behind	20/30
ret	BRITISH GP	Silverstone	10	Team Rothmans International	G	3.0 March 761B-Cosworth V8		spun off	24/30
ret	GERMAN GP	Hockenheim	10	Team Rothmans International	G	3.0 March 761B-Cosworth V8		clutch	18/30
ret	AUSTRIAN GP	Österreichring	10	Team Rothmans International	G	3.0 March 761B-Cosworth V8		spun off	24/30
10	DUTCH GP	Zandvoort	10	Team Rothmans International	G	3.0 March 771-Cosworth V8		2 laps behind	25/34
ret	ITALIAN GP	Monza	10	Team Rothmans International	G	3.0 March 771-Cosworth V8		transmission	17/34
ret	US GP EAST	Watkins Glen	10	Team Rothmans International	G	3.0 March 771-Cosworth V8		crashed at chicane	21/34
ret	CANADIAN GP	Mosport Park	10	Team Rothmans International	G	3.0 March 771-Cosworth V8		engine	18/27

GP Starts: 18   GP Wins: 0   Pole positions: 0   Fastest laps: 0   Points: 0

JODY SCHECKTER

WORLD CHAMPION: 1979

JODY SCHECKTER

Jody was a prodigy who burst upon the motor racing scene in much the same manner as Ricardo Rodriguez had done a decade earlier. Immensely talented, brave almost to the point of being foolhardy and blindingly quick in any car he chose to drive, Jody somehow managed to avoid the 'Grim Reaper' in those wild early days to become a dry-humoured, somewhat world-weary elder statesman who had got the risks under control and knew his destiny.

Jody started his racing early, running a go-kart at 12 before moving on to motor cycles and then saloons by the age of 18. His home-built Renault proved to be tremendously successful in the youngster's hands, and he scored numerous victories before his racing took a back seat to a spell of National Service. Towards the end of 1970, Team Lawson entrusted their Mazda to the youngster in the Springbok series, and he finished fifth in the Bulawayo 3 Hours and won his class in the Goldfields 9 Hours. His immediate ambition, though, was to do well in the Formula Ford Sunshine series and thus win the 'Driver to Europe' prize that went with it. Sure enough, young Jody in his Lola T200 Formula Ford did exactly that and was on his way to England early in 1971.

The headstrong Scheckter got himself into a Merlyn at Brands, and sensationally led the race until he spun. This set the pattern for his short Formula Ford career. Spin or win seemed to be the order of the day until, after a few races, he felt he needed the tougher challenge of Formula 3, jumping into the deep end with an EMC and then a works Merlyn. By the end

of the year he was winning at this level, in addition to hustling a Ford Escort Mexico indecently quickly. McLaren were first in with their pen, and Jody was signed to race for their Formula 2 team in 1972.

Generally his luck was out with the McLaren M21, but he did manage one win in the Greater London Trophy at Crystal Palace. As a bonus the team gave him his Grand Prix debut at Watkins Glen, where he kept the lid on things and finished a creditable ninth. McLaren kept him on for the 1973 season, though with Revson and Hulme on board they didn't really have room to accommodate him. Perhaps they wished they hadn't when his 1973 Grand Prix season turned into a succession of accidents, the most serious incident being his infamous spin at the beginning of the British GP which not only halted the race but wiped out a good proportion of the field. Ever the paradox at this stage of his career, Jody also raced for Sid Taylor in America, winning the L & M F5000 series in a Trojan, and competed in Can-Am with a Porsche 917 – completely without mishap.

With McLaren unable to offer Jody a firm deal for 1974, Ken Tyrrell stepped in and signed the South African to head his team, newly shorn of the retired Jackie Stewart and deceased François Cevert. It was to prove an inspired choice as the still relatively inexperienced charger took two Grand Prix wins and finished third in the championship table. Jody found it hard to maintain his scintillating form the following season, but he did

Jody left Tyrrell for the newly created Walter Wolf Racing team in 1977 and scored a sensational first-race win with the Wolf WR1 in Argentina.

have the wonderful bonus of winning the South African GP. In 1976 Tyrrell launched the bizarre but effective six-wheel P34 car. In Scheckter's hands this became a serious machine, Jody taking it to a historic victory in Sweden and racking up the points regularly elsewhere to finish a creditable third in the World Championship behind Hunt and Lauda. It was also a year when Scheckter achieved another ambition by wininng the Wynn's 1000 Km at Kyalami in a BMW with Nilsson and Grohs.

Out of sync with the Tyrrell philosophy, Jody took a big gamble in joining Wolf for 1977, but it paid off immediately when he gave the restructured team a winning debut in the Argentine GP. The car wasn't consistently good at every circuit, but Jody never let that become a problem. Two more wins were to follow and second place to Lauda in the championship was his reward. His 1978 season was not so productive, the new Wolf chassis being far more troublesome than the relatively straightforward machine of the previous year. An offer from Ferrari for 1979 was too good to refuse, and the wild man of the early days was now but a distant memory. Indeed, incredible though it may seem, he was now driving almost conservatively. Certainly he had everything weighed up and his performances were the model of economy, Scheckter doing just enough and no more, but he was able to clinch the World Championship in style, with a win at Monza.

His ambition realised, Jody planned just one more year. As it happened it was easily the worst of his career, leaving the South African frustrated and a little bemused. The ultimate humiliation came at Montreal where he failed to qualify; he knew it was just one of those things, that circumstances had conspired against him, but it hurt his pride none the less. Scheckter came in with a bang but went out with a whimper, but he walked away unhurt and there were a few people who didn't believe that possible in 1973.

Ever his own man, after retiring Jody settled in the United States and began a new life without even mentioning his achievements. Most of his new acquaintants knew nothing of Scheckter the Formula 1 World Champion, and that's exactly the way he wanted it as he built a highly successful business. However, Jody has now returned to Europe and over the past couple of years he has been much in evidence at races once more. His sons, Thomas and Toby, are making names for themselves in the junior single-seater formulae and 'dad' regularly casts his paternal eye over their upward progress.

SCHECKTER, Jody (ZA) b 29/1/1950, East London

	1972			Championship position: Unplaced				
	Race	Circuit	No	Entrant	Tyres	Car/Engine	Comment	Q Pos/Entries
9	US GP	Watkins Glen	21	Yardley Team McLaren	G	3.0 McLaren M19A-Cosworth V8	1 lap behind	8/32

	1973			Championship position: Unplaced				
9/ret	SOUTH AFRICAN GP	Kyalami	7	Yardley Team McLaren	G	3.0 McLaren M19C-Cosworth V8	engine/4 laps behind	3/25
ret	FRENCH GP	Paul Ricard	8	Yardley Team McLaren	G	3.0 McLaren M23-Cosworth V8	collision-Fittipaldi/suspension	2/25
ret/dns	BRITISH GP	Silverstone	30	Yardley Team McLaren	G	3.0 McLaren M23-Cosworth V8	caused multiple accident 1st start	6/29
ret	CANADIAN GP	Mosport Park	0	Yardley Team McLaren	G	3.0 McLaren M23-Cosworth V8	accident with Cevert	3/26
ret	US GP	Watkins Glen	0	Yardley Team McLaren	G	3.0 McLaren M23-Cosworth V8	suspension	11/28

	1974			Championship position: 3rd Wins: 2 Pole positions: 0 Fastest laps: 2 Points scored: 45				
ret	ARGENTINE GP	Buenos Aires	3	Elf Team Tyrrell	G	3.0 Tyrrell 006-Cosworth V8	cylinder head gasket	12/26
13	BRAZILIAN GP	Interlagos	3	Elf Team Tyrrell	G	3.0 Tyrrell 006-Cosworth V8	1 lap behind	14/25
8	SOUTH AFRICAN GP	Kyalami	3	Elf Team Tyrrell	G	3.0 Tyrrell 006-Cosworth V8		8/27
5	SPANISH GP	Jarama	3	Elf Team Tyrrell	G	3.0 Tyrrell 007-Cosworth V8	2 laps behind	– / –
dns	"	"	3	Elf Team Tyrrell	G	3.0 Tyrrell 006-Cosworth V8	brake problems-set grid time	9/28
3	BELGIAN GP	Nivelles	3	Elf Team Tyrrell	G	3.0 Tyrrell 007-Cosworth V8		2/32
2	MONACO GP	Monte Carlo	3	Elf Team Tyrrell	G	3.0 Tyrrell 007-Cosworth V8		=4/28
1	SWEDISH GP	Anderstorp	3	Elf Team Tyrrell	G	3.0 Tyrrell 007-Cosworth V8		2/28
5	DUTCH GP	Zandvoort	3	Elf Team Tyrrell	G	3.0 Tyrrell 007-Cosworth V8		5/27
4	FRENCH GP	Dijon	3	Elf Team Tyrrell	G	3.0 Tyrrell 007-Cosworth V8	FL	7/30
1	BRITISH GP	Brands Hatch	3	Elf Team Tyrrell	G	3.0 Tyrrell 007-Cosworth V8		3/34
2	GERMAN GP	Nürburgring	3	Elf Team Tyrrell	G	3.0 Tyrrell 007-Cosworth V8	FL	4/32
ret	AUSTRIAN GP	Österreichring	3	Elf Team Tyrrell	G	3.0 Tyrrell 007-Cosworth V8	engine	5/31
3	ITALIAN GP	Monza	3	Elf Team Tyrrell	G	3.0 Tyrrell 007-Cosworth V8		12/31
ret	CANADIAN GP	Mosport Park	3	Elf Team Tyrrell	G	3.0 Tyrrell 007-Cosworth V8	brake failure/accident	3/30
ret	US GP	Watkins Glen	3	Elf Team Tyrrel	G	3.0 Tyrrell 007-Cosworth V8	fuel pipe	6/30

	1975			Championship position: 7th= Wins: 1 Pole positions: 0 Fastest laps: 0 Points scored: 20				
11	ARGENTINE GP	Buenos Aires	3	Elf Team Tyrrell	G	3.0 Tyrrell 007-Cosworth V8	1 lap behind	9/23
ret	BRAZILIAN GP	Interlagos	3	Elf Team Tyrrell	G	3.0 Tyrrell 007-Cosworth V8	oil tank	8/23
1	SOUTH AFRICAN GP	Kyalami	3	Elf Team Tyrrell	G	3.0 Tyrrell 007-Cosworth V8		3/28
ret	SPANISH GP	Montjuich Park	3	Elf Team Tyrrell	G	3.0 Tyrrell 007-Cosworth V8	engine	13/26
7	MONACO GP	Monte Carlo	3	Elf Team Tyrrell	G	3.0 Tyrrell 007-Cosworth V8	1 lap behind	7/26
2	BELGIAN GP	Zolder	3	Elf Team Tyrrell	G	3.0 Tyrrell 007-Cosworth V8		9/24
7	SWEDISH GP	Anderstorp	3	Elf Team Tyrrell	G	3.0 Tyrrell 007-Cosworth V8	1 lap behind	8/26
16/ret	DUTCH GP	Zandvoort	3	Elf Team Tyrrell	G	3.0 Tyrrell 007-Cosworth V8	engine/8 laps behind	4/25
9	FRENCH GP	Paul Ricard	3	Elf Team Tyrrell	G	3.0 Tyrrell 007-Cosworth V8		2/26
3/ret	BRITISH GP	Silverstone	3	Elf Team Tyrrell	G	3.0 Tyrrell 007-Cosworth V8	spun off in rainstorm/-1 lap	6/28
ret	GERMAN GP	Nürburgring	3	Elf Team Tyrrell	G	3.0 Tyrrell 007-Cosworth V8	tyre failure/accident	3/26
8	AUSTRIAN GP	Österreichring	3	Elf Team Tyrrell	G	3.0 Tyrrell 007-Cosworth V8	1 lap behind	10/30
8	ITALIAN GP	Monza	3	Elf Team Tyrrell	G	3.0 Tyrrell 007-Cosworth V8	1 lap behind	4/28
6	US GP	Watkins Glen	3	Elf Team Tyrrell	G	3.0 Tyrrell 007-Cosworth V8		10/24

	1976			Championship position: 3rd Wins: 1 Pole positions: 1 Fastest laps: 1 Points scored: 49				
5	BRAZILIAN GP	Interlgos	3	Elf Team Tyrrell	G	3.0 Tyrrell 007-Cosworth V8		13/22
4	SOUTH AFRICAN GP	Kyalami	3	Elf Team Tyrrell	G	3.0 Tyrrell 007-Cosworth V8		12/25
ret	US GP WEST	Long Beach	3	Elf Team Tyrrell	G	3.0 Tyrrell 007-Cosworth V8	suspension	11/27
ret	SPANISH GP	Jarama	3	Elf Team Tyrrell	G	3.0 Tyrrell 007-Cosworth V8	oil pump belt	14/30
4	BELGIAN GP	Zolder	3	Elf Team Tyrrell	G	3.0 Tyrrell P34-Cosworth V8		7/29
2	MONACO GP	Monte Carlo	3	Elf Team Tyrrell	G	3.0 Tyrrell P34-Cosworth V8		5/25
1	SWEDISH GP	Anderstorp	3	Elf Team Tyrrell	G	3.0 Tyrrell P34-Cosworth V8		1/27
6	FRENCH GP	Paul Ricard	3	Elf Team Tyrrell	G	3.0 Tyrrell P34-Cosworth V8		9/30
2*	BRITISH GP	Brands Hatch	3	Elf Team Tyrrell	G	3.0 Tyrrell P34-Cosworth V8	* 1st place car disqualified	8/30
dns	"	"	3	Elf Team Tyrrell	G	3.0 Tyrrell 007-Cosworth V8	practice only	– / –
2	GERMAN GP	Nürburgring	3	Elf Team Tyrrell	G	3.0 Tyrrell P34-Cosworth V8	FL	8/28
ret	AUSTRIAN GP	Österreichring	3	Elf Team Tyrrell	G	3.0 Tyrrell P34-Cosworth V8	suspension/accident	10/25
5	DUTCH GP	Zandvoort	3	Elf Team Tyrrell	G	3.0 Tyrrell P34-Cosworth V8		8/27
5	ITALIAN GP	Monza	3	Elf Team Tyrrell	G	3.0 Tyrrell P34-Cosworth V8		2/29
4	CANADIAN GP	Mosport Park	3	Elf Team Tyrrell	G	3.0 Tyrrell P34-Cosworth V8		7/27
2	US GP EAST	Watkins Glen	3	Elf Team Tyrrell	G	3.0 Tyrrell P34-Cosworth V8		2/27
ret	JAPANESE GP	Mount Fuji	3	Elf Team Tyrrell	G	3.0 Tyrrell P34-Cosworth V8	overheating	5/27

It was the switch to Ferrari that brought Scheckter his World Championship in 1979. *Right:* He leads team-mate Gilles Villeneuve on his way to victory at Monaco in the Ferrari 312T4.

1977

Championship position: 2nd   Wins: 3   Pole positions: 1   Fastest laps: 2   Points scored: 55

1	ARGENTINE GP	Buenos Aires	20	Walter Wolf Racing	G	3.0 Wolf WR1-Cosworth V8		11/21
ret	BRAZILIAN GP	Interlagos	20	Walter Wolf Racing	G	3.0 Wolf WR1-Cosworth V8	engine	15/22
2	SOUTH AFRICAN GP	Kyalami	20	Walter Wolf Racing	G	3.0 Wolf WR1-Cosworth V8		5/23
dns	"	"	20	Walter Wolf Racing	G	3.0 Wolf WR2-Cosworth V8	practice only	– /–
3	US GP WEST	Long Beach	20	Walter Wolf Racing	G	3.0 Wolf WR2-Cosworth V8	puncture when 1st	3/22
3	SPANISH GP	Jarama	20	Walter Wolf Racing	G	3.0 Wolf WR2-Cosworth V8		5/31
1	MONACO GP	Monte Carlo	20	Walter Wolf Racing	G	3.0 Wolf WR1-Cosworth V8	FL	2/26
dns	"	"	20	Walter Wolf Racing	G	3.0 Wolf WR3-Cosworth V8	practice only	– /–
ret	BELGIAN GP	Zolder	20	Walter Wolf Racing	G	3.0 Wolf WR3-Cosworth V8	engine	4/32
dns	"	"	20	Walter Wolf Racing	G	3.0 Wolf WR2-Cosworth V8	practice only	– /–
ret	SWEDISH GP	Anderstorp	20	Walter Wolf Racing	G	3.0 Wolf WR1-Cosworth V8	hit Watson	4/31
dns	"	"	20	Walter Wolf Racing	G	3.0 Wolf WR3-Cosworth V8	practice only	– /–
ret	FRENCH GP	Dijon	20	Walter Wolf Racing	G	3.0 Wolf WR3-Cosworth V8	hit by Regazzoni	8/30
ret	BRITISH GP	Silverstone	20	Walter Wolf Racing	G	3.0 Wolf WR1-Cosworth V8	engine	4/36
2	GERMAN GP	Hockenheim	20	Walter Wolf Racing	G	3.0 Wolf WR2-Cosworth V8		1/30
ret	AUSTRIAN GP	Österreichring	20	Walter Wolf Racing	G	3.0 Wolf WR3-Cosworth V8	spun off	8/30
dns	"	"	20	Walter Wolf Racing	G	3.0 Wolf WR1-Cosworth V8	practice only	– /–
3	DUTCH GP	Zandvoort	20	Walter Wolf Racing	G	3.0 Wolf WR2-Cosworth V8	1 lap behind	15/34
ret	ITALIAN GP	Monza	20	Walter Wolf Racing	G	3.0 Wolf WR1-Cosworth V8	engine	3/34
3	US GP EAST	Watkins Glen	20	Walter Wolf Racing	G	3.0 Wolf WR2-Cosworth V8		9/27
1	CANADIAN GP	Mosport Park	20	Walter Wolf Racing	G	3.0 Wolf WR1-Cosworth V8		9/27
10	JAPANESE GP	Mount Fuji	20	Walter Wolf Racing	G	3.0 Wolf WR3-Cosworth V8	pit stop/tyres/FL/-2 laps	6/23

1978

Championship position: 7th   Wins: 0   Pole positions: 0   Fastest laps: 0   Points scored: 24

10	ARGENTINE GP	Buenos Aires	20	Walter Wolf Racing	G	3.0 Wolf WR4-Cosworth V8		– /–
dns	"	"	20	Walter Wolf Racing	G	3.0 Wolf WR1-Cosworth V8	set grid time in car	15/26
ret	BRAZILIAN GP	Rio	20	Walter Wolf Racing	G	3.0 Wolf WR1-Cosworth V8	collision-Tambay/suspension	12/28
ret	SOUTH AFRICAN GP	Kyalami	20	Walter Wolf Racing	G	3.0 Wolf WR1-Cosworth V8	engine cut out/accident	5/30
dns	"	"	20	Walter Wolf Racing	G	3.0 Wolf WR3-Cosworth V8	practice only	– /–
ret	US GP WEST	Long Beach	20	Walter Wolf Racing	G	3.0 Wolf WR3-Cosworth V8	hit by Tambay	10/30
dns	"	"	20	Walter Wolf Racing	G	3.0 Wolf WR1-Cosworth V8	practice only	– /–
3	MONACO GP	Monte Carlo	20	Walter Wolf Racing	G	3.0 Wolf WR1-Cosworth V8		9/30
dns	"	"	20	Walter Wolf Racing	G	3.0 Wolf WR5-Cosworth V8	practice only	– /–
ret	BELGIAN GP	Zolder	20	Walter Wolf Racing	G	3.0 Wolf WR1-Cosworth V8	spun off	5/30
4	SPANISH GP	Jarama	20	Walter Wolf Racing	G	3.0 Wolf WR5-Cosworth V8		=9/29
ret	SWEDISH GP	Anderstorp	20	Walter Wolf Racing	G	3.0 Wolf WR5-Cosworth V8	overheating	6/27
6	FRENCH GP	Paul Ricard	20	Walter Wolf Racing	G	3.0 Wolf WR5-Cosworth V8		7/29
ret	BRITISH GP	Brands Hatch	20	Walter Wolf Racing	G	3.0 Wolf WR5-Cosworth V8	gearbox	3/30
dns	"	"	20	Walter Wolf Racing	G	3.0 Wolf WR6-Cosworth V8	practice only	– /–
2	GERMAN GP	Hockenheim	20	Walter Wolf Racing	G	3.0 Wolf WR5-Cosworth V8		4/30
ret	AUSTRIAN GP	Österreichring	20	Walter Wolf Racing	G	3.0 Wolf WR5-Cosworth V8	spun off in first part of race	7/31
12	DUTCH GP	Zandvoort	20	Walter Wolf Racing	G	3.0 Wolf WR6-Cosworth V8	handling problems/-2 laps	15/33
dns	"	"	20	Walter Wolf Racing	G	3.0 Wolf WR5-Cosworth V8	practice only	– /–
12	ITALIAN GP	Monza	20	Walter Wolf Racing	G	3.0 Wolf WR5-Cosworth V8	did not practice this car/-1 lap	– /–
dns	"	"	20	Walter Wolf Racing	G	3.0 Wolf WR6-Cosworth V8	car damaged at first start	9/32
3	US GP EAST	Watkins Glen	20	Walter Wolf Racing	G	3.0 Wolf WR6-Cosworth V8		11/27
2	CANADIAN GP	Montreal	20	Walter Wolf Racing	G	3.0 Wolf WR6-Cosworth V8		2/28

1979

Championship position: WORLD CHAMPION   Wins: 3   Pole positions: 1   Fastest laps: 0   Points scored: 60

ret/dns	ARGENTINE GP	Buenos Aires	11	Scuderia Ferrari SpA SEFAC	M	3.0 Ferrari 312T3 F12	hurt wrist in first start	5/26
6	BRAZILIAN GP	Interlagos	11	Scuderia Ferrari SpA SEFAC	M	3.0 Ferrari 312T3 F12	1 lap behind	6/26
2	SOUTH AFRICAN GP	Kyalami	11	Scuderia Ferrari SpA SEFAC	M	3.0 Ferrari 312T4 F12	pit stop/tyres when 1st	2/26
2	US GP WEST	Long Beach	11	Scuderia Ferrari SpA SEFAC	M	3.0 Ferrari 312T4 F12		3/26
4	SPANISH GP	Jarama	11	Scuderia Ferrari SpA SEFAC	M	3.0 Ferrari 312T4 F12		5/27
1	BELGIAN GP	Zolder	11	Scuderia Ferrari SpA SEFAC	M	3.0 Ferrari 312T4 F12		=6/28
1	MONACO GP	Monte Carlo	11	Scuderia Ferrari SpA SEFAC	M	3.0 Ferrari 312T4 F12		1/25
7	FRENCH GP	Dijon	11	Scuderia Ferrari SpA SEFAC	M	3.0 Ferrari 312T4 F12	pit stop/tyres/1 lap behind	5/27
5	BRITISH GP	Silverstone	11	Scuderia Ferrari SpA SEFAC	M	3.0 Ferrari 312T4 F12	1 lap behind	11/26
4	GERMAN GP	Hockenheim	11	Scuderia Ferrari SpA SEFAC	M	3.0 Ferrari 312T4 F12		5/26
4	AUSTRIAN GP	Österreichring	11	Scuderia Ferrari SpA SEFAC	M	3.0 Ferrari 312T4 F12		9/26
2	DUTCH GP	Zandvoort	11	Scuderia Ferrari SpA SEFAC	M	3.0 Ferrari 312T4 F12		5/26
1	ITALIAN GP	Monza	11	Scuderia Ferrari SpA SEFAC	M	3.0 Ferrari 312T4 F12		3/28
4	CANADIAN GP	Montreal	11	Scuderia Ferrari SpA SEFAC	M	3.0 Ferrari 312T4 F12	pit stop/tyres/1 lap behind	9/29
ret	US GP EAST	Watkins Glen	11	Scuderia Ferrari SpA SEFAC	M	3.0 Ferrari 312T4 F12	tyre failure/suspension	16/30

1980

Championship position: 19th   Wins: 0   Pole positions: 0   Fastest laps: 0   Points scored: 2

ret	ARGENTINE GP	Buenos Aires	1	Scuderia Ferrari SpA SEFAC	M	3.0 Ferrari 312T5 F12	engine	11/28
ret	BRAZILIAN GP	Interlagos	1	Scuderia Ferrari SpA SEFAC	M	3.0 Ferrari 312T5 F12	engine	8/28
ret	SOUTH AFRICAN GP	Kyalami	1	Scuderia Ferrari SpA SEFAC	M	3.0 Ferrari 312T5 F12	engine/electrics	9/28
5	US GP WEST	Long Beach	1	Scuderia Ferrari SpA SEFAC	M	3.0 Ferrari 312T5 F12	pit stop/tyres/1 lap behind	16/27
8	BELGIAN GP	Zolder	1	Scuderia Ferrari SpA SEFAC	M	3.0 Ferrari 312T5 F12	2 laps behind	14/27
ret	MONACO GP	Monte Carlo	1	Scuderia Ferrari SpA SEFAC	M	3.0 Ferrari 312T5 F12	handling	17/27
12	FRENCH GP	Paul Ricard	1	Scuderia Ferrari SpA SEFAC	M	3.0 Ferrari 312T5 F12	2 pit stops/tyres	19/27
10	BRITISH GP	Brands Hatch	1	Scuderia Ferrari SpA SEFAC	M	3.0 Ferrari 312T5 F12	pit stop/nose cone/-3 laps	23/26
13	GERMAN GP	Hockenheim	1	Scuderia Ferrari SpA SEFAC	M	3.0 Ferrari 312T5 F12	pit stop/tyres/1 lap behind	21/26
13	AUSTRIAN GP	Österreichring	1	Scuderia Ferrari SpA SEFAC	M	3.0 Ferrari 312T5 F12	pit stop/tyres/1 lap behind	22/25
9	DUTCH GP	Zandvoort	1	Scuderia Ferrari SpA SEFAC	M	3.0 Ferrari 312T5 F12	2 pit stops/tyres/-1 lap	12/28
8	ITALIAN GP	Imola	1	Scuderia Ferrari SpA SEFAC	M	3.0 Ferrari 312T5 F12	1 lap behind	16/28
dnq	CANADIAN GP	Montreal	1	Scuderia Ferrari SpA SEFAC	M	3.0 Ferrari 312T5 F12		26/28
11	US GP EAST	Watkins Glen	1	Scuderia Ferrari SpA SEFAC	M	3.0 Ferrari 312T5 F12	3 laps behind	23/27

GP Starts: 110 (112)   GP Wins: 10   Pole positions: 3   Fastest laps: 5   Points: 255

HARRY SCHELL

Born in Paris but of American parents, Harry O'Reilly Schell was a fun-loving extrovert who was one of the great characters of the fifties motor racing scene. His childhood during the thirties was filled by racing, for his father Laury was the patron of Ecurie Bleue, a team which raced Delahayes and Talbots. His mother Lucy took over the running of the team following the death of her husband in a road accident and ran René Dreyfus at Indianapolis just before the war. Young Harry was on that trip, and resolved to race himself once old enough.

The war saw him serving in the US military in Finland, and by the late forties he was taking his first steps in racing. In 1949 he managed a second place with a Talbot in the Coupe du Salon at Montlhéry but it was the following year, when he raced a Cooper-JAP, that brought him success. Schell handled the little car with great verve, frequently embarrassing Formula 2 opposition. At the Circuit du Lac, in Aix-les-Bains, he succeeded in beating the works Ferrari in his heat and comfortably led the final before being forced into retirement. He managed to gain an entry for the Monaco GP that year but was eliminated in the first-lap multiple crash, but at Bremgarten he enjoyed his first taste of a real Grand Prix machine, taking a Talbot into eighth place.

Schell mainly raced Maseratis entered by Ecurie Platé in 1951 and 1952, but started to gain solid results only when he joined forces with Simca Gordini. A second place in the Cadours GP of 1952 encouraged both parties to continue together the following year, when Harry was out of luck in the championship Grands Prix, but took a string of good finishes in the French championship rounds. Schell ran his own Maserati A6GCM in 1954, taking second place at Castelfusano and thirds at Pescara and Aintree, but by the end-of-season Spanish GP he had his own Maserati 250F and caused something of a stir as he drove off into the distance at the start, only losing the lead to Fangio after a spin and eventually retiring with transmission failure. There was talk of the American running on half-tanks to break up the opposition, but he had certainly made his mark, for both Vanwall and Ferrari used his services in 1955, and he won some minor events for Tony Vandervell. Schell showed the green machines' startling potential in 1956 when he put on a marvellous show at Reims, snapping at the heels of the works Ferraris, and scored a win in the Caen GP before taking his leave to join the works Maserati team in 1957.

Harry fulfilled a useful subordinate role to Fangio, recording a number of good results, including a fine if distant third place at Pescara. He also took second place at Pau and third at Modena before arranging to join BRM for the 1958 and 1959 seasons. Harry proved an excellent acquisition for the Bourne team, his second place at Zandvoort being the closest the American would ever get to that elusive Grand Prix win. At the end of the 1959 season he purchased a Cooper-Climax which he raced under the Ecurie Bleue banner as a privateer. He also raced the car at the beginning of 1960 before joining the Yeoman Credit team. It was while practising one of their cars for the International Trophy in the wet at Silverstone that he was to lose his life, crashing after the Cooper got away from him on one of the circuit's fast bends. Harry was an immensely popular character, and his death was a great loss to the racing scene as it moved into a new era.

SCHELL, Harry (F/USA) b 29/6/1921, Paris, France – d 13/5/1960, Silverstone Circuit, Northamptonshire, England

1950 — Championship position: Unplaced

	Race	Circuit	No	Entrant	Tyres	Car/Engine	Comment	Q Pos/Entries
ret	MONACO GP	Monte Carlo	8	Horschell Racing Corp	D	1.1 Cooper T12-JAP V2	multiple accident	20/21
8	SWISS GP	Bremgarten	44	Ecurie Bleue	D	4.5 Lago-Talbot T26C 6	3 laps behind	18/18

1951 — Championship position: Unplaced

| 12 | SWISS GP | Bremgarten | 32 | Enrico Platé | P | 1.5 s/c Maserati 4CLT/48 4 | 4 laps behind | 17/21 |
| ret | FRENCH GP | Reims | 20 | Enrico Platé | P | 1.5 s/c Maserati 4CLT/48 4 | overheating engine | 22/23 |

1952 — Championship position: Unplaced

ret	SWISS GP	Bremgarten	40	Enrico Platé	P	2.0 Maserati 4CLT/Platé 4	engine	18/21
ret	FRENCH GP	Rouen	18	Enrico Platé	P	2.0 Maserati 4CLT/Platé 4	gearbox	12/20
ret	"	"	16	Enrico Platé	P	2.0 Maserati 4CLT/Platé 4	took de Graffenried's car /brakes	– / –
17	BRITISH GP	Silverstone	33	Enrico Platé	P	2.0 Maserati 4CLT/Platé 4	7 laps behind	32/32

1953 — Championship position: Unplaced

7*	ARGENTINE GP	Buenos Aires	28	Equipe Gordini	E	2.0 Gordini Type 16 6	* took Trintignant' car/-6 laps	– / –
ret	DUTCH GP	Zandvoort	20	Equipe Gordini	E	2.0 Gordini Type 16 6	transmission	10/20
7	BELGIAN GP	Spa	20	Equipe Gordini	E	2.0 Gordini Type 16 6	3 laps behind	12/22
ret	FRENCH GP	Reims	6	Equipe Gordini	E	2.0 Gordini Type 16 6	engine	20/25
ret	BRITISH GP	Silverstone	28	Equipe Gordini	E	2.0 Gordini Type 16 6	magneto	9/29
ret	GERMAN GP	Nürburgring	11	Equipe Gordini	E	2.0 Gordini Type 16 6	head gasket	10/35
9	ITALIAN GP	Monza	38	Equipe Gordini	E	2.0 Gordini Type 16 6	5 laps behind	15/30

1954 — Championship position: Unplaced

6	ARGENTINE GP	Buenos Aires	28	Harry Schell	P	2.5 Maserati A6GCM/250F 6	3 laps behind	11/18
ret	FRENCH GP	Reims	48	Harry Schell	P	2.5 Maserati A6GCM/250F 6	fuel pump	21/22
12	BRITISH GP	Silverstone	3	Harry Schell	P	2.5 Maserati A6GCM/250F 6	7 laps behind	16/31
7	GERMAN GP	Nürburgring	15	Harry Schell	P	2.5 Maserati A6GCM/250F 6	1 lap behind	14/23
ret	SWISS GP	Bremgarten	34	Officine Alfieri Maserati	P	2.5 Maserati 250F 6	oil pump	13/16
ret	SPANISH GP	Pedralbes	24	Harry Schell	P	2.5 Maserati 250F 6	transmission-rear axle	4/22

1955 — Championship position: Unplaced

6*	ARGENTINE GP	Buenos Aires	28	Officine Alfieri Maserati	P	2.5 Maserati 250F 6	* Behra took over/- 5 laps	7/22
7*	"	"	22	Officine Alfieri Maserati	P	2.5 Maserati 250F 6	* Mantovani/Musso/-13 laps	– / –
ret*	"	"	26	Officine Alfieri Maserati	P	2.5 Maserati 250F 6	Bucci/Menditéguy/* fuel starvation	– / –
ret	MONACO GP	Monte Carlo	46	Scuderia Ferrari	E	2.5 Ferrari 555 4	engine	18/22
dns	BELGIAN GP	Spa	4	Scuderia Ferrari	E	2.5 Ferrari 555 4	Trintignant drove car	– / –
ret	BRITISH GP	Aintree	30	Vandervell Products Ltd	P	2.5 Vanwall 4	accelerator	7/25
nc*	"	"	28	Vandervell Products Ltd	P	2.5 Vanwall 4	took Wharton's car/-18 laps	– / –
ret	ITALIAN GP	Monza	42	Vandervell Products Ltd	P	2.5 Vanwall 4	suspension	13/22

1956 — Championship position: 12th= Wins: 0 Pole positions: 0 Fastest laps: 0 Points scored: 3

ret	MONACO GP	Monte Carlo	16	Vandervell Products Ltd	P	2.5 Vanwall 4	spun off avoiding Fangio	5/19
4	BELGIAN GP	Spa	10	Vandervell Products Ltd	P	2.5 Vanwall 4	1 lap behind	6/16
ret	FRENCH GP	Reims	22	Vandervell Products Ltd	P	2.5 Vanwall 4	engine	4/20
10*	"	"	24	Vandervell Products Ltd	P	2.5 Vanwall 4	* took Hawthorn's car/-5 laps	– / –
ret	BRITISH GP	Silverstone	16	Vandervell Products Ltd	P	2.5 Vanwall 4	fuel pipe	5/28
ret	GERMAN GP	Nürburgring	12	Scuderia Centro Sud	P	2.5 Maserati 250F 6	overheating	12/21
ret	ITALIAN GP	Monza	18	Vandervell Products Ltd	P	2.5 Vanwall 4	transmission	10/26

1957 — Championship position: 7th= Wins: 0 Pole positions: 0 Fastest laps: 0 Points scored: 8

4	ARGENTINE GP	Buenos Aires	22	Scuderia Centro Sud	P	2.5 Maserati 250F 6	2 laps behind	9/16
ret*	MONACO GP	Monte Carlo	38	Officine Alfieri Maserati	P	2.5 Maserati 250F 6	king pins	8/21
ret	"	"	34	Officine Alfieri Maserati	P	2.5 Maserati 250F 6	* took Scarlatti's car/mechanical	– / –
6	FRENCH GP	Rouen	6	Officine Alfieri Maserati	P	2.5 Maserati 250F 6	7 laps behind	4/15
ret	BRITISH GP	Aintree	6	Officine Alfieri Maserati	P	2.5 Maserati 250F 6	water pump	7/19
7	GERMAN GP	Nürburgring	3	Officine Alfieri Maserati	P	2.5 Maserati 250F 6		6/24
3	PESCARA GP	Pescara	6	Officine Alfieri Maserati	P	2.5 Maserati 250F 6		5/16
ret	ITALIAN GP	Monza	4	Officine Alfieri Maserati	P	2.5 Maserati 250F 6	fuel pump	6/19
5*	"	"	8	Officine Alfieri Maserati	P	2.5 Maserati 250F 6	* took Scarlatti's car/-3 laps	– / –

1958 — Championship position: 5th= Wins: 0 Pole positions: 0 Fastest laps: 0 Points scored: 14

6	ARGENTINE GP	Buenos Aires	8	Joakim Bonnier	P	2.5 Maserati 250F 6	3 laps behind	8/10
5	MONACO GP	Monte Carlo	8	Owen Racing Organisation	D	2.5 BRM P25 4	9 laps behind	11/28
2	DUTCH GP	Zandvoort	15	Owen Racing Organisation	D	2.5 BRM P25 4		7/17
5	BELGIAN GP	Spa	10	Owen Racing Organisation	D	2.5 BRM P25 4	1 lap behind	7/20
ret	FRENCH GP	Reims	16	Owen Racing Organisation	D	2.5 BRM P25 4	overheating	3/21
5	BRITISH GP	Silverstone	20	Owen Racing Organisation	D	2.5 BRM P25 4		2/21
ret	GERMAN GP	Nürburgring	6	Owen Racing Organisation	D	2.5 BRM P25 4	brakes	8/26
6	PORTUGUESE GP	Oporto	10	Owen Racing Organisation	D	2.5 BRM P25 4	1 lap behind	7/15
ret	ITALIAN GP	Monza	10	Owen Racing Organisation	D	2.5 BRM P25 4	collision-Von Trips on grid	9/21
5	MOROCCAN GP	Casablanca	16	Owen Racing Organisation	D	2.5 BRM P25 4		10/25

1959 — Championship position: 10th= Wins: 0 Pole positions: 0 Fastest laps: 0 Points scored: 5

ret	MONACO GP	Monte Carlo	16	Owen Racing Organisation	D	2.5 BRM P25 4	crash-damaged radiator	9/24
ret	DUTCH GP	Zandvoort	6	Owen Racing Organisation	D	2.5 BRM P25 4	gearbox	6/15
7	FRENCH GP	Reims	6	Owen Racing Organisation	D	2.5 BRM P25 4	3 laps behind	9/22
4	BRITISH GP	Aintree	8	Owen Racing Organisation	D	2.5 BRM P25 4	1 lap behind	3/30
nc	GERMAN GP	AVUS	10	Owen Racing Organisation	D	2.5 BRM P25 4	5th heat 1/nc heat 2/-11 laps	8/16
5	PORTUGUESE GP	Monsanto	6	Owen Racing Organisation	D	2.5 BRM P25 4	3 laps behind	9/16
7	ITALIAN GP	Monza	2	Owen Racing Organisation	D	2.5 BRM P25 4	2 laps behind	7/21
ret	US GP	Sebring	19	Ecurie Bleue	D	2.2 Cooper T51-Climax 4	clutch	3/19

1960 — Championship position: Unplaced

| ret | ARGENTINE GP | Buenos Aires | 34 | Ecurie Bleue | D | 2.2 Cooper T51-Climax 4 | fuel pump | 9/22 |

GP Starts: 56 GP Wins: 0 Pole positions: 0 Fastest laps: 0 Points: 30

TIM SCHENKEN

With 42 wins in Formula Ford and a Grovewood Award in 1968, Tim Schenken was obviously a man to watch, and in 1969 he continued the good work in Rodney Bloor's Sports Motors Formula 3 Brabham at home and abroad, winning the French Craven A title.

For 1970 Tim and the Sports Motors team took the step up to Formula 2 and had an up-and-down season, the best results being second at Paul Ricard, and third at Pau and Mantorp Park. Schenken also made his Grand Prix debut, coming into a Williams team still reeling from the loss of Piers Courage, but he could do nothing with the de Tomaso.

The following season he appeared to have made the big breakthrough. Signed as number two to Graham Hill in the Brabham team, Tim was restricted to the old BT33 (possibly an advantage, as it was an easier car to set up than the 'lobster-claw' BT34) but overshadowed the former World Champion for much of the year. Schenken's two points finishes were not really just reward for his efforts, though in non-title races he took third place in the International Trophy and fourth in the Race of Champions.

In 1972 he made what turned out to be the biggest mistake of his career, joining Team Surtees for a season which effectively sabotaged his long-term Grand Prix ambitions. There was some solace, for he had been leading the Rondel Formula 2 outfit with distinction and was invited to join the Ferrari sports car team, for whom he scored a win in the Buenos Aires 1000 Km and the Nürburgring 1000 Km in addition to four second places, all paired with Peterson.

After ambitious plans to race a Formula 1 Rondel failed to materialise in 1973 and the Trojan project with his old Brabham boss Ron Tauranac turned into an embarrassing failure in 1974, poor Tim must have thought things couldn't get worse, but they did when he was invited to handle a Lotus 76 in the 1974 US GP and found the car almost undriveable, his one race for the Hethel team ending in non-qualification.

Schenken then embarked on a programme of sports car and GT racing for George Loos, racing his stable of Porsches during 1975-77 and winning the Nürburgring 1000 Km with Hezemans and Stommelen in 1977. Tim also shared the Jaguar XJ12C with John Fitzpatrick in the 1977 European GT championship, before retiring to concentrate on his Tiga racing car business with partner Howden Ganley.

Tim now represents the Australian motor sport federation and acts as clerk of the course for the Grand Prix in Melbourne.

SCHENKEN, Tim (AUS) b 26/9/1943, Gordon, Sydney, New South Wales

	1970			Championship position: Unplaced					
	Race	Circuit	No	Entrant	Tyres	Car/Engine		Comment	Q Pos/Entries
ret	AUSTRIAN GP	Österreichring	26	Frank Williams Racing Cars	D	3.0 de Tomaso 505-Cosworth V8		engine	18/24
ret	ITALIAN GP	Monza	54	Frank Williams Racing Cars	D	3.0 de Tomaso 505-Cosworth V8		engine	22/27
nc	CANADIAN GP	St Jovite	10	Frank Williams Racing Cars	D	3.0 de Tomaso 505-Cosworth V8		p stop/shock absorber-11 laps	17/20
ret	US GP	Watkins Glen	30	Frank Williams Racing Cars	D	3.0 de Tomaso 505-Cosworth V8		rear suspension	20/27
	1971			Championship position: 14th= Wins: 0 Pole positions: 0 Fastest laps: 0 Points scored: 5					
9	SPANISH GP	Montjuich Park	8	Motor Racing Developments	G	3.0 Brabham BT33-Cosworth V8		3 laps behind	21/22
10	MONACO GP	Monte Carlo	8	Motor Racing Developments	G	3.0 Brabham BT33-Cosworth V8		pit stop-wheel change/-4 laps	18/23
ret	DUTCH GP	Zandvoort	25	Motor Racing Developments	G	3.0 Brabham BT33-Cosworth V8		collision with Pescarolo	19/24
12/ret	FRENCH GP	Paul Ricard	8	Motor Racing Developments	G	3.0 Brabham BT33-Cosworth V8		engine-oil pressure/-5 laps	14/24
12/ret	BRITISH GP	Silverstone	8	Motor Racing Developments	G	3.0 Brabham BT33-Cosworth V8		gearbox/5 laps behind	7/24
6	GERMAN GP	Nürburgring	25	Motor Racing Developments	G	3.0 Brabham BT33-Cosworth V8			9/23
3	AUSTRIAN GP	Österreichring	8	Motor Racing Developments	G	3.0 Brabham BT33-Cosworth V8			7/22
ret	ITALIAN GP	Monza	11	Motor Racing Developments	G	3.0 Brabham BT33-Cosworth V8		rear subframe	9/24
ret	CANADIAN GP	Mosport Park	8	Motor Racing Developments	G	3.0 Brabham BT33-Cosworth V8		transistor box	17/27
ret	US GP	Watkins Glen	23	Motor Racing Developments	G	3.0 Brabham BT33-Cosworth V8		valve	16/32
	1972			Championship position: 19th= Wins: 0 Pole positions: 0 Fastest laps: 0 Points scored: 2					
5	ARGENTINE GP	Buenos Aires	19	Brooke Bond Oxo/R Walker/Team Surtees	F	3.0 Surtees TS9B-Cosworth V8			11/22
ret	SOUTH AFRICAN GP	Kyalami	16	Brooke Bond Oxo/R Walker/Team Surtees	F	3.0 Surtees TS9B-Cosworth V8		engine	=8/27
8	SPANISH GP	Jarama	12	Brooke Bond Oxo/R Walker/Team Surtees	F	3.0 Surtees TS9B-Cosworth V8		2 laps behind	18/26
ret	MONACO GP	Monte Carlo	10	Team Surtees	F	3.0 Surtees TS9B-Cosworth V8		hit barrier	13/25
ret	BELGIAN GP	Nivelles	35	Team Surtees	F	3.0 Surtees TS9B-Cosworth V8		engine	21/26
17	FRENCH GP	Clermont Ferrand	27	Flame Out-Team Surtees	F	3.0 Surtees TS9B-Cosworth V8		pit stop/fuel pressure/-2 laps	5/29
ret	BRITISH GP	Brands Hatch	22	Flame Out-Team Surtees	F	3.0 Surtees TS9B-Cosworth V8		rear suspension mounting	5/27
14	GERMAN GP	Nürburgring	15	Team Surtees	F	3.0 Surtees TS9B-Cosworth V8		pit stops/tyre/electrical/-1 lap	12/27
11	AUSTRIAN GP	Österreichring	24	Team Surtees	F	3.0 Surtees TS9B-Cosworth V8		pit stop/tyres/2 laps behind	8/26
ret	ITALIAN GP	Monza	8	Team Surtees	F	3.0 Surtees TS9B-Cosworth V8		hit chicane	22/27
7	CANADIAN GP	Mosport Park	22	Team Surtees	F	3.0 Surtees TS9B-Cosworth V8		1 lap behind	=12/25
ret	US GP	Watkins Glen	22	Team Surtees	F	3.0 Surtees TS14-Cosworth V8		oil leak	32/32
	1973			Championship position: Unplaced					
14	CANADIAN GP	Mosport Park	26	Frank Williams Racing Cars	F	3.0 Iso Williams 1R-Cosworth V8		pit stop/tyres/5 laps behind	24/26
	1974			Championship position: Unplaced					
14/ret	SPANISH GP	Jarama	23	Trojan-Tauranac Racing	F	3.0 Trojan T103-Cosworth V8		spun off/8 laps behind	26/28
10	BELGIAN GP	Nivelles	41	Trojan-Tauranac Racing	F	3.0 Trojan T103-Cosworth V8		2 laps behind	23/32
ret	MONACO GP	Monte Carlo	23	Trojan-Tauranac Racing	F	3.0 Trojan T103-Cosworth V8		multiple accident	24/28
dnq	DUTCH GP	Zandvoort	23	Trojan-Tauranac Racing	F	3.0 Trojan T103-Cosworth V8			26/27
ret	BRITISH GP	Brands Hatch	23	Trojan-Tauranac Racing	F	3.0 Trojan T103-Cosworth V8		suspension	=25/34
dnq	GERMAN GP	Nürburgring	23	Trojan-Tauranac Racing	F	3.0 Trojan T103-Cosworth V8			28/32
10	AUSTRIAN GP	Österreichring	23	Trojan-Tauranac Racing	F	3.0 Trojan T103-Cosworth V8		4 laps behind	19/31
ret	ITALIAN GP	Monza	29	Trojan-Tauranac Racing	F	3.0 Trojan T103-Cosworth V8		gear selection	20/31
dsq	US GP	Watkins Glen	31	John Player Team Lotus	G	3.0 Lotus 76-Cosworth V8		started unofficially-2nd reserve	27/30

GP Starts: 34   GP Wins: 0   Pole positions: 0   Fastest laps: 0   Points: 7

On the pace. Schenken's best Grand Prix result came driving for Brabham in Austria in 1971. *Left:* **He leads the Lotus of Emerson Fittipaldi during the course of his drive to third place.**

ALBERT SCHERRER

This Swiss was strictly an amateur national racer who competed from the late forties through until the mid-fifties. His Jaguar XK 120 provided some top-three finishes, either outright or in class, at such circuits as Bremgarten and Geneva. He was also a stalwart of the well-supported and popular Swiss hill-climbs of that period.

His only major race was in the 1953 Swiss Grand Prix, hiring one of John Heath's HWM-Altas. Despite a shunt he made it to the finish but did not complete enough laps to be classified.

Subsequently Scherrer competed domestically in a Mercedes 300SL, winning the over-2600 cc production sports class in the 1956 Ollon-Villars hill-climb.

DOMENICO 'MIMMO' SCHIATTARELLA

Schiattarella is another driver to have found his way onto the Grand Prix grid in the nineties by dint of finance rather than a track record of major successes.

'Mimmo' began racing in Italian Formula 4 back in 1985. He won that championship the following term and graduated to Italian Formula 3, where he was to spend the next three years. By 1991 he was a leading runner along with the likes of Badoer and Jacques Villeneuve, but threw away his chance of becoming the champion in the final round at Vallelunga when he pushed his title rival Giambattista Busi off the circuit and was black-flagged.

Schiattarella then spent part of the next year in the Sud-Am championship before making an end-of-year appearance in the Macau F3 race, where he finished fifth.

A couple of outings in the Project Indy Lola tested the Indy Car waters, but the chance to drive for Simtek at the end of the 1994 season whetted his appetite for more in 1995. Apparently hs contract was for the first half of the year only, with Hideki Noda laying down his wedge of cash for the balance of the season. In the event 'Mimmo' failed to get past round five at Monaco as Simtek, despite possessing a very promising car, were in such financial difficulties that they could no longer carry on.

Subsequently Schiattarella has, in the main, concentrated on sports car racing. In 1996 he won the Vallelunga 6 Hours in a Ferrari F40 against moderate opposition, and he shared a Lotus GT1 with Luca Badoer on a couple of occasions the following year. The 1998 season saw the briefest of returns to single-seaters in CART with Project Indy after Moreno quit the team. A race at Long Beach was to be their final outing of the year as a lack of funding forced them out.

'Mimmo' found a competitive ride at last in 1999 driving Team Rafanelli's Riley & Scott MkII sports car in the American Le Mans Series. Teamed with Eric van de Poele, he won the opening round at Road Atlanta and placed well elsewhere. Schiattarella also joined Caffi and Montermini at Le Mans, where the Italian trio took a Courage-Nissan into a fine sixth place.

SCHERRER, Albert (CH) b 28/2/1908 – d 5/7/1986

	1953	Championship position: Unplaced						
	Race	Circuit	No	Entrant	Tyres	Car/Engine	Comment	Q Pos/Entries
nc	SWISS GP	Bremgarten	18	HW Motors	D	2.0 HWM-Alta 4	16 laps behind	18/23

GP Starts: 1   GP Wins: 0   Pole positions: 0   Fastest laps: 0   Points: 0

SCHIATTARELLA, Domenico 'Mimmo' (I) b 17/11/1967, Milan

	1994	Championship position: Unplaced						
	Race	Circuit	No	Entrant	Tyres	Car/Engine	Comment	Q Pos/Entries
19	EUROPEAN GP	Jerez	32	MTV Simtek Ford	G	3.5 Simtek S941-Ford HB V8	5 laps behind	26/28
ret	AUSTRALIAN GP	Adelaide	32	MTV Simtek Ford	G	3.5 Simtek S941-Ford HB V8	gear selection	26/28
	1995	Championship position: Unplaced						
ret	BRAZILIAN GP	Interlagos	11	MTV Simtek Ford	G	3.0 Simtek S195-Ford ED V8	steering box	26/26
9	ARGENTINE GP	Buenos Aires	11	MTV Simtek Ford	G	3.0 Simtek S195-Ford ED V8	4 laps behind	20/26
ret	SAN MARINO GP	Imola	11	MTV Simtek Ford	G	3.0 Simtek S195-Ford ED V8	suspension	23/26
15	SPANISH GP	Barcelona	11	MTV Simtek Ford	G	3.0 Simtek S195-Ford ED V8	4 laps behind	22/26
ret/dns	MONACO GP	Monte Carlo	11	MTV Simtek Ford	G	3.0 Simtek S195-Ford ED V8	accident at first start	(20)/26

GP Starts: 6 (7)   GP Wins: 0   Pole positions: 0   Fastest laps: 0   Points: 0

HEINZ SCHILLER

Heinz was a Swiss speedboat champion before turning to four-wheeled sport, making a good start in a 1500 cc Porsche GT and RS sports. He took numerous placings and wins with the car in the mid-fifties, including second in class in the 1957 Mille Miglia. Early in 1958 Schiller was allowed to race his Porsche RS at the Formula 2 Pau GP, circulating steadily to earn a distant sixth place.

After hill-climbing in the Porsche Carrera Abarth in 1961, the Swiss tasted some real single-seater competition with Ecurie Filipinetti in 1962 partnering Jo Siffert. Heinz mainly handled the team's Porsche 718, but had a single chance in the more competitive Lotus 24-BRM V8 at the German GP.

He made just one more open-wheeled appearance for the team, back in the old Porsche at Pau in 1963, and finished third, albeit five laps behind the Lotus duo of Clark and Taylor. He continued to race Filipinetti's GT cars, taking second in class at the Nürburgring 1000 Km and also a class win at the Ollon-Villars hill-climb in the Porsche Carrera Abarth.

In 1964 he raced his Porsche 904 in long-distance events with Jo Siffert, and took tenth place (and third in class) at Le Mans in the works car with Gerhard Koch.

JEAN-LOUIS SCHLESSER

A nephew of the late Jo Schlesser, Jean-Louis is a driver who missed the Formula 1 boat, and unfortunately the immensely popular Frenchman will be best remembered for inadvertently tangling with Ayrton Senna near the end of the 1988 Italian GP as the Brazilian was about to lap his Williams.

A graduate of Formule Renault, Schlesser got bogged down in French Formula 3 and production racing before turning to the European F3 championship in 1981. However, his Martini was saddled with the wrong brand of tyres and the undoubted high spot of the year was a terrific second place at Le Mans, sharing a Rondeau with Jacky Haran and Philippe Streiff. Still determined to succeed in single-seaters, Jean-Louis joined the Maurer F2 team alongside Bellof in 1982, but it was another season of frustration, as he did not enjoy the best of equipment.

In 1983 Schlesser began work as a test driver for Williams, and attempted to qualify the RAM for the French GP. He then returned to production cars, winning the French championship in 1985, before Tom Walkinshaw signed him for the TWR Jaguar sports car team in 1986. Disappointingly, finishes were thin on the ground and he was released, ultimately joining the Kouros Sauber team, which, in 1988, became the official representative of the Mercedes factory.

Schlesser scored two wins and finished second to Martin Brundle in the points standings that year, and the following season he made no mistake, winning five rounds (Suzuka, Jarama, the Nürburgring, Donington and Mexico City) to claim the World Sports Car Championship, a feat he repeated in 1990, when he shared the title with Mauro Baldi.

Throughout the nineties, Jean-Louis has been tackling another branch of the sport, the gruelling cross-desert marathons. In 1999, at the eleventh attempt, he finally won the Paris–Dakar Rally driving his own Schlesser-buggy.

SCHILLER, Heinz (CH) b 25/1/1930, Frauenfeld

	1962	Championship position: Unplaced							
	Race	Circuit	No	Entrant	Tyres	Car/Engine		Entrant	Q Pos/Entries
ret	GERMAN GP	Nürburgring	28	Ecurie Filipinetti	D	1.5 Lotus 24-BRM V8		oil pressure	20/30

GP Starts: 1   GP Wins: 0   Pole positions: 0   Fastest laps: 0   Points: 0

SCHLESSER, Jean-Louis (F) b 12/9/1948

	1983	Championship position: Unplaced							
	Race	Circuit	No	Entrant	Tyres	Car/Engine		Comment	Q Pos/Entries
dnq	FRENCH GP	Paul Ricard	18	RAM Automotive Team March	P	3.0 March-RAM 01-Cosworth V8			29/29
	1988	Championship position: 0 Wins: 0 Pole positions: 0 Fastest laps: 0 Points scored: 0							
11	ITALIAN GP	Monza	5	Canon Williams Team	G	3.5 Williams FW12-Judd V8		collided with Senna/2 laps	22/31

GP Starts: 1   GP Wins: 0   Pole positions: 0   Fastest laps: 0   Points: 0

SCHLESSER, Jo (F) b 18/5/1928, Liouville – d 7/7/1968, Rouen Circuit

	1966			Championship position: Unplaced				
	Race	Circuit	No	Entrant	Tyres	Car/Engine	Comment	Q Pos/Entries
10*	GERMAN GP (F2)	Nürburgring	33	Matra Sports	D	1.0 Matra MS5-Cosworth 4 F2	* 3rd in F2 class/-1 lap	20/30
	1967			Championship position: Unplaced				
ret	GERMAN GP (F2)	Nürburgring	23	Ecurie Ford-France	D	1.6 Matra MS5-Cosworth 4 F2	clutch	18/25
	1968			Championship position: Unplaced				
ret	FRENCH GP	Rouen	18	Honda Racing (France)	F	3.0 Honda RA302 V8	fatal accident	17/18

GP Starts: 3   GP Wins: 0   Pole positions: 0   Fastest laps: 0   Points: 0

JO SCHLESSER

A true all-rounder and as brave as they come, Schlesser loved every form of motor sport and competed in as many of them as he possibly could during a career that started in 1952, when he rallied a Panhard. He tried the current French vogue of monomill racing in 1954, but his serious competition activities were then put on hold for three years while he was working in Madagascar. Back in Europe in 1957, he finished second in the Liège-Rome-Liège Rally with a Mercedes, which he soon replaced with a Ferrari 250 GT, but success did not really come until 1960 when he took second in class at the Nürburgring 1000 Km, and second overall in the Rouen GP. This was in contrast to his rather disappointing year in a Formula 2 Cooper, a sixth place at Syracuse his only result worth mentioning. His 1961 season was curtailed by a very big accident during the practice days at Le Mans which left him with a badly broken arm and leg, but he was back in action the following year with a Formula Junior Brabham, putting in some superb drives to become one of the formula's leading protagonists.

The advent of the 1-litre Formula 2 in 1964 gave Jo the chance to pit himself against some of racing's top names, and he became a respected member of the Continental F2 fraternity, joining the Matra works team in 1966 and running the same car under the Ford France banner the following season before setting up a team with his great friend Guy Ligier to race McLarens in 1968. Since 1965 Schlesser had also made something of name for himself at the wheel of powerful sports cars including a Shelby Cobra and then the Ford France GT40, winning the Reims 12-hour race in 1967, paired with Ligier.

However, his Grand Prix experience was limited to just two outings in the Formula 2 class of the German GP when he was invited to race the totally unproven air-cooled Honda in the 1968 French GP – it must be said, much against the wishes of John Surtees. In the opening laps of the race, Schlesser lost control of the car in pouring rain, crashing it into an earth bank, whereupon it burst into flames, swiftly claiming the life of its 41-year-old driver.

BERND SCHNEIDER

A graduate of Formula Ford 1600 and FF2000, Schneider finished equal third in his first year of German F3 in 1986, but when he came back to slaughter the opposition in 1988, winning seven of the eight rounds he contested, many watchers were convinced that here at last was a German with a big future. Little did they realise that it would be at the wheel of Mercedes touring and sports cars that he would taste success rather than in Grand Prix racing, where two miserable seasons with Zakspeed and a couple of drives with Arrows unfairly left him washed up as a Grand Prix driver at the age of 26.

Bernd drove a Kremer Porsche in Interserie racing in 1990 and then raced in IMSA for the Joest team, before reviving his career in the DTM with a Zakspeed Mercedes. He switched to an AMG works car for 1992 and was soon considered the fastest driver in the Mercedes squad, but the scintillating form of Larini and the Alfas in 1993 meant his quest for the championship would have to wait a little longer. After enduring the frustration of often leading but hitting mechanical problems in 1994, Bernd's luck changed and everything came together a year on. In the AMG Mercedes the German regularly blitzed the opposition, taking 11 wins from 23 starts to claim both the DTM and ITC titles. Nobody could have deserved his success more, and he rightly became the key driver in the Stuttgart giant's racing programme. The final year of the ITC in 1996 yielded only four wins, but his consistent finishes brought him second in the final standings behind Manuel Reuter's Opel. With the high-tech formula scrapped, Mercedes unleashed their CLK-GTR on the FIA GT series and Bernd shared in six wins from the eleven races to emerge as clear drivers' champion. Despite five wins from ten starts, the German had to settle for second place behind AMG team-mates Ludwig and Zonta in 1998.

Since Mercedes concentrated solely on Le Mans for 1999, Bernd was without a regular racing schedule, but with the revised German Super Touring series in place for 2000 he will surely relish the chance to fight for the championship with the stunning new V8-engined CLK.

SCHNEIDER, Bernd (D) b 20/7/1964, Saarbrücken

	1988	Championship position: Unplaced							
	Race	Circuit	No	Entrant	Tyres	Car/Engine		Comment	Q Pos/Entries
dnq	BRAZILIAN GP	Rio	10	West Zakspeed Racing	G	1.5 t/c Zakspeed 881 4			30/31
dnq	SAN MARINO GP	Imola	10	West Zakspeed Racing	G	1.5 t/c Zakspeed 881 4			30/31
dnq	MONACO GP	Monte Carlo	10	West Zakspeed Racing	G	1.5 t/c Zakspeed 881 4			28/30
ret	MEXICAN GP	Mexico City	10	West Zakspeed Racing	G	1.5 t/c Zakspeed 881 4		engine	15/30
dnq	CANADIAN GP	Montreal	10	West Zakspeed Racing	G	1.5 t/c Zakspeed 881 4			30/31
dnq	US GP (DETROIT)	Detroit	10	West Zakspeed Racing	G	1.5 t/c Zakspeed 881 4			29/31
ret	FRENCH GP	Paul Ricard	10	West Zakspeed Racing	G	1.5 t/c Zakspeed 881 4		gearbox	21/31
dnq	BRITISH GP	Silverstone	10	West Zakspeed Racing	G	1.5 t/c Zakspeed 881 4			30/31
12	GERMAN GP	Hockenheim	10	West Zakspeed Racing	G	1.5 t/c Zakspeed 881 4		1 lap behind	22/31
dnq	HUNGARIAN GP	Hungaroring	10	West Zakspeed Racing	G	1.5 t/c Zakspeed 881 4			28/31
13/ret	BELGIAN GP	Spa	10	West Zakspeed Racing	G	1.5 t/c Zakspeed 881 4		gearbox/5 laps behind	25/31
ret	ITALIAN GP	Monza	10	West Zakspeed Racing	G	1.5 t/c Zakspeed 881 4		engine	15/31
dnq	PORTUGUESE GP	Estoril	10	West Zakspeed Racing	G	1.5 t/c Zakspeed 881 4			30/31
dnq	SPANISH GP	Jerez	10	West Zakspeed Racing	G	1.5 t/c Zakspeed 881 4			27/31
ret	JAPANESE GP	Suzuka	10	West Zakspeed Racing	G	1.5 t/c Zakspeed 881 4		unwell after practice accident	25/31
dnq	AUSTRALIAN GP	Adelaide	10	West Zakspeed Racing	G	1.5 t/c Zakspeed 881 4			30/31
	1989	Championship position: Unplaced							
ret	BRAZILIAN GP	Rio	34	West Zakspeed Racing	P	3.5 Zakspeed 891-Yamaha V8		collision with Cheever	25/38
dnpq	SAN MARINO GP	Imola	34	West Zakspeed Racing	P	3.5 Zakspeed 891-Yamaha V8			38/39
dnpq	MONACO GP	Monte Carlo	34	West Zakspeed Racing	P	3.5 Zakspeed 891-Yamaha V8			33/38
dnpq	MEXICAN GP	Mexico City	34	West Zakspeed Racing	P	3.5 Zakspeed 891-Yamaha V8			35/39
dnpq	US GP (PHOENIX)	Phoenix	34	West Zakspeed Racing	P	3.5 Zakspeed 891-Yamaha V8			37/39
dnpq	CANADIAN GP	Montreal	34	West Zakspeed Racing	P	3.5 Zakspeed 891-Yamaha V8			35/39
dnpq	FRENCH GP	Paul Ricard	34	West Zakspeed Racing	P	3.5 Zakspeed 891-Yamaha V8			34/39
dnpq	BRITISH GP	Silverstone	34	West Zakspeed Racing	P	3.5 Zakspeed 891-Yamaha V8			36/39
dnpq	GERMAN GP	Hockenheim	34	West Zakspeed Racing	P	3.5 Zakspeed 891-Yamaha V8			39/39
dnpq	HUNGARIAN GP	Hungaroring	34	West Zakspeed Racing	P	3.5 Zakspeed 891-Yamaha V8			34/39
dnpq	BELGIAN GP	Spa	34	West Zakspeed Racing	P	3.5 Zakspeed 891-Yamaha V8			35/39
dnpq	ITALIAN GP	Monza	34	West Zakspeed Racing	P	3.5 Zakspeed 891-Yamaha V8			34/39
dnpq	PORTUGUESE GP	Estoril	34	West Zakspeed Racing	P	3.5 Zakspeed 891-Yamaha V8			38/39
dnpq	SPANISH GP	Jerez	34	West Zakspeed Racing	P	3.5 Zakspeed 891-Yamaha V8			34/38
ret	JAPANESE GP	Suzuka	34	West Zakspeed Racing	P	3.5 Zakspeed 891-Yamaha V8		engine on lap 1	21/39
dnpq	AUSTRALIAN GP	Adelaide	34	West Zakspeed Racing	P	3.5 Zakspeed 891-Yamaha V8			33/39
	1990	Championship position: Unplaced							
12	US GP (PHOENIX)	Phoenix	10	Footwork Arrows Racing	G	3.5 Arrows A11-Cosworth V8		2 laps behind	20/35
dnq	SPANISH GP	Jerez	10	Footwork Arrows Racing	G	3.5 Arrows A11B-Cosworth V8			29/33

GP Starts: 9   GP Wins: 0   Pole positions: 0   Fastest laps: 0   Points: 0

RUDOLF SCHOELLER

Schoeller was a Swiss veteran who tagged along with Fischer's Espadon team in 1952. Apart from his one German GP drive, he was a reserve (but not used) at non-championship Formula 2 races at both Rouen and AVUS.

At the end of the year he apparently bought the team's old 212 car to race in minor events at home.

SCHOELLER, Rudolf (CH) b 27/4/1902 – d 7/3/1978

	1952	Championship position: 0		Wins: 0	Pole positions: 0	Fastest laps: 0	Points scored: 0		
	Race	Circuit	No	Entrant	Tyres	Car/Engine		Comment	Q Pos/Entries
ret	GERMAN GP	Nürburgring	118	Ecurie Espadon	P	2.0 Ferrari 212 V12		shock absorber	24/32

GP Starts: 1   GP Wins: 0   Pole positions: 0   Fastest laps: 0   Points: 0

SCHROEDER, Rob (USA) b 11/5/1926

	1962	Championship position: 0		Wins: 0	Pole positions: 0	Fastest laps: 0	Points scored: 0		
	Race	Circuit	No	Entrant	Tyres	Car/Engine		Comment	Q Pos/Entries
10	US GP	Watkins Glen	26	John Mecom	D	1.5 Lotus 24-Climax V8		hired Rob Walker's car/-7 laps	17/20

GP Starts: 1   GP Wins: 0   Pole positions: 0   Fastest laps: 0   Points: 0

MICHAEL SCHUMACHER

WORLD CHAMPION: 1994 & 1995

MICHAEL SCHUMACHER

When Michael Schumacher burst upon the Grand Prix stage with a sensational qualifying performance on his debut for Jordan at Spa, the Grand Prix hype-machine went into overdrive, billing this young 'unknown' as the next Senna. In truth Michael's racing career had been very carefully planned before he ever stepped into a Formula 1 car, and he had the comforting prospect of major manufacturer and commercial backing with which to develop his top-level career. However, he has since proved beyond doubt that he is the supreme driver of the current era, and the target for the others to aim at.

A former karting star with but a single season of Formula Ford 1600 and Formula König in 1988 behind him, Schumacher was signed by leading German F3 team OTS to support Heinz-Harald Frentzen in 1989. It was a closely contested season, with the pair both finishing just one point behind series winner Karl Wendlinger. It was then that Mercedes sporting director Jochen Neerpasch stepped in with his junior-driver scheme which placed all three drivers in the Sauber-Mercedes Group C programme for 1990. Under the wise tutelage of Jochen Mass, the trio were schooled in the art of handling big, powerful cars in a very disciplined and professional framework. In parallel to his sports car drives, Michael was back in German F3, and this time won the series comfortably. He also took in two end-of-season races at Fuji and Macau, and confirmed his talent by winning them both.

Most drivers would be wanting to try their hand at F3000 by this time, but Michael was happy to stay within the confines of the Mercedes team. This second season saw a change of emphasis with the young lions Schumacher and Wendlinger paired together and allowed their heads. Both did an excellent job, but the consensus was that Michael had the edge, the pair's reward after a trouble-strewn year being victory in the round at Autopolis. With a Formula 1 drive inevitable sooner (as it would turn out) or later, nothing was left to chance and Neerpasch arranged for Schumacher to race a Formula 3000 car at Sugo, well away from the glare of publicity. He finished second and enjoyed the different experience of racing a powerful single-seater.

A month later came the Jordan drive at Spa which, after his stirring deeds in practice, ended disappointingly when Michael's clutch failed at the start. Suddenly Schumacher was a hot property and after much legal wrangling the somewhat bemused driver was whisked off to join the Benetton team in time for the next race at Monza. Three points-scoring finishes in his first three races were more than enough evidence for Flavio Briatore to plan the team's future around the German star and he was not to disappoint. In his first full Grand Prix season Michael proved to be not only very quick but also remarkably consistent, rarely making costly mistakes and putting in some scintillating performances such as his second place to Mansell in the rain at Barcelona and his climb through the field to third at Monza after being left at the start. Of course, the supreme moment was his fully deserved, if slightly fortunate, win at Spa where he made his own luck – and reaped the rewards.

The 1993 season provided more evidence of Schumacher's increasing maturity. Only Williams' dominance stood between him and the top step of the podium on numerous occasions and he took a superbly thought-out win at Estoril. Much work was done over the winter months, and when the new Benetton B194, mated with the Ford Zetec-R V8 engine, was placed in Schumacher's hands he left Senna and Williams struggling in his wake in the opening two races. It seemed that the balance of power might be about to shift, and tragically it did so at Imola, leaving Michael with the prospect of chasing a World Championship which he felt would be much devalued by the loss of the Brazilian. From then on his season was to be surrounded by controversy. Amid rumblings that the team were running some form of traction control, Schumacher won six of the first seven Grands Prix, but he was excluded at Silverstone for ignoring the black flag, which was later to earn him a two-race ban, and this, together with the loss of his crushing win at Spa when he was disqualified for having an illegal skid-block, left the door open for Damon Hill to make a late challenge for the title. When the pair collided in Adelaide, Schumacher became Germany's first World Champion, but the manner of his triumph can have brought him little inner satisfaction.

The following season was to be a different matter entirely as Schumacher, given superb support by the whole Benetton squad, ruthlessly exposed the shortcomings of both the Williams team and their drivers. From the Spanish Grand Prix onwards Michael upped the stakes to put in a succession of brilliant performances. His dominant wins in Monaco, France and Germany looked almost routine, especially when compared with his extraordinary displays at Spa (where he drove through the field from a lowly 16th place on the grid) and in the European GP at the Nürburgring, where, quite frankly, the rest of the field, Alesi apart, were made to look like novices. It was fitting that Michael and Benetton had the opportunity to win the 1995 championship in a manner which reflected their talent and commitment.

It was natural that Ferrari, so long in the doldrums, should look to Schumacher to return them to the top and they were prepared to stump up a massive retainer to capture his signature. With a huge amount of restructuring needed, his immediate championship prospects for 1996 were not deemed bright, but the German still produced drives of genius, such as in the wet in Spain, and later in the season at Spa and Monza. It was much the same story the following year as Michael took the fight to the superior Williams of Jacques Villeneuve, brilliant wins in the wet at both Monaco and Spa and on slicks on a treacherous track at Magny Cours emphasising his mesmeric car control. His refusal to concede defeat was to lead to an inglorious end to his title challenge in a Jerez gravel trap after an outrageous manoeuvre on his title rival. Schumacher was subsequently stripped of his points and his second place in the championship.

With the slate wiped clean for 1998, Ferrari were still the underdog, as McLaren Mercedes now boasted the fastest machine on the track. Michael again ruthlessly took advantage of any weakness shown by his rivals and some of his drives (such as in Hungary, and at Spa before he ran into the back of Coulthard's ambling McLaren) were on a different plane from the rest. In the end stalling the Ferrari on the grid at Suzuka effectively stymied his title chances for the third time in as many years, but it would be churlish to criticise the German too harshly for his error, as it was only his brilliance that had extended the title fight to the end.

Schumacher and Ferrari were left facing a fourth attempt to clinch a championship which by now must have seemed like the holy grail. Dominant performances at Imola and in Monaco provided a satisfactory start, but a relatively low-speed shunt on the first lap of the British Grand Prix left the unlucky German with a broken leg. His title chances were gone but Michael still had a major part to play in the championship battle. Having seen Eddie Irvine take over Maranello's challenge and carry the fight to McLaren with tremendous effect, the German was back in action at the penultimate race in Malaysia to aid his number two driver. Not only did he claim pole position but he also dominated the race, allowing Irvine to win and at the same time blunting Häkkinen's challenge in a brilliant but controversial display of team tactics. At Suzuka he seemed unable to match the pace of the Finn, who duly took a well-deserved second title. For Michael, the dream of being the first Ferrari driver to win the World Championship since 1979 still remains. Providing he retains his motivation, and Ferrari can continue to give him the equipment, 2000 might be a 21st anniversary for them to celebrate.

SCHUMACHER Michael (D) b 3/1/1969, Hürth-Hermühlheim

	Race	Circuit	No	Entrant	Tyres	Car/Engine	Comment	Q Pos/Entries
	1991	Championship position: 12th=		Wins: 0	Pole positions: 0	Fastest laps: 0	Points scored: 4	
ret	BELGIAN GP	Spa	32	Team 7UP Jordan	G	3.5 Jordan 191-Ford HB V8	clutch at start	7/34
5	ITALIAN GP	Monza	19	Camel Benetton Ford	P	3.5 Benetton B191-Ford HB V8		7/34
6	PORTUGUESE GP	Estoril	19	Camel Benetton Ford	P	3.5 Benetton B191-Ford HB V8		10/34
6	SPANISH GP	Barcelona	19	Camel Benetton Ford	P	3.5 Benetton B191-Ford HB V8		5/33
ret	JAPANESE GP	Suzuka	19	Camel Benetton Ford	P	3.5 Benetton B191-Ford HB V8	engine	9/31
ret	AUSTRALIAN GP	Adelaide	19	Camel Benetton Ford	P	3.5 Benetton B191-Ford HB V8	collision with Alesi	6/32
	1992	Championship position: 3rd		Wins: 1	Pole positions: 0	Fastest laps: 2	Points scored: 53	
4	SOUTH AFRICAN GP	Kyalami	19	Camel Benetton Ford	G	3.5 Benetton B191B-Ford HB V8		6/30
3	MEXICAN GP	Mexico City	19	Camel Benetton Ford	G	3.5 Benetton B191B-Ford HB V8		3/30
3	BRAZILIAN GP	Interlagos	19	Camel Benetton Ford	G	3.5 Benetton B191B-Ford HB V8	1 lap behind	5/31
2	SPANISH GP	Barcelona	19	Camel Benetton Ford	G	3.5 Benetton B192-Ford HB V8		2/32
ret	SAN MARINO GP	Imola	19	Camel Benetton Ford	G	3.5 Benetton B192-Ford HB V8	spun-suspension damage	5/32
4	MONACO GP	Monte Carlo	19	Camel Benetton Ford	G	3.5 Benetton B192-Ford HB V8		6/32
2	CANADIAN GP	Montreal	19	Camel Benetton Ford	G	3.5 Benetton B192-Ford HB V8		5/32
ret	FRENCH GP	Magny Cours	19	Camel Benetton Ford	G	3.5 Benetton B192-Ford HB V8	accident-collision Senna	5/30
4	BRITISH GP	Silverstone	19	Camel Benetton Ford	G	3.5 Benetton B192-Ford HB V8		4/32
3	GERMAN GP	Hockenheim	19	Camel Benetton Ford	G	3.5 Benetton B192-Ford HB V8		6/32
ret	HUNGARIAN GP	Hungaroring	19	Camel Benetton Ford	G	3.5 Benetton B192-Ford HB V8	collision-lost rear wing/spun off	4/31
1	BELGIAN GP	Spa	19	Camel Benetton Ford	G	3.5 Benetton B192-Ford HB V8	FL	3/30
3	ITALIAN GP	Monza	19	Camel Benetton Ford	G	3.5 Benetton B192-Ford HB V8	clutch	6/28
7	PORTUGUESE GP	Estoril	19	Camel Benetton Ford	G	3.5 Benetton B192-Ford HB V8	started from back/puncture/-2 laps	5/26
ret	JAPANESE GP	Suzuka	19	Camel Benetton Ford	G	3.5 Benetton B192-Ford HB V8	gearbox	5/26
2	AUSTRALIAN GP	Adelaide	19	Camel Benetton Ford	G	3.5 Benetton B192-Ford HB V8	FL	5/26
	1993	Championship position: 4th		Wins: 1	Pole positions: 0	Fastest laps: 5	Points scored: 52	
ret	SOUTH AFRICAN GP	Kyalami	5	Camel Benetton Ford	G	3.5 Benetton B192B-Ford HB V8	collision with Senna	3/26
3	BRAZILIAN GP	Interlagos	5	Camel Benetton Ford	G	3.5 Benetton B192B-Ford HB V8	FL	4/26
ret	EUROPEAN GP	Donington	5	Camel Benetton Ford	G	3.5 Benetton B193B-Ford HB V8		3/26
2	SAN MARINO GP	Imola	5	Camel Benetton Ford	G	3.5 Benetton B193B-Ford HB V8		3/26
3	SPANISH GP	Barcelona	5	Camel Benetton Ford	G	3.5 Benetton B193B-Ford HB V8	FL	4/26
ret	MONACO GP	Monte Carlo	5	Camel Benetton Ford	G	3.5 Benetton B193B-Ford HB V8	active hydraulics/fire	2/26
2	CANADIAN GP	Montreal	5	Camel Benetton Ford	G	3.5 Benetton B193B-Ford HB V8	FL	3/26
3	FRENCH GP	Magny Cours	5	Camel Benetton Ford	G	3.5 Benetton B193B-Ford HB V8	FL	7/26
2	BRITISH GP	Silverstone	5	Camel Benetton Ford	G	3.5 Benetton B193B-Ford HB V8		3/26
2	GERMAN GP	Hockenheim	5	Camel Benetton Ford	G	3.5 Benetton B193B-Ford HB V8	FL	3/26
ret	HUNGARIAN GP	Hungaroring	5	Camel Benetton Ford	G	3.5 Benetton B193B-Ford HB V8	fuel pump drive	3/26
2	BELGIAN GP	Spa	5	Camel Benetton Ford	G	3.5 Benetton B193B-Ford HB V8		3/25
ret	ITALIAN GP	Monza	5	Camel Benetton Ford	G	3.5 Benetton B193B-Ford HB V8	engine	5/26
1	PORTUGUESE GP	Estoril	5	Camel Benetton Ford	G	3.5 Benetton B193B-Ford HB V8		6/26
ret	JAPANESE GP	Suzuka	5	Camel Benetton Ford	G	3.5 Benetton B193B-Ford HB V8	collision-Hill/suspension	4/24
ret	AUSTRALIAN GP	Adelaide	5	Camel Benetton Ford	G	3.5 Benetton B193B-Ford HB V8	engine	4/24
	1994	Championship position: WORLD CHAMPION		Wins: 8	Pole positions: 6	Fastest laps: 9	Points scored: 92	
1	BRAZILIAN GP	Interlagos	5	Mild Seven Benetton Ford	G	3.5 Benetton B194-Ford Zetec-R V8	FL	2/28
1	PACIFIC GP	T.I. Circuit	5	Mild Seven Benetton Ford	G	3.5 Benetton B194-Ford Zetec-R V8	FL	2/28
1	SAN MARINO GP	Imola	5	Mild Seven Benetton Ford	G	3.5 Benetton B194-Ford Zetec-R V8	FL	2/28
1	MONACO GP	Monte Carlo	5	Mild Seven Benetton Ford	G	3.5 Benetton B194-Ford Zetec-R V8	FL	1/24
2	SPANISH GP	Barcelona	5	Mild Seven Benetton Ford	G	3.5 Benetton B194-Ford Zetec-R V8	car stuck in 5th gear/FL	1/27
1	CANADIAN GP	Montreal	5	Mild Seven Benetton Ford	G	3.5 Benetton B194-Ford Zetec-R V8	FL	1/27
1	FRENCH GP	Magny Cours	5	Mild Seven Benetton Ford	G	3.5 Benetton B194-Ford Zetec-R V8		2/28
2/dsq*	BRITISH GP	Silverstone	5	Mild Seven Benetton Ford	G	3.5 Benetton B194-Ford Zetec-R V8	*later dsq for ignoring black flag	2/28
ret	GERMAN GP	Hockenheim	5	Mild Seven Benetton Ford	G	3.5 Benetton B194-Ford Zetec-R V8	engine	4/28
1	HUNGARIAN GP	Hungaroring	5	Mild Seven Benetton Ford	G	3.5 Benetton B194-Ford Zetec-R V8	FL	1/28
1/dsq*	BELGIAN GP	Spa	5	Mild Seven Benetton Ford	G	3.5 Benetton B194-Ford Zetec-R V8	*later dsq-skidblock wear	2/28
1	EUROPEAN GP	Jerez	5	Mild Seven Benetton Ford	G	3.5 Benetton B194-Ford Zetec-R V8	FL	1/28
2	JAPANESE GP	Suzuka	5	Mild Seven Benetton Ford	G	3.5 Benetton B194-Ford Zetec-R V8		1/28
ret	AUSTRALIAN GP	Adelaide	5	Mild Seven Benetton Ford	G	3.5 Benetton B194-Ford Zetec-R V8	collision with Hill/FL	2/28
	1995	Championship position: WORLD CHAMPION		Wins: 9	Pole positions: 4	Fastest laps: 8	Points scored: 102	
1	BRAZILIAN GP	Interlagos	1	Mild Seven Benetton Renault	G	3.0 Benetton B195-Renault V10	FL	2/26
3	ARGENTINE GP	Buenos Aires	1	Mild Seven Benetton Renault	G	3.0 Benetton B195-Renault V10	FL	3/26
ret	SAN MARINO GP	Imola	1	Mild Seven Benetton Renault	G	3.0 Benetton B195-Renault V10	accident-crashed	1/26
1	SPANISH GP	Barcelona	1	Mild Seven Benetton Renault	G	3.0 Benetton B195-Renault V10		1/26
1	MONACO GP	Monte Carlo	1	Mild Seven Benetton Renault	G	3.0 Benetton B195-Renault V10		2/26
5	CANADIAN GP	Montreal	1	Mild Seven Benetton Renault	G	3.0 Benetton B195-Renault V10	led-gearbox/throttle trouble/FL	1/24
1	FRENCH GP	Magny Cours	1	Mild Seven Benetton Renault	G	3.0 Benetton B195-Renault V10	FL	2/24
ret	BRITISH GP	Silverstone	1	Mild Seven Benetton Renault	G	3.0 Benetton B195-Renault V10	collision with Hill	2/24
1	GERMAN GP	Hockenheim	1	Mild Seven Benetton Renault	G	3.0 Benetton B195-Renault V10	FL	2/24
11/ret	HUNGARIAN GP	Hungaroring	1	Mild Seven Benetton Renault	G	3.0 Benetton B195-Renault V10	fuel pump/4 laps behind	3/24
1	BELGIAN GP	Spa	1	Mild Seven Benetton Renault	G	3.0 Benetton B195-Renault V10		16/24
ret	ITALIAN GP	Monza	1	Mild Seven Benetton Renault	G	3.0 Benetton B195-Renault V10	run into by Hill	2/24
2	PORTUGUESE GP	Estoril	1	Mild Seven Benetton Renault	G	3.0 Benetton B195-Renault V10		3/24
1	EUROPEAN GP	Nürburgring	1	Mild Seven Benetton Renault	G	3.0 Benetton B195-Renault V10	FL	3/24
1	PACIFIC GP	T.I. Circuit	1	Mild Seven Benetton Renault	G	3.0 Benetton B195-Renault V10	FL	3/24
1	JAPANESE GP	Suzuka	1	Mild Seven Benetton Renault	G	3.0 Benetton B195-Renault V10	FL	1/24
ret	AUSTRALIAN GP	Adelaide	1	Mild Seven Benetton Renault	G	3.0 Benetton B195-Renault V10	collision with Alesi	3/24
	1996	Championship position: 3rd		Wins: 3	Pole positions: 4	Fastest laps: 2	Points scored: 59	
ret	AUSTRALIAN GP	Melbourne	1	Scuderia Ferrari	G	3.0 Ferrari F310-V10	brakes	4/22
3	BRAZILIAN GP	Interlagos	1	Scuderia Ferrari	G	3.0 Ferrari F310-V10	1 lap behind	4/22
ret	ARGENTINE GP	Buenos Aires	1	Scuderia Ferrari	G	3.0 Ferrari F310-V10	debris damage to rear wing	2/22
2	EUROPEAN GP	Nürburgring	1	Scuderia Ferrari	G	3.0 Ferrari F310-V10		3/22

2	SAN MARINO GP	Imola	1	Scuderia Ferrari	G	3.0 Ferrari F310-V10		1/22
ret	MONACO GP	Monte Carlo	1	Scuderia Ferrari	G	3.0 Ferrari F310-V10	crashed on lap 1	1/22
1	SPANISH GP	Barcelona	1	Scuderia Ferrari	G	3.0 Ferrari F310-V10	FL	3/22
ret	CANADIAN GP	Montreal	1	Scuderia Ferrari	G	3.0 Ferrari F310-V10	driveshaft	3/22
dns	FRENCH GP	Magny Cours	1	Scuderia Ferrari	G	3.0 Ferrari F310-V10	engine on parade lap	1/22
ret	BRITISH GP	Silverstone	1	Scuderia Ferrari	G	3.0 Ferrari F310-V10	hydraulic leak	3/22
4	GERMAN GP	Hockenheim	1	Scuderia Ferrari	G	3.0 Ferrari F310-V10		3/20
9/ret	HUNGARIAN GP	Hungaroring	1	Scuderia Ferrari	G	3.0 Ferrari F310-V10	throttle/7 laps behind	1/20
1	BELGIAN GP	Spa	1	Scuderia Ferrari	G	3.0 Ferrari F310-V10		3/20
1	ITALIAN GP	Monza	1	Scuderia Ferrari	G	3.0 Ferrari F310-V10	FL	3/20
3	PORTUGUESE GP	Estoril	1	Scuderia Ferrari	G	3.0 Ferrari F310-V10		4/20
2	JAPANESE GP	Suzuka	1	Scuderia Ferrari	G	3.0 Ferrari F310-V10		3/20

1997   Championship position: Unplaced   Wins: 5   Pole positions: 3   Fastest laps: 2   Points scored: 0 (78 points disallowed by FIA)

2	AUSTRALIAN GP	Melbourne	5	Scuderia Ferrari Marlboro	G	3.0 Ferrari F310B-V10		3/24
5	BRAZILIAN GP	Interlagos	5	Scuderia Ferrari Marlboro	G	3.0 Ferrari F310B-V10	lack of grip	2/22
ret	ARGENTINE GP	Buenos Aires	5	Scuderia Ferrari Marlboro	G	3.0 Ferrari F310B-V10	collision with Barrichello	4/22
2	SAN MARINO GP	Imola	5	Scuderia Ferrari Marlboro	G	3.0 Ferrari F310B-V10		3/22
1	MONACO GP	Monte Carlo	5	Scuderia Ferrari Marlboro	G	3.0 Ferrari F310B-V10	FL	2/22
4	SPANISH GP	Barcelona	5	Scuderia Ferrari Marlboro	G	3.0 Ferrari F310B-V10		7/22
1	CANADIAN GP	Montreal	5	Scuderia Ferrari Marlboro	G	3.0 Ferrari F310B-V10	race shortened after Panis crash	1/22
1	FRENCH GP	Magny Cours	5	Scuderia Ferrari Marlboro	G	3.0 Ferrari F310B-V10	FL	1/22
ret	BRITISH GP	Silverstone	5	Scuderia Ferrari Marlboro	G	3.0 Ferrari F310B-V10	wheel bearing	4/22
2	GERMAN GP	Hockenheim	5	Scuderia Ferrari Marlboro	G	3.0 Ferrari F310B-V10		4/22
4	HUNGARIAN GP	Hungaroring	5	Scuderia Ferrari Marlboro	G	3.0 Ferrari F310B-V10		1/22
1	BELGIAN GP	Spa	5	Scuderia Ferrari Marlboro	G	3.0 Ferrari F310B-V10		3/22
6	ITALIAN GP	Monza	5	Scuderia Ferrari Marlboro	G	3.0 Ferrari F310B-V10		9/22
6	AUSTRIAN GP	A1-Ring	5	Scuderia Ferrari Marlboro	G	3.0 Ferrari F310B-V10	stop & go penalty	9/22
ret	LUXEMBOURG GP	Nürburgring	5	Scuderia Ferrari Marlboro	G	3.0 Ferrari F310B-V10	collision damage	5/22
1	JAPANESE GP	Suzuka	5	Scuderia Ferrari Marlboro	G	3.0 Ferrari F310B-V10		2/22
ret	EUROPEAN GP	Jerez	5	Scuderia Ferrari Marlboro	G	3.0 Ferrari F310B-V10	collision with Villeneuve	2/22

1998   Championship position: 2nd   Wins: 6   Pole positions: 3   Fastest laps: 6   Points scored: 86

ret	AUSTRALIAN GP	Melbourne	3	Scuderia Ferrari Marlboro	G	3.0 Ferrari F300-V10	engine	3/22
3	BRAZILIAN GP	Interlagos	3	Scuderia Ferrari Marlboro	G	3.0 Ferrari F300-V10		4/22
1	ARGENTINE GP	Buenos Aires	3	Scuderia Ferrari Marlboro	G	3.0 Ferrari F300-V10		2/22
2	SAN MARINO GP	Imola	3	Scuderia Ferrari Marlboro	G	3.0 Ferrari F300-V10	FL	3/22
3	SPANISH GP	Barcelona	3	Scuderia Ferrari Marlboro	G	3.0 Ferrari F300-V10		3/22
10	MONACO GP	Monte Carlo	3	Scuderia Ferrari Marlboro	G	3.0 Ferrari F300-V10	collision with Würz/2 laps behind	4/22
1	CANADIAN GP	Montreal	3	Scuderia Ferrari Marlboro	G	3.0 Ferrari F300-V10	FL	3/22
1	FRENCH GP	Magny Cours	3	Scuderia Ferrari Marlboro	G	3.0 Ferrari F300-V10		2/22
1	BRITISH GP	Silverstone	3	Scuderia Ferrari Marlboro	G	3.0 Ferrari F300-V10	stop & go pen/FL	2/22
3	AUSTRIAN GP	A1-Ring	3	Scuderia Ferrari Marlboro	G	3.0 Ferrari F300-V10		4/22
5	GERMAN GP	Hockenheim	3	Scuderia Ferrari Marlboro	G	3.0 Ferrari F300-V10	lack of grip	9/22
1	HUNGARIAN GP	Hungaroring	3	Scuderia Ferrari Marlboro	G	3.0 Ferrari F300-V10	FL	3/22
ret	BELGIAN GP	Spa	3	Scuderia Ferrari Marlboro	G	3.0 Ferrari F300-V10	collision with Coulthard/FL	4/22
1	ITALIAN GP	Monza	3	Scuderia Ferrari Marlboro	G	3.0 Ferrari F300-V10		1/22
2	LUXEMBOURG GP	Nürburgring	3	Scuderia Ferrari Marlboro	G	3.0 Ferrari F300-V10		1/22
ret	JAPANESE GP	Suzuka	3	Scuderia Ferrari Marlboro	G	3.0 Ferrari F300-V10	started from back of grid/puncture/FL	1/22

1999   Championship position: 5th   Wins: 2   Pole positions: 3   Fastest laps: 5   Points scored: 44

8	AUSTRALIAN GP	Melbourne	3	Scuderia Ferrari Marlboro	B	3.0 Ferrari F399-V10	started from back/puncture/- 1 lap/FL	3/22
2	BRAZILIAN GP	Interlagos	3	Scuderia Ferrari Marlboro	B	3.0 Ferrari F399-V10r		4/22
1	SAN MARINO GP	Imola	3	Scuderia Ferrari Marlboro	B	3.0 Ferrari F399-V10r	FL	3/22
1	MONACO GP	Monte Carlo	3	Scuderia Ferrari Marlboro	B	3.0 Ferrari F399-V10		2/22
3	SPANISH GP	Barcelona	3	Scuderia Ferrari Marlboro	B	3.0 Ferrari F399-V10	FL	4/22
ret	CANADIAN GP	Montreal	3	Scuderia Ferrari Marlboro	B	3.0 Ferrari F399-V10	crashed	1/22
5	FRENCH GP	Magny Cours	3	Scuderia Ferrari Marlboro	B	3.0 Ferrari F399-V10		6/22
ret/dns	BRITISH GP	Silverstone	3	Scuderia Ferrari Marlboro	B	3.0 Ferrari F399-V10	accident-broken leg did not restart	2/22
2	MALAYSIAN GP	Sepang	3	Scuderia Ferrari Marlboro	B	3.0 Ferrari F399-V10	allowed Irvine to win/FL	1/22
2	JAPANESE GP	Suzuka	3	Scuderia Ferrari Marlboro	B	3.0 Ferrari F399-V10	FL	1/22

GP Starts: 127 (128)   GP Wins: 35   Pole positions: 23   Fastest laps: 39   Points: 492 (570)

Schumacher put on a dominant performance to win the 1998 French Grand Prix for Ferrari. With team-mate Eddie Irvine backing him up, the pair took Maranello's first 1-2 finish since Prost and Mansell filled the top two positions in Spain in 1990.

RALF SCHUMACHER

If the 1999 season buried the reputation (and possibly the F1 career) of the popular Alex Zanardi, then it was the making of the previously unpopular Ralf, who by the end of the year had earned a respect that went far beyond mere acceptance that he was on the Grand Prix grid on his own merits. As the younger brother of the prodigiously talented Michael Schumacher, it would have been perfectly understandable if he had opted for a profession as diametrically opposed to his sibling's as could be found, but Ralf had other ideas.

The younger Schumacher first made an impression in German Formula 3 during the 1994 season: driving the ubiquitous Dallara, he only scored a single victory but posted an additional nine top-three finishes to claim third place in the final standings behind runaway winner Jörg Müller and Alexander Wurz. The following year saw Ralf embroiled in a battle with Norberto Fontana for the crown but, despite a run of three wins from four races in mid-season, he was eventually beaten into second place by the diminutive Argentinian.

Although courted by Opel for a drive in the ITC series in 1996, Ralf and his manager Willy Weber decided that he should race in Formula Nippon in Japan as the next stage of his career development. It was a successful move for the young German, who posted three victories in the Le Mans Co. Reynard 96D to take the title. In addition he shared a Toyota Supra with Naoki Hattori in the All-Japan GT championship.

His year in Japan was crucial to his personal development – and Ralf certainly needed all his resilience when he stepped up to F1 with Jordan in 1997. He was paired with the equally ambitious and inexperienced Giancarlo Fisichella, and the two young turks slugged it out in a battle for supremacy within the team which was to be counter-productive for everyone. Ralf simply overdrove in his attempts to impress. A podium finish in Argentina should have been cause for major celebration, but it was tainted by his crassness in pushing his team-mate into premature retirement. The prevailing feeling was that Schumacher was wasting the natural speed that even his hardened critics had to admit he possessed in abundance.

For 1998 the German was joined by Damon Hill and both drivers spent the first part of the season vainly looking for an answer to seemingly insoluble problems, but Ralf's superb drive into sixth place in the wet at Silverstone was to prove the turning point for the team. Schumacher seemed to grow in confidence race by race and was deeply frustrated to have to hold station behind Hill at Spa when Jordan's first Grand Prix win was achieved. By then, however, he had already decided to accept an offer from Williams for 1999, much to Eddie Jordan's disappointment.

The conventional wisdom was that it was going to be a year of bedding-in for Ralf, with the planned BMW engine tie-up coming on tap in 2000. Nobody expected fireworks with the team consigned to running Supertec-engined cars, but they were wrong. Schumacher was the revelation of the season and could have won both the Italian and European Grands Prix if circumstances had played into his hands. More than anything, however, he had finally proved that he didn't need 'big brother' at all. He was very much his own man.

SCHUMACHER, Ralf (D) b 30/6/1975, Hürth-Hermüthlheim

	1997	Championship position: 11th	Wins: 0	Pole positions: 0	Fastest laps: 0	Points scored: 13		
	Race	Circuit	No	Entrant	Tyres	Car/Engine	Comment	Q Pos/Entries
ret	AUSTRALIAN GP	Melbourne	11	B&H Total Jordan Peugeot	G	3.0 Jordan 197 Peugeot V10	gearbox	12/24
ret	BRAZILIAN GP	Interlagos	11	B&H Total Jordan Peugeot	G	3.0 Jordan 197 Peugeot V10	electrics	10/22
3	ARGENTINE GP	Buenos Aires	11	B&H Total Jordan Peugeot	G	3.0 Jordan 197 Peugeot V10	collided with Fisichella	6/22
ret	SAN MARINO GP	Imola	11	B&H Total Jordan Peugeot	G	3.0 Jordan 197 Peugeot V10	driveshaft	5/22
ret	MONACO GP	Monte Carlo	11	B&H Total Jordan Peugeot	G	3.0 Jordan 197 Peugeot V10	crashed	6/22
ret	SPANISH GP	Barcelona	11	B&H Total Jordan Peugeot	G	3.0 Jordan 197 Peugeot V10	engine	9/22
ret	CANADIAN GP	Montreal	11	B&H Total Jordan Peugeot	G	3.0 Jordan 197 Peugeot V10	accident	7/22

6	FRENCH GP	Magny Cours	11	B&H Total Jordan Peugeot	G	3.0 Jordan 197 Peugeot V10		3/22
5	BRITISH GP	Silverstone	11	B&H Total Jordan Peugeot	G	3.0 Jordan 197 Peugeot V10		5/22
5	GERMAN GP	Hockenheim	11	B&H Total Jordan Peugeot	G	3.0 Jordan 197 Peugeot V10		7/22
5	HUNGARIAN GP	Hungaroring	11	B&H Total Jordan Peugeot	G	3.0 Jordan 197 Peugeot V10		14/22
ret	BELGIAN GP	Spa	11	B&H Total Jordan Peugeot	G	3.0 Jordan 197 Peugeot V10	started from pits/spun off	6/22
ret	ITALIAN GP	Monza	11	B&H Total Jordan Peugeot	G	3.0 Jordan 197 Peugeot V10	hit Herbert-collision damage	8/22
5	AUSTRIAN GP	A1-Ring	11	B&H Total Jordan Peugeot	G	3.0 Jordan 197 Peugeot V10		11/22
ret	LUXEMBOURG GP	Nürburgring	11	B&H Total Jordan Peugeot	G	3.0 Jordan 197 Peugeot V10	collision with Fisichella-lap 1	8/22
9*	JAPANESE GP	Suzuka	11	B&H Total Jordan Peugeot	G	3.0 Jordan 197 Peugeot V10	*5th place car dsq	13/22
ret	EUROPEAN GP	Jerez	11	B&H Total Jordan Peugeot	G	3.0 Jordan 197 Peugeot V10	alternator	16/22

1998 Championship position: 10th   Wins: 0   Pole positions: 0   Fastest laps: 0   Points scored: 14

ret	AUSTRALIAN GP	Melbourne	10	B&H Jordan Mugen Honda	G	3.0 Jordan 198-Mugen Honda V10	collision with Magnussen-lap 1	9/22
ret	BRAZILIAN GP	Interlagos	10	B&H Jordan Mugen Honda	G	3.0 Jordan 198-Mugen Honda V10	spun off	8/22
ret	ARGENTINE GP	Buenos Aires	10	B&H Jordan Mugen Honda	G	3.0 Jordan 198-Mugen Honda V10	suspension failure-spun off	5/22
7	SAN MARINO GP	Imola	10	B&H Jordan Mugen Honda	G	3.0 Jordan 198-Mugen Honda V10	low air valve pressure/-1 lap	9/22
11	SPANISH GP	Barcelona	10	B&H Jordan Mugen Honda	G	3.0 Jordan 198-Mugen Honda V10	2 laps behind	11/22
ret	MONACO GP	Monte Carlo	10	B&H Jordan Mugen Honda	G	3.0 Jordan 198-Mugen Honda V10	collision damage after shunt	16/22
ret	CANADIAN GP	Montreal	10	B&H Jordan Mugen Honda	G	3.0 Jordan 198-Mugen Honda V10	clutch	5/22
ret	FRENCH GP	Magny Cours	10	B&H Jordan Mugen Honda	G	3.0 Jordan 198-Mugen Honda V10	collision damage/3 laps behind	6/22
6	BRITISH GP	Silverstone	10	B&H Jordan Mugen Honda	G	3.0 Jordan 198-Mugen Honda V10	1 lap behind	10/22
5	AUSTRIAN GP	A1-Ring	10	B&H Jordan Mugen Honda	G	3.0 Jordan 198-Mugen Honda V10		9/22
6	GERMAN GP	Hockenheim	10	B&H Jordan Mugen Honda	G	3.0 Jordan 198-Mugen Honda V10		4/22
9	HUNGARIAN GP	Hungaroring	10	B&H Jordan Mugen Honda	G	3.0 Jordan 198-Mugen Honda V10	1 lap behind	10/22
2	BELGIAN GP	Spa	10	B&H Jordan Mugen Honda	G	3.0 Jordan 198-Mugen Honda V10		8/22
3	ITALIAN GP	Monza	10	B&H Jordan Mugen Honda	G	3.0 Jordan 198-Mugen Honda V10		6/22
ret	LUXEMBOURG GP	Nürburgring	10	B&H Jordan Mugen Honda	G	3.0 Jordan 198-Mugen Honda V10	brake disc	6/22
ret	JAPANESE GP	Suzuka	10	B&H Jordan Mugen Honda	G	3.0 Jordan 198-Mugen Honda V10	engine	7/22

1999 Championship position: 6th   Wins: 0   Pole positions: 0   Fastest laps: 1   Points scored: 35

3	AUSTRALIAN GP	Melbourne	6	Winfield Williams	B	3.0 Williams FW21-Supertec V10		8/22
4	BRAZILIAN GP	Interlagos	6	Winfield Williams	B	3.0 Williams FW21-Supertec V10	1 lap behind	11/22
ret	SAN MARINO GP	Imola	6	Winfield Williams	B	3.0 Williams FW21-Supertec V10	throttle	9/22
ret	MONACO GP	Monte Carlo	6	Winfield Williams	B	3.0 Williams FW21-Supertec V10	accident	16/22
5	SPANISH GP	Barcelona	6	Winfield Williams	B	3.0 Williams FW21-Supertec V10		10/22
4	CANADIAN GP	Montreal	6	Winfield Williams	B	3.0 Williams FW21-Supertec V10		13/22
4	FRENCH GP	Magny Cours	6	Winfield Williams	B	3.0 Williams FW21-Supertec V10		16/22
3	BRITISH GP	Silverstone	6	Winfield Williams	B	3.0 Williams FW21-Supertec V10		8/22
ret	AUSTRIAN GP	A1-Ring	6	Winfield Williams	B	3.0 Williams FW21-Supertec V10	spun off on lap 1	8/22
4	GERMAN GP	Hockenheim	6	Winfield Williams	B	3.0 Williams FW21-Supertec V10		11/22
9	HUNGARIAN GP	Hungaroring	6	Winfield Williams	B	3.0 Williams FW21-Supertec V10	1 lap behind	16/22
5	BELGIAN GP	Spa	6	Winfield Williams	B	3.0 Williams FW21-Supertec V10		5/22
2	ITALIAN GP	Monza	6	Winfield Williams	B	3.0 Williams FW21-Supertec V10	FL	5/22
4	EUROPEAN GP	Nürburgring	6	Winfield Williams	B	3.0 Williams FW21-Supertec V10	puncture-lead race	4/22
ret	MALAYSIAN GP	Sepang	6	Winfield Williams	B	3.0 Williams FW21-Supertec V10	spun off	8/22
5	JAPANESE GP	Suzuka	6	Winfield Williams	B	3.0 Williams FW21-Supertec V10		9/22

GP Starts: 49   GP Wins: 0   Pole positions: 0   Fastest laps: 1   Points: 62

VERN SCHUPPAN

After a few successful years in karting, this tall, blond Australian came to Britain in 1969 to race in Formula Ford, but it was when he moved into Formula Atlantic with a works Palliser in 1971 that he made the breakthrough, winning the Yellow Pages championship. After a Tyrrell test, Vern was contracted as a junior driver for BRM, but his opportunities were restricted to a couple of non-title events – in which he did well, taking fifth place in the Gold Cup and fourth in the John Player Challenge at Brands Hatch. It was much the same the following year, with Vern kicking his heels in F1, so he accepted an offer to join the Gulf/Wyer team to replace the injured Watson, taking second place in the Spa 1000 Km with Ganley.

For 1974, Schuppan settled into an F5000 programme with Theodore Racing, and although a Grand Prix chance came with Ensign he dropped out after a few races. His later F1 outings with Hill and Surtees were equally unproductive, but he was already concentrating on building a career in sports cars and F5000, joining Dan Gurney's Eagle team in 1975.

In 1976, Vern hit the USAC trail, earning the 'Rookie of the Year' award at Indianapolis that year, but his best finish was to be third at Indy in 1981. In the early eighties Schuppan became heavily involved in endurance racing, winning the Le Mans 24 Hours in 1983 for the powerful Rothmans Porsche factory team with Holbert and Haywood. Thereafter Vern became a successful Porsche entrant in the FIA and Japanese sports car series, developing the basic 962 design on behalf of customers around the world.

Most recently Schuppan has been a partner in Stefan Johansson's successful Indy Lights team, which is hoping to move up to the CART series when the necessary budgets are in place.

SCHUPPAN, Vern (AUS) b 19/3/1943, Booleroo, Whyalla, South Australia

	1972	Championship position: Unplaced						
	Race	Circuit	No	Entrant	Tyres	Car/Engine	Comment	Q Pos/Entries
dns	BELGIAN GP	Nivelles	26	Marlboro BRM	F	3.0 BRM P153B V12	*Marko raced car*	(26)/26
	1974	Championship position: Unplaced						
15	BELGIAN GP	Nivelles	22	Team Ensign	F	3.0 Ensign N174-Cosworth V8	*pit stop/fuel feed/-3 laps*	14/32
ret	MONACO GP	Monte Carlo	22	Team Ensign	F	3.0 Ensign N174-Cosworth V8	*spun off*	25/28
dsq	SWEDISH GP	Anderstorp	22	Team Ensign	F	3.0 Ensign N174-Cosworth V8	*started unofficially*	27/28
ret/dsq*	DUTCH GP	Zandvoort	22	Team Ensign	F	3.0 Ensign N174-Cosworth V8	*fuel line/*tyre change outside pits*	17/27
dnq	FRENCH GP	Dijon	22	Team Ensign	F	3.0 Ensign N174-Cosworth V8		23/30
dnq	BRITISH GP	Brands Hatch	22	Team Ensign	F	3.0 Ensign N174-Cosworth V8		30/34
ret	GERMAN GP	Nürburgring	22	Team Ensign	F	3.0 Ensign N174-Cosworth V8	*transmission*	22/32
	1975	Championship position: Unplaced						
ret	SWEDISH GP	Anderstorp	22	Embassy Racing with Graham Hill	G	3.0 Hill GH1-Cosworth V8	*driveshaft*	– / –
dns	"	"	22T	Embassy Racing with Graham Hill	G	3.0 Lola T370-Cosworth V8	*set grid time in this car*	26/26
	1977	Championship position: Unplaced						
12	BRITISH GP	Silverstone	18	Team Surtees	G	3.0 Surtees TS19-Cosworth V8	*2 laps behind*	23/36
7	GERMAN GP	Hockenheim	18	Team Surtees	G	3.0 Surtees TS19-Cosworth V8	*1 lap behind*	19/30
16	AUSTRIAN GP	Österreichring	18	Team Surtees	G	3.0 Surtees TS19-Cosworth V8	*pit stop/tyres/2 laps behind*	25/30
dnq	DUTCH GP	Zandvoort	18	Team Surtees	G	3.0 Surtees TS19-Cosworth V8		29/34

GP Starts: 9   GP Wins: 0   Pole positions: 0   Fastest laps: 0   Points: 0

ADOLFO J SCHWELM-CRUZ

This enthusiastic Argentinian drove a Jaguar XK120 and then an Alfa Romeo Monza in sports car and road races at home, but made trips to Europe along with a large contingent of his fellow countrymen for a limited programme of miscellaneous events from 1949 through to 1951, when he scored his best result on foreign soil, taking sixth in the Gran Premio di Roma at Caracalla driving a Maserati A6G.

At the beginning of 1953 he made his only Grand Prix appearance in one of the works Cooper-Bristols, which broke a stub axle and then shed a wheel. He fared no better in the Buenos Aires City Libre GP when the same car suffered a broken camshaft.

Subsequently Schwelm-Cruz returned to competition in his ancient Alfa, and was later seen in a Maserati sports.

ARCHIE SCOTT-BROWN

Archie was a tiny Scot who made light of the disabilities caused by his mother having contracted German measles when he was in the womb. As a baby he underwent no fewer than 22 operations to repair and add as much function as possible to his partly formed right arm and badly deformed legs and feet. Determined to lead as full a life as the next man, he was always bursting with vitality and exuberance, and earned a living as a travelling salesman in order to fund his motor sport ambitions.

Scott-Brown began racing in 1950 in a minor way in an MG TD, but it was 1954 before he began to make his mark, forming a great partnership with Brian Lister to race his Lister-Bristol. Soon Archie was winning club and national events all over the country with the car, and he earned himself a chance in the Connaught F1 team for 1956, taking part in the British Grand Prix and finishing second in the International Trophy race. His performances drew admiration from everyone for the amazing way he handled any type of machinery – Fangio for one thought his car control was phenomenal.

In 1957, he had the opportunity to race the works BRM in the British GP but, after a brake problem in testing and discussions with friends, he was persuaded to decline the offer. However, he continued to race in sports cars and was now back with Lister, handling his ferocious Lister-Jaguar.

By this time Scott-Brown was greatly frustrated by his inability to gain an international licence, which stopped him competing abroad. He did obtain permission to race in New Zealand early in 1958, winning the Lady Wigram Trophy, but the following May, when competing in a big sports car race at Spa, he lost control of his Lister on a piece of damp track while dicing with Masten Gregory. He crashed into a field and the car burst into flames, the luckless Scot dying from his injuries the following day.

SCHWELM-CRUZ, Adolfo J (RA) b 28/6/1923, Buenos Aires

	1953	Championship position: Unplaced						
	Race	Circuit	No	Entrant	Tyres	Car/Engine	Comment	Q Pos/Entries
ret	ARGENTINE GP	Buenos Aires	24	Cooper Car Co	D	2.0 Cooper T20-Bristol 6	*broken stub axle-lost wheel*	13/16

GP Starts: 1   GP Wins: 0   Pole positions: 0   Fastest laps: 0   Points: 0

SCOTT-BROWN, Archie (GB) b 13/5/1927, Paisley, Renfrewshire, Scotland – d 19/5/1958, Heusy, Belgium

	1956	Championship position: Unplaced						
	Race	Circuit	No	Entrant	Tyres	Car/Engine	Comment	Q Pos/Entries
ret	BRITISH GP	Silverstone	19	Connaught Engineering	P	2.5 Connaught-Alta B Type 4	*stub axle-lost wheel*	10/28

GP Starts: 1   GP Wins: 0   Pole positions: 0   Fastest laps: 0   Points: 0

SCOTTI, Piero (I) b 11/11/1909, Florence – d 14/2/1976

	1956	Championship position: Unplaced						
	Race	Circuit	No	Entrant	Tyres	Car/Engine	Comment	Q Pos/Entries
ret	BELGIAN GP	Spa	28	Piero Scotti	P	2.5 Connaught-Alta B Type 4	*oil pressure*	12/16

GP Starts: 1   GP Wins: 0   Pole positions: 0   Fastest laps: 0   Points: 0

SEIDEL, Wolfgang (D) b 4/7/1926 – d 1/3/1987

	1953	Championship position: Unplaced						
	Race	Circuit	No	Entrant	Tyres	Car/Engine	Comment	Q Pos/Entries
16	GERMAN GP	Nürburgring	22	Wolfgang Seidel	–	2.0 Veritas RS 6	*4 laps behind*	29/35
	1958	Championship position: Unplaced						
ret	BELGIAN GP	Spa	32	Scuderia Centro Sud	P	2.5 Maserati 250F 6	*rear axle*	17/20
ret	GERMAN GP (F2)	Nürburgring	22	R R C Walker Racing Team	D	1.5 Cooper T43-Climax 4 F2	*suspension*	22/26
ret	MOROCCAN GP	Casablanca	26	Scuderia Centro Sud	P	2.5 Maserati 250F 6	*accident*	20/25
	1960	Championship position: Unplaced						
9	ITALIAN GP	Monza	10	Wolfgang Seidel	D	1.5 Cooper T45-Climax 4		13/16
	1961	Championship position: Unplaced						
dns	BELGIAN GP	Spa	48	Scuderia Colonia	D	1.5 Lotus 18-Climax 4	*car raced by Bianchi*	(21)/25
17	BRITISH GP	Aintree	52	Scuderia Colonia	D	1.5 Lotus 18-Climax 4	*17 laps behind*	22/30
ret	GERMAN GP	Nürburgring	26	Scuderia Colonia	D	1.5 Lotus 18-Climax 4	*steering*	23/27
ret	ITALIAN GP	Monza	56	Scuderia Colonia	D	1.5 Lotus 18-Climax 4	*engine*	28/33
	1962	Championship position: Unplaced						
nc	DUTCH GP	Zandvoort	16	Ecurie Maarsbergen	D	1.5 Emeryson 1006-Climax 4	*28 laps behind*	20/20
ret	BRITISH GP	Aintree	44	Autosport Team Wolfgang Seidel	D	1.5 Lotus 24-BRM V8	*brakes/overheating*	21/21
dnq	GERMAN GP	Nürburgring	34	Autosport Team Wolfgang Seidel	D	1.5 Lotus 24-BRM V8		28/30

GP Starts: 10   GP Wins: 0   Pole positions: 0   Fastest laps: 0   Points: 0

PIERO SCOTTI

Scotti was an Italian businessman who raced Ferrari sports cars in the early fifties, taking third place in the 1951 Mille Miglia, and sharing a works car with Farina to win the Casablanca 12 Hours. He continued to find success in minor events before trying his hand at Formula 1 in 1956.

He bought an F1 Connaught on hire-purchase and took seventh in the International Trophy, but after the Belgian Grand Prix at Spa he returned the car to the factory and gave up racing.

WOLFGANG SEIDEL

An enthusiastic German, Seidel raced intermittently in Grands Pix for a decade without any success, despite campaigning some quite decent machinery on occasion.

He competed regularly in sports car events as a privateer, but sometimes drove for the works Ferrari and Porsche teams. Seidel's best result was a victory in the 1959 Targa Florio, sharing with Barth, but he was placed on numerous occasions, including second in the 1957 Reims 12 Hours with Phil Hill and third at Sebring in 1958 with Behra.

AYRTON SENNA

The wonder of the age, Senna's colossal talent bestrode Grand Prix racing for a decade. He had virtually made it his own personal fiefdom (in the widest sense) with a frightening intensity and commitment that could be viewed as bordering on arrogance. Yet Senna's creed was simplicity itself; his innate talent, just like that of a great musician, was to be continually developed day by day, year after year. To achieve this goal everything else must match his expectations: the machine and organisation at his disposal had to perform to his exacting standards or they served no useful purpose. Toleman, Lotus and then McLaren were blessed by his gifts, but immediately discarded when no longer of use. At the beginning of 1994 Ayrton, having finally landed the Williams-Renault drive he had long coveted, stood poised on the edge of another period of success. Then, with the new partnership having barely begun, came that blackest of weekends at Imola . . .

From a well-to-do Brazilian family, Ayrton was racing karts from a very early age and in fact had amassed eight seasons' experience before coming to Britain to make his Formula Ford debut in 1981. Twelve wins ensured the FF1600 title was won, and the Brazilian returned the following year to continue his climb to fame and fortune in the FF2000 series. A tally of 21 wins from 27 starts tells its own story. In 1983 Ayrton joined the West Surrey Racing F3 team and became embroiled in a fabulous tussle for the Marlboro championship with Martin Brundle. In the end Senna's early-season run of wins kept him in front when the title was decided, and after testing for both Williams and McLaren he agreed to drive for Toleman in Formula 1 in 1984.

The phenomenal talent was soon in evidence, with his drive in the wet at Monaco outstanding. Senna was poised to challenge Prost for the lead when the race was controversially stopped, but he had made his mark on an event he was to win for a staggering sixth time in 1993. When it became clear that Toleman were not able to provide Ayrton with the means to win, the Brazilian engineered his way out of his contract and joined Lotus. Almost immediately his first Grand Prix victory arrived, his skills in the wet at Estoril provoking memories of the great Jacky Ickx. Over the next three seasons Senna proved to be the fastest man around, certainly in qualifying, where he amassed 16 pole positions, but he scored only six wins, due in part to the fragility of the Lotus. It was crystal clear to Senna that to win the championship he needed a Honda engine, but definitely not a Lotus, and for 1988 he joined the McLaren team to partner Alain Prost.

Senna was supremely confident of his ability to outdrive the Frenchman, and was as good as his word. In a season which saw McLaren take victory in all bar one of the 16 races, Ayrton emerged triumphant in a manner more convincing than the eight-wins-to-seven margin suggests. Relationships between the two superstars were never more than cordial at best, and they broke down completely in 1989 as both drivers waged war within the confines of the team. This time the championship battle ended in Prost's favour after the Brazilian was deftly taken out by the Frenchman at the Suzuka chicane. By this time, of course, Prost had nothing to lose, having already decided to take his leave of McLaren, though he and Senna were to be embroiled in further controversy the following season. With Prost needing points at Suzuka to maintain Ferrari's challenge, Ayrton seemed to take his revenge, driving into the back of Prost's car at the first corner. It was an unworthy way for the title to be decided, wiping away the memory of some great performances earlier in the season.

In many ways 1991 was Senna's finest championship triumph. The new V12 Honda was not initially markedly superior to its lighter predecessor, despite the impression given by Ayrton's four straight wins from the start of the season. In fact these had been extremely hard-won triumphs that had demanded every ounce of the Brazilian's skill and guile. The following season found Senna in the unusual position of underdog, Williams and Renault finally having found the edge and the ability to sustain it. Ayrton predictably gave his all, winning at Monaco, Hungary and Monza, but perceived shortcomings at McLaren were already irking him and his frustration was probably not helped by his inability to muscle into a Williams drive alongside Prost in 1993.

During the winter months McLaren were having to come to terms with the loss of Honda power and hoping that the replacement Ford engine would be sufficiently promising to tempt the unhappy Brazilian to continue. In the event Senna deigned to drive – initially on a race-by-race basis for a reported fee of $1 million per race. Luckily for us lesser beings, he served up a number of superlative performances which can seldom have been bettered at any time in the history of motor racing. Brazil, Donington and Adelaide showed us all why he truly was one the sport's all-time greats.

When it was announced that Senna would be joining the all-conquering Williams-Renault team for 1994, it was difficult to see how anybody was going to beat him, Mansell and Prost having taken the previous two titles with comparative ease. Things did not start well for the Brazilian, with the latest FW16 car proving troublesome to sort, although Ayrton somehow managed to assert his authority in practice, exploring the outer edges of the car's performance to take pole position.

But in the first two races he struggled to match Schumacher's Benetton, and in the third at Imola his lead in the early stages of the restarted race was looking extremely tenuous. Then came disaster. Possibly the steering column on the Williams sheared or perhaps the car became unsettled on the bumpy track surface, but the Brazilian appeared helpless as it speared into the concrete wall at the Tamburello corner. As fate would have it, part of the suspension came back and struck poor Senna, who then stood no chance of survival, being officially pronounced dead in a Bologna hospital later that afternoon.

The aftermath of Senna's death caused shock waves to ripple through the sport. Additional safety measures, some sound and others less so, were introduced as Grand Prix racing tried to come to terms with the loss of its premier talent. For his legion of fans, he was irreplaceable and things would never be the same again. For the sport at large that awful day ushered in a new era but, although time would heal the wounds, the scars would always remain.

AYRTON SENNA

WORLD CHAMPION: 1988, 1990 & 1991

SENNA, Ayrton (BR) b 21/3/1960, São Paulo – d 1/5/1994, Bologna, Italy

1984
Championship position: 9th= Wins: 0 Pole positions: 0 Fastest laps: 1 Points scored: 13

	Race	Circuit	No	Entrant	Tyres	Car/Engine	Comment	Q Pos/Entries
ret	BRAZILIAN GP	Rio	19	Toleman Group Motorsport	P	1.5 t/c Toleman TG183B-Hart 4	turbo boost pressure	17/27
6	SOUTH AFRICAN GP	Kyalami	19	Toleman Group Motorsport	P	1.5 t/c Toleman TG183B-Hart 4	3 laps behind	13/27
6*	BELGIAN GP	Spa	19	Toleman Group Motorsport	P	1.5 t/c Toleman TG183B-Hart 4	* 6th place car dsq/-2 laps	19/27
dnq	SAN MARINO GP	Imola	19	Toleman Group Motorsport	P	1.5 t/c Toleman TG183B-Hart 4	tyre problems	28/28
ret	FRENCH GP	Dijon	19	Toleman Group Motorsport	M	1.5 t/c Toleman TG184-Hart 4	turbo	13/27
2*	MONACO GP	Monte Carlo	19	Toleman Group Motorsport	M	1.5 t/c Toleman TG184-Hart 4	race stopped/rain/FL/*half points	13/27
7	CANADIAN GP	Montreal	19	Toleman Group Motorsport	M	1.5 t/c Toleman TG184-Hart 4	2 laps behind	9/26
ret	US GP (DETROIT)	Detroit	19	Toleman Group Motorsport	M	1.5 t/c Toleman TG184-Hart 4	broken wishbone/crashed	7/27
ret	US GP (DALLAS)	Dallas	19	Toleman Group Motorsport	M	1.5 t/c Toleman TG184-Hart 4	driveshaft	6/27
3	BRITISH GP	Brands Hatch	19	Toleman Group Motorsport	M	1.5 t/c Toleman TG184-Hart 4		7/27
ret	GERMAN GP	Hockenheim	19	Toleman Group Motorsport	M	1.5 t/c Toleman TG184-Hart 4	rear wing failure/accident	9/27
ret	AUSTRIAN GP	Österreichring	19	Toleman Group Motorsport	M	1.5 t/c Toleman TG184-Hart 4	oil pressure	10/28
ret	DUTCH GP	Zandvoort	19	Toleman Group Motorsport	M	1.5 t/c Toleman TG184-Hart 4	engine	13/27
ret	EUROPEAN GP	Nürburgring	19	Toleman Group Motorsport	M	1.5 t/c Toleman TG184-Hart 4	hit Rosberg	12/26
3	PORTUGUESE GP	Estoril	19	Toleman Group Motorsport	M	1.5 t/c Toleman TG184-Hart 4		3/27

1985
Championship position: 4th Wins: 2 Pole positions: 7 Fastest laps: 3 Points scored: 38

	Race	Circuit	No	Entrant	Tyres	Car/Engine	Comment	Q Pos/Entries
ret	BRAZILIAN GP	Rio	12	John Player Special Team Lotus	G	1.5 t/c Lotus 97T-Renault V6	electrics	4/25
1	PORTUGUESE GP	Estoril	12	John Player Special Team Lotus	G	1.5 t/c Lotus 97T-Renault V6	FL	1/26
7/ret	SAN MARINO	Imola	12	John Player Special Team Lotus	G	1.5 t/c Lotus 97T-Renault V6	out of fuel	1/26
ret	MONACO GP	Monte Carlo	12	John Player Special Team Lotus	G	1.5 t/c Lotus 97T-Renault V6	engine	1/26
16	CANADIAN GP	Montreal	12	John Player Special Team Lotus	G	1.5 t/c Lotus 97T-Renault V6	p stop/turbo pipe loose/FL/-5 laps	2/25
ret	US GP (DETROIT)	Detroit	12	John Player Special Team Lotus	G	1.5 t/c Lotus 97T-Renault V6	hit wall/FL	1/25
ret	FRENCH GP	Paul Ricard	12	John Player Special Team Lotus	G	1.5 t/c Lotus 97T-Renault V6	engine/accident	2/26
10/ret	BRITISH GP	Silverstone	12	John Player Special Team Lotus	G	1.5 t/c Lotus 97T-Renault V6	fuel injection problems/-5 laps	4/26
ret	GERMAN GP	Nürburgring	12	John Player Special Team Lotus	G	1.5 t/c Lotus 97T-Renault V6	driveshaft c.v. joint	5/27
2	AUSTRIAN GP	Österreichring	12	John Player Special Team Lotus	G	1.5 t/c Lotus 97T-Renault V6		14/27
3	DUTCH GP	Zandvoort	12	John Player Special Team Lotus	G	1.5 t/c Lotus 97T-Renault V6		4/27
3	ITALIAN GP	Monza	12	John Player Special Team Lotus	G	1.5 t/c Lotus 97T-Renault V6		1/26
1	BELGIAN GP	Spa	12	John Player Special Team Lotus	G	1.5 t/c Lotus 97T-Renault V6		2/24
2	EUROPEAN GP	Brands Hatch	12	John Player Special Team Lotus	G	1.5 t/c Lotus 97T-Renault V6		1/27
ret	SOUTH AFRICAN GP	Kyalami	12	John Player Special Team Lotus	G	1.5 t/c Lotus 97T-Renault V6	engine	4/21
ret	AUSTRALIAN GP	Adelaide	12	John Player Special Team Lotus	G	1.5 t/c Lotus 97T-Renault V6	engine	1/25

1986
Championship position: 4th Wins: 2 Pole positions: 8 Fastest laps: 0 Points scored: 55

	Race	Circuit	No	Entrant	Tyres	Car/Engine	Comment	Q Pos/Entries
2	BRAZILIAN GP	Rio	12	John Player Special Team Lotus	G	1.5 t/c Lotus 98T-Renault V6	incident with Mansell	1/25
1	SPANISH GP	Jerez	12	John Player Special Team Lotus	G	1.5 t/c Lotus 98T-Renault V6		1/25
ret	SAN MARINO GP	Imola	12	John Player Special Team Lotus	G	1.5 t/c Lotus 98T-Renault V6	wheel bearing	1/26
3	MONACO GP	Monte Carlo	12	John Player Special Team Lotus	G	1.5 t/c Lotus 98T-Renault V6		3/26
2	BELGIAN GP	Spa	12	John Player Special Team Lotus	G	1.5 t/c Lotus 98T-Renault V6		4/25
5	CANADIAN GP	Montreal	12	John Player Special Team Lotus	G	1.5 t/c Lotus 98T-Renault V6	1 lap behind	2/25
1	US GP (DETROIT)	Detroit	12	John Player Special Team Lotus	G	1.5 t/c Lotus 98T-Renault V6		1/26
ret	FRENCH GP	Paul Ricard	12	John Player Special Team Lotus	G	1.5 t/c Lotus 98T-Renault V6	spun off on oil	1/26
ret	BRITISH GP	Brands Hatch	12	John Player Special Team Lotus	G	1.5 t/c Lotus 98T-Renault V6	gearbox	3/26
2	GERMAN GP	Hockenheim	12	John Player Special Team Lotus	G	1.5 t/c Lotus 98T-Renault V6		3/26
2	HUNGARIAN GP	Hungaroring	12	John Player Special Team Lotus	G	1.5 t/c Lotus 98T-Renault V6		1/26
ret	AUSTRIAN GP	Österreichring	12	John Player Special Team Lotus	G	1.5 t/c Lotus 98T-Renault V6	engine misfire	8/26
ret	ITALIAN GP	Monza	12	John Player Special Team Lotus	G	1.5 t/c Lotus 98T-Renault V6	transmission at start	5/27

Deadly rivals. Senna in the McLaren leads Mansell in the Williams in 1992. There was never any love lost between the two men, but each held a grudging respect for the other's talent as a driver.

4	PORTUGUESE GP	Estoril	12	John Player Special Team Lotus	G	1.5 t/c Lotus 98T-Renault V6	*out of fuel/1 lap behind*	1/27
3	MEXICAN GP	Mexico City	12	John Player Special Team Lotus	G	1.5 t/c Lotus 98T-Renault V6		1/26
ret	AUSTRALIAN GP	Adelaide	12	John Player Special Team Lotus	G	1.5 t/c Lotus 98T-Renault V6	*engine*	3/26

1987   Championship position: 3rd   Wins: 2   Pole positions: 1   Fastest laps: 3   Points scored: 57

ret	BRAZILIAN GP	Rio	12	Camel Team Lotus Honda	G	1.5 t/c Lotus 99T-Honda V6	*engine*	3/23
2	SAN MARINO GP	Imola	12	Camel Team Lotus Honda	G	1.5 t/c Lotus 99T-Honda V6		1/27
ret	BELGIAN GP	Spa	12	Camel Team Lotus Honda	G	1.5 t/c Lotus 99T-Honda V6	*accident with Mansell*	3/26
1	MONACO GP	Monte Carlo	12	Camel Team Lotus Honda	G	1.5 t/c Lotus 99T-Honda V6	*FL*	2/26
1	US GP (DETROIT)	Detroit	12	Camel Team Lotus Honda	G	1.5 t/c Lotus 99T-Honda V6	*FL*	2/26
4	FRENCH GP	Paul Ricard	12	Camel Team Lotus Honda	G	1.5 t/c Lotus 99T-Honda V6	*1 lap behind*	3/26
3	BRITISH GP	Silverstone	12	Camel Team Lotus Honda	G	1.5 t/c Lotus 99T-Honda V6	*1 lap behind*	3/26
3	GERMAN GP	Hockenheim	12	Camel Team Lotus Honda	G	1.5 t/c Lotus 99T-Honda V6	*1 lap behind*	2/26
2	HUNGARIAN GP	Hungaroring	12	Camel Team Lotus Honda	G	1.5 t/c Lotus 99T-Honda V6		6/26
5	AUSTRIAN GP	Österreichring	12	Camel Team Lotus Honda	G	1.5 t/c Lotus 99T-Honda V6	*2 laps behind*	7/26
2	ITALIAN GP	Monza	12	Camel Team Lotus Honda	G	1.5 t/c Lotus 99T-Honda V6	*FL*	4/28
7	PORTUGUESE GP	Estoril	12	Camel Team Lotus Honda	G	1.5 t/c Lotus 99T-Honda V6	*pit stop-throttle/2 laps behind*	5/27
5	SPANISH GP	Jerez	12	Camel Team Lotus Honda	G	1.5 t/c Lotus 99T-Honda V6	*tyre problems*	5/28
ret	MEXICAN GP	Mexico City	12	Camel Team Lotus Honda	G	1.5 t/c Lotus 99T-Honda V6	*clutch-spun off*	7/27
2	JAPANESE GP	Suzuka	12	Camel Team Lotus Honda	G	1.5 t/c Lotus 99T-Honda V6		8/27
dsq*	AUSTRALIAN GP	Adelaide	12	Camel Team Lotus Honda	G	1.5 t/c Lotus 99T-Honda V6	*2nd-dsq* oversize brake ducts*	4/27

1988   Championship position: WORLD CHAMPION   Wins: 8   Pole positions: 13   Fastest laps: 3   Points scored: 94

dsq	BRAZILIAN GP	Rio	12	Honda Marlboro McLaren	G	1.5 t/c McLaren MP4/4-Honda V6	*changed cars illegally at start*	1/31
1	SAN MARINO GP	Imola	12	Honda Marlboro McLaren	G	1.5 t/c McLaren MP4/4-Honda V6		1/31
ret	MONACO GP	Monte Carlo	12	Honda Marlboro McLaren	G	1.5 t/c McLaren MP4/4-Honda V6	*hit barrier when 1st/FL*	1/30
2	MEXICAN GP	Mexico City	12	Honda Marlboro McLaren	G	1.5 t/c McLaren MP4/4-Honda V6		1/30
1	CANADIAN GP	Montreal	12	Honda Marlboro McLaren	G	1.5 t/c McLaren MP4/4-Honda V6	*FL*	1/31
1	US GP (DETROIT)	Detroit	12	Honda Marlboro McLaren	G	1.5 t/c McLaren MP4/4-Honda V6		1/31
2	FRENCH GP	Paul Ricard	12	Honda Marlboro McLaren	G	1.5 t/c McLaren MP4/4-Honda V6		2/31
1	BRITISH GP	Silverstone	12	Honda Marlboro McLaren	G	1.5 t/c McLaren MP4/4-Honda V6		3/31
1	GERMAN GP	Hockenheim	12	Honda Marlboro McLaren	G	1.5 t/c McLaren MP4/4-Honda V6		1/31
1	HUNGARIAN GP	Hungaroring	12	Honda Marlboro McLaren	G	1.5 t/c McLaren MP4/4-Honda V6		1/31
1	BELGIAN GP	Spa	12	Honda Marlboro McLaren	G	1.5 t/c McLaren MP4/4-Honda V6		1/31
10/ret	ITALIAN GP	Monza	12	Honda Marlboro McLaren	G	1.5 t/c McLaren MP4/4-Honda V6	*collision-Schlesser/-2 laps*	1/31
6	PORTUGUESE GP	Estoril	12	Honda Marlboro McLaren	G	1.5 t/c McLaren MP4/4-Honda V6	*collision-Mansell/pit stop*	2/31
4	SPANISH GP	Jerez	12	Honda Marlboro McLaren	G	1.5 t/c McLaren MP4/4-Honda V6	*pit stop/tyres/*	1/31
1	JAPANESE GP	Suzuka	12	Honda Marlboro McLaren	G	1.5 t/c McLaren MP4/4-Honda V6	*FL/then record 8th win of year*	1/31
2	AUSTRALIAN GP	Adelaide	12	Honda Marlboro McLaren	G	1.5 t/c McLaren MP4/4-Honda V6		1/31

1989   Championship position: 2nd   Wins: 5   Pole positions: 13   Fastest laps: 3   Points scored: 60

11	BRAZILIAN GP	Rio	1	Honda Marlboro McLaren	G	3.5 McLaren MP4/5-Honda V10	*lap 1 collision/4 p stops/-2 laps*	1/38
1	SAN MARINO GP	Imola	1	Honda Marlboro McLaren	G	3.5 McLaren MP4/5-Honda V10	*aggregate of two parts*	1/39
1	MONACO GP	Monte Carlo	1	Honda Marlboro McLaren	G	3.5 McLaren MP4/5-Honda V10		1/38
1	MEXICAN GP	Mexico City	1	Honda Marlboro McLaren	G	3.5 McLaren MP4/5-Honda V10		1/39
ret	US GP (PHOENIX)	Phoenix	1	Honda Marlboro McLaren	G	3.5 McLaren MP4/5-Honda V10	*electrics/FL*	1/39
7/ret	CANADIAN GP	Montreal	1	Honda Marlboro McLaren	G	3.5 McLaren MP4/5-Honda V10	*engine/3 laps behind*	2/39
ret	FRENCH GP	Paul Ricard	1	Honda Marlboro McLaren	G	3.5 McLaren MP4/5-Honda V10	*transmission at start*	2/39
ret	BRITISH GP	Silverstone	1	Honda Marlboro McLaren	G	3.5 McLaren MP4/5-Honda V10	*gearbox-spun off*	1/39
1	GERMAN GP	Hockenheim	1	Honda Marlboro McLaren	G	3.5 McLaren MP4/5-Honda V10	*FL*	1/39
2	HUNGARIAN GP	Hungaroring	1	Honda Marlboro McLaren	G	3.5 McLaren MP4/5-Honda V10		2/39
1	BELGIAN GP	Spa	1	Honda Marlboro McLaren	G	3.5 McLaren MP4/5-Honda V10		1/39
ret	ITALIAN GP	Monza	1	Honda Marlboro McLaren	G	3.5 McLaren MP4/5-Honda V10	*engine*	1/39
ret	PORTUGUESE GP	Estoril	1	Honda Marlboro McLaren	G	3.5 McLaren MP4/5-Honda V10	*collision with Mansell*	1/39
1	SPANISH GP	Jerez	1	Honda Marlboro McLaren	G	3.5 McLaren MP4/5-Honda V10	*FL*	1/38
dsq*	JAPANESE GP	Suzuka	1	Honda Marlboro McLaren	G	3.5 McLaren MP4/5-Honda V10	** 1st but dsq-push start*	1/39
ret	AUSTRALIAN GP	Adelaide	1	Honda Marlboro McLaren	G	3.5 McLaren MP4/5-Honda V10	*collision with Brundle*	1/39

1990   Championship position: WORLD CHAMPION   Wins: 6   Pole positions: 10   Fastest laps: 2   Points scored: 78

1	US GP (PHOENIX)	Phoenix	27	Honda Marlboro McLaren	G	3.5 McLaren MP4/5B-Honda V10		5/35
3	BRAZILIAN GP	Interlagos	27	Honda Marlboro McLaren	G	3.5 McLaren MP4/5B-Honda V10	*p stop/collision with Nakajima*	1/35
ret	SAN MARINO GP	Imola	27	Honda Marlboro McLaren	G	3.5 McLaren MP4/5B-Honda V10	*wheel rim damage spun off*	1/34
1	MONACO GP	Monza	27	Honda Marlboro McLaren	G	3.5 McLaren MP4/5B-Honda V10	*FL*	1/35
1	CANADIAN GP	Montreal	27	Honda Marlboro McLaren	G	3.5 McLaren MP4/5B-Honda V10		1/35
20/ret	MEXICAN GP	Mexico City	27	Honda Marlboro McLaren	G	3.5 McLaren MP4/5B-Honda V10	*puncture/6 laps behind*	3/35
3	FRENCH GP	Paul Ricard	27	Honda Marlboro McLaren	G	3.5 McLaren MP4/5B-Honda V10		3/35
3	BRITISH GP	Silverstone	27	Honda Marlboro McLaren	G	3.5 McLaren MP4/5B-Honda V10	*spun at Copse*	2/35
1	GERMAN GP	Hockenheim	27	Honda Marlboro McLaren	G	3.5 McLaren MP4/5B-Honda V10		1/35
2	HUNGARIAN GP	Hungaroring	27	Honda Marlboro McLaren	G	3.5 McLaren MP4/5B-Honda V10	*pit stop-puncture*	4/35
1	BELGIAN GP	Spa	27	Honda Marlboro McLaren	G	3.5 McLaren MP4/5B-Honda V10		1/33
1	ITALIAN GP	Monza	27	Honda Marlboro McLaren	G	3.5 McLaren MP4/5B-Honda V10	*FL*	1/33
2	PORTUGUESE GP	Estoril	27	Honda Marlboro McLaren	G	3.5 McLaren MP4/5B-Honda V10	*pit stop-tyres*	3/33
ret	SPANISH GP	Jerez	27	Honda Marlboro McLaren	G	3.5 McLaren MP4/5B-Honda V10	*punctured radiator/engine*	1/33
ret	JAPANESE GP	Suzuka	27	Honda Marlboro McLaren	G	3.5 McLaren MP4/5B-Honda V10	*collision with Prost*	1/30
ret	AUSTRALIAN GP	Adelaide	27	Honda Marlboro McLaren	G	3.5 McLaren MP4/5B-Honda V10	*missed 2nd gear-crashed*	1/30

1991   Championship position: WORLD CHAMPION   Wins: 6   Pole positions: 8   Fastest laps: 2   Points scored: 96

1	US GP (PHOENIX)	Phoenix	1	Honda Marlboro McLaren	G	3.5 McLaren MP4/6-Honda V12		1/34
1	BRAZILIAN GP	Interlagos	1	Honda Marlboro McLaren	G	3.5 McLaren MP4/6-Honda V12	*lost 3rd-5th gears*	1/34
1	SAN MARINO GP	Imola	1	Honda Marlboro McLaren	G	3.5 McLaren MP4/6-Honda V12		1/34
1	MONACO GP	Monte Carlo	1	Honda Marlboro McLaren	G	3.5 McLaren MP4/6-Honda V12		1/34
ret	CANADIAN GP	Montreal	1	Honda Marlboro McLaren	G	3.5 McLaren MP4/6-Honda V12	*electrics/alternator*	3/34
3	MEXICAN GP	Mexico City	1	Honda Marlboro McLaren	G	3.5 McLaren MP4/6-Honda V12		3/34
3	FRENCH GP	Magny Cours	1	Honda Marlboro McLaren	G	3.5 McLaren MP4/6-Honda V12		3/34
4/ret	BRITISH GP	Silverstone	1	Honda Marlboro McLaren	G	3.5 McLaren MP4/6-Honda V12	*out of fuel/1 lap behind*	2/34
7/ret	GERMAN GP	Hockenheim	1	Honda Marlboro McLaren	G	3.5 McLaren MP4/6-Honda V12	*out of fuel/1 lap behind*	2/34

	Race	Circuit	No	Entrant	Tyres	Car/Engine	Comment	Q Pos/Entries
1	HUNGARIAN GP	Hungaroring	1	Honda Marlboro McLaren	G	3.5 McLaren MP4/6-Honda V12		1/34
1	BELGIAN GP	Spa	1	Honda Marlboro McLaren	G	3.5 McLaren MP4/6-Honda V12		1/34
2	ITALIAN GP	Monza	1	Honda Marlboro McLaren	G	3.5 McLaren MP4/6-Honda V12	*FL*	1/34
2	PORTUGUESE GP	Estoril	1	Honda Marlboro McLaren	G	3.5 McLaren MP4/6-Honda V12		3/34
5	SPANISH GP	Barcelona	1	Honda Marlboro McLaren	G	3.5 McLaren MP4/6-Honda V12	*spin*	3/33
2	JAPANESE GP	Suzuka	1	Honda Marlboro McLaren	G	3.5 McLaren MP4/6-Honda V12	*allowed Berger to win/FL*	2/31
1*	AUSTRALIAN GP	Adelaide	1	Honda Marlboro McLaren	G	3.5 McLaren MP4/6-Honda V12	*rain shortened race/*half points*	1/32

1992 Championship position: 4th Wins: 3 Pole positions: 1 Fastest laps: 1 Points scored: 50

	Race	Circuit	No	Entrant	Tyres	Car/Engine	Comment	Q Pos/Entries
3	SOUTH AFRICAN GP	Kyalami	1	Honda Marlboro McLaren	G	3.5 McLaren MP4/6B-Honda V12		2/30
ret	MEXICAN GP	Mexico City	1	Honda Marlboro McLaren	G	3.5 McLaren MP4/6B-Honda V12	*transmission*	6/30
ret	BRAZILIAN GP	Interlagos	1	Honda Marlboro McLaren	G	3.5 McLaren MP4/7A-Honda V12	*electrics*	3/31
dns	"	"	1	Honda Marlboro McLaren	G	3.5 McLaren MP4/6B-Honda V12	*practice only*	–/–
9/ret	SPANISH GP	Barcelona	1	Honda Marlboro McLaren	G	3.5 McLaren MP4/7A-Honda V12	*spun off/3 laps behind*	3/32
3	SAN MARINO GP	Imola	1	Honda Marlboro McLaren	G	3.5 McLaren MP4/7A-Honda V12		3/32
1	MONACO GP	Monte Carlo	1	Honda Marlboro McLaren	G	3.5 McLaren MP4/7A-Honda V12		3/32
ret	CANADIAN GP	Montreal	1	Honda Marlboro McLaren	G	3.5 McLaren MP4/7A-Honda V12	*electrics*	1/32
ret	FRENCH GP	Magny Cours	1	Honda Marlboro McLaren	G	3.5 McLaren MP4/7A-Honda V12	*collision damage lap 1*	3/30
ret	BRITISH GP	Silverstone	1	Honda Marlboro McLaren	G	3.5 McLaren MP4/7A-Honda V12	*transmission*	3/32
2	GERMAN GP	Hockenheim	1	Honda Marlboro McLaren	G	3.5 McLaren MP4/7A-Honda V12		3/32
1	HUNGARIAN GP	Hungaroring	1	Honda Marlboro McLaren	G	3.5 McLaren MP4/7A-Honda V12		3/31
5	BELGIAN GP	Spa	1	Honda Marlboro McLaren	G	3.5 McLaren MP4/7A-Honda V12	*gambled to stay on slicks*	2/30
1	ITALIAN GP	Monza	1	Honda Marlboro McLaren	G	3.5 McLaren MP4/7A-Honda V12		2/28
3	PORTUGUESE GP	Estoril	1	Honda Marlboro McLaren	G	3.5 McLaren MP4/7A-Honda V12	*pit stops-handling/-1 lap/FL*	3/26
ret	JAPANESE GP	Suzuka	1	Honda Marlboro McLaren	G	3.5 McLaren MP4/7A-Honda V12	*engine*	3/26
ret	AUSTRALIAN GP	Adelaide	1	Honda Marlboro McLaren	G	3.5 McLaren MP4/7A-Honda V12	*ran into back of Mansell*	2/26

1993 Championship position: 2nd Wins: 5 Pole positions: 1 Fastest laps: 1 Points scored: 73

	Race	Circuit	No	Entrant	Tyres	Car/Engine	Comment	Q Pos/Entries
2	SOUTH AFRICAN GP	Kyalami	8	Marlboro McLaren	G	3.5 McLaren MP4/8-Ford HB V8		2/26
1	BRAZILIAN GP	Interlagos	8	Marlboro McLaren	G	3.5 McLaren MP4/8-Ford HB V8		3/26
1	EUROPEAN GP	Donington	8	Marlboro McLaren	G	3.5 McLaren MP4/8-Ford HB V8	*FL*(set via pit lane)*	4/26
ret	SAN MARINO GP	Imola	8	Marlboro McLaren	G	3.5 McLaren MP4/8-Ford HB V8	*hydraulic failure*	4/26
2	SPANISH GP	Barcelona	8	Marlboro McLaren	G	3.5 McLaren MP4/8-Ford HB V8		3/26
1	MONACO GP	Monte Carlo	8	Marlboro McLaren	G	3.5 McLaren MP4/8-Ford HB V8	*6th Monaco win-new record*	3/26
18/ret	CANADIAN GP	Montreal	8	Marlboro McLaren	G	3.5 McLaren MP4/8-Ford HB V8	*electrics/7 laps behind*	8/26
4	FRENCH GP	Magny Cours	8	Marlboro McLaren	G	3.5 McLaren MP4/8-Ford HB V8		5/26
5/ret	BRITISH GP	Silverstone	8	Marlboro McLaren	G	3.5 McLaren MP4/8-Ford HB V8	*out of fuel-last lap/1 lap behind*	4/26
4	GERMAN GP	Hockenheim	8	Marlboro McLaren	G	3.5 McLaren MP4/8-Ford HB V8	*collision-spin lap 1*	4/26
ret	HUNGARIAN GP	Hungaroring	8	Marlboro McLaren	G	3.5 McLaren MP4/8-Ford HB V8	*throttle*	4/26
4	BELGIAN GP	Spa	8	Marlboro McLaren	G	3.5 McLaren MP4/8-Ford HB V8		5/25
ret	ITALIAN GP	Monza	8	Marlboro McLaren	G	3.5 McLaren MP4/8-Ford HB V8	*ran into back of Brundle*	4/26
ret	PORTUGUESE GP	Estoril	8	Marlboro McLaren	G	3.5 McLaren MP4/8-Ford HB V8	*engine*	4/26
1	JAPANESE GP	Suzuka	8	Marlboro McLaren	G	3.5 McLaren MP4/8-Ford HB V8		2/24
1	AUSTRALIAN GP	Adelaide	8	Marlboro McLaren	G	3.5 McLaren MP4/8-Ford HB V8		1/24

1994 Championship position: Unplaced Pole positions: 3

	Race	Circuit	No	Entrant	Tyres	Car/Engine	Comment	Q Pos/Entries
ret	BRAZILIAN GP	Interlagos	2	Rothmans Williams Renault	G	3.5 Williams FW16-Renault V10	*spun off and stalled*	1/28
ret	PACIFIC GP	T.I. Circuit	2	Rothmans Williams Renault	G	3.5 Williams FW16-Renault V10	*hit by Häkkinen-spun out*	1/28
ret	SAN MARINO GP	Imola	2	Rothmans Williams Renault	G	3.5 Williams FW16-Renault V10	*fatal race accident*	1/28

GP Starts: 161   GP Wins: 41   Pole positions: 65   Fastest laps: 19   Points: 614

DORINO SERAFINI

This ex-Gilera motor cycle racer's career prospects on four wheels were spoilt by a very serious accident in the 1947 Comminges GP when the steering column failed on his Maserati. It put him out of action for some time, and he was never quite the same prospect subsequently.

Joining Ferrari for 1950, Serafini shared the second-place Ferrari with Ascari in his only Grand Prix start, and took a number of other second places – notably at Pedralbes, in the F1 car, and in the Eva Peron Cup race at Buenos Aires and the Circuit of Garda with the F2 T166.

It was much the same story in 1951 with second places again in both the Syracuse and San Remo GPs, before another big accident – this time in the Mille Miglia – left him with a broken arm and leg. Thereafter Dorino raced less frequently but he returned to contest the 1954 Brescia-Rome-Brescia classic, taking seventh place overall and first in the GT class with his Lancia.

SERAFINI, Dorino (I) b 22/7/1909, Pesaro

1950 Championship position: Unplaced

	Race	Circuit	No	Entrant	Tyres	Car/Engine	Comment	Q Pos/Entries
2*	ITALIAN GP	Monza	48	Scuderia Ferrari	P	4.5 Ferrari 375F1 V12	** car taken over by Ascari*	6/27

GP Starts: 1   GP Wins: 0   Pole positions: 0   Fastest laps: 0   Points: 3

CHICO SERRA

A contemporary and bitter rival of fellow countryman Nelson Piquet, Serra enjoyed an outstanding Formula Ford season in 1977, winning the Townsend Thoresen FF1600 championship, before stepping into Formula 3 with the Ron Dennis-run Project Four March. It was a strong year, with Piquet and Warwick among the opposition, but Chico was unflustered, escaping a huge accident at Mallory Park to finish third in the Vandervell series and joint second with Warwick in the BP championship.

Back in Formula 3 in 1979, Serra made no mistake, winning the 20-round Vandervell championship, taking five victories and seven second places, and putting his Project Four March on the front row no fewer than 16 times. Moving into Formula 2 along with the team, Chico found the going tough, being very much the number two driver to Andrea de Cesaris.

Joining Emerson Fittipaldi to race his fading team's cars in Grands Prix, Serra again struggled, but when he managed to get the car onto the grid he more often than not brought it home to the finish, gaining his only championship point at Zolder in 1982. After the team closed its doors, Serra briefly raced the Arrows while Alan Jones prevaricated over the prospect of a GP comeback with the team, before losing out to Thierry Boutsen.

A dispirited Serra returned to his homeland, no doubt ruefully watching Piquet's latest successes. He didn't turn his back on the sport, however, and continues to race saloons to this day in his native Brazil.

SERRA, Chico (Francisco) (BR) b 3/2/1957, São Paulo

	1981			Championship position: Unplaced					
	Race	Circuit	No	Entrant	Tyres	Car/Engine		Comment	Q Pos/Entries
7	US GP WEST	Long Beach	21	Fittipaldi Automotive	M	3.0 Fittipaldi F8C-Cosworth V8		2 laps behind	18/29
ret	BRAZILIAN GP	Rio	21	Fittipaldi Automotive	M	3.0 Fittipaldi F8C-Cosworth V8		startline collision	22/30
ret	ARGENTINE GP	Buenos Aires	21	Fittipaldi Automotive	M	3.0 Fittipaldi F8C-Cosworth V8		gearbox	20/29
dnq	SAN MARINO GP	Imola	21	Fittipaldi Automotive	A	3.0 Fittipaldi F8C-Cosworth V8			28/30
ret	BELGIAN GP	Zolder	21	Fittipaldi Automotive	M	3.0 Fittipaldi F8C-Cosworth V8		engine	20/31
dnq	MONACO GP	Monte Carlo	21	Fittipaldi Automotive	A/M	3.0 Fittipaldi F8C-Cosworth V8			24/31
11	SPANISH GP	Jarama	21	Fittipaldi Automotive	M	3.0 Fittipaldi F8C-Cosworth V8		1 lap behind	21/30
dns	FRENCH GP	Dijon	21	Fittipaldi Automotive	M	3.0 Fittipaldi F8C-Cosworth V8		accident in warm-up	(24)/29
dnq	BRITISH GP	Silverstone	21	Fittipaldi Automotive	M	3.0 Fittipaldi F8C-Cosworth V8			25/30
dnq	GERMAN GP	Hockenheim	21	Fittipaldi Automotive	M	3.0 Fittipaldi F8C-Cosworth V8			30/30
dnq	DUTCH GP	Zandvoort	21	Fittipaldi Automotive	P	3.0 Fittipaldi F8C-Cosworth V8			28/30
dnq	ITALIAN GP	Monza	21	Fittipaldi Automotive	P	3.0 Fittipaldi F8C-Cosworth V8			30/30
dnq	CANADIAN GP	Montreal	21	Fittipaldi Automotive	P	3.0 Fittipaldi F8C-Cosworth V8			26/30
dnq	CAESARS PALACE GP	Las Vegas	21	Fittipaldi Automotive	P	3.0 Fittipaldi F8C-Cosworth V8			26/30
	1982			Championship position: 26th Wins: 0 Pole positions: 0 Fastest laps: 0 Points scored: 1					
17	SOUTH AFRICAN GP	Kyalami	20	Fittipaldi Automotive	P	3.0 Fittipaldi F8D-Cosworth V8		5 laps behind	25/30
ret	BRAZILIAN GP	Rio	20	Fittipaldi Automotive	P	3.0 Fittipaldi F8D-Cosworth V8		spun off	25/31
dnq	US GP WEST	Long Beach	20	Fittipaldi Automotive	P	3.0 Fittipaldi F8D-Cosworth V8			29/31
6	BELGIAN GP	Zolder	20	Fittipaldi Automotive	P	3.0 Fittipaldi F8D-Cosworth V8		3 laps behind	25/32
dnpq	MONACO GP	Monte Carlo	20	Fittipaldi Automotive	P	3.0 Fittipaldi F8D-Cosworth V8			30/31
11	US GP (DETROIT)	Detroit	20	Fittipaldi Automotive	P	3.0 Fittipaldi F8D-Cosworth V8		3 laps behind	26/28
dnq	CANADIAN GP	Montreal	20	Fittipaldi Automotive	P	3.0 Fittipaldi F8D-Cosworth V8			29/29
ret	DUTCH GP	Zandvoort	20	Fittipaldi Automotive	P	3.0 Fittipaldi F8D-Cosworth V8		fuel pump	19/31
ret	BRITISH GP	Brands Hatch	20	Fittipaldi Automotive	P	3.0 Fittipaldi F8D-Cosworth V8		accident with Jarier	21/30
dnq	FRENCH GP	Paul Ricard	20	Fittipaldi Automotive	P	3.0 Fittipaldi F9-Cosworth V8			29/30
11	GERMAN GP	Hockenheim	20	Fittipaldi Automotive	P	3.0 Fittipaldi F9-Cosworth V8		2 laps behind	26/30
7	AUSTRIAN GP	Österreichring	20	Fittipaldi Automotive	P	3.0 Fittipaldi F9-Cosworth V8		2 laps behind	20/29
dnq	SWISS GP	Dijon	20	Fittipaldi Automotive	P	3.0 Fittipaldi F9-Cosworth V8			27/29
11	ITALIAN GP	Monza	20	Fittipaldi Automotive	P	3.0 Fittipaldi F9-Cosworth V8		3 laps behind	26/30
dnq	CAESARS PALACE GP	Las Vegas	20	Fittipaldi Automotive	P	3.0 Fittipaldi F9-Cosworth V8			30/30
	1983			Championship position: Unplaced					
9	BRAZILIAN GP	Rio	30	Arrows Racing Team	G	3.0 Arrows A6-Cosworth V8		1 lap behind	23/27
ret	FRENCH GP	Paul Ricard	30	Arrows Racing Team	G	3.0 Arrows A6-Cosworth V8		gearbox	26/29
8	SAN MARINO GP	Imola	30	Arrows Racing Team	G	3.0 Arrows A6-Cosworth V8		2 laps behind	20/28
7	MONACO GP	Monte Carlo	30	Arrows Racing Team	G	3.0 Arrows A6-Cosworth V8		2 laps behind	15/28

GP Starts: 18   GP Wins: 0   Pole positions: 0   Fastest laps: 0   Points: 1

DOUG SERRURIER

A mainstay of the South African motor racing scene as driver, constructor and later entrant, Doug – a former grass track and speedway rider both at home and abroad – began his circuit racing career driving a Triumph TR2 in 1956, before starting work on the first of his home-built LDS specials, the initials being derived from his full name (Louis Douglas Serrurier).

A trip to Europe saw Doug initially purchase a Cooper T51 from Alan Brown, and further machines ordered from the factory were soon to follow, including the lowline T53 which provided the inspiration for his own LDS Mk2 of 1961. Powered by an Alfa Romeo engine, this was just one of a gradually evolving series of cars that were developed during the early sixties, later models being based upon Brabham designs (much to the chagrin of Jack Brabham). They were driven, for the most part, by Serrurier himself and another veteran, Rhodesian star Sam Tingle.

By 1966 it was becoming increasingly impractical to compete with the major constructors so, after sharing Roy Pierpoint's Lola T70 to take second place in the Cape Town 3 Hours, Serrurier decided to buy one of these cars, which he then shared with Jackie Pretorious, winning the Roy Hesketh 3 Hours in 1967. After more or less retiring from racing at the end of 1969, Serrurier entered Pretorious in the South African F1 series with a Surtees, but still had occasional road and rally outings himself as well as trying his hand at powerboat racing.

Until he was well into his seventies, Serrurier continued to build and rebuild fast cars such as the AC Cobra and the Ferrari Daytona to his usual superb standards in his backyard workshop near Johannesburg, often incorporating his own suspension designs.

JOHNNY SERVOZ-GAVIN

Georges 'Johnny' Servoz-Gavin was a handsome, blond playboy racer who loved the good life, but significantly he also possessed a great deal of talent.

After being thrown out of the Winfield driving school in 1963, 'Johnny' did a little rallying in 1964, before spending all his money on a Brabham for 1965. He was wild but fast, taking fourth place in the French F3 series to earn a drive with Matra in 1966. Although he was promoted to the Matra Formula 2 team for 1967, his results were moderate, and only a splendid fourth in the F1/F2 non-title Spanish GP kept him on board.

An accident to Jackie Stewart early in 1968 brought the Frenchman a glorious opportunity to show his ability. In Ken Tyrrell's Matra he sensationally led the Monaco GP, but clipped a barrier which broke a driveshaft. Later in the season he redeemed himself with a superb second place in the Italian GP, but he still lacked a full-time Grand Prix ride.

For 1969 he concentrated on the European F2 championship, and with victory in the Rome GP took the title of top non-graded driver. In Grands Prix, he was mainly entrusted with the Matra MS84, and succeeded in gaining a point with it at Mosport, the only time any 4WD car achieved this feat.

The following season, 'Johnny' was paired with Jackie Stewart in the Tyrrell team, running the difficult March 701. He finished fifth in the Spanish GP, but failed to qualify at Monaco, which caused him suddenly to announce his retirement.

Ultimately he had decided that the risks inherent in racing at the time were not worthwhile, but there was also, apparently, a problem with his vision, which may have been the deciding factor.

SERRURIER, Doug (ZA) b 9/12/1920, Germiston, Transvaal

	1962			Championship position: Unplaced					
	Race	*Circuit*	*No*	*Entrant*	*Tyres*	*Car/Engine*		*Comment*	*Q Pos/Entries*
ret	SOUTH AFRICAN GP	East London	21	Otelle Nucci	D	1.5 LDS Mk2-Alfa Romeo 4		*radiator leak*	=13/17
	1963			Championship position: Unplaced					
11	SOUTH AFRICAN GP	East London	16	Otelle Nucci	D	1.5 LDS MK2-Alfa Romeo 4		*7 laps behind*	18/21
	1965			Championship position: Unplaced					
dnq	SOUTH AFRICAN GP	East London	21	Otelle Nucci	D	1.5 LDS Mk2-Climax 4			23/25

GP Starts: 2   GP Wins: 0   Pole positions: 0   Fastest laps: 0   Points: 0

SERVOZ-GAVIN, 'Johnny' (Georges) (F) b 18/1/1942, Grenoble

	1967			Championship position: Unplaced					
	Race	*Circuit*	*No*	*Entrant*	*Tyres*	*Car/Engine*		*Comment*	*Q Pos/Entries*
ret	MONACO GP	Monte Carlo	2	Matra Sports	D	1.6 Matra MS7-Cosworth 4 F2		*fuel injection unit drive*	11/18
	1968		Championship position: 12th= Wins: 0 Pole positions: 0 Fastest laps: 0 Points scored: 6						
ret	MONACO GP	Monte Carlo	11	Matra International	D	3.0 Matra MS10-Cosworth V8		*hit chicane-broken driveshaft*	=2/18
ret	FRENCH GP	Rouen	32	Cooper Car Co	F	3.0 Cooper T86B-BRM V12		*spun off-hit tree*	16/18
2	ITALIAN GP	Monza	5	Matra International	D	3.0 Matra MS10-Cosworth V8			14/24
ret	CANADIAN GP	St Jovite	15	Matra International	D	3.0 Matra MS10-Cosworth V8		*spun off*	13/22
ret	MEXICAN GP	Mexico City	23	Matra International	D	3.0 Matra MS10-Cosworth V8		*engine-ignition/8 laps behind*	16/21
	1969		Championship position: 16th= Wins: 0 Pole positions: 0 Fastest laps: 0 Points scored: 1						
ret	GERMAN GP (F2)	Nürburgring	27	Matra International	D	1.6 Matra MS7-Cosworth 4 F2		*engine/FL(F2 class)*	11/26
6	CANADIAN GP	Mosport Park	19	Matra International	D	3.0 Matra MS84-Cosworth V8 4WD		*6 laps behind*	15/20
nc	US GP	Watkins Glen	16	Matra International	D	3.0 Matra MS84-Cosworth V8 4WD		*2 stops-wheel bearing/-16 laps*	15/18
8	MEXICAN GP	Mexico City	16	Matra International	D	3.0 Matra MS84-Cosworth V8 4WD		*2 laps behind*	14/17
	1970		Championship position: 19th= Wins: 0 Pole positions: 0 Fastest laps: 0 Points scored: 2						
ret	SOUTH AFRICAN GP	Kyalami	2	Tyrrell Racing Organisation	D	3.0 March 701-Cosworth V8		*engine*	17/24
5	SPANISH GP	Jarama	16	Tyrrell Racing Organisation	D	3.0 March 701-Cosworth V8			17/22
dnq	MONACO GP	Monte Carlo	20	Tyrrell Racing Organisation	D	3.0 March 701-Cosworth V8		*car not seeded*	14/21

GP Starts: 12   GP Wins: 0   Pole positions: 0   Fastest laps: 0   Points: 9

TONY SETTEMBER

A Californian of Italian descent, Tony raced Corvettes and a Mercedes 300SL in the States before coming to Europe, where, initially driving a WRE-Maserati sports car, he took a win in the Naples GP at Posillipo but achieved little else before returning home.

After persuading his wealthy friend Hugh Powell to provide suitable funding, Settember commissioned Emeryson to build a chassis for the 1962 season, but the driver did not fit the car properly and relationships in the team became strained when no success was achieved. In the event Paul Emery departed before the season was out, and the two Americans formed the Scirocco-Powell team for 1963, using BRM power. The car was attractive but slow, Settember being flattered by an inherited second-place finish in the non-championship Austrian GP, some five laps down.

When Powell finally called a halt to proceedings, Settember continued his racing activities in the US with Lotus 23 and 30 sports cars, and then an AC Cobra, before trying his hand at Can-Am in the late sixties with a Lola T70. He reappeared in the early seventies in the L & M F5000 series between 1972 and 1974, but never seriously threatened the front-runners.

SETTEMBER, Tony (USA) b 1930, California

	1962			Championship position: Unplaced					
	Race	*Circuit*	*No*	*Entrant*	*Tyres*	*Car/Engine*		*Comment*	*Q Pos/Entries*
11	BRITISH GP	Aintree	40	Emeryson Cars	D	1.5 Emeryson 1004-Climax 4		*4 laps behind*	19/21
ret	ITALIAN GP	Monza	48	Emeryson Cars	D	1.5 Emeryson 1004-Climax 4		*cylinder head gasket*	21/30
	1963			Championship position: Unplaced					
8/ret	BELGIAN GP	Spa	24	Scirocco Powell (Racing Cars)	D	1.5 Scirocco 01-BRM V8		*accident/5 laps behind*	19/20
ret	FRENCH GP	Reims	38	Scirocco Powell (Racing Cars)	D	1.5 Scirocco 01-BRM V8		*rear hub bearing*	20/21
ret	BRITISH GP	Silverstone	15	Scirocco Powell (Racing Cars)	D	1.5 Scirocco 01-BRM V8		*ignition*	18/23
ret	GERMAN GP	Nürburgring	23	Scirocco Powell (Racing Cars)	D	1.5 Scirocco 01-BRM V8		*accident*	22/26
dnq	ITALIAN GP	Monza	34	Scirocco Powell (Racing Cars)	D	1.5 Scirocco 01-BRM V8			23/28

GP Starts: 6   GP Wins: 0   Pole positions: 0   Fastest laps: 0   Points: 0

'HAP' SHARP

A Texan involved in the oil-drilling business, Sharp was a long-time associate of Jim Hall who became closely involved in the Chaparral project, mainly racing in the USRRC series. In 1964, 'Hap' was fifth overall

in the championship and also won the Nassau Trophy teamed with Roger Penske. Improving on this the following year, he took third overall in the series and won the Sebring 12 Hours with Hall, recording six other big wins including another Nassau victory.

A great Formula 1 enthusiast, Sharp had the wherewithal to arrange a succession of Grand Prix drives on the North American continent in the early sixties, coming close to scoring a point in Mexico City in 1963 in Reg Parnell's Lotus-BRM. After retiring from the sport, Sharp suffered from personal problems which resulted in his suicide in May 1993.

BRIAN SHAWE-TAYLOR

A garage proprietor from Gloucestershire, Shawe-Taylor gained some success before the war, winning the 1939 Nuffield Trophy, and after the hostilities he reappeared with a B-Type ERA. When his entry for the 1950

British GP was refused on the grounds that his car was too old, he shared Joe Fry's Maserati instead. He was developing a reputation as a very quick driver, and in 1951 he practised Tony Vandervell's Ferrari at Reims, but in the event Parnell raced the car after his BRM failed to show.

Having scored some good placings with the ERA at Goodwood (second in both the Richmond Trophy and the Chichester Cup), Brian was granted an entry for the British GP, and succeeded in finishing eighth, the first privateer home. He shared a works Aston Martin with Abecassis at Le Mans and finished fifth, before his progress was halted by an accident in the Daily Graphic Trophy at Goodwood, when he spun the ERA and was hit by Branca's car. Seriously injured, this promising driver recovered, but never raced again.

CARROLL SHELBY

This hard-bitten Texan began racing in 1952 with an MG TC, winning his first event. He soon progressed to more potent machinery with an Allard-Cadillac and a Ferrari in 1953, and the following season he competed abroad for the first time, racing in Argentina before coming over to Europe to drive David Brown's Aston Martin DB3S.

In 1955 Shelby continued to race in sports car events, sharing a Ferrari with Phil Hill to take second place in the Sebring 12 Hours, and also made his F1 debut for Maserati with a sixth place in the Syracuse GP. Staying in the US for 1956, Carroll virtually swept the board in SCCA circles, winning 27 races – 19 of them consecutively – in his Ferrari. Driving a Ferrari for John Edgar in 1957, Shelby finished second to Fangio in the Cuban GP, and he continued his winning ways in SCCA, overcoming a nasty crash at Riverside in which he sustained facial injuries.

Tempted back to Europe in 1958, Shelby raced the outdated Maserati 250F, and was unfortunate to be stripped of his points at Monza after taking over Gregory's car to earn a fourth-place finish. He also renewed his association with Aston Martin, finishing third with Lewis-Evans in the Tourist Trophy at Goodwood to set up a full season in both Formula 1 and sports cars in 1959.

The Grand Prix project was a huge disappointment. Although the front-engined cars were beautifully made, their reliability was suspect and they were unable to compete with the fleet little Coopers. In direct contrast, the sports car programme went well and the Feltham team eventually took the World Sports Car Championship, Carroll playing his part by winning the Le Mans 24 Hours with Salvadori, and the Tourist Trophy at Goodwood with Moss and Fairman.

In 1960 Shelby competed in SCCA events once more, but by this time he was suffering from heart trouble, and retired at season's end. It was the beginning of a new chapter, though, as Shelby was to gain even greater fame, first developing the AC Cobra, and then overseeing Ford's massive and ultimately successful assault on the Le Mans 24-hour race.

After many years of failing health, Carroll was literally given a new lease of life in 1990, receiving a successful heart transplant which has since offered him the freedom to travel the world once more and relive his racing days with many old friends and acquaintances.

SHARP, 'Hap' (James R) (USA) b 1/1/1928, Tulsa – d 5/1993

	1961		Championship position: Unplaced					
	Race	Circuit	No Entrant	Tyres	Car/Engine	Comment	Q Pos/Entries
10	US GP	Watkins Glen	3 'Hap' Sharp	D	1.5 Cooper T53-Climax 4	3rd works car/7 laps behind	17/19
	1962		Championship position: Unplaced				
11	US GP	Watkins Glen	24 'Hap' Sharp	D	1.5 Cooper T53-Climax 4	9 laps behind	15/20
	1963		Championship position: Unplaced				
ret	US GP	Watkins Glen	22 Reg Parnell (Racing)	D	1.5 Lotus 24-BRM V8	engine	18/21
7	MEXICAN GP	Mexico City	22 Reg Parnell (Racing)	D	1.5 Lotus 24-BRM V8	4 laps behind	16/21
	1964		Championship position: Unplaced				
nc	US GP	Watkins Glen	23 Rob Walker Racing Team	D	1.5 Brabham BT11-BRM V8	long stop engine/-45 laps	18/19
13	MEXICAN GP	Mexico City	23 Rob Walker Racing Team	D	1.5 Brabham BT11-BRM V8	5 laps behind	19/19

GP Starts: 6   GP Wins: 0   Pole positions: 0   Fastest laps: 0   Points: 0

SHAWE-TAYLOR, Brian (GB) b 29/1/1915, Dublin, Republic of Ireland – d 6/1999

	1950		Championship position: Unplaced				
	Race	Circuit	No Entrant	Tyres	Car/Engine	Comment	Q Pos/Entries
10*	BRITISH GP	Silverstone	10 Joe Fry	D	1.5 s/c Maserati 4CL 4	* took over from Fry/-6 laps	–/–
	1951		Championship position: Unplaced				
dns	FRENCH GP	Reims	26 G A Vandervell	P	4.5 Ferrari 375/Thinwall Special F1	Parnell drove car	–/–
8	BRITISH GP	Silverstone	9 Brian Shawe-Taylor	D	1.5 s/c ERA B Type 6	6 laps behind	12/20

GP Starts: 2   GP Wins: 0   Pole positions: 0   Fastest laps: 0   Points: 0

SHELBY, Carroll (USA) b 11/1/1923, Leesburg, Texas

	1958		Championship position: Unplaced				
	Race	Circuit	No Entrant	Tyres	Car/Engine	Comment	Q Pos/Entries
ret	FRENCH GP	Reims	28 Scuderia Centro Sud	P	2.5 Maserati 250F 6	engine	17/21
9	BRITISH GP	Silverstone	5 Scuderia Centro Sud	P	2.5 Maserati 250F 6	3 laps behind	15/21
ret	PORTUGUESE GP	Oporto	28 Temple Buell	P	2.5 Maserati 250F 6	crashed-brakes	10/15
ret	ITALIAN GP	Monza	34 Temple Buell	P	2.5 Maserati 250F 6	engine	17/21
4*	"	"	32 Scuderia Centro Sud	P	2.5 Maserati 250F 6	Gregory's car/*no points awarded	–/–
	1959		Championship position: Unplaced				
ret	DUTCH GP	Zandvoort	5 David Brown Corporation	A	2.5 Aston-Martin DBR4/250 6	engine	10/15
ret	BRITISH GP	Aintree	4 David Brown Corporation	A	2.5 Aston-Martin DBR4/250 6	magneto	6/30
8	PORTUGUESE GP	Monsanto	9 David Brown Corporation	A	2.5 Aston-Martin DBR4/250 6	4 laps behind	13/16
10	ITALIAN GP	Monza	26 David Brown Corporation	A	2.5 Aston-Martin DBR4/250 6	2 laps behind	19/21

GP Starts: 8   GP Wins: 0   Pole positions: 0   Fastest laps: 0   Points: 0

SHELLY, Tony (NZ) b 2/2/1937, Wellington

	1962		Championship position: Unplaced				
	Race	Circuit	No Entrant	Tyres	Car/Engine	Comment	Q Pos/Entries
ret	BRITISH GP	Aintree	48 John Dalton	D	1.5 Lotus 18/21-Climax 4	cylinder head gasket	18/21
dnq	GERMAN GP	Nürburgring	29 John Dalton	D	1.5 Lotus 18/21-Climax 4		27/30
dnq	ITALIAN GP	Monza	60 Autosport Team Wolfgang Seidel	D	1.5 Lotus 24-BRM V8		22/30

GP Starts: 1   GP Wins: 0   Pole positions: 0   Fastest laps: 0   Points: 0

TONY SHELLY

A popular New Zealander who made a promising start to his career by winning the first big race he contested at Teretonga with a Cooper in 1958, Shelly became a leading driver down-under before coming to Europe in 1962 to race, mainly in non-championship events, for John Dalton.

Considering his unfamiliarity with the tracks, Tony acquitted himself very well, taking his four-cylinder Lotus 18 into fifth place in the Lombank Trophy, and following that with a third in the Lavant Cup.

He went back to New Zealand at the end of the season and never returned, racing down-under in 1963-64 before retiring to concentrate on his thriving car dealerships, though he did have occasional outings in later years.

JO SIFFERT

Siffert could be a wild and hairy driver, but how the fans loved him, perhaps because he was a man who chanced his arm a little more than most. Chiefly remembered for the 1968 British Grand Prix when, in Rob Walker's dark-blue Lotus 49, he withstood all Chris Amon's attempts to pass in the Ferrari to take a fairy-tale victory, 'Seppi' was a very underrated Grand Prix driver, having spent the bulk of his

career uncomplainingly in second-rank equipment. He had the heart of a lion and, despite his frail appearance, was an immensely tough and doughty competitor – no doubt born of his motor cycling career, during which he won the 350 cc Swiss championship on a Gilera and passengered Edgar Strub in the 1959 sidecar World Championship.

Siffert's first competition on four wheels came in 1960 when he raced in Formula Junior, but he really came to prominence the following year when, driving a Lotus 21, he won the Eifelrennen race among others to emerge as joint European Formula Junior champion with Tony Maggs. For 1962, Siffert decided to step up to Formula 1 with Ecurie Filipinetti. No results of note were achieved but he plugged away into 1963, buying the Filipinetti Lotus 24-BRM to run as an independent. He finally took a championship point at Reims and also won a poorly supported Syracuse GP and took second in the Imola GP.

Purchasing a Brabham for 1964 increased his Grand Prix competitiveness and he scored a superb win in the Mediterranean GP, in which even the great Jim Clark had to take second best, the final margin being a tenth of a second. Amazingly 'Seppi' was to repeat the victory in 1965 when he again saw off the great Scot, this time by the huge margin of three-tenths of a second! Jo had joined the Walker team at the beginning of the year and was to strike up a wonderful relationship with Rob which saw them through the many tough times that were to follow.

The 1966-67 seasons were a period of struggle when Siffert scraped the occasional point but top-three finishes were achieved only in non-title races. Hopes were high for 1968 when Walker persuaded Colin Chapman to provide him with a Lotus 49, and after the team's wonderful day at Brands Hatch 'Seppi' was a front-runner for the rest of the year and sometimes quicker than the works car of Graham Hill. He was to stay with Rob for one more season which, after a bright start, faded disappointingly. By this time Siffert had established himself as a star of the Porsche sports car team, having won five major races in the 1969 season alone. A tempting offer from Ferrari was dangled in front of him but Porsche, desperate not to lose his services, paid for him to join the STP March team for 1970. It was an absolutely disastrous Grand Prix year for 'Seppi', only partly salvaged by success in Formula 2 with the works BMW and in sports car racing with the Gulf Porsche team, for whom he won the Targa Florio, the Spa 1000 Km and the Österreichring 1000 Km, all with Brian Redman.

Siffert set out on a hectic racing programme in 1971. He joined the BRM Formula 1 team, purchased a Chevron to race in F2 and a Porsche 917 for Can-Am and continued to race the works Porsche with Gulf/John Wyer. The season was a very successful one for 'Seppi'. Apart from his dominant BRM triumph in the Austrian GP, he took plenty of top-three finishes in the other formulae and the popular Swiss had much to look forward to in 1972 when he arrived at Brands Hatch for the season's finale, the Rothmans Victory Race. However, during the race a suspension failure sent the BRM P160 hurtling into a bank, the car bursting into flames. Poor Siffert was trapped in the wreckage and when he was finally extricated was found to have died of asphyxia, having survived the initial impact with a broken leg. Coming so soon after the loss of Pedro Rodriguez, the death of another of the sport's great 'tigers' was hard to bear.

SIFFERT, Jo (CH) b 7/7/1936, Fribourg – d 24/10/1971, Brands Hatch Circuit, Kent, England

	1962			Championship position: Unplaced					
	Race	Circuit	No	Entrant	Tyres	Car/Engine		Comment	Q Pos/Entries
dnq	MONACO GP	Monte Carlo	46	Ecurie Nationale Suisse	D	1.5 Lotus 21-Climax 4		faster than 5 seeded drivers	13/21
10	BELGIAN GP	Spa	22	Ecurie Filipinetti	D	1.5 Lotus 21-Climax 4		3 laps behind	17/20
ret	FRENCH GP	Rouen	40	Ecurie Filipinetti	D	1.5 Lotus 24-BRM V8		clutch	15/17
dns	"	"	40	Ecurie Filipinetti	D	1.5 Lotus 21-Climax 4		practice only	– / –
12	GERMAN GP	Nürburgring	19	Ecurie Filipinetti	D	1.5 Lotus 21-Climax 4			17/30
dnq	ITALIAN GP	Monza	42	Ecurie Filipinetti	D	1.5 Lotus 24-BRM V8			26/30

	1963			Championship position: 15th Wins: 0 Pole positions: 0 Fastest laps: 0 Points scored: 1					
ret	MONACO GP	Monte Carlo	25	Siffert Racing Team	D	1.5 Lotus 24-BRM V8		engine	12/17
ret	BELGIAN GP	Spa	28	Siffert Racing Team	D	1.5 Lotus 24-BRM V8		crashed in rain storm	14/20
7	DUTCH GP	Zandvoort	36	Siffert Racing Team	D	1.5 Lotus 24-BRM V8		3 laps behind	=17/19
6	FRENCH GP	Reims	36	Siffert Racing Team	D	1.5 Lotus 24-BRM V8		1 lap behind	10/21
ret	BRITISH GP	Silverstone	25	Siffert Racing Team	D	1.5 Lotus 24-BRM V8		gearbox	15/23
9/ret	GERMAN GP	Nürburgring	18	Siffert Racing Team	D	1.5 Lotus 24-BRM V8		differential/5 laps behind	9/26
ret	ITALIAN GP	Monza	54	Siffert Racing Team	D	1.5 Lotus 24-BRM V8		oil pressure	16/28
ret	US GP	Watkins Glen	14	Siffert Racing Team	D	1.5 Lotus 24-BRM V8		gearbox	=13/21
9	MEXICAN GP	Mexico City	14	Siffert Racing Team	D	1.5 Lotus 24-BRM V8		6 laps behind	9/21

	1964			Championship position: 10th Wins: 0 Pole positions: 0 Fastest laps: 0 Points scored: 7					
8	MONACO GP	Monte Carlo	24	Siffert Racing Team	D	1.5 Lotus 24-BRM V8		pit stops-misfire etc/-22 laps	16/20
nc	DUTCH GP	Zandvoort	36	Siffert Racing Team	D	1.5 Brabham BT11-BRM V8		pit stops-misfire/-25 laps	18/18
ret	BELGIAN GP	Spa	17	Siffert Racing Team	D	1.5 Brabham BT11-BRM V8		engine	13/20
ret	FRENCH GP	Rouen	30	Siffert Racing Team	D	1.5 Brabham BT11-BRM V8		clutch	17/17
11	BRITISH GP	Brands Hatch	20	Siffert Racing Team	D	1.5 Brabham BT11-BRM V8		4 laps behind	=16/25
4	GERMAN GP	Nürburgring	19	Siffert Racing Team	D	1.5 Brabham BT11-BRM V8			10/24
ret	AUSTRIAN GP	Zeltweg	20	Siffert Racing Team	D	1.5 Brabham BT11-BRM V8		accident	12/20
7	ITALIAN GP	Monza	12	Siffert Racing Team	D	1.5 Brabham BT11-BRM V8		1 lap behind	6/25
3	US GP	Watkins Glen	22	Rob Walker Racing Team	D	1.5 Brabham BT11-BRM V8		1 lap behind	12/19
ret	MEXICAN GP	Mexico City	22	Rob Walker Racing Team	D	1.5 Brabham BT11-BRM V8		fuel pump	13/19

	1965			Championship position: 11th Wins: 0 Pole positions: 0 Fastest laps: 0 Points scored: 5					
7	SOUTH AFRICAN GP	East London	12	Rob Walker Racing Team	D	1.5 Brabham BT11-BRM V8		2 laps behind	14/25
6	MONACO GP	Monte Carlo	14	Rob Walker Racing Team	D	1.5 Brabham BT11-BRM V8		2 laps behind	=10/17
8	BELGIAN GP	Spa	21	Rob Walker Racing Team	D	1.5 Brabham BT11-BRM V8		1 lap behind	8/21
6	FRENCH GP	Clermont Ferrand	36	Rob Walker Racing Team	D	1.5 Brabham BT11-BRM V8		1 lap behind	14/17
9	BRITISH GP	Silverstone	16	Rob Walker Racing Team	D	1.5 Brabham BT11-BRM V8		2 laps behind	18/23
13	DUTCH GP	Zandvoort	28	Rob Walker Racing Team	D	1.5 Brabham BT11-BRM V8		pit stop-fuel feed/-25 laps	=10/17
ret	GERMAN GP	Nürburgring	17	Rob Walker Racing Team	D	1.5 Brabham BT11-BRM V8		engine	11/22
ret	ITALIAN GP	Monza	44	Rob Walker Racing Team	D	1.5 Brabham BT11-BRM V8		gearbox	10/23
11	US GP	Watkins Glen	16	Rob Walker Racing Team	D	1.5 Brabham BT11-BRM V8		pit stop clutch slip/-11 laps	11/18
4	MEXICAN GP	Mexico City	16	Rob Walker Racing Team	D	1.5 Brabham BT11-BRM V8			11/18

	1966			Championship position: 14th Wins: 0 Pole positions: 0 Fastest laps: 0 Points scored: 3					
ret	MONACO GP	Monte Carlo	14	Rob Walker Racing Team	D	2.0 Brabham BT11-BRM V8		clutch	13/16
ret	BELGIAN GP	Spa	21	Rob Walker Racing Team	D	3.0 Cooper T81-Maserati V12		engine	14/18
ret	FRENCH GP	Reims	38	Rob Walker Racing Team	D	3.0 Cooper T81-Maserati V12		overheating	6/17
nc	BRITISH GP	Brands Hatch	20	Rob Walker Racing Team	D	3.0 Cooper T81-Maserati V12		pit stop-overheating/-10 laps	11/20
ret	DUTCH GP	Zandvoort	28	Rob Walker Racing Team	D	3.0 Cooper T81-Maserati V12		engine	11/18
ret	ITALIAN GP	Monza	36	Rob Walker Racing Team	D	3.0 Cooper T81-Maserati V12		engine	17/22
4	US GP	Watkins Glen	19	Rob Walker Racing Team	D	3.0 Cooper T81-Maserati V12		3 laps behind	13/19
ret	MEXICAN GP	Mexico City	19	Rob Walker Racing Team	F	3.0 Cooper T81-Maserati V12		suspension bolt	11/19

	1967			Championship position: 11th Wins: 0 Pole positions: 0 Fastest laps: 0 Points scored: 6					
ret	SOUTH AFRICAN GP	Kyalami	12	Rob Walker/Jack Durlacher Racing	F	3.0 Cooper T81-Maserati V12		engine	16/18
ret	MONACO GP	Monte Carlo	17	Rob Walker/Jack Durlacher Racing	F	3.0 Cooper T81-Maserati V12		engine	=9/18
10	DUTCH GP	Zandvoort	20	Rob Walker/Jack Durlacher Racing	F	3.0 Cooper T81-Maserati V12		pit stop-overheating/-7 laps	16/17
7	BELGIAN GP	Spa	34	Rob Walker/Jack Durlacher Racing	F	3.0 Cooper T81-Maserati V12		1 lap behind	16/18
4	FRENCH GP	Le Mans	18	Rob Walker/Jack Durlacher Racing	F	3.0 Cooper T81-Maserati V12		3 laps behind	11/15
ret	BRITISH GP	Silverstone	17	Rob Walker/Jack Durlacher Racing	F	3.0 Cooper T81-Maserati V12		engine	18/21
ret	GERMAN GP	Nürburgring	14	Rob Walker/Jack Durlacher Racing	F	3.0 Cooper T81-Maserati V12		fuel pump	13/25
dns	CANADIAN GP	Mosport Park	14	Rob Walker/Jack Durlacher Racing	F	3.0 Cooper T81-Maserati V12		starter ring on way to grid	(13)/19
ret	ITALIAN GP	Monza	6	Rob Walker/Jack Durlacher Racing	F	3.0 Cooper T81-Maserati V12		crashed-puncture	13/18

A great day for both Jo Siffert and Rob Walker as the Swiss driver in the Lotus 49B leads Chris Amon's Ferrari *en route* to a momentous victory in the 1968 British Grand Prix at Brands Hatch.

	Race	Circuit	No	Entrant	Tyres	Car/Engine	Comment	Q Pos/Entries
4	US GP	Watkins Glen	15	Rob Walker/Jack Durlacher Racing	F	3.0 Cooper T81-Maserati V12	*2 laps behind*	12/18
12/ret	MEXICAN GP	Mexico City	15	Rob Walker/Jack Durlacher Racing	F	3.0 Cooper T81-Maserati V12	*engine-no water/-6 laps*	10/19
1968	Championship position: 7th	Wins: 1	Pole positions: 1			Fastest laps: 3	Points scored: 12	
7	SOUTH AFRICAN GP	Kyalami	19	Rob Walker/Jack Durlacher Racing	F	3.0 Cooper T81-Maserati V12	*3 laps behind*	16/23
ret	SPANISH GP	Jarama	16	Rob Walker/Jack Durlacher Racing	F	3.0 Lotus 49-Cosworth V8	*transmission vibration*	=9/14
ret	MONACO GP	Monte Carlo	17	Rob Walker/Jack Durlacher Racing	F	3.0 Lotus 49-Cosworth V8	*transmission*	=2/18
7/ret	BELGIAN GP	Spa	3	Rob Walker/Jack Durlacher Racing	F	3.0 Lotus 49-Cosworth V8	*oil pressure/3 laps behind*	9/18
ret	DUTCH GP	Zandvoort	21	Rob Walker/Jack Durlacher Racing	F	3.0 Lotus 49-Cosworth V8	*gear selectors*	13/19
11	FRENCH GP	Rouen	34	Rob Walker/Jack Durlacher Racing	F	3.0 Lotus 49-Cosworth V8	*6 laps behind*	12/18
1	BRITISH GP	Brands Hatch	22	Rob Walker/Jack Durlacher Racing	F	3.0 Lotus 49B-Cosworth V8	*FL*	4/20
ret	GERMAN GP	Nürburgring	16	Rob Walker/Jack Durlacher Racing	F	3.0 Lotus 49B-Cosworth V8	*wet ignition*	9/20
ret	ITALIAN GP	Monza	20	Rob Walker/Jack Durlacher Racing	F	3.0 Lotus 49B-Cosworth V8	*shock absorber mounting*	9/24
ret	CANADIAN GP	St Jovite	12	Rob Walker/Jack Durlacher Racing	F	3.0 Lotus 49B-Cosworth V8	*oil leak/FL*	=3/22
5	US GP	Watkins Glen	16	Rob Walker/Jack Durlacher Racing	F	3.0 Lotus 49B-Cosworth V8	*pit stop-fuel/3 laps behind*	12/21
6	MEXICAN GP	Mexico City	16	Rob Walker/Jack Durlacher Racing	F	3.0 Lotus 49B-Cosworth V8	*pit stop-throttle/FL/-1 lap*	1/21
1969	Championship position: 9th	Wins: 0	Pole positions: 0			Fastest laps: 0	Points scored: 15	
4	SOUTH AFRICAN GP	Kyalami	4	Rob Walker/Jack Durlacher Racing	F	3.0 Lotus 49B-Cosworth V8		=12/18
ret	SPANISH GP	Montjuich Park	10	Rob Walker/Jack Durlacher Racing	F	3.0 Lotus 49B-Cosworth V8	*engine*	6/14
3	MONACO GP	Monte Carlo	9	Rob Walker/Jack Durlacher Racing	F	3.0 Lotus 49B-Cosworth V8		6/16
2	DUTCH GP	Zandvoort	10	Rob Walker/Jack Durlacher Racing	F	3.0 Lotus 49B-Cosworth V8		10/15
9	FRENCH GP	Clermont Ferrand	3	Rob Walker/Jack Durlacher Racing	F	3.0 Lotus 49B-Cosworth V8	*pit stop-damaged nose/-4 laps*	9/13
8	BRITISH GP	Silverstone	10	Rob Walker/Jack Durlacher Racing	F	3.0 Lotus 49B-Cosworth V8	*pit stop-fuel/3 laps behind*	9/17
5*/ret	GERMAN GP	Nürburgring	11	Rob Walker/Jack Durlacher Racing	F	3.0 Lotus 49B-Cosworth V8	*accident/*11th on road/-2 laps*	4/26
8/ret	ITALIAN GP	Monza	30	Rob Walker/Jack Durlacher Racing	F	3.0 Lotus 49B-Cosworth V8	*engine/4 laps behind*	8/15
ret	CANADIAN GP	Mosport Park	10	Rob Walker/Jack Durlacher Racing	F	3.0 Lotus 49B-Cosworth V8	*driveshaft*	=8/20
ret	US GP	Watkins Glen	10	Rob Walker/Jack Durlacher Racing	F	3.0 Lotus 49B-Cosworth V8	*fuel metering unit drive belt*	5/18
ret	MEXICAN GP	Mexico City	10	Rob Walker/Jack Durlacher Racing	F	3.0 Lotus 49B-Cosworth V8	*collision with Courage*	5/17
1970	Championship position: Unplaced							
10	SOUTH AFRICAN GP	Kyalami	16	March Engineering	F	3.0 March 701-Cosworth V8	*pit stop-broken exhaust/-5 laps*	9/24
dnq	SPANISH GP	Jarama	14	March Engineering	F	3.0 March 701-Cosworth V8	*not seeded*	16/22
8	MONACO GP	Monte Carlo	19	March Engineering	F	3.0 March 701-Cosworth V8	*engine misfire/4 laps behind*	11/21
7	BELGIAN GP	Spa	9	March Engineering	F	3.0 March 701-Cosworth V8	*engine fuel feed/2 laps behind*	10/18
ret	DUTCH GP	Zandvoort	9	March Engineering	F	3.0 March 701-Cosworth V8	*engine*	17/24
ret	FRENCH GP	Clermont Ferrand	12	March Engineering	F	3.0 March 701-Cosworth V8	*accident-locked brakes*	16/23
ret	BRITISH GP	Brands Hatch	15	March Engineering	F	3.0 March 701-Cosworth V8	*rear suspension bracket*	21/25
8/ret	GERMAN GP	Hockenheim	12	March Engineering	F	3.0 March 701-Cosworth V8	*engine/3 laps behind*	4/25
9	AUSTRIAN GP	Österreichring	3	March Engineering	F	3.0 March 701-Cosworth V8	*1 lap behind*	19/24
ret	ITALIAN GP	Monza	50	March Engineering	F	3.0 March 701-Cosworth V8	*engine*	7/27
ret	CANADIAN GP	St Jovite	21	March Engineering	F	3.0 March 701-Cosworth V8	*engine*	14/20
9	US GP	Watkins Glen	11	March Engineering	F	3.0 March 701-Cosworth V8	*pit stop-tyre/3 laps behind*	23/27
ret	MEXICAN GP	Mexico City	11	March Engineering	F	3.0 March 701-Cosworth V8	*engine*	16/18
1971	Championship position: 4th=	Wins: 1	Pole positions: 1			Fastest laps: 1	Points scored: 19	
ret	SOUTH AFRICAN GP	Kyalami	17	Yardley-BRM	F	3.0 BRM P153 V12	*overheating*	=16/25
ret	SPANISH GP	Montjuich Park	15	Yardley-BRM	F	3.0 BRM P160 V12	*gear linkage*	10/22
ret	MONACO GP	Monte Carlo	14	Yardley-BRM	F	3.0 BRM P160 V12	*engine-oil line*	=3/23
6	DUTCH GP	Zandvoort	9	Yardley-BRM	F	3.0 BRM P160 V12	*2 laps behind*	8/24
4	FRENCH GP	Paul Ricard	14	Yardley-BRM	F	3.0 BRM P160 V12		6/24
9	BRITISH GP	Silverstone	16	Yardley-BRM	F	3.0 BRM P160 V12	*2 p stops-condenser/-2 laps*	2/24
ret	GERMAN GP	Nürburgring	21	Yardley-BRM	F	3.0 BRM P160 V12	*coil failure*	3/23
1	AUSTRIAN GP	Österreichring	14	Yardley-BRM	F	3.0 BRM P160 V12	*FL*	1/22
9	ITALIAN GP	Monza	20	Yardley-BRM	F	3.0 BRM P160 V12	*stuck in gear for final laps/-2 laps*	3/24
9	CANADIAN GP	Mosport Park	14	Yardley-BRM	F	3.0 BRM P160 V12	*p stop dirt in nose of car/-3 laps*	2/27
2	US GP	Watkins Glen	14	Yardley-BRM	F	3.0 BRM P160 V12		7/32

GP Starts: 96   GP Wins: 2   Pole positions: 2   Fastest laps: 4   Points: 68

SIMON, André (F) b 5/1/1920, Paris

1951	Championship position: Unplaced							
	Race	Circuit	No	Entrant	Tyres	Car/Engine	Comment	Q Pos/Entries
ret	FRENCH GP	Reims	34	Equipe Gordini	E	1.5 s/c Simca-Gordini Type 15 4	*engine*	21/23
ret	GERMAN GP	Nürburgring	83	Equipe Gordini	E	1.5 s/c Simca-Gordini Type 15 4	*engine*	12/23
6	ITALIAN GP	Monza	48	Equipe Gordini	E	1.5 s/c Simca-Gordini Type 15 4	*6 laps behind*	11/22
ret	SPANISH GP	Pedralbes	16	Equipe Gordini	E	1.5 s/c Simca-Gordini Type 15 4	*engine*	10/20
1952	Championship position: Unplaced							
ret*	SWISS GP	Bremgarten	32	Scuderia Ferrari	P	2.0 Ferrari 500 4	** Farina took over/magneto*	4/21
6	ITALIAN GP	Monza	8	Scuderia Ferrari	P	2.0 Ferrari 500 4	*1 lap behind*	7/35
1955	Championship position: Unplaced							
ret	MONACO GP	Monte Carlo	4	Daimler Benz AG	C	2.5 Mercedes-Benz W196 8	*drove Herrmann's car/valve*	10/22
dns	"	" "	16	Ecurie Rosier	P	2.5 Maserati 250F 6	*practice only-drove Mercedes*	–/–
ret	BRITISH GP	Aintree	8	Officine Alfieri Maserati	P	2.5 Maserati 250F 6	*gearbox*	8/25
1956	Championship position: Unplaced							
ret	FRENCH GP	Reims	42	André Simon	P	2.5 Maserati 250F 6	*engine*	20/20
9	ITALIAN GP	Monza	12	Equipe Gordini	E	2.5 Gordini Type 16 6	*5 laps behind*	25/26
1957	Championship position: Unplaced							
dnq	MONACO GP	Monte Carlo	4	Scuderia Centro Sud	P	2.5 Maserati 250F 6		19/21
nc*	ITALIAN GP	Monza	28	Ottorino Volonterio	P	2.5 Maserati 250F 6	** Volonterio took over/-15 laps*	16/19

GP Starts: 11   GP Wins: 0   Pole positions: 0   Fastest laps: 0   Points: 0

ANDRE SIMON

Now a somewhat forgotten figure, Simon was a key member of the Simca-Gordini team in 1950, taking a string of second-place finishes (German GP, Aix-les-Bains, Angoulême, Reims, Geneva and Périgueux) that year. He continued to race the light-blue cars in both Grands Prix and Formula 2 the following season, winning at Les Sables d'Olonne. For 1952 Simon joined Ferrari but raced in only a few events, although he did share the winning T500 with Ascari at Comminges, and took second place in the Paris GP and the Autodrome GP at Monza, and fourth in the Monaco sports car race.

From 1953 on, André raced intermittently as an independent in both Grands Prix and sports car events, taking a third for Gordini in the 1954 International Trophy. In 1955 he replaced the injured Herrmann in the Mercedes at short notice at Monaco and also raced the German team's sports cars, taking third in the Tourist Trophy. Driving a Maserati 250F, Simon won the Albi GP in 1955, but it was by then a much less important event than in previous years. He raced in a few more Grands Prix without success, his last decent placing being second in the rain-soaked 1956 Caen GP in a Gordini.

Turning to sports car and GT racing, Simon was third in the Paris 1000 Km at Montlhéry in Schlesser's Ferrari, and third in the Auvergne Trophy and Coupe de la Marne Debouteville at Rouen in 1961, also in a Ferrari. In 1962 he won the Tour de France with co-driver Dupeyren – his last major win, though he continued racing through until 1965 when he finished 12th in the Nürburgring 1000 Km in a Ford France AC Cobra with his old friend Jo Schlesser.

MOISES SOLANA

Solana was first and foremost an expert exponent of the sport of jai-alai, and so good was he at this that it provided him with the means to go motor racing, though he rarely competed outside Mexico.

In 1962 he arranged to drive a Bowmaker Lola in the non-championship F1 race there, but he rejected the car in practice, claiming it was not satisfactory. From then on he found the cars he drove acceptable, but was unable to score any worthwhile results, despite some excellent qualifying performances, which included seventh fastest for the 1967 United States Grand Prix.

Most of his sorties outside Mexico were across the border in USRRC races, but he did come to Europe once to race a Lotus 48 F2 car at the Madrid GP in 1967, when he finished eleventh.

Solana was killed in 1969 while competing in the Valle de Bravo hill-climb when he lost control of his McLaren M6B, which crashed into a bridge and caught fire.

SOLANA, Moises (MEX) b 1936 – d 27/7/1969, Valle de Bravo, nr Mexico City

	1963	Championship position: Unplaced						
	Race	Circuit	No	Entrant	Tyres	Car/Engine	Comment	Q Pos/Entries
11/ret	MEXICAN GP	Mexico City	13	Scuderia Centro Sud	D	1.5 BRM P57 V8	cam follower/8 laps behind	11/21
	1964	Championship position: Unplaced						
10	MEXICAN GP	Mexico City	17	Team Lotus	D	1.5 Lotus 33-Climax V8	2 laps behind	14/19
	1965	Championship position: Unplaced						
12	US GP	Watkins Glen	18	Team Lotus	D	1.5 Lotus 25-Climax V8	15 laps behind	=15/18
ret	MEXICAN GP	Mexico City	18	Team Lotus	D	1.5 Lotus 25-Climax V8	ignition	9/18
	1966	Championship position: Unplaced						
ret	MEXICAN GP	Mexico City	9	Cooper Car Co	F	3.0 Cooper T81-Maserati V12	overheating	16/19
	1967	Championship position: Unplaced						
ret	US GP	Watkins Glen	18	Team Lotus	F	3.0 Lotus 49-Cosworth V8	electrics-ignition	7/18
ret	MEXICAN GP	Mexico City	18	Team Lotus	F	3.0 Lotus 49-Cosworth V8	front suspension	9/19
	1968	Championship position: Unplaced						
ret	MEXICAN GP	Mexico City	12	Gold Leaf Team Lotus	F	3.0 Lotus 49B-Cosworth V8	collapsed wing	11/21

GP Starts: 8   GP Wins: 0   Pole positions: 0   Fastest laps: 0   Points: 0

SOLER-ROIG, Alex (E) b 29/10/1932, Barcelona

	1970			Championship position: Unplaced				
	Race	Circuit	No	Entrant	Tyres	Car/Engine	Comment	Q Pos/Entries
dnq	SPANISH GP	Jarama	23	Garvey Team Lotus	F	3.0 Lotus 49C-Cosworth V8		21/22
dnq	BELGIAN GP	Spa	22	World Wide Racing	F	3.0 Lotus 72-Cosworth V8	insufficient practice	18/18
dnq	FRENCH GP	Clermont Ferrand	9	World Wide Racing	F	3.0 Lotus 49C-Cosworth V8		23/23
	1971			Championship position: Unplaced				
ret	SOUTH AFRICAN GP	Kyalami	26	STP March	F	3.0 March 711-Cosworth V8	engine	25/25
ret	SPANISH GP	Montjuich Park	19	STP March	F	3.0 March 711-Cosworth V8	fuel line	20/22
dnq	MONACO GP	Monte Carlo	18	STP March	F	3.0 March 711-Cosworth V8		22/23
ret	DUTCH GP	Zandvoort	19	STP March	F	3.0 March 711-Cosworth V8	engine	17/24
ret	FRENCH GP	Paul Ricard	18	STP March	F	3.0 March 711-Cosworth V8	fuel pump	22/24
	1972			Championship position: Unplaced				
ret	ARGENTINE GP	Buenos Aires	6	España Marlboro BRM	F	3.0 BRM P160B V12	accident-stuck throttle	21/22
ret	SPANISH GP	Jarama	28	España Marlboro BRM	F	3.0 BRM P160B V12	accident-no gears	22/26

GP Starts: 6   GP Wins: 0   Pole positions: 0   Fastest laps: 0   Points: 0

ALEX SOLER-ROIG

From a wealthy background, this sophisticated Spaniard had the means to try his hand at Formula 1 over a three-year period but it was obvious that he lacked the hunger or speed to be truly competitive.

He won his first event, a hill-climb, in 1960, and continued to race in his own country, usually with a Porsche, until he joined the European Formula 2 circus in 1967 for his first sustained attempt at professional racing. His season with the Lola was not too successful, so in 1968 he switched to sports car and GT racing, winning the Jarama 6 Hours with Rindt, and finishing fourth in the Sebring 12 Hours with Lins, both in Porsches. Alex finished second in the Buenos Aires 1000 Km in 1970 with his Porsche 908, again teamed with Rindt, and cleaned up in Spanish G5/6 races with his Porsche 917.

After failing to qualify for a Grand Prix in three attempts with Lotus, Soler-Roig joined March for the 1971 season, but although he made the grids he felt dissatisfied with the engines he was given and quit in mid-season, preferring to concentrate on his drive in the European touring car championship with Ford Germany, which yielded two victories in the Capri, co-driving with Glemser. His short spell in the Marlboro BRM team at the beginning of 1972 was a disaster, but a return to touring cars brought further wins at Zandvoort and Jarama with the help of such talents as Glemser, Mass and Larrousse before Alex called it a day at the end of the season.

RAYMOND SOMMER

Given the format of this book, Raymond Sommer's entry is brief, and unfortunately lack of space prevents me from writing more fully about this truly exceptional individual, who surely epitomised all that is good about motor racing – courage, tenacity, enthusiasm, persistence and sportsmanship.

He first came to fame by defeating the works Alfas in his private machine at Le Mans in 1932, driving for all but three of the 24 hours. The following year he won again, this time with the legendary Nuvolari. Raymond was soon racing in Grands Prix, usually as an independent, for he could not bear the constraints teams might impose. Thus he had to make do with whatever machinery was available, and always drove it to its limits, taking great delight when he managed to beat a car from the mighty Scuderia Ferrari or Mercedes teams. In this context, his record of successes was remarkable, even if he failed to win a monoposto Grand Prix outright before the war, though he did win the French sports car GP with Wimille in 1936.

After the war, Sommer was soon back in action, and in 1946 he enjoyed his best season, which included a famous victory in the GP of St Cloud, when the works Alfa 158s failed. In 1947 he was out of action after inadvertently swallowing some methanol at the Pau GP, but he returned with a semi-works Ferrari the following year, winning the Reims F2 race. Equipping himself with a big Talbot, Sommer was like a cat among the pigeons in 1949, hammering the car for all it was worth and frequently mixing it with the Italians, who viewed his on-the-edge, no-quarter-asked-or-given style with some concern.

He was driving as well as ever in 1950, scoring a fourth place at Monaco in his nimble Formula 2 Ferrari (with which he also took F2 wins at Roubaix, Aix-les-Bains and Bremgarten). He reverted to his Talbot for the later championship Grands Prix, where power was all, but no points were gained. It came as a huge shock when the motor racing world learned of his death while competing in a minor end-of-season 500 cc race at Cadours when, it is thought, a wheel bearing seized on his Cooper.

SOMMER, Raymond (F) b 31/8/1906, Paris – d 10/9/1950, Cadours Circuit, nr Toulouse

	1950	Championship position: 10=		Wins: 0	Pole positions: 0	Fastest laps: 0	Points scored: 3		
	Race	Circuit	No	Entrant	Tyres	Car/Engine	Comment	Q Pos/Entries
4	MONACO GP	Monte Carlo	42	Scuderia Ferrari	P	1.5 s/c Ferrari 125 V12	3 laps behind	9/21
ret	SWISS GP	Bremgarten	20	Scuderia Ferrari	P	2.0 Ferrari 166 V12 F2	suspension	13/18
ret	BELGIAN GP	Spa	6	Raymond Sommer	D	4.5 Lago-Talbot T26C 6	engine	5/14
ret	FRENCH GP	Reims	12	Automobiles Talbot-Darracq	D	4.5 Lago-Talbot T26C-GS 6	engine	17/20
ret	ITALIAN GP	Monza	12	Raymond Sommer	D	4.5 Lago-Talbot T26C 6	gearbox	8/27

GP Starts: 5   GP Wins: 0   Pole positions: 0   Fastest laps: 0   Points: 3

'SPARKEN, Mike' (Michel Poberejsky) **(F)** b 16/6/1930, Neuilly sur Seine, nr Paris

	1955	Championship position: Unplaced						
	Race	Circuit	No	Entrant	Tyres	Car/Engine	Comment	Q Pos/Entries
7	BRITISH GP	Aintree	26	Equipe Gordini	E	2.5 Gordini Type 16 6	9 laps behind	23/25

GP Starts: 1   GP Wins: 0   Pole positions: 0   Fastest laps: 0   Points: 0

'MIKE SPARKEN'

This Frenchman was a great amateur enthusiast who raced sports cars under a pseudonym. In 1952 he ran an Aston Martin DB2 and won his class at Montlhéry, but much of his success came in North African events. He won the 1955 sports car race at Agadir in his 3-litre Ferrari T750S, which he brought to England and drove impressively in the British Empire Trophy before the clutch failed, and at Goodwood, where he placed second.

His only single-seater drive of any note was at the wheel of the works Gordini at the British GP that year.

MIKE SPENCE

Spence overcame polio as a child with no ill effects, and from a young age he harboured dreams of becoming a racing driver. After his Army service was finished he took up club racing in 1958 with a Turner, before going into Formula Junior in 1960 with a Cooper-Austin. He made his Formula 1 debut the following year with an Emeryson-Climax at Solitude, and won the minor Commander York Trophy at Silverstone in the same car. For 1962, Spence entered his own Formula Junior Lotus under the wing of Ian Walker's team, with Mike preparing the car himself in the evenings after his day job was done. He had only one big win – at Reims – but scored many placings and was taken on by Lotus on a three-year contract in 1963.

The fair-haired Englishman drove in the Formula Junior team, but the car proved difficult to handle and Mike's confidence dropped. However, things gradually came round when the car was made more competitive, and he enjoyed a late-season boost when he stood in for the injured Trevor Taylor at Monza. In 1964 Mike was planning a season of Formula 2 and the occasional Grand Prix when he found himself thrust into the F1 team after Arundell's accident.

For one so inexperienced he coped well, especially as Peter had made such a big impression in his few starts. Colin Chapman had no hesitation in keeping Spence in the team with Jim Clark for 1965, and he soon repaid that faith by winning the Race of Champions and performing well on other occasions. With Arundell fit to return for 1966, Mike was out of a drive, but he bade farewell by winning the non-championship South African GP on New Year's Day, before spending the rest of the year marking time with Tim Parnell's team. Joining the works BRM line-up for 1967 was a step back up, but he was given the task of sorting the troublesome BRM H16 car and did superbly to bring it to five points finishes. He also raced the fabulous winged Chaparral with Phil Hill, which was quick but fragile, suffering repeated transmission failures, but at Brands Hatch in the BOAC 500 the car had its great day, crushing the Ferraris.

In 1968, Mike Spence had been racing for ten years; it had been a long haul to the top, but suddenly his talent had begun to flower, and he was about to take his rightful place among the very top echelon of his profession. Yet fate would decree otherwise. The shadow of Jim Clark, which had, perhaps inevitably, held him back throughout his years at Lotus, passed over him once more as he took over the late Scotsman's Lotus for the forthcoming Indianapolis 500. In qualifying everything had gone well, but when Spence took a team-mate's car out for a few shakedown laps, he lost control and crashed into the wall. The right-front wheel flew back and struck the driver's head, and poor Spence died in hospital a few hours later.

SPENCE, Mike (GB) b 30/12/1936, Croydon, Surrey – d 7/5/1968, Indianapolis Speedway, Indiana, USA

	1963			Championship position: Unplaced					
	Race	Circuit	No	Entrant	Tyres	Car/Engine		Comment	Q Pos/Entries
13/ret	ITALIAN GP	Monza	6	Team Lotus	D	1.5 Lotus 25-Climax V8		oil pressure/13 laps behind	9/28
	1964			Championship position: 12th=	Wins: 0	Pole positions: 0	Fastest laps: 0	Points scored: 4	
9	BRITISH GP	Brands Hatch	2	Team Lotus	D	1.5 Lotus 25-Climax V8		3 laps behind	=12/25
8	GERMAN GP	Nürburgring	2	Team Lotus	D	1.5 Lotus 33-Climax V8		1 lap behind	17/24
dns		"	23	Team Lotus	D	1.5 Lotus 33-Climax V8		practice only-Mitter's car	– / –
ret	AUSTRIAN GP	Zeltweg	2	Team Lotus	D	1.5 Lotus 33-Climax V8		driveshaft	8/20
6	ITALIAN GP	Monza	10	Team Lotus	D	1.5 Lotus 33-Climax V8		1 lap behind	8/25
7/ret	US GP	Watkins Glen	2	Team Lotus	D	1.5 Lotus 33-Climax V8		fuel feed/Clark took car/-8 laps	6/19
ret	" "	" "	1	Team Lotus	D	1.5 Lotus 33-Climax V8		fuel injection/given Clark's car	– / –
4	MEXICAN GP	Mexico City	2	Team Lotus	D	1.5 Lotus 25-Climax V8			5/19
dns	" "	" "	1	Team Lotus	D	1.5 Lotus 33-Climax V8		practice only	– / –
	1965			Championship position: 8th	Wins: 0	Pole positions: 0	Fastest laps: 0	Points scored: 10	
4	SOUTH AFRICAN GP	East London	6	Team Lotus	D	1.5 Lotus 33-Climax V8			=3/25
7	BELGIAN GP	Spa	18	Team Lotus	D	1.5 Lotus 33-Climax V8		1 lap behind	12/21
7	FRENCH GP	Clermont Ferrand	8	Team Lotus	D	1.5 Lotus 33-Climax V8		1 lap behind	=10/17
4	BRITISH GP	Silverstone	6	Team Lotus	D	1.5 Lotus 33-Climax V8			6/23
dns	"	"	77	Team Lotus	D	1.5 Lotus 25-Climax V8		practice only	– / –
8	DUTCH GP	Zandvoort	8	Team Lotus	D	1.5 Lotus 25-Climax V8		1 lap behind	8/17
ret	GERMAN GP	Nürburgring	2	Team Lotus	D	1.5 Lotus 33-Climax V8		driveshaft	6/22
11/ret	ITALIAN GP	Monza	26	Team Lotus	D	1.5 Lotus 33-Climax V8		alternator/13 laps behind	8/23
dns	"	"	28	Team Lotus	D	1.5 Lotus 25-Climax V8		practice only-Geki's car	– / –
ret	US GP	Watkins Glen	6	Team Lotus	D	1.5 Lotus 33-Climax V8		engine	4/18
dns	" "	" "	18	Team Lotus	D	1.5 Lotus 25-Climax V8		practice only-Solana's car	– / –
3	MEXICAN GP	Mexico City	6	Team Lotus	D	1.5 Lotus 33-Climax V8			6/18
	1966			Championship position: 12th=	Wins: 0	Pole positions: 0	Fastest laps: 0	Points scored: 4	
ret	MONACO GP	Monte Carlo	6	Reg Parnell Racing Ltd	F	2.0 Lotus 25-BRM V8		rear suspension	12/16
ret	BELGIAN GP	Spa	16	Reg Parnell Racing Ltd	F	2.0 Lotus 25-BRM V8		accident in rain storm	7/18
ret	FRENCH GP	Reims	32	Reg Parnell Racing Ltd	F	2.0 Lotus 25-BRM V8		clutch	10/17
ret	BRITISH GP	Brands Hatch	17	Reg Parnell Racing Ltd	F	2.0 Lotus 25-BRM V8		oil leak	9/20
5	DUTCH GP	Zandvoort	32	Reg Parnell Racing Ltd	F	2.0 Lotus 25-BRM V8		3 laps behind	12/18
ret	GERMAN GP	Nürburgring	15	Reg Parnell Racing Ltd	F	2.0 Lotus 25-BRM V8		electrics	14/30
5	ITALIAN GP	Monza	42	Reg Parnell Racing Ltd	F	2.0 Lotus 25-BRM V8		1 lap behind	14/22
ret	US GP	Watkins Glen	18	Reg Parnell Racing Ltd	F	2.0 Lotus 25-BRM V8		electrics	12/19
dns	MEXICAN GP	Mexico City	18	Reg Parnell Racing Ltd	F	2.0 Lotus 25-BRM V8		accident in practice	(12)/19
	1967			Championship position: 10th	Wins: 0	Pole positions: 0	Fastest laps: 0	Points scored: 9	
ret	SOUTH AFRICAN GP	Kyalami	6	Owen Racing Organisation	D	3.0 BRM P83 H16		oil pipe	13/18
6	MONACO GP	Monte Carlo	5	Owen Racing Organisation	D	3.0 BRM P83 H16		4 laps behind	=12/18
8	DUTCH GP	Zandvoort	10	Owen Racing Organisation	F	3.0 BRM P83 H16		gearbox problems/-3 laps	12/17
5	BELGIAN GP	Spa	12	Owen Racing Organisation	G	3.0 BRM P83 H16		1 lap behind	11/18
dns	"	14	Owen Racing Organisation	G/D	2.1 BRM P261 V8		practice only	– / –
ret	FRENCH GP	Le Mans	11	Owen Racing Organisation	G	3.0 BRM P83 H16		driveshaft	12/15
ret	BRITISH GP	Silverstone	4	Owen Racing Organisation	D	3.0 BRM P83 H16		ignition	11/21
ret	GERMAN GP	Nürburgring	12	Owen Racing Organisation	G	3.0 BRM P83 H16		transmission	12/25
5	CANADIAN GP	Mosport Park	16	Owen Racing Organisation	G	3.0 BRM P83 H16		3 laps behind	10/19
5	ITALIAN GP	Monza	36	Owen Racing Organisation	G	3.0 BRM P83 H16		1 lap behind	12/18
ret	US GP	Watkins Glen	8	Owen Racing Organisation	G	3.0 BRM P83 H16		engine	13/18
5	MEXICAN GP	Mexico City	8	Owen Racing Organisation	G	3.0 BRM P83 H16		2 laps behind	11/19
	1968			Championship position: Unplaced					
ret	SOUTH AFRICAN GP	Kyalami	12	Owen Racing Organisation	G	3.0 BRM P115 H16		boiling fuel	13/23
dns	" "	"	11	Owen Racing Organisation	G	3.0 BRM P126 V12		Rodriguez raced car	– / –

GP Starts: 36 GP Wins: 0 Pole positions: 0 Fastest laps: 0 Points: 27

ALAN STACEY

Stacey made his competition debut in 1955 and spent three years in club racing – almost exclusively at the wheel of Lotus XI sports cars. He won seven races with his own car in 1956, before gaining an invitation to drive for the works during the following season.

Alan had the handicap of an artificial lower right leg, but this proved no obstacle to his racing, nor did it seem to limit his competitiveness, otherwise Colin Chapman would certainly not have signed him to race his sports cars full-time for 1958. He won the Farningham Trophy at Brands Hatch, and scored another victory at Crystal Palace, also taking third place in the Rouen GP. Stacey made his Grand Prix debut at Silverstone that year but, in common with his team-mates Innes Ireland and Graham Hill, he was to suffer a frustrating 1959 season as a lack of reliability undermined the Lotus team's efforts in F1, F2 and sports car racing.

With Hill departing for BRM, Alan was promoted to the position of Ireland's number two in 1960, and once the European season started he had one of Chapman's stunning rear-engined Lotus 18s to drive. He finished fourth in the International Trophy race, but retired at both Monaco and Zandvoort, where he lay in third place before transmission trouble. However, during the Belgian GP at Spa, it is thought the luckless Stacey was hit full in the face by a bird, the stunned driver losing control and suffering fatal injuries after being flung from the car when it hit a bank.

STACEY, Alan (GB) b 29/8/1933, Broomfield, nr Chelmsford, Essex – d 19/6/1960, Spa-Francorchamps Circuit, Belgium

	1958			Championship position: Unplaced					
	Race	Circuit	No	Entrant	Tyres	Car/Engine		Comment	Q Pos/Entries
ret	BRITISH GP	Silverstone	18	Team Lotus	D	2.0 Lotus 16-Climax 4		overheating	20/21
	1959			Championship position: Unplaced					
8	BRITISH GP	Aintree	30	Team Lotus	D	2.5 Lotus 16-Climax 4		4 laps behind	12/30
ret	US GP	Sebring	11	Team Lotus	D	2.5 Lotus 16-Climax 4		clutch	12/31
	1960			Championship position: Unplaced					
ret	ARGENTINE GP	Buenos Aires	22	Team Lotus	D	2.5 Lotus 16-Climax 4		driver exhaustion-sunstroke	14/22
ret	MONACO GP	Monte Carlo	24	Team Lotus	D	2.5 Lotus 18-Climax 4		engine mountings	13/24
ret	DUTCH GP	Zandvoort	5	Team Lotus	D	2.5 Lotus 18-Climax 4		transmission	8/21
ret	BELGIAN GP	Spa	16	Team Lotus	D	2.5 Lotus 18-Climax 4		fatal accident	17/18

GP Starts: 7   GP Wins: 0   Pole positions: 0   Fastest laps: 0   Points: 0

STARRABBA, Prince Gaetano (I) b 3/12/1932, Palermo, Sicily

	1961			Championship position: Unplaced					
	Race	Circuit	No	Entrant	Tyres	Car/Engine		Comment	Q Pos/Entries
ret	ITALIAN GP	Monza	72	Prince Gaetano Starrabba	D	1.5 Lotus 18-Maserati 4		engine	30/33

GP Starts: 1   GP Wins: 0   Pole positions: 0   Fastest laps: 0   Points: 0

STEWART, Ian (GB) b 15/7/1929, Edinburgh, Scotland

	1953			Championship position: Unplaced					
	Race	Circuit	No	Entrant	Tyres	Car/Engine		Comment	Q Pos/Entries
ret	BRITISH GP	Silverstone	15	Ecurie Ecosse	D	2.0 Connaught A Type-Lea Francis 4		engine	20/29

GP Starts: 1   GP Wins: 0   Pole positions: 0   Fastest laps: 0   Points: 0

GAETANO STARRABBA

This Italian nobleman enjoyed a long competitition career, mainly within the confines of his home shores. In the mid-fifties the Count raced a 2-litre Maserati sports, before replacing it with a Ferrari Testa Rossa 500, which he drove into seventh place in the 1957 Targa Florio.

With the 1.5 litre formula in full swing by mid-1961 and plenty of races in which to take part, Gaetano purchased a Lotus 18 chassis powered by a four-cylinder Maserati unit. His best finishes with the car came in 1963 when he took sixth place at Syracuse and fifth in the Rome GP.

After a brief spell with the F3 Giannini-Brabham in 1964, Starrabba returned to sports and GTs, taking 13th and a class win in the 1966 Targa Florio with a Ferrari 250LM. Subsequently he raced both a Porsche Carrera '6' and a 911.

IAN STEWART

Not related to the brothers Jackie and Jimmy, this young Scot mainly raced his Jaguar XK120 north of the border in 1951, before coming to prominence as a founder member of the Ecurie Ecosse team in 1952, winning the Jersey Road Race, the Wakefield Trophy and other sports car events in their Jaguar C-Type.

For 1953, the team laid more ambitious plans, running a Formula 2 Connaught, which Ian handled in the British GP and Libre events, and contesting Continental sports car races, Stewart finishing second in the Nürburgring 1000 Km, with Salvadori, and fourth at Le Mans, with Peter Whitehead.

The following season began with an accident in the Buenos Aires 1000 Km in the team's D-Type from which he escaped with minor injuries, and when he got married shortly afterwards Ian decided to retire from the sport and concentrate on his business interests.

JACKIE STEWART

WORLD CHAMPION: 1969, 1971 & 1973

JACKIE STEWART

Jackie Stewart was the driving force behind the transformation of motor racing from a sport where death was almost routine. When Stewart began racing, the risks were blithely accepted with a shrug of the shoulders as an occupational hazard. But the determined little Scot, who was to see many of his friends and colleagues perish, pursued his campaign with remarkable fervour long after his own retirement and he more than any other individual is responsible for the emergence of the highly organised and remarkably safe sport we know today. As if this weren't enough, Stewart was also a truly great racing driver, a triple World Champion who was a more than worthy successor to his great idol Jim Clark.

Motor racing was part of the family as the young Jackie was growing up, for his brother Jimmy – eight years his senior – was a driver for Ecurie Ecosse. However, young Jackie was more interested in clay pigeon shooting. He was an excellent shot, winning many tournaments at home and abroad, and was hoping to take part in the 1960 Rome Olympics, but missed the team when he had an 'off day' at the final trials. It was to be the biggest disappointment of his sporting life, worse than anything that he ever suffered during his racing days. Jackie's circuit career began in a casual way, at the wheel of a Healey Sprite and a Marcos, before he joined Ecurie Ecosse in 1963. Driving the team's GT and touring cars, Stewart virtually swept the board. While still racing for Ecosse, Jackie came under the guidance of Ken Tyrrell to race a Cooper-BMC in Formula 3, where he set about thrashing the opposition. Colin Chapman tried him in his Ron Harris Formula 2 team and liked what he saw, putting the Scot into a Formula 1 Lotus for the Rand GP at Kyalami, where he retired in the first heat but won the second.

Offered a seat alongside Jim Clark for 1965, Stewart wisely declined, preferring to join BRM, where he could learn his trade with Graham Hill and not face the pressure of being compared directly with his fellow Scot. A second place in the Race of Champions and a win in the International Trophy gave fair notice that here was a special talent, and his Grand Prix performances went from strength to strength, culminating in his first World Championship win at Monza. In the 1966 Tasman series Stewart took the BRM to four victories, and he then won the opening Grand Prix of the year at Monaco in the 2-litre car. Then his luck changed. Victory seemed certain at the Indianapolis 500 until an engine failure close to the finish, and on his return to Europe he crashed the BRM in a rainstorm at Spa. Lying trapped in the car for some time soaked in petrol with a cracked collar-bone was an experience that the Scot would never forget, and no doubt acted as a catalyst for his subsequent safety crusade.

Jackie stayed with BRM for a third season in 1967, but it was a disappointing year with the H16 car proving woefully unreliable. His second place with it in Belgium was a remarkable achievement, especially as he was obliged to hold it in gear for much of the race. The only compensation was a drive for Ferrari in the BOAC 500 at Brands Hatch, where he shared a P4 with Chris Amon, the pair taking second place and clinching the championship for Maranello. Of more importance, however, was his developing working partnership with Ken Tyrrell and Matra, Jackie taking the French Formula 2 car to victory in four of the last five races of the season as a prelude to a Formula 1 effort in 1968.

At last Stewart was in a competitive car, and following the death of Jim Clark he looked the favourite to take the title. Unfortunately his season was interrupted by a crash in a Formula 2 race which sidelined him with a wrist injury. Though he missed only two Grands Prix, it was enough to crucially blunt his title challenge. A feature of the year was his brilliant win in the German GP in the most appalling conditions, truly one of his greatest drives, and there was no stopping him in 1969 as he swept to his first championship with six Grand Prix wins in the Matra MS80, a car he loved to drive.

For the 1970 season Tyrrell was forced to resort to a March chassis, for Matra were running their own operation once more. However, despite a promising start with wins in the Race of Champions and the Spanish GP and a second place in the International Trophy, all was not well. The car was not up to the expectations of a World Champion, and therefore not of the required standard, and Tyrrell secretly set Derek Gardner to work building his own Grand Prix challenger at the greatest possible speed. The new car was unveiled at the Canadian GP where Stewart took pole position. The future was now clear and Tyrrell was henceforth to build his own cars. The 1971 season saw Jackie back at his brilliant best, using the new Tyrrell to devastating effect, winning six Grands Prix and easily taking his second World Championship. He was much in demand that year and undertook the ten-round Can-Am series for Carl Haas. Stewart won two rounds in the Lola, but the strain of trans-Atlantic travel was already taking its toll.

Jackie's health was to suffer in 1972 due to an ulcer which caused him to miss six weeks of the season, enough to see his title chances disappear as an ebullient Emerson Fittipaldi made the most of his opportunities with his Lotus 72. Not that Stewart was about to let his title slip away without a fight. He won the French GP on his return and finished the year on a winning note with back-to-back wins at Mosport and Watkins Glen to sound a warning that he would not be so easy to beat in 1973. And so it was to prove. By this time Stewart was the complete driver, mentally and physically prepared to cope with every eventuality. He won as he pleased at Kyalami, Monte Carlo, Zandvoort and the Nürburgring, thus passing the late Jim Clark's number of wins to set a new record total of 27. His last race in Europe was one of his greatest. As he climbed through the field after a puncture at Monza to take fourth place, it was a stirring sight to see him forced to drive at the limit lap after lap, picking off one car after another.

Jackie had decided to retire after the US GP at Watkins Glen and what would have been his 100th Grand Prix start, but the weekend was to be clouded by tragedy as his team-mate François Cevert was killed in practice. The Tyrrell team withdrew their cars, and the wonderful career of John Young Stewart was over. Since then, of course, Jackie has worked harder than ever. He was seen regularly at the circuits, imparting his wisdom to a new generation of racers, and his son Paul, much against his parents' wishes, raced with some success, before setting up his own team, Paul Stewart Racing. The near-dominance of the operation in the junior formulae during the early nineties led to an ambitious move into Formula 1 in 1997. With a five-year engine deal from Ford, and Jackie's business acumen and vast experience, Stewart Grand Prix was clearly going to be a force to be reckoned with. Having the necessary funding to compete properly was a crucial factor in persuading Stewart to take the plunge. A second-place finish at Monaco in the organisation's first season was an early peak, to be followed by the inevitable troughs as the young team found their feet in the white-hot cauldron of Formula 1.

Without doubt, 1999 was a momentous year for Jackie, who reached his 60th birthday, saw Stewart Grand Prix achieve their maiden victory at the European Grand Prix, and took the decision to sell the Formula 1 team he had built up to Ford. Henceforth the organisation will race under the Jaguar banner, but Stewart maintains that the single victory he achieved as a constructor means more to him than any of the 27 wins he took when he was a driver.

STEWART, Jackie (John Young) (GB) b 11/6/1939, Milton, Dunbartonshire, Scotland

1965 — Championship position: 3rd Wins: 1 Pole positions: 0 Fastest laps: 0 Points scored: 34

	Race	Circuit	No	Entrant	Tyres	Car/Engine	Comment	Q Pos/Entries
6	SOUTH AFRICAN GP	East London	4	Owen Racing Organisation	D	1.5 BRM P261 V8	2 laps behind	11/25
3	MONACO GP	Monte Carlo	4	Owen Racing Organisation	D	1.5 BRM P261 V8		3/17
2	BELGIAN GP	Spa	8	Owen Racing Organisation	D	1.5 BRM P261 V8		3/21
2	FRENCH GP	Clermont Ferrand	12	Owen Racing Organisation	D	1.5 BRM P261 V8		2/17
5	BRITISH GP	Silverstone	4	Owen Racing Organisation	D	1.5 BRM P261 V8		=3/23
2	DUTCH GP	Zandvoort	12	Owen Racing Organisation	D	1.5 BRM P261 V8		6/17
ret	GERMAN GP	Nürburgring	10	Owen Racing Organisation	D	1.5 BRM P261 V8	suspension	2/22
1	ITALIAN GP	Monza	32	Owen Racing Organisation	D	1.5 BRM P261 V8		3/23
ret	US GP	Watkins Glen	4	Owen Racing Organisation	D	1.5 BRM P261 V8	suspension	6/18
ret	MEXICAN GP	Mexico city	4	Owen Racing Organisation	D	1.5 BRM P261 V8	clutch	8/18

1966 — Championship position: 7th Wins: 1 Pole positions: 0 Fastest laps: 0 Points scored: 14

	Race	Circuit	No	Entrant	Tyres	Car/Engine	Comment	Q Pos/Entries
1	MONACO GP	Monte Carlo	12	Owen Racing Organisation	D	2.0 BRM P261 V8		3/16
ret	BELGIAN GP	Spa	15	Owen Racing Organisation	D	2.0 BRM P261 V8	spun off in rainstorm-injured	3/18
dns	"	"	15	Owen Racing Organisation	G/D	3.0 BRM P83 H16	practice only	–/–
ret	BRITISH GP	Brands Hatch	4	Owen Racing Organisation	D	3.0 BRM P83 H16	engine	8/20
4	DUTCH GP	Zandvoort	14	Owen Racing Organisation	G	2.0 BRM P261 V8	2 laps behind	8/18
5	GERMAN GP	Nürburgring	6	Owen Racing Organisation	D	2.0 BRM P261 V8		3/30
ret	ITALIAN GP	Monza	28	Owen Racing Organisation	G	3.0 BRM P83 H16	fuel leak	9/22
ret	US GP	Watkins glen	4	Owen Racing Organisation	G	3.0 BRM P83 H16	engine	6/19
ret	MEXICAN GP	Mexico City	4	Owen Racing Organisation	G	3.0 BRM P83 H16	oil leak	10/19

1967 — Championship position: 9th Wins: 0 Pole positions: 0 Fastest laps: 0 Points scored: 10

	Race	Circuit	No	Entrant	Tyres	Car/Engine	Comment	Q Pos/Entries
ret	SOUTH AFRICAN GP	Kyalami	5	Owen Racing Organisation	D	3.0 BRM P83 H16	engine	9/18
ret	MONACO GP	Monte Carlo	4	Owen Racing Organisation	F	2.1 BRM P261 V8	transmission	6/18
dns	"	"	4T	Owen Racing Organisation	F	3.0 BRM P83 H16	practice only	–/–
ret	DUTCH GP	Zandvoort	9	Owen Racing Organisation	G	3.0 BRM P83 H16	brakes	11/17
2	BELGIAN GP	Spa	14	Owen Racing Organisation	G	3.0 BRM P83 H16		6/18
dns	"	"	12	Owen Racing Organisation	G/D	2.1 BRM P261 V8	practice only	–/–
3	FRENCH GP	Le Mans	10	Owen Racing Organisation	G	2.1 BRM P261 V8	1 lap behind	10/15
dns	"	"	10	Owen Racing Organisation	G/D/F	3.0 BRM P83 H16	practice only	–/–
ret	BRITISH GP	Silverstone	3	Owen Racing Organisation	G	3.0 BRM P83 H16	transmission	12/21
ret	GERMAN GP	Nürburgring	11	Owen Racing Organisation	G	3.0 BRM P115 H16	transmission	4/25
dns	"	"	11	Owen Racing Organisation	G/D	3.0 BRM P83 H16	practice only	–/–
ret	CANADIAN GP	Mosport Park	15	Owen Racing Organisation	G	3.0 BRM P115 H16	throttle slides-spun off	9/19
ret	ITALIAN GP	Monza	34	Owen Racing Organisation	G	3.0 BRM P115 H16	engine	7/18
ret	US GP	Watkins Glen	7	Owen Racing Organisation	G	3.0 BRM P115 H16	fuel metering unit belt	10/18
ret	MEXICAN GP	Mexico City	7	Owen Racing Organisation	G	3.0 BRM P115 H16	engine vibration	12/19

1968 — Championship position: 2 Wins: 3 Pole positions: 0 Fastest laps: 2 Points scored: 36

	Race	Circuit	No	Entrant	Tyres	Car/Engine	Comment	Q Pos/Entries
ret	SOUTH AFRICAN GP	Kyalami	16	Matra International	D	3.0 Matra MS9-Cosworth V8	engine	3/23
dns	"	"	26	Matra International	D	1.6 Matra MS7-Cosworth 4	practice only	–/–
4	BELGIAN GP	Spa	7	Matra International	D	3.0 Matra MS10-Cosworth V8	pit stop-fuel/1 lap behind	2/18
1	DUTCH GP	Zandvoort	8	Matra International	D	3.0 Matra MS10-Cosworth V8		5/19
3	FRENCH GP	Rouen	28	Matra International	D	3.0 Matra MS10-Cosworth V8	pit stop-tyres/1 lap behind	2/18
6	BRITISH GP	Brands Hatch	14	Matra International	D	3.0 Matra MS10-Cosworth V8	2 laps behind	=6/20
1	GERMAN GP	Nürburgring	6	Matra International	D	3.0 Matra MS10-Cosworth V8	FL	6/20
ret	ITALIAN GP	Monza	4	Matra International	D	3.0 Matra MS10-Cosworth V8	engine	6/24
6	CANADIAN GP	St Jovite	14	Matra International	D	3.0 Matra MS10-Cosworth V8	p stop-suspension/-7 laps	=10/22
1	US GP	Watkins Glen	15	Matra International	D	3.0 Matra MS10-Cosworth V8	FL	2/21
7	MEXICAN GP	Mexico City	15	Matra International	D	3.0 Matra MS10-Cosworth V8	fuel feed problems/-1 lap	7/21

1969 — Championship position: WORLD CHAMPION Wins: 6 Pole positions: 2 Fastest laps: 5 Points scored: 63

	Race	Circuit	No	Entrant	Tyres	Car/Engine	Comment	Q Pos/Entries
1	SOUTH AFRICAN GP	Kyalami	7	Matra International	D	3.0 Matra MS10-Cosworth V8	FL	4/18
dns	"	"	20	Matra International	D	3.0 Matra MS80-Cosworth V8	practice only	–/–
1	SPANISH GP	Montjuich Park	7	Matra International	D	3.0 Matra MS80-Cosworth V8		4/14

Stewart, driving the Tyrrell 006, wins the Monaco GP for the third and last time in 1973.
He retired at the season's end with three world titles and 27 Grand Prix victories from just 99 starts.

Pos	Race	Circuit	No	Team		Car	Notes	
ret	MONACO GP	Monte Carlo	7	Matra International	D	3.0 Matra MS80-Cosworth V8	*driveshaft/FL*	1/16
1	DUTCH GP	Zandvoort	4	Matra International	D	3.0 Matra MS80-Cosworth V8	*FL*	2/15
dns	"	"	4T	Matra International	D	3.0 Matra MS84-Cosworth V8 4WD	*practice only*	–/–
1	FRENCH GP	Clermont Ferrand	2	Matra International	D	3.0 Matra MS80-Cosworth V8	*FL*	1/13
dns	"	"	2T	Matra International	D	3.0 Matra MS84-Cosworth V8 4WD	*practice only*	–/–
1	BRITISH GP	Silverstone	3	Matra International	D	3.0 Matra MS80-Cosworth V8	*FL*	2/17
dns	"		30	Matra International	D	3.0 Matra MS84-Cosworth V8 4WD	*practice only*	–/–
2	GERMAN GP	Nürburgring	7	Matra International	D	3.0 Matra MS80-Cosworth V8		2/26
dns	"		7T	Matra International	D	3.0 Matra MS84-Cosworth V8 4WD	*practice only*	–/–
1	ITALIAN GP	Monza	20	Matra International	D	3.0 Matra MS80-Cosworth V8		3/15
dns	"		24	Matra International	D	3.0 Matra MS84-Cosworth V8 4WD	*practice only*	–/–
ret	CANADIAN GP	Mosport Park	17	Matra International	D	3.0 Matra MS80-Cosworth V8	*hit by Ickx*	=2/20
ret	US GP	Watkins Glen	3	Matra International	D	3.0 Matra MS80-Cosworth V8	*engine*	3/18
dns	"	"	3	Matra International	D	3.0 Matra MS84-Cosworth V8 4WD	*practice only*	–/–
4	MEXICAN GP	Mexico City	3	Matra International	D	3.0 Matra MS80-Cosworth V8		3/17

1970 Championship position: 5th= Wins: 1 Pole positions: 4 Fastest laps: 0 Points scored: 25

Pos	Race	Circuit	No	Team		Car	Notes	
3	SOUTH AFRICAN GP	Kyalami	1	Tyrrell Racing Organisation	D	3.0 March 701-Cosworth V8		1/24
1	SPANISH GP	Jarama	1	Tyrrell Racing Organsiation	D	3.0 March 701-Cosworth V8		3/22
ret	MONACO GP	Monte Carlo	21	Tyrrell Racing Organisation	D	3.0 March 701-Cosworth V8	*engine*	1/21
ret	BELGIAN GP	Spa	11	Tyrrell Racing Organisation	D	3.0 March 701-Cosworth V8	*engine*	1/18
2	DUTCH GP	Zandvoort	5	Tyrrell Racing Organisation	D	3.0 March 701-Cosworth V8		2/24
9	FRENCH GP	Clermont Ferrand	1	Tyrrell Racing Organisation	D	3.0 March 701-Cosworth V8	*pit stop-ignition*	4/23
ret	BRITISH GP	Brands Hatch	1	Tyrrell Racing Organisation	D	3.0 March 701-Cosworth V8	*melted clutch line-fire*	8/25
ret	GERMAN GP	Hockenheim	1	Tyrrell Racing Organisation	D	3.0 March 701-Cosworth V8	*engine*	7/25
ret	AUSTRIAN GP	Österreichring	1	Tyrrell Racing Organisation	D	3.0 March 701-Cosworth V8	*split fuel line*	4/24
2	ITALIAN GP	Monza	18	Tyrrell Racing Organisation	D	3.0 March 701-Cosworth V8		4/27
dns	"	"	18	Tyrrell Racing Organisation	D	3.0 Tyrrell 001-Cosworth V8	*practice only*	–/–
ret	CANADIAN GP	St Jovite	3	Tyrrell Racing Organisation	D	3.0 Tyrrell 001-Cosworth V8	*broken stub axle*	1/20
dns	"	" "	1	Tyrrell Racing Organisation	D	3.0 March 701-Cosworth V8	*practice only*	–/–
ret	US GP	Watkins Glen	1	Tyrrell Racing Organisation	D	3.0 Tyrrell 001-Cosworth V8	*engine-oil leak*	2/27
dns	"		33	Tyrrell Racing Organisation	D	3.0 March 701-Cosworth V8	*practice only*	–/–
ret	MEXICAN GP	Mexico City	1	Tyrrell Racing Organisation	D	3.0 Tyrrell 001-Cosworth V8	*steering-hit dog*	2/18

1971 Championship position: WORLD CHAMPION Wins: 6 Pole positions: 6 Fastest laps: 3 Points scored: 62

Pos	Race	Circuit	No	Team		Car	Notes	
2	SOUTH AFRICAN GP	Kyalami	9	Elf Team Tyrrell	G	3.0 Tyrrell 001-Cosworth V8		1/25
dns	"	"	10	Elf Team Tyrrell	G	3.0 Tyrrell 002-Cosworth V8	*practice only-Cevert's car*	–/–
1	SPANISH GP	Montjuich Park	11	Elf Team Tyrrell	G	3.0 Tyrrell 003-Cosworth V8		3/22
dns	"	" "	11T	Elf Team Tyrrell	G	3.0 Tyrrell 003-Cosworth V8	*practice only*	–/–
1	MONACO GP	Monte Carlo	11	Elf Team Tyrrell	G	3.0 Tyrrell 003-Cosworth V8	*FL*	1/23
dns	"	" "	11T	Elf Team Tyrrell	G	3.0 Tyrrell 001-Cosworth V8	*practice only*	–/–
11	DUTCH GP	Zandvoort	5	Elf Team Tyrrell	G	3.0 Tyrrell 003-Cosworth V8	*spin in rain/5 laps behind*	3/24
dns	"	"	5T	Elf Team Tyrrell	G	3.0 Tyrrell 001-Cosworth V8	*practice only*	–/–
1	FRENCH GP	Paul Ricard	11	Elf Team Tyrrell	G	3.0 Tyrrell 003-Cosworth V8	*FL*	1/24
dns	"	" "	11T	Elf Team Tyrrell	G	3.0 Tyrrell 001-Cosworth V8	*practice only*	–/–
1	BRITISH GP	Silverstone	12	Elf Team Tyrrell	G	3.0 Tyrrell 003-Cosworth V8	*FL*	=1/24
1	GERMAN GP	Nürburgring	2	Elf Team Tyrrell	G	3.0 Tyrrell 003-Cosworth V8		1/23
dns	"	"	2T	Elf Team Tyrrell	G	3.0 Tyrrell 001-Cosworth V8	*practice only*	–/–
ret	AUSTRIAN GP	Österreichring	11	Elf Team Tyrrell	G	3.0 Tyrrell 003-Cosworth V8	*lost wheel*	2/22
dns	"		11T	Elf Team Tyrrell	G	3.0 Tyrrell 001-Cosworth V8	*practice only*	–/–
ret	ITALIAN GP	Monza	30	Elf Team Tyrrell	G	3.0 Tyrrell 003-Cosworth V8	*engine*	7/24
1	CANADIAN GP	Mosport Park	11	Elf Team Tyrrell	G	3.0 Tyrrell 003-Cosworth V8		1/27
dns	"	" "	11T	Elf Team Tyrrell	G	3.0 Tyrrell 001-Cosworth V8	*practice only*	–/–
5	US GP	Watkins Glen	8	Elf Team Tyrrell	G	3.0 Tyrrell 003-Cosworth V8	*chunking tyres*	1/32

1972 Championship position: 2nd Wins: 4 Pole positions: 2 Fastest laps: 4 Points scored: 45

Pos	Race	Circuit	No	Team		Car	Notes	
1	ARGENTINE GP	Buenos Aires	21	Elf Team Tyrrell	G	3.0 Tyrrell 003-Cosworth V8	*FL*	2/22
ret	SOUTH AFRICAN GP	Kyalami	1	Elf Team Tyrrell	G	3.0 Tyrrell 004-Cosworth V8	*gearbox*	1/27
dns	" "		1T	Elf Team Tyrrell	G	3.0 Tyrrell 004-Cosworth V8	*practice only*	–/–
ret	SPANISH GP	Jarama	1	Elf Team Tyrrell	G	3.0 Tyrrell 003-Cosworth V8	*spun-holed radiator*	4/26
dns	"		1T	Elf Team Tyrrell	G	3.0 Tyrrell 004-Cosworth V8	*practice only*	–/–
4	MONACO GP	Monte Carlo	1	Elf Team Tyrrell	G	3.0 Tyrrell 003-Cosworth V8	*2 spins/misfire/2 laps behind*	=8/25
dns	"	" "	1T	Elf Team Tyrrell	G	3.0 Tyrrell 004-Cosworth V8	*practice only*	–/–
1	FRENCH GP	Clermont Ferrand	4	Elf Team Tyrrell	G	3.0 Tyrrell 003-Cosworth V8		3/29
2	BRITISH GP	Brands Hatch	1	Elf Team Tyrrell	G	3.0 Tyrrell 003-Cosworth V8	*FL*	4/27
dns	"		1	Elf Team Tyrrell	G	3.0 Tyrrell 005-Cosworth V8	*accident in practice*	–/–
11/ret	GERMAN GP	Nürburgring	1	Elf Team Tyrrell	G	3.0 Tyrrell 003-Cosworth V8	*collision-Regazzoni/-1 lap*	2/27
7	AUSTRIAN GP	Österreichring	1	Elf Team Tyrrell	G	3.0 Tyrrell 005-Cosworth V8	*handling problems*	3/26
ret	ITALIAN GP	Monza	1	Elf Team Tyrrell	G	3.0 Tyrrell 005-Cosworth V8	*transmission*	3/27
dns	"	"	1T	Elf Team Tyrrell	G	3.0 Tyrrell 004-Cosworth V8	*practice only*	–/–
1	CANADIAN GP	Mosport Park	1	Elf Team Tyrrell	G	3.0 Tyrrell 005-Cosworth V8	*FL*	=4/25
dns	"	" "	1T	Elf Team Tyrrell	G	3.0 Tyrrell 004-Cosworth V8	*practice only*	–/–
dns	"	" "	2T	Elf Team Tyrrell	G	3.0 Tyrrell 006-Cosworth V8	*practice only*	–/–
1	US GP	Watkins Glen	1	Elf Team Tyrrell	G	3.0 Tyrrell 005-Cosworth V8	*FL*	1/32

1973 Championship position: WORLD CHAMPION Wins: 5 Pole positions: 3 Fastest laps: 1 Points scored: 71

Pos	Race	Circuit	No	Team		Car	Notes	
3	ARGENTINE GP	Buenos Aires	6	Elf Team Tyrrell	G	3.0 Tyrrell 005-Cosworth V8	*slow puncture*	4/19
2	BRAZILIAN GP	Rio	3	Elf Team Tyrrell	G	3.0 Tyrrell 005-Cosworth V8		8/20
1	SOUTH AFRICAN GP	Kyalami	(4) 3	Elf Team Tyrrell	G	3.0 Tyrrell 006-Cosworth V8		16/25
dns	" "		4	Elf Team Tyrrell	G	3.0 Tyrrell 005-Cosworth V8	*practice crash-brake failure*	(3)/25
ret	SPANISH GP	Montjuich Park	3	Elf Team Tyrrell	G	3.0 Tyrrell 006-Cosworth V8	*disc brake mounting*	4/22
dns	"	"	3T	Elf Team Tyrrell	G	3.0 Tyrrell 005-Cosworth V8	*practice only*	–/–
1	BELGIAN GP	Zolder	5	Elf Team Tyrrell	G	3.0 Tyrrell 006-Cosworth V8		6/23
1	MONACO GP	Monte Carlo	5	Elf Team Tyrrell	G	3.0 Tyrrell 006-Cosworth V8		1/26
dns	"	" "	5T	Elf Team Tyrrell	G	3.0 Tyrrell 005-Cosworth V8	*practice only*	–/–

5	SWEDISH GP	Anderstorp	5	Elf Team Tyrrell	G	3.0 Tyrrell 006-Cosworth V8	*brake problems*	3/22
dns	"	"	5T	Elf Team Tyrrell	G	3.0 Tyrrell 005-Cosworth V8	*practice only*	–/–
4	FRENCH GP	Paul Ricard	5	Elf Team Tyrrell	G	3.0 Tyrrell 006-Cosworth V8		1/25
dns	"	" "	5T	Elf Team Tyrrell	G	3.0 Tyrrell 005-Cosworth V8	*practice only*	–/–
10	BRITISH GP	Silverstone	5	Elf Team Tyrrell	G	3.0 Tyrrell 006-Cosworth V8	*pit stop to remove debris/-1 lap*	=4/29
dns	"	"	42	Elf Team Tyrrell	G	3.0 Tyrrell 006-Cosworth V8	*practice only*	–/–
1	DUTCH GP	Zandvoort	5	Elf Team Tyrrell	G	3.0 Tyrrell 006-Cosworth V8		2/24
dns	"	"	5T	Elf Team Tyrrell	G	3.0 Tyrrell 005-Cosworth V8	*practice only*	–/–
1	GERMAN GP	Nürburgring	5	Elf Team Tyrrell	G	3.0 Tyrrell 006-Cosworth V8		1/23
dns	"	"	5T	Elf Team Tyrrell	G	3.0 Tyrrell 005-Cosworth V8	*practice only*	–/–
2	AUSTRIAN GP	Österreichring	5	Elf Team Tyrrell	G	3.0 Tyrrell 006-Cosworth V8		7/25
4	ITALIAN GP	Monza	5	Elf Team Tyrrell	G	3.0 Tyrrell 006-Cosworth V8	*pit stop-tyres/FL*	6/25
5	CANADIAN GP	Mosport Park	5	Elf Team Tyrrell	G	3.0 Tyrrell 006-Cosworth V8	*1 lap behind*	9/26
dns	US GP	Watkins Glen	5	Elf Team Tyrrell	G	3.0 Tyrrell 006-Cosworth V8	*withdrawn after Cevert's death*	(6)/28

GP Starts: 99   GP Wins: 27   Pole positions: 17   Fastest laps: 15   Points: 360

JIMMY STEWART

After cutting his teeth on hill-climbs and scratch races in 1951-52 with a Healey, Jimmy became an integral part of the Ecurie Ecosse team the following year, racing both the Jaguar C-Type and XK120 with great success. He was then given the chance to race the team's Cooper-Bristol in that year's British GP and ran in sixth place, going very quickly indeed, before spinning out.

Back with the Ecosse C-Type in 1954, Stewart continued to build a reputation as a very fast and fearless driver. He won three races in one meeting at Goodwood, but his season was soon cut short by injury when he was involved in a collision at Le Mans and thrown from the car, suffering a fractured elbow.

He was back in 1955, but another crash in practice for a major sports car race at Silverstone left him badly injured. This time he retired but could later enjoy the many fabulous successes of his younger brother Jackie.

SIEGFRIED STOHR

Born in Rimini of an Italian mother and a German father, Stohr won the 1978 Italian F3 championship with a Chevron, a title which at that time was very much secondary to the European crown. Nevertheless the former karting ace moved into Formula 2 for 1979, taking second places at Vallelunga and Pau with a Chevron before switching less successfully to a March.

Securing sponsorship from Beta, Stohr joined the Alan Docking team to race a Toleman in 1980 and did a sound job, scoring a win at Enna and earning fourth place in the championship.

Taking his sponsorship along to Arrows the following season, Stohr never really got to grips with things in his one shot at Grand Prix racing, being very much the number two to Riccardo Patrese.

STEWART, Jimmy (GB) b 6/3/1931, Bowling, Dunbartonshire, Scotland

	1953	Championship position: Unplaced						
	Race	*Circuit*	*No*	*Entrant*	*Tyres*	*Car/Engine*	*Comment*	*Q Pos/Entries*
ret	BRITISH GP	Silverstone	18	Ecurie Ecosse	D	2.0 Cooper T20-Bristol 6	*spun off*	15/29

GP Starts: 1   GP Wins: 0   Pole positions: 0   Fastest laps: 0   Points: 0

STOHR, Siegfried (I) b 10/10/1952, Rimini

	1981	Championship position: Unplaced						
	Race	*Circuit*	*No*	*Entrant*	*Tyres*	*Car/Engine*	*Comment*	*Q Pos/Entries*
dnq	US GP WEST	Long Beach	30	Arrows Racing Team	M	3.0 Arrows A3-Cosworth V8		28/29
ret	BRAZILIAN GP	Rio	30	Arrows Racing Team	M	3.0 Arrows A3-Cosworth V8	*collision with Tambay*	21/30
9	ARGENTINE GP	Buenos Aires	30	Arrows Racing Team	M	3.0 Arrows A3-Cosworth V8	*1 lap behind*	19/29
dnq	SAN MARINO GP	Imola	30	Arrows Racing Team	M	3.0 Arrows A3-Cosworth V8		25/30
ret/dns	BELGIAN GP	Zolder	30	Arrows Racing Team	M	3.0 Arrows A3-Cosworth V8	*ran into Patrese at first start*	13/31
ret	MONACO GP	Monte Carlo	30	Arrows Racing Team	M	3.0 Arrows A3-Cosworth V8	*electrics*	14/31
ret	SPANISH GP	Jarama	30	Arrows Racing Team	M	3.0 Arrows A3-Cosworth V8	*engine*	23/30
dnq	FRENCH GP	Dijon	30	Arrows Racing Team	M	3.0 Arrows A3-Cosworth V8		25/29
ret	BRITISH GP	Silverstone	30	Arrows Racing Team	P	3.0 Arrows A3-Cosworth V8	*collision with Rebaque*	18/30
12	GERMAN GP	Hockenheim	30	Arrows Racing Team	P	3.0 Arrows A3-Cosworth V8	*1 lap behind*	24/30
ret	AUSTRIAN GP	Österreichring	30	Arrows Racing Team	P	3.0 Arrows A3-Cosworth V8	*spun off-could not restart*	24/28
7	DUTCH GP	Zandvoort	30	Arrows Racing Team	P	3.0 Arrows A3-Cosworth V8	*3 laps behind*	21/30
dnq	ITALIAN GP	Monza	30	Arrows Racing Team	P	3.0 Arrows A3-Cosworth V8		28/30

GP Starts: 8 (9)   GP Wins: 0   Pole positions: 0   Fastest laps: 0   Points: 0

ROLF STOMMELEN

While both Kurt Ahrens and Gerhard Mitter promised much but failed to make a permanent mark on Grand Prix racing, Rolf Stommelen became the first German driver since Wolfgang von Trips to appear regularly on the F1 starting grids.

After campaigning his private Porsche 904 GTS in 1964-65, Rolf was invited to join the works team for endurance racing. He soon became a key member of the team, winning the 1967 Targa Florio with Paul Hawkins, and the Daytona 24 Hours and Paris 1000 Km in 1968, as well as taking many placings. He was also successfully involved in Porsche's European mountain-climb programme with the 2-litre Bergspyder.

After dipping his toe into the water by competing in the 1969 German GP with a hired F2 Lotus, Stommelen gained sponsorship for a full F1 season in 1970 with a works Brabham and showed distinct promise, highlighted by a brilliant drive in Austria when he drove from 18th to finish third. He was also busy making his mark in Formula 2 with the Eifelland Caravans-backed Brabham, and was a works driver for the Alfa Romeo sports car team, for whom he drove until 1974.

For 1971, Stommelen took his sponsorship money to Surtees, but the partnership produced little and relationships were strained, so it was no surprise when he branched out on his own for 1972 with the curious-looking March-based Eifelland-Ford, which performed even more lamely than its appearance promised. Temporarily on the Formula 1 sidelines after this fiasco, Stommelen grabbed the lifeline of a Brabham drive after de Adamich's accident at Silverstone in 1973, and was then called up to replace Guy Edwards in the Embassy Hill Lola in mid-1974.

Rolf got on well with Hill and secured a seat for 1975, but his first race in the new Hill GH1 at the trouble-torn Spanish GP ended in disaster when a wing stay failed while he was leading the race. The car was pitched into the crowd, killing four spectators and seriously injuring the driver. Happily Rolf soon recovered and returned later in the year, but by that time Tony Brise had emerged as Hill's prize asset.

For 1976 Stommelen returned to sports car racing with Martini Porsche, winning at Enna and Watkins Glen, and this helped him to a couple of rides in the works Brabham that season. The following year he won the Nürburgring 1000 Km for Porsche, and also took the German national touring car title in the Gelo Racing 935 turbo.

With Warsteiner backing the Arrows team in 1978, Rolf was given the second seat and a chance to renew his Grand Prix career, but the season was a severe disappointment and Stommelen returned to sports car and GT racing, where he was still a competitive runner. In 1980 he won the Daytona 24 Hours and the Nürburgring 1000 Km in a Porsche, and he continued to race for top endurance teams such as Porsche, Lancia and Rondeau, as well as trying his hand at IMSA.

It was racing a Porsche 'replica' 935 in this category that he lost his life after crashing in a race at Riverside in April 1983.

STOMMELEN, Rolf (D) b 11/7/1943, Siegen – d 24/4/1983, Riverside Circuit, California, USA

	Race	Circuit	No	Entrant	Tyres	Car/Engine	Comment	Q Pos/Entries
	1969	Championship position: Unplaced						
8*	GERMAN GP (F2)	Nurburgring	22	Roy Winkelmann Racing Ltd	F	1.6 Lotus 59B-Ford 4 F2	* 4th in F2 class	22/26
	1970	Championship position: 11th	Wins: 0	Pole positions: 0		Fastest laps: 0	Points scored: 10	
ret	SOUTH AFRICAN GP	Kyalami	14	Auto Motor Und Sport	G	3.0 Brabham BT33-Cosworth V8	engine	15/24
ret	SPANISH GP	Jarama	24	Auto Motor Und Sport	G	3.0 Brabham BT33-Cosworth V8	engine	20/22
dnq	MONACO GP	Monte Carlo	6	Auto Motor Und Sport	G	3.0 Brabham BT33-Cosworth V8	car not seeded	15/21
5	BELGIAN GP	Spa	19	Auto Motor Und Sport	G	3.0 Brabham BT33-Cosworth V8		7/18
dnq	DUTCH GP	Zandvoort	19	Auto Motor Und Sport	G	3.0 Brabham BT33-Cosworth V8		22/24
7	FRENCH GP	Clermont Ferrand	22	Auto Motor Und Sport	G	3.0 Brabham BT33-Cosworth V8		14/23
dns	BRITISH GP	Brands Hatch	18	Auto Motor Und Sport	G	3.0 Brabham BT33-Cosworth V8	accident in practice	(10)/25
5	GERMAN GP	Hockenheim	21	Auto Motor Und Sport	G	3.0 Brabham BT33-Cosworth V8	1 lap behind	11/25
3	AUSTRIAN GP	Österreichring	11	Auto Motor Und Sport	G	3.0 Brabham BT33-Cosworth V8		16/24
5	ITALIAN GP	Monza	46	Auto Motor Und Sport	G	3.0 Brabham BT33-Cosworth V8		20/27
ret	CANADIAN GP	St Jovite	12	Auto Motor Und Sport	G	3.0 Brabham BT33-Cosworth V8	steering	18/20
12	US GP	Watkins Glen	16	Auto Motor Und Sport	G	3.0 Brabham BT33-Cosworth V8	pit stop-brakes/4 laps behind	19/27
ret	MEXICAN GP	Mexico City	16	Auto Motor Und Sport	G	3.0 Brabham BT33-Cosworth V8	fuel system	17/18
	1971	Championship position: 18th=	Wins: 0	Pole positions: 0		Fastest laps: 0	Points scored: 3	
12	SOUTH AFRICAN GP	Kyalami	21	Auto Motor Und Sport-Team Surtees	F	3.0 Surtees TS7-Cosworth V8	2 laps behind	15/25
ret	SPANISH GP	Montjuich Park	25	Auto Motor Und Sport-Team Surtees	F	3.0 Surtees TS9-Cosworth V8	fuel pressure release valve	19/22
6	MONACO GP	Monte Carlo	24	Auto Motor Und Sport-Team Surtees	F	3.0 Surtees TS9-Cosworth V8	1 lap behind	=15/23
dsq	DUTCH GP	Zandvoort	29	Auto Motor Und Sport-Team Surtees	F	3.0 Surtees TS9-Cosworth V8	spun off-push start	10/24
11	FRENCH GP	Paul Ricard	24	Auto Motor Und Sport-Team Surtees	F	3.0 Surtees TS9-Cosworth V8	2 laps behind	10/24
5	BRITISH GP	Silverstone	24	Auto Motor Und Sport-Team Surtees	F	3.0 Surtees TS9-Cosworth V8	1 lap behind	12/24
10	GERMAN GP	Nürburgring	12	Auto Motor Und Sport-Team Surtees	F	3.0 Surtees TS9-Cosworth V8	handling problems/-1 lap	12/23
7	AUSTRIAN GP	Österreichring	24	Auto Motor Und Sport-Team Surtees	F	3.0 Surtees TS9-Cosworth V8		12/22
dns	ITALIAN GP	Monza	8	Auto Motor Und Sport-Team Surtees	F	3.0 Surtees TS9-Cosworth V8	accident in practice	(23)/24
ret	CANADIAN GP	Mosport Park	24	Auto Motor Und Sport-Team Surtees	F	3.0 Surtees TS9-Cosworth V8	oil pressure	23/27
	1972	Championship position: Unplaced						
13	SOUTH AFRICAN GP	Kyalami	25	Team Eifelland Caravans	G	3.0 Eifelland 21/March 721-Cosworth V8	2 laps behind	25/27
ret	SPANISH GP	Jarama	16	Team Eifelland Caravans	G	3.0 Eifelland 21/March 721-Cosworth V8	spun-hit barrier	17/26
10	MONACO GP	Monte Carlo	27	Team Eifelland Caravans	G	3.0 Eifelland 21/March 721-Cosworth V8	poor handling in rain/-3 laps	25/25
11	BELGIAN GP	Nivelles	6	Team Eifelland Caravans	G	3.0 Eifelland 21/March 721-Cosworth V8	2 laps behind	20/26
16	FRENCH GP	Clermont Ferrand	10	Team Eifelland Caravans	G	3.0 Eifelland 21/March 721-Cosworth V8	pit stop-puncture/-1 lap	=17/29
10	BRITISH GP	Brands Hatch	33	Team Eifelland Caravans	G	3.0 Eifelland 21/March 721-Cosworth V8	5 laps behind	25/27
ret	GERMAN GP	Nürburgring	22	Team Eifelland Caravans	G	3.0 Eifelland 21/March 721-Cosworth V8	electrics	14/27
15	AUSTRIAN GP	Österreichring	27	Team Eifelland Caravans	G	3.0 Eifelland 21/March 721-Cosworth V8	pit stops-bodywork /-6 laps	=17/26
	1973	Championship position: Unplaced						
11	GERMAN GP	Nürburgring	9	Ceramica Pagnossin Team MRD	G	3.0 Brabham BT42-Cosworth V8		16/23
ret	AUSTRIAN GP	Österreichring	9	Ceramica Pagnossin Team MRD	G	3.0 Brabham BT42-Cosworth V8	front wheel bearing	17/25
12	ITALIAN GP	Monza	9	Ceramica Pagnossin Team MRD	G	3.0 Brabham BT42-Cosworth V8		9/25
12	CANADIAN GP	Mosport Park	9	Ceramica Pagnossin Team MRD	G	3.0 Brabham BT42-Cosworth V8	4 laps behind	18/26
	1974	Championship position: Unplaced						
ret	AUSTRIAN GP	Österreichring	27	Embassy Racing with Graham Hill	F	3.0 Lola T370-Cosworth V8	tyre punctured-accident	13/31
ret	ITALIAN GP	Monza	27	Embassy Racing with Graham Hill	F	3.0 Lola T370-Cosworth V8	suspension mounting plate	14/31
11	CANADIAN GP	Mosport Park	27	Embassy Racing with Graham Hill	F	3.0 Lola T370-Cosworth V8	2 laps behind	11/30
12	US GP	Watkins Glen	27	Embassy Racing with Graham Hill	F	3.0 Lola T370-Cosworth V8	2 pit stops-tyres/-5 laps	21/30
	1975	Championship position: Unplaced						
13	ARGENTINE GP	Buenos Aires	23	Embassy Racing with Graham Hill	G	3.0 Lola T370-Cosworth V8	pit stop-tyre/2 laps behind	19/23
14	BRAZILIAN GP	Interlagos	23	Embassy Racing with Graham Hill	G	3.0 Lola T370-Cosworth V8	1 lap behind	23/23
7	SOUTH AFRICAN GP	Kyalami	23	Embassy Racing with Graham Hill	G	3.0 Lola T371-Cosworth V8		14/28
ret	SPANISH GP	Montjuich Park	22	Embassy Racing with Graham Hill	F	3.0 Hill GH1-Cosworth V8	lost rear wing-accident	9/26
16	AUSTRIAN GP	Österreichring	22	Embassy Racing with Graham Hill	G	3.0 Hill GH1-Cosworth V8	2 laps behind	26/30
ret	ITALIAN GP	Monza	22	Embassy Racing with Graham Hill	G	3.0 Hill GH1-Cosworth V8	accident at chicane	23/28
	1976	Championship position: 19th=	Wins: 0	Pole positions: 0		Fastest laps: 0	Points scored: 1	
6	GERMAN GP	Nürburgring	77	Martini Racing	G	3.0 Brabham BT45-Alfa Romeo F12		15/28
dns	"	"	32	RAM Racing	G	3.0 Brabham BT44B-Cosworth V8	practice only	– / –
12	DUTCH GP	Zandvoort	25	Hesketh Racing with Rizla/Penthouse	G	3.0 Hesketh 308D-Cosworth V8	3 laps behind	25/27
ret	ITALIAN GP	Monza	7	Martini Racing	G	3.0 Brabham BT45-Alfa Romeo F12	engine-fuel system	11/29
	1978	Championship position: Unplaced						
9	SOUTH AFRICAN GP	Kyalami	36	Arrows Racing Team	G	3.0 Arrows FA1-Cosworth V8	pit stop-fuel/1 lap behind	22/30
9	US GP WEST	Long Beach	36	Arrows Racing Team	G	3.0 Arrows FA1-Cosworth V8	1 lap behind	18/30
ret	MONACO GP	Monte Carlo	36	Arrows Racing Team	G	3.0 Arrows FA1-Cosworth V8	driver unwell-rib injury	=18/30
ret	BELGIAN GP	Zolder	36	Arrows Racing Team	G	3.0 Arrows FA1-Cosworth V8	crashed	17/30
14	SPANISH GP	Jarama	36	Arrows Racing Team	G	3.0 Arrows FA1-Cosworth V8	2 pit stops/4 laps behind	19/29
14	SWEDISH GP	Anderstorp	36	Arrows Racing Team	G	3.0 Arrows FA1-Cosworth V8	3 laps behind	24/27
15	FRENCH GP	Paul Ricard	36	Arrows Racing Team	G	3.0 Arrows FA1-Cosworth V8	1 lap behind	21/29
dnq	BRITISH GP	Brands Hatch	36	Arrows Racing Team	G	3.0 Arrows FA1-Cosworth V8		27/30
dsq	GERMAN GP	Hockenheim	36	Arrows Racing Team	G	3.0 Arrows FA1-Cosworth V8	took back entrance to pits	17/30
dnpq	AUSTRIAN GP	Österreichring	36	Arrows Racing Team	G	3.0 Arrows A1-Cosworth V8		31/31
dnpq	DUTCH GP	Zandvoort	36	Arrows Racing Team	G	3.0 Arrows A1-Cosworth V8		33/33
dnpq	ITALIAN GP	Monza	36	Arrows Racing Team	G	3.0 Arrows A1-Cosworth V8		31/33
16	US GP EAST	Watkins Glen	36	Arrows Racing Team	G	3.0 Arrows A1-Cosworth V8	pit stop-brakes/5 laps behind	22/27
dnq	CANADIAN GP	Montreal	36	Arrows Racing Team	G	3.0 Arrows A1-Cosworth V8		27/28

GP Starts: 54   GP Wins: 0   Pole positions: 0   Fastest laps: 0   Points: 14

PHILIPPE STREIFF

This tall, intense French driver came to the fore in 1980, when an acrimonious Formula 3 season ended with a splendid win at the final European round at Zolder. The following year he concentrated on winning the French F3 championship in his Martini, and took fourth in the European series, joining the two-car AGS Formula 2 team for 1982. Streiff's season was up and down, due in part to the arguments that raged over the technical regulations, but he finished the year strongly to take sixth place in the final standings.

In 1983, AGS and Streiff really got to work, despite the team's chronic shortage of funds, and the Frenchman carried the fight to the dominant Ralts, though he had to wait until the very end of the 1984 season before scoring a long overdue and well earned win. He did, however, have the fillip of a Grand Prix outing for Renault in the 1984 Portuguese GP. His F3000 campaign with AGS in 1985 was well funded yet strewn with mechanical failures, but by now he had been elevated to the Grand Prix ranks, taking over the Ligier of de Cesaris in mid-season and scoring a fine third place in the end-of-year Australian GP. With Ligier missing the South African GP because of the political situation, Philippe drove for Tyrrell, and he joined the Ockham team full time in 1986 to handle their Renault-engined cars. He drove well enough on occasions during the next two seasons, but was generally outpaced by his team-mates Brundle and Palmer, the latter claiming the non-turbo honours after a switch to Cosworth power in 1987.

Streiff was taking a gamble when he joined the tiny AGS GP team for 1988, but at least it was an environment with which the Frenchman was familiar, and early in the season he caught the eye with some spirited performances, most notably at Imola, where he qualified and raced superbly, only for engine problems to intervene. Philippe was looking forward to another season with the team in 1989, but in a pre-season test at Rio he crashed heavily, sustaining serious back injuries which, possibly due to a lack of prompt medical assistance, resulted in him being left totally paralysed.

STREIFF, Philippe (F) b 26/6/1955, La Tronche, nr Grenoble

	1984			Championship position: Unplaced					
	Race	Circuit	No	Entrant	Tyres	Car/Engine		Comment	Q Pos/Entries
ret	PORTUGUESE GP	Estoril	33	Equipe Renault Elf	M	1.5 t/c Renault RE50 V6		driveshaft	13/27
	1985			Championship position: 15th= Wins: 0 Pole positions: 0 Fastest laps: 0 Points scored: 4					
10	ITALIAN GP	Monza	25	Equipe Ligier Gitanes	P	1.5 t/c Ligier JS25-Renault V6		2 laps behind	19/26
9	BELGIAN GP	Spa	25	Equipe Ligier Gitanes	P	1.5 t/c Ligier JS25-Renault V6		1 lap behind	18/24
8	EUROPEAN GP	Brands Hatch	25	Equipe Ligier Gitanes	P	1.5 t/c Ligier JS25-Renault V6		2 laps behind	5/27
ret	SOUTH AFRICAN GP	Kyalami	4	Tyrrell Racing Organisation	G	1.5 t/c Tyrrell 014-Renault V6		accident	18/21
3	AUSTRALIAN GP	Adelaide	25	Equipe Ligier Gitanes	P	1.5 t/c Ligier JS25-Renault V6			18/25
	1986			Championship position: 13th Wins: 0 Pole positions: 0 Fastest laps: 0 Points scored: 3					
7	BRAZILIAN GP	Rio	4	Data General Team Tyrrell	G	1.5 t/c Tyrrell 014-Renault V6		2 laps behind	18/25
ret	SPANISH GP	Jerez	4	Data General Team Tyrrell	G	1.5 t/c Tyrrell 014-Renault V6		engine-lost oil	20/25
ret	SAN MARINO GP	Imola	4	Data General Team Tyrrell	G	1.5 t/c Tyrrell 014-Renault V6		transmission	22/26
11	MONACO GP	Monte Carlo	4	Data General Team Tyrrell	G	1.5 t/c Tyrrell 015-Renault V6		hit by Jones-spin/-4 laps	13/26
12	BELGIAN GP	Spa	4	Data General Team Tyrrell	G	1.5 t/c Tyrrell 014-Renault V6		3 laps behind	18/25
11	CANADIAN GP	Montreal	4	Data General Team Tyrrell	G	1.5 t/c Tyrrell 014-Renault V6		4 laps behind	17/25
9	US GP (DETROIT)	Detroit	4	Data General Team Tyrrell	G	1.5 t/c Tyrrell 015-Renault V6			18/26
dns	"	"	4	Data General Team Tyrrell	G	1.5 t/c Tyrrell 014-Renault V6		practice only	– / –
ret	FRENCH GP	Paul Ricard	4	Data General Team Tyrrell	G	1.5 t/c Tyrrell 015-Renault V6		fuel leak-fire	17/26
6	BRITISH GP	Brands Hatch	4	Data General Team Tyrrell	G	1.5 t/c Tyrrell 015-Renault V6		3 laps behind	16/26
ret	GERMAN GP	Hockenheim	4	Data General Team Tyrrell	G	1.5 t/c Tyrrell 015-Renault V6		engine	18/26
8	HUNGARIAN GP	Hungaroring	4	Data General Team Tyrrell	G	1.5 t/c Tyrrell 015-Renault V6		2 laps behind	18/26
ret	AUSTRIAN GP	Österreichring	4	Data General Team Tyrrell	G	1.5 t/c Tyrrell 015-Renault V6		engine	20/26
9	ITALIAN GP	Monza	4	Data General Team Tyrrell	G	1.5 t/c Tyrrell 015-Renault V6		2 laps behind	23/27
ret	PORTUGUESE GP	Estoril	4	Data General Team Tyrrell	G	1.5 t/c Tyrrell 015-Renault V6		engine	23/27
ret	MEXICAN GP	Mexico City	4	Data General Team Tyrrell	G	1.5 t/c Tyrrell 015-Renault V6		turbo	19/26
5/ret	AUSTRALIAN GP	Adelaide	4	Data General Team Tyrrell	G	1.5 t/c Tyrrell 015-Renault V6		out of fuel/2 laps behind	10/26

	1987	Championship position: 14th		Wins: 0	Pole positions: 0	Fastest laps: 0	Points scored: 4	
11*	BRAZILIAN GP	Rio	4	Data General Team Tyrrell	G	3.5 Tyrrell DG 016-Cosworth V8	*2nd non-turbo/4 laps behind	20/23
8*	SAN MARINO GP	Imola	4	Data General Team Tyrrell	G	3.5 Tyrrell DG 016-Cosworth V8	*1st non-turbo/2 laps behind	22/27
9*	BELGIAN GP	Spa	4	Data General Team Tyrrell	G	3.5 Tyrrell DG 016-Cosworth V8	*2nd non-turbo/4 laps behind	23/26
ret	MONACO GP	Monte Carlo	4	Data General Team Tyrrell	G	3.5 Tyrrell DG 016-Cosworth V8	hit barrier	23/26
ret	US GP (DETROIT)	Detroit	4	Data General Team Tyrrell	G	3.5 Tyrrell DG 016-Cosworth V8	lost wheel-hit wall	14/26
6*	FRENCH GP	Paul Ricard	4	Data General Team Tyrrell	G	3.5 Tyrrell DG 016-Cosworth V8	*1st non-turbo/4 laps behind	25/26
ret	BRITISH GP	Silverstone	4	Data General Team Tyrrell	G	3.5 Tyrrell DG 016-Cosworth V8	engine	23/26
4*	GERMAN GP	Hockenheim	4	Data General Team Tyrrell	G	3.5 Tyrrell DG 016-Cosworth V8	*1st non-turbo/1 lap behind	22/26
9*	HUNGARIAN GP	Hungaroring	4	Data General Team Tyrrell	G	3.5 Tyrrell DG 016-Cosworth V8	*2nd non-turbo/2 laps behind	14/26
ret/dns	AUSTRIAN GP	Österreichring	4	Data General Team Tyrrell	G	3.5 Tyrrell DG 016-Cosworth V8	accident in first start	25/26
12*	ITALIAN GP	Monza	4	Data General Team Tyrrell	G	3.5 Tyrrell DG 016-Cosworth V8	*1st non-turbo/3 laps behind	24/28
12*	PORTUGUESE GP	Estoril	4	Data General Team Tyrrell	G	3.5 Tyrrell DG 016-Cosworth V8	*3rd non-turbo/4 laps behind	21/27
7*	SPANISH GP	Jerez	4	Data General Team Tyrrell	G	3.5 Tyrrell DG 016-Cosworth V8	*2nd non-turbo/1 lap behind	15/28
8*	MEXICAN GP	Mexico City	4	Data General Team Tyrrell	G	3.5 Tyrrell DG 016-Cosworth V8	*3rd non-turbo/3 laps behind	25/27
12*	JAPANESE GP	Suzuka	4	Data General Team Tyrrell	G	3.5 Tyrrell DG 016-Cosworth V8	*2nd non-turbo/2 laps behind	26/27
ret	AUSTRALIAN GP	Adelaide	4	Data General Team Tyrrell	G	3.5 Tyrrell DG 016-Cosworth V8	spun off	18/27
	1988	Championship position: Unplaced						
ret	BRAZILIAN GP	Rio	14	Automobiles Gonfaronaise Sportive	G	3.5 AGS JH23-Cosworth V8	brakes-spun off	19/31
10	SAN MARINO GP	Imola	14	Automobiles Gonfaronaise Sportive	G	3.5 AGS JH23-Cosworth V8	2 laps behind	13/31
dns	MONACO GP	Monte Carlo	14	Automobiles Gonfaronaise Sportive	G	3.5 AGS JH23-Cosworth V8	throttle cable before start	12/30
12	MEXICAN GP	Mexico City	14	Automobiles Gonfaronaise Sportive	G	3.5 AGS JH23-Cosworth V8	4 laps behind	19/30
ret	CANADIAN GP	Monteal	14	Automobiles Gonfaronaise Sportive	G	3.5 AGS JH23-Cosworth V8	rear suspension	10/31
ret	US GP (DETROIT)	Detroit	14	Automobiles Gonfaronaise Sportive	G	3.5 AGS JH23-Cosworth V8	suspension	11/31
ret	FRENCH GP	Paul Ricard	14	Automobiles Gonfaronaise Sportive	G	3.5 AGS JH23-Cosworth V8	fuel leak	17/31
ret	BRITISH GP	Silverstone	14	Automobiles Gonfaronaise Sportive	G	3.5 AGS JH23-Cosworth V8	broken rear wing-crashed	16/31
ret	GERMAN GP	Hockenheim	14	Automobiles Gonfaronaise Sportive	G	3.5 AGS JH23-Cosworth V8	throttle cable	16/31
ret	HUNGARIAN GP	Hungaroring	14	Automobiles Gonfaronaise Sportive	G	3.5 AGS JH23-Cosworth V8	lost wheel	23/31
10*	BELGIAN GP	Spa	14	Automobiles Gonfaronaise Sportive	G	3.5 AGS JH23-Cosworth V8	*3rd & 4th cars dsq/-1 lap	18/31
ret	ITALIAN GP	Monza	14	Automobiles Gonfaronaise Sportive	G	3.5 AGS JH23-Cosworth V8	gearbox	23/31
9	PORTUGUESE GP	Estoril	14	Automobiles Gonfaronaise Sportive	G	3.5 AGS JH23-Cosworth V8	2 laps behind	21/31
ret	SPANISH GP	Jerez	14	Automobiles Gonfaronaise Sportive	G	3.5 AGS JH23-Cosworth V8	engine	13/31
8	JAPANESE GP	Suzuka	14	Automobiles Gonfaronaise Sportive	G	3.5 AGS JH23-Cosworth V8	1 lap behind	18/31
11/ret	AUSTRALIAN GP	Adelaide	14	Automobiles Gonfaronaise Sportive	G	3.5 AGS JH23-Cosworth V8	electrics	16/31

GP Starts: 52 (54)   GP Wins: 0   Pole positions: 0   Fastest laps: 0   Points: 11

STUCK, Hans (A) b 27/12/1900, Warsaw, Poland – d 8/2/1978, Grainau, nr Garmisch-Partenkirchen, Germany

	1951	Championship position: Unplaced						
	Race	Circuit	No	Entrant	Tyres	Car/Engine	Comment	Q Pos/Entries
dns	ITALIAN GP	Monza	32	BRM Ltd	D	1.5 s/c BRM P15 V16	tried car in practice only	– / –
	1952	Championship position: Unplaced						
ret	SWISS GP	Bremgarten	2	AFM	–	2.0 AFM 4-Kuchen V8	engine	14/21
dnq	ITALIAN GP	Monza	20	Ecurie Espadon	P	2.0 Ferrari 212 V12		33/35
	1953	Championship position: Unplaced						
ret	GERMAN GP	Nürburgring	21	Hans Stuck	–	2.0 AFM 4-Bristol 6		23/35
nc	ITALIAN GP	Monza	48	Hans Stuck	–	2.0 AFM 4-Bristol 6	23 laps behind winner	29/30

GP Starts: 3   GP Wins: 0   Pole positions: 0   Fastest laps: 0   Points: 0

HANS STUCK

Stuck's competition career spanned some 39 years – from 1924 to 1963 – during which he took part in more than 700 events. Most of his success was gained in hill-climbs, of which he became the undisputed master during the 1920s in his Austro-Daimlers, and he remained dominant in the early 1930s with a Mercedes SSK sports, by which time he was also winning on the circuits, taking the 1931 Rio de Janeiro GP. In 1934 Stuck joined the Auto Union team to win the German, Swiss and Czech GPs, adding the Italian GP to his tally in 1935, as well as an unending run of hill-climb successes.

After the war, Stuck got back into action with a little 1100 cc Cisitalia, before racing the AFM Formula 2 car, which was fast but fragile. He took a third place in the 1950 Solitude GP, and won a minor race at Grenzlandring in 1951, but on the hills, of course, he was still a regular winner. By the end of the 1952 season the AFM was totally outclassed, and he briefly raced an Ecurie Espadon Ferrari, taking fifth at AVUS, and ninth at Modena.

Stuck later joined BMW and raced their cars successfully until the early 1960s.

HANS-JOACHIM STUCK

As the son of the famous pre-war Auto Union ace, it was perhaps natural that Hans Jnr should follow his father into a career in motor racing, especially as he had driven karts and small-capacity BMWs long before he was eligible for a racing licence. After driving a BMW 2002 in national hill-climbs, he graduated to the works European touring car championship team, winning the Nürburgring 24-hour race in 1969. Stuck then took over from Jochen Mass in the Ford Germany Capri in the national series for 1972, and won the Spa 24 Hours with Mass as co-driver.

His single-seater career began properly in 1973 when he raced the works March in Formula 2, graduating to the Grand Prix team the following year, but he proved to be somewhat inconsistent, very quick on some occasions, but mysteriously lacklustre on others. He did well in F2, however, finishing second in the championship with four wins (at Barcelona, Hockenheim, Rouen and Enna).

Initially dropped from the March Grand Prix team for 1975, Stuck made a successful sortie into IMSA with BMW, but was then recalled to the Bicester ranks to replace the out-of-favour Lella Lombardi. He remained with the team in 1976, but it was the same infuriating mixture of the brilliant and the banal once more. At Watkins Glen Hans finished fifth, after being 23rd on the first lap, and occasional Formula 2 outings with the 762 produced three wins in only five starts.

Given the chance to race the Brabham-Alfa in 1977 following the death of Carlos Pace in an air crash, Hans scored superb third places in Germany and Austria, and led the US GP at Watkins Glen before blotting his copybook by sliding off the circuit. From then on it was downhill all the way as far as Formula 1 was concerned, a season with Shadow bringing only one points finish, and an even more dispiriting year with ATS yielding the same return.

Hans then turned his back on F1, but certainly not on motor sport, for he was soon immersed in a huge schedule of sports, GT and touring car racing. He joined the Rothmans Porsche team in 1985, sharing the drivers' crown with Derek Bell in both 1985 and 1986, and won Le Mans with Bell and Holbert in 1986 and '87. After a switch to Audi, his presence spiced up IMSA's GTO class in 1989, and back at home he won the 1990 DTM championship in the awesome 3.6-litre V8 quattro.

As the nineties unfolded Stuck was still racing competitively in German Super Touring for Audi and was a Le Mans regular. In 1994 he finished third with Sullivan and Boutsen in a Dauer Porsche 962LM, and the following year he was placed sixth, this time in a Kremer Porsche with Boutsen and Bouchut. Just as his career seemed to be winding down came the surprise news that he was forsaking Audi to join Opel's squad to contest the Class 1 ITC series in 1996. Driving the Team Rosberg car, he could still show the youngsters a thing or two, winning both rounds in Helsinki. He was also part of the factory Porsche team, taking second at Le Mans with Boutsen and Wollek in the 911 GT1. In 1997 Hans teamed up with Boutsen to contest the FIA GT championship in one of the works cars but, despite a number of top-six placings, the experienced duo were deemed too old, and dropped at season's end.

The immensely popular Stuck shows no sign of hanging up his helmet and remains a quick and spectacular driver, mainly racing a BMW M3 in the GT3 class in the American Le Mans Series.

STUCK, Hans-Joachim (D) b 1/1/1951, Grainau, nr Garmisch-Partenkirchen

	1974	Championship position: 16th=		Wins: 0	Pole positions: 0		Fastest laps: 0	Points scored: 5		
	Race	Circuit	No	Entrant		Tyres	Car/Engine		Comment	Q Pos/Entries
ret	ARGENTINE GP	Buenos Aires	9	March Engineering		G	3.0 March 741-Cosworth V8		transmission	23/26
ret	BRAZILIAN GP	Interlagos	9	March Engineering		G	3.0 March 741-Cosworth V8		seized constant-velocity joint	13/25
5	SOUTH AFRICAN GP	Kyalami	9	March Engineering		G	3.0 March 741-Cosworth V8			7/27
4	SPANISH GP	Jarama	9	March Engineering		G	3.0 March 741-Cosworth V8		2 laps behind	14/28
ret	BELGIAN GP	Nivelles	9	March Engineering		G	3.0 March 741-Cosworth V8		clutch	10/32
ret	MONACO GP	Monte Carlo	9	March Engineering		G	3.0 March 741-Cosworth V8		collision with Hunt	9/28
ret	DUTCH GP	Zandvoort	9	March Engineering		G	3.0 March 741-Cosworth V8		collision while braking	22/27
dnq	FRENCH GP	Dijon	9	March Engineering		G	3.0 March 741-Cosworth V8			26/30

ret	BRITISH GP	Brands Hatch	9	March Engineering	G	3.0 March 741-Cosworth V8	spun off	9/34
7	GERMAN GP	Nürburgring	9	March Engineering	G	3.0 March 741-Cosworth V8		20/32
11/ret	AUSTRIAN GP	Österreichring	9	March Engineering	G	3.0 March 741-Cosworth V8	suspension-spun off/-6 laps	15/31
ret	ITALIAN GP	Monza	9	March Engineering	G	3.0 March 741-Cosworth V8	engine mounting bolts	18/31
ret	CANADIAN GP	Mosport Park	9	March Engineering	G	3.0 March 741-Cosworth V8	engine-fuel pressure	23/30
dnq	US GP	Watkins Glen	9	March Engineering	G	3.0 March 741-Cosworth V8		28/30

1975   Championship position: Unplaced

ret	BRITISH GP	Silverstone	10	Lavazza March	G	3.0 March 751-Cosworth V8	spun off in rain-hit barrier	14/28
ret	GERMAN GP	Nürburgring	10	Lavazza March	G	3.0 March 751-Cosworth V8	engine	7/26
ret	AUSTRIAN GP	Österreichring	10	Lavazza March	G	3.0 March 751-Cosworth V8	spun off in rain-hit barrier	4/30
ret	ITALIAN GP	Monza	10	Lavazza March	G	3.0 March 751-Cosworth V8	hit chicane	16/28
8	US GP	Watkins Glen	10	Lavazza March	G	3.0 March 751-Cosworth V8	took flag in pits-puncture/-1 lap	13/24

1976   Championship position: 13th   Wins: 0   Pole positions: 0   Fastest laps: 0   Points scored: 8

4	BRAZILIAN GP	Interlagos	34	March Racing	G	3.0 March 761-Cosworth V8		14/22
12	SOUTH AFRICAN GP	Kyalami	34	March Racing	G	3.0 March 761-Cosworth V8	2 laps behind	17/25
ret	US GP WEST	Long Beach	34	Theodore Racing	G	3.0 March 761-Cosworth V8	collision with Fittipaldi	18/27
ret	SPANISH GP	Jarama	34	March Racing	G	3.0 March 761-Cosworth V8	gearbox	17/30
ret	BELGIAN GP	Zolder	34	March Racing	G	3.0 March 761-Cosworth V8	suspension	15/29
4	MONACO GP	Monte Carlo	34	March Racing	G	3.0 March 761-Cosworth V8	1 lap behind	6/25
ret	SWEDISH GP	Anderstorp	34	March Racing	G	3.0 March 761-Cosworth V8	engine	20/27
7	FRENCH GP	Paul Ricard	34	March Racing	G	3.0 March 761-Cosworth V8		17/30
ret	BRITISH GP	Brands Hatch	34	March Racing	G	3.0 March 761-Cosworth V8	collision-Peterson & Depailler	17/30
ret/dns	GERMAN GP	Nürburgring	34	March Racing	G	3.0 March 761-Cosworth V8	clutch in first start	4/28
ret	AUSTRIAN GP	Österreichring	34	March Racing	G	3.0 March 761-Cosworth V8	fuel pressure	11/25
ret	DUTCH GP	Zandvoort	34	March Racing	G	3.0 March 761-Cosworth V8	engine	18/27
ret	ITALIAN GP	Monza	34	March Racing	G	3.0 March 761-Cosworth V8	collision with Andretti	6/29
ret	CANADIAN GP	Mosport Park	34	March Racing	G	3.0 March 761-Cosworth V8	handling	8/27
5	US GP EAST	Watkins Glen	34	March Racing	G	3.0 March 761-Cosworth V8		6/27
ret	JAPANESE GP	Mount Fuji	34	March Racing	G	3.0 March 761-Cosworth V8	electrics	18/27

1977   Championship position: 11th   Wins: 0   Pole positions: 0   Fastest laps: 0   Points scored: 12

ret	SOUTH AFRICAN GP	Kyalami	10	Team Rothmans International	G	3.0 March 761B-Cosworth V8	engine	18/23
ret	US GP WEST	Long Beach	8	Martini Racing	G	3.0 Brabham BT45B-Alfa Romeo F12	brakes	17/22
6	SPANISH GP	Jarama	8	Martini Racing	G	3.0 Brabham BT45B-Alfa Romeo F12	1 lap behind	13/31
ret	MONACO GP	Monte Carlo	8	Martini Racing	G	3.0 Brabham BT45B-Alfa Romeo F12	fire-electrical fault	5/26
6	BELGIAN GP	Zolder	8	Martini Racing	G	3.0 Brabham BT45B-Alfa Romeo F12	1 lap behind	18/32
10	SWEDISH GP	Anderstorp	8	Martini Racing	G	3.0 Brabham BT45B-Alfa Romeo F12	1 lap behind	5/31
ret	FRENCH GP	Dijon	8	Martini Racing	G	3.0 Brabham BT45B-Alfa Romeo F12	collision with Laffite	13/30
5	BRITISH GP	Silverstone	8	Martini Racing	G	3.0 Brabham BT45B-Alfa Romeo F12		7/36
3	GERMAN GP	Hockenheim	8	Martini Racing	G	3.0 Brabham BT45B-Alfa Romeo F12		5/30
3	AUSTRIAN GP	Österreichring	8	Martini Racing	G	3.0 Brabham BT45B-Alfa Romeo F12		4/30
7	DUTCH GP	Zandvoort	8	Martini Racing	G	3.0 Brabham BT45B-Alfa Romeo F12	2 laps behind	19/34
ret	ITALIAN GP	Monza	8	Martini Racing	G	3.0 Brabham BT45B-Alfa Romeo F12	engine	11/34
ret	US GP EAST	Watkins Glen	8	Martini Racing	G	3.0 Brabham BT45B-Alfa Romeo F12	crashed-car jumped out of gear	2/27
ret	CANADIAN GP	Mosport Park	8	Martini Racing	G	3.0 Brabham BT45B-Alfa Romeo F12		13/27
7	JAPANESE GP	Mount Fuji	8	Martini Racing	G	3.0 Brabham BT45B-Alfa Romeo F12	1 lap behind	4/23

1978   Championship position: 18th   Wins: 0   Pole positions: 0   Fastest laps: 0   Points scored: 2

17	ARGENTINE GP	Buenos Aires	16	Shadow Racing Team	G	3.0 Shadow DN8-Cosworth V8	handling problems/-2 laps	18/27
ret	BRAZILIAN GP	Rio	16	Shadow Racing Team	G	3.0 Shadow DN8-Cosworth V8	fuel pump	9/28
dnq	SOUTH AFRICAN GP	Kyalami	16	Shadow Racing Team	G	3.0 Shadow DN8-Cosworth V8		30/30
dns	US GP WEST	Long Beach	16	Shadow Racing Team	G	3.0 Shadow DN9-Cosworth V8	practice accident	(23)/30
ret	MONACO GP	Monte Carlo	16	Shadow Racing Team	G	3.0 Shadow DN9-Cosworth V8	collision-Keegan-steering	17/30
ret	BELGIAN GP	Zolder	16	Shadow Racing Team	G	3.0 Shadow DN9-Cosworth V8	spun off-stalled	20/30
ret	SPANISH GP	Jarama	16	Shadow Racing Team	G	3.0 Shadow DN9-Cosworth V8	broken rear suspension	24/29
11	SWEDISH GP	Anderstorp	16	Shadow Racing Team	G	3.0 Shadow DN9-Cosworth V8	2 laps behind	20/27
11	FRENCH GP	Paul Ricard	16	Shadow Racing Team	G	3.0 Shadow DN9-Cosworth V8	1 lap behind	20/29
5	BRITISH GP	Brands Hatch	16	Shadow Racing Team	G	3.0 Shadow DN9-Cosworth V8	1 lap behind	18/30
ret	GERMAN GP	Hockenheim	16	Shadow Racing Team	G	3.0 Shadow DN9-Cosworth V8	collision with Mass	24/30
ret	AUSTRIAN GP	Österreichring	16	Shadow Racing Team	G	3.0 Shadow DN9-Cosworth V8	spun off in rain	23/31
ret	DUTCH GP	Zandvoort	16	Shadow Racing Team	G	3.0 Shadow DN9-Cosworth V8	differential	18/33
ret/dns	ITALIAN GP	Monza	16	Shadow Racing Team	G	3.0 Shadow DN9-Cosworth V8	crash at first start-concussion	17/32
ret	US GP EAST	Watkins Glen	16	Shadow Racing Team	G	3.0 Shadow DN9-Cosworth V8	fuel pump	14/27
ret	CANADIAN GP	Montreal	16	Shadow Racing Team	G	3.0 Shadow DN9-Cosworth V8	hit by Fittipaldi	8/28

1979   Championship position: 19th=   Wins: 0   Pole positions: 0   Fastest laps: 0   Points scored: 2

dns	ARGENTINE GP	Buenos Aires	9	ATS Wheels	G	3.0 ATS D2-Cosworth V8	car unprepared	26/26
ret	BRAZILIAN GP	Interlagos	9	ATS Wheels	G	3.0 ATS D2-Cosworth V8	broken steering wheel	24/26
ret	SOUTH AFRICAN GP	Kyalami	9	ATS Wheels	G	3.0 ATS D2-Cosworth V8	spun off	24/26
dsq	US GP WEST	Long Beach	9	ATS Wheels	G	3.0 ATS D2-Cosworth V8	push start after spin	23/26
14	SPANISH GP	Jarama	9	ATS Wheels	G	3.0 ATS D2-Cosworth V8	2 pit stops-tyres/-6 laps	21/27
8	BELGIAN GP	Zolder	9	ATS Wheels	G	3.0 ATS D2-Cosworth V8	pit stop-puncture/-1 lap	20/28
ret	MONACO GP	Monte Carlo	9	ATS Wheels	G	3.0 ATS D2-Cosworth V8	broken wheel	12/25
dns	FRENCH GP	Dijon	9	ATS Wheels	G	3.0 ATS D2-Cosworth V8	tyre dispute-withdrawn	(23)/27
dnq	BRITISH GP	Silverstone	9	ATS Wheels	G	3.0 ATS D2-Cosworth V8		25/26
ret	GERMAN GP	Hockenheim	9	ATS Wheels	G	3.0 ATS D2-Cosworth V8	broken suspension	23/26
ret	AUSTRIAN GP	Österreichring	9	ATS Wheels	G	3.0 ATS D3-Cosworth V8	engine	18/26
dns	"	"	9	ATS Wheels	G	3.0 ATS D2-Cosworth V8	practice only	– / –
ret	DUTCH GP	Zandvoort	9	ATS Wheels	G	3.0 ATS D3-Cosworth V8	driveshaft	15/26
11	ITALIAN GP	Monza	9	ATS Wheels	G	3.0 ATS D3-Cosworth V8	1 lap behind	15/28
ret	CANADIAN GP	Montreal	9	ATS Wheels	G	3.0 ATS D3-Cosworth V8	accident with Arnoux	12/29
5	US GP	Watkins Glen	9	ATS Wheels	G	3.0 ATS D3-Cosworth V8		14/30

GP Starts: 72 (74)   GP Wins: 0   Pole positions: 0   Fastest laps: 0   Points: 29

DANNY SULLIVAN

Sullivan is now a multi-millionaire, thanks to his fabulous success in Indy Car racing, but it wasn't always that way, for the Kentucky kid spent a good few hard seasons in England climbing the ladder towards a top-line career. Without any financial help, Danny somehow clung on in various junior formulae, scoring the occasional success, only to be knocked back by some misfortune. Eventually he went back to the States to get his career moving again, making a good impression in Can-Am with an old Lola in 1980, and returned the following year, winning a race at Las Vegas and taking fourth in the championship. Suddenly the momentum was building; an Indy Car debut for Forsythe-Newman at Atlanta brought third place, and after he had been bumped from the team by Rebaque and his bank balance Danny returned to Can-Am to finish third in the standings.

For 1983 he took the plunge into Formula 1 with Tyrrell, a fifth place at Monaco and second in the Race of Champions showing what he could do, but the lure of a more competitive drive in Indy cars took Danny back across the Atlantic. In Shierson's team he took three wins in 1984, before joining Roger Penske's crack team to win a famous victory at Indy in 1985 which made him a household name in the US. Subsequently he went on to win the Indy Car title in 1988, with four wins and eight pole positions, before joining the ultimately unsuccessful Patrick Racing Alfa Romeo effort. He then moved to the Galles team with substantial backing from Molson, taking his total of wins to 17 by the end of the 1993 season.

Danny was out of an Indy Car drive at the start of 1994, but he did quite well in a couple of guest outings for Alfa Romeo in the 'DTM on tour' rounds at Donington and Mugello. He also took third place at Le Mans in a Dauer Porsche with Boutsen and Stuck, before the chance came to resurrect his Indy Car career with the fledgling PacWest team. His experience was invaluable as he tested the car late in the year, and he was taken on for a full-time ride in 1995. Apart from a bright performance in the opening round at Miami, the season was largely unrewarding and was cut short when he suffered a nasty crash at Michigan which left him suffering a broken pelvis.

Happily he made a full recovery, but there was no realistic prospect of his making another return to Indy Car competition. Taking up a TV commentary role, Sullivan continued to make selected appearances in sports car events, posting an eighth place at Le Mans in 1998 in the Team Bigazzi McLaren F1 GTR with Piquet and Cecotto.

SULLIVAN, Danny (USA) b 9/3/1950, Louisville, Kentucky

	1983	Championship position: 17th	Wins: 0	Pole positions: 0	Fastest laps: 0	Points scored: 2		
	Race	Circuit	No	Entrant	Tyres	Car/Engine	Comment	Q Pos/Entries
11	BRAZILIAN GP	Rio	4	Benetton Tyrrell Team	G	3.0 Tyrrell 011-Cosworth V8	1 lap behind	21/27
8	US GP WEST	Long Beach	4	Benetton Tyrrell Team	G	3.0 Tyrrell 011-Cosworth V8	severe tyre vibration/-2 laps	9/28
ret	FRENCH GP	Paul Ricard	4	Benetton Tyrrell Team	G	3.0 Tyrrell 011-Cosworth V8	clutch	24/29
ret	SAN MARINO GP	Imola	4	Benetton Tyrrell Team	G	3.0 Tyrrell 011-Cosworth V8	spun off	22/28
5	MONACO GP	Monte Carlo	4	Benetton Tyrrell Team	G	3.0 Tyrrell 011-Cosworth V8	2 laps behind	20/28
12	BELGIAN GP	Spa	4	Benetton Tyrrell Team	G	3.0 Tyrrell 011-Cosworth V8	1 lap behind	23/28
ret	US GP (DETROIT)	Detroit	4	Benetton Tyrrell Team	G	3.0 Tyrrell 011-Cosworth V8	electrics	16/27
dsq*	CANADIAN GP	Montreal	4	Benetton Tyrrell Team	G	3.0 Tyrrell 011-Cosworth V8	9th on road/*car underweight	22/28
14	BRITISH GP	Silverstone	4	Benetton Tyrrell Team	G	3.0 Tyrrell 011-Cosworth V8	2 laps behind	23/29
12	GERMAN GP	Hockenheim	4	Benetton Tyrrell Team	G	3.0 Tyrrell 011-Cosworth V8	2 laps behind	21/29
ret	AUSTRIAN GP	Österreichring	4	Benetton Tyrrell Team	G	3.0 Tyrrell 011-Cosworth V8	multiple collision on lap 1	23/29
ret	DUTCH GP	Zandvoort	4	Benetton Tyrrell Team	G	3.0 Tyrrell 011-Cosworth V8	engine	26/29
ret	ITALIAN GP	Monza	4	Benetton Tyrrell Team	G	3.0 Tyrrell 011-Cosworth V8	fuel pump drive	22/29
ret	EUROPEAN GP	Brands Hatch	4	Benetton Tyrrell Team	G	3.0 Tyrrell 012-Cosworth V8	fire-broken fuel line	20/29
7	SOUTH AFRICAN GP	Kyalami	4	Benetton Tyrrell Team	G	3.0 Tyrrell 012-Cosworth V8	2 laps behind	19/26

GP Starts: 15   GP Wins: 0   Pole positions: 0   Fastest laps: 0   Points: 2

MARC SURER

Something of a late starter in motor racing, Surer graduated from karts and Super Vee to the German F3 championship with the KWS team, taking the runner-up slot in 1976. The following year he made the move into Formula 2, gathering valuable experience. He had also been signed by Jochen Neerpasch to race a BMW 320i in the up-to-2-litre division of the German touring car championship for BMW's 'Junior Team', but his season was somewhat overshadowed by a clash with Hans Heyer which saw him suspended for two months.

Despite this unfortunate incident, Marc was promoted to the BMW Team Polifac Formula 2 squad for 1978, as number two to Bruno Giacomelli, who went on to dominate proceedings. However, Surer backed his team-mate superbly, taking a clear second place in the championship with six second-place finishes. In 1979 he was promoted to team leader and duly took the honours, but serious doubts over his pedigree were already being voiced, as he seemed unable to stamp his authority on races in the manner of true champions.

Nevertheless Marc had already been given his Grand Prix baptism by Ensign, and he signed to drive for ATS in 1980, but his season had barely begun when he crashed in practice for the South African GP, sustaining broken ankles, which kept him sidelined until mid-season. For 1981, Surer joined the little Ensign team, and really began to come out of his shell, taking a superb fourth place and fastest lap in Brazil, and sixth at Monaco, before moving to Teddy Yip's Theodore set-up.

In 1982 his progress was once more halted by injury, when a crash at Kyalami left him with leg injuries which delayed his Arrows debut. Fit again, he was somewhat overshadowed by the emerging Boutsen and his chances to shine were restricted by the late development of the turbo car in 1984. When François Hesnault quit the Brabham team early in 1985, Marc finally got the opportunity to show his ability, and he enjoyed his best-ever season as team-mate to Nelson Piquet. In 1986 the tough Swiss was back with Arrows but, taking part in a German rally, he crashed his Ford into a tree; his co-driver was killed and Surer sustained serious injuries and burns which ended his competitive racing career.

Since then he has kept close links with the sport on a number of fronts. Not only has Marc acted as a commentator for Swiss TV and headed up the competitions department at BMW, looking after their drivers, but he was also able to enjoy following the excellent progress of his wife Yolanda as she proved to be a formidable competitor in the German Super Touring series.

SURER, Marc (CH) b 18/9/1951, Aresdorf

	1979	Championship position: Unplaced						
	Race	Circuit	No	Entrant	Tyres	Car/Engine	Comment	Q Pos/Entries
dnq	ITALIAN GP	Monza	22	Team Ensign	G	3.0 Ensign N179-Cosworth V8		26/28
dnq	CANADIAN GP	Montreal	22	Team Ensign	G	3.0 Ensign N179-Cosworth V8		26/29
ret	US GP EAST	Watkins Glen	22	Team Ensign	G	3.0 Ensign N179-Cosworth V8	engine	21/30
	1980	Championship position: Unplaced						
ret	ARGENTINE GP	Buenos Aires	9	Team ATS	G	3.0 ATS D3-Cosworth V8	fire-brake fluid on disc	21/28
7	BRAZILIAN GP	Interlagos	9	Team ATS	G	3.0 ATS D3-Cosworth V8	1 lap behind	20/28
dnq	SOUTH AFRICAN GP	Kyalami	9	Team ATS	G	3.0 ATS D4-Cosworth V8	practice crash-broken ankle	26/28
ret	FRENCH GP	Paul Ricard	9	Team ATS	G	3.0 ATS D4-Cosworth V8	gearbox	11/27
ret	BRITISH GP	Brands Hatch	9	Team ATS	G	3.0 ATS D4-Cosworth V8	engine	15/27
12	GERMAN GP	Hockenheim	9	Team ATS	G	3.0 ATS D4-Cosworth V8	1 lap behind	13/26
12	AUSTRIAN GP	Österreichring	9	Team ATS	G	3.0 ATS D4-Cosworth V8	1 lap behind	16/25
10	DUTCH GP	Zandvoort	9	Team ATS	G	3.0 ATS D4-Cosworth V8	pit stop-fuel/3 laps behind	20/28
ret	ITALIAN GP	Imola	9	Team ATS	G	3.0 ATS D4-Cosworth V8	engine	23/28
dnq	CANADIAN GP	Montreal	9	Team ATS	G	3.0 ATS D4-Cosworth V8		25/28
8	US GP EAST	Watkins Glen	9	Team ATS	G	3.0 ATS D4-Cosworth V8	2 laps behind	17/27

1981		Championship position: 16th	Wins: 0	Pole positions: 0	Fastest laps: 1	Points scored: 4			
ret	US GP WEST	Long Beach	14	Ensign Racing	M	3.0 Ensign N180B-Cosworth V8		electrics	19/29
4	BRAZILIAN GP	Rio	14	Ensign Racing	M	3.0 Ensign N180B-Cosworth V8		FL	18/30
ret	ARGENTINE GP	Buenos Aires	14	Ensign Racing	M	3.0 Ensign N180B-Cosworth V8		engine	16/29
9	SAN MARINO GP	Imola	14	Ensign Racing	M	3.0 Ensign N180B-Cosworth V8		pit stop-tyres/1 lap behind	21/30
11	BELGIAN GP	Zolder	14	Ensign Racing	M	3.0 Ensign N180B-Cosworth V8		2 laps behind	15/31
6	MONACO GP	Monte Carlo	14	Ensign Racing	M	3.0 Ensign N180B-Cosworth V8		2 laps behind	19/31
12	FRENCH GP	Paul Ricard	33	Theodore Racing Team	M	3.0 Theodore TY01-Cosworth V8		2 laps behind	21/29
11/ret	BRITISH GP	Silverstone	33	Theodore Racing Team	A	3.0 Theodore TY01-Cosworth V8		fuel pressure/7 laps behind	24/30
14/ret	GERMAN GP	Hockenheim	33	Theodore Racing Team	A	3.0 Theodore TY01-Cosworth V8		spun off last corner/-2 laps	22/30
ret	AUSTRIAN GP	Österreichring	33	Theodore Racing Team	A	3.0 Theodore TY01-Cosworth V8		distributor	23/28
8	DUTCH GP	Zandvoort	33	Theodore Racing Team	A	3.0 Theodore TY01-Cosworth V8		3 laps behind	20/30
dnq	ITALIAN GP	Monza	33	Theodore Racing Team	A	3.0 Theodore TY01-Cosworth V8			25/30
9	CANADIAN GP	Montreal	33	Theodore Racing Team	A	3.0 Theodore TY01-Cosworth V8		2 laps behind	19/30
ret	CAESARS PALACE GP	Las Vegas	33	Theodore Racing Team	A	3.0 Theodore TY01-Cosworth V8		rear suspension	23/30
1982		Championship position: 20=	Wins: 0	Pole positions: 0	Fastest laps: 0	Points scored: 3			
7*	BELGIAN GP	Zolder	29	Arrows Racing Team	P	3.0 Arrows A4-Cosworth V8		* 3rd place car dsq/-4 laps	24/32
9	MONACO GP	Monte Carlo	29	Arrows Racing Team	P	3.0 Arrows A4-Cosworth V8		6 laps behind	19/31
8	US GP (DETROIT)	Detroit	29	Arrows Racing Team	P	3.0 Arrows A4-Cosworth V8		1 lap behind	19/28
5	CANADIAN GP	Montreal	29	Arrows Racing Team	P	3.0 Arrows A4-Cosworth V8		1 lap behind	16/29
10	DUTCH GP	Zandvoort	29	Arrows Racing Team	P	3.0 Arrows A4-Cosworth V8		pit stop-tyres/1 lap behind	17/31
ret	BRITISH GP	Brands Hatch	29	Arrows Racing Team	P	3.0 Arrows A4-Cosworth V8		engine	22/30
13	FRENCH GP	Paul Ricard	29	Arrows Racing Team	P	3.0 Arrows A4-Cosworth V8		2 laps behind	20/30
6	GERMAN GP	Hockenheim	29	Arrows Racing Team	P	3.0 Arrows A4-Cosworth V8		1 lap behind	27/30
ret	AUSTRIAN GP	Österreichring	29	Arrows Racing Team	P	3.0 Arrows A4-Cosworth V8		air lock in fuel system	21/29
15	SWISS GP	Dijon	29	Arrows Racing Team	P	3.0 Arrows A5-Cosworth V8		pit stop-tyres/4 laps behind	14/29
ret	ITALIAN GP	Monza	29	Arrows Racing Team	P	3.0 Arrows A5-Cosworth V8		engine	19/30
7	CAESARS PALACE GP	Las Vegas	29	Arrows Racing Team	P	3.0 Arrows A5-Cosworth V8		1 lap behind	17/30
1983		Championship position: 15th	Wins: 0	Pole positions: 0	Fastest laps: 0	Points scored: 4			
6	BRAZILIAN GP	Rio	29	Arrows Racing Team	G	3.0 Arrows A6-Cosworth V8			20/27
5	US GP WEST	Long Beach	29	Arrows Racing Team	G	3.0 Arrows A6-Cosworth V8		1 lap behind	16/28
10	FRENCH GP	Paul Ricard	29	Arrows Racing Team	G	3.0 Arrows A6-Cosworth V8		1 lap behind	21/29
6	SAN MARINO GP	Imola	29	Arrows Racing Team	G	3.0 Arrows A6-Cosworth V8		1 lap behind	12/28
ret	MONACO GP	Monte Carlo	29	Arrows Racing Team	G	3.0 Arrows A6-Cosworth V8		accident with Warwick	12/28
11	BELGIAN GP	Spa	29	Arrows Racing Team	G	3.0 Arrows A6-Cosworth V8		started from pitlane/-1lap	10/28
11	US GP (DETROIT)	Detroit	29	Arrows Racing Team	G	3.0 Arrows A6-Cosworth V8		2 laps behind	5/27
ret	CANADIAN GP	Montreal	29	Arrows Racing Team	G	3.0 Arrows A6-Cosworth V8		transmission	14/28
17	BRITISH GP	Silverstone	29	Arrows Racing Team	G	3.0 Arrows A6-Cosworth V8		3 laps behind	19/29
7	GERMAN GP	Hockenheim	29	Arrows Racing Team	G	3.0 Arrows A6-Cosworth V8		1 lap behind	20/29
ret	AUSTRIAN GP	Österreichring	29	Arrows Racing Team	G	3.0 Arrows A6-Cosworth V8		accident-Ghinzani & Laffite	22/29
8	DUTCH GP	Zandvoort	29	Arrows Racing Team	G	3.0 Arrows A6-Cosworth V8		2 laps behind	14/29
10	ITALIAN GP	Monza	29	Arrows Racing Team	G	3.0 Arrows A6-Cosworth V8		1 lap behind	20/29
ret	EUROPEAN GP	Brands Hatch	29	Arrows Racing Team	G	3.0 Arrows A6-Cosworth V8		engine	17/29
8	SOUTH AFRICAN GP	Kyalami	29	Arrows Racing Team	G	3.0 Arrows A6-Cosworth V8		2 laps behind	22/26
1984		Championship position: 20th	Wins: 0	Pole positions: 0	Fastest laps: 0	Points scored: 1			
7*	BRAZILIAN GP	Rio	17	Barclay Nordica Arrows BMW	G	3.0 Arrows A6-Cosworth V8		* 5th place car dsq/-2 laps	25/27
9	SOUTH AFRICAN GP	Kyalami	17	Barclay Nordica Arrows BMW	G	3.0 Arrows A6-Cosworth V8		4 laps behind	23/27
8*	BELGIAN GP	Zolder	17	Barclay Nordica Arrows BMW	G	3.0 Arrows A6-Cosworth V8		* 6th place car dsq/-2 laps	24/27
ret	SAN MARINO GP	Imola	17	Barclay Nordica Arrows BMW	G	1.5 t/c Arrows A7-BMW 4		turbo	16/28
ret	FRENCH GP	Dijon	17	Barclay Nordica Arrows BMW	G	3.0 Arrows A6-Cosworth V8		accident with Warwick	20/27
dnq	MONACO GP	Monte Carlo	17	Barclay Nordica Arrows BMW	G	3.0 Arrows A6-Cosworth V8			21/27
ret	CANADIAN GP	Montreal	17	Barclay Nordica Arrows BMW	G	3.0 Arrows A6-Cosworth V8		engine	23/26
ret/dns	US GP (DETROIT)	Detroit	17	Barclay Nordica Arrows BMW	G	3.0 Arrows A6-Cosworth V8		hit Piquet-1st start/did not restart	22/27
ret	US GP (DALLAS)	Dallas	17	Barclay Nordica Arrows BMW	G	1.5 t/c Arrows A7-BMW 4		hit wall	22/27
11*	BRITISH GP	Brands Hatch	17	Barclay Nordica Arrows BMW	G	1.5 t/c Arrows A7-BMW 4		* 11th place car dsq/-4 laps	15/27
ret	GERMAN GP	Hockenheim	17	Barclay Nordica Arrows BMW	G	1.5 t/c Arrows A7-BMW 4		turbo	14/27
6	AUSTRIAN GP	Österreichring	17	Barclay Nordica Arrows BMW	G	1.5 t/c Arrows A7-BMW 4		1 lap behind	19/28
ret	DUTCH GP	Zandvoort	17	Barclay Nordica Arrows BMW	G	1.5 t/c Arrows A7-BMW 4		wheel bearing	19/27
ret	ITALIAN GP	Monza	17	Barclay Nordica Arrows BMW	G	1.5 t/c Arrows A7-BMW 4		engine	15/27
ret	EUROPEAN GP	Nürburgring	17	Barclay Nordica Arrows BMW	G	1.5 t/c Arrows A7-BMW 4		accident-Berger, Fabi & Ghinzani	16/26
ret	PORTUGUESE GP	Estoril	17	Barclay Nordica Arrows BMW	G	1.5 t/c Arrows A7-BMW 4		electrics	16/27
1985		Championship position: 13=	Wins: 0	Pole positions: 0	Fastest laps: 0	Points scored: 5			
15	CANADIAN GP	Montreal	8	Motor Racing Developments Ltd	P	1.5 t/c Brabham BT54-BMW 4		3 laps behind	20/25
8	US GP (DETROIT)	Detroit	8	Motor Racing Developments Ltd	P	1.5 t/c Brabham BT54-BMW 4		1 lap behind	11/25
8	FRENCH GP	Paul Ricard	8	Motor Racing Developments Ltd	P	1.5 t/c Brabham BT54-BMW 4		1 lap behind	14/26
6	BRITISH GP	Silverstone	8	Motor Racing Developments Ltd	P	1.5 t/c Brabham BT54-BMW 4		2 laps behind	15/26
ret	GERMAN GP	Nürburgring	8	Motor Racing Developments Ltd	P	1.5 t/c Brabham BT54-BMW 4		engine	11/27
6	AUSTRIAN GP	Österreichring	8	Motor Racing Developments Ltd	P	1.5 t/c Brabham BT54-BMW 4		1 lap behind	11/27
10/ret	DUTCH GP	Zandvoort	8	Motor Racing Developments Ltd	P	1.5 t/c Brabham BT54-BMW 4		exhaust/5 laps behind	9/27
4	ITALIAN GP	Monza	8	Motor Racing Developments Ltd	P	1.5 t/c Brabham BT54-BMW 4			9/26
8	BELGIAN GP	Spa	8	Motor Racing Developmetns Ltd	P	1.5 t/c Brabham BT54-BMW 4		1 lap behind	12/24
ret	EUROPEAN GP	Brands Hatch	8	Motor Racing Developments Ltd	P	1.5 t/c Brabham BT54-BMW 4		turbo	7/27
ret	SOUTH AFRICAN GP	Kyalami	8	Motor Racing Developments Ltd	P	1.5 t/c Brabham BT54-BMW 4		engine	5/21
ret	AUSTRALIAN GP	Adelaide	8	Motor Racing Developments Ltd	P	1.5 t/c Brabham BT54-BMW 4		engine	6/25
1986		Championship position: Unplaced							
ret	BRAZILIAN GP	Rio	17	Barclay Arrows BMW	G	1.5 t/c Arrows A8-BMW 4		engine	20/25
ret	SPANISH GP	Jerez	17	Barclay Arrows BMW	G	1.5 t/c Arrows A8-BMW 4		fuel system	22/25
9/ret	SAN MARINO GP	Imola	17	Barclay Arrows BMW	G	1.5 t/c Arrows A8-BMW 4		out of fuel/3 laps behind	15/26
9	MONACO GP	Monte Carlo	17	Barclay Arrows BMW	G	1.5 t/c Arrows A8-BMW 4		3 laps behind	17/26
9	BELGIAN GP	Spa	17	Barclay Arrows BMW	G	1.5 t/c Arrows A8-BMW 4		2 laps behind	21/25

GP Starts: 81 (82)   GP Wins: 0   Pole positions: 0   Fastest laps: 1   Points: 17

JOHN SURTEES

WORLD CHAMPION: 1964

JOHN SURTEES

John Surtees is widely honoured as the only World Champion on two wheels and four, a remarkable achievement of which he can justly be proud. But that tag tends to be used so often that it is easy to forget what a brilliant all-round racing driver he really was. Born into a motor cycling background – his father Jack was an amateur racer – the young Surtees began racing on two wheels seriously in 1951, becoming a star on Nortons through to the mid-fifties when he switched to the Italian MV Agusta concern. From 1956 to 1960 Surtees was the outstanding rider of the day, winning seven world titles in the 350 cc and 500 cc classes. He had some promising trials with both Vanwall and Aston Martin in 1959 and, when his bike commitments allowed, embarked on his car racing career early in 1960.

A win first time out at Goodwood in Ken Tyrrell's Cooper Formula Junior marked him down as a special talent. No sooner had he purchased his own F2 Cooper than he received an invitation from Lotus to race their Formula 1 Lotus 18. At this point Colin Chapman was adroitly juggling with a number of drivers, a situation of which John was unaware. Nevertheless he proved staggeringly quick for one so inexperienced. In his second Grand Prix he was second only to Brabham, and he led in Portugal before an error cost him dear. Not so worldly-wise in those early days, John shied away from signing to drive alongside Jim Clark for the 1961 season, unhappy with Chapman's somewhat cavalier attitude towards his contract with Innes Ireland. In the short term at least, it proved to be the wrong decision. Joining the Yeoman Credit-backed team running off-the-shelf Coopers for 1961, Surtees recorded only mediocre results, the sole minor success being a win in the Glover Trophy. Things improved when the team, now under the Bowmaker banner, aligned themselves with Lola, and Surtees, deeply involved in the development of the car, came close to a Grand Prix victory. He did win a non-title race at Mallory Park, but at the end of the year could resist the overtures of Ferrari no longer.

John had a galvanising effect on the team, not only as a driver but also as a source of technical input, particularly in the development of the monocoque chassis. Prior to his arrival at Maranello, Ferrari had completely lost their way but by mid-1963 Surtees had won both the German GP and Mediterranean GP to re-establish the Scuderia as a potent force once more. When the team introduced the 158 V8 engine early in 1964, Surtees at last found the car in which he could make a realistic championship bid. Mid-season victories in Germany and Italy enabled him to travel to the final round in Mexico with a chance of the title, and luck was on his side as his two rivals, Clark and Hill, both hit trouble. It may not have been one of the most convincing championship wins, but in a year when all the cars were evenly matched it was still thoroughly deserved.

The 1965 season found Ferrari bogged down with their flat-12 engine project, and most of Surtees' success came in the older 158 V8 at the beginning of the season. Apart from his sports car commitments, which brought victory in the Nürburgring 1000 Km, John was now running his own Lola T70 on the North American sports car scene, but in practice for a race at Mosport he suffered a massive accident which he was very lucky to survive – as it was he lay in hospital with serious back injuries for many weeks before making a brave comeback the following spring. Ironically 1966 was probably his finest year despite the bitter disagreement which caused him to leave Ferrari in mid-term. Before the split, John had won the Belgian GP, the Syracuse GP and the Monza 1000 Km sports car race, but afterwards he scored victories in the Mexican GP for Cooper and a whole succession of sports car races back in his Lola.

The 1967 season was another busy one. Surtees joined the Honda F1 effort but development proved to be a slow and painful process, though some reward came when the hastily prepared Lola-based 'Hondola' won a sensational Italian GP by a hair's-breadth from Jack Brabham. John's involvement with Lola was deep. Running their Formula 2 car, he broke the Brabham dominance on occasion, which was a not inconsiderable feat, but the Lola-Aston Martin sports car project was best forgotten. Meanwhile his transatlantic journeys to bag some of the lucrative purse-money on offer in Can-Am went on unhindered. With little headway being made during the second year of the Surtees-Honda alliance, the project was abandoned at the end of the season, and for 1969 John joined BRM but it was to become a nightmarish season for both parties. His Can-Am drives for Chaparral that year were also less than satisfactory when the narrow 2H car proved to be the most difficult machine he had ever handled.

The logical decision was to follow the example of his fellow drivers Brabham and McLaren and build his own Formula 1 car. He was obliged to run a McLaren while his own challenger was being prepared, but a superb drive and fastest lap in South Africa proved he could still cut it behind the wheel. There was even a brief and successful return to Ferrari for three sports car races, before development of the Surtees TS7 took over, an aggregate win in the end-of-season Gold Cup race at Oulton Park boosting his morale. The 1971 season proved tougher than expected as the new TS9 made only an occasional impression on the Grand Prix elite. In the less rarefied atmosphere of non-championship races, John scored some useful placings, again winning the Gold Cup, but there was no denying it had been a disappointing season for a man who had been used to much greater things.

Mike Hailwood's drive at Monza, coupled with a realisation that he could no longer fulfil all the roles in his team effectively, saw Surtees take a back seat in 1972. His third place in the International Trophy was his last Formula 1 success, while in Formula 2 he signed off his racing career with wins in the Japanese GP at Mount Fuji and the Shell GP at Imola. Thenceforth he concentrated on running his team, with a succession of drivers good, bad and indifferent filling the cockpit depending on the exigencies of the times.

Certainly few of them could meet the exacting standards required by this hardest of taskmasters. When suitable sponsorship dried up and medical problems which had dogged him intermittently as a result of his 1965 Mosport accident resurfaced, he quit the racing scene somewhat disillusioned. Happily, having remarried and become a contented family man, John now enjoys the historic racing scene in both cars and bikes, where he is a major attraction demonstrating many of the machines he handled with such brilliance in the past.

SURTEES, John (GB) b 11/2/1934, Tatsfield, Surrey

1960
Championship position: 11th=   Wins: 0   Pole positions: 1   Fastest laps: 1   Points scored: 6

	Race	Circuit	No	Entrant	Tyres	Car/Engine	Comment	Q Pos/Entries
ret	MONACO GP	Monte Carlo	26	Team Lotus	D	2.5 Lotus 18-Climax 4	transmission	15/24
2	BRITISH GP	Silverstone	9	Team Lotus	D	2.5 Lotus 18-Climax 4		11/25
ret	PORTUGUESE GP	Oporto	18	Team Lotus	D	2.5 Lotus 18-Climax 4	radiator/FL	1/16
ret	US GP	Riverside	11	Team Lotus	D	2.5 Lotus 18-Climax 4	spun-hit by Clark	6/23

1961
Championship position: 11th=   Wins: 0   Pole positions: 0   Fastest laps: 0   Points scored: 4

	Race	Circuit	No	Entrant	Tyres	Car/Engine	Comment	Q Pos/Entries
ret	MONACO GP	Monte Carlo	22	Yeoman Credit Racing Team	D	1.5 Cooper T53-Climax 4	head gasket	=12/21
7	DUTCH GP	Zandvoort	12	Yeoman Credit Racing Team	D	1.5 Cooper T53-Climax 4		9/17
5	BELGIAN GP	Spa	24	Yeoman Credit Racing Team	D	1.5 Cooper T53-Climax 4		4/25
ret	FRENCH GP	Reims	40	Yeoman Credit Racing Team	D	1.5 Cooper T53-Climax 4	suspension-accident	=6/26
ret	BRITISH GP	Aintree	34	Yeoman Credit Racing Team	D	1.5 Cooper T53-Climax 4	transmission	10/30
5	GERMAN GP	Nürburgring	18	Yeoman Credit Racing Team	D	1.5 Cooper T53-Climax 4		10/27
ret	ITALIAN GP	Monza	42	Yeoman Credit Racing Team	D	1.5 Cooper T53-Climax 4	accident	19/33
ret	US GP	Watkins Glen	18	Yeoman Credit Racing Team	D	1.5 Cooper T53-Climax 4	engine	=9/19
dns	"	" "	26	Frank J Harrison	D	1.5 Lotus 18-Climax 4	Lloyd Ruby's car-practice only	– / –

1962
Championship position: 4th   Wins: 0   Pole positions: 1   Fastest laps: 0   Points scored: 19

	Race	Circuit	No	Entrant	Tyres	Car/Engine	Comment	Q Pos/Entries
ret	DUTCH GP	Zandvoort	19	Bowmaker Racing Team	D	1.5 Lola 4-Climax V8	suspension	1/20
4	MONACO GP	Monte Carlo	28	Bowmaker Racing Team	D	1.5 Lola 4-Climax V8	1 lap behind	11/21
5	BELGIAN GP	Spa	5	Bowmaker Racing Team	D	1.5 Lola 4-Climax V8	1 lap behind	11/20
5	FRENCH GP	Rouen	18	Bowmaker Racing Team	D	1.5 Lola 4-Climax V8	3 laps behind	5/17
2	BRITISH GP	Aintree	24	Bowmaker Racing Team	D	1.5 Lola 4-Climax V8		2/21
dns	"	" "	24	Bowmaker Racing Team	D	1.5 Lola 4A-Climax V8	practice only	– / –
2	GERMAN GP	Nürburgring	14	Bowmaker Racing Team	D	1.5 Lola 4-Climax V8		4/30
dns	"	"	14	Bowmaker Racing Team	D	1.5 Lola 4A-Climax V8	practice only	– / –
ret	ITALIAN GP	Monza	46	Bowmaker Racing Team	D	1.5 Lola 4A-Climax V8	engine	8/30
dns	"	"	46	Bowmaker Racing Team	D	1.5 Lola 4-Climax V8	practice only	– / –
ret	US GP	Watkins Glen	18	Bowmaker Racing Team	D	1.5 Lola 4-Climax V8	crankcase plug	20/20
ret	SOUTH AFRICAN GP	East London	6	Bowmaker Racing Team	D	1.5 Lola 4-Climax V8	engine	5/17

1963
Championship position: 4th   Wins: 1   Pole positions: 1   Fastest laps: 3   Points scored: 22

	Race	Circuit	No	Entrant	Tyres	Car/Engine	Comment	Q Pos/Entries
4	MONACO GP	Monte Carlo	21	Scuderia Ferrari SpA SEFAC	D	1.5 Ferrari 156 V6	FL	=3/17
ret	BELGIAN GP	Spa	9	Scuderia Ferrari SpA SEFAC	D	1.5 Ferrari 156 V6	fuel injection pipe	10/20
3	DUTCH GP	Zandvoort	2	Scuderia Ferrari SpA SEFAC	D	1.5 Ferrari 156 V6	1 lap behind	5/19
ret	FRENCH GP	Reims	16	Scuderia Ferrari SpA SEFAC	D	1.5 Ferrari 156 V6	fuel pump	=4/21
2	BRITISH GP	Silverstone	10	Scuderia Ferrari SpA SEFAC	D	1.5 Ferrari 156 V6	FL	5/23
1	GERMAN GP	Nürburgring	7	Scuderia Ferrari SpA SEFAC	D	1.5 Ferrari 156 V6	FL	2/26
ret	ITALIAN GP	Monza	4	Scuderia Ferrari SpA SEFAC	D	1.5 Ferrari 156 V6	engine	1/28
9/ret	US GP	Watkins Glen	23	Scuderia Ferrari SpA SEFAC	D	1.5 Ferrari 156 V6	engine-valve spring/-28 laps	3/21
dsq	MEXICAN GP	Mexico City	23	Scuderia Ferrari SpA SEFAC	D	1.5 Ferrari 156 V6	push start at pit stop	2/21
ret	SOUTH AFRICAN GP	East London	3	Scuderia Ferrari SpA SEFAC	D	1.5 Ferrari 156 V6	engine	4/21

1964
Championship position: WORLD CHAMPION   Wins: 2   Pole positions: 2   Fastest laps: 2   Points scored: 40

	Race	Circuit	No	Entrant	Tyres	Car/Engine	Comment	Q Pos/Entries
ret	MONACO GP	Monte Carlo	21	Scuderia Ferrari SpA SEFAC	D	1.5 Ferrari 158 V8	gearbox	=3/20
dns	"	"	21	Scuderia Ferrari SpA SEFAC	D	1.5 Ferrari 156 V6	practice only	– / –
2	DUTCH GP	Zandvoort	2	Scuderia Ferrari SpA SEFAC	D	1.5 Ferrari 158 V8		4/18
ret	BELGIAN GP	Spa	10	Scuderia Ferrari SpA SEFAC	D	1.5 Ferrari 158 V8	engine	5/20
ret	FRENCH GP	Rouen	24	Scuderia Ferrari SpA SEFAC	D	1.5 Ferrari 158 V8	oil pipe	3/17
3	BRITISH GP	Brands Hatch	7	Scuderia Ferrari SpA SEFAC	D	1.5 Ferrari 158 V8		5/25
dns	"	" "	7	Scuderia Ferrari SpA SEFAC	D	1.5 Ferrari 156 V6	practice only	– / –
1	GERMAN GP	Nürburgring	7	Scuderia Ferrari SpA SEFAC	D	1.5 Ferrari 158 V8	FL	1/24
ret	AUSTRIAN GP	Zeltweg	7	Scuderia Ferrari SpA SEFAC	D	1.5 Ferrari 158 V8	rear suspension	2/20
1	ITALIAN GP	Monza	2	Scuderia Ferrari SpA SEFAC	D	1.5 Ferrari 158 V8	FL	1/25
2	US GP	Watkins Glen	7	North American Racing Team	D	1.5 Ferrari 158 V8		2/19
dns	"	" "	7T	North American Racing Team	D	1.5 Ferrari 156 V6	practice only	– / –
dns	"	" "	8T	North American Racing Team	Tyres	1.5 Ferrari 1512 F12	practice only	– / –
2	MEXICAN GP	Mexico City	7	North American Racing Team	D	1.5 Ferrari 158 V8		4/19

1965
Championship position: 5th   Wins: 0   Pole positions: 0   Fastest laps: 0   Points scored: 17

	Race	Circuit	No	Entrant	Tyres	Car/Engine	Comment	Q Pos/Entries
2	SOUTH AFRICAN GP	East London	1	Scuderia Ferrari SpA SEFAC	D	1.5 Ferrari 158 V8		2/25
4/ret	MONACO GP	Monte Carlo	18	Scuderia Ferrari SpA SEFAC	D	1.5 Ferrari 158 V8	out of fuel/1 lap behind	5/17

After joining Ferrari in 1963, Surtees was the pivotal figure in the revival of Maranello's declining fortunes.
Right: **Championship year: John taking the Ferrari 156 V6 to second place in the 1964 Dutch Grand Prix.**

ret	BELGIAN GP	Spa	1	Scuderia Ferrari SpA SEFAC	D	1.5 Ferrari 158 V8	engine	6/21
3	FRENCH GP	Clermont Ferrand	2	Scuderia Ferrari SpA SEFAC	D	1.5 Ferrari 158 V8		=3/17
3	BRITISH GP	Silverstone	1	Scuderia Ferrari SpA SEFAC	D	1.5 Ferrari 1512 F12		=3/23
dns	"	"	71	Scuderia Ferrari SpA SEFAC	D	1.5 Ferrari 158 V8	practice only	–/–
7	DUTCH GP	Zandvoort	2	Scuderia Ferrari SpA SEFAC	D	1.5 Ferrari 1512 F12	1 lap behind	=2/17
dns	"	"	2	Scuderia Ferrari SpA SEFAC	D	1.5 Ferrari 158 V8	practice only	–/–
ret	GERMAN GP	Nürburgring	7	Scuderia Ferrari SpA SEFAC	D	1.5 Ferrari 1512 F12	gearbox	4/22
ret	ITALIAN GP	Monza	8	Scuderia Ferrari SpA SEFAC	D	1.5 Ferrari 1512 F12	clutch	2/23

1966 Championship position: 2 Wins: 2 Pole positions: 2 Fastest laps: 3 Points scored: 28

ret	MONACO GP	Monte Carlo	17	Scuderia Ferrari SpA SEFAC	D	3.0 Ferrari 312/66 V12	transmission	2/16
1	BELGIAN GP	Spa	6	Scuderia Ferrari SpA SEFAC	D	3.0 Ferrari 312/66 V12	FL	1/18
ret	FRENCH GP	Reims	10	Cooper Car Co	D	3.0 Cooper T81-Maserati V12	overheating	2/17
ret	BRITISH GP	Brands Hatch	12	Cooper Car Co	D	3.0 Cooper T81-Maserati V12	transmission	6/20
ret	DUTCH GP	Zandvoort	24	Cooper Car Co	D	3.0 Cooper T81-Maserati V12	electrics	10/18
2	GERMAN GP	Nürburgring	7	Cooper Car Co	D	3.0 Cooper T81-Maserati V12	FL	2/30
ret	ITALIAN GP	Monza	14	Cooper Car Co	F	3.0 Cooper T81-Maserati V12	fuel leak	4/22
3	US GP	Watkins Glen	7	Cooper Car Co	F	3.0 Cooper T81-Maserati V12	spin-pit stop/FL/1 lap behind	4/19
1	MEXICAN GP	Mexico City	7	Cooper Car Co	F	3.0 Cooper T81-Maserati V12		1/19

1967 Championship position: 4th Wins: 1 Pole positions: 0 Fastest laps: 0 Points scored: 20

3	SOUTH AFRICAN GP	Kyalami	11	Honda Racing	G	3.0 Honda RA273 V12	tyre problems/1 lap behind	6/18
ret	MONACO GP	Monte Carlo	7	Honda Racing	F	3.0 Honda RA273 V12	engine	3/18
ret	DUTCH GP	Zandvoort	7	Honda Racing	F	3.0 Honda RA273 V12	sticking throttle slides	=6/17
ret	BELGIAN GP	Spa	7	Honda Racing	F	3.0 Honda RA273 V12	engine	10/18
6	BRITISH GP	Silverstone	7	Honda Racing	F	3.0 Honda RA273 V12	2 laps behind	7/21
4	GERMAN GP	Nürburgring	7	Honda Racing	F	3.0 Honda RA273 V12		7/25
1	ITALIAN GP	Monza	14	Honda Racing	F	3.0 Honda RA300 V12	Lola developed chassis	9/18
ret	US GP	Watkins Glen	3	Honda Racing	F	3.0 Honda RA300 V12	alternator-flat battery	11/18
4	MEXICAN GP	Mexico City	3	Honda Racing	F	3.0 Honda RA300 V12	1 lap behind	7/19

1968 Championship position: 7th Wins: 0 Pole positions: 1 Fastest laps: 1 Points scored: 12

8	SOUTH AFRICAN GP	Kyalami	7	Honda Racing	F	3.0 Honda RA300 V12	2 pit stops-misfire/-5 laps	6/23
ret	SPANISH GP	Jarama	7	Honda Racing	F	3.0 Honda RA301 V12	gearbox	7/14
ret	MONACO GP	Monte Carlo	8	Honda Racing	F	3.0 Honda RA301 V12	gearbox	4/18
ret	BELGIAN GP	Spa	20	Honda Racing	F	3.0 Honda RA301 V12	rear suspension/FL	4/18
ret	DUTCH GP	Zandvoort	7	Honda Racing	F	3.0 Honda RA301 V12	alternator drive-flat battery	9/19
2	FRENCH GP	Rouen	16	Honda Racing	F	3.0 Honda RA301 V12	pit stop-tyres	7/18
5	BRITISH GP	Brands Hatch	7	Honda Racing	F	3.0 Honda RA301 V12	rear wing fell off/2 laps behind	9/20
ret	GERMAN GP	Nürburgring	7	Honda Racing	F	3.0 Honda RA301 V12	overheating-ignition	7/20
ret	ITALIAN GP	Monza	14	Honda Racing	F	3.0 Honda RA301 V12	crashed avoiding Amon	1/24
ret	CANADIAN GP	St Jovite	8	Honda Racing	F	3.0 Honda RA301 V12	transmission	=6/22
3	US GP	Watkins Glen	5	Honda Racing	F	3.0 Honda RA301 V12	1 lap behind	9/21
ret	MEXICAN GP	Mexico City	5	Honda Racing	F	3.0 Honda RA301 V12	overheating	6/21

1969 Championship position: 11th Wins: 0 Pole positions: 0 Fastest laps: 0 Points scored: 6

ret	SOUTH AFRICAN GP	Kyalami	10	Owen Racing Organisation	D	3.0 BRM P138 V12	engine	=9/18
5	SPANISH GP	Montjuich Park	14	Owen Racing Organisation	D	3.0 BRM P138 V12	2 pit stops-fuel feed/-6 laps	9/14
ret	MONACO GP	Monte Carlo	14	Owen Racing Organisation	D	3.0 BRM P138 V12	gearbox-accident with Brabham	7/16
9	DUTCH GP	Zandvoort	14	Owen Racing Organisation	D	3.0 BRM P138 V12	pit stop-fuel/3 laps behind	12/15
dns	"	"	14T	Owen Racing Organisation	D	3.0 BRM P139 V12	practice only	–/–
ret	BRITISH GP	Silverstone	14	Owen Racing Organisation	D	3.0 BRM P139 V12	collapsed front suspension	6/17
dns	GERMAN GP	Nürburgring	14	Owen Racing Organisation	D	3.0 BRM P139 V12	suspension problems	(12)/26
11	ITALIAN GP	Monza	14	Owen Racing Organisation	D	3.0 BRM P139 V12	2 pit stops-various/-8 laps	10/15
ret	CANADIAN GP	Mosport Park	14	Owen Racing Organisation	D	3.0 BRM P139 V12	engine	14/20
3	US GP	Watkins Glen	14	Owen Racing Organisation	D	3.0 BRM P139 V12	2 laps behind	11/18
ret	MEXICAN GP	Mexico City	14	Owen Racing Organisation	D	3.0 BRM P139 V12	gearbox	10/17

1970 Championship position: 17th Wins: 0 Pole positions: 0 Fastest laps: 1 Points scored: 3

ret	SOUTH AFRICAN GP	Kyalami	7	Team Surtees	F	3.0 McLaren M7C-Cosworth V8	engine/FL	=7/24
ret	SPANISH GP	Jarama	8	Team Surtees	F	3.0 McLaren M7C-Cosworth V8	gearbox	14/22
ret	MONACO GP	Monte Carlo	14	Team Surtees	F	3.0 McLaren M7C-Cosworth V8	oil pressure	16/21
6	DUTCH GP	Zandvoort	16	Team Surtees	F	3.0 McLaren M7C-Cosworth V8	1 lap behind	14/24
ret	BRITISH GP	Brands Hatch	20	Team Surtees	F	3.0 Surtees TS7-Cosworth V8	oil pressure	20/25
9/ret	GERMAN GP	Hockenheim	7	Team Surtees	F	3.0 Surtees TS7-Cosworth V8	engine/4 laps behind	15/25
ret	AUSTRIAN GP	Österreichring	15	Team Surtees	F	3.0 Surtees TS7-Cosworth V8	engine	=11/24
ret	ITALIAN GP	Monza	14	Team Surtees	F	3.0 Surtees TS7-Cosworth V8	electrics	=10/27
5	CANADIAN GP	St Jovite	4	Team Surtees	F	3.0 Surtees TS7-Cosworth V8	pit stop-misfire/1 lap behind	=5/20
ret	US GP	Watkins Glen	17	Team Surtees	F	3.0 Surtees TS7-Cosworth V8	flywheel	8/27
8	MEXICAN GP	Mexico City	17	Team Surtees	F	3.0 Surtees TS7-Cosworth V8	1 lap behind	15/18

1971 Championship position: 18th Wins: 0 Pole positions: 0 Fastest laps: 0 Points scored: 3

ret	SOUTH AFRICAN GP	Kyalami	20	Brooke Bond Oxo/R. Walker/Team Surtees	F	3.0 Surtees TS9-Cosworth V8	gearbox	=5/25
dns	"	"	20T	Brooke Bond Oxo/R. Walker/Team Surtees	F	3.0 Surtees TS7-Cosworth V8	practice only	–/–
11	SPANISH GP	Montjuich Park	24	Brooke Bond Oxo/R. Walker/Team Surtees	F	3.0 Surtees TS9-Cosworth V8	2 pit stops-body damage/-8 laps	22/22
7	MONACO GP	Monte Carlo	22	Brooke Bond Oxo/R. Walker/Team Surtees	F	3.0 Surtees TS9-Cosworth V8	1 lap behind	=9/23
5	DUTCH GP	Zandvoort	23	Brooke Bond Oxo/R. Walker/Team Surtees	F	3.0 Surtees TS9-Cosworth V8	2 laps behind	7/24
8	FRENCH GP	Paul Ricard	22	Brooke Bond Oxo/R. Walker/Team Surtees	F	3.0 Surtees TS9-Cosworth V8		13/24
6	BRITISH GP	Silverstone	23	Brooke Bond Oxo/R. Walker/Team Surtees	F	3.0 Surtees TS9-Cosworth V8	1 lap behind	18/24
7	GERMAN GP	Nürburgring	22	Brooke Bond Oxo/R. Walker/Team Surtees	F	3.0 Surtees TS9-Cosworth V8		15/23
ret	AUSTRIAN GP	Österreichring	22	Brooke Bond Oxo/R. Walker/Team Surtees	F	3.0 Surtees TS9-Cosworth V8	engine	18/22
ret	ITALIAN GP	Monza	7	Brooke Bond Oxo/R. Walker/Team Surtees	F	3.0 Surtees TS9-Cosworth V8	engine	15/24
11	CANADIAN GP	Mosport Park	22	Brooke Bond Oxo/R. Walker/Team Surtees	F	3.0 Surtees TS9-Cosworth V8	4 laps behind	14/27
17	US GP	Watkins Glen	18	Brooke Bond Oxo/R. Walker/Team Surtees	F	3.0 Surtees TS9-Cosworth V8	pit stop-ignition/5 laps behind	14/32

1972 Championship position: Unplaced

ret	ITALIAN GP	Monza	7	Team Surtees	F	3.0 Surtees TS14-Cosworth V8	fuel vaporisation	19/27
dns	US GP	Watkins Glen	24	Team Surtees	F	3.0 Surtees TS14-Cosworth V8	engine shortage	(25)/32

GP Starts: 111 GP Wins: 6 Pole positions: 8 Fastest laps: 11 Points: 180

AGURI SUZUKI

To date Suzuki is Japan's most successful Grand Prix contender, and the only one to stand on the podium, courtesy of his excellent third place in the 1990 Japanese GP. His father was the founder of the Japanese karting association, and the young Suzuki naturally became involved in the sport, winning the title in 1981. He then moved into F3 and finished second in the 1983 championship, which brought an offer to race for Nissan in sports and touring cars, Aguri taking the 1986 Group A championship.

Single-seaters were still his first priority, and in 1987 Suzuki went into the All-Japan F3000 series, finishing runner-up, before finishing the job the following year by taking the title. His eyes were now on Grand Prix racing and he briefly came to Europe to race the Footwork-backed March in the F3000 series, before being given a race in the Japanese GP with the Larrousse team in place of the indisposed Dalmas. Having previously been associated with Yamaha, Aguri joined the Zakspeed team which was runnning the Japanese manufacturer's engines for 1989, but Suzuki drew a complete blank, failing even to pre-qualify the hopeless device at every one of the 16 Grands Prix.

This could have sunk many a driver's career, but luckily he was able to find a drive with Larrousse in 1990, when he became a points-scorer on three occasions, including his splendid drive at Suzuka, which cemented his future. Unfortunately the precarious financial position at Larrousse, and consequent lack of testing and development, blunted his progress the following year, and for 1992 Aguri joined the Footwork team, which was itself regrouping, but armed with the Mugen Honda V10. Suzuki's season was disappointing, his form not helped by the problems he had fitting into the cockpit, and he was completely overshadowed by team-mate Michele Alboreto. For 1993, he remained with the team, paired with Derek Warwick, but once again finishes in the points eluded him. The year was punctuated by a worryingly high number of spins and collisions, and apart from sixth place on the grid at Spa, which seemed to suit the Footwork's active suspension system, there was precious little to cheer the Japanese driver, who lost his drive when the restructured Arrows team under Jack Oliver were no longer in receipt of finance from the Far East.

Aguri then returned home to race for Nissan, perhaps thinking his F1 career was behind him, but, with Eddie Irvine suspended, he was brought into the Jordan team at the Pacific GP. Suzuki was uneasy about this because of his lack of preparation and fitness and was to be proved right when he spun out. It did not hurt his long-term plans, however, and, with Mugen Honda's backing, he signed to race for Ligier in 1995 in a season shared with Martin Brundle. Sixth place at Hockenheim apart, the Japanese driver looked less than convincing when compared with his team-mates. Aguri had already decided to retire from Formula 1 after the Japanese GP, but a practice accident at Suzuka left him with cracked ribs and unable to take any further part in proceedings.

For 1996 Suzuki signed a contract with Nissan to return to the All-Japan GT championship to race their revised Skyline and he was a member of the crew of the TWR-run Nissan R390 which finished third at Le Mans in 1998. He has subsequently formed his own Formula Nippon team and continues to race with a Toyota Supra in the All-Japan GT series.

SUZUKI, Aguri (J) b 8/9/1960, Tokyo

	1988	Championship position: Unplaced							
	Race	Circuit	No	Entrant	Tyres	Car/Engine		Comment	Q Pos/Entries
16	JAPANESE GP	Suzuka	29	Larrousse Calmels	G	3.5 Lola LC88-Cosworth V8		3 laps behind	20/31
	1989	Championship position: Unplaced							
dnpq	BRAZILIAN GP	Rio	35	West Zakspeed Racing	P	3.5 West Zakspeed 891-Yamaha V8			36/38
dnpq	SAN MARINO GP	Imola	35	West Zakspeed Racing	P	3.5 West Zakspeed 891-Yamaha V8			37/39
dnpq	MONACO GP	Monte Carlo	35	West Zakspeed Racing	P	3.5 West Zakspeed 891-Yamaha V8			37/38
dnpq	MEXICAN GP	Mexico City	35	West Zakspeed Racing	P	3.5 West Zakspeed 891-Yamaha V8			36/39
dnpq	US GP (PHOENIX)	Phoenix	35	West Zakspeed Racing	P	3.5 West Zakspeed 891-Yamaha V8			38/39
dnpq	CANADIAN GP	Montreal	35	West Zakspeed Racing	P	3.5 West Zakspeed 891-Yamaha V8			38/39
dnpq	FRENCH GP	Paul Ricard	35	West Zakspeed Racing	P	3.5 West Zakspeed 891-Yamaha V8			37/39
dnpq	BRITISH GP	Silverstone	35	West Zakspeed Racing	P	3.5 West Zakspeed 891-Yamaha V8			38/39
dnpq	GERMAN GP	Hockenheim	35	West Zakspeed Racing	P	3.5 West Zakspeed 891-Yamaha V8			38/39
dnpq	HUNGARIAN GP	Hungaroring	35	West Zakspeed Racing	P	3.5 West Zakspeed 891-Yamaha V8			38/39
dnpq	BELGIAN GP	Spa	35	West Zakspeed Racing	P	3.5 West Zakspeed 891-Yamaha V8			36/39
dnpq	ITALIAN GP	Monza	35	West Zakspeed Racing	P	3.5 West Zakspeed 891-Yamaha V8			36/39
dnpq	PORTUGUESE GP	Estoril	35	West Zakspeed Racing	P	3.5 West Zakspeed 891-Yamaha V8			37/39
dnpq	SPANISH GP	Jerez	35	West Zakspeed Racing	P	3.5 West Zakspeed 891-Yamaha V8			36/38
dnpq	JAPANESE GP	Suzuka	35	West Zakspeed Racing	P	3.5 West Zakspeed 891-Yamaha V8			34/39
dnpq	AUSTRALIAN GP	Adelaide	35	West Zakspeed Racing	P	3.5 West Zakspeed 891-Yamaha V8			36/39

1990
Championship position: 10th= Wins: 0 Pole positions: 0 Fastest laps: 0 Points scored: 6

ret	US GP (PHOENIX)	Phoenix	30	Espo Larrousse F1	G	3.5 Lola LC89-Lamborghini V12	brakes	18/35
ret	BRAZILIAN GP	Rio	30	Espo Larrousse F1	G	3.5 Lola LC89-Lamborghini V12	suspension	18/35
ret	SAN MARINO GP	Imola	30	Espo Larrousse F1	G	3.5 Lola 90-Lamborghini V12	clutch	16/34
ret	MONACO GP	Monte Carlo	30	Espo Larrousse F1	G	3.5 Lola 90-Lamborghini V12	electrics	15/35
12	CANADIAN GP	Montreal	30	Espo Larrousse F1	G	3.5 Lola 90-Lamborghini V12	collision-Martini pit stop/-4 laps	18/35
ret	MEXICAN GP	Mexico City	30	Espo Larrousse F1	G	3.5 Lola 90-Lamborghini V12	collision with Nakajima	19/35
7	FRENCH GP	Paul Ricard	30	Espo Larrousse F1	G	3.5 Lola 90-Lamborghini V12	1 lap behind	14/35
6	BRITISH GP	Silverstone	30	Espo Larrousse F1	G	3.5 Lola 90-Lamborghini V12	1 lap behind	9/35
ret	GERMAN GP	Hockenheim	30	Espo Larrousse F1	G	3.5 Lola 90-Lamborghini V12	clutch	11/35
ret	HUNGARIAN GP	Hungaroring	30	Espo Larrousse F1	G	3.5 Lola 90-Lamborghini V12	engine	19/35
ret/dns	BELGIAN GP	Spa	30	Espo Larrousse F1	G	3.5 Lola 90-Lamborghini V12	crash at first start/did not restart	11/33
ret	ITALIAN GP	Monza	30	Espo Larrousse F1	G	3.5 Lola 90-Lamborghini V12	electrics	18/33
14/ret	PORTUGUESE GP	Estoril	30	Espo Larrousse F1	G	3.5 Lola 90-Lamborghini V12	collision with Caffi/-3 laps	11/33
6	SPANISH GP	Jerez	30	Espo Larrousse F1	G	3.5 Lola 90-Lamborghini V12		15/33
3	JAPANESE GP	Suzuka	30	Espo Larrousse F1	G	3.5 Lola 90-Lamborghini V12		10/30
ret	AUSTRALIAN GP	Adelaide	30	Espo Larrousse F1	G	3.5 Lola 90-Lamborghini V12	differential	24/30

1991
Championship position: 18th= Wins: 0 Pole positions: 0 Fastest laps: 0 Points scored: 1

6	US GP (PHOENIX)	Phoenix	30	Larrousse F1	G	3.5 Larrousse Lola L91-Cosworth V8	2 laps behind	21/34
dns	BRAZILIAN GP	Interlagos	30	Larrousse F1	G	3.5 Larrousse Lola L91-Cosworth V8	no fuel pressure on dummy grid	17/34
ret	SAN MARINO GP	Imola	30	Larrousse F1	G	3.5 Larrousse Lola L91-Cosworth V8	spun off	20/34
ret	MONACO GP	Monte Carlo	30	Larrousse F1	G	3.5 Larrousse Lola L91-Cosworth V8	brake problems-crashed	19/34
ret	CANADIAN GP	Montreal	30	Larrousse F1	G	3.5 Larrousse Lola L91-Cosworth V8	fire-broken fuel line	22/34
ret	MEXICAN GP	Mexico City	30	Larrousse F1	G	3.5 Larrousse Lola L91-Cosworth V8	gearbox	19/34
ret	FRENCH GP	Magny Cours	30	Larrousse F1	G	3.5 Larrousse Lola L91-Cosworth V8	clutch	22/34
ret	BRITISH GP	Silverstone	30	Larrousse F1	G	3.5 Larrousse Lola L91-Cosworth V8	collision with Alesi	22/34
ret	GERMAN GP	Hockenheim	30	Larrousse F1	G	3.5 Larrousse Lola L91-Cosworth V8	started from pitlane/engine	22/34
ret	HUNGARIAN GP	Hungaroring	30	Larrousse F1	G	3.5 Larrousse Lola L91-Cosworth V8	engine	22/34
dnq	BELGIAN GP	Spa	30	Larrousse F1	G	3.5 Larrousse Lola L91-Cosworth V8		27/34
dnq	ITALIAN GP	Monza	30	Larrousse F1	G	3.5 Larrousse Lola L91-Cosworth V8		30/34
ret	PORTUGUESE GP	Estoril	30	Larrousse F1	G	3.5 Larrousse Lola L91-Cosworth V8	gearbox	25/34
dnq	SPANISH GP	Barcelona	30	Larrousse F1	G	3.5 Larrousse Lola L91-Cosworth V8		27/33
ret	JAPANESE GP	Suzuka	30	Larrousse F1	G	3.5 Larrousse Lola L91-Cosworth V8	engine	25/31
dnq	AUSTRALIAN GP	Adelaide	30	Larrousse F1	G	3.5 Larrousse Lola L91-Cosworth V8		27/32

1992
Championship position: Unplaced

8	SOUTH AFRICAN GP	Kyalami	10	Footwork Mugen Honda	G	3.5 Footwork FA13-Mugen Honda V10	2 laps behind	16/30
dnq	MEXICAN GP	Mexico City	10	Footwork Mugen Honda	G	3.5 Footwork FA13-Mugen Honda V10		27/30
ret	BRAZILIAN GP	Interlagos	10	Footwork Mugen Honda	G	3.5 Footwork FA13-Mugen Honda V10	oil system	22/31
7	SPANISH GP	Barcelona	10	Footwork Mugen Honda	G	3.5 Footwork FA13-Mugen Honda V10	2 laps behind	19/32
10	SAN MARINO GP	Imola	10	Footwork Mugen Honda	G	3.5 Footwork FA13-Mugen Honda V10	2 laps behind	11/32
11	MONACO GP	Monte Carlo	10	Footwork Mugen Honda	G	3.5 Footwork FA13-Mugen Honda V10	2 laps behind	19/32
dnq	CANADIAN GP	Montreal	10	Footwork Mugen Honda	G	3.5 Footwork FA13-Mugen Honda V10		27/32
ret	FRENCH GP	Magny Cours	10	Footwork Mugen Honda	G	3.5 Footwork FA13-Mugen Honda V10	slid off avoiding Grouillard	15/30
12	BRITISH GP	Silverstone	10	Footwork Mugen Honda	G	3.5 Footwork FA13-Mugen Honda V10	2 laps behind	17/32
ret	GERMAN GP	Hockenheim	10	Footwork Mugen Honda	G	3.5 Footwork FA13-Mugen Honda V10	spun off lap 1	15/32
ret	HUNGARIAN GP	Hungaroring	10	Footwork Mugen Honda	G	3.5 Footwork FA13-Mugen Honda V10	collision with Gachot	14/31
9	BELGIAN GP	Spa	10	Footwork Mugen Honda	G	3.5 Footwork FA13-Mugen Honda V10	1 lap behind	25/30
ret	ITALIAN GP	Monza	10	Footwork Mugen Honda	G	3.5 Footwork FA13-Mugen Honda V10	spun off	19/28
10	PORTUGUESE GP	Estoril	10	Footwork Mugen Honda	G	3.5 Footwork FA13-Mugen Honda V10	started from pit lane/-3 laps	17/26
8	JAPANESE GP	Suzuka	10	Footwork Mugen Honda	G	3.5 Footwork FA13-Mugen Honda V10	1 lap behind	16/26
8	AUSTRALIAN GP	Adelaide	10	Footwork Mugen Honda	G	3.5 Footwork FA13-Mugen Honda V10	2 laps behind	18/26

1993
Championship position: Unplaced

ret	SOUTH AFRICAN GP	Kyalami	10	Footwork Mugen Honda	G	3.5 Footwork FA13B-Mugen Honda V10	ran into Barbazza-suspension	20/26
ret	BRAZILIAN GP	Rio	10	Footwork Mugen Honda	G	3.5 Footwork FA13B-Mugen Honda V10	crashed in rainstorm	19/26
ret	EUROPEAN GP	Donington	10	Footwork Mugen Honda	G	3.5 Footwork FA14-Mugen Honda V10	gearbox	23/26
9	SAN MARINO GP	Imola	10	Footwork Mugen Honda	G	3.5 Footwork FA14-Mugen Honda V10	stop & go penalty/brakes/-7 laps	21/26
10	SPANISH GP	Barcelona	10	Footwork Mugen Honda	G	3.5 Footwork FA14-Mugen Honda V10	2 laps behind	19/26
ret	MONACO GP	Monte Carlo	10	Footwork Mugen Honda	G	3.5 Footwork FA14-Mugen Honda V10	spun off	18/26
13	CANADIAN GP	Montreal	10	Footwork Mugen Honda	G	3.5 Footwork FA14-Mugen Honda V10	gearbox trouble/spin/-3 laps	16/26
12	FRENCH GP	Magny Cours	10	Footwork Mugen Honda	G	3.5 Footwork FA14-Mugen Honda V10	stalled at pit stop/-2 laps	13/26
ret	BRITISH GP	Silverstone	10	Footwork Mugen Honda	G	3.5 Footwork FA14-Mugen Honda V10	spun off	10/26
ret	GERMAN GP	Hockenheim	10	Footwork Mugen Honda	G	3.5 Footwork FA14-Mugen Honda V10	gearbox	8/26
ret	HUNGARIAN GP	Hungaroring	10	Footwork Mugen Honda	G	3.5 Footwork FA14-Mugen Honda V10	spun off	10/26
ret	BELGIAN GP	Spa	10	Footwork Mugen Honda	G	3.5 Footwork FA14-Mugen Honda V10	hydraulic failure	6/25
ret	ITALIAN GP	Monza	10	Footwork Mugen Honda	G	3.5 Footwork FA14-Mugen Honda V10	collision-Warwick spun off lap 1	8/26
ret	PORTUGUESE GP	Estoril	10	Footwork Mugen Honda	G	3.5 Footwork FA14-Mugen Honda V10	spin/gearbox	16/26
ret	JAPANESE GP	Suzuka	10	Footwork Mugen Honda	G	3.5 Footwork FA14-Mugen Honda V10	spun off	9/24
7	AUSTRALIAN GP	Adelaide	10	Footwork Mugen Honda	G	3.5 Footwork FA14-Mugen Honda V10	1 lap behind	10/24

1994
Championship position: Unplaced

ret	PACIFIC GP	T.I. Circuit	15	Sasol Jordan	G	3.5 Jordan 194-Hart V10	steering problem-crashed	20/28

1995
Championship position: 17th= Wins: 0 Pole positions: 0 Fastest laps: 0 Points scored: 1

8	BRAZILIAN GP	Interlagos	25	Ligier Gitanes Blondes	G	3.0 Ligier JS41-Mugen Honda V10	2 laps behind	15/26
ret	ARGENTINE GP	Buenos Aires	25	Ligier Gitanes Blondes	G	3.0 Ligier JS41-Mugen Honda V10	collision with Salo	19/26
11	SAN MARINO GP	Imola	25	Ligier Gitanes Blondes	G	3.0 Ligier JS41-Mugen Honda V10	3 laps behind	16/26
6	GERMAN GP	Hockenheim	25	Ligier Gitanes Blondes	G	3.0 Ligier JS41-Mugen Honda V10	1 lap behind	18/24
ret	PACIFIC GP	T.I. Circuit	25	Ligier Gitanes Blondes	G	3.0 Ligier JS41-Mugen Honda V10	spun off	13/24
dns	JAPANESE GP	Suzuka	25	Ligier Gitanes Blondes	G	3.0 Ligier JS41-Mugen Honda V10	accident in practice	(13)/24

GP Starts: 63 (64) GP Wins: 0 Pole positions: 0 Fastest laps: 0 Points:8

TOSHIO SUZUKI

In 1993 Toshio Suzuki took part in a Grand Prix for the first time at the age of 38, having arranged a two-race deal with Larrousse in place of Philippe Alliot. His aim was to finish, and in that he succeeded, but just to compete at this level must have been a source of great satisfaction for this very popular driver, who had been Japanese Formula 3 champion as far back as 1979. He raced in Europe during 1980-81, and was a leading contender in the Japanese F2 and F3000 series for more than a decade but enjoyed little luck until the 1995 season when at last things went his way, Suzuki winning the All-Japan F3000 series at the last gasp for Hoshino Racing.

It was in sports car racing that Toshio found his greatest success. After driving Toyotas, he joined Nissan to team up with Kazuyoshi Hoshino, the pair becoming a formidable combination not only at home but also on the international stage, their proudest triumph coming in the 1992 Daytona 24 Hours when, with Masahiro Hasemi, they became the first all-Japanese crew to win a major race.

The veteran has recently been a regular in the All-Japan GT championship, racing a Toyota Supra, and a member of the driver line-up for the Japanese giant's Le Mans assault. After finishing ninth in the 1998 Le Mans 24 Hours with the Toyota GT-One, Toshio teamed up again with Ukyo Katayama and Keiichi Tsuchiya to finish a fine second a year later.

JACQUES SWATERS

A great enthusiast, Swaters made his racing debut in the 1948 Spa 24 Hours in an MG shared with his friend Paul Frère. In 1950, he was one of the founders of Ecurie Belgique and initially handled a Veritas, but when Pilette was injured in the team's Talbot at the 1951 Dutch GP, Jacques stepped in to take his place. For 1952, the team bought a Ferrari T500, which was mainly raced by de Tornaco, but Swaters drove it in two Grands Prix the following year and also won the AVUS F2 race. For 1954, Jacques raced the Ferrari fitted with a 625 engine, but found greater success in sports car events with the team's recently acquired Jaguar C-Type, taking fourth at Le Mans and third in the Reims 12 Hours with Laurent. Swaters then concentrated on sports cars, taking the team's D-Type to third place at Le Mans with Claes in 1955, and finishing fourth in 1956 with the same car, partnered by Rousselle. By this time he was busy with the management of Ecurie Francorchamps, and his thriving Ferrari concession, and retired from racing after a final appearance in the Sarthe classic in 1957.

SUZUKI, Toshio (J) b 10/3/1955, Saitama

	1993	Championship position: Unplaced						
	Race	Circuit	No	Entrant	Tyres	Car/Engine	Comment	Q Pos/Entries
12	JAPANESE GP	Suzuka	19	Larrousse F1	G	3.5 Larrousse LH93-Lamborghini V12	*spin/2 laps behind*	23/24
14	AUSTRALIAN GP	Adelaide	19	Larrousse F1	G	3.5 Larrousse LH93-Lamborghini V12	*5 laps behind*	24/24

GP Starts:2 GP Wins: 0 Pole positions: 0 Fastest laps: 0 Points: 0

SWATERS, Jacques (B) b 30/10/1926, Woluwe-St-Lambert, Brussels

	1951	Championship position: Unplaced						
	Race	Circuit	No	Entrant	Tyres	Car/Engine	Comment	Q Pos/Entries
10	GERMAN GP	Nürburgring	93	Ecurie Belgique	D	4.5 Lago-Talbot T26C 6	*2 laps behind*	22/23
ret	ITALIAN GP	Monza	28	Ecurie Belgique	D	4.5 Lago-Talbot T26C 6	*overheating*	22/22
	1953	Championship position: Unplaced						
dns	BELGIAN GP	Spa	42	Ecurie Francorchamps	E	2.0 Ferrari 500 4	*practised only*	– / –
7	GERMAN GP	Nürburgring	18	Ecurie Francorchamps	E	2.0 Ferrari 500 4	*1 lap behind*	19/35
ret	SWISS GP	Bremgarten	2	Ecurie Francorchamps	E	2.0 Ferrari 500 4	*crashed*	13/23
	1954	Championship position: Unplaced						
ret	BELGIAN GP	Spa	2	Ecurie Francorchamps	E	2.5 Ferrari 500/625 4	*engine*	14/15
8	SWISS GP	Bremgarten	2	Ecurie Francorchamps	E	2.5 Ferrari 500/625 4	*8 laps behind*	16/16
ret	SPANISH GP	Pedralbes	30	Ecurie Francorchamps	E	2.5 Ferrari 500/625 4	*engine*	19/22

GP Starts: 7 GP Wins: 0 Pole positions: 0 Fastest laps: 0 Points: 0

TORANOSUKE TAKAGI

A protégé of Satoru Nakajima, Takagi has an apt forename since, in part, it means 'tiger' in Japanese, which fits this aggressive hard-charger's racing style. Conversely, off the track he is low-key, and is of a retiring and shy disposition.

After a brilliant karting career and a season in Formula Toyota, Takagi was picked by TOM'S to succeed Jacques Villeneuve in their F3 squad when he was aged just 18 back in 1993. He caught the eye of Nakajima, who gave him a chance to race in his F3000 team late the following year.

Three seasons were then spent in Formula Nippon, where he was a regular top-six runner and an occasional winner. The 1997 campaign also saw the Japanese driver clock up over 2000 km of testing in preparation for his inclusion in the Tyrrell line-up the following year.

Unfortunately he stepped into a team that was going through the motions, having been purchased by British American Racing. However, the year gave him a useful opportunity to learn the circuits and provided a good platform to build on when he took his sponsorship to Arrows for 1999. As at Tyrrell, Takagi impressed with a fair turn of speed but as often as not was found wanting when it came to putting everything together in the races.

One day, surely, a superstar driver will emerge from the Far East. On the basis, admittedly, of two years spent in poor cars, Takagi appears to be just the latest in a long line of Japanese hopefuls, and it seems that he will be returning to Formula Nippon with the Nakajima team in 2000.

TAKAGI, Toranosuke (J) b 12/2/1972, Shizouka

	1998			Championship position: Unplaced				
ret	AUSTRALIAN GP	Melbourne	21	Tyrrell Ford	G	3.0 Tyrrell 026- Ford Zetec-R V10	collision on first lap	13/22
ret	BRAZILIAN GP	Interlagos	21	Tyrrell Ford	G	3.0 Tyrrell 026- Ford Zetec-R V10	engine	17/22
12	ARGENTINE GP	Buenos Aires	21	Tyrrell Ford	G	3.0 Tyrrell 026- Ford Zetec-R V10	2 laps behind	13/22
ret	SAN MARINO GP	Imola	21	Tyrrell Ford	G	3.0 Tyrrell 026- Ford Zetec-R V10	engine	15/22
13	SPANISH GP	Barcelona	21	Tyrrell Ford	G	3.0 Tyrrell 026- Ford Zetec-R V10	2 laps behind	21/22
11	MONACO GP	Monte Carlo	21	Tyrrell Ford	G	3.0 Tyrrell 026- Ford Zetec-R V10	2 laps behind	20/22
ret	CANADIAN GP	Montreal	21	Tyrrell Ford	G	3.0 Tyrrell 026- Ford Zetec-R V10	transmission	16/22
ret	FRENCH GP	Magny Cours	21	Tyrrell Ford	G	3.0 Tyrrell 026- Ford Zetec-R V10	engine	20/22
9	BRITISH GP	Silverstone	21	Tyrrell Ford	G	3.0 Tyrrell 026- Ford Zetec-R V10	4 laps behind	19/22
ret	AUSTRIAN GP	A1-Ring	21	Tyrrell Ford	G	3.0 Tyrrell 026- Ford Zetec-R V10	spun off on first corner	20/22
13	GERMAN GP	Hockenheim	21	Tyrrell Ford	G	3.0 Tyrrell 026- Ford Zetec-R V10	1 lap behind	15/22
14	HUNGARIAN GP	Hungaroring	21	Tyrrell Ford	G	3.0 Tyrrell 026- Ford Zetec-R V10	3 laps behind	18/22
ret	BELGIAN GP	Spa	21	Tyrrell Ford	G	3.0 Tyrrell 026- Ford Zetec-R V10	spun off	19/22
9	ITALIAN GP	Monza	21	Tyrrell Ford	G	3.0 Tyrrell 026- Ford Zetec-R V10	1 lap behind	19/22
16	LUXEMBOURG GP	Nürburgring	21	Tyrrell Ford	G	3.0 Tyrrell 026- Ford Zetec-R V10	3 laps behind	19/22
ret	JAPANESE GP	Suzuka	21	Tyrrell Ford	G	3.0 Tyrrell 026- Ford Zetec-R V10	collision with Tuero	17/22
	1999			Championship position: Unplaced				
7	AUSTRALIAN GP	Melbourne	15	Arrows	B	3.0 Arrows A20-V10		17/22
8	BRAZILIAN GP	Interlagos	15	Arrows	B	3.0 Arrows A20-V10	3 laps behind	19/22
ret	SAN MARINO GP	Imola	15	Arrows	B	3.0 Arrows A20-V10	fuel pressure	20/22
ret	MONACO GP	Monte Carlo	15	Arrows	B	3.0 Arrows A20-V10	engine	19/22
12	SPANISH GP	Barcelona	15	Arrows	B	3.0 Arrows A20-V10	3 laps behind	20/22
ret	CANADIAN GP	Montreal	15	Arrows	B	3.0 Arrows A20-V10	transmission	19/22
11/dsq	*FRENCH GP	Magny Cours	15	Arrows	B	3.0 Arrows A20-V10	*used illegal tyres	22/22
16	BRITISH GP	Silverstone	15	Arrows	B	3.0 Arrows A20-V10	2 laps behind	19/22
ret	AUSTRIAN GP	A1-Ring	15	Arrows	B	3.0 Arrows A20-V10	engine	20/22
ret	GERMAN GP	Hockenheim	15	Arrows	B	3.0 Arrows A20-V10	engine	22/22
ret	HUNGARIAN GP	Hungaroring	15	Arrows	B	3.0 Arrows A20-V10	gearbox	21/22
ret	BELGIAN GP	Spa	15	Arrows	B	3.0 Arrows A20-V10	clutch	19/22
ret	ITALIAN GP	Monza	15	Arrows	B	3.0 Arrows A20-V10	spun off	22/22
ret	EUROPEAN GP	Nürburgring	15	Arrows	B	3.0 Arrows A20-V10	spun off	21/22
ret	MALAYSIAN GP	Sepang	15	Arrows	B	3.0 Arrows A20-V10	driveshaft	22/22
ret	JAPANESE GP	Suzuka	15	Arrows	B	3.0 Arrows A20-V10	gearbox	19/22

GP Starts:32   GP Wins: 0   Pole positions: 0   Fastest laps: 0   Points: 0

NORITAKE TAKAHARA

Though not as fast a driver in the seventies as his rivals, Masahiro Hasemi and Kazuyoshi Hoshino, Takahara nevertheless got the results that mattered, winning the Japanese F2 title and the Grand Champion sports car series – for the third time – in 1976.

He began racing in 1969 in a Honda S800 coupé, and was a successful March driver in Japan in the early seventies. In 1973 he appeared very briefly in European Formula 2 with a GRD and the following season saw him race a works March 741 in the International Trophy, where he drove steadily and sensibly into 11th place. His ninth-place finish in a rented Surtees at Fuji in 1976 earned him the distinction of being the first Japanese driver to finish a World Championship Grand Prix.

Much to the chagrin of Hasemi, Takahara took over his seat in the Kojima team in 1977, racing in that year's Grand Prix. He was a leading contender in the Japanese Formula 2 series for the rest of the decade, driving Nova, Martini and March chassis, and like his aforementioned rivals continued to race, though much less regularly, throughout the eighties.

KUNIMITSU TAKAHASHI

Takahashi began his career on two wheels as a motor cycle racer, gaining the distinction of being the first Japanese rider to win a World Championship Grand Prix on a 250 cc Honda in 1961, when aged just 21. A serious accident in 1962 during the Isle of Man TT races halted his progress and he eventually switched to four wheels.

A regular competitor in the Japanese sports car series in the 1970s, he raced the old Tyrrell that had been used by Hoshino the previous year in the 1977 Japanese GP and took a distant ninth place, though satisfyingly he was ahead of the Kojima driven by Hoshino.

He subsequently joined the Kojima team for the domestic Formula 2 series and later also ran a Toleman TG280 with backing from Yokohama tyres.

Takahashi was Japanese sports car champion four times in the eighties: 1985 and '86 (with Kenji Takahashi), 1987 (with Kenneth Acheson) and 1989 (with Stanley Dickens).

He subsequently competed regularly in the Japanese F3000 championship and in recent years has formed his own GT team to successfully race a Honda NSX GT2 in the All-Japan GT championship.

TAKAHARA, Noritake (J) b 6/6/1951, Tokyo

	1976	Championship position: Unplaced						
	Race	Circuit	No	Entrant	Tyres	Car/Engine	Comment	Q Pos/Entries
9	JAPANESE GP	Mount Fuji	18	Team Surtees	G	3.0 Surtees TS19-Cosworth V8	3 laps behind	24/27
	1977	Championship position: Unplaced						
ret	JAPANESE GP	Mount Fuji	51	Kojima Engineering	B	3.0 Kojima KE009-Cosworth V8	crash-avoiding Andretti's wheel	19/23

GP Starts: 2   GP Wins: 0   Pole positions: 0   Fastest laps: 0   Points: 0

TAKAHASHI, Kunimitsu (J) b 29/1/1940, Tokyo

	1977	Championship position: Unplaced						
	Race	Circuit	No	Entrant	Tyres	Car/Engine	Comment	Q Pos/Entries
9	JAPANESE GP	Mount Fuji	50	Meiritsu Racing Team	D	3.0 Tyrrell 007-Cosworth V8	2 laps behind	22/23

GP Starts: 1   GP Wins: 0   Pole positions: 0   Fastest laps: 0   Points: 0

PATRICK TAMBAY

Easy-going and impeccably mannered, the general consensus is that Patrick was just too nice a guy to succeed in the cut-throat world of Grand Prix racing. Certainly the cosmopolitan Frenchman had a lot of talent, but maybe he lacked the single-minded determination which is a crucial part of any true champion's armoury.

Patrick's career got off to the brightest of starts when he won the Pilote Elf scheme, which was the passport to Formule Renault in 1973. Finishing runner-up in the series, he leap-frogged straight into the European F2 championship with the Elf team for 1974 and won a round at Nogaro to cap a consistent first season at this level. A seat in the Elf-backed works March team the following year should have brought Tambay more success than a singleton victory. Although he scored four second places to take the runner-up position in the series, worryingly he was involved in a series of silly accidents. Competing in the series with Elf backing for a third year in 1976 but this time running a Martini chassis, he once again scored just a single victory – remarkably, like his two previous wins, it came at Nogaro – but finishing third in the championship was regarded as a failure by the French oil company, who dropped him in favour of Didier Pironi.

Tambay's career was in limbo at the start of 1977 until he was offered the Carl Haas/Jim Hall Can-Am car in place of the badly injured Brian Redman. Though the opposition was in the main modest, he made the most of the opportunity and won six of the seven rounds in which he competed to take the championship easily. His luck had turned for the better for, after a fiasco at Dijon where he was dumped into a Surtees at short notice in a desperate attempt to get him into the race, he finally made his Grand Prix debut in Teddy Yip's Ensign at Silverstone. Given the previous poor reliability record of the N177, the inexperienced Tambay did well to score points in three races, and even a massive practice crash at Monza failed to dent the Frenchman's new-found confidence.

Joining the McLaren team in 1978 should have seen Patrick make the big breakthrough, but unfortunately their star was temporarily on the wane, and although he took five points-scoring finishes that year his second season was something of a disaster. Failing to qualify at both Zolder and Monaco was the nadir of a year in which McLaren plumbed the depths. So in 1980 he was back across 'the pond', making hay in Can-Am once more and taking a second title in the Carl Haas Lola T530.

Teddy Yip still had faith in the Frenchman and signed him for his Theodore F1 outfit for 1981. A sixth place in the US GP first time out was way beyond the little team's expectations, but Patrick performed so well in the car subsequently that he was an obvious candidate to replace Jean-Pierre Jabouille when he decided to retire from Ligier in mid-season. However, Tambay's short stay with the French team was a desperately unhappy one, ending in a string of accidents which could have beached his Grand Prix career for good.

In motor racing one man's misfortune is another's opportunity, however, and in the saddest of circumstances Patrick was brought into the Ferrari line-up in place of the late Gilles Villeneuve. He soon found his feet and after yet another dreadful setback for the team at Hockenheim, when Pironi was injured so terribly in practice, he rose to the occasion magnificently by winning the race. For the rest of the season he carried the weight of the team manfully despite a painful back problem which caused him to miss two races. Tambay was joined by René Arnoux for 1983, and the two Frenchmen had the equipment to launch a championship assault. Although Arnoux came closer in terms of results, Patrick's all-round performances were the more convincing, and it was a major surprise when he was the one released at the end of the year to make way for Alboreto.

Moving to Renault for the 1984 season, Tambay failed to find any sort of continuity as minor problems constantly undermined his efforts. This led to an inconsistency which was scarcely helped by the introduction of the disappointing RE60 in 1985. Patrick made a solid start but the car could never be persuaded to offer a truly satisfactory level of performance on a regular basis, which must have driven both Tambay and Warwick to distraction as they gave their all. At the end of the year the Renault factory team closed their doors to lick their wounds, leaving Tambay seeking employment once more. He found it with the Haas Lola team, who were embarking on a full season with the Ford turbo engine. As an exercise in wasting money, this was as good as any, and both Tambay and Alan Jones were forced to spend the season in midfield mediocrity before the team folded.

Subsequently Patrick joined the TWR Jaguar team for the 1989 season, gaining some good placings with Jan Lammers. He has since worked in Grand Prix racing once more, both as a TV commentator and, briefly during 1994, in a PR role with the now defunct Larrousse team.

TAMBAY, Patrick (F) b 25/6/1949, Paris

	1977	Championship position: 17th=		Wins: 0	Pole positions: 0		Fastest laps: 0	Points scored: 5	
	Race	Circuit	No	Entrant	Tyres	Car/Engine		Comment	Q Pos/Entries
dnq	FRENCH GP	Dijon	18	Team Surtees	G	3.0 Surtees TS19-Cosworth V8		*Ensign not ready/1 session only*	29/30
ret	BRITISH GP	Silverstone	23	Theodore Racing Hong Kong	G	3.0 Ensign N177-Cosworth V8		*electrics*	16/36
6	GERMAN GP	Hockenheim	23	Theodore Racing Hong Kong	G	3.0 Ensign N177-Cosworth V8			11/30
ret	AUSTRIAN GP	Österreichring	23	Theodore Racing Hong Kong	G	3.0 Ensign N177-Cosworth V8		*engine*	7/30
5/ret	DUTCH GP	Zandvoort	23	Theodore Racing Hong Kong	G	3.0 Ensign N177-Cosworth V8		*out of fuel/2 laps behind*	12/34
ret	ITALIAN GP	Monza	23	Theodore Racing Hong Kong	G	3.0 Ensign N177-Cosworth V8		*engine*	21/34
dnq	US GP EAST	Watkins Glen	23	Theodore Racing Hong Kong	G	3.0 Ensign N177-Cosworth V8		*engine problems in practice*	27/30
5	CANADIAN GP	Mosport Park	23	Theodore Racing Hong Kong	G	3.0 Ensign N177-Cosworth V8			16/27
ret	JAPANESE GP	Mount Fuji	23	Theodore Racing Hong Kong	G	3.0 Ensign N177-Cosworth V8		*engine*	16/23
	1978	Championship position: 13th=		Wins: 0	Pole positions: 0		Fastest laps: 0	Points scored: 8	
6	ARGENTINE GP	Buenos Aires	8	Marlboro Team McLaren	G	3.0 McLaren M26-Cosworth V8			9/27
ret	BRAZILIAN GP	Rio	8	Marlboro Team McLaren	G	3.0 McLaren M26-Cosworth V8		*hit by Scheckter-spun off*	5/28
ret	SOUTH AFRICAN GP	Kyalami	8	Marlboro Team McLaren	G	3.0 McLaren M26-Cosworth V8		*spun-radiator & rear wing damage*	4/30
12/ret	US GP WEST	Long Beach	8	Marlboro Team McLaren	G	3.0 McLaren M26-Cosworth V8		*hit by Laffite/6 laps behind*	11/30
7	MONACO GP	Monte Carlo	8	Marlboro Team McLaren	G	3.0 McLaren M26-Cosworth V8		*1 lap behind*	11/30
ret	SPANISH GP	Jarama	8	Marlboro Team McLaren	G	3.0 McLaren M26-Cosworth V8		*spun off*	14/29
4	SWEDISH GP	Anderstorp	8	Marlboro Team McLaren	G	3.0 McLaren M26-Cosworth V8		*1 lap behind*	15/27
9	FRENCH GP	Paul Ricard	8	Marlboro Team McLaren	G	3.0 McLaren M26-Cosworth V8		*pit stop-rear end problems*	6/29
6	BRITISH GP	Brands Hatch	8	Marlboro Team McLaren	G	3.0 McLaren M26-Cosworth V8		*1 lap behind*	20/30
ret	GERMAN GP	Hockenheim	8	Marlboro Team McLaren	G	3.0 McLaren M26-Cosworth V8		*puncture-crashed*	11/30
ret	AUSTRIAN GP	Österreichring	8	Marlboro Team McLaren	G	3.0 McLaren M26-Cosworth V8		*spun off*	14/31
9	DUTCH GP	Zandvoort	8	Marlboro Team McLaren	G	3.0 McLaren M26-Cosworth V8		*1 lap behind*	14/33
5	ITALIAN GP	Monza	8	Marlboro Team McLaren	G	3.0 McLaren M26-Cosworth V8			19/32
6	US GP EAST	Watkins Glen	8	Marlboro Team McLaren	G	3.0 McLaren M26-Cosworth V8			18/27
8	CANADIAN GP	Montreal	8	Marlboro Team McLaren	G	3.0 McLaren M26-Cosworth V8			17/28
	1979	Championship position: Unplaced							
ret/dns	ARGENTINE GP	Buenos Aires	8	Marlboro Team McLaren	G	3.0 McLaren M28-Cosworth V8		*accident-first start/did not restart*	9/26
ret	BRAZILIAN GP	Interlagos	8	Marlboro Team McLaren	G	3.0 McLaren M26-Cosworth V8		*accident with Regazzoni*	18/26
dns	"	"	8	Marlboro Team McLaren	G	3.0 McLaren M28-Cosworth V8		*crashed in practice*	– / –
10	SOUTH AFRICAN GP	Kyalami	8	Marlboro Team McLaren	G	3.0 McLaren M28-Cosworth V8		*pit stop-tyres/2 laps behind*	17/26
ret	US GP WEST	Long Beach	8	Löwenbräu Team McLaren	G	3.0 McLaren M28-Cosworth V8		*accident with Lauda*	19/26
13	SPANISH GP	Jarama	8	Marlboro Team McLaren	G	3.0 McLaren M28-Cosworth V8		*pit stop-fuel/3 laps behind*	20/27
dnq	BELGIAN GP	Zolder	8	Marlboro Team McLaren	G	3.0 McLaren M28-Cosworth V8			25/28
dnq	MONACO GP	Monte Carlo	8	Marlboro Team McLaren	G	3.0 McLaren M28-Cosworth V8			22/25
10	FRENCH GP	Dijon	8	Marlboro Team McLaren	G	3.0 McLaren M28-Cosworth V8		*2 laps behind*	20/27
7/ret	BRITISH GP	Silverstone	8	Marlboro Team McLaren	G	3.0 McLaren M28-Cosworth V8		*out of fuel/2 laps behind*	18/26
ret	GERMAN GP	Hockenheim	8	Marlboro Team McLaren	G	3.0 McLaren M28-Cosworth V8		*broken rear suspension*	15/26
10	AUSTRIAN GP	Österreichring	8	Marlboro Team McLaren	G	3.0 McLaren M29-Cosworth V8		*1 lap behind*	14/26
ret	DUTCH GP	Zandvoort	8	Marlboro Team McLaren	G	3.0 McLaren M29-Cosworth V8		*engine*	14/26
ret	ITALIAN GP	Monza	8	Marlboro Team McLaren	G	3.0 McLaren M29-Cosworth V8		*engine*	14/28
ret	CANADIAN GP	Montreal	8	Marlboro Team McLaren	G	3.0 McLaren M29-Cosworth V8		*engine*	20/29
ret	US GP EAST	Watkins Glen	8	Marlboro Team McLaren	G	3.0 McLaren M29-Cosworth V8		*engine*	22/30
	1981	Championship position: 18th=		Wins: 0	Pole positions: 0		Fastest laps: 0	Points scored: 1	
6	US GP WEST	Long Beach	33	Theodore Racing Team	M	3.0 Theodore TY01-Cosworth V8		*1 lap behind*	17/29
10	BRAZILIAN GP	Rio	33	Theodore Racing Team	M	3.0 Theodore TY01-Cosworth V8		*1 lap behind*	19/30
ret	ARGENTINE GP	Buenos Aires	33	Theodore Racing Team	M	3.0 Theodore TY01-Cosworth V8		*engine-lost oil*	14/29
11	SAN MARINO GP	Imola	33	Theodore Racing Team	M	3.0 Theodore TY01-Cosworth V8		*pit stop-tyres/2 laps behind*	16/30
dnq	BELGIAN GP	Zolder	33	Theodore Racing Team	M	3.0 Theodore TY01-Cosworth V8			28/31
7	MONACO GP	Monte Carlo	33	Theodore Racing Team	M	3.0 Theodore TY01-Cosworth V8		*4 laps behind*	16/31
13	SPANISH GP	Jarama	33	Theodore Racing Team	M	3.0 Theodore TY01-Cosworth V8		*2 laps behind*	16/30
ret	FRENCH GP	Dijon	25	Equipe Talbot Gitanes	M	3.0 Ligier JS17-Matra V12		*seized rear wheel bearing*	16/29
ret	BRITISH GP	Silverstone	25	Equipe Talbot Gitanes	M	3.0 Ligier JS17-Matra V12		*ignition*	15/30
ret	GERMAN GP	Hockenheim	25	Equipe Talbot Gitanes	M	3.0 Ligier JS17-Matra V12		*rear wheel bearing*	11/30

Wearing Gilles Villeneuve's number 27, Patrick Tambay took a highly emotional win in the 1983 San Marino Grand Prix for Ferrari.

TAMBAY

Pos	Race	Circuit	No	Team	Tyre	Engine	Notes	Result
ret	AUSTRIAN GP	Österreichring	25	Equipe Talbot Gitanes	M	3.0 Ligier JS17-Matra V12	engine	17/28
ret	DUTCH GP	Zandvoort	25	Equipe Talbot Gitanes	M	3.0 Ligier JS17-Matra V12	accident with Pironi	11/30
ret	ITALIAN GP	Monza	25	Equipe Talbot Gitanes	M	3.0 Ligier JS17-Matra V12	puncture	15/30
ret	CANADIAN GP	Montreal	25	Equipe Talbot Gitanes	M	3.0 Ligier JS17-Matra V12	spun off	17/30
ret	CAESARS PALACE GP	Las Vegas	25	Equipe Talbot Gitanes	M	3.0 Ligier JS17-Matra V12	crashed	7/30

1982 Championship position: 7th Wins: 1 Pole positions: 0 Fastest laps: 0 Points scored: 25

Pos	Race	Circuit	No	Team	Tyre	Engine	Notes	Result
8	DUTCH GP	Zandvoort	27	Scuderia Ferrari SpA SEFAC	G	1.5 t/c Ferrari 126C2 V6	tyre problems/1 lap behind	6/31
3	BRITISH GP	Brands Hatch	27	Scuderia Ferrari SpA SEFAC	G	1.5 t/c Ferrari 126C2 V6		13/30
4	FRENCH GP	Paul Ricard	27	Scuderia Ferrari SpA SEFAC	G	1.5 t/c Ferrari 126C2 V6		5/30
1	GERMAN GP	Hockenheim	27	Scuderia Ferrari SpA SEFAC	G	1.5 t/c Ferrari 126C2 V6		5/30
4	AUSTRIAN GP	Österreichring	27	Scuderia Ferrari SpA SEFAC	G	1.5 t/c Ferrari 126C2 V6	pit stop-tyre/1 lap behind	4/29
dns	SWISS GP	Dijon	27	Scuderia Ferrari SpA SEFAC	G	1.5 t/c Ferrari 126C2 V6	w/drawn-Sun a.m.-bad back	(10)/29
2	ITALIAN GP	Monza	27	Scuderia Ferrari SpA SEFAC	G	1.5 t/c Ferrari 126C2 V6		3/30
dns	CAESARS PALACE GP	Las Vegas	27	Scuderia Ferrari SpA SEFAC	G	1.5 t/c Ferrari 126C2 V6	w/drawn, Sun a.m.-bad back	(8)/30

1983 Championship position: 4th Wins: 1 Pole positions: 4 Fastest laps: 1 Points scored: 40

Pos	Race	Circuit	No	Team	Tyre	Engine	Notes	Result
5	BRAZILIAN GP	Rio	27	Scuderia Ferrari SpA SEFAC	G	1.5 t/c Ferrari 126C2/B V6		3/27
ret	US GP WEST	Long Beach	27	Scuderia Ferrari SpA SEFAC	G	1.5 t/c Ferrari 126C2/B V6	accident with Rosberg	1/28
4	FRENCH GP	Paul Ricard	27	Scuderia Ferrari SpA SEFAC	G	1.5 t/c Ferrari 126C2/B V6	pit stop-tyres	11/29
1	SAN MARINO GP	Imola	27	Scuderia Ferrari SpA SEFAC	G	1.5 t/c Ferrari 126C2/B V6		3/28
4	MONACO GP	Monte Carlo	27	Scuderia Ferrari SpA SEFAC	G	1.5 t/c Ferrari 126C2/B V6		4/28
2	BELGIAN GP	Spa	27	Scuderia Ferrari SpA SEFAC	G	1.5 t/c Ferrari 126C2/B V6		2/28
ret	US GP (DETROIT)	Detroit	27	Scuderia Ferrari SpA SEFAC	G	1.5 t/c Ferrari 126C2/B V6	stalled at start	3/27
3	CANADIAN GP	Montreal	27	Scuderia Ferrari SpA SEFAC	G	1.5 t/c Ferrari 126C2/B V6	FL	4/28
3	BRITISH GP	Silverstone	27	Scuderia Ferrari SpA SEFAC	G	1.5 t/c Ferrari 126C3 V6		2/29
ret	GERMAN GP	Hockenheim	27	Scuderia Ferrari SpA SEFAC	G	1.5 t/c Ferrari 126C3 V6	engine	1/29
ret	AUSTRIAN GP	Österreichring	27	Scuderia Ferrari SpA SEFAC	G	1.5 t/c Ferrari 126C3 V6	engine	1/29
2	DUTCH GP	Zandvoort	27	Scuderia Ferrari SpA SEFAC	G	1.5 t/c Ferrari 126C3 V6		2/29
4	ITALIAN GP	Monza	27	Scuderia Ferrari SpA SEFAC	G	1.5 t/c Ferrari 126C3 V6		2/29
ret	EUROPEAN GP	Brands Hatch	27	Scuderia Ferrari SpA SEFAC	G	1.5 t/c Ferrari 126C3 V6	fluid leak, lost brakes-accident	6/29
ret	SOUTH AFRICAN GP	Kyalami	27	Scuderia Ferrari SpA SEFAC	G	1.5 t/c Ferrari 126C3 V6	turbo	1/26

1984 Championship position: 11th Wins: 0 Pole positions: 1 Fastest laps: 0 Points scored: 11

Pos	Race	Circuit	No	Team	Tyre	Engine	Notes	Result
5*/ret	BRAZILIAN GP	Rio	15	Equipe Renault Elf	M	1.5 t/c Renault RE50 V6	out of fuel/*5th place car dsq	8/27
ret	SOUTH AFRICAN GP	Kyalami	15	Equipe Renault Elf	M	1.5 t/c Renault RE50 V6	fuel metering unit/FL	4/27
7*	BELGIAN GP	Zolder	15	Equipe Renault Elf	M	1.5 t/c Renault RE50 V6	spin/*6th place car dsq/-2 laps	12/27
ret	SAN MARINO GP	Imola	15	Equipe Renault Elf	M	1.5 t/c Renault RE50 V6	hit by Cheever	14/28
2	FRENCH GP	Dijon	15	Equipe Renault Elf	M	1.5 t/c Renault RE50 V6		1/27
ret	MONACO GP	Monte Carlo	15	Equipe Renault Elf	M	1.5 t/c Renault RE50 V6	collision with Warwick-hurt leg	6/27
dns	CANADIAN GP	Montreal	15	Equipe Renault Elf	M	1.5 t/c Renault RE50 V6	unfit-w/drew after untimed practice	-/-
ret	US GP (DETROIT)	Detroit	15	Equipe Renault Elf	M	1.5 t/c Renault RE50 V6	transmission	9/27
ret	US GP (DALLAS)	Dallas	15	Equipe Renault Elf	M	1.5 t/c Renault RE50 V6	hit wall	10/27
8/ret	BRITISH GP	Brands Hatch	15	Equipe Renault Elf	M	1.5 t/c Renault RE50 V6	turbo	10/27
5	GERMAN GP	Hockenheim	15	Equipe Renault Elf	M	1.5 t/c Renault RE50 V6		4/27
ret	AUSTRIAN GP	Österreichring	15	Equipe Renault Elf	M	1.5 t/c Renault RE50 V6	engine	5/28
6	DUTCH GP	Zandvoort	15	Equipe Renault Elf	M	1.5 t/c Renault RE50 V6	1 lap behind	5/27
ret	ITALIAN GP	Monza	15	Equipe Renault Elf	M	1.5 t/c Renault RE50 V6	throttle cable	8/27
ret	EUROPEAN GP	Nürburgring	15	Equipe Renault Elf	M	1.5 t/c Renault RE50 V6	fuel feed	3/26
7	PORTUGUESE GP	Estoril	15	Equipe Renault Elf	M	1.5 t/c Renault RE50 V6	1 lap behind	7/27

1985 Championship position: 11th= Wins: 0 Pole positions: 0 Fastest laps: 0 Points scored: 11

Pos	Race	Circuit	No	Team	Tyre	Engine	Notes	Result
5	BRAZILIAN GP	Rio	15	Equipe Renault Elf	G	1.5 t/c Renault RE60 V6	2 laps behind	11/25
3	PORTUGUESE GP	Estoril	15	Equipe Renault Elf	G	1.5 t/c Renault RE60 V6	1 lap behind	12/26
3	SAN MARINO GP	Imola	15	Equipe Renault Elf	G	1.5 t/c Renault RE60 V6	1 lap behind	11/26
ret	MONACO GP	Monte Carlo	15	Equipe Renault Elf	G	1.5 t/c Renault RE60 V6	hit Johansson on lap 1	17/26
7	CANADIAN GP	Montreal	15	Equipe Renault Elf	G	1.5 t/c Renault RE60 V6	1 lap behind	10/25
ret	US GP (DETROIT)	Detroit	15	Equipe Renault Elf	G	1.5 t/c Renault RE60 V6	spun off	15/25
6	FRENCH GP	Paul Ricard	15	Equipe Renault Elf	G	1.5 t/c Renault RE60B V6		10/26
ret	BRITISH GP	Silverstone	15	Equipe Renault Elf	G	1.5 t/c Renault RE60B V6	spun-hit by Johansson	13/26
ret	GERMAN GP	Nürburgring	15	Equipe Renault Elf	G	1.5 t/c Renault RE60B V6	spun off	16/27
10/ret	AUSTRIAN GP	Österreichring	15	Equipe Renault Elf	G	1.5 t/c Renault RE60B V6	engine/6 laps behind	8/27
ret	DUTCH GP	Zandvoort	15	Equipe Renault Elf	G	1.5 t/c Renault RE60B V6	started from pit lane/transmission	6/27
7	ITALIAN GP	Monza	15	Equipe Renault Elf	G	1.5 t/c Renault RE60B V6	1 lap behind	8/26
ret	BELGIAN GP	Spa	15	Equipe Renault Elf	G	1.5 t/c Renault RE60B V6	gearbox	13/24
12	EUROPEAN GP	Brands Hatch	15	Equipe Renault Elf	G	1.5 t/c Renault RE60B V6	3 laps behind	17/27
ret	AUSTRALIAN GP	Adelaide	15	Equipe Renault Elf	G	1.5 t/c Renault RE60B V6	transmission	8/25

1986 Championship position: 15th= Wins: 0 Pole positions: 0 Fastest laps: 0 Points scored: 2

Pos	Race	Circuit	No	Team	Tyre	Engine	Notes	Result
ret	BRAZILIAN GP	Rio	16	Team Haas (USA) Ltd	G	1.5 t/c Lola THL1-Hart 4	flat battery	13/25
8	SPANISH GP	Jerez	16	Team Haas (USA) Ltd	G	1.5 t/c Lola THL1-Hart 4	6 laps behind	18/25
ret	SAN MARINO GP	Imola	16	Team Haas (USA) Ltd	G	1.5 t/c Lola THL1-Hart 4	engine	11/26
ret	MONACO GP	Monte Carlo	16	Team Haas (USA) Ltd	G	1.5 t/c Lola THL2-Cosworth V6	accident with Brundle	8/26
ret	BELGIAN GP	Spa	16	Team Haas (USA) Ltd	G	1.5 t/c Lola THL2-Cosworth V6	accident with Fabi	10/25
dns	CANADIAN GP	Montreal	16	Team Haas (USA) Ltd	G	1.5 t/c Lola THL2-Cosworth V6	accident-Sun a.m.warm-up	(14)/25
ret	FRENCH GP	Paul Ricard	16	Team Haas (USA) Ltd	G	1.5 t/c Lola THL2-Cosworth V6	brakes	13/26
ret	BRITISH GP	Brands Hatch	16	Team Haas (USA) Ltd	G	1.5 t/c Lola THL2-Cosworth V6	gearbox	17/26
8	GERMAN GP	Hockenheim	16	Team Haas (USA) Ltd	G	1.5 t/c Lola THL2-Cosworth V6	1 lap behind	13/26
7	HUNGARIAN GP	Hungaroring	16	Team Haas (USA) Ltd	G	1.5 t/c Lola THL2-Cosworth V6	2 laps behind	6/26
5	AUSTRIAN GP	Österreichring	16	Team Haas (USA) Ltd	G	1.5 t/c Lola THL2-Cosworth V6	2 laps behind	13/26
ret	ITALIAN GP	Monza	16	Team Haas (USA) Ltd	G	1.5 t/c Lola THL2-Cosworth V6	accident with Patrese	15/27
nc	PORTUGUESE GP	Estoril	16	Team Haas (USA) Ltd	G	1.5 t/c Lola THL2-Cosworth V6	3 pit stops-brakes/-8 laps	14/27
ret	MEXICAN GP	Mexico City	16	Team Haas (USA) Ltd	G	1.5 t/c Lola THL2-Cosworth V6	hit by Arnoux on lap 1	8/26
nc	AUSTRALIAN GP	Adelaide	16	Team Haas (USA) Ltd	G	1.5 t/c Lola THL2-Cosworth V6	hit Dumfries/gearbox/-12 laps	17/26

GP Starts: 113 (114) GP Wins: 2 Pole positions: 5 Fastest laps: 2 Points: 103

GABRIELE TARQUINI

This pleasant and underrated Italian caused quite a stir back in 1985 when, as reigning world karting champion and with almost no Formula 3 experience to speak of, he became an instant front-runner in F3000. He finished his first year a very creditable sixth in the standings, but his 1986 season was less startling as the newly formed Coloni team struggled to find its feet, though he did score third places at Enna and the Österreichring.

Joining Lamberto Leoni's FIRST racing ream for 1987, Gabriele was once again a 'nearly-man' in terms of ultimate success, but he made his Formula 1 debut for Osella at Imola, and then rejoined Enzo Coloni for a testing first Grand Prix season in 1988.

With poor Philippe Streiff gravely injured in a Brazilian testing accident, Tarquini came into the AGS line-up for the 1989 San Marino GP, soon gaining a priceless point for the little team in Mexico. Over the next three seasons, the ever-cheerful Italian plugged away against insurmountable odds as the debt-ridden team headed towards extinction, but before the end came he had been allowed to sign for Fondmetal (formerly Osella). With Ford HB engines at his disposal for 1992, Tarquini had easily his best opportunity to shine but the team was hampered by a lack of adequate funding – the Italian was under strict instructions to conserve the car at all costs – and any promise it had possessed soon evaporated, resulting in the outfit's withdrawal before the season was out.

Tarquini then joined the horde of famous names in the Italian touring car championship in 1993, taking third place in the series with a works Alfa Romeo. He was chosen to spearhead the Italian manufacturer's move into the BTCC series in 1994 and enjoyed a highly successful season, winning eight of the 21 rounds to take the championship crown. Gabriele also gained well-earned plaudits from all for his off-track demeanour and was a credit to the series and his sport.

It was going to be tough to follow this success in 1995, and so it proved as Alfa lost their advantage. Gabriele was initially racing in Italy, but the company's sudden decision to withdraw from their domestic championship saw him back in Britain for the balance of the year. The sudden transition from being the dominant force to midfield strugglers was quite a shock but Tarquini always gave of his best.

Partly due to his links with Fondmetal, he had been an occasional test driver for Tyrrell, and was drafted in to deputise for the indisposed Katayama at the Nürburgring, though his one-off F1 return was not a particularly distinguished one.

In 1996 Gabriele stepped up to the high-profile International Touring Car series as a works driver alongside the experienced Larini and Nannini in the Alfa 155 V6 TI and scored a big win at Silverstone, but endured a thin time otherwise.

So it was back to the Super Touring category in 1997, the Italian switching his allegiance to Honda. Although Gabriele's three seasons driving the Accord in both the BTCC and the German Super Touring series have produced no more than the occasional win, the driver himself is still regarded as one of the class's most accomplished performers.

TARQUINI, Gabriele (I) b 2/3/1962, Giulianova Lido, nr Pescara, Teramo

	1987			Championship position: Unplaced				
	Race	Circuit	No	Entrant	Tyres	Car/Engine	Comment	Q Pos/Entries
ret	SAN MARINO GP	Imola	22	Osella Squadra Corse	G	1.5 t/c Osella FA1G-Alfa Romeo V8	gearbox	27/27
	1988			Championship position: Unplaced				
ret	BRAZILIAN GP	Rio	31	Coloni SpA	G	3.5 Coloni FC188-Cosworth V8	rear upright bearing	25/31
ret	SAN MARINO GP	Imola	31	Coloni SpA	G	3.5 Coloni FC188-Cosworth V8	throttle cable	17/31
ret	MONACO GP	Monte Carlo	31	Coloni SpA	G	3.5 Coloni FC188-Cosworth V8	suspension	24/30
14	MEXICAN GP	Mexico City	31	Coloni SpA	G	3.5 Coloni FC188-Cosworth V8	5 laps behind	21/30
8	CANADIAN GP	Montreal	31	Coloni SpA	G	3.5 Coloni FC188-Cosworth V8	2 laps behind	26/31
dnpq	US GP (DETROIT)	Detroit	31	Coloni SpA	G	3.5 Coloni FC188-Cosworth V8		31/31

dnpq	FRENCH GP	Paul Ricard	31	Coloni SpA	G	3.5 Coloni FC188-Cosworth V8		31/31
dnpq	BRITISH GP	Silverstone	31	Coloni SpA	G	3.5 Coloni FC188-Cosworth V8		31/31
dnpq	GERMAN GP	Hockenheim	31	Coloni SpA	G	3.5 Coloni FC188-Cosworth V8		31/31
13	HUNGARIAN GP	Hungaroring	31	Coloni SpA	G	3.5 Coloni FC188-Cosworth V8	rear suspension/-5 laps	22/31
nc	BELGIAN GP	Spa	31	Coloni SpA	G	3.5 Coloni FC188-Cosworth V8	steering rack problem/-7 laps	22/31
dnq	ITALIAN GP	Monza	31	Coloni SpA	G	3.5 Coloni FC188-Cosworth V8		29/31
11	PORTUGUESE GP	Estoril	31	Coloni SpA	G	3.5 Coloni FC188B-Cosworth V8	5 laps behind	26/31
dnpq	SPANISH GP	Jerez	31	Coloni SpA	G	3.5 Coloni FC188B-Cosworth V8		31/31
dnpq	JAPANESE GP	Suzuka	31	Coloni SpA	G	3.5 Coloni FC188B-Cosworth V8		31/31
dnq	AUSTRALIAN GP	Adelaide	31	Coloni SpA	G	3.5 Coloni FC188B-Cosworth V8		27/31
1989		Championship position: 26th=	Wins: 0	Pole positions: 0		Fastest laps: 0 Points scored: 1		
8	SAN MARINO GP	Imola	40	Automobiles Gonfaronaise Sportive	G	3.5 AGS JH23B-Cosworth V8	1 lap behind	18/39
ret	MONACO GP	Monte Carlo	40	Automobiles Gonfaronaise Sportive	G	3.5 AGS JH23B-Cosworth V8	electrics	13/38
6	MEXICAN GP	Mexico City	40	Automobiles Gonfaronaise Sportive	G	3.5 AGS JH23B-Cosworth V8	1 lap behind	17/39
7/ret	US GP (PHOENIX)	Phoenix	40	Automobiles Gonfaronaise Sportive	G	3.5 AGS JH23B-Cosworth V8	engine last lap/2 laps behind	24/39
ret	CANADIAN GP	Montreal	40	Automobiles Gonfaronaise Sportive	G	3.5 AGS JH23B-Cosworth V8	collision with Arnoux	25/39
ret	FRENCH GP	Paul Ricard	40	Automobiles Gonfaronaise Sportive	G	3.5 AGS JH23B-Cosworth V8	engine	21/39
dns	"	" "	40	Automobiles Gonfaronaise Sportive	G	3.5 AGS JH24-Cosworth V8	practice only-new car	– / –
dnq	BRITISH GP	Silverstone	40	Automobiles Gonfaronaise Sportive	G	3.5 AGS JH24-Cosworth V8		29/39
dnpq	GERMAN GP	Hockenheim	40	Automobiles Gonfaronaise Sportive	G	3.5 AGS JH23B-Cosworth V8		33/39
dnpq	HUNGARIAN GP	Hungaroring	40	Automobiles Gonfaronaise Sportive	G	3.5 AGS JH24-Cosworth V8		35/39
dnpq	BELGIAN GP	Spa	40	Automobiles Gonfaronaise Sportive	G	3.5 AGS JH24-Cosworth V8		– / –
dnpq	"	"	40	Automobiles Gonfaronaise Sportive	G	3.5 AGS JH23B-Cosworth V8		34/39
dnpq	ITALIAN GP	Monza	40	Automobiles Gonfaronaise Sportive	G	3.5 AGS JH24-Cosworth V8	brake problems	31/39
dnpq	PORTUGUESE GP	Estoril	40	Automobiles Gonfaronaise Sportive	G	3.5 AGS JH24-Cosworth V8		36/39
dnpq	SPANISH GP	Jerez	40	Automobiles Gonfaronaise Sportive	G	3.5 AGS JH24-Cosworth V8		30/38
dnpq	JAPANESE GP	Suzuka	40	Automobiles Gonfaronaise Sportive	G	3.5 AGS JH24-Cosworth V8		37/39
dnpq	AUSTRALIAN GP	Adelaide	40	Automobiles Gonfaronaise Sportive	G	3.5 AGS JH24-Cosworth V8		38/39
1990		Championship position: Unplaced						
dnpq	US GP (PHOENIX)	Phoenix	17	Automobiles Gonfaronaise Sportive	G	3.5 AGS JH24-Cosworth V8		31/35
dnpq	BRAZILIAN GP	Interlagos	17	Automobiles Gonfaronaise Sportive	G	3.5 AGS JH24-Cosworth V8		31/35
dnpq	SAN MARINO GP	Imola	17	Automobiles Gonfaronaise Sportive	G	3.5 AGS JH25-Cosworth V8	no time recorded	– /34
dnpq	MONACO GP	Monte Carlo	17	Automobiles Gonfaronaise Sportive	G	3.5 AGS JH25-Cosworth V8		31/35
dnpq	CANADIAN GP	Montreal	17	Automobiles Gonfaronaise Sportive	G	3.5 AGS JH25-Cosworth V8		31/35
dnpq	MEXICAN GP	Mexico City	17	Automobiles Gonfaronaise Sportive	G	3.5 AGS JH25-Cosworth V8		32/35
dnq	FRENCH GP	Paul Ricard	17	Automobiles Gonfaronaise Sportive	G	3.5 AGS JH25-Cosworth V8		28/35
ret	BRITISH GP	Silverstone	17	Automobiles Gonfaronaise Sportive	G	3.5 AGS JH25-Cosworth V8	engine	26/35
dnpq	GERMAN GP	Hockenheim	17	Automobiles Gonfaronaise Sportive	G	3.5 AGS JH25-Cosworth V8		31/35
13	HUNGARIAN GP	Hungaroring	17	Automobiles Gonfaronaise Sportive	G	3.5 AGS JH25-Cosworth V8	pit stop-tyres/3 laps behind	24/35
dnq	BELGIAN GP	Spa	17	Automobiles Gonfaronaise Sportive	G	3.5 AGS JH25-Cosworth V8		28/33
dnq	ITALIAN GP	Monza	17	Automobiles Gonfaronaise Sportive	G	3.5 AGS JH25-Cosworth V8		27/33
dnq	PORTUGUESE GP	Estoril	17	Automobiles Gonfaronaise Sportive	G	3.5 AGS JH25-Cosworth V8		29/33
ret	SPANISH GP	Jerez	17	Automobiles Gonfaronaise Sportive	G	3.5 AGS JH25-Cosworth V8	electrics	22/33
dnq	JAPANESE GP	Suzuka	17	Automobiles Gonfaronaise Sportive	G	3.5 AGS JH25-Cosworth V8		28/30
ret	AUSTRALIAN GP	Adelaide	17	Automobiles Gonfaronaise Sportive	G	3.5 AGS JH25-Cosworth V8	oil fire	26/30
1991		Championship position: Unplaced						
8	US GP (PHOENIX)	Phoenix	17	Automobiles Gonfaronaise Sportive	G	3.5 AGS JH25-Cosworth V8	pit stop-tyres/misfire/-4 laps	22/34
ret	BRAZILIAN GP	Interlagos	17	Automobiles Gonfaronaise Sportive	G	3.5 AGS JH25-Cosworth V8	spun off on first lap	24/34
dnq	SAN MARINO GP	Imola	17	Automobiles Gonfaronaise Sportive	G	3.5 AGS JH25-Cosworth V8		27/34
ret	MONACO GP	Monte Carlo	17	Automobiles Gonfaronaise Sportive	G	3.5 AGS JH25-Cosworth V8	gearbox	20/34
dnq	CANADIAN GP	Montreal	17	Automobiles Gonfaronaise Sportive	G	3.5 AGS JH25-Cosworth V8		28/34
dnq	MEXICAN GP	Mexico City	17	Automobiles Gonfaronaise Sportive	G	3.5 AGS JH25-Cosworth V8		28/34
dnq	FRENCH GP	Paul Ricard	17	Automobiles Gonfaronaise Sportive	G	3.5 AGS JH25B-Cosworth V8		29/34
dnq	BRITISH GP	Silverstone	17	Automobiles Gonfaronaise Sportive	G	3.5 AGS JH25B-Cosworth V8		30/34
dnq	GERMAN GP	Hockenheim	17	Automobiles Gonfaronaise Sportive	G	3.5 AGS JH25B-Cosworth V8		29/34
dnpq	HUNGARIAN GP	Hungaroring	17	Automobiles Gonfaronaise Sportive	G	3.5 AGS JH25B-Cosworth V8		31/34
dnpq	BELGIAN GP	Spa	17	Automobiles Gonfaronaise Sportive	G	3.5 AGS JH25B-Cosworth V8		32/34
dnpq	ITALIAN GP	Monza	17	Automobiles Gonfaronaise Sportive	G	3.5 AGS JH27-Cosworth V8		32/34
dnpq	"	"	17	Automobiles Gonfaronaise Sportive	G	3.5 AGS JH27-Cosworth V8		– / –
dnq	PORTUGUESE GP	Estoril	17	Automobiles Gonfaronaise Sportive	G	3.5 AGS JH27-Cosworth V8		28/34
12	SPANISH GP	Barcelona	14	Fondmetal F1 SpA	G	3.5 Fomet F1-Cosworth V8	2 laps behind	22/33
11	JAPANESE GP	Suzuka	14	Fondmetal F1 SpA	G	3.5 Fomet F1-Cosworth V8	3 laps behind	24/31
dnpq	AUSTRALIAN GP	Adelaide	14	Fondmetal F1 SpA	G	3.5 Fomet F1-Cosworth V8		31/32
1992		Championship position: Unplaced						
ret	SOUTH AFRICAN GP	Kyalami	15	Fondmetal F1 SpA	G	3.5 Fondmetal GR01-Ford HB V8	engine	15/30
ret	MEXICAN GP	Mexico City	15	Fondmetal F1 SpA	G	3.5 Fondmetal GR01-Ford HB V8	clutch	14/30
ret	BRAZILIAN GP	Interlagos	15	Fondmetal F1 SpA	G	3.5 Fondmetal GR01-Ford HB V8	radiator overheating	19/31
ret	SPANISH GP	Barcelona	15	Fondmetal F1 SpA	G	3.5 Fondmetal GR01-Ford HB V8	spun off	18/32
ret	SAN MARINO GP	Imola	15	Fondmetal F1 SpA	G	3.5 Fondmetal GR01-Ford HB V8	overheating	22/32
ret	MONACO GP	Monte Carlo	15	Fondmetal F1 SpA	G	3.5 Fondmetal GR01-Ford HB V8	overheating	25/32
ret	CANADIAN GP	Montreal	15	Fondmetal F1 SpA	G	3.5 Fondmetal GR02-Ford HB V8	gearbox failed at start	18/32
ret	FRENCH GP	Magny Cours	15	Fondmetal F1 SpA	G	3.5 Fondmetal GR02-Ford HB V8	throttle cable	23/30
14	BRITISH GP	Silverstone	15	Fondmetal F1 SpA	G	3.5 Fondmetal GR02-Ford HB V8	2 laps behind	15/32
ret	GERMAN GP	Hockenheim	15	Fondmetal F1 SpA	G	3.5 Fondmetal GR02-Ford HB V8	engine	19/32
ret	HUNGARIAN GP	Hungaroring	15	Fondmetal F1 SpA	G	3.5 Fondmetal GR02-Ford HB V8	collision-van de Poele-lap 1	12/31
ret	BELGIAN GP	Spa	15	Fondmetal F1 SpA	G	3.5 Fondmetal GR02-Ford HB V8	engine	11/30
ret	ITALIAN GP	Monza	15	Fondmetal F1 SpA	G	3.5 Fondmetal GR02-Ford HB V8	gearbox	20/28
1995		Championship position: Unplaced						
14	EUROPEAN GP	Nürburgring	3	Nokia Tyrrell Yamaha	G	3.0 Tyrrell 023-Yamaha V10	6 laps behind	19/24

GP Starts: 38   GP Wins: 0   Pole positions: 0   Fastest laps: 0   Points: 1

PIERO TARUFFI

Originally a successful motor cycle racer, Taruffi first tasted four-wheel competition in the 1930 Mille Miglia, and was soon showing promise with his Itala. That brought him to the attention of Ferrari, who provided him with a 2.3 Alfa Romeo to beat Biondetti in the Coppa Frigo hill-climb. He was still racing on two wheels but took second place in the 1932 Rome GP behind Fagioli in an Alfa Monza, and third in the 1933 Eifelrennen.

By 1934 he was driving works Maseratis but crashed badly at Tripoli, and in 1935 he moved to the Bugatti team, taking a third at Turin. Taruffi was still involved in motor cycling, and though he stopped racing in 1937 he continued to manage the Gilera team both before and after the war.

Between 1947 and 1949, Piero drove Dusio's Cisitalias with great success and, guesting for Alfa Romeo, he took fourth in the Monza GP in 1948. Joining Scuderia Ferrari in 1949, Taruffi took second place in the Rome GP at Caracalla with the Tipo 166. In 1950 he occasionally represented both Alfa Romeo, taking third in the Grand Prix of Nations in Geneva, and Ferrari, his third in the end-of-year Penya Rhin GP at Barcelona bringing an invitation to join the works team on a regular basis in 1951. This was the final year of Alfa's dominance, but Piero finished second in the Swiss GP and third in the non-title Bari GP at Lungomare. In sports cars he took second place in the Tour of Sicily and, sharing a 4.1-litre with Chinetti, won the Carrera Panamericana.

Taruffi enjoyed his finest year in 1952. With the Tipo 500 now the car to beat, he backed the brilliant Ascari superbly, winning the Swiss GP at Bremgarten, and with some other excellent drives finished third in the drivers' championship. In other important single-seater races, Piero won the Paris GP at Montlhéry, and was second at both Syracuse and Naples, while in the big-capacity cars he took second in Turin and won the Libre Silverstone race in Vandervell's Ferrari 'Thinwall Special'. For 1953 he joined the Lancia team, racing their sports cars without great success, though he did finish second in the Carrera Panamericana in a 3.3 Lancia. Things improved in 1954, as victories in the Targa Florio and the Tour of Sicily demonstrate, the latter success being repeated the following year, this time at the wheel of a Ferrari.

Taruffi was still an occasional Grand Prix driver who could be relied upon to do a good job, and Mercedes brought him into their team after Hans Herrmann had put himself out of action, Piero bringing the silver car to excellent finishes in his two outings. For 1956 he joined Maserati's sports car team, sharing the winning car with Moss, Schell and Behra in the Nürburgring 1000 Km, and taking second in the Targa Florio, the Circuit of Sicily and the Pescara GP. His final F1 race came in the 1957 Syracuse GP when, driving a Scuderia Centro Sud Maserati 250F, he finished fourth, despite a broken shock absorber. Soon after, and at his 13th attempt, Taruffi achieved his great ambition, by taking victory in the ill-fated Mille Miglia in a works Ferrari as a late replacement for Musso. With this, he announced his retirement from racing, and set up a racing drivers' school.

TARUFFI, Piero (I) b 12/10/1906, Albone Laziale, Rome – d 12/1/1988, Rome

	1950	Championship position: Unplaced						
	Race	Circuit	No	Entrant	Tyres	Car/Engine	Comment	Q Pos/Entries
ret	ITALIAN GP	Monza	54	Alfa Romeo SpA	P	1.5 s/c Alfa Romeo 158 8	* Fangio took over/engine	7/27
	1951	Championship position: 6th=	Wins: 0	Pole positions: 0	Fastest laps: 0	Points scored: 10		
2	SWISS GP	Bremgarten	44	Scuderia Ferrari	P	4.5 Ferrari 375F1 V12		6/21
ret	BELGIAN GP	Spa	12	Scuderia Ferrari	P	4.5 Ferrari 375F1 V12	transmission	5/13
5	GERMAN GP	Nürburgring	73	Scuderia Ferrari	P	4.5 Ferrari 375F1 V12		6/23
5	ITALIAN GP	Monza	8	Scuderia Ferrari	P	4.5 Ferrari 375F1 V12	2 laps behind	6/22
ret	SPANISH GP	Pedralbes	8	Scuderia Ferrari	P	4.5 Ferrari 375F1 V12	lost wheel	7/20
	1952	Championship position: 3rd	Wins: 1	Pole positions: 0	Fastest laps: 1	Points scored: 22		
1	SWISS GP	Bremgarten	30	Scuderia Ferrari	P	2.0 Ferrari 500 4	FL	2/21
ret	BELGIAN GP	Spa	6	Scuderia Ferrari	P	2.0 Ferrari 500 4	spun-hit by Behra	3/22
3	FRENCH GP	Rouen	12	Scuderia Ferrari	P	2.0 Ferrari 500 4	2 laps behind	3/20
2	BRITISH GP	Silverstone	17	Scuderia Ferrari	P	2.0 Ferrari 500 4	1 lap behind	3/32
4	GERMAN GP	Nürburgring	103	Scuderia Ferrari	E	2.0 Ferrari 500 4	1 lap behind	5/32
7	ITALIAN GP	Monza	14	Scuderia Ferrari	P	2.0 Ferrari 500 4	3 laps behind	6/35
	1954	Championship position: Unplaced						
6	GERMAN GP	Nürburgring	4	Scuderia Ferrari	P	2.5 Ferrari 625 4	1 lap behind	13/23
	1955	Championship position: 6th	Wins: 0	Pole positions: 0	Fastest laps: 0	Points scored: 9		
8*	MONACO GP	Monte Carlo	48	Scuderia Ferrari	E	2.5 Ferrari 555 4	* Frere took over car/-14 laps	15/22
4	BRITISH GP	Aintree	50	Daimler Benz AG	C	2.5 Mercedes Benz-W196 8	1 lap behind	5/25
2	ITALIAN GP	Monza	14	Daimler Benz AG	C	2.5 Mercedes Benz-W196 8		9/22
	1956	Championship position: Unplaced						
ret	FRENCH GP	Reims	8	Officine Alfieri Maserati	P	2.5 Maserati 250F 6	engine	16/20
ret	ITALIAN GP	Monza	16	Vandervell Products Ltd	P	2.5 Vanwall 4	suspension	4/26

GP Starts: 18   GP Wins: 1   Pole positions: 0   Fastest laps: 1   Points: 41

HENRY TAYLOR

A farmer, Taylor entered club racing in 1954 with a Cooper-Vincent, taking the Autosport championship the following year. He added to his experience racing a Jaguar D-Type, taking third in the 1957 Belgian sports car GP, but it was 1958 before he began to make his mark in single-seaters, winning the GP de Paris in a Cooper. He continued to make good progress in Formula 2, taking a superb second place at the 1959 Auvergne Trophy, ahead of McLaren's works car, and second in class at the British GP at Aintree.

For 1960 Taylor signed to race Ken Tyrrell's Cooper-Austin in Formula Junior, winning the prestigious Monaco race, and made his debut in the Yeoman Credit Cooper, scoring a morale-boosting fourth place at Reims for a team still reeling from Bristow's fatal accident at Spa. He continued under the UDT Laystall banner in 1961, racing the team's Lotus 18/21 F1 car as well as a Lotus 19 in sports car events. Taylor gained a few minor placings outside Grands Prix, until a nasty crash in the British GP left him injured and trapped in his car. He recovered to compete again at the ill-fated Monza race when, perhaps with the tragic events of the day in mind, he decided to retire from circuit racing to concentrate on farming.

Taylor was soon back in action, rallying for Ford, and became the first man to compete in the Cortina. He later returned to the tracks occasionally in 1963 and 1964, when he finished second at both Zolder and Brands Hatch and third at the Nürburgring in Alan Mann's Lotus-Cortina. After finally retiring in 1966, he became competitions manager at Ford.

TAYLOR, Henry (GB) b 16/12/1932, Shefford, Bedfordshire

	1959	Championship position: Unplaced						
	Race	Circuit	No	Entrant	Tyres	Car/Engine	Comment	Q Pos/Entries
11*	BRITISH GP (F2)	Aintree	58	R H H Parnell	D	1.5 Cooper T51-Climax 4 F2	* 2nd in F2 class/-6 laps	21/30
	1960	Championship position: 16th=	Wins: 0	Pole positions: 0	Fastest laps: 0	Points scored: 3		
7	DUTCH GP	Zandvoort	10	Yeoman Credit Racing Team	D	2.5 Cooper T51-Climax 4	5 laps behind	14/21
4	FRENCH GP	Reims	46	Yeoman Credit Racing Team	D	2.5 Cooper T51-Climax 4	1 lap behind	12/23
8	BRITISH GP	Silverstone	15	Yeoman Credit Racing Team	D	2.5 Cooper T51-Climax 4	3 laps behind	16/25
dns	PORTUGUESE GP	Oporto	10	Yeoman Credit Racing Team	D	2.5 Cooper T51-Climax 4	practice accident-injured	– /16
14	US GP	Riverside	8	Yeoman Credit Racing Team	D	2.5 Cooper T51-Climax 4	pit stop/7 laps behind	14/23
	1961	Championship position: Unplaced						
dnq	MONACO GP	Monte Carlo	34	UDT-Laystall Racing Team	D	1.5 Lotus 18-Climax 4		17/21
dnp	BELGIAN GP	Spa	16	UDT-Laystall Racing Team	D	1.5 Lotus 18/21-Climax 4	car crashed by Allison	– / –
10	FRENCH GP	Reims	30	UDT-Laystall Racing Team	D	1.5 Lotus 18/21-Climax 4	3 laps behind	25/26
ret	BRITISH GP	Aintree	30	UDT-Laystall Racing Team	D	1.5 Lotus 18/21-Climax 4	accident in rain	17/30
11	ITALIAN GP	Monza	20	UDT-Laystall Racing Team	D	1.5 Lotus 18/21-Climax 4	4 laps behind	23/33

GP Starts: 8   GP Wins: 0   Pole positions: 0   Fastest laps: 0   Points: 3

JOHN TAYLOR

A protégé of Bob Gerard, Taylor raced extensively in Formula Junior during 1962-63 with the Midlander's Cooper-Ford, gaining quite a bit of success, mainly at club level, and also took part in the British non-championship Formula 1 races of the period. In 1964 John was fifth in the Aintree 200 with a four-cylinder car and seventh in the Mediterranean GP at Enna in Gerard's Cooper-Climax V8, which he drove in three more non-championship races in 1965.

Having finished sixth in the 1966 International Trophy, Taylor took David Bridges' Brabham-BRM to the French GP and, despite his limited experience, scored a priceless point. However, in the German GP, he spun on the first lap and was involved in a collision with Ickx's F2 Matra. His car crashed off the track and burst into flames, leaving the poor driver badly burned. Though he seemed to be making a slow recovery, he died in hospital a few weeks later.

MIKE TAYLOR

An amateur racer who showed a great deal of skill in the Lotus XI sports car in 1958, winning a number of club races, Taylor continued to race the car in 1959, taking victory in the GP des Frontières at Chimay. He also campaigned a Formula 2 Cooper-Climax and won the BARC 200 at Aintree against moderate opposition, before making his GP debut at the same venue in July. Late in the season, Taylor planned to compete in the US GP, but had to stand down after contracting jaundice.

For the 1960 season, Mike's syndicate bought one of Colin Chapman's latest Lotus 18s, which – after an outing in the International Trophy – he took to Spa for the Belgian GP. In a meeting which saw Moss badly injured and Stacey and Bristow killed, the car careered off the track into the woods during practice after the steering column failed, leaving Taylor with multiple injuries but lucky to have survived. He successfully sued Lotus for damages, but never raced again, instead turning to property speculation.

TAYLOR, John (GB) b 23/3/1933, Leicester – d 8/9/1966, Koblenz, Germany

	1964			Championship position: Unplaced					
	Race	Circuit	No	Entrant	Tyres	Car/Engine	Comment		Q Pos/Entries
14	BRITISH GP	Brands Hatch	22	Bob Gerard Racing	D	1.0 Cooper T73-Ford 4	long stop-gearbox/-24 laps		20/25
	1966			Championship position: 17th= Wins: 0 Pole positions: 0 Fastest laps: 0 Points scored: 1					
6	FRENCH GP	Reims	44	David Bridges	G	2.0 Brabham BT11-BRM V8	3 laps behind		15/17
8	BRITISH GP	Brands Hatch	22	David Bridges	G	2.0 Brabham BT11-BRM V8	4 laps behind		16/20
8	DUTCH GP	Zandvoort	38	David Bridges	G	2.0 Brabham BT11-BRM V8	6 laps behind		18/18
ret	GERMAN GP	Nürburgring	16	David Bridges	G	2.0 Brabham BT11-BRM V8	accident-later proved fatal		26/30

GP Starts: 5   GP Wins: 0   Pole positions: 0   Fastest laps: 0   Points: 1

TAYLOR, Mike (GB) b 24/4/1934, London

	1959			Championship position: Unplaced					
	Race	Circuit	No	Entrant	Tyres	Car/Engine	Comment		Q Pos/Entries
ret	BRITISH GP (F2)	Aintree	50	Alan Brown Equipe	D	1.5 Cooper T45-Climax 4 F2	transmission		24/30
	1960			Championship position: Unplaced					
dns	BELGIAN GP	Spa	20	Taylor-Crawley Racing Team	D	2.5 Lotus 18-Climax 4	broken steering-crashed		– / –

GP Starts: 1   GP Wins: 0   Pole positions: 0   Fastest laps: 0   Points: 0

TAYLOR, Trevor (GB) b 26/12/1936, Gleadless, nr Sheffield, Yorkshire

	1959			Championship position: Unplaced					
	Race	Circuit	No	Entrant	Tyres	Car/Engine	Comment		Q Pos/Entries
dnq	BRITISH GP (F2)	Aintree	44	Ace Garage (Rotherham)	D	1.5 Cooper T51-Climax 4			– /30
	1961			Championship position: Unplaced					
13	DUTCH GP	Zandvoort	16	Team Lotus	D	1.5 Lotus 18-Climax 4	2 laps behind		16/17
	1962			Championship position: 10th Wins: 0 Pole positions: 0 Fastest laps: 0 Points scored: 6					
2	DUTCH GP	Zandvoort	5	Team Lotus	D	1.5 Lotus 24-Climax V8			10/20
dns	"	"	5	Team Lotus	D	1.5 Lotus 24-Climax 4	practice only		– / –
ret	MONACO GP	Monte Carlo	20	Team Lotus	D	1.5 Lotus 24-Climax V8	oil leak		17/21
dns	"	" "	20	Team Lotus	D	1.5 Lotus 24-BRM V8	practice only		– / –
ret	BELGIAN GP	Spa	17	Team Lotus	D	1.5 Lotus 24-Climax V8	accident with Mairesse		3/20
8	FRENCH GP	Rouen	14	Team Lotus	D	1.5 Lotus 25-Climax V8	hit Trintignant at finish/-6 laps		12/17
8	BRITISH GP	Aintree	22	Team Lotus	D	1.5 Lotus 24-Climax V8	1 lap behind		10/21
ret	GERMAN GP	Nürburgring	6	Team Lotus	D	1.5 Lotus 24-Climax V8	engine problems-accident		26/30
ret	ITALIAN GP	Monza	22	Team Lotus	D	1.5 Lotus 25-Climax V8	gearbox		16/30
12	US GP	Watkins Glen	9	Team Lotus	D	1.5 Lotus 25-Climax V8	pit stop-oil pressure/-15 laps		8/20
ret	SOUTH AFRICAN GP	East London	2	Team Lotus	D	1.5 Lotus 25-Climax V8	gearbox		9/17

	1963	Championship position: 15th=		Wins: 0	Pole positions: 0	Fastest laps: 0	Points scored: 1			
6	MONACO GP	Monte Carlo	10	Team Lotus	D	1.5 Lotus 25-Climax V8	gearchange problems/-2 laps	9/17
ret	BELGIAN GP	Spa	2	Team Lotus	D	1.5 Lotus 25-Climax V8	leg injury after practice accident	11/20
10	DUTCH GP	Zandvoort	8	Team Lotus	D	1.5 Lotus 25-Climax V8	pit stop-misfire/-14 laps	10/19
13/ret	FRENCH GP	Reims	20	Team Lotus	D	1.5 Lotus 25-Climax V8	transmission/12 laps behind	7/21
ret/dsq*	BRITISH GP	Silverstone	5	Team Lotus	D	1.5 Lotus 25-Climax V8	fuel pump/*push start at pit stop	=10/23
8	GERMAN GP	Nürburgring	4	Team Lotus	D	1.5 Lotus 25-Climax V8	1 lap behind	18/26
ret	US GP	Watkins Glen	9	Team Lotus	D	1.5 Lotus 25-Climax V8	transistor box	=7/21
ret	MEXICAN GP	Mexico City	9	Team Lotus	D	1.5 Lotus 25-Climax V8	engine	12/21
8	SOUTH AFRICAN GP	East London	2	Team Lotus	D	1.5 Lotus 25-Climax V8	spin/pit stop-gearchange/-4 laps	=7/21
	1964	Championship position: 197h=		Wins: 0	Pole positions: 0	Fastest laps: 0	Points scored: 1			
ret	MONACO GP	Monte Carlo	15	British Racing Partnership	D	1.5 BRP 1-BRM V8	fuel leak	14/20
7	BELGIAN GP	Spa	4	British Racing Partnership	D	1.5 BRP 2-BRM V8	1 lap behind	12/20
ret	FRENCH GP	Rouen	18	British Racing Partnership	D	1.5 BRP 2-BRM V8	brakes-accident	12/17
ret	BRITISH GP	Brands Hatch	12	British Racing Partnership	D	1.5 Lotus 24-BRM V8	unwell after practice crash	=16/25
dns	"	" "	12	British Racing Partnership	D	1.5 BRP 2-BRM V8	practice accident	–/–
ret	AUSTRIAN GP	Zeltweg	15	British Racing Partnership	D	1.5 BRP 1-BRM V8	rear suspension	16/20
dnq	ITALIAN GP	Monza	44	British Racing Partnership	D	1.5 BRP 1-BRM V8		22/25
6	US GP	Watkins Glen	12	British Racing Partnership	D	1.5 BRP 2-BRM V8	4 laps behind	15/19
ret	MEXICAN GP	Mexico City	12	British Racing Partnership	D	1.5 BRP 2-BRM V8	overheating	18/19
	1966	Championship position: Unplaced						
ret	BRITISH GP	Brands Hatch	23	Aiden Jones/Paul Emery	D	3.0 Shannon-Climax Godiva V8	split fuel tank	18/20

GP Starts: 27   GP Wins: 0   Pole positions: 0   Fastest laps: 0   Points: 8

TREVOR TAYLOR

Even this gritty and determined Yorkshireman was eventually battered into submission by a catalogue of crashes which would have frightened a lesser man from the cockpit of a racing car for ever. As it was, he returned from a bombed-out Formula 1 career to later establish himself as a top-line F5000 campaigner, which says a lot for the qualities he possessed.

The son of a garage proprietor, Trevor was given much encouragement in his early racing days by his father, who bought a Triumph TR2 for him to race in 1955. This was soon replaced by a succession of 500 cc F3 cars, one of them the ex-Lewis-Evans Cooper-Norton. Progress was slow initially, but by 1958 Trevor was good enough to take the British F3 championship. The garage purchased an F2 Cooper for him to race in 1959, but apart from a minor Libre win at Rufforth little of note was achieved. Colin Chapman offered to run Taylor as part of his Junior team in 1960 if he purchased a Lotus 18, and it proved to be a sound decision for both parties. Taylor shared the championship that year with Jim Clark, and was taken into the team proper for 1961, when he again won the title, this time on his own. With Ireland injured at Monaco, Trevor was given his Grand Prix debut at Zandvoort where he finished 13th, and last, in a race unique for its complete lack of a pit stop or retirement.

There were a few other Formula 1 outings that year, his best results being a second place in the Rand GP at Kyalami, followed by a win in the Cape GP at Killarney early in 1962. By this time Chapman had placed his faith in the youngster, putting him into the Formula 1 team at the expense of Innes Ireland. A second place at Zandvoort was a great start, but he was shaken up at Spa when a duel with Willy Mairesse left both cars wrecked and the Belgian in hospital. This was followed by an 80 mph crash-test into the back of Trintignant's stalled car at Rouen which left him bruised from head to foot, and at the Nürburgring he was the victim of an engine malady which sent him through a hedge. His confidence was restored at the end of the year, however, when he shared the winning car in the Mexican GP with Clark and then won the Natal GP at Westmead.

Retained for 1963, Taylor took second places at Pau and Karlskoga, but apart from a single point at Monaco was out of luck in championship events. The Mediterranean GP at Enna supplied perhaps Taylor's most astounding escape, when he was pitched from his Lotus at over 100 mph, rolling some 50 yards down the circuit as his car hurtled to destruction. Amazingly he emerged with just grazes and bruising. With Peter Arundell knocking at the door, Taylor was released to join the BRP team in 1964, but apart from a sixth place at Watkins Glen there was little to enthuse about in the performances of the pale-green cars. Trevor raced a Brabham in Formula 2 during 1965-66, and was briefly involved in the amateurish Shannon project, which represented the nadir of his career. From 1967 he went back to basics, first running a Lotus 47 with encouraging results before moving up to a Lola T70 to win the 1969 Tourist Trophy at Oulton Park. This was the inaugural year of F5000, and Trevor took his Surtees TS5 right to the brink of a championship win before losing out to Peter Gethin after the pair collided in the final round at Brands Hatch. Trevor continued in the formula throughout the next three seasons, always a competitive proposition but never quite the force of that first year. At the end of 1972 he brought the curtain down on a sometimes unlucky career, but the fact that he had emerged intact after some of those early mishaps was probably cause enough for him to count his blessings.

MIKE THACKWELL

In 1980, at the age of 19, Thackwell became the youngest-ever starter in a World Championship Grand Prix, when he left the grid at Montreal only to be involved in a multiple collision which halted the race. Mike's car was hors de combat and the race restarted without him. So there's the conundrum: technically, did he start or not? In the event, it was to be nearly four years before another Grand Prix chance came his way, and by that time his career had lost momentum – and the driver, perhaps, the necessary determination.

Mike's early career was meteoric. In 1979, aged just 18, he contested the Vandervell F3 series in a works March, finishing third in the championship with five wins. In 1980 he raced the ICI March 802, putting in some brilliant drives without gaining the reward he deserved, turned down the chance to race the works Ensign, practised an Arrows at Zandvoort, and then joined the Tyrrell team for Montreal.

A hot favourite for the Formula 2 title in 1981, Thackwell started the season with a win at Silverstone, but a heavy crash at Thruxton left him on crutches and his title hopes evaporated. Ron Tauranac, unconvinced about Mike's fitness, dropped him from the F2 team just before the start of the 1982 season, and his confused driver was left in the lurch, eventually scraping a deal together which saw him living from race to race. Fortunately the New Zealander was back in the Ralt fold for 1983, though a slowish start meant he had to play second fiddle to team-mate and champion-elect Palmer. However, 1984 was to be his year and, showing a new resolve, he dominated proceedings, winning seven of the 11 rounds, taking six poles and nine fastest laps, and leading an incredible 408 of the 580 laps run.

Still without a Formula 1 ride, and eyeing Indy Car racing, Thackwell moved somewhat unwillingly into F3000 with Ralt in 1985. Having proved beyond doubt that he was the best driver in the series but failed to clinch the title through sheer bad luck, he understandably felt dissatisfied with his lot and refused to commit himself to a full season in 1986. When he did compete, notably at Pau, he showed what talent was being wasted, subsequently running around – albeit quite successfully – in endurance racing with Sauber and Brun before a brief reunion with Ralt in F3000 in 1988. Disillusioned, he then walked away from the sport before the age of 30.

ALFONSE THIELE

With the exception of his single-seater drive in the 1960 Italian GP, Thiele was exclusively a sports car pilot, and a pretty good one at that.

He spent most of the late fifties campaigning the little Fiat Abarth (taking a 750 cc class win in the 1957 Mille Miglia), before graduating to a more potent proposition with the Ferrari 250GT, winning his class at the 1959 Monza GT meeting with this car.

In the early sixties he was a works driver for both the Fiat Abarth and Alfa Romeo teams. With the latter he took a fine fourth place in the 1964 Targa Florio, just behind team-mate Businello.

THACKWELL, Mike (NZ) b 30/3/1961, Auckland

	1980	Championship position: Unplaced						
	Race	Circuit	No	Entrant	Tyres	Car/Engine	Comment	Q Pos/Entries
dnq	DUTCH GP	Zandvoort	30	Warsteiner Arrows Racing Team	G	3.0 Arrows A3-Cosworth V8		27/28
ret/dns	CANADIAN GP	Montreal	43	Candy Tyrrell Team	G	3.0 Tyrrell 010-Cosworth V8	accident-first start/did not restart	(24)/28
dnq	US GP EAST	Watkins Glen	43	Candy Tyrrell Team	G	3.0 Tyrrell 010-Cosworth V8		26/27
	1984	Championship position: Unplaced						
ret	CANADIAN GP	Montreal	10	Skoal Bandit Formula 1 Team	P	1.5 t/c RAM 02-Hart 4	broken turbo wastegate	25/26
dnq	GERMAN GP	Hockenheim	4	Tyrrell Racing Organisation	G	3.0 Tyrrell 012-Cosworth V8		27/27

GP Starts: 1 (2)   GP Wins: 0   Pole positions: 0   Fastest laps: 0   Points: 0

THIELE, Alfonse (I/USA) b 1922

	1960	Championship position: Unplaced						
	Race	Circuit	No	Entrant	Tyres	Car/Engine	Comment	Q Pos/Entries
ret	ITALIAN GP	Monza	34	Scuderia Centro Sud	D	2.5 Cooper T51-Maserati 4	gearbox	9/16

GP Starts: 1   GP Wins: 0   Pole positions: 0   Fastest laps: 0   Points: 0

ERIC THOMPSON

Life as a Lloyds broker left Eric Thompson with less time to race than he would have liked, but he still managed to make his mark as a member of the Aston Martin sports car team between 1949 and 1953. He enjoyed some excellent results with David Brown's équipe, finishing third at Le Mans in 1951 with Macklin and second at Dundrod in the 1953 Tourist Trophy, and winning the BARC 9 Hours at Goodwood with Reg Parnell.

His single-seater outings were largely confined to minor Formula Libre events in Rob Walker's Connaught but, given a works machine for the 1952 British GP, Eric did extremely well to bring the car home in fifth place and secure two championship points in his only Grand Prix appearance.

LESLIE THORNE

Leslie was a chartered accountant by profession who raced extensively in trials and hill-climbs both before and after the war.

After some impressive performances in a Formula 3 Cooper-Norton during 1953, his friend David Murray (the owner of Ecurie Ecosse) persuaded him to try his hand with the team's Connaught Formula 2 car in 1954.

Thorne raced the Connaught in that year's British Grand Prix, but otherwise drove mainly in Formula Libre events, with his best finish being sixth in the Chichester Cup at Goodwood.

SAM TINGLE

A great enthusiast, this Rhodesian began racing in his homeland in 1947, at the wheel of an old Bentley. This was replaced with a succession of cars, mainly MGs, before he accquired the ex-Claes, ex-Gibson Connaught which brought him the Rhodesian championship.

Sam contested the South African championship with great verve throughout the 1960s in one of Doug Serrurier's Cooper-based LDS-Alfas, scoring his first big win in the 1966 Border Trophy at East London, although he took many other good placings.

By 1968 Sam was perhaps past his prime, but still managed to stay competitive in his final seasons in the sport by getting his hands on an ex-works Brabham BT24-Repco entered by Team Gunston.

THOMPSON, Eric (GB) b 4/11/1919, Ditton Hill, Surbiton, Surrey

	1952	Championship position: 11th=		Wins: 0	Pole positions: 0	Fastest laps: 0	Points scored: 2		
	Race	Circuit	No	Entrant	Tyres	Car/Engine		Comment	Q Pos/Entries
5	BRITISH GP	Silverstone	5	Connaught Engineering	D	2.0 Connaught A Type-Lea Francis 4		3 laps behind	9/32

GP Starts: 1   GP Wins: 0   Pole positions: 0   Fastest laps: 0   Points: 2

THORNE, Leslie (GB) b 23/6/1916, Greenock, Renfrewshire, Scotland – d 13/7/1993, Troon, Ayrshire, Scotland

	1954	Championship position: Unplaced							
	Race	Circuit	No	Entrant	Tyres	Car/Engine		Comment	Q Pos/Entries
nc	BRITISH GP	Silverstone	26	Ecurie Ecosse	D	2.0 Connaught A Type-Lea Francis 4		12 laps behind	23/31

GP Starts: 1   GP Wins: 0   Pole positions: 0   Fastest laps: 0   Points: 0

TINGLE, Sam (RSR) b 24/8/1921, Manchester, England

	1963	Championship position: Unplaced							
	Race	Circuit	No	Entrant	Tyres	Car/Engine		Comment	Q Pos/Entries
ret	SOUTH AFRICAN GP	East London	20	Sam Tingle	D	1.5 LDS Mk1-Alfa Romeo 4		driveshaft	17/21
	1965	Championship position: Unplaced							
13	SOUTH AFRICAN GP	East London	25	Sam Tingle	D	1.5 LDS Mk1-Alfa Romeo 4		12 laps behind	20/25
	1967	Championship position: Unplaced							
ret	SOUTH AFRICAN GP	Kyalami	18	Sam Tingle	F	2.7 LDS Mk3-Climax 4		burst tyre-accident	14/18
	1968	Championship position: Unplaced							
ret	SOUTH AFRICAN GP	Kyalami	18	Team Gunston	F	3.0 LDS Mk3-Repco V8		ignition/fuel	22/23
	1969	Championship position: Unplaced							
8	SOUTH AFRICAN GP	Kyalami	17	Team Gunston	F	3.0 Brabham BT24-Repco V8		7 laps behind	18/18

GP Starts: 5   GP Wins: 0   Pole positions: 0   Fastest laps: 0   Points: 0

DESMOND TITTERINGTON

The Ulsterman may have driven in only a single Grand Prix but he was a very fine driver indeed, and had he not chosen to suddenly retire from competition at the end of the 1956 season would quite probably have become a household name. Having gained experience in an Allard in novice trials and handicaps from 1951, Titterington joined Ecurie Ecosse for the 1953 Tourist Trophy at Dundrod, finishing sixth with Dickson in an Aston Martin. Early the following year he showed his versatility by taking sixth place in the Monte Carlo Rally in a Jaguar and then raced his own Triumph TR2 before receiving an invitation to rejoin Ecurie Ecosse, who had lost the services of the injured Jimmy Stewart. Racing the Scottish team's Jaguar, he was second in the BARC 9 Hours at Goodwood in 1955, and also won a number of national events for them. In addition he drove for Mercedes in the 1955 Targa Florio, finishing fourth with John Fitch. So impressed were Jaguar that they signed him as a works driver for major sports car races, Desmond taking third place at Reims in 1956.

In Formula 1, he scored a superb third at Oulton Park in 1955 on his debut for Vanwall, and also took third in the 1956 International Trophy for Connaught, for whom he drove in that year's British GP. What a pity that business and family reasons deprived the racing world of the chance to see how his career might have developed.

MAURICE TRINTIGNANT

Maurice was the youngest of the five sons of a prosperous vineyard owner and followed three of his brothers into racing. Despite the death of Louis at Péronne in 1933, he could not resist the urge to try his hand at the sport five years later at the wheel of the Bugatti used by his unfortunate sibling. He took it to fifth place in the Pau GP, and won the 1939 GP des Frontières at Chimay before the war caused the cessation of racing activities. When the first post-war motor race was held in the Bois de Boulogne, Trintignant was there with his trusty Bugatti. Unfortunately his car suffered fuel starvation which was later found to have been caused by rat droppings (les petoules) left in the tank from its wartime lay-up. This was the cause of much merriment and Maurice was henceforth given the sobriquet 'Le Petoulet', which he accepted in fine spirit.

He soon replaced the Bugatti with an Amilcar, winning at Avignon in 1947, and after half a season in the Gersac team's Delage joined the Simca Gordini team. The 1948 season started well with wins at Perpignan and Montlhéry, but he was seriously injured in the tragic Swiss GP at Bremgarten in which three drivers were killed. Maurice was more fortunate. He spun his car and was flung into the middle of the track and only split-second reactions by the approaching Farina, Bira and Manzon enabled them to miss his unconscious body, the three brave pilots eliminating themselves in avoidance. In hospital Maurice's life hung by a thread as he lay in a coma for eight days. At one stage he was pronounced dead, but his pulse returned and a slow recovery began. He was back in action at the beginning of 1949 for Simca, winning the Circuit des Ramparts at Angoulême. Showing no ill-effects from his accident, Trintignant remained with Gordini to the end of the 1953 season, taking the little pale-blue car to victories at Geneva in 1950, Albi and Cadours in 1951 and Cadours again in 1953, the year he was crowned racing champion of France. The Gordinis were, of course, notorious for their fragility, and in World Championship Grands Prix he could achieve no better than three fifth places.

After winning the Buenos Aires GP in Rosier's Ferrari, he joined the works team for the bulk of 1954, which brought an immediate improvement in results. Regularly placing in World Championship events, Trintignant won F1 races at Caen and Rouen and was second at Syracuse and Bari. He also shared the winning 4.9-litre Ferrari with Gonzalez to win the Le Mans 24-hour race. In 1955 a steady drive at Monaco brought him his first-ever World Championship win, and in sports cars he won the Messina 10 Hours with Castellotti. He continued to race the Scuderia's sports cars successfully in 1956, winning the Agadir, Dakar and Swedish GPs. But in Formula 1 the picture was less happy, Trintignant having a dismal time in the Vanwall and the ambitious but ill-fated Bugatti. He drove less frequently in 1957, but won the F2 Coupe de Vitesse at Reims in Ferrari's Dino V6, and took third in the Moroccan GP in BRM's P25.

Maurice was back at the forefront again in 1958 when, with Rob Walker's little Cooper, he won the Monaco GP once more and also took victories at Pau and Clermont Ferrand. He was to enjoy his two-year association with the Walker équipe and, despite being 'number two' to Moss, provided them with some excellent Grand Prix results in 1959, as well as another victory at Pau. After finishing second at Le Mans in the Aston Martin that year, Maurice found his outings with David Brown's Formula 1 team in 1960 restricted by the project's myriad problems and he was forced to find rides with Centro Sud. He also ran his own Cooper in Formula 2 that season, plenty of solid placings bringing excellent remuneration. He was also awarded the Légion d'honneur for his services to French motor racing, but he had no intention of resting on his laurels. After a thin time in 1961, he was back with Rob Walker in 1962 following the Goodwood accident which was to end the career of Stirling Moss. Though now past his best, Trintignant could still teach Jim Clark a thing or two, as he showed when he took a third win at Pau.

Maurice raced very little in 1963 and retirement seemed imminent, but he purchased a BRM V8 for 1964 and drove exceedingly well in the German GP to be classified fifth, thus taking two championship points at the age of 47. Although this was his final season in Grands Prix, his farewell came at Le Mans in 1965, ending a remarkable career during which – his Bremgarten crash apart – he had perhaps been one of the safest drivers around. Rarely involved in accidents, his mechanical sympathy ensured a great many finishes, which was much appreciated by team managers.

In his final race 'Le Petoulet' drove a Ford GT, which was quite a long way down the chain of motor racing evolution from a Type 35 GP Bugatti, and the cause of his retirement from the 24 Hours certainly wasn't rat droppings!

TITTERINGTON, Desmond (GB) b 1/5/1928, Cultra, nr Holywood, Co Down, Northern Ireland

1956 — Championship position: Unplaced

	Race	Circuit	No	Entrant	Tyres	Car/Engine	Comment	Q Pos/Entries
ret	BRITISH GP	Silverstone	20	Connaught Engineering	P	2.5 Connaught B Type-Alta 4	engine	11/28

GP Starts: 1   GP Wins: 0   Pole positions: 0   Fastest laps: 0   Points: 0

TRINTIGNANT, Maurice (F) b 30/10/1917, Sainte Cécile-les-Vignes, Vaucluse

1950 — Championship position: Unplaced

	Race	Circuit	No	Entrant	Tyres	Car/Engine	Comment	Q Pos/Entries
ret	MONACO GP	Monte Carlo	12	Equipe Gordini	E	1.5 s/c Simca Gordini Type 15 4	multiple accident	13/21
ret	ITALIAN GP	Monza	42	Equipe Gordini	E	1.5 s/c Simca Gordini Type 15 4	water pipe	12/27

1951 — Championship position: Unplaced

	Race	Circuit	No	Entrant	Tyres	Car/Engine	Comment	Q Pos/Entries
ret	FRENCH GP	Reims	32	Equipe Gordini	E	1.5 s/c Simca Gordini Type 15 4	engine	18/23
ret	GERMAN GP	Nürburgring	81	Equipe Gordini	E	1.5 s/c Simca Gordini Type 15 4	engine	14/23
dns*	ITALIAN GP	Monza	50	Equipe Gordini	E	1.5 s/c Simca Gordini Type 15 4	*Behra apparently drove car	12/22
ret	SPANISH GP	Pedralbes	12	Equipe Gordini	E	1.5 s/c Simca Gordini Type 15 4	engine	11/20

1952 — Championship position: 11th=   Wins: 0   Pole positions: 0   Fastest laps: 0   Points scored: 2

	Race	Circuit	No	Entrant	Tyres	Car/Engine	Comment	Q Pos/Entries
dns	SWISS GP	Bremgarten	14	Ecurie Rosier	P	2.0 Ferrari 166 V12 F2	engine trouble	–/–
5	FRENCH GP	Rouen	44	Equipe Gordini	E	1.5 Simca Gordini Type 15 4	5 laps behind	6/20
ret	BRITISH GP	Silverstone	25	Equipe Gordini	E	2.0 Gordini Type 16 6	gearbox	21/32
ret	GERMAN GP	Nürburgring	109	Equipe Gordini	E	2.0 Gordini Type 16 6	brakes/suspension	3/32
6	DUTCH GP	Zandvoort	12	Equipe Gordini	E	2.0 Gordini Type 16 6	3 laps behind	5/18
ret	ITALIAN GP	Monza	4	Equipe Gordini	E	2.0 Gordini Type 16 6	engine	4/35

1953 — Championship position: 9th=   Wins: 0   Pole positions: 0   Fastest laps: 0   Points scored: 4

	Race	Circuit	No	Entrant	Tyres	Car/Engine	Comment	Q Pos/Entries
7*	ARGENTINE GP	Buenos Aires	28	Equipe Gordini	E	2.0 Gordini Type 16 6	* Schell took over/-6 laps	7/16
6	DUTCH GP	Zandvoort	24	Equipe Gordini	E	2.0 Gordini Type 16 6	3 laps behind	12/20
5	BELGIAN GP	Spa	18	Equipe Gordini	E	2.0 Gordini Type 16 6	1 lap behind	8/22
ret	FRENCH GP	Reims	4	Equipe Gordini	E	2.0 Gordini Type 16 6	transmission	23/25
ret	BRITISH GP	Silverstone	29	Equipe Gordini	E	2.0 Gordini Type 16 6	transmission	8/29
ret	GERMAN GP	Nürburgring	10	Equipe Gordini	E	2.0 Gordini Type 16 6	differential	5/35
ret	SWISS GP	Bremgarten	8	Equipe Gordini	E	2.0 Gordini Type 16 6	transmission	4/23
5	ITALIAN GP	Monza	36	Equipe Gordini	E	2.0 Gordini Type 16 6	1 lap behind	8/30

1954 — Championship position: 4th   Wins: 0   Pole positions: 0   Fastest laps: 0   Points scored: 17

	Race	Circuit	No	Entrant	Tyres	Car/Engine	Comment	Q Pos/Entries
4	ARGENTINE GP	Buenos Aires	26	Ecurie Rosier	P	2.5 Ferrari 625 4	1 lap behind	5/18
2	BELGIAN GP	Spa	8	Scuderia Ferrari	P	2.5 Ferrari 625 4		6/18
dns	"	"	8	Scuderia Ferrari	P	2.5 Ferrari 553 4	practice only	–/–
ret	FRENCH GP	Reims	4	Scuderia Ferrari	P	2.5 Ferrari 625 4	engine	9/22
5	BRITISH GP	Silverstone	10	Scuderia Ferrari	P	2.5 Ferrari 625/555 4	3 laps behind	8/31
3	GERMAN GP	Nürburgring	2	Scuderia Ferrari	P	2.5 Ferrari 625 4		7/23
ret	SWISS GP	Bremgarten	26	Scuderia Ferrari	P	2.5 Ferrari 625/555 4	engine	4/16
5	ITALIAN GP	Monza	30	Scuderia Ferrari	P	2.5 Ferrari 625/555 4	5 laps behind	11/21
ret	SPANISH GP	Pedralbes	40	Scuderia Ferrari	P	2.5 Ferrari 625/555 4	gearbox	8/22

1955 — Championship position: 4th   Wins: 1   Pole positions: 0   Fastest laps: 0   Points scored: 11.33

	Race	Circuit	No	Entrant	Tyres	Car/Engine	Comment	Q Pos/Entries
ret	ARGENTINE GP	Buenos Aires	14	Scuderia Ferrari	E	2.5 Ferrari 625/555 4	engine	14/22
2*	"	"	12	Scuderia Ferrari	E	2.5 Ferrari 625/555 4	* González/Farina also drove	–/–
3*	"	"	10	Scuderia Ferrari	E	2.5 Ferrari 625/555 4	* Farina/Maglioli co drove/-2 laps	–/–
1	MONACO GP	Monte Carlo	44	Scuderia Ferrari	E	2.5 Ferrari 625/555 4		9/22
6	BELGIAN GP	Spa	4	Scuderia Ferrari	E	2.5 Ferrari 555 4	1 lap behind	10/14
ret	DUTCH GP	Zandvoort	4	Scuderia Ferrari	E	2.5 Ferrari 555 4	gearbox	8/16
dns	"	"	4	Scuderia Ferrari	E	2.5 Ferrari 625/555 4	practice only	–/–
ret	BRITISH GP	Aintree	18	Scuderia Ferrari	P	2.5 Ferrari 625/555 4	overheating	13/25
8	ITALIAN GP	Monza	8	Scuderia Ferrari	E	2.5 Ferrari 555 4	3 laps behind	15/22

1956 — Championship position: Unplaced

	Race	Circuit	No	Entrant	Tyres	Car/Engine	Comment	Q Pos/Entries
ret	MONACO GP	Monte Carlo	14	Vandervell Products Ltd	P	2.5 Vanwall 4	overheating after accident	6/19
ret	BELGIAN GP	Spa	12	Vandervell Products Ltd	P	2.5 Vanwall 4	fuel pipe	7/16
ret	FRENCH GP	Reims	28	Automobiles Bugatti	E	2.5 Bugatti 251 8	throttle pedal	18/20
ret	BRITISH GP	Silverstone	17	Vandervell Products Ltd	P	2.5 Vanwall 4	fuel line	16/28
ret	ITALIAN GP	Monza	20	Vandervell Products Ltd	P	2.5 Vanwall 4	rear suspension	=11/26

1957 — Championship position: 10th=   Wins: 0   Pole positions: 0   Fastest laps: 0   Points scored: 5

	Race	Circuit	No	Entrant	Tyres	Car/Engine	Comment	Q Pos/Entries
5	MONACO GP	Monte Carlo	30	Scuderia Ferrari	E	2.5 Lancia-Ferrari 801 V8	5 laps behind	6/21
ret	FRENCH GP	Rouen	16	Scuderia Ferrari	E	2.5 Lancia-Ferrari 801 V8	magneto	8/15
4*	BRITISH GP	Aintree	16	Scuderia Ferrari	E	2.5 Lancia-Ferrari 801 V8	* Collins took over/-2 laps	9/19

1958 — Championship position: 7th   Wins: 1   Pole positions: 0   Fastest laps: 0   Points scored: 12

	Race	Circuit	No	Entrant	Tyres	Car/Engine	Comment	Q Pos/Entries
1	MONACO GP	Monte Carlo	20	R R C Walker Racing Team	D	2.0 Cooper T45-Climax 4		5/28
9	DUTCH GP	Zandvoort	9	R R C Walker Racing Team	D	2.0 Cooper T45-Climax 4	3 laps behind	8/17
7	BELGIAN GP	Spa	28	Scuderia Centro Sud	P	2.5 Maserati 250F 6	1 lap behind	16/20
ret	FRENCH GP	Reims	18	Owen Racing Organisation	D	2.5 BRM P25 4	broken camshaft gear	7/21
8	BRITISH GP	Silverstone	4	R R C Walker Racing Team	D	2.0 Cooper T43-Climax 4	2 laps behind	12/21
3	GERMAN GP	Nürburgring	11	R R C Walker Racing Team	D	2.2 Cooper T45-Climax 4		7/26
8	PORTUGUESE GP	Oporto	12	R R C Walker Racing Team	D	2.2 Cooper T45-Climax 4	2 laps behind	9/15
ret	ITALIAN GP	Monza	2	R R C Walker Racing Team	D	2.2 Cooper T45-Climax 4	gearbox	13/21
dns	"	"	2	R R C Walker Racing Team	D	2.0 Cooper T43-Climax 4	practice only	–/–
ret	MOROCCAN GP	Casablanca	38	R R C Walker Racing Team	D	2.2 Cooper T45-Climax 4	engine	9/25

1959 — Championship position: 5th Wins: 0 Pole positions: 0 Fastest laps: 1 Points scored: 19

	Race	Circuit	No	Entrant	Tyres	Car/Engine	Comment	Q Pos/Entries
3	MONACO GP	Monte Carlo	32	R R C Walker Racing Team	D	2.5 Cooper T51-Climax 4	2 laps behind	6/24
8	DUTCH GP	Zandvoort	10	R R C Walker Racing Team	D	2.5 Cooper T51-Climax 4	2 laps behind	11/15
nc	FRENCH GP	Reims	14	R R C Walker Racing Team	D	2.5 Cooper T51-Climax 4	spun and stalled/-14 laps	8/22
5	BRITISH GP	Aintree	18	R R C Walker Racing Team	D	2.5 Cooper T51-Climax 4	1 lap behind	4/30
4*	GERMAN GP	AVUS	8	R R C Walker Racing Team	D	2.5 Cooper T51-Climax 4	* 6th Heat 1/4th Heat 2/-1 lap	12/16
4	PORTUGUESE GP	Monsanto	5	R R C Walker Racing Team	D	2.5 Cooper T51-Climax 4	2 laps behind	4/16
9	ITALIAN GP	Monza	16	R R C Walker Racing Team	D	2.5 Cooper T51-Climax 4	2 laps behind	13/21
2	US GP	Sebring	6	R R C Walker Racing Team	D	2.5 Cooper T51-Climax 4	FL	5/19

1960 — Championship position: Unplaced

	Race	Circuit	No	Entrant	Tyres	Car/Engine	Comment	Q Pos/Entries
3*	ARGENTINE GP	Buenos Aires	38	R R C Walker Racing Team	D	2.5 Cooper T51-Climax 4	* Moss took car-no points allowed	8/22
ret	MONACO GP	Monte Carlo	44	Scuderia Centro Sud	D	2.5 Cooper T51-Maserati 4	gearbox	16/24
ret	DUTCH GP	Zandvoort	18	Scuderia Centro Sud	D	2.5 Cooper T51-Maserati 4	transmission	17/21
ret	FRENCH GP	Reims	38	Scuderia Centro Sud	D	2.5 Cooper T51-Maserati 4	hit by G Hill on grid	18/23
11	BRITISH GP	Silverstone	19	David Brown Corporation	D	2.5 Aston Martin DBR5/250 6	5 laps behind	21/25
15	US GP	Riverside	18	Scuderia Centro Sud	D	2.5 Cooper T51-Maserati 4	9 laps behind	19/23

1961 — Championship position: Unplaced

	Race	Circuit	No	Entrant	Tyres	Car/Engine	Comment	Q Pos/Entries
7	MONACO GP	Monte Carlo	42	Scuderia Serenissima	D	1.5 Cooper T51-Maserati 4	5 laps behind	16/21
ret	BELGIAN GP	Spa	26	Scuderia Serenissima	D	1.5 Cooper T51-Maserati 4	gearbox	19/25
dns	"	"	26	Scuderia Serenissima	D	1.5 Cooper T43-Climax 4	practice only	–/–
13	FRENCH GP	Reims	32	Scuderia Serenissima	D	1.5 Cooper T51-Maserati 4	11 laps behind	23/26
dns	"	"	34	Scuderia Serenissima	D	1.5 de Tomaso F1-001-OSCA 4	practice only	–/–
ret	GERMAN GP	Nürburgring	20	Scuderia Serenissima	D	1.5 Cooper T51-Maserati 4	engine	21/27
9	ITALIAN GP	Monza	48	Scuderia Serenissima	D	1.5 Cooper T51-Maserati 4	2 laps behind	22/33

1962 — Championship position: Unplaced

	Race	Circuit	No	Entrant	Tyres	Car/Engine	Comment	Q Pos/Entries
ret	MONACO GP	Monte Carlo	30	Rob Walker Racing Team	D	1.5 Lotus 24-Climax V8	first corner accident	7/21
8	BELGIAN GP	Spa	18	Rob Walker Racing Team	D	1.5 Lotus 24-Climax V8	2 laps behind	16/20
7	FRENCH GP	Rouen	28	Rob Walker Racing Team	D	1.5 Lotus 24-Climax V8	hit by T Taylor after finish	13/17
ret	GERMAN GP	Nürburgring	17	Rob Walker Racing Team	D	1.5 Lotus 24-Climax V8	gearbox	11/30
ret	ITALIAN GP	Monza	36	Rob Walker Racing Team	D	1.5 Lotus 24-Climax V8	electrics	19/30
ret	US GP	Watkins Glen	6	Rob Walker Racing Team	D	1.5 Lotus 24-Climax V8	brakes-fluid leak	19/20

1963 — Championship position: Unplaced

	Race	Circuit	No	Entrant	Tyres	Car/Engine	Comment	Q Pos/Entries
ret	MONACO GP	Monte Carlo	17	Reg Parnell (Racing)	D	1.5 Lola 4A-Climax V8	raced Amon's car-clutch	–/–
dns	"	" "	17	Reg Parnell (Racing)	D	1.5 Lola 4-Climax V8	practice only-blown engine	14/17
8	FRENCH GP	Reims	28	Reg Parnell (Racing)	D	1.5 Lotus 24-Climax V8	3 laps behind	15/21
9	ITALIAN GP	Monza	66	Scuderia Centro Sud	D	1.5 BRM P57 V8	3 laps behind	20/28

1964 — Championship position: 16th= Wins: 0 Pole positions: 0 Fastest laps: 0 Points scored: 2

	Race	Circuit	No	Entrant	Tyres	Car/Engine	Comment	Q Pos/Entries
ret	MONACO GP	Monte Carlo	4	Maurice Trintignant	D	1.5 BRM P57 V8	overheating	13/20
11	FRENCH GP	Rouen	28	Maurice Trintignant	D	1.5 BRM P57 V8	5 laps behind	16/17
dnq	BRITISH GP	Brands Hatch	25	Maurice Trintignant	D	1.5 BRM P57 V8		25/25
5/ret	GERMAN GP	Nürburgring	22	Maurice Trintignant	D	1.5 BRM P57 V8	flat battery/1 lap behind	14/24
ret	ITALIAN GP	Monza	48	Maurice Trintignant	D	1.5 BRM P57 V8	fuel injection	21/25

GP Starts: 80 (81) GP Wins: 2 Pole positions: 0 Fastest laps: 1 Points: 72.33

TRULLI, Jarno (I) b Pescara, Italy 13/7/1974

1997 — Championship position: 15th Wins: 0 Pole positions: 0 Fastest laps: 0 Points scored: 3

	Race	Circuit	No	Entrant	Tyres	Car/Engine	Comment	Q Pos/Entries
9	AUSTRALIAN GP	Melbourne	21	Minardi Team	B	3.0 Minardi M197-Hart V8	3 laps behind	17/24
12	BRAZILIAN GP	Interlagos	21	Minardi Team	B	3.0 Minardi M197-Hart V8	1 lap behind	17/22
9	ARGENTINE GP	Buenos Aires	21	Minardi Team	B	3.0 Minardi M197-Hart V8	1 lap behind	18/22
dns	SAN MARINO GP	Imola	21	Minardi Team	B	3.0 Minardi M197-Hart V8	gearbox hydraulic pump	20/22
ret	MONACO GP	Monte Carlo	21	Minardi Team	B	3.0 Minardi M197-Hart V8	accident-slid off	18/22
15	SPANISH GP	Barcelona	21	Minardi Team	B	3.0 Minardi M197-Hart V8	2 laps behind	18/22
ret	CANADIAN GP	Montreal	21	Minardi Team	B	3.0 Minardi M197-Hart V8	engine	20/22
10	FRENCH GP	Magny Cours	14	Prost Gauloise Blondes	B	3.0 Prost JS45-Mugen Honda V10	2 laps behind	6/22
8	BRITISH GP	Silverstone	14	Prost Gauloise Blondes	B	3.0 Prost JS45-Mugen Honda V10	1 lap behind	13/22
4	GERMAN GP	Hockenheim	14	Prost Gauloise Blondes	B	3.0 Prost JS45-Mugen Honda V10	collision-Villeneuve 1 lap behind	11/22
7	HUNGARIAN GP	Hungaroring	14	Prost Gauloise Blondes	B	3.0 Prost JS45-Mugen Honda V10		12/22
15	BELGIAN GP	Spa	14	Prost Gauloise Blondes	B	3.0 Prost JS45-Mugen Honda V10	started in spare from pits/-2 laps	14/22
10	ITALIAN GP	Monza	14	Prost Gauloise Blondes	B	3.0 Prost JS45-Mugen Honda V10		16/22
ret	AUSTRIAN GP	A1-Ring	14	Prost Gauloise Blondes	B	3.0 Prost JS45-Mugen Honda V10	engine-led race	3/22

1998 — Championship position: 15th= Wins: 0 Pole positions: 0 Fastest laps: 0 Points scored: 1

	Race	Circuit	No	Entrant	Tyres	Car/Engine	Comment	Q Pos/Entries
ret	AUSTRALIAN GP	Melbourne	12	Gauloises Prost Peugeot	B	3.0 Prost AP01-Peugeot V10	gearbox	15/22
ret	BRAZILIAN GP	Interlagos	12	Gauloises Prost Peugeot	B	3.0 Prost AP01-Peugeot V10	fuel pressure	12/22
11	ARGENTINE GP	Buenos Aires	12	Gauloises Prost Peugeot	B	3.0 Prost AP01-Peugeot V10	2 laps behind	16/22
ret	SAN MARINO GP	Imola	12	Gauloises Prost Peugeot	B	3.0 Prost AP01-Peugeot V10	throttle	16/22
9	SPANISH GP	Barcelona	12	Gauloises Prost Peugeot	B	3.0 Prost AP01-Peugeot V10	2 laps behind	16/22
ret	MONACO GP	Monte Carlo	12	Gauloises Prost Peugeot	B	3.0 Prost AP01-Peugeot V10	gearbox	10/22
ret	CANADIAN GP	Montreal	12	Gauloises Prost Peugeot	B	3.0 Prost AP01-Peugeot V10	multiple collision on lap 1	14/22
ret	FRENCH GP	Magny Cours	12	Gauloises Prost Peugeot	B	3.0 Prost AP01-Peugeot V10	spun off	12/22
ret	BRITISH GP	Silverstone	12	Gauloises Prost Peugeot	B	3.0 Prost AP01-Peugeot V10	spun off	15/22
10	AUSTRIAN GP	A1-Ring	12	Gauloises Prost Peugeot	B	3.0 Prost AP01-Peugeot V10	1 lap behind	16/22
12	GERMAN GP	Hockenheim	12	Gauloises Prost Peugeot	B	3.0 Prost AP01-Peugeot V10	1 lap behind	14/22
ret	HUNGARIAN GP	Hungaroring	12	Gauloises Prost Peugeot	B	3.0 Prost AP01-Peugeot V10	electronics	16/22
6	BELGIAN GP	Spa	12	Gauloises Prost Peugeot	B	3.0 Prost AP01-Peugeot V10	2 laps behind	13/22
13	ITALIAN GP	Monza	12	Gauloises Prost Peugeot	B	3.0 Prost AP01-Peugeot V10	3 laps behind	10/22
ret	LUXEMBOURG GP	Nürburgring	12	Gauloises Prost Peugeot	B	3.0 Prost AP01-Peugeot V10	gearbox	14/22
12/ret	JAPANESE GP	Suzuka	12	Gauloises Prost Peugeot	B	3.0 Prost AP01-Peugeot V10	engine/3 laps behind	14/22

1999			Championship position: 11th=	Wins: 0	Pole positions: 0	Fastest laps: 0	Points scored: 7		
ret	AUSTRALIAN GP	Melbourne	19	Gauloises Prost Peugeot	B	3.0 Prost AP02-Peugeot V10	collision with Géne	12/22
ret	BRAZILIAN GP	Interlagos	19	Gauloises Prost Peugeot	B	3.0 Prost AP02-Peugeot V10	gearbox	13/22
ret	SAN MARINO GP	Imola	19	Gauloises Prost Peugeot	B	3.0 Prost AP02-Peugeot V10	collision-broken suspension	14/22
7	MONACO GP	Monte Carlo	19	Gauloises Prost Peugeot	B	3.0 Prost AP02-Peugeot V10	1 lap behind	7/22
6	SPANISH GP	Barcelona	19	Gauloises Prost Peugeot	B	3.0 Prost AP02-Peugeot V10	1 lap behind	9/22
ret	CANADIAN GP	Montreal	19	Gauloises Prost Peugeot	B	3.0 Prost AP02-Peugeot V10	collision with Alesi on lap 1	9/22
7	FRENCH GP	Magny Cours	19	Gauloises Prost Peugeot	B	3.0 Prost AP02-Peugeot V10		8/22
9	BRITISH GP	Silverstone	19	Gauloises Prost Peugeot	B	3.0 Prost AP02-Peugeot V10		14/22
7	AUSTRIAN GP	A1-Ring	19	Gauloises Prost Peugeot	B	3.0 Prost AP02-Peugeot V10	1 lap behind	13/22
ret	GERMAN GP	Hockenheim	19	Gauloises Prost Peugeot	B	3.0 Prost AP02-Peugeot V10	engine	9/22
8	HUNGARIAN GP	Hungaroring	19	Gauloises Prost Peugeot	B	3.0 Prost AP02-Peugeot V10	1 lap behind	13/22
12	BELGIAN GP	Spa	19	Gauloises Prost Peugeot	B	3.0 Prost AP02-Peugeot V10		12/22
ret	ITALIAN GP	Monza	19	Gauloises Prost Peugeot	B	3.0 Prost AP02-Peugeot V10	gearbox	12/22
2	EUROPEAN GP	Nürburgring	19	Gauloises Prost Peugeot	B	3.0 Prost AP02-Peugeot V10		10/22
dns	MALAYSIAN GP	Sepang	19	Gauloises Prost Peugeot	B	3.0 Prost AP02-Peugeot V10	engine failure on parade lap	(18)/22
ret	JAPANESE GP	Suzuka	19	Gauloises Prost Peugeot	B	3.0 Prost AP02-Peugeot V10	engine	7/22

GP Starts: 45 (46)   GP Wins: 0   Pole positions: 0   Fastest laps: 0   Points: 11

JARNO TRULLI

Jarno was a star in karting from 1983 and by the time he moved into cars the slightly built Italian had racked up successes all around the world. His mid-1995 debut in German F3 was sensational: in his half-season he amassed enough points to place fourth in the final rankings, signing off the year with wins in the last two rounds at Hockenheim.

It is not surprising, therefore, that Trulli was the hot favourite for the title with his KMS Motorsport Dallara in 1996. The little Italian delivered with six wins and it was only the late-season appearance of Nick Heidfeld that gave him cause for concern.

Benetton boss Flavio Briatore had the Formula 3 star under contract and duly found him a seat in the Minardi team for 1997. Paired with the experienced Ukyo Katayama, Jarno soon proved the faster driver and his already astonishing rise towards the top was further fast-tracked when he was moved into the Prost line-up to replace the injured Olivier Panis.

Sixth place on the grid on his debut for the team at the French Grand Prix was a sign of good things in the offing, and a fourth-place finish in Germany was followed by a brilliant performance in Austria where he led the race before his engine failed.

Naturally impatient for success, Trulli had to endure a largely barren season in 1998 when his car was overweight and unreliable. The frustrated driver hardly got a decent run throughout the year and his motivation was given another searching examination at the beginning of 1999, when the Prost was still a midfield runner at best.

It is fair to say that the Prost team was not the happiest of ships during the year, both Trulli and Panis having their differences with the demanding proprietor. Trulli, not unnaturally, grabbed his big chance by signing for Jordan for 2000, and relationships subsequently soured to the point that Jarno's second place in the European Grand Prix was dismissed by Prost as 'lucky'.

Trulli has thus far been a bit-part player and now he has been handed a leading role. It will be interesting to see whether the Italian has what it takes to be a star.

ESTEBAN TUERO

If Conan Doyle had penned a short story entitled 'The Strange Case of the Disappearing Racing Driver', it would have been entirely appropriate to Esteban Tuero, a young Argentinian who was assiduously groomed for stardom. Sent around the world at great expense, he was found a place in a Grand Prix car only to end up back in his homeland racing a VW Polo within a year.

After an apprenticeship in the Sud-Am F3 series, Esteban travelled to Italy in 1996 to race in the national F3 championship but before long he had been elevated to F3000 with Draco. Plans had already been laid for his graduation to F1 with Minardi and the following season he headed off to Japan to compete in Formula Nippon alongside Norberto Fontana. Precious little was achieved in the way of results, but it did not stop the still inexperienced Tuero from gaining the superlicence required to take up a Grand Prix drive with the Italian team in 1998.

His one season in the big time went well enough. Proving a quick learner, he was evenly matched with team-mate Nakano, but in the last race of the year in Japan he tangled with Takagi's Tyrrell and injured vertebrae in his neck. Esteban went home to convalesce and never returned. He later announced his retirement from Formula 1 on 'irrevocable personal grounds', mysteriously adding that he was sworn to secrecy on his reasons for taking such a decision.

TUERO, Esteban b 22/4/1978

	1998			Championship position: Unplaced					
ret	AUSTRALIAN GP	Melbourne	23	Fondmetal Minardi Ford	B	3.0 Minardi M198-Ford Zetec R V10	engine	17/22
ret	BRAZILIAN GP	Interlagos	23	Fondmetal Minardi Ford	B	3.0 Minardi M198-Ford Zetec R V10	gearbox	19/22
ret	ARGENTINE GP	Buenos Aires	23	Fondmetal Minardi Ford	B	3.0 Minardi M198-Ford Zetec R V10	accident	20/22
8	SAN MARINO GP	Imola	23	Fondmetal Minardi Ford	B	3.0 Minardi M198-Ford Zetec R V10	2 laps behind	19/22
15	SPANISH GP	Barcelona	23	Fondmetal Minardi Ford	B	3.0 Minardi M198-Ford Zetec R V10	2 laps behind	19/22
ret	MONACO GP	Monte Carlo	23	Fondmetal Minardi Ford	B	3.0 Minardi M198-Ford Zetec R V10	crashed on lap 1	21/22
ret	CANADIAN GP	Montreal	23	Fondmetal Minardi Ford	B	3.0 Minardi M198-Ford Zetec R V10	electrics	21/22
ret	FRENCH GP	Magny Cours	23	Fondmetal Minardi Ford	B	3.0 Minardi M198-Ford Zetec R V10	hydraulics	22/22
ret	BRITISH GP	Silverstone	23	Fondmetal Minardi Ford	B	3.0 Minardi M198-Ford Zetec R V10	spun off	20/22
ret	AUSTRIAN GP	A1-Ring	23	Fondmetal Minardi Ford	B	3.0 Minardi M198-Ford Zetec R V10	spun off	19/22
16	GERMAN GP	Hockenheim	23	Fondmetal Minardi Ford	B	3.0 Minardi M198-Ford Zetec R V10	2 laps behind	21/22
ret	HUNGARIAN GP	Hungaroring	23	Fondmetal Minardi Ford	B	3.0 Minardi M198-Ford Zetec R V10	gearbox	21/22
ret	BELGIAN GP	Spa	23	Fondmetal Minardi Ford	B	3.0 Minardi M198-Ford Zetec R V10	electrics	22/22
11	ITALIAN GP	Monza	23	Fondmetal Minardi Ford	B	3.0 Minardi M198-Ford Zetec R V10	2 laps behind	22/22
nc	LUXEMBOURG GP	Nürburgring	23	Fondmetal Minardi Ford	B	3.0 Minardi M198-Ford Zetec R V10	11 laps behind	21/22
ret	JAPANESE GP	Suzuka	23	Fondmetal Minardi Ford	B	3.0 Minardi M198-Ford Zetec R V10	collision-Takagi-injured neck	21/22

GP Starts: 16   GP Wins: 0   Pole positions: 0   Fastest laps: 0   Points: 0

GUY TUNMER

This South African amateur racer began competing in Minis in the late sixties, then racing an Alfa with brother Derek before turning to single-seaters regularly in 1973 with a March 722.

In 1975 he drove for Team Gunston in both the Grand Prix and the local F1 series with their Lotus 72E, winning the False Bay 100 at Killarney. Guy also raced in Europe in John Lepp's March at the Monza 1000 Km.

When the premier domestic single-seater class switched to Formula Atlantic, Tunmer raced his own front-running Chevron B34 in 1976.

He died at the age of 50 in 1999, from injuries he had received some time previously in a motor cycle accident.

TONI ULMEN

The outstanding Veritas driver, Ulmen was the German F2 champion in 1949 and always posed a real threat in his Veritas-Meteor. In 1950 he was third at Erlen, less than ten seconds behind two Ferraris led by Villoresi, second in the Eifelrennen and fourth in the German GP. In 1951 he took second place and fastest lap at AVUS, and third at the ultra-fast Grenzlandring circuit.

For 1952 Toni entered his sports-bodied Veritas in two World Championship events without success, but took a fifth place at the Eifelrennen, and won the the Formula 2 high-speed thrash at Grenzlandring and a 2-litre sports car race at the Nürburgring. Despite announcing his retirement in early 1953, he was soon back, albeit briefly, sharing Roosdorp's Jaguar in sports car events and finishing third in the Spa 24 Hours.

BOBBY UNSER

The exploits of the Unser racing dynasty are legendary. Bobby's uncle Louis won the famous Pikes Peak hill-climb nine times, and his brother Al and nephew Al Junior have also achieved enormous success in USAC/Indy Car racing.

Bobby enjoyed an equally illustrious racing career: twice the USAC champion (1968 and 1974) and three times the Indianapolis 500 winner (1968, 1975 and 1981), he stands among the all-time greats with a total of 35 Indy Car victories to his credit.

His Grand Prix appearance with the works BRM team could hardly have been less auspicious: not allowed to race at Monza due to clashing race schedules, Unser managed to crash his car in practice at Watkins Glen and also blew a couple of engines. All in all an expensive exercise best forgotten.

ALFREDO URIA

Uria was another of the local drivers who very much made up the numbers in the international events held in the Argentine at the beginning of 1955 and 1956.

A Uruguayan, he crossed the River Plate with his elderly Maserati A6GCM fitted with a 250F engine, but could only manage a distant 14th on aggregate in the 1955 Buenos Aires City Grand Prix.

The following season he shared the car with Oscar Gonzalez, trailing home sixth on the road. The pair, however, were not classified, being ten laps adrift.

TUNMER, Guy (ZA) b Fricksburg, Transvaal 1/12/1948 – d 6/1999

	1975			Championship position: Unplaced					
	Race	Circuit	No	Entrant	Tyres	Car/Engine		Comment	Q Pos/Entries
11	SOUTH AFRICAN GP	Kyalami	34	Team Gunston	G	3.0 Lotus 72-Cosworth V8		2 laps behind	25/28

GP Starts: 1   GP Wins: 0   Pole positions: 0   Fastest laps: 0   Points: 0

ULMEN, Toni (D) b Düsseldorf 12/1/1906 – d 4/11/1976, Düsseldorf

	1952			Championship position: Unplaced					
	Race	Circuit	No	Entrant	Tyres	Car/Engine		Comment	Q Pos/Entries
ret	SWISS GP	Bremgarten	4	Toni Ulmen	–	2.0 Veritas-Meteor 6 sports		fuel tank	16/21
8	GERMAN GP	Nürburgring	125	Toni Ulmen	–	2.0 Veritas-Meteor 6 sports		2 laps behind	15/32

GP Starts: 2   GP Wins: 0   Pole positions: 0   Fastest laps: 0   Points: 0

UNSER, Bobby (USA) b 20/2/1934, Colorado Springs, Colorado

	1968			Championship position: Unplaced					
	Race	Circuit	No	Entrant	Tyres	Car/Engine		Comment	Q Pos/Entries
dns	ITALIAN GP	Monza	25	Owen Racing Organisation	G	3.0 BRM P126 V12		racing USAC event 24 hours	(20)/24
ret	US GP	Watkins Glen	9	Owen Racing Organisation	G	3.0 BRM P138 V12		engine	–/–
dns	"	" "	9	Owen Racing Organisation	G	3.0 BRM P126 V12		accident in practice-grid time	19/21

GP Starts: 1   GP Wins: 0   Pole positions: 0   Fastest laps: 0   Points: 0

URIA, Alfredo (U)

	1955			Championship position: Unplaced					
	Race	Circuit	No	Entrant	Tyres	Car/Engine		Comment	Q Pos/Entries
ret	ARGENTINE GP	Buenos Aires	30	Alberto Uria	–	2.5 Maserati A6GCM/250F 6		fuel starvation	21/22
	1956			Championship position: Unplaced					
6*	ARGENTINE GP	Buenos Aires	16	Alberto Uria	–	2.5 Maserati A6GCM/250F 6		* shared - Oscar González/-10 laps	13/15

GP Starts: 2   GP Wins: 0   Pole positions: 0   Fastest laps: 0   Points: 0

VACCARELLA, Nino (I) b 4/3/1933, Palermo, Sicily

	1961			Championship position: Unplaced					
	Race	Circuit	No	Entrant	Tyres	Car/Engine		Comment	Q Pos/Entries
ret	ITALIAN GP	Monza	50	Scuderia Serenissima	D	1.5 de Tomaso F1 003-Alfa Romeo 4		engine	20/33
	1962			Championship position: Unplaced					
dnq	MONACO GP	Monte Carlo	42	Scuderia SSS Republica di Venezia	D	1.5 Lotus 18/21-Climax 4			21/21
15	GERMAN GP	Nürburgring	26	Scuderia SSS Republica di Venezia	D	1.5 Porsche 718 F4			15/30
9	ITALIAN GP	Monza	24	Scuderia SSS Republica di Venezia	D	1.5 Lotus 24-Climax V8		2 laps behind	14/30
	1965			Championship position: Unplaced					
12/ret	ITALIAN GP	Monza	6	Scuderia Ferrari SpA SEFAC	D	1.5 Ferrari 158 V8		engine/8 laps behind	15/23

GP Starts: 4   GP Wins: 0   Pole positions: 0   Fastest laps: 0   Points: 0

NINO VACCARELLA

A Sicilian lawyer, Vaccarella was almost deified by the local fans after some superb drives in the Targa Florio, a race which he won three times – and it could have been more. His first victory came in 1965 in a works Ferrari 275 P2 shared with Bandini, the next in 1971, this time driving an Alfa Romeo T33/3 with Toine Hezemans. He came out of retirement in 1975 to record his third triumph, though this time the Alfa T33 T12 he shared with Merzario was pitted against poor opposition.

A top sports car driver from 1962 to 1975, Nino also won Le Mans in 1964 for Ferrari with Guichet, the Nürburgring 1000 Km (again in 1964) with Scarfiotti, and the 1970 Sebring 12 Hours with Andretti and Giunti. He also scored many other placings, and was a very reliable practitioner, rarely damaging the car and enjoying a remarkable ratio of finishes in this punishing category.

His Formula 1 career started brightly with Scuderia Serenissima in 1961, when he took a third in the Coppa Italia at Vallelunga, and he finished sixth in the 1962 Pau GP, but that was as far as it went, his 'one-off' Ferrari drive at Monza in 1965 being literally just that.

ERIC van de POELE

This popular Belgian began his career in French Formula 3 in 1984, before a season in Belgian Group N and the Benelux Formula Ford championships. Eric then briefly tasted the German F3 series but really made a name for himself in the Zakspeed BMW Junior team, winning the German championship, with the added highlight of a victory in the Spa 24 Hours with Theys and Martin.

After another season of touring cars with Schnitzer BMW, Eric made the break into single-seaters at last with an F3000 drive with GA Motorsports in 1989. He was to enjoy two happy years with the team, taking second place in the 1990 championship after three wins (Pau, Birmingham and Nogaro).

With long-time sponsors Lease Plan behind him, Eric joined the newly formed Lambo team for a crack at Grands Prix in 1991. The car was never a competitive proposition, but mysteriously it ran very well at Imola, van de Poele holding a secure fifth place until a fuel pump failure on the last lap. For 1992 Eric threw in his lot with the by now distinctly shaky Brabham team for another frustrating string of non-qualifications, before jumping out of the frying pan and into the fire with a Fondmetal team also facing imminent extinction.

He was on the sidelines for much of 1993, but landed a deal to lead the Nissan Primera challenge in the 1994 British touring car championship. It was to be a tough old season as the team struggled to optimise the car. Frustrated at the lack of progress, Eric quit the series in mid-season, though it was not to harm his long-term prospects with the Japanese manufacturer.

Early in 1995, sharing a Ferrari 333SP with Fermin Velez, he won the Sebring 12 Hours (also taking a stint in the Baldi/Alboreto fourth-place car). When the season got into full swing Eric was back behind the wheel of a Primera, this time in the Spanish touring car championship. With the car now a much more serious contender, van de Poele enjoyed two competitive seasons in the series, but another win at Sebring (this time with a Riley & Scott) left him itching for a return to the more potent prototype classes.

The Belgian joined Wayne Taylor in the Doyle Risi Racing Ferrari 333SP to contest the Professional Racing Series in America in 1998 and won rounds at Las Vegas and Road Atlanta. Teaming up with Schiattarella at Team Rafanelli for 1999, Eric won the opening round of the American Le Mans Series at Atlanta, but his season was then dealt a serious blow when a jammed throttle caused a heavy crash when he was testing the works Nissan in preparation for the Le Mans 24-hour race, which left him sidelined for three months with cracked vertebrae.

van de POELE, Eric (B) b 30/9/1961, Verviers, nr Spa

	Race	Circuit	No	Entrant	Tyres	Car/Engine	Comment	Q Pos/Entries
	1991	Championship position: Unplaced						
dnpq	US GP (PHOENIX)	Phoenix	35	Modena Team SpA	G	3.5 Lambo 291-Lamborghini V12		34/34
dnpq	BRAZILIAN GP	Interlagos	35	Modena Team SpA	G	3.5 Lambo 291-Lamborghini V12		31/34
9/ret	SAN MARINO GP	Imola	35	Modena Team SpA	G	3.5 Lambo 291-Lamborghini V12	fuel pump/4 laps behind	21/34
dnpq	MONACO GP	Monte Carlo	35	Modena Team SpA	G	3.5 Lambo 291-Lamborghini V12		32/34
dnpq	CANADIAN GP	Montreal	35	Modena Team SpA	G	3.5 Lambo 291-Lamborghini V12		33/34
dnpq	MEXICAN GP	Mexico City	35	Modena Team SpA	G	3.5 Lambo 291-Lamborghini V12		32/34
dnpq	FRENCH GP	Magny Cours	35	Modena Team SpA	G	3.5 Lambo 291-Lamborghini V12		33/34
dnpq	BRITISH GP	Silverstone	35	Modena Team SpA	G	3.5 Lambo 291-Lamborghini V12		33/34
dnq	GERMAN GP	Hockenheim	35	Modena Team SpA	G	3.5 Lambo 291-Lamborghini V12		30/34
dnq	HUNGARIAN GP	Hungaroring	35	Modena Team SpA	G	3.5 Lambo 291-Lamborghini V12		29/34
dnq	BELGIAN GP	Spa	35	Modena Team SpA	G	3.5 Lambo 291-Lamborghini V12		30/34
dnq	ITALIAN GP	Monza	35	Modena Team SpA	G	3.5 Lambo 291-Lamborghini V12		29/34
dnq	PORTUGUESE GP	Estoril	35	Modena Team SpA	G	3.5 Lambo 291-Lamborghini V12		30/34
dnq	SPANISH GP	Barcelona	35	Modena Team SpA	G	3.5 Lambo 291-Lamborghini V12		30/33
dnq	JAPANESE GP	Suzuka	35	Modena Team SpA	G	3.5 Lambo 291-Lamborghini V12		29/31
dnq	AUSTRALIAN GP	Adelaide	35	Modena Team SpA	G	3.5 Lambo 291-Lamborghini V12		29/32
	1992	Championship position: Unplaced						
13	SOUTH AFRICAN GP	Kyalami	7	Motor Racing Developments Ltd	G	3.5 Brabham BT60B-Judd V10	4 laps behind	26/30
dnq	MEXICAN GP	Mexico City	7	Motor Racing Developments Ltd	G	3.5 Brabham BT60B-Judd V10		28/30
dnq	BRAZILIAN GP	Interlagos	7	Motor Racing Developments Ltd	G	3.5 Brabham BT60B-Judd V10		29/31
dnq	SPANISH GP	Barcelona	7	Motor Racing Developments Ltd	G	3.5 Brabham BT60B-Judd V10		28/32
dnq	SAN MARINO GP	Imola	7	Motor Racing Developments Ltd	G	3.5 Brabham BT60B-Judd V10		30/32
dnq	MONACO GP	Monte Carlo	7	Motor Racing Developments Ltd	G	3.5 Brabham BT60B-Judd V10		27/32
dnq	CANADIAN GP	Montreal	7	Motor Racing Developments Ltd	G	3.5 Brabham BT60B-Judd V10		28/32
dnq	FRENCH GP	Magny Cours	7	Motor Racing Developments Ltd	G	3.5 Brabham BT60B-Judd V10		29/30
dpq	BRITISH GP	Silverstone	7	Motor Racing Developments Ltd	G	3.5 Brabham BT60B-Judd V10		30/32
dnq	GERMAN GP	Hockenheim	7	Motor Racing Developments Ltd	G	3.5 Brabham BT60B-Judd V10		28/32
ret	HUNGARIAN GP	Hungaroring	14	Fondmetal	G	3.5 Fondmetal GR02-Ford HB V8	multiple collision-spun off	18/31
10	BELGIAN GP	Spa	14	Fondmetal	G	3.5 Fondmetal GR02-Ford HB V8	1 lap behind	15/30
ret	ITALIAN GP	Monza	14	Fondmetal	G	3.5 Fondmetal GR02-Ford HB V8	clutch	25/28

GP Starts: 5   GP Wins: 0   Pole positions: 0   Fastest laps: 0   Points: 0

ANDRE van der LOF

'Dries' was a lively and enthusiastic competitor who took part in both circuit racing and rallies in the Netherlands in the early fifties.

When the inaugural Dutch Grand Prix was given championship status in 1952, the organisers arranged for Dries and his compatriot Jan Flinterman to take part. Van der Lof was found a place in one of John Heath's HWMs, but much of his race was spent visiting the pits with magneto trouble.

Dries continued to take an active interest in motor sport thereafter and was still occasionally competing in historic events into his early sixties.

GIJS van LENNEP

A much respected driver, Gijs always gave a good account of himself whenever his occasional Grand Prix opportunities arose, and scored a point for both Williams and Ensign when their cars were hardly at their most competitive.

Beginning in Formula Vee in 1965, van Lennep soon took up sports car racing to such effect that he was in the Porsche factory team in 1967, taking third place with Elford in the Circuit of Mugello. After concentrating on Formula 3 in 1968, Gijs returned to sports cars and was awarded the Porsche Cup for the best private entrant in 1970.

The 1971 season found him much in demand. He won the Le Mans 24 Hours with Helmut Marko for Martini Porsche and the Paris 1000 Km for Gulf/Wyer, and took second place in the Targa Florio for Alfa Romeo, as well as hiring a Surtees to make his GP debut.

Adding F5000 to his already hectic schedule, van Lennep won the 1972 Rothmans title in a Surtees, and enjoyed continued sports car success with Martini Racing, winning the 1973 Targa Florio with Herbert Muller and the 1976 Le Mans with Jacky Ickx, after which he announced his retirement.

van der LOF, Andre (NL) b 23/8/1919, Emmen – d 24/5/1990 Enschede

	1952	Championship position: Unplaced						
	Race	Circuit	No	Entrant	Tyres	Car/Engine	Comment	Q Pos/Entries
nc	DUTCH GP	Zandvoort	30	HW Motors Ltd	D	2.0 HWM-Alta 4	*pit stop/20 laps behind*	14/18

GP Starts: 1   GP Wins: 0   Pole positions: 0   Fastest laps: 0   Points: 0

van LENNEP, Gijs (NL) b 16/3/1942, Bloemendaal

	1971	Championship position: Unplaced						
	Race	Circuit	No	Entrant	Tyres	Car/Engine	Comment	Q Pos/Entries
8	DUTCH GP	Zandvoort	30	Stichting Autoraces Nederland	F	3.0 Surtees TS7-Cosworth V8	*5 laps behind*	21/24
dns	US GP	Watkins Glen	19	Team Surtees	F	3.0 Surtees TS9-Cosworth V8	*Posey drove car*	29/32
	1973	Championship position: 19th= Wins: 0 Pole positions: 0 Fastest laps: 0 Points scored: 1						
6	DUTCH GP	Zandvoort	26	Frank Williams Racing Cars	F	3.0 Iso Williams 1R-Cosworth V8	*2 laps behind*	20/24
9	AUSTRIAN GP	Österreichring	26	Frank Williams Racing Cars	F	3.0 Iso Williams 1R-Cosworth V8	*2 laps behind*	24/25
ret	ITALIAN GP	Monza	26	Frank Williams Racing Cars	F	3.0 Iso Williams 1R-Cosworth V8	*overheating*	23/25
	1974	Championship position: Unplaced						
14	BELGIAN GP	Nivelles	21	Frank Williams Racing Cars	F	3.0 Williams FW02-Cosworth V8	*3 laps behind*	30/32
dnq	DUTCH GP	Zandvoort	21	Frank Williams Racing Cars	F	3.0 Williams FW01-Cosworth V8		27/27
	1975	Championship position: 19th= Wins: 0 Pole positions: 0 Fastest laps: 0 Points scored: 1						
10	DUTCH GP	Zandvoort	31	HB Bewaking Team Ensign	G	3.0 Ensign N174-Cosworth V8	*pit stop-tyres/4 laps behind*	22/25
15	FRENCH GP	Paul Ricard	31	HB Bewaking Team Ensign	G	3.0 Ensign N175-Cosworth V8	*1 lap behind*	22/26
6	GERMAN GP	Nürburgring	19	HB Bewaking Team Ensign	G	3.0 Ensign N175-Cosworth V8		24/26

GP Starts: 8   GP Wins: 0   Pole positions: 0   Fastest laps: 0   Points: 2

BASIL van ROOYEN

Having shown his talent as early as 1963, when he beat Lotus Cortina ace John Whitmore in an identical machine, Basil was a dominant force in saloons in South Africa for many years, handling a variety of cars including Ford Mustangs and Alfa Romeo GTs. With backing from STP he also moved into national single-seaters in 1968 with a Brabham BT24, although he had to make do with John Love's old Cooper for the Grand Prix.

In 1969, van Rooyen had a McLaren M7A at his disposal, but afer a couple of wins in the car he wrote it off in a big way at Kyalami, returning to the more comfortable environment of saloon cars until 1973, when he virtually retired from racing. However, when Formula Atlantic was introduced in 1975, Basil was tempted back into single-seaters with a Chevron for a couple of seasons.

JOS VERSTAPPEN

Despite his tender years and lack of racing experience, Verstappen has certainly seen plenty of highs and lows in his intermittent Grand Prix career, and he might have blossomed into a major talent had he found an environment in which his abilities were nurtured. At the time of writing, his Formula 1 prospects look bleak, the Dutchman having failed to make the most of the chances that have come his way.

The young Jos might not have pursued the path of motor sport at all after he was hospitalised following a bad crash in his first-ever kart race as a ten-year-old. Soon, however, the passion to compete was all-consuming, and he quickly became one of Europe's outstanding kart racers, before moving to Formula Opel Lotus in 1992. He demolished the opposition in the Benelux series, then turned his attention to the Euroseries, immediately putting the cat among the pigeons with his forceful and brilliant driving.

Naturally much sought after, he opted to race a WTS Dallara-Opel in the German F3 championship in 1993 and cut a swathe through the opposition in this class as well, winning eight races on his way to the title. Victory in the Marlboro Masters at Zandvoort helped attract the Formula 1 teams to his door and a test at Estoril for Footwork was so impressive that Benetton immediately moved to sign him on a long-term contract.

An injury to JJ Lehto meant that Verstappen's debut was not long in coming. Being thrown in at the deep end as number two to Michael Schumacher is not the easiest way to start a Grand Prix career, but Jos did well in the first two Grands Prix before Lehto returned. After the Finn's confidence had quickly been sapped, Verstappen was brought back into the team and soon made headline news worldwide when he escaped from a fiery inferno when his Benetton caught fire at a refuelling stop during the German GP. Luckily he suffered only minor burns and in the next race scored his first podium finish. His meteoric rise came to an abrupt halt when Benetton decided a proper learning season with Simtek was in order, but he once again caught the eye with some impressive qualifying performances in his short spell with the team before it folded.

In 1996 the young Dutchman restarted his GP career at Arrows, and caused quite a stir in the early-season races when he took the unfancied car into the top half of the timing sheets. Inevitably, as the year wore on, Verstappen struggled to impress as the Footwork, lacking in development, was overhauled by others. A move to Tyrrell should have brought more reward, but the team were plainly uncompetitive in 1997, and the hard-charging Verstappen could only take satisfaction that he was mostly the equal of his team-mate Mika Salo. Ken Tyrrell was impressed enough to want to retain the Dutchman's services for the following year and, having sold out to Craig Pollock, the former team owner resigned from the organisation when Jos was passed over in favour of pay-driver Ricardo Rosset. Luckily another F1 chance soon presented itself when Verstappen replaced the out-of-favour Jan Magnussen in the Stewart line-up in mid-1998. In his half-season with the outfit Jos fared little better than his hapless predecessor, and it seems that there was friction with team owner Jackie Stewart.

Harvey Postlethwaite certainly thought highly of Verstappen's talents and employed him to help in the development of Honda's Grand Prix challenger. Sadly the former Tyrrell guru's untimely death brought proceedings to a halt, and contributed to an about-face by the Japanese car giant, which took the project to British American Racing. For Verstappen, it was a return to his father's karting centre in Holland, where he was left tinkering with his beloved machines and waiting in hope for the phone call that might resurrect his career.

van ROOYEN, Basil (ZA) b 19/4/1939, Johannesburg

1968 — Championship position: Unplaced

	Race	Circuit	No	Entrant	Tyres	Car/Engine	Comment	Q Pos/Entries
ret	SOUTH AFRICAN GP	Kyalami	25	John Love	F	2.7 Cooper T79-Climax 4	head gasket	20/23

1969 — Championship position: Unplaced

ret	SOUTH AFRICAN GP	Kyalami	18	Team Lawson	D	3.0 McLaren M7A-Cosworth V8	brakes	=9/18

GP Starts: 2   GP Wins: 0   Pole positions: 0   Fastest laps: 0   Points: 0

VERSTAPPEN, Jos (NL) b 4/3/1972, Montfort

1994 — Championship position: 10th   Wins: 0   Pole positions: 0   Fastest laps: 0   Points scored:10

	Race	Circuit	No	Entrant	Tyres	Car/Engine	Comment	Q Pos/Entries
ret	BRAZILIAN GP	Interlagos	6	Mild Seven Benetton Ford	G	3.5 Benetton B194-Ford Zetec-R V8	hit by Irvine-multiple accident	9/28
ret	PACIFIC GP	T.I. Circuit	6	Mild Seven Benetton Ford	G	3.5 Benetton B194-Ford Zetec-R V8	spun off after making pitstop	10/28
ret	FRENCH GP	Magny Cours	6	Mild Seven Benetton Ford	G	3.5 Benetton B194-Ford Zetec-R V8	spun off-brake trouble	8/28
8*	BRITISH GP	Silverstone	6	Mild Seven Benetton Ford	G	3.5 Benetton B194-Ford Zetec-R V8	*2nd place car dsq/-1 lap	10/28
ret	GERMAN GP	Hockenheim	6	Mild Seven Benetton Ford	G	3.5 Benetton B194-Ford Zetec-R V8	car caught fire in refuelling	19/28
3	HUNGARIAN GP	Hungaroring	6	Mild Seven Benetton Ford	G	3.5 Benetton B194-Ford Zetec-R V8		12/28
3*	BELGIAN GP	Spa	6	Mild Seven Benetton Ford	G	3.5 Benetton B194-Ford Zetec-R V8	*1st place car dsq	6/28
ret	ITALIAN GP	Monza	6	Mild Seven Benetton Ford	G	3.5 Benetton B194-Ford Zetec-R V8	puncture on lap 1	10/28
5	PORTUGUESE GP	Estoril	6	Mild Seven Benetton Ford	G	3.5 Benetton B194-Ford Zetec-R V8		10/28
ret	EUROPEAN GP	Jerez	6	Mild Seven Benetton Ford	G	3.5 Benetton B194-Ford Zetec-R V8	spun off	12/28

1995 — Championship position: Unplaced

ret	BRAZILIAN GP	Interlagos	12	MTV Simtek Ford	G	3.0 Simtek S195-Ford ED V8	clutch	24/26
ret	ARGENTINE GP	Buenos Aires	12	MTV Simtek Ford	G	3.0 Simtek S195-Ford ED V8	gearbox	14/26
ret	SAN MARINO GP	Imola	12	MTV Simtek Ford	G	3.0 Simtek S195-Ford ED V8	gearbox	17/26
12	SPANISH GP	Barcelona	12	MTV Simtek Ford	G	3.0 Simtek S195-Ford ED V8	2 laps behind	16/26
ret/dns	MONACO GP	Monte Carlo	12	MTV Simtek Ford	G	3.0 Simtek S195-Ford ED V8	gearbox at first start	(23)/26

1996 — Championship position: 16th   Wins: 0   Pole positions: 0   Fastest laps: 0   Points scored: 1

ret	AUSTRALIAN GP	Melbourne	17	TWR Arrows	G	3.0 Footwork FA17-Hart V8	engine	12/22
ret	BRAZILIAN GP	Interlagos	17	TWR Arrows	G	3.0 Footwork FA17-Hart V8	engine	13/22
6	ARGENTINE GP	Buenos Aires	17	TWR Arrows	G	3.0 Footwork FA17-Hart V8		7/22
ret	EUROPEAN GP	Nürburgring	17	TWR Arrows	G	3.0 Footwork FA17-Hart V8	gearbox	13/22
ret	SAN MARINO GP	Imola	17	TWR Arrows	G	3.0 Footwork FA17-Hart V8	refuelling accident	14/22
ret	MONACO GP	Monte Carlo	17	TWR Arrows	G	3.0 Footwork FA17-Hart V8	slid into barrier on lap 1	12/22
ret	SPANISH GP	Barcelona	17	TWR Arrows	G	3.0 Footwork FA17-Hart V8	spun off	13/22
ret	CANADIAN GP	Montreal	17	TWR Arrows	G	3.0 Footwork FA17-Hart V8	engine	13/22
ret	FRENCH GP	Magny Cours	17	TWR Arrows	G	3.0 Footwork FA17-Hart V8	detached steering arm	16/22
10	BRITISH GP	Silverstone	17	TWR Arrows	G	3.0 Footwork FA17-Hart V8	1 lap behind	15/22
ret	GERMAN GP	Hockenheim	17	TWR Arrows	G	3.0 Footwork FA17-Hart V8	ran into Katayama on lap 1	17/20
ret	HUNGARIAN GP	Hungaroring	17	TWR Arrows	G	3.0 Footwork FA17-Hart V8	spun off	17/20
ret	BELGIAN GP	Spa	17	TWR Arrows	G	3.0 Footwork FA17-Hart V8	crashed-broken stub axle	16/20
8	ITALIAN GP	Monza	17	TWR Arrows	G	3.0 Footwork FA17-Hart V8	1 lap behind	15/20
ret	PORTUGUESE GP	Estoril	17	TWR Arrows	G	3.0 Footwork FA17-Hart V8	engine	16/20
11	JAPANESE GP	Suzuka	17	TWR Arrows	G	3.0 Footwork FA17-Hart V8	1 lap behind	17/20

1997 — Championship position: Unplaced

ret	AUSTRALIAN GP	Melbourne	18	Tyrrell	G	3.0 Tyrrell 025-Ford ED4 V8	incident with Katayama-crashed	21/24
15	BRAZILIAN GP	Interlagos	18	Tyrrell	G	3.0 Tyrrell 025-Ford ED4 V8	2 laps behind	21/22
ret	ARGENTINE GP	Buenos Aires	18	Tyrrell	G	3.0 Tyrrell 025-Ford ED4 V8	fuel pressure	16/22
10	SAN MARINO GP	Imola	18	Tyrrell	G	3.0 Tyrrell 025-Ford ED4 V8	2 laps behind	21/22
8	MONACO GP	Monte Carlo	18	Tyrrell	G	3.0 Tyrrell 025-Ford ED4 V8	2 laps behind	22/22
11	SPANISH GP	Barcelona	18	Tyrrell	G	3.0 Tyrrell 025-Ford ED4 V8	1 lap behind	19/22
ret	CANADIAN GP	Montreal	18	Tyrrell	G	3.0 Tyrrell 025-Ford ED4 V8	air valve	14/22
ret	FRENCH GP	Magny Cours	18	Tyrrell	G	3.0 Tyrrell 025-Ford ED4 V8	stuck throttle-crashed	18/22
ret	BRITISH GP	Silverstone	18	Tyrrell	G	3.0 Tyrrell 025-Ford ED4 V8	engine	20/22
10	GERMAN GP	Hockenheim	18	Tyrrell	G	3.0 Tyrrell 025-Ford ED4 V8	1 lap behind	20/22
ret	HUNGARIAN GP	Hungaroring	18	Tyrrell	G	3.0 Tyrrell 025-Ford ED4 V8	pneumatic leak	18/22
ret	BELGIAN GP	Spa	18	Tyrrell	G	3.0 Tyrrell 025-Ford ED4 V8	spun off	21/22
ret	ITALIAN GP	Monza	18	Tyrrell	G	3.0 Tyrrell 025-Ford ED4 V8	engine	20/22
12	AUSTRIAN GP	A1-Ring	18	Tyrrell	G	3.0 Tyrrell 025-Ford ED4 V8	2 laps behind	20/22
ret	LUXEMBOURG GP	Nürburgring	18	Tyrrell	G	3.0 Tyrrell 025-Ford ED4 V8	engine	21/22
13*	JAPANESE GP	Suzuka	18	Tyrrell	G	3.0 Tyrrell 025-Ford ED4 V8	*5th place car dsq/-1 lap	21/22
16	EUROPEAN GP	Jerez	18	Tyrrell	G	3.0 Tyrrell 025-Ford ED4 V8	1 lap behind	22/22

1998 — Championship position: Unplaced

12	FRENCH GP	Magny Cours	19	Stewart Ford	B	3.0 Stewart SF2-Ford Zetec-R V10	2 laps behind	15/22
ret	BRITISH GP	Silverstone	19	Stewart Ford	B	3.0 Stewart SF2-Ford Zetec-R V10	engine	17/22
ret	AUSTRIAN GP	A1-Ring	19	Stewart Ford	B	3.0 Stewart SF2-Ford Zetec-R V10	engine	12/22
ret	GERMAN GP	Hockenheim	19	Stewart Ford	B	3.0 Stewart SF2-Ford Zetec-R V10	transmission	19/22
13	HUNGARIAN GP	Hungaroring	19	Stewart Ford	B	3.0 Stewart SF2-Ford Zetec-R V10	3 laps behind	17/22
ret	BELGIAN GP	Spa	19	Stewart Ford	B	3.0 Stewart SF2-Ford Zetec-R V10	engine	17/22
ret	ITALIAN GP	Monza	19	Stewart Ford	B	3.0 Stewart SF2-Ford Zetec-R V100	gearbox	17/22
13	LUXEMBOURG GP	Nürburgring	19	Stewart Ford	B	3.0 Stewart SF2-Ford Zetec-R V10	2 laps behind	18/22
ret	JAPANESE GP	Suzuka	19	Stewart Ford	B	3.0 Stewart SF2-Ford Zetec-R V10	gearbox	19/22

GP Starts: 56 (57)   GP Wins: 0   Pole positions: 0   Fastest laps: 0   Points: 11

GILLES VILLENEUVE

GILLES VILLENEUVE

To this day opinions are sharply divided about Gilles Villeneuve. To many he was simply what motor racing was all about. To the more dispassionate he was an accident waiting to happen, and when the end came, well, they were proved right, weren't they?

In soccer, if the ball goes to a Pele or Best, or now Giggs, there is a collective sense of anticipation, a feeling that something special could be about to happen . . . It was like that with Gilles. As an ordinary punter denied access to the inner sanctum of pit or paddock, you could stand on any corner, at any circuit and wait for his Ferrari to scream into view. Then came the reward. With a glint of wildness in his eyes, and the car at some wicked angle – more often than not at its very limit and then some – Villeneuve would pass and you could sense the thrill.

Gilles raced snowmobiles for several years and tried drag racing before turning to Formula Ford in 1973. Winning seven out of ten races seemed to indicate that a move into Formula Atlantic would be needed to test his powers, but he was soon sidelined, but only for a month, by a fractured leg sustained in an accident at Mosport. Once back in the groove, he started to be noticed, especially after a race at Trois Rivières in 1976 when James Hunt, no less, was soundly thrashed. Typically James told McLaren to sign this man up as soon as possible. The following July, the French-Canadian was in a McLaren – at Silverstone – but for only one race. He was to make the most of it, indulging in countless spins, which to most onlookers seemed to indicate he was in over his head. Gilles knew better; he was just finding the limits in a Grand Prix car and the only way to do that was to go up to and beyond the point of adhesion. Amazingly, Teddy Mayer felt that he could pass on Villeneuve, and so he was picked up by Ferrari. It could all have ended after just two races, for at Fuji he ran into the Tyrrell of Ronnie Peterson and his car somersaulted wildly into a prohibited area, killing two spectators. This time Gilles walked away. . .

He was to be involved in a string of shunts at the start of 1978, some of his own making, some not. But he was undoubtedly quick and as the year wore on he got quicker. At Monza he and Andretti battled for the win, only for both drivers to be penalised for jumping the start. The last race of 1978 was in Canada, and Gilles finally scored his first Grand Prix win, but only after Jarier's Lotus had hit trouble. He felt that his triumph was somehow devalued by that – not having won the race on merit took the gloss off the victory. In statistical terms 1979 was the season he could have won the World Championship, but it went instead to team-mate Jody Scheckter and Gilles supported the South African all the way. There were, of course, the moments of genius, such as his battle with Arnoux at Dijon, or his qualifying performance at Watkins Glen in the rain when he was eleven seconds quicker than Scheckter. There was also controversy, with his notorious return to the pits at Zandvoort with the rear wheel hanging off the Ferrari following a blown tyre and spin. Pure Gilles!

Pure Gilles. The Canadian the way he will always be remembered, taking the Ferrari to the limits of its adhesion.

In 1980 his efforts were handicapped by the truly awful handling of the Ferrari 312T5, which even the matchless skill of Villeneuve could do little to tame, but the new 126CK V6 car was a different proposition. Sure the chassis still needed to be refined, but the turbo power gave him a chance to compete on more equal terms with the Williamses and Brabhams. He took only two wins that year, but they were both memorable. At Monaco he pounced on Alan Jones' faltering Williams to take an unlikely win when many would have long given up the race for lost. Then came an unforgettable performance at Jarama when he kept the snarling pack of cars in his wake for the bulk of the race to take a win one would not have believed possible.

Certainly the cars of the period did a driver like Villeneuve no favours and by the time the 1982 season came round, he hated ground-effect and all it stood for. But he was being paid to drive and just got on with the job in typical fashion. At Imola, the Ferraris had it all their own way and Gilles had the race under control, until team-mate Pironi 'stole' the victory from him on the last lap. Villeneuve was shocked, outraged and suffered every other conceivable hurt over the Fenchman's underhand tactics. He would not speak to him again – ever.

Two weeks later at Zolder, Gilles was hardly any less anguished. He went out for practice, 100 per cent committed as usual, but this time he was not to return, for having touched the March of Jochen Mass his Ferrari cartwheeled across the track in an accident of sickening ferocity. The hapless driver was thrown from the car, receiving terrible injuries. There was no hope of survival, but while the little man had gone, the legend he left behind would never die.

VILLENEUVE, Gilles (CDN) b 18/1/1950, Saint-Jean-sur-Richelieu, Chambly, Quebec – d 8/5/1982, Zolder Circuit, Belgium

	1977			Championship position: Unplaced					
	Race	Circuit	No	Entrant	Tyres	Car/Engine		Comment	Q Pos/Entries
11	BRITISH GP	Silverstone	40	Marlboro Team McLaren	G	3.0 McLaren M23-Cosworth V8		faulty temperature gauge/-2 laps	9/36
12/ret	CANADIAN GP	Mosport Park	21	Scuderia Ferrari SpA SEFAC	G	3.0 Ferrari 312T2 F12		driveshaft	17/27
ret	JAPANESE GP	Mount Fuji	11	Scuderia Ferrari SpA SEFAC	G	3.0 Ferrari 312T2 F12		collision-Peterson-crashed	20/23

	1978			Championship position: 9th	Wins: 1	Pole positions: 0	Fastest laps: 1	Points scored: 17	
8	ARGENTINE GP	Buenos Aires	12	Scuderia Ferrari SpA SEFAC	M	3.0 Ferrari 312T2 F12		FL	7/27
ret	BRAZILIAN GP	Rio	12	Scuderia Ferrari SpA SEFAC	M	3.0 Ferrari 312T2 F12		spun off	6/28
ret	SOUTH AFRICAN GP	Kyalami	12	Scuderia Ferrari SpA SEFAC	M	3.0 Ferrari 312T3 F12		oil leak	8/30
ret	US GP WEST	Long Beach	12	Scuderia Ferrari SpA SEFAC	M	3.0 Ferrari 312T3 F12		collision with Regazzoni	2/30
ret	MONACO GP	Monte Carlo	12	Scuderia Ferrari SpA SEFAC	M	3.0 Ferrari 312T3 F12		tyre failure-accident	8/30
4	BELGIAN GP	Zolder	12	Scuderia Ferrari SpA SEFAC	M	3.0 Ferrari 312T3 F12			4/30
10	SPANISH GP	Jarama	12	Scuderia Ferrari SpA SEFAC	M	3.0 Ferrari 312T3 F12		pit stop-tyres/1 lap behind	5/29
9	SWEDISH GP	Anderstorp	12	Scuderia Ferrari SpA SEFAC	M	3.0 Ferrari 312T3 F12		pit stop-tyres/1 lap behind	7/27
12	FRENCH GP	Paul Ricard	12	Scuderia Ferrari SpA SEFAC	M	3.0 Ferrari 312T3 F12		pit stops-tyres/1 lap behind	9/29
ret	BRITISH GP	Brands Hatch	12	Scuderia Ferrari SpA SEFAC	M	3.0 Ferrari 312T3 F12		driveshaft	13/30
8	GERMAN GP	Hockenheim	12	Scuderia Ferrari SpA SEFAC	M	3.0 Ferrari 312T3 F12		pit stop-tyres	15/30
3	AUSTRIAN GP	Österreichring	12	Scuderia Ferrari SpA SEFAC	M	3.0 Ferrari 312T3 F12			11/31
6	DUTCH GP	Zandvoort	12	Scuderia Ferrari SpA SEFAC	M	3.0 Ferrari 312T3 F12			5/33
7*	ITALIAN GP	Monza	12	Scuderia Ferrari SpA SEFAC	M	3.0 Ferrari 312T3 F12		*2nd but-1 min pen-jumped start	2/32
ret	US GP EAST	Watkins Glen	12	Scuderia Ferrari SpA SEFAC	M	3.0 Ferrari 312T3 F12		engine	4/27
1	CANADIAN GP	Montreal	12	Scuderia Ferrari SpA SEFAC	M	3.0 Ferrari 312T3 F12			3/28

	1979			Championship position: 2nd	Wins: 3	Pole positions: 1	Fastest laps: 6	Points scored: 53	
12/ret	ARGENTINE GP	Buenos Aires	12	Scuderia Ferrari SpA SEFAC	M	3.0 Ferrari 312T3 F12		engine/5 laps behind	10/26
5	BRAZILIAN GP	Interlagos	12	Scuderia Ferrari SpA SEFAC	M	3.0 Ferrari 312T3 F12		1 lap behind	5/26
1	SOUTH AFRICAN GP	Kyalami	12	Scuderia Ferrari SpA SEFAC	M	3.0 Ferrari 312T4 F12		FL	3/26
1	US GP WEST	Long Beach	12	Scuderia Ferrari SpA SEFAC	M	3.0 Ferrari 312T4 F12		FL	1/26
7	SPANISH GP	Jarama	12	Scuderia Ferrari SpA SEFAC	M	3.0 Ferrari 312T4 F12		pit stop-tyres/FL	3/27
7/ret	BELGIAN GP	Zolder	12	Scuderia Ferrari SpA SEFAC	M	3.0 Ferrari 312T4 F12		out of fuel/FL/-1 lap	=6/28
ret	MONACO GP	Monte Carlo	12	Scuderia Ferrari SpA SEFAC	M	3.0 Ferrari 312T4 F12		transmission	2/25
2	FRENCH GP	Dijon	12	Scuderia Ferrari SpA SEFAC	M	3.0 Ferrari 312T4 F12			3/27
14/ret	BRITISH GP	Silverstone	12	Scuderia Ferrari SpA SEFAC	M	3.0 Ferrari 312T4 F12		fuel vaporisation/-5 laps	13/26
8	GERMAN GP	Hockenheim	12	Scuderia Ferrari SpA SEFAC	M	3.0 Ferrari 312T4 F12		pit stop-rear wing/FL/-1 lap	9/26
2	AUSTRIAN GP	Österreichring	12	Scuderia Ferrari SpA SEFAC	M	3.0 Ferrari 312T4 F12			5/26
ret	DUTCH GP	Zandvoort	12	Scuderia Ferrari SpA SEFAC	M	3.0 Ferrari 312T4 F12		blown tyre-suspension damage/FL	6/26
2	ITALIAN GP	Monza	12	Scuderia Ferrari SpA SEFAC	M	3.0 Ferrari 312T4 F12			5/28
2	CANADIAN GP	Montreal	12	Scuderia Ferrari SpA SEFAC	M	3.0 Ferrari 312T4 F12			2/29
1	US GP EAST	Watkins Glen	12	Scuderia Ferrari SpA SEFAC	M	3.0 Ferrari 312T4 F12			3/30

	1980			Championship position: 10th=	Wins: 0	Pole positions: 0	Fastest laps: 0	Points scored: 6	
ret	ARGENTINE GP	Buenos Aires	2	Scuderia Ferrari SpA SEFAC	M	3.0 Ferrari 312T5 F12		accident-suspension-steering	8/28
16/ret	BRAZILIAN GP	Interlagos	2	Scuderia Ferrari SpA SEFAC	M	3.0 Ferrari 312T5 F12		jammed throttle/4 laps behind	3/28
ret	SOUTH AFRICAN GP	Kyalami	2	Scuderia Ferrari SpA SEFAC	M	3.0 Ferrari 312T5 F12		transmission	10/28
ret	US GP WEST	Long Beach	2	Scuderia Ferrari SpA SEFAC	M	3.0 Ferrari 312T5 F12		driveshaft	10/27
6	BELGIAN GP	Zolder	2	Scuderia Ferrari SpA SEFAC	M	3.0 Ferrari 312T5 F12		1 lap behind	12/27
5	MONACO GP	Monte Carlo	2	Scuderia Ferrari SpA SEFAC	M	3.0 Ferrari 312T5 F12		pit stop-tyre/1 lap behind	6/27
8	FRENCH GP	Paul Ricard	2	Scuderia Ferrari SpA SEFAC	M	3.0 Ferrari 312T5 F12		pit stop-tyres/1 lap behind	17/27
ret	BRITISH GP	Brands Hatch	2	Scuderia Ferrari SpA SEFAC	M	3.0 Ferrari 312T5 F12		engine	19/27
6	GERMAN GP	Hockenheim	2	Scuderia Ferrari SpA SEFAC	M	3.0 Ferrari 312T5 F12		pit stop-tyres	16/26
8	AUSTRIAN GP	Österreichring	2	Scuderia Ferrari SpA SEFAC	M	3.0 Ferrari 312T5 F12		pit stop-tyres/1 lap behind	15/25
7	DUTCH GP	Zandvoort	2	Scuderia Ferrari SpA SEFAC	M	3.0 Ferrari 312T5 F12		pit stop-tyres/1 lap behind	7/28
ret	ITALIAN GP	Imola	2	Scuderia Ferrari SpA SEFAC	M	3.0 Ferrari 312T5 F12		puncture-accident	8/28
5	CANADIAN GP	Montreal	2	Scuderia Ferrari SpA SEFAC	M	3.0 Ferrari 312T5 F12			22/28
ret	US GP EAST	Watkins Glen	2	Scuderia Ferrari SpA SEFAC	M	3.0 Ferrari 312T5 F12		hit chicane	18/27

	1981			Championship position: 7th	Wins: 2	Pole positions: 1	Fastest laps: 1	Points scored: 25	
ret	US GP WEST	Long Beach	27	Scuderia Ferrari SpA SEFAC	M	1.5 t/c Ferrari 126CK V6		driveshaft	5/29
ret	BRAZILIAN GP	Rio	27	Scuderia Ferrari SpA SEFAC	M	1.5 t/c Ferrari 126CK V6		turbo wastegate	7/30
ret	ARGENTINE GP	Buenos Aires	27	Scuderia Ferrari SpA SEFAC	M	1.5 t/c Ferrari 126CK V6		driveshaft	7/29
7	SAN MARINO GP	Imola	27	Scuderia Ferrari SpA SEFAC	M	1.5 t/c Ferrari 126CK V6		pit stop-tyres/FL	1/30
4	BELGIAN GP	Zolder	27	Scuderia Ferrari SpA SEFAC	M	1.5 t/c Ferrari 126CK V6			7/31
1	MONACO GP	Monte Carlo	27	Scuderia Ferrari SpA SEFAC	M	1.5 t/c Ferrari 126CK V6			2/31
1	SPANISH GP	Jarama	27	Scuderia Ferrari SpA SEFAC	M	1.5 t/c Ferrari 126CK V6			7/30
ret	FRENCH GP	Dijon	27	Scuderia Ferrari SpA SEFAC	M	1.5 t/c Ferrari 126CK V6		electrics	11/29
ret	BRITISH GP	Silverstone	27	Scuderia Ferrari SpA SEFAC	M	1.5 t/c Ferrari 126CK V6		spun off	8/30
10	GERMAN GP	Hockenheim	27	Scuderia Ferrari SpA SEFAC	M	1.5 t/c Ferrari 126CK V6		pit stop-tyres/1 lap behind	8/30
ret	AUSTRIAN GP	Österreichring	27	Scuderia Ferrari SpA SEFAC	M	1.5 t/c Ferrari 126CK V6		accident	3/28
ret	DUTCH GP	Zandvoort	27	Scuderia Ferrari SpA SEFAC	M	1.5 t/c Ferrari 126CK V6		accident-Giacomelli & Patrese	16/30
ret	ITALIAN GP	Monza	27	Scuderia Ferrari SpA SEFAC	M	1.5 t/c Ferrari 126CK V6		turbo	9/30
3	CANADIAN GP	Montreal	27	Scuderia Ferrari SpA SEFAC	M	1.5 t/c Ferrari 126CK V6			11/30
dsq*	CAESARS PALACE GP	Las Vegas	27	Scuderia Ferrari SpA SEFAC	M	1.5 t/c Ferrari 126CK V6		*started from wrong grid position	3/30

	1982			Championship position: 15th=	Wins: 0	Pole positions: 0	Fastest laps: 0	Points scored: 6	
ret	SOUTH AFRICAN GP	Kyalami	27	Scuderia Ferrari SpA SEFAC	G	1.5 t/c Ferrari 126C2 V6		turbo	3/30
ret	BRAZILIAN GP	Rio	27	Scuderia Ferrari SpA SEFAC	G	1.5 t/c Ferrari 126C2 V6		spun off	2/31
dsq*	US GP WEST	Long Beach	27	Scuderia Ferrari SpA SEFAC	G	1.5 t/c Ferrari 126C2 V6		3rd on road/*wing infringement	7/31
2	SAN MARINO GP	Imola	27	Scuderia Ferrari SpA SEFAC	G	1.5 t/c Ferrari 126C2 V6		overtaken by Pironi on last lap	3/14
dns	BELGIAN GP	Zolder	27	Scuderia Ferrari SpA SEFAC	G	1.5 t/c Ferrari 126C2 V6		fatal practice accident	(8)/32

GP Starts: 67   GP Wins: 6   Pole positions: 2   Fastest laps: 8   Points: 107

JACQUES VILLENEUVE

WORLD CHAMPION: 1997

JACQUES VILLENEUVE

The modern-day racing driver is an incredibly glamorous figure in a sport where image is everything. Yet F1's corporate culture and the hawkish nature of some sections of the media have now perhaps turned these superstars into comparatively bland individuals whose thoughts and opinions are screened and shaped before being made public via non-controversial press releases or media conferences. Whether naturally or by intention, the one man who stands out as the exception to the stereotype on all counts is Jacques Villeneuve. His grunge look, complete with bleached hair, appeals to the younger pop-culture generation and his outspoken views on Formula 1 have caused agitation within the portals of the FIA. Indeed young Master Jacques' maverick streak got him into hot water back in 1997 when he criticised the new technical regulations in his own inimitable style.

Being the son of such a legendary father naturally helped Jacques to get his fledgling career off the ground, but after a none-too-impressive three seasons spent in Italian Formula 3 between 1989 and 1991 it seemed that his 'name' was greater than his talent. However, he was soon to prove the doubters wrong when a move to Japan to race in Formula 3 saw him score three victories and take second place in the series. Luck can play a huge part in the shaping of any driver's career and in Villeneuve's case it came in the form of an invitation to compete in the 1992 Player's Trois Rivières race in Quebec. Then an unknown quantity, Jacques took a fine third place and his new mentor Craig Pollock set in motion a deal for him to race in Formula Atlantic full-time in 1993.

The young French-Canadian fought out a three-way battle for the title but, despite seven poles and five wins from fifteen starts, made just a few errors too many and came up short. Crucially, though, Jerry Forsythe and Barry Green decided Jacques was the driver to stick with when they made the move up to the Indy Car championship in 1994. Villeneuve took to the series like a duck to water, and winning a race at Elkhart Lake and finishing a very close second in the Indy 500 contributed to an impressive sixth place in the final standings. The destination of the 'Rookie of the Year' award was a foregone conclusion. Things were to get even better the following year, as Jacques not only became the youngest-ever PPG Cup champion but also scooped the Indy 500 after being two laps down at one stage. His stock was at its highest, and astutely Villeneuve and Pollock decided that the chance of a dream move to Formula 1 with Williams-Renault for 1996 was much too good to pass up.

Jacques blew into the new F1 season like a full-force gale. He could easily have won his maiden Grand Prix in Australia and as the season progressed he grew an ever-stronger threat to Damon Hill. In fact he came closer to beating his more experienced team-mate than the final points table showed. Crucially, Villeneuve's performances convinced the Williams management that they could dispense with the services of their loyal stalwart and put their faith in the bouncy, self-assured enfant terrible.

Villeneuve duly delivered in 1997 when, with a cocktail of brilliance and some notable gaffes (both on and off track) he squared up to the challenge of Michael Schumacher and Ferrari, and slugged it out right up to the thrilling finale at Jerez, where the German attempted his outrageous blocking manoeuvre. To win the World Championship is hard enough in itself, but to achieve such a feat in only his second year in F1 was a truly remarkable performance. Jacques had to win the title that season, for with Renault pulling out of racing Williams knew they would no longer be the leading force of yore.

In 1998 Jacques hustled the garishly liveried Williams FW20 for all it was worth, often placing it above quicker cars. After spending the previous two seasons eyeing up the silverware, the French-Canadian's expectations were now lowered to a scramble for points-scoring finishes and the odd podium placing. If nothing else, it proved Villeneuve's calibre as a top-notch performer, with an added bonus being his realistic acceptance of the position Williams were in.

Certainly Patrick Head would have liked to hold on to Jacques for a fourth year, but the attraction of the British American Racing project headed up by his mentor Craig Pollock was irresistible. Of course, history now records that the first year for the cocksure new team was one of self-inflicted humiliation as the acquisition of even a single World Championship point proved beyond them. In fairness to Villeneuve, he extracted the very maximum from the car, which on a number of occasions was quite useful. Crucially, he never became disheartened, always gave 100 per cent commitment and absolutely never gave up trying – the qualities of a champion who will surely be back among the winners again.

Jacques Villeneuve leads David Coulthard during the 1997 Hungarian Grand Prix. The race produced a lucky win for the Williams driver, who took full advantage when Damon Hill's Arrows ran into trouble.

VILLENEUVE, Jacques (CDN) b 9/4/1971, Saint-Jean-sur-Richelieu, Chambly, Quebec

1996
Championship position: 2nd   Wins: 4   Pole positions: 3   Fastest laps: 6   Points scored: 78

	Race	Circuit	No	Entrant	Tyres	Car/Engine	Comment	Q Pos/Entries
2	AUSTRALIAN GP	Melbourne	6	Rothmans Williams Renault	G	3.0 Williams FW18-Renault V10	led debut race until oil leak/FL	1/22
ret	BRAZILIAN GP	Interlagos	6	Rothmans Williams Renault	G	3.0 Williams FW18-Renault V10	spun off	3/22
2	ARGENTINE GP	Buenos Aires	6	Rothmans Williams Renault	G	3.0 Williams FW18-Renault V10		3/22
1	EUROPEAN GP	Nürburgring	6	Rothmans Williams Renault	G	3.0 Williams FW18-Renault V10		2/22
11/ret	SAN MARINO GP	Imola	6	Rothmans Williams Renault	G	3.0 Williams FW18-Renault V10	broken suspension/-6 laps	3/22
ret	MONACO GP	Monte Carlo	6	Rothmans Williams Renault	G	3.0 Williams FW18-Renault V10	collision with Badoer	10/22
3	SPANISH GP	Barcelona	6	Rothmans Williams Renault	G	3.0 Williams FW18-Renault V10		2/22
2	CANADIAN GP	Montreal	6	Rothmans Williams Renault	G	3.0 Williams FW18-Renault V10	FL	2/22
2	FRENCH GP	Magny Cours	6	Rothmans Williams Renault	G	3.0 Williams FW18-Renault V10	FL	6/22
1	BRITISH GP	Silverstone	6	Rothmans Williams Renault	G	3.0 Williams FW18-Renault V10	FL	2/22
3	GERMAN GP	Hockenheim	6	Rothmans Williams Renault	G	3.0 Williams FW18-Renault V10		3/20
1	HUNGARIAN GP	Hungaroring	6	Rothmans Williams Renault	G	3.0 Williams FW18-Renault V10		3/20
2	BELGIAN GP	Spa	6	Rothmans Williams Renault	G	3.0 Williams FW18-Renault V10		1/20
7	ITALIAN GP	Monza	6	Rothmans Williams Renault	G	3.0 Williams FW18-Renault V10	suspension damage/-1 lap	2/20
1	PORTUGUESE GP	Estoril	6	Rothmans Williams Renault	G	3.0 Williams FW18-Renault V10	FL	2/20
ret	JAPANESE GP	Suzuka	6	Rothmans Williams Renault	G	3.0 Williams FW18-Renault V10	lost wheel after pitstop/FL	1/20

1997
Championship position: WORLD CHAMPION   Wins: 7   Pole positions: 10   Fastest laps: 3   Points scored: 81

	Race	Circuit	No	Entrant	Tyres	Car/Engine	Comment	Q Pos/Entries
ret	AUSTRALIAN GP	Melbourne	3	Rothmans Williams Renault	G	3.0 Williams FW19-Renault V10	collision with Irvine and Herbert	1/24
1	BRAZILIAN GP	Interlagos	3	Rothmans Williams Renault	G	3.0 Williams FW19-Renault V10	FL	1/22
1	ARGENTINE GP	Buenos Aires	3	Rothmans Williams Renault	G	3.0 Williams FW19-Renault V10		1/22
ret	SAN MARINO GP	Imola	3	Rothmans Williams Renault	G	3.0 Williams FW19-Renault V10	gear selection	1/22
ret	MONACO GP	Monte Carlo	3	Rothmans Williams Renault	G	3.0 Williams FW19-Renault V10	accident damage	3/22
1	SPANISH GP	Barcelona	3	Rothmans Williams Renault	G	3.0 Williams FW19-Renault V10		1/22
ret	CANADIAN GP	Montreal	3	Rothmans Williams Renault	G	3.0 Williams FW19-Renault V10	hit wall	2/22
4	FRENCH GP	Magny Cours	3	Rothmans Williams Renault	G	3.0 Williams FW19-Renault V10		4/22
1	BRITISH GP	Silverstone	3	Rothmans Williams Renault	G	3.0 Williams FW19-Renault V10		1/22
ret	GERMAN GP	Hockenheim	3	Rothmans Williams Renault	G	3.0 Williams FW19-Renault V10	tangled with Trulli- spun off	9/22
1	HUNGARIAN GP	Hungaroring	3	Rothmans Williams Renault	G	3.0 Williams FW19-Renault V10		2/22
5*	BELGIAN GP	Spa	3	Rothmans Williams Renault	G	3.0 Williams FW19-Renault V10	*3rd place car dsq/FL	1/22
5	ITALIAN GP	Monza	3	Rothmans Williams Renault	G	3.0 Williams FW19-Renault V10		4/22
1	AUSTRIAN GP	A1-Ring	3	Rothmans Williams Renault	G	3.0 Williams FW19-Renault V10	FL	1/22
1	LUXEMBOURG GP	Nürburgring	3	Rothmans Williams Renault	G	3.0 Williams FW19-Renault V10		2/22
dsq*	JAPANESE GP	Suzuka	3	Rothmans Williams Renault	G	3.0 Williams FW19-Renault V10	*5th dsq after appeal	1/22
3	EUROPEAN GP	Jerez	3	Rothmans Williams Renault	G	3.0 Williams FW19-Renault V10		1/22

1998
Championship position: 5th   Wins: 0   Pole positions: 0   Fastest laps: 0   Points scored: 21

	Race	Circuit	No	Entrant	Tyres	Car/Engine	Comment	Q Pos/Entries
5	AUSTRALIAN GP	Melbourne	1	Winfield Williams	G	3.0 Williams FW20-Mechachrome V10	1 lap behind	4/22
7	BRAZILIAN GP	Interlagos	1	Winfield Williams	G	3.0 Williams FW20-Mechachrome V10	1 lap behind	10/22
ret	ARGENTINE GP	Buenos Aires	1	Winfield Williams	G	3.0 Williams FW20-Mechachrome V10	collision with Coulthard	7/22
4	SAN MARINO GP	Imola	1	Winfield Williams	G	3.0 Williams FW20-Mechachrome V10		6/22
6	SPANISH GP	Barcelona	1	Winfield Williams	G	3.0 Williams FW20-Mechachrome V10	1 lap behind	10/22
5	MONACO GP	Monte Carlo	1	Winfield Williams	G	3.0 Williams FW20-Mechachrome V10	1 lap behind	13/22
10	CANADIAN GP	Montreal	1	Winfield Williams	G	3.0 Williams FW20-Mechachrome V10	collision lost rear wing/-6 laps	6/22
4	FRENCH GP	Magny Cours	1	Winfield Williams	G	3.0 Williams FW20-Mechachrome V10		5/22
7	BRITISH GP	Silverstone	1	Winfield Williams	G	3.0 Williams FW20-Mechachrome V10	1 lap behind	3/22
6	AUSTRIAN GP	A1-Ring	1	Winfield Williams	G	3.0 Williams FW20-Mechachrome V10		11/22
3	GERMAN GP	Hockenheim	1	Winfield Williams	G	3.0 Williams FW20-Mechachrome V10		3/22
3	HUNGARIAN GP	Hungaroring	1	Winfield Williams	G	3.0 Williams FW20-Mechachrome V10		6/22
ret	BELGIAN GP	Spa	1	Winfield Williams	G	3.0 Williams FW20-Mechachrome V10	spun off	6/22
ret	ITALIAN GP	Monza	1	Winfield Williams	G	3.0 Williams FW20-Mechachrome V10	spun off	2/22
8	LUXEMBOURG GP	Nürburgring	1	Winfield Williams	G	3.0 Williams FW20-Mechachrome V10	1 lap behind	9/22
6	JAPANESE GP	Suzuka	1	Winfield Williams	G	3.0 Williams FW20-Mechachrome V10		6/22

1999
Championship position: Unplaced

	Race	Circuit	No	Entrant	Tyres	Car/Engine	Comment	Q Pos/Entries
ret	AUSTRALIAN GP	Melbourne	22	British American Racing	B	3.0 BAR 01-Supertec V10	lost ear wing	11/22
ret	BRAZILIAN GP	Interlagos	22	British American Racing	B	3.0 BAR 01-Supertec V10	hydraulics/practice time disallowed	21/21
ret	SAN MARINO GP	Imola	22	British American Racing	B	3.0 BAR 01-Supertec V10	transmission	5/22
ret	MONACO GP	Monte Carlo	22	British American Racing	B	3.0 BAR 01-Supertec V10	oil leak	8/22
ret	SPANISH GP	Barcelona	22	British American Racing	B	3.0 BAR 01-Supertec V10	transmission	6/22
ret	CANADIAN GP	Montreal	22	British American Racing	B	3.0 BAR 01-Supertec V10	accident	16/22
ret	FRENCH GP	Magny Cours	22	British American Racing	B	3.0 BAR 01-Supertec V10	spun off	12/22
ret	BRITISH GP	Silverstone	22	British American Racing	B	3.0 BAR 01-Supertec V10	gearbox	9/22
ret	AUSTRIAN GP	A1-Ring	22	British American Racing	B	3.0 BAR 01-Supertec V10	broken driveshaft	9/22
ret	GERMAN GP	Hockenheim	22	British American Racing	B	3.0 BAR 01-Supertec V10	collision with Diniz	12/22
ret	HUNGARIAN GP	Hungaroring	22	British American Racing	B	3.0 BAR 01-Supertec V10	clutch	9/22
15	BELGIAN GP	Spa	22	British American Racing	B	3.0 BAR 01-Supertec V10r	1 lap behind	9/22
8	ITALIAN GP	Monza	22	British American Racing	B	3.0 BAR 01-Supertec V10		11/22
ret/10	EUROPEAN GP	Nürburgring	22	British American Racing	B	3.0 BAR 01-Supertec V10	clutch/5 laps behind	8/22
ret	MALAYSIAN GP	Sepang	22	British American Racing	B	3.0 BAR 01-Supertec V10	hydraulics	10/22
9	JAPANESE GP	Suzuka	22	British American Racing	B	3.0 BAR 01-Supertec V10	1 lap behind	11/22

GP Starts: 65   GP Wins: 11   Pole positions: 13   Fastest laps: 9   Points: 180

LUIGI VILLORESI

Success and tragedy in equal measure marked the 25-year career of 'Gigi' Villoresi, the silver-haired Italian who was at his zenith in the immediate post-war era. He began racing back in 1931 with Fiats before turning to the marque that would make his name: Maserati. That was in 1936, and by then he and his brother Emilio had established a reputation as a pretty wild pair. Nevertheless Luigi won the voiturette Brno GP in Czechoslovakia in 1937 to earn promotion to the Maserati Grand Prix team. He became the 1500 cc Italian champion in 1938 and 1939, and took wins in the Albi, Pescara and South African GPs. He also won the Targa Florio in both 1939 and 1940, again in a Maserati, but the period was clouded by the death of Emilio, who was by now racing as a rival in the Alfa Romeo team.

During the war Villoresi was held as a prisoner of war, but upon his release he was immediately looking to race again. He and Farina soon vied for the title of Italy's fastest driver, and with Wimille he was regarded as the world's best. In 1946 he scored victories in Nice and the Circuit of Voghera with his Maserati and took a 3-litre 8CL to Indianapolis, where he finished seventh, and the following season he notched up wins at Buenos Aires, Mar del Plata, Nimes, Nice, Strasbourg and Luxembourg. The 1948 season saw him suffer a major crash at Bremgarten which he was lucky to survive, though he was to triumph as Italian champion for the second successive year. Wins were recorded at Buenos Aires in two races, Comminges, Albi, Silverstone (the first post-war British GP) and Barcelona. After winning the Libre races at Interlagos and Gavea, Villoresi finally forsook his beloved Maserati to join Ferrari along with Ascari, to whom he passed on much of his racecraft. He was soon winning races for the Scuderia at Zandvoort in the supercharged car and in Formula 2 at Brussels, Luxembourg, Rome and Garda.

The 1950 and 1951 seasons were spent chasing the Alfa Romeos, but Villoresi still found success aplenty; wins at Buenos Aires and Rosario were followed by more success at Marseilles, Erlen and Monza in 1950, while the following year saw a very consistent championship campaign with the Type 375, which he took to victory at Syracuse and Pau in non-title events. It was a good year for 'Gigi', for he won the Mille Miglia and was second in the Carrera Panamericana, and shared a Lancia with Ascari to win the Sestrieres Rally. During 1952-53 he was forced sit in the shadow of his brilliant pupil Ascari, but could still do the job when required, taking wins at Turin and Modena.

Villoresi signed for Lancia for the 1954 season along with Ascari, but they were forced to wait for their Formula 1 car, which failed to appear until the last Grand Prix of the season. 'Gigi' raced for Maserati in the interim, but a crash in the Mille Miglia had dulled his edge. He continued with the Lancia concern in 1955 but, after the death of Ascari and the subsequent amalgamation of the team with Ferrari, found himself out of a works drive when the 1956 season began. By now well past his best, he drove privateer Maseratis and the works OSCA in sports car events. It was in this form of racing, driving a Maserati, that he suffered yet another serious injury when he crashed at Castelfusano and broke his leg very badly. Begged by his family to retire, he deferred to their wishes, but couldn't resist taking part in the 1958 Acropolis Rally, which he won in a Lancia.

VILLORESI, Luigi (I) b 16/5/1909, Milan – d 8/1997

	1950								
	Championship position: Unplaced								
	Race	Circuit	No	Entrant	Tyres	Car/Engine	Comment	Q Pos/Entries
ret	MONACO GP	Monte Carlo	38	Scuderia Ferrari	P	1.5 s/c Ferrari 125 V12	transmission/rear axle	6/21
ret	SWISS GP	Bremgarten	22	Scuderia Ferrari	P	1.5 s/c Ferrari 125 V12	transmission	4/18
6	BELGIAN GP	Spa	2	Scuderia Ferrari	P	1.5 s/c Ferrari 125 V12	2 laps behind	4/14
dns	FRENCH GP	Reims	8	Scuderia Ferrari	P	1.5 s/c Ferrari 125 V12	withdrawn to race in F2 support	– / –

	1951								
	Championship position: 5th Wins: 0 Pole positions: 0 Fastest laps: 0 Points scored: 18								
ret	SWISS GP	Bremgarten	18	Scuderia Ferrari	P	4.5 Ferrari 375F1 V12	crashed in rain	3/21
3	BELGIAN GP	Spa	10	Scuderia Ferrari	P	4.5 Ferrari 375F1 V12		3/13
3	FRENCH GP	Reims	10	Scuderia Ferrari	E	4.5 Ferrari 375F1 V12	3 laps behind	4/23
3	BRITISH GP	Silverstone	10	Scuderia Ferrari	P	4.5 Ferrari 375F1 V12	2 laps behind	5/20
4	GERMAN GP	Nürburgring	72	Scuderia Ferrari	P	4.5 Ferrari 375F1 V12		5/25
4	ITALIAN GP	Monza	4	Scuderia Ferrari	P	4.5 Ferrari 375F1 V12	1 lap behind	5/22
ret	SPANISH GP	Pedralbes	4	Scuderia Ferrari	P	4.5 Ferrari 375F1 V12	ignition	5/20

	1952								
	Championship position: 7th= Wins: 0 Pole positions: 0 Fastest laps: 0 Points scored: 8								
3	DUTCH GP	Zandvoort	6	Scuderia Ferrari	P	2.0 Ferrari 500 4		4/18
3	ITALIAN GP	Monza	16	Scuderia Ferrari	P	2.0 Ferrari 500 4		2/35

	1953								
	Championship position: 5th Wins: 0 Pole positions: 0 Fastest laps: 1 Points scored: 17								
2	ARGENTINE GP	Buenos Aires	14	Scuderia Ferrari	P	2.0 Ferrari 500 4	1 lap behind	3/16
ret	DUTCH GP	Zandvoort	4	Scuderia Ferrari	P	2.0 Ferrari 500 4	throttle cable/FL	4/20
2	BELGIAN GP	Spa	8	Scuderia Ferrari	P	2.0 Ferrari 500 4		5/22
6	FRENCH GP	Reims	12	Scuderia Ferrari	P	2.0 Ferrari 500 4		3/25
ret	BRITISH GP	Silverstone	7	Scuderia Ferrari	P	2.0 Ferrari 500 4	transmission	6/29
ret*	GERMAN GP	Nürburgring	4	Scuderia Ferrari	P	2.0 Ferrari 500 4	* Ascari took over/engine	6/35
8*	"	"	1	Scuderia Ferrari	P	2.0 Ferrari 500 4	* took over Ascari's car/-1 lap	– / –
6	SWISS GP	Bremgarten	28	Scuderia Ferrari	P	2.0 Ferrari 500 4	3 laps behind	6/23
3	ITALIAN GP	Monza	2	Scuderia Ferrari	P	2.0 Ferrari 500 4	1 lap behind	5/30

	1954								
	Championship position: 15th= Wins: 0 Pole positions: 0 Fastest laps: 0 Points scored: 2								
5	FRENCH GP	Reims	14	Officine Alfieri Maserati	P	2.5 Maserati 250F 6	on loan from Lancia/-3 laps	14/22
ret*	BRITISH GP	Silverstone	32	Officine Alfieri Maserati	P	2.5 Maserati 250F 6	* Ascari took over/oil pressure	27/31
dns	GERMAN GP	Nürburgring	5	Officine Alfieri Maserati	P	2.5 Maserati 250F 6	w/drawn after Marimón's death	(10)/23
ret	ITALIAN GP	Monza	22	Officine Alfieri Maserati	P	2.5 Maserati 250F 6	clutch	6/21
ret	SPANISH GP	Pedralbes	36	Scuderia Lancia	P	2.5 Lancia D50 V8	brakes	5/22

	1955								
	Championship position: 12th= Wins: 0 Pole positions: 0 Fastest laps: 0 Points scored: 2								
ret	ARGENTINE GP	Buenos Aires	34	Scuderia Lancia	P	2.5 Lancia D50 V8	fuel pump	11/22
ret	"	"	36	Scuderia Lancia	P	2.5 Lancia D50 V8	took Castellotti's car-crashed	– / –
5	MONACO GP	Monte Carlo	28	Scuderia Lancia	P	2.5 Lancia D50 V8	1 lap behind	7/22
dns	ITALIAN GP	Monza	10	Scuderia Ferrari	P	2.5 Lancia D50 V8	tyre problems in practice	(8)/22

	1956								
	Championship position: 15th= Wins: 0 Pole positions: 0 Fastest laps: 0 Points scored: 2								
5	BELGIAN GP	Spa	22	Scuderia Centro Sud	P	2.5 Maserati 250F 6	2 laps behind	11/16
ret	FRENCH GP	Reims	38	Luigi Piotti	P	2.5 Maserati 250F 6	brakes	10/20
6	BRITISH GP	Silverstone	11	Luigi Piotti	P	2.5 Maserati 250F 6	5 laps behind	19/28
ret	GERMAN GP	Nürburgring	18	Luigi Piotti	P	2.5 Maserati 250F 6	engine	– /20
ret*	ITALIAN GP	Monza	34	Officine Alfieri Maserati	P	2.5 Maserati 250F 6	*Bonnier took over/engine	8/26

GP Starts: 31 GP Wins: 0 Pole positions: 0 Fastest laps: 1 Points: 49

OTTORINO VOLONTERIO

A lawyer from Locarno, Volonterio raced a Maserati sports car with a modicum of success, taking second place in the Coupe de Paris at Montlhéry in 1955. He shared Baron de Graffenried's Maserati at Pedralbes in 1954, but when he acquired the car for 1955 he was usually slow or hopelessly slow.

In 1957 he purchased a Maserati 250F, but in the main he wisely left it to others to race; Mackay-Fraser practised the car for the GP de Reims, but was killed in the F2 supporting race. Ottorino did make one final appearance, at Monza, where he shared the car with André Simon, the pair finishing 15 laps behind.

VOLONTERIO, Ottorino (CH) b 7/12/1917, Orselina

	1954								
	Championship position: 0 Wins: 0 Pole positions: 0 Fastest laps: 0 Points scored: 0								
	Race	Circuit	No	Entrant	Tyres	Car/Engine	Comment	Q Pos/Entries
ret*	SPANISH GP	Pedralbes	22	Baron de Graffenried	P	2.5 Maserati A6GCM/250F 6	* took de Graffenried,s car/engine	– /22
	1956								
	Championship position: 0 Wins: 0 Pole positions: 0 Fastest laps: 0 Points scored: 0								
nc	GERMAN GP	Nürburgring	22	Ottorino Volonterio	P	2.5 Maserati A6GCM/250F 6	6 laps behind	19/21
	1957								
	Championship position: 0 Wins: 0 Pole positions: 0 Fastest laps: 0 Points scored: 0								
nc*	ITALIAN GP	Monza	28	Ottorino Volonterio	P	2.5 Maserati 250F 6	* shared with Simon/-15 laps	– /19

GP Starts: 3 GP Wins: 0 Pole positions: 0 Fastest laps: 0 Points: 0

RIKKY von OPEL

An heir to the Opel automobile fortune, von Opel began his racing career under the pseudonym 'Antonio Bronco', but soon reverted to his true name after a successful introduction to Formula Ford in 1970.

He jumped staight into F3 the following year with a Lotus and showed much promise, which was realised in 1972 when, driving the Iberia-sponsored works F3 Ensign, he took the Lombard North Central title and was so impressed with Mo Nunn's little team that he commissioned a Formula 1 car to go Grand Prix racing in 1973.

Inevitably with such an inexperienced pairing, success was thin on the ground and von Opel was damned as a playboy racer, which was unfair as he took the whole project very seriously indeed. When the oportunity arose to drive a pukka works Brabham at the beginning of the European season in 1974, Rikki grabbed it, reasoning that he could learn much in this established team.

After he was unable qualify the car at Dijon for the French GP, von Opel turned his back on the sport, having tried but failed to make the grade, to pursue other interests.

von OPEL, Rikky (FL) b 14/10/1947, New York, USA

1973 — Championship position: Unplaced

	Race	Circuit	No	Entrant	Tyres	Car/Engine	Comment	Q Pos/Entries
15	FRENCH GP	Paul Ricard	29	Team Ensign	F	3.0 Ensign N173-Cosworth V8	3 laps behind	25/25
13	BRITISH GP	Silverstone	28	Team Ensign	F	3.0 Ensign N173-Cosworth V8	p stop-temperature gauge/-6 laps	21/29
dns	DUTCH GP	Zandvoort	28	Team Ensign	F	3.0 Ensign N173-Cosworth V8	suspension pick up failure	(14)/24
ret	AUSTRIAN GP	Österreichring	28	Team Ensign	F	3.0 Ensign N173-Cosworth V8	fuel pressure	19/25
ret	ITALIAN GP	Monza	28	Team Ensign	F	3.0 Ensign N173-Cosworth V8	overheating	17/25
nc	CANADIAN GP	Mosport Park	28	Team Ensign	F	3.0 Ensign N173-Cosworth V8	2 pit stops-off road/-12 laps	26/26
ret	US GP	Watkins Glen	28	Team Ensign	F	3.0 Ensign N173-Cosworth V8	stuck throttle	28/28

1974 — Championship position: Unplaced

	Race	Circuit	No	Entrant	Tyres	Car/Engine	Comment	Q Pos/Entries
dns	ARGENTINE GP	Buenos Aires	22	Team Ensign	F	3.0 Ensign N174-Cosworth V8	handling problems in practice	26/26
ret	SPANISH GP	Jarama	8	Motor Racing Developments	F	3.0 Brabham BT44-Cosworth V8	oil leak	25/28
ret	BELGIAN GP	Nivelles	8	Motor Racing Developments	F	3.0 Brabham BT44-Cosworth V8	oil pressure	22/32
dnq	MONACO GP	Monte Carlo	8	Motor Racing Developments	F	3.0 Brabham BT44-Cosworth V8		28/28
9	SWEDISH GP	Anderstorp	8	Motor Racing Developments	F	3.0 Brabham BT44-Cosworth V8	1 lap behind	20/28
9	DUTCH GP	Zandvoort	8	Motor Racing Developments	F	3.0 Brabham BT44-Cosworth V8	2 laps behind	23/27
dnq	FRENCH GP	Dijon	8	Motor Racing Developments	F	3.0 Brabham BT44-Cosworth V8		28/30

GP Starts: 10   GP Wins: 0   Pole positions: 0   Fastest laps: 0   Points: 0

von TRIPS, Wolfgang (D) b 4/5/1928, Horrem, nr Cologne – d 10/9/1961, Monza Circuit, Italy

1956 — Championship position: Unplaced

	Race	Circuit	No	Entrant	Car/Engine	Comment	Q Pos/Entries
dns	ITALIAN GP	Monza	50	Scuderia Ferrari	E 2.5 Lancia-Ferrari D50 V8	accident in practice	(=11)/26

1957 — Championship position: 12th=   Wins: 0   Pole positions: 0   Fastest laps: 0   Points scored: 4

	Race	Circuit	No	Entrant	Car/Engine	Comment	Q Pos/Entries
6*	ARGENTINE GP	Buenos Aires	18	Scuderia Ferrari	E 2.5 Lancia-Ferrari D50A V8	* Perdisa & Collins co drove/-2 laps	– /16
7/ret*	MONACO GP	Monte Carlo	24	Scuderia Ferrari	E 2.5 Lancia-Ferrari 801 V8	engine/*Hawthorn drove for 4 laps	9/21
3	ITALIAN GP	Monza	36	Scuderia Ferrari	E 2.5 Lancia-Ferrari 801 V8	2 laps behind	8/19

1958 — Championship position: 10th   Wins: 0   Pole positions: 0   Fastest laps: 0   Points scored: 9

	Race	Circuit	No	Entrant	Car/Engine	Comment	Q Pos/Entries
ret	MONACO GP	Monte Carlo	40	Scuderia Ferrari	E 2.4 Ferrari Dino 246 V6	engine	12/28
3	FRENCH GP	Reims	6	Scuderia Ferrari	E 2.4 Ferrari Dino 246 V6		21/21
ret	BRITISH GP	Silverstone	3	Scuderia Ferrari	E 2.4 Ferrari Dino 246 V6	engine	11/21
4	GERMAN GP	Nürburgring	4	Scuderia Ferrari	E 2.4 Ferrari Dino 246 V6		5/26
5	PORTUGUESE GP	Oporto	24	Scuderia Ferrari	· E 2.4 Ferrari Dino 246 V6	1 lap behind	6/15
ret	ITALIAN GP	Monza	16	Scuderia Ferrari	E 2.4 Ferrari Dino 246 V6	collision with Schell-broken leg	6/21

1959 — Championship position: Unplaced

	Race	Circuit	No	Entrant	Car/Engine	Comment	Q Pos/Entries
ret	MONACO GP (F2)	Monte Carlo	6	Dr Ing hcf Porsche KG	D 1.5 Porsche 718 F4 F2	multiple accident	12/24
dns	GERMAN GP (F2)	AVUS	14	Dr Ing hcf Porsche KG	D 1.5 Porsche 718 F4 F2	w/dawn after Behra's accident	– / –
6	US GP	Sebring	4	Scuderia Ferrari	D 2.4 Ferrari Dino 246 V6	4 laps behind	6/19

1960 — Championship position: 6th=   Wins: 0   Pole positions: 0   Fastest laps: 0   Points scored: 10

	Race	Circuit	No	Entrant	Car/Engine	Comment	Q Pos/Entries
5	ARGENTINE GP	Buenos Aires	30	Scuderia Ferrari	D 2.4 Ferrari Dino 246 V6	1 lap behind	5/22
8/ret	MONACO GP	Monte Carlo	38	Scuderia Ferrari	D 2.4 Ferrari Dino 246 V6	clutch/39 laps behind	8/24
5	DUTCH GP	Zandvoort	2	Scuderia Ferrari	D 2.4 Ferrari Dino 246 V6	1 lap behind	15/21
dns	"	"	2	Scuderia Ferrari	D 2.4 Ferrari Dino 246P V6	practice only	– / –
ret	BELGIAN GP	Spa	26	Scuderia Ferrari	D 2.4 Ferrari Dino 246 V6	transmission	11/18
11/ret	FRENCH GP	Reims	4	Scuderia Ferrari	D 2.4 Ferrari Dino 246 V6	transmission/-19 laps	5/23
6	BRITISH GP	Silverstone	11	Scuderia Ferrari	D 2.4 Ferrari Dino 246 V6	2 laps behind	7/25
4	PORTUGUESE GP	Oporto	28	Scuderia Ferrari	D 2.4 Ferrari Dino 246 V6		9/16
5	ITALIAN GP	Monza	22	Scuderia Ferrari	D 1.5 Ferrari Dino 246P V6 F2	2 laps behind	6/16
9	US GP	Riverside	26	Scuderia Centro Sud	D 2.5 Cooper T51-Maserati 4	3 laps behind	16/23

1961		Championship position: 2nd		Wins: 2	Pole positions: 1	Fastest laps: 0	Points scored: 33		
4/ret	MONACO GP	Monte Carlo	40	Scuderia Ferrari SpA SEFAC	D	1.5 Ferrari 156 V6		engine failed-crashed/-2 laps	6/21
1	DUTCH GP	Zandvoort	3	Scuderia Ferrari Spa SEFAC	D	1.5 Ferrari 156 V6			2/17
2	BELGIAN GP	Spa	2	Scuderia Ferrari SpA SEFAC	D	1.5 Ferrari 156 V6			2/25
ret	FRENCH GP	Reims	20	Scuderia Ferrari SpA SEFAC	D	1.5 Ferrari 156 V6		engine	2/26
1	BRITISH GP	Aintree	4	Scuderia Ferrari SpA SEFAC	D	1.5 Ferrari 156 V6			=1/30
2	GERMAN GP	Nürburgring	3	Scuderia Ferrari SpA SEFAC	D	1.5 Ferrari 156 V6			5/27
ret	ITALIAN GP	Monza	4	Scuderia Ferrari SpA SEFAC	D	1.5 Ferrari 156 V6		collision-Clark, fatal accident	1/33

GP Starts: 27   GP Wins: 2   Pole positions: 1   Fastest laps: 0   Points: 56

WOLFGANG von TRIPS

This dashing, handsome and immensely popular German aristocrat stood on the verge of the drivers' World Championship at Monza on a sunny September day in 1961. Everything was going to plan; his red Ferrari sat on pole position at the head of a two-by-two grid, cunningly arranged by the organisers to help reduce the chances of any fast non-Italian machines gaining the all-important tow. However, when the flag dropped Trips was not the quickest away and was enmeshed in the leading bunch which hammered around the banking to complete the first lap. The German was under pressure from the Lotus of Jim Clark and when the young Scot pulled out of the Ferrari's slipstream in an attempt to pass, Trips moved over too. . .

Clipping the front wheel of the Lotus sent the number four Ferrari out of control and it crashed up a bank and along a fence packed with spectators before rolling back down to the track. The driver lay on the circuit, flung like a rag doll; Jim Clark was wandering around unhurt but in shock as the cars sped past on their third lap; and one driver and 14 spectators were to pay the sport's ultimate price. The race went on, and team-mate Phil Hill was crowned World Champion, but Wolfgang von Trips was dead. Such were the stark realities of motor racing.

The German had always lived on the edge. His first Grand Prix appearance at Monza was ended by a practice crash when the steering failed, but he escaped serious injury this time around. In 1958 he collided with Schell on the opening lap and ended up with a broken leg. Returning to action at the start of 1959 he spun the works F2 Porsche at Monaco and eliminated the rest of his class. This sorry tally makes him seem a liability, but that was far from the case, for from the earliest days, when he took a third place in the 1955 Tourist Trophy in a Mercedes 300SLR at Dundrod, Trips was a fearless and skilled driver, particularly in sports cars. He was European hill-climb champion in 1958 in a works Porsche RSK, and in 1959 drove a brilliant race in the small-capacity Porsche in the Tourist Trophy at Goodwood to finish second ahead of Brooks' Ferrari.

By 1960 von Trips was emerging as a trusty and reliable single-seater exponent. Apart from his placings in the championship races, he won at Syracuse and Solitude for Ferrari, and took second in the F2 German GP for Porsche. His work with the rear-engined prototype car set him up for the 1961 season, and with the new 156 'sharknose' Ferrari he took his first Grand Prix win at Zandvoort in masterly style. In sports cars, the Targa Florio was won with Gendebien, and then back in F1 he coped with the early wet conditions at Aintree to extend his championship lead. Even a second place behind the genius of Moss in the German Grand Prix seemed to be sufficient, for the next race was at Monza and, surely, the title would be his . . .

JO VONLANTHEN

A car trader from Frauenfeld in Switzerland, Vonlanthen began racing in Formula Vee in 1968 and, driving a Tecno, won the 1972 Swiss F3 championship. He went into Formula 2 in 1973 with a GRD, taking a third place in the Rome GP, but this was easily his best result until he came second in the opening round of the 1975 series at Estoril in a March 742-BMW, when most of the front-runners fell by the wayside.

His brief Formula 1 career lasted just three races in 1975, Jo driving a works Ensign in the International Trophy before switching to Williams for the Swiss GP at Dijon. After taking a distant 14th place in this non-championship race, Vonlanthen made the grid in his Williams for the Austrian GP only because both Henton and Wilson Fittiplaldi had practice mishaps. He returned to Formula 2 on an irregular basis in 1976, but never really featured.

DAVE WALKER

This rugged Australian trained to be an accountant until a chance meeting with some motor sport enthusiasts took him hill-climbing. Dave came to Britain in 1962 dreaming of emulating the likes of Brabham, but soon realised that he was too inexperienced to make it at this stage and hitch-hiked home to go about racing in a more serious manner. By 1966 he was back to begin an on-off Formula 3 career which saw him slowly climb the ladder. In 1967 he took the European trail in a Merlyn, winning a race at Ojatia, but during 1968-69 Walker was stuck in Formula Ford in the works Alexis. However, he joined the works Lotus F3 team in 1970, winning the Lombank F3 championship, and in 1971 he was back for more, securing both the Shell and Forward Trust titles. Although a Grand Prix outing in the Lotus turbine was unhappy, he was chosen to partner Fittipaldi in 1972, but apart from a fifth place in the non-title Brazilian GP the year was a personal disaster for Walker, while the Brazilian stormed to his first World Championship. Set to race for GRD in Formula 2 in 1973, Dave suffered two separate road accidents, breaking a leg in one and an arm in the other, but came back to race in 2-litre sports car events. He then had a brief stab at F5000 in 1975, before trying his hand at Canadian Formula Atlantic.

FRED WACKER Jnr

An SCCA racer from Chicago who competed regularly at the wheel of an Allard-Cadillac, and a member of the Cunningham team at Le Mans in 1951, the wealthy Wacker raced for Gordini on a number of occasions, taking a third place at Chimay in 1953 and fourth in the minor Cadours GP the following season.

In World Championship Grands Prix, he was extremely lucky to escape with a lightly fractured skull after crashing the Gordini in practice for the 1953 Swiss GP. After his European adventures, he continued racing sports cars in the States.

VONLANTHEN, Jo (CH) b 31/5/1942, St Ursen

	1975	Championship position: Unplaced						
	Race	Circuit	No	Entrant	Tyres	Car/Engine	Comment	Q Pos/Entries
ret	AUSTRIAN GP	Österreichring	20	Frank Williams Racing Cars	G	3.0 Williams FW03-Cosworth V8	engine	29/30

GP Starts: 1   GP Wins: 0   Pole positions: 0   Fastest laps: 0   Points: 0

WACKER (Jnr), Fred (USA) b 10/7/1918, Chicago, Illinois

	1953	Championship position: Unplaced						
	Race	Circuit	No	Entrant	Tyres	Car/Engine	Comment	Q Pos/Entries
dns	DUTCH GP	Zandvoort	40	Equipe Gordini	E	2.0 Gordini Type 16 6	engine needed by Schell	– /20
9	BELGIAN GP	Spa	38	Equipe Gordini	E	2.0 Gordini Type 16 6	4 laps behind	15/22
dns	SWISS GP	Bremgarten	44	Equipe Gordini	E	2.0 Gordini Type 16 6	practice crash-fractured skull	– /23
	1954	Championship position: Unplaced						
ret	SWISS GP	Bremgarten	14	Equipe Gordini	E	2.5 Gordini Type 16 6	transmission	15/16
6	ITALIAN GP	Monza	42	Equipe Gordini	E	2.5 Gordini Type 16 6	5 laps behind	18/21

GP Starts: 3   GP Wins: 0   Pole positions: 0   Fastest laps: 0   Points: 0

WALKER, Dave (AUS) b 10/6/1941, Sydney, New South Wales

	1971	Championship position: Unplaced						
	Race	Circuit	No	Entrant	Tyres	Car/Engine	Comment	Q Pos/Entries
ret	DUTCH GP	Zandvoort	15	Gold Leaf Team Lotus	F	Turbine Lotus 56B-Pratt & Witney	crashed in the rain	22/24
dns	"	"	12	Gold Leaf Team Lotus	F	3.0 Lotus 72D-Cosworth V8	practice only	– / –
	1972	Championship position: Unplaced						
dsq	ARGENTINE GP	Buenos Aires	12	John Player Team Lotus	F	3.0 Lotus 72D-Cosworth V8	outside assistance	20/22
10	SOUTH AFRICAN GP	Kyalami	9	John Player Team Lotus	F	3.0 Lotus 72D-Cosworth V8	1 lap behind	=18/27
9/ret	SPANISH GP	Jarama	21	John Player Team Lotus	F	3.0 Lotus 72D-Cosworth V8	out of fuel/3 laps behind	24/26
14	MONACO GP	Monte Carlo	9	John Player Team Lotus	F	3.0 Lotus 72D-Cosworth V8	pit stop-handling/-5 laps	14/25
14	BELGIAN GP	Nivelles	33	John Player Team Lotus	F	3.0 Lotus 72D-Cosworth V8	2 stops-tyres-oil pressure/-6 laps	12/26
18/ret	FRENCH GP	Clermont Ferrand	6	John Player Team Lotus	F	3.0 Lotus 72D-Cosworth V8	gearbox/4 laps behind	26/29
ret	BRITISH GP	Brands Hatch	9	John Player Team Lotus	F	3.0 Lotus 72D-Cosworth V8	rear suspension	=14/27
ret	GERMAN GP	Nürburgring	25	John Player Team Lotus	F	3.0 Lotus 72D-Cosworth V8	oil tank	23/27
ret	AUSTRIAN GP	Österreichring	21	John Player Team Lotus	F	3.0 Lotus 72D-Cosworth V8	engine	19/26
ret	US GP	Watkins Glen	11	John Player Team Lotus	F	3.0 Lotus 72D-Cosworth V8	engine	31/32

GP Starts: 11   GP Wins: 0   Pole positions: 0   Fastest laps: 0   Points: 0

PETER WALKER

Walker gained a certain notoriety for his aggressive, sliding style in Peter Whitehead's ERA before the war, and in the late forties became one of the few drivers to glean much success in the E-Type ERA both on the circuits and on the hills, where he put in some stunning performances in 1948. He raced the ERA at the 1950 British GP with Rolt, but it soon failed. He did well to finish the race the following year, however, when he brought the hitherto unreliable BRM into seventh place despite extreme discomfort from a burning-hot exhaust.

Signed by Jaguar in 1951 to race their sports cars, he shared his greatest triumphs with his old friend Peter Whitehead, the pair winning Le Mans and finishing second at Dundrod in the Tourist Trophy. In addition, Walker took second place at Le Mans in 1953, this time with Moss. Moving to Aston Martin, Peter won the Goodwood 9 Hours with Dennis Poore in 1955, and raced single-seaters once more at Zandvoort (for Moss) and Aintree (for Rob Walker). After escaping a nasty accident at Le Mans in 1956 relatively lightly, Walker decided to retire, though he was tempted back one more time, to race Rob Walker's Connaught at Syracuse in 1957.

HEINI WALTER

A Swiss amateur who raced Porsche Carrera and RSK models both on the circuits and in hill-climbs, Walter was an extremely able driver who was 1961 European mountain-climb champion and drove the Filipinetti Porsche at the German GP, his only major appearance in a single-seater.

He later concentrated on hill-climbs with a Ferrari 250 LM, before returning to a Porsche.

RODGER WARD

Ward perhaps holds the unwanted distinction of having raced the most unsuitable machine ever to appear in a Grand Prix when he ran a Kurtis Midget at Sebring in 1959. After years of trying, he had just won the Indianapolis 500, starting a run of successes at the Brickyard (first/second/third/first/fourth/second) that extended through to 1964. With a total of 26 USAC career victories, Ward is one of Indy Car racing's all-time greats.

In 1963 Rodger made another Formula 1 appearance in the US GP, this time with more suitable machinery – a Lotus 24-BRM V8.

WALKER, Peter (GB) b 7/12/1912, Leeds, Yorkshire – d 1/3/1984, Newtown

	1950	Championship position: Unplaced						
	Race	Circuit	No	Entrant	Tyres	Car/Engine	Comment	Q Pos/Entries
ret*	BRITISH GP	Silverstone	9	Peter Walker	D	1.5 s/c ERA E Type 6	* shared with Rolt/gearbox	10/21
	1951	Championship position: Unplaced						
7	BRITISH GP	Silverstone	7	BRM Ltd	D	1.5 s/c BRM P15 V16	burnt by exhaust/-6 laps	19/20
	1955	Championship position: Unplaced						
ret	DUTCH GP	Zandvoort	26	Stirling Moss Ltd	D	2.5 Maserati 250F 6	wheel bearing	10/16
ret	BRITISH GP	Silverstone	36	R R C Walker Racing Team	D	2.5 Connaught B-Alta 4	* shared with Rolt/throttle cable	– /25

GP Starts: 4   GP Wins: 0   Pole positions: 0   Fastest laps: 0   Points: 0

WALTER, Heini (CH) b 28/7/1927, Rüti

	1962	Championship position: Unplaced						
	Race	Circuit	No	Entrant	Tyres	Car/Engine	Comment	Q Pos/Entries
14	GERMAN GP	Nürburgring	32	Ecurie Filipinetti	D	1.5 Porsche 718 F4	1 lap behind	14/30

GP Starts: 1   GP Wins: 0   Pole positions: 0   Fastest laps: 0   Points: 0

WARD, Rodger (USA) b 10/1/1921, Beloit, Kansas

	1959	Championship position: Unplaced						
	Race	Circuit	No	Entrant	Tyres	Car/Engine	Comment	Q Pos/Entries
ret	US GP	Sebring	1	Leader Cards Incorporated	–	1.75 Kurtis Kraft-Offenhauser 4	clutch/car outclassed	19/19
	1963	Championship position: Unplaced						
ret	US GP	Watkins Glen	18	Reg Parnell (Racing)	D	1.5 Lotus 24-BRM V8	gear selection	17/21

GP Starts: 2   GP Wins: 0   Pole positions: 0   Fastest laps: 0   Points: 0

DEREK WARWICK

Sometimes there seems to be no justice in motor racing. For a driver as committed and talented as Derek Warwick to have toiled for more than a decade and taken part in nearly 150 Grands Prix without even a single victory must be particularly galling. Yet there is no bitterness from the down-to-earth Hampshireman, who in the early days of his Formula 1 career looked a likelier prospect than Nigel Mansell.

After the hurly-burly of stock car racing, Derek funded his own early career in Formula Ford. He took second place in the 1976 DJM championship in his Hawke, before moving into Formula 3 the following year with a Chevron. In 1978 Warwick became embroiled in a terrific three-way battle with Piquet and Serra, winning the Vandervell F3 championship and emerging as runner-up to Nelson in the BP series. Moving to Formula 2 in 1979 with a Theodore Racing-entered March brought little cheer, but a switch to Toleman for 1980 signalled the start of a great relationship with the emerging team. That first year was in Formula 2, and he won two races (at Silverstone and Monza) as his more experienced team-mate Brian Henton took the coveted European title. Flushed with their success, Toleman made the jump to Formula 1 the following year but it proved to be a tough baptism for Derek, who managed to qualify only at the season's final race.

Things could only get better, and they did. In 1982 and 1983 Warwick battled away in the Pirelli-shod turbo car, scrapping ferociously for every place, no matter how far down the field. This fighting spirit no doubt helped to earn him his chance when the call came from Renault to race for them in 1984. Derek was never to get closer to that elusive Grand Prix win than on his debut for the team at Rio, where he was leading comfortably when the suspension collapsed. Somehow that blow seemed to set the tone for a season which failed to meet expectations of both the car and the driver. Then came the worst decision of Warwick's career – to stay with Renault in 1985. The year was a personal disaster, and the offer of a seat at Williams which he rejected and was taken by Mansell instead must always haunt him. When the French team pulled the plug on their Formula 1 effort, Derek was an out-of-work Grand Prix driver. A Jaguar sports car ride was his only realistic option for 1986 but he did a fine job for the team, missing the drivers' championship by just one point. However, the tragic death of Elio de Angelis found Warwick making a swift return to the Grand Prix scene with the difficult 'lowline' Brabham BT55, a car with which nobody could have found success.

Warwick then joined Arrows, who, like their new driver, were still looking for their first Grand Prix victory, and this was their tenth season of trying. In the three years he was to stay with the team, a few worthwhile results were achieved, but the cars were mediocrity personified. A switch to the well-funded but disorganised Lotus team in 1990 was probably the bottom of the barrel for poor Derek, who showed incredible bravery at Monza, where he crashed spectacularly at the exit of the Parabolica, only to calmly walk back to the pits to take the spare car for the inevitable restart, and then at Jerez, where he raced despite Donnelly's disturbing accident in practice.

Derek then took another Formula 1 sabbatical to return to sports car racing, first with Jaguar in 1991 and then the following year with Peugeot, with whom he was to enjoy the sweet taste of victory at Le Mans and also share the drivers' championship with team-mate Yannick Dalmas. However, Warwick's cheerful presence was to be found in the Formula 1 paddocks yet again in 1993, as he teamed up with Jack Oliver once more in the renamed Footwork team. The year was better than the team had experienced for some time but, even with the expensive acquisition of the TAG/McLaren active suspension system, the cars were top-six runners at best.

At the end of the season, rightly no longer interested in Formula 1 if he could not have a competitive car, Warwick stepped back to consider his options, which as it turned out were none, or none that excited him. So he took a year out before signing to drive for Alfa Romeo in the 1995 BTCC. Unfortunately once again it was the story of Derek's career: right car – wrong time.

Warwick (apart from sharing a Courage at Le Mans with Jan Lammers and Mario Andretti) then took another sabbatical to set up his own BTCC team, Triple Eight Race Engineering, which was to run the works Vauxhall Vectras. Two seasons driving one of the cars brought more frustration than success, though a win at Knockhill in 1998 gave Derek the satisfaction of claiming a BTCC victory before standing down from driving duties to continue in a management role with his team.

WARWICK, Derek (GB) b 27/8/1954, Alresford, Hampshire

	1981	Championship position: Unplaced							
	Race	Circuit	No	Entrant	Tyres	Car/Engine		Comment	Q Pos/Entries
dnq	SAN MARINO GP	Imola	36	Candy Toleman Motorsport	M	1.5 t/c Toleman TG181-Hart 4			29/30
dnq	BELGIAN GP	Zolder	36	Candy Toleman Motorsport	P	1.5 t/c Toleman TG181-Hart 4			29/31
dnq	MONACO GP	Monte Carlo	36	Candy Toleman Motorsport	P	1.5 t/c Toleman TG181-Hart 4			31/31
dnq	SPANISH GP	Jarama	36	Candy Toleman Motorsport	P	1.5 t/c Toleman TG181-Hart 4			29/30
dnq	FRENCH GP	Dijon	36	Candy Toleman Motorsport	P	1.5 t/c Toleman TG181-Hart 4			29/29
dnq	BRITISH GP	Silverstone	36	Candy Toleman Motorsport	P	1.5 t/c Toleman TG181-Hart 4			29/30
dnq	GERMAN GP	Hockenheim	36	Candy Toleman Motorsport	P	1.5 t/c Toleman TG181-Hart 4			28/30

dnq	AUSTRIAN GP	Österreichring	36	Candy Toleman Motorsport	P	1.5 t/c Toleman TG181-Hart 4		26/28
dnq	DUTCH GP	Zandvoort	36	Candy Toleman Motorsport	P	1.5 t/c Toleman TG181-Hart 4		30/30
dnq	ITALIAN GP	Monza	36	Candy Toleman Motorsport	P	1.5 t/c Toleman TG181-Hart 4		27/30
dnq	CANADIAN GP	Montreal	36	Candy Toleman Motorsport	P	1.5 t/c Toleman TG181-Hart 4		29/30
ret	CAESARS PALACE GP	Las Vegas	36	Candy Toleman Motorsport	P	1.5 t/c Toleman TG181-Hart 4	*gearbox*	22/30

1982   Championship position: Unplaced   Fastest laps: 1

ret	SOUTH AFRICAN GP	Kyalami	35	Candy Toleman Motorsport	P	1.5 t/c Toleman TG181C-Hart 4	*accident*	14/30
dnq	BRAZILIAN GP	Rio	35	Candy Toleman Motorsport	P	1.5 t/c Toleman TG181C-Hart 4		30/31
dnpq	US GP WEST	Long Beach	35	Candy Toleman Motorsport	P	1.5 t/c Toleman TG181C-Hart 4		31/31
dns	SAN MARINO GP	Imola	35	Toleman Group Motorsport	P	1.5 t/c Toleman TG181C-Hart 4	*electrics on parade lap*	(8)/14
ret	BELGIAN GP	Zolder	35	Toleman Group Motorsport	P	1.5 t/c Toleman TG181C-Hart 4	*driveshaft*	21/32
dnq	MONACO GP	Monte Carlo	35	Toleman Group Motorsport	P	1.5 t/c Toleman TG181C-Hart 4		24/31
ret	DUTCH GP	Zandvoort	35	Toleman Group Motorsport	P	1.5 t/c Toleman TG181C-Hart 4	*engine/FL*	13/31
ret	BRITISH GP	Brands Hatch	35	Toleman Group Motorsport	P	1.5 t/c Toleman TG181C-Hart 4	*driveshaft-c.v. joint*	16/30
15	FRENCH GP	Paul Ricard	35	Toleman Group Motorsport	P	1.5 t/c Toleman TG181C-Hart 4	*pit stop/4 laps behind*	14/30
10	GERMAN GP	Hockenheim	35	Toleman Group Motorsport	P	1.5 t/c Toleman TG181C-Hart 4	*pit stop/2 laps behind*	15/30
ret	AUSTRIAN GP	Österreichring	35	Toleman Group Motorsport	P	1.5 t/c Toleman TG181C-Hart 4	*rear suspension*	15/29
ret	SWISS GP	Dijon	35	Toleman Group Motorsport	P	1.5 t/c Toleman TG181C-Hart 4	*engine*	21/29
ret	ITALIAN GP	Monza	35	Toleman Group Motorsport	P	1.5 t/c Toleman TG183-Hart 4	*spin-hit by Henton*	16/30
ret	CAESARS PALACE GP	Las Vegas	35	Toleman Group Motorsport	P	1.5 t/c Toleman TG183-Hart 4	*misfire-plugs*	10/30

1983   Championship position: 14th   Wins: 0   Pole positions: 0   Fastest laps: 0   Points scored: 9

8	BRAZILIAN GP	Rio	35	Candy Toleman Motorsport	P	1.5 t/c Toleman TG183B-Hart 4	*1 lap behind*	5/27
ret	US GP WEST	Long Beach	35	Candy Toleman Motorsport	P	1.5 t/c Toleman TG183B-Hart 4	*tyre failure-accident*	6/28
ret	FRENCH GP	Paul Ricard	35	Candy Toleman Motorsport	P	1.5 t/c Toleman TG183B-Hart 4	*split water pipe-engine*	9/29
ret	SAN MARINO GP	Imola	35	Candy Toleman Motorsport	P	1.5 t/c Toleman TG183B-Hart 4	*spun off*	14/28
ret	MONACO GP	Monte Carlo	35	Candy Toleman Motorsport	P	1.5 t/c Toleman TG183B-Hart 4	*accident with Surer*	10/28
7	BELGIAN GP	Spa	35	Candy Toleman Motorsport	P	1.5 t/c Toleman TG183B-Hart 4	*2 pit stops-tyre-fuel*	22/28
ret	US GP (DETROIT)	Detroit	35	Candy Toleman Motorsport	P	1.5 t/c Toleman TG183B-Hart 4	*water leak-engine*	9/27
ret	CANADIAN GP	Montreal	35	Candy Toleman Motorsport	P	1.5 t/c Toleman TG183B-Hart 4	*engine-turbo*	12/28
ret	BRITISH GP	Silverstone	35	Candy Toleman Motorsport	P	1.5 t/c Toleman TG183B-Hart 4	*gearbox*	10/29
ret	GERMAN GP	Hockenheim	35	Candy Toleman Motorsport	P	1.5 t/c Toleman TG183B-Hart 4	*engine*	9/29
ret	AUSTRIAN GP	Österreichring	35	Candy Toleman Motorsport	P	1.5 t/c Toleman TG183B-Hart 4	*turbo*	10/29
4	DUTCH GP	Zandvoort	35	Candy Toleman Motorsport	P	1.5 t/c Toleman TG183B-Hart 4	*pit stop-fuel*	7/29
6	ITALIAN GP	Monza	35	Candy Toleman Motorsport	P	1.5 t/c Toleman TG183B-Hart 4	*pit stop-fuel*	12/29
5	EUROPEAN GP	Brands Hatch	35	Candy Toleman Motorsport	P	1.5 t/c Toleman TG183B-Hart 4	*pit stop-fuel*	11/29
4	SOUTH AFRICAN GP	Kyalami	35	Candy Toleman Motorsport	P	1.5 t/c Toleman TG183B-Hart 4	*pit stop-fuel/1 lap behind*	13/26

1984   Championship position: 7th   Wins: 0   Pole positions: 0   Fastest laps: 1   Points scored: 23

ret	BRAZILIAN GP	Rio	16	Equipe Renault Elf	M	1.5 t/c Renault RE50 V6	*hit by Lauda-suspension*	3/27
3	SOUTH AFRICAN GP	Kyalami	16	Equipe Renault Elf	M	1.5 t/c Renault RE50 V6	*1 lap behind*	9/27
2	BELGIAN GP	Zolder	16	Equipe Renault Elf	M	1.5 t/c Renault RE50 V6		4/27
4	SAN MARINO GP	Imola	16	Equipe Renault Elf	M	1.5 t/c Renault RE50 V6	*1 lap behind*	4/28
ret	FRENCH GP	Dijon	16	Equipe Renault Elf	M	1.5 t/c Renault RE50 V6	*accident with Surer*	7/27
ret	MONACO GP	Monte Carlo	16	Equipe Renault Elf	M	1.5 t/c Renault RE50 V6	*accident with Tambay*	5/27
ret	CANADIAN GP	Montreal	16	Equipe Renault Elf	M	1.5 t/c Renault RE50 V6	*loose underbody*	4/26
ret	US GP (DETROIT)	Detroit	16	Equipe Renault Elf	M	1.5 t/c Renault RE50 V6	*gearbox/FL*	6/27
2	US GP (DALLAS)	Dallas	16	Equipe Renault Elf	M	1.5 t/c Renault RE50 V6	*spun off*	3/27
3	BRITISH GP	Brands Hatch	16	Equipe Renault Elf	M	1.5 t/c Renault RE50 V6		6/27
ret	GERMAN GP	Hockenheim	16	Equipe Renault Elf	M	1.5 t/c Renault RE50 V6		3/27
ret	AUSTRIAN GP	Österreichring	16	Equipe Renault Elf	M	1.5 t/c Renault RE50 V6	*engine*	6/28
ret	DUTCH GP	Zandvoort	16	Equipe Renault Elf	M	1.5 t/c Renault RE50 V6	*spun off on oil*	4/27
11/ret	ITALIAN GP	Monza	16	Equipe Renault Elf	M	1.5 t/c Renault RE50 V6	*oil pressure*	12/27
ret	EUROPEAN GP	Nürburgring	16	Equipe Renault Elf	M	1.5 t/c Renault RE50 V6	*engine/6 laps behind*	7/26
	PORTUGUESE GP	Estoril	16	Equipe Renault Elf	M	1.5 t/c Renault RE50 V6	*gearbox*	9/27

1985   Championship position: 13th=   Wins: 0   Pole positions: 0   Fastest laps: 0   Points scored: 5

10	BRAZILIAN GP	Rio	16	Equipe Renault Elf	G	1.5 t/c Renault RE60 V6	*2 pit stop-plugs-tyres/-4 laps*	10/25
7	PORTUGUESE GP	Estoril	16	Equipe Renault Elf	G	1.5 t/c Renault RE60 V6	*2 laps behind*	6/26
10	SAN MARINO GP	Imola	16	Equipe Renault Elf	G	1.5 t/c Renault RE60 V6	*spin/pit stop-electrics/-4 laps*	14/26
5	MONACO GP	Monte Carlo	16	Equipe Renault Elf	G	1.5 t/c Renault RE60 V6	*1 lap behind*	10/26
ret	CANADIAN GP	Montreal	16	Equipe Renault Elf	G	1.5 t/c Renault RE60 V6	*accident*	6/25
ret	US GP (DETROIT)	Detroit	16	Equipe Renault Elf	G	1.5 t/c Renault RE60 V6	*transmission*	6/25
7	FRENCH GP	Paul Ricard	16	Equipe Renault Elf	G	1.5 t/c Renault RE60 V6		11/26
5	BRITISH GP	Silverstone	16	Equipe Renault Elf	G	1.5 t/c Renault RE60B V6	*1 lap behind*	12/26
ret	GERMAN GP	Nürburgring	16	Equipe Renault Elf	G	1.5 t/c Renault RE60B V6	*ignition*	20/27
ret	AUSTRIAN GP	Österreichring	16	Equipe Renault Elf	G	1.5 t/c Renault RE60B V6	*engine*	13/27
ret	DUTCH GP	Zandvoort	16	Equipe Renault Elf	G	1.5 t/c Renault RE60B V6	*gearbox*	12/27
ret	ITALIAN GP	Monza	16	Equipe Renault Elf	G	1.5 t/c Renault RE60B V6	*transmission*	12/26
6	BELGIAN GP	Spa	16	Equipe Renault Elf	G	1.5 t/c Renault RE60B V6	*1 lap behind*	14/24
ret	EUROPEAN GP	Brands Hatch	16	Equipe Renault Elf	G	1.5 t/c Renault RE60B V6	*fuel injection*	8/27
ret	AUSTRALIAN GP	Adelaide	16	Equipe Renault Elf	G	1.5 t/c Renault RE60B V6	*transmission*	12/25

1986   Championship position: Unplaced

ret	CANADIAN GP	Montreal	8	Motor Racing Developments Ltd	P	1.5 t/c Brabham BT55-BMW 4	*engine*	10/25
10	US GP (DETROIT)	Detroit	8	Motor Racing Developments Ltd	P	1.5 t/c Brabham BT55-BMW 4	*pit stop-tyres/3 laps behind*	15/26
9	FRENCH GP	Paul Ricard	8	Motor Racing Developments Ltd	P	1.5 t/c Brabham BT55-BMW 4	*gearbox trouble/3 laps behind*	14/26
8	BRITISH GP	Brands Hatch	8	Motor Racing Developments Ltd	P	1.5 t/c Brabham BT55-BMW 4	*2 pit stops-tyres/3 laps behind*	9/26
7	GERMAN GP	Hockenheim	8	Motor Racing Developments Ltd	P	1.5 t/c Brabham BT55-BMW 4	*1 lap behind*	20/26
ret	HUNGARIAN GP	Hungaroring	8	Motor Racing Developments Ltd	P	1.5 t/c Brabham BT55-BMW 4	*accident with Alboreto*	19/26
dns	AUSTRIAN GP	Österreichring	8	Motor Racing Developments Ltd	P	1.5 t/c Brabham BT55-BMW 4	*Patrese took car for race*	(10)/26
ret	ITALIAN GP	Monza	8	Motor Racing Developments Ltd	P	1.5 t/c Brabham BT55-BMW 4	*brakes-spun off*	7/27
ret	PORTUGUESE GP	Estoril	8	Motor Racing Developments Ltd	P	1.5 t/c Brabham BT55-BMW 4	*electrics*	12/27
ret	MEXICAN GP	Mexico City	8	Motor Racing Developments Ltd	P	1.5 t/c Brabham BT55-BMW 4	*engine*	7/26
ret	AUSTRALIAN GP	Adelaide	8	Motor Racing Developments Ltd	P	1.5 t/c Brabham BT55-BMW 4	*brakes*	20/26

1987   Championship position: 16th=   Wins: 0   Pole positions: 0   Fastest laps: 0   Points scored: 3

ret	BRAZILIAN GP	Rio	17	USF&G Arrows Megatron	G	1.5 t/c Arrows A10-Megatron 4		engine	8/23
11/ret	SAN MARINO GP	Imola	17	USF&G Arrows Megatron	G	1.5 t/c Arrows A10-Megatron 4		out of fuel/4 laps behind	11/27
ret	BELGIAN GP	Spa	17	USF&G Arrows Megatron	G	1.5 t/c Arrows A10-Megatron 4		water hose	12/26
ret	MONACO GP	Monte Carlo	17	USF&G Arrows Megatron	G	1.5 t/c Arrows A10-Megatron 4		gear linkage	11/26
ret	US GP (DETROIT)	Detroit	17	USF&G Arrows Megatron	G	1.5 t/c Arrows A10-Megatron 4		hit wall	10/26
ret	FRENCH GP	Paul Ricard	17	USF&G Arrows Megatron	G	1.5 t/c Arrows A10-Megatron 4		turbo	10/26
5	BRITISH GP	Silverstone	17	USF&G Arrows Megatron	G	1.5 t/c Arrows A10-Megatron 4			13/26
ret	GERMAN GP	Hockenheim	17	USF&G Arrows Megatron	G	1.5 t/c Arrows A10-Megatron 4		turbo	13/26
6	HUNGARIAN GP	Hungaroring	17	USF&G Arrows Megatron	G	1.5 t/c Arrows A10-Megatron 4		2 laps behind	9/26
ret	AUSTRIAN GP	Österreichring	17	USF&G Arrows Megatron	G	1.5 t/c Arrows A10-Megatron 4		engine	11/26
ret	ITALIAN GP	Monza	17	USF&G Arrows Megatron	G	1.5 t/c Arrows A10-Megatron 4		electrics	12/28
13	PORTUGUESE GP	Estoril	17	USF&G Arrows Megatron	G	1.5 t/c Arrows A10-Megatron 4		2 spins/4 laps behind	12/27
10	SPANISH GP	Jerez	17	USF&G Arrows Megatron	G	1.5 t/c Arrows A10-Megatron 4		2 laps behind	12/28
ret	MEXICAN GP	Mexico City	17	USF&G Arrows Megatron	G	1.5 t/c Arrows A10-Megatron 4		hit by Nakajima	11/27
10	JAPANESE GP	Suzuka	17	USF&G Arrows Megatron	G	1.5 t/c Arrows A10-Megatron 4		1 lap behind	14/27
ret	AUSTRALIAN GP	Adelaide	17	USF&G Arrows Megatron	G	1.5 t/c Arrows A10-Megatron 4		transmission	12/27

1988   Championship position: 17th=   Wins: 0   Pole positions: 0   Fastest laps: 0   Points scored: 17

4	BRAZILIAN GP	Rio	17	USF&G Arrows Megatron	G	1.5 t/c Arrows A10B-Megatron 4			11/31
9	SAN MARINO GP	Imola	17	USF&G Arrows Megatron	G	1.5 t/c Arrows A10B-Megatron 4		2 laps behind	14/31
4	MONACO GP	Monte Carlo	17	USF&G Arrows Megatron	G	1.5 t/c Arrows A10B-Megatron 4		1 lap behind	7/30
5	MEXICAN GP	Mexico City	17	USF&G Arrows Megatron	G	1.5 t/c Arrows A10B-Megatron 4		1 lap behind	9/30
7	CANADIAN GP	Montreal	17	USF&G Arrows Megatron	G	1.5 t/c Arrows A10B-Megatron 4		2 laps behind	16/31
ret	US GP (DETROIT)	Detroit	17	USF&G Arrows Megatron	G	1.5 t/c Arrows A10B-Megatron 4		stuck throttle-crashed	9/31
ret	FRENCH GP	Paul Ricard	17	USF&G Arrows Megatron	G	1.5 t/c Arrows A10B-Megatron 4		spun off avoiding Nakajima	11/31
6	BRITISH GP	Silverstone	17	USF&G Arrows Megatron	G	1.5 t/c Arrows A10B-Megatron 4		1 lap behind	9/31
7	GERMAN GP	Hockenheim	17	USF&G Arrows Megatron	G	1.5 t/c Arrows A10B-Megatron 4		1 lap behind	12/31
ret	HUNGARIAN GP	Hungaroring	17	USF&G Arrows Megatron	G	1.5 t/c Arrows A10B-Megatron 4		brakes	12/31
5*	BELGIAN GP	Spa	17	USF&G Arrows Megatron	G	1.5 t/c Arrows A10B-Megatron 4		*3rd & 4th place cars dsq	10/31
4	ITALIAN GP	Monza	17	USF&G Arrows Megatron	G	1.5 t/c Arrows A10B-Megatron 4			6/31
4	PORTUGUESE GP	Estoril	17	USF&G Arrows Megatron	G	1.5 t/c Arrows A10B-Megatron 4		severe vibration problems	10/31
ret	SPANISH GP	Jerez	17	USF&G Arrows Megatron	G	1.5 t/c Arrows A10B-Megatron 4		slid over kerb-chassis damage	17/31
ret	JAPANESE GP	Suzuka	17	USF&G Arrows Megatron	G	1.5 t/c Arrows A10B-Megatron 4		spun off	7/31
ret	AUSTRALIAN GP	Adelaide	17	USF&G Arrows Megatron	G	1.5 t/c Arrows A10B-Megatron 4		engine	7/31

1989   Championship position: 10th   Wins: 0   Pole positions: 0   Fastest laps: 0   Points scored: 7

5	BRAZILIAN GP	Rio	9	Arrows Grand Prix International	G	3.5 Arrows A11-Cosworth V8			8/38
5	SAN MARINO GP	Imola	9	Arrows Grand Prix International	G	3.5 Arrows A11-Cosworth V8		1 lap behind	12/39
ret	MONACO GP	Monte Carlo	9	Arrows Grand Prix International	G	3.5 Arrows A11-Cosworth V8		electrical short-circuit	6/38
ret	MEXICAN GP	Mexico City	9	Arrows Grand Prix International	G	3.5 Arrows A11-Cosworth V8		electrics	10/39
ret	US GP (PHOENIX)	Phoenix	9	Arrows Grand Prix International	G	3.5 Arrows A11-Cosworth V8		ran into de Cesaris-suspension	10/39
ret	CANADIAN GP	Montreal	9	Arrows Grand Prix International	G	3.5 Arrows A11-Cosworth V8		engine	12/39
9	BRITISH GP	Silverstone	9	Arrows Grand Prix International	G	3.5 Arrows A11-Cosworth V8		2 laps behind	19/39
6	GERMAN GP	Hockenheim	9	Arrows Grand Prix International	G	3.5 Arrows A11-Cosworth V8		no clutch/1 lap behind	17/39
10	HUNGARIAN GP	Hungaroring	9	Arrows Grand Prix International	G	3.5 Arrows A11-Cosworth V8		collision-Nakajima/-1 lap	9/39
6	BELGIAN GP	Spa	9	Arrows Grand Prix International	G	3.5 Arrows A11-Cosworth V8			10/39
ret	ITALIAN GP	Monza	9	Arrows Grand Prix International	G	3.5 Arrows A11-Cosworth V8		fuel flow-engine cut out	16/39
ret	PORTUGUESE GP	Estoril	9	Arrows Grand Prix International	G	3.5 Arrows A11-Cosworth V8		accident	22/39
9	SPANISH GP	Jerez	9	Arrows Grand Prix International	G	3.5 Arrows A11-Cosworth V8		despite collisions/-2 laps	16/38
6*	JAPANESE GP	Suzuka	9	Arrows Grand Prix International	G	3.5 Arrows A11-Cosworth V8		* 1st place car dsq/-1 lap	25/39
ret	AUSTRALIAN GP	Adelaide	9	Arrows Grand Prix International	G	3.5 Arrows A11-Cosworth V8		engine cut in and out-crashed	20/39

1990   Championship position: 14th   Wins: 0   Pole positions: 0   Fastest laps: 0   Points scored: 3

ret	US GP (PHOENIX)	Phoenix	11	Camel Team Lotus	G	3.5 Camel Lotus 102-Lamborghini V12		rear suspension	24/35
ret	BRAZILIAN GP	Rio	11	Camel Team Lotus	G	3.5 Camel Lotus 102-Lamborghini V12		electrics	24/35
7	SAN MARINO GP	Imola	11	Camel Team Lotus	G	3.5 Camel Lotus 102-Lamborghini V12		1 lap behind	11/34
ret	MONACO GP	Monte Carlo	11	Camel Team Lotus	G	3.5 Camel Lotus 102-Lamborghini V12		brakes/spun-stalled	13/35
6	CANADIAN GP	Montreal	11	Camel Team Lotus	G	3.5 Camel Lotus 102-Lamborghini V12		part-detached undertray/-2 laps	11/35
10	MEXICAN GP	Mexico City	11	Camel Team Lotus	G	3.5 Camel Lotus 102-Lamborghini V12		low on revs/1 lap behind	11/35
11	FRENCH GP	Paul Ricard	11	Camel Team Lotus	G	3.5 Camel Lotus 102-Lamborghini V12		1 lap behind	16/35
ret	BRITISH GP	Silverstone	11	Camel Team Lotus	G	3.5 Camel Lotus 102-Lamborghini V12		engine	16/35
8	GERMAN GP	Hockenheim	11	Camel Team Lotus	G	3.5 Camel Lotus 102-Lamborghini V12		severe vibration/1 lap behind	16/35
5	HUNGARIAN GP	Hungaroring	11	Camel Team Lotus	G	3.5 Camel Lotus 102-Lamborghini V12			11/35
11	BELGIAN GP	Spa	11	Camel Team Lotus	G	3.5 Camel Lotus 102-Lamborghini V12		misfire/1 lap behind	18/33
ret	ITALIAN GP	Monza	11	Camel Team Lotus	G	3.5 Camel Lotus 102-Lamborghini V12		clutch	12/33
ret	PORTUGUESE GP	Estoril	11	Camel Team Lotus	G	3.5 Camel Lotus 102-Lamborghini V12		throttle jammed	22/33
ret	SPANISH GP	Jerez	11	Camel Team Lotus	G	3.5 Camel Lotus 102-Lamborghini V12		gearbox	10/33
ret	JAPANESE GP	Suzuka	11	Camel Team Lotus	G	3.5 Camel Lotus 102-Lamborghini V12		gearbox	12/30
ret	AUSTRALIAN GP	Adelaide	11	Camel Team Lotus	G	3.5 Camel Lotus 102-Lamborghini V12		gearbox	11/30

1993   Championship position: 15th=   Wins: 0   Pole positions: 0   Fastest laps: 0   Points scored: 4

7/ret	SOUTH AFRICAN GP	Kyalami	9	Footwork Mugen Honda	G	3.5 Footwork FA13B-Mugen Honda V10		spun off/3 laps behind	22/26
9	BRAZILIAN GP	Interlagos	9	Footwork Mugen Honda	G	3.5 Footwork FA13B-Mugen Honda V10		2 laps behind	18/26
ret	EUROPEAN GP	Donington	9	Footwork Mugen Honda	G	3.5 Footwork FA14-Mugen Honda V10		gearbox	14/26
ret	SAN MARINO GP	Imola	9	Footwork Mugen Honda	G	3.5 Footwork FA14-Mugen Honda V10		spun off	15/26
13	SPANISH GP	Barcelona	9	Footwork Mugen Honda	G	3.5 Footwork FA14-Mugen Honda V10		2 spins/3 laps behind	16/26
ret	MONACO GP	Monte Carlo	9	Footwork Mugen Honda	G	3.5 Footwork FA14-Mugen Honda V10		throttle failure	12/26
16	CANADIAN GP	Montreal	9	Footwork Mugen Honda	G	3.5 Footwork FA14-Mugen Honda V10		poor handling/4 laps behind	18/26
13	FRENCH GP	Magny Cours	9	Footwork Mugen Honda	G	3.5 Footwork FA14-Mugen Honda V10		2 laps behind	15/26
6	BRITISH GP	Silverstone	9	Footwork Mugen Honda	G	3.5 Footwork FA14-Mugen Honda V10		1 lap behind	8/26
17	GERMAN GP	Hockenheim	9	Footwork Mugen Honda	G	3.5 Footwork FA14-Mugen Honda V10		spin-wing damage/-3 laps	11/26
4	HUNGARIAN GP	Hungaroring	9	Footwork Mugen Honda	G	3.5 Footwork FA14-Mugen Honda V10		1 lap behind	9/26
ret	BELGIAN GP	Spa	9	Footwork Mugen Honda	G	3.5 Footwork FA14-Mugen Honda V10		electrical failure	7/25
ret	ITALIAN GP	Monza	9	Footwork Mugen Honda	G	3.5 Footwork FA14-Mugen Honda V10		collision with Suzuki on lap 1	11/26
15/ret	PORTUGUESE GP	Estoril	9	Footwork Mugen Honda	G	3.5 Footwork FA14-Mugen Honda V10		taken off by Patrese/-8 laps	9/26
14/ret	JAPANESE GP	Suzuka	9	Footwork Mugen Honda	G	3.5 Footwork FA14-Mugen Honda V10		hit by Irvine-spun off/-5 laps	7/24
10	AUSTRALIAN GP	Adelaide	9	Footwork Mugen Honda	G	3.5 Footwork FA14-Mugen Honda V10		driver unwell/spin/-2 laps	17/24

GP Starts: 146 (147)   GP Wins: 0   Pole positions: 0   Fastest laps: 2   Points: 71

JOHN WATSON

'Wattie' has perhaps not been given the credit that is his due, which may sound strange when you consider he holds the MBE. But because his successes in Grand Prix racing were not concentrated into one great spell, his long and in the main very successful career, which spanned more than twenty years, tends to be overlooked.

In fact he started racing way back in 1963-64 in his native Northern Ireland with an Austin Healey Sprite, before graduating to single-seaters. Outstanding in Irish Formula Libre, he soon crossed the water to try his hand against sterner opposition. In 1970 he took his Brabham BT30 into the European F2 championship, but a heavy crash at Rouen left him with a broken arm and leg. Undaunted, he was back the following year and, competing as a privateer in his elderly car, put to shame many more vaunted names. His persistence was about to bring rewards, for in 1972 a sixth place in the John Player Trophy race at Brands Hatch in a March 721, plus some excellent drives in Alan McCall's F2 Tui, caught the eye of both Brabham and Gulf, who were to give the then bearded Ulsterman his first real breaks. The 'luck of the Irish' certainly deserted him when, in the Race of Champions early in 1973, he broke his leg once more after the throttle stuck open on the new Brabham BT42. With typical quiet determination he was back to make his Grand Prix debut at Silverstone, and by the end of the year he had set up a full F1 season with Hexagon Racing's private Brabham. A great drive to sixth place at Monaco was followed by some terrific performances once he had the use of the BT44 chassis, headed by a brilliant drive into fourth in Austria after a pit stop.

Sadly the team were unable to continue in 1975, and Watson, having previously driven in a few Formula 2 races for Surtees, joined 'Big John's outfit. A second place in the Race of Champions and fourth in the International Trophy were as good as it was going to get in a year fraught with mechanical difficulties. Just before the end of the season Surtees withdrew to regroup his efforts, leaving 'Wattie' unemployed. Fortunately he soon picked up a ride in the Penske team at Watkins Glen and, after taking ninth place with a car not set up for the track, he was offered a contract for the 1976 season. The team were to suffer something of an up-and-down year, but John's magnificent victory in Austria gave him the confidence that comes from being a winner. The only thing he lost that day was his famous beard, as a result of a wager with Roger Penske!

When Penske decided to call it a day at the end of the year, Bernie Ecclestone lost no time in signing John to join Carlos Pace in his Brabham-Alfa team for 1977. Tragically, the Brazilian was soon killed in an air crash, leaving Watson to carry the burden of development in an unproven car. He nearly won at Paul Ricard until fuel pick-up problems took away his last-lap lead. The season ended up as a major disappointment after beginning with so much promise, but things improved in 1978, when at least he was a regular points scorer, although teamed with Niki Lauda his performances seemed a trifle erratic. When James Hunt became disillusioned with McLaren, Watson was the man chosen to take his place. Initially it seemed to be a disastrous move, for the team were at a low ebb under the declining Teddy Mayer regime. The following season was frustrating, with points scraped here and there in a difficult car, and 1980 was to bring even less cheer, Watson being out-driven in the early part of the year by newcomer Alain Prost. Some observers were tempted to write him off but John fought back, and his confidence and speed began to return – particularly when he was installed in the John Barnard-designed MP4 under McLaren's new Ron Dennis regime in 1981. He scored a lucky win at Silverstone when Arnoux's Renault faltered, and generally re-established his standing as one of the leading drivers which had seemed under threat.

Joined by Niki Lauda in 1982, Watson answered the Austrian's Long Beach challenge with a well-taken win at Zolder, but overall his season was hampered by unpredictable lapses in form which led to some lacklustre showings. In 1983 he came through the field to take an unexpected win at Long Beach, but was generally handicapped by the lack of turbo power until late in the season. He fully expected to remain paired with Lauda for a third year in 1984, but protracted negotiations worked against him when Alain Prost came onto the scene after being released by Renault. With no other options open, 'Wattie' was left to find a seat in sports car racing, driving occasionally for Rothmans Porsche over the next couple of years and taking a win at Fuji in 1984 with Bellof. A last-minute call-up by McLaren to deputise for the injured Lauda in the European GP merely emphasised how two seasons out can take away the edge, and there was to be no more Formula 1.

Instead he returned to endurance racing with the Silk Cut Jaguar team and later with Toyota, before retiring from the track to concentrate on his Silverstone-based Performance Driving School and his role as a commentator, firstly for the satellite channel Eurosport and currently for the BBC, covering the British touring car championship.

WATSON, John (GB) b 4/5/1946, Belfast, Northern Ireland

	1973	Championship position: Unplaced							
	Race	Circuit	No	Entrant	Tyres	Car/Engine		Comment	Q Pos/Entries
ret	BRITISH GP	Silverstone	29	Ceramica Pagnossin-Team MRD	G	3.0 Brabham BT37-Cosworth V8		seized fuel metering unit	=23/29
ret	US GP	Watkins Glen	9	Ceramica Pagnossin-Team MRD	G	3.0 Brabham BT42-Cosworth V8		engine	25/28

1974

Championship position: 14th= Wins: 0 Pole positions: 0 Fastest laps: 0 Points scored: 6

Result	Race	Circuit	No.	Team		Car	Notes	
12	ARGENTINE GP	Buenos Aires	28	John Goldie Racing with Hexagon	F	3.0 Brabham BT42-Cosworth V8	pit stop-nose cone/-4 laps	20/26
ret	BRAZILIAN GP	Interlagos	28	John Goldie Racing with Hexagon	F	3.0 Brabham BT42-Cosworth V8	clutch	15/25
ret	SOUTH AFRICAN GP	Kyalami	28	John Goldie Racing with Hexagon	F	3.0 Brabham BT42-Cosworth V8	fuel union	13/27
11	SPANISH GP	Jarama	28	John Goldie Racing with Hexagon	F	3.0 Brabham BT42-Cosworth V8	pit stop-tyres/4 laps behind	16/28
11	BELGIAN GP	Nivelles	28	John Goldie Racing with Hexagon	F	3.0 Brabham BT42-Cosworth V8	pit stop-tyres/2 laps behind	19/32
6	MONACO GP	Monte Carlo	28	John Goldie Racing with Hexagon	F	3.0 Brabham BT42-Cosworth V8	1 lap behind	=21/28
11	SWEDISH GP	Anderstorp	28	John Goldie Racing with Hexagon	F	3.0 Brabham BT42-Cosworth V8	3 laps behind	14/28
7	DUTCH GP	Zandvoort	28	John Goldie Racing with Hexagon	F	3.0 Brabham BT42-Cosworth V8		13/27
16	FRENCH GP	Dijon	28	John Goldie Racing with Hexagon	F	3.0 Brabham BT42-Cosworth V8	pit stop-exhaust/4 laps behind	14/30
11	BRITISH GP	Brands Hatch	28	Goldie Hexagon Racing	F	3.0 Brabham BT44-Cosworth V8	pit stop-puncture/-2 laps	13/34
ret	GERMAN GP	Nürburgring	28	Goldie Hexagon Racing	F	3.0 Brabham BT42-Cosworth V8	accident damage	14/32
dns	"	"	28	Goldie Hexagon Racing	F	3.0 Brabham BT42-Cosworth V8	practice only	– / –
4	AUSTRIAN GP	Österreichring	28	Goldie Hexagon Racing	F	3.0 Brabham BT44-Cosworth V8		11/31
7	ITALIAN GP	Monza	28	Goldie Hexagon Racing	F	3.0 Brabham BT44-Cosworth V8	1 lap behind	4/31
ret	CANADIAN GP	Mosport Park	28	Goldie Hexagon Racing	F	3.0 Brabham BT44-Cosworth V8	broken suspension-accident	15/30
5	US GP	Watkins Glen	28	Goldie Hexagon Racing	F	3.0 Brabham BT44-Cosworth V8		7/30

1975

Championship position: Unplaced

Result	Race	Circuit	No.	Team		Car	Notes	
dsq	ARGENTINE GP	Buenos Aires	18	Team Surtees	G	3.0 Surtees TS16-Cosworth V8	repairs outside of pit area	15/23
10	BRAZILIAN GP	Interlagos	18	Team Surtees	G	3.0 Surtees TS16-Cosworth V8	slow puncture	13/23
ret	SOUTH AFRICAN GP	Kyalamia	18	Team Surtees	G	3.0 Surtees TS16-Cosworth V8	clutch	10/28
8	SPANISH GP	Montjuich Park	18	Team Surtees	G	3.0 Surtees TS16-Cosworth V8	pit stop-flat spotted tyre/-3 laps	6/26
ret	MONACO GP	Monte Carlo	18	Team Surtees	G	3.0 Surtees TS16-Cosworth V8	spun off	17/26
10	BELGIAN GP	Zolder	18	Team Surtees	G	3.0 Surtees TS16-Cosworth V8	collision-new nose cone/-2 laps	18/24
16	SWEDISH GP	Anderstorp	18	Team Surtees	G	3.0 Surtees TS16-Cosworth V8	3 laps behind	10/26
ret	DUTCH GP	Zandvoort	18	Team Surtees	G	3.0 Surtees TS16-Cosworth V8	severe vibration	14/25
13	FRENCH GP	Paul Ricard	18	Team Surtees	G	3.0 Surtees TS16-Cosworth V8	1 lap behind	14/26
11/ret	BRITISH GP	Silverstone	18	Team Surtees	G	3.0 Surtees TS16-Cosworth V8	spun off in rainstorm/-2 laps	18/28
ret	GERMAN GP	Nürburgring	6	John Player Team Lotus	G	3.0 Lotus 72F-Cosworth V8	broken front suspension	14/26
10	AUSTRIAN GP	Österreichring	18	Team Surtees	G	3.0 Surtees TS16-Cosworth V8	1 lap behind	18/30
9	US GP	Watkins Glen	28	Penske Cars	G	3.0 Penske PC1-Cosworth V8	went off at chicane/-2 laps	– / –
dns	"	"	28	Penske Cars	G	3.0 Penske PC3-Cosworth V8	practice only-set grid time	12/24

1976

Championship position: 7th Wins: 1 Pole positions: 0 Fastest laps: 0 Points scored: 20

Result	Race	Circuit	No.	Team		Car	Notes	
ret	BRAZILIAN GP	Interlagos	28	Citibank Team Penske	G	3.0 Penske PC3-Cosworth V8	fire-broken fuel line	8/22
5	SOUTH AFRICAN GP	Kyalami	28	Citibank Team Penske	G	3.0 Penske PC3-Cosworth V8	1 lap behind	3/25
nc	US GP WEST	Long Beach	28	Citibank Team Penske	G	3.0 Penske PC3-Cosworth V8	stops-nose cone-exhaust/-11 laps	9/27
ret	SPANISH GP	Jarama	28	Citibank Team Penske	G	3.0 Penske PC3-Cosworth V8	engine	13/30
7	BELGIAN GP	Zolder	28	Citibank Team Penske	G	3.0 Penske PC3-Cosworth V8	1 lap behind	17/29
10	MONACO GP	Monte Carlo	28	Citibank Team Penske	G	3.0 Penske PC3-Cosworth V8	2 laps behind	17/25
ret	SWEDISH GP	Anderstorp	28	Citibank Team Penske	G	3.0 Penske PC3-Cosworth V8	accident-throttle stuck open	17/27
3*	FRENCH GP	Paul Ricard	28	Citibank Team Penske	G	3.0 Penske PC4-Cosworth V8	*dsq-but reinstated on appeal	8/30
3	BRITISH GP	Brands Hatch	28	Citibank Team Penske	G	3.0 Penske PC4-Cosworth V8	1 lap behind	11/30
7	GERMAN GP	Nürburgring	28	Citibank Team Penske	G	3.0 Penske PC4-Cosworth V8		19/28
1	AUSTRIAN GP	Österreichring	28	Citibank Team Penske	G	3.0 Penske PC4-Cosworth V8		2/25
ret	DUTCH GP	Zandvoort	28	Citibank Team Penske	G	3.0 Penske PC4-Cosworth V8	gearbox	4/27
11	ITALIAN GP	Monza	28	Citibank Team Penske	G	3.0 Penske PC4-Cosworth V8		29/29
10	CANADIAN GP	Mosport Park	28	Citibank Team Penske	G	3.0 Penske PC4-Cosworth V8	1 lap behind	14/27
6	US GP EAST	Watkins Glen	28	Citibank Team Penske	G	3.0 Penske PC4-Cosworth V8		8/27
ret	JAPANESE GP	Mount Fuji	28	Citibank Team Penske	G	3.0 Penske PC4-Cosworth V8	engine	4/27

1977

Championship position: 13th= Wins: 0 Pole positions: 1 Fastest laps: 2 Points scored: 9

Result	Race	Circuit	No.	Team		Car	Notes	
ret	ARGENTINE GP	Buenos Aires	7	Martini Racing	G	3.0 Brabham BT45-Alfa Romeo F12	sheared suspension mounting	2/21
ret	BRAZILIAN GP	Interlagos	7	Martini Racing	G	3.0 Brabham BT45-Alfa Romeo F12	crashed	7/22
6	SOUTH AFRICAN GP	Kyalami	7	Martini Racing	G	3.0 Brabham BT45-Alfa Romeo F12	FL	11/23
dsq	US GP WEST	Long Beach	7	Martini Racing	G	3.0 Brabham BT45B-Alfa Romeo F12	outside assistance	6/22
ret	SPANISH GP	Jarama	7	Martini Racing	G	3.0 Brabham BT45B-Alfa Romeo F12	fuel metering unit	6/31
ret	MONACO GP	Monte Carlo	7	Martini Racing	G	3.0 Brabham BT45B-Alfa Romeo F12	gearbox	1/26
ret	BELGIAN GP	Zolder	7	Martini Racing	G	3.0 Brabham BT45B-Alfa Romeo F12	hit by Andretti	2/32
5	SWEDISH GP	Anderstorp	7	Martini Racing	G	3.0 Brabham BT45B-Alfa Romeo F12		2/31
2	FRENCH GP	Dijon	7	Martini Racing	G	3.0 Brabham BT45B-Alfa Romeo F12	out of fuel on last lap when 1st	4/30
ret	BRITISH GP	Silverstone	7	Martini Racing	G	3.0 Brabham BT45B-Alfa Romeo F12	engine-fuel feed	2/36
ret	GERMAN GP	Hockenheim	7	Martini Racing	G	3.0 Brabham BT45B-Alfa Romeo F12	engine	2/30
8	AUSTRIAN GP	Österreichring	7	Martini Racing	G	3.0 Brabham BT45B-Alfa Romeo F12	FL/1 lap behind	12/30
ret	DUTCH GP	Zandvoort	7	Martini Racing	G	3.0 Brabham BT45B-Alfa Romeo F12	engine-lost oil damaged sump	8/34
ret	ITALIAN GP	Monza	7	Martini Racing	G	3.0 Brabham BT45B-Alfa Romeo F12	accident-hit kerb	14/34
12	US GP EAST	Watkins Glen	7	Martini Racing	G	3.0 Brabham BT45B-Alfa Romeo F12	3 pit stops-tyres/2 laps behind	3/27
ret	CANADIAN GP	Mosport Park	7	Martini Racing	G	3.0 Brabham BT45B-Alfa Romeo F12	hit Peterson	10/27
ret	JAPANESE GP	Mount Fuji	7	Martini Racing	G	3.0 Brabham BT45B-Alfa Romeo F12	gearbox	3/23

1978

Championship position: 6th Wins: 0 Pole positions: 1 Fastest laps: 0 Points scored: 25

Result	Race	Circuit	No.	Team		Car	Notes	
ret	ARGENTINE GP	Buenos Aires	2	Parmalat Racing Team	G	3.0 Brabham BT45C-Alfa Romeo F12	engine	4/27
8	BRAZILIAN GP	Rio	2	Parmalat Racing Team	G	3.0 Brabham BT45C-Alfa Romeo F12	2 laps behind	21/28
3	SOUTH AFRICAN GP	Kyalami	2	Parmalat Racing Team	G	3.0 Brabham BT46-Alfa Romeo F12		10/30
dns	"	"	2	Parmalat Racing Team	G	3.0 Brabham BT45C-Alfa Romeo F12	practice only	– / –
ret	US GP WEST	Long Beach	2	Parmalat Racing Team	G	3.0 Brabham BT46-Alfa Romeo F12	oil tank	5/30
4	MONACO GP	Monte Carlo	2	Parmalat Racing Team	G	3.0 Brabham BT46-Alfa Romeo F12		2/30
ret	BELGIAN GP	Zolder	2	Parmalat Racing Team	G	3.0 Brabham BT46-Alfa Romeo F12	spun and damaged chassis	9/30
5	SPANISH GP	Jarama	2	Parmalat Racing Team	G	3.0 Brabham BT46-Alfa Romeo F12		7/29
ret	SWEDISH GP	Anderstorp	2	Parmalat Racing Team	G	3.0 Brabham BT46B-Alfa Romeo F12	fan car/stuck throttle after spin	2/27
4	FRENCH GP	Paul Ricard	2	Parmalat Racing Team	G	3.0 Brabham BT46-Alfa Romeo F12		1/29
3	BRITISH GP	Brands Hatch	2	Parmalat Racing Team	G	3.0 Brabham BT46-Alfa Romeo F12		9/30
7	GERMAN GP	Hockenheim	2	Parmalat Racing Team	G	3.0 Brabham BT46-Alfa Romeo F12		5/30
7	AUSTRIAN GP	Österreichring	2	Parmalat Racing Team	G	3.0 Brabham BT46-Alfa Romeo F12	pit stop-tyres/1 lap behind	10/31
4	DUTCH GP	Zandvoort	2	Parmalat Racing Team	G	3.0 Brabham BT46-Alfa Romeo F12		8/33
2*	ITALIAN GP	Monza	2	Parmalat Racing Team	G	3.0 Brabham BT46-Alfa Romeo F12	*after 1st & 2nd cars given 1 min pen	7/32
ret	US GP EAST	Watkins Glen	2	Parmalat Racing Team	G	3.0 Brabham BT46-Alfa Romeo F12	engine	7/27
ret	CANADIAN GP	Montreal	2	Parmalat Racing Team	G	3.0 Brabham BT46-Alfa Romeo F12	collision with Andretti	4/28

1979
Championship position: 9th= Wins: 0 Pole positions: 0 Fastest laps: 0 Points scored: 15

3	ARGENTINE GP	Buenos Aires	7	Marlboro Team McLaren	G	3.0 McLaren M28-Cosworth V8		6/26
8	BRAZILIAN GP	Interlagos	7	Marlboro Team McLaren	G	3.0 McLaren M28-Cosworth V8	1 lap behind	14/26
ret	SOUTH AFRICAN GP	Kyalami	7	Marlboro Team McLaren	G	3.0 McLaren M28-Cosworth V8	ignition	=14/26
ret	US GP WEST	Long Beach	7	Löwenbräu Team McLaren	G	3.0 McLaren M28-Cosworth V8	fuel injection unit	18/26
ret	SPANISH GP	Jarama	7	Marlboro Team McLaren	G	3.0 McLaren M28-Cosworth V8	engine	18/27
6	BELGIAN GP	Zolder	7	Marlboro Team McLaren	G	3.0 McLaren M28-Cosworth V8		19/28
4	MONACO GP	Monte Carlo	7	Marlboro Team McLaren	G	3.0 McLaren M28-Cosworth V8		=13/25
11	FRENCH GP	Dijon	7	Marlboro Team McLaren	G	3.0 McLaren M28-Cosworth V8	pit stop-tyres/2 laps behind	15/27
4	BRITISH GP	Silverstone	7	Marlboro Team McLaren	G	3.0 McLaren M29-Cosworth V8	1 lap behind	7/26
5	GERMAN GP	Hockenheim	7	Marlboro Team McLaren	G	3.0 McLaren M29-Cosworth V8		12/26
9	AUSTRIAN GP	Österreichring	7	Marlboro Team McLaren	G	3.0 McLaren M29-Cosworth V8	1 lap behind	16/26
ret	DUTCH GP	Zandvoort	7	Marlboro Team McLaren	G	3.0 McLaren M29-Cosworth V8	engine	12/26
ret	ITALIAN GP	Monza	7	Marlboro Team McLaren	G	3.0 McLaren M29-Cosworth V8	accident with Jarier	19/28
6	CANADIAN GP	Montreal	7	Marlboro Team McLaren	G	3.0 McLaren M29-Cosworth V8	pit stop-fuel/2 laps behind	17/29
6	US GP EAST	Watkins Glen	7	Marlboro Team McLaren	G	3.0 McLaren M29-Cosworth V8	pit stop-tyres/1 lap behind	13/30

1980
Championship position: 10th= Wins: 0 Pole positions: 0 Fastest laps: 0 Points scored: 6

ret	ARGENTINE GP	Buenos Aires	7	Marlboro Team McLaren	G	3.0 McLaren M29-Cosworth V8	gearbox oil leak	17/28
11	BRAZILIAN GP	Interlagos	7	Marlboro Team McLaren	G	3.0 McLaren M29-Cosworth V8	1 lap behind	23/28
11	SOUTH AFRICAN GP	Kyalami	7	Marlboro Team McLaren	G	3.0 McLaren M29-Cosworth V8	2 laps behind	21/28
4	US GP WEST	Long Beach	7	Marlboro Team McLaren	G	3.0 McLaren M29-Cosworth V8	1 lap behind	21/27
nc	BELGIAN GP	Zolder	7	Marlboro Team McLaren	G	3.0 McLaren M29-Cosworth V8	2 pit stops-brakes/-11 laps	20/27
dnq	MONACO GP	Monte Carlo	7	Marlboro Team McLaren	G	3.0 McLaren M29-Cosworth V8		21/27
7	FRENCH GP	Paul Ricard	7	Marlboro Team McLaren	G	3.0 McLaren M29-Cosworth V8	1 lap behind	13/27
8	BRITISH GP	Brands Hatch	7	Marlboro Team McLaren	G	3.0 McLaren M29-Cosworth V8	pit stop-tyres/2 laps behind	12/27
ret	GERMAN GP	Hockenheim	7	Marlboro Team McLaren	G	3.0 McLaren M29-Cosworth V8	engine	20/26
ret	AUSTRIAN GP	Österreichring	7	Marlboro Team McLaren	G	3.0 McLaren M29-Cosworth V8	engine	21/25
ret	DUTCH GP	Zandvoort	7	Marlboro Team McLaren	G	3.0 McLaren M29-Cosworth V8	engine	9/28
ret	ITALIAN GP	Imola	7	Marlboro Team McLaren	G	3.0 McLaren M29-Cosworth V8	brakes/wheel bearing	14/28
4	CANADIAN GP	Montreal	7	Marlboro Team McLaren	G	3.0 McLaren M29-Cosworth V8		7/28
nc	US GP EAST	Watkins Glen	7	Marlboro Team McLaren	G	3.0 McLaren M29-Cosworth V8	pit stop-shock absorber/-9 laps	9/27

1981
Championship position: 6th Wins: 1 Pole positions: 0 Fastest laps: 1 Points scored: 27

ret	US GP WEST	Long Beach	7	McLaren International	M	3.0 McLaren M29F-Cosworth V8	engine	23/29
8	BRAZILIAN GP	Rio	7	McLaren International	M	3.0 McLaren M29F-Cosworth V8	1 lap behind	15/30
ret	ARGENTINE GP	Buenos Aires	7	McLaren International	M	3.0 McLaren M29F-Cosworth V8	transmission	11/29
10	SAN MARINO GP	Imola	7	McLaren International	M	3.0 McLaren MP4-Cosworth V8	pit stop-nose cone/-2 laps	7/30
7	BELGIAN GP	Zolder	7	McLaren International	M	3.0 McLaren MP4-Cosworth V8	gearbox problems	5/31
ret	MONACO GP	Monte Carlo	7	McLaren International	M	3.0 McLaren MP4-Cosworth V8	engine	10/31
3	SPANISH GP	Jarama	7	McLaren International	M	3.0 McLaren MP4-Cosworth V8		4/30
2	FRENCH GP	Dijon	7	McLaren International	M	3.0 McLaren MP4-Cosworth V8		2/29
1	BRITISH GP	Silverstone	7	McLaren International	M	3.0 McLaren MP4-Cosworth V8		5/30
6	GERMAN GP	Hockenheim	7	McLaren International	M	3.0 McLaren MP4-Cosworth V8	1 lap behind	9/30
6	AUSTRIAN GP	Österreichring	7	McLaren International	M	3.0 McLaren MP4-Cosworth V8		12/28
ret	DUTCH GP	Zandvoort	7	McLaren International	M	3.0 McLaren MP4-Cosworth V8	electrics	8/30
ret	ITALIAN GP	Monza	7	McLaren International	M	3.0 McLaren MP4-Cosworth V8	crashed	7/30
2	CANADIAN GP	Montreal	7	McLaren International	M	3.0 McLaren MP4-Cosworth V8	FL	9/30
7	CAESARS PALACE GP	Las Vegas	7	McLaren International	M	3.0 McLaren MP4-Cosworth V8	pit stop-tyres	6/30

1982
Championship position: 2nd= Wins: 2 Pole positions: 0 Fastest laps: 1 Points scored: 39

6	SOUTH AFRICAN GP	Kyalami	7	Marlboro McLaren International	M	3.0 McLaren MP4B-Cosworth V8		9/30
2*	BRAZILIAN GP	Rio	7	Marlboro McLaren International	M	3.0 McLaren MP4B-Cosworth V8	*after 1st & 2nd place cars dsq	12/31
6	US GP WEST	Long Beach	7	Marlboro McLaren International	M	3.0 McLaren MP4B-Cosworth V8	1 lap behind	11/31
1	BELGIAN GP	Zolder	7	Marlboro McLaren International	M	3.0 McLaren MP4B-Cosworth V8	FL	12/32
ret	MONACO GP	Monte Carlo	7	Marlboro McLaren International	M	3.0 McLaren MP4B-Cosworth V8	oil leak/battery	10/31
1	US GP (DETROIT)	Detroit	7	Marlboro McLaren International	M	3.0 McLaren MP4B-Cosworth V8		17/28
3	CANADIAN GP	Montreal	7	Marlboro McLaren International	M	3.0 McLaren MP4B-Cosworth V8		6/29
9	DUTCH GP	Zandvoort	7	Marlboro McLaren International	M	3.0 McLaren MP4B-Cosworth V8	pit stop-tyres/1 lap behind	11/31
ret	BRITISH GP	Brands Hatch	7	Marlboro McLaren International	M	3.0 McLaren MP4B-Cosworth V8	spun off avoiding Jarier/Serra	12/31
ret	FRENCH GP	Paul Ricard	7	Marlboro McLaren International	M	3.0 McLaren MP4B-Cosworth V8	battery lead	12/30
ret	GERMAN GP	Hockenheim	7	Marlboro McLaren International	M	3.0 McLaren MP4B-Cosworth V8	front suspension	11/30
ret	AUSTRIAN GP	Österreichring	7	Marlboro McLaren International	M	3.0 McLaren MP4B-Cosworth V8	engine-split water hose	18/29
13	SWISS GP	Dijon	7	Marlboro McLaren International	M	3.0 McLaren MP4B-Cosworth V8	pit stop-broken skirt/-3 laps	11/29
4	ITALIAN GP	Monza	7	Marlboro McLaren International	M	3.0 McLaren MP4B-Cosworth V8		12/30
2	CAESARS PALACE GP	Las Vegas	7	Marlboro McLaren International	M	3.0 McLaren MP4B-Cosworth V8		9/30

1983
Championship position: 6th= Wins: 1 Pole positions: 0 Fastest laps: 1 Points scored: 22

ret	BRAZILIAN GP	Rio	7	Marlboro McLaren International	M	3.0 McLaren MP4/1C-Cosworth V8	engine	16/27
1	US GP WEST	Long Beach	7	Marlboro McLaren International	M	3.0 McLaren MP4/1C-Cosworth V8		22/28
ret	FRENCH GP	Paul Ricard	7	Marlboro McLaren International	M	3.0 McLaren MP4/1C-Cosworth V8	throttle linkage	14/29
5	SAN MARINO GP	Imola	7	Marlboro McLaren International	M	3.0 McLaren MP4/1C-Cosworth V8	1 lap behind	24/28
dnq	MONACO GP	Monte Carlo	7	Marlboro McLaren International	M	3.0 McLaren MP4/1C-Cosworth V8		23/28
ret	BELGIAN GP	Spa	7	Marlboro McLaren International	M	3.0 McLaren MP4/1C-Cosworth V8	accident with Jarier	20/28
3	US GP (DETROIT)	Detroit	7	Marlboro McLaren International	M	3.0 McLaren MP4/1C-Cosworth V8	FL	21/27
6	CANADIAN GP	Montreal	7	Marlboro McLaren International	M	3.0 McLaren MP4/1C-Cosworth V8	pit stop-tyres/1 lap behind	20/28
9	BRITISH GP	Silverstone	7	Marlboro McLaren International	M	3.0 McLaren MP4/1C-Cosworth V8	pit stop-tyres/1 lap behind	24/29
5	GERMAN GP	Hockenheim	7	Marlboro McLaren International	M	3.0 McLaren MP4/1C-Cosworth V8	pit stop-tyres/1 lap behind	23/29
9	AUSTRIAN GP	Österreichring	7	Marlboro McLaren International	M	3.0 McLaren MP4/1C-Cosworth V8	pit stop-tyres/2 laps behind	17/29
3	DUTCH GP	Zandvoort	7	Marlboro McLaren International	M	3.0 McLaren MP4/1C-Cosworth V8	pit stop-tyres	15/29
ret	ITALIAN GP	Monza	7	Marlboro McLaren International	M	1.5 t/c McLaren MP4/1E-TAG V6	engine	15/29
ret	EUROPEAN GP	Brands Hatch	7	Marlboro McLaren International	M	1.5 t/c McLaren MP4/1E-TAG V6	accident-rear wing failure	10/29
dsq	SOUTH AFRICAN GP	Kyalami	7	Marlboro McLaren International	M	1.5 t/c McLaren MP4/1E-TAG V6	overtook cars on warm-up lap	15/26

1985
Championship position: Unplaced

7	EUROPEAN GP	Brands Hatch	1	Marlboro McLaren International	G	1.5 t/c McLaren MP4/2B-TAG V6	2 laps behind	21/27

GP Starts: 152 GP Wins: 5 Pole positions: 2 Fastest laps: 5 Points: 169

KARL WENDLINGER

Racing was in Wendlinger's blood, for both his father and grandfather had competed in the past, and naturally Karl followed suit. After some karting experience the Austrian was helped greatly by Gerhard Berger (an old family friend) to get started in FF1600 in 1987.

Assisted by the former Grand Prix driver Dr Helmut Marko, he came to the fore in the 1989 German F3 championship with some excellent drives in a Ralt and took the title, edging out Schumacher and Frentzen after the closest fought of battles.

This trio of young talent was then selected by Mercedes-Benz to be groomed in their Group C programme as possible candidates for a future Formula 1 return. Paired with Jochen Mass, the best possible tutor, the young Austrian learned quickly and helped the company achieve its goal of winning the teams' championship with a win at Spa and second places at Suzuka and Monza. However, the necessity of having top-class equipment at his disposal was brought home when he endured a rather lacklustre time in Formula 3000 that year with a Helmut Marko-run Lola, taking only two championship points. The 1991 season saw the two star pupils Wendlinger and Schumacher paired together in the same Mercedes, and they performed splendidly in the somewhat less than previously dominant silver cars. A win at Autopolis was the high point of the season, and Karl was found a place in the Leyton House team for the final two races of the year. All eyes were really opened in South Africa at the beginning of 1992, when he qualified the largely unregarded car in seventh place on the grid. A brilliant fourth place in Canada gave some indication of the driver's potential, but the season was largely inconclusive due to reliability problems with the Ilmor V10. It had been a useful preparatory year for Karl, and for

1993 he moved to the new Sauber team as Mercedes had foreseen. In its first season the Swiss entrant made excellent progress and Wendlinger scored points on four occasions, though he was unfortunately involved in a number of on-track incidents which blotted his copybook somewhat.

The 1994 season saw Karl partnered by his ex-Mercedes Group C team-mate Heinz-Harald Frentzen, and it was immediately apparent that the newcomer meant business. Everything started satisfactorily for Wendlinger with points-scoring finishes in Brazil and at Imola, but then he was involved in a relatively low-speed crash during practice for the Monaco GP, the impact resulting in a brain contusion and swelling. He was immediately hospitalised and kept in a stable condition by means of a medically induced coma for almost three weeks, but thankfully he was soon on the road to recovery, although it was not until near the end of the season that he returned to the cockpit. Unfortunately after testing in Barcelona he was not well enough to race and he had to wait until the beginning of 1995 to resume his career. Somehow the old spark was missing, and Wendlinger visibly struggled to come to terms with the sheer speed of Frentzen. Eventually Sauber took the tough decision to rest him from the team in favour of Jean-Christophe Boullion, and it was only at season's end, when the Frenchman had seen his star wane in the wake of some poor performances, that Karl was brought back for a final chance to show he could still do the business. Sadly it seems that when he withdrew from the Australian GP suffering the effects of a practice crash, his fate was sealed.

Instead of looking back on a lost career, Karl started to build a new one. A two-year contract with Audi saw Wendlinger compete in both the German and Italian Super Touring series, before he was invited to join the ORECA team for 1998 to drive their Chrysler Viper. A win in the GT2 class with Justin Bell at the A1-Ring brought his first victory of any kind since his Group C Mercedes days in 1991 and, with the Austrian teaming up with Olivier Beretta for 1999, the Viper pair stormed to the newly formed Sports Racing World Cup, winning six of the nine rounds. Wendlinger also found time to successfully compete in the American Le Mans Series with the same car.

WENDLINGER, Karl (A) b 20/12/1968, Kufstein

	1991	Championship position: Unplaced						
	Race	Circuit	No	Entrant	Tyres	Car/Engine	Comment	Q Pos/Entries
ret	JAPANESE GP	Suzuka	16	Leyton House Racing	G	3.5 Leyton House CG911-Ilmor V10	*multiple collision lap 1*	22/32
20	AUSTRALIAN GP	Adelaide	16	Leyton House Racing	G	3.5 Leyton House CG911-Ilmor V10	*rain shortened race/-2 laps*	26/31
	1992	Championship position: 12th Wins: 0 Pole positions: 0 Fastest laps: 0 Points scored: 3						
ret	SOUTH AFRICAN GP	Kyalami	16	March F1	G	3.5 March CG 911-Ilmor V10	*overheating*	7/30
ret	MEXICAN GP	Mexico City	16	March F1	G	3.5 March CG 911-Ilmor V10	*collision with Capelli on lap 1*	19/30
ret	BRAZILIAN GP	Interlagos	16	March F1	G	3.5 March CG 911-Ilmor V10	*clutch*	9/31
8	SPANISH GP	Barcelona	16	March F1	G	3.5 March CG 911-Ilmor V10	*2 laps behind*	9/32
12	SAN MARINO GP	Imola	16	March F1	G	3.5 March CG 911-Ilmor V10	*3 laps behind*	12/32
ret	MONACO GP	Monte Carlo	16	March F1	G	3.5 March CG 911-Ilmor V10	*gearbox*	16/32

4	CANADIAN GP	Montreal	16	March F1	G	3.5 March CG 911-Ilmor V10		*1 lap behind*	12/32
ret	FRENCH GP	Magny Cours	16	March F1	G	3.5 March CG 911-Ilmor V10		*gearbox*	21/30
ret	BRITISH GP	Silverstone	16	March F1	G	3.5 March CG 911-Ilmor V10		*gearbox*	21/32
16	GERMAN GP	Hockenheim	16	March F1	G	3.5 March CG 911-Ilmor V10		*3 laps behind*	10/32
ret	HUNGARIAN GP	Hungaroring	16	March F1	G	3.5 March CG 911-Ilmor V10		*collision with Grouillard*	23/31
11	BELGIAN GP	Spa	16	March F1	G	3.5 March CG 911-Ilmor V10		*1 lap behind*	18/30
10	ITALIAN GP	Monza	16	March F1	G	3.5 March CG 911-Ilmor V10		*3 laps behind*	17/28
ret	PORTUGUESE GP	Estoril	16	March F1	G	3.5 March CG 911-Ilmor V10		*oil cooler/gearbox*	22/26

1993   Championship position: 1th=   Wins: 0   Pole positions: 0   Fastest laps: 0   Points scored: 7

ret	SOUTH AFRICAN GP	Kyalami	29	Sauber	G	3.5 Sauber C12-Ilmor V10	*electronics*	10/26
ret	BRAZILIAN GP	Interlagos	29	Sauber	G	3.5 Sauber C12-Ilmor V10	*overheating*	8/26
ret	EUROPEAN GP	Donington	29	Sauber	G	3.5 Sauber C12-Ilmor V10	*hit by Andretti on lap 1*	5/26
ret	SAN MARINO GP	Imola	29	Sauber	G	3.5 Sauber C12-Ilmor V10	*engine*	5/26
ret	SPANISH GP	Barcelona	29	Sauber	G	3.5 Sauber C12-Ilmor V10	*engine*	6/26
13	MONACO GP	Monte Carlo	29	Sauber	G	3.5 Sauber C12-Ilmor V10	*collision-Lehto-pit stop/-4 laps*	8/26
6	CANADIAN GP	Montreal	29	Sauber	G	3.5 Sauber C12-Ilmor V10	*1 lap behind*	9/26
ret	FRENCH GP	Magny Cours	29	Sauber	G	3.5 Sauber C12-Ilmor V10	*gearbox*	11/26
ret	BRITISH GP	Silverstone	29	Sauber	G	3.5 Sauber C12-Ilmor V10	*spun off*	18/26
9	GERMAN GP	Hockenheim	29	Sauber	G	3.5 Sauber C12-Ilmor V10	*1 lap behind*	14/26
6	HUNGARIAN GP	Hungaroring	29	Sauber	G	3.5 Sauber C12-Ilmor V10	*1 lap behind*	17/26
ret	BELGIAN GP	Spa	29	Sauber	G	3.5 Sauber C12-Ilmor V10	*engine*	12/26
4	ITALIAN GP	Monza	29	Sauber	G	3.5 Sauber C12-Ilmor V10	*1 lap behind*	15/26
5	PORTUGUESE GP	Estoril	29	Sauber	G	3.5 Sauber C12-Ilmor V10	*1 lap behind*	13/26
ret	JAPANESE GP	Suzuka	29	Sauber	G	3.5 Sauber C12-Ilmor V10	*stuck throttle*	16/24
15/ret	AUSTRALIAN GP	Adelaide	29	Sauber	G	3.5 Sauber C12-Ilmor V10	*brake disc-spun off/-5 laps*	11/24

1994   Championship position: 18th=   Wins: 0   Pole positions: 0   Fastest laps: 0   Points scored: 4

6	BRAZILIAN GP	Interlagos	29	Sauber Mercedes	G	3.5 Sauber C13-Mercedes Benz V10	*2 laps behind*	7/28
ret	PACIFIC GP	T.I. Circuit	29	Sauber Mercedes	G	3.5 Sauber C13-Mercedes Benz V10	*accident-hit by Alboreto*	19/28
4	SAN MARINO GP	Imola	29	Sauber Mercedes	G	3.5 Sauber C13-Mercedes Benz V10	*broken exhaust*	10/28
dns	MONACO GP	Monte Carlo	29	Sauber Mercedes	G	3.5 Sauber C13-Mercedes Benz V10	*practice accident*	– / –

1995   Championship position: Unplaced

ret	BRAZILIAN GP	Interlagos	29	Red Bull Sauber Ford	G	3.0 Sauber C14-Ford Zetec-R V8	*electrics*	19/26
ret	ARGENTINE GP	Buenos Aires	29	Red Bull Sauber Ford	G	3.0 Sauber C14-Ford Zetec-R V8	*collision with Gachot*	21/26
ret	SAN MARINO GP	Imola	29	Red Bull Sauber Ford	G	3.0 Sauber C14-Ford Zetec-R V8	*stuck wheel nut*	21/26
13	SPANISH GP	Barcelona	29	Red Bull Sauber Ford	G	3.0 Sauber C14-Ford Zetec-R V8	*2 laps behind*	20/26
10	JAPANESE GP	Suzuka	29	Red Bull Sauber Ford	G	3.0 Sauber C14-Ford Zetec-R V8	*2 laps behind*	16/24
ret	AUSTRALIAN GP	Adelaide	29	Red Bull Sauber Ford	G	3.0 Sauber C14-Ford Zetec-R V8	*withdrew/driver unwell*	18/24

GP Starts: 41   GP Wins: 0   Pole positions: 0   Fastest laps: 0   Points: 14

WESTBURY, Peter (GB) b 26/5/1938, South London

1969   Championship position: Unplaced

	Race	Circuit	No	Entrant	Tyres	Car/Engine	Comment	Q Pos/Entries
9*	GERMAN GP (F2)	Nürburgring	31	Felday Engineering Ltd	F	1.6 Brabham BT30-Cosworth 4 F2	**5th in F2 class/1 lap behind*	18/26

1970   Championship position: Unplaced

dnq	US GP	Watkins Glen	32	Yardley Team BRM	D	3.0 BRM P153 V12		25/27

GP Starts: 1   GP Wins: 0   Pole positions: 0   Fastest laps: 0   Points: 0

PETER WESTBURY

Westbury's career fell neatly into two halves, the first as a top-notch hill-climber, the second as a true circuit racer. He took to the hills in 1962 with a Cooper-Daimler, and when the V8 was dropped into his own Felday chassis in 1963 his first British hill-climb championship was duly attained. For the following year Westbury got his hands on the Ferguson 4WD, which proved almost unbeatable.

Although he continued to compete in 1965, Peter was busy building up his Felday Engineering firm, but he made a successful transition to Formula 3 in 1967 with a Brabham BT21. He won races at Silverstone, Chimay and Cermont Ferrand, and took further victories at Chimay again and Reims in 1968.

That year saw a couple of Formula 2 drives, before a full season in 1969 with his own Brabham BT30 which yielded second place in the Lottery GP at Monza and fifth in the F2 class of the German GP.

Peter was given a chance to try a pukka F1 machine when he joined BRM for the 1970 US GP, but the car suffered a blown engine and the disappointed driver failed to qualify. He was a consistent top-six finisher in Formula 2 during 1970-71 but results sagged the following year, and early in 1973 Westbury announced his retirement.

KEN WHARTON

A Smethwick garage owner, Wharton was a versatile all-rounder who began racing immediately before the war in an Austin Seven special, but it was not until the late forties that he began to make his mark in a number of motor sport arenas. In trials he won successive RAC championships, and his special was much copied by his competitors, while in rallies he campaigned a Ford Pilot, winning the Tulip Rally on three occasions.

In 1950 Wharton won at Zandvoort with a Cooper-JAP, while in 1951 he went hill-climbing, winning the first of four successive championships. Meanwhile he had taken up circuit racing in a big way, initially competing in Grands Prix with a large and old-fashioned Frazer-Nash. It ran reliably on its debut at Bremgarten in 1952, and Wharton took it to fourth place, his best-ever World Championship finish. This car was replaced by a more competitive Cooper-Bristol by the end of the season, but he could gain no major success with it the following season. He was kept busy by BRM, who were still racing their V16 car in Libre events, and joined the Owen team for 1954 to handle their Maserati 250F in Grands Prix and their V16 in Libre races, winning the Glover Trophy.

As if he wasn't already sufficiently stretched by his commitments, Wharton also tried his hand at sports car racing with the works Jaguar, winning the 1954 Reims 12 Hours with Peter Whitehead. For 1955, Ken joined the Vanwall team, suffering a nasty accident in the International Trophy at Silverstone which resulted in burns to his arms and neck. It was generally an unproductive year, and Wharton freelanced in 1956, taking a third place in the Australian Tourist Trophy in Melbourne with a Ferrari Monza. However, early in 1957 he was killed after crashing this car in a sports car race at Ardmore, New Zealand.

WHARTON, Ken (GB) b 21/3/1916, Smethwick, Worcestershire – d 12/1/1957, Ardmore Circuit, New Zealand

	1952	Championship position: 10=	Wins: 0		Pole positions: 0	Fastest laps: 0	Points scored: 3		
	Race	Circuit	No	Entrant	Tyres	Car/Engine		Comment	Q Pos/Entries
4	SWISS GP	Bremgarten	22	Scuderia Franera	D	2.0 Frazer Nash FN48-Bristol 6		2 laps behind	13/21
ret	BELGIAN GP	Spa	36	Scuderia Franera	D	2.0 Frazer Nash FN48-Bristol 6		spun off	7/22
ret	DUTCH GP	Zandvoort	34	Scuderia Franera	D	2.0 Frazer Nash 421-Bristol 6		transmission	7/18
9	ITALIAN GP	Monza	40	Scuderia Franera	D	2.0 Cooper T20-Bristol 6		4 laps behind	15/35
	1953	Championship position: Unplaced							
ret	DUTCH GP	Zandvoort	32	Ken Wharton	D	2.0 Cooper T23-Bristol 6		rear suspension	18/20
ret	FRENCH GP	Reims	40	Ken Wharton	D	2.0 Cooper T23-Bristol 6		engine	14/25
8	BRITISH GP	Silverstone	16	Ken Wharton	D	2.0 Cooper T23-Bristol 6		10 laps behind	11/29
7	SWISS GP	Bremgarten	20	Ken Wharton	D	2.0 Cooper T23-Bristol 6		3 laps behind	9/23
nc	ITALIAN GP	Monza	30	Ken Wharton	D	2.0 Cooper T23-Bristol 6		23 laps behind	19/30
	1954	Championship position: Unplaced							
ret	FRENCH GP	Reims	42	Owen Racing Organisation	D	2.5 Maserati 250F 6		transmission	16/22
8	BRITISH GP	Silverstone	8	Owen Racing Organisation	D	2.5 Maserati 250F 6		4 laps behind	9/31
dns	GERMAN GP	Nürburgring	17	Owen Racing Organisation	D	2.5 Maserati 250F 6		withdrawn during practice	– /23
6	SWISS GP	Bremgarten	18	Owen Racing Organisation	D	2.5 Maserati 250F 6		2 laps behind	8/16
8	SPANISH GP	Pedralbes	28	Owen Racing Organisation	D	2.5 Maserati 250F 6		6 laps behind	14/22
	1955	Championship position: Unplaced							
nc*	BRITISH GP	Aintree	28	Vandervell Products Ltd	P	2.5 Vanwall 4		* Schell took over car/-18 laps	15/25
ret	ITALIAN GP	Monza	44	Vandervell Products Ltd	P	2.5 Vanwall 4		fuel injection pump mounting	17/22

GP Starts: 15   GP Wins: 0   Pole positions: 0   Fastest laps: 0   Points: 3

WHITEHEAD, Graham (GB) b 15/4/1922, Harrogate, Yorkshire – d 15/1/1981, Lower Basildon, nr Reading, Berkshire

	1952	Championship position: Unplaced							
	Race	Circuit	No	Entrant	Tyres	Car/Engine		Comment	Q Pos/Entries
12	BRITISH GP	Silverstone	1	Peter Whitehead	D	2.0 Alta F2 4		5 laps behind	12/32

GP Starts: 1   GP Wins: 0   Pole positions: 0   Fastest laps: 0   Points: 0

GRAHAM WHITEHEAD

Graham began racing Peter's ERA in 1951, and then drove his F2 Alta in the 1952 British GP, before a long and generally successful period when he competed in Jaguar and Aston Martin sports cars, often paired with his half-brother. Their greatest success together was second place in the 1958 Le Mans 24 Hours, only weeks before the crash in the Tour de France in which Peter was killed. Graham escaped serious injury and returned to competition racing an Aston Martin and then a Ferrari 250GT until the end of the 1961 season.

PETER WHITEHEAD

A throwback to the age of the truly amateur driver, Whitehead, a wealthy businessman, had the means with which to indulge his passion for motor sport in the best possible fashion. He began racing in 1934 and was soon making a name for himself in an ERA. He took the car to Australia in 1938 and won the Grand Prix at the Bathurst circuit.

His trusty ERA was back in action after the war and took second place in the 1947 British Empire Trophy at the Isle of Man. The following year he was seriously injured – not racing, but in an air crash at Croydon aerodrome when preparing to fly to Milan to arrange the purchase of a Ferrari 125. It was the 1949 season before he was able to put the green-painted machine through its paces in competition. He looked set to win the French GP at Reims, until gearbox problems dropped him to third place, but he did triumph in Czechoslovakia, becoming the first Briton to win a major race abroad since Seaman. His successes with the Ferrari continued into the 1950 season when he took the Jersey Road Race and the Ulster Trophy. Despite his amateur status, Peter was certainly no slouch as a driver and he scored some excellent Continental placings in the 1951 season with the Ferrari, but the highlight of his year was undoubtedly a glorious Le Mans win with Peter Walker for Jaguar.

The 1952 and 1953 seasons saw Whitehead campaigning an Alta and a Cooper-Alta in addition to his Ferrari, but he was now finding it more rewarding to race sports cars, where the chances of success were greater. In 1953, with a D-Type Jaguar, he won the Reims 12 Hours with Moss and the Hyères 12 Hours with Tom Cole. He triumphed again in the Reims 12 Hours the following season, sharing a works Jaguar with Ken Wharton, but after his last British GP appearance, Peter was little seen in Formula 1, preferring to concentrate on his newly acquired Cooper-Jaguar sports car and Libre events with his Ferrari 3-litre – particularly in the Antipodes, where he often raced during the English winter.

His last great performance came in the 1958 Le Mans 24 Hours, when he shared the second-placed Aston Martin with his half-brother Graham. Just a couple of months later Peter lost his life during the Tour de France when the pair's Jaguar, with Graham at the wheel, crashed over a bridge parapet into a ravine, injuring the driver but killing his unfortunate passenger.

WHITEHEAD, Peter (GB) b 12/11/1914, Menstone, nr Ilkley, Yorkshire – d 21/9/1958, Lasalle, nr Nimes, France

	Race	Circuit	No	Entrant	Tyres	Car/Engine	Comment	Q Pos/Entries
	1950	Championship position: 9= Wins: 0 Pole positions: 0 Fastest laps: 0 Points scored: 4						
dns	MONACO GP	Monte Carlo	28	Peter Whitehead	D	1.5 s/c Ferrari 125 V12	3 engine failures in practice	(21)/21
3	FRENCH GP	Reims	14	Peter Whitehead	D	1.5 s/c Ferrari 125 V12	3 laps behind	19/20
7	ITALIAN GP	Monza	8	Peter Whitehead	D	1.5 s/c Ferrari 125 V12	8 laps behind	18/27
	1951	Championship position: Unplaced						
ret	SWISS GP	Bremgarten	16	Scuderia Ferrari	D	1.5 s/c Ferrari 125 V12	crashed-cut face	9/21
ret	FRENCH GP	Reims	24	Graham Whitehead	D	1.5 s/c Ferrari 125 V12	cylinder head gasket	20/23
9	BRITISH GP	Silverstone	14	G A Vandervell	P	4.5 Thinwall Ferrari 375F1 V12	7 laps behind	8/20
ret	ITALIAN GP	Monza	16	Peter Whitehead	D	1.5 s/c Ferrari 125 V12	engine	19/22
	1952	Championship position: Unplaced						
ret	FRENCH GP	Rouen	26	Peter Whitehead	D	2.0 Alta F2 4	clutch	13/20
10	BRITISH GP	Silverstone	21	Peter Whitehead	D	2.0 Ferrari 125 V12 F2	4 laps behind	20/32
dnq	ITALIAN GP	Monza	68	Peter Whitehead	D	2.0 Ferrari 125 V12 F2		29/35
	1953	Championship position: Unplaced						
9	BRITISH GP	Silverstone	20	Atlantic Stable	D	2.0 Cooper T24-Alta 4	brake problems/-11 laps	14/29
	1954	Championship position: Unplaced						
ret	BRITISH GP	Silverstone	21	Peter Whitehead	D	2.5 Cooper T24-Alta 4	engine	24/31

GP Starts: 10 GP Wins: 0 Pole positions: 0 Fastest laps: 0 Points: 4

WHITEHOUSE, Bill (GB) b 1/4/1909, London – d 14/7/1957, Reims Circuit, France

	1954	Championship position: Unplaced						
	Race	Circuit	No	Entrant	Tyres	Car/Engine	Comment	Q Pos/Entries
ret	BRITISH GP	Silverstone	22	Bill Whitehouse	D	2.0 Connaught A Type-Lea Francis 4	fuel system	19/31

GP Starts: 1   GP Wins: 0   Pole positions: 0   Fastest laps: 0   Points: 0

WIDDOWS, Robin (GB) b 27/5/1942, Cowley, nr Uxbridge, Middlesex

	1968	Championship position: Unplaced						
	Race	Circuit	No	Entrant	Tyres	Car/Engine	Comment	Q Pos/Entries
ret	BRITISH GP	Brands Hatch	16	Cooper Car Co	F	3.0 Cooper T86-BRM V12	ignition	18/20

GP Starts: 1   GP Wins: 0   Pole positions: 0   Fastest laps: 0   Points: 0

BILL WHITEHOUSE

One of the top 500 cc F3 Cooper drivers in the early 1950s, 'Big Bill' raced Gordon Watson's F2 Alta briefly in 1951 before breaking out of the tiddler class in 1954 with his own F2 Connaught, sensibly keeping to Libre and national events with the exception of the British GP.

After an accident, Bill retired but, once fit, the lure of the track proved too great for this enthusiast. In 1957, he bought an F2 Cooper-Climax, which he raced at Syracuse, and when his car suffered engine trouble at Reims he was delighted to be loaned the works Bob-tail 'streamliner' for the race. Tragically, he was to meet his death when a tyre appeared to burst as he approached Thillois, the car somersaulting and bursting into flames.

ROBIN WIDDOWS

An Olympic-standard bobsleigh rider, Robin raced an MG Midget and a Lotus 23, winning the Autosport Class C championship in 1965, before successfully moving up to Formula 3 the following year. A syndicate of friends financed a season of Formula 2 in 1967 in a Brabham BT23, the highlight of which was a surprise win in the Rhine Cup at Hockenheim. For 1968, he joined the Chequered Flag team to drive a McLaren M4A, and took second place at Pau with a superb display.

Cooper gave him his only Grand Prix outing at that year's British GP, and he was back in Formula 2 with Bob Gerard in 1969. He did well once more, winning the Lottery GP and taking second at Reims, and also raced sports cars for Matra, finishing seventh at Le Mans with Galli. In 1970 he raced Alistair Walker's Brabham, again in F2, until suddenly retiring from racing in mid-season.

EPPIE WIETZES

One of Canada's most enduring and successful drivers at national level, Wietzes began racing as far back as 1958, and by the early 1960s was a leading sports and GT contender with such diverse cars as AC Cobras, Ford Mustangs and a Ford GT40.

In 1967 he hired the third works Lotus to race alongside Clark (pictured left) and Hill in the first World Championship Canadian GP. Switching to single-seaters, he was Canadian FA champion with a Lola T142 in 1969, and again the following year, this time with a McLaren M10. Eppie then became one of the leading privateers on the US F5000 circuit in the early seventies.

He won a round at Donnybrooke in 1972 in his Lola T300 and drove superbly in 1974, generally being beaten only by Andretti and Redman. Wietzes ran a hired Brabham in the 1974 Grand Prix, without success, and after the demise of F5000 Stateside re-appeared in Trans-Am. In 1981 he took the CRC Championship with some stylish drives in Garretson Enterprises' Chevrolet Corvette.

WIETZES, Eppie (CDN) b 28/5/1938

	1967	Championship position: Unplaced						
	Race	*Circuit*	*No*	*Entrant*	*Tyres*	*Car/Engine*	*Comment*	*Q Pos/Entries*
ret	CANADIAN GP	Mosport Park	5	Team Lotus/Comstock Racing Team	F	3.0 Lotus 49-Cosworth V8	wet ignition	17/19
	1974	Championship position: 0 Unplaced						
ret	CANADIAN GP	Mosport Park	50	Team Canada Formula 1 Racing	G	3.0 Brabham BT42-Cosworth V8	transmission	26/30

GP Starts: 2   GP Wins: 0   Pole positions: 0   Fastest laps: 0   Points: 0

WILDS, Mike (GB) b 7/1/1946, Chiswick, London

	1974	Championship position: Unplaced						
	Race	*Circuit*	*No*	*Entrant*	*Tyres*	*Car/Engine*	*Comment*	*Q Pos/Entries*
dnq	BRITISH GP	Brands Hatch	35	Dempster International Racing Team	F	3.0 March 731-Cosworth V8		33/34
dnq	AUSTRIAN GP	Österreichring	22	Team Ensign	F	3.0 Ensign N174-Cosworth V8		29/31
dnq	ITALIAN GP	Monza	25	Team Ensign	F	3.0 Ensign N174-Cosworth V8		29/31
dnq	CANADIAN GP	Mosport Park	22	Team Ensign	F	3.0 Ensign N174-Cosworth V8		28/30
nc	US GP	Watkins Glen	22	Team Ensign	F	3.0 Ensign N174-Cosworth V8	pit stop-fuel pump/-9 laps	22/30
	1975	Championship position: Unplaced						
ret	ARGENTINE GP	Buenos Aires	14	Stanley BRM	G	3.0 BRM P201 V12	oil scavenge pump drive belt	22/23
ret	BRAZILIAN GP	Interlagos	14	Stanley BRM	G	3.0 BRM P201 V12	electrics-damaged by loose nut	22/23
	1976	Championship position: Unplaced						
dnq	BRITISH GP	Brands Hatch	40	Team P R Reilly	G	3.0 Shadow DN3-Cosworth V8		29/30

GP Starts: 3   GP Wins: 0   Pole positions: 0   Fastest laps: 0   Points: 0

WILLIAMS, Jonathan (GB) b 26/10/1942, Cairo, Egypt

	1967	Championship position: Unplaced						
	Race	*Circuit*	*No*	*Entrant*	*Tyres*	*Car/Engine*	*Comment*	*Q Pos/Entries*
8	MEXICAN GP	Mexico City	12	Scuderia Ferrari SpA SEFAC	F	3.0 Ferrari 312/67 V12	2 laps behind	16/19

GP Starts: 1   GP Wins: 0   Pole positions: 0   Fastest laps: 0   Points: 0

MIKE WILDS

A former Firestone employee, Mike spent seven years in club racing before hitting the Formula 3 trail in 1972. With backing from a loyal sponsor in Dempster Developments, Wilds was a leading runner and occasional winner in F3 before opting to race in F5000 in 1974, but in mid-season he was given the chance to race in Formula 1, initially with a March and then with Ensign. Invited to lead the BRM team for 1975, poor Wilds only lasted two races before the Stanley axe fell.

Shortly afterwards Mike split from his long-time sponsor, and rejoined the F5000 trail, racing an ex-works Shadow in 1976. Driving a Ralt, he took the F2 class championship in the 1978 Aurora AFX series, and since then he has been a star of club racing once more, enjoying himself immensely in historic and sports cars.

In 1994 he was invited to demonstrate the ex-Gilles Villeneuve Ferrari 312T3 at the Goodwood Festival of Speed. Unfortunately he crashed the car quite heavily, sustaining a broken leg and other serious injuries.

Undeterred, Mike was back on the tracks once more in 1995, and has since been a champion in historic racing events driving a Chevron B31/36 sports car.

JONATHAN WILLIAMS

An Englishman abroad. Williams, based in Italy, was plucked from the relative obscurity of the de Sanctis F3 team to join Ferrari in 1967, competing in but one Grand Prix and a single F2 race, in addition to a handful of sports and Can-Am outings, before being discarded as casually as he seemed to have been signed.

Certainly Jonathan had been amazingly successful in European F3 in 1965-66, but his sojourn at Maranello did his career prospects no favours. A Formula 1 project for Abarth proved abortive, leaving him scratching for rides thereafter.

He did some Formula 2 in 1968, winning the Rhine Cup race for his old F3 partner Frank Williams, and then raced the works Serenissima and various other privateer sports cars into the early seventies before retiring to pursue a career as a pilot based in the south of France.

ROGER WILLIAMSON

Williamson is remembered as a smashing bloke, completely without pretension, and a terrific talent, who was needlessly to pay the ultimate price in front of millions of TV viewers that tragic day at Zandvoort in 1973.

Roger had a successful karting career behind him when, with encouragement from his father, he took up circuit racing in an 850 Mini, winning 14 races in 1968. Deciding to try single-seaters, he purchased a Cooper T71, which was unfortunately burnt out in a garage fire. However, Roger took the engine and fitted it to a Ford Anglia and it proved to be a potent combination. In 1970 he won the 1000 cc class of the Hepolite Glazier championship with ease, and decided to try Formula 3 the following year. Despite his inexperience, he was soon a front-runner, with his spectacular driving in a March 713 catching the eye. He was fortunate at this time to be helped financially by local businessman and racing enthusiast Tom Wheatcroft, and the pair became firm friends, with Tom guiding his rise towards the top.

Having won the Lombank F3 championship, Williamson stayed in the formula for a further year and convincingly took both the major F3 titles that season. His foray into Formula 2 was not so happy, but it was good experience for a planned season in 1973 with GRD. The car turned out to be no match for the dominant March chassis, and Wheatcroft swiftly provided his charge with the equipment he needed. Almost immediately Roger won the Lottery GP at Monza, and would have taken another victory at Misano but for engine problems, establishing himself as a truly serious talent. A season in Formula 1 was the goal in 1974, and to this end Wheatcroft hired an STP March for a couple of races to allow Williamson to become acclimatised. At Silverstone he was eliminated in the now notorious Jody Scheckter-induced carnage, and then came Zandvoort. It is thought a tyre failed, sending his car into an inadequately secured barrier which launched it across the track. The March came to rest upside down and on fire, with poor Roger trapped in the cockpit. Scandalously, nobody came to his help, apart from the brave David Purley, who single-handedly attempted to right the inverted machine. Then the fire caught hold and a truly nightmarish scenario was complete. For poor Williamson it was a cruel and gruesome end.

VIC WILSON

Vic was born in England, but spent his teens living in South Africa. He began racing in Rhodesia in the late fifties, finding success with a variety of MGs and then a Lotus XI. Plans to race a Lotus in England went awry when the car was written off, but he then approached Dick Gibson, who was languishing in hospital after recently crashing his almost new Cooper. Having repaired the machine, Wilson went racing along with Bruce Halford and Keith Ballisat, competing in the boycotted Italian GP of 1960.

Settling in Yorkshire, Vic did not race at all between 1961 and 1963, but at the behest of his wealthy cousin Bernard White he returned late in 1964, before a busy season racing a Lotus 30 and a Ferrari 250LM in 1965. Team Chamaco Collect then planned a full season of Grands Prix in 1966 with a couple of BRMs, but after Vic took a distant fourth at the Syracuse GP and practised briefly at Spa Bob Bondurant became the team's sole driver, leaving Wilson in the cold.

WILLIAMSON, Roger (GB) b 2/2/1948, Leicester – d 29/7/1973, Zandvoort Circuit, Netherlands

	1973	Championship position: Unplaced							
	Race	Circuit	No	Entrant	Tyres	Car/Engine	Comment		Q Pos/Entries
ret/dns	BRITISH GP	Silverstone	14	STP March Racing/Wheatcroft Racing	G	3.0 March 721G/731-Cosworth V8	multiple accident-1st start		22/29
ret	DUTCH GP	Zandvoort	14	STP March Racing Team	G	3.0 March 731-Cosworth V8	fatal accident		18/24

GP Starts: 1 (2)   GP Wins: 0   Pole positions: 0   Fastest laps: 0   Points: 0

WILSON, Vic (GB) b 14/4/1931, Drypool, Kingston-upon-Hull

	1960	Championship position: Unplaced							
	Race	Circuit	No	Entrant	Tyres	Car/Engine	Comment		Q Pos/Entries
ret	ITALIAN GP	Monza	30	Equipe Prideaux/Dick Gibson	D	1.5 Cooper T43-Climax 4	engine-oil sump		16/16
	1966	Championship position: Unplaced							
dns	BELGIAN GP	Spa	8	Team Chamaco-Collect	G	2.0 BRM P261-V8	practice only-Bondurant raced		17/18

GP Starts: 1   GP Wins: 0   Pole positions: 0   Fastest laps: 0   Points: 0

MANFRED WINKELHOCK

Manfred was a likeable man, friendly and unassuming, for whom Formula 1 was not the be-all-and-end-all of his life. He was quite content to enjoy his racing in sports-prototypes and touring cars, happy to be part of the Grand Prix scene while it wanted him.

He started racing in the Scirocco Cup in 1976, but soon began a long and happy association with BMW which saw him rapidly progress through their junior team from saloons to Formula 2. He was to spend three seasons in the formula, coming close to victory at Hockenheim in 1981, when his troubled Ralt was overhauled almost within sight of the finish.

An abortive drive for Arrows apart, Manfred's Grand Prix career began with the ATS team at the start of 1982. There were those who thought his style harsh and crude, but there was no doubting either his commitment or bravery as he manhandled the cars for all they were worth. Unfortunately, as the statistics show, his Formula 1 efforts were largely frustrated by a catalogue of retirements and he was no doubt glad to be able to go racing properly in the Kremer Porsche – particularly in 1985, when the season had started so brightly with a second place at Mugello and then a win at Monza, with Marc Surer.

Tragedy was to strike at Mosport, however, when in an unexplained accident Manfred's Porsche left the track at high speed. The driver was finally freed from the wreckage, and taken to hospital critically injured. Though no bones were broken, his head injuries were severe, and he died some 24 hours later.

WINKELHOCK, Manfred (D) b 6/10/1951, Waiblingen, nr Stuttgart – d 12/8/1985, Toronto, Canada

	1980	Championship position: Unplaced						
	Race	Circuit	No	Entrant	Tyres	Car/Engine	Comment	Q Pos/Entries
dnq	ITALIAN GP	Imola	30	Warsteiner Arrows Racing Team		3.0 Arrows A3-Cosworth V8		26/28
	1982	Championship position: 22nd=	Wins: 0	Pole positions: 0	Fastest laps: 0	Points scored: 2		
10	SOUTH AFRICAN GP	Kyalami	9	Team ATS	A	3.0 ATS D5-Cosworth V8	2 laps behind	20/30
5*	BRAZILIAN GP	Rio	9	Team ATS	A	3.0 ATS D5-Cosworth V8	* 1st & 2nd cars dsq/-1 lap	15/31
ret	US GP WEST	Long Beach	9	Team ATS	A	3.0 ATS D5-Cosworth V8	collision with Borgudd	25/31
dsq	SAN MARINO GP	Imola	9	Team ATS	A	3.0 ATS D5-Cosworth V8	under weight limit	12/14
ret	BELGIAN GP	Zolder	9	Team ATS	A	3.0 ATS D5-Cosworth V8	clutch	14/32
ret	MONACO GP	Monte Carlo	9	Team ATS	M	3.0 ATS D5-Cosworth V8	differential	14/31
ret	US GP (DETROIT)	Detroit	9	Team ATS	M	3.0 ATS D5-Cosworth V8	steering arm-accident	5/28
dnq	CANADIAN GP	Montreal	9	Team ATS	M	3.0 ATS D5-Cosworth V8		27/29
12	DUTCH GP	Zandvoort	9	Team ATS	M	3.0 ATS D5-Cosworth V8	delayed start/2 laps behind	18/31
dnq	BRITISH GP	Brands Hatch	9	Team ATS	M	3.0 ATS D5-Cosworth V8		27/30
11	FRENCH GP	Paul Ricard	9	Team ATS	M	3.0 ATS D5-Cosworth V8	2 laps behind	18/30
ret	GERMAN GP	Hockenheim	9	Team ATS	M	3.0 ATS D5-Cosworth V8	clutch/gearbox	17/30
ret	AUSTRIAN GP	Österreichring	9	Team ATS	M	3.0 ATS D5-Cosworth V8	spun off	25/29
ret	SWISS GP	Dijon	9	Team ATS	M	3.0 ATS D5-Cosworth V8	engine mounting	20/29
dnq	ITALIAN GP	Monza	9	Team ATS	M	3.0 ATS D5-Cosworth V8		28/30
nc	CAESARS PALACE GP	Las Vegas	9	Team ATS	M	3.0 ATS D5-Cosworth V8	2 pit stops-misfire/-13 laps	22/30
	1983	Championship position: Unplaced						
16	BRAZILIAN GP	Rio	9	Team ATS	G	1.5 t/c ATS D6-BMW 4	pit stop-fuel feed/-4 laps	25/27
ret	US GP WEST	Long Beach	9	Team ATS	G	1.5 t/c ATS D6-BMW 4	mechanical breakage-hit wall	24/28
ret	FRENCH GP	Paul Ricard	9	Team ATS	G	1.5 t/c ATS D6-BMW 4	exhaust-engine	10/29
11	SAN MARINO GP	Imola	9	Team ATS	G	1.5 t/c ATS D6-BMW 4	3 laps behind	7/28
ret	MONACO GP	Monte Carlo	9	Team ATS	G	1.5 t/c ATS D6-BMW 4	accident with Boesel	16/28
ret	BELGIAN GP	Spa	9	Team ATS	G	1.5 t/c ATS D6-BMW 4	lost rear wheel	7/28
ret	US GP (DETROIT)	Detroit	9	Team ATS	G	1.5 t/c ATS D6-BMW 4	hit wall	22/27
9*/ret	CANADIAN GP	Montreal	9	Team ATS	G	1.5 t/c ATS D6-BMW 4	* 9th car dsq/2 pit stops/-3 laps	7/28
ret	BRITISH GP	Silverstone	9	Team ATS	G	1.5 t/c ATS D6-BMW 4	overheating	8/29
dnq	GERMAN GP	Hockenheimq	9	Team ATS	G	1.5 t/c ATS D6-BMW 4		29/29
ret	AUSTRIAN GP	Österreichring	9	Team ATS	G	1.5 t/c ATS D6-BMW 4	overheating	13/29
dsq	DUTCH GP	Zandvoort	9	Team ATS	G	1.5 t/c ATS D6-BMW 4	overtook cars on parade lap	9/29

ret	ITALIAN GP	Monza	9	Team ATS	G	1.5 t/c ATS D6-BMW 4	broken exhaust	9/29
8	EUROPEAN GP	Brands Hatch	9	Team ATS	G	1.5 t/c ATS D6-BMW 4	pit stop-tyres/1 lap behind	9/29
ret	SOUTH AFRICAN GP	Kyalami	9	Team ATS	G	1.5 t/c ATS D6-BMW 4	engine	8/26

1984 Championship position: Unplaced

excl	BRAZILIAN GP	Rio	14	Team ATS	P	1.5 t/c ATS D7-BMW 4	push started against regs	(15)/27
ret	SOUTH AFRICAN GP	Kyalami	14	Team ATS	P	1.5 t/c ATS D7-BMW 4	engine/battery	12/27
ret	BELGIAN GP	Zolder	14	Team ATS	P	1.5 t/c ATS D7-BMW 4	electrics/exhaust	6/27
ret	SAN MARINO GP	Imola	14	Team ATS	P	1.5 t/c ATS D7-BMW 4	turbo	7/28
ret	FRENCH GP	Dijon	14	Team ATS	P	1.5 t/c ATS D7-BMW 4	clutch	8/27
ret	MONACO GP	Monte Carlo	14	Team ATS	P	1.5 t/c ATS D7-BMW 4	spun off	12/27
8	CANADIAN GP	Montreal	14	Team ATS	P	1.5 t/c ATS D7-BMW 4	2 laps behind	12/26
ret	US GP (DETROIT)	Detroit	14	Team ATS	P	1.5 t/c ATS D7-BMW 4	accident	14/27
8	US GP (DALLAS)	Dallas	14	Team ATS	P	1.5 t/c ATS D7-BMW 4	3 laps behind	13/27
ret	BRITISH GP	Brands Hatch	14	Team ATS	P	1.5 t/c ATS D7-BMW 4	spun off	11/27
ret	GERMAN GP	Hockenheim	14	Team ATS	P	1.5 t/c ATS D7-BMW 4	turbo boost/gearbox	13/27
dns	AUSTRIAN GP	Österreichring	14	Team ATS	P	1.5 t/c ATS D7-BMW 4	gearbox in Sun a.m.warm-up	(14)/28
ret	DUTCH GP	Zandvoort	14	Team ATS	P	1.5 t/c ATS D7-BMW 4	spun off	16/27
ret/dns	ITALIAN GP	Monza	14	Team ATS	P	1.5 t/c ATS D7-BMW 4	gearbox on warm-up lap	(21)/27
10	PORTUGUESE GP	Estoril	2	MRD International	M	1.5 t/c Brabham BT53-BMW 4	1 lap behind	19/27

1985 Championship position: Unplaced

13	BRAZILIAN GP	Rio	9	Skoal Bandit Formula 1 Team	P	1.5 t/c RAM 03-Hart 4	4 laps behind	16/25
nc	PORTUGUESE GP	Estoril	9	Skoal Bandit Formula 1 Team	P	1.5 t/c RAM 03-Hart 4	tyre problems/17 laps behind	15/26
ret	SAN MARINO GP	Imola	9	Skoal Bandit Formula 1 Team	P	1.5 t/c RAM 03-Hart 4	engine	23/26
dnq	MONACO GP	Monte Carlo	9	Skoal Bandit Formula 1 Team	P	1.5 t/c RAM 03-Hart 4		24/26
ret	CANADIAN GP	Montreal	9	Skoal Bandit Formula 1 Team	P	1.5 t/c RAM 03-Hart 4	hit by de Cesaris-hit wall	14/25
ret	US GP (DETROIT)	Detroit	9	Skoal Bandit Formula 1 Team	P	1.5 t/c RAM 03-Hart 4	turbo	20/25
12	FRENCH GP	Paul Ricard	9	Skoal Bandit Formula 1 Team	P	1.5 t/c RAM 03-Hart 4	3 laps behind	20/26
ret	BRITISH GP	Silverstone	9	Skoal Bandit Formula 1 Team	P	1.5 t/c RAM 03-Hart 4	turbo	18/26
ret	GERMAN GP	Nürburgring	9	Skoal Bandit Formula 1 Team	P	1.5 t/c RAM 03-Hart 4	engine	22/27

GP Starts: 46 (47)   GP Wins: 0   Pole positions: 0   Fastest laps: 0   Points: 2

WISELL, Reine (S) b 30/9/1941, Motal, nr Linköping

1970 Championship position: 15th=   Wins: 0   Pole positions: 0   Fastest laps: 0   Points scored: 4

	Race	Circuit	No	Entrant	Tyres	Car/Engine	Comment	Q Pos/Entries
3	US GP	Watkins Glen	23	Gold Leaf Team Lotus	F	3.0 Lotus 72C-Cosworth V8		9/27
nc	MEXICAN GP	Mexico City	23	Gold Leaf Team Lotus	F	3.0 Lotus 72C-Cosworth V8	3 pit stops-oil line/-9 laps	12/18

1971 Championship position: 9th=   Wins: 0   Pole positions: 0   Fastest laps: 0   Points scored: 9

4	SOUTH AFRICAN GP	Kyalami	3	Gold Leaf Team Lotus	F	3.0 Lotus 72C-Cosworth V8		=13/25
nc	SPANISH GP	Montjuich Park	3	Gold Leaf Team Lotus	F	3.0 Lotus 72C-Cosworth V8	pit stop-gearbox/-17 laps	=16/22
ret	MONACO GP	Monte Carlo	2	Gold Leaf Team Lotus	F	3.0 Lotus 72C-Cosworth V8	rear hub bearing	12/23
dsq	DUTCH GP	Zandvoort	14	Gold Leaf Team Lotus	F	3.0 Lotus 72D-Cosworth V8	reversed into pits	6/24
6	FRENCH GP	Paul Ricard	2	Gold Leaf Team Lotus	F	3.0 Lotus 72D-Cosworth V8		15/24
nc	BRITISH GP	Silverstone	3	Gold Leaf Team Lotus	F	Turbine Lotus 56B-Pratt & Whitney	2 pit stops/11 laps behind	19/24
8	GERMAN GP	Nürburgring	9	Gold Leaf Team Lotus	F	3.0 Lotus 72D-Cosworth V8	left on grid-fuel pressure	17/23
4	AUSTRIAN GP	Österreichring	3	Gold Leaf Team Lotus	F	3.0 Lotus 72D-Cosworth V8		10/22
5	CANADIAN GP	Mosport Park	3	Gold Leaf Team Lotus	F	3.0 Lotus 72D-Cosworth V8	1 lap behind	=7/27
ret	US GP	Watkins Glen	3	Gold Leaf Team Lotus	F	3.0 Lotus 72D-Cosworth V8	brakes-hit barrier	10/32

1972 Championship position: Unplaced

ret	ARGENTINE GP	Buenos Aires	4	Marlboro BRM	F	3.0 BRM P153 V12	water leak	=16/22
ret	SPANISH GP	Jarama	10	Austria Marlboro BRM	F	3.0 BRM P160B V12	went off at end of straight	10/26
ret	MONACO GP	Monte Carlo	28	Marlboro BRM	F	3.0 BRM P160B V12	engine	16/25
ret	FRENCH GP	Clermont Ferrand	24	Marlboro BRM	F	3.0 BRM P160B V12	gear linkage	=19/29
ret	GERMAN GP	Nürburgring	18	Marlboro BRM	F	3.0 BRM P160C V12	engine seized	17/27
12	ITALIAN GP	Monza	24	Marlboro BRM	F	3.0 BRM P160C V12	pit stop-gearbox/-4 laps	10/27
ret	CANADIAN GP	Mosport Park	6	John Player Team Lotus	F	3.0 Lotus 72D-Cosworth V8	engine	16/25
10	US GP	Watkins Glen	12	John Player Team Lotus	F	3.0 Lotus 72D-Cosworth V8	2 laps behind	16/32

1973 Championship position: Unplaced

dns	SWEDISH GP	Anderstorp	27	Team Pierre Robert	G	3.0 March 731-Cosworth V8	suspension in warm-up	(14)/22
ret	FRENCH GP	Paul Ricard	15	Clarke-Mordaunt-Guthrie-Durlacher	G	3.0 March 721G/731-Cosworth V8	engine-fuel vaporisation	22/25

1974 Championship position: Unplaced

ret	SWEDISH GP	Anderstorp	9	March Engineering	G	3.0 March 741-Cosworth V8	suspension	16/28

GP Starts: 22   GP Wins: 0   Pole positions: 0   Fastest laps: 0   Points: 13

WUNDERINK, Roelof (NL) b 12/12/1948

1975 Championship position: Unplaced

	Race	Circuit	No	Entrant	Tyres	Car/Engine	Comment	Q Pos/Entries
ret	SPANISH GP	Montjuich Park	31	HB Bewaking Team Ensign	G	3.0 Ensign N174-Cosworth V8	driveshaft c.v. joint	19/26
dnq	MONACO GP	Monte Carlo	31	HB Bewaking Team Ensign	G	3.0 Ensign N174-Cosworth V8		23/26
dnq	BRITISH GP	Silverstone	31	HB Bewaking Team Ensign	G	3.0 Ensign N175-Cosworth V8		27/28
nc	AUSTRIAN GP	Österreichring	33	HB Bewaking Team Ensign	G	3.0 Ensign N174-Cosworth V8	pit stop-tyres/4 laps behind	28/30
dnq	ITALIAN GP	Monza	31	HB Bewaking Team Ensign	G	3.0 Ensign N174-Cosworth V8		27/28
ret	US GP	Watkins Glen	31	HB Bewaking Team Ensign	G	3.0 Ensign N175-Cosworth V8	gearbox	22/24

GP Starts: 3   GP Wins: 0   Pole positions: 0   Fastest laps: 0   Points: 0

REINE WISELL

A contemporary and rival of Ronnie Peterson in Scandinavian Formula 3, Wisell did not quite have the talent to make a top-line career, despite a most promising start in 1970 when, thrust into the Lotus team at Watkins Glen, he took the 72C into third place.

His career had begun as far back as 1962 with an unreliable Mini Cooper and he then switched to an Anglia, which was similarly troublesome, but Reine plugged away, returning to a Mini in 1965 to take the runner-up position in the Swedish Group 5 championship. Early in 1966 he swapped his saloon for a Cooper F3 car and soon began to show a great deal of flair. By the end of that season he had done well enough to progress to a Brabham bought from his experienced rival Picko Troberg, and he was the man to watch in 1967, comfortably taking the Swedish F3 title, but more importantly making an impression in his occasional appearances in European events. It was now time to spread his wings and compete outside Scandinavia on a regular basis. He travelled down to Bologna with Ronnie Peterson and the two Swedes each ordered themselves a new F3 Tecno for the 1968 season. Reine gained valuable experience racing abroad that year and scored 11 wins in total, while his younger rival concentrated on racing at home and took the Swedish crown.

In 1969 Wisell took up an offer to race F3 and GT cars for Chevron, but generally endured a disappointing time. Feeling that he now needed to find a more challenging arena, Reine was persuaded to join Jo Bonnier's sports car team in 1970, and also took over the Sid Taylor F5000 McLaren with great success, winning three of the final four rounds towards the end of the year. Of course, by then his big chance had arrived, his performance and that of Emerson Fittipaldi ensuring their places in the Lotus team for 1971. It was to be a hectic year for the Swede, who did a full Formula 2 programme highlighted by a splendid win in the Pau GP. His performances in Formula 1 were solid but not inspired, and Chapman decided to promote his then current hot-shot Dave Walker into the team for 1972.

Wisell moved to BRM who were running a multi-car squad which spread the available resources too thinly. Nothing worthwhile was achieved and Reine even made a brief return to the Lotus fold in place of the luckless Walker for the Canadian GP. Wisell, no longer considered to have sufficient Grand Prix potential, drifted into other forms of the sport. His superb win in the F2 Eifelrennen was a timely reminder of the talent that still lurked, but his subsequent occasional Grand Prix appearances brought no joy.

After sharing a Gulf/John Wyer GR7 with Vern Schuppan in 1974, but gaining little success, Wisell raced a Porsche Carrera with distinction in 1975 before drifting out of the sport.

ROELOF WUNDERINK

Roelof began his racing career in a Simca in 1970, before progressing to Formula Ford and winning the Dutch championship in 1972. With the benefit of strong sponsorship from HB alarm systems, Wunderink rushed through Formula 3 and F5000 during the next two seasons, and found himself in a works-backed Ensign for 1975 without showing anything like the form to justify such a chance.

Nevertheless, he bravely got on with the job, hampered at first by having to make do with the '74 car and then being sidelined with a broken cheekbone and concussion after a testing accident in an F5000 car. At the end of the season, having tried but failed, the quiet Dutchman stepped out of the racing limelight.

ALEXANDER WURZ

A BMX champion and kart graduate, Alex made a massive impression in the 1994 German F3 championship when he took the runner-up slot behind Jörg Müller and finished ahead of both Ralf Schumacher and Norberto Fontana. Results dipped somewhat the following season but his talent was spotted by Team Joest, who placed him in their Opel Calibra for the 1996 ITC season. This gave the Austrian a chance to gain experience in a high-profile environment, and his career received an unexpected but massive boost when he shared Joest's Porsche WSC95 at Le Mans with Manuel Reuter and Davy Jones to become the youngest-ever winner of the Sarthe classic.

With healthy personal sponsorship, Wurz not only gained a foothold on the Grand Prix ladder with a testing contract with Benetton in 1997 but also had a seat in the works Mercedes squad to race their CLK-GTR alongside Bernd Schneider in the FIA GT championship. When the lanky Austrian stepped into the big time, replacing sinusitis victim Gerhard Berger in Montreal, he was still, however, largely an unknown quantity. Benetton's faith in their test driver was not without foundation, though, as he had already proved to be a fast, thoughtful and reliable performer with over 2700 km of track time behind the wheel of an F1 car.

His three-race stint, which culminated in a fine third place in the British Grand Prix, naturally sealed a full-time drive for 1998. Teamed with Italian hot-shot Giancarlo Fisichella, the quiet but tough Wurz showed he was no soft touch as he banged wheels with Michael Schumacher in Monaco and emerged from a roll into the gravel in Montreal seemingly completely unperturbed. A string of solid drives into the points increased Alex's credibility, but his inexorable rise to the top was about to come to an end in 1999 when the Austrian found the inherent characteristics of the B199 at odds with his particular driving style.

Huge changes in both management and design personnel cannot have helped Benetton in their quest to get back to the top, but Wurz stays on board for another season in 2000 hoping to re-establish his front-line credentials.

WURZ, Alexander (A) b 15/2/1974, Waidhofen, Austria

	Race	Circuit	No	Entrant	Tyres	Car/Engine	Comment	Q Pos/Entries
	1997	Championship position: 14th		Wins: 0	Pole positions: 0	Fastest laps: 0	Points scored: 4	
ret	CANADIAN GP	Montreal	8	Mild Seven Benetton Renault	G	3.0 Benetton B197-Renault V10	transmission	11/22
ret	FRENCH GP	Magny Cours	8	Mild Seven Benetton Renault	G	3.0 Benetton B197-Renault V10	spun off	7/22
3	BRITISH GP	Silverstone	8	Mild Seven Benetton Renault	G	3.0 Benetton B197-Renault V10		8/22
	1998	Championship position: 7th=		Wins: 0	Pole positions: 0	Fastest laps: 1	Points scored: 17	
7	AUSTRALIAN GP	Melbourne	6	Mild Seven Benetton Playlife	B	3.0 Benetton B199-Playlife V10	1 lap behind	11/22
4	BRAZILIAN GP	Interlagos	6	Mild Seven Benetton Playlife	B	3.0 Benetton B199-Playlife V10		5/22
4	ARGENTINE GP	Buenos Aires	6	Mild Seven Benetton Playlife	B	3.0 Benetton B199-Playlife V10	FL	8/22
ret	SAN MARINO GP	Imola	6	Mild Seven Benetton Playlife	B	3.0 Benetton B199-Playlife V10	engine	5/22
4	SPANISH GP	Barcelona	6	Mild Seven Benetton Playlife	B	3.0 Benetton B199-Playlife V10		5/22
ret	MONACO GP	Monte Carlo	6	Mild Seven Benetton Playlife	B	3.0 Benetton B199-Playlife V10	accident	6/22
4	CANADIAN GP	Montreal	6	Mild Seven Benetton Playlife	B	3.0 Benetton B199-Playlife V10	rolled car at first start	11/22
5	FRENCH GP	Magny Cours	6	Mild Seven Benetton Playlife	B	3.0 Benetton B199-Playlife V10	1 lap behind	10/22
4	BRITISH GP	Silverstone	6	Mild Seven Benetton Playlife	B	3.0 Benetton B199-Playlife V10	1 lap behind	12/22
9	AUSTRIAN GP	A1-Ring	6	Mild Seven Benetton Playlife	B	3.0 Benetton B199-Playlife V10	1 lap behind	17/22
11	GERMAN GP	Hockenheim	6	Mild Seven Benetton Playlife	B	3.0 Benetton B199-Playlife V10		7/22
ret	HUNGARIAN GP	Hungaroring	6	Mild Seven Benetton Playlife	B	3.0 Benetton B199-Playlife V10	gearbox	9/22
ret	BELGIAN GP	Spa	6	Mild Seven Benetton Playlife	B	3.0 Benetton B199-Playlife V10	collision with Coulthard	11/22
ret	ITALIAN GP	Monza	6	Mild Seven Benetton Playlife	B	3.0 Benetton B199-Playlife V10	gearbox	7/22
7	EUROPEAN GP	Nürburgring	6	Mild Seven Benetton Playlife	B	3.0 Benetton B199-Playlife V10		8/22
9	JAPANESE GP	Suzuka	6	Mild Seven Benetton Playlife	B	3.0 Benetton B199-Playlife V10	1 lap behind	9/22
	1999	Championship position: 13th=		Wins: 0	Pole positions: 0	Fastest laps: 0	Points scored: 3	
ret	AUSTRALIAN GP	Melbourne	10	Mild Seven Benetton Playlife	B	3.0 Benetton B199-Playlife V10	suspension	10/22
7	BRAZILIAN GP	Interlagos	10	Mild Seven Benetton Playlife	B	3.0 Benetton B199-Playlife V10	1 lap behind	9/21
ret	SAN MARINO GP	Imola	10	Mild Seven Benetton Playlife	B	3.0 Benetton B199-Playlife V10	collision with de la Rosa	17/22
6	MONACO GP	Monte Carlo	10	Mild Seven Benetton Playlife	B	3.0 Benetton B199-Playlife V10	1 lap behind	10/22
10	SPANISH GP	Barcelona	10	Mild Seven Benetton Playlife	B	3.0 Benetton B199-Playlife V10	1 lap behind	18/22
ret	CANADIAN GP	Montreal	10	Mild Seven Benetton Playlife	B	3.0 Benetton B199-Playlife V10	driveshaft on lap 1	11/22
ret	FRENCH GP	Magny Cours	10	Mild Seven Benetton Playlife	B	3.0 Benetton B199-Playlife V10	spun off	13/22
10	BRITISH GP	Silverstone	10	Mild Seven Benetton Playlife	B	3.0 Benetton B199-Playlife V10		18/22
5	AUSTRIAN GP	A1-Ring	10	Mild Seven Benetton Playlife	B	3.0 Benetton B199-Playlife V10		10/22
7	GERMAN GP	Hockenheim	10	Mild Seven Benetton Playlife	B	3.0 Benetton B199-Playlife V10		13/22
7	HUNGARIAN GP	Hungaroring	10	Mild Seven Benetton Playlife	B	3.0 Benetton B199-Playlife V10		7/22
14	BELGIAN GP	Spa	10	Mild Seven Benetton Playlife	B	3.0 Benetton B199-Playlife V10		7/22
ret	ITALIAN GP	Monza	10	Mild Seven Benetton Playlife	B	3.0 Benetton B199-Playlife V10	electrics	14/22
ret	EUROPEAN GP	Nürburgring	10	Mild Seven Benetton Playlife	B	3.0 Benetton B199-Playlife V10	collision with Diniz	11/22
8	MALAYSIAN GP	Sepang	10	Mild Seven Benetton Playlife	B	3.0 Benetton B199-Playlife V10		7/22
10	JAPANESE GP	Suzuka	10	Mild Seven Benetton Playlife	B	3.0 Benetton B199-Playlife V10	1 lap behind	15/22

GP Starts: 35   GP Wins: 0   Pole positions: 0   Fastest laps: 1   Points: 24

ALESSANDRO ('ALEX') ZANARDI

The fall and rise of Alex Zanardi is one of motor sport's most heartening stories of the nineties. Sadly, there was to be no happy ending, as a cruel epilogue found the Italian all but crushed after a nightmare return to Grand Prix racing with Williams in 1999 which yielded not a single points finish, having gloried in three seasons of almost unbroken success racing for Chip Ganassi in the CART series.

The first chapter in the career of this untypically quiet and unassuming Italian began with seven seasons spent racing karts before he contested the national Formula 3 series in 1988. His promise shone through the following year but his Racing for Italy Ralt RT33 was handicapped when a change to unleaded fuel in mid-season hobbled his Toyota engine and his results inevitably suffered. However, switching to a Dallara chassis in 1990, Alessandro finished second in the championship just three points adrift of Roberto Colciago, winning two of the series' 12 rounds.

Having made an inauspicious debut in F3000 at the tail-end of the 1989 season, nothing much was expected of Zanardi when he took his place in the new Il Barone Rampante team for the start of the 1991 campaign. Extensive pre-season testing gave the Italian an early advantage, but despite victories at Vallelunga and Mugello he eventually lost the championship to the more consistent finishing record of Christian Fittipaldi. Not that it really mattered, for by this time Zanardi had been chosen to fill the Jordan seat vacated by Michael Schumacher for the final three races of the season. His hopes of a place in the Tyrrell line-up for 1992 were dashed when the team opted for de Cesaris, but he secured a testing contract with Benetton and ultimately made three unhappy appearances for Minardi in place of his former F3000 adversary Fittipaldi, who had injured his back.

Alessandro was offered a chance to prove himself in 1993 when Mika Häkkinen left Lotus for McLaren, and Peter Collins was to be pleased with the Italian's early form. He drove a storming race at Monaco, where he was unlucky to miss the points, and his contribution to the development of the team's highly complex active suspension programme drew warm praise, but his season came to a premature end after an extremely violent 150 mph accident at Spa's notorious Eau Rouge which finished with his car destroyed and Zanardi in hospital with severe concussion. While he recovered from this shaking, he was rested in favour of Pedro Lamy for the remaining Grands Prix. The Portuguese hot-shot retained the ride for the 1994 season, although Zanardi was kept on in the role of test driver. As fate would have it, Lamy was subsequently badly injured in a testing accident at Silverstone, putting Alessandro back in for the balance of a dispiriting season as the once great Team Lotus heaved its dying breath.

Zanardi was forced to sit out the 1995 season, save for an occasional Lotus GT drive, but at the end of the year he secured a deal to compete in the Indy Car series with Target/Chip Ganassi Racing after glowing recommendations from Adrian Reynard and Rick Gorne. Alex adapted to CART in sensational manner. The brilliant Italian won 15 races from his 51 starts and claimed successive PPG Cup championships in 1997 and 1998. It is all the more perplexing, therefore, that, thus far, he has been unable to translate his considerable skills to any telling effect in a Formula 1 car. At the time of writing his place at Williams seems under threat, but if he keeps his seat perhaps a revitalised figure will reappear. Certainly no one would begrudge him another chance.

ZANARDI, Alessandro (I) b 23/10/1966, Bologna

	1991	Championship position: Unplaced							
	Race	Circuit	No	Entrant	Tyres	Car/Engine		Comment	Q Pos/Entries
9	SPANISH GP	Barcelona	32	Team 7UP Jordan	G	3.5 Jordan 191-FordHB V8		1 lap behind	20/33
ret	JAPANESE GP	Suzuka	32	Team 7UP Jordan	G	3.5 Jordan 191-FordHB V8		gearbox	13/31
9	AUSTRALIAN GP	Adelaide	32	Team 7UP Jordan	G	3.5 Jordan 191-FordHB V8		race stopped-14 laps-rain	16/32
	1992	Championship position: Unplaced							
dnq	BRITISH GP	Silverstone	23	Minardi Team	G	3.5 Minardi M192-Lamborghini V12			27/32
ret	GERMAN GP	Hockenheim	23	Minardi Team	G	3.5 Minardi M192-Lamborghini V12		clutch on first lap	24/32
dnq	HUNGARIAN GP	Hungaroring	23	Minardi Team	G	3.5 Minardi M192-Lamborghini V12			29/31
	1993	Championship position: 20th	Wins: 0	Pole positions: 0	Fastest laps: 0	Points scored: 1			
ret	SOUTH AFRICAN GP	Kyalami	11	Team Lotus	G	3.5 Lotus 107B-Ford HB V8		collision with Hill	16/26
6	BRAZILIAN GP	Interlagos	11	Team Lotus	G	3.5 Lotus 107B-Ford HB V8		1 lap behind	15/26
8	EUROPEAN GP	Donington	11	Team Lotus	G	3.5 Lotus 107B-Ford HB V8		4 laps behind	13/26
ret	SAN MARINO GP	Imola	11	Team Lotus	G	3.5 Lotus 107B-Ford HB V8		spun into wall-lost wheel	20/26
14/ret	SPANISH GP	Barcelona	11	Team Lotus	G	3.5 Lotus 107B-Ford HB V8		engine/5 laps behind	15/26
7	MONACO GP	Monte Carlo	11	Team Lotus	G	3.5 Lotus 107B-Ford HB V8		2 laps behind	20/26
11	CANADIAN GP	Montreal	11	Team Lotus	G	3.5 Lotus 107B-Ford HB V8		spin/2 laps behind	21/26
ret	FRENCH GP	Magny Cours	11	Team Lotus	G	3.5 Lotus 107B-Ford HB V8		active suspension failure	17/26
ret	BRITISH GP	Silverstone	11	Team Lotus	G	3.5 Lotus 107B-Ford HB V8		lost body panel-spun off	14/26
ret	GERMAN GP	Hockenheim	11	Team Lotus	G	3.5 Lotus 107B-Ford HB V8		spun off	15/26
ret	HUNGARIAN GP	Hungaroring	11	Team Lotus	G	3.5 Lotus 107B-Ford HB V8		gearbox failure	21/26
dns	BELGIAN GP	Spa	11	Team Lotus	G	3.5 Lotus 107B-Ford HB V8		accident in Fri a.m. practice	–/–

	1994			Championship position: Unplaced				
9	SPANISH GP	Barcelona	11	Team Lotus	G	3.5 Lotus 107C-Mugen Honda V10	3 laps behind	23/27
15/ret	CANADIAN GP	Montreal	11	Team Lotus	G	3.5 Lotus 107C-Mugen Honda V10	7 laps behind/engine	23/27
ret	FRENCH GP	Magny Cours	11	Team Lotus	G	3.5 Lotus 109-Mugen Honda V10	engine on fire	23/28
ret	BRITISH GP	Silverstone	11	Team Lotus	G	3.5 Lotus 109-Mugen Honda V10	started from pit lane/engine	19/28
ret	GERMAN GP	Hockenheim	11	Team Lotus	G	3.5 Lotus 109-Mugen Honda V10	multiple accident at start	21/28
13	HUNGARIAN GP	Hungaroring	11	Team Lotus	G	3.5 Lotus 109-Mugen Honda V10	5 laps behind	22/28
ret	ITALIAN GP	Monza	11	Team Lotus	G	3.5 Lotus 109-Mugen Honda V10	collision-Morbidelli on lap 1	13/28
16	EUROPEAN GP	Jerez	12	Team Lotus	G	3.5 Lotus 109-Mugen Honda V10	2 laps behind	21/28
13	JAPANESE GP	Suzuka	12	Team Lotus	G	3.5 Lotus 109-Mugen Honda V10	2 laps behind	17/28
ret	AUSTRALIAN GP	Adelaide	12	Team Lotus	G	3.5 Lotus 109-Mugen Honda V10	throttle	14/28
	1999			Championship position: Unplaced				
ret	AUSTRALIAN GP	Melbourne	5	Winfield Williams	B	3.0 Williams FW21-Supertec V10	accident	15/22
ret	BRAZILIAN GP	Interlagos	5	Winfield Williams	B	3.0 Williams FW21-Supertec V10	transmission	16/21
11/ret	SAN MARINO GP	Imola	5	Winfield Williams	B	3.0 Williams FW21-Supertec V10	spun off/4 laps behind	10/22
8	MONACO GP	Monte Carlo	5	Winfield Williams	B	3.0 Williams FW21-Supertec V10	2 laps behind	11/22
ret	SPANISH GP	Barcelona	5	Winfield Williams	B	3.0 Williams FW21-Supertec V10	transmission	17/22
ret	CANADIAN GP	Montreal	5	Winfield Williams	B	3.0 Williams FW21-Supertec V10	accident	12/22
ret	FRENCH GP	Magny Cours	5	Winfield Williams	B	3.0 Williams FW21-Supertec V10	engine	15/22
11	BRITISH GP	Silverstone	5	Winfield Williams	B	3.0 Williams FW21-Supertec V10		13/22
ret	AUSTRIAN GP	A1-Ring	5	Winfield Williams	B	3.0 Williams FW21-Supertec V10	out of fuel	14/22
ret	GERMAN GP	Hockenheim	5	Winfield Williams	B	3.0 Williams FW21-Supertec V10	differential	14/22
ret	HUNGARIAN GP	Hungaroring	5	Winfield Williams	B	3.0 Williams FW21-Supertec V10	differential	15/22
8	BELGIAN GP	Spa	5	Winfield Williams	B	3.0 Williams FW21-Supertec V10		15/22
7	ITALIAN GP	Monza	5	Winfield Williams	B	3.0 Williams FW21-Supertec V10	loose undertray	4/22
ret	EUROPEAN GP	Nürburgring	5	Winfield Williams	B	3.0 Williams FW21-Supertec V10	transmission	18/22
10	MALAYSIAN GP	Sepang	5	Winfield Williams	B	3.0 Williams FW21-Supertec V10	1 lap behind	16/22
ret	JAPANESE GP	Suzuka	5	Winfield Williams	B	3.0 Williams FW21-Supertec V10	electrics	16/22

GP Starts: 41   GP Wins: 0   Pole positions: 0   Fastest laps: 0   Points: 1

RICARDO ZONTA

When British American Racing launched their new challenger at the beginning of 1999 all eyes were quite naturally on Jacques Villeneuve, and Ricardo Zonta's Grand Prix debut in the second car went largely unheralded. The disastrous season that BAR were to endure provided the Brazilian with the toughest of baptisms in the big time. Ricardo was injured in a practice crash at his home track which forced him to miss three races, and then emerged unscathed from a massive off at Eau Rouge during practice for the Belgian Grand Prix at Spa later in the year. Through all this, his self-confidence remained unshakeable, for the ambitious Brazilian has been a champion in every major category in which he has competed.

His father was a racer on the local dirt tracks around his native Curitiba and the young Ricardo was soon bitten by the racing bug. In 1986 his dad bought him his first kart and the following year his competition career began. By 1991 he was Brazilian champion, and after a season in Formula Chevrolet Zonta moved up to Formula 3 in the Sud-Am series. Six victories in the 1995 season brought him the South American championship and with it the opportunity to go to Europe and race in the F3000 series with the Italian Draco Engineering team.

Wins at Mugello and Estoril marked him out as a man to watch and, switching to the crack Super Nova team for 1997, he had the equipment and the talent to take the F3000 title after a tremendous battle with Juan Montoya. Grand Prix teams had already been alerted to his ability and a highly promising F1 test for Jordan brought a testing contract with McLaren in 1998. Mercedes placed him alongside the experienced Klaus Ludwig in their CLK-GTR to contest the FIA GT championship and the pair duly shared the drivers' crown after five wins in the ten-round series.

Zonta now looks forward to a second year in Formula 1 with BAR. His philosophy is: 'being the best in everything I do'. Don't bet against him reaching the very top in the future.

ZONTA, Ricardo (BR) b 23/3/1976, Curitiba

	Race	Circuit	No	Entrant	Tyres	Car/Engine	Comment	Q Pos/Entries
	1999			Championship position: Unplaced				
ret	AUSTRALIAN GP	Melbourne	23	British American Racing	B	3.0 BAR 01-Supertec V10	engine	19/22
dns	BRAZILIAN GP	Interlagos	23	British American Racing	B	3.0 BAR 01-Supertec V10	practice accident-injured foot	– / –
ret	CANADIAN GP	Montreal	23	British American Racing	B	3.0 BAR 01-Supertec V10	accident	17/22
9	FRENCH GP	Magny Cours	23	British American Racing	B	3.0 BAR 01-Supertec V10		10/22
ret	BRITISH GP	Silverstone	23	British American Racing	B	3.0 BAR 01-Supertec V10	suspension	16/22
15/ret	AUSTRIAN GP	A1-Ring	23	British American Racing	B	3.0 BAR 01-Supertec V10	clutch/ 8 laps behind	15/22
ret	GERMAN GP	Hockenheim	23	British American Racing	B	3.0 BAR 01-Supertec V10	engine	18/22
13	HUNGARIAN GP	Hungaroring	23	British American Racing	B	3.0 BAR 01-Supertec V10	2 laps behind	17/22
ret	BELGIAN GP	Spa	23	British American Racing	B	3.0 BAR 01-Supertec V10	gearbox	17/22
ret	ITALIAN GP	Monza	23	British American Racing	B	3.0 BAR 01-Supertec V10	wheel bearing	18/22
8	EUROPEAN GP	Nürburgring	23	British American Racing	B	3.0 BAR 01-Supertec V10	1 lap behind	17/22
ret	MALAYSIAN GP	Sepang	23	British American Racing	B	3.0 BAR 01-Supertec V10	engine	13/22
12	JAPANESE GP	Suzuka	23	British American Racing	B	3.0 BAR 01-Supertec V10	1 lap behind	18/22

GP Starts: 12   GP Wins: 0   Pole positions: 0   Fastest laps: 0   Points: 0

ZORZI, Renzo (I) b 12/12/1946, Ziano di Fiemme, nr Turin

	1975	Championship position: Unplaced						
	Race	Circuit	No	Entrant	Car/Engine	Comment		Q Pos/Entries
14	ITALIAN GP	Monza	20	Frank Williams Racing Cars	G 3.0 Williams FW03-Cosworth V8	6 laps behind		22/28
	1976	Championship position: 0 Wins: 0 Pole positions: 0 Fastest laps: 0 Points scored: 0						
9	BRAZILIAN GP	Interlagos	21	Frank Williams Racing Cars	G 3.0 Williams FW04-Cosworth V8	1 lap behind		17/22
	1977	Championship position: 0 Wins: 0 Pole positions: 0 Fastest laps: 0 Points scored: 0						
ret	ARGENTINE GP	Buenos Aires	17	Shadow Racing Team	G 3.0 Shadow DN5-Cosworth V8	gearbox		21/21
6	BRAZILIAN GP	Interlagos	17	Shadow Racing Team	G 3.0 Shadow DN5-Cosworth V8	1 lap behind		18/22
ret	SOUTH AFRICAN GP	Kyalami	17	Shadow Racing Team	G 3.0 Shadow DN8-Cosworth V8	engine		20/23
ret	US GP WEST	Long Beach	16	Shadow Racing Team	G 3.0 Shadow DN8-Cosworth V8	gearbox		20/22
ret	SPANISH GP	Jarama	16	Shadow Racing Team	G 3.0 Shadow DN8-Cosworth V8	engine		24/31

GP Starts: 7 GP Wins: 0 Pole positions: 0 Fastest laps: 0 Points: 1

ZUNINO, Ricardo (RA) b 13/4/1949, Buenos Aires

	1979	Championship position: Unplaced						
	Race	Circuit	No	Entrant	Tyres	Car/Engine	Comment	Q Pos/Entries
7	CANADIAN GP	Montreal	5	Parmalat Racing Team	G	3.0 Brabham BT49-Cosworth V8	pit stop-gear linkage/-4 laps	19/29
ret	US GP EAST	Watkins Glen	5	Parmalat Racing Team	G	3.0 Brabham BT49-Cosworth V8	spun off	9/30
	1980	Championship position: Unplaced						
7	ARGENTINE GP	Buenos Aires	6	Parmalat Racing Team	G	3.0 Brabham BT49-Cosworth V8	2 laps behind	16/28
8	BRAZILIAN GP	Interlagos	6	Parmalat Racing Team	G	3.0 Brabham BT49-Cosworth V8	1 lap behind	18/28
10	SOUTH AFRICAN GP	Kyalami	6	Parmalat Racing Team	G	3.0 Brabham BT49-Cosworth V8	1 lap behind	17/28
ret	US GP WEST	Long Beach	6	Parmalat Racing Team	G	3.0 Brabham BT49-Cosworth V8	hit wall avoiding Mass	18/27
ret	BELGIAN GP	Zolder	6	Parmalat Racing Team	G	3.0 Brabham BT49-Cosworth V8	clutch/gearbox	22/27
dnq	MONACO GP	Monte Carlo	6	Parmalat Racing Team	G	3.0 Brabham BT49-Cosworth V8		25/27
ret	FRENCH GP	Paul Ricard	6	Parmalat Racing Team	G	3.0 Brabham BT49-Cosworth V8	clutch	22/27
	1981	Championship position: Unplaced						
13	BRAZILIAN GP	Rio	4	Tyrrell Racing	M	3.0 Tyrrell 010-Cosworth V8	5 laps behind	24/30
13*	ARGENTINE GP	Buenos Aires	4	Tyrrell Racing	M	3.0 Tyrrell 010-Cosworth V8	* 1 lap pen-overshot chicane/-2 laps	24/29

GP Starts: 10 GP Wins: 0 Pole positions: 0 Fastest laps: 0 Points: 0

RENZO ZORZI

Zorzi has the same date of birth as Emerson Fittipaldi, but not the same racing pedigree. A graduate of Italian Formula 3 while acting as a test driver at Pirelli, Renzo shot to prominence with a surprise win in the 1975 Monaco F3 support race, after Conny Andersson had been given a one-minute penalty and the other front-runners had eliminated each other.

His immediate reward was a Williams seat for the Italian GP, where he drove sensibly to the finish. Zorzi started the 1976 season in the newly constituted Wolf-Williams équipe, but was dropped after just one Grand Prix, being replaced by Michel Leclère. For Zorzi, it was back to F3 in a Modus while he waited for a further opportunity, which came in 1977, when Francesco Ambrosio sponsored his drive in the Shadow team. A sixth place in the Brazilian GP was achieved mainly because of a high rate of attrition, and soon Renzo himself was to become a Formula 1 casualty, losing his drive after falling out with Ambrosio. He reappeared towards the end of the decade in occasional rounds of the World Championship of Makes, and then in the 1980 Aurora AFX Monza Lottery GP in Charles Clowes' Arrows A1B, retiring after a collision.

RICARDO ZUNINO

During two seasons with a March-BMW in Formula 2 (1977-78), this Argentine driver's performances were nothing more than thoroughly ordinary, despite his having access to competitive machinery. A lacklustre start to his third year in the formula convinced him a switch to the less demanding world of the Aurora F1 championship would be beneficial, and he was right. Racing an Arrows in the final nine rounds of the series, Zunino won one race and finished five others in the top six.

Somewhat ambitiously, he managed to step into Grand Prix racing at the end of 1979, when Lauda suddenly quit at Montreal, and he started 1980 still driving the second Brabham BT49, but was eased out of the team in mid-season when Rebaque took his place. Ricardo was back with Brabham at the start of 1981, but only for the non-championship South African GP, in which he finished eighth.

He then joined Tyrrell to contest the two South American rounds, before giving way to a shining new talent by the name of Michele Alboreto.

GIOVANNA AMATI   GIANFRANCO BRANCATELLI   BERNIE ECCLESTONE   NAOKI HATTORI   'LUCIENBONNET'   CLIVE PUZEY   DENIS TAYLOR

MICHAEL BARTELS   COLIN CHAPMAN   CARLO FACETTI   TOM JONES   PERRY McCARTHY   JEAN-CLAUDE RUDAZ   TONY TRIMMER

ASDRÉBAL BAYARDO   PEDRO CHAVES   WILLIE FERGUSON   JUAN JOVER   BRIAN McGUIRE   STEPHEN SOUTH   JACQUES VILLENEUVE

ENRICO BERTAGGIA   KEVIN COGAN   GIORGIO FRANCIA   DAVID KENNEDY   BILL MOSS   VINCENZO SOSPIRI   VOLKER WEIDLER

JEAN-MANUEL BORDEU   ALAIN de CHANGY   HIROSHI FUSHIDA   BRUCE KESSLER   JAC NELLEMAN   OTTO STUPPACHER   DESIRÉ WILSON

GARY BRABHAM   BERNARD de DRYVER   DIVINA GALICA   MASAMI KUWASHIMA   ALFREDO PIÁN   ANDY SUTCLIFFE   JOACHIM WINKELHOCK

'TINO' BRAMBILLA   PIERO DUSIO   HELMUT GLÖCKLER   CLAUDIO LANGES   ERNESTO PRINOTH   LUIGI TARAMAZZO   EMILIO ZAPICO

AMATI, Giovanna (I) b 20/7/1962, Rome

1992

	Race	Circuit	No	Entrant	Tyres	Car/Engine	Comment	Pos/Entries
dnq	SOUTH AFRICAN GP	Kyalami	8	Motor Racing Developments Ltd	G	3.5 Brabham BT60B-Judd V10		30/30
dnq	MEXICAN GP	Mexico City	8	Motor Racing Developments Ltd	G	3.5 Brabham BT60B-Judd V10		30/30
dnq	BRAZILIAN GP	Interlagos	8	Motor Racing Developments Ltd	G	3.5 Brabham BT60B-Judd V10		30/31

Lady driver who competed regularly in Italian national racing before reaching the limit of her abilities in European F3000

BARTELS, Michael (D) b 8/3/1968, Plettenberg

1991

	Race	Circuit	No	Entrant	Tyres	Car/Engine	Comment	Q Pos/Entries
dnq	GERMAN GP	Hockenheim	12	Team Lotus	G	3.5 Lotus 102B-Judd V8		28/34
dnq	HUNGARIAN GP	Hungaroring	12	Team Lotus	G	3.5 Lotus 102B-Judd V8		30/34
dnq	ITALIAN GP	Monza	12	Team Lotus	G	3.5 Lotus 102B-Judd V8		28/34
dnq	SPANISH GP	Barcelona	12	Team Lotus	G	3.5 Lotus 102B-Judd V8		29/33

Star of German F3 in the late eighties, subsequently left in the shadows of Schumacher and Wendlinger, but successfully competed in the saloon car DTM/ITC series

BAYARDO, Asdrébal Fontes (U) b 1922

1959

	Race	Circuit	No	Entrant	Tyres	Car/Engine	Comment	Q Pos/Entries
dnq	FRENCH GP	Reims	36	Scuderia Centro Sud	D	2.5 Maserati 250F 6	no practice time recorded	–/–

BERTAGGIA, Enrico (I) b 19/9/1964, Noale, nr Venice

1989

	Race	Circuit	No	Entrant	Tyres	Car/Engine	Comment	Q Pos/Entries
dnpq	BELGIAN GP	Spa	32	Coloni SpA	P	3.5 Coloni C3-Cosworth V8		39/39
dnpq	ITALIAN GP	Monza	32	Coloni SpA	P	3.5 Coloni C3-Cosworth V8		38/39
dnpq	PORTUGUESE GP	Estoril	32	Coloni SpA	P	3.5 Coloni C3-Cosworth V8		39/39
dnpq	SPANISH GP	Jerez	32	Coloni SpA	P	3.5 Coloni C3-Cosworth V8		38/38
dnpq	JAPANESE GP	Suzuka	32	Coloni SpA	P	3.5 Coloni C3-Cosworth V8	no practice time recorded	–/39
dnpq	AUSTRALIAN GP	Adelaide	32	Coloni SpA	P	3.5 Coloni C3-Cosworth V8		39/39

1992

	Race	Circuit	No	Entrant	Tyres	Car/Engine	Comment	Q Pos/Entries
dnp	SOUTH AFRICAN GP	Kyalami	35	Andrea Moda Formula	G	3.5 Coloni C4B-Judd V10	team excluded from meeting	–/–
dnp	MEXICAN GP	Mexico City	35	Andrea Moda Formula	G	3.5 Moda S921-Judd V10	cars not ready-entry withdrawn	–/–

BORDEU, Jean-Manuel (RA) b 1934 – d 12/1990

1961

	Race	Circuit	No	Entrant	Tyres	Car/Engine	Comment	Q Pos/Entries
dns	FRENCH GP	Reims	28	UDT Laystall Racing Team	D	1.5 Lotus 18/21-Climax 4	car raced by Bianchi	–/–

*A protégé of Fangio, Bordeu was very successful in Formula Junior, but suffered a bad testing accident at Goodwood which ended his Grand Prix aspirations.
He subsequently raced again, very competitively, in the mid-sixties Temporada Series and after retirement in 1973 he represented Argentina as a delgate of FISA;
with a seat on the World's Motorsport Council.*

BRABHAM, Gary (AUS) b 29/3/1961, Wimbledon, London, England

1990

	Race	Circuit	No	Entrant	Tyres	Car/Engine	Comment	Q Pos/Entries
dnpq	US GP (PHOENIX)	Phoenix	39	Life Racing Engines	P	3.5 Life L190 W12		34/35
dnpq	BRAZILIAN GP	Interlagos	39	Life Racing Engines	P	3.5 Life L190 W12		35/35

*Second son of Sir Jack. After an excellent British F3 record, found his career blighted after the Life fiasco. One-off appearance in Indy cars (at Surfers Paradise) in
1994, followed by touring car appearances (also down-under) in 1995*

BRAMBILLA, Tino (Ernesto) (I) b 31/1/1934, Monza

1963

	Race	Circuit	No	Entrant	Tyres	Car/Engine	Comment	Q Pos/Entries
dnq	ITALIAN GP	Monza	62	Scuderia Centro Sud	D	1.5 Cooper T53-Maserati 4		26/28

1969

	Race	Circuit	No	Entrant	Tyres	Car/Engine	Comment	Q Pos/Entries
dns	ITALIAN GP	Monza	10	Scuderia Ferrari SpA SEFAC	F	3.0 Ferrari 312/68/69 V12	Pedro Rodriguez raced car	–/–

Notoriously hard racer and elder brother of Vittorio. Tino raced works Formula 2 Ferraris with some success, but was never given a real F1 chance

BRANCATELLI, Gianfranco (I) b 18/1/1950

1979

	Race	Circuit	No	Entrant	Tyres	Car/Engine	Comment	Q Pos/Entries
dnq	SPANISH GP	Jarama	36	Willi Kauhsen Racing Team	G	3.0 Kauhsen WK-Cosworth V8		27/27
dnq	BELGIAN GP	Zolder	36	Willi Kauhsen Racing Team	G	3.0 Kauhsen WK-Cosworth V8		28/28
dnpq	MONACO GP	Monte Carlo	24	Team Merzario	G	3.0 Merzario A2-Cosworth V8		25/25

1970s Formula Italia and F3 star, who after his unhappy failures in F1 turned to a solid career in touring cars and Group C

CADE, Phil (USA) b 12/7/1916, Charles City, Iowa

1959

	Race	Circuit	No	Entrant	Tyres	Car/Engine	Comment	Q Pos/Entries
dns	US GP	Sebring	22	Phil Cade	D	2.5 Maserati 250F 6	engine problems	(18)/19

Amateur enthusiast who raced a Chrysler-engined 1936 Maserati in SCCA events during the 1950s

CHAPMAN, Colin (GB) b 19/5/1928, Richmond, Surrey – d 16/12/1982, East Carelton, nr Norwich, Norfolk

1956

	Race	Circuit	No	Entrant	Tyres	Car/Engine	Comment	Q Pos/Entries
dns	FRENCH GP	Reims	26	Vandervell Products Ltd	P	2.5 Vanwall 4	practice accident-car damaged	(5)/20

Founder of Lotus, a true innovator whose designs changed the shape of Formula 1. Also a very good sports car driver, who could mix it with the best

CHAVES Pedro (P) b 27/2/65, Porto

1991

	Race	Circuit	No	Entrant	Tyres	Car/Engine	Comment	Q Pos/Entries
dnpq	US GP (PHOENIX)	Phoenix	31	Coloni Racing Srl	G	3.5 Coloni C4-Cosworth V8		32/34
dnpq	BRAZILIAN GP	Interlagos	31	Coloni Racing Srl	G	3.5 Coloni C4-Cosworth V8		33/34
dnpq	SAN MARINO GP	Imola	31	Coloni Racing Srl	G	3.5 Coloni C4-Cosworth V8		34/34
dnpq	MONACO GP	Monte Carlo	31	Coloni Racing Srl	G	3.5 Coloni C4-Cosworth V8		33/34
dnpq	CANADIAN GP	Montreal	31	Coloni Racing Srl	G	3.5 Coloni C4-Cosworth V8		34/34
dnpq	MEXICAN GP	Mexico City	31	Coloni Racing Srl	G	3.5 Coloni C4-Cosworth V8		33/34
dnpq	FRENCH GP	Magny Cours	31	Coloni Racing Srl	G	3.5 Coloni C4-Cosworth V8		34/34
dnpq	BRITISH GP	Silverstone	31	Coloni Racing Srl	G	3.5 Coloni C4-Cosworth V8		34/34
dnpq	GERMAN GP	Hockenheim	31	Coloni Racing Srl	G	3.5 Coloni C4-Cosworth V8		34/34
dnpq	HUNGARIAN GP	Hungaroring	31	Coloni Racing Srl	G	3.5 Coloni C4-Cosworth V8		34/34
dnpq	BELGIAN GP	Spa	31	Coloni Racing Srl	G	3.5 Coloni C4-Cosworth V8		33/34
dnpq	ITALIAN GP	Monza	31	Coloni Racing Srl	G	3.5 Coloni C4-Cosworth V8	no time recorded	34/34
dnpq	PORTUGUESE GP	Estoril	31	Coloni Racing Srl	G	3.5 Coloni C4-Cosworth V8		34/34

1990 British F3000 champion, now a successful mainstay of Indy Lights after his moribund 1991 season with Coloni

COGAN, Kevin (USA) b 31/3/1956, Culver City, California

1980

	Race	Circuit	No	Entrant	Tyres	Car/Engine	Comment	Q Pos/Entries
dnq	CANADIAN GP	Montreal	51	RAM/Rainbow Jeans Racing	G	3.0 Williams FW07B-Cosworth V8		28/28

1981

	Race	Circuit	No	Entrant	Tyres	Car/Engine	Comment	Q Pos/Entries
dnq	US GP WEST	Long Beach	4	Tyrrell Racing	M	3.0 Tyrrell 010-Cosworth V8		25/29

One-time IndyCar winner whose later career was been blighted by injury after a succession of major accidents

COLOMBO, Alberto (I) b 23/2/1946, Veredo, nr Milan

1978

	Race	Circuit	No	Entrant	Tyres	Car/Engine	Comment	Q Pos/Entries
dnq	BELGIAN GP	Zolder	10	ATS Racing Team	G	3.0 ATS HS1-Cosworth V8		28/30
dnq	SPANISH GP	Jarama	10	ATS Racing Team	G	3.0 ATS HS1-Cosworth V8		28/29
dnpq	ITALIAN GP	Monza	34	Team Merzario	G	3.0 Merzario A1-Cosworth V8		32/32

CRESPO, Alberto (RA) b 16/1/1930 – d. 14/8/1991 Buenos Aires

1952

	Race	Circuit	No	Entrant	Tyres	Car/Engine	Comment	Q Pos/Entries
dnq	ITALIAN GP	Monza	58	Enrico Platé	P	2.0 Maserati 4CLT/48-Maserati/Platé 4		26/35

de CHANGY, Alain (B)

1959

	Race	Circuit	No	Entrant	Tyres	Car/Engine	Comment	Q Pos/Entries
dnq	MONACO GP	Monte Carlo	12	Equipe Nationale Belge	D	1.5 Cooper T51-Climax 4		19/24

de DRYVER, Bernard (B) b 19/9/1952, Brussels

1977

	Race	Circuit	No	Entrant	Tyres	Car/Engine	Comment	Q Pos/Entries
dnq	BELGIAN GP	Zolder	38	British Formula 1 Racing	G	3.0 March 761-Cosworth V8		31/32

1977

	Race	Circuit	No	Entrant	Tyres	Car/Engine	Comment	Q Pos/Entries
dnc	BELGIAN GP	Zolder	–	Bernard de Dryver	G	3.0 Ensign N177-Cosworth V8	did not qualify for official practice	

de RIU, Giovanni (I)

1954

	Race	Circuit	No	Entrant	Tyres	Car/Engine	Comment	Q Pos/Entries
dnq	ITALIAN GP	Monza	2	Giovanni de Riu	P	2.5 Maserati A6GCM/250F 6	*too slow*	21/21

DOCHNAL, Frank J (USA)

1963

	Race	Circuit	No	Entrant	Tyres	Car/Engine	Comment	Q Pos/Entries
dns	MEXICAN GP	Mexico City	20	Frank J Dochnal	D	1.5 Cooper T53-Climax 4	*crashed in unofficial practice*	–/–

Along with Tom Jones, perhaps the most obscure character in this book, whose fleeting appearance above seems to be the sum total of his achievements

DUSIO, Piero (I) b 13/10/1899, Scurzolengo D'Asti – d 7/11/1975, Buenos Aires, Argentina

1952

	Race	Circuit	No	Entrant	Tyres	Car/Engine	Comment	Q Pos/Entries
dnq	ITALIAN GP	Monza	44	Piero Dusio	P	Cisitalia D46	*engine-no time set*	–/–

Italian amateur pre-war champion who built the little Cisitalia D46 racers which found wide favour – unlike the later Porsche-based Tipo 360 Grand Prix car

ECCLESTONE, Bernie (GB) b 28/10/1931, St Peters, Suffolk

1958

	Race	Circuit	No	Entrant	Tyres	Car/Engine	Comment	Q Pos/Entries
dnq	MONACO GP	Monte Carlo	12	B C Ecclestone	A	2.5 Connaught B-Alta 4	*not a serious attempt*	28/28
dnq	BRITISH GP	Silverstone	14	B C Ecclestone	D	2.5 Connaught B-Alta 4	*car driven by Fairman*	21/21

Subsequently owned Brabham team, and in his capacities with FOCA and the FIA has been the driving force shaping the development of Grand Prix racing

FACETTI, Carlo (I) b 26/6/1935, Cormano, Milan

1974

	Race	Circuit	No	Entrant	Tyres	Car/Engine	Comment	Q Pos/Entries
dnq	ITALIAN GP	Monza	31	Scuderia Finotto	G	3.0 Brabham BT42-Cosworth V8		27/31

FERGUSON, Willie (ZA) b 6/3/1940, Johannesburg

1972

	Race	Circuit	No	Entrant	Tyres	Car/Engine	Comment	Q Pos/Entries
dns	SOUTH AFRICAN GP	Kyalami	28	Team Gunston	F	3.0 Brabham BT33-Cosworth V8	*engine in practice*	27/27
dns	"	"	27T	Team Gunston	F	3.0 Surtees TS9-Cosworth V8	*car driven by Love in race*	–/–

FISCHER, Ludwig (D)

1952

	Race	Circuit	No	Entrant	Tyres	Car/Engine	Comment	Q Pos/Entries
dns	GERMAN GP	Nürburgring	131	Ludwig Fischer	–	2.0 AFM BMW 6		31/32

FRANCIA, Giorgio (I) b 8/11/1947, Bologna

1977

	Race	Circuit	No	Entrant	Tyres	Car/Engine	Comment	Q Pos/Entries
dnq	ITALIAN GP	Monza	21	Martini Racing	G	3.0 Brabham BT45B-Alfa Romeo F12	*withdrawn after first practice*	34/34

1981

dnq	SPANISH GP	Jarama	32	Osella Squadra Corse	M	3.0 Osella FA1B-Cosworth V8		30/30

Alfa Romeo stalwart, who raced for well over two decades in most categories.

FUSHIDA, Hiroshi (J) b 1946

1975

	Race	Circuit	No	Entrant	Tyres	Car/Engine	Comment	Q Pos/Entries
dns	DUTCH GP	Zandvoort	35	Maki Engineering	G	3.0 Maki F101C-Cosworth V8	*blown engine in practice*	(25)/25
dnq	BRITISH GP	Silverstone	35	Maki Engineering	G	3.0 Maki F101C-Cosworth V8		28/28

GALICA, Divina (GB) b 13/8/1946, Bushey Heath nr Watford, Hertfordshire

1976

	Race	Circuit	No	Entrant	Tyres	Car/Engine	Comment	Q Pos/Entries
dnq	BRITISH GP	Brands Hatch	13	Shellsport/Whiting	G	3.0 Surtees TS16-Cosworth V8		28/30

1978

dnq	ARGENTINE GP	Buenos Aires	24	Olympus Cameras with Hesketh	G	3.0 Hesketh 308E-Cosworth V8		27/27
dnq	BRAZILIAN GP	Rio	24	Olympus Cameras with Hesketh	G	3.0 Hesketh 308E-Cosworth V8		28/28

Determined lady racer and international skier who made her mark in the mid-seventies Shellsport G8 series

'GIMAX' (FRANCHI Carlo) (I) b c.1935

1978

	Race	Circuit	No	Entrant	Tyres	Car/Engine	Comment	Q Pos/Entries
dnq	ITALIAN GP	Monza	18	Team Surtees	G	3.0 Surtees TS20-Cosworth V8		28/32

Veteran Italian racer who managed to get his hands on works Surtees, and managed tnothing more than to get in the way of everyone else

GLÖCKLER, Helmut (D) b – d 1993 .

1953

	Race	Circuit	No	Entrant	Tyres	Car/Engine	Comment	Q Pos/Entries
dns	GERMAN GP	Nürburgring	39	Equipe Anglaise	D	2.0 Cooper T23-Bristol 6	engine threw rod in practice	– /35

GUBBY, Brian (GB) b 17/4/1934, Epsom, Surrey

1965

	Race	Circuit	No	Entrant	Tyres	Car/Engine	Comment	Q Pos/Entries
dnq	BRITISH GP	Silverstone	26	Brian Gubby	D	1.5 Lotus 24-Climax V8		23/23

HATTORI, Naoki (J) b 13/6/1966

1991

	Race	Circuit	No	Entrant	Tyres	Car/Engine	Comment	Q Pos/Entries
dnpq	JAPANESE GP	Suzuka	31	Coloni Racing Srl	G	3.5 Coloni C4-Cosworth V8		31/31
dnpq	AUSTRALIAN GP	Adelaide	31	Coloni Racing Srl	G	3.5 Coloni C4-Cosworth V8		32/32

Japanese F3 champion in 1990 and a front-runner in the All-Japan F3000 championship. Made an abortrve attempt to find success in CART in 1999

HEYER, Hans (D) b 16/3/1943, Mönchengladbach *(also included in main statistics)*

1977

	Race	Circuit	No	Entrant	Tyres	Car/Engine	Comment	Q Pos/Entries
dnq/ret	GERMAN GP	Hockenheim	35	ATS Racing Team	G	3.0 Penske PC4-Cosworth V8	started illegally/gear linkage	27/30

JONES, Tom (CDN)

1967

	Race	Circuit	No	Entrant	Tyres	Car/Engine	Comment	Q Pos/Entries
dnq	CANADIAN GP	Mosport Park	41	Tom Jones	–	2.0 Cooper T82-Climax V8	not allowed to start-too slow	19/19

A group of enthusiasts from Cleveland, Ohio entered the unknown Jones, but unfotunately the inexperienced pilot was 20 seconds off the pace of Mike Fisher

JOVER, Juan (E) b 1903, Barcelona, – d 28/6/1960, Sitges, Catalunya

1951

	Race	Circuit	No	Entrant	Tyres	Car/Engine	Comment	Q Pos/Entries
dns	SPANISH GP	Pedralbes	46	Scuderia Milano	–	1.5 s/c Maserati 4CLT/48 4	engine in practice	18/20

KAVANAGH, Ken (AUS) b 1922

1958

	Race	Circuit	No	Entrant	Tyres	Car/Engine	Comment	Q Pos/Entries
dnq	MONACO GP	Monte Carlo	50	Ken Kavanagh	–	2.5 Maserati 250F 6		19/28
dns	BELGIAN GP	Spa	34	Ken Kavanagh	–	2.5 Maserati 250F 6	engine in practice	(20)/28

Very successful Norton and Moto-Guzzi motor cycle racer, who dabbled briefly in four-wheeled competition

KENNEDY, David (IRL) b 15/1/1953, Sligo

1980

	Race	Circuit	No	Entrant	Tyres	Car/Engine	Comment	Q Pos/Entries
dnq	ARGENTINE GP	Buenos Aires	18	Shadow Cars	G	3.0 Shadow DN11-Cosworth V8		25/28
dnq	BRAZILIAN GP	Interlagos	18	Shadow Cars	G	3.0 Shadow DN11-Cosworth V8		26/28
dnq	SOUTH AFRICAN GP	Kyalami	18	Shadow Cars	G	3.0 Shadow DN11-Cosworth V8		27/28
dnq	US GP WEST	Long Beach	18	Shadow Cars	G	3.0 Shadow DN11-Cosworth V8		25/27
dnq	BELGIAN GP	Zolder	18	Shadow Cars	G	3.0 Shadow DN11-Cosworth V8		26/27
dnq	MONACO GP	Monte Carlo	18	Theodore Shadow	G	3.0 Shadow DN11-Cosworth V8		27/27
dnq	FRENCH GP	Paul Ricard	18	Theodore Shadow	G	3.0 Shadow DN12-Cosworth V8		27/27

Note: qualified and raced in 1980 Spanish GP – subsequently deprived of championship status

1976-77 Formula Ford champion who switched to sports cars after his brief F1 career failed to take off. Raced regularly with Mazda in the late eighties

KESSLER, Bruce (USA)

1958

	Race	Circuit	No	Entrant	Tyres	Car/Engine	Comment	Q Pos/Entries
dnq	MONACO GP	Monte Carlo	12	B C Ecclestone	A	2.5 Connaught B-Alta 4		21/28

KOZAROWITSKY, Mikko (SF) b 17/5/1948, Helsinki

1977

	Race	Circuit	No	Entrant	Tyres	Car/Engine	Comment	Q Pos/Entries
dnq	SWEDISH GP	Anderstorp	32	RAM Racing/F & S Properties	G	3.0 March 761-Cosworth V8		31/31
dnpq	BRITISH GP	Silverstone	32	RAM Racing/F & S Properties	G	3.0 March 761-Cosworth V8		36/36

KRAKAU, Willi (D) d 6/1995

1952

	Race	Circuit	No	Entrant	Tyres	Car/Engine	Comment	Q Pos/Entries
dns	GERMAN GP	Nürburgring	133	Willi Krakau	--	2.0 AFM 6		28/32

KUHNKE, Kurt (D)

1963

	Race	Circuit	No	Entrant	Tyres	Car/Engine	Comment	Q Pos/Entries
dnq	GERMAN GP	Nürburgring	27	Kurt Kuhnke	D	1.5 BKL Lotus 18-Borgward 4		26/26

KUWASHIMA, Masami (J) b 14/9/1950

1976

	Race	Circuit	No	Entrant	Tyres	Car/Engine	Comment	Q Pos/Entries
dns	JAPANESE GP	Mount Fuji	21	Walter Wolf Racing	G	3.0 Williams FW05-Cosworth V8	sponsors withdrew	26/27

LANGES, Claudio (I) b 20/7/1960, Brescia

1990

	Race	Circuit	No	Entrant	Tyres	Car/Engine	Comment	Q Pos/Entries
dnpq	US GP (PHOENIX)	Phoenix	34	EuroBrun Racing	P	3.5 EuroBrun ER189-Judd V8		33/35
dnpq	BRAZILIAN GP	Interlagos	34	EuroBrun Racing	P	3.5 EuroBrun ER189-Judd V8		34/35
dnpq	SAN MARINO GP	Imola	34	EuroBrun Racing	P	3.5 EuroBrun ER189B-Judd V8		32/34
dnpq	MONACO GP	Monte Carlo	34	EuroBrun Racing	P	3.5 EuroBrun ER189B-Judd V8		33/35
dnpq	CANADIAN GP	Montreal	34	EuroBrun Racing	P	3.5 EuroBrun ER189B-Judd V8		34/35
dnpq	MEXICAN GP	Mexico City	34	EuroBrun Racing	P	3.5 EuroBrun ER189B-Judd V8		34/35
dnpq	FRENCH GP	Paul Ricard	34	EuroBrun Racing	P	3.5 EuroBrun ER189B-Judd V8		33/35
dnpq	BRITISH GP	Silverstone	34	EuroBrun Racing	P	3.5 EuroBrun ER189B-Judd V8		33/35
dnpq	GERMAN GP	Hockenheim	34	EuroBrun Racing	P	3.5 EuroBrun ER189B-Judd V8		34/35
dnpq	HUNGARIAN GP	Hungaroring	34	EuroBrun Racing	P	3.5 EuroBrun ER189B-Judd V8		34/35
dnpq	BELGIAN GP	Spa	34	EuroBrun Racing	P	3.5 EuroBrun ER189B-Judd V8		32/33
dnpq	ITALIAN GP	Monza	34	EuroBrun Racing	P	3.5 EuroBrun ER189B-Judd V8		32/33
dnpq	PORTUGUESE GP	Estoril	34	EuroBrun Racing	P	3.5 EuroBrun ER189B-Judd V8		32/33
dnpq	SPANISH GP	Jerez	34	EuroBrun Racing	P	3.5 EuroBrun ER189B-Judd V8		32/33

Gave a number of good performances in junior formulae and F3000, but his task with the EuroBrun was hopeless. Since succesfully raced touring cars

'LUCIENBONNET', (BONNET, Jean Lucien) (F) b Nice – d 19/8/1962, Sicily, Italy

1959

	Race	Circuit	No	Entrant	Tyres	Car/Engine	Comment	Q Pos/Entries
dnq	MONACO GP	Monte Carlo	14	Jean Lucienbonnet	D	2.0 Cooper T45-Climax 4 F2		23/24

A motor and motorboat dealer by trade, 'Lucienbonnet' rallied Alfa Romeos, and raced in GT and Formula Junior formulas. Killed in a Formula Junior race in Sicily

McCARTHY, Perry (GB) b 3/3/1963, Stepney, London

1992

	Race	Circuit	No	Entrant	Tyres	Car/Engine	Comment	Q Pos/Entries
dnpq	SPANISH GP	Barcelona	35	Andrea Moda Formula	G	3.5 Moda S921-Judd V10	did not practice	– /32
dnpq	SAN MARINO GP	Imola	35	Andrea Moda Formula	G	3.5 Moda S921-Judd V10		32/32
dnpq	MONACO GP	Monte Carlo	35	Andrea Moda Formula	G	3.5 Moda S921-Judd V10	did not practice	– /32
dnpq	CANADIAN GP	Montreal	35	Andrea Moda Formula	G	3.5 Moda S921-Judd V10	did not practice	– /32
dnpq	BRITISH GP	Silverstone	35	Andrea Moda Formula	G	3.5 Moda S921-Judd V10		32/32
excl*	GERMAN GP	Hockenheim	35	Andrea Moda Formula	G	3.5 Moda S921-Judd V10	* missed car weight check	32/32
dnpq	HUNGARIAN GP	Hungaroring	35	Andrea Moda Formula	G	3.5 Moda S921-Judd V10	no time recorded	– /31
dnq	BELGIAN GP	Spa	35	Andrea Moda Formula	G	3.5 Moda S921-Judd V10		29/30

Ever enthusuiatic but impecunious racer, whose tilt at F1 was mainly confined to the pitlane

McGUIRE, Brian (AUS) b 13/12/1945, Melbourne, Victoria – d 29/8/1977, Brands Hatch Circuit, Kent, England

1976

	Race	Circuit	No	Entrant	Tyres	Car/Engine	Comment	Q Pos/Entries
dnc	BRITISH GP	Brand Hatch	41	Brian McGuire	G	3.0 Williams FW04-Cosworth V8	reserve entry-not allowed to compete	

1977

	Race	Circuit	No	Entrant	Tyres	Car/Engine	Comment	Q Pos/Entries
dnpq	BRITISH GP	Silverstone	45	Brian McGuire	G	McGuire BM1-Cosworth V8		35/36

Travelled over from Oz with Alan Jones to seek fame and fortune. Killed practising his own car during a national meeting at Brands Hatch

MERKEL, Harry (D)

1952

	Race	Circuit	No	Entrant	Tyres	Car/Engine	Comment	Q Pos/Entries
dns	GERMAN GP	Nürburgring	134	Willi Krakau	–	2.0 BMW-Eigenbau 6	no time set	–/–

MOSS, Bill (GB) b 1933

1959

	Race	Circuit	No	Entrant	Tyres	Car/Engine	Comment	Q Pos/Entries
dnq	BRITISH GP (F2)	Aintree	56	United Racing Stable	D	1.5 Cooper T51-Climax 4 F2		–/30

NELLEMAN, Jac (DK)

1976

	Race	Circuit	No	Entrant	Tyres	Car/Engine	Comment	Q Pos/Entries
dnq	SWEDISH GP	Anderstorp	33	RAM Racing	G	3.0 Brabham BT42-Cosworth V8		27/27
dnq	"	"	33	RAM Racing	G	3.0 Brabham BT44B-Cosworth V8		–/–

OPPITZHAUSER, Karl (A)

1976

	Race	Circuit	No	Entrant	Tyres	Car/Engine	Comment	Q Pos/Entries
dnp	AUSTRIAN GP	Österreichring	40	Sports Cars of Austria	G	3.0 March 761-Cosworth V8	No F1 experience-not allowed to run	

PIÀN, Alfredo (RA) b 1912

1950

	Race	Circuit	No	Entrant	Tyres	Car/Engine	Comment	Q Pos/Entries
dns	MONACO GP	Monte Carlo		Scuderia Achille Varzi	–	1.5 s/c Maserati 4CLT/48 4	practice accident	(18)/21

PRINOTH, Ernesto (I) b 1924 – d 1981

1962

	Race	Circuit	No	Entrant	Tyres	Car/Engine	Comment	Q Pos/Entries
dnq	ITALIAN GP	Monza	54	Scuderia Jolly Club	D	1.5 Lotus 18-Climax 4		27/30

PUZEY, Clive (RSR)

1965

	Race	Circuit	No	Entrant	Tyres	Car/Engine	Comment	Q Pos/Entries
dnpq	SOUTH AFRICAN GP	East London	24	Clive Puzey Motors	D	1.5 Lotus 18-Climax 4		–/–

RICHARDSON, Ken (GB)

1951

	Race	Circuit	No	Entrant	Tyres	Car/Engine	Comment	Q Pos/Entries
dns	ITALIAN GP	Monza	32	BRM Ltd	D	1.5 s/c BRM P15 V16	did not possess correct licence	(10)/22

Test and development driver on the drawn-out and largely unsuccessful BRM V16 project of the early fifties

ROLLINSON, Alan (GB) b 15/5/1943, Walsall, Staffordshire

1965

	Race	Circuit	No	Entrant	Tyres	Car/Engine	Comment	Q Pos/Entries
dnq	BRITISH GP	Silverstone	25	Gerard Racing	D	1.5 Cooper T71/73-Ford 4		22/23

Talented British F5000 runner who never made a Grand Prix start, but enjoyed a long and successful career in other formulae

RUDAZ, Jean-Claude (CH)

1964

	Race	Circuit	No	Entrant	Tyres	Car/Engine	Comment	Q Pos/Entries
dns	ITALIAN GP	Monza	60	Fabre Urbain	D	1.5 Cooper T60-Climax V8	engine in practice	(20)/25

SEIFFERT Günther (D)

1962

	Race	Circuit	No	Entrant	Tyres	Car/Engine	Comment	Q Pos/Entries
dnq	GERMAN GP	Nürburgring	34	Autosport Team Wolfgang Seidel	D	1.5 Lotus 24-BRM V8	shared car with Seidel	30/30